# ENCYCLOPEDIA OF PROFESSIONAL MANAGEMENT

*Editor-in-Chief*
## LESTER ROBERT BITTEL

*School of Business, James Madison University*
*formerly Director of Information Systems, McGraw-Hill Publishing Company*

*Managing Editor*
## MURIEL ALBERS BITTEL

## McGRAW-HILL BOOK COMPANY

*New York   St. Louis   San Francisco   Auckland   Bogotá   Düsseldorf   Johannesburg*
*London   Madrid   Mexico   Montreal   New Delhi   Panama   Paris*
*São Paulo   Singapore   Sydney   Tokyo   Toronto*

*Library of Congress Cataloging in Publication Data*

Main entry under title:

Encyclopedia of professional management.

Includes index.
1. Management—Dictionaries.  2. Business—
Dictionaries.  I. Bittel, Lester R.  II. Bittel,
Muriel Albers.
HD30.15.E5     658.4′003     78-17215
ISBN 0-07-005478-9

1234567890   KPKP   78654321098

The editors for this book were W. Hodson Mogan and
Beatrice Carson, the designer was Naomi Auerbach, and the
production supervisor was Frank Bellantoni. It was set in
Janson by University Graphics, Inc.

Printed and bound by The Kingsport Press

# CONTENTS

# PREFACE

The purpose of this encyclopedia is to provide managers in all kinds of organizations with (1) clear explanations of fundamental concepts and widely practiced techniques and (2) specific advice about how to apply them successfully. The material was selected and shaped to serve managers and potential managers in both the private and public sectors, and they will find here not only *why* a particular principle is accepted but also *how* to use it effectively. The emphasis is primarily on business usage, but adequate attention is given to management practices in public administration and not-for-profit organizations.

Whatever its values or its shortcomings—and it is to be hoped that the former prevail—this encyclopedia reflects the considered judgment of many qualified individuals about a number of pivotal factors. These are elaborated on below.

**Scope**   Three intimately related areas were considered in selecting subject matter:

1. *Primary management functions*, such as planning, organizing, activating, controlling, and decision making

2. *Major business activities*, such as finance and accounting, operations and production, marketing and sales, and information management

3. *Environmental resources and constraints*, such as human resources, materials, funds, equipment and facilities, consumer demand, economic conditions, natural resources, community influences, and government regulations

The management process and the business system are examined in each of their parts, from assembling resources to converting them into value-added outputs as products and services. These, in turn, are placed in context with the various environments in which they operate. Thus, the reader will find definitions, explanations, and application instructions on most significant aspects of management as it applies to business and resources conversion. Figure 1 graphically illustrates the process involved, and the encyclopedia includes almost everything that the advisory board decided was of value for the practice of professional management.

Historical information about a concept or technique is included only where it

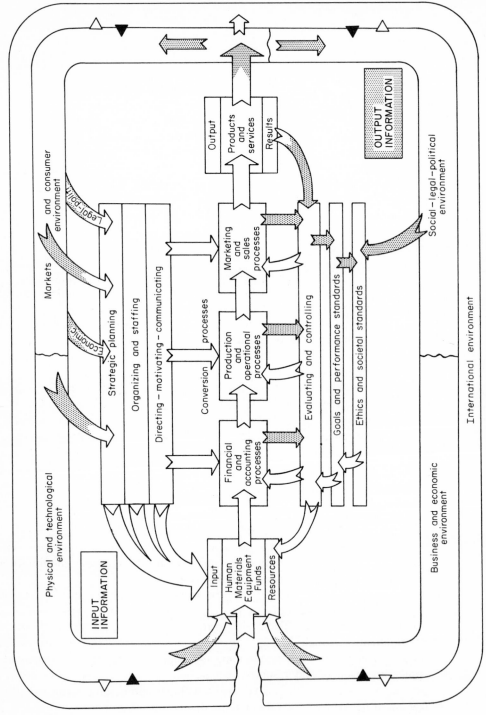

Fig. 1. Conceptual rationale for determining scope of subject matter.

contributes to understanding some application. Specific figures and statistics that may be quickly outdated are included only when absolutely necessary to provide a frame of reference for immediate usage.

A difficult decision, arrived at with the help of the editorial advisors, was to eliminate biographical sketches of significant managers or contributors to managerial theories and practices. Some coverage is given to individuals, however, under the entries MANAGEMENT, HISTORICAL DEVELOPMENT OF, HALL OF FAME OF BUSINESS LEADERSHIP, and GANTT MEDAL AWARDS. Throughout the text, reference is also made to notable contributors, but no biographical sketches as such are included.

**Entry Coverage**  In this work there are over 250 comprehensive entries, which contain nearly 2300 specific definitions. In general, each major entry provides: (1) a definition of the underlying principle or concept; (2) application opportunities, techniques, procedures, and examples; (3) an evaluation of the usefulness of the concept or technique; and (4) a list of other sources of information either in the encyclopedia or available elsewhere. The key definitions in the major entries are highlighted in italics.

**Perspective**  Regardless of how abstract the subject, contributors were encouraged to use simple language and to furnish practical examples. Most important, the authors emphasized the place of every subject within the managerial purview. Because of this, in the eyes of some specialists, depth may seem to be lacking in some areas. If this be the case, it has not been accidental. With such breadth of subject matter, the controlling guideline throughout has been to demonstrate the techniques of managerial usage and the suitability for management application.

**Disciplines**  Many terms and subjects appear under more than one subject heading. This reflects the multidisciplinary nature of many managerial and business activities. Inevitably, and intentionally, there are areas of overlap. Occasionally there are differing points of view. This reflects the nature of management, which precludes flat statements of conclusions and unqualified prescriptions for behavior without first taking the nature of the situation and the various forces at play fully into account. In many management areas, the study is fragmented because of the specialized attitudes, training, and experience of those who practice it. From an academic view, broad disciplines enter into its discussion, such as sociology, psychology, information sciences, communications theory, economics, statistics, mathematics, physics and engineering. From an experiential view, various business disciplines prevail, such as accounting, finance, marketing, and operations—based also on the individual's experience in a particular industry such as construction, manufacturing, banking, insurance, public administration, or not-for-profit institutions.

**Topic Selection**  Some two dozen basic reference texts, specialized handbooks, and encyclopedias were scanned for commonly used management and business terms. Additionally, the curricula of leading graduate schools of business, commerce, administration, and management were searched for key subject matter in commonly required courses. This study yielded 2300 terms and subjects. These were arranged systematically according to field and compiled in a 50-page planning booklet which was distributed to the 30 business leaders, consultants, and academic authorities who make up the advisory board. Subjects and terms were rated by the board according to an ABC classification: A, absolutely necessary; B, probably worthy of inclusion; and C, optional. All A subjects and most B subjects were selected for comprehensive treatment as major entries. The remainder of the B and a large percentage of the C terms were selected for definitions to be included within the major entries. As the development of the encyclopedia progressed, new terms were added and other terms dropped on the advice of the contributors themselves.

**Terminology**   No claim is made that the definitions presented represent standard terminology. At best, they reflect popular business usage and academic consensus. Lt. Col. L. F. Urwick, our most senior editorial advisor, has for over half a century deplored the absence of standard terminology and has labored nearly that long to correct this condition, but with little success. His colleague from Australia on the board, Sir Walter Scott, has also challenged our terminology, but on the basis that it represents North American rather than international usage. Admittedly, as Lord Kelvin observed in 1899, "When you can measure what you are speaking about, and express it in numbers, you know something about it. But when you cannot measure it, cannot express it in numbers, your knowledge is a meagre and unsatisfactory kind." H. B. Maynard, father of predetermined time standards, commented similarly in 1959: "Before you can control, you must be able to measure what you want done." It should follow, then, that if we cannot precisely define a subject we cannot properly classify it and accurately rationalize it. Happily, this conclusion does not necessarily follow in the management field. Managers and students of management alike *do* muddle through. One way or another, they find sufficient agreement about meanings so as to establish universal principles and broadly useful practices and techniques.

It is especially difficult to reach a standard (or consensus) for management terms because of their unique origin. Management is widely practiced and has its source in many countries and cultures and languages. Furthermore, it is derived from and grows from many disciplines or fields such as the social and physical sciences, mathematics and statistics, economics and philosophy, and language and communications. It is truly multidisciplinary in character and thus resists the efforts to place its elements under universal restraints, even those imposed by terminology.

Where possible, however, the contributors have respected the efforts to standardize management terms. They have drawn on the works of those professional societies that have developed glossaries of terms acceptable to their members (notably the American Institute of Industrial Engineers, which has a published standard) and on the efforts of the accounting profession to develop standard practices based upon agreement on definitions of terms. They have also consulted the hundreds of textbooks and occasional management dictionaries which have separately tried to solve the problem. In the main, however, the standard for a great many terms remains the basic dictionaries of the English language. Our instruction to authors was to define only those terms for which the established dictionary definition was inadequate or misleading. Accordingly, most terms with a meaning unique to management or its practice are italicized in the text (or appear as free-standing entries), with their definition following immediately.

**Indexing**   The arrangement of entries is alphabetical and is self-indexing. This is based upon the original decision to arrange this work alphabetically rather than according to disciplines or functional fields. Because of the many disciplines involved, it makes sense, but it cannot be denied that management and business subjects do not lend themselves easily to alphabetizing. For this reason, every effort has been made to assist the reader in finding the specific subject matter desired.

*Lester R. Bittel*

# HOW TO FIND WHAT YOU ARE LOOKING FOR

Terms, definitions, subjects, and subject "fields" can be located by following one, or all, of four different search approaches.

1. *Search the main pages of the text alphabetically.* Some 2000 major entries and reference entries are arranged in alphabetical sequence. You will find the term or subject you are seeking listed

    *a.* as a major entry, for example:

**Network planning methods**

    *b.* or as a reference entry, for instance:

**Dummy activities**   (*See* NETWORK PLANNING METHODS)

2. *Check the "See also" listing at the end of each entry.* The items set in small capital letters direct you to other closely related entries in which similar terms or subjects are discussed from another point of view. The items set in italic type refer you to the Table of Contents and Subject Locator Guide (item 3 below).

3. *Consult the Table of Contents and Subject Locator Guide.* This appears on pages x–xxi. There are 48 locators covering the most important subject fields in management and business. Under each heading are given the major entries that are particularly relevant to the subject field. For example, under *Budgets and Budgeting*, 19 entries are suggested as being especially useful. Other entries also contain pertinent information for this field, and they can be found by looking in the index.

4. *Search the comprehensive index in the back of the book.* Approximately 25,000 items are listed there. They are cross-referenced in about every reasonable variation of term or subject matter, including proper names of people, organizations, and places.

# TABLE OF CONTENTS AND SUBJECT LOCATOR GUIDE

This table lists in alphabetical order 48 vital areas of managerial concern. Under each of the 48 headings is a list of the major entries in the encyclopedia that contain information most relevant to the heading. Entries in the list are found in alphabetical sequence within the main pages of this volume.

## Budgets and Budgeting

## Communications, Internal and External

## Compensation and Incentive Plans

## Controls and Control Systems

## Costs and Cost Improvement

## Customer Relations

## Data Processing Management

## Decision Making and Problem Solving

## Health and Health Management

## Human Resources Management

## Improvement Methods and Techniques

## Information Systems

# ACKNOWLEDGMENTS

Underlying the content and quality of this encyclopedia is the dedicated effort of an unusually talented staff. It includes:

*Research and Contributing Editors*
Pavey L. Hoke, coordinator, learning laboratory
   Lord Fairfax Community College
Alice Smith, editorial assistant to Ernest Dale

*Editorial Assistants*
Lillian Bryant Mason
Helen Turner Royall
Amy Bittel Calabrese

*Special Consultant*
Arthur G. Bedeian, Auburn University

*McGraw-Hill Liaison*
Mildred W. Hetherington

This work was greatly assisted by a number of individuals who participated in the search for the best-qualified contributors. Those who aided the editor in this search were: Paul Abramson of Intelligence for Education, Inc.; Russel L. Ackoff of the Wharton School; Susan Alt of *Business Insurance*; Arthur E. Aronson of the Industrial Management Society; Robert A. Abbott of American Society for Quality Control; Robert W. Albert of *Sales Management and Marketing*; Alvin L. Arnold of *Real Estate Review*; Donald Bacon of Gulf and Western Industries; Doris Baldwin of *Job Safety and Health*; Lawrence Bass; Lester Bernstein of RCA; D. F. Berry of INSTEAD;

Herbert H. Blevins of Merck; Courtney Brown of Columbia University; Louis P. Bucklin; Robert G. Butler of the American Management Associations; Thomas Christofel of the Lord Fairfax Planning Commission; Ray W. Crawley of the National Academy of Public Administrators; Frank Deastlov of the Bank of New York; John W. Enell of the American Management Associations; Herbert Fajors of National Urbanonics, Inc.; Joseph J. Famularo of McGraw-Hill, Inc.; Robert C. Freeman of *Hotel & Motel Management*; Charles C. Glasgow of the American Society of Traffic and Transportation; Eli Ginzberg of Columbia University; C. Jackson Grayson of Southern Methodist University; Mack Hanan; John W. Hannon of Maynard Research Council; Wayne Kirton of the American Society for Training and Development; Harry Levinson; Robert A. Linciocome of *Electric Light & Power*; Donald Lundberg of Colorado State Polytechnic University; Thomas O. McGinn; Colin Macpherson of The World Trade Institute; Edward J. Marien of the University of Wisconsin—Oshkosh; William Matuszeski of the U.S. Council on Environmental Quality; Lynn G. Merritt of Life Office Management Association; Carrol M. Mickey; Ted Mills of National Quality of Work Center; John F. O'Connor of *Purchasing World*; John M. Paulson of A. B. Dick Company; Miles J. Rowan of *Modern Materials Handling*; Eli Shapiro of Travelers Insurance Companies; Lyle Schertz of the U.S. Department of Agriculture; William W. Sihler of the University of Virginia; Floyd A. Smith of Union Carbide; Leo E. Smith of Commercial Law League of America; Leo F. Spector of *Plant Engineering*; William Stocker of *American Machinist*; M. A. Tatter of the National Association of Suggestion Systems; Robert C. Walter of Administrative Management Society; Robert Wall of Morgan Adhesives; Alan Weiss; Collin H. Weschke; Charles A. Whittingham of *Fortune*; and Daniel A. Wren of the University of Oklahoma.

I am particularly indebted to my colleagues of the School of Business at James Madison University who volunteered consultation on technical matters and advice in assembling bibliographies. They include, especially: Thomas M. Bertsch, John Bilon, James G. Fox, Joseph E. Hollis, Paul H. Kipps, Ross Johnson, Joseph T. Kosnick, R. Lawrence LaForge, Philip Maxwell, Kevin G. Miller, Jackson E. Ramsey, Morton Schnabel, Thomas C. Stanton, and D. Kent Zimmerman.

*Lester R. Bittel*

# EDITORIAL ADVISORY BOARD

This distinguished panel is composed of leading businesspersons, specialized management consultants, and academic authorities. Board members devoted endless hours to nominating contributors, recommending and selecting subject matter for coverage, and reviewing and evaluating the entries. The board is listed alphabetically.

# CONTRIBUTORS

This unusually qualified group of 232 authors, selected from over 3000 nominees, includes businesspersons of outstanding managerial achievement, management consultants who are the leaders in their specialized professions, and academic figures who are recognized authorities in their fields. The entries are original and were prepared, with few exceptions, expressly for this encyclopedia. These articles were reviewed by their colleagues and by selected members of the editorial advisory board. The contributors are listed alphabetically, and the titles of their entries are given.

**Roy Abel, P.E.**
Vice-President
Albert Ramond and Associates, Inc.
Management Consultants
Chicago, Illinois
WORK MEASUREMENT

**Earl W. Adams, Ph.D.**
Andrew Wells Robertson Professor of Economics
Allegheny College
Meadville, Pennsylvania
MARKETS, PUBLIC

**Ichak Adizes, Ph.D.**
Associate Professor of Managerial Studies
Graduate School of Management
University of California
Los Angeles, California
CODETERMINATION AND INDUSTRIAL DEMOCRACY

**Robert Albanese, Ph.D.**
Professor of Management
College of Business Administration

Texas A & M University
College Station, Texas
OBJECTIVES AND GOALS

**Willard Allan, A.M., F.S.C.A., C.F.A.**
Vice-President, Finance
Alaska Airlines
Seattle, Washington
FINANCIAL MANAGEMENT, SHORT-TERM, INTERMEDIATE, AND LONG-TERM FINANCING

**H. Igor Ansoff, M.E., M.S., Ph.D.**
Professor, European Institute for Advanceed Studies in Management, Brussels, Belgium
Professor, Stockholm School of Economics
Senior Partner, Ansoff-Joeb Associates, Brussels, Belgium
PLANNING, PLANNED MANAGEMENT OF TURBULENT CHANGE

**James M. Apple, P.E.**
School of Industrial and Systems Engineering
Georgia Institute of Technology

Atlanta, Georgia
MATERIAL HANDLING

**Roger M. Atherton, Jr., Ph.D.**
Baldwin Associate Professor of Management
College of Business Administration
University of Oklahoma
Norman, Oklahoma
YOUNGER EMPLOYEES, MANAGEMENT OF

**Charles F. Axelson**
Vice-President, Chief Financial Officer
Lawry's Foods, Inc.
Los Angeles, California
INFORMATION SYSTEMS, MANAGEMENT (MIS), APPLIED

**Guy J. Bacci, II, P.E.**
Manager, Corporate Industrial Engineering
International Harvester Company
Chicago, Illinois
COMPENSATION, WAGE AND SALARY POLICY ADMINIS-
TRATION

**Alexander Bally, IDSA**
Bally Design, Inc.
Industrial Design Consultants
Carnegie, Pennsylvania
DESIGN, INDUSTRIAL

**Dean J. Barron, J.D., C.P.A.**
Attorney at Law
Fairfax, Virginia
TAX MANAGEMENT, MANAGERIAL RESPONSIBILITY FOR
FEDERAL INCOME TAX REPORTING

**Patricia R. Barrow**
Consultant
Booz·Allen and Hamilton, Inc.
Chicago, Illinois
JOB ANALYSIS; JOB EVALUATION

**Douglas C. Basil, Ph.D.**
Professor of Management
Graduate School of Business Administration
University of Southern California
Los Angeles, California
MARKETING OF SERVICES; PLANNING UNDER UNCER-
TAINTY

**Lawrence W. Bass**
Vice-President, retired
Arthur D. Little, Inc.
Cambridge, Massachusetts
PROJECT AND TASK FORCE MANAGEMENT

**Arthur G. Bedeian, D.B.A.**
Associate Professor, Department of Management
School of Business

Auburn University
Auburn, Alabama
MANAGEMENT, HISTORICAL DEVELOPMENT OF

**David D. Bedworth, Ph.D.**
Chairman and Professor, Faculty of Industrial and
Management Systems Engineering
College of Engineering and Applied Sciences
Arizona State University
Tempe, Arizona
AUTOMATION

**Howard A. Berrian**
President, Berrian Associates, Inc., and
Principal of Greenhouse Corporation
Hilton Head Island, South Carolina
SALES MANAGEMENT

**John E. Biegel, Ph.D.**
Professor, Industrial Engineering and Operations
Research
Syracuse University
Syracuse, New York
PRODUCTION PROCESSES

**Lester R. Bittel, M.B.A.**
Associate Professor
School of Business
James Madison University
Harrisonburg, Virginia
CENTRALIZATION AND DECENTRALIZATION; CONFER-
ENCE LEADERSHIP; COUNSELING, EMPLOYEE; DISCI-
PLINE; EXCEPTION, MANAGEMENT BY; FINANCIAL
RATIO ANALYSIS; GANTT CHARTS; MANUALS, POLICY
AND PROCEDURES; SYSTEMS AND PROCEDURES

**Paul W. Bockley**
Director of Labor Relations
Honeywell, Inc.
Minneapolis, Minnesota
LABOR-MANAGEMENT RELATIONS

**Paul M. Bons, Ph.D.**
Associate Professor
Department of Behavioral Sciences and Leadership
United States Military Academy
West Point, New York
LEADERSHIP

**Donald D. Bowen, Ph.D.**
Associate Professor of Management
College of Business Administration, Marketing, and
Management
University of Tulsa
Tulsa, Oklahoma
DEVELOPMENT AND TRAINING, CAREER PATH PLAN-
NING FOR MANAGERS

**Charles Boyer**
Assistant Editor, *Industrial Engineering*
American Institute of Industrial Engineers, Inc.
Norcross, Georgia
ENGINEERING, INDUSTRIAL

**George W. Bricker, S.B., M.B.A., J.D.**
Management Consultant
Publisher of *Bricker's International Directory of University-Sponsored Executive Development Programs*
South Chatham, Massachusetts
DEVELOPMENT AND TRAINING, UNIVERSITY EXECUTIVE PROGRAMS

**Dr. William L. Brockhaus**
Chairman of the Board and Chief Executive Officer
Edward Hyman Company
Los Angeles, California
Partner, Brockhaus, Carlisle & Associates
Consultants to Management
Los Angeles, California
ACQUISITIONS AND MERGERS

**R. Lee Brummet, Ph.D., C.P.A.**
Willard J. Graham Professor of Business Administration
School of Business Administration
University of North Carolina
Chapel Hill, North Carolina
ACCOUNTING, HUMAN RESOURCES (ASSETS)

**Jim N. Bruno**
Director of Communication
Administrative Management Society
Willow Grove, Pennsylvania
ADMINISTRATIVE MANAGEMENT

**Louis P. Bucklin, Ph.D.**
Professor of Business Administration
Schools of Business Administration
University of California
Berkeley, California
MARKETS, CLASSIFICATIONS AND MARKET ANALYSIS

**Victor P. Buell**
Professor of Marketing
Editor, *Handbook of Modern Marketing*
School of Business Administration
University of Massachusetts
Amherst, Massachusetts
MARKETING, CONCEPTS AND SYSTEMS

**Elmer H. Burack, Ph.D.**
Professor of Management and Management Head
College of Business
University of Illinois, Chicago Circle
Chicago, Illinois
ORGANIZATION STRUCTURES AND CHARTING

**Marian W. Byers**
Office of Public Information
United States Small Business Administration
Washington, D.C.
SMALL BUSINESS ADMINISTRATION

**William C. Byham, Ph.D.**
President
Development Dimensions, Inc.
Pittsburgh, Pennsylvania
ASSESSMENT CENTER METHOD

**William P. Camp, M.D.**
Director
Friends Hospital
Philadelphia, Pennsylvania
VALUE SYSTEMS, MANAGEMENT OF

**Bruce A. Campbell**
Manager, Industrial Systems
Science Research Associates, Inc.
Chicago, Illinois
ATTITUDE SURVEYS

**A. William Capone**
Vice-President, Chief Financial Officer and Treasurer
Koppers Company, Inc
Pittsburgh, Pennsylvania
FINANCIAL MANAGEMENT, CAPITAL STRUCTURE AND DIVIDEND POLICY

**D. R. Carmichael, Ph.D., C.P.A.**
Vice-President, Technical Services
American Institute of Certified Public Accountants
New York, New York
AUDITING, FINANCIAL

**Ronald E. Carrier, Ph.D.**
President
James Madison University
Harrisonburg, Virginia
COLLEGE AND UNIVERSITY ADMINISTRATION

**Archie B. Carroll, D.B.A.**
Associate Professor of Management
College of Business Administration
University of Georgia
Athens, Georgia
ETHICS, MANAGERIAL

**Richard E. Cheney**
Executive Vice-President
Hill and Knowlton, Inc.
Public Relations/Public Affairs Counsel
New York, New York
SHAREHOLDER RELATIONSHIPS

**Bruce S. Childers**
Vice-President, Research
Meldrum and Fewsmith, Inc.
Cleveland, Ohio
MARKETING RESEARCH

**H. Weston Clarke, Jr., Ph.D.**
Vice-President, Human Resources
American Telephone and Telegraph Company
New York, New York
WORK, CONCEPT AND IMPLICATIONS

**John L. Cobbs**
Editor, *Business Week*
McGraw-Hill Publications Company
New York, New York
EGALITARIANISM

**John W. Cogger, Ph.D.**
Senior Training Associate
The Psychological Corporation
New York, New York
EMPLOYMENT PROCESS

**Stephen D. Cohen, Ph.D.**
Associate Professor
School of International Service
American University
Washington, D.C.
INTERNATIONAL TRADE

**Richard A. Connor, Jr., M.Ed., C.M.C.**
President
Professional Services Research/Marketing
Division of Synergy Corporation
Springfield, Virginia
MARKETING OF SERVICES, PROFESSIONAL

**Marcel Corstjens**
Schools of Business Administration
University of California
Berkeley, California
MARKETS, CLASSIFICATIONS AND MARKET ANALYSIS

**Philip B. Crosby**
Vice-President, Director–Quality
International Telephone and Telegraph Corporation
New York, New York
QUALITY MANAGEMENT

**Philip T. Crotty, M.B.A., Ed.D.**
Associate Dean
College of Business Administration
Northeastern University
Boston, Massachusetts
OLDER EMPLOYEES, MANAGEMENT OF

**David A. Cunningham, Ph.D.**
Associate Professor
Faculty of Physical Education and Department of Physiology
University of Western Ontario
London, Canada
HEALTH, EXECUTIVE, MANAGING STRESS AND JOB TENSION

**Tim Cunningham, IDSA**
Bally Design, Inc.
Industrial Design Consultants
Carnegie, Pennsylvania
DESIGN, INDUSTRIAL

**Virgil B. Day**
Attorney at Law
Vedder, Price, Kaufman, Kammholz and Day
New York, New York, and Washington, D.C.
LABOR LEGISLATION

**Burton V. Dean, Ph.D.**
Professor, Department of Operations Research
Case Western Reserve University
Cleveland, Ohio
NETWORK PLANNING METHODS; ZERO-BASE BUDGETING

**Kenyon B. De Greene, Ph.D.**
Associate Professor
Human Factors Department, Institute of Safety and Systems Management
University of Southern California
Los Angeles, California
HUMAN FACTORS ENGINEERING

**M. Wayne DeLozier, Ph.D.**
Associate Professor of Marketing
College of Business Administration
University of South Carolina
Columbia, South Carolina
ADVERTISING CONCEPTS

**Robert H. Doktor, Ph.D.**
College of Business Administration
University of Hawaii
Honolulu, Hawaii
INTERPERSONAL RELATIONSHIPS

**John D. Donnell, J.D., D.B.A.**
Professor of Business Administration and Chairperson of Business Law
Former Editor in Chief, *American Business Law Journal*
Graduate School of Business
Indiana University
Bloomington, Indiana

BOARDS OF DIRECTORS, LEGAL LIABILITY GUIDELINES;
LEGAL AFFAIRS, MANAGEMENT OF CORPORATE

**Stahrl W. Edmunds**
Dean
Graduate School of Administration
University of California
Riverside, California
ENVIRONMENT, PHYSICAL

**Joseph Eisenberg**
President
Profit-Improvement, Inc.
Management Consultants
New York, New York
PROFIT IMPROVEMENT

**Bruce R. Ellig**
Corporate Director, Compensation and Benefits
Pfizer, Inc.
New York, New York
COMPENSATION, EMPLOYEE BENEFIT PLANS

**James C. Emery**
President
EDUCOM
Princeton, New Jersey
CONTROL SYSTEMS, MANAGEMENT

**Anthony X. Farmer, Ph.D.**
Professional Development Consultant
The Personnel Laboratory, Inc.
New York, New York
EMPLOYMENT PROCESS

**Fred E. Fiedler, Ph.D.**
Professor of Psychology and of Management and
    Organization
Department of Psychology
University of Washington
Seattle, Washington
LEADERSHIP

**Alan C. Filley, Ph.D.**
Professor, Department of Management
Graduate School of Business
University of Wisconsin
Madison, Wisconsin
ORGANIZATION ANALYSIS AND PLANNING

**William M. Fox, Ph.D.**
Professor of Industrial Relations and Management
College of Business Administration
University of Florida
Gainesville, Florida
COMPENSATION, SPECIAL PLANS

**Jack P. Friedman, Ph.D., C.P.A.**
Associate Professor
The University of Texas at Arlington
Arlington, Texas
REAL ESTATE MANAGEMENT, CORPORATE

**Sheldon J. Fuchs, P.E.**
Director–Facility Maintenance Institute
Hofstra University
Hempstead, New York
MAINTENANCE MANAGEMENT

**Robert M. Fulmer, Ph.D.**
Distinguished Professor of Management
College of Business Administration
Memphis State University
Memphis, Tennessee
SUPERVISORY MANAGEMENT

**Ralph M. Gaedeke, Ph.D.**
Professor of Marketing
School of Business and Public Administration
California State University
Sacramento, California
CONSUMERISM AND CONSUMER PROTECTION LEGISLA-
TION

**William F. Glueck, Ph.D.**
Distinguished Professor of Management
College of Business Administration
The University of Georgia
Athens, Georgia
POLICY FORMULATION AND IMPLEMENTATION

**William Gomberg, Ph.D.**
Professor of Management and Industrial Relations
The Wharton School
University of Pennsylvania
Philadelphia, Pennsylvania
LABOR (TRADE) UNIONS

**Arthur S. Graham, Jr.**
Vice-President
A. T. Kearney, Inc.
Management Consultants
New York, New York
PLANNING, STRATEGIC PLANNING MODELS

**Ben S. Graham, Jr., Ph.D.**
President
The Ben Graham Corporation: Paperwork Simplifi-
    cation Division
Tipp City, Ohio
PAPER WORK SIMPLIFICATION

**Mary Jane Grant**
School of Business Administration
University of Western Ontario

London, Canada
HEALTH, EXECUTIVE MANAGING STRESS AND JOB
  TENSION

**James H. Graves**
Vice-President, Banking
First National Bank in Dallas
Dallas, Texas
FINANCIAL MANAGEMENT, BANK RELATIONSHIPS

**Jack Gray, M.B.A., Ph.D., C.P.A.**
Professor of Accounting and Management Informa-
  tion Systems
College of Business Administration
University of Minnesota
Minneapolis, Minnesota
ACCOUNTING, COST ANALYSIS AND CONTROL

**E. T. Grether, Ph.D., LL.D., ekon.dr. (hon.c.)**
Flood Professor of Economics, Emeritus
Dean Emeritus, School of Business Administration
Dean Emeritus, Graduate School of Business Ad-
  ministration, Teaching, Research
University of California
Berkeley, California
COMPETITION

**Frank K. Griesinger**
President
Frank K. Griesinger and Associates, Inc.
Suite 1412, Superior Building
Cleveland, Ohio
LEASING, EQUIPMENT; TELECOMMUNICATIONS

**Paul J. Grogan**
Professor of Engineering
Department of Engineering
University of Wisconsin–Extension
Madison, Wisconsin
CONTINUING EDUCATION UNIT (CEU)

**Bernard S. Gutow**
Principal
A. T. Kearney, Inc.
Management Consultants
Chicago, Illinois
ENERGY RESOURCES, MANAGEMENT OF

**Bernard J. Hale, M.B.A.**
Corporate Vice President, Distribution Planning
Bergen Brunswig Corporation
Carson, California
DISTRIBUTION, PHYSICAL

**Douglas T. Hall, Ph.D.**
Earl Dean Howard Professor of Organizational Be-
  havior
Graduate School of Managment

Northwestern University
Evanston, Illinois
DEVELOPMENT AND TRAINING, CAREER PATH PLAN-
  NING FOR MANAGERS

**Arthur J. Hamilton, J.D.**
Assistant Professor
School of Business
James Madison University
Harrisonburg, Virginia
GOVERNMENT REGULATIONS, BUSINESS LAW; GOVERN-
  MENT RELATIONS, FEDERAL REGULATION OF COM-
  PETITION

**H. T. S. Heckman**
Director of Advertising
Republic Steel Corporation
Cleveland, Ohio
ADVERTISING MANAGEMENT, INDUSTRIAL

**Roger W. Hill, Jr.**
Vice-President, Pension Fund Investments
National Distillers and Chemical Corporation
New York, New York
FINANCIAL MANAGEMENT, WORKING CAPITAL CON-
  TROL

**Dorothy Hogan**
Deputy Managing Director, Communications
American National Standards Institute, Inc.
New York, New York
STANDARDS AND STANDARDIZATION PROGRAMS

**Pavey L. Hoke, M. Ed.**
Coordinator of Learning Laboratory
Lord Fairfax Community College
Middletown, Virginia
(contributor of selected definitions)

**Frank Holladay, CPE**
Vice-President, Plant Engineering Department
Southwire Corporation
Carrollton, Georgia
PLANT ENGINEERING MANAGEMENT

**Michael E. Hora**
Principal
A. T. Kearney, Inc.
Management Consultants
Chicago, Illinois
ENERGY RESOURCES, MANAGEMENT OF

**John H. Howard, D.B.A.**
Associate Professor of Business Administration
University of Western Ontario
London, Ontario
HEALTH, EXECUTIVE, MANAGING STRESS AND JOB
  TENSION

**Wardwell Howell**
Chairman
Ward Howell Associates, Inc.
New York, New York
SEARCH AND RECRUITMENT, EXECUTIVE

**Elbert W. Hubbard, Ph.D.**
Associate Professor
Department of Real Estate and Urban Affairs
School of Business Administration
Georgia State University
Atlanta, Georgia
REAL ESTATE MANAGEMENT, CORPORATE

**John S. Jenness, M.B.A.**
Director, Human Resources Planning and Development
Consolidated Edison Company of New York, Inc.
HUMAN RESOURCES (WORK FORCE) PLANNING

**Alton C. Johnson, Ph.D.**
Professor
Graduate School of Business
University of Wisconsin
Madison, Wisconsin
HEALTH INSTITUTIONS, MANAGEMENT OF

**Frank J. Johnson, P.E., C.V.S.**
Johnson Management Corporation
Smyrna (Atlanta), Georgia
VALUE ANALYSIS

**Howard W. Johnson**
Chairman of the Corporation
Massachusetts Institute of Technology
Cambridge, Massachusetts
TECHNOLOGY, MANAGEMENT IMPLICATIONS

**Rodney Johnson, Ph.D.**
Deputy Director of Finance
City of Philadelphia
Philadelphia, Pennsylvania
STATISTICAL ANALYSIS FOR MANAGEMENT

**David A. Jones**
Citicorp
San Francisco, California
BUDGETING, CAPITAL, SPECIAL PROBLEMS OF

**Anthony F. Jurkus, Ph.D.**
Associate Professor of Management
College of Administration and Business
Louisiana Tech University
Ruston, Louisiana
PROFESSIONALISM IN MANAGEMENT

**Robert N. Katz**
Managing Editor, *California Management Review*
University of California
Berkeley, California
GOVERNMENT RELATIONS AND SERVICES

**Stephen H. Kaufman**
Editor
The Research Institute of America, Inc.
New York, New York
CONSULTANTS, MANAGEMENT

**Barry P. Keating, Ph.D.**
Assistant Professor of Finance and Business Economics
Department of Finance and Business Economics
University of Notre Dame
South Bend, Indiana
ECONOMIC CONCEPTS

**John W. Kendrick, Ph.D.**
Professor of Economics
George Washington University
Washington, D.C.
Formerly Chief Economist
U.S. Department of Commerce
PRODUCTIVITY

**Donald L. Kirkpatrick, Ph.D.**
Professor of Management Development
University of Wisconsin–Extension
Milwaukee, Wisconsin
DEVELOPMENT AND TRAINING, MANAGEMENT

**Blair J. Kolasa, Ph.D.**
Dean, School of Business and Administration
Duquesne University
Pittsburgh, Pennsylvania
CONFORMITY IN MANAGEMENT

**Harold Koontz, Ph.D.**
Mead Johnson Professor of Management
Graduate School of Management
University of California
Los Angeles, California
MANAGEMENT THEORY, SCIENCE, AND APPROACHES

**Philip Kotler, Ph.D.**
The Harold T. Martin Professor of Marketing
Graduate School of Management
Northwestern University
Evanston, Illinois
MARKETING OF SERVICES, PROFESSIONAL

**Seymour D. Kramer**
President
Revere Business Graphics, Inc.
New York, New York
FORMS DESIGN AND CONTROL

**William A. W. Krebs**
Vice-President
Arthur D. Little, Inc.
Cambridge, Massachusetts
DEVELOPING COUNTRIES, MANAGEMENT IN

**Donald W. Kroeber, Ph.D.**
Assistant Professor, School of Business
James Madison University
Harrisonburg, Virginia
INFORMATION SYSTEMS, MANAGEMENT (MIS), IN LARGE
   ORGANIZATIONS

**Howard C. Launstein, Ph.D.**
Professor of Accounting and Finance
Director, National Institute on Consumer Credit
   Management
The Robert A. Johnston College of Business Ad-
   ministration
Marquette University
Milwaukee, Wisconsin
CREDIT MANAGEMENT

**John C. Lere, Ph.D.**
Assistant Professor of Accounting
University of Minnesota
Minneapolis, Minnesota
PRODUCT AND SERVICE PRICING

**Richard L. Lesher, Ph.D.**
President
Chamber of Commerce of the United States
Washington, D.C.
NOT-FOR-PROFIT ORGANIZATIONS, MANAGEMENT OF

**Stanley H. Lieberstein**
Attorney at Law
Partner, Ostrolenk, Faber, Gerb and Soffen
New York, New York
PATENTS AND VALUABLE INTANGIBLE RIGHTS

**William E. Linane, S.I.R.**
President
Linane & Company, Inc.
Industrial Real Estate
Rosemont, Illinois
SITE SELECTION

**Paul A. Lodato**
Office of Public Information
United States Small Business Administration
Washington, D.C.
SMALL BUSINESS ADMINISTRATION

**George C. Lodge**
Professor Of Business Administration
Graduate School of Business Administration

Harvard University
Boston, Massachusetts
SOCIAL RESPONSIBILITY OF BUSINESS

**Wallace G. Lonergan, Ph.D.**
Director, Industrial Relations Center
University of Chicago
Chicago, Illinois
APPRAISAL, PERFORMANCE

**Marvin D. Loper, Ph.D.**
College of Business Administration
University of Hawaii
Honolulu, Hawaii
INTERPERSONAL RELATIONSHIPS

**James P. Low**
President
American Society of Association Executives
Washington, D.C.
ASSOCIATIONS, TRADE AND PROFESSIONAL

**James M. Lyneis, Ph.D.**
Assistant Professor of Management
Alfred P. Sloan School of Management
Massachusetts Institute of Technology
Cambridge, Massachusetts
SYSTEM DYNAMICS

**William K. McAleer**
President
Peter F. Loftus Corporation
Consulting and Design Engineers
Pittsburgh, Pennsylvania
ENGINEERING MANAGEMENT

**Dalton E. McFarland, Ph.D.**
University Professor
School of Business
University of Alabama in Birmingham
Birmingham, Alabama
BOARDS OF DIRECTORS; COMMITTEES; MANAGEMENT,
   DEFINITIONS OF; MANAGER, DEFINITIONS OF; OFFI-
   CERS, CORPORATE

**David J. McLaughlin**
Principal
McKinsey and Company, Inc.
New York, New York
COMPENSATION, EXECUTIVE

**Randolph B. McMullen**
Executive Vice-President
McCormick and Company
Consulting Engineers
Scarsdale, New York
MARGINAL INCOME ANALYSIS

**Keith L. McRoberts, Ph.D., P.E.**
Professor and Chairman, Department of Industrial
  Engineering
Iowa State University
Ames, Iowa
INVENTORY CONTROL, PURCHASING AND ACCOUNTING
  ASPECTS

**Peter J. McTague, J.D., P.E., C.F.A.**
President and Chief Executive Officer
Green Mountain Power Corporation
Burlington, Vermont
REGULATED INDUSTRIES, MANAGEMENT OF

**Edward O. Malott, Jr.**
Vice-President for Planning and Development
American Management Associations
New York, New York
CONFERENCES AND MEETINGS, PLANNING FOR

**Daniel R. Mandelker, J.S.D.**
Howard A. Stamper Professor of Law
School of Law
Washington University
St. Louis, Missouri
COMMUNITY PLANNING LEGISLATION

**Burton H. Marcus, Ph.D.**
Associate Professor of Marketing
Graduate School of Business Administration
University of Southern California
Los Angeles, California
MARKETING OF SERVICES

**Charles J. Mathey**
Member, Senior Staff
The Futures Group
Glastonbury, Connecticut
Formerly Group Division Manager: Product Sourc-
  ing
Communications Division: Motorola Inc.
PRODUCT PLANNING AND DEVELOPMENT

**Edward G. Mayers**
Senior Economist, Department of Economics
McGraw-Hill Publications Company
New York, New York
ECONOMIC MEASUREMENTS

**John F. Mee, Ph.D., LL.D.**
Mead Johnson Professor of Management
Graduate School of Business
Indiana University
Bloomington, Indiana
MANAGEMENT, FUTURE OF

**Dileep R. Mehta, Ph.D.**
Professor of Finance
College of Business Administration
Georgia State University
Atlanta, Georgia
RISK ANALYSIS AND MANAGEMENT

**Taulman A. Miller, Ph.D.**
Professor of Economics
Indiana University
Bloomington, Indiana
EMPLOYMENT AND UNEMPLOYMENT

**John B. Miner, Ph.D.**
Research Professor
Department of Management
Georgia State University
Atlanta, Georgia
COMMUNICATIONS, ORGANIZATIONAL

**Mary Green Miner**
Director of Surveys
Bureau of National Affairs, Inc.
Washington, D.C.
COMMUNICATIONS, ORGANIZATIONAL

**Allan H. Mogensen**
Work Simplification Conferences
Lake Placid, New York
WORK SIMPLIFICATION AND IMPROVEMENT

**John O. Morris, B.A., J.D.**
Vice President, Language Training
Siegel & Gale
445 Park Avenue
New York, New York
WRITING FOR BUSINESS

**David G. Muller, A.E.P.**
Vice-President and Personnel Director
Ohio National Life Insurance Company
Cincinnati, Ohio
PERSONNEL ADMINISTRATION

**Edward A. Nelson, Ph.D.**
Associate Professor of Management
The American University in Cairo
Cairo, Egypt
EXCHANGE, FOREIGN, MANAGEMENT OF

**Chester A. Newland, Ph.D.**
Professor
School of Public Administration
University of Southern California
Los Angeles, California
USC Washington Public Affairs Center
Washington, D.C.

Formerly Director, Federal Executive Institute
PUBLIC ADMINISTRATION

**Herbert L. Newmark**
Planning Consultant
Pompano Beach, Florida
OFFICE SPACE PLANNING AND DESIGN

**John W. Newstrom, Ph.D.**
Professor of Management
School of Business and Economics
University of Minnesota–Duluth
Duluth, Minnesota
DEVELOPMENT AND TRAINING, EMPLOYEE

**Gerard I. Nierenberg, Esq.**
President
Negotiation Institute, Inc.
New York, New York
COMMUNICATIONS, NONVERBAL; NEGOTIATING

**Peter V. Norden, Ph.D., P.E.**
International Business Machines Corporation
White Plains, New York
Columbia University
New York, New York
COMPUTER SYSTEMS

**David Novick**
David Novick Associates
Consultants in Economics
Santa Monica, California
PROGRAM BUDGETING (PPBS)

**Otto H. Nowotny**
Manager, Economic Adviser
F. Hoffman-La Roche and Company, Ltd.
Basle, Switzerland
WESTERN EUROPE, MANAGEMENT IN

**David W. Nylen, Ph.D.**
Vice President
Booz·Allen Venture Management, Inc.
New York, New York
INNOVATION AND CREATIVITY

**George S. Odiorne, Ph.D.**
Professor, School of Business Administration
University of Massachusetts
Amherst, Massachusetts
OBJECTIVES, MANAGEMENT BY (MBO)

**Tai K. Oh, Ph.D.**
Professor of Management
School of Business Administration and Economics
California State University at Fullerton
JAPANESE INDUSTRIES, MANAGEMENT IN

**Jerry H. Opack**
Attorney at Law
Washington, D.C.
Former President and Chief Administrative Officer
   (1971–1977)
International Franchise Association
FRANCHISING

**Neil Orloff, J.D.**
Associate Professor
Program on Science, Technology, and Society
Cornell University
Ithaca, New York
ENVIRONMENTAL PROTECTION LEGISLATION

**Lonnie L. Ostrom, Ph.D.**
Assistant Dean and Professor of Marketing
College of Business Administration
Arizona State University
Tempe, Arizona
PRODUCT LIABILITY

**James A. Parsons, Ph.D.**
Manager, Materials Management
International Division
American Cyanamid Company
Wayne, New Jersey
PRODUCTION/OPERATIONS MANAGEMENT

**Walter W. Perlick, Ph.D.**
Associate Professor, Finance
College of Business
Colorado State University
Fort Collins, Colorado
OWNERSHIP, LEGAL FORMS OF

**Richard O. Peterson, Ph.D.**
Human Resources Manager
American Telephone and Telegraph Company
Basking Ridge, New Jersey
WORK, CONCEPT AND IMPLICATIONS

**Victor H. Pooler, P.E., C.P.M.**
Director of Purchasing
Carrier Air Conditioning Group
Carrier Corporation
Syracuse, New York
PURCHASING MANAGEMENT

**Avner M. Porat, Ph.D.**
Partner
Hay Associates
Management Consultants
Philadelphia, Pennsylvania
COMPENSATION, SALES

**Walter J. Primeaux, Jr., Ph.D.**
Professor of Business Administration
College of Commerce and Business Administration
University of Illinois at Urbana
Urbana, Illinois
PROFITS AND PROFIT MAKING

**Harold F. Puff, D.B.A., C.P.M.**
Professor of Management
School of Business Administration
Miami University
Oxford, Ohio
COST IMPROVEMENT

**Reverend Theodore V. Purcell, S.J., Ph.D.**
Research Professor
Jesuit Center for Social Studies
Georgetown University
Washington, D.C.
MINORITIES, MANAGEMENT OF AND EQUAL EMPLOY-
MENT OPPORTUNITY

**Inez L. Ramsey, M.L.S.**
Department of Library Science and Educational
Media
James Madison University
Harrisonburg, Virginia
INFORMATION SEARCH

**Jackson E. Ramsey, Ph.D., P.E.**
Associate Professor and Director of the MBA Pro-
gram
School of Business
James Madison University
Harrisonburg, Virginia
LEARNING (EXPERIENCE) CURVES

**Peter A. Rechnitzer, M.D.**
Clinical Professor of Medicine
University of Western Ontario
London, Canada
HEALTH, EXECUTIVE, MANAGING STRESS AND JOB
TENSION

**Larry D. Redinbaugh, Ph.D.**
Associate Professor
University of Montana
Graduate School of Business
Malmstrom Air Force Base, Montana
RETAILING MANAGEMENT

**Robert Redinger**
Graduate School of Industrial Administration
Carnegie-Mellon University
Pittsburgh, Pennsylvania
CONSUMER BEHAVIOR, MANAGERIAL RELEVANCE OF

**Frank K. Reilly, Ph.D., C.F.A.**
Professor of Finance
College of Commerce and Business Administration
University of Illinois at Urbana
Urbana, Illinois
MARKETS, SECURITIES; MARKETS, STOCK INDICATOR
SERIES

**James W. Rice, Ph.D.**
Associate Professor
College of Business Administration
University of Wisconsin–Oshkosh
Oshkosh, Wisconsin
PRODUCTION PLANNING AND CONTROL

**Wallace J. Richardson**
Professor of Industrial Engineering
Department of Industrial Engineering
Lehigh University
Bethlehem, Pennsylvania
WORK SAMPLING

**J. Robin Roark, Ph.D.**
Partner
Hay Associates
Management Consultants
Philadelphia, Pennsylvania
WAGES AND HOURS LEGISLATION

**Ralph W. Rogers, CMC**
President
Rogers & Company, Strategic Planning
Greenwich, Connecticut
MARKETING MANAGEMENT

**J. Wesley Rosberg**
Senior Vice-President, Marketing Services
Meldrum and Fewsmith, Inc.
Cleveland, Ohio
MARKETING RESEARCH

**Stuart Rosenthal, M.S., M.D.**
Associate, The Levinson Institute
Cambridge, Massachusetts
Associate Clinical Professor of Psychiatry
Tufts University School of Medicine
Boston, Massachusetts
HEALTH, MENTAL

**Joel E. Ross, D.B.A.**
Professor of Management
Florida Atlantic University
Boca Raton, Florida
INFORMATION SYSTEMS, MANAGEMENT (MIS)

**Carol A. Ruth**
Vice-President
Hill and Knowlton, Inc.

Public Relations/Public Affairs Counsel
New York, New York
SHAREHOLDER RELATIONSHIPS

**Burt K. Scanlan, Ph.D.**
Professor of Management
College of Business Administration
University of Oklahoma
Norman, Oklahoma
YOUNGER EMPLOYEES, MANAGEMENT OF

**Fred L. Schmidt**
Safety Manager
Bristol-Myers Company
New York, New York
SAFETY AND HEALTH MANAGEMENT, EMPLOYEE

**Rockwell Schulz, Ph.D.**
Associate Professor, Preventive Medicine
Director, Program in Health Services Administration
Center for Health Sciences
University of Wisconsin
Madison, Wisconsin
HEALTH SERVICES, PLANNING FOR

**Donald P. Schwab, Ph.D.**
Professor of Business and Industrial Relations
Graduate School of Business and Industrial Relations Research Institute
University of Wisconsin
Madison, Wisconsin
MOTIVATION IN ORGANIZATIONS

**Eleanor Brantley Schwartz, D.B.A.**
Associate Dean
The James J. Nance College of Business Administration
Professor of Marketing
Cleveland State University
Cleveland, Ohio
WOMEN IN INDUSTRY; WOMEN IN MANAGEMENT

**Rex A. Sebastian**
Senior Vice-President, Operations
Dresser Industries, Inc.
Dallas, Texas
INTERNATIONAL OPERATIONS AND MANAGEMENT IN MULTINATIONAL COMPANIES

**Robert E. Seiler, Ph.D.**
Professor and Chairman, Department of Accounting
College of Business Administration
University of Houston
Houston, Texas
ACCOUNTING FOR MANAGERIAL CONTROL

**Robert E. Shannon, Ph.D.**
Professor
School of Science and Engineering
Department of Industrial and Systems Engineering
University of Alabama
Huntsville, Alabama
OPERATIONS RESEARCH AND MATHEMATICAL MODELING

**Jagdish N. Sheth, Ph.D.**
I.B.A. Distinguished Professor and Research Professor
College of Commerce and Business Administration
University of Illinois at Urbana-Champaign
Urbana, Illinois
CONSUMER BEHAVIOR, MANAGERIAL RELEVANCE OF

**Robert A. Shiff, M.A., C.M.C., C.R.M.**
President
Naremco Services, Inc.
Management Consultants
New York, New York
RECORDS MANAGEMENT

**Julian L. Simon**
Professor of Economics and Marketing
College of Commerce and Business Administration
University of Illinois
Urbana, Illinois
PROFITS AND PROFIT MAKING

**E. Ralph Sims, Jr., P.E., C.M.C.**
President
E. Ralph Sims, Jr. and Associates, Incorporated
Consulting Industrial Engineers/Management Consultants
Lancaster, Ohio; London, England
MATERIALS MANAGEMENT

**George L. Sing**
EMDEX, Division of Exxon Enterprises, Inc.
Milford, Connecticut
AUDIT, MANAGEMENT

**Bernard R. Siskin, Ph.D.**
Professor
Temple University
Philadelphia, Pennsylvania
STATISTICAL ANALYSIS FOR MANAGEMENT

**Alice Smith**
Business Writer and Editor (Annual Plant Engineering Conference Techniques; Ernest Dale's *Readings in Management: Landmarks and New Frontiers;* and various American Management Associations publications)
New York, New York
(contributor of selected definitions)

# Contributors

**C. Ray Smith**
Professor and Associate Dean
The Colgate Darden Graduate School of Business
    Administration
University of Virginia
Charlottesville, Virginia
BUDGETING, CAPITAL

**William A. Smith, Jr., D. Eng. Sc., P.E.**
Head, Department of Industrial Engineering
North Carolina State University
Raleigh, North Carolina
SYSTEM CONCEPT, TOTAL

**Edwin H. Sonnecken**
Vice-President, Corporate Business Planning
The Goodyear Tire and Rubber Company
Akron, Ohio
BRANDS AND BRAND NAMES

**Rajendra K. Srivastava**
Assistant Professor
Department of Marketing Administration
Graduate School of Business
University of Texas at Austin
Austin, Texas
MARKET ANALYSIS

**Steven J. Stanard, Ph.D.**
Personnel and Management Consulting
Chicago, Illinois
TESTING, PSYCHOLOGICAL

**Thomas C. Stanton, D.B.A.**
Vice-President for Academic Affairs
James Madison University
Harrisonburg, Virginia
ACCOUNTING, FINANCIAL

**George A. Steiner, Ph.D.**
Professor of Management and Public Policy
Director, Center for Research and Dialogue on
    Business in Society
Graduate School of Management
University of California
Los Angeles, California
PLANNING, STRATEGIC MANAGERIAL

**Lawrence L. Steinmetz, Ph.D.**
President
High Yield Management, Inc.
Boulder, Colorado
DELEGATION

**David C. Stewart, P.E., P.C.M.M.**
President
Carlisle Engineering Management, Inc.
Carlisle, Massachusetts
FACILITIES AND SITE PLANNING AND LAYOUT

**Morris Stone**
Vice-President and Editorial Director
American Arbitration Association
New York, New York
ARBITRATION, COMMERCIAL; ARBITRATION, LABOR

**Paul J. Stonich**
Senior Vice-President
MAC, Inc., Management Analysis Center
Northbrook, Illinois
BUDGETS AND BUDGET PREPARATION

**Richard J. Stull, F.A.C.H.A.**
President
American College of Hospital Administrators
Chicago, Illinois
HOSPITAL ADMINISTRATION

**C. Ian Sym-Smith**
General Partner
Hay Associates
Management Consultants
Philadelphia, Pennsylvania
COMPENSATION, SALES

**Daniel A. Tagliere**
President
Organization Development Services, Inc.
Chicago, Illinois
ORGANIZATION DEVELOPMENT (OD)

**Robert L. Taylor, D.B.A., Lt. Col., U.S.A.F.**
Tenure Associate Professor
Department of Economics, Geography, and Man-
    agement
United States Air Force Academy, Colorado
PROGRAM PLANNING AND IMPLEMENTATION

**Weldon J. Taylor, Ph.D.**
Professor of Marketing
Dean Emeritus, College of Business
Brigham Young University
Provo, Utah
MARKETING, CHANNELS OF DISTRIBUTION

**Frederick A. Teague, C.M.C.**
Vice-President
Booz·Allen and Hamilton, Inc.
Chicago, Illinois
JOB ANALYSIS; JOB EVALUATION

**L. Ruth Thomas, Ph.D.**
Management Information Officer
United States Immigration and Naturalization Ser-
    vice
Washington, D.C.
Formerly Chief, Standards Developing Branch
National Archives and Records Service
WORD PROCESSING

**Curtis J. Tompkins, Ph.D.**
Professor and Chairman
Department of Industrial Engineering
West Virginia University
Morgantown, West Virginia
FORECASTING BUSINESS CONDITIONS

**Paul E. Torgersen, Ph.D.**
Dean, College of Engineering
Virginia Polytechnic Institute and State University
Blacksburg, Virginia
SIMULATIONS, BUSINESS AND MANAGEMENT

**Benjamin B. Tregoe, Ph.D.**
Chairman
Kepner-Tregoe, Inc.
Organization Development and Research
Princeton, New Jersey
DECISION-MAKING PROCESS

**Joseph M. Trickett, Ph.D.**
Professor of Management
Graduate School of Business and Administration
University of Santa Clara
Santa Clara, California
AUTHORITY, RESPONSIBILITY, AND ACCOUNTABILITY

**Jon A. Turner**
Director of Advanced Systems
University Center for Computing Activities and
Adjunct Assistant Professor, Graduate School of
   Business
Columbia University
New York, New York
COMPUTER SYSTEMS

**Jerome J. Vallen, Ph.D.**
Dean, College of Hotel Administration
University of Nevada
Las Vegas, Nevada
HOSPITALITY MANAGEMENT

**Walter Bernhard Waetjen, Ed.D.**
President
Cleveland State University
Cleveland, Ohio
WOMEN IN MANAGEMENT

**Loren E. Waltz, D.B.A.**
Professor of Business Administration and
Director, Management Development Programs
Division of Business and Economics
Indiana University
South Bend, Indiana
SOCIETIES, PROFESSIONAL

**A. John Ward**
President
Management Research and Planning, Inc.

Management Counsel–Marketing Research
Evanston, Illinois
MARKETING, INDUSTRIAL

**David Warren, C.P.C.U.**
Warren, McVeigh and Griffin
Risk Management Consultants
San Francisco, California
INSURANCE AND RISK MANAGEMENT

**Howard Way**
Howard Way and Associates, Inc.
Consultant, Warehousing and Physical Distribution
   Management
Editor, *Distribution/Warehouse Cost Digest*
Alexandria, Virginia
INVENTORY CONTROL, PHYSICAL AND STOCKKEEPING

**Norman Weissman**
President
Ruder and Finn, Inc.
New York, New York
PUBLIC AND COMMUNITY RELATIONS

**Suzanne Welborn**
Environmental Policy Analyst
U.S. Department of Energy
Washington, D.C.
COMMUNITY PLANNING LEGISLATION

**Merle T. Welshans, Ph.D.**
Vice-President, Finance
Union Electric Company
St. Louis, Missouri
FINANCIAL MANAGEMENT

**Robert M. Wendlinger**
Assistant Vice-President–Communications
Bank of America
San Francisco, California
COMMUNICATIONS, EMPLOYEE

**J. Fred Weston, Ph.D.**
Professor of Managerial Economics and Finance
Graduate School of Management
University of California
Los Angeles, California
FINANCIAL STATEMENT ANALYSIS

**George M. Whitmore, Jr.**
Vice-President and Director
Cresap, McCormick and Paget, Inc.
Management Consultants
New York, New York
AUDIT, MANAGEMENT

**David A. Whitsett, Ph.D.**
Associate Professor of Psychology
Department of Psychology

University of Northern Iowa
Cedar Falls, Iowa
WORK DESIGN, JOB ENLARGEMENT, JOB ENRICHMENT,
  JOB DESIGN, AND AUTONOMOUS WORK GROUPS

**George W. Wilson, Ph.D.**
Professor of Economics and Business Administration
Graduate School of Business
Indiana University
Bloomington, Indiana
ECONOMIC SYSTEMS

**Bruce J. Wright**
Manager
Systematics, Inc.
Salt Lake City, Utah
DATA PROCESSING PRINCIPLES AND PRACTICES

**Gerald Zaltman, Ph.D.**
Albert Wesley Frey Professor of Marketing
Graduate School of Business
University of Pittsburgh
Pittsburgh, Pennsylvania
MARKET ANALYSIS

**Carle C. Zimmerman, Jr., Ph.D.**
Denver Research Center
Marathon Oil Company
Littleton, Colorado
RESEARCH AND DEVELOPMENT MANAGEMENT

**D. Kent Zimmerman, M.B.A.**
School of Business
James Madison University
Harrisonburg, Virginia
POWER AND INFLUENCE

# A

**ABC analysis** (*See* INVENTORY CONTROL, PHYSICAL AND STOCKKEEPING; INVENTORY CONTROL, PURCHASING AND ACCOUNTING ASPECTS; PRODUCTION PLANNING AND CONTROL.)

**Ability tests, general** (*See* TESTING, PSYCHOLOGICAL.)

**Absence** (*See* PERSONNEL ADMINISTRATION.)

**Acceptance, product** (*See* QUALITY MANAGEMENT.)

**Acceptance financing** (*See* FINANCIAL MANAGEMENT, SHORT-TERM, INTERMEDIATE, AND LONG-TERM FINANCING.)

**Accident prevention programs** (*See* SAFETY AND HEALTH MANAGEMENT, EMPLOYEE.)

**Accident reports** (*See* SAFETY AND HEALTH MANAGEMENT, EMPLOYEE.)

**Accountability** (*See* AUTHORITY, RESPONSIBILITY, AND ACCOUNTABILITY.)

**Accountability, true and accurate** (*See* TAX MANAGEMENT, MANAGERIAL RESPONSIBILITY FOR FEDERAL INCOME TAX REPORTING.)

## Accounting, cost analysis and control

What is generally called cost accounting serves two fairly distinct purposes. Confusion of these purposes can lead to using inappropriate information in decision making and uneconomic decisions. Two illustrations will suffice. Your accountants report that the average cost per unit of a product produced in the month of July is $4, while in the month of July last year the cost was $4.50. Does this mean that production has been more efficient this year than last? Not necessarily. In another company, accountants report that the average cost of producing a subassembly is $15 per unit, while the purchasing department reports that the identical subassembly can be purchased from a subcontractor for $11 per unit. Does this mean that the subassembly

1

should be purchased from the subcontractor rather than produced internally? Not necessarily. Both cases illustrate situations in which information produced for one purpose might be used for another inappropriate purpose.

**Domain of Cost Accounting** The two distinct areas served by cost accounting are sometimes called cost finding and management accounting. *Cost finding* was originally the sole interest of cost accounting. Its purpose is to calculate the average cost per unit of products produced by a manufacturer. The accounting rules for determining the average cost per unit are established to facilitate preparation of income statements and balance sheets. Generally accepted accounting principles require that inventories be reported on the basis of their cost. When the same units are sold, they are reported in the income statement as cost of goods sold at this same cost. In a manufacturing organization, this cost must be determined by an averaging process which satisfies generally accepted accounting principles.

*Management accounting* is the newer interest of cost accounting. Its purpose is to provide managers with information which aids decision making. There are no generally accepted principles which specify how management accounting information is to be reported. While systems such as direct costing and standard costing exist in management accounting, each accounting report should be tailored to the needs of the decision and the decision maker. The most effective systems result when the manager–decision maker and the accountant work together until the accountant understands the decision to be made and the manager understands the source of the information that the accountant will report.

## COST-VOLUME RELATIONS

The relation of total cost to volume of operations has its most important application in management accounting, but is also used in cost finding. It is important in management accounting because managers frequently face decisions involving changes in volume of operations (along with other changes). To determine the profit impact of a decision, it is necessary to predict the resulting changes in cost level. This requires knowledge of existing cost-volume relations. As will be noted in the discussion of cost finding, a predetermined overhead rate (burden rate) can be calculated only after the total amount of overhead cost for the year has been predicted. Since the volume of output is important to the amount of variable costs which should be expected, it is neces-

sary to know the cost-volume relation to predict the total amount of overhead cost.

The relation of cost to volume generally falls into two categories, fixed and variable, explained below. Other possibilities exist, and the most important one—semivariable costs—will also be discussed.

**Fixed Costs** A fixed cost is one for which the total amount of the cost per period is independent of the volume of operations, within a relevant range of volume. Graphically, it can be shown as indicated in Fig. A-1. The graph shows that as the volume of operations fluctuates within the relevant range, as

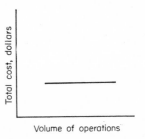

Fig. A-1. Graph of a fixed cost.

shown by the length of the line, the total amount of this expense, as measured on the vertical scale, remains constant. Examples include, among many others, the salary of the factory manager, property taxes, and insurance on the factory building and equipment. Note that the definition does not say that a fixed cost will not change. Managers know that salaries, taxes, and insurance do change. The significant point is that the amount of the fixed cost is not directly changed by changes in volume. It would be most unusual, for example, if a factory manager's salary were to fluctuate from month to month based on the production volume of the factory. (If this were to happen, the salary would no longer be an example of a fixed expense.) If there is a significant expansion of the factory capacity, the factory manager's salary might be increased at the next salary review. In addition, the expansion of factory capacity would probably increase the amount of insurance and taxes. However, these changes would not make these costs variable costs. Rather, the amount of cost would have changed from one fixed level to another fixed level. The new line on the graph would be higher than the old line, but it would still be horizontal. If this were to happen, management would have to replan a variety of activities and also alter the overhead rate used in this factory.

**Variable Costs** A variable cost is one in which the total amount varies in direct proportion to the volume of operations but where the per unit cost remains constant within a relevant range. This can be illustrated as shown on the graph in Fig. A-2. To

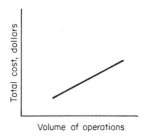

Fig. A-2. Graph of a variable cost.

meet this rather strict definition, the line of the variable cost must be pointed so that it would pass through the origin of the graph (0,0), if the relevant range extended that far back. A prime example of a variable cost is raw materials used in the production of a product. Increasing production by 10 percent will increase the amount of raw materials used by 10 percent. Further, one should expect that a reduction in volume of operations by, say 15 percent, would reduce the amount of raw materials required by 15 percent. This is because the amount of raw materials used per unit of product is constant.

The idea of a relevant range is important because experience probably tells a person that if a manager were to consider doubling volume or cutting volume by two-thirds, cost levels might change in a somewhat erratic manner. But such large changes are the exceptions; dealing with them requires a special study. In the normal situation, managers have found that costs can be expected to fluctuate in a predictable manner within the relevant range in which most decisions are made.

**Semivariable Costs** If a cost increases as a result of volume changes, it cannot, by definition, be a fixed cost. But there are instances where a cost would increase as a result of volume changes but would not fit the rather strict definition of variable cost. Maintenance cost or electricity cost would be likely examples. These costs often fall into the category of semivariable costs. Within the relevant range, a semivariable cost will increase as a result of changes in the volume of operations but not in direct proportion to volume. A graph of a semivariable cost is shown in Fig. A-3. Note that the line slopes upward as volume increases but that it would not

extend back through the origin if the relevant range extended back that far.

Semivariable costs present no new problems in analysis, however, because they can be broken into a fixed component and a variable component. This can probably be most easily seen by referring to the graph in Fig. A-4. The graph is the same as Fig. A-3 except that the dashed line is added to illustrate that the semivariable cost can be thought of as a variable

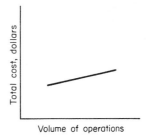

Fig. A-3. Graph of a semivariable cost.

cost with a fixed amount added on top. The dashed line shows the variable-cost component. The amount added on top is a fixed amount, the same at all volumes, thus fitting the definition of a fixed cost. For analysis, a semivariable expense is broken into its fixed and variable components.

Considering the examples of maintenance and

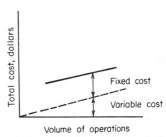

Fig. A-4. Graph of a semivariable cost showing fixed and variable components.

electricity, one can understand why a fixed and variable component would exist. The routine preventive maintenance is the fixed component. The balance of the maintenance could be expected to increase or decrease as the volume of operations resulted in greater or less use of the machines. Electricity used in lighting would likely be a fixed cost. The plant must be lighted whether it operates at 70 percent capacity or 80 percent capacity, the lighting cost does not vary with volume. The electricity used to power the machines, however, could be expected to increase or decrease as the volume of operations resulted in greater or less use of the machines. Thus the total electricity cost would have a fixed and variable component and therefore be a semivariable cost.

## COST FINDING

One of the important generally accepted accounting principles (*See* ACCOUNTING, FINANCIAL.) is that assets, including inventories, shall be reported at their cost. As the inventory items are sold, the inventory asset account is reduced by the cost of the item sold, and that cost is reported in the income statement as an expense, cost of goods sold. For a retailing or wholesaling firm, the inventory cost can generally be taken from a purchase invoice, adjusted for transportation costs to the warehouse and perhaps some minor preparation costs. In other words, determining the cost of inventory items (and the subsequent cost-of-goods-sold expense) is relatively easy. But in a manufacturing concern, raw material is purchased and converted through the use of production labor, supplies, equipment, plant facilities, supervision, etc., into the finished inventory ready for sale. The cost of the finished-goods inventory cannot be determined by referring to a purchase invoice. Many other items are a part of the cost. The major task of cost finding is to take the total pool of manufacturing costs and find an average cost of each unit of product produced.

The determination of the average cost per unit is done as follows: The total costs of operating the production facility for a month or year are determined. If a single product is produced, the total number of units produced is also counted. The average cost per unit is calculated by dividing the total cost by the total number of units. In other words,

Average cost per unit

$$= \frac{\text{total product costs for the period}}{\text{total units produced during the period}}$$

**Cost Definitions**   For a single product company the only serious problem in determining the average cost per unit is distinguishing between product costs and period costs. By looking at the formula above, to obtain the average cost per unit, only product costs are divided by units produced. Of course most manufacturing organizations produce more than one product, and so they have other problems in cost finding. But all firms must distinguish between product and period costs.

*Product Costs.*   Certain costs are physically traceable to a product and are generally agreed to be a part of the cost of the product. The major examples of these product costs are raw materials and direct labor. *Raw materials* are the materials incorporated into the product. They may be basic materials like steel, sand, and ore, or they may be sophisticated subassemblies such as engines and computer modules. In like manner, some production labor is performed directly on the product (perhaps using machinery and equipment). Direct labor is also physically traceable to the product since one can observe and time the work done on a particular product. Thus *direct labor* is that production labor which is performed directly on the product and which can be observed being performed on the product.

Supplies, electricity, heating of the plant, and property taxes and insurance on the plant and equipment are examples of the production costs and are included as part of the average cost of a product. Any cost incurred solely because the firm is in manufacturing is a product cost.

*Period Costs.*   Costs which are not product costs are period costs. Period costs are *not* included in the average cost of the product produced; rather they are considered an expense in the income statement of the period. Generally speaking, period costs include the selling expenses and general administrative expenses. A wholesaler or retailer incurs selling expenses and general administrative expenses. Of course the nature and amount of selling and general administrative expenses depend on the nature of the company, its products, and how they are sold. But these types of costs are incurred by all businesses; therefore it cannot be argued that these costs are incurred solely as a result of being in manufacturing.

*Overhead Costs.*   One further definition is needed before the ideas of product and period costs can be summarized. Overhead costs are all product costs other than raw materials and direct labor. Notice that a rather special definition is applied. In general conversation, general administration such as sales management, credit management, customer billing, and similar items might be considered overhead. Not so in this definition. All these items are examples of period costs. They are not product costs and therefore are not overhead. Any organization, retail, wholesale, or manufacturing, would have them.

Schematically, the distinctions and definitions

just discussed can be illustrated as shown in Fig. A-5. The significance of the distinctions is that period costs are accounted for as income statement expense items for all retailers, wholesalers, and manufacturers. Product costs would not exist in a retailing or

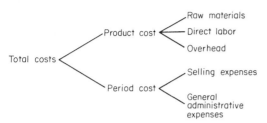

Fig. A-5. Relationships of various cost definitions.

wholesaling organization. For the manufacturer, they are added together and divided by the number of units produced during the period to determine the average cost per unit of manufactured product. This average cost per unit is first accounted for as an addition to the inventory asset account. When the product is sold, the inventory (asset) is reduced and the expense (cost of goods sold) is increased.

**Overhead Rates**  In the single product firm, the process of cost finding—determining the average cost per unit—consists of the following three steps:

1. Determine which of the costs incurred by the firm during a year are product costs.

2. Determine the number of units of product produced during the year.

3. Divide the total product costs for the year by the number of units produced.

But what if the company produces several products in a single plant? A new problem exists. The same three-step process cannot be followed because it does not make sense to add units of different products as if they were the same. For example, a company produces color and black-and-white television sets in the same factory. Further, there are several models of each type of television. If product costs were totaled and divided by the total number of television sets produced, all units would be found to have the same cost, a conclusion which is obviously erroneous. Each type and model uses some different parts, requires different direct labor time to produce, and makes use of some different facilities.

*Direct Measurement.*  How does cost accounting find a more reasonable answer? Since the raw material is physically incorporated into the product, it is possible to ask production workers to record the amount of material used in producing each model

and type of set. Also, the direct labor workers can be asked to record on their timecards the amount of time spent producing each model and type of set. If questions arise about the accuracy of either raw material or direct labor cost, it is possible to send someone into the factory to observe the production process and to record the material and direct labor going into each model and type of set. The resulting figures should agree with records kept by the production workers, since the raw materials are physically incorporated into the set and the direct labor is performed on a particular set. Although it requires some careful record-keeping, this is the easy part of the accounting process.

*Overhead Measurement.*  The accounting for the overhead, however, presents three different problems.

1. Most of the overhead costs will be incurred for the benefit of several or all the products rather than for a single product. There is no physical link to the product as there is in the case of raw materials and direct labor. It is plain that if the product is to be produced, the plant must be heated during the cold months of the year. The heating of the factory is a product cost and must be included in the average cost of the products produced. But the heat cost benefits not a particular set but all sets produced. There is no way of tracing the amount of heat going into each set as can be done with direct labor.

2. Many costs are cyclical. For example, the heating cost is seasonal. It will be incurred in cold months and not in warm months. But should physically identical sets which were produced in the month of January be said to cost more than the same set produced in June? The accounting answer is no. If the sets were produced in the same facilities, by the same methods, and with the same general level of production efficiency, accountants argue that the sets should have the same average cost. So the heat costs should be averaged over all sets produced during the year.

3. Much production is cyclical. This is similar to the seasonality problem but relates to the fact that the number of units produced from month to month will vary because of seasonal sales patterns. This presents no serious problems with raw materials and direct labor because these are usually variable costs, and the cost per unit is constant at any volume in the relevant range. Many overhead costs are fixed, however. What happens if the fixed total monthly costs are divided by varying monthly production totals? The average cost per unit varies from month to month for physically identical products. This is illustrated below.

| | June | September |
|---|---|---|
| Monthly total fixed costs | $35,000 | $35,000 |
| Monthly total production of sets | 10,000 sets | 14,000 sets |
| Average fixed cost per unit | $3.50 | $2.50 |

Again accountants argue that these cost variations should be averaged out in cost finding.

*Burden Rates.* All three problems are solved by use of predetermined overhead rates which average the fixed costs and serve as a basis for dividing common costs among different products. These rates are also called burden rates. A predetermined overhead rate is calculated and used as follows:

1. A decision is made to allocate the overhead in proportion to some base, often direct labor hours, direct labor cost, or machine hours. This decision solves the common cost problem.

2. The total expected production volume for the next year is estimated. The volume is converted to units of the base selected in step 1.

3. The total overhead cost to be incurred for the next year is estimated.

4. The predetermined overhead rate is determined by dividing the total estimated overhead cost for next year by the total estimated production volume, estimated in step 2. The annual estimates used in this step solve the seasonality problems mentioned earlier.

5. Overhead cost is applied to each product by multiplying the predetermined overhead rate times the amount of base (direct labor hours, etc.) contained in the product.

Here is an example of the process. Vinz Corporation produces three products. The expected material and labor content of each product is given below.

| | Product R | Product C | Product D |
|---|---|---|---|
| Materials | $11 | $8 | $17 |
| Direct labor @ $6 per hour | $3 (½ hour) | $4 (⅔ hour) | $6 (1 hour) |

For next year, Vinz estimates sales of R will be 18,000 units, C will be 15,000 units, and D will be 6000 units. It is further estimated that the fixed overhead costs will total $50,000 for the year. Variable overhead is estimated to be $5 per direct labor.

How is the predetermined overhead rate found? Management examines the nature of the overhead items and discovers that the largest part of the overhead consists of supervision, fringe benefits, and other personnel-related costs. Further, the accounting system is already recording and totaling

direct labor hours incurred. Thus management decides to base the predetermined overhead rate on direct labor hours. Had the production process been more automated and the overhead costs primarily machine-related costs such as property taxes, insurance, maintenance, and depreciation, management might have decided to base the overhead rate on machine hours. If there had been heavy components of both personnel-related costs and machine-related costs, management might have considered using two predetermined rates, one based on direct labor hours and the other based on machine hours. Most often a single rate is used.

The total production volume had already been estimated in units. All that was needed was to convert the volume estimate to direct labor hours, the base of the predetermined overhead rate. It was done as follows:

| Product R | 18,000 units @ ½ hour per unit | 9,000 hours |
|---|---|---|
| Product C | 15,000 units @ ⅔ hour per unit | 10,000 |
| Product D | 6,000 units @ 1 hour per unit | 6,000 |
| Total estimated volume for next year | | 25,000 hours |

Next the total overhead cost for next year was estimated as follows:

| Fixed overhead | $50,000 |
|---|---|
| Variable overhead 25,000 hours @ $5 per hour | 125,000 |
| Total estimated overhead for next year | $175,000 |

The predetermined overhead rate is then

$$\frac{\text{Total estimated overhead for next year}}{\text{Total estimated volume for next year}} = \frac{\$175,000}{25,000}$$
$$= \$7 \text{ per direct labor hour}$$

**Determining the Average Unit Cost** The Vinz Corporation example is used to complete the illustration of how the average cost per unit is calculated. During the first month of the new year, the company produced 1200 units of R, 1000 units of C, and 500 units of D. The raw materials used for each product were determined by totaling of requisitions from the raw materials storeroom. The direct labor cost incurred on each product was identified on time tickets prepared by the direct labor workers.

| | Product R | Product C | Product D |
|---|---|---|---|
| Raw materials used | $13,464 | $7,840 | $9,010 |
| Direct labor cost incurred | $3,852 (647 hours) | $4,200 (706 hours) | $3,013 (506 hours) |

(The reader who recalls the expected direct labor content given earlier in the entry may note that Vinz Corporation used more hours than should have been used for the number of units of products R, C, and D produced. Further, the average cost per direct labor hour was slightly below the expected rate. In a standard cost system—to be discussed later—these facts would give rise to an unfavorable direct labor price variance.)

The average direct labor cost and raw materials cost per unit are determined by dividing the total cost for each product by the number of units produced in the period. The overhead cost per unit is determined by calculating the overhead cost applied to each product during the first month and then dividing it by the number of units produced. The overhead cost applied is the predetermined overhead rate of $7 per direct labor hour times the number of direct labor hours spent on each product during the month.

Product R $7 per hour × 647 hours  =  $4529
Product C $7 per hour × 706 hours  =  $4942
Product D $7 per hour × 506 hours  =  $3542

The average cost per unit of product R is

| Raw materials $13,464/1200 units | = | $11.22 | per unit |
| Direct labor $3,852/1200 units | = | 3.21 | per unit |
| Overhead $4,529/1200 units | = | 3.77 | per unit |
| Average cost | | $18.20 | per unit |

In like manner, the average cost of the other two products produced in the first month is

| | Product C | Product D |
| --- | --- | --- |
| Raw materials | $7.84 | $18.02 |
| Direct labor | 4.20 | 6.03 |
| Overhead | 4.94 | 7.08 |
| Average cost | $16.98 per unit | $31.13 per unit |

**Standard Costs**  Standard costs are estimates of what the material, direct labor, and overhead cost per unit *should* be. They are often determined by adjusting past cost levels, as shown in the accounting records, for any inefficiencies discovered in discussions with production workers and production supervisors. Industrial engineering estimates, though expensive, are also helpful. Sometimes engineering estimates can be obtained as a by-product of designing or redesigning the product or designing the production process.

In the initial Vinz Corporation example, expected material and labor content of the products were given. They were not labeled as standard costs, but were in fact standard costs. A standard overhead cost per unit was not given, but it is usually included in the standard cost for completeness. The standard overhead cost per unit is determined by applying the predetermined overhead rate to the standard direct labor content in hours. Vinz' predetermined overhead rate is $7 per direct labor hour. The standard direct labor hour content of product R is ½ hour. Thus the standard overhead cost per unit of product R would be $3.50 (½ hour × $7 per hour). In like manner, the standard overhead cost per unit of product C is $4.67; of product product D, $7.

*Advantages.* The system for determining average cost, discussed prior to this section, could be referred to as an *actual cost* or *historical cost* system. The primary advantage of a standard cost system over an actual cost system is that the standard cost system with up-to-date standards produces variances which signal the possible need for corrective management action. Of course if the standards do not reflect attainable performance, the variances become mixed in meaning and difficult to interpret.

Another important advantage of the standard cost system is that it simplifies certain bookkeeping problems by recording all inventories at their standard cost rather than their actual cost. Actual costs will fluctuate from month to month because of variations in production efficiency. Because units are entering inventory at differing costs per unit, one must follow an inventory method such as first in, first out (FIFO) average, last in, first out (LIFO) average, or some other method. In a standard cost system, the ending inventories are determined by multiplying the number of units on hand times the standard cost per unit. The cost-of-goods-sold expense is determined by multiplying the number of units sold by the standard cost per unit.

These advantages of standard costs must be weighed against the cost of establishing the standards and updating them when significant changes in production methods or prices occur.

**Job Order Cost versus Process Cost Systems**  The discussions thus far have implicitly assumed that cost finding (either actual or standard costing) followed the process costing system. It has been assumed that the average cost per unit was determined by taking the product costs for a *period of time* and dividing them by the number of units produced during that *period of time*. While no great attention has been given to the appropriate period of time, most of the discussion has implied that the appropriate period of time for determining raw material and direct labor costs is a month. For overhead, the appropriate period of time has been implied to be a year (through the predetermined overhead rate). But the time period selected is arbitrary. A month was used in the discussion because it corresponds to the reporting cycle of many manufacturers. But occasionally a time period of a day, a week, a quarter, or a year is used for raw materials and direct labor. In a situation where a certain product is produced in a more or less continuous process, such as a production line, continuous molding, or mixing, there is no natural dividing line and a process cost system is applied.

In other production situations, products are produced in batches or jobs. A machine shop is a good example where an order may come in for 100 units of a certain machined piece. The production of the order or batch is scheduled, and the units are produced. The batches provide a natural basis for determining the average material and direct labor cost per unit. Materials requisitions show the quantity of raw material requisitioned for the batch of production. Timecards show the amount of direct labor spent on the batch. When the batch is completed, it is easy to count the number of good pieces which result (which might be slightly different from the 100 ordered, depending on spoilage). Then the average raw material cost is determined in the usual manner:

Average raw material cost per unit
$$= \frac{\text{total cost of raw material used for this batch}}{\text{total number of good units in this batch}}$$

The same approach can be followed for direct labor cost. The overhead cost is applied to the batch by using the predetermined overhead rate, and the average overhead cost per unit is then also determined by dividing the total overhead cost applied to this batch by the number of good units in the batch.

*Differences.* In a *job order cost system*, the average cost per unit is determined by taking the total product costs incurred in producing the *batch or job* and dividing them by the total number of good units in the batch or job. In a *process cost system*, the average cost per unit is determined by dividing the total product cost incurred for a *period of time* by the number of good units produced during that period of time. In other words, the differences between the systems is not very profound. If the product is produced in batches or jobs, then the batch or job is a convenient basis for calculating the average cost per unit. In a more or less continuous process, time is the most convenient basis for calculating the aver-

age cost per unit. Both job order and process costing can be done on an actual cost basis or a standard cost basis. Most complex manufacturing companies use both job order and process costing in different departments of the company, depending on the production process in that department. Further hybrid systems are often found.

## MANAGEMENT ACCOUNTING

The purpose of management accounting is to provide managers with information which aids decision making. It is convenient to classify management decisions into two categories: planning decisions and control decisions.

*Planning Decisions.* These are made at all levels but have the objectives of finding a course of action which is feasible and which also accomplishes organizational objectives. Feasibility implies that the plan is workable and that the organization has the resources to implement the plan. Since a major set of resources are financial resources, accounting information is useful in determining the feasibility of plans. Cash budgets, capital budgets, and projected balance sheets are examples of contributions which accounting can make to resource planning.

A major organizational objective is usually that some minimum level of profit be achieved. In a profit-directed organization, the achievement of a minimum profit is necessary to provide investors the incentive to invest in the company. A not-for-profit organization may seek to break even or to limit losses in various activities in order that funding sources will provide the resources necessary for the continuance of the organization. A symphony orchestra might anticipate operating at a loss during a year, but a loss which was twice the anticipated loss might make it impossible for the orchestra to continue. Outside funding is anticipated, but it is limited in amount, and careful planning may be necessary to limit the operating losses to levels which can be covered by donations. Thus profit planning is important to most organizations because one objective normally relates to achieving a specified level of profit (or loss). Accounting statements, including projected income statements, are important in this planning activity.

One profit-planning decision which frequently arises is whether to make or buy a component of a company product. The decisions to sell a by-product in its raw state or to process it further before selling are similar. Another decision is whether to sell existing products to private label merchandisers. A decision with major profit and resource implications is the addition of a new product line. Finally, the annual profit plan, incorporating the results of both continuing operations and new operations, is a significant part of the planning process in which management accounting plays a major role.

*Control Decisions.* These naturally follow the planning decisions. With a feasible plan developed which meets organizational objectives, management action is required to implement the plan. Accounting reports provide feedback for control to signal situations in which management action may be required. Control reports inform managers when activities which are part of their responsibility are deviating from the plan.

**Accounting in Planning Decisions** The focus of accounting here comes from the particular decision itself. The data to be reported should be relevant to the decision being considered. The only data relevant to a decision are those data which will change as a result of the decision. Any data which will not change as a result of a decision are not relevant to the decision and can be safely ignored in making the decision.

Suppose a company is in the business of making poster-size enlargements from ordinary-size photographs. They have an east and west sales location, but the processing equipment is at the east location and serves both locations. The company's annual volume is 1000 posters. The cost of making the 1000 posters is as follows:

| | |
|---|---:|
| Photographic paper and chemicals | $900 |
| Fixed annual rental of equipment | 400 |
| Insurance | 120 |
| Maintenance contract ($200 per year plus 10 cents per poster) | 300 |
| Total | $1,720 |

*Sales and Promotion.* Management is considering a promotional plan that might increase sales by 400 posters per year. The management accountant was asked to predict the increase in cost of making the posters. It was concluded that the relevant costs were the variable paper and chemical costs and the variable portion of the semivariable maintenance cost. Photographic paper and chemicals were estimated to be 90 cents per poster ($900/1000), and the variable component of the maintenance contract was noted to be 10 cents per poster. Thus the cost of making the posters would increase by $1 per poster, and the total cost of making the 1400 posters was predicted to increase by $400, to $2120. Management weighed these costs and the cost of the added promotion against the added sales revenue which

could be achieved and decided that the promotion would add to company profits.

*Facilities and Location.* At another time, the manager of the west location suggested that it would be convenient to have poster-making equipment at both locations. It was assumed that the number of posters to be made and sold would be unchanged. Since qualified operators were already available at both locations, the management accountant concluded that the relevant expenses were the fixed expenses of renting and insuring the added machine and the fixed component of a second maintenance contract. It was reasoned that the total paper and chemical usage would remain unchanged since the total number of posters to be produced would be unchanged. These variable costs would be incurred at two locations, but the total for the two locations would be the same as the total at the present single location. Thus the relevant cost increases were $400 per year additional machine rental, $120 per year additional insurance, and $200 per year fixed maintenance. Management decided that $720 per year was too much to pay for the convenience of having a machine at each location. It was suggested that if added sales could be generated by having two machines and providing quicker service, the decision could be reconsidered.

Notice that if the accountant had taken the cost-finding approach of determining the average cost per poster, the result would have been $1.72 per poster ($1720 total annual cost divided by 1000 posters per year). But the $1.72 per poster would not have been useful information for either decision. It is important not to confuse cost-finding information with management-accounting information.

**Accounting in Control Decisions** There are two key elements in accounting for control. First is responsibility accounting, and second is management by exception.

*Responsibility Accounting.* This requires that a manager's financial responsibilities be defined in advance. Any revenues, expenses, and assets which the manager is responsible for controlling must be identified. The management accountant then establishes a system of regular reports which show the planned results in one column, the actual results in an adjoining column, and the variances in a third column. The important point is that the report is tailored to the responsibilities of the particular manager. Items which are not the responsibility of the manager are generally not included on the report of that manager. The reason is that the report should focus the manager's attention on those items for which he or she is responsible.

*Management by Exception.* The variance column of the accounting control report accomplishes management by exception by indicating the items which have deviated from the plan. Managers usually add most to profitability by spending their control efforts on the exceptional items where variances have occurred.

*Application.* Probably the most widely applied accounting control reports are based on standard costs, and the following example will illustrate how a standard cost system is used to compute variances which are reported to the responsible manager. While a standard cost system produces variances for both raw materials and direct labor costs, the example will consider only direct labor cost since raw material variances are calculated in exactly the same manner.

There are only two reasons for an actual direct labor cost to exceed planned or standard direct labor costs. One is that the hourly rate paid for the direct labor was higher than the standard rate. The second is that the number of direct labor hours used were more than the standard allowed for the work done during the period. Since the type of management action called for might differ depending on which reason caused the variance, a standard cost system reports both a rate and a use variance.

The *rate variance* simply asks what the total dollar cost was of paying a higher than standard rate. Suppose that a standard allowed paying $5 per hour for labor in a certain department but that the rate actually paid was $5.30 per hour. Assume further that during the month in question 800 hours of labor were used. The direct labor rate variance would then be ($5.30 − $5.00) × 800 hours, or $240, unfavorable. In this month, the cost of paying 30 cents an hour above standard totaled $240 because 800 hours of direct labor were used. The variance was unfavorable because the actual rate exceeded the standard rate.

More information is needed to compute the *use variance*. Suppose that the standard allowed ¼ hour per unit of product produced, and accounting records show that 2800 units were produced during the month. According to the standard, 700 hours should have been used in producing 2800 units (2800 units × ¼ hour per unit). 800 hours were actually used, or an excess of 100 hours. The dollar cost is found by multiplying this excess by the standard labor rate; in this example $5 per hour times 100 excess hours equals $500. The standard suggests that this unfavorable labor use variance might have been avoided. The job of management is to find the causes of the variance and to seek means of avoiding a similar variance in the future.

*See also* ACCOUNTING FOR MANAGERIAL CONTROL; BUDGETS AND BUDGET PREPARATION; CONTROL SYSTEMS, MANAGEMENT; MARGINAL INCOME ANALYSIS; PRODUCT AND SERVICE PRICING.

### REFERENCES

Gray, Jack, and Kenneth S. Johnson: *Accounting and Management Action*, 2d ed., McGraw-Hill Book Company, New York, 1977.

Horngren, Charles T.: *Cost Accounting: A Managerial Emphasis*, 4th ed., Prentice-Hall, Inc., Englewood Cliffs, N.J., 1977.

Lynch, Richard M., and Robert W. Williamson: *Accounting for Management Planning and Control*, 2d ed., McGraw-Hill Book Company, New York, 1976.

Meigs, Walter B., Charles E. Johnson, and Robert F. Meigs: *Accounting: The Basis for Business Decisions*, 4th ed., McGraw-Hill Book Company, New York, 1977.

Moore, Carl L., and Robert K. Jaedicke: *Management Accounting*, 4th ed., South-Western Publishing Company, Incorporated, Cincinnati, 1976.

Shillinglaw, Gordon: *Cost Accounting Analysis and Control*, 4th ed., Richard D. Irwin, Inc., Homewood, Ill., 1977.

JACK GRAY, *University of Minnesota*

# Accounting, financial

Financial accounting identifies, classifies, records, and summarizes the monetary aspects of business transactions in a sufficiently systematic way to permit managers, investors, and creditors to measure and evaluate an entity's activities. Although double-entry bookkeeping was described as early as 1494 by the Franciscan friar Luca Pacioli, the most determinant force in the development of modern accounting was the industrial revolution and the use of the corporate form of organization that was occasioned by it. In the United States, some twentieth century influences have been (1) the growth in the government's tendency to tax economic activity and (2) the government's determination to regulate business.

Whether performed for a fifteenth century Italian merchant or for a twentieth century conglomerate, accounting deals with questions concerning the firm's stocks and flows of wealth. To answer the stock question, "What is the entity's financial position at a particular point in time?", a statement of financial condition, or a balance sheet, is prepared. To answer the flow question, "What profit (or loss) has the entity realized over some period of time?", a statement of income is prepared.

**Generally Accepted Accounting Principles** For these statements to have predictive value and to be otherwise useful to the decision makers for whom they are prepared, a body of knowledge has evolved concerning the standards, assumptions, measuring methods, and reporting procedures that the accounting profession will follow. Taken together, these are referred to as *generally accepted accounting principles* (GAAP), which by definition are principles that enjoy substantial authoritative support.

Under the securities laws of 1933 and 1934, the U.S. Congress empowered the Securities and Exchange Commission (SEC) to establish the accounting principles to be followed by companies issuing their securities to the public or having them traded on organized stock exchanges. For over a generation, the SEC chose not to use its powers and instead allowed the accounting profession to take the lead in establishing GAAP. The most influential voice of the profession during this period was the American Institute of Certified Public Accountants (AICPA), which prior to 1957 was the American Institute of Accountants (AIA). In the 1960s and especially in the 1970s, however, the SEC showed a growing willingness to direct a particular practice when the profession faltered or permitted wide areas of difference in GAAP.

Nevertheless, the work done by the AICPA through its Committee on Accounting Procedures, established in the mid 1930s, and subsequently by its Accounting Principles Board (APB), established in 1959 to advance the written expression of GAAP, has been substantial. Until it was superseded in 1973 by the Financial Accounting Standards Board (FASB), the APB issued 31 opinions and 4 statements and other letters and bulletins that served to shape the financial accounting profession. In spite of its success, the APB came increasingly under criticism from investors and the public at large because of the large number of alternatives allowed in the acceptable methods of accounting for business transactions. A significant criticism was that the APB was dominated by Certified Public Accountants who, according to some, gave inadequate weight to the full range of accounting problems confronting investors and managers.

In an attempt to correct the deficiencies expressed by these critics, the FASB was formed to include membership from business, government, and industry. Some of its work has dealt with clarifying previously issued APB opinions and extending the work that was done by this precedent body. In spite of its broader membership, the FASB was unable to avoid controversies similar to those that troubled the APB, thus giving evidence to the observation that accounting principles, being pragmatic as opposed to self-evident, will always be open to criticism.

**The Measurement Problem** Financial accounting is concerned with the application of GAAP to the analysis of economic transactions in a sufficiently consistent manner that an entity's stock of wealth, its flows of wealth, and the changes in the resulting obligations can be accurately measured and reliably reported. The problems associated with the efforts to make these measurements and to report the results of economic transactions can be appreciated through a description of two of the more important financial statements, the balance sheet and the income statement.

## BALANCE SHEET

The balance sheet reflects the fundamental accounting model which describes the financial position of a firm in terms of an equality between its assets on one side and its liabilities plus owner's equities on the other ($A = L + OE$). Hence, the balance sheet is a widely used term but is somewhat less descriptive than the more appropriate designation, statement of financial position.

*Assets* are economic resources and benefits owned by an entity, valued generally at acquisition cost less accumulated write-offs.

*Liabilities* are the debts of the entity and other claims against its assets which may oblige the firm to provide goods or services. Usually, liabilities are measured at their current cash equivalent or the maturity value of a debt.

*Owner's equities* are the residual amounts, $A - L = OE$, but bear little resemblance to the current market value of an entity.

The components of the fundamental accounting model are defined by GAAP, which in turn are defined by the accountants. Managers and investors, irked by this implied circularity, press for more realism in the measurement and reporting process. Nowhere is this pressure more intense than in the problem of accounting for the effects of inflation. For example, productive assets such as buildings, machinery, and other equipment have traditionally been carried on a firm's books at the acquisition cost less the accumulated depreciation to date.

**Inflation Accounting** Alternatives to this historical cost method have been proposed to account for inflation.

*Price level adjustments* can be made to balance sheet values by applying to them a price index designed to measure the impact of inflation on a firm's financial statements. Both the FASB and the SEC have examined this issue. The problem is dramatized by the separate directions taken by these two bodies; i.e., the FASB sought a solution in general price level adjustments (GPLA), while the SEC was concerned with the specific price changes. The FASB ap-

11

proach is the easiest for the accountant to take since it retains historical costs and makes adjustments based on changes in the purchasing power of the dollar, using readily available indexes such as the *GNP implicit price deflator* or the *wholesale price index*. But the GPLA may produce results as misleading as the historical cost method it seeks to improve since a particular company's experience may be totally unrelated to general trends in the economy. On the other hand, the SEC's approach deals with the firm's specific experience, but in so doing, it may risk a loss in objectivity and comparability.

*Replacement cost accounting*, as an alternative to historical cost accounting, addresses the problem from two slightly different views: (1) the cost of replacing the asset as such or (2) the cost of maintaining a comparable productive capacity. Dangers persist. Suppose a firm is using a converted castle for a garment factory. What is the cost of replacing the asset as such? How are the highly subjective assumptions for maintaining a productive capacity handled in industries experiencing rapid changes in technology? While there are no answers to these questions, the mere raising of them serves to explain the pressure accountants endure in attempting to cope with inflation accounting using this method.

*Current (fair) value accounting* has a conceptual potential for dealing with the problem of inflation accounting, even though its origin is found in legal proceedings where it is defined as an exchange price that a willing and well-informed buyer and an equally willing and well-informed seller would reach through negotiation. Theoretically, the best way to estimate the fair value of an asset is to calculate the *present value* of the net cash inflows attributable to the asset, using a discount factor that takes into account the effects of inflation as well as the time value of money and the asset's risks and rewards characteristics. That this method is not more widely used is due to the great difficulty involved in estimating future net cash inflows and the highly subjective nature of the choice of a rate at which these inflows should be discounted.

## INCOME STATEMENT

Accountants avoid using the word *profit* on the grounds that it applies so generally to a wide variety of concepts that precision is lost; e.g., profit for tax purposes is not defined the same as profit for internal decision making. This problem of definition can be illustrated with the economist and the accountant, both of whom agree with the fundamental idea that revenues minus costs equal profit ($R - C = P$).

The economist holds that a cost is that payment which keeps resources out of alternative employment; therefore, profit is the amount remaining after all costs (including opportunity costs) have been substracted from revenues. The accountant maintains that profit is determined on the basis of completed transactions; therefore, profit is the amount remaining after all verifiable costs have been subtracted from revenues.

The actual profitability of a firm can be determined by subtracting its net worth at inception from its net worth at termination. Owners and investors are not usually willing to wait such a long period of time to participate in the returns from their investments; therefore, financial accounting must attempt to measure net income, the designation preferred by accountants to the more general term *profit*, over a specific segment of time. This attempt necessarily introduces a degree of arbitrariness, but the measurement problem is handled by preparing an income statement that summarizes all transactions of revenue and expenses according to GAAP for a particular period of time, usually a business year ($R - E = NI$).

The first obstacle to income measurement is to determine when revenues and expenses are to be recognized. Basically, there are two methods.

1. The *cash basis* of accounting recognizes revenue and expenses when cash or some other assets are exchanged in completed transactions.

2. Under the *accrual method*, the *realization principle* is followed; i.e., revenues and expenses are recognized when goods are exchanged or when services are provided and the right to revenues is realized.

The next obstacle to income measurement lies in the difficulty in determining what expenses should be matched with what revenues during a period. For example, the calculation of cost of goods sold for a merchandising firm enjoying stable prices would be made by subtracting the ending inventory from the sum of the beginning inventory and the purchase of new merchandise during the period. Because prices are not stable, and because business conditions affect firms differently, GAAP allow certain assumptions to be made concerning the flow of inventories. In choosing from these alternative assumptions, the accountant considers their effects not only on a periodic net income but also on the inventory valuations remaining at the end of the period.

**Last In, First Out (LIFO)** This method assumes that goods most recently purchased will be sold first. During periods of rising prices, this method tends to match current revenues with the costs of replacing merchandise and, consequently, produces a more accurate income statement.

**First In, First Out (FIFO)**  This method assumes that the oldest goods in stock are sold first, an assumption that usually corresponds to reality. During periods of rising prices, however, this method produces inventory profits because current revenue is matched against costs that are below prices being paid for inventory replacements.

**Weighted-Average Method**  This method assumes that goods in inventory are so intermixed that stocks are withdrawn at random. Thus, the cost of goods sold is calculated first by stating inventories at average prices paid, weighted according to the quantity purchased at each price, and then subtracting the ending inventory from the cost of goods available for sale. Results produced by this method lie between those obtained by the LIFO and FIFO methods.

**Specific-Identification Method**  This method allows management to identify sales with specific purchases. While this method is essential and practical for high-cost items such as boats, cars, jewelry, and serially numbered items, it opens avenues for profit manipulation when applied to commodities and other goods that are comingled in inventories.

The third obstacle to income measurement involves distinguishing between income or losses obtained from normal operations and those caused by windfalls or disasters. Two fundamentally different approaches for dealing with this obstacle are possible.

1. The *all-inclusive concept of income*, holding to the view that income is the aggregate of all transactions affecting an entity's equity over a period of time, reports both recurrent and nonrecurrent operations as income.

2. The *current operating performance approach*, seeking to separate the normal earning power of the firm from its extraordinary gains and losses, reports only the results of recurrent operations on the income statement and makes direct adjustments to retained earnings for extraordinary items.

The APB's Opinion No. 9 of 1966 mandated the all-inclusive concept for reporting income but allowed for the segregation of extraordinary items from the results of normal operations on the income statement. In 1973, the APB issued Opinion No. 30 which made more stringent the conditions an event must satisfy to be regarded as extraordinary; i.e., it must be unusual in nature and not expected to recur in the foreseeable future. Under these rules, losses from an earthquake, since it is both unusual and

unforeseeable, would be an extraordinary item; devaluation of foreign currencies, unforeseeable but not unusual, would not qualify as extraordinary.

## CONCEPTUAL FRAMEWORK

The development of accounting has been characterized by pragmatism. The practice of dealing with single issues and the problems at hand has created a system of GAAP that lacks conceptual underpinnings. Contemporary problems created by conceptual deficiencies include the following areas troublesome to management.

*Accounting for Human Resources.*  Clearly, one of the most critical factors for the success of an enterprise is the personnel who work for it. These people represent a cost to the firm, a value to it, and an investment that it must maintain. Yet, financial accounting has not accepted the concepts needed to account for a firm's human resources.

*Income Tax Accounting.*  Governed by law rather than GAAP, income tax accounting presents some features that dramatize the need for a conceptual framework to support financial accounting.

*Accounting for Installment Sales.*  Tax laws allow dealers in personal property to spread income from their installment sales over the years in which collections are made. GAAP require revenues to be accounted for at the time the transaction is made.

*Investment Tax Credits.*  Accepting the idea of economics that investments in plants and equipment have an accelerator effect on the economy as a whole, Congress often includes provisions in tax laws to give businesses incentives to make these investments. Although the rate varies from time to time, the laws allow a percentage of the investment to be deducted from the firm's income taxes. How to account for this "gain" is an accounting problem. Two alternatives are available, either of which is permissible under current tax laws.

1. The *flow-through method* takes the view that the investment tax credit is intended to reduce taxes in the year of the investment only.

2. The *cost reduction method* holds to the position that it is the use, not acquisition, of assets that produces benefits to a firm; therefore, the investment tax credit is prorated over the productive life of the asset, and a proportionate amount is deducted from the taxes due each year.

While the FASB has taken the lead in developing a conceptual framework for accounting, the success of that undertaking depends on cooperation from all segments of society—business, industry, government, academia, and the professions.

See also ACCOUNTING, COST ANALYSIS AND CONTROL; ACCOUNTING; HUMAN RESOURCES (ASSETS); ACCOUNTING, WHOLE-DOLLAR; ACCOUNTING FOR MANAGERIAL CONTROL; ACQUISITIONS AND MERGERS; AUDITING, FINANCIAL; BUDGETS AND BUDGET PREPARATION; CONTROL SYSTEMS, MANAGEMENT; FINANCIAL MANAGEMENT; FINANCIAL MANAGEMENT, CAPITAL STRUCTURE AND DIVIDEND POLICY; FORECASTING BUSINESS CONDITIONS; INFORMATION SYSTEMS, MANAGEMENT (MIS), APPLIED; INVENTORY CONTROL, PURCHASING AND ACCOUNTING ASPECTS; LEASING, EQUIPMENT; MARGINAL INCOME ANALYSIS; PROGRAM PLANNING AND IMPLEMENTATION; RISK ANALYSIS AND MANAGEMENT; TAX MANAGEMENT, MANAGERIAL RESPONSIBILITY FOR FEDERAL INCOME TAX REPORTING.

### REFERENCES

Carey, John L.: *The Rise of the Accounting Profession*, 2 vols., American Institute of Certified Public Accountants, New York, 1969–1970.

Davidson, Sidney, and Roman L. Weil: *Handbook of Modern Accounting*, 2d ed., McGraw-Hill Book Company, New York, 1970.

*Federal Income Tax Course*, Commerce Clearing House, Chicago, issued annually.

Financial Accounting Standards Board, High Ridge Park, Stamford, Conn. 06905, *Financial Accounting Standards*, Commerce Clearing House, Chicago, August 1976.

Haase, Paul: *Financial Executives Institute: The First Forty Years*, Financial Executives Institute, New York, 1971.

Kohler, Eric L.: *Dictionary for Accountants*, 5th ed., Prentice-Hall, Inc., Englewood Cliffs, N.J., 1975.

THOMAS C. STANTON, *James Madison University*

# Accounting, human resources (assets)

Within the most recent decade, accountants, financial managers, personnel managers, and general managers have reflected a new and increasing interest in the subject of human resource accounting. A logical extension of the scope of enterprise accounting, it is the process of measuring and reporting the human dynamics of an organization. It is an assessment of the condition of human resources within an organization and a measurement of the change in this condition through time. It is also the method by which information about individuals and groups of individuals within an organization can be provided to both internal and external decision makers.

In *Accounting: The Language of Business* Davidson et al. define human resource accounting as "a term used to describe a variety of proposals that seek to report and emphasize the importance of human resources—knowledgeable, trained and loyal employees—in a company's earning process and total assets."[1] Human resource accounting involves the concept of human resources as assets, determines invested costs and related cost expirations, and in some instances estimates and provides surveillance over the economic value of the human organization.

**The Concept of Human Capital**  The concept of human capital, which is basic to human resource accounting at the enterprise level, is not of recent origin. Investment in human capital is considered in the writings of Adam Smith. As economists and other social scientists have sought to understand the nature and causal aspects of industrial growth, the human factor has been given increasingly greater recognition. The concepts of human capital have clear relevance for policy makers in the public sector, as evidenced by the numerous macro studies on the relative impact of various economic factors on human resources. On the national level, human capital is becoming an operational concept, but its use at the enterprise level is very much in its infancy.

**Historical Development**  Although the significance of human resources in organizations has long been recognized in management theory and practice, traditional accounting has limited itself largely to financial and physical resources. In 1964, suggesting that human resources constitute the most significant operational asset of most organizations, Hermanson[2] argued that financial statements would be more complete and more useful to managers and investors if they included such resources. Hekimian and Jones,[3] writing in the *Harvard Business Review* in 1967, emphasized the importance of human resources in the planning process and particularly in resource allocation decisions. Also in 1967, Likert published *The Human Organization: Its Management and Value*,[4] devoting one chapter to human asset accounting. Likert emphasized the importance of the human element in organizations and the significant failure of accountants to deal with it as an asset. Calling attention to the magnitude of this omission in corporate balance sheets, as indicated by large differences between market and book values of the owners equity in many corporations, he argued that managers make inappropriate decisions due to lack of information about the firm's human assets.

On a more operational level, Brummet et al.,[5] in 1968 and 1969, published several articles dealing with the ongoing assessment or an up-to-date monitoring of these resources; an integration of human resource accounting within the framework of the conventional accounting model.

The possibilities for human resource accounting may be dichotomized into historical cost-based approaches and replacement, or value-based, methods.

**Cost-based Human Resource Accounting** Techniques for cost-based human resource accounting are analogous to those for accounting for plant or other physical resources. They involve (1) recording of investments in human resources through a capitalization process; (2) recording of routine expirations of such capitalized items using an established amortization procedure; (3) recording of losses to recognize special expirations due to obsolescence of investments in certain skills or knowledge capabilities or the turnover of personnel; and (4) reporting or communicating to interested parties on the dynamics and condition of human resources in terms of investments therein. Figure A-6 shows the fundamental aspects and some of the classification possi-

bilities for a cost-level system. The two best-known examples of cost-based human resource accounting in practice are the R. G. Barry Corporation of Columbus, Ohio, and Touche Ross & Co. of Canada.

Historically cost-based accounting for human resources has serious limitations, just as it does for financial or physical resources. Ideally, a balance sheet should reflect the economic significance of an organization's assets and claims, and income measurement should assess the changes in these economic phenomena for specific time periods. In this setting cost-based human resource accounting suits the purpose only to the extent that cost inputs are fair representations of the economic significance of value. One can hardly claim any great validity of such a representation of human resources.

**Valuation Models** Numerous models have been suggested for use in estimating the value of human resources of an organization. These models involve

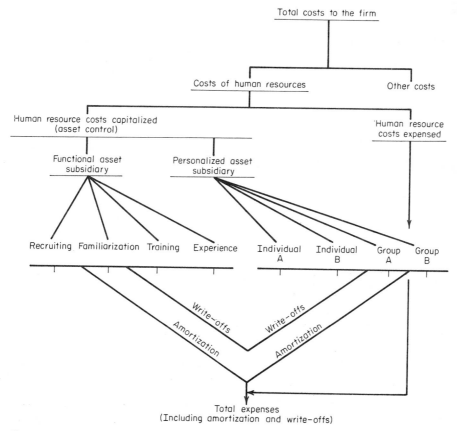

Fig. A-6. A generalized model of a cost-based human resource accounting system.

some similarities, but they do vary somewhat in both concept and in choice of surrogates.

Hermanson[6] suggests that the value of human resources of an organization may be assessed by capitalizing earnings in excess of normal earnings for the industry or group of companies of which the firm is a part. He calls the approach the unpurchased goodwill method.

Hermanson[7] also suggests the discounting of future compensation with an adjustment, using an efficiency ratio to determine the value of an individual.

Hekimian and Jones[8] propose a procedure by which profit center managers bid for the services of valuable employees of their divisions. The maximum bid would be used as the "value" of the individual, since it would represent the estimated current equivalent of the optimum use of the individual's services among the profit centers.

Lev and Schwartz consider the use of the economic concept of human capital in financial statements and conclude from Irving Fisher's theory that "capital is thus defined as a source of income stream and its worth is the present value of future income discounted by a rate specific to the owner of the source."[9]

In an early work, Brummet et al.,[10] suggest multiple measures of human resources, including an economic-value concept involving the forecasting of future earnings, the discounting of these forecasted future earnings, and the pro rata association of this amount with all assets, including human resources. This suggestion is similar to Hermanson's proposal but places human resources on a level with the other resources in their contribution to earnings rather than relating only an excess of normal earnings to human assets.

Flamholtz[11] visualizes the movement of individuals through different roles or positions in the organization as a stochastic process depending on prior roles or service states held by the individual in the system. This model, with some variations, has been operationalized at Lester Witte & Co., CPAs in Chicago, and is reported as a case study in some detail in the book by Caplan and Landekich.[12]

On a conceptual and theoretical level Flamholtz[13] has tried to identify the key variables that determine an individual's value to an organization and the interrelationships of such variables. He recognizes that these determinants may lend themselves to monetary or nonmonetary indicators. Drawing to some extent on his earlier work and on a limited field test with a major international firm of Certified Public Accountants, he has developed the model shown in Fig. A-7.

Most of the models suggested in the previous paragraphs emphasize the assessment of individual values to a firm and do not deal with the group or interactive process among people. Likert's[14] model is based on measured relationships among causal, intervening, and end-result variables to explain interactive conditions.

Myers and Flowers[15] propose a procedure for assessing the work force of an organization and estimating costs of various inputs to improve the effectiveness of the human organization. Dimensions of human assets are suggested to include knowledge, skills, health, availability, and attitudes. Assessments using checklists and subjective appraisal are suggested for measurement of the first four of these attributes, and perception surveys are used for an assessment of attitudes. Decisions, as a result of this procedure, should be based on cost effectiveness of each of the five dimensions.

With only minor exceptions the valuation models considered thus far emphasize human resource contributions to the firm, ignoring the costs to the firm of retaining such resources. From the proprietary viewpoint of the organization, this is inadequate. Ogan[16] proposes a model which includes explicit consideration of both the cost and benefit aspects of the value of human resources to an organization. The model is used to sum the discounted *certainty equivalent net benefits*.

Suggesting that a knowledge of the dynamics of human resource values in an organization is more important than a knowledge of an estimate of value at a particular point in time, Brummet and Taylor[17] propose the development of a human resource value index. The initial value of an organization's human resources may be estimated and then "tracked" with successive calculations of this human resource value index. This model may be used to assess human resources as currently allocated in an organization and readily lends itself to the application of optimization techniques to learn how personnel may be assigned better, and thus the cost of the present allocation may be determined.

**Integration of Cost-based and Value-based Systems** A clear analogy may be drawn between the problem of cost-based and value-based data for human resources and similar data for other resources included in the conventional accounting model. Value-based data defy, or at best strain, the facility of the conventional accounting model as an ongoing dynamic construct for the entity. Assessment of human resources and human resource value dynamics of an organization may, within the constraints of the conventional accounting model, take the form of periodic human resource inventory adjustment with the attendant limitations of lack of timeliness and certainty with which cause and effect relationships may be inferred.

Figure A-8 portrays this relationship. Conventional accounting systems assess the end-result phenomena captured in the current period and relate them to incomplete measures of investment dynamics information (a potential product of cost-based human resource accounting) and interspacing measures of human resource condition (a potential product of value-based human resource accounting). Concepts of return on investment may be refined, and concepts of return on human resource building investments and return on human resource utilization may be introduced into management thinking and, in turn, may make an impact on management decisions.

Table A-1 illustrates, in vastly simplified form, the substance of such possibilities within the con-

ventional accounting constraint. One may note that during the first quarter of 19X0, a new investment of $95,000 was made, while the estimated value of human resources increased $96,000, and book value write-offs amounted to $60,000. These figures account for the $61,000 increase of the excess of estimated value of human resources over their book value. By separating the representations that are cost-based and those that are value-based, readers are put on guard to make their own interpretations of each set of figures, based on a knowledge of the measurement techniques that produced them.

**HRA Information for Management Decisions**  The failure of organizations to capitalize certain investments in human resources causes profit to be significantly understated in periods of rapid human resource building and significantly overstated in periods of human resource deterioration. In this way managers, stockholders, and the public are

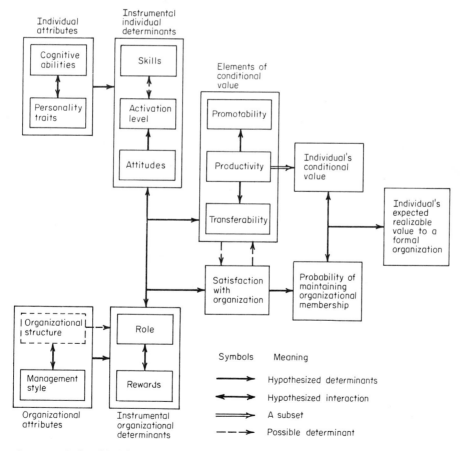

**Fig. A-7. Revised model of the determinants of an individual's value to a formal organization.**

# Accounting, human resources (assets)

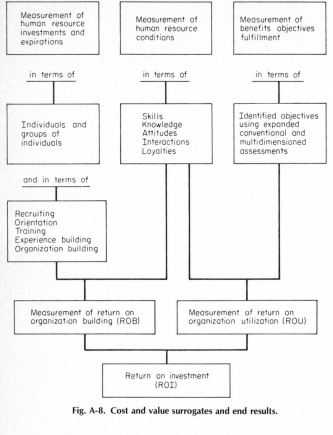

**Fig. A-8. Cost and value surrogates and end results.**

misled and perhaps caused to make counterproductive decisions. The dangers in this area are particularly great for segment performance reports using profit center accounting.

A significant aspect of performance measurement is the use of a return on assets or return on investment. Using human resource accounting this measure or performance index becomes

$$\frac{\text{(Conventional profit or profit contribution}}{\text{(Conventional assets or investment}} \\ \pm \text{ change in human resources)} \\ + \text{ human assets)}$$

Used as a critical measure, new decision areas are highlighted and different decisions may be made. An interesting possibility exists for intracompany "transfer pricing" of people. As individuals move from one segment to another, the asset bases of these calculations change so that responsibility heads are charged with or released from an incre-

**TABLE A-1  Example of Financial Statements That Incorporate Human Resources Accounting**

### EXAMPLE COMPANY
Balance Sheet, January 1, 19X0

| | | |
|---|---:|---:|
| Current assets | | $ 700,000 |
| Plant | | 1,300,000 |
| Investment in human resources | $500,000 | |
| Excess of estimated value over cost of human resources | 300,000 | |
| Estimated value of human organization | | 800,000 |
| TOTAL ASSETS | | $2,800,000 |
| Current liabilities | | $ 300,000 |
| Capital stock | | 1,000,000 |
| Retained earnings: | | |
| Financial, product, and plant resources | $700,000 | |
| Human resources—cost | 500,000 | |
| Human resources—additional value | 300,000 | 1,500,000 |
| TOTAL LIABILITIES AND CAPITAL | | $2,800,000 |

### EXAMPLE COMPANY
Income Statement, for Quarter Ending March 31, 19X0

| | | |
|---|---:|---:|
| Sales | | $2,000,000 |
| Expenses: | | |
| Depreciation of plant | $ 82,000 | |
| Human resource expenditures | 715,000 | |
| Other expenses | 913,000 | 1,710,000 |
| | | $ 290,000 |
| Income tax charges (48%) | | 139,200 |
| Income before recognizing investment on human resources. | | $ 150,800 |
| Additions to human resources | $ 95,000 | |
| Less: Amortization | $45,000 | |
| Write-offs | 15,000 | 60,000 |
| Net increase in investment in human resources | | 35,000 |
| Net increase in excess of estimated value of human resources over cost | | 61,000 |
| Income including investment in human resources | | $ 246,800 |

### EXAMPLE COMPANY
Balance Sheet, March 31, 19X0

| | | |
|---|---:|---:|
| Current assets | | $ 832,800 |
| Plant | | 1,318,000 |
| Investment in human resources | $535,000 | |
| Excess of estimated value of human resources | 361,000 | |
| Estimated value of human organization | | 896,000 |
| TOTAL ASSETS | | $3,046,800 |
| Current liabilities | | $ 300,000 |
| Capital stock | | 1,000,000 |
| Retained earnings: | | |
| Financial, product, and plant resources | $850,000 | |
| Human resources—cost | 535,000 | |
| Human resources—additional value | 361,000 | 1,746,800 |
| TOTAL LIABILITIES AND CAPITAL | | $3,046,800 |

mental amount of profit expectation. This practice could encourage more effective assignment and utilization of personnel.

The conventional practice of "expensing" all human resource expenditures has deterred managers from giving close scrutiny to these costs. Human resource accounting, when fully implemented, can give managers criteria for determining the optimum amount and mix of its human resource expenditures. This must involve measures of return on investments in recruiting, training, experience building, and other personnel areas and the related trade-offs. It can encourage managers to extend well-known capital budgeting procedures to human resource investments and to develop postaudit techniques to provide experience data for making new decisions.

One of the most usual concerns of personnel directors is employee turnover. Human resource accounting can assist by identifying unrecovered investments in exiting employees and by providing continuously updated cost information for those activities, such as recruiting and training, that are occasioned by personnel turnover. It can provide information that will assist in determining wage and salary and fringe benefit policies that may be appropriate to optimize the rate and nature of personnel turnover.

Human resource accounting can also help to bring under close surveillance the costs and results (benefits) of a personnel department. Cost and result standards may be set up for several activities of the personnel department and actual performance measured in relation to them.

**Impact on Management Concepts and Behavior** The conventional accounting model and the performance signals that it produces have come to influence, if not direct, managements' efforts to accomplish its objectives, particularly in the primary area of profitability. Accordingly the inclusion or exclusion within the accounting model of potential bits of information will condition the views of decision makers and affect the decisions made.

Managers tend to emphasize the maintenance of assets that are represented regularly on balance sheets as opposed to "off balance sheet" items. To the extent that this is true, human resource accounting may direct managers' attention and emphasis to the personnel of the organization and encourage maintenance and upgrading programs and experiences for this resource that might otherwise fail to be given consideration.

Further, human resource accounting is in itself a way of communicating to the people of an organization that their role is considered critical and that managers are going to be evaluated, at least in part, on the basis of their contribution to the development of the human resources under their control. If this communication is effective, it will certainly affect decisions and behavior.

The assessment of human resource conditions through either cost-based or value-based data should encourage managers to take a longer-run view of their decisions. The impact of human resource investments as well as other decisions and management styles are now represented as a human resource condition precedent to the ultimate productivity or effectiveness of the organization. Human resources become the first-order effect, and conventional profit or cash flows become the second- or third-order results.

Human resource accounting may provide a new basis for management thought and action. Wright observes that

a new way of thinking about the human resource is emerging. It is apparent that the reconceptualization of the only vital factor of production will have a profound impact on the way managers manage. The new set of concepts is coming as an outgrowth of the design of accounting systems adequate to measure the costs of human resources and to report manpower as a capital asset. Though of itself the revised accounting system will not improve the management of . . . people, it will provide substantive evidence of . . . their value and, therefore, act to emphasize that . . . each person *is a unique entity requiring individualized consideration.* [18]

**Implementation** The major problem in implementing a cost-based human resource accounting system may be one of cost justification since it is difficult, if not impossible, to justify the cost of any human resource accounting effort without some experimentation based on faith and conviction—a condition not uncommon in organization decision making.

The technical problems of value-based human resource accounting are substantial. Recognizing this, accountants and business managers may be expected to innovate with great caution. Neither the typical general manager nor the trained accountant has the measurement expertise to implement a value-based system. The technical aspects of the measurement practices should come from the psychologist, the psychometrician, and the behavioralist. An interdisciplinary effort is critical for success.

**Public Reporting and Attestation** Published corporate reports have begun to show increased emphasis upon personnel or human resource information, but dollar representations are very seldom reported. Some exceptions may be noted.

With apparent approval of its external auditors, Electronic Data Systems has reported the capitalization and related amortization of certain training costs.

Several professional athletic organizations have capitalized player development costs and purchased player contracts and have reported such amounts with related amortizations in their published reports.

In 1967, the Flying Tiger Line Inc. included in its published balance sheet an item, "initial training and preoperating costs." Although the company changed its practice in 1969, the capitalization of this item was part of an unqualified opinion by the external auditors.

Other companies such as Abt and Associates, Inc. and The R. G. Barry Corporation have integrated human resource accounting with their conventional accounting systems; however, the human resource data generated are currently not attested to by their external auditors.

Notwithstanding the various possibilities and the instances of usage that have been noted, there appears to be little prospect for the inclusion of human resource accounting as an integral part of generally accepted accounting principles within the next several years.

*See also* ACCOUNTING, COST ANALYSIS AND CONTROL; ACCOUNTING, FINANCIAL; COST-BENEFIT ANALYSIS; *Development and Training;* FINANCIAL STATEMENT ANALYSIS; PRODUCTIVITY.

## NOTES

[1]Sidney Davidson, Clyde P. Stickney, James S. Schindler, and Roman L. Weil, *Accounting: The Language of Business,* 2d ed., Thomas Horton and Daughters, Inc., Glen Ridge, N.J., 1975, p. 25.

[2]Roger H. Hermanson, *Accounting for Human Assets,* Michigan State University, Graduate School of Business Administration, Bureau of Business and Economic Research, Occasional Paper No. 14, East Lansing, Mich. 1964.

[3]James S. Hekimian and Curtis H. Jones, "Put People on Your Balance Sheet," *Harvard Business Review,* January–February 1967.

[4]Rensis Likert, *The Human Organization: Its Management and Value,* McGraw-Hill Book Company, New York, 1967.

[5]R. Lee Brummet, William C. Pyle, and Eric G. Flamholtz, "Accounting for Human Resources," *Michigan Business Review,* March 1968; R. Lee Brummet, Eric G. Flamholtz, and William C. Pyle. "Human Resource Measurement—A Challenge for Accountants," *The Ac-*

*counting Review,* April 1968; R. Lee Brummet, Eric G. Flamholtz, and William C. Pyle, "Human Resource Accounting: A Tool to Increase Managerial Effectiveness," *Management Accounting,* August 1969; R. Lee Brummet, William C. Pyle, and Eric G. Flamholtz, "Human Resource Accounting in Industry," *Personnel Administration,* July–August 1969; R. Lee Brummet, Eric G. FLamholtz, and William C. Pyle (eds.), *Human Resource Accounting: Development and Implementation in Industry,* Foundation for Research in Human Behavior, Ann Arbor, Mich., 1969.

[6]Roger H. Hermanson, op. cit., pp. 7–11.

[7]Ibid.

[8]James S. Hekimian and Curtis H. Jones, op. cit.

[9]Baruch Lev and Aba Schwartz, "On the Use of the Economic Concept of Human Capital in Financial Statements," *The Accounting Review,* January 1971.

[10]R. Lee Brummet et al., "Human Resource Accounting: A Challenge for Accountants," op. cit., pp. 222–223.

[11]Eric G. Flamholtz, "The Theory and Measurement of an Individual's Value to an Organization," Ph.D. dissertation, University of Michigan, 1969; "A Model for Human Resource Valuation: A Stochastic Process with Service Rewards," *The Accounting Review,* April 1971, pp. 253–267.

[12]Edwin H. Caplan and Stephen Landekich, *Human Resources Accounting: Past, Present, and Future,* National Association of Accountants, New York, 1974, pp. 109–120.

[13]Eric G. Flamholtz, *Human Resource Accounting,* Dickenson Publishing Company, Inc., Encino, Calif., 1974, pp. 168–169.

[14]Rensis Likert, *The Human Organization: Its Management and Value,* McGraw-Hill Book Company, New York, 1967; "Human Organizational Measurements: Key to Financial Success," *Michigan Business Review,* May 1971; with William C. Pyle, "A Human Organization Measurement Approach," *Financial Analysis Journal,* January–February 1971; with David G. Bowers, "Improving the Accuracy of P/L Reports by Estimating the Change in Dollar Value of the Human Organization," *Michigan Business Review,* March 1973.

[15]M. Scott Myers and Vincent S. Flowers, "A Framework for Measuring Human Assets," *California Management Review,* Summer 1974, pp. 5–16.

[16]Pekin Ogan, *A Human Resource Value Model and its Operationalization in a CPA Firm,* Doctoral Dissertation, University of North Carolina, 1974.

[17]R. Lee Brummet and Robert Taylor, "Human Resource Accounting—A Completed Model," from an unpublished work, University of North Carolina, Chapel Hill, N.C., 1974.

[18]Robert Wright, "Managing Man as a Capital Asset," *Personnel Journal,* April 1970, p. 290.

## REFERENCES

Alexander, Michael O.: "Investments in People," *The Canadian Chartered Accountant,* July 1971.

Brummet, R. Lee: "Accounting for Human Resources,"

*The Journal of Accountancy*, December 1970, pp. 62–66.

Brummet, R. Lee, William C. Pyle, and Eric G. Flamholtz: "Human Resource Accounting: A Tool to Increase Managerial Effectiveness," *Management Accounting*, August 1969, pp. 12–15.

Brummet, R. Lee, William C. Pyle, and Eric G. Flamholtz: "Human Resource Accounting: A Tool to Increase Managerial Effectiveness," *Management Accounting*, August 1969, pp. 12–15.

Brummet, R. Lee, William C. Pyle, and Eric G. Flamholtz: "Human Resource Accounting in Industry," *Personnel Administration*, July–August 1969, pp. 34–46.

Elias, Nabil S.: *Elias' Experimental Study of the Effects of Human Asset Statements on the Investment Decision*, Research Summary 8-1, University of Minnesota, 1969.

Flamholtz, Eric G.: *Human Resource Accounting*, Dickenson Publishing Company, Inc., Encino, Calif., 1974.

Flamholtz, Eric G.: "A Model for Human Resource Valuation: A Stochastic Process with Service Rewards," *The Accounting Review*, April 1972, pp. 148–152.

Flamholtz, Eric G.: "Towards a Theory of Human Resource Value in Formal Organization," *The Accounting Review*, October 1972, pp. 666–678.

Gambling, Trevor: "How to Put the Accounting into Human Resource Accounting," University College of North Wales, Bangor, Gwynedd, occasional paper presented at the Human Resource Accounting Seminar, European Institute for Advanced Studies in Management, Brussels, November 28–29, 1974.

Glautier, M. W. E.: "Human Resource Accounting: A Critique of Research Objectives for the Development of Human Resource Accounting Models," University College of North Wales, Bangor, Gwynedd, occasional paper presented at the Human Resource Accounting Seminar, European Institute for Advanced Studies in Management, Brussels, November 28–29, 1974.

Hermanson, Roger H., et al.: "Human Resource Accounting" supplement to *The Accounting Review*, 1973, pp. 169–184.

Jaggi, Bikki, and Hon-Shiang Lau: "Toward a Model for Human Resource Valuation," *The Accounting Review*, vol. 49, no. 2, pp. 321–329, April 1974.

Kiker, B. F.: "The Historical Roots of the Concept of Human Capital," *Journal of Political Economy*, vol. 74, no. 5, pp. 481–499, 1966.

Patten, Thomas H., Jr.: *Manpower Planning and the Development of Human Resources*, Wiley-Interscience, a division of John Wiley & Sons, Inc., New York, 1971.

Pyle, William C.: "Monitoring Human Resources 'On Line,'" *Michigan Business Review*, July 1970, pp. 19–32.

Pyle, William C.: "Human Resource Accounting," *The Financial Analysts Journal*, September–October 1970, pp. 69–78.

Saunders, D. A.: "Human Resource Accounting," Ashridge Management College, Berkhamsted, Hertfordshire HP4 1NS, occasional paper presented at the Human Resource Accounting Seminar, European Institute for Advanced Studies in Management, Brussels, November 28–29, 1974.

Schultz, T. W.: "Investment in Human Capital," *American Economic Review*, vol. 51, pp. 1–17, March 1969.

Thurow, L.: *Investment in Human Capital*, Wadsworth Publishing Company, Inc., Belmont, Calif., 1970.

Woodruff, R. L., Jr.: "Human Resource Accounting," *The Canadian Chartered Accountant*, September 1970, pp. 156–161.

Zacks, Gordon: *How We Rebuilt our Company*, R. G. Barry Corporation, Columbus, Ohio.

Zacks, Gordon: "People are Capital Investments at R. G. Barry Corporation," *Management Accounting*, November 1971.

Zacks, Gordon: "Report of the American Accounting Association Committee on Human Resource Accounting," *The Accounting Review*, supplement to vol. 49, 1974.

R. Lee Brummet, *University of North Carolina*

## Accounting, internal (See ACCOUNTING FOR MANAGERIAL CONTROL.)

## Accounting, management (See ACCOUNTING FOR MANAGERIAL CONTROL.)

## Accounting, replacement cost (See FINANCIAL STATEMENT ANALYSIS.)

## Accounting, responsibility (See ACCOUNTING, COST ANALYSIS AND CONTROL; ACCOUNTING FOR MANAGERIAL CONTROL.)

## Accounting, whole-dollar

In *whole-dollar*, or centless, *accounting* cents are eliminated by rounding off amounts to the nearest dollar. If a figure includes 50 cents or more, the cents are eliminated and the figure is raised to the next higher dollar. If a figure includes less than 50 cents, the cents are dropped and only the dollar amount is included.

The theory is, of course, that the changes will cancel each other and the final sums will not differ greatly from what they would have been if the exact number of cents had been added in every case.

REFERENCE

Young, M. S.: "Centless Accounting," *Administrative Management*, May 1968, pp. 38–42.

STAFF/SMITH

# Accounting for managerial control

The accounting process is the primary vehicle within a company for capturing and reporting data on a systematic basis. These data are summarized for the organization as a whole, thus providing a measure of enterprise profitability and financial position; for better-managed companies, data are also accumulated by subsegments of the business to provide a basis for more detailed operational control.

**Enterprise Measurement**  The profitability of the organization as a whole is reported in the income statement (also called the profit and loss statement), while the financial position of the firm is reported in the balance sheet (also called the statement of financial position). When these two statements are released to stockholders, creditors, governmental agencies, or other groups outside the immediate management of the company, they must conform with generally accepted accounting principles. Although the data which these two reports contain are used by management at the upper levels of the organization and are thus an integral part of the top management control process, their complexity and the need for uniformity warrant separate discussions in this encyclopedia. (*See* ACCOUNTING, FINANCIAL; FINANCIAL STATEMENT ANALYSIS.)

**Segment Measurement**  Data for sound operational control, detailed planning, and day-to-day decisions are accumulated for each major segment of the business. Segments in this context include any of the fractional parts into which the business may be divided. Examples of the type of segmentation most frequently used are cost centers, departments, products or product lines, territories, manufacturing processes or activities, and customer outlets. The organization may be divided into segments in an almost infinite number of ways, and while many businesses have utilized too few, it is possible to utilize too many. Ascertaining the appropriate subdivisions for data accumulation purposes is the foundation of the accounting control process, since too much detail is costly and at times obscures the more significant points, while too little detail does not provide sufficient facts for proper operational planning and control.

**Relationship to Other Accounting Processes**  *Management accounting*, also referred to as *internal accounting*, is directed primarily toward the needs of managers and provides the data needed for controlling their specific activities. The same data-gathering processes which are utilized for financial reports to external groups (*see* ACCOUNTING, FINANCIAL) are employed to gather the data which appear in management control reports, and separate information systems for these two related, but different, reporting processes are not normally required. Thus the detailed internal data concerning segments of the business are accumulated upward to provide the data contained in reports submitted to outsiders concerning the enterprise as a whole.

The federal and state tax returns which must be filed are also prepared from the same data base as is used for financial and managerial reports. A large number of adjustments to these data are necessary to satisfy the statutory tax regulations, but a separate accounting system for tax purposes is rarely maintained.

Budgetary plans for the coming months also follow the same format as the basic financial data-gathering system. Plans for future periods are expressed in dollar amounts through the budget plan; following the same format as is used for financial and managerial reports permits actual costs to be compared with the budget plan on a regular basis.

## FITTING THE ACCOUNTING SYSTEM TO THE ORGANIZATION

The management accounting system must be designed to fit the organizational structure of the company, including the responsibility centers of individual managers. Each revenue and cost must be recorded and traced to the manager who has primary responsibility for it. The terms *responsibility accounting*, *activity accounting*, and *profitability accounting* are used interchangeably to describe this type of accounting framework.

**Responsibility Accounting Systems**  An accounting system built around managerial responsibilities must be based upon a sound organizational structure with well-defined responsibilities. Each cost must be separately studied to ascertain which executive has primary responsibility for its incurrence or has the strongest influence over its incurrence. This is not an easy task, for few costs are clearly the responsibility of a single individual. Where several persons influence the amount of a cost, the temptation to prorate that cost is strong, but should be resisted. Prorations frequently lead to conflicts concerning their fairness and equity and thus weaken the control framework.

Since supervisors are responsible for both the costs that they and their subordinates incur, a responsibility accounting system accumulates costs upward. Lower-level reports at the first-line supervisory level show only the costs for that individual's activities, but a plant superintendent's reports will contain aggregate costs of all the supervisors under his or her control. A vice-president of manufacturing, in turn, will receive reports reflecting the activities of all superintendents or other managers under his or her supervision. In this way a pyramid of cost reports is constructed to follow the organizational framework of the company.

**Controllable and Uncontrollable Costs** A controllable cost can not be neatly defined, since costs are controllable only over time and usually by the combined efforts of several persons. The raw material costs entering into a product are affected (1) by their price, which may be the purchasing officer's responsibility, and (2) by the efficiency of use, which may be the responsibility of the production officers. A general guide is to assign a cost which cannot be causally separated to that one person who has primary control responsibility for it or who most closely supervises the day-to-day actions which influence it. The control reports which are submitted to that individual should ideally contain only those costs considered controllable at that level. Should any costs considered uncontrollable at that level be included in the report, such as an allocated amount for building depreciation appearing on a production supervisor's report, those costs should be clearly separated and designated as uncontrollable.

**Cost Centers** A cost center is an activity within the organization to which costs are assigned. While responsibility centers are established for individuals, cost centers may be established for a machine, a group of machines, a process, or any physical activity for which separate cost information is needed. A single responsibility center sometimes contains a number of cost centers. Information about a physical activity, accumulated through cost centers, is used primarily to accumulate the cost of producing individual products or performing specific services for customers.

**Profit Centers** A profit center exists where both cost and revenue data can be directly traced to an activity. Each retail outlet of a chain store is a profit center since both sales revenues and cost may be recorded for each outlet separately. Internal billing, sometimes of an arbitrary nature, makes artificial

profit centers out of such activities as the data processing center, the equipment repairs activity, or similar service arms of the organization. The justification for these arbitrary profit centers is that they utilize the profit motive as a motivation device. Any resulting artificial profit is eliminated when a true profit or loss for the company is calculated.

**Investment Centers** An investment center exists where the investment required to create and operate a profit center is separable and a return on investment can be calculated. The rate of return earned by the divisions or profit centers within a company is carefully monitored in most instances to provide a measure of divisional performance. The differences in the investment base which result from varying depreciation methods on fixed properties, from different inventory valuation methods, or from leased instead of owned assets must be taken into account when comparing the rates of return.

**Intracompany Pricing** Where investment centers or profit centers exist and one center provides products or services for another center, an intracompany pricing system must be established. Methods used to determine the *transfer price* of products or services between autonomous divisions of the same company may be based upon (1) the full cost, (2) the variable cost, (3) the market price if sold to outside customers, or (4) a negotiated price. Variations of these methods are often used, and in all cases care must be exercised when interpreting the resulting profit, especially if a return-on-investment calculation is used as a performance measure.

**Direct and Indirect Costs** Many cost analyses require a distinction between those costs which are direct and those which are indirect to the segment being studied. The concept of controllable or uncontrollable, discussed earlier, is related to the managerial control process; the concept of direct or indirect relates to the question of whether the cost is necessary to support a given segment of the company.

*Direct Costs.* A direct cost is one which is directly traceable to the particular segment of the business under study and is incurred specifically for that segment. In a retail establishment the salaries of salesclerks are direct expenses of the departments in which they work, but these same salaries would be indirect to the several product lines sold in the department. A direct cost is usually one which could be eliminated if that segment of the business were to be eliminated.

*Indirect Costs.* An indirect cost is one that is not directly traceable to specific segments and probably could not be eliminated if that segment of the business were terminated. Since these costs are not directly traceable or could not in many cases be eliminated, they are sometimes allocated or pro-rated, utilizing an appropriate allocation base. Many allocation bases exist, and the only criterion which must be satisfied when selecting an allocation base is that a reasonable relationship exist between the expense and the selected base. Building occupancy costs, such as rent, depreciation, property taxes, and insurance, may be allocated to departments or processes on a cubic space basis, on a square footage basis, or on a percentage basis, calculated to take into account the value of strategic locations near doors or passageways. When indirect costs are allocated to segments, the resulting costs are open to serious question and care must be exercised in interpreting the results. The *contribution margin approach*, discussed later in this section, is a more reliable method and is basically a subtraction of only direct costs from revenues to arrive at the contribution margin produced by that segment. Any indirect or allocated costs are then considered, but only to the extent that they increase or decrease as a result of the specific action being considered.

**Internal Control** A company's system of internal control consists of all the measures taken to protect the company's assets against irregularities, to insure the accuracy of recorded transactions, and to assure management that the information on which it must base decisions is authentic and reliable. The system includes the arrangement of duties and the flow of paper work which ensure a minimum of clerical errors and maximum security against theft and embezzlement.

*Internal Check.* The system of internal checks is based upon two basic principles:

1. Responsibilities of all personnel must be fixed and clearly communicated.

2. Each clerical activity in the organization should to the extent possible be checked automatically by another clerical activity with a minimal duplication of effort.

The following example illustrates the importance of these two principles: When sales are registered in a cash register on the sales floor of a retail establishment, a locked-in tape accumulates the amounts registered. At the end of the day a person *who is other than the salesclerk and who does not have access to cash* will remove the tapes from the registers and check the tape totals with the total of the cash transferred to the cashier for deposit. These two amounts must match, and thus the salesclerks and the cashier operate under a system where they know

their work is monitored. Note that the duties of the persons involved must be fixed, and one person automatically checks the work of another with a minimum duplication of effort.

*Separation of Functions.* The construction of sound systems of internal checks are based upon the separation of three functions. These are (1) the authority to move or transfer assets, (2) physical control of the asset itself, and (3) the record-keeping process. Only when these three activities are separated will the internal-check system be strong.

*Fixed Property Controls.* An internal-check system for fixed properties such as equipment, machinery, tools, and office furniture illustrates the separation of duties discussed above.

1. A permanent record is established for each individual asset and is maintained in the accounting department. A permanently affixed number of identification is placed on the record and on the asset itself. These records constitute the record-keeping process.

2. Each asset is placed under the responsibility of a specific person who has physical custody over it. This person is identified on the permanent records.

3. The asset may not be transferred to some other person and must remain in the custody of the one who has responsibility for it. The asset may not be sold or scrapped without the approval of a responsible person, who must be someone other than the record keeper and the individual who currently has physical custody.

4. The final step in the control process is to complete an inventory every 6 months or each year to ensure that the assets are where they should be. In this way missing assets or unauthorized transfers will be identified and responsibility for the asset is maintained.

**Analysis of Cost Behavior** Knowledge of the reaction of individual costs and expenses to changes in the volume of activity is the foundation for (1) planning the amount of costs to be incurred in future periods; (2) estimating profits from future activities; and (3) determining whether costs have been adequately controlled by those responsible for their incurrence. The relation between changes in a cost and changes in the volume of activity result in a classification of variable, fixed, and semivariable (also called semifixed or mixed) costs.

*Variable costs* are those which will fluctuate in close relation to a selected activity or volume measure. Units sold, dollars of sales, units produced, labor hours, and labor costs are the more frequently used volume measures. When volume increases, the amount of a variable cost will increase proportionately. The raw material used in the manufacture of a finished product is almost always a variable cost. The expense for wrapping paper, twine, shopping bags, or other supplies will usually vary with the amount of sales activity in a retail store. Sales commissions, when based upon a percentage of sales, are another example of an expense which is completely variable.

*Fixed Costs* are those which are related to the passage of time and have only a minimal relationship to the volume of activity which has or is expected to be undertaken. An annual lease expense which is incurred for building space will be fixed in amount regardless of the manufacturing or sales volume. Depreciation expense is usually fixed, as are many types of insurance; office salaries and property taxes are also examples of costs which are in most cases fixed and have little relationship to the volume of activity. Most fixed costs are committed or programmed costs. Given a long enough time period, all fixed costs would appear variable, and their fixed nature, usually within a 1-year planning period, is the result of management decisions which have committed the company to incur the cost. Depreciation on equipment, certain types of insurance coverage, and salaries of key personnel are examples of *committed costs. Programmed costs* are the result of appropriation decisions and include such costs as advertising and research and development. A programmed cost can be any sum which management wishes, but once it has been budgeted, it must be considered a fixed cost for the period.

*Semivariable (or mixed)* costs are those which change when volume changes, but not in exact proportion. Salaries of salesclerks in retail stores are an example of this type of expense. When the store's sales are expected to increase, as they are prior to Easter or Christmas, additional salesclerks will be employed, so that the total salaries paid to salesclerks will move up or down with the amount of sales. The change will not be in exact proportion, however, for a minimum number of salesclerks will be necessary to all times, and at peak times all clerks will be busier and will produce a larger dollar volume of sales.

The three types of cost behavior are shown graphically in Fig. A-9.

**Methods of Measuring Cost Behavior** Methods utilized to measure the behavior of a cost range from simple estimation methods to sophisticated mathematical formulas. Where historical records are available, they may be the basis for utilizing the (1) scattergraph (or graphic method), (2) the high-low points method, or (3) the least-squares method. Where no past history is available, the high-low points method may be utilized, with the points being carefully selected estimates of two cost amounts.

*Scattergraph.* Historical cost data, usually by monthly periods, is plotted on a graph, with the volume index on the horizontal axis and the cost amounts on the vertical axis (Fig. A-10). Unusual cost amounts which arise from nonrecurring events, such as a fire, labor strike, or major equipment failure, should be eliminated. After the data are plotted, a trend line is drawn through the points to reflect the general movement. The fixed portion of the cost would be that point where the trend line intersects the vertical axis. The variable portion is stated in terms of cost per unit volume and is calculated by relating the change in cost between any two points on the trend line with the change in volume between the same two points.

*High-Low Points Method.* Since two points determine a straight line, the trend line can be determined by selecting any two volume levels and estimating the cost which would be incurred at those two levels. The points selected should be represen-

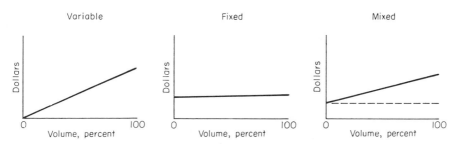

Fig. A-9. Graphical representation of variations in cost behavior.

tative high and representative low levels. The two points may be based upon historical data but must be estimated where no prior history exists. Determining the fixed and variable portions of the cost would then be done in the same way as in the scattergraph method.

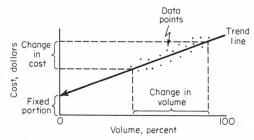

**Fig. A-10. Scattergraph.**

*Least-Squares Method.* This method is based upon a mathematical computation to fit the line to a set of data points. Historical amounts must be available. The method is based upon the solution to a set of simultaneous equations. The amounts which go into the two equations are $\Sigma X$ (total of all individual volume amounts), $\Sigma Y$ (total of all individual cost amounts), $\Sigma X^2$ (total of each volume amount multiplied by itself), $N$ (number of data points), and $\Sigma XY$ (total of each volume point multiplied by its related cost amount). The formulas, which are solved for $a$ and $b$, are

$$\Sigma Y = Na + \Sigma Xb$$
$$\Sigma XY = \Sigma Xa + \Sigma X^2 b$$

The calculation can easily be done on a computer or on a hand calculator which is able to store a simple program. The $a$ value, once determined, is the fixed portion of the expense, and the $b$ value, which will be stated as a cost per unit of volume, will be the variable portion.

**The Contribution Margin** A company's overall cost structure is made up of the total of all its fixed costs and the total of all its variable costs. The mixed costs, once analyzed into their fixed and variable components, can be included in the summation of these totals. Knowledge of this overall cost-behavior structure provides a powerful information base for major planning decisions. This is the result of having isolated and measured the variable costs, which move with the volume, and separated them from the fixed costs, which will not change. The projected profit from a contemplated

course of action is thus readily determined by subtracting the expected variable costs from the anticipated revenues, thus determining the contribution margin. The *contribution margin* is, simply stated, the contribution which a particular segment makes toward covering the general pool of fixed costs. If a unit sells for $1 per unit, and the variable costs of manufacturing and selling the unit are 80 cents, then each unit contributes 20 cents toward the company's fixed costs. The concept of contribution margin is both logical and easily applied and is one of the most universal applications of variable- and fixed-cost data. Determining the level of sales where losses stop and profits start, for example, can be accomplished by calculating the sales volume which will produce the amount of contribution margin necessary to cover exactly the firm's total fixed costs.

Another example of the use of this concept is found in calculating the point at which a company should temporarily cease operations. When a company is incurring losses, it may minimize these losses in the short run by continuing in operations, rather than temporarily closing down, so long as it has a contribution margin on present sales to cover a part of its fixed costs, which would continue.

**Break-Even Analysis** *Break-even analysis* is the analysis of a company's cost, volume, and profit relationships to determine the amount of revenue it must earn to break even exactly with neither a profit or a loss. The analysis is dependent upon knowledge of the firm's fixed and variable costs and is based upon the concept of the contribution margin. For example, if a company has $1 million of fixed costs and variable costs equal to 60 percent of sales, the break-even point would be calculated as follows:

$$\text{Total revenues} = \text{fixed expenses} + \text{variable expenses}$$
$$+ \text{ zero profit}$$
$$R = \$1,000,000 + 0.6R + 0$$
$$R - 0.6R = \$1,000,000$$
$$0.4R = \$1,000,000$$
$$R = \$2,500,000$$

Stated verbally, each dollar of revenue received must be used to pay 60 cents of variable costs, leaving 40 cents to cover fixed costs. At this 40-cent rate of contribution the company must have $2,-500,000 of sales to exactly cover $1 million of fixed costs.

*Estimating the Effect of Future Actions.* Break-even analysis is a useful tool to measure the effect of future actions. The following questions illustrate how answers are determined for complex questions utilizing the break-even–analysis technique:

| Question | Answer |
|---|---|
| Assuming the cost structure given above, what level of sales must be realized to produce a profit of $200,000? | $0.4S = \$1,000,000 + \$200,000$ <br> $S = \$3,000,000$ |
| What amount must sales be to cover a $50,000 increase in fixed costs and still produce a profit of $200,000? | $0.4S = \$1,000,000 + \$50,000 +$ <br> $\$200,000$ <br> $S = \$3,125,000$ |
| What amount of sales will be needed to break-even if variable costs can be reduced to 55% but with an increase in fixed costs to $1,100,000? | $0.45S = \$1,100,000$ <br> $S = \$2,444,444$ |

*The Break-Even Graph.* The cost-volume-profit relationships which are inherent in break-even analysis may be shown graphically, as in Fig. A-11. When this is done, the total fixed costs are shown separately from the total variable costs, usually with the fixed costs in the lower position. The point at which the revenue line crosses the total cost line will represent the break-even point. *See also* MARGINAL INCOME ANALYSIS.

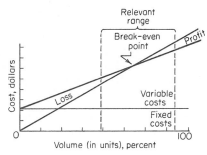

Fig. A-11. Break-even graph.

An additional concept, that of the *relevent range*, has been superimposed upon the illustrative break-even chart. The analysis of fixed and variable costs which underlies the break-even concept will be valid only within a certain volume range; that is, the assumption is made that costs will be linear and will not hold at very high or very low ranges of activity. The relevant range must be considered when the fixed- and variable-cost analysis is originally undertaken and is therefore implicit in break-even analysis.

*Margin of Safety.* One measure which is utilized in the analysis of the financial affairs of a company is the margin of safety. This may be defined as the amount by which present sales exceed the break-even point. When two companies or two divisions of the same company are being compared, their relative margins of safety will indicate which is in the most vulnerable profit position.

*Limiting Assumptions.* The break-even analysis is based upon a number of assumptions, and its use must be undertaken with awareness of them. The most important assumption is that cost behavior is linear. The behavior of each cost will approach linearity, but careful study will reveal that few costs are actually linear. Another assumption is that the relationship of cost change is sufficiently causal; there may be forces other than volume which produce changes in cost. Finally, if several products are manufactured or sold, the analysis assumes that the product mix will remain constant and that sales prices will not shift. Should this occur, the revenue line will not be correctly portrayed and the relationship of revenue to cost will no longer hold. However, these assumptions are usually not so overpowering that they preclude the use of the technique for overall broad analysis of the effect of contemplated managerial actions. (*See* MARGINAL INCOME ANALYSIS.)

*See also* ACCOUNTING, COST ANALYSIS AND CONTROL; ACCOUNTING, FINANCIAL; ACCOUNTING, HUMAN RESOURCES (ASSETS); *Accounting for Managerial Control*; BUDGETING, CAPITAL; BUDGETS AND BUDGET PREPARATION; CONTROL SYSTEMS, MANAGEMENT; CREDIT MANAGEMENT; DATA PROCESSING PRINCIPLES AND PRACTICES; FINANCIAL MANAGEMENT; FINANCIAL STATEMENT ANALYSIS; INFORMATION SYSTEMS, MANAGEMENT (MIS); MARGINAL INCOME ANALYSIS; PRODUCT AND SERVICE PRICING; TAX MANAGEMENT, MANAGERIAL RESPONSIBILITY FOR FEDERAL INCOME TAX REPORTING; ZERO-BASE BUDGETING.

### REFERENCES

Anthony, Robert N.: *Management Accounting Text and Cases,* 4th ed., Richard D. Irwin, Inc., Homewood, Ill., 1970.

Bierdman, Harold, and Allan R. Dreblin: *Managerial Accounting: An Introduction,* 2d ed., The Macmillan Company, New York, 1972.

Horngren, Charles T.: *Cost Accounting: A Managerial Emphasis,* 3d ed., Prentice-Hall, Inc., Englewood Cliffs, N.J., 1972.

Matz, Adolph, and Milton F. Usury: *Cost Accounting: Planning and Control,* 6th ed., South-Western Publishing Company, Incorporated, Cincinnati, 1975.

Moore, Carl L., and Robert K. Jaedicke: *Managerial Accounting*, 3d ed., South-Western Publishing Company, Incorporated, Cincinnati, 1972.

Seiler, Robert F.: *Accounting Principles for Management*, 2d ed., Charles E. Merrill, Inc., Englewood Cliffs, N.J., 1975.

ROBERT E. SEILER, *University of Houston*

# Accounting Principles Board (APB)

(*See* ACCOUNTING, FINANCIAL.)

# Accounting profit   (*See* PROFITS AND PROFIT MAKING.)

# Accounts payable management   (*See* FINANCIAL MANAGEMENT.)

# Achievement tests   (*See* TESTING, PSYCHOLOGICAL.)

# Acquisitions, international   (*See* INTERNATIONAL OPERATIONS AND MANAGEMENT IN MULTINATIONAL COMPANIES.)

# Acquisitions and mergers

Most companies seek growth, and those that do grow, do so in one of two ways: (1) through internal expansion or (2) through external growth, that is, by acquisition of or merger with another company. In common business parlance, an *acquisition* is the purchase of one company by another company with either (1) the purchasing company surviving as the only entity or (2) the acquired company becoming a division or unit of the acquiring company. A *merger* can be simply defined as the combination or consolidation of two companies based upon an exchange of stock, with the identity of only one of the companies surviving or with the creation of an entirely new resultant company.

**PLANNING**

To determine which method of growth makes sense for a given firm, its overall purpose must first be clearly established: *who* it is as an entity, and *where* it is headed. Its management should formulate specific objectives, and these should be targeted goals that can be attained within 3 to 5 years. Next, a strategy or approach to the achievement of the objectives must be set forth. Finally, such strategy must be operationalized by long- and short-range business planning. Of course, certain objectives can be best achieved through internal, rather than external, expansion. It is far better to reach this conclusion early. In any event, this kind of business planning will ensure that a company's true operating needs and future capital requirements are known. In a time of active corporate growth, it will also help avoid the pitfalls of an exciting but dangerous venture into a misguided acquisition or merger.

**Purpose**   Reasons for external expansion may be many: additional plant capacity, better channels of distribution, new technology, new product or service lines, or extra working capital. Such external growth programs are useful in achieving synergistic effects. For example, products of the new firm may be distributed through the other firm's existing distribution system for only a slight cost increase. On the other hand, large companies often focus upon specific financial, as opposed to operating, objectives.

The three major periods of high acquisition and merger activity in the United States in this century reveal the kinds of objectives and gains most commonly sought through intercompany consolidation. Between 1889 and 1902, most consolidations took place within a single industry, usually railroad, metal, and mining companies. During the second period, 1919 to 1931, companies sought to develop organizational forms (such as holding companies) for the purpose of control, rather than for operating reasons. The third period, running from World War II into the 1960s, showed a notable increase in consolidations of commercial banks, in vertical acquisitions and mergers, and in the number of conglomerate marriages.

**Types of Consolidations**   A *vertical* acquisition or merger occurs when a company unites with one of its suppliers or customers. A *backward-vertical* acquisition or merger is one with a supplier, whereas a *forward-vertical* consolidation would be one with a customer. A *conglomerate* is a company comprised of several component companies which are in different fields of business and tend to have certain financial, administrative, and managerial systems as their only common denominator. In addition, there are *horizontal* acquisitions and mergers wherein two or more companies within the same field combine, such as a merging of two canneries. Still another way of categorizing these combinations is whether they are *taxable* or *tax-free* transactions, tax-free meaning that the tax consequences are not incurred at the time of closing but are deferred. In order to be tax-free, any exchanges or distributions must be made in accordance with any of several types of reorganizations defined as A, B, and C by the Internal Revenue Code.

**Objectivity in Planning** Approaching growth by means of acquisition or merger requires the conscientious, rigorous application of sound business logic. The intrigue and sense of excitement surrounding acquisitions and mergers must be removed from the decision-making process so that the pride or ego of the owners and managers is not the prime motivating factor to acquire or merge. Professionalism and logic should determine which growth strategy is best suited to achieve the firm's stated objectives.

**Public Securities Markets** Since salaries and dividends accruing to business executives are customarily limited and highly taxed, external growth of a company is often viewed as an attractive alternative means to achieve personal wealth. Consequently, a primary trigger for acquisition and merger activity is a rising public securities market. During a rising market, privately held companies often seek to become publicly owned and actively traded. Publicly held companies, realizing the difficulties in sustaining a corporate image of dramatic increases in earnings per share and an associated increasing price-earnings ratio through internal growth alone, may initiate a program of external expansion. A combined program of internal and external growth can allow for rapid increases in earnings per share, which are then actively communicated to the investment community. Ideally, this results in an increased price-earnings ratio, which promotes corporate capital accumulation and personal wealth through the sale of the company's stock at much higher prices.

There is nothing inherently inappropriate about the program described above, but, unfortunately, for many firms these are often only paper transactions. They may bring about temporary increases in corporate and personal wealth, but they may do so in a manner that does not serve the long-term development of a sound company. For this reason, many firms often find themselves with acquired or merged concerns that they do not really understand or know how to operate profitably.

## SELECTION CRITERIA

When a company knows what it wants to achieve and has developed its objectives, strategies, long- and short-range plans, and operating objectives, then the necessary acquisition or merger candidate-selection criteria will evolve naturally. Some overly opportunistic companies, instead, set out to locate firms which may simply be ripe, or merely available, for consolidation—without first having developed overall corporate aims and plans. This approach is rarely successful.

Well-developed selection criteria facilitate a design by which candidate companies may be identified, and such criteria also serve as a screen in the examination of those concerns. Moreover, properly formulated criteria are highly useful in minimizing the enormous time commitments involved in a program of external growth by reducing the time spent on investigating companies which in retrospect should never have been considered as candidates.

**Nature of Criteria** Criteria may be general in nature, dealing with basic considerations; or they may be exact and restrictive, depending upon the needs of the initiating firm. For a company with highly specific criteria and a potentially large number of candidate companies, a quantitative method for expressing acquisition or merger criteria can be used. The selection criteria may include such considerations as desirable industries or fields of business; geographical locations; range of sales volume; profitability and return on investment; range of investment funds available, and whether the funds are in the form of cash, notes, or stock; preference for publicly or privately owned firms; necessary stage of company development; and degree of control desired.

**Sellers' Rationale** It is helpful if the selection criteria reflect not only the needs of the company pursuing external growth but also the desirability of the proposed acquisition or merger from the viewpoint of the owners of the candidate companies. Some owners, for instance, want to sell their firms for personal or health reasons; others because of current or projected industry or market conditions; and still others because of financial difficulties, technological obsolescence, or the lack of successor management.

## SEARCH

Identifying viable companies is one of the most difficult steps in the acquisition or merger process. Unless secrecy is important, it is usually best for the company to let it be known that it is interested in a consolidation and is looking for available candidates.

**Sources**  Typical sources for locating candidate companies include banks, investment bankers, accounting firms, lawyers, finders and business brokers, suppliers, sales representatives, factoring companies, bankruptcy specialists, venture capitalists, consultants, corporate development directors, trade journals, and business acquaintances.

**Fees**  Some professionals charge a fee for assisting in identifying candidates; others do it as a courtesy. Some *finders* or *business brokers,* who are professional matchmakers, may require a retainer fee whether or not they are successful in locating a suitable company. Others work on a *contingency fee* basis, whereby they are paid only if a suitable company is found and the consolidation is completed. Still others employ a combination of these methods. Care must be taken to avoid paying unjustified or multiple finders' fees to several brokers, and legal counsel should be employed to work out the fee agreement. Such search services can be critical to the success of the effort, and, consequently, professional finders' fees should simply be considered as part of the overall cost of a given acquisition or merger.

**Corporate Raids and Divestitures**  Candidate companies can also be identified through either an analysis of the stock prices of publicly traded companies or the monitoring of the corporate development plans of large holding companies and conglomerates. When the public securities markets are depressed, it is possible to acquire (i.e., *raid*) a company whose stock is selling below its book value by using the public exchange to quietly purchase a controlling interest. A second approach is to identify candidates which are *spin-off companies*—firms which larger holding companies and conglomerates seek periodically to dispose of as part of their corporate development program. These are termed *divestitures*. The reason for a divestiture is often one inherent in, and peculiar to, the divesting firm. For instance, there may be a change in the direction of the parent company which as no affect on the worth or anticipated performance of the divested company. Other times, a divestiture is prompted simply because the company is too small to justify its current demand upon the time and talent of the parent concern. Often, such companies are available on very attractive terms.

## EVALUATION

The process of evaluating (i.e., *due diligence*) acquisition and merger candidates is generally an extremely time-consuming, costly, and imperfect process. Not just one, but sometimes dozens of companies must be investigated and examined.

**Multiphase Evaluation**  The systematic approach of a multiphase evaluation process is the most efficient and effective. A good evaluation plan will include a comprehensive assessment of all the major facets of a candidate company—financial, marketing, operations, general management, organization, and personnel—and will serve to focus attention on the primary issues involved. Too often, companies lose perspective and become immersed in endless detail and concerns of relatively little importance.

For the first phase, the initiating company should develop a set of eight or ten questions requiring affirmative answers before subsequent phases of evaluation may proceed. The principal purpose is to eliminate as many inappropriate candidate companies as possible from further consideration and thereby minimize or preclude wasted effort and money at each stage. Evaluation questions that might be asked during the early phases of the screening process include: What risks exist based upon technological change? Will key company personnel remain? Why is the company really being sold? How can the company's profitability be increased? What is the outlook of the company's industry? What are the key functional areas for the company's success? What degree of dependence exists on a few suppliers or customers? What can each firm contribute to the other? What degree of compatibility is anticipated between the management of both companies?

Various checklists (e.g., *see references* for Baumer, Burstein, Choka, Hennessy, Hilton, and Scharf) are available which can serve as a stimulus in the formulation of detailed and specific questions for the later phases of the evaluation process. Examples of questions that might be asked during the later phases include: Are any inventory items on consignment? Have reserves been established for warranties and rework? What are the remaining lives of key patents? What is the status of current union agreements? What is the amount of any unfunded pension liability? Will key contacts survive a change in ownership of the company? In the final stages, detailed pro forma balance sheets, income statements, and cash flow statements should be prepared to reflect the anticipated financial structure and performance of the consolidated companies. This costly and time-consuming work, however, should be reserved for only those candidate companies which have passed the prior phases of the selection process.

**Special Problems** The problems involved in evaluating a given company as an acquisition or merger candidate are many. First, the secrecy of the negotiations may preclude more than a limited view of internal management activities. Second, unless the acquiring company is knowledgeable in the field of business of the candidate company, important aspects of the firm may be easily overlooked or improperly considered. In this regard, it is useful to employ consultants familiar with the field to contribute to the evaluation. Third, some companies are deliberately prepared and "window-dressed" for a sale and have eliminated or substantially reduced such normal operating expenditures as preventive maintenance, research and development efforts, managerial development programs, and managerial systems in order to enhance their financial statements. Fourth, small or closely held firms often do not have certified financial statements, and this may mean a statement based upon inaccurate data or improper accounting procedures.

**Representations, Warranties, and Recourse** Since no evaluation process, however systematic and detailed, can eliminate every possibility of mistake or misjudgment, the sellers are usually asked to give a written warranty of certain facts, conditions, and other representations which protect the buyer even after the consolidation has been consummated. Since legal remedies may not always provide adequate pragmatic recourse, some buyers will structure the payment of the purchase price over a period of time—thereby permitting the withholding of remaining payments in case misrepresentations or negative eventualities materialize.

## VALUATION

The valuation of a company, despite systematic and sophisticated methods, is a highly subjective process. Depending upon which firm is considering it, a candidate company may be perceived to have various values; therefore, one must look to the benefits accruing to a particular firm to determine an appropriate value.

While there are many techniques for valuing a given concern, the classic approaches are: (1) valuation based primarily upon the assets and liabilities of a company; (2) valuation based upon the earnings of a company; and (3) the "gut feeling" of a seller.

**Stock versus Assets** A given transaction may involve the purchase of all or part of a company's stock or assets. Generally, buyers prefer to purchase assets, leaving the seller responsible for the firm's liabilites. Sellers, however, usually want to dispose of liabilities and, therefore, wish to sell the company's stock. In certain cases, however, these general preferences are not manifested. A buyer may desire, for example, to preserve a net operating loss carry forward for tax purposes, or the seller may not wish to incur the recapture of prior years' depreciation or investment tax credits.

**Book Value** Clearly, the book value of a company's stock or assets does not always reflect an appropriate value for the company. Some concerns capitalize certain costs, whereas others expense them. The age of a company will also affect book value. For example, an older company's depreciable and amortizable assets may have almost no book value, and other assets—such as land—may be drastically undervalued. For these and other reasons, book value is often adjusted. Sometimes the original cost is used, or only the tangible assets are included in the valuation, or the adjusted value of tangible assets is used. An appraiser may be employed to place a current market value on the assets of a company. This figure may vary widely, however, depending upon whether the valuation is on the basis of (1) a forced liquidation, (2) an orderly liquidation, (3) a going concern, (4) the replacement cost of tangible assets, or (5) the cost of reproducing a similar company under current conditions.

**Projected Earnings** Valuation based upon earning potential takes the current or projected earnings and capitalizes them by multiplying the earnings by a price-earnings ratio. If projected earnings are used, they should reflect the effect of the anticipated acquisition or merger. If a candidate company is publicly traded, it has a price-earnings ratio established by the securities market. A private corporation does not have such a ratio, and, therefore, a capitalization ratio may be chosen based upon an analysis of the prevailing ratios for similar publicly traded companies in the same industry. Other variations of this approach include (1) calculating the present value of a selected future-earnings stream of a company or (2) applying an agreed-upon price-earnings ratio to whatever future earnings actually materialize. This latter method has been termed the *contingent purchase price* or *earn-out* arrangement. Other modifications may involve return on investment (ROI), return on equity (ROE), or payback period—all of which effectively reflect a capitalization ratio.

**Intuition** With the third approach, "gut feeling," it is assumed that there will be no acquisition or merger unless the seller gets his price, however arbitrary that price may be.

**Other Considerations** Whichever method is chosen, other factors come into play:

1. Tax considerations in most acquisitions and mergers are highly complex matters of critical importance. As a result of taxation, the price the buyer pays will not necessarily be the price the seller receives.

2. Risk is also a factor in negotiating a suitable valuation. The buyer is acquiring or merging to some extent with an unknown entity, and there are inherently different levels of risk in various fields of business. The seller also assumes a risk if there is a contingent purchase price or if certain forms of payment are accepted. Payment, for example, can take the form of unsecured as well as secured notes, cash, or stock in another company, all of which can have differing values in a given situation. Often the term *goodwill* is mentioned in negotiations. It is simply the premium paid for the perceived value of a going concern over its net worth.

3. It is also a common strategy of a buyer to allow the seller to name a price and then for the buyer to effectively change the price by setting the terms and conditions of the acquisition or merger. Typically, the buyer draws up the agreement, and the seller negotiates and redrafts the document.

## IMPLEMENTATION PROCEDURES

Management must make critical decisions concerning the financial structuring of any consolidation. A company with an aggressive program of external growth will often seek to leverage the use of its own financial resources either (1) through an increased value of its own stock (because of a rising public market) or (2) by means of the acquisition of a company employing that company's own financial resources.

Buying a company with its own financial resources usually occurs when owners must sell their interests for such reasons as a death, a divorce, or a desire to retire. In such situations, it may be possible to persuade the seller to accept a very small down payment with notes secured by the business to be acquired for the balance of the purchase price; thus, the seller provides a large part of the financing

for the acquisition. Usually the seller is offered a higher price as an inducement to accept such terms. This approach reduces the initial capital outlay of the buyer and, therefore, is referred to as a *bootstrap purchase.* Another incentive for the seller to accept such a bootstrap purchase is the installment sale provision of the Internal Revenue Code. This provision provides beneficial tax incentives to the seller if he or she accepts only a limited payment of the total purchase price within the first tax year after the acquisition.

Since acquisition or merger is often an unfamiliar process for both companies, the process should be carefully planned and managed. Authority should be delegated for specific functions and responsibility fixed for their successful completion. Planning should also include (1) the establishment of time-based performance standards coupled with (2) a good system of accountability to ensure effective control.

## LEGAL AND TAX CONSIDERATIONS

The typical consolidation involves highly complex legal issues including governmental regulations, the acquisition or merger agreement per se, and a review of the prior legal affairs of a candidate company. Governmental regulations may involve antitrust laws, Securities and Exchange Commission regulations, state securities "Blue-Sky" laws, and other legislation. A prudent review of a candidate's legal affairs could include such considerations as corporate minutes, prior issuance of stock, transferability of contracts, and pension fund liabilities.

It is helpful if the principals reach a fundamental agreement, a meeting of the minds, before legal advisors and tax counsel are engaged to perform detailed analysis and structuring of the proposed consolidation. Toward this end, a *letter of intent* may be used. This optional document sets forth the basic proposed agreement, thereby assuring that the parties understand each other. Beyond this step, however, professional advice and counsel, including attorneys and accountants, should be sought and extensively utilized to structure and draft the agreement and to guide the parties through the necessary steps. The actual acquisition or merger agreement often contains selective outs for both parties, affording a retreat from the agreement should facts or conditions substantially change in the interim before the deal is closed.

Proper structuring of the acquisition or merger can enhance the tax positions of both parties, allowing the seller to reap greater financial rewards and the buyer to pay a reduced price. Special care must be exercised to avoid the necessity of either party having to pay an immediate and large tax liability before receiving the proceeds of the transaction in a negotiable form.

## PITFALLS

While acquisitions and mergers afford a viable and powerful means of achieving corporate objectives, they must be approached with caution and with an awareness of such potential pitfalls as those highlighted below:

1. No decision can have a greater affect on a company than a decision to be acquired or merged with or to acquire or merge. These are often highly charged, emotional decisions, particularly for the seller. It is, therefore, not uncommon for a seller to attempt to terminate a proposed agreement at the last moment simply because it is psychologically difficult to part with a company which constitutes a life's work and investment.

2. Often, there is an inability to effect a successful integration of the two companies. Usually, it is "people problems" which undo that which has been legally accomplished. In assessing the likelihood of a successful integration, the degree of decentralization, the similarity of structure in terms of product line, functional, and geographic divisions, and the similarity in the number of authority levels should be considered. Differences in size, leadership styles, and management philosophies should also be assessed. Compensation packages and personnel practices, as well as the overall manner in which the integration of the two companies is planned, will have a major impact upon the success of the venture.

3. Another pitfall centers upon the initiating firm's choice of the representative of the candidate company with whom to negotiate. It must be determined early in the negotiation whether the representative of the candidate company is in fact the individual with the authority to obligate the company. The problem of whom to deal with might, for example, occur when the owner of a company is recently deceased.

It is an unfortunate commentary that since World War II, about half of all acquisitions and mergers in the United States have been unsuccessful for some reason and one-third of all consolidations have turned out to be such poor business ventures that they have since been spun-off or dissolved. Proper planning coupled with objective, cautious, and carefully controlled implementation are key safeguards in the prevention of these misfortunes.

*See also* AUDIT, MANAGEMENT; AUDITING, FINANCIAL; BUDGETING, CAPITAL, SPECIAL PROBLEMS OF; FINANCIAL STATEMENT ANALYSIS; PLANNING, PLANNED MANAGEMENT OF TURBULENT CHANGE; POLICY FORMULATION AND IMPLEMENTATION; SHAREHOLDER RELATIONSHIPS.

### REFERENCES

Baumer, William H., and Leo J. Northart: *Buy, Sell, Merge: How To Do It*, Prentice-Hall, Inc., Englewood Cliffs, N.J., 1971.

Brockhaus, William L.: "A Model for Success in Mergers and Acquisitions," *S. A. M. Advanced Management Journal*, Winter 1975.

Brockhaus, William L.: "How to Develop a Plan for Securing Venture Capital," *Business Horizons*, June 1976.

Burstein, Milton B.: *Acquisitions and Mergers*, Oceana Publications, Inc., Dobbs Ferry, N.Y., 1973.

Choka, Allen D.: *Buying, Selling and Merging Businesses*, Joint Committee on Continuing Legal Education for the American Law Institute and the American Bar Association, Philadelphia, Pa., 1965.

Hennessy, J. H., Jr.: *Acquiring and Merging Businesses*, Prentice-Hall, Inc., Englewood Cliffs, N.J., 1966.

Hilton, Peter: *Planning Corporate Growth and Diversification*, McGraw-Hill Book Company, New York, 1970.

Mace, Myles L., and George G. Montgomery, Jr.: *Management Problems of Corporate Acquisitions*, Harvard University Press, Cambridge, Mass. 1962.

McCarthy, George D., and Robert E. Healy: *Valuing a Company*, The Ronald Press Company, New York, 1971.

Scharf, Charles A.: *Acquisitions, Mergers, Sales and Takeovers: A Handbook with Forms*, Prentice-Hall, Inc., Englewood Cliffs, N.J., 1971.

WILLIAM L. BROCKHAUS, *Edward Hyman Company and Brockhaus, Carlisle and Associates*

## Action-event areas   (*See* STATISTICAL ANALYSIS FOR MANAGEMENT.)

## Action-indicator chart   (*See* EXCEPTION, MANAGEMENT BY.)

## Actions, statistical   (*See* STATISTICAL ANALYSIS FOR MANAGEMENT.)

## Activities   (*See* NETWORK PLANNING METHODS.)

**Activities, maintenance** (*See* INTERPER-SONAL RELATIONSHIPS.)

**Activities, task-related** (*See* INTERPER-SONAL RELATIONSHIPS.)

**Activities chart** (*See* SCHEDULING, SHORT-INTERVAL.)

**Activities management** (*See* MANAGE-MENT, FUTURE OF.)

**Adaptation, lag time** (*See* PLANNING, PLANNED MANAGEMENT OF TURBULENT CHANGE.)

**Adjustable funding line** (*See* BUDGETS AND BUDGET PREPARATION.)

**Administration** (*See* MANAGEMENT, DEFINI-TIONS OF.)

**Administration, hospital** (*See* HOSPITAL ADMINISTRATION.)

**Administration, marketing** (*See* MARKET-ING, INDUSTRIAL.)

**Administration, public** (*See* PUBLIC AD-MINISTRATION.)

## Administrative management

Every business, whether product- or service-oriented, has major functions to perform: production or operations, sales or marketing, finance, and administration. It is easy to see how the first three functions relate to an improved profit picture. On the other hand, the support that administration provides to the first three functions is often thought of as a necessary evil that diminishes profits. By definition, however, administration or management is es-

sential in every aspect of a business operation. Because its home is an office environment, administrative management is often mistaken as an entity quite separate from marketing, manufacturing, and finance.

Though administration is commonly thought of as those expenses that subtract directly from the bottom line, they are the same expenses that, when minimized, give back to the bottom line. If, for example, ABC company operates on a 5 percent net profit basis, a decrease of $10,000 in administrative costs is equal to an increase in gross sales of $200,000.

*Typical Responsibilities.* Administration is carried out by a mix of people and machines. The tasks administrative managers perform are as varied as the companies in which they work. The administrative manager might be accountable for responsibilities as diverse as secretarial services and in-house food services. Other responsibilities typically include record and file maintenance, print shop and mailroom operations, and building maintenance (see Table A-2).

TABLE A-2   Typical Responsibilities of Managers of Administration

Building maintenance
Car fleet operations
Clerical support
Copying/duplicating
Data processing
File and records maintenance
In-house food services
Micrographics
Office design
Office equipment/supplies
Printshop
Purchasing
Secretarial services
Security
Telecommunications
Word processing/administrative support

It is not the intent of this entry to investigate these diverse duties. Instead, this entry will concentrate on the tools administrative managers use to keep administrative costs down: personnel incentives, work measurement and performance analysis, mechanization, and office systems.

*Employee Attitudes.* Because administration is so often viewed as a necessary evil, employees who work in administration occasionally have a dim view of their role in the organization. Being relegated to support functions, they find it hard to envision themselves as the movers and shakers. They settle into routines. Consequently, problems arise. Administration for the sake of administration can begin.

**Incentive Plans**   To minimize problems of complacency and, perhaps, unnecessary work, incentives are an effective managerial technique.

Because of the integrated systems employed and the cooperative effort required, it is not individuals who must be motivated as much as it is groups of individuals—those people who make up the system's teams. When considering any type of group incentive, some basic questions should be asked.

Do employees really believe they can increase their productivity through this or another program?

Have incentives worked here in the past? Why or why not?

Is there a feeling of teamwork present?

What do employees think about the present state of labor-management relations?

Will employees view management's approach as manipulative, or relevant and rational?

If management cannot answer these questions positively, preliminary work must be done to improve employees' outlooks before the incentive program can be effective. Only after attitudes are changed can a manager proceed to establish performance standards and/or sample work with a minimum of employee resentment and fear.

*Plan Requirements.*   The incentive plan must be deemed by employees to be fair and equitable, especially as it relates to work measurement. The plan should have a consensus of approval by all levels of employees involved, who must also feel that their rewards will be just.

It is important in office situations that the program be placed within a time frame, i.e., 6 months, 1 year, etc. Plans that go on indefinitely cause problems. A time frame enables management to compare present results with past performance for rewards. If the plan continues after initial rewards are given, employee interest can wane. At this point it is necessary to establish new goals and to change incentives—in effect, start a new plan. Simply calling a close to the program can evoke counterproductive results. But if the plan is given a time frame at the onset, once it has run its course, management can decide whether or not to recycle it, start another plan with new rewards, or discontinue it, without the pressure of employees feeling something has been taken away from them.

**Work and Performance Measurement**   Work measurement examines the jobs being done. Performance analysis examines the employees performing the work. The object is to determine whether the work is being done efficiently and whether it should

be done at all. Work and performance measurement may be conducted in conjunction with, or independent of, an incentive plan.

Employees, upon realizing work is being scrutinized, tend to fear a change in their work patterns, or worse, job displacement. To counter this, a work measurement program should not only identify weaknesses; it should also show how these weaknesses can be overcome. Emphasis should be on improving employees' jobs, perhaps even making them easier.

*Performance Standards.*   Two basic types of performance standards are

1. *General standards,* which cover a broad range of jobs (always more than one). For this reason, they are less expensive to develop and are usually easier to explain to employees. The major weakness of these standards is that they do not isolate a specific task or job. General standards are most beneficial in measuring overall effectiveness; they are least beneficial in measuring specific task efficiency.

2. *Isolated standards,* which focus on a specific job or task, such as the number of envelopes labeled in an hour. Costs for developing these standards are much higher because each task has to be studied independently, their implications are limited to the particular task being studied, and it is time-consuming to explain each standard individually to the employees performing it.

Jobs that are complex in nature usually lend themselves to general standards, while isolated standards favor simple tasks.

Performance standards should (1) emphasize goals, (2) be specific, (3) identify measurable job traits, and (4) show the employee ways of improving.

*Measurement Techniques.*   In order to apply standards, performance (or work) must first be measured. Traditionally, this has meant *time studies,* which require large numbers of timed observations to find a norm. A shorter but less precise approach is *work sampling,* which involves randomized observations of how employees occupy their time (i.e., productively or nonproductively). A third method uses *predetermined elemental times* for performing work as obtained from various proprietary sources. (*See* WORK MEASUREMENT.)

**Impact of Equipment**   In addition to integrating people within different departments, today's administrator must also consider equipment, which can help increase work capacity and minimize costs while maintaining high standards of customer satisfaction—the quality of output.

The rapid advances in office equipment and related technology, however, both solve and create problems. Conversion to laborsaving equipment often forces a complete realignment of the labor force. Moreover, the rapidly approaching *total system* office which integrates word processing, data processing, micrographics, reprographics, telecommunications, and mail systems, not only threatens to realign the office work force, it may also change the knowledge and skill requirements of the workers themselves. What used to be done by 10 secretaries, for example, is now accomplished by machines and two or three highly skilled technicians.

*Shifting Standards Base.* Because of the complexity of today's administrative environment, isolated standards are often found to be too rigid. With general standards, management must look to employees for input on measuring because intangibles such as interdepartmental interaction have to be taken into account. Hard-and-fast standards fall by the wayside, deferring to an objective of working toward an optimal level or standard.

For this type of standard, precise piecemeal measurements are often impractical. Instead, output data of the total operation are collected and observed. Productivity trends emerge from these data. These trends lend themselves to comparisons that help management to make systems decisions which,

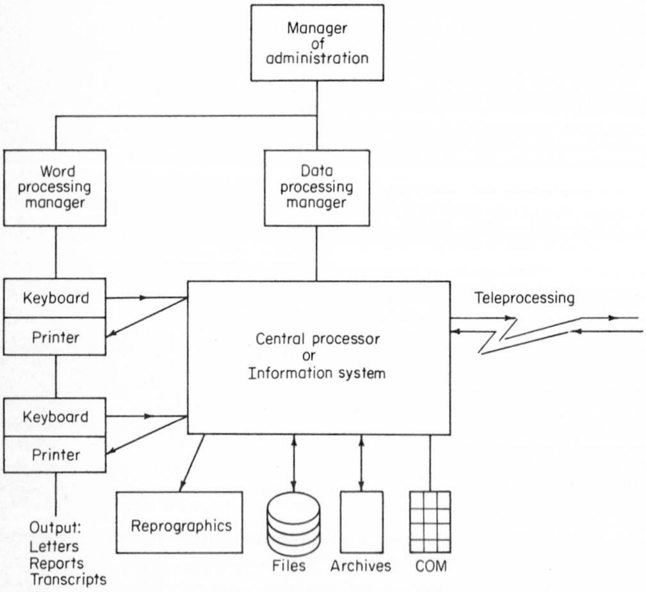

in turn, may entail introduction of new equipment and realignment of the office force.

*Word Processing.* One restructuring brought about by automation is evident in word processing. When some companies in the early seventies traded in their electric typewriters for automatic word processing equipment, more than just equipment changed. The "one-secretary-to-one-principal" institution changed as well. Initially, the secretarial function was split into two jobs: (1) the typing specialist, or correspondence secretary, and (2) the administrative secretary. Typing specialists were located in the *word processing center.* Staffed by correspondence secretaries only, the center handled the entire typing workload. Administrative secretaries, on the other hand, supported two or more principals, handling all their nontyping support activities. Later, due to necessity, there was an evolution into cluster and satellite formations, where word processing centers handled all the secretarial work for the principals surrounding them.

Presently both configurations are in operation and, in some instances, adaptations of both. In any arrangement, however, the automatic typewriter already has forced a realignment of office labor.

*Total System Development.* The automatic typewriter, which presaged the word processing system, is now beginning to merge with data processing. Simple keyboard operations can handle typing, data processing, filing in-memory, or, in the case of computer output to micrographics (COM), microfilming. Simultaneously, reprographics as well as facsimile transmission are merging into the system. As electronic mail becomes more cost-effective, a total system will support many of the functions of administration (see Fig. A-12).

The cost-savings potential of the total system approach is still largely untapped. Enormous savings will be found at *crossover* points—points at which it becomes cost-effective to automate.

*See also* COMPUTER SYSTEMS; CONTROL SYSTEMS, MANAGEMENT; DATA PROCESSING PRINCIPLES AND PRACTICES; FORMS DESIGN AND CONTROL; INFORMATION SYSTEMS; OFFICE SPACE PLANNING AND DESIGN; PAPER WORK SIMPLIFICATION; RECORDS MANAGEMENT; TELECOMMUNICATIONS; WORD PROCESSING.

## REFERENCES

Further information on office administration is available from the Administrative Management Society, a nonprofit professional management association, at its Management Information Center, AMS, Maryland Road, Willow Grove, Pennsylvania 19090.

**Fig. A-12. The total administrative system.**

Journals regularly covering the field include:

*Administrative Management*, Geyer-McAllister Publications, 51 Madison Avenue, New York, New York 10010.

*Information and Records Management*, 250 Fulton Avenue, Hempstead, New York 11550.

*Infosystems*, Hitchcock Building, Wheaton, Illinois 60187.

*Management World*, Administrative Management Society, Maryland Road, Willow Grove, Pennsylvania 19090.

*Personnel Journal*, 1131 Olympic Boulevard, Santa Monica, California 90404.

*Purchasing*, Cahner's Publishing Co., 1600 North Main Street, Pontiac, Illinois 61764.

*Reproductions Review and Methods*, North American Publishing Co., 401 North Broad Street, Philadelphia, Pennsylvania 19108.

JIM N. BRUNO, *Administrative Management Society*

# Administrative (office) management   *(See heading in Table of Contents for complete listing.)*

# Administrative managers   *(See* MANAGER, DEFINITIONS OF.*)*

# Administrative manuals   *(See* MANUALS, POLICY AND PROCEDURES.*)*

# Administrative organization   *(See* ORGANIZATION ANALYSIS AND PLANNING.*)*

# Adoption process   *(See* CONSUMER BEHAVIOR, MANAGERIAL RELEVANCE OF.*)*

# Ad-readership research   *(See* MARKETING RESEARCH.*)*

# Advertising concepts

This entry examines the economic value and cost of advertising, the functions of advertising, how advertising goals and strategies are developed, basic advertising appeals, and the functions and characteristics of media.

## ECONOMIC VALUES AND COSTS

There are three ways to view the economic value and costs of advertising. One way is to view advertising's aggregate effect on the economy of a nation. The second is to view the value and cost to the individual firm. The third is to look at the value and cost to the consumer.

*Aggregate Effect.* There is much debate on the value and cost of advertising to an economy. Critics believe that advertising is wasteful by adding to product costs, misallocating billions of dollars to unproductive use rather than to production of goods and services, setting up barriers by large firms to the entry of new firms into an industry, and making consumers buy products they do not really need.

Advocates of advertising feel that advertising plays an important role in lessening the negative effects of a recession, extending product life cycles, supporting the media from which we obtain news and entertainment, reducing the prices of products by increasing demand and realizing economics of scale in production, informing consumers of product improvements and new products and thereby contributing to economic growth, and helping to satisfy psychological needs of consumers (e.g., status). Although the debate over the costs and benefits of advertising to an economy has not been, nor is it likely to be, resolved, it probably is fair to say that both sides of the issue have merit.

*Individual Firm.* Firms benefit from advertising in different ways and to a different extent, depending upon several factors. A company that is unknown or whose brands are unknown is likely to benefit most from advertising. Where products are physically similar, advertising can create a psychological differentiation for a brand in the minds of consumers and increase company sales and profits. Advertising also is more beneficial to a company which is in an industry with expanding sales as opposed to one in which sales are declining. For example, companies which sell citizen band radios will benefit from advertising more than ones selling slide rules. Companies which manufacture products having "hidden" or unobservable qualities will tend to benefit more from advertising than companies in which product features are more apparent.

Advertising also provides a relatively inexpensive means of informing consumers about a company's brands, especially when compared with the cost of a sales force performing the same function. Advertising also benefits a company by making its sales representatives more efficient. That is, advertising provides an entrée for the sales representative. The prospective customer is made aware of the company and its product offerings through advertising. Good advertising may have created an interest in the brand and have stimulated questions about the brand. Thus, advertising can help open the door for sales representatives, inform prospective buyers of product features, and stimulate interest and desire for a product, all of which make sales representatives more efficient.

*The Consumer.* Advertising is certainly a cost which consumers incur; however, when we consider the alternatives, the benefits of advertising outweigh the cost. To make a product and brand choice, a consumer must have some knowledge of what is available. Advertising is an economical way for consumers to reduce their search time for products and brands which can satisfy a need or solve a problem. Advertising also helps create images and psychological values which can help satisfy the psychological and social needs of consumers. In the United States economy, psychological needs are very important, since basic physiological needs of food, clothing, and shelter have been generally met.

It is generally agreed that many companies do waste some of their money in advertising. Some companies either spend too little on advertising to gain significant economic benefits or spend too much, incurring negative marginal returns. The net effect of advertising in the United States, however, is beneficial to the economy by stimulating demand for new products and by helping firms achieve mass production, economies of scale, and higher employment. The consumer benefits from reduced search costs and psychological and social satisfaction. The firms benefit from higher sales and profits through an efficient means of informing consumers of product offerings.

## FUNCTIONS OF ADVERTISING

Advertising performs at least seven basic functions for a company.[1]

*Information.* Advertising informs consumers of the existence of a brand, its characteristics and benefits, its price, where it can be purchased, and the terms of purchase.

*Entertainment.* Advertising is very often entertaining. The humor of Alka Seltzer and Benson and Hedges commercials and the adventuresomeness of the Schlitz commercials are examples of how advertising can entertain consumers.

*Persuasion.* Advertising attempts to create or change consumer attitudes toward the company brand. To influence consumer attitudes, companies use celebrities (credible sources), consumer testimonials, two-sided messages, comparison advertising, logical-factual argumentation, and psychological or social benefits which will accrue to the purchasers of the brand.

*Reminder.* Because of its repetitive nature, advertising continually reminds consumers of the product and its benefits. Furthermore, heavy reminder advertising tends to create consumer confidence for a brand because of increased familiarity.

*Reassurance.* Advertising serves to reduce post-purchase doubt for products which require a large investment, such as an automobile. Consumers seek out information which supports a major purchase decision they have made. Advertising is one source which helps to alleviate the doubt they have after a purchase decision.

*Assistance to Other Company Efforts.* Advertising facilitates other company efforts. Advertising can generate leads for sales representatives, provide an entry to clients for sales representatives, help consumers to identify more easily product packages in the store, desensitize consumers to the higher than average price of a brand, enhance the image and reputation of the firm and stores carrying the brand, improve employee morale, and create a favorable image among present stockholders and potential investors and lending institutions.

*Addition of Value.*[2] Advertising adds value to a product by associating intangible attributes with the brand. A cigarette is "masculine" (Marlboro) or "feminine" (Virginia Slims) because of the meanings which advertisers associate with the brand names. Thus, advertisers influence consumers' perceptions of products by attributing socially significant values to brands, such as status, sex appeal, and elegance.

## ADVERTISING STRATEGY[3]

There are five basic steps in developing a strategy.
1. Assess opportunities.
2. Analyze corporate resources.
3. Set objectives.
4. Develop and evaluate alternative strategies.
5. Assign specific tasks.

**Environmental Factors** The initial step in developing an advertising strategy is to identify and evaluate market opportunities. Market opportunities are created and destroyed by changes in environmental factors. The major environmental factors an advertiser must consider are (1) technological factors, (2) economic factors, (3) sociocultural factors, and (4) legal-political factors.

1. *Technological changes* affect the kinds of media that can be used and how these media can be used. A relatively recent innovation in media is the shopper-talker. It is a device that shows films or slides to consumers at the point of purchase while playing a recorded message about the product. It can be located on counters in department stores or in thoroughfares within shopping malls. As previously mentioned, microfragrance and vinyl sound sheets have been used in magazines to bring the dimension of smell and sound to the print medium. A development on the horizon is the "television newspaper." Because of newsprint shortages and other factors, consumers may only have to push a button on their television to read the comics, the sports page, or Dear Abby. This prospect could have serious implications for the future of newspaper advertising.

2. *Economic changes* can both create and destroy opportunities for advertisers. When economic times are prosperous and discretionary income increases, the demand for amusements, travel, high-quality products, and status goods increases. Advertisers of these goods and services must be ready to increase their effort in times of prosperity. The energy crisis of 1973 to 1974 is an example of how advertisers adapted to a change in the economic environment. Automobile manufacturers began to advertise economy and gas efficiency; gasoline cap locks and anti-siphoning devices were advertised; AT&T advertised the energy-saving usage of telephone conferences as opposed to travel by plane or other transportation methods. Electric and gas companies provided consumers with fuel-saving suggestions through their advertising.

3. Changes in the *social* and *cultural* behavior of consumers create and destroy advertising opportunities. The women's liberation movement provided an opportunity for advertisers to develop a new theme associating women's liberation with their products, e.g., cigarettes. Changing societal attitudes toward feminine hygiene deodorants and condoms opened up opportunities for advertising these and other products.

4. Changes in the *legal-political* environment affect what can be advertised and how it can be advertised. Cigarettes and liquor are two prime examples of products for which the federal government regulates advertising. Claims advertisers can make about mouthwashes is another example. Changes in the political relations with foreign countries, such as Russia and China, affect where advertisements can be shown. Another influence of government on advertising has been the Federal Trade Commission's (FTC) encouragement of comparison advertising (discussed later). During the 1970s the FTC has caused many firms (e.g., in the mouthwash industry) to spend money on corrective advertising.

Advertisers must continually monitor environmental changes, such as those cited above, to adapt and create their advertising messages.

**Product-Oriented Strategy** There are two broad categories of advertising strategies—those which use a product-oriented approach and those which use a consumer-oriented approach.[4] At least three advertising strategies use a product-oriented approach. They are (1) *feature-oriented* strategy, where the advertising campaign stresses specific attributes or characteristics of a brand, such as "our cigarette has only 2 milligrams of tar and 0.2 milligrams of nicotine"; (2) *use-oriented* strategy, where the advertising campaign stresses the in-operation and/or post-operation benefits of a brand, such as "Auto-wax is easier to apply in half the time"; and (3) *product comparison–oriented* strategy, where the advertising campaign stresses differences between a client's brand and a competing brand. Comparative advertising, a form of the product-comparison approach, became popular in the 1970s. This strategy has its critics and its advocates. Critics believe that comparative advertising reduces the credibility of claims, creates greater consumer awareness of competitors, and confuses consumers. Advocates claim that comparative advertising increases sales of better brands, informs consumers, and forces competitors to upgrade their brands.[5]

**Consumer-Oriented Strategy** The second broad set of advertising strategies uses a consumer-oriented approach. At least four strategies use this approach. The first is an *attitude-oriented* strategy, which presents a message consistent with the consumer's attitude-value-belief structure. The second is a *significant group-oriented* approach, which stresses the group that uses or approves of the client's brand. The group must be important to the target market and is usually a reference or social group. The third is a *life-style–oriented* strategy, which develops its theme around the life-style of a distinct target market. Finally, some advertisers use a *subconsciously oriented* approach by appealing to subconscious (or unconscious) consumer needs through symbolism. This approach uses veiled appeals to repressed human desires.

**Image-Oriented Strategy** This strategy cannot be classified exclusively under the product- or consumer-oriented approaches. Although all advertising strategies create some kind of brand image in the mind of consumers, an image-oriented strategy is a conscious attempt on the part of advertisers to create a brand "personality" or to develop a brand image consistent with a consumer's self-image.

**Positioning** One last strategy which may be categorized as either product- or consumer-oriented creates a "position," or brand niche in the consumer's mind by relating the client's brand to those of its competitors or by attaching the brand to something already in the consumer's mind. This strategy, which became popular in the 1970s, is *product positioning.*[6] Avis positioned itself as second to Hertz, Volkswagen created the "ugly" position, and 7-Up positioned itself as an "uncola" against the colas. Supporters of product positioning say the strategy has become successful because of the high noise level and clutter resulting from the enormous volume of advertising and the volume of products and brands. The positioning approach allows consumers to hang the brand on a product ladder or attach it to something with which they are familiar and therefore able to remember the brand more easily.

The advertising strategy which a company selects depends upon the product type as well as the market segment to whom it chooses to sell.

## APPEALS, MESSAGES, AND COMMUNICATIONS

Communication is an inherent part of advertising. To advertise effectively, advertisers should adhere to basic communications principles, such as stating the message in terms familiar to the target audience. A message which is successful in the white Anglo-Saxon market will very likely not appeal to the black subculture.

From communications research several basic advertising principles have evolved. The following are a few of these principles:

1. A *two-sided advertising message* (i.e., one in which strengths and weaknesses of a brand are brought out or where strengths of a competitive brand are mentioned) is more effective than a one-sided message if (*a*) the audience is well-educated, and (*b*) the audience uses a competing brand.[7]

2. *Fear appeals* are an effective means of persuading an audience. Mouthwashes, breath mints, and toothpaste are among the product categories which use this appeal by communicating fear of ostracism.

3. *Pleasant forms of distraction* presented with the advertised message can increase the effectiveness of persuasive appeals.

4. A *message which actively involves the audience* can increase effectiveness. Camera angles can place the audience in a position of vicariously trying the product. Permitting the audience to complete a jingle will actively involve audience members. An example is the earlier television commercial, "You can take Salem out of the country, but. . . ."

5. Advertising practitioners believe that *emotional appeals* are more successful than rational appeals.

6. *Humor* has not proven to be an effective persuasive appeal, but it can be effective in gaining audience attention and in aiding consumer recall of the brand and its message.

7. *Nonverbal communications* are often more important than the verbal message. Facial expressions, voice qualities, dress, gestures, music, and eye movement are examples.

## THE MEDIA: AN OVERVIEW

Communications research provides us with several characteristics of the broadcast and print media. Some of the more important are the following:

1. An audience will retain complex factual material better when it is presented in print as opposed to oral presentation. On the other hand, the broadcast media are more effective for simple material.

2. The print media permit easy reexposure, whereas the broadcast media are fleeting.

3. The broadcast media offer consumers a greater sense of realism than the print media.

4. Print allows the reader to develop the topic in depth, because the reader can control the time, pace, and direction of the exposure.

5. Multiple-channel messages are more effective than single-channel presentations. That is, advertising is more effective when the message stimulates more than one sense. The idea helps to explain the powerful effects of television.

Each medium has its strengths and weaknesses. The media mix which an advertiser selects should be based upon the objectives, the advertising strategy used, the characteristics of the product, and the characteristics of the target market.

**Print Media** Some of the distinguishing *strengths of a newspaper* are the following:

1. Has high geographic flexibility, i.e., ads can be placed in some markets to the exclusion of others and therefore have copy tailored to each.

2. Has short closing time; ads usually can be placed in newspapers within a 24 to 48 hour period.

3. Read most widely by well-educated and high socioeconomic groups.

4. Has highly involved readers.
5. Is used as a shopping guide.
6. Is a habitual (daily) activity.[8]

Some of the *newspaper's major weaknesses* are poor reproduction quality and a short life-span; i.e., they are usually kept in the home for one day and do not permit frequent reexposure.

Over the past several years, *magazines,* the other major print medium, have become very specialized in order to survive. *Life* and *Look* magazines, once very popular general magazines, have died. One of the major strengths of magazines is their *long life-span.* They are retained in the home for long periods of time (often several months) and permit frequent reexposure.

Magazines which have survived into the seventies have done so because of their high degree of *audience selectivity.* Advertisers can zero in on consumers with specific product interests (e.g., *Golf Digest*) and specific sex, income, and age groups. Magazines also have increased their geographic flexibility by offering regional editions. Thus, some ads can run in the Northeast which have little relevance to people in the Southeast. Magazines also have advantages of high quality in reproduction and a high level of credibility and prestige.

*Business publications,* such as *Purchasing* and *Advertising Age,* are high-interest publications to which industry and professionals look, for information relevant to their businesses. Other print media available to advertisers are the *Yellow Pages* of telephone books which 92 million Americans use an average of 40 times a year.[9] *Outdoor advertising,* a very inexpensive means of delivering a message, and *transit advertising,* found on buses, trains, taxicabs, etc., are also important print media for advertisers.

**Broadcast Media** *Television* has the highest overall impact of any media. Television can reach an enormous audience with a single advertisement, yet cost per exposure is relatively low. Because television uses sight, sound, motion, and color, it delivers a message with great realism. Even though television reaches extremely large audiences, it still maintains a good degree of audience selectivity due mostly to programming. A major advantage of television is *psychology of attention;* that is, an audience will continue to watch a commercial message rather than get up to switch channels.[10]

Among the disadvantages of television are the large absolute (versus relative) cost of a national advertisement, the poor availability of desired times or programs to air the commercial, and the lack of easy reexposure (as opposed to print).

Even with these disadvantages television has high psychological impact because it is realistic and has a multichannel nature, it provides manufacturers with an opportunity to demonstrate their products, and it has the ability to build strong brand images.

*Radio* was the most pervasive medium until the advent of television. Since the arrival of television, radio has undergone great change. Technologically, radio developed into a highly portable medium as the transistor was ushered in. Now radio can be found in the home, car, factory, beach, stores, and office. Although radio has a very massive audience, it is still a very highly selective medium. Its selectivity (well-defined target audience) is due to the plethora of program formats. Advertisers can select nearly any age, race, or socioeconomic class they wish with radio. Radio attracts a larger audience than television until 6:00 P.M. It offers geographic and time flexibility and is less expensive than television or newspapers.

It has, however, the major disadvantage of all broadcast media. It is fleeting, thereby lacking in easy reexposure, and, moreover, it cannot deliver the visual impact of television. Finally, radio lacks the prestige of television and is subject to a higher degree of message distortion.

**Media Planning** As we can see, each medium possesses its strengths and weaknesses. To aid the advertiser in making a media-mix decision, a media-planning matrix (Fig. A-13) should be evaluated. Below is a partial representation of a media-planning matrix.[11]

To use the matrix, one should place some value or weight on each dimension for each medium. The

| Media characteristics and functions / Media | Reputation | Life span | Target market/ Total audience | Cost | Flexibility | Reseller support | Message reproduction | Editorial climate | Availability | Psychological impact |
|---|---|---|---|---|---|---|---|---|---|---|
| Newspapers | | | | | | | | | | |
| Magazines | | | | | | | | | | |
| Radio | | | | | | | | | | |
| Television | | | | | | | | | | |
| Yellow pages | | | | | | | | | | |
| Outdoor | | | | | | | | | | |
| Transit | | | | | | | | | | |

Fig. A-13. A media-planning matrix.

following are brief descriptions of each medium characteristic or function:

1. *Reputation:* the credibility, trustworthiness, or prestige of the medium.

2. *Life-span:* the length of time a medium remains in the home to permit reexposure.

3. *Target market/total audience:* the proportion of total audience which are prime prospects for the firm's product. Thus, *total* circulation and listener or viewer figures are not good criteria.

4. *Cost:* at least two costs must be considered—*absolute* and *relative* costs. The relative cost (cost per prime contact) might be low, but the absolute cost of the medium prohibitive.

5. *Flexibility:* should be judged in terms of *timing* (when the message will be exposed to the audience), *geography* (the physical location of the audience), and *lead time* (advance notice time to the medium).

6. *Reseller support:* the degree of importance that resellers perceive that a medium gives them in selling a product. The producer often needs to obtain shelf space, and this dimension becomes very important.

7. *Message reproduction:* the level of quality in producing a client's message in a medium; for example, color reproduction in magazines versus newspapers.

8. *Editorial climate:* the philosophy or tone of programs or articles which appear within the medium.

9. *Availability:* the degree of ease or difficulty in obtaining media space or time.

10. *Psychological impact:* the level of impression and emotion with which a medium imparts the advertiser's message.

Not only each medium but also the specific vehicles within each medium (i.e., *Golf* magazine versus *Golf Digest*, or *Stereo* versus *Stereo Today*) should be evaluated with a media-planning matrix.

After evaluating the media using the media-planning matrix, management should develop the media mix which will achieve stated advertising objectives.

*See also* ADVERTISING MANAGEMENT, INDUSTRIAL; BRANDS AND BRAND NAMES; CONSUMER BEHAVIOR, MANAGERIAL RELEVANCE OF; CONSUMERISM AND CONSUMER PROTECTION LEGISLATION; FORECASTING BUSINESS CONDITIONS; MARKETING RESEARCH; PATENTS AND VALUABLE INTANGIBLE RIGHTS; PUBLIC AND COMMUNITY RELATIONS.

### NOTES

[1]M. Wayne DeLozier, *The Marketing Communications Process*, McGraw-Hill Book Company, New York, 1976, pp. 216–219.

[2]Ivan L. Preston, "Theories of Behavior and the Concept of Rationality in Advertising," *Journal of Communication*, vol. 17, no. 3, pp. 211–222, September 1967.

[3]DeLozier, op. cit., pp. 272–281.

[4]Ibid., pp. 232–234, for more in-depth discussion.

[5]"Tannenbaum: Comparative Ads Can Work; Kershaw Says No," *Advertising Age*, May 17, 1976.

[6]Jack Trout, and Al Ries, "The Positioning Era Cometh," *Advertising Age*, April 24, May 1, and May 8, 1972.

[7]E. W. J. Faison, "Effectiveness of One-sided and Two-sided Mass Communications in Advertising," *The Public Opinion Quarterly*, vol. 25, pp. 468–469, 1961.

[8]*Advertising Age*, November 21, 1973, p. 66.

[9]"The *Yellow Pages* in Marketing and Advertising," American Telephone and Telegraph Company, 1970, pp. 6–7.

[10]J. F. Engel, H. G. Wales, and M. R. Warshaw, *Promotional Strategy*, revised ed., Richard D. Irwin, Inc., Homewood, Ill., 1971, p. 261.

[11]DeLozier, op. cit., pp. 245–247.

M. WAYNE DELOZIER, *University of South Carolina*

# Advertising management, industrial

Industrial advertising is a means for a manufacturing company to promote the sale of its products to industrial buyers. These are the products consumed by the industrial buyers in their own conversion processes or incorporated as components of the products they produce. Advertising in support of this promotion is directed to the manufacturing, construction, and mining industries in particular and their various distribution segments.

The industrial advertising function, when structured properly, involves product development, market research, product publicity, and sales. Only through the coordination of these activities can a truly successful industrial advertising program be formulated. It is vitally important that corporate objectives be translated into commercial objectives, which, in turn, can be translated into advertising objectives. Selling more product is not a proper industrial advertising objective, although advertising is an important part of the equation that makes that objective attainable. To be able to maximize its contribution to the marketing function, advertising should have responsibility and authority for (1) agency selection, supervision, and compensation; (2) media selection; and (3) creativity.

## A FORMER STEPCHILD

Industrial advertising has come of age only in the last half of the twentieth century. The fault for this late blooming lies equally between industrial management and academia. In the former instance, the tendency used to be to assign the advertising responsibility to the son-in-law or to "good old Charlie" who couldn't quite cut it but has been around too long to fire. At best, the function was assigned to someone in the sales department as an additional duty. Obviously, this approach did little to develop professionalism or competence.

On the academic side, students were taught for decades about the big difference between consumer and industrial *advertising* when, in fact, the emphasis should have been on the difference between the consumer and industrial *purchase*. Academia generally overlooked the fact that purchasing agents, when they enter their offices, do not shed all human emotions. Their attention can be drawn in the same manner as it can in the consumer field. The difference, of course, is that the purchasing agent does not have to account for an impulse purchase but must justify the reason for buying a half-million dollar machine tool. So the "stopping" techniques of consumer and industrial ads can be similar. However, the ad must also provide the industrial buyer with solid reasons for the purchase.

A large portion of the credit for the emerging professionalism of industrial advertising can be attributed to three associations: Association of National Advertisers (ANA), American Business Press (ABP), and the Business/Professional Advertising Association (B/PAA). ANA commissioned several landmark texts (*see* references), and the other two associations have for years sponsored contests in which industrial advertising is measured against advertising objectives.

## CREATIVITY

Modern industrial advertising employs virtually every medium: magazines, newspapers, broadcasting, direct mail, trade shows, outdoor. Regardless of the medium, nothing is accomplished without first attracting the buyer's attention. This is where the creative people come in. Few things can be more detrimental to advertising effectiveness than to have the creative team feel, "The client will never stand still for that." Inasmuch as nearly everyone is a self-appointed advertising expert, it is incumbent upon the advertising manager to remind the top management that the ads are being directed not to the chairman of the board but to the company's customers and prospects. This author has repeatedly said in speeches and articles that about 30 percent of the ads he approves do not particularly appeal to him, but they do very well in the marketplace. Indeed, some of the most effective advertising will be the kind that makes management a bit uncomfortable.

There is a companion to this problem. It occurs when top management tires of a campaign just about the time the customers and prospects are beginning to notice it. Part of the problem is that most managements have seen the campaign several times before it even sees the light of day. The other part of the problem is that it is not generally recognized that repeated advertising can be most effective. [*See* McGraw-Hill and IARI (now CMC) studies mentioned in the references.] A corollary to this problem is the penchant for starting new campaigns with the beginning of each fiscal year. Campaigns should begin when they are *needed*, whether it be Bastille Day, Valentine's Day, or, by coincidence, the beginning of the fiscal year.

Another creative aspect is color. It is demonstrable that four-color is most effective, but it is also the most expensive process. Advertisers who cannot budget four-color work should go to black and white, unless two-color can be used functionally. In the first half of the century, two-color advertisers always used red, probably because of its dominant promotional hue. Subsequently, research indicated that a second color enhanced an ad only if it was used functionally—to show a product's color or to emphasize a point. The principle is: When using a second color, there should be a specific reason other than just decorating the border for the ad.

## THE ADVERTISING BUDGET

The greatest ad ever prepared will not do any good unless it is displayed or broadcast somewhere. Therefore, budgets are as important as creativity. Although there are almost as many approaches to advertising budgets as there are advertisers, they can be resolved into two basic concepts: (1) percentage of sales and (2) task method. In the industrial field, almost everyone prefers the *task method* wherein the product managers set forth their marketing goals, the advertising people determine what kinds of ads and campaigns are needed to assist in achieving these goals, and then a cost estimate is made. If this estimate is unrealistic, adjustments have to be made, but, with that exception, the advertising people should request the funding necessary to do the prescribed job. If top management feels the request to be too high, it should determine which projects or campaigns must be eliminated. Flat percentage cuts, such as 10 percent budget reduction, are not the way to approach an advertising budget. After all, how does one run 10.8 pages, reduced from a proposed 12-page schedule?

**Continuity** Far too many companies fail to provide for continuity in their advertising campaigns. Because most companies are on a calendar year basis, this accounts for the thin publication issues in January and February. Actually, there is nothing magical about January 1, except for the fact that many companies have not finalized their budgets. On the other hand, they know that they will be advertising; it is only the numbers that are not yet firm. Enlightened managements allow their advertising people to take advantage of the thin January-February issues, while the numbers are being hammered out. This way they obtain maximum exposure, while less-foresighted companies run the risk of ganging their advertising in fewer, thicker issues.

## MEDIA

The selection of media is a specialized function which should be handled between the ad manager and the agency. Good salespeople are aggressive, and occasionally a space salesperson will find access to top management. Obviously, top management has a right to inject itself into any aspect of the corporation's activities. If this occurs, the ad manager should insist that the corporate officer see competitive salespeople as well. After all, any good salesperson can make a publication look like the best product, and the only way to put the whole thing in perspective is to hear from the other sides.

**Selection** There are more than 2500 media listed in the business publication section of *Standard Rate and Data*. This presents a considerable selection problem. Four fundamental guidelines are used in selecting media.

*Audit.* Review of a publication which is not audited by one of the tripartite nonprofit audit bureaus (Audit Bureau of Circulations, Business Publications Audit of Circulation, Canadian Circulations Audit Board) should cause one to hesitate. There are many excuses advanced for books that are not audited but none really holds water. One is the expense of the audit. This is not true. All three audit bureaus readily provide audit charge schedules to show how extremely reasonable they are. A more valid excuse is that it would be too costly to get the

records in order for an audit. Any publication in this situation is probably in trouble and does not know it. The final reason, of course, is that the publication has something to hide.

*Media Data Form.* This is a publication of the Media Comparability Council (MCC), and it complements the media form. The MCC is an organization of 14 leading advertising-oriented associations: Advertising Research Foundation, American Association of Advertising Agencies, Inc., American Business Press, Inc., Association of Canadian Advertisers, Association of National Advertisers, Inc., Audit Bureau of Circulations, Business/Professional Advertising Association, Business Publications Audit of Circulation, Inc., Canadian Advertising Research Foundation, Canadian Business Press, Canadian Circulations Audit Board, Inc., Center for Marketing Communications, Institute of Canadian Advertising, and Society of National Association Publications.

Although the MCC delves into a wide-ranging number of topics through its various committees (Comparability Committee, Research Committee, Standards and Practices Committee), the principal thrust is through the Media Data Form Committee. The data form serves two purposes. Because it standardizes reporting, it eliminates the necessity for media people to refigure publishers' statements in order to make them comparable. It also serves to reduce to a minimum the questionnaires sent by advertisers and advertising agencies to over 500 publishers who file forms.

*Association Membership.* A third criterion in media selection might well be whether the publication belongs to its trade association. In most cases in the industrial field this would be the American Business Press (ABP). However, the ABP excludes some notable publications such as *Business Week, Dun's Review, Forbes, Fortune, Harvard Business Review, Nation's Business, Wall Street Journal,* and the news weeklies. The reason is that their primary listing is not in the Business Publication section of *Standard Rate and Data*. Obviously, if a publication is not eligible for ABP, the third criterion does not apply.

*Bleed Charges.* A fourth criterion that more and more advertisers and agencies are applying to media is the matter of bleed charges. (*Bleed* is any portion of an ad that extends to the edge of the page.) Before the advent of offset lithography, printers assessed publications an additional charge for bleed. This charge was passed on to the advertisers in the form of a 10 to 15 percent additional charge. Most publications today are printed by offset lithography, and the printers no longer charge the publisher for bleed. Yet many publications retain the bleed charge. Doubtless the publication needs the revenue provided by the anachronistic bleed charge. Advertisers, however, are taking the position that the publisher should raise general advertising rates sufficiently that there would be no discrimination against an advertiser who inserts a better-looking ad. More and more publications are coming around to this point of view. Those who are still resisting cite these principal reasons:

1. Pagination, date of issue, and logo: If the charge for bleed was dropped, everyone would use bleed, and there would be no place for page numbers. *Answer:* If everyone paid for bleed, there would still have to be place for page numbers, and so the publisher must figure out a way to accommodate this situation.

2. Space: Bleed provides 32 percent additional space. *Answer:* A page is sold and bought as a page, not as 68 percent of a page. If publishers wish to take this approach, they will have to adjust to a different argument to accommodate 7 by 10-inch versus 8½ by 11-inch pages.

3. Nonbleed advertisers would subsidize bleed advertisers. *Answer:* On the contrary, because there are no true bleed costs, the bleed advertisers now subsidize the nonbleed.

## RESEARCH

Consumer advertisers do a great deal of pretesting and posttesting as well as other types of advertising research. This is an area in which the industrial advertiser has been extremely slow in catching up. Possibly the most significant step was taken in 1951 when the National Industrial Advertisers Association (now B/PAA) founded the Industrial Advertising Research Institute [now the Center for Marketing Communications (CMC)]. Any company that spends an appreciable amount on advertising should earmark a portion of that sum to determine whether the job is being done properly. Membership in CMC would help, but beyond that, specific research projects should be undertaken. As a point of departure, the company (or its agency) should purchase all readership studies for all publications in which the company's ads appear. This gives the advertiser a fix on how well the company's ads are doing vis-á-vis others in its category and all others in the publication. The advertiser should go further, of course. He or she should commission independent research to determine whether the company's sales message is actually getting through. Not surprisingly, the more successful advertisers who have taken this approach more often come up with results which indicate that everything is fine. In these instances, the question has been raised as to whether the research money was wasted. This ignores the possibility that the ads had *not* been on the right track. After all, few people want to collect on fire insurance or life insurance.

## AGENCY RELATIONS

Agency selection is possibly the most difficult aspect of the advertising function. Because the advertising manager will have to live with the agency, he or she should have the principal role in the selection. There is a wide selection of competent advertising agencies offering industrial services but not necessarily specializing in industrial advertising. This is good because there is much the industrial people can borrow from the consumer people.

**Agency Selection** Obviously, the agency should be chosen first for its competence. Next would be its size. Does the advertiser want to be a big frog in a little pond, or vice versa? And finally, its location, although today's fast transportation makes location less important than formerly.

Another alternative is the in-house agency. In earlier years, this approach was used because of transportation problems. Today, it is done mainly for economic reasons. Those who feel they can do a better job are not realistic. Only the largest of companies, however, can justify an in-house agency, and even there one wonders what they do with payroll artists during slack periods.

**Agency Compensation** Although agency compensation is a much debated issue, the principles are fairly simple: Advertisers may get less than they are paying for, but it is highly unlikely that they will get more. As a result, many industrial advertisers embrace the fee system. Everyone wants to make a profit: enlightened companies expect their suppliers to make a *reasonable* profit. In this perspective, it becomes obvious that an agency cannot assign a top creative person to a $300 ad (agency commission is $45). As more industrial companies take the stance that any ad run over their logotype should be the best ad possible, more of these companies are drawn to the fee system. Although there are many versions of the fee system, the simplest is to have the agency charge for the hours on the account, deduct the media commissions, and invoice for the differential.

**Agency Evaluation** Among major advertisers concern has grown about the need to evaluate advertising agencies on a formalized basis. This is particularly true of multidivision companies which use two or more agencies. Historically, all advertisers, knowingly or not, have evaluated their agencies on a day-to-day basis, based on the kind of service rendered and on the agency's creative efforts. In recent years, however, many advertisers have felt the need to formalize the evaluation process for two specific purposes: (1) to analyze performance in order to detect and correct any weaknesses before a situation may be created which would force an agency change; (2) to compare the strengths and weaknesses of several agencies serving the same client in order to determine which of several agencies might recieve new or changed assignments.

If an evaluation system is established, the guidelines should be carefully spelled out and then reviewed with the principal of the agency so that there is a clear understanding on both sides concerning the ground rules of the valuation. Moreover, recognizing that the basic purpose of an evaluation is not to criticize but rather to foster better agency-client relationships, consideration should be given to allow the agency to simultaneously evaluate the client. In any event, the main purpose of the evaluation system is to reinforce the client-agency relationship. If entered into as a systematic critique of an agency's shortcomings, the evaluation will end in disaster.

### EVALUATION PROCEDURE

Those advertisers who use a formalized system typically employ questionnaires with a simple four-step grading system, i.e., excellent, good, average, unsatisfactory. These grades are then applied to

1. Functional services, such as
    Creative
    Research
    Sales promotion
    Media
    Account contact
    Public relations
2. Operation criteria, such as
    Interest in our account
    Knowledge of our business
    Ability to present new ideas
    Overall leadership
    Financial stability

This approach is especially suitable at the lower end of the advertising department structure. The formalized evaluation sheet should provide room for comments and a closing statement by the evaluator in response to the question, "What can I do to improve our relationship with the agency in the future?"

The evaluation form for the advertising director, or other management person responsible for coordi-

nating the evaluations, should provide room for the executive in charge to evaluate the agency on such criteria as management involvement in the account, agency interest, total coordination of creative efforts, and media plans.

After all the assigned people have completed their evaluations, they should be reviewed with the appropriate management person(s) who will then have the responsibility for the review with the agency personnel. This review, of course, will be a face-to-face meeting of appropriate client personnel and an agency principal who may be accompanied by a management supervisor and/or the account supervisor. At that time, if the agency has also been accorded the privilege of evaluating the client, agency personnel should be equally prepared to review the client-agency relationship as its staff perceives it.

*See also* ADVERTISING CONCEPTS; MARKETING, INDUSTRIAL; MARKETING MANAGEMENT; MARKETING RESEARCH; MARKETING OF SERVICES.

### REFERENCES

"Defining Advertising Goals for Measured Advertising Results," Association of National Advertisers, Inc., New York, 1961.

"Effective Marketing Management," Association of National Advertisers, Inc., New York, 1973.

Grosse, W. H.: "How Industrial Advertising and Promotion Can Increase Marketing Power," American Management Association, New York, 1973.

"How Much to Spend for Advertising," Association of National Advertisers, Inc., New York, 1969.

"How Repeat Advertisements Affect Readership," *McGraw-Hill Laboratory of Advertising Performance Reports 3041, 3041.1, and 3040.2*, McGraw-Hill Publications, New York, 1962, 1971, and 1974.

"Management and Advertising Problems in Advertiser-Agency Relationships," Association of National Advertisers, Inc., New York, 1965.

"The Management of the Marketing Function," Association of National Advertisers, Inc., New York, 1973.

"Repeat Ad Study, Report No. 9, Industrial Advertising Research Institute, Princeton, N.J., 1962.

"Trade Shows and Exhibits," Association of National Advertisers, Inc., New York, 1968.

H. T. S. HECKMAN, *Republic Steel Corporation*

## Affiliation (*See* INTERPERSONAL RELATIONSHIPS.)

## Affirmative action

*Affirmative action* is positive action taken to ensure nondiscriminatory treatment of all groups protected by legislation forbidding discrimination in employment because of race, religion, sex, age, or national origin.

The criterion for determining whether affirmative action is needed is not by what the intent of the employment practices are but by what the results are. If company statistics (e.g., on pay or promotion) indicate that the current status of a protected group is inferior to that of the general run of employees, affirmative action may be ordered, including preferential hiring and promotion.

All companies with federal contracts or subcontracts over $50,000 and more than 50 employees are required to have written affirmative action plans. Monitoring is by the Office of Federal Contract Compliance, and violations may result in loss of the contracts. Other companies are monitored by the Equal Employment Opportunity Commission, which may resort to the courts to enforce the demand for affirmative action.

*See also* LABOR LEGISLATION; MINORITIES, MANAGEMENT OF AND EQUAL EMPLOYMENT OPPORTUNITY; PERSONNEL ADMINISTRATION; WOMEN IN INDUSTRY.

### REFERENCES

*Affirmative Action and Equal Employment: A Guidebook for Employers*, U.S. Equal Employment Opportunity Commission, vol. 1, January 1974. (Volume 2 provides specific reference materials.)

Churchill, Neil C., and John K. Shank: "Affirmative Action and Guilt-edged Goals," *Harvard Business Review.* March–April, 1976, pp. 111–116.

"Hartford's Suburban Crunch: Four Towns Are Cited for Lack of Affirmative Action to Shoulder City Burdens," *Business Week*, May 10, 1976.

*How to Eliminate Discriminatory Practices: A Guide to EEO Compliance*, Staff of Humanic Designs Division, Information Science Incorporated, American Management Association, New York, 1975, pp. 31–33.

"A New Boss Breathes Life into Affirmative Action," *Business Week*, May 10, 1976, p. 98.

STAFF/SMITH

## Age discrimination in employment act (ADEA)   (*See* OLDER EMPLOYEES, MANAGEMENT OF.)

## Agency   (*See* GOVERNMENT REGULATIONS, BUSINESS LAW.)

## Agency, advertising   (*See* ADVERTISING MANAGEMENT, INDUSTRIAL.)

## Agendas, hidden   (*See* INTERPERSONAL RELATIONSHIPS.)

## Agents, change   (*See* ORGANIZATION DEVELOPMENT (OD).)

## Agents, merchandise   (*See* MARKETING, CHANNELS OF DISTRIBTION.)

## Air act, clean   (*See* ENVIRONMENTAL PROTECTION LEGISLATION.)

## American Institute of Certified Public Accountants (AICPA)   (*See* ACCOUNTING, FINANCIAL.)

## American National Standards Institute (ANSI)   (*See* STANDARDS AND STANDARDIZATION PROGRAMS.)

## Analysis, job   (*See* JOB ANALYSIS.)

## Analysis, market   (*See* MARKET ANALYSIS.)

## Antitrust   (*See* PATENTS AND VALUABLE INTANGIBLE RIGHTS.)

## Anxiety   (*See* HEALTH, MENTAL.)

## Application, research   (*See* RESEARCH AND DEVELOPMENT MANAGEMENT.)

## Application area, MIS   [*See* INFORMATION SYSTEMS, MANAGEMENT (MIS); IN LARGE ORGANIZATIONS.]

## Appraisal, enterprise  (*See* POLICY FORMULATION AND IMPLEMENTATION.)

## Appraisal, performance

Top management in the United States generally agrees that one of the key factors in developing a smoothly functioning and efficient organization is the full utilization of its human resources. Management of the work force is no different from other areas of operation. Effective policies cannot be formulated nor effective action taken without first obtaining reliable and relevant information. Accurate information is needed about each employee's present performance on the job, potential for other jobs, and promotability, and about the requirements of the organization in relation to the talents which an individual can offer.

Appraisal of an employee's performance is but one step in a developmental sequence for strengthening the total organization. It is a crucial step which, unfortunately, has often been carried out with only indifferent success. This indifferent success is largely a result of the sensitivity of the process to human errors of judgment, aggravated by a lack of clarity as to just what it is that is being appraised and why.

*Objective Appraisal.* Too many appraisal programs have been launched without a clear definition of the objective to be achieved. Worse, they may be planned with the vague expectation of achieving a number of overlapping objectives at once. For example, appraisal of performance on the present job is often undertaken in order to

Identify people who need training.

Determine wage and salary increases.

Compare the effectiveness of two departments performing the same operation.

Determine transfers and policies for internal reorganization.

Identify people who deserve promotion.

*Objectives Should Be Realistic.* It is doubtful whether appraisal programs could validly provide the primary criterion for most of the objectives mentioned above. For example, if performance on the present job were the only criterion for promotion, then all employees performing satisfactorily could rightfully expect to be promoted regardless of age, experience, length of service, availability of positions, talent for other and different occupations, and the general financial position of the company. Again, if excellent performance on the present job

were a prerequisite for promotion, then many a misplaced individual with talent and potential for other, possibly more responsible and specialized, jobs would be lost to the company.

*Objectives Should Be Positive and Constructive.* Appraisal programs are doomed to failure if employees associate them with determination of firing and layoffs. Such negative associations not only engender resentment and distrust on the part of employees but also put the assessing supervisor on the spot. Similarly, if appraisal programs become associated with favorable management action, a supervisor, wishing to show the department in a good light, might understandably upgrade an employees' ratings, thus adding deliberate distortion to already biased human judgment.

*Objectives Should Be Unitary.* If appraisal programs cannot, on their own, validly accomplish a single objective, it is unlikely that they will be effective in serving different or overlapping objectives.

For example, suppose that one objective of an appraisal program is to determine salary increases. In this case, assessing supervisors frequently emphasize the strengths of an employee if they feel that the employee deserves an increase. Suppose also that at the same time the appraisal program is being used to improve performance. With this objective in mind, the assessing supervisor may feel obligated to point out an employee's relative weaknesses in order to identify areas for improvement. Inevitably, the assessing supervisors will find themselves in a frustrating, if not untenable, position in attempting to use the assessments for these differing purposes.

*Individual Development as an Objective.* Using appraisal as a basis for purely administrative decision making is generally unsatisfactory. A far better utilization of it is for the development of the individual employee. Setting individual development as the objective of an appraisal program has a number of advantages.

1. The program is likely to be more acceptable to employees and to gain their support rather than arouse their resentment.

2. There is less obvious reason for the assessing supervisors to introduce deliberate distortion into the assessments to achieve their own ends.

3. Feelings of stress and strain on the part of both the assessing supervisors and the employees are lessened.

4. Assessments will probably better reflect the facts.

**Approaches to Appraisal**  There are two clearly definable approaches in making an appraisal.

*The Work-centered Approach.* In this approach, the *content* of the appraisal is limited to the way in which the person actually performs the significant functions of the job. The items to be evaluated consist of concrete job elements, such as the ability to meet scheduled deadlines. Some of the advantages of the work-centered approach are as follows:

1. It focuses on concrete and observable behavior.

2. The supervisor can cite observable behavior.

3. It supplies an objective basis for discussion between supervisor and employee.

4. It is likely to arouse less resentment and be less damaging to the employee's ego than a discussion of the employee's personality deficiencies and shortcomings.

5. It is amenable to concrete plans for corrective action. Coaching an employee on how to schedule his or her work more realistically is an easier task than advising the employee to cooperate better.

*The Person-centered Approach.* In this approach, the *content* of the appraisal concerns the personal characteristics of the person involved. The items to be evaluated consist of personality traits, such as an ability to cooperate.

These approaches sometimes overlap, and some appraisal forms in current use contain items of both types scattered throughout in apparently random order. Certainly, the assessment of behavior traits *and* personality characteristics is an important aspect of determining an employee's potential and formulating plans for personal development. The latter should not be a responsibility of the line supervisor, however. It is a job for a specialist, assisted by the discriminating use of psychological measuring instruments.

**Content of Appraisal**  To obtain maximum benefit from the work-centered approach, a careful clarification of the functions and responsibilities of the job should be undertaken before the appraisal procedure is initiated. It is clearly unfair to assess a person in terms of how well he or she is doing the job if a person's concept of the job and the superior's expectations of what should be achieved on the job do not coincide. The superior and subordinate should be in agreement on the major functions of the job, the order of their importance, and the degree of responsibility and authority that the subordinate has with respect to each.

When the objectives, approach, and content of an appraisal program have been defined, the final preliminary step is the selection of the technique to be used in making the assessments. Techniques of appraisal may be divided into two major types according to the criteria which are used in making the judgments about performance on the job.

## APPRAISAL TECHNIQUES EMPLOYING OBJECTIVE CRITERIA

Appraisal techniques of the first type employ objective criteria. The person's performance on the job is judged solely in terms of some measurable index associated with the work, computed for a given period of time. For example, indices include amount produced, amount of avoidable scrap, or the number of assembled parts found defective. Objective criteria can also be more complex, for example, labor turnover in a supervisor's department or volume of sales adjusted for market potential in different geographical areas. Where such indices are available, they fulfill a useful purpose. They do, however, suffer from a number of deficiencies, such as the emphasis on quantity rather than quality of work performed. Also it is difficult to combine quantitative ratings, unless you take into consideration the operating conditions for different plants or market conditions in different sales territories. In spite of these limitations, the concept of applying objective criteria to present performance is a popular one and has become an integral part of many management-by-objectives programs. Used in this way, the manager or rater serves as the human link between quantitative data and qualitative judgments or evaluations based upon an analysis of quantitative results. Raters are able to take account of rapidly changing circumstances and conditions which affect quantitative measures of work performance. For example, a sales manager for a chemical company was able to take into account the adverse impact of a specific ruling made by the Environmental Protection Agency on the sales of a specific pesticide in different regions of the country with different markets and crop cycles. In another study of sales behavior, it was clearly shown that food sales territories differed markedly in their potential, and that viewing dollar volume sold as a direct measure of sales success greatly oversimplified the sales evaluation process.

## APPRAISAL TECHNIQUES BASED ON HUMAN JUDGMENT

Appraisal techniques of the second type are based on human judgment. These range all the way from completely unquantified subjective judgments to ones based on data from refined instruments employing psychometric methods. No real substitute has been found for the practice of accepting the judgment of peers or supervisors in attempting to determine how well a person is performing the job. The history of appraisal techniques consists, basically, of various attempts to make these judgments quantitative, objective, and reliable.

**The Graphic Rating Scale**   Typical items from a graphic rating scale are shown in Fig. A-14. The scale has two features which earlier rating methods lacked. First, the scale in descriptive, and there is no need for the rater to make quantitative judgments.

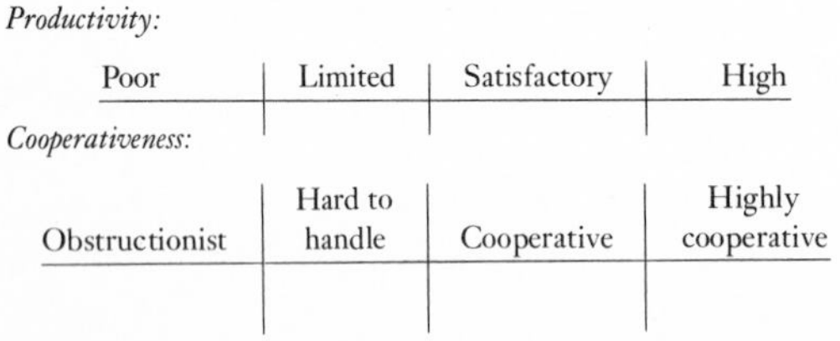

*Productivity:*

| Poor | Limited | Satisfactory | High |
|------|---------|--------------|------|

*Cooperativeness:*

| Obstructionist | Hard to handle | Cooperative | Highly cooperative |
|----------------|----------------|-------------|--------------------|

**Fig. A-14   Example of graphic rating scale**

Second, the fact that raters can indicate their assessment at any point along the scale line means that they could discriminate as finely as they choose. It has become evident, however, that even though supervisors place the same person in the same general rank order, they use different standards of assessment. Such different standards result in what the psychologists have called constant errors of judgment. This is a major weakness of this technique.

**Forced-Distribution Technique**   This method improves on the graphic rating technique. An illustration of it is given in Fig. A-15. Supervisors are forced to allocate a definite percentage of their assessments to each point on the scale. Generally, a five-point scale is used with 10:20:40:20:10 distribution of assessments. This procedure obviates the necessity of applying statistical adjustments to ensure uniform standards. It forces raters to place only 10 percent of their subordinates as top performers

| Poorest | | | Best | |
|---------|--|--|------|--|
| 10%   20% | | 40% | 20%   10% | |

Job performance

| Unlikely promotable | | | Likely promotable | |
|---------------------|--|--|-------------------|--|
| 10%   20% | | 40% | 20%   10% | |

Promotability

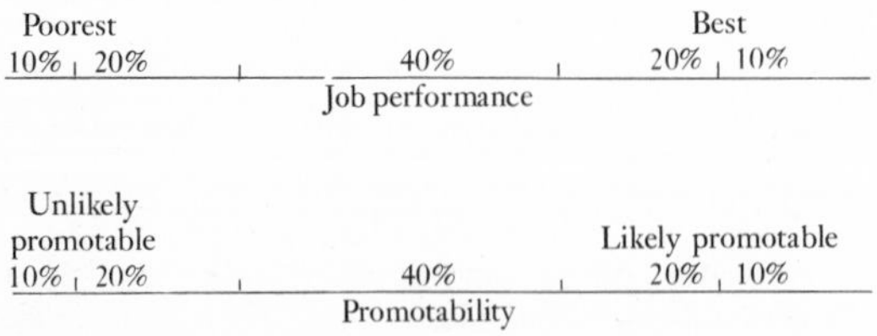

**Fig. A-15   Example of a forced distribution report**

and 10 percent as poor performers, with the other 80 percent distributed normally. The same concept can be applied to promotability as well. Since most employees want to know why they are given a high or low job performance rating, supervisors are given a previously prepared checklist of traits and simply check off those that apply to the employee's performance. The disadvantages of this technique are that it assumes either a normal or at least a comparable distribution of proficiency or performance in each rating group. Also it is a relative rather than an absolute measure of performance, and no reasons or explanations are given for the ratings which are made. Because of these limitations, it becomes unwieldy with large groups of employees.

**Forced-Choice Technique**   In this performance report, instead of indicating how much or how little of each characteristic a person possesses, the rater is required to select from several sets of four adjectives or phrases, one which is *most* characteristic and one which is *least* characteristic of the person being rated. The sets of four adjectives, known as tetrads, are so constructed that each contains two favorable and two unfavorable characteristics.

Only one of the favorable statements in each tetrad will yield a point on the report if it is chosen as "most characteristic" of the person being rated. Similarly, only one of the unfavorable statements will yield a point if it is selected as "least characteristic." The reason for this lies in the construction of the tetrads. In each tetrad, the two favorable items are matched with respect to their preference index but differ with respect to their discrimination index. The same holds true for the two unfavorable items. In other words, although the favorable items in each pair appear equally favorable to the rater, and the unfavorable items in each pair appear equally unfavorable, only one item in each pair has been demonstrated to discriminate between good and poor performers. An example of this technique is given in Table A-3.

**TABLE A-3   Example of a Forced-Choice Performance Report**

| | | |
|---|---|---|
| a. Always criticizes, never praises. | M | L |
| b. Carries out orders by "passing the buck." | M | L |
| c. Knows the job and performs it well. | M | L |
| d. Plays no favorites. | M | L |
| a. Commands respect by his or her actions. | M | L |
| b. Cool-headed. | M | L |
| c. Indifferent. | M | L |
| d. Overbearing. | M | L |

Which is *most* and *least* characteristic of the employee?

Although forced-choice ratings have not lived up to their first bright promise, they are still successfully used for specific purposes and populations. A large law enforcement agency has used the forced-choice rating technique for a number of years. The implementation of the technique was based upon essays describing the most effective and successful agent known to respondents. Scale items were developed which were matched for social desirability or preference value but which had high differentiation in separating above-average and below-average employee groups. The continuing success of this implementation of the forced-choice technique is due to strong support from top management, limiting access to the scale scoring key to personnel division staff, periodically updating the content of the scale, and using selected items to form diagnostic subscales for coaching and counseling employees to help them improve their performance.

When the use of forced-choice techniques declined, the search for objective ratings of performance branched off in two rather disparate directions, as characterized by ratings of observable behavior and in the refinement of the classical psychometric, or ranking, or pairing.

**Critical Incident Ratings** Ratings of observed behavior which depend upon the identification of incidents of behavior which indicate either exceptionally good or exceptionally poor performance have been grouped under the broad category known as *critical* incident ratings. These ratings assume that the supervisor, who is in daily contact with employees, will be able to observe and identify critical incidents or occurrences that represent either effective or ineffective performance and will record them in an objective manner. It also presumes that supervisors can be trained to identify critical job requirements and specify the kind of behavior incidents which contribute to each requirement. For certain types of work, this can be a very effective method. In the opinion of many who have used it, the greatest contribution, however, has been in establishing a good basis for supervisors' appraisal interviews with their people. It points the way to constructive dialogue about performance. It is equally clear. however, that its claims to objectivity are overdrawn. While it is true that the procedure deals with concrete behavior incidents, what is actually reported will be only that which appears in the eye of the observer.

In contrast to methods employing critical incident ratings which are of fairly recent origin, the application of classical psychometric methods goes back to about the middle of the nineteenth century. Those

most often employed today are the method of rank order and the method of paired comparisons.

**Method of Rank Order** When this is applied to appraisal of job performance, the supervisor is required to rank the people in order from the best to the poorest performer according to their overall worth to the organization. A popular variation, called the alternation ranking method, requires that the supervisor first select the best performer and then, from the people remaining, the poorest performer. After this, the supervisor selects the next best and the second poorest, and so on, in sequence, until all employees have been ranked. A typical ranking could look like the example in Fig. A-16.

The comparisons which are made by the supervisor or supervisors in determining the rankings in the method of rank order are made explicitly and more systematically in what is known as the method of paired comparisons.

| Employees to be ranked | | Rank |
|---|---|---|
| Art | ↑ | 1—Highest_____ |
| Bill | | 2—Next highest _____ |
| Bob | | 3—Next highest _____ |
| Carla | | 4—Next highest _____ |
| Charlie | | 5—Next highest _____ |
| Dan | | 6—Next highest _____ |
| Edward | | 7—Next highest _____ |
| Frances | | 8—Next highest _____ |
| Fred | | 9—Next highest _____ |
| George | | 10—Next highest _____ |
| Mary | | 10—Next lowest _____ |
| Ora | | 9—Next lowest _____ |
| Paul | | 8—Next lowest _____ |
| Ralph | | 7—Next lowest _____ |
| Rose | | 6—Next lowest _____ |
| Sam | | 5—Next lowest _____ |
| Ted | | 4—Next lowest _____ |
| Verna | | 3—Next lowest _____ |
| Walter | | 2—Next lowest _____ |
| Yvonne | ↓ | 1—Lowest _____ |

Fig. A-16　Example of alternation ranking report

**Method of Paired Comparisons** The principles underlying this method require that every individual to be assessed be compared with every other individual and an explicit judgment made as to who is the better performer. If five employees were to be assessed on job performance, the comparisons required would be those shown in Table A-4.

Comparisons are not made sequentially as presented here, but in random order, and precautions are taken to ensure that no employee is involved in two successive judgments.

In spite of the reliability and validity of assessments made with the paired-comparisons technique, the method has not been widely used. The reasons

TABLE A-4 Example of Comparative Judgments Required by the Method of Paired Comparisons in Assessing Performance of Five Employees

| 1 vs. 2 | 2 vs. 3 | 3 vs. 4 | 4 vs. 5 |
|---------|---------|---------|---------|
| 1 vs. 3 | 2 vs. 4 | 3 vs. 5 | |
| 1 vs. 4 | 2 vs. 5 | | |
| 1 vs. 5 | | | |

$$\text{Total} = \frac{5 \times 4}{2} = 10 \text{ judgments}$$

for this are twofold: (1) the time and effort required of the judges and (2) the computational labor called for in obtaining the scale values. The problem of the raters' time and effort is particularly acute when large groups of employees are involved, since the number of comparisons which must be made rises as an exponential function of the number of individuals being assessed.

The consistency of the results obtained in validation studies corroborate the long-held belief that the paired-comparisons technique minimizes the influence of personal bias in subjective judgments, thereby increasing objectivity, reliability, and validity. Mechanization of this technique, using computer programs, has resulted in considerable savings of time and effort in the administration and scoring of the results.

## PERFORMANCE APPRAISAL INTERVIEW

Any discussion of appraisal would be incomplete if it did not conclude with a discussion of the performance interview, since the appraisal is primarily developmental in nature. It is based on the belief that individual improvement will ultimately lead to organization improvement. Managers should be cautioned, however, that there are a few rules that, if followed, lead to a successful relationship. This is particularly true of the appraisal interview, which involves highly sensitive relationships; nevertheless here is how an effective interview might develop:

1. The superior makes it clear that he or she is not taking over the subordinate's problem. It is still the subordinate who has the responsibility for and who must think about the problem. The individual may resent not getting an immediate solution, but the superior helps the subordinate see that only the individual can solve the problem.

2. The superior indicates in many ways that the subordinate is neither stupid nor unusual for having a problem. The individual is not made to feel a failure.

3. The superior helps the subordinate see the value and importance of working on the problem, pointing out that it would be very much worthwhile to seek the best answer to the problem. An atmosphere of encouragement must prevail.

4. The superior may be aware of reasons for the subordinate's difficulty, but guards against telling what is wrong. The superior helps the employee find a positive approach to the problem so as to recognize faulty or short-sighted thinking.

5. The superior then asks insightful questions about the nature of the problem, why it occurred, and what symptoms of it are evident. This helps the subordinate see the need for diagnosing the problem before developing solutions for it.

6. As the two talk further, the superior helps set up criteria for selecting a solution from among the alternatives.

**Principles Involved** A review of this ideal appraisal interview highlights some important elements:

1. The purpose of the interview was made clear from the beginning.

2. Nothing was done to emphasize differences in power or authority.

3. The two did not argue.

4. The superior did not tell the subordinate what to do or how to do it.

5. The subordinate helped to solve the problem. Both superior and subordinate gained in self-confidence and in problem-solving skills.

6. Both came out with their own self-respect intact. Their motivation to work on the problem was increased.

The temptation is always present for the superior to take the ball and run with it. If the superior does, however, he or she is playing the game and not coaching. The ability to observe accurately and objectively is left on the bench when the boss joins the contest.

Appraising people is a complex job. It involves understanding other people and the processes of individual change. It also involves understanding ourselves and how we affect others. It requires that manager and managed control and modify their own behavior as required. Above all, it involves establishing relationships between people in which help can be both given and received most effectively.

*See also* COMPENSATION, WAGE AND SALARY POLICY AND ADMINISTRATION; COUNSELING EMPLOYEE; DEVELOPMENT AND TRAINING, EMPLOYEE; MOTIVATION IN ORGANIZATIONS; WORK, CONCEPT AND IMPLICATIONS.

## REFERENCES

Cummings, Larry L., and Donald P. Schwab: *Performance in Organizations: Determinants and Appraisal*, Scott, Foresman and Company, Glenview, Ill., 1973.

Kearney, William J.: "The Value of Behaviorally Based Performance Appraisals," *Business Horizons*, vol. 19, pp. 75–83, June 1976.

Kellogg, Marion S.: *What To Do About Performance Appraisal*, revised ed., American Management Association, New York, 1975.

Kellogg, Marion S.: *Career Management*, American Management Association, New York, 1972.

Koontz, Harold: *Appraising Managers as Managers*, McGraw-Hill Book Company, New York, 1971.

Koontz, Harold: "Making Managerial Appraisal Effective," *California Management Review*, vol. 15, pp. 46–55, Winter 1972.

Lazer, Robert L.: "The 'Discrimination' Danger in Performance Appraisal," *Conference Board Record*, vol. 13, pp. 60–64, March 1976.

Lee, M. Blaine, and William L. Zwerman: "Designing A Motivation and Team Building Employee Appraisal System," *Personnel Journal*, vol. 55, pp. 354–357, July 1976.

Levinson, Harry: "Appraisal of *What* Performance," *Harvard Business Review*, vol. 54, pp. 30–36, July–August 1976.

Patz, Alan L.: "Performance Appraisal: Useful but Still Resisted," *Harvard Business Review*, vol. 53, pp. 74–80, May–June 1975.

Rowland, Virgil K.: *Evaluating and Improving Managerial Performance*, McGraw-Hill Book Company, New York, 1970.

Zawacki, Robert A., and Robert L. Taylor: "A View of Performance Appraisal from Organizations Using It," *Personnel Journal*, vol. 55, pp. 290–292, June 1976.

WALLACE G. LONERGAN, *University of Chicago*

## Appraisal, real estate (*See* REAL ESTATE MANAGEMENT, CORPORATE.)

## Apprenticeship (*See* DEVELOPMENT AND TRAINING, EMPLOYEE.)

## Arbitrage (*See* EXCHANGE, FOREIGN, MANAGEMENT OF.)

## Arbitration, commercial

With few exceptions, any controversy which might be the subject of civil litigation may be submitted by the disputing parties to an impartial person for final and binding determination. Essentially, *commercial arbitration* is a business executive's court—an alternative to the more complex and time-consuming procedures of the official court system.

This process is used mostly where issues turn on questions of fact, such as the quality of merchandise, rather than law. In such cases, parties may want a decision made by one who is familiar with trade customs rather than by a judge who may or may not be knowledgeable in such areas.

Other reasons for resorting to arbitration are that informal procedures can be put in motion quickly and result in decisions which are not subject to appeal on the merits. Even if an arbitrator should err on matters of fact or law, the decision would be final. Under federal law and the arbitration statutes of 38 states, awards are subject to reversal only if the arbitrator was biased or committed gross procedural errors which prejudiced the rights of a party.

No one can be compelled to arbitrate unless they have in some manner agreed to forego the right to litigate the issue in court. The agreement to arbitrate is commonly expressed in a future-dispute arbitration clause of a contract. It may also be expressed in a submission agreement signed by both parties, who affirm their willingness to abide by the decision.

Most commercial arbitration in the United States is conducted through the American Arbitration Association (AAA), a nonprofit organization that is available to parties in all industries and fields of activity. AAA charges an administrative fee, based upon the amount claimed, but its arbitrators generally serve without fee, except where a case involves many days of hearings. Arbitration is also administered by some organized trades, but these procedures are usually available only to members of the trade association.

Although arbitration is less formal than litigation, hearings follow the conventional pattern of opening statements, examination and cross-examination of witnesses, summations, and occasional post-hearing briefs. Unlike labor arbitrators, who usually write opinions setting forth the arguments and explaining how they reached their decision, commercial arbitrators write only a brief award, telling the disputants what they must do to resolve the controversy.

Arbitration decisions seldom have meaning for persons other than the parties themselves, and awards are therefore not published.

Many years ago, it was common for judges to disapprove of commercial arbitration on the ground that it "ousted the courts" of jurisdiction. Many lawyers were hostile because they feared that basic concepts of due process would be lost for the sake of speed and economy. Moreover, some advocates of arbitration, hostile to lawyers, urged procedures which would bar legal counsel from participating.

But those attitudes have changed in the wake of laws which, while enforcing agreements to arbitrate and awards, provide remedies if arbitrators should exceed their authority. Lawyers, too, have accepted arbitration as a form of law practice. Today, it is only in cases involving very small sums of money that parties enter into arbitration without the guidance of lawyers.

*See also* CONSUMERISM AND CONSUMER PROTECTION LEGISLATION; CREDIT MANAGEMENT; GOVERNMENT REGULATIONS, UNIFORM COMMERCIAL CODE; LEGAL AFFAIRS, MANAGEMENT OF CORPORATE; PATENTS AND VALUABLE INTANGIBLE RIGHTS; PRODUCT LIABILITY.

### REFERENCES

Bernstein, Merton C.: *Private Dispute Settlement: Cases and Materials on Arbitration*, The Free Press, New York, 1968, vol. 14.
Domke, Martin: *Commercial Arbitration*, Prentice-Hall, Inc., Englewood Cliffs, N.J., 1965, vol. 11.
Lazarus, Steven, et al.: *Resolving Business Disputes: The Potential of Commercial Arbitration*, American Management Association, Inc., New York, 1965.

MORRIS STONE, *American Arbitration Association*

## Arbitration, labor

Virtually every union contract in the United States contains a provision called an *arbitration clause*, providing for final and binding resolution of employee grievances. Although strikes over alleged violations of existing contracts still occur, work stoppages have for the most part been supplanted by arbitration as the conventional way to deal with disputes over interpretation or the application of collective agreements.

The situation is different with respect to new contract terms. Most private employers and unions prefer not to let an "outsider" determine basic wages and working conditions. They negotiate to a conclusion, even if this means enduring a strike on occasion. In public employment, however, there is a growing trend toward third-party intervention in contract impasses, under the impact of laws which forbid strikes and provide machinery for alternative methods of settlement—binding arbitration, advisory arbitration, fact-finding, etc.

Most employers and unions use ad hoc, or case-by-case, procedures for arbitration. They anticipate too few cases to warrant making full-time arrangements. Instead, they select an arbitrator when he or she is needed, although this does not exclude the possibility that they will make the same selection in the future. Each call to service is for the specific grievance or group of grievances with which the parties are momentarily concerned.

In some industries, however—steel, auto, airlines, construction, for example—companies and unions set up permanent machinery and name arbitrators or a rotating panel of arbitrators who will be called upon for the life of the contract. In this way, they are assured of decisions that follow established precedents, a circumstance that does not necessarily prevail when a different arbitrator is chosen for each case.

For companies and unions favoring ad hoc procedures, there are two major sources of arbitrators. One is the American Arbitration Association (AAA), a private organization which functions through regional offices throughout the country. AAA charges each party $50 for each case it administers. The other major source is the Federal Mediation and Conciliation Service (FMCS), which operates from Washington, and which does not charge for submitting lists of proposed arbitrators.

Although there are some differences in the way the two organizations operate, they are basically alike in the arbitrators on its panels and in procedures by which a mutual choice of arbitrator is determined from proposed lists. Arbitrators tend to charge about $200 per day of hearing and day of study (study time also includes the writing of an opinion explaining the reason for the decision), and this figure is likely to be the same whether the arbitrator was appointed by the AAA, the FMCS, or directly by the parties, who may have called upon the arbitrator without the assistance of any agency.

The most common subject of labor grievance arbitration is discipline and discharge. Most union contracts forbid disciplinary action by management except for *just cause*. But just cause is seldom defined so completely as to preclude controversy in particular cases. It is then left to the arbitrator to determine whether, in the light of past practice, contract language, and the factual situation, the penalty was appropriate.

Another source of conflict centers around the phrase *seniority versus ability*. A chief objective of unions is to favor senior employees over juniors in matters of promotion, layoff, selection of shifts, and other terms of employment. But the exercise of seniority rights is usually dependent upon the employee having sufficient ability, and contracts seldom are explicit in their definition of terms. Whether a grievant had the contractually required ability to "bump" a junior during a reduction of the work force is a common subject in arbitration.

For decades, labor arbitration awards and opinions have been published by several commercial award-reporting services and by the American Arbitration Association. There is also a considerable amount of interchange of awards within the labor movement and among management groups. Thus, despite the absence of any requirement that ad hoc arbitrators follow precedents, the total body of published decisions has created what the U.S. Supreme Court called "the common law of the shop." These awards, offering insight into practical problems of the workplace, have had a profound influence on American industrial relations.

*See also* LABOR LEGISLATION; LABOR-MANAGEMENT RELATIONS; LABOR (TRADE) UNIONS.

### REFERENCES

Elkouri, Frank, and Edna Asper Elkouri: *How Arbitration Works,* Bureau of National Affairs, Washington, D.C., 1952, vol. 12; revised ed., 1960, vol. 17; 3d ed., 1973, vol. 25.

Stone, Morris: *Managerial Freedom and Job Security,* Harper & Row, Publishers, Incorporated, New York, 1964, vol. 8.

Publishers of labor arbitration award reporting services: Bureau of National Affairs, Washington, D.C. Commerce Clearing House, Chicago, Illinois. Amercian Arbitration Association, New York, New York.

MORRIS STONE, *American Arbitration Association*

# Articles of copartnership  (*See* OWNERSHIP, LEGAL FORMS OF.)

# Assembly line or process  (*See* PRODUCTION PROCESSES.)

# Assertiveness training

*Assertiveness Training* is instruction in practical techniques for communicating effectively with others from a basis of self-assurance and conviction of self-worth. Training is intended to enhance both self-expression and listening skills, as well as resistance to intimidation.

First expounded in 1970 by psychologists Robert Alberti and Michael Emmons, its popular growth as a training technique began about 1975 with an increasing number of corporate training courses. It was initially viewed as especially useful for women, but managers project its increasing importance to men as well.

Based on the principles of behavior modification, training typically aims at the ground halfway between aggressiveness and passivity, using role-modeling and critiquing of role-playing in real-life simulations. Small-group sessions generally last several days and are usually conducted by an outside consultant.

Managerial exponents claim that training improves employees' usefulness to the company by leading to calculated risk-taking, higher productivity, and the individual's sense of personal value to the firm. Problems arise from too-high employee expectations of being able, after training, to get what they want. It is also accused of being superficial and potentially dangerous in encouraging intimidation.

*See also* WOMEN IN INDUSTRY; WOMEN IN MANAGEMENT.

### REFERENCES

Alberti, Robert E., and Michael L. Emmons: *Your Perfect Right: A Guide to Assertive Behavior,* 2d ed., Impact Press, San Luis Obispo, Calif., 1974.

"Assignment: Assertion," *Time Magazine,* May 19, 1975.

Franke, Linda Bird, and Martin Kasindorf: "Coming on Strong," *Newsweek,* October 13, 1975.

*Kramarsky, David: "Management Learns to Assert Itself," Adminstrative Management,* March 1976.

Smith, Manuel J.: *When I Say No, I Feel Guilty,"* The Dial Press, Inc., New York, 1975.

STAFF/HOKE

# Assessment center method

The assessment center method is used by many business, government, and nonprofit organizations to improve the accuracy of personnel selection and of development decisions. It has a threefold purpose: (1) to evaluate the potential of candidates for supervisory, sales, or management positions; (2) to help determine training and development needs of individual employees; and (3) to facilitate more accurate work force planning.

An *assessment center* is a method, not a place. Assessment center participants engage in a variety of job-related simulations designed to bring out behavior relevant to skills or dimensions determined by the organization to be critical to success in a target job or jobs. Managers familiar with the requirements of the target-level jobs, and who have been trained in the assessment process, observe and evaluate this behavior.

By placing participants in situations similar to the ones in which they will be required to perform after promotion or assignment, the process is made relevant and fair to all participants. The odds for the accurate prediction of future job success are improved by (1) training the manager-assessors, (2) providing a structured method for observing and analyzing behavior, and (3) subjecting each participant to the same treatment.

The end result of an assessment center is a written report summarizing the strengths and weaknesses of the individual and, depending upon the center, an estimate of the candidate's potential for a higher level position. This report usually becomes part of the individual's personnel file and serves as a basis for discussion between the individual and the center administrator. Assessment center feedback discussions are unique in their emphasis on behavioral observations. Specific observations, which lead assessors to make certain decisions about dimensions, are shared with the participant.

In addition to rational arguments, the increased accuracy of this technique in comparison with supervisory ratings and tests has been demonstrated in more than 25 well-controlled research studies conducted in both large and small organizations.[1]

Dimensions often measured in assessment centers include

| | |
|---|---|
| Impact | Planning and |
| Creativity | organization |
| Stress tolerance | Judgment |
| Leadership | Decisiveness |
| Sales ability | Use of delegation |
| Sensitivity | Flexibility |
| Initiative | Tenacity |
| Independence | Management control |
| Problem analysis | Risk-taking |

**Affirmative Action** Recent research findings indicate that the assessment center method is valid for minority and nonminority group members. Many companies use the method as a component of their program for achieving affirmative action goals. The landmark 1973 EEOC/AT&T compliance agree-

ment established AT&T's assessment centers as the means for identifying management potential among previously overlooked employees.[2]

Other organizations use the method to identify the management potential of minority groups and women early in their business careers so that development can be accelerated. The method also has proven useful in diagnosing training and developmental needs, thus maximizing the impact of training expenditures.

**Flexibility** Assessment centers should be designed as solutions to specific problems. Details of these problems and the environments in which they occur differ greatly from organization to organization; therefore, so do the assessment centers designed to aid in solving the problems. Experience has shown the assessment center method to be flexible and effective in generating valid data under a variety of different situations and circumstances. In addition, assessment center format may be easily changed in order to evaluate candidates individually rather than in groups.

**Objectives** The most frequent reason for initiating an assessment center program is to provide additional sources of data for making promotional decisions. Many other reasons also exist, but the most common program goals are: (1) aid in making immediate promotional decisions; (2) early determination of potential so that an individual can be placed in special training and development programs; and (3) diagnosis of individual strengths and weaknesses in order to devise targeted training and developmental activities.

**Application** Small and large organizations of all types use the assessment center method to make a wide variety of personnel decisions. Selection, identification of supervisory-managerial potential, and the diagnosis of an individual's strengths and weaknesses relative to present and future positions are the most popular applications. Initial selection of salespeople, management trainees, stationary engineers, police and fire fighters, and highly skilled blue-collar workers is an increasingly popular application.

**Length** The number of exercises and the total time required vary greatly with the assessment center purpose and the organizational level of the target job for which it is used. First-line supervisory centers and centers designed to select salespeople, management trainees, or blue-collar employees typically last for a day or less. High-level executive centers can involve 2½ days of exercises. Generally, centers designed to generate developmental recommendations last longer than those designed primarily to yield selection or promotion recommendations.

**Size** Typically, six or twelve people are assessed simultaneously, although centers designed for initial selection often assess only one person at a time. Most centers involve one assessor to every two participants; some operate on a one-to-one ratio.

**Steps in Starting an Assessment Center** Methods vary, of course, but the following steps ought to be included in most programs:

*Establish Goals.* The purposes of an assessment center must be clearly defined prior to planning. Several goals may be accomplished by the same center, but the more goals an organization sets for it, the longer and more expensive the program will be. The most fundamental decision is the relative weight to be assigned to the goals of selection versus identification of training and developmental needs.

*Plan Program.* Planning must concern all aspects of the center, from identification of dimensions to feedback of assessment information to the participants and to management. Fitting the center program into current programs and practices and the need to be sensitive to the attitudes of center participants and nonparticipants in the organization often require many difficult decisions.

*Identify Dimensions of Job Performance.* Some or all of the following steps should be taken to determine the dimensions to be observed in the assessment center: (1) Examine professional literature and company records. (2) Conduct a systematic job analysis. (3) Observe a sampling of individuals performing the job, and interview higher management about the needed dimensions. (4) Conduct a questionnaire survey of management's views of job requirements. (5) Arrange a "brainstorming" meeting of key managers familiar with the position or positions for which the candidates are being assessed. (6) Obtain critical incidents of behavior leading to particularly successful or unsuccessful performance. (7) Focus not only on present job requirements but also on future ones. (8) Eliminate those dimensions that can be assessed adequately on a person's present job. (9) Obtain a rough ranking of remaining dimensions.

*Select Exercises.* More than 100 specially developed and tested assessment center exercises are commercially available.[3] They include such techniques as business games, in-baskets, leaderless group discussions (nonassigned roles and assigned roles), analysis (presentation and/or group discussion), individual fact-finding and decision-making exercises, interview simulations, and written presentation and oral presentation exercises.

Exercises should be selected according to the following criteria: (1) level of sophistication and education of the assessees; (2) relative importance of the various dimensions; (3) actual job content of the target position(s); (4) need to observe the participants in a variety of situations; (5) need to observe critical dimensions in several different exercises; and (6) time available for assessment.

*Train Assessors.* Minimum training should include (1) discussion of the definitions of the dimensions; (2) practice in observing and recording behavior and in writing reports on at least one of each type of exercise used in the center; (3) practice in conducting interviews; and (4) familiarization with the procedure for reaching final decisions.

As an aid in assessor training, videotapes of exercises, sample exercises, and sample final reports are frequently used.

*Conduct Center.* Centers may be conducted at an organization's own facilities, a conveniently located motel, or other similar locations. The role of the administrator is critical, and the individual performing this function should be thoroughly trained in the process beforehand.

**Operational Considerations** Assessment centers are usually initially designed by a trained psychologist familiar with the method but are generally administered by representatives of the organization's training or personnel department who are not psychologists. This representative must administer the exercises, write a final report summarizing the consensus of the assessors on each participant, and, usually, be responsible for feeding back assessment center information to the participants. Administrators must go through assessor training and must have had additional training for their special responsibilities prior to serving in this function.

Most organizations end the administrator's role with the feedback discussion. In some highly developmentally oriented programs, the administrator has continued to be involved in counseling the participant and the participant's supervisor regarding appropriate developmental action and acts as a catalyst to ensure that development actions take place.

The percentage of candidates who do well in assessment centers varies markedly between and within organizations. In general, at the presupervisory level approximately one-third of those individuals assessed are thought to have supervisory potential. The percentage goes up in higher-level centers, where there is more opportunity for preselection of the assessees.

Management is, of course, always concerned with the effect of assessment center findings on participants who do poorly. They fear possible morale or turnover implications. Although there are few published research studies in this area, a number of organizations have collected sufficient data to disprove any specific negative reaction. The apparent key to minimizing the negative effects of assessment center reports is in providing effective feedback of the data. Proper feedback stresses that the assessment center is designed to predict potential for a specific job, not a generalized area of potential. It also stresses the training and developmental aspects of center results.

Many small organizations have considered forming a consortium where they can pool resources to operate a cooperative assessment center. To this author's knowledge, this has never worked out. The organizations disagree on the dimensions to be sought and on the scheduling of centers. The advent of new techniques which apply the assessment center method to individual selection has somewhat diminished the motivation of smaller companies to consider cooperative centers.

*Consulting Specialists.* Most assessment centers have been installed with the advice of consulting specialists. Organizations deem the use of specialists to be advisable in order to establish an effective program which is job-related and thus acceptable to the Equal Employment Opportunity Commission. The EEOC guidelines stress the need for professionally conducted job analyses. A properly qualified outside consultant provides this service and helps the organization choose the most appropriate job-related exercises and design the most efficient assessment. Assessment centers require a great deal of management time, and an investment in qualified assistance can more than pay off by freeing-up executive time.

*See also* DEVELOPMENT AND TRAINING, CAREER PATH PLANNING FOR MANAGERS; DEVELOPMENT AND TRAINING, MANAGEMENT; LABOR LEGISLATION; LEADERSHIP; MINORITIES, MANAGEMENT OF AND EQUAL EMPLOYMENT OPPORTUNITY; SEARCH AND RECRUITMENT; EXECUTIVE; SUPERVISORY MANAGEMENT; TESTING, PSYCHOLOGICAL.

### NOTES

[1] B. Cohen, J. L. Moses, and W. C. Byham, "The Validity of Assessment Centers: A Literature Review," *Monograph II*, Development Dimensions, Inc., Pittsburgh, 1974.

[2] D. F. Hoyle, "AT&T Completes Assessment of Nearly 1700 Women Under Consent Agreement," *Assessment and Development*, vol. 12, pp. 4–5.

[3] *Catalog of Assessment and Development Exercises*, Development Dimensions, Inc., Pittsburgh, 1977.

### REFERENCES

Huck, J. R.: "Assessment Centers: A Review of the External and Internal Validities," *Personnel Psychology*, vol. 26, pp. 191–212.

Huck, J. R. and D. W. Bray: "Management Assessment Center Evaluations and Subsequent Job Performance of White and Black Females," *Personnel Psychology*, vol. 29, pp. 13–30.

WILLIAM C. BYHAM, *Development Dimensions, Inc.*

## Asset management, fixed  (See FINANCIAL MANAGEMENT.)

## Assets  (See ACCOUNTING, FINANCIAL.)

## Assignment, patent  (See PATENTS AND VALUABLE INTANGIBLE RIGHTS.)

## Associated Credit Bureau, Inc.  (See CREDIT MANAGEMENT.)

## Associations, trade and professional

America's trade associations and professional societies are a powerful force in the private sector—representing more than 40 million organized individuals and business firms that use their organizational machinery, work force, and resources to help solve business, economic, and social problems. There are some 15,000 national, state, and local trade and professional associations. Most have full-time paid executives.

Although the central purpose of the voluntary association has always been to serve the needs and to protect the interests of the industry or profession it represents, the present trend is for the trade association to broaden its purpose and to serve the overall needs of the nation.

Associations traditionally have performed services in marketing, education, and other areas that business people understand and support. But in carrying out these activities, business executives have traditionally expected the association to take a low profile. Much of this has changed as a result of government initiatives in health and safety, consumerism, the environment, and the economy. Business executives today demand help from associations in explaining new laws and administrative rulings that affect their companies. They look to associations to take public stands they do not want to take individually. More and more the operation of the association is the responsibility of a paid executive rather than of volunteers. The business executive members are too busy running their own businesses. The government, too, relies on associations to present a single voice for an industry or profession. In other words, if there is to be a finger pointed by someone, the association philosophy is: Let it be pointed at the industry as a whole and not at the individual firm.

## SCOPE OF SERVICES

Voluntary associations are widening their scope of services and raising their sights. A nationwide survey conducted by the American Society of Association Executives shows that 73 percent of all associations in the United States are involved in helping resolve economic, social, and human problems. Nearly half the associations conduct programs designed to improve consumer satisfaction. More than a third of the associations have programs aimed at safeguarding and improving the environment, and more than a third have programs aimed at aiding the disadvantaged.

**Improving Consumer Satisfaction** In this area, associations engage in such activities as

Publishing and putting into operation a code of ethics that includes requirements for consumer protection.

Encouraging the buying public to report to the association about unsatisfactory products and services.

Educating and urging members to adhere strictly to truth in advertising.

Working closely with federal, state, and local offices of consumer affairs.

Maintaining a task force of members and consumers to study and analyze consumer problems and to find ways to correct them.

Conducting tests and inspection and grading services to help ensure consumer satisfaction.

Developing standards of grade-and-quality labeling to help others choose the right products to meet their needs.

Operating consumer relations committees on the local level to deal with consumer complaints and to correct the causes.

**Improving the Environment** In this area, associations, in increasing numbers, engage in such activities as

Working for legislation, state and national, to establish standards for environmental control.

Maintaining a task force of members to study sound ways to reduce air, water, and land pollution.

Conducting research to devise better methods of waste disposal on the part of industry.

Conducting educational programs to reduce waste and pollution on the part of users.

Sponsoring programs to encourage clean-up campaigns.

**Aiding the Disadvantaged** In this area, associations, as never before, engage in such activities as

Encouraging members to hire the disadvantaged.

Helping members provide on-the-job training.

Expanding apprentice training.

Working with government, federal and state, to aid in job training and creating new job opportunities.

Encouraging entrepreneur programs for minority groups.

Operating placement services for the disadvantaged.

Providing scholarships for disadvantaged students.

Setting up training courses in vocational schools.

Providing accounting, merchandising, and other business assistance to minority and underprivileged business firms and individuals.

**Government Relations** Although government relations have always been a key association function, it is now dominant, according to the ASAE survey. Ninety-two percent of the associations surveyed say they keep their members informed about federal legislative developments. (*See* Table A-5.) Some 96 percent of ASAE's members see a likelihood that association expenditures for government relations will increase significantly in the coming years.

**Legislative Activities of Associations** Many associations engage in legislative activities on both the state and federal levels. In fact, many legislators prefer to deal with an association representative rather than deal individually with member companies. In turn, member companies often prefer to deal through an association.

There is nothing sinister about lobbying activities of associations. The United States has a representative government, and the open struggle among special interests is precisely what marks democracy as a system resting on the consent of the governed.

One problem which arises in connection with lobbying is whether an association must register under the Federal Regulation of Lobbying Act. The act requires that any person engaged in attempting

59

TABLE A-5 Government Relations Programs Offered by Associations and Percent of Associations Conducting Them

| Program | Percent |
|---|---|
| Informs members of congressional developments | 92 |
| Equips members to express views to representatives and senators | 87 |
| Informs members of federal administrative actions | 87 |
| Informs members of state and local legislative developments | 81 |
| Testifies before Congress or state legislatures | 76 |
| Maintains a committee to study and make recommendations on state and national legislation | 71 |
| Provides data to state governments | 66 |
| Convention programs include speakers on national legislation | 57 |
| Drafts legislation | 55 |
| Lobbies | 54 |
| Provides data to federal government | 49 |
| Reports federal court decisions | 46 |
| Trains members to become active in politics | 29 |
| Collects and distributes political funds to candidates | 27 |
| Arranges plant tours to help government demonstrate United States industry to foreign visitors | 23 |
| Sponsors courses on political participation | 15 |
| Assists members with customs, tariffs, and trade agreements | 12 |
| Represents industry in tariff negotiations | 9 |
| Assists government in foreign trade fair participation | 8 |

to influence the passage or defeat of any federal legislation (1) must register with the clerk of the House of Representatives and the secretary of the Senate and (2) must periodically disclose certain information about his or her activities. In view of the fact that there are very few associations whose principal purpose is influencing the passage or defeat of federal legislation, it is arguable that the lobbying act does not require multipurpose organizations such as associations to register. Since the act is ambiguous on this point, most cautious associations do register.

Another troublesome area to associations in regard to the present concept of lobbying lies in the difficulty of distinguishing between *influencing* and *informing* members of Congress. Since associations are engaged in activities which are informational in character, they are conduits of business information. They collect information from their members, from government agencies, from related agencies, and from other sources. The material collected is ordinarily distributed to anyone who has an interest in it—to members primarily, but also to government officials, including members of Congress. Certainly legislators desire to have access to all sources of information so that they can continue to perform their legislative functions intelligently.

If informing a legislator were to become tantamount to influencing that individual, then all persons seeking to assist in making information available to elected representatives would have to register as lobbyists under the act. Such a reading of the present act would certainly prove counterproductive because it would result in blocking the flow of information to federal legislators. Accordingly, if new lobbying legislation were forthcoming, it would appear beneficial if it provided an exemption for those activities which serve to inform as opposed to attempting to influence.

## MEMBERSHIP COSTS AND RETURNS

Each association in a particular field of business offers a variety of valuable services which are obtained at a reasonable cost through payment of company or individual membership dues and by company and individual participation in the work of the association.

Business people expect a return for their dues investment. Many not only lean on their association's representation and guidance, they also look upon the association as one of their business departments. Confirmation of this view came during the early 1970s business downturns. At a time when many companies traditionally cut back on association participation, some 82 percent of the associations surveyed by ASAE asked for—and got—a dues increase to fund their increased activity.

Association dues vary according to the group and the amount of services it offers. Generally, dues are a fraction of 1 percent on the member's annual volume of business. Some associations charge a uniform fee. A few use a combination figure derived from the rate based on volume plus a specific flat charge. Many groups also have a ceiling on the dues they charge.

Among state and national associations, annual assessment dues are most common. Local associations often assess dues by the month instead of annually or semiannually.

*See also* COMPETITION; CREDIT MANAGEMENT; GOVERNMENT RELATIONS AND SERVICES; SOCIETIES, PROFESSIONAL.

## REFERENCES

*Association Activities*, American Society of Association Executives, Washington, 1972.

Low, James P.: *Association Services for Small Business*, U.S. Small Business Administration, Washington, 1976.

*Members Appraise Their Associations*, American Society of Association Executives, Washington, 1972.

*Motivating Participation in Voluntary Membership Associations*, The Foundation of the American Society of Association Executives, Washington, 1970.

*Policies and Procedures of Associations*, American Society of Association Executives, Washington, 1974.

*Principles of Association Management*, American Society of Association Executives and the U.S. Chamber of Commerce, Washington, 1975.

Webster, George D.: *The Law of Associations*, Matthew Bender, New York, 1975.

Webster, George D., and Arthur L. Herold: *Antitrust Guide for Association Executives*, American Society of Association Executives, Washington, 1976.

JAMES P. LOW, *American Society of Association Executives*

## Attendance bonus (See COMPENSATION, EMPLOYEE BENEFIT PLANS.)

## Attention time (See WORK MEASUREMENT.)

## Attitude surveys

Employee morale is considered an important and quantifiable indicator of the success of employer-employee relationships. Early industrial surveys of morale were called inventories and were based on the idea that management should inventory human resources as it does raw materials and finished goods. Such inventories, now called morale scales, opinion surveys, or *attitude surveys* are a valuable management tool providing a systematic measure of how employees view and react to various policies of management. At the same time they provide employees with an opportunity to share opinions and activate change.

Attitude surveys are not tests; there are no right or wrong answers, only reactions or opinions, indicating how a particular individual regards an action or condition.

Management commonly uses three methods to survey employee attitudes: (1) questioning the employee's immediate supervisor; (2) interviewing employees; (3) administering professionally constructed and normed attitude surveys. The latter is the most economical, efficient, and objective source of information. Questions can be quickly adminis-

tered to large groups, readily scored and interpreted, and the responses provide an objective measure of attitudes concerning both general and particular work situations, as well as providing a basis for comparison useful to management.

**Criteria for Effective Use** The ultimate goal of an attitude survey program is positive—to increase awareness and understanding of employee feelings and to initiate the changes necessary to improve company working conditions and relationships.

An attitude survey should be professionally developed for effective use. It must be reliable, with standardized items and normed results to permit meaningful comparisons between various groups of employees. The survey should be designed to allow individual companies to insert supplementary items on subjects of special concern to that company's management. The program should allow for feedback discussion of the results between employees and management so that each may more fully understand the other's point of view and so that the appropriate action may be initiated. This is crucial because *the decision to initiate an attitude survey carries with it the commitment from management that it is ready and willing to do something*. The attitude survey properly used is a visible sign to employees that management values their opinions: Steps must be taken to ensure employee participation in feedback discussions; plans must be made to change (or attempt to change) objectionable conditions; employees should be informed of actions taken and progress made.

**Program Benefits** The attitude survey program is a self-critical process—measuring a company's strengths and weaknesses—to a constructive end—improvement of that company. The information derived is useful on many levels: It can measure the impact of a benefit or policy adjustment, build goodwill, provide information about company operations, ease scheduled mergers through transition phases, and elicit information related to existing or potential unions; it can be used to assess sources and reasons for such costly problems as low morale, high turnover, absenteeism, and substandard production; it can confirm problem areas but also measure the magnitude and therefore the priority of problems; it can be used to evaluate and promote communication in a company; and it can help management discover how their company compares with others like it across the country.

Well-designed and administered surveys can uncover areas of discontent *before* they become major issues. Thus, often, employees can warn management when equipment is malfunctioning before it actually breaks down, when customers are reacting unfavorably to a product before sales results reflect this, when safety hazards are becoming serious before major accidents occur, or even when employees are becoming disenchanted with a company action, program, or condition *before* organized resistance or a strike results. Surveys provide an early warning to management while there is still time to act. Conversely, such a program can also reassure management that programs are working properly and are serving the purpose for which they were designed.

**Survey Components and Procedures** A typical attitude survey might have three components: a core survey, a section for write-in comments, and a tailor-built survey. The core survey is composed of a number of items or questions that have been tested and retested for validity, reliability, and clarity. For example, "The people I work with get along well together." Typical survey categories are working conditions, pay, benefits, relations with fellow employees and supervisors, effectiveness of management, and adequacy of intracompany communication. Standardization of items permits comparison of a company's results with national, industrial, occupational, or other norms compiled from responses of thousands of employees and employee groups.

Experts find that the most useful survey provides both (1) standardized items, to permit comparisons between companies based on statistical norms, and (2) custom-made items, designed to meet the needs of the specific company. Areas of concern that might be included in a custom-built survey are company benefits, personnel policies, plant changes, parking, unions, and quality controls.

*Procedure.* The survey program normally proceeds as follows: (1) Appoint survey administrator. (2) Determine date, time, and place for survey. (3) Assign code numbers for various groups in the company taking the survey to facilitate eventual analysis and to reassure employees that their responses are anonymous. (4) Determine norm groups for comparison with the particular company. (5) Conduct survey in a positive psychological climate, making employees feel that the survey is important to them. (6) When finished, have employees put materials in locked box, for mailing to administrative company for scoring.

*Interpretation.* When survey results are returned to the company, management reviews and interprets the summarized results. The idea is to look first at organization problems and then at significant variations in the various coded groups, observing general morale level, noting specific strong and weak points, and interpreting profile patterns for each coded group. They also take note of favorable and unfavorable comments. Where profiles are uniformly low, employees probably have unfavorable attitudes toward the organization, apathy toward their jobs, or depressed attitudes about working conditions. Job satisfaction is often found to be related to productivity, and conversely there is strong evidence that a relationship exists between low morale and turnover and absenteeism.

*Feedback.* After top management has reviewed the findings, they discuss them with middle management. The information can then be sent back to employees via written report or, more effectively, through departmental employee meetings, which provide an opportunity to discuss personally the problems revealed by the survey. Session leaders are sometimes managers of the department, sometimes outside supervisors. Ideally, session leaders are trained to draw out group comments with sensitivity and maturity. These *feedback sessions are considered the crucial part of an attitude survey,* for it is here that a sharing of management decisions takes place. It is here also that suggestions and creative solutions to acknowledged problems are born. Feedback is beneficial in several ways: It builds employee morale and confidence in management, making every member feel important to the organization; the person-to-person discussion is valuable, for it is one of the few times the average employee has the opportunity to discuss working conditions, benefits, and other concerns with a responsible company executive; it stimulates upward and downward communication between management and employees; and it often provides the first step in solving problems revealed by the attitude survey.

A one-time survey is of some immediate value, but a continuous program, with follow-up surveys 1 to 2 years later, serves better to monitor the effectiveness of a company's action plan, as well as employee reactions to management's activities. The initial survey provides a benchmark; succeeding surveys indicate improvement or deterioration.

**Applications in Business and Industry** Attitude surveys are in extensive use: Medium and small-sized companies tend to use standardized surveys developed and constructed by outside testing companies; large corporations often develop their own individualized surveys. Many companies using attitude surveys cultivate their own nuances of use. (The following four examples are excerpted from SRA's Employee Attitude Surveys cassette program.)

*Reynolds Metals* suggests that a representative of the group being surveyed be involved in initial planning of the program to gain cooperation of all employees. They use an outside expert to administer the survey and train feedback leaders, thus emphasizing the import of the survey and giving credibility to the anonymous nature of the survey. No decisions are made at the feedback sessions; changes, if any, are made by top management after thorough study of all feedback sessions.

At *Parke-Davis*, they prepare tables of critical and favorable written comments by subject. All agreed-upon changes (resulting from feedback sessions and management review) are put into effect immediately. A highly effective aspect of their feedback program is that employees are told that their comments are read, not only by their own line supervisor and plant management, but also by the president of the company and several vice-presidents as well, emphasizing the importance top management places on the attitude survey results. Examples of matters learned about and corrected as a result of surveys and feedback meetings are: customer service at distribution centers not up to par; sales promotion material late getting to sales representatives; training programs not achieving objectives; some departments overstaffed, while others overworked.

*Sears, Roebuck and Co.* uses several versions of an extensive questionnaire in each of their different locations. Each version is question-specific for particular work groups. As internal conditions change or such things as new government regulations are introduced, new questions are introduced. A core group of general items remains as a permanent measure of employee feelings and expressed motivation. This portion, identical in all versions, provides a comparative base measure of all groups within the organization. The local manager gets results ahead of the next lower level, to allow the manager time to digest the report and to indicate that the situation, positive or negative, is his or her responsibility. Numerous individual meetings with employee groups are then held to discuss the findings. This is considered the heart of the program—time-consuming but effective and important. The whole program is designed to encourage continuous attention to the human organization. Because the program is long established, numerous senior executives have participated in it, and therefore are confident of it. In addition, supervisory training programs are specifically related to the issues and needs indicated in the survey.

At *IBM*, they have found that administering the questionnaires on company time rather than mailing them home increases participation 15 to 20 percent. Acceptance and use of the survey by first-level man-

agers improved when they were given report results for their own department; it makes survey data relevant to their unique management situation. Employees' perceptions of management's use of survey findings were influenced by whether or not they received feedback. In IBM's attitude survey, 50 percent of the questions in any questionnaire are specific to a particular program, policy, or practice of concern to the unit being surveyed. They resurvey approximately every $1\frac{1}{2}$ to 2 years to give managers feedback on the effectiveness of the actions taken.

**Evaluation**  In evaluating an attitude survey program it appears that it is correct management attitude and usage that makes such a program successful and incorrect attitude and usage that dooms it to fail.

1. For a survey to "work," support and involvement of all line and staff managers must be real and explicit. Management must see the program as a constructive tool. The tacit committment by management to accept and respect the results and to respond or act upon them where possible is the backbone of the program. Using the survey simply as a means for employees to "get it off their chests" is of temporary value and can actually lower morale.

2. The survey should seek out information specifically relevant to the needs of the users.

3. Feedback of information must be done in a timely and skillful manner, informing employees of survey results and what progress is being made toward realization of changes.

4. The commitment to anonymity must not be violated. Subordinates should not be questioned about their answers to survey questions or comments. Supervisors must be convinced that the intention of the survey is positive, not punitive, that there will be no recriminations; they must be made to feel that the survey is their tool also, to provide them with the knowledge to deal more effectively with their superiors, peers, and subordinates.

The increased use of attitude surveys reflects growing concern with the assessment and management of human resources. They keep responsible management in touch with large numbers of people, and in a time of fast-paced technological and social change, they provide a way for policy makers to take the pulse among different occupation groups and different generations so that they can respond in a responsible manner. These needs, together with the increasingly available technology of computers—permitting processing and analysis of thousands of questionnaires quickly and skillfully, create an atmosphere receptive to an attitude survey program.

*See also* COMMUNICATIONS, ORGANIZATIONAL; COUNSELING, EMPLOYEE; HYGIENE FACTORS; INTERPERSONAL RELATIONSHIPS; MOTIVATION IN ORGANIZATIONS; SUGGESTION SYSTEMS; WORK, CONCEPT AND IMPLICATIONS.

## REFERENCES

Erdos, Paul L.: "Employee Surveys," *Personnel Journal*, vol. 53, pp. 294–300, April 1974.

Goode, Robert V.: "How to Get Better Results from Attitude Surveys," *Personnel Journal*, vol. 52, pp. 87–92, March 1973.

Klein, Stuart M., Allen I. Kraut, and Alan Wolfson: "Employee Reactions to Attitude Survey Feedback: A Study of the Impact of Structure and Process," *Administrative Science Quarterly*, vol. 16, pp. 497–514, December 1971.

Pritchett, Price: "Employee Attitude Surveys: A Natural Starting Point for Organization Development," *Personnel Journal*, vol. 54, pp. 202–205, April 1975.

Roberts, Karlene H., and Frederick Savage: "Twenty Questions: Utilizing Job Satisfaction Measures," *California Management Review*, vol. 15, pp. 82–90, Spring 1973.

Sirota, David, and Alan D. Wolfson: "Pragmatic Approach to People Problems," *Harvard Business Review*, vol. 51, pp. 120–128, January 1973.

Smith, Frank J., R. A. Dunnington, David J. McNamara, Hugh Moltzau, Robert N. Ford, and Victor K. Schuster: "Employee Attitude Surveys," a series of six cassettes, Science Research Associates, Inc., 1975.

Wheatley, Bruce C. and William B. Cash: "Employee Survey: Correcting Its Basic Weakness," *Personnel Journal* vol. 52, pp. 456–459, June 1973.

Yoder, Dale: *Personnel Management and Industrial Relations*, 6th ed., Prentice-Hall, Inc., Englewood Cliffs, N.J., 1970.

BRUCE A. CAMPBELL, *Science Research Associates, Inc.*

## Attitude tests (*See* TESTING, PSYCHOLOGICAL.)

## Attitudes (*See* DEVELOPMENT AND TRAINING, EMPLOYEE.)

## Attitudes, personal (*See* INTERPERSONAL RELATIONSHIPS.)

## Attitudinal theories (*See* CONSUMER BEHAVIOR, MANAGERIAL RELEVANCE OF.)

## Attribute-listing technique (*See* PRODUCT PLANNING AND DEVELOPMENT.)

## Attributes measurement (*See* STATISTICAL ANALYSIS FOR MANAGEMENT.)

## Audit, communication (*See* COMMUNICATIONS, ORGANIZATIONAL.)

## Audit, energy (*See* ENERGY RESOURCES, MANAGEMENT OF.)

## Audit, environmental (*See* ENVIRONMENTAL PROTECTION LEGISLATION.)

## Audit, management

The concept of an audit, while by no means new, is still evolving. In particular, there is still a good deal of confusion about the scope and objectives of a management audit as compared with its predecessor forms (such as the financial audit, the internal audit, or the operational audit). It seems appropriate, therefore, to begin with a brief review of the historical evolution of the audit concept, followed by a discussion of the characteristics which distinguish the management audit from other types.

### HISTORICAL EVOLUTION OF THE AUDIT

The concept of the audit arose primarily from the need for information. As long as 5000 years ago, auditors in the royal courts of Egypt reported the net cost of the harvest to Pharaoh so that taxes could be levied. There were also provisions for having one official's records audited by another, for supporting disbursements with written evidence and for certifying the receipt of transported goods. Similar provisions for auditing have been noted in early Persian, Hebrew, Greek, and Roman history.

**The Financial Audit** In the thirteenth and fourteenth centuries, the nature of private enterprise began to change as individual traders entered into joint ventures and partnerships. These new relationships precipitated the need for better controls.

For example, double-entry bookkeeping was evolved during this period, with its use noted in Genoa as early as 1340. Subsequently, the growth of international trade, and the impact of wars on this trade, intensified the need for independent examination of business records. The American and French Revolutions caused many British bankruptcies and made it necessary to determine the interests of the owners and creditors of these firms.

The rise of joint stock companies, together with the separation of ownership from control, further intensified the need for financial auditing. In the late nineteenth century, a group of leading public accountants in the United States attempted to establish standards for the accounting practice, ultimately resulting in the enactment, by New York State in 1896, of a law setting forth the requirements for use of the title of Certified Public Accountant. Within 30 years thereafter, all states and territories had enacted similar laws.

Since World War I, financial audits have been required on government contracts to ensure adequate profit and cost controls for the protection of the public. As a result, the financial audit has become a basic element of modern business practice. Publicly held companies are now required to have annual financial audits conducted by individual Certified Public Accountants (CPAs). The CPA is expected to assess the integrity of the company's financial statement and of the data on which it is based, and to render an opinion. This includes determining whether a company's financial reports are prepared in accordance with generally accepted accounting principles. The development of the financial audit can be measured by the growth of the public accounting profession: whereas there were fewer than 300 CPAs in 1900, there were more than 50,000 in the mid-1950s, and more than 100,000 currently.

**The Internal Audit** Internal auditing can be viewed as a natural extension of financial auditing, the major distinction being that an internal audit is performed by a company's own employees, rather than by an outside independent auditor. The internal audit may also be broader in scope. Initially, the role of the internal auditor was to undertake a detailed review and examination of financial transactions on behalf of the company's management, as an element of control. More recently, the scope of the internal auditing function has been expanded to include operational as well as financial matters, with the additional objective of identifying opportunities for profit improvement. In many firms, internal auditing has developed into a major staff function.

**The Operational Audit** Extension of the internal auditing function into the area of operations is commonly termed *operational auditing*. While the two terms may be considered virtually synonymous for practical purposes, there is a subtle distinction in that *internal auditing* connotes an ongoing task performed by people within the company who are specifically assigned to that function. *Operational auditing*, on the other hand, may be undertaken either by a special task force made up of people within the company or by outside independent analysts.

Since the early 1950s there have been numerous seminars and conferences concerned with the principles and procedures to be employed in operational auditing. There is general agreement, however, that an operational audit should embrace the financial, production, marketing, and staff service functions.

**The Management Audit** Since the middle of the twentieth century, particularly with the advent of automation and other technological innovations, there has been a rapid increase in business complexities, increasing attention to business from governmental regulatory agencies, shifting and expanding markets, and the establishment of active public bodies concerned with the conduct of businesses. These factors have had substantial impact on the structure and practices of most industries and of the enterprises operating within those industries. Many new management tools and techniques have been developed to deal with this rapidly changing business environment—among them, the development of the total marketing concept and rapid expansion of the use of computers in the 1950s and 1960s, together with the refinement of long-range planning and strategic planning in the 1960s and 1970s.

There has thus emerged a need for an audit even broader in scope than the operational audit—one which would evaluate the performance of management and the effectiveness of new management tools and techniques, within the context of environmental considerations. This impending situation was recognized by T. G. Rose as early as 1932 in his paper entitled "Management Audit." Rose stated that insofar as a business's financial position is concerned, the managing director of a business enterprise is

... relieved of any fear of error or misdirection here owing to the annual financial audit which is carried out by an independent firm of auditors. . . . But in the matters relating to the technical and business side, in the equally complex problems of organization and management that permeate the whole of the selling and manufacturing branches, he has no similar annual survey, nor the help of any such impartial experts. . . . I suggest that what could help him more than anything else—if such a thing were possible—would be something like an annual "audit" or examination of the management. If this existed, it would enable him to feel as satisfied in his mind with regard to the detail organization of the company as he is with the detail arrangement of the accounts.[1]

The need for a management audit was also presaged by William P. Leonard, who in 1959 defined this term as a

. . . comprehensive and constructive examination of an organizational structure of a company, institution, or branch of government, or of any component thereof, such as a division or department, and its plans and objectives, its means of operation, and its use of human and physical facilities.[2]

Although the management audit thus was conceptualized as early as 1932, it began to be put into practice only in the 1960s and 1970s. A good illustration of the historical development of the management audit is provided by activities of the U.S. General Accounting Office (GAO), an independent federal agency which, in its role as congressional watchdog, has considerably expanded the scope of its examinations in recent years. The Budget and Accounting Act of 1921 established the GAO and empowered the comptroller general of the United States to make independent examinations into the manner in which governmental agencies discharge their financial responsibilities. This law and other federal legislation enacted from 1945 through 1950 have steadily broadened the scope of the GAO's audits, extending them far beyond traditional accounting and financial matters. Nowadays, the GAO

. . . audits or reviews department or agency financial controls and accountability, efficiency of management and use of resources, and effectiveness of program results, [*and also*] . . . suggests ways and means for financial management improvement, including principles and standards for accounting in the federal agencies.[3]

## DISTINGUISHING CHARACTERISTICS

The various forms of the audit discussed thus far have been essentially audits *for* management. In recent years, there has been a rapidly growing demand for audits *of* management, requested by such nonmanagement groups as investors, bankers, boards of directors, financial analysts, governmental regulatory agencies, and the like. For example, several state public service commissions have imposed

mandatory management audits on the public utilities they are charged with regulating. Also, boards of directors generally, not only in business enterprises but also in health care, cultural, educational, and religious institutions, are becoming more actively concerned with the performance of management and are looking to management audits to furnish them with useful information in this area. Furthermore, the boards of directors and top management of business enterprises are finding that management audits are highly useful tools in evaluating major acquisition candidates.

The characteristics of a management audit which distinguish it from its predecessor forms lie primarily in the areas of (1) the scope of the audit (the functional areas covered) and (2) its objectives (the audience addressed and the extent to which findings are developed into specific recommendations).

**Scope** The scope of the management audit is considerably broader than that of other types of audits. It embraces all functions and systems as well as corporate strategy and business objectives within the context of the corporation's unique environment. (For convenience, in this entry the management audit is described in terms of a corporate structure; it should be kept in mind, however, that it can be applied to any type of organization.)

The major elements investigated in a management audit (depending on the type of enterprise) can include organization structure, the planning process, budgeting and the allocation of resources (human, financial, physical), the management decision-making process, research and development, marketing, physical operations, internal controls, and management information systems.

The management audit also has a broader time horizon than the other types, in that it views past, present, and future; by comparsion, the financial audit has essentially only a past perspective. While the main focus of the management audit is on the present and the future, the past is also significant because it often reveals causative factors contributing to a corporation's present situation.

The scope of a management audit should encompass both the internal aspects of the corporation and the external environment. A full analysis should include consideration of all the forces that may affect the corporation and its achievement of business objectives.

**Objectives** Among the objectives of the management audit, perhaps the most important is to increase knowledge of corporate affairs through the identification of both strengths and weaknesses. A balanced picture will identify areas in which management has been effective as well as those in which improvements are required.

A second objective is to develop recommendations for capitalizing on opportunities for improvement, and a third is to develop the credibility of the auditing process and hence acceptance of the results. Top management's acceptance and support of the management audit are critical to the successful implementation of the resulting recommendations. In addition, the findings of a management audit are often used to set future performance standards, both for the corporation and for its management.

In the case of a management audit of a candidate for acquisition, additional objectives will be (1) to help put a value on the company and (2) to determine what resources may have to be infused into the company.

## PROCEDURE FOR MANAGEMENT AUDIT

The individual steps to be carried out in conducting a management audit are described below, more or less in sequence, although a number of these steps may overlap and some may be conducted concurrently.

**Orientation and Initial Interviews**  In this first step, the study team charged with conducting the management audit solicits inputs from corporate management regarding the individuals to be interviewed, the locations to be visited, the types of information to be gathered, and the like. This step also enables members of the study team to become acquainted with key members of management, to meet the persons specifically designated to serve as liaison with them, and to make arrangements for other administrative matters.

As part of this step, the study team defines the scope of the audit, in terms of subject areas and/or functions to be covered, and the depth of investigation, through interviews with top officers of the enterprise. In addition, the study team initiates the collection of a wide variety of documentation on organization, activities, and systems. The documentation requested may include plans, budgets, financial statements, operating reports, organization manuals, statements of policies and procedures, systems manuals, minutes of key committee meetings, reports resulting from prior studies, biographical data (including work histories) on key employees, and so forth.

From these initial interviews and a review of the documentation assembled, the study team determines which areas of study are likely to be most productive and consequently should receive concentrated attention during the audit.

**Preparation of a Plan of Study**  On the basis of information obtained and analyzed in the preceding step, the study team prepares a detailed plan of study and time schedule, specifying the individuals to be interviewed (both within and outside the enterprise), the specific facilities to be visited, and other fact-finding required. This detailed plan of study usually is reviewed with corporate management to obtain its approval before pursuing subsequent steps.

**Internal Fact-Finding**  This step, which is concerned with investigations within the corporation itself, entails interviews, review of documentation, and observation of facilities and work processes. Interviews usually are the most important source of information; they may be conducted with all officers, key managers, and selected lower-level personnel in all functions of the business, with the depth of interviewing varying among levels and functions as determined to be appropriate in preparing the play of study.

These interviews generally have several purposes: (1) to develop a clear picture of each person's responsibilities, authorities, and relationships, involvement in key management and administrative processes, and specific functions; (2) to solicit the interviewee's ideas about opportunities for improvement in organization and operations, and any suggestions for solutions of the problems that have been identified; and (3) to obtain (in confidence) opinions concerning the availability of qualified candidates to succeed to specific management positions under the alternative circumstances of an emergency or the normal retirement of the incumbent.

Through these interviews, along with observations of facilities and work processes and review of documentation, the study team can be expected to gain a thorough understanding of the enterprise's organizational structure, its human, physical, and financial resources, and its operations.

**External Fact-Finding**  This step (which usually overlaps those that precede and follow it) consists mainly of interviews with outside people who have some kind of relationship with the enterprise and/or particular knowledge of it, for example, board members (if they have not requested the audit), representatives of customer firms, financial institutions, external auditors, government agencies at the federal, state, and local levels, unions, and vendors.

In these external interviews, the main purpose is to develop a thorough understanding of how the enterprise relates to its external environment so that the study team may make realistic assessments of the enterprise's performance and of opportunities for improvement. Specific matters that may be explored in this context include sourcing, product policy, manufacturing policy, distribution, market share, profitability, and overall strategy.

**Analysis** At this stage, all the data gathered—through interviews, review of documentation, and observation of facilities and work processes—will be analyzed to develop a profile of the enterprise's performance. In general, the criteria used for performance evaluation provide comparisons on the basis of efficiency or effectiveness. Although many of these criteria can be measured quantitatively (in terms of dollars or units of production), it is necessary to keep in mind the difficulties inherent in finding truly comparable benchmarks. For this reason, particular attention should be given to evaluating the enterprise's performance within the context of its unique environment. Seasoned judgment should be applied in tempering quantitative evaluations and also in measuring the less-tangible elements of performance, such as the enterprise's impact on the general public or the attitude of the management.

*Levels of Examination.* An enterprise may be viewed as a collection of interrelated functions and systems that are guided by an overall strategy in seeking to achieve a set of business objectives. In this light, a conceptual framework for the analysis phase of a management audit could include three levels of examination, as follows:

1. Appraisal of the efficiency, effectiveness, necessity, and flexibility of each function and system.

2. Assessment of the interrelationships and linkages between dependent or related functions and systems.

3. Appraisal of the congruence of all functions and systems to the overall strategy of the enterprise. All functions and systems should operate synergistically to achieve the desired business objectives. Substrategies and unit-level objectives within the enterprise should mesh with the overall strategy and objectives.

Implicit in each of the three levels of examination is the appraisal of management effectiveness. Because the kinds of management tasks differ at each level of examination, however, different sets of performance measures may have to be developed.

**Development of Conclusions and Recommendations** On the basis of the comprehensive analysis undertaken at this stage in the management audit, interpreted in the light of the study team's background and experience, conclusions are drawn regarding the efficiency and effectiveness of the enterprise's management and operations. To the extent that the enterprise is found to be sound, the study team will confirm this. If any significant opportunities for improvement have been identified, the study team will document each such opportunity, describing the apparent sources of the difficulty, the potential consequences if the problem is not resolved, and the course of action recommended.

**Communication of the Results of the Audit** Typically, the study team holds a series of meetings with the corporation's management (and/or the group that actually authorized the audit, such as the board of directors or a government agency) to review and discuss findings, conclusions, and recommendations informally as they evolve. To the extent that there is agreement on the need to take specific improvement steps, these steps may be initiated immediately instead of waiting until the final report is submitted. Depending on the scope and depth of the management audit and the conclusions reached, a second phase may or may not be required to explore further some of the opportunities for improvement that have been identified.

The final report is usually presented first in draft form to the corporation's management, to ensure accuracy and completeness. It is then revised as necessary and submitted officially—preceded or supplemented by oral-visual presentations as required. The formal plan of action should detail recommendation priorities, the individual actions and the persons or units responsible for carrying them out, the timing projected for each action, the personnel and other resources required, and the benefits to be anticipated.

## SIGNIFICANT ISSUES THAT MAY ARISE

This description of the management audit would not be complete without some discussion of certain issues which commonly arise.

**Audience to Be Addressed** Frequently, the management group which is being audited is also the group that requested and authorized the study and consequently is the only audience to which findings will be reported. In this situation, management may ask the study team to concentrate its efforts on those areas which need improvement, with little emphasis on confirming the strengths of the enterprise.

As noted earlier, however, there are growing

pressures on boards of directors to assume more active roles in their respective enterprises (as opposed to the days in which they were content merely to ratify the actions of management). The trend is to make more constructive use of outside directors in overseeing the performance of management. An effective tool for this purpose is authorization of a management audit on behalf of the board of directors, since this can provide the kind of independent overview of the corporation that the board will find helpful in appraising management's effectiveness. In this situation, the concerns of the board must outweigh the desires of the management group being audited—although that management group is *always* a part of the audience to which a report on the audit will be addressed.

In the case of an audit requested by a governmental regulatory agency, the final report must be oriented primarily to the special concerns of that agency, and also the general public. For example, it was noted earlier that there is a growing tendency for some state public service commissions to impose mandatory management audits on the public utilities for which they are responsible, to ensure that any conditions potentially detrimental to the interests of ratepayers are identified and eliminated. Because the final report on such an audit is often made available to the public, the report must present, fairly and objectively, both the strengths and the weaknesses of the utility, since a report citing only weaknesses would distort the picture.

**Scope of the Audit**   This issue is closely related to the question of the audience to be addressed, but there is a broad range of viewpoints. At one extreme, it is suggested that any management audit should have an unrestricted scope, on the grounds that the management of an enterprise should be flexible enough to deal with any situations that may arise. Others feel that the scope should be restricted to findings only, without conclusions or recommendations. (This point of view adheres closely to the traditional definition of an audit as no more than a review or examination.) Nonetheless, it is generally agreed that the identification of opportunities for improvement at least implies the eventual development of recommendations for capitalizing on them.

The scope of a management audit may include appraisal of the methods employed by management, in addition to the results achieved through those methods. One view limits the scope specifically to the *results* achieved, on the grounds that only results which can be quantified and compared are useful. A less-widely held view limits the audit solely to an appraisal of the *methods* used by management. The

general view is that both the methods and the results should be assessed.

As defined here, the *scope* of a management audit involves analysis of the internal aspects of an enterprise in the light of its external environment. There is, however, a view that the analysis should be limited entirely to the internal aspects of an enterprise. The objection to internal analysis only is that it disregards the impact of environmental forces and obviates the use of any external standards of comparison.

**Timing of the Audit**   The issue of when a management audit should be conducted is also subject to widely varying views. This is understandable, since no two enterprises are exactly alike. Some prescribe a preventive maintenance, an ongoing approach, whereby audits are performed continuously by internal auditors and/or external auditors. Others advocate a comprehensive management audit every 2 to 5 years. Currently, however, the majority still feel that a management audit should be undertaken on an as-needed basis.

The frequency with which management audits are voluntarily conducted tends to be closely related to the precise nature of the enterprise as well as to the attitudes and expectations of management regarding the benefits that may be derived.

**Evaluation Criteria to Be Used**   There are two main schools of thought regarding evaluation criteria. One advocates a set of standard criteria; the other prefers a more flexible approach. The advantage of standard criteria is the ease of comparing different companies on a uniform basis. On the other hand, it is argued that the characteristics of any two companies differ enough to make true comparisons impossible and that evaluation criteria therefore should be determined for each enterprise.

In most situations, these opposing points of view can be combined, at least to some extent, using standard criteria where they can be applied and interpreting them according to the particular circumstances affecting the enterprise under study.

**The Study Team's Relationships with the Management Group Being Audited**   Some people feel that an arm's-length relationship is proper, while others argue that a close working relationship leads to more effective results. The first group holds that maintaining a distant relationship ensures greater objectivity. The basic contention of the second group is that a close working relationship promotes management's understanding of the study team's thinking as it develops, as well as subsequent acceptance of the findings.

In any event, management is expected to cooperate with the study team, making its people available for interviews, supplying the data requested, and arranging for members of the study team to observe facilities and work processes. For its part, the study team, through its thoroughness, professionalism, and sensitivity to the concerns of different constituencies, is expected to promote the credibility of the auditing process and the resulting recommendations.

**Study Team Membership and Qualifications** Whether internal or external analysts are selected to conduct the audit depends on four main considerations: (1) the degree of independence sought; (2) the skills required; (3) the timing of the audit; and (4) the scope and objectives set for it. External analysts are used if a completely independent appraisal is desired, if management lacks the internal resources or the time to carry out the audit, or if an external study is required to supplement the work of the internal auditing function.

Regardless of who conducts the audit, there are certain qualifications which every member of the study team should possess. Each should have a broadly based conceptual understanding of the total management process, together with analytical skills and sound judgment to complement this conceptual understanding. Management auditing is primarily a judgmental process, unlike financial auditing, which involves mainly the verification of quantifiable data. Accordingly, the study team must be able to develop new methods of examination and evaluation, as required. In addition, of course, the study team as a whole must possess a degree of in-depth functional experience which at least matches the prescribed scope of the audit.

Thus, there should be a balance of conceptual understanding, broad management perspective, analytical skills, creativity, and sound, practical judgment. Furthermore, every member of the study team must be able to deal with people at all levels in the enterprise, since the information obtained through interviews is a key factor governing the success of the audit.

## BENEFITS TO BE ANTICIPATED

There are significant benefits to be anticipated from the conduct of a management audit. It will determine the extent of an enterprise's compliance with established policies, plans, and procedures, and how well assets are safeguarded. The quality of the management group is evaluated in terms of its performance of assigned tasks and its discharge of responsibilities. Recommendations are developed to capitalize on potential cost reductions and other opportunities for improvement. Information flows are reviewed to determine whether adequate information is being channeled to management to enable it to make effective operating and strategic decisions.

The management audit is particularly effective as a strategic tool since it presents an overview of the enterprise in relation to its environment, identifying relative strengths and weaknesses. If the audit report is generally favorable, management can retain the established strategy and use the findings as a guide in building on strengths and eliminating weaknesses to achieve the desired objectives. Alternatively, management can use the assessment of strengths and weaknesses as input in formulating a new set of objectives and a strategy for accomplishing them.

Whether management audits are conducted voluntarily or are imposed, it is likely that there will be many more of them in the future. The forces encouraging increasing use of them include growing management recognition of the potential benefits, the mandating of audits through laws or regulations, requests by boards of directors for better information about corporate affairs, and the rapidly growing use of the management audit as a key element in investigating a candidate for acquisition.

Ultimately, of course, the future of the management audit depends directly on proven past accomplishments. The key factors contributing to a successful management audit are thorough and objective fact-finding, analysis based on conceptual understanding and sound judgment, the development of recommendations that are practical and hence implementable, and acceptance of the audit results by the management group being audited. All these factors, in turn, are directly influenced by the quality of the study team's performance.

*See also* AUDITING, FINANCIAL; BOARDS OF DIRECTORS, LEGAL LIABILITY GUIDELINES; CONSULTANTS, MANAGEMENT; CONTROL SYSTEMS, MANAGEMENT; *Information Systems;* ORGANIZATION ANALYSIS AND PLANNING; POLICY FORMULATION AND IMPLEMENTATION.

## NOTES

[1]Robert E. Gobeil, "The Management Audit—A Service to Management," *Cost and Management*, May–June 1972, pp. 30–31.

[2]William P. Leonard, *The Management Audit, An Appraisal of Management Methods and Performance*, Prentice-Hall, Inc., Englewood Cliffs, N.J., 1962.

[3]GAO, U.S. General Accounting Office, November 1970. [Italics supplied.]

REFERENCE

Lindberg, Roy A., and Theodore Cohn: *Operations Auditing*, American Management Association, New York, 1972.

GEORGE M. WHITMORE, JR., *Cresap, McCormick and Paget Inc.*
GEORGE L. SING, *formerly Cresap, McCormick and Paget Inc.; now Emdex, A Division of Exxon Enterprises, Inc.*

## Audit, material handling (See MATERIAL HANDLING.)

## Audit, MBO [See OBJECTIVES, MANAGEMENT BY (MBO).]

## Audit, media (See ADVERTISING MANAGEMENT, INDUSTRIAL.)

## Audit, operational (See AUDIT, MANAGEMENT.)

## Audit, quality (See QUALITY MANAGEMENT.)

## Audit, situation (See PLANNING, STRATEGIC MANAGERIAL.)

## Audit, social (See SOCIAL RESPONSIBILITY OF BUSINESS.)

## Audit, tax (See TAX MANAGEMENT, MANAGERIAL RESPONSIBILITY FOR FEDERAL INCOME TAX REPORTING.)

# Auditing, financial

A *financial audit* is an objective investigation to validate the representations in financial statements by obtaining reasonable assurance of the integrity and reliability of the underlying accounting system.

Since management has a personal interest in the way that its performance is measured in financial statements, the custom has developed of having those statements audited by an independent firm of auditors to provide an outside expert opinion of management's representations.

## THE AUDITOR'S STANDARD REPORT

The *auditor's report* is a formal communication by a firm of independent auditors, describing its examination of financial statements and expressing its professional opinion on those statements.

The typical report contains two paragraphs. The first paragraph identifies the financial statements examined—typically, comparative balance sheets, income statements, statements of retained earnings, and changes in financial position—and describes the nature and scope of the examination made by the auditor. The second (the opinion) paragraph states whether the financial statements identified in the scope paragraph fairly present the company's financial position, results of operations, and changes in financial position in conformity with generally accepted accounting principles and whether those principles have been consistently applied.

Much of the significance that users of financial statements attach to the report comes from the underlying meaning of two key phrases: generally accepted auditing standards and generally accepted accounting principles.

**Generally Accepted Auditing Standards** Independent auditors typically distinguish auditing procedures from auditing standards. *Auditing procedures* are acts performed by auditors to gather evidential matter concerning the underlying accounting data and corroborating data supporting financial statements. *Generally accepted auditing standards* is a technical term that defines accepted auditing practice at a particular time. It includes broad objectives to be achieved in the audit and more detailed technical guidance.

The membership of the American Institute of Certified Public Accountants (AICPA) has officially adopted 10 formal standards—divided into general standards, standards of fieldwork, and standards of reporting.

The general standards broadly describe the qualifications of an independent auditor and the quality his or her work should achieve. The fieldwork standards describe in general terms the minimum requirements of a financial audit, and the reporting standards describe the essential requirements for the form and content of the auditor's report.

The 10 formal standards provide only broad guidance. The AICPA's Auditing Standards Division issues Statements on Auditing Standards (SAS) that provide interpretation of the 10 formal standards. SASs have been referred to in many court cases as the minimum requirements for financial audits.

**Generally Accepted Accouting Principles** The first standard of reporting requires the independent auditor's report to state whether the financial statements conform with generally accepted accounting principles. Like generally accepted auditing standards, *generally accepted accounting principles* is a technical term that describes the guidance necessary to define accepted accounting practice at a particular time. The task of developing generally accepted accounting principles now rests principally with the Financial Accounting Standards Board (FASB)—an independent organization in the private sector. The Council of the AICPA has designated the FASB as the authoritative source of accounting principles for AICPA members.

**Modifications of the Standard Report** The standard report described is referred to as an unqualified opinion. It communicates the fact that the auditor has gathered evidence to support the validity of the events and transactions underlying the statements and that in the auditor's judgment those events and transactions are adequately presented and disclosed in accordance with their economic substance. Anything less than an unqualified opinion is usually considered undesirable by management and may be unacceptable to users of the financial statements. An independent auditor, however, may be forced to express something other than an unqualified opinion if the financial statements depart in a material manner from generally accepted accounting principles, the auditor's examination is not adequate to support an opinion, or the financial statements are affected by a material uncertainty that may at a future date require adjustment of financial statements.

## AUDITING PRACTICE AND METHODS

The audit report is signed by a CPA firm rather than by the individual auditor or auditors who conduct the examination.

**CPA Firms** A management's choice of a CPA firm can be expected to receive scrutiny by users of financial statements who rely chiefly on the reputation of the CPA firms. Underwriters of large public offerings of securities may demand an international or national firm of wide-known reputation. Bankers and other credit grantors are known to keep lists of acceptable CPA firms based on their own and other creditors' experience.

**The Audit Examination** The first examination of a new client is normally extensive. In subsequent audits the end of one engagement blends into the beginning of the next, and each engagement builds on the experience of prior ones. An audit depends heavily on the independent auditor's understanding of the accounting system in use and the controls over it as well as the accounting principles used.

The auditor must be familiar with the characteristics of the company's operations that could have an accounting effect and of the management's policies and procedures that have an effect on the reliability of the accounting records and the financial statements prepared from them. The auditor must also consider the effect of changes in the business environment, in the company, and its operations, and the legal requirements under which the company must operate.

An audit normally begins with a *preliminary review* and evaluation of the client's operations and controls. The auditor may conduct initial interviews with the client's management and supervisory personnel, tour the offices and principal plants, read company manuals on practices and procedures, and in other ways become familiar with the client, its industry, and its particular problems.

The *study and evaluation of internal control* play a significant part in modern audits. The first step is normally a review of the system to obtain an understanding of the controls that are supposed to be in effect. A preliminary evaluation is then made of those controls to see if the auditor can rely on them to assure the integrity and reliability of the accounting records. If the auditor plans to rely on particular controls, he or she will then test compliance with them by (1) observing controls, such as separation of key functions in operation, and (2) sampling transactions by inspection of supporting documents.

The study and evaluation of internal control is correlated with analytic review procedures and tests of transactions and balances on a sample basis. *Analytic review procedures* include (1) reading important documents, looking for matters of financial and accounting significance; (2) scanning the activity in accounts and summary entries, looking for unusual items; and (3) comparing account balances in one or more other accounting periods or in the budget, looking for unusual or unexpected deviations. Tests of transactions and balances include such procedures as (1) confirming receivables and bank balances with outside parties, (2) physically inspecting assets and comparing asset counts with accounting records, and (3) scrutinizing the documents supporting transactions.

## CLIENT-AUTOR RELATIONS AND COMMUNICATIONS

Because independent auditors must have contact with many levels in the organization, it is advisable to fix responsibility on some one individual for coordinating these matters.

**Establishing Responsibility within the Organization** Generally, it is the chief financial officer or chief internal auditor who is charged with coordination. The chief executive officer, however, should know the independent auditor well enough to consult with him or her in advance as frequently as necessary on significant matters involving the presentation of the company's financial statements or on significant transactions that are being planned.

*Letters of Representation.* A generally accepted auditing procedure is to obtain a letter of representation from a company's legal counsel concerning litigation, contingent liabilities, and, in some cases, interpretation of specific contracts and agreements. If a company has a general counsel, it would be common practice for the auditor to work with that person in obtaining the necessary information and representation.

Another common audit procedure is to obtain a representation letter from top officers of the corporation concerning significant representations in the financial statements. Representations obtained from management are not a substitute for audit procedures. They are used by the independent auditor to make a record of significant inquiries and responses during the engagement and to record management's belief that the auditor has been informed of all matters within their knowledge that could have a material bearing on the work.

*Audit Committees.* Many companies have established audit committees composed primarily of the outside directors of the board of directors. The existence of an audit committee helps to demonstrate that the board of directors is fulfilling its responsibility to shareholders concerning financial reporting and disclosure. Through the audit committee, the board of directors is able to evaluate the work of the independent auditor and understand the nature and limitations of a financial audit.

**CPA Firm Selection and Termination** For many companies, the selection of the independent auditor is approved by the board of directors and often ratified by its shareholders. Top management should take the initiative in seeing that the board of directors is adequately informed to make an appropriate selection. CPA firms should be expected to make a proposal explaining their qualifications and abilities to conduct the audit and provide other services.

Just as the company should conduct an investigation in the selection of auditors, independent auditors commonly investigate the reputation and business standing of potential clients. An auditor considering the acceptance of an engagement must also communicate with the independent auditor who preceded him or her on the engagement. In addition, a regulation of the Securities and Exchange Commission may require a company to disclose any dispute with the predecessor auditor about accounting principles or disclosures in a filing.

**Working Relations During the Audit** A client's staff may often assist the independent auditor by preparing schedules and analyses of accounts and by searching files for needed information and documents. The cost of an audit can be reduced if this assistance is provided.

If a company has an internal audit department, the independent auditor can be expected to obtain an understanding of the work of the internal audit staff and may be able to make use of the work normally done by the internal audit staff in his or her study and evaluation of internal control. The independent auditor may also be able to get direct assistance from members of the internal audit staff in portions of the examination.

**Conferences During the Audit** From time to time during the audit, the partner in charge of the engagement must meet with the chief financial officer or the chief executive officer or the audit committee to discuss accounting policies and controls and the company's financial reporting practices. The level of the communication usually depends on the nature and significance of the matter in question. Important decisions about accounting matters should not be put off until the end of the year, and communications should take place continuously during the audit. The independent auditor and top management should adopt the policy of mutual nonsurprise.

Top management will want to consult with the independent auditor, for example, prior to engaging in major transactions, such as the acquisition of another corporation, to find out how the transaction will be reflected in the financial statements and about prospective changes in accounting principles and prospective changes in accounting systems or controls.

If the auditor and top management cannot reach agreement on accounting principles or disclosures, it may be necessary for the matter to be resolved by the audit committee or the board of directors itself. Some matters of significance such as major weaknesses in controls may need to be brought to the attention of the board of directors in any event.

**Written Communications from the Auditor** Independent auditors may prepare a number of reports for use within the client organization—the most frequent form is the so-called "management letter." *Management letters* draw attention to weaknesses in accounting systems and related controls, make constructive suggestions about correcting weaknesses, and explore other possibilities for improvements.

**Annual Meetings** It is desirable for the independent auditor to be available at annual meetings to answer the questions of shareholders. Independent auditors are frequently able to explain the safeguards that the company has adopted to prevent common financial problems from receiving press coverage. Also, independent auditors are able to answer questions concerning the accounting policies followed by the company and how those policies compare with those of other companies in the industry.

*See also* ACCOUNTING, COST ANALYSIS AND CONTROL; ACCOUNTING, FINANCIAL; ACCOUNTING FOR MANAGERIAL CONTROL; ACQUISITIONS AND MERGERS; AUDIT, MANAGEMENT; CONTROL SYSTEMS, MANAGEMENT; EXCHANGE, FOREIGN, MANAGEMENT OF; FINANCIAL MANAGEMENT; FINANCIAL STATEMENT ANALYSIS; INFORMATION SYSTEMS, MANAGEMENT (MIS); OMBUDSMAN; SHAREHOLDER RELATIONSHIPS; TAX MANAGEMENT; MANAGERIAL RESPONSIBILITY FOR FEDERAL INCOME TAX REPORTING.

### REFERENCES

Auditing Standards Division, *Statements on Auditing Standards*, American Institute of Certified Public Accountants, New York: Codification of Statements on Auditing Standards, nos. 1 to 7, January 1976; "Other Information in Documents Containing Audited Financial Statements," no. 8, December 1975; "The Effect of an Internal Audit Function on the Scope of the Independent Auditor's Examination," no. 9, December 1975; "Limited Review of Interim Financial Information," no. 10, December 1975; "Using the Work of a Specialist," no. 11, December 1975; "Inquiry of a Client's Lawyer Concerning Litigation, Claims, and Assessments," no. 12, January 1976; "Reports on Limited Review of Interim Financial Information," no. 13, May 1976.

Carmichael, D. R., and John J. Willingham: *Perspectives in Auditing*, 2d ed., McGraw-Hill Book Company, New York, 1975.

Defliese, Philip L., Kenneth P. Johnson, and Roderick K. Macleod: *Montgomery's Auditing*, 9th ed., The Ronald Press Company, New York, 1975.

Mautz, R. K., and F. L. Neumann: *Corporate Audit Committees*, Bureau of Economic and Business Research, University of Illinois, Urbana, Ill., 1970.

Solomon, Kenneth I., Charles Chazen, and Barry S. Augenbraun: "Who Judges the Auditor, and How?" *The Journal of Accountancy*, vol. 142, no. 2, pp. 67–74, August 1976.

"Symposium on Accounting and the Federal Securities Laws," *Vanderbilt Law Review*, vol. 28, no. 1, January 1975.

D. R. CARMICHAEL, *American Institute of Certified Public Accountants*

## Auditing, internal (*See* FINANCIAL MANAGEMENT.)

## Auditor's report (*See* AUDITING, FINANCIAL.)

## Authority, functional (*See* MANAGEMENT THEORY, SCIENCE AND APPROACHES.)

## Authority, responsibility, and accountability

Authority encompasses the concepts of power, responsibility, accountability, delegation, and decentralization; it is "the key to the management job."[1] The changing applications and implications of authority have concerned and confused many managers. The current tendency is to criticize past meanings of the concept, to impute new interpretations, and to suggest new applications in management practice. Several approaches, however, can be used by today's managers to achieve an integrated view of authority. They are those based upon (1) status and rank, (2) function or job, and (3) subordinate acceptance. In this entry, responsibility and accountability are considered in their relationship to authority. Delegation, its role in decentralized authority, and its importance to effective management are also considered.

## MEANINGS AND RELATIONSHIPS

Authority and responsibility have long been linked in management theory—usually with the admonition that they must be coincidental, corresponding, coequal, coterminous, coexistent, and, often, delegated simultaneously.

*Accountability* is a concommitant, a derivative, or an adjunct of responsibility.

Power is considered by some to be an element of authority; by others, as related to but different from authority. Still others view authority as an aspect, type, or derivative of power and use the terms interchangeably. Power has not always been freely discussed in management literature, but it needs to be recognized, and its role as an activator in organizations needs to be explored. Such recognitions and investigations are already in progress.[2] In this discussion, *power* is defined as an ingredient of all organizational activities and as an underlying basis for the sharing of responsibility and the granting of authority. (*See also* POWER.)

*Authority* is derived from the Latin word *auctoritas*, indicating one who increases or produces. How it should be interpreted and applied in a modern organization depends upon the orientation of the person who is wielding it.

## AUTHORITY

Authority will be considered from three points of view, followed by a synthesis of these (*see* Table A-6) and a consideration of its relationship to responsibility and its role in the essential managerial act of delegation.

**Authority Based upon Power, Status, or Rank** This is the traditional or classical concept. It stresses two elements: (1) a *right* to do something (issue orders, make decisions, command, demand obedience) and (2) the *power* to enforce compliance. It is often stated quite boldly as "the right to tell other people what you want them to do and the power to see that they do it." This interpretation presumes that total, final, or complete authority within each organization resides at some top level where it was placed by a sovereign authority (witness the divine right of kings). In a democracy, the analogy would be the citizenry through their elected representatives. This top level (group, position, person) has been granted the authority to use property or things in an approved way. It then passes parts of this authority downward in the organization, through prescribed channels or paths, to the persons

who must take the intended action. The right and power of these action-level people to perform, hence, can be traced upward to its ultimate source within the organization—the charter or grant. Traditional authority has had many exponents and still retains quite a few, as indicated in Table A-6.

*Authority Based upon Position.* Within an organizational hierarchy, this kind of authority is actually a part of traditional authority and sometimes is considered to be a subset thereof. It is closely related to status or rank and is spoken of as a level of authority within the organization. In all organizations, people become quite conscious of these levels and refer to top management, middle management, and first-line management as indicative of these respective levels of authority. Thus, a certain position, at a certain level, is presumed to be endowed with a certain amount or degree of authority.

**Authority Based upon Function or Job** In this approach, the authority to act is essentially another part of whatever job is committed to take the final or intended action. In other words, the capacity to act resides in and is part of the job. There is no continuing pathway of delegation other than the assignment of the job. Once the job assignment has been accepted, full or complete authority resides in the job and with the person on the job. M. P. Follett is recognized as the first management theorist to propose this concept and to point out that the person on a job and the job itself are interdependent ("authority belongs to the job and stays with the job"[3]). She was objecting to a supreme or final authority which then delegated bits and pieces downward throughout the organization. Thus, the *immediate* source of authority becomes the assignment-acceptance of a job, and the only *ultimate* source is the one who determined and assigned the work.

*Staff Authority and Functional Authority.* Closely akin to the concept of job authority, staff authority is related directly to and is based solely upon the specialized knowledge and capabilities of a particular staff member (e.g., an attorney). This professional-staff specialization puts such a person in the position to say, "When you do thus and so, do it *this* way." In some cases, there are various levels or locations of staff within a specialized field (e.g., personnel). Here, the top-level staff member is sometimes granted staff authority or functional authority over corresponding functions at lower levels in the organization. Such top-level staff may be given authority for surveillance of lower-level performance and for directing work-level personnel. This is frequently the cause of conflict with the local or immediate line authority involved (e.g., account-

**TABLE A-6  Concepts of Authority—A Comparison and an Integration**

| Type and basis | Elements of meaning | Characteristics and assumptions | Immediate source | Ultimate source and path of delegation | Exponents* |
|---|---|---|---|---|---|
| Traditional authority—based on power, status, rank | A right and power: to enforce, to require obedience, to demand compliance, to make decisions, to issue orders, to command, to control the action of others | Stems from ownership and use of property  Paths or lines of delegation downward through organization to work level  Person viewed as passive and inert, an instrument of production or of the organization  Manager issues orders or commands and makes decisions | Organizational superordinate | Citizens ↓ Government ↓ Organizational charter ↓ Owners ↓ Officers ↓ Managers ↓ Supervisors ↓ Workers | Alford Davis Fayol Hopf Koontz Mooney Schell Taylor Terry |
| Functional authority—based on function or job | Inherent in function or work  In effect, created by the offer and acceptance of a work assignment | Resides in and is a part of a function, responsibility, job  Moves with job assignment—stays with the job—no path  Person and work interdependent | A work assignment or job | One who determines and assigns work—no path | Follett |
| Behavioral authority—based on acceptance, consent, assent | Acceptance of another's right to direct  An interpersonal relationship  A communication  A set of behaviors—interaction between persons | Resides with subordinate, granted to superordinate; subordinate consents to perform  Path of authority upward, conferred on boss when subordinate assents to orders  Person viewed as independent of organization  Manager gets acceptance of proposed action and decisions | The individual subordinate | Owners ↑ Officers ↑ Managers ↑ Supervisors ↑ Workers | Argyris Barnard Fromm Mayo Roethlisberger Simon |
| Intergrational authority—based on pertinent elements from all the above | Freedom to act, to decide—requiring permission and ability  Permission to take action  Opportunity to perform  Opportunity to innovate  Comes into being with the specification of responsibility and its acceptance | Resides with but one person at work, *at any one time*  No path or channel; monolithic, unitary, indivisible, integrated  Optimum self-direction  Person and work interdependent  Manager as a transfer agent transfers authority to those who are to take action (work)  Combines freedom and opportunity for self-direction with organizational objectives and job goals | When responsibility is offered to and accepted by a subordinate, he or she is delegated the authority to perform | An organization's permission to exist and operate—its charter, license, etc.; no path | Golembiewski Mandeville Trickett |

*Named exponents are merely a sampling of some of the management theorists who have espoused all or parts of the respective interpretations of authority.

ing versus production). A number of students of management have analyzed these causes of conflict and sought ways to alleviate them.[4] There is no foolproof solution to this specialist-generalist authority problem, although openness, frankness, and joint responsibility for results can alleviate much of it.

**Authority Based upon Acceptance, Consent, or Assent** Increasingly popular since Chester Barnard's[5] monumental contribution to the field in 1938, this approach avers that authority resides with the subordinate who is to take the prescribed action and that the subordinate grants an authority to the superordinate by consenting to perform. In short, subordinates *accept* the boss's right to direct them. Thus, as Barnard pointed out, this acceptance is based upon an interpersonal relationship, a communication between persons, and, therefore, is actually passed upward in the organization—just the reverse of the traditional idea of a downward passage. Most exponents of this concept have been classed as *behaviorists* and the authority relationship seen as a set of behaviors or interactions, hence the appellation *behavioral authority* in Table A-6.

**An Integrated Approach to Authority** Authority based upon an integration of applicable elements from each of the previous approaches would seem most practicable for modern managers. Each has its merits, and some of the elements of each are needed in today's organizations. Observers have pointed out that those who espouse traditional authority have viewed the employee (who does the work and takes the action) as passive and inert, as an instrument of the organization; that M. P. Follett and the adherents of authority based upon function or job saw the employee and his or her work as interdependent; and that the behavioral approach considered the employee as separate and apart from the organization. The first approach has been labeled as considering organizations without people; the second, as only observing people within organizations; and the third, as studying people without organizations.

Practicing managers can integrate or combine today's beliefs concerning individual freedom, worth, and opportunities with current developments in human work behavior (including the growing awareness of a person's capacity for self-direction) and with historical evidence and experience in effective organizational functioning. Now, authority can be seen as freedom or opportunity to act, to decide, to perform; the essential elements being *permission* (the consent to do or use something) and *ability* (the capability to take the action). This, of course, requires the manager not only to give permission for the proposed action but also to see that the one who will perform is ready and prepared to act. This will require further that there be agreement as to just *what* is to be done, *how* it is to be done, and *the acceptance* by the subordinate of these objectives. This acceptance equals the responsibility to perform, and it is from this acceptance that the authority to act arises. Thus, this authority is unitary or monolithic and resides with the one who is to perform, whereas the responsibility for action is shared and pluralistic. That is, the responsibility for effective action is shared among the actor, the superordinate, the superordinate's superordinate, and so forth, to the very top of the organization.

## RESPONSIBILITY AND ACCOUNTABILITY

Responsibility and accountability are terms that are often confused and are frequently used synonymously. *Responsibility*, from the French *responsable*, means liable to respond, answerable. In common parlance, it implies an accountability or answerability to a person or body imposing a task or duty. A number of management theorists, however, have distinguished between responsibility and accountability.[6] More-current thinkers have said that this may be an unnecessary and even confusing distinction.[7] *If* responsibility has to be accepted (not imposed) and if this acceptance creates an obligation to perform, to do something, then there is an implicit answerability or *accountability*. It is this acceptance and sharing of responsibility which causes the accountability for results that is the very essence of the superordinate-subordinate reporting relationship. With the relationship agreed to and established, the permission to take the intended action naturally follows. And this permission, involving preparation to perform and the inducement to do what has to be done, is the substance of authority as a derivative of responsibility. What, then, *is* delegated by a manager?

## DELEGATION

Delegation has been called the essence of the manager's job, and some observers have claimed that the greatest cause of manager failure is the inability or unwillingness of a manager to delegate. *Delegate*, from the Latin *delegatus*, means to send one with a commission, hence to empower or trust another person to take action or to perform. Managerial inadequacy in delegation appears to come from the fact that managers are selected to be managers because they are effective doers; whereas, when they become managers, they must get things done through other persons. Henry Taylor's 1832 admonition, published in *The Statesman*, could well be directed to today's managers:

The most important qualification of an executive is his ability to act through others, since the value of his operations vicariously effected ought to predominate greatly over the importance of his direct activity. But it is a snare into which men in business and statesmen are apt to fall, that in attaching weight to the immediately visible effects of their efforts they lose sight of what they might accomplish if they applied their powers through the widest possible instrumentalities.

It should be clear by now that managers delegate authority—as permission and inducement to take some action—but that they do *not* delegate responsibility which they *share* with subordinates. Thus, responsibility, as accepted by the one to take the action, exists and is shared from this point of acceptance upward, level by level, to the top of the organization. Is it this acceptance of accountability for results that the behaviorists find passing upward within the organization (see Table A-6)?

*Decentralized* authority results from delegation. Decentralization is the keynote of Jethro's ancient advice to Moses (*Exodus* 18:17) that implemented two of the oldest of management precepts—that decisions affecting the work of the organization should be made as close as possible to the level (and location) at which the action is to be taken and that only unusual or exceptional problems should be passed upward for decision—i.e., the principle of decentralized authority and the principle of management by exception.

*See also* DELEGATION; EXCEPTION, MANAGEMENT BY; LEADERSHIP; MANAGEMENT, DEFINITIONS OF; MANAGEMENT, THEORY, SCIENCE, AND APPROACHES; ORGANIZATION ANALYSIS AND PLANNING.

### NOTES

[1] H. Koontz and C. O'Donnell, "The Functions and Authority of the Manager," *Principles of Management: An Analysis of Managerial Functions*, 5th ed., McGraw-Hill Book Company, New York, 1972, chap. 3.

[2] B. M. Gross, "The Power-Authority-Responsibility Triangle," *Organizations and Their Managing*, The Free Press, New York, 1968, p. 74; B. E. Kline and N. H. Martin, "Freedom, Authority, and Decentralization," *Harvard Business Review*, vol. 36, no. 3, p. 71, May–June 1958; M. Korda, *Power: How to Get It, How to Use It*, Random House, Inc., New York, 1975; D. C. McClelland and D. H. Burnham, "Power is the Great Motivator,"

*Harvard Business Review*, vol. 54, no. 2, p. 100, March–April 1976; R. N. McMurry, "Power and the Ambitious Executive," *Harvard Business Review*, vol. 51, no. 6, p. 140, November–December 1973; A. Zaleznik and M. F. R. Kets de Vries, *Power and the Corporate Mind*, Houghton Mifflin Company, Boston, 1975.

[3] M. P. Follett, "The Basis of Authority," *Freedom and Coordination*, Management Publications Trust, Ltd., 1949, p. 1.

[4] D. E. McFarland, *Management: Principles and Practices*, 4th ed., The Macmillan Company, New York, 1974.

[5] C. I. Barnard, *The Functions of the Executive*, Harvard University Press, Cambridge, Mass., 1938, p. 183.

[6] R. C. Davis, *The Fundamentals of Top Management*, Harper & Brothers, New York, 1951, p. 293; B. J. Hodge and H. J. Johnson, *Management and Organizational Behavior*, John Wiley & Sons, Inc., New York, 1970, p. 404.

[7] H. Koontz and C. O'Donnell, loc. cit.

### REFERENCES

Bennis, W. G.: "Leadership Theory and Administrative Behavior: The Problem of Authority," *Administrative Science Quarterly*, December 1959, p. 263.

Golembiewski, R. T.: "Authority as a Problem in Overlays: A Concept for Action and Analysis," *Administrative Science Quarterly*, vol. 9, p. 23, 1964–1965.

Mandeville, M. J.: "The Nature of Authority," *Academy of Management Journal*, August 1960, p. 107.

Petersen, E., E. G. Plowman, and J. M. Trickett: "The Changing Role of Authority," *Business Organization and Management*, Richard D. Irwin, Inc., Homewood, Ill., 1962, chap. 4.

Satow, R. L.: "Value-Rational Authority and Professional Organizations," *Administrative Science Quarterly*, vol. 20, p. 526, December 1975.

Trickett, J. M.: "An Integrated Concept of Authority," *Management Recrod*, vols. 24–25, p. 19, May 1962.

Zaleznik, A.: "Power and Politics in Organizational Life," *Harvard Business Review*, vols. 48–43, p. 47. May–June 1970.

JOSEPH M. TRICKETT, *University of Santa Clara*

# Automatic balance accounts, bank
(*See* FINANCIAL MANAGEMENT.)

# Automation

Automation is a broadly inclusive term that encompasses all facets of accomplishing tasks with little or no human assistance. Applications are as varied as human imagination, ranging in scope from control of the Alaskan pipeline to automatically marking the correct identifier on miniature electronic components that are so small that the marking is barely visible to the human eye.

**Rapid Development** The development of automation has been one of steady progression and can be marked by

Inception of mass production by Henry Ford in 1909.

Acceleration of mechanization in World Wars I and II.

Machine tool sequencing by numerical control in 1952.

Digital computer control of an oil refinery's catalytic cracker in 1959.

Since 1959, digital computer control has become an essential element in processes such as steel rolling, power generation, cement production, and oil and chemical processing. The sizable decrease in computer costs, some 10 to 15 percent a year for a while, spurred a corresponding increase in automation applications, a phenomenon that will accelerate even more with the development of the microcomputer.

**Need for Automation** Application of automation should be dictated by a need which, in turn, should be supported by a potential return. While return is commonly measured in terms of dollars and cents, the need for automation is frequently initiated by one of the following compelling reasons:

*Noneconomic Labor.* In many instances, automation is mandated by the high costs of labor. This has brought about its most-feared effect—the potential for job reduction and elimination. In actual fact, in many cases more jobs have been created than lost.

*Lack of Manufacturing Feasibility.* Many production operations simply cannot be performed feasibly without automation. These would include (1) product and component size too big or too little for effective human operation; (2) production rates too high for human capability; (3) safety requirements that prohibit use of a human operator; and (4) production environment not conducive to human tolerance, such as a frozen food warehouse.

*Competition.* Elimination of production downtime is especially critical when the profit margin per production unit is low due to keen competition. This is claimed as a prime reason for widespread use of digital computer control of cement production.

*Multi-Parameter Control.* Several processes have interacting parameters that affect the end product. The exothermic reaction required in a cement kiln, for example, is affected by kiln rotation speed, fuel characteristics, and draft setting, to name just three. Changes may not have an effect on the resultant product for a half hour or more. While it is difficult for a human operator to keep track of response changes, especially those with slow response times, it is a simple matter for a control digital computer to monitor past changes and to correlate these changes with current product characteristics.

## AUTOMATION HIERARCHY

An understanding and application of automation is made simpler by structuring its various techniques into a hierarchy in the following order: (1) mechanization; (2) numerical control; (3) digital computer control, *(a)* microprocessor control, *(b)* minicomputer control, and *(c)* large-scale computer control.

**Mechanization** The accomplishment of tasks with machines or mechanical aids is classified as *mechanization.* An original differentiation between automation and mechanization lies in *feedback,* the concept of self-correction. An automated system is assumed to be self-correcting, while one mechanized is not. The feedback relationship is currently not a major item in separating automation from mechanization. A mechanized process is not necessarily completely automatic and may require operator setup and intervention. For hierarchical purposes an automation system may contain one or more mechanized processes, although many purists do not consider a mechanized process to be automation.

In the assembly of electronic diodes at rates of thousands per hour, for example, minute positioning of leads and bonding of the leads to a microscopic die are accomplished by mechanized means. This logically is an automated process even though certain aspects of lot material handling are accomplished by an operator. Machine tool operations are also naturally considered a part of mechanization. Automatically stepping a mechanized process through a series of operations by a tape- or card-controlled process, however, is a higher-order of automation, classified as numerical control.

**Numerical Control** With numerical control (N/C), machining operations are directed by numerical instructions either from a punched card, punched paper tape, or from magnetic tape. One of the first applications of numerical control was in airplane wing–spar milling, a large and complex task with tight tolerances. The tape control contained cutter-positioning information for one master spar. Duplicate spars could then be produced from the same tape with tolerance uniformity among all the spars.

In addition to machine tool operations, numerical control is utilized for parts positioning and component insertion and assembly, such as in the manufactur of computer circuit boards where many components are required in extremely tight tolerance locations.

*Input Instructions.* These direct the operations being controlled. A general-purpose computer with an N/C compiler generates the tape or cards. A commercial computer center or in-house computer facility may perform this function. Some N/C equipment is available with integrated computer equipment.

*Positioning Operation.* Two types of positioning exist with N/C: (1) point-to-point and (2) continuous path.

*Point-to-point* positioning is for discrete-type operations such as hole drilling, hole punching, part insertion, wrapping wire to terminal posts, and so on. The interpretive logic is much simpler than for *continuous-path* positioning which interpolates motion for the continuous cutting of material, as in the cutting of cams by a milling process. Regardless of positioning technique, typical linear resolution accuracy is on the order of a thousandth of an inch or better.

*Advantages.* These include

Elimination of lengthy lead times needed for setting up a particular operation.

Higher accuracy than with operator control.

Tolerance maintainability between parts and minimal rejections.

Long machining runs (frequently in terms of hours), thus allowing a single operator to handle a bank of machines efficiently and effectively.

One disadvantage of conventional N/C is the inflexibility of the device. Once a tape is prepared, machine actuations will conform exactly and only to that tape's specifications. N/C can, therefore, be construed as a nonflexible fixed program piece of equipment. It does not, for example, allow linking several machines together to enable production of several parts through varying sequences of machines.

*Machining Center Concept.* An advanced concept in numerical control that has been available for several years is that of the machining center, such as the one shown in Fig. A-17. The machining center allows tooling to be changed and actuated automatically. The center shown allows up to 69 tools in a tool magazine. Tool-to-tool changing times are under 4 seconds, and chip-to-chip is rated at 10 seconds.[1] Further flexibility is achieved with the addition of a computerized controller, shown in the rear center of the illustration. The system may be linked to a master computer to allow automatic load from the host device. Theoretically, several machines could be integrated for optimal system operation through the master computer, a step leading to full digital computer control.

**Digital Computer Control** A digital computer used for controlling processes has the same basic central processor as a scientific or business computer. The greatest differences occur due to the fact that a control digital computer must (1) operate in real time and (2) communicate with physical processes.

Thousands of digital signals and many analog signals may be checked at specified intervals by the computer to determine process status. Feedback information may then be sent back to the process to correct imperfect conditions and to attempt to obtain process optimality. A *digital signal* is one that is discrete in nature, such as a relay that closes upon detecting high temperatures. An *analog signal* is a voltage that represents a state in the process. For example, this might be a voltage that represents motor speed or a voltage that is proportional to a device's angular position.

Many control digital computer systems are gigantic in scope. Cement-plant control from a single computer, for example, encompasses cement-blending control and analysis, with blending optimized by a mathematical algorithm; kiln control, with up to three independent kilns; determination of efficiency values for management reports and the printing of those reports; an alarm when abnormal conditions occur; and performance of off-line calculations, such as quarry-digging optimization. To accomplish this a system of ordered priorities and interrupt controls are required to allow queuing of functions when many must be performed in a very short time period. Timing is accomplished internally by *priority interrupt*. Interrupts may be triggered by (1) physical occurrences, such as a power failure and process start and stop; and (2) print and other input-output peripherals so that the computer only works on these devices when an interrupt indicates that they are ready. The interrupts used for real time control can operate in frequencies of the order of millionths of a second.

*Minicomputers.* A control digital computer system that is very broad in scope is classified as large-scale, or a maxicomputer. Smaller systems, called *minicomputers,* can be used for less-demanding (but still highly complex) control activities and at much lower cost. A minicomputer in 1978 could generally be purchased for less than $25,000.

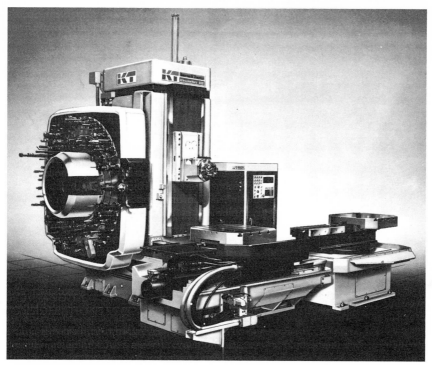

**Fig. A-17** A large-scale numerical control machining center. *(Courtesy of Kearney and Trecker Corporation, Milwaukee, Wisconsin.)*

*Microcomputer and Microprocessor.* The *microcomputer* is an extremely small, low cost, but complete, computer with peripheral input and output. A *microprocessor* is the heart of the microcomputer and does not possess the peripherals; thus it costs even less than the microcomputer. Microprocessors can be used where the process requires control on a repetitive basis once the program has been inserted. Microprocessor control is usually reserved for specialized applications, such as positioning leads for transistor die connections. The microprocessor is difficult to program, however, and has relatively slow operation speeds; thus it is best for small local applications.

## EXAMPLES OF APPLICATION

The following cases broadly demonstrate the need, equipment used, and benefits of automation.

**Discrete Production** The automation of discrete-unit production processes is extremely difficult. It requires innovation and ingenuity as well as possible large expenditures for equipment that is primarily mechanization-oriented. Computers are often used to integrate and control the various mechanized components of the discrete system.

*Microprocessor Control.*[2] In the fabrication of certain transistors it is necessary to bond extremely small wires (in the order of ten-thousandths of an inch diameter) to a die which has the required electrical properties of the transistor on one end and a post (which is the device lead) on the other end. The small size of the components is shown in Fig. A-18.

Problems associated with this job include parts handling into and out of the bonding machine, material handling within the machine to locate the required bonding points on the die and lead, the actual bonding of wires to both die and lead, and an integrity test to assure proper bonding. An operator can perform these functions with optical and mechanical aids, but the production rate is variable and slow compared with a microprocessor-controlled system which controls the necessary function sequence as well as controlling the lead-to-die positioning. With no operator, the automation system operates consistently at a production rate 5 times faster than with an operator.

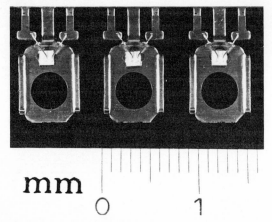

Fig. A-18. Transistor leads bonded through microprocessor control. Two 10-mil leads have to be bonded to specific locations on the 1.55 by 1.55 millimeter circuit die. *(Courtesy of Motorola Semiconductor Products Division, Phoenix, Arizona.)*

Advantages for this automation system are increased production rates, improved quality, and decreased labor cost per unit. In order for the company to stay competitive, all three advantages had to be realized: This was only possible through automation.

*Minicomputer Control.*[3] The testing and sorting of power transistors by Motorola is accomplished with the aid of a PDP-11 minicomputer, as shown in Fig. A-19. The sequence for testing and sorting includes picking up and orienting the devices, inserting them into a testing machine for a series of electrical tests, performing and recording the results of the tests, and then sorting the devices into the correct containers. Operator control would entail an unbelievable amount of paper work, to say nothing of the cost and time requirements for required sorting rates in the order of thousands per hour.

The PDP-11 controls acquisition of devices from bulk or tray storage and routes the devices to be tested under test heads, where they undergo series or parallel tests for several parameters. The computer stores the test results as required, classifies the device, and then routes the device to the proper container. The automation system performs all functions at testing rates of over 5000 devices per hour.

Automation was mandatory in this case. Operator control was not feasible. Small components and high production rates dictated operator aids or even operator elimination. The objective of automation here was not to displace labor but to allow production to occur.

*Maxicomputer Control.*[4] The Rochester Products Division of General Motors Corporation has 97 carburetor test stands controlled by a GE/PAC 4060 control digital computer system. Operators place carburetors on test stands, as shown in Fig. A-20, and the control computer then directs from 9 to 13 tests of carburetor operation from idle to full throttle. The adjustment of carburetor metering screws is automatically driven by the computer to allow compliance with requirements for automotive exhaust

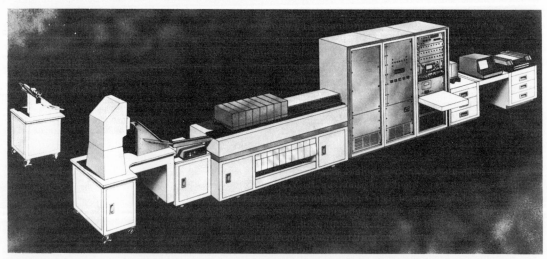

Fig. A-19. Minicomputer-controlled sorting system. *(Courtesy of Motorola Semiconductor Products Division, Phoenix, Arizona.)*

Fig. A-20. Inspector inserting carburetor in computer-controlled test stand. *(Courtesy of General Motors' Rochester Products Division and Honeywell Process Computer Operations—formerly General Electric Process Computer.)*

*Indirect Control.* The control of an electric furnace in the production of high-grade steel illustrates a unique benefit of computer control. Carbon control is especially difficult to attain because the needed carbon content must be determined just as the steel temperature hits a specified level. Using a computer, input temperature taken by a destructible thermocouple can be matched with the carbon content computed by subtracting (1) the carbon content (analyzed by the computer) from the smoke venting the process from (2) the carbon content in the steel which is analyzed prior to heating. This is a case of *indirect* measurement provided by computer control. Instrumentation to accomplish this control directly would be prohibitively expensive.

**Mechanization**[5] Thousands of examples could be cited. Pretzel forming, for example, requires intricate mechanical operations and is now a completely mechanized process. Packing materials in boxes and cartons—from candy to soap powder—is another example of complex mechanization. A particularly good example of assembly mechanization is provided at Motorola. Thousands of diodes per hour are assembled by manipulating the pin-head size parts which make up the device. The market price of a single diode is so small that it must be produced in huge quantities at an extremely low piece-part cost. The solution has been to employ in-line handling of devices and multiple stations within the lines. Each assembly step is then performed on hundreds of devices at one time. Labor associated with the assembly is limited to material handling.

**Water Resource Allocation** Examples of automation in nonmanufacturing include airplane control, rapid transit control, and automatic point-of-sale inventory analysis and control in retail stores. The Salt River Project[6] has some 138 miles of canals carrying irrigation water through metropolitan Phoenix from its central Arizona watershed area. A Hewlett-Packard 2116B control digital computer controls and monitors 206 canal gates in the system. Flows are regulated and alarm conditions monitored throughout the system, with information transmitted to and from the computer over leased telephone lines. The control room for this system is shown in Fig. A-22. Distances within the irrigation system create a situation which is extremely difficult to control manually. Other long-distance automation systems include the California Water Project which spans over 300 miles and the Alaskan Oil Pipeline Project. Moreover these systems require extremely rapid action in emergencies, which is only feasible with large-scale computer control.

emission. Each function of each test machine is monitored every quarter of a second, and 20,000 carburetors are handled each day of operation. Figure A-21 shows several test stations.

This case is representative of one where external regulations forced a move to automation. Setting of carburetors by hand could have been accomplished by an army of operators, of course, but the time and cost requirements would have been prohibitive. This is also an instance where high-speed production dictates a need for automation. As production rates of discrete units approach those of a continuous process, the need for automation and benefits from automation increases.

**Continuous-Process Automation** Prior to using the control computer, the process industries employed a large amount of "local" automation. Instrumentation costs were high. Accordingly, integration of these components by computer was a natural evolution. Moreover, elimination of labor is rarely the paramount justification in process automation. The major objectives have been reduced waste, improved tolerances, better control, and optimization of throughput.

Fig. A-21. Ninety-seven test stands controlled by digital computer. *(Courtesy of General Motors' Rochester Products Division and Honeywell Process Computer Operations—formerly General Electric Process Computer.)*

**Warehouse Automation**   With a computer keeping track of inventory items and their storage locations, it is possible to store items randomly rather than in fixed locations reserved for specific items. A 20 percent reduction in volume is typical for automatic warehousing when compared with conventional storage. Automatic systems also minimize errors in order picking, reduce thefts, lessen handling damage, and increase operation speed.

The Genesco shoe warehouse in Nashville, for example, allowed storage of up to 90,000 possible pairs of shoes with one unique combination of style, size, and width for each pair.[7] A fixed storage system is not feasible for this type of operation. Sara Lee operates a bakery warehouse with temperatures of $-10°F$. This precludes continual use of operators in the warehouse.[8] Automation is the *only* answer to these storage systems.

Fig. A-22. Control room for digital computer–controlled irrigation system. *(Courtesy of the Salt River Project, Phoenix, Arizona.)*

*Cost Comparison.* When comparing automatic stacking and picking systems with traditional fork-lift trucks and associated storage hardware, fixed costs for automatic warehousing are found to be much higher. The variable costs, however, tend to favor automatic systems, and it is there that the potential payback occurs.[9]

## ECONOMICS OF AUTOMATION

Complex automation equipment can be extremely expensive. If it is not to be used for a long period of time, the payoff period must also be extremely short. For this reason, any automation project should be studied carefully before it is implemented. In every case, management should strongly consider the alternative effects revealed by the analyses.

*Technological Implications.* Where technology is changing rapidly, automation investment should pay for itself in less than a year. Even large-scale projects in the hundreds of thousands of dollars should show a return within this time span under the technology constraint. It is doubtful that the payoff period for *any* automation project should ever be greater than 3 years, regardless of the technology involved.

*Sources of Savings.*[10] While labor savings draw the most attention, the payoff for automation often comes from other sources. For example,

1. A 2 million barrel-per-year cement plant saves $205,000 annually, primarily from reduced power and fuel use, savings in kiln-lining maintenance, and insurance of product uniformity.

2. For an electric power company a control digital computer saves millions of dollars annually in its 20,000 square mile service area by calculating costs of alternate generating sources and transmission routes and by filling load demands with the most economical power.

3. A single steel-rolling mill saves over 1 million dollars per year through reduction in rejects, scrap, power, and maintenance.

Each installation must be evaluated on its own merits, of course.

## IMPACT ON MANAGEMENT AND SOCIETY

Automation is directly responsible for the increased productivity that has made it easier for individuals to purchase luxury items as well as basic necessities. One of the early fears of automation was the fear of dehumanization by machines. To a large part, this fear has not become a reality. Automation has the power to take away a large amount of tedious work from the operator—allowing the human to do what the human can do best and the machine to do what the machine can best accomplish. There is little doubt, however, that automation can make a certain class of worker nonemployable. These are typically workers who are disadvantaged by education, training, or environment.

Management has several responsibilities in this regard. If automation is to be considered, management must

1. Understand the consequences of its decisions. This not only applies to potential worker displacement, it also means that management has to be able to understand the economic trade-offs between implementation and nonimplementation.

2. Be able to talk to the control engineers and be able to follow all facets of the automation decision.

3. Have a talking knowledge of mechanization, digital computers, automation equipment, and similar topics.

Comments on automation and management's responsibility can best be summed in the following statement:

Today, and in the future, the real power of America will be the power of the intellect and the power of the human being to triumph over his environment. The human being is our basic resource. Automation is merely a tool of the human race—and a good tool. Used wisely, it will continue to be of benefit to all of us. Explained carefully, it will be much accepted by employees. Planned properly, it will remove much of the opportunity for building fear into employees by misguided or opportunistic publicists. In short: 1. Use automation. 2. Explain automation. 3. Plan automation.[11]

*See also* COMPUTER SYSTEMS; CONTROL SYSTEMS, MANAGEMENT; DATA PROCESSING PRINCIPLES AND PRACTICES; FACILITIES AND SITE PLANNING AND LAYOUT; HUMAN FACTORS ENGINEERING; INFORMATION SYSTEMS, MANAGEMENT (MIS); LINE BALANCING; MATERIALS REQUIREMENTS PLANNING (MRP); OFFICE SPACE PLANNING AND DESIGN; PRODUCTION PROCESSES; SYSTEM CONCEPT, TOTAL; SYSTEM DYNAMICS; TECHNOLOGY, MANAGEMENT IMPLICATIONS.

## NOTES

[1]Information courtesy of the Kearney and Trecker Corporation, Milwaukee, Wisconsin.

[2]Example courtesy of the Motorola Semiconductor Products Division, Phoenix, Arizona.

[3]Example courtesy of the Motorola Semiconductor Products Division, Phoenix, Arizona.

[4]Example courtesy of Honeywell Process Computer Operations, Phoenix, Arizona, and Rochester Products Division of General Motors Corporation.

[5]Example courtesy of the Motorola Semiconductor Products Division, Phoenix, Arizona.

[6]Example courtesy of the Salt River Project, Phoenix, Arizona.

[7]"Warehousing Shoes Under Computer Control," *Automation*, vol. 12, July 1965.

[8]"Plant of 1970 Is Here in '64," *Factory*, February 1964.

[9]Roy W. Ferrari, "Automated High Rise Storage Systems," *Industrial Engineering*, vol. 8, no. 3, March 1976.

[10]David D. Bedworth, "Systems Concepts for Control Digital Computers," *Industrial Engineering*, vol. 5, no. 3, March 1973.

[11]Louis T. Rader, "Manpower Policy and Labor," *Automation*, vol. 13, pp. 103–125, January 1965.

## REFERENCES

Ampula, R. F.: "Keep the Bugs Out of Your Computerized Warehouse," *Automation*, vol. 22, no. 12, December 1975.

Bittel, L. R., M. G. Melden, and R. S. Rice, *Practical Automation*, McGraw-Hill Book Company, New York, 1957.

Boyer, C. H.: "Putting Small Computers to Work," *Industrial Engineering*, vol. 8, no. 10, October 1976.

Grabbe, E. M. (ed.): *Automation in Business and Industry*, John Wiley & Sons, Inc., New York, 1957.

Harrison, T. J. (ed.): *Handbook of Industrial Control Computers*, Interscience Publishers, a division of John Wiley & Sons, Inc., New York, 1972.

Hegland, D. E.: "Computerized Material Handling Comes of Age," *Automation*, vol. 22, no. 11, November 1975.

Lee, T. H., G. E. Adams, and W. M. Gaines: *Computer Process Control: Modeling and Optimization*, John Wiley & Sons, Inc., New York, 1968.

Leone, W. C.: *Production Automation and Numerical Control*, The Ronald Press Company, New York, 1967.

Luke, H. D.: *Automation for Productivity*, John Wiley & Sons, Inc., New York, 1972.

Reed, R. E.: "Guidelines for DNC," *Automation*, vol. 18, no. 5, May 1971.

"Robots: Off-the-Shelf-Automation," *Automation*, vol. 23, no. 5, May 1976.

Savas, E. S.: *Computer Control of Industrial Processes*, McGraw-Hill Book Company, New York, 1965.

Zollinger, H. A.: "Take Control of Material Handling," *Industrial Engineering*, vol. 8, no. 10, October 1976.

DAVID D. BEDWORTH, *Arizona State University*

## Autonomous working groups (See CO-DETERMINATION AND INDUSTRIAL DEMOCRACY.)

## Autoregressive-moving-average (ARMA) schemes (See FORECASTING BUSINESS CONDITIONS.)

## Averages, long-run (See STATISTICAL ANALYSIS FOR MANAGEMENT.)

**B**

**Backlog report**  (*See* MAINTENANCE MANAGE-
MENT.)

**Balance, economic**  (*See* PRODUCTION/OPER-
ATIONS MANAGEMENT.)

**Balance of trade**  (*See* EXCHANGE, FOREIGN,
MANAGEMENT OF; INTERNATIONAL TRADE.)

**Balance sheet**  (*See* ACCOUNTING, FINANCIAL;
ACCOUNTING FOR MANAGERIAL CONTROL; FINAN-
CIAL STATEMENT ANALYSIS.)

**Bank loans**  (*See* FINANCIAL MANAGEMENT.)

**Bank relationships**  (*See* FINANCIAL MAN-
AGEMENT, BANK RELATIONSHIPS.)

**Bankruptcy**  (*See* GOVERNMENT REGULATIONS,
BUSINESS LAW.

**Bargaining process, collective**  (*See* LA-
BOR-MANAGEMENT RELATIONS.)

**Basket orders, purchase**  (*See* PURCHASING
MANAGEMENT.)

**Batch process**  (*See* PRODUCTION PROCESSES.)

**Bayesian analysis**  (*See* STATISTICAL ANALY-
SIS FOR MANAGEMENT.)

**Behavior, individual and group**  (*See*
INTERPERSONAL RELATIONSHIPS.)

**Behavior, organizational**  (*See* MOTIVA-
TION IN ORGANIZATIONS.)

**Behavior in organizations**  (*See heading in*
*Table of Contents for complete listing.*)

## Behavioral authority  (*See* AUTHORITY, RE-SPONSIBILITY, AND ACCOUNTABILITY.)

## Behavioral models

*Behavioral models*, generally in the form of diagrams, are developed by behavioral scientists to explain their theories—to show, for example, possible patterns of communication.

One example is the management grid developed by Robert Blake and Jane S. Mouton, which is used in management seminars. The aim of the management grid is to have managers exhibit maximum concern for both people and production instead of emphasizing one or the other or compromising between the two.

Another is the Johari window (*see* Fig. B-1), named for its originators Joseph Luft and Harry Ingham. This model may be used by managers to develop greater self-awareness. A questionnaire enables them to diagnose their own attitudes. Then an attempt is made to enlarge area 1 at the expense of area 2. Several variations of this have been used in managerial development.

| 1<br>Known to one's<br>self and to<br>others | 2<br>Known to others<br>but not to one's self |
|---|---|
| 3<br>Known to one's<br>self alone | 4<br>Known neither to<br>one's self nor to<br>others |

Fig. B-1. Behavioral model for personality or managerial style: Johari window.

A more recent development has been a spate of written, audio, and filmed examples (models) of effective managerial behavior for handling a variety of employee problems such as absenteeism, tardiness, work habits, disciplinary action, delegation, and for handling customer grievances. One proprietary technique called *interaction modeling* (Development Dimensions) has been used with demonstrable success in supervisory training programs at AT&T, General Electric Company, and Agway, Inc. In effect, supervisors observe effective behavior in common situations and then are given an opportunity to imitate that behavior in role-playing sessions and, later on, in actual occurrences on the job. Provision is made for a high degree of personal involvement, feedback, and professional counseling. Other proprietary programs include *Telos*, offered by Kepner-Tregoe, and *Teleological Feedback*, by Teleometrics International.

*See also* INTERPERSONAL RELATIONSHIPS; MOTIVATION IN ORGANIZATIONS.

REFERENCES

Byham, William, and James Robinson: "Interaction Modeling: A new Concept in Supervisory Training," *Training and Development Journal*, February 1976.

"Grid Puts Executives on the Griddle," *Business Week*, October 18, 1969, pp. 168–170.

Reddin, William J.: *Managerial Effectiveness*, McGraw-Hill Book Company, New York, 1970.

STAFF/SMITH

## Benchmark  (*See* WORK SAMPLING.)

## Benchmark advertising studies  (*See* MARKETING RESEARCH.)

## Benefits, employee  (*See* COMPENSATION, EMPLOYEE BENEFIT PLANS.)

## Bid list, approved  (*See* PURCHASING MANAGEMENT.)

## Bid pricing  (*See* PRODUCT AND SERVICE PRICING.)

## Bidders, responsible  (*See* MARKETS, PUBLIC.)

## Bids  (*See* PURCHASING MANAGEMENT.)

## Bill of materials, manufacturing of (*See* MATERIALS MANAGEMENT; PRODUCTION PLANNING AND CONTROL.)

## Biomechanics  *See* HUMAN FACTORS ENGINEERING.)

## Blanket orders, purchase  (*See* PURCHASING MANAGEMENT.)

## Blue Cross and Blue Shield  (*See* COMPENSATION, EMPLOYEE BENEFIT PLANS.)

## Board, chairman of the  (*See* OFFICERS, CORPORATE.)

## Board, officer of  (*See* OFFICERS, CORPORATE.)

## Boards, advisory  (*See* COMPENSATION, SPECIAL PLANS.)

## Boards, supervisory  (*See* CODETERMINATION AND INDUSTRIAL DEMOCRACY.)

## Boards of directors

The *board of directors* is the highest level of management in the modern corporation. Over three-fourths of the state laws of the United States under which corporations are chartered require corporations to be managed by a board of directors. Although corporations are legal entities with attributes of their own, actual persons, such as directors, are responsible for their management.

Board members are elected by stockholders to represent them as a group. Legally they are not agents required to carry out the direct orders of stockholders. They are more akin to elected government officials, such as members of Congress, who represent their constituents but make decisions according to their own best judgment.

**Authority and Responsibilities of the Board**  It is the board's duty to manage the business in the best interests of the owners, whom they represent, but it also has the responsibility of recognizing the associated interests of other groups, such as employees, customers, and the public.

Directors have the necessary authority to run the corporation, subject to the restrictions of state and federal laws and limitations of the corporate charge and bylaws. These limitations, however, are very general, giving the board a wide scope of authority.

Charters typically specify broad and general corporate purposes, and except where stockholder approval is required, boards have the power to change the bylaws.

Directors are guided by procedures for governance and operations by corporate bylaws, which typically include statements concerning the rights of stockholders, the powers, qualifications, and responsibilities of the directors, and procedures for conducting corporation affairs. Directors are free to exercise their best judgment in running the company, but they must do so lawfully and prudently in the best interests of the owners.

**The Balance of Interests**  While the primary responsibility for owner (stockholder) interests is widely recognized, boards must also face the demands and pressures from other interested parties, such as employees, customers, and the public. Difficult decisions must be made where the various interests appear to be in conflict.

Two opposing views of these contending influences prevail: (1) that the sole responsibility is toward owners or (2) that the board should take a balanced approach to the issues posed by the various interest groups involved. The first view is prevalent where the principal owners are also the top management group and are few in number and where the directors are "insiders" whose jobs depend on pleasing the owners. The second view, the most widely held, does not regard responsibilities toward the other groups as necessarily incompatible with stockholder interests. This approach recognizes that acting in socially responsible ways and in awareness of the interests of the various claimant groups is feasible and desirable. In the main, this balanced view is generally consistent with actions in the best interests of the owners.

**Specific Tasks, Duties, and Responsibilities**  The board is responsible for six major activities: trusteeship, determination of objectives, selection of officers and executives, approval of plans and policies, decision making, and monitoring results.

*Trusteeship.*  A central responsibility, known as trusteeship, is to safeguard and husband the corporation's assets and resources and to use them in the best interests of the stockholders. The idea of trusteeship includes the balanced view noted above, where obligations to society and to other constituent groups are regarded as consistent with the primary obligations to stockholders.

*Objectives.*  Boards also determine the corporation's general objectives and a number of corporation-wide specific objectives. Boards identify and authenticate major goals, providing priorities and clarification thereof. They are concerned with the corporation's long-term stability and growth, with a consequent need to keep objectives matched to changing conditions inside the organization and arising from the environment.

*Selecting Officers and Executives.* The board elects the corporate officers and assigns their general responsibilities. This is the beginning of the delegation process. Some officers are primarily concerned with board matters; most are delegated operating responsibilities through the chief executive officer. Most boards allow the chief executive officer a wide scope for choosing those who serve under him or her, but may reserve a ratifying power over the selection of all key executives who may or may not be elected as officers.

*Plans and Policies.* Major plans and policies having corporation-wide significance are approved by the board. This has the effect of attesting to their importance and reinforcing the commitments of operating managers. Budgets are developed to assist in planning and controlling the company's activities.

*Deciding.* Major decisions result in the adoption of objectives, plans, and policies. In addition, major operating decisions are often made. Major decisions often represent critical turning points for the company, such as mergers, expansions, or commitments of investment capital. Resource allocation decisions are extremely vital. These include declaring dividends, investing profits, and acquiring or disposing of assets. Major organizational design problems are often decided by boards.

*Monitoring Results.* To fulfill their responsibilities for the stability, success, and welfare of the corporation, boards continuously exercise control through reviewing operating results, executive performance, market and economic conditions, and the extent to which objectives, plans, and policies are succeeding. The monitoring of production, financial, and other performance data is important, as is the surveillance of conditions in the external environment. Reviews of financial statements, the cash position, revenues and expenses, and budgetary control are needed. Financial and management audits are conducted.

**Board Operations** The chairman of the board is the key executive in board operations and is responsible for planning board meetings, agendas, and proposals. He or she has a leadership role and a strong voice in determining the matters that come before the board for action. The chairman may also be the chief executive officer, but if not, the president and/or the chief executive officer share a joint

work load with the chairman. Sometimes the position is an honorary one, or one where contacts with outside agencies or groups are important.

Running board meetings requires parlimentary and conference-discussion leading skills, as well as substantive knowledge of the problems discussed and the information being provided. As leader, the chairman must deal with a diversity of persons and interests, guide deliberations, handle arguments and dissent, and cope with conflict and divisiveness.

Such matters as the frequency and duration of meetings, the obtaining and handling of information and staff support work, and the use of committees are important for board operations. Boards generally meet quarterly, but in large firms they may meet monthly, and in small firms, annually.

**Directors** There is no standard ideal size for the board of directors. The needs of companies vary, and the board size may depend on the range of experience and talent required. Five to six members appears to be a minimum, while fifteen members approaches the upper limit of most boards. The board needs to be large enough to provide the managerial capabilities required but compact enough to function as a reasonably efficient committee.

*Time Requirements.* Most board members are part time, but some large companies utilize full-time directors. In addition to attending regular board meetings, directors may perform committee work, and must have additional time for studying documents and reports in preparation for board meetings. Directors must be able to devote enough time to their responsibilities to make an effective contribution.

*Qualifications.* Boards need a variety of capabilities, depending on the nature of the company and its operations. Experience, intelligence, proven capability for making judgments, and analytical skills are highly important for all directors. In addition, particular directors may be chosen for their expertise in certain areas of management. It is important for a board to be composed of a good balance of the capabilities needed. A record of success, maturity, community standing, and interests in the company or industry are also often taken into account in choosing directors. Other qualities of extreme importance include those of independence—the willingness and ability to speak out on issues of importance—of character, integrity, and ethical behavior.

*Insiders versus Outsiders.* A much-debated issue regarding directors is what the balance should be between inside and outside directors. An inside director is generally defined as one having a full-time employment commitment with the firm. A part-time director does not have a full-time appointment with the firm. Too much reliance on inside directors runs the risks of inbreeding and lack of independence. On the other hand, inside directors rate high on commitment and on knowledge of the company and its operations. Outside directors, on the other hand, can be relatively independent and bring into consideration fresh points of view and the influence of outside factors. They may, however, lack intimate knowledge of the firm's operations and may also be overcommitted by serving on other boards.

In recent years there has been substantial pressure in corporations to elect some board members as representatives of interest groups, such as consumers, employees, or the general public. While many are ready to acknowledge the wisdom and benefit of having at least some outside directors, the practice of requiring boards to have directors representing nonstockholder groups is not widely accepted. In a sense, an outside director, if truly independent, can be viewed as representative of the public interest.

*Compensation.* Board memberships generally have a high status in society. Directors may be paid by per diem fees or by annual retainers. Some companies also provide directors with fringe benefits, such as company-paid insurance programs and reimbursement for travel and other expenses.

*Legal Liabilities.* Those accepting directorship appointments thereby are subject to complex legal obligations and legal risks. Before accepting an appointment on a board of directors, the individual should consult a personal attorney for a review of obligations and possible risks.

*See also* AUDIT, MANAGEMENT; BOARDS OF DIRECTORS, LEGAL LIABILITY GUIDELINES; ETHICS, MANAGERIAL; MANAGEMENT, DEFINITIONS OF; MANAGEMENT THEORY, SCIENCE, AND APPROACHES; ORGANIZATION STRUCTURES AND CHARTING; OWNERSHIP, LEGAL FORMS OF; SHAREHOLDER RELATIONSHIPS.

### REFERENCES

Brown, Courtney: *Putting the Corporate Board to Work*, The Macmillan Company, New York, 1976.
*Corporate Directorship Practices: Compensation 1975*, National Industrial Conference Board, Inc., New York, 1975.
Juran, J. M., and Keith J. Louden: *The Corporate Director*, American Management Association, New York, 1966.
Koontz, Harold: *The Board of Directors and Effective Management*, McGraw-Hill Book Company, New York, 1967.
Little, Arthur D., Inc.: *The Corporate Director: New Roles, New Responsibilities*, Cahners Books, Boston, 1975.
Mace, Myles L.: *Directors: Myth and Reality*, Harvard Business School, Division of Research, Boston, 1971.
Vance, Stanley C.: *The Corporate Director: A Critical Evaluation*, Dow Jones-Irwin, Inc., Homewood, Ill., 1968.

DALTON E. MCFARLAND, *University of Alabama in Birmingham*

# Boards of directors, legal liability guidelines

In the United States the basic law that establishes the duties and liabilities of directors is the law of the state of incorporation. The federal securities laws also impose duties on corporate directors, especially those of the larger corporations. What follows is relevant to outside, or nonemployee, directors who are not direct participants in corporate wrongdoing.

Almost all state laws declare that the directors shall manage the business. Delaware has recently amended its statute to recognize the reality of management in most corporations. It states that the business shall be "managed by or under the direction of" the directors. Presently no state has a more specific law. The courts, in resolving disputes where the behavior of directors has been at issue, have developed three duties of directors. Under these common-law rules, directors have a duty (1) to act in loyalty and good faith, that is, to act in the best interests of the corporation and not for their own personal interests if the two interests clash; (2) to act diligently and with due care in conducting the affairs of the corporation, that is, to act without negligence; and (3) to act within designated authority and with the powers given the corporation, that is, not to approve taking the corporation into lines of business not authorized by the charter (articles of incorporation) nor to assume powers reserved to the shareholders either by statute or in the articles. Judges have tended to state the second duty in terms of acting with the diligence, care, and skill that a prudent person would give to his or her own affairs, although the courts in some states have related the duty to the conduct of a prudent person acting in a like position under similar circumstances.

Clearly the ordinary, upper middle class person whom most judges would identify as the prudent person would know a great deal more about his or her personal affairs than a director of General Motors (or even a corporation one thousandth that size) would know about corporate matters. With few exceptions, however, courts have tended to hold outside corporate directors to a rather low standard of care, seldom imposing liability regardless of the phrasing of the standard.

**Federal Law**   The greatest concern of directors should be for the duties imposed upon them by the federal securities laws, the Securities Act of 1933 and the Securities Exchange Act of 1934. These statutes, and especially SEC Rule 10b-5, have been the basis for what has been labeled an explosion of court actions, many of them including outside directors as defendants. The number of reported cases that have gone to trial and resulted in a judgment against one or more outside directors is extremely small, but these cases have established a level of duty substantially more onerous than that established by courts interpreting state statutes and the common law.

Generally, the approach of the federal securities laws is to require disclosure of all information about the corporation that might affect an investor's investment decisions. This applies not only to the prospectus and registration statement but also to all documents filed with the SEC. In addition, there are several overlapping provisions prohibiting misleading statements and omissions in general, all of which are given the general and disquieting label of *fraud*. Contrary to a common impression, the fraud portions of these laws are not limited just to securities listed on exchanges or being traded regularly over the counter; they have been applied to many ills that have only a tangential relationship to security trading, for example, the failure of a company to report bribes paid to officials of foreign countries.

In the 1960s and early 1970s there had been a clear trend in the decisions of the federal courts involving the federal securities laws to hold directors to a higher level of conduct than earlier. There was evidence that at least some state courts were following this trend. Rule 10b-5 of the Securities and Exchange Commission was becoming what some called a new federal corporation law under the expanding interpretations of the SEC and the courts. Several courts were declaring that mere negligence by a director or others could be the basis of liability under SEC Rule 10b-5. Decisions handed down by the U.S. Supreme Court in 1975 and 1976 not only required "scienter" or intent to deceive but limited plaintiffs under the rule to buyers and sellers of securities. This slowed expansion, if not entirely reversing the trend of recent decisions. Only a lack of due diligence or simple negligence, however, is sufficient for director liability for false or misleading prospectuses, registrations, and other SEC filings by the corporation, and for any false or misleading statements made in connection with the sale of securities. Currently, a number of critics of corporate practices are urging Congress to adopt new legislation that would impose specific new duties on directors as well as raise further the level of conduct expected of them.

**Guidelines for Director Conduct**   In 1973 and 1974 the Securities and Exchange Commission indicated it was preparing to issue guidelines for director conduct under the federal securities laws. This project was terminated in December 1974. The following guidelines attempt to state norms under both state and federal laws. The effort is to prescribe a prudent path that goes beyond minimum conduct as delineated in court decisions holding directors liable. Although there is no way a director can escape the possibility of being sued, following the guidelines should minimize the chances of suit and assure that the director would prevail if suit is brought. They are arranged under the headings of the common-law duties, although a number of them are based upon federal laws.[1]

*Loyalty to the Corporation.*   These include:

1. Do not join a board, or resign promptly if you are already a member, if you are or become an officer, director or influential shareholder in a corporation that competes in any material way with the corporation in question or if you, as an individual or partner, are engaged in a business that competes in any material way.

2. If, in any particular transaction, you have, or may appear to have, an interest that is in conflict with that of the corporation, advise the chief executive officer and the board about the nature of your conflicts and neither participate in the board's discussion nor vote on any matter that involves that interest.

3. Do not personally compete with the corporation in any transaction nor enter a competing line of business, nor permit a firm in which you have a controlling interest to do so.

4. Do not buy or sell securities of the corporation nor knowingly permit your spouse, children, parents or others (including foundations and trust funds) in whom you have a personal interest to do so when you have information that might affect the price or salability of the stock and that information has not been publicly disclosed.

5. Do not buy and resell within six months (or vice versa) any equity security of the corporation.

6. Do not discuss the plans and prospects of the corporation, nor material new developments concerning it, except with other directors and top officers and with as few others as required to con-

duct necessary or desirable corporate business on a confidential and "need to know" basis.

*Diligence and Care.* These include:

7. Attend board meetings regularly and participate actively in the discussion. Make a special effort to attend meetings where matters of extraordinary importance to the corporation and its investors are involved.

8. Insist upon the establishment of a system of providing information to directors appropriate to their needs. Study this information and not only vote on resolutions proposed by management but assume the initiative in seeking additional information and in taking action if management appears to be incompetent, dishonest, self-serving or to be unwittingly following a policy or making a decision that will result in probable loss to the corporation.

9. Insist upon the establishment of an audit committee and such other committees as seem appropriate.

10. Read every word of any prospectus prepared for an issue of securities and any proxy statement to be used to solicit votes of shareholders on any transaction involving the corporation. If you have any doubt as to its accuracy or completeness, make a reasonable investigation to settle that doubt. If there is a failure to disclose material information or the document is misleading to an investor, get it changed or have your disapproval recorded.

11. Prior to voting on a declaration of a dividend or other distribution by the corporation, obtain an opinion from its general counsel and auditors declaring such a distribution is permissible under the applicable corporation law and any restrictive covenants in its financing or other agreements.

*Act Within Authority.* These include:

12. Be familiar with and do not permit the corporation to exceed the powers granted to it and be familiar with any limitations placed on the authority of directors in its articles of incorporation.

**Outlook** A number of suits have been brought against directors after their corporations have been found guilty of antitrust practices. Conceivably, directors could be held liable for negligence in not insisting on the establishment of programs and practices that would avoid other statutory or even common-law wrongs, such as environmental pollution or the sale of unsafe products. Apparently, no such suit has been won thus far. Directors are potentially liable as fiduciaries under the Employment Retirement Income Security Act of 1974 (ERISA), and this act is likely to spawn a multitude of suits in the future. There are also specific duties imposed on directors under some of the state incorporation laws.

They include making directors liable for loans made by the corporation to its officers and directors, for purchase by the corporation of its own shares under certain prohibited circumstances, and for other prohibited acts.

Although such protection is under attack by critics, corporations can indemnify their directors against liability for at least negligence and can insure this obligation as well as provide insurance protecting the directors themselves under specific statutory authority or court decision in most states. Since most suits against directors end in settlement, director and officer (D&O) insurance is particularly valuable because it provides funds to undertake the legal defense and to provide much, if not all, of the settlement fund.

*See also* AUDIT, MANAGEMENT; AUDITING, FINANCIAL; BOARD OF DIRECTORS; ETHICS, MANAGERIAL; *Government regulations and laws affecting management and business; Ownership;* SHAREHOLDER RELATIONSHIPS.

### NOTES

[1] Permission has been granted for use here of portions of the author's article, "Sixteen Commandments for Corporate Directors," *Business Horizons*, vol. 20, February 1976, p. 45. Copyright 1976 by the Foundation for the School of Business, Indiana University.

### REFERENCES

Caplin, Mortimer: "Outside Directors and Their Responsibilities: A Program for the Exercise of Due Care," *The Journal of Corporate Law*, vol. 1, 1975, p. 57.

Feuer, Mortimer: (revised by Joseph F. Johnston, Jr.) *Personal Liabilities of Corporate Officers and Directors*, 2d ed., Prentice-Hall, Inc., Englewood Cliffs, N.J., 1974.

Knepper, William E.: *Liability of Corporate Officers and Directors*, 2d ed., The Allen Smith Co., Indianapolix, 1973.

*See* the following cases holding outside directors liable: *Escott v. BarChris Construction Corp.*, 283 F. Supp. 643 (S.D.N.Y. 1968); *Gould v. American Hawaiian S.S. Co.*, 351 F. Supp. 853 (D.Del. 1972); *Blakely v. Lisac*, 357 F. Supp. 255 (D.Ore. 1972). See also *Ernst & Ernst v. Hochfelder*, 425 U.S. 185 (1976); *Lanza v. Drexel & Co.*, 479 F.2d 1277 (2d Cir. 1973); and *SEC v. Texas Gulf Sulphur Co.*, 401 F.2d 833 (2d Cir. 1968).

JOHN D. DONNELL, *Indiana University; former Editor in Chief, American Business Law Journal*

# Bond ratings (*See* FINANCIAL MANAGEMENT, SHORT-TERM, INTERMEDIATE, AND LONG-TERM FINANCING.)

**Bonds, debenture** (*See* FINANCIAL MANAGE-MENT.)

**Bonds, industrial revenue** (*See* REAL ES-TATE MANAGEMENT, CORPORATE.)

**Bonds, mortgage** (*See* FINANCIAL MANAGE-MENT.)

**Bonus, executive incentive** (*See* COM-PENSATION, EXECUTIVE.)

**Bootstrap purchase** (*See* ACQUISITIONS AND MERGERS.)

**Borrowing, corporate** (*See* FINANCIAL MANAGEMENT, SHORT-TERM, INTERMEDIATE, AND LONG-TERM FINANCING.)

**Borrowing, secured** (*See* FINANCIAL MAN-AGEMENT, SHORT-TERM, INTERMEDIATE, AND LONG-TERM FINANCING.)

**Borrowing, unsecured** (*See* FINANCIAL MANAGEMENT, SHORT-TERM, INTERMEDIATE, AND LONG-TERM FINANCING.)

**Bottom-up planning** (*See* PLANNING, STRA-TEGIC MANAGERIAL.)

**Brainstorming** (*See* COST IMPROVEMENT; PRODUCT PLANNING AND DEVELOPMENT.)

**Brainstorming conferences** (*See* CON-FERENCE LEADERSHIP.)

**Brand loyalty** (*See* PRODUCT AND SERVICE PRICING.)

**Brand management** (*See* PRODUCT PLAN-NING AND DEVELOPMENT.)

**Brand managers** (*See* MARKETING, INDUS-TRIAL.)

## Brands and brand names

Brand names are to products or services what personal names are to humans. They distinguish or set apart each individual product offering. They are the means by which users or purchasers can identify a product or service of a specific origin, with a reputation or characteristic which is unique or distinct.

Brand names differ from generic names. A *generic* name denotes a category of product or service. A *brand name* identifies a particular version of a generic product or service offered by a particular seller. The analogy to humans is also useful here. The term *woman* applies to a certain category of humans. *Sue Smith* identifies a specific individual within the generic category of *woman*. The word *automobile* denotes a generic product, a vehicle with four wheels usually propelled by an internal combustion engine. The words *Ford Thunderbird* denote a specific version of an automobile offered by the Ford Motor Company.

**Value of Brand Names**  The reputation, or image, of brands has potentially great value to users and purchasers as well as to those who offer the product or service. Here, again, a fundamental distinction emerges between a brand name and a generic name. A *generic name* denotes a category of product or service which may be defined in tangible terms (dimensions, chemical makeup, performance). A *brand name* stands for something else: It represents the total image or reputation of the company or individual offering the product or service. Two different brands may, in fact, apply to products or services which, by tangible measurements, are identical. Yet users may view them differently for a host of reasons. They may bear different prices. They may be sold through different outlets. The advertising and promotion may differ in quantity or quality. Users' experience in obtaining service or adjustments may vary.

Thus, the brand or brand name synthesizes the entire complex of physical and psychological factors that affect attitudes toward the product or service which bears that name. Just as Sue Smith stands for a specific image or reputation among those who know her, so too Ford Thunderbird evokes an attitudinal response among individuals who have an awareness of that product.

**Families of Names** Brand names, like human names, may embrace an entire family, or they may apply to an entity within the family. In the case of Sue Smith, Sue is an individual in the Smith family. So too Thunderbird is an individual entity in the Ford family of automobiles.

*Collective Policy.* One aspect of brand policy is a decision to use the family name on all products offered by a seller, such as Del Monte for canned fruits and vegetables. Another decision is whether differing products of the same seller should bear brand names in addition to the family name or be given a combination of a family name and a generic name. For example, under the family name of General Electric, the General Electric Company offers General Electric washers, General Electric refrigerators, General Electric irons, and so on. On the other hand, a company like Sunbeam Electric offers its electric mixer under the name Sunbeam Mixmaster rather than Sunbeam mixer. Eastman offers Kodak Instamatic cameras.

*Modified Policy.* Sometimes the family name is dropped altogether. Certain products or services may be so different in nature or character that it would be unwise or inappropriate to apply the family name. (This policy can be compared with that of individuals who enter the public forum as actors and decide their family name is inappropriate for the personality they are selling the public and therefore adopt a different name for their public life.) Classic examples of this are found in the products of the Johnson & Johnson Company. The Johnson & Johnson family of products includes a wide line of health and beauty aids, such as Johnson & Johnson bandages and Johnson & Johnson baby powder. Under this family name are products which also bear their own brand names, such as Johnson & Johnson Bandaids.

*Concealment Policy.* The options may extend further. For example, Johnson & Johnson has also elected to offer a series of products which carry no Johnson & Johnson identity. These include feminine hygiene products sold under the brand name Modess by a subsidiary known as the Personal Products Company. They include pressure-sensitive tapes sold under the name Texcel by a subsidiary known as the Industrial Tape Company; and they include specialty products for women sold under the Ortho name by the Ortho Products Company. This brand strategy is based on the belief that it is more beneficial to conceal the family relationship of these products than to disclose it.

A reason for this decision may be the belief that these products are so different from the basic family line that they would not benefit from the family name and would have greater acceptance with a name more suited to the character of the product or service. The reasoning may be the other way, of course. It may be felt that some products might adversely affect the reputation or image of the basic family product members. If so, it would be better that users or purchasers did not know of the association between the two.

**Selecting Brand Names** Several options are open to a marketer in selecting a brand name.

*Personal Identification.* When marketing was less sophisticated (and perhaps less competitive) than today, many individuals bestowed their personal family names on their companies and on their products. Henry Ford and Walter Chrysler did so. B. F. Goodrich and Harvey Firestone gave their names to tire companies. But personal names are not always easy to pronounce. They seldom carry an image that relates to the product being sold. Sometimes they are less than appealing. The advertising agency which was asked to promote a line of jams and jellies called Smucker's felt its client's name was more of a handicap than an advantage. To turn this handicap into a benefit, it coined the slogan, "With a name like Smucker's, it has to be good," implying that the product was so superior it overcame the name.

*Generic Implications.* Some entrepreneurs saw that there was far more to be gained by preempting a name with broad generic implications rather than by trying to glorify their personal names. These marketing-oriented businesspeople opted for corporate cognomens, like The General Electric Company, Radio Corporation of America, International Harvester Corporation, and International Business Machines.

*Value by Association.* Sometimes companies were named after famous inventors, to lend an aura of scientific authority to the products or services. Bell Telephone System is a widely known example. Consolidated Edison in New York and Commonwealth Edison in Chicago are regional utilities capitalizing on the name of the famous inventor. When the Seiberling brothers decided to enter the rubber manufacturing business, they concluded that the name Seiberling stood for nothing in rubber, but Charles Goodyear was renowned for discovering vulcanization of rubber. So in his honor they named their new company The Goodyear Tire and Rubber Company. They judged correctly that while a name like Seiberling might eventually acquire a reputation for outstanding rubber products, their marketing task would be eased with a name like Goodyear that would readily be perceived as standing for quality and innovation in the types of products they were selling.

*Investigative Selection.* As products proliferate and brand names multiply, the hunt for names that will be appropriate, favorable, and distinctive becomes more difficult but more necessary. This hunt has spawned a corps of specialists, both as consultants and within the marketing concerns themselves. These specialists utilize psychologists, consumer researchers, computers, graphic designers, and allied professionals and techniques to solve the brand name equation.

**Abstract versus Relevant Names** A constant dilemma confronts those charged with finding the right name: If the name is descriptive enough to convey quickly the product characteristics, it may not be protectable under U.S. trademark law. Corporate executives frequently seek an abstract name, like Kodak, which is distinctive yet has wide recognition as denoting a brand of photographic products. Such a choice tends to overlook or minimize the fact that a major marketing investment was required to give Kodak the status it achieved.

Given the enormous levels of advertising required today to give meaning to abstract words, a marketer who can find a product name with meaning can get off the starting blocks faster in the race against competition. Two refrigerator makers made such an effort. One named his product after Lord Kelvin, who discovered the principles on which refrigeration is based. While Kelvinator may have had meaning to some learned prospective buyers, Frigidaire probably said it more quickly to those who wanted to get rid of their drippy ice boxes. Finding names like Frigidaire which are protectable is an arduous task, however.

So, despite examples of success in finding distinctive names which project correct images of products or services, many marketers have adopted a policy of creating names which, like Kodak, are meaningless in themselves. Du Pont has stated that it follows such a policy, although its adoption of the names Zerone and Zerex for antifreeze are apparent exceptions. Names for synthetic fibers such as Dacron, Qiana, and Kevlar—which indicate neither the corporate origin or generic nature of the product—are an outgrowth of this policy. In contrast, Eastman Kodak's name for its polyester fiber Kodel indicates an effort to associate the product with the parent Kodak company.

**Trademarks** Trademarks are synonymous with brand names. They are not to be confused with trade names. *Trade names* are sometimes called the "commercial name," for they represent the name of the company that makes the product. The name of the product is its brand or trademark. For example, General Motors Corporation makes Cadillacs.

There are exceptions—Johnson & Johnson and Polaroid are examples—where the trade name is the same or is the major part of the trademark. In general, however, the trade name identifies the company, and the trademark or brand is the name of the product. A trade name, unlike a brand name, cannot be registered. Handled separately, as in the Johnson & Johnson case where it is used on products as a trademark, it can qualify for registration for the company's products.

The visual treatment of a brand or trademark plays a vital role in making that name distinctive and meaningful. The use of design, including logotypes, lettering styles, type faces, package layout, and the like plays a key role in communicating the essence of the offering. (*See* Fig. B-2.) This is a marketing aspect which goes far beyond trademarks and trade names.

**Legal Requirements** Distinction in the name is one means of legal protection for the name—but only one! Legal pitfalls abound for the unwary marketer who seeks to reserve for exclusive use a brand name for a company's product. Some marketers have lost the use of names which they believed to be well-established properties of their company. A classic case was Du Pont's loss of the rights to cellophane as a brand name for a variety of transparent packaging film. The courts ruled that by calling the product simply cellophane, with no generic designation, Du Pont had made the word *cellophane* a generic term. For this reason, it lost the rights to the word *cellophane*, and other producers could describe their product as cellophane. Since this ruling, users of brand names must accompany the name with a generic description of the product or service. *Frigidaire* is not enough. It must be a Frigidaire refrigerator.

Under United States trademark law, registration of a name is no guarantee of a right to its use. Prior use is a vital consideration, even though registration has not been accomplished. It is possible that some obscure local user will turn up, claiming infringement of rights. Ownership must also be preserved

**Fig. B-2. Examples of well-known trademarks:** (A) CBS; (B) White Rock Psyche; (C) McDonald's arch symbol; (D) Seagram's 7 Crown; (E) Green Giant; (F) Safeway; (G) Morton International umbrella girl; (H) Maxwell House Div. of General Foods, cup and drop symbol; (I) Hallmark crown symbol; (J) Checkerboard Square of Ralston Purina Co.; (K) Bell symbol of American Telephone and Telegraph; (L) Lawry's; (M) Cotton bud symbol of Cotton Incorporated; (N) Gerber Baby; (O) Singer Company; (P) Quaker Oats; (Q) Mister Donut; (R) Circle "W" of Westinghouse Electric Corp.; (S) Frigidaire crown symbol; (T) Woolmark of The Wool Bureau Inc. *(Source: U.S. Trademark Association.)*

by regular use of the mark. In short, registration alone should not be relied on to protect a trademark. Not only is constant use important, but so is constant vigilance in challenging unauthorized use. Companies like Coca-Cola and Xerox police this territory intensively.

**Private Brands**  Throughout this entry, the term offered has been used to describe the ownership of the brand or brand name. This is because the ownership of the name may be vested in a variety of parties in the chain, from the original producers of

the product or service to the final purchaser. It may be a manufacturer's brand or wholesaler's brand or a distributor's brand. The brand may be owned by one party and rented, leased, or franchised to another party. A widespread example of this is found in the franchising of retail or service establishments, such as fast food restaurants, or gasoline service stations.

The essential fact to keep in mind is that the owner of the brand is the party to whom the purchaser looks for satisfaction. Today, many so-called "private brands" exist. Generally this means they are not brands owned by the manufacturer of the product but instead are owned by some reseller—either at the wholesale or at the retail level. This says nothing about the quality, the value, or the price of the product. Many examples may be found of private brands, retailers' brands, distributors' brands, custom brands (or whatever they may be called) which sell for higher prices than manufacturers' brands. Exclusive retail shops, for example, frequently put their own labels on merchandise manufactured by others and obtain premium prices for such goods. The reason is clear. The consumer has great confidence in the establishment whose name is on the merchandise and feels the fashion or the quality will be superior. Therefore, the consumer does not insist on knowing the name of the manufacturer.

On the other hand, some consumers patronize establishments in which they have little confidence and are reluctant to purchase goods which do carry only the retailer's label and not the manufacturer's brand. They would like to resolve their dilemma by knowing the name of the manufacturer, while still paying the low prices of the retailer, Having one's cake and eating it too is a common desire, and it exists in the world of brands.

To the extent that manufacturers of brands with high consumer acceptance also supply comparable products to private brands, and such merchandise is represented to consumers as being identical to the brand product, sales of the higher-priced brand product will suffer. A Gresham's law of brand policy might be stated as follows:

To the extent that consumers perceive a lower-priced private brand to be from the same source and/or of the same quality as a higher-priced manufacturer's brand, the private brand will drive out the manufacturer's brand.

**Outlook for Name Marketing**   In the age of consumerism, there appears to be constant pressure to wipe out purchasing by brand and to foster purchasing of generically described merchandise. Yet closer examination suggests that brand buying is far from extinct. What is really occurring is that as product categories mature, more and more generic purchasing occurs. Products become commodities rather than specialties, and the progression from manufacturer's brands to private brands to no brands may occur. But the market is constantly entered by new and distinctive products, by innovations in technology, fashion, or function. So new manufacturer's brands win popularity and achieve user preference.

It is not atypical for the same individuals who purchase some items on a near-generic basis to pay significant premium prices for manufacturer's brands in other categories of products. The lesson for marketers is that purchasers continue to seek and pay for distinction and quality in products that are important in their ever-changing scale of values. Identifying those wants, fulfilling them, and labeling products with brand names that enable consumers to differentiate their product selections thus continues to be an important factor in marketing success.

*See also* ADVERTISING CONCEPTS; CONSUMER BEHAVIOR, MANAGERIAL RELEVANCE OF; DESIGN, INDUSTRIAL; MARKETING RESEARCH; PATENTS AND VALUABLE INTANGIBLE RIGHTS; PRODUCT PLANNING AND DEVELOPMENT; PRODUCT AND SERVICE PRICING.

### REFERENCES

Barach, Arnold B: *Famous American Trademarks*, Public Affairs Press, Washington 1971.
Carter, David E.: *Book of American Trademarks*, Century Communications, Ashland, Ky., 1972.
Cook, Victor, and Thomas Shutte: *Brand Policy Determination*, Allyn and Bacon, Inc., Boston, 1967.
Crowley, Ellen T.: *Trade Names Dictionary*, Gale Research Company, Detroit, 1976.
Kamekura, Yusaku: *Trademarks and Symbols of the World*, Reinhold Book Corporation, New York, 1967.
Marquette, Arthur F.: *Brands, Trademarks and Good Will*, McGraw-Hill Book Company, New York, 1967.
Offner, Eric: *International Trademark Protection*, Fieldston Press, New York, 1965.
Rosen, Ben: *The Corporate Search for Visual Identity*, Van Nostrand Reinhold Company, New York, 1970.
*Trademark Management*, U.S. Trademark Association, New York, 1968.
*Trademarks in the Market Place*, U.S. Trademark Association, New York, 1964.
Uhr, Ernest, and William Wallace: *Brands: A Selected Bibliography*, American Marketing Association, Chicago, 1972.
Wildbur, Peter: *Trademarks: A Handbook of International Designs*, Reinhold Book Corporation, New York, 1966.

EDWIN H. SONNECKEN, *The Goodyear Tire and Rubber Company*

**Break-even analysis**   (*See* ACCOUNTING FOR MANAGERIAL CONTROL; FINANCIAL MANAGEMENT.)

**Break-even charting**   (*See* MARGINAL INCOME ANALYSIS.)

**Brokers** (*See* MARKETING, CHANNELS OF DISTRI-BUTION.)

**Budget, advertising** (*See* ADVERTISING, IN-DUSTRIAL.)

**Budgetary process** (*See* FINANCIAL MANAGE-MENT.)

**Budgeting** (*See* FINANCIAL MANAGEMENT.)

## Budgeting, capital

Expenditures for property, plant, and equipment, known as capital expenditures, are major decisions for most companies. The money involved is significant, the management time involved is significant, the investment is permanent and not easily reversible, and the company's future profitability is at stake. Therefore, the process of evaluating capital expenditures, called capital budgeting, is extremely important.

**Capital Budgeting** *Capital budgeting* is a loosely used term to describe the process of allocating cash expenditures to investments which have a life longer than the operating period—normally 1 year. Traditionally, capital investments have been thought of as those involving *capitalized assets,* or property, plant, and equipment. Actually, property, plant, and equipment comprise only 30 to 40 percent of the total balance sheet assets of the typical manufacturing company. The percentage is greater for process industries and less for service-oriented industries. A certain amount of permanent investment in cash, receivables, and inventory is just as necessary to support an increase in sales, for example, as is the investment in property, plant, and equipment. If one commits $100,000 to buy a new machine to produce "tingler," a new product just approved by the marketing department, the additional working capital requirements to support the new sales are just as much a part of the company's investment portfolio as is the new equipment.

*Methods Used to Make Investment Decisions.* A number of methods are used in business today to allocate a company's limited resources to the most profitable investments. The three most widely used methods are payback, accounting return, and present value.

### PAYBACK

Payback is the most widely used measure in business for making investment decisions. Payback is computed as follows:

$$\frac{\text{Cash outlay}}{\text{Net annual cash inflow}} = x \text{ years}$$

For example, a company has an opportunity to invest $10,000 in a new machine which will result in annual cash savings of $2000. Payback is

$$\frac{\$10,000}{2000} = 5 \text{ years}$$

The same company has an opportunity to invest $10,000 in a piece of equipment which will return $2500 per year. If the company has only $10,000 to invest, presumably, using the payback criteria, it will take the opportunity to invest $10,000/2500 = 4 year payback in preference to the 5-year payback.

**Advantages** Payback, given a cash outlay and cash inflow, is easy to compute and easily understood. The worker on the shop floor understands that if one invests $5 and gets back $1 per year, the investment will be returned in 5 years. It is a measure which is especially suited to the early stages of an investment decision when the figures will necessarily be rough. For a project with a long life, the reciprocal of the payback gives a reasonable estimate of return on investment.

**Disadvantages** Payback does not take into consideration the following:

1. Life of the project. For how many years will the cash flow be received? If $10,000 is invested and $2500 received each year for 4 years and if the machine only lasts 4 years, then the investment is returned but nothing more. Payback gives return *of* investment, not return *on* investment.

2. Uneven cash flow. Many cash outlays are made in anticipation of future net cash inflows which vary from year to year. For example, there may be heavy start-up costs, and positive cash flow may not occur until several years in the future. Another project may generate high positive cash flow for 2 or 3 years and then decrease rapidly.

To illustrate these problems, consider the question of which of the following projects is the best investment.

| Year / Cash flow | 0 | 1 | 2 | 3 | 4 | 5 |
|---|---|---|---|---|---|---|
| A | −$10,000 investment | +1000 | +1000 | +1000 | +7000 | +4000 |
| B | −$10,000 investment | +3000 | +3000 | +3000 | +1000 | +4000 |

Each of these projects involves the outlay of $10,000 today in return for $14,000 over 5 years. Each project has a payback of 4 years. Common sense indicates that project B is the better investment because more dollars are received earlier. If project

The return on project A is $2000/$10,000 = 20 percent. The return on project B is $2500/$10,000 = 25 percent.

Using the accounting return as a measure, if the company had only $10,000 to invest, it would take project B.

**Advantages**   The major advantage of the accounting return is that it is consistent with the way in which many managers have their performance measured. If managers are held responsible for and their bonus is based on getting a 15 percent ROI defined as income/investment, they will be inclined to take only investments which will deliver at least this return.

**Disadvantages**   The accounting return is similar to payback in that it does not consider the life of a project or the time flow of money. For example:

| Year / Cash flow | 0 | 1 | 2 | 3 | 4 | 5 | 6 to 10 |
|---|---|---|---|---|---|---|---|
| A | −$10,000 | +$2500 | +$2500 | +$2500 | +$2500 | +$2500 | 0 |
| B | −$10,000 | +$2000 | +$2000 | +$3000 | +$3000 | +$2500 | +$2500 |

A continued to return cash flows of $4000 for years 6 to 10 and project B ends at year 5, one would not have to make too many calculations to know that project A would be preferable to project B.

## ACCOUNTING OF UNADJUSTED RETURN

Many companies measure the performance of operating units by accounting return (unadjusted), better known as examining the *return on investment* (ROI). This is calculated as follows:

$$ROI = \frac{income}{investment}$$

There are a number of variations to this formula. Some companies use operating income (income before interest, taxes, and corporate overhead). Others use net income. Some use gross investment; others use net investment (after accumulated depreciation). Some use average investment.

ROI, however calculated, is also used in making investment decisions. For example, suppose a company has two investment alternatives,

1. $10,000 investment with $2000 income
2. $10,000 investment with $2500 income

The average return for both projects A and B is $2500/$10,000 = 25 percent. Project A has a life of 5 years, and project B has a life of 10 years. Again, common sense indicates that one would rather invest in project B. Yet, the accounting return, literally applied, would indicate no difference between the two projects because each has an average return on investment of 25 percent.

## PRESENT VALUE

Analysis of capital expenditures, using the concept of present value, is becoming widely used. It is a rather new approach, significant application in the United States being developed only in the late 1950s. Present value is the reciprocal of compound interest. The *present value* of a dollar to be received at a future date is the amount which, if invested today at a specified rate, would grow to a dollar at the future date. Present value is used when there is an opportunity to invest x dollars today in return for y dollars in the future.

In applying the present-value concept to capital investment decisions, four items are involved. They are

1. Investment—cash outlay
2. Savings—cash inflow
3. Life—economic life of the project

4. Rate of return—rate desired or computed rate on a specific project

A discussion of each item follows:

**Investment**  Investment represents the incremental cash outlay required to install a machine, build a plant, or whatever the capital investment involves. For example, the cash outlay for a new machine to reduce labor costs would involve the purchase price of the equipment, the freight in, and the cost of installation and start-up.

**Savings**  Savings represents the incremental cash inflow to be realized by making the investment. This would be the additional cash flow associated with a new product. For a new machine, the savings would be the net labor and other savings to be realized if the machine is installed. The savings are computed for each year of the estimated useful life of the investment.

**Life**  The life to be used in computing the return on investment is the useful or economic life of the project. This would be the shortest physical life, technological life, or market life. For example, if a special-purpose machine is purchased, its physical life may be estimated at 20 years and its technological life at 12 years, but if the product produced on the machine is estimated to have a life of only 10 years, then the useful life is market life—10 years.

**Rate of Return**  A company must determine what is an acceptable rate of return on a specific project, a class of projects, or an overall rate. In computing rates of return, present-value tables are used. (*See* Tables B-1, B-2, B-3, and B-4.) Today, with many computer programs easily available, the computer is often used to perform the calculations.

EXAMPLE: Assume the following situation:

Invest $10,000 in a laborsaving machine.
Labor savings = $2500 per year.
Useful life = 10 years.
Company desires 10 percent return on investment.
Machine will be depreciated over 10 years on a straight-line basis.
Company has 50 percent tax rate.
Machine will have no salvage value.

*Annual Cash-Flow Computations.*  Compute the annual cash flow as follows: (In this example, the savings are the same each year.)

| | |
|---|---|
| Cash in from labor savings | $2500 |
| Cash out for taxes | 750* |
| Annual net cash inflow | $1750 |

*Income subject to tax = $2500 − $1000 depreciation = $1500 at 50 percent = $750.

*Rate-of-Return Calculations.*  The investment outlay is $10,000. The annual cash savings is $1750. A 10 percent return is desired. Look at Table B-4. Under the 10 percent column, read down to 10 years. The factor is 6.44. Multiply 6.44 by the annual savings of $1750. The result is $11,270. This means that the present value of the future cash inflows of $1750 per year is worth $11,270 today if a 10 percent return on investment is desired. Since the investment is only $10,000 and the present value of future inflow is $11,270, the investment would be made.

If the actual return is desired, divide the investment by the annual savings, $10,000/$1750 = 5.71. Again, look at Table B-4 and read across from year 10. The factor 5.71 is between 12 and 14 percent or about a 13 percent return on investment.

The future cash inflow discounted at 13 percent will be equal to the $10,000 investment today. Finding the rate of return, rather than discounting at a predetermined rate, is called the discounted cash-flow (DCF) method or the internal rate-of-return method.

Based on the example above, one can see that the mechanics of computing the rate of return on a project are relatively easy, given the information for the four items of investment, savings, life, and desired return.

*Judgment.*  The difficult part in the decision-making process is the judgment involved in estimating the savings and the useful life and determining the rate of return desired. It is usually easier to get a fairly accurate figure for the investment—especially for equipment purchased when there is a firm price. Estimating savings for a cost-reduction project is easier than estimating savings involved in producing a new product.

*Complexities.*  Variable annual savings, the cash savings generated from a capital project, are seldom the same for each year of the life of the project. The savings may be different because of the use of accelerated depreciation, varying production levels, changes in tax rates, and other related items. The discounted cash-flow concept can be used with varying annual savings in two ways, as illustrated in the following example: A company has the opportunity to invest $1000 in one of four alternative projects. Each project has an estimated life of 6 years and a total return of $1800. The flow of the savings is as shown at the top of page 102.

**Internal Rate of Return**  One approach is to calculate the rate of return on each project. The *internal rate of return* is that rate which is being

| Year Project | 1 | 2 | 3 | 4 | 5 | 6 | Total |
|---|---|---|---|---|---|---|---|
| A—$1000 | +300 | +300 | +300 | +300 | +300 | +300 | $1800 |
| B—$1000 | +400 | +400 | +400 | +200 | +200 | +200 | $1800 |
| C—$1000 | +200 | +200 | +200 | +400 | +400 | +400 | $1800 |
| D—$1000 | +400 | +400 | +400 | +0 | +0 | +600 | $1800 |

earned on the unamortized balance of the investment, such as the rate on a home mortgage. Using Table B-4, the calculation is made using a trial-and-error approach. What rate will bring the future cash flow back to $100 today? The rates are

Project A: 25 + percent
Project B: 30 + percent
Project C: 16 percent
Project D: 25 percent

Thus, project B gives the highest rate of return because more dollars are received in the early years.

**Net Present Value** The *net present value* of an investment is the difference between future cash inflows discounted at a specified rate and the amount of the original investment. If a desired rate of return is known, the present value of the future flow can be determined. Assume the company wants a 20 percent return on investment. The present-value factors for 20 percent for each year are given in Table B-2. Applying these factors to the flows for the four projects, a present value for each project is as follows:

| Project | Investment | Present Value @ 20% | Net Present Value |
|---|---|---|---|
| A | $1000 | $1092 | $92 |
| B | 1000 | $1188 | $188 |
| C | 1000 | $996 | −$4 |
| D | 1000 | $1142 | $142 |

Using the net-present-value (NPV) approach, we see that project B has the highest net present value. Projects A, B, and D all have positive net present values, which means that these projects all return over 20 percent. Project B has the highest NPV, which makes it the most attractive alternative. Project C, with a negative NPV, returns slightly less than 20 percent.

How would you rank projects if the original outlay is different? The one with the highest invest-

ment is likely to have the highest absolute dollar NPV but may be a smaller return. Projects of this nature can be ranked by the use of a profitability index.

**Profitability Index** The profitability index is applied as follows:

| Project | Investment | Present Value @ 20% | NPV @ 20% | Profitability Index |
|---|---|---|---|---|
| A | $10,000 | $11,200 | $1200 | $\dfrac{11,200}{10,000} = 1.12$ |
| B | $20,000 | $22,000 | $2000 | $\dfrac{22,000}{20,000} = 1.10$ |
| C | $80,000 | $84,000 | $4000 | $\dfrac{84,000}{80,000} = 1.05$ |

Project A has the lowest dollar NPV. It also has the lowest investment outlay. The index shows, however, that it has the highest return; i.e., the dollars received discounted at 20 percent are higher relative to the investment than either project B or C.

**Uneven Lives** In making a decision to replace an existing piece of equipment with a new one, the differential cash flows must be computed to arrive at the cash savings. If the existing equipment will last as long as the economic life of the proposed new piece of equipment, the cash flows are computed each year over the economic life. If, however, the existing equipment would have to be replaced before the end of the economic life of the new equipment, then there would be no savings for the period after the existing equipment is replaced.

One way to handle this problem is to estimate a terminal value for the new equipment at the end of the comparable period of the two pieces of equipment. The least amount of the terminal value would be the tax savings on the write-off of the unallocated cost of the new equipment.

An example follows:

| Year | 1 | 2 | 3 | 4 | 5 | 6 | 7 | 8 |
|---|---|---|---|---|---|---|---|---|
| Existing cash cost | $3000 | 3000 | 4000 | 4000 | 5000 | Replace | | |
| New cash cost | $1500 | 1500 | 1500 | 2000 | 2000 | 2000 | 2000 | 2000 |
| Savings | $1500 | 1500 | 2500 | 2000 | 3000 + terminal value | | | |

If the cost of the new piece of equipment is $8000 and it is depreciated over 8 years on a straight-line basis, there would be $3000 unallocated cost at the end of 5 years. The tax write-off terminal value, at a 50 percent tax rate, would be $1500 at the end of 5 years. Thus, savings to be compared with the $8000 investment would be the operating savings for 5 years plus the terminal value of the new equipment at the end of the fifth year.

**MAPI**   The Machinery and Allied Products Institute (MAPI) published a MAPI study and manual *Business Investment Management* in 1967. This book and accompanying charts have been widely used in business, especially for equipment-replacement problems. The approach used by MAPI approximates DCF return, yet it is based on short-cut procedures. The MAPI methodology handles the problem of uneven lives which is more common in equipment-replacement situations than in most other capital budgeting problems.

## POSTAUDIT

In practice, more emphasis has been put on the techniques of financial analysis than on an audit of a project after completion to see if it is in fact giving the estimated return. A good postaudit procedure should aid in refining the methodology used in appraising capital expenditures and help in isolating further investment opportunities.

There are a number of more specific reasons for an organized postaudit effort. Several reasons mentioned in Research Report 43, *Financial Analysis to Guide Capital Expenditures Decisions*, published by the National Association of Accountants, are:

1. To develop information about the pattern of error that is associated with different project organization or organizational units which submit investment proposals.

2. To learn lessons from project exposure which can be used in increasing estimating proficiency and to improve estimating procedures.

3. To measure the ability of project engineers, planning analysts, or others who are directly concerned with project organization and evaluation.

4. To provide an overall framework of control so that project origination, approval, and implementation will be a disciplined management process; and to advise both manager and specialists in advance that their project work will be subject to review.

Without a disciplined postaudit procedure, there is a tendency for project proposals to show a satis-factory return in order to justify the project when, in fact, the assumptions used may be faulty.

## LEASE/PURCHASE ANALYSIS

Leasing on a long-term noncancelable basis is a means of financing an asset, e.g., building or equipment. A commitment to make lease payments on a long-term noncancelable lease is similar to a commitment to make payments on a term loan.

Most sophisticated lenders today look at a company's lease commitments as well as its other debt obligations in appraising the company's ability to carry additional debt.

After a company has made an investment decision to obtain an asset, how does it decide whether it is cheaper to borrow and buy or to lease the asset? There are two basic approaches:

1. Determine the effective rate of interest paid for lease financing and compare this rate with the borrowing rate.

2. Determine the present-value cash outlay for leasing compared with the present-value outlay for purchasing.

In approaching a lease/purchase analysis, certain assumptions are made:

1. The lease commitment is substantially equivalent to a debt obligation.

2. Depreciation tax savings associated with the purchase alternative and tax savings associated with the lease payments are similar in their certainty. The certainty of tax savings depends upon the certainty that the company will pay taxes in the future. If it is highly probable that the company will pay income taxes in the future, the appropriate rate to use to discount both depreciation tax savings (under purchase) and after-tax lease payments (under leasing) is the company's after-tax interest cost of a term loan.

**Effective Rate of Interest**   In order to find the effective rate of interest paid for leasing, it is first necessary to compute the after-tax present-value cost of the purchase alternative. The following example will be used:

| | |
|---|---|
| Cost of equipment today | $100,000 |
| Estimated life | 15 years |
| Before-tax cost of borrowing | 8% |
| Tax rate | 50% |
| Depreciable life | 20 years |
| Method of depreciation | Straight line |
| Lease payments for 15 years | $12,550 annually |
| Salvage value of equipment at end of 15 years (conservative) | -0- |

**TABLE B-1  Present Value of $1 Received at End of Year Indicated**

$P. V. = 1 \div (1 + i)^n$

| End of year | 2% | 4% | 6% | 8% | 10% | 12% | 14% | 16% | 18% | 20% | 25% | 30% |
|---|---|---|---|---|---|---|---|---|---|---|---|---|
| 1 | .98 | .96 | .94 | .93 | .91 | .89 | .88 | .86 | .85 | .83 | .80 | .77 |
| 2 | .96 | .92 | .89 | .86 | .83 | .80 | .77 | .75 | .71 | .70 | .64 | .59 |
| 3 | .94 | .89 | .84 | .79 | .75 | .71 | .67 | .64 | .61 | .58 | .51 | .46 |
| 4 | .93 | .86 | .79 | .73 | .68 | .63 | .59 | .55 | .52 | .48 | .41 | .35 |
| 5 | .90 | .82 | .75 | .68 | .62 | .57 | .52 | .47 | .44 | .40 | .33 | .27 |
| 6 | .89 | .79 | .71 | .63 | .56 | .51 | .46 | .41 | .37 | .34 | .26 | .20 |
| 7 | .87 | .76 | .66 | .59 | .51 | .45 | .40 | .36 | .31 | .28 | .21 | .16 |
| 8 | .85 | .73 | .63 | .54 | .47 | .41 | .35 | .30 | .27 | .23 | .17 | .12 |
| 9 | .84 | .70 | .59 | .50 | .42 | .36 | .31 | .26 | .22 | .19 | .13 | .10 |
| 10 | .82 | .68 | .56 | .46 | .39 | .32 | .27 | .23 | .19 | .16 | .11 | .07 |
| 11 | .81 | .65 | .52 | .43 | .35 | .29 | .23 | .20 | .16 | .14 | .09 | .06 |
| 12 | .79 | .63 | .50 | .40 | .32 | .26 | .21 | .17 | .14 | .11 | .07 | .04 |
| 13 | .77 | .60 | .47 | .37 | .29 | .23 | .18 | .14 | .12 | .09 | .05 | .03 |
| 14 | .76 | .58 | .44 | .34 | .26 | .20 | .16 | .13 | .10 | .08 | .04 | .03 |
| 15 | .74 | .55 | .42 | .31 | .24 | .18 | .14 | .11 | .08 | .07 | .04 | .02 |
| 20 | .67 | .45 | .31 | .22 | .15 | .10 | .07 | .05 | .04 | .03 | .01 | .01 |
| 25 | .61 | .37 | .23 | .15 | .09 | .06 | .04 | .03 | .02 | .01 | * | * |
| 30 | .55 | .31 | .17 | .10 | .06 | .03 | .02 | .01 | .01 | * | * | * |
| 35 | .50 | .25 | .13 | .07 | .04 | .02 | .01 | .01 | * | * | * | * |
| 40 | .45 | .21 | .10 | .05 | .02 | .01 | * | * | * | * | * | * |

**TABLE B-2  Present Value of $1 Received at Middle of Year Indicated**

$P. V. = 1 \div (1+i)^{n-1/2}$

| Middle of year | 2% | 4% | 6% | 8% | 10% | 12% | 14% | 16% | 18% | 20% | 25% | 30% |
|---|---|---|---|---|---|---|---|---|---|---|---|---|
| 1 | .99 | .98 | .97 | .96 | .95 | .95 | .94 | .93 | .92 | .91 | .89 | .88 |
| 2 | .97 | .94 | .92 | .89 | .87 | .84 | .82 | .80 | .78 | .76 | .72 | .67 |
| 3 | .95 | .91 | .86 | .83 | .79 | .75 | .72 | .69 | .66 | .63 | .57 | .52 |
| 4 | .93 | .87 | .82 | .76 | .72 | .67 | .63 | .60 | .56 | .53 | .46 | .40 |
| 5 | .92 | .84 | .77 | .71 | .65 | .60 | .55 | .51 | .48 | .44 | .37 | .31 |
| 6 | .90 | .81 | .72 | .65 | .59 | .54 | .49 | .44 | .40 | .37 | .29 | .23 |
| 7 | .88 | .77 | .69 | .61 | .54 | .48 | .43 | .38 | .34 | .31 | .23 | .18 |
| 8 | .86 | .75 | .64 | .56 | .49 | .43 | .37 | .33 | .29 | .25 | .19 | .14 |
| 9 | .84 | .71 | .61 | .52 | .44 | .38 | .33 | .28 | .24 | .21 | .15 | .11 |
| 10 | .83 | .69 | .58 | .48 | .40 | .34 | .29 | .25 | .21 | .18 | .12 | .08 |
| 11 | .81 | .66 | .54 | .45 | .37 | .31 | .25 | .21 | .18 | .15 | .10 | .07 |
| 12 | .80 | .64 | .51 | .41 | .33 | .27 | .22 | .18 | .15 | .12 | .07 | .05 |
| 13 | .78 | .61 | .48 | .38 | .30 | .24 | .20 | .15 | .12 | .10 | .06 | .04 |
| 14 | .76 | .59 | .46 | .36 | .28 | .22 | .17 | .14 | .11 | .09 | .05 | .03 |
| 15 | .75 | .57 | .43 | .33 | .25 | .19 | .15 | .11 | .09 | .07 | .04 | .02 |
| 20 | .68 | .47 | .32 | .22 | .16 | .11 | .08 | .05 | .04 | .03 | .01 | * |
| 25 | .61 | .38 | .24 | .15 | .10 | .06 | .04 | .03 | .02 | .02 | * | * |
| 30 | .56 | .31 | .18 | .10 | .06 | .04 | .02 | .01 | .01 | .01 | * | * |
| 35 | .50 | .26 | .13 | .07 | .04 | .02 | .01 | .01 | * | * | * | * |
| 40 | .46 | .21 | .10 | .05 | .02 | .01 | * | * | * | * | * | * |

**TABLE B-3  Present Value of $1 Received at End of Each Year for "N" Years**

| Period in years | 2% | 4% | 6% | 8% | 10% | 12% | 14% | 16% | 18% | 20% | 25% | 30% |
|---|---|---|---|---|---|---|---|---|---|---|---|---|
| 1 | .98 | .96 | .94 | .93 | .91 | .89 | .88 | .86 | .85 | .83 | .80 | .77 |
| 2 | 1.94 | 1.88 | 1.83 | 1.79 | 1.74 | 1.69 | 1.65 | 1.61 | 1.56 | 1.53 | 1.44 | 1.36 |
| 3 | 2.88 | 2.77 | 2.67 | 2.58 | 2.49 | 2.40 | 2.32 | 2.25 | 2.17 | 2.11 | 1.95 | 1.82 |
| 4 | 3.81 | 3.63 | 3.46 | 3.31 | 3.17 | 3.03 | 2.91 | 2.80 | 2.69 | 2.59 | 2.36 | 2.17 |
| 5 | 4.71 | 4.45 | 4.21 | 3.99 | 3.79 | 3.60 | 3.43 | 3.27 | 3.13 | 2.99 | 2.69 | 2.44 |
| 6 | 5.60 | 5.24 | 4.92 | 4.62 | 4.35 | 4.11 | 3.89 | 3.68 | 3.50 | 3.33 | 2.95 | 2.64 |
| 7 | 6.47 | 6.00 | 5.58 | 5.21 | 4.86 | 4.56 | 4.29 | 4.04 | 3.81 | 3.61 | 3.16 | 2.80 |
| 8 | 7.32 | 6.73 | 6.21 | 5.75 | 5.33 | 4.97 | 4.64 | 4.34 | 4.08 | 3.84 | 3.33 | 2.92 |
| 9 | 8.16 | 7.43 | 6.80 | 6.25 | 5.75 | 5.33 | 4.95 | 4.60 | 4.30 | 4.03 | 3.46 | 3.02 |
| 10 | 8.98 | 8.11 | 7.36 | 6.71 | 6.14 | 5.65 | 5.22 | 4.83 | 4.49 | 4.19 | 3.57 | 3.09 |
| 11 | 9.79 | 8.76 | 7.88 | 7.14 | 6.49 | 5.94 | 5.45 | 5.03 | 4.65 | 4.33 | 3.66 | 3.15 |
| 12 | 10.58 | 9.39 | 8.38 | 7.54 | 6.81 | 6.20 | 5.66 | 5.20 | 4.79 | 4.44 | 3.73 | 3.19 |
| 13 | 11.35 | 9.99 | 8.85 | 7.91 | 7.10 | 6.43 | 5.84 | 5.34 | 4.91 | 4.53 | 3.78 | 3.22 |
| 14 | 12.11 | 10.57 | 9.29 | 8.25 | 7.36 | 6.63 | 6.00 | 5.47 | 5.01 | 4.61 | 3.82 | 3.25 |
| 15 | 12.85 | 11.12 | 9.71 | 8.56 | 7.60 | 6.81 | 6.14 | 5.58 | 5.09 | 4.68 | 3.86 | 3.27 |
| 20 | 16.35 | 13.59 | 11.47 | 9.82 | 8.51 | 7.47 | 6.62 | 5.93 | 5.35 | 4.87 | 3.95 | 3.32 |
| 25 | 19.52 | 15.62 | 12.78 | 10.68 | 9.08 | 7.85 | 6.88 | 6.09 | 5.47 | 4.95 | 3.99 | 3.33 |
| 30 | 22.40 | 17.30 | 13.76 | 11.26 | 9.43 | 8.06 | 7.01 | 6.18 | 5.52 | 4.98 | 4.00 | 3.33 |
| 35 | 25.00 | 18.67 | 14.49 | 11.65 | 9.64 | 8.18 | 7.07 | 6.21 | 5.54 | 4.99 | 4.00 | 3.33 |
| 40 | 27.36 | 19.80 | 15.04 | 11.92 | 9.78 | 8.25 | 7.11 | 6.23 | 5.55 | 5.00 | 4.00 | 3.33 |

**TABLE B-4  Present Value of $1 Received at Middle of Each Year for "N" Years**

| Period in years | 2% | 4% | 6% | 8% | 10% | 12% | 14% | 16% | 18% | 20% | 25% | 30% |
|---|---|---|---|---|---|---|---|---|---|---|---|---|
| 1 | .99 | .98 | .97 | .96 | .95 | .95 | .94 | .93 | .92 | .91 | .89 | .88 |
| 2 | 1.96 | 1.92 | 1.89 | 1.85 | 1.82 | 1.79 | 1.76 | 1.73 | 1.70 | 1.67 | 1.61 | 1.55 |
| 3 | 2.91 | 2.83 | 2.75 | 2.68 | 2.61 | 2.54 | 2.48 | 2.42 | 2.36 | 2.30 | 2.18 | 2.07 |
| 4 | 3.84 | 3.70 | 3.57 | 3.44 | 3.33 | 3.21 | 3.11 | 3.02 | 2.92 | 2.83 | 2.64 | 2.47 |
| 5 | 4.76 | 4.54 | 4.34 | 4.15 | 3.98 | 3.81 | 3.66 | 3.53 | 3.40 | 3.27 | 3.01 | 2.78 |
| 6 | 5.66 | 5.35 | 5.06 | 4.80 | 4.57 | 4.35 | 4.15 | 3.97 | 3.80 | 3.64 | 3.30 | 3.01 |
| 7 | 6.54 | 6.12 | 5.75 | 5.41 | 5.11 | 4.83 | 4.58 | 4.35 | 4.14 | 3.95 | 3.53 | 3.19 |
| 8 | 7.40 | 6.87 | 5.39 | 5.97 | 5.60 | 5.26 | 4.95 | 4.68 | 4.43 | 4.20 | 3.72 | 3.33 |
| 9 | 8.24 | 7.58 | 7.00 | 6.49 | 6.04 | 5.64 | 5.28 | 4.96 | 4.67 | 4.41 | 3.87 | 3.44 |
| 10 | 9.07 | 8.27 | 7.58 | 6.97 | 6.44 | 5.98 | 5.57 | 5.21 | 4.88 | 4.59 | 3.99 | 3.52 |
| 11 | 9.88 | 8.93 | 8.12 | 7.42 | 6.81 | 6.29 | 5.82 | 5.42 | 5.06 | 4.74 | 4.09 | 3.59 |
| 12 | 10.68 | 9.57 | 8.63 | 7.83 | 7.14 | 6.56 | 6.04 | 5.60 | 5.21 | 4.86 | 4.16 | 3.64 |
| 13 | 11.46 | 10.18 | 9.11 | 8.21 | 7.44 | 6.80 | 6.24 | 5.75 | 5.33 | 4.96 | 4.22 | 3.68 |
| 14 | 12.22 | 10.77 | 9.57 | 8.57 | 7.72 | 7.02 | 6.41 | 5.89 | 5.44 | 5.05 | 4.27 | 3.71 |
| 15 | 12.97 | 11.34 | 10.00 | 8.90 | 7.97 | 7.21 | 6.56 | 6.00 | 5.53 | 5.12 | 4.31 | 3.73 |
| 20 | 16.51 | 13.86 | 11.81 | 10.20 | 8.93 | 7.91 | 7.07 | 6.38 | 5.81 | 5.33 | 4.42 | 3.78 |
| 25 | 19.72 | 15.93 | 13.16 | 11.09 | 9.52 | 8.30 | 7.34 | 6.56 | 5.94 | 5.42 | 4.45 | 3.80 |
| 30 | 22.62 | 17.64 | 14.18 | 11.70 | 9.88 | 8.53 | 7.48 | 6.65 | 5.99 | 5.46 | 4.46 | 3.80 |
| 35 | 25.25 | 19.04 | 14.93 | 12.11 | 10.11 | 8.66 | 7.55 | 6.69 | 6.02 | 5.47 | 4.46 | 3.80 |
| 40 | 27.63 | 20.19 | 15.50 | 12.39 | 10.26 | 8.73 | 7.58 | 6.71 | 6.03 | 5.48 | 4.47 | 3.80 |

The present value cost of purchasing is

| | |
|---|---|
| Cash outlay today ................................ | $100,000 |
| Depreciation tax savings ($5000 × 0.50) = $2500 per year for 15 years, present valued at 4%, factor 11.34 = 2500 × 11.34 = ................ | (28,350) |
| Write-off of unallocated cost at end of 15 years = $25,000 × 0.50 × 0.55 (present-value factor for 4% at end of 15 years) ...................... | (6875) |
| Present-value cost of purchasing ................. | $64,775 |

In order to find the effective cost of leasing, the rate which will bring the lease payments to a present value of $64,775 must be calculated.

| | |
|---|---|
| Gross lease payment ................... | $12,550 |
| After-tax lease payment ............... | $ 6275 |

What rate will bring 15 annual after-tax lease payments of $6275 back to $64,775?

$$\frac{64,775}{6275} = 10.33 \text{ factor for 15 years is something slightly more than 6%}$$

Therefore, the after-tax cost of leasing is about 6 percent compared with an after-tax cost of borrowing of 4 percent. In this case it is more attractive to purchase.

**Present-Value Outlays** Using the example given above, the net-present-value outlay if the asset is purchased is $64,775.

What is the present value of the lease payments? First, it is necessary to state the discount rate which is to be used to discount the lease payments. This rate is the after-tax cost of debt rate, applied to the after-tax lease payments, if the same rate is deemed to be applicable to the tax savings associated with the lease payments.

Using the example above, the after-tax lease payments are $6275 annually. The 15 year 4 percent discount factor is 11.34. Thus, the present value of the lease alternative is

$$\$6275 \times 11.34 = \$71,160$$

Thus, the same conclusion is reached: It is less expensive to purchase than it is to lease—$64,775 compared with $71,160.

**Exceptional Cases** An abbreviated explanation of two methods of approaching a straightforward lease versus purchase analysis has been presented. But not all lease/purchase situations are as simple as that illustrated. Some of the more common exceptional cases are

1. Under the purchase alternative, the company owns an asset which at the end of the estimated life, used for comparative purposes, is "worth" something, i.e., land or a building useful for other purposes. In the illustration used above, it was assumed that the asset had no terminal value, and consequently it was written off for tax purposes. If it is probable that the asset has some value at the end of the estimated life, the situation can be handled in two ways;

a. Estimate the value at the end of the useful life, consider taxable gains or write-offs, apply a present-value factor, and bring the present-value amount back to reduce the purchase cost. Continuing with the example used above, if it is assumed that the equipment would be salable for $50,000 at the end of 15 years, this would result in a $25,000 gain on sale ($50,000 sales price less $25,000 unallocated cost). If the gain is taxed at 25 percent, the net cash inflow at the end of the 15 years would be $50,000 − $6250 taxes, or $43,750. Applying a present-value factor of 0.55 (4 percent, 15 years) would result in $24,063. The present-value cost of purchasing would then be:

| | |
|---|---|
| Same ..................................... | $100,000 |
| Same ..................................... | (28,350) |
| Present value of salvage value ............. | (24,063) |
| Present value cost of purchasing ............ | $ 47,587 |

b. If it is difficult to estimate a precise figure for the salvage (or terminal) value, it is possible to determine what this value would have to be in order to make the purchase alternative as attractive as the lease alternative, assuming the lease alternative had a lower cost without considering salvage value. (This was not the case in the previous example.)

Examine another case with the following situation:

| | |
|---|---|
| Present-value cost of purchasing, before considering salvage value ...................... | $50,000 |
| Present-value cost of leasing ...................... | $40,000 |

What would the after-tax salvage value of the asset owned under the purchase alternative have to be to make purchasing as attractive as leasing? There is a present-value difference of $10,000 ($50,000 − 40,000). Using the 4 percent present-value factor for the fifteenth year, the after-tax salvage value would have to be

$$\frac{\$10,000}{0.55} = \$18,182$$

Using this method, it is possible to highlight the unknown, i.e., by determining what the value has to be, rather than by attempting to assign a definite figure.

2. A second type of exceptional case is involved where a company is a marginal credit risk or for some reason appears to have access to more lease than debt capacity. A company in this category may not be able to get term loans, yet it may be able to lease assets, particularly if it can lease equipment from the company manufacturing the equipment. If leasing is the only alternative, and the asset is a good investment, then a lease/buy analysis is not applicable.

### NEW TECHNIQUES

Companies today are combining other quantitative techniques with capital project analysis. Some of them are:

**Sensitivity Analysis** This method, in effect, uses different sets of assumptions relative to the projected savings to look at a proposed project. What would the savings be if the selling price of the product produced on the machine increased by 10 percent? Decreased by 10 percent? What would the savings be if volume decreased by 20 percent? Increased by 20 percent? It is useful to apply sensitivity analysis when any of the factors involved in the savings calculation are likely to be unstable.

**Probability** Sensitivity analysis can be combined with the use of probability theory. What is the probability that prices may increase or decrease by 10 percent? The probability factors can be applied to the various price alternatives to get an expected return. A simple example:

| Price | Probability | Expected Price |
|-------|-------------|----------------|
| $12   | 25%         | $3.00          |
| $10   | 50%         | 5.00           |
| $ 8   | 15%         | 1.20           |
| $ 6   | 10%         | 0.60           |
|       |             | $9.60          |

The use of probability analysis provides a disciplined way of injecting subjective hunches into the analysis process.

### SUMMARY

Various methods are used in practice to appraise the desirability of long-term investments. The three most commonly used are payback, accounting return, and discounted cash flow. Each of these methods has its advantages and disadvantages.

*See also* ACCOUNTING, COST ANALYSIS AND CONTROL; ACCOUNTING, FINANCIAL; ACCOUNTING FOR MANAGERIAL CONTROL; BUDGETING, CAPITAL, SPECIAL PROBLEMS OF; BUDGETS AND BUDGET PREPARATION; ENERGY RESOURCES, MANAGEMENT OF; FACILITIES AND SITE PLANNING AND LAYOUT; FINANCIAL MANAGEMENT, CAPITAL STRUCTURE AND DIVIDEND POLICY; MARGINAL INCOME ANALYSIS; RISK ANALYSIS AND MANAGEMENT; TAX MANAGEMENT, MANAGERIAL RESPONSIBILITY FOR FEDERAL INCOME TAX REPORTING.

### REFERENCES

Davey, Patrick J.: *Capital Investments: Appraisals and Limits,* National Industrial Conference Board, Inc., New York, 1974.

*Financial Analysis to Guide Capital Expenditure Decisions,* Research Report 43, National Association of Accountants, New York, 1967.

Frengen, James N.: "Capital Budgeting Practices: A Survey," *Management Accounting,* May 1973, p. 19.

Johnston, Robert Willard: *Capital Budgeting,* Wadsworth Publishing, Company, Inc., Belmont, Calif., 1970.

Quirin, G. David: *The Capital Expenditure Decision,* Richard D. Irwin, Inc., Homewood, Ill., 1967.

Terbough, George W.: *Business Investment Management,* Machinery and Allied Products Institute, Washington, 1967.

C. RAY SMITH, *University of Virginia*

# Budgeting, capital, special problems of

Capital budgeting represents the process of planning and evaluating capital expenditures. Most literature on capital budgeting tends to focus on techniques of analysis rather than on the entire decision process. Analytical techniques are critical to an understanding of capital budgeting and are well explained in the entry on BUDGETING, CAPITAL. This entry attempts to integrate those techniques into an overall decision framework with specific discussion of these issues: (1) limitations and procedures; (2) problems related to use of capital budgeting techniques in financing rather than investment decisions; (3) working capital considerations; and (4) corporate acquisition analysis.

### DECISIONS: LIMITATIONS AND A PROCEDURE

Most firms have come to accept the time-weighted or discounted cash-flow techniques as the most useful, consistent, and accurate method of planning and evaluating capital expenditure proposals. Regardless of the techniques employed, they merely represent "number-crunching" models. The models generate answers that are only as valid as the input data.

**Decisions**   With that in mind, consider the role of such models in the entire decision process which could look something like the following:

1. What are the goals and objectives of the company/division? Does the proposed expenditure fit? Is there risk compatibility?

2. Where did the proposal originate: senior management, production, marketing, etc.? Does the proposal, as conceived by the originating unit, meet the constraints of the other units that have to live with it? For example, does a senior executive's desire for the acquisition of a company fit the objectives and capabilities of the division manager who would have line responsibility for managing the newly acquired company?

3. If a proposal seems to fit overall goals and objectives, can existing talent and capacity absorb it?

4. Is adequate financing really available? (Capital budgeting models always assume so).

5. Have the projections (used in the capital budgeting models) been adequately tested at all levels: engineering, production, quality control, and economic and marketing research?

6. Finally, do appropriate capital budgeting models indicate that the proposal is satisfactory, given predetermined acceptance criteria?

**Limitations**   Most capital budgeting literature focuses on question 6 alone and leaves the first five questions to the imagination. The first four questions seem fairly obvious and perhaps can be easily answered. Question 5, however, is the single most-critical determinant of the success of the models. Without tested input data, capital budgeting techniques are not only useless but also dangerous. It is axiomatic that capital budgeting models can make any marginal proposal look good. Analysts (and managers) are remiss if they do not isolate and evaluate those factors which make or break the project.

There is a common anecdote told among financial staff members about a proposal package submitted by a senior executive with an attached memorandum instructing the analysts to generate a favorable NPV and IRR. No capital budgeting model will screen out such projects, no matter how marginal. However, knowledge of weaknesses in the input data could very well provide the stroke necessary to kill the proposal.

**Recommended Procedure**   There are a number of ways to implement a capital budgeting program. Many, however, do not adequately protect against loose assumptions. Below is one simple, reliable way that does:

STEP 1: Generate proposal (of a certain minimum size) at the operating division level. Gather engineering, production, and marketing information in support of the idea.

STEP 2: Secure preliminary approval from senior management in light of existing objectives, risk patterns, etc.

STEP 3: Analyze input data. This is performed independently by economic and marketing research staffs.

STEP 4: Analyze the project from the standpoint of (a) available financing and (b) investment evaluation through the use of capital budgeting models.

## CAPITAL BUDGETING TECHNIQUES IN FINANCING DECISIONS[1]

Capital budgeting, by definition, attempts to solve investment problems, not financing problems; nevertheless, capital budgeting techniques, such as the NPV and IRR, can be very useful in solving financing problems, such as lease versus purchase decisions. It is very tempting—especially if the financing source of a proposed investment is known in advance—to analyze both investment and financing problems simultaneously. One should be cautioned that simultaneous analyses almost always result in distorted conclusions about the economic merit of the investment. Thus, it is imperative that investment and financing decisions be assessed independently of each other.

**Leasing**   Take the case of a firm that wishes to purchase a small plant for $150,000. After-tax cash flows over the next 10 years, exclusive of financing payments, are expected to be $20,000 per year. The firm plans to finance the plant by a lease agreement which called for payments of $25,227 per annum (equivalent to a 14 percent rate paid in advance) for 10 years. The plant can be repurchased at the end of 10 years at fair market value, which is expected to be nominal. The firm considers its cost of capital to be 10 percent.

The firm evaluates this problem by deducting its after-tax lease payments (50 percent tax rate × $25,-228 = $12,614) from the expected cash flows (see Table B-5). Analyzed in this manner, the internal rate of return on the project was well over 50 percent.

**TABLE B-5  Leasing: Internal Rate of Return Calculations**

| Year | Expected cash flow | − | After-tax rental | = | Net cash flow | × | Present-value factors at 10% | Present value |
|------|------|------|------|------|------|------|------|------|
| Present | $     0 | | $12,614 | | $(12,614) | | 1 | ($12,614) |
| 1 | 20,000 | | 12,614 | | 7,386 | | | |
| 2 | 20,000 | | 12,614 | | 7,386 | | | |
| 3 | 20,000 | | 12,614 | | 7,386 | | | |
| 4 | 20,000 | | 12,614 | | 7,386 | | | |
| 5 | 20,000 | | 12,614 | | 7,386 | | 5.759 | 42,536 |
| 6 | 20,000 | | 12,614 | | 7,386 | | | |
| 7 | 20,000 | | 12,614 | | 7.386 | | | |
| 8 | 20,000 | | 12,614 | | 7.386 | | | |
| 9 | 20,000 | | 12,614 | | 7,386 | | | |
| 10 | 20,000 | | | | 20,000 | | 0.386 | 7,720 |
| | | | | | | Net present value at 10% | | $37,642 |

Calculation for internal rate of return (IRR):

$$I = \sum_{1}^{10} \frac{C}{(1 + R)^n}$$

$I$ = initial outlay of $12,614
$C$ = cash flow per period
$n$ = time periods 1 to 10
$R$ = the rate that equates the present value of the cash flows to the initial outlay, i.e., the IRR

Thus, solve for $R$ (the IRR). The tipoff is the positive NPV of $37,642, which indicates that the IRR is greater than the cost of capital of 10%. In this case, the IRR exceeds 50%.

This case provides a typical example of how financing decision analyses can be mixed with investment decision analyses. By negotiating for rental payments in arrears rather than in advance, the project can be made to show an infinite IRR! But is the project really any better?

**Debt Financing**  Without examining the question of whether or not leases conserve borrowing power, consider the same investment when financed, at least in part, by straight debt. Assume that payment terms call for $50,000 down and $10,000 per year for 10 years (for simplicity's sake assume that an interest rate need not be imputed in the installments).

From a straight cash-flow/time standpoint, this project would be analyzed as shown in Table B-6. The analysis indicates a positive NPV and an IRR (15 percent) that exceeds the cost of capital (10 percent). However, this approach fails to consider the real reason why the financing could be obtained and the impact on future opportunities created by the utilization of this financing. In other words, *the availability and specific cost of financing* for a particular investment is generally not a function of that investment alone but the investing company's overall financing power as derived from its profitability, asset structure (liquidity), and equity base. Furthermore, the inclusion of financing costs in the cash flows, either directly or indirectly, represents double counting because such costs are already imputed in the discount factor (cost of capital).

**Utilization of Spending Power**  The real issue is to compare the present value of total inflows with the present value of total spending power utilized. Spending power is obtained from both equity sources and borrowing capacity. If the firm acquires the plant with a $50,000 down payment and a $100,000 loan, it has actually used $150,000 in spending power—$50,000 in cash or equity and $100,000 in the reduction of its debt capacity. Stated another way, the *firm reduced its ability to borrow for investment* in other projects by $100,000 due to the loan of an equal amount taken for the plant.

Ideally, this proposal should have been analyzed by deducting the present value of the expected cash inflows (not net of financing payments) from the purchase price of $150,000. The results would be a negative NPV of ($27,100) and an IRR of about 6 percent.

$$\text{NPV:}\quad 150,000 - \sum_{1}^{10} \frac{20,000}{(1.10)^n} = (27,100)$$

$$\text{IRR:}\quad 150,000 = \sum_{1}^{10} \frac{20,000}{(1.06)^n}$$

IRR = 6 percent solution found through trial and error

TABLE B-6    Debt-Financing Calculations

| Year | Expected cash inflow | – | Financing payments | = | Net cash flow | Present-value factor at 10% | Present value |
|------|-----|---|-----|---|-----|-----|-----|
| Present | $      0 | | $50,000 | | $(50,000) | 1 | (50,000) |
| 1 | 20,000 | | 10,000 | | 10,000 | | |
| 2 | 20,000 | | 10,000 | | 10,000 | | |
| 3 | 20,000 | | 10,000 | | 10,000 | | |
| 4 | 20,000 | | 10,000 | | 10,000 | | |
| 5 | 20,000 | | 10,000 | | 10,000 | | |
| 6 | 20,000 | | 10,000 | | 10,000 | 6.145 | 61,450 |
| 7 | 20,000 | | 10,000 | | 10,000 | | |
| 8 | 20,000 | | 10,000 | | 10,000 | | |
| 9 | 20,000 | | 10,000 | | 10,000 | | |
| 10 | 20,000 | | 10,000 | | 10,000 | | |
| | | | | | | Net present value @ 10% | $11,450 |

IRR calculation:

$$I = \sum_1^{10} \frac{C}{(1 + R)^n}$$

Solve for $R$ (trial and error indicates that 15% is approximately correct). Again, the positive NPV generated above indicates that the IRR exceeds 10%.

$$50,000 = \sum_1^{10} \frac{10,000}{(1 + 15)^n}$$

Admittedly, this approach defies traditional concepts of looking at the cost of capital and time value of money. However, distorted conclusions about the real value of a proposed investment will generally be avoided when financing decision information is excluded. In other words, (1) the total purchase price (not the down payment) should be considered the initial outlay; and (2) financing payments, including interest expense, should not be deducted from the expected inflow.

## WORKING CAPITAL CONSIDERATIONS[2]

Many capital investments create the need for investments in complementary short-term assets, e.g., receivables and inventory. These increased outlays for working capital–related assets should be included in the calculation of the initial outlay when analyzing the proposed investment. Ideally, periodic increases in working capital should be deducted from the cash flows. Residual value should include the return of working capital to the firm's pool of capital. To exclude working capital expenditures from the analysis implies that such outlays are invested independently of the investment in plant and equipment. In reality, however, the working capital expenditures and fixed assets are often joint investments. One would not take place without the other. Exclusion of the cash-flow impact of working capital from the analysis may result in an internal rate of return that is arbitrary and in some cases unrealistically high.

Consider the case of a company analyzing the purchase of a plant that costs $1.5 million. If the company makes the acquisition, it will also have to acquire and maintain about $1 million in raw materials inventory. The acquiring company has cash available to purchase the plant. It also has an unused credit line of about $1 million (short term notes available at 8 percent p.a.) which could be used to finance the increased raw materials requirement.

The firm estimates that it will receive $320,000 in annual after-tax cash flows for 10 years if the plant is purchased (residual value is not considered, for purposes of simplicity). It was suggested by management that the raw materials financed by short-term debt should be excluded from the initial outlay. This reasoning was based on the argument that the working capital assets are so liquid that the inherent risk does not require the same rate of return as a commitment to plant and equipment; therefore, most or all should be excluded from the initial outlay for purposes of calculating the NPV. Consequently, the project was analyzed in the manner shown in Table B-7. (The firm considered its cost of capital to be 10 percent.)

Using this approach, the firm finds the plant investment to have an NPV of over $220,600 which is, of course, quite attractive. However, the $1 million in working capital was excluded from the analysis, except for interest expense. This repre-

**TABLE B-7**

| Year | Cash inflow | Cash outflow | Net cash flow | Present-value factor at 10% | Present value |
|------|------------|--------------|---------------|----------------------------|---------------|
| Present | $    0 | $1,500,000 | $(1,500,000) | 1 | $(1,500,000) |
| 1 | 320,000 | 40,000* | 280,000 | | |
| 2 | 320,000 | 40,000 | 280,000 | | |
| 3 | 320,000 | 40,000 | 280,000 | | |
| 4 | 320,000 | 40,000 | 280,000 | | |
| 5 | 320,000 | 40,000 | 280,000 | 6.145 | 1,720,600 |
| 6 | 320,000 | 40,000 | 280,000 | | |
| 7 | 320,000 | 40,000 | 280,000 | | |
| 8 | 320,000 | 40,000 | 280,000 | | |
| 9 | 320,000 | 40,000 | 280,000 | | |
| 10 | 320,000 | 40,000 | 280,000 | | |
| | | | | Net present value @ 10% | $220,600 |

*Approximate after-tax interest expense of 8% on $1 million (tax rate = 50%).

sents a mixing of financing data with investment data; such a treatment distorts the analysis. The firm used $1 million of its limited borrowing capacity and thus its spending power. A more realistic approach to this problem would show a substantially negative net present value, as indicated in Table B-8. Note that the initial outlay now includes the working capital as well as plant costs, and that annual interest charges have been deleted. Under this approach the financing decision information has been totally excluded from investment decision data, and, consequently, the project is very marginal.

In summary, working capital requirements should always be included in the capital budgeting analysis; the cost of financing working capital

**TABLE B-8**

| Year | Cash inflow | Cash outflow | Present-value factor at 10% | Present value |
|------|------------|--------------|----------------------------|---------------|
| Present | $    0 | $(2,500,000)* | 1 | $(2,500,000) |
| 1 | 320,000 | | | |
| 2 | 320,000 | | | |
| 3 | 320,000 | | | |
| 4 | 320,000 | | | |
| 5 | 320,000 | | 6.145 | 1,966,400 |
| 6 | 320,000 | | | |
| 7 | 320,000 | | | |
| 8 | 320,000 | | | |
| 9 | 320,000 | | | |
| 10 | 320,000† | | | |
| | | | Net present value @ 10% | $(533,600) |

Since the NPV is negative, the IRR must be less than the cost of capital of 10%.

*$1.5 million for plant and $1 million for inventory.
†A more comprehensive approach would consider the return of working capital to the firm's pools of funds upon termination of the project. However, the return of funds in this example would not make the project acceptable.

should be excluded. To do otherwise risks generating seriously distorted answers.

## CAPITAL BUDGETING FOR CORPORATE ACQUISITIONS

Determining the financial acceptability of a corporate acquisition is as much a capital budgeting problem as the acquisition of a machine tool. However, there are significant new wrinkles in determining relevant cash flows. These variables should be given special attention:

1. *Net cash flow.* This is defined as net earnings plus all noncash charges (such as depreciation, deferred taxes, and amortization of intangibles) less incremental investments. Net income does not generally provide a good proxy for the actual funds generated by the firm.

2. *Financing method ignored.* A company can be purchased with cash, straight debt instruments, convertible securities, stock swaps, or combinations. To include the financing mechanism in the capital budgeting analysis can distort the real economic merit of the company to be acquired.

3. *Working capital requirements included.* Working capital injections by the acquiring company represent incremental investments which are best handled by deducting them from expected cash flow.

4. *Residual Value.* Most companies are assumed to have perpetual life, but the nature of forecasting calls for an intermediate-term horizon. If, for example, forecasts are only considered realistic for a 5-year period, an estimate of residual value must be included with the fifth year cash-flow projection. There are several methods for calculating residual value, all must be considered "seat of the pants" methods. Two such methods follow:

**TABLE B-9**
($000's omitted)

| Time | Purchase price | Working capital | + | Fixed capital investment | = | Incremental investment | Net income | + | Depreciation | = | Gross cash flow | − | Incremental investment | = | Net cash flow |
|------|------|------|---|------|---|------|------|---|------|---|------|---|------|---|------|
| Present | $1500 | 250 | | | | | | | | | | | | | |
| 1 | | 13 ⎫ | | 200 | | 213 | 300 | | 200 | | 500 | | 213 | | 287 |
| 2 | | 26 ⎪ | | 210 | | 236 | 330 | | 200 | | 530 | | 236 | | 294 |
| 3 | | 39 ⎬ * | | 220 | | 259 | 363 | | 200 | | 563 | | 259 | | 304 |
| 4 | | 54 ⎪ | | 230 | | 284 | 399 | | 200 | | 599 | | 284 | | 315 |
| 5 | | 69 ⎭ | | 240 | | 309 | 439 | | 200 | | 639 | | 309 | | 330 |
| | Cumulative | 319 | | | | | 1831 | | | | | | | | |

Initial outlay
Purchase price ............................ $1,500,000
Working capital ............................ 250,000
$1,750,000

Residual value
Working capital ............................ $ 319,000
Book value† ............................ 3,431,000
Investment ............................ $3,750,000

An alternative to the book value approach would be to assume that the fifth year cash flow remains constant into perpetuity.

*Represents 5% annual increase in cumulative amounts.
†Purchase price ........................................ $1,500,000
Cumulative net income ................................ 1,831,000
Incremental fixed investment (above replacement costs) ..... 100,000
$3,431,000

*a.* Assume the company is sold in the fifth year at book value or a multiple of average earnings.

*b.* Calculate the present value of the fifth year cash flow assuming it remains constant for perpetuity.

EXAMPLE: The following example illustrates how a corporate acquisition could be analyzed. Critics of the illustration will argue that certain treatments are either missing, distorted, or superfluous. The example should not be considered a definitive treatment of the subject, but merely as an illustrative framework for considering the relevance of capital budgeting techniques.

The company under consideration can be acquired for a price of $1,500,000. Additionally, the acquiring firm will have to make an immediate working capital injection of $250,000. Since sales are expected to increase, annual working capital increases of 5 percent are expected. The acquiring firm feels that forecast revenue and earnings are reliable for a 5-year period. First year net income is projected to be $300,000 with 10 percent annual growth thereafter. Annual depreciation will be $200,000. Incremental fixed assets (above replacement costs) are estimated to increase by $10,000 per year. See Table B-9.

With the above information the NPV and IRR can be computed. Assume the acquiring company's

acceptance rate or cost of capital is 15 percent. See Table B-10.

By applying the present-value factors of a 30 percent rate to the cash flows, the NPV would be approximately zero. In other words, the IRR is about 30 percent.

From the financial standpoint, the project is obviously acceptable since the NPV≥0 and the IRR≥cost of capital.

*See also* ACQUISITIONS AND MERGERS; BUDGETING, CAPITAL; FINANCIAL MANAGEMENT, SHORT-TERM, INTERMEDIATE, AND LONG-TERM FINANCING; FINANCIAL MANAGEMENT, WORKING CAPITAL CONTROL; LEASING, EQUIPMENT; TAX MANAGEMENT, MANAGERIAL RESPONSIBILITY FOR FEDERAL INCOME TAX REPORTING.

**TABLE B-10**

| Time | Cash flow | Present-value factors @ 15% | = | Present value |
|------|------|------|---|------|
| Present | (1,750,000) | 1.0 | | (1,750,000) |
| 1 | 287,000 | 0.870 | | 249,690 |
| 2 | 294,000 | 0.756 | | 222,264 |
| 3 | 304,000 | 0.658 | | 200,032 |
| 4 | 315,000 | 0.572 | | 180,180 |
| 5 | 330,000 | 0.497 | | 164,010 |
| Residual | 3,750,000 | 0.497 | | 1,863,750 |
| | | Net present value @ 15% | | 1,129,926 |

NOTES

[1]David A. Jones, "Capital Budgeting: Mixing Up the Balance Sheet," *Financial Executive*, April 1976, pp. 45–48.

[2]Ibid.

REFERENCES

Johnson, Robert W. *Capital Budgeting*, Wadsworth Publishing Company, Inc., Belmont, Calif., 1970.

Philippatos, George C.: *Financial Management Theory and Techniques*, Holden-Day, Inc., Publisher, San Francisco, 1973.

DAVID A. JONES, *Citicorp*

## Budgeting, program [*See* PROGRAM BUDGETING (PPBS); PROGRAM PLANNING AND IMPLEMENTATION.]

## Budgets (*See* MANAGEMENT THEORY, SCIENCE, AND APPROACHES.)

# Budgets and budget preparation

Budgeting is the process by which costs are assigned to specific functions or activities that are planned within a designated upcoming period (usually 12 months). Budgeting is a widely used management tool that facilitates utilization of the vast amounts of information available today. Effective budgeting can improve decision making, provide a benchmark to measure and control performance, increase general communication and analysis within the organization, and establish an understanding between managers about goals and objectives. The budgeting process draws on planning input, such as long-range plans and goals; and economic, industry, and market-share forecasts. The three components of budgeting dealt with in this entry are (1) sales and volume budgets, (2) variable-cost budgets, and (3) overhead budgets. (These three components are the core of a basic budgeting system. There are, of course, special other components, such as project budgets, which do not have the same degree of general applicability, and those will not be presented here.)

## EFFECT OF THE BUDGETING PROCESS

All organizations have a limited amount of resources. Decisions must be made about how to allocate the available resources to meet the organization's objectives most effectively. The quality of those decisions can be greatly enhanced by a good planning and budgeting process—one that emphasizes input from all levels of management and rationalizes each allocation along the way.

Budgeting measures and controls performance. Goals must be set before any budgeting begins. As the budgeting process unfolds, feedback tells if the partial results are leading in the appropriate direction. Corrective action can be undertaken at this point if the thrust seems off target.

A good budgeting process improves communication within the organization. Budgeting encourages managers to think analytically. Improved analysis and communication ultimately lead to better decision making at the grass roots of the organization, as well as at the general manager level.

**Interrelationship of Planning and Budgeting** Planning and budgeting are interrelated in that the budget assigns dollar costs to the activities planned in the upcoming year. Prior to the budgeting process, several planning activities must be undertaken, as shown in Fig. B-3. Economic, industry, and market-share forecasts are prepared as long-range plans and goals are established. These serve as cornerstones upon which the budget is built.

Budgeting is merely a portion of broader management systems. Management systems are administrative tools used to accomplish the organization's objectives. These include management by objectives, planning systems, reward systems, organizational systems, and communications systems. As one of these management systems, budgeting concentrates on resource allocation and quantification of the costs required to fund certain activities. Budgeting, however, is closely linked to other systems in the following ways:

The determination of *objectives* comes first. Objectives precede plans which, in turn, precede budgets. The plans and budgets state *how* and *how much* in more detail than the objectives.

*Plans* define what will be done and how the task will be accomplished. Budgets outline the costs associated with the plans. Planning tends to be a more nearly top-down process; budgeting, bottom-up.

*Budgets* provide data upon which performance can be controlled and upon which rewards can be determined.

*Budgeting* encourages communications and uses the communications systems established in the organization.

*Organization structure* helps determine how the budgeting process will work.

**Budgeting Involves Three Processes** The budget is completed in three major processes which result in

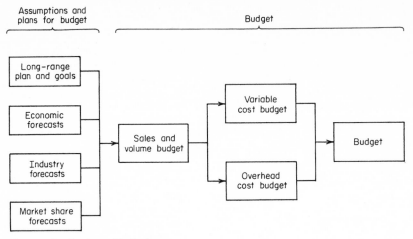

**Fig. B-3. The planning and budgeting process.**

1. Sales and volume budgets
2. Variable-cost budgets
3. Overhead-cost budgets

The components of budgeting are accomplished sequentially. Sales and volume budgets are prepared prior to the other two components because the volume forecast serves as input to the other budgets. A description of each of these budgets follows.

## SALES AND VOLUME BUDGETING

*Sales and volume budgeting* is a process by which revenues and the quantity of goods to be produced are forecast for the upcoming year. Usually, the budget is broken down by product lines, by month, and by producing location.

Different types of sales and volume budgets are produced for a variety of uses. Sales quotas are generally developed as a means to measure and motivate sales personnel. The sales quota may differ from the budget since quotas are meant to motivate the employees. General sales forecasts usually are based on estimated economic conditions and generally are produced by economists or others not directly involved in line management. Sales budgets, on the other hand, are produced by line management. They become a part of the overall company budget and are used by others as input to their budgets.

The sales and volume budget is necessary for three reasons:

1. Line executives responsible for sales need to be involved in planning their activities and the ex-

pected results. The act of budgeting increases their analytical involvement in planning sales activities.

2. A benchmark for measuring results and monitoring performance should be established.

3. Sales and volume budgets are a necessary and vital input to the variable-cost budgets and overhead-cost budgets.

Table B-11 shows examples of sales and volume budgets. Note that the budget is broken down by product line and by region within each product line. The needs of various organizations may dictate other breakdowns, but these are the most common.

**TABLE B-11   Example of Sales Budget**

| Sales Budget Summary | | |
|---|---|---|
| Product line | Sales | |
| | $000 | Volume (units) |
| Widgets ← | 1000 | 12,000 |
| Buggy whips | 525 | 15,500 |
| Hoola hoops | 610 | 13,250 |
| | 2135 | |

| Widget Sales Budget by Region | | |
|---|---|---|
| Region | Sales by region | |
| | $000 | Volume (units) |
| Midwest | 500 | 6000 |
| West | 250 | 3000 |
| East | 200 | 2500 |
| South | 50 | 500 |
| | 1000 | 12,000 |

**Four Major Steps** The sales and volume budgeting process is composed of the following four major steps.

1. Overall sales goals are prepared and provided to the manager responsible for sales. These goals are established through (*a*) an economists's sales outlook, (*b*) sales forecasts prepared via forecasting models, (*c*) historical sales trends, and (*d*) the chief executive's judgment. The goals are somewhat arbitrary at this point and are prepared on a top-down basis with little input from the sales force manager. *See also* FORECASTING BUSINESS CONDITIONS.

2. The product line managers or their counterparts prepare their sales budgets. This process involves a series of substeps: (*a*) examination of industry, economic, and market-share data; (*b*) examination of historical trends; (*c*) determination of the market approach in terms of use of sales force, advertising, promotion, pricing, channels of distribution, packaging, product modifications, etc.; and (*d*) estimation of sales by month by major product line.

3. Sales management and manufacturing management estimate production requirements and inventory levels. An estimate of production volume for each plant and for each product is prepared.

4. The finance group works with sales and manufacturing to develop estimates and ensure that the production volume estimates, inventory level estimates, and sales forecasts tie in.

The final sales and volume plan is approved only after significant interaction among many levels of management.

Since many factors influence sales volume, a range of sales volume should be provided, indicating pessimistic, most likely, and optimistic assessments. This contingency budget provides management with data to deal effectively with uncertainty.

**Pitfalls of the Sales and Volume Budgeting Process** Perhaps the greatest hazard of this process is the tendency of some organizations to budget sales without first carefully planning the marketing approach. Well-thought-out marketing plans behind the numbers are a prerequisite to meaningful budgets.

Another pitfall involves the diverse use of budgets. If the salesperson's quota is based on the same budget prepared for company planning purposes, trouble can arise. The salesperson may want a low quota; the sales manager may want a high or a low quota, depending upon the motivation involved. Such pressures can cause the budget to be unrealistic.

A third pitfall is overreliance on economic and forecasting models for sales budgeting. The common denominator in most successful modeling applications is the use of practical models that are responsive to the manager's own perspective.

*Design and Use of Decision Models.* There are at least seven critical ingredients in the successful design and use of decision models:

1. Closing the designer-user gap. There is usually a gulf between the model designer and the model user that must be explicitly resolved to avoid failure. The model designer has a technical knowledge that is likely to be far greater than that of the user. The user, on the other hand, has a finer appreciation of the problems that he or she must face and the operating or policy decisions that he or she must make.

2. Defining the problem before selecting a solution. Much time and effort is wasted finding a problem to fit a solution. Implicit in not allowing the management scientist to predetermine the solution is the recognition that there are many problems for which models are not useful.

3. Being willing to sacrifice technical efficiency for communication. It is more important for the user to understand the model than it is to save computing time.

4. Building models for people and not for organization charts. Models are used by people and not by titles, positions, or job descriptions.

5. Making the model small enough to be manageable and to address specific well-defined problems.

6. Assuring that the problem addressed by the model is large (in potential impact on profits) and/or repetitive so that the model can prove its value.

7. Utilizing management judgment as well as hard data in the model. The model should complement management judgment but not replace judgment. The successful model uses a small number of critical pieces of data which more often than not must be estimated by judgment and/or special studies rather than accounting or other regularly collected data.

In summary, people, rather than models, make decisions, and the people who generally make the best decisions are those who are closely involved in the marketing function. Thus it is vital that the sales budgeting responsibility is not abrogated to a model.

## VARIABLE-COST BUDGETS

Variable costs are those that vary directly with increases and decreases in the volume of goods manufactured. Variable costs traditionally are associated with three categories of expense:

Direct material expense

Direct labor expense

Portions of manufacturing or plant overhead expense which vary with volume.

Other departmental expenses (such as corporate administrative, marketing, and research and development) are generally considered fixed overhead expenses. These, together with the nonvariable portions of plant overhead, are addressed more fully in this entry in the section on Overhead Budgets.

Variable-cost budgeting begins with the development of the sales forecast, since inventory and production cost estimates are related to the anticipated sales volume. Completion of the forecast enables management to proceed to the production budget (by product and expressed in units). The production budget is based on the expected level of sales for the year, plus expected inventory additions for the year. The completion of these steps allows management to establish budgets for

1. Material usage and purchases
2. Direct labor costs
3. A portion of manufacturing or plant overhead costs

**Budgeting for Direct Costs of Production** The budgeting process for material usage and purchases and that for direct labor costs is similar. Standard costs are generally considered unit costs, while budgeted costs typically refer to the standard or unit costs multiplied by the expected production for the year. When variable budgets are used, the use of multiple production levels results in multiple budgets for each standard or unit cost, as shown in Table B-12.

**TABLE B-12  Example of Flexible Budget**
Flexible Budgeting for Direct Costs for Widgets

| | | Budgeted Cost for Indicated Volume Levels | | |
|---|---|---|---|---|
| Cost category | Standard cost | 20,000 hours 10,000 units | 22,000 hours 11,000 units | 24,000 hours 12,000 units |
| Direct labor cost | $ 5.00/hour | $100,000 | $110,000 | $120,000 |
| Material cost | $15.00/unit | $150,000 | $165,000 | $180,000 |
| Total direct cost | | $250,000 | $275,000 | $300,000 |

The budget for the direct costs of production is developed through establishing standards for both labor and material factors.

*Labor Standards.* Direct labor costs are composed of two factors: the quantity of labor utilized and the rate paid to the productive work force.

Labor rates are generally not controllable by a company since they are most often the result of union contract negotiations and/or local conditions of labor supply-and-demand factors. The rates to be used for standard-setting purposes are those that are anticipated for the forthcoming year.

The quantity of labor utilized, on the other hand, is of much greater importance, for actual labor efficiency measured by the labor-efficiency standard is largely controllable by management.

Time and motion studies and associated work-measurement techniques are the most widely used method of setting labor standards. Meaningful method studies evaluate both the operation and the environment in arriving at realistic objectives. Critical questions to answer are these: "Is the standard to be an average of expected production so as to most accurately price inventory and allow for overachievement as well as underachievement? Is the standard to be established as a goal for the work force to strive toward, and hence be set more stringently than management's expectation of actual performance?" For planning and budgeting purposes, the standard should reflect what manufacturing management expects to happen. Other standards can be used for motivational purposes.

Other methods utilized as a basis for establishing labor-efficiency standards involve evaluation of past standards and actual times, times used in similar operations, and industry guidelines.

*Material Standards.* The various costs for raw material entering into the product are comprised of both a price and a usage factor.

The price factor is generally determined by a purchasing group within the corporation and is based upon either the current prices or upon average expected prices during the forthcoming year. Price budgeting is mainly a predictive task, since the major variation in price is usually an external phenomenon. Nonetheless, wise purchase timing, lot ordering, discount planning, and alternative transportation evaluations all can produce better prices. In budgeting for prices, the possible economics available through effective purchasing management, particularly within the current economic climate, should be recognized.

Budgets for material quantities are prepared through the development of the standard bill of materials. The preparation of the standard bill of materials (see Table B-13) is based upon formal engineering test standards, trial runs, historical experience when the job is already in production, and industry experience. The responsibility for setting the material standards is generally that of the engineering department, with the assistance of the production and accounting staffs.

In order to arrive at a unit material budget, for each raw material or part entering into the production of an item, the quantity of material or number of parts required per unit produced (taken from the standard bill of materials) is multiplied by the estimated price for that type of material or part. Once this has been done for all materials, parts, and components that make up the item being manufactured, the unit material budgets are added to a total material budget for the production of one item. (In Table B-12, this is the $15.00 per unit shown as the material cost.)

**Budgeting for Variable Indirect Costs of Production**  In addition to direct material and labor costs, a number of other plant, or manufacturing, costs vary with volume. Examples of these include *portions of* maintenance, utilities, expendable supplies, and certain indirect labor costs. An analysis of numerous corporate budgets would show that these particular indirect product costs are often mixed in with managed or overhead costs for budgeting and expense-reporting purposes. Separate reporting is preferable due to the varied nature of the controllability of these costs.

Three characteristics of indirect product costs are important:

1. Like direct material and labor, a quantity required per unit of production can be established on the basis of engineering studies (utility expense for heavy machinery, for example).

2. Some items may have a fixed element of cost as well as a variable element.

3. Like managed costs, levels or organizational efficiency can be identified with various levels of expenditures for indirect product costs.

The most common approach to the evaluation of these costs is through the flexible budgeting technique, where volume-cost relationships are established (see Fig. B-4). While individual items may not bear direct relationships to production, the aggregate departmental relationships often do.

*Hazards in Flexible Budgeting.*  A word of caution is in order, however, since flexible budgeting does not address the following questions:

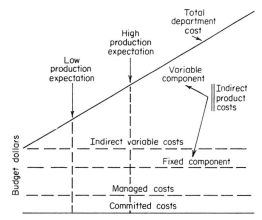

**Fig. B-4.  A simple flexible budget for departmental costs.**

1. What is the excess cost built into the standard or budgeted indirect costs that have been used in the past?

2. How much lower could the variable budgeting line be set (by reducing the fixed component of indirect costs, managed costs, and committed costs) and still meet production schedules in the short run or in the long run?

These questions can be answered better by evaluating the relative necessity of various service levels per unit of production for different departments or categories of indirect variable expense. A fuller explanation of this service-level approach (zero-base planning and budgeting) is presented in the section of this entry on Overhead Budgets.

### OVERHEAD BUDGETS

Overhead budgets are prepared for all costs that do not vary directly with volume. There are two major types of overhead costs, as shown in Fig. B-4.

**Committed Costs**  Committed costs are expenses that the organization will incur in the short term no matter what decisions are made, e.g., depreciation, insurance, rental charges, and certain taxes. Obviously, these costs can be changed by drastic action or in the long term.

**TABLE B-13  Example of Bill of Material**
Standard Bill of Materials for Superwidgets

| Part number | Quantity required per unit | Description |
| --- | --- | --- |
| X1416 | 140 cubic inches | Cement block |
| X2372 | 3 ounces | Epoxy |
| Q0002 | 10 pieces | Catch lever |
| K1000 | 2 boxes | Expansion bolt kit |

**Managed Costs** Managed costs do not vary directly with volume, but they can be changed. Examples include all overhead activities such as finance, research, development, office services, quality control, production planning, and engineering. The difference between these costs and committed costs is that decisions can be made about the level of service and cost that can be provided in the current year. Note that some manufacturing and plant overhead costs (e.g., the fixed component of indirect product costs shown in Fig. B-3) vary directly with volume and can be changed.

The managed costs are important for two reasons: (1) management can make decisions about what level of service and cost is provided, and (2) the increases or decreases in these costs have a dramatic impact on profit. Table B-14 shows how a 5 percent reduction in managed costs has a 20 percent positive impact on profits before taxes.

**TABLE B-14**  Impact of Managed Costs on Profits

|  | ($000) | Change |
| --- | --- | --- |
| Sales | 750,000 | |
| Variable costs | 496,000 | |
| Managed costs | 204,200 | (10,210) − (5%) |
| Profit before taxes | 49,800 | 60,010 + 20% |

**Overhead Costs Pose Problems** Traditionally, organizations have had a difficult time dealing with overhead costs. No neat standard cost formulas can be developed readily, and managers have felt uneasy about determining the relative merits of various overhead activities. Thus the usual approach is to concentrate in one of the following ways:

1. Examine new overhead activities very carefully.

2. Examine particular line items, such as travel, with a fine tooth comb.

3. Reduce or expand all overhead activities across the board.

The problem with this approach, of course, is that overhead costs are not scrutinized in terms of their value to the organization. Furthermore, the *base* activities that have gone on for years are not examined systematically. These flaws result in management's inability to reallocate resources intelligently to the uses most appropriate to the organization.

**Zero-Base Planning and Budgeting** A new approach for overhead budgeting, called zero-base planning and budgeting, attacks overhead in a different way. The effects of the zero-base planning and budgeting process include (1) selective cost and activity reductions or expansions, (2) reallocations of resources among overhead activities, and (3) a variety of analytical and communication benefits.

Zero-base planning and budgeting is a tool that helps cost center managers analyze their operations better and allows general managers to allocate resources more effectively through:

Examination of expected work loads.

Proper compartmentalization of overhead costs.

Rigorous analysis of each overhead-cost compartment.

Allocation of critical resources to appropriate activities.

Preparation of detailed budgets.

The process can be briefly summarized in four steps.

*Proper Identification of Decision Units.* The decision unit is the grouping of activities around which analysis is centered. In many cases, the decision unit corresponds to the traditional cost center or budget unit. In other cases, the decision unit encompasses a group of activities that can be analyzed effectively by management. Decision units may include special projects or programs, activities that apply across the organization (e.g., marketing), objects of expense, or services rendered.

It is important to note that decision units are established so that units of activities can be analyzed and discretionary trade-off decisions can be made. While managed costs are broken into decision units, committed costs are separated and not analyzed through zero-base planning and budgeting.

*Rigorous Analysis of Each Decision Unit.* The zero-base process is designed to involve all levels of management in the analysis. After the managers analyze their decision units, higher-level managers use the information to make resource allocation decisions.

Each decision unit is analyzed in three different ways: (1) the managers examine the purpose of their functions and their current methods of operation; (2) alternative ways of operating are examined; (3) incremental cost-benefit analysis is performed once the method of operation is determined.

A decision-unit manager usually begins the analysis by specifying exactly how he or she currently operates and by describing the number of people and dollars involved in the activity. Performance measures are developed to examine the strengths and weaknesses of the manager's current approach.

The manager then considers alternative ways of operating. After reviewing the alternatives (including the current method), the manager chooses the best method of operation. To begin the incremental analysis, the decision-unit manager determines, from a base of zero, which is the most important service need provided by the unit. These highest-priority needs constitute the first or minimum increment of service. In all cases, the first increment requires lower expenditure than is currently provided and offers either a narrower range of services than is presently provided or a reduced quality or quantity of service. Additional increments of service and cost are developed, with each successive increment containing those services which are next in order of priority. Several increments may be required before the cumulative total approximates or exceeds current service levels.

Performance measures are included in each analysis since they identify meaningful quantitative measures that assist in evaluating the effectiveness and efficiency of each increment. Measures may include workload (e.g., divisions served, number of work units, or tasks performed), performance (e.g., cost effectiveness, unit cost), or other pertinent data.

*Allocation of Critical Resources.* The increments developed by decision-unit managers provide the basic information from which higher-level managers allocate critical resources to high-priority activities.

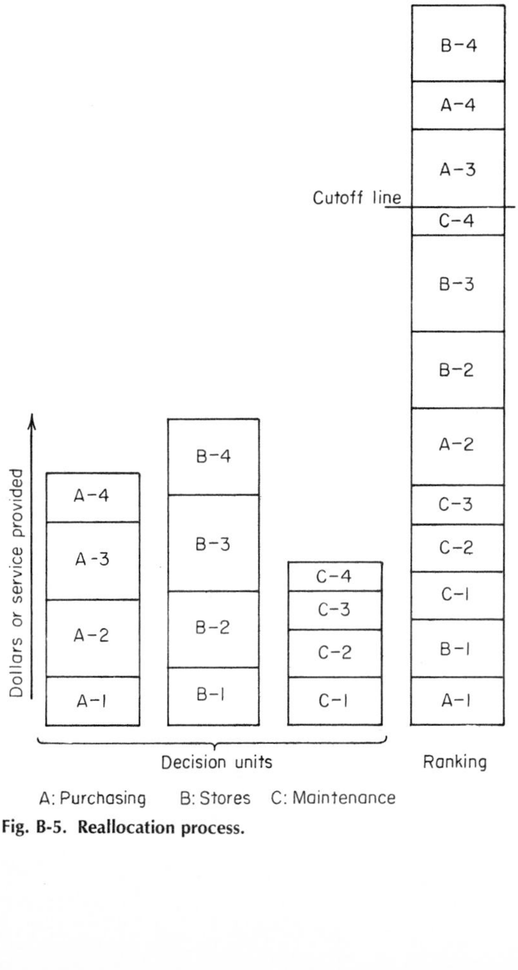

Figure B-5 shows how the reallocation process works. Suppose a corporate division is divided in three decision units: purchasing, A; stores, B; and maintenance, C. Further assume that each decision unit is broken down into four increments. After analysis is provided by the decision-unit manager, the division head ranks the 12 increments in priority order. The diagram shows that A-1, B-1, and C-1, the minimum increments, are ranked first. Then the manager ranks C-2 and C-3 before approving A-2 and B-2. If the current level of expenditure for each decision unit is between 2 and 3, it is obvious that the manager prefers funding a new increment for C before funding the current increments for A and B.

Furthermore, if the total budget available is represented by the cutoff line, the manager would have approved expenditures through increment C-4. Note that different amounts of cost and service were approved for each decision unit. This tool, therefore, can be used to allocate resources to the highest payoff activities.

How are the trade offs made? The ranking manager examines increments and analysis for each decision unit and makes the decision on the basis of the cost-benefit analysis by increment. Of course, the decision is made in consultation with the decision-unit managers.

The initial ranking of increments occurs at the organization level, where the analysis is developed to allow each manager to evaluate the relative importance of his or her own operations. Thus, the managers are able to make trade offs between discrete levels of services, optimizing the return on expenditures. This ranking is reviewed at higher organizational levels and used as a guide for merging those rankings.

*Preparation of Detailed Budgets.* Once the allocation decisions have been made, detailed budgets are prepared. The ranking table prepared by management provides the basis for this clerical function.

## PREPARING THE FINAL BUDGET

The sales and volume budgets, variable-cost budgets, and overhead budgets are the three major components of the total final budget. Top management must review each of the budgets, determine the effect on the organization, and make decisions leading to the preparation of the final budget.

Figure B-6 shows that top management first examines the three components separately. Reviews of the plans and budgets should be conducted for each individual component. Then the three should be

Fig. B-5. Reallocation process.

A: Purchasing   B: Stores   C: Maintenance

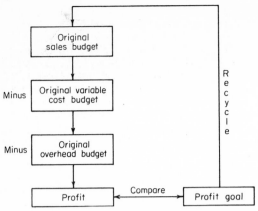

**Fig. B-6. Integrating budgets with profit goals.**

combined to determine the likely profit. A comparison is made with the profit goal for the organization.

Management then simulates various effects of sales levels. It is relatively simple to simulate variable-cost margins at different sales levels. (Computer simulation models are useful for this exercise.) Given a certain level of overhead, the break-even points and profit levels are developed. (*See* MARGINAL INCOME ANALYSIS.)

Once a good estimate of revenue minus variable costs is determined, overhead costs can be established. Figure B-7 indicates that overhead is not fixed. The zero-base analysis, for example, ends with a ranking of overhead activities. Management can adjust the funding line to level A, B, or C, as shown in Fig. B-7, to increase or decrease the profit levels.

*See also Accounting for Managerial Control;* BUDGETING, CAPITAL; CONTROL SYSTEMS, MANAGEMENT;

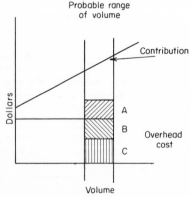

**Fig. B-7. Adjustable funding line.**

FORECASTING BUSINESS CONDITIONS; MARGINAL INCOME ANALYSIS; PLANNING, STRATEGIC MANAGERIAL; PROGRAM PLANNING AND IMPLEMENTATION; TAX MANAGEMENT, MANAGERIAL RESPONSIBILITY FOR FEDERAL INCOME TAX REPORTING; WORK MEASUREMENT; ZERO-BASE BUDGETING.

## REFERENCES

Anthony, Robert N., John Dearden, and Richard F. Vancil: *Management Control Systems,* Richard D. Irwin, Inc., Homewood, Ill., 1965, chap. 5.

Benninger, Lawrence J.: "Standard Costs," *Financial Executive's Handbook,* edited by Richard F. Vancil, Dow Jones-Irwin, Inc., Homewood, Ill., 1970.

Bump, Jack A.: "Profit Planning and Budgeting," *Financial Executive's Handbook,* edited by Richard F. Vancil, Dow Jones-Irwin, Inc., Homewood, Ill., 1970.

Bunge, Walter R.: "Budgeting," *Handbook of Modern Accounting,* edited by Sidney Davidson, McGraw-Hill Book Company, New York, 1970.

Ferrara, William L.: "Production Costs," *Handbook of Modern Accounting,* edited by Sidney Davidson, McGraw-Hill Book Company, New York, 1970.

Funari, Mario R.: "Control of Manufacturing Costs," *Financial Executive's Handbook,* edited by Richard F. Vancil, Dow Jones-Irwin, Inc., Homewood, Ill., 1970.

Hart, John N.: "Inventory Management and Control," *Financial Executive's Handbook,* edited by Richard F. Vancil, Dow Jones-Irwin, Inc., Homewood, Ill., 1970.

Helfert, Erich A.: "Responsibility Accounting," *Financial Executive's Handbook,* edited by Richard F. Vancil, Dow Jones-Irwin, Inc., Homewood, Ill., 1970.

Horngren, Charles T.: *Cost Accounting: A Managerial Emphasis,* Prentice-Hall, Inc., Englewood Cliffs, N.J., 1972, chaps. 5, 7–9.

Kotler, Philip: *Marketing Management,* Prentice-Hall, Inc., Englewood Cliffs, N.J., 1967.

Leininger, David L., and Ron C. Wong: *Zero-Based Budgeting in Garland, Texas,* 1975, Management Analysis Center, Inc., 1120 Nineteenth Street, NW, Suite 316, Washington, 20036.

Pyhrr, Peter A.: "Zero-Base Budgeting," *Harvard Business Review,* November–December 1970.

Pyhrr, Peter A.: *Zero-Base Budgeting,* John Wiley & Sons, Inc., New York, 1973, chap. 6.

Singleton, David W., Bruce A. Smith, and James R. Cleaveland: "Zero-Based Budgeting in Wilmington, Delaware," *Government Finance,* August 1976.

Stonich, Paul J.: "Formal Planning Pitfalls and How to Avoid Them," *Management Review,* June 1975.

Stonich, Paul J.: "Zero-Base Planning: A Management Tool," *Managerial Planning,* July–August 1976.

Stonich, Paul J., and Frederick W. Harvey: "The New Look for Budgeting: Zero-Base Planning," *Today's Manager,* May–June 1976.

Stonich, Paul J., and MAC, Inc.: *Zero-Base Planning and Budgeting: Improved Cost Control and Resource Allocation,* Dow Jones-Irwin, Inc., Homewood, Ill., June 1977.

Stonich, Paul J., and William H. Steeves: "Zero-Base Planning and Budgeting for Utilities," *Public Utilities Fortnightly*, September 1976.

PAUL J. STONICH, *MAC, Inc., Management Analysis Center*

**Budgets and budgeting**   (*See heading in Table of Contents for complete listing.*)

**Burden rate**   (*See* ACCOUNTING, COST ANALYSIS AND CONTROL.)

**Business climate analysis**   (*See* PRODUCT PLANNING AND DEVELOPMENT.)

**Business cycle**   (*See* FORECASTING BUSINESS CONDITIONS.)

**Business forms**   (*See* FORMS DESIGN AND CONTROL.)

**Business information system**   [*See* INFORMATION SYSTEMS, MANAGEMENT (MIS), APPLIED.]

**Business logistics**   (*See* LOGISTICS, BUSINESS.)

**Business plan, retailing**   (*See* RETAILING MANAGEMENT.)

**Business policy**   (*See* POLICY FORMULATION AND IMPLEMENTATION.)

**Business-we-are-in strategy**   (*See* PLANNING, PLANNED MANAGEMENT OF TURBULENT CHANGE.)

**Businesses**   (*See* OWNERSHIP, LEGAL FORMS OF.)

**Buying, forward**   (*See* PURCHASING MANAGEMENT.)

**Buying habits**   (*See* CONSUMER BEHAVIOR, MANAGERIAL RELEVANCE OF.)

**Buying-power index**   (*See* RETAILING MANAGEMENT.)

# C

**Cafeteria compensation plans** (*See* COMPENSATION, EMPLOYEE BENEFIT PLANS.)

**Candidate description** (*See* SEARCH AND RECRUITMENT, EXECUTIVE.)

**Capability, managerial** (*See* PLANNING, PLANNED MANAGEMENT OF TURBULENT CHANGE.)

**Capability profile, sales** (*See* SALES MANAGEMENT.)

**Capacity utilization** (*See* ECONOMIC MEASUREMENTS.)

**Capital, cost of** (*See* FINANCIAL MANAGEMENT.)

**Capital, working** (*See* FINANCIAL MANAGEMENT, CAPITAL STRUCTURE AND DIVIDEND POLICY.)

**Capital budgeting** (*See* BUDGETING, CAPITAL; BUDGETING, CAPITAL, SPECIAL PROBLEMS OF.)

**Capital expenditures** (*See* BUDGETING, CAPITAL.)

**Capital goods, procurement** (*See* PURCHASING MANAGEMENT.)

**Capital spending** (*See* ECONOMIC MEASUREMENTS.)

**Capital structure** (*See* FINANCIAL MANAGEMENT, CAPITAL STRUCTURE AND DIVIDEND POLICY.)

**Capitalism** (*See* ECONOMIC SYSTEMS.)

**Captive financing** (*See* FINANCIAL MANAGEMENT, SHORT-TERM, INTERMEDIATE, AND LONG-TERM FINANCING.)

**Career**  (*See* DEVELOPMENT AND TRAINING, CAREER PATH PLANNING FOR MANAGERS.)

**Career paths**  (*See* DEVELOPMENT AND TRAINING, CAREER PATH PLANNING FOR MANAGERS.)

**Career planning workshop**  (*See* DEVELOPMENT AND TRAINING, CAREER PATH PLANNING FOR MANAGERS.)

**Carriers, motor**  (*See* DISTRIBUTION, PHYSICAL.)

**Carry-back and carry-forward**  (*See* TAX MANAGEMENT, MANAGERIAL RESPONSIBILITY FOR FEDERAL INCOME TAX REPORTING.)

**Cash budgets**  (*See* FINANCIAL MANAGEMENT.)

**Cash distribution plans**  (*See* COMPENSATION, SPECIAL PLANS.)

**Cash flow management**  (*See* FINANCIAL MANAGEMENT, WORKING CAPITAL CONTROL.)

**Cash management**  (*See* FINANCIAL MANAGEMENT.)

**Cash payout**  (*See* FINANCIAL MANAGEMENT, CAPITAL STRUCTURE AND DIVIDEND POLICY.)

**Caveat emptor**  (*See* REAL ESTATE MANAGEMENT, CORPORATE.)

**Censor-taskmaster**  (*See* HEALTH, MENTAL.)

## Centralization and decentralization

*Centralization* is a gathering together of organizational elements. It shortens the span of management

124

(or control) and makes the organization deeper and more rigid. This added depth extends the channels of command and communication by increasing the number of organization levels between rank and file employees and top management. Centralization is characteristic of functional and line and staff organizations. Its particular advantages are that it (1) helps to strengthen managerial control and to improve the effectiveness of specialized staff and service functions, especially where the staff people report at very high levels and over the heads of most operating (marketing and production) divisions; (2) enables an organization to concentrate authority in the hands of a few relatively rare energetic, brilliant, and knowledgeable individuals; (3) facilitates coordination and unity in large, complex organizations; and (4) protects the confidentiality of organizational strategies and plans.

*Decentralization* is, in most ways, just the opposite of centralization. It broadens the span of control and loosens the ties between the organizations elements. Such organization structures are relatively flat with fewer levels between the top and the bottom. Communications between highest and lowest levels are more direct as a result. Decentralization is characteristic of organizations structured around independent product or service groups rather than around functions. Decentralization is often advantageous because it (1) forces a realistic, planned delegation of authority, which might otherwise occur only on paper in large organizations; (2) places organizational units closer to their markets and keeps them small enough to be managed effectively; (3) facilitates a more rapid response to changing environments; and (4) provides opportunity and motivation for a greater number of managers, thus building a larger reservoir of managerial talent.

Both centralization and decentralization have their favored applications. The choice depends upon the nature of the business, its products and market, its stage of development, and the managerial styles of those involved. An intensely competitive company, or one in its early stages of development, or a manufacturing company with only one product line are all likely to benefit from centralization. A company still in the hands of its original entrepreneur is unlikely to decentralize effectively. On the other hand, large, diversified, and mature companies tend to benefit from decentralization.

Many companies find themselves cycling over a period of decades between centralization and decentralization. As a centralized organization becomes rigid, stifling to its managers and poorly responsive to its environment, it may find itself pressed to loosen the degree of its controls so as to encourage initiative and reflexiveness. Over a period of years, however, the decentralized organization invites laxness of control and an unprofitable erosion of unity. Accordingly, its management (often a new management brought in to restore order and liquidity) may seek to tighten the reins and move toward greater centralization and control.

*See also* CONTROL SYSTEMS, MANAGEMENT; DELEGATION; ORGANIZATION ANALYSIS AND PLANNING; ORGANIZATION STRUCTURES AND CHARTING.

### REFERENCES

Chapple, Eliot, and Leonard R. Sayles: *The Measure of Management*, The Macmillan Company, New York, 1960.

Dale, Ernest, and L. F. Urwick: *Staff in Organization*, McGraw-Hill Book Company, New York, 1960.

Heflebower, Richard B.: "Observations of Decentralization in Large Enterprises," *The Journal of Industrial Economics*, Oxford, 1960.

Negandhi, A. R., and B. C. Reimann: "Correlates of Decentralization: Closed and Open System Perspectives," *Academy of Management Journal*, vol. 16, no. 4, 1973.

STAFF/BITTEL

**Centralization strategy** (*See* ORGANIZATION STRUCTURES AND CHARTING.)

**Centralized maintenance** (*See* MAINTENANCE MANAGEMENT.)

**Certainty** (*See* STATISTICAL ANALYSIS FOR MANAGEMENT.)

**Certainty and uncertainty** (*See* RISK ANALYSIS AND MANAGEMENT.)

**Certificate of competency (COC)** (*See* SMALL BUSINESS ADMINISTRATION.)

**Certification of managers** (*See* PROFESSIONALISM IN MANAGEMENT; SUPERVISORY MANAGEMENT.)

**Certified public accounting firms** (*See* AUDITING, FINANCIAL.)

**Chain store** (*See* MARKETING, CHANNELS OF DISTRIBUTION.)

**Chain stores retailing** (*See* RETAILING MANAGEMENT.)

**Chairman of the board** (*See* BOARDS OF DIRECTORS.)

**Change, strategic** (*See* PLANNING, PLANNED MANAGEMENT OF TURBULENT CHANGE.)

**Channels, communications** (*See* COMMUNICATIONS, ORGANIZATIONAL.)

**Channels of distribution** (*See* MARKETING, CHANNELS OF DISTRIBUTION.)

**Charts, organization** (*See* ORGANIZATION STRUCTURES AND CHARTING.)

**Chief executive officer** (*See* OFFICERS, CORPORATE.)

**Chief financial executive** (*See* OFFICERS, CORPORATE.)

**Choice and chance, areas of** (*See* STATISTICAL ANALYSIS FOR MANAGEMENT.)

**Chronological stabilization plans, insurance** (*See* RISK ANALYSIS AND MANAGEMENT.)

**Circulation factors, office** (*See* OFFICE SPACE PLANNING AND DESIGN.)

**Classical school** (*See* MANAGEMENT THEORY, SCIENCE, AND APPROACHES.)

## Classification of jobs  (*See* JOB EVALUATION.)

## Classifications of product markets  (*See* MARKETS, CLASSIFICATIONS AND MARKET ANALYSIS.)

## Clayton Act  (*See* GOVERNMENT REGULATIONS, FEDERAL REGULATION OF BUSINESS.)

## Coaching  (*See* DEVELOPMENT AND TRAINING, EMPLOYEE.)

# Codetermination and industrial democracy

Codetermination and industrial democracy are two examples of workers' management participative systems. Other terms used to describe such participative systems are workplace democracy, autonomous working groups, economic democracy, industrial community, cooperative systems, self-management, and self-government.

While codetermination specifically refers to the systems of workers' mangement participation in the Federal Republic of Germany, the other terms are not so specifically identified with any one country or with any particular method of participation; i.e., they are more generic. They are applied worldwide, such as in the Scandinavian countries (industrial democracy), in the United States (cooperatives, autonomous working groups, and workplace democracy), in Israel (cooperative systems and kibbutz and moshav movements), in Peru (industrial community and self-management), in Yugoslavia (self-management and self-government), and lately in Jamaica (the cooperative and self-management system).

The common denominator of all these systems is that the process of managing organizations is expected to be more democratic than in the typical hierarchical corporate system.

**Hierarchical versus Democratic Organizations**  In a hierarchical corporate system the distribution of power, authority, duty, and reward is hierarchical: the higher one ascends the organizational hierarchy, the greater is the authority, the power, the duty, and the reward. In a hierarchical system *management* stands for planning, organizing, controlling, directing, getting the job done through people, deciding, governing, dominating, and even manipulating. Management is a theory of how to make decisions *for* an organization and to secure compliance of the followers to the organizational goals selected by management. The success of management is then measured by the efficiency and effectiveness with which the plans are carried out.

In a democratic system, on the other hand, the distribution of authority, power, duty, and reward is shared; there are no exclusive prerogatives of management that exclude workers. The workers themselves or their elected representatives decide with management on, for example, production methods and goals, organizational changes, modernization, and salary scales. The role of managers is to recommend, present, convince, and influence. They make recommendations to decision-making bodies of the organization which are composed of workers and managers alike. The success of management is measured in terms which go beyond economic efficiency and effectiveness: the quality of life of the membership (in terms of art, education, and housing, for instance) and the growing capability of individuals in the organization to be responsible participants in decision making are taken into account.

These democratic systems are different from the participative systems of the human relations school and from collective bargaining. They are not dependent on the whims and style of a willing manager, as human relations theories propagate. The system has increased the legal managerial prerogatives of the workers. Democratic systems also differ from collective bargaining, which is based on adversary relationships between management and unionized workers. The aim of the participative systems described above is to encourage and nourish direct cooperation among the members of an organization.

**Degrees of Participation**  The different systems of worker-management cooperation differ in their scope of application of workers' participation. In autonomous work groups and workplace democracy the participative system is applied on the production line at the shift or plant level of the organization. Workers make decisions on how to organize their working environment (at Volvo in Sweden, for example) and in some cases elect their own supervisors. In industrial democracy (Norway and Sweden) and in codetermination (Germany), the scope is enlarged; workers are elected to be members of the board of directors and have voting rights.

*Profit Sharing.*  In addition to the sharing of tasks and the authority to decide, in some participative systems workers and managers share in the proceeds of their cooperative work, i.e., gains sharing. An example is the industrial community system of Peru where the workers, as a group, share in up to 14 percent of the profits of the company.

*Ownership.* Another scope of participation is in ownership of company assets. The Peruvian industrial community allows workers, as a group, to invest part, or all, of their 14 percent share of profits for incremental ownership of the company. In Israeli cooperatives, as in the transportation cooperative Egged, each worker has a share of ownership, which, if he or she wants to leave, can be sold to another qualified worker who is willing to join. The Yugoslav self-management system applies the social ownership concept where no one individual or one particular institution, such as the government, exclusively owns the production assets. All members of any organization thus have an equal right to enjoy the proceeds of working with those assets, and no absent owner can request any rental benefits.

*Legal-Political Aspects.* The systems further differ in scope of application to different organizations. While autonomous work groups and workplace democracy are usually limited experiments in a few chosen plants within a company, self-management in Yugoslavia is a legally required system in all organizations with 10 or more members in the profit and not-for-profit sectors. Also, the scope of application differs on the political-economic-social dimension. While industrial democracy focuses its participation mainly on the economic side of the enterprise and on some social variables as they relate to the technology of the production system in the organization, in an Israeli kibbutz the democratic organization is an all-encompassing socioeconomic-political entity; most members of a kibbutz share the same political convictions and participate fully in the planning of their social activities.

## EXAMPLE OF
## CODETERMINATION

Codetermination refers to a system of workers' participation in decision making as applied in the Federal Republic of Germany. The vehicles for participation are (1) works councils at the production-line level of the organization and (2) supervisory boards at the top of the organization hierarchy.

**Works Councils** According to the law, any company with more than five employees can have a works council if the employees wish to do so. All large, and most medium-sized, companies have works councils; about 25,000 were operating in 1976. The council is composed of workers' representatives which are elected separately by the blue- and white-collar workers. The workers serve for 3 years, and membership varies from 5 to 50. In large companies, each plant will have its own works council, which sends its representatives to the corporate-level works council. The candidates for election run in slates, which are mostly suggested by the blue- and white-collar unions respectively. Frequently, there are slates of nonunion employees.

*Rights of the Works Council.* The works councils have either information and consultative rights or joint decision-making rights, depending on the decision.

Works councils have the right to be informed or consulted about building new plants, purchasing technical equipment and machinery, adopting production methods, planning for personnel, hiring top and middle management, and extending or closing plants.

The works council has joint decision-making powers with management on labor relations issues, such as working time, vacation plans, wage administration, incentive system, hiring, firing, transfer of employees, safety rules, design of workplace, time and motion studies application, occupational training, grievance handling, and special compensation during mass layoffs.

**Supervisory Board** This is the organization vehicle for workers' participation at the top level of the organizational hierarchy, and as of May 1976, most companies in the Federal Republic of Germany with more than 2000 employees must have supervisory boards in addition to works councils. In 1976 there were about 650 companies to whom the law applied. The composition of the supervisory board differs in the coal, steel, and iron industry from the rest of the industry. In general, the white-collar and the blue-collar workers, middle management, and the stockholders have representatives on the supervisory board. A 50:50 representation between employees and stockholders is being sought.

The supervisory board determines and approves major organization decisions such as policies and plans concerning mergers, mass layoffs, modernization, major investments, and dividends to stockholders. Furthermore, it elects the executive committee that manages the company. The executive committee is composed of the president and vice-presidents of the company. No member of the supervisory board can be a member of the executive committee.

The employee representatives in the coal, steel, and iron industry have a right to veto the election of the labor director, who holds the title of vice-president, is a member of the executive committee, and is in charge of all aspects of personnel management, including bargaining with the unions on wages.

## ASSESSMENT

In the Federal Republic of Germany, codetermination has been in existence for about 20 years. By and large, the system has worked well. The elections to supervisory boards are usually coordinated with the unions, and most decisions on the board are made unanimously. Management usually discusses matters with employee representatives before presenting anything for a vote. Empirical research shows that employee representatives are concerned about the long-term survival of the company and neither profits nor the amount of dividends paid to stockholders nor modernization has suffered in a manner that can be attributed to the system.

*Layoffs.* When new technology is introduced, workers' representatives usually try to minimize layoffs. If layoffs are absolutely necessary, they attempt to secure substantial compensation to those laid off.

*Industrial Peace.* Some of the industrial peace in Federal Republic of Germany can be attributed to the continuously open channels of dialogue between workers and managers.

*Labor Goals.* The initiatives of labor representatives focus mainly on fringe benefits and working conditions; however, some initiatives concerning investments and restructuring of companies have been reported.

*Representation.* The participative system of codetermination is based on representation. As such, participation is limited to those elected. A "credibility gap" between the constituency and their elected representatives has been reported. This gap is less acute between the works council and the people on the production line since the works council deals with the day-to-day problems, in which there is constant interest. There is more of a gap between workers on the line and representatives on the supervisory boards. This observation might be attributed to the facts that (1) the topics discussed at the board level are of less immediate interest to workers; (2) secrecy is requested on board decisions and deliberations; and (3) workers' representatives on the board were elected indirectly (by the works councils and unions) and not directly by the people on the line.

## UNIVERSAL GOALS

In general, some of the goals of workers' management participative systems are the humanization of the workplace, increased productivity, and the democratization of society. It is claimed that participation humanizes work because it enables people to control their working environment; that is, they are not just human extensions of machines, employed to achieve employers' goals. Furthermore, it is claimed that participation will increase productivity, and politically, it is hypothesized that a person who participates in controlling his or her working environment will have a greater tendency to participate in political activity as well.

*Political Impact.* Workers' management participative systems have, by and large, achieved their humanistic, productivity, and political goals. In their political sphere, they have been even too successful, i.e., they have posed a threat to those in power, whether those in power were managers or politicians in one-party countries.

*Labor Expectations.* In Yugoslavia, self-management has created expectations in people for democratization of the political ideology and thus has threatened the only party in power. In the United States, workers' management systems have been usually limited to experimental sites and have not gone beyond the production-line level. By and large, management has not shown a deep desire to share its managerial prerogatives voluntarily.

*Ideological Support.* The workers' management participative systems, in order to work, need the socioideological convictions of the people where the system is applied. In Peru, these systems encountered serious difficulties since there was no sufficient political leverage to maintain the system for the necessary long run. Since such a system requires organizational and cultural change, like education, it needs a long range of application before yielding results. When economic conditions require short-range results and there is pressure for short-run productivity, those systems which require vast amounts of time for meetings and education of the participants are usually considered counterproductive and not deemed worth following by those in power.

*Educational Requirements.* The system requires retraining of (1) the workers to be able to participate and (2) the managers to be democratic leaders of their organizations rather than hierarchical autocrats. Many attempts to democratize organizations fail, either because there is no cultural or ideological support or because there is pressure for short-term economic results or because management did not care to know how to share information and power and subsequently make the democratic system work.

*Technology and Productivity.* Sociotechnical systems have been one of the approaches used to introduce and apply industrial democracy on the production line. Sociotechnical design analyzes the technological process of production, isolates the critical variables that need to be controlled, and searches social variables that can be introduced to control those variables. The sociotechnical design, for instance, will recommend group responsibility, team work, and rewards for a technology where the technological variables require high interdependency in performing the task.

*Limitations.* Its limitations are (1) the preoccupation with production technology, (2) insufficient attention given to the technology of decision making that top management has to do, and (3) the lack of political ideological support for it. Sociotechnical systems run the danger of becoming another fad that will end up only increasing productivity without changing the internal legal rights of workers to share the managerial prerogatives of the organization.

*See also* COMMITTEES; COMPENSATION, SPECIAL PLANS; EUROPE, MANAGEMENT IN WESTERN; INTERNATIONAL OPERATIONS AND MANAGEMENT IN MULTINATIONAL COMPANIES; OMSBUDSMAN; RUCKER PLAN; SCANLON PLAN.

### REFERENCES

Adizes, Ichak: *Industrial Democracy: Yugoslav Style*, The Free Press, New York, 1971.
Adizes, Ichak, and Elizabeth Mann Borgese, eds.: *Self-Management: New Dimensions to Democracy*, ABC-CLIO, Santa Barbara, Calif., 1975.
Agervold, Mogens: "Swedish Experiments in Industrial Democracy," in Louis E. Davis and Albert B. Cherns, eds., *The Quality of Working Life*, vol. II, The Free Press, New York, 1975.
Foy, Nancy, and Herman Gadow: "Worker Participation: Contrasts in Three Countries," *Harvard Business Review*, May–June 1976.
Garson, David: *On Democratic Administration and Socialist Self-Management; A Comparative Survey Emphasizing the Yugoslav Experience*, Sage Publications, Inc., Beverly Hills, Calif., 1974.
Garson, David, Gerry Hunnius, and John Case (eds.): *Workers' Control: A Reader on Labor and Social Change*, Random House, Inc., New York, 1973.
Hartmann, H.: "Co-Determination in Western Germany," *Industrial Relations*, vol. 9, no. 2, February 1970.
"Humanization of the Workplace: The Swedish Experience," *Proceedings of the Seminar on the Quality of Working Life*, Oct. 8, 1974, Institute of Industrial Relations of the University of California, Los Angeles.
Pateman, Carol: *Participation and Democratic Theory*, Cambridge University Press, London, 1970.
Sussman, Gerald I.: *Autonomy of Work*, Frederick A. Praeger, Inc., New York, 1976.

ICHAK ADIZES, *University of California, Los Angeles*

## Coding of parts (*See* MATERIALS MANAGEMENT.)

## Coffee break (*See* COMPENSATION, EMPLOYEE BENEFIT PLANS.)

## Collaboration (*See* INTERPERSONAL RELATIONSHIPS.)

## Colleague management (*See* ORGANIZATION STRUCTURES AND CHARTING.)

## Collection ratio, credit (*See* CREDIT MANAGEMENT.)

## Collective bargaining (*See* LABOR LEGISLATION; LABOR UNIONS.)

## College and university administration

While a college or university surely cannot be considered in the same manner as a large corporation, there can be no doubt that higher education in this country today is indeed a business—a very big business.

Statistics concerning higher education in this country are staggering. In the fall of 1976, there were some 11.7 million full-time and part-time students enrolled in the nation's 3000 colleges and universities. The number of students represented some 5.5 percent of the entire population of the United States. In other words, about 1 person in each 18 was enrolled as a college student.

Total enrollment increased in 1976 some 4.5 percent over the previous year, equal to an additional half-million students. The increase in 1976 had been preceded the year before by a 9.4 percent increase, the sharpest such jump since the mid 1960s when the post–World War II "Baby Boom" hit the campus.

Budgetary figures also clearly point out the magnitude—and big business characteristics—of higher education. For the school year 1973–1974, higher education in America had expenditures totaling some $31 billion. In the entire world, only one corporation, Exxon Corporation, had revenues exceeding the expenditures of higher education. The total spent by higher education is roughly equal to the annual sales of General Motors Corporation or Royal Dutch Shell.

About half the total expenditures in higher education went directly to instructional programs. Other major expenditures went, however, into areas such as plant operation ($2.5 billion); operation of dormitories, dining facilities, etc. ($3.6 billion); and extension and public service programs ($742 million). Massive expenditures also went into research on college campuses, which continued to be the chief spawning ground for scientific breakthroughs and innovative approaches to problems. More than $3.5 billion was spent in sponsored research during 1973–1974, in addition to several billion dollars within regular academic programs.

On a balance sheet, higher education certainly resembles a gargantuan corporation, and to varying degrees, each of the nation's institutions of higher learning is similar to a business or corporation.

But higher education poses special problems of management—problems that are unlike those faced on the corporate level. Foremost among these is the fact that each college and university has a broad-based constituency, one composed of many distinct groups with each viewing the institution in a different light. The job of managing the institution then is to maintain a proper balance among each of these groups and to attempt to satisfy each group.

**Constituent Relations** The major constituent groups that each college or university must serve are alumni, students, faculty, and the general public, including legislators for the state-supported institutions.

Each of these groups views the institution through glasses of varying tints. Each has its own distinct idea on how the institution should be run,

on what it should be doing, and what it should not be doing. Alumni, for example, tend to view the institution the way it was "back then." As a rule, they are reluctant to accept change or to fully support any move that would alter the institution from the way it was in their undergraduate days. Most frequently, students represent the opposite end of the spectrum. They carry a philosophy advocating change that would fulfill their aims of the moment. In terms of change, faculty generally are split, with younger faculty members resembling students in seeking change and older faculty members paralleling alumni concerns about change. Faculty members are united, however, in their desire to carry out their jobs with as little interference as possible from the management level. Their concern is for total academic freedom in their classrooms without influences from the outside. As would be expected, concerns of the general public run the widest possible range and all must be considered. These range from the strictly parochial concerns of the college's neighbors over parking regulations to the broader concerns of state legislators over accountability for expenditure of public funds.

From this complexity of desires, the college administrator has a job which is simple in description but highly difficult in practice: he or she must balance the objectives of all these diverse groups into a common direction for the institution. In simplest terms, the best solution is a utilitarian one, as expressed by John Stuart Mill: the greatest happiness for the greatest number of people. In practice, however, equal weight cannot possibly be given strictly on the basis of numbers. Additional importance must be assigned to the feelings of students and faculty in particular, for it is they who constitute the living fiber of the institution.

For the purpose of determining the mission and role of the institution and for carrying out the functions of the institution, a precise plan must be adopted.

**Plan Development** The first, and by far the most important, portion of the plan should deal with the institution's purpose. Purposes of different institutions of higher learning vary widely. Is the institution a major university with a multitude of undergraduate and graduate programs? Is it a small, single-purpose college? Is it primarily for lower-level undergraduate work, upper-level undergraduate work, or graduate work? Is its appeal mainly to urban students? Is it a residential campus? All these questions, and many more, must be answered before the institution's true purpose can be ascertained. And not only does the purpose of today need to be determined, but the purposes of 10, 20, and 30 years in the future must also be projected.

One method of answering the questions of purpose and objectives is through action of a blue-ribbon committee composed of representatives of all constituent groups: alumni, students, faculty, public, and legislators.

Once the plan is developed, it is essential that it be fully understood by all members of the college or university community. It must be asserted and reasserted. Of particular importance is that the institution's board of trustees must be in full support of the plan and completely understand the plan and its purposes.

Carrying out the plan, however, depends not on the institution's constituent groups but on its administrators. The next important job of the college chief executive is similar to that of his or her corporate colleagues: to select able lieutenants. It is crucial for the president of the institution to have efficient and conscientious assistants in carrying out the institution's plan.

**Organization Development** First attention in the organization of the college or university should go to the budget and personnel areas. Staff members in these areas must have the expertise to handle problems and establish budgets, as they would were they employed by industry. However, they must also have the ability to realize that while institutions of higher learning must be operated in a businesslike manner, they have special characteristics that business firms do not have. Budget and personnel staff members must recognize these differences and keep in mind that the primary mission of an institution of higher learning is the teaching of young men and women.

Another vital prerequisite for good college management is for the president to have a solid cadre of experienced and knowledgeable vice-presidents. Each distinct area of the college or university's operation should be headed by a divisional head or vice-president. The number of divisions and vice-presidents will, of course, vary greatly, depending upon the size of the institution. A larger institution, for example, might have vice-presidents in academic, business, administrative, public service, student service, and development areas as well as in any major specialized area such as medicine. The vice-presidents must be given sufficient authority and latitude to handle the day-to-day decisions in their respective areas, and they should meet frequently with the president to determine answers to broader questions.

Above all, there must be active and easily accessible means of communication between the president and the vice-presidents and among the vice-presidents themselves. The entire organization system could easily collapse if vice-president A did not know which areas were being handled by vice-president B. The president cannot expect—and should not want—complete agreement among all the vice-presidents on all matters. He or she should, however, demand full and frank input from all key aides on every pressing matter.

In many institutions of higher education, the computer, personnel, budgeting, auditing, and institutional research are generally placed under a vice-president who has line responsibility in the organization. These functions can be carried out more effectively if they are under a division head or a vice-president who reports directly to the president and has staff responsibility in the organization.

By and large, these functions are being performed to assist the other vice-presidents in planning for resource utilization within the institution. The president should be directly involved in this type of planning. The allocation of resources to accomplish the mission of the institution is paramount in the responsibilities of the president. After the plans are made and the budget is established, the vice-presidents responsible for operating divisions can carry out the mission of the institution within the resources allocated by the president's budget advisers. A division of administrative services and systems development enables the president to stay involved in the important responsibility of planning and resource allocation, but gives the vice-presidents the responsibility for the day in and day out conduct of the affairs of the institution. This administrative structure allows the president to have input from the various constituents of the campus in developing the mission and objectives of the institution and in allocating the resources to achieve these objectives.

**Unique Aspects** Even if all the institution's objectives are set forth clearly and the organization is established in flawless fashion, there are unique difficulties of management which must be faced in higher education.

As mentioned before, there is a general resistance to change, particularly among alumni and older faculty members. But when change is indicated, change must take place. And it is the singular role of the institution's chief executive officer to effect this change.

An important ingredient in a college or university environment is trust among the different constituencies. The faculty, the students, the alumni, and the public who trust each other will be able to carry through on projects more effectively than if there is a feeling of anxiety, uncertainty, and fear.

In order to establish an environment where there is mutual trust, the president must believe he or she is dealing with intelligent and competent individuals who can make a contribution to the institution, not only in handling classroom instruction and research but also in helping to delineate and to achieve the purpose and the mission of the institution. There must be a formal structure for the ideas of faculty and students to emerge in the institution. It is essential that faculty and student organizations exist and that these organizations have a degree of autonomy in their operations. It is by having these organizations that the faculty and students can feel that they are making an input into the direction and operation of the institution. Their input not only contributes to a feeling of involvement but also can be very beneficial to the president and the vice-presidents of the institution because of the insight which faculty and students have in regard to program development.

In addition to the formal organization for the faculty and students, an institution can also combine representatives from these two groups with administrators and will benefit from the combined efforts of the three groups involved in the operation of the institution. The president, then, has the full benefit of views on the college from various sections of the campus, and the various sections of the campus will feel that they have been heard in regard to their interest in the institution. There should be a faculty senate and a student senate, and these organizations should act on matters of concern to them. In addition, there should be a body that brings representatives from these two groups into contact with administrators for discussion of broader issues of the campus. This provides full involvement of all the groups and helps to create an environment that is responsive to change.

**Curriculum Development**  At the core of the success of the college is the curriculum. The curriculum of a college or university must reflect the needs of society in given areas; however, there is a time lag problem. The students of today must meet the needs of a society that is 1 to 4 years in the future. Therefore, it is the role of the institution not only to recognize society's needs of today but also to forecast correctly the needs of the future. The curriculum must be geared to fill future voids in professional and vocational markets. One way of tackling this problem is to establish a department which deals with the future society and the curriculum needed to accommodate that society, as well as the scholarly and professional talents needed by faculty members for the new curriculum. The institution can deal with the instructional changes that will come about in the future if it involves the faculty and students in describing the curriculum of the future. It can also provide the resources and assistance whereby faculty members can make changes in their own scholarly efforts in order to accommodate the new instructional requirements.

**Commitment and Change**  Colleges and universities face severe problems in the future—declining enrollments and a shortage of resources. These problems can be more easily managed if there is a feeling on the campus that all the constituents are committed to the institution and its mission. In the absence of an orderly process for change, the pressures of declining enrollment and resources will engender fear and hostility. The campus which does not overcome these problems becomes less effective in terms of its pursuit of scholarship, freedom, and the expansion of learning. It is this matter that is the most important to effective management of an institution—recognizing the need to deal with change and to involve faculty and students in the process of change. After all, the institution of higher education is essentially one which deals with the human factor.

*See also* NOT-FOR-PROFIT ORGANIZATIONS, MANAGEMENT OF; ORGANIZATION ANALYSIS AND PLANNING; PROGRAM PLANNING AND IMPLEMENTATION; PUBLIC ADMINISTRATION.

## REFERENCES

Carnegie Commission on Higher Education Reports, McGraw-Hill Book Company, New York, 1968–1973.

Hughes, John F., and Olive Mills: *Formulating Policy in Post-secondary Education*, American Council on Education, Washington, 1975.

Meeth, L. Richard: *Quality Education for Less Money*, Jossey-Bass Inc., Pubs., San Francisco, 1974.

Schmuck, Richard A., and Matthew B. Miles: *Organization Development in Schools*, National Press Books, Palo Alto, Calif., 1973.

Sikes, Walter W., Lawrence E. Schlesinger, and Charles N. Seashore: *Renewing Higher Education from Within*, Jossey-Bass Inc., Pubs., San Francisco, 1974.

Simons, Joseph H.: *Problems of the American University*, The Christopher Publishing House, Boston, 1967.

Taylor, Harold: *How to Change Colleges*, Holt, Rinehart and Winston, Inc., New York, 1971.

Wilson, Logan, and Olive Mills: *Universal Higher Education*, American Council on Education, Washington, 1972.

RONALD E. CARRIER, *James Madison University*

**Commercial code, uniform**  (*See* GOVERNMENT REGULATIONS; UNIFORM COMMERCIAL CODE.)

**Commercial paper**  (*See* FINANCIAL MANAGEMENT, SHORT-TERM, INTERMEDIATE, AND LONG-TERM FINANCING; GOVERNMENT REGULATIONS, BUSINESS LAW.)

**Commission plans, sales**  (*See* COMPENSATION, SALES.)

**Commitment, management**  [*See* OBJECTIVES, MANAGEMENT BY (MBO).]

**Committee, organization-based**  (*See* COMMITTEES.)

**Committee, patent**  (*See* PRODUCT PLANNING AND DEVELOPMENT.)

**Committee, permanent**  (*See* COMMITTEES.)

**Committee, temporary (ad hoc)**  (*See* COMMITTEES.)

## Committees

The use of committees is widespread in all organizations. In some, permanent committees are established, but temporary committees of various types are the most numerous.

Deploring or disparaging committees is fashionable, both because they entail an extra burden for their members and because they are often poorly directed and hence ineffectual. Properly managed, however, committees are an effective way of coping with special tasks and problems, particularly of the kind that cut across more than one organizational unit.

### ADVANTAGES

Committees are useful for directly working on problems where integration and coordination are required for better linkages between otherwise separate units. If left to their own devices, the individual units would have to rely on a weaker strategy—that of cooperation—or on the coercive coordinating decision of a higher manager.

The most outstanding advantage is that committees bring together the special human capabilities that each problem or activity area requires.

Another advantage is that a committee can focus intensely on a problem area. It can concentrate its efforts in a shorter time span. Decisions needing quick action can be sped up. By contrast, problems that continue over long periods of time can be kept under constant review. Thus committees provide flexibility for meeting a wide range of needs.

A further benefit occurs for the individual members themselves. It provides a means of involvement and participation. Members learn skills needed for working with other people in a less structured way, removed, usually, from direct boss-subordinate roles. Both written and oral communication skills can be developed through practice and observation. Members often learn interpersonal and group skills and acquire technical insight and practice not possible to them in their regular jobs.

### DISADVANTAGES

Most of the possible disadvantages stem from inept handling of the committee's deliberations or problems in the way a committee is set up. Such drawbacks may include an excessive amount of time spent to complete the work, a failure of communications among members, and the possibility that a committee will prevent or delay action rather than accelerate it. Committees may be unable to accomplish worthwhile results. Such difficulties add unnecessarily to an organization's costs.

### ROLES AND TYPES OF COMMITTEES

*Permanent Committees.* These include standing committees and committees integrated into the organization's basic structure. Standing committees may be at any level, and they deal with problems that continue to exist over time. The safety committee in an organization is a good example.

*Organization-Based Committees.* These are permanent committees usually consisting of high-level officers of the corporation and continuing over substantial periods of time. The executive committee of the board of directors is an example. Since the board may meet only quarterly, the day-to-day policy actions may be entrusted to an executive committee. Another common type is the finance committee, given the responsibility for long-range financial planning and the financial security of the enterprise. The board of directors of a corporation also functions much like a permanent organization committee.

Voluntary associations make wide use of permanent committees, which include advisory or administrative groups. The conceptual difference between committees, boards, councils, and advisory groups is often unclear.

*Temporary Committees.* These committees provide maximum flexibility and adaption to changing needs. Most organizations employ an enormous variety of them. They are also called ad hoc committees.

The roles and tasks of such committees should be specifically stated in an initial written charge to the committees. The charge details the purposes, aims, or intended uses of the work. Among the common tasks are (1) investigating problem areas; (2) making recommendations to managers or action units; (3) planning new activities or programs; (4) doing research to support new plans, policies, or programs; and (5) evaluating or auditing practices, programs, or procedures. A terminal date is usually indicated, so that a temporary committee knows when it should be disbanded. A moderator may be appointed or elected from the group by committee members.

### SETTING UP COMMITTEES

It is important to provide permanent, standing, or ad hoc committees with a specific, clearly written charge which gives the scope and purpose of their work. The creating authority should establish the committee's authority and designate the individual or group to which it reports or refers its results. A target date of completion is important for ad hoc committees.

The selection of members is a key element. The criteria include the capabilities of individuals, the specific interests or constituencies of each member, the balance of power resulting from the association of group members, and the amount of the members' time to be required.

The committee should make sure its tasks, goals, and authority are understood by members. A mini-

mum structure is achieved by electing or appointing a moderator. Subcommittees may be needed to divide the work into related parts. Meeting schedules should be worked out.

Chairing a committee requires skill in conference leading, group discussion, and human relations. Special training in small-group leadership may be given to those who frequently are chosen to chair committees.

*See also* BOARDS OF DIRECTORS; INTERPERSONAL RELATIONSHIPS; MANAGEMENT, DEFINITIONS OF; MANAGER, DEFINITIONS OF; OFFICERS, CORPORATE; ORGANIZATION STRUCTURES AND CHARTING; PROJECT AND TASK FORCE MANAGEMENT.

### REFERENCES

Davis, Keith: *Human Behavior at Work,* 4th ed., McGraw-Hill Book Company, New York, 1972.

Miner, John B.: *The Management Process: Theory, Research, and Practice,* The Macmillan Company, New York, 1973.

Redfield, Charles E.: *Communication in Management,* rev. ed., The University of Chicago Press, Chicago, 1969.

Steiner, George A., and William G. Ryan: *Industrial Project Management,* The Macmillan Company, New York, 1968.

Trewatha, Robert L., and M. Gene Newport: *Management: Functions and Behavior,* Business Publications, Inc., Dallas, 1976.

DALTON E. MCFARLAND, *University of Alabama in Birmingham*

## Committees, plant safety (*See* SAFETY AND HEALTH MANAGEMENT, EMPLOYEE.)

## Common Market (European Economic Community) (*See* INTERNATIONAL TRADE.)

## Commodity markets

Commodity markets are exchanges for the sale and purchase of commodities (raw materials, such as grain and metals) and for trading in futures contracts. Commodity exchanges exist in a number of cities in the United States, and several cities have more than one exchange, each handling different commodities.

*See also* MARKETS, SECURITIES.

### REFERENCES

Arthur, Henry B.: *Commodity Futures as a Business Management Tool,* Division of Research, Graduate School of

Business·Administration, Harvard University, Boston, Mass., 1971, 392 pp.

"Hot to Trade in Commodities," Personal Business Supplement, *Business Week*, Sept. 20, 1976, pp. 129–131, 133, 136, 138.

Munn, Glenn G.: *Encyclopedia of Banking and Finance*, 7th ed., rev. and enl. by F. L. Garcia, Bankers Publishing Company, Boston, Mass., 1973, pp. 208–209.

STAFF/SMITH

# Communications, advertising (*See* ADVERTISING CONCEPTS.

# Communications, employee

Employee communications can be described as the exchange of information and attitudes within an organization. In fact, communications are the very essence of organization. All organizations communicate effectively to some degree or they would not exist.

While employee communications are the responsibility of the individual manager, the manager's work may be supplemented through specialized services offered by a staff employee communications department. It may be charged with disseminating mainstream corporate information through various media, maintaining channels for more effective listening to staff concerns, and offering communications advice and counsel to organizational units.

## COMMUNICATIONS CHANNELS AND BARRIERS

The manager's objective is to plan, organize, and control flows of information within an organization so that the organization will function more effectively. Communications encourage the effective use and coordination of human resources. More effective communications—a better exchange of ideas, feelings, and attitudes for the organization's benefit—can improve work quality and productivity.

For the communications activity to be successful, it must take into account the different directions information flows within an organization. Each direction poses different problems and possibilities.

**Downward Communications** Most exchanges of information within an organization move from the top downward, through face-to-face transactions and written materials. An overreliance on this aspect of communications can impair an organization's

effectiveness, since communications often breaks down the farther a message gets from its source.

Downward communications most often serve two purposes: (1) informing employees of their job responsibilities and of their importance within the total organizational structure and (2) enlisting the understanding and support of employees about management objectives.

Barriers to downward communications often hinge on manager-subordinate relationships. The person responsible for communicating downward may believe that the subordinate has no right to certain information. The employee may fail to understand the message or may not listen well. Employees often get information that is irrelevant to their needs (called *information overload*) and do not get information that they do need (called *underload*). As organizations grow in size and geographic scope, message distribution practices often break down, and information is not received in time to be useful. So a message "sent" is not necessarily a message "received."

Managers sometimes do not appreciate that the person on the receiving end has the ultimate power to ignore or distort a message that does not meet his or her immediate needs. Consciously or unconsciously, a "receiver" may block an intended message for various reasons. An employee who distrusts management, for example, is not inclined to believe what management says.

The completeness, candor, and credibility of management messages have concerned younger employees particularly. Better educated, more mobile, and with higher expectations than older generations, the "under 30s" often demand more openness and sharing of information by senior managers and supervisors.

When communicating downward, there are two points to remember:

1. Messages that consider the interests of the person receiving them as well as the sender's have the best chance of getting through.

2. If told the reasoning behind a management decision or action, employees are more likely to accept and support it.

**Upward Communications** As the term implies, *upward communications* describe a flow of information from bottom up—from subordinate to supervisor and, when appropriate, up the line to management. The most important person in upward communications is the first-line supervisor, management's representative to the largest number of employees. Ideally, information should pass freely from subordinates to supervisors and on up the chain of command so that management gets the feedback needed to evaluate results and initiate improvements.

In practice, upward communications along formal lines of organization are often haphazard and unreliable. While good news tends to filter upward fairly easily, bad news moves slowly and often gets blocked altogether or is never communicated at all. This can have costly consequences for the organization. If management, at any level, is unaware of an impending crisis, it cannot prepare to meet it.

Obstacles to upward communications are most common when there is a climate of mistrust or apathy in the organization. If employees feel management is not interested in their ideas, they will not offer them. If they think that dissent or criticism is not tolerated in their unit or organization, they will not openly express their opinions.

Without feedback, i.e., a two-way exchange of information, most managers will overrate the effectiveness of their communications. Managers are often too removed from work and relationships at lower levels of the organization to observe directly the problems, ill will, and wasted resources that can result from poor communication. Consequently, they may often be unaware of the relationship between communication and such factors as operating effectiveness, morale, and turnover.

Accurate feedback allows managers to make objective and realistic evaluations. Problems can be detected and solved earlier.

**Horizontal Communications**  The flow of information among peers at equal levels in the organization is referred to as *horizontal communications*. While much of the horizontal communications process takes place in one-to-one interactions, it often takes the form of intradepartmental meetings or of committees made up of representatives from a number of departments.

One obstacle to horizontal communications can be the conflicting interests and objectives of those involved. Another is the organizational structure itself, since organizations are designed for communicating along vertical lines, i.e., downward and upward, rather than horizontal ones. Organizations that do not overcome this shortcoming through interlocking small-group structures suffer from duplicated efforts, poor use of resources, and lack of coordination.

Conventional meeting structures can also discourage full participation of group members, creativity in problem solving, and the effective use of members' time.

## A SYSTEMATIC APPROACH

Perhaps the major obstacle to more effective employee communications is the absence of a systematic approach that incorporates senior management support, communications objectives, adequate budget and staff monitoring, and specific communications responsibilities and resources at every level of the organization.

A systematic approach to employee communications can be visualized as a circle divided into four sections: evaluation, objectives and strategies, budget, and implementation.

At the top of the circle is evaluation, the starting line for establishing a communications system or subsystem. This is the phase for gathering information about existing practices and problems. Tools commonly used here are surveys of employee and management attitudes toward employee communications, group panels, surveys of distribution practices, and task forces.

Next come objectives and strategies, where information gathered during the evaluation phase is used to develop specific improvement objectives and concrete ways of attaining them.

This, in turn, leads to financial considerations, which pose two questions: (1) How much will the proposed improvements cost? (2) What can be afforded in money and human resources?

After the budget comes implementation, although this does not signal an end to the systematic process. Following the circle, the focus quickly returns to evaluation. Are the objectives that were set earlier still meaningful? Is the strategy working? Has the environment for communications changed? No communications effort, however sophisticated, can be regarded as finished.

The principles and approach outlined here can be applied to a wide variety of situations. They can be used to build the framework for a corporate-wide communications program embracing thousands of people or to solve specific communications problems within a small company or department.

## CASE STUDY

To illustrate these principles in action, consider their application within a hospital.

*Evaluation.* Through a survey, the hospital was made aware of accumulating grievances affecting employee morale.

*Objectives.* It therefore became evident that a

method was needed to bring specific grievances to management's attention quickly so they could be resolved.

*Strategy*. An Employee Communications Committee was formed, consisting of nonsupervisory employees from various departments. Its specific objective was to propose questions that might be answered in the hospital's monthly publication.

*Implementation*. Several meetings were held during a 3-week period. Guests from various departments were invited to answer questions from committee members. Typical questions involved the grievance procedure, merit ratings, unpaid overtime, shift problems, and current methods of communicating with staff. The questions revealed that many hospital policies and procedures were not understood and that current methods of communicating with staff were unsatisfactory. One suggestion led to a new column in each issue of the "house" publication, in which the administrator explained hospital plans, interesting developments, and employee benefits.

The assistant administrator held a series of meetings for *all* employees. Questions already raised were answered, and discussions were held about action that could not be taken immediately. New questions were raised in a two-way exchange with participants.

In a memorandum to his superior, the assistant administrator summarized and analyzed employee questions and complaints. He included a timetable for action on various matters. This was forwarded to the committee.

In a separate meeting, supervisors were told that hospital policies and procedures had been widely misunderstood and were themselves given a quiz to test their knowledge of these policies and procedures. When the results showed misunderstanding among the supervisory group, policies were again explained to them. During the question period, administration agreed to reconsider some policies.

These suggestions were communicated to the hospital's personnel policies committee and to the administrator for review.

Department heads now conduct follow-up discussions with all their supervisors to make certain that policies have been understood and can be explained clearly to employees. Before a performance appraisal, each subordinate is given a multiple-choice quiz about employee benefits. The subordinate and his or her superior then discuss all the questions which the employee answered incorrectly. The Employee Communications Committee now meets once a month to provide questions, news, and employee reactions for the monthly magazine.

## NEW TECHNIQUES AND MEDIA

Professional communicators and managers can draw upon a broad range of communications principles and techniques that go far beyond the "house organs" of former years. Here are some that have gained acceptance in recent years.

**Task Forces** A task force is a temporary project team, usually appointed by a senior officer and often made up of line and staff officers representing various areas of the organization. Some organizations have used them to overhaul existing communications or to lay the foundation for new ones.

This approach offers several advantages. The task force's credibility is high because it does not have a vested interest in the outcome. Its existence can demonstrate senior management's commitment to communications. Members serving on the task force gain valuable exposure to communications problems and possibilities. As a result they tend to support communications specialists during the implementation phase.

**"Speak-Up" Programs** To "unblock" upward communications to management and to offer a "safety valve" to employees with grievances, many organizations have created special channels through which employees can "by-pass" their supervisors and send questions and complaints directly to management. Employees direct their comments to a coordinator or ombudsman who will protect their identity. Ideally, the responses to questions will be signed by members of senior management. To be successful, the procedure must guarantee the anonymity of those employees who use it. The single, most important ingredient for such a program's success is the support of senior management and the candor and completeness of the answers.

**Training in Interpersonal Relations** A large percentage of communications problems are interpersonal, and a manager's style of communicating with subordinates often reflects basic assumptions about people and the psychological needs of others. Sometimes these assumptions are based on old information that is no longer appropriate in an organizational environment which requires the cooperation of all its members.

For these reasons, the psychological theories of Maslow, McGregor, and Herzberg are taught in communications training sessions. The theory of transactional analysis, as developed by Eric Berne, is being widely used by corporations to develop interpersonal relationships that will help to achieve company objectives.

**Meeting-Process Management** Some organizations find that they can enhance creativity, group participation, and accomplishment of objectives through a different approach to meetings. A specially trained meeting facilitator does not assume the role of a chairperson, i.e., someone who contributes and makes decisions. Instead, the facilitator is concerned only with *how* the meeting is conducted.

The facilitator's tools are a knowledge of group dynamics and various problem-solving tools. These may range from brainstorming to force-field analysis and are used when appropriate in the various stages involved in problem solving.

**New Technology** Technology is rapidly expanding the horizons of organizational communications and is helping to solve the problems of timeliness and communications overload. Some companies are turning to computer-based document distribution systems which can channel information only to those specific groups of employees who need it. To reduce overload, it is also possible to provide information "on call" through cathode-ray terminals (CRTs) linked to computerized libraries that supply citations and abstracts about various subjects.

In addition, closed-circuit and video-cassette television equipment is now supplementing the printed page in many organizations. This offers communicators a new medium that is credible and entertaining and particularly attractive to younger employees.

**Communications Research** With modern sampling methods, data about the effectiveness of communications can be derived from a small percentage of the total employee group. Specialized surveys can be used to pretest proposed articles in employee publications as well as proposed communications services. This data may be collected by communications departments, marketing research groups, or outside consultants.

Some organizations are using *network analysis* to discover where people go to get information. Researchers study actual interpersonal communications patterns within an organization and how they compare with the communications relationships that would be expected if the formal table of organization were followed. These studies may provide clues to reorganization and new policies that would better satisfy actual information needs.

*See also* ATTITUDE SURVEYS; COMMUNICATIONS, ORGANIZATIONAL; CONFERENCE LEADERSHIP; DEVELOP-MENT AND TRAINING, EMPLOYEE; HUMAN RESOURCES (WORK FORCE) PLANNING; MOTIVATION IN ORGANIZATIONS; PERSONNEL ADMINISTRATION.

### REFERENCES
Carter, Robert M.: *Communication in Organizations: An Annotated Bibliography and Sourcebook*, Gale Research Company, Detroit, 1972.

Doyle, Michael, and David Strauss: *How to Make Meetings Work: The Interaction Method*, Wyden Books, New York, 1976.

Farace, Richard V., Peter R. Monge, and Hamish M. Russell, *Communicating and Organizing*, Addison-Wesley Publishing Company, Inc., Reading, Mass., 1977.

Gildea, Joyce, and Peter Haas (eds): *Case Studies in Organizational Communication*, Industrial Communication Council, P.O. Box 3970, Grand Central Post Office, New York, N.Y. 10017.

Jongeward, Dorothy, et al.: *Everybody Wins: Transactional Analysis Applied to Organizations*, rev. ed., Addison-Wesley Publishing Company, Inc., Reading, Mass., 1976.

Koehler, J. W., K. W. E. Anatol, and R. L. Applebaum: *Organizational Communication: Behavioral Perspectives*, Holt, Rinehart and Winston, Inc., New York, 1976.

Wendlinger, Robert M.: "Using a Task Force to Improve Employee Communications: Bank of America's Approach," *Management Review*, August 1975, pp. 25–30.

ROBERT M. WENDLINGER, *Bank of America*


# Communications, internal and external (See heading in Table of Contents for complete listing.)


# Communications, nonverbal

Nonverbal communications are probably the oldest human communications system. It has many facets: acting, art, communicating with the deaf, zoology, anthropology, psychology, psychiatry, linguistics, general semantics, etc. The study of nonverbal communications has also been given many names: gestures, kinesics, kinetics, body movements, body language, and pantomime.

Current theory on how nonverbal communication takes place emphasizes empathy. The viewer of a nonverbal communication or gesture imagines being in the position of the person observed, remembers how he or she felt in a similar situation, attributes personal reactions to the other person, and responds accordingly. This is not done consciously. It comes naturally; for the first two years of life, children communicate with their mothers in largely nonverbal ways.

Nonverbal communications are "evanescent," unlike spoken words, which can be remembered more easily and can be written down. In describing ballet, the quintessential example of gestures as a fine art, one can rely only on relatively crude notations to recreate a particular work. A pioneering study of nonverbal communications attempts to deal with the problem by breaking gestures down into minute movements, thus permitting a more accurate classification.[1] Two other observers have moved the study from the microscopic to the macroscopic level.[2] Instead of studying discrete fragments of movements, they consider gesture clusters—a whole complex of movements that expresses a particular attitude. The original method of notations might be compared with individual letters, the latter with paragraphs.

*Signs.* A large percentage of nonverbal communications can be classified as *signs.* These gestures have explicit denotations in a particular culture. For example, in the United States the sign made with the circle of the thumb and forefinger indicates A-OK. In many other cultures this would be an obscene gesture. Or if you were to put your feet on the desk and show your shoe sole to an Arab or Indonesian businessman, he would be offended by the sight and would probably terminate the conversation.

It should be emphasized that a gesture, like a word, has no absolute meaning. Words, gestures, and other elements of communication are ambiguous. Thoughts, emotions, and beliefs cannot fit into an exact formula. Gestures must be considered along with the user-observer and also in context: what went before and what comes after. Verbal verification of a gesture can be of great assistance. When the nose is touched in a "doubt" gesture, one might ask, "Do you feel certain about that?"

*Business Implications.* In many business situations, it is essential that the participants understand the whole communications process. Understanding the nonverbal aspects of communications can add about one-third to the understanding of the message that is being presented. In cases where the nonverbal communication contradicts the verbal communication, the nonverbal communication is a more accurate expression of the situation and may prevail.

Businesspeople typically use nonverbal communications to indicate attitudes. Sometimes a manager will consciously attempt to present an open attitude while subconsciously revealing by gestures a closed attitude. It is easy to portray an attitude that is considered by the communicator to be positive. It is much less easy to *control* the nonverbal communications that one might wish to conceal. Employees, associates, customers, and vendors are often skilled at reading nonverbal communications. For this reason, if no other, managers are finding that nonmanipulating, open communications on all levels produce closer and longer-lasting relationships. Actions, to many people, do speak louder—and often more truthfully—than words.

*Hidden Verbal Communications.* In many business or organizational discussions, words or phrases may be introduced that have hidden meanings. They do not say what they seem on the surface to say. An executive, for example, may try to conceal a sense of self-importance with statements that minimize personal ability or power: "In my humble opinion . . . "; "May I make a modest suggestion?"; "Far be it from me to disagree." The statements are attempts to "hide the halo," and these "grand deceivers" have been referred to as "meta-talk."[3] Probably no careful listener is fooled by them.

Finally, in the communications cycle, a manager can become more skillful in relating to people by changing from "You did . . . " to "I feel. . . . " People tend to use talk flavored with their judgments as their defense, but it exposes their weakness. These present barriers to honest communications. People see through them. When a manager acknowledges indecision or emotional bias by saying, "I feel . . . ," meaningful relationships can result. Reapplying the energy used to hide from one another to understanding ourselves and each other leads to better communicating, verbal as well as nonverbal.

*See also* COMMUNICATONS, EMPLOYEE; COMMUNICATIONS, ORGANIZATIONAL; NEGOTIATING.

## NOTES

[1]Ray L. Birdwhistell, *Kinesics and Context,* University of Pennsylvania Press, Philadelphia, 1970.

[2]Gerard I. Nierenberg and Henry Calero, *How to Read a Person like a Book,* Hawthorn Books, Inc., New York, 1971.

[3]Gerard I. Nierenberg and Henry Calero: *Meta-Talk,* Simon and Schuster, New York, 1973.

## REFERENCES

Davis, Flora: *Inside Intuition: What We Know about Nonverbal Communication,* McGraw-Hill Book Company, New York, 1971.

Weitz, Shirley: *Nonverbal Communication: Readings with Commentary*, Oxford University Press, New York, 1974.

GERARD I. NIERENBERG, ESQ., *Negotiation Institute, Inc.*

# Communications, organizational

The communications processes within organizations are vital for the achievement of organizational goals. They are the processes that link the various components of the organization together; they are found at all levels of the organization, and they affect every individual working for the organization in one way or another. The effectiveness of the communications system—the way in which it is managed—has a significant impact on the ultimate effectiveness of the total organization.

Communications have a major influence on both types of organizational goals—task and maintenance. With respect to *task (or productivity) goals*, without some means for downward communications, employees would not know what work they were expected to perform and when and how to do their work. Without adequate provision for upward communications, managers would not have the information needed to decide what to tell employees to do in the future. As organizations grow and become more complex, communications related to the organizational *maintenance goal* become increasingly important. Employees, including those at managerial levels, want to know how their work and their departments fit into the total operation, and they want to be informed about changes that might have some effect on their jobs or job environment. Thus in very large organizations, the management effort involved in communications processes can, and should, be considerable.

**Communications Policy** While the extent of the management effort in the area of communications is important, the most crucial ingredient for the success of the communications program is the attitude of top management. Perhaps more than in any other aspect of management, the communications system requires the involvement and support of the highest levels of the organization. Unless there is a climate of trust and sincerity from the top, little real communication is likely to occur, no matter how much time and money are spent on formal communications techniques.

The basic requirements for effective organizational communications may be summarized as follows:

1. Top management must recognize the need for and benefits of good communications throughout the organization and take the steps necessary to provide a climate conducive to effective communication.

2. Managers at all levels need to be aware of their role in the communications system and, if necessary, be given training to help them in this role.

3. Professionals in the field of organizational communications should be called upon to assist management in planning the communications system, in implementing it, and in measuring its effectiveness.

## COMMUNICATIONS SYSTEMS

Essentially, communication is the transmission of a *message* from one person (referred to as the *source)* to one or more other persons *(receivers)*. In the organizational context, the message may involve a directive or order to do something; it may be a suggestion for changing a procedure; it may be an expression of approval or disapproval for the way a job has been performed, and so forth. The vehicle for transmitting the message is called the *channel*. Communication channels may be oral or written, formal, or informal, and one-to-one or one-to-many. A supervisor's casual conversation with one of his or her subordinates uses an oral, informal, one-to-one channel; a letter from the company president mailed to all employees' homes is a written, formal, one-to-many channel.

For successful transmission of messages, there has to be some assurance that the source and the receiver have some common basis for understanding the message—that it means the same thing to the person sending the message as to the person or persons receiving it. To achieve this, communications systems frequently include *feedback mechanisms*, which in essence send another message from the receiver to the source saying the original message has been received and understood. One common mechanism is a question-and-answer period at the end of a meeting in which an executive reports on the company's financial situation or on plans for new products.

**Communications Networks** Within organizations, communication, or the transmission of messages, occurs through formal structures or through informal processes, both of which involve communications *networks*. A network, essentially, is a pattern of channels for the communication of messages to and from, or among, a specific group of people.

Figure C-1 illustrates five possible networks involving five persons; these networks are commonly found in the literature on communication because they have been widely studied by researchers on communication effectiveness. In the wheel network, person A is the central position through which messages from B, C, D, and E must be transmitted. In the chain network, person A also is in a central position for transmitting messages, but messages to person C must go through person B, and messages to person E must go through person D. In the Y network, person C is in a central position with respect to persons A, B, and D, but messages to person E must go through person D. In the circle, each person can communicate with the persons on either side, and in the all-channel network, messages can be transmitted by each person from and to all other persons.

In ongoing organizations, it is unlikely that exact replicas of such networks will be found to any degree. The networks, both formal and informal, in the typical company usually involve many more than five people, and often they are a combination of two or more of the ones illustrated. One important concept that is illustrated by three of the networks—the wheel, chain, and Y—is that of the *gatekeeper*, or a person who is in a position to decide what messages should, or need to be, transmitted to others. In the wheel, person A is the gatekeeper

with respect to all other persons, and in the chain, person A is the gatekeeper for persons B and D, while B is the gatekeeper for C, and D is the gatekeeper for E.

**The Formal Communications System** In most large organizations, the formal communications system is based on a chain of command from the top of the organization down, and the communications network can be depicted in the form of an organization chart, as shown in Fig. C-2. Within the formal system, messages are transmitted through the channels specified, and there are gatekeepers at each level of the organization for the persons at the next lower level. In the formal organizational context, these people also have been referred to as *linking pins*. Thus, in Fig. C-2, supervisor K is the linking pin between the supervisory level and employees 1 through 8.

The formal communications system is used for all official messages, including directives, procedures, policies, explanatory memorandums, job instructions, and so forth. It is predominantly a downward system, although there usually are provisions for some upward communications through the formal system in the form of production and sales reports, performance appraisals, and the like. In the case of upward communications, the person at the lower level is the gatekeeper for messages being transmitted upward. In Fig. C-2 for example, the head of

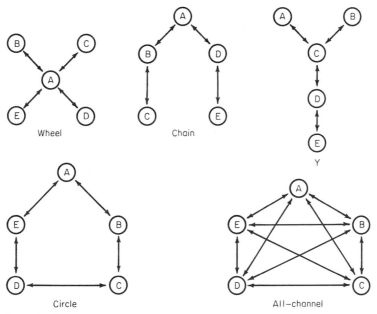

**Fig. C-1. Communications networks.**

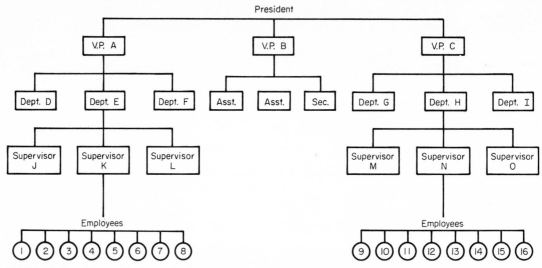

**Fig. C-2. The formal communications system.**

department E is the gatekeeper for information concerning work units directed by supervisors J, K, and L that is transmitted to vice-president A.

For purposes of efficiency, there are frequent instances where horizontal communication is desirable. For example, if the job assignment of employee 5 requires communication with employee 12, the formal network in its strictest sense would require communication from employee 5 through supervisor K, department head E, vice-president A, to the president and then back down through vice-president C, department head H, and supervisor N. It is generally recognized that in such a situation, horizontal communication should be encouraged as long as it is authorized by the immediate superiors. In the situation described, supervisors K and N would be what are called the *authorizing agents* for the creation of a *bridge* of horizontal communication between employees 5 and 12. This process frequently is referred to as *Fayol's bridge* after management theorist Henri Fayol, who first discussed this principle of management.

**The Informal Communications System**  As any manager knows, there are many messages transmitted in organizations every day that do not go through the formal channels. In contrast to the formal system, which relies predominantly on written channels, the informal communications system is primarily oral. Furthermore, much of the information transmitted through the informal system is not crucial to the functioning of the organization; often it is "scuttlebutt." The opportunity to engage

in such communication may serve a purpose insofar as organizational maintenance is concerned and have a positive effect on the company's reputation as a place to work, but it does not contribute directly to the achievement of task goals.

There are some informal communications, however, that do affect organizational productivity, either positively or negatively; thus, the informal system cannot be ignored. The networks of the informal system can be very complex, and usually they involve relationships outside the formal hierarchy. A car pool can be the basis of a communications network; perhaps employees 3, 4, and 8 are in a car pool with supervisor N and one of the assistants to president B. Another opportunity for informal communication is the golf or tennis match that might involve supervisor J, department heads F and H, and vice-president B. These situations provide an opportunity for the transmission of information in channels not accounted for in the formal system. Furthermore, the persons involved who receive messages through the informal system are in a position to transmit the message to the persons directly above or below them in the formal system. Thus, the informal networks can become very extensive.

*The Grapevine.* An informal communications network found in nearly all organizations is the *grapevine*, so called because of its tendency to wander in and out of the formal, hierarchical lines of communication. The grapevine is the channel, usually an oral, one-to-one channel, through which rumors can spread throughout the organization extremely rapidly. When the rumors involve possible changes in company policies, production plans, or top-level personnel, their effect on both productivity and organization climate can be devastating. Because of this, the grapevine generally is viewed negatively by employees although it often is perceived as influential since the rumors frequently have an element of truth to them. However, most messages transmitted through the grapevine are either groundless or distorted in some way.

It has been suggested that the best way to deal with the grapevine is to try to identify the persons in the organization who are the active transmitters on the grapevine, and who may constitute about 10 percent of the total personnel of the company. These people can then be "used" by top management to transmit messages quickly. This is a risky approach, however, because there is such frequent distortion on the grapevine and because there usually are many persons who are completely isolated from the grapevine and would never receive the

messages. It is generally conceded that there is no way to eliminate the grapevine, and there may actually be some positive aspects to its existence. Probably the most effective approach for offsetting the harmful effects of the grapevine is to make sure that formal channels are established and used for all information managers and employees need or want to know.

## COMMUNICATIONS TECHNIQUES

A variety of techniques or methods are used in most companies to transmit information through the formal communications system. They may be oral or written or a combination of the two, and they usually are described in terms of downward techniques or upward techniques. Communications methods commonly used in organizations are listed in Table C-1.

Many of the oral methods listed may involve both

**TABLE C-1   Communications Methods**

| Direction | Oral | Written |
|---|---|---|
| Downward: Among managerial levels | Directives over the telephone<br>One-to-one conferences or interviews<br>Staff meetings<br>Committee meetings<br>Lunch or dinner meetings | Policy and procedure manuals<br>Job descriptions<br>Organization charts<br>Memoranda<br>Reports of committee meetings and decisions reached<br>Progress and planning reports<br>Management newsletters |
| Downward: To all employees | Job instructions from supervisor or trainer<br>Appraisal interviews<br>Orientation and training meetings<br>Departmental or work-unit meetings<br>Mass meetings or annual meetings of all employees<br>Closed-circuit TV addresses<br>Public address systems<br>Videotapes or cassettes<br>Open house and plant tours<br>Recorded telephone messages | Assignment sheets or lists of job duties<br>Bulletin board notices<br>Posters<br>Memos or announcements<br>Employee publications<br>Pay inserts<br>Letters to employees' homes<br>Handbooks, pamphlets or brochures on company policies, benefits, etc.<br>Annual reports<br>News stories and/or advertisements in the local press or TV |
| Upward: | Informal discussions with employees, first-level supervisors, union representatives<br>Employee or staff meetings<br>Counseling sessions<br>Exit interviews<br>Telephone "hot lines" for employee questions | Formal attitude surveys<br>Written grievances or complaints filed<br>Company performance reports on production, sales, finances, personnel, etc.<br>Suggestion systems<br>Question and answer column in employee publications<br>Gripe boxes |

downward and upward communications; one-to-one telephone conversations or interviews typically provide an opportunity for information to be transmitted upward. Of the more formal oral communications methods, meetings frequently are used for two-way communications, particularly such meetings as those of an executive with his or her immediate staff or those of a supervisor with his or her work group. Most written communications, however, are strictly one way—either downward or upward.

**Downward Communications** As noted, communications from the top of the organization down are essential to any operation; they translate management policy planning and decision making into orders directing employees on their jobs. It is not surprising, therefore, that most organizations spend much more time and effort on downward than on upward communications. As the methods listed in Table C-1 indicate, however, much of the communications effort involves information designed to enhance the organizational climate and build a loyal group of employees and managers. Many of the written methods used for all employees, particularly employee publications, have no direct bearing on productivity.

Where it is essential for information to be communicated downward, the same message may be transmitted by several methods. This approach provides for a certain amount of *redundancy*, but it has been found that some redundancy may be necessary for effective communication. Research studies involving employee communications have reinforced the notion that a combination of communication methods, including both oral and written, are the best assurance that information will be received.

To determine which downward technique to use for a particular type of information, a number of factors are relevant. Some techniques are much faster than others; some are appropriate only for certain levels of employees; some are viewed as more authoritative than others. Another factor that should be considered is whether the information is likely to be viewed as positive or negative.

The figures in Table C-2 indicate the methods used most frequently by more than 200 companies for communicating three different types of information to employees. For information on changes in pay, which usually is viewed positively, the most frequently used method is an individual verbal communication between the employee and the immediate supervisor. To communicate changes in operations, where the information may be negative, the most frequent method is a group meeting, which usually provides an opportunity for answering em-

ployees' questions and presenting more information on future prospects. For information of a relatively neutral variety, such as changes in top-level personnel, the more impersonal, written techniques are used most frequently.

*Employee Publications.* In many companies, particularly large ones with a number of work locations, considerable time and money are spent on employee publications. These may take the form of a newsletter, a newspaper, or a magazine complete with color photographs. They are published as frequently as weekly or as infrequently as quarterly with a monthly publication schedule being most common. Distribution most often is by mail to employees' homes, although sometimes the publications are distributed at work—sent through the company mail system, handed out by supervisors, or picked up at the plant gate or other distribution points. Frequently the publications are prepared by professional journalists on the company staff; another approach is for the company's advertising agency to do the final layout and artwork with company personnel writing the material to be included.

In view of the expense of the employee publica-

**TABLE C-2  Methods Used for Communicating Different Types of Information**

| Type of information/method of communication | Percent of 219 companies using method indicated |
|---|---|
| *Changes in wage or salary levels* | |
| Individual oral communication | 45 |
| Memos or letters to employees | 31 |
| Group meetings | 29 |
| Articles in employee publications | 14 |
| Through union/union contract | 13 |
| Posted on bulletin boards | 12 |
| Other (cassette recordings, public address sytem, local press) | 5 |
| *Changes in operations that might result in layoffs, transfers, etc.* | |
| Group meetings | 44 |
| Individual oral communication | 31 |
| Memos or letters to employees | 21 |
| Articles in employee publications | 13 |
| Posted on bulletin boards | 12 |
| Through union/union contract | 8 |
| *Changes in top-level personnel* | |
| Memo or letters to employees | 44 |
| Articles in employee publications | 43 |
| Posted on bulletin boards | 36 |
| Group meetings | 13 |
| Local news media | 8 |
| Individual oral communication | 5 |

SOURCE: Adapted from *Employee Communications*, Bureau of National Affairs, Inc., Personnel Policies Forum Survey, no. 110, Washington, 1975, p. 16.

tion effort in most companies, often little is done to find out if management is getting its money's worth from its efforts. In some companies, management is reluctant to use employee publications for other than chitchat or announcements about retirements and service anniversaries. In cases where companies have conducted readership surveys of their employee publications, however, they have found that employees generally are interested in material that is more company-oriented and gives them information on company progress and future plans.

**Upward Communications**   While most communication in organizations is downward from the top of the hierarchy, upward communication is essential as well. The two most important aspects of upward communication are that it (1) provides management with some feedback indicating whether messages communicated downward have been received and (2) transmits upward the information needed for higher-level decisions. It is also important because it gives lower-level managers and employees an opportunity to ask questions, make complaints, express satisfaction or dissatisfaction with the way things are being managed, and make suggestions for improvements in methods or changes in policies.

As indicated in Table C-1, there are fewer methods for upward communications than for downward; furthermore, the methods that generally are considered most effective for upward communications are informal discussions with employees or first-level supervisors. In one survey of personnel executives, the formal upward method considered most effective was the attitude survey; however, less than one-third of the companies participating in the survey had ever conducted a formal employee attitude survey. Because of the time and expense involved in conducting such surveys, it is usually the larger companies that use them as a means for upward communications.

A major problem in upward communications is associated with the hierarchical system of most business organizations. Supervisors and department heads, in essence, are the gatekeepers with respect to messages upward, and in many cases they can effectively stifle employee complaints or reports of dissatisfaction. Many of the formal upward channels are designed to get around this problem in that they set up a channel around the immediate superior. This is true, for example, of attitude surveys, formal grievance procedures, gripe boxes, and suggestion systems. In recent years, a number of companies have established private "hot line" systems to provide a method for employees to communicate anonymously on any matter of concern with the com-

pany official best qualified to discuss the issue. Inquiries may be made through a special telephone line or company mail forms. One such program is in operation at New England Telephone Company, which has a coordinating staff to transmit the inquiries to the appropriate person for reply. The employee making the inquiry receives a direct response, and questions that are of general interest are discussed in the company newspaper. In this way, both upward and downward communications are served.

*Employee Meetings.* Employee meetings also provide a method for both upward and downward communications. Some meetings are almost all downward in nature; this is true, for example, of meetings held to present information on the company's environmental position, to explain a new safety procedure, or to train a group of employees in a new method of handling orders. For these types of meetings, there often are elaborate visual aids, such as slides, videotapes, or films, and a good deal of preparation. While there may be some opportunity for feedback in the way of questions related to the subject at hand, these meetings are not aimed at providing a general channel of upward communication.

In some companies, a general upward channel is provided through special employee meetings on a regular basis. One example of how such meetings may be arranged is shown in Table C-3, taken from the policy and procedure bulletin of a large manufacturing company with a number of plants in different locations.

**Management Information Systems**   With the advent of computer technology in the 1950s, business organizations began to develop management information systems (MIS). These systems are in essence a complex communications network linking all parts of an organization no matter how geographically dispersed they may be. Such a system permits input of data from any point within the organization, data transmission, data processing, and information storage and retrieval; in effect, it is capable of gathering and processing all the data needed to provide information for planning, operating, and controlling the organization. *See* INFORMATION SYSTEMS, MANAGEMENT (MIS).

While the potential value of MIS as a communications channel is great, the technology appears to be far ahead of actual or effective application to date. Most organizations have not yet developed their systems to the extent possible. In part, this is because many top-level managers are reluctant to put certain data into the computer data bank for fear it

**TABLE C-3   An Example of Upward Communications**

Employee Discussion Groups—Hourly

1. The Plant will conduct bi-monthly (more often if necessary) employee discussion groups.

2. The group representation will consist of 8–10 hourly employees, the Plant Manager and Personnel Manager.

3. The selection will include both sexes, all races and a mixture of old and new employees to assure representation from each operating segment of the plant.

4. The notice of each group discussion will be posted on all bulletin boards two days prior to the meeting. The notice will include the employee's name, department, time and location of the meeting. Copies of the notice will be mailed to Department Heads and to each individual employee's supervisor.

5. Discussion groups will cover all shifts. It is recommended the discussions begin 1½ hours before shift end and conclude at shift end. The meeting will be held in the Plant Manager's office.

6. The meeting will be opened by the Plant Manager introducing himself and informing the group that all statements made by himself or the Personnel Manager may be repeated throughout the plant. The group will be assured that their statements, suggestions, and complaints will not be repeated except where follow-up is required. The group will then introduce themselves and the discussion will begin.

7. The purpose of these group discussions is to allow the employee an opportunity to register complaints regarding working conditions, equipment, wages, classifications, overtime, etc., either for himself or fellow workers. The Plant Manager and Personnel Manager will answer questions and explain management's position.

8. Immediately following the meeting the Personnel Manager will follow up on all items and instigate corrective action if warranted. The action taken will be reported back to the employee registering the complaint or suggestion. A written record of reported items and corrective action will be maintained by the Personnel Department.

SOURCE: *Employee Communications*, Bureau of National Affairs, Inc., Personnel Policies Forum Survey, no. 110, Washington, 1975, pp. 25–26.

will become available to unauthorized persons. There are many applications, however, where management information systems have proved worthwhile, particularly in such areas as production planning and sales forecasting. A major benefit of the use of computer networks for communications is that the information can be transmitted directly from the operating levels of the organization to the highest levels without having to be processed through the several hierarchical levels in between. This both saves time and reduces the chances of distortion of the information transmitted.

## BARRIERS TO EFFECTIVE COMMUNICATIONS

In any type of communication, there are inherent difficulties associated with the different perceptions, values, experiences, standards, and biases of the sender and the receiver of the message involved. In the organizational context, these problems are amplified by such factors as physical distance between the sender and the receiver, emotional distance resulting from status differences between higher management and the lower levels, fears and anxieties related to boss-subordinate roles, and so forth.

**Communications Breakdown** Probably the most common problem in organizational communications is the failure to transmit the message intended to those who should receive it: a communications breakdown. Studies in ongoing organizations indicate that often only about 50 percent of the communicational interactions between people result in real communication. In other words, as many as half the people for whom a message is intended either do not receive it at all or else receive a distorted version of the message.

There are two major approaches to reducing the incidence of communications breakdown. The first is repetition or redundancy: the same message is sent to the same people through more than one channel and using various methods. The more often a message is transmitted and the more ways it is sent, the more likely it will in fact reach the intended receivers without error or distortion. The drawback to this approach is that it reduces the amount of information that can be communicated at any point in time. There also is the possibility that some persons may, in effect, "tune out" the communications channel when they perceive the message is redundant.

Another approach to preventing communications breakdown is to provide a means for the receiver of a message to verify it through some feedback process or two-way interaction. Studies consistently have shown that two-way communication is viewed as more accurate and more satisfying to the parties involved; however, it is more time-consuming (about 50 percent longer on the average) and thus not feasible for all kinds of information.

**Distortion in Upward Communications** The breakdown in communications is of particular concern in the downward system because it is essential for those at lower levels to know what management expects them to do. In the upward system, the major difficulty involves distortion. This may involve the transmission upward of only "good" news and suppression of bad performance reports, employee complaints, and the like. In some instances, superiors may completely block the upward transmission of information—either because it might be interpreted to reflect negatively on the superior or because it does not appear sufficiently important to bother higher-level management with it.

As noted earlier, some formal upward communications channels, such as attitude surveys and employee complaint procedures, may permit the by-passing of lower-level managers. Computerized information systems also tend to transmit information directly to top management. Unless these programs are administered effectively and considered legitimate communications channels, there may be considerable resentment on the part of the lower-level managers who are by-passed in the process.

**Information Overload**  A problem, particularly for those at the highest levels of management, is that of information overload. Full information on every detail of the company's operation and the activities of every employee is more than most executives can cope with. The information-producing capabilities of the computer have added greatly to the overload problem.

This is one area where each manager has to decide for himself or herself what information is really needed and how frequently it should be updated. Often, information processing can be delegated; where delegation and decentralization are used as a means of avoiding overload, however, there has to be some means to assure that crucial messages get through. It is important that decision makers have all the relevant information before deciding the future course of the organization.

As noted, top management has to set the stage for effective organizational communications. In many organizations, unfortunately, management thinks of communications only in terms of orders downward and progress reports upward; frequently managers fail to communicate because they assume everyone knows as much as they do. A relatively new approach to assessing the communications climate in organizations is the *communications audit.* Through a variety of procedures including questionnaires and interviews, the audit provides a comprehensive picture of the organization's communications system, including the sources and causes of communications failure. Such an audit, in addition to suggesting areas where more formal communications techniques may be needed, also can indicate points in the organization where management needs to concentrate on providing a more effective communications climate.

*See also* ATTITUDE SURVEYS; COMMUNICATIONS, EMPLOYEE; COMMUNICATIONS, NONVERBAL; CONFERENCE LEADERSHIP; CONFERENCES AND MEETINGS, PLANNING FOR; INFORMATION SYSTEMS, MANAGEMENT (MIS); INTERPERSONAL RELATIONSHIPS; NEGOTIATING; PUBLIC AND COMMUNITY RELATIONS.

### REFERENCES

*Employee Communications,* Bureau of National Affairs, Inc., Personnel Policies Forum Survey, no. 110, July 1975.

Harriman, Bruce: "Up and Down the Communications Ladder," *Harvard Business Review,* vol. 52, no. 5, pp. 143–151, September-October 1974.

Huseman, Richard C., Cal M. Logue, and Dwight I. Freshley: *Readings in Interpersonal and Organizational Communication,* 2d. ed., Holbrook Press, Inc., Boston, Mass., 1973.

*Case Studies in Organizational Communication,* Industrial Communication Council, 1975.

Lewis, Philip V.: *Organization Communications,* Grid, Inc., Columbus, Ohio, 1975.

Miner, John B.: *The Management Process,* 2d. ed., Macmillan Publishing Co., Inc., New York, 1978, chaps. 8 and 9.

Rogers, Everett M., and Rekha Agarwala-Rogers: *Communication in Organizations,* The Free Press, New York, 1976.

MARY GREEN MINER, *Bureau of National Affairs, Inc.*
JOHN B. MINER, *Georgia State University*

## Communications, telephone  (*See* TELECOMMUNICATIONS.)

## Communications industry management  (*See* REGULATED INDUSTRIES.)

## Communications paths, R&D  (*See* RESEARCH AND DEVELOPMENT MANAGEMENT.)

## Community planning legislation

Community planning legislation is the enabling legislation that provides local units of government with the authority to develop and adopt plans that guide the pattern of development and redevelopment in the community. During the 1920s, states began to pass enabling legislation that delegated authority to units of government to create planning boards and commissions which would be responsible for preparation and adoption of a comprehensive or master land use plan and capital improvements program. This legislation was based on a model state planning act prepared at that time by the U.S. Department of Commerce. Many states still have legislation based on this model act, but some have made significant innovations. Community planning was optional with the municipality under the Department of Commerce model act, but several states—including California, Florida, and Oregon—have now made community planning mandatory.

**Municipal Agencies** Community planning legislation has created various types of organizations for planning and managing growth and redevelopment, including municipal planning boards and county planning commissions. It is the function of the commission to prepare a community plan for consideration by the community's council or legislative body. Many statutes then provide that the plan is not binding until adopted by the community legislative body.

**Plan Elements** Community planning legislation indicates what the community plan must contain. Under the Department of Commerce model act and many state statutes, the legislation merely contains a "shopping list" of elements that ultimately must be included in the plan. These elements always include a land use element, a capital improvements element, and a transportation element. Some states also include additional elements, such as an open space element and a housing element. These statutes do not specify what planning policies must be included in each of these elements; they merely indicate what elements must be in the plan, leaving the development of policy for each element to the community. A few states have now placed specific planning policies for housing in their planning legislation, and require the plan to include policies for housing for all sectors of the community. California and Florida are notable examples. Florida also requires that a growth management element contain policies for managing growth. This trend toward including substantive housing policies and growth management policies will probably be spurred by the federal Housing and Community Development Act of 1974, which requires communities receiving federal financial assistance for planning to include both these elements.

**Zoning** Zoning is the major community tool to regulate development and manage growth and thus implement the plan. Through the use of zoning regulations, the community can control the height, number of stories and size of buildings, the percentage of lot that may be occupied, the size of yards, courts and other open spaces, the density of popula-

tion, the setback of buildings, and the type of land use, such as industrial, commercial/retail, residential, recreational, critical area, or open space.

Although zoning is a major technique for the implementation of the community plan, the relationship between the planning and zoning has not been clear. A model zoning act published by the U.S. Department of Commerce at the same time as the model planning act provided that zoning must be "in accordance with a comprehensive plan." Most state zoning acts still contain this language; however, practically all courts at first read this requirement out of the legislation. The courts did not require that the zoning ordinance be based on an independently prepared and adopted comprehensive *plan*, but read the requirement to mean merely that the zoning ordinance had to be adopted as part of a rational and comprehensive *process*. This interpretation may have been justified by ambiguities in the original Department of Commerce model legislation. Some state courts now require, however, that zoning actually be "consistent with an adopted comprehensive plan," and several statutes also contain a similar consistency requirement. As this requirement is increasingly enforced by the courts, the relationship between planning and zoning will be significantly improved.

**Impact on Development** Community planning legislation is thus an important tool for controlling and guiding development. It offers a flexible approach to designating and regulating land uses and protecting critical, natural resource areas. An increasing number of states are expanding the traditional roles of their planning agencies to respond to the growing demands for growth management, energy facility siting, and environmental management. Community planning legislation is becoming more complex in response to these needs and remains the primary means for influencing growth. In many communities, for example, new growth may not occur unless it is served by adequate public facilities as indicated by the plan.

**New Directions** Community planning legislation, however, has not always provided for a consideration of the environmental impact of community planning, although many communities are increasingly paying attention to environmental concerns in their planning activities. A new model planning act prepared as part of a comprehensive revision of planning and zoning legislation by the American Law Institute contains a requirement that the environmental impacts of planning be considered.

This model planning act, which was approved by the institute in 1975, retains the stipulation that planning is optional with communities. Planning is mandatory, however, if the community wants to use certain regulatory measures to implement the plan, particularly those conferring regulatory discretion on the community. The institute's model act improves on community planning legislation by (1) providing greater flexibility in the form and content of the plan that may be adopted and (2) requiring communities to give attention to the problems actually considered by community plans and the solutions that reasonably can be developed to solve them. It should be noted that in 1977 the *Report of the American Bar Association's Advisory Commission on Housing and Urban Growth Housing for All Under Law* adopted a position contrary to that of the institute and urged that community planning be made mandatory.

**National Involvement** Community planning is also becoming an important part of some state planning programs that are required by national legislation, such as the National Coastal Zone Management Act of 1972. This act requires a state coastal zone management program which closely resembles a community plan. In some states, as in California and North Carolina, planning for state coastal areas has been delegated to the communities in the coastal zone subject to state guidelines and policies for coastal zone planning.

**Impact on Managerial Decisions** Management should be aware of applicable state and local planning efforts and develop methods for participating in this process. The involvement of management in the planning process can lead to more effective evaluation, decision making, cooperation, and coordination between business operations and the public sector.

The regulations adopted by local units of government and state agencies for implementation of community planning legislation may require a cumbersome and time-consuming application review and approval process. Any delays in this process often result in escalating the costs of a project; these costs are eventually transferred to the consumer. A prolonged delay may force a developer to terminate the project as a result of high front-end costs which the developer may no longer be able to carry. Some states and municipalities are now experimenting with coordinated review procedures to simplify this process. It is in the area of expediting review procedures that management's input can be most effective.

*See also* EGALITARIANISM; ENVIRONMENT, PHYSICAL; ENVIRONMENTAL PROTECTION LEGISLATION; FACILITIES AND SITE PLANNING AND LAYOUT; PUBLIC AND COMMUNITY RELATIONS; SOCIAL RESPONSIBILITY OF BUSINESS; TECHNOLOGY, MANAGEMENT IMPLICATIONS; VALUE SYSTEMS, MANAGEMENT: SOCIAL AND CULTURAL.

### REFERENCES
Boulder Area Growth Study Commission: *Exploring Options for the Future: A Study of Growth in Boulder County*, 10 vols., Municipal Government Reference Center, Boulder Public Library, P.O. Drawer H, Boulder, Colo. 80302. November 1973.
Chapin, F. Stuart, Jr.: *Urban Land Use Planning*, The University of Illinois Press, Urbana, 1965.
Einsweiler, Robert C., Inc.: *Planning and Development Systems*, prepared for Metropolitan Washington Council of Governments, National Technical Information Service, 2285 Port Royal Road, Springfield, Va., 22151, August 1973.
Freund, Eric C., and William I. Goodman (eds.): *Principles and Practice of Urban Planning*, ICMA, Washington, 1968.
Mandelker, Daniel R.: "The Role of the Local Comprehensive Plan in Land Use Regulation," *Michigan Law Review*, vol. 74, 1976, p. 899.
Mandelker, Daniel R.: *The Zoning Dilemma*, American Society of Planning Officials, Chicago, Ill., 1971.

DANIEL R. MANDELKER, *Washington University*
SUZANNE WELLBORN, *U.S. Department of Energy*

## Communism (*See* ECONOMIC SYSTEMS.)

## Community relations (*See* PUBLIC AND COMMUNITY RELATIONS.)

## Comparative advantage (*See* INTERNATIONAL TRADE.)

## Compensation plans, cafeteria (*See* COMPENSATION, EMPLOYEE BENEFIT PLANS.)

## Compensation, employee benefit plans

Originally identified as fringe benefits because of their minimal role, forms of indirect compensation for work have become popularly known as employee benefits as their importance has increased relative to direct compensation (i.e., wages, salaries, and bonuses in the form of cash and/or stock payments). Defined most simply, an *employee benefit* is compensation in cash or its equivalent which is not paid directly or specifically for time spent discharging work assignments.

For about the first hundred years of this country's growth, the only form of pay was for time actually worked. The hours were long, and in most instances the work was hard. Near the turn of the century a number of new concepts were introduced (e.g., pensions, paid vacations, and profit sharing to name a few). But because companies were slow to recognize what citizens considered to be employer obligations, a number of laws were enacted to spur the development of employee benefits.

Among the first (Wisconsin, 1911) was a statutory requirement to compensate a worker who lost time because of a work injury (i.e., workmen's compensation). When state laws were inadequate or nonexistent, the federal government stepped in. For example, the massive unemployment of the early thirties lead to the Social Security Act of 1935. This law provided a federal-state system of unemployment insurance, and it also established a federal program for pension benefits to workers retiring from industry. This law has been amended frequently both to improve benefits and to add new coverage (e.g., survivors benefits in 1939, disability benefits in 1956, and Medicare in 1966). Also, the tax rate and the tax base on which both employee and employer pay the federal government to support benefits have continued to increase from the original 1 percent on the first $3000 of employee earnings.

Today, basically all forms of employee benefits may be classified into one of six categories: time off with pay, employee services, nonperformance awards, health care, survivor protection, and retirement.

## EMPLOYEE BENEFIT CATEGORIES

**Time Off with Pay** As the phrase implies this is payment for hours not worked (thereby differentiating it from wage or salary, which is pay for time worked). Basically, time off with pay covers pay while not at the work site, but it may also cover pay for not working while on the company premises.

Included in this grouping of payments for time not spent at the work site are pay for leisure time (e.g., holidays and vacations), for meeting social and civic responsibilities (e.g., funeral leave, jury duty, and military reserve training allowance), for accident or illness which incapacitates a person (e.g., workers' compensation and disability), and for termination of employment (e.g., unemployment compensation and severance pay).

*Rest-Period Pay.* Probably the most widely known recuperation period is the coffeebreak—a scheduled stoppage in work for 10 or 15 minutes while the individual is paid to enjoy a drink and the companionship of fellow workers. Other short paid periods of time not worked include wash and cleanup at the end of the day and a meal period taken at the work station (often required by state law when insufficient time is given for one meal during a shift).

*Leisure-Time Pay* Many companies now provide about 10 paid holidays each year. In addition to what is referred to as the "basic six" (i.e., New Year's Day, Memorial Day, Fourth of July, Labor Day, Thanksgiving, and Christmas), the other popular holidays are Good Friday, Washington's Birthday, Columbus Day, Veteran's Day, and the employee's own birthday. Normally an employee is eligible for holiday pay after a minimum period of employment (e.g., 1 month).

Vacation pay on the other hand normally increases with additional years of company service (e.g., 2 weeks after 1 year, 3 weeks after 5 years, 4 weeks after 15 years and 5 weeks after 25 years employment).

The sabbatical is a more restricted form of time off with pay, whereby the recipient receives 6 months or more to accomplish a specific objective. Sabbaticals are used to meet specific educational needs of the individual (e.g., completing doctorate work in a technical discipline), to respond to social needs (e.g., working with a worthy nonprofit organization such as a drug rehabilitation center), or simply to allow a person a longer period to "get away from it all" in order to return with renewed enthusiasm.

Because of the cost, sabbaticals are usually very limited in number. Recipients are chosen typically on the basis of organizational level and/or some form of competitive examination.

*Social Responsibility Pay.* A death in the immediate family normally allows the employee a maximum number of days of paid absence (e.g., 3) for funeral leave—time off for bereavement.

Jury duty pay is usually the difference between normal pay and what the individual receives from the court for serving as a juror.

A military reserve training allowance is payment

for all or a portion of the time off which an employer is required to give an employee to fulfill military training commitments.

*Disability Pay.* Another paid absence, which may be for a long time, is a period of inability to work due to accident or illness. If the disability is work-related, payment is covered under workers' compensation. Today all states have laws requiring employers to be responsible for all costs of work-related disabilities, regardless of who is at fault. All disabilities are categorized as either permanent or temporary and either total or partial. Benefits are either in the form of lump sum awards and/or weekly payments for a specified period of time.

Only five states (California, Hawaii, New Jersey, New York, and Rhode Island) have statutes covering nonoccupational accident or illness absences. These provide limited payments usually for a maximum of 6 months and are called disability pay plans. In spite of the lack of legislated benefits, most companies have instituted voluntary programs to provide benefits similar to workers' compensation. In most companies this is split into two different programs: short term and long term. As the words denote, the difference is in the duration of benefits.

Short-term disability benefits normally cover the first 6 (maybe 12) months of the disability: such programs are usually self-insured in larger companies. Long-term plans pick up where short-term plans end and are normally more formally insured. In most instances long-term disability plans are integrated with disability benefits provided by Social Security.

*Unemployment and Termination Pay.* Unemployment compensation is pay to a person no longer employed. Provision for such programs was established in the Social Security Act of 1935. This law made the individual states responsible for setting up and administering their own programs. Although there is a federal tax to the employer on a portion of each employee's earnings, 90 percent of this will be refunded to the state if its program meets certain minimum requirements. Among these are the following: a threshold eligibility period (met by earning a minimum amount of pay and/or working for a specified period of time), a right to a hearing if benefits are denied, the requirement that the individual register at a public employment office indicating availability for work, and the right to refuse work unsuitable to the individual's training and background.

The level and extent of benefits vary significantly by state, although most states provide up to 26 weeks, depending upon eligibility. Some provide higher benefits depending on the number of dependents, and a few include workers who are on strike. A number also provide automatic extension of benefits during periods of high unemployment.

The amount of tax each employer will pay on covered compensation is based on an experience rating formula which penalizes those companies with an unstable work force. The formulas, while similar, do vary from state to state.

In addition to statutory unemployment, a few unions have negotiated supplemental unemployment benefits (SUBs). Under such plans, company benefits are normally combined with unemployment pay to provide a weekly maximum (e.g., 95 percent of take-home pay).

Termination or severance pay is the final form of pay for time not worked. In many instances, it is pay for time not worked in lieu of notice. Under such conditions the employee may receive notice on Friday of being terminated, effective immediately, and of being given two additional weeks of pay. The assumption is that during the next 2 weeks he or she can find employment elsewhere and therefore not suffer any loss of income.

Some companies differentiate between individual terminations and plant closings. When they do, greater termination or severance pay benefits are given in the latter situation—often scaled upward in relation to years of service (e.g., 2 weeks plus 1 additional week for every year of service).

Severance pay for higher-paid employees is often more generous than that for lower-paid individuals—probably a reflection that higher-paid employees may have fewer suitable employment opportunities available elsewhere.

**Employee Services** This covers a wide range of items which are either provided at no cost to the employee or made available at a discounted price. Included in this category are a company cafeteria, parking facilities, recreation programs, company medical facilities, clothing, and company products.

Many companies are offering additional services in response to social pressures. These services include providing day-care facilities, thus enabling mothers to work, scheduling car pools and sometimes providing minibuses to reduce commuting cost and fuel consumption, and providing a full array of protective clothing for those who might be exposed to health-threatening gases and substances.

Another service is making employee-authorized deductions through the company's payroll system. These run the range from mass-merchandised insurance programs for automobile and homeowner policies to credit unions. The latter are employee organizations in which members agree to save their money and make low-interest loans to each other in accordance with standards prescribed by the Bureau of Federal Credit Unions or similar state leagues. In addition to serving as a collection agency for the credit union, the company often provides low-cost or no-cost office materials and facilities.

Relatively new on the benefit scene are the following: legal insurance (where legal services are paid for in whole or part by the employer); auto insurance (with the company passing on group rates to its employees, who usually pay through a payroll deduction); homeowners' insurance (similar in operation to auto insurance); and liability insurance (normally provided only to officers and directors to protect them from legal actions arising out of performance of their duties).

Counseling is another service which is provided by a number of companies and which can take many forms. Financial counseling for executives normally includes advice on estate building as well as estate conservation (including tax aspects). A more broadly based benefit is preretirement counseling. Under such a program, employees who are several years away from retirement are invited to a number of company-sponsored seminars and lectures focusing on the use of increased leisure time and the benefits available from the company programs and from Social Security and Medicare. Subscriptions to magazines directed toward this portion of the employee population are also available.

**Nonperformance Awards**  These are cash benefits paid in recognition of certain events. An example is the attendance bonus (paid either in cash or in paid time off) for specified periods of perfect attendance (e.g., week, month, or year). An extension of this is the length of service bonus which increases with every additional year of company service (e.g., $25 for 1 year of service, $50 for 2 years, etc). A more common modification is the service award program where 5-year milestones are commemorated with a special pin or other item displaying the company emblem. Normally a special recognition is taken of 25 years of service. Many companies sponsor a quarter-century club with annual dinners for past and new members at company expense.

Special-event gifts are common, especially among smaller companies. The Thanksgiving turkey, the Christmas ham, the wedding cake knife, and the baby sweater are among the more common examples.

*Educational Assistance.* Company recognition of the importance of continued education is often reinforced with an educational assistance program for its employees. This usually takes the form of reim-

bursement of a percentage of college tuition (e.g., 75 percent), although it usually does not include other expenses such as books. Some will graduate payment in relation to course grades (e.g., 50 percent for a C, 75 percent for a B, and 100% for an A). Usually the course has to be approved prior to enrolling and in many instances has to be related to the individual's current or possible future work assignments.

In providing scholarships for dependents of employees, a company will invariably specify the number it is prepared to give each year. Often the employee's dependent is required to submit a formal application and take a competitive examination.

Another educational benefit is the matching gift program, whereby the company will match (possibly to a stated individual maximum amount) a contribution by the employee to a qualified institute of higher learning.

*Relocation Reimbursement.* Relocation expenses are often reimbursed to a significant extent when the company wishes an individual to move to a different company location. Usually such coverage is only provided to management-level employees, but there are instances of coverage of lower-paid employees who possess unique technical skills. In addition to paying the actual moving costs, many companies will pay all or part of the selling costs of a house (including loss against appraised value), travel and lodging costs while the employee seeks new accommodations (or waits for a new home to become available) carrying costs on a former residence until sold, and low-cost or no-cost loans until the former residence is sold.

Reimbursement for travel, meals, and lodging in conjunction with business responsibilities are covered under expense accounts, not employee benefits, and usually are limited to sales representatives and management personnel. Many companies, however, pay blue-collar and lower-paid office employees a supper allowance if their work extends into a meal period which is after normal working hours.

*Overtime and Premiums.* Some authorities consider penalty pay as a form of benefit. The most significant form of penalty pay is overtime pay. In 1938, the federal Fair Labor Standards Act became law. Among its provisions was the requirement that all employees who could not be exempted from the act (i.e., outside salespeople, executives, professionals, and administrators) had to be paid time and one-half for all hours worked in excess of 40 hours per week if the company was engaged in interstate commerce. Previously, in 1936, the Walsh-Healey Act stated that similar people must be compensated at the rate of time and one-half for all hours worked in excess of 8 hours per day, if the employer had a federal government contract of $10,000 or more.

In addition to overtime pay, most companies will pay a premium if the employee works on a company-paid holiday or on Sunday. A number of companies also pay a special premium for Saturday, regardless of the number of hours the employee otherwise works.

Especially disagreeable work often commands an additional hourly premium (dirty money). Similarly a guarantee of 2 to 4 hours is used by many when the employee is called back to the site after having left for the day or called in on a nonscheduled workday. This assures the individual of a minimum amount of pay, even though the task may take only a few minutes. A similar approach is used to cover the employee who reports in on a regularly scheduled workday and finds there is no work (possibly owing to an unforseen calamity, such as a power failure). In each case the difference between the pay for hours actually worked versus those paid can be considered a benefit.

**Health Care**   Reimbursement for various types of medical expenses is a prevalent employee benefit. Employers have a great deal of flexibility in designing programs to ease the financial burden that can be imposed on the employee through varying types of health care expenses. Nonetheless, the employer must comply with the requirements of the Employee Retirement Income Security Act (commonly called ERISA). Although this act deals primarily with pension plans, it supercedes the earlier Welfare and Pension Plans Disclosure Act as it relates to reporting financial and other information on health care plans.

The major portion of employer-provided health care coverage is provided under group health insurance plans. As implied, the word *group* indicates that the contract covers a designated group of employees, rather than a specific person. Financing ranges from a fully insured program (the typical group contract placed with an insurance company) to a self-insured plan (whereby the company directly assumes the risk). The premium paid to insurance companies covers benefit payments, claim expenses, taxes, commissions, and the insurance company profits.

Since the premium of an insured plan is generally experience-rated for each group, there can be differences in cost from one group to another. The inherent efficiencies of a large group generally provide lower premiums than comparable coverage under an individual policy.

Well known in the area of health care protection are Blue Cross and Blue Shield—independent, non-profit membership corporations. The first provides protection against the cost of hospital charges; the second focuses on surgical and other medical care items.

Another form of community-rated health care plan is the health care maintenance organization (HMO). For a fixed monthly charge every covered employee and his or her family receive no-cost health care instead of pay-for-repair health care. The incentive to those responsible for administering health care is to diagnose problems early and treat them before they become major problems, which require more time and expense to treat. This concept of prepaid health care was essentially the model for the Health Maintenance Organization Act of 1973.

The normal group insurance contract providing health care is either a comprehensive or a schedule plan (usually with a major medical override). A comprehensive plan lumps all reimbursable expenses under one payment formula, which normally has a corridor or deductible (e.g., $100), which the employee pays in full. The plan then pays a percentage (e.g., 80 percent) of all remaining expenses in a calendar year up to maximum (e.g., $100,000). The advantage of this plan is its simplicity.

The schedule plan identifies each covered expense and the maximum amount that will be paid. Normally, such a plan also has a major medical feature, which, after a deductible (e.g., $100), will pay a percentage of all remaining expenses (e.g., 80 percent). While more complicated than a comprehensive type, a schedule plan makes possible for the individual to get full reimbursement of all expenses if the charges are equal to or less than the allowable schedule.

Since July 1966, a major role in health care for disabled and retired employees has been played by Medicare, under title XVIII of the Social Security law. This program specifies two types of coverage: (1) basic coverage (providing benefits to cover the cost of hospital and related care) and (2) a voluntary supplement to cover certain doctor charges and other medical services not covered by the basic plan. Eligible employees receive basic benefits at no cost and are automatically enrolled in the supplemental plan at a monthly premium set by the government (although they can of course withdraw from the voluntary portion).

Title XIX of the Social Security Act is also significant in the discussion of health care, for it introduced Medicaid—a program which provides matching federal funds to those states granting a specified minimum degree of health care protection to defined low-income people. Since these medical benefits are

153

provided to those normally on welfare, they should not be considered part of a company employee benefit program.

Since most medical insurance programs cover prescription drugs only if administered as part of hospital care, a number of companies have also set up prescription care plans. Under such plans the employee normally pays the first 50 cents or $1 and the plan will cover the remaining expenses.

In addition, vision care insurance (a plan which covers all or part of eye examinations, prescription lenses, and frames) is becoming an established benefit.

Probably the most dramatic change in health care insurance has been the rapid rise to popularity of dental insurance. As recently as 1965 this type of coverage was estimated to include about 2 million employees—mainly on the West Coast. In 10 years this number has increased over tenfold. Most such plans reimburse a higher percentage of charges for preventive oral care (e.g., checkups, cleaning, and x-rays) than charges for repair and replacement. Thus the plan provides a financial incentive to seek early care, which is likely to be less expensive.

**Survivor Protection**  This includes all forms of compensation paid to survivors. The most common is provided under group life insurance plans. A majority of these plans (especially for salaried employees) provide an amount equal to a specified portion of salary (e.g., 2 times). In many companies this cost is paid, at least in part, by the employee, though the trend is to company-pay-all coverage.

Many companies also have an accidental death and dismemberment (AD&D) policy. The former pays an additional amount of insurance if the death is accidental; the latter, specified amounts for loss of various members or limbs.

An additional form of survivor protection is business travel accident insurance. Normally, such programs provide for death benefits equal to some multiple of salary if death occurs while traveling on company business. For cost considerations, some plans will exclude high-exposure risks (e.g., salespersons traveling within their territory).

**Retirement**  Benefits included in this category are all deferred payments which commence with the date the employee leaves the active employment of the company (and usually the work force). Such benefits may be supplemented by deferred bonuses to management employees, but since these are deferred compensation payments (which usually could have been taken while still employed), they are not really benefits as defined here.

*Defined Benefit Plans.* Retirement plans are either defined benefit or defined contribution plans.

The former indicates the annuity amount that the individual will receive upon attaining certain age and/or service requirements. Such plans are subdivided into career service (e.g., $15 per month per year of service), career earnings (e.g., 1.4 percent per $1000 earned with the company), and final pay (e.g., 1.1 percent per $1000 of the average compensation during the highest paid 5 years of the 10 years immediately preceeding retirement, multiplied by the years of service).

With most defined benefit plans, benefits are scheduled to begin at age 65 (although a number of plans now specify 62, and some, age 60). If benefits begin before this normal retirement date, there is a discount for each year, the rationale being that the individual probably will receive benefits for a longer period of time because of this early retirement.

Additionally, many plans will integrate benefits with those provided under Social Security. This allows the company to minimize the possibility of the employee retiring with combined net income (Social Security benefits are tax-free) greater than that while employed. Additionally, it allows the company to provide greater plan benefits to the higher-paid individuals (since it gives lesser benefits to the lower-paid) at the same cost.

Integrated plan formulas are essentially of two types and are used with both career earnings and final-pay-type plans. The more common is the carve-out or step-up approach. This uses one value for all earnings up to the Social Security tax base (e.g., 1 percent) and a higher value for all earnings in excess of that amount (e.g., 1.5 percent). The other approach employs an offset formula which uses one value (e.g., 1.5 percent) for all earnings but then subtracts a percentage (e.g., 50 percent) of the primary Social Security benefit at age 65. Although there is a considerable amount of flexibility in designing integrated pension plans, there are a number of specific Internal Revenue Service rules that must be followed in developing the plan.

Defined benefit plans falling under the jurisdiction of ERISA need to have provisions to ensure that the benefits will be available when payment is to commence. To discharge this obligation, companies either contract with an insurance company to provide insured benefits or set up a trust. The former is most common with smaller companies; the latter is used by the bigger plans.

Under a trusteed plan an actuary determines each year how much the company must contribute. This determination is made by making a number of assumptions regarding such items as mortality, salary increases, turnover, and investment gains in the portfolio as well as by adjusting for earlier errors in judgment. Once the money has been paid to the trustee, it can never be recaptured by the company.

*Defined Contribution Plans.* These plans indicate the amount that will be set aside each year for purposes of retirement. The value at time of retirement is usually dependent upon the market value of the investments at that later date. Such plans are usually described as either thrift (or savings) plans or profit-sharing programs. A critical difference is that with the former, the employee must set aside a certain portion from his or her paycheck (e.g., 5 percent of salary) and the company will match this on a formula basis (e.g., 50 cents on the dollar). While employees usually have a choice of how their contributions will be invested (e.g., fixed income, common stocks excluding the company's, and/or the company's own stock), the company contribution is normally in the form of company stock.

Under a profit-sharing plan the company agrees to take a percentage of profits (generally not to exceed 15 percent of covered payroll) and set it aside for the employee's termination. It should be noted that some plans pay off in shorter cycles, but these are not really directed toward providing retirement income.

Another form of defined contribution plan is the employee stock ownership plan (ESOP). Under such a plan the company makes a contribution of company stock to a trust (i.e., an ESOT). The value credited to each employee's account is normally in relation to earnings.

If these plans are not discriminatory in favor of higher-paid people (other than in relation to direct compensation) and meet certain other requirements (e.g., ensuring payments will accrue only to employees and only at time of retirement), the plans will be able to qualify under Section 401 of the Internal Revenue Code. This means that deductions can be taken by the company in the year in which it makes contributions either to the trust or insurance carrier whereas the employees usually have no tax liabilities until they actually receive payments.

Additional requirements dealing with disclosure, fiduciary responsibility, funding requirements, reinsurance, and vesting (i.e., the nonforfeitable right), among other items, are covered in the 1974 Employee Retirement Income Security Act. The provisions of this act should be studied very carefully to ensure that a retirement plan conforms to its provisions.

Another form of deferred income which is often used to supplement retirement annuities is the qualified stock purchase plan, described in Section 423 of the Internal Revenue Code. This is somewhat similar in appearance, but is not to be confused with the qualified stock option, described in Section 422 of the same code. Under the qualified stock purchase plan, the employee contracts with the company to purchase, normally on an installment basis, a specified number of shares at a price as low as 85 percent of market at the time of each installment. Under a qualified stock option, a form which will disappear on May 21, 1981, as a result of legislation, the company agrees to allow the individual to buy up to a specified number of shares of stock not later than 5 years from the date of option at a price equal to the fair market value at the date of grant. While the company may pick and choose who will be eligible in a qualified stock option plan, essentially all employees must be afforded the opportunity to join if a qualified stock purchase plan is established.

## COST OF EMPLOYEE BENEFIT PROGRAMS

Recognizing the rising value of indirect compensation, the U.S. Chamber of Commerce in 1967 officially changed the name of its periodic analysis from the Fringe Benefits Report to the Employee Benefits Report.

*To Company.* In addition to calculating the annual total cost of each benefit, it is common to calculate three indicators of the cost per employee: (1) dollars per year per employee (total benefit dollars divided by average number of employees on the payroll during the year); (2) cents per payroll hour (total benefit dollars divided by total hours paid, thereby giving a percentage for every hour paid, or by total hours worked, thereby giving a percentage for every hour worked); and (3) percent of pay (total benefit dollars divided by total payroll or total base payroll).

Following these approaches it is possible to cost not only the total benefit program but also each of the components. Results can be compared with the U.S. Chamber of Commerce's biennial benefit survey. The most recent results are for 1975 covering 761 employers, and they are $3984 per year per employee, 193.2 cents per hour paid, and 35.4 percent of total payroll. To dramatize the rise in importance of employee benefits relative to total compensation, the same report indicates that benefit payments for 152 identical companies increased from 22.7 percent in 1955 to 40.3 percent in 1975.

*To Employees.* Employee costs fall into two categories: payroll deductions and noncovered costs. A payroll deduction is the amount the employee pays in order to participate in the program, an amount taken from each paycheck. When the employee pays a portion of the cost in this way, the plan is said to

**155**

be contributory (i.e., the employee contributes toward part of the cost). When the company does not charge the employee for coverage, the plan is said to be noncontributory. In addition to the payroll deductions to support membership in various company benefit plans, the employee, of course, has various statutory deductions (e.g., Social Security and income tax withholding for federal, state, and possibly city taxes).

The second category, noncovered cost, is the amount in excess of plan benefits (e.g., the deductible and the coinsurance feature in a health care plan).

Because of the combined impact of all deductions, it is important that the benefits be considered worthwhile by the employee. It is this concern that has led to what some call cafeteria or customized compensation. This pick-and-choose benefit planning by the individual is present to some extent in almost every company. The various stages include the following: (1) the employee decides whether he or she wishes plan coverage; (2) the employee determines the extent of coverage by authorizing one of several possible payroll deductions; and (3) the employee chooses whether to waive normal protection with one benefit (thereby receiving lower minimum no-cost coverage), applying the value difference to obtain greater coverage in other benefits.

Developing various levels of benefit programs to meet the cost trade-off considerations inherent in a cafeteria plan has proved sufficiently challenging so that very few organizations have yet to move from the discussion stage to implementation.

## SUMMARY

Employee benefits are a part of the whole—one segment of the compensation an individual receives in return for his or her work efforts. Their prominence is due to a combination of factors: (1) at several times in the last 40 years or so there have been periods when it was easier to grant benefit improvements than to provide direct compensation improvements (i.e., during World War II, the Korean Conflict, and the periods of wage controls during the early 1970s); (2) a number of benefits can be provided at less cost on a group basis than on an individual basis; and (3) timing and extent of income tax liability, if any, provides additional appeal for such forms of compensation.

Because benefit plans are very visible, unlike salaries and incentive plans, they are easy reference points for a person considering alternative career opportunities. However, since the level of participation in employee benefit programs is usually not correlated with performance, they have very little motivational impact for most. Justification for adding new programs and improving features of existing plans essentially stems from competitive pressures (i.e., what other companies are doing). For some the competitive pressure is very direct, namely, in the bargaining sessions.

## PERQUISITES

Unlike employee benefits in general, which extend to all or most employees in the organization, perquisites are special "benefits" that apply only to a few executives at the pinnacle of the organization. They include such items as a chauffered limousine, a company jet, additional expense account allowances, fully paid medical expenses, tuition allowances for children, country club memberships, vacation retreat, sumptuous office, and financial counseling.

The reason for perquisites is to show that there is a difference between the very top executive level and everyone else in the organization. In some organizations these differences are openly flaunted; in most they are more discreetly observed. Their motivational value is directed toward those top executives who do *not* have these special benefits. It is a carrot in front of their noses, a specific "here's what you will get if you are good enough to become a vice-president."

Some authorities have identified perquisites as a form of psychic income, inasmuch as many of the forms are identified with the highest standard of living. But there has been another real value to these special benefits. For a while many of these items, which are deductible by the company as business expenses, were not considered to be income by the individual but rather to be business-related services. In recent years, however, the U.S. Internal Revenue Service has continued to strike down more and more on the "nonincome" aspect. Companies are being asked to calculate the economic benefit to the executive of these perquisites—an amount which is fully taxable.

*See also* COMPENSATION, SPECIAL PLANS; COMPENSATION, WAGE AND SALARY POLICY AND ADMINISTRATION; PERSONNEL ADMINISTRATION; WAGES AND HOURS LEGISLATION.

### REFERENCES

Coffin, Richard M., and Michael S. Shaw: *Effective Communication of Employee Benefits*, American Management Association, New York, 1971.

Eilers, Robert D., and Robert M. Crowe: *Group Insurance Handbook*, Richard D. Irwin, Inc., Homewood, Ill., 1965.

Ellig, Bruce R.: "Determining Competitiveness of Employee Benefit Systems," *Compensation Review*, American Management Association, New York, 1974.

*Employee Benefits 1973*, Chamber of Commerce of the United States, Washington, 1974.

Gersh, Harry, and Robert D. Paul: *Employee Benefits Factbook 1972*, Martin E. Segal Company, New York, 1972.

McCaffery, Robert M.: *Managing the Employee Benefits Program*, American Management Association, New York, 1972.

Melone, Joseph J., and Everett T. Allen: *Pension Planning*, Richard D. Irwin, Inc., Homewood, Ill., 1972.

BRUCE R. ELLIG, *Pfizer Inc.*

# Compensation, executive

*Executive compensation plans* are those special pay vehicles developed to motivate and reward an organization's key management employees. The five principal vehicles are the incentive bonus, executive stock plans, deferred compensation, executive insurance, and perquisites.

1. The incentive bonus is a plan under which executives are eligible for annual bonus awards in addition to their salaries. The amount of the award varies with performance. The plan is designed to stimulate executives to improve company profitability.

2. Executive stock plan(s) are various types of stock option, stock purchase, or stock bonus plans that, taken alone or in combination, enable key personnel to acquire their own company's stock over time. The purpose of these plans is to align executives' interests with those of the stockholders, give them a long-term incentive to improve company performance, and build their net worth.

3. Deferred compensation is an arrangement under which executives earn (or in some cases voluntarily defer) income that is payable in the future. The purpose is to minimize current taxes and provide a source of retirement income or capital accumulation.

4. Executive insurance is special company-paid or subsidized insurance to (*a*) cover the perceived protection needs of key executives, or (*b*) extend the amount of insurance available to executives beyond the coverage limits of the benefit plans available to all employees.

5. Perquisites are those special benefits or privileges that provide indirect, and sometimes tax-fa-vored, compensation for key executives. In many instances, they connote status.

**Basic Concepts** The typical executive compensation program consists of from three to six special plans. Underlying this program are a number of concepts, some of which affect all forms of executive compensation; others relate to specific types of pay or common design approaches.

1. Compensation should be hierarchical; that is, at each successively higher postion level, the total pay opportunity should increase. Executive compensation plans provide a means of achieving a more hierarchical pay structure since they restrict eligibility to executives at a certain salary or title level. Moreover, the use of several plans can create a "tiered" approach to compensation, thus motivating individuals to progress in the organization where not only will their salary increase, but they will become eligible for extra rewards.

2. Executive pay should vary with performance in a given year and over time and do so more sharply than is possible through salaries alone. This concept helps explain the popularity of the incentive bonus and executive stock plans, which with varying degrees of precision, match reward with performance.

3. At successively higher levels of responsibility, more of the executive's total reward should be at risk. This concept affects the design and award patterns of most plans, increasing the size of the target bonus or stock award at each higher level and thereby reinforcing the hierarchical concept of pay.

4. The professional manager should have a proprietary stake in the business, and his or her interests should be aligned directly with those of the stockholder. This concept provides one of the principal rationales for the adoption of an executive stock plan.

5. An executive's compensation should facilitate the building of personal net worth. This concept helps explain the prevalence of executive stock plans and deferred compensation plans that provide capital accumulation opportunities.

6. The compensation vehicles used by the company should be cost effective in a way that has the least impact on company earnings; that is, they should take advantage of those provisions of the law that enable corporations to provide tax-free or tax-favored compensation—thus delivering more net after-tax reward for every dollar of compensation expenditure. This concept has contributed to the popularity of certain forms of executive stock options and perquisites.

7. Compensation plans should be used to re-

tain key executives. This concept has led to the development of plans that make the realization of actual gain or payout contingent on the recipient's continued employment. Some form of exercise or vesting provision is particularly common in most executive stock and deferred compensation plans.

8. Because of their position, executives have unique needs that the company should help them meet in order to spare them concern about personal affairs and free them for company matters. This concept underlies some of the additional indirect rewards that come as part of a total pay package; for example, special forms of insurance such as kidnap insurance and perquisites such as free assistance in personal tax preparation.

9. Executive compensation needs to be competitive both in the level of total reward and in the types of plans that are made available. In applying this concept, most companies attempt to relate their executive compensation program to that of companies within their industry.

In addition to these broad principles and concepts, one other factor has affected the evolution of executive compensation programs in the United States: the considerable and growing body of tax legislation and regulation. This consideration has affected the mix of pay, the popularity of specific pay vehicles, and often the design of plans and provisions. To a lesser extent, accounting rulings and precedents have had a similar result. Occasionally these tax and accounting considerations will be given more importance than basic principles, often to the detriment of good plan design.

## THE INCENTIVE BONUS

The incentive bonus is a highly individualized form of executive compensation used in approximately 8 out of 10 companies today. This was not always the case. Originally, incentive bonus plans were, for the most part, limited to those industries where the business cycle is relatively short-term and where management decisions in a given year can affect profits substantially, such as in the automobile and retail trade industries. Rarely were they used in heavily regulated industries or in industries where results can only be measured over several years. In the past decade, however, large corporations in industries that do not meet all these criteria—e.g., commercial banks, property and casualty insurance companies, oil companies, and airlines—have increasingly adopted incentive bonus plans. In many instances, the plans in these industries (or poorly designed or administered plans in any company) do not provide a true incentive but rather a yearly "lump sum" salary payment.

**Variable Features**  Most incentive bonus plans are tailored to the organization structure and profit economics of the business. Five features, taken together, help characterize a given plan.

1. An incentive bonus is either formal (that is, the amount and basis of payout are defined and communicated to participants) or judgmental. The E. I. Du Pont plan, for example, is quite formal, with the plan text itself taking 11 pages in the proxy. It is submitted at least once every 5 years to stockholders.

2. The aggregate monies available for payout (called the *bonus pool*) are based on corporate performance (usually profits before or after taxes), unit performance (operating income of a business group, division, or subsidiary), or a combination of both. The American Can Company, for example, has a key employees' incentive plan based on corporate-wide earnings, and a separate incentive plan for profit units based on unit operating income.

3. The degree of leverage also distinguishes plans. Leverage in the aggregate pool is usually achieved by (*a*) setting a minimum performance hurdle or "set aside" that must be met before any bonuses can be paid, and then accruing a percentage of profits above that level, or (*b*) accruing the bonus pool with a variable percentage of profits that increases at successively higher levels of performance. As an example of pool leverage, the Texaco plan develops available bonus monies based on 3 percent of the company's net income in excess of 6 percent of employed capital. Individual leverage is achieved by varying the size of a participant's bonus on the basis of his or her accomplishments during the plan year. Some plans are highly leveraged, with individual awards that can range from 0 to 2 or 3 times a "normal" award. The 1975 A&P plan, adopted as part of the company's turnaround efforts, provides a good example of highly leveraged individual awards. In plans without individual leverage awards vary only slightly from year to year.

4. Some plans are fixed formulas. The 1975 Campbell Soup Company plan, for example, sets out a very specific and complex formula for the calculation of the fund. Others are target- or goal-based; that is, management and the board set a target related to their annual budget or profit plan, and the degree of attainment of this target governs the fund payout that year. The 1976 Nabisco incentive compensation plan uses this approach. Some companies combine the two approaches by using a fixed formula that determines the maximum payout

(often called an umbrella fund or stockholder protection formula), and then setting specific targets to guide the actual payout each year.

5. An incentive plan can be designed to complement the base salary program so that the salary plus the normal bonus provides competitive cash compensation. This is sometimes referred to as a *discounted plan* because the salary structure is set on a discounted basis; that is, it is lower than it would be normally. Alternatively, a plan can be designed as an extra incentive to provide compensation opportunities substantially above competitive levels when results are superior.

**Program Design** Because of these variable features, few incentive bonus plans, even within the same industry, are identical, and designing an effective plan is a complex task. It involves:

1. Evaluating the competitiveness of existing pay levels and ensuring that the base salary plan is sound (otherwise the incentive could compound inequities in base pay).

2. Determining eligibility criteria and selecting participants. The principal criteria should be (*a*) the impact of the position on business results, and (*b*) the ability to measure the individual's contribution in a plan year.

3. Determining the magnitude of the award in a normal plan year for each level of participant. This award is often referred to as the target award or normal bonus. It is the dollar payment or percentage of salary that the company will award if it achieves its target profit objective and individual performance is standard. The sum total of these normal awards constitutes the target bonus pool.

4. Developing a formula for generating the bonus pool and varying its size at different levels of performance. This step should involve a detailed analysis of past performance, comparisons of the company's results with those of its competition, and a thorough review of different methods of measuring corporate or unit results. The decisions made in this step will affect the plan leverage discussed above.

5. Developing stockholder protection features. Many companies set other control features beyond the basic formula; for example, they limit the aggregate bonuses that can be paid to a percentage of common stock dividends.

6. Determining how individual performance will be judged and what the degree of leverage will be in individual awards.

7. Deciding on all award provisions, such as the form (usually cash) and timing of awards (most companies pay awards in full at the end of the plan year, but some pay the earned award over several years or defer a portion until retirement). Other decisions have to be made on how individual accrued awards will be handled in the event of promotion, death, or termination during the plan year.

8. Describing the bonus plan in detail in a formal plan text and administration guide; reviewing this guide with appropriate legal counsel.

9. Securing approval of the board of compensation committee and the full board of directors. (Unlike an executive stock plan, an incentive bonus usually does not require stockholder approval—although some companies take this step.)

10. Implementing the plan, i.e., setting a specified profit target and individual goals for the first plan year, communicating the details of the plan to participants, and establishing all necessary administrative procedures.

**Operational Considerations** A well-designed and effectively administered incentive bonus plan can be a powerful motivation for the key executive group. It also adds a variable element to the company's compensation cost. An incentive bonus is, however, one of the most difficult forms of executive compensation to develop and manage. It is not uncommon, for example, for the actual award process to become somewhat arbitrary and therefore lose its motivating power, or for the plan to evolve over a few years into a type of group profit sharing, with limited year-to-year variation. Further, studies have shown that most incentive plans increase total cash compensation 15 to 20 percent above the compensation levels prevailing in companies with just a salary plan.

An incentive bonus plan should not be adopted for vague philosophical reasons or for any me-too reasons. Unless executive decisions can substantially affect business results, unless management performance can be fairly evaluated on an annual basis, and unless senior management has the discipline to make the tough administrative decisions required, a company will not benefit from an incentive bonus.

## EXECUTIVE STOCK PLANS

Plans that help executives acquire their own company's common stock have been a fixture in United States industry for more than a quarter-century. At present they are used by approximately 80 percent of publicly held companies and about one-third of privately held. For some 14 years (1950 to 1963), the restricted stock option was virtually the only executive stock plan in use. This plan permitted the granting of 10-year options on company stock to key executives at 85 percent of the market price at the time of the award. Upon exercise, the stock had to be held for only 6 months, and the gains qualified for capital gains tax treatment. When this type of plan was eliminated in the 1964 tax law, industry began to experiment with other types of plans to meet the program objectives. This experimentation started slowly and then accelerated after the 1969 Tax Reform Act.

**Basic Plans**  Eight types of plans are currently in use.

*Qualified Stock Options.*  Executives are granted the right to buy stock during a 5-year period at the fair market value at the time of the grant, with appreciation in value taxed at capital gains rates. Upon exercise, the stock then has to be held an additional 3 years. Originally authorized in 1964, qualified stock options were for a time the most popular executive stock plan, but their use began to decline after 1969. The 1976 Tax Reform Act has phased them out totally. After May 21, 1976, no new qualified stock option plans could be adopted, and all options granted under an extant plan must be exercised by May 21, 1981.

*Nonqualified Stock Options.*  Executives are granted the right to buy stock during a period up to 10 years, usually at the fair market value at the time of the grant, although a lower price can be set. Because no special IRS requirements need be met, capital gains tax treatment is not available on gains at exercise; in most circumstances, any gain is taxed as earned income. Nonqualified stock options are currently the most prevalent executive stock plan, and many companies amended an existing qualified stock option plan to permit the granting of either qualified or nonqualified awards. This type of plan is sometimes used alone (for example, the 1976 National Gypsum Company plan) or in combination with other types of executive stock plans (as it is, for example, at Xerox).

*Stock Appreciation Rights (Linked to Nonqualified Options).*  Executives may elect to receive payment of all or part of the appreciation on the underlying option in lieu of exercising the option. About one-third of all nonqualified stock options now include this additional feature. For example, the 1976 Dow Chemical plan permits "incentive rights" to be granted at the time of an option award or subsequently.

*Phantom Stock.*  Executives are granted units, the value of which is tied to future stock price; payout of any appreciation on the underlying units is deferred

for a specific period. An example of this type of plan is the 1976 Inland Container plan (called a unit performance plan), which reserves 250,000 "phantom units" for rewards, with any gain "converted" into real stock or cash over a period of up to 72 months.

*Restricted Stock.*  Executives receive outright grants of company stock, but ownership is subject to risk of forfeiture and the right to sell is restricted for a specific period. The three-part 1975 American Express executive stock program contained such a plan aimed primarily at middle management, with awards vesting over 4 years.

*Book-Value Shares.*  Executives buy shares, or are granted shares outright, at a price equal to book value rather than market price; subsequently the company either repurchases the stock at a price equal to book value at the time or makes cash or stock payments in the amount of the book-value appreciation. Citibank recently adopted a book-value stock purchase plan and Kimberly Clark a book-value phantom award plan.

*Performance Shares.*  Executives are awarded shares of common stock subject to earn-out some time later if a specified corporate performance objective is achieved. The most common vesting method is to relate the ultimate number of units paid out to an EPS growth target. For example, the Del Monte performance share plan relates payout to a cumulative earnings per share goal over 4 years, with a sliding payout scale starting at 0 if EPS growth drops below 6 percent and increasing to 100 if EPS growth gets up to 12 percent.

*Long-Term Performance Bonus.*  Executives are awarded long-term dollar bonus opportunities, with earn-out depending on achievement of a specified corporate performance objective. The 1976 Xerox executive stock program contained a long-term performance bonus along with stock options and stock appreciation rights.

**Program Design**  The range of available plans and the many possible combinations complicate the task of selecting the right vehicle(s) and designing a program that meets the unique needs of a given company. For example, one company may need to emphasize the holding power of a program, while another needs to reinforce long-term growth objectives. More often than not, a company's program has several needs to meet. In developing an executive stock program, a company should take the following steps:

1. Analyze the need the program should satisfy and clearly define program objectives. This step

usually requires reviewing the existing stock plan and the *total* executive compensation program; comparing the form, timing, and level of reward with competitive patterns, and determining the changes required.

2. Decide on the specific design requirements that will be used to screen available types of plans, and review and test various plans against them. Often two or three alternatives will be considered.

3. Establish eligibility ground rules and estimate the likely number of participants initially and over the term of the plan.

4. Concurrently, develop award guidelines and estimate the total share, or share equivalent, requirements.

5. To further narrow the plans being considered, make a detailed evaluation of them, comparing their inherent characteristics with the needs of the corporation, developing cost estimates, and projecting the potential gain for various levels of participants under a number of performance assumptions.

6. Select a specific plan and describe it in detail in a formal plan text and an administrative guide.

7. Submit the proposed plan to a thorough legal review.

8. Present the plan to a board compensation committee (and often the full board).

9. Upon approval of the plan by this group, prepare proxy material describing the new plan and send it to shareholders for their approval.

10. After final plan approval, make the initial awards and implement appropriate administrative procedures.

**Risks of Stock Plans** Any corporation considering the adoption of an executive stock plan should recognize that this type of reward and incentive carries risks as well as benefits. One risk is that the cost will be excessive and out of proportion to the benefits. Since most executive stock plans increase the total amount of common stock outstanding, they have a dilution impact. Moreover, with the exception of stock options granted at market, all executive stock plans involve a cost to the corporation and thus can reduce reported earnings. Often this cost is not fixed; for example, where basis for gain is related to stock price in the future, the total cost can escalate sharply.

Another risk of stock plans is that they are not always effective long-term incentives. For example, factors outside the company's control or unrelated to its program (such as overall stock market trends) may wipe out the gain or payout to participants. This situation can lead to executive dissatisfaction and even contribute to turnover, particularly if other companies have better designed plans or have moved more promptly to update their plan as circumstances change.

Finally, there is a particularly acute risk for both the company and the individual executives if they adopt a plan that requires participant investment (as all option plans do, for example). If the stock price drops precipitously after the executive exercises the option, the individual can suffer a substantial loss if unable to dispose of the stock. Corporate officers and other insiders are especially vulnerable to this risk under applicable SEC rules. If they have taken out loans to acquire the stock, as is customary, the personal financial risk is obviously much greater.

In summary, although executive stock plans can be an effective long-term incentive and benefit both the stockholders and the individual executive, they do involve some risk. Since it is increasingly difficult to design an effective overall program, this type of executive compensation should be adopted only after intense study.

### DEFERRED COMPENSATION

A premise underlying most deferred compensation plans is that an executive with high current income, taxed at the maximum rates, will benefit from the deferral of some of that income until retirement. Presumably his or her tax rate will then be lower, particularly if payout of the deferred funds is spread over a number of years. With the lowering of the maximum federal tax rates in the 1964 and 1969 acts, this tax savings rationale was weakened, since deferred compensation payouts initially did not qualify for the new lower maximum rates. However, the Tax Reform Act of 1976 made deferred compensation eligible for earned income tax treatment (currently a maximum rate of 50 percent). Because of this development and the fact that deferral arrangements can be designed to make up for inadequate pensions, to help hold key executives, or to provide an additional type of reward, they may become more popular. Currently, about 40 percent of corporations have some form of deferred compensation plan in effect for an individual or group of individuals.

**Basic Plans** The basic types of deferred compensation plans in use today are:

*Voluntary Deferral Plans.* Under these plans, the company permits certain executives (usually at a stated position or earnings level) to defer a portion of the income they would normally be paid currently (in salary or an annual bonus). Generally, this voluntary deferral is specified annually, before each tax year. A large textile company, for example, permits all executives earning over $50,000 to defer up to 100 percent of their bonus until retirement; then the deferred amounts, plus earnings thereon (at 9 percent) are paid out over 10 to 15 years.

*Incentive Deferrals.* These plans are integrated with an incentive bonus under which a portion of the annual bonus is mandatorily deferred. Often under an incentive deferral, the basis of appreciation is related to company performance, and return on stockholders' equity or growth in earnings per share, for example, is used to determine the annual change in the value of the deferred funds. The plan can be set up to defer a portion of the bonus the executive earns (as at E. I. du Pont de Nemours & Co.) or it can involve an extra award. For example, in a large oil company, an additional award, equal to 25 percent of each executive's cash bonus, is set aside and can be forfeited if the executive leaves the company.

*Nonqualified Pensions.* Under these plans, eligible executives accrue additional retirement benefits each year based on their earnings level. Since the 1974 Employee Retirement Income Security Act (ERISA) placed a maximum (initially set at $75,000) on qualified pension benefits, these plans have become increasingly popular. Often the nonqualified pension is set up with the same formula as the company's basic pension—an annual accrual of a stated percentage of earnings (e.g., 1.5 percent). Eligibility and vesting on the additional benefits are not subject to the strict requirements applicable to a "qualified" plan, which must conform to IRS regulations, ensuring that the benefit is paid only to those who retire. An example of this arrangement is the supplemental plan adopted in 1976 by Allegheny Ludlum Industries for its executives to "pay the difference, if any, between the benefits they would otherwise be entitled to receive under the retirement plan of the corporation and the annual benefits they are permitted to receive under the plan pursuant to ERISA."

*Other Retirement Deferral Plans.* Among the other arrangements used to provide an additional source of retirement income, the most common are the following:

1. The stipulation of flat amount. A New Jersey bank that does not have a qualified pension plan sets aside $15,000.

2. Purchase of life insurance and annuities. Clark Equipment Company has this type of deferral plan for 63 key employees.

3. Guarantee of an annual retirement benefit from all sources. For example, Briggs & Stratton, in 1975 guaranteed an aggregate benefit of $70,000 to its president and $60,000 to another senior officer, less the amounts received from the company's basic pension plan.

4. Provision for the accrual of a deferred sum each year (usually a stated dollar amount) based on continued employment. This technique is often used by a new company to recruit senior executives at older ages who will not have long enough to accrue an adequate retirement benefit. For example, a large New York textile company recently recruited a new president and agreed to set aside $50,000 each year for him beyond his base salary and other incentives.

In assessing the applicability of deferred compensation, companies should first consider whether there is a need. A need can arise, for example, because of a shortfall in the basic retirement plan, or a demand for such a provision from older senior executives whose cash needs have already been met, or the unique problems of recruiting a new executive.

**Program Design** The steps to be taken in designing and implementing a deferred compensation plan are similar to those outlined in the preceding sections. Three steps are particularly critical, however, in most deferral arrangements:

1. Determining the basis of appreciation of the deferred funds in voluntary or incentive deferral plans. Some companies use a variable external return measure (e.g., the prime rate or AAA bond rates); others set a fixed rate, which is reviewed periodically; still others use some measure of company performance. If this provision is not thought through carefully in the context of current interest rate trends, a deferral decision can be a poor *investment* decision for the individual.

2. Carefully analyzing all the income tax and estate tax consequences. This step is particularly important in deciding who should be eligible and in setting forfeiture and payout provisions.

3. Integrating the deferred plan with other compensation vehicles that pay off in the future, such as executive stock plans, pensions, and qualified profit sharing or savings plans.

**Program Risks** Deferred compensation can meet legitimate executive compensation objectives and be of value to older executives who are close enough to retirement to estimate their future income and tax situation with some reliability. Even for these executives, however, most deferral plans involve individual risk. If the corporation goes into bankruptcy, the accrued deferred funds can disappear (as happened at Penn Central). If the income tax structure changes after the deferral decision has been made, the inherent economics of the decision may be altered or an individual's projected income may vary sharply from that which was assumed.

Even where the circumstances are right or the benefit seems worth some risk, participation in a deferred compensation plan is, in the final analysis, an investment decision and should be evaluated against other investment choices.

## EXECUTIVE INSURANCE

With the proliferation of company paid or subsidized insurance for all employees, corporations have been adopting more and varied types of insurance to meet the needs of key executives. Among the most prevalent forms of executive insurance are the following:

*Excess Life Insurance.* Most basic company life insurance plans provide two to three times pay in coverage for all salaried employees, often with a dollar limit. Many corporations have adopted additional group plans, restricted to a certain salary or position level, that provide group term coverage substantially in excess of this basic amount. For example, one large New York law firm provides $600,000 additional term insurance for all its partners; a large chemical company provides an additional three times current earnings for all corporate officers.

*Split-Dollar Insurance.* This is a life insurance arrangement involving permanent insurance written under an individual contract with an executive. In this plan, the company pays the portion of premium each year equal to the increase in the policy's cash value and the executive pays the balance, if any. In the event of the executive's death, his or her beneficiaries receive the insurance benefits in excess of the cash value. The General Electric Company has a form of split-dollar insurance program covering about 90 key personnel.

*Personal Liability Insurance.* This form of insurance is usually provided to certain levels of executives to protect them against personal liability up to a stated maximum, generally a million dollars or more. It is designed to cover executives against suits growing out of a car accident, for example, or some other liability they could incur as individuals. It is distinguished from director or officer liability coverage, which protects key executives from stockholder or consumer suits growing out of their role in the corporation.

*Kidnap Insurance.* As the term implies, this insurance provides a source of funds for the payment of a ransom in the event an executive is abducted. It is set up as an individual or group policy.

**Evaluation of Need** In evaluating the need for one or more forms of executive insurance, a company should carefully review the income and age profiles of the executive group and the extent of benefit coverage under other company plans. Often it faces difficult trade-off decisions between improving the basic coverage for all categories of employees and responding to the special requirements of key executives. Another consideration is cost. Unlike bonuses and executive stock plans, insurance is not performance related and thus, in most instances, cannot justify a large proportion of the corporation's executive compensation expenditure. Because of these circumstances, individual company philosophy has a greater bearing on the prevalence of executive insurance (and perquisites) than it has on other compensation vehicles. Companies reach different decisions on the amount of protection to provide (which, it can be argued, is an individual responsibility) or the extent to which they should discriminate in favor of higher level employees in matters of insurance.

**Program Design** Should a company decide that some executive insurance is appropriate, it should take care to:

1. Select the right insurance carrier and negotiate the best rate possible (wide variations in cost are not unusual).

2. Coordinate the coverage with other company plans and see that the individual recipient gets proper advice on integrating the company coverage with the policies he or she may own. For example, most personal liability plans require certain stated amounts of basic automobile liability and homeowners' coverage.

3. Examine the plan's annual cash flow requirements and the impact of any special insurance on the company's asset and liability structure. Since permanent insurance can require substantial cash outlays, the financial implications for the company need professional analysis, particularly in a smaller company.

In summary, insurance can play a special, but limited, role in the total executive compensation program. The most common mistakes companies make are to adopt plans that they do not need or that respond poorly to their total requirements and priorities. Thus they increase costs unnecessarily or perpetuate more basic weaknesses in their overall compensation program.

## EXECUTIVE PERQUISITES

Long before the advent of the corporate form, human institutions were granting special privileges to key personnel to meet perceived needs and often to denote rank in the organization. With the coming of the income tax, these special privileges or "perks" began to multiply rapidly. Under United States tax laws and regulations, a corporation can deduct legitimate business expenses. Even if the executive gains some personal benefit, he or she is often not taxed or not taxed fully on it. Thus an executive can receive tax-favored, indirect "compensation."

Among the more common executive perks used by corporations today are the following:

*Company Loans.* The corporation either lends an executive money directly or guarantees a bank loan, usually at a low interest rate and with liberal repayment terms. A relatively recent compensation form, this device is most commonly used to help an executive finance stock options and build personal net worth. In 1973, Heublein, for example, guaranteed $3 million in personal loans for four of its key executives, reimbursing them for any interest payable in excess of 6 percent per year.

*Company-Sponsored Tax Shelter.* This is a fairly rare compensation device under which the company organizes a special limited partnership for its executives, usually to provide them with both a tax shelter and an opportunity to build personal net worth. The device is most often used in privately held companies.

*Executive Dining Room.* Many organizations make an on-premise company eatery available to certain levels of executives as both a perquisite and a convenience. In commercial banks, for example, three or four classes of dining rooms can often be found, ranging from a cafeteria to private dining suites for senior officers.

*Executive Housing.* Company-provided housing is typically offered when executives are on temporary assignments away from their home base or when they can be expected to encounter unusual costs or difficulty in finding accommodations. Occasionally, executive housing, such as an in-town apartment or permanent hotel suite, is offered as an indirect form of compensation for high-level executives. For example, the Fabergé Company provides the head of one of its subsidiaries a New York apartment costing $30,000 a year.

*Executive Physical Program.* Executives are provided free periodic physical examinations. Frequently the policies and procedures governing the program become more liberal with rank.

*Personal Financial Counseling.* An independent professional firm advises an individual executive or a group of executives on financial matters under a plan organized and/or partially paid for by the company. The couselor analyzes financial affairs, suggests investment strategies, and gives advice on specific financial decisions. This perquisite is now offered by about 20 percent of companies.

*Company Cars.* Under this perquisite, an automobile (and on occasion a driver) is provided for the individual's use. Usually the company pays all insurance, maintenance, and operating expenses.

*Tax Preparation Assistance.* The corporation, through its staff or an outside professional firm, assists the executive in preparing their personal tax returns. A New York chemical company limits this "perk" to officers, for whom it pays up to $2000 in tax preparation fees.

*Direct Medical Reimbursement.* The company pays all medical and dental expenses not covered by group medical insurance for the executive and his or her dependents, usually up to an annual maximum. Montford of Colorado, for example, reimburses some of its key executives up to $2500 a year.

*Special Expense Accounts.* This is a plan or individual arrangement under which executives are permitted more liberal reimbursement of business-related expenses (including entertainment) or are given a specific sum for expenses each year which they need not account for.

*Education Reimbursement.* Funds are set aside for self-development, the education of one's dependents, or educational leaves. Kimberly-Clark established such a plan in 1974.

*Personal Services.* This category of perquisites covers the many, and occasionally special, personal services provided executives at company cost, including a company barber, free clothing, free tickets to cultural or sporting events, free checking accounts, etc.

*Company Plane.* An executive can use corporate aircraft for both business and personal reasons but must generally reimburse the corporation for at least part of the cost. The chairman and chief executive of the Seagram Company, Ltd., has such an arrangement.

*Spouse Travel.* Spouses are permitted to accompany executives on business trips, conventions, etc., at company expense.

In general, a company should not adopt a perquisite unless it fills a clear and justifiable business need. Moreover, before implementing any such arrangement, a corporation should seek legal counsel. There is an extensive body of IRS rules and regulations governing most perquisites, and individual executives may find themselves liable for additional taxes. And there are proposed new SEC disclosure rules that would require additional information on perquisites in proxies. Even where business rationale and precedent in other companies support adoption of perquisites, a corporation should assess their impact on the business environment. Many corporations maintain that perquisites create too hierarchical a structure, reduce cost consciousness within the company, and engender adverse reactions from employees.

*See also* COMPENSATION, SPECIAL PLANS; COMPENSATION, SALES; COMPENSATION, WAGE AND SALARY POLICY AND ADMINISTRATION; MOTIVATION IN ORGANIZATIONS; SEARCH AND RECRUITMENT, EXECUTIVE; TAX MANAGEMENT, MANAGERIAL RESPONSIBILITY FOR FEDERAL INCOME TAX REPORTING; WAGES AND HOURS LEGISLATION.

### REFERENCES

Babson, Stanley M., Jr.: *Fringe Benefits*, John Wiley & Sons, Inc., New York, 1974.
Cheeks, James E.: *How to Compensate Executives*, Dow Jones-Irwin, Inc., Homewood, Ill., 1974.
Crystal, Graef S.: *Financial Motivation for Executives*, American Management Association, New York, 1970.
McLaughlin, David J.: *The Executive Money Map*, McGraw-Hill Book Company, New York, 1975.
Patton, Arch: *Men, Money and Motivation*, McGraw-Hill Book Company, New York, 1961.
Sibson, Robert E.: *Wages And Salaries*, 2d ed., American Management Association, New York, 1974.

DAVID J. MCLAUGHLIN, *McKinsey and Company, Inc.*

# Compensation, sales

A company may have sound product lines, appropriate marketing strategies, and a well-positioned sales organization, but without a motivated sales force, it will have difficulty accomplishing its sales goals. An integral part of a motivational system is a sales compensation package that complements and reinforces the overall marketing objectives. While the best sales compensation package will not overcome poor products or ineffective pricing, a well-designed package can have a direct impact on sales volume, profit margins, or market penetration.

The choices of sales compensation plans are wide, and the final design should always be tailored to support the overall marketing strategy of the company. The specific package should also be coordinated with the overall compensation policy of the company. As such, it should combine functional inputs from both marketing and personnel.

Historically, there are two basic methods of rewarding salespersons: straight salary and straight commission. Straight salary is simple to administer, but it provides limited incentives for greater sales productivity and generates a largely fixed cost of a sales force rather than a variable one. Straight commission, traditionally on volume, encourages the sales force to hustle but at the cost of decreasing the company's control over field salespersons, since it impacts on only one factor and gives rise to personal anxiety because there is no assurance of income. Beyond volume, neither system encourages the achievement of specific multimarketing and sales objectives. Consequently, enterprises typically develop combinations of base salary and incentives to get "the best of both worlds."

To develop an appropriate sales compensation plan, a number of distinct phases must be considered:

1. Review marketing objectives, analyzing them for clarity and consistency, getting agreement, and spelling out in detail the sales aims. Vague generalizations about increasing sales and reducing selling costs will not suffice; neither will exhorting salespersons, e.g., "to concentrate on the most profitable products." Rather, concise written statements of all the marketing goals and strategies which management agrees are desirable and attainable within a reasonable time are called for. For example, one large agricultural equipment concern predicated its sales reward plan on the following corporate objectives:

To increase the utilization of available production capacity through upgrading of sales volume and product mix

To upgrade the marketing and sales force effectiveness through improved goal setting, performance measurement, and communication processes

To upgrade the coordination and utilization of the various sales forces leading to improved market share

To lead to increased motivation of the sales force through emphasis on a reward system that balances the compensation rewards with career development rewards, within the marketing and workforce strategies of the company

2. Study marketing-related areas, each of which can present important issues and complex variables which must be addressed. Of particular importance is an evaluation of the marketplace, the

internal climate, the organization, and its competition.

3. Establish the internal worth of a sales position to the company. To this end, job evaluation, such as the Hay Guide Chart-Profile Method, which rates jobs according to their know-how, problem-solving, and accountability content, is often utilized.

4. Reconcile the inputs from the earlier phase so that the sales compensation plan is one in which total earnings opportunity is established, base salary levels set, methods of incentive payment determined, and the timing of payouts agreed upon.

5. Follow through with implementation, communication, and administration. The plan must be "built up" and communicated to the sales force. Its legal ramifications should be gauged; an employee may successfully sue for the recovery of earned incentives under certain conditions.

6. Once the plan has been put in effect, evaluate it routinely and update it to reflect changes in the strategies and the marketplace.

### THE SALES FORCE CLIMATE

The design of a sales compensation program will be mechanical and often ineffective if it is not based on a sound understanding of the sales force's environment. Furthermore, management must be aware of the perceptions of each level in the sales organization so that reward structures responsive to their specific needs can be planned. A not infrequent misconception of top executives who used to be salespeople is that every salesperson is motivated the same way they were when salespeople. What they forget is that they belong not to the average but to a minority who made it to the top.

Recent climate surveys have revealed contradictions to conventional wisdom regarding the character and compensation preferences of salespeople. It appears that most salespeople, when thinking about their own compensation, have a reasonably clear perception of what an equitable income is. They appear to know what they want; to some extent, "how they get there" is secondary.

Further survey data suggest that the traditional notion of the salesperson as a risk-oriented entrepreneur has to be substantially revised. In fact, the average field salesperson is much more security-oriented and noninnovative than is generally assumed. Sales forces are intensely interested in security and stability. There are salespeople, of course, who are highly achievement-oriented. For them, however, the earning of substantial incentive rewards appears to be sought as much for the purpose of personal fulfillment and recognition as it is for increasing income per se.

It is possible that economic downturns are a factor influencing salespeople to favor security. A substantial economic upturn might create more enthusiasm for compensation structures with a high ratio of incentives to base salary. No one, therefore, least of all salespeople, suggests doing away with incentive compensation. But in managing a force of more security-oriented salespeople, design of the base salary and perquisite aspects of a compensation program have become important.

### WHERE INCENTIVES WORK BEST

An early decision in developing a compensation package is to establish the basic compensation approach. The five most common ones are the following:

*Entrepreneurial Plans.* In this approach, the company provides a product or know-how in return for part of the revenues. Typically, such plans cover general insurance agency, real estate, and manufacturing representatives. The company has only limited control in the marketing efforts of the participants.

*Straight Commissions* (with or without a draw against commission). These are typically provided from "dollar one" on volume of sales with occasional adjustment for profit margins. Real estate and encyclopedia salespeople are often paid this way. The changing social and marketing environment makes it less common elsewhere.

*Basic Salary Plus a Managed Variable Incentive.* Such plans are increasing in number. Incentive plans, whose purpose is to stimulate and motivate action, are causal in nature and contractual in a formula that equates individual incentive earnings to predetermined levels of performance. Incentive award levels are set before the effort is expended, resulting in motivational pull toward desired earnings levels.

*Base Salary Plus Bonuses.* This differs from managed variable incentives in that bonuses are determined after the fact; consequently the judgments on which they are based can be perceived as subjective by the recipient. Thus, they are often of questionable motivational value and most applicable where long-time employment is prevalent.

*Variable Base Salary.* This approach is an attempt to reward performance through periodic increases in the base salary. In the right sales environment this can be the preferred approach, and appropriately it is widely used where the sales situation is complex. *See* Fig. C-3.

In selecting a specific approach, the eligibility issue has to be raised. A good rule is to restrict incentive plan participation to those postions with line accountabilities designed to impact directly on the desired end results of sales volume, sales profitability, market penetration, or other clearly defined sales goals. To extend a plan beyond the sales force can rarely be justified; it generally weakens the program through confusion of, and difficulty in, setting objectives. Temptation to do so should be resisted.

Field sales-force incentives imply the need for variable compensation for all ranks of sales management. Aside from logic, an incentive program for management is a practical necessity in order to avoid creating problems of career development and promotion, as well as equity of total compensation.

## RELATION TO THE MARKET LIFE CYCLE

A principal concern in designing incentives is the nature of the market served combined with the fundamental sales challenge. A rapidly expanding market with limited competition is one thing; a mature market fully exploited by a number of competitors is another. Such factors have a bearing on total earnings opportunity, base salary levels, and the degree of plan elasticity. A general view of the applicability of the ratio of incentives to base salary may be seen in Fig. C-4, which represents a normal growth curve as it might apply to a product line, market segment, or company growth.

During a *start-up period* (phase A), competition is usually light, there is no track record, and forecasts are likely to be highly inaccurate. Ideally, this period calls for a relatively high base salary (to attract high performance staff), with some discretionary-type, after-the-fact bonus. Phase B is the period of *high growth* acceleration. This is the phase of the high commission plan, with a market responsive to sales efforts. At this point, minimum performance levels may be established. In the United States economy, many companies and products are in phase C, that of *decelerating growth rates* where exceptionally high earnings for star performers are no longer justified. Other companies find themselves, or their products, in phase D, that of *market maturity*, calling for stiff, sustained competition in maintaining market share. Typically, phases C and D

|  | Influencing Factors | |
|---|---|---|
| Use incentives as <u>less</u> of a percentage of total compensation | | Use incentives as <u>more</u> of a percentage of total compensation |
| No ⟵ | Clear goal setting and monitoring process | ⟶ Yes |
| High ⟵ | Number of different objectives | ⟶ Low |
| Yes ⟵ | Multiproducts | ⟶ No |
| Very long ⟵ | Time span between interest, booking, and shipment | ⟶ Short |
| Large ⟵ | Size of order or unit sale | ⟶ Small |
| Mature ⟵ | Market maturity | ⟶ Developing |
| Low ⟵ | Salesperson independence | ⟶ High |
| No ⟵ | Defined selling territories | ⟶ Yes |
| High ⟵ | Need for repeat business | ⟶ Low |
| Significant ⟵ | Continuous service to accounts | ⟶ Limited |
| High ⟵ | Special support by staff (engineering, finance, technical service) | ⟶ Low |
| High ⟵ | Technical know-how required | ⟶ Low |

**Fig. C-3. The applicability of incentives.**

call for either a "managed" incentive plan or emphasis on base salary.

The general evidence suggests that sales incentives should be modified as market conditions evolve, rather than being fixed for long periods of time.

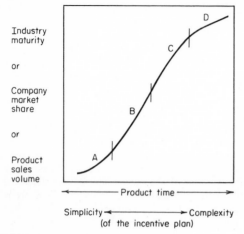

Industry maturity

or

Company market share

or

Product sales volume

Product time

Simplicity ◄──────► Complexity
(of the incentive plan)

**Fig. C-4. Product life cycle.**

## PLAN ELASTICITY AND EARNINGS OPPORTUNITY

In designing sales incentives, income variability and earnings levels appropriate for the various performance levels are closely related. As a rule, the higher the earnings opportunity and the more variable an individual's income, the greater the motivation. Following this heuristic, high performers may attain comparably high earnings but must continuously perform at this level to maintain them. If the volume of business generated justifies such earnings, a workable plan can be accomplished. Conversely, the more secure a salesperson's income is, the lower the maximum earnings opportunity should be. Additionally, total incomes must be externally competitive as well as internally equitable. Special sales compensation surveys conducted within an industry or a geographic area will reveal appropriate earnings levels as well as industry peculiarities regarding the weight given the various components of cash compensation. An industry survey, in fact, is a good place to start when undertaking the design of an incentive plan, after which the company must get down to setting earnings levels.

Maximum earnings opportunity sets the top income level that the highest performers can achieve. It should strike a balance between how much the additional business is worth to the company and the amount of incentive it is reasonable to pay as a cost of acquiring it. Usually, the more responsive the market is to direct sales effort, the higher the earnings opportunity may be without loss of sales productivity, i.e., ratio of incentives paid (the cost of generating additional sales volume) to the volume of business produced.

Average earnings opportunity varies in most cases directly with the degree of maximum incentive opportunity and should be communicated to the participants. To establish proper maximum and projected average incentive levels the following must be considered: industry practice, flexibility of the market, nature of the sales event, considerations of internal and external equity, and productivity factors.

Base salaries for salespeople are commonly adjusted downward when incentive plans are installed. National surveys which compare salaries for field salespersons with those of other employees in the organization (e.g., the Hay Compensation Comparison) often disclose a tendency to discount salary levels when sales incentive plans are in use. Many companies find it useful to retain a portion of a salary range to recognize the junior-senior nature of some sales organizations.

## PERFORMANCE STANDARDS AND SALES GOALS

A significant overall objective for many incentive plans is management's desire to focus clearly the attention of the sales force on a few well-established goals critical to the enterprise's marketing plans and to amply reward their attainment.

**Performance Standards** The most prevalent component of incentive payout is the achievement of *sales volume objectives* either on a quota or absolute volume basis. In an intensely competitive environment, or in those industries subject to major cyclical changes, *overall market position/market penetration* is often a much better indicator of the success of the field sales force than is volume or growth. The problem with its use as the primary objective is the timeliness and accuracy of measurement.

Other incentive components include new business, customers, new product introduction, repeat business, profit and margins volume, and ROI. As competition increases and the available share of the remaining market decreases, considerations of profitability shift from volume alone to the selective marketing of more profitable product lines.[1] Multiple-rate commission plans, featuring different rates for different products or territories, are often applicable to such situations.

As long as an essential objective can be clearly defined and measured, there appears to be no limit to the sophistication of incentive plans.

**Sales Goals**  Several methods are available to define sales goals.

*Sales forecasts* commit the sales force to obtaining precalculated volumes. Of course, sales forecasting is a critical management process essential to market planning and should be kept as objective as possible. A substantial advantage is gained if calculations of incentive remuneration are divorced from the process of sales forecasting. A salesperson becomes a natural pessimist when asked to forecast future volumes if he or she is aware that one use for the forecast will be to establish sales objectives which will determine future incentive earnings.

*Sales quotas* are more autocratic. Required total sales volume is set on the basis of (1) amount of available business and (2) desired profit margins implying a certain level of plant utilization.

*Sales bogeys* begin incentive payments "one step off par." Incentive earnings commonly commence between 70 and 90 percent below planned territorial objectives. The bogey system can be utilized to allow salespersons to increase income as they build their territories. This provides a long-term motivation and increases career opportunity for the salespersons.

*Territorial standards* are generally used in well-established markets. Territories are grouped into small, medium, and large categories whose volume levels are fixed for an extended period of time. Incentives may be paid to the degree that actual sales exceed certain norms or sales volume.

Whatever the goals a company selects, it is important to review and adjust them periodically to reflect changes in the market, objectives, or strategies.

1. In determining the proper components and rates for incentive payout, the overriding considerations are simplicity and the ability of the individual salesperson to compute quickly and accurately future incentive earnings on the basis of assumed performance levels.

2. An appropriate variable may be derived by relating desired incentive earnings levels to anticipated territorial volumes which have been adjusted to compensate for a sales goal or quota.

3. An important general rule is this: The lower the sales goal, the lower the variable rate required and the more stable the plan. As an illustration of this principle, assume the following two incentive plans, A and B (Fig. C-5).

Plan A had a high minimum sales objective and consequently a high variable rate to ensure the required planned average payout (assumed to occur at the median volume level). An unstable situation occurred because incentive earnings increased at too rapid a pace relative to increased sales volume. Too many individuals ordinarily got no commissions for a given period (approximately 35 percent of the sales force), and too many (those with sales above the 75th percentile, or about 25 percent) earned top dollar. For the latter, a "cap," or maximum earnings level, was established. This was a poor incentive plan because it put 60 percent of the sales force at the extremes of income potential. Salespeople were provoked by what they considered an illogical earnings cap, and some encouraged customers to delay bookings until the outset of the following sales period. This created havoc in planning and even customer unrest.

The company reacted to the problem by returning to the general rule: sales goals were lowered, and so were commission rates to stabilize the plan. The company adopted plan B, with a lower sales objective (now called a *bogey*) fixed at 70 percent of the normal sales goal, and a reduced commission rate. It found that the cap could be eliminated under the new system, since only about 10 percent would be expected to achieve high earnings and at a much slower rate of increase in earnings. Normal incentive awards in each case turned out to be about the same.

4. Commission rates do not necessarily have to be linear (e.g., proportional). A much sharper motivation program will result if the commission rate is allowed to increase in steps as higher volume levels are achieved. Such plans may prove useful, but they usually are more unstable and tougher to control than single rate plans.

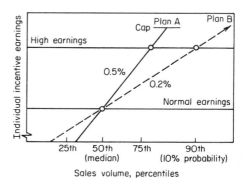

**Fig. C-5. Determining incentive rates.**

## PAYOUT PERIODS

As a rule, the payout should be as close as possible to the event generating the reward. A highly variable compensation plan combined with a relatively short incentive payout period provides the highest motivation levels. The limiting factor is practicality determined by administrative procedure. Monthly incentive plans are quite common; even biweekly plans are not unusual in the case of straight commissions. Many firms quite sensibly choose to pay base salaries in weekly or biweekly increments, supplemented by quarterly payment of incentive earnings. If variable earnings levels are determined to some extent by overall corporate or divisional performance, a common practice is to split incentive payouts, with the bulk of variable earnings paid quarterly and the portion that relates to overall performance paid annually.

The larger the portion of an individual's total earnings tied to incentives is, the shorter the payout period should be. Deferred payment of part of earned incentives is a common practice, however, wherever a contingency exists on the part of full customer commitment or where true sales performance cannot be fully determined until some later date.

**Evaluation**  Design of a sales compensation plan is not without pitfalls. The following, in particular, should be avoided: overly complex plans; quota-based plans; straight percentage commission plans; plans with high risk; plans which reward too few or too many results; plans which set unrealistic goals; plans which are wrong for the life cycle of the product; and plans which encourage counterproductive behavior. Other mistakes are (1) to have a plan at all where it is not possible to forecast, (2) not to change the plan when the business itself changes, and (3) not to have and properly use salary ranges.

*See also* COMPENSATION, EMPLOYEE BENEFIT PLANS; COMPENSATION, WAGES AND SALARY POLICY AND ADMINSTRATION; FORECASTING BUSINESS CONDITIONS; MOTIVATION IN ORGANIZATIONS; SALES MANAGEMENT; WAGES AND HOURS LEGISLATION.

### NOTES

[1]*See* Michael Reynolds, "Keying Compensation to Profits," *Sales Management*, November 1970.

### REFERENCES

Carey, James F.: "Cost and Value in Salesmen's Pay," *Compensation Review*, first quarter 1975.

*Compensating Salesmen and Sales Executives*, National Industrial Conference Board, Report #579, New York, 1972.

Davis, Kenneth L.: "Are Your Salesmen Paid Too Much?" in Edward C. Bursk and G. Scott Hutchinson (eds.), *Salesmanship and Sales Force Management*, Harvard University Press, Cambridge, Mass., 1971, pp. 10–18.

Ellig, Bruce R.: "Salesmen's Compensation: A Systematic Approach," *Compensation Review*, fourth quarter 1969.

Fletcher, F. L., and Edwin R. Mead: "Designing Incentives for Sales Personnel," in Milton L. Rock (ed.), *Handbook of Wage and Salary Administration*, McGraw-Hill Book Company, New York, 1972, pp. 7-28—7-739.

Stanton, William F., and Richard H. Buskirk: *Management of the Sales Force*, Richard D. Irwin, Inc., Homewood, Ill., 1969.

C. IAN SYM-SMITH, *Hay Asociates*
AVNER M. PORAT, *Hay Associates*

# Compensation, special plans

Four special plans, profit sharing, the Lincoln incentive management plan, multiple management plan, and the guaranteed annual wage plan will be discussed in this entry.

## PROFIT SHARING

In its simplest form profit sharing involves the payment of part of profits to employees in addition to regular wages. All plans are variations of cash and/or deferred types. The trend today is away from strictly cash plans toward the establishment of combination plans.

Experience shows that profit sharing will not work as a substitute for sound management and good relationships with employees. Though profit sharing companies tend to outperform nonsharers, the advantages of the approach in comparison with other large-group, team-oriented approaches do not derive primarily from incentive value.

**Definitions**  In Paris in 1889 the International Cooperative Congress defined *profit sharing* as "an agreement freely entered into by which the employees receive a share, fixed in advance, of the profits." However, a Senate subcommittee which made an exhaustive study of United States practice in 1938[1] regarded it as "all payments to employees, regardless of the form in which they are allocated or distributed, which are in addition to the market or basic wage rate." The Proft Sharing Council of America sees profit sharing as "payment, in addition to regular pay, of current or deferred sums based on the profitability of the enterprise as a whole." This is similar to the definition used by the National

Industrial Conference Board, which published five reports on profit sharing between 1920 and 1948.

More rigorous definition is associated with the present trend toward the establishment of deferred plans which can qualify for tax benefits under the requirements of Section 401(a) of the Internal Revenue Code. Among these requirements are the following: There must be a definite formula for allocating the employer contribution among participants; the plan cannot discriminate in favor of higher-level personnel; benefits must bear a consistent relationship to employee compensation; the plan must meet the requirements of relevant state and federal laws (e.g., the Equal Pay Act of 1963, the Civil Rights Act of 1964, the Age Discrimination in Employment Act of 1967, and the Employee Retirement Income Security Act of 1974).

**Types of Plans** Basically, there are cash or current distribution plans (cash or stock is paid to participants monthly, quarterly, semiannually, or most often yearly) and deferred distribution plans (shares are put into a fund to be distributed to participants at some later time and/or contingency). All other plans stem from these two types. For example, there are plans that (1) combine both cash and deferred elements; (2) require or do not require employee contributions; (3) have either limited or broad employee coverage; or (4) operate in concert with a separate pension plan.

According to the Profit Sharing Council of America,[2] there were 700 known profit sharing plans in the United States in 1938. As of 1974 there were some 225,000, of which approximately 50,000 were cash and 175,000 were deferred distribution plans, with the former tapering off and the latter growing at the rate of some 25,000 plans per year. The pure cash plan is the simplest form of profit sharing and is established primarily for its incentive value. Properly designed deferred plans, in addition to incentive value and significant tax advantages, offer greater flexibility in meeting employee security needs than most other employee benefit programs, especially when they are integrated with existing medical, disability, group life, and pension plans.

**Employer Contribution and Allocation** On the basic of its survey of 505 plans of council members in 1974 the PSCA found that 32.2 percent base employer contributions solely on the discretion of the employer, 47.7 percent base them on a specific percentage of profits or reserved profits, 11.4 percent combine a specific percentage with a discretionary addition, and the remainder of the plans provide for a specific percentage of participant deposits or combine this with a specified profit percentage. Employer contributions (expressed as a percentage of participant pay) varied significantly with company size and type of plan. Contributions as a percent of net profits also varied significantly according to company size.

The most common methods used by PSCA members for allocating profit shares to participants are based (under cash plans) upon compensation, length of service, and individual performance and (under deferred plans) upon compensation, length of service, and participant money contribution. The council feels that 5 percent of compensation is a minimum objective for incentive purposes.

**Requirements for Success** Of some 900 predominately cash plans adopted in England over a 100-year period, almost half were dropped within 20 to 30 years. An even higher attrition rate was experienced by American plans established before 1900.[3] An analysis by Industrial Relations Counselors Inc. in 1949 turned up a 42 percent mortality rate for 78 plans established during the profitable war years. On the other hand, the PSCA reports several studies conducted in 1960, 1969, and 1971 which show that profit sharing companies clearly outperformed nonprofit sharers. Generally, the mortality rate for cash plans is much higher than for other types.

One theme that comes through from all analyses is that profit sharing will not work as a substitute for competitive wages and benefits, coupled with competent management and good employer-employee relations. A plan launched solely to fight unionism or to exempt management from having to deal effectively with employees is almost doomed from the start. It is likely to aggravate suspicions rather than alleviate them. Many employees will see it as a gimmick to get something for nothing out of them and will resolve to withhold rather than increase their efforts. Some may try to embarrass management with insistent questions about "excessive" executive compensation which denies them greater profit shares.

Profits depend on so many factors other than the efforts of individual employees: for example, market demand as it affects price and volume of sales; the effectiveness of management in getting orders and in supplying appropriate materials; organizational arrangements and up-to-date technology, and the quality of cooperation required of fellow workers.

As part of a viable company-wide team effort profit sharing can work very well, though for incentive purposes alone there are other company-wide programs which better insulate employees from factors beyond their control.

Prior to launching a profit sharing plan management should provide competitive benefits and develop mutual trust. Also, management must anticipate adequate profits and be willing to share relevant information and decision making with employees. If there is a bargaining agent, the provisions of the profit sharing plan are bargainable unless the collective bargaining agreement contains an explicit waiver by the union.

**Steps in Establishing a Plan** Given the important preconditions discussed above:

1. Management should define specific objectives for the plan in the light of existing benefit programs and needs and a survey of experience to learn what can reasonably be expected in the way of results.

2. On the basis of these objectives, the nature of the business, the composition of the work force (age, sex, length of service, etc.), and employee preferences, a particular type of plan should be chosen and adapted (e.g., how much will be shared, who will share, on what basis, will there be partial withdrawal privileges for deferred funds and investment options, will the participant have some say-so in how much is deferred, how will employee contributions and vesting rights be handled, and so on).

3. The program and its implications need to be discussed thoroughly with each employee, not merely presented, so that the philosophy as well as the mechanics of the program are genuinely understood and appreciated.

4. In addition to provisions for continuing publicity about the program, management should make definite arrangements for meaningful employee inputs about it and for periodic assessment of its effectiveness in the light of its objectives.

The major trend today is toward deferred plans with increased flexibility to accommodate individual needs and preferences. From the standpoint of incentive value, the most important factor is employee involvement. Employees must feel like accepted and active partners in dealing with matters which affect profits. If management's primary concern is incentive value, it should give serious consideration to alternate types of programs, as was suggested earlier.

**Sources of Information** There is a wealth of information to draw upon in the publications of the Profit Sharing Council of America, Chicago, Illinois; the Profit Sharing Research Foundation, Evanston, Illinois; and the Center for the Study of Productivity Motivation of the Graduate School of Business at the University of Wisconsin.

**History** It is said that Albert Gallatin, secretary of the Treasury under Presidents Jefferson and Madison, used profit sharing in his New Geneva Pennsylvania glassworks in the 1790s, but details are not available.[4] This is one of the first reported instances, though it seems likely that profit sharing is as old as the concept of computing profit.

The first schemes to receive much publicity were launched in France. Among the earliest were those introduced by the French National Fire Insurance Company in 1820 and the house painting and decorating firm, Maison Leclaire, in 1842. Other firms followed these leads, and by 1891 there were estimated to be 108 French companies engaged in profit sharing. In 1879 the Society for the Practical Study of the Participation of Working People in Profits was established in Paris, the first such employer association of which there is any record.

These developments in France came to the attention of employers across the channel. During the period 1880–1910 some 240 profit sharing plans are known to have been started in England, some in the form of *copartnership* whereby employees were given the opportunity to participate in profits as shareholders through options to buy stock on particularly favorable terms.

From 1889 until nationalization of the gas industry in 1948, there was significant growth in the adoption of cash plans, especially by gas companies in the London area. Most of these plans evolved into combination plans with half of the profit share being used to buy stock and the other half being funded for later payment. In 1920 a law was passed requiring the gas companies to use three-fourths of surplus profits (after payment of prescribed rates on capital) for rate reductions and to divide the remaining quarter evenly between stockholders and employees (as a percentage of their compensation).[5] One of the British management movement's greatest pioneers, Benjamin S. Rowntree, thoroughly investigated profit sharing and introduced a plan in his Cocoa Works in 1923 that became widely regarded as a model.[6]

In 1892, 14 years after the establishment of the employer profit sharing association in Paris, the American Association for the Promotion of Profit Sharing was founded. Among its first officers were the U.S. commissioner of labor as president and the president of MIT as vice-president. Though this association lasted only 4 years, its periodical and other publications did much to acquaint employers with American and European experience.

Well over 40 firms in the United States experimented with profit sharing prior to 1900.[7] Some current plans have been remarkably durable, as is indicated by the following dates of establishment: Procter and Gamble, 1886; Pillsbury Mills, 1880s;

Eastman Kodak, 1912; and Sears, Roebuck and Co., 1916.

A real impetus to growth occurred during World War II. In 1942, Section 165(h) of the Internal Revenue Code made employer contributions to qualified profit sharing funds tax deductible. Many employers responded because of virtually frozen wage rates and an acute labor shortage. For those in the excess profits category, the cost was only 15 cents on the dollar.

Most of the plans spawned during this period had little prospect for long-term survival, because management interest and involvement did not go much beyond the tax aspects. The mortality rate of cash plans was some 10 times higher than that of deferred plans.

Early French and English experience sparked experimentation with profit sharing in many other countries of Western Europe, such as Belgium, Germany, Italy, the Netherlands, and Switzerland. Modest development has occured in Australia and New Zealand. Among countries today which legally require some form of profit sharing are Brazil, Chile, and Venezuela.

## LINCOLN INCENTIVE MANAGEMENT PLAN

The Lincoln Plan is a classic approach to profit sharing that emphasizes employee responsibility and self-direction. The Lincoln Electric Company is the world's largest manufacturer and price leader for arc welding equipment, manufacturing some 100 different types. It makes 75 types of electrodes, 60 models of AC motors, and 20 types of battery chargers, along with a line of welding fluxes and accessories. The engineering department makes some 2000 engineering changes per year in existing products alone.

By 1962 the company's 2000 employees had achieved a productivity of $46,936 in annual sales per employee compared with an average for all manufacturing of $24,420. Yet the average employee, paid going base community wages, enjoys an annual bonus equal to 100 percent base pay and is quaranteed 50 weeks of work per year (minimum of 32 hours per week) with 3 weeks paid vacation. These results are generally attributed to Lincoln's unusual incentive plan.

**Profit Sharing**  After the board of directors determines a certain percent return on net worth and "seed" money requirements, the remaining profit is available for distribution to both exempt and nonexempt employees on the basis of individual merit ratings. These merit-based bonuses typically range from 50 to 150 percent of base pay (using base rate for those on piece work).

Though merit ratings are due twice a year, most supervisors go over the performance of their subordinates monthly or bimonthly. Ratings are made against four factors on a percentage basis and every department's ratings must average 100 percent. The four factors are:

1. Ideas and cooperation
2. Workmanship and attitude toward quality
3. Supervision required
4. Output

Ratings are made by the immediate supervisor in conjunction with representatives from various departments such as time study, inspection, and production control.

**Advisory Boards**  An advisory board comprising representatives of each department, the supervisior, the office force, and women factory employees meets with the president, the plant superintendent, and the personnel manager every 2 weeks to bring up any matter desired and to provide feedback to top management. In addition, there is a junior board of directors drawn from department heads and others considered to have executive potential, which meets once a month to draw up recommendations for the board. At the top level there is a senior policy committee of nine to advise the president with regard to new products, etc.

**One-Worker Shops**  Lincoln has its own version of job enrichment in the form of one- or two-worker "shops" which do complete subassembly jobs, much like a subcontractor on a piecework basis. They not only complete the work but inspect and "sign" it, taking great pride in low returns due to defective workmanship.

**Other Features**  As far as possible, promotions are made from within and there is no compulsory retirement age. As older workers slow down, many seek and get less demanding jobs rather than go on pension. A cost-of-living wage adjustment is made on the basis of the U.S. Department of Labor consumer price index. Upon challenge by an employee, the time study expert must perform that employee's job for a day; whatever he or she "earns" becomes the new job standard.

**Management Philosophy**  Many of the specific features discussed above have experienced only limited success elsewhere, but not at Lincoln. Employees have repeatedly rejected outside attempts to unionize them. In addition to unusually high productivity, the company enjoys absenteeism of 0.5 percent and turnover of under 1 percent. The key to this success lies in company-wide commitment to high standards and team effort in a climate of open communications, trust, and mutual respect. As much as any company, Lincoln Electric satisfies the requirements for viable profit sharing.

James F. Lincoln, who led the company from 1914 to 1954, was the one person most responsible for creating this system. He installed the employee advisory board in 1914 and the present merit-based profit distribution plan in 1933. These were the six principles which guided him:

1. It is management's job to help the worker develop himself and increase his pride in himself. The greatest incentive is recognition.
2. The worker must be made to feel that he is in partnership with management and that in helping management he helps himself.
3. The success of a plan depends on the desire of all parties to cooperate for the good of all.
4. Details of a plan must work themselves out. The main thing is to make the beginning.
5. The goal of the organization must be to make a better and better product at a lower and lower price. Profit cannot be the *goal*; it must be a by-product. An organization with this philosophy cannot help making profits.
6. Industry must attempt to develop the human being—our greatest natural resource.

The conscientiousness and self-direction at Lincoln are expressions of personal values shared by personnel from top to bottom. In all likelihood, a newcomer lacking this orientation will not feel at home or last out the probationary period. The motto over the entrance is taken quite literally: "It's a good place to work if you like to work."

## MULTIPLE MANAGEMENT

*Multiple Management* is the term given to a system of advisory boards of employees at various levels created to serve as sources of new ideas and policy recommendations, facilitate vertical and horizontal communication, and identify and develop managerial potential. Profit sharing and compensation factors are subordinate to the main purpose of multiple management, which is to motivate and develop employees by letting them participate meaningfully in the decision-making process.

Typically, organizations have established one or more of the following boards of 7 to 15 members each: plant or factory board, sales board, and junior board of directors. Boards usually meet once or twice a month to consider organizational problems and opportunities. When three-fourths or better voting support is obtained for a particular proposal, it is referred to the appropriate authority. Periodic peer evaluations of each member's board perfor-

mance are usually made with provision for replacing the lowest-rated 20 to 30 percent of the board with newly elected members. Often, board members are given extra monthly compensation while serving.

Though such advisory boards were established as early as 1842 in France[8] and 1914 in America, the seminal development work on the concept was begun in 1932 by Charles P. McCormick of the Baltimore spice firm.[9] Of 2109 recommendations made unanimously by his junior board during its first 5 years of existence, only 6 were turned down by top management. Today, it is estimated that 80 percent of the ideas generated at the junior board level at McCormick are adopted by the corporate board.

The firm has grown from 500 employees with sales of $4 million in 1932 to 4669 employees with sales of $251 million in 1975, made throughout the world by seven divisions and 14 subsidiaries (not counting sales by five affiliates and six licensees). Seventeen of McCormick's eighteen directors have come up through the junior boards. Some version of McCormick's highly successful multiple management system has been adopted by hundreds of companies here and abroad.

The detailed duties and procedures for a McCormick junior board of directors (now called a corporate multiple management board) are clearly defined in writing and are, as much as any other factor, responsible for the company's success.

## GUARANTEED ANNUAL WAGE

The guaranteed annual wage (GAW) is a plan provided by an employer to assure eligible employees a minimum amount of work or pay during the year, provided they meet certain requirements such as willingness to change jobs and to work overtime when needed.

**Relation to SUB** In the post–World War II period, American unionism advanced the cause of GAW. For the most part, this effort resulted in settlements in the late 1950s for supplemental unemployment benefits (SUB), defined as a "private plan of unemployment benefits whose eligibility or benefit requirements are linked directly with the public program of unemployment insurance."[10] The seminal agreement was signed by the Ford Motor Company with the UAW in 1955.

No fundamental changes have had to be made in the core SUB plans of the auto and steel industries as a result of experience, and relatively few GAW plans have been established since the advent of SUB. Although SUB has been negotiated as an alternative to GAW, the two can be complementary. An eligible employee under such a combined program would be assured a minimum amount of yearly work until circumstances forced the employer to lay him or her off, then the employee would be eligible for a year or more of unemployment benefits. In 1967 Ford and the UAW negotiated something similar to this with a plan involving guaranteed annual income credit units (GAICU).

**Typical GAW Plans**  The Lincoln Electric Company guarantees 32 hours of work 50 weeks a year for employees with 2 or more years of service. No specific rate of pay is assured, and the employee must be willing to transfer from one job to another and work overtime during periods of peak activity.[11]

George A. Hormel and Company guarantees 36 to 40 hours of pay per week (depending on the department), 52 weeks a year, at the eligible employee's base rate. When the day's fluctuating livestock receipts are processed, employees are permitted to go home regardless of hours worked. Within limitations of the Fair Labor Standards Act, overtime hours required by peak days are balanced against released time on light days.[12]

Other well-known companies with GAW plans are Armstrong Cork, Eastman Kodak, Nunn Bush, Procter and Gamble, Sears, Roebuck and Co., and William Wrigley, Jr.

**Requirements for Success**  Most companies with successful GAW plans produce and sell consumer goods since there are greater opportunities for stability of operations associated with such activity. Even so, the "guarantee" lies more in the performance potential of the organization than in any other factor. A Hormel spokesman emphasized:

This guarantee of ours is designed not as a protection to the employees through the medium of the guarantee, but rather as a compulsion of management to so conduct itself so that the guarantee is never invoked. Certainly, our company is wholly unable to redeem the money consideration in such a guarantee unless we can keep the people actually and profitably employed. The entire capital value of our company, cashing everything we own, would only be sufficient to redeem a ten month's guarantee.[13]

*See also* CODETERMINATION AND INDUSTRIAL DEMOCRACY; COMPENSATION, WAGE AND SALARY POLICY AND ADMINISTRATION; COST IMPROVEMENT; ERISA; MOTIVATION IN ORGANIZATIONS; RUCKER PLAN; SCANLON PLAN; WAGES AND HOURS LEGISLATION.

### NOTES

[1] "Survey of Experiences in Profit Sharing and Possibilities of Incentive Taxation," Subcommittee of the Committee on Finance, United States Senate, Washington, 1939.

[2] "Guide to Modern Proft Sharing, 1973," "Profit Sharing and How It Can Help You," and "The 1975 Profit Sharing Experience," Profit Sharing Council of America, Chicago, Ill.

[3] R. Marriott, *Incentive Payment Systems*, Staples Press, Ltd., London, 1957.

[4] Nicholas P. Gilman, *Profit Sharing*, Houghton Mifflin Company, Boston, 1889.

[5] *Encyclopedia Britannica*, vol. 18, 1970, pp. 601–602.

[6] L. Urwick, *The Golden Book of Management*, Newman Neame Ltd., London, 1956, p. 156.

[7] Gilman, op. cit., pp. 365–366, 386–389.

[8] Gilman, op. cit., pp. 77–105.

[9] Charles P. McCormick, *Multiple Management*, Harper & Brothers, New York, 1949.

[10] Joseph M. Becker, *Guaranteed Income for the Unemployed*, The Johns Hopkins Press, Baltimore, 1968, p. 6.

[11] Materials in the archives of the Lincoln Electric Company, Cleveland, Ohio.

[12] "Guaranteed Annual Wage," in Carl Heyel *The Encyclopedia of Management*, 2 nd ed., Van Nostrand Reinhold Company, New York, 1973, pp. 296–297.

[13] *Profit Sharing Manual*, Council of Profit Sharing Industries, Edwards Brothers, Ann Arbor, Mich., 1948, pp. 464–465 and 571–620.

### REFERENCES

Fein, Mitchel: *Motivation for Work*, American Institute of Industrial Engineers, Altanta, Ga., 1971.

Latimer, Murray W.: "Guaranteed Wages," in E. Wight Bakke, Clark Kerr, and Charles W. Anrod (eds.), *Unions, Management, and the Public*, 2d ed., Harcourt, Brace and Company, Inc., New York, 1960.

Lincoln, James F.: *A New Approach to Industrial Economics*, The Devin-Adair Company, Inc., New York, 1962.

Lincoln, James F.: *Incentive Management*, Lincoln Electric Company, Cleveland, Ohio, 1951.

*Lincoln's Incentive System and Approach to Manufacturing*, Lincoln Electric Company, Cleveland, Ohio, undated.

Moley, Raymond: *The American Century of John C. Lincoln*, Duell, Sloan & Pearce, Inc., New York, 1962.

*Revised Profit Sharing Manual*, Council of Profit Sharing Industries, Edwards Brothers, Ann Arbor, Mich. 1953.

WILLIAM M. FOX, *University of Florida*

# Compensation, wage and salary policy and administration

The primary purpose of wage and salary administration is to assure both management and employees of equitable compensation for services rendered. This purpose, although simply stated, is difficult to translate into a practical program for implementation. Equitable compensation is fundamental to modern enterprise, however. As Smyth and Murphy observed long ago:

Monetary income is the most important phase of the employee-employer relationship. As prerequisites to sound industrial relations, the individual employee (1) should receive an absolute amount of income sufficient to sustain him and his dependents adequately, and (2) should feel generally satisfied with the relationship between his income and the income of other persons performing the same class of work in the concern and in the community or industry.[1]

Wage and salary administration, of course, is not entirely an internal company matter. The design and function of the compensation plan is influenced greatly by outside forces such as the government and labor unions. *See* WAGES AND HOURS LEGISLATION; LABOR-MANAGEMENT RELATIONS

## PURPOSE AND OBJECTIVES

The skillful management of wage and salary compensation is essential to assure the attaining of cost or profit objectives. The achieving of these cost or profit objectives is accomplished through maintaining proper balance between the input costs and the resultant income from output. An immediate conflict of objective arises, since the wage administrator's aim is to satisfy employer, owner or stockholder, employees, and outside interests such as suppliers and consumers.

**Work Force Aspects**  A key ingredient to solving this conflict rests on the understanding and acceptance of the wage and salary program by the employee. Regardless of whether the industry contains a large or a small degree of labor content, the importance of good management of labor is apparent. Even with sophisticated automation, a well-engineered, smooth-functioning compensation program contributes greatly to harmonious labor relations. Lawrence A. Appley, for example, emphasized that "A fair day's pay for every job well done, from the least skilled to the most complex, is a fundamental goal and responsibility of good management and a foundation stone of industrial peace."[2]

**Employer Aspects**  To assure the proper balance between expenses and income, an understanding of the inherent factors of operational cost is essential. A sound and equitable compensation program is influenced to a great degree by many factors, the most important among which are the following:

General economic climate of the industry

Anticipated rate of return on investment as compared to other companies in the industry

Governmental influence: legislation and taxation

Effects of collective bargaining

**Program Objectives**  With these factors clearly in mind, the objective of a sound wage and salary administration program can be subdivided into specific subgoals that represent milestones along the path to successful and equitable wage and salary compensation:

1. Equitable wage and salary payment in proportion to each person's relative worth to the organization

2. Consistency of wages between comparable occupations

3. Adjustment of wages in relation to changes in the labor market

4. Recognition of individual capability and proficiency

5. Comprehension of the plan by supervision and management

6. Procedure to solve compensation problems rationally

## ORGANIZATIONAL STATUS

The organizational form of wage and salary administration varies, depending on the industry and the emphasis placed on the function by executive management. It is normally an integral part of the industrial relations department and plays an important role in total policy making of this department. The principal responsibilities of wage and salary administration are (1) establishing policies and procedures, (2) researching new and changing concepts in this field, and (3) auditing the operational levels of wage and salary administration to assure adherence to policies and procedures.

## COMPENSATION SYSTEMS

There are numerous types of compensation systems. They cover the entire spectrum: straight hourly wages, salaried scales for clerical employees, productivity plans, daywork and measured daywork, and individual and organization-wide incentive plans. Each of these plans requires a different management style, which must be recognized and incorporated in the overall corporate training and development of supervision and employees. For example,

1. A pure daywork plan has no relationship between compensation and output. It does not utilize work measurement or formal labor control. To maintain productivity, pure daywork requires an excellent relationship between employee and supervisor. This relationship has been enhanced in recent years by incorporation of the concepts of job en-

largement, job enrichment, work design, and other motivational aspects.

2. A measured daywork plan also does not have a direct relationship between compensation and output. This plan does, however, utilize close supervision, work measurement, and formal labor controls.

3. An incentive plan, whether group or individual, compensates employees based on output. This plan strongly utilizes work measurement and formal labor controls. It offers financial incentives for improvement of output or productivity goals. Profit sharing plans are a form of incentive plan based on the measurement of the improvement of profits (*see* COMPENSATION, SPECIAL PLANS). Most incentive plans, whether group or individual, are based on output easily measured and distinguishable such as total units shipped or number of production parts produced. The concept of incentive plans is based on the motivational effect of more pay for more work. However, many incentive plans lose effectiveness after a number of years owing to the pressures from employees, union, or supervision. The inclusion of an incentive plan in the overall compensation structure of the company must be considered over the long term since the compensation relationship between employees is difficult to maintain in the face of annual increases and cost of living increases. (*See* WORK MEASUREMENT.)

4. The salaried compensation plan is similar to the pure daywork plan with little or no relationship between compensation and output. However, motivational plans have had great success in these areas. And there still are a number of companies that pay extra compensation in the form of year-end bonuses

based on attainment of company profit objectives. Only in companies using broad forms of incentive plans (such as profit sharing, Scanlon Plan, etc.) would a salaried compensation system for technical engineering, and professional employees be incentive-oriented. And typically, these plans are not based on measured individual output or contribution.

*Employee Benefits.* In recent years the importance of benefits other than wages and salary has come to the forefront. These are now considered an integral part of the overall compensation system and must be maintained in line with changing living conditions and competition. *See* COMPENSATION, EMPLOYEE BENEFIT PLANS.

## PROGRAM COMPONENTS

A sound wage and salary program can only materialize when the plan is well thought out, thoroughly understood by employees at all levels, properly executed by management and flexible to the requirements of the personnel involved. The typical wage plan is complex when viewed in its entirety, but the key to comprehension for the manager is knowledge and understanding of the components it comprises. These components, along with the important core of the program, namely, the necessary planning, the fundamental policies, and the operational procedures, are illustrated in Fig. C-6.

**Planning** The planning for implementation of a new or revised wage and salary plan must be carefully executed. The success or failure of the program depends heavily on this foundation. A number of questions require immediate answers:

Who will develop the program?
What jobs will be included?
Which specific plan should be selected?

Answers to these questions will take many forms, depending on the character of the company and the environment in which it operates. In most organizations—and following the thoughts developed previously—the wage and salary administration department will be responsible for developing the program. To achieve the objective of equitable compensation, it is imperative to include *all* hourly and salary paid jobs in the program. The form of the plan will vary considerably, depending on type of work performed, skills required, availability of labor, etc.

**Policies and Procedures** The development of the plan requires competent wage and salary administration personnel. The approval and implementation of the plan requires equally competent and

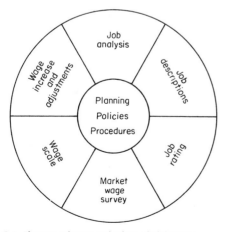

Fig. C-6. Elements of wage and salary administration.

dedicated top management and supervision. The importance of comprehension and effective decision making in wage and salary matters cannot be over-emphasized. This point is well made by Charles W. Brennan:

The formulation of policies and the establishment of procedures is a difficult and complex undertaking, requiring careful study, analysis and judgment. They should be worked out by the person in charge of the program who recommends them to top management for review and authorization. However, while the policies are formulated by the person in charge of the program, the communication or the major decisions should originate in top management.[3]

Policies and procedures are normally reviewed and approved by a wage committee consisting of the wage administrator and other members of management. In cases where specific coverage is included in the labor contract, union officials may also serve in this capacity. The policies and procedures must be clear and understandable and permit quick reaction to questions and problems by supervision and workers. To assist in the communication of policy, all new employees are normally given an orientation that includes wage and salary matters. To augment this, training classes are conducted for supervision on the subject.

**Job Analysis**  Job analysis is the step that follows planning, and it initiates the mechanics of the wage plan. During this process, all the pertinent factors are collected and analyzed by the job analyst. To help the analyst to procure the necessary information, a questionnaire or work sheet is normally utilized. This work sheet is designed specifically to stimulate the analyst's approach by investigating the four basic aspects of the job, namely:

1. What work is performed?
2. How is this work performed?
3. Why is it performed?
4. What are the skills required to perform it?

An illustration of a typical job analysis work sheet is shown in Fig. C-7.

The job analysis function is well summarized in a statement by Lawrence C. Lovejoy:

Job analysis is defined as the process of ascertaining and recording information about a specific job. This information will include the nature of, and time spent on, job duties; equipment and materials used; the responsibilities, authorities and relationships involved; the qualifications of a suitable employee; and the conditions under which the work is performed.[4]

**Job Descriptions**  The end result of the job analysis function is a clear and concise job description,

which must accurately portray the basic and necessary information inherent in performing the job. This information is found in many forms in industry. But whatever the form, the following basic items must be covered:

*Job Title.*  The title should briefly describe the job and be definitive in nature. A typical example of a job title would be "Drill Press Operator—Multiple Spindle."

*Summary of the Job.*  The summary should be in the form of a brief statement covering the purpose and function. A summary of the job titled above could be the following: "Set up and operate a multiple spindle drill press to machine gray iron casting parts, including drilling, reaming, boring, tapping, etc., to close tolerances."

*Job Duties and Work Performed.*  This should include an accurate description of the specific tasks of work performed and the occurrence factor associated with them.

*Equipment, Tools, and Material.*  A good description of equipment tools and material is essential to indicate the nature and complexity of the job.

*Working Conditions.*  The physical surroundings and job-related hazards should be carefully described.

*Job Requirements.*  The general requirements of education and experience necessary for job performance should be stated. A typical job description is illustrated in Fig. C-8.

**Job Rating**  The process of job rating establishes the relative worth of the job. This is a beginning point for the eventual determination of rates of pay. The criteria for determining relative worth can be classified as either quantitative or nonquantitative.

*Quantitative Methods.*  Typical of the quantitative types of job rating is the job evaluation technique. This technique subdivides each job into its essential job factors. These factors are then weighted in accordance with a rating scale. Other types of evaluation plans include the comparison of these factors of each job and the ranking of these factors between jobs (*see* JOB EVALUATION).

*Nonquantitative Methods.*  The main difference between this form of job rating and the quantitative method approach is that the latter determines the essential factors which constitute the job, while the former compares one job with another on the basis of a total approach of job content. Each separate job is ranked by the overall evaluation of all its elements and is ranked with the other jobs. The chief advantage of this method is its simplicity and ease of application.

The choice of either of these methods should

Form No. _____   **JOB ANALYSIS SHEET**

Job Title _____ Set up Automatic Screw Machine _____

Dept. No. ___40___ Job No. ___201___ Date __Sept. 20, 1977__

Code No. _____

Dept. Name _____ Miscellaneous Machining _____

A. Job Duties

Works from simple drawings. Sets up single and multiple spindle automatics. Uses precision measuring instruments. Selects feeds and speeds. Makes daily inspection of equipment, minor adjustments. Assists operator in maintaining production standards. Repetitive work

B. Working Conditions                                          Analyst's Value

| 1. | Job Condition | Ordinary shop conditions. | |
| 2. | Safety for Others | None | |
| 3. | Hazards | Possibility of infection from screw cutting oil. | |
| 4. | Responsibility of Equipment and Material | Possibility of machine damage due to setting. Loss of approx. $250. | |

C. Skilled Job Requirements

| 1. | Knowledge | | |
| | Equipment and tools | Expert knowledge of average to complex tools. | |
| | Method | Knowledge of average method of doing work. | |
| | Material | Working knowledge of wide variety of materials (ferrous). | |
| 2. | Education | 8 years of school. Read simple drawings. Knowledge of speeds and feeds. Write simple reports. | |
| 3. | Experience | 3 years of diversified experience as a screw machine operator. | |
| 4. | Trust and Confidence | Minor. | |
| 5. | Supervision | Indirect supervision. | |
| 6. | Judgment and Initiative | Requires judgment of average nature, some degree of initiative. | |
| 7. | Mental Capability | Decisions to maintain standard average initiative. | |
| 8. | Physical Skill | Reaction time of worker is not a factor within reasonable limits. | |

**Fig. C-7. Job analysis work sheet.**

---

**JOB DESCRIPTION SHEET**

JOB TITLE: _____Power Truck Operator_____ JOB SYMBOL: _____

DEPARTMENT: _____Plant Engineering_____ DATE OF ANALYSIS: _____

CODE NO.: _____

---

SUMMARY:
Under immediate supervision, to operate industrial power trucks such as lift trucks, trailer and tractor type, in moving, hauling, and transporting material inside and outside the building.

DUTIES:
Load and unload materials, transporting them by power truck to and from various locations. Operate lifting and elevating mechanisms of the truck in storing and tiering materials according to approved practices.

Perform minor adjustments and repairs to power trucks, fueling and checking operations periodically, reporting major failures when such become apparent. Perform related work as assigned.

EDUCATION:
Graduation from high school, or equivalent educational training and study.

TRAINING AND EXPERIENCE:
Previous satisfactory experience in the operation of industrial power trucking equipment.

EQUIPMENT, TOOLS, AND MATERIAL:
Lift trucks, trailers or a tractor type, up to a maximum of 2 1/2 tons rated capacity.

A well-lighted and ventilated plant. Job subject to traffic hazards and noise, requires special clothes.

PROMOTION TO:
No formal line of promotion.

SUPERVISED BY:
Foreman of the department.

---

Fig. C-8. Job description sheet.

reflect management's knowledge of the particular working environment of the company.

**Market Wage Survey** Once the internal relative worth of the job has been established, it becomes necessary to compare this worth with the prevailing wage for comparable jobs in the industry or community. This is accomplished by a survey of the labor market to determine current compensation rates and practices.

*Methods and Format.* The formats used are as numerous as the industries they survey, but some basic information is inherent in each form. Because the survey cannot be exhaustive, it becomes extremely important to select *key* jobs for comparison.

In addition to key jobs, a truly representative sample of companies must be selected and this sample should include companies having similar wage policies and objectives. The survey can be conducted by personal contact (including telephone) or by mail. Other important sources of wage and salary information are organizations that periodically conduct compensation surveys. Typical of these are personnel associations, chambers of commerce, trade and employee associations, and various governmental organizations such as the Department of Labor. An example of a wage market survey form is shown in Fig. C-9.

The primary use of the information obtained in the market survey is to establish a comparison between similar jobs in different companies. There are, however, many additional uses for this information. These include (1) establishment of minimum hiring rates, (2) current assessment of pay rate trends and their effect on product cost, and (3) the determination of nonwage benefits offered in industry.

**Wage Scales** The final step in the determination of the relative worth of the particular job requires a review of some of the important parameters inherent in the company's business picture such as the following:

1. The current anticipated profit potential
2. The availability of an adequate labor supply
3. The effects of collective bargaining
4. The benefits of paying a leading wage
5. The important effects of nonwage benefits

After careful review and study, the information compiled in all the preceding steps can be correlated to formulate an equitable wage scale designed to accomplish the overall objectives of the company or organization.

*Graphical Method.* A graphical method for developing the wage and salary curve starts with the selection of key comparison jobs that cover the entire wage structure from nonskilled laboring jobs to highly skilled apprenticable trades and upward to technical, engineering, and professional positions. The midpoints of each key job become a graphical point of comparison to the ascending wage scale. In this manner the range of labor grades can be determined graphically; the smoothness of the wage curve can be ascertained by using mathematical correlation methods. A typical wage and salary curve is illustrated in Fig. C-10.

**Wage Increases and Adjustments** The culmination of the preceding steps in the wage process is the equitable distribution of wages. The vehicle for

achieving this result is a thorough understanding of the process by supervision and employees. This should be augmented by fair and equitable compensation on an individual basis where possible. Although many jobs are paid on a single-rate basis and leave no room for merit consideration, individual performance on these jobs should be given definite consideration toward future promotion.

There are a number of causes for wage adjustments, such as a change in internal relative worth of a job or a change in job worth in outside companies; however, the most common type of adjustment comes from changes in the general structure of the economy. As technological advances occur, the benefits of total productivity gains are usually shared with the wage earners in the form of periodic wage increases. In addition or conjunction with this, wage increases or decreases have also been related to changes in the general cost of living. These usually stem from formulas based on the consumer price index published by the U.S. Department of Labor.

**Automatic Wage Increases** In many of the jobs assigned to rate ranges, the beginning portion of the rate range is used for automatic wage increases. These occur on the basis of time spent on the job and often bear no relationship to skill or ability. This concept began with the lower-rated occupations but has spread even to those requiring apprenticable trades and salaried positions.

**Supplementary Compensation Methods** In addition to the real wage received by employees, the effect of supplemental pay policies has become increasingly important. Payment for the employee benefits of paid vacation, holidays, life insurance, hospitalization, pension, etc., has a definite effect on product costs and the resultant profit. Therefore the wage administrator must remain cognizant of this effect and take employee benefits into consideration when altering or instituting the wage plan.[5] *See* COMPENSATION, EMPLOYEE BENEFIT PLANS.

## CONTROL AND APPRAISAL

A compensation program must be constantly surveyed and appraised. The conditions that affect its important factors are dynamic and change almost continuously. New product or service models are introduced and processes change, these cause changes in work requirements, materials, specifications, and methods. In turn, these changes cause shifting values of job skills and job conditions, which influence job descriptions and standards.

---

### WAGE MARKET SURVEY DATA SHEET

Name of Participating Company _____

Address _____

Nature of Business _____

Survey No. _____

Data Furnished by _____ Title _____ Date _____

---

|  |  | Hourly | Incentive | Salary |
|---|---|---|---|---|
| 1. | No. of employes in your company: | _____ | _____ | _____ |
| 2. | Minimum hiring rate: | _____ | _____ | _____ |
| 3. | Average no. of hours worked | | | |
|  | per week: | _____ | _____ | _____ |
|  | per year: | _____ | _____ | _____ |
| 4. | Do you use single rate for each job? | _____ | _____ | _____ |
|  | Do you use rate range for each job? | _____ | _____ | _____ |
| 5. | Method for progression | | | |
|  | within the range: | _____ | _____ | _____ |
|  | automatic increase: | _____ | _____ | _____ |
|  | merit increase: | _____ | _____ | _____ |
|  | part automatic: | _____ | _____ | _____ |
| 6. | Are you granting rest periods? | _____ | _____ | _____ |
| 7. | Method of overtime payment: | _____ | _____ | _____ |
| 8. | Percentage of base rate paid as supplemental wages: | _____ | _____ | _____ |
| 9. | Do you use a wage incentive plan? If so, describe: | _____ | _____ | _____ |
| 10. | What are the average incentive earnings as percentage of base rate? | _____ | _____ | _____ |
| 11. | Do you guarantee employees an annual income? | _____ | _____ | _____ |
| 12. | Do you have night shifts? | _____ | _____ | _____ |
| 13. | Is cleanup time granted at the end of each shift? | _____ | _____ | _____ |

Fig. C-9. Wage market survey data sheet.

**WAGE MARKET SURVEY DATA SHEET cont.**

|  | Hourly | Incentive | Salary |
|---|---|---|---|

14. If sick leave is granted with pay, how is it paid?

    full pay: _____

    % base rate: _____

15. Holiday observed:

    Jan. 1  Feb. 12  Feb. 22  May 30  July 4  L.D.  Th.  G.  Dec. 25

    Hourly

    Incentive

16. Do you pay supplemental wages (fringe benefits)? Name the fringe benefits: _____

17. If you have employee benefit plans, excluding social security and workman's compensation, how are they financed?

|  | Yes | No | Company Only | Employee Only | Both Company % | Employee % |
|---|---|---|---|---|---|---|
| Death | | | | | | |
| Accident | | | | | | |
| Sickness | | | | | | |
| Hospitalization | | | | | | |
| Pension | | | | | | |
| Savings | | | | | | |
| Other | | | | | | |

18. Do you have a suggestion system? If yes, how are employees rewarded? _____

19. Do you pay a separation allowance at the time of termination? If yes, explain the basis: _____

20. Do you supply work clothes and laundry? _____

**Internal Implications** A constant appraisal is mandatory to maintain the goal of equitable wage and salary compensation. This appraisal can be accomplished by an active program of internal company wage surveys. These surveys must be estab-

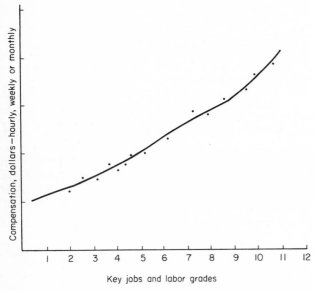

**Fig. C-10. Wage and salary curve. Determination of line of best fit to wage data of key jobs.**

lished in accordance with a firm schedule to review all job assignments at least once a year. The survey itself takes the form of a continuous job analysis, with the check sheet serving as the means of assessing the success of the program. As changes are discovered in job content, immediate reaction should be forthcoming. Rapid feedback goes a long way toward assuring employee understanding and cooperation.

**Legal Implications** In addition to constant internal knowledge of changing conditions, the wage administrator must maintain complete cognizance of government regulations and other legal aspects. As new legislation becomes law, the wage administrator must immediately react to implement the necessary changes. At the same time, the cost effects of these changes must be evaluated and reported to executive management.

**Labor Contract Implications** Wage matters are being included in labor contract coverage at a rapid pace. With the increase in national labor contract negotiations and wage pattern setting, the results of the collective bargining become an integral part of

**TABLE C-4  Typical Wage Contractual Language Found in the Majority of Labor Contracts**

Article XII—Section 1 (*b*)
JOB CLASSIFICATION

If an appropriate classification does not exist in the appropriate Works Occupational Rating Book of the Works involved for new daywork or piecework, and in the case of changed daywork or piecework if the change has made the former classification inappropriate under the principles of the arbitration awards on classification under the prior Contract, the Company shall initially determine the classification, job description and wage group, including those cases under Article VII of this Contract in which an Arbitrator has decided that no appropriate classification exists. Such determination by the Company shall become final unless challenged by the Union within a thirty (30) day period after the Company informs the Local Union and the International Union of such determination. If challenged by the Union within such period, the issue shall become the subject of collective bargaining between the Company and the Local Union without undue delay. However, at the request of either the International Union or the Labor Relations Department of the Company, negotiations will be conducted on a central level. The Company's determination shall continue to be applied unless changed as the result of such collective bargaining.

the labor contract. These often include the procedural aspects of wage matters. An example of this coverage is illustrated in Table C-4.

As this coverage is extended, more collective bargaining sessions are likely to include details of the wage and salary administration plan. This will necessitate including the administrator in many of the face-to-face negotiation sessions.

*See also* COMPENSATION, EMPLOYEE BENEFIT PLANS; COMPENSATION, EXECUTIVE; COMPENSATION, SALES; COMPENSATION, SPECIAL PLANS; PERSONNEL ADMINISTRATION; WAGES AND HOURS LEGISLATION; WORK MEASUREMENT.

### NOTES

[1]Richard C. Smyth and Matthew J. Murphy, *Job Evaluation and Employe Rating*, McGraw-Hill Book Company, New York, 1946, p. 3.

[2]Joseph M. Dooher and Vivienne Marquis, *The AMA Handbook of Wage and Salary Administration*, American Management Association, New York, 1950.

[3]Charles W. Brennan, *Wage Administration*, Richard D. Irwin, Inc., Homewood, Ill. 1963, p. 73.

[4]Lawrence C. Lovejoy, *Wage and Salary Adminitration*, The Ronald Press Company, New York, 1959, p. 122.

[5]Adolph Langsner and Herbert G. Zollitsch, *Wage and Salary Administration*, South-Western Publishing Co., Incorporated, Cincinnati, Ohio, 1961, p. 593–632.

### REFERENCES

Belcher, David W.: *Wage and Salary Administration*, Prentice-Hall, Inc., Englewood Cliffs, N.J., 1962.

Bradfield, E.G.: *Wage and Salary Administration: Meeting the Challenge of Changing Conditions*, American Management Association, Personnel Series, no. 157, New York, 1954.

Dunlop, John T.: *The Theory of Wage Determination*, Macmillan & Co., Ltd., London, 1957.

Dunn, J. D., and Frank M. Rachel: *Wage and Salary Administration: A System Approach*, McGraw-Hill Book Company, New York, 1971.

Lanham, Elizabeth: *Administration of Wages and Salaries*, Harper & Row, Publishers, Incorporated, New York, 1963.

GUY J. BACCI, II, P. E. *International Harvester Company*

# Compensation and incentive plans
*(See heading in Table of Contents for complete listing.)*

# Competition

Competition, in the sense of rivalry, is inherent in all social organizations and throughout the biological world. This basic rivalry can be enhanced, directed, utilized, and guided to assist in achieving the goals and objectives of the organizations.

**Regulated Rivalry**  The focus here is upon competition between business and enterprises in countries, such as the United States and other western nations, which have national economic policies of competition. In such countries, all business enterprises, unless specifically exempted, are to some degree under "the rule of competition" along with governmental rules and regulations. Competition in this sense expresses itself in market forms of organizations as opposed to bureaucratic, centrally directed operations. It springs almost spontaneously out of private property rights, the freedom and guarantee of contracts, and freedom of choice and of enterprise. The competitive market system through which free choices and enterprise are expressed and coordinated is inherently a highly flexible, adaptable, interacting system. It responds both to internal interactions and to its numerous environments, including governmental rules and regulations. The competitive market system, while regulating and enforcing its own discipline, is also under the rules of the game enunciated by government and to some extent, of course, customs and conventions.

Competition is not a simple or single force, set of forces, or form of organization. The variety of expression is so great as to defy precise, universal definition and would require a long list of adjectival qualifications, depending upon the special interests, vantage points, or purposes of the users of the term. In this entry the interest is essentially in competition as rivalry under the rules of the game established by government.

**Competition Rather than Cooperation**  The Supreme Court of the United States in the Philadelphia Bank case in 1963 reiterated clearly that "subject to narrow qualifications, it is surely the case that competition is our fundamental economic policy, offering as it does the only alternative to the cartellization or governmental regimentation of large portions of the economy." But how and why did this come about in the United States and other Western nations that have a national economic policy of competition?

The answer lies only in part in the rationalizations of competition as to its presumed benefits: better allocations of resources, increased efficiency, higher qualities of goods and services, lower prices, and so on. The answer in the United States may be found in the complex of institutions and ideologies which the early settlers brought from Western Europe, especially Great Britain. Most important, for competition policy, were the bodies of intermeshed common laws of restraint of trade and of unfair competition, which had emerged slowly, case by case, out of the adjudication of private grievances. This body of judge-made law was peculiarly appropriate to the conditions in the New World. Early settlers and later immigrants came to the new continent in search of freedom and individual opportunity; the common-law doctrine against restraints of trade could not have found more fertile soil. Consequently, the United States became the magnificent success story of the transition from a society based on feudal status to one based on contract and free private enterprise and choice. It was a remarkable coincidence that Adam Smith's *Wealth of Nations* appeared also in 1776, the year the United States of America was founded.

*From Trading and Rural Society to Modern Industrial Society.*  The rule of competition in the United States can no longer be understood merely in terms of its common-law origin and tradition. Following the Civil War of the 1860s, the United States quickly began to move away from a relatively loose rural society into an integrated, complex industrial society. The Interstate Commerce Act of 1887 and the Sherman Antitrust Law of 1890 represented the first stages of the increasingly complex set of regulations imposed by the federal government in reaction to the new industrialization. The Sherman Act of 1890 was not a radical law, for it merely gave federal statutory form to the common law. It was symptomatic, however, of the intrusion of the federal government into the regulation of competition. This intrusion has continued step by step, statue by statute, tribunal by tribunal, and case by case ever since. As a consequence, the diverse expressions of market competition are now under the aegis of a labyrinth of federal and state regulations, intended both to (1) maintain and enhance competition and to (2) establish its plane and its essential quality and characteristics.

The two leading enforcement agencies are the Antitrust Division of the Department of Justice and the Federal Trade Commission. There are, in addition, numerous other agencies with overlapping responsibilities and numerous areas of special jurisprudence and of limited and partial exemption, plus the varied laws and regulations of the 50 states. The traditional negative requirements—the "thou shalt nots"—are increasingly being supplemented by positive, affirmative requirements. There is also a growing host of rules and regulations arising out of consumer, conservation, ecology, and broad welfare needs and issues. In retrospect, the relatively simple rules of the common-law tradition arising out of the adjudication of private grievances are overlaid by a complex variety of governmental regulations and requirements in the ceaseless efforts to adapt to the full needs of our democracy under the conditions of modern, complex, industrial society. A curious, almost paradoxical, development in recent years, however, has been the tremendous increase of private actions reminiscent of common-law procedures.

## APPLICATION TO MANAGEMENT

To live under the rule of competition involves two sets of interlinked rules:

1. Business policies and practices of a given firm in relation to those of its actual and potential competitors are expressions of the rule of competition between competitors. These policies must be effective in terms of the requirements of each product line, division, geographical area, situation, and so on. All business firms are in continuing processes of gathering the market and other intelligence data essential for appraising and adjusting their product lines, policies, and practices in relation to those of (a) direct and indirect competitors and (b) the needs and wants of buyers and users. The benefits to economic society accrue out of these continuing competitive compulsions.

2. All firms must also live under the rules enunciated by the various governmental agencies as interpreted by the courts. The fact findings and interpretations in this second area require a different form of expertise, including the advice of legal counsel supported by legal intelligence sources and services.

For large, diversified, national and multinational enterprises, the provision of adequate market and legal intelligence is an enormous task. Fortunately, the computer has come to the rescue, almost as if timed to coincide with the increasing complexities of the burden of fact finding and interpretation. It appears that we are moving into a regulative state of affairs in which the two great bodies of intelligence, market and legal, are becoming better integrated both by business enterprises and in law and regulation. The portents are that Western nations are about to emerge out of the common-law tradition with its rules and regulations derived under simpler conditions into a coordinated pattern more appropriate to the complexities of modern industrial society.

**Internal Organization and Decision Rules in Relation to Those of Law and Regulation** The United States economic policy of competition effectuated through the competitive market system cannot survive in recognizable form unless the rules of acceptable, effective private competition and those of governmental law and regulation complement each other, instead of thwarting each other. This does not mean that governmental regulations must play merely secondary or passive roles. It does mean that both sets of rules must be appropriate to (1) the basic tenets of a national economic policy of competition and (2) the circumstances and conditions of markets. This can happen only if there are basic understandings and appropriate working relations between the private and public sectors. There are some reasons for optimism as to the possible outcome. Business management increasingly is expected to explain in federal courts the internal organization and policies and practices of their enterprises in terms of the rationale of effective competition. Increasingly, business executives are being deposed and appear as witnesses in trial cases. Discovery procedures digging deeply into internal organization and policies are an accepted part of corporate life. And there is an enormous stress on more adequate disclosure.

Out of the present sound and fury it is likely that established procedures better understood both on the private sides and by government will emerge, and these procedures will aid in bringing the regulation of competition more fully into the modern world. If this occurs, market intelligence and legal intelligence will, for the most part, run together. Business management will be reasonably expected to explain and interpret its organization, policies, and practices in the framework and setting of the market action.

**The Market Structure Framework of Analysis** The framework appropriate to such interpretation has become well recognized in recent years under the guise of so-called "market structure analysis." In this analysis, the elements of the setting of the market action are portrayed as the basis for interpreting the nature and results of market competition. These elements include (1) the number and size distribution of the market participants in both buying and selling, (2) the degree of product and enterprise differentiation, and (3) the conditions of entry into the market, including potential competition. In a complete approach, the vertical channel structures and relations and geographical submarkets and competition are also brought into the analysis. In this setting and perspective, allowance can be made for unique historical episodes, for basic trends, and especially for internal organization and decision factors.

*Competition among the Few.* One must not underemphasize, however, the problems and difficulties in the use of this type of analysis, especially in the great areas of "competition among the few," or *oligopoly*, and the case of broadly diversified enterprises. When there are only a few competitors, then some uniformities in pricing (and in other vectors of competition) may appear out of the recognition of interdependence, without formal agreement. This is all the more reason for careful, detailed, conjoined analyses of structure and internal organization. There are many possible variations of oligopolistic market structures as well as those of product, price, service, and territory policies and practices. The basic issues have to do with possible violations of the established, so-called "rules against cartel-type agreements." A careful analysis of the record over a number of years usually provides evidence as to whether there was active, effective competition or explicit or tacit agreements.

*Diversification and Merger.* Cases arising out of the diversification and conglomeration of assortments and of enterprises, especially in merger cases, also require a similar type of market structure analysis by product lines, divisions, or whatever internal organizational breakdowns are employed. Insofar as there are relatively discrete product lines or divisons, it is possible to relate the market categories

reasonably to the internal organizational accounting. A difficult problem arises when, in managed and planned diversification, product line and other relationships with possible synergistic effects are emphasized. As yet, very little solid analysis and evidence have emerged in this area. It is likely, however, that market economies or advantages arising out of such planned relatedness would lead to the development of similar competitive enterprises, as has occurred historically in the case of department stores and supermarkets. In this event, the regulative issues would usually be those of competition among the few (oligopoly).

Furthermore, the increasing diversification of enterprises has raised regulatory issues that are unique to such enterprises. Allegedly, firms with wide assortments are able to employ practices such as cross-subsidization (out of so-called "deep pockets" of profits), coercive reciprocity, predatory pricing, tying arrangements, and so on, whereby specialized competitors are placed under unfair handicaps. Although such potentialities exist, they need not be exercised in fact. Regulations appropriate to unfair forms of competition are in the process of development or are already in effect. For example, coercive, organized reciprocity through trade relations departments has largely disappeared from the American scene. This whole set of problems beautifully illustrates the great need for updating the regulation of competition from its more simple, common-law base.

## OUTLOOK

The vitality of competition and of the competitive market system derives from the ceaseless processes of dynamic innovation and flexible adjustments to the needs of buyers and to the policies and practices of competitors. This is in sharp contrast to the rigidities of governmental-state–directed bureaucracies. Although one cannot be certain, the present portents are that emerging conjoined rules of private competition and of governmental rules and regulations will aid and complement each other instead of subverting or thwarting each other. In these conjoined sets of rules, however, management must be prepared and able to explain and interpret its internal organization and decision processes in relation to the requirements of law and regulation. This can have a sobering, salutary effect on management. In any event, looking ahead, there will be important learning processes on both sides that should, with goodwill, assist in maintaining and enhancing competition as our national economic policy, while updating the panoply of private and governmental rules from its common-law base to the requirements of complex industrial society. If this occurs, then a national economic policy of competition, in terms of the dictum of the Supreme Court of the United States, will continue as the alternative to "the cartellization or governmental regimentation of large portions of the economy."

*See also* ACQUISITION AND MERGERS; ECONOMIC CONCEPTS; ECONOMIC SYSTEMS; EGALITARIANISM; GOVERNMENT REGULATION, BUSINESS LAW; GOVERNMENT REGULATION, UNIFORM COMMERCIAL CODE; POLICY FORMULATION AND IMPLEMENTATION; PRODUCT AND SERVICE PRICING; PROFITS AND PROFIT MAKING; REGULATED INDUSTRIES, MANAGEMENT OF; RISK ANALYSIS AND MANAGEMENT.

### REFERENCES

Clark, J. M.: *Competition as a Dynamic Process*, The Brookings Institution, Washington, 1961.

Grether, E. T.: "Marketing and Public Policy: A Contemporary View," *Journal of Marketing*, vol. 38, no. 3, July 1974.

Jacoby, Neil, E. T. Grether, Lee E. Preston et al., "Competition Policy: Looking Ahead Worldwide," *California Management Review*, vol. XVI, no. 4, Spring 1974, pp. 52–130.

Kintner, Earl, W.: *An Antitrust Primer*, Macmillan Publishing Co., Inc., New York, 1973.

Scherer, F. M.: *Industrial Market Structure and Economic Performance*, Rand McNally & Co., Chicago, 1970.

Van Cise, Jerrold G.: *Understanding the Antitrust Laws*, Practising Law Institute, New York, 1973.

Williamson, Oliver E.: *Corporate Control and Business Behavior*, Prentice-Hall, Inc., Englewood Cliffs, N.J., 1970.

E. T. GRETHER, *University of California, Berkeley*

## Competition, nonprice (*See* MARKETING, CHANNELS OF DISTRIBUTION.)

## Competition, pure (*See* ECONOMIC CONCEPTS.)

## Competitive niche (*See* PLANNING, PLANNED MANAGEMENT OF TURBULENT CHANGE.)

## Competitive strategy (*See* PLANNING, PLANNED MANAGEMENT OF TURBULENT CHANGE.)

## Compliance through consensus (*See* JAPANESE INDUSTRIES, MANAGEMENT IN.)

## Computer control of processes (*See* PRODUCTION PROCESSES.)

## Computer generations (*See* INFORMATION SYSTEMS, MANAGEMENT (MIS), IN LARGE ORGANIZATIONS.)

## Computer systems

More and more managers in industry at all levels are required to make decisions concerning computers—their selection and their use. This entry provides basic, relevant information, using nontechnical terms as much as possible, and focuses on the key decisions executives make pertaining to computers rather than on how computers work. These decisions revolve around determining whether computers should be used at all, and if so, deciding how to use them properly.

Several background observations are first in order. The application of computers is diverse, spanning such activities as administration, management, scientific applications, education, and process control. A number of industries and government agencies have become heavily dependent upon computing for their day-to-day operations. Banking, telephone switching, typesetting, and the Social Security Administration are prominent examples. Computers, in their own right, represent a very large industry with annual sales in the United States in excess of 15 billion dollars and growing at a rate of approximately 15% per year. Finally, social concerns such as those associated with the privacy of data have been in public discussion and have resulted in legislation such as the Privacy Act of 1974.

Computers and computer-based information systems are a relatively new and large field. It is a field that has grown so quickly that many of the orderly, underlying principles and structures, which normally exist in other fields, have not yet developed. Thus, what constitutes common practice is only now beginning to be understood, and the field is still in a state of change.

## ELEMENTS AND FUNCTIONS OF COMPUTER SYSTEMS

To fully comprehend computer usage, one must consider a number of related elements and functions.

**Functional Parts** Computers consist of four functional parts: memory, an arithmetic or logic unit, a control unit, and an input-output unit. The *memory* stores data and instructions in specific locations called *addresses*. The storage of data is accomplished by changing numbers coded in decimal form to binary form—a base 2 number system—and storing them in a logical element which can either be turned on or off. (A binary character is termed a *bit*.) The *arithmetic unit* performs functions such as addition and multiplication based on the value of an *operations code* in the instruction. The *control unit* fetches successive instructions from memory, decodes them, and notifies the other units of the computer what to do. By determining the memory location of the next instruction in a string of instructions, the control unit establishes the sequence of instructions executed. The *input-output unit* connects the central part of the computer to tape drives, disk drives, printers, and other peripheral equipment. The memory, control, and arithmetic units together are often called the *central processing unit (CPU)*.

**Programs and Language** A string of instructions which, when executed by a computer results in performing a given operation, is termed a *program*. To write an actual application processing program, e.g., payroll or accounting, the programmer often uses a higher-level computer *language* such as COBOL or FORTRAN. Since the programmer must also identify the computer resources, e.g., amount of main memory, the peripheral devices, the computer languages, and the data sets needed to run the program, the programmer writes another program in the *control language* of the computer to obtain these resources. Thus actual programs consist of two parts: one dealing with the computer resources and protocols required for the job, and the other which does the job.

**Physical Equipment** The physical equipment such as the CPU, tape drives, disk storage units, and displays are commonly termed *hardware*, while the control system program and the individual information system programs are colloquially known as *software*. Although at one time the boundary between hardware and software was quite clear, the difference has become less distinct owing to the use of small programmable computers within the control unit to decode instructions and the fact that most control system program functions can also be performed by specialized hardware.

**Dimensions** Computer systems differ along many dimensions. "Size" usually refers to the amount of memory and the number of peripheral equipments in a particular configuration. "Speed" refers to the amount of time the CPU requires to perform instructions, with the faster machines requiring less time to execute a given set of instructions than the slower ones. "Power" refers to the number of different instructions in the machine's instruction set, to their strength, (i.e., the number of operations that can be "made to happen" with a single instruction), and to the "machine's organization" (i.e., whether or not some things can proceed in parallel).

**Distinctions** Computers are distinctly different from other machines, although not because of "mechanization" or "automation," which is characteristic of many devices. Computers are unique machines in that they store both their program and data in a memory and can modify the contents of this memory under the control of their program. This allows computers to have a variable program and enables them to be "general" in their area of use. Other machines, if they have a program at all, have a "fixed" program. For example, an automatic record changer and an automatic coffee maker are specific in their use; while each embodies a similar sort of logic, record changers can not make coffee. Furthermore, the instructions executed in a program are deterministic. That is, when the computer is functioning correctly there is no ambiguity in the execution of an instruction, and the execution of the same program will give the same results each time, unless intentional variations is "built in" by use of a random-number generator or similar device. Thus, questions of choice and judgment must be resolved prior to writing the computer program, and the resulting assertions are declared by that program.

**Computer Generations** The first stored-program computer was designed and built by Professors Eckert and Mauchly at the University of Pennsylvania in 1946. It was called the ENIAC, and it contained over 18,000 vacuum tubes as switching elements. This machine was followed closely by computers at Cambridge, England, and at Massachusetts Institute of Technology. The M.I.T. machine, the WHIRLWIND, was notable for its use of small magnetic cores as the memory storage element and a formal diagram describing the machine logic.

The first commercial computer was the UNIVAC made by Remington Rand for the U.S. Census Bureau in 1951. It had magnetic tape drives which could read tape moving in either direction, i.e., forward and backward, and buffered input-output operations which enabled computation to go on while input-output was being performed.

IBM's first commercial computer, the 701, was introduced in 1953. Although not so large nor so powerful as the Univac, it was available and well supported. The 701 was followed by a number of other machines culminating in the 704, which was first delivered in 1956. It had 4096 words of magnetic core memory and a special form of number representation (floating point), which was particularly well suited to scientific work involving very large and very small numbers. The 704 was followed by the 709, which became the standard for scientific computing.

The "generation" to which a computer belongs is usually determined by the components used to build the CPU. Thus, the UNIVAC I and the IBM 701 and 704, which used vacuum tubes as the logical element, were considered the first generation. Computers such as the IBM 7000 series, which used transistor circuits as the logical elements, were considered the second generation. In the early 1960s IBM embarked on the design of a new family of computers, to be called the 360 series. This system used integrated circuits as logical elements and was considered third generation. Newer computers such as the 370 use large-scale integrated circuit technology as the basic logic element, so they might rightfully be considered as "fourth" generation machines.

## FACTORS INFLUENCING COMPUTER SYSTEMS SELECTION

The following factors have proven useful in guiding the selection of computer systems:

**General to Special Purpose** Most computers are general purpose in that the program in execution at a particular time determines what task the machine is performing. Economies of scale permit a low unit-cost of computing. However, some machines are special purpose in that they have only one program, which is always resident and performs only one activity. An example would be a computer controlling the ratio of compounds in a chemical process. With the advent of microcomputers, or CPUs completely contained on an integrated circuit chip, special systems are becoming more attractive since they are simpler; that is, they do not have to take all possible conditions into account. On the other hand, the general purpose machine (or more recently, distributed network of interconnected machines) permits greater flexibility and customization.

**Dedicated to Shared** A disk drive that is used by only one application at a time is considered *dedicated*. If it can be used by more than one application program at a time it is considered *shared*. All resources—hardware, software, and even people—can be either dedicated or shared. Although sharing resources creates more complexity, it permits more efficient use of resources.

**Batch to On-line** *Batch* systems use a preassembled queue of input jobs so that a good mix of jobs can be running on the computer at any one time. With the correct choice of memory and CPU size, extremely efficient operation can be achieved, i.e., few of the system's facilities stand idle. These systems, however, are somewhat inconvenient to use since it is necessary to be physically present at the card reader to run a program. *On-line* systems allow many users to access the computer at one time via typewriter or cathode-ray tube (CRT) displays. In some systems the user gets a prescribed fraction of the available processing facility, e.g., 1/100; in others, such as airline reservation systems, the terminals generate small messages (transactions) which are processed in sequence and the result is returned to the terminal. In both cases, the user perceives that he or she alone is using the complete computer system. On-line systems are more costly than batch systems. However, for certain applications such as instruction, interactive problem solving, computer program design and "debugging," and reservation systems, they provide considerably better service.

These three concepts can be summarized as follows:

1. The dimension of "general to special purpose" corresponds to the sequential use of a resource—are there one or many uses for the system?

2. The "dedicated to shared" dimension concerns the concurrent use of a resource.

3. The "batch–on-line" dimension represents a trade off between resource efficiency and user convenience.

## ORGANIZATIONAL USES OF COMPUTERS

Usage of computers can be viewed by level of organizational application or by the type of administrative system in which they are employed.

**Levels of Application** Although the range of computer applicatons is large, well over half are involved with managerial and administrative tasks in business and government. Organizational use can be broadly characterized as occurring at three levels. On the bottom level are the operational activities such as manufacturing, marketing, and the various support functions including accounting and personnel. In the middle are the managerial/administrative activities such as directing, controlling, supervising, and short-range planning. At the top are the executive/policy functions of strategy selection, long-range planning, and complex decision making.

*Bottom Level.* Tasks at the bottom level are primarily operational and transactional in nature, such as keeping a ledger or making a particular part. Most of these tasks are preplanned; each step is known in advance, and there is often a prescribed way to handle every situation. These tasks could be thought of as being deterministic or programmed, having little variability, and requiring no judgment on the part of the individual performing them.

Most recorded successful uses of computers in business have been at the operational level. Almost all large corporations in the United States have transferred their major administrative record-keeping systems from manual to computer systems. Examples of such systems are personnel information systems, payroll systems, inventory control systems, and accounting systems. Note that for each of these system types, the correct response to a particular situation is, in principle, completely known in advance; that is, the proper system response is predetermined. In general, computer information systems at the operational level have slightly reduced administrative costs, even including the cost of system development (amortized over a number of years). The real benefits of these systems have been the reduction of human error (which often required considerable retroactive correction), improved customer service through better and more rapidly received knowledge of what is happening, and the ability to handle great increases in transactional volume. For instance, the volume of checks cleared in the United States today could no longer be handled manually.

*Middle Level.* In the middle level, the managerial tasks are not nearly so well structured: they require gathering a considerable amount of data on a subject and analyzing it. These tasks require judgment, and there is much variability and uncertainty in their performance.

Systems to support managerial control and decision making are just coming into being. Although there are fewer successful examples of these than operational systems, there is evidence that consider-

able gains are being made. Systems of this sort scan large amounts of data in search of patterns of regularity and abnormal conditions—for instance, systems which do exception reporting. Many of these systems contain models of, for example, the market in which the company is engaged. They enable the analyst to forecast the probable results of different operational decisions, such as the anticipated change in product demand as a result of a product pricing change. In most cases these systems, instead of recommending decisions, provide a framework for evaluating alternative actions. Note that these systems are only as good as the data with which they operate and the validity of the model used.

*Top Level.* At the top level, tasks are almost without structure. Here politics, style, timing, information beyond the boundary of the company, and *judgment* are crucial.

Few, if any, successful computerized systems have been built to aid top or executive level decision making—probably because we do not yet understand precisely what goes on at this level and what distinguishes a truly outstanding executive from an average one.

**Types of Systems** Another useful way to classify computer information systems is by the type of administrative activity they perform. Five categories, in particular, merit description.

*Record-Keeping Systems.* These accept data, validate them, store them on a master file, and produce various reports from the file. The systems are distinguished by the presence of the master file and are essentially independent of any particular application area. *Batch* record-keeping systems perform these steps sequentially, while *on-line* systems perform them concurrently. In a batch system, movement of data from the validation to the file maintenance phase is distinct, usually involving the submittal of another program to the computer system. In an on-line system, input transactions are validated and applied to the file as part of a single process. Record keeping encompasses both the structure of the information processing system and the purpose for which the system is to be used. Modern on-line systems increasingly feature remote-access, interactive capabilities, which permit the creation, updating, and querying of files in a conversational mode.

*Operational Control Systems.* These interact with an operational process and provide control via a feedback mechanism. Examples of such systems are the process control systems used for the distillation of petrochemicals, in which sensors measure parameters such as the temperature of a mixture or flow rate through a pipe. These measurements are then fed to a computer, which summarizes the readings, compares them with expected values, and issues commands to a regulating mechanism, such as a valve, when deviations are noted.

*Planning Systems.* These are distinguished by the presence of a model of activities and their relationships. Examples include a marketing model of a firm's competitors or a model for production scheduling. Either model would be used to evaluate the potential effects of different strategies. For instance, different production schedules could be tried to determine which one would provide the most efficient use of the physical plant or minimize the cost of production. These systems typically have some sort of forecasting capability and a limited number of users.

*Management Control Systems.* These monitor another system, usually looking for conditions which depart from the expected or intended. Examples of such systems are expenditure control systems and budget-exception reporting systems. These systems often accomplish both record keeping and modeling. They are characterized by providing some type of feedback for performance improvement. They can be programmed to give early warning of imminent, unacceptable deviations from approved plans, and to "flag" and report on exceptions that have already occurred.

*Personal Systems.* These systems are used by only one person for private purposes. They can be a record-keeping, a modeling, or any other type of system.

All these system types can be either structured or ad hoc. A *structured* system produces predefined reports either periodically, on demand, or triggered by an event within the system (i.e., the updating of a file triggering the creation of an audit trail report). In an *ad hoc* system, a portion of the system is specifically configured and controlled by the user. For instance, a sales analyst may use monthly sales data collected by another information system to produce ad hoc reports of sales activity. The analyst does not know in advance which reports will be produced, for that depends on the sales figure relationships for that period. Furthermore, these reports may be produced only once.

Information systems can also be classified by the functional area of the company using the system. There are financial systems, purchasing systems, and payroll systems—in fact, as many different systems as there are functional areas in the company. Unfortunately, the difference between company A's and company B's payroll systems is likely to be considerable, largely because of the different

meanings of common terms such as employee and pay cycle. These differences make the sharing of common systems difficult.

## FACTORS RELATED TO INFORMATION SYSTEMS

Data processing began long before the widespread use of computers. Traditionally, nine basic steps or functions of data processing have been recognized. They are the following:

Original recording (data entry)
Classifying
Sorting
Calculating
Summarizing
Storing
Retrieving
Reproducing
Communicating

In effect, all computer-based information systems can be thought of as being constructed from these nine building blocks. For instance, applying verified transactions to a master file consists of *sorting* the transactions into the same order as the file, taking the first transaction and *retrieving* the proper master file record, *calculating* what changes should be made to the record, and *storing* the modified record back in the master file.

**Information System Selection**   One of the most important decisions that an executive must make with regard to computing concerns the development of information systems. How does one determine which of numerous possible information systems to develop, given limited resources? Intuitively, one would expect formal evaluations involving the identification of opportunities, a detailed cost-benefit analysis, and selection of the most advantageous system for development. In practice, however, for a variety of reasons including human frailty, these decisions are often made without objective evaluation. Nevertheless, managers concerned with this activity should insist that a formal evaluation be performed and a report produced, setting forth the rationale for the selection. This can then be used as the basis for evaluating the developed system.

**Information System Development Cycle**   The information system development cycle involves seven processes or phases which are generally the same from project to project and firm to firm.

*Opportunity Identification.* This phase involves identifying the objective—the major business opportunity—toward which the information system is directed. It normally includes some form of business analysis in which alternative information systems are identified and evaluated. Both the operational and technical feasibility of the system should be determined prior to proceeding. A proposal should be prepared describing the system in some detail. This should include (1) a preliminary system design; (2) an identification of system benefits and development and operating costs; (3) a description of the work tasks necessary to build the system; and (4) a task schedule. The proposal should also include a cost-benefit analysis using ROI or another accepted evaluation procedure, and it should clearly identify the criteria by which the resulting system will be judged successful. Any assumptions, broad objectives, constraints, or problems—such as policy decisions which must be made prior to the system being built—should be included in the proposal.

*Preliminary Design.* This phase includes the establishment of general and detailed user requirements. Detailed requirements are often displayed in decision tables—an unambiguous method of specifying how the system is to react in each decision situation. The general processing design is also done at this point. This includes determining the type of processing approach to be used, partitioning the system into subsystems and then into programs, and assigning each function to a subsystem and then to a program. Data elements are also identified, and a definition is created for each element.

*Detailed Design.* This includes (1) selecting file structures; (2) specifying error message, report, and input document formats; and (3) determining the specific logical structure for each program. Common functions should be performed by subroutines—small programs which are callable from other programs.

Good procedures can dramatically improve project productivity. Thus, the establishment of libraries for the storing of programs (in source code form), the creation of project conventions (e.g., program names, documentation content), and the generation of test data should be done at this point. Also included in this phase should be the design of manual procedures necessary to route data into the system and to distribute information from the system. These consist of processing and auditing controls, security measures, document routing, data input procedures, and user staff training.

*Implementation.* This is the actual building phase of the project, including the coding and debugging of computer programs, actual forms layout, and procedure writing. On a large business system project, the amount of effort needed for computer program building and for manual procedure writing

is often approximately equal. Testing of each program is performed using test data; tests are also made of each form and data entry procedure. If the system is to replace an existing manual or computer-based system, a conversion plan should be worked out. This identifies each data element, describes the source of the initial value of the element, and identifies the acceptable element values for editing. Often, additonal computer programs must be written to edit data from a manual system and translate it to the form required for entry into the new system. For instance, a new accounting system may have a new account-numbering scheme. Thus, each old account number must be assigned a new account number. In this case it would probably be a good idea to verify each account balance and account header at the time the new account number is assigned.

*System Testing.* The individual working programs must be tied together into a system and thoroughly tested. This involves using simulated and live test data in the form of input transactions to exercise each function of the system. Internal points are monitored to assure that the proper action is taking place, i.e., the updating of a field on a file based on a certain input to the system. Improper data should then be submitted to the system to ensure that it is recognized and rejected.

System testing is an iterative process. Initially many problems are found among the programs and then among the subsystems. As these are resolved, more problems are uncovered until finally the number of remaining problems decreases and the system stabilizes.

*Conversion.* Data from the previous system is used to initialize the new system. Editing programs are run on the old data, and errors are corrected. Often this phase involves considerable time while the incorrect data is researched, gathered, and entered. If the file to be converted is large, it must be partitioned and converted sequentially. Provision must be made for queuing activity to the old system during the conversion period.

*System Support.* Needs to change the system may come from many sources, e.g., a new government regulation, or from a better understanding of how the system should operate. System changes are of two types: (1) maintenance and (2) modificaton. Maintenance changes are changes required because a portion of the system does not work. These changes are of highest priority. Modification changes usually improve or enhance the system and thus are of lower priority. Each change made to the system must be reflected in the many different documentation forms. For instance, changing the system to produce a new report may require—besides the design work of laying out the report and its programming—changing the on-line program libraries, program documentation, running instructions, and system description.

It should be pointed out that the phases of the project development cycle are not necessarily distinct or performed serially. In practice, preliminary and detailed design have a tendency to overlap, and implementation often begins before detailed design is complete. The object is to determine when detailed design has progressed far enough to allow implementation to proceed. The phases are also interrelated. Often a logical inconsistency found at one stage affects work done in a previous stage, requiring the previous work to be redone. This is why projects move so quickly to the 90 percent completion point and then take so long to go the remaining 10 percent.

During the opportunity identification phase, when implementation strategies are being worked out, it is a good idea to plan the project with clearly defined intermediate "milestones." In this manner, progress to a point can be assessed and, if it does not meet expectations or if the project is no longer desirable, the project can be canceled. It is also a good idea to implement a series of small projects rather than one large one. Successful completion of a small project is easier than a large one because there are fewer uncertainties. A completed project adds credibility to the work in progress. Intermediate milestones and incremental system enhancement are strategies for reducing the risk in system development.

## PROJECT MANAGEMENT

The development and installation of a computerized information system involves instituting planned change in the internal organization. Development activities of this scope must be managed consciously. Thus, there should be a written plan for the development activity, the project must be staffed, the proper leadership and direction must be provided, and there must be a way to measure progress against the plan and to take corrective action when deviation from the plan is noted. These activities usually are termed *project management*.

Because of the necessity of building the system in parts, a considerable amount of time must be spent in integrating the various subsystems to ensure that they work together. Thus, it is often advantageous to assign responsibility for this function specifically to an individual or group.

When the written status reports show that a project is failing to meet the schedule, several recovery strategies can be used: (1) the composition or the sequence of tasks can be altered; (2) the number and assignments of staff can be changed, although the addition of staff increases the communication needed; or (3) the scope of the project can be changed.

The major cost elements in developing a computer-based information system are labor and computer accounting units. Consequently, every development project represents a trade off between these factors. For instance, if there is a surplus of computer accounting units, i.e., the computer system is not fully loaded, then programmers can do less desk checking of programs and more computer testing. Although the computing cost will be higher, the labor cost will be lower and the total development cost might be lower. The proper operating point for any situation depends on the quality and experience of the available staff, the loading of the computer system, and the complexity of the task.

Over the course of time a number of indicators of project failure have been observed. Consistently missed target dates and cost overruns are two of the earliest signs of a project in trouble. Often they indicate that the project was improperly planned or that unforeseen technical difficulties exist. In both cases, the reasons for the discrepancy should be investigated. Absence of regular status reporting (e.g., a written periodic status report and periodic technical/managerial review) might indicate a project out of control. If a detailed review uncovers unforeseen problems or status substantially different than anticipated, controls of this nature should be instituted. Absence of end-user and top-management involvement with the project at a detailed and policy level respectively are signs that the system will not meet objectives. By the middle of the implementation phase of the project, a fairly detailed conversion plan should exist. If not, conversion probably has not been thought through.

The system should not be made operational—that is, operational activities of the enterprise should not be committed to the system—until the system has been thoroughly tested. This includes running the system in parallel with the manual system and reconciling the outputs.

## MANAGERIAL ISSUES RELATED TO COMPUTING

Although most of the activities pertaining to computers, computer-based information systems, and computer-related personnel involve managerial decisions, a few decision areas have proved to be particularly troublesome and they require special managerial attention.

**The Computer Selection Process**  The specifications of computer equipment are usually determined solely by the manufacturer. Thus, the process of equipment evaluation concentrates largely on finding equipment which meets requirements without modification.

Candidate computer systems are usually evaluated formally. First the work load—the amount and type of computing to be done—is estimated. Then a set of qualitiative and quantitative requirements is determined. Each requirement is weighted, and the candidate systems are scored on their abilities to meet the requirements. The highest total score is presumed to indicate the best system. There are a number of difficulties with this process. First, it is extremely difficult to place relative weights on qualitative items such as the responses of the manufacturers' service personnel or the reliability of the equipment. Who is to say whether field service or reliability is more important and deserves a greater weight? Second, it is difficult to rate the candidate systems in the qualitative areas. These evaluations are, by their nature, judgmental, and their accuracy depends both on the skill of the person making the judgment and on current circumstances. Finally, it is difficult to forecast accurately future computing demand, since this depends partly on present availability and partly on future events. Thus it is hard to gauge the ideal size of a system to be obtained today.

Since the success of the evaluation depends mainly on the persons involved, it is best to form a task group composed of competent, senior members of the groups most affected—data processing (technical), finance, operating management, users, and executive management. The use of a committee reduces the chance that one person will have excessive control or distort the process. Management should structure the process to ensure that an evaluation rather than a rationalization is performed. Thus the objectives should be clearly defined by management, and biases or prejudgments should be discouraged.

**Contracting for Equipment and Services**  Contracts for computer equipment and services should contain the following: (1) description of the equipment or service (often by reference to a spec sheet); (2) delivery date; (3) charges including the amount, commencement date, and payment terms; (4) conditions of acceptance; (5) period extensions and purchase options (if leased); (6) lease termination procedure; (7) maintenance, including the method of contacting the service representative, service call response time, the service coverage period, and charges; (8) training and documentation; (9) warranty; and (10) definition of terms used.

Computer contracts rarely include warranties that the equipment will perform in an intended use, credits for malfunctions, and penalties for nonperformance, e.g., software bugs, equipment failure, missed delivery dates, etc. Although a smaller supplier might be persuaded to negotiate a special contract, most large companies are unwilling to alter their standard terms and conditions.

**Management of the Data Processing Department**  Commercial data processing departments serve two basic functions:

1. To provide a reliable, easy-to-use computational resource

2. To design, implement, and maintain computer-based information system

The dual nature of the data processing department, namely, the operational aspect of providing the computational resource and the research aspect of developing information systems, creates particular managerial problems. First, different types of staff are involved. The production activity is staffed mostly by operatives while information systems development is staffed by designers and engineers. Second, the objectives of the two groups are different: production is concerned with stability and service while development is concerned with effecting change. These two groups require different managerial techniques, style, and organizational structure.

*Department Activities.*  The data processing department consists of the following functional areas:

1. Operations: is responsible for running the computer, setting up tape and disk volumes (files), reading cards into card readers, separating output, and storing data volumes.

2. Production: schedules and submits repetitive data processing programs to the computer; reviews completed programs to ensure that they are executed properly; maintains logs of work completed and in progress; performs input-output control.

3. Control systems support: maintains the operating system program by applying "fixes" distributed by the computer manufacturer; plans and installs new versions of the operating system.

4. User service: performs consulting services for users of the computer; installs and maintains frequently used computer languages (e.g., COBOL and FORTRAN), package programs (e.g., CROSTABS), and on-line libraries; produces documentation and provides information and administrative services.

5. Information system design: performs feasibility studies, preliminary and detailed information system design, implementation, testing, and conversion; includes training of users, documentaton, and manual procedures and forms.

6. Information system support: performs maintenance and modification of information systems.

7. Management and administration: responsible for policy determination, planning, budgeting, cost recovery (including pricing for services), purchasing, accounting, personnel adminstration, and general management.

*Department Organizational Structure.* There are a number of internal data processing department organizational structures, the two most popular being *functional* and *project.*

1. The functional structure is organized along either technical specialty or business system lines. For instance, information system design can be subdivided into a programming and an analytical group, or the programmers and analysts doing information systems design may be part of a user department such as accounting. The main advantage of the functional department is that it promotes the specialty of the department.

2. The project organization combines all the specialities needed to perform a given project. Its primary focus is on the project itself rather than on a particular discipline or user activity. The advantage of this organizational form is that it is goal-oriented and that it naturally contributes to subsystem integration.

Typically, operations, production, control systems, and user service are functionally organized while information system development and support use the project form. As a guide, the more unstructured the work and decisions are in a given area, the more suited it is to a project-type organization.

The most important organizational issue concerning the use of computers in business is the question of centralization. Centralization permits economies of scale, promotes specialization, and facilitates integration of ideas by grouping people together. Decentralization promotes greater interest and motivation on the local level. Centralization can apply to physical computer systems, to the staff, or to information system development. It can also apply to data and to authority or administrative control.

The other important structural element is the reporting level of the data processing department. If the department reports too low in the organization, it will not have sufficient power to compete for resources. It also will not be in a position to mediate if a resource conflict arises—for example, a conflict

over data sharing. If the department reports too high in the organization, it directly competes with the main business activities of the enterprise.

**Personnal Recruitment, Development, and Training** The personnel involved with data processing and management information systems can be divided into four groups:

*The End User.* This group is rapidly growing to encompass almost everyone in the organization. Specifically, it includes everyone who is a recipient or user of business or technical reports, analysts, forecasters, problem solvers, managers, planners, policy makers and many more. These individuals do not, in the strictest sense, require formal training, although they will need to be increasingly familiar (and comfortable) with computer terminals, graphic devices, and general capabilities.

*Computer and Information System Analysts and Programmers.* This group comprises the designers, architects, and reducers-to-practice of computer application systems. Their job is to design, develop, and implement the information systems for the organization or its subdivison.

*Operators of Machines and Managers of Data Processing Centers.* To this group is entrusted the physical operation (sometimes also the responsibility for evaluation and acquisition) of the hardware and software that constitutes the "capital equipment" of the data processing function and its efficient utilization.

*The DP and Information Systems Managers.* This group includes all those managers, at every level of the hierarchy, who have to make design or operating decisions concerning the data processing function. They are found to be increasingly diffused throughout modern enterprises, as more and more people and functions become involved with information handling. Attention should be called to one particularly important individual of this group, the data base manager, whose function has emerged with the trend toward on-line data base systems. Typically, the data base manager has jurisdiction over what data the organization stores, in what formats, with what file organizations, using what sort of hardware devices and access methods, for how long a time, and with what distribution.

As in many other training situations, the best way to acquire the necessary skills for each of the positions mentioned above is to serve in an "apprentice" role alongside an experienced individual. Since this is often impractical, formal training must be sought. Some of the best formal training is offered by vendors of hardware and software in the data processing industry. Both large computer manufacturers and small software houses offer a wide variety of excellent courses and workshops. The major advantages of this form of education are the economy of time and the focused presentation of the subject matter: you get exactly what you need and only that. Other sources of training are associations, such as the American Management Association, and special tutorials periodically conducted by professional societies. In addition, colleges, universities, and trade schools are offering more and more courses in computer science, programming, information systems design and implementation.

Finally, it is worth looking into self-study opportunities, such as those provided by programmed texts, independent study kits featuring everything from audio cassettes, slide films, and motion pictures to video tapes. Of special note in the self-study area is the method which employs computers themselves to train users on the very devices they are expected to work with later or has users deal with the machines in an interactive (sometimes called "Socratic") mode. IBM's Interactive Instructional System (IIS) and its successor programs are an example of the latter.

## TRENDS AND CONCLUSIONS

Computers and information systems not only are continually increasing in size, speed and number, but tend more and more to pervade the entire organization. In addition to being prodigious "number crunchers," i.e., processors of numerical and mathematical information, they are increasingly being utilized for text processing. This comprises entering words, pages, and whole manuscripts into computers; editing; electronically distributing documents; abstracting and listing; and formatting and driving devices such as photocomposers and printers capable of delivering camera-ready copy for the publishing industries. The whole field of office automation is becoming increasingly computerized.

The trend is toward proliferaton in a mode that has been called *distributed computing*. This trend manifests itself in two ways:

1. The increasing use of minicomputers and microcomputers, small machines of relatively low cost but with increasing capability and virtuosity, which may be placed in many departments of a business. These small computers are generally operated in a *stand-alone* mode, i.e., isolated and independent from one another.

2. The parallel trend toward connecting computers into networks, in which many central processing units (*host machines*) can communicate with many terminal input-output devices, via telephone lines, private wires, microwave or satellite links.

These data base/data communication (DB/DC) systems are becoming more "transparent" to the user; that is, the user does not know which host machine or special application program is servicing his or her current requests or transactions. Such systems are becoming increasingly user-friendly, in that they can thus be used by people with less and less special training.

Finally, the kingfish of the information systems world will increasingly be the end user. As evolving technology makes these systems more versatile, powerful, and easy to use, and as more and more people interact directly with information systems, their use will become more pervasive in all the endeavors of enterprise.

*See also* DATA PROCESSING PRINCIPLES AND PRACTICES; FORMS DESIGN AND CONTROL; INFORMATION SYSTEMS, MANAGEMENT (MIS); INFORMATION SYSTEMS, MANAGEMENT (MIS), APPLIED; INFORMATION SYSTEMS, MANAGEMENT (MIS), IN LARGE ORGANIZATIONS; RECORDS MANAGEMENT; SYSTEM DYNAMICS.

### REFERENCES

Blackman, M.: *The Design of Real Time Applications*, Wiley-Interscience, a divison of John Wiley & Sons, Inc., New York, 1975.

Davis, G.: *Management Information Systems*, McGraw-Hill Book Company, New York, 1974.

Gore, Marvin, and John Stubbe: *Elements of Systems Analysis for Business Data Processing*, Wm. C. Brown Company Publishers, Dubuque, Iowa, 1975.

Haidinger, T. P., and D. R. Richardson: *A Manager's Guide to Computer Time Sharing*, Wiley-Interscience, a division of John Wiley & Sons, Inc., New York, 1975.

Lyon, J. K.: *The Database Administrator*, Wiley-Interscience, a division of John Wiley & Sons, Inc., New York, 1976.

McFarlan, F. W., and R. L. Nolan: *The Information Systems Handbook*, Dow Jones-Irwin, Inc., Homewood, Ill., 1974.

Mader, C., and R. Hagin: *Information Systems: Technology, Economics, Applications*, Science Research Associates, Inc., Chicago, 1974.

Nolan, R. D.: *Managing the Data Resource Function*, West Publishing Company, St. Paul, Minn., 1974.

Sanders, Donald H.: *Computers in Business*, 2d ed., McGraw-Hill Book Company, New York, 1975.

Vaszonyi, Andrew: *Introduction to Electronic Data Processing*, rev. ed., Richard D. Irwin, Inc., Homewood, Ill., 1977.

Weiss, Eric, ed.: *Computer Usage/Fundamentals*, 2d ed., McGraw-Hill Book Company, New York, 1975.

PETER V. NORDEN, *International Business Machines Corporation, and Columbia University*
JON A. TURNER, *Columbia University Center for Computing Activities and Graduate School of Business*

# Computerized relationship layout planning (CORELAP) (*See* FACILITIES AND SITE PLANNING AND LAYOUT.)

# Computerized relative allocation of facilities techniques (CRAFT) (*See* FACILITIES AND SITE PLANNING AND LAYOUT.)

# Concept coordination (*See* RECORDS MANAGEMENT.)

# Conference leadership

The effectiveness of conference leadership depends as much upon preparation and procedure as upon personal communications skills.

**Preparation** Seven factors should receive careful attention, whether the conference is formal or informal, intraorganization or public:

1. *Location.* Convenience to participants, atmosphere, adequacy of size, and other accommodations should be reviewed for appropriateness of the conference's purpose.

2. *Purpose.* Like all organizational activities, a conference's objectives should be clearly identified as a first step and provide the basis for all other factors.

3. *Frequency.* Executives and employees alike complain of being "meetinged to death." Obviously, there can be too much of even a good thing; but regularity of organizational conferences helps to establish their relevance to programs of which they are a part.

4. *Duration.* Single-purpose meetings can be of any duration, but experience suggests that 1 to 2 hours is optimum for most purposes.

5. *Participants.* A conference implies participation. Those invited should be in a position either to contribute information and join in problem solving or to benefit from exposure to the communications and interactions.

6. *Agenda.* Whether agendas are published or not, the conference should proceed on the basis of a carefully thought out sequence that anticipates the information participants will need and the subjects and issues to be covered.

*Checklist.* Any number of major and minor elements may contribute to a conference's success or failure. A key aid to planning its effectiveness is a detailed checklist such as the one shown in Table C-5.

**Procedure** Conferences typically proceed according to one of five basic plans.

*Informational Conferences.* These are selected to convey information and to assure an understanding of its content and implications. Four steps contribute to this understanding:

1. Make the announcement. This can be a straightforward statement of the information to be conveyed, but it should always emphasize why the information is important and how it will affect the participants.

2. Ask for, and stimulate, questions. If the announcement stage has been handled empathetically, participants usually will not need to be prodded for questions. If questions are not forthcoming, they can be stimulated by the speaker's own questions directed toward individuals and phrased as follows: *How* will you go about making this change effective in your department? In *what* way will this affect your operating procedures? *Which* part of the new directive is least clear?

3. Summarize. Before closing the conference, the leader should restate the main points of the announcement and any clarifying information that developed during the question period.

4. Follow up. In instances where the background data is voluminous or complex or where confirmation seems desirable, the information presented should be reproduced for distribution or publication.

*Problem-Solving Conferences.* These are selected to deal with operational or planning problems in situations where involvement in planning and decision making is genuinely desired. These conferences should follow a fairly inflexible sequence in order not to short-circuit the course to valid conclusions:

1. Decide on the real problem. General problems should be narrowed down to specific ones. A problem of high costs, for example, should pin down exactly which costs are high and what *high* actually means in those instances.

2. Present and discuss the facts. All relevant information should be gathered beforehand by the leader or his or her staff. It should be stated precisely—together with its date and source. At this point, participants should be invited to challenge the information if they wish.

3. List advantages of solving the problem. This step is mainly motivational in that it provides participants with some idea of how much it may be worth to them to solve the problem.

4. List obstacles to solving the problem. These are the *causes*—apparent or hidden—that seem re-

TABLE C-5  Checklist for Conference Leader Preparation and Planning

| Have you | Yes | No |
|---|---|---|
| 1. Fixed in your mind the objectives to be attained through the conference discussion? | ___ | ___ |
| 2. Secured, prepared, or thoroughly familiarized yourself with the necessary conference aids: | | |
|    *a.* Charts ready? | ___ | ___ |
|    *b.* Case studies prepared? | ___ | ___ |
|    *c.* Check sheets to be distributed ready in sufficient quantities? | ___ | ___ |
|    *d.* Demonstrations predetermined? | ___ | ___ |
|    *e.* All special materials obtained? | ___ | ___ |
|    *f.* Visual aids to be used previewed and a plan made for their use? | ___ | ___ |
| 3. Prepared your opening talk? | ___ | ___ |
| 4. Carefully studied your conference agenda or outline? | ___ | ___ |
|    *a.* Determined the important points to be emphasized? | ___ | ___ |
|    *b.* Considered anticipated responses and group reactions? | ___ | ___ |
|    *c.* Determined points at which quick summaries will be made? | ___ | ___ |
|    *d.* Considered experiences and stories to be used for emphasis? | ___ | ___ |
|    *e.* Determined ways and means of getting conferee participation, stimulating thinking, and creating interest? | ___ | ___ |
|    *f.* Considered what the summary of the group's thinking might be? | ___ | ___ |
| 5. Planned carefully to be sure adequate time has been allotted? | ___ | ___ |
| 6. Notified everyone concerned of time and place of meeting? | ___ | ___ |
| 7. Checked physical requirements for conducting meeting? | ___ | ___ |
|    *a.* Blackboard or chart paper available? | ___ | ___ |
|    *b.* Seating arrangement conforms to good conference procedure? | ___ | ___ |
|    *c.* Facilities for showing films in readiness? | ___ | ___ |
|    *d.* Ashtrays provided if smoking is permissible? | ___ | ___ |
|    *e.* Chalk, crayon, scotch tape, thumb tacks, erasers, paper, pencils, etc., on hand? | ___ | ___ |
|    *f.* Ventilation, heat, light, conferee comfort adequate? | ___ | ___ |

sponsible for the problem's existence. Typically, there are many causes, although only one may be truly critical.

5. Suggest possible solutions. These are the ideas or programs that might remove or overcome the obstacles or causes. The solutions should match up with the obstacles developed, either singly or collectively.

6. Decide what to do. This is the decision, or choice, step. The action or program chosen as a solution should be as specific as possible. It should identify those responsible for carrying out the action and establish definite timetables for implementation.

7. Follow up. This stage should never be omitted. A written summary of the conference highlights should be prepared and distributed—with special attention to action plans, responsibilities, and timetables.

*Open-Agenda Conferences.* These are selected to provide a medium of information or problem exchange where group involvement is especially beneficial. Such a conference can deal with vague intuitions about morale, the market, changing environments, and the like. If such is the case, they provide an opportunity for participants to ask general questions for which there is no other forum, to make general observations, or to invite suggestions for uncertain projects or conditions. Formats for this kind of conference stress informality. The leader simply senses interests, and issues, and moves the discussion only so long as direction seems necessary or desired.

*Brainstorming Conferences.* These are selected to stimulate ideas for a particular problem, project, or product. Ideally, a brainstorming conference should adopt the following four guidelines:

1. Do not criticize ideas. Negative thinking is

discouraged, and its expression is penalized. Any idea, thought, or suggestion is accepted without judgment.

2. Encourage serendipity. Sometimes, the wilder the idea, the more provocative it will be to other participants. The theme should be: "Can you top this?" Participants should use others' ideas as jumping-off places.

3. Strive for quantity. Experience shows that the more ideas there are generated, the better they are likely to be. Even seemingly remote ideas often contain the seed for more fruitful thoughts.

4. Combine and improve. Ideas are like building blocks. Participants should be encouraged to suggest how others' ideas can be improved—how two or more ideas can be combined into a single one that is better than either.

*On-Record Conferences.* These are the strictly formal ones required to conduct official business such as to establish goals and policies, appropriate funds, elect officers, or take any sort of certified action requiring recorded minutes. Seven factors are typically included:

1. Opening, such as a call to order.

2. Quorum, in which the minimum number of officially designated participants is verified.

3. Agenda, of old business, new business, and an invitation to place issues in registry for "old" business at the next meeting.

4. Reading of the record, or minutes, of last meeting.

5. Controlled procedure (often using Robert's Rules of Order) as a guide, in which (*a*) the leader or chairperson only may recognize speakers and invite or cut off discussion, and (*b*) action is taken and/or decisions are made only after a supporting motion is made and seconded and relevant discussion is permitted, followed by a vote to accept or reject.

6. Closing, only upon a formally introduced and approved motion.

7. Records, or minutes, prepared and distributed, of main items of discussion and their disposition, especially issues voted upon.

**Personal Skills** Conference leadership is not public speaking. Instead, it depends upon interpersonal skills in developing rapport with participants so that each individual makes his or her greatest contribution and derives the maximum benefit from participation. Neither should the conference leader become an entertainer. Often this role is most effective when it is least discernable to participants. Several techniques will contribute to this effectiveness:

1. Draw out reticent or inarticulate individuals. Do not press for participation immediately.

**200**

Wait until the conference has warmed up; then ask open-ended questions of them directly. For example: "Sam, *where* have you observed that trouble has occurred in the past?" "Mary, *what* do you feel is the reason for poor sales this month?"

2. Try not to answer questions. If there is someone else of authority present, direct the question to him or her, or try turning the question back to the group.

3. Ask open-ended questions, those that cannot be answered by a simple yes or no. Ask questions that begin with *why, where, in what way, when,* or *how.*

4. Do not argue. Let others reply to challenges. Disagreements are best cleared up by participants, not the conference leader. Arguing destroys rapport and free discussion.

5. Do not try to cover too much ground. People will participate and make conferences productive if the conferences are pointed and results are obtained. Better to hold a second or third meeting than to try to accomplish too much in one.

6. Start and finish on time. Respect for participants' other time commitments puts them at ease and helps to assure continuing attendance.

**Audiovisual Aids and Support Material** The major purpose of audio and/or visual aids such as charts, three-dimensional models, sound tapes, slides, and motion pictures is to help the conference leader to:

1. Demonstrate and clarify complex or difficult concepts

2. Reduce presentation time

3. Dramatize and reinforce major elements

4. Provide additional interest or change of pace

Aids should be selected for their contribution to the above objectives. They are often expensive and time-consuming to design and prepare, although there is an abundance of materials and equipment that can simplify and reduce their cost of construction. Unless properly rehearsed, aids can be cumbersome to manipulate and distracting to the leader's main purpose. Simplicity and ease of use are usually good criteria to establish in their application.

*See also* COMMUNICATIONS, EMPLOYEE; COMMUNICATIONS, ORGANIZATIONAL; CONFERENCES AND MEETINGS, PLANNING FOR; DEVELOPMENT AND TRAINING, EMPLOYEE.

### REFERENCES

Bittel, Lester R.: "How to Hold Group Discussions and Lead Conferences," *What Every Supervisor Should Know,* 3d ed., McGraw-Hill Book Company, New York, 1974, chap. 36.

Gulley, Arthur T.: *Discussion, Conference, and Group Process*, 2d ed., Holt, Rinehart and Winston, Inc., New York, 1968.

Morgan, John S.: *Practical Guide to Conference Leadership*, McGraw-Hill Book Company, New York, 1966.

Reith, Jack: "Group Meetings: Conferences, Meetings, Workshops, Seminars," in R. L. Craig (ed.), *Training & Development Handbook*, 2d ed., McGraw-Hill Book Company, New York, 1976, chap. 34.

Sager, Arthur W.: *Speak Your Way to Success: A Guide to Effective Speaking in Business and the Professions*, McGraw-Hill Book Company, New York, 1968.

Zelko, Harold P.: *The Business Conference: Leadership and Participation*, McGraw-Hill Book Company, New York, 1969.

STAFF/BITTEL

# Conferences and meetings, planning for

The meeting in its many forms is one of the most valuable tools of communication available to managers in any type of organization. They are often maligned because they are misused—held for the wrong reasons, poorly planned, or ineptly conducted.

**Meeting Objectives**  Certain conditions indicate meetings as the "tool of choice." They are indicated when other major communications tools (personal action, memos, or phone calls) are not practical or cannot do the job. They are particularly indicated when speed of communication with several people is essential, where it is important that many people be exposed to the same information in exactly the same way, and where quick feedback is important. For instance, in a meeting it is much easier to determine whether clarification is needed or whether response is favorable or unfavorable than it would be if a memo were the medium.

The major reasons for holding a meeting are to:
1. Inform
2. Get information
3. Provide direction or give orders
4. Identify and/or solve problems
5. Create and/or develop ideas
6. Plan
7. Provide a training experience

*Nonsubstantive Dimensions of Meetings.* Objectives represent one axis of a matrix. Meetings designed to serve these objectives also have other dimensions, each of which can be identified on a continuum, and each of which represents special problems (Fig. C-11). These are:

1. Size, from small to large
2. Degree of structure, from low to high
3. Degree of participation desired, from active to passive
4. Behavior of chairperson, from permissive to autocratic

It is absolutely essential in planning a meeting to have the objective clearly in mind and to be prepared to deal with the special problems posed by the session's position on each of the four continua.

**Advance Preparation**  After determining objectives, the first step in preparing for any meeting is to inform those who are to attend and to let them know the purpose. The advance expectations of those who are to take part have a very direct bearing on their participation and (to the extent that this is important) their ultimate satisfaction.

1. If the meeting is one of which action is expected, it may be very important to have some involvement of the group in doing the planning. For instance, either in person or by questionnaire, the participants might be asked for agenda items related to the objective from the standpoint of their special knowledge or interest. This gives them a stake in the outcome and ensures a degree of interest. An attempt to involve participants in advance, however, must be genuine and must be followed through. Otherwise, it will be seen as manipulative and the backlash will defeat the entire purpose.

2. The person in charge should set a realistic schedule to ensure that time is properly distributed within the allotted time frame. The schedule should admit a degree of flexibility; no one can really tell in

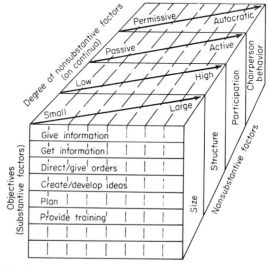

**Fig. C-11. Meeting planning matrix.**

advance just how much time will be required, especially if group participation is required.

3. It is absolutely essential, however, that the meeting start on time and adjourn no later than the announced time. It is a matter of simple courtesy to the attendees, makes it possible for them to plan their time efficiently, and establishes a certain kind of credibility for the chairperson. Also, attendees are more apt to be prompt (and enthusiastic) at future meetings. One way to preserve flexibility is to allow somewhat more time for breaks than will be necessary; another is to allocate discussion time, which can be abbreviated.

4. An agenda should be worked out in advance and circulated so that attendees can effectively prepare themselves. The sequence of the agenda should be thought through rather than occurring by chance. More time should be allotted to the more complex items. Items which contribute to the understanding of other items should come first. Controversial items may be placed first so that the group will be fresh; on the other hand, they may be placed just before a break or adjournment so that discussion can be cut off gracefully.

5. Sometimes the time of a group can be conserved by sending out prework to stimulate advance thought about the substance and thus bring about more informed participation. At the other end of the meeting, carry-over value may be extended and implementation improved by the provision of postwork.

6. It is important that members of a meeting group know each other or be able to identify each other. Where members are not already acquainted and the group is small, place cards (with names in large block letters) are helpful. An opening routine in which each member also states his or her name and organizational identification is a convenient icebreaker and helps others to identify faces and voices with names. In large groups, badges with names and identification in nothing smaller than jumbo typewriter type are appropriate.

7. Attendance lists are usually not feasible for very large groups. However, if a group of as many as 75 to 100 people are to be together for as long as a week it may be well worth the time and effort to provide an accurate list. That way, attendees with similar vocational or geographical backgrounds will be able to seek each other out. In smaller groups meeting for a shorter time, even as briefly as a half-day, such a list is a useful summary of those present and serves the purpose of increasing cohesion.

**Special Problems of Small Groups** Small groups—usually 7 to 15 members, and not over

20—have to be treated differently from larger assemblies. It is almost always desirable that members sit facing each other, generally around a table. A round table is ideal, but it does not use space economically or lend itself to flexible arrangements; i.e., it cannot be expanded or made smaller or set up in a different shape. Therefore a round table is used only in unusual situations (*see* Fig. C-12 for other arrangements).

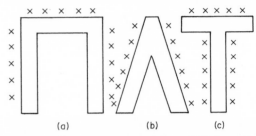

Fig. C-12. Table arrangements. (*a*) U shape; (*b*) V shape; (*c*) T shape.

More commonly, a rectangular conference table is used or is made up of combinations of square or rectangular tables. The first problem here is to avoid having legs so located that they constrict the spacing and movement of group members. Tables are available with legs near the center, rather than around the perimeter. Most people do not sit still in any meeting, nor do they sit neatly facing the center of the table. They tend to move and shift their bodies in keeping with the focus of discussion. Therefore, swivel chairs are preferred over straight chairs and in either event should be as well padded, seat and back, as possible. Because people shift positions (seat directions) even in straight chairs, adequate space provision must be made for this. Simply allowing the width of one chair for each person will result in intolerable cramping. Twice the width of a chair is a more reasonable allocation of space. By all means, make certain that there is room between occupied chairs and the walls so that members may enter and leave without inconveniencing the others.

At U- and V-shaped tables, do not seat members on the inside, because they will then have their backs to at least part of the group. In some training situations, the trainer may be tempted to walk into the "slot." This may provide an effective change of pace but must be done quickly (in and out) because obviously the trainer, too, will be facing only part of the group.

There are certain housekeeping details which must not be overlooked: place cards if indicated (and crayons for filling them out), ashtrays and matches, fresh water and glasses or paper cups, provision for emptying ashtrays and refreshing water at major breaks, and note paper and pencils.

**Small-Group Leadership**    If an autocratic leadership style is adopted in the small group, it tends, by definition, to take care of itself. However, in most small-group meetings a degree of participation by the group members—ranging from *some* to *full*—may be desired, and this poses many problems for the group leader. Certain fundamental principles stand out. This means that the leader puts aside the traditional assumptions that the leader must know more than anybody else or that the leader must have all the answers. Instead, the leader performs certain functions—or makes sure that they are performed by members of the group—such as gatekeeping (making sure that each member has a fair chance to speak), pacing, stimulating, summarizing, and avoiding premature voting or polarization. The leader also protects the members, not only by assuring them "entry to the board" by gatekeeping, but by decreasing any threat which might result from participation and by avoiding or deflecting "put-downs." In this role, the leader is very much an "officer of the court"—in favor of justice but neither for nor against either side.

Frequently, the leader will operate through the use of questions, either direct or overhead. *Direct* questions are aimed at a specific individual and are intended to elicit a specific response. ("Bill, why do you believe that more service calls will reduce overall sales expense?") However, in order to get a group moving there may be heavy reliance on *overhead* questions; these are questions directed to the group as a whole and designed to provoke general discussion because they cannot be answered by a flat opinion or a simple yes or no. ("*To what extent* do you feel that . . .?" *In what ways do you think* the new procedure might be helpful?")

A great deal has been written about problem members of a group. There are an infinite number of these, but the most common are the overly vocal member and the silent member. Given time, the group may in its own way silence the vocal member. If not, the leader can (1) avoid eye contact with him or her, thus decreasing opportunity for admission to discussion; (2) deliberately call on other members of the group; or (3) say, "Frank, we've heard a great deal from you—let's hear some other viewpoints." If all else fails, the leader can take the vocal member aside at a break and suggest privately that others have contributions to make, which he or she is inhibiting. To encourage a silent member, it is helpful to know the reasons for the silence. Does he or she feel too inexperienced? The leader can suggest, "Let's hear from someone who has a fresh viewpoint." Does the silent member feel "above it all"? One solution is to say, "Frances has had a great deal of experience in this. Could you give us some of your views, Frances?" Or maybe the silent member just doesn't feel like participating at the moment. He or she should be left alone for a while.

**Special Problems of Large Meetings**    The large meeting—75 to 100 or even several hundred—also has its own special problems.

The first problem is simple logistics. Has consideration been given to the traffic flow of people into and out of the main meeting room? Is the route clearly marked with direction signs? Are there bottlenecks in the form of narrow hallways or hallways blocked by desks, chairs, signs, or exhibits? Are there enough aisles in the room so that latecomers can get in without walking over an undue number of early arrivals? In large, auditorium-size meetings, it is useful to have one or more ushers for each aisle to indicate open seats to late arrivals. Many registrants will prefer to cluster, standing, in the rear rather than look for seats but will take them willingly when they are pointed out.

The second problem is the registration procedure. If it is necessary, set it up so that it is convenient but does not impede the traffic flow. Make sure that all related records and pieces of equipment such as typewriters are ready at hand and that there are enough staff to handle the peak loads. If large numbers are antipated, break the registration area up alphabetically to avoid jams. Provide a staff phone where outside inquiries can be answered. Make adequate provision for hats and coats, either through formal checking facilities or hat and coat racks in individual rooms. The "nitty gritty" of seemingly endless, petty, and thankless details is unfortunately a major influence in the perception of the effectiveness of a meeting—frequently as important as the substance and presentation.

The third problem is the necessity for briefing attendees. They should know the time schedule (if it is not in a printed program, notebook, or handout), the location of phones, rest rooms, and meal service, if any. Operating procedures should be set forth, such as how phone messages will be handled, how questions will be dealt with, how supplies such as notepads and pencils may be obtained, etc. A conference planner may think these matters are adequately covered if they are put in writing as part of a notebook or handouts. Unfortunately, this runs counter to human nature; as a generalization, people cannot be counted on to read material. If it is something they should know, it should be presented orally, even if it is summarized in print. It is also desirable that staff members responsible for the program and/or facilities be identified by a distinctive badge so that attendees will know where to get information or make requests.

The fourth problem is the need to adhere closely to the announced time schedule. Sessions that start late and run overtime convey an atmosphere of sloppiness, lack of planning, and lack of concern for the audience. There are many ways to control this. They start with *clear advance briefing* of the chairperson and the speakers. The chairperson should start on time and if he or she realizes a speaker is running overtime, a note should be slipped to the podium to that effect. A speaker should know in advance what the assigned time is and how much is for speaking and how much for questions and answers, if that is the pattern. A question-and-answer period provides a measure of flexibility since it can be shortened, if necessary. Scheduled midmorning and midafternoon breaks provide similar flexibility. A 20-minute break can be shortened by 10 minutes; however, a clear announcement should be made to that effect, and the following session should start on time without waiting for stragglers. Similarly, the time allotted for lunch can be shortened, provided the lunch service can accommodate it. If an afternoon program has run long, it is possible to adhere to the schedule at the end of the last presentation by announcing, "This concludes the formal part of our day, but Ms. So-and-so has kindly consented to stay here for those of you who want to ask questions."

The fifth problem is the consideration of whether to break the meeting up into smaller groups. This provides for more intimate, face-to-face communication. Although there are many names for this procedure, *subgrouping* and *buzz-grouping* are most common. Subgrouping, admittedly, has become almost a ritual, undertaken as a matter of routine without real thought. Executed in this way, it may cause more harm than good. *Do not* subgroup unless there is a good reason for it. *Do* make sure that group assignments are clearly stated and will have value to the members: superficial or "make-work" assignments will be seen as just that and will lower the standard of the entire meeting.

Not all buzz-group discussions need to be reported back to the entire group; many have their greatest value within themselves. If there is to be reporting back, however, the method must be carefully considered; nothing is more deadly than a succession of repetitive reports. There are ways to counter this: (1) announce in advance that not all groups will report but those that do will be picked at random; (2) be sure that a time limit is set for each report; and (3) after about the third report, ask if other groups have *different* or *additional* conclusions.

**Visual Aids** Visual aids are a complicated enough problem to justify a full volume devoted only to them, and that is where to look for technical information. However, there are general caveats that should be observed.

1. By far the greatest crime is to have aids which are too small. Texts on the subject of visuals contain tables specifying the minimum size of letters or numbers for visibility at varying distances.[1] An illegible visual is not only useless but irritating to the audience. To achieve the proper size, cut the length of the copy or split the copy into more segments. In very rare cases—a mathematical table, for instance—breaking up the material might destroy the point of the table. The best thing to do in such an instance is to have the material reproduced and distributed as a handout. The projected or poster chart can still be exhibited; the speaker may draw attention to specific areas with a pointer while the audience then looks at the precise detail on the individual copies.

2. The second greatest crime is to use visual aids just to be using them—or to use aids which are not directly relevant to the subject.

3. Another crime is to place a poster or the projection screen in a position where not everyone in the audience can see it—where heads or pillars are in the way. It must be remembered also that the illumination intensity on certain types of projection screens falls off drastically when viewed from angles of less than 90 to 45°.

**Meticulous Attention to Detail** It is probable that the single most significant factor in the success of meetings and conferences—large or small—is meticulous attention to detail. Take *nothing* for granted; make no assumptions! The hotel has assured you that coffee will be served at 10:45 A.M.? At 10:15 A.M., be on the phone, reminding the floor captain. (And be sure to have the extension number and name of the floor captain who will be on duty *that day*.) The facilities manager tells you your meeting room will be ready when you want it by 8:30 A.M.? At 7:00 A.M., be there yourself and check to see that action is taking place. Count the number of chairs at the speakers' table; count the number of glasses, pitchers of water, and ashtrays. Are the table coverings clean and properly centered? Snap your fingers on the public address mike—is it working? *Always* check far enough in advance to allow time for remedial action if necessary.

Check beforehand to assure that speakers' and chairpersons' arrangements are complete. Check the correspondence files. All arrangements should have been confirmed in writing. If arrangements were set more than 3 or 4 weeks before—even if in writing—a phone call to ask if everything is all right represents a tactful reminder and may spare many an ulcer. The name of the meetings' game is check, check, and double-check.

**Evaluation of Meetings**   The needs for evaluation—and therefore the methods used—vary widely. For most in-company staff meetings, there is no need for evaluation. As the content becomes more complex, however, and the group more numerous or diverse, the need increases.

At the very least, the evaluation should provide information as to the extent to which the meeting's objectives were attained. The kinds of feedback received constitute part of a life-long learning experience for meeting conveners, because even though responses may be the same over time, there is often some new element in each situation. Soliciting comments about a meeting, either orally or in writing, is evidence to the group of the convener's interest in the session and in them. Again, this interest must be genuine. If it is simply part of a routine, used manipulatively, it will do more harm than good. To state it bluntly, don't ask questions if you are not prepared to live with the answers.

At least three categories should be evaluated:

1. *Substance.* Questions should deal with the subject matter, its coverage in breadth and depth, its relevance to the attendee's needs, its clarity, its internal consistency, and its logical development. It may be desirable to find out which elements were strongest, which were weak, and where there were gaps or overlaps.

2. *Methods.* Comments should be solicited on the methods of presentation, the effectiveness of presenters, and the usefulness of visual aids and supplemental materials.

3. *Logistics.* This concerns the schedule itself, the physical comfort of the meeting facilities, the meals, clarity of instructions, and adequacy of arrangements.

In addition to whatever detailed questions there are, it is useful to have an overall "umbrella" question dealing with the respondent's reaction to the meeting as a whole. This type of question is desirable because the response may turn out to be much more than the sum of the responses to the specific questions. Conscientious respondents may give only moderate "scores" to individual parts of the session when in fact they are really quite satisfied with the *overall* result. Therefore, the general rating is a very useful measure to include.

Rated questionnaires are often criticized on the grounds that they are subjective. But subjective feeling is real to the respondent and will govern his or her subsequent behavior, no matter how many statistics may argue otherwise.

**Effectiveness**   All that has been said in this entry may be summarized as follows:

An effective meeting is one in which the subject matter is relevant to the participants' concerns and is logically developed, internally consistent, and competently presented within a logistical environment which is smooth and unobtrusive.

A final word should be said regarding the role of participants' expectations in their evaluation of a meeting. Some years ago the American Management Associations analyzed the comment sheets turned in by a sample of 2000 registrants in its meetings in an attempt to isolate those factors associated with highly regarded meetings and those associated with poorly regarded meetings. Although many factors were predictable, the single factor with the highest correlation to both good and bad meetings was the degree to which advance expectations were realized. This reinforces the need for clear objectives for a meeting—any kind of a meeting. If the objectives are not clear in the mind of the convener, it is unlikely that they will be realized. And unless clear objectives are clearly communicated and then lived up to, an attendee has every right to be frustrated.

*See also* COMMUNICATIONS, EMPLOYEE; CONFERENCE LEADERSHIP; INTERPERSONAL RELATIONSHIPS; LEADERSHIP.

### NOTE
[1]B. Y. Auger, *How to Run Better Business Meetings*, American Management Associations, New York, 1962.

### REFERENCES
Bradford, Leland: *Making Meetings Work: A Guide for Leaders of Group Meetings*, University Associates, Inc., La Jolla, Calif., 1976.

Burke, W. Warner, and Richard Beckhard: *Conference Planning*, 2d ed., University Associates, Inc., La Jolla, Calif., 1962.

Finkel, Coleman, *Professional Guide to Successful Meetings*, Herman Publishing Co., Boston, 1976.

Miller, Ernest, (ed.): *Conference Leadership*, rev., American Management Associations, New York, 1972

EDWARD O. MALOTT, *American Management Associations*

# Conflict and resolution  [*See* INTERPER-SONAL RELATIONSHIPS; ORGANIZATION DEVELOPMENT (OD).]

# Conformity in management

A major problem with conformity is that the term often has a negative image. Some may believe that conformity is bad but that following the rules is all right; such simple positions often influence discussion of the topic and hinder an understanding of it. It should be made clear, first of all, that conformity is a neutral concept and must be considered as such without the value judgments that often color the use of the term.

*Conformity* is, to put it simply, the adherence of the individual to group norms through the influence of that group. The key word is *influence*, but people in a society seldom, if ever, act without being influenced by a group of others with whom they live and work. Analysis of any social activity—in business as elsewhere—must therefore focus upon the nature of the group, its norms, and the roles of individuals within it.

**Response Differentiation**  Students of behavior should also be cautioned to differentiate between types of human response.

1. Adherence can be in behavior only—without underlying attitudes and beliefs.

2. Actions may represent true feelings that fit and support the situation.

Obviously, the recognition and measurement of behavior is much easier than the determination of attitude and the beliefs supporting it. Behavior *without* congruent attitudes can be called *compliance*. The fuller state of behavior *with* attitudes is often referred to as *acceptance*. It is possible to analyze a situation further as to whether (1) compliance or acceptance is created by the situation or (2) it has been there below the surface all along waiting to emerge. Conclusions from scientific studies differ considerably as a result.

**Group Differentiation**  Groups were described long ago as "basic units of interacting personalities"[1] and later as units "with an interdependent sharing of an ideology."[2] Members of groups are aware of this belonging with others and of their sharing of attitudes and values with those in the group. A true group differs from casual aggregates or a crowd with no cohesive forces; a group is composed of individuals who interact in a meaningful and knowing way.

Groups exist because they provide a means of fulfilling needs—individual and group needs. If membership in a group provides something positive for the persons in it, there should be no surprise in the fact that the influence of a group is an important factor in society.

Groups are of many types. The first that usually come to mind are those groups officially organized under some authority, that is, *formal* groups. Beyond the official groupings, and often more important, are the *informal* groupings that can arise in an organization. Aggregates structured outside of regular channels can exert an influence even if they do not appear on the organization chart. Based upon intimacy or intensity of interaction, the distinction may also be made between primary and secondary groups. *Primary* groups are those with persons in close, face-to-face relationships, as in families or work teams. *Secondary* groups are broader, and there is less intense interaction in them. Universities or corporations in the aggregate are a bit more remote in their impact upon individuals and are typically secondary groups. *Membership* groups are the actual entities to which persons belong; *reference* groups are those toward which individuals may be drawn or which they may wish to join.

**Group Norms**  Norms are simply the rules or guidelines for behavior in connection with group activity. These may vary (1) from the very simple to the more complex and (2) from ones of little importance to those that are critical to the continued existence of the group. At whatever level, norms indicate to group members what should or should not be done. In addition, they provide a system of rewards and punishments which is assimilated by the individual who identifies with the group. In an industrial setting, the determination of a fixed number of units produced per day by a work group as a *fair day's work* (a norm) carries with it sanctions if that norm is either exceeded or not met. Higher up, in the executive suite, the norms may be more numerous and more complex, ranging from the appropriate color for a manager's socks to the elaborate patterns of deference to the president of the company at a meeting. These behavior guidelines may seem facetious to the outside observer when compared with the practical rules for organizational functioning, but they play a significant part in the process.

**Group Influence**  The influence of the group toward conformity to social norms has often been demonstrated. One of the earliest experiments to show this was conducted by Asch.[3] A task called for members of a group to make simple judgments involving matching of one of three lines with a standard. Ordinarily, people by themselves got perfect scores; when accomplices were put into a group of naïve subjects and instructed to give occasional wrong responses, the pattern of responses changed dr natically. While there were variations by individual or number in the group, the number of choices that agreed with the incorrect ones given by the accomplices increased greatly. If not supported by another member, however, the incorrect responses were given less often, or ceased entirely. The strong lesson that emerges is that if the group induces conformity in such obvious choice situations, it can easily be deduced that the influence is even greater in work and social situations where the "correct" choices are not so easily identifiable.

**Differences in Conformity** Are there any differences between individuals in the extent to which they conform? Some researchers have found that authoritarian personalities conform more than non-authoritarians and strong needs for social approval, as well as authoritarian leanings, induce conformity more often.[4] Females, younger subjects, and those at lower intellectual or educational levels tended to conform more than others.[5] The structure of groups and the kind of situation are also important factors. Influence of the group is greater when it is cohesive. This may be based upon attractiveness of the group for its members. The more cohesive and homogeneous the group is, the more consistent the criteria for behavior; that is, the clearer the norms. This reduces anxiety and provides greater security for individuals since the "right" responses are more easily identifiable. The fewer the changes in membership, the stronger the cohesiveness, and the greater the membership communication, the closer the bond. All these factors reinforce each other and tend to continue the pressure toward conformity.

There is more of a tendency to conform to group norms when an individual is required to take a public stand than when asked to come to a conclusion in private. An early study[6] showed that listeners to a speech tended more to agree with a speaker when told that the results of a questionnaire on their views would be publicized. More recent research[7] found similar definite differences in the extent of conformity between private and public settings.

**Participative Influences** Much interest in work situations over the years has focused upon participation by members in group activity. The classic "Hawthorne Studies"[8] started out as research on the effect of physical factors upon work output. The surprised experimenters discovered that social factors were much more important in work performance. The workers, involved as they were in every

phase of the development of the work process, adhered easily to group norms and worked effectively. Productivity and satisfaction both were at high levels. While the studies are characterized as research on participation and productivity, the interrelationship of these factors and norms is clear. Participation in structuring the rules and procedures makes for more cohesiveness of a group in adhering to those norms.

A final look at factors in conformity in organizations might come full circle to the beginnings of membership in those groupings. Selection processes often involve the very norms that are prominent in group functioning. Personnel officers and supervisors are apt to choose those candidates who already display the behavior desired on the job. Conformity *in* organizations is preceded by conformity *for* organizations.

**Productive and Nonproductive Conformity** At times, statements are made to the effect that conformity to group norms means a reduction of individual fulfillment with a concomitant decline in societal well-being. That can and does happen, but those simple statements miss the valuable, or even necessary, features of conformity. The pressures for conformity provide stability in the functioning of the group because the norms give the members an idea of the information they need to reach a goal. Adherence of the group members to the "correct" information builds that stability.

At the same time it must be pointed out that norms can be so complex or contradictory that they hinder the group, not help it. Norms can be counterproductive in an additional way if there is so much emphasis on adhering to the norms that the main purpose of the group—reaching the goal—is subordinated to the conformity to group norms. This phenomenon is often seen in business and other organizations. The insistence upon sticking to the rules may overshadow the real reason for those rules; it often interferes with getting the job done. Purists for rules miss this implication and often stand in the way of having informal methods do the work more effectively.

*See also* AFFIRMATIVE ACTION; AUTHORITY, RESPONSIBILITY, AND ACCOUNTABILITY; CONTROL SYSTEMS, MANAGEMENT; DISCIPLINE; INNOVATION AND CREATIVITY; INTERPERSONAL RELATIONSHIPS; ORGANIZATION STRUCTURES AND CHARTING; LEADERSHIP; MOTIVATION IN ORGANIZATIONS.

### NOTES
[1]E. Burgess, "The Family: A Unit of Interacting Personalities," *Family*, vol. 7, pp. 3–9.

[2]D. Krech et al., *Individual in Society*, McGraw-Hill Book Company, New York, 1962.

[3]S. Asch, *Social Psychology*, Prentice-Hall, Englewood Cliffs, Inc., N.J., 1952.

[4]B. Strickland, and D. Crowne, "Conformity under Conditions of Simulated Group Pressure as a Function of the Need for Social Approval," *The Journal of Social Psychology*, vol. 58, 1962, pp. 171–181.

[5]F. Di Vesta and L. Cox, "Some Dispositional Correlates of Conformity Behavior," *The Journal of Social Psychology*, vol. 52, 1960, pp. 259–268.

[6]H. Kelley and E. Volkart, "The Resistance to Change of Group-Anchored Attitudes," *American Sociological Review*, vol. 17, 1952, pp. 453–465.

[7]T. Nosanchuk and J. Lightstone, "Canned Laughter and Public and Private Conformity," *Journal of Personality and Social Psychology*, vol. 29, 1974, no. 1, pp. 153–156.

[8]F. Roethlisberger and W. Dickson, *Management and the Worker*, Harvard University Press, Cambridge, Mass., 1939.

BLAIR J. KOLASA, *Duquesne University*

## Conglomerate (See ACQUISITIONS AND MERGERS.)

## Conglomerate organization (See ORGANIZATION STRUCTURES AND CHARTING.)

## Congruency of goals (See OBJECTIVES AND GOALS.)

## Consensus building (See NOT-FOR-PROFIT INSTITUTIONS, MANAGEMENT OF.)

## Conservation, energy (See ENERGY RESOURCES, MANAGEMENT OF.)

## Conservation/conversion evaluation (See ENERGY RESOURCES, MANAGEMENT OF.)

## Conservation measures (See ENVIRONMENT, PHYSICAL.)

## Consortium

A *consortium* is any temporary partnership formed for a large-scale investment in industry. In practice, it is usually a meld of several "foreign" companies in a jointly owned local venture or a combination of both foreign and national companies. The term is also applied to an agreement by several nations or their financial institutions (or to the body formed by them) to join together for a common purpose, usually to help one of the member nations.

*See also* LEASING, EQUIPMENT; OWNERSHIP, LEGAL FORMS.

STAFF/HOKE

## Consultants, management

Management consultants are professional men or women, or groups of such individuals, who—for a fee—lend their services, expertise, experience, objectivity, and skills to client companies to help analyze management problems, recommend solutions, and, if needed, help implement their findings and suggestions. Their methods generally involve moving in with the client company, almost on an on-staff basis, to observe, question, analyze, and make conclusions.

Their fields of specialty run the gamut of management activity: acquisitions and mergers, advertising, annual reports, aptitude testing, audiovisual aids, automation, budgeting, career guidance, community relations, computer and data processing, contest planning and management, costing and pricing, credit and collection, direct mail marketing, employee selection and training, equipment and transportation leasing, estate planning, executive compensation, executive development, executive recruitment, export-import, financial management, foreign licensing, fund raising, government relations, human relations, industrial relations, insurance, investment counseling, marketing, material handling, methods engineering, new product introduction, new ventures, office layout and design, office management, operations research, opinion pools, packaging, pension planning, plant layout and design, plant security, pollution control, product design, production management, profit sharing, public relations, purchasing, quality control, records management, research and development, safety engineering, sales forecasting, sales management, sales meetings and conventions, sales policy, sales training, sales staff recruiting, small business development, stockholder relations, tax, traffic and shipping, urban and social problems, wages and salary administration, warehousing, etc. There are also consultants and consulting groups that specialize along industry lines—in apparel, plastics, chemicals, publishing, and so forth.

The wide spectrum of specialties makes the job of selecting the right consultant a staggering one for companies that feel the need for a consultant's help. Complicating that selection process is the fact that consulting "firms" come in all sizes and shapes—from one-person shops to conglomerate corporations with offices all over the world.

There is also, unfortunately, a wide variation in consultants' skills and abilities. "Management engineers," such as Frederick W. Taylor, Henry Gantt, and Frank and Lillian Gilbreth, helped pioneer the consultant's role in American business around the turn of the century. There were many others, however, who were anxious to trade on the success of the early legitimate consultants. Some so-called "efficiency experts," equipment peddlers, and schemers with get-rich-quick promises lowered the quality of the profession and made businesses wary of anyone hanging out a "consultant" shingle.

In the 1930s, an attempt was made to separate the legitimate consultants from the charlatans by forming nonprofit membership associations with standards, codes of ethics, and strict membership requirements. One of the first was the Association of Consulting Management Engineers (ACME), formed in 1933 by 12 leading consulting firms. ACME was followed shortly by several other similar associations. Four predominant ones survive to this day representing the industry: ACME, the Association of Management Consultants (AMC), the Institute of Management Consultants (IMC), and the Society of Professional Management Consultants (SPMC).

These groups have made a determined effort to upgrade the consulting profession. Not mere dues-collectors, they screen applicants and base membership on such requirements as length of service, good record of accomplishment, solid client list, participation in certain types of services, demonstration of competence, reliability, integrity, and adherence to a code of ethics. Members of these groups—whether they are firms or individual practitioners—prominently display their association affiliations as symbols of their professionalism, good standing, and reputation in the consulting fraternity.

There is, nevertheless, no certification or seal of approval in the consulting profession. Because of the subjective nature of each and every job a consultant may take, membership in any of the professional societies is no guarantee of a happy ending; nor should nonmembership be an absolute knockout factor in the selection process. Rather, the selection process is—or should be—a thorough and complex effort that rests heavily on the businessperson's shoulder.

**Selecting a Consultant**  Not only is there a wide variety of consultants' abilities, experience, specialties, and methods, but companies have nearly as wide a variety of reasons for calling on consultants for help. A company must be certain it has identified its problem and its reason for summoning a consultant before it can match that problem to the person or organization it needs.

"Bad" or "wrong" reasons for calling in consultants often lead to poorly organized jobs and time and money wasted. Bad reasons include the following: using a consultant as a scapegoat for unpopular decisions or unpleasant changes that have to be made; using a consultant to shake things up within the company; using a consultant to help manage the company; using a consultant to support some executive's point of view; using a consultant to impress the board of directors; or depending on a consultant for some magic formula to help make vague problems disappear.

On the other hand, a management consultant might be the very person for the job in the following situations: when a company needs more know-how or expertise in a particular area than it has on staff; when there's a big job to be done quickly; when a company is heading into major growth or diversification and needs the objectivity and perspective provided by a qualified outsider; or when a company is fighting for its survival and needs help in identifying and analyzing opportunities for rebuilding or improving profitability.

There are about 4000 consulting firms in the United States, with the membership of these firms totaling an estimated 50,000 individuals. Including the college professors, retired executives, insurance agents and accountants, lawyers, moonlighters, computer programmers, businesspeople between jobs, and part-timers who carry the title of "consultant," that figure approaches 80,000 practitioners. The effort to narrow down the selection process becomes a big one.

*Where to Start.*  The various consultant associations are a good source of names. Also helpful are consultant directories, trade associations, local banks, chambers of commerce, law firms, accounting firms, advertising agencies, and other executives and companies. The consultants themselves will, of course, supply names of references, but those must be dealt with gingerly.

*Dealing with References.* Naturally, any consultant is going to provide the names of references who will attest to his or her abilities. Proper questioning, done by an executive qualified to investigate the quality of work and assess the conditions under which it was done, can probe deeper and glean more than simply superficial recommendations.

Good questions, likely to get the reference talking, include: Would you use the consultant again? What were the consultant's main strengths and weaknesses? Were the consultant's recommendations carried out? With what success? What were the disappointing aspects, if any, in the work done? Was there much disruption in your plant while the consultant was there? Did you have any trouble maintaining control over the project? Did the consultant help implement the recommendations made? Were there any real benefits from the work done? What can you tell me so that I can get maximum efficiency from my association with this consultant?

*Narrowing down the Choice.* Once a company has isolated a group of the most qualified prospects, narrowing down the choice to the single best consultant or consulting group to do the job at hand requires an equally thorough and well-thought-out plan. After a discussion of the problem in the initial interview, the consultant will generally submit a proposal. The proposal, or letter of understanding, should be the final instrument in the selection process. It should include the objectives, scope, and nature of the engagement; the general plan, approach, and methods to be used; the supervision and staffing for the project; an estimate of the time necessary to accomplish the work; an estimate of professional fees and other costs; the results and benefits which can be expected from the completed project; the type of report to be submitted upon completion of the work; the degree to which the consultant will participate in implementing any new systems, equipment, or change; the approximate date when the consultant can begin the assignment; and a description of the consultant's billing methods.

*Fees.* Consultants' fees generally consist of charges for time worked on the engagement by all consulting personnel; out-of-pocket expenses for travel and living away from the headquarters city and for services such as stenography, charting, printing, report typing, statistical work, and special research for the project; general overhead expenses; and margin of profit added on to the foregoing groups of costs.

If the proposal seems to indicate a sufficient understanding of the company's situation and the problem at hand—and the fee seems reasonable in view of the work to be done—the company should be able to finalize the selection and choose a consultant. If, after proposals and fees have been submitted, there are still several equally attractive finalists, a company would do well to give some consideration to personal chemistry. The consultant will be spending a good deal of time on company premises, and so the company needs someone with whom it feels it can build a good personal relationship.

**Preparing the Company for the Consultant** For many companies, the trouble does not begin until the consultant has been selected and moves onto the premises to do the job. Rumors often begin to circulate among employees, spreading every notion from the idea that their jobs are in danger to the expectation that the company is in serious trouble. To stop rumors quickly and gain maximum cooperation between employees and consultants, managers should inform the department heads who will be directly or indirectly involved about the project immediately. Verbal announcements, in which the nature of the consultant's assignment and the procedures to be used are discussed, are generally preferred. Emphasis should be on the positive benefits of the project— greater efficiency, better working conditions, and profitability. If a union is involved, the project should be discussed with the shop steward, especially since many unions have rules about outsiders questioning its members.

**Dealing with the Consultant's Recommendations** Because companies often decide to use consultants without carefully considering their reasons for doing so, they have trouble dealing with the consultant's recommendations when the job is over. One pitfall is automatically accepting whatever the consultant suggests. The other extreme is resisting the suggestions—either because of a basic resistance to change or because the consultant's findings did not agree with the executive's own analyses.

The best approach to dealing with consultants' findings and recommendations is to analyze the proposed course of action against such yardsticks as: How likely is success? How much net gain can be reasonably expected? How likely is failure? How much net loss is possible in case of failure? If doubts persist, the consultant should be confronted. He or she should be asked how the final recommendations were reached and how well documented they are.

*Who Should Implement?* There is varied opinion on whether the consultant should implement his or her own recommendations. The advantage of doing so is that it guarantees that those recommendations do not end up in a desk drawer. The disadvantage is that the company must, of course, pay for the extra time the consultant stays around, and it is delaying the time when its own personnel actually get involved in, and take charge of, the new process or system.

Regardless of who implements the recommendations, however, the consultant should be expected to oversee or supervise the process; discuss fully the "what to do," "how to do it," and "what to expect" aspects of any new plan of action; resolve such questions as "What other parts of the company are directly affected by the new change?" and "What sorts of instructions and policy statements are needed?"; and leave the company's personnel with the idea that their jobs have really been improved, lest they go back to their old ways as soon as the consultant has left.

**After the Consultant Leaves** Most good consultants will not abandon a client company until they are absolutely certain that things are working properly. Most good ones will also include some sort of postassignment check-up procedure as part of their service. Depending on the nature of the arrangement, and the complexity of the change to be enforced, the consultant should make spot checks on the client's system for up to a year. For some jobs, one postinstallation review after 3 months is regarded as sufficient. For others, once a month for 6 months is necessary. In any case, an advance arrangement should be made that the consultant will come back and give a hand if problems develop, if certain personnel changes require reinstruction, or if developments outside the company make it necessary to update the system or program.

*See also* AUDIT, MANAGEMENT; SEARCH AND RECRUITMENT, EXECUTIVE.

### REFERENCES

Blake, Robert R., and Jane Srygley Mouton: *Consultation,* Addison-Wesley Publishing Company, Inc., Reading, Mass., 1976.

Boettinger, Henry M.: "New Directions for Management and Consultants," *Conference Board Record,* March 1975, pp. 53–56.

Flaster, Stephen R., and Stanley C. Hollander: *Management Consultants and Clients,* Michigan State University School of Business, East Lansing, 1972.

Fuchs, Jerome H.: "Making the Most of Management Consulting Services," American Management Association, New York, 1975.

"Just Managing: On the Uses of Experts by Management," *Conference Board Record,* March 1976, pp. 53–54.

STEPHEN H. KAUFMAN, *The Research Institute of Amercia, Inc.*

## Consultative selling   (*See* SALES MANAGEMENT.)

## Consumer   (*See* ECONOMIC MEASUREMENTS.)

## Consumer affairs unit   (*See* CONSUMERISM AND CONSUMER PROTECTION LEGISLATION.)

## Consumer behavior, managerial relevance of

In developing different strategies to achieve the marketing task, management can adopt one of three different orientations: a selling orientation, a product orientation, and a consumer orientation. In adopting a *selling orientation,* management presumes that consumers will not buy the product unless there is a substantial promotional and selling effort. This approach is based on the "if you can make it, I can sell it" school of thought. Emphasis is on advertising, promotion, personal selling, and point of purchase displays. The second orientation, the *product orientation,* is embodied in the "build a better mousetrap" school of thought. Characteristic of this approach are heavy research and development costs, an emphasis on higher technology, and frequent product failures. Consequently, the marketing mix variables receive minimal attention, and almost no consumer research is undertaken. The third orientation is the *consumer orientation,* which arises from the "find out what they want and give it to them" school of thought. The key tasks in this orientation are (1) the determination of the wants, needs, and desires of the consumers within the target market and (2) the shaping of the company so as to deliver the wants more effectively and efficiently than the competitors do. The primary emphasis is on consumer research, but product development, promotion, and the other marketing mix variables are equally important. Thus a fully integrated marketing plan is utilized in the consumer-oriented philosophy of marketing management.

**Benefits of a Consumer Orientation** Several specific and tangible benefits result from the adoption of a consumer orientation:

1. The company obtains a better picture of the structure of its market. Because consumer needs are more durable than products, they will reveal the true substitutability and "complementarity" of products. These relationships based on consumer needs often transcend the traditional industry viewpoint of competition.

2. There will be less waste and greater efficiency of the marketing effort, thereby decreasing marketing costs and increasing profitability. By providing the consumers with what they want, persuasion is not necessary. Further, receptivity of marketing communications will increase, reducing the amount of promotion necessary.

3. Product development stems from changes in the wants of consumers rather than from changes in technology. Product research becomes more structured and meaningful, and product failure is less likely.

4. Products that are no longer desired in the marketplace are more easily discarded and replaced by new, more quickly successful products. The company becomes a leader instead of a follower.

5. Customer satisfaction is increased because customers have been provided with what they want. This increased satisfaction leads to favorable word-of-mouth communications, probably the most effective form of promotion for the generation of new demand. Increased satisfaction also leads to brand loyalty and a more positive public opinion.

## DEFINING CONSUMER BEHAVIOR

Consumer behavior is not merely the use of goods and services marketed by profit-seeking companies and individuals; nor is it restricted to the actual act of consumption, such as the eating of french fries; nor is it restricted to the individual consumer. To more fully understand the complete scope and complex nature of consumer behavior, its three aspects need to be examined separately.

**Objects of Consumption** The most typical objects of consumption are those products and services provided by companies or individuals who have a profit motive. Included among these are (1) nondurable goods such as groceries, personal care items, and household cleaning supplies; (2) semidurable goods such as clothing; (3) consumer durables such as furniture, appliances, and automobiles; and (4) private services such as doctors, lawyers, and beau-

ticians. Additionally, the products and services of companies regulated by government, exemplified by the utility and transportation industries, should be included in this group.

However, people also consume public services provided by "nonprofit" organizations catering to such needs as health and recreation. Also included are those goods and services freely provided by the public sector such as highways, personal safety services, and educational facilities. The last, and the most subtle, addition are those goods and services satisfying the political, moral, and religious values of society. Included in these are the marketing of churches, politicians, and astrology.

This expansion to less traditional goods and services is relevant for management because they are all competing for pieces of the same well-defined pie, namely, the consumer's time, interest, and money.

**Consuming Units** It is insufficient to consider only individuals when discussing consumption behavior. Such a limitation results in misleading estimates of actual and potential markets. Other living creatures also consume vast quantities of goods and services. Household pets and other animals, domesticated and wild, require such diverse things as food, shelter, and medical services just as people themselves do. In addition, households and related consumer durables are also consuming units because they result in the use of products and services not otherwise required by individuals. Included in this group are such items as gasoline and repair services for the family automobile, home maintenance products, and special types of soap for dishwashers. It is frequently forgotten, but this derived demand represents a considerable share of all the goods and services demanded in a society. Finally, industries, organizations, and institutions must be considered consuming units with three major categories of consumption objects: (1) capital goods, (2) consumable goods such as raw materials, and (3) maintenance goods and services. The single most important, and largest, member of this group of consuming units is the national government.

**Behavioral Roles** Having delineated the *who* (consumers) and the *what* (goods and services), it now remains to classify the *how* and the *why* (activities and processes) to complete the complex picture of consumer behavior. Consumer behavior can be broadly categorized in two distinct ways: (1) by the nature of the activities and processes (behavioral roles) and (2) by the underlying motives and characteristics (behavioral types). Within the activities and processes, four behavioral roles can be identified: information gathering, decision making, purchasing, and consuming. These roles are important because they represent distinct parts of the total process, parts that permit specialization enabling them to be performed by different people in a household or organization in different places at different times.

The role of *information gathering* includes all activities regarding the collection, sorting, and evaluation of information concerning the benefits, risks, and consequences of the different alternatives. Information may be actively sought or passively received, and can be obtained from many sources including advertisements, point-of-purchase displays, word-of-mouth communications, and so on. Of importance to management is the ability of the decision maker to be selective in information gathering. This selectivity can result in perceptual biases of the information received, causing a difference between the objective information presented and the information perceived. For example, many consumers believe that there is a qualitative difference between national brands and store brands even though they are made by the same company.

Another behavioral role is *decision* or *choice making*. The process of choice making can be represented as a series of sequential steps. First, the decision maker must decide whether or not the product should be bought, depending on existence of the need, desire, and ability to buy the product. Second, he or she must narrow down the number of alternatives to a manageable few. Next, a choice of brands must be made from among the selected set of alternatives. Finally, he or she must decide on the place and method of purchase.

While the decision maker, purchaser, and user may all be the same person, frequently this is not the case. Almost always in organizational buying, the three roles are separated. For example, in the consumption of raw materials, the decision is made by the quality control department, the procurement by the purchasing department, and the consumption by the production department. This separation is also frequently evidenced in family buying behavior, most notably in the case of goods consumed by children where the decision making and purchasing are usually performed by the parents.

*Purchasing* refers to all the activities related to the procurement of the product or service. The most common activities include going to the store, physically searching for the product, picking up the product off the shelf, paying for the product, and transporting the product to the place of consumption. Consuming and purchasing do not have to occur at the same place or at the same time. Goods are frequently stockpiled for later consumption, and

while usually purchased at the seller's place of business, they are most often consumed elsewhere. This discontinuity in time and place is important because the satisfaction obtained at the time of consuming may not equal the expectations at the time of purchase.

*Consuming* includes all the activities related to the actual utilization of the product or service. It can occur instantaneously or over a period of years. For example, an automobile burns gasoline, a child eats a candy bar, and a family wears out their living room rug.

*Types of Behavior.* In addition to separating behaviors into different activities, they can also be categorized by the underlying motives of the buying process. The six most common types of buying behavior are described below. Each type of behavior has different implications for marketing management.

1. *Impulse purchasing* is the simplest type of buying behavior. It is completely unplanned and involves no previous search, deliberation, or systematic choice. For example, a person randomly selects a candy bar while waiting at the checkout counter. While the marketer has less direct influence over this type of buying behavior, the most relevant aspects of the marketing mix are point-of-purchase displays and package designs.

2. *Habitual buying behavior* refers to those purchases that have become routinized and are performed almost mechanistically. The behavior is fully learned, involves highly repetitive purchases, and occurs over short time cycles. While it is somewhat more involved than impulse purchasing, there is no information gathering or decision making involved on the part of the consumer. A common example is the consumer who always buys the same type, size, and brand of bread at the grocery store. The most relevant marketing strategy is to ensure good distribution so that the product is always available.

3. *Problem-solving behavior* refers to the deliberative and calculated decision-making approach to purchasing and includes the following steps: (*a*) the recognition of needs, (*b*) the establishment of goals to meet the needs, (*c*) the collection of information, (*d*) the determination of a set of alternatives, (*e*) the calculation of the potential of each of the alternatives to meet the goals, (*f*) a decision rule for choosing one of the alternatives, and (*g*) the purchase of the chosen alternative. The purchase of a home for most people involves problem-solving behavior. The total integrated marketing concept becomes most relevant in this type of buying behavior.

4. *Curiosity-motivated buying behavior* arises from a state of satiation or boredom with existing situations which creates a need for change, a need for increased complexity. This behavior is most susceptible to environmental stimuli (information). The product is tried because it is new or different. Many new products in a test market attain substantial first-time purchases but not enough repeat purchases to sustain the product because people buy the product owing to its novelty rather than its intrinsic superiority over existing products.

5. *Innovative buyer behavior* refers to the adoption of a new product or idea which may result in fundamental changes in the individual's life style. The activities involved are similar to those of the problem-solving behavior but refer primarily to new areas of consumption. Because of the fundamental change required, adoption is more difficult than ordinary problem solving. The adoption process will be more fully developed later.

6. *Collective decision making* is jointly performed by several people. It requires special attention, for in addition to the previously discussed activities involved in the decision-making process, two new aspects result. First, the roles are often more differentiated, indicating a separation of the marketing strategies. Second, interpersonal conflict results, making conflict resolution relevant for the marketing manager. Two specific types of collective purchasing, family buying and organizational buying, will be more fully developed later.

## EXPLANATIONS OF CONSUMER BEHAVIOR

Within the last several decades, many theories have been developed in an attempt to explain and predict consumer behavior. Often derived from different discipline perspectives, all have resulted in varying degrees of success, each with its own advantages and disadvantages. Although highly divergent in nature and scope, most theories can be classified into one of the following categories: learning theory and habit formation, demographic and socioeconomic theories, cultural and reference group theories, motivation research, perceived risk, cognitive dissonance, and attitude theories.

**Learning and Habit Formation**  One of the most intriguing phenomena in consumer behavior is brand, store, or supplier loyalty. A variety of approaches have been introduced in an attempt to explain this phenomenon of repeat purchasing, and while differing substantially in their formulations, they are all derived from the psychological theories of learning and conditioning. Learning, in psychology, refers to the change in an individual's response pattern which results from past experience. Thus, learning implies that the future purchases of an individual will be determined by his or her past purchases. Past experience can affect future responses in two ways. Based on the classical conditioning theory, the first approach postulates that the individual "learns" to make the same responses when confronted with the same stimuli by doing them over and over. For example, in the checkout line at the supermarket when the clerk asks for money, the consumer gives the amount requested, rather than making a counter offer and then bargaining for the price to be paid. The consumer does this because it is what he or she has always done.

Furthermore, the outcomes of past behavior also have an effect on future behavior. Based on the operant conditioning theory (reinforcement theory), a suggestion has been made that past behaviors that have resulted in favorable outcomes are more likely to recur than those resulting in less or unfavorable outcomes. If a consumer buys a brand of detergent and finds that it gets clothes very clean, he or she is more likely to buy it again than if it did not get clothes clean.

Thus, the amount of learning will depend on both the habit strength—the number of previous stimulus-response associations—and on the incentive motivation—the expectation of reward based on past experience. In addition, both the internal state of the individual and the strength of the stimulus will affect the response tendency. It has been found, for example, that people tend to purchase more unplanned groceries when they are hungry (e.g., right before lunch) than when they are not hungry. Similarly, the aroma of fresh pastries that is coming from a bakery with open doors is more likely to bring about the puchase of some bakery products than would a billboard advertisement several blocks away.

**Socioeconomic and Demographic Factors**  One of the more traditional approaches to explaining consumer behavior is the use of socioeconomic and demographic (SED) factors. SED variables are characteristics by which an individual may be described, and they include physical characteristics, social characteristics, and economic characteristics. Generally, they can be separated into two categories: those that are ascribed, i.e., outside the control of the consumer for the most part, and those that are attainable, i.e., within the control of the indivdual. The ascribed SED variables include sex, race, religion, ethnic origin, physical characteristics, health, age, and intelligence. The attainable SED variables include income, education, occupation, marital status, home ownership, family occupation, and place of residence.

The theory holds that various aspects of consumer behavior such as brand choices and preferences, media habits, and shopping habits can be explained through differences in the SED characteristics of consumers. That is, people with the same SED characteristics are more likely to behave in the same manner.

SED models have several advantages. First, they are easy data to collect and communicate. Respondents have a better understanding of what is being asked than they do with questions involving attitudes, beliefs, and values. Second, because they are objective, SED variables generally elicit more reliable responses. Finally, because this type of data is collected by the Census Bureau, results can be easily generalized to entire populations.

*Limitations.* SED variables present two major problems in explaining consumer behavior, however. First, they have proven to be poor correlates of brand choice in the past, and second, they are outside the control of marketing management. Therefore, SED variables should be used in the explanation of consumer behavior with the following considerations:

1. They are probably more relevant at the product level. While not differentiating well between brand users, they may help explain differences in product usage.

2. Owing to the increasing affluence of the lower classes, some SED variables are becoming obsolete. This is true for income, for example; however, race, sex, age, and religion are still very relevant SED variables.

3. Finally, these variables will at best provide only a partial explanation; hence idealistic models developed using only SED variables will be unrealistic.

**Culture and Reference Groups**  The consumption behavior of an individual is determined in part by the social forces acting on her or him. The two major social forces in consumer behavior are culture and reference groups.

*Culture.* This is the learned response patterns and feelings of a homogeneous group of individuals which collectively reflect the values and their meaningful symbols as they are transmitted from one generation to the next. Thus, culture is an attempt of each society to adapt to its particular environment.

The most common identification of culture is with national boundaries. However, culture can transcend national boundaries. More than one nation may belong to the same relevant culture, as for example the industrialized Western European nations, or more than one culture may be found within the same country—especially true in the United States, where there are many large ethnic groups, each with its own culture and traditions.

Culture has a twofold effect on consumer behavior. First, the same product or promotion as symbols of values may not be equally acceptable to all cultures. Products geared for the independent working woman would not be relevant in less-developed countries where the role of woman is still more traditional. Apart from this obvious effect, culture may also affect the actual decision-making process of the consumer; that is, culture may in part determine the extent to which individuals engage in problem-solving behavior, in curiosity behavior, or in habitual behavior.

*Reference Groups.* A social force with a more direct impact on consumption behavior is the reference group. A *reference group* can be defined as any aggregation of people that influences an individual's attitudes or behaviors by serving as a point of reference. While reference groups may be classified in many ways, the most relevant types are membership groups, aspirational groups, dissassociative groups, and primary groups.

*Membership* groups, those groups to which an individual belongs by a voluntary choice, are the most general form of reference group. *Aspirational* groups are groups to which an individual desires to belong, as for example, the local country club. In such instances, the individual will emulate the members of this group, especially in the consumption of conspicuous products. The impact of aspirational groups is best demonstrated by the effectiveness of advertising endorsements. Just the opposite, *disassociative* groups represent those groups with which an individual does not want to be identified. Consequently, the individual will go out of his or her way to avoid using products and brands that would indicate membership in that particular group. Finally, *primary* groups are those groups whose members all have face-to-face interaction. They represent the most forceful social influence on patterns of consumption. Their influence is exerted through pressures of conformity. Group members who deviate too far from group norms are ostracized by the group for their deviant behavior.

**Motivation Research**  While culture, reference group, and SED explanations of consumer behavior involve the identification of external consumer characteristics, motivation research refers to the understanding of human motives which are hidden, deep-rooted, and otherwise not obvious, but at the same time are determinants of product choices. Relying on the theory and methodology of clinical psychology, motivation research has evolved into three major types in studying consumption behavior:

1. *Psychoanalytic theory* seeks hidden motives. It postulates that the human personality structure is composed of the id, the ego, and the superego. The id represents the force acting in the body to satisfy the biological needs, the ego acts as the mediator between the demands of the id and the person's environment by determining behaviors that can satisfy the needs, and the superego provides the societal and personal norms that constrain behavior. Behavior is a result of the unconscious motivation resulting from the interaction of these three parts. Psychoanalytic theory has prompted the use of sexuality in the design of both products and promotion.

2. *Projective techniques* represent a method whereby the hidden and socially unacceptable or objectionable motivations of an individual can be determined. It assumes that in addition to sex, a human being can be motivated by such things as the need for power, achievement, money, and social acceptance. The technique consists of having an individual playact, for example, describing what he or she sees in a picture, or complete a short story. The individual's motives are then determined through the subjective analysis of his or her responses.

The purpose of these first two types of motivation research can be seen as only exploratory. They provide a means for pretesting and developing new ideas. They are too costly to perform in large numbers, highly subjective, and difficult to quantify.

3. *Personality characteristics* represent the major influence of motivation research on consumer behavior. Personality traits are those characteristics that cause two people to behave differently in the same situation. Thus, personality is an individual difference variable. For the theory to be useful, it is necessary to assume that many individuals will have the same personality characteristics, that these characteristics will be stable over time, and that they will consistently influence a wide variety of behaviors.

Personality traits can be measured through the use of specially designed instruments called personality tests. The traits are then used as independent variables in an attempt to find the relationship between them and product or brand choice.

**Perceived Risk and Cognitive Dissonance** Two distinct cognitive theories that attempt to explain a consumer's choice behavior are (1) perceived risk theory and (2) cognitive dissonance theory.

*Perceived Risk.* This refers to the individual's evaluation of the negative consequences which are likely to arise if he or she makes a wrong choice among available alternatives. Thus, perceived risk is a function of two components: (1) aversive consequences and (2) degree of uncertainty. The theory posits that the consumer will act in such a way as to reduce the risk involved in the choice situation.

Three general types of risk have been identified in the product choice situation: personal risk, economic risk, and social risk. *Personal risk* is the risk that something may happen to harm the individual physically: for example, injury due to product failure. *Social risk* refers to the undesirable social effects resulting from a wrong choice: for example, ridicule for wearing outlandish clothes. Finally, *economic risk* can result from either loss of money or loss of time.

Because people will act to decrease risk, the theory has the following implications for consumer behavior:

1. The greater the perceived risk, the more likely the development of brand loyalty. People will stick with something they are sure of.

2. The greater the perceived risk, the more extensive the individual's search for information, hence the greater the impact of advertising.

3. The greater the perceived risk, the greater the importance of word-of-mouth communications.

4. The greater the perceived risk, the more thorough the deliberation an individual will engage in; therefore, impulse purchasing is less likely to occur.

*Cognitive Dissonance.* This refers to the psychological discomfort experienced immediately following a choice decision between two or more attractive alternatives. While perceived risk is relevant to predecision behavior, cognitive dissonance is more applicable to postdecision activities. In order for cognitive dissonance to occur, the following antecedant conditions are necessary:

1. There must be a number of desirable alternatives; that is, a choice exists.

2. The unchosen alternatives must in fact have some desirable features that are not obtainable in the chosen alternative.

3. There must be some commitment to the choice, and the choice must be seen as irrevocable.

4. The individual must not feel forced into the particular decision, but rather must believe that the choice was of his or her own volition.

Under such circumstances, the individual will experience mental discomfort and will act in such a way as to reduce this tension after making the choice. The methods of dissonance reduction are very relevant for marketing management. First, the individual may psychologically decrease the attractiveness of the unchosen alternative and increase the attractiveness of the chosen. Thus, cognitive dissonance should lead to the development of brand loyalty. The individual can also search for information to support the choice. Thus, he or she will prefer consonant to discrepant information. This implies that marketing should not stop with the act of purchase but also continue to *reinforce* the decisions of those customers who have bought the product. Consumers will want to rationalize their choices. Advertising's greatest impact is often on loyal customers.

**Attitudinal Theories** An attitude may be defined as some mental state of the individual which reflects favorableness or unfavorableness toward an object and includes his or her predisposition to behave in specific ways toward that object. Because attitudes represent prior predispositions, they can be used to predict future behavior. An individual's choice among products or brands will be determined by personal attitudes toward them, resulting in a choice of the most favorable. Thus, the key to understanding choice behavior is the understanding of the underlying attitudes.

Attitudes are presumed to be determined by a number of factors. This determination of attitudes has been a major source of controversy in social psychology, resulting in four major schools of thought: the behavioral school, the perceptual school, the functional school, and the cognitive consistency school.

1. The behavioral school hypothesizes that attitudes are a direct result of the experiences of past behaviors. Attitudes are the result of behaviors rather than the cause.

2. The perceptual school holds that attitudes are determined by the relative position of products to each other and to an ideal product within some defined product space. An individual's attitudes are estimated from this product space by comparing the distances between different products and the individual's ideal point. The individual is said to have the most favorable attitude toward that product which lies closest to his or her ideal point. Attitude change is brought about by changing the individual's perception of the products in the product space.

3. The functional school deals with the possibility that many people have the same attitude toward a particular product but for different reasons. The functional school posits that attitudes serve four

functions for the individual. The utilitarian function of an attitude is to express a feeling about the usefulness of an object for satisfying an individual's functional and physical needs. The knowledge function of an attitude is to help individuals cope with a complex world. This function permits the stereotyping of objects into categories of like or dislike so that when confronted with them in future situations, the individual will not have to engage in extensive decision making. The expressive function of an attitude is to reflect the individual's self-concept. It is this function which often results in purchase of products not so much for their functional utility as for the expression of social psychological needs by conspicuous consumption behavior. The final function of an attitude is to protect the individual from internal anxieties. In this sense, the attitude serves as an ego-defensive mechanism, often leading to the perceptual biasing of information.

4. The last school of thought, the cognitive consistency school, has had the greatest influence on consumer behavior theory and research. This theory posits that attitudes are based on three factors: a cognitive factor, an affective factor, and a conative factor. The cognitive factor represents an individual's information about an object, consisting of two basic types of beliefs: beliefs in the existence of an object (awareness) and beliefs about the object (evaluative beliefs). The affective dimension of attitude is the overall feeling of like or dislike. In consumer behavior it is generally believed that this overall affect is a direct function of the person's evaluative beliefs. Specifically, affect for a product is hypothesized to be the sum of the evaluative beliefs (weighted according to their importance) over all the relevant product attributes. Research in this area has focused on the method of selecting salient product attributes, the method of measurement of both the evaluative beliefs and the importance of those beliefs, the inclusion or exclusion of the weights in the model, and the manner in which the beliefs are combined to form the overall affect toward the product.

The apparent uncertainty is due in part to the inability of evaluative beliefs to predict exactly affect and hence product choice. It has thus been suggested that the conative factor mediates affect and behavior. This conative factor is the gross behavioral intention of the individual.

A comprehensive picture of the attitude behavior relationship (Sheth, 1974) is presented in Fig. C-13. Behavior will depend on the behavioral intentions (what a person plans to do) as well as events that could not have been planned for. What a person

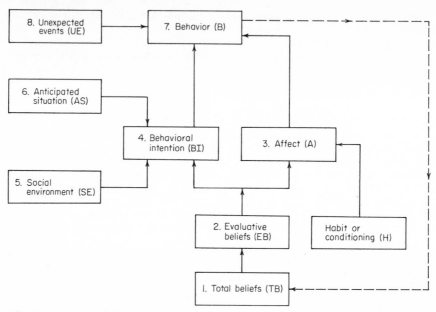

Fig. C-13. A conceptual theory of attitude structure and attitude-behavior relationship.

plans to do with respect to a product will depend on (1) the overall affect (like-dislike) of the individual toward the product, (2) the expected situation surrounding the purchase and use of the product, and (3) the social image surrounding the purchase and use of the product. Finally, affect for the product will be determined by the individual's beliefs about the capability of product to satisfy his or her needs (evaluative beliefs).

## A COMPREHENSIVE MODEL OF CONSUMER BEHAVIOR

Like most marketing managers' theories of their customers' behavior, the previous explanations of consumer behavior are partial explanations at best. Consequently, several attempts have been made to combine all the relevant aspects of consumer behavior into one framework. A well-known comprehensive theory of consumer behavior is the Howard-Sheth (1969) theory of buyer behavior (Fig. C-14). It is concerned with the buying process in the context of repetitive choice decisions. The buying process starts with a brand choice decision which is based on a set of motives the buyer has, a set of alternatives that might satisfy those motives, and a set of choice criteria to aid in making the choice. The consumer

must have reasons for buying any brand in a particular product class; that is, the product will be purchased in an attempt to satisfy a set of motives. Having identified personal motives and the product class relevant for satisfying those motives, the consumer must locate within that product class a set of alternatives from which a choice can be made. In instances when the number of brands within a product class is small, the set of alternatives considered may include all the brands available. More frequently, the number of brands is quite large, so the consumer must first select a subset of brands from which to make the ultimate choice. This subset is called the evoked set and will normally not exceed six or seven brands. Finally, having obtained a set of suitable alternative brands, the consumer must evaluate the brands in terms of their potential to satisfy personal motives and thus provide maximum satisfaction.

As the consumer gains familiarity with a product class, the decision-making process will become more routinized and requires less effort and time. This psychology of simplication progresses through identifiable stages. During the initial purchase within a product class, the consumer engages in extensive problem solving. During this state he or she has little knowledge of the product class and must develop the choice criteria by which to evaluate potential alternatives. Thus, generalizations will be made from past similar experiences. The consumer is most susceptable to external information at this state.

After the initial purchase, the consumer gains experience and the choice criteria become well entrenched. During this stage, limited problem solving is engaged in because the consumer only needs to obtain brand information. Usually the number of alternatives in the evoked set is small at this stage, only three to five, each with a relatively equal probability of being purchased.

Finally, the consumer reaches the stage of routinized response behavior. During this last stage in the simplification process, no decision making occurs. After many purchases, not only are the choice criteria well established, but brand familiarity is so strong that the individual does not decide among alternatives at each purchase. Brands are purchased from habit. For example, the consumer writes "coffee" on a shopping list, but in fact knows exactly which brand and size he or she will purchase.

## THE DIFFUSION OF INNOVATIONS

While the Howard-Sheth theory of buyer behavior is concerned primarily with the decision process of an individual in a repeat purchasing situation, diffusion theory is concerned with the adoption of new products.

The major components of theories of diffusion, from a marketing perspective, are (1) the innovation and its characteristics, (2) the process by which the new product is accepted, (3) the sources of communication relevant for the adoption process, and (4) the characteristics of different types of adopters.

**Defining an Innovation**  The most important of these elements is the innovation. Most marketers define an *innovation* as any new product, but this definition is misleading. A better definition of innovation is a product which is *perceived* as new by the potential adopters.

There are several characteristics of an innovation which determine whether or not the product will be

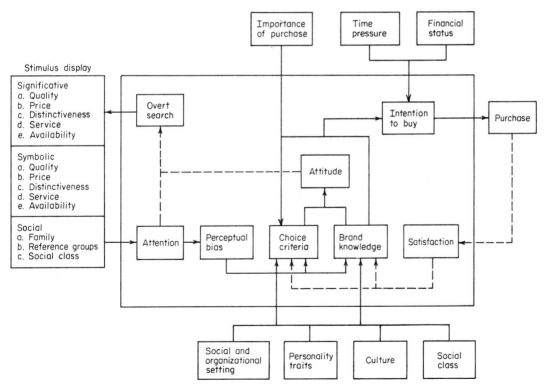

Fig. C-14.  Howard-Sheth theory of buyer behavior.

adopted, and if it is adopted, the rate of adoption—the speed at which it is diffused throughout the society.

1. Compatibility refers to the extent the new product blends in with current behavior patterns, values, beliefs, and attitudes. The less disruptive of current life an innovation is, the faster it will be adopted.

2. Perceived relative advantage of a new product is the extent to which it is perceived as being superior to existing alternatives. Relative advantage is a multidimensional concept based on many factors including initial cost, maintenance costs, risk, time and effort savings, discomfort reductions, and the speed of gratification.

3. Complexity of a product refers to the amount of knowlege necessary for the use and understanding of a new product. If a new product is too complex, and therefore very difficult to understand, relatively few people will be able to adopt initially, and the rate of diffusion will be very slow. Furthermore, more complex products are more difficult to communicate.

4. Trialability refers to the extent the consumer can experience the product firsthand before a decision to adopt must be made. Innovations that must be accepted without trial will diffuse more slowly than those that can be tried. Trial can occur through a division of the product into smaller units (such as in the adoption of new food products) or through use without commitment to adopt (such as the test driving of a new automobile).

5. Finally, the more easily the new product can be communicated to individuals, the faster it will be adopted. Communication can be of three forms: demonstration of the product itself, pictorial descriptions of the product, or verbal descriptions. Of these, demonstration will have the greatest effect.

**Process of Adoption**  There are several theories describing the process an individual goes through in accepting a new product. The best-known theory of adoption process is that developed by Rogers and Shoemaker (1971). Their paradigm consists of four stages in the individual's acceptance process. The first stage, *knowledge*, consists of the individual's awareness of the product's existence and knowledge about its characteristics. The second stage, *persuasion*, refers to the process of forming an attitude or opinion toward the product. The attitude may be either positive or negative. In the third stage of the adoption process, the *decision*, the individual will decide either to adopt the product or to reject it. However, the decision need not be final. In some

instances it is possible to discontinue use after adoption, and in some instances it is possible merely to postpone the decision.

Because of the lack of finality, the adoption process does not stop with the decision. If the consumer does accept the product, he or she will desire support for the decision. Therefore, in the fourth stage, *confirmation*, the consumer seeks reinforcement for the decision to adopt, and this reinforcement can come from actual use of the product, from social sources, or from commercial sources.

**Sources of Communication**  Sources of communication affecting the adoption process can be either interpersonal or mass media. Because of the nature of the adoption process, interpersonal communication, especially from a social source, is often crucial in the acceptance of new products. However, it is impossible for everyone to obtain information from social sources prior to adoption; hence a two-step flow of communication has been proposed to explain the communication process. The fundamental principle of the two-step flow process is that some people will rely more on mass media and commercial sources for information regarding a new product while the rest will depend more on interpersonal and social sources. The people who use mass media are the ones whom the rest of society relies upon for information and are called the opinion leaders. They constitute a fundamental part of the diffusion process.

**Adopter Characteristics**  Because many new product adoption curves follow a cumulative normal distribution (the so-called "S-shaped curve"), the most common classification system of adopters is based on the time (relative to others) of adoption and consists of innovators, early adopters, early majority, late majority, and laggards.

*Innovators* are the first people to adopt a new product and represent the first 3 to 5 percent of the population. They are venturesome, like to take risks, and generally have control of their financial resources and are able to withstand a possible financial loss. They are also able to easily understand the use and nature of the new product.

*Early adopters* are more respectable in the community than innovators and are the next 13 to 15 percent of the population. They are more integrated into the social structure and often serve as models for the rest of society. They exhibit the greatest amount of opinion leadership.

Members of the *early majority* (the next 35 percent) are more deliberate. They want more information, especially from a social source; hence they have more frequent social interactions. However, their social interactions seldom occur outside their own area.

The last two categories, *late majority* and *laggards*, comprise the remaining 45 to 50 percent of the population. These individuals are more tradition-oriented and exhibit a high degree of brand loyalty. The demonstration of the perceived advantages of the new product is necessary for these individuals to adopt a new product.

## FAMILY BUYING BEHAVIOR

The most relevant aspect of the family buying process, as opposed to the individual process, is that the decision may be made either autonomously by a single individual or jointly by two or more members of the family. It is, therefore, necessary to separate those instances when a joint decision is more likely from those when an autonomous decision will be made (Sheth, 1974).

There are three *family determinants* of the decision-making process: (1) social class, (2) life cycle, and (3) role orientation. It is found that there is more joint decision making among members of the middle class than among families in either the upper or lower classes. Similarly, joint decision making tends to be more prevalent as the family moves up the family life cycle. Newly marrieds without children are less likely to make joint decisions than are couples with young children. Finally, the more separated the family role structure is, the more likely family members are to make autonomous decisions.

In addition to the family determinants of the decision-making process, there are three *product determinants:* (1) time pressure (2) perceived risk, and (3) importance of purchase. As the amount of time available for a decision decreases, the likelihood of an autonomous decision increases. However, as the perceived risk inherent in a product increases, and as the importance of the purchase increases, the likelihood becomes greater that the decision making will be joint.

A second and more important part of the theory revolves around the *concept of conflict*. Conflict will occur in the family decision process if first, there is a felt need for a joint decision, and second, if there is a difference in goals or perceptions among family members. The type of conflict resolution depends on the reason for the conflict.

When conflict occurs because of a disagreement on the evaluation of different brands to satisfy the motives, its resolution will be by the *problem-solving*

*process*. The consequences of problem-solving resolution is that family members will seek additional information from outside to support or refute the alternatives. They may even search for new alternatives.

However, the disagreement may be deeper than just the evaluation of the alternative brands. The members may disagree as to the criteria with which they should be evaluating the alternatives. Resolution in this instance occurs through a *process of persuasion*. For example, the teenage son may want a car of his own for reasons of prestige, but the other family members may persuade him that he will need his money for college, which is much more important to him. Thus, in effect, they demonstrate to him the inconsistency of his motives.

If two members have motives that are irreconcilable, then resolution involves a *process of bargaining*. In this type of situation one member of the family may be given the permission to make an autonomous decision in return for some favor granted to the other members. Thus, the father gets to buy a new set of golf clubs for recreation if he takes the whole family on a vacation.

Finally, the disagreement may go beyond even differences in motives. Conflict may occur over the very style of life. When disagreement is this deep, resolution is only possible through the *process of politicking*. This style of resolution usually involves the formation of coalitions and subgroups within the family, but may also result in the dissolution of the family.

## ORGANIZATIONAL BUYER BEHAVIOR

Organizational buying behavior is the other major instance of collective decision making and shares many similarities with family buying behavior. Like family buying behavior, organizational buying consists of three major aspects: (1) the different perspectives of the individuals engaged in the decision-making process, (2) conditions that precipitate either a joint or an autonomous decision, and (3) conflict and methods of conflict resolution.

A popular notion holds that the organizational buyer is a more rational decision maker than the consumer. However, a significant amount of evidence indicates just the opposite: the organizational buyer is far from rational (Sheth, 1973).

Probably the biggest difference between organizational buyer behavior and family buyer behavior is the predominance of conflict within the organizational buying process. Conflict is almost always a part of organizational buying because of the fundamental differences between the groups that normally engage in the decision-making process. The buying decisions are usually made by members of the purchasing department, the quality control department, and the manufacturing department. Conflict arises because of the fundamental differences in the purchasing criteria of these groups. The purchasing agent is most concerned about the price of the product, desiring to minimize costs. Quality control wants the best quality product on the market. And manufacturing wants the product to be the safest and the easiest to use. These criteria are often mutually exclusive, and, therefore, conflict arises.

In order to better explain and integrate this process of organizational buyer behavior, a model of the process is depicted in Fig. C-15. The model consists of four major parts: first are the expectations of the different groups involved; second is the actual deci-sion-making process—whether it will be joint or autonomous; third is the method of conflict resolution; and fourth are those variables already discussed that inhibit the systematic choice process.

## CONCLUSION

Consumer behavior is highly complex and full of variety. The manager who believes that she or he fully understands consumer behavior for an organization's products and services is often in the same situation as the proverbial seven blind men and the elephant. It is best to hold a conservative view about the mystique of consumer behavior. Not only is consumer behavior complex, but it is also a dynamically changing phenomenon. What the manager knows about the firm's customers today may not necessarily hold true in the future.

*See also* ADVERTISING CONCEPTS; ADVERTISING MANAGEMENT, INDUSTRIAL; BRANDS AND BRAND-

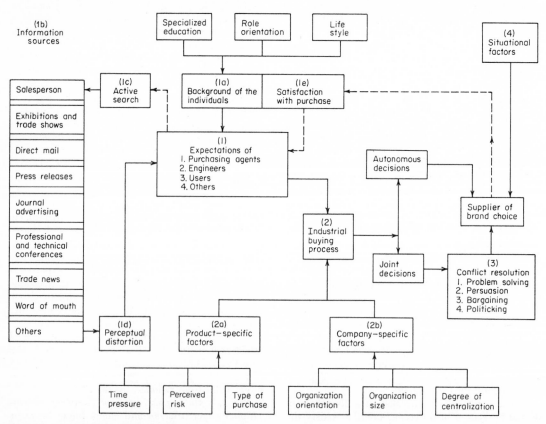

**Fig. C-15. A model of industrial buyer behavior.**

NAMES; CONSUMERISM AND CONSUMER PROTECTION LEGISLATION; CREDIT MANAGEMENT; DESIGN, INDUSTRIAL; MARKET ANALYSIS; MARKETING, CONCEPTS AND SYSTEMS; MARKETING RESEARCH; PRODUCT AND SERVICE PRICING; PRODUCT PLANNING AND DEVELOPMENT.

### REFERENCES

Bourne, Francis: *Group Influences in Marketing and Public Relations,* Foundation for Research on Human Behavior, Ann Arbor, Mich., 1956.

Cox, Donald F.: *Risk Taking and Information Handling in Consumer Behavior,* Division of Research, Harvard Business School, Cambridge, Mass., 1967.

Engel, James F., David T. Kollak, and Roger D. Blackwell: *Consumer Behavior,* 2d ed., Holt, Rinehart and Winston, Inc., New York, 1973.

Festinger, Leon: *A Theory of Cognitive Dissonance,* Stanford University Press, Palo Alto, Calif., 1957.

Fishbein, Martin, ed.: *Attitude Theory and Measurement,* John Wiley & Sons, Inc., New York, 1967.

Hansen, Flemming: *Consumer Behavior: A Cognitive Approach,* The Macmillan Company, New York, 1971.

Howard, John A., and Jagdish N. Sheth: *The Theory of Buyer Behavior,* John Wiley & Sons, Inc., New York, 1969.

Kassarjian, Harold, and Thomas Robertson, eds.: *Perspectives in Consumer Behavior,* rev. ed., Scott, Foresman and Company, Boston, 1973.

Kotler, Philip: *Marketing Management,* 3d ed., Prentice-Hall, Inc., Englewood Cliffs, N.J., 1976.

Rogers, Everett, and F. Floyd Shoemaker: *Communication of Innovations,* The Free Press, New York, 1971.

Sheth, Jagdish N.: "A Model of Industrial Buyer Behavior," *Journal of Marketing,* vol. 37, October 1973, pp. 50–56.

Sheth, Jagdish N., ed.: *Models of Buyer Behavior,* Harper & Row, Publishers, Incorporated, New York, 1974.

Sheth, Jagdish N.: "Role of Demographics in Consumer Behavior," College of Commerce, University of Illinois, Faculty Working Paper, no. 218, Urbana, November 1974.

Woodside, Arch, Peter D. Bennet, and Jagdish N. Sheth, eds.: *Consumer and Industrial Buying Behavior,* American Elsevier Publishing Company, Inc., 1977.

Worcester, Robert M., ed.: *Consumer Market Research Handbook,* McGraw-Hill Publishing Company, Ltd., London, 1972.

JAGDISH N. SHETH, *University of Illinois at Urbana*
ROBERT REDINGER, *Carnegie-Mellon University*

## Consumer education  (*See* CONSUMERISM AND CONSUMER PROTECTION LEGISLATION.)

## Consumer goods  (*See* MARKETS, CLASSIFICATIONS AND MARKET ANALYSIS.)

## Consumer income and spending  (*See* ECONOMIC MEASUREMENTS.)

## Consumer Product Warranties Act  (*See* CONSUMERISM AND CONSUMER PROTECTION LEGISLATION.)

## Consumer sovereignity  (*See* ECONOMIC CONCEPTS.)

## Consumerism and consumer protection legislation

Consumerism provides business with a challenge to take the offensive and to reexamine its marketing philosophy, practices, and programs which affect short- and long-run customer satisfaction in a manner consistent with the public welfare. So enduring is today's consumer protection movement that it can be counted on to operate as a major force of influence in the years ahead.

**Persistent Activity** Consumerism is a form of advocacy that seeks to protect and broaden the rights and powers of consumers. Since its inception in the early 1960s, the scope and impact of this modern day consumer movement continues to evolve. It encompasses basic consumer rights which were first articulated in 1962 by President Kennedy as the right to safety, the right to be informed, the right to choose, and the right to be heard. In the intervening years, other presidents have restated them, while Congress has acted on them through consumer protection legislation (*see* Appendix at end of this entry). Indications point to continuing legislative activity in the foreseeable future at the federal, state, and local level alike.

Corporate managers and executives no longer ask whether consumerism is here to stay, but rather how to respond constructively to the problems and dissatisfactions of consumers. To an increasing number of executives, consumerism is viewed as an opportunity in the market arena, rather than as a threat. Correspondingly, new programs designed to meet the challenges of consumerism need to be analyzed, planned, and implemented.

**Widening Parameters** The challenge of consumerism today includes not only the demands of consumers for safer, higher quality, and more effective goods and services, but also an insistence upon corporate responsibility in meeting a host of noneconomic and social concerns. Such matters as pollution of the environment, quality-of-life considerations, and even multinational business relations frequently appear under the banner of consumerism. In short, the parameters of consumerism continue to expand in response to ever-escalating consumer demands and expectations. The increased sophistication of consumers, the growing gap between product performance and marketing claims, the depersonalized nature of the marketplace (consumers repeatedly decry the lack of personal attention to their problems), and the failure of normal marketplace operations to satisfy consumers pose tremendous challenges to management operating in an environment that is characterized by *caveat venditor*.

**Continuing Surveillance** If management is to address basic consumer issues, rather than surface symptoms, it must have an information system that enables management to identify and predict underlying consumer issues and discontent. To understand the problems facing a company's customers and to stay current with consumer opinion trends, many companies have found it useful to conduct surveys, even if informally, on a periodic basis. From the responses of such surveys, important problem areas and worthwhile opportunities can be identified and compared with survey findings from trade associations, public opinion polls, and academic efforts. While the relative importance of consumer issues varies among and within manufacturing, retail, and service industries, corporate responses in terms of constructive consumer programs need to be developed by all firms. This requires top management commitment, not only in budget resource support but also in terms of philosophy and personal attitude.

**Top Management Commitment** Management's basic attitudinal requirement is to accept consumerism and reject the notion that since "we have always been customer-oriented," there is really nothing new about today's consumer protection movement. Additionally, adequate funding for specific, ongoing consumer programs should become part of the annual budget. These requirements pose a formidable task since direct corporate benefits may be difficult to measure, appear nonexistent, and are generally deferred. Consequently, there is a need to establish operational objectives and performance measures for improving or establishing on a first-time basis a consumer affairs program.

## ESTABLISHING A CONSUMER AFFAIRS UNIT*

A specialized consumer affairs unit now appears on the organization chart of a number of companies in different industries. This unit is given various titles, including Office of Consumer Affairs (RCA, Motorola), Department of Consumer Affairs (Firestone, Grand Union), Consumer Services Office (Nabisco), Customer Relations Department (Westinghouse, Hertz, Scott Paper), Consumer Affairs Department (National Can Company), or simply Customer Services Department (Polaroid, Gillette). While these units are virtually new entities in many companies and are not always concerned with the same range of responsibilities, they are usually directly involved in one or more of the following activities: (1) responding to consumer complaints; (2) disseminating consumer education materials; (3) dealing with outside consumer interest groups; (4) coordinating programs and developing standards with respective trade associations; and (5) advising management on consumerism issues. The overall purpose of such consumer affairs units is to improve relations and communications with consumers and to make the company more responsive to the needs and problems of consumers, thereby helping to increase customer prepurchase, purchase, and postpurchase satisfaction.

**Organizational Considerations** The organizational placement of the consumer affairs unit within a company depends on the magnitude, nature, and diversity of the company's operations, as well as the importance top management attaches on the unit. A 1973 survey by The Conference Board Inc., based on the experiences of 149 companies having formal, full-time consumer affairs units, shows that nearly two-thirds of them enjoy separate organizational status. The consumer affairs unit's status and relative organizational independence is further demonstrated in that 62 percent of the units report directly to general management, e.g., the company president, executive vice-president, or operating division head. When the unit is placed in some other depart-

*This section draws on the works of E. Patrick McGuire, *The Consumer Affairs Department: Organizations and Functions*, The Conference Board Inc., New York, 1973. Granted with permission.

ment, it is usually either in the public relations or the marketing department.

In practice, most firms have established a single consumer affairs unit located at corporate headquarters. This placement helps give the unit maximum status, visibility, and direct access to management. Furthermore, consumer affairs directors are thus in a position to participate actively in the marketing planning process, to influence basic corporate policies, and to ensure that the input of customers is represented in the corporate decision-making process.

**Handling and Resolving Consumer Complaints** For the companies that have separate consumer affairs units, handling and resolving customer complaints or establishing policies and procedures to be followed by others is of primary concern. Regardless of which units have final responsibility for consumer complaints, however, all firms should establish a formal complaint control system. Unfortunately, some companies continue to harbor a negative attitude toward consumer complaints. They are often accorded a low-budget priority and viewed as outside the mainstream of the firm. A constructive complaint-handling system, on the other hand, not only receives and then responds to consumer complaints, but actually seeks complaints and uses them as an early warning system. Knowing what bothers customers should point the company in new directions.

*Policy and Procedures.* It is important to specify in written form policies and procedures regarding customer complaints. In particular, the following aspects should be spelled out:

1. Who is responsible for receiving, processing, and resolving consumer complaints

2. How much authority for resolving complaints is possessed by various individuals and functional units

3. Who is to receive copies of the complaints within the company

4. What the time limit is on responding to and settling complaints

5. What control or follow-up procedures should be taken to ensure that complaints have, in fact, been satisfactorily resolved

6. How frequently summaries of complaints should be compiled and submitted to management

Complaint-handling procedures are often the single most important corporate action affecting customer goodwill and satisfaction. Complaints can easily be mishandled by delaying responses, using computers or distributors as scapegoats, and, most

important, failing to use a personalized response. Nothing irritates a customer more than receiving a form letter response. Indeed, consumer affairs directors find it ironic that many companies continue to respond to complaints via form postcard or letter replies, thus further depersonalizing contact with customers at the worst possible time. Lengthy response delays also help assure additional alienation. Most firms set a response time limit of 5 days, while some attempt to respond within 48 hours.

**Consumer Education** Company-sponsored consumer education programs and materials have become an integral part of consumer protection. Numerous companies publish and distribute buying guides, pamphlets and booklets, posters, charts, and "fact sheets" for home use and/or educational programs administered by others. Additionally, films, newspaper features, television film clips, and public service radio announcements are prepared to keep consumers better informed and thereby more knowledgeable in shopping and consumption alike.

Concentrated efforts are made increasingly to deal with the problems facing specific groups of consumers, especially children, the economically disadvantaged, and the elderly. These groups should be the focus of special corporate consumer protection efforts. Reliance on existing or proposed consumer protection legislation and industry guidelines or codes is insufficient. Special educational and research efforts are called for, directed to such consumer problems of children as sweetened foods and nutrition, toy safety and promotion, and television programming. Similarly, tailored consumer protection efforts via educational programs need to be directed toward the poor and the elderly.

It should also be recognized that educational programs can easily be viewed as being too self-serving, and thus they become self-defeating. This occurs when undue emphasis is placed on promoting the firm's own products and brands.

## MARKETING OPPORTUNITIES

Increasingly, executives view consumerism as representing new opportunities and profit potential, notably in the firm's marketing efforts. The basic consumer rights to have a choice, to be safe, to be informed, and to be heard suggest a framework for specific corporate actions to fulfill customer needs and create satisfied consumers.

**New Product Opportunities** Today's consumer protection climate brings into focus new product opportunities aimed at protecting the consumer's short- and long-run health and safety. As more consumers express concern for their own and society's long-run welfare, totally new products or reformulations of existing products that fulfill both immediate satisfaction and long-run benefits will find a profitable niche in the marketplace.

New product opportunities may be identified by creating special task forces which continually monitor products on the basis of suggestions coming from the Consumer Products Safety Commission, congressional and regulatory agencies' hearings and investigations, consumer groups, and customers. Efforts might also be directed to the active solicitation of ideas from various experts, including nutritionists, home economists, safety engineers, chemists, etc. Bringing "outsiders," including customers, into the decision-making process is recommended.

**Advertising Guidelines** Responsible, informative advertising benefits the consumer and contributes to a positive image among the buying public. All too frequently, however, advertising creates expectations about the performance of products that are not (or cannot be) fulfilled. To be sure, in a survey conducted by the Council of Better Business Bureaus, a majority of those polled responded that the business practices which annoyed them most were products not performing as represented and advertisements making exaggerated claims.

It is essential that a company determine its advertising credibility from a consumer's point of view and develop its advertising policy accordingly. In developing such policy, management should listen to consumer complaints and cooperate with outside industry and consumer groups.

The flow of persuasive information needs to emphasize not only what the consumer wants to know, but also what should be known to make intelligent choices in the marketplace. For example, there are many examples of advertising which contain information directed at consumer education. Such advertising can be especially efficacious as a substitute for the present appeals to self-esteem and irrationality.

While advertising materials are in preparation, they are normally reviewed by the legal department for conformity to all relevant laws and regulations. In addition, a company's advertising policy should deal with accuracy, completeness, and usefulness of advertisements and other promotional materials. Those responsible for corporate consumer affairs should participate in periodic review of policy and in the ongoing assessment of specific advertising campaigns.

**Product Information** There are a number of ways in which customers can be provided with useful product information. Among the methods currently employed are buying guides (nutritional information, performance criteria, open dating, unit pricing, etc.), installation and assembly guides, and product use and care instructions. The objective is to provide information that helps customers choose the "right" product in the first place so as to achieve better and prolonged product use. Accomplishing the task of providing the proper product information requires a coordinated effort between marketing, advertising, and consumer affairs.

To make it easier for consumers to receive timely product information, a number of companies have established or are experimenting with toll-free telephone arrangements. For instance, Whirlpool has successfully used its Cool Line program since 1967 when it first began experimenting with a toll-free telephone system for possible use by consumers having questions or complaints about Whirlpool products. Other firms (General Motors, American Motors, ITT, Polaroid, etc.) have similarly helped narrow the communication gap between a company and the ultimate user of its products and services.

**Consumer Warranties** A major problem facing consumers pertains to existing warranty practices. Congressional hearings and consumer complaints have repeatedly shown that sellers have been too preoccupied with the precision of the legal language used in warranties, rather than with the extent to which the document communicates to the buyer. The ongoing problems of customer understanding of difficult legalities and the existing loopholes continue to lead to customer dissatisfaction.

According to a study by the staff of the House Commerce and Finance Subcommittee, consumer product warranties were no better in 1974 than they were in 1969 when a presidential task force told manufacturers to improve warranty service or face tighter federal controls. After reviewing 200 warranties from 51 companies, the staff concluded that warranties continued to be riddled with ambiguities that misled and frustrated consumers while providing loopholes for manufacturers and sellers. It was largely to correct this problem that in 1975 Congress passed the Consumer Product Warranties Act (*see* Appendix at end of this entry). This consumer protection legislation introduces several new dimensions to the provision of postsale customer satisfaction.

Whether or not the Consumer Product Warranties Act will accomplish its objective of resolving warranty problems remains to be seen. Final FTC warranty rules, which will not take effect until the end of 1978, will govern the scope of service contracts, the dealer's duty to replace rather than repair faulty products, the depreciation of products for which cash refunds are offered, and the customer's obligation when a product is defective. In the meantime, considerable progress can be made by adopting a concise, straightforward warranty, rather than continuing to add to the confusion with legal jargon and complicated loopholes. Whirlpool Corporation, for example, has simplified the language of its warranties so that they clearly explain what is to be done and who will do it. Similarly, General Electric moved in the direction of warranty simplification by removing the restrictions and legal language and replacing them with clear and concise statements. Corning Corporation has even dropped the words *warranty* and *guarantee* and has replaced them by the term *promise*.

It is useful for management to reflect upon the functional role of warranties in today's marketplace and to recognize that a warranty (or guarantee) is essentially an assurance made by the seller to the customer. It should not be perceived as a legal instrument that limits the seller's obligation to the consumer according to the terms of the warranty. In short, a warranty should give consumers some assurance, prior to sale, that the product will perform up to the claims indicated in the advertising and sales promotion. If, for whatever reason, the product does not perform up to the customer's expectations, recourse should be readily available.

## A CORPORATE PROGRAM

The decade since the mid 1960s has been marked by a growing maturity of consumerism and a more enlightened business attitude toward the movement. Increasingly, consumerism is recognized by management as representing an opportunity which, if fully exploited, can yield corporate dividends through increased consumer confidence and satisfaction.

On the whole, consumerism is a positive development for consumers and business alike. As an enduring force in the marketplace, consumerism is responsible for far-reaching changes in business orientation and practice. Some generalizations as to how to bring about constructive, positive corporate responses are the following:

1. It is necessary to adopt the proper managerial orientation and to listen conscientiously to consumer proposals. The role of consumerism should be viewed in terms of long-run corporate, consumer, and public welfare.

2. It is useful to establish a corporate mechanism, such as a consumer affairs unit, which represents the consumer interest in product planning, implementation of marketing programs, and review of customer policies. This unit should be an independent corporate entity reporting directly to top management.

3. Consumer complaints should be processed promptly and properly. Special effort should be undertaken to see that correspondence with customers is personalized and that complaints have indeed been satisfactorily resolved.

4. An effective response to consumerism calls for an integrated program of quality products, meaningful consumer information, and reliable postpurchase service. Product performance should match customer expectations; advertising and promotion should yield more factual and usable product information; warranty and service policies should be clear and comprehensive.

5. A control system should be established to help prevent corporate practices that inadvertently produce consumer complaints when product performance and buyer expectations are not harmonious.

6. A consumer information system should periodically inform top management of consumer problems which are the derivative of the firm's marketing practices and products.

7. Management should recognize that immediate, measurable results from its consumerism-oriented initiatives may not be forthcoming. Measuring dividends in terms of increased customer satisfaction and long-run welfare calls for extended information systems and new interpretations of existing data.

*See also* ADVERTISING CONCEPTS; CONSUMER BEHAVIOR, MANAGERIAL RELEVANCE OF; EGALITARIANISM; ENVIRONMENTAL PROTECTION LEGISLATION; ETHICS, MANAGERIAL; GOVERNMENT REGULATIONS, BUSINESS LAWS; GOVERNMENT REGULATIONS, UNIFORM COMMERCIAL CODE; INSURANCE AND RISK MANAGEMENT; PRODUCT LIABILITY; PRODUCT PLANNING AND DEVELOPMENT; PRODUCT AND SERVICE PRICING; PUBLIC AND COMMUNITY RELATIONS; SOCIAL RESPONSIBILITY OF BUSINESS; VALUE SYSTEMS, MANAGEMENT: SOCIAL AND CULTURAL.

## REFERENCES

Aaker, David A., and George S. Day, eds.: *Consumerism: Search for the Consumer Interest*, 2d ed., The Free Press, New York, 1974.

*The Consumer Affairs Department: Organizations and Functions*, The Conference Board, Inc., Report, no. 609, New York, 1973.

Feldman, Lawrance P.: *Consumer Protection: Problems and Prospects*, West Publishing Company, New York, 1976.

*Fulfilling Consumer Rights*, Chamber of Commerce of the United States, Washington, 1972.

Gaedeke, Ralph M., and Warren W. Etcheson, eds.: *Consumerism: Viewpoints from Business, Government, and the Public Interest*, Canfield Press, San Francisco, Calif., 1972.

Greyser, Stephen A., and Steven L. Diamond: "Business is Adapting to Consumerism," *Harvard Business Review*, September-October 1974, pp. 38–58.

*Initiatives in Corporate Responsibility*, A Report of the Committee on Commerce, U.S. Senate, Oct. 2, 1972, Washington, 1972.

Peterson, Esther: "Consumerism as a Retailer's Asset," *Harvard Business Review*, May-June 1974, pp. 91–101.

*Responsive Approaches to Consumer Complaints and Remedies*, Report of the Sub-Council on Complaints and Remedies of the National Business Council for Consumer Affairs, Washington, October 1972.

Webster, Frederick E., Jr.: "Does Business Misunderstand Consumerism?" *Harvard Business Review*, September-October 1973, pp. 89–97.

## APPENDIX

### Significant Consumer Protection Legislation

1872  *Mail Fraud Act:* made it a federal crime to defraud through the use of mail.

1906  *Food and Drugs Act:* regulated interstate commerce in misbranded and adulterated foods, drinks, and drugs.

1914  *Federal Trade Commission Act:* established the Federal Trade Commission and declared "unfair methods of competition" illegal.

1938  *Food, Drug, and Cosmetic Act:* strengthened the Food and Drugs Act (1906) by extending coverage to cosmetics and therapeutic devices; authorized standards of identity and quality for food product.

1938  *Wheeler-Lea Act:* amended the Federal Trade Commission Act by making it possible to prosecute for deceptive advertising or sales practices.

1939  *Wool Products Labeling Act:* provided for proper labeling of the kind and percentage of each type of wool used in products.

1951  *Fur Products Labeling Act:* provided that all furs show the true name of the animal from which they were produced.

1953  *Flammable Fabrics Act:* prohibited the shipment in interstate commerce of any wearing apparel or material which is highly flammable.

1958  *Automobile Information Disclosure Act:* required automobile manufacturers to post the suggested retail price on all new passenger vehicles.

1958  *Food Additives Amendment:* amended the Food, Drug, and Cosmetic Act (1938) by prohibiting use of new food additives until manufacturer establishes safety for human consumption and FDA issues regulations specifying conditions for use.

1959  *Textile Fiber Products Identification Act:* required identification of most textile products not covered by the Wool or Fur Products Labeling Acts.

1960  *Hazardous Substances Labeling Act:* required prominent warning labeling on hazardous household chemicals.

1960  *Color Additives Amendment:* amended the Food, Drug, and Cosmetic Act (1938) by allowing the FDA to establish by regulations the conditions of safe use for color additives used in foods, drugs, and cosmetics.

1962  *Kefauver-Harris Drug Amendments:* required drug manufacturers to file all new drugs with the FDA, to label all drugs by generic name, and to require pretesting of drugs for safety and efficacy.

1965  *Fair Packaging and Labeling Act* ("Truth-in-Packaging"): regulated the packaging and labeling of consumer goods and provided that voluntary uniform packaging standards be established by industry.

1966  *National Traffic and Motor Vehicle Safety Act:* authorized the Department of Transporation to establish compulsory safety standards for new and used tires and automobiles.

1966  *Child Safety Act:* strengthened the Hazardous Substances Labeling Act (1960) by preventing the marketing of potentially harmful toys and permitting the FDA to remove inherently dangerous products from the market.

1966  *Cigarette Labeling Act:* required cigarette manufacturers to label cigarettes: "Caution: cigarette smoking may be hazardous to your health."

1967  *Wholesome Meat Act:* required states to upgrade their meat inspection systems to stringent federal standards and to clean up unsanitary meat plants.

1968  *Wholesome Poultry Products Act:* required states to develop inspection systems for poultry and poultry products which meet federal standards.

1968  *Consumer Credit Protection Act* ("Truth-in-Lending"): required full disclosure of annual interest rates and other finance charges on consumer loans and credit buying including revolving charge accounts.

1968  *Hazardous Radiation Act:* required the secretary of HEW to establish performance standards for electronic products in order to limit or prevent the emission of radiation.

1969  *Child Protection and Toy Safety Act:* amended the Hazardous Substances Labeling Act (1960) to broaden its coverage to provide for the banning of toys and other articles used by children that pose electrical, mechanical, or thermal hazards.

1970  *Fair Credit Reporting Act:* stated conditions for the maintenance and dissemination of consumer credit records.

1970  *Poison Prevention Packaging Act:* authorized the establishment of standards for child-resistant packaging of hazardous substances.

1972  *Consumer Product Safety Act:* established the Consumer Product Safety Commission to protect consumers against unsafe products. Empowered the commission to set safety standards for a broad range of consumer products and to levy fines for failure of compliance.

1975 *Consumer Product Warranties Act:* set federal standards for consumer product warranties and established procedures for FTC rule making and legal action. FTC warranty rules, expected to take effect by the end of 1978, will govern:
1. The customer's obligation when a product is defective
2. The scope of service contracts
3. The dealer's duty to replace rather than repair faulty products
4. Depreciation of products for which cash refunds are offered

RALPH M. GAEDEKE, *California State University, Sacramento*

# Content theories of motivation (*See* MOTIVATION IN ORGANIZATIONS.)

# Contingency concept (*See* ORGANIZATION STRUCTURES AND CHARTING.)

# Contingency management (*See* MANAGEMENT THEORY, SCIENCE, AND APPROACHES.)

# Contingency model of leadership (*See* LEADERSHIP.)

# Contingency theory, in planning (*See* PLANNING, STRATEGIC MANAGERIAL.)

# Contingent purchase price (*See* ACQUISITIONS AND MERGERS.)

# Continuing education [*See* CONTINUING EDUCATION UNIT (CEU).]

# Continuing education unit (CEU)

The *continuing education unit* (CEU) is the comparatively recent development nationally of a uniform module applicable to noncredit learning experiences. The following sequence of steps is intended

to take both the *sponsors thereof* and interest groups *served by* continuing education along the path of commitment to the concept of measuring and recognizing noncredit learning experiences. The steps are graduated in such a manner that any sponsor of continuing education may exercise judgment in adopting the recommendations of the National Task Force on the CEU in this regard.[1]

Latitude also applies to any user group that seeks to build a recognition program based, in part, on the accumulation of CEU. In accepting CEU for recognition purposes, the user group may also exercise discretion with respect to the particular source, content, level, purpose, and the extent to which evaluation has been used by sponsoring organizations to determine satisfactory performance by individuals.

## PHASE 1: CONTINUING EDUCATION DEFINED

The first requirement in defining the CEU is to identify and refer consistently to *continuing education* as all significant examples of postsecondary-level learning experiences for which degree credit *is not* earned. The exclusion applies whether credit is real and immediate, as typical, or it is either probationary or earned on a deferred basis.

The definition is intended to encompass the great wealth and diversity of educational opportunities that have been referred to variously as noncredit courses, state-of-the-art courses, short courses, institutes, conferences, extension activities, refreshers, evening division offerings, clinics, professional updating, off-campus instruction, certificate programs, etc. This terminology still applies wherever desirable or appropriate. Yet all of the above are simply continuing education by the definition adopted here. All are amenable to use with the CEU, virtually without regard to distinctions of nomenclature or format. Continuing education may be thought of as paralleling the spectrum of diploma- and degree-oriented education that is available through secondary, technical, undergraduate, and postgraduate programs. At the same time, continuing education serves purposes not served by these programs by virtue of its meeting more immediate needs.

## PHASE 2: CONTINUING EDUCATION UNIT NEEDED

Given the broad definition of continuing education, as stated above, it then becomes feasible and desirable to refer to all learning activities under that definition in terms of the number of continuing education units associated with the learning experience. These units of continuing education have since become known as CEU, pronounced "q."

Adopting this simple convention asks no more than a change in state of mind vis-à-vis the planning and conduct of continuing education. Use of CEU makes it possible to drop the use of the innocuous term *noncredit* from the lexicon of education. The same convention also avoids giving offense to those who wish to reserve and apply the term *credit* exclusively to formal learning activities that traditionally culminate in a diploma or a degree.

The continuing education unit is not intended to apply toward diplomas or degrees under ordinary circumstance. Formal education is served ably, both in breadth and in depth, by the institutions and their curricula that have been long established exclusively for such purposes.

## PHASE 3: CONTINUING EDUCATION UNIT DEFINED

The next step in the evolution of a uniform measure is to define the continuing education unit. The CEU is defined effectively as the equivalent of 10 hours of participation in the classroom recitation mode of instruction. Implicit in a collegiate level and approach to the organized learning experience for the purposes of CEU are the additional requisites: (1) a bona fide sponsor; (2) a level and content appropriate, respectively, to the principal audience and objective served; and (3) a workable teaching-learning format and qualified persons in responsible charge, respectively, of (a) the instructional activity, (b) the overall course direction, and (c) the administration of the educational program by the sponsoring organization. These are the minimum criteria essential to the validity of the continuing education unit regardless of the source or the specific purpose to which it may be applied later by user groups of whatever identity.[2]

The CEU may be compared with the quarter-hour of credit in terms of both the nominal number of classroom instructional hours required and the presumption of an equivalent amount of learning taking place. The quarter-hour of credit is both well established and accepted as a significant level of individual effort in the acquisition of knowledge. The CEU exists in its own spectrum at a similar level of effort.

The use of CEU makes it possible to measure (1) curriculum concepts, in the sense of there being an organized or goal-oriented body of knowledge acquired through a sequence of learning experiences;

(2) work loads, equally applicable to individuals, instructors, and institutions; (3) use of facilities; (4) evidences of meaningful achievement; etc. These are done according to the needs and preferences of sponsors of and user groups served by continuing education.

## PHASE 4: WIDE USE ENCOURAGED FOR RECOGNITION PURPOSES

The CEU takes on universal meaning outside of academe once large numbers of professional societies, all other forms of membership organizations, trade associations, certificating agencies, placement activities, employers, personnel managers, counselors, licensing boards, etc., begin to establish standards and incentives for personal and professional development, each in its own terms. User groups, in all such categories as listed immediately above, are urged to establish acceptable content, learning objectives, format, and level pertinent to the learning experience as well as qualifying standards for those producers who would become recognized sources of sponsorship in the service of society.[3]

These standards, as set by users, serve the purposes of accreditation. The suggestion that recognition be external to the sponsoring organization should help ward off the specter of "diploma mills" coming into existence. These operations are potentially made possible, should the conferring of "recognition" ever be vested solely among sponsors. Recognition should be (1) for the individual and (2) from a user group with whom the person to be recognized is affiliated.

Maintenance of this dichotomy between "producer" and "user" serves to avoid the adverse criticism that noncredit operations of greater or lesser intensity, duration, and on-the-spot evaluation might encounter if they were to identify with either "credits" or "degrees" that are neither in the eyes of academe. The proposed system also permits, indeed encourages, the typical individual to marshal and utilize a host of continuing education resources in the realization of immediate goals or retraining needs.

Included with the great number and variety of college and university programs are such diverse sources of continuing education as in-plant courses; the educational programs of membership organizations, whether professional, technical, or trade association in nature; the output of the newly recognized "knowledge industry" and educational consultants; proprietary schools and organizations; the direct involvement of publishers in the delivery of education;

the programs of community, service, and religious organizations; etc. These sources of continuing education may be used jointly to serve particular needs in well-formulated career objectives, whether established by one or another of the many groups to which the individual belongs at any given time.

## PHASE 5: STANDARDIZED DESCRIPTIONS ENCOURAGED

Given the market potentials of phase 4, above, it now becomes feasible and desirable to describe continuing education programs insofar as is possible in terms of audience, content, purpose, implied level, format, duration, prerequisites, qualifying requirements, evaluation techniques to be employed, etc. These data make it possible for intelligent judgments to be made by others at removed locations and at later times as to what the educational experience amounted to in terms of the new learning or skill potentially acquired by the participant. The CEU makes this possible.

Sponsors are therefore obligated to maintain in their permanent records, say for 10 years, abstracts of essential information of the nature referenced above. These records may be accessed later by interested users wishing to consider the learning experiences of individuals who have been granted CEU. Indeed, the need to maintain a reasonably permanent and highly transferable record is one of the principal obligations imposed upon the sponsor of continuing education activities when awarding CEU. Therefore, the record is in two parts: *substantive*, as described immediately above, and *individual*, as described in phases 6 and 7, below.

Course evaluation should be made by the user group being served whenever CEU are to be used for recognition purposes. This contrasts with having as much done by the sponsors, often in their own interest and behalf, when they are engaged in a for-credit enterprise; or as much may be done for sponsors by their immediate counterparts in the form of accrediting organizations. The use of CEU should fit the need. "The utility of the CEU is in the eyes of the beholder" has often been stated in the literature on the CEU.[4]

## PHASE 6: TRANSFER OF INDIVIDUAL RECORDS FACILITATED

Sponsors are therefore encouraged to establish a machine-readable and easily transferable individual record for all CEU on file in the current context of, say, the past 5 or 10 years of service. These records should be maintained more or less indefinitely, in the manner and time frame suggested above as well as by Social Security number and the learning experience (phase 5) in which each individual participated. This machine record should be readily transferable to any inquirer (*see* phase 4) who wishes to recognize or otherwise reward the individual for consistence and excellence in the pursuit of continuing education. Both the personal and substantive records merge as CEU takes on meaning through the recognition obtained by individuals.

## PHASE 7: INDIVIDUAL EVALUATION MAINTAINED OPTIONAL

Sponsors of CEU may exercise their own discretion in the establishment and maintenance of personally evaluated records of individuals in continuing education. Appropriate mechanisms may include, but are not limited to, the following:[5]

1. *Enrollee*, perhaps with grade designated as X, simply to denote "presence only," with attendance verified insofar as is practicable by the sponsor's records.

2. *Participant*, with grade of *satisfactory* or *incomplete* (S or I, respectively), after the fashion of pass–no pass or the pass-fail option that is currently in vogue in undergraduate instruction and which also applies here readily and naturally for the grading of the majority of continuing education programs. Requirements for a satisfactory mark could be *(a)* good attendance, *(b)* active participation in discussions, and *(c)* the filing of a course appraisal form by the participant upon conclusion of the learning experience.

3. *Participant*, with conventional letter or numerical grades, for example, A through F or their numerical equivalents. These grades could be used whenever the typical standards of instruction and evaluation for academic credit are maintained in terms of *(a)* attendance, *(b)* responsiveness in class, *(c)* performance of outside reading and problem assignments, and *(d)* the periodic and final evaluation of individual performance by examination, whether with or without notes.

## SUMMARY

The proposed system set forth here of a uniform unit of measurement of participation in noncredit continuing education does not detract in any way from the traditional operation of continuing education in either its simplicity or its appeal. It is expected, however, that the more meaningful forms of

231

individual recognition—each built upon its own requirements for participation in continuing education—will also carry their own stipulations as to how individual performance is to be evaluated. For example, national-level proficiency or equivalency examinations may eventually come into being, career by career, so as to remove any reasonable doubt about the competency an individual may claim to have gained, in substantial part, through continuing education. The requisite knowledge and skill may also be demonstrated by local examination or other aspects of proven performance on the job or in the practice of the particular vocation.

The potential for these developments, as with all other forms of recognition through education, depends upon the existence of a basic module by which that education is measured for purposes of records' transfer. The CEU, based on the equivalent of 10 hours spent in the classroom recitation mode of instruction, is the much-needed module upon which to establish the basis for recognition programs serving all sectors of society. This is particularly true of the often informally acquired and recognized skill of management.

*See also* DEVELOPMENT AND TRAINING, CAREER PATH PLANNING FOR MANAGERS; DEVELOPMENT AND TRAINING, EMPLOYEE; DEVELOPMENT AND TRAINING, MANAGEMENT; DEVELOPMENT AND TRAINING, UNIVERSITY EXECUTIVE PROGRAMS.

## NOTES

[1] Anne C. Kaplan and Clive C. Veri, "The Continuing Education Unit," *ERIC Clearinghouse in Career Education*, Information Series, no. 1, Northern Illinois University, DeKalb, August 1974, pp. 4–7.
[2] "National Task Force on the Continuing Education Unit," *The CEU—Criteria and Guidelines*, National University Extension Association, Suite 360, One Dupont Circle, Washington, D.C. 20036, May 1975, pp. 10–14. $2.50.
[3] Paul J. Grogan, "Continuing Education for the Professions," *Proceedings of the Association for Continuing Higher Education*, c/o Howell W. McGee, University of Oklahoma, Norman, Oklahoma 73069, 1974, pp. 12–17. $5.
[4] Paul J. Grogan, "Future of the CEU—Who, What, Why, When, Where and How," *Continuing Education Study Series*, Conference Report, no. 8, American Society for Engineering Education, Suite 400, One Dupont Circle, Washington, D.C. 20036, 1974, p. 55. $3.
[5] Paul J. Grogan, "Elements of a System for the Uniform Measurement of Participation in Continuing Education," *Proceedings of the National Association of Boards of Pharmacy and the American Association of Colleges of Pharmacy*, 1969.

PAUL J. GROGAN, *University of Wisconsin— Extension, Madison*

**Continuous process**   (*See* AUTOMATION.)

**Contract** (*See* GOVERNMENT REGULATIONS, BUSINESS LAW.)

**Contract, consultant-client** [*See* ORGANIZATION DEVELOPMENT (OD).]

**Contracting, call program** (*See* SMALL BUSINESS ADMINISTRATION.)

**Contracting, systems** (*See* PURCHASING MANAGEMENT.)

**Contribution margin** (*See* ACCOUNTING FOR MANAGERIAL CONTROL.)

**Contribution to profit concept** (*See* PROFITS AND PROFIT MAKING.)

**Control, accounting** (*See* ACCOUNTING FOR MANAGERIAL CONTROL.)

**Control, business forms** (*See* FORMS DESIGN AND CONTROL.)

**Control, cost** (*See* ACCOUNTING, COST ANALYSIS AND CONTROL.)

**Control, management** (*See* MANAGEMENT THEORY, SCIENCE, AND APPROACHES.)

**Control, managerial** (*See* CONTROL SYSTEMS, MANAGEMENT.)

**Control, operational** (*See* MANAGEMENT THEORY, SCIENCE, AND APPROACHES.)

# Control, production (*See* MATERIALS MANAGEMENT; PRODUCTION PLANNING AND CONTROL.)

# Control, sources of (*See* SOCIAL RESPONSIBILITY OF BUSINESS.)

# Control lag (*See* MANAGEMENT THEORY, SCIENCE, AND APPROACHES.)

# Control systems, management

A management control system is concerned with the comparison of actual versus planned performance and the initiation of steps to correct any significant deviations from the plan. Such systems operate at all levels of an organization. At the lower operating levels the control system deals with detailed plans, while at the higher levels of the organization the system deals with broad, aggregate plans.

## MANAGEMENT CONTROL CONCEPTS

**Development of Plans and Standards** A measurement of performance is meaningful only when it can be compared to a standard. In some instances a standard may only be implicit and informal, but the emphasis in designing a management control system should be placed on explicit and formal standards. Ideally, every control variable should have a corresponding standard or plan against which it can be compared. For example, output of a manufacturing plant should be measured against scheduled production, actual sales should be compared with forecasted sales, and the actual cost of raw materials should be compared with standard costs.

Control standards are established through the organization-wide planning process. For example, production schedules are created through a complex process of forecasting the needs for products and determining planned outputs that meet these needs consistent with available capacities, existing inventories, relative costs of production, production lead times, and the like. Schedules are generated in increasingly fine detail through a hierarchical planning process in which each level adds details to higher-level plans. Many variables do not necessarily change during each planning period; for instance, standard material costs and policy-determined operating standards (such as the target inventory) remain

in effect until conditions change or policies are revised.

**Control as a Feedback Process** Planning is a forward-looking process, and therefore some uncertainty always exists as to the degree of attainment of a plan. Actual performance never matches plans exactly. Deviations arise because of unpredictable and uncontrollable factors in the environment of the organization, errors in execution, or imperfections in the plans themselves.

If a deviation becomes significant enough, corrective action should be taken. The corrective action may call for lower-level steps to bring performance back to the plan—such as working on overtime to make up for a schedule slippage. A large deviation may require revision in the plan itself, rather than action aimed at achieving the plan. If, for example, an equipment failure in the factory causes a major delay in production, a revised shipping schedule may be the best way of coping with the deviation.

The greater the deviation from a current plan, the greater the potential penalty. The exposure to serious penalty can be reduced by maintaining tighter control. An important means of achieving such control is by reducing the *time interval* between the measurement of performance and the reporting of deviations. Fig. C-16 illustrates how more frequent

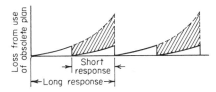

Fig. C-16. Effect of more frequent planning.

monitoring can reduce the penalties of deviations from plans. When a plan is created, it incorporates available information about internal and external conditions, such as current rates of sales, existing inventory levels, and raw material prices. As time goes on, deviations accumulate between the actual and planned conditions; the corresponding penalty similarly grows over this interval. If replanning takes place more frequently, the penalty is reduced. The shaded area in Fig. C-16 shows the total reduction in the penalty when the planning interval is cut in half.

Tighter control can also come from reducing the *size of the deviation* that is permitted before initiating more detailed scrutiny. In an "exception reporting system" (discussed more fully below), a deviation is not reported at all unless it exceeds some threshold

(10 percent of the planned value of a variable, say). If the threshold is reduced (to 5 percent, for example), a review of the situation is more likely to occur and thus tighter control is exercised.

The *level of detail* of reporting also affects the degree of control. In a highly decentralized organization, top management might monitor only aggregate financial data pertaining to each autonomous unit; detailed variables dealing with such physical quantities as production output and inventory levels would not be reported. In a centralized organization, on the other hand, detailed physical and financial variables may be reported for purposes of coordinating action among lower-level units of the organization.

**Trade-off between Loose and Tight Control** Setting the proper degree of control involves a complex trade-off between the pros and cons of tight control. On the one hand, if control is too loose, a deviation between actual and planned performance may result in poor coordination among organizational subunits and the failure to respond in time to unforeseen problems or opportunities. Loose control may also reduce some of the incentives for managers to meet their plans.

On the other hand, tighter control generally calls for additional data collection, information processing, and management reporting. The cost and inconvenience of the "red tape" associated with tight control is likely to be resented by the persons being controlled. Tight control may restrict the ability of lower-level managers to exercise imagination and initiative in response to changed conditions. Close monitoring of detailed performance may also lead to behavior that is not in the best interest of the organization as a whole. For example, an organization that closely watches the travel expenses of its employees may prevent needed face-to-face coordination among geographically dispersed activities.

The improved coordination of a tight control system may sometimes prove to be more apparent than real. For example, the seemingly tight control provided by more detailed and frequent monitoring may in fact be spurious. A control system deluged with masses of data may not be able to screen out the trivia from the significant information. In the presence of random fluctuations in variables being monitored, frequent reporting may not provide a sufficient sample of events on which to draw valid inferences. For example, daily sales reporting for a national distribution system would rarely make any sense, since the sales figure for a particular day is subject to random variation in the market and vagaries in the shipping and billing cycles. The "noise"

component of daily sales data tends to be smoothed out when the data are aggregated over periods of a week or longer.

A trade-off obviously exists between tight and loose control. The ideal is to strike the proper balance between the risks and penalties of insufficent control and the costs and disruption of overly tight control. The correct choice in any specific case depends on a variety of considerations, but in general the following factors should be taken into account.

*Factors Favoring Tight Controls.* These include:

1. Strong interrelations between organizational subunits (e.g., one unit supplying another with a basic raw material)

2. Significant potential penalties from deviations in plans

3. The existence of an integrated computer-based planning system that reduces the incremental cost of close monitoring and frequent replanning

*Factors Favoring Loose Controls.* These include:

1. Organizational subunits that are relatively independent of one another (e.g., selling in separate markets; using no common raw materials, technology, or manufacturing facilities)

2. Profit figures or a few other aggregate financial variables that provide adequate measures of performance and incentives for lower-level managers to behave in a way that contributes to the performance of the organization as a whole

3. Unpredictable changes in the environment that have significant effect on performance, and call for rapid responses on the part of managers closely involved in the activities affected by the changes. (In an uncertain environment, lower-level managers may require tight controls to detect significant changes and trigger a response. Higher-level managers, however, need not be made aware of the changes if they are not involved in replanning.)

## DESIGN ISSUES

The design of a management control system basically comes down to the questions of what should be measured, what should be reported, and what the timing should be.

**What to Measure** The management control system deals primarily in quantitative variables that can be measured and processed. Typical examples are sales in dollars or physical units, dollars of various categories of expense, number of employees hired, and the current volume of back orders. The objective in designing a control system is to choose the minimum set of variables that conveys the essence of what is going on of relevance to management.

The choice of variables depends in part on the level of management. At the lower operating levels of the organization, the variables are highly detailed, such as the sale of five units of item X to customer Y. The higher levels, on the other hand, deal in summary or aggregate variables, such as $5 million sales of product group ABC.

A variable may give either status or operating information (also called *level* or *rate* variables, respectively). A *status* variable defines a condition as of a given point in time, such as a cash balance of $17,000 at the end of the year. An *operating* variable defines a rate of activity during a given time period, such as sales of $73,000 during the month of April. A financial balance sheet typifies status or level variables, and an income statement illustrates operating or rate variables.

The proper choice of variable to describe a given condition requires a great deal of thought. Consider, for example, a variable (or set of variables) to describe *delivery performance* in a manufacturing plant that produces custom-ordered products. Performance might be described in terms of the percent of jobs shipped on time. Such a variable ignores, however, the amount of lateness for a job shipped after its scheduled time. A variable such as *average days late per shipment*, or perhaps a composite variable weighted by a nonlinear function of lateness, gives a more complete, yet concise, measure of delivery performance. Similar variables must be chosen for all other aspects of performance that management deems relevant.

**What to Report**  Reporting occurs when a variable is displayed on a printed report or a transient display device (such as a cathode-ray tube). Not every measurement should necessarily be reported. Ideally, a variable should be reported only when it requires the attention of a decision maker. If a system monitors a large number of variables, it is desirable that the system filter out the insignificant data and only report information that will lead to improved decision making. In practice, however, it is impossible to identify all the relevant information and nothing but the relevant information. A compromise must be made between reporting too much (and hence not filtering out all insignificant data) and reporting too little (and hence overlooking significant information).

**Timing Considerations**  Measurement of a status variable occurs when the data base of which it is a function is updated. In a batch processing system, various transactions that affect the data base are accumulated over a time interval (such as a day or a week). At the end of the interval, the transactions are processed together and the results are reflected in the data base records. For example, inventory transactions (withdrawals, receipts, etc.) are processed against inventory records, with the resulting inventory balances reflecting the net addition to or reduction of inventory levels.

The age of status information depends on two components: (1) the batch processing interval and (2) the processing lag (the time period from the end of the batch interval until the updating is complete). If $I$ is the processing interval and $L$ is the processing lag, the minimum age is $L$, the maximun is $L + I$, and the average is $L + \frac{1}{2}I$. The average age of status information can thus be reduced by reducing the processing interval (i.e., by updating more frequently, perhaps even in "real time" as transactions enter the system) or by reducing the processing lag (e.g., by collecting the data more quickly and transmitting them more rapidly to the processing point).

Similar reasoning applies in determining the age of operating information, except that in this case the age is increased by half the length of the operating time period (since some of the events being reported occur toward the beginning of the operating period, others occur toward the end, and the average occurs halfway into the period). Thus, even with instantaneous processing, the average age of sales reported monthly will be a half-month.

If events of relevance to the system occur frequently and unpredictably, reducing the average age of information will give a more faithful representation of actual conditions. This, in turn, permits better coordination and faster response to unexpected conditions. In an airline reservation system, for example, events occur frequently, and so the value of up-to-the-minute information is very considerable. If, on the other hand, the situation changes relatively slowly or in predictable ways, more timely data may not be of much value. This is true, for example, of the typical inventory system, where daily updating is usually quite adequate.

## BEHAVIORAL ISSUES

Measurement and reporting of performance always have behavioral effects. Their purpose is, of course, to motivate behavior consistent with the goals of the organization. Unless great care is taken, however, the control system may motivate dysfunctional behavior.

**Compatibility of Individual Goals with Organizational Goals**  When a variable is given serious attention, a manager will tend to behave in a way that makes the performance measure appear favorable. If improved performance in terms of the variable contributes to the achievement of the organization's goals, then compatibility exists and the control system induces desirable behavior. If, on the other hand, "improvement" in terms of the measured variable actually reduces performance of the organization as a whole, the control system provides undesirable incentives. Although compatibility between control variables and the organization's goals is an obvious design objective, in practice it is impossible to achieve perfect compatibility.

It is not difficult to find examples of incompatibility. For example, a sales manager might be measured in terms of sales revenue, which induces behavior aimed at increasing sales rather than selling products having a favorable profit margin. Similarly, a production superintendent whose delivery performance is measured in terms of the percent of jobs completed on schedule might be motivated to slight jobs already late and instead concentrate on jobs that can be completed on time. Flagrant incompatibilities such as these can usually be avoided, but more subtle examples exist throughout almost any management control system.

**Multiple Goals** A manager must deal simultaneously with multiple, and often conflicting, goals. Even in a private firm, in which a profit goal normally predominates, variables in addition to short-term accounting profit have to be considered. Undue attention to profit might motivate a manager to ignore the longer-term health of the firm, i.e., growth in sales, expenditures for research and maintenance, product quality, and personnel training and development. If trade-offs between accounting profit and the other variables were known, everything could be translated into a profit measure. Such relationships are not known in general, however, and so multiple goals must be established.

*Surrogate Goals.* A strong bias exists in favor of quantifiable goal variables. Thus, in order to measure progress in personnel development, the organization may use such surrogate goal variables as expenditures for training, number of training courses attended, or the number of advanced degrees earned by employees. A surrogate goal tends to take on an importance of its own, independent of its relation to the underlying real (but unmeasurable) goal. For example, the personnel manager may become more concerned with the number of course offerings than with the quality of instruction or the relevance of material learned in furthering the long-term interests of the organization.

*Limited Numbers of Goals.* The goal variables that apply to a given manager should be limited to a relatively small number—perhaps a half-dozen or so. Beyond that number, goals cease to have much meaning as a guide to action; the manager would instead have to deal simultaneously with only a limited subset. It is therefore desirable to identify a few of the most critical goal dimensions for each manager. For a manufacturing vice-president, for example, the critical dimensions might be cost, product quality, schedule performance, personnel development, and long-term improvements; for a dean of a community college, the critical dimensions might be the number and quality of entering students, the quality of teaching, salary costs of instruction, other costs of instruction, and contribution to the community.

*Critical Goals.* An effort should be made to choose a set of critical goals that are incommensurable and exhaustive. If an explicit trade off could be established between two goals, a single composite goal should be used instead of the two separate goals, since this would reduce the number of goals with which a manager would have to deal. An exhaustive set of goals is needed to prevent undue attention to measured goals at the expense of unmeasured ones. For example, if an inventory manager were controlled only in terms of dollars of investment, the tendency would be to reduce stocks at the expense of poorer stock-out performance.

Each critical goal should, in general, be defined in terms of a composite variable. This is relatively straightforward in the case of profit or cost goals that can be broken down into components that have a monetary measure. Other goals, however, may require judgments concerning the weighting of goal components—such as a weighting of late jobs according to their lateness in measuring delivery performance. Since the trade offs among components of a goal define desired performance of the organization, it is critical that they reflect the best combined thinking of the personnel most closely concerned with the goal in question. In the case of delivery performance, for example, the views of marketing and production control managers should certainly be considered.

## INCREASING THE USEFULNESS OF CONTROL INFORMATION

Control information has value to the extent that it (1) provides some "surprise," (2) causes a decision maker to take action that otherwise would not have been taken, and (3) leads to improved performance. The ideal control system would thus report only unexpected situations that call for management action.

The information reported in a management control system always reflects a compromise between too much and too little information. If the system is too selective, it will fail to report valuable information; if it is not selective enough, it will report data with little surprise content and with little relevance to action. The proper balance depends on the relative penalties of overlooking relevant information versus reporting irrelevant data. The bias in most systems is toward reporting too much information, on the (often mistaken) grounds that the recipient of a report can always filter out useless data. In fact, valuable information immersed in a sea of irrelevant data might just as well not exist if the recipient does not have an efficient means of selection. A well-designed reporting system can significantly increase the selectivity of displayed information.

**Condensing Detailed Data**  Transaction data are typically far too detailed to be useful for control purposes; they must first be condensed in various ways. The most common means is simple aggregation of detailed items within a broader category. Figure C-17 shows a typical summary report, in which detailed inventory items are aggregated within such product categories as "Major Appliances" (refrigerators, washers, etc.).

*Summary Reports.* A control system should allow the comparison of actual performance against a standard. A summary report should therefore give an aggregate standard corresponding to the aggregate actual value of a variable. If standards are available for the detailed items that make up an aggregation, the standard for the aggregation can be calculated by summing the detailed standards (the

standard inventory level for all major appliances, say). In other cases, the standard may be a function of an aggregate variable (for example, a standard inventory of major appliances equal to 3 months' supply at the current aggregate rate of sales).

*Supporting Detail.* Summary reports always run the risk of hiding useful details. In order to reduce this risk, it is desirable for the system to provide easy access to the details that are included in a summary report. Figure C-18, for example, shows the breakdown of major appliances into dryers, freezers, refrigerators, and washers. The two reports are properly "nested," in the sense that each entry in the high-level report has a corresponding sum in the lower-level report. This nesting of reports might continue several levels down to the most detailed level (individual products in an inventory system, for example). A hierarchy of nested reports thus provides condensed information, while still allowing a user to penetrate into the level of detail necessary to identify and deal with a problem.

An improper choice of aggregation categories may wash out significant information. In Fig. C-17, for example, the aggregate inventory is shown to be 106 percent of standard, with no product category seemingly in any significant trouble. In fact, however, the aggregation process may simply balance items with surplus inventory with items suffering from short supply. In order to avoid this problem, the aggregation categories could be defined in terms of the current inventory status of each individual item, as illustrated in Fig. C-19. Thus, the current balance of items in short supply (defined as less than half their standard) are aggregated separately; a similar process is used for surplus items and those items "in control" (that is, neither short nor surplus). Such

|  |  | INVENTORY REPORT | | | |
|  |  | 23 April 197**X** | | | |
| Status | Number of products | Balance, $000 | Standard, $000 | Deviation from standard, $000 | Percent of standard |
| In Control | 9,242 (84%) | 2,330 (71%) | 2,405 | − 75 | 97 |
| Short (<50%) | 1,025 ( 9%) | 135 ( 4%) | 415 | − 280 | 33 |
| Surplus (>200%) | 779 ( 7%) | 822 (25%) | 271 | + 551 | 303 |
| Total | 11,046 (100%) | 3,287 (100%) | 3,091 | +196 | 106 |

Fig. C-17.  A typical summary report.

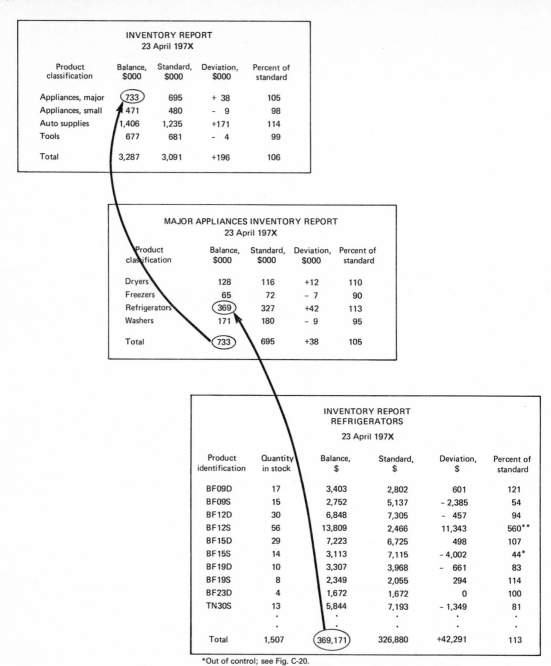

### INVENTORY REPORT
### 23 April 197X

| Product classification | Balance, $000 | Standard, $000 | Deviation, $000 | Percent of standard |
|---|---|---|---|---|
| Appliances, major | (733) | 695 | + 38 | 105 |
| Appliances, small | 471 | 480 | − 9 | 98 |
| Auto supplies | 1,406 | 1,235 | +171 | 114 |
| Tools | 677 | 681 | − 4 | 99 |
| Total | 3,287 | 3,091 | +196 | 106 |

### MAJOR APPLIANCES INVENTORY REPORT
### 23 April 197X

| Product classification | Balance, $000 | Standard, $000 | Deviation, $000 | Percent of standard |
|---|---|---|---|---|
| Dryers | 128 | 116 | +12 | 110 |
| Freezers | 65 | 72 | − 7 | 90 |
| Refrigerators | (369) | 327 | +42 | 113 |
| Washers | 171 | 180 | − 9 | 95 |
| Total | (733) | 695 | +38 | 105 |

### INVENTORY REPORT
### REFRIGERATORS
### 23 April 197X

| Product identification | Quantity in stock | Balance, $ | Standard, $ | Deviation, $ | Percent of standard |
|---|---|---|---|---|---|
| BF09D | 17 | 3,403 | 2,802 | 601 | 121 |
| BF09S | 15 | 2,752 | 5,137 | − 2,385 | 54 |
| BF12D | 30 | 6,848 | 7,305 | − 457 | 94 |
| BF12S | 56 | 13,809 | 2,466 | 11,343 | 560** |
| BF15D | 29 | 7,223 | 6,725 | 498 | 107 |
| BF15S | 14 | 3,113 | 7,115 | − 4,002 | 44* |
| BF19D | 10 | 3,307 | 3,968 | − 661 | 83 |
| BF19S | 8 | 2,349 | 2,055 | 294 | 114 |
| BF23D | 4 | 1,672 | 1,672 | 0 | 100 |
| TN30S | 13 | 5,844 | 7,193 | − 1,349 | 81 |
| | . | . | . | . | . |
| | . | . | . | . | . |
| Total | 1,507 | (369,171) | 326,880 | +42,291 | 113 |

*Out of control; see Fig. C-20.
**Out of control; see Fig. C-20.

Fig. C-18. A hierarchical nesting.

INVENTORY REPORT

23 April 197X

| Product classification | Balance, $000 | Standard, $000 | Deviation, $000 | Percent of standard |
|---|---|---|---|---|
| Appliances, major | 733 | 695 | + 38 | 105 |
| Appliances, small | 471 | 480 | − 9 | 98 |
| Auto supplies | 1,406 | 1,235 | +171 | 114 |
| Tools | 677 | 681 | − 4 | 99 |
| Total | 3,287 | 3,091 | +196 | 106 |

Fig. C-19. Aggregation within decision-oriented categories.

a report provides a concise picture of inventory status and illustrates the importance of choosing relevant aggregation categories.

**Exception Reports** If the deviation is small between the actual value of a control variable and its standard or desired value, a report of this fact is unlikely to lead to new action and therefore it has little value. It is only when the deviation becomes significant that action is likely and information about the deviation becomes valuable. An exception report only displays the variables having a large enough deviation for the information to have potential value. Figure C-20 shows an inventory report that only lists the items having either a shortage or surplus of inventory.

*Standards for Comparison.* One of the requiremens for exception reporting is the availability of a standard with which a control variable can be com-

pared. The standard should be the same as used in planning. Any planning variable can be subjected to exception reporting, whether it is an input variable or a planning outcome. For example, in a production scheduling system, standard raw material costs and standard processing times are basic input variables used in generating a schedule; an exception reporting system could therefore report when actual material costs or processing times deviate from the standard. The system could also report when actual production deviates significantly from the schedule. The control system thus monitors significant changes in the environment as well as failures in the execution of a plan.

*Significance of Deviation.* The second requirement for exception reporting is a means of determining when a deviation is significant enough to report. In principle, the threshold should be set at the point

INVENTORY REPORT
REFRIGERATORS
Items Out of Control
(Below 50% of standard or above 200%)

| Product identification | Quantity in stock | Balance, $ | Standard, $ | Deviation, $ | Percent of standard |
|---|---|---|---|---|---|
| BF 12S | 56 | 13,809 | 2,466 | 11,343 | 560** |
| BF 15S | 14 | 3,113 | 7,115 | 4,002 | 44* |

Fig. C-20. An exception report.

at which the penalty of not replanning when a deviation occurs is just matched by the cost of replanning. In practice, however, these costs can seldom be estimated with any accuracy. Normally a simple percentage threshold is set more or less arbitrarily.

In a sophisticated exception reporting scheme, standards can be determined dynamically by a model that takes changing conditions into account. For example, an inventory model might determine the optimal inventory balance based on current costs and current sales forecasts.

*Adjustable Criteria.* A system should allow the recipient of a report to define the (perhaps complex) criteria by which an exception is defined; furthermore, the recipient should be able to change the criteria as conditions or interests change. For example, when working capital becomes tight a manager may want to reduce the control limits that govern the reporting of items having surplus inventory. Rather than defining a surplus inventory item solely in terms of its percent surplus (over 25 percent of standard, say), the manager may also want to know about all items having a surplus dollar amount that exceeds some threshold (e.g., $5000), whether or not it is over 25 percent surplus. By permitting a manager to adjust exception criteria, the system provides an effective filter between the detailed data base and the decision makers.

**Ad Hoc Reports** Most control reports require someone to define in advance the information that will be reported (either in terms of content or exception criteria); the designers then implement a system that provides the specified information. Subsequent changes in report content are often expensive and time-consuming to make.

This inflexibility is guaranteed to cause problems. By the very nature of many unstructured management tasks, it is impossible to anticipate all desirable ways of reporting information. Even if designers could correctly determine future information needs, the variety of requirements would be large enough to preclude the routine preparation of anything other than the most commonly used reports. Information needs not satisfied by the standard periodic reports can usually not be satisfied at all within reasonable cost and response time limits.

*Information System.* The solution to this problem is to implement an information system capable of responding to unanticipated, or ad hoc, requests for information. The person entering a request expresses the desired information in terms of a retrieval language. For example, an ad hoc inventory report might be expressed as

LIST PRODUCT, BALANCE, STANDARD,
    BALANCE − STANDARD
WHERE BALANCE/STANDARD > 1.25
OR BALANCE − STANDARD > 5000

Such a request is then translated into a program that a computer executes to generate the specified report. The system may allow "on-line" retrieval, in which case the report is prepared almost immediately, or (more often) it can be processed in batch fashion and the results returned within, say, one working day.

An obvious requirement of such a system is a data base that contains the necessary raw data to process an inquiry—detailed inventory data, in the above example. In order to provide flexibility in preparing a wide variety of reports, the data should be maintained in disaggregated form; they can then be aggregated according to each specific ad hoc inquiry. Because of this flexibility, it is only necessary to anticipate the general nature of inquiries in order to provide the necessary raw data. This is much easier than trying to anticipate the exact nature of a report. Since the output from an ad hoc inquiry is in direct response to a specific request for information, the likelihood of its being useful is much greater than the case of a standard periodic report (just as the response from a telephone directory assistance operator is much more likely to be used than a randomly selected name from a telephone book).

**Use of Decision-Support Models** A decision-support model can be viewed as a particularly effective filter between the detailed data base and the decision maker. Output from the model might be either an optimal decision (such as the optimal production schedule) or, in the case of an interactive person-machine system, the predicted consequences of a proposed alternative plan (the cash flow consequences of a proposed budget, say). In either case, the output displayed to the decision maker is very much more condensed than the input data used by the model. By its very nature, model output is decision-oriented and therefore likely to lead to (desirable) action. As information systems evolve toward more direct decision support, decision makers will be less subject to the flood of irrelevant data that many current systems still inflict upon them.

**Other Issues** The reporting system serves as the interface between the information system and decision makers. It is important, therefore, that reports take account of the principles of good human engineering. For example, careful attention should be given to the labeling of reports. When possible, a standard format should be used so that a recipient can more quickly grasp the content of a report. Graphical displays, rather than tubular formats, are becoming increasingly common. They are particularly valuable when displaying complex relationships among variables that need not be presented with great precision—a common requirement for information needed to support decision making.

*See also* ACCOUNTING FOR MANAGERIAL CONTROL; AUDIT, MANAGEMENT; AUDITING, FINANCIAL; BUDGETS AND BUDGET PREPARATION; EXCEPTION, MANAGEMENT BY; INFORMATION SYSTEMS; MARGINAL INCOME ANALYSIS; STANDARDS AND STANDARDIZATION PROGRAMS; WRITING FOR BUSINESS.

### REFERENCES

Anthony, Robert N., and John Dearden: *Management Control Systems*, 3rd ed., Richard D. Irwin, Inc., Homewood, Ill., 1976.

Dermer, Jerry: *Management Planning and Control Systems*, Richard D. Irwin, Inc., Homewood, Ill., 1977.

Emery, James C.: *Organizational Planning and Control Systems: Theory and Technology*, The Macmillan Company, New York, 1969.

Jones, Reginald L., and H. George Trentin: *Management Controls for Professional Firms*, American Management Association, New York, 1968.

Prince, Thomas R.: *Information Systems for Management Planning and Control*, Richard D. Irwin, Inc., Homewood, Ill., 1975.

JAMES C. EMERY, *EDUCOM*

## Control systems, merchandise (*See* RETAILING MANAGEMENT.)

## Control techniques (*See* MANAGEMENT THEORY, SCIENCE, AND APPROACHES.)

## Controlling (*See* MANAGEMENT THEORY, SCIENCE, AND APPROACHES.)

## Controls and control system (*See* heading in Table of Contents for complete listing.)

## Convenience goods (*See* MARKETS, CLASSIFICATIONS AND MARKET ANALYSIS; RETAILING MANAGEMENT.)

## Conversion (*See* EXCHANGES, FOREIGN, MANAGEMENT OF; PRODUCTION PROCESSES.)

## Cooperative systems (*See* CODETERMINATION AND INDUSTRIAL DEMOCRACY.)

## Cooperatives (*See* FRANCHISING; OWNERSHIP, LEGAL FORMS OF.)

## Copyrights (*See* PATENTS AND VALUABLE INTANGIBLE RIGHTS.)

## Corporate officers (*See* OFFICERS, CORPORATE.)

## Corporation (*See* OWNERSHIP, LEGAL FORMS OF.)

## Correspondence training (*See* DEVELOPMENT AND TRAINING, EMPLOYEE.)

## Cost, full (*See* PRODUCT AND SERVICE PRICING.)

## Cost, incremental (*See* PRODUCT AND SERVICE PRICING.)

## Cost, marginal (*See* PRODUCT AND SERVICE PRICING.)

## Cost, overhead (*See* ACCOUNTING, COST ANALYSIS AND CONTROL; BUDGETS AND BUDGET PREPARATION.)

## Cost, product (*See* ACCOUNTING, COST ANALYSIS AND CONTROL.)

## Cost, replenishment (*See* INVENTORY CONTROL, PURCHASING AND ACCOUNTING ASPECTS.)

**Cost, stock-out**  (*See* INVENTORY CONTROL, PURCHASING AND ACCOUNTING ASPECTS.)

**Cost, storage**  (*See* INVENTORY CONTROL, PURCHASING AND ACCOUNTING ASPECTS.)

**Cost, variable**  (*See* ACCOUNTING, COST ANALYSIS AND CONTROL.)

**Cost accounting**  (*See* ACCOUNTING, COST ANALYSIS AND CONTROL.)

**Cost benefit work sheet**  (*See* PAPER WORK SIMPLIFICATION.)

**Cost balance model, inventory**  (*See* INVENTORY CONTROL, PURCHASING AND ACCOUNTING ASPECTS.)

## Cost-benefit analysis

*Cost-benefit analysis* is the determination of the ratio of the benefits of a given project to its costs, taking into account the benefits and costs that cannot be directly measured in dollars.

Techniques exist for translating the more intangible benefits into units comparable with the dollar costs. For example, the benefits of a new personnel program might be measured in such things as decreased absenteeism, lower employee turnover, and fewer grievances, which, in turn, could be assigned monetary values.

Much of the literature on cost-benefit analysis, however, deals with public projects, and here there are likely to be both intangible social costs and intangible social benefits. (It is becoming increasingly necessary for business to take these into account also.)

Closely related to cost-benefit analysis is *cost-effectiveness analysis*, which is defined as a way of finding the least expensive means of reaching an objective or a way of obtaining the greatest possible value from a given expenditure (e.g., a budgeted amount).

*See also* ACCOUNTING, HUMAN RESOURCES (ASSETS); ACCOUNTING FOR MANAGERIAL CONTROL; BUDGETING, CAPITAL, SPECIAL PROBLEMS OF; COLLEGE AND UNIVERSITY ADMINISTRATION; HEALTH SERVICES, PLANNING FOR; PROGRAM PLANNING AND IMPLEMENTATION; PUBLIC ADMINISTRATION; SOCIAL RESPONSIBILITY OF BUSINESS; VALUE SYSTEMS, MANAGEMENT: SOCIAL AND CULTURAL.

### REFERENCES

Clay, M. J.: "Cost Benefit Analysis," *Work Study and Management Services*, July 1970, pp. 557–560.
Dewhurst, R. F. J.: *Business Cost-Benefit Analysis*, McGraw-Hill Book Company, New York, 1971.
Layard, R. (comp.): *Cost-Benefit Analysis: Selected Readings*, Penguin Books, Inc., London, 1974.
Mishan, E. J.: *Elements of Cost-Benefit Analysis*, George Allen & Unwin, Ltd., London, 1972.

STAFF/SMITH

**Cost centers**  (*See* ACCOUNTING FOR MANAGERIAL CONTROL.)

## Cost improvement

Cost improvement is a positive approach to a continuous problem of all companies, that of reducing and keeping costs down through efficient and effective operations in all phases of management.

### FUNDAMENTAL ELEMENTS

A systematic approach to improving work methods and procedure can best be accomplished through the problem-solving techniques which are variations of the scientific method—analysis, hypothesis, testing, synthesis, and application. The early scientific management pioneers advocated "seeking the one best way." Later, the attack was on "waste," with the admonition to "work smarter, not harder." Early techniques were first applied by specialized "efficiency experts" or by industrial engineers and consultants. Today, the trend is to train the workers themselves to apply the more conceptual techniques of work improvement, work design, and the total systems approach. Workers, aided by specialists, put work simplification techniques into practice on the job, thereby enhancing the quality of working life through participation.

**Work Design**  From a cost improvement point of view, work design is a systematic analysis of the work performed in order to formulate the most effective way to approximate an ideal system of utilizing people, machines, and materials in the working environment. The four areas for improved utilization are (1) space and environment, (2) technology and energy, (3) product and raw material, and (4) time and people.

*Space and Environment.* This encompasses physical facilities, the plant itself, the layout, material handling, the workplace, and the flow of work. The social environment is equally important, including attitudes and interpersonal relationships of workers among their peers and with their supervisors.

*Technology and Energy.* This involves utilizing the most appropriate technology and equipment so that the human resource uses minimum effort to yield high energy.

*Product and Raw Material.* This area encourages the introduction of new ideas for the product, product mix, or raw materials that can change operations and work activities. The specific effects of changes in raw materials or maintenance and operating supplies can be evaluated through value analysis, value engineering, and standardization.

*Time and People.* Examination of these elements can reveal needs to (1) minimize time lost in waiting and traveling and (2) increase production through better methods, technology, or use of the human resource. Behavioral approaches also focus on motivation methods to build job satisfaction, high morale, and self-fulfillment.

**Planning** Planning for work design encompasses all the following:

1. Design of the product, including size, shape, weight, material, and ultimate use

2. Design of the process, since this determines the production system, the operations required and their sequences, dimensions and tolerances, machine tools, gauges, and equipment required

3. Design of the work method, which establishes worker-job relationships by determining how the work is to be performed, the workplace, flow, and economic considerations

4. Design of tools and equipment, which determines the fixtures, dies, gauges, tools, and machines needed to perform the operations

5. Design of plant layout, which determines the total space required in terms of overall location of equipment, inventory service centers, work space, material-handling equipment, and worker/machine relationship

6. Determination of the standard time for the accomplishment of the work, which makes control of the job possible

*Organization.* The planning process for work design may be organized by a team, or matrix organization, composed of design engineers, industrial engineers, and manufacturing and production specialists, to arrive at some optimal operation involving the above six factors. The broad functional areas of marketing, finance, and purchasing may be added to the matrix organization for coordination.

*Installation.* Following this phase, preproduction trials may be made before establishing the continuing production system involving people, machines, and tools for the most effective accomplishment of the work. This applies to either product or service installations.

*Control.* The control function should indicate when methods deteriorate from planned methods so that corrective improvement action can be taken. Thus a constant analysis of current methods is required to follow up the improvement and installation.

*Staff Role.* The role of the industrial engineer or other staff specialist is to reduce costs by increasing productivity through continuing improvements. The role is that of the creator, motivator, innovator, trainer, facilitator, and catalyst.

**Management of Cost Improvement** Planning, organizing, and controlling cost improvement programs should originate from top management, emphasizing an awareness of work improvement as a tool of management and promoting a company-wide positive attitude and support. To this end, a training program taught by qualified industrial engineers should be available. Middle management should be offered an intensive course in techniques of methods study and its practical application for results. Supervisors should study work simplification and all its ramifications—work measurement, process planning, and managerial and motivational techniques.

*Rank and File Employees.* Motivational and behavioral research has found that employees involved in the improvement of their own jobs derive self-satisfaction and fulfillment with ready adoption and little or no resistance to changes. Therefore many companies, such as Texas Instruments Company, teach work simplification methods to production and clerical workers for participative improvements to their own jobs. Other techniques such as job enlargement and job enrichment are becoming increasingly popular for creating positive attitudes about work and jobs and thus greater productivity.

## TECHNIQUES

Cost improvement typically follows a seven-part approach, as illustrated in Fig. C-21.

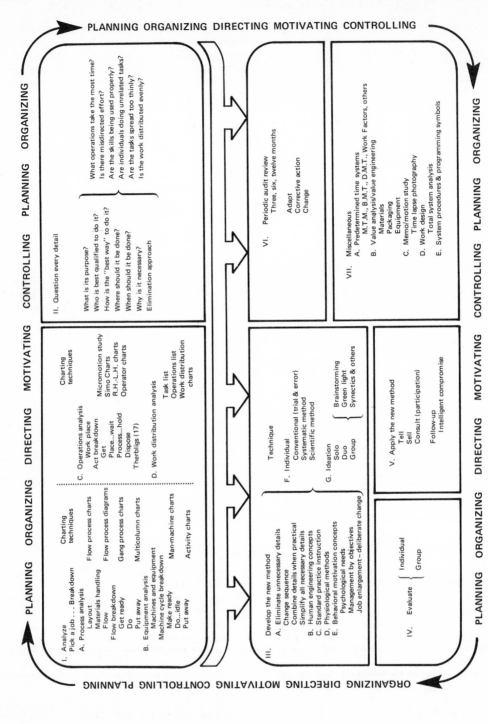

I. Analyze
Pick a job. . . . Breakdown

A. Process analysis

| | Charting techniques |
|---|---|
| Layout | Flow process charts |
| Materials handling | Flow process diagrams |
| Flow | Gang process charts |
| Flow breakdown | Multicolumn charts |
| Get ready | |
| Do | |
| Put away | |

B. Equipment analysis
Machine cycle breakdown

| Make ready | Man-machine charts |
|---|---|
| Do...idle | Activity charts |
| Put away | |

C. Operations analysis

| Work place | Charting techniques |
|---|---|
| Act breakdown | Micromotion study |
| Get | Simo Charts |
| Place...wait | R.H.-L.H. charts |
| Process...hold | Operator charts |
| Dispose | |
| Therbligs (17) | |

D. Work distribution analysis

Task list
Operations list
Work distribution charts

II. Question every detail

What is its purpose?
Who is best qualified to do it?
How is the "best way" to do it?
Where should it be done?
When should it be done?
Why is it necessary?
Elimination approach

What operations take the most time?
Is there misdirected effort?
Are the skills being used properly?
Are individuals doing unrelated tasks?
Are the tasks spread too thinly?
Is the work distributed evenly?

III. Develop the new method

A. Eliminate unnecessary details
   Change sequence
   Combine details when practical
   Simplify all necessary details
B. Human engineering concepts
C. Standard practice instruction
D. Physiological methods
E. Behavioral motivation concepts
   Psychological needs
   Management by objectives
   Job enlargement – deliberate change

F. Technique

Individual
   Conventional (trial & error)
   Systematic method
   Scientific method

G. Ideation
   Solo
   Duo
   Group { Brainstorming
           Green light
           Synectics & others }

IV. Evaluate { Individual
               Group }

V. Apply the new method
   Tell
   Sell
   Consult (participation)
   Follow-up
   Intelligent compromise

VI. Periodic audit review
    Three, six, twelve months
    Adapt
    Corrective action
    Change

VII. Miscellaneous
   A. Predetermined time systems
      M.T.M., B.M.T., D.M.T., Work Factors, others
   B. Value analysis/value engineering
      Materials
      Packaging
      Equipment
   C. Memo/motion study
      Time lapse photography
   D. Work design
   E. Total system analysis
      System procedures & programming symbols

Fig. C-21. Management of improvement - problem-solving master chart.

**Analyze** After the problem is defined, a systematic analysis is made based upon the scientific method. This reveals the overall effectiveness of the total process and its flow. *Charting techniques* help to arrange detailed information and observations systematically so that the work study can easily be managed. Graphic analysis may take the form of a flow process, flow diagram, gang, or multicolumn chart. *Equipment analysis* using worker/machine charting and activity charts visualizes the relationship between workers and the equipment they are utilizing. In very precise and/or complex studies (from macromotion to micromotion) the workplace operation is analyzed through action-work breakdown, presented on micromotion, simultaneous (right-hand and left-hand), and operator charts. *Work distribution charts* help to show how well the work is allocated to individuals, particularly on clerical and service tasks.

**Question Every Detail** Evaluation of the analysis requires asking the following questions: What is its purpose? Who is best qualified to do it? What is the "best way" to do it? Where should it be done? When should it be done? And especially, why is it necessary? This last question often provides the starting point for elimination of tasks or parts.

For work distribution, further questions are appropriate: Which operations take the most time? Is this effort misdirected? Are skills being used properly? Are the individuals doing unrelated tasks? Are the tasks spread too thinly? Is the work distributed evenly?

**Develop the New Method** When all information has been systematically detailed, essential procedures will stand out, clarifying the following options: (1) elimination of the whole task, (2) elimination of unnecessary work, (3) utilization of the most effective sequence of operations, (4) combining of steps, and (5) simplified work.

*Sources.* In developing the new method, human engineering concepts (motion economy principles) along with new discoveries in biomechanics involving physiological needs can emerge as deliberate change is continuously sought out. Knowledge of models and statistical and mathematical techniques can be applied creatively to work flow, layout, material handling, and other functional activities for highest productivity. Once an improvement is identified, standard practice instructions, materials, tools and equipment, working conditions, and procedures should be formalized and followed.

*Brainstorming.* To bring forth ideas for improvements of all kinds, one may apply such creativity techniques as brainstorming, Mogenson's

Green Light (Go Signal), synectics, and other applied imagination methods, either on an individual, a duo, or a group ideation basis.

**Evaluate** Evaluation and testing of improvement ideas may be an individual or a group team effort. After approval or synthesizing of many components, a report is necessary, either to reject or to promote acceptance of the idea. Reports made on successful accomplishments, as well as on failures, indicate where more attention should be concentrated. Specifically, reports compare, review, evaluate, and provide feedback so that plans can be made to improve departmental operations.

**Apply the New Method** Assuming approval of the work improvement plan, acceptance by members of the organization depends on the philosophy of management toward bringing about changes in behavior. Resistance to change can be expected and anticipated. Employees fear the unknown, especially the possibility of job elimination. This fear can foment insecurity and worries about whether change may entail new skills, new habits, different hours, or different work environment. Antagonisms are often aroused when employees are shifted into a new area where their acceptance may be in doubt.

Managerial personnel may silently feel that the training and attention necessary to promote and plan the program is time-consuming, and may fail to acknowledge any gains in adopting a new idea or program. It is easier for many to "let things ride," to feel that "if things are going all right, why change?"

Union opposition must be anticipated, particularly where "changes" are part of the work rules contract provisions. Discussing program objectives and techniques and securing union cooperation in advance are very important.

Authoritarian directives should be avoided. Diplomatic "selling" of the change may be effective, but participation by inviting consultation and requesting input of ideas from users of the improvements will yield greater acceptance with the least resistance. Behavioral research favors participation in the decision process at all levels, and the development of work improvement is no exception. Workers vitally involved with decisions about their day-to-day work activities tend to accept changes more readily when job security is guaranteed and incentives provided for cooperation.

*Follow-up.* Once changes are installed, follow-up must be made to ensure success. The departments and people affected may have objections and challenge the adoption of changes. Intelligent compromise may be good strategy. Negotiations or even waiting for better timing may be justified. A follow-up at this point may reveal that a proposed change would have an adverse effect on other operations and departments. For this reason, the total system should be reexamined.

**Periodic Audit Review**  In a dynamic organization changes are constant. A periodic audit will reveal whether methods and products, materials and equipment are obsolete or improperly utilized. Adaptations, corrective improvements and changes can be instituted to keep the organization dynamic and viable to meet current demands of the market and competition.

**Miscellaneous**  Work measurement—with all its techniques of time study, standard data, predetermined time systems, work sampling, etc.—can be used for setting standards, scheduling work, estimating costs, and installing incentive systems. The use of these techniques points up areas for improvement, revealing inefficient methods and unnecessary work. The micromotion approach, using predetermined time systems, also reveals inefficiencies so that improvements can be adopted as a by-product.

*Value analysis* and value engineering, on a more technical level, can be of great help in reducing costs in materials, packaging, and equipment.

*Memo-motion study* will reveal inefficiencies of work effort over longer periods of time which are too time-consuming for individual monitoring. Also called time-lapse photography and generally known as production study, the slow film sequences of this technique record the everpresent occurrences of wasted effort and wrong methods.

*Work design*, as conceived by Gerald Nadler, is a total systems analysis intended to crystallize an ideal system which may then be suboptimized. This is the opposite of breaking down individual parts for examination. Instead, the individual parts are integrated in a total operating system for a synergistic effect.

## COST IMPROVEMENT PROGRAMS

Using all the management techniques described above, an optimum work design may be put in operation. There still exists, however, a need for improvement to offset rising wage and materials costs. Typically, a cost improvement program should be initiated simultaneously in order to maintain resilience and flexibility in constantly changing economic times. At its core, a cost improvement program is one of increasing productivity, a need so great that the United States government has established the National Center for Productivity and Quality of Working Life.

**Communications**  A philosophy of work improvement must be communicated to all levels of management and labor to assure success of the program. The expected benefits and goals should be specified so that understanding and appreciation will lead to shared enthusiasm and better employer-employee relationship. Emphasis should be placed on achieving goals of better and faster service through lower costs of materials and labor.

**Suggestion Systems**  For a cost reduction program to be fruitful, top management should initiate and completely support channels and procedures for an ongoing suggestion system. A responsible review committee with authority to reward and implement worthy suggestions can cut across departments and across levels of management, in order to elicit participation. *See* SUGGESTION SYSTEMS.

Training of employees by industrial engineers in techniques of value analysis and creativity can be helpful to implant awareness of possible improvements and to establish a receptive climate for suggestions. Specialized forms (Fig. C-22), comparing present method and proposed method, with estimated cost savings, simplify the effort for workers proposing an improvement, by spelling out the correct procedure for submitting ideas with supportive drawings or sketches.

**Successful Programs**  The National Center for Productivity and Quality of Working Life, in a monograph of December 1975, found that in companies successfully utilizing programs to improve productivity, a pattern emerged: (1) company support for the effort at top management levels; (2) recognition of the key role of the company's employees; (3) a full understanding at all levels of the purposes and objectives of the productivity improvement program; (4) establishment of goals and the development of valid measurements to reveal whether, and to what extent, the goals were being met; and (5) improvement in productivity sought to the extent possible without impairing job security.

Although company approaches differ, Beech Aircraft Corporation typifies what an all-out program of cost reduction can accomplish. The overall improvement program at Beechcraft is under the direction of the controller–cost management. The budget for each phase must be procured from savings accomplished. A work simplification administrator has plant-wide responsibility to organize, train, direct, and follow up the program. Training in work simplification techniques makes all employees aware

## COST—REDUCTION REPORT

DESCRIPTION OF ITEM INVOLVED      FILE     11-B
    DEPT.   Finished stock & shipping      DEPT. NO.    64      DATE
    OPERATION   Marking with name and address of cosignee    PRODUCT   Cartons to be shipped
    OBJECT OF ANALYSIS   To determine possible savings through stamping instead of stenciling

### Comparison

| Present method | | Proposed method | |
|---|---|---|---|
| Machine | | Machine | |
| Tools: Fountain stencil brush and precut stencil | | Tools: Rubber stamp and stamp pad | |
| Description: Stencils are prepared in advance and kept on file for all major cosignees, and name and address are stenciled on each carton | | Description: Rubber stamps would be made up for all major cosignees, and name and address are stamped on each carton | |
| Cost of operations involved: | $ per | Cost of operations involved: | $ per |
| Labor | carton | Labor | carton |
| 0.16 minute per carton @ $3.00 per labor-hour | 0.0080 | 0.05 minute per carton @ $3.00 per labor-hour | 0.0025 |
| Materials | | Materials | |
| Miscellaneous | | Miscellaneous | |
| Total of above items | 0.0080 | Total of above items | 0.0025 |

Estimate of savings:
       Saving with proposed change ($0.0080 − $0.0025) equals $0.0055 per carton
       Probable yearly requirements 1,250,000 cartons     Estimated by    Sales dept.
       Estimated savings per year (based on 1,250,000 per year) . . . . . . . . . . . . . . $6875.00

Estimated cost of change:

| | | |
|---|---|---|
| Design | $ | est. by |
| Equipment | $500 | " " |
| Installation | $ | " " |
| | $ | " " |
| | $ | " " |
| Total cost of change | $500.00 | |

Probable savings per year . . . . . . . . . . . . . . . $6500.00
Less total cost of change . . . . . . . . . . . . . . . . $ 500.00
Net savings first year . . . . . . . . . . . . . . . . . $6000.00
New method would pay for itself in months . . . . . . .     1

Note:     100 rubber stamps required at $5.00 each

Suggested by   John Ryan

Report prepared by   T. A. Wilson

| cc to | Attached are | | Date | Date |
|---|---|---|---|---|
| | 1 Sheets drawings | First considered | Expen. appr. | |
| | Sheets prints | Investgn. started | Installed | |
| | 2 Sheets details | Rept. submitted | Final rept. | |

Fig. C-22. Cost-reduction report. (Ralph M. Barnes, "Motion and Time Study," 6th ed., John Wiley & Sons, Inc., 1968, New York, p. 39.)

of the possibilities of job improvements. After employees learn the basic tools, they achieve results that amount to as much as a half-million dollars a year. Beechcraft also has a separate suggestion program, headed by its own administrator, with monthly and semiannual awards made by a committee reviewing and evaluating the suggestions. A strong program of management by objectives, with work measurement for control standards, is another factor in successful cost improvement programs.

*See also* ACCOUNTING, COST ANALYSIS AND CONTROL; FORMS DESIGN AND CONTROL; MARGINAL INCOME ANALYSIS; PAPERWORK SIMPLIFICATION; PRODUCTIVITY; PROFIT IMPROVEMENT; RECORDS MANAGEMENT; SYSTEMS AND PROCEDURES; WORK SIMPLIFICATION AND IMPROVEMENT.

## REFERENCES

Barnes, Ralph, M: *Motion and Time Study, 6th ed.*, John Wiley & Sons, Inc., New York, 1968.

*BLS Publications on Productivity and Technology*, Bureau of Labor Statistics, Washington, 1975.

Burnham, Donald C.: *Productivity Improvement*, Columbia University Press, New York, 1973.

*Fourth Annual Report of the National Commission on Productivity and Work Quality*, National Center For Productivity and Quality of Working Life, Washington, 1975.

Greenberg, Leon: *A Practical Guide to Productivity Measurement*, Bureau of National Affairs, Inc., Washington, 1973.

*Improving Productivity, A Description of Selected Company Programs*, National Center For Productivity and Quality of Working Life, Washington, 1975.

*Job Satisfaction: Is There a Trend?* U.S. Department of Labor, Manpower Research Monograph, no. 30, Washington, 1975.

Moore, Franklin G.: *Production Management (6th ed.)*, Richard D. Irwin, Inc., Homewood, Ill., 1973.

Nadler, Gerald: *Work Design: A System Concept*, Richard D. Irwin, Inc., Homewood, Ill., 1970.

Niebel, Benjamin W.: *Motion and Time Study* (5th ed.), Richard D. Irwin, Inc., Homewood, Ill., 1972.

Rush, H. M. F.: "Motivation through Job Design," *Conference Board Record*, January 1971.

HAROLD F. PUFF, *Miami University*

## Cost price review   (*See* INTERNATIONAL OPERATIONS AND MANAGEMENT IN MULTINATIONAL COMPANIES.)

## Cost reduction   (*See* COST IMPROVEMENT.)

## Cost-volume-profit relationships   (*See* MARGINAL INCOME ANALYSIS.)

## Costs, committed   (*See* BUDGETS AND BUDGET PREPARATION.)

## Costs, direct   (*See* ACCOUNTING FOR MANAGERIAL CONTROL.)

## Costs, fixed   (*See* ACCOUNTING, COST ANALYSIS AND CONTROL; ACCOUNTING FOR MANAGERIAL CONTROL; MARGINAL INCOME ANALYSIS.)

## Costs, indirect   (*See* ACCOUNTING FOR MANAGERIAL CONTROL.)

## Costs, managed   (*See* BUDGETS AND BUDGET PREPARATION.)

## Costs, mixed   (*See* ACCOUNTING FOR MANAGERIAL CONTROL.)

## Costs, one-time   (*See* OFFICE SPACE PLANNING AND DESIGN.)

## Costs, period   (*See* ACCOUNTING, COST ANALYSIS AND CONTROL.)

## Costs, recurring   (*See* OFFICE SPACE PLANNING AND DESIGN.)

## Costs, semivariable   (*See* ACCOUNTING FOR MANAGERIAL CONTROL; MARGINAL INCOME ANALYSIS.)

## Costs, standard   (*See* WORK MEASUREMENT.)

## Costs, variable   (*See* ACCOUNTING FOR MANA-GERIAL CONTROL; MARGINAL INCOME ANALYSIS.)

## Costs and cost improvement   (*See heading in Table of Contents for complete listing.*)

## Costs budgets, variable   (*See* BUDGETS AND BUDGET PREPARATION.)

## Counseling, employee

*Employee counseling* is an interviewing technique used to help emotionally troubled or frustrated employees to adjust to the causal condition. Counseling may be carried on by an interested manager or by a professionally trained counselor.

Emotionally troubled employees demonstrate their worries or frustrations by such displays as a sudden change in behavior, preoccupation, irritability, increased accidents or absences, unusual fatigue, or by excess alcohol or drug usage. When such behavior represents only a mild degree of disturbance, it probably is indicative of a neurotic condition, one from which most humans suffer either regularly or occasionally. If the displays are exaggerated, bizarre, or violent, the condition may be psychotic, requiring the attention of a professionally certified individual such as a psychologist or psychiatrist. It is important that the manager be sensitive to this distinction and not pursue the counseling if relief is not apparent by the second or third interview.

Most troubled employees will be helped just by knowing the degree to which this behavior is affecting their job and the extent to which it can be tolerated. This knowledge provides a guideline for the individual who is attempting to manage his or her own behavior. The approach, in any event, should be supportive and empathetic rather than critical, judicial, or instructive. In essence, the interview should be *nondirective;* that is, it should allow the counseled employee to explore the problem only as far or as deeply as the individual wishes, with no pressure from the interviewer for revelations, confessions, or conclusions.

The principal technique used in the counseling interview is listening, often described as *nonevaluative listening.* This calls for the counselor to listen actively but without passing or indicating approval or disapproval. Typically, the counselor follows six guidelines:

1. Listen patiently to what an employee has to say while offering the minimum of comments.

2. Refrain from criticizing or offering advice on the employee's problem. This interview is an opportunity for the employee to "ventilate."

3. Never argue with an employee while counseling. This is threatening and works counter to the interview's objectives.

4. Give undivided attention to the employee. Cut off telephone calls and block any other kind of interruption.

5. Look beyond the mere words of what the employee says. Listen and "feel" for those things that are deeper than when appears on the surface.

6. If the employee does not calm down or becomes agitated, try to conclude the interview and seek professional advice on how to proceed for referral of the employee to a qualified professional counselor. Tact in handling referrals is essential and may best be approached by advising the employee to see his or her personal physician.

Counseling in industry is an outgrowth of the Hawthorne Studies at the Western Electric Company in the late 1920s and early 1930s. What started out as an investigation to relate working environment to productivity led to the observation that workers who were personally involved in their jobs and encouraged in that direction by management performed better than those who were not. An integral part of this research involved nondirective interviewing of employees by the research team, which ultimately detected a beneficial side effect upon employees from the interviews themselves. As a result, many companies began to, and still do, offer employee counseling either as a routine, optional, on-site service or on a referral basis.

*See also* INTERVIEWING, EMPLOYEE; LABORATORY (SENSITIVITY) TRAINING.

### REFERENCES

Dickson, William J., and F. J. Roethlisberger: *Counseling in an Organization: A Sequel to the Hawthorne Researches,* Graduate School of Business Administration, Division of Research, Harvard University, Cambridge, Mass., 1966.

Maier, Norman R. F.: *Psychology in Industry,* 3d ed., Houghton Mifflin Company, Boston, 1965.

Rogers, Carl R.: *Counselling and Psychotherapy,* Houghton Mifflin Company, Boston, 1942.

STAFF/BITTEL

**Counseling, financial** (*See* COMPENSATION, EMPLOYEE BENEFIT PLANS.)

**Craft organization** (*See* ORGANIZATION ANALYSIS AND PLANNING.)

**Creativity** (*See* INNOVATION AND CREATIVITY.)

**Credit accounts classification** (*See* CREDIT MANAGEMENT.)

**Credit Bureau Reports, Inc.** (*See* CREDIT MANAGEMENT.)

**Credit check, employee** (*See* PERSONNEL ADMINISTRATION.)

**Credit, lines of** (*See* FINANCIAL MANAGEMENT.)

**Credit, trade** (*See* FINANCIAL MANAGEMENT; FINANCIAL MANAGEMENT, SHORT-TERM, INTERMEDIATE, AND LONG-TERM FINANCING.)

## Credit management

Business activity in most Western economic systems is based, to a large degree, on the use of credit. Credit instruments or devices such as checks, notes, credit cards, and line-of-credit are basic for both business and individual trade transactions. The Securities and Exchange Commission estimates in the *Federal Reserve Bulletin* (July 1976, p. A41) show: (1) notes and accounts receivable, in the nonfinancial sector of the economy, constituted approximately 41 percent of total current assets in 1975, and notes and accounts payable represented approximately 63 percent of total current liabilities; and (2) creditors supplied $152.6 billion of the growth of $239.3 billion in current assets from 1970 through 1975, while the owners supplied only $86.7 billion. The ability of management to generate these funds, from both within and outside the firm, is affected by the ability of its credit department to collect its outstanding receivables.

### DEFINITION OF CREDIT MANAGEMENT

The Latin term *credere* means to believe or to trust. The term *credit* in an economic sense, as used by business, means to give or extend economic value to someone else now, on faith or trust that the economic equivalent will be returned to the extender in the future. The term *management* is concerned with planning, organizing, and administering the functions and resources of a firm so as to accomplish its basic and established objectives and policies. *Credit management* might therefore be defined as planning, organizing, and administering the resources and functions pertaining to the act of providing economic value to someone now on the faith that a given economic equivalent will be returned to the provider in the future. A well-conceived credit management program is based on preestablished objectives and policies.

### OBJECTIVES AND POLICIES

An effective operation of the credit function presupposes that the objectives and policies of the firm are clearly defined and understood by the personnel who are to make the decisions. Efficient credit management is fundamental in today's business operations. It cannot be emphasized too strongly that the success or failure of a firm, where credit is an important instrument within the operation, is dependent on the collection of the receivables. A good credit policy has to incorporate courses of action to be followed under recurring situations dealing with creditworthiness, terms of sale, collection time intervals, and nonroutine special problems such as "write-offs." The procedures to be followed in implementing the company's credit policies are usually left up to the credit department or with an individual where there is a common understanding of the firm's objectives and policies.

### RESPONSIBILITY AND ORGANIZATION OF CREDIT DEPARTMENT

**Responsibility** Finance, sales, and other major functional managers all share responsibility for credit decisions within the overall objectives and operation of the firm. The actual day-to-day credit operations are usually the responsibility of a credit manager, an individual (within management) who has been assigned the duties and responsibilities of planning, organizing, and administering the credit function. The number of persons within the credit function will vary with the size of the firm and the relative importance of the credit service. Even decentralized business operations have credit personnel overseeing the credit function at the local or regional level. The home office credit manager will normally evaluate the performance of the regional credit offices.

**Organizational Structure** The organizational structures of most credit departments are usually classified as follows: line, line and staff, and functional.

*Line Structure.* Under the line form, each person reports to only one superior and is given authority over the work assigned to the position. The line structure normally works best when a company is small.

*Line and Staff Structure.* The line and staff structure inserts one or more staff positions between functional areas; e.g., the personnel function is between the vice-president–sales and vice-president–finance. Each functional position reports to a supervisor, yet receives specialized services from the personnel department in the areas of selecting, hiring, training, etc., of all personnel. The line and staff structure appears to be the best all-around organization for all but small businesses.

*Functional Structure.* The functional structure, for the sake of simplicity, has each person, except for the top management levels, reporting to more than one superior according to a specific phase of his or her authority. A local credit manager would report on sales matters to the local sales manager; on financial matters to the company financial officer, e.g., the treasurer; and on employee matters to the personnel function.

**Location** In most firms, the credit function is placed under the finance (treasury or controller) department, although there are some firms who look on credit as a sales function. Regardless of the position of the credit function within the company, a close working relationship must be maintained with the treasurer's office because of mutual interests and responsibilities in the areas of cash forecasting, handling of collateral in connection with a customer's account, deposit of receipts, relationships with banks, and the overall financial position of the firm. All these relationships are simpler and less time-consuming where the credit function is directly under the treasurer's authority.

In its operation, the credit function must be independent of, yet cooperate at all times with, the sales function in developing profitable business within the financial constraints of the firm. Even if a firm is sales-oriented and the credit function is under the sales manager, there is no advantage to the firm in entering into a sale if the company cannot later collect from the customer.

## APPLICATION PROCEDURES

**Retail** The retail credit application is a self-generated, written form of credit information, providing the creditor with facts about the applicant which may or may not be obtainable elsewhere. This information is generally supplemented by credit reports and occasionally by interviews. Application forms are made available to potential customers through promotional mailings, distribution boxes throughout retail stores, general advertisements, and in response to customer requests. The consumer application form usually contains the following information: the correct full name of applicant with address, marital status, married and maiden names, social security number or numbers, residential ownership, length of current and prior employment, current indebtedness and scheduled payments, and other data such as bank accounts.

**Mercantile** With mercantile credit, there is less use of credit applications. New customers are derived from solicitation by sales representatives and product promotion activities wherein the sales person fills out the information form and the complex credit details are obtained later by a credit specialist. In addition, the prospective customer is often asked for the company's balance sheet and other operating reports.

**Interviews** Compared with application forms, interviews are very personal because they are held solely for the purpose of assessing the credit worthiness of the potential customer. The interview will yield information that cannot be totally ascertained from the application. Personal contact with an applicant, for example, provides useful observations of character, integrity toward debt, and attitudes toward credit service. It also gives a general impression of the individual's economic philosophy and competence.

Equally important is the vendor's opportunity to inform the potential customer of the firm's credit terms, policies, and business procedures. The interview for mercantile credit is often held when the credit manager visits the customer. In retailing, the applicant visits the creditor's place of business. Telephone conversations often provide a less expensive substitute for the personal interview and afford a rapport with the potential customer which routine correspondence does not give.

## CREDIT INVESTIGATION

The investigation is used to provide and verify vital information which is desirable in making a credit decision. It is important to know when adequate or sufficient credit information is available relative to the credit line. Excessive information increases the cost without providing any economic benefit.

**Information Needed**  A credit investigation is performed to determine the buyer's *four C's of credit:* character, capacity, capital, and conditions. The four C's of credit are only guides. The credit department cannot usually sort all accumulated information into these general terms. Facts which bear on character, for example, also bear on capacity.

*Character.*  Character may be defined as the reputation or personal attributes others sense about a person or a firm. It is an assessment of attitudes regarding, for example, professional conduct, payment on time, return of goods without cause, and debt obligations. In seeking information in this area it is usually better to ask specific questions; general questions tend to invite general answers that provide little predictive information about the future.

*Capacity.*  Capacity is a measure of the person's or firm's ability to pay from stated or known sources. While capacity reflects earning power, it is important that the adequacy of the applicant's income above present debt commitments be determined as well as the applicant's expenditure patterns.

*Capital.*  The adequacy of capital (owner's net investment in the firm or the net personal assets of an individual) must be considered when establishing credit limits, although economic conditions and the relative adequacy of earning power would affect the actual authorization and limits of credit.

*Conditions.*  Conditions represent the economic environment in which the business concern or credit applicant operates. Conditions which affect credit should be examined by asking: Are there strikes looming now or in the future? Has the weather been too dry or too wet? Is the applicant in a declining industry? The credit manager must be familiar with

the line of business and the community of the applicant and/or debtor.

It is important to remember that credit judgments are judgments of individuals. Even a firm's credit reflects a judgment of the personal activities of the individual or individuals in charge.

**Sources of Credit Information**  Sources are of two kinds—specialized and nonspecialized.

*Nonspecialized Sources.*  These sources of information, other than the application (formal or informal), include interviews by the firm's own salespersons or representatives, banks, and direct trade interchanges.

1. A firm's own salespersons, when properly trained and with knowledge of the vendor's overall corporate objectives, can be a valuable source of information. Commercial salespersons who call on customers can develop a rapport that the credit manager may not have. By developing the proper relationships between the credit department and the field salespersons, the credit manager can determine how the information supplied by the salespersons can best be used.

2. An inquiry directed by a vendor through the firm's own bank will often produce more valuable information than a vendor's inquiry to the buyer's bank. The reason for this is the close relationships between banks. Questions which can provide valuable information are:

   *a.* How long has the bank been dealing with the buyer? If the account is relatively new, who initiated it? What is the buyer's average balance?

   *b.* Has the bank granted any loans to the applicant? What were the largest sums and what is the buyer's current loan status? What was the reason for the loan?

   *c.* Were the loans secured or unsecured? If secured, what was the security? If unsecured, was the loan *cosigned*, etc.?

   *d.* What is the bank's general attitude toward the account? The general attitudes of banks often provide information as to the buyer's reputation and managerial abilities.

Although a direct inquiry with the buyer's bank is not always productive, it can be. A credit manager can often obtain information from the buyer's bank if he or she is also willing to share some information which is valuable to the bank; e.g., the failure of the buyer to take discounts, or possibly the revelation that many merchants are overstocked with certain types of merchandise inventory.

*Specialized Sources.*  Specialized consumer credit agencies include the Associated Credit Bureaus,

Inc. (ACB), Credit Bureau Reports, Inc., Independent Credit Bureau Managers (ICMB), and local retail credit bureaus.

1. ACB is an international trade association. Its Collection Service Division helps locate "skip" debtors, and the Medical Credits Division handles collection problems for physicians, dentists, and hospitals.

2. Credit Bureau Reports, Inc., is a centralized reporting service, which is engaged in the wholesale distribution of consumer credit reports to national concerns. To qualify for membership, the grantor of credit must meet the requirements of the Fair Credit Reporting Act and have need for consumer credit reports from outside localities. A minimum order charge of $200 per month is also required.

3. Independent Credit Bureau Managers (ICBM) is a trade organization of credit bureaus and collection service managers. It arose because of a conflict between the management of Associated Credit Bureaus, Inc., and Credit Bureau Reports, Inc., as to "the right of a bureau to charge for its services a price that is equal and consistent for all bona fide users."

4. Local retail credit bureaus are owned and operated by a coalition of local business firms—retail, financial, and service—which offer consumer credit, although a substantial number are privately owned. Most of the local bureaus charge fees based on the use made of their services. All rely on the creditors to contribute information to the pool.

Under good credit management procedures, it is the responsibility of the user of a credit bureau report to interpret and apply the facts contained within and to form his or her own opinion on the credit applicant. It is, therefore, imperative that a credit bureau distinguish between fact and opinion. Standardization of the terms within the credit industry has been a problem, and the prudent user must be aware of any ambiguous statements within the data.

*Service Value.* Credit bureaus provide valuable credit information, which can be exchanged economically. Without credit bureaus, credit decisions would have to be made without the quantity or quality of data that is currently available to a credit manager within a short period of time. The economy would be affected by credit-granting delays or by an increase in uncollectable accounts. Credit bureaus are only as good as the cooperation of their members in pooling information, the efficiency of their personnel, and promptness in handling inter-bureau reports. Credit managers who are reluctant to pay for good credit reports will find that the reports they do receive are often of poor quality. Poor reports are of little value when dealing with new customers, whether locally or in distant cities.

**Legal and Regulatory Restrictions** The Fair Credit Reporting Act (Title VI Amendment of the Consumer Credit Protection Act) became effective in April 1971. The act states that an individual's report from a consumer reporting agency may not contain any of the following information:

1. Bankruptcies which, from date of adjudication of most recent bankruptcy, antedate the report by more than fourteen years.

2. Suits and judgments which from date of entry, antedate the report by more than seven years or until the governing statute of limitations has expired, whichever is the longer period.

3. Paid tax liens which from date of payments, antedate the report by more than seven years.

4. Accounts placed for collection or charged to profit and loss which antedate the report by more than seven years.

5. Records of arrest, indictment, or conviction of crime which, from date of disposition, release, or parole, antedate the report by more than seven years.

6. Any other adverse item of information which antedates the report by more than seven years.

The Federal Trade Commission has the responsibility for enforcement of the act, and in February 1973, it announced six additional interpretations. These interpretations were:

1. Prohibit publication and distribution by credit bureaus of books containing consumers' credit rating, called "credit guides" unless encoded to insure consumers' anonymity.

2. Allow the use of certain kinds of "protective bulletins" which identify check forgers, swindlers and the like, provided no information in them is used in establishing the subjects' eligibility for credit, insurance, or employment.

3. Require that consumers be informed by prospective lenders when they are denied credit on the basis of information furnished by loan exchanges.

4. Require that when an insurance company uses a state motor vehicle report to deny or increase the cost of a consumer's insurance, it must inform him or her of that fact and of the state agency's identity.

5. Permit consumer reporting agencies to pre-screen prospects' names for creditworthiness for di-

rect-mail solicitations, so long as the user certifies that every person on the list furnished by the credit bureau will receive the solicitation.

6. Conclude that reporting activities of Federal agencies such as the Civil Service Commission will not be included within the scope of the Fair Credit Reporting Act.

It is mandatory under the law for retail or service-oriented firms to provide the consumer with the name and address of the credit bureau if the individual is denied credit based wholly or partially on that information. It is recommended that a preprinted form with the name and address of the credit bureau be given the customer at this time.

*Credit Denials.* Denial of credit based on information from a source or sources other than a credit bureau requires the retail or service-oriented firm to inform the consumer, at the time of denial, that he or she has the right to request in writing, within 60 days, the nature of the information causing the rejection. The intent of the law is to provide the consumer with enough facts so that he or she is able to refute or challenge the accuracy of the information. Under the law, retailers and service-oriented firms reporting credit information to another, which in turn uses that information to reject a customer credit application, have to be careful that the data supplied is based on their own records and not information reported by others. Otherwise, the firm supplying the credit data is considered a consumer-reporting agency and is subject to the provisions of the act regarding consumer reporting agencies.

## COLLECTIONS

The purpose of collection operations is to maximize collections and minimize the loss of future trade. The aims and policies of the collector affect the speed of collection. If there are conflicting collection goals and policies—such as to retain goodwill, rehabilitate the debtor, encourage prompt payment, and carry out an economical operation—the difficulty of making collections is increased. Collection effectiveness is mainly influenced, however, by (1) the classification of debtors; (2) credit policy as influenced by the type of business and its goods, profit margin, and competition; and (3) the type of records to be used to monitor collection procedures.

**Classification of Debtors** Classification of debtors attempts to identify the reasons for failure to pay promptly. Typical debtor nonpayment classifications include those who have (1) misunderstood

terms, (2) disputed balances, (3) a temporary lack of funds but normally good paying habits, (4) slow paying habits by nature, (5) poor money management, (6) the financial ability to pay but must be forced to pay, (7) taken discounts, even though payments are only partial or late, or (8) dishonest intentions (possible fraud).

Many other debtor classifications have also been used by creditors over the years; e.g., some debtors (1) do not worry about settling small balances or (2) are careless about such matters as signing checks, inserting the right check in the payment envelope, and avoiding other breakdowns in office procedures.

*Simple Misunderstandings.* A simple misunderstanding of credit terms can be handled by a clarification of the terms, but a lack of coordination between sales and the credit department will cause customer ill will. The latter situation requires reselling the customer, as well as making sure that the customer is aware of the true credit terms. It might also mean the establishment of a common understanding of the credit terms among the firm's salespersons.

*Disputed Balances.* These usually result from dissatisfaction with quality, allowances, or other credits which have not been honored. The buyer withholds payment until an agreement has been reached. Disputed balances should not be left open indefinitely.

*Lack of Funds.* A temporary lack of funds can be due to overbuying, local business conditions, or the need for additional working capital. The credit manager should be on top of these situations and make sure that they are not long-term marginal accounts.

*To Collect or Not?* The credit manager must be able to assess and determine whether it is worthwhile to expend the extra effort needed to make collections from customers with slow pay habits or poor management and from firms who are able but must be forced to pay. The nuisance and trouble involved in collecting small amounts are not always worth the extra effort. Larger accounts or an account that could be developed are worth the added effort. Good relationships are often developed with customers who can be educated through persuasion and other collection procedures.

*Fraud.* The dishonest debtor requires little sympathy, and every effort should be made to force payment, including hiring a collection agency or filing legal suit. An early determination should be made in these cases; time is of the utmost importance in collection activities.

*Chronic Offenders.* The debtor who continually takes discounts on late or partial payments leaves the creditor with one course of action; namely, issuing to the debtor a clear, concise statement of the firm's credit terms. The chronic offender should be given a warning that future offenses will be considered a violation of the credit agreement and will be handled in a clearly stated manner. The payment might be returned; some keep the check and bill for the balance due. The profitability of the account and the desire for future business will affect the credit procedure to be followed.

**Developing a Collection Policy** A good collection policy must have a plan of action to be followed in collecting past-due accounts. Modifications are necessary to keep the policy alive and up to date. Any change should be introduced slowly so that salespersons, customers, and interested parties are abreast of the changes. All credit and collection policies lie somewhere between (1) liberal credit and liberal collection and (2) strict credit and strict collection. Many firms have learned from experience that it is wise to indoctrinate new customers with an understanding that prompt payment is expected and that every effort will be made to collect overdue accounts. New accounts, which have been properly indoctrinated as to the firm's credit and collection policies, are often considered half-collected.

**Factors Affecting Collection Policy** There are five factors which influence a firm's collection policy: (1) capital, (2) competition, (3) type of goods or services, (4) class of debtors, and (5) legal restrictions.

1. A firm operating on limited capital is forced to adopt strict credit and collection policies. A firm blessed with capital can usually afford to be more liberal.

2. Naturally, what the competition does affects this policy. There is usually room for different policies among competitors in large cities, but it is not usually so among small-town competitors.

3. The type of goods or services—such as perishable, hard versus soft, and essential versus deferable—affects a firm's collection policy.

4. Many firms learn early which customers pay their accounts automatically, which need reminders, and which may require pressure. Between the prompt payers and uncollectable accounts are debtors for whom judgment and experience set the collection method to be used. It is among the in-between parties that the firm's credit policy becomes important in solving collection problems and developing future business.

5. Credit managers must be familiar with the Equal Opportunity Credit and Consumer Protection Acts as well as the bankruptcy laws so as to not violate the law or endanger possible collections.

## INTEREST RATES

Basically there are three primary methods of computing finance charges on loans or contracts, namely, the simple interest, add-on, and discount methods. Some rate structures use a combination of two of the primary methods, while others include initial or periodic fees. All three methods use the formula: $I = PRT$ (Interest equals Principal times Rate times Time).

**Definition of Principal** This varies with the method being used as illustrated below.

| Method | Principal |
|---|---|
| 1. Simple Interest | Declining periodic balances of original amount financed (original balance minus the total of periodic payments applicable to the principal to date). |
| 2. Add-on | Amount financed (original total of all proceeds to be paid). |
| 3. Discount | Total of all payments (face of note). |

The Truth in Lending Regulation Z has aided in standardizing terminology in the credit industry. The terms or components of any loan or contract are

Total payments
= amount financed plus finance charges

Some commonly used synonyms for these terms are
*Total of payments:* face of note or original gross balance
*Amount financed:* proceeds or principal
*Finance charge:* interest and fees

**Simple Interest** The best example of a simple interest agreement is a loan or contract calling for one payment at the end of the year:

| | |
|---|---|
| Principal | $100.00 |
| 6% interest | 6.00 |
| Total payment | $106.00 |

Another example is a 6 percent simple interest compounded quarterly:

| | 1st Qtr. | 2d Qtr. | 3d Qtr. | 4th Qtr. |
|---|---|---|---|---|
| Principal | $100.00 | $101.50 | $103.02 | $104.57 |
| 6% interest | 1.50 | 1.52 | 1.55 | 1.57 |
| Principal plus interest | $101.50 | $103.02 | $104.57 | $106.14 |

A simple interest installment loan agreement, where there are six equal principal payments and a 1 percent monthly interest charge is illustrated as follows:

| Month | Principal balance | Payment: Int. @ 1% per mo | Principal | Total |
|---|---|---|---|---|
| 1 | $100.00 | $1.00 | $16.67 | $17.67 |
| 2 | 83.33 | .83 | 16.67 | 17.50 |
| 3 | 66.66 | .67 | 16.67 | 17.34 |
| 4 | 49.99 | .50 | 16.67 | 17.17 |
| 5 | 33.32 | .33 | 16.67 | 17.00 |
| 6 | 16.65 | .17 | 16.65 | 16.82 |
| Total | | $3.50 | $100.00 | $103.50 |

Other examples of simple interest rate structures are (1) the flat or equal payments plan and (2) the whole, or round-dollar, payment plan. These plans are used in scheduling periodic equal-installment payments and make use of annuity tables for a variety of rates and periods.

An *abbreviation rate*, such as 3–2–1% (150–300), is translated as 3 percent per month on that portion of each periodic principal balance which is not greater than $150, 2 percent on that portion of the balance over $150 and not greater than $300, and 1 percent on the balance over $300.

Table C-6 is an example of the schedule of payments under a *graduated interest* situation.

**TABLE C-6 Schedule of Interest and Principal Payments Collected Each Month on Actual Declining Balances under a Graduated Rate**

| Month | Principal balance | Payment: Interest | Payment: Principal | Payment: Total | Cumul. int. | True rate/mo |
|---|---|---|---|---|---|---|
| 1 | $800.00 | 12.50 | 62.62 | 75.12 | 12.50 | 1.56 |
| 2 | 737.38 | 11.87 | 63.25 | 75.12 | 24.37 | 1.59 |
| 3 | 674.13 | 11.24 | 63.88 | 75.12 | 35.61 | 1.61 |
| 4 | 610.25 | 10.60 | 64.52 | 75.12 | 46.21 | 1.64 |
| 5 | 545.73 | 9.96 | 65.16 | 75.12 | 56.17 | 1.67 |
| 6 | 480.57 | 9.31 | 65.81 | 75.12 | 65.48 | 1.70 |
| 7 | 414.76 | 8.65 | 66.47 | 75.12 | 74.13 | 1.74 |
| 8 | 348.29 | 7.98 | 67.14 | 75.12 | 82.11 | 1.78 |
| 9 | 281.15 | 7.12 | 68.00 | 75.12 | 89.23 | 1.82 |
| 10 | 213.15 | 5.76 | 69.36 | 75.12 | 94.99 | 1.86 |
| 11 | 143.79 | 4.31 | 70.81 | 75.12 | 99.30 | 1.89 |
| 12 | 72.98 | 2.19 | 72.98 | 75.17* | 101.49 | 1.91 |

*If all payments are made precisely on the scheduled payment dates, the final payment in the example will be 5 cents more than the standard payment amount; the total interest collected will also be 5 cents more than the disclosed finance charge of $101.44.

*Note:* Amount financed = $800; Finance charge = $101.44; Monthly payment = $75.12; Rate = 3.–2.–1% (150–300)

**Add-on Interest** The add-on interest represents the rate applied to the original amount financed. For example, assume the following information: amount financed, $1000; term, 24 months; and rate, 10 percent per annum add-on. The finance charge is (24/12)(.10)(1000) or $200. Total of payments equals $1000 plus $200 or $1200. The amount of the individual payments can be determined simply by dividing $1200 by the number of payments; e.g., $1200 ÷ 24 = $50/mo.

The *graduated* add-on interest method with rates of 12–10–8% (300–500) means a 12 percent per annum add-on on the first $300 of the original amount financed, 10 percent of the next $200, and 8 percent of any amount over $500. If the same information used in the basic add-on interest method above were applied, the finance charges would be (24/12)(.12)(300) plus (24/12)(.10)(200) plus (24/12)(.08)(500), or $72 plus $40 plus $80 or $192. Total payment equals $1000 plus $192, or $1192. The monthly payment would be $1192 ÷ 24 or $49.67 per month.

**Discount Rate** The discount rate method (rate applied to total of payments) provides for the calculation of the finance charges. Assume that total of payments (face) equals $1200; term equals 1 year; rate equals 10 percent per annum discount. The computations are as follows:

1. (0.10)($1200) = $120
2. $1200 = amount financed + $120. The amount financed is $1080, and the monthly payment is $100 ($1200 ÷ 12).

The discount rate *graduated by amount* with rates of 8–5%(400) and assuming the other information given above, would be computed as follows: (12/12)(0.08)($400) plus (12/12)(0.05)($800) = $72. The amount financed equals $1200 minus $72 or $1128. It is also similarly possible to discount amounts *graduated by maturity*, such as 8–6% (12 months), which means 8 percent for the first 12 months and 6 percent after 12 months to maturity.

**The Annual Percentage Rate** The *true* rate, or APR (annual percentage rate as required by Regulation Z), can be defined as the flat simple interest rate which will produce a given total amount of finance charges when each scheduled payment is applied first to the interest at the true rate and the remainder to the principal. The principal represents the declining balances of the amount financed. The add-on and discount rates are not true rates. They are applied to the original amount of the loan rather than to the declining unpaid balances. As a result, the equivalent true rates are roughly double the stated rates. True rates on discount charges are always higher in relation to the stated rate than true rates on add-on rates.

Finding the APR, or true rate, requires the following contract details:

1. Amount financed, and date loan was made (or contract written).

2. Repayment schedule (date and amount of each payment). The APR for a contract requires periodic payments that are equal in amount. The method used originally to compute the finance charge, whether it be the simple interest, add-on, or discount methods, is of no importance insofar as the APR is concerned. The amount of the finance charge alone with the repayment schedule is all that is needed. Suppose, for example, the amount financed is $1000, the finance charge is $200, and the term is one year. This can be illustrated as follows (two payments of $600):

| Date | Principal balance | Payment | | |
|---|---|---|---|---|
| | | Interest 13.07% | Principal | Total |
| 1–1–77 | $1,000.00 | | | |
| 7–1–77 | 530.70 | $130.70 | $ 469.30 | $ 600.00 |
| 1–1–78 | 0 | 69.30 | 530.70 | 600.00 |
| | | $200.00 | $1,000.00 | $1,200.00 |

$$APR = 2 \times 13.07 = 26.14\% \text{ annum}$$

Table C-7 illustrates how a flat rate equivalent (average interest rate of 1.886 percent) schedule of interest and principal payments compares with the graduated rate schedule shown in Table C-6. The same data, otherwise, are used in both schedules and the APR is 22.632 percent; therefore the flat simple interest rate for this data, as required by Regulation Z, is illustrated.

**Precomputation** Precomputation is the computation in advance of simple interest on scheduled declining periodic balances. The term also applies to the determination of the finance charges for installment loans and contracts where the add-on and discount methods are used. The basic assumption for precomputing simple interest is that all monthly or periodic payments are made in full and remitted on the scheduled dates. When the debtor's actual payments differ from the schedule, adjustments have to be made in the total finance charge to maintain the scheduled yield.

The laws of most states require refunds of the excess finance charges only if the prepayments, i.e., all remaining payments on the loan, are made prior to their due date. Under sales finance laws, acquisition charges are sometimes deducted before refunds

TABLE C-7 Schedule of Interest and Principal Payments and APR Computation, Flat Rate Equivalent

| Month | Principal balance | Payment | | |
|---|---|---|---|---|
| | | Int. @ 1.886% per mo | Principal | Total |
| 1 | $800.00 | 15.09 | 60.03 | 75.12 |
| 2 | 739.97 | 13.96 | 61.16 | 75.12 |
| 3 | 678.81 | 12.80 | 62.32 | 75.12 |
| 4 | 616.49 | 11.63 | 63.49 | 75.12 |
| 5 | 553.00 | 10.43 | 64.69 | 75.12 |
| 6 | 488.31 | 9.21 | 65.91 | 75.12 |
| 7 | 422.40 | 7.97 | 67.15 | 75.12 |
| 8 | 355.25 | 6.70 | 68.42 | 75.12 |
| 9 | 286.83 | 5.41 | 69.71 | 75.12 |
| 10 | 217.12 | 4.09 | 71.03 | 75.12 |
| 11 | 146.09 | 2.76 | 72.36 | 75.12 |
| 12 | 73.73 | 1.39 | 73.73 | 75.12 |
| | | 101.44 | 800.00 | 901.44 |

$$APR = 12 \times 1.886\% = 22.632\%$$

are computed. Refunds of the excess finance charges are usually calculated under one of the following two methods:

*Rule of 78s.* This gets its name from a 12-month contract in which the sum of the numbers 1 through 12 is 78. Refunds are the total of the proportionate sum of interest charges calculated each month on the declining face-of-note balances stated or scheduled in the contract. The rule of 78s is not restricted to 12 payments; e.g., the sum of 20 payments is 210 and 30 payments is 465; thus the description *sum of the digits* is often used. Based on the fact that 12 payments are outstanding the first month, 12/78 of the total finance charge is earned for the first month, 11/78 for the second month, etc. Refunds at the end of the first month would be 66/78 of the finance charges; at the end of second month they would be 55/78, etc. Table C-8 illustrates monthly precomputation interest charges and refunds for payments in full, prior to due dates.

The following data are used in Table C-8 to demonstrate the declining balance rate: The amount financed is $600; the term is 12 months; the precomputed finance charge is $103.80; the total of payments is $703.80 with a monthly payment of $58.65; and APR is 30.54 percent. Actuarial refunds on a discount rate, day counting, etc., would show similar amounts.

*Actuarial Refund Method.* This method and its variations has arisen from criticism of the higher effective finance charges for prepayments of the loans under the rule of 78s. Since Iowa has incorporated such a feature into its loan laws, Iowa will be used as a model to illustrate actuarial refunds on

**TABLE C-8   Schedule of Interest and Principal Payments, Cumulative Interest, and Prepayment Refunds**

**PART A   Rule of 78s Method**

| Month | Beginning prin. bal. | Payment Total | Payment Prin. | Interest Earned* Ratio | Interest Earned* Amount | Cumulative interest | Refund for repayment† Ratio | Refund for repayment† Amount |
|---|---|---|---|---|---|---|---|---|
| 1 | $600.00 | $58.65 | $42.68 | 12/78 | $15.97 | $ 15.97 | 66/78 | $87.83 |
| 2 | 557.32 | 58.65 | 44.01 | 11/78 | 14.64 | 30.61 | 55/78 | 73.19 |
| 3 | 513.31 | 58.65 | 45.34 | 10/78 | 13.31 | 43.92 | 45/78 | 59.88 |
| 4 | 467.97 | 58.65 | 46.67 | 9/78 | 11.98 | 55.90 | 36/78 | 47.90 |
| 5 | 421.30 | 58.65 | 48.00 | 8/78 | 10.65 | 66.55 | 28/78 | 37.25 |
| 6 | 373.30 | 58.65 | 49.33 | 7/78 | 9.32 | 75.87 | 21/78 | 27.93 |
| 7 | 327.97 | 58.65 | 50.67 | 6/78 | 7.98 | 83.85 | 15/78 | 19.95 |
| 8 | 273.30 | 58.65 | 52.00 | 5/78 | 6.65 | 90.50 | 10/78 | 13.30 |
| 9 | 221.30 | 58.65 | 53.33 | 4/78 | 5.32 | 95.82 | 6/78 | 7.98 |
| 10 | 167.97 | 58.65 | 54.66 | 3/78 | 3.99 | 99.81 | 3/78 | 3.99 |
| 11 | 113.31 | 58.65 | 55.99 | 2/78 | 2.66 | 102.47 | 1/78 | 1.33 |
| 12 | 57.32 | 58.65 | 57.32 | 1/78 | 1.33 | 103.80 | 0 | .00 |

*12/78 × $103.80 = $15.97
†66/78 × $103.80 = $87.83

**PART B   Actuarial Refund Method**

| Month | Beginning prin. bal. | Payment Total | Payment Prin. | Interest at 2.545% per mo‡ | Cumulative interest | Refund for prepayment |
|---|---|---|---|---|---|---|
| 1 | $600.00 | $58.65 | $43.38 | $15.27 | $ 15.27 | 88.53 |
| 2 | 556.62 | 58.65 | 44.48 | 14.17 | 29.44 | 74.36 |
| 3 | 512.14 | 58.65 | 45.62 | 13.03 | 42.47 | 61.33 |
| 4 | 466.52 | 58.65 | 46.78 | 11.87 | 54.34 | 49.46 |
| 5 | 419.74 | 58.65 | 47.97 | 10.68 | 65.02 | 38.78 |
| 6 | 371.77 | 58.65 | 49.19 | 9.46 | 74.48 | 29.32 |
| 7 | 322.58 | 58.65 | 50.44 | 8.21 | 82.69 | 21.11 |
| 8 | 272.14 | 58.65 | 51.72 | 6.93 | 89.62 | 14.18 |
| 9 | 220.42 | 58.65 | 53.04 | 5.61 | 95.23 | 8.57 |
| 10 | 167.38 | 58.65 | 54.39 | 4.26 | 99.49 | 4.31 |
| 11 | 112.99 | 58.65 | 55.77 | 2.88 | 102.37 | 1.43 |
| 12 | 57.22 | 58.65 | 57.22§ | 1.43§ | 103.80 | .00 |

‡APR of 30.54% ÷ 12 = 2.545% monthly rate
§Adjustment of $0.03 made in month 12; arises due to rounding

declining balances. The actuarial refund method assumes prepayment on the payment due date, and the Iowa law specifies an actuarial refund utilizing the APR (annual percentage rate).

## PERFORMANCE

Any attempt to measure the effectiveness of credit operations must start with a precise definition of the responsibilities and objectives of the credit department. The credit manager and/or department cannot be held responsible for operating decisions which are outside their assigned authority.

There are three immediate objectives which relate to a credit department's net contribution. They are (1) to maximize sales, (2) to minimize bad debt losses, and (3) to minimize the cost of carrying accounts receivable. The problem is that these objectives compete with one another; e.g., maximum sales can only be realized by approving credit for marginal risks, which means a larger investment in the receivables and greater bad debt losses. By not accepting marginal risks, sales are lower.

No statistical measure such as the bad-debt loss ratio or the collection ratio can by itself indicate the effectiveness of the credit department. Credit operations are interdependent, and measures of performance tend to reflect more than one functional area. Judgment of results must be based on a group of related ratios which are compared to some predetermined standards. Even then, ratio trends may only indicate the area or areas where further analysis and evaluation need to be made. If the interrelationships and possible ambiguities associated with the various measures of performance are understood, a great deal of information can be realized relating to the effectiveness of the credit department. The following discussion of the performance of the credit department will be organized along functional lines: (1) the extension of credit, (2) collection performance, (3) the contribution to sales, and (4) the effectiveness of cost data.

**Extension of Credit** The extension of credit can be measured as to the following: lost sales, types of accounts accepted, and the net results. Lost sales, in their simplest form, consist of the sum of sales from credit applications which have been refused credit during a stated period. When refusals involve specific orders, a cumulative dollar volume and number can be computed. If the credit department turns down only a few requests for credit and still holds bad debt losses to a nominal figure, it is usually thought that the credit department has done an excellent job. The fact that bad debt losses are kept under control allows for a simple dollar-measure of lost sales. It contributes to a direct comparison of the cost of refusing and accepting marginal credit risks. It must be remembered that the number of applications and the total amount of the orders will vary from month to month; therefore, the number and dollar amounts may be expected to vary without any basic change in the credit department's standards. It is the long-run objectives that are important.

Since the absolute figures do not lend themselves to comparisons, many firms use a percentage of total applications and/or a percentage of dollar volume to all credit sales for evaluation purposes. These comparisons assume that there is a sufficient number of new credit applications being received to provide reliable periodic percentages. Even though a would-be customer has been refused credit, the credit manager may attempt to negotiate a sale on safer terms. Records need to be kept on the number and volume of sales that were made on other terms which could not be made on the open account basis. These would-be customers might some day become eligible for regular credit.

**Collection Performance** A statement of amount and number of bad debt losses is the simplest measure of results. When losses are small, there may be no reason to show results in any other form. It is usually difficult to make comparisons between different companies because of the differences in timing and composition; e.g., losses are not always written off when the accounts reach a predetermined age, nor are recoveries of losses recorded in the same manner.

*Classification of Accounts.* An analysis of collections from accepted accounts provides a useful measure of the potential loss in the various customer classifications. Customer accounts may be classified in various catagories such as (1) government; (2) prime or excellent: large, well-established firms; (3) good: firms that are not large and have not yet established excellent credit reputations; (4) restricted: firms that are limited to a definite credit line; and (5) marginal: high-risk accounts which must be watched. Any classification or measure of this type is dependent on the care taken in rating the accounts. All pertinent information available to credit departments including Dun and Bradstreet, credit agencies, financial statements, and the like should be used when rating the individual accounts, whether initially or during their periodic reviews.

Most account classifications start with a balance-sheet-type breakdown or a number and dollar-volume account breakdown relative to sales. The balance-sheet-type breakdown is used to detect significant changes in the pattern of credit decisions from period to period. It gives management the opportunity to assign experienced credit personnel to the more risky accounts.

The number, or dollar-volume, account breakdown relative to sales classifications highlights customers who are marginal or whose line-of-credit is restricted. Management should know how many sales, number and dollar volume, are in these catagories, and what percentage these risky accounts are of the actual sales above the company's break-even point. Risk distributions of the type described above have proved extremely useful to those individuals who are responsible for the periodic revaluation of credit policy. Partial breakdowns for a specific group of accounts are made at regular intervals while comprehensive breakdowns are usually prepared periodically.

Efficient collection operations presuppose a constant supervision of the credit accounts. Only credit managers of the smaller companies will have personal knowledge of individual customer's accounts; therefore, in most companies collection performance can be judged only by knowing the following: (1) the aging of accounts receivable, (2) the ratio of credit sales to accounts receivable, and (3) the ratio of collections to accounts receivable.

*Aging of Accounts Receivable.* This is basically a distribution of outstanding accounts by time periods. The time classifications are usually current, overdue—less than 30 days, 30 to 60 days, 60 to 90 days, and over 90 days. These reports are usually prepared monthly, although some firms increase the frequency, especially for the extended overdue accounts. The basic reason for aging accounts is to develop a file of customers who require special attention either in the form of statements, letters, or other collection activity. It also provides a receivable condition report and data for evaluating credit operations of the company. The department's main function is to prevent the tie-up of funds in uncollectable accounts.

The aging and collection ratios are of limited value when there are sizable amount differences in the individual accounts. These ratios are affected by large account balances; therefore, the relative number of overdue accounts may be a better measure of collection performance. The second limitation has to do with the cost of aging numerous small accounts. The value of each account does not warrant the expenditure of large sums of money. Broad, undifferentiated groupings of accounts, such as slow governmental accounts and deferred payment term accounts in with ordinary open accounts, can create a false impression of poor performance on officials who do not have personal knowledge of the situation.

*Accounts Receivable Turnover Ratio.* This is widely used by credit and financial analysts in evaluating the efficiency of collection activities. It is usually used in one of two forms: (1) credit sales divided by ending accounts receivable and (2) accounts receivable divided by credit sales times 365 days. The first formula gives the number of times the current balance of receivables is collected during the year, while the second formula gives the average number of days the current balance is expected to remain outstanding before it is collected. Either formula can be affected by changes in prepayments, which mask an increase in delinquent accounts.

*Collection Ratio.* This is the ratio of monthly collections to the accounts receivable outstanding at the first of the month; it yields the number of times, or fraction thereof, that beginning accounts are collected during the month. This ratio, like the accounts receivable turnover, is sometimes stated as an average collection period: the number of days represented by the cumulative collection figure divided by the collection ratio.

The two ratios, namely, sales to receivables and collections to receivables, are closely related. Both ratios tend to cover up a growing volume of delinquent accounts. The only time there may be discrepancies in the results between these ratios is when there are abrupt and relatively sizable changes in the data used. Except for the above situation and the availability and use of comparative data, there is no major reason why one ratio is better than another.

There are a number of other ratios which can be used to judge performance including (1) the ratio of collections to sales for the preceding month and (2) the ratio of collections to total realizable collections. The collections to sales ratio for the preceding month has the limitation of being affected by uncollected sales from earlier periods. The ratio of collections to total realizable collections is used more by firms which offer several different sets of credit terms. It, too, tends to cover up past-due accounts when prepayments increase.

*Ratio Drawbacks.* Ratios on collection performance tend to report collection trends in overdue accounts, rather than reporting the cause of the performance. It is easy to infer that an increase in these ratios means poor collection performance, but in reality, poor performance cannot be determined from collection data alone. It may be due to improper extension of credit.

*Contribution to Sales.* The credit department's responsibility in promoting sales is completely different from its responsibilities of credit extension and collection. The sales efforts of the credit personnel are based on the objectives of the sales department. There are no measures or ratios similar to those stated for credit extension and collection performance that can be used in judging contribution to sales. There are records, however, which provide an indication of its contribution. The credit department's correspondence file often provides clues as to the customers' reaction to past-due credit letters or to some form of managerial assistance; it may also contain personal letters from customers expressing appreciation for the manner in which their accounts were handled. Another contribution is the periodic estimates which the credit department may compile of the additional sales potential of active and inactive accounts. Although none of these represents reliable measures of performance, each demonstrates how credit personnel can help sales.

**Effectiveness of Cost Data** The operating costs of the credit function in many companies are a part of the treasurer's office or the sales department's budget and are not specifically identified. Even where actual and budgeted credit department costs are identified, there is no common agreement among companies as to the appropriate costs to be included in the budget; e.g., overhead, bad debt losses, and legal expenses for nonroutine collections. The relatively fixed nature of most credit department costs tends to give little indication of the efficiency of the credit operation.

*Collection Costs Comparisons.* An attempt to indicate the efficiency factor by relating the credit department's total collections gives the average cost of collecting a dollar of sales. Some companies restrict their budget cost comparisons to immediate operating expenses, such as salaries and wages, travel expenses, special legal collection costs, and bad debt losses. Average cost figures tend to obscure the actual costs experienced with marginal customers; therefore, the cost of accepting marginal credit customers is not truly evaluated.

*Profit Contributions.* The effectiveness of credit department operations can only be judged by the department's net contribution to company profits. Marginal accounts affect the end results; the problem is to compare the costs of doing business with each group and the contributions to the overhead and/or profit of each group. The contribution to overhead from sales—the difference between sales and cost of production and distribution—can be determined for each group. It is then possible to look at the department's controllable costs, namely, bad debt losses, cost of financing the receivables, and the department's operating expenses. A bad debt loss is never known until the final settlement. It could affect unrelated accounting periods, e.g., early write-offs and extended recoveries. The going rate of interest for any firm could be used in computing the cost of financing the receivable balance in each category. If financed by long-term capital, it would be reasonable to use the long-term cost-of-capital figure. The apportionment of the department's operating costs may become difficult because of the time factor, while other costs, such as legal fees, might be directly identifiable with the accounts collected. All costs which are fixed in nature, without regard to the type of account, should not be considered in the above calculations because they are incurred irrespective of the type of sales.

*Expense Analysis.* Any summation of credit department activities should include cost figures. Bad debts are only one item in the operation of a credit department. Wages and salaries represent one of the most important single categories of credit expense. Other expenses include the interest on outstanding accounts, fees and dues for credit information, outside assistance in making collections, legal and other supplies, and equipment expenses. Costing out individual credit operations is complex. Much attention has been directed toward (1) measuring costs

against sales for various catagories of customers, (2) developing methods of explaining certain results in credit department accounts, and (3) forecasting performance. The human factor, as well as clearly defined credit goals and objectives, is important in establishing effective credit management procedures and practices. Practicing credit managers and personnel must be alert to the modern tools of credit management and recognize their use in establishing credit policy and making decisions. The more conscious credit management becomes of the need to evaluate its own performance, the better its credit decisions will be.

*See also* ACCOUNTING FOR MANAGERIAL CONTROL; CONSUMERISM AND CONSUMER PROTECTION LEGISLATION; CONTROL SYSTEMS, MANAGEMENT; FINANCIAL MANAGEMENT; FINANCIAL MANAGEMENT, BANK RELATIONSHIPS; FINANCIAL MANAGEMENT, SHORT-TERM, INTERMEDIATE, AND LONG-TERM FINANCING.

## REFERENCES

Cole, Robert H.: *Consumer and Commercial Credit Management*, 5th ed., Richard D. Irwin, Inc., Homewood, Ill., 1976.

Committee, Thomas C.: *Managerial Finance for the Seventies*, McGraw-Hill Book Company, New York, 1972.

Credit Research Foundation: *Credit Management Handbook*, 2d ed., Richard D. Irwin, Inc., Homewood, Ill., 1965.

Heiser, Edward J., Jr.: "Federal Regulations Affecting Consumer Credit Lenders," *National Institute on Consumer Credit Management*, Marquette University, Milwaukee, Wis., June 1976, unpublished.

Johnson, Robert W.: "Better Way to Monitor Accounts Receivable," *Harvard Business Review*, vol. 50, May–June 1972.

Nemmers, Erwin Esser, and Alan E. Grunewald: *Basic Managerial Finance*, 2d ed., West Publishing Company, St. Paul, Minn., 1975.

Smith, E. W.: "Efficient Credit Management with Time Sharing," *Financial Executive*, vol. 39, March 1971.

Wesselink, David D.: "Rates and Precomputation," *National Institute on Consumer Credit Management*, Marquette University, Milwaukee, Wis., June 1976, unpublished.

Weston, J. Fred, and Eugene F. Brighan: *Managerial Finance*, 5th ed., The Dryden Press, Inc., New York, 1975.

HOWARD C. LAUNSTEIN, *Marquette University*

## Credit unions (*See* COMPENSATION, EMPLOYEE BENEFIT PLANS.)

## Critical incident rating (*See* APPRAISAL, PERFORMANCE.)

**Critical path method** (*See* NETWORK PLANNING MODELS.)

**Cultural values** (*See* VALUE SYSTEMS, MANAGEMENT: SOCIAL AND CULTURAL.)

**Current rate method** (*See* EXCHANGES, FOREIGN, MANAGEMENT OF.)

**Custom manufacture** (*See* PRODUCTION PROCESSES.)

**Customer relations** (*See heading in Table of Contents for complete listing.*)

**Customs union** (*See* INTERNATIONAL TRADE.)

**Cybernetics** (*See* SYSTEM CONCEPT, TOTAL.)

# D

**Data, input** (*See* DATA PROCESSING PRINCIPLES AND PRACTICES.)

**Data, raw** (*See* DATA PROCESSING PRINCIPLES AND PRACTICES.)

**Data bank, materials** (*See* MATERIALS MANAGEMENT.)

**Data base** (*See* INFORMATION SYSTEMS, MANAGEMENT (MIS), APPLIED.)

**Data processing management** (*See* heading in Table of Contents for complete listing.)

## Data processing principles and practices

*Data processing* is the collection, manipulation, analysis, and dissemination of information useful to managers in the operation of their organizations. It can be accomplished manually, mechanically, or automatically. Techniques have changed radically in the past quarter century, but the basic principles remain the same. Emphasis, however, has shifted from a management of people to the management of information that people use. In its ultimate stage, the objective of data processing is to provide the right information for handling the opportunities and problems that the dynamics of business and society create. This places a premium on the prevention of problems rather than just on their solution.

As data processing techniques have improved, the information generated has become increasingly cumbersome. Much of this problem has little to do with technique. It results from the essentially short-term nature of many management operations. Information prepared without adequate planning tends to pile up layer upon layer of information that is redundantly used for short-range decisions. The vital information needed for strategic decisions is usually there, but it is buried in the pile and is often difficult and costly to extract.

**Decision Analysis** A primary requirement of management is to make decisions based upon the flow and substance of information. The "hands on" people in the organization are placed where they are because of decisions made concerning the use and value derived from information. Accordingly, it is the decisions made on the information within a manager's sphere of control that dictates how and where personnel will be employed. This basic fact must be taken into consideration when examining

263

information and data processing. The focus should not be on information bulk but upon the information and the related decisions concerning that information.

Take, for example, a simple inventory control system. The information needed to control inventory begins with what is actually the end result—the volume of product placed in storage. From that endpoint, analysis steps backward. At each step, an examination must be made of the decisions concerning the parts that make up the product. These decisions include: (1) use-life of the components; (2) availability of materials; (3) control needed to protect against pilferage or component damage; and (4) any other decisions that affect the creation and control of the end product. Regardless of activity, function, or objective, a similar type of analysis should be conducted. Whether for a service or physical product, the principle is to start with the desired result and then analyze the flow of information and the decisions that are progressively made to change the initial information into information that goes to make up that final product or service. This process is *decision analysis*. It is one of the most important principles to follow in data processing. Without a thorough evaluation of the decisions and changes in information that take place throughout a business, nothing connected with the use of computers or any other machines will improve upon what is already being done. Machines may do it faster, but they will not improve the value of the information.

**To Automate or Not to Automate** This is probably the question most often asked about data processing and least often answered correctly. The common practice, unfortunately, is to look at the problem areas and automate them with the hope that automation will clear up the problems. More often than not, this does not happen.

Before the decision to automate is considered, a complete decision analysis should be made of the areas under examination. This will uncover many of the present inefficiencies in handling information and allow for a clear understanding of the information flow and change. With this knowledge, it is much easier to evaluate the advantages that automation can offer: (1) speed, (2) accuracy, and (3) discipline. Each of these should be considered separately—and then collectively—when making the automation decision.

*Speed.* The use of modern data processing systems should result in communicating knowledge as it is needed. Without speed, knowledge has little practical use in the making of day-to-day, on-the-spot business decisions. The business environment

in the United States is one that heavily stresses time and its cost. For a business to survive in such a competitive system, executive decisions must be made rapidly and on as sound a basis as possible. Many split-second decisions are required daily. These decisions require reliable and accurate information, presented in an understandable form at the time it is needed. For these reasons, care should be taken to consider speed in true relation to its value to the particular operation.

Once the advantages of speed are established, a value should be placed on those advantages. Values can often be measured very accurately and should be put in a perspective that everyone understands, that of money. After this is done, a correct evaluation of the desirability of automation can be made from the standpoint of speed.

*Accuracy.* Because machines do not think and because they do things in rote repetition, once a routine is established, the machine will do the same thing over and over again. This means that once a routine is established properly, the machine will handle it exactly the same each time. The solution or analysis of a problem, once learned, requires little creative thinking. However, because it seems to be human nature to think and make decisions in performing each task, there is a wide margin for error, especially if the steps offer exceptions. For example, in computing the pay for a full-time salesclerk working on salary plus commission, a payroll clerk must look up the base pay for each salesclerk and add it to the commission based on a percentage of items sold. After a while, this job becomes routine and the steps seem mechanical and dull. Errors occur and multiply as the payroll clerk repeats the same computations. This can be disturbing to the salesclerk if the pay is miscalculated too low and costly to the company if too high. When automated, this operation is very simple and is handled the same every time, no matter how many times. Here again, however, a comparison of the savings brought through increased accuracy versus the cost of obtaining that accuracy should be made—and the results should be used to determine the value of the data processing effort.

*Discipline.* Disciplining of information refers to the requirement of the computer for consistent information kept in an organized manner. All information relating to one end product will be placed in a single grouping; thus it causes a discipline of information to the point that it is easy to review the information kept and to weigh the value of the information against the cost of keeping that information. Discipline also provides a means of assuring that all pertinent information that relates to a given product or function is gathered and stored. Internal and external factors force this information discipline on companies. This need for discipline requires building a data processing system efficient enough to present all necessary reports accurately and economically with as little waste of time as possible.

## MACHINE SYSTEMS

The introduction of a machine into a data processing system does not change the fact that the information (or data) flows through decisions and/or changes resulting from these decisions. The main difference is that a machine, instead of a person, will process those decisions that can be identified and quantified.

With machine systems, the processing of information follows the same general pattern as with manual systems. Raw data are found on original papers, usually called *source documents*. *Raw data* become *input data*, which consist of original or source transactions that require processing.

**Recording**   Proper recording of data involves

1. Editing. This involves deciding on the kind of information that requires processing and checking that information for conformance to predetermined levels of usability.

2. Verifying. This requires checking on the validity and accuracy of the data.

3. Recording and grouping. This is done by categorizing or classifying the data for use in later operations. With machines, recording is usually done on cards, magnetic tapes, or magnetic disks and is performed by a group called data entry.

**Processing**   Typically the processes include (1) sorting, (2) calculating and recording, (3) summarizing, (4) reporting or communicating, and (5) storing. These operations are also accomplished with cards, magnetic tapes, or magnetic disks used in conjunction with a program or set of instructions that has been written to conform with the desired decisions from previous analysis.

All these steps can be accomplished manually, but with the great bulk of information required by business in most modern organizations, it would be very time-consuming. It can also be a serious problem to maintain the integrity of the information through multiple recording, processing, and reporting cycles. This is why most companies that have large processing requirements use computers.

**Programming**   A *program* is essentially a series of quantified decisions placed in a logical sequence so that a machine can execute the decisions the same way each time—but with an increase of speed and

accuracy over manual processing. Before a program (or set of instructions for the computer) can be written, a complete analysis of the data must be made. Care must be taken beforehand by the manager who will use the resultant information to make sure that the programmed decisions are correct. A program is no better than the analyst or programmer who wrote it. If this is kept in mind, checks and balances can be set up to assure that the program is written efficiently and correctly.

**Computer Functions**   In principle, all that has been done so far is to examine a manual method and, after decison analysis, to set up a machine to perform a corresponding group of decisions. The computer is just a very high-powered machine, a tool in the hands of those who write the programs and those who operate it. A computer itself has absolutely no power; it accomplishes desired goals only through the expertise of those who operate and control it. The origin of errors can, in almost all instances, be traced to (1) improper analysis of the decisions made concerning the data involved or (2) incorrect data being placed in the machine.

**Manager and Specialist Functions**   Analysis of these decisions and the correctness of the information is the responsibility of the user-manager. A systems analyst or programmer can provide assistance in the area of how the computer might be used in processing the data, but responsibility for decisons, for data, and for control lie with the operating manager. The analyst and/or programmer has an important additional assignment, however. He or she should be charged with making sure that as the data flow from one manager's jurisdiction to another through the total system, (1) that the data be controlled and coordinated so that nothing is lost and (2) that the continuity of the data not be disturbed.

**Data Capture to Data Return**   Because of the discipline factor associated with the computer, it is usually best to capture data at the first point that they become available in the company. This would typically be on the receiving dock of a manufacturing plant or at the teller's window in a bank. Moreover, the idea is to collect the data at the earliest possible point and keep the data as pure as possible through processing. This changes the manager's responsibility; the manager no longer directly manages the flow of information as it passes through his or her area of responsibility. Instead, through a series of reports, the manager controls the information as it flows through the computer system. This highlights the real value of management by exception: a manager who wants to see and evaluate everything that is on the computer will almost always misuse it. It is not unusual for an uninformed manager to try to examine every line on a computer printout or to require that all the information pertaining to his or her area of responsibility be printed on a report. More often, all that is really needed is the information on the *total* lines. Most of the information between can be ignored until a problem arises. It is when a problem arises that the computer should react and notify the manager so that the appropriate action can be taken. A computer can store and print information at such a rapid rate that it could inundate a department in paper. Paper does not contribute to efficiency; in fact, it detracts from all three advantages of the computer: speed, accuracy, and discipline.

**Information on Exceptions** The time between data capture and return of the data to the final resting place should be filled with reports to the various operations managers that show the exceptions to the standard decisions that have been established. In effect, a good data processing system will remain silent until

1. Possible exceptions occur.

2. Decisions occur that are not quantifiable or that require human judgment.

3. Information is required for audit and control or for decisions outside the system, including the final storage of information for government purposes.

The information discipline changes the nature of the manager's responsibility from one requiring the direct application of people to problems to (1) analysis of critical decisions and (2) determination of the exception and control information needed to effectively manage the change that takes places within the department and the data processing environment. A manager still has full responsibility for the manner in which the data are processed. The data processing group has the responsibility to make certain the systems are run properly and that all data are processed.

## INTEGRATED SYSTEMS

As data processing becomes more sophisticated and crosses more company lines, the job of managing the data becomes increasingly difficult and complex. Lines of responsibility become less clear; it is hard to see where one department ends and another department begins. It is also more difficult to determine who has the responsibility for generating and controlling the data.

The capability of putting decisions of a routine nature into a machine does not release those in-

volved with the information from their responsibility. It is the management of the information and the structure of the programs that take on a different perspective.

**Media and Methods** Integration of data implies that there are three distinct operations that data go through: (1) input and edit, (2) processing, and (3) reporting.

*Input and Edit.* At this stage, data are collected, analyzed, and their correctness and validity checked. Often, data from several sources are combined and placed under the same edit criterion; this can create a change in the management of the data. The data are combined, and a manager is placed in charge of the operations connected with making sure the data are correct. This is sometimes referred to as *data base management*, although this term also has other meanings such as the programming of the information within a given data base. It is important at this point in an integrated system that the person performing a particular function knows how it fits in with the rest of the system.

The methods and media can be anything from a form that is filled out manually and sent to the proper place for key entry to a cathode-ray tube that allows direct entry of the information to the system. The particular input system does not really make any significant difference to the success or failure of the data processing effort: it is the completeness of the information edit once it reaches that first stage.

*Processing.* Once the data are captured and proven correct, the second operation is to process the data according to the formulas and decision criteria established earlier. With an integrated system, the passing of data from department to department and its associated multiple handling are eliminated. From that identical input point, the same data can be used in accounting, sales, marketing, or manufacturing.

A system of this nature requires that programs that control the information be prepared in a modular, or building block, manner. Each block stands alone and can be changed independently of the other blocks. Without a clear distinction between modules, management of the system is difficult, and it is almost impossible to maintain accountability for the data processed in the various functional areas. Operating managers blame data processing and data processing blames operating managers for problems generated in the system.

*Reporting.* Because modules are used, each report from an information group is separate and distinct and can be looked upon as a separate entity that can be changed without affecting either input and edit or processing. Management of this system area is especially complex when one report must serve in several different operating areas. Coordination of the information on the report often represents a compromise between several wants and needs. However, these needs are usually best served by concise, well thought out information that can be formatted for use among several managers.

## GUIDELINES

In summary, there are eight keys to a successful data processing system:

1. Make sure the application is sound. Use decision analysis and the expertise of both user and data processing personnel.

2. Keep the system simple. The payoffs are in mass manipulation, not mathematical optimization. Put prices on the advantages, and look keenly at the results desired.

3. Make a clear assignment of responsibility. Users should develop the systems with the assistance of the systems people.

4. Educate all personnel affected by the system. Do not overlook the little people.

5. Design the system for people. Do not think that the system will control the people. This is especially true with integrated systems.

6. Prepare regular progress reports. Make sure a good line of communication is set up between all users and the systems team.

7. Do homework where it really counts. Be sure (*a*) that transactions will be handled properly, (*b*) that basic documents are correct, and (*c*) that proper numbering systems are established.

8. Audit results at agreed dates. Plans should call for periodic audits. This not only keeps the team sharp, it also allows midcourse correction of a system gone wrong. Another important audit time is at the replacement of a system so that mistakes made in one system can be avoided in another.

*See also* COMPUTER SYSTEMS; FORMS DESIGN AND CONTROL; INFORMATION SYSTEMS, MANAGEMENT (MIS), APPLIED; PAPER WORK SIMPLIFICATION; RECORDS MANAGEMENT; SYSTEMS AND PROCEDURES.

### REFERENCES

Condon, Robert J.: *Data Processing Systems Analysis and Decisions*, Reston Publishing Company, Reston, Va., 1975.

Gore, Marvin, and John Stubbe: *Elements of System Analysis for Business Data Processing*, Wm. C. Brown Company Publishers, Dubuque, Iowa, 1975.

Leeson, Marjorie: *Basic Concepts in Data Processing*, Wm. C. Brown Company Publishers, Dubuque, Iowa, 1975.

Murach, Mike: *Business Data Processing and Computer Programming*, Science Research Associates, Inc., Chicago, 1973.

Walton, Thomas F.: *Communications and Data Management*, John Wiley & Sons, Inc., New York, 1976.

BRUCE J. WRIGHT, *Systematics, Inc.*

**Daywork plan** (*See* COMPENSATION, WAGE AND SALARY POLICY AND ADMINISTRATION.)

**Debentures** (*See* FINANCIAL MANAGEMENT, SHORT-TERM, INTERMEDIATE, AND LONG-TERM FINANCING.)

**Debt financing** (*See* FINANCIAL MANAGEMENT, SHORT-TERM, INTERMEDIATE, AND LONG-TERM FINANCING.

**Debt management** (*See* FINANCIAL MANAGEMENT.)

**Debt ratios** (*See* FINANCIAL MANAGEMENT, CAPITAL STRUCTURE AND DIVIDEND POLICY.)

**Debt structures** (*See* FINANCIAL MANAGEMENT, CAPITAL STRUCTURE AND DIVIDEND POLICY.)

**Debtors, classification of** (*See* CREDIT MANAGEMENT.)

**Decentralization and centralization** (*See* CENTRALIZATION AND DECENTRALIZATION.)

**Decentralized authority** (*See* AUTHORITY, RESPONSIBILITY, AND ACCOUNTABILITY.)

**Decentralized decision making** (*See* DELEGATION.)

**Decision, system** (*See* SYSTEM DYNAMICS.)

## Decision analysis (*See* DECISION-MAKING PROCESS.)

## Decision flow (*See* PLANNING, PLANNED MANAGEMENT OF TURBULENT CHANGE.)

## Decision making, in groups (*See* INTERPERSONAL RELATIONSHIPS.)

## Decision making and problem solving (*See heading in Table of Contents for complete listing.*)

# Decision-making process

*Rational thought processes* are those skills that allow a manager to apply a uniform set of mental processes to every situation encountered on the job. They enable him or her to gather and utilize data successfully, regardless of environment and content, through a sequence of systematic questioning and analytic steps. The advantages of such an approach lie in these elements:

Proficiency that results from utilizing a consistent approach.

Ability to extract the relevant data from the superfluous.

Facility in communicating with others when using a common terminology.

As the individual manager becomes responsible for more and more content areas, the manager's ability to survive as a "content expert" diminishes severely. Few people are capable of mastering the various aspects of accounting, law, inventory, personnel, sales, and so forth that are components of the modern manager's responsibilities. The successful manager is forced to rely on specialists in these fields, some of whom are subordinates, peers, and superiors, and even people who do not work for the same organization. This does not diminish the fact, of course, that the manager is held accountable for the results expected from his or her position. As a consequence, the manager must still gather data from a variety of sources and then organize and analyze the data. A rational process for accomplishing this task is shown in Table D-1.

High-quality results can be achieved only if the raw material and mental process are of equally high quality.

**TABLE D-1  An Example of Rational Thought Process**

| Raw material (input) | Mental process | Goal (output) |
|---|---|---|
| Data from various sources | Organizing and analyzing the data | High-quality results (meeting objectives) |

Experience indicates that sound results can be generated from three kinds of managerial activities:

1. Determine why someone or something is not performing as expected, commonly known as *problem solving.*

2. Select some course of action from among a range of options, which is usually termed *decision making.*

3. Anticipate events so that potential benefit can be maximized and threat minimized, which is generally called *planning.*

The first activity deals with resolving an event which has occurred in the past. The second addresses a choice that must be made in the present. The third provides for protection in the future. The thought processes employed will be different in each activity, since the successful resolution of concerns in the past, present, and future require significantly distinct approaches.

## SITUATION APPRAISAL

If differing approaches are needed to solve problems, make decisions, and protect plans, then a unique technique is also required to enable the manager to determine into precisely which of these areas a particular conern falls. This technique is *situation appraisal.* In appraising a situation, a manager should accomplish the following:

Recognize the number and range of concerns to be resolved.

Separate those concerns into manageable segments.

Establish their priority.

Determine whether each is a problem, decision, or planning (past, present, or future) type of concern so that the appropriate analytic process can be applied.

A *concern* is anything that prompts a manager to action. Such concerns are generated by telephone calls, standard operating procedures, organizational changes, employee grievances, and a variety of other sources, not the least of which is the manager's own motivation to seize opportunity and maximize personal contribution to the organization. The need to recognize concerns consciously and deliberately is created by

The necessity of considering *all* concerns before deciding how time and resources will be allocated for their resolution.

The pitfall of overlooking necessary evils as legitimate concerns to be resolved (the noise of a poorly working air-conditioner or the inconvenience of habitually receiving a report late are not conditions that one has to live with; all too often they are considered one's normal burdens in life).

The desirability of consciously attempting to exploit every potential opportunity that might present itself.

**Separation**   Having determined what a manager's concerns are, it is important to separate them into manageable pieces. Generalized and ambiguous statements such as "personality clash," "communications breakdown," "morale problem," and "distribution situation" are insufficient in describing the specific concerns inherent in a situation. Separation is used to establish discrete problems, decisions, and plans by seeking to determine what *exactly* is prompting the manager to take action. For example, if a morale problem is examined by asking what is prompting you to take action in that situation, or what evidence there is that indicates you should take action, it might reveal that employee grievances are up 2 percent over last month, turnover has increased by 10 percent this year, three people are requesting transfers to other departments, and a new union contract is due to be signed.

Upon examination of these individual concerns, the manager might determine that the first two are problems to be solved, the third involves a decision to be made, and the fourth requires some anticipation of future problems. Consequently, three distinct approaches will have to be utilized to resolve what was originally termed a morale problem.

**Priorities**   Having separated the generalized concern into specific ones, the manager can establish priorities, determining which need to be personally handled, which can be delegated, and what resources to allocate for the resolution of each. By applying such factors as seriousness, urgency, and growth to these concerns, the manager can determine which require immediate action, which can be delayed for a while, and which must be tolerated.

**Selection of Process**   Having identified the concerns that exist, what their individual components are, and which represent the greatest opportunity or threat, the manager can choose which of the analytic processes apply: problem analysis, decision analysis, or potential-problem analysis. Up to this point

the manager has been engaged in a process of clarification. The manager is now ready to embark upon a process of resolution.

## PROBLEM ANALYSIS

*Problem analysis* is a search for a cause. A problem exists when there is deviation from an expected performance norm, or "should," the cause for that deviation is unknown, and the situation is of concern to us, as established in the situation appraisal process. (This last point is critical, since a problem to one manager might not be a problem to another, as one is prompted to action by it and the other is not.) The relationship is shown graphically in Fig. D-1.

**Fig. D-1. Deviation from an expected performance norm.**

The steps in the problem-solving process may be simply stated as

1. Recognizing the problem (deviation).
2. Describing the problem (definition).
3. Determining causes of the problem (distinction).
4. Verifying the cause (testing) and eliminating the problem (correction).

The recognition step is accomplished when the manager perceives that there is a deviation of "actual" from "should," for which the cause is not known and about which the manager is concerned. The description of the problem entails defining the problem in terms of its identity, location, timing, and magnitude in two dimensions: (1) where the problem is actually occurring, and (2) where it could have been expected to occur but in fact did not.

**Changes and Causes**   In comparing the problem's existence—the "is"—with what might have been its existence—the "is not"—one can develop distinctions about the person, process, or machine that constitute the problem. One can then search for changes that affected those distinctions, because if nothing had changed, then the problem would never have come into being. Some change had to have occurred at or before the point at which the deviation was observed. Since thousands of changes occur to all managers everyday, the distinctions allow us to focus only on *relevant* changes, changes that only affected the characteristics of the "is" data and, therefore, could be responsible for the problem.

Changes that impact *both* the "is" and "is not" dimensions could not be responsible for the problem described only in the "is." This relationship is shown in Fig. D-2.

The search for a cause, then, is a search for the change responsible for driving performance off the "should."

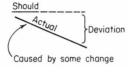

**Fig. D-2. How distinctions focus on relevant changes.**

**Testing and Verifying** As these causes are developed, they are tested against the facts contained in the "is" and "is not" data. Causes which fail to explain why only the "is" was affected and not the "is not" are eliminated from consideration. The cause which best explains the description provided by the "is" and "is not" data is the most probable cause and is then verified in the real world. Once the verification has proved that the most-probable cause emerging from the process is actually the cause, appropriate steps are taken to remove the cause and eliminate the problem.

**Problem Elimination** Eliminating a problem's effects can only be accomplished by finding and eliminating the *cause* of the problem. This is called *corrective action*. In seeking to live with or mitigate the effects while the cause is sought, or because corrective action is impossible or too expensive, a manager can take adaptive action. (For example, NASA has had a long-standing problem with thunderstorms during launches. Corrective action—changing the launch or stopping the storm—is impossible. The adaptive actions of lightning arrestors, last-minute fueling, and minimum personnel exposure have saved the day.) The critical point is that a manager's best action can *only* be adaptive until and unless the cause of the problem is determined.

Problem analysis is not confined to hardware and machine problems. It applies to a diverse array of conditions, particularly in the area of human performance. In fact, in situations where there are fewer tangibles and few hard facts, the ability to focus on "hard data" is doubly important. Clear "shoulds" are critical to the manager if standard operating procedures are to be realistic and achieved. Too few people address this need. Instead, they squander time and money trying to correct situations for which no standards exist.

## DECISION ANALYSIS

Choosing courses of action that provide maximum benefit within acceptable limits of risk is the purpose of decision analysis. It is intended to provide the manager with an objective tool with which to analyze fact and opinion. While it may be used as a result of finding cause in problem analysis, it is more often applied to the vast number of decision-making situations encountered everyday.

There are three major components to decision making:

1. *Establishment of objectives.* Objectives are the goals which the selected course of action seeks to achieve. The degree to which these goals are missed, met, or surpassed will determine the success of the course of action chosen.

2. *Generation of alternatives.* Alternatives represent the various routes available to reach the goal. Processes for generation and evaluation of alternatives identify the alternative that best meets the objectives.

3. *Examination of adverse consequences.* This entails an evaluation of the risks inherent in each alternative. It establishes peril, enabling the manager to determine if the risk is prohibitive.

**Decision Levels** A key determinant in the process is to establish the correct level of the decision. This *level* does not refer to stratum in the organizational hierarchy, but rather to the range of alternatives that will be under consideration. For example, the simple decision to buy a new car implies that several prior decisions have already been made: The car will be new, and it will be purchased. Originally, it was determined that there was a need for transportation. For example, a major insurance company entered the casualty field not long ago. Its entry was the result of a strategic decision to increase profits. Its *decision chain* might have looked like this:

1. Need to increase profits.
   Raise premiums
   Cut staff
   *Enter new line*
   Cut dividends
2. Select a new line.
   Marine
   *Casualty*
   Variable annuity
3. How to enter casualty business.
   Retain staff
   *Buy out casualty company*
   Hire new people

The next step in its decision sequence might be to select which company to buy. Note that as a manager moves down the chain, the alternatives become less global. In the example, management has moved from broad profit-generating alternatives to specific plans to purchase a company. Examining the level of the decision will also keep managers out of a rut. By asking, "Why are we making *this* decision?" a manager can determine whether or not the level ought to be raised.

**Establishing Objectives** Once the proper level has been set, objectives can be established. Two sources should be considered for these: (1) the *resources*, and the limits on those resources, to which the manager has access; and (2) the *results* that the manager expects from the decision. By considering both resources and results, the manager is in a position to try to maximize the latter with minimum investment of the former.

*Musts and Wants.* Objectives should also be classified into what are called "musts" and "wants." The "musts" are absolute minimum standards that are critical to the success of the decision. Any alternative that fails to meet a "must" cannot provide a satisfactory degree of success, no matter how well it may meet other objectives. The "musts" are the objectives that should always reflect the budgetary limits involved (i.e., maximum expenditure of $x$ dollars), time constraints (i.e., available within $x$ days), and so on.

The "wants" are those objectives which are noncritical but desirable for any alternative to achieve. Sometimes they might reflect a minimum standard established in the "musts" (i.e., minimum expenditure), and somtimes they will represent entirely new goals (i.e., increase corporate image in the community).

**Generating Alternatives** Alternatives should not be considered until after objectives have been established and classified. Alternatives are not generated earlier in order to avoid the pitfall of establishing objectives around a pet alternative. Common sources for the generation of alternatives include: experience, superiors, subordinates, consultants, creativity, competition, research, peers, technical literature, and government regulations.

An alternative that does not meet the "must" objectives is immediately eliminated from further study, since it cannot meet goals critical to the success of the decision. Those that do meet "must" objectives are then compared against the "wants" to determine which do the best job of meeting these desirable goals.

**Examination of Adverse Consequences** Those alternatives that meet the "must" objectives and are most successful in meeting "want" objectives are then examined for adverse consequences. Each alternative will probably entail some risk. The manager now assesses that risk, determining how probable and serious it is and what might be done to eliminate or minimize it.

The final decision will result in that alternative that provides the most benefit (best meets the "want" objectives) while entailing acceptable risk (adverse consequences that the manager is willing to accept). Consequently, the final decision involves more than just a paper exercise. The manager must exercise judgment as to the degree of risk that the organization and the manager are willing to undertake in return for various benefits.

**Other Applications** Another key aspect of decision analysis is the degree to which various parts of the process can be utilized.

*Conflict Resolutions.* When conflict among individuals or departments occurs, the immediate question should be, "Is this conflict over alternatives or over objectives?" This will separate the conflict into one of two more manageable concerns which require different approaches.

1. If the conflict is over alternatives, it is helpful to refocus back on the objectives. Since, presumably, there is agreement on objectives, this will defuse the hostility by concentrating on common ground. In so doing, it is possible to attempt to combine the best features of the alternatives that were in conflict or perhaps generate a new alternative upon which all parties can agree. In any case, conflict over alternatives should be handled by reestablishing the agreement on objectives and working toward compromise from there.

2. Conflict over objectives, however, requires a more basic approach. An assessment must be made as to the proper origin of the objectives. Is it up to the parties involved to establish them, or are they to accept objectives from a third party or superior? If objectives originate elsewhere, it is a matter of rechecking with the source. If objectives are to be established by the parties in conflict, then it is necessary to examine critically the level of the decision and what is to be accomplished. In many cases, an impartial third party might be needed.

*Meetings Design.* While most meetings have an agenda, few have *results objectives* to guide participants to what results need to be achieved (rather than merely to activities performed). This element of decision making also enables participants to consider the proper resources to be invested in consideration of the results desired, including knowing who to involve in the meeting and what their role should be. Finally, results objectives also allow the manager to track and monitor progress and to determine when the meeting is over.

## POTENTIAL-PROBLEM ANALYSIS

Potential-problem analysis is used for the implementation and protection of a plan. In using this technique while examining the sequence of steps in any plan, a manager will be able to identify threats lurking along the way (perhaps as a result of the adverse consequence elements in decision analysis). *Potential-problem analysis*, then, is a process designed to enable the manager to systematically identify and plan actions to deal with those risks.

When the actions discussed in problem analysis are carried into the future, (1) corrective action becomes *preventive action*—intended to eliminate the likely cause of a future problem; and (2) adaptive action becomes *contingent action*—intended to mitigate the effects of a future problem. This relationship is shown in Fig. D-3.

|        | Past       | Future     |
|--------|------------|------------|
| Cause  | Corrective | Preventive |
| Effect | Adaptive   | Contingent |

Fig. D-3. Potential-problem analysis.

Once the manager identifies future, or potential, problems, he or she then establishes what the likely causes of those problems might be. This step is undertaken because, just as in problem analysis, the effects of a problem cannot be eliminated unless the cause is removed. Hence, likely causes are established so that preventive actions can be taken.

For example, if a potential problem is fire, two likely causes might be smoking in dangerous areas and electrical malfunction. Preventive actions might be "no smoking" signs and electrical provisions which exceed normal safety standards. But if the fire occurs anyway, either because preventive action failed or some unanticipated cause started it, the contingent actions which would minimize the effects might be a sprinkler system, emergency exits, and first-aid facilities. Note that the contingent actions address the effects of the fire itself, since the effects will be the same no matter which cause was responsible.

Two other concepts of special usefulness in potential-problem analysis are triggers and mileposts.

*Triggers.* A trigger is the activating agent for contingent action. In the example of the fire, the fire alarm might be the trigger which prompts the emergency first-aid facilities to be set up by the designated personnel. In the case of the sprinklers, the trigger is automatic since heat activates the device. Triggers are employed to ensure that contingent action will occur at the appropriate time.

*Mileposts.* Mileposts are used to keep track of the plan and the status of the actions proposed. In the example of the fire, mileposts might include "install sprinkler system by March 1" or "check for presence of 'no smoking' signs of the first of each month." Perhaps more importantly, they are useful in determining when contingent actions are no longer needed. For example, if insurance is one of the contingent actions against fire on a building, the milepost might be the monthly insurance premium which keeps this action in effect. If the building is sold, then the contingent action is no longer needed. The next insurance premium—the milepost—reminds that this action should be discontinued. By alerting a manager that contingent actions have outlived their usefulness, mileposts can be extremely valuable in conserving scarce resources.

**Summary** Most of the time in most of their activities, managers are dealing with data. There is a need for processes which enable the manager to systematically deal with these data, both in terms of personal consistency and the ability to speak a common language with subordinates and peers. The concepts embodied in situation appraisal, problem analysis, decision analysis, and potential-problem analysis provide those abilities.

*See also* COST IMPROVEMENT; INFORMATION SYSTEMS, MANAGEMENT, (MIS); PAPER WORK SIMPLIFICATION; RISK ANALYSIS AND MANAGEMENT; STATISTICAL ANALYSIS FOR MANAGEMENT; VALUE ANALYSIS; WORK SIMPLIFICATION AND IMPROVEMENT.

BENJAMIN B. TREGOE, *Kepner-Tregoe, Inc., Organization Development and Research*

# Decision-making theory (*See* LEADERSHIP.)

# Decision making under uncertainty
(*See* STATISTICAL ANALYSIS FOR MANAGEMENT.)

# Decision matrix (*See* STATISTICAL ANALYSIS FOR MANAGEMENT.)

**Decision point, union** (*See* LABOR-MANAGEMENT RELATIONS.)

**Decision support, MIS** [*See* INFORMATION SYSTEMS, MANAGEMENT (MIS), IN LARGE ORGANIZATIONS.]

**Decision theory** (*See* MANAGEMENT THEORY, SCIENCE, AND APPROACHES.)

**Decision tree** (*See* OPERATIONS RESEARCH AND MATHEMATICAL MODELING; STATISTICAL ANALYSIS FOR MANAGEMENT.)

**Decision unit, in budgeting** (*See* BUDGETS AND BUDGET PREPARATION.)

**Decision variables** (*See* PRODUCTION/OPERATIONS MANAGEMENT.)

**Deed, real estate** (*See* SITE SELECTION.)

**Defects, foreseeable product** (*See* PRODUCT LIABILITY.)

**Deferred compensation** (*See* COMPENSATION, EXECUTIVE.)

**Deferred distribution plans** (*See* COMPENSATION, SPECIAL PLANS.)

**Definition, business** (*See* POLICY FORMULATION AND IMPLEMENTATION.)

**Delay symbol** (*See* WORK SIMPLIFICATION AND IMPROVEMENT.)

# Delegation

Delegation is essentially the task of farming out one's work to one's subordinates and of making sure that the subordinates successfully accomplish the projects or tasks thus assigned. Being proficient at the art and skill of delegation is probably the single most useful management tool for the person attempting to get work done through other people.

Many people make a complex issue of the subject of delegation by focusing their attention on the methods used in delegation rather than on the concept itself. In its simplest form, the art of delegation is the process of establishing and maintaining effective working arrangements between a manager and the people who report to him or her. Delegation takes place when the performance of specified work is entrusted to another and the expected results are mutually understood.

**Decentralized Decision Making** The basic principle behind delegating work to one's subordinates is that of decentralizing decision-making responsibility throughout the organization. There are many reasons to decentralize such decision making:

1. It reduces costs throughout the organization.

2. It enables the executives to devote time to executive-level work (rather than the "doing" activities which would otherwise constitute the executive's workaday functions).

3. It often results in a better decision because in most cases people who are on the spot have closer insights and more relevant information.

4. It tends to get the best out of people, since most people like to have some say in how they are going to do their job.

**Roadblocks to Delegation** While many people understand very well the *need* for decentralization of decision making within an organization, many managers still find it difficult to delegate. At the root of this difficulty are certain mental blocks that managers frequently have toward making subordinates responsible for activities for which the manager bears the ultimate responsibility. These include:

1. *The need to be needed.* A person who has an intense desire to make or keep subordinates dependent will find it difficult to give free rein to subordinates for job achievement.

2. *Fear of losing control.* When a manager delegates responsibility and authority to a subordinate, the manager runs the risk of the subordinate's not doing the job well or otherwise failing to perform as required. In such instances, the manager feels that

delegation has removed control of performance for which he or she is accountable.

3. *The desire for reward.* Many managers enjoy the rewards that are usually associated with the achievement of functional, "doing" work. Delegating such work to one's subordinate necessarily means that the subordinate will get the reward— particularly the self-satisfaction from performing a task with "hands on" application.

4. *The feeling of a need to work.* Many managers have the notion that being weary at the end of the day from having worked hard is an indicator of meritorious job performance. They fail to recognize that the intellectual work of activating others effectively is far more productive of results than having done the work themselves.

5. *Fear of competition.* Still other managers are afraid that if they assign work for which they are responsible to their subordinates, their subordinates may, in fact, outperform them and, indeed, possibly end up becoming their supervisors.

**Managerial Attitudes**  Most managers who are ineffective delegators of work have yielded to one or more of the above mental blocks. Perhaps a still more fundamental reason for the inability of some managers to make effective work assignments is their latent feeling about people themselves. In short, many bosses fail at delegation because they do not have an effective attitude toward working with other people, especially their employees. The basic requirements for developing the appropriate attitude in the matter of delegation include:

1. *Receptiveness to other people's ideas.* A good delegator does not feel that his or her ideas are necessarily better than anyone else's or, more specifically, that other people's ideas are unworkable.

2. *A sufficiently placid disposition.* A good manager must be able to accept others doing things in a way that he or she would not do them. This does not mean that the manager will accept absolute mistakes on a subordinate's part. It does mean that the manager must be willing to see others attempt to do things their way. Futher, the manager must be willing to forego prejudging that way as unworkable when it in fact is still viable.

3. *A forebearance for mistakes.* An effective manager must forego the luxury of irate criticism of subordinates. Wreaking havoc is futile when a subordinate has erred. Good delegation means encouraging people to do things their way. This implies, of course, encouraging them to do them in an operable manner. It does *not*, however, imply insisting that one's own way, no matter how effective, is the *only* way to accomplish a task.

4. *Powers of self-restraint.* The good delegator must resist the temptation of stepping in and taking over even though the subordinate's way of doing things seems inconsistent with what the manager thinks would be an optimal procedure.

**Essential Requirements**  Effective delegation of work is based upon six essentials. These include:

1. *Policies must be stated clearly and explicity.* The subordinate must understand the operational guidelines within which he or she must operate. This requires that the manager clearly state what authority the subordinate has and the limits of the subordinate's responsibilities for task performance.

2. *Jobs and tasks must be carefully defined.* Nothing is more destructive of effective delegation than the manager's failure to define succinctly the performance expected of the individual on the delegated task. Failure to be explicit in this regard is confusing to the subordinate who may then become frustrated. Such poor practice often results in the subordinate's inability or unwillingness to shoulder the delegated responsibility.

3. *Specific goals for completion of job performance must be established.* Job or task performance objectives should contain specific deadlines as to when, how good, how much, and under what governing restraints the task will be done.

4. *Ideas must be communicated to one's subordinates.* Effective delegation implies effective communication. This usually requires discussion and an exchange of ideas as to what the manager expects the subordinate to accomplish. This is particularly true, for example, when there are unique requirements for material handling or for relating the project to factors outside the manager's control. Without such guidance, both the superior and the subordinate may be frustrated. Often a subordinate will be disappointed at the superior's seeming unappreciativeness for the work which is done.

5. *Controls must be established to monitor progress toward the accomplishment of objectives.* It would be a mistake to delegate if there were no way to ensure that the work delegated is actually going to be (or has been) accomplished. If, for example, the sky diver has no way of determining whether the parachute rigger who has packed the diver's chute has done so correctly, then sky divers must either pack their own chutes or not make the jump. But when controls are established (riggers of parachutes are trained specifically in the art of packing the chute, and control efforts exerted by requiring riggers to jump some chutes they have packed), a degree of control is also exerted over the individual's motivation to accomplish the objectives. This is an extreme

example, but, in business, control would normally be executed by the manager making use of various techniques including: requiring progress reports on work performed; making comparisons of planned budgets against actual expenditures; analyzing indicators of performance against established norms (e.g., comparing scrap reports against standard scrap rates or comparing customer complaints or requests for adjustments on poor merchandise against the normal level of such complaints).

6. *Whole tasks must be delegated rather than pieces of tasks.* It is impractical for any individual to accept an incomplete assignment of work. This is particularly true when someone else is to be working on the assignment, especially if that individual is also unaware of the desired end result. No individual can be expected to function effectively on any job task if it must become an integral part of someone else's total job responsibility, or if the end outcome desired is not known. Indeed, assigning pieces of one job to many people can, in fact, violate the basic rule of unity of command.

Figure D-4 is an example of the steps of delegation which might be taken by a company's personnel department manager in developing a personnel policy manual. Note that each level in the delegation chain breaks out in greater detail the "doing" tasks necessary for the satisfactory completion of the whole project. The unseen factor is the control (also time and length of statement requirements) and other constraints which the personnel department manager would level on each subordinate in ensuring that the work will be accomplished on time as required by the board of directors.

**Pros and Cons of Delegation** The principal advantages of effective delegating include: freeing up executive time to work on more important projects; leveraging one's talents throughout a whole organization; and making it possible to accomplish functional details which exceed the limits and capabilities of any one person in that organization. The disadvantages to delegation are essentially mental rather than instrumental. Some managers simply cannot stand what they perceive to be loss of control over their own work. Primarily, they cannot tolerate to rely upon other people for results for which they retain ultimate responsibility. Because of this, many managers live in constant fear that a subordinate will botch an assignment, or that work will not be done on time, or that other embarrassing circumstances will occur.

Effective managers recognize that one cannot live in today's society without accepting the need to delegate tasks effectively to other people. In an

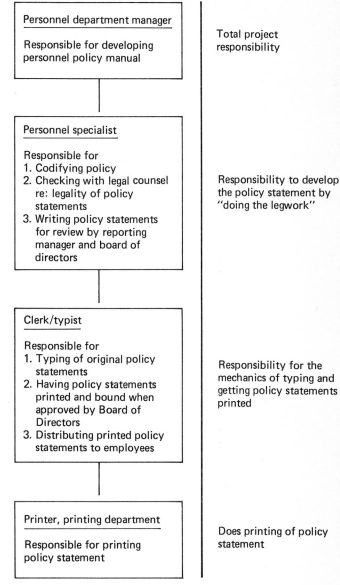

Fig. D-4. Example of how work is delegated through an organization.

ultimate sense, no one is self-sufficient. All people, in the final analysis, depend upon others to produce their food, provide their medication, supply their heat, light, and water, and the like. Modern organizations are built on that premise. Effective delegation relies on the fact that everyone can do something useful. Failure to delegate is not only unintelligent behavior upon the part of a manager who wishes to be self-sustaining only in his or her own right, it is also an abuse of the law of comparative advantage. It is clear that no matter how limited a person is, he or she can do some one thing better than others. That person's time, therefore, should be devoted to doing that task. This makes that person a productive citizen.

See also AUTHORITY, RESPONSIBILITY, AND AC-COUNTABILITY; EXCEPTION MANAGEMENT BY INTER-PERSONAL RELATIONSHIPS; MANAGEMENT THEORY, SCIENCE, AND APPROACHES; OBJECTIVES, MANAGE-MENT BY (MBO); ORGANIZATION ANALYSIS AND PLAN-NING; WORK, CONCEPT AND IMPLICATIONS; WORK DE-SIGN, JOB ENLARGEMENT, JOB ENRICHMENT, JOB DESIGN, AND AUTONOMOUS WORK GROUPS.

### REFERENCES

Dalton, Gene W.: *The Distribution of Authority in Formal Organizations,* The M.I.T. Press, Cambridge, Mass., 1973.

McConkey, Dale D.: *No-Nonsense Delegation,* American Management Association, New York, 1974.

Steinmetz, Lawrence L.: *The Art and Skill of Delegation,* Addison-Wesley Publishing Company, Inc., Reading, Mass., 1976.

Valentine, Raymond F.: *Initiative in Managerial Power,* American Management Association, New York, 1973.

LAWRENCE L. STEINMETZ, *High Yield Management, Inc.*

## Delphi method   (See FORECASTING BUSINESS CONDITIONS.)

## Delphi technique   (See PRODUCT PLANNING AND DEVELOPMENT.)

## Demand, economic   (See ECONOMIC CON-CEPTS.)

## Demand curve   (See PRODUCT AND SERVICE PRICING.)

## Demand elasticity   (See PRODUCT AND SER-VICE PRICING.)

## Democracy, industrial   (See CODETERMI-NATION AND INDUSTRIAL DEMOCRACY.)

## Demotion   (See PERSONNEL ADMINISTRATION.)

## Department store retailing   (See RETAIL-ING MANAGEMENT.)

## Department stores   (See MARKETING, CHAN-NELS OF DISTRIBUTION.)

## Department maintenance   (See MAINTE-NANCE MANAGEMENT.)

## Depreciation policy   (See TAX MANAGE-MENT, MANAGERIAL RESPONSIBILITY FOR FEDERAL INCOME TAX REPORTING.)

## Depressive response   (See HEALTH, MEN-TAL.)

## Descriptors   (See RECORDS MANAGEMENT.)

## Design, business forms   (See FORMS DESIGN AND CONTROL.)

## Design, industrial

As with many other new professions, there are probably as many interpretations of the term *industrial design* as there are people who call themselves industrial designers. In broad terms, a *designer* organizes and directs a process which is aimed at producing a preconceived result or change. Implied in the word *industrial* is the designer's concern with products made by machine, whether they are one-of-a-kind assemblies for use in a specific situation or mass produced by the thousands for a large market of consumers. The difficulty in reaching a precise definition for what an industrial designer does stems from the complex nature of the product development cycle. The development of any product involves, from its conception until it reaches the marketplace, people of many diverse skills who are all responsible in part for the final form that a product takes.

**The Industrial Designer**   Of the team of skilled people needed to develop a product, it is the industrial designer who is most concerned with the fit between the end product and the person who has to use it. The industrial designer is concerned with the shape and form of the product, how it feels and handles, how it is used and operated, and how it is visually perceived and understood by people. All these concerns overlap the responsibilities of other specialists—from research to marketing—who are equally interested in seeing a product reach the marketplace. Because of these shared interests it is difficult to isolate the industrial designer's contribution from that of the product development team as a whole. The main difference between the industrial designer and the other members of the team is one of emphasis: (1) engineering is interested in the mechanical function of the product, making sure that it will work; (2) marketing is concerned with getting a product that can be sold; (3) industrial design attends to whether people can actually use the product comfortably and easily.

## BACKGROUND

Prior to the industrial revolution, most utilitarian objects were custom-made by artisans dealing directly with the customer. In this one-to-one relationship, goods could be tailor-made to the specific needs of the user. With the advent of mass production, the manufacturer became increasingly remote from the ultimate user of the items produced. Direct communication between the producer and consumer was no longer possible. Today, the industrial designer has become the liaison between the end user of a product and the manufacturer, bridging the gap created between the product's maker and user by the technology of the industrial revolution.

Industrial design as a distinct profession is only about a half-century old. During the 1920s, Walter Gropius founded the Bauhaus, a German school devoted to preparing students to combine an understanding of technology with the sensitivity of the artist and the skill of the craftworker. These students were trained to work with other disciplines to solve problems of industry. During the 1930s, many people associated with the Bauhaus emigrated to the United States where their ideas provided much of the theoretical basis for today's design education. At the same time as the Bauhaus was flourishing in Europe, a more pragmatic view of design was developing in the United States. Men like Henry Dreyfuss and Norman Bel Geddes, trained as stage-set designers, began to apply their talents to consumer items. Raymond Loewy, an engineer, and Walter Dorwin Teague, a typographic designer, opened offices to provide design services to industry. Manufacturers were looking for anything that might separate their products from the competition and achieve more customer acceptance. In response to this need, these early designers skillfully and often flamboyantly changed the look, feel, and function of mass-produced items.

**Styling**   Much of the early work attributed to industrial designers, and much of what is done today, can be called styling. *Styling* implies the superficial alteration of a product's exterior form to enhance its market appeal. It is the deliberate imposition of a preconceived form on an object regardless of its function or use. Few designers, though, are immune to the natural development of a style, which is the unique character or look of the forms of any particular time period.

**Human Requirements**   The more perceptive industrial designers realized that there was more to the design process than the streamlining of objects that were not going to go anywhere anyway. Human needs became the starting point for each new product. In addition to the natural skills as a visualizer of form through drawings and models, the designer reinforced his or her ideas by using information from the growing science of human factors engineering, or "ergonomics," as it is called in Europe. *Human factors engineering* deals with the human/machine interface, attempting to integrate the biological characteristics of humans with the mechanical functions of the machine.

**Production Requirements**   Human factors engineers achieved early success with the use of anthropometric data to arrange the instruments and controls in the cockpits of military aircraft during World War II in an effort to minimize pilot error and fatigue. While both the industrial designer and the human factors engineer share a common concern with the human/machine interface, the industrial designer is equally interested in the production processes necessary to make the machine. By focusing on the human component of any product or system, the industrial designer and the human factors engineer work to make the points of contact between the product/system and the people who use it as frictionless as possible. Jointly, they are particularly effective in developing information about people which can be used as a basis for making intelligent design decisions where no precedents exist.

**Product Requirements**   Depending upon the nature of the product and its complexity, the industrial designer plays a greater or lesser role in its development. Many simple low-technology consumer items with a high style or fashion emphasis (furniture or household accessories) might be controlled entirely by the designer; while a complex piece of electronic equipment or transportation vehicle would require the industrial designer to become part of a team which includes other specialists.

## DESIGN PROCESS

In any project, the industrial designer follows a process that considers human requirements as its starting point. The function of a product is not considered in a narrow mechanistic way; instead, it is appraised in light of perceptual, emotional, and physical needs of the user of that product.

**Perceptual Factors** Even in the most complex projects where functional and structural requirements must be rigorously adhered to, there is room for esthetic decisions that relate more to the user's spiritual needs than physical requirements. In fact, the only way many complicated products, such as computers, can be comprehended and understood by the majority of us is by their appearance. Appearance is always the first thing that is noted in a product; it is evaluated immediately, while the other properties may only be discovered after prolonged use and testing. The only indication one gets of the operation and function of much of today's complex machinery is through the product's external form, because the actual working elements are hidden behind protective housings. Even if one could look behind the cover of a product like an electronic calculator, it would be difficult for anyone not schooled in electronics to discern the operation of each piece of microcircuitry.

In other products, like a chair, for example, the function is readily understandable; yet most chairs are sold for reasons other than the basic need to accommodate a sitting person. The classic chair designs express much more to the buyer than their use as support. In fact, some chairs that continue to be sold by the thousands are not very comfortable at all, but the visual statement their design makes about sitting—through its form, material, and construction—creates a demand for the product. Therefore, one of the most important means available to a manufacturer to communicate the worth of a product to the potential buyer and user is through its appearance and perceived operating qualities. There are numerous cases of products which failed to achieve consumer acceptance even though they worked well, just because the public failed to understand and appreciate the function. Any product is a

symbol for the forces that shaped it and the task it is to perform. If unity is not attained between the dynamic requirements of the machine and the human anatomical, physiological, and perceptional needs, the product will be less than successful.

The full application of the design process is necessary for any project. An attempt to apply design to a product that is on its way to the production line will result in superficial styling. Every product should be considered in its own right, with its design developed from a given set of factors that are unique to that product. Through advocacy of the human needs in any development project, the industrial designer can contribute significantly to the definition of a product concept in its earliest beginnings and throughout the course of its development.

**Definition and Constraints** The first stage in the design process is the accumulation of information and establishment of design constraints. The designer can (1) work from a brief or specification provided by the manufacturer or (2) help in the writing of that specification. Answers must be provided to questions about the need for the new product or the change to an existing product, its function and use, means of production, distribution, and maintenance. The designer will survey the existing competition and become familiar with the operation of similar kinds of products. He or she might use film or other means to document the operation of the product in its environment. Observation of the potential users of the product and interviews with them are important sources of information.

**Criteria Ranking** The next stage in the process is to sort out the collected data and give them relevance. This usually involves the establishment, with other team members, of a set of ranked criteria which the product should meet, such as, (1) operating efficiency and control, (2) safety, (3) optimum size, (4) fabrication method, (5) maintainability, (6) appearance, and (7) cost. Value will be attributed to the product by the consumer to the degree that the design successfully meets the desired criteria.

**Unifying Factors** The industrial designer is apt to take a more holistic look at the criteria than the other members of the development team and seek a solution that conveys a visual unity and order between the components. The designer tends to regard a product or system in much the same way as the user, seeking a gestalt, or wholeness, that expresses the quality of the object through its form. In contrast, the engineer is more likely to examine the technical problems initially, considering each in turn and then linking them together into a complete product or system. While the engineer is analyzing the physical components in detail, the industrial designer is looking at the system in behavioral and human terms. The designer is interested in how the finished product will relate to other things in its environment, such as, "What operator tasks are required to make it function? How well does it represent the overall image of the manufacturer?"

**Alternative Solutions**  The industrial designer also tends to broaden the overall problem and to consider many alternative solutions rather than look for the single best answer to any subproblem. For any given set of restraints, the industrial designer is likely to generate many divergent solutions but in less detail than other members of the development team. At this stage, the design process is both rational and intuitive. In a sense, the designer considers all the criteria simultaneously, seeking a definition to what is really an ill-defined problem with many possible answers. As with innovation of all kinds, the designer weighs matters of value against matters of fact, looking beyond the data to reach conclusions.

**Model Building**  The special mystique of designers arises from the tools and skills they utilize. Invariably, as the designer thinks about the problem, he or she tries to visualize the characteristic properties of the final product with sketches or models which are more or less abstractions of the end result of the process. The designer begins a series of successive approximations or models, which may take the form of perspective sketches or increasingly realistic three-dimensional simulations made from cardboard, wood, and plastic. With these models, the designer integrates the technical black-box information provided by the engineers into a configuration that can be appreciated and evaluated by everyone on the development team. Models are usually accompanied by mechanical drawings which specify the appearance-related details. Renderings, scale mockups, and finished models help focus the development group's attention at any particular phase of the projects, allowing the team to adjust and alter the product concept without a great amount of risk or expense. In many ways, this aspect of the process is roughly equivalent to the artisan of the preindustrial revolution who made an item for sale and then modified it to suit the individual needs of the customer. Because the designer is producing only a model or simulation (often using the services of a skilled model maker) of the final product, and not a working prototype, the concept can be easily changed and modified as the technical information becomes more specific or as the development team's perceptions of the end result

become clearer. A surprising amount of information can be shared and communicated by having a model of the product to discuss, no matter how simple the model may be.

**Market Preparation**  The last stage of the design process involves taking the product to market. In this stage, the production drawings are finished, final colors and finishes are specified, product graphics and sales literature are completed, prototypes are constructed and tested, the tooling is purchased, and the lines of distribution are set up. Last minute changes are handled, and the production lines spew forth the product to await the verification of the marketplace. In this period, the industrial designer provides supervision and quality-control checks on the work in progress, making sure that any changes are in keeping with the original design concept and helping in the selection of vendors and suppliers.

## PRACTICE

The field of industrial design is commonly subdivided into areas of special emphasis, such as product design, graphic design, packaging design, or interior design. While these areas share the definition of the terms *industrial* and *design*, they vary in the means of production utilized and the scale of the final product.

*Product design*, which is central to industrial design, deals with three-dimensional objects or systems which are produced by means of "hard" industrial manufacturing methods, like molding, welding, or stamping. Any manufactured item which has a high degree of interaction with the user would be of interest to the product designer. This could range from consumer products, such as an automobile or a toaster, to medical and scientific instrumentation, as well as to production machinery itself.

*Graphic design* concentrates on visual communication. The two-dimensional printed word or visual image is the center of this specialty, and the printing press and photographic camera are its dominant production tools. The graphic designer works with all forms of printing, audiovisual materials, and information systems, including signs, exhibits, product graphics, films, and packaging.

*Interior design* is concerned with the working or living environment. The design of furniture, specialized work stations, space-dividing systems for offices, or mass-produced enclosures belongs to this specialty.

Industrial designers can be found practicing their

profession in a variety of situations. Many large manufacturers with an ongoing need for design services employ internal staffs to concentrate on the company's particular requirements. An equal number of designers are found in consultant offices, which may range in size from one or two individuals to a hundred or more personnel. Many of these consultants have capabilities that range far afield from pure product design. Packaging, graphics, corporate identification, exhibits, interior space planning, market research, and engineering are among their services.

Neither the in-house designer nor the consultant designer has a monopoly on good design. The decision for a manufacturer to add an industrial designer to the staff or to hire a consultant is a complex one. It should be treated with the same degree of concern as the consideration of "make or buy." Most designers will represent themselves with a portfolio which should give a good indication of their experience, working methods, and quality of completed projects. A consultant designer can be expected to develop a written proposal for any project, specifying the designer's output (reports, sketches, models, drawings, etc.), schedule, and fees.

The Industrial Designers Society of America (IDSA), with headquarters in McLean, Virginia, has chapters in most major metropolitan areas. The society provides information about the profession and a listing of members in any particular location.

Many major universities have degree programs in industrial design which, depending upon the institution, may be found associated with schools of engineering, fine arts, or architecture. Several museums, such as the Walker Art Center in Minneapolis or the Museum of Modern Art in New York, have permanent industrial design collections. A number of European nations have national design centers, Britain's being the most noted, which promote the services of designers and the importance of good design.

A well-designed product is a most effective means for a manufacturer to communicate with the customer. The product is the crucial interface between the buyer and seller. The industrial designer contributes to the perceived value of merchandise by helping perfect the relationship between the purchaser and the product. By carefully considering all the user's needs, both utilitarian and emotional, and expressing them appropriately in the form and function of the manufactured item, the industrial designer can maximize the product's impact in the marketplace.

*See also* HUMAN FACTORS ENGINEERING; PRODUCT LIABILITY; PRODUCT PLANNING AND DEVELOPMENT; PRODUCTION PROCESSES; THERBLIGS; VALUE ANALYSIS; WORK SIMPLIFICATION AND IMPROVEMENT.

## REFERENCES

Archer, L. Bruce: *"Systematic Method for Designers," Design Magazine*, London, 1963.
Archer, L. Bruce: *Technolgical Innovation: A Methodology*, Inforlink, Surrey, England, 1971.
Dreyfuss, Henry: *Designing for People*, Van Nostrand Reinhold Company, New York, 1973.
Dreyfuss, Henry: *The Measure of Man, Human Factors In Design*, Whitney Library of Design, New York, 1967.
Jones, J. Christopher: *Design Methods*, Interscience Publishers, a division of John Wiley & Sons, Inc., London, 1974.
Mayall, W. H.: *Machines and Perception in Industrial Design*, Studio Vista, Reinhold Book Corporation, London, 1968.
Middleton, Michael: *Group Practice in Design*, George Braziller, Inc., New York, 1969.
Nelson, George: *Problems of Design*, Whitney Library of Design, New York, 1965.
Rowland, Kurt: *A History of the Modern Movement: Art, Architecture and Design*, Van Nostrand Reinhold Company, New York, 1973.
Ryckman, Peter: *Integrating Design Into the Business Process*, Ryckman Design, Pittsburgh, 1976.

TIM CUNNINGHAM, *Bally Design, Inc., Industrial Design Consultants*

ALEXANDER BALLY, *Bally Design, Inc., Industrial Design Consultants*

## Design patent  (*See* PATENTS AND VALUABLE INTANGIBLE RIGHTS.)

# Developing countries, management in (management in the lesser-developed countries)

Managers in the lesser-developed countries (LDCs) face challenges which surpass in complexity and severity most of those met by their counterparts in the technologically more advanced societies. These challenges include

> Capital scarcity
> Lack of a trained work force
> Inadequate access to technology
> Poorly articulated, often politicized, legal systems

Government intervention in the private sector

Limited consumer markets

Underdeveloped supporting services: banking, insurance, accounting, communications, transport, engineering, technical, secretarial

Legal and physical constraints on access to raw materials, components, and supplies, and to information of all kinds

None of these is entirely missing from the daily concerns of managers in more advantageous settings, but their omnipresence and intractability in many LDCs give to management in these societies a distinctive difficulty. This difficulty is only partially offset by the presence of some unique resources and opportunities.

**Definition of Lesser-Developed Countries** While there is no universally accepted classification of countries as lesser developed, an authoritative list is that of the World Bank which in 1976 identified 103 nations as "developing."[1] Thus defined, the *LDCs*, sometimes referred to as the *developing nations* or *the Third World*, are to be contrasted with 21 industrialized countries with market economies *(the First World)*[2] and with 13 countries having centrally planned economies.[3]

**Managerial Environment of the LDCs** The variation among the LDCs in the conditions which affect management is enormous; only a little imagination is needed to visualize the differing managerial environments of, say, Upper Volta, Brazil, Saudi Arabia, Yugoslavia, and the Philippines—each of them is on the World Bank list. Nonetheless some generalizations are valid. In most of these countries annual per capita incomes are low (in the range of $100), population growth is rapid (2 to 3 percent per annum), disparities among the highest and the lowest income groups are wide and still growing, average educational attainment is limited. Legacies (some helpful) from prior colonial status abound— in legal systems, language, cultural orientations, educational structure, and international market relationships. Growth since the 1950s in international telecommunications, in the availability of other mass media, and in air travel is breaking down intellectual isolation and stimulating aspirations previously dormant. Manifold interdependencies in economic and political relationships with other countries are emerging.

Amid this welter of ideas, interests, aspirations, demands, and frustrations, national governments in most LDCs must struggle to maintain political and social stability. The depth of poverty in many countries makes resort to extensive government intervention in the economy nearly inevitable. Strongly felt nationalism and the related demand for national economic and political autonomy lead to government intervention in any event, since it would be seen as required to constrain the power of foreign capital and technology. Authoritarian rule is widespread. Independence of the judiciary is the exception. These circumstances shape management practice.

**Management Practice in LDCs** Most domestic firms in the private sector are small and usually family-owned, which limits the scale of operations, career opportunities for professional managers, and the growth of a managerial class. Large-scale operations are usually in the control of government or multinational corporations.

Finance from domestic sources tends to be short term and high cost. Securities markets are thin and largely unregulated. Coupled with high rates of inflation, these conditions frequently demand that a large share of management attention be focused on rolling-over short-term financing. Government plans and expenditures are often crucially important in market forecasts and marketing programs.

Technological research is rarely performed within the firm, and reliance on foreign technology available under license is the usual practice. Imported technology is often poorly adapted to LDC conditions, having been conceived in societies where labor cost outweighs other factors. In the limited instances when government supports research, it tends to do so in laboratories oriented strongly to academic rather than practical interests. Domestic consulting firms are small and tend to stress accounting, industrial engineering, or market research.

With important exceptions, education for management as a profession is available only abroad, and the social status of managers—in comparison with that of doctors, lawyers, engineers—is low. As in other professions, the relative attractiveness of careers in management in the countries where advanced management training is available has induced management talent to emigrate.

**Opportunities for LDC Managers** This litany of difficulty is partially offset by unique positive factors and opportunities for the LDC manager. Bilateral and multilateral foreign-aid agencies and development banks provide capital resources and technical assistance of kinds not usually available in the industrialized countries. A generation of managers equipped with powerful tools such as systems analysis and operations research, backed up by growing computer power, is entering the scene. Management by task force is replacing, in some organizations and countries, the more traditional, hierarchical methods.

Managers in the private sector in the LDCs often have access to government-sponsored financial incentives for investment and growth in the form of tax holidays, capital grants for plant and equipment, subsidized personnel training programs, preferential financing terms, and other cost-reducing privileges, provided their enterprises are in activities to which government gives priority. In many countries, development banks and similar institutions offer subsidized technical assistance in connection with financing. There is a special opportunity for managers of business in some LDCs because natural resources in minerals, forests, and agricultural land have only recently been opened for development; they are usually reserved for exploitation by nationals. For the well-trained manager in the LDC, an advantage of great importance is the fact that the competition is thin; this can mean more than normal opportunity both for the manager and for the enterprise.

*See also* CODETERMINATION AND INDUSTRIAL DEMOCRACY; ECONOMIC SYSTEMS; INTERNATIONAL OPERATIONS AND MANAGEMENT IN MULTINATIONAL COMPANIES; INTERNATIONAL TRADE; TECHNOLOGY, MANAGEMENT IMPLICATIONS; VALUE SYSTEMS, MANAGEMENT.

## NOTES

[1]See World Bank, *Annual Report 1976*, p. 97, Table 1, footnote, which lists the following as "developing countries":

Africa South of the Sahara—Benin (People's Republic of), Botswana, Burundi, Cameroon, Central African Republic, Chad, Congo (People's Republic of the), East African Community, Ethiopia, Gabon, Gambia (The), Ghana, Guinea, Ivory Coast, Kenya, Lesotho, Liberia, Madagascar, Malawi, Mali, Mauritania, Mauritius, Niger, Nigeria, Rwanda, Senegal, Sierra Leone, Somalia, Sudan, Swaziland, Tanzania, Togo, Uganda, Upper Volta, Zaire, Zambia.

East Asia and Pacific—Cambodia, China (Republic of), Fiji, Indonesia, Korea (Republic of), Laos, Malaysia, Papua New Guinea, Philippines, Singapore, South Vietnam (now part of the Socialist Republic of Vietnam—see footnote 3), Thailand, Western Samoa.

Latin America and the Caribbean—Argentina, Bahamas, Barbados, Bolivia, Brazil, Chile, Colombia, Costa Rica, Dominican Republic, Ecuador, El Salvador, Grenada, Guatemala, Guyana, Haiti, Honduras, Jamaica, Mexico, Nicaragua, Panama, Paraguay, Peru, Trinidad and Tobago, Uruguay, Venezuela.

North Africa and Middle East—Afghanistan, Algeria, Cyprus, Egypt (Arab Republic of), Iran, Iraq, Jordan,

Kuwait, Lebanon, Libyan Arab Republic, Morocco, Oman, Saudi Arabia, Syrian Arab Republic, Tunisia, Yemen Arab Republic, Yemen (People's Democratic Republic of).

South Asia—Bangladesh, Burma, India, Nepal, Pakistan, Sri Lanka.

More advanced Mediterranean countries—Greece, Israel, Malta, Portugal, Spain, Turkey, Yugoslavia.

The sharp increase in price of imported petroleum which occurred initially in October 1973, has forced a new division among the LDCs into what one commentator has called "the rich-poor" (e.g., Oman) and "the poor-poor" (e.g., Sri Lanka), based primarily on whether the LDC must import a substantial part of its energy requirements. See Irving S. Friedman, "The New World of the Rich-Poor and the Poor-Rich," *Fortune*, May 1975.

[2]Australia, Austria, Belgium, Canada, Denmark, Finland, France, Germany (Federal Republic of), Iceland, Ireland, Italy, Japan, Luxembourg, Netherlands, New Zealand, Norway, South Africa, Sweden, Switzerland, United Kingdom, United States.

[3]Albania, Bulgaria, the People's Republic of China, Cuba, Czechoslovakia, the German Democratic Republic (East Germany), Hungary, Democratic People's Republic of Korea, Poland, Rumania, the USSR, and the Socialist Republic of Vietnam. Presumably these constitute a "Second World," although this term does not seem to be widely used.

## REFERENCES

Bass, Lawrence W.: *Management by Task Forces*, Lomond Books, Mt. Airy, Md., 1975.

Davis, Stanley M.: *Comparative Management: Organizational and Cultural Perspectives*, Prentice-Hall, Inc., Englewood Cliffs, N.J., 1971.

Higgins, Benjamin: *Economic Development, Problems, Principles, and Policies*, W. W. Norton & Company, Inc., New York, 1968.

Kindleberger, Charles P.: *Economic Development*, 2d ed., McGraw-Hill Book Company, New York, 1965.

Samuelson, Paul A.: *Economics*, 10th ed., McGraw-Hill Book Company, New York, 1976, chap. 38.

*Systems Analysis and Operations Research: A Tool for Policy and Program Planning for Developing Countries*, National Academy of Sciences—National Research Council, Washington, 1976.

Vernon, Raymond, and Louis T. Weeks, Jr.: *Managers in the International Economy*, Prentice-Hall, Inc., Englewood Cliffs, N.J., 1976, especially chap. 7.

World Bank, *Development Finance Companies*, Sector Policy Paper, April 1976.

WILLIAM A. W. KREBS, *Arthur D. Little, Inc.*

## Development (See RESEARCH AND DEVELOPMENT MANAGEMENT.)

# Development, organization (OD) [*See* ORGANIZATION DEVELOPMENT (OD).]

# Development and training *(See heading in Table of Contents for complete listing.)*

## Development and training, career path planning for managers

The term *career* suffers from surplus meaning. To some people it means advancement up the organizational pyramid. To others, a career entails a certain class of occupations: professions such as medicine, law, engineering, or management. A third view is that a career is a person's experience in one particular organization or occupation, so that changing jobs means changing careers. In most management writings and in this entry, however, the term *career* is defined as follows:

The career is the individually perceived sequence of attitudes and behaviors associated with work related experiences and activities over the span of the person's work life.[1]

It is important to note that in this context, a career involves (1) work experiences, not other facets of a person's life; (2) a long period of time, the person's entire work life; (3) both attitudes (e.g., job involvement and satisfaction) and behaviors (e.g., performance and decision making); and (4) the person's own perceptions of career processes, rather than an external observer's description.

Although there is a great deal of current interest in life-styles, career path planning does not entail as broad a concern as life planning. The latter includes planning for family, leisure, community, and other activities, as well as work. There are legitimate questions about the right of an organization to get involved in an employee's entire life, and, therefore, this entry is restricted to career planning applied to the field of work.

**Impact on Operations** Careers are important because they affect an employee's job behavior significantly. A job may provide the features many management analysts prescribe—motivation, specific performance expectations, a well-designed organization structure, a clear reward system, good communications, good supervision, etc. If the employee sees no career growth opportunities, however, positive attitudes and performance will eventually decline among those employees most inclined to seek greater opportunities for responsibility and contribution to the organization's objectives.

Organizations pay a price for poor career growth opportunities in two important ways:

1. *High turnover among recently hired employees.* One company hired 120 new MBAs each year in order to have 20 left at the end of the year.[2] The cost of such turnover is enormous, considering recruiting expenses, travel, testing, lost output before replacement, reduced performance during orientation of new employees, etc. One authority has estimated the cost of replacing a middle manager at around $25,000.[3] Therefore, a company which loses 40 good managers each year, adds an extra $1 million to operating expenses just to stay even with last year's operation.

2. *Decreasing employee involvement.* In a declining economy and job market, some people may remain on the job in the face of poor growth opportunities, but they will adapt by "turning off" (becoming less involved in their work), with a corresponding drop in the quality of their work performance.

**Responsibility** Management might ask, "Should career planning be something people do for themselves?" Perhaps, but in practice, people tend to give little attention to planning their own careers, in spite of the importance of career fulfillment to them. In one study of executives and other professionals who had recently switched jobs, the researchers were surprised to see how few people made the change at their own initiative. Most of the changes were externally initiated—e.g., better job offers elsewhere, termination, job transfers, family problems which required relocation. The study found very little evidence of career planning, even among these high-powered people who practiced corporate planning and planning for subordinates all the time—but not for themselves.[4]

**Personal Values** Careers are also important because career fulfillment is more important now. Life-styles are changing, and more employees are willing to turn down transfers or promotions in order to stay in desirable geographical areas such as Seattle, San Diego, Minneapolis, or Houston. Self-fulfillment is becoming more important to many people, even if it has to come at the expense of salary, position, or status.

### DEVELOPING CAREER COMPETENCE IN THE ORGANIZATION

For a management determined to provide assistance to employees in their career planning, a number of options are possible. A firm may establish its program independently. A smaller firm which cannot afford an internal program may wish to hire a consultant. Even larger firms may benefit from a consultant's assistance, especially in designing their program.

**Career Planning Workshop**  A 2- to 5-day career planning workshop is a basic approach. The focus here is on an organized internal program; the basic elements of any comprehensive program will be similar in purpose, while the activities pursued will usually vary substantially between programs. The framework employed is Crites's[5] five components of career competence.

*Self-appraisal.*  The first step, the most crucial by far, and the one most frequently overlooked, is self-appraisal. There are few occupations which provide opportunities for people to assess themselves systematically, and most relationships at work are too impersonal to provide the candid, insightful feedback necessary to encourage self-appraisal. The career planning program, then, usually begins with some combination of occupational interest tests and small-group interaction to generate the data needed for self-assessment. It is in this phase that professional counseling assistance is most essential. Interpreting scores, designing group experiences to facilitate open feedback, and leading the group are all skills requiring professional expertise.

*Occupational Review.*  As participants pursue their self-appraisal, they develop a need to obtain occupational information. There are a few publications (the *Dictionary of Occupational Titles* and the Department of Labor's *Occupational Outlook Handbook*) which may prove useful for persons seeking general vocational information. Within the organization, job descriptions or discussions with job incumbents may be the most practical sources. Deciding which of these sources will be most suitable will largely depend upon management's objectives in sponsoring the program. General information may encourage people to consider career changes to jobs not available within the organization.

*Goal Selection.*  This is the central focus, once participants have achieved a tentative notion about the optimal job-person fit feasible. Argyris[6] identified four key characteristics of goals which produce genuine personal development. Goals are more effective to the extent that they are (1) challenging (but attainable), (2) related to more central psychological needs, (3) chosen by the person involved (rather than imposed), and (4) achieved by the person's own efforts. Setting such goals requires thorough self-awareness and knowledge of occupational opportunities. Goals should be chosen with the expectation

that some will be achieved, some not, and some changed as needs and the situation change. Hence, the career planning program needs to be designed to encourage revising or setting new goals from time to time.

Several career planning exercises have been developed to facilitate the goal-setting process. Working with others is an important adjunct to the goal-setting activity. Making a public commitment to achieve the goal makes it more likely that the goal will be pursued. Furthermore, a support group can be developed to provide encouragement to persevere when the goal is truly challenging. Coworkers can provide much of this support, but increasing recognition is being paid to the role of the participant's family as the most crucial support group in most instances. Goal-setting modules in the career planning program should be structured so that participants' families can be active in the decision making.

*Planning.*  Having selected their goals, the participants next enter the planning phase, the development of action steps to achieve the goal. Again, working in a group is helpful for the same reasons that the group improves the goal-setting process. Moreover, the group can be a useful source of ideas for alternative strategies which might be otherwise overlooked. Development of skills in planning, per se, is one of the most valuable things that participants may learn from the planning exercises usually assigned. *Force-field analysis*, a technique for identifying factors which discourage or encourage progress, is typical of the techniques employed at this point.[7]

*Problem Solving.*  The resolution of problems encountered in achieving the career plan is the last step. Problem solving occurs largely after participants leave the career planning workshop. The problem solving, however, should be based upon the self-awareness, job information, and plans developed in the workshop. The workshop can further subsequent problem solving to the extent that participants are encouraged to develop contingency plans, support groups are established, and a system of progress charting is provided. Organizational superiors can also be of substantial assistance, where participants are encouraged to seek their aid in pursuing the career plan.

## EXAMPLES OF SUCCESSFUL APPLICATIONS

The *management assessment program* (MAP) at the 3M Company uses assessment centers not just for employee selection but also for identifying (1) career goals, (2) developmental needs, and (3) placement opportunities. Normally, young, nonmanagerial employees who have completed 3 years of employment meet in groups of 15 for 2 days. During this time, they complete various tests, exercises, and interviews, and are also evaluated by a staff of professional psychologists. After 2 days, each participant then has a private feedback interview with a staff member, who provides the general results and suggests specific areas for development efforts by the employee. This information is also available to management for future career counseling and guidance. Here the focus is on the individual, with the resulting information made available to the company.[8]

The Travelers Insurance Company uses *career planning conferences*, where the stress is also on the individual but the information is not used for corporate personnel decisions. In fact, the information is not made available to anyone in the company. Employees who have completed 3 to 7 years of employment (who are often found to be at an initial plateau) first complete a battery of interest, personality, skill, and ability tests. Then people meet in a university setting, with trained professionals from outside the company, for 8 days. Much of the time is spent with participants and professionals in one-to-one counseling sessions. Class sessions discuss peoples' perceptions of what goes on in the company, the realities and imperfections of everyday organizational life, how to cope with the boss, strategies a person can build into his or her own behavior, etc. These discussions also cover issues such as family relationships and work versus family tensions.

Each participant develops a 6-month plan, with a follow-up contact made 6 months later. These experiences are shared anonymously with all participants and provide for more learning from peers. The results seem to include more personal self-direction and an increased sense of personal achievement, according to Dr. Andrew Souerwine of the University of Hartford, Director of the program.[9]

AT&T puts more stress on the work environment than the 3M and Travelers approaches. One program for high-potential employees involves first completing the company's regular *assessment center*. Based on the results of the assessment center, the employee, the boss, and a corporate staff person draw up a career plan, which includes: a target job, training needed, interim assignments, and a time frame. This plan is reviewed by all three parties every 3 months.

Other career programs also utilize assessment center data for input and are based on the following principles:[10]

1. Emphasize the development of high-potential people only. Do not try to change people who lack management potential.

2. Set specific developmental objectives. Identify specific job experiences and specific skills the person needs to acquire (e.g., supervise a central office PBX group).

3. Train the supervisor to provide day-to-day job experiences (e.g., job challenge, performance appraisal) which promote development.

4. Structure and monitor a *process* of career planning and development, but allow the supervisor and the employee to provide the *content*. Thus, a personnel staff member responsible for the program often plays a third-party, nondominant role in the process.

## CONSIDERATIONS IN IMPLEMENTATION

Organizations interested in sponsoring career planning need to be aware of several considerations:

1. Travelers Insurance, despite generally favorable results, found that some employees attending decided to leave the organization.

2. Out-of-pocket costs are determined largely by the number of employees participating, since the primary cost is usually the wages of the participants.

3. There is presently an almost total lack of empirical research on the effectiveness of career planning, save for a number of case studies reporting positive results in the sponsoring organizations.

4. Management must be willing to follow through and integrate the career planning program with other related activities. In order to assure that career planning does not become just another isolated program advocated by the personnel department, management should at the very least *(a)* provide training in coaching skills for managers and supervisors and systematically reward those who encourage employees to pursue their career goals; *(b)* revise work force planning and performance appraisal systems to provide meaningful opportunities for employees to pursue and achieve their career goals; and *(c)* provide for periodic refresher activities at 2 or 3 year intervals to assure that employees reassess and revise their objectives. Ideally, the program should also be tailored to the unique concerns of employees at different stages of their careers. New management trainees and older managers approaching retirement will have different interests and priorities.

5. A job-posting system may be appropriate to ensure that employees know when opportunities to achieve their career goals are available. The career planning process tends to raise employees' aspirations, and if opportunities to fulfill these aspirations are not available in the organization, they may look elsewhere.

Career planning as a means of developing a more involved and committed work force appears to be a powerful tool. It should only be undertaken by a management willing to assume the added risks when employees begin to seek greater opportunities to take initiative and responsibility and desire greater opportunities for achievement and personal growth in their work.

See also APPRAISAL, PERFORMANCE; ASSESSMENT CENTER METHOD; CONTINUING EDUCATION UNIT (CEU); COUNSELING, EMPLOYEE; DEVELOPMENT AND TRAINING, MANAGEMENT; DEVELOPMENT AND TRAINING, UNIVERSITY EXECUTIVE PROGRAMS; HEALTH, EXECUTIVE, MANAGING STRESS AND JOB TENSION; HEALTH, MENTAL; LEADERSHIP; PROGRAMMED INSTRUCTION.

## NOTES

[1]D. T. Hall, *Careers in Organizations*, Goodyear, Santa Monica, Calif., 1976, p. 4.

[2]Ibid., p. 75.

[3]D. T. Hall and F. S. Hall, "What's New in Career Management," *Organizational Dynamics*, vol. 5, pp. 17–33.

[4]A. Roe and R. Baruch, "Occupational Changes in the Adult Years," *Personnel Administration*, vol. 4, pp. 212–217, 1957.

[5]J. O. Crites, *Theory and Research Handbook, Career Maturity Inventory*, McGraw-Hill Book Company, New York, 1973.

[6]C. Argyris, *Integrating the Individual and the Organization*, John Wiley & Sons, Inc., New York, 1964.

[7]A. Blumberg and R. T. Golembiewski, "Laboratory Goal Attainment and the Problem Analysis Questionnaire," *Journal of Applied Behavioral Science*, vol. 5, pp. 597–600, 1969.

[8]Hall, op. cit., pp. 165–166.

[9]Hall, op. cit., pp. 167–169.

[10]Hall, op. cit., p. 167.

## REFERENCES

Haldane, Bernard: *Career Satisfaction and Success: A Guide to Job Freedom*, American Management Association, New York, 1974.

Pearse, Robert F., and B. Purdy Pelzer: *Self-Directed Change for the Mid-Career Manager*, American Management Association, New York, 1975.

DONALD D. BOWEN, *University of Tulsa*
DOUGLAS T. HALL, *Northwestern University*

# Development and training, employee

The solution to the productivity problem facing western economy in the decade ahead lies in two areas—technological advances and a better work force. Improved productivity from the labor force itself will occur from either better-trained workers or better-motivated workers. This entry addresses the question of how employees can be better trained so as to increase their potential for greater productivity.

*Employee training programs* are designed to provide the knowledge, attitude, or job skills that will help employees perform their present jobs. Training has immediate practical application on the job.

*Employee development programs* are designed to assist employees in preparing themselves for future responsibilities of a different nature, or a higher degree of proficiency in their present jobs. Whereas training has an early and often visible payoff, development is future-oriented. Consequently, development programs represent an investment, with the attendant risks of uncertain returns.

*Basic guidelines* governing the area of employee training and development have been distilled below from experience and research. These are presented in prescriptive form as principles, followed by brief explanations and illustrations. Four topical areas encompass the field of training: (1) needs analysis, (2) learning principles, (3) training techniques, and (4) evaluation of effectiveness.

### NEEDS ANALYSIS

*All training should be justified on the basis of a prior needs analysis.* This is true of both new and existing programs. The reason is obvious: too often organizational training programs have been created and perpetuated for the wrong reasons. Examples of poor justification include: because a supervisor asked for it, because there were resources available that we wanted to use, because our competitor initiated a program like this first, or (worst of all) because we thought there was a need for it.

A good needs analysis provides data relevant to five issues. It identifies the trainee group (or individual), the type of change desired, the topical area (content) of the training, the degree of improvement desired, and the overall priority placed upon this particular program.

**Knowledge, Attitudes, and Skills** It is important to clarify here the difference between (and interrelatedness of) the three types of change. *Knowledge* includes the fundamental information needed to understand the job adequately. It describes what is to be done, under what conditions, with which resources, and with whom. It is the acquisition of technical facts prerequisite to effective job performance.

*Attitudes* are predispositions of employees to view their jobs and work environment either favorably or unfavorably. A positive frame of reference is an important prerequisite to using job knowledge effectively. Common examples include employee attitudes toward the value of safe work habits, attitudes toward a superior or coworker, and attitudes toward the organization in general.

*Skill* is the capacity to perform a task at an acceptable level of speed and quality. Adequate job knowledge and proper job attitudes are normally viewed as prerequisites to skill development. All three must be considered in a satisfactory needs analysis program.

**Techniques of Needs Analysis** Many techniques of needs analysis have been developed and used successfully. Those described below represent the most practical ones.

*Data Analysis.* This is a technique that uses existing records and requires minimal expertise. The process involves examination of job descriptions for entry-level positions to determine the knowledge, skills, and attitudes required of new employees. This information is then compared with data describing the actual (or probable) qualifications of new employees. The difference between these two levels, if significant, represents a training need from which training programs can be designed.

*Observation.* This is an approach that requires a trained observer. This person, either a line supervisor or a staff specialist in training, physically observes the job behavior of the employee to determine whether upgrade training is necessary and, if so, what kind. A hybrid of observation and data analysis exists when records of an employee's behavior are examined (e.g., productivity, rejects, or absenteeism) and from this secondary information, a training need is inferred.

*Surveys.* These may take at least two forms.

1. *Written questionnaires* may be distributed to employees asking them to identify problems in their jobs, areas in which they wished they had more expertise, or their desires for future advancement. A key assumption is that the employees have an accurate perception of their needs and will report those perceptions honestly.

2. *Structured interviews* are surveys in which a staff specialist explores similar needs-oriented questions with each employee. The questionnaire has the merits of objective data that are recorded for later analysis and are often collected anonymously. Its greatest constraint is the tight structure it often places on the respondent. The interview is more flexible in that it can adapt to emerging information. The results are difficult to record and often subjective in their interpretation, however.

An example of the written questionnaire often used in business and government organizations is the *skills inventory*. This may take the form of a checklist for employees to indicate the skills in which they have various degrees of proficiency. As an illustration, a clerk-typist may designate skill with a manual typewriter and 10-key adding machine, familiarity with an electric typewriter and electronic calculator, and no knowledge of how to operate a mimeograph machine. The data from this self-record of skills may then be used to assess training needs.

## LEARNING PRINCIPLES

*Training programs should incorporate as many fundamental principles of learning as are relevant.* Extensive research, both in experimental settings and in organizations, has validated the utility of several basic principles of learning. Each of these, when understood and carefully applied, will increase the effectiveness of a given training program. Learning will generally tend to be facilitated when:

1. *Multiple senses are stimulated.* The most probable ones are sight, sound, and touch, with smell and taste used far less often. It is for this reason that visual aids become a critical factor in training-program success, for they stimulate the sense of sight during what might otherwise be a boring presentation. Examples of *visual aids* include the chalkboard, overhead transparency projector, felt board, flip chart, and movie projector.

2. *Objectives of training are delineated in advance and are known by both trainer and trainee.* Objectives allow the participants to anticipate what comes next and relate the content and methodology to an overriding purpose.

3. *Trainee desires to learn.* This will occur more readily when the need for training has been made apparent to the employees. They can then better understand how the training program relates to more effective job performance and/or personal satisfaction.

4. *Content of the course is arranged in ascending order of difficulty and logical order.* This allows the trainee to absorb the easy material first and build upon it as the material becomes more complex. It also allows for the existence of natural *plateaus in learning* or times when no new skill development seems to take place.

5. *Trainees receive feedback on their progress.* They need to know how they are doing. That information should be specific, relevant, timely, and accurate. This allows the trainees to organize their thoughts or generate a new burst of enthusiasm for the program.

6. *Trainees are reinforced for appropriate behavior in the training program.* A word of praise or encouragement from the trainer or peers can be highly effective at solidifying the learning that has taken place and stimulating future effort.

7. *Trainees are given adequate time to practice.* Repetition of a new skill facilitates its retention and improvement. The old axiom "practice (tends to) make perfect" captures the essence of this principle.

8. *Trainees are actively involved in the training process.* Techniques that require at least intellectual involvement (e.g., question and answer discussion periods) if not also physical participation (e.g., practice transactions on a simulated bank-teller computer) are far more effective than those that allow passivity by the trainees.

9. *The skill to be learned is challenging, yet within the range of achievement.* The task must be difficult enough to stimulate interest and arouse a competitive spirit, but not so demanding that it is out of reach of the trainee.

10. *The training program is personalized to fit individual needs.* Trainees vary in terms of their background, experience, and capacity to learn. An ideal training program has entry capacity at different skill levels, as well as a flexible pace to accommodate varying speeds of learning.

## TRAINING TECHNIQUES

*Careful analysis of the pros and cons should precede the selection and use of any training technique.* One of the most critical decisions to be made by the trainer concerns the selection of the appropriate training technique. Effective trainers utilize a more rigorous decision process in their selection decisions. One approach is to classify, in advance, the various training techniques according to the degree to which they match a set of relevant criteria.[1] These criteria might include, but not be limited to, the following:

1. Whether the technique is oriented toward knowledge, attitudes, or skills.

2. Whether the technique is generally applied on the job or off the job.

3. The degree to which the technique incorporates the major principles of learning.

4. The relative expense involved in development and administration of the program.

5. The flexibility inherent in the technique in terms of the size of training group that can be simultaneously accommodated.

6. The unique trainer skills required.

7. The extent to which specialized equipment or facilities are necessary (and available).

8. The degree to which the technique lends itself to evaluation by some of the more sophisticated criteria of effectiveness (as outlined later).

9. The time duration over which the training technique usually extends.

Several of the more common employee training techniques are briefly described below and evaluated by application of the above criteria.

**Off-the-Job Techniques**   The trainee is typically not producing a product or service while engaged in these forms of training.

*Orientation Training.* Objectives of this technique vary from firm to firm but typically include an attempt to develop a positive attitude toward the firm (loyalty). The length of formal orientation programs ranges from less than 1 to several days' duration. Orientation usually precedes the beginning of any productive work experience. Its content includes such diverse topics as the history of the organization, company policies and procedures, employee benefits, career paths available, a tour of organizational facilities, a review of resources (counseling, cafeteria, recreational programs), and major organizational philosophies and programs (e.g., the use of transactional analysis at American Airlines.)

Two major issues pervade the design of orientation programs. One is the question of how much material should be included and in what form (written, verbal, or visual). The answer to this question depends heavily on the trainer's assessment of how much content will likely be retained (if that is the objective) or how much "selling" must be done to develop a positive attitude. Experience suggests that short, rather than long, orientation programs are better received by most employees, who are probably anxious to begin work and demonstrate their usefulness to the organization. Later (perhaps after 2 weeks) they can be scheduled for a second session, at which time the more extraneous material can be presented and their questions can be answered.

The other major issue concerns the ease of evaluating the effectiveness of orientation programs. If the objective is to communicate content-oriented materials, then it is possible to test the new employees on their retention at the end of the training seminar (or later). Alternatively, if the objective is to reduce future employee turnover by developing more loyal employees, then not only will the evaluation be delayed substantially, but so many other factors intervene as to make objective evaluation almost worthless.

*Vestibule Training.* Used almost exclusively for skill development, vestibule programs involve setting up realistic production-like equipment and materials away from the actual workplace. It reproduces the workplace tasks in an environment conducive to close observation and individualized instruction. Many of the learning principles are incorporated (participation, practice, feedback), and the assessment of skills developed is readily observable or measurable. The time required is typically flexible, depending on the learner's pace of development and the job's complexity. The costs of development and operation may both be high, however, and prohibitive for the small firm. Vestibule training is most appropriate for those positions requiring use of mechanical equipment, ranging from the use of punch-press machines to key-punch machines.

*Films.* Films are often used to demonstrate appropriate supervisory behaviors, to communicate the essential elements of a procedure, or even to convince the viewers to change their perspective on a given issue. Purchased commercially, films typically cost $400 to $500, or rent for approximately 10 percent of that amount. They have frequently been misused organizationally, as fillers or as entertainment rather than for true learning purposes. A projector, screen, and suitable room are required, as is a trainer who has, at a minimum, previewed the film, prepared introductory comments, and developed a thoughtful plan for stimulating focused discussion subsequent to the showing. A critique of films by learning theorists shows them to be among the poorer techniques for incorporating learning concepts.[2]

*Videotape.* A technique closely aligned with films is the use of videotape equipment, available in either black and white or color playback, with sound. This equipment is typically used to provide feedback to trainees on their actual behavior; therefore, it is more clearly skill-oriented. Costs can range up to several thousand dollars of initial investment, but the operating costs are relatively low and the uses limited only by the trainer's imagination. Several learning concepts are directly incorporated, such as participation, feedback, and reinforcement. A dysfunction is that the technique is most effective when applied to each individual trainee (as in the development of personal selling skills) and less effective as simply a group demonstration device. An outstanding example of the use of videotape is by the Armour-Dial Management Institute, which uses this technique in a vestibule setting to conduct its weeklong Professional Salesman Workshops.[3]

*Lecture.* The lecture is singularly useful for transmitting knowledge and impractical for attitude change or skill development. It is widely used, economical to develop, flexible in application both with regard to time required and group size, and its effectiveness can be readily assessed by objective tests of knowledge. It incorporates very little of good learning theory, and perhaps is most blatant in its violation of the concept of trainee involvement. Although no special facilities other than an auditorium or classroom are required, the importance of platform presentation skills are often underestimated, thereby depreciating the value of the technique in practice.

*Programmed Instruction.* This technique (PI) has acquired increasing popularity. Oriented primarily toward knowledge acquisition, PI most clearly (of all techniques discussed) incorporates the major principles of learning. Its highlights are self-pacing, individualized entry at the appropriate background level, immediate feedback, correction and reinforcement, active involvement of the trainee, and arrangement of the material in ascending order of complexity. The essence of the PI technique is the systematic presentation of small units of material (one or more sentences) coupled with the requirement of an overt response (fill in the blank or choose one of several alternative answers) from the trainee. After self-checking the response, the individual is directed on to the next material. Mastery at one level, then, is a prerequisite to further learning.

Programmed instruction requires minimal trainer supervision, but it is time-consuming to properly prepare materials. PI texts can be used with almost any size group. A PI program is inexpensive to administer, although relatively costly to develop. Its effectiveness, particularly in reducing the total time required for learning, has been well documented. Honeywell Information Systems, for example, incorporated programmed instruction texts into their courses in basic COBOL computer programming— and reduced their training costs for 40,000 students by 25 percent per year.[4] Many observers feel that the uses of PI have not yet been fully explored and will expand rapidly in the years ahead.

*Correspondence.* This method involves the receipt of input (texts, manuals, instructional guides) by mail and requires the student to absorb the material and usually submit a completed examination before receiving the subsequent phases of the material. The objectives are typically twofold: (1) acquisition of knowledge and (2) development of basic skills. Frequently a certain amount of technical equipment (e.g., electronic test devices) will be included as part of the package so that the trainee can practice the skill while at home. Training costs are fixed (the cost of the course is known in advance), supervision required is minimal or absent, and any number of trainees can be simultaneously handled. Trainee participation, self-pacing, and feedback are typically incorporated. The most serious weakness is probably the difficulty (time lag) in obtaining answers to student questions. In other words, the student can become extremely frustrated at the lack of on-the-spot supportive feedback and redirection when needed. Effective correspondence courses are often expensive to develop (especially for small groups of employees or in specialized areas), and, therefore, many organizations rely on commercial programs or those offered by colleges and universities or by trade schools.

**On-the-Job Techniques** These techniques are defined as those that allow the worker to produce a product or provide a service simultaneously as the training takes place. This "learn as you earn" approach has great appeal to organizations and trainees alike, from the dual perspectives of cost effectiveness and motivation of the student (feeling of contribution). In general, total training time using on-the-job techniques is quite extended. Also, the usual orientation of the programs is toward skill development, in sharp contrast to several off-the-job approaches.

*Apprenticeship.* As typically practiced, apprenticeship programs combine the features of on-the-job and off-the-job techniques. New workers joining the organization (and entering the craft, trade, or occupation for the first time) are provided with a balance of the theoretical and practical through both instruction and experience. Persons in sales, clerical, managerial, or professional occupations would normally not participate in apprenticeship programs. Examples of apprenticeship programs of 1 to 5 years' duration abound in careers such as mechanics, hairdressing, drafting, plumbing, and printing.[5]

The administrative cost of apprenticeship programs is a function of several factors, but primarily the length of the program, the proportion of class-room hours to work hours, the number of individuals enrolled, and the expected level of productivity of the trainees while they are working. The training staff includes trained workers in the occupation who supervise the trainees while they work. This can be a strength or weakness of the program, depending upon the technical knowledge and ability of these trained workers to effectively develop subordinate workers. Little, if any, specialized training equipment is needed. The learning principles highlighted are participation, logical progression from step to step, feedback, the use of multiple senses, and adequate practice time.

*Job Instruction.* This method (JIT) of training trainers to train workers has been used for over three decades. Appropriate for both white- and blue-collar workers, the prerequisites to JIT are evaluation of the trainees prior to instruction, thorough job analysis to determine the important components, and a detailed schedule of instruction.

There are four major steps in JIT: (1) The trainer explains the task thoroughly. (2) The trainer demonstrates the performance of the skill. (3) The trainee is asked to explain the steps involved. (4) The trainee is asked to perform the operation. Steps 3 and 4 may be repeated as many times as necessary until the frequency of mistakes reaches a satisfactory level.

The costs of JIT can be substantial in terms of both the analysis required, and the high ratio of trainers to trainees in the early phases. Time usage is quite efficient, however, since the trainer can gauge the progress of the trainee through direct observation. Skill development is the primary objective, although the existence of proper job attitudes (e.g., safety) can also be evaluated. In terms of learning principles, JIT utilizes feedback, correct sequencing of tasks, practice time, communication of learning objectives, and the opportunity for reinforcement of appropriate behavior.

*Job Rotation.* This technique involves the *systematic* movement of an individual from one job to another after sufficient time intervals to allow for basic competency (if not proficiency) in each succeeding job. The jobs may or may not be arranged in ascending order of difficulty or skill requirements. The purpose is to acquaint the employee with the nature of, and interrelationship between, each of several jobs. This can have a motivational effect in terms of developing the trainee's skill in several areas (job enlargement). It also has a beneficial effect on the organization in that it produces backup employees who can be called upon when other employees are ill, are on vacation, are terminated, or when extra workload demands arise.

All three training objectives may be accomplished

through job rotation. Multiple skills are developed, the trainees accumulate knowledge of several jobs, and the trainees' attitudes are expected to improve by virtue of better understanding and variety of jobs. The primary expense factor is the relative inefficiency (low productivity, disruption of work flow, possible safety threat) of the workers as they become acclimated to the new position. Little or no direct expenses are involved, nor is a formal trainer required. In terms of time, some job rotation programs are almost endless; however, the more structured ones typically last 1 to 2 years, with rotation taking place at intervals of 2 weeks to 6 months.

Unless carefully constructed, job rotation programs seldom fit neatly into a format of planned progression from simple to complex. Also, the limited amount of time spent in each position virtually precludes the opportunity to practice newly acquired skills adequately. Objectives of each phase must be carefully delineated to each trainee and reviewed at the conclusion. Although job rotation has the capacity to individualize itself to fit personal needs, it typically disregards trainee backgrounds and preferences, and instead forces each person into each phase in lock-step fashion. On the positive side, the factors of feedback, active participation, and opportunity for reinforcement may be present.

*Coaching.* This method involves the formal pairing of a skilled person with an unskilled trainee, and making the coach responsible for the trainee's skill development. This has the merit of being inexpensive from a direct cost standpoint, and it effectively utilizes the years of experience that older workers may have. It is highly personalized from the standpoint of teacher-student ratio (often 1:1) and requires no special equipment or facilities. It is similar to job rotation in its multiple objectives of skill, knowledge, and attitude development.

Coaching incorporates the use of multiple senses, makes it easier to gauge the trainee's desire to learn (because of the extensive degree of coach-trainee contact), and provides opportunity for feedback, reinforcement, involvement, and practice. Perhaps the single biggest drawback is the difficulty of discovering or developing persons with effective coaching skills who can not only demonstrate but also explain why they work as they do.

## EVALUATION OF TRAINING

*All training programs should be evaluated.* As Kirkpatrick has stated, "All training professionals agree: evaluation should be done."[6] Few persons argue with the desirability of evaluation; they do, however, disagree regarding the method to use, or else

contend that the cost of evaluation exceeds the benefits to be gained.

The reasons for evaluation are clear cut. The trainer and the organization wish to know whether or not the objectives have been achieved (and if not, why not?); the trainer also seeks information on how the program (or trainer) can be improved.

Training can be evaluated at any of three stages: input, throughput, or output. In terms of input, the costs (expense) of training can be assessed, either in comparison with other programs or against a budgeted figure. In terms of throughput, organizations often assess the numbers of trainees processed in a given time period. Far more effective, however, is the evaluation of output, which can be assessed by one of four criteria.[7]

1. *Reaction* measures the emotional response of the trainees to the program. This is done through attitude surveys, typically immediately after the program.

2. *Learning* measures the acquisition of knowledge. This is measured by objective or subjective tests administered to the trainees.

3. *Behavior* measures the change in skills that occurs as a result of training. It is often assessed by direct observation of the trainee or by self-report.

4. *Result* measures the organizational effect of training. This is assessed through direct calculation of costs, sales, profits, etc.

With the exception of reaction (which by definition follows the training) the criteria can be assessed before, during, and after the training program, and again at a follow-up date. The ultimate purpose of evaluation is to demonstrate whether a change occurred in the positive direction—one that is significant, practical, and can reasonably be assumed to have occurred as a direct product of the training program.

*See also* APPRAISAL, PERFORMANCE; ASSESSMENT CENTER METHOD; ATTITUDE SURVEYS; COMMUNICATIONS, EMPLOYEE; CONTINUING EDUCATION UNIT (CEU); DEVELOPMENT AND TRAINING, CAREER PATH PLANNING FOR MANAGERS; DEVELOPMENT AND TRAINING, MANAGEMENT; HUMAN RESOURCES (WORK FORCE) PLANNING; PERSONNEL ADMINISTRATION; PROGRAMMED INSTRUCTION; TESTING, PSYCHOLOGICAL.

### NOTES

[1]John W. Newstrom, "Selecting Training Methods: A Contingency Approach," *Training and Development Journal*, October 1975, pp. 12–16. See also Chip R. Bell, "Criteria for Selecting Instructional Strategies," *Training and Development Journal*, October 1977, pp. 3–7.

[2]Bernard M. Bass and James A. Vaughan, *Training in Industry: The Management of Learning*, Wadsworth Publishing Company, Inc., Belmont, Calif., 1966, p. 131.

[3]Richard Cooper, "Simulated Supermarket," *Training*, November 1974, pp. 37–40.

[4]John L. Shahdanian and John J. Walsh, "Self-Instruction Saves," *Training*, January 1975, pp. 38 ff.

[5]*The National Apprenticeship Program*, U.S. Department of Labor: Manpower Administration, 1972, 32 pp.

[6]Donald L. Kirkpatrick, ed., *Evaluating Training Programs*, American Society for Training and Development, Madison, Wis., 1975.

[7]Ibid.

### REFERENCES

Craig, Robert L., ed.: *Training and Development Handbook*, 2d ed., McGraw-Hill Book Company, New York, 1976.

Hammer, Mark: "A Promising Innovation in Pedagogical Technology: The Personalized System of Instruction," *Collegiate News & Views*, Spring 1976.

Tracey, William R.: *Managing Training and Development Systems*, American Management Association, New York, 1974.

JOHN W. NEWSTROM, *University of Minnesota*

# Development and training, management

Management development is the process of gradual, systematic improvement in the knowledge, skills, attitudes—and performance—of those individuals in an organization who carry management responsibilities. Management development is generally acknowledged as essential for improved results as well as the growth of an organization. In principle, it is noncontroversial. It does become controversial, however, as soon as an organization faces up to six fundamental questions that are critical to the implementation of management development programs. These are:

1. Who should be developed?
2. For what purpose?
3. Whose responsibility is it?
4. What should be done?
5. How and where should it be done?
   a. On the job or off the job?
   b. In-house or by sending managers to outside programs?
6. How can management development efforts be evaluated?

**Who Are Managers?**   According to Lawrence Appley, former president of the American Management Association, a manager is one who gets things done through others. For management development purposes, a *manager* may be defined as a person who supervises one or more other people. It would include a staff person who supervises a secretary, but it would not include a district sales manager who manages a district with no one else there. By this definition, then, a first-line supervisor is just as much a manager as the president of the organization.

**For What Purpose?**   Management development is done for two different (but often related) reasons. *First*, and most common and most important, managers are developed to perform their present job as effectively as possible. Their present job may be changing for one reason or another (more complicated, computer involved, etc.), but the basic job is essentially the same. The *second* purpose for management development is to prepare people for higher-level management jobs. These are the special cases. Even though many of the same principles and approaches apply, this entry is devoted to the first purpose—to help managers perform their present job most effectively.

**Whose Responsibility?**   Some organizations suggest that all development is self-development, and the initiative is up to the individual. This view is rarely sufficient for the effective development of managers. It is far better for an organization to adopt a philosophy (and write a policy) that includes three areas of responsibility for management development:

1. Each manager is responsible for his or her own development. This means that some effort, time, energy, and possibly money should be spent by each manager for self-development.

2. Each manager is responsible for the training and development of subordinates. This means that middle-level managers have a responsibility for the development of lower-level managers (first-line supervisors), and top executives have a responsibility for the development of middle-level managers. This responsibility can be discharged informally through coaching or formally through such programs as performance review and management by objectives.

3. The organization itself has a responsibility for the training and development of its managers. This means that the organization must provide time, money, and other resources to help the development take place. Examples of such help are tuition refund plans for attendance at evening classes, hiring outside consultants to conduct in-house training courses, sending people to outside seminars and workshops, and hiring a full- or part-time training and development staff to plan, coordinate, and teach in-house management development courses. Also, a library of management books should be maintained.

**What Should Be Done?**   Management development programs and activities should be planned and developed to meet the needs of each organization.

Many different approaches can be used to determine the needs. Each organization should use those approaches that are practical and effective.

1. *Universal needs.* Most organizations can safely assume that their managers can stand improvement in such areas as planning, communications, motivations, and decision making.

2. *Ask the managers themselves.* Interviews and surveys can be used to find out the needs that managers feel they have. If this is done well, valuable quantitative data about these felt needs can be obtained.

3. *Ask the bosses.* Interviews and surveys can also be made of the bosses of those managers to be trained. They may or may not agree with the managers themselves. There is no guarantee which of them will be right. If there is agreement, this is a good indication that the need does exist. If there is a difference of opinion, someone must make the decision. If the managers who are being trained do not feel the need, then special efforts should be made to sell them on the value of such training.

4. *Ask the subordinates.* Probably the best source of information about the training needs of managers is their subordinates. Managers, understandably, are not usually enthusiastic and are easily alienated by this approach. Therefore, confidential attitude surveys made by outside organizations on an indirect basis may be effective. Results of attitude surveys, however, must be interpreted to indicate management training needs. Exit interviews of people who are leaving an organization may also be helpful.

5. *Analyze the manager's job.* Some organizations (EXXON for example) carefully analyze the job functions and responsibilities of each manager to determine the knowledges, skills, and attitudes necessary to do the job. Training needs are then determined on the basis of specific performance requirements. Where indicated, performance deficiencies can be converted to training needs.

6. *Use an advisory committee.* One of the most effective ways of determining needs is to use an internal advisory committee representing different departments and levels in an organization. These people can provide input from a number of different points of view. In using an advisory committee, the person who makes the final decision on needs (usually the training professional) should first provide the committee with ample quantitative data to consider in making their recommendations.

7. *Use performance appraisal information.* If an organization has an effective performance review procedure, information from appraisal forms can provide valuable indicators. The needs of each manager can be identified and tabulated to determine group training needs.

8. *Analyze problems and records.* An analysis of problems and records can provide some valuable clues regarding training needs. Examples include too much scrap, too much turnover, costs over budget, lack of productivity, and too many accidents.

## DEVELOPMENT PROGRAMS

The question of on-the-job versus off-the-job training has been debated widely in the training and development profession. In almost all cases, the same conclusion is reached: Both are necessary.

**On-the-Job Development** One thing is sure: On-the-job training is taking place all the time. Lower-level managers are learning from middle-level managers, and middle-level managers are learning from higher-level managers. The question is, how *effective* is this training? The answer, of course, is that it varies from excellent to poor. Some managers do an excellent job of developing their subordinates. Others do a poor job—either by setting a poor example or by teaching and coaching the wrong things, or the right things improperly. Many of the reasons for poor on-the-job development can be attributed to the manager's immediate supervisor. For example,

Bosses who do not want to develop subordinates. Often, they are afraid the subordinate will become too good and will outperform (and perhaps be promoted over) the present supervisor.

Bosses who do not feel that development is important. They believe only in self-development and thereby leave the subordinate alone.

Bosses who do not get around to do it. They are too busy with seemingly more important functions, such as report writing, decision making, attending or conducting meetings, planning, putting out fires, and keeping on top of everything.

Bosses who do not know how to develop subordinates effectively. They are willing but not able.

Analysis of these conditions make it obvious that effective on-the-job training requires

1. Bosses who *want* to develop subordinates.
2. Bosses *who will find the time* to do it.
3. Bosses who *know how* to do it.

*Performance-Oriented Development.* Two currently popular approaches include both a philosophy and a set of procedures for effective on-the-job development. They are closely related and sometimes used or interpreted almost interchangeably. They are called *management by objectives* and *performance standards, appraisal and review.* In either case, a similar approach is followed:

STEP 1: Agreement is reached in advance between the manager and the superior of what the manager is expected to accomplish. It may also include what to do to accomplish these objectives, goals, or standards.

STEP 2: After a designated period of time, a comparison is made between the manager's performance and the objectives, goals, or standards that were set in advance.

STEP 3: An analysis is made of areas where standards and objectives were not met. Plans for improved performance are established and agreed on, and the superior coaches the subordinate to help implement these plans.

**Off-the-Job Development** A great variety of options for training and development take the manager away from the job, the office, or the regular workplace. These include:

1. *Job rotation.* Some organizations (AT&T, for example) make extensive use of job rotation as a training and development approach. Managers are moved into responsible positions in other departments where they must learn by doing the new job. Their coaching comes from supervisors, subordinates, and peers.

2. *Reading.* Hundreds of management books and thousands of articles are available which provide information on philosophy, approaches, and procedures that managers might follow to be effective.

3. *Programmed instruction.* Although programmed instruction is used most extensively by nonmanagerial people, there are programmed instruction courses for managers. These are available with or without program learning machines and allow an individual to study and learn at the individual's own pace. The main difference between programmed instruction and reading is that the former has a built in requirement that the individual learn the material before continuing.

4. *Correspondence courses.* This, too, is an individualized approach. The manager selects a course and pursues it by mail—studying the material, completing papers and tests, and receiving grades from the instructor. This approach, like programmed instruction, is seldom used by managers. Many who begin a correspondence course do not finish it.

5. *Professional societies.* Some managers in professional and/or specialized areas like accounting, engineering, data processing, marketing, personnel, and purchasing learn by active participation in the related professional society. Not only do these managers learn from speakers at meetings, but they also learn by exchanging ideas and experiences with other managers in their profession. They may also learn management skills by "doing"—by becoming a local or national officer in the society. There is, of course, one professional society in particular that is devoted exclusively to human resource development. It is the American Society for Training and Development, P.O. Box 5307, Madison, WI 53705.

6. *Evening classes.* Some managers take advantage of evening classes to improve their management knowledge and skills. They select courses that will help them improve their performance on their present job and/or enhance their chances for promotion to higher-level management. This is a demanding approach and requires dedication on the individual's part.

Far more popular than any of the above are in-house courses and outside seminars, both of which are discussed in detail below.

**In-House Courses** For off-the-job training and development of managers there is the in-house training program. The term *in-house* indicates that the program is restricted to managers from the same organization. The instructors may be from inside or outside the organization, and the program may be held on or off the premises of the organization. Programs for lower-level managers generally use in-house facilities if adequate conference rooms are available. Programs for middle and top-level managers are more frequently held off the premises.

Generally, the organization employs full-time training and development professionals who become instructors for in-house programs for lower-level managers. Where the participants are middle- or top-level managers, the instructors are frequently hired from outside the organization.

Scheduling of these programs varies, depending on the availability of the participants as well as the preferences of those who plan the programs. There seems to be no pattern as to the timing or the length of the training and development course. In general, however, in-house courses are held on company time, although some organizations schedule the programs on Saturdays. In some cases managers are paid for attending on their own time, and in other cases they are not.

Effectiveness of these programs depends on a number of factors—listed here in order of importance:

1. Subjects that meet the needs of participants.
2. Leaders who are effective as instructors.
3. Scheduling that fits the participants.
4. Physical facilities that are adequate.

In addition to these four basic requirements, the effectiveness of in-house courses is enhanced by top-management support, a favorable job climate, effective audiovisual aids, and related handouts and other prescribed reading materials.

**Outside Seminars and Conferences**   These outside programs vary from 1 day to as much as 13 weeks. The University of Wisconsin Management Institute, for example, specializes in programs of 1, 2, or 3 days. Northwestern University offers a 4-week course for managers, while Harvard University offers a 13-week management development course.   (*See* DEVELOPMENT AND TRAINING, UNIVERSITY EXECUTIVE PROGRAMS.)

Outside seminars are costly, from an out-of-pocket view, at least. Are the benefits worth the costs? The obvious answer is sometimes yes and sometimes no. In order to be sure that benefits exceed costs, it is important to do the following:

1. Carefully select programs of verifiable quality. Examine the cost of the program, content of the bulletin (the promised benefits and subjects to be covered), and the brochure description relating to the effectiveness of the instructor. Investigate the reputation of the organization offering the program and, if possible, check with people who have previously attended.

2. Carefully select the participants. Most important qualities are (*a*) a desire to attend and (*b*) the subject content that will help improve the manager's performance.

3. Orient the participant beforehand to program details and the opportunities it affords. Also, explain what is expected when the participant returns—such as a written or oral report, discussion with the participant and supervisor, and on-the-job application of what was learned.

4. Discuss the program with the participant after the program is over. This can be done by the individual's supervisor and/or the training professional to determine the value of the course and to encourage on-the-job application.

5. Provide encouragement and help in getting the participant to apply the practical ideas that were learned.

6. Use the feedback from the participant to decide whether to send other participants to the same program or other programs offered by the same organization.

## EVALUATING MANAGEMENT DEVELOPMENT

Evaluation of on-the-job development is difficult to accomplish, but every effort should be made to do so. For example, a main objective of most performance appraisal programs is to improve the performance of those being appraised. If the program is properly planned and implemented, evidence should be sought to document improved performance. Likewise, a management by objectives program should be studied rigorously to determine whether the time and money spent is paying off in improved performance and results.

Four possible ways to evaluate management development programs, especially in-house classroom training, are listed here.

**Reaction**   How do the participants feel about the program? Are they satisfied customers who feel that their time and effort was well spent? Those managers who have participated are in a good position to judge to what extent they have been helped. Use the following guidelines to evaluate their reaction:

1. Determine what you want them to react to. (For example, subject, leader, facilities, schedule, meals, etc.)

2. Use a written comment sheet including factors determined in item 1 above.

3. Get quantitative reactions that can be tabulated and quantified. Ask participants to check boxes such as, ☐ Excellent ☐ Very good ☐ Good ☐ Fair ☐ Poor instead of asking open-ended questions such as, "How did you like the leader?"

4. Encourage written comments to explain and amplify the boxes that were checked. A simple but effective question is, "What suggestions do you have for improvement?"

5. Seek honest reactions. This usually requires that the forms be anonymous because many participants are fearful of giving frank and critical reactions if they can be identified.

**Learning**   To what extent did the participants learn the facts, principles, and skills that were taught? Use the following guidelines to evaluate learning:

1. The learning of each participant should be measured.

2. The learning should be measured *objectively* (i.e., compare what participants knew after the course with what they knew before). Use such techniques as a pretest and posttest. Sometimes a standardized test such as Kirkpatrick's *Supervisory Inventories* on "Human Relations," "Communications," or "Safety" can be used. If standardized tests are not related to the subject content of the course, a pretest and posttest must be developed. If skills, such as oral communications or interviewing are being taught, actual performance tests must be used on a before and after basis.

**Behavior**   To what extent did the job behavior of the participant change because of the course? This area is more difficult to evaluate because so many factors cause changes in behavior. Use the following guidelines to evaluate behavior:

1. The before and after behavior of the *participants* should be measured. This is preferred to an approach that only measures behavior *after* the program and determines how your present behavior differs from what you were doing before you attended the program.

2. The before and after behavior of a *control group* (those not attending the training program) should also be measured. These results should be compared with the participant (experimental) group in order to identify, and then eliminate, behavior changes that came from sources other than the training program.

**Results**   What final results were achieved because of the training course? This is the most significant and most difficult type of evaluation. It implies an evaluation on a cost versus benefit basis, where benefits include such desired results as reduced costs of operations, improved productivity, improved quality, reduction of accidents, reduction of absenteeism, reduction of turnover, improved sales, increase in profits, and improved return on investments.

Desired results such as these are affected by so many different factors that it is difficult, if not impossible, to relate the training course directly to the improved results. Efforts should constantly be made to do so, however, and the following guidelines may prove helpful:

1. Desired results should be established before the training program is presented.

2. Before and after measurements should be made and compared.

3. The before and after results of a control group should be made and compared with the experimental group.

## SELECTING AND TRAINING FUTURE MANAGERS

Selection of managers is, of course, the foundation upon which future development is based. It is evident, too, that many current managers should not be managers at all. Many were selected because of one or more of the following qualifications: a good performer as a doer (production worker, salesworker, engineer, accountant, researcher, etc.); seniority within the organization; and cooperation with higher management—i.e., doing what the boss

asks without asking why or suggesting a better way. Many organizations, accordingly, are faced with the impossible task of trying to develop unsuitable people into efficient managers.

The solution to this common problem lies in preventing the same thing from happening in the future. In other words, an organization should carefully select its future managers on the basis of more and better criteria than past performance, seniority, and cooperation. It should look for generally accepted indicators of management potential. These qualification criteria could include such identifiable qualities as a desire to be a manager, communications skills, intelligence, desire to work with people, emotional stability, and demonstrable leadership effectiveness. Each organization should first determine the qualities its managers need to be successful. Then it should develop a selection process for identifying the qualities and potential of candidates for managerial jobs.

More and more organizations are using the assessment center approach to determine qualifications for various levels of management. This approach utilizes interviews, stress situations, decision-making exercises, tests, and other techniques for measuring management potential. (*See* ASSESSMENT CENTER METHOD.)

Once a candidate has been screened and selected for promotion from doer to manager, at least some minimal management training should be provided before the candidate takes over the job. This can be accomplished by working along with a present manager (as at General Motors Corporation), or those selected can be given classroom training while they are still hourly workers. A combination of both approaches is better than either one.

*See also* APPRAISAL, PERFORMANCE; ASSESSMENT CENTER METHOD; DEVELOPMENT AND TRAINING, CAREER PATH PLANNING FOR MANAGERS; DEVELOPMENT AND TRAINING, UNIVERSITY EXECUTIVE PROGRAMS; HUMAN RESOURCES (WORK FORCE) PLANNING; LEADERSHIP; OBJECTIVES, MANAGEMENT BY (MBO); ORGANIZATION DEVELOPMENT (OD); PROFESSIONALISM IN MANAGEMENT; SEARCH AND RECRUITMENT, EXECUTIVE; SUPERVISORY MANAGEMENT; TESTING, PSYCHOLOGICAL.

### REFERENCES

Allhiser, Norman: *Self-Development for Supervisors and Managers,* The University of Wisconsin Press, Madison, 1971.

Batten, J. D.: *Beyond Management By Objectives,* American Management Association, New York, 1966.

Bennett, Willard E.: *Manager Selection, Education and Training,* McGraw-Hill Book Company, New York, 1951.

Craig, Robert L.: *Training and Development Handbook*, 2d ed., McGraw-Hill Book Company, New York, 1976.

Cummings, L. L., and Donald P. Schwab: *Performance in Organizations: Determinants and Appraisal*, Scott, Foresman and Company, Glenview, Ill., 1973.

Davis, Larry: *Planning, Conducting and Evaluating Workshops*, Learning Concepts, Inc., Austin, Tex., 1975.

Desatnick, Robert L.: *A Concise Guide to Management Development*, American Management Association, New York, 1970.

Goldstein, Irwin I.: *Training: Program Development and Evaluation*, Brooks/Cole Publishing Company, Belmont, Calif., 1974.

Hendershot, Carl H.: *Programed Learning*, 4th ed., Carl H. Hendershot, Bay City, Mich., 1967.

House, Robert J.: *Management Development: Design, Evaluation, and Implementation*, The University of Michigan Press, Ann Arbor, 1967.

Humble, John: *Improving Business Results*, McGraw-Hill Book Company, New York, 1968.

Kellogg, Marion S.: *What to Do About Performance Appraisal*, American Management Association, New York, 1965.

Kirkpatrick, Donald: *Evaluating Training Programs*, American Society for Training and Development, Madison, Wis.. 1976.

Kirkpatrick, Donald: *How to Plan and Conduct Productive Business Meetings*, The Dartnell Corporation, Chicago, 1976.

Kirkpatrick, Donald: *Obtaining Maximum Benefit from Outside Management Development Programs*, The University of Wisconsin Press, Madison, 1968.

Kirkpatrick, Donald: *A Practical Guide for Supervisory Training and Development*, Addison-Wesley Publishing Company, Inc., Reading, Mass., 1971.

Kirkpatrick, Donald: *Selecting and Training Potential Foremen and Supervisors* (Case studies of Bendix and Inland Steel), The University of Wisconsin Press, Madison, 1967.

Koontz, Harold: *Appraising Managers as Managers*, McGraw-Hill Book Company, New York, 1971.

Mager, R. F., and Peter Pipe: *Analyzing Performance Problems*, Fearon Publishers, Inc., Palo Alto, Calif., 1970.

Maier, Norman, Allen Solem, and Ayesha Maier: *Supervisory and Executive Development: A Manual for Role Playing*, John Wiley & Sons, Inc., New York, 1957.

McConkey, Dale D.: *How to Manage By Results*, American Management Association, New York, 1965.

McConkey, Dale D.: *No-Nonsense Delegation*, American Management Association, New York, 1974.

Morrisey, George: *Management By Objectives and Results*, Addison-Wesley Publishing Company, Inc., Reading, Mass., 1970.

Odiorne, George S.: *Management By Ojbectives*, Pitman Publishing Corporation, New York, 1965.

Pfeiffer, J. William, and John E. Jones: *A Handbook of Structured Experiences for Human Relations Training*, vol. 2, University Associates Press, La Jolla, Calif., 1972.

Raia, Anthony: *Managing By Objectives*, Scott, Foresman and Company, Glenview, Ill., 1974.

Rowland, Virgil K.: *Evaluating and Improving Managerial Performance*, McGraw-Hill Book Company, New York, 1970.

Schleh, Edward C.: *Management By Results*, McGraw-Hill Book Company, New York 1961.

Sperry, Len, and Lee R. Hess: *Contact Counseling*, Addison-Wesley Publishing Company, Inc., Reading, Mass., 1974.

Universal Training Systems Co.: *Successful In-Company Training Programs*, The Dartnell Corporation, Chicago, 1974.

Varney, Glenn: *Management By Objectives*, The Dartnell Corporation, Chicago, 1971.

Wikstrom, Walter: *Managing By-and With-Objectives*, National Industrial Conference Board, Inc., New York, 1970.

Wright, Moorhead: *How Do People Grow in a Business Organization*, Industrial Relations Division, National Association of Manufacturers, New York.

Zelko, H. P.: *Successful Conference and Discussion Techniques*, McGraw-Hill Book Company, New York, 1957.

DONALD L. KIRKPATRICK, *University of Wisconsin—Extension, Milwaukee*

# Development and training, university executive programs

University executive management programs are residential nondegree programs at least 2 weeks in length, dealing with various aspects of general business management, and conducted under the auspices of a department of a university, usually its school of business.

## HISTORICAL PERSPECTIVE

The need for teaching management to executives already engaged in some phase of business management was recognized 50 years ago by Erwin Schell at M.I.T. With the help and support of Alfred P. Sloan, an experimental 1-year course for young executives of high potential was started in 1931. By 1938 the course had become the present Sloan Fellowship Program.

At the close of World War II, the United States Office of Education asked the Harvard Business School to set up the so-called "War Production Retraining Course" for executives returning from war service. This course operated for seven sessions in 1943, 1944, and the spring of 1945 under the auspices of the government. In the fall of that year full responsibility for the course was assumed by Harvard, and it became the Harvard Advanced Management Program, generally conceded to be the start of the university executive management program movement.

Success of the Harvard program, which accepted 160 participants from the beginning and operated twice a year, caused many business schools and others to take a look at this phenomenon. One year later the National Association of Credit Management started a management program for executives in the credit and financial functions of both industry and banking. This was a split program of 2 weeks a year over 3 years, held at Dartmouth, and taught by business school professors, primarily from the Amos Tuck School of Business. Two years later, in 1948, the University of Western Ontario started its Management Training Course, using the faculty of the Harvard Business School in its early years. In 1949 the University of Pittsburgh joined the parade, and from then on to the mid 1950s the number of executive management programs, most frequently called *executive development programs*, grew rapidly in North America. During the 1950s a relatively small number of programs fell by the wayside, but most of those started in that period and since are still in existence.

By the end of the 1950s there were 47 such residential programs in North America of 2 to 4 weeks in length, some of which were split programs scheduled by single weeks or weekends during 1 year, or by 2 or 3 weeks each year for two or three summers. By 1976 there were 48 programs in the United States, 8 in Canada, 10 in Continental Europe, 24 in the United Kingdom, 2 in Scandinavia, 4 in Australia, and 1 in South America, many held more than one session a year, and all were conducted in the English language.

## DESCRIPTION OF PROGRAMS

Executive management programs differ in many ways—not only in subject matter but also in length, number of participants, methods of instruction, size of class, type of living accommodations, and cost. Although the basic purpose of all executive management programs is to broaden the horizons of the participants and to build an appreciation of the inherent interaction between various functions of a business and the inevitable effect of internal and external environments, the methods by which these objectives are accomplished vary in considerable degree. At one end of the scale, some programs concern themselves primarily with certain aspects of the external environment as it affects the day-to-day operations and long-range strategy of business. At the other extreme, some programs deal primarily

with various techniques of functional management, such as decision making, operations management, marketing management, and financial control. In between, there is an infinite combination of approaches to the strategic and practical problems of business management.

Executive management programs are neither the equivalent of nor a substitute for an MBA degree. With one or two exceptions, they deal primarily with the problems of establishing business policy or strategy (depending on the level of management to which the particular program is addressed) and the implementation of those policies and strategies by means of various techniques which are currently available, such as quantitative approaches, use of the computer, and recognition of the part played by interpersonal reactions among executives.

Three of the longer programs follow the format of their own school's MBA programs, but the material used is more advanced and appropriate to the business experience of the participants.

**Length of Programs**   In North America, length varies from 13 or 14 weeks at Harvard to as little as 2 weeks at a dozen different programs in other parts of the continent. This range does not include the 1-year Sloan program at M.I.T. or the 9-month Sloan program at Stanford. (There is also a 9-month Sloan program at the London Business School, started in 1972.) Generally speaking, the longer programs tend to limit participation to the higher levels of management, while the shortest programs tend to be geared to the lower levels of management. This is not universally true, and the participants in several 4- and 6-week programs, including Columbia, Northwestern, and Southern California, are of managerial levels comparable with those of the Harvard Advanced Management Program, the Stanford Executive Program, and M.I.T.'s Program for Senior Executives.

**Methods of Instruction**   Methods vary from primarily case method[1] to primarily lecture or seminar discussion. Most programs use business case discussions to at least some extent. Some programs, including the Dartmouth Institute and California's Executive Program at Berkeley, devote most of their time to seminar discussions of various philosophical concepts and environmental dilemmas, such as the limits to growth, and their application to and effect upon the current and developing business situation. About half the programs use some form of computerized simulation or business game. A few use this type of learning experience as a central activity of the program.

Further variations in instructional methods concern the scheduling of instructors. Some programs utilize a relatively limited group of instructors, primarily from the sponsoring institution, who teach in parallel through all or most of the program. In some other programs, a limited number of instructors from a number of institutions each teach one subject in a block of time—2 or 3 days is usual—without overlap. In still other programs, a relatively large number of lecturers from industry, consulting firms, and the academic world treat individual facets of management in one or more class periods. Still other programs use combinations of these three methods. Only a few programs require any written work by the participants, but in most programs there is a heavy reading and study workload in preparation for class discussions.

**Number of Participants** The number in each program in North America ranges from as low as 20 to a maximum of 180 at Stanford. (In Great Britain there are a number of programs which take only 12 participants, and one that takes only six.) Most of the larger programs are divided into two or three sections so that actual class size is no more than 80. Almost all programs use small study groups of four to twelve persons for some class preparation. More than half the North American programs have classes of 35 or less, but nine programs with classes larger than 50 account for 35 percent of total attendance. Of these, five programs which accept over 100 in each session account for more than one-quarter of the annual attendance.

**Living Accommodations** Accommodations vary from strictly functional shared dormitory rooms with down-the-hall bathroom facilities, to oppulent country residence rooms with shared or private baths. The trend over the last 10 years has been definitely toward single rooms with bath, but not all programs are yet in a position to provide such accommodations. Some programs are housed in local hotels or motels within walking distance of the classroom.

**Costs** Costs for executive management programs have been going up along with every other type of service operation. Tuition, including room and board, now ranges from $940 for one 2-week program to $9750 for the 9-week M.I.T. program for senior executives. A better way to compare cost of programs may be the investment per week. On this basis costs range from $392 to $1500, with a median weekly rate of $667. Eighteen years ago this range was $125 to $350, with a median of $225. The Sloan programs are not included in this comparison because, in those programs, the participants almost invariably bring their families and live in local ac-

commodations of their own choosing. Tuition alone in these programs is $11,200 for M.I.T. and $11,450 for Stanford, compared with $2900 and $2000, respecitvely, in 1960.

## SELECTION OF PROGRAM

To get the greatest value out of executive management programs, a company should first define its own broad objectives in sending executives to such programs. Are those objectives merely to provide a general broadening of perspective? Or do they include an expansion of skills in certain broad areas such as financial and accounting control, quantitative methods, decision-making techniques, international business relationships, social responsibilities of business, or even increased awareness of interpersonal relationships?

Selection of individuals to be sent to executive management programs is a matter which should be given careful consideration and should be planned well in advance. Much is to be gained by recognizing high-potential managerial ability as early as it becomes apparent, based on periodic performance appraisals and the observations of superiors in their daily contact with young executives engaged in performing their assigned functions. Planned exposure to several increasingly sophisticated executive management courses over a period of 10 to 15 years is a concept worth considering early in the development of future key personnel.

In choosing programs for selected candidates, consideration should be given first to what the company feels will be helpful to the individual, based on an assessment of the specific development needs of the particular candidate as seen by his or her superiors, in view of the individual's background, managerial experience to date, performance on the present job, requirements for immediate promotion, and requirements for future progress envisioned by the company.

At the same time consideration should be given to development needs as seen by the individual candidate in such areas as specific knowledge, management skills, interpersonal relations, and special types of personal contacts.

After these determinations, and not before, should come selection of those programs which appear to meet the requirements of the candidate, giving due regard to the types of instruction provided, length of time involved, time of year, geographic location, and management level of the participants. Recognition should be given to the fact that continuous programs of 4 weeks or more enable the participant to become more detached from day-to-day business routines, and become more completely involved in the educational experience which he or she is undergoing. On the other hand, split programs offer the advantages of requiring less time away from the job at one time, allowing the participant to put to work some of the principles learned in one session before returning to the next session of the program, and spreading the learning process over a longer period of time.

A comprehensive description of all executive management programs appears in *Bricker's International Directory of University-Sponsored Executive Development Programs*,[2] published annually each December for the year ahead. If the executive responsible for administering the company's executive development program needs help in selecting the programs best suited for certain individuals, advice can be sought from the directors of the programs under consideration and from independent consultants who have knowledge of the various programs available.

## VALUE OF PROGRAMS

There has been, and probably will continue to be, much speculation about the value of executive management programs to the participant's company in terms of demonstrable return on its investment. A number of inconclusive studies have been undertaken to determine this value, the most comprehensive of which was the Andrews study in 1959 to 1960 (published in 1966)[3] based on over 6000 replies to an extensive questionnaire sent to 10,000 graduates of 42 university executive management programs, of which 16 programs were analyzed in depth. The study measured the reactions of individuals to their experiences at the programs they attended and resulted in an overwhelmingly favorable evaluation by the participants. Professor Andrews himself recognized that further research using other methods would undoubtedly be stimulated by his study and would throw more light on many aspects of the impact of executive education upon individual behavior. It was not until 1975, however, that a first attempt was made to measure under controlled conditions the changes brought about in that behavior in terms of subject area knowledge (by before-and-after tests of the individual) and managerial behavior (as observed before and after by all direct subordinates of the individual participant). The results of this study at the University of Houston have not yet been published.

Most senior executives who have been through one or more executive management programs seem to believe that attendance at a carefully chosen executive program will be of constructive value in the participant's future judgments, decisions, and managerial actions. The growth in number of programs and the increasing number of participants attending annually over the last 30 years bears witness to this belief.

*See also* APPRAISAL, PERFORMANCE; ASSESSMENT CENTER METHOD; DEVELOPMENT AND TRAINING, CAREER PATH PLANNING FOR MANAGERS; DEVELOPMENT AND TRAINING, MANAGEMENT.

## NOTES

[1] The case method, a teaching technique pioneered by the Harvard Business School and now widely used in business education, involves presenting participants with a series of actual, sometimes disguised, situations drawn from business, but often also from labor unions and the government. The cases are prepared by professors and their case-writing assistants after careful field research to assure immediacy, reality, and accuracy. They are also carefully developed to illuminate particular problems or to establish a sequence of problems and issues of mounting difficulty for a pattern of cumulative learning. (Extracted from the brochure "Executive Education" of the Harvard Business School.)

[2] George W. Bricker, *Bricker's International Directory of University-Sponsored Executive Development Programs*, annually 1969–, Bricker Publications, South Chatham, Mass.

[3] Kenneth R. Andrews, *The Effectiveness of University Management Development Programs*, Harvard Business School, Division of Research, Boston, 1966.

## REFERENCES

Andrews, Kenneth R.: *The Effectiveness of University Management Development Programs*, Harvard Business School, Division of Research, Boston, 1966.

Bricker, George W.: *Bricker's International Directory of University-Sponsored Executive Development Programs*, Bricker Publications, South Chatham, Mass., annually 1969–.

Crotty, Phillip T.: "Development Programs for Mature Managers," *Business Horizons*, December 1974.

Lee, Sang M., and Charles C. Dean: "University Management Training Programs: An Empirical Evaluation," *Training and Development Journal*, American Society for Training and Development, January 1971.

Livingston, J. Stirling: "Myth of the Well-Educated Manager," *Harvard Business Review*, January–February 1971.

Pearse, Robert F.: *Manager to Manager—What Managers Think of Management Development*, American Management Association, New York, 1974.

Powell, Reed M., and Charles S. Davis: "University Executive Development Programs Pay Off?," *Business Horizons*, 1973.

GEORGE W. BRICKER, *Management Consultant, South Chatham, Massachusetts*

**Development programs, employee** (*See* DEVELOPMENT AND TRAINING, EMPLOYEE.)

**Deviation, standard** (*See* RISK ANALYSIS AND MANAGEMENT.)

**Dewey decimal system** (*See* RECORDS MANAGEMENT.)

**Diagram, bubble** (*See* OFFICE SPACE PLANNING AND DESIGN.)

**Dictation inputs** (*See* WORD PROCESSING.)

**Differentiation, horizontal** (*See* ORGANIZATION STRUCTURES AND CHARTING.)

**Digital computer control** (*See* AUTOMATION.)

**Diminishing marginal utility** (*See* ECONOMIC CONCEPTS.)

**Directors** (*See* BOARDS OF DIRECTORS.)

**Dirty money** (*See* COMPENSATION, EMPLOYEE BENEFIT PLANS.)

**Disability pay** (*See* COMPENSATION, EMPLOYEE BENEFIT PLANS.)

**Disadvantaged employees** (*See* MINORITIES, MANAGEMENT OF AND EQUAL EMPLOYMENT OPPORTUNITY.)

**Disaster control** (*See* INSURANCE AND RISK MANAGEMENT.)

**Discharge** (*See* PERSONNEL ADMINISTRATION.)

# Discipline

*Discipline* (as a formal managerial control device) describes those measures or sanctions used to penalize, and thus control and influence, employee behavior. Typically, these measures include (1) suspension (such as time off without pay); (2) discharge; (3) assignment of unpleasant or undesirable tasks; (4) withholding of promotion or advancement; or (5) direct or indirect criticism (warnings and reprimands), either orally or in writing.

The basic purpose of discipline is to regulate employee behavior so as to direct it toward the best interests of the organization and its objectives. The mechanisms for discipline stem from the organization's policies and programs (as well as those imposed upon the organization by outside influences such as the government, customers, or suppliers) and usually takes the form of regulations and rules.

*Regulations* prescribe the way in which activities, functions, duties, and tasks should be carried out in conformance with operating procedures. They are best when they are positive in language and intent. *Rules* tend to be more restrictive and are thus more likely to be negative in concept and expression. Rules cover a wide range of subjects, including attendance, theft, drinking and drugs, gambling, and safety.

Excessive discipline destroys motivation and invites resistance and defiance, either open or covert. Laxity in discipline tends to erode an organization's unity and purpose. Over the short term, strict discipline may succeed with some leaders in some situations. Over the long haul, however, a more reasonable, participative approach is likely to be more effective.

*Disciplinary Failures.* Attempts by management to discipline employees are increasingly subject to review, either internally by labor unions or externally by various federal agencies, especially those concerned with equal employment opportunities and its ramifications. Failure to sustain disciplinary decisions are often attributable to the following:

1. *Absence of clear-cut breach of a rule.* Rules must be specific and their infractions demonstrable.

2. *Inadequate warning.* Rules and regulations should be published in writing and be made part of routine employee orientation and training.

3. *Lack of positive evidence.* Opinions and inferences may be correct, but they hold little weight in arbitration proceedings.

4. *Acting on prejudices.* Real or imagined discrimination or favoritism weakens a disciplinary ruling.

5. *Inadequate records.* The value of written records cannot be overemphasized. An accumulation of warnings and reprimands helps to support the "final straw" incident.

6. *Too severe punishment.* Especially for a first offense, a severe penalty may be viewed as unjust. Arbitrators tend to favor progressive discipline, which grows increasingly severe with subsequent infractions.

*Positive Objectives.* Most discipline is, in fact, negative, but to be judged effective, it should have a long-term positive effect upon employee behavior. A number of generally accepted guidelines support that objective:

1. The act, rather than the employee who performs it, should be the focus of the disciplinary decision.

2. The disciplinary action should provide a guideline to all employees for future behavior.

3. Application of rules and regulations should be consistent and uniform. Conversely, an element of flexibility should be incorporated in the discipline policy so as to allow for extenuating circumstances when they are validly present.

4. Disciplinary action should not be taken hastily in the heat of the moment, but it should be prompt. Delays dull the employee's acceptance of the connection between the infraction and the penalty.

5. The procedure should attempt to allow the individual to save face with his or her peers. Negative discipline—especially personal criticism—is best handled in private.

6. Disciplinary interviews should be conducted in the sense of ultimate employee development, so far as is possible, with the overriding view that most employees desire to perform effectively and to conform to reasonable standards of organizational behavior.

*See also* LABOR-MANAGEMENT RELATIONS; MOTIVATION IN ORGANIZATIONS; PERSONNEL ADMINISTRATION; POWER AND INFLUENCE.

### REFERENCES

Bittel, Lester R.: *What Every Supervisor Should Know*, 3d ed., McGraw-Hill Book Company, New York, 1974, chap. 17.

Shull, Fremont A., Jr., and L. L. Cummings: "Enforcing the Rules: How Do Managers Differ?," *Personnel*, March–April, 1966.

Stessin, Lawrence: *Employee Discipline*, Bureau of National Affairs, Washington, 1960.

STAFF/BITTEL

**Discount house** (*See* MARKETING, CHANNELS OF DISTRIBUTION.)

**Discount retailing** (*See* RETAILING MANAGEMENT.)

**Discounted cash-flow method** (*See* BUDGETING, CAPITAL.)

**Discounting** (*See* PURCHASING MANAGEMENT.)

**Discounts, cash** (*See* FINANCIAL MANAGEMENT, SHORT-TERM, INTERMEDIATE, AND LONG-TERM FINANCING.)

**Discovery** (*See* RESEARCH AND DEVELOPMENT MANAGEMENT.)

**Discrete production** (*See* AUTOMATION.)

**Discrimination, minority** (*See* MINORITIES, MANAGEMENT OF AND EQUAL EMPLOYMENT OPPORTUNITY.)

**Dissonance, cognitive** (*See* CONSUMER BEHAVIOR, MANAGERIAL RELEVANCE OF.)

**Distribution, extensive** (*See* MARKETING, CHANNELS OF DISTRIBUTION.)

**Distribution, intensive** (*See* MARKETING, CHANNELS OF DISTRIBUTION.)

**Distribution, one-step** (*See* MARKETING, INDUSTRIAL.)

# Distribution, physical

In its most elementary form, physical distribution is concerned with overcoming the inherent problems of distance between production and consumption. As late as mid 1976, the National Council of Physical Distribution Management (Chicago) broadly described the activity as relating to the efficient movement of finished goods from producer to consumer. The council updated the definition that year, however, to reflect the increased breadth of the function and the many activities it encompasses:

*Physical distribution management* is the term describing the integration of two or more activities for the purpose of planning, implementing, and controlling the flow of new materials, in-process inventory, and finished goods from point of origin to point of consumption. These activities may include, but are not limited to, customer service, demand forecasting, distribution communications, inventory control, material handling, order processing, parts and service support, plant and warehouse site selection, procurement, packaging, return goods handling, salvage and scrap disposal, traffic and transportation, warehousing and storage.[1]

This new definition helps to explain why the term *business logistics* has come to be used interchangeably with physical distribution. It also is an indication of the impact of the marketing concept philosophy on corporate orientation in general and upon distribution in particular. (*See* MARKETING, CONCEPTS AND SYSTEMS.)

*Components.* No two firms or organizations are likely to find their precise physical distribution system requirements exactly alike. In general, however, the components that make up the typical physical distribution system are (1) location of production and distribution warehouse facilities, (2) type of transportation mode used between those facilities as well as from them to the consumer, (3) communications system, (4) allocation of inventories, (5) material handling system, and (6) the personnel operating the components of the system.

*Design and Objectives.* The objective of a physical distribution or business logistics system for an industrial firm is simple to state but hard to practice. Its goal is to achieve the optimal balance between providing the necessary service to customers while holding costs to a minimum. It can achieve this only by coordination of inbound raw materials, raw materials storage, the handling of work-in-process, packaging of finished goods, warehousing of those finished goods, and the transportation of such goods through the various channels of distribution and ultimately to the consumer.

Care must be taken to constantly monitor and update various elements of the physical distribution system. It is not something done once and then forgotten. It must be fine-tuned regularly to keep pace with the dynamics of a firm's customers, markets, competition, or the firm's strategies themselves. It is these factors of geomarket location and penetration, of marketing and production capabilities, of strategies, and financial resources that determine the type of physical distribution system used.

*Relationship to Other Functions.* Physical distribution is most concerned with the creation of time and place utility in a business system. Thus, a binding and natural relationship exists with marketing and manufacturing. Both require physical distribution to get the right product or supplies to the right place, at the right time, and in the right condition. Obviously, this mission must be done within the financial limitations of the enterprise.

**Physical Distribution Management** The management and updating of the elements of a physical distribution system should be administered by an individual competent in the logistics of physical distribution. Acceptance of this view has led many large firms to organize their distribution functions around a centralized alignment of all related departmental functions. The purpose is simply to attain the maximum from cost trade offs in attempting to achieve the optimal service level to the customers at the lowest price.

## WAREHOUSING

Managers can chose from three alternative types of warehouses:

1. *Private warehouses* are operated and managed by the firm that owns the merchandise handled through the facility. These warehouses may be owned or leased.

2. *Public warehouses* are operated by an independent contractor who controls the building. The independent contractor provides a wide range of service to a number of different firms for a fee.

3. The *contract warehouse* is a combination of a private and public facility. In such a warehouse, an independent contractor provides warehouse services to a firm under a formal agreement; either party can exercise varying degrees of control over space and labor, depending upon the terms of the agreement.

**Services** Public warehouses offer an important advantage in that they allow the user to expand and contract requirements for service and space on short notice. Public warehouses can provide a wide range of services, including storage, order picking, local pick-up or delivery, rail car loading and unloading, inventory control, product line sorting, break bulk and assembly operations, and in-transit mixing. Some public warehouses offer even more complete services, such as temperature control, in-bond storage, and price tagging. Public warehouses may also be classified according to the primary service offered, such as general merchandise, cold storage, special commodity, bonded, household goods and furniture, and bulk commodity. Many offer combinations of these services.

Contract warehouses can offer one or all of the above services under a formal agreement. A user, however, must bear an additional risk because the contract will provide a basis for fixed revenue to the warehouse operator. On the other hand, the user has far more control over the operator than in a public warehouse.

**Planning, Organizing, and Operating** Great care must be given such physical factors as site selection, the material handling system, layout, and structural design. Once the physical factors have been determined, the same care must be extended to operational factors. These include plans for stocking and control of stock, table of organization, selecting and training the personnel, and work procedure. A typical organization for a large warehouse operation is shown in Fig. D-5.

*Controlling.* Control of the warehouse operations is best done through the establishment and close monitoring of productivity measurement systems. Productivity is usually expressed as the number of pieces, pallet loads, line items, or pounds which can normally be handled in a worker-hour. These are referred to as throughput measurements.

Other factors also deserve a close watch in a well-controlled warehouse operation. These include (1) backlog of orders on a daily basis; (2) back-order levels, with particular emphasis on items that were omitted but were actually in stock; (3) utilization of space; (4) fleet efficiency; and (5) overall performance of the operational departments against expense budgets.

*Functions Performed.* Most warehouse operations include such functions as receiving, stocking, order selection, shipping, and inventory control. Often, added functions, such as the assembly of parts, packaging, customer service and repair, and salvage and scrap disposal also take place.

*Automation.* A great variety of automated material handling systems and/or equipment is now

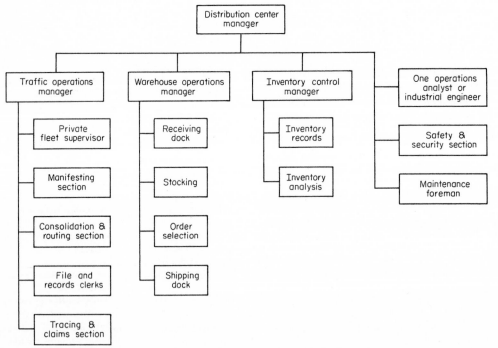

Fig. D-5. Organization and structure of a large warehousing operation or distribution center.

available for the warehouse. The user is cautioned, however, to keep a number of things in mind before committing substantial investments to automated systems. These points are:

1. There is really no such thing as a totally automatic system. The degree of automation, however, can be mind boggling.

2. There is an inverse relationship between automation and flexibility. Adaptation to future change is, therefore, a factor to consider.

3. No matter how automated a warehouse system may be, a back-up system will also be needed. What the risks are when a breakdown occurs in the automated system should be a major determinant of the type of back-up system required.

4. When comparing conventional and automated equipment costs, the cost of back-up systems, maintenance, management time, spare parts inventory, and the cost of capital should be included.

All too often, automated systems are adopted without first exploring the degree of productive movement that could have been obtained through such conventional management principles as standard operating procedures, work standards, removal of bottlenecks, improvement in work flow, and better training of both workers and supervisors.

**Safety and Security**  No matter what the size of the warehouse operation is, attention must be given to adequate safety and security measures. The multitude of federal and state Occupational Safety and Health Administration regulations makes it essential that these measures not be haphazard. A good warehouse *safety program* should include proper work assignments to well-trained people, good housekeeping procedures, safety practices, the use of safe devices, and a good means of communication. *Fire risk* is a particularly important area of concern, and constant attention must be given to vigilance in this area. Sprinkler systems, fire extinguishers, smoking regulations, fire-fighting training, fire drills, and related factors must be included.

*Security Measures.*  These also must be carefully planned and rigorously exercised. Most warehouse experts agree that the security risk manifests itself most often in one of the following five ways:

1. Removal of goods by warehouse employees.

2. Breaking and entering the warehouse.

3. Breaking and entering company-operated transportation equipment.

4. Deliberate overloading of freight vehicles in collusion with truckers or with other persons outside the warehouse or firm.

5. Fraudulent documentation of warehouse releases.

The most effective safeguards against some of these practices include a thorough background check of all employees selected for the warehouse, good exterior fencing and lighting, and electronic protection systems.

## TRANSPORTATION

Alternative modes of transportation include air carriers, railroads, motor carriers, freight forwarders, and water carriers.

In considering each alternative the objective of a physical distribution system must be kept in mind: *deliver* the *right product* at the right *time*, at the right *place*, in the right *condition*, and at the right *cost*. The two main factors in selecting the mode of transportation are delivery time and cost.

**Motor Carriers**  These include common, contract, private, and exempt carriers. The basis for these groupings is one of regulation. Each type of motor carrier is subject, in varying degrees, to federal and state regulations.

Common and contract motor carriers are considered *for-hire* carriers in the United States. They are subject to the most direct controls by federal and state regulations. Exempt carriers do, indeed, operate on a for-hire basis, but the nature of their operations is of such a restrictive degree that it is felt by the governmental authorities that they require a relatively small degree of direct regulation. Private carriers cannot legally operate on a for-hire basis.

*Common carriers* are those that offer transport service to all shippers (commonly referred to as "the public") on a tariff basis. They must apply for and obtain from the appropriate regulatory agency a certificate of public convenience and necessity. That certificate authorizes them to operate as common carriers. Certificates are of two different types: (1) general commodities and (2) special commodities. Common specialized commodity certificates cover petroleum products and household goods. The common carrier assumes full responsibility for safe delivery of shipments as part of the mandate under the operating authority or certificate.

*Contract motor carriers* are those that obtain a permit from the Interstate Commerce Commission for the right to transport shipments between states under specific contracts between themselves and a limited number of shippers. These contracts must be filed with the Interstate Commerce Commission and are normally for a time period of at least 6 months. Contract carriers can only (1) serve a limited number of shippers (not specifically defined by the ICC but generally accepted as no more than eight to ten), (2) carry a restricted number of commodities, and (3) serve a limited geographic area.

*Private carriage* is the term applied to shipper-operated truck fleets. The regulations stipulate that shippers must have ownership or lease on the transport equipment, must have control over the drivers and equipment, and that the merchandise shipped in the equipment must be owned in a bona fide manner by the shipper.

*Exempt carriers* are exempt from direct regulation and fall into three major categories:

1. Exempt commodities: These are most commonly agricultural commodities, and they may be transported by any legal means with no regulation as to rates.

2. Exempt areas: Certain geographic areas, such as the metropolitan area surrounding a larger city, are often defined as exempt from rate regulation by the Interstate Commerce Commission.

3. Exempt associations: Groups of shippers may join together under certain provisions of the Interstate Commerce Act to reduce transport costs and may do so on an exempt basis. Agricultural cooperatives are the biggest users of this type of exemption.

**Intermodal Services** These are transport services in which the equipment of one mode moves in joint transport for part of a route via another mode. As an example, a shipper may ship a commodity from Tokyo, Japan, to an inland point, such as Denver, Colorado. The original load can be loaded in a container van supplied by a water carrier providing service between Tokyo and the West Coast of the United States. Once that container load arrives in a West Coast port, such as Los Angeles, it can then be transloaded on to trailer chassis and trucked via highway to Denver. It also might be set down on the bed of a railroad flat car and shipped via rail to Denver. In either case, this is known as an intermodal service. Often, through rates from a foreign port to an inland United States destination apply on such services.

Intermodal services are also used for export shipments and domestic shipping. Motor carriers and shippers often ship their trailers in piggy-back service, officially known as *Trailer-on-Flat-Car* service, or TOFC. Air carriers commonly provide shippers with small to medium-size containers for shipments which often require services of motor carriers for at least part of the delivery route.

Users can often find substantial economic benefits by using intermodal service because it allows them to benefit from the inherent advantages of each mode of transport, e.g., economy of water or rail, flexibility of motor carrier, speed of air.

**Comparative Evaluation** General services offered vary widely by mode. A brief recap of comparative services and the relative advantages and disadvantages of each mode follows.

*Motor Carriage.* This is by far the most-used mode in the United States and is the result of intensive and widespread development of motor carrier service ever since the motor carriers came under the Interstate Commerce Act in 1935.

Motor carriage has a number of *advantages*. These include

1. Flexibility and maneuverability. They can haul shipments of nearly any size and dimension into almost any reasonable geographic point.

2. Relatively shorter delivery time on shipments than via rail.

3. For shorter distances (generally 400 to 500 miles), rates that are generally more advantageous than rail.

4. Service on small (less than truckload, or LTL) shipments.

5. Availability.

6. An incidence of cargo damage somewhat less than via rail.

Motor carriers have *disadvantages*, too. These include

1. On longer distances where rail service or TOFC service is offered, truck rates will be more expensive on large loads. On significant volume, in fact, rail costs can be so much lower that motor carriage may be economically unfeasible.

2. While truckers generally offer to handle very small shipments (100 to 500 pound range), they profess that such shipments are not profitable to handle. Many carriers do not enthusiastically seek, nor expeditiously handle, such shipments if that is the only type of shipment a particular shipper has to offer. The same thing often happens on very light density commodities, even full loads of such items. Although regulations call for common carriers to provide shippers with service on such items, experienced traffic managers attest to being told by a carrier dispatcher that the carrier is simply out of equipment.

3. Because of ease of entry into the field, shippers must be cautious about the motor carriers selected for use. An occasional motor carrier may not be financially sound and able to provide consistent service or prompt claims settlement.

*Rail Carriage.* This was the major means of transport in the United States until shortly after

World War II, when motor carriers began to become dominant. Railroads have, in the main, done a creditable job of upgrading equipment, tracks, switching procedures, car control programs, and damage control over the past few years. Many of the Western and Southern railroads are financially sound and very well-managed. The railroad service in the Northeastern quadrant of the United States is where most of the serious problems have been, and still are, concentrated. On April 1, 1976 federally assisted ConRail assumed the rail operations of six bankrupt railroads in the Northeast and Midwest, and this action offers renewed hope of improved service in that area.

Railroad service offers a shipper notable *advantages*. These include (1) cost advantages over motor carrier rates on larger shipments, (2) greater flexibility in loading and unloading time, (3) larger carrying capacity, (4) specialized equipment often designed for specific commodities, and (5) surprising maneuverability for both rail service and TOFC service. Transit times have improved significantly the past few years, in large measure due to truck competitors; coast-to-coast service of 5½ to 6 days is now consistently offered between Southern California and the New York/New Jersey metropolitan area.

*Disadvantages* of rail include (1) slower transit time than truck, (2) less flexibility, (3) poor rates and service on short-haul shipments, and (4) higher frequency of damage. No single railroad serves coast-to-coast, although a number of major motor carriers do. As a result, care must be taken in routing shipments. This two-or-more carrier route often leads to claims problems, interchange delays, and slowness in car returns of private rail boxcars. The problems are most aggravated in shipping to and from the Northeast. The larger shippers can greatly benefit from a traffic manager skilled in anticipating and overcoming such problems.

*Air Transportation.* This mode has grown significantly since 1960. Air cargo service is offered by all regular passenger airlines on their regularly scheduled flights. Many such airlines offer special cargo aircraft, and many more are using "quick-change" aircraft for combined passenger cargo service. There are also a number of all-cargo airlines that specialize in cargo transportation between major cities throughout the United States and between United States points and foreign cities. Smaller air taxi service is now offered to remote and small communities throughout the country.

*Advantages* of air transportation include (1) speed, (2) simplified tariffs, (3) a high variety of rates that

often can compete favorably with motor carriage, and (4) a low incidence of cargo damage. *Disadvantages* include (1) higher costs, as a general rule; (2) weather restrictions; (3) dimensional restrictions, particularly on passenger aircraft; and (4) geographic restrictions where air service is not available.

*Freight Forwarders.* This is a mode often misunderstood by the nontransportation-oriented distributor. This type of carrier is regulated by federal regulatory bodies and operates its own terminals and fleets of trucks for pick-up and delivery service. Freight forwarders *do not* provide transport service between cities on their own transport equipment. Instead, they use the equipment of regular common carriers. There are surface as well as air freight forwarders. They concentrate their main efforts on the consolidation of smaller shipments into larger loads and then tender those loads to the line-haul carriers for intercity transport to another of that same forwarder's terminals, where the larger shipments are then sorted and delivered. They can offer big advantages in lower costs, and do actively solicit small, as well as large, shipments. Air freight forwarders do a particularly fine job in pick-up and delivery services and in tracing of shipments. Their main disadvantage is that they do not have direct control over the line-haul transport service on shipments tendered to them.

*Water Carriers.* These offer the lowest-cost transportation generally available. Ocean water carriers now offer consistent bulk cargo and containerized cargo service between most major ports in the world. On a domestic basis, barge lines offer bulk cargo service and are now expanding container service over the country's inland waterways. The disadvantages are often related to geography. Water access is a necessity for direct water carrier service. Container shipping has greatly reduced pilferage and damage, but transferring of such containers between ship and land can lead to damage.

## REGULATION OF TRAFFIC AND TRANSPORTATION

A basic understanding of the effects of regulation on transportation greatly assists in deciding which alternative modes to employ. A brief synopsis of some of the more pertinent aspects of this regulation follows, but the reader should be cautioned that such regulation is, indeed, a very complicated matter and that laws, court and regulatory-body decisions, and a multitude of dissertations on the subject fill a vast number of books. For specific in-depth knowledge about such regulations, one should consult a qualified traffic manager, the regulatory agencies themselves, or an attorney knowledgeable in transportation law.

**The Federal Regulatory Bodies** Three major regulatory bodies deal with transportation regulation on interstate and international commerce in the United States:

1. The *Interstate Commerce Commission (ICC)* is responsible for the regulation of railroads, motor carriers, freight forwarders, shipper associations, and the interstate commerce activities of pipelines and water carriers.

2. The *Civil Aeronautics Board (CAB)* is responsible for the regulation of air carriers and air freight forwarders.

3. The *Federal Maritime Commission* is responsible for the regulation of international rates and services for water carriers.

These three bodies operate under federal acts approved by Congress. Although the Department of Transportation (DOT) does not have direct power over the enforcement of regulations by those bodies, it certainly influences changes in regulation by advocating regulatory changes before the regulatory bodies themselves do and by introducing law reforms before Congress.

**Impact of Regulations on Management Policies and Decisions** Regulations govern the actions of both carriers and shippers regarding transportation. Fines for violations of the regulatory acts can be assessed by the regulatory bodies against both carriers and shippers. Shippers, then, must indeed conform to such regulations and set internal policies and make decisions accordingly.

*Transportation Costs.* The biggest single impact on management relates to transportation costs. Contrary to a popular misconception, regulatory bodies, such as the ICC, do not set rates. The rates, in fact, are set by the carriers. Common carriers generally set rates through group action via Rate Bureaus. (The Department of Transportation has announced its intention to seek legislation to eliminate Motor Carrier Rate Bureaus' antitrust immunity as part of the Motor Carrier Reform Act of 1975. Hearings are under way.) This group action is specifically excluded from certain antitrust provisions by law. Such carriers retain a right of independent action, however, if they do not agree with the group action.

Shippers and carriers may protest changes in rates or regulations if they can base such protests upon evidence such as harmful competition or noneconomic return on investment. The regulatory bodies have the right to decide whether to approve or disapprove such changes.

While regulations that affect private carriers can have a direct bearing on shippers' decisions, shippers must also consider that regulatory decisions of any widespread magnitude have a major impact upon the economic well-being of entire segments of the transportation industry. This can affect a mode's service abilities, costs, and, thus, freight rates and equipment supply. This could, in turn, have a direct bearing on plant or distribution center locations, private industry service, and ultimately on a shipper's own profitability.

*Freight Classification and Rating.* Virtually every type of item shipped is described by common-carrier classification books. Some items are specifically described; others are covered only in broad terms. *Classification* categorizes items in alphabetical sequence, generally under generic descriptions. The description of each item is given a rating based upon that item's shipping characteristics (key shipping characteristics include density, value, propensity to damage, and degree of danger involved in handling). The *rating* is a particular class into which an item falls. The basic rating is Class 100, and other classes are expressed as percentages of this amount.

*FOB Points.* The letters FOB signify *free on board*, which means that a shipment will be delivered free of charge on the mode of transport to the FOB point indicated. This term designates who will pay the freight charges. It *does not* indicate when title of goods passes. If a shipment moves on an "FOB shipper's plant," the shipper (or seller) would be responsible for loading the goods, but the freight charges to destination would be on a "collect" basis. If the terms were "FOB destination," then the seller would prepay the freight but not pay for unloading of the material or equipment at the destination if unloading charges were involved.

*Freight Claims.* If a shipment suffers pilferage, loss, or damage due to wrongful action on the part of the carrier, then a *freight claim* for the value of the loss can be filed. Carriers will provide shippers or recipients of such shipments with the appropriate claims forms when asked to do so. Many shippers use their own forms. Such forms require that some basic information be listed, such as a copy of the carrier delivery receipt, a statement of the items lost or damaged, and statement of demand for the value of such loss. Carriers will also inspect or arrange to inspect damaged shipments of any significant size.

Freight claims must be filed within certain prescribed time limits or a carrier is prohibited from paying them. This is commonly referred to as the *freight claim statute of limitations*. For railroads, motor carriers, and most other surface carriers, the time limit is fixed at 9 months following the delivery date of the shipment, or 9 months following the date whereby delivery should have been made. Water carriers restrict the time period to only 30 days.

If a carrier refuses to pay a claim, the claimant may file suit, but there is a time limit for this action, within 2 years and 1 day from the date of a carrier's rejection of the claim. Water carriers have a 1-year time limit for filing suit.

*Overcharge Claims.* Carriers subject to the Interstate Commerce Act must publish their rates in tariffs. If a shipper feels that the charge has been more than the applicable tariff rate, then the shipper may file an overcharge claim within 3 years after the date of the shipment and may seek ICC's interpretation of applicable rates in cases of dispute.

**Traffic and Transportation Management** The objective of a traffic and transportation department is to provide a transport service that meets the various requirements of a firm's physical distribution system. There are two major functional areas in which an effective traffic and transportation management department can contribute to the achievement of a firm's physical distribution objectives. One is through administrative functions, and the second is through research.

*Traffic Administration.* This includes (1) freight classification, (2) obtaining the lowest legal rates possible consistent with service levels needed, (3) scheduling equipment, (4) shipping documentation, (5) routing shipments, (6) tracing and expediting shipments, (7) auditing freight bills, and (8) filing claims.

*Traffic and Transportation Research.* This consists of studying various transport service alternatives, negotiating rates with carriers, and analyzing ways in which overall distribution costs can be affected by changes in transportation service.

*See also* FACILITIES AND SITE PLANNING AND LAYOUT; INVENTORY CONTROL, PHYSICAL AND STOCKKEEPING; INVENTORY CONTROL, PURCHASING AND ACCOUNTING ASPECTS; LOGISTICS, BUSINESS; MARKETING, CHANNELS OF DISTRIBUTION; MATERIAL HANDLING; MATERIALS MANAGEMENT; PLANNING, STRATEGIC PLANNING MODELS.

## NOTE
[1]*N.C.P.D.M. What It's All About,* The National Council of Physical Distribution Management, Chicago, Ill., 1977, pg. 2.

## REFERENCES

Ackerman, Gardner, and Thomas: *Understanding Today's Distribution Center*, The Traffic Service Corporation, Washington, 1976.

Arbury, James N., et al., *A New Approach to Physical Distribution*, American Management Association, New York, 1967.

*A Bibliography on Physical Distribution Management*, published annually by the National Council of Physical Distribution Management, Chicago.

Bowersox, Smykay, and LaLonde,: *Physical Distribution Management*, Macmillan & Co., Ltd., London, 1969.

Davis, Bob L.: *Information Sources in Transportation Material Management, and Physical Distribution, An Annotated Bibliography and Guide*, Greenwood Press, Westport, Conn., 1976.

Jenkins, Creed H.: *Modern Warehouse Management*, McGraw-Hill Book Company, New York, 1968, pp. 29, 95, 129, 132–137.

Johnson, James C.: *Readings in Contemporary Physical Distribution*, The Commerce Press, Tulsa, Okla., 1974.

McElhiney, Paul T., and Charles L. Hilton: *Introduction to Logistics and Traffic Management*, Wm. C. Brown Company Publishers, Dubuque, Iowa, 1968, p. 68–75.

"What Is the Right Name for Us?" *Handling and Shipping Magazine*, May 1976, pp. 46–48.

BERNARD J. HALE, *Bergen Brunswig Corporation*

**Distribution, selective** (*See* MARKETING, CHANNELS OF DISTRIBUTION.)

**Distribution, two-step** (*See* MARKETING, INDUSTRIAL.)

**Distribution and transportation** (*See* heading in Table of Contents for complete listing.)

**Distribution channels** (*See* MARKETING, CHANNELS OF DISTRIBUTION.)

**Distribution facilities** (*See* PLANNING, STRATEGIC PLANNING MODELS.)

**Distribution of services** (*See* MARKETING OF SERVICES.)

**Distributions** (*See* RISK ANALYSIS AND MANAGEMENT.)

**Distributors, industrial** (*See* MARKETING, INDUSTRIAL.)

**Diversification** (*See* ACQUISITIONS AND MERGERS.)

**Divestiture** (*See* ACQUISITIONS AND MERGERS.)

**Dividend policy** (*See* FINANCIAL MANAGEMENT, CAPITAL STRUCTURE AND DIVIDEND POLICY.)

**Dividend reinvestment** (*See* SHAREHOLDER RELATIONSHIPS.)

**Divisionalized organizations** (*See* ORGANIZATION STRUCTURES AND CHARTING.)

**Do** (*See* WORK SIMPLIFICATION AND IMPROVEMENT.)

**Document, transaction** (*See* RECORDS MANAGEMENT.)

**Door-to-door retailing** (*See* MARKETING, CHANNELS OF DISTRIBUTION; RETAILING MANAGEMENT.)

**Dow-Jones industrial average** (*See* MARKETS, STOCK INDICATOR SERIES.)

**Down time reports** (*See* PLANT ENGINEERING MANAGEMENT.)

**Drafts, bank** (*See* INTERNATIONAL TRADE.)

**Drug abuse** (*See* HEALTH, MENTAL.)

**Dummy activities** (*See* NETWORK PLANNING METHODS.)

**Durable goods** (*See* MARKETS, CLASSIFICATIONS AND MARKET ANALYSIS.)

**Dynamics, system** (*See* SYSTEM DYNAMICS.)

E

**Earn-out arrangement**  (*See* ACQUISITIONS AND MERGERS.)

**Earned hours**  (*See* WORK MEASUREMENT.)

**Earnings, retained**  (*See* FINANCIAL MANAGEMENT.)

**Ecological concepts**  (*See* ENVIRONMENT, PHYSICAL.)

**Econometric models**  (*See* FORECASTING BUSINESS CONDITIONS.)

## Economic concepts

Economics may be defined as the social science which deals with scarcity and choice. While economics is not the only social science to deal with these two items, it is the only social science which presumes rational behavior on the part of individuals when they interact with one another to make choices through the social mechanism of the market.

*Rational Behavior*.  By the term *rational behavior* an economist means an individual's actions designed to achieve self-interest. Rational behavior tends to be systematic, while irrational behavior tends to be unpredictable. Economists assume that individuals recognize the constraint of their scarce resources and that they will seek to select situations that best advance their own interest. Rational individuals will seek to accomplish their objectives at the least possible cost. When choosing among alternatives that yield equal benefit, a rational individual will select the cheapest option. Rationality assumes that individuals have some knowledge on which to base their evaluation of possible outcomes.

*Self-Interest*.  Economists are sometimes criticized for assuming that individuals are self-interested, because many equate this with saying that individuals are completely selfish. Such a criticism is unfair. Charity is certainly an important feature in many individuals' lives, but overall charity accounts for only a very small part of the aggregate expenditures of individuals. The assumption of self-interest does not rest upon empirical study by psychologists, but rather upon a process that might be called *intelligent introspection*. That is, economists justify their principle of self-interest by assuming that their own experiences represent "typical" experiences.

**Human Wants and Resources**  While the definition of economics focuses on the way in which scarce resources are allocated to satisfy human wants, a perfectly satisfactory definition must include the meanings of scarce resources and human wants. *Resources* are those items which can be used to produce economic goods. They include machines, natural resources, land, and any other productive factors. These resources are scarce because nature provides far less of them than human beings in the aggregate would like to have. *Human wants* are the goods and services, situations and things that people desire. They vary from individual to individual as well as over time. While economists assume that the desire for any particular good over a period of time is not infinite, they also assume that human wants in the aggregate are indeed infinite.

**Microeconomics versus Macroeconomics** A distinction is often drawn between microeconomics and macroeconomics. *Microeconomics*, often called *price theory*, used to be all there was to economics. The term *macroeconomics* refers to examining the aggregate level of activity of the economy. Macroeconomics developed in the 1930s with the ideas of John Maynard Keynes. The meanings of the prefixes *micro-* and *macro-* imply that microeconomics is a close-up look at the field, while macroeconomics is a broad overview of a much larger field. The distinction between microeconomics and macroeconomics can be described as the difference between (1) a detailed study of the behavior of individual decision-making units in the economy and (2) a study of the behavior of the broad aggregates in the economy: inflation, unemployment, and gross national product.

**Tasks of an Economic System** It is not very likely that the human race would still be on planet Earth if each individual or each family unit had merely tried to remain self-sufficient over time. Instead there is a great deal of variety and ingenuity in the techniques people have devised to perform the economic function of allocating scarce resources to competing uses. Each economic system has its own way to solve this particular problem. Three distinct categories of economic systems characterized by their institutional mechanisms can be identified: (1) decision by a central authority, (2) decision by tradition, and (3) decision by some automatic control mechanism. Economies of the twentieth century are most realistically described as combining all three of these forms of control.

Regardless of the method of control, however, each economy must solve the central economic problem and perform related functions dealing with production and distribution of the goods and services. The economic decisions facing all economies are what to produce, how to produce it, and for whom to produce it. Answering these questions requires some understanding of how goods are chosen and how resources are allocated and organized in a particular society. In societies controlled by a central authority, the economic decisions are dictated to the separate firms, families, and individuals by the central authority. In those societies dominated by tradition, previous experience offers the solution to current economic decisions. In most economies, including the United States, many of the economic decisions are made through (1) the decentralized market system and (2) the centralized public sector. Goods and services desired by consumers are the ends toward which the private economy is directed. Resources are allocated in this private economy according to the dictates of *consumer sovereignty*, which means the consumer guides the determination of which goods are to be produced, how they are to be produced, and for whom they are to be produced. If all resources were available in abundance, that is, if they were not scarce, the tasks of economics in terms of choosing alternatives would disappear. The procedure by which decisions are made in a decentralized economy is, of course, of great significance. Economics is important as a social science because it is a process by which the ends are chosen and the scarcity of the resources examined relative to those ends. While there are a number of qualifications, the United States economy is primarily market-oriented; that is, the composition of goods and services provided is largely the result of private decisions exercised in a network of private markets where free choice is permitted within limits.

**Problem Solving with Economics** Economics as a social science deals with the problem of predicting the impact of changes in economic variables. When these predictions are considered to be value-free, the economic approach is strictly *positive*. *Normative* issues are those that include value judgments about "what ought to be." Normative issues also require economic analysis. *Positive economic statements* may take the form "A will surely follow B" or "If the price of automobiles rises, all other things being equal, people will buy fewer automobiles." *Normative economic statements* emphasize a particular point of view and will normally only advocate one side of a proposition. These statements may be of the form "A should follow B" or "The federal government should support higher education." Observers of economic policy statements should be aware of the difference between positive and normative economics. Positive economic statements rely on facts to determine whether the statement is correct or incorrect. Normative economic statements are often philosophical and cannot be "proven" or "disproven" by reference to the facts.

*Experimentation.* The facts in economics are not oftentimes established through experimentation similar to the laboratory experiments in the natural sciences. The reason these experiments are not performed is that they would be unreasonably costly. In order to observe economic phenomena in a laboratory situation, the economic incentives facing individuals would have to be similar to real world incentives. Such reproduction would, in all probability, be exceedingly costly. In lieu of laboratory experiments then, economists most often determine facts by means of statistical inference through model building.

**Models** An economist's model is an abstraction that is simple enough to understand and manipulate and yet close enough to reality to yield correct predictions. In most cases, it is simply not possible to represent an entire economic system in all its complexity. Abstraction is the hallmark of model building. A theory and a model are in many ways synonomous. Each attempts to identify key variables and establish relationships between these variables. Each provides a framework which allows scientists to examine the complexities of a real world situation with greater insight than if they were to try to work with all the variables and relationships at a single point in time. Models are tested by returning to the real world and examining whether the predictions of the model conform to observed events.

The models used by economists in problem solving may be models of individual markets where the prices of individual consumer goods are determined and the quantities provided of those individual consumer goods are examined. Models dealing with individual consumer goods or factor markets would be termed *microeconomic* models. *Macroeconomic* models, on the other hand, concentrate on the employment level, the rate of inflation, and the total amount of goods and services produced in the economy as a whole. Macroeconomic models often lead to prescriptions for policy to be followed in order to achieve stable prices, low unemployment, and reasonable economic growth.

Figure E-1 is an economic model by which the relationship between macroeconomics and microeconomics may be described. The model shows how "consumption" goods flow from firms to individuals and "factor" inputs flow from individuals to firms. In the opposite direction, money flows from individuals to firms and back again to individuals. There

are opposite circular flows of money and goods as indicated by the arrows. This model incorporates both macroeconomic and microeconomic descriptions.

*Macroeconomic Interpretation.* It is possible on the one hand to view the overall opposite flows of money and of goods and to describe the situation in which the flow of dollars increases relative to the flow of goods as inflation. If the model were made more complicated, it would be possible to break down the individuals' incomes into the portions saved and portions spent and to insert into the stream of money the effects of actions by the central bank to increase or decrease the flow of money. It would also be possible to show the government as a purchaser of factor inputs or of consumer products and also as a tax claimant upon individuals' incomes. Finally, it would be possible to incorporate into the model the effects of international trade on the flow of goods and on the flow of money. Each of these matters is the domain of macroeconomics, which deals with the system as a whole.

Microeconomics, or price theory, on the other hand, concerns itself with the individual aspects of the system and generally assumes that the system as a whole is operating at the full employment level. Microeconomics would seek to determine prices of the factor inputs and of the consumer products and how these prices and outputs are affected by the degree of competition. Instead of taking an overall view of the system, microeconomics considers its parts.

## MICROECONOMICS

The basic economic model, illustrated in Fig. E-1, shows that the economic problem of an individual is twofold. The individual faces the product market as a demander of consumer goods and he or she must decide how to spend that income over the consumer goods and services which are available in the market. At the same time, the consumer's income must be derived from the factor market where he or she is a supplier of resources. Viewing the economic model in this way, the concentration is on the individual as consumer and as resource owner. Economists classify this view of the economic problem as microeconomics.

**Utility** Each individual in this economic model attempts to maximize self-interest within the limits of the information available. Each consuming unit establishes hierarchies that indicate the order in which the needs and desires of the individual are to

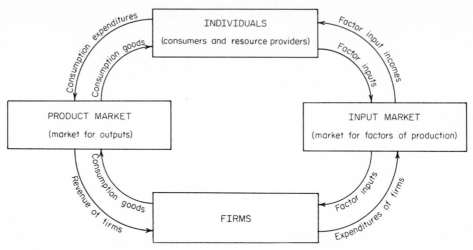

Fig. E-1. Economic model.

be met. A well-known hierarchy of human needs frequently cited in the literature of industrial psychology is given by Abraham H. Maslow. Economists, however, abstract from such observations and hypothesize the existence of something called *utility*, which represents the satisfaction derived by individuals from the various goods and services which they consume. The *law of diminishing marginal utility* has been derived from observations that after a certain amount of a good or service has been consumed, additional units of the good or service will yield diminishing increments of utility. A consumer existing in a world of diminishing marginal utility will maximize self-satisfaction by exchanging money for commodities that yield greater utility than holding on to his or her money would yield, such that additional utility per dollar spent is equal for each of the commodities purchased. Economists do not actually measure utility because the concept is wholly abstract. The only objective gauge of utility available to the economist is the *price measure*; that is, the amount of money, time, effort, or other commodities which an individual is willing to sacrifice to obtain an item. Models predicting the amounts of a commodity that would be purchased by consumers in a market over a period of time and at different prices are consumer demand models.

**Demand** Consumer demand for a particular item is a schedule of the amounts that consumers would purchase at various prices. The relationship between the rate of purchase of a commodity and the price of a commodity is often diagramed as a demand curve. Figure E-2 depicts the relationship

that the quantity demanded as a function of price. Demand curves for an individual consumer simply describe his or her willingness to make certain rates of purchase at a particular time as some function of price. This inverse relationship between price and quantity demanded has been observed so often that the negative slope of the demand curve is referred to as the *law of demand*. A market demand curve is the sum of individual rates of purchase at various market prices. The negative slope of the market demand curve has also been verified empirically. The analy-

Fig. E-2. Demand and supply.

sis of consumer demand is of critical importance to business managers in pursuing the firm's goals of maximizing profits, sales, the value of the firm, earnings per share, share of the market, or some combination of these goals.

Three different approaches are used by researchers to estimate market demand empirically. First, direct interviews are sometimes undertaken in order to secure information about consumer preferences. Second, market experiments can be conducted to obtain information about a product's demand function. The most commonly used market experiment involves a series of price changes over time in one market to determine how these changes affect demand. Finally, the most often used technique to estimate market demand is regression analysis of existing data.

**Supply** Just as individuals face a budget constraint, according to consumer demand theory, when they make decisions concerning which items and what quantities of those items to purchase, so do firms face technical constraints in producing the goods and services which individuals are willing and able to purchase. These technical constraints are exhibited in production functions which outline the physical relationships between a firm's input of factors and its output of goods and services over a given period of time. A firm's production function relates the magnitude of a flow of output to the magnitude of the corresponding flow of input which is required to generate it. Economists assume that the profit motive induces firms to utilize the production function which is most efficient. A firm is assumed to employ this production function in such a way as always to obtain the greatest output from each alternative combination of inputs. Knowledge of the production function is of particular importance to a firm because it is the production function from which the supply curves of firms and product markets and the demand curves of firms and factor markets are derived.

The supply curve of a firm focuses on the price-quantity relationship—the rate at which a producer is willing to supply a product as a function of the expected market price of the product. A supply curve applies principally to competitive markets where price responds freely to market forces and where individual producers react to the price established by the market. In market situations which are not competitive but rather are dominated by a few large producers, the functional relationship economists call supply may cease to be meaningful. The supply function is then the quantity a producer

would be willing to supply in a given period of time as a function of price. The positive slope of the supply curve in Fig. E-2 represents the empirical fact that sellers will offer more of their product as the price increases. A *market equilibrium* in Fig. E-2 is represented by the intersection of the demand and supply curves whose coordinates are $P$, the price, and $Q$, quantity demand of the item. The economists' justification that the intersection of supply and demand is an equilibrium position for the market is that there is no tendency for either suppliers or consumers to move from such a position. Such a position is acceptable to both parties because it lies on their respective schedules.

**Markets** Economists use the term *market* to define certain aspects of an individual firm's external environment within which the firm must operate in order to fulfill its objectives. A market is a process by which buyers and sellers interact for the purpose of (1) obtaining information about what they are willing to buy and sell and (2) determining prices. Most markets involve transactions on a continuing basis. Often there are technical problems in trying to determine where one market ends and another begins. The *perfectly efficient market* is one where adjustments in terms of price and quantity are instantaneous as the result of perfect knowledge of market conditions by buyers and sellers and of perfect factor mobility.

*Pure Competition.* A purely competitive market is one in which price and output determination are the result of the impersonal forces of supply and demand, not the result of individual actions of buyers and sellers. Economists refer to an individual firm in a purely competitive market as a *price taker*. Market demand and supply are defined as separate and distinct, interacting to determine the price-quantity combination which is the equilibrium of the market. The demand curve in Figure E-1 may be viewed as the industry demand for a particular item, and the supply curve may be viewed as the industry's supply for a particular item. The price $P$ and quantity $Q$ would be the equilibrium price and quantity for this competitive market. An individual firm in this competitive market would be required to sell at price $P$. If the firm chose to raise its price, buyers would defect to the other firms in the market. If it chose to lower its price, it would sell its entire output at less than the price it would be able to get. For a market to be purely competitive a number of conditions must prevail:

1. There must be many firms in the market, each acting independently and each unimportant

enough relative to the size of the market so that a single firm's decision either to cease producing entirely or to produce to capacity will not have a noticeable change on market supply or cause a change in market price.

2. Firms must be allowed to enter or exit the market at will.

3. The products offered for sale in this market are assumed to be homogeneous; that is, the output of any one firm is the same as the output of any other firm in the market.

4. There are also assumed to be many individual buyers in the market—so many, in fact, that individual buyers and sellers are assumed to act independently. That is, there is no collusion between buyers and sellers.

*Real-World Competition.* The purely competitive market is an abstraction from the real world. It is a particular way of looking at the operation of market forces and is often used as the standard by which to judge real-world markets. Most economists agree that under rather restrictive assumptions the resource allocation within the purely competitive market is ideal from society's point of view. In a competitive market, sellers are induced to produce efficiently, and rewards are offered to those sellers who produce what consumers desire. The abstract idea of a purely competitive market is important to economists precisely because it explains why competitive forces are consistent with economic efficiency.

In a purely competitive market, price alone determines the basis for competition. In the real world, however, the basis for competition may be product quality, convenience of location, quickness of service or any of a number of nonprice variables. Nonprice competition in the real world may be just as intense as the price competition in the prefectly competitive model.

**Monopoly** One real-world variation from the competitive market is monopoly. This is the situation in which only one firm produces and sells a particular product. The study of monopoly focuses on situations where the barriers to entry into the industry are high and the existing firms have some protection from the competition of new firms entering the industry. In a monopoly market the consumer must either buy from the monopolist or do without the product. Economists view this reduction in the choices available to the consumer as less efficient than the purely competitive situation.

**Oligopoly** Oligopoly is the term used to describe a market in which there are only a few sellers. There are a number of real-world industries which

could qualify as oligopolistic. While economics has a general theory of perfectly competitive markets and a general theory of monopoly, there is no general theory of oligopoly because of the possibility of close interaction between firms.

## MACROECONOMICS

Macroeconomics deals with aggregate measurements which are the result of individual decisions made in the economy. The most often used measure of the nation's pulse is the *gross national product (GNP)*. GNP is the measure of the market value of all the goods and services produced in the United States over a specific period of time, usually a year. The importance of GNP is that it acts as an indicator of short-term changes in productive activity. Without some measure of business fluctuations, government policy could not be formulated and long-run prescriptions could not be made. The focus in macroeconomics is clearly on income and expenditure flows rather than on individual markets.

**Keynesian Influence** John Maynard Keynes probably had more influence on macroeconomic analysis than any other economist. His book *The General Theory of Employment, Interest and Money* was published in 1935 after 5 years of severe economic depression in the United States. While many points Keynes made in the book had been mentioned previously, and while the book was confusing and contradictory in some sections, the book transformed modern economic theory. The two important contributions of the book were that (1) it explained the existence in equilibrium of involuntary unemployment in a competitive economy like the United States economy, and (2) it suggested policy tools for eliminating that involuntary unemployment. Keynes suggested that industralized economies like the United States could suffer from high unemployment and large underproduction and be unable to rid themselves of the unemployment unless they were bailed out by government action in the form of public works. The mainstream economists of Keynes's day felt that the economy would pull itself out of a depression with little or no government interference. Their prescription then was to do nothing, i.e., *laissez faire.*

**Keynesian versus Monetarist** There are two approaches to studying the aggregate level of income and output in the economy. These two approaches are referred to as the Keynesian model and the monetarist model.

*Keynesian Approach.* The Keynesian model of income determination concentrates on the behavior of households and their consumption-saving choices and on the behavior of firms in their investment decisions. The quantity of money in the economy is not ignored by the Keynesians, but its effect on income and output is indirectly felt as a result of its altering the behavior of economic agents. The determination of consumption expenditures, that is, expenditures by households for goods and services, is central to the Keynesian model. Personal consumption expenditures by households are the largest component of the United States gross national product. In the Keynesian model, great importance is placed on the proposition that the consumption function is stable. Aggregate consumption, according to Keynes, is a stable function of aggregate disposable income. That is, as the rule and on the average, as individuals find their income increasing, they will also increase their consumption but not by as much as their income increases. This stability of the consumption function indicates the important influence of income as a determinant of both consumption and its counterpart, saving.

*Monetarist Approach.* The monetarist approach to studying the level of income and output in the economy is often called the *quantity theory of money*, and the approach concentrates on measuring the quantity of money and the velocity of money, that is, the speed with which money is spent or changes hands. The link in the monetarist model between the quantity of money and the level of income is the velocity of money, which is defined as the level of income divided by the quantity of money in the economy. The monetarist model rests on the assumption that velocity is either constant or very stable and predictable. If this is true, then the quantity of money will be a very important policy variable determining the level of income and output in the economy.

Keynesians believe that the major cause of unemployment and inflation in the economy is the instability of the investment function—that is, the private business sector. Monetarists believe that the major source of the business cycle is inappropriate monetary policy. The Keynesian view of an economy assumes that the macro system is inherently unstable. Keynes's prescriptions and those of his followers were that government could play the role of stabilizer in the economy by adopting (1) proper tax and expenditure policies called *fiscal policy* and (2) appropriate monetary growth called *monetary policy*. The monetarists, on the other hand, view the macro system as inherently stable and attribute most of the disturbances in the form of inflation or unemployment to government intervention in the market

economy. Their often expressed proposal for stabilization involves a stable and predictable rate of growth in the money supply.

**Impact on Managerial Decisions** Macroeconomic models today are well suited to serve management decision makers in large American corporations. Managers often deal with decisions which involve assumptions about the future aggregate level of economic activity, tendencies towards consumer saving, the intentions of corporations to increase their level of investment, and the liquidity preferences of firms and individuals. These same variables and others are included in most analytical models in the United States economy. Thus, macroeconomic models are a highly relevant tool for organizing and using economic information and forecasts in decision making. Perhaps the most important aspect of economic models is that they help to explain economic phenomena. In most business problems, management has some degree of control over a number of variables which are present in the relationship being examined. When forecasting the sales of a product for instance, a firm must take into account the price of the product; it is the firm itself, however, which will set that price. Only when management clearly understands the interrelationships involved in an economic situation can it hope to forecast accurately and make optimal decisions by selecting correct values for the variables over which it has control.

## SPECIAL INFLUENCES

Public finance and money and banking are two special areas in economics which do not clearly fall into either the microeconomic or the macroeconomic category.

**Public Finance** Public finance is the study by economists of government considered as a unit. The objective of the field of public finance is to explain how the collective decision-making process operates. Public finance economists develop theories which link individual choices to collective action and analyze the implications of that theory. Just as microeconomists have traditionally studied the pricing mechanism and how it works, so do public finance economists explain how public choices are made. An individual makes private choices while going about ordinary personal business. He or she makes public choices when selecting among alternatives for others as well as for himself or herself. Traditional economic theory in the sense of microeconomics and macroeconomics is narrowly defined to interpret only the private choices of individuals in a market process. Public finance concentrates on the outcome of collective decisions even as they influence outcomes in the market.

Public finance economists view the government as a means of aggregating individual preferences. In addition to studying the social goals for aggregated preferences of individuals, public finance also studies the decision process used to arrive at such goals. Fiscal policy, that is, the expenditure and taxation policies of the government, is also the domain of public finance.

**Money and Banking** Money and banking is the study of the role of money in the economy with the emphasis on monetary process. It is not the study of bank management or financial institution management. The study of money and banking involves the study of monetary process including (1) the institutions which make up the monetary sector, (2) monetary theory, and (3) monetary policy prescriptions.

*See also* COMPETITION; ECONOMIC MEASUREMENTS; ECONOMIC SYSTEMS; EMPLOYMENT AND UNEMPLOYMENT; FINANCIAL MANAGEMENT; FORECASTING BUSINESS CONDITIONS; MARGINAL INCOME ANALYSIS; MARKETS FOR PRODUCTS AND SERVICES; PLANNING AND POLICY MAKING; PRODUCTIVITY; PROFITS AND PROFIT MAKING; REGULATED INDUSTRIES, MANAGEMENT OF; RISK ANALYSIS AND MANAGEMENT; VALUE-ADDED TAX.

### REFERENCES

Buchanan, James M., and Marilyn R. FLowers: *The Public Finances*, 4th ed., Richard D. Irwin, Inc., Homewood, Ill., 1975.

Friedman, Milton, and Walter Heller: *Monetary Versus Fiscal Policy*, W. W. Norton & Company, Inc., New York, 1969.

Keating, Barry P., and Dolores Martin: *Cases and Problems in Political Economy*, McGraw-Hill Book Company, New York, 1978.

Klein, John J.: *Money in the Economy*, 2d ed., Harcourt Brace Jovanovich, Inc., New York, 1974.

Laidler, David J.: *Introduction to Microeconomics*, Basic Books, Inc., Publishers, New York, 1976.

Leftwich, Richard H.: *The Price System and Resource Allocation*, The Dryden Press, Inc., Hinsdale, Ill., 1973.

McGuigan, James R., and Charles R. Moyer: *Managerial Economics*, The Dryden Press, Inc., Hinsdale, Ill., 1975.

Ritter, Lawrence S., and William R. Silber: *Money*, 2d ed., Basic Books, Inc., New York, 1973.

Samuelson, Paul A.: *Economics*, 10th ed., McGraw-Hill Book Company, New York, 1976.

Tullock, Gordon, and Richard McKenzie: *Modern Political Economy*, McGraw-Hill Book Company, New York, 1978.

BARRY P. KEATING, *University of Notre Dame*

## Economic factors (*See heading in Table of Contents for complete listing.*)

## Economic forecasting (*See* FORECASTING BUSINESS CONDITIONS.)

# Economic measurements

Various indicators are available which are routinely used to predict economic conditions. These indicators will be discussed in this entry.

### PERSONAL INCOME

The term *personal income* is generally regarded as nearly synonymous with the term *consumer income* but, because it has been assigned a very precise meaning, is preferred to the latter. As defined by the U.S. Department of Commerce, *personal income* refers to the amount of income received by individuals from all sources during a specified conventional period of time such as a week, month, or year.[1] It includes money income from private businesses, professions, wages and salaries, rental income, dividends, interest, and the difference between transfer payments (social security benefits, unemployment insurance, etc.) and personal contributions for Social Security.

The statistical series on personal income is reported prior to allowance for personal tax and nontax payments, and it is of interest to the business community primarily as a reliable indicator of general business trends. Personal income figures are the only United States income and product series currently estimated on a monthly basis. These data are published in a monthly news release by the U.S. Department of Commerce, Bureau of Economic Analysis, and subsequently in the monthly publication of the U.S. Department of Commerce, the *Survey of Current Business*.

In a recent normally prosperous year, personal income amounted to slightly more than 80 percent of gross national product in the United States. The difference between personal income and gross national product consists of depreciation allowances (capital consumption allowances) and indirect tax and nontax liability.[2] (A nontax liability is a payment such as a fine or a royalty.) Since the turning points (changes in the direction of trends) of this statistical series coincide with turning points in general business,[3] the series has limited application to business forecasting.

The term *disposable personal income* refers to the income remaining in the hands of individuals after payment of all taxes levied directly on the individual.[4] Such taxes include federal, state, and local income taxes, property taxes, school taxes, etc. Hence, disposable personal income is essentially the same as *take-home pay* and is the amount of income that individuals are free to spend or save as they see fit. Disposable personal income is the pool of private consumer purchasing power for which all members of the business community (including banks and other financial institutions) compete. Total United States disposable personal income amounts to slightly more than 85 percent of total United States personal income and to about 70 percent of total United States gross national product.

*Real disposable personal income* is computed when figures for disposable personal income are deflated (divided by a price index, usually the U.S. Bureau of Labor Statistics, *Consumer Price Index*.[5]) When the general price level rises faster than disposable personal income during any given time period, real income (effective purchasing power and, therefore, the volume of final demand) declines and when disposable personal income rises faster than the general price level, real income (effective purchasing power and the volume of potential demand) increases. The statistical series representing total United States real disposable personal income and real disposable personal income per capita are of vital interest to management since increases or decreases in real purchasing power influence both the amount of money spent (rather than saved) and the composition of goods and services that are purchased by consumers.

## PERSONAL CONSUMPTION EXPENDITURES

The term *personal consumption expenditures* refers to the portion of personal income after taxes that is spent for goods and services. Hence, disposable personal income minus interest paid by individuals, personal transfer payments to foreigners, and personal savings (in any of the various possible forms) equals personal consumption expenditures. The changes in trends in personal consumption expenditures (up or down) tend to coincide with turning points in general business as measured by estimates of gross national product. Therefore, the statistical series representing personal consumption expenditures is not useful in business forecasting although it ranks among the most important economic statistical variables that must be forecast. The value of total United States personal consumption expenditures is estimated quarterly by the U.S. Department of Commerce on a seasonally adjusted, annual rate basis and is published when available in the *Survey of Current Business*,[5] in monthly publication *Economic Indicators*,[6] and elsewhere.

Expressed in terms of market prices (prices actually paid), total United States personal consumption expenditures in a typical year are equal to about 62 percent of gross national product, the largest single category within gross national product. Similarly, total United States personal savings for the 5 years 1972–1976, inclusive, averaged 7.1 percent of disposable income and during that period ranged from a low of 6.2 percent of disposable personal income to a high of 7.8 percent.

The typical United States consumer is reluctant to reduce his or her standard of living or that of his or her family (that is, reduce the amounts, kinds, and qualities of goods and services consumed), and a consumer who feels economically secure is apt to (in fact, expected to) reduce liquid assets and/or use installment credit or borrow money to maintain or raise a given standard of living.

Increases in disposable personal income over the years have tended to be associated with predictable shifts in patterns of personal consumption expenditures first toward the purchase of relatively more luxury items (durable goods) and later, chronologically, toward the purchase and consumption of relatively more services such as education, medical care, or entertainment. For example, in 1946, personal consumption expenditures were distributed as follows: 11 percent on durable goods, 58 percent on nondurable goods and 31 percent on services; whereas the 1976 distribution was as follows: 14 percent on durable goods, 41 percent on nondurable goods, and 45 percent on services.[7]

Consumers' decisions on whether to save or to borrow money and, when they spend, on which goods and services to purchase are influenced by their assessments of trends in general business and their expectations concerning their personal future economic and financial conditions. The consumers' changing moods are measured on a quarterly basis by indexes of consumer confidence.[8] When consumers become pessimistic, they defer purchases of durable goods, reduce outstanding installment credit, and increase savings (and the inverse). Probably because consumers are quick to respond to changes in their own economic and financial conditions and also because a shift (up or down) in final demand is often the first sign of a change in general business conditions, consumer confidence indexes are classified as leading economic indicators and, hence, are useful in business forecasting. Their record of accuracy at forecasting major swings in general business activity, however, is not particularly good; that is, changing trends in consumer confidence often signal changes in general business conditions that do not occur.

## PRICE(S)

In modern, developed economies, the price of an object (or service) is stated as an amount of money a seller is willing to accept in exchange for the object (or service). When the supply of an object is scarce relative to the volume of demand for the object, the price of the object is high relative to other similar objects and often (as, for example, in the case of a rare art object) also relative to the intrinsic value of the materials out of which the object is made. Under more normal conditions, a high price is said to ration a small supply. Any related high profit is expected to attract new producers into the field and bring the shortage to an end. In general, an increase in supply relative to effective demand is accompanied by reductions in price often made possible by the shift to large-scale production and the introduction of new, labor-saving technology. This holds true even when the increase in supply occurs along with significant improvements in product quality, e.g., color television.

In free enterprise, capitalist economies, the price of an object (or service) is usually set by the seller (exceptions are auctions, barter, and special cases where buyers tender offers to buy specified objects or services at a stated price) but can be influenced by consumers' response to price changes as measured by their market behavior. Normally the price of a given object (or service) consists of the sum of all costs of production (labor, raw materials, power, tax and nontax payments, overhead costs, etc.) and an allowance for profit. Comprehensive statistical data concerning corporate profits are published quarterly by the Federal Trade Commission.[9]

## PRICE INDEXES

A price index is a ratio that expresses the relationship between the price of a given object (or service) at a specific time and the price of the same object during a period selected as a base year. A price index is derived by dividing the current or given period price by the base year price and adding 100 to the quotient. An index number larger than 100 indicates an increase in the price under study (e.g., an index of 110 indicates a 10 percent increase over the base year) and an index number less than 100 indicates a decrease from the base year level (e.g., 95 indicates a 5 percent decline.)

A price index may measure changes in the price of a single item or the weighted average change over time in a group of products. Typically, price changes are not related to changes in general business conditions; for example, recently prices have continued to rise while the volume of output has declined. However, movements in price indexes are predictable in the sense that a change in the price of one or more raw materials is, as a rule, reflected with a time lag in the Bureau of Labor Statistics *Wholesale Price Index* and after a further time lag, in the *Consumer Price Index*.

The *Wholesale Price Index* and its components are of interest to the business community for the role they may play in product price contract escalation clauses. Similarly, the *Consumer Price Index* (often erroneously called the cost-of-living index) often plays a role in wage contract negotiations.

## INFLATION

Most economists do not describe a price increase that can be traced to a specific, temporary cause (e.g., a crop failure) as inflation. The term *inflation* usually refers to a persistent rise in the general price level of a nation. Inflation is described as being "cost push" when it can be traced to increases in the costs of key inputs and as "demand pull" when it can be traced to existing monetary purchasing power that exceeds the total value of goods available for sale at a given point in time.

Inflation is considered undesirable because it erodes the purchasing power of people living on fixed incomes (such as pensions) and because it renders the involved nation's products less competitive in world trade. The following figures represent changes that have occurred in the general price levels (as measured by implicit deflators of gross national product) of the nations shown as of the year 1976 where 1967 = 100, the base year.[10]

| | |
|---|---|
| Australia | 208.3 |
| Austria | 174.3 |
| Belgium | 183.3 |
| Canada | 179.8 |
| Denmark | 219.4 |

| | |
|---|---|
| France | 189.8 |
| Italy | 219.7 |
| Japan | 199.5 |
| Mexico | 267.1 |
| Netherlands | 194.7 |
| Norway | 184.4 |
| South Africa | 183.1 |
| Spain | 225.9 |
| Sweden | 182.3 |
| Switzerland | 160.3 |
| United Kingdom | 243.6 |
| United States | 169.0 |
| West Germany | 163.7 |

## MONEY SUPPLY

The term *money supply* is synonymous with the term *money stock* and has five definitions that are currently in use. The narrowest definition appropriately designated (M-1) includes the total amount of coin and paper money in circulation and the total of all demand deposits (checking account balances) in banks. The second definition (M-2) consists of M-1 plus time and savings deposits in banks. The third definition (M-3) consists of M-2 plus deposits at mutual savings banks, savings and loan associations, and credit union shares. The fourth definition (M-4) consists of M-2 plus large negotiable certificates of deposit. The final definition (M-5) consists of M-3 plus large negotiable certificates of deposit. The actual dollar amounts of the various definitions of the money supply are published monthly in the *Federal Reserve Bulletin*.[11] There are two crucial points to remember in regard to the money supply:

1. It includes the proceeds of borrowing (loans); that is, when a bank extends credit (makes a loan), it creates a demand deposit and thereby increases the money supply (and the inverse).

2. The central bank of any nation (in the United States it is the Federal Reserve Banking System) has the power to regulate changes in the money supply (total purchasing power at a given point in time) to permit economic growth without inflation.

## INTEREST ON LOANS AND DEPOSITS

Interest is the price paid for the use of money for a specific period of time. Hence, an interest rate is the cost of using borrowed money expressed as a percentage of the amount of money borrowed and applicable to a specific time period indicated in the contract drawn up at the time a loan is negotiated. The actual rates charged (percentages per year or some portion thereof) depend upon such factors as the term of the loan, the credit rating of the borrower, the use to which the borrowed money is to be put, etc. A schedule of prevailing interest rates on borrowed money is published in the *Federal Reserve Bulletin*.

Banks and other financial institutions charge interest on loans and pay interest on money placed at their disposal by depositors. There is a schedule of interest rates paid by financial institutions and the rates vary in relation to the length of time depositors agree to leave the money in their accounts. For example, many banks pay no interest at all on small demand deposits (checking account balances).

Because the supply of money and changes in it are commonly regarded as causal factors in the general business cycle, the statistical series covering the money supply are ranked among leading indicators and are an aid in business forecasting. In contrast, trends in interest rates have not shown consistent responses to the ups and downs of general business activity and remain unclassified as to their normal cyclical behavior. Hence, they are of no help in forecasting. Interest rates reflect changes in the money supply.

## CREDIT

When a bank loans money, it extends credit to the borrower. In more common usage, however, the term *credit* refers to a business transaction in which a seller delivers a product or someone performs a service in exchange for a promise of future payment whether or not a formal contract is involved.

In the past, credit was a form of competition, extended by sellers to purchasers to attract and hold their business, and the involved costs were included (hidden) in prices charged. At present, most vendors limit interest-free credit to a relatively brief period and thereafter charge a fee similar to interest and based on the amount of credit outstanding. Third parties (e.g., banks and others) are now involved in consumer credit via the growing popularity and proliferation of credit cards. Paying for expensive consumer goods, especially automobiles, is commonly accomplished via installment credit where payments are made according to a predetermined schedule and include clearly specified interest charges.

When consumers feel economically secure, they assume debt in various forms (borrowing money to buy a car). When consumers turn pessimistic in response to early signs of an economic slowdown, particularly increases in unemployment, they attempt to reduce outstanding credit, stop taking out new loans, and in some cases are unable to make (default on) installment payments. Therefore, consumer credit and defaults are ranked among leading indicators and are useful in business forecasting. However, no forecasting statistical series are infallible whether used alone or as components of complex econometric models.

## SAVING(S)

While the term *saving* is most commonly associated with the finances of private individuals, it also applies to corporations. In the case of individuals, saving is the amount of disposable personal income (income after taxes) that is not spent on consumption and may be allowed to accumulate in the form of cash and/or negotiable securities. In the case of corporations, savings consist of after-tax corporate profit that is retained by the corporation in the form of cash or liquid assets rather than distributed to the corporation's owners in the form of dividends. State banking laws regulate the investment practices of savings banks while no restraints are imposed on the uses to which corporate retained earnings may be put.

## MONETARY POLICY

The term *monetary policy* refers to the actions of a nation's central bank in controlling the money supply and, through control of the money supply, influencing the level of short-term and long-term interest rates. Monetary policy (increasing the money supply) is a powerful weapon against business recession since it can be used to stimulate economic activity (and the inverse). Similarly, reducing the money supply or preventing it from increasing can slow the pace of demand-pull inflation by bringing the supply of money into closer balance with the volume of goods and services available for purchase. A gradual increase in the money supply is necessary to accommodate growth in the volume of a nation's production of goods and services.

As a rule, Western nations attempt to maintain balanced economic growth with minimum inflation by a combination of monetary policy, as described above, and fiscal policy—maintaining surplus or deficit government budgets—with, say, monetary policy acting to reinforce (or contain) the impact of central government fiscal policy.

## CIVILIAN LABOR FORCE

In the United States, the civilian labor force is defined as the nation's noninstitutional population

16 years of age and over that either is employed or is actively looking for work, excluding, obviously, the armed forces serving in the United States or elsewhere. The number of persons satisfying the above qualifications normally amounts to about 60 percent of the nation's total population.

Statistical data concerning the labor force, employment, unemployment, wages, etc., are collected and published routinely by the U.S. Department of Labor, Bureau of Labor Statistics, and are available from the Superintendent of Documents, Washington, D.C. The main sources of data are the *Monthly Labor Review* and the monthly publication *Employment and Earnings*. A catalog of Department of Labor publications is available from the Superintendent of Documents, Washington, D.C. 20402.

Employment statistics in general are among the first to reflect changes in trends in general business activity and six statistical series covering job vacancies, employment, and unemployment are listed by the U.S. Department of Commerce among leading economic indicators. As such, they should be of value in business forecasting. In practice, however, employment statistics are of limited value in forecasting trends for any particular industry.

## WAGES AND HOURS

Similarly, the existence of unemployment in any given industry (or in general) no longer signals a reduction in pay levels or necessarily elicits moderation in demands for pay increases and more generous employee benefits. Industry-wide contract negotiations have greatly weakened the individual employer's bargaining power in wage contract negotiations. As a rule, union pay levels and employee benefits are the main determinants of wage trends although there are still some regional pay differentials for the same kind of work in the United States.[12] The Bureau of Labor Statistics publishes detailed information concerning pay rates, average weekly hours of work, overtime hours worked, etc., for the various major industries. These data permit businesses to compare their own pay schedules with the averages prevailing in the industry of which they are a member.[13]

The entire area of employment (wages, hours of work, working conditions, hiring practices, employee benefits, unemployment insurance, social security contributions, etc.) has tended over the past four decades to fall under the influence of government regulations and union bargaining power and to become less subject to control by private managers. Hence, data covering wages and hours and the like now play roles chiefly as variables in decisions as to whether and when to adopt new laborsaving technology.

## PRODUCTIVITY

The term *productivity* refers to the volume of goods or services produced per unit of labor input (worker-hour) or capital or both. The most popular measure of productivity is the ratio of any given volume of output to total worker-hours of labor input. The U.S. Bureau of Labor Statistics calculates and publishes statistics on rates of productivity and changes therein for the United States as a whole and for various major industries, as well as special reports, monthly in the United States *Department of Labor News.* [14]

Efficiency, as measured by rates of change in output per unit of input, tends to decrease as maximum levels of output are approached and to remain low during the initial stages of a general business slowdown because employers are reluctant to discharge workers in response to short-term declines in output. In contrast, efficiency tends to increase during the upswing after a general business slowdown because rehiring lags behind increases in output.

In today's computer-oriented business world, the concepts of output per worker-hour (or per unit of capital) and dollar costs per unit of output can be examined in the light of various assumptions as to future costs of inputs (factors of production) and to possible combinations of manpower and machinery. This analysis permits direct comparisons of alternatives that are open to corporate management and is of great value in planning and decision making.

## BUSINESS AND PRODUCTION ACTIVITY

The terms *business* and *production activity* are virtually synonymous in common usage. They refer to the primary function of management: bringing together all the human skills, tools, and raw materials (including energy) to enable the performance of a service or the creation of a product for which there is a ready market and which can be sold at a profit to its creator.

## SERVICE INDUSTRIES

The volume or value of services is usually measured in terms of the incomes of those who supply the services and/or the amounts of money spent by consumers to obtain and use the services during a specified period of time. The use of money as the common denominator of the service industries is made necessary by the many difficulties encountered in attempting to measure the volume and intrinsic value of services that may in themselves be ephemeral, e.g., a symphony concert. The wealthier a society, the larger the portion of its consumers' disposable income that is likely to be devoted to services.

Another way of measuring the importance of the service industries in any nation is to determine the share of total employment that is devoted to the service industries. If one includes in the service category, employment in wholesale and retail trade, finance, insurance, and real estate, government, and the conventional services such as laundries, more than half the total United States employment has been in the service sector since 1953. In 1976 the share has risen to almost two-thirds of nonagricultural employment. For some time, service industry employment has been the fastest growing area while employment in manufacturing has not really increased since 1969 in spite of significant increases in manufacturing output. [15]

## INDUSTRIAL PRODUCTION

Because physical units of output are involved, measuring the nation's manufacturing output presents far fewer problems. The most popular measure of industrial output is the Federal Reserve Board's Index of Industrial Production where 1967 = 100. It is published monthly in greatest detail in a special report released by the FRB toward the middle of each month. The report contains historical monthly data for a full year. The index also appears in the *Federal Reserve Bulletin* and the *Survey of Current Business* [16]

The volume of output measured by the FRB index turns down at the same time general business conditions weaken, while upturns tend to occur before improvements in overall business conditions are apparent. Even so, the usefulness of the index in forecasting upturns is limited by the fact that it represents the average of diverse trends. Furthermore, preliminary data are at times subject to rather substantial revision. By means of the FRB index, management can compare its own performance with that of the industry of which it is a member and it can obtain valuable information about trends in supplier and customer industries that is not available elsewhere.

## MANUFACTURERS' SALES, INVENTORIES, AND UNFILLED ORDERS

Data covering the dollar value of manufacturers' sales, inventories, and unfilled orders are collected and published monthly by the U.S. Department of Commerce in a special report and subsequently in the *Survey of Current Business*. Data are shown with and without seasonal adjustment for the standard two-digit SIC classifications, by stage of fabrication and for several special market groupings. The main value to management of this body of data lies in a continuing study of the relationship between trends in sales, inventories, and unfilled orders since these data can signal, at a fairly early date, the accumulation of burdensome inventories (overproduction relative to effective demand) or emerging shortages as evidenced by growing order backlogs.

## MANUFACTURING PROFITS

The term *profit* is defined as an amount of money that remains (a residual) after all costs of production have been recovered. Profits tend to decline at peaks of economic activity when output is pushed above optimum rates and to improve when rates of production are increased from low levels. So profits are regarded as a leading indicator relative to trends in general business. In economic theory, profit represents payment for the use of owners' money to conduct the business while variations in the level of profits from one industry to another are said to reflect variations in the risk assumed by owners in investing in the various industries.

## CAPACITY UTILIZATION RATES

A capacity utilization rate represents the percentage of a company's or an industry's plant and equipment that is actually being used to produce goods and services during a specific period of time (e.g., the average for a month) or at a given point in time (e.g., as of a given date). Statistical data for capacity utilization are published monthly by the U.S. Department of Commerce[17] and by McGraw-Hill Publications, Department of Economics,[18] and quarterly in the *Federal Reserve Bulletin*. Capacity utilization rates are a leading indicator at cyclical peaks while upturns tend to coincide with upturns in general business. When the overall industrial operating rate reaches 85 percent of capacity an upturn in business capital spending may be expected.

## BUSINESS CAPITAL SPENDING

Business spending for new plant and equipment is regarded as a lagging indicator, tending to rise after the need for new capacity has ceased and to remain low for a while after an upturn in general business and operating rates has occurred. Data relative to capital spending are regularly collected and reported by the U.S. Department of Commerce[19] and by McGraw-Hill Publications, Department of Economics.[20]

*See also* ECONOMIC CONCEPTS; ECONOMIC SYSTEMS; EMPLOYMENT AND UNEMPLOYMENT; FORECASTING BUSINESS CONDITIONS; INPUT-OUTPUT ANALYSIS; MARKETS, CLASSIFICATIONS AND MARKET ANALYSIS; MARKETING RESEARCH; PRODUCTIVITY.

## NOTES

[1]*Dictionary of Economic and Statistical Terms*, U.S. Department of Commerce, Social and Economic Statistics Administration, Washington, 1972.

[2]*Economic Report of the President*, Washington, Jan. 1977.

[3]*Business Conditions Digest*, U.S. Department of Commerce, Bureau of Economic Analysis, Washington, monthly.

[4]*Dictionary of Economic and Statistical Terms*.

[5]*The Consumer Price Index* is available in a special monthly release; in the Bureau of Labor Statistics, *Monthly Labor Review*, and in the U.S. Department of Commerce, *Survey of Current Business*.

[6]*Economic Indicators*, prepared for the Joint Economic Committee by the Council of Economic Advisers, Washington, monthly.

[7]*Economic Report of the President*.

[8]*Business Conditions Digest*.

[9]*Quarterly Financial Report for Manufacturing, Mining and Trade Corporations*, Federal Trade Commission, Washington, annual subscription only.

[10]As estimated in *World Business Outlook*, McGraw-Hill Publications, Department of Economics, Dec. 17, 1976.

[11]*Federal Reserve Bulletin*, Division of Administrative Services, Board of Governors of the Federal Reserve System.

[12]*Employment and Earnings*, U.S. Department of Labor, Bureau of Labor Statistics, Washington, monthly. *Employment and Earnings by States and Areas*, U.S. Department of Labor, Bureau of Labor Statistics, Bulletin 1370, Washington, annual. Includes historical data.

[13]*Employment and Earnings* (monthly).

[14]*United States Department of Labor News*, Office of Information, Washington.

[15]*Economic Report of the President*.

[16]*Survey of Current Business*, U.S. Department of Commerce, Bureau of Economic Analysis, Washington.

[17]Ibid.

[18]*Monthly Calculation of Industrial Operating Rate*, McGraw-Hill Publications, Department of Economics, New York.

[19]*Survey of Current Business.*
[20]*Annual Survey of U.S. Business' Plans for New Plant and Equipment*, McGraw-Hill Publications, Department of Economics, New York.

EDWARD G. MAYERS *McGraw-Hill Publications Company*

## Economic order quantity (*See* INVENTORY CONTROL, PURCHASING AND ACCOUNTING ASPECTS.)

## Economic-oriented managers (*See* MANAGEMENT, FUTURE OF.)

## Economic systems

Economic systems are distinguished from one another by the way they answer the three basic questions that every economy must answer, namely:

1. *What to produce and in what quantities.* All economies have to decide the kinds of things they want to produce both in general (such as consumer goods, military goods, and capital goods) and specifically within each category (the kinds of consumer goods, whether football fields, beverages, wheat, automobiles, television sets, medical services, and the like; the kind of capital equipment required to produce consumer and defense output that society wants). All these decisions must, of course, be made within the constraints of the resources available for productive activity. In addition to decisions about what kinds of things to produce, every economy must decide the relative quantities of each, again within the limits of the resources available.

2. *How to produce each category of goods and services.* The questions here are what technology to adopt, whether to use much labor and little capital or much capital and little labor, and whether to use the latest techniques available or so-called "secondhand" techniques.

3. *Who should get what.* In its traditional form, this is the problem of income distribution. Goods and services go to those who have the income to purchase them in a money economy, and the distribution of income determines the claims against the output of the economy.

**Custom, Command, and Demand Economies** Prior to the industrial revolution (during the last quarter of the eighteenth century and throughout much of the nineteenth century), these kinds of questions were answered at various times and in various places by a mixture of what may be referred to as *custom and command*. Thus the answers could be provided by following traditions and customs passed along from generation to generation. Feudal society in Western Europe (tenth to thirteenth centuries) and many past (and some present) primitive economies operated largely on this basis. On the other hand, the questions of what, how, and to whom could also be answered by command or the dictates of (1) a single person in the form of a monarch, commissar, dictator, or religious leader or (2) a group (usually relatively small) such as a military junta, ruling elite based on royalty, wealth or age, a politburo, etc.

It was only following the early phases of the agricultural and industrial revolutions in England that differentiation started to develop between types of economic systems, and terms with a more contemporary ring came into use, namely, capitalism, socialism, communism, and fascism. All involved variants of custom and command, although applied to *nation* states. Capitalism was unique in that it added a third way to answer the basic economic questions, namely, by the demands of the citizens of the society in their roles as suppliers of services or products and consumers thereof.

All actual economies, of course, employ mixtures of custom, command, and demand. Distinctions among economies then rest upon the extent to which the basic economic questions rely mainly on one or another of these methods. Though all economies have substantial elements of custom or tradition embedded in economic (and especially noneconomic) processes, almost all economies strive for rapid economic growth and thus seek to overcome the inertia (or stability) of traditional productive processes; most seek to "modernize," to raise output per head and change both the quantity and quality of human wants. We may therefore exclude custom in the economies of contemporary nation states as a major and deliberate way to answer the questions what, how, and to whom, even though the desirability or even the possibility of continuous economic growth and change is being questioned.

The two dominant forms of economic organization thus involve demand and command.

**Capitalism** In its pure or theoretical form, a demand-oriented (capitalistic) economy relies upon the institutions of private property, the profit motive, competitive markets, free consumer choice, and minimal role of government to answer the three basic questions.

1. *What?* In such a system the prices of goods and services relative to their costs of production,

which in turn represent the prices and quantities of the resources required to produce them, determine the absolute and relative profitability of particular products. The profit motive ensures that only those goods yielding a positive profit will be produced, with the relative quantities depending upon relative profitability. If consumer tastes and preferences change, their demands will change, thereby altering the profitability of particular commodities. Producers will respond to such price changes under the profit motive. The price mechanism, determined as it is in the pure form by the impersonal forces of supply and demand, provides the signals to which producers respond. This is the meaning of a consumer sovereignty economy—the monetary votes (demands) of the consumers determine what will be produced and in what quantities.

2. *How?* How things will be produced depends largely upon the profit incentive as well. Each producer has an incentive to reduce production costs. A producer who succeeds in so doing will increase profits. Other producers will be induced to adopt the more efficient production technique (unless barred by such things as patent laws, entry restrictions, secrecy, and the like). Thus, over time, least cost techniques tend to remain consistent with the factor endowments of the economy.

3. *To whom?* To whom such output goes depends upon incomes generated in the productive process. If factor prices (i.e., wage rates, interest rates, rents, and profit rates) are determined in competitive markets, claims against the output of society are equivalent to one's productive contribution to society.

In short, the things that people want (as determined by their willingness to pay a price equal or above the costs occasioned) are produced in the appropriate amounts by methods which are least costly.

Such, in crude summary form, is the message that Adam Smith presented in 1776, which provided the *economic* rationale for the private enterprise, or capitalistic, system. The message included much more, of course, such as scathing attacks on monopoly, private or public, a political justification of an atomistic organization of industry in terms of maximum dispersal of economic and thus political power, and so on. But in its strictly economic message, Smith demonstrated not only (1) that government controls, planning, and intervention were unnecessary and contributed to inefficiency but also (2) that a completely unregulated economy, *if competitively organized*, would maximize output consistent with consumer tastes, preferences, and incomes—the latter

being a measure of the consumer's productive contribution.

*The Rise of Other Isms.* Smith's rationale was heeded increasingly by the British government as it came to be influenced by the interests of the rising commercial and business class. Capitalism, accompanied by the industrial revolution in England— and later North America—put great stress on individualism (itself a product of the American and French revolutions and developments in political philosophy), private property, the profit motive, and the minimum role of government. The results, in terms of total growth of output, were spectacular in the United Kingdom. Indeed, growth rates some 5 times higher than in previous centuries were recorded. Why the industrial revolution and the capitalist form of economic organization developed first in England is unknown. However, it soon spread to other countries in Western Europe as well as North America, Australia, and New Zealand with similar results in terms of overall growth of output.

*Modern Problems.* Even before 1850, certain problems of such an economic system as it was developing were perceived. Three principal problems came to dominate the concern of social thinkers, as well as major segments of society, especially labor. These were (1) periodic instability in the sense that the society was subject to waves of expansion and contraction, or as we would now refer to it, the business cycle; (2) apparently growing inequality of income distribution which led to a few extremely wealthy persons and a very large mass of poor people, with, however, a growing middle class (rising inequality seemed, indeed, to be part of the economic system that was evolving during this time period); (3) persistent poverty related to inequality in the sense that if an economy is expanding rapidly overall and at the same time exhibits a growing inequality, this must mean that most of the fruits of economic growth end up in the hands of a relatively few people, leaving large numbers at a fairly low level of living.

*Protest and Dissent.* The awareness of these problems, whether due to the capitalist system itself or due to the very process of rapid industrialization, led to various forms of protest, dissent, and ultimately alternative systems. These took the highly ambiguous terms *socialism* and *communism* with several versions of each, such as guild socialism, scientific socialism, syndicalism, anarchism, and the like. The two major versions persist: socialism and communism. Socialism and communism, however, did not differ fundamentally from command systems as they had existed in previous centuries except to the extent that they were more rationally conceived and systematically applied to nation-state systems as a whole. In their more modern form, socialism and communism are essentially reactions against (1) the specific problems of capitalism noted above as well as (2) the growing concentration of industry and (3) the apparent decline of markets that were perfectly or workably competitive.

**Communism** As used in reference to *economic* planning in some contemporary nation states, communism refers mainly to the *goal* of a classless society with public ownership of the means of production where the distributive ethic of "from each according to his abilities and to each according to his needs" *can* be realized. Achievement of this goal requires not only a high level of production per head and nearly equal distribution of income but a change in human attitudes away from self-interest toward the larger interests of society as a whole, toward "community." Ultimately, the state, viewed as an instrument of coercion especially under capitalism, will wither away: it will no longer be needed to maintain social order once human nature has been transformed within an economy of abundance.

*Transformation of Human Nature.* As a goal, proclaimed by various contemporary nations, this transformation presupposes a path along which the economy as well as the entire social order should be propelled. There is, however, little agreement concerning the nature of such a path. Clearly, it calls for more than simply economic planning, essential as that may be under a system of widespread public ownership. To transform human nature may require either coercion or a set of novel inducements. Capitalist theory, à la Adam Smith, viewed human nature as "essentially selfish" and sought to create or maintain a set of institutions—the competitive market system and private property—which channeled selfish motivations along lines that contributed to the public well-being. Not so is the path to communism: prices and outputs are to be centrally or administratively determined, production for use rather than for exchange and private profit is to prevail, selfishness is to be eradicated, and a new spirit is to be generated through education or reeducation.

*Ambiguities of Approach.* The ambiguities concerning the appropriate route to communism have quite naturally given rise to sharp differences in the approach among those nations proclaiming the same or similar goals. This is true even for those nations professing to be Marxist or to follow Marxist-Leninist principles. Indeed, the work *communism* in this sense was introduced in England as late as 1841 and was then used to define the more militant and radical wing of the socialist movement rather than to specify any blueprint for economic planning. The *Communist Manifesto* of 1848 was so designated by Marx and Engels to distinguish it from the various socialist movements they believed to be "utopian" and inadequate to overthrow or replace the capitalistic institutions.

*Similarities and Differences.* Centralized economic planning that specifies what will be produced even in very broad terms is, of course, a form of command economy, the details of which vary sharply from nation to nation aspiring to communist objectives. But, as indicated above, both socialism and communism were reactions against the perceived problems of England and Western Europe during the industrial revolution. Furthermore, they involved beliefs that the system designated as capitalism could not resolve the problems of poverty, inequality, and instability without radically changing its basic institutions and in a sense transforming itself into a different "ism." Communists at the time believed strongly that capitalism sooner or later would destroy itself but sought to hasten the process by fomenting revolution and violence. Socialists tended to be somewhat less militant.

**Socialism** Those believing in communism as a goal view public ownership and operation of the instruments of production as merely one step "beyond" capitalism. Socialism sometimes has this meaning, which implies that much work remains to be done to complete the voyage to communism. In the meantime, under this view of socialism, certain amounts of productive assets can be left in private hands, some reliance upon market forces may be necessary, and pecuniary incentives may still be required with their resultant income inequalities. This view also contends that until the productive power of the economy has expanded greatly, human greed eliminated, and self-discipline and restraint inculcated, it will not be possible to realize the goal of "to each according to his needs." Thus the Soviet Union and China continue to rely upon coercion and monetary incentives, in varying degrees, in order to create the new "socialist man," who is cooperative, not competitive; honest; hardworking; disciplined; and incorruptible. Until this is achieved, some coercion and regimentation will be required to eliminate the last vestiges of bourgeois or capitalistic attitudes.

The Western world is liable to view societies holding the above views as *communist* even though Russia refers to itself as "socialist" and China calls itself a "People's Democratic Republic." Other nations—such as Cuba, Albania, the Indochina

States, and those in Eastern Europe—are also designated as communist, although internally the adjective *socialist* is used more often.

*"Democratic" Socialist States.* There are, however, many other nations and political parties designated as socialist that differ sharply from the above vision and even more sharply in terms of their actual economic, social, and political policies and procedures. Sweden and the United Kingdom under the British Labour party are examples. In virtually all countries of the Western world, there are socialist parties that periodically come to power via the electoral process instead of revolution. The distinction between communism and this view of socialism is less one of economic planning and administration than it is of the extent to which coercion is exercised to realize centrally established economic and noneconomic objectives. Indeed, Russian communism may best be defined as totalitarianism dedicated to economic growth and is vastly different from Swedish socialism.

There are many so-called "democratic" socialist states—democratic in the sense that alternative political parties exist, dissent is tolerated, elections are regularly held, and the results are accepted. In economic terms, such socialist nations emphasize the traditional problems of capitalism. They stress, however, the need for more detailed planning, more public ownership of industrial assets, or at least more public participation in price, output, and investment decisions of major industries, especially those producing capital goods and those providing "basic" services. The goals of democratic socialism are usually less radical than communists aspire to and more concerned with problems of inequality, instability, and poverty. The goals, in short, are more confined to economic matters under the belief that only a higher degree of deliberate intervention in the market place, more progressive taxation combined with more publicly provided services (health, education, power, transport, communication, etc.), and more control over investment will suffice to redress the defects of a full-blown market system. There are, of course, serious concerns with efficiency in publicly owned and operated industries and in investment decisions in the public sector (as is also true in the Soviet Union though much less so in China). But it is believed that better decisions can be made using *social* cost-benefit analysis rather than relying on private profit as a guide. This belief is especially strong where markets are not "workably" competitive and where external effects are large, such as when pollution and other social costs are not considered by the private firm in making price and output decisions.

In addition, democratic socialism leaves a good deal more of society's productive activity in private hands, especially in the consumer goods sector, than communism and retains some (often substantial) reliance upon market forces where these seem to be functioning well or satisfactorily.

**The Isms in Reality** As should be apparent, it is no easy task to define economic systems with much precision, even in the abstract. If one examines the isms as actually practiced, the difficulties of definition and distinctions among them mount rapidly. One should not study communism, capitalism, etc., in the abstract when attempting to unravel basic differences. Instead, one should examine Russian, Chinese, or Yugoslav communism, all of which differ substantially as is true of United States, German, or Canadian capitalism; British, Swedish, or French socialism; Spanish, Argentinian, or German (under Hitler) fascism. Forms of economic organization vary with any nation's history, culture, and traditions. Indeed, "the economy" is not something separate from the whole society: it is part of an entire social, legal, political, and religious system. Collectivism in the Soviet Union, the "rights" of private property in England, and individualism in the American colonies, for example, all antedated the beginnings of industrialization.

*Coercion and Repression.* The degree of coercion or repression in any economy also depends partly upon the means by which a new regime comes to power. If it is by revolution, coercion is liable to be greater and last longer than if it is by peaceable transition. Most of the present regimes in the communist bloc acquired power after internal struggle and thus continue with a higher degree of coercion and centralized administration than socialist regimes democratically elected. This has obviously different implications in terms of economic planning and ensuring that plans are fulfilled in a communist or socialist economy, even though both may loosely be called command economies. It is particularly the case that democratic socialist regimes pay more attention to consumer sovereignty and individual rights than do highly centralized communist regimes.

*Economic Convergence.* Not only are all the industrialized economies shaped by the whole set of past and present institutions, values and customs, as well as the method of political power transference, but all industrialized economies are also mixed. This is in the sense that central governments now play a substantially greater role in capitalistic economies than envisioned by the original rationale while central governments often take a somewhat lesser role in socialist or communist economies than originally thought desirable or necessary. Many of the changes that have taken place since the late nineteenth century, and especially since the 1930s, within capitalistic economies have constituted attempts to redress the problems associated with instability, inequality, and poverty. These have involved a considerable expansion in the role of government and, to a lesser extent, its size. Similarly attempts to administer a socialist or communist state have run into increasing problems of bureaucracy, inefficiency, and excessive centralization, which may retard the overall rate of economic growth. Attempts to redress these problems have pushed such economies to a greater or lesser extent in the direction of decentralization, or market socialism, as it is sometimes called. These general tendencies have given rise to a belief in the confluent or convergent economies. The industrialized, capitalistic economies of the Western world and Japan and the industrialized communist countries of Eastern Europe and the Soviet Union have in fact moved away from the extremes of individualism and collectivism, respectively, in the economic sphere. To the extent that these trends continue, the *economic* distinctions among the isms become even more blurred.

Political, social, and cultural distinctions, however, are far less convergent, but these relate more to specific nation-states rather than to any general form of economic organization. Indeed, economic systems have become less generalizable and exhibit rather unique characteristics better explained by national history, national values, and so on.

*Variance in Nonindustrialized Nations.* The relevance of the terms *capitalism, socialism, communism,* and *fascism* is even more questionable when applied to nonindustrialized states. India refers to itself as a socialist state, yet little of its industry is publicly owned. China refers to itself as a communist state, yet little detailed planning takes place at the center. So-called "communist" regimes have recently been installed in Laos, Khmer, and Vietnam, yet the approach to economic planning and organization differs sharply in each. Several of the Central American republics refer to themselves as "market-oriented" if not capitalistic, but given the political systems, the large role of the military, and the high concentration of property ownership in a few families, *fascist* would be a somewhat more descriptive term. Likewise, South Korea and the Philippines,

while stressing private property and the market system, have political regimes that tend to be more dictatorial than democratic, and so on.

**Categorization Difficulties** The present realities therefore suggest that economic systems cannot be so neatly categorized as implied by the terms *capitalism, socialism, communism,* and *fascism.* Indeed, these designations appear to be far more polemical and emotive than descriptive. This is true even in the purely conceptual and economic aspects. With reference to particular nation-states, the terms are not only nondescriptive but misleading. All countries "plan" in one way or another. All countries have "markets" that are more or less free and extensive. To what degree either mix exists in any economy is more the result of circumstances and the immediate past than any ideological principles associated with economics. Freedom, coercion, tradition, the level of economic development, the extent and kind of natural resources, the quality of human resources, the extent of inequality, aspirations, and so on are more determinative of the specific mix and forms of demand and command than ideologies of capitalism, communism, and socialism developed more than 100 years ago.

**Political Differentiation** It is in the noneconomic realm that sharp differences exist to some extent in concepts but especially in real situations. For example, the states that are designated as capitalist or market-oriented tend to be the political democracies of the Western world. They have two or more political parties and conduct elections at more or less regular intervals. They frequently bring to power a socialist or a labor party. In some local or provincial elections, communist parties are elected. A communist party achieving power by such processes is likely to behave in a much different fashion from one achieving power by war or revolution.

The states designed as communist, on the other hand, tend to be one-party states or even subject to one-person or small-group rule. There may be considerable dissent *within* the party or group on economic issues, but once decisions are made, dissent ceases. Virtually every existing communist state arose following a revolution or external takeover by an existing communist power. Some sought, or are seeking, a radical transformation of previous social relations. The collective farms, the communes, the people's courts, the one-party press, political indoctrination, and so on, are pushed at various times and with varying degrees of ruthlessness among communist states. The attempt is to create a "new" order to replace the old, which all too often was identified with repression, exploitation for private gain, enormous inequality, colonial status, and so on. Some states go to great lengths to eradicate the institutions of the past, such as China in the "Great Leap Forward," Russia in de-kulakizing the kulaks, and more recently, the Khmers in forcibly depopulating Phnom Penh, abolishing money, and establishing a harsh, repressive regime. Other communist states work more pragmatically at the process of social and economic transformation.

**Misleading Economic Labels**  Whether public or private ownership of industrial assets is emphasized, whether economic decision making is centralized or decentralized, and whether coercion or incentives are used to ensure production are more matters of pragmatic judgment for any nation at any point of time. Furthermore, these (and other) attributes are not uniquely related to each other. Indeed, it is possible to have widespread public ownership of assets and, at the same time, decentralized decision making and reliance upon incentives. Similarly, private ownership is consistent with centralized decision making and coercion.

Unfortunately, the terms *capitalism, socialism, communism,* and *fascism* have had much more than economic matters attributed to them. Since it is possible to have varying political, social, and religious institutions associated with any given set of economic institutions, the isms have become nondescriptive and not only fail to distinguish between economic and noneconomic matters but also neglect important differences in the economic sphere itself.

Late twentieth century capitalism bears little resemblance to the system so effectively analyzed by Adam Smith 200 years ago. In fact, the major specific proposals for economic reform made by the *Communist Manifesto* in 1848 have been almost completely adopted by the present market-oriented economies of the Western world. Since socialism and communism were largely reactions to the real and apparent defects of the early phases of industrialization of the West, their contemporary relevance is severely attenuated as is the Smithian rationale of the capitalistic system. Economic systems cannot therefore be meaningfully distinguished by use of such terms.

*See also* ECONOMIC CONCEPTS; ECONOMIC MEASUREMENTS; EGALITARIANISM; EMPLOYMENT AND UNEMPLOYMENT; EXCHANGES, FOREIGN, MANAGEMENT OF; FORECASTING BUSINESS CONDITIONS; INTERNATIONAL OPERATIONS AND MANAGEMENT IN MULTINATIONAL CORPORATIONS; PRODUCTIVITY; PROFITS AND PROFIT MAKING; TECHNOLOGY, MANAGEMENT IMPLICATIONS; VALUE SYSTEMS, MANAGEMENT: SOCIAL AND CULTURAL.

### REFERENCES

Campbell, Robert W.: *Soviet Economic Power: Its Organization Growth and Challenge,* 2d. ed., Houghton Mifflin Company, Boston, 1966.

Grossman, Gregory: *Economic Systems,* Foundations of Modern Economic Series, Prentice-Hall, Inc., Englewood Cliffs, N.J., 1967.

Marx, Karl, and Friedrich Engels: *The Communist Manifesto,* various sources. No contemporary U.S. business people should miss reading this classic if they want to understand something about communism as an ideology.

Schumpter, Joseph A.: *Capitalism, Socialism and Democracy,* 1942, various editions.

GEORGE W. WILSON, *Indiana University*

## Economical order quantity (EOQ) (See INVENTORY CONTROL; PURCHASING AND ACCOUNTING ASPECTS; PRODUCTION PLANNING AND CONTROL.)

## Economical production quantity (EPQ) See PRODUCTION PLANNING AND CONTROL.)

## Economics, production (See PRODUCTION/OPERATIONS MANAGEMENT.)

## Educational assistance (See COMPENSATION, EMPLOYEE BENEFIT PLANS.)

## Effectiveness measures (See PRODUCTION/OPERATIONS MANAGEMENT.)

## Efficiency, building (See OFFICE SPACE PLANNING AND DESIGN.)

## Efficiency, economic (See EGALITARIANISM.)

## Efficiency, floor (See OFFICE SPACE PLANNING AND DESIGN.)

# Efficiency, labor  (*See* WORK MEASUREMENT.)

# Efficiency, principles of  (*See* MANAGEMENT, HISTORICAL DEVELOPMENT OF.)

# Efficiency, purchasing  (*See* PURCHASING MANAGEMENT.)

# Egalitarianism

The "one man one vote" ruling of the Supreme Court in 1964 climaxed two centuries of evolution toward political equality in the United States. In doing so, it strengthened a parallel but less visible movement toward economic equality. As a result, today's corporate managers face a serious challenge not just to their traditional prerogatives but also to some of the basic goals of their organizations.

There is no egalitarian party in American politics, but there is an effective working alliance between the politicians who represent urban areas and the organizations representing minorities or groups that have reason to think they have been assigned a secondary place in American society. Specific measures, such as affirmative action hiring and promotion programs, have been supported by coalitions of members of Congress from low-income districts, by women, and by minority groups. Transfer payments designed to shift income from the upper to the lower brackets have generally been supported by the elderly as well as by the cities, where low-income recipients are concentrated.

**Equal Rights versus Equal Results**  The intellectual foundations of egalitarianism go back to John Locke and Jean Jacques Rousseau. The modern statement of these principles by philosophers such as John Rawls and Christopher Jencks make a strong appeal to young people who see American society as grossly materialistic and callous about noneconomic values.

The modern egalitarian movement began as a demand for equal rights—the right to vote, the right to employment and promotion, and the right to equal pay for equal work. Equality before the law, however, rarely satisfies today's egalitarians. They press for equality of results—equal incomes, equal job satisfaction, equal housing, and equal recognition from the community. John Rawls states the proposition in his book *A Theory of Justice* that soci-

ety must offset unequal distribution of abilities with a "principle of redress." It must "give more attention to those with fewer native assets and to those born into less favorable social positions."[1]

**Conflict with Organizational Objectives**  The drive for equality of condition rather than just equality of opportunity brings the egalitarian movement into increasing conflict with the corporation, the primary apparatus that the United States has developed to handle its economic activities. The corporation is essentially hierarchical. It generates not only wide differences in income among its employees but also significant differences in authority and recognition. Moreover, these differences are essential to the effective operation of the United States economy. A free enterprise system depends on differentials in wages, profits, and interest to allocate its resources and its work force, to determine what products are made, where they are sold, and who is able to buy them.

Egalitarian thinking has shown a growing hostility toward corporations and corporate management. This reflects an increasing sense of frustration, for a structural weakness in the egalitarian philosophy is its failure to provide practical alternatives to income differentials as a means of making the economy work. In a changing world, any effective economic system must provide (1) a device to shift workers out of declining industries into ones where demand is rising and (2) a way of rewarding efficient output and penalizing wasteful work.

**Equality versus Efficiency**  It is unlikely that today's egalitarian movement will succeed in imposing equality of incomes and democratic governance on corporations. The danger is that hostility toward the corporation and dissatisfaction with the distribution of incomes will lead to more and more arbitrary regulation of the economy by federal and state governments. Proposals for intensive government planning, for government-dictated wage scales, and for tax schedules to equalize spendable incomes often gain their main support from groups that do not trust the American economy to achieve the results they desire.

Management's best defense against such an abridgment of its authority is not to make a counterclaim of "private rights." Since the corporation is granted its powers by the state, the corporation is likely to lose any contest that sets corporate interests against those of the public. Instead, the case against egalitarian intervention must rest on one simple proposition: as long as efficiency matters to a society, differences in rewards are inevitable.

Arthur Okun of the Brookings Institution offers an objective appraisal of this problem in his book *Equality and Efficiency, The Big Tradeoff*. Okun sums it up: "Any insistence on carving the pie into equal slices would shrink the size of the pie. That fact poses the tradeoff between economic equality and economic efficiency."[2]

*See also* COMPETITION; ECONOMIC CONCEPTS; ECONOMIC SYSTEMS; PRODUCTIVITY; PROFITS AND PROFIT MAKING; SOCIAL RESPONSIBILITY OF BUSINESS; VALUE SYSTEMS, MANAGEMENT: SOCIAL AND CULTURAL.

### NOTES

[1]John Rawls, *A Theory of Justice*, Harvard University Press, Cambridge, Mass., 1971, p. 100.

[2]Arthur M. Okun, *Equality and Efficiency, The Big Tradeoff*, The Brookings Institution, Washington, 1975, p. 48.

### REFERENCES

Cobbs, John: "*Egalitarianism*," a series of three articles, *Business Week*, Dec. 1, Dec. 8, Dec. 15, 1975.

Jencks, Christopher: *Inequality: A Reassessment of the Effect of Family & Schooling in America*, Basic Books, Inc., Publishers, New York, 1972.

Nisbet, Robert: *Twilight of Authority*, Oxford University Press, New York, 1975.

Thurow, Lester C.: *Generating Inequality: Mechanisms of Distribution in the U.S. Economy*, Basic Books, Inc., Publishers, New York, 1975.

JOHN L. COBBS, *Business Week, McGraw-Hill Publications Company*

## Electronic data processing  (See COMPUTER SYSTEMS; DATA PROCESSING PRINCIPLES AND PRACTICES.)

## Emerson, Harrington  (See MANAGEMENT, HISTORICAL DEVELOPMENT OF.)

## Empathy  (See INTERPERSONAL RELATIONSHIPS.)

## Empirical approach  (See MANAGEMENT THEORY, SCIENCE, AND APPROACHES.)

## Employee benefits  (See COMPENSATION, EMPLOYEE BENEFIT PLANS.)

## Employee communications  (See COMMUNICATIONS, EMPLOYEE; COMMUNICATIONS, ORGANIZATIONAL.)

## Employee discipline  (See DISCIPLINE.)

## Employee handbook  (See PERSONAL ADMINISTRATION.)

## Employee minorities  (See MINORITIES, MANAGEMENT OF AND EQUAL EMPLOYMENT OPPORTUNITY.)

## Employee relations management  (See PERSONNEL ADMINISTRATION.)

## Employee selection, uniform guidelines  (See TESTING, PSYCHOLOGICAL.)

## Employee training  (See DEVELOPMENT AND TRAINING, EMPLOYEE.)

## Employees, older  (See OLDER EMPLOYEES, MANAGEMENT OF.)

## Employment and unemployment

The amounts of employment and unemployment existing within a nation, a state, or a community are widely regarded as key indicators of its economic well-being. *Full employment*, a term which defies precise definition, has been proclaimed as a major policy goal in virtually all industrialized nations, and the right of equal access to employment for all who desire to work has been widely acclaimed and underscored by specific legislation prohibiting discrimination. Professional management needs precise knowledge of the available data on employment and unemployment and the concepts underlying them in order to carry out its responsibility, to understand the economic environment in which it operates, and to exercise its forecasting, planning, and policy-making functions. The most widely accepted definitions of employment and unemployment are actually drawn from the measurement process.

**Measurement** In the United States, the official national estimates of employment and unemployment are prepared jointly by the Bureau of Census and the Bureau of Labor Statistics and are published monthly by the latter agency in *Employment and Earnings*. These national estimates are based on a monthly sample survey of the *labor force*, which is conceived as that portion of the total population which is "economically active," i.e., either at work for pay or profit or desiring work. The division between the total population and the labor force is thus determined by individual decisions to participate in or remain outside of the labor force. *Employed* in turn becomes that portion of the labor force which is at work, and *unemployed*, those individuals who are seeking work. The boundary lines between these paired groups, i.e., labor force and nonlabor force, employed and unemployed, are difficult to establish with precision. Classification rules, however, which have developed over many years in the conduct of the monthly survey provide meaningful and operational data in considerable detail.

The basis of classification is the reported activity during a specified week in the given month of each person included in the survey sample. Those classified as *employed* include:

1. All persons who worked (an hour or more) for pay or profit and those who worked 15 hours or more without pay in a family-operated enterprise

2. Those with a job but not at work because of one of the following:
   a. Vacation
   b. Illness
   c. Involvement in an industrial dispute
   d. Bad weather
   e. Time off for personal reasons

The *unemployed* component of the labor force includes:

1. Those who actively sought work during the previous 4 weeks (the tests of active search for work include registering at an employment office, interviewing with potential employers, placing or answering advertisements, writing letters of application, and being listed in a professional or union employment register)

2. Those waiting to start a new job within 30 days

3. Those waiting to be recalled from layoff

To be classified as unemployed, the individual must, in all cases be currently available for work.

The widely quoted *unemployment rate* is simply the volume of unemployment expressed as a percentage of the civilian labor force. As generated by the process described, however, published unemployment rates have been criticized by various groups as both "too high" and "too low." Critics in the first category argue that the estimating procedure gives equal weight to experienced, skilled workers with dependents and to young persons with no dependents seeking part-time or vacation employment. Acceptance of this point of view would imply the incorporation of some sort of judgment of need for work as a criterion for classifying an individual as unemployed, an almost impossible task. Those who contend that unemployment is understated point to the fact that those whose workweeks are less than full time are counted as employed and those who have been unable to find work and have given up an active search for jobs are considered to be outside the labor force and hence not unemployed.

*Data Analysis.* Criticisms of the key summary statistics, the monthly unemployment rate, lose much of their force when the analyst examines the detailed data available in the monthly reports and the annual summaries. For example, if one is convinced that the published unemployment rate is inflated because it includes young people and so-called "secondary workers" (those whose employment is less than essential to family support), one may examine unemployment rates by age group, by sex, or by duration of unemployment and may concentrate upon those who have been without work for 15 weeks or more, unemployed heads of households, or unemployed full-time workers. On the other hand, information is also available on the number of part-time workers who prefer full time jobs and the number of "discouraged workers," i.e., those who want jobs but have given up the search for work because they believe it is impossible to find. Although the unemployment data are sufficiently detailed to accommodate several concepts of unemployment, they must be studied in depth and over time. In the first place, there are seasonal variations; more importantly, changes and trends in unemployment (and employment) are influenced by shifts and changes within the labor force as well as by changes in the aggregate demand for labor. As population grows, the labor force grows and the number of new entrants and reentrants either directly into employment or into the ranks of the unemployed fluctuates over time. For example, civilian employment rose by approximately 1 million from August 1975 to February 1976. It had risen by almost the same amount in the previous 6 months. The labor force increased by 1.7 million, however, between February and August 1975, but by only 0.2 million in the next 6 months. This phenomenon was in part responsible for the rise in the unemployment rate over the first 6-month period and its decline during the second.

**Trends** Unemployment is by no means a purely contemporary problem in the industrialized world, nor indeed is it a problem only of the past 50 years. Unemployment became a matter of central, massive concern, however, during the worldwide depression that began in 1929. In the decade of the 1930s unemployment rates reached unprecedented heights and levels that, fortunately, have not since been equaled (Table E-1).

Despite widespread concern that unemployment, which had receded to very low levels during the World War II years, would rebound to intolerably high levels immediately following the end of the war, it did not do so. Except for the peaks reached in six postwar recessions, unemployment rates were for the most part below 5 percent of the civilian labor force over the years 1947–1975. During the same period, the civilian labor force expanded from 60 million to 92 million. The postwar recessions, however, of which the most recent was the most severe, underline the fact that unemployment remains a problem of continuing concern. Table E-2 sets forth the record and also indicates the differences in unemployment rates among various segments of the labor force.

**TABLE E-1  U.S. Unemployment Rates, 1929–1939**

| Year | Rate | Year | Rate |
|------|------|------|------|
| 1929 | 3.2  | 1935 | 20.1 |
| 1930 | 8.7  | 1936 | 16.9 |
| 1931 | 15.9 | 1937 | 14.3 |
| 1932 | 23.6 | 1938 | 19.0 |
| 1933 | 24.9 | 1939 | 17.2 |
| 1934 | 21.7 |      |      |

SOURCE: *Economic Report of the President*, January 1969.

These differences, particularly in the percentage distribution of unemployment, reflect long-term changes in the composition of the labor force, particularly the growing proportion of women among those working or seeking employment.

The severity of the 1974–1975 recession gave new emphasis to discussions of the problem of unemployment in the economy. Not only did unemployment rates reach the highest levels of the postwar years, but the average duration of unemployment lengthened and the number of discouraged workers increased substantially. The data show clearly that loss of jobs, rather than a major flow of new entrants and reentrants into the labor market was responsible for the upsurge in unemployment. Construction workers and workers in manufacturing showed the highest unemployment rates. Unemployment rates for black workers in all subgroups of the labor force continued to exceed those for whites.[1]

**Causes of Unemployment** It is obvious that the proximate cause for the unemployment of any individual may be the act of discharge or layoff by an

**TABLE E-2  Unemployment Highs in Postwar Recessions**

| Age and sex | Quarterly averages, seasonally adjusted, percent | | | | | |
|---|---|---|---|---|---|---|
| | IV 1949 | III 1954 | II 1958 | II 1961 | III 1971 | II 1975 |
| All workers | 7.0 | 6.0 | 7.4 | 7.0 | 6.0 | 8.9 |
| Both sexes, 16–19 years old | 15.0 | 13.7 | 16.3 | 16.3 | 16.9 | 20.5 |
| Males, 20–24 years old | 11.1 | 11.0 | 13.7 | 11.9 | 10.3 | 15.1 |
| Males, 25 years old and over | 5.9 | 4.9 | 6.2 | 5.5 | 3.5 | 5.8 |
| Females, 20–24 years old | 8.6 | 7.8 | 9.9 | 11.0 | 9.1 | 12.8 |
| Females, 25 years old and over | 5.3 | 4.8 | 6.2 | 6.1 | 5.0 | 7.5 |
| | Percent distribution | | | | | |
| Total unemployment | 100.0 | 100.0 | 100.0 | 100.0 | 100.0 | 100.0 |
| Both sexes, 16–19 years old | 15.1 | 14.1 | 13.9 | 16.1 | 25.3 | 21.8 |
| Males, 20–24 years old | 12.1 | 8.9 | 10.3 | 10.0 | 12.9 | 13.6 |
| Males, 25 years old and over | 50.5 | 49.6 | 48.7 | 44.2 | 29.2 | 30.5 |
| Females, 20–24 years old | 5.4 | 5.0 | 5.0 | 6.0 | 9.3 | 9.5 |
| Females, 25 years old and over | 16.9 | 22.3 | 22.1 | 23.7 | 23.3 | 24.6 |

*Note:* These are the actual highs of the seasonally adjusted unemployment rates and do not necessarily reflect the National Bureau of Economic Research troughs.

SOURCE: *Employment and Unemployment During 1975*, Special Labor Force Report 185, U.S. Department of Labor, Bureau of Labor Statistics, 1976.

employer or the act of quitting by an employee. Any serious reflection on the problem of unemployment, however, would require more than study of proximate or precipitating causes. Yet it is interesting to note that frequent commentary on the causes of unemployment imply acceptance of the notion that the responsibility for unemployment is somehow personal in nature. Management is criticized either for creating unemployment or for failing to provide a sufficient number of jobs; on the other hand, unemployed workers are often alleged to be either lazy or incompetent or unwilling to make a vigorous search for work. Actually, however, serious analysis of the causes of unemployment accepts the view that unemployment is the product of a constantly shifting market economy with broad economic, political, and social forces as its basic causes.

It is convenient to consider the causes of unemployment as falling into two main categories: those associated with insufficient demand for labor, and those associated with the structure and functioning of the labor market itself. Both categories may be further subdivided into short-term and long-term phenomena.

*Cyclical Unemployment.* Perhaps the most familiar type of unemployment is that associated with periodic recessions or depressions, often referred to as cyclical unemployment. Although there are many complex theories of the cyclical behavior of general economic activity, there is reasonable agreement that cyclical unemployment is the result of short-term inadequacy of total demand for goods and services. From time to time production falls short of the level necessary to utilize the existing labor force. Elimination of the gap requires increased business investment, government spending, or sales to foreign countries or else a rise in total consumer spending relative to income—one or the other or a combination. Unemployment arising out of inadequacies in total demand also has a long-run aspect. Over time, population and the labor force grow, and there is continuing improvement in production efficiency. Thus, in the long run, the volume of unemployment depends upon the rate of growth of the labor force, the rate of increase in output per worker-hour (the actual amount of labor required to produce a given quantity of product), the annual average number of hours worked, and the growth in aggregate demand for goods and services. In order to maintain an acceptable rate of unemployment over the long-run including periods of high-level business activity, aggregate demand must grow at a rate equal to the rate of growth in the labor force plus the rate of increase in productivity (output per unit of labor

employed) minus the rate at which average annual hours of work decline.

*Labor Market Dynamics.* The other major category of causes of unemployment is associated with the structure and functioning of labor markets. Full employment in the broadest terms means equating the demand for labor with the supply of labor. But both of these phenomena are, in reality, enormously complex. The demand for labor is a demand for individuals with hundreds if not thousands of different skills, experience, education and training, and personal characteristics in millions of different business units in different industries distributed over a very large country. Similarly, the supply of labor is a complex of millions of individuals possessing varied skills, experience, education, and personal traits; having markedly different preferences with respect to employment; and living in localities that may or may not correspond to areas of active demand for labor. It would indeed be miraculous if these complex structures meshed with each other perfectly and continously. Thus, full employment is not zero unemployment, and the residual of continuing unemployment attributable to less than perfect adjustments within labor markets is called frictional unemployment.

*Frictional Unemployment.* Not a matter of an insufficient number of job vacancies, frictional unemployment results because instantaneous adjustments to continuous, dynamic change in labor markets simply do not take place. As the tomato canning season ends, many of the workers employed drop out of the labor force; some, however, may start a search for work and are unemployed during the period of job search. Workers voluntarily leave jobs for a variety of reasons; others are separated for disciplinary reasons or because of an inability to meet the requirements of the job. Some businesses fail and close their doors; others begin operations. In all these cases, unemployed, displaced individuals do not immediately find a new job because (1) they lack complete and accurate information on job vacancies; (2) there may be no vacancies in the community in which they live, although employment opportunities may exist in other communities; or (3) despite a number of inquiries, they fail to locate opportunities that match their qualifications. For the same series of reasons, persons who enter the labor force for the first time, or those who reenter, may also experience periods of unemployment of varying duration. These spells of unemployment last until the individual either finds a job that matches personal qualifications and preferences or decides to leave the labor force. The frictionally unemployed group does not consist of the same individuals over time, for each day persons shift from employment to unemployment or from unemployment to employment. Similarly there are continuous shifts back and forth between employment and unemployment and the various groups of the population outside the labor force. The residual of all these shifts, assuming no deficiency in aggregate demand, on a given day or during a given week is frictional unemployment. In a very real sense this type of unemployment exists because there is individual freedom of choice in labor markets. Frictional unemployment, however, does impose costs in the form of lost wages for individuals, and its existence leaves the question of how much unemployment of this kind is necessary to assure flexibility in labor markets.

*Structural Unemployment.* Structural unemployment stems from a different but related set of circumstances. It resembles frictional unemployment in that it is associated with the structure and functioning of labor markets rather than aggregate demand, but it comes about over long periods of time. The composition of the demand for labor is not fixed but changes over time as technologies change and a different mix of individual skills and abilities among workers is required. Sometimes the changes take place slowly and imperceptibly; sometimes they have dramatic impact. Involved in this process are the rise of new industries, the industrial development of new areas, and the need for new occupations, new skills, and abilities coupled with the corresponding decline of older industries, areas, and skills. Thus the severity of structural unemployment depends on a number of variables. The rapidity of shifts in the composition of the demand for labor is an important factor, for it must be matched by equivalent changes in the composition of the labor supply if unemployment of potentially long duration is to be avoided. The possibility of timely adjustments within the labor supply in turn depends upon such matters as the flexibility of the skill requirements of jobs and the possibility of transferability of skills already possessed by workers in the labor force. The amount of education, training, and experience required in expanding industries, occupations, and areas is another important variable. Finally, the inability of workers to move geographically arising out of inadequate information about opportunities and moving costs, as well as a frequent reluctance to move, has created areas or pockets of unemployment that is structural in character.

There are obvious interactions between the two major causes of unemployment, deficiency in aggregate demand and frictional-structural factors. For example, the rate of frictional unemployment varies with the level of total demand for labor; i.e., the fewer job vacancies there are, the more rapidly those vacancies are filled. In the longer run, if the total demand for labor is inadequate, solutions to the problems of structural unemployment will not by themselves be able to bring about high levels of employment. Considerations of deficiency of aggregate demand and the best way to remove the deficiency are also intimately associated with contemporary discussion and debate over the relationship between price inflation and unemployment. Without attempting to summarize the complex and highly theoretical controversies involved, it seems clear that direct efforts to stimulate the economy, including tax reductions, increases in government spending, or significant increases in the money supply, will very likely reduce unemployment, but may simultaneously bring about significant increases in the level of prices.

**Responsibilities of Management** Management has the basic responsibility to operate a business enterprise efficiently, to produce a salable product, to market it effectively, and in so doing to make the most efficient use possible of both human and material resources. Although there are some opinions to the contrary, it is generally asserted that management, especially of a large enterprise, also has a significant social responsibility to the communities in which its plants are located and to the economy at large.

Management's initial responsibility with respect to unemployment is to seek understanding of the problem as one of continuing national concern. More specifically, management has the responsibility to analyze and take cognizance of the impact of its decisions upon the levels and fluctuations of employment and unemployment in its own plants and within the communities in which they are located. With appropriate consideration of external effects, management's effort to achieve maximum efficiency in the use of human resources may in a variety of ways help to improve the functioning of labor markets. For example, both voluntary and involuntary separations have the potential for producing periods of unemployment. Careful hiring practices to make sure that job applicants are a good "fit" for existing job vacancies, maintenance of a safe, healthy working environment, and responsible supervision should contribute to a reduction in job separations. By diligently applying policies of nondiscrimination in hiring and advancement, management may make some contribution to a reduction of the high rates of unemployment of minority groups. Private business firms carry on a very substantial amount of on-the-job training especially for new employees, which contributes to the development of skills and experience. Participation in apprenticeship training programs where appropriate has the same effects. All these activities have the potential for improving the functioning of labor markets. To serve the same objective, management should extend its full cooperation to federal and state employment services, particularly in the form of specific and detailed listings of all job vacancies.

In conjunction with the development of unemployment insurance legislation in the United States, there were strong views that business management, given sufficient incentive, could prevent unemployment. These views were in part responsible for the incorporation of experience rating in state unemployment insurance laws. While it is true that, in addition to the personnel practices previously noted, management in many enterprises has done a great deal to regularize employment through careful production planning and scheduling, management of inventories, and improvement of marketing methods, it is also true that the fundamental determinant of employment in a given business firm, large or small, is the level of demand for the firm's products. The level of demand for products and services is very closely correlated with the general level of business activity. If recession develops, declines in the demand for all kinds of products will take place, resulting in rising unemployment. Management therefore, cannot be held responsible for unemployment arising out of a short-term deficiency in aggregate demand or the failure of aggregate demand to grow at a sufficient rate over a longer term. The resulting unemployment is the result of broad complex economic forces.

The social responsibilities of management do not permit it, however, to ignore the phenomena of recession or inadequate growth. Managers must always seek to understand the economic environment in which they function and should be ready to offer thoughtful advice, consultation, and cooperation in governmental efforts to develop appropriate economic policies for dealing with unemployment. Regarding action as opposed to advice, management should certainly do everything in its power to avoid inflationary price increases at a time when the economy faces the risk of an excessive rate of growth. It might also reexamine the feasibility of price reductions, rather than reductions in output, during the early stages of a recession.

*See also* COMPENSATION, EMPLOYEE BENEFIT PLANS; ECONOMIC CONCEPTS; ECONOMIC MEASUREMENTS; ECONOMIC SYSTEMS; PRODUCTIVITY; WAGES AND HOURS LEGISLATION.

## NOTES
[1]For further details, *see* Stephen M. St. Marie and Robert W. Bednarzik, "Employment and Unemployment during 1975," *Monthly Labor Review*, February 1976, pp. 11–20.

## REFERENCES
Gilpatrick, Eleanor: "On the Classification of Unemployment: A View of the Structural-Inadequate Demand Debate," *Industrial and Labor Relations Review*, vol. 19, no. 2, January 1966, pp. 201–212.

Hamermesh, Daniel S.: *Manpower Policy and the Economy*, General Learning Press, New York, 1971.

Kalacheck, Edward D.: *Labor Markets and Unemployment*, Wadsworth Publishing Company, Inc., Belmont, Calif., 1973.

Marshall, F. Ray, Allan M. Carter, and Allan G. King: *Labor Economies: Wages, Employment and Trade Unionism*, 3d ed., Richard D. Irwin, Inc., Homewood, Ill., 1976.

Reynolds, Lloyd G.: *Labor Economies and Labor Relations*, 6th ed., Richard D. Irwin, Inc., Homewood, Ill., 1976.

Shiskin, Julius: "Employment and Unemployment: The Doughnut or the Hole?" *Monthly Labor Review*, vol. 99, no. 2, February 1976, pp. 3–10.

TAULMAN A. MILLER, *Indiana University*

## Employment office (*See* PERSONNEL ADMINISTRATION.)

## Employment process

The employment process can be conceptualized as consisting of eight essential steps. If these are observed, job misfits can be avoided, and equally important, good potential employees will not be overlooked. It provides a procedure for matching applicants and jobs which is thorough, expeditious, and objective. It is a positive process, which aims to put persons in the jobs for which they are best qualified in terms of what they *can* do and what they *will* do. It requires, however, that the interviewer have a thorough knowledge of the job demands, the human environment on the job, and the quantity and quality of supervision needed and given. Thus, the interviewer first makes a diagnosis, then a prognosis of possible job success.

*Establishing Specifications.* Formal job descriptions and specifications give only a superficial picture of what a job actually entails. In addition, the following questions must be considered:

How often is this person supervised?

What type of supervision will be provided?

How does the supervisor wish to see the job done?

Is the supervision provided by someone with the same specialty?

Is there a rule book to go by?

What are the practical possibilities for promotion?

With what types of people must the new employee get along?

How much pressure does the job entail?

How much interference is there with normal family life?

To what extent is initiative desirable?

To what extent is creativity essential?

How much does the job involve exercise of authority over people?

To what degree is administrative know-how required?

What is the most difficult aspect of this particular job?

What are the political aspects of the job?

*Recruiting.* The one fundamental rule for successful recruiting is this: the more candidates there are for any available job, the greater the opportunity is to fill that job with the right person the first time. There is no "one best" recruiting technique for all firms for all situations. Many methods can be used, including newspaper classified and display ads, radio announcements, handbills, company bulletin boards, the state employment service, private employment agencies, college and university placement bureaus, industrial and professional organizations, billboards, job offers to present employees, the company publication, trade and technical magazine advertising, and motion picture and TV advertising. Each, or all, of the methods should be used experimentally until the most appropriate and best one is found.

*Screening.* An applicant screening form should be compiled for each job opening. It is designed to get the factual information needed to make judgments about qualifications. The form should request the applicant's name, address, telephone number, past three jobs (over three jobs in the past 5 years often indicates instability), present employed status, availability to begin work, earning requirements, ability to travel, freedom to relocate, driver's license number, bonding history, etc. The specification sheet should be reviewed for factors which may prove to be "knockout" factors. To expedite the

screening process much can be done on the telephone to screen out unqualified candidates.

*Testing.* Tests are of value, particularly in helping to evaluate what a person *can do* based on intelligence, aptitudes, and proficiency. Tests are also of value in evaluating *will-do* factors, which are based on personality, temperament, and motivation. Projective techniques are helpful if a qualified professional psychologist interprets the test results in the light of job conditions and demands. Tests and testing procedures must meet EEOC requirements.

*Reference Checking.* Consciously or unconsciously, people are not always truthful in telling about themselves. They tend to put the most favorable interpretation upon whatever has happened to them in the past. At least three telephone reference checks should be conducted, and it is best to check with the person's former supervisor or operating official rather than with persons in the personnel department. Also, utilize college transcripts, credit reports (with the person's permission as required by law), a bonding company, and the individual's W-2 form. Checking personal or character references is almost uniformly futile.

*Interviewing.* A *guided interview form* should be utilized to aid in eliciting all the information needed about a particular person. It differs from the screening form in that it is far more comprehensive, for it is designed to learn about the attitudes and feelings of the person and is used only with previously screened prospects. The interview lends itself to analysis of what the individual will do by reviewing what the candidate has done in the past.

*Evaluating the Candidate.* Interpreting the guided interview information enables the interviewer to forecast what an individual will do. Behavior patterns that are important (in variable degrees) in most jobs relate to job tenure, work habits, tenacity, competitive spirit, loyalty, planning, organizing activity, relations with others, and the ability to lead.

*Selecting the Right Person.* At this point the several qualified candidates may be rated on a four-level scale:

1. Almost perfectly qualified
2. Well qualified—no serious deficiencies
3. Marginally qualified—seriously deficient in at least one will-do requirement
4. Unqualified

The question of whether or not a particular applicant should be employed depends also upon certain factors outside his or her qualifications. For example, if there are a large number of 1s, the firm can afford to be selective. Urgency in filling the position without delay may necessitate hiring a 3. One should not, however, be tempted to raise the rating to a 2. Instead, the individual who was given the 3 rating should be hired with the total understanding that the chance for success and permanence is the same as the individual's qualifications: marginal.

*Summary.* Shortcuts are not advisable. The important thing is to go through all the eight steps. There is no substitute for systematic thoroughness.

*See also* COMPENSATION, WAGE AND SALARY ADMINISTRATION; INTERVIEWING, EMPLOYEE; JOB ANALYSIS AND EVALUATION; PERSONNEL ADMINISTRATION; TESTING, PSYCHOLOGICAL.

### REFERENCES

Farmer, Anthony X.: "How to Hire the Right Person the First Time," *Training Management and Motivation,* Spring 1976.

Fear, Richard A.: *The Evaluation Interview,* 2d ed., McGraw-Hill Book Company, New York, 1973.

Lopez, Felix M.: *Personnel Interviewing,* 2d ed., McGraw-Hill Book Company, New York, 1975.

Miner, John B., and Mary Green Miner: "Screening and Selection," *Personnel and Industrial Relations: A Managerial Approach,* 2d ed., Macmillan Publishing Co., Inc., New York, 1973, part IV.

ANTHONY X. FARMER, *The Personnel Laboratory, Inc.*

# Employment system, permanent (*See* JAPANESE INDUSTRIES, MANAGEMENT IN.*)

# Energy resources, management of

Most managers readily accept the long-term view that conservation of energy resources is needed to ensure that sources of power will be available to meet future needs. This view discounts our ability, however, to innovate technologically. It is therefore suggested that a shorter-term view be taken as the basis for energy management. Astute business people can, and should, manage their resources for profit.

Unlike other business inputs, the effort required to manage energy resources is not always commensurate with the profits to be obtained. This must be determined on a case-by-case basis. "Energy crunches" may strike at any time, and curtailments of electrical power, gas, and oil are not an aberration of the past. These events can be expected to be repeated in the near term as demand for energy continues to escalate and the world moves from the petroleum age to the nuclear and solar age. The impact of these transitory problems will best be resolved by those who comprehend and manage their energy resources.

**Essential Elements** Four basic elements should be integrated into an energy resources management program:

1. Determination of areas where opportunities for improvement exist. Note that opportunity does not necessarily result in direct savings. A savings of energy represents one kind of improvement opportunity, but an increase in production with a substantially smaller increase in energy input is also an opportunity.

2. Decision as to whether implementation of corrective action makes economic and financial sense.

3. Consideration of the impact of energy decisions on the health and safety of employees. Allowing building temperatures to drop to intolerable levels in the interest of saving energy is folly, of course, but there are other, more subtle traps that are easy to fall into.

4. Management's continuing commitment. This implies far more than keeping a report on a shelf for interested people to read. Management continuity (*a*) implies a commitment of company talent and resources to maintaining an environment of energy awareness and (*b*) extends to encouraging employees in energy conservation at home. It also involves making hard economic choices to demonstrate to employees that management believes this activity to be important.

## IMPROVEMENT OPPORTUNITIES

Five basic steps to manage energy resources and determine conservation potential are as follows:

1. The energy audit
2. Conservation/conversion evaluation
3. The energy availability forecast
4. Progress measurement
5. Repetition of the steps

The key is the energy audit and the conservation/conversion evaluation.

### THE ENERGY AUDIT

The energy audit provides a systematic method for management to get on top of the energy situation. The understanding gained from an analysis of energy application may not eliminate all risks from energy-related decisions, but it will identify current and basic ramifications of the problem.

An energy audit is not to be an engineering study. The audit is a management tool, and once the purpose is clearly stated the detailed engineering study can follow.

**Purpose**  The first step in an energy audit is to establish the purpose clearly. This ensures that all participants understand the goal toward which they are working. In addition, it helps to keep the objectives clearly in focus as the study proceeds.

The purpose of an energy audit is to size up a plant's energy situation quickly so as to provide a firm foundation for profitable decisions. The audits should point to energy reduction potential, potential for avoiding a shutdown, a methodology for reducing energy use, and documentation of an action plan. Documentation is an important step, as evidenced by legislative requirements of federal and state governments.

**Foundation Studies**  Expected energy activity can be effectively defined by studying a 5-year history and making 5-year projections.

*Historical Data.*  Several factors should be examined in the 5-year history: monthly usage, costs per period, cost per unit of energy, and production levels. Relationships can be developed to show production units per 1000 Btu's of energy input and energy cost as a percent of product cost. The form shown in Table E-3 is typical of those used to collect this data.

*Projections.*  Five-year projections should include projected production levels; energy requirements; total costs per period; future productions per 1000 Btu's; energy costs as a percent of product costs; purchasing factors, such as expected availability and expected unit cost changes; and other aspects, such as alternative considerations and possible governmental impact.

*Analysis.*  The final step in developing the foundation elements is to detail current energy use *by type*. A pie chart indicating the amount of each energy form used in a particular operation helps to visualize this analysis. It is also desirable to estimate usage. This is a management study and need not be as accurate as an engineering audit. The pie chart shown in Fig. E-3 is representative of the output of this step.

**Reduction Potential**  The largest energy users in the facility can be isolated by examining the significant portions of each slice of the pie chart. Generally, the traditional ABC curve will be the rule; that is, 20 percent of the operations will account for 80 percent of the energy used.

Each large energy user should be examined to determine if utilization patterns can be altered. Several approaches may be considered: for example, reduction of fuel input, increase in equipment productivity, alternative fuels, more modern technology, improved metallurgical consciousness, the use of waste heat recovery, use of regulatory devices such as thermostats, and preventive maintenance.

**Course of Action**  A study without a recommendation for action is a waste of time. The recommendation, of course, may simply be to do nothing. The key, however, is to arrive at a decision based on an analysis of facts economically available and the good business judgment of the people responsible for a profitable operation. The final decision should fall into one of three general categories:

1. Specific action is deferred until a later date when conditions are more suitable.

2. A simple conservation program should be implemented.

3. Development of a definite capital expenditure program is deemed desirable for any of several reasons.

*Major Considerations.*  Several major considerations should play a role in making the decision. First, the return on investment should meet minimum company financial requirements. While social considerations cannot be ignored, no business can survive long without a satisfactory profit.

Second, deferment of a potential curtailment of the facility's energy supply should be considered. If positive action to conserve resources can place a company in a favorable light with local utilities or government agencies, then expenditure of funds may be wise. While this decision may not be readily convertible into a return-on-investment analysis, it falls into a category of need that cannot be ignored.

Third, the practices of the company's neighbors should be considered. If the facility is the only one in a community practicing conservation, it will probably be subject to curtailment, no matter how much fuel is saved, since curtailment is a function of total demand in a specified time period in a specific geographic area.

Finally, a company should consider the consumer and/or political benefits which may accrue because of its favorable actions and reputation in the community.

In short, the decision to take action must be based on long-run needs for profitable operations but must also take into account what is expected from a responsible citizen in the community.

**Taking Action**  Documentation should support two objectives. First, the foundation methods and future implications must be clearly and concisely recorded so that others may readily grasp the signif-

**TABLE E-3   Data Collection Form**

**PART A**

MONTHLY DEPARTMENT ENERGY USE

| | Raw material "A" | | | Raw material "B" | | | Raw material "C" | | | Total raw material Btu | Raw material Btu per unit of production | Total conversion and raw material Btu per unit of production |
|---|---|---|---|---|---|---|---|---|---|---|---|---|
| | k lb | Btu/k lb | Btu | k lb | Btu/k lb | Btu | k lb | Btu/k lb | Btu | | | |
| Jan. | | | | | | | | | | | | |
| Feb. | | | | | | | | | | | | |
| Mar. | | | | | | | | | | | | |
| Apr. | | | | | | | | | | | | |
| May | | | | | | | | | | | | |
| June | | | | | | | | | | | | |
| July | | | | | | | | | | | | |
| Aug. | | | | | | | | | | | | |
| Sep. | | | | | | | | | | | | |
| Oct. | | | | | | | | | | | | |
| Nov. | | | | | | | | | | | | |
| Dec. | | | | | | | | | | | | |

**PART B**

MONTHLY DEPARTMENT ENERGY USE

| | psig steam | | | psig steam | | | Condensate used or lost | | | Water | | | Total conversion Btu | Number of units produced | Conversion Btu per unit of production |
|---|---|---|---|---|---|---|---|---|---|---|---|---|---|---|---|
| | k lb | Btu/k lb | Btu | k lb | Btu/k lb | Btu | k lb | Btu/k lb | Btu | k lb | Btu/k lb | Btu | | | |
| Jan. | | | | | | | | | | | | | | | |
| Feb. | | | | | | | | | | | | | | | |
| Mar. | | | | | | | | | | | | | | | |
| Apr. | | | | | | | | | | | | | | | |
| May | | | | | | | | | | | | | | | |
| June | | | | | | | | | | | | | | | |
| July | | | | | | | | | | | | | | | |
| Aug. | | | | | | | | | | | | | | | |
| Sep. | | | | | | | | | | | | | | | |
| Oct. | | | | | | | | | | | | | | | |
| Nov. | | | | | | | | | | | | | | | |
| Dec. | | | | | | | | | | | | | | | |

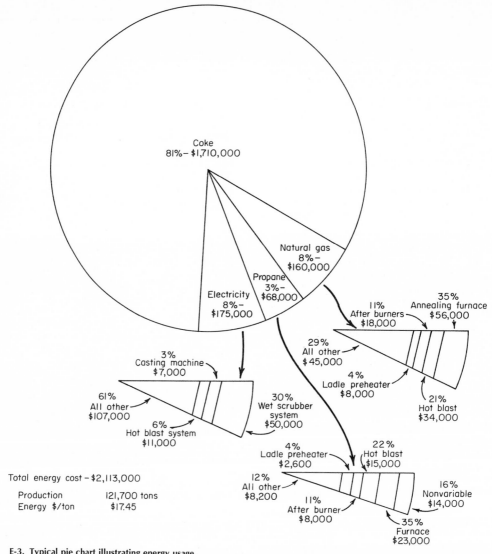

Coke
81%– $1,710,000

Natural gas
8%–
$160,000

Propane
3%–
$68,000

Electricity
8%–
$175,000

11%
After burners–
$18,000

35%
Annealing furnace
$56,000

3%
Casting machine–
$7,000

29%
All other–
$45,000

4%
Ladle preheater–
$8,000

61%
All other–
$107,000

6%
Hot blast system
$11,000

30%
Wet scrubber
system
$50,000

21%
Hot blast
$34,000

4%
Ladle preheater–
$2,600

22%
Hot blast
$15,000

12%
All other–
$8,200

16%
Nonvariable
$14,000

11%
After burner–
$8,000

35%
Furnace
$23,000

Total energy cost – $2,113,000

Production         121,700 tons
Energy $/ton      $17.45

**E-3. Typical pie chart illustrating energy usage.**

icance of the study. Second, the plan of action must clearly define paths to be taken to achieve the desired goals. The successful implementation plan has four basic elements:

1. The task
2. The deadline
3. The person(s)
4. The leader(s)

Studies of this type can normally be accomplished in 3 to 6 weeks depending on the complexity of the situation and the experience of the personnel assigned. The technology employed, while not so-

phisticated, is adequate for reliable preliminary indications.

**Other Audit Ideas** A valuable addition to the literature was made in March 1976 when the Office of Energy Conservation, Department of Energy, Mines and Resources, of the government of Canada produced a publication entitled *First Steps to Energy Conservation for Business*. It suggested multiple surveys, or different types of surveys, as follows:

1. Survey of housekeeping conditions such as inadequate insulation, machinery functioning when not in use, and steam leaks.

2. General survey of processes, departments, and products, with the purpose of developing an energy report for each of them. This report might specify total input of energy in Btu's, total number of units of product turned out, and total Btu's per unit of product.

3. Analysis of surveyed processes, departments, and products to determine just how waste energy can be recovered, how processes may be altered, what inefficient equipment might be replaced, and how often energy sources might be used most profitably.

4. Weekend and night audits when the plant or business is not operational. This will isolate the amount of energy wasted during nonworking hours.

5. Survey of specific processes and equipment, such as the heating and air-conditioning system, the steam system, and the electric motors.

## FINANCIAL ANALYSIS

It is important that economic evaluations of energy conservation opportunities be consistent. An energy investment, like all others, should be tested by some quantitative measure of profitability so that its expected return can be compared with alternative investment opportunities.

Energy conservation opportunities which directly generate benefits greater than costs are profitable and attractive. Other opportunities requiring an initial capital outlay can be amortized by the energy savings generated over their anticipated lifetime.

The basic tools of financial analysis apply to the economic evaluation of each conservation opportunity as follows:

**Levels of Analysis** Energy investment decisions should be based on more than simple rates of return, or return on investment (ROI). Factors such as risk, cash flow, taxation schedules, and long- versus short-term investment preferences must be considered. In actual application, however, these factors vary greatly among companies and are not introduced in the measurement criteria presented here. The analysis discussed will be at various levels of financial sensitivity.

The first level allows for a rapid screening of conservation measures and rejection due to low or negative ROI. The second-level measures incorporate an allowance for the time value of money. The third-level of performance deals with marginal analysis for those opportunities whose ROI decrease as the investment increases.

The information needed to perform financial analysis consists of the following:

First cost of the conservation measure: dollars
Operating cost of the measure: dollars/year
Energy savings: MBtu/year
Fuel price: dollars/MBtu
Lifetime of the measure: years
Corporate discount rate: percent

For simplicity, salvage value of the investment is disregarded here.

**First-Level Measures** The measurement criteria included here are payback period and return-on-investment. In general, these criteria should not be used for justifying major investments for energy conservation projects since they do not reflect the time value of money. These criteria are useful, however, in screening out opportunities without application of more sophisticated criteria.

*Return on investment*
$$\text{ROI} = \frac{\text{savings} - \text{depreciation}}{\text{first cost}} \times 100\%$$

where savings = (energy savings × fuel price)
− annual operating cost

$$\text{depreciation} = \frac{\text{first cost}}{\text{lifetime of measure}}$$
(assuming straight line method)

Note that annual operating costs include the ongoing cost of maintenance and operating costs that reduce the gross annual savings.

Where the ROI is less than 15–20 percent, second-level measures are required.

*Payback period*
$$\text{Payback period} = \frac{\text{first cost}}{\text{savings}}$$

Comparing the payback period with the expected lifetime of the investment provides a quick judgment as to its potential for recoupment.

**Second-Level Measures** These measurement criteria incorporate an allowance for the time value of money, generally in the form of a discount factor.

The criteria to be discussed at this level are the following three: (1) cost-benefit, (2) capital investment recovery, and (3) internal rate of return.

*Cost-Benefit Analysis.* This analysis compares the present value benefits of the lifetime savings generated by a given investment with the first cost. A ratio greater than unity implies that such an investment is profitable.

The present worth factor (PWF) for an investment with a given discount rate and project life can be found in present value tables in this volume, or from the equation

$$\text{PWF} = \frac{1 - (1 + r)^n}{r}$$

where $r$ = discount rate, percent/100
$n$ = project life, years

$$\text{Cost benefit} = \frac{\text{present value}}{\text{first cost}}$$

where present value = savings $\times$ PWF

*Capital Investment Recovery.* This analysis is similar to that of the payback period except that the break-even period takes into consideration the discount rate and the cost of foregone investment opportunities. If the appropriate discount rate has been applied, any investment which is recouped in a period less than its lifetime should be considered profitable. The break-even period can be calculated from the equation

$$\text{PWF} = \frac{1 - (1 + r)^{-n}}{r}$$

simply by substituting the payback period for the expression PWF and solving for $n$.

*Internal Rate of Return.* The internal rate of return (IRR) is that discount rate which reduces the savings associated with an investment to a present value of zero; that is, the present value equals the first cost. The IRR is often considered to be the appropriate discount rate for evaluating investment opportunities. If the IRR is below the true borrowing rate then the discount rate must be at least as high as the borrowing rate.

The solution for IRR is not straightforward but requires an iterative approach for those investments which have an unequal stream of benefits. If the stream of benefits (savings) are constant each year over the life of the investment, the IRR can be computed relatively easily.

$$\text{First cost} = \text{savings} \times \text{PWF}$$

where $\text{PWF} = \dfrac{1 - (1 + r)^{-n}}{r}$

Solving for $r$ yields the internal rate of return.

This criterion indicates if the discounted value of the benefits using the required discount rate is greater than or equal to the first cost.

**Marginal Investment** Many conservation opportunities have returns which decrease as the investment increases, such as the application of insulation. Each increment of insulation generates less savings than the last.

These investments can be considered by determining the investment level beyond which no savings are generated which offset the cost, that is, the marginal savings equals the marginal cost.

$$\text{MS} = \text{MC}$$

where MS = the present value savings generated by the last increment of the project
MC = the present value cost of the last increment

The use of marginal analysis will aid in determining the point at which adding investment ceases to be profitable. It also will indicate the reduction in investment levels in a proposed project that is unprofitable to a point where the project may indeed be made profitable.

**Project Evaluation Summary** Each project under consideration should be summarized for evaluation purposes. A typical evaluation summary form is illustrated in Table E-4. Sample calculations are shown in Table E-5.

## SAFETY AND HEALTH CONSIDERATIONS

As a facility's energy conservation program progresses, it will inevitably interface with the pollution control program, and certain conservation actions will affect the safety and health conditions within the plant. In some cases, measures designed to conserve or recover energy may create a local pollution problem unless appropriate actions are taken as the changes are made.

Better elimination of hot surfaces and containment of energy losses in escaping hot fluids may result in a gain in plant safety. In other cases, where closer attention to process equipment requires more frequent operator or maintenance actions, opportunities for accidents may increase.

In any event, energy conservation programs should be examined as to their specific advantages and precautions as they affect safety and health. Advantages, in some cases, may be credited as a cost savings while disadvantages may require the extra expense of appropriate countermeasures. Such savings and costs should be included in evaluating the economics of alternative energy conservation measures.

**Pollution Control** Energy conservation opportunities which result in reduced material losses, recovery of heat, or a more optimal process may also have environmental benefits, such as the following:

1. Process leaks cause losses in chemicals and heat and increase basic material and fuel costs. If these leaks find their way into the environment or to a waste treatment system, they cause either environmental degradation or increased waste treatment costs. Repairs, as part of an energy conservation program, minimize these side effects.

**TABLE E-4   Project Analysis Form**

**PART A**

ENERGY CONSERVATION PROJECT
EVALUATION SUMMARY

Capital_____ or Expense_____

Department _____

Date_____

Project No. _____ Person responsible _____

Project title _____

Description of project _____

_____

_____

_____

_____

_____

_____

Location _____

*Financial Evaluation*

Estimated

Energy saving (electric power, kilowatthour per year; steam pound per year etc.)

Utility or raw material

_____    _____ /year

_____    _____ /year

_____    _____ /year

Total energy saving _____    _____ MBtu/year

Total energy cost saving _____    _____ $/year

Other cost saving due to

_____    _____ $/year

Additional cost due to

_____    _____ $/year

Net cost saving _____    _____ $/year

Cost of project _____    _____ $

**PART B**

ENERGY CONSERVATION PROJECT
EVALUATION SUMMARY

Calculated

Return on investment _____ %

Payback period_____ months

Other_____

Btu/unit of production: Now _____ After project    implemented _____

*Benefits/Problems*

Product quality _____

Product yield _____

Production rate _____

Safety _____

Pollution_____

Maintenance-work force/materials_____

Utilities_____

Working conditions_____

Employee attitude_____

Community _____

Other benefits/problems connected with implementation

_____

_____

_____

Comments _____

Project rating _____

_____

Planned authorization request date_____

**TABLE E-5  Example of Project Analysis Calculations**

Project financial information
First cost = $75,000
Operating cost = $2,500/year
Energy savings = 30,000 MBtu/year
Fuel price = $1/MBtu, projected over project life
Life of project = 10 years
Corporate discount rate = 20%

Return on investment

$$\text{Depreciation} = \frac{\$75,000}{10} = \$7,500/\text{year}$$

$$\text{Savings} = 30,000 \times \text{Btu/year} \times \$1/\text{MBtu} - \$2,500$$
$$= \$27,500/\text{year}$$

$$\text{ROI} = \frac{\$27,500/\text{year} - \$7,500/\text{year}}{\$75,000} \times 100\% = 27\%$$

Payback period

$$\text{Payback period} = \frac{\$75,000}{\$27,500} = 2.7 \text{ years}$$

Cost benefit

$$\text{PWF} = \frac{1 - (1 + .20)^{-10}}{0.20} = 4.192$$

$$\text{Present value} = \$27,500/\text{year} \times 4.192 = \$115,280$$

$$\text{Cost benefit} = \frac{\$115,280}{\$75,000} = \$1.54$$

Note: Ratio is greater than unity; therefore project is profitable.

Capital investment recovery

$$2.7 = \frac{1 - (1 + 0.20)^{-n}}{0.20}$$
$$n = 4.3 \text{ years}$$

Internal rate of return

$$\$75,000 = \$27,500 \times \frac{1 - (1 + r)}{r}$$
$$r = 34\%$$

2. Returning condensate to the boiler plant eliminates discharging high-quality water and needless waste treatment.

Although the majority of energy-saving measures have beneficial environmental effects, there are certain conservation practices that might have unfavorable local effects.

1. Reduction in building exhausts and make-up air usually results in decreased air pollution costs and energy savings. This action, however, might cause ventilation to drop below OSHA requirements for the nature of materials handled in the plant.

2. Regular cleaning of fouling from water lines is a good practice; however, care must be taken so that the cleaning compounds used are compatible with the waste treatment system and will not overload the system when discharging large, concentrated amounts of cleaning solutions at one time.

**Safety and Health**  Energy conservation progress may require changes in operating and maintenance procedures. This may result in changes to existing equipment and/or the installation of new equipment. Plant safety engineers responsible for identifying unsafe conditions should be called upon to review these changes.

Management must also be on guard for actions that might result in a conflict with applicable safety and health standards or insurance requirements. A warehouse storing flammable materials, for example, may have been designed for a specific number of air changes per hour based upon safety requirements involving the insurance carrier, regulatory agency, and OSHA. Reducing the ventilation to save energy without considering the safety factors would be a serious error. Safety personnel included on the energy conservation team assure an early consideration of safety in planning each conservation project.

## MANAGEMENT CONTINUITY

As energy is used more effectively, product costs can be reduced and profits improved. This can be accomplished, however, only by a long-term, continuing effort on the part of management. Energy conservation must become part of the everyday plant functions and must receive the support of everyone from top management on down the organization chart. A new box on the organization chart devoted to energy conservation will *not* get the energy conservation job accomplished. A commitment must be made at all levels in the organization.

**Management Organization**  Initiation of an aggressive energy conservation program must start at the top, and top management should appoint a single person to act as the energy coordinator.

The role of the coordinator will be to provide continuity and control to the program. He or she will develop plans, establish channels of communication between plant departments and employees, acquire and disseminate information, and develop various outside contacts on conservation.

To assist the coordinator, a committee can be formed from representatives of the various departments. Committee members provide the communication link between the committee and key supervisors. It is the responsibility of top management to provide the committee with guidelines as to what is expected of them and to set goals in energy savings.

Top management must also stand ready to assist in implementing approved conservation measures.

**Employee Involvement** Energy conservation is achieved through line management, but it must receive the cooperation and commitment of all employees. It can be successful only if it arouses and maintains the interest and participation of all employees.

Employee involvement can be increased on the job in a number of ways including the use of newsletters, bulletin boards, posters emphasizing energy conservation, and periodic progress reports from top management. Participation can be encouraged by suggestion awards for successful ideas on energy savings opportunities. Competition between departments or processes (as measured in terms of savings of Btu's used per unit of production) also stimulates more active involvement.

To maintain full-time employee involvement, off-the-job energy conservation should also be encouraged. The use of car pools and home energy conservation should be stressed.

The two basic elements of employee participation are communication and education. These must be a continuing effort. Conservation literature readily available from government agencies and utilities can aid in both activities.

*See also* BUDGETING, CAPITAL; COST-BENEFIT ANALYSIS; ENVIRONMENT, PHYSICAL; ENVIRONMENTAL PROTECTION LEGISLATION; REGULATED INDUSTRIES, MANAGEMENT OF; TECHNOLOGY, MANAGEMENT IMPLICATIONS; VALUE SYSTEMS: MANAGEMENT: SOCIAL AND CULTURAL.

### REFERENCES

Cotz, Victor J.: *Plant Engineer's Manual and Guide*, Prentice-Hall, Inc., Englewood Cliffs, N.J., 1974.

*How to Start an Energy Management Program*, Office of Energy Programs, U.S. Department of Commerce, Washington, October 1973.

Lund, Herbert F.: *Handbook of Industrial Pollution Control*, McGraw-Hill Book Company, New York, 1970.

*33 Money-Saving Ways to Conserve Energy in Your Business*, Office of Energy Programs, U.S. Department of Commerce, Washington, November 1973.

*United States Energy: A Summary Review*, U.S. Department of the Interior, Washington, January, 1972.

BERNARD S. GUTOW, *A. T. Kearney, Inc., Management Consultants*
MICHAEL E. HORA, *A. T. Kearney, Inc., Management Consultants*

## Engineer, plant (*See* PLANT ENGINEERING MANAGEMENT.)

## Engineering, application (*See* MARKETING, INDUSTRIAL.)

## Engineering, industrial

Industrial engineers, trained in the principles of work study, operations research, ergonomics, behavioral science, computer science, administration, economics, systems analysis and design, statistics, value engineering, quality control, and many other specialized fields, apply their unique skills in every type of business and manufacturing and service industry.

In the service industries industrial engineers use operations research techniques to (1) schedule traffic and maintenance in the transportation industry, (2) improve the flow of work in large offices, (3) develop more efficient methods for distributing the mail and retail goods, and (4) allocate city services.

In the manufacturing industries industrial engineers (1) locate and lay out new facilities, (2) select processes and methods, (3) develop work standards, (4) design and install management information and data processing systems and materials requirement planning systems, (5) perform economic analyses, (6) make job evaluations, and (7) institute adequate safety and health procedures.

Depending on the area of specialization, an industrial engineer may work under many different titles, including methods engineer, systems engineer, and sometimes manufacturing or production engineer. Regardless of title, the industrial engineering profession is best distinguished by the confluence of historical and modern engineering principles creatively applied to the improvement of productivity. Although the principles of industrial engineering were applied long before the industrial revolution when civilized people first began to organize and improve their labor efforts, the definition adopted by the 30,000-member American Institute of Industrial Engineers reflects the work of many industrial engineers, scientists, and academicians, beginning with the work of Frederick C. Taylor in about 1890. This definition reads:

Industrial Engineering is concerned with the design, improvement, and installation of integrated systems of people, material, equipment, and energy. It draws upon the specialized knowledge and skills in the mathematical, physical and social sciences together with the principles and methods of engineering analysis and design to specify, predict, and evaluate the results to be obtained from such systems.

Taylor, the father of scientific management, began a systematic study of ways to improve labor productivity among steelworkers in the late 1890s. He eventually developed a series of principles of scientific management. During the early 1900s many pioneers in the scientific approach to management added to the body of knowledge, forming the foundation of modern industrial engineering. Henry Gantt developed management procedures and principles and a humanistic approach to management. Frank and Lillian Gilbreth worked extensively with motion study and methods improvement. Harrington Emerson evolved a set of efficiency and organization principles and a bonus payment incentive plan.

*See also* ACCOUNTING, COST ANALYSIS AND CONTROL; COMPENSATION, WAGE AND SALARY POLICY AND ADMINISTRATION; COST IMPROVEMENT; JOB ANALYSIS; PAPER WORK SIMPLIFICATION; PRODUCTION/OPERATIONS MANAGEMENT; PRODUCTION PROCESSES; SYSTEM CONCEPT, TOTAL; SYSTEMS AND PROCEDURES; THERBLIGS; VALUE ANALYSIS; WORK, CONCEPT AND IMPLICATIONS; WORK DESIGN, JOB ENLARGEMENT, JOB ENRICHMENT, JOB DESIGN, AND AUTONOMOUS WORK GROUPS; WORK MEASUREMENT; WORK SAMPLING; WORK SIMPLIFICATION AND IMPROVEMENT.

## REFERENCES

Emerson, Harrington: *The Twelve Principles of Efficiency*, The Engineering Magazine Company, New York, 1912.

Rathe, Alex W., ed.: *Gantt on Management*, American Management Association and American Society of Mechanical Engineers, New York, 1961.

Taylor, Frederick W.: *The Principles of Scientific Management*, Harper & Brothers, New York, 1911.

CHARLES BOYER, *Industrial Engineering, American Institute of Industrial Engineers, Inc.*

## Engineering, plant   (*See* PLANT ENGINEERING MANAGEMENT.)

## Engineering, quality   (*See* QUALITY MANAGEMENT.)

## Engineering, safety   (*See* SAFETY AND HEALTH MANAGEMENT, EMPLOYEE.)

## Engineering, systems   (*See* SYSTEM CONCEPT, TOTAL.)

## Engineering management

Engineering, which can be defined as the adaptation of natural forces and materials to their beneficial use

by human beings, is practiced in a wide range of industrial, institutional, and governmental organizations. In the normal industrial firm, engineering may be found in the organization structure in facilities design, product design, service engineering, and maintenance or plant engineering. In institutions such as hospitals, universities, and public school systems, facility and maintenance engineering also play a key role. Another important area is consulting and design engineering provided by professional firms. *Engineering News-Record* reported that its listing of the top 415 design firms in 1975 represented billings of approximately $3 billion and staffs of 86,000 people. These firms engage primarily in the construction design of new facilities and in planning and economic feasibility studies. In addition, there are numerous firms in the "design-construct" classification which provide turnkey services from initial design of a plant or facility through construction and start-up.

While the broad concepts of managing these activities are the same as those for management in general, some special conditions and tools of managing must be recognized and used by the successful engineering manager. Professional engineering resources are available as time, such as worker-hours, worker-days, etc. They cannot be stored or inventoried. They must be used effectively or they are wasted. The engineering manager's principal goal is to optimize the utilization of the professional and technical resources in an organization when guiding that organization toward meeting its objectives.

While the specific examples that follow are based upon the management of a professional consulting and design firm, the concepts and approaches apply to engineering activities in all types of organizations.

### OVERALL PLANNING

The first step in planning is to establish the broad goals and objectives of the engineering organization. For a professional design firm, the broad objective may be stated as follows: to provide multidisciplined consulting engineering and design services of the highest quality to a wide range of industrial, utility, health care, and institutional clients, on a profitable basis. This broad objective may then be made more detailed by establishing dollar-volume goals of billings and profit over a 5-year period. This first year's planning activity breaks down the totals by type of client (*see* Table E-6).

**Organization Structures**   To achieve this projected level of operation requires an organization and staffing plan. Figure E-4 shows the type of organization for a typical design firm that would be

**TABLE E-6  Example of an Engineering Firm's Objectives**

|  XYZ Design Inc.—1977 Objectives | | | | |
| --- | --- | --- | --- | --- |
| Total Billings ................................ $4,500,000 | | | | |
| Profits (net after taxes) ......................... $  300,000 | | | | |

Breakdown of Billings and Profit

| Type of client | Billings | % | Profit | % |
| --- | --- | --- | --- | --- |
| Industrial clients | $1,575,000 | 35 | $120,000 | 40 |
| Utility clients | $1,125,000 | 25 | $ 90,000 | 30 |
| Institutional clients | $1,800,000 | 40 | $ 90,000 | 30 |
| Totals | $4,500,000 | 100 | $300,000 | 100 |

**TABLE E-7  Example of a Position Guide**

POSITION: Director of Engineering

REPORTS TO: President

PURPOSE OF POSITION: To provide overall technical and administrative control of corporate engineering activities.

DUTIES: 1. To provide overall technical direction and coordination of engineering design activities—mechanical, electrical, structural-civil, and environmental.

2. To maintain overall cost control of all engineering design activities through administration of project budgets, cost reports, and other similar tools.

3. To maintain top quality of engineering design work through procedures to eliminate errors and omissions in design, calculators, specifications, and drawing.

4. To improve efficiency of engineering operations through procedures to eliminate errors and omissions in design, calculations, specifications, and drawings.

5. To maintain schedules and ensure completion of work on schedule.

6. To administer and implement engineering personnel policies and procedures such as job classifications, merit reviews, hiring procedures, worker utilization, and training.

7. To maintain liaison with project engineers on project schedules, costs, quality of work, and client problems.

8. To deal with clients as required.

9. To undertake business development and promotional activities as required.

needed to attain these objectives. Position descriptions, as shown in Table E-7 supplement the organization chart. An engineering organization, however, needs to be flexible. Rigid adherence to the organization chart can create problems rather than avoid them. Organizational changes may be necessary to meet special conditions.

For carrying out major projects, a project-type organization, as shown in Fig. E-5, may be used. The project engineer or project manager assembles a multidisciplined team to provide the talents and resources needed for the project. The project manager has responsibilities for successful technical completion as well as for cost control and adherence to schedule. The project-type organization is used within the more traditional organization structure. *See* PROJECT AND TASK FORCE MANAGEMENT.

Total worker needs to meet the billing and profit objectives are determined by using billings per employee. If experience indicates that $30,000 per year per employee represents normal billings and produces a net profit of 6.6 percent, an average staff of 150 would be required to produce the target of $4,500,000 shown in Table E-6. The specific mix of manpower among the functional departments will depend upon the mix represented by the typical work level, tempered by any prospects for new projects which may represent a bias toward one particular discipline.

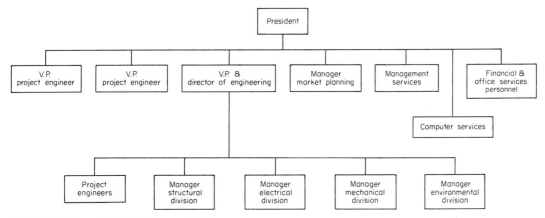

**Fig. E-4. Typical consulting-design firm organization.**

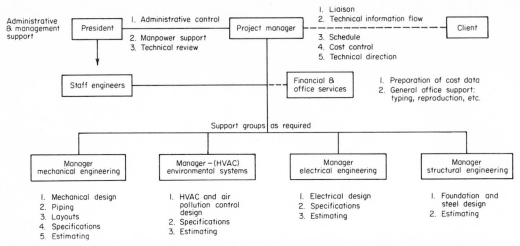

**Fig. E-5. Example of a project organization.**

**Detailed Planning** One of the first requirements is to see that job schedules and budgets are established for individual projects. For each project, an analysis must be made to determine the total number of worker-hours of engineering and technical (usually drafting) time required to complete the project. These requirements are broken down by the various disciplines, i.e., mechanical, electrical, structural, civil, and the like. As part of this procedure, a detailed list of drawings, with worker-hour estimates required, is prepared by each department manager. Also, he or she prepares estimates of the time required for preparation of the necessary specifications and cost estimates. The project manager or project engineer for the project then assembles these into a composite drawing list and composite worker-hour requirement. The drawing list is prepared in such a fashion that it then becomes the basis for the departmental schedules for a specific project. Figure E-6 shows a typical drawing schedule which is commonly used in construction-design engineering activities.

The project manager, with the detailed information developed for scheduling, then prepares a budget for the specific project indicating the hours and costs allocated to each department. Once this budget is established, this becomes a key tool in the process of controlling the costs and progress of the particular project.

## EXECUTION AND CONTROL

It is difficult to separate the execution and control stages of engineering management as these two work

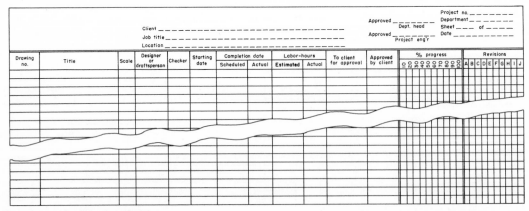

**Fig. E-6. Example of drawing schedule.**

together in conjunction with planning in a feedback-type system. The following, however, will outline some of the more significant steps involved in the execution and control of engineering projects.

**Work Flow** Individual work assignments are prepared from the detailed schedules. The engineering or project manager has the responsibility of coordinating the sequence of work and interrelationship of work carried out by the various disciplines. For example, on a project involving the construction design for an industrial steam plant, the first step is to develop the flow sheet for the plant and determine and specify the major items of equipment such as the boilers, feedwater pumps, coal-handling equipment, stokers, and the like. A general arrangement drawing is then prepared, usually by the mechanical department, showing the relative positioning of the items of equipment and piping for the plant. As this general arrangement drawing is being completed, information is passed to the structural department so that it can begin to develop the design of the foundations, supporting structures, and the housing for the complete plant. As this work progresses, the electrical engineering department is working to develop the power distribution design based upon mechanical information giving the sizes and types of motors and controls required throughout the plant, as well as the details on the necessary instrumentation which may require electrical design and drafting work.

**Progress Controls** In a typical operation, biweekly meetings with all key management personnel are held to discuss project progress and any particular problems that may arise in the course of design. These progress meetings provide an opportunity for the various department heads to ask questions regarding particular design problems or lack of information from other departments. Also on a biweekly basis, estimates of percentage of completion are prepared by each of the engineering department managers. These estimates are then incorporated in the biweekly budget control printout (Table E-8) so that the project manager and the director of engineering have an indication of how the job is progressing, from the standpoint of both cost and hours expended. These estimates of percentage completion are made prior to the printout or distribution of information on *actual* hours spent or cost incurred, so that the percent completion figure is a genuine estimate of progress rather than an arithmetic calculation based upon ratio of hours expended to total hours available for the job. This report gives the engineering manager an effective, short-interval tool for taking action before costs get too far out of line by providing an indicator of project progress against the actual cost and hours expended to date.

## WORK FORCE UTILIZATION

In order to utilize a professional work force effectively, overall detailed projections of work force requirements must be made at least monthly—with overall projections for a minimum forward period of 3 months and possibly 6 months. These projections then can be revised on a monthly basis to incorporate new projects that have been received during the previous month and to allow for projects that have been completed and will no longer require the work force.

**Projections** Figure E-7 shows a typical chart for such projection made on a monthly basis by individual projects with totals on a departmental basis being compared against available work force resources. The net result may indicate a balance or a

**TABLE E-8 Example of Project Budget Control Report Through 10/31/7X**

PROJECT NO. 448-6  TITLE: Plant Addition
PHASE WORKING DRAWINGS  FEE: $102,530  PROJECT ENGINEER: John Doe

| Department | Budget hours | Budget cost | Percent complete | Budget to date | | Actual to date | | Variance | |
|---|---|---|---|---|---|---|---|---|---|
| | | | | Hours | Cost | Hours | Cost | Hours | Cost |
| Electrical | 6100 | 32500 | 30 | 1830 | 9840 | 1216 | 6505 | 614 | 3335 |
| Environmental | 5700 | 34000 | 25 | 1425 | 8500 | 1599 | 9275 | −174 | −775 |
| Mechanical | 3300 | 18740 | 30 | 990 | 5622 | 755 | 4229 | 235 | 1393 |
| Structural | 440 | 2400 | 30 | 132 | 720 | 39 | 249 | 93 | 471 |
| Computer | 70 | 350 | 15 | 10 | 52 | 70 | 346 | −60 | −294 |
| Staff | 780 | 5200 | 30 | 234 | 1560 | 299 | 2046 | −65 | −486 |
| Others | 0 | 9040 | 25 | 0 | 2260 | 0 | 1596 | 0 | 664 |
| Totals | 16390 | 102230 | | 4621 | 28554 | 3978 | 24246 | 643 | 4308 |

Remarks:

Electrical Department
Year 197X as of January 7

| Project no. | Client | Jan | Feb | Mar | April | May | June | July | Aug | Sept | Oct | Nov | Dec | Jan | Feb | Mar | April | May |
|---|---|---|---|---|---|---|---|---|---|---|---|---|---|---|---|---|---|---|
| 1 | "A" | (Hold) | | | | | | | | | | | | | | | | |
| 2 | "B" | 1 | 2 | 3 | 3 | 2 | 2 | | | | | | | | | | | |
| 3 | "C" | 19 | 19 | 19 | 19 | 19 | 19 | 19 | | | | | | | | | | |
| 4 | "D" | 20 | 20 | 20 | 20 | 20 | 20 | 20 | 20 | | | | | | | | | |
| 5 | "E" | 2 | 2 | 2 | 2 | 2 | 2 | 2 | 2 | | | | | | | | | |
| 6 | "F" | 4 | 4 | 4 | 4 | 4 | 4 | 4 | 4 | | | | | | | | | |
| 7 | "G" | (Hold) | | | | | | | | | | | | | | | | |
| 8 | "H" | 2 | 2 | | | | | | | | | | | | | | | |
| 9 | "I" | | 1 | 1 | | | | | | | | | | | | | | |
| | Vacations | | | 1 | 1 | 1 | | | | | | | | | | | | |
| | Workers required | 48 | 49 | 49 | 49 | 48 | 48 | 46 | 45 | | | | | | | | | |
| | Workers available | 50 | 50 | 50 | 50 | 50 | 50 | 50 | 50 | (Including 1 on loan from Structural Department) | | | | | | | | |
| | Worker surplus | 2 | 1 | 1 | 1 | 1 | 2 | 2 | 4 | 5 | | | | | | | | |
| | Worker shortage | | None | | | | | | | | | | | | | | | |

Fig. E-7. Example of work force projection schedule.

surplus or a deficit. A deficit, particularly on a continuing basis, indicates the need for additional workers. It alerts the engineering manager to secure the additional work force required either by new hirings or scheduling of overtime. On the other hand, a surplus indicates the need for additional projects. If the prospects for additional projects are not forthcoming, some steps may have to be taken by the engineering manager to reduce staff to bring it in line with the job work force requirements.

**Nonproductive Time** Another tool that is extremely useful to the engineering manager in controlling work force utilization is a daily report of standby, or nonproductive, time. This records the available professional, or technical, time that is not chargeable to specific jobs or projects either because of the lack of available work or because of inadequacies in departmental scheduling and work force assignment. The daily standby report time provides an immediate signal to the engineering manager to begin to determine why the available engineering time was not utilized. With a computerized system, this information can be available the day following that on which stand-by time occurred.

**Work Sampling** Many times, even though time is reported as chargeable to a job and is considered productive, the engineering manager may wish to determine exactly how the professionals and technician are really spending their time. The technique of work sampling is a most effective tool for seeking areas for improvement in engineering and drafting operations (see WORK SAMPLING). Table E-9 shows

the results of work sampling of engineers and draftpersons in the design and application groups of a machine tool engineering department. The significant results of this work sampling study showed that 42.3 percent of the available time was spent in activities which were not directly productive. Investigation of nonproductive activities indicated that a certain portion were directly associated with the engineers' jobs. Some were caused by confusion with customer requirements, particularly the high percentage of discussion with others (32 percent). Information retrieval was another problem area

TABLE E-9  Work Sampling Study

| Results of Work Sampling of Engineers and Draftpersons in Design and Applications Groups | | |
|---|---|---|
| Productive elements . . . . . . . . . . . . . . . . . . . . . . . . . . . . . . . . | | 57.7% |
| Drafting | 30.4% | |
| Study customer information, specifications | 19.9% | |
| Write | 6.8% | |
| Calculate | 0.6% | |
| Nonproductive elements . . . . . . . . . . . . . . . . . . . . . . . . . . . | | 42.3% |
| Discussion with others | 32.0% | |
| Discussion with engineers | 22.1% | |
| Discussion with shop | 6.0% | |
| Discussion with supervisors | 1.7% | |
| Discussion with sales | 1.6% | |
| Discussion with methods | 0.3% | |
| Discussion with planning | 0.3% | |
| Get information from vault or files | | 7.5% |
| Personal and miscellaneous | | 2.8% |

since 7.5 percent of the overall time was spent in getting information from the vault or files.

**Personnel Administration**  One of the key factors in engineering personnel administration is the use of a sound job evaluation program. Position descriptions should be developed for the various functions in the organization, and appropriate wage or salary scales should be developed for each position. Job evaluation should be supplemented by a merit review program in which each individual in the organization is reviewed at periodic intervals.

Professional performance can be encouraged by one or all of the following: providing an education allowance for advanced study, paying for membership in professional societies, encouraging professional engineering registration, permitting and encouraging presentation and publication of technical papers, keeping professionals working on professional work, and maintaining good lines of communication.

### QUALITY CONTROL

A successful and well-managed engineering organization must provide a finished product—a construction design package, a product design, or a design for plant modifications—of the highest quality. Quality can be achieved in a number of ways. An unequivocal definition of the scope of the specific engineering project is important so that all involved have a clear concept of what is expected as the final result. Detailed departmental checklists of design items and factors that should be inspected and verified will limit design errors and omissions. Adequate checking of design calculations, design drawings, and specifications is as critical to the control of quality in an engineering operation as is inspection and checking of components and finished products to quality in a manufacturing operation.

### METHODS AND PROCEDURES

Of considerable importance in an efficient and well-managed engineering operation are the methods and procedures employed in achieving the output of completed design as well as the equipment that is made available to the personnel. Sound engineering standards for making drawings—which include such items as dimensioning, lettering, preparing title blocks, issuing drawing numbers, processing vendor and purchased equipment drawings—are factors of importance. The specific standards and methods employed will vary from one type of engineering operation to another.

Of growing importance in achieving quality and better utilization of the work force is the use of computer-aided design. Computer programs are available for solving a wide range of structural, civil, electrical, mechanical, and HVAC design problems. The use of computer programs greatly reduces design time and ensures a higher degree of accuracy in calculations. The average engineering organization does not need an in-house computer to obtain this kind of assistance. A time-sharing terminal may be used. If larger and more complex programs are used, a remote card entry terminal providing access to large computers on a remote, batch basis are available for a modest cost on a per-use basis.

Specifications can also be prepared on the computer or on advanced work-processing equipment such as tape-controlled typewriters. Many parts of a typical construction design specification can be standardized and stored either in a computer or on the word-processing tapes. Duplication of those parts of the specification by the specification writer is avoided, and the time required for the actual typing or reproduction of the specification is reduced.

The use of modern drafting equipment including drafting machines (which automatically prepare electrical schematics and mechanical piping drawings), tilt-top tables, reference tables, and chair-type seats contribute to improved drafting output.

*See also* HUMAN RESOURCES (WORK FORCE) PLANNING; PROGRAM PLANNING AND IMPLEMENTATION; PROJECT AND TASK FORCE MANAGEMENT; WORK SAMPLING.

### REFERENCES

Joint Engineering Societies Management Conference, "Creating Second Sources of Engineering Manpower," *Proceedings of the IEEE*, 1966.

"Reshaping the EE for the Seventies," *Electronics*, June 7, 1971.

Seiler, Robert E.: *Improving the Effectiveness of Research and Development*, McGraw-Hill Book Company, New York, 1965.

Weinberger, Arthur J.: "Improving R&D's Batting Average," *Chemical Engineering*, Oct. 28, 1963.

WILLIAM K. MCALEER, *Peter F. Loftus Corporation*

## Entrepreneural management  (*See* MANAGEMENT, DEFINITIONS OF.)

## Entrepreneural sales plans  (*See* COMPENSATION, SALES.)

**Entries check-off list** (*See* PAPER WORK SIMPLIFICATION.)

**Entropy consequences** (*See* ENVIRONMENT, PHYSICAL.)

# Environment, physical

Management concerns regarding the physical environment center mainly on material supplies, chemical pollutants, and energy conversion residuals. Material and fuel supplies are essential inputs for the industrial process. Pollutants and residuals load the physical environment with added wastes, which must be assimilated or transferred to an ultimate sink. As added waste loads, these residuals may alter the ecology or nutrient cycles upon which living species depend for survival.

Ecology is concerned with the interactions by which energy is transferred into materials or nutrients through successive living processes. As such, ecology covers a wide range of human and biological activity, as well as disciplines. Basically, ecological processes may be viewed as successive stages of development from energy or material sources to biological species, populations, and communities. Thus, a simplified view of ecological systems may be obtained by tracing the flow and balance of materials, or nutrients, as they are embodied successively in species or return as residuals to the earth, air, or water. For example:

The parent material of all living processes is the geochemical composition of the earth, from which all biological species draw their chemical and mineral requirements.

The primary energy source for converting geochemicals into cellular nutrient material is solar radiation. The biological conversion efficiency of solar radiation into usable energy is generally low, amounting to a few percent or less of the incoming radiation, with the balance of the sun's rays being reradiated back into the atmosphere.

The most basic of the energy converters are the autotrophs, such as green plants on land and photoplankton in the sea, which have the ability to fix carbon by photosynthesis into carbon molecules (living cells) with the use of solar energy and carbon dioxide in the atmosphere. The residuals of this process are respired back into the ecosystem as oxygen, water vapor, heat, and unassimilated gases.

The herbivores, such as rodents, deer, and cattle, consume the autotrophic species; then they combust the carbon nutrient and energy in them by digestion and oxidation. The residuals are carbon dioxide, vapor, heat, and solid waste.

The carnivores utilize the nutrients in herbivores by a similar consumption-combustion process and use a large part of the energy to maintain their own movement and respiration.

**Entropy** In this process, energy moves through these ecological linkages and material forms from a higher to a lower energy state, from more concentrated to more diffused, in accordance with the second law of thermodynamics. This diffusion of energy state is called entropy. Living species temporarily reverse the entropic process by storing or concentrating nutrient energy reserves in their cells by high rates of consumption.

The consequence of energy diffusion in ecology has two important implications for management: (1) the cost of energy or materials increases the farther it moves through successive stages, thus the protein cost of beef is higher than of soybeans, just as the energy cost of carbon steel is higher than of iron; (2) the concentration of chemicals in cellular structure increases as energy is diffused (i.e., energy is being converted into materials), with the result that low levels of pollution in the environment may concentrate into high levels of chemical pollution in successive species higher in the food chain.

Or more simply, the ecological system confronts management with (1) cost problems for energy conversion of all types and (2) chemical contamination problems for residuals that concentrate to toxic levels in living species, thus causing health damage or death.

**Management Implications** Management of an industrial economy compounds these physical phenomena multifold by pumping into the ecosystem (1) additional industrial heat with its added residuals and (2) synthetic chemicals which are not biodegradable, with the result that they concentrate as pollutants in the food chain. For example, an oyster concentrates materials 70,000 times; thus one part per billion of DDT or PCBs (polychlorinated biphenyls) in sea water becomes 70 parts per million in the oyster. Eagles, as carnivorous birds of prey at the high end of the food chain, have been measured with 240 parts per million of PCBs in their muscle.

The management problems regarding the physical environment essentially come down to trying to (1) reduce the residuals from manufactured combustion, either by reducing the emissions or the intensity of energy use, (2) reducing the concentration of hazardous chemicals as pollutants, and (3) at the same time, maintaining adequate material supplies.

## ENVIRONMENTAL RESOURCE FORECASTS

An industrial economy operates by intensive use of energy for high rates of materials conversion. Hence, management is interested in future availability of materials and fuel supplies. A forecast of resource requirements depends upon (1) available energy sources and use rates, (2) availability or scarcity of raw materials, (3) the pollution damage effects constraining ecosystem productivity, and (4) the human population and consumption growth rate. Or in economic terms, the withdrawal rate and supply of any given resource depends upon the following variables: energy costs, material costs, damage costs, and price (human demand).

The world population in 1975 reached 4 billion people. The population doubled in the prior 45 years and is expected to double again in the next 35 years. Ninety percent of this growth was in the developing countries of the world, and only ten percent in the industrial nations. Of the 3 billion persons in the developing countries, 20 percent do not receive the daily requirement of calories or proteins, 60 percent are illiterate, and 85 percent have no access to basic health or family planning service.

**Food** On the supply side, the food available per person has increased only by 4 percent in 20 years. World grain output is about 1.2 billion tons. People in developing nations consume about 300 to 500 pounds of grain per year, mostly as grain. The United States consumption of grain is 1650 pounds per person per year: 200 as grain and 1450 as meat. To produce 1 pound of meat, animals eat from 2 to 10 pounds of grain. By the year 2000, world grain production will have to increase to 2 billion tons to keep up with population with no improvement in diets. In 1972 the world experienced a slight decline in food production with massive crop failures in Russia and Eastern Europe. Since then, disappointing crops have been experienced in India, Ethiopia, the Sahel of West Africa, and to a lesser extent, in Western Europe. Some climatologists speculate that the weather is becoming more variable because of a cooling and drying trend in world climate. Other causes of food shortages are the high birth rates, high oil prices limiting power for food production, and leveling off of the production stimulus from the Green Revolution with its high yielding wheat and rice. The countries of the world have turned to the United States and Canada to fill their food deficits. The consequence has been rising domestic and world food prices.

**Materials** The consumption rate of materials in the world is growing faster than population by a ratio of about $2\frac{1}{2}$:1 as all nations seek to raise production and living standards. From 1975 to the year 2000, world population is expected to increase by 60 percent, materials consumption, as reflected in the gross domestic product, by 150 percent, and fuel requirements by 170 percent. The United States has large reserves or potential for the production of foods, fiber, coal, feldspar, gypsum, copper, magnesium, titanium, molybdenum, and iron. The United States currently has scarce reserves of or imports substantial aluminum, antimony, asbestos, bismuth, cobalt, fluorine, gold, lead, mercury, nickel, petroleum, phosphorus, platinum, potassium, sulfur, thorium, tungsten, uranium, vanadium, and zinc.

**Energy** The United States used 60 quadrillion ($10^{15}$) Btu's of energy in 1975, which is projected to become 140 quadrillion by 2000. The current supply of energy is 46 percent from petroleum, 30 percent natural gas, 18 percent coal, 4 percent hydropower, and 2 percent nuclear. The new energy supplies are expected to come from nuclear energy, low-sulfur Western coal, high-sulfur Eastern coal, oil shale, and geothermal energy, in that order of importance. With nuclear and coal being the major new sources of fuels, environmental pollution will be aggravated by more particulates, nitrogen oxides, sulfur dioxide, solid wastes, and radiation hazards. Petroleum will continue to provide approximately the same supply of energy, about 35 quadrillion Btu's, with 40 percent of the oil imported.

**Land** The land supply in the United States comprises 2.3 billion acres, of which the federal government owns one-third, mainly in Western states and Alaska. Of the total United States acreage, 57 percent is classified as agricultural, but only 17 percent is cropland; the remainder is mostly grassland and grazed forest. Of the 43 percent nonagricultural land, more than half is in forest, and the balance in marsh, open swamp, desert, tundra, and the like. Urban land comprises 60 million acres, 3 percent of the total, and is the most valuable commercially. The land area for human settlement has been increasing at a rate 1.7 times faster than the population growth, with the result that population densities (at 3376 persons per square mile) have been declining by about 1.3 percent per year. Metropolitan areas have experienced a slower growth rate than nonmetropolitan counties since 1970, and the suburban growth has shifted to the nonfarm segment of rural areas. About 1¼ million acres of rural land, one-third of which is cropland, is withdrawn from agricultural use annually for more intensive settlement use.

**Water** The water resources of the United States originate in the 4750 million acre-feet of rainfall which fall annually. Of this, 70 percent falls on nonirrigated lands: about 30 percent on cropland and the balance on forest and open land vegetation. The rest of the precipitation (30 percent or 1370 million acre-feet) enters the streamflows. About 1000 million acre-feet are not withdrawn from streams and flow to the sea. Of the water withdrawn from streams approximately 160 million acre-feet are used for irrigation, 160 million acre-feet for industry, and 30 million acre-feet for municipal water. While these withdrawals appear small relative to the total, very little of the water is consumed (100 million acre-feet) and the balance is discharged back into streamflows as effluent. There are 22 major river basins, which drain 70 percent of the nation's land area, into which these effluents are repeatedly discharged, with the result that stream qualities deteriorate under the wasteloads of nitrates, phosphates, pesticides, and nutrients from agriculture; chemicals and trace metals from industry; and fecal coliform bacteria and carbonaceous wastes from municipalities. The carbonaceous wastes impose a biochemical oxygen demand upon the stream for their decomposition, which tends to deplete the oxygen supply in the water for aquatic life.

**Solid Waste** The solid waste, or gross discard, generated annually amounted to 150 million tons in 1975, or 3.8 pounds per person per day. The gross discard of solid waste by 1990 is expected to rise to 225 million tons annually, or 5 pounds per person per day. About 6 percent of the solid waste is currently recovered, mostly as paper, glass, metals, or rubber. The recycling by 1990 is projected at a 25 percent resource recovery. However, many of the voluntary and commercial recycling activities went out of operation in the mid 1970s with the fall in waste paper and scrap metal prices. The bulk of solid waste is disposed of by landfill, which is the lowest-cost disposal method. However, close-in landfill sites are becoming scarce, and transportation is a major disposal cost. The result may be rising landfill costs, which would make alternative forms of disposal such as pyrolisis or recycling more competitive.

## CONSERVATION MEASURES

Conservation measures, such as resource recovery from solid waste, have been encouraged by government as all forms of material have become scarce. However, the economic incentives have not always encouraged the degree of conservation expected by government goals. This has been true in energy conservation, in land conservation, as well as in solid waste recycling. The government's role as conservationist has been more effective through regulation or public ownership, as is the case of public lands.

The conservation movement began in the late nineteenth century primarily to preserve timberland. The national forest reserves, national parks, grazing regulation on public lands, mining regulations, and wildlife preserves have tended to regulate multiple uses and sustainable yields on the public domain. The clear-cutting of private forest lands is still common among small operators, although large timber companies practice sustained yield timber harvesting for their own long-run interest. The timber case illustrates that conservation is effective either when government is the proprietor and regulator, or when economic incentives make conservation a self-interest in the private sector. These conditions do not regularly exist in the new areas in which conservation is currently attempted, such as solid waste, energy, land use, or materials conservation.

**Energy** Rising fuel prices caused a temporary conservation of energy following the oil crisis of 1973, but energy consumption since then has tended to return to its historic growth rates. Residential and personal transportation consumptions of energy have returned to normal. Industry has tended to reduce its intensity of energy use in response to higher prices by utilization of waste heat or materials substitutions when possible. The hoped-for conservation of energy in construction or home maintenance by better insulation, tighter windows, new designs, or lower thermostat temperatures has generally not materialized. The construction or remodeling costs in many cases impose an added capital investment which is too high and long term, when amortized over the years, compared to paying higher current energy costs. Thus, the internalized economic incentive to conserve energy has not materialized for the most part, except in those industry cases where waste heat or materials with cheaper processing can be utilized at favorable cost trade offs compared to energy at higher prices. The rising price of energy may turn out to be a conservation stimulus as industrial substitutions are made to offset its cost. The preembargo cost of electricity was of the order of 10 mills per kilowatt-hour at the busbar for fossil fuel plants. This has risen to 30 mills per kilowatthour at 1976 prices for oil-fired plants, in which the cost of oil itself at $12 per barrel accounts for 20 mills of operating cost. The new energy sources are likely to range in cost (at 1976 prices) from 25 to 30 mills per kilowatthour for geothermal and 30 to 35 mills per kilowatthour for coal and nuclear plants.

**Water**  Water conservation by recycling is occurring under the permit system and the Water Pollution Control Act Amendments of 1972 as industry effluents are controlled by regulation. Industry must obtain permits for water withdrawal and effluent discharge into streams, and the level of effluent discharges is controlled by water quality standards. The effect is to impose on industry the investment cost required to abate effluents to the tolerable standard. This internalization of waste water disposal costs within industry has tended to produce gradual improvement in stream quality.

**Land**  Land conservation is being attempted through open-space, estuary, wildlife, and coastal zone regulations, much of which is experimental under state law rather than federal legislation. Such land conservation is selective in area and restrictive as to purpose. The broad use of land conservation measures is yet to be developed. Only 9 of the 50 states (as of 1975) even have a land-use plan for inventorying land use and identifying uses of more than local concern. Meanwhile, research studies by the Environmental Protection Agency have shown that better land use (i.e., 0.3 acres per housing unit rather than 0.6 acres) could reduce private and public investment in housing by 44 percent, reduce operating costs by 18 percent, energy usage by 40 percent, and pollution by 50 percent.

## POLLUTION CONTROL AND ABATEMENT

The incremental resource abatement costs amount to 1.1 to 1.5 percent of gross national product (GNP) in the 1974 to 1983 period, which include the investment in pollution control equipment plus operating and maintenance costs. These costs average about $50 per capita, and for a median income family this amounts to 2 to 2.5 percent of gross family income. Two-thirds of these costs are for air pollution control, 30 percent for water pollution abatement, 3 percent for solid waste, and minor amounts for radiation, surface mining, and noise abatement. Industry bears the highest incremental costs for water and air quality improvement. The federal government costs are mainly in water treatment through matching grants to state and local government.

**Distribution of Cost**  The distribution of environmental abatement costs by industry shows the heaviest burden for utilities, petroleum refining, metals, paper, chemicals, stone, clay, and glass. For the most part, these abatement costs correspond with the energy intensity of the industry. Those industries with high pollution and energy intensity characteristics are encountering abatement costs ranging from 0.2 to 1 percent of the value of their shipments.

The citizenry, of course, ultimately pay all these costs as they are passed on by industry or government in higher prices or taxes. The automobile pollution abatement costs, for example, are $5 billion per year to consumers, made up of about $1 billion in car price or investment, $1½ billion in maintenance, and $2½ billion in the fuel penalty cost. The retail price increase for air pollution control on automobiles amounts to about $200 per car.

The net impact of these costs on the citizenry is somewhat regressive, bearing more heavily on the lower-income groups. The environmental costs are progressively distributed to the extent that the federal income tax is the transfer media. But federal pollution control costs amount to only about 4 percent of the total. The balance of the cost is distributed mainly by price increases or sales and property taxes, which tend to be regressive.

**Impact on Growth**  The effect of environmental costs upon economic growth is a source of opposition to environmental regulation because growth is seen as necessary to improve productivity and living standards. Here the argument by industry is that the capital markets will be strained in the future to meet energy requirements, capacity expansion, and productivity needs. Thus, pollution control expenditures could potentially displace normal private investment for productive purposes.

The counter argument is that pollution control expenditures are small, averaging only about 4.6 percent of total private investment in the next decade. Moreover, a Brookings study concludes that the capital demands of industry can be met in the next decade to satisfy normal growth.

Also, according to a macroeconomic analysis sponsored by the Council for Environmental Quality, pollution control expenditures at mid-decade with underemployment have stimulated the economy so that GNP is higher than it would otherwise have been. In the future as the rate of pollution control investment slows and slightly higher prices result, environmental costs will have a minor depressing effect on the economy. However, this minor depressing effect will disappear as incomes adjust to prices, and GNP will end up at the same level it would have been without environmental improvement programs.

**Impact on Inflation**  The extra inflation rates attributable to pollution control costs are about 0.3 to 0.5 percent per year, which are small compared with the general inflation rates running from 6 to 12 percent during the decade. The effect of the extra inflation rate for pollution abatement upon the wholesale price index is projected at about one-tenth of the price increase.

**Unemployment**  Unemployment which is attributable to environmental costs has occurred by plant closings among older and small facilities, which were only marginally profitable in any case. An EPA study indicates that, from 1971 to 1975, 75 plants closed because of environmental costs affecting 13,600 workers (0.0015 percent of the labor force). Offsetting these unemployment impacts, moreover, are new jobs created by producing equipment for pollution control investment. For example, about 85,000 additional jobs have been created by the construction of sewage treatment plants alone, plus additional jobs for other water and air quality improvement equipment. On balance, it would appear that the immediate impact of environmental regulation has been to create more jobs than those terminated. However, those reemployed in newly created pollution control jobs are not the same persons as those who were unemployed in plant closings, and therein lies the individual and political sensitivity of environmental unemployment.

In summary, then, the direct and indirect economic costs of environmental regulation amount to about 1 percent of GNP, plus very small effects on economic growth, inflation, and unemployment.

## HEALTH AND DAMAGE EFFECTS OF POLLUTION

The most serious, sensitive, and elusive effects of pollution damage are upon human health. A variety of studies have attempted to assess health damage to human beings. The valuations are based mainly upon medical costs and income losses due to excess morbidity and mortality. Such costs total at least $4.5 billion per year, comprising $1.8 billion for cancer, $2.1 billion for respiratory diseases from air pollution, and $0.6 billion for drinking water diseases.

**Materials**  The identifiable damage to materials and property is about $6½ billion per year, and the additional loss in property values due to air pollution is from $1½ to $5 billion per year. Roughly, the total losses are about $10 billion annually. The material damage losses are the following: For rubber products, $0.2 billion; textile fibers and dyes, $0.2 billion; metals, $1.5 billion; paints, $0.7 billion; and other materials, $3.8 billion.

Much of this damage comes from sulfur oxides in the presence of particulates and moisture, forming sulfuric acid, which is corrosive to metals and many materials. The balance is attributable to ozone, which oxidizes materials and turns them into oxides such as ferric oxide or iron rust.

**Biota**  Ozone also oxidizes living tissue, such as human lung tissue, causing it to harden and age. The effects of oxidation are most easily seen on delicate plant leaves such as lettuce or grape leaves, where oxidation of cell tissue results in a brownish scaling of the surface.

The crop and ornamental damage in the nation from pollution is estimated to be over $130 million.

Of biota, generally, the economic costs are more difficult to estimate than the species count. The species count is indicative of the size and range of the gene pool from which future evolution may occur.

The Department of Interior estimates that 1 out of every 10 species native to the United States may be endangered or threatened. Hawaii, with a smaller species set, already finds 12 percent of its species extinct and another 38 percent endangered or threatened.

Among wildlife animals the situation is much the same. Among the animal species, 85 have become extinct. In the United States, 185 will probably be extinct by the year 2000, and another 718 may possibly become extinct by 2000. Some species nearing extinction have been recovering as a result of hunting regulations or wildlife management, but the list of recovering species is small compared to the endangered.

## COPING WITH SOCIAL, POLITICAL, AND REGULATORY PRESSURES

Environmental decisions represent a conflict, in many cases, between economic goals and health or ecological goals. The parties involved include business and labor on the economic side against factional interests in health, consumerism, environmentalism, conservation, recreation, and ecology and adversely affected property groups. These factional interests combine on some issues to press for tightening environmental standards or enforcement. Coalitions are most likely to be successful when demonstrable dangers exist to human health or wildlife or when there is local property owner opposition.

The focus for these pressures within the political structure usually occurs within the framework of (1) environmental impact cases, (2) regulatory hearings, or (3) jurisdictional disputes.

**Environmental Impact Cases** Environmental impact cases may be heard in the courts when a plaintiff seeks to show that environmental damage is demonstrable in order to obtain an award of monetary damages or to obtain an injunction preventing the defendant from taking an environmental action until further facts or proofs are established. An award of monetary damages is usually difficult to obtain because the direct causation of adverse impacts is hard to prove in anything so interlinked as ecological networks. However, environmental groups have been relatively successful in delaying projects by obtaining injunctions. Often these delays so compound the costs and uncertainties that the project is abandoned.

An administrative method of examining environmental impact cases takes the form of prepared statements, clearances, and hearings under the National Environmental Policy Act of 1970 (NEPA) or its state counterparts. Section 102 of NEPA provides that federal agencies shall prepare environmental impact statements on all projects, particularly construction, which have ecological consequences. These statements are to describe the nature of the work to be done, its effects upon the ecology, its probable impacts on health or species, means of avoidance or abatement of impacts, and alternative courses of action. Environmental impact statements once prepared are circulated among governmental agencies or constituencies concerned for recommendations. The environmental impact statement and its comments form the basis of a hearing in which interest parties can further argue their cases prior to an administrative ruling.

Environmental impact statements have proved to be time-consuming, costly, and voluminous. Some federal agencies, such as the Army Corps of Engineers with many construction projects throughout the country, estimate that 1 to 2 percent of their total expenditures go into the preparation of environmental impact statements. Business has also encountered the costs and delays of environmental impact statements as state laws have required state or local government to review the environmental impacts of new projects, particularly construction. Electric utilities especially have found that environmental requirements, along with new fuel technologies, have stretched out the lead time on siting new power plants from 5 to 7 or 10 years.

Although the environmental impact statement is not a precise decision document and is prone to costliness and delays, it does serve the purpose of airing and resolving conflicts among the many interest parties over environmental issues.

**Regulatory Hearings** The regulatory hearings of environmental protection agencies serve somewhat the same purpose of reconciling conflicts. Regulatory hearings occur when an agency proposes new environmental standards or enforcement procedures; for example, automotive engine emission controls, banning DDT, offshore drilling, or the Alaskan oil pipeline. Here the agency proposes a compromise stand, business appears as proponents for a more favorable ruling, and environmentalists appear for more stringent rulings. These hearings or administrative deliberations may go on for several years before resolution.

**Jurisdictional Disputes** The jurisdictional issues regarding environmental affairs occur most frequently among federal, state, and local government. Most environmental decisions, particularly those involving construction, are highly localized and ecological conditions are unique to each biome or biological community. Moreover, land-use decisions have historically been in the jurisdiction of local governments. The federal government, in attempting to enforce environmental programs or standards, has sought to delegate much of the implementation to state or local government, for reasons of both practical politics and administrative necessity. Indeed, the environmental program has brought a number of innovations and new dimensions to intergovernmental relations, but conflicts do occur since a state or local government is expected to implement federal regulations or legislation. Local governments frequently feel, however, that the regulatory measures are not applicable to the local case, that communication is poor in clarifying standards or procedure, that financial and administrative support is not adequate, that decisions are not forthcoming, or that local politics runs counter to federal practice. Thus, jurisdictional conflicts, apathy, or counterproductive practices develop.

On the whole, environmental problems present a

wide order of social, political, and regulatory pressures among diverse groups throughout the private and public sectors as people try to learn to live together under the limits which resources and ecology impose as population densities increase.

## TECHNICAL HEALTH AND OPERATIONAL IMPLICATIONS

The technical and operational problems imposed by environmental regulations include (1) establishing the biological and medical research base from which to adequately measure ecological damage for the purpose of setting environmental quality standards; (2) developing the technical instrumentation and monitoring networks which will measure ambient environmental quality against the standards; (3) developing new industrial technology to reduce emissions or effluence in products or equipment; and (4) devising the administrative incentives and penalties which will encourage individuals and business to modify their behavior toward the reduction of pollution. These several operational problems are perhaps best illustrated by examining the trends in environmental quality, which demonstrate some of the standards setting, monitoring, research, and administrative problems which occur.

**Air Pollution**  Air quality has shown some improvement in recent years in particulates, sulfur dioxide, and carbon monoxide, but rather little improvement in nitrogen oxides or hydrocarbons. The problem is, of course, that the average nitrogen oxide emissions of automobiles have not decreased very much owing to technical obstacles, and the number of cars continues to increase.

The air pollution problem is very general and pervasive throughout the United States, despite common impressions that the problem is limited to a few cities such as Chicago for sulfur dioxide or Los Angeles for nitrogen oxides. At least 80 cities, large and small, throughout the United States exceed national standards for oxidants. Indeed, even rural areas are not immune. EPA monitors unexpectedly found rural oxidant levels exceeding 1-hour standards in western Maryland and eastern West Virginia while studying air pollution damage to Christmas trees. Additional studies showed air pollution to be significant throughout rural Maryland, Ohio, Pennsylvania, and West Virginia.

**Water Pollution**  Water quality has improved over the past decade for drinking purposes, but less so for aquatic life protection. In 1961, a third of the drinking water was poor or worse; by 1974 this category was down to 10 percent of the potable water supplies. During the same period for aquatic

life protection, the poor or worse water was 40 percent in 1961 and was still at 25 percent in 1974.

The nature of the water pollution is indicated by the frequency of observed violations of EPA's proposed standards. The highest rates of violation were observed for fecal coliform bacteria (67 percent of observations), ammonia (11 percent), and sulfate (18 percent). For trace metals, the highest violation rates were for iron, lead, maganese and zinc.

**Hazardous Pollutants**  Among the hazardous pollutants, environmental regulation has focused upon four—DDT, aldrin/dieldrin, PCBs and mercury—as scientists have attempted to find the dose rates at which these pollutants become carcinogens or damaging to human health.

The dietary intake of DDT from meat, fish, poultry, and dairy products has been declining since restrictions on production and use were established. The older population, aged 50 years and over, still retain about 8 to 9 parts per billion of DDT in human fatty tissue from applications and usage of DDT 20 to 30 years ago. The young age population, below 15 years of age, have only half the body weight of DDT of their elders.

Aldrin/dieldrin, which is used as a pesticide, is of concern because it is carcinogenic, i.e., cancer inducing, in human beings. The dietary intake of aldrin/dieldrin is declining slightly as sales of the pesticide are restricted; but the levels of dieldrin in surface waters, and as residues in fish, continue to rise.

Polychlorinated biphenyls (PCBs) have been widely used since the 1930s as coolants, insulators, inks, adhesives, hydraulic fluids, and pesticide extenders. PCBs have no natural counterpart in nature and, therefore, are not biodegradable, which makes them very persistent in nature. Their persistence causes them to cumulate in the food chain. PCBs, up to 20 parts per million have been observed in seal blubber and 240 parts per million in muscle of the white-tailed eagle. PCBs are toxic to wildlife at varying dosages, as low as 0.1 parts per million to young shrimp. PCBs have been correlated with mortality in game birds and reduced reproduction among fish-eating mammals. Recent studies indicate they may be carcinogens. PCBs in surface waters of the North Atlantic have been measured at around 30 parts per million in recent years; PCB residues in Lake Michigan fish range from 5 to 20 parts per million. About 4 percent of all human foods had traces of PCBs in 1974. The dietary intake of PCBs ranges from 1 to 3 parts per million. The health implications of these data are not yet known.

Mercury occurs in natural state in rocks and minerals whose decomposition produces background mercury measurements of 0.03 to 2 parts per billion. In addition, 60,000 to 70,000 flasks of mercury are produced annually for such uses as agricultural biocides, paint, electrical apparatus, and electrolytic processes. Mercury circulates readily through air, land, water, and living things. Mercury poisoning affects aquatic life, animals, and human beings by attacking the nervous system and is fatal in varying dosages. The mercury level in surface United States waters is about 1 part per billion, with similar levels as residues in freshwater fish. The human dietary intake of mercury in foods is now about 2.8 micrograms per day, down one-third from 1972 when mercury was banned for agricultural biocides.

**Cancer** The presence of hazardous pollutants in the environment is a significant factor in rising cancer death rates. From 60 to 90 percent of all cancers are related to environmental factors, such as exposures to chemicals, cigarette smoking, natural and induced radiation, and asbestos fiber. The death rate from cancer has doubled since 1900, until now it is the no. 2 killer in the United States after heart disease.

Of some 2 million known chemicals, only about 6000 have been laboratory tested for carcinogenicity. Several thousand new chemicals are discovered annually, and several hundred go on the market each year without testing. The known chemical classes of carcinogens include aromatic amines, chlorinated hydrocarbons, tars, radioactive elements, metal dusts, and steroids. Federal agencies are sponsoring research models to speed up and reduce the cost of testing from 2 to 3 years at tens of thousands of dollars to 1 week at perhaps $1000 per compound.

Meantime, the rise in cancer death rates since 1950 has offset the reduction in mortality from other diseases so that for 25 years there has been no improvement in life expectancy.

## MANAGEMENT RESPONSIBILITIES

The management responsibilities for environmental affairs are manifold in both private and public institutions because ecology is complex. Management has responsibility for organizing the decision information needed on all the problems discussed in previous sections, namely, (1) to forecast accurately its own resource requirements in the light of available energy sources, materials availability, pollution damage costs, and human consumption rates; (2) to minimize the cost of energy in materials by more efficient energy utilization or by substituting materials lower in the successive nutrient chains; (3) to reduce the concentration of chemicals in their ambient state; (4) to recycle water and materials; (5) to reduce land use costs in terms of social investment, energy usage, or pollution; (6) to ascertain pollution abatement costs and make trade-offs against product development or health damage costs; (7) to help develop an objective basis for environmental decisions by better research inputs into environmental impact statements and hearings; (8) to undertake research which will establish the biological and medical base for environmental standard setting and monitoring; (9) to direct industrial research toward compliance with environmental standards as well as maximizing near-term demand; and (10) to devise incentives and administrative implementation which will modify human behavior toward reducing ecological damage. These substantial responsibilities are a recognition that management and its institutions, as well as individuals, survive in the long run by living compatibly within an ecology which has limits and constraints to its waste assimilation capabilities. The ecological limits and constraints impose rising costs upon materials and fuels. Management, therefore, has both short- and long-term interests in ecology, namely, to minimize costs in the short term and to survive over the long run.

*See also* COMMUNITY PLANNING LEGISLATION; ENERGY RESOURCES, MANAGEMENT OF; ENVIRONMENTAL PROTECTION LEGISLATION; FACILITIES AND SITE PLANNING AND LAYOUT; TECHNOLOGY, MANAGEMENT IMPLICATIONS.

### REFERENCES

Edmunds, Stahrl W., and John Letey: *Environmental Administration*, McGraw-Hill Book Company, New York, 1973.

*Environmental Quality, Annual Reports,* Council on Environmental Quality, Washington, 1970–1975.

Massachusetts Institute of Technology: *Man's Impact on the Global Environment*, The M.I.T. Press, Cambridge, Mass., 1970.

*Material Needs and the Environment*, National Commission on Materials Policy, Washington, June 1973.

National Academy of Sciences, *Resources and Man*, W. H. Freeman and Company, San Francisco, 1969.

Price, Victoria S.: *State and Regional Implementation of Pollution Controls*, monogram, Committee on Environmental Decision Making, National Academy of Sciences, Washington, June 1976.

*Project Independence*, Federal Energy Administration, Washington, November 1974.

*The Role of Ecology in the Federal Government*, Council on Environmental Quality and Federal Council for Science and Technology, Washington, December 1974.

STAHRL W. EDMUNDS, *University of California, Riverside*

### Environmental factors  *(See heading in Table of Contents for complete listing.)*

### Environmental health  *(See HEALTH INSTITUTIONS, MANAGEMENT OF.)*

### Environmental health programs  *(See HEALTH SERVICES, PLANNING FOR.)*

## Environmental protection legislation

Since the first Earth Day in April 1970, the United States government has enacted far-reaching environmental laws covering air pollution, water pollution, toxic chemicals, and pesticides. It has also enacted a number of statutes of more limited impact covering areas such as noise pollution, solid waste, public lands, the coastal zone, and occupational health and safety. Together, these laws have established major constraints on the types of products which may be sold and the manner in which they may be produced.

A few examples, all drawn from a single 30-day period in 1976, illustrate some of the impacts which these environmental laws have had on business. Allied Chemical was fined $13 million for discharging Kepone into the James River, and two executives of a subcontractor to the company were criminally prosecuted in connection with the discharge. United States Steel agreed with the Environmental Protection Agency (EPA) to spend $155 million for pollution control equipment at the corporation's Clairton Coke Works. EPA ordered the General Motors Corporation to recall 330,000 Pontiacs in order to correct a defect in the vehicles' emission control system. EPA also accepted a plan proposed by the state of Mississippi to end all use by 1978 of the controversial pesticide Mirex. Hooker Chemical, the sole producer of the pesticide, had announced earlier, however, that it would refuse to sell Mirex to Mississippi, or to any other party, unless it would agree to indemnify Hooker against financial losses from possible lawsuits. Voters in Michigan and Maine approved a bill which imposed a 5-cent mandatory deposit on beverage containers, including nonreturnables, and which banned the use of pull-tops. These examples are not typical; they are cases of unusually far-reaching effect. They do reflect, though, the magnitude and breadth of the problems for business which recent environmental laws have created.

### ENVIRONMENTAL LEGISLATION

There are currently four major federal environmental laws in effect.

The Clean Air Act was passed in its current form in 1970 and amended in 1974 and 1977. It establishes national ambient air-quality standards and requires each state to impose emission limitations on sources of air-pollution within the state. A state is given almost unlimited discretion to decide on the mix of emission limitations imposed on sources within its boundaries, provided the net effect is the attainment and maintenance of the national standards by the time set in the statute. A state is not permitted to postpone attainment of these national standards or to establish alternative ones. Moreover, neither economic hardship nor social disruption legally excuses a state from its responsibility to meet the standards set under the act.

The Federal Water Pollution Control Act was enacted in its current form in 1972. It prohibits all discharges into waterways without a permit. It requires industrial sources to apply, by 1977, "best practicable control technology" to their discharges, and by 1983, "best available technology economically achievable." Unlike the Clean Air Act, in which the restrictions imposed on the same type of plant may vary from state to state, the Federal Water Pollution Control Act establishes nationally uniform discharge limitations. The only exception to this is a case where the dischargers on a stretch of waterway are so numerous that even with the national limitations, the water will not be usable for the purposes desired for it. In such a case, more stringent standards may be established for the dischargers over that stretch of waterway.

The Federal Insecticide, Fungicide, and Rodenticide Act—the "pesticide law"—was passed in 1972 and amended in 1975. It requires the presale registration of pesticides and empowers EPA to refuse to register a potentially harmful pesticide. It also permits EPA to restrict the people to whom hazardous pesticides may be sold.

The Toxic Substances Control Act was enacted on October 11, 1976. It gives EPA comprehensive regulatory authority over industrial chemicals. It permits EPA to order a manufacturer to hold a new chemical off the market until premarket testing is done, and it empowers EPA, if the manufacturer objects to the agency's order, to go to court to obtain an injunction. It also empowers EPA to require testing of existing chemicals and to regulate the production, use, distribution, and disposal of hazardous chemicals.

**Related Legislation** In addition to these four laws, there are a myriad of other federal environmental statutes of more limited application and impact. These include the National Environmental Policy Act, the Noise Control Act, the Resource Conservation and Recovery Act, the Occupational Safety and Health Administration Act, the Coastal Zone Management Act, and the Safe Drinking Water Act. While Congress may enact several additional environmental laws, most observers do not foresee any major new laws for at least the next 5 to 10 years.

Since 1970, there has also been a proliferation of state and local laws aimed at protecting the environment. These laws, along with the creation of state environmental agencies, have introduced a sustained environmental perspective into state and local government.

**Common Features** All the major federal statutes have several features in common:

1. They are all based, at least in part, on very optimistic notions of what the country can do. For example, the Clean Air Act assumes that carbon monoxide in even extremely polluted and automobile-dependent cities such as Los Angeles can be reduced to the level of the national standard. The Federal Water Pollution Control Act assumes that all municipalities will find the financial resources to construct advanced sewage treatment facilities by 1983. Most observers readily concede that not all the requirements of the statutes are attainable.

2. The legislation delegates substantial discretion to EPA and state environmental agencies. Part of this is due to the congressional tradition of establishing the broad outlines of a program and then leaving the details of its implementation up to the regulatory agency in charge. A more important factor operating here, however, was (and is) the limitations of our knowledge of the proper way to arrest and reverse environmental deterioration. Congress responded to this situation by vesting substantial discretion in agencies to establish how pollution limits set by the acts were to be achieved.

3. The acts have all grown into very complicated programs. There are a number of reasons for this. One is the inherent complexity of environmental issues. Another is the large amounts of money involved and the provision of elaborate procedures to ensure due process. A third is the coordination

among federal, state, and local governments and the involvement of citizen groups which the statutes require. The programs have become so complicated, and the provisions under them change so quickly, that it takes a team of people just to stay abreast of their specific requirements.

## DEVELOPING AN
## ENVIRONMENTAL STRATEGY

There is no master plan integrating these various pieces of environmental legislation. There is also no consistent theme in their implementation. Environmental legislation is a patchwork quilt of programs. There is overlap among them, large holes in their coverage, and occasionally serious conflicts. Moreover, it seems very unlikely that this pattern will change in the foreseeable future.

*Coping with Continual Change.* What is likely to change, however, is the nature of the specific requirements. While six pollutants may be regulated one year under the Clean Air Act, seven or eight pollutants may be regulated the next year, as new scientific evidence is produced on the health hazards associated with air pollution. The legislation empowers, and in some cases requires, the government to respond to this new information as it becomes available. Requirements also change as the considerable volume of litigation challenging the government's interpretation of the statutes works its way through the judicial system. Further, requirements change as Congress "fine-tunes" the statutes. In mid-1977, Congress amended the Clean Air Act, and as of November 1977 the outlook was for amendments to the Federal Water Pollution Act and the federal pesticides law before the year's end.

In this fluid situation, involving large amounts of money and substantial government restrictions, "fire fighting" does not work well as an approach for dealing with changes in environmental requirements. It misses major opportunities afforded by anticipating future restrictions and adapting products and processes accordingly. It limits the options that are ultimately available, and it invites mistakes in reacting haphazardly and hurriedly to new developments.

A longer-term approach—a corporate environmental strategy—is needed to respond effectively to this situation. While the content and detail of the strategy will vary from company to company, its development should include three major components, beginning with a clear understanding of the environmental consequences of the company's present operations.

**Part 1: The Environmental Audit** This is an analysis of the environmental consequences of the company's operations. It should cover each plant and product line. It should highlight the extent to which the company is currently complying with existing pollution control requirements. Since requirements change rapidly, however, the audit should not be limited to establishing the company's degree of compliance with their present terms. It should also alert management to potential environmental problems.

*Implementation.* The implementation of the audit is complex, and no simple prescription is possible. There are, though, a few guideposts which can be offered:

1. The company needs to determine where responsibility lies for compliance with environmental requirements. Responsibility can be centralized to achieve the efficiency that results from having a relatively small, expert group interpret and decide on the company's obligations. Alternatively, responsibility can be decentralized to the plant or product level to bring the costs of compliance directly under the control of the person in charge of the operation.

2. Those who implement the audit need a general corporate policy to guide them. Does the company intend, for example, to be a leader in pollution control, to do only what is immediately required, or to bring legal challenges to government-imposed standards? Is the chosen approach consistent with the corporate image which the company is trying to present? Is it consistent with the company's financial resources? Is it consistent with the practice followed in promoting middle managers?

3. Top management must establish a reporting system to enable it to keep track of progress and problems. It needs sufficient information to know when to intervene. For example, major problems may arise in getting equipment in time to comply with environmental requirements; top management needs to be alerted to such delays. It also needs information on the general environmental posture of the company's operations to assist it in exercising judgment on other corporate matters.

*Rules of Thumb.* There are several rules of thumb for evaluating the choices which are frequently involved:

1. The best solution to abating a pollution discharge may *not* be to add on a major treatment facility at the end of the pipe. A change in the production process may be more cost effective. It may reduce the wastes that must be treated and simultaneously increase the efficiency of production and the overall quality of output. Alternatively, wastes might be pretreated and then discharged into a municipal facility. Major end-of-the-pipe additions are frequently not the best solution.

2. Similarly, the best solution may not be the one with the lowest initial cost. Operation and maintenance expense over the life of the facility may be higher than the initial capital outlay. Industrial revenue bonds, on which interest payments are tax-free, might be available to fund some proposed solutions but not others. The selection of an alternative should be viewed as a complex investment decision, with the same financial sophistication exercised as is used in other corporate decisions.

**Part 2: Participating in the Formulation of Rules** In the first part of the environmental strategy—the environmental audit—a company basically looks at the extent to which it is in compliance with existing requirements. In the second part, a company steps beyond these requirements and participates in the process through which new ones are established.

The United States' environmental programs are in a state of flux. Legislation is being amended. Scientific and legal problems are being discovered. Major court decisions are being handed down. Government officials are continually revising their programs to keep them up to date with these developments.

During such a revision, an opportunity exists to explore new approaches to complying with the law. Requirements that were rigid may temporarily become flexible. Moreover, most companies are in a unique position to influence the outcome of the deliberations, because they have a vast reservoir of information regarding the feasibility of complying with alternative proposals for their industry. Indeed, they may have more information on the costs and benefits of the proposals than do those who are responsible for setting the requirements. Government officials need this information; it is frequently in a company's best interest to provide it.

There is, however, a major hurdle here. Many individuals perceive business, accurately or not, as having avoided assumption of responsibility for environmental protection. Accordingly, a company must first establish its credibility, particularly in the minds of those who are involved in the revision process, if its contribution to the dialogue is to be seriously considered. The extent to which a company is able to do this will determine whether government officials will look to it for its views.

Presentation of a company's views depends on a number of factors, such as its size and the type of business it is in. A large company may work *directly* with federal and state legislators and their staffs and with officials of federal and state agencies. It may meet informally with them. It may submit comments on proposed amendments to legislation, on agencies' "program strategy papers," and on proposed regulations. It may testify at public hearings. It may submit background information to the press and to environmental and other citizen organizations. It may conduct briefings and organize site visits.

A smaller company can more easily participate *indirectly* in this process. It can support the activities of its trade association and industry representatives through financial contributions and through the provision of information on the effect of environmental requirements on its operations.

**Part 3: New Business Operations** The last component of the corporate environmental strategy deals with the development of new business ventures. There are two facets here.

First, a company needs to include environmental analysis as an early, integral part of its project planning. Regardless of what is being considered—a new plant, a new product, or a change in the manufacturing process—a company must assess the environmental consequences and the costs of abatement. It should explicitly identify not only measures required by law but also those dictated by local public opinion, and it should weigh them in the decision on the project.

Second, a company should turn environmental problems around and capitalize on them. New opportunities have been created by environmental legislation. The more obvious ones are substantial. The pollution control equipment market has mushroomed. According to the Council on Environmental Quality (CEQ), capital expenditures associated with pollution control exceeded $5 billion in 1975 and are expected to reach more than $19 billion in 1984. CEQ forecasts that almost $250 billion will be spent in the United States on some sort of environmental protection between 1975 and 1984.

In addition to these direct effects, companies should consider the indirect effects of a new national environmental consciousness. Recent environmental laws reflect a change in public attitudes, and new types of products and services are likely to be demanded. For example, consumers have been rejecting aerosol sprays with fluorocarbons and are switching to products packaged with other types of applicators. The use of parks and forests is expanding and is creating a corresponding increase in demand for camping and other outdoor recreational equipment. Over the long run, opportunities created by these more subtle shifts may be more beneficial and enduring than those created by direct expenditures for pollution control.

*See also* COMMUNITY PLANNING LEGISLATION; CONSUMERISM AND CONSUMER PROTECTION LEGISLATION; EGALITARIANISM; ENERGY RESOURCES, MANAGEMENT OF; ENVIRONMENT, PHYSICAL; OMSBUDSMAN; SAFETY AND HEALTH MANAGEMENT, EMPLOYEE; SOCIAL RESPONSIBILITY OF BUSINESS; TECHNOLOGY, MANAGEMENT IMPLICATIONS; VALUE SYSTEMS, MANAGEMENT: SOCIAL AND CULTURAL.

### REFERENCES

"Air Program Strategy for Attainment and Maintenance of Ambient Air Quality Standards and Control of Other Pollutants," Environmental Protection Agency, Washington, 1976.

Butler, William A: "Federal Pesticides Law," in *Federal Environmental Law*, West Publishing Company, St. Paul, Minn., 1974.

Jorling, Thomas: "The Federal Law of Air Pollution Control," in *Federal Environmental Law*, West Publishing Company, St. Paul, Minn., 1974.

Leung, Kenneth Ch'uan'k'ai and Jeffrey A. Klein: "The Environmental Control Industry: An Analysis of Conditions and Prospects for the Pollution Control Equipment Industry," U.S. Department of Commerce, National Technical Information Service, Washington, 1976.

*The Seventh Annual Report*, Council on Environmental Quality, Washington, 1976.

Zener, Robert: "The Federal Law of Water Pollution Control," in *Federal Environmental Law*, West Publishing Company, St. Paul, Minn., 1974.

NEIL ORLOFF, *Cornell University*

# Environmental uncertainty, organizational (*See* ORGANIZATION STRUCTURES AND CHARTING.)

# Equal employment opportunity (EEO)
(*See* MINORITIES, MANAGEMENT OF AND EQUAL OPPORTUNITY.)

# Equal Pay Act (*See* WAGES AND HOURS LEGISLATION; WOMEN IN INDUSTRY.)

# Equal rights (*See* EGALITARIANISM.)

**Equality, economic**   (*See* EGALITARIANISM.)

**Equilibrium, market**   (*See* ECONOMIC CONCEPTS.)

**Equipment analysis**   (*See* COST IMPROVEMENT.)

**Equipment expenditures, long-term** (*See* BUDGETING, CAPITAL.)

**Equipment layout**   (*See* FACILITIES AND SITE PLANNING AND LAYOUT.)

**Equipment, material handling**   (*See* MATERIAL HANDLING.)

**Equity financing**   (*See* FINANCIAL MANAGEMENT OF SHORT-TERM, INTERMEDIATE, AND LONG-TERM FINANCING.)

**Equity, trading on**   (*See* FINANCIAL MANAGEMENT.)

**Ergonomics**   (*See* HUMAN FACTORS ENGINEERING.)

## ERISA

The Employee Retirement Income Security Act (ERISA) is the United States federal law designed to ensure that employees do not lose their pensions because they leave a company before retirement age or because the pension funds are insufficient.

The law, which took effect in January 1975, requires vesting under one of three plans. One requires full vesting after 10 years of service, and the other two result in full vesting after 15 years, generally with partial vesting before that.

The law also covers funding, and pension fund trustees may be held personally liable for misuse of their powers. In addition, it requires annual reports to employees and the Department on Labor on the status of the plans, and "willful failure" to report may be punishable by jail sentences.

*See also* COMPENSATION, EMPLOYEE BENEFIT PLANS; LABOR LEGISLATION; WAGES AND HOURS LEGISLATION.

### REFERENCES
Carlson, Donald G.: "Responding to the Pension Reform Law," *Harvard Business Review*, November–December 1974, pp. 133–144.

Employee Retirement Income Security Act (Public Law 93–406), *Congressional and Administrative News*, 93d Congress, Second Session, 1974, vol. 1, pp. 935–1187, West Publishing Company, St. Paul, Minn. Text of the law. Text may also be obtained from the U.S. Chamber of Commerce.

"Pension Reform's Expensive Ricochet," Special Report, *Business Week*, March 24, 1975, pp. 144–155.

Scala, Bea: "ERISA: Administrative Nightmare," *Administrative Management*, June 1976, pp. 24–25 and 52.

STAFF/SMITH

**Error, forecast**   (*See* FORECASTING BUSINESS CONDITIONS.)

**Error-cause removal**   (*See* QUALITY MANAGEMENT.)

**Escalation clause**   (*See* REAL ESTATE MANAGEMENT, CORPORATE.)

## Ethics, managerial

Managerial ethics are concerned with what is deemed acceptable or unacceptable—and by whom—in the realm of business action (behavior) and decision making. Ethics are the collection of moral principles or views about acceptable or unacceptable actions in a given field of human activity. Thus medical ethics or legal ethics indicate what is acceptable or unacceptable behavior in the fields of medicine and law. The term *management ethics* refers to the collection of ideas or thoughts about acceptable or unacceptable behavior by managers. The focus for examination here is on managers in business organizations, keeping in mind that much applies also in government, education, and other types of organizations in our society.

## ETHICAL ISSUES

Degrees of acceptability of management behavior suggest other terms also: that which is good or bad, fair or unfair, just or unjust. Taken together these terms clearly identify managerial ethics as a concern with what behavior and decision making of managers is considered *right* or *wrong*.

**Judgments** Judgments about what is right or wrong, moreover, are the crux of the problem in talking about ethics. An individual may agree that the subject of managerial ethics is precisely as described, but *who decides* what is right or wrong, acceptable or unacceptable? Herein lies the problem. Value judgments of people—as individuals or, most usually, as groups—make the determination. They make this determination by comparing managerial actions against standards or norms. Standards or norms evolve from group consensus or agreement.

**Consensus** The clearest case of group consensus might be said to be a country's laws. Though it is true that some in any society do not agree with or like its laws, the legal process is the method by which a people formally establish norms or standards of acceptability. Thus, judgments about managerial ethics are made by value-based comparisons of behavior or actions with standards or norms (which in the final analysis are themselves based upon a set of values).

Unfortunately there is no clear consensus in our society as to what is acceptable or unacceptable regarding all the situations managers face. There are laws, of course, but laws cover only the grossest violations. In many decision arenas no laws exist at all. For example, there are no clear-cut guidelines of acceptability in such "grey" areas as: What constitutes deceptive or misleading advertising? What responsibility does the manager have with respect to hidden product dangers? What about using company services for personal use? What about taking longer than necessary to do a job?

**Guidelines** The real quandary in business, then, is that there are no clear-cut guidelines for behavior and decision making. Faced with this dilemma, the manager frequently responds to those guidelines which are clear. As an illustration, take the case of the spate of overseas bribery scandals by business firms in the late 1970s. Many business people felt—perhaps rightly—that society had not made clear what is acceptable or unacceptable behavior in the international business arena. Thus, when in doubt managers tend to respond to the norms of competition and profit, which, unlike ethics, are quite clear.

**Level of Abstraction** While society may reach consensus on certain values at a high level of abstraction, this consensus tends to break down as the issues move from the general to the specific. At a high level of abstraction, for example, all agree that one should not take another person's life. As one moves to particular situations, however, there are circumstances under which we rationalize killing as justifiable, e.g., self-defense and war.

As another example, at a high level of abstraction most tend to agree that one should not take another person's property. When examining specifics, once again, there is trouble drawing the line. Is it all right to take home pencils? pens? paper? staples? adding machines? One recent cartoon illustrates a similar dilemma. In the first panel a father speaks to his son, who stands before him with a load of pencils in his hands. The father says, "You know how I feel about stealing, Wilberforce! Now tomorrow I want you to return every one of those pencils to school!" In the second panel the father says: "I'll bring you all the pencils you need from work."

So the problem develops. The manager has no clear-cut standard or norm as to what is acceptable and unacceptable. In the absence of such guidelines, the manager applies personal standards to the predicament, which sometimes mean "no standards" or standards motivated by self-gain, expediency, or perhaps fear of reprisal by superiors.

## CURRENT STATE OF MANAGERIAL ETHICS

It is difficult to pinpoint whether the state of managerial ethics has indeed deteriorated over the past several years, or whether renewed interest in ethics has been stimulated by the dramatic events of the last 5 years or so. Beginning with revelations of illegal corporate giving traceable to the 1972 presidential election in the United States, news accounts have reported large-scale questionable business practices ranging from kickbacks and fraud schemes to bribes to foreign officials in order to induce business abroad.

Though a few studies have tried in recent years to assess the current state of managerial ethics, the results are never conclusive. The main difficulties seem to stem from (1) the lack of clear-cut standards of measurement and (2) the problem of distinguishing between what managers say they believe and what they actually believe (and do). Related to this, one finding which frequently seems to emerge in studies is that managers usually believe their colleagues to be more unethical than they perceive themselves to be.

One study conducted by Carroll in 1975 posed the question directly for managers to evaluate the current period with earlier periods in terms of business ethics. The managers surveyed were asked to indicate the extent of their agreement or disagreement with the following proposition: "Business ethics today are far superior to ethics of earlier periods." The survey results from 238 managers were as follows:

| Response | No. | Percent |
|----------|-----|---------|
| Disagree | 60 | 25.2 |
| Somewhat disagree | 52 | 21.8 |
| Somewhat agree | 78 | 32.8 |
| Agree | 48 | 20.2 |
| Totals | 238 | 100.0 |

The responses were extremely varied: 47 percent disagreed and 53 percent agreed.[1] It is unlikely, however, that clear consensus on this type of assessment would ever result. It is somewhat like asking the nation's Monday morning quarterbacks to compare the current Super Bowl champions with the Green Bay Packers under the leadership of Vince Lombardi. Even in the light of recent highly publicized questionable business acts, however, and the general impression given by the press that moral decay of business has set in, a slightly higher number of managers feel that today's ethics are far superior to the ethics of earlier periods.

Several conclusions did come out of the Carroll study which are relevant to an assessment of the current state of managerial ethics. First, the study indicated that a majority of the managers surveyed felt that "managers today feel under pressure to compromise personal standards to achieve company goals." It was further substantiated that these pressures were perceived most prevalently at the lower management level. That is, 84 percent of the managers at the lower level indicated they perceived pressure to compromise, 65 percent at the middle level, and only 50 percent at the top level.

A second item from the Carroll survey lent support to the above. The managers were posed the following proposition: "The junior members of Nixon's reelection committee who confessed that they went along with their bosses to show their loyalty is just what young managers would have done in business." The results:

| Response | No. | Percent |
|----------|-----|---------|
| Disagree | 58 | 24.6 |
| Somewhat disagree | 38 | 16.1 |
| Somewhat agree | 84 | 35.6 |
| Agree | 56 | 23.7 |
| Total | 236 | 100.0 |

These data show that 60 percent of the managers surveyed agreed that young managers in business would have done just what Nixon's subordinates had done. Like the earlier findings, these data displayed an interesting pattern when examined by managerial level: 37 percent of top managers agreed with the proposition, while 61 percent of middle managers agreed, and 85 percent of the lower managers agreed.

These findings are consistent with earlier findings in that they suggest that the lower one is in the management hierarchy, the more one believes that unethical pressures or practices exist. Several likely implications stem from this: (1) top level managers are insulated from organizational reality with respect to ethical issues; (2) top managers just do not understand how far their subordinates will go to please them—perhaps out of a misguided sense of loyalty or fear of reprisal; (3) a serious problem exists with respect to the current state of managerial ethics.

## IMPROVING MANAGERIAL ETHICS

Though some adhere to the belief that good ethics cannot be taught or improved by management, there are a number of levels on which the problem can be effectively addressed: (1) the individual level, (2) the organizational level, (3) the association level, and (4) the societal level. These levels must be approached simultaneously, however, rather than in the sequential order presented here.

**Individual Level** It is frequently asserted that ultimately good ethics depend on the individual. Ethical decision making may be improved by carefully engaging in self-analysis with respect to the following tests that business managers have suggested have been useful in recent years:

1. Test of common sense. Does the action I am getting ready to engage in make sense? That is, is it an action a reasonably responsible person would take?

2. Test of negative impact. Will the action harm others or have an irresponsible negative impact on them?

3. Test of self-concept. Does the action conform with my best concept of myself?

4. Watergate TV test. Could my action stand up under close public scrutiny? Would I be embarrassed if what I am getting ready to do became public?[2]

5. Test of ventilation. Would my actions hold up under the scrutiny of ventilation with my colleagues?[3] That is, if I got divergent views in a grey area would my proposed behavior hold up as acceptable?

6. Test of the purified idea. Am I simply hiding behind my superior's judgments—assuming that the idea is "purified" or made acceptable by a superior's approval?[4]

**Organizational Level** There are a number of actions which can be taken by management at the organizational level to improve ethical performance and climate:

1. Exercise of leadership by top management. L. W. Foy, chairman of Bethlehem Steel, recently suggested, "It is a primary responsibility of business management to instruct, motivate, and inspire their employees to conduct themselves with honesty, probity, and fairness. Starting at the top, management has to *set an example* for the others to follow." Foy elaborates, " . . . management has to *make company policy absolutely clear* to all employees. People have to be told and re-told, in unmistakable terms, that the company is firmly committed to integrity in all its activities."[5] Fred T. Allen, chairman and president of Pitney-Bowes, Inc., adds, "It is up to the leader to make sure that ethical behavior permeates the entire company. Employees must know exactly what is expected of them in the moral arena and how to respond to warped ethics."[6]

2. Establishment of realistic sales and profit goals. Allen remarks, "Under the stress of patently unrealistic goals, otherwise responsible subordinates will often take the attitude that 'anything goes.'" Goals should be set that are *realistic* and *achievable* within accepted business practices.

3. Development of codes of ethics. Codes which transcend the lip-service level of commitment can be established. These codes then must be communicated, adhered to, and made into "living documents."

4. Encourage of "whistle blowing." An effective ethical climate is contingent upon employees having a *mechanism* for and top management *support* of blowing the whistle on violators of the organization's codes of ethics.

5. Creation of an ethical ombudsman or advocate. Theodore Purcell advocates that ethical expertise be institutionalized at the executive level by creating a position of "ethics advocate."[7] The primary responsibility of this individual would be to identify the general questions of an ethical nature that should be constantly brought to the attention of top management along with the conventional marketing, financial, and legal questions.

6. Dismissal of unethical managers. Responding to the question "How should the corporation respond to the individual who is guilty of deliberately and flagrantly violating its ethical code?" Fred T. Allen asserts, "From the pinnacle of the corporate pyramid to its base, there can only be one action: dismissal. . . . When a company fails to take strong action against an employee—at whatever level—most people think the employee had the implicit—if not the explicit—consent of management."[8]

**Association Level** Associations are groups of businesses that have a common interest based upon membership in the same trade, industry, or profession. Associations can take leadership in the ethical arena by the development of professional codes of ethics which are designed to bring about norms of behavior and ethical uniformity among a group of businesses: for example, the codes of ethics of the American Institute of Certified Public Accountants, the American Psychological Association, and the American Bar Association.

Efforts to provide leadership in other ways are also recommended. For example, the Chamber of Commerce of the United States' Institute for Organization Management offers courses on "ethics for association executives."

**Societal Level** Law is the primary instrument of ethical advocacy at the societal level, but management should not view law as the means of ensuring ethical behavior and practices. A section of the Code of Worldwide Business Conduct issued by Caterpillar Tractor Co. is cogent here. It reads, "The law is a floor. Ethical business conduct should normally exist at a level well above the minimum required by law."[9]

*See also* COMPETITION; OBJECTIVES AND GOALS; PROFITS AND PROFIT MAKING; SOCIAL RESPONSIBILITY OF BUSINESS; VALUE SYSTEMS, MANAGEMENT: SOCIAL AND CULTURAL; WORK, CONCEPT AND IMPLICATIONS.

## NOTES

[1]Archie B. Carroll, "Managerial Ethics: A Post-Watergate View," *Business Horizons*, vol. XVIII, April 1975, pp. 75–80.

[2]"Stiffer Rules for Business Ethics," *Business Week*, Mar. 30, 1974, pp. 87–92.

[3]Ibid, p. 88.

[4]Ibid.

[5]L. W. Foy, "Business Ethics: A Reappraisal," Distinguished Leaders Lecture Series, Columbia University Graduate School of Business, New York, Jan. 30, 1975. (Italics added.)

[6]Fred T. Allen, "Corporate Morality: Is the Price Too High?" *Wall Street Journal*, Oct. 17, 1975, p. 16 (Italics added.)

[7]Theodore V. Purcell, "A Practical Guide to Ethics in Business," *Business and Society Review*, no. 13, Spring 1975, pp. 43–50.

[8]Allen, loc. cit.

[9]Ibid.

### REFERENCES

Adair, John E.: *Management and Morality: The Problems and Opportunities of Social Capitalism*, David and Charles, London, 1974.

Baumhart, Raymond: *Ethics in Business*, Holt, Rinehart and Winston, Inc., New York, 1968.

Berlo, David K.: "Morality or Ethics? Two Approaches to Organizational Control," *Personnel Administrator*, vol. 20, April 1975, pp. 16–19.

Crawford, C. M., and C. S. Goodman: "Young Executives: A Source of New Ethics?" *Personnel Journal*, March 1974, pp. 180–187.

Newstrom, John W., and William A. Ruch: "The Ethics of Management and the Management of Ethics," *MSU Business Topics*, vol. XXIII, Winter 1975, pp. 29–37.

ARCHIE B. CARROLL, *University of Georgia*

# Europe, management in Western

There is nothing so clear cut as a single managerial style which is uniformly adhered to by all American or by all European business leaders. Yet underlying the behavior and attitudes of these two different groups of executives are certain general characteristics or common denominators which can be identified.

**Past Versus Future**   The most striking difference between the outlooks of Europeans and Americans lies in their orientation toward time. It is as if they were standing back to back, with the European inclined to look at the past and present and the American seeing the present and future.

The Europeans' attachment to the past accounts for their respect for such characteristics as wisdom, stability, convention, necessity, quality, and diversity. The Americans' more futuristic outlook leads them to respect vitality, mobility, informality, abundance, quantity, and organization. Unless Europeans abandon some of their excessive attachment to the past and Americans their more or less profound disregard for it, little change can be expected.

**Wisdom Versus Vitality**   Though neither continent can claim to have a monopoly on vitality or wisdom, it is reasonably true to say that American management philosophy is, in general, more vital than wise, while Europe's is more wise than vital. Here is an example:

One of the most rigorous belt-tightening operations by a major corporation was undertaken by Chrysler Corp. in 1961. It fired 7,000 of 36,000 white collar employees, from secretaries to high-ranking executives. The action helped lower Chrysler's break-even point to 725,000 cars and trucks from a million units. President Lynn A. Townsend says the cutback didn't impair efficiency.[1]

Obviously, some very wasteful things must have been allowed to happen in the past, or else the company could not have cut its white-collar work force by 20 percent without a loss of efficiency. Vitality (the urge to expand) not moderated by wisdom had resulted in an extremely uneconomic situation which only equally extreme countermeasures could correct. But—and this again is a proof of vitality—the necessary measures were taken.

*Slow Growth.*   In Europe the moderating influence of wisdom (that is, top management's preference for slow, organic growth) prevents many production and clerical jobs from being mechanized. But at the middle-management level and, even more, at the top-management level, in comparison with America, *under*staffing rather than *over*staffing seems to be the rule. Important decisions are still made by single individuals or at least by a much smaller group of top executives than in the United States.

With most of the strategic decisions concentrated at the top, there is also a pronounced tendency not to communicate the reasoning behind these decisions to those at lower management levels. Obviously, European top executives try to save a part of the time American executives spend on communications, though they do so somewhat at the expense of middle management "learning." This fact, indeed, is reflected by the smaller percentage of key positions in European business held by executives aged 40 or less. The theory that a good wine requires many years of aging in a dark, coolish cellar has been extended to the business executive and seems to have become an integral part of European management philosophy.

This particular way of thinking explains the relatively small interest European top executives still show for training their potential managers in American or American-style business schools. In addition, many are convinced that only the more technical aspects, and not the *essence* or the *style* of executive leadership, can be learned there.

As a result of this attitude, climbing up the corporate ladder in Europe takes the aspiring executive, generally speaking, more time than in North America. But once the executive reaches the top, the risk of coming down again is also much smaller.

Many examples of course, could be cited to reveal how wisdom and vitality are given different weights in the American and European management philosophies. But they would all lead us to the same conclusion: to optimize our business performance it is necessary to combine the advantages of both characteristics. How can this be done?

In Europe large reserves of vital energy could certainly be released by dropping some of the most outdated conventions. Examples are those conventions that require most decisions to be made at the top rather than at the lowest possible level in the organization, or those that hold an executive responsible to a superior but do not require the superior to bother about *actively* developing the subordinate's capacities. Many of these conventions need close questioning so that the weight given presently to different values can be redistributed more logically.

To put a conscious break between *stimulus* and *reaction*—as Napoleon is said to have done when he once decided to leave his mail unopened for a certain time, only to find that at the end of it most of the letters had taken care of themselves and so did not have to be answered—is one of the particular privileges and duties top management must make more liberal use of. For wisdom requires deliberation, and deliberation requires time.

**Stability Versus Mobility**  It is not surprising to find that stability and mobility are two other typical opposing characteristics of the respective management philosophies.

Accordingly, intercompany job changes in the higher echelons are much less frequent in Europe than in America. In part this is a matter of language and geographical barriers; however, it is also the result of Europeans being more skeptical about human nature than Americans. They prefer to let several years of observation pass before giving high-level responsibility to a new member of management, who, by the time he (or she) gets it, is of course no longer new. Switching companies at a frequency customary in America would normally lead to an intolerable loss of time in the career of a European executive.

Similarly, changing jobs within companies in the sense of job rotation has never been as fully accepted by big business in Europe as it has been in America. This is due partly to the fact that specialization on lower and middle management levels has not been pushed as far ahead as in America; thus, job rotation seems less urgent. It is also due partly to top management's belief that rotating people through various jobs is costly and can lead to situations where a great number of employees have had experience in a lot of areas but lack solid competence in any one. With all strategic and many tactical decisions still being made at or at least close to the top, there is also less need for vision on the lower levels. There is, however, more demand for highly competent "spade work" on which European top management can solidly build its decisions without having to resort to double and triple checking through extensive committee work. Committees are, therefore, far less important in the European than they are in the American management process.

**Status Versus Title**  Another illustration of stability and mobility can be found in the area of job titles. Business on the European continent uses, in general, a very limited number of official titles—much the same way that the military forces employ a relatively small number of different ranks. Thus, knowing a European executive's title and the size of the company he (or she) works for makes it fairly easy to estimate the executive's responsibility as well as earnings. The latter are rarely, if ever, spoken of openly, contrary to the practice in America where knowing the earnings of an executive is often the only way to measure his (or her) responsibility—the number of titles being so great as to make quick orientation a rather hopeless affair.

European top executives believe that the widespread use of custom-tailored titles to compensate for a lack of job satisfaction is a short-range expedient which merely starts a vicious circle, forcing top management to dole out ever more status symbols and leading ultimately to the highly sophisticated and eventually costly kind of human relations being practiced by large corporations in America.

**Convention Versus Informality**  Although an open-door policy and a first-name basis are both widely accepted practices in American business, they are but two exterior signs of how American management philosophy has given preference to informality. This is, of course, contrary to practices in Europe, where numerous conventions are still strictly adhered to. But the roots of different convictions go much deeper, and it seems as if in the external dilemma of all executives—having to exercise authority and trying to be liked—European top management has constantly preferred to put more weight on the former and American top management more on the latter quality.

Thus, American managers seem to feel that human relations in Europe have an authoritarian and paternalistic flavor, and consider the social distance between individuals a remnant from feudal times. Europeans, in turn, believe Americans to be guilty of promoting excessive egalitarianism and status stripping, which in their eyes not only is naïve and unrealistic but must inevitably destroy management effectiveness in the long run.[2]

Thus human relations in European business lack the outer nonchalance and friendliness found in America; on the other hand, the Europeans do not seem to share the inner tensions which are often apparent on the other side of the Atlantic. American tensions stem, it seems, largely from trying to adhere to the overly idealistic point of view that one must like everybody or, if that cannot be done, at least pretend to do so.

Between the extremes of bullying and loving people there is ample room for the less spectacular but more effective way of simple *respecting* them. How good a balance can finally be struck between convention and informality will always depend on the maturity of the individual top executive.

**Necessity Versus Abundance**  The relative lack of natural resources in Europe and their abundance in America have had profound impact on the management philosophies of the two continents. Thus, the tendency toward thrift and the desire to avoid waste are evident in the thinking of European executives.

Surprise and particularly its cause, secrecy, are a natural part of European management philosophy. American financial analysts often complain about the rudimentary information given by European companies in their balance sheets and profit and loss statements. But the smaller amount of information published is in strict accordance with local government rules. And if no voluntary supplements are handed out to the general public, it is only partly to seek additional protection from foreign competition behind the smoke screen of secrecy. It is also caused by the general conviction that the more information a company releases, the more explanations it has to give.

**Quality Versus Quantity**  European management has always found it necessary to stress quality much more than quantity. How else—to cite one extreme example—could a small country like Switz-

erland, with hardly any natural resources, have become a prosperous nation than by simply doing a few things better than anybody else would do them? "Quality, not quantity" is, therefore, the outstanding characteristic of European management philosophy.

A typical facet is the fairly general tendency of Europeans to *think before trying*. As a leading European businessman once said, "We are not in the habit of increasing through wastefulness the chance of a random hit."

And so the technique of brainstorming, which has been given much publicity in America, has never really been accepted in Europe. Preference has always been given to high-quality, individual thinking rather than to group thinking, which explains why the managements of European companies seem to be relatively understaffed.

Another technique which has never made much impression in Europe is speed reading. Although the quantity of reading matter has increased as much for the European as it has for the American executive, the former has in general refused the *speed* solution, believing that it necessarily leads to an accent on quantity (at the expense of quality). The European has relied more on *selectivity* to solve the reading problem.

In addition, the European has applied this same principle in his (or her) community and public activities, which seem to be a fraction of what many American executives have accepted. The reasoning behind this consistent refusal to get too involved outside the immediate sphere of work is the European conviction that each individual should, above all, concentrate on his (or her) job, because nobody aiming at top performance can afford to dissipate energy. Thus, by preferring quality to quantity, European management is forced necessarily to favor selectivity and a concentration of efforts.

But by saying *yes* to quantity, one cannot say *no* to standardization, because these two characteristics of managerial philosophy are linked like Siamese twins. Quantity per se is certainly not bad. On the contrary, it has considerable social benefits, such as the increase in the standard of living resulting from mass production. But there are always the attendant dangers of excessive standardization trailing in its wake and of overorganization stifling individual initiative.

**Diversity Versus Organization**  Overorganization, the European believes, is a particularly threatening consequence. The ideal of all national economies and individual businesses is, of course, to arrive at a proper balance between organized, controlled activity and that which offers an incentive for a freer use of individual initiative. The European achieves order through definite status levels in the organization but does not try to structure a person's every effort.

There can be too little organization, that is, too much diversity. In many instances European business performance could be improved if there were more of it. But executives must be aware of the fact that good organization is always in a state of unstable equilibrium, needing slight but constant corrective action from the top.

The basic characteristics of American and European management philosophies are strikingly complementary. A combination of what is best in both might lead to an improvement in the conduct of the Euro-American free enterprise economics.

*See also* CODETERMINATION AND INDUSTRIAL DEMOCRACY; INTERNATIONAL OPERATIONS AND MANAGEMENT IN MULTINATIONAL COMPANIES; INTERNATIONAL TRADE; OMBUDSMAN.

### NOTES

Excerpted and updated by the author from "American vs European Management Philosophy," *Harvard Business Review*, March–April 1964. Copyright © 1964 by the president and Fellows of Harvard College.

[1]"White Collar Cutback," *The Wall Street Journal*, Jan. 3, 1963, p. 19.

[2]*See*, for example, Abraham Zaleznik, "The Human Dilemmas of Leadership," *Harvard Business Review*, July–August 1963, p. 51. (For a contrary point of view, *see* Robert N. McMurry. "The Case for Benevolent Autocracy," *Harvard Business Review*, January–February 1958, p. 82.)

OTTO H. NOWOTNY, *F. Hoffman-La Roche and Company, Ltd.*

## Evaluation, applicant (*See* EMPLOYMENT PROCESS.)

## Evaluation, job (*See* JOB EVALUATION.)

## Evaluation of training (*See* DEVELOPMENT AND TRAINING, EMPLOYEE.)

## Events (*See* NETWORK PLANNING METHODS.)

## Events, statistical (*See* STATISTICAL ANALYSIS FOR MANAGEMENT.)

## Exception, control of (*See* CONTROL SYSTEMS, MANAGEMENT.)

## Exception, management by

Management by exception is an information and control technique that provides management with signals that tell when a condition or operation is within its prescribed standards and when it is not. Certain refinements may enable the system to indicate the degree of variance and the particular level of management attention required, as shown in Fig. E-8 (page 374). The principle, as conceived by Frederick W. Taylor, provides leverage for the use of management time and enables managers to accomplish far more than if they were to apply themselves indiscriminately to every problem that arose.

Management by exception implies the use of delegation, since subordinates typically handle conditions that are within the lower ranges of variance. Frank B. Gilbreth suggested that various control levels—or zones of variance—be established for each key condition and that responsibilities for appropriate action within each zone be prearranged, as shown in Fig. E-9 (page 375).

Most budget and variance reports incorporate some form of management by exception in their information system. These range widely in (1) degree of specificity (some reports simply indicate under or over budget); (2) speed of reporting (instantaneous with on-line process controls and daily, weekly, or monthly with typical budgetary controls); and (3) format (ranging from handposted quality control charts to computer printouts to visual CRT indicators.)

*See also* ACCOUNTING, COST ANALYSIS AND CONTROL; AUTHORITY, RESPONSIBILITY AND ACCOUNTABILITY; DELEGATION.

### REFERENCES

Bittel, Lester R.: "Manage By Exception," *The Nine Master Keys of Management*, McGraw-Hill Book Company, New York, 1972, chap. 6.

Bittel, Lester R.: *Management by Exception*, McGraw-Hill Book Company, New York, 1964.

Gilbreth, Frank B.: "Graphical Control on the Exception Principle for Executives," Paper 1573a, American Society of Mechanical Engineers, New York, December 1916.

Starr, Martin K.: "Control Models: Forecasting and Feedback," *Production Management: Systems and Synthesis*, 2d ed., Prentice-Hall, Inc., Englewood Cliffs, N.J., 1972, chap. 5.

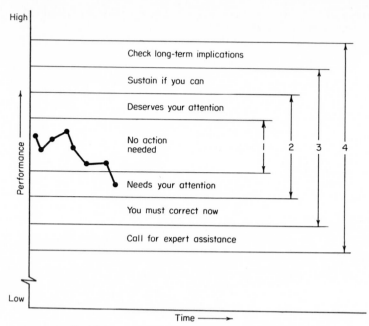

Establishment of zone limits is key to performance control.

Zone 1 — Expected and acceptable performance.

Zone 2 — Unusual performance. On the low side, needs surveillance. On the high side, needs verification.

Zone 3 — Unacceptable performance. On the low side, needs action to correct now. On the high side, look for evidence of changed conditions that indicate standards should be raised.

Zone 4 — Vitally disturbed performance. On the low side, ask for staff help to analyze and correct. On the high side, full-scale investigation indicated to assure that performance isn't being attained at expense of long-term goals.

**Fig. E-8. Action-indicator chart.**

Taylor, Frederick W.: "Shop Management," reprinted in *Scientific Management,* Harper & Row, Publishers, Incorporated, New York, 1947, p. 126.

STAFF/BITTEL

## Exception point [*See* OBJECTIVES, MANAGEMENT BY (MBO).]

## Exception principle (*See* EXCEPTION, MANAGEMENT BY.)

## Exchange, foreign, management of

The necessity for dealing with matters concerning foreign exchange is one of the principal dimensions that distinguishes international business transactions from their domestic counterparts. *Foreign exchange* deals with the relationships of the monies of one country to those of another; it is a generic term, used in conjunction with procedures and documents as well as prices and institutions. The actual purchase of the money of one nation with that of another is called *conversion.* The price at which the sale takes place is the *exchange rate.* If no actual purchase or sale takes place, merely the changing of accounting statements from an expression of values in one money to equivalent values in another, the process is called *translation. Money* refers to anything that is generally accepted to make payments for goods or services or to discharge obligations; it includes bills of exchange and bank drafts as well as bank notes (currency). Business assets and liabilities are expressed in the monetary units, or the *units of account*, of a particular country. If an eventual conversion must take place, the possibility of a change in the value of exchange rates gives rise to potential gain or loss of assets, or to a *foreign exchange risk*. The total amount of money subject to foreign exchange risk is called the foreign exchange *exposure*.

## EXCHANGE RATE VARIATION

Consideration of the shifting values of foreign exchange rates should begin with a recognition that any quoted rate, unless otherwise qualified, could represent an official rate or a free-market rate. The *official rate* is the value that the issuing government places on its own currency. The assignment of this value by a government can be quite arbitrary, but the use of that value can be enforced by the government's control of the banking system, with severe penalties for trading outside of prescribed channels.

The *free-market rate*, as the term implies, is the value determined by the forces of supply and demand. However, the greatest single force in the market affecting supply or demand is often a government action, even for currencies that are designated as freely convertible. A *convertible* currency is

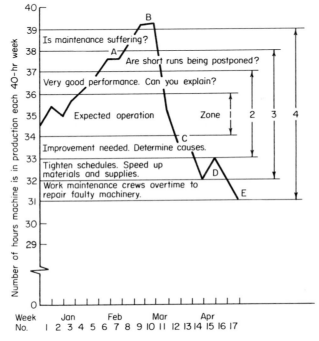

A. High degree of machine utilization.
   Could reflect a favoring of long runs at expense of short runs, which must be scheduled later, and will reduce utilization rate.

B. Exceptional utilization.
   Could reflect seriously deferred maintenance or equipment run at excessive speeds.

C. Marginally acceptable utilization.
   Cause should be found immediately. Action should be taken if this performance persists.

D. Low degree of machine utilization.
   Could reflect supply or scheduling deficiencies rather than maintenance or poor operation.

E. Unacceptable utilization.
   If attributable to machine downtime, requires immediate action.

**Fig. E-9. Machine utilization analysis using an action-indicator chart.**

one that may be freely exchanged or converted into other foreign currencies.

**Amount of Rate Variation** Some exchange rates do not vary at all over long periods, but other currencies may fluctuate widely over short periods of time. The United States dollar is legal tender in Panama, on par with their own balboa; therefore one dollar has equaled one balboa since the inception of the balboa in 1904. On the other hand, the French franc fell about 5½ percent in value relative to the Japanese yen between the end of February and the middle of March 1976.[14]

A change can also come quickly in both directions, as illustrated by the performance of the Italian lire and the French franc, where the franc appreciated about 12½ percent between the end of February and the end of April 1976, only to fall back more than 8 percent of its peak value the following month.[14] Rapid price variations such as these are not unusual in free markets for commodities, including those for the commodity of foreign exchange. But the official rates of controlled currencies usually maintain their values, changing seldom but changing precipitously when the governments involved are finally forced to act.[5] The United States dollar for example, was devalued 7.89 percent in December 1971, and another 10 percent in February 1973, after having maintained its previous official value in terms of gold since 1934.

**Fixed Versus Floating Exchange Rates** Most Western nations do not now attempt to maintain a stable value of their currencies solely by edict and the exercise of police power, since this results in the development of black markets or it chokes off desirable commerce. Instead, they take part in elaborate economic measures that include direct operations by government in the exchange markets,[7] working arrangements between central banks, and participation in international agreements such as the International Monetary Fund (IMF) or the European Monetary Agreement. There exists considerable literature on international monetary agreements, especially the IMF.[16] The fundamental objectives of these agreements are to promote commerce by providing exchange stability and orderly markets and a sufficient supply of foreign exchange (*international liquidity*). The choices of available means for establishing a new world monetary order fit on a continuum between administratively determined *fixed exchange rates*, on the one hand, and flexible or *floating exchange rates* established by the marketplace, on the other.

Fixed exchange rates have the advantage of stability: businesses have assurances that foreign money will cost the same next month regardless of market conditions. But fixed rates, if different from what free markets would dictate, must be maintained by government action. This means restrictions,[3] with concomitant evasive behavior by citizens, or it could be accomplished by *pegging*, or direct government intervention in the market to maintain a particular rate of exchange (the *parity* rate). When governments, or more precisely their agents, the central banks, peg the market by buying or selling the currency in question, they make the transaction with gold (especially in the past) or reserves. *Reserves* are drawable funds held by central banks or other financial institutions such as the IMF. Thus, in the fixed exchange rate system, rates remain fairly constant, but there is a fluctuation in the level of available reserves. In situations where the conditions underlying the market pressures are chronic, a central bank may exhaust its supply of available reserves. If this happens, a sharp adjustment of exchange rates becomes necessary. Floating rates, therefore, adjust daily and reflect the market at any moment; fixed rates are stable in the short run but risk precipitous changes in the long run.

**Spot and Forward Exchange Rates** Foreign exchange resembles other commodities in an important respect besides price fluctuations. Exchange transactions may take place on the basis of a spot or forward contract defined as in commodities trading. A *spot* transaction is one where immediate delivery of, and payment for, the currency takes place; because of procedural delays "immediate" is generally taken to mean within two business days of the trade date. A *forward* transaction is a contract wherein the currency is to be delivered, and payment made, at a designated future date at a price set at the time when the contract is drawn. The period of the contract can be of any length, but 30, 60, or 90 days are the most common.

The spot and forward exchange rates are related to one another. At least two theories are currently available to explain the magnitude of the premium or discount at which the forward sells relative to the spot value: (1) *the interest rate parity theory*,[6] which holds that the difference in forward and spot prices is determined by the differences in short-term interest rates in the respective financial centers; and (2) the *interest parity plus speculation theory*,[6] which holds that in addition to the above, the forward rate reflects the expected future value of the spot rate, with speculators entering the market to shift the prices away from their "natural" interest parity values. The interest parity idea makes sense because when banks take one side of a forward contract they typically, and must in some instances (such as is the case with British banks), offset the contract by a second transaction to cover any exposed position. For example, if an American bank sells a client a 90-day forward contract for British pounds, it has acquired an obligation to come up with a designated number of pounds in 90 days; to ensure that the pounds will be available 90 days hence without suffering an exchange loss, the bank can offset the forward contract by purchasing a British treasury bill (denominated in pounds). The bank earns interest at London rates on that British treasury bill; but it likewise has sacrificed the opportunity to put the same funds in a U.S. Treasury bill at New York interest rates. Therefore, if New York interest rates were higher, the client must reimburse the bank for this loss, or pay a premium equal to the difference in the rates, when buying the forward contract; conversely, if London interest rates are higher, the client's promise to deliver dollars in 90 days provides the bank with the opportunity to take advantage of the higher London rates without incurring exposure, hence the forward contract would sell at a discount. Speculators, however, by the very nature of that operation do take *open* (i.e., uncovered) positions; therefore, to the degree that the forward market is represented at any time by open positions, the interest parity plus speculation theory is reasonable. Also, since a forward contract depends upon the ability of the participants to deliver, credit standing of participants could be reflected in the price of a given transaction.

**Why Spot Rates Fluctuate**  Granting the above relationship between spot and forward rates, the question still remains as to the determinants of the spot rates of any two currencies. The most immediate impact on the supply and demand for currencies is produced by the *balance of trade* between the respective nations, or more precisely the *balance of payments*, which includes in addition to the difference between exports and imports, the net of all other money flows. This flow of payments is in turn affected by the differences in inflation rates (one of the best leading indicators), productivity, available reserves, interest rates, trader's attitudes, taxes, money supply, restrictions, and political considerations, all of which are to some extent interdependent.

## FOREIGN EXCHANGE MARKETS

The very word *marketplace* denotes a location where trading takes place. And indeed, the New York Stock Exchange, the Chicago Board of Trade, and Billingsgate in London all call up visions of specific

buildings or areas with their own unique sights and sounds and character. Physically, the major portion of a foreign exchange market can best be described as a mass of telephone lines, cable, and radio systems located within and connecting the major financial centers of the world.[10] The closest thing to a "place" in the foreign exchange market would be the trading room of a major bank, wherein the bank's currency trading specialists are congregated for convenience and greater efficiency, along with their desks, telephones, and perhaps posting boards or electronic terminals. But the bank trading room usually represents only a part of any given transaction; the other parts of the transaction involve the participants on the other ends of the telephone wires. These participants are, aside from the ultimate buyer and seller, another bank and often a broker specialist who connects the bank that has currency to buy with the one that has currency to sell. A central bank could also be a participant as a buyer or seller, and in countries with exchange controls, it may be a required link in clearing any transaction.

**The One World of Foreign Exchange**  Because of the capabilities of modern communications, the connection between financial centers in effect creates a single world marketplace for currencies. A businessperson in a small town in Alabama can place an order for Spanish pesetas with a local banker. The local banker probably does not have foreign exchange trading facilities, or even published market reports on currencies, but this doesn't matter. The order is relayed through a correspondent, or perhaps placed directly, with a major New York or Chicago commercial bank that executes the order. All this can be done within minutes.

This capacity for communication also serves to keep the rates in one financial center in line with those at another. If the pesetas sold for a cheaper price in Frankfurt than in Chicago, a trader would make a quick profit by buying pesetas cheaply in Frankfurt and immediately selling them dearly in Chicago, thereby affecting the supply-demand relationships in both centers and bringing about equilibrium. This simultaneous purchase in one market and sale in another to take advantage of price discrepancies is called *arbitrage*.

Arbitrage also takes place to make the exchange rates mutually consistent among the various currencies. That is, if the British pound sells for $1.80, and the French franc sells for $0.20, a British pound should also buy 9 French francs, or the ratio of $1.80:$0.20. The relationship of the exchange rates of two currencies derived from their values in terms of a third currency is called *cross rate*. Because of arbitrage transactions, principally by commercial bank traders, cross rates would not usually maintain significant differences for more than a few minutes.

The worth of a particular currency can be determined daily by a local banker by checking his or her bank's own internal daily rate sheet, or by making a phone call to the trading room if it is a large bank or through a correspondent if it is not. Exchange dealers in the trading rooms of some of the large commercial banks also give up-to-the-minute information directly to their more important clients. For most clients, the information on currency rates supplied by various publishers and advisory services should suffice.[14] The most widely available daily reporting of exchange rates in the English language appears in the *Wall Street Journal* and the *London Financial Times*.

## TRANSLATING ACCOUNTS AND MEASURING EXPOSURE

There are a number of different ways of translating accounts for consolidation purposes, or of calculating exposure to determine how much is at risk. The following four methods are illustrated in Table E-10, assuming a balance sheet of a British subsidiary

of an American firm with all entries denominated in pounds sterling.

**Current Rate Method**  Sometimes referred to as the *closing rate method*, this procedure translates all items on the balance sheet at the current (i.e., closing) rate of exchange. Since the past is dead, this method has considerable appeal to the practioner and is indeed favored by British firms and many European firms. With this philosophy, only net equity is exposed, since losses on assets are compensated for by corresponding gains on liabilities if the foreign currency depreciates and vice versa.

The major problem with this approach is that it is not usually valid to assume all classes of assets and liabilities represent the same risks, either under inflation or exchange fluctuation. Fixed assets such as plant and equipment would tend to increase in money terms if the unit of account were depreciated, as would their replacement costs. Also, the use of this method disturbs accountants since it departs from the traditional cost basis of valuation.

**Working Capital Method**  For translation, consider current assets and liabilities at current rates, fixed assets and liabilities at historical rates. Since this method has an application of rates and accounting classification that appears to be consistent in time frame, it likewise has appeal to many firms,

**TABLE E-10**  Comparison of Methods of Measuring Foreign Exchange Exposure

| Example, Ltd. Balance sheet as of Dec. 31, 1977 (in pounds sterling) | | | Exposed Item | | | |
|---|---|---|---|---|---|---|
| | | | Current rate method | Working capital method | Monetary-nonmonetary method | Temporal method |
| Assets: | | | | | | |
| Cash | | 150 | 150 | 150 | 150 | 150 |
| Accounts receivable | | 200 | 200 | 200 | 200 | 200 |
| Inventory | | 400 | 400 | 400 | | |
| Prepaid expenses | | 50 | 50 | | 50 | |
| Plant & equipment | 1000 | | | | | |
| Less depreciation | 100 | 900 | 900 | | | |
| Goodwill | | 80 | 80 | | | |
| Total assets = | | 1780 | 1780 | | | |
| Liabilities: | | | | | | |
| Accounts payable | | 170 | 170 | 170 | 170 | 170 |
| Short-term debt | | 120 | 120 | 120 | 120 | 120 |
| Long-term debt | | 700 | 700 | | 700 | 700 |
| Total liabilities | | 990 | 990 | | | |
| Net worth: | | 790 | | | | |
| Total liabilities & NW = | | 1780 | | | | |
| Total exposure | | | 790 Net assets | 460 Net assets | (590) Net liability | (640) Net liability |
| Definition of exposure | | | Total assets less total liabilities | Current assets less current liabilities | Monetary assets less monetary liabilities | Temporal assets less temporal liabilities |

*Note:* Preferred stock, if any, would have been a monetary liability.

especially in the United States. *Current*, of course, means within a 1-year period. It is called the working capital method because the exposure is defined as current assets less current liabilities, or the firm's *working capital*.

The argument here is that it is the short-term items that are subject to rate fluctuation. But with this method, inventory becomes an exposed item where long-term debt does not. Yet inventory is only carried on the balance sheets as a value near current costs when first in, first out (FIFO) inventory valuation is used; and the trend in inflation-prone environments is away from FIFO procedures.[12] And long-term debt remains an obligation whose ultimate payment changes with rate fluctuations; hence a risk is involved.

**Monetary-Nonmonetary Method** Exposure equals monetary assets less monetary liabilities. In translating accounts, monetary assets and liabilities are translated at current rates, nonmonetary assets and liabilities at historical rates. This method divides assets and liabilities according to their nature: physical or financial. It is based on the concept that physical items have an economic value that is independent of the unit of account; if inflation (or currency depreciation) occurs, physical items merely obtain a proportionately higher value in the depreciated currency. A classification of balance sheet items is as follows:

| *Monetary Assets* | *Monetary Liabilities* |
|---|---|
| Cash | Accounts payable |
| Marketable securities | Short-term notes |
| Accounts receivable | Long-term debt |
| Prepaid expenses | Preferred stock[12] |

This method is based on good economic logic, and it is internally consistent if inventory is valued on last in, first out (LIFO) accounting procedures, hence carried on the balance sheet at historical cost. The method does increase exposure sharply for firms with high debt to equity ratios. Today, this is the method recommended by most authorities for exchange exposure measurement[9,12] but not for accounting translation.[8]

**Temporal Method** This method, introduced by the Financial Accounting Standards Board and mandatory for consolidating financial statements for United States reporting that requires auditor approval, is defined as follows: "The temporal method translates cash, receivables and payables, and assets and liabilities carried at present or future prices at current rate and assets and liabilities carried at past prices at applicable historical rates."[8] That is, if an item (such as inventory) is carried on the balance sheet at historical rates (which it is under LIFO), it should be translated at historical rates. Since most monetary items are carried on most firms' balance sheets at what amounts to current or future rates in a foreign exchange context, and nonmonetary items are carried at historical rates, the results of the temporal method will usually coincide with those of the monetary-nonmonetary method. One exception, as seen in Table E-10, is prepaid expenses. The temporal method emphasizes consistency at accounting principles and usage; the monetary-nonmonetary method emphasizes economic decision making.

Comparison of the four methods with the example in Table E-10 illustrates the wide divergence in total exposure that can result. The first two show a risk of loss if the pound depreciates but a chance to gain if the pound increases in value relative to the dollar; the last two indicate the reverse! Here is an example where the international monetary manager would be expected to take entirely different protective actions depending on which exposure measurement system were in use. Which would be correct?

As mentioned above, the monetary-nonmonetary method is the method of measuring exchange exposure that is most *generally* appropriate for *economic* decisions. But it is worth remembering that this economic validity is based on a number of assumptions, so the following are among the questions that should be asked: Can you really raise prices in your markets if currency depreciates? Are your fixed assets a good inflation hedge, and does their value really go up as much as the value of the currency goes down? Are debts really debts when owed to the parent or a sister subsidiary? Do tax effects alter the picture? Do exchange restrictions limit repatriation of funds? What is the actual cost of replacing inventories, and other assets, today?

## DEALING WITH EXCHANGE EXPOSURE

Once the method of measuring exposure most appropriate to the situation has been selected, and the magnitude of the exposure calculated, the question remains: How best to deal with it? Several of the more popular devices are outlined below.[4]

**Hedging** A *hedge* is an offset. The term can be used generally to indicate any offsetting action, but in the context of foreign exchange, hedging generally refers to the use of a purchase or sale of a currency in the forward markets to offset an exposed position. For example, if an American exporting firm signed a contract for which it would be paid 1 year hence in Italian lira, it has a risk of loss if the lira declines in value. So the firm can sell the lira forward at a price known today, and thereby remove the exchange risk. Two parties such as a parent and subsidiary can lend each other currencies by a simultaneous spot purchase and forward sale or vice versa; this form of the hedge is called a *swap* transaction. For example, the American exporter could lend its Italian subsidiary lira by buying lira spot and making the loan; this creates an open position that is immediately covered by the simultaneous forward sale.

Hedging is a direct financial device for reducing exchange risk. Its use has minimal interference with operational considerations. However, hedging can be expensive; the forward contract will probably cost at least as much as the interest rate differential between the two centers, as discussed previously. And hedging can increase the credit risk. Note what would happen in the example above if the exporter were not paid for its goods; it is out its payment and must also deliver lira according to the conditions of the forward contract!

Forward contracts are readily available for most major European currencies. The International Monetary Market of the Chicago Mercantile Exchange also regularly trades in forward Mexican pesos. But forward markets in minor currencies, especially in underdeveloped countries with chronic inflation and balance of payments problems, can be thin or nonexistent.

**Monetary Balance** The previous discussion of methods for measuring exposure, and the illustration in Table E-10, show the offsetting effects of assets and liabilities. Exposure can be managed by eliminating it, with actions that alter the magnitudes of the balance sheet items themselves. Such actions include:

Credit policy, to adjust accounts receivable
Payments policy, to adjust accounts payable
Factoring, to dispose of accounts receivable
Cash management, to reduce soft currency assets
Inventory management and pricing
Local borrowing of soft currency
Refinancing debt denominated in hard currency

A number of the above can be considered good management practices to be followed regardless of the foreign exchange issue. Some companies routinely use credit policy, for example, as a source of funds by (1) slow remittance on accounts payable and (2) pressure for quick payment on receivables. This may also be useful in currency management; however, when the payables and receivables are denominated in currencies subject to appreciation, the reverse policy is followed. Speeding or slowing payments and receipts is called *leading* and *lagging* in money management vernacular.

Problems associated with altering monetary balance include financing costs, such as the interest required in obtaining soft currency loans (where interest is normally high), and disruption of a firm's financial structure, which can affect not only cost of capital but also return on investment. Inventory reduction to reduce exposure can cause stock-outs and loss of sales. Tight credit policy and price rises to compensate for currency depreciation can lose sales. Factoring can be expensive and is not available in many countries. In countries where currency fluctuations are expected, borrowing is likely to be difficult. And leads and lags in payments and receipts are harder to orchestrate when everyone is doing it. In addition many nations now regulate leads and lags.[13]

**Netting** Multinational companies have an important advantage: with branches in many locations, exposed assets in one branch can be offset by exposed liabilities in another, thereby reducing the *net* exposure for the multinational entity. Also, payments may actually flow between branches, and the cost of these transfers may be reduced if only net amounts are involved. Exposure netting need not rely exclusively on matching identical currencies among branches; currencies that are tied together by the respective governments can be used as equivalents.

Netting can save substantial sums in exchange commissions and provide the advantages of centrally controlled money management, optimizing at the corporate level. But a large volume of transactions is usually required to justify the executive time required. Netting is also legally curtailed in many countries.[13]

**Dollar Invoicing** A simple means for an exporter to avoid foreign exchange risk is to invoice in dollars or, more generally, in the currency of its home country. This is the most common procedure for American exporters, for reasons of tradition and lack of knowledge, as well as currency risk aversion. This method presents obvious legal and operational problems for companies with subsidiaries abroad. Competitive marketing pressures and dollar weaknesses may make this procedure less attractive in the future, even to exporters.

**Accepting Risk** The ultimate alternative for dealing with foreign exchange risk should always be considered by the international money manager, and that is simply to accept it.

A final caveat applicable to all the above discussions of measuring and dealing with foreign exchange exposure regards taxation. The necessity of integrating foreign exchange management with tax strategy is illustrated by the fact that tax rate *differences* can be as high as 48 percent for American corporations; this is considerably higher than the overwhelming majority of exchange rate fluctuations within a year. Therefore, although foreign exchange management is an important topic for the multinational manager, tax considerations can easily predominate.

*See also* ECONOMIC SYSTEMS; FINANCIAL MANAGEMENT; FINANCIAL MANAGEMENT, BANK RELATIONSHIPS; INTERNATIONAL OPERATIONS AND MANAGEMENT IN MULTINATIONAL COMPANIES; INTERNATIONAL TRADE.

## REFERENCES

1. *IMF Survey*, International Monetary Fund, Washington. Newsletter published twice monthly, $5 per year. Economic and monetary events, exchange rates.

2. *International Financial Statistics*, International Monetary Fund. Published monthly, $12 per year. Statistics on exchange transactions, international reserves, interest rates, world trade, balance of payments, and other data, by country.

3. *Annual Report on Exchange Restrictions*, International Monetary Fund. Summary of restrictive practices by country.

4. *Operating in a Floating Rate World*, New York, Business International Corp., One Dag Hammerskjold Plaza, 1976.

5. Paul Einzig, *This History of Foreign Exchange*, Macmillan & Co., Ltd., London, 1970.

6. Paul Einzig, *A Dynamic Theory of Forward Exchange*, Macmillan & Co., Ltd., London, 1968.

7. Eric B. Chalmers (ed.), *Forward Exchange Intervention, the British Experience 1964–67*, Hutchinson Educational Ltd., London, 1971.

8. *Statement No. 8—Accounting for the Translation of Foreign Currency Transactions and Foreign Currency Financial Statements*, Financial Accounting Standards Board, October 1975.

9. Andreas R. Prindl, *Foreign Exchange Risk*, John Wiley & Sons, Ltd., London, 1976.

10. Max J. Wasserman, Andreas R. Prindl, and Charles C. Townsend, Jr., *International Money Management*, American Management Association, New York, 1972.

11. H. E. Evitt, *A Manual of Foreign Exchange*, Sir Isaac Pitman & Sons, Ltd., London. Seventh edition by Raymond F. Pither, 1971.

12. J. Fred Weston and Bart W. Sorge, *International Managerial Finance*, Richard D. Irwin, Inc., Homewood, Ill., 1972.

13. *Solving International Financial & Currency Problems*, New York: Business International, One Dag Hammerskjold Plaza, June 1976.

14. *International Currency Review*, published bimonthly by Currency Journals Ltd., 11 Regency Place, London. Also available from same source: *Economic Data Service*, with monthly updates of data pertinent to currency; *London Currency Reports*, with charts, data, and significant events affecting major world currencies.

15. Franz Pick, *Pick's Currency Yearbook*, Pick Publishing Corp., New York. Annual encyclopedia of the world's currencies, $120 per year. Includes historical data on black market rates, currency in circulation, currency restrictions, data on gold, and a monthly update, *Pick's World Currency Report*, on official and black market rates.

16. Brian Tew, *International Monetary Cooperation 1945–1970*, Hutchinson & Co., Ltd., London, 1970.

17. *Survey of Current Business*, U.S. Department of Commerce, Washington. Published monthly.

18. *International Reports on Finance and Currencies*, International Reports, Inc., 200 Park Avenue South, New York, NY 10003. Published weekly.

19. *Monthly Review*, Federal Reserve Bank of New York. Free. Contains articles by Alan R. Holmes and Scott E. Pardee in every third issue, which discuss Federal Reserve foreign exchange operations, and developments in the markets for major world currencies.

EDWARD A. NELSON, *The American University in Cairo*

## Exchange, Security Commission (SEC)

[*See* SECURITIES AND EXCHANGE COMMISSION (SEC).]

## Exchange rates (*See* EXCHANGE, FOREIGN, MANAGEMENT OF.)

## Executive compensation (*See* COMPENSATION, EXECUTIVE.)

## Executive development (*See* DEVELOPMENT AND TRAINING, MANAGEMENT.)

## Executive development programs (*See* DEVELOPMENT AND TRAINING, UNIVERSITY EXECUTIVE PROGRAMS.)

## Executive managers (*See* MANAGER, DEFINITIONS OF.)

## Executive Order 11246 (*See* WOMEN IN INDUSTRY.)

**Executive orders (EEO)** (*See* MINORITIES, MANAGEMENT OF AND EQUAL EMPLOYMENT OPPORTUNITY.)

**Executive search firms** (*See* PERSONNEL ADMINISTRATION; SEARCH AND RECRUITMENT, EXECUTIVE.)

**Executive stock plans** (*See* COMPENSATION, EXECUTIVE.)

**Expectancy theory** (*See* MOTIVATION IN ORGANIZATIONS.)

**Expected-value technique** (*See* OPERATIONS RESEARCH AND MATHEMATICAL MODELING.)

**Expediting, purchase** (*See* PURCHASING MANAGEMENT.)

**Experience curve** [*See* LEARNING (EXPERIENCE) CURVES.]

**Export-import bank** (*See* INTERNATIONAL TRADE.)

**Exporting** (*See* INTERNATIONAL TRADE.)

**Extrinsic factors, Herzberg's** (*See* MOTIVATION IN ORGANIZATIONS.)

**F**

**Fabrication** (*See* PRODUCTION PROCESSES.)

**Facilities, distribution** (*See* PLANNING, STRATEGIC PLANNING MODELS.)

**Facilities, office planning** (*See* OFFICE SPACE PLANNING AND DESIGN.)

**Facilities engineering** (*See* PLANT ENGINEERING MANAGEMENT.)

**Facilities and equipment management**
(*See heading in Table of Contents for complete listing.*)

**Facilities management** (*See* REAL ESTATE MANAGEMENT, CORPORATE.)

## Facilities and site planning and layout

Facilities planning and layout encompasses the conceptual planning of the new plant, office, institution, and/or warehouse. The principles discussed herein are fundamental to the effective transition from objectives and goals to the completion of plans and layouts for an operating unit. It is essential to planning and layout procedures that objectives and parameters be set forth and that certain standards of performance for the project itself (the planning and implementation process) be established. With the completion of this work those charged with the architectural engineering design phase will have clear and accurate directions.

The vital relationship of buildings, site, and equipment represents the total environment in planning of facilities. The site must accommodate immediate and long-term requirements for the proposed operating unit in terms of: (1) traffic, access, utilities, services, (2) adherence to governing covenants and regulations, and (3) provisions for flexibility and growth in later site developments. The buildings must accommodate production operations effectively, represent the desired corporate image, and be adaptable to revisions in use and requirements for expansion. Layouts of equipment must reflect the same factors plus the need for efficiency of operations, effective employee and administrative services, and provisions for security and quality control. It is popular to observe that a facility should be designed from the inside out, that production equipment determines the building configuration; in practice, building design and plant layout are mutually dependent. The ideal layout in terms of production flow can be costly in terms of supervision, security, or lack of flexibility. Although the process will govern, facility planning prepares for the demands of future product and business needs.

## PROGRAM DIRECTION PHASE

Facilities planning is the key to the success of the capital investment opportunities; any significant allocation of funds and energy requires detailed goal setting and establishment of parameters for the program. Management (1) directs in general, but clear, terms the size of the facility in reference to production capacity or similar measure, relating this to return on investment (ROI) policy and (2) establishes the order of magnitude of anticipated capital investments. The project manager proceeds to identify equipment, plant, services, staffing, and estimated costs. The ROI policy is the basic checkpoint and is monitored throughout the planning process.

It is essential that policy be established both for initial cost versus operating cost considerations and for utilitarian versus quality image determinations. This addresses the question of low-cost startup versus high energy consumption and inordinate maintenance costs. Complete estimates of project operating costs should be included in the ROI statement, as poor judgment in equipment and materials selection can cut deeply into profit margins of even a new plant.

**Objectives** The basic objectives of planning and layout are set forth prior to the planning process. These objectives relate to performance levels for the facility and the role of the facility within the corporate structure. Growth policy determines what provision is to be made for expansion and added capacity.

**Data Base** It is essential that data be compiled, correlated, and subscribed to, in order that the planning process can be based upon factual information. The data will be in many forms and cover a wide range of material. The content depends upon the type of facility being planned, the complexity of the process, and whether the facility is a modification or addition to existing facilities or a new one. Typical forms of data are suggested by the following:

1. Capacity or production rate(s) of the facility.
2. Number of product lines or areas of service of the facility. Planning must include a close evaluation of the performance goals and the equipment and services that will be required.
3. Identification of assemblies represented and manufactured and purchased parts. This informa-

tion leads to assessments of production and storage requirements.
4. Estimates of the percentage of the product falling into active versus occasional classifications, that is, the approximately 20 percent of the products that usually provide 80 percent of sales versus the 80 percent that provide little profit.
5. Equipment requirements. Planners must determine what existing equipment can be reused and what must be purchased (with special reference to technologically advanced equipment).
6. Number of employees (by classifications) initially and as anticipated over the foreseeable life of the facility. This should also include an evaluation of visitor access to and activity in the property or facility.
7. Utilities and services. This should include comprehensive listings of utility and service requirements with usage rates, quantities by period and characteristics, and the amount and physical description of wastes to be discharged.
8. Criteria for special building services such as air-conditioned areas, clean rooms, high-pressure steam service, and compressed air service.
9. Fire prevention requirements in detail, developed in consultation with the underwriting agency.
10. Reference data for governing restrictions, as required by building codes, zoning, the Environmental Protection Agency (EPA), and the Occupational Safety and Health Act (OSHA). A widening range of special requirements must be followed, and the only reasonable approach is to learn of the requirements at an early date, move to meet them, and arrange to discuss or appeal requirements which could abort the program.

These are but samples of the data that must be developed for analysis. Specialized handbooks will provide checklists, and company staff must furnish special data for specific operations of the company. The pertinence and accuracy of the information will determine in a large measure the efficiency of the total planning picture.

## TECHNICAL PHASE

The technical phase relates policy, objectives, and data needed to serve proposed production requirements by department and function. This work develops the optimum-sized facility with equipment, systems, and staffing for what can be considered a model of the proposed facility. Against this model, all considerations of alternatives and trade offs will be measured.

**Flow Diagrams** The first step in the plant layout process is the development of flow diagrams of principal operations. Flow diagrams show relationships of individual processing and production operations in sequence and with interacting functions. Although an established set of symbols is used to indicate operation, transportation, storage, delay, and inspection, the technique is less important than an understanding of the diagramming exercise. The diagrams' graphic representation of steps in a manufacturing and materials flow procedure, including interdependent functions, uncovers inefficiencies and, more important, opportunities for improvement.

**Relationship Charts** The second major step is the preparation of a relationship chart showing relative importance of proximity between departments and functions. Essentially, a relationship chart will list each area on an $X$ and $Y$ axis similar to the mileage chart in a road atlas. In the intersecting square opposite two areas, the relative value of a close proximity between the areas is noted using a scale from 1 to 10 (for "no importance" to "very critical"). The values are determined by priority factors such as difficulty in product movement, quality control considerations in any moves, necessity of joint supervision or coordination between certain departments, and common use of critical services. A second set of indicators (usually letters) can be used to indicate types of moves. Color coding of similar values (using high-importance values) will further illustrate key relationships. Thus a pattern emerges indicating key areas for close (or remote) proximity, and trade-off judgments on location priorities can be made from this factual data.

The application of materials handling systems in conjunction with the plant layout work, and with special reference to the relationship values among functions, is most important. (*See* MATERIALS HANDLING.)

**Block Layouts** The flow diagrams, relationship chart, and an understanding of material handling system opportunities are preludes to the actual plant layout work. A series of general block layouts can now be accomplished. The blocks should be to a scale that indicates the floor area required for each function. By their shape, they may also indicate a production line or other special configuration.

The blocks, in template form and to common scale (representing departments, operations, and functions) can be assembled to represent the total plant. The blocks are then arranged and adjusted to reflect the flow of material and information, relationships, and other factors governing efficient oper-

ation. The general layout of the plant will emerge from the practical procedure of study, critique, and refinement.

**Overlays** A further tool in this phase is the use of overlays to represent services, distribution, and management patterns. With the general layout as a base plan, a series of transparent overlays will indicate distribution systems for services and utilities, employee population of each department and function, and traffic patterns of employees and visitors, that is, between entrance points, employee services, and work stations. Overlays will represent the principal traffic patterns of material, supplies, and parts from receiving, through the operations, and into storage and shipping. The overlays (and the relationship chart) test the layouts and demonstrate where adjustments are required.

By working with the plant layout, it may be possible to modify the operating sequences (and the flow diagrams) if new problems and opportunities are uncovered. Changes can sometimes be made in sequences to assist in layout solutions without adverse effect on production. An existing procedure should not dictate against improvements, and the plant layout effort is the ideal time for such evaluation.

**Office Planning** A parallel operation, as work on the production areas takes shape, is the planning of office areas. The relationship of manufacturing, warehousing, and employee services to the office is integrated into the total facilities planning effort. (*See* OFFICE SPACE PLANNING AND DESIGN.)

**Computer Programs for Plant Layout** Several computer programs are available to accomplish the plant layout process described. Notably, these include computerized relative allocation of facilities techniques (CRAFT) and computerized relationship layout planning (CORELAP). Their input is area (space) and relationship data. Generally, they tend to lack capability for judgments and trade-off considerations, and their graphic printouts require considerable massaging. For complex plants, however, a computer program can reduce a mass of data to comprehensible forms and can also provide a useful check for many manual efforts.

**Equipment Layouts** The final step in planning the facility involves developing detailed layouts by working from revised plant layouts and overlays. This planning is usually done with 1/4-inch scale templates, available commercially for most production machines, equipment, and furniture. All significant machines and equipment are shown, and layouts are carefully analyzed (1) for the ability to operate and serve the equipment efficiently, and (2) to ensure that aisle widths are generous and that provisions are advantageous for maintenance and housekeeping work. A reproducible print of the equipment layout is used to indicate specific services required for each machine and locations of connections. This information again checks the layout and is used by engineers for design of distribution systems.

Use of *three-dimensional models* may be worth considering where there are questions of clearly demonstrating interaction of equipment, personnel, and services. Models are invaluable when dealing with management people who have difficulty visualizing from plans and diagrams.

### SITE PLANNING

It is now possible to relate the plant requirements to the site. Here, even to a greater extent than in the plant itself, plans are totally critical to the long-term usefulness of the facility investment.

**Nonproductive Areas**   For effective use of land, an effort must be made to minimize nonproductive areas, as in setbacks and excessive landscaping. Locating a building in the center of a site may not leave surrounding areas of suitable size for expansion. It is usually better practice to locate the buildings forward and to one side, providing optimum alternatives to future planners.

**Critical Factors**   Several factors should be considered in approaching the site-planning phase:

1. The total site and facility (whether a plant, distribution center, or headquarters) should convey to the public the functional and favorable image the company wishes to project.

2. Landscaping, roads, and parking areas must provide for ready identification of visitor destinations, clear views for security and safety, and screening for trucking and yard storage areas.

3. Access to the site should be planned for separation of dissimilar traffic, as far as practical. Parking areas should be convenient to building entrances. It is realistic to provide a parking space for each employee unless there is public transportation and existing car pools. The EPA is working to mandate the reduction of available parking, and these regulations should be carefully researched.

A *preliminary site plan* is developed showing principal uses on the site for study. The buildings (with expansion shown as a dotted extension), shipping and receiving, roads, parking, railroad siding, utilities, fire prevention systems, etc., all can be sketched into the plan. The site plan is related to the building plans so as to indicate clearly relationships of employee parking and building access.

A *completed site plan* will provide sufficient direction for the designers (engineers, architects, and landscape architects) to execute the detailed plans.

### EXPANSION AND FLEXIBILITY

A 5-year forecast is about the limit for accuracy in specific planning of equipment layouts. In fact, a totally efficient layout for a high-production operation can be justified on a short-term basis, even allowing for extensive changeover costs on completion of the production run. Product changes, new marketing programs, and technology breakthroughs may put unforeseen pressure on the facility. Good facility planning provides diverse opportunities for the future planner, as specific future requirements can only be theorized. It is in the present planning effort that the future viability of the plant is established. Later changes in the functions will be reasonable or costly, on the basis of the alternatives provided in the original plan.

To provide for expansion and flexibility, the more permanent operations and services should be so located as to avoid blocking options for change. Power plants, substations, and equipment requiring special foundations or underfloor services should also receive special attention. Requirements for contiguous location of departments can be overcome through the use of conveyor systems and other accommodations. It is often wise to locate departments with the common characteristics of immobility in a central core area—even when such a choice may not be indicated in the flow diagrams or relationship charts.

Growth and flexibility factors apply to site planning as well as to production areas. Parking areas provide logical expansion space if the road system has foreseen this eventuality. Underground water mains should be located away from areas that seem logical for building expansion. Railroad sidings and truck docks require special attention.

### MANAGERIAL CONTROL

Planning requires the continuous analysis of all available cost data.

**Cost Control**   An early development of policy for return on investment combined with performance specifications for the facility is a basic requirement. It will help management ascertain that the facility, as it emerges in greater detail, falls within the mandated economic guidelines. While cost estimates will be rough and generally will be provided only on a square-foot and unit cost basis, these figures suffice for warning or confirmation purposes. Estimates should always be developed within a plus or minus 10 percent of actual cost.

**Monitoring the Planning Process**  The planning functions are cyclical in nature, running from policy determination and data collection through a series of exercises in design and refinement, reevaluation of data, review of policy, and further refinements. It is essential that management monitor these cycles of effort and that participation of all staff functions and manufacturing and operating interests be ensured, so that planning of the facility is consistent with the interests of those charged with its operation. It is a severe error to expect a planning group, no matter how expert, while developing a solution for the long-term, or even short-term interests of the company, to work in a vacuum. The planning process is a total concern for the company.

*See also* INVENTORY CONTROL, PHYSICAL AND STOCK-KEEPING; MATERIAL HANDLING; OFFICE SPACE PLANNING AND DESIGN; PROJECT AND TASK FORCE MANAGEMENT; REAL ESTATE MANAGEMENT, CORPORATE.

### REFERENCES

Buffa, Elwood: *Basic Production Management*, 2d ed., John Wiley & Sons, Inc., New York, 1975, chaps. 9 and 10.

Corman, Joel: *Managing the Productive Process*, General Learning Press, Morristown, N.J., 1974, chap. 9.

Lewis, Bernard T., and J. P. Marron, eds.: *Facilities and Plant Engineering Handbook*, McGraw-Hill Book Company, New York, 1974.

Moore, Franklin G.: *Production Management*, 6th ed., Richard D. Irwin, Inc., Homewood, Ill., 1973, sec. 3.

Muther, Richard: *Practical Plant Layout*, McGraw-Hill Book Company, New York, 1956.

Zimmerman, Hans-Jurgen, and Michael G. Sovereign: *Quantitative Methods for Production Management*, Prentice-Hall, Inc., Englewood Cliffs, N.J., 1974, chap. 7.

DAVID C. STEWART, *Carlisle Engineering Management, Inc.*

**Facility planning committee**  (*See* OFFICE SPACE PLANNING AND DESIGN.)

**Fact-finding, audit**  (*See* AUDIT, MANAGEMENT.)

**Factor analysis**  (*See* MARKET ANALYSIS.)

**Factor comparison**  (*See* JOB EVALUATION.)

**Factoring**  (*See* FINANCIAL MANAGEMENT, SHORT-TERM, INTERMEDIATE, AND LONG-TERM FINANCING.)

**Fair Credit Reporting Act**  (*See* CREDIT MANAGEMENT.)

**Fair Labor Standards Act**  (*See* WAGES AND HOURS LEGISLATION.)

**Fair trade laws**  (*See* GOVERNMENT REGULATIONS: FEDERAL REGULATION OF BUSINESS.)

**Fair value accounting**  (*See* ACCOUNTING, FINANCIAL.)

**Fayol, Henry**  (*See* MANAGEMENT, HISTORICAL DEVELOPMENT OF.)

**Fayol's bridge**  (*See* COMMUNICATIONS, ORGANIZATIONAL.)

**Fear**  (*See* HEALTH, MENTAL.)

**Feasibility**  (*See* SYSTEM CONCEPT, TOTAL.)

**Feasibility appraisal**  (*See* PROJECT AND TASK FORCE MANAGEMENT.)

**Federalism**  (*See* PUBLIC ADMINISTRATION.)

**Feedback**  (*See* AUTOMATION.)

**Feedback, communications**  (*See* COMMUNICATIONS, ORGANIZATIONAL.)

**Feedback, organization** [*See* ORGANIZATION DEVELOPMENT (OD).]

**Feedback loop, negative** (*See* SYSTEM DYNAMICS.)

**Feedback loop, positive** (*See* SYSTEM DYNAMICS.)

**Feedback theory** (*See* SYSTEM DYNAMICS.)

**Fiduciary management** (*See* MANAGEMENT, DEFINITIONS OF.)

**FIFO** (*See* PROFITS AND PROFIT MAKING; ACCOUNTING, FINANCIAL.)

**Files** (*See* OFFICE SPACE PLANNING AND DESIGN.)

**Files, dictionary pattern** (*See* RECORDS MANAGEMENT.)

**Files, functional classification** (*See* RECORDS MANAGEMENT.)

**Finance charges** (*See* CREDIT MANAGEMENT.)

**Financial accounting** (*See* ACCOUNTING, FINANCIAL.)

**Financial Accounting Standards Board (FASB)** (*See* ACCOUNTING, FINANCIAL.)

**Financial audit** (*See* AUDITING, FINANCIAL.)

**Financial industry management** (*See* REGULATED INDUSTRIES, MANAGEMENT OF.)

**Financial and investment management** (*See heading in Table of Contents for complete listing.*)

## Financial management

Modern financial management is concerned primarily with the commitment of funds to various uses in the business and with the best possible combination of types of financing. It serves to maximize the profitability of the firm within the limits of prudent risk exposure. To the extent that management of financial affairs contributes to this goal, the total value of the firm is increased. In earlier years, in contrast, the financial manager typically had as basic functions the custody of funds and the obtaining of money for the firm's operations and expansion. The increasing complexity of operations has dictated a vast increase in responsibility for financial management; mounting pressure on the nation's capital markets indicates that this responsibility will continue to grow. The establishment of profit goals, the direction of cost control programs, and the measurement of results have fallen primarily to the finance function. In short, financial management is now directly related to active profit seeking through participation in the planning, organization, administration, and control of company affairs.

### SCOPE AND ORGANIZATION

An indication of the breadth of the finance function is reflected in Table F-1. This table, based on a survey of the nation's leading corporations, indicates the extent to which various business functions report to the chief financial officers of the firms. The organizational structure of the finance function may take many forms. Not only do the size and nature of the business enterprise influence the organizational arrangement, but there is also a wide diversity among firms within similar industries and among businesses of the same size. Each business attempts to establish a structure that will best serve its purposes. Typically, however, the chief financial officer reports directly to a company's chief executive officer and, in some cases, to the board of directors or committee of the board. The chief financial officer may carry the title of financial vice-president, treasurer, or controller. A common arrangement is for both the treasurer and the controller to report to a financial vice-president. For companies with several operating divisions the purchasing, production, and marketing functions may be carried out with a high

TABLE F-1 Functions Reporting to the Chief
Financial Officer

| | |
|---|---|
| Cash control | 93.4 |
| Bank relations | 93.0 |
| Financing | 92.8 |
| Tax accounting | 77.1 |
| Custody of assets | 75.4 |
| Insurance management | 74.4 |
| General accounting | 71.4 |
| Auditing | 69.9 |
| Credit management | 69.3 |
| Budgetary control | 66.9 |
| Capital expenditures control | 65.0 |
| Investor relations | 64.4 |
| Cost accounting | 56.1 |
| Management information system | 53.2 |
| Mergers and acquistions | 40.9 |
| Corporate planning | 37.9 |
| Real estate management | 28.6 |
| Pensions | 7.0 |
| Legal staff | 4.2 |
| Purchasing | 3.2 |
| Investments | 2.3 |
| Other | 28.6 |

SOURCE: *Profile of a Chief Financial Officer*, Heidrick & Struggles, Inc., New York, 1975, p. 5.

degree of independence of central headquarters. The financial executives of these divisions, however, rely heavily upon corporate headquarters for direction of their activities, and, although they may report directly to division heads, there remains in most instances a divided responsibility between the division and corporate headquarters.

## SYSTEM DEVELOPMENT

The advent of electronic data processing has introduced a wide range of planning and control devices little known in earliest times. Through the use of the computer it is now possible for managements to base their decisions upon information that may be only a few hours old. Not only is planning enhanced, but deviations from plans may be quickly noted and corrective action taken. *Budgeting* has become far more meaningful as a plan for action and as a control device in noting departures from financial plans. The *budgetary process* may be described as the itemizing of planned expenditures along with the expected sources of funds from which expenditures are to be met. The *cash budget* is a special budgeting process designed to show how much cash the firm will have on hand by days, weeks, or months, and the timing of financing necessary to supplement cash flows. The cash budgeting process has become of increasing importance as interest rates have increased and as the availability of loan funds has become more

restricted. For many firms the availability of cash may govern the overall operations of the firm, dictating the amount and timing of purchasing and work processing activities and, in some cases, the nature of the production itself. The *internal auditing* function of businesses is that of preventing and disclosing error and fraud. This has been made particularly effective through the use of modern financial systems. Further, the effectiveness of the internal auditing function facilities the work of independent auditors and reduces the cost of independent audits. Finally, periodic reports to top management are now available on a more timely and useful basis.

## SPECIFIC ASPECTS OF FINANCIAL MANAGEMENT

Beyond the aspects of planning, organizing, administering, and controlling for finance, it is helpful to explore specific activities of finance as they relate to business operations. It is important to keep in mind that there is a constant search in these activities for an optimum balance between profit maximizing and prudent risk assumption. The language of finance is most conveniently reflected in the financial statements of the firm. Although the modern balance sheet has a host of special accounts, the basic items as shown below will serve our purpose in describing specific financial activities.

Current assets     Current liabilities
    Cash             Accounts payable
    Receivables       Short-term borrowing
    Inventory
Fixed assets
Long-term debt
Ownership capital
    Preferred stock
    Common stock
    Retained earnings

**Cash Management** Cash management is a most important function and one that is capable of significant contribution to the dynamic management of business affairs. As for any asset, the more efficient the use made of cash, the smaller the necessary investment therein. Cash management functions may be classified as custodial, flow of funds control, obtaining banking services, and investment of surplus cash.

*Custodial Functions.* Perhaps the oldest reponsibility of cash management is that of protection of company funds. This remains an important function and involves the careful selection of banking facilities, vault depositories, and internal auditing controls. As in the case of the loss of any asset, a major cash loss may endanger the existence of the firm.

*Controlling Cash Flows.* To the extent that collection of cash from customers can be speeded, the cash balances of the firm are increased. The wire transfer of funds from divisional banks to headquarters banks and among the banks of the nation enables firms to minimize their bank balances. Just as an acceleration of the collection of money reduces the amount of required cash, so, too, a carefully devised plan of disbursements may make a similar contribution. The most obvious of these plans is to make payments at the latest possible moment compatible with obtaining discounts on purchases and otherwise maintaining a reputation for payment of obligations on schedule. Although the clearance of checks among banks has been speeded, it is still true that until a check is presented for payment at the bank on which it is written, the firm's deposit balance in that bank is not reduced. It is the balance shown on the bank's books that determines the services to which the business is entitled. Under special circumstances, so-called *zero accounts* or *automatic balance accounts* may be useful. Under these systems dual accounts are maintained at the bank, with one of the accounts being drawn upon to maintain specified balances in the account on which checks are drawn. By such a system, a single general bank account may serve to prevent several special clearing accounts from falling below specified levels. Some firms make extensive use of *drafts* in paying bills. Under this arrangement the business is not required to have funds on hand to meet the drafts until they are presented for payment. The daily cash report is the principal tool by which cash balances are managed most effectively.

*Bank Services.* Banks, of course, provide a host of services for their customers, not the least of which is the handling of the firm's payment and disbursement transactions through check clearance. Such services are typically paid for by the firm through credits received for balances maintained at the bank. Thus, if the firm has two or more banks of deposit on which checks may be drawn, it is important to allocate balances among the banks in such a way that credits offset the cost of each bank's services to the firm. Some banks are in a position to provide a greater variety of services than other banks, and a careful choice among banks may expand the range of services to which the firm is entitled by virtue of the balances it maintains. Finally, most banks require balances to support lines of credit. It is important to choose banks with lending capacities adequate for the needs of one's firm, and this, in turn, requires a careful distribution of deposits among the banks so that the balances are maintained at agreed-upon levels.

*Investment of Surplus Cash.* At certain times cash balances may be far in excess of needed levels. If these balances are not too large, they may be offset by below-normal balance levels at other times. Most banks are willing to measure bank balances on an average rather than a minimum balance basis. It is often to the advantage of a firm to invest excess cash balances until they are needed. To this end, the manager of the cash account must be familiar with the types of investments available and the methods by which these investments can be made. Ordinarily, temporary excesses of cash are invested in high-quality short-term obligations such as Treasury bills, commercial paper notes, bankers' acceptances, bank certificates of deposit, and other highly liquid short-term obligations.

**Receivables Management** Accounts and notes receivable are the second most liquid form of assets of the firm. These receivables come into being as a result of credit sales and constitute one of the largest assets of most firms. Studies have revealed that of all determinable causes of bankruptcy, one of the most important is the inability to collect receivables. Skillful administration of the receivables account is, therefore, of prime importance to the business. As in the case of cash management, however, the goal is not simply to minimize losses on receivables but to contribute to the overall profitability of the firm. The very reason for credit sales is to expand sales volume, and if too tight a rein is maintained by the credit manager in the approval of customer credit purchases, many sales may be lost that would otherwise contribute to the profits of the firm. It is the responsibility of credit management to effect a strategic balance between preservation of the investment in receivables and the maximizing of profitable sales.

**Inventory Management** Although the finance function typically has complete control of cash and receivables management, it plays only a supportive role in inventory management. Inventory accumulation is primarily a purchasing and production function, but the finance function must make payment for the inventories. To this end, close cooperation between the purchasing and finance functions is called for. At times when there is extreme pressure on cash resources, the financial executive may substantially influence the timing and extent of purchases. Ordinarily, however, such cooperation is manifested by a constant exchange of information concerning cash position and inventory accumulation plans.

**Fixed-Asset Management** As for inventory management, the financial executive plays a supportive role in the determination of expenditures for fixed assets. This general process is referred to as *capital budgeting*. The importance of skillful fixed-asset expenditures is due to the fact that such expenditures are typically large and the economic lives of the assets quite long. Mistakes, therefore, must be lived with for many years.

The special contribution of the finance function to capital budgeting is in the determination of prospective rates of return on alternative investment projects and the establishment of minimum return levels. Further, since most firms will have more investment alternatives than their resources will accommodate, it is important to choose among the alternative proposals in such a way as to maximize the overall profitability. A key factor in the investment selection process is a consideration of the *timing* of the revenue flows from each investment proposal. While the relative speed with which an investment may pay back the capital committed to it is important, profits can be maximized only if the prospective returns over the economic life of the investment can be appropriately analyzed. Basic to the finance function in this respect is the determination of the firm's cost of capital. The *cost of capital* may be described as the composite cost of the forms of financing on which the firm relies for expansion.

Many firms continue to use a simple *payback* measure of investment attractiveness—that is, a determination of the relative speed with which the capital committed to the project will be recaptured over the years. More sophisticated techniques such as the *net present-value* method or the *internal rate of return* method usually provide a better basis for evaluation of long-term investments. Although these techniques add a measure of complexity to the analysis, the importance of proper decisions warrants all possible constructive effort. The *net present-value* method of investment analysis involves the discounting of cash flows. This is accomplished first by a determination of the firm's cost of capital and the use of this cost for purposes of determining the present value of all expected net cash flows from an investment. If the present value of a series of net cash flows over the years discounted at the firm's cost of capital is in excess of the cost of the investment, then it is assumed that the project will provide a positive return. If the present value of the stream of net cash flows is equal to or less than the necessary investment to implement the project, then

the project must be rejected or justified on some basis other than prospective profitability. The *internal rate of return* method involves the determination of that interest rate that equates the amount of the project investment with the current value of the anticipated net cash receipts. This rate, then, may be compared with the firm's cost of capital to determine whether the project has the potential for a return greater than that currently being experienced by the firm. While the net present-value method and the internal rate of return method have much in common, the circumstances involved in a particular decision may cause one technique to be more satisfactory than the other.

It is also important to recognize that the risk characteristics of alternative investment proposals will differ widely. Thus a group of projects with similar return expectations may have different degrees of attractiveness based upon the riskiness of the project. The introduction of risk adjustment in the capital budgeting process is complex, but procedures are available to accommodate such adjustments.

**Current Liabilities** Obligations of the business that must be satisfied within a period of 1 year are classified as current liabilities.

*Accounts payable* are the first form of current liability and derive primarily from the purchase of goods by a business on credit terms. The term *trade credit* is customarily used to describe this form of financing and is by far the most substantial form of short-term liability for most businesses. Careful administration of accounts payable requires that discounts offered by the supplier be taken but that payments be scheduled in such a manner that as little advance payment as possible is made. Payments made beyond due dates, of course, may quickly be reflected in a reduced credit rating by suppliers and credit rating agencies.

The second principal form of current liability is *short-term borrowing*. For most businesses this takes the form of borrowing from commercial banks on a line of credit. *Lines of credit* are established in advance on the basis of the prospective borrowing requirements of the business during seasonal peak demands of the year. Short-term funds are also obtained from commercial finance companies, ordinarily on the basis of a pledge of the firm's receivables as collateral. Large business firms may issue *commercial paper* notes directly or through dealers for purposes of short-term financing. Dealers, or commercial paper houses, purchase the promissory notes of the business and resell them to other banks or businesses, charging a fee based upon the amount of the notes. Short-term financing in the commercial paper market is not a substitute for bank credit, but rather a supplement to it. Ordinarily, purchasers of commercial notes insist that the issuers maintain an unused bank line of credit to back such commercial paper notes.

**Long-Term Debt Management** Some businesses borrow on a long-term basis because it is the only form of financing available to them to support investments in long-term assets. Beyond the matter of availability, however, long-term borrowing is used for other reasons. Long-term debt contracts usually include "call" provisions to make retirement of the debt possible if the need for the funds should cease to exist or if advantageous refunding opportunities should occur. It is also true that long-term lenders to the business do not have voting rights. Long-term borrowing may be carried out at times when the stock market is depressed and management wishes to avoid the sharing of ownership interests with new stockholders at depressed stock prices.

Most important, however, in the matter of strategic management of long-term borrowing is cost, especially as it affects *income taxes*. The interest paid on debt capital is a financial expense for tax purposes in contrast with earnings on the equity capital of the firm. For most businesses, therefore, the after-tax cost of interest payments on long-term borrowing is approximately half of the nominal rate. This assumes, of course, that the firm has taxable profits against which interest expense may be charged.

Beyond the tax advantage is the *financial leverage* that may be exerted on the earnings of the stockholders if the cost of long-term borrowing is less than the return on the total assets of the firm. This relationship is sometimes referred to as *trading on the equity*.

*Hazards.* While long-term debt financing may offer a substantial cost advantage to the firm, it should be recognized as a two-edged weapon. Just as the return on capital invested by the common stockholders may be benefited through the use of leverage financing, so too, their return may be severely depressed if the overall earnings on the company's assets fall below the cost of the long-term debt financing. There is a limit beyond which debt financing should not be carried. By way of generalization, it may be said that leverage financing—that is, financing with long-term debt capital or other fixed cost types of capital—should be utilized to the fullest possible extent compatible with the safety of the firm. The level of long-term debt financing, of course, will differ with the type of business. Some firms with stable revenues find it possible to borrow

as much as 60 or 65 percent of their asset requirements without undue risk to the stockholders. Other businesses find that long-term borrowing should be limited to a very modest level.

*Form.* The forms of long-term debt financing will also differ among businesses. Smaller firms will ordinarily arrange long-term borrowing on the basis of a *mortgage* placed with a single lender. Larger firms may issue *mortgage bonds* based on the collateral value of a mortgage, such bonds being sold to many investors. *Debenture bonds* differ from mortgage bonds in that they are secured by the general credit of the firm rather than by the backing of a mortgage on specific assets.

*Term Loans and Leases.* Commercial banks may provide long-term debt financing to a business in the form of term loans. *Bank term loans* usually have maturities from 1 to 10 years and may provide for installment payments throughout the life of the loans. Unlike mortgage and bond financing, term loans usually have floating rates, that is, rates that vary in relation to the prime bank rate. Bank term loans are especially useful to the firm as an intermediate form of financing. The *lease of fixed assets* is not a form of long-term debt financing, yet it bears a resemblance. The use of lease financing has grown to large proportions in recent years as a result of pressure on the capital markets. Many firms have found it possible to obtain long-term assets for expansion or replacement purposes only through the lease device. Substantial tax advantages may at times arise from a properly drawn lease arrangement.

**Ownership Capital Management** The second form of long-term financing is that arising from the owners' investment in the business. For the sole proprietorship and partnership this may involve little more than the contribution of owners' capital to the firm along with appropriate bookkeeping entries. For the corporation, on the other hand, ownership interest is represented by the issuance of stock. *Preferred stock* generally carries a limited dividend specified as either a percentage of par or as a fixed number of dollars a year. It ordinarily has priority over common stock shares upon the liquidation of the business. *Common stock*, on the other hand, represents the basic ownership in the business and has a residual claim on profits after creditors' obligations have been met and the dividends on preferred stock shares have been paid. If the firm experiences losses, the common stockholders bear the initial brunt of such losses. Common stockholders of the corporation ordinarily exercise control over the policies of the firm through the election of a board of directors. *Retained earnings* in the business result from the declaration of dividends in an amount less than that of earnings. Such earnings retained in the firm are invested for the benefit of the firm's operations and are classified as a part of the common stockholders' ownership interest. Dividend payout policies differ widely among types of businesses.

## SPECIAL FINANCIAL RESPONSIBILITIES

The nature of the finance function is such that many new responsibilities have been added to financial managers' traditional activities. The financial manager, by training and by activity, has been in the best position to assume the responsibility for the growing importance of financial relations, mergers and acquisitions, multinational matters, and pension and profit sharing management.

**Financial Relations** The financial manager must spend a significant amount of time developing and maintaining good relations with all facets of the capital markets. To this end, frequent reports are made to commercial banks, dealers in commercial paper, and investment bankers. Not the least of the responsibilities of the financial manager is that of communicating with and maintaining constant contact with rating agencies. Among these rating agencies are Dun & Bradstreet, Inc., primarily for short-term credit ratings, Moody's Investor Service, Inc., and Standard & Poor's Corporation for long-term ratings.

**Mergers and Acquisitions** Mergers and acquisitions may be carried out for a variety of reasons. Among these may be diversification of product lines, acquisition of management talent, or improvement of operating incomes as a result of economies of scale of operation. As a result of growth through merger and acquisition, financing may be made easier as access is gained to the public securities market. Financial management plays a key role in negotiations for merger or acquisition and also must make recommendations as to how such mergers and acquisitions are to be financed.

**Multinational Financial Management** Many corporations have engaged in worldwide business operations for generations. In recent years, however, there has been a vast increase in multinational operations by firms that have heretofore limited their operations entirely to domestic affairs. It has become necessary for the financial manager not only to study specific foreign business activities and their prospective profitability, but also to analyze the governmental processes of the nations in which business operations are to be carried out. In addition to the general attitude of governments toward foreign business interests, much attention must be given to the matter of duties and taxes imposed by foreign countries. The repatriation of profits and restrictions on reinvestment vary greatly from one country to another, and changes in attitudes with changing administrations must also receive careful attention. The decision as to how foreign operations are to be financed is a key problem for the financial manager. Finally, almost daily attention must be given to exchange rates between nations for purposes of protecting bank balances and other short-term investments. The expectation of a devaluation typically demands quick action to prevent the loss of value of bank deposits.

**Pension and Profit Sharing Fund Management** The rate of growth of pension funds and profit sharing funds has dwarfed that of all other investment forms. Many companies manage such funds internally and maintain large staffs for purposes of analysis and fund allocation among bonds, stock, real estate, and other investments. More common, however, is the use of banks, insurance companies, or individual investment managers to handle these funds. The placement of funds with professional money managers, however, does not relieve the corporation or the financial manager of responsibility. It remains an important function to work with the money managers in evaluating their performance, as well as in determining the degree to which the objectives of the funds are being carried out.

The Employee Retirement Income Security Act (ERISA) signed into law by the President on Labor Day, 1974, has added significantly to the financial manager's responsibility. Among other things, this act provides that pension claims are not limited to pension assets and that under certain circumstances up to 30 percent of a company's net assets may be legally claimed for pension liabilities.

## FINANCIAL ANALYSIS

All financial analysis begins with the study of the basic financial statements of the firm. These statements—the balance sheet and the income statement—however, are only a starting point in the analytical process. It is important, for example, to know how the balance sheet and the income sheet were prepared and the assumptions made therein. In analyzing the statements of other businesses for purposes of granting trade credit or for other reasons, it is necessary to engage in much research in order to have a clear understanding of the statements.

**Trend Analysis** The most common form of financial analysis is that of studying the trend of individual accounts over a period of years. By so doing, one can identify changing conditions. Following the trend of a single item may provide information relating to that particular item, but it fails to reveal interactions that may be taking place with respect to other items in the financial statements; hence, what may appear to be a deteriorating condition in one respect may be completely offset by a close analysis of other items. To this end, the financial manager often resorts to ratio analysis in addition to trend analysis.

**Ratio Analysis** Although it is possible to express hundreds of relationships among accounts in the balance sheet and the income statement, the challenge has been to identify especially significant ratios. To do this, financial managers may compare certain well-defined ratios for their own business with those of similar businesses for purposes of determining possible problem areas. It is important to look at a group of ratios to form a composite profile of the position of the firm. Ratio analysis, of course, does nothing to correct a weakness in business operations, but diagnosis is a critical step in any corrective process. The financial manager has many sources of financial ratios which can be used for comparative purposes. Perhaps the best known of these sources is Dun & Bradstreet. This firm has for many years compiled a group of 14 ratios for 125 lines of business activities including manufacturing, wholesaling, and retailing enterprises. Ratios are reported for the median and quartile ranges. Another useful source is provided by Robert Morris Associates in their annual statement studies. The Federal Trade Commission has for many years published quarterly financial reports which present composite figures for a large sample of manufacturing corporations in ratio form and by asset size. Many commercial banks also provide such information. Trade associations have found that the preparation of financial ratios for their members is an important service. It is important to remember that ratio analysis is only one tool in the process of analysis. As an illustration of the types of ratios available to the financial manager, a small section of the Dun & Bradstreet *Ratios for Selected Industries* report is shown in Table F-2.

**Analysis of Return on Investment** Of special interest in studying the return on investment is the relationship between the margin of profit on sales and the turnover of the firm's net operating assets. If the margin of profit on sales is multiplied by the number of times the net operating assets turn over during a specified period, the result is the earning power of the firm for the period under study. More precisely stated, the margin times the turnover equals the return on investment. Of special interest in this relationship, however, is the derivation of these individual components, as shown in Fig. F-1. The return on investment may have the benefit of leverage, as discussed earlier, giving rise to an increasing percentage return to the common stockholders of the business. The leverage contributed by each class of preference capital (current liabilities, long-term debt, and preferred stock) is shown in this chart as a hypothetical example.

**Sources and Uses of Funds Statement** Study of the balance sheet and the income statement of a firm will usually fail to provide a clear picture of all the sources of funds acquired by the business during a particular period of time and of the disposition of these funds. The source and use of funds statement serves to provide this particular information. It is particularly valuable to the financial manager attempting to determine the credit characteristics of a customer to which trade credit is to be extended, or to a lending officer in a commercial bank attempting to determine the probability of repayment of a prospective loan to a customer of the bank. Ordinarily, an applicant for credit will be required to provide not only a current source and use of funds statement but also a projection or pro forma statement.

**Break-even Analysis** This interesting type of analysis relates fixed costs and variable costs to total revenues for purposes of determining the level of revenues that must be achieved if the firm is to operate successfully. Break-even analysis not only provides a knowledge of the revenue level required to break even but also may reveal the point at which operations of the business should cease. Firms may at times operate at a substantial loss, however, in anticipation of prospective improvements in business conditions and in order to avoid the loss of skilled employees and other operating essentials dependent upon continuous business activity. Basically, the theoretical shutdown point for a business is that point at which revenues fail to cover the variable costs of operation. The presumption is that fixed costs are sunk and will exist irrespective of the level of sales. Break-even analysis, then, may serve to identify levels of revenues that will minimize losses as well as those levels that will maximize profits.

*See also* ACCOUNTING, FINANCIAL; AUDITING, FINAN-

**TABLE F-2  Types of Ratios Available to the Financial Manager**

| Line of business (and number of concerns reporting) | Current assets to current debt (Times) | Net profits on net sales (Per cent) | Net profits on tangible net worth (Percent) | Net profits on net working capital (Percent) | Net sales to tangible net worth (Times) | Net sales to net working capital (Times) | Collection period (Days) | Net sales to inventory (Times) | Fixed assets to tangible net worth (Percent) | Current debt to tangible net worth (Percent) | Total debt to tangible net worth (Percent) | Inventory to net working capital (Percent) | Current debt to inventory (Percent) | Funded debts to net working capital (Percent) |
|---|---|---|---|---|---|---|---|---|---|---|---|---|---|---|
| *Retailing* | | | | | | | | | | | | | | |
| 5531 Auto & home supply stores (56) | 3.72 **1.90** 1.39 | 3.82 **1.88** 0.61 | 16.76 **7.63** 2.91 | 31.11 **12.17** 3.95 | 6.04 **4.32** 2.79 | 9.50 **5.48** 3.57 | | 7.4 **5.7** 4.0 | 10.3 **27.4** 64.9 | 35.2 **81.4** 151.5 | 72.6 **99.0** 223.5 | 60.0 **115.6** 151.1 | 71.5 **104.7** 172.8 | 13.4 **44.5** 113.9 |
| 5641 Children's & infants' wear stores (47) | 4.30 **2.18** 1.55 | 3.58 **1.92** 0.39 | 14.06 **8.16** 2.27 | 20.48 **10.07** 2.85 | 6.19 **4.56** 3.35 | 8.30 **5.15** 3.91 | | 7.3 **4.9** 3.8 | 5.7 **22.7** 34.2 | 33.3 **58.0** 113.6 | 65.5 **90.6** 152.1 | 73.6 **106.4** 188.8 | 40.0 **76.2** 98.4 | 13.0 **26.9** 41.7 |
| 5611 Clothing & furnishings, men's & boys' (212) | 4.23 **2.83** 1.85 | 3.70 **1.79** 0.60 | 12.69 **6.11** 1.73 | 14.65 **7.69** 1.94 | 4.72 **3.32** 2.41 | 5.56 **3.69** 2.62 | | 5.7 **4.2** 3.1 | 4.8 **11.1** 27.4 | 28.0 **50.5** 108.2 | 57.6 **103.7** 203.4 | 66.7 **96.4** 132.0 | 37.8 **65.9** 96.7 | 10.0 **34.0** 51.2 |
| *Wholesaling* | | | | | | | | | | | | | | |
| 5075 & 78 Air condtg. & refrigtn. equipt. & supplies (41) | 3.47 **2.04** 1.44 | 3.43 **2.24** 1.31 | 17.00 **11.16** 6.42 | 18.84 **12.89** 7.55 | 8.30 **5.31** 2.96 | 9.76 **5.51** 3.48 | 40 **50** 65 | 7.5 **5.4** 4.1 | 8.1 **17.7** 32.1 | 27.1 **72.7** 214.1 | 67.4 **147.0** 267.9 | 64.5 **98.3** 154.8 | 48.9 **90.8** 136.9 | 8.5 **24.5** 48.0 |
| 5013 Automotive parts & supplies (135) | 4.02 **2.83** 2.04 | 4.02 **2.88** 1.46 | 15.18 **10.83** 5.84 | 19.03 **12.90** 7.40 | 4.94 **3.92** 2.99 | 6.39 **4.54** 3.38 | 26 **34** 46 | 7.1 **4.6** 3.7 | 7.5 **14.6** 28.6 | 26.9 **46.4** 83.2 | 50.2 **92.0** 117.8 | 72.3 **94.1** 116.8 | 44.8 **61.7** 98.6 | 11.0 **19.3** 46.9 |
| 5181 & 82 Beer, wine & alcoholic beverages (92) | 2.97 **1.86** 1.39 | 2.36 **1.19** 0.51 | 17.70 **9.51** 4.46 | 27.12 **13.29** 5.96 | 12.03 **8.55** 5.23 | 18.01 **11.57** 7.57 | 5 **19** 33 | 13.4 **8.0** 6.3 | 9.2 **24.3** 42.9 | 37.2 **78.1** 171.9 | 61.9 **136.3** 238.9 | 82.6 **114.7** 221.5 | 64.4 **93.8** 128.8 | 18.4 **38.4** 70.3 |
| *Manufacturing and Construction* | | | | | | | | | | | | | | |
| 2873-74-75-79 Agricultural chemicals (46) | 3.14 **2.26** 1.66 | 8.25 **5.20** 2.08 | 28.44 **18.53** 11.68 | 52.27 **33.73** 18.44 | 5.56 **3.57** 2.85 | 8.65 **5.27** 4.08 | 23 **36** 61 | 15.3 **8.6** 5.6 | 18.9 **32.4** 52.2 | 37.8 **51.2** 103.2 | 48.9 **117.3** 172.0 | 38.9 **72.1** 143.1 | 86.1 **137.9** 211.2 | 5.8 **35.9** 122.9 |
| 3724-28 Airplane parts & accessories (68) | 3.09 **2.23** 1.77 | 6.39 **4.50** 1.43 | 17.92 **11.75** 5.43 | 25.88 **16.49** 6.20 | 4.27 **2.90** 1.79 | 5.72 **3.94** 2.67 | 41 **52** 65 | 7.3 **4.6** 3.2 | 25.2 **46.9** 71.4 | 32.6 **59.5** 102.2 | 60.8 **116.8** 202.2 | 51.0 **95.2** 126.2 | 65.8 **92.8** 121.7 | 26.4 **54.5** 74.0 |
| 2051-52 Bakery products (54) | 2.92 **1.72** 1.34 | 2.63 **1.47** 0.51 | 12.35 **5.77** 3.04 | 38.31 **16.51** 7.01 | 8.04 **4.73** 3.66 | 27.30 **14.88** 7.88 | 19 **24** 35 | 33.8 **24.5** 15.2 | 55.5 **72.0** 98.7 | 22.0 **45.5** 71.3 | 46.5 **76.4** 159.1 | 35.9 **77.1** 138.0 | 116.5 **181.9** 249.5 | 18.0 **52.5** 172.8 |

SOURCE: Dun & Bradstreet, Inc., *Key Business Ratios*, 1974.

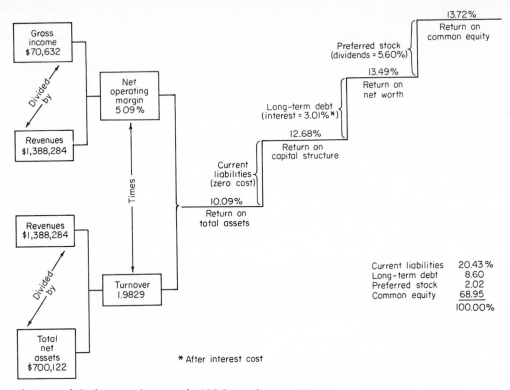

Current liabilities    20.43%
Long-term debt      8.60
Preferred stock     2.02
Common equity     68.95
                100.00%

\* After interest cost

**Fig. F-1. Analysis of return on investment for ABC Corporation, year 1978.**

CIAL; BUDGETING, CAPITAL; BUDGETS AND BUDGET PREPARATION; CREDIT MANAGEMENT; ERISA; EXCHANGE, FOREIGN, MANAGEMENT OF; FINANCIAL MANAGEMENT, BANK RELATIONSHIPS; FINANCIAL MANAGEMENT, CAPITAL STRUCTURE AND DIVIDEND POLICY; FINANCIAL MANAGEMENT, SHORT-TERM, INTERMEDIATE, AND LONG-TERM FINANCING; FINANCIAL STATEMENT ANALYSIS; INTERNATIONAL TRADE; MARGINAL INCOME ANALYSIS; PROFIT IMPROVEMENT; RISK ANALYSIS AND MANAGEMENT; SHAREHOLDER RELATIONSHIPS.

## REFERENCES

*Cash Management:* Conference Board Report No. 580, National Industrial Conference Board, Inc., New York, 1973.

Curran, Ward S.: *Principles of Financial Management.* McGraw-Hill Book Company, New York, 1970.

Dauten, Carl A., and Merle T. Welshans: *Principles of Finance,* 4th ed., South-Western Publishing Company, Incorporated, Cincinnati, 1975.

Johnson, Robert W.: *Financial Management,* 4th ed., Allyn and Bacon, Inc., Boston, 1971.

Van Horne, James C.: *Financial Management and Policy,* 3d ed., Prentice-Hall, Inc., Englewood Cliffs, N.J., 1974.

Weston, J. Fred, and Eugene F. Brigham: *Managerial Finance,* 5th ed., The Dryden Press, Inc., Hinsdale, Ill., 1975.

MERLE T. WELSHANS, *Union Electric Company*

# Financial management, bank relationships

The quality of a financial relationship can often determine a company's capital structure, interest cost, and competitive position. Even the best-managed corporation may overlook simple ways to get more from its banking ties. Every business, large or small, should continually seek to establish a more profitable bank relationship while maintaining flexibility and alternative sources.

## THE BANK'S VIEWPOINT

In the banker's eye, credit worthiness is a composite snapshot, a mixture of both quantitative and subjective facts. Nearly all lenders intuitively follow the same thought process to arrive at a final picture. By understanding the key elements of this process, a company can assess its own standing.

**Relationship Profitability** A bank makes money from a business account in three ways: (1) fees, (2) interest on loans, and (3) reinvestment of deposits. Money market conditions will often determine which of the three is more profitable. For example, in periods of high interest rates (tight money), deposits will be worth more than in periods of lower rates. To improve its own profit and liquidity, the bank will often ask its borrowers to keep deposits equal to a prenegotiated percentage of the loan rather than charge the borrower a higher rate. Historically, the percentage has been around 20 percent; however, risk, length of maturity, and money market conditions can alter the balance arrangement.

Operating services are often paid for by balances. The bank should provide a monthly statement of services used, the service cost, and the balances required to pay for them. When comparing banks, a company should check both the price of the service and the rate that is used to convert its balances into a fee. Both the price and the rate vary from bank to bank. The industry trend is to fully price all services, including credit. The implications of this are far-reaching. In the past, bankers sometimes shrouded their prices in mystery by suggesting that some unquantifiable amount of surplus balance was necessary to keep the relationship profitable. But with full pricing, a bank's profit is built into the price, and so the corporate customer knows exactly how much it has paid and that the bank has been fairly compensated. No business should settle for some vague understanding of the price. It should know in advance how much it will be charged for credit or services: if more convenient, the customer should ask if it can pay in fees. A good lender does not necessarily provide the most efficient operating services, so the client should place its business accordingly.

Full-product pricing applies to credit as well as services. Sophisticated banks will guarantee the availability of money (subject to continuing credit worthiness) even in capital-short markets. The usual cost is a commitment fee of ½ percent on the amount of funds to be reserved. In spite of recent attempts to price every product, banks still have some services which defy the cost accountant's calculator; credit information and financial consulting are examples. A business may wish to keep some surplus

deposits at the bank to ensure that these and other intangibles are fairly covered.

**Management Capability** Executive skill is an elusive and broad category which cannot be totally dissected. In general, however, the two most important qualities of good management are depth and dependability. On special problem is worth noting, however. Many banks have experienced loan losses among a particular kind of manager—the self-important entrepreneur. Steady turnover in the lower management ranks of a business usually confirms this problem.

**Financial Position** Traditional measures of financial risk, such as excessive leverage and earnings volatility, have not changed over the years. However, several analytical trends have recently emerged which underscore the need to support credit worthiness in depth:

1. Off–balance sheet financing per se will not increase borrowing capacity. If it does, the company lives with the risk of an inopportune reassessment when its capital structure is finally understood.

2. Subordinated debt is not equity. Too often, senior and junior positions in liquidation confuse the right of any creditor to accelerate because of a missed payment.

3. Deferred taxes are not equity. They are a legitimate obligation which, in an earnings slump, may compete for corporate cash with any other liability.

4. The current ratio is only a weak proxy for more reliable measures of liquidity. Management should regularly assess the permanency of both current assets and bank lines. Growing companies often find that inventory and receivables are really fixed investments, which should be financed on a permanent basis. Too often lines of credit are thought of as term loans—rolled over on an annual basis ad infinitum. In fact, the bank has no legal obligation to lend money under a line of credit, and most lines can be extinguished at the bank's option. If a company cannot "clean up" its line at least annually, it may be in trouble. More bankers are looking beyond the current ratio to test liquidity, and an annual current-debt retirement is one such test.

**Controls and Information** The best management in the world would be helpless without reliable information about its business—not minutia, but expressive data. A massive and complex system is not necessary. The lender wants to see the reports firsthand to be assured that they fit into the corporation's overall objectives and represent a simple, manageable picture. An accounting firm can provide

provide valuable assistance in this process. In fact, most banks will expect a complete audit by a recognized public accountant when borrowings exceed $1 million.

**Planning Process and Capability**  Planning flows from the information base. If borrowing is on a term basis, projections covering the loan period should be provided. A detailed cash budget is the foundation of this process. Forecasting is inherently subjective, but well-managed companies seem to have monotonous luck in their ability to predict their financial future. The most common indicator of poor planning is an *urgent* need for funds.

**Corporate Structure**  Complex legal structures frequently cloud and impede borrowing relationships. Holding companies that own operating companies that own holding companies, for example, can accidentally create several classes of creditors, which forces the bank to rely on more comprehensive loan agreements. For the best borrowing posture the corporate structure should be kept clean and simple.

**Openness and Honesty**  Honesty is the cornerstone of the credit system. It is uncompromising. The lender should be told the good with the bad and at regular intervals. Openness is a form of honesty. Company management must be prepared to discuss every facet of the business and to provide supporting information. This does not mean that the client should not question the reasonableness of any information request that seems unnecessary. Lenders are usually sympathetic to adversity when they have been apprised of all events as they occurred. The lender may, in fact, be able to offer constructive suggestions as well as money.

## LOAN APPLICATIONS

When preparing an application for a term loan, a company should incorporate its response to the bank's viewpoint into an information package. This package should include the following: (1) amount; (2) purpose; (3) repayment plans and source; (4) organizational and legal structure; (5) business description in a 10-K format; (6) historical financial statements with sales and profits by business line; (7) financial forecast; (8) background of key management; and (9) accountant's management letter.

The entire credit process requires something more than a series of cold, analytical steps. The essence of credit is a relationship—a working understanding between the bank and the borrower. In a sense, it is the summary of all the factors just mentioned but placed in the context of a company's personality. Unless the lender knows and understands that personal side of a business, it is difficult to seal the relationship. Making sure that the banker knows and interacts with several levels of management within the client company is a very sound practice.

## HOW MANY BANKS?

Competition is healthy. Even though most companies work hard to maintain multiple vendors, the philosophy is not always extended to their bank— one of their most important suppliers. When does a company reach the critical mass required to justify a multibank relationship? Two guidelines might be useful:

1. Does the bank sell part of your loan to another bank?

2. Does your company borrow more than $1 million?

On the surface, the cost of establishing two profitable relationships may appear to outweigh the advantages. However, that cost will easily be eliminated as each institution scrambles to justify its position.

When a company diversifies its banking ties, it should consider several points.

*Geographic Location.*  Sometimes banks in the same city find it difficult to compete constructively. Likewise, regional economic factors can shut off funds in one area and not in another.

*Bank Size.*  This can affect both the quality of attention and availability of funds; however, at a minimum, each bank should be capable of handling a significant portion of the customer's financial needs.

*Operating Capability.*  This varies from institution to institution. Basic services like money transfer or cash management can be prohibitively expensive if the bank makes repeated mistakes or overcharges. It is sometimes a good idea to split a company's operating services until one organization proves to be superior.

*Reputation.*  Successful banks rarely achieve their position by default. A better-managed bank will readily reflect its skill through the income statement. It makes sense to seek out the leaders in the field.

## THE CUSTOMER'S VIEWPOINT

It is vital for the chief financial officer (CFO), at least, to know the basic workings of the company's bank. At the minimum, the CFO should know:

1. Who makes the credit decisions and how fast?

2. Is there quality and depth among the bank's key personnel?

3. How does the bank prioritize the importance of the company's account?

4. What kind of business is appreciated?

Whether the answers to these questions are favorable or not, the company's reactions should be communicated to bank officials. The CFO should visit with the account manager at least 4 to 6 times each year. The CFO, accompanied on occasion by other top management personnel, should meet with senior bank managers biannually—if they are in any way involved in the decision process.

The ideal relationship is one of balance: honest and open, but competitive. The borrower should negotiate pricing or credit with candor and know what issues are important and where a compromise may be struck. Overkill is counterproductive. In the end, the most profitable relationship will be well balanced between the bank's interests and those of the lender.

*See also* ACCOUNTING, FINANCIAL; AUDIT, MANAGEMENT; AUDITING, FINANCIAL; CREDIT MANAGEMENT; FINANCIAL MANAGEMENT, SHORT-TERM, INTERMEDIATE, AND LONG-TERM FINANCING.

JAMES H. GRAVES, *First National Bank in Dallas*

# Financial management, capital structure and dividend policy

Planning the capital structure of a company poses two basic questions: What portion debt (borrowings)? What portion equity (stockholder purchases)? In the past the decision-making process which structured a company's financing was relatively simple. Equity was good; debt was bad. Contemporary times have changed all this and have also made the science and art of planning a capital structure one of the fundamental decisions in business management.

*Capital Needs.* As a company grows and as the nature of its business changes, so will its capital needs. Technological advances and increased labor costs can change a labor-intensive industry with little need for debt into a capital-intensive industry greatly dependent on debt financing. Optimum debt-to-equity ratios will vary with each corporation's unique capabilities to service a debt while still paying a reasonable dividend. What is right for one

business will not necessarily solve another's problems. The level and type of debt at one point in time may not be proper in the future.

*Debt Ratios.* The debt ratio of a company is an important indicator of its financial soundness. Too high, and investors and lenders both become concerned with the borrower's ability to service the debt in periods of low business activity. Too low, and the capital structure is heavily weighted with higher after-tax cost equity. In either case, additional capital for growth may be costly and difficult to find.

*Debt Structure.* Another major consideration must be the structure of the debt. Just a few of the possibilities include: bank loans, private placement of debt with financial institutions such as insurance companies and pension funds, public issues of debentures (both convertible and straight debt), and lease financing. Bank loans are further divided into revolving credit agreements, new types of term loans, and international currency loans.

When the debt strategy is effective, the income-producing base of the company is expanded, and the earnings generated by this added debt capital will prove to be substantially higher than the interest payments on the debt.

**Planning for Capital Requirements** Every organization should formulate plans to manage growth and at the same time cope with the shocks of variations in business cycles. Some key factors in establishing a financing plan are:

1. *Suitability of capital.* The types of funds obtained must be in harmony with the operating assets employed.

2. *Risk.* Fluctuations in business cycles affect the ability to service debt already incurred or ability to incur new debt.

3. *Income.* A major objective is to provide a reasonable current yield to the shareholders as well as potential appreciation.

4. *Maneuverability.* An ability to be selective as to sources of future capital requirements (debt or equity) will depend on maintaining debt levels below acceptable peaks.

5. *Timing.* Stock, bond, and money markets change constantly, making "when to act" an important criterion.

## CAPITAL STRUCTURE

**Leverage** Equity shareholders benefit from the ability of a company to borrow funds and invest them at a rate of return higher than the cost of borrowing. Doing this results in increased earnings per share of stock outstanding and is commonly known as *leverage*.

Leverage should be carefully planned since the impact on earnings per share when business declines can be substantial. Some unfortunate examples of lack of forward planning were demonstrated by highly leveraged conglomerates finding themselves in financial crises during the 1974–1975 recession.

**Debt Levels** Financial decision making determines what debt level is optimum for a particular industry or corporation. There are no clear-cut rules or formulas to make this determination. In Koppers Company, Inc., for example, parameters have been established of between 25 and 35 percent of debt to total capitalization. The company feels this level gives the shareholder the advantages of leverage without an undue risk in the event of a business turndown. As debt levels approach the targeted peak, sources of equity financing are explored. Means of accomplishing this are (1) acquisitions of other business in exchange for equity securities and (2) public marketing of equity securities.

Generally, while a business is expanding and until a determination is reached as to the amount of capital that will be permanently invested in such expansions, medium-term financing can be used to advantage. The funds permanently invested in fixed assets (i.e., plant equipment, buildings) should be covered by long-term financing, both equity and debt in the agreed-upon proportion.

*Working Capital.* The funds invested in working capital should be divided into two categories: (1) a minimum base load and (2) the additional amounts required to support levels of high business activity. Admittedly, this division is somewhat arbitrary but nevertheless necessary. The minimum base load should be financed on a long-term basis. However, the working capital required during high levels of business activity should be financed with debt which can be liquidated in the event of a business decline.

*Seasonal Aspects.* Another factor to be taken into account in financing working capital is one of a seasonal nature. Where peak working capital requirements occur during certain periods of a year, short-term debt such as commercial paper or short-term bank loans should be used. This allows for complete liquidation of this liability during the off-peak season.

**Capital Stock** The prudent use of a company's equity securities can reap considerable advantages for both the company and its shareholders. The company can generate funds to finance future growth, and from this growth the individual investor can receive income and appreciation gains.

An obvious way to obtain a more favorable debt-equity ratio is to issue more stock. This is usually a practice in times when market enthusiasm is high and the company's earnings performance is good. Adverse consequences are that: (1) new stock issues can potentially dilute earnings per share, and (2) they must be serviced with dividends. Long-range planning should take into account these possible drains on earnings from new stock issues.

**Tax Considerations** Income taxes are an important consideration in sourcing financing (i.e., debt or equity). Interest payments on debt securities are tax deductible while dividends are not. While there is considerable movement to eliminate or reduce the double taxation of dividends, several years probably will pass before any meaningful relief is granted. Therefore, for the immediate future, debt financing, used judiciously, will remain the least costly, after provision for taxes.

**Analyzing the Capital Structure** The return on investment (ROI) approach to earnings analysis is the most widely used method of analyzing performance. The earnings before interest charges and income tax expenses are related to the total investment (i.e., total assets minus current liabilities). This calculation measures the return in relation to all the assets employed regardless of the source of financing—debt or equity. This is a sounder approach than measuring performance on earnings per share of stock outstanding or as a return only on the equity employed.

Another important measurement is the cash payout (the sum of after-tax earnings plus depreciation) related to the total investment. This measurement is extremely important during times of high inflation. The more rapidly an investment can be recouped, the less deterioration there is in the money received as a result of inflation.

## DIVIDEND POLICY

Two characteristics dominate the image of a stock and its owner's reasons for investing—income and appreciation in market value.

In establishment of a dividend policy, an eye to the future is of paramount importance. Investors usually will seek both current yield and long-term appreciation, but in varying degrees. In an inflationary economy, current yield becomes more important. On the other hand, an enterprise exists on profits; it grows only when those profits are reinvested wisely. A high dividend payout ratio can rapidly deplete the base that provides such profits.

A continuing dividend payout without frequent retractions is fundamental. Current payout should take into account current yield of other investment opportunities available to the investor, needs for growth of the company, and ability to sustain such a payout except in times of protracted adversity. As the earnings record of the corporation improves, increases in dividends should follow. Such a pattern reflects concern by management for a reasonable payment for the use of the stockholders' money as well as confidence in the corporation's future earnings potential. Proper consideration of these two factors should result in dividend increases being made on the basis of sound financial decisions and not wishful thinking.

**Dividend Payout Ratio**  Because of the dynamic changes experienced in business conditions—both advances and declines—percentage payout targets should be avoided. Much of the profit reported by corporations in recent years has been of an inflationary nature and not a sound basis on which to structure a percentage payout target. Depreciation charges based upon current and future costs of replacing fixed assets are not properly reflected in such reported profits; targeted payout ratios based upon these inflated profits would lead to eventual liquidation of the corporation's assets. Contemporary conditions have produced a financial climate with inflation as an integral part. While shareholders may delight in immediate income, they will not be happy if in a few years the company has not retained sufficient earnings to support future growth and to maintain its position in the marketplace.

The basic rule is to determine the character of your business and its future capital requirements. Measure these against the competitive money markets and attempt to arrive at a solution to satisfy both dividend and growth capital demands. One possible solution is to fix dividends at a competitive yield based on the current market price of the company's stock, rather than as a fixed percent of earnings. This also provides for regularity of dividend payments—a vital concern to investors seeking income.

**Extras**  Extra dividends (those paid above the regularly stated dividend) are another tool for the financial manager. They allow for a temporary boost in dividends—reflecting unusually high temporary earnings or those of a cyclical nature. It is important to reserve extra dividends only as an occasional issue. When declared too often, they lose their impact, and the marketplace will regard failure to declare them tantamount to a dividend cut.

**Stock Dividends and Splits**  The general distinction between a stock dividend and a stock split is that the former generally refers to smaller distributions made as a supplement to, or substitute for, a cash dividend. The stock dividend requires that an amount equal to the fair market value of the stock distributed be transferred from the retained earnings account to the common capital stock and capital surplus accounts. A stock split reduces the par value per share with no change in the capital stock or capital surplus accounts.

Some reasons for stock dividends are to conserve cash, permit shareholders to defer income taxes, and increase future dividends to shareholders. Normally in a stock dividend, the cash dividend per share remains unchanged and is paid in the future on the additional shares issued as a stock dividend.

Reasons for stock splits include reducing a high-priced stock to a more popular selling range (around $20 to $40 per share), making round-lot purchases (increments of 100 shares) easier for individual investors, increasing or broadening the shareholder base—this creates more marketability for the stock and normally increases trading activity, and facilitating sale of new offerings because of broadened ownership.

**Dividend Administration**  The authority to declare dividends is usually vested in the board of directors. Practically, however, the administration of dividend policy depends on company management input and advice.

Several factors should be considered in establishing dividend policies:

1. Both the historical record of earnings and the future prospects should be examined in setting a dividend policy.

2. Maintenance of a stable rate of dividends per share is generally advisable. Where earnings fluctuate substantially, a minimum regular dividend can be established with extra dividend payouts added when appropriate.

3. Cash flow, current cash positions, and anticipated need for asset replacement funds should be taken into consideration in determining whether a dividend should be paid in cash or stock or possibly a combination of both.

4. Also of importance are restrictions in current loan agreements, income tax considerations, and excess accumulation of earnings penalties and factors relating to the stock market.

## STOCK REPURCHASES

A company buys its own stock usually to employ a cash surplus at a favorable rate of return. However, doing this has a negative implication: it can indicate that a company has run out of growth opportunities and new ideas for employing its funds. There may be times, however, when such an action is justified, such as buying one's shares for: (1) future stock option or profit sharing plan requirements and (2) an acquisition program which may require stock.

*See also* BUDGETING, CAPITAL; FINANCIAL MANAGEMENT, SHORT-TERM, INTERMEDIATE, AND LONG-TERM FINANCING; FINANCIAL STATEMENT ANALYSIS; RISK ANALYSIS AND MANAGEMENT; SHAREHOLDER RELATIONSHIPS.

### REFERENCES

Committe, Thomas C.: *Managerial Finance for the Seventies*, McGraw-Hill Book Company, New York, 1972.

Davey, Patrick J.: *Dividend Reinvestment Programs*, The Conference Board, Inc., New York, 1976.

Donaldson, Gordon: *Corporate Debt Capacity, A Study of Corporate Debt Policy and the Determination of Corporate Debt Capacity*, Harvard Graduate School of Business Administration, Cambridge, Mass., 1961.

Harkins, Edwin P., and Francis J. Walsh: *Corporate Debt Management*, The Conference Board, Inc., New York, 1968.

Walsh, Francis J., Jr.: *Planning Corporate Capital Structures*, The Conference Board, Inc., New York, 1972.

A. WILLIAM CAPONE, *Koppers Company, Inc.*

# Financial management, international

(*See* INTERNATIONAL OPERATIONS AND MANAGEMENT IN MULTINATIONAL COMPANIES.)

# Financial management, short-term, intermediate, and long-term financing

As used here, *financing* refers to actions undertaken to supply an enterprise with the money and/or credit it wants or needs in order to carry out its affairs. Financing, therefore, is a necessity. Effective financing requires craftsmanship and intuitive apperception so that a company is financed at the least possible total cost over the longest significant period of time. According to period of time or source, financing may be classified five ways: (1) short term, (2) intermediate term, (3) long term, (4) government, and (5) off-book. Each is examined separately below.

The financial officer must know more about the financing goals of the company than anyone else. Strategic counsel or technical advice may be obtained from many sources, but financing decisions should be those of the chief financial executive. This responsibility stems from his or her conception of the financing profile of the company.

## FINANCING PROFILE

The basic purpose of financing is to contribute to the maximum extent toward corporate objectives, specifically to increase profit after tax by minimizing the direct and indirect costs of money and credit.

**Rank Order of Company Objectives**  There are circumstances, however, in which the immediate or intermediate corporate objective bears little direct resemblance to long-term profit. Examples include the following:

1. The need to stay in business at almost any cost.

2. A desire to pay for a very large call upon debt so as to be able in the future to take some important corporate step, such as investing in a new product or service or acquiring a new division.

3. Improving balance sheet ratios to meet existing loan covenants or to give the company a "healthier" look.

4. A plan to weaken the balance sheet with a heavy burden of expensive debt in order to make the company less vulnerable to an expected take-over bid.

Since these purposes can be antithetical to one another, and more than one can exist at the same time, the fundamental and paramount requirements of the financing officer are complete understanding of company objectives and the ability to rank-order them where necessary.

**Impact on Company Capital**  All financing becomes a part of the capital structure of a company. For this reason, it is important that financing alternatives be evaluated against their effect on company capital as reflected in the balance sheet.

Capital consists of equity and debt, with some capital instruments embracing attributes of both. Examples of the latter include convertible debentures issued with warrants for the purchase of common stock and cumulative preferred stock. *Equity* capital consists of common stock, which may exist in more than one class, perhaps with differing voting rights, and/or preferred stock in various forms, including participating and convertible. *Debt* may appear on the balance sheet as long term or short term; it may be mentioned only in a footnote, or—depending upon its form and significance—it may be unmentioned. Since potential lenders and investors are likely to examine the balance sheet and the footnotes to the financial statements closely, the underlying capital therein reflected should be assembled to appeal to those whose support is important.

*Trial-and-Error Testing.* Unfortunately, the building of a corporate structure cannot be preprogrammed with precision, because the financial environments in which a company operates are in a continuous state of flux. Equity markets ebb and flow. Long-term and short-term interest rates go up and down, not always in concert. The rate of inflation and the absolute availability of funds vary. Sources of capital change their business cycle expectations, and various means of financing (or investing) swing fadlike into and out of favor. For these reasons, financing plans must be tested like tax plans on a trial-and-error basis. The financing officer must define the alternatives, establish the limits within which they appear realistic, and then apply each one in turn to the company's operations as they may develop in the future. The better the company's forward plan, the more likely its financing proposals will prove appropriate, but trial-and-error testing against ranges of possible operating performance may prove better than no attempt to foresee the future.

**Checklist for Borrowing** The desirability of pretesting a financing alternative suggests the importance not only of profit and cash forecasts, but also of the use of checklists. Many bank and institutional lenders use and frequently update a *loan agreement checklist*, and a similar reminder will prove helpful to most financing officers. Since such a list should be tailored specifically to the industry, geographic location, company, and financial structure involved, it is not practical to try to develop here a checklist which would meet the needs of every reader, or even readers in general. The illustrative listing in Table F-3 may prove useful, however. The list refers only to borrowing, but a similar list can be drawn up when equity capital is being considered. The entries in Table F-3 have been listed compactly in order to save space; in practice, the table will require several pages to make room for all the information.

### SHORT-TERM FINANCING

Short-term financing traditionally is used for seasonal purposes, for example, to build up inventory. If a business is healthy enough to be able to repay its short-term borrowing each year, as after the sale of the inventory, it will be able to obtain all the short-term money it needs. But when short-term funds are asked to meet long-term needs, difficulties arise.

**Trade Credit** One normal source of short-term financing for all businesses is trade credit. Unfortunately for the cash-short company, it works both ways: a company can increase its working capital by not paying its suppliers, but it may also have to let its customers use some of the money they owe it.

**TABLE F-3  Illustrative Borrowing Checklist**

1. General
   a. Purpose of loan
   b. Amount desired
      Minimum
      Maximum
   c. Preferred term
      Minimum
      Optimum
      Maximum
   d. Type of loan preferred
2. Useful background data
   a. Summary of existing indebtedness
   b. Covenants presently in force
      Affirmative
      Negative
   c. Current working capital
   d. Major ratios at present
      Current
      Debt/equity
      Coverage of fixed charges
3. Alternatives available
   a. Loan elements
      Placement costs
      Commitment fee
      Compensating balance
      Prepayment
      Sinking fund
      Collateral
      No financial call
      Affirmative covenants
      Negative covenants
      Apparent effective cost
   b. Forecast of major ratios at year-end
      19XX
         Current
         Debt/equity
         Coverage of fixed charges
      19XX
         Current
         Debt/equity
         Coverage of fixed charges
      19XX
         Current
         Debt/equity
         Coverage of fixed charges

Attachment: 5-year summary forecast, prior to loan, with space in which to insert effect of alternative loan possibilities.

*Leads and Lags.* The phrase *leads and lags* is used to describe the use of trade credit, but the term at times implies some manipulation. A company which extends only 30-day credit but pays on 60-day terms may be ahead, depending on the value it adds to the products it buys, but this is not practical in many instances. Indeed, if a company knows in advance that it is facing a tight cash situation, it probably is well advised to discuss payment expectations with each supplier in order to reach an understanding on the use of trade credit before serious questions can arise.

The one area in which leads and lags may have

**403**

substantial merit is that involving multicurrency cash flows. Here there is special reason for prepaying or withholding payments if one can anticipate changes in currency parities.

*Cash Discounts.* A subordinate question related to trade credit involves cash discounts: should or should not one take the "1 percent, 10 days" or "2 percent, 20 days" offered by some suppliers for prompt payment? The answer devolves from discounted cash flow analysis of the cost or saving involved. Usually, the discounts offered are greater than the company's cost of capital, which suggests that they should be taken and, conversely, should not be offered.

**Secured Borrowing**   Secured borrowing is likely to provide more money to most companies than trade credit. A secured loan involves borrowing against accounts receivable, inventory, machinery, equipment, vehicles, construction, buildings, or a contract of some type. Such loans are available from banks, commercial finance companies, and (in the medium-term range) a few other financial intermediaries.

*Commercial Finance Companies.* Since every company has a banker and every banker can explain the secured and unsecured financing offered by the bank, it seems desirable to shape this discussion primarily in terms of the less familiar services of a commercial finance company. As a general statement, a finance company often is willing to consider secured lending to a potential borrower who cannot arrange bank borrowing. The reason for the borrower's difficulty may be that it is in an undercapitalized seasonal business, has an insufficiently clear track record with the banking community, wants to make an acquisition of which the borrower's banker does not approve, or simply needs to be tided over a bad period. The finance company charges something on the order of 6 percent over the prime rate (more or less, depending upon circumstances), but this need not necessarily be considered exorbitantly high, particularly if alternative borrowing from a bank would cost the same borrower 2 or 3 percent over prime, plus compensating balances (and if the bank would not lend the money anyway).

*Factoring.* Finance companies are particularly known for factoring. This involves the buying of accounts receivable, with the assumption of the credit risk by the purchaser, or *factor*. There normally are three aspects to the arrangement:

1. The factoring company advances the face amount of selected invoices prior to their maturity.

2. It may take over the ancillary bookkeeping and collection services required.

3. It also may provide credit insurance where it establishes credit limits for selected customers.

*Accounts Receivable Financing.* This involves lending against accounts receivable that are secured by a floating loan registered under the Uniform Commercial Code. In this case, the lender does not collect the accounts directly nor assume credit risk, and the account debtors are not aware that the accounts have been assigned. Accounts receivable financing is limited to a percentage of the total receivable, perhaps 80 percent, with the cushion established to provide allowance for disputed items, past-due accounts, and errors.

*Inventory Financing.* In the normal course of events not many loans are made against inventory alone. For companies with sharp seasonal businesses, however, a straight inventory loan may be particularly appropriate.

**Unsecured Borrowing**   All the foregoing forms of lending also may be offered by commercial banks which provide, in addition, unsecured short-term loans, lines of credit, and revolving loans. These may be called "unsecured loans," but they are unsecured only in the sense that they are not tied to a specific asset or group of assets. In fact, of course, "unsecured credit" *is secured* by the general financial and operating strength of the borrower as evaluated by the lender. Since this general strength consists in large measure of specific assets such as receivables, inventory, and equipment, no company should be able to borrow twice against the same security; that is, a company may be able to get unsecured credit from its bank, or it may be able to borrow against its assets, but it should not be able to do both, excepting in part. The trade-off from the point of view of the financing officer will devolve from an evaluation of the alternative costs involved as well as from the value put upon the flexibility and comfort of unsecured borrowing.

**Paper and Notes**   Short-term money is also available through two-name and three-name paper of various types.

*Acceptance Financing.* The most common such paper, which can be used for illustrative purposes, is the bankers' acceptance. To borrow money through this mechanism, the borrower arranges a line of credit with a banker and then issues a series of notes payable in 30, 60, 90, 120, or 180 days. These notes are payable to bearer at a competitive interest rate published in financial papers each day. The borrower delivers each note to the bank, normally paying the bank an additional 1/8 percent per month for its assistance. The bank endorses, or "accepts," the note and may retain it in its own portfolio or sell it to the investing public. In the latter case, the purchaser of the note looks in the first instance to the credit worthiness of the accepting bank rather than to that of the issuing company. The borrower, in effect, is paying the bank for the privilege of borrowing against the bank's credit.

The bank may charge a commission or a facility fee, in addition to the interest surcharge, but to date banks have not attempted to obtain compensating balances for acceptance financing. While acceptance financing, therefore, often is less expensive to a borrower than bank borrowing, the financing officer should recognize that the bank in offering an acceptance facility may be undercutting its own more profitable straight-loan business. Acceptance financing, therefore, should be considered only as one part of a financing package, since a business that insists on the cheapest possible borrowing when it can get away with it may find, when conditions are more competitive, that it has no borrowing opportunity at all.

*Commercial Paper.* Large, well-run companies also may be able to raise short-term funds by issuing commercial paper. This consists of unsecured promissory notes broadly similar to those which form the basis of acceptance financing, except that they are not countersigned or "accepted" by anyone. Commercial paper is sold by a corporation to or through a dealer, or directly to an institutional investor, at a discount (similar to a treasury bill), for a maximum term of 9 months. A company considering the issuance of commercial paper (which also means entering the market in competition with its banker) should obtain counsel from one of the half-dozen or so major brokerage firms which act as dealers in the commercial paper market. Typical commercial paper and other short-term interest rates are set forth in Table F-4.

**Captive Financing** Large companies which sell products against installment, lease, or rental payments may wish to consider establishing their own ("captive") finance companies. While such a company initially will be lending rather than borrowing,

a captive finance company with a good record of 5 years or more will be able to obtain highly leveraged borrowing against its own name, rather than that of the parent company. The argument probably never will be settled as to whether the use of a captive finance company increases or fails to increase the total debt capacity of the parent (removal of much of or all the receivables from the parent reduces its borrowing capacity as the capacity of the captive increases), but there are, nevertheless, instances in which a captive can prove profitable. There also may be nonfinancial benefits in a subsidiary finance company. For example, a parent company with imprecise credit, collection, and bookkeeping records may be able to "start afresh" and reduce the size of its problems by channeling new time payment business through a captive. Similarly, a captive finance company may be structured to offer marketing and new business advantages.

## INTERMEDIATE-TERM FINANCING

Most intermediate-term financing in the United States is handled by the commercial banking system through lines of credit extending for periods longer than 1 year and term loans up to 5 or 7 years. An amalgam of these two financing vehicles also is common. An example would be a line of credit for 2 or 3 years which then becomes a 3- or 4-year term loan, either automatically or at the option of the borrower. Intermediate banking facilities of this nature cost more than shorter-term facilities and usually are priced higher for the later than for the earlier years.

*Custom-Tailored.* Intermediate loans depend in large measure upon predictions of the business climate, company operations, and cash flow. The extent to which lenders have confidence in the managerial control and forecasting abilities of borrowers is, therefore, crucial. Since each loan is essentially tailormade for a specific situation, there is no reason for the borrower or the lender to start with any preconception about term, price level, or interest escalation, prepayment penalty, or any other aspect of the proposed arrangement. If the two parties are intelligent and have confidence in one another, the borrower should be able to obtain the amounts needed at costs and under conditions that can be sustained, and the lender should be able to earn a reward sufficient to pay for tying up funds for an intermediate period of time.

*International Sources.* Institutions other than banks may make intermediate-term loans in special circumstances, but traditionally in the United States

TABLE F-4   Selected Short-Term Interest Rates

| | 1974 High, % | 1975–1976 Low, % | June 30, 1977, % |
|---|---|---|---|
| Prime rate of major New York City banks | 11.0 | 6.50 | 6.75 |
| One-month bankers' acceptances | 12.25 | 4.65 | 5.35 |
| Three-month commercial paper | 12.25 | 5.00 | 5.51 |
| Euro-dollars: London interbank 6-month asking rate | 13.75 | 4.78 | 6.13 |

nonbank lenders have been in either the short-term market (a year or less) or the long-term market (15 years or more). The situation has not been quite the same internationally. Intermediate funding possibilities abroad include the placement of 5- or 10-year bonds through major Swiss or other banks, the occasional availability of 5- to 10-year money directly from noncommercial banking institutions, and possible Eurocurrency loans. Three- or five-year Euro-dollar commitments are not uncommon, and there have been many 7-year loans. Unfortunately for the inflation-conscious borrower, it has become next to impossible to borrow intermediate-term Euro-dollars on anything but a floating-rate basis.

Since the specific requirements and ramifications of foreign borrowing are quite complex, as well as changeable, the potential lender should approach foreign money through an intermediary in the banking, merchant banking, or underwriting community.

**Leasing** One of the more popular methods of obtaining intermediate or long-term financing involves the use of leases. The principles involved are sufficiently complex to suggest some definitions:

A *lease* is an instrument which permits a lessee to use something (equipment or a building) in return for payments which are made regularly, over time, to the owner.

A *finance lease* permits the lessee to use an asset for most of—but not all—its life. The user must maintain the asset, pay taxes and insurance, and also make lease payments to the owner. The lease payments over the life of the lease repay the owner for the cost of the asset and the interest costs to own it, as well as providing a profit.

A *net lease* is any lease which stipulates payments to be made to the owner net of any deductions. For example, taxes, insurance, and maintenance are paid by the user. Most finance leases are of this type.

An *operating lease* is an arrangement, usually short-term, through which the lessee uses an asset for only a small portion of its life. Examples include 1-year leases of data processing equipment or copying machines.

A *true lease* is one which, by meeting selected IRS criteria, permits the user to obtain a tax deduction for lease payments while at the same time permitting the owner to claim the tax benefits of ownership, such as investment tax credit and depreciation.

A *leveraged lease* is the most complex of the leasing arrangements. It involves three parties: the owner, who provides less than half the cost of the asset; an institutional investor, who provides most of the cost

on a nonrecourse basis to the owner; and the user. The interest of the institutional investors is secured both by a first lien on the asset and by the assignment of the lease.

Leasing arrangements can prove beneficial to all parties. In many instances, for example, it is possible to structure the arrangement in such a way that tax benefits go to the party who can use them most advantageously. In return for these benefits, that party may be willing to share some of their effect with the other party, to whom they otherwise might have been of no direct benefit.

It should not be inferred from the foregoing that leasing is a magical financing vehicle or that it is always desirable. In fact, a cash purchase is always cheaper than leasing on a pretax basis, if for no other reason than that it avoids the need for profit by the lessor. On the other hand, leasing may offer useful options, including the possibilities of saving capital, of borrowing advantageously through another's credit, and of introducing tax flexibility.

## LONG-TERM FINANCING

The longest-term financing is with equity capital, which occurs when investors turn over cash in return for a part ownership in the company. Evidence of the latter takes the form of a certificate of stock. There are various types of stock, but the fundamental difference is between common and preferred. *Preferred stock* has a first, but limited, call upon earnings in the form of dividends, and perhaps upon payout in the case of liquidation. *Common stock* represents residual ownership after the company has met its obligations to creditors of all types and to holders of preferred stock.

Companies may raise money by placing equity with friends or institutions, but by far the most usual practice in the United States is to engage a brokerage firm to advise on the timing and amounts of equity which can be raised in specific markets, to help the company comply with government and exchange regulations, and, one hopes, to guarantee to "take" or "place" the stock in question. (Equity is discussed more fully in FINANCIAL MANAGEMENT, CAPITAL STRUCTURE AND DIVIDEND POLICY.)

**Debentures** By far the largest volume of long-term funds is made available to companies in the form of term loans, either unsecured or secured. Unsecured borrowing, such as that represented by debentures placed privately or sold to the public, essentially is secured by the general credit and financial strength of the issuing company. For this reason, debentures normally contain covenants to protect the holders against loss or diminution of their security. In addition, there normally is a trustee to check upon the financial well-being of the corporation on behalf of the holders and to be prepared, if necessary, to cry "default" on their behalf. Long-term debt secured by assets, such as buildings and equipment, is similar to intermediate-term debt of the same nature, and the applicable covenants normally refer to the care and use of the underlying surety rather than to general corporate strength.

**Conditions of Agreement** The documentation which sets forth the terms and conditions of any long-term borrowing must be examined with considerable care, since the obligation is long term in nature and the borrower wants a document which (1) will allow flexibility and (2) is unlikely to become burdensome in the not-quite-foreseeable and varying circumstances of the years ahead. If there is any general forewarning which is likely to prove helpful to all borrowers, it probably is this: *Nothing is absolutely necessary, nothing is free, there is a trade off for everything, and the smallest things may cost the most.* This somewhat laconic stricture refers to the many considerations included in a long-term loan document, among them the positive and negative covenants, the sinking fund, the commitment fee, the prepayment penalty, the interest cost, and the call provision.

Even the novice at borrowing knows that one prefers a lower to a higher rate of interest, but the careful borrower will remain alert to every aspect of the agreement and to the fact that anything one wants will cost one something. A 5-year no-financial-call provision (the borrower cannot for 5 years pay off the loan by borrowing at a lower rate of interest) may mean a higher prepayment penalty or a less attractive restriction on the payment of cash dividends; keeping the stated interest rate below a predetermined level may be possible, but if this means selling the bond at a discount, foregoing a call provision, or agreeing to a sinking fund schedule which does not synchronize well with the company's long-term cash forecast, then the cost of that appealing rate of interest may be too high. In short, almost any specific provision is possible, even if it is said to be "not customary," but everything has its price. It is the total long-term cost of the borrowing, including indirect and contingent or potential costs, which should be the primary concern of the borrower.

**Bond Ratings** Since in practice most executives will turn to a specialized financial intermediary for full and up-to-date information on how to borrow long-term money through bonds and how to add an

*equity kicker* (a conversion feature or warrants) when appropriate, more will not be written on the subject here. Because of their importance, however, some comment on bond ratings is advisable.

Many investors—the buyers of the bonds the company wants to sell—rely heavily on bond ratings to help them evaluate security, quality, and risk. Bond ratings not only have a significant effect on the cost of borrowing, they also serve to some extent as indications of a company's general investment quality, including the value of its common stock.

There are three major rating agencies: Moody's Investor Service, Inc., Standard & Poor's Corporation, and Fitch Investors' Service, Inc. All have been publishing ratings for at least 50 years, and all now charge for their ratings. The rating agencies have slightly different ways of differentiating among rated issues to identify those which are of the highest grade, those which lack the qualities of a desirable investment, and those which fall in between.

Rating agencies have maintained consistently that ratings cannot be deduced by formula, that the application of personal judgment to each company (for example, in the evaluation of management) is crucial; nevertheless, a few key ratios have been proved over time to give a good hint as to the rating likely to be achieved. The most important data are: (1) interest coverage, (2) debt/equity ratio, (3) absolute size of the company, (4) earnings volatility, and (5) relationship between funded debt and earnings. A company considering the issuance of rated indebtedness should be able to approximate the rating it is likely to receive by reviewing the aforementioned data on a reasonable basis, comparing the ratios derived objectively with those of other companies in its industry of similar size which have rated debt, and listening carefully to its external financial advisors.

The interest differential between debt rated at different levels varies from time to time—sometimes markedly—and over the last 50 years in the area above B each rating improvement has saved the borrower from one-fourth to a full percent. See Table F-5.

## GOVERNMENT FINANCING

No financial officer looking for short-, intermediate-, or long-term money in the United States at the present time should fail to search out programs of the federal government which may prove helpful. There are so many of these—probably hundreds— that it would be an encyclopedic effort simply to

TABLE F-5  1975 Yield Spreads on Rated Corporate Bonds, in basis points*

|  |  | Average | Maximum | Minimum |
|---|---|---|---|---|
| Utilities | Aa vs. Aaa | 25 | 35 | 10 |
|  | A vs. Aa | 45 | 100 | 25 |
| Industrials | A vs. Aa | 28 | 70 | 20 |

Additional Interest Paid over the Life of a 25-Year $50 Million Bond with no Sinking Fund

| Incremental interest, in basis points* | Aggregate cash cost, dollars |
|---|---|
| 10 | 1,250,000 |
| 25 | 3,125,000 |
| 50 | 6,250,000 |
| 75 | 9,375,000 |
| 100 | 12,500,000 |

*A *basis point* is 1/100th of 1%, or 0.01%; 50 basis points are 1/2%.

catalog them. Some programs provide guarantees, some include interest subsidy, some involve nonrecourse loans, and there are no doubt many other special attributes in one program or another.

**Federal Sources**  Specific examples include the following:

1. The Bureau of Indian Affairs makes nonrecourse, low-interest loans for individuals and organizations qualifying as natives or native groups.

2. The Economic Development Administration of the Department of Commerce makes business development and trade adjustment assistance loans to companies located in "redevelopment areas" or harmed by foreign competition.

3. The Farmers' Home Administration of the Department of Agriculture makes business and industrial loans available for nonagricultural projects in rural areas.

4. From time to time, the Federal Aviation Administration has offered government guarantees to support long-term loans to small air carriers for the purchase of aircraft.

5. The Small Business Administration makes available sums of money and loan guarantees (generally under $1 million).

6. The Agency for International Development of the Department of State offers guarantees for investment abroad.

Most financial intermediaries are familiar with a few of these programs, and a persistent borrower probably can uncover leads to many of them.

In addition to direct government involvement, there are government programs which facilitate borrowing in other ways, such as by providing government subsidized or supervised insurance programs.

Flood insurance is a domestic example, as are the export credit insurance programs of various countries (ECGD in Great Britain, Hermes in Germany, COFACE in France, MITI in Japan, and the Export-Import Bank in the United States).

**State and Local Sources**  The most important programs below the federal level are those handled under state regulations by counties, other subdivisions, or especially established authorities to facilitate the issuance of industrial revenue bonds to finance industrial development, including antipollution expenditures. While the formalities differ by geographic location and to some extent with the purpose of the funding, the arrangements in general permit a company to raise money on a tax-free basis, thereby saving from 2 to 4 percent as compared with its normal cost of raising such funds. The procedures are somewhat burdensome in some cases, and the costs in an issue below $1 million to $2 million might eat up the savings, but industrial revenue bonds always merit consideration. Assistance is available from underwriters, several of whom specialize in this type of financing.

**Surveillance**  There is no easy, guaranteed way of knowing without omission where one can borrow money most readily. This means that every financial officer must find some way to keep reasonably current on the subject, preferably personally, but at least through a staff. The only way this can be done is by reading a flow of reports on financing from a number of sources and maintaining personal contacts with financial intermediaries of various types and in several locations.

## OFF-BOOK FINANCING

This term refers to financing which does not appear on a balance sheet. For example, a relatively strong corporation may guarantee the indebtedness of a subsidiary or of a weaker company with which it has a business relationship. The debt appears on the balance sheet of the company for which the guarantee is issued, but the guarantee is not recorded on the balance sheet of the issuing corporation; it may or may not be mentioned in a footnote, depending upon the materiality of all guarantees or related contingent liabilities in the aggregate.

Such a guarantee may be desirable for the guaranteeing corporation, particularly if its alternatives are to lend the funds itself directly, to take a risky equity position in the smaller firm, or to forego a profitable business relationship. Guarantees may be in various forms, ranging from legally binding documents which explicitly state "we hereby irrevocably guarantee . . ." to implications of guarantee (sometimes called "monkey letters") in which the guaranteeing corporation advises the lender by letter that it is "aware" of a loan or proposed loan. The overriding need is to remember that each guarantee is a call upon financing, however indirect or improbable any actual cash outflow may seem, and that it therefore represents a diminution in the overall debt capacity of the guaranteeing corporation.

## INFORMATION SOURCES

The financial officer has many sources to tap in the continual search for the most current information about financing opportunities. These include the following:

1. The most important source of information on *short-term borrowing*, and possibly on loans of up to 10 years, is the company's banker. It is from this person, or from a more sophisticated banker to whom the company's own banker will introduce the financing officer, that the officer can learn (with one exception) what short-term financing alternatives are available. The exception is that a company for which commercial paper is a viable alternative will have to turn for practical advice on the subject to one of the half-dozen or so brokerage firms which are prepared to act as intermediaries in selling such paper to the investing public.

2. Useful, up-to-date information on *long-term borrowing* may be obtained from the corporate finance department of any major, money center bank, or from a similar department in the office of a major or regional broker. Sound companies with substantial needs may find it practical to talk directly with institutional investors, such as insurance companies.

3. Advice on the *placement of equity* is available from members of the underwriting fraternity.

4. In the area of *background reading*, excellent periodical and occasional papers are disseminated by leading banks and underwriters, usually gratis, and each financing officer should endeavor to receive a selection of these regularly. Examples include the following:

    *a. Bond and Money Market Comments*, A. G. Becker & Co., New York, N.Y., 10005.

    *b. Comments on Credit*, Salomon Brothers, New York, N.Y., 10005.

    *c. Financial Digest*, Manufacturers Hanover Trust, New York, N.Y., 10022.

    *d. Leveraged Leasing, a New Alternative in Financing*, 1973, First Chicago Leasing Corporation, Chicago.

    *e. Market Memo*, Investment Banking Division, First Company Bank, Atlanta, Ga., 30304.

    *f. Monetary and Fixed Income Policy*, Smith Barney, Harris Upham & Co., New York, N.Y., 10005.

    *g. Money Markets*, First Pennsylvania Corporation, Philadelphia, Pa., 19101.

    *h. The Rating of Corporate Debt Issues*, 1973, Irving Trust Company, New York.

    *i. Securities Industry Trends*, Economic Research Department, Securities Industry Association, 20 Broad Street, New York, N.Y., 10005.

    *j. Short Term Money Memo*, Commercial Credit Company, 300 St. Paul Place, Baltimore, Md., 21202.

    *k. Weekly Economic Package*, Economic Research Department, Chemical Bank, New York, N.Y., 10005.

*See also* ACCOUNTING, FINANCIAL; BUDGETING, CAPITAL; CREDIT MANAGEMENT; FINANCIAL AND INVESTMENT MANAGEMENT; FINANCIAL MANAGEMENT, CAPITAL STRUCTURE AND DIVIDEND POLICY; RISK ANALYSIS AND MANAGEMENT; SECURITY AND EXCHANGE COMMISSION (SEC); TAX MANAGEMENT, MANAGERIAL RESPONSIBILITY FOR FEDERAL INCOME TAX REPORTING.

### REFERENCES

Childs, John F.: *The Encyclopedia of Long-Term Financing and Capital Management*, Prentice-Hall, Inc., Englewood Cliffs, N.J., 1976.

Hutchinson, G. Scott: *The Streategy of Corporate Financing*, Presidents Publishing House, New York, 1971.

Lebowitz, Martin L.: *The Analysis of Intermediate Term Bond Financing*, Salomon Brothers, New York, 1976.

WILLARD ALLAN, *Alaska Airlines*

# Financial management, working capital control

*Working capital* may be defined as the current liquid resources required to operate a business comprising cash, short-term marketable securities, accounts receivables, and inventory. The evaluation of working capital is not meaningful unless viewed in conjunction with *current liabilities* which may be defined as financial obligations that must be paid within 1 year under normal operating conditions. The excess of current assets over current liabilities is the general definition of net working capital. The evaluation of net working capital is paramount in estimating the adequacy of a given level of working capital for the operation of a business.

**Broad Measures of Working Capital**  Over the years, two broad measures of corporate liquidity have been developed to evaluate the relationship between current assets and current liabilities. The first broad measure of liquidity and the one most universally used is the *current ratio*, the relationship of current assets to current liabilities. The general rule indicates that in a sound business enterprise current assets should be equal to at least twice the current liabilities. It should be remembered that this is a benchmark or a starting point for measuring liquidity and that the indiscriminate application of this rule to particular businesses may be tenuous at best. There are services such as Robert Morris Associates and Dun & Bradstreet, Inc., that prepare analyses of various industries and subgroups within industries which may be more useful for comparing and evaluating individual companies. Also, since this ratio is developed from the balance sheet, it measures liquidity only at a given point in time and does not measure the flow of funds, the quality of future earnings, or inflows of funds into the current asset portion of the balance sheet. Nevertheless, over longer periods of time, the deterioration or improvement of this broad measure has given a good indication of the financial health of the corporate sector of the economy.

A second measure of liquidity is referred to as the "quick ratio" or "acid test"; it measures a company's ability to survive under the most adverse conditions because in it no value is assigned to inventories. This ratio values cash, government securities, other readily marketable short-term securities, and accounts receivables against current liabilities. The general rule assumes that in a sound enterprise these assets equal or exceed the current liabilities, and so they would enable a company to meet its current liabilities without the sale of inventories. As with the current ratio, while corporations within given industries may have their own peculiarities, this rule tends to be a valid measure of liquidity over periods of time as seen in Table F-6.

The 1970s have been somewhat difficult for the corporate sector and, in this period, both ratios have gone below their minimum historical benchmarks of 2:1 for the current ratio and 1:1 for the quick ratio.

Table F-7 indicates the current ratios of those companies that compose the Dow Jones Industrial Average with the exception of American Telephone and Telegraph Company. This table shows that 22 of 29 companies in the average had a current ratio of 1.8 or better in 1975. However, the current ratios of the oil companies illustrate the peculiarities of a given industry. All three oil companies had current ratios significantly less than 2.0 although they enjoy an outstanding credit rating as indicated by the Moody's bond ratings.

**TABLE F-6   Current Assets and Liabilities of Nonfinancial Corporations**

| Year | Government securities* | Receivables* | Assets Inventories and other* | Total* | Current ratio | Quick ratio |
|------|------------------------|--------------|-------------------------------|--------|---------------|-------------|
| 1940 | 15.0 | 24.0 | 21.3 | 60.3 | 1.83 | 1.19 |
| 1945 | 42.8 | 25.9 | 28.7 | 97.4 | 2.13 | 1.50 |
| 1950 | 47.9 | 56.8 | 56.8 | 161.5 | 2.02 | 1.31 |
| 1955 | 58.1 | 88.9 | 77.0 | 224.0 | 1.80 | 1.21 |
| 1960 | 57.3 | 129.3 | 102.4 | 289.0 | 1.80 | 1.16 |
| 1965 | 57.2 | 134.1 | 144.7 | 336.0 | 1.88 | 1.06 |
| 1970 | 57.9 | 206.1 | 228.3 | 492.3 | 1.61 | .86 |
| 1975 | 87.5 | 298.3 | 345.8 | 731.6 | 1.60 | .75 |
| 6/1976 | 94.1 | 321.8 | 359.5 | 775.4 | 1.63 | .87 |

| Year | Payables* | Liabilities Federal tax liability* | Other* | Total* | Capital* | Ratio to NWC |
|------|-----------|------------------------------------|--------|--------|----------|--------------|
| 1940 | 23.2 | 2.5 | 7.1 | 32.8 | 27.5 | 1.29 |
| 1945 | 25.7 | 10.4 | 9.7 | 45.8 | 51.9 | 1.96 |
| 1950 | 48.3 | 16.7 | 14.9 | 79.8 | 81.6 | 1.48 |
| 1955 | 76.1 | 19.3 | 25.7 | 121.0 | 103.0 | 1.41 |
| 1960 | 106.8 | 13.5 | 40.1 | 160.4 | 128.6 | 1.40 |
| 1965 | 121.5 | 18.3 | 39.0 | 178.8 | 157.2 | 1.41 |
| 1970 | 211.3 | 10.0 | 83.6 | 304.9 | 187.4 | .97 |
| 1975 | 288.0 | 20.7 | 148.8 | 457.5 | 274.1 | .96 |
| 6/1976 | 293.8 | 22.0 | 160.1 | 475.9 | 299.5 | 1.01 |

*In billions of dollars.

**TABLE F-7** Current Ratios of Companies that Compose the Dow Jones Industrial Average*

| | Current ratio | | Bond rating† |
|---|---|---|---|
| | 1970 | 1975 | |
| Allied Chemical | 2.0 | 2.2 | A |
| Aluminun Company of America | 2.7 | 2.7 | A |
| American Brands | 2.1 | 2.2 | Aa |
| American Can Company | 2.1 | 2.0 | A |
| Bethlehem Steel | 1.7 | 1.9 | A |
| Chrysler Corporation | 1.4 | 1.3 | Baa |
| E. I. du Pont de Nemours & Co. | 3.6 | 2.0 | Aaa |
| Eastman Kodak Company | 2.4 | 2.4 | Est. Aaa |
| Esmark | 2.4 | 1.8 | A |
| Exxon | 1.5 | 1.5 | Aaa |
| General Electric | 1.3 | 1.4 | Aaa |
| General Foods | 2.0 | 1.9 | Aa |
| General Motors | 2.0 | 2.0 | Aaa |
| Goodyear | 2.0 | 1.8 | A |
| Inco | 2.5 | 2.1 | Aa |
| International Harvester | 2.2 | 2.1 | Baa |
| International Paper | 2.2 | 1.9 | Aa |
| Johns Manville | 2.8 | 1.9 | Aa |
| Minnesota Mining & Mfg. Co. | 2.5 | 2.6 | Aaa |
| Owens Illinois | 1.6 | 2.0 | A |
| Procter & Gamble | 2.5 | 2.4 | Aaa |
| Sears Roebuck and Co. | 1.6 | 1.6 | Aaa |
| Standard Oil of Ohio | 1.5 | 1.2 | Aaa |
| Texaco | 1.7 | 1.4 | Aaa |
| Union Carbide | 2.2 | 2.5 | Aa |
| United Tech. | 1.5 | 2.2 | A |
| U.S. Steel | 1.6 | 1.8 | Aa |
| Westinghouse Electric Corp. | 1.8 | 1.4 | A |
| F. W. Woolworth Co. | 1.8 | 2.1 | A |

*American Telephone and Telegraph Co. omitted.
†By Moody's Investor Service, Inc.

**Other Measures of Working Capital**  Other ratios that assist in determining the short-term liquidity of a company are:

1. A comparison of a company's net fixed assets to net worth will indicate how much equity is available for working capital. A high ratio indicates a smaller amount of equity in working capital.

2. A comparison of net sales to working capital indicates the turnover of, or efficient use of, working capital. Net sales to receivables and cost of sales to inventory ratios are a means of measuring the efficient use of, or turnover of, receivables and inventory.

3. The ratio of net sales to net worth gives an indication of adequacy of capitalization. A high ratio could indicate that a company is undercapitalized and too dependant upon creditors for financing. The ratio of debt to net worth is another means of determining whether a company has sufficient equity.

4. Cash flow ratios measure the relationship of the income statement to the balance sheet. Since current liabilities must be paid in cash, it is impor-

tant that a sufficient flow of cash is generated to meet these expenses. The most common expression of this measure is the ratio of current liabilities to the yearly cash flow. Another ratio which measures cash flow, in the same way as the quick ratio, is the relationship of cash and receivables to the year's cash expenditures.

**Determining Adequate Working Capital**  Working capital may be thought of as a circular flow of liquid assets required in the normal day-to-day operations from cash for the purchase of raw materials, to inventory to be sold for accounts receivables, which are paid in cash (Fig. F-2). Some factors that may influence the level of working capital required are:

1. Type of business the company is engaged in
2. Rate of inventory and/or receivable turnover
3. Terms of trade as they apply to the purchase of materials and the collection of receivables
4. Seasonal requirements
5. Time and cost in the manufacturing process
6. Impact of inflation upon the costs of production and maintaining inventory
7. Currency regulations and exchange fluctuations
8. Growth of the company

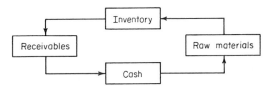

**Fig. F-2. Cash flow diagram.**

Some companies require larger working capital because of the nature of their business. The large retail chain stores have a need for greater working capital than do companies that sell only a service. The ability to turn over receivables and inventory reduces the amount of working capital required and enables a company to grow without increasing working capital. Measuring this ability has also become a standard way to evaluate management ability in many industries. In certain industries, set patterns of terms for payments of materials have emerged such as paying bills for materials on the 10th of the following month or invoicing in terms of 2 percent 10, net 30. Other industries may give terms of 45 or 90 days. A few industries have peak seasonal demands (Christmas sales) that cause a sharp increase in demand for working capital for relatively brief periods. In a few industries, among them distilling, inventories must be held for several years, which requires a heavy investment in working capital.

Inflation and currency regulations and fluctuations have caused a need for substantial increases in working capital because sales expressed in nominal dollars have increased sharply in relation to the growth in equity and retained earnings. Currency difficulties have reduced efficiency in carrying on multinational trade and have increased the needs in working capital for hedging currencies and ensuring the availability of various local currencies to pay for materials and services. The growth of a company's sales has been a common cause for the increase in the need for working capital as inventory, receivables, and payables expand to accommodate it.

**Monitoring Changes in Working Capital**   As business conditions change or as a company continues to grow, the requirements for working capital change materially. Two methods used for monitoring the changes in working capital are forecasts which analyze receipts and disbursements and the adjusted net income for a given period.

The forecast using estimates of expected cash receipts and disbursements is normally for short periods (a year or less) that take into consideration seasonal requirements. Such forecasts indicate the latest actual results for a particular period and give estimates for that stipulated forecasted period. This type of forecast lists, by major classification, those items that will produce cash during the period and those that must be paid for in cash. The excess of receipts over disbursements is added to the cash balance to arrive at a projected cash balance for the end of the forecasted period. If the disbursements are greater than the receipts, the difference is subtracted from the cash beginning balance to arrive at a balance for the end of the forecasted period. If this balance is negative, the need becomes evident for additional funds to maintain a given level of cash. Thus forecast of cash receipts and disbursements forces recognition of cash requirements, but it does not highlight the subtle changes that may take place in the buildup of inventory or receivables. Table F-8 indicates a format that may be used to estimate receipts and disbursements.

In order to identify increases or decreases in the current assets more accurately, a forecast using an adjusted net income method is made. Such a forecast is similar to a source and application of funds statement. The forecast is used to adjust a company's estimated income, its working capital accounts, depreciation, and other noncash charges to a cash basis. Table F-9 shows a format that may be used to estimate adjusted net income.

**TABLE F-8   Receipts and Disbursement Forecast**

|  | Comparable period actual | Period estimate |
|---|---|---|
| Cash receipts |  |  |
| Collections on receivables |  |  |
| Collections on notes |  |  |
| Dividend income |  |  |
| Sales of assets |  |  |
| Other |  |  |
| Total cash receipts |  |  |
| Cash disbursements |  |  |
| Operating expenses |  |  |
| Income taxes |  |  |
| Capital expenditures |  |  |
| Payroll |  |  |
| Advertising |  |  |
| Insurance |  |  |
| Repayment of debt |  |  |
| Interest expense |  |  |
| Dividends |  |  |
| Other |  |  |
| Total cash disbursements |  |  |
| Excess receipts over disbursements |  |  |
| Cash period beginning |  |  |
| Cash period ending |  |  |

**Need to Raise Working Capital**   From estimates of receipts and disbursements and from analysis of the source and application of funds, a pattern in the flow and the need, if any, for raising working capital will develop. If the need for increased working capital is of a temporary or seasonal nature, some

**TABLE F-9   Adjusted Net Income Forecast**

|  | Comparable periods actual | Period estimate |
|---|---|---|
| Sources of cash |  |  |
| Net profit |  |  |
| Income tax provision |  |  |
| Depreciation |  |  |
| Dividends |  |  |
| Other |  |  |
| Total cash provided |  |  |
| Uses of cash |  |  |
| Increase in accounts receivable |  |  |
| Increase in inventory |  |  |
| Increase in property and plant |  |  |
| Decrease in accounts payable |  |  |
| Income taxes paid |  |  |
| Total uses of cash |  |  |
| Excess cash provided (required) |  |  |
| Cash period beginning |  |  |
| Cash period ending |  |  |

method of short-term financing may be used. The specific methods of short-term financing developed by some industries have been standardized. Factoring, the selling of receivables, is a standard way of doing business in the textile industry; in another industry the sale of accounts receivable would be considered a sign of financial weakness. Use of bills of lading and warehouse receipts is a means of financing inventories that is common practice in certain businesses. The most universal means of securing short-term financing for periodic working capital needs is by unsecured commercial loans which should be a part of the company's overall banking activities. In order to secure credit, a company should state to its banker the amounts of credit needed, the duration of the need, and the means it will use to compensate the bank. The means for securing credit lines are normally compensating bank balances that represent a lower percentage of the credit line when not in use (10 percent) and of the amounts borrowed under the line (20 percent). At times a more formal contract for credit facilities is agreed to whereby a commitment fee or small percentage is paid ($\frac{1}{4}$ to $\frac{1}{2}$ percent) to ensure that the credit is available. In recent years more companies have used bank credit lines as a backup to the issuance of short-term commercial or industrial paper. A company sells its unsecured notes for short periods (1 to 9 months) in the money markets directly or through an investment banker. Many times market conditions are such that a company's interest expense is less when it issues commercial paper than when it borrows from a bank. The increase in the use of corporate short-term paper can be seen in the fourfold rise since 1960 in other liabilities in Table F-6 of which short-term commercial paper issued by corporations is a substantial part.

Monies required for longer periods should not be derived from short-term sources but should come from an increase in the equity of a corporation or the sale of longer-term securities that can be repaid over the life of a fixed asset through depreciation. The use of short-term money for longer-term purposes can cause a financial crisis for a corporation, threatening its growth or even its survival. The corporations that seem to remain healthy over long periods of time are those that protect their credit by maintaining adequate working capital for their operations and fund longer-term capital needs with more permanent funds.

*See also* ACCOUNTING, FINANCIAL; ACCOUNTING FOR MANAGERIAL CONTROL; BUDGETS AND BUDGET PREPARATION; CREDIT MANAGEMENT; FINANCIAL MANAGEMENT; FINANCIAL MANAGEMENT: SHORT-TERM, INTERMEDIATE, AND LONG-TERM FINANCING; FINANCIAL RATIO ANALYSIS; FINANCIAL STATEMENT ANALYSIS.

### REFERENCES

Bradley, Joseph F.: *Administrative Financial Management*, 3d ed., Holt, Rinehart and Winston, Inc., New York, 1974, part III.

Engler, George N.: *Business Financial Management*, Richard D. Irwin, Inc., Homewood, Ill., 1975, part V.

Meigs, Walter B., Charles E. Johnson, and A. N. Mosich: *Financial Accounting*, McGraw-Hill Book Company, New York, 1970, chaps. 9 to 11.

Van Horne, James C.: *Fundamentals of Financial Management*, 2d ed., Prentice-Hall, Inc., Englewood Cliffs, N.J., 1972, part II.

Weston, J. Fred, and Eugene F. Brigham: *Managerial Finance*, 4th ed., Holt, Rinehart and Winston, Inc., New York, 1972, part VI.

ROGER W. HILL, JR., *National Distillers and Chemical Corporation*

## Financial ratio analysis

Financial ratio analysis is a simple mathematical technique for appraising the financial condition of an organization. It utilizes figures that routinely appear in one or more of the various financial statements and in stock exchange reports. Once calculated, the ratios may be compared with (1) ratios derived from the firm's previous statements in order to detect trends and estimate improvement, stability, or erosion of the measured conditions, and (2) ratios from similar firms or industry averages, which are judged as desirable standards. Financial ratios for various industries are published by such firms as Dun & Bradstreet, Inc., and Robert Morris Associates and by the Securities and Exchange Commission and the Federal Trade Commision and are selectively available from credit agencies and trade associations.

Ratios typically measure financial strength and operating efficiency of the subject firm. The more common ratios are listed below according to an arbitrary set of classifications.

**Liquidity Ratios**   These indicate how well a firm could meet all its short-term obligations if called upon to do so. These ratios include

$$\text{Current ratio} = \frac{\text{current assets}}{\text{current liabilities}} \qquad (1)$$

The larger the ratio, the better able is the firm to pay its maturing debts out of current assets.

**413**

$$\text{Quick (acid test) ratio} = \frac{\text{current assets} - \text{inventory}}{\text{current liabilities}} \tag{2}$$

This is a more rigorous measure since it indicates the ability of the firm to pay its current debts without selling its inventory.

$$\text{Cash ratio} = \frac{\text{cash} + \text{marketable securities}}{\text{current liabilities}} \tag{3}$$

This ratio tells whether the firm could pay current obligations out of pocket immediately.

**Leverage and Coverage Ratios**  These provide: (1) a comparison between the owners' present investment in the firm and that of the creditors and (2) a measure of how well a firm can cover its fixed charges (mainly interest and debt reduction commitments) from its operating profits.

$$\text{Debt (or debt/equity) ratio} = \frac{\text{total debt}}{\text{stockholder's equity}} \tag{4}$$

The higher the ratio, the greater the leverage, i.e., the use of borrowed funds to finance the business. Total debt may also be compared with net worth or to assets.

Times interest earned
$$= \frac{\text{profit before taxes} + \text{interest charges}}{\text{interest charges}} \tag{5}$$

The higher the ratio, the more favorable the firm's structure will appear to creditors. Other ratios may make similar comparisons utilizing rent and lease expenses in the denominators.

**Profitability Ratios**  These provide measures of the relative value of a firm's profits as compared with various bases, particularly sales and investment.

$$\text{Gross profit margin} = \frac{\text{sales} - \text{cost of goods sold}}{\text{net sales}} \tag{6}$$

This illustrates operating margins only, without considering fixed charges.

$$\text{Net operating profit} = \frac{\text{net operating profit}}{\text{net sales}} \tag{7}$$

This considers profit only from the mainstream of the business.

$$\text{Net income on sales} = \frac{\text{net income}}{\text{net sales}} \tag{8}$$

This is the true "bottom line" profit figure paid after all expenses are paid, including income taxes.

Return on assets
$$= \frac{\text{net profit after taxes (net income)}}{\text{total tangible assets}} \tag{9}$$

This is the firm's financial earning power.

Return on investment
$$= \frac{\text{net profit after taxes (net income)}}{\text{net worth}} \tag{10}$$

This is the return on the owner's investment. It may also be calculated on the basis of long-term capital (long-term debt + stockholder's equity) or on common stockholder's equity.

Earnings per share [(EPS) of common stock]
$$= \frac{\text{income after preferred dividends}}{\text{number of common shares outstanding}} \tag{11}$$

This is the income earned (not necessarily paid in dividends) per share of common stock.

$$\text{Dividend yield} = \frac{\text{dividend paid per share per year}}{\text{average market price}} \tag{12}$$

This indicates the present average profitability of the firm's stock as an investment.

$$\text{Price-earnings ratio} = \frac{\text{average market price}}{\text{earnings per share}} \tag{13}$$

This indicates the number of times greater than a firm's EPS investors are presently willing to pay for a share of stock.

**Activity or Operating Efficiency Ratios**  These measure how effectively a firm manages the various resources available to it.

$$\text{Asset turnover ratio} = \frac{\text{net sales}}{\text{total tangible assets}} \tag{14}$$

The higher the ratio, the greater the trading activity and the greater efficiency of the assets. It may also be computed using fixed assets as a base.

$$\text{Cash turnover ratio} = \frac{\text{net sales}}{\text{cash} + \text{marketable securities}} \tag{15}$$

This measures the efficiency of cash usage.

$$\text{Inventory turnover} = \frac{\text{net sales}}{\text{inventory}} \tag{16}$$

This measures the efficiency of funds invested in materials and inventory and how often inventory is liquidated. Cost of goods sold may also be used as the numerator.

$$\text{Receivables turnover} = \frac{\text{net sales}}{\text{accounts receivable}} \quad (17)$$

This measures the average liquidity of capital invested in receivables and its efficiency.

$$\text{Collection period} = \frac{360 \text{ days}}{\text{receivables turnover}} \quad (18)$$

This shows average age of receivables or number of days that sales are carried before collection.

**Interpretation** Financial ratios are numerical indicators only and should be subjected to rigorous analysis before conclusions about a firm's resources and activities are drawn. Many other aspects should be studied, especially the notes that accompany the public financial statements as required by the Securities and Exchange Commission.

*See also* ACCOUNTING, FINANCIAL; AUDITING, FINANCIAL; FINANCIAL STATEMENT ANALYSIS.

### REFERENCES

Davidson, Sidney, James S. Schindler, and Roman L. Weil: *Accounting: The Language of Business,* Thomas Horton and Daughters, Inc., Glen Ridge, N.J., 1974.

Van Horne, James C.: *Fundamentals of Financial Management,* 2d ed., Prentice-Hall, Inc., Englewood Cliffs, N.J., 1974.

Weston, J. Fred, and Eugene F. Brigham: *Managerial Finance,* 4th ed., Holt, Rinehart and Winston, Inc., New York, 1972.

STAFF/BITTEL

# Financial statement analysis

Financial statement analysis, like other tools of financial analysis, is based on a logical relationship between underlying business operations and the accounting or financial representation of those activities. Analysis of the cash flow cycle, for example, demonstrates how various business activities, such as the purchase of raw materials, production and manufacturing activity, the sale of goods on credit, and the collection of accounts receivable, all are reflected in corresponding changes in the financial statements. In a like manner, the operations of a business firm generally follow the same logic in that the underlying production, sales, personnel, and the other operations of the firm are reflected in their financial consequences. Five types of ratios tend to measure these consequences: activity, cost structure, leverage, liquidity, and profitability.

**Logic of Financial Analysis** The logical relation between the financial ratios is shown in Fig. F-3.

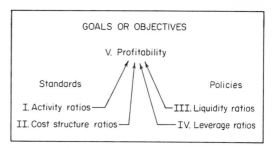

Fig. F-3. Relationships between financial ratios.

The top goal or objective which represents the keystone in the arch of planning and control is overall profitability (in its broadest sense). This is a result of two broad sets of forces.

1. *Standards.* The first set represents standards of performance (or operating) ratios. The activity ratios measure how effectively the firm is managing its investments in assets. The cost-structure ratios measure how effectively the firm is managing the control of its costs.

2. *Policies.* Leverage ratios measure the extent to which the firm finances its investments and operations by the use of debt. Liquidity ratios measure the balance in the firm's cash flows.

Profitability ratios measure the overall effectiveness of both the operations and policies of the firm. The liquidity and leverage ratios reflect management policies. Up to a point, decreasing liquidity and increasing leverage will increase the profitability of the firm. But if carried too far, leverage and illiquidity can lead to losses and insolvency of the firm. Therefore, each individual ratio is first explained in this entry, and then a broad view of the use of ratios in the effective management and valuation of the firm is discussed.

## COMPUTATION PROCEDURES

For each financial ratio, (1) the method of measurement or calculation is described, (2) the nature of the information conveyed by the financial ratio is explained, and (3) the consequences of ratios that depart from industry averages are discussed.

To provide a concrete illustration of the calculations, the Jones Company is assumed to have been in operation for several years and to have reached a level of sales of $4 million per year. The financial statements of a firm are strongly influenced by its industry classification and by its size. In this initial presentation, the influences of size on the financial characteristics of a firm are emphasized. The ratios calculated for the Jones Company are based on the data in Table F-10 which presents the balance sheet data as of December 31, 1977, and the income statement for the year ending December 31, 1977.

The balance sheet composition and the income statement relationships presented in Table F-10 reflect the characteristic or "normal" pattern for a firm whose sales are in the $1 to $5 million range. (The sources utilized were the Federal Trade Commis-

sion—Securities and Exchange Commission, *Quarterly Financial Report for Manufacturing Companies, U.S. Government Printing Office; Robert Morris Associates, Annual Statement Studies,* Philadelphia.)

**Activity Ratios** These measure how effectively the firm is managing the investment in its assets. The underlying logic is that to manufacture goods a firm necessarily uses plant and machinery, represented by fixed assets. The firm must also have some inventories in advance of making sales. Usually there is some lag between making sales and the actual receipt of cash, resulting in accounts receivable for some period of time. Thus the investments of business firms and assets are all required by the sales activity of the firm, and so all activity ratios

**TABLE F-10   Jones Company Financial Data**

Balance Sheet, Dec. 31, 1977

| ASSETS | Amount | Percent | CLAIMS ON ASSETS | | Amount | Percent |
|---|---|---|---|---|---|---|
| Cash | $200,000 | 10 | Accounts payable | | $300,000 | 15 |
| Receivables, net | 500,000 | 25 | Notes payable 8% | | 200,000 | 10 |
| Inventories | 500,000 | 25 | Accruals | | 80,000 | 4 |
| | | | Provisions for federal income taxes | | 20,000 | 1 |
| TOTAL CURRENT ASSETS | $1,200,000 | 60 | TOTAL CURRENT LIABILITIES | | $600,000 | 30 |
| Gross plant and equipment .. 1,500,000 | | | Long-term debt at 8% | $300,000 | | 15 |
| Less reserve for depreciation ... 700,000 | | | Total debt | | 900,000 | |
| Net plant and equipment | 800,000 | 40 | Common stock | 300,000 | | |
| TOTAL ASSETS | $2,000,000 | 100 | Retained earnings | 800,000 | | |
| | | | Net worth | | $1,100,000 | 55 |
| | | | TOTAL CLAIMS ON ASSETS | | $2,000,000 | 100 |

Income Statement, for Year Ending Dec. 31, 1977

| | | Amount | Percent |
|---|---|---|---|
| Net sales | | $4,000,000 | 100 |
| Cost of sales excluding depreciation | | 2,800,000 | 70 |
| Gross profit | | $1,200,000 | 30 |
| Less operating expenses: | | | |
| Selling and delivery expense | $400,000 | | 10 |
| Officer's salaries | 120,000 | | 3 |
| Other general and administrative expenses | 200,000 | | 5 |
| Lease rentals | 40,000 | | 1 |
| Total operating expenses excluding depreciation | | $760,000 | |
| Net operating profit excluding depreciation | | 440,000 | |
| Depreciation (8% of gross plant and equipment) | | 120,000 | 3 |
| Net operating income | | $320,000 | 10 |
| Add: Other income | | | 1 |
| Royalties | | 40,000 | 9 |
| Earnings before interest and taxes | | $360,000 | |
| Less: | | | |
| Interest on notes payable | $16,000 | | |
| Interest on long-term debt | 24,000 | 40,000 | 1 |
| Earnings before income tax | | 320,000 | 8 |
| Tax at 40% | | 128,000 | |
| Net income available to stockholders | | $192,000 | 4.8 |

measure a relationship to sales. The amount of sales represents the basic forecasting, or causal variable, in financial ratio analysis, budgeting, and financial forecasting.

*Inventory Turnover.* The inventory turnover is measured by dividing inventories into sales:

$$\text{Inventory turnover} = \frac{\text{sales}}{\text{inventory}}$$
$$= \frac{\$4,000,000}{\$500,000} = 8 \text{ times}$$

Two technicalities are involved in making this calculation. One is that while sales are made over some period of time such as a year, the inventory figure is a balance sheet item determined at the balance sheet date. Theoretically, if the turnover is calculated on an annual basis, the inventory figure for each day of the year would be averaged and this average figure would be divided into sales for the year. This is unnecessarily cumbersome, so a number of alternatives are available. If inventories do not fluctuate greatly during the year, using the end-of-year inventory figure is accurate. If there is an upward trend in both sales and inventory each year, this trend will be reflected in both sales and inventories and can be approximated by averaging the beginning-of-year inventory with the end-of-year figure. If there is a strong seasonal pattern within the year in the firm's inventories, it will be desirable to calculate an inventory turnover at the time of the peak level of inventory and an inventory turnover at the time of the lowest level of inventory, then to calculate an average between the two for analysis.

A second technicality is that inventories are measured at cost. Logically, inventories at cost should be related to the cost of goods sold rather than to sales, but the published financial statements of many firms do not divulge the cost of goods sold. Therefore, the compilations of financial ratio statistics (such as those by Dun & Bradstreet) measure the inventory turnover on the basis of sales. Since one of the methods of evaluating the performance of an individual firm is to compare it with data for its industry, a firm's ratio should be calculated in such a way as to make possible the desired comparison.

If inventory turnover is low, there may be at least two possible causes, both undesirable. One is that inventories are excessive, indicating that the firm is inefficient in inventory control. This will have a depressing effect on profitability. If inventory turnover is low, the risk is higher that some obsolete or otherwise unsaleable inventories continue to be carried. If some inventories are obsolete, the current

asset figure, which includes inventories and which is an overall indicator of liquidity, would be overstated.

On the other hand, if the sales inventory ratio is unusually high in relationship to the average for the industry, the firm may be losing sales because of lack of adequate inventory stocks on hand. Undesirable consequences would include reduced sales and underutilization of fixed assets.

*Average Collection Period.* The accounts receivable turnover is expressed as an average collection period because this number can be compared with the customary terms of sales in the industry. The degree of divergence is a measure of a firm's credit and collection performance. For example, if the general terms of credit in the industry are sales on net 30 days credit and a firm has an average collection period of 60 days, then the accounts of the firm were on the average 1 month overdue.

To measure the average collection period, one first determines credit sales per day by dividing total credit sales by 360. Then the resulting figure is divided into accounts receivable. The result is the average collection period.

$$\text{Sales per day} = \frac{\$4,000,000}{360} = \$11,111$$

$$\text{Average collection period} = \frac{\text{receivables}}{\text{sales per day}}$$
$$= \frac{\$500,000}{\$11,111} = 45 \text{ days}$$

An alternative convenient method of calculation is to find the accounts receivable turnover and divide this into 360 to determine the average collection period.

$$\text{Receivables turnover} = \frac{\text{sales}}{\text{accounts receivables}}$$
$$= \frac{\$4,000,000}{\$500,000} = 8 \text{ times}$$

$$\text{Average collection period} = \frac{360}{\text{receivables turnover}}$$
$$= \frac{360}{8} = 45 \text{ days}$$

The main basis for comparison, of course, is the general credit terms of the industry. An average collection period in substantial excess of the industry average term or duration of credit suggests the possibility that unsound credit policies exist or that the firm is experiencing serious collection problems with at least some of its accounts. An average collection period in excess of the industry average will be associated with a low receivables turnover. This may be an indicator of two potentially unfavorable developments. One is that bad debt writeoffs may occur; the other is that if some of the receivables are in fact uncollectible, the balance sheet value of the accounts receivable is overstated. Therefore, the firm may not be as liquid as the total current assets figure would ostensibly indicate.

*Fixed Asset Turnover.* The fixed asset turnover is measured by dividing the total net value of plant and equipment into sales.

$$\text{Fixed asset turnover} = \frac{\text{sales}}{\text{net fixed assets}}$$
$$= \frac{\$4,000,000}{\$800,000} = 5.0 \text{ times}$$

Decisions on investment of individual assets are made by the use of capital budgeting techniques. As a rough overall measure of the soundness of capital budgeting decisions, the fixed asset turnover ratio compared with the industry average is a useful guide. One other important consideration needs to be taken into account. To the extent that a firm leases its plant or equipment, a substantial portion of its fixed assets will not show up on the balance sheet. Therefore, without a consideration of lease rentals in conjunction with other financial ratios, the fixed asset turnover of the firm cannot properly be evaluated. One method of taking into account the role of leases is to capitalize lease rentals and add the resulting figure to the firm's fixed assets and to its debt.

*Total Asset Turnover.* The total asset turnover ratio obviously reflects the resultant of all the preceding ratios.

$$\text{Total assets turnover} = \frac{\text{sales}}{\text{total assets}}$$
$$= \frac{\$4,000,000}{\$2,000,000} = 2 \text{ times}$$

The total asset turnover will be greatly influenced by both the size of the firm and the nature of the industry. The largest firms tend to be found predominantly in capital-intensive industries—industries that require heavy investments in plant and machinery to make their products. Examples of such industries are petroleum, chemicals, automobiles, and steel.

Small firms predominate in the least capital-intensive industries, so the ratios for small firms are likely to reflect their smaller use of fixed assets and their greater use of leased assets. Small firms would be expected to have a total asset turnover of 2 times

or more. Large firms are more likely to have total asset turnovers of between 1 and 1½ times.

**Cost-Structure Ratios** These ratios are the most critical of all financial ratios. Costs represent a continuous flow which, if out of control, can quickly lead to an erosion of profitability and result in bankruptcy for the firm. However, costs are also amenable to corrective actions by the firm's managers. While relatively little information is provided on the structure of the income statement, analysis of the structure of costs is highly important in internal operations. (Information on cost structures for a relatively large number of industries is provided in the *Annual Statement Studies* of Robert Morris Associates.) The four cost ratios presented are discussed as a group because their logic is intertwined:

*Gross profit margin* = sales less cost of sales (excluding depreciation and rentals) to sales
$$= \frac{\$4,000,000 - 2,800,000}{\$4,000,000} = 30 \%$$

*Selling expense ratio* = selling expenses to sales
$$= \frac{\$400,000}{\$4,000,000} = 10\%$$

*General & administration ratio*
= general and administration expenses to sales
$$= \frac{\$320,000}{\$4,000,000} = 8\%$$

*Depreciation plus lease rentals ratio*
= depreciation plus lease rentals to sales
$$= \frac{\$120,000 + 40,000}{\$4,000,000} = 4\%$$

The first of the four cost-structure ratios is the gross profit margin. Since this figure is obtained by deducting the cost of sales from the total sales figure of the firm, it indicates the margin available for covering all the other functions that have to be performed to achieve the final sale of the goods. For most lines of business the gross profit margin must be in the area of 30 percent, as is indicated for the Jones Company, because the other functions whose costs are not included in the cost of sales remain to be performed. Obviously, the required gross profit margin figures will vary widely among industries. For firms too small to have their own selling operations and who must pay 15 to 25 percent for the use of sales representatives of sales agents, the gross profits are to remain. For those particular industries in which research and development as well as considerable selling effort have to be performed, the gross profit margin may need to be as high as 50 percent.

The selling and delivery expense ratio is likely to be about 10 percent for most lines of business. If the firm has its own sales organization and the volume is high, and if technical engineering expenses involved in sales are relatively modest, the selling expense ratio may be somewhat less than 10 percent.

The general and administrative expense ratio measures the cost of the overall corporate level functions to be performed in the firm. It includes such items as officers' salaries, travel, and telephone. The control of general and administrative expenses is important because it involves a degree of self-regulation by the officers of the firm. Hence, it is a critical ratio to outsiders seeking to appraise the firm's performance.

All depreciation expenses have been separated from the previous income statement items. Depreciation plus lease rentals represents major elements of expense involved in the utilization of the firm's fixed assets. If most fixed assets have long lives, the ratio of depreciation to gross plant and equipment and to sales will be somewhat lower. The rentals have been added to the depreciation figure to account both for methods of obtaining the use and for utilization of assets.

In the Jones Company, for example, the figures for selling expenses, general administrative expense, and depreciation plus lease rentals total 22 percent. Thus, of the 30 percent gross profit margin, 8 percent remains as the before-tax profit margin.

**Leverage Ratios** Leverage and liquidity policies are influenced by the extent to which the firm has utilized its assets and to which it has managed the control of its costs. To some degree, the liquidity and leverage ratios are interrelated. For example, if a firm uses a considerable amount of current debt, this will decrease the current ratio, but it will also increase the total debt unless long-term debt is offset to an equal degree. This also illustrates the fact that liquidity ratios are not the same as leverage ratios. If a firm substitutes long-term debt for short-term debt, its current ratio will be increased; but if it has an excessive amount of long-term debt, it may face insolvency problems because of large fixed-interest requirements.

Short-term creditors of the firm are most concerned with liquidity ratios because they provide the key to the firm's ability to meet its maturing short-term obligations. Longer-term creditors of the firm are more concerned about the firm's total debt and the performance of the activity and cost-structure ratios which will greatly influence the firm's long-term profitability—the ultimate source of paying its long-term obligations.

Fundamentally, leverage ratios measure the relative degree to which the owners versus the creditors have financed the firm's investments. The use of debt enables owners to utilize leverage in the sense that the firm is able to obtain the use of assets in excess of the amount that could be purchased by the owners' funds. This leverage of controlling a larger quantity of assets also results in amplifying the returns to the owners. For example, if assets earn 10 percent and debt costs 6 percent, the 4 percent differential benefits the owners of the firm. However, if the cost of debt remains 6 percent and the earnings on total assets fall to 4 percent, the returns to the owners of the firm will be less than 4 percent. Thus, when assets earn more than the cost of debt, leverage is favorable to the owners, and conversely.

Creditors also have a direct interest in leverage ratios because the percent of total assets financed by the owners represents the margin of safety by which the value of total assets can decline on liquidation and still meet the obligations to creditors. The Jones Company balance sheet shows that the owners' funds have financed 55 percent of total assets. Therefore, on liquidation, total assets could decline in value by 55 percent and still meet all obligations to creditors. Creditors are also interested in the ability of the firm to meet its fixed obligations, which explains the use of two leverage ratios: (1) a leverage ratio based on balance sheet relations alone and (2) the fixed-charge coverage ratio.

*Leverage Ratio.* The debt ratio, or the degree of leverage employed by the firm, is the ratio of total debt to total assets. It measures the percent of the firm's total investment that has been provided by creditors.

$$\text{Leverage ratio} = \frac{\text{total debt}}{\text{total assets}} = \frac{\$900,000}{\$2,000,000} = 45\%$$

A broad rule of thumb is that the owners should have at least as much funds in the business as the creditors. The Jones Company is approaching this limit. Creditors obviously prefer lower debt ratios since they provide a greater cushion against losses in the event of liquidation. Owners may seek high leverage in order to control more assets and to magnify earnings. Extremely high debt ratios may result in irresponsible "shoestring" operations by the owners. Thus, while owners may seek to have very high debt ratios, the financial market may be unwilling to provide debt beyond a safe limit.

*Fixed-Charge Coverage.* The fixed-charge coverage ratio is calculated by dividing the income available for meeting fixed charges by the total fixed charges. The total fixed charges include interest payments, lease payments, and before-tax sinking-fund payments. It is assumed that the sinking-fund requirement on the Jones Company long-term debt is $15,000 per year.

A *sinking fund* is a requirement of a bond issue; it consists of an annual amount set aside in connection with the repayment of the bond. Sinking-fund payments represent repayment of a debt and therefore are not deductible for income tax purposes. Therefore, the firm must earn enough profit before taxes to be able to pay its taxes and then be able to meet the sinking-fund requirements with the remainder. With a tax rate of 40 percent, $25,000 must be earned to meet the sinking-fund requirement of $15,000:

Before-tax income required for sinking-fund

$$\text{payment} = \frac{\text{sinking-fund payment}}{1.0 - \text{tax rate}}$$
$$= \frac{\$15,000}{1.0 - 0.4} = \frac{\$15,000}{0.6} = \$35,000$$

The numerator in the ratio represents earnings before interest and taxes plus fixed charges such as lease rentals. The before-tax sinking-fund requirement which appears in the denominator is not added back to earnings before interest and taxes in the numerator.

Fixed-charge coverage

$$= \frac{\text{income available for meeting fixed charges}}{\text{fixed charges}}$$
$$= \frac{\text{EBIT} + \text{rentals}}{\text{interest} + \text{rental} + (\text{before-tax sinking-fund payment})}$$
$$= \frac{\$360,000 + \$40,000}{\$40,000 + \$40,000 + \$25,000}$$
$$= \frac{\$400,000}{\$105,000} = 3.8 \text{ times}$$

A broad rule of thumb of fixed-charge coverage for a manufacturing company is that it should range from 4 to 7 times. This allows for some decline in gross income before financial embarrassment is encountered from inability to meet fixed charges.

**Liquidity Ratios** These measure the firm's ability to meet its maturing obligations. A large number of liquidity ratios could be employed, but most aspects of liquidity are conveyed by two ratios, the current and the quick ratios.

*Current Ratio.* This ratio is current assets divided by current liabilities:

$$\text{Current ratio} = \frac{\text{current assets}}{\text{current liabilities}}$$
$$= \frac{\$1,200,000}{\$600,000} = 2.0 \text{ times}$$

A widely employed "bankers" rule of thumb is that the current ratio should be at least 2. This provides for a shrinkage in the value of the current assets by 50 percent before the firm is unable to meet its maturing short-term obligations. Such a rule of thumb, however, should not be used inflexibly—it is more of a checkpoint. Wide departures from the appropriate norm of a financial ratio are a signal for further investigation by the analyst.

*Quick Ratio.* In calculation of the quick ratio, inventories are deducted from current assets and the remainder is divided by current liabilities. The logic of this calculation is that inventories are likely to be the least liquid of a firm's current assets in that the loss ratio is likely to be higher on inventories if forced liquidation is required.

$$\text{Quick ratio} = \frac{\text{current assets} - \text{inventories}}{\text{current liabilities}}$$
$$= \frac{\$700,000}{\$600,000} = 1.2 \text{ times}$$

A widely used rule of thumb for the quick ratio is 1. This implies that inventories are normally about half of current assets, and a comparison between the norm of 1 and the actual quick ratio provides a guide for further judgment.

**Profitability Ratios** These ratios reflect the results of the preceding four sets of ratios. They measure the joint effects of the extent to which the firm has met its standards with regard to activity and cost structure performance, balanced against the policies the firm selects with regard to liquidity and leverage ratios. These four sets of ratios are interrelated, since if the firm fails to meet its objectives with regard to asset turnover and cost control, the levels it had set as policies for liquidity and leverage may be inappropriate at the altered levels of activity and costs. At least three profitability measures should be utilized because of variability in accounting measures of revenues and costs as well as in the measurement of balance sheet values: profit margin on sales, return on investment, and return on net worth.

*Profit Margin on Sales.* The profit margin on sales is net income after taxes available to the owners of the firm divided by total sales. It is shown in Table F-10 as the last item in the income statement presented in both absolute and percentage terms.

The profit margin on sales measures the percent by which the selling price of the firm's products could decline before the firm suffers losses:

$$\text{Profit margin on sales} = \frac{\text{net income}}{\text{sales}}$$

$$= \frac{\$192,000}{\$4,000,000} = 4.8\%$$

*Return on Investment.* The return on investment is measured by adding back interest to net income after taxes and dividing by total assets. It is a measure of the after-tax profitability with which the firm's total resources have been employed.

$$\text{Return on investment} = \frac{\text{net income} + \text{interest}}{\text{total assets}}$$

$$= \frac{\$192,000 + \$40,000}{\$2,000,000} = 11.6\%$$

*Return on Net Worth.* The return on net worth measures the overall results of operations from the owners' standpoint:

$$\text{Return on net worth} = \frac{\text{net income}}{\text{net worth}}$$

$$= \frac{\$192,000}{\$1,100,000} = 17.4\%$$

The return on net worth reflects both the profitability with which total investment or total assets have been employed and the effectiveness with which the firm has utilized leverage. Since leasing assets involves the simultaneous use of assets and the payment for them through lease payments, the net result of the use of leverage through leasing activity is also reflected in return on net worth. In analyzing two firms, one of which leases a substantial proportion of its fixed assets while the other does not, comparisons of profitability will require either the use of the measurement of return on net worth or the capitalization of lease rentals to include them both in total assets and in debt.

## EVALUATION OF FINANCIAL RATIOS

Two broad measures for the evaluation of the ratios for individual companies are used. One is to compare them with industry composites; a second is to analyze historical trends.

**Industry Composites** A comparison of individual ratios with industry composites, as illustrated in the previous section, is useful as a starting point. It is not determinate, however. The product charac-

teristics of the individual firm may differ somewhat from those of the industry as a whole. In addition, the firm may follow specific policies which make its situation somewhat different from that of the industry. An important value of comparing the individual firm with the industry, however, is that if differences are observed, they form a basis for raising the significant analytical questions. Why are the ratios different? What distinct and different policies are being followed? What is the basis for these different policies? Under what economic conditions would these policies be particularly advantageous? Under what economic and financial circumstances would different policies of the firm be undesirable or unfavorable? These are the kinds of questions that can be raised by a comparison of the individual firm's ratios with those of industry composites.

**Analysis of Historical Trends** The use of the industry composites for historical analysis may be illustrated with reference to the Jones Company. For each of the five categories of ratios described, there is set out graphically in Fig. F-4 the pattern of composite ratios for the industry. These are the solid lines drawn in Fig. F-4, which charts 11 of the 15 ratios. To illustrate the idea in connection with planning, the years 1973 to 1976 are shown. The ratios are given slight time trends to avoid the implication that the industry ratios would not change. Starting with the ratios for the Jones Company in 1973, aspects of the use of industry composites can be seen by considering the effects of management performance on the ratios.

Suppose, for example, that the average collection period for the Jones Company went up sharply owing to the lengthening of credit terms or to slow collections in 1974, as illustrated in panel a, Fig. F-4. The inventory turnover shown in panel b would not be affected, but the total asset turnover would decline. With the excessive investment in receivables, the gross profit margin would probably decline, as shown in panel c of Fig. F-4. Excessive receivables are likely to result in a higher bad-debt ratio and possibly increased office personnel expenses in the effort to return collections to normal. Thus, the general and administrative expense ratio, panel d, might also rise.

If the excessive receivables were financed by current debt, the current ratio, panel e, would also decline, even if receivables and current debt increased by the same amount. To illustrate this point, assume that the current ratio was 2:1 to start. If the same amount were added (for example, 1) to both the numerator and the denominator, the ratio

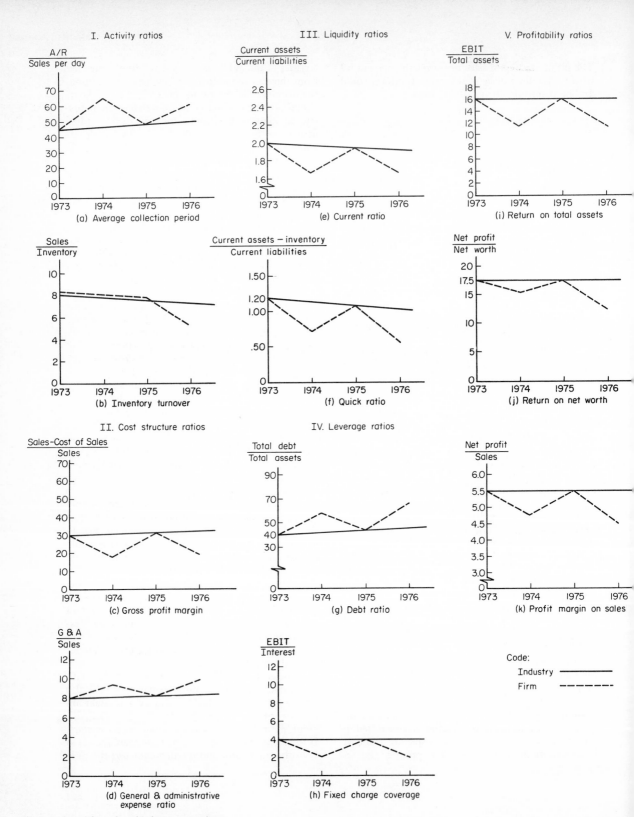

**Fig. F-4. Financial trends and industry comparisons.**

would decline to 1.5:1. The quick ratio, panel f, would also decline for similar reasons. The total debt–total assets ratio, panel g, would increase because current debt would have increased without a corresponding increase in equity. Furthermore, if the gross profit margin, panel c, has decreased and the amount of debt (and therefore the amount of interest) have increased, it is likely that the times-interest-earned ratio (h) will also decline. With the lower profit margins, the return on total assets (i) will also decline, and in addition the ratio of net profits to sales (k) will decline. Whether the return on net worth (j) declines depends upon the influence of the two opposing pressures. If profit margins decrease, it will tend to reduce the return on net worth (j). On the other hand, if the firm is earning more on total assets than after-tax cost of debt, the increased leverage the firm is utilizing may increase the return on net worth. This analysis assumes a slight decline in the net-worth-to-net-profit ratio.

In Fig. F-4 it is assumed that collections return to normal by 1975. If so, all the firm's ratios return to coincide with industry ratios. Thus, the charts illustrate graphically how unsound management policies in a single area can be reflected throughout many other financial ratios. In Fig. F-4 a substantial increase in the collection period, for example, was reflected in 9 of the 10 other ratios illustrated.

In a similar fashion, the impact of excessive inventories can be demonstrated. If this occured in 1976, the impact of a decline in inventory turnover would be even more pervasive than that of excessive receivables. Indeed, attempts to sell obsolete inventory might lead to dissatisfied customers and make collection of receivables even more difficult. As a consequence, the average collection period might rise. Warehousing costs of holding the larger inventories and other additional expenses would cause the gross profit margin to decline. Also, the general administrative expense ratio, panel d, would rise as the average collection period, panel a, rose for the reasons indicated previously. In addition, insurance costs of holding larger inventories and expenses for additional warehouse and supervisory personnel would cause the general and administrative expense ratio, panel d, to increase. The excessive inventories are likely to be financed in part with increased accounts payable. To the extent that the current debt increases, the current ratio, panel e, would decline. The quick ratio, panel f, would decline even further than the current ratio because inventories are subtracted from current assets to obtain the numerator for calculating the quick ratio. Furthermore, since one or more forms of current debt have

increased, the debt ratio, panel g, would rise. Hence, the fixed-charge coverage ratio, panel h, would decline. As in the analysis of the impact of excessive receivables, the consequences of inadequate control of inventories would result in a decline in all the profitability ratios, panels i to k.

Comparisons with industry composites need not be determinative. Since there may be valid reasons for the financial ratios of a firm to depart from those of its industry, such divergences will not necessarily indicate a pathological condition in the firm. However, in such an instance, greater emphasis would be placed on the time trend of the individual firm's ratios. If over time the ratios are deteriorating independent of their relationship to the industry composites, the need for analysis and inquiry is increased.

## FINANCIAL MARKET TESTS

Profitability may be an incomplete measure of performance. The financial markets may capitalize the earnings stream of companies differently when their capital structures differ. Different leverage and liquidity policies may result in different capitalization ratios.

Related to the measures of profitability discussed in the preceding sections are four financial market tests which are often employed. These are: (1) growth in earnings per share, (2) growth in market price per share, (3) the price-earnings ratio, and (4) the ratio of market to book value.

Any growth figure, of course, is greatly influenced by the choice of base period. From the early 1950s to 1965, earnings per share (EPS) for any stock index grew at about the same rate as the economy as a whole, 6 to 8 percent per annum. The growth in the market price per share, however, was at a somewhat higher rate, in the range of 8 to 12 percent per annum. This higher growth rate in market price per share for any group of companies reflects a rise in the price-earnings ratio on common stocks since the early 1950s. For a long period, the normal price-earnings ratio was about 10 times; this was its level in the 1950s. However, by the middle 1950s the standard price-earnings ratio moved up to about 14 times. From the late 1950s to 1965, price-earnings ratios fluctuated in the range of 18 to 20.

Finally, there is the consideration of the ratio between the market price of stocks and their book values. Since book values reflect historical costs and earnings retention, they reflect in part the timing of asset purchases and earnings-retention policies. Although the ratios of market to book values fluctuate among firms, a well-managed firm should expect a market value from 1½ to 2 times its book value per share.

For a growth firm, the performance measures would be higher. The growth in earnings per share could be expected to be over 10 percent per annum. The growth in market price per share might be 15 percent or more per annum. The price-earnings ratio would be 25 to 30 times or better. Finally, the ratio of market to book value for growth companies reaches as high as 3 times or more. These ratios for growth companies represent the upper ranges of financial market tests by which management may gauge the performance of its own company.

## MARKET POSITION TESTS

Much can be learned from an analysis of the firm's position in its own industry—market position tests. The relevant measures are: (1) trends in share of market, (2) trends in quality of product, (3) productivity trends, (4) cost reduction trends, and (5) trends in relative selling price.

One of the performance measures frequently employed is the firm's share of its industry. The firm's industry reveals what the market potential for the firm may be. How well the firm exploits that opportunity is measured by its share of its total industry. Trends in the firm's share of its industry represent a significant measure of performance in comparison with its competitors.

The other market position tests help determine the firm's share of its industry. One of the important factors is the firm's reputation for leadership in quality and performance of its products. For the producer of durable goods, reliability of performance and the availability of service are particularly important.

Productivity measures the efficiency with which the firm utilizes labor and capital inputs. Productivity measures are output per unit of labor input, output per unit of capital input, and output per unit of total inputs. Over a long period of years, productivity in the American economy as a whole increased over 3½ percent per annum. Although variation among individual industries occurs, a firm should aim at an increase in productivity of at least 3½ to 4 percent per annum if it is to compare favorably with the economy as a whole.

Related to productivity performance is cost reduction. Unit costs reflect the prices paid for labor and capital as well as their productivity. Characteristically, as an industry or a product line matures, many cost reductions are achieved. Hence, if a firm is to maintain its position in an industry or product line, cost reduction is necessary.

As an industry matures, the rise of new and increased competition can be expected to put increased pressure on prices. Thus, cost reduction is related to selling price. The performance of a product line or company is likely to be greatly influenced by the ability to reduce prices over time.

These five factors are a part of and reflect a firm's market position over time. They are significant indicators, or barometers, of what is likely to show up in the more quantitatively oriented ratios discussed in the preceding sections.

## MEASURE OF STRATEGIC PERFORMANCE

Related to the measures of the firm's market position are measures of the strategic performance of the firm. The strategic performance measures discriminate among the causes of differential performance by the firm. Strategic planning emphasizes comparisons with individual close competitors rather than with industry standards. An industry is an average of a set of firms; some of these will be good, some poor. The aspiring firm seeks to compare itself with its close competitors.

The other important orientations of ratios for strategic production market planning are distinctive in two respects. First, the ratios are oriented to the future. Second, emphasis is on economic characteristics of the product-market environment rather than the internal performance measures of the firm. Conventional financial ratio analysis focuses on the internal operations of the firm. Financial ratios for evaluation of the strategic position of the firm emphasize characteristics of the firm's external environment, are oriented to the future, and emphasize proper modeling of the characteristics of the firm to survival and growth in its economic environment.

**Economic Environment** The tests of the firm's strategic position emphasize the economic environment. The economic variables considered should include the following:
   1. Industry demand
       *a.* Growth
       *b.* Stability
       *c.* Stage in life-cycle
   2. Competitive trends
       *a.* Entry
       *b.* Size structure
       *c.* Growth-to-capacity relationships

3. Impact of dynamic change
   a. Political
   b. Technological
   c. Economic
   d. Social

The third set of factors overlaps the first two. The distinction is that in going through the appraisal for the first two, analysts make the best probabilistic judgments about the future as they see it. In analyzing the third set of factors, they take into account the fact that the environment, as viewed under the first set (with particular reference to the stage of the life-cycle of the environment), and the capabilities which the firm possesses are other statements of the firm's strategic gap. One remedy for a strategic gap is found in diversification studies.

## ACCOUNTING FOR CHANGES IN PRICE LEVELS AND FOR CURRENT VALUES

Double-digit inflation as measured by the wholesale or consumer price indices has been an actuality or a threat in the United States for more than a decade. As a consequence, proposals have been made to modify accounting procedures to recognize that the traditional postulate of a stable measuring unit is no longer valid. In December 1974, the Financial Accounting Standards Board (FASB) issued an exposure draft of a proposed statement entitled "Financial Reporting in Units of General Purchasing Power." On March 23, 1976, the Securities and Exchange Commission issued Accounting Series Release No. 190. This release requires disclosure of replacement costs for inventory items and depreciable plant from registrants with $100 million or more (at historical cost) of gross plant assets and inventories constituting 10 percent or more of their total assets. For 1977 and thereafter, the SEC will require additional details on the replacement costs of plant assets and inventories.

In its Status Report No. 37, issued June 4, 1976, FASB announced that action was being deferred on the issuance of a statement on financial reporting in units of general purchasing power. The board stated that the action did not have any implications for the merits of the proposal. Rather, the board stated, " . . . general purchasing power information is not now sufficiently well understood by preparers and users and the need for it is not now sufficiently well demonstrated to justify imposing the cost of implementation upon all preparers of financial statements at this time."

Thus, while the requirement for disclosure of current replacement costs is now effective, the proposal for general purchasing power accounting is still under development. Nevertheless, both approaches have implications for financial statement analysis.

In a period of inflation, distortions will result from the use of the historical cost postulate. Assets are recorded at cost, but revenue and other expense flows are in dollars of different purchasing power. The amortization of fixed costs does not reflect the current cost of these assets.[1] Furthermore, net income during periods when assets are held do not reflect the effects of management's decision to hold the assets rather than to sell them. Assets are not stated on the balance sheet at their current values, and so the firm's financial position cannot be accurately evaluated. And when assets are sold, gains or losses are reported during that period even though these results reflect decisions in prior periods to hold the assets.[2]

**Replacement Cost Accounting** In replacement cost accounting, two major categories of problems must be solved. One is to decide upon a measure of the current value of assets. A second is to measure income after the first problem is solved.

*Measuring the Current Value of Assets.* Three methods have been identified:

1. Current replacement costs. This has been referred to as an entry value and may be defined as the current cost of an identical asset or of an asset equivalent in capacity and service. The SEC requirement is not of current values in general, but one specific measure of current values—replacement costs. Other measures of current value may be disclosed in addition to, but not as a substitute for, replacement costs.

2. Realizable value. If a company were to be liquidated by selling off its assets, the relevant measure of value is the net realizable values of the individual assets. But in applying this approach, the only assets for which current market values are quoted are those continuously traded, such as marketable securities. Conceptually, exit values are hardly relevant for a going concern for which liquidation is not contemplated.

3. Present value of future cash flows (or the discounted cash flows). These are considered by many to represent economic values. The practical implementation of this method requires dependable forecasts and the selection of the applicable discount rates. Most companies continue to make new investments, seeking to add to the earning power of exist-

ing assets. Hence it becomes difficult to segregate the future cash flows of the firm from its existing assets and its new investments. Thus the discounted cash flow method, while widely and effectively used in evaluating individual investment projects, is more difficult to apply in placing values upon the physical assets of the firm as a whole.

It has been stated that in judging the ability of a business to perform in the future as in the past and to pay dividends or to finance expansion without requiring new external financing, "replacement costs are perhaps the most useful measure of current value."[3] It might also be argued that the discounted cash flow method, soundly applied, yields results consistent with current replacement values.

*Measuring Income and Financial Position.* A number of concepts of income are involved. The simplified illustration presented by Falkenstein and Weil is utilized here. Their illustration and three concepts of income are reproduced in Table F-11.[3]

**TABLE F-11  Replacement Cost Income Statement: Simple Illustration**

|  | Assumed data | |
| --- | --- | --- |
|  | Acquisition (historical) cost | Replacement cost |
| Inventory, 1/1/76 .................... | $ 900 | $1100 |
| Inventory, 12/31/76 .................. | 1200 | 1500 |
| Cost of goods sold for 1976 ........... | 4000 | 4500 |
| Sales for 1976 ................... $5,200 | | |
| *Income Statement for 1976* | | |
| Sales ............................ | | $5200 |
| Cost of goods sold, replacement cost basis | | 4500 |
| (1) Distributable income ............... | | $ 700 |
| Realized holding gains ................ | | 500* |
| (2) Realized income .................. | | $1200 |
| Unrealized holding gains ............. | | 150† |
| (3) Economic income ................. | | $1350 |

*Realized holding gain during a period is replacement cost of goods sold less historical cost of goods sold; for 1976 the realized holding gain is $500 = $4500 − $4000.

†The total unrealized holding gain at any time is replacement cost of inventory on hand at that time less historical cost of that inventory. The unrealized holding gain during a period is the unrealized holding gain at the end of the period less the unrealized holding gain at the beginning of the period. The unrealized holding gain prior to 1976 is $200 = $1100 − $900. The unrealized holding gain during 1976 = ($1550 − $1200) − ($1100 − $900) = $350 − $200 = $150.

SOURCE: Falkenstein and Weil, p. 49.

*Pretax distributable income* is defined as revenues less expenses based on replacement costs. This figure is a measure of income that can be distributed as taxes and returns to owners without impairing the firm's physical capacity to remain in business at current levels.

*Realized income* is distributable income plus holding gains that have been realized during the period. The realized holding gain is the replacement value of goods sold less their historical costs. The sum of the distributable income and the realized holding gain is the realized income. This is the same as the conventional measure of income, which is based on the realization principle. Replacement cost data make it possible to separate distributable income and realized holding gains.

The sum of realized income plus unrealized holding gains has been called *economic income*. One view holds that an increase in the value of assets is economic income whether or not the asset has been sold. The economic measure of income has been defined as the income that can be consumed during the period leaving the person as well off at the end of the period as at the beginning. This leads to an emphasis on the physical capacity of the firm. A company may be said to be as well off at the end of the period as at the beginning only if it has sufficient physical assets to carry on the same level of business activity. Under this view, holding gains, whether or not realized, are tied up in the net assets required to conduct the operations of the firm at the current physical levels of activity. Thus it might be more appropriate to label the third measure of income "realized plus unrealized income unadjusted for general purchasing power changes."

Taking distributable income as the most relevant measure of income, Falkenstein and Weil make comparisons with the use of income as conventionally reported for the Dow Jones industrials for 1975. Income as conventionally reported approximated $14.5 billion. Using replacement costs, the cost of goods sold increases by $2.2 billion and depreciation by $6.5 billion. Distributable income drops to somewhat under $6 billion, representing 40 percent of the conventionally measured income.

While dividends were about 50 percent of conventional income, they were 127 percent of distributable income. Income taxes currently payable were 63 percent of pretax conventional income but almost 81 percent of distributable income. A wide variation was found among the individual companies reflecting variations in the economic characteristics of their industries, the extent of use of LIFO accounting methods, and other individual circumstances. Thus the impacts of inflation varied among companies.

The preceding discussion shows that the use of current replacement costs in calculating a distributable income measure can result in substantial changes in income results as well as in financial position. When economic changes are so large that current values of assets differ greatly from their historical values, it is argued that major distortions will result if these changes are not considered in accounting procedures and practices.

**General Purchasing Power Reporting** Because both the realized and unrealized holding gains in the use of replacement accounting may simply reflect a declining value of the unit of account, it has been proposed that more general adjustments are needed. These adjustments would recognize that the assumption of a stable unit of account are no longer valid in most parts of the world. As a result proposals have been made for general purchasing power reporting (GPPR) along the lines of the FASB draft proposal of December 1974.

The GPPR would seek to adjust the current value of nonmonetary items by a general price index. The historical cost basis of accounting is retained but adjusted by a price index. GPPR adjusts original cost data to compensate for changes in the purchasing power of the dollar and capital consumption expenses, and the value of goods sold from inventory are adjusted accordingly. A new entry would be introduced to financial reports, net holding gains on monetary items. Operationally, monetary and nonmonetary items must be separated in financial statements and a price index must be selected. Cash, claims to cash, and claims on cash fixed in terms of dollars are designated as monetary items.

While the adjustments can be quite detailed, some simplifications can be made. When income and expenses are spread relatively uniformly throughout the year, a roughly accurate measure of monetary gain or loss can be calculated on the basis of the average balance of monetary items rather than on the transactions which created them. Consider the following balance sheets; the general price level rose 10 percent between the two balance sheet dates.

### GPPR Company
#### Balance Sheets for 19X1 and 19X2

| Monetary assets | 19X1 | 19X2 |
|---|---|---|
| Cash | $8000 | $10,000 |
| Receivables | 12,000 | 20,000 |
| Nonmonetary assets | | |
| Inventories | 30,000 | 40,000 |
| Net fixed assets | 50,000 | 60,000 |
| Total assets | $100,000 | $130,000 |
| Monetary liabilities | | |
| Current liabilities | $10,000 | $15,000 |
| Deferred income taxes | 2000 | 3000 |
| Long-term debt | 28,000 | 36,000 |
| Net holding gains on monetary items | | 2000 |
| Nonmonetary liabilities | | |
| Net worth | 60,000 | 74,000 |
| Total claims | $100,000 | $130,000 |

The net balance of monetary items was ($20,000) in 19X1 and ($24,000) in 19X2. The average net monetary liability was $22,000. The rate of inflation during the year was 10 percent. Hence the value of the net monetary liability at the end-of-the-year price index was $22,000 divided by 1.10, or $20,000. Thus the constant dollar value of the net monetary liabilities decreased by $2000, and the net holding gains on monetary items was $2000.

The broad significance of the two major forms of adjustments can be indicated by some aggregate measures. Table F-12 shows the effects on selected financial ratios for U.S. nonfinancial corporations over 11 years from utilizing current-value reporting as contrasted to conventional reporting. Note that debt-to-equity ratios, which are over 130 percent by conventional reporting, fall below 100 percent by current value reporting.

However, the operating income coverage of interest liability drops from somewhat less than 2 to approximately 1. This is because the operating-income-to-equity ratio drops from about 12 percent to 6 percent in recent years. The ratio of taxes to operating income, which has been in the region of 42 percent by conventional reporting, rises to 60 percent or more by current value.

This illustrates how the use of current value reporting can have a substantial impact on ratios involving the operating performance and financial position of business firms. Given the substantial changes that have taken place in the U.S. economy during the past decade and that the inflation rate has been in the two-digit range, supplemental accounting information is necessary. Without taking into account changes in the purchasing power of the monetary unit and changes in the relative values of assets held by different business firms in the same industry and the differential impact of change on various industries, conventional accounting reporting based on historical cost postulates can be seriously misleading. A reworking of financial ratio analysis based on current values, therefore, becomes a highly desirable check on financial ratio analysis utilizing conventional accounting reports.

**Sources and Uses of Funds Statement** This statement performs an important analytical function in conjunction with standard ratio analysis. On a historical basis, the sources and uses of funds statement indicates where the cash came from and how it was used. With it, the firm is able to answer the question often posed by possible lenders, "How has the firm used the funds it obtained in the past?"

Sources and uses analysis is also employed on a pro forma, or budget, basis for planning. It can

**TABLE F-12**   Selected Financial Ratios for U.S. Nonfinancial Corporations

| | Conventional reporting | | | | Current-value reporting | | | |
|---|---|---|---|---|---|---|---|---|
| Debt/<br>equity | Operating<br>income/<br>interest<br>liability | Operating<br>income/<br>equity | Taxes/<br>operating<br>income | Debt/<br>equity | Operating<br>income/<br>interest<br>liability | Operating<br>income/<br>equity | Taxes/<br>operating<br>income | |
| | (1) | (2) | (3) | (4) | (5) | (6) | (7) | (8) |
| 1965 | .97 | 5.3 | .15 | .42 | .91 | 5.4 | .15 | .41 |
| 1966 | 1.02 | 4.8 | .15 | .42 | .92 | 4.4 | .14 | .42 |
| 1967 | 1.08 | 3.9 | .13 | .43 | 1.02 | 3.4 | .13 | .43 |
| 1968 | 1.14 | 3.7 | .14 | .47 | .96 | 3.0 | .12 | .49 |
| 1969 | 1.21 | 2.7 | .12 | .50 | .94 | 2.1 | .09 | .53 |
| 1970 | 1.28 | 1.8 | .09 | .49 | 1.01 | 1.4 | .07 | .57 |
| 1971 | 1.30 | 2.0 | .10 | .47 | 1.06 | 1.6 | .08 | .54 |
| 1972 | 1.29 | 2.2 | .11 | .44 | 1.07 | 1.9 | .09 | .48 |
| 1973 | 1.32 | 2.1 | .13 | .43 | 1.00 | 1.7 | .08 | .52 |
| 1974 | 1.36 | 1.8 | .13 | .42 | .95 | 0.9 | .05 | .77 |
| 1975 | 1.34 | 1.7 | .12 | .42 | .92 | 1.1 | .06 | .60 |

SOURCE: R. W. Kopcke, "Current Accounting Practices and Proposals for Reform," *New England Economic Review*, Federal Reserve Bank of Boston, September–October 1976, p. 23.

explain the way funds will be employed in the future. Subsequently, the budgeted sources and uses statement can be used to determine whether funds were employed according to plan.

In constructing this statement, the category *uses* of funds includes increases in asset items or decreases in liability items. The category *sources* of funds includes decreases in asset items or increases in liability items. Depreciation is a noncash outlay. Since it is deducted from revenues to calculate net income, it is added back as a source of funds in addition to net income. The financial statements in the annual reports of major corporations ordinarily will provide a sources and uses of funds statement for analysis along the lines indicated.

**Footnotes to Statements** SEC and FASB requirements make the footnotes to financial statements of increased importance. For example, SEC Accounting Series Release No. 190 requires disclosure of replacement costs. FASB 13 on leasing requires footnote information on lease obligations over a period of years. Hence, footnotes are vital parts of the overall analysis and deserve careful reading.

## LIMITATIONS OF FINANCIAL STATEMENT ANALYSIS

For a number of reasons, managers and analysts cannot place absolute reliance upon the results of financial ratio analysis. In general, "window dressing" practices which will improve profitability in the short run may be utilized. Such practices include the postponement of the maintenance of fixed assets which will decrease costs and increase profitability in the short run, but which will impact the firm

severely when machine breakdowns occur and production processes are interrupted. A policy of delaying the purchase of modern equipment will decrease capital outlays and reduce depreciation expenditures in the short run. However, failure to keep pace with competitors who are installing modern, efficient, and low-cost machinery will result in a cost disadvantage at some point in time.

In addition, changing price levels and changes in the current values of assets can produce distortions in accounting measures of performance and financial position. It is desirable, therefore, to have made available the kinds of additional information that will be forthcoming under the SEC's Accounting Release No. 190 requiring information on current replacement values. Additional information would be provided by the FASB's program for general purchasing power reporting.

Nevertheless, even with the additional supplementary information, financial ratio analysis is not the complete answer to evaluating the performance of a firm. When financial ratio analysis indicates that the patterns of a firm depart from industry norms, this is not an absolutely certain indication that something is wrong with the firm. Departures from industry norms provide a basis for raising questions and further investigation and analysis. Additional information and discussions may establish sound explanations for the differences between the pattern for the individual firm and industry composite ratios. Or the differences may reveal forms of mismanagement calling for correction.

Conversely, conformance to industry composite ratios does not establish with certainty that the firm is performing normally and is managed well. In the short run, many tricks can be used to make the firm "look good" in relation to industry standards. The analyst must develop firsthand knowledge of the operations of the firm and of its management to provide a check on the financial ratios. In addition, the analyst must develop a sense, a touch, a smell, and a feel of what is going on in the firm. Sometimes it is this "sixth sense" that uncovers weaknesses in the firm. The analyst should not be anesthetized by financial ratios that appear to conform with normality. Thus, financial ratios are a useful part of an investigative and analytic process, but they are not the complete answer to questions about the performance of any firm.

*See also* ACCOUNTING, FINANCIAL; AUDIT, MANAGEMENT; AUDITING, FINANCIAL; FINANCIAL MANAGEMENT; FINANCIAL MANAGEMENT, CAPITAL STRUCTURE AND DIVIDEND POLICY; FINANCIAL RATIO ANALYSIS; MARKETS, SECURITIES; MARKETS, STOCK INDICATOR SERIES.

### NOTES
[1]Thompson and Koons, "Accounting for Changes in General Price Levels and Current Values," in Edwards and Black (eds.), *Modern Accountant's Handbook*, chap. 26, Dow Jones-Irwin, Inc., Homewood, Ill., 1976, pp. 560–561, 580–581.
[2]Davidson, Schindler, Stickney, and Weil, *Financial Accounting*, The Dryden Press, Inc., Hinsdale, Ill., 1975, p. 441.
[3]A. Falkenstein and R. L. Weil, "Replacement Cost Accounting," *Financial Analysts Journal*, January–February, 1977, pp. 47–48.

### REFERENCES
Foulke, Roy A.: *Practical Financial Statement Analysis*, 6th ed., McGraw-Hill Book Company, New York, 1968.
Helfert, Erich A.: *Techniques of Financial Analysis*, Richard D. Irwin, Inc., Homewood, Ill., 1972.
Lerner, Eugene M., and Willard T. Carleton: *A Theory of Financial Analysis*, Harcourt Brace Jovanovich, Inc., New York, 1966.
Weston, J. Fred, and Eugene F. Brigham: *Managerial Finance*, 4th ed., Holt, Rinehart and Winston, Inc., New York, 1972.

J. FRED WESTON, *University of California, Los Angeles*

**Financial summary form** (*See* PLANNING, STRATEGIC MANAGERIAL.)

**Financing, government** (*See* FINANCIAL MANAGEMENT, SHORT-TERM, INTERMEDIATE, AND LONG-TERM FINANCING; GOVERNMENT RELATIONS AND SERVICES; SMALL BUSINESS ADMINISTRATION.)

**Financing, intermediate-term** (*See* FINANCIAL MANAGEMENT, SHORT-TERM, INTERMEDIATE, AND LONG-TERM FINANCING.)

**Financing, long-term** (*See* FINANCIAL MANAGEMENT, SHORT-TERM, INTERMEDIATE, AND LONG-TERM FINANCING.)

**Financing, short-term** (*See* FINANCIAL MANAGEMENT, SHORT-TERM, INTERMEDIATE, AND LONG-TERM FINANCING.)

**Finishing processes** (*See* PRODUCTION PROCESSES.)

**First-in, first-out (FIFO)** (*See* ACCOUNTING, FINANCIAL; PROFITS AND PROFIT MAKING.)

**First-level management** (*See* SUPERVISORY MANAGEMENT.)

**First-level managers** (*See* MANAGER, DEFINITIONS OF.)

**First world countries** (*See* DEVELOPING COUNTRIES, MANAGEMENT IN.)

**Flexible budgets** (*See* BUDGETS AND BUDGET PREPARATION.)

**Flexitime** (*See* WORK HOURS, FLEXIBLE.)

**Float** (*See* INTERNATIONAL TRADE.)

**Float** (*See* NETWORK PLANNING METHODS.)

**Flow diagram** (*See* PAPER WORK SIMPLIFICATION; WORK SIMPLIFICATION AND IMPROVEMENT.)

**Flow diagram, layout**   (*See* FACILITIES AND SITE PLANNING AND LAYOUT.)

**Flow of materials**   (*See* MATERIAL HANDLING.)

**Flow process chart**   (*See* WORK SIMPLIFICATION AND IMPROVEMENT.)

**FOB points**   (*See* DISTRIBUTION, PHYSICAL.)

**Forced distribution technique**   (*See* APPRAISAL, PERFORMANCE.)

**Forced relationship technique**   (*See* PRODUCT PLANNING AND DEVELOPMENT.)

**Force-field analysis**   [*See* DEVELOPMENT AND TRAINING, CAREER PATH PLANNING FOR MANAGERS; ORGANIZATION DEVELOPMENT (OD).]

**Forecast, market**   (*See* PRODUCT PLANNING AND DEVELOPMENT.)

**Forecast, stochastic**   (*See* PRODUCT PLANNING AND DEVELOPMENT.)

## Forecasting business conditions

Forecasting is an essential managerial function that should be a continuing activity in any organization that produces goods or services. The executive responsible for corporate forecasting should consider the purposes, premises, priorities, and performance measures of the forecasting activities in the company and should conduct a periodic audit or review of those activities. Successful forecasting involves more than simply choosing and applying the best forecasting method. This entry presents pertinent management considerations and describes several of the most useful forecasting techniques.

## MANAGEMENT OF FORECASTING

Forecasting should be considered an organizational function deserving careful managerial attention. This section briefly discusses five key aspects that require adequate, balanced attention to ensure satisfactory performance of a corporate forecasting system.

**Purposes of the Forecast**   The needs of management to be filled by forecasting should be clearly understood by all involved in the forecasting activities. Obvious as this may appear, in many cases the purpose of a forecast is not understood, and consequently the real needs of management are not filled completely or appropriately. The forecasting function may be an integral part of the *planning* process of an organization; on the other hand, forecasting methods may be used in management *control* systems to establish performance standards or to determine as early as possible when a process or pattern has shifted in some undesirable direction.

*Planning.*   In a competitive environment, correct anticipation of future circumstances can give a corporation significant advantage. Resource allocation decisions in marketing, capital budgeting, cash management, manpower planning, raw materials procurement, and production scheduling are often based in part on "anticipated circumstances." By analyzing historical trends and patterns in demand for products and services and by investigation of relevant economic data, a forecaster may project patterns and relationships into the future as a basis for product mix, promotion and advertising, plant expansion (or contraction), and other policies. The level of detail and precision of a forecast should be responsive to the intended purpose of the forecast; the manager should avoid the pitfall of using a forecast created for one purpose for a significantly different purpose.

*Control.*   Budgetary control and product quality control may be assisted by analytic methods which are able to predict and recognize changes in basic patterns at an early stage. A good example of this is presented by Bradley.[1]

**Premises of the Forecast**   It is usually vitally important for the manager to recognize and understand the underlying assumptions or premises of a forecast, both at the time the forecast is made and afterward. In addition to explicitly stated premises, there may be implicit, unstated assumptions; if managers are not aware of some of the implicit premises underlying forecasts upon which they are basing their decisions, they may not be adequately sensitive to shifts in factors that will affect the actual results. Premises are themselves "quasi-forecasts" often based on some earlier statistical work or investigation.

*Internal* premises concerning conditions within the corporation (e.g., "wages will increase annually by 7 percent" or "production yields on a particular product will improve by $X$ percent during each of the next 2 years") may receive more attention from many managers than do the external premises. *External* premises usually include assumptions about economic, governmental, general environmental, market, and supply conditions that will affect the corporation.

A forecast should always be accompanied by an explicit list of internal and external premises. Successful use of a forecast will usually be enhanced by a systematic, timely, and satisfactorily dependable way of monitoring the status of internal and external premises.

**Priorities for Forecasting** In many companies a large number of variables and factors are amenable to forecasting, but to try to forecast all of them is often not economically reasonable. In a large corporation, it is a significant management task to decide upon the priorities for the forecasting function on the bases of the *value* of analysis on the one hand and the *cost* of the analysis on the other hand.

The value of a forecast is a function of the *usefulness* of the forecast (in terms of its accuracy, appropriateness, and timeliness) and the *importance* of the forecast to the firm. The cost of a forecast is composed of the cost of developing the associated forecasting process for a variable or factor, data acquisition and storage, and operating and maintaining the forecasting process.

**Performance Measures** No matter how fancy and sophisticated a forecasting process, it is essentially worthless if the decision maker lacks confidence in it. Therefore, in developing performance measures for forecasting, one should first attempt to identify those aspects of the forecast that affect the decision maker's confidence in the forecast.

There should be a "performance assessment component" in every corporate forecasting system. The usual basic measure in this regard is simply the difference between forecast results and actual results; this is designated the *forecast error*. Several other measures are often used to adjust the forecasting system to produce more accurate or more precise forecasts; some of these are the mean absolute deviation, the mean percentage error, the mean absolute percentage error, and the mean squared error.

One of the pitfalls of forecasting is to evaluate a forecasting method's performance relative only to the data used in constructing the forecast. To gain a fair assessment, one should evaluate a forecasting method with respect to data *not* used in developing the forecast.

**Periodic Review** Considerable benefit can be derived from a periodic audit or review of an ongoing forecasting system to ensure that:

1. The value-cost considerations are still valid

2. The priorities are still reasonable and consistent

3. The premises of the forecasts continue to be correct

4. Persons involved in forecasting are competent to perform their jobs

5. The organizational structures and processes for forecasting are still appropriate and effective

6. The data collection activities are supplying valid, reliable data for forecasting in a timely manner

7. The correct forecasting methods are being employed

8. The forecasts are being communicated effectively to management

9. The predictive performances of the forecasts are being adequately assessed, and the necessary actions are being taken to adjust the forecasting process when forecast performance is unsatisfactory

10. The needs of management are being filled by the forecasting function

11. Corrective actions are taken as warranted by analysis of items 1 to 10 above

Unfortunately, too many companies casually pass over this concept of a periodic review of their forecasting activities. This may be a result of the feeling that such a review is a "luxury" or that the current forecasting practice is adequate without a full-blown review. Nevertheless, it is strongly recommended that every corporation systematically subject its forecasting to a periodic review (annually or every other year).

## FORECASTING METHODS

A wide range of forecasting methods has been developed to help the manager anticipate future circumstances so that production, marketing, financial, and personnel decisions can be made as intelligently as possible. With the capability supplied by modern electronic computers and with the theoretically sound body of knowledge that now exists, forecasting methods are widely used and have practical value.

**Subjective Assessments Using Experts** One of the practical challenges of forecasting involves the incorporation of expert judgment into the forecast. Judgment is certainly required in the use of many of the so-called objective forecasting methods to be described in later sections; however, the specific focus of this section is on ways to develop forecasts based entirely on expert judgment. There are numerous ways of doing this, and the present brief summary does not purport to mention them all. A good survey of judgmental forecasting methods is presented by Gross and Peterson.[2]

Some of the many reasons for using subjective assessment methods in addition to or instead of objective methods of forecasting are these:

1. Past behavior patterns for the variable being forecast have changed: new influences have emerged or old influences have changed.

2. Sufficient data are not available, or the data are incomplete or unreliable.

3. Data are available, but none of the quantitative methods work well in the specific forecasting situation.

4. The planning horizon is too far in the future to rely on time series or causal methods.

5. New technology is expected to exist in the future period being examined.

*Probability Assessment Methods.* Some companies have used probability assessment methods to forecast sales volume, market share, size of an aggregate market, and other variables. In one approach an expert within the company is questioned about the most likely sales volume, what level of sales there is less than a 1 percent chance of going above, what level there is less than a 1 percent chance of going below, what level of sales there is a 25 percent chance of exceeding, and what level there is a 25 percent chance of going below. These estimates can be translated into a cumulative probability curve by plotting on graph paper the 1, 25, 50, 75, and 99 percent estimates obtained above and connecting these points with a smooth curve. The curve can then be used as an aid in forecasting. There are several variations on this probability assessment approach.

Figure F-5 illustrates the cumulative probability curve assessed by a product manager for annual sales of a new product during that product's first year on the market. The product manager thought it was equally likely that annual sales would be greater or less than $5 million and also felt that there was a 25 percent chance that sales would be less than $3,500,000 and a similar likelihood that they would exceed $6 million. In no case did the manager feel that the first year's sales of the product would fall below $2,500,000 or exceed $7,500,000.

In using subjective estimation procedures, the

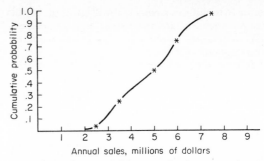

**Fig. F-5. Cumulative probability curve for first year's sales of a new product.**

executive should try to "calibrate" the bias of the estimator by comparing the subjective forecasts with actual outcomes. If the estimator's bias can be determined, either allowances can be made for the bias or the estimator can be trained to reduce the bias of future estimates. Methods for calibrating a forecast are discussed in chapter 13 of Wheelwright and Makridakis.[3]

*PERT Method of Estimating.* The program evaluation and review technique (PERT) requires estimates of optimistic (O), pessimistic (P), and most likely (ML) future circumstances. These three estimates are weighted to form an expected value as follows:

$$\text{Expected value} = \frac{O + P + 4ML}{6}$$

The relative weights of 1 for O and P and 4 for ML are typically used; other weighting schemes are rarely used in this context. The corresponding standard deviation is computed as follows:

$$\text{Standard deviation} = \frac{O - P}{6}$$

This PERT-derived technique has been used in some companies to convert an expert's estimates of most likely and extreme values into measures of central tendency and dispersion. One rationale for using this approach is that many people find it easier to provide optimistic, pessimistic, and most likely values than to estimate a specific value. A second rationale is that the computed standard deviation enables the forecaster to estimate a confidence interval around the expected value.

The PERT approach is obviously only an approximation; however, it is quick and easy to use. It can often be valuable as a way to take expert opinion into account quickly as a check on estimates produced by other methods.

*The Delphi Method.* An Air Force-sponsored Rand Corporation study, called Project Delphi, concerning the use of expert opinion was started in the early 1950s. Naturally, the earliest applications of the Delphi method dealt with defense questions, and later applications were aimed at research and development (R & D) questions where expert opinions were processed to gain better perspectives of long-range future circumstances. In recent years, there have been numerous business applications of the Delphi method in marketing and R&D long-term forecasting.

The Delphi method of forecasting operates as in the following example:

1. A panel of experts, whose members are kept physically remote from one another, is asked to respond in writing to a questionnaire dealing with a specific question, such as one asking for an estimate of sales of a product in some future year.

2. Each panel member is informed of the median (middle value) response (and perhaps is given other information about the responses), and if the panel member's forecast is significantly different from the median, he or she is asked to state his or her reasons for the significant difference in opinions. The panel members are asked to submit answers to the questionnaire again.

3. Step 2 is repeated until the median and the twenty-fifth (or twentieth) and seventy-fifth (or eightieth) percentile values stabilize so that further rounds do not greatly change the results of those which preceded.

The Delphi method excludes many aspects of group behavior such as social pressure, domination by a few members, undue optimism or conservatism, or argumentation. The result is usually a spread of opinions that can be used in decision making. Descriptions of applications of the Delphi method are provided by Jolson and Rossow[4] and Linstone and Turoff.[5]

**Causal Models** When the forecast variable can be explained as a function of explanatory or causal variables, a causal model may provide better forecasts than those generated by other forecasting techniques. The basic method used in causal models is usually *regression analysis*, which statistically describes the response of the forecast variable to changes in one or more explanatory variables. Beyond single-equation regression models, multiple-equation simulation models are used to forecast national, industry, company, or product variables. This latter approach is known as *econometric modeling*.

*Regression Analysis.* A regression model mathematically describes "an average relationship" between a variable (usually called the *dependent* variable) and one or more explanatory variables (usually called the *independent* variables). While the actual relationship among the variables will deviate from the "average" relationship, the regression model serves to explain some portion of the variance of the forecast (dependent) variable.

The *method of least squares* is used in regression analysis to fit the regression model to the historical data. It is worthwhile understanding that this method produces the best possible fit in terms of minimizing the sum of the squares of the errors (actual minus fitted values). Symbolically, for each historical observation of the variable being forecast there is a "fitted" value (produced by the regression model) such that

$$\text{Error (e)} = \text{actual (A) minus fitted (F)}$$

of, for the $i$th observation,

$$e_i = A_i - F_i$$

Where there were $n$ historical observations, the corresponding errors may be symbolized as $e_1$, $e_2$, ..., $e_n$. The method of least squares minimizes the sum of the squares of these errors; that is, $e_1^2 + e_2^2 + \cdots + e_n^2$ is minimized (thus, the term *least squares*). A primary measure of performance in most forecasting systems is the *mean squared error*, which is simply the *mean* of the squared errors; i.e.,

$$\text{Mean squared error} = \frac{e_1^2 + e_2^2 + \cdots + e_n^2}{n}$$

Typically, the best forecasting method for a given situation is one that minimizes the mean squared error.

The *coefficient of determination* (usually symbolized as $R^2$) indicates the proportion of the variance (a common measure of dispersion) of the forecast variable that is explained by the regression model. When given a choice of two or more regression models, the forecaster generally will select the model which maximizes this coefficient of determination, for this is tantamount to minimizing the mean squared error.

The independent or explanatory variables in a regression model may include leading indicators, time, marketing variables (such as price or advertising expenditures), demographic factors, or other indicators or variables that exhibit explanatory relationships with the forecast variable. One way to identify a possible relationship between variables is to plot a *scatter diagram* of one variable *versus* the other variable. Another way is to calculate the *correlation coefficient* which measures the degree of linear association between the variables. Most good computer programs for regression analysis will plot the scatter diagrams and calculate the correlation coefficients for a specified set of variables.

Consider, for example, the regression model for annual sales of a glass company in terms of two explanatory variables, building contracts awarded and number of automobiles produced, as follows:

Sales = 38.02 + 10.59 (building contracts awarded)
+ 33.25 (automobile production)

where annual sales are in millions of dollars, building contracts are in billions of dollars, and automobile production is in millions of automobiles. The coefficient of determination ($R^2$) for this model was calculated to be .9479, meaning that the model explained nearly 95 percent of the variance in annual glass sales. (Again, any good computer program for regression analysis will calculate key coefficients, such as $R^2$; the manager should ask for this information in order to better judge the usefulness of the model.)

A measure of the statistical contribution of a variable to a regression model's explanatory power is called the *beta index* or the *beta coefficient*. This coefficient indicates the *relative* importance of each of the explanatory variables in the regression model. When there are several explanatory variables, the beta coefficients can be used to decide which variables to retain in the model and which to exclude. For example, in the annual glass sales model above, the beta coefficients were computed to be .8215 for building contracts awarded and .2496 for automobile production; thus, building contracts appear to be more than three times as important as automobile production in explaining annual glass sales for the company being studied. It would follow that one would prefer to retain building contracts awarded as an explanatory variable over automobile production if one of the variables were to be dropped from the model. (The forecaster is often motivated to delete variables from a regression model to simplify the model or because reliable data are not available for the deleted variables.)

In interpreting the regression model for annual glass sales, one would say that *on average* for each billion dollars of building contracts awarded, annual glass sales would be expected to increase by 10.59 million dollars. Similarly, for each million automobiles produced, annual glass sales would be expected to increase 33.25 million dollars. The coefficients 10.59 and 33.25 in the model are called *regression coefficients*.

There is one particular trap in using regression models into which some executives unknowingly

fall; it is caused by a phenomenon called *multicollinearity*. This phenomenon occurs when one explanatory (independent) variable is correlated with one or more of the other explanatory variables in a regression model. For example, if building contracts and automobile production were associated statistically, they would be said to be *collinear*. The simplest way to recognize collinearity is to have the computer calculate correlation coefficients for pairs of explanatory variables. An undesirable effect of multicollinearity is that it reduces the reliability of the regression coefficients and the beta coefficients defined above. On the other hand, multicollinearity generally enhances the predictive capability of a regression model. The main point here is to avoid interpreting literally the regression and beta coefficients as we did above if multicollinearity exists to any considerable extent. This problem can sometimes be eliminated by dropping some of the collinear variables from the regression model.

*Econometric Models.* Some forecasting models contain more than one equation. When the dependent variable in one equation is used as an independent variable in one or more of the other equations, the model is said to be a *simultaneous system* of equations and is often called an *econometric model*. Not only does each equation describe the relationship of a dependent variable with several independent variables, but the set of equations describes the *interactions* of these interrelationships.

The use of econometric models requires a good deal of knowledge about the process being modeled. Because of the complex technical aspects of this approach, econometric modeling is practiced only in the largest corporations and banks, in governments, and in federally supported university research centers. Forecasts of gross national product (GNP) and its components are produced by several organizations, among them Wharton Econometric Forecasting Associates (University of Pennsylvania), the Brookings Institute, Chase Econometrics, Inc., Data Resources, Inc., the Economic Research Department of Chemical Bank, Kent Econometric Associates, Inc., General Electric Company, Goldman, Sachs and Company, Irving Trust Company, and Townsend-Greenspan & Company, Inc.[6]

An increasing amount of work is being done in applying econometric approaches to company and product forecasting. Claycamp and Liddy[7] developed a model for predicting new-product performance using three simultaneous regression equations. Some companies, including General Foods, Inc., have experimented with the Claycamp-Liddy approach; specifically, decisions related to introducing the freeze-dried coffee Maxim were modeled using this approach.

Thorough explanations of regression analysis and econometric modeling are provided by Pindyck and Rubinfeld.[8]

**Time-Series Methods**  When past behavior of a variable (for example, sales of a particular product) can be used to infer something about the future behavior of that variable, a time-series method may produce satisfactory forecasts for that variable. Time-series methods do not explicitly account for causal relationships that may exist between the variable of interest and other factors; rather, historical patterns (sometimes obscure to the human eye) are projected into the future. These methods are generally applicable to relatively short-term forecasting situations in which the planning horizon is less than 6 months, whereas causal methods often are used to forecast as far as 2 years into the future.

*Characteristics of Time-Series Data.*  Many series of consecutive data over time contain trend, seasonal, cyclical, and random components. A *horizontal* pattern exists when there is no trend in the data; there is no tendency for the series either to increase or decrease in any systematic way. Patterns that over several years exhibit a definite trend sometimes might be assumed to have a horizontal pattern over a short period of time (e.g., during a 2- or 3-month period).

A recurring *seasonal* pattern exists when a series fluctuates according to some seasonal influence. The "seasons" may be the days of the week, the days of the month, the months of the year, or the quarters of the year. Sales of fertilizer, paint, air conditioners, new cars, heating oil, and soft drinks and visits to hospital emergency rooms typically exhibit seasonal patterns.

A *cyclical* pattern is very similar to a seasonal pattern in some ways; however, the length of a single cycle is generally longer than 1 year, and cycles will often vary in length. Various economic indices have cyclical patterns; forecasting the business cycle has challenged businesspersons and economists for several decades.[9]

A *trend* pattern exists when there is a pervasive increase or decrease in the value of a variable over a specified period of time. The sales of a company, the gross national product, and many other business and economic indicators follow a trend pattern. The underlying trend is often not linear; the life-cycle of a product is an example of an underlying trend pattern that is not a straight line.[10]

In many cases, time series data will contain a combination of trend, seasonality, and cyclicality; it

may be desirable to "decompose" the raw series into its underlying "components."

*Classical Decomposition Method.*  Two phases are involved in the decomposition method: (1) seasonal, trend, and business cycle components are separated from the random aspects of a historical time series, and (2) a time series model is chosen on the basis of the information gained in the first phase to forecast future behavior of the variable. (It should be emphasized at this point that while many time series methods are cumbersome to use manually, inexpensive computer programs are available from most computer vendors to accomplish all the necessary computation.) *At least* 3 years' monthly data or 4 years' quarterly data are needed if a decomposition method is being used.

Each of the components of a time series is symbolized with the first letter of that component; that is, trend $T$, seasonality $S$, cyclicality $C$, and randomness $R$, where $Y$ denotes the time series data. Symbolically, each point of the time series data is represented as the product of its components:

$$Y = T \times S \times C \times R$$

*Subscripts* are used to designate the time series value for a particular period. For example, $Y_8$ refers to the observed value in period 8, and $Y_{15}$ refers to the observed value in period 15. Thus, the time series value in some period $t$ can be represented as

$$Y_t = T_t \times S_t \times C_t \times R_t$$

The classical decomposition method proceeds as follows:

1.  Determine the *seasonal indices* ($S$) by dividing each raw data value by the corresponding moving average composed of 1 year's observations, half of which occurred prior to and half after the period whose seasonal index is being calculated. (If annual data are used, there is no seasonality; the raw data would then be of the form $Y = T \times C \times R$, and one could begin the procedure at step 2.) Detailed computational methods for doing this are presented by Dauten and Valentine.[11] Divide the raw data by the corresponding seasonal indices to produce seasonally adjusted or deseasonalized data. In symbols,

$$\frac{Y_t}{S_t} = \frac{T_t \times C_t \times S_t \times R_t}{S_t} = T_t \times C_t \times R_t$$

For example, consider the monthly sales of the Roanoke Corporation (name disguised at the request of the subject company) for 1972 through 1976 as shown in Table F-13. Figure F-6 presents a graph of these actual sales and corresponding 12-month moving averages; Table F-14 shows the monthly sales,

**TABLE F-13** Monthly Sales of Roanoke Corporation, 1972–1976*

| Month | 1972 | 1973 | 1974 | 1975 | 1976 |
|---|---|---|---|---|---|
| January | 48.78 | 45.82 | 47.96 | 50.10 | 60.19 |
| February | 35.94 | 43.58 | 43.98 | 49.18 | 54.04 |
| March | 37.03 | 44.91 | 45.21 | 48.96 | 58.49 |
| April | 42.01 | 55.32 | 52.06 | 53.55 | 68.12 |
| May | 48.60 | 59.56 | 57.05 | 62.08 | 80.73 |
| June | 50.83 | 60.90 | 58.84 | 64.90 | 80.77 |
| July | 50.23 | 55.69 | 54.31 | 58.01 | 75.46 |
| August | 49.88 | 57.12 | 57.27 | 63.69 | 80.89 |
| September | 54.04 | 57.99 | 59.92 | 65.90 | 83.51 |
| October | 48.38 | 50.95 | 53.60 | 60.59 | 74.01 |
| November | 41.77 | 44.02 | 48.61 | 52.69 | 67.37 |
| December | 44.70 | 44.76 | 47.30 | 51.71 | 68.49 |

*Sales in thousands of dollars.

corresponding 12-month moving averages, and the ratios of actual sales to moving averages. Figure F-7 illustrates the ratios of actual sales to moving averages, thereby giving a clearer picture of the seasonal behavior of sales with the effects of trend and cyclicality removed. The ratios for a particular month (say, January) are then averaged; these average ratios are recorded in column 1 of Table F-15. Finally, the average ratios are adjusted to sum to 1200; these adjusted average ratios (shown in column 2 of Table F-15) are called the *seasonal indices*. The January index of 92.7 means that, *on average*, January sales are about 92.7 percent of the sales level the Roanoke Corporation expects to achieve in a "normal" month (i.e., a month in which no seasonal effect is experienced). On the other hand, the June

index indicates that, *on average*, June sales have been about 115.17 percent of the "normal" sales level.

2. Determine the trend pattern $T$ in the deseasonalized data by fitting a curve or a straight line through those data. One popular mathematical technique for doing this, the *method of least squares*, was discussed earlier in the section on causal methods.

3. Determine the cyclical component in the historical time series data by dividing each deseasonalized data point by the corresponding trend component (determined in step 2) and then fit a polynomial curve through this series of ratios to smooth out the effects of randomness. Thus,

$$\frac{T_t \times C_t \times R_t}{T_t} = C_t \times R_t$$

where for any point in time $t$, the corresponding *cyclical index* $C_t$ can be determined from the fitted polynomial. A plot of the resultant series of cyclical indices should describe the cycle underlying the particular variable being analyzed.

The three steps outlined above comprise phase 1 of the classical decomposition method. This method provides *approximations* for seasonal and cyclical indices and for an underlying trend in the historical data. No claims are made regarding the precision and accuracy of this approach. It stands to reason that the forecaster's confidence in the results of the decomposition analysis will increase as more historical data are employed in the analysis.

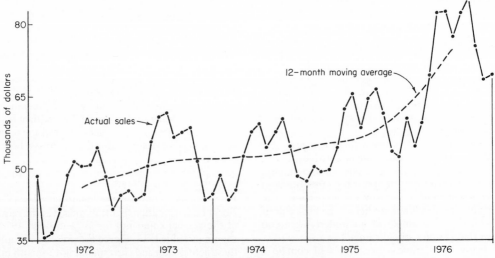

**Fig. F-6. Monthly sales of the Roanoke Corporation, 1972–1976 (thousands of dollars).**

**TABLE F-14  Monthly Sales of Roanoke Corporation Divided by Corresponding Moving Average, 1972–1976**

| Year | Month | Monthly sales, thousands of dollars (1) | 12-Month moving average (2) | Ratio: (1) ÷ (2) × 100 (3) |
|------|-------|------|------|------|
| 1972 | January | 48.78 | | |
| | February | 35.94 | | |
| | March | 37.03 | | |
| | April | 42.01 | | |
| | May | 48.60 | | |
| | June | 50.83 | | |
| | July | 50.23 | 46.015 | 109.155 |
| | August | 49.88 | 45.768 | 108.975 |
| | September | 54.04 | 46.404 | 116.456 |
| | October | 48.38 | 47.060 | 102.797 |
| | November | 41.77 | 48.169 | 86.709 |
| | December | 44.70 | 49.082 | 91.065 |
| 1973 | January | 45.82 | 49.921 | 91.775 |
| | February | 43.58 | 50.376 | 86.502 |
| | March | 44.91 | 50.979 | 88.089 |
| | April | 55.32 | 51.309 | 107.809 |
| | May | 59.56 | 51.523 | 115.592 |
| | June | 60.90 | 51.711 | 117.769 |
| | July | 55.69 | 51.716 | 107.676 |
| | August | 57.12 | 51.895 | 110.060 |
| | September | 57.99 | 51.928 | 111.681 |
| | October | 50.95 | 51.954 | 98.070 |
| | November | 44.02 | 51.682 | 85.175 |
| | December | 44.76 | 51.474 | 86.952 |
| 1974 | January | 47.96 | 51.302 | 93.485 |
| | February | 43.98 | 51.187 | 85.912 |
| | March | 45.21 | 51.200 | 88.308 |
| | April | 52.06 | 51.361 | 101.362 |
| | May | 57.05 | 51.581 | 110.605 |
| | June | 58.84 | 51.963 | 113.228 |
| | July | 54.31 | 52.175 | 104.084 |
| | August | 57.27 | 52.354 | 109.392 |
| | September | 59.92 | 52.787 | 113.521 |
| | October | 53.60 | 53.099 | 100.936 |
| | November | 48.61 | 53.223 | 91.329 |
| | December | 47.30 | 53.642 | 88.185 |
| 1975 | January | 50.10 | 54.147 | 92.521 |
| | February | 49.18 | 54.455 | 90.305 |
| | March | 48.96 | 54.990 | 89.026 |
| | April | 53.55 | 55.488 | 96.507 |
| | May | 62.08 | 56.071 | 110.711 |
| | June | 64.90 | 56.412 | 115.040 |
| | July | 58.01 | 56.779 | 102.165 |
| | August | 63.69 | 57.619 | 110.542 |
| | September | 65.90 | 58.025 | 113.564 |
| | October | 60.59 | 58.820 | 103.017 |
| | November | 52.69 | 60.034 | 87.770 |
| | December | 51.71 | 61.588 | 83.960 |
| 1976 | January | 60.19 | 62.911 | 95.668 |
| | February | 54.04 | 64.365 | 83.960 |
| | March | 58.49 | 65.799 | 88.897 |
| | April | 68.12 | 67.266 | 101.272 |
| | May | 80.73 | 68.384 | 118.054 |
| | June | 80.77 | 69.607 | 116.031 |
| | July | 75.46 | 71.006 | 106.274 |
| | August | 80.89 | | |
| | September | 83.51 | | |
| | October | 74.01 | | |
| | November | 67.37 | | |
| | December | 68.49 | | |

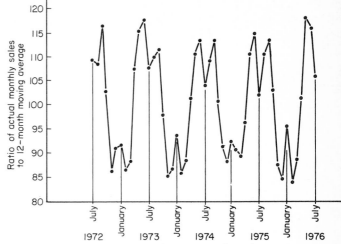

**Fig. F-7. Ratio of actual monthly sales to 12-month moving averages, the Roanoke Corporation, 1972–1976.**

A computer program, known as Census II, and instructions for decomposition analysis are available from the U.S. Bureau of the Census; this is probably the most generally used computer program for the decomposition type of time series analysis.

In order to forecast (phase 2 of the decomposition method), each of the components of the data must be reconstructed as follows:

4. Using a trend model, project deseasonalized $T_t$ into the future. Often this trend model is the one developed in step 2 above; it is possible, however, that the trend will change and another trend model may be more appropriate. At this stage, the forecast should be adjusted for accounting-period changes, holidays, and abnormal events to the extent possible.

5. Multiply the trend component for a future

**TABLE F-15  Seasonal Indices for Roanoke Corporation**

| Month | Average ratio (1) | Seasonal index (2) |
|-------|------|------|
| January | 93.003 | 92.712 |
| February | 86.207 | 85.937 |
| March | 88.603 | 88.325 |
| April | 101.317 | 101.000 |
| May | 113.151 | 112.797 |
| June | 115.536 | 115.174 |
| July | 106.011 | 105.679 |
| August | 109.726 | 109.382 |
| September | 113.543 | 113.187 |
| October | 101.866 | 101.547 |
| November | 87.240 | 86.966 |
| December | 87.569 | 87.294 |
| Total | 1203.771 | 1200.000 |

time period $t$ by the seasonal index corresponding to that period, that is, $T_t \times S_t$.

6. Decide on an estimate of cyclicality for the future period and multiply the value from step 5 by this cyclical index, thus, $T_t \times S_t \times C_t$. This produces a *point estimate* or *point forecast* for the future time period $t$. Random effects may be incorporated by describing an *interval* around the point forecast.

The last step of the decomposition method, namely, estimating the future impact of the cyclical influences, is usually the most challenging one in this forecasting method. Failing to anticipate a turn in the cycle correctly can result in the forecast overestimating ("overshooting") or underestimating the forecast variable. In this regard, the use of *leading economic indicators* to anticipate changes in the cycle is practiced by virtually every major U.S. corporation.

*Economic Indicators.* For a specific time series, it is usually possible to identify *leading, coincident,* and *lag indicators.* These indicators are statistics that tend to change value ahead of, at approximately the same time as, or after a change in the series being forecast. Of course, primary attention is generally focused on identifying and monitoring *leading* indicators pertinent to the forecast variable.

Many carefully prepared economic indicators are available from governmental, trade association, and university sources. Among the most used sources are the Bureau of the Census (especially the *Business Conditions Digest*), the Department of Commerce (especially the *Survey of Current Business*), the Bureau of Labor Statistics (especially the *Monthly Labor Review*), F. W. Dodge (especially dealing with construction contracts awarded), *Business Week* (weekly data on production, trade, prices, and finance), the Council of Economic Advisors (monthly *Economic Indicators* publications), and the 12 Federal Reserve banks.[12] There are many, many more, and each business should identify those sources pertinent to its particular activities.

*Business Cycle Indicators.* The indicator approach to business cycle analysis was developed at the National Bureau of Economic Research (NBER) by analyzing the U.S. economy from the early 1800s to the present time. Researchers at NBER defined a business cycle as consisting of "expansions occurring at about the same time in many economic activities, followed by similarly general recessions, contractions and revivals which merge into the expansion phase of the next cycle." Business cycles relate to aggregate economic activity as distinguished from the cycle of an individual series discussed earlier. A relationship may exist between an aggregate business cycle and the cycle of the time-series data of a particular variable; it is in such matters that an executive should be advised by highly trained, experienced economists and other business forecast experts.[13]

*Smoothing Methods.* Many companies of every kind and size use smoothing techniques for short-term forecasting, especially for purposes of production and inventory control. Three categories of smoothing methods are moving average, exponential smoothing, and adaptive filtering methods. These methods essentially remove the effects of randomness by averaging several consecutive data points together.

In the *moving-average* methods, a specified (constant) number of consecutive data points are averaged; as each new observation in the series becomes available, the oldest observation is dropped and a new average is computed. The latest moving average is used as the forecast for the next period. Table F-14 and Fig. F-6 illustrated moving averages. The 12-month moving average listed for July 1972, for example, was the average of sales for January 1972 through December 1972; as described in this present section, this average would be used as the simple moving-average forecast for January 1973. Table F-16 shows 12-month moving-average forecasts for the Roanoke Corporation.

A common trait of the numerous versions of the moving-average method is that they respond more rapidly to changes in the value of the variable as the number of periods used in the moving average decreases; conversely, as the number of periods increases, the moving-average estimates become more stable. A comparison of the relative merits of the responsiveness and the stability of the moving-average (and other smoothing) methods should be made in terms of the accuracy of the forecast. Stability is obviously an important attribute in situations in which sudden changes in production, labor force, or inventory levels are not desirable or tolerable.

Whereas simple moving averages place the same amount of weight on each of the components of the average, one may desire to put more weight on more recent data; *exponential smoothing* is an easy-to-use, economical approach to forecasting where exponentially decreasing weights are given to older observed values.

Exponential smoothing methods are probably the most commonly used time series methods. They are widely accepted because they place more weight on recent occurrences and because they require only the most recent value of the variable being forecast

**TABLE F-16  Twelve-Month Moving-Average Forecasts for Monthly Sales of Roanoke Corporation**

| Year | Month | Monthly sales, thousands of dollars (1) | 12-Month moving average (2) |
|------|-------|------|------|
| 1972 | January | 48.78 | |
| | February | 35.94 | |
| | March | 37.03 | |
| | April | 42.01 | |
| | May | 48.60 | |
| | June | 50.83 | |
| | July | 50.23 | |
| | August | 49.88 | |
| | September | 54.04 | |
| | October | 48.38 | |
| | November | 41.77 | |
| | December | 44.70 | |
| 1973 | January | 45.82 | 46.015 |
| | February | 43.58 | 45.768 |
| | March | 44.91 | 46.404 |
| | April | 55.32 | 47.060 |
| | May | 59.56 | 48.169 |
| | June | 60.90 | 49.082 |
| | July | 55.69 | 49.921 |
| | August | 57.12 | 50.376 |
| | September | 57.99 | 50.979 |
| | October | 50.95 | 51.309 |
| | November | 44.02 | 51.523 |
| | December | 44.76 | 51.711 |
| 1974 | January | 47.96 | 51.716 |
| | February | 43.98 | 51.895 |
| | March | 45.21 | 51.928 |
| | April | 52.06 | 51.954 |
| | May | 57.05 | 51.682 |
| | June | 58.84 | 51.474 |
| | July | 54.31 | 51.302 |
| | August | 57.27 | 51.187 |
| | September | 59.92 | 51.200 |
| | October | 53.60 | 51.361 |
| | November | 48.61 | 51.581 |
| | December | 47.30 | 51.963 |
| 1975 | January | 50.10 | 52.175 |
| | February | 49.18 | 52.354 |
| | March | 48.96 | 52.787 |
| | April | 53.55 | 53.099 |
| | May | 62.08 | 53.223 |
| | June | 64.90 | 53.642 |
| | July | 58.01 | 54.147 |
| | August | 63.69 | 54.455 |
| | September | 65.90 | 54.990 |
| | October | 60.59 | 55.488 |
| | November | 52.69 | 56.071 |
| | December | 51.71 | 56.412 |
| 1976 | January | 60.19 | 56.779 |
| | February | 54.04 | 57.619 |
| | March | 58.49 | 58.025 |
| | April | 68.12 | 58.820 |
| | May | 80.73 | 60.034 |
| | June | 80.77 | 61.588 |
| | July | 75.46 | 62.911 |
| | August | 80.89 | 64.365 |
| | September | 83.51 | 65.799 |
| | October | 74.01 | 67.266 |
| | November | 67.37 | 68.384 |
| | December | 68.49 | 69.607 |
| 1977 | January | | 71.006 |

(whereas the moving-average methods require storage of data from several periods).

In its simplest form, the exponential smoothing formula is as follows:

Forecast for next period
$\quad = \alpha$ (actual value for the most recent period)
$\quad + (1 - \alpha)$ (forecast value for most recent period)

where $\alpha$ (the Greek letter *alpha*) is the *smoothing constant* (weight), a number between 0 and 1. The larger $\alpha$ becomes, the more responsive the forecast will be to changes in the value of the variable being forecast. The value for $\alpha$ in exponential smoothing (and the value for $n$, the number of periods included in a moving average) should be chosen so that the mean squared error is minimized. (Experience has shown that smoothing constant values between .1 and .5 work best in most applications of exponential smoothing.) Higher-order exponential smoothing methods have been developed to handle underlying trends and seasonality.[14]

One of the most recently developed methods for business forecasting is called *adaptive filtering*. The basic concept of adaptive filtering is to extend the smoothing techniques described earlier in order to determine the optimum set of weights to apply to past observations. While at least 5 years' data should be available to use this method effectively, it is an easy method to use in practice (with a computer) and will probably become one of the most-used time series methods. A good explanation of generalized adaptive filtering is given by Wheelwright and Makridakis.[15]

*Autoregressive-Moving-Average Methods.* The so-called Box-Jenkins autoregressive-moving-average (ARMA) methods of time series forecasting are probably the most powerful of all the time series methods. At least 5 years' data should be used as the historical basis for the Box-Jenkins approach if it is to work effectively. The basic concept of the Box-Jenkins technique is that various classes of forecasting models are tested to determine which one minimizes the sum of the squared forecast errors; the challenge to the forecaster is to interpret skillfully the data patterns that are produced by alternative models so that incremental improvements can be made in the forecast.[16]

The ARMA approach essentially expresses the current value $(Y_t)$ of the forecast variable as a function of previous values $(Y_{t-1}, Y_{t-2}, \ldots, Y_{t-k})$ of that same variable. Systematic analysis of the characteristics of the time series data is accomplished by computing, graphing, and interpreting the *autocorrelation coefficients* of the data. Autocorrelation coefficients indicate the simple correlation between a particular variable value $Y_t$ and some previous (lagged) value $Y_{t-j}$ of that same (auto) variable; the meaning of autocorrelations is exactly the same as that of simple correlation coefficients computed in regression analysis. For example, the autocorrelation of $Y_t$ and $Y_{t-1}$ indicates how variables $Y_t$ and $Y_{t-1}$ are related to each other. If monthly data are seasonal, data for periods that are 12 months apart would be related to each other so that autocorrelations between $Y_t$ and $Y_{t-12}$ would show positive correlation. On the other hand, if the autocorrelation of 12 time lags is close to zero, this would indicate the absence of a relationship between the same months of successive years and, therefore, the lack of a seasonal pattern.

*Stationarity.* This refers to the absence of a trend in the data; i.e., stationary data fluctuate around a constant mean, independent of time. The characteristic of stationarity in a data series can be easily identified by examining a graph of the autocorrelation coefficients. The autocorrelations of stationary data essentially drop to zero after the second or third time lag, while for a nonstationary series they are significantly different from zero for several time periods. A graphical representation of the autocorrelation coefficients of nonstationary data shows a trend, indicating that successive values are highly correlated with each other. The *method of differencing* is used to remove trend from data in the ARMA scheme, thus transforming nonstationary data to stationary data.

A *series of first differences* is created by subtracting the most recent previous value from the current value of the forecast variable; symbolically,

$$Y'_t = Y_{t+1} - Y_t$$

and $Y'_t$ represents the series of first differences. If this new series still exhibits nonstationarity (trend), the method of differencing must be applied again to produce a *series of second differences*, symbolized as

$$Y''_t = Y'_{t+1} - Y'_t$$

For most practical purposes, a maximum of two differences will transform the data into a stationary series.

If a stationary series has significant autocorrelations of lag greater than 3, there is a seasonal pattern whose length corresponds to the time lag with the largest autocorrelation. When seasonality is combined with other patterns such as trend, the stronger the trend, the less obvious the seasonality will be. This problem can be avoided by determin-

ing seasonality only when the data are stationary. As a rule, the presence of a trend in the data indicates that the data should be transformed to a stationary series using the method of differencing before determining seasonality.

A comparison of the ARMA and decomposition methods shows that many of the same things are accomplished by these two different approaches. The decomposition method removes trend by dividing trended data by a moving average to obtain a series without trend. The ARMA method accomplishes this in a more computationally efficient manner by using the method of differencing. The ARMA approach incorporates a seasonal component into the model if there is a seasonal pattern in the data. The decomposition method develops a set of seasonal indices which are used to adjust forecasts for the seasonality attributed to each forecast period. The ARMA method uses autocorrelation analysis to reveal the underlying characteristics of the data; existing computer programs make autocorrelation analysis computationally relatively easy. On the other hand, decomposition methods, while much less sophisticated (and therefore considerably less precise) than ARMA methods, are generally easier to apply. During the next decade, ARMA methods will very probably become increasingly popular for business forecasting, even though these are the most expensive time series methods currently available, and the technical competence required to use them successfully is considerably more than is required for other time series methods.

*Multivariate ARMA Models.* A highly promising development in business forecasting recently has been in the area of multivariate ARMA models (sometimes called *transfer functions*) as contrasted with the time series methods previously described, which pertained only to univariate *(single)* time series. Multivariate ARMA (MARMA) methods combine the time series approach with the causal (regression) approach to forecasting. The main aim of the MARMA approach is to identify some leading indicators of the series to be forecast that can be used to improve the predictions over those attainable with a univariate model; this will prove to be especially valuable when sudden cyclical changes occur.

*Intervention analysis,* an extension of the MARMA approach, is aimed at identifying the type of response a forecast variable will exhibit, given some step or impulse change in an explanatory variable. A purpose of intervention analysis is to answer such questions as how sales will be affected if a promotional campaign is initiated on January 1 or how sales will be affected if a price is increased by 25 percent. Whereas these questions could be considered using multiple regression analysis, regression analysis does not depict what happens during the transition period before a new equilibrium is reached. Rather, regression assumes that a new steady state (of sales, for example) is immediately achieved. In practice, the businessperson is often more interested in the transition period than in periods in which new equilibrium has been reached. Thus, intervention analysis, while still in the developmental stage, should prove to be an important forecasting method in future years.

**Other Methods** While most forecasting methods used in business planning have been described in previous sections, several other forecasting approaches deserve brief mention in the concluding section of this entry.

*Indirect Methods.* Most of the attention in the discussion of time series, causal, and subjective assessment methods was spent on directly forecasting variables such as sales. Another approach is to base a forecast on estimates of national, regional, or industrial economic activity where the company's share of the larger activity is estimated. We briefly mention a few of these so-called "indirect" methods; a good discussion may be found in Gross and Peterson.[17] It should be noted that time series, causal, and judgmental methods are often used in conjunction with the indirect approach.

When a purchaser is a manufacturer or some other intermediate consumer unit, forecasts for demand for goods or services purchased by that unit may be based on demand for the unit's output. For example, the demand for glass may be derived from the demand for new automobiles and building contracts awarded.

Sometimes it is helpful to be able to gauge the "complementary consumption" of goods or services where the utilization of one product is related to that of another. Typical examples are such complementary products as beer and pretzels, tires and automobiles, grass seed and lawn fertilizer, and baseball bats and baseballs.

Some goods and services exhibit cycles of obsolescence or replacement such that forecasts can be based on knowledge of these replacement patterns. Publishers of textbooks, manufacturers of automobiles, and aircraft producers are examples of corporations that have attempted to use the concept of a replacement cycle to forecast future sales volumes. Time series and causal models have been used to analyze the replacement cycle phenomenon.

Closely related to derived demand and replacement cycle analysis, input-output analysis traces the flows of goods and services from one country to another, from one industry to another, from one sector of an economy to another, or conceivably between parts of a corporation. By understanding the magnitudes and paths of such flows, a forecaster can sometimes draw conclusions upon which to base forecasts. However, because of lack of data, technical limitations, and the expense involved, it is doubtful that input-output analysis will be useful to many corporate executives for forecasting purposes in the forseeable future.

*Survey Methods.* Consumer surveys and test markets are widely used for forecasting in cases where historical data are not adequate. (See MARKETING RESEARCH.)

*Normative Models.* Policies are normative in nature, aimed at achieving specific objectives; that is, policies indicate what should be done to accomplish the goals of an organization. Thus, *normative models* are prescriptive in nature. Most of the methods and models discussed in this chapter are *not* prescriptive; rather, their usefulness is generally confined to assisting the forecaster to anticipate what *may* happen given certain assumptions and premises, *not* what *should* happen. In that sense, the methods discussed thus far could be called descriptive and diagnostic models. These descriptive and diagnostic models rely on previous experience and/or historical data.

Mathematical programming techniques and decision tree approaches could be considered to be normative methods, and certain uses of computer simulation and the Delphi approach could be considered to be normative.[18] These are also sometimes referred to as *rational* methods. Normative or rational methods are used to best advantage when the uncontrollable variables have been forecasted and constraints (such as budget limitations) are known. If the uncontrollable variables and constraints can be assumed to be known with certainty, it may be possible to use a mathematical programming approach (such as linear programming) to make future resource allocation decisions and thus to project optimal policies.

If the future values of uncontrollable variables and constraints are not known with certainty, one may be able to use a decision tree approach (or other decision analysis) or a Monte Carlo simulation model to determine the best policies in the face of the uncertainties surrounding the decision maker.

*See also* DECISION MAKING PROCESS; ECONOMIC MEASUREMENTS; INPUT-OUTPUT ANALYSIS; MARKET ANALYSIS; OPERATIONS RESEARCH AND MATHEMATI-

CAL MODELING; PRODUCTION PLANNING AND CONTROL; STATISTICAL ANALYSIS FOR MANAGEMENT.

## NOTES

[1]Hugh E. Bradley, "Setting and Controlling Budgets with Regression Analysis," *Management Accounting*, November 1969, pp. 31–34.

[2]Charles W. Gross and Robin T. Peterson, *Business Forecasting*, Houghton Mifflin Company, Boston, 1976, chap. 2.

[3]Steven C. Wheelwright and Spyros Makridakis, *Quantitative and Technological Methods of Forecasting and Planning*, Wiley-Hamilton, New York, 1976.

[4]Marvin A. Jolson and Gerald L. Rossow, "The Delphi Process in Marketing Decision Making," *Journal of Marketing Research*, vol. 8, no. 4, pp. 443–448, November 1971.

[5]Harold A. Linstone and Murray Turoff, *The Delphi Method: Techniques and Applications*, Addison-Wesley Publishing Company, Inc., Reading, Mass., 1975.

[6]*Business Forecasts, 1976*, Federal Reserve Bank of Richmond, Richmond, Va., 1976.

[7]Henry J. Claycamp and Lucien E. Liddy, "Prediction of New Product Performance: An Analytical Approach," *Journal of Marketing Research*, vol. 6, pp. 414–420, November 1969.

[8]Robert S. Pindyck and Daniel L. Rubinfeld, *Econometric Models and Economic Forecasts*, McGraw-Hill Book Company, New York, 1976.

[9]Carl A. Dauten and Lloyd M. Valentine, *Business Cycles and Forecasting*, 4th ed., South-Western Publishing Company, Inc., Cincinnati, 1974.

[10]N. K. Dhalla and Sonia Yuspeh, "Forget the Product Life Cycle Concept," *Harvard Business Review*, vol. 54, no. 1, pp. 102–112, January–February 1976.

[11]Dauten and Valentine, op. cit.

[12]*Business Forecasts, 1976*, op. cit.

[13]Elizabeth W. Angle, *Keys for Business Forecasting*, Federal Reserve Bank of Richmond, Richmond, Va., June 1975.

[14]Wheelwright and Makridakis, op. cit.

[15]——— and ———, op. cit., chap. 9.

[16]Vincent A. Mabert, *An Introduction to Short Term Forecasting Using the Box-Jenkins Methodology*, American Institute of Industrial Engineers Monograph, Atlanta, 1975.

[17]Gross and Peterson, op. cit., chap. 9.

[18]John W. Sutherland, "Architecting the Future: A Delphi-Based Paradigm for Normative System-Building," in Linstone and Turoff, op. cit.

## REFERENCES

Chambers, John C., Satinder K. Mullick, and Donald D. Smith: *An Executive's Guide to Forecasting*, John Wiley & Sons, Inc., New York, 1974.

Chisolm, Roger K., and Gilbert R. Whitaker, Jr.: *Forecasting Methods*, Richard D. Irwin, Inc., Homewood, Ill., 1971.

*Forecasting Series Reprint*, no. 21215, *Harvard Business Review*, Cambridge, Mass., 1971.

*Sales Forecasting*, The Conference Board, Inc., New York, 1976.

Wheelwright, Steven C., and Spyros Makridakis: *Forecasting Methods for Management*, 2d ed., Interscience Publishers, a division of John Wiley & Sons, Inc., New York, 1976.

——— and ———, *Interactive Forecasting*, Holden-Day, Inc., Publisher, San Francisco, 1976.

(The author acknowledges the guidance provided by Professor Steven Wheelwright, Harvard Business School; Mr. Louis P. Pante, American Can Company; Professors John Forbes, Robert Landel, and Willis Ryckman, The Darden School, University of Virginia.)

Curtis J. Tompkins, *West Virginia University*

## Forecasts, environmental  (*See* ENVIRONMENT, PHYSICAL.)

## Foreign exchange  (*See* EXCHANGE, FOREIGN, MANAGEMENT OF.)

## Foreign trade  (*See* INTERNATIONAL TRADE.)

## Forms analysis  (*See* PAPER WORK SIMPLIFICATION.)

## Forms design and control

Business forms cover the entire spectrum of paper work used to collect, process, record, and communicate organizational information in a standard or uniform way. Regardless of organization size, the cost of preparing, processing, and using business forms constitutes a sizable, ongoing investment in employee time. How productively that time is spent is largely determined by how well or poorly the forms are designed. Studies in government and private industry have shown that the costs of forms themselves are only 5 percent of the true, overall cost of the typical clerical operation. The remaining 95 percent is the employee time required to process and use them.

Poorly designed forms are more expensive to process and invariably cost more than they should. If forms are not constantly reevaluated, they soon become obsolete; if their introduction is not closely supervised, forms tend to increase rapidly in number. In either case, the result is greater clerical cost. Clearly, all these factors point to the need for effective forms design and control.

## PRINCIPLES OF FORMS DESIGN

The ideal form serves its function with a minimum of effort, expense, and waste. To achieve this goal, an analysis conducted by a forms designer (internally employed or a qualified vendor) must precede the design of a new form or the redesign of an existing one.

With the exact purpose of the form clearly in mind, and with nothing assumed, every aspect of it is questioned and examined. Those who wish to initiate a new form as well as those who will process it are interviewed. The flow of each part of the form is traced from the time it is prepared until it is either sent out, filed, or discarded.

Some of the key factors to be considered are:

1. *Is the form truly necessary?* There is always the possibility that the information the new form would provide is available on an existing form.

2. *Does the form have more or fewer parts than are actually needed?* All too often forms are routinely reordered with the same number of parts, although one or more no longer serve any purpose. Eliminating only one part from an order for 10,000 multiple-part carbon-interleaved forms saves the cost of shipping, storing, processing, and filing 10,000 pieces of paper, in addition to the cost of the paper and carbon itself. Too few parts, on the other hand, result in costly trips to the copier.

3. *Is all the information on the form necessary?* Any data not required for a specific purpose should be eliminated. If not, the time and effort spent in gathering and recording that information are wasted.

4. *Can the form be combined with another form?* Dramatic savings of employee time and forms cost can be realized if two or more forms with similiar information can be combined.

5. *Have all possible manual operations been eliminated by "building" them into the form?* Information or numbering that is repetitively written or stamped onto a form can be preprinted. Hand stapling can be eliminated by pregluing parts that eventually must be joined. File holes can be punched during form manufacture.

6. *What would be the most advantageous construction?* The volume of usage and the application, among other factors, will point to the best of a number of possible constructions. For instance, unit sets (multiple-part forms which come with carbons between parts) free the clerical worker of the tedious, time-consuming task of manually inserting carbons into each form before typing it. For larger volumes, the continuous construction does away with the need to insert, adjust, and eject each individual form. Only the first need be inserted and lined up in the machine. The rest follow one another in perfect alignment.

Upon completion of the analysis, the forms designer creates a form that reflects the answers to these and numerous other questions.

## CASE HISTORIES

The benefits and savings to be realized from these principles and procedures can best be illustrated by a series of actual case histories.

CASE HISTORY NO. 1: Each of the approximately 150,000 shipments made annually by a large coffee company required a three-part bill of lading form which was prepared by hand in the shipping department. Shipments were subsequently billed on six-part continuous invoice forms prepared on computer terminals in the billing department. *Improvement:* Both the bill of lading and invoice forms are combined into a nine-part invoice/bill of lading form and continue to be prepared on the billing department terminals. A special type of very thin, carbonless paper is used to ensure legibility of all parts.

This change eliminates the time and expense of writing 150,000 bill of lading forms per year. Also gone are problems caused by illegible handwriting.

CASE HISTORY NO. 2: A large percentage of applications for new policies received by an insurance company required additional information from the agents who sent them in. The request for additional information came in a letter dictated by a sales executive and typed by a secretary. *Improvement:* A three-part unit set "request for additional information" form was designed. It lists those items of information which an analysis of past letters revealed to be most frequently requested. To the left of each item is a check box; to the right, enough space for an answer. By using this form, the executive need only check one or more boxes for the information required of the agent. One copy is kept for follow-up, and the remaining two copies, with carbon intact, are sent to the agent. No additional typing of an envelope is required; the form is designed to be used with a no. 10 window envelope, which reveals the agent's name and address after the form has been folded and inserted. Upon receipt of the form, the agent simply fills in the items of information requested, removes the carbon, keeps one copy for the files, and returns the completed original to the insurance company. This form not only reduces executive and secretarial time; it speeds up replies.

CASE HISTORY NO. 3: A small but rapidly growing jewelry manufacturer had found that its forms failed to keep pace with the company's volume of orders. Each sales order required the preparation of a two-part production order, packing list, shipping label, and multiple-part invoice, each of which was individually prepared at different points and times in the operation. *Improvement:* All forms were combined into an eight-part typewritten unit set. At the start, the form is completely filled out except for the quantity shipped, extensions, and final totals. The production order copies, packing list, and shipping label are removed from the set as needed during the operation while the invoice section, with carbons intact, remains on file until final shipment of the order is made. At this point, with final quantities and shipping charges known, the invoice section is reinserted into the typewriter and completed.

CASE HISTORY NO. 4: A bottled water distributor had a collection system consisting of three different 8½- by 11-inch continuous-form dunning statements. There were 30-, 60-, and 90-day past-due notifications. Large volumes of statements in each category were processed by computer each month, requiring a separate run for each of the three forms. After print-out, the forms were separated from one another, folded, inserted into mailing envelopes along with a return remittance envelope, sealed, stamped and mailed. *Improvement:* Through major revisions in layout and a more economical use of space, the length of the form was reduced from 11 to 5½ inches. The three different forms were redesigned into a single form so that all three categories are prepared in one pass through the computer, with the computer print-out making the differentiation between the 30-, 60-, and 90-day statements. In addition, a continuous-mailer construction was introduced; the statements are manufactured so that each has already been sealed into its stamped mailing envelope, along with a return-remittance envelope, prior to being run through the computer. Now, after computer processing, these continuous envelopes need only be separated from one another and mailed. Form size is cut by 50 percent; monthly computer runs for the system are reduced from three to one; postcomputer processing is cut from 2 days to less than ½ day (thereby also improving cash flow), and the company has to order and store only one form instead of three.

## MANAGEMENT AND FORMS DESIGN

The price that must be paid for using inefficient forms is too high to be ignored. Effectively designed forms should be considered a necessity, not an option. Still, the mistaken notion persists that anyone can design a form, with paper and pencil the only prerequisites. Truly effective design, however, calls for professional knowledge and experience in the areas of systems analysis, layout, paper, carbon, printing, and forms manufacture, as well as the ability to deal with the capabilities and limitations of an everexpanding array of equipment for processing forms.

## FORMS CONTROL

An organization with an awareness of the true cost of its forms (initial *plus* processing costs) and a desire to keep these expenses to a minimum can realize appreciable savings by initiating a forms control program. The size and scope of such a program will vary among companies, depending upon organization size, number of forms involved, and the degree of management's commitment to such an effort. A forms control program, on any scale, must have the total support of the highest levels of management if it is to succeed.

For smaller-sized companies, a forms control program carried out by a qualified design and systems-oriented forms vendor will serve the purpose. Larger organizations, however, require an internal forms control unit, which can range in size from a single person to a full staff of analyst/designers headed by a forms manager.

**Objectives** Ideally, the forms control group should have the necessary authority and staff to deal with and administer every aspect of the organization's paperwork and carry out these major objectives:

1. Collection and review of every form being used within the organization.

2. Elimination of all unnecessary forms, combination of forms wherever possible, redesign of existing forms as required for maximum efficiency and cost savings, and responsibility for analysis and design of all new forms.

3. Attainment of economies in purchasing by means of standardizing sizes wherever possible and combining purchases.

4. Assurance that forms are available as needed while inventories are kept at a minimal level.

**Implementation.** In order to implement and maintain a forms control program, the following steps are required:

1. Prepare and distribute a collection letter throughout the organization as a means of collecting samples of every form in use, along with a fully detailed account of how the form is presently being used and its volume of usage.

2. Set up and maintain a *numerical file*, by initially devising an appropriate numbering system and then using it as the basis for assigning a number to each new form.

3. Set up and maintain a *functional file* as a means of sorting forms by function, such as "authorize," "acknowledge," "bill," "report." This file will uncover existing duplication of forms and act as a tool to prevent future duplication as well. It is also a valuable reference file in which all forms which deal with a particular function or area can readily be found.

4. Establish the forms control unit as the sole authority in handling requests to initiate new forms and reorder existing ones, as well as in determining whether a form is to be supplied by an outside vendor or produced by an in-house printing facility.

5. Set up procedures and controls for procurement, inventory, storage, and distribution.

Initiating a forms control unit requires an investment of time, effort, and personnel, but there is a potential saving of from 30 to 50 percent of the total spent on forms and their usage. Initial savings are the most dramatic; subsequent savings tend to level off, however. For this reason care should be taken that forms control remains a permanent concern of the organization to ensure that economies gained and controls established are not lost.

*See also Information Systems;* PAPER WORK SIMPLIFICATION; RECORDS MANAGEMENT; SYSTEMS AND PROCEDURES.

## REFERENCES

Carey, L. Chester: "The Quality Form," *Journal of Systems Management,* June 1972, p. 28.

Hunt, Don E., Sr.: "Many Forms Are Not Working as They Should," *The Office,* January 1973.

Kramer, Seymour D.: "10 Ways to Improve Your Sales Control Forms," *Sales Management,* Special Report on Sales Control Forms, August 1975, p. 2.

Myers, Gibbs: "Forms as a Symptom of Business Health," *Journal of Systems Management,* February 1976, p. 16.

Osteen, Carl E.: *Forms Analysis, A Management Tool for Design and Control,* Office Publications, Inc., Stamford, Conn., 1969.

Pemberton, Roy F.: "Organizing the Forms Management Program," *Information-Records Management Magazine,* August 1975, p. 8.

SEYMOUR D. KRAMER, *Revere Business Graphics, Inc.*

## Four C's of credit  (*See* CREDIT MANAGEMENT.)

## Four-day week

A schedule that compresses the normal working week into four days instead of five is termed a four-day week. The most usual plan where the normal workweek is 40 hours is to have the employees work four 10-hour days.

Four-and-a-half- and three-day weeks have also been introduced in some cases. For example, one schedule calls for two 12-hour days and one 11-hour day.

Four-day weeks have been used in both the United States and Europe. In the United States only a minority of companies have scheduled compressed workweeks, and some of those that have done so have later abandoned the plan. A Bureau of Labor Statistics report, drawn from a Bureau of the Census survey of 47,000 households (in May 1974) showed that of full-time employees (those working 35 hours or more a week) 82 percent were working 5 days, 16 percent 5½ to 7 days, and only 2 percent 3 to 4½ days.

Some companies have found that longer working days and shorter working weeks have improved morale and reduced costs. Others have experienced scheduling difficulties, higher costs, and problems with employee fatigue.

*See also* WORK-HOURS, FLEXIBLE.

## REFERENCES

Evans, Archibald A.: *Hours of Work in Industrialized Countries,* International Labour Office, Geneva, 1975, pp. 91–93.

Gannon, Martin J.: "Four Days, Forty Hours: A Case Study," *California Management Review,* Winter 1974, pp. 74–81.

Hedges, Janice Neipert: "How Many Days Make a Workweek?" *Monthly Labor Review,* April 1975, pp. 29–36.

Wheeler, Kenneth E., Richard Gurman, and Dale Tarnowieski: *The Four-Day Week* (an AMA research report), American Management Association, New York, 1972.

STAFF/SMITH

## Fourth market, securities  (*See* MARKETS, SECURITIES.)

## Franchise contract  (*See* RETAILING MANAGEMENT.)

# Franchising

Franchising is both a distinctive form of organizing a business and a method of doing business. It is a way of marketing a product and/or service which has been adopted and used in a wide variety of industries and businesses. More than 1200 companies, representing over 40 distinct industries, use the franchising method.

Franchising is perhaps the only form of business organization that, by its very nature, tends to create new business units. When the franchisee joins the franchise system, his or her new trade name, the acquisition of a distinctive business appearance, and the standardization of products, services, and operating procedures lead to the birth of a new enterprise for the express purpose of marketing the franchiser's products and/or services.

There is no simple, single definition of franchising. In its basic form, franchising is a system characterized by a continuing relationship in which the franchiser grants to the franchisee a licensed privilege to do business and provides assistance in organizing, training, merchandising, and managing, usually in return for a consideration from the franchisee. In many cases, the franchisee, with or without an agreed-upon consideration, gains the right to sell a certain product or service and to use a certain brand name, trademark, business technique, or technical process as developed by the franchiser.

Franchise arrangements can be subdivided into two broad classes:

1. Product distribution arrangements in which the dealer is to some degree, but not entirely, identified with the manufacturer/supplier

2. Entire business format franchising, in which there is complete identification of the dealer with the buyer

Some prefer a subdivision into three broad classes:

1. Establishment of a selective and limited distribution system for particular products (for example, automobiles, bicycles, gasoline, tires, appliances, cosmetics) to be distributed under the manufacturer's name and trademark

2. Trademark and brand name licensing for

processing plants, for example, soft drink bottlers, which combine some elements of 1 and 3

3. Franchising of an entire retail business operation, including the license of a trademark, tradename, method and format of doing business, sometimes called "pure," "comprehensive," or "entire business format" franchising (for example, fast-food restaurants and stores, motels, car rental firms, personnel businesses, and schools)

A franchising business generally develops into an organization consisting of supporting units, created and administered by the franchiser, which are designed to expand the distribution of products and/or services under uniformity controls over quality, format, and technique.

Judging from the wide variety of business and industries employing the franchise system, one might well conclude that practically anything is franchiseable. There are certain basic requirements, however. It is essential that the product or service be capable of complete systemization. It also is essential that the system be easily taught to others in a comparatively brief time—say, 2 to 3 weeks. And the system must be one for which an individual identity can be effectively created and maintained.

A franchise concept should be tested and proved through the establishment of prototype units before it is expanded into a franchise network. One should carefully plan and consider the important characteristics of real estate location, the building to be erected on the property, the fixturization of the premises to accommodate the kind of operation or service being offered, effective signs for the business, advertising, training of employees, accounting, marketing, promotion, financing, and a host of other items.

## HISTORY OF FRANCHISING

Franchise distribution in the United States has existed for nearly 100 years. The earliest, and still among the largest, franchise networks were based on sewing machines (Singer), automobiles, gasoline, soft drinks (Pepsi-Cola and Coca-Cola), and food (Howard Johnson and A&W Root Beer). The last two decades, however, have seen a virtual explosion of this marketing method, particularly in the retail and service fields. Franchising in the industrial markets has not grown as extensively. Industrial marketers have usually resorted to the issuance of licenses for product distribution—but a franchise is not simply a license. Inherent in a franchise system is the degree of operational control over the franchisee that a true licenser seldom seeks.

Franchising may also be divided into traditional and newer types. Automobile and truck dealers, gasoline service stations, and soft drink bottlers are the traditional types. The newer types of franchising include fast food, lodging, rentals, business aids, personnel services, bicycle shops, lawn services, real estate, and wholesaling.

The traditional types of franchising for many years have dominated the franchising scene, accounting for some 75 percent of all franchise sales, according to the U.S. Department of Commerce.

The adoption of the method by a wide variety of other businesses during the 1950s and 1960s resulted in a remarkable growth in the newer types of franchising during these two decades, giving rise to the modern-day giants such as McDonald's, 7-Eleven, Manpower, and Midas Muffler, to name only a few.

## TRADEMARK LICENSING

This practice, once an integral part of the law of trademark assignments and generally prohibited, is today legally permissible, in widespread use, and uniquely adaptable to a broad variety of business situations. A trademark may be licensed to a single licensee or to thousands.

The trademark is ordinarily the "cornerstone of a franchise system." It is its most dominant, unifying element, that which identifies the particular product or services to the purchasing public and guarantees a uniform standard of quality.

Trademark franchising is the purest form of franchising. Nearly every franchise operation of this form establishes and supports an entirely new business. The franchisee is highly dependent on the franchiser for training, promotion, marketing, and equipment supply. In turn, the franchiser is totally dependent on the franchisee (unless company-owned operations exist) for revenue. In this system, the ongoing relationship between franchiser and franchisee and the enforcement of quality control standards become very important to the success of the operation. Because a franchiser's trademark provides identification, customer attraction, and quality assurance, the franchiser must police the uniformity of the system and the trademark or trade name under which it operates.

## ECONOMICS OF FRANCHISING

In 1977, franchise sales of goods and services by all franchising companies were estimated at $238 billion, 31 percent of all retail sales, and more than double the level of sales at the start of the 1970s. In the same year, the number of establishments associated with franchise businesses was estimated to total 460,000, employing 3.5 million people.

Traditional types of franchising—automobile and truck dealers, gasoline service stations, and soft drink bottlers—continue to account for a major portion of franchising activity, accounting for 79 percent of all franchise sales in 1977. The traditional types of franchising establishments have seen a decline since 1972 in the number of outlets, while the newer types of franchises—fast food, convenience stores, hotel-motel, recreation, and entertainment—have shown an increase in the number of establishments.

Today the newer areas of franchising are enjoying a substantial growth, far outpacing the growth rate in the traditional sectors, according to the Department of Commerce. For 1977, the Department predicts that sales in the newer or nontraditional types of franchising will move up to $50.6 billion, 13 percent over the 1976 level. The growth rate of these establishments "showed an impressive climb of almost 12 percent in 1976 over 1974, from 209,727 to 234,166 establishments," the Department reports.

Among those companies with dual operations, franchised and company-owned, the trend is toward greater growth in franchising, and there is little doubt that the growth exhibited between 1974 and 1976 will continue.

## REASONS BEHIND THE GROWTH

Franchising has charisma. It has a fascination and an appeal to the entrepreneurial spirit which remains vibrant in our free enterprise system. Franchising has been termed the last, best hope for independent business in an era of growing vertical integration. It helps small business to compete with the giants. The Small Business Administration (SBA) has stated, "Franchisees have a good chance to survive and prosper in a highly competitive society, offering an opportunity to those individuals who have only a limited amount of capital and experience. It is a system that offers an economically feasible alternative to the vertically integrated, centrally owned organizations, and one also that can provide a vehicle for greater minority entry into business." "Without franchising," the SBA has stated, "thousands of small businessmen would never have had the opportunity of owning their own businesses."

## FRANCHISING'S APPEAL

When planning to market a new product, service, or concept, a firm has a choice of several alternative distribution routes. The firm can (1) convince independent outlets, distributors, or manufacturers to take on the company's offering as an additional item in their line; (2) find individuals interested in establishing a new business to sell the product; (3) establish a network of company-owned outlets staffed by company employees. However, assuming that a product can support full-scale distributive operations in different localities with owner/managers, then a company may consider a fourth option—franchising.

A most important reason for adopting franchised distribution is to conserve or acquire capital while at the same time attempting to establish an effective distribution network as quickly as possible. Naturally, other financing techniques are available; but borrowing creates a heavy burden with its associated high risk, especially for a new product, while equity financing dilutes ownership. The acquisition of funds through franchising, by contrast, does not dilute ownership and, in fact, creates a self-liquidating debt liability.

The franchise marketing concept includes more than rapid expansion at low cost. It includes the ability to control and coordinate the product's movement from production to retail marketing, the standardization of promotion practices, messages, and techniques, and the establishment of quality control processes. In essence, a well-managed and conceived franchised distribution system and the adjoining marketing concept will result in a synergistic organization.

Franchising reduces the costs of distribution. The franchise company creates a marketing system in which the elements of distribution usually pay for the right to market its product or services. If the company were to rely on distribution through its own outlets or manufacture in one large plant or several dispersed facilities, then it might be saddled with high fixed overhead expenses, especially in the product's early life-cycle.

Managerial motivation is a second major advantage, especially over company-owned outlets. Franchisees are often more sensitive to the needs of the local market, more sensitive to the need for controlling operating costs, and more likely to work hard at developing their markets than a salaried employee.

## THE FRANCHISE CONTRACT

The relationship between franchiser and franchisee is set by the franchise contract. A noted legal expert,

Jerrold G. Van Cise, poses three principles that should guide the franchiser in preparing a contract. The first is that the contract should be frank. "Complete disclosure of a proposed relationship between franchisor and franchisee is desirable in order to ensure that neither party may reasonably charge that thereby he was deceived by the other." Van Cise secondly holds that the provisions of the contract should be fair. "This franchise relationship should be so equitable that no party may convincingly claim that thereunder he was dominated by the other." Thirdly, Van Cise declares that the contract should be enforceable. "If either the franchisor or the franchisee should be tempted to breach the covenants thus openly and equitably entered into, he should not be in the position of a pot entitled to call the other an equally black kettle."

Obviously, drafting a franchise contract in accordance with these principles is not a simple task. The franchiser should seek out a skilled and knowledgeable legal craftsman for the job.

## FRANCHISING AND THE LAW

The last decade has seen an emergence of a highly specialized body of franchise law. The focus primarily has been in defining the franchiser's ability to control the operational aspects of the business and the activities of franchise owners who are legally independent businessmen.

Today, legal considerations are part of the fabric of franchising. No company contemplating franchising can ignore them. This discussion considers state and federal regulations and judicial decisions.

**State Regulations**  The era of state regulation of franchising began in earnest when California enacted a franchise investment law in 1970. Today more than a dozen states have registration and disclosure laws regulating presale disclosure of all information pertaining to the franchise offering, and a number of other state legislatures have similar laws under consideration. This means that the franchiser must register and submit extensive disclosure statements in each of those states with such laws. The lack of uniformity between the disclosure laws has been a major problem for franchising companies and has sharply increased the cost of entering franchising. The problem has been eased considerably recently, however, with the introduction of the Uniform Franchise Offering Circular which, with minor changes, now is accepted by all states requiring disclosure. Another problem with state regulation has been the tendency to impose upon all franchisers restrictions designed to halt practices in a particular industry. For example, because of the short-term leases prevalent in the gasoline industry, legislatures have been turning increasing attention to regulating franchise termination and nonrenewal.

**Federal Regulations**  Disclosure and termination have not been ignored by the federal government. As of this writing, the Federal Trade Commission has before it a trade regulation rule on franchising. This rule would regulate the sale of franchises, making disclosure mandatory nationwide. In both the U.S. Senate and House, bills have been introduced which would restrict the circumstances under which a franchiser could terminate a franchisee or fail to renew the franchise upon expiration of the contract.

**Judicial Decisions**  Franchise law as established by the courts has emerged from cases brought under the federal antitrust laws. A number of landmark court decisions have established the parameters under which franchisers may operate. It has been found illegal, for example, for franchisers to require franchisees to purchase all types of products or services from them, to restrict the franchisees' territory or class of customers, to consult with one franchisee before granting a franchise to another, and to require franchisees to adhere to price levels.

In addition to state and federal laws and judicial decisions applicable generally, there are laws which regulate the franchiser-franchisee relationship within specific industries, and there are laws intended to regulate other business relations which have an impact on franchising.

It is essential that any franchising company be well aware of all the laws, rules, and regulations affecting franchising, for violations—even though they be inadvertent—can trigger ruinous lawsuits, and the resulting judgments can involve treble money awards and even criminal sanctions.

## CONCLUSION

Clearly, franchising offers tremendous rewards and advantages to a producer in terms of financing, growth, and management motivation. Modern-day franchising, however, is not for companies who do not have a well-thought-out concept, who do not have sufficient capital, or who do not avail themselves of competent and current legal advice and information.

*See also* MARKETING, CHANNELS OF DISTRIBUTION; OWNERSHIP, LEGAL FORMS OF; RETAILING MANAGEMENT.

## REFERENCES

Fels, Jerome L.; *Franchising and the Law*, International Franchise Association, Washington, 1976.

————and Lewis G. Rudnick: *Investigate before Investing*, International Franchise Association, Washington, 1976.

*Franchised Distribution*, The Conference Board, Inc., New York, 1971.

Gilson, Jerome: *Trademark Protection and Practice*, Matthew Bender, New York, 1974.

Kaul, Donald A.: *Protecting Your Franchise Trademark*, International Franchise Association, Washington, 1974.

Thompson, Donald N.: *Franchise Operations and Antitrust*, D. C. Heath and Company, Lexington, Mass., 1971.

U.S. Department of Commerce, *Franchise Opportunities Handbook*, 1976.

U.S. Department of Commerce, *Franchising in the Economy*, 1975–1977, December 1976.

Van Cise, Jerrold G.: *A Franchise Contract*, International Franchise Association, Washington, 1974.

JERRY H. OPACK, *Attorney at Law,*
*Washington, D.C.*

## FRANCHISING: APPENDIX

Franchising is a method of distribution that formally links two members in a distribution channel. The relationship is usually a carefully prescribed legal one in which the firm at or near the source of the product or service (such as a manufacturer) agrees to license, allow, and assist a firm closer to the customer (such as a distributor or retailer) to operate in the former's behalf for certain considerations such as fees, commissions, and royalties.

Franchising had its origins in the automobile industry, but it has extended to almost every conceivable kind of business, product, or service. In the United States, there are nearly 500,000 franchisees whose collective sales amount to over $200 billion annually and account for more than 30 percent of the country's retail sales. Of this total, auto and truck dealers account for about 60 percent, gasoline stations 22 percent, commercial food markets 2 percent, and fast-food outlets over 5 percent. The fastest growing segments include autos and auto products, business services and aids, convenience stores, educational products and services, fast-food establishments, recreation, travel, entertainment, rental and leasing services, and tax preparation. Franchising is by no means limited to the United States. Growth in the number of franchisers and outlets overseas has been greatest in Canada, Australia, and Japan—with the pattern of products and services roughly following that in the United States.

**Approaches**  Franchising arrangements take several forms. They may be grouped, however, into two major classes:

1. *Association franchising.* In this approach, a wholesaler may initiate a *voluntary chain* of independent retailers for the purpose of ensuring the whole-

saler of profitable outlets for its merchandise. A notable example is the Independent Grocers' Alliance (IGA). In such wholesaler-sponsored chains, the wholesaler offers services to franchised retailers who agree to buy all or almost all their merchandise from the wholesaler. A retail cooperative chain differs from the preceding form in that it is typically sponsored by its retail members who jointly own and operate a warehouse in their own behalf, with themselves as franchisees.

2. *Manufacturer-sponsored franchising.* This is the form more usually identified as franchising. The manufacturer of a product or the owner of a proprietary form of service sets up a network of retail outlets by contracting with "independent" owners who operate according to the terms of the franchising agreement. This arrangement may include *(a)* one product, such as a line of cookies sold on a special rack in a grocery store; *(b)* a single department such as consumer electronic items within a department store; or *(c)* a complete retail outlet such as dealerships for John Deere's farm equipment, Pizza Hut fast-food restaurants, Holiday Inn motels, Avis or Hertz car rentals, H&R Block tax services, and Fred Astaire dance studies.

**Franchise Advantages**   The advantages of franchising to the franchiser are many. Principally, they include the following:

1. The parent company obtains greater control of marketing, especially pricing, advertising, and inventory quality and service maintenance.

2. The parent company can expand its markets and grow faster, since the franchisees provide the operating organization and its local management.

3. The franchiser attains greater leverage from both investment and management. Typically, the franchisee must invest a substantial portion of his or her money, although this may be only a small portion of the total investment required in a particular outlet. This investment, in turn, provides an incentive for economies and astute management at the local level.

4. Both parties can make more effective use of cooperative advertising and promotion.

5. Group purchasing power offers economies of scale, which can be turned into lower retail prices and/or higher profits for parent and operator.

6. The operator has available better, more sophisticated administrative services such as *(a)* employment, training, and operation standards, and *(b)* purchasing, inventory, accounting, and control procedures.

7. The franchisee's liability may be limited to that specified in the contractual agreement.

8. The retailer gains from affiliation with an established organization whose public reputation is greater than the outlet might obtain independently.

**Franchise Disadvantages**   The disadvantages of franchising are often the obverse of its advantages. Additionally, there are these limitations:

1. Increased buying power is not necessarily the key to retailing success. It is more likely to be the ability to develop and use specialized services and controls usually available only to larger organizations.

2. The desire to extend control often inhibits not only profitability at the local level but also the kind of marketing flexibility needed to keep the outlet viable in the face of increasing and varied competition.

3. The franchise system depends ultimately upon the quality and dedication of the outlet owners. Financial rewards tend to be small in proportion to the time and effort required. Thus, it is difficult to attract and hold effective operators.

4. Profitability squeezes tend to foster "buyback" of outlets, which often puts the franchiser in competition with franchisees and can lead to operation by the corporation itself, with dependence upon its own staff for local management.

**Affiliation Guidelines**   The potential franchisee, who is usually in a position of less bargaining strength, should assess the affiliation carefully in terms of (1) demonstrated salability of product or service, (2) services offered by the parent company, especially those the outlet cannot provide itself, (3) ratio of operator investment to the total startup cost, (4) and profitability of the arrangement in terms of both hours of owner input and return on capital. Additionally, the operator prospect should determine (through organizations like the International Franchise Association, the Council of Better Business Bureaus, and the Small Business Administration) the reputation and the financial strength of the parent company. The product itself warrants particular scrutiny in terms of its intrinsic quality, its competitive stance, its pricing, and its long-term viability in the market.

The franchiser must be just as careful in the selection of affiliates, and most successful ones are. Successful outlet operators tend to be thrifty, healthy, hard-working, marketing-oriented, and capable of carefully following prescribed specifications and instructions.

**Legal Concerns**   Franchising, like many rapidly growing fields, has had its share of problems stemming from both inexperience and disreputable promoters. Over and above the risks inherent in any business venture, the franchising field has often been characterized by overpromising and overexpansion. Franchising is especially vulnerable to the abuse of "pyramiding," in which a promoter is more interested in the fees obtained from opening new franchises than with their operation or potential for success. Accordingly, careful attention should be given by both parties to the prospectus, the market assessment, and the affiliation contract. Under particular legal scrutiny should be the following:

1. The franchiser's power over contract renewal.

2. The extent to which pricing is determined by the parent company.

3. The extent to which the operator must purchase supplies from the franchiser or a designated supplier.

STAFF/BITTEL

**Free trade area**   (*See* INTERNATIONAL TRADE.)

**Friction, in profit making**   (*See* PROFITS AND PROFIT MAKING.)

**Fringe benefits**   (*See* COMPENSATION, EMPLOYEE BENEFIT PLANS.)

**Function**   (*See* VALUE ANALYSIS.)

**Functional authority**   (*See* AUTHORITY, RESPONSIBILITY, AND ACCOUNTABILITY.)

**Functional management**   (*See* MANAGEMENT, HISTORICAL DEVELOPMENT OF.)

**Functional organizations**   (*See* ORGANIZATION ANALYSIS AND PLANNING; ORGANIZATION STRUCTURES AND CHARTING.)

**Functions, production**   (*See* PRODUCTION/OPERATIONS MANAGEMENT.)

**Funds, sources and uses statement**   (*See* FINANCIAL MANAGEMENT; FINANCIAL STATEMENT ANALYSIS.)

# G

## Games, management and business
(*See* SIMULATIONS, BUSINESS AND MANAGEMENT.)

## Gaming, operational
(*See* SYSTEM CONCEPT, TOTAL.)

## Gaming theory
(*See* OPERATIONS RESEARCH AND MATHEMATICAL MODELING.)

## Gantt, Henry L.
(*See* MANAGEMENT, HISTORICAL DEVELOPMENT OF.)

## Gantt charts

The *Gantt chart* is a graphic method for planning and controlling production quantities and times. Originated prior to World War I by the industrial engineer Henry Laurence Gantt, the chart is widely used today in a variety of forms in every kind of organization.

The unique value of the Gantt chart is demonstrated in Fig. G-1 which deals with five production orders, stamped serially from 101 to 105. These orders indicate what machines the work must be processed on, the sequence that must be followed, and the estimated number of hours each machine will require to complete its work.

If the schedule planner were to load the machines with the assumption that each order must be finished before another one was begun (straight-line or point-to-point scheduling), the planner would come up with a schedule something like chart A in Fig. G-1. The flow of work would be orderly, but the equipment would be underutilized. Worse still, a great many orders would be delayed. To correct these deficiencies, Gantt *overlapped* orders, disregarding the sequence in which they were accepted while still rigidly adhering to the *operation* sequence that each order specifies. Chart B in Fig. G-1 shows how the scheduler can juggle orders, starting no. 105 on machine B and no. 102 on machine C while at the same time beginning no. 101 on machine A. If the jobs are rearranged and overlapped, all five orders can be finished by Friday afternoon. Furthermore, the scheduler has greatly increased the overall machine utilization. Machine A is now scheduled to be in operation 18 of the first 24 hours of the week (through Wednesday). It works 4 hours on no. 101, 4 hours on no. 104, is idle for 2 hours, then works 4 hours on no. 102, 6 hours on no. 105, and is idle again until the close of the shift on Wednesday. Machine B utilizes 22 hours during the same period:

Chart A

| | Monday | Tuesday | Wednesday | Thursday | Friday | Monday | Tuesday |
|---|---|---|---|---|---|---|---|
| Machine A | 101 | | | 102 | | 103 | |
| Machine B | | 101 | | 102 | 103 | | |
| Machine C | | | 101 102 | | | 103 | |

Log of orders for Charts A and B

| Order no. | 101 (mask) | | | 102 (knob) | | | 103 (optic) | | | 104 (pan) | | | 105 (quoit) | | |
|---|---|---|---|---|---|---|---|---|---|---|---|---|---|---|---|
| Operation sequence | 1 | 2 | 3 | 1 | 2 | 3 | 1 | 2 | 3 | 1 | 2 | 3 | 1 | 2 | 3 |
| Machine no. | A | B | C | C | A | B | B | A | C | A | C | B | B | C | A |
| Machine time (hr) | 4 | 8 | 2 | 10 | 4 | 8 | 6 | 4 | 8 | 4 | 10 | 12 | 4 | 2 | 6 |

Chart B

| | Monday | Tuesday | Wednesday | Thursday | Friday | Monday | Tuesday |
|---|---|---|---|---|---|---|---|
| Machine A | 101 104 | 102 105 | | 103 | | | |
| Machine B | 105 101 | | 102 103 104 | | | | |
| Machine C | 102 105 101 104 | | | 103 | | | |

Fig. G-1. Development of a Gantt chart from a series of production orders. Chart A shows jobs lined up in sequence as they were received. Chart B shows jobs rearranged (overlapped) for maximum machine loading, with prescribed sequences of operations for each job maintained. Each day represents 8 hours.

4 hours on no. 105, 8 hours on no. 101, idle for 2 hours, 6 hours on no. 102, and 4 hours on no. 103. Machine C utilizes all 24 hours: 10 hours on no. 102, 2 hours on no. 105, 2 hours on no. 101, and 10 hours on no. 104. This schedule predicts utilization rates of 75 percent, 92 percent, and 100 percent. While the scheduler might not be able to juggle the work so efficiently all week long, this sequence is an indication of what judicial overlapping of jobs can accomplish.

*Reserved-Time and Progress Control Chart.* Gantt took his chart one step further in order to make it the basis for following progress of work through a shop and providing each worker with a detailed schedule. The Gantt reserved-time and progress control chart in Fig. G-2 is identical in arrangement to the one in chart B of Fig. G-1. It applies the same data in the same way but is different in the way in which the individual rectangles are prepared. For each job scheduled on each machine, the scheduler lightly draws an open-topped rectangle. Inside the rectangle the name (and sometimes the part number) of the job to be run is marked. Where there are open, or unassigned work, blocks, the scheduler inserts an X in pencil that can be quickly found if a new job comes up which might fill the space. During the course of the week as each job progresses, the scheduler draws a heavy line across

the bottom of the rectangle. This progress line is proportional to the *amount produced*, not to the time blocked out for its production. For example, on machine B, job no. 102 has been running since Tuesday afternoon; it is now Wednesday noon and the job should have been completed, but the heavy line at the bottom of the rectangle shows that the job is only two-thirds done (it has made only 450 of the 675 pieces scheduled). Examination of this chart, as of Wednesday noon, shows the following:

Jobs nos. 101 and 105 have been completed.

Job no. 102 is still running on machine B and is behind schedule.

Job no. 104 is running on machine C and is ahead of schedule.

Job. no. 103 has not been begun, but it is on schedule.

Finding that some jobs run behind and others run ahead of schedule is not unusual. This is one reason machines cannot be scheduled for 100 percent utilization. The scheduler, in this example, will have to keep modifying the reserved-time chart to take into account the realities of day-to-day operations. The scheduler also continually adds new orders as well as cancels others.

*Order-of-Work Sheet.* Figure G-3 shows how the scheduler can transfer the planned schedule on the reserved-time chart to an order-of-work sheet. This

454

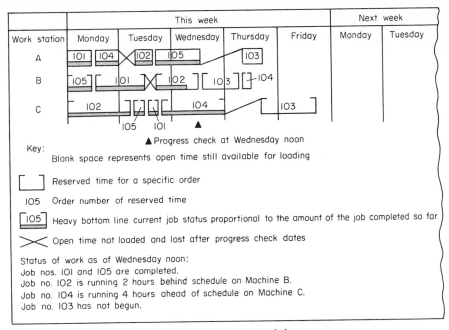

Key:

Blank space represents open time still available for loading

☐ Reserved time for a specific order

105 Order number of reserved time

☐105 Heavy bottom line current job status proportional to the amount of the job completed so far

✕ Open time not loaded and lost after progress check dates

Status of work as of Wednesday noon:
Job nos. 101 and 105 are completed.
Job no. 102 is running 2 hours behind schedule on Machine B.
Job no. 104 is running 4 hours ahead of schedule on Machine C.
Job no. 103 has not begun.

**Fig. G-2. Reserved-time production planning and progress control chart.**

Dept. no.: ___135___    Date originated: Monday, Sept. 6
Period: Week of Sept. 6

| Machine, operation, or bench | | | Part | | | No. of |
| Name | No. | Order no. | Part name | Part no. | Operator's name | pieces to make |
| --- | --- | --- | --- | --- | --- | --- |
| Machine | A | 101 | Mask | 276 | Randolph | 280 |
| | | 104 | Pan | 654 | " | 410 |
| | | 102 | Knob | 410 | " | 675 |
| | | 105 | Quoit | 832 | " | 318 |
| | | 103 | Optic | 721 | " | 1500 |
| Machine | B | 105 | Quoit | 832 | Santo | 318 |
| | | 101 | Mask | 276 | " | 280 |
| | | 102 | Knob | 410 | " | 675 |
| | | 103 | Optic | 721 | " | 1500 |
| | | 104 | Pan | 654 | " | 410 |
| Machine | C | 102 | Knob | 410 | Trosk | 675 |
| | | 105 | Quoit | 832 | " | 318 |
| | | 101 | Mask | 276 | " | 280 |
| | | 104 | Pan | 654 | " | 410 |
| | | 103 | Optic | 721 | " | 1500 |

**Fig. G-3. Order-of-work sheet.**

455

sheet becomes the detailed schedule for each machine and for each operator. It tells *what* will be run, *how much*, and *in what sequence*. Santo, for example, knows that she will operate machine B, that she will work on job nos. 105, 101, 102, 103, and 104 in that sequence. She also knows what *parts* she will work on and *how many* of each she must make to complete her portion of the order.

*See also* NETWORK PLANNING METHODS; PAPERWORK SIMPLIFICATION; PRODUCTION/OPERATIONS MANAGEMENT; PRODUCTION PLANNING AND CONTROL.

### REFERENCES
Bittel, Lester R.: *Improving Supervisory Performance*, McGraw-Hill Book Company, New York, 1976, chap. 10.
Clark, Mrs. Wallace: "The Gantt Chart," chap. 7-3 in H. B. Maynard (ed.), *Industrial Engineering Handbook*, 2d ed., McGraw-Hill Book Company, New York, 1963.
Gantt, Henry Laurence: "A Graphical Daily Balance in Manufacture," *Transactions*, vol. 24, American Society of Mechanical Engineers, 1903.

STAFF/BITTEL

## Gantt Medal awards

Since 1929 the Gantt Medal has been awarded jointly by the American Society of Mechanical Engineers and the American Management Associations to individuals for "distinguished achievement in management as a service to the community." Specifically, the award's criteria recognizes: significant economic and social advancement; imaginative innovation or refinement of management concepts; unique leadership to inspire others; and evidence of major contributions in service to the community. Over the years, recipients have included a wide variety of particularly effective businesspersons and educators who have also made outstanding contributions to society through public service. The medalists, in chronological order, are as follows:

*Henry Laurence Gantt* (1929, posthumously), management engineer, industrial leader, and advocate of corporate social responsibility.

*Fred J. Miller* (1930), editor (*American Machinist*), manager Remington Typewriter Company, industrial engineer.

*Leon Pratt Alford* (1931), engineer, editor (*Industrial Management*), and educator, New York University.

*Henry Sturgis Dennison* (1932), president Dennison Manufacturing Company, progressive in employee benefits and personnel policies.

*Wallace Clark* (1933), international consultant and practitioner of scientific management.

*Horace B. Cheney* (1934), sponsor of Gantt's pioneering work at Cheney Brothers manufacturing company.

*Arthur Howland Young* (1935), pioneer in safety and industrial relations for United States Steel Corporation.

*Morris Evans Leeds* (1936), instrument inventor and public humanitarian, founder of Leeds & Northrup Company.

*William Loren Batt* (1940), president SKF Industries and leading administrator of United States production effort in World War II.

*Paul Eugene Holden* (1941), economist and educator (Stanford University) noted for concepts of organization and control.

*Dexter Simpson Kimball* (1943), educator (Cornell University) and writer on industrial organizations and plant management.

*Lillian Moller Gilbreth and Frank Bunker Gilbreth* (1944), consulting engineers, time and motion innovations (therbligs).

*John Milton Hancock* (1945), creative financier (Jewel Tea Co. and Lehman Brothers), contributor to national policy.

*Paul Gray Hoffman* (1946), progressive management and labor relations at Studebaker Corporation, contributor to national policy.

*Alvin E. Dodd* (1947), founder of American Management Associations, adult educator.

*Fowler McCormick* (1948), corporate organizer, president of International Harvester Company.

*Arthur Clinton Spurr* (1949), leader in rural electrification, utility executive, Monongahela Power Company.

*Charles R. Hook, Sr.* (1950), proponent of incentives and industrial peace at Armco Steel Corporation.

*Thomas Roy Jones* (1951), innovative manufacturing management at ATF, Inc.

*Frank H. Neely* (1952), retailer (Rich's Incorporated), banker, and community leader.

*Thomas E. Millsop* (1953), humanist, industrialist (Weirton Steel Company), and public official.

*Clarence Francis* (1954), educator, executive (General Foods Corporation), administrator of national welfare programs.

*Walker Lee Cisler* (1955), corporate executive (Detroit Edison Company) and developer of international policy.

*Henning Webb Prentis, Jr.* (1956), inspirational private (Armstrong Cork Company) and public leader.

*Harold F. Smiddy* (1957), organization architect (General Electric Company) and teacher of management practices.

*Richard Redwood Deupree* (1958), innovator of guaranteed annual wage at Proctor & Gamble Company.

*Charles Perry McCormick* (1960), exponent of multiple management at McCormick & Company.

*Lyndall Fownes Urwick* (1961), international consultant, proponent of professional status for managers.

*Austin Joseph Tobin* (1962), outstanding public administrator, The Port of New York Authority.

*Lawrence A. Appley* (1963), outstanding management educator, developer of American Management Associations.

*Harold Bright Maynard* (1964), consulting engineer, developer of predetermined time standards and techniques for work measurement and the improvement of productivity.

*Ralph J. Cordiner* (1965), proponent of decentralized corporate management, president of General Electric Company.

*John Erik Jonsson* (1968), corporate innovator (Texas Instruments, Inc.), mayor of Dallas, Texas.

*David Packard* (1969), pioneering electronics executive (Hewlett-Packard Company) and Assistant Secretary of Defense of the United States.

*Frederick R. Kappel* (1970), developer of systems concept as chairman of AT&T and reorganizer of United States Postal Service.

*Donald C. Burnham* (1971), developer of manufacturing productivity improvement at Westinghouse Electric Corporation.

*Robert E. Booker* (1972), growth-oriented merchandiser, president of Whirlpool Corp. and later of Marcor, Inc.

*John T. Connor* (1973), research administrator, chief executive officer of Merck & Co. and later Allied Chemical Corp., Secretary of Commerce of the United States.

*Willard F. Rockwell*, Jr. (1974), architect of creative mergers and technology transfer at Rockwell International Corporation.

*Patrick E. Haggerty* (1975), human relations innovator as chairman of Texas Instruments, Inc.

*Kenneth R. Daniel* (1976), environmentally oriented executive and exponent of value added by technology, American Cast Iron Pipe Company.

*See also* HALL OF FAME OF BUSINESS LEADERSHIP; MANAGEMENT, HISTORICAL DEVELOPMENT OF.

STAFF/BITTEL

## Gatekeeper, communications (*See* COMMUNICATIONS, ORGANIZATIONAL.)

## General Agreement on Tariffs and Trade (GATT) (*See* INTERNATIONAL TRADE.)

## General purchasing power reporting (*See* FINANCIAL STATEMENT ANALYSIS.)

## General staff (*See* ORGANIZATION ANALYSIS AND PLANNING.)

## General systems theory (*See* SYSTEM CONCEPT, TOTAL.)

## Generally accepted accounting principles (GAAP) (*See* ACCOUNTING, FINANCIAL; AUDITING, FINANCIAL.)

## GERT (*See* NETWORK PLANNING METHODS.)

## Gesture clusters (*See* COMMUNICATIONS, NONVERBAL.)

## Gifts, matching (*See* COMPENSATION, EMPLOYEE BENEFIT PLANS.)

## Gilbreth, Frank K. (*See* MANAGEMENT, HISTORICAL DEVELOPMENT OF.)

## Gilbreth, Lillian M. (*See* MANAGEMENT, HISTORICAL DEVELOPMENT OF.)

## Goal-oriented organizations (*See* ORGANIZATION ANALYSIS AND PLANNING.)

## Goals, formal and informal (*See* OBJECTIVES AND GOALS.)

## Goals, hierarchy (*See* OBJECTIVES AND GOALS.)

## Goals, individual and group  (*See* OBJECTIVES AND GOALS.)

## Goals, multiple  (*See* CONTROL SYSTEMS, MANAGEMENT.)

## Goals and objectives  (*See* OBJECTIVES AND GOALS.)

## Goals, official  (*See* OBJECTIVES AND GOALS.)

## Goals, operational  (*See* OBJECTIVES AND GOALS.)

## Goals, surrogate  (*See* CONTROL SYSTEMS, MANAGEMENT.)

## Government assistance  (*See* GOVERNMENT RELATIONS AND SERVICES.)

## Government financing  (*See* FINANCIAL MANAGEMENT, SHORT-TERM, INTERMEDIATE, AND LONG-TERM FINANCING; GOVERNMENT REGULATIONS AND SERVICES; SMALL BUSINESS ADMINISTRATION.)

## Government markets  (*See* MARKETS, PUBLIC.)

## Government regulations, business law

Business law includes a multitude of laws affecting the rights and obligations of those persons and organizations who engage in business. This entry is by no means encompassing, especially in view of the dynamic state of laws and legislation in the United States. The entry does include, however, basic but not exhaustive insights into selected elements of law that are most vital to business transactions.

### COMMON LAW AND EQUITY

**Common Law** At the heart of the American legal system is the body of law which originated with William the Conqueror in 1066: the common law. This system, or body, of law is composed of the decisions of judges in resolving real disputes. The distinguishing characteristic of the common law is the *doctrine of precedent* which holds that prior decisions involving the same or similar facts should be followed in resolving present disputes. The United States adopted the common law as it had developed in England up to the time of the Revolution; since that time the United States has carried on the tradition of common law in its own courts. The common law is also described as the *law of cases* and is to be distinguished from the acts of the various legislatures. This is not to say, however, that the two are unrelated, as any court decision which defines or interprets a statute is a part of the body of common law.

In a broader sense, common law distinguishes the jurisprudence in the United States and Great Britain from that of other nations and cultures.

**Equity** Equity, or chancery, is—in the strictest sense—a system of law administered by courts separate and distinct from the common-law courts. The equity courts evolved to hear cases the common-law courts were unable to resolve, and they render justice unimpaired by the strict limitations imposed by the common-law courts. The distinguishing characteristics of the law of equity is the flexibility and broad range of remedies available, which include, for example, injunctions and decrees of specific performance. In the broader sense, equity has come to denote the ethical as opposed to the strictly legal resolution of disputes.

### TORTS

A tort is a private injury or wrong arising from a breach of duty owed by one member of society to a fellow member. It is a wrong to person or property not arising out of a contractual relationship. A wrongful act may be a tort and a crime at the same time, if the act transgresses the law. Torts may be classified as intentional and unintentional, and the later group may be further divided into negligence and strict liability.

**Intentional Torts** Intentional torts include assault, battery, defamation, false imprisonment, fraud, invasion of privacy, and infliction of emotional distress.

*Against Persons.* *Assault* is the intentional act of putting another in reasonable apprehension of the possibility of immediate bodily contact. *Battery* is the intentional act of touching another without justification or consent.

*Defamation* is the publication of false statements which impute some disreputable or immoral conduct to another. *Libel* is written defamation, whereas *slander* is spoken. Truth is a complete defense to an action of defamation.

*False imprisonment* is the wrongful denial of the physical liberty of another; the denial may be brought about by either acts or words.

*Invasion of privacy* is the unwarranted infringement upon a person's private life to include the unpermitted use of a person's endorsement in an advertisement. Because one's peace of mind is being protected, the truth is not a defense in an action for invasion of privacy.

*Emotional distress* is actionable when a person has acted with the intention of causing the emotional disturbance of another. There need be no bodily contact in order to recover, but the plaintiff must demonstrate that defendant's conduct has caused some illness.

*Against Property.* Tort for interfering with the property rights of another include: (1) trespass to land, (2) trespass to personal property, (3) conversion, and (4) fraud. *Trespass* is any unpermitted interference with another's possession of his or her land. The plaintiff need not demonstrate monetary loss; the interference alone is sufficient. The simple act of throwing a rock onto the property of another is a trespass. In an action for trespass to personal property, the plaintiff normally must prove that some damage has been done to the property. The distinguishing characteristics of *conversion* is the unlawful dominion of the personal property of another so as to deny the owner possession of the property. A person is guilty of conversion if he or she wrongfully, though mistakenly, takes goods belonging to another. *Fraud* is the knowing misrepresentation of a fact for the purpose of deceiving another person. Silence does not usually constitute fraud, but the law does impose a duty to speak when one occupies a position of trust. A statement of opinion or a prediction as to the future is not usually construed as the representation of a fact.

**Unintentional Torts** These generally fall into two classifications.

1. *The law of negligence* imposes on every person the duty to act in such a way as not to harm others. The plaintiff in a negligence action must prove that the defendant has been negligent and that the negligent conduct was the cause of the plaintiff's injuries. Unlike the intentional torts, in an action for negligence there must be actual injury to the plaintiff. The duty the law imposes is to conduct oneself as a reasonable person in the same or similar circumstance. Ignorance and honest mistakes are no excuse.

The *doctrine of respondent superior* dictates that an employer is responsible for the torts of his or her employees as long as committed in the course of performing their normal duties.

Defenses to an action for negligence are contributory negligence and assumption of risk. In *contributory negligence*, the plaintiff through his or her own negligent conduct contributed to the cause of the accident. In *assumption of risk*, the plaintiff voluntarily enters into a situation where he or she knows there is a risk of injury. For example, a person attending a hockey game may have assumed the risk of being hit by a flying puck.

2. *Strict liability* means that the defendant, even though not negligent, can still be held liable for any damage resulting from his or her conduct. The law imposes strict liability upon a person when engaging in activities which are inherently dangerous yet provide a beneficial service. The spraying of crops from airplanes and the use of dynamite are traditional examples of strict liability. Recent years have witnessed the expansion of the doctrine of strict liability to sales of defective consumer products when the consumer is exposed to reasonable risks.

## CONTRACTS

A contract is a binding agreement between two or more people to do or not to do some particular thing which is enforceable in a court of law. There are four requisites to every contract: (1) mutual assent, (2) capacity of parties, (3) consideration, and (4) legality of subject matter.

**Mutual Assent** Mutual assent is arrived upon through an offer made by the offeror to the offeree who accepts the offer. The offer must be definite and certain, must be more than an invitation to negotiate, must be serious, and must be communicated to the offeree. The offeror may revoke the offer any time before it is accepted. An offer is terminated at the end of the time expressly stated or, if not stated, at the end of a reasonable period of time. The offeror determines the manner of acceptance, and acceptance of an offer must be in accordance with the terms of the offer. An offeree who does not accept the offer as communicated has rejected it; an offeree who attempts to accept but materially changes the terms has made a counteroffer.

Fraud, duress, and undue influence render a contract unenforceable by the guilty party. Salesperson's talk or "puffing" does not constitute fraud. Compelling a person to make a contract against his or her will is duress, whereas the improper use of power over the mind of another is undue influence. A contract is also unenforceable if there has been a mutual mistake as to the existence, but not value, of the subject matter.

**Capacity** A contract with a party lacking capacity to contract is voidable, at the option of the party under the incapacity. Infants, mental incompetents, and drunkards, when the party is so intoxicated as not to be able to understand the nature of the transaction, lack legal capacity to contract. However, one lacking capacity is liable for the reasonable value (not the contract price) of "necessaries" furnished him or her. "Necessaries" are defined in terms of the party's normal needs for items such as food, clothing, and shelter. Upon reaching majority, an infant may ratify contracts either by a new promise or an act in which he or she recognizes contractual liability.

**Consideration** Consideration is the price bargained and paid for a promise; it is the element of exchange in a contract; it induces another to enter into the contract. It may be an act, a forbearance to act, or a promise given in exchange for a promise. Past consideration or a moral obligation will not support a promise. In the absence of fraud, the courts will not look into the value of the consideration.

**Legality** An agreement is illegal whenever the agreement itself or the performance called for is illegal. Common examples include contracts made in violation of gambling, usury, and licensing statutes, as well as restraint of trade. Not all contracts in restraint of trade are illegal; restraint of trade is permissible when it gives necessary and reasonable protection to the benefiting party.

**Other Factors** The essentials of an enforceable contract having been set out, there are two additional considerations of which businesspersons should be aware, the statute of frauds and the parol evidence rule.

*Statute of Frauds.* As a general rule, an oral contract is in every way as enforceable as a written one. However, the statute of frauds requires certain classes of contracts to be in writing signed by the party to be charged. The statute of frauds does not pertain to fraud as such, but rather was designed to prevent fraud in certain types of contracts. Some of the more important contracts within the statute are these: Contract for the sale of land or any interest therein; a promise to answer for the debt of another; agreements not to be performed within 1 year; con-

tracts to sell goods of a value of from $50 to $2500, depending on state law.

*Parol Evidence Rule.* The term *parol evidence* refers to any oral or written evidence which is extrinsic to the written contract. The parol evidence rule prohibits either party in a lawsuit from introducing any evidence which would change or contradict the written contract. The rule is designed to give effect only to those terms which the parties considered important enough to include in the writing.

The rule does not apply to:

1. Contracts partially in writing and partially oral.

2. Sales receipts which do not purport to be contracts.

3. Gross typographical errors.

4. Evidence which tends to prove incapacity or fraud, duress, or undue influence.

The parol evidence rule will never prevent the introduction of evidence which would explain or resolve an ambiguity in the contract.

## SALES

Article 2 of the Uniform Commercial Code governs the sale of *personal* property; the sale of *real* property is covered in the section on property.

**Contract of Sale** A *sale*, as the term is used in the Uniform Commercial Code, is the transfer of ownership of goods from the seller to the buyer for a price. The code defines "goods" as all things which are movable at the time of the identification to the contract, excluding money, investment securities, and *choses in action*. Rules governing the formation and requirements of contracts, discussed earlier, generally apply to contracts of sale. The courts will attempt to give effect to the intention of the parties as gleaned from the contract and the circumstances surrounding its formation. The code requires no particular form for a sales contract, nor does the code require the contract to be in writing unless the statute of frauds so specifies. A contract for the sale of goods may be made in any manner sufficient to show agreement, including conduct by both parties which recognizes the existence of the contract.

The code differs from the general law of contracts in several areas:

1. An *acceptance*, which states terms additional to or different from those stated in the offer, will still form a contract.

2. An *agreement modifying a contract* of sale needs no consideration.

3. The code also establishes *separate rules which apply to transactions involving one or more merchants as a*

*party.* There are 15 sections of the code regulating these transactions which demand a higher standard of conduct because of a merchant's presumed knowledge of the practices of commerce. If a court, for example, finds a contract of sale or any clause of the contract to have been unconscionable at the time it was made, the court may refuse to enforce the contract, or it may enforce the remainder of the contract without the unconscionable clause.

4. *Risk of loss, insurable interest, and other rights and liabilities* under the code are no longer solely determined on the basis of who is the holder of the title to the goods. Title may still be determinative, but only if the code expressly so states.

5. If not set out in the terms of the contract, *title passes when the seller has completed his or her performance.* If the contract calls for "delivery" by the seller, title passes upon delivery and tender to the buyer at the place designated in the contract. Where the contract calls for "shipment" by the seller, title passes to the buyer upon delivery to the carrier. If a buyer should reject goods, title revests in the seller.

**Warranties** A warranty is a statement or representation made by the seller at the time of sale for the quality or suitability of the goods. A seller who limits statements to "sales talk" such as, "This is an excellent buy" has not made a warranty, nor is the seller responsible for a mere opinion as to the quality of the goods. The seller must still be cautious, however, about any statements made to induce a sale.

In certain situations, the seller is considered to have such a strong advantage over the buyer that the law imposes implied warranties. Responsibility for these warranties exists even when the seller does not make any representation as to the quality of the goods. Under the code, there are two implied warranties: (1) the implied warranty of fitness for a particular purpose and (2) the implied warranty of merchantability.

The *implied warranty of merchantability* applies only to merchants dealing in goods of the kind sold. Six criteria for merchantability are set out in the code; they basically require that the goods must be of "fair, average quality."

The *implied warranty of fitness* for a particular purpose is based on (1) the seller's having reason to know any particular purpose for which the goods are needed and (2) the buyer's reliance on the seller's skill or judgment to select suitable goods. This warranty will be implied to any seller, whether or not he or she is a merchant. Unless the seller expressly excludes or modifies an implied warranty, it becomes a part of the sales contract by operation of law. Both implied warranties may be excluded through express language of disclaimer.

## AGENCY AND PARTNERSHIP

**Agency Relationship** When one person, the *agent,* is authorized to perform some transaction for the benefit of another, the *principal,* an agency relationship arises. No particular formalities are required to create an agency; it may or may not involve a contract. Either party may be a corporation.

The law of agency governs the relationship of master and servant and that of principal and agent. Agents may be distinguished from servants in that agents represent the principal in business transactions while servants, or employees, perform physical activities under the control of the master or employer. The distinction is important in that it will determine the principal's liability for the torts of the agent. An *independent contractor* is neither an agent nor an employee; he or she does specified work for the employer but determines his or her own methods. The employer is not liable for the torts of an independent contractor.

The principal is liable for the authorized acts of the agent. The agent has the *express authority* to do as the principal has directed and also has the *implied authority* to do acts reasonably necessary in performing the express purpose of the agency. Furthermore, an agent's authority includes that which has apparently been delegated to him or her. If a principal intentionally or negligently allows the agent to lead third persons to believe justifiably that the agent has authority to act in the name of the principal, the principal is responsible for these acts of the agent.

*Ratification* is the subsequent approval of the unauthorized act of one person claiming to represent another. Ratification is the granting of authority after the act and relates back to the time at which the act was done.

An agent has a *fiduciary duty,* one of utmost loyalty and good faith, to the principal. In addition to fiduciary duties an agent must obey all instructions, act with skill and care, and maintain proper accountings of all business done in the principal's behalf.

The principal owes a duty to pay the agent any compensation due, and the principal must reimburse the agent for all expenditures made in the performance of the principal's business.

An agency may be terminated

1. At the will of either party, though this may be a breach of contract.

2. At the accomplishment of the purpose of the agency.

3. By the terms of the agreement.

4. By the death or insanity of either the principal or the agent.

5. By impossibility of performance.

Upon termination of an agency, the principal should personally notify all persons who have dealt with the agent.

**General Partnership**   A partnership is the association of two or more persons to conduct a business for profit. No formalities are required to form a partnership. In determining whether a partnership exists, the courts will look for evidence of sharing of profits and having a voice in the management of the business. A corporation may become a member in a partnership.

In the absence of agreements to the contrary,

1. Each partner has an equal voice in the management of the business.

2. Each partner shares equally in the profits and losses of the business.

3. A simple majority can make everyday business decisions (unanimity is required for fundamental changes).

4. A partner is not entitled to wages for services rendered to the partnership.

5. Every partner is an agent of the partnership for the purpose of its business.

The law imposes a *fiduciary relationship* between the members of a partnership; this is a duty of utmost loyalty and good faith in all dealings with the partnership. A partner, for instance, may not take a partnership opportunity for himself or herself. The law also imposes equal liability on all partners for contracts of the partnership. Partners are liable jointly and severally for the torts of the partnership.

A partnership is not a legal entity; rather, it is merely an aggregation of its members. Partnerships, unlike corporations, have limited existence. Death or bankruptcy of a member will cause a partnership to dissolve automatically. The effects of the admission of a new partner and the withdrawal or retirement of a partner depend on the laws of the various states. A partner has the power to dissolve a partnership, although this may amount to a breach of contract. A partner may ask a court to dissolve a partnership on the grounds that (1) there are irreconcilable differences; (2) it is impossible to carry on the business at a profit; (3) a partner suffers from some incapacity.

After dissolution, a partnership continues to exist for the sole purpose of winding up and termination. A partnership will normally be wound up by the partners themselves. If a partnership has been dissolved by court decree, a receiver will be appointed to wind up the business. As a general rule each partner must give actual notice of the dissolution to all persons who have done business with the partnership.

*Limited Partnership.* A limited partnership is a hybrid between the general partnership and the corporation. State statutes provide for the limited liability of one or more partners so long as the limited partner's name does not appear in the firm name and the limited partner does not participate in the management or control of the business. The limited partner does have the right to examine the books and may demand an accounting of partnership affairs.

## REAL PROPERTY

Real property is land and that which is erected or growing upon it.

**Interests in Real Property**   The law recognizes different degrees of ownership interest in real property:

1. *Fee simple.* This form entitles the owner to the entire property for an indefinite period of time. The owner may sell the property or devise it to another in his or her will. However, the owner of a fee simple is limited in the use of the land by the state's power of eminent domain and by zoning and building ordinances.

2. *Life estates.* The owner of a fee simple may create a life estate in the property whereby the owner gives another the right to occupy, use, and enjoy the land so long as he or she lives. The life tenant is obligated to maintain the property in the condition received and may use the land's natural resources only as necessary to keep up the property. The life tenant must pay all taxes and continue any mortgage payments due on the property. Unless the terms of the life estate state otherwise, the interest may be sold or mortgaged, but the purchaser or mortgagee will receive only that which the tenant has himself or herself—an interest which terminates when the tenant dies. A *life estate pur autre vie* is a life estate measured by the life of someone other than the tenant. A *reversion* occurs when, at the end of the life estate, the property returns to the original owner or his or her heirs. If the property is to go to someone other than the owner or heirs at the end of the life estate, it is called a *remainder*.

3. *Leasehold.* A leasehold is the right to occupy and possess property for a fixed term of years. Leases may be oral or written, but where the period

of the lease is to be in excess of 1 year, the statute of frauds in most jurisdictions requires the lease to be written. An *estate for years* runs for a certain number of weeks, months, or years from a specific date; it has a definite beginning and end. The lease terminates automatically; no notice is required. A *periodic tenancy* is a lease which continues automatically for periods of weeks, months, or years until terminated by proper notice by either party. The notice required to terminate the periodic tenancy varies from state to state—it is usually 30 days. A *tenancy at will* covers no specific time period and can be terminated by either party giving proper notice.

4. *Easements.* An *easement* is the right to use the land of another for a particular purpose. Two examples are a right of way over land and the right to extend power lines over land. An easement may be acquired by an express writing, by implication, necessity, or prescription. A *license* is oral permission to use the land of another and may be revoked at any time.

**Coownership of Real Property** Coownership falls into two classes.

1. *Tenancy in common.* A tenancy in common is created whenever two or more persons take an ownership interest in the same piece of property. Tenants in common need not own equal percentages of the property. When a tenant in common dies, the interest in the property passes to his or her heirs. In most states, property taken by two or more persons is presumed to be a tenancy in common.

2. *Joint tenancy.* A joint tenancy is property taken by two or more persons by the same instrument and at the same time who share equal rights to its use and enjoyment. The distinguishing characteristic of a joint tenancy is that the interest of one tenant, upon death, goes to the survivor or survivors. A *severence* occurs when one of the joint tenants conveys his or her interest to some third person. The third person becomes a tenant in common with the remaining joint tenants. *Tenants by the entirety* are joint tenants who are husband and wife; however, neither the husband nor wife has the power to sever by his or her individual actions. *Community property* is a statutory type of ownership for husband and wife recognized in several states.


## COMMERCIAL PAPER

Article 3 of the Uniform Commercial Code covers instruments known as *commercial paper*. The code recognizes two major classes of commercial paper: drafts and notes.

**Drafts** A draft is an order to pay which involves three parties: one party, the drawer, orders a second party, the drawee, to pay a third party, the payee. The ordinary bank check is the most popular type of draft. A check is a draft drawn on a bank payable upon demand. Other types of drafts are bank drafts, trade acceptances, and cashier's checks.

**Notes** A note is a promise to pay which involves two parties: one party, the maker, promises to pay to the order of a second party, the payee or bearer, a stated sum of money on demand or at some future date. Types of notes are simple promisory notes, collateral notes, installment notes, and mortgage notes. Article 3 treats certificates of deposit as if they were notes.

**Negotiability** If an instrument satisfies certain strict requirements, it will become *negotiable* and obtain certain characteristics which make it distinguishable from simple contracts. Article 3 specifies the following requirements of negotiability:

1. The instrument must be in writing.
2. The instrument must be signed.
3. The instrument must contain a promise to pay, if a note, or an order to pay, if a check or draft.
4. The promise or order must be unconditional.
5. The payment required must be of a definite amount.
6. The payment required must be in money only.
7. The instrument must contain no other promise or order.
8. The instrument must be payable on demand or at a definite time.
9. The instrument must be payable to order of bearer.

The holder of a negotiable instrument acquires distinct advantages over a person who is the mere assignee of a contract. If the holder is one of the original parties, the holder has certain procedural advantages such as not having to prove consideration.

*Negotiation* is a special type of transfer whereby the transferee becomes a *holder*. The two requisites for a valid negotiation are delivery and endorsement. *Delivery* is the voluntary transfer of possession; *endorsement* is a writing on the back of an instrument.

A *holder* is a person in possession of an instrument payable to the person, to the person's order, or to bearer. The holder does not need to have given value in obtaining the instrument and may or may not be a holder in due course. A holder may transfer or negotiate an instrument in his or her possession.

A *holder in due course* is one who is a holder and who also meets certain additional requirements, which are the following:

1. The holder must have given value.
2. The holder must have taken in good faith.
3. The holder must have taken without notice of claim or defense.
4. The holder must have taken without notice that the instrument is overdue.
5. The holder must have taken without notice that the instrument has been dishonored.

A holder in due course takes the instrument free from personal defenses that one party to the instrument may have against another party. However, the holder takes the instrument subject to any real defenses. *Real defenses* are those which go to the very existence of the contract or which render it null or void. The defenses which may be raised against a holder in due course are:

1. Infancy.
2. Other incapacity, duress, or illegality.
3. Misrepresentation of the nature or terms of the instrument.
4. Discharge in insolvency proceedings.
5. Any other discharge of which the holder has notice when taking the instrument.

The holder who does not meet the qualifications of a holder in due course takes the instrument subject to any defense which could be asserted under the general law of contracts.

Makers of notes and acceptors of drafts are primarily liable for making payment. All other parties such as endorsers are secondarily liable.

## BANKRUPTCY

The United States Constitution provides that the federal government has sole jurisdiction in bankruptcy proceedings. There are two basic types of bankruptcy.

**Voluntary Bankruptcy**  This type of bankruptcy is available to any person, partnership, or corporation with some exceptions. A petition must be made to the federal district court setting forth four items: a list of assets, a list of creditors, a list of exemptions claimed by the debtor, and a financial statement of the debtor. The debtor need not allege insolvency.

**Involuntary Bankruptcy**  An involuntary petition in bankruptcy may be filed by (1) any three or more creditors with an aggregate claim of $1500 or more or; (2) any one creditor with a claim of $1500 or more, if there are fewer than 12 creditors of the debtor.

In order for an involuntary petition to succeed, the debtor must either (1) consent to it or (2) have committed an act of bankruptcy within 4 months of the date of filing.

The Acts of Bankruptcy as set forth in the Bankruptcy Act are:

1. A transfer of property with the intent of defrauding creditors.
2. A transfer of property while insolvent, in preference of one or more creditors.
3. Failure, while insolvent, to have discharged a lien within 30 days of filing.
4. Making a general assignment for the benefit of creditors.
5. Allowing while insolvent, either voluntarily or involuntarily, a receiver to take charge of one's property.
6. Admitting in writing an inability to pay one's debts and a willingness to be judged a bankrupt.

After adjudication of bankruptcy the case is given to a referee in bankruptcy. The first meeting of creditors is called, and a trustee in bankruptcy is elected. The trustee obtains possession and title to the bankrupt's property. The trustee's duties are to set aside the bankrupt's exemptions, collect the claims, liquidate the assets, and distribute the proceeds.

Anyone who is to share in the bankrupt's estate must first demonstrate a *provable claim*. Virtually all claims, except unliquidated tort claims, are *provable claims*. Certain claimants have priority in that they must be paid in full before the other claimants receive any payment. The order of priority is

1. Costs and expenses of administration
2. Wages due employees not to exceed $600
3. Taxes due to the United States or any state

Additionally, valid lien claims of secured creditors have priority over the claims of unsecured creditors. Any claimant wishing to share in the bankrupt's estate must file a claim within 6 months of the first meeting of creditors.

*See also* BOARDS OF DIRECTORS, LEGAL LIABILITY GUIDELINES; GOVERNMENT REGULATIONS, UNIFORM COMMERCIAL CODE; LEGAL AFFAIRS, MANAGEMENT OF CORPORATE.

## REFERENCES

Burby, W.: *Handbook of the Law of Real Property*, 3d ed., West Publishing Company, St. Paul, Minn., 1965.

Crane, J., and A. Bromberg: *Law of Partnership*, West Publishing Company, St. Paul, Minn., 1968.

Kimbrough, R.: *Summary of American Law*, Lawyer Cooperative Publishing Co., Rochester, N.Y., 1974.

McLaughlin, William P.: *American Legal Process*, John Wiley & Sons, Inc., New York, 1977.

Moore, Russell F.: *Law for Executives*, American Management Association, New York, 1966.

Nordstrom, R.: *Handbook of the Law of Sales*, West Publishing Company, St. Paul, Minn., 1970.

Prosser, W.: *Handbook of the Law of Torts*, 4th ed., West Publishing Company, St. Paul, Minn., 1971.

Seavy, W.: *Handbook of the Law of Agency*, West Publishing Company, St. Paul, Minn., 1964.

Simpson, L.: *Cases on the Law of Contracts*, 2d ed., West Publishing Company, St Paul, Minn., 1965.

White, J. and R. Summers: *Handbook of the Law under the Uniform Commercial Code*, West Publishing Company, St. Paul, Minn., 1972.

ARTHUR J. HAMILTON, *James Madison University*

# Government regulations, community planning (*See* COMMUNITY PLANNING LEGISLATION.)

# Government regulations, consumer protection (*See* CONSUMERISM AND CONSUMER PROTECTION LEGISLATION.)

# Government regulations, environmental legislation (*See* ENVIRONMENTAL PROTECTION LEGISLATION.)

# Government regulations: federal regulation of competition

The United States federal government, state governments, and local governments have the power to regulate business activity. This power is exercised through the lawmaking power of the legislative branch, and it is enforced by various administrative agencies. The Congress has enacted legislation to protect competition, prevent monopolies, and outlaw price discrimination; this area of law is known as *antitrust law*. The federal acts which are the basis of antitrust law are the Sherman Act, the Clayton Act, the Robinson-Patman Act, and the Federal Trade Commission Act.

*Restraint of trade* refers to business practices which tend to lessen free competition. Certain business combinations, such as monopolies and cartels, tend to restrain trade. Price fixing among competitors also tends to restrain trade. Antitrust law has made many such activities illegal, but not all restraints of trade are illegal.

**The Sherman Act** In 1890, Congress, under its power to regulate interstate commerce, passed the Sherman Antitrust Act. The Sherman Act had two main provisions: (1) contracts, combinations, and conspiracies in restraint of trade were made illegal; and (2) monopolies and attempts to monopolize were made illegal. Restraints within the purview of the act include contract combinations or conspiracies to fix prices, limit production, and divide markets or clients. Still other activities may be illegal if, in light of the particular transaction and surrounding economic circumstances, the activity is found to unreasonably restrain competition. A common example of a permissible contract in restraint of trade is the covenant not to compete found in many contracts for the sale of a business.

The Sherman Act provides for three types of sanctions: (1) Fines not to exceed $50,000, imprisonment not to exceed 1 year, or both; (2) injunctions to prevent violations; and (3) civil remedies of treble damages plus costs and attorney's fees to persons injured by violations of the act.

**The Clayton Act** Soon after passage of the Sherman Act the need for a more specific law was realized. Congress enacted the Clayton Act in 1914 to dispel confusion in the minds of businesspersons subject to the antitrust laws. The Clayton Act was broader in scope than the Sherman Act and attempted to prevent the harm to competition before it was done. The Clayton Act contained three major provisions:

1. Section 2 of the act made price discrimination between different buyers of commodities illegal "where the effect of such discrimination may be substantially to lessen competition or tend to create a monopoly in any line of commerce." Price discrimination is not illegal, however, if it is due to *(a)* legitimate differences in grade, quality, or quantity; *(b)* differences in cost of transportation; or *(c)* a good faith attempt to meet the price of the competitor. This section was amended and strengthened by the Robinson-Patman Act (discussed below).

2. Section 3 of the act applies to exclusive-dealing contracts and to tying contracts. It prohibits a seller or lessor of a highly desirable product from forcing a buyer to purchase or lease a less desirable product in order to obtain the highly desired product. Section 3 applies only to sales of commodities and not to sales of services.

3. Section 7 as amended prohibits the acquisition by a corporation of the stock of another corporation engaged in interstate or foreign commerce when the effect substantially lessens competition or tends to create a monopoly. As long as there exists a

reasonable probability that the merger will have anticompetitive effects, it will be prohibited under Section 7. However, purchases merely for investment are not prohibited. Additionally, a person may not be a director of two competing corporations if either corporation has assets in excess of $1 million.

**The Robinson-Patman Act** In 1936 Congress amended Section 2 of the Clayton Act through passage of the Robinson-Patman Act. It was designed to ensure equality of treatment to all buyers of a particular seller. It prohibits price discrimination in commodities of like grade and quality shipped in interstate commerce. To be in violation, the price discrimination must substantially lessen competition or tend to create a monopoly. Section 2 of the Clayton Act allowed sellers to discriminate if they could justify their action on the grounds that their selling or transportation costs were greater for some buyers or that they were selling at a lower price to meet the price of competitors. These shortcomings of the earlier legislation were eliminated in part by the Robinson-Patman Act.

The act applies only to commodities; it does not cover services or radio and newspaper advertising, for example. The act is also limited to commodities of like grade and quality. The act also prohibits discounts, rebates, and allowances that are tantamount to discrimination.

The price of a commodity within the meaning of the act is the delivered price. Before a sale can be ruled as discriminatory, it must be shown to have been relatively close in time to a nondiscriminatory sale. The relevant time period will depend on the nature of the commodity, that is, whether it is perishable or seasonal in nature.

The act not only prohibits discrimination among customers, it also prohibits discriminatory pricing to eliminate a competitor.

The act does permit (1) price differentials which reflect differences in the cost of manufacturing, selling, and delivery that are caused by differences in methods or quantities involved; (2) price differentials made in good faith to meet the price of a competitor so long as the competitor is not guilty of price discrimination; and (3) price differentials because of the deterioration of goods or when the seller is closing out a particular line of goods.

Finally, a buyer who knowingly accepts a discriminatory price is in violation of the act.

**The Federal Trade Commission Act** In 1914 the Federal Trade Commission was created through the Federal Trade Commission Act. The commission is charged with preventing "unfair methods of competition in commerce and unfair or deceptive acts or practices in commerce."

The commission has the responsibility of investigating both violations of antitrust laws and unfair or deceptive trade practices. The commission has the power to issue cease and desist orders and levy fines. However, private suits for treble damages are not allowed. A cease and desist order by the commission has the force of an injunction and becomes final unless appealed to the U.S. Court of Appeals.

**Fair Trade Laws** In 1937 Congress enacted the Miller-Tydings Act amending the Sherman Act to permit "fair trade" contracts where permissible under state law. A fair trade law allows a manufacturer of a brand name to enter into a contract with a retailer whereby the retailer agrees to sell the product at or above a minimum price set by the manufacturer. The purpose of the statute is to allow manufacturers to protect the image of their brand name products.

A unique aspect of many states' fair trade laws is the nonsigner clause. Under this provision one contract between a manufacturer and a retailer agreeing to a minimum retail price will bind all other retailers in that state whether or not they are a party to such a contract themselves.

If a state has no fair trade law, any agreement to maintain prices is a violation of the Sherman Act. Any price maintenance scheme between businesses on the same level, as for example between wholesalers, is not covered by the fair trade law and is a violation of the Sherman Act.

*See also* BOARD OF DIRECTORS, LEGAL LIABILITY GUIDELINES; GOVERNMENT REGULATIONS, BUSINESS LAW; GOVERNMENT REGULATIONS, UNIFORM COMMERCIAL CODE; LEGAL AFFAIRS, MANAGEMENT OF CORPORATE.

## REFERENCES

Anderson, Ronald A.: *Government and Business*, 3d ed., South-Western Publishing Company, Inc., Cincinnati, 1966.

Gellhorn, R.: *Antitrust Law and Economics in a Nutshell*, West Publishing Company, St. Paul, Minn., 1976.

Raphael, Jesse S.: *Government Regulation of Business*, The Free Press, Glencoe, Ill., 1966.

Reid, Samuel R.: *The New Industrial Order: Coordination, Regulation, and Public Policy*, McGraw-Hill Book Company, New York, 1976.

Weiss, Leonard W. and Allyn Strickland: *Regulation: A Case Approach*, McGraw-Hill Book Company, New York, 1976.

ARTHUR J. HAMILTON, *James Madison University*

# Government regulations, labor laws

(*See* LABOR LEGISLATION.)

# Government regulations and laws affecting management and business (*See heading in Table of Contents for complete listing.*)

# Government regulations, patent law

(*See* PATENTS AND VALUABLE INTANGIBLE RIGHTS.)

# Government regulations, pricing legislation (*See* PRODUCT AND SERVICE PRICING.)

# Government regulations, product liability (*See* PRODUCT LIABILITY.)

# Government regulations, safety and health (OSHA) (*See* SAFETY AND HEALTH MANAGEMENT¿ EMPLOYEE.)

# Government regulations, taxes (*See* TAX MANAGEMENT, MANAGERIAL RESPONSIBILITY FOR FEDERAL INCOME TAX REPORTING.)

# Government regulations, Uniform Commercial Code

The *Uniform Commercial Code* is a unified, comprehensive set of laws describing legal guidelines and limits for all business transactions from the time raw materials are purchased until finished merchandise is sold to a consumer. The code has been enacted in every state except Louisiana (as of this writing).

Generally considered one of the major legal developments of this century in the United States, and clearly the most important legislative measure in United States Commerce, the code is an attempt to systematize and bring uniformity to the voluminous, enormously complicated, confusing, and often contradictory and inequitable body of 800-year-old common law and statute laws of the various states. As this country became a single economic unit for the first time in the closing years of the nineteenth century, discrepancies among the laws of the different states had become a serious barrier to commercial intercourse. The National Conference of Commissioners on Uniform State Laws (organized in 1891 by cooperation of several states) made attempts at uniformity in specific areas (the Uniform Sales Act, the Uniform Partnership Act, and many others). These acts failed to attain widespread adoption by the states, however; they were interpreted with wide differences by the various state courts, or simply became outmoded by changing commercial practices between the two World Wars. The need for a single enactment to encompass the broad area of commercial law became critical.

**Development** In 1945 the Commissioners on Uniform State Laws and the American Law Institute began the monumental task of drafting a Uniform Commercial Code (UCC) by reviewing and synthesizing laws of the various states. In 1957 the official edition was finally completed; it has since been adopted by 49 of the states, the District of Columbia, and the Virgin Islands. The code expressly provides that, where adopted, it will replace the following uniform acts: Uniform Negotiable Instrument Law, Uniform Sales Act, Uniform Trust Receipts Act, Uniform Warehouse Receipts Act, Uniform Stock Transfer Act, Uniform Conditional Sales Act, and Uniform Bills of Lading Act. Additionally it repeals any acts regulating bank collections, bulk sales, chattel mortgages, conditional sales, factors' liens, farm storage of grain and similar acts, and assignment of accounts receivable.

**Objectives** Specifically the purposes of the code are to: (1) simplify, clarify, and modernize the law governing commercial transactions, (2) permit expansion of commercial practices through custom, usage, and agreement of the parties, and (3) make uniform the laws among the states and legal jurisdictions. In addition, the code asserts two important new legal concepts: (1) the duty of *good faith* imposed on every contract of duty subject to the code, and (2) the concept that the ordinary rules of contract law frequently need modification when applied to sales transactions involving one or more merchants, who are presumably possessed of special "knowledge and skill" in the area of the transaction.

**Scope** The code covers the following areas of commercial law: sales, commercial paper and banking, letters of credit, bulk sales, documents of title, investment securities, and secured transactions. In addition, it deals with related transactions, such as movement of merchandise from one point to another, storage of goods, financing of commercial transactions, payments for merchandise, and the deposit and collection of checks, notes, and drafts.

The UCC contains 10 articles. Article 1, General Provisions, deals with general principles and definitions. Article 2, Sales, is the longest and possibly most radical article. It deals with contracts, their formation and obligations; with title, creditors, and good faith purchasers; with breach and remedies, etc. Article 3, Commercial Paper. Article 4, Bank Deposits and Collections. Article 5, Letters of Credit, codifies law on this subject for the first time. Article 6, Bulk Transfers, covers situations where a person or business transfers a major portion of its assets; it is designed to protect creditors of the transferer. Article 7, Warehouse Receipts, Bills of Lading, and Other Documents of Title, is of especial significance to shippers and storers of goods. Article 8, Investment Securities, governs the issuance, transfer, purchase, and registration of investment securities. Article 9, Secured Transactions, Sales of Accounts, Contract Rights and Chattel Paper, states the law relating to personal property security. Article 10 gives the effective date of the statute and lists prior laws that it specifically repeals.

**Impact** The drafting of the Uniform Commercial Code represents an ambitious and commendable attempt by persons serving no self-interest to bring certainty into the hitherto prodigiously complex and inconsistent body of statutory and common law governing United States commercial transactions and to bring it into practicable conformity with the great changes in the country's economy and business practices. Experience has already indicated that close attention to the code's provisions, and particularly to the rules concerning the content and filing of financial statements, can usually prevent the problems of litigation and frequently serious losses of money.

The code is a living document, not a final statement, and therein lies its vulnerability as well as its strength. Business persons are cautioned to be alert to changes, to keep themselves well-informed, and to express their views actively whenever interpretive or legislative trends impinge on areas of their particular concern.

*See also* GOVERNMENT REGULATIONS, BUSINESS LAW.

### REFERENCES

Anderson, Ronald A., and Walter A. Kumpf: *Business Law*, 8th ed., South-Western Publishing Company, Inc., Cincinnati, 1968.

Craver, Theodore R.: "On the Road to Regulation," *The Conference Board Record*, vol. 12, October 1975.

Frascona, Joseph L.: *C.P.A. Law Review: Under the Uniform Commercial Code*, 3rd ed., Richard D. Irwin, Inc., Homewood, Ill., 1966.

Hawkland, William D.: *A Transactional Guide to the Uniform Commercial Code*, 2 vols., The American Law Institute and American Bar Association, Philadelphia, 1964.

Silberfeld, Eli S.: "Legislative and Judicial Developments in 1975," *Journal of Commercial Bank Lending*, vol. 58, February 1976.

Votaw, Dow: *Legal Aspects of Business Administration*, 3rd ed., Prentice-Hall, Inc., Englewood Cliffs, N.J., 1969.

STAFF/HOKE

## Government regulations, wages and hours law (*See* WAGES AND HOURS LEGISLATION.)

## Government relations and services

Government regulation of business has historically been indirect in the United States. Adam Smith asserted that government fostering of unhindered action of individuals, controlled only by competition, was the best means of increasing the wealth of a nation. Thus the role of government in the economic sphere was historically limited in the United States to (1) maintaining a safe environment for business; (2) providing for judicial relief for common law and statutory wrongs inflicted upon business; and (3) providing certain public works and institutions. Government regulation of business is provided for by Article I, Section 8, of the Constitution, vesting in Congress the power "to regulate Commerce with foreign nations, among the several States, and with the Indian Tribes."

The nature of the role of government initially in the United States was that of protector of business. Thus early tariffs were designed to protect infant industry. Government provision of public works was limited. Fire departments were financed by private fees; toll roads were common. As society became more complex, government was looked to for more public works, and government undertook to provide services in areas where the risk or capital need was beyond the reasonable capability of the private sector.

Rather than assume the role of provider of public services and public works, the government developed the policy of providing direct and indirect subsidy to the private sector. The limited role of government as a protector and promoter of business is consistent with a long-held implicit consensus that private decision making was the best way to accomplish economic gain for society generally. With passage of the Employment Act of 1946, the increased roles and responsibility of government in shaping the direction of economic activity, however, became a recognized and accepted policy.

Thus the impact of government relations upon management decisions and policies is felt as a result of government acting for the following aims:

1. Protect business.
2. Regulate to: (*a*) maintain competition, (*b*) maintain health and safety, and (*c*) implement public policy.
3. Promote and subsidize by furnishing: (*a*) information, (*b*) services, (*c*) financing, (*d*) insurance against various risks, (*e*) a source of supply, and (*f*) a source of sales. As a result, government relations have an impact daily on the firm's decision making.

## RELATIONS WITH GOVERNMENT

**The Executive Branch** There are few restrictions on, or guides to, relations with the executive branch. The Federal Election Campaign Act Amendments of 1976 (2 USC 431) provide restrictions upon contributions to candidates, political parties, and political committees. 2 USC 441a *et seq.* sets forth restrictions applicable to specific groups such as national banks and government contractors.

Regulations by some executive agencies against conflicts of interest provide limitations upon employment by industry of former employees of those agencies when employment would involve work on projects directly related to the employee's previous duties.

Influencing general and specific policies of government is vital to major industries, companies, and associations. Many companies and industries maintain an office in Washington. While some of the activity of these offices may involve lobbying, an important aspect is furnishing of regular access to the executive branch. This is done by frequent communication with staff personnel in the agencies that may affect the specific company. Most government offices desire whatever information their industry constituency can provide to resolve mutual problems. The astute Washington representative makes regular visits to the appropriate agency even when there are no immediate problems facing the company. (*See* ASSOCIATIONS, TRADE AND PROFESSIONAL.) The Department of Commerce is the advocate of industry and commerce within the cabinet.

The role of the Office of Management and Budget (OMB) is substantial in developing the executive department's approaches to economic and fiscal policy and in formulating the positions of the executive branch and White House on legislation. Thus many Washington representatives seek to persuade staff of the OMB of the legitimacy of the company or industry position. Most representatives seek a continuing dialogue.

**The Legislative Branch** This arm of government requires that any person who seeks to influence legislation file reports disclosing financial expenditures. The influence upon specific legislation is a small part of lobbyists activities. The stating of company position, problems, and needs, and information exchange is the major function of the lobbyist.

**The Regulatory Agencies** The Administrative Procedure Act serves to insulate the Commissioners and Administrative Law Judges from *ex parte* attempts to influence the outcome of specific hearings. These hearings are quasijudicial in nature, and all presentations must be a matter of record. It is important and proper, however, for industry to provide information to aid the independent regulatory commission to reach policy directions or positions.

## FEDERAL REGULATORY COMMISSIONS

The 1976–1977 United States Government Manual lists 58 agencies in addition to many boards, committees, commissions, and quasiofficial agencies, all of which operate to some extent independently of the executive branch. Many are rarely heard from, but a few have substantial impact upon practically all business in the nation. The principal agencies impacting upon business decision making are shown in Table G-1, as are some of the regulatory functions of these agencies. A substantial amount of industry and business regulation is performed by the executive departments. Their activities range from antitrust enforcement by the Department of Justice to regulation of packers and stockyards by the Department of Agriculture, from regulation by the Food and Drug Administration within the Department of Health, Education, and Welfare to requirements for statistical reporting by the Department of Commerce.

## GOVERNMENT AS A SOURCE OF ASSISTANCE

Government, today, is a major source of assistance to business. The business that does not utilize this

TABLE G-1   Regulatory Agencies and Commissions

| Name of commission | Year of formation | Number of members | Purpose |
|---|---|---|---|
| **TRANSPORTATION** | | | |
| Interstate Commerce Commission | 1887 | 11 | To regulate interstate surface transportation, to approve routes, grant certification, and ensure that rates and services are fair and reasonable. |
| Civil Aeronautics Board | 1938 | 5 | To promote and regulate civil air transportation, and to approve rates, routes, and agreements involving air carriers. |
| Federal Maritime Commission | 1961 | 5 | To regulate waterborne foreign and domestic offshore shipping of the United States and to ensure financial responsibility for indemnification of passengers and for cleanups of oil spills. |
| **UTILITIES** | | | |
| Federal Communications Commission | 1934 | 7 | To regulate interstate and foreign communications by radio, television, wire, and cable. The commission grants operating authority and approves interstate communication rates. |
| Federal Power Commission | 1920 | 5 | To regulate interstate aspects of electric power and natural gas to ensure reasonable rates and adequate supply. |
| **CONSUMER PROTECTION AND COMPETITION REGULATION** | | | |
| Federal Trade Commission | 1914 | 5 | To promote fair competition in interstate commerce, to prevent false advertising and deceptive practices, and to ensure true credit cost disclosure. |
| Consumer Product Safety Commission | 1972 | 5 | To protect the public against unreasonable risks of injury from consumer products, to establish product safety standards, and to ban hazardous products. |
| **EMPLOYMENT** | | | |
| Equal Employment Opportunity Commission | 1964 | 5 | To investigate charges of employment discrimination and to bring actions before the appropriate Federal District Court. |
| National Labor Relations Board | 1935 | 5 | To investigate and settle labor disputes and to prevent unfair labor practices. |
| Occupational Safety and Health Review Administration | 1970 | 3 | To adjudicate cases from the Department of Labor respecting safety and health inspections. |
| **ENVIRONMENT AND TECHNOLOGY** | | | |
| Environmental Protection Agency | 1970 | Administrator | To abate and control pollution through standard setting and monitoring. |
| Energy Research and Development Administration | 1974 | Administrator | To consolidate federal activities relating to research and development on the various sources of energy, to achieve self-sufficiency in energy. |
| Federal Energy Administration | 1974 | Administrator | To ensure a sufficient supply of energy to the United States, to evaluate allocation, to plan storage and rationing. |
| National Aeronautics and Space Administration | 1958 | Administrator | To conduct research on space flight and exploration. |

| Name of commission | Year of formation | Number of members | Purpose |
|---|---|---|---|
| FINANCE AND INTERNATIONAL COMMERCE | | | |
| Commodity Futures Trading Commission | 1974 | 5 | To strengthen the regulation of trading in futures and all commodities traded on commodity exchanges, to protect market users from fraud and other abuses. |
| Export-Import Bank | 1934 | President of the bank | To grant loans and issue guarantees and insurance so that exportation may be undertaken without undue risk. |
| Federal Deposit Insurance Corporation | 1933 | Chairman | To promote confidence in banks and to provide insurance coverage for bank deposits. |
| Securities and Exchange Commission | 1934 | 5 | To protect investors and the financial community against wrongful practices in the securities markets. The SEC relies on disclosure requirements to, as well as regulation of, securities dealers. |
| U.S. International Trade Commission (formerly U.S. Tariff Commission) | 1916 | 6 | To provide studies and recommendations concerning international trade and tariffs to the President, Congress, and other government agencies; to conduct investigations especially with respect to import relief for domestic industry and antidumping. |

assistance to the greatest extent practicable is being competitively disadvantaged. The Department of Commerce is the source of most assistance to business in the form of services and information. A number of agencies have grant programs which aid business. Most programs are administered by grants to state or local governments or to nonprofit organizations. Industry cooperation with grant recipients, such as universities, is encouraged by some agencies, among them the National Science Foundation.

**Loans** Some representative sources of loans are these:

1. The Agency for International Development grants loans to certain foreign countries for development projects. These projects often utilize U.S. industry.

2. The Agricultural Stabilization and Conservation Service (within the Agriculture Department) grants crop loans through county offices.

3. The Overseas Private Investment Corporation provides for some direct loans for United States investors in overseas projects. Such loans range from $50,000 to $2 million and run from 5 to 20 years.

4. The Small Business Administration provides various types of loans to qualified small business concerns and to disaster victims (see below).

Most loan programs provide for guarantee of loans made by or through commercial lending institutions. Loan applications, under either a direct loan or a guaranteed loan program, are processed through the district or regional office of the involved agency.

**Insurance** Various agencies insure against certain risks too substantial for industry, itself, to bear. In most instances the agency guarantees through usual commercial channels. For example,

1. The Small Business Administration reinsures or guarantees surety companies against the major portion of losses on construction bonds issued for minority-owned businesses.

2. The Export-Import Bank guarantees repayment to commercial banks which finance medium-term transactions for exports.

3. The Overseas Private Investment Corporation insures U.S. lenders against both commercial and political risks by guaranteeing payment of principal and interest.

In addition to the indirect insurance, direct insurance is provided by the above agencies as well as others, such as the Federal Crop Insurance Corporation (within the Department of Agriculture) which insures crops against unavoidable losses. For domestic programs, applications are made through the local offices of the agency. For international programs, application is made through the Washington offices of the agency.

The consensus of most observers is that borrowers should first pursue all regular commercial sources of financing before seeking federal loans. This view prevails for several reasons:

1. In most instances the lending or guaranteeing agency requires that the applicant demonstrate nonavailability of customary commercial sources of financing.

2. Substantial time is involved in the processing of applications by a government agency.

3. The government agency frequently requires personal guarantees from the borrower even though the loan is for business purposes.

**Management and Research Assistance** The major source of government assistance to the business entity is found in the Department of Commerce. The Department states that its purpose is to encourage, serve, and promote the nation's economic development and encourage the competitive, free enterprise system. The Department is a source of substantial aid and information. It is the first place to which business decision makers might look for market data. The Domestic and International Business Administration (DIBA) maintains field offices in over three dozen cities in the United States. The DIBA provides data on export opportunities, production, pricing, materials availability, and a myriad of other data. In addition, the Department conducts other programs of aid to business. The National Bureau of Standards, the Economic Development Administration, the National Technical Information Service, the Patent and Trademark Office, the Bureau of the Census, the Office of Minority Business Enterprise, and the Economic Development Administration, all have programs of assistance to business, by way of either information, research data, or financial aid.

The Small Business Administration provides financial assistance to small business through guaranteed direct or lender participation loans. It also provides financial assistance to and regulation of small business investment companies (SBICs) and grants licenses (minority enterprise SBICs). In addition, it provides management assistance through conferences, workshops, publications, and courses. It maintains 10 regional and more than 80 local offices. (*See* SMALL BUSINESS ADMINISTRATION.)

## GOVERNMENT AS A CUSTOMER

The government is the largest single customer of business in the United States. The two agencies through which most procurement takes place are the General Services Administration (GSA) and the Department of Defense. Procurement for the nonmilitary agencies is subject to provisions of the Federal Procurement Regulation. Military procurement is covered by the Armed Service Procurement Regulation. Within the General Services Administration, the Federal Supply Service is the buying agent for standard or "off-the-shelf" items used by all government agencies.

The GSA also maintains business service centers in 10 major cities. These centers provide guidance to business interested in selling to or buying from the government. Another source of information is the *Commerce Business Daily* published by the Department of Commerce. In addition to requesting to be placed on the GSA bidders' lists, one may request to be placed on the bidders' list of other agencies which procure for government simply by writing to the Director of Procurement for the agency.

The General Accounting Office (GAO) is the Congressional "watchdog" over the integrity of federal expenditures and procurement practices. For an unsuccessful bidder on a government contract, a protest to the GAO is one form of recourse.

## MEANINGFUL RELATIONS

Any business of any size finds itself faced with the need to file significant numbers of reports with various federal agencies. These range from annual reports to the Securities and Exchange Commission and Internal Revenue Service to personnel practice reports. There is always the question of how much information one should voluntarily provide to a regulatory body which might eventually invoke sanctions upon one's business activities. Answers to this question are varied.

The channels of communication to government agencies are opened more widely than is generally recognized, both formally and informally. With respect to formal channels, for example, on antitrust or trade practices both the Federal Trade Commission and the Department of Justice will render advisory opinions to guide business in advance of deciding upon a course of action. The IRS provides opinions concerning tax treatment of various transactions. These are obtained by request for a tax ruling. Informal channels are provided by trade associations and through one's representative in Congress. Many businesses fail to utilize fully the resources to be found in the offices of their congressional representative or senator. The administrative or legislative aid in a Capitol Hill office is quite often a great source of information for the business decision maker.

There has been considerable discussion of the encroachment of government agencies upon business freedom in decision making. Frequently there are moves to reduce the role of government, to deregulate or partially deregulate the regulated industries, and to revise antitrust laws either by repeal or by exemptions. Regardless of the ebb and flow of criticism of the governmental role in the management of economic enterprise, it is a fact of life that government will continue to have a meaningful role, as a regulator, as a partner, or as an adversary.

*See also* EGALITARIANISM; *Government Relations and Services;* MARKETS, PUBLIC; PUBLIC ADMINISTRATION; SMALL BUSINESS ADMINISTRATION; TAX MANAGEMENT, MANAGERIAL RESPONSIBILITY FOR FEDERAL INCOME TAX REPORTING.

### REFERENCES

*The Budget of the U.S. Government,* U.S. Government Printing Office, 1976.
*The Government Organization Manual,* U.S. Government Printing Office, 1976.
Katz, Robert N.: "Business Impact upon Regulatory Agencies," *California Management Review,* summer 1974, pp. 102–108.
Kohlmeier, Louis: *The Regulators,* Harper & Row, Publishers, Inc., New York, 1969.
Wiedenbaum, Murray: *Business, Government and the Public,* Prentice-Hall, Inc., Englewood Cliffs, N.J., 1977.

ROBERT N. KATZ, *Editor, California Management Review*

## Government relations with small businesses (*See* SMALL BUSINESS ADMINISTRATION.)

## Government sales (*See* MARKETS, PUBLIC.)

## Graphic-rating scale (*See* APPRAISAL, PERFORMANCE.)

## Grid, analytical marketing (*See* MARKETING MANAGEMENT.)

## Grid, managerial (*See* MANAGERIAL GRID.)

## Grievances (*See* PERSONNEL ADMINISTRATION.)

## Gross national product (GNP) (*See* ECONOMIC CONCEPTS.)

## Group norms (*See* CONFORMITY IN MANAGEMENT.)

## Groups (*See* INTERPERSONAL RELATIONSHIPS.)

## Groups, formal and informal (*See* CONFORMITY IN MANAGEMENT.)

## Groups, membership (*See* CONFORMITY IN MANAGEMENT.)

## Groups, primary and secondary (*See* CONFORMITY IN MANAGEMENT.)

## Groups, reference (*See* CONFORMITY IN MANAGEMENT.)

## Groups, reference and culture (*See* CONSUMER BEHAVIOR, MANAGERIAL RELEVANCE OF.)

## Growth strategy (*See* POLICY FORMULATION AND IMPLEMENTATION.)

## Guaranteed annual wage (GAW) (*See* COMPENSATION, SPECIAL PLANS.)

# Hall of fame of business leadership

Since 1975, Junior Achievement, Inc., has sponsored an annual recognition program for business leaders to be selected by the editors of *Fortune* magazine. Annual selections include historical as well as contemporary persons. The criterion for selection of the laureates is "outstanding and enduring contributions to improving the products, the processes, the efficiencies, or the human relations of business." Laureates include:

Historical figures:

*Henry Ford* (1863–1947), developer of the automobile, father of mass production.

*John D. Rockefeller* (1839–1937), aggressive corporate entrepreneur, monopolist, Standard Oil Company.

*J. Pierpont Morgan* (1837–1913), extraordinary financier, especially in railroading and mining.

*Alfred P. Sloan, Jr.* (1875–1966), formalized policy making and corporate control at General Motors Corporation.

*A. P. Giannini* (1870–1949), pioneer in branch banking and consumer loans, founder of Bank of America.

*George Washington* (1732–1799), systematic appraiser and developer of farmland and real estate.

*Eli Whitney* (1765–1825), mechanic who conceived the principle of interchangeable parts.

*Cyrus H. McCormick* (1809–1884), fathered installment selling and money-back guarantees of agricultural equipment.

*Andrew Carnegie* (1835–1919), steel entrepreneur, exponent of cost accounting, and powerful motivator of subordinates.

*Theodore N. Vail* (1845–1920), advocate of service in support of profit, President of AT&T.

*Alexander T. Stewart* (1803–1876), innovator of retailing practice of "one price for all," credit purchases.

*Thomas A. Edison* (1847–1931), inventor and technological entrepreneur, founder of Edison General Electric Company.

*J. Edgar Thomson* (1808–1874), railroad (Pennsylvania) construction and cost control leader.

*David Sarnoff* (1891–1971), visionary founder of RCA.

*George Eastman* (1854–1932), leader in vertical integration and corporate research, Eastman Kodak Company.

*James Cash Penney* (1875–1971), innovator of the retail chain store with a "manager-partner."

*Charles Edward Merrill* (1885–1956), investment banker and broker, founder of the firm now named Merrill Lynch Pierce Fenner & Smith, Inc.

*William Cooper Procter* (1862–1934), soapmaker, pioneer in equitable treatment of employees, Procter & Gamble Company.

*Albert Davis Lasker* (1880–1952), father of modern advertising, Foote, Cone and Belding.

*Walter Elias Disney* (1901–1966), innovative film maker and developer of entertainment parks.

*James Jerome Hill* (1838–1916), transportation magnate, "the empire builder," Great Northern Railroad.

*Benjamin Franklin* (1706–1790), creator of economic maxims in *Poor Richard's Almanac*.

*Henry Robinson Luce* (1898–1967), innovative magazine publisher, founder of Time, Inc.

*Florence Nightengale Graham* (1878–1966), founder of beauty salon chain Elizabeth Arden.

*Henry John Kaiser* (1882–1967), ship, road, and dam builder; founder of steel and aluminum companies and 100 more.

Contemporary figures (date is year of award):

*M. J. Rathbone* (1975), corporate strategist for integrated oil company, now Exxon.

*J. Erik Jonsson* (1975), electronic products entrepreneur, Texas Instruments, Inc.

*Royal Little* (1975), father of conglomerates, Textron.

*William M. Allen* (1975), sales-oriented risk analyst, chairman, Boeing Company.

*Thomas John Watson, Jr.* (1976), spearheaded development of computer and electronic data processing, IBM Corporation.

*George Stevens Moore* (1976), proponent of extended banking services, chairman, Citibank.

*Stephen Davison Bechtel, Sr.* (1976), master of processing plant construction and project management.

*Cyrus Rowlett Smith* (1976), developer of passenger aviation (American Airlines) and United States Secretary of Commerce.

*Robert Winship Woodruff* (1977), advocate of business definition, Coca-Cola, civic leader.

*John J. McCloy* (1977), sponsor of merger which formed Chase Manhattan Bank, Assistant Secretary of War of the United States.

*William Blackie* (1977), advocate of international manufacturing installations, Caterpillar Tractor Company.

*Joyce Clyde Hall* (1977), innovator of unique inventory systems, founder of Hallmark Cards, Inc.

See also GANTT MEDAL AWARDS; MANAGEMENT, HISTORICAL DEVELOPMENT OF.

STAFF/BITTEL

**Hardware** (*See* INFORMATION SYSTEMS, MANAGEMENT (MIS), APPLIED.)

## Hawthorne studies and effect (*See* MANAGEMENT, HISTORICAL DEVELOPMENT OF.)

## Hawthorne study (*See* INTERPERSONAL RELATIONSHIPS.)

## Health, employee (*See* SAFETY AND HEALTH MANAGEMENT, EMPLOYEE.)

## Health, executive, managing stress and job tension

A manager's first responsibility is to become effective. The second responsibility is to maintain that effectiveness. In the maintenance of managerial effectiveness, stress is an increasingly significant threat. Stress is not new to managers, but there are at least three reasons for a new and enlightened concern.

*First*, there is the issue of change and adaptation. Organizations must respond continuously to a changing environment. They adjust, adapt, attempt to find new structures and new policies to meet changing constraints and opportunities. The need to adapt induces stress; and when organizations are under stress, managers are under stress.

The *second* reason for concern is that, over the past 50 years, the nature of disease and disorder has changed. Chronic diseases are now the principal contributors to morbidity and mortality, and each day new evidence reveals the relationship of stress to chronic disease.

A *third* factor is that management jobs have become more complex, more difficult—because of global changes. Harlan Cleveland described three such changes:

1. The coming of the "horizontal society."
2. The blurring of what is public and what is private.
3. The need for systems thinking, systems action.[1]

These and other changes forebode more uncertainty and ambiguity in the future. They also require adjustment and adaptation, with resultant stress.

For managers and organizations, the issue of stress has many dimensions. The most obvious is simply health and longevity. The personal tragedy in premature death is obvious. The corporate loss is also significant. Many managers, having just risen to the point of assuming key positions, die of coronary heart disease. Thus, the bench strength dies on the brink of making its most significant contributions. Organizations must learn to nurture and be vigilant of such a valuable resource. Corporations must respond to stress-related issues. Should managers have annual medical examinations? Do they know what they should about alcoholism, nutrition, exercise, and stress? Do they know how to survive in the twentieth century?

**The Meaning of Stress**  Most managers understand stress intuitively. It is usually an emotional discomfort accompanied by feelings of not being able to cope, that things are falling apart, that one is not in control. Or it may be just a general unease that all is not well, without an apparent cause. At the physical level, it includes loss of appetite, sleeplessness, sweating, ulcers, and other signs and symptoms.

In general, *stress is the result of the body's preparing itself for activity without the activity following*. As a consequence the body's systems are thrown out of balance. Excess acid is secreted in the stomach. Adrenalin appears in the blood. Heart rates increase, and there are other inappropriate reactions. *Chronic* physiological preparation for action, without the action, leads to disease and disorder. Stress, then, is fundamentally a psychophysiological phenomenon. It has to do with our feelings and emotions and the way our body reacts to them.

Intense feelings and emotions are often the result of experiences we encounter within organizations. In addition, some types of experience are more stressful than others, and the same type of experience can be more stressful to one person and less to another. Thus the *stress potential* of a situation can be defined as a function of two elements, (1) the situation and (2) the individual. Individuals, however, tend to differ in their abilities to cope with stress and job tension. In addition, some techniques for coping tend to be more effective than others.

**Coping with Job Tension**  In studies we have done on job tensions, managers were asked to indicate the various methods by which they coped with potentially stressful job situations. Their answers were grouped into the 10 categories listed below:

1. Build resistance by regular sleep, exercise, and good health habits.
2. Compartmentalize work and nonwork life.
3. Engage in physical exercise.
4. Talk through with peers on the job.
5. Withdraw physically from the situation.
6. Change to a different work activity.
7. Change strategy of attack on work.
8. Work harder.

9. Talk through with spouse.
10. Change to a nonwork activity.

*Most Effective Techniques*.  In follow-up studies, the effectiveness of each technique was determined by relating the usage of the technique to the incidence of stress symptoms. In terms of the average number of stress symptoms reported, the five best techniques for coping with job tensions were as follows:

1. Build resistance by regular sleep, exercise, and good health habits.
2. Compartmentalize work and nonwork life.
3. Engage in physical exercise.
4. Talk through with peers on the job.
5. Withdraw physically from the situation.

The most effective mechanism, building physical resistance, is highly significant in designing an action plan for coping with stress. It reflects an awareness of the demands of the job, a sensitivity to one's own limited physical resources, and a readiness to deal with tension as it arises. Individuals who have a preventive concern about their health will have energy available that they can use to help deal with problems rationally and effectively. Individuals who are healthy and alert have a much greater success potential as "managers of stress" than do the managers who neglect their health and, thus, their readiness to deal with stress.[2]

**Managing the Stress of Change**  Change is a principal source of stress in the life of a manager, and coping effectively with *change* often requires a reassessment of attitudes and life-style. Research by the authors has shown that some individuals are more "change-prone" and that this same group is less efficient in dealing with the stress resulting from change. To become an effective "manager of stress," the individual must maintain "change events" within tolerable limits. This is not to say that one should suppress change, as change constitutes the dynamics of life itself. Rather, one can consciously *plan* those events that are controllable so as to maintain a firm grasp on the events and activities of day-to-day living. At the same time, the manager who is aware of the fact that the unexpected does occur prepares himself or herself by retaining a "reserve" of energy to cope with unanticipated events.

**Active Participation versus Passive Reaction**  One *can* make a conscious decision either to experience life as a series of inevitable, uncontrollable events or to actively control and anticipate occurrences in the present and in the future. The two extremes in attitude may be described as *active participation* and *passive reaction*.

The active participators simplify their life-styles

by consciously selecting and timing the occurrences of specific milestones in their lives. They are aware of, and consider, their personal energy level (psychological and physical capacity) and do not judge personal success by the number of activities and new events they can handle without first "breaking down" or "burning out." They leave a reservoir of untapped time and energy for those unexpected events that otherwise might cause disruption and distress. They are "managers of change."

On the other hand, the passive reactors tend to leave their lives to fate. They seem to pride themselves on the number of activities and new undertakings they can cram into an already busy schedule. They do not anticipate the fact that, sooner or later, the one unexpected event will occur that is too large to fit into their chaotic and overburdened life-styles. "Change," therefore, not only occurs more frequently (from a self-inflicted source) but also tends to hit harder since it is often unanticipated.

From evidence collected in research by the authors, a continuum has been constructed, representing at its extremes the least and most effective attitudes toward life and change, and the subsequent mechanisms used to cope and adapt. The ends of the continuum may be imagined as two hypothetical individuals composed of polar extremes in attitudes, actions, and coping dispositions. The summary of these constructs is presented in Table H-1.

If a manager is to cope successfully with a constantly changing environment and to adapt within the dynamics of an evolving life-style, he or she should attempt to consciously move toward the right-hand extreme of this continuum.

**Development of Stress Management** A concerned manager can begin immediately a personal development program in the management of stress. Eight steps are particularly appropriate.

1. Consciously assess your own pace of life at present. Take inventory of all recent changes; include current or upcoming change events. Analyze job situations and identify those which you find particularly stressful. Ask yourself if you feel generally tense, overloaded, unsure about your job status, or confused by your state of affairs.

2. Try to become aware of your own psychophysiological threshold. Practice sensitivity in detecting stress symptoms (e.g., heart palpitations, headaches, rapid pulse, insomnia). Learn to identify a state of stress within yourself so you can begin to deal with it directly.

3. Simplify your life. Attempt to foresee the occurrence of specific stress-producing job events and try to schedule these so they do not occur simultaneously. In the same way, budget change events in such a way that they remain within *your* perception of controllable limits. Do not suppress all change and tensions; merely "manage" them. Leave

TABLE H-1  Styles of Coping With Change

| The passive reactor<br>(least effective) | The active participator<br>(most effective) |
| --- | --- |
| 1. Reacts passively to life's events. | 1. Participates actively in life. |
| 2. Leaves life to "fate." Tends to "cram" rather than "plan" activities. | 2. Maintains change events within tolerable limits by making a conscious selection of controllable activities. |
| 3. Shows little foresight or anticipation of events. | 3. Anticipates and prepares for likely events in the foreseeable future. Has good foresight. |
| 4. Allows events to accumulate until unable to cope when the unexpected arises. | 4. Builds and maintains a reservoir of untapped time and energy to deal with unexpected events. |
| 5. Perceives the environment and most change events as generally threatening. | 5. Views the environment objectively. Sorts events into categories of importance, urgency, and degree of actual threat. |
| 6. When faced with potentially stressful change, tends to react compulsively, most often in a stereotyped manner. | 6. When faced with potentially stressful change, takes time out to evaluate alternative strategies, perhaps even adopting a novel solution to a novel problem. |
| 7. May unconsciously choose a coping mechanism that actually increases stress reaction through adverse consequences. | 7. After careful evaluation, tries to adopt the mechanism of coping most apt to reduce potential stress and aid in successful adaptation. |
| 8. Continues to tax his or her psychophysiological capacity to the limit. Stress symptoms accumulate. | 8. Effectively eliminates or reduces stress. Continues to operate well within an adaptive range, and avoids overtaxing his or her psychophysiological capacity. |

job tensions *at* the office; compartmentalize work and home life. Become an active participator in controlling your life rather than a passive reactor to fate.

4. Leave room within your coping range for those unanticipated stress situations. Do not load your time and budget your energy completely to its quota. Maintain a state of readiness by staying healthy and alert. Be prepared! Develop a preventive concern about your health.

5. When an unexpected stress situation or major change event arises, *stop* and think about it. Is it really as serious as it appears to be on the surface? Is it worth the expenditure of valuable energy resources in worrying and tension? Or, with the application of a little imagination and flexibility, can you adapt quite easily and readily?

6. Evaluate the various alternative mechanisms at hand for coping with tension. Are the old ways still working effectively? Or is it time to take a break, get away from it all, and evaluate new courses of action objectively? Begin to design and apply a broad repertoire of alternate responses. Be flexible and imaginative; shy away from stereotyped reactions. Follow through by analyzing the implications and range of consequences in your responses.

7. Above all, be in conscious control of your life. Participate actively, imaginatively, and with flexibility. Remember that you, as a manager, are particularly exposed to tension and susceptible to stress.

8. Remember also that stress is not all bad. Some stress is both necessary and desirable. The basic issue is not its elimination but its containment and allocation—the management of stress.

*See also* HEALTH, MENTAL; HUMAN FACTORS ENGINEERING.

## NOTES

[1] Harlan Cleveland, *The Future Executive; A Guide for Tomorrow's Managers*, Harper & Row, Publishers, Inc., New York, 1972.

[2] The value of good health habits was recently demonstrated by Dr. Lester Breslow in a 5½-year study with 7000 people. The seven habits studied were: 8 hours sleep per day, breakfast every morning, no snacks, maintaining weight within limits, no smoking, moderate alcohol consumption, and moderate exercise. Dr. Breslow found that at age 45, those following six or seven of these habits had an additional life expectancy of 33.1 years, while those at age 45 following three or less of the habits had an additional life expectancy of only 21.6 years. Dr. Breslow also found the effect to be cumulative—the more health habits one follows, the better one's health. N. B. Belloc and L. Breslow, "The Relationship of Physical Health Status and Health Practices," *Preventive Medicine*, no. 1, pp. 409–421, 1972.

## REFERENCES

Howard, John H.: "Management Productivity: Rusting Out or Burning Out?" *The Business Quarterly*, summer 1975.

———: "What Is Our Capacity to Cope with Stress?," *The Business Quarterly*, winter 1973.

———, Peter A. Rechnitzer, and D. A. Cunningham: "Coping with Job Tension—Effective and Ineffective Methods," *Public Personnel Management*, September–October 1975.

———, ———, and ———: "Stress Inoculation for Managers and Organizations," *The Business Quarterly*, winter 1975.

Selye, Hans: *The Stress of Life*, McGraw-Hill Book Company, New York, 1956.

JOHN H. HOWARD, PETER A. RECHNITZER, DAVID A. CUNNINGHAM, and MARY JANE GRANT, *University of Western Ontario*

# Health, mental

This entry describes the symptoms of emotional stress and distress, their impact upon the work organization, and the strategies employed to prevent, abort, or ameliorate them. It views occupational stress in the context of people's continuous efforts to maintain their psychological equilibrium by balancing the forces which impinge upon them from within and without. When the "executive" function of the personality fails in the balancing-stabilizing process, the ensuing disease and distress are labeled *mental illness*. Executives at all levels of the organization must understand the process of change and the psychology of motivation if they are to perform the crucial managerial tasks of leading, motivating, and integrating human resources toward achieving mutual purpose. This understanding will help channel policies, goals, and decisions toward managing the stress of individual and organizational change.

## THE MEANING OF WORK

Work is a vehicle through which one maintains contact and interaction with the human and physical environment. It facilitates a productive expression of innermost drives and deep aspirations. To the matrix of work a person brings a lifetime of experience with its attendant attitudes, expectations, and modes of behaving. In short, people enter the workaday world carrying their psychological baggage with them. The shift of focus from the economic to the psychological model of motivation implies that work serves different purposes for different people, as each "marches to a different drummer," and is a major device for maintaining psychological balance.

## ON BALANCING

"What makes people tick?" They do not—tick, that is—they feel! All strive to maximize pleasure and minimize pain. To accomplish this, one must manage the feelings—love, hate, fear, dependency, and self-esteem—arising from the interfaces between one's desires and aspirations, reality's imperatives, societal and family rules, values and expectations, and one's standards and principles. Normal behavior is a compromise between these competing forces within and without and requires constant balancing; this is the executive function of the personality.

The executive of the personality utilizes the functions of perception, thinking, memory, calculation, concentration, judgment, and planning to organize the intellectual and emotional spheres of life. We are most familiar with this function through its interface with reality where rational problem-solving supposedly predominates. When rational thinking delays gratification of present desires in the interests of more effective long-term adaptation to reality, the personality is functioning on the *reality principle*. This is a difficult mode to maintain because there exist the buried remnants of unsolved and unresolved developmental tasks of childhood which incessantly press for time in conscious awareness, threatening to upset the delicate balance. The executive function must expend considerable energy in maintaining a constant vigil and in keeping out of awareness the painful skeletons in one's psychological closet. To complicate matters further, external events can, and often do, activate or escalate these buried emotional conflicts which are latent in all of us. Giving these conflicts such force are the powerful feelings, forged in childhood, which accompany them. These feelings can color our perceptions and result in thinking and behavior more appropriate to yesteryear. What distinguishes the emotionally disordered person from the average is not so much the presence of imbalance, per se, as is the tipping of the psychological scales toward repetitive constellations of maladaptive modes for managing stress, or exaggerations of normally occurring responses. To a greater or lesser degree everyone at one time or another is "off balance."

**Signals** The executive function manages stress via its own early warning system linked to a variety of mental mechanisms designed either to channel, divert, contain, or reverse the two major drives of affectionate attachment on the one hand and assertive mastery and self-preservation on the other. The signaling system scans the internal and external environments for signs of danger and sounds an "audible" alarm—*fear*, when the threat is external and known—and a silent alarm when forbidden impulses from the drives or painful memories of early conflict threaten to surface. Fear provokes a constellation of physiological responses which prepares one for fight or flight. The silent alarm initiates one or several unconscious mechanisms, each having different consequences and import for the balancing process. For most of us most of the time, no blips appear on our psychological radar; when they do, defenses are initiated. If defenses prove inadequate at a given time resulting in the imminent eruption of buried conflict and feelings, a general alarm is signaled—*anxiety*.

**Defenses** A cardinal principle of the Oriental martial arts and of the science of conservation is to channel a potentially destructive force into constructive outlets. This is also the most constructive and efficient means of managing primitive impulses: channeling them into problem solving—*sublimation*. When this does not occur, the executive function contains impulses and memories through the process of "forgetting"—*repression*. In moderation, repression maintains a defense against internal threat with no difficulty; when abused, spontaneity of feelings is lost, and psychosomatic symptoms may appear in susceptible persons. Diverting feelings and impulses to alternate targets results in scapegoating or "kicking the cat," while reversing the impulse onto oneself can produce self-condemnation, self-punishment, accidents, or even suicide at the extreme. These latter modes of maintaining psychological balance along with the excessive application of repression are inefficient uses of energy and suggest the magnitude of the forces that the executive function is dealing with.

Defenses also ward off a special form of anxiety—guilt. This painful feeling arises from a part of the personality closely allied to the executive function, the censor-taskmaster.

**The Censor-Taskmaster** This psychological "structure" is the repository of the moral and spiritual values of one's culture, the rules and regulations from family, and the "mind's-eye" attitudes toward oneself which are in part acquired from the reflected appraisal of others. Earlier, the mention of aspirations referred not only to one's explicit and acknowledged goals, but also to that inner hidden taskmaster who drums out a measured beat, chastising us with pangs of guilt for errors of omission and commission alike. Each of us takes the measure of the distance between the way we perceive ourselves—our self-image—and the way we feel we ideally ought to be—our future best. The greater that distance, the lower is the self-esteem; the lower the self-esteem, the greater the incidence of illness. One strives toward one's future best along a road marked by the restraints and constraints of internalized ethics and values of parents and significant others that are grafted onto one's own personality. In order to understand the psychology of motivation, one must appreciate that the most vital motivating force for any human being is that person's insistent and persistent striving to attain the ideal self—one's future best. Often one perceives only dimly, if at all, the tune to which one marches.

**Change and Loss** In addition to losing control of buried conflicts and feelings, and censure for running afoul of the "dos" and "don'ts," a major pervasive threat from within is the process of aging. It limits the rate at which new information can be acquired and dampens energy levels. One tends to become more inflexible in coping behavior and to become less innovative. The greater the inflexibility, the greater the potential for becoming and remaining obsolete with its resulting lowered self-esteem. Lowered self-esteem makes one overly sensitive to rejection and defeat with an attendant unwillingness to take risks. Learning requires that we risk failure; failure to learn produces obsolescence—the cycle is complete.

We all have emotional conflicts which can be activated by an environmental event. The common denominator in most occupational stress is *change*. In this regard Levinson's three axioms are pertinent: all change involves loss—"promotion, transfer, demotion, reorganization, merger, retirement, and most other managerial actions produce change"; losses in general and particularly those which are long-standing and accompanied by feelings of hopelessness often trigger significant illness which may be life-threatening; lastly, people will try to compensate for their losses and can be aided in this process by management to the benefit of the organization.

*Loss.* People insistently and persistently minimize their attachments to faces, places, things, and ways of thinking and doing. The losses of affection, supportive milieu, information networks, and of being "on top" of one's world are often the consequences of moving, career changes, and the severing of close work relationships. Loss requires a process

of grieving before old attachments can be relinquished and new ones made. Appreciation of this process is essential to the management of loss and the stress of change.

## OFF BALANCE

Normal psychological growth is a continuous process of conflict resolution. One's personality is distinguished by the repertoire of methods employed. These methods apply to threats in the real world and to the ways we deal with buried unresolved early conflicts and those aspects of current reality which threaten to uncover them. When the response to stress is so severe or frequent as to be disruptive, it is called a *symptom;* it can be present as feelings, behavior, or bodily dysfunction. In all instances, the capacity to love and/or work is impaired.

The executive must be concerned with the task at hand and must hold a worker accountable for resolving behavior that interferes with work; referral to a professional may be indicated.

**Fear-Anxiety Response** "Butterflies in the stomach, white as a ghost, sweating bullets, the runs, nervousness" and heart palpitations describe the body's expression of this emotion. When severe, concentration and overall intellectual efficiency are impaired; if mild, performance may be improved. When this response occurs in the absence of a palpable source of danger, we can infer the presence of unconscious conflict. In the milder cases executives can help by calling the sufferer's attention to the events which preceded the onset of the distress and by facilitating discussion; it is always of some comfort to learn that one's emotional reactions are not unique.

When the severity of fear-anxiety reaches a level that is grossly disorganizing—*panic*—professional help should be sought through the organization's medical department or private sources. Under these circumstances the superior should take the initiative.

Sometimes, fear-anxiety is so predominant over time and situation that it is part of the character—such persons are called "high-strung." More complex are symptoms of irrational fear and avoidance of experiences which have a neutral tone for most people—animals, heights, open spaces, elevators, etc. Professional help is indicated when the phobia limits the accomplishment of the task or becomes unacceptable to the sufferer.

*Organizational Impact.* The exercise of power inherent in executive functioning militates against being affectionately regarded. Those who are overly anxious about a loss in popularity avoid the use of power in order to please, thereby subverting their authority and position and creating further anxiety.

The anxiety of not being "on top" or in control of one's job results from responsibility-without-authority and not knowing what one is supposed to do, how it is to be done, or how one is performing—*role ambiguity*. This anxiety may lead to anger and/or withdrawal.

*Executive Action.* Efforts should promote collaborative planning to reduce fear of the unknown; make problem solving and the task the competitive focus instead of internecine rivalry; initiate and maintain contact with subordinates to support them and to define job boundaries, and provide time daily to become aware of feelings and to talk them out.

**Depressive Response** Sadness, dejection, pessimism, and loss of energy, interest, appetite, and sleep are all part of this most common of psychological symptoms. Actual or threatened loss underlies depression; loss is the "flip side" of attachment. When depression is of such severity and duration as to preclude involvement in work or other everyday activities of living, professional assistance is mandatory. This is imperative if the person voices suicidal intent, or more seriously, has a plan and the means at hand to execute it. If the sufferer cries, allow it by waiting patiently; this communicates acceptance and understanding.

More commonly we note individuals who consistently become angry with themselves over minor errors. One can infer that they hold themselves to very strict inner standards and suffer guilt and self-recrimination when they do not meet them. "Minor" events with major symbolic meaning can precipitate symptoms. One can help by lending a sympathetic ear, sharing one's own "goofs," or making contact with an outstretched arm; such efforts will often relieve some of the immediate burdens imposed by conscience. To be avoided is the tendency to prescribe "vacations" for depressed people; guilt is increased because they do not feel deserving. Exaggerated praise also increases guilt for the same reason; praise in moderation gives the approval sought and a sense of earned recognition.

The strict standards, high expectations, and strivings for perfection also make for very good employees and executives; one's strengths can often be one's point of vulnerability.

*Organizational Impact.* Many of even the most successful executives have feelings of inadequacy. This ubiquitous feeling can handicap a career if it leads to a paralyzing doubt of one's ability to assume greater responsibility. Also, a sense that one is in an occupational cul-de-sac is common is early middle-age and may lead to compulsive competitive activities to assuage self-doubt. Such digressions prevent a necessary midlife reappraisal of goals.

When self-doubt turns to guilt and the need to expiate it, one may seek punishment via accidents, performance failure, aggression-provoking behavior, or behavior that invites imprisonment. When organizations act in ways that violate the consciences of workers, expiation may take the form of "leaks" to consumer or government agencies.

*Executive Action.* This requires an awareness of the prevalence of self-doubt and, if indicated, discussing an alternate career path with a person versed in that alternative. If, after consulting with vocational guidance experts, talking with a trusted friend or spouse, and developing a course of action, one is still plagued by doubt, professional help should be sought.

**Hostility Responses** A fearful, cornered animal will fight. A wild-animal trainer maintains a critical distance between self and animal in order to effect fearful retreat or compliance knowing that "trespass" will invite attack. When one feels that one's "turf" or boundaries have been invaded or threatened, fear is evoked and anger follows. Note that although two feelings are present, overt behavior may express either or both of them.

The tendency to ascribe to others what one does not want to acknowledge in oneself is universal. In the extreme, some deal with their underlying feelings of helplessness and low self-esteem by attributing to others persecutory intent and responsibility for failure while maintaining for themselves a grossly distorted image of their own self-importance and omnipotence. Psychiatric intervention is mandatory in these cases and should be sought also when there is constant hostility in the absence of provocation.

*Organizational Impact.* People are most threatened by the possibility of losing control of their feelings, autonomy, power, and self-esteem. Such loss may result from change, rivalry with superiors, peers, or subordinates, increased responsibility, role ambiguity, and conflicting superiors. Anger often ensues in the forms of hostile withdrawal, irritability, or tension, becoming a "workaholic" to expend feelings, channeling it into productive competition, or boss-induced destructive intraorganizational rivalry expressed as defensiveness, refusal to communicate, guarding of territory, and fighting. At times anger is "staged" to manipulate others or is displaced onto innocent, helpless substitute targets via scapegoating.

*Executive Action.* Be aware of your "flash points" and responses. Delay expression of your anger to avoid "shooting from the hip"; ask yourself, "What am I afraid of? What or who hurt my feelings?"

If you or your subordinates become the objects of displaced feelings, do not fire back, placate, or withdraw. If the other person seems embarrassed by the outburst, cushion the person's guilt by acknowledging that there *might* be a reason for it and that one also feels angry at times. Remind the person that the joint concern is the task. When anger is explosive, insist that such loss of control must not be repeated but that discussion of grievances is welcome. Immediately abort destructive expressions of anger in the work group and search for causes, not culprits, by promoting an airing of problems.

Placing yourself in your "attacker's" shoes will provide a mirror of recognition and maintain perspective. One's anger can be defused in hobbies, sports, travel; it can be productively vented toward subordinates and associates in response to limit testings, and it can be used to accent one's position to help move the problem-solving process forward.

**Withdrawal Response** Not uncommonly, people withdraw after a major life crisis; we all need privacy at times to recoup. But when one severs all contact with colleagues, friends, and usual activities, gradually or abruptly, it is cause for alarm, all the more so if there is no discernible precipitant.

*Organizational Impact.* Illness, accidents, absenteeism, apathy, high turnover, and frequent changes of employment may be disguised withdrawal. Fear of failure and of success can lead to avoidance of competition—slumps. The latter has its roots in threatening childhood competition with siblings and father, when unacceptable hostile impulses stimulated fear of retaliation. Those who have difficulty with rivalry feelings may be unable to work for others and elect to become entrepreneurs.

*Executive Action.* Be alert to the symptoms. Maintain contact by communicating caring and a desire to keep in touch. Pressuring the person to be more sociable or active is counterproductive. Though childlike behavior may surface, avoid treating the person as a child since this further reduces self-esteem. If withdrawal is a personality style, do not put the person into a position requiring continual or close relationships with others.

**Drug Abuse** Overall decrements in performance, Friday/Monday absences, or erratic performance and emotional lability may signal drug abuse. Performance should be discussed with the worker; if alcohol or other abuse surfaces in these talks, treatment should be mandated as a condition of continued employment, or sick leave provided during treatment. As with cancer, failure to act promptly will lead to progressive and possibly irretrievable physical, psychological, and social impairment. Close liaison between the medical department and a community drug treatment program is crucial.

### SUMMARY

Psychological forces are just beginning to be appreciated by management, as is the potency of unconscious motivation. It is not what you do *to* people but what you do *with* them that matters. We have learned, painfully, that one meddles with the balance of nature at one's peril and that we must "court," not conquer, our physical environment. Managerial policies, goals, and decisions *must* be consonant with the ecology of the emotional environment.

*See also* ASSERTIVENESS TRAINING; CONFORMITY IN MANAGEMENT; HEALTH, EXECUTIVE, MANAGING STRESS AND JOB TENSION; HUMAN FACTORS ENGINEERING; INTERPERSONAL RELATIONSHIPS; MOTIVATION IN ORGANIZATIONS; TRANSACTIONAL ANALYSIS.

### REFERENCES

Cass, E., and F. Zimmer (eds.): *Man and Work in Society*, Van Nostrand Reinhold Co., New York, 1975.

Claiborne, C. and L. Shapiro: *You are not Alone*, Little, Brown and Company, Boston, 1976; paperback, Consumers Union Edition, 1976.

Levinson, H.: *Emotional Health: In the World of Work*, Harper & Row, Publishers, Inc., New York, 1964.

———: *The Exceptional Executive*, Harvard University Press, Cambridge, Mass. 1968; paperback, New American Library, Inc., New York, 1971.

———: *Executive Stress*, Harper & Row, Publishers, Inc., New York, 1972; paperback, New American Library, Inc., New York, (revised and updated), 1975.

———: *The Great Jackass Fallacy*, Harvard University Press, Boston, 1973 (paperback).

———: *Psychological Man*, The Levinson Institute, Cambridge, Mass., 1976.

———, J. Molinari, and A. Spohn: *Organizational Diagnosis*, Harvard University Press, Cambridge, Mass., 1972 (paperback).

Rosenthal, S.: "The Economy and Human Dignity—The Dehumanizing Consequences of Inflation and Unemployment and the Social Responsibilities of Big Business," *A Report on the Bicentennial Conference on Human Dignity and American Democracy*, St. Louis University Press, 1976.

STUART ROSENTHAL, *The Levinson Institute,*
*Tufts University School of Medicine*

**Health care** (*See* COMPENSATION, EMPLOYEE BENEFIT PLANS.)

**Health care maintenance organizations (HMOs)** (*See* COMPENSATION, EMPLOYEE BENEFIT PLANS.)

**Health care system** (*See* HEALTH INSTITUTIONS, MANAGEMENT OF.)

**Health delivery system** (*See* HEALTH SERVICES, PLANNING FOR.)

**Health and health management** (*See* heading in Table of Contents for complete listing.)

## Health institutions, management of

As it increases in magnitude and significance, the health care system in the United States is becoming more and more complex. Its major components are personal health, public health, and environmental health. *Personal health* is provided by physicians, hospitals, long-term care facilities, etc. *Public health* has traditionally been the concern of government at various levels. *Environmental health* copes with health problems stemming from water and air pollution, occupational hazards, sanitation, and waste disposal. Of the three components, personal health care represents the greatest proportion of health expenditures, and the hospital is often thought of as the major component of the personal health care system.[1]

*Health Care Units.* As the health care system has developed, a great variety of units or combined specialized groups have come into being to provide health services. Some examples of these are: hospitals, clinics, prepaid group health units, health maintenance organizations, nursing homes, medical centers, convalescent hospitals, mental and psychiatric institutions, federal, state, and local governmental units, third-party payers (the Blue Cross Associations), professional standards review organizations, business and industry components, and educational institutions. Each of these units has a role to play in the health system, and each has its individualized goals or objectives. In turn, each of these units requires management and managerial personnel.

Each of the health care system units has its own specific characteristics. For example, hospitals tend to concentrate on the short-term care of patients, whereas the nursing home is concerned with long-term care. Different skills are needed, too, particularly among medical personnel. Most units in the health care system, however, tend to be both independent and nonprofit. Costs are important, but patient care is more important. On the one hand, each unit derives the bulk of its income from payments by those served. On the other hand, each is dedicated to providing attention to all people presenting themselves for care so long as rooms and time are available. Given the complex nature of these health care units, managers must develop and implement a framework within which medical personnel can provide the needed services.

### MANAGERIAL RESPONSIBILITIES

In any health care unit, the role of the manager is to plan, organize, and control resources in order to achieve (1) the objectives of the individual unit and, in turn, (2) those objectives of the total health system. Specifically, the manager's responsibility is to apply leadership ability in such a manner that the inputs of human and material resources are combined to produce the desired outputs or goals.

Managerial positions in the health care system have three basic components: the managerial component itself, a general health aspect, and an institutional or environmental component.

**The Managerial Component** This component involves the basic managerial functions of planning, organizing, and controlling. The manager is also concerned with organizational development and, more specifically, with the way people and the organization interact. Related managerial activities include determination of goals and objectives, financial management, personnel management, coordinating department operations, program review and evaluation, and planning—including both facility and program, public and community activities, health industry activities, and educational development. These activities all have similar basic performance aspects, although the implementation will vary in terms of the specific health care unit.[2]

**The General Health Component** This component is concerned with knowledge about the health industry and the specific nature of promoting and maintaining good health. In part, this component relates to a social responsibility concept, as well as information about the nature of health itself. The administrator, unless he or she is a physician, is generally not expected to be a certified expert in the field of health, since the role is one of management. On the other hand, the administrator needs to be knowledgeable about such matters as the nature of the health industry itself and changes occurring within it, factors affecting health, commonly used medical terms, approaches to improving health, health delivery systems, and the relationships involved in the "health delivery" team. There is a situational aspect to this basic component in that specific knowledge of the health industry, as it relates to the unit in which the manager is located, is a necessity.

Each individual unit in the health care system has its own characteristics and state of development. The manager must relate to these characteristics and work toward the achievement of the goals of the unit managed.

**The Environmental Component** Several changes are occurring in the manager's role. As is true with almost all management positions, the role is becoming more complex. This complexity is the result of many factors, including increased use of medical technology in the diagnosis and treatment of illness, larger units, extension of health care to increasing numbers of citizens, increase in third-party payers, changes in government controls, and increased knowledge by, and expectations from, people themselves. These and other related forces have caused managers of health institutions to become increasingly concerned with external forces. No longer can they be involved exclusively in the day-to-day procedural internal operations but must become involved with external planners, evaluators, and controllers. In this sense, they perform a boundary-spanning link between the health care unit and the external units of the health care system including the government with whom the managers are in contact.

**Integrated Systems** Another factor in the increasing complexity of the manager's role is the development of integrated health care systems. These integrated systems are organized either on a horizontal or vertical basis.

1. *Vertical integration* involves different kinds of health care delivery units such as clinics, hospitals, ambulatory care institutions, long-term care, and/or mental health facilities (product lines). Combinations of different "product delivery lines" are involved in this arrangement as well as the combination of administrative and medical technology in an integrated arrangement.[3]

2. *Horizontal integration* involves the combining of similar health care units, such as a number of hospitals or long-term care facilities, in order to share administrative and medical technology. The relationship may be somewhat informal, although in instances the individual units are combined or merged so that either a large organization results or new and complex organizational structures become necessary. Another form of relationship similar to vertical integration is the sharing among hospitals of services such as data processing and laundry facilities. This is a *cooperative* arrangement, and no merger or combination takes place.

Both horizontal and vertical models have business prototypes. In fact, the corporate form of organization and management is involved. The chief executive officer of a health unit may carry the title of president and sit on the board of directors, thus having policy-making authority and being in a position to influence directly the particular organizational institution. Furthermore, the chief executive is responsible for a vast array of human and technical resources involving, in certain situations, some of the most brilliant physicians and complicated technical machines as well as an expensive physical plant. This level of manager has a profound social responsibility to patients and society in general.[4]

Societal pressures, oftentimes implemented through federal legislation, have changed the role of the administrator so that he or she must give more attention to external forces. The administrator must look at the needs of the geographic area wherein the organization is situated and is expected to meet these needs. Planning groups have been established to ensure that the needs of citizens are met. These review committees examine the proposed plans of the health care unit in order to meet needs and ensure utilization of medical skills for all citizens.

**Situational Management** Given the complex nature of the health care system and the need for managerial skills and knowledge appropriate to the unit in question, it is necessary to utilize a concept of management which will meet these goals. Called the *contingency* or *situational concept of management*,[5,6] it begins with the assumption that organizations are complex arrangements and that, therefore, no single approach to management is necessarily universally best. Instead, the manager must deal with relationships and subsystems in such a way that the goals of the particular unit are attained. This concept im-

485

plies that there are few, if any, universally applicable principles but there are situational principles which are useful and applicable once the manager has determined the environmental characteristics within which he or she is operating.

The situational concept is very useful in the health industry because it enables the manager to develop skills in management and health generally, as well as to develop expertise in applying these to the specific health unit he or she manages. It implies that the manager must be able to influence policy decisions rather than merely to administer or implement the policies determined by others. In addition, a team approach, as opposed to a hierarchical, authoritarian method is more appropriate. Most health care units combine the skills and abilities of a wide range of professionals. As health technology increases, the impact of this diversification on organizational units will be ever greater. An effective manager, consequently, must be a person who can weld together working teams of professionals so that the technology may be adequately delivered to those in need.

*See also* HEALTH SERVICES, PLANNING FOR; HOSPITAL ADMINISTRATION; NOT-FOR-PROFIT ORGANIZATIONS, MANAGEMENT OF; PUBLIC ADMINISTRATION.

### NOTES

[1]Rockwell Schulz and Alton C. Johnson, *Management of Hospitals*, McGraw-Hill Book Company, New York, 1976, chap. 1.

[2]Charles J. Austin, "Emerging Roles and Responsibilities of Health Administration," in The Report of the Commission on *Education for Health Administration: Vol. 1*, Health Administration Press, Ann Arbor, Mich., 1975.

[3]Rockwell Schulz and Alton C. Johnson, *Management of Hospitals*, McGraw-Hill Book Company, New York, 1976, chap. 16.

[4]Thomas F. Treat, "The Performance of Merging Hospitals," *Medical Care*, vol. XIV, no. 3, pp. 199–209, March 1976.

[5]Paul R. Lawrence and Jay W. Lorsch, *Organization and Environment*, Richard D. Irwin, Inc., Homewood, Ill., 1969.

[6]Robert J. Mockler, "Situational Theory of Management," *Harvard Business Review*, vol. 49, no. 3, pp. 146–155, May–June, 1971.

ALTON C. JOHNSON, *University of Wisconsin, Madison*

# Health services, planning for

Health care represents a major cost to industry and to the nation. For example, General Motors reportedly spends more for employee health care than it spends on metal for its automobiles. Furthermore, in addition to health care being a direct cost to employees, productivity is directly related to employees' health status. Health is also one of the more important issues facing the United States today. Providing access to health care for those who need it, improving the quality of health services, and containing rapidly rising health care costs are primary concerns to the nation. Health care, in itself, is one of the largest industries in the United States: it employs over 4½ million individuals, and in 1976 involved expenditures of $139 billion or over 8.6 percent of the gross national product.

Managers professionally and as concerned citizens have much to contribute through an understanding of the underlying factors that relate to health and the efficient delivery of services to improve health.

## INPUTS TO HEALTH

Good health is the result of many factors. Figure H-1 illustrates the health spectrum (or inputs to health) of environment, behavior, heredity, and health care services as inputs to psychosocial (emotion and mental) and somatic (physical) health or well-being. These four inputs relate to and affect one another through ecological balance, natural resources, population characteristics, cultural systems, and mental health.

**Environment**  Physical characteristics of the environment such as climate, social conditions, and topography relate to health directly as well as interacting to affect the other forces that contribute to a state of healthfulness. Manufactured aspects of the environment have an increasing influence on health. Inadequate housing, for example, contributes to disease. Inadequacies in transportation and communication often present major barriers to the adequate delivery of health services. While advances in technology have had a major impact on health improvement, they sometimes lead to new hazards, such as the noise pollution associated with airplanes.

Sociocultural factors are also inputs to health. For example, cultural patterns affect nutrition, exercise, personal habits, and other health-related factors. Social stress and responses to cardiovascular, respiratory, gastrointestinal, and other systems have been widely researched and indicate relationships. There is increasing evidence that life-style contributes in a major way to health status in developed countries, more so than income or medical care. Politics, as reflected in laws on alcohol and safety, for example, contributes to health. The reduction of

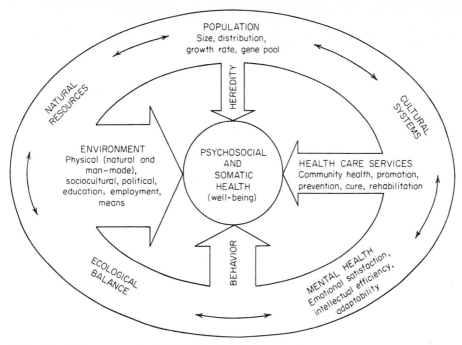

**Fig. H-1. The health spectrum. The width of the four huge input-to-health arrows indicates assumptions about the relative importance of the inputs to health. The four inputs are shown as relating to and affecting one another by means of an encompassing matrix which would be called the "environment" of the health system.** *From Rockwell Schulz and Alton Johnson, Management of Hospitals, McGraw Hill Book Company, New York, 1976, p. 5.*

deaths on the road as the result of setting highway speed limits is an example.

There is increasing evidence, also, that an individual's educational level is correlated with health. Income levels and occupations show relationships to health as well.

**Behavior** Personal behavior and habits such as smoking, drinking, dangerous driving, overeating, abuse of drugs, lack of personal hygiene, and delay in seeking medical care are major influences on health and well-being. The effect of personal behavior on individual health in turn reflects on the way in which a person reacts to environmental hereditary and health care services.

**Heredity** Heredity, or genetic endowment (the intrinsic nature of the individual), is recognized as the primary influence on susceptibility to, as well as inheritance of, disease. Genetic endowment reacts with environment, mental, and behavioral factors. Cultural considerations, such as ethnic or racial probities, limit the choice of marital partners and so influence the genetic potential of all offspring and their susceptibility to certain diseases. Problems arising from genetic factors may be controlled

through (1) screening, (2) increasingly thorough genetic counseling, and (3) potentially, genetic engineering.

**Health Care Services** These services include the community health services delivered by both the environmental agencies and the public health agencies. Environmental services can intervene in problems of pollution, occupational safety, housing conditions, etc. Health promotion activities relate to improvement of exercise, rest, attitudes, nutrition, etc. Prevention of disease requires health screening, early diagnosis, and good personal habits.

The cure factors or "diagnosis and treatment"— that is, services typically provided by physicians and hospitals—receive primary attention when health is studied. Of the $139 billion spent on health in 1976, nearly 95 percent was spent for personal health services, construction, and supplies, primarily for hospital and physician services. The balance, some $7 billion or about 5 percent, was spent on public health services and research. These figures indicate that the bulk of health expenditures is made to *correct* the problems *caused* by demographic, behavioral, physical, and genetic factors. Medical and hospital services receive the most public attention since they represent crisis care, sometimes referred to as "heroic medicine" or "too-late medicine": they are concerned with illness, not health.

This emphasis on cure rather than prevention is due partly to (1) health insurance, which encourages crisis care, and (2) the lack of promotion in prevention services. It is also due to (3) personal attitudes: people respond only when they have to. Moreover, as one author notes, "No matter what is done, most patients get well most of the time. Therefore, anything done in the name of health (cure) will be successful most of the time. This includes prayer, incantations, copper bracelets, manipulation of joints, special foods, prescription drugs, anything at all."[1]

*Rehabilitation*, or restorative services, designed to return patients to their maximum state of health is increasingly provided through hospitals, extended care facilities, and rehabilitation centers. *Custodial care* delivered by institutions and home health services also provides inputs to health.

In summary, therefore, managers concerned with improving health and providing more efficient health services need to look well beyond the traditional medical care services. They need to look especially toward incentives and behavioral modifications that would emphasize promotion of health—with less reliance upon and utilization of the expensive, traditional care services.

## HEALTH DELIVERY SYSTEM

The responsibility for delivery of health services in the total health spectrum has been fragmented among environmental, public, and personal health groups.

**Environmental Health Programs** These relate to public health and are carried out through a number of governmental and private agencies. This fragmentation has handicapped the development of effective and efficient programs. Environmental health programs include water supply and pollution control, solid waste disposal, insect and rodent control, milk and food sanitation, air pollution control, noise pollution control, control of radiological hazards, housing and land use, and occupational health.

**Public Health Services** These are concerned with populations and have traditionally included communicable (infectious) disease control, sanitation, maternal and child health, public health nursing, public health education, and vital statistics. These programs have been administered through state, county, and local health districts. Increasingly, public health services provided by govern-

ment go beyond the services listed above. They now include programs and activities for health planning and policy determination, health maintenance, continuous assessment of community ecology and resource, reduction of health hazards, and research.

**Personal Health Care** This is usually provided by the individual, by private physicians, hospitals, nursing homes, and so forth. These activities fall into four categories.

1. *Promotion of health* is usually considered the responsibility of the individual. In most cases, information and prescriptions related to such factors as diet, exercise, and rest are provided by the individual's cultural environment, family, and schools, and through the mass media. Management is usually by the individual. Increasingly, however, there is more emphasis on the promotion of health, and it is probable that employers will become more involved in promoting the psychosocial and somatic health of their workers and families as a way to reduce costs and improve productivity.

2. *Early detection of disease* through mass screening services among high-risk populations is a component of preventive medicine, although there is considerable difference of opinion about its effectiveness. Prevention of disease by controlling personal habits (for example, refraining from smoking, halting alcoholism) is an individual matter, but here, too, employers can help to modify an individual's behavior.

3. *Cure services*, that is, diagnosis and treatment services, can be categorized as ambulatory, outpatient, or inpatient care. *Outpatient services* are usually provided in physician's offices or clinics. In the private sector over 18 percent of the nation's physicians practice in medical groups or clinics. There are approximately 8000 group practices: nearly 53 percent of these are single specialty groups with an average of five physicians per group, nearly 35 percent are multispecialty groups with an average of 13 physicians, and about 12 percent are in general or family practice groups. With the increasing complexities of delivering physician services, there has been a rapid growth in both the number and size of group practices. Hospitals, too, provide outpatient services, with university hospitals and large public teaching hospitals having formalized clinics for services (primarily to indigents).

Specialized diagnostic and treatment services have also attracted ambulatory patients such as alcoholics and drug abusers to hospitals. *Home care* services provided by hospitals offer an alternative that has potential for more development.

*Inpatient* care is that provided within the hospital facility itself. Over 7000 hospitals are registered by the American Hospital Association. Over 3000 of these are nongovernment, not-for-profit hospitals which contain more than 600,000 short-term hospital beds, about 62 percent of the total.

Other commonly used terms include primary, secondary, and tertiary care hospital services. *Primary care* involves the site of entry into the health system—and coordination through it. It is obtained through the family physicain who may be a general practitioner, internist, pediatrician, or general surgeon. Primary care services are usually provided on an ambulatory or office visit basis. *Secondary care* services are consultant services. The services of a classically educated general internist or a general surgeon fit into this category. *Tertiary care* services are those of a subspecialty or categorical referral service provided in a regional medical center such as a university hospital.

*Mental health ambulatory treatment* services, such as those offered by community mental health centers, are frequently organized within community hospitals. *Dental health* is another important, but frequently segregated, component of health care.

4. *Restorative and long-term (or custodial) care services* are organized in a variety of institutions, such as hospitals, convalescent centers, group practice clinics, separate rehabilitation centers, and public agencies. Convalescent, long-term extended custodial care services are provided primarily by private and governmental institutions.

*A Pluralistic System.* Each of the above components of personal health care services involves a wide variety of specialists. More than 225 health vocations are listed by the U.S. Department of Labor, and they are represented by more than 300 professional organizations which some people classify as guilds. In addition to the diversity of professions and location within the health system, health services are controlled by a variety of governmental, proprietary, voluntary, and church groups. The financing of health services is just as diverse, with governmental programs of Medicare and Medicaid, nonprofit insurance programs, such as Blue Cross and Blue Shield, and commercial insurance plans, in addition to payments by individuals themselves.

Because of the diversity in health service delivery in the United States, some refer to it as a "nonsystem." Certainly it is a pluralistic one. Traditionally it has been fragmented within and among environmental, public health, and personal health delivery services. Frequently, there has been considerable overlap and duplication as well as substantial gaps in services. In recent years, however, efforts have been made to provide comprehensive services in a continuum through neighborhood health centers, health maintenance organizations (HMOs), and regional planning and regulation of health services.

## RESTRAINING FACTORS

Objectives of the health care system might be summarized on the basis of (1) access to appropriate services, (2) appropriate quality service to meet the individual's need, and (3) control over unnecessary costs. Within each of these objectives not only is there considerable room for debate over definitions, but also a concern as to levels of appropriateness.

**Access to Care** One of the changing values of recent years is the conviction by most people that health care is a right, i.e., that they should have access to medical services. But adequate health care involves far more than medical services. Accordingly, most of the problems associated with access to health care have centered on needs of the poor. It is evident that such barriers as income, education, race, and location present problems in attaining good health or in gaining access to health care. In recent years, however, some progress toward removing these barriers has been made through governmental insurance (Medicare, Medicaid), establishment of a National Health Services Corps which places physicians in areas having a scarcity of health services, setting up of neighborhood health centers, screening programs, and so forth.

In 1973, a study was made of the barriers to access, quality, and cost in the health field by the Commission on Education for Health Administrators.[2] Selected experts in the delivery of health services representing administrators, policy makers, researchers, planners, and health care providers developed a list of barriers and ranked them using a Delphi technique. There tended to be agreement on the following as major barriers to access to health care: Consumer problems in financing their health care; lack of incentives for physicians to locate in rural or ghetto areas; services not reimbursed by third-party payers are not sought; legal and educational barriers to use of paramedical personnel; inability to agree on health goals; fee for service system encourages an increase in the volume of services provided, but not in the quality of services; and lack of understanding by consumers of availability of services.

From this list it is clear that if managers wish to improve access to better health, they must consider a number of factors beyond the availability and cost of medical services.

**Quality** While quality of health care can be viewed very broadly, this evaluation is limited to quality of medical services. Donabedian suggested that "good" medical care is based on "articles of faith." Good medical care, he said, is limited to the practice of rational medicine based on medical science; emphasizes prevention; requires intelligent cooperation between lay public and the practitioners of scientific medicine; treats the individual as a whole; maintains a close and continuing personal relation between the physician and patient; is coordinated with social welfare work; coordinates all types of medical services; and implies the application of all necessary services of modern scientific medicine to the needs of all people.[3]

While the quality of medical care in the United States is recognized throughout the world as outstanding,[4] there is room for improvement. Studies show that (1) medical mismanagement contributes significantly to deaths from trauma,[5] (2) chances for survival appear to be greater in larger and particularly teaching hospitals,[6] and (3) unnecessary surgery is a major problem in the United States as well as in other countries.

The health field, itself, has been very active in attempting to improve quality of care through such programs as the Joint Commission on Accreditation of Hospitals, certification of specialists, quality review activities aided by mechanisms developed by the Commission on Professional and Hospital Activities, and numerous educational programs developed by health professionals and universities. Government, too, has been concerned with the quality of care through such activities as licensing of health professionals (which many feel has not been very effective) and the recently developed Professional Standards Review Organization (PSRO), which requires physicians' (peer) review of quality and utilization of health services on patients funded from federal sources.

In his study, Gustafson[7] lists the major barriers to quality of care as: consumers lack understanding of preventive measures and do not know when services are needed; third-party payment policies do not discriminate between poor and good quality care; organization and coordination of all health services is inadequate; consumers and providers use services as a reactive rather than a preventive function; incentive for quality care provided by competitors, governing boards, third-party payers and consumers is minimal; standards of quality care are lacking; information of measures causally relating treatment interventions to outcomes is largely absent.

**Containment of Rising Costs**  National expenditures for health care increased from $12 billion or $82 per person in 1950 to over $139 billion or $638 per person in 1976. Inevitably, the question arises, "Are current expenditures too much or too little?" Answers to that complex question relate to trade offs on other expenditures, social priorities, and what appear to be individual preferences. One might conclude that if less were spent on health care, more could be put into education and into environmental factors that cause poor health. On the other hand, it must be noted that billions of dollars are spent annually on tobacco, alcohol, and other indulgences that contribute to health problems.

By far the largest component in the rising health care costs has been hospital costs. The average cost per patient day in 1960 was less than $16; by 1975 it had exceeded $133. Factors contributing to rising hospital costs have been rising wage rates in a labor-intensive industry, a significant increase in malpractice insurance, and other inflationary factors.

Larger and more elaborate facilities that presumably improve the quality of care also contribute to rising hospital costs, as has the increasing scope of services per patient. Unfortunately, there are few, if any, incentives to contain rising hospital costs. Hospitals are generally reimbursed on the basis of costs and are thereby rewarded for expansion of facilities (even though this frequently means unnecessary duplication of services). Patients generally have not complained about rising costs because third-party payers (such as Blue Cross or Medicare) pay the bulk of them.

Gustafson[8] found the following to be major barriers to containing costs of health care: organization of coordination of health services is inadequate; evaluation skills of providers or proposed innovations are lacking; consumers lack understanding of when services are needed; information and measures causally relating treatment interventions to outcomes are largely absent; incentives for efficiency provided by competitors, governing boards, third-party payers, and consumers are minimal; consumers lack means of providing incentives to reduce costs; inflation; the increasing and changing nature of demand for services; consumers lack understanding of preventive measures; and the medical mystique causes consumers and trustees to hesitate to take issue with physicians.

To contain the rising costs, many are arguing for governmental controls over health services. And indeed, as the government assumes an increasing portion of support for health care and services, it demands more control over such services. Nevertheless, studies comparing costs and increases in United States with other Western nations suggest that governmental controls have done little to mollify such increases.

**Planning and Regulation** Attitudes and opinions toward health care regulation and centralized planning vary.

*Proponents.* Individuals favoring more regulation of the health industry tend to cite the following reasons: the health services industry is too large and too important to be unregulated; health care is a right; economists will point out that the health industry is a classic example of market failure and that the free enterprise system is inoperable in the health industry; there are increasing concerns over rising health care costs, and with centralized financing, controls are more feasible; current reimbursement plans are based on reimbursement of costs or charges and consequently there are no incentives to contain costs—that is, health services with higher costs will obtain higher reimbursement; and the public is aroused about examples of waste, of duplication of expensive services, and of high incomes of health providers.

*Opponents.* Those opposed to increased regulations point toward the progress made by the health industry in providing superior quality services and aver that quality and cost controls are being exercised by providers on a voluntary basis. They argue that while increased regulation may be more effective in controlling costs and access, it will result in lower quality. Moreover, when regulations are imposed on everyone, the unique needs and expectations of individuals are compromised.

*Trend.* While the debate over increased regulations continues, it is obvious that the health industry is currently highly regulated. Many of the regulations are voluntary—such as the Joint Commission on Accreditation of Hospitals to evaluate the quality of services provided in institutions—while others are governmental. Governmental and voluntary cost controls, such as Blue Cross Rate Review Programs and prospective reimbursement schemes, are in use in a number of states.

*Need.* Most will agree, however, that there is a need for a more rationalized health care system. Since 1946 with the Hill-Burton legislation (providing federal funds for hospital construction), the federal government has attempted to plan for a more effective and efficient health care system. In 1966, the Partnership for Health Acts (to accomplish comprehensive health planning) was passed to provide for state and regional health planning agencies. This fell short of expectations and in 1974, presumably in preparation for a national health insurance, Public Law 93-641, the National Health Planning and Re-

source Development Act, was passed. This act puts considerably more force behind the planning process and the adherence of plans, and in addition it consolidates a number of other programs.

*Future.* To date, most of the planning activities have centered on inventorying health services in the area and reacting to hospitals' proposals for expansion or replacement of facilities. In the future, as health planning becomes more sophisticated, one can expect to see improved application of quantitative techniques to identify health needs and evaluate effectiveness of alternatives for meeting these needs. Examples of approaches for evaluating need include: (1) Multiattributed utility analysis[9] to predict scarcity of health services as determined by experts, (2) regression analysis to project trends and relationships, (3) nominal group techniques[10] to provide for consumer inputs and health status indicators,[11] and (4) systems analysis, cost-benefit analysis, simulation techniques, and the like.

## CONCLUSION

In summary, professional managers, in or out of the health care arena, can make important contributions toward health care costs. These include:

1. Conducting consumer education programs to remove the barriers described above.

2. Evaluating hazards of the work environment and taking steps to remove these hazards.

3. Evaluating needs of employees and aiding them to meet these needs by, for example, referring the illiterate to appropriate reading programs (the illiteracy rate in communities even with high socioeconomic status is shockingly high); establishing, or referring workers to, alcohol prevention and treatment programs; developing programs to reduce smoking; and setting up exercise programs within the work environment.

4. Establishing incentives for employees to reduce utilization of health services by, for example, requiring the employee to pay a portion of health care costs.

5. Educating the employee as to when it is appropriate and when not appropriate to seek health care services.

6. Taking an active role in the community to evaluate the need for health care services and promote activities to reduce unnecessary costs.

7. Arguing for the application of quantitative techniques for the evaluation of community needs and allocation of resources.

8. Being on guard against adoption of bureaucratic structures that cost too much for benefits that may be denied.

See also COST-BENEFIT ANALYSIS; HEALTH INSTI-
TUTIONS, MANAGEMENT OF; NOT-FOR-PROFIT ORGA-
NIZATIONS; PUBLIC ADMINISTRATION; VALUE SYSTEMS,
MANAGEMENT.

## NOTES

[1] Nevin Scrimshaw, "Myths and Realities in International Health Planning," *American Journal of Public Health*,
vol. 64, no. 8, pp. 792–797, August 1974.

[2] David H. Gustafson, Glenwood Rowse, and Nancy J.
Howes, "Roles in Training for Future Health Systems
Engineers," in *Education for Health Administration*, vol. 2,
Health Administration Press, Ann Arbor, Mich., 1975.

[3] Avedis Donabedian, *A Guide to Medical Care Administration, vol. 2: Medical Care Appraisal—Quality and Utilization*, American Public Health Association, Washington,
1969.

[4] Harry Schwartz, *The Case for American Medicine*, David
McKay Company, Inc., New York, 1972.

[5] Harold R. Gertner, Jr., et al., "Evaluation of the Management of Vehicular Fatalities Secondary to Abdominal
Injury," *The Journal of Trauma*, vol. 12, no. 5, pp. 425–
431, 1972.

[6] Osler Peterson, "The Importance of Obtaining High
Quality Medical Care," in *The Hospital's Role in Assessing the
Quality of Medical Care*, Proceedings of the 15th Annual
Symposium on Hospital Affairs, University of Chicago,
May 1973.

[7] Gustafson, op. cit.

[8] Gustafson, op. cit.

[9] Wisconsin Health Services Research Group, "The Development of an Index of Medical Underservedness,"
*Health Services Research*, vol. 11, no. 2, summer 1975.

[10] Andre L. Delbecq, "Critical Problems in Health Planning," paper presented at the 32d Annual Meeting of the
Academy of Management, Aug. 13–16, 1972.

[11] Donald L. Patrick, J. W. Bush, and Milton Chin,
"Toward an Operational Definition of Health," *Journal of
Health and Social Behavior*, March 1973, pp. 6–23.

## REFERENCE

Schulz, Rockwell, and Alton Johnson: *Management of Hospitals*, McGraw-Hill Book Company, New York, 1976.

ROCKWELL SCHULZ, *University of Wisconsin*

**Hedging**   (*See* EXCHANGE, FOREIGN, MANAGE-
MENT OF; PURCHASING MANAGEMENT.)

**Herzberg's theory**   (*See* MOTIVATION IN
ORGANIZATIONS.)

**Heuristic methods**   (*See* OPERATIONS RE-
SEARCH AND MATHEMATICAL MODELING; PLANNING,
STRATEGIC PLANNING MODELS.)

**492**

**Hierarchical corporate system**   (*See* CO-
DETERMINATION AND INDUSTRIAL DEMOCRACY.)

**Hierarchy, organizational**   (*See* ORGANI-
ZATION STRUCTURES AND CHARTING.)

**Hierarchy of goals**   (*See* OBJECTIVES AND
GOALS.)

**Hierarchy of needs**   (*See* MOTIVATION IN
ORGANIZATIONS.)

**Hierarchy of production policies**   (*See*
PRODUCTION/OPERATIONS MANAGEMENT.)

**High-low point method**   (*See* ACCOUNTING
FOR MANAGERIAL CONTROL.)

**History of management**   (*See* MANAGE-
MENT, HISTORICAL DEVELOPMENT OF.)

## Hospital administration

Hospital administration is the application of generic
principles and techniques of management to the
most complex organizational component of the system for providing professional health and medical
services. The combination of factors affecting the
organization and management of the hospital is sufficiently unique as to require a specialized complement of administrative knowledge and skills. Hospital administration has emerged as a substantive field
of professional endeavor with special requirements
of education and competence in the management of
health care institutions.

The uniqueness of hospital administration is attributable to the purposes, structural characteristics,
and external relationships which distinguish the
contemporary hospital as a social institution. The
mission of the hospital encompasses the values of
humanistic care and community service which are
rooted deeply in a charitable and altruistic tradition.
The hospital is an integral component of the system
for providing individualized professional health services, with an organizational structure adapted to
the exacting requirements of medical knowledge and

technology. As a localized concentration of resources for medical care, the hospital is exposed to a multiplicity of pressures and constraints emanating from the medical professions, the community it serves, and the larger social, economic, and political environment. Administrative decision making in the hospital is subject to a variety of normative prescriptions, professional standards, and regulatory controls applicable specifically to the organization and management of institutional resources for the delivery of personal health services.

**Ownership Implications** Widely diverse forms of ownership and control are found in the hospital system of the American society. There are networks of hospitals operated by the federal government to serve segments of the population for which it assumes a special obligation. There are also many publicly owned hospitals operated under the control of state and local governments. For the most part, however, the ownership of hospitals serving the general community is in the private sector. The great majority of community general hospitals are voluntary, not-for-profit institutions, and many are operated under religious sponsorship. The private sector includes also a significant number, but relatively small proportion, of proprietary, investor-owned institutions. Despite these differences in hospital ownership and control, administrative functions are similar. The service orientation of both public and private institutions makes financial viability of the hospital a limiting condition rather than the dominant goal of policy and managerial decisions.

**Multipurpose Aspects** Hospitals differ markedly in size and in the scope and complexity of services, but all are multipurpose organizations. Medical knowledge and techniques are intensely specialized, and their assimilation by the hospital results in a proliferation of programs of patient care and ancillary services. Added to diagnostic, therapeutic, and restorative functions are correlative programs of clinical research and programs of education for professional and technical personnel. Full-scale development of these functions is best exemplified by large medical centers closely affiliated with medical schools. These serve as regional or national resources for teaching, research, and highly specialized medical care. Local community hospitals also respond to advances in health care technology by adding new programs of service, and many are engaged in teaching and research. The development of the hospital as a multipurpose community health center is accompanied and facilitated by an enlargement of the administrative function at both executive and program management levels.

**Authority Structure** Administrative authority in the hospital is based in the organization of the institution as a legally constituted corporate entity. In the typical community hospital responsibility for governance resides in a board of trustees whose members represent community interests and serve without compensation. The governing body appoints an administrator who serves as chief executive officer. As operating head of the organization, the administrator is responsible for management of the institution and is accountable to the governing authority.

The provision of medical services to individual patients is based on professional authority, exercised according to the license and mandate conferred on physicians. Practice in the hospital is contingent on the granting of privileges, but physicians enjoy a high degree of autonomy due to their status as independent professionals who commonly receive payment for services from sources other than the hospital. Within the hospital the organized medical staff is an instrument for reviewing the professional qualifications and performance of individual physicians and for developing and maintaining standards of quality in medical care. While professional standards are derived from medical science and technology, the medical staff is formally accountable to the governing authority of the hospital for quality control. By legal precedent, ultimate responsibility for the quality of care in the hospital is lodged in the board of trustees.

**Professional Orientation** The hospital is the prototype of a professionally oriented organization. The organizational pattern encompasses a system of overall administrative control and a system of professional control of the performance of key tasks. Accommodative relationships between the systems take many forms, but institutional and professional perspectives must be incorporated in decision-making processes. There is a trend toward expansion of the jurisdiction of administrative authority. The specialization of medical services, along with the functional differentiation of professional and paraprofessional roles, generates multiple, often competing, demands for hospital-based resources. The problem of balancing these demands within the capacity of the hospital to respond requires administrative solutions. The accountability of the hospital to the community it serves adds another dimension to the administrative task. Responsiveness to community needs requires decisions on strategies and programs at the institutional and executive level.

**Financial Planning and Cost Containment** Financial relationships between the hospital and its clients are mediated commonly by third parties:

private health insurance organizations and governmental programs of health services financing. Insurance plans differ widely, but a common approach involves the underwriting of health services and direct reimbursement of providers. The hospital has come to be dependent for revenue on contractual ties and financial transactions with external third-party entities. By minimizing the effect of price on decisions to utilize medical services, mechanisms of collective financing raise the level and affect the pattern of demand. By concentrating the means of payment for services, these mechanisms also put third parties in a position of great influence with respect to providers. As government has enlarged its role in the financing of health services in the private sector, it has also adopted measures to implement an explicit policy of cost containment. At the same time, since borrowing has come to be the principal means whereby the hospital meets its growing capital requirements, capital costs account for an ever-larger share of hospital expenses. Financial planning and budgetary control in the hospital must be accomplished within a complex framework of externally imposed constraints. Increasingly the administration of the hospital is held accountable to outside agencies for decisions related to costs, charges, and capital expenditures.

**Public Policies**   Public confidence in the efficacy of medical services is expressed in a national policy affirming a universal right of access to health care according to need. Governmental programs to implement this policy are directed largely to lowering financial barriers to medical and hospital services. Increasingly, however, governmental programs are being developed with the specific aim of improving the distribution and organization of resources for delivering health services. Current legislation has instituted a system of comprehensive health planning and integration in which community hospitals have long been engaged voluntarily. In effect, the community hospital has come to be an instrument for the fulfillment of public policy, accountable to public agencies for decisions on programs of service and investments in plant and equipment.

**Role of Chief Executive**   As the most resource-intensive center of community health services, the hospital is at the vortex of change in the health care delivery system. One consequence is the development of an administrative structure capable of providing strong executive leadership as well as effective internal management. The hospital's chief executive officer has become the focal point of strategic planning, the primary source of guidance to the governing board in formulating long-range goals

and policies compatible with the function of the institution as the locus of community health services. The chief executive is the principal representative of the institution in an intricate network of external relationships involving other health care institutions, sources of funding, and regulatory agencies. The responsibilities and accountabilities of the hospital chief executive are analogous to those of the corporate chief executive in other enterprises.

*Staff Dependency.*   The emergence of a corporate form of administrative organization involves an extension of the management structure below the chief executive level. Effective administration is increasingly dependent on the expertise of specialists in financial management, information processing, quality control, systems engineering, personnel management, and labor relations. In addition, the internal operation of the hospital requires management personnel to coordinate ongoing programs and participate in tactical program planning. Expansion of the scope and complexity of administrative responsibilities is accompanied by the development of a coherent management system. At the top executive level decision-making strategy is essentially judgmental but increasingly entails formal analysis of quantitative data. At staff and operational levels the use of the specialized skills and tools of management technology is required.

*Extended Responsibilities.*   As the role of the hospital is in transition, so is the role of the chief executive. Among contemporary hospitals there are significant differences in the organizational relationships of the chief executive to the governing authority and to the medical staff. Executive roles differ with respect to levels of accountability for formulating institutional objectives and policies, monitoring the quality of medical services, acquiring and allocating institutional resources, and shaping external relationships. In hospitals which retain a historically conventional pattern of organization, the chief executive serves mainly as the administrator of internal operations, with a narrowly circumscribed freedom of action and a limited responsibility for decisions on the mission and policies of the institution. Among hospitals in a transitional stage of organizational change, the chief executive's role is broader in scope. The principal task is to define and gain support for short-range goals of program development consonant with policies established by the governing authority. In contemporary hospitals at the leading edge of organizational development, the executive officer is the chief strategist of the institution. While the chief executive is specifically accountable to the governing authority for the conduct of the hospital, the challenge is to chart the long-range development of the institution in accordance with the principle of accountability to the larger community.

**Coordinated Health Care**   The concept of effectiveness in the delivery of health services encompasses criteria of accessibility, comprehensiveness, continuity, and quality of personal and community health services. Fulfillment of these demands is contingent on the development of a health services system which includes and integrates multiple sources of medical and hospital services. Because the pursuit of effectiveness necessarily proceeds within the constraints of limited resources, the critical issues for public policy as well as hospital administration concern the achievement of optimal balance between requirements of effectiveness and efficiency in use of health care resources. Efforts to cope with these issues are manifested in the development of coordinative arrangements among health care institutions designed to improve the delivery of services and to take advantages of economies of scale. Interinstitutional relationships among hospitals cover a wide spectrum: consolidation by merger, multiple hospitals under common management, voluntary consortia for joint planning and program operation, and contractual arrangements for sharing management, clinical, and supportive services. Adoption of comprehensive health planning as a tenet of public policy adds impetus to a well-established trend toward the development of organizational linkages among hospitals and toward the development of more inclusive systems of management.

*See also* HEALTH INSTITUTIONS, MANAGEMENT OF; HEALTH SERVICES, PLANNING FOR; NOT-FOR-PROFIT INSTITUTIONS, ORGANIZATIONS, MANAGEMENT OF; PUBLIC ADMINISTRATION.

### REFERENCES

Austin, Charles J.: "What Is Health Administration?" *Hospital Administration*, vol. 19, no. 3, summer 1974.
Levey, Samuel, and N. Paul Loomba: *Health Care Administration: A Managerial Perspective*, J. B. Lippincott Company, Philadelphia, 1973.
Shuler, Cyril O.: "Some Unique Characteristics in Health Administration," *Hospital Administration*, vol. 17, no. 1, winter 1972.
Stull, R. J.: "Professionalism in Health Care Administration," in *The Future of Health Care Delivery*, United States Army Medical Field Service School, Brooks Army Medical Center, Fort Sam Houston, Tex., 1969.

RICHARD J. STULL, *American College of Hospital Administrators*

# Hospitality management

Hospitality management is a frequently used, but ill-defined, term to umbrella the lodging and food service industries. Included in lodging are hotels, motels, and motor inns with all their unique management problems. Food service encompasses an even broader scope of operations: clubs, institutions, restaurants, stadium food services, shipboard, fast food, and catering. Tourism and recreation are on the fringe. While the timing is not completely clear, the term *hospitality management* appears to be a recent euphemism for the earlier term *hotel/restaurant/institutional (HRI) management*. Obviously the term is in some ways a misnomer, since one is hard pressed to identify the hospitable aspects of many types of institutional care despite their inclusion in the lodging and food service business.

Enough historical support exists to explain the unity of what are, in fact, two disparate industries. For one, food service was an integral part of the American lodging industry until the early part of the nineteenth century when independent restaurants first began to appear. More important, their unity provided strength during the period when service industries as a group lacked legitimacy or economic credibility. Now, suddenly, demographers, economists, government planners, and others have discovered the service industries. Enter the tertiary age. It is in this new era of economic development that the demand for professional management in the hospitality industry has exploded. This demand manifests itself in accelerating professional opportunities and developing educational offerings.

**Size and Specialization**   The service age is to the hospitality industry what the industrial age was to heavy industry: a period of growth and specialization; an era of heavy capitalization and market creation. With such dramatic changes, it is no wonder that the industry has come to recognize the importance of and dependence on the professional manager.

*Large-Scale Industry.*   Several interesting characteristics have emerged as the industry metamorphosed from a "mom-and-pop business" toward a conglomerate specialty. Expressed another way, small business is in transition to large-scale industry. No longer do hotelier-restauranteurs passively await the pleasure of passing guests. They have, instead, aggressively entered the market place, aping the techniques of demand creation set by industrial models. For the lodging industry this has meant a gradual, vertical integration of marketing elements. Airlines, hotels, ground and baggage movers, travel agents, and destination sites are a mixture of interlocking ownerships, arrangements, and affiliations as travel adopts to new market horizons, especially mass merchandising and handling. The travel intermediary (wholesaler and travel agent) has achieved its own identity as a new element in the distribution chain.

*Bottom-Line Orientation.* On the opposite side of the coin the hospitality industry is in the role of buyer. As the size of the operating unit grows (rooms per hotels, seats per dining room) and equity interests shift from single proprietorship and small partnerships to corporations and conglomerates (for example, ITT, Ralston-Purina, United Airlines, General Foods), both the need for, and the capability to buy, capital goods grow. Management becomes concerned with finance and taxation, break-even points, and constant volume. Today's hospitality manager knows the cue words of productivity and bottom line. Cognizant of their components, managers no longer view their patrons as guests of the smiling Boniface, but encourage them through clever merchandising to take on by self-service, many of the high operational costs and marginal earners. What has been old hat to the production industries is just now being discovered by managers in the lodging/food service field. The corner restaurant is now part of a big company run by a professional manager.

**Scope of Management** Traditionally, management for the hospitality field has been divided into "back" and "front" of the house, that is, divided between (1) those areas that service but do not encounter the guest and (2) those that require a face-to-face involvement. Cooking, engineering, and accounting are examples of one; front desk, table service, and uniformed services are examples of the other. These operational distinctions grow less significant as hospitality management moves away from the basic line decisions that preoccupied its attention a decade ago. From the simple, line organizational problems of a handful of employees, hospitality management has exploded into international business.

It is the opinion of most industry observers that management for the hospitality industry calls on a multitude of interdisciplinary skills not always required in other industries. These range from organizational behavioral problems to food science; from engineering and plant management to knowledge of fixed asset depreciation; from systems management (food, reservation) to advertising and merchandising techniques.

*Special Problems.* Today, several special problems beset the industry. For one, food service has had a unique combination of on-premise manufacturing and retailing. Although there is an increasing amount of off-premise preparation (so-called "convenience foods"), the *need to balance production and sales* remains a particularly problemsome area for food management.

*Service,* in the traditional meaning of the industry's terms, is a second bugaboo. Management is faced with a dilemma. Historically, the industry has sold service. In all its advertising and representation, this is the product still being touted. But, in fact, few American workers accept the role of service as a function of their job descriptions, and fewer customers still can afford to pay for it. Service as a career never came to the United States from Europe. The hotel/restaurant industry hawks that product, nevertheless, along with some of the other traditional by-products of European hoteldom.

*Labor* remains the major problem area of hospitality management. The lack-of-service syndrome is compounded by: wages that are sometimes less than unemployment/welfare benefits; dead-end, unchallenging types of domestic drudgery; and floater-type employees who run turnover up to 500 times per year. Superimposed on this difficult position is the character of the operation. It is one that responds to demand. Unfortunately, people do not eat and sleep on a continuous 24-hour basis, although legally hotels must operate around the clock. There are great peaks and valleys of demand, production, and labor utilization. None of this makes for the accurate scheduling of labor, the single highest cost item with which management contends. The situation is more acute in those areas subject to unionization, and it faces additional crises as social/labor legislation expands to cover the hospitality field.

*Energy* management is a new concern of hospitality managers, as it is for other industry executives. The pinch in this industry is twofold, however. Rising operational costs for such mundane items as shower water or hall lighting are precariously balanced by threats of declining traffic as tourists are frightened off by rising fuel costs. Omnipresent is government's threat to declare such energy use nonessential. The foretoken of this was the disastrous financial period of 1973 to 1974, when many units closed and many real estate investment trusts took back their mortgages.

*Equity Ownership.* Repossession of many small properties accelerated a change that was already evident by the start of the 1970s: a movement toward management alone, a modificator of the traditional small business concept that identifies ownership and management as one. Even the largest of the hotel chains have concentrated on the management of the property, leaving the equity interests to others. Numerous management companies have appeared because trusts, insurance companies, and banks sought means of converting repossessions into viable operations and because profitable real estatement investment still requires good management.

Actually, the trend started with the franchise movement. Franchising was the first step in separating hospitality management from hospitality equity. It was a transition movement that saw the creation of a professional management cadre larger than the industry had ever before experienced. The movement is just now gathering momentum.

**Outlook** Strange as it seems, the ancient hospitality industry—predating the Roman Empire—is a growth industry of the final quarter of the twentieth century. As it becomes a mature industry, it begins to encounter the kinds of problems that its small business posture had protected it from previously. Even as the market of the food industry prospers from working-wives, rising income, and smaller families, it faces the specter of consumerism: truth in menus, no-smoking designations, stringent health and sanitation regulations. Even as the lodging industry rebounds from its worst period since the depression, it encounters threats of (1) federal restrictions on travel, (2) governmental intrusions on tips and wages, and (3) overbooking legislation.

These are picayune now, but they represent a trend: a greater partnership of government and industry. School food programs, housing for the elderly, meals-on-wheels, and preschool nurseries are the start of a closer affiliation of government-sponsored services managed by the industry professional.

Changing recreation and leisure patterns suggest similar shifts for the lodging industry. The predominance of the convention hotel is likely to give way to hotels as centers of activity. The rebirth of the core city in plazas and malls, the possible restriction of gasoline for travel, and the increasing demand for entertainment and recreation offer a scenario that finds the community hotel of colonial times reborn in a new form.

This much is clear: hospitality management is caught up in major changes even though the profession is still taking shape.

*See also* MARKETING OF SERVICES, PROFESSIONAL; RETAILING MANAGEMENT.

## REFERENCES

Dukas, P.: *Planning Profits in the Food and Lodging Industry*, Cahners Publishing Co., Boston, 1976.

Fay, Clifford, et al.: *Managerial Accounting of the Hospitality Service Industries*, 2d ed., Wm. C. Brown Company Publishers, Dubuque, Iowa, 1976.

Kreck, Lothar, and John McCracken, eds.: *Dimensions of Hospitality Management*, 2 vols., Cahners Publishing Co., Boston, 1975.

Levinson, Charles: *Food and Beverage Operation: Cost Control and Systems Management*, Prentice-Hall, Inc., Englewood Cliffs, N.J., 1976.

Lundberg, Donald: *The Hotel and Restaurant Business*, rev. ed., Cahners Publishing Co., Boston, 1974.

McConnell, J. P.: *Hospitality Management: Avoiding Legal Pitfalls*, Cahners Publishing Co., Boston, 1975.

Vallen, Jerome J.: *Check-in; Check-out. Principle of Front Office Management*, Wm. C. Brown Company Publishers, Dubuque, Iowa, 1974.

———— et al.: *HRI: The Art and Science of Hospitality Management*, Ahrens Publishing Company, Inc., New York, 1977.

JEROME J. VALLEN, *University of Nevada, Las Vegas*

## Hostility response  (*See* HEALTH, MENTAL.)

## Hotel, restaurant, and institutions  (*See* HOSPITALITY MANAGEMENT.)

## Human assets accounting  [*See* ACCOUNTING, HUMAN RESOURCES (ASSETS).]

## Human factors engineering

Human factors engineering consists of a body of theories, experimental and empirical data, and methodology devoted to bridging the gap between human capabilities and limitations on the one hand and design of equipment, systems, and products on the other. Human factors engineering operates within the context of the development of systems or of products. It is an integral part of systems science and engineering; it interfaces with a number of other fields associated with the processes of analysis and design. As such it cannot and must not be viewed out of context.

Human factors engineering is not a perfectly delineated field, and considerable controversy exists as to its exact content and boundaries. Controversy stems from the recency of the field, from its origins both in the United States and in Europe, from the nature of the practitioners, and from the nature of problems dealt with. Difficulties with definition and terminology in no way diminish the fundamental importance of human factors engineering in designing equipment, products, and systems that are operable, maintainable, safe, comfortable, and consonant with human needs. Experience has shown that, in the absence of effective human factors engineering, economic costs and costs in accidents and loss of life can be high.

*Human factors engineering* is an American term. Its history, methodology, and the problems chosen for study have been strongly influenced by experimental psychology; hence, there has been a strong emphasis on sensory, perceptual, and perceptual-motor processes. Human factors engineering received a strong boost from American military and space programs and has developed in the context of large and complex systems. Thus, implicit in the meaning of the term are considerations not only of worker/machine interrelationships but of environmental considerations, staffing, and training. Related terms are *engineering psychology*, referring to a branch of psychology covering essentially the same breadth as does human factors engineering, and *human engineering*, which often refers to design only without also including staffing and training.

*Ergonomics* is a European term now widely used throughout the world. As its Greek roots indicate, it places a strong emphasis on the study and measurement of work, strength, and fatigue. Many of the problems originally studied by ergonomists were more physiological and medical than psychological. Ergonomics tended to be practiced in an industrial rather than in a military or space systems context. Today these distinctions between human factors engineering and ergonomics are blurring, because of the retrenchment of the U.S. aerospace industry; the concern over civil systems problems, relevance, and the quality of life; and the holding of international meetings and the exchange of scholars in recent years.

*Systems psychology* studies human behavior *and* experience in complex systems. It includes the domain of engineering psychology, but in addition is more concerned with societal systems and with the study of motivational, affective, cognitive, and group behavior than is engineering psychology. *Sociotechnical systems* are analogous to worker/machine systems but operate at a higher hierarchical level. Studies deal with the interactions among groups, organizations, and societies; technologies as a whole (rather than separate pieces of equipment); and the natural and social environments.

## HUMAN FACTORS ENGINEERING IN SYSTEMS DEVELOPMENT

Human factors engineering in the practical setting of systems development consists of a dynamic, iterative sequence of analysis, data gathering, design, test, and evaluation. At each stage the human factors engineer interfaces as appropriate with other specialists such as the program planner; systems manager; systems analyst; electrical and electronics, reliability, mechanical, or aeronautical engineer; and computer expert. The term *personnel subsystem* has been utilized to describe this situation wherein the operator-maintainer or crew subsystem (the personnel subsystem) is developed in parallel with, and in interaction with, the development of the structural, power, communications, support, and other subsystems. *Personnel subsystem* connotes a number of interacting elements including analysis and data base, human engineering, life support, staffing, training, and test and evaluation. Unfortunately, the term is passing into disuse.

Systems development can be divided into a number of stages. Although authorities differ in their subdivisions, the following are representative:

1. *Conceptual stage.* A need for the system is perceived, stemming, for example, from a new perception of enemy threat, societal deterioration, or technological change, or from pressures by powerful interests in government, the military, or industry. Economic costing is made and schedules laid out. Determination is made of the gross nature of system structure, that is, how people as well as other systems constituents will be incorporated into the system. Analyses, computer simulation, trade-off studies, and reference to human factors experimental findings and data banks help ensure that human performance will be the best possible, considering constraints of money and schedule and the needs and limitations of the other subsystems; nevertheless, many systems do not get beyond this first stage.

2. *Initial design stage.* The ideas, analysis results, and other documentation produced in the conceptual stage now begin to be translated into design sheets, drawings, and specifications and into actual hardware components and subsystems. Human and human/machine performance requirements and constraints and functions are specified in greater

detail. *Task descriptions* are begun. Testing is made of proposed alternative designs, using mock-ups and simulations if available.

3. *Major design stage.* An addition or change in the major contractor(s) may be made. Components and modules are fabricated or acquired from vendors or subcontractors and assembled into subsystems. Test and evaluation continues. Human factors engineers engage in one of their principal activities, *task analysis.* Task analysis involves determining the behavioral consequences of the tasks required to operate, maintain, control, and manage the system. It is a bridge between the world of psychology, physiology, medicine, and anthropometry on the one hand and that of operating systems on the other. Although the literature details a number of steps in performing task analyses, the following captures the essence of this indispensable process: (*a*) Treat the person and machine as a closed-loop system, relating each machine display output as a stimulus to a human sense organ such as the eye or the ear and each human hand or foot response as an input to a machine control such as a lever or pedal; (*b*) starting with the task descriptions which are typically outcomes of preliminary equipment design, back up and ask, "Given this task, what decisions must the person make before performing the task effectively and what information must the person have before making the correct decision?"; (*c*) determine task criticalities, priorities, interdependencies, loadings, and constraints; (*d*) determine environmental requirements and features leading to performance degradation; (*e*) determine presence of feedback of satisfactory task performance; and (*f*) determine special skills needed.

Task analysis data can be expressed on sequential sheets, as flow diagrams, and in quantitative reliability form. Task analysis is a prerequisite to effective human engineering design of equipment, determining the kinds and number of people required to staff the system, and determining training requirements.

As the relative length of this section suggests, a preponderance of the human factors engineering effort typically occurs at the major design stage. The collective output of this stage is a prototype. Development may terminate at this stage, or in some cases the prototype may be put directly into operation.

4. *Production stage.* Should the prototype pass critical tests and evaluations and reviews, and should funding be available, the system can enter production. The human factors engineer is concerned with late design changes, quality control, and selection and training of personnel, including the development of the associated manuals.

5. *Operations stage.* Following final system test and evaluation incorporating user personnel, the system becomes operational. The human factors engineer continues to play an important role in the monitoring of operations, collection and analysis of error and accident data, and preparation for model changes and new generations of the system.

## MANAGEMENT OF THE HUMAN FACTORS ENGINEERING PROGRAM

Successful management of a human factors engineering program requires a systems understanding of hierarchy, interfaces, and interrelationships, and an awareness of educational and personality differences among engineering and human factors specialists. This is in addition to the expected cognizance of procedures, methodology, and data, and is independent of whether the formal organization is line, staff, or matrix. Several features that can make or break a human factors program are reviewed below.

**Personnel Subsystem** Whether the formal, somewhat obsolescent term *personnel subsystem* or a substitute or no term is employed, the requirements of the user must be borne in mind from the earliest time of system conceptualization. User requirements must be progressively met in parallel with and interacting with the design of hardware and software. In actual practice just the opposite has often been the case—the human factors effort has come in too late when design is essentially frozen and at too low a system hierarchical level to have any significant effect. The single most important contribution of the human factors engineer will be answers to the question, "What will people *actually* do in the system?" "Knobs and dials" human engineering—concern only with simple displays and controls and front-panel design—does not constitute effective human factors work.

**Management's Understanding** The human factors engineering program will be severely crippled by the absence of understanding and full backing by top management. Management is increasingly aware that human factors engineering transcends "knobs and dials" work and that poorly human factored systems, programs, and products can be associated with immense human, operational, economic—and, increasingly, legal—costs. This new understanding has been advanced by publicity given to dramatic accidents associated with human error and by lawsuits in which corporate negligence or lack of product safety was interpreted in terms of the absence of consideration of human factors.

**Costs and Benefits**   The costs of a human factors *program* always entail the salaries and support of the human factors professionals. The costs of having a human factored system or product may entail substituting more expensive for less expensive (e.g., government furnished or off-the-shelf) equipment. Costs *may* entail abandoning a tight schedule.

Benefits can be determined from both negative and positive events. The literature now documents numerous examples of costly system or operational failures associated with human factors deficiencies. For example, the crash of a DC-9 jetliner on Sept. 11, 1974, at Charlotte, North Carolina, was the result of the pilot's misreading his altimeter by 1000 feet. The crash cost 72 lives. And the crash of a Turkish Airlines DC-10 on March 3, 1974, near Paris, which took 346 lives, was due to another display deficiency—the special instructions for proper closing of a design-deficient cargo door could not be read by an illiterate crewman.

Alternatively, the presence of good human factors work has greatly improved many operations. Applications include aircraft, spacecraft, ships, command and control systems, the home, and products such as tools, stoves, the push-button telephone, biomedical instrumentation, and television sets. Benefits can often be defined in terms of applications beyond those originally intended, that is, in terms of *technological transfer*. For example, a number of tools designed for the National Aeronautics and Space Administration (NASA) for the weightless conditions of space will find use in underwater operations and in confined or limited spaces. And techniques for detecting crew motions and limb positions in spacecraft can be applied to motions, space, and forces required in work, emergency, and recreational behavior on earth.

## WORKER/MACHINE INTERRELATIONSHIPS

The determination of worker/machine interrelationships is the heart of human factors engineering. At the highest level, the integration of the following major activities is involved.

**Theory and Research**   Human factors engineers use and contribute to theories as varied as general systems theory, queuing theory, cybernetic theory, physiological theories of sensory function, information theory, decision theory, control theory, and reliability theory. For example, signal detection theory and the relative operating characteristic help determine the probability that a blip on a radar screen will be detected and whether vigilance will decrease over time spent looking at the screen. Control theory helps explain the flight behavior of pilots. And human reliability theory helps predict the probabilities of task success or failure.

Research continues actively in the traditional areas of display, control, and work station design. Representative new vistas include several areas of research on the worker/computer interface: how workers and computers interact to solve problems, the automatic recognition of handwriting, and the automatic recognition of speech. The last area involves not only syntactic and semantic interpretation of speech sounds, but electromyographic analysis of the muscles used in vocalization and subvocalization (thinking the words) and electroencephalographic analysis of the associated brain waves.

**Analysis and Simulation**   The indispensable role of task analysis should be mentioned here. Human factors engineers engage in a number of other systems analyses and trade-off studies. These may involve, for example, alternative presentations of information visually or aurally, comparisons of manual and automatic control of vehicles, and trade offs between design for operability and design for maintainability. Mathematical models have been derived for dynamic man-in-the-loop situations and for motions of the human body. Computer simulation models have been developed for people flying airplanes and for the behavior of multiperson crews. Simulators are invaluable in substituting less expensive simulator training time for more expensive training time spent actually flying. Without simulation for zero gravity and lunar landing, the Apollo moon landings might never have been possible.

**Data Gathering and Use**   Representative areas include errors, accidents, incidents, failures, and safety. Static and dynamic anthropometric data, used, for instance, in the design of work spaces, cockpits, escape hatches, ejection seats, and space suits, have long been available for healthy young men. The changing social picture now requires that more data be collected on women, children, the aged, the handicapped, and different races. There is a need for more base line data from physiological measures. Human factors *data banks* contribute to a faster evolution of the field and lessen the redundancy of effort.

**Findings and Principles**   Human factors principles, derived from over three decades of work in both experimental and practical but largely military settings, are well documented in the design criterion literature. Good guides are DOD Military Standard 1472B, "Human Engineering Design Criteria for Military Systems, Equipment and Facilities"; Air Force Systems Command Design Handbook 1-3, "Human Factors Engineering"; and the guide edited by Van Cott and Kinkade (see References). These and similar works describe design principles applicable to traditional military situations. Most of them illustrate good (and sometimes for comparison, poor) designs and present underlying theoretical arguments and quantitative data corroborating the recommended designs. These guides find their best use as applied to visual and auditory displays, noise and speech, controls, work spaces, anthropometry, and maintainability. Systems concepts and methods, computer systems, and nonmilitary situations require additional sources.

**Evaluation of Practices**    Human engineering designs are successively *tested* throughout the systems development process. *Evaluation* is a broader-scale effort, involving criteria taken from the real world, not from the experimental laboratory. Representative criteria include performance measures of time and accuracy, economic costs, cost/effectiveness and benefit/cost ratios, and satisfaction.

## BIOMECHANICS

*Biomechanics* deals with the mechanical properties of the movement of organisms and with the effects of mechanical forces on organisms. Differentiation between this term and *biodynamics* does not appear necessary. A related field is *engineering anthropometry*, which treats of the static and dynamic dimensions of people. Data on people, nude and clothed, are available for the various positions, standing, sitting, crouching, and reaching. These data are applied to the design of such things as doorways, emergency exits, hallways, farm machinery, cockpits, rooms in homes, and furniture. Data are also applied to the design of special clothing such as arctic wear, pressure suits, and space suits. In all three cases, anthropometric data must apply not only directly to suit design, but also secondarily to the design of controls and work space.

Biomechanical studies are made under conditions of normal gravitation, acceleration, deceleration, impact, vibration, and weightlessness. These forces, or lack thereof, affect both the whole body and specific organs and tissues.

Mathematical models and associated sensing equipment can be used to study limb and body motion and position, forces exerted on the body and required of the body, and work space required of the body during the performance of various tasks in normal work, recreational, and especially stressful settings. Instrumented vehicles, such as automobiles, used in conjunction with anthropometric dummies, are employed to study crashworthiness and the design of restraint systems and other protective devices. Rocket sleds are also used in studying the effects of acceleration, deceleration, and impact on body structure and function and on performance.

High gravitational forces and weightlessness can have major effects on the skeletal, muscular, cardiovascular, sensory, and nervous systems. For example, normal limb movements may be distorted or become impossible. Higher gravitational forces may lower the visual capability of pilots or cause them to lose consciousness or develop vertigo. The effects of environmental degradation must be compensated for in the design of the total worker/machine system. These areas are typically studied by physiologists and physicians trained in the specialty of *aerospace medicine*.

## ENVIRONMENTAL CONSIDERATIONS

A major principle of human factors engineering could be called *five-part interaction*, that is, the interactions among human, machine, medium, mission, and management. Here *medium* substitutes for *environment*. The principle holds that the performance of a human/machine ensemble will be a function of its environment, the phase of the mission profile (e.g., takeoff, climb to altitude, cruise, descent, or landing of an aircraft), and the management of system resources.

The operating or working environment can be considered from two interrelated points of view: (1) normal environmental factors, the *extremes* of which greatly reduce or preclude normal body functioning and performance, and (2) atypical environmental factors, the *presence* of which greatly stresses both physiology and performance.

**Limited-Range Environmental Factors**    Human life itself can exist only within certain ranges of many environmental factors. Health and effective performance may require even narrower ranges. Examples are atmospheric composition and pressure, electromagnetic radiation, and acceleration and gravitation. Representative effects of the last have already been discussed. Temperature is also in this category, but its effects are well known, and it will not be discussed here.

*Atmospheric Composition and Pressure.* The chemical composition and pressure of atmospheres are interrelated. Thus, at high pressures, both oxygen and nitrogen are toxic. Anoxia is fatal after about 4 minutes, and hypoxia can lead progressively to visual difficulties, poor judgment and memory, and death. Aerospace and undersea operations require special breathing mixtures, not only to provide oxygen, but to eliminate or reduce the possibility of "bends" when nitrogen comes out of solution in the blood as a person goes from a higher to a lower atmospheric pressure. One hundred percent oxygen enhances combustion. In January 1967 three astronauts were killed in a fire in an Apollo Command Module, leading to severe repercussions throughout the main contracting and monitoring agencies. This provides a striking instance of the need for management to think in systems terms.

Explosive decompressions, depending on the altitude, may lead to loss of consciousness, rupturing of internal organs, or even boiling of the blood.

*Electromagnetic Radiation.* Extremes of electromagnetic radiation—x-rays, gamma rays, and microwaves (and perhaps radio waves)—can be dangerous to health and even fatal. Microwaves and infrared radiation produce the effects of heating. Ultraviolet radiation may lead to the production of cancers. Ionizing radiation progressively affects blood cell production, the skin and gastrointestinal tract, the central nervous system, and the testes. The composition of visible light must incorporate factors of brightness, contrast, target size, location, and distance. Red lighting, used to maintain dark adaptation in some aircraft cockpits and ship command centers, precludes the use of color codes in documents and color codes painted on surfaces. Visible light may be a stressor in the form of glare, illusions, flicker, or as a disruption of psychophysiological rhythms. All these forms of radiation have design implications in terms of level and placement of source(s), shielding, sensors, warning devices, and so on.

**Stressors in the Environment**  The main factors in this category are toxic chemicals and acoustic noise. Some substances are toxic when present in concentrations as low as a few parts per million or even a few parts per billion. Sources include pesticides, paints, engine emissions, mined materials, and fabrics. The effects of carbon monoxide are well known, as are black lung disease, silicosis, and asbestos poisoning. In some airplane crashes, survivors have been killed by hydrogen cyanide released by burning upholstery.

*Acoustic noise* is defined as unwanted sound; hence, there is a strong subjective component in what any one person considers to be noise. Never-

theless, noise can produce distraction and annoyance, distort or mask speech, and at higher decibel levels and longer exposure times cause temporary or permanent hearing loss.

The results of noise provide an excellent representative example to management of the effects of technology on occupational health and safety and on the external environment. Airport operations have been curtailed in many countries, and in some places (e.g., Los Angeles) billions of dollars in lawsuits have been generated because of airport noise. Other large lawsuits have been concerned with the release of pollutants into the environment. Thus, the environment may not only be a stressor on people but is itself stressed by human activities.

*See also* HEALTH, MENTAL; JOB EVALUATION; THERBLIGS; WORK, CONCEPT AND IMPLICATIONS; WORK DESIGN, JOB ENLARGEMENT, JOB ENRICHMENT, JOB DESIGN, AND AUTONOMOUS WORK GROUPS.

### REFERENCES

Behan, Robert A., and H. W. Wendhausen: *Some NASA Contributions to Human Factors Engineering*, U.S. Government Printing Office, 1973.

De Greene, Kenyon B.: *Sociotechnical Systems: Factors in Analysis, Design, and Management*, Prentice-Hall, Inc., Englewood Cliffs, N.J., 1973.

——: *Systems Psychology*, McGraw-Hill Book Company, New York, 1970.

Grandjean, Etienne: *Ergonomics of the Home*, Taylor and Francis, London, 1973.

McCormick, Ernest J.: *Human Factors in Engineering and Design*, 4th ed., McGraw-Hill Book Company, New York, 1976.

Meister, David: "Systems Development: The Future of Ergonomics as a System Discipline," *Ergonomics*, vol. 16, no. 3, pp. 267–280, 1973.

National Aeronautics and Space Administration: *Bioastronautics Data Book*, U.S. Government Printing Office, 1973.

Shackel, Brian, and L. Klein: "ESSO London Airport Refuelling Control Centre Redesign—an Ergonomics Case Study, *Applied Ergonomics*," vol. 7, no. 1, pp. 37–45, 1976.

Sheridan, Thomas B., and William R. Ferrell: *Man-Machine Systems: Information, Control, and Decision Models of Human Performance*, The M.I.T. Press, Cambridge, Mass., 1974.

Van Cott, Harold P., and Robert G. Kinkade, eds.: *Human Engineering Guide to Equipment Design*, U.S. Government Printing Office, 1972.

KENYON B. DE GREENE, *University of Southern California*

# Human relations  (*See* MOTIVATION IN ORGANIZATIONS.)

# Human resources development  [*See* ORGANIZATION DEVELOPMENT (OD).]

# Human resources management  (*See heading in Table of Contents for complete listing.*)

# Human resources management  (*See* PERSONNEL ADMINISTRATION.)

# Human resources (work force) planning

Effective human resources planning in an organization provides for continuous and proper staffing and ensures that appropriate skills are available within the work force to meet the organization's changing needs. It also ensures that the organization meets its human resource obligations to society at large.

In its simplest forms human resources planning—or manpower planning, as it used to be known—has been practiced for centuries. Whenever a boss needed more "hands" on the following day and made arrangements for them to be taken on, or whenever a superintendent recognized the need for an additional crew or shift to start the next week, crude manpower planning was taking place. Today's dynamic economic and social environment makes highly evident the need for more sophisticated planning for human resources in industry. Additionally, it is being widely practiced in the public sector as an aid in ameliorating existing social ills. Within industry, it is—or should be—a part of the total resources planning of the enterprise, on a par with the planning devoted to financial affairs, capital development, materials and equipment purchases, and market development.

**Plan Characteristics**  An effective human resources plan must include (1) a mechanism for periodic *monitoring* and revision to compensate for changes in the organization's objectives or either internal or external factors; (2) established *responsibility* for its accomplishment; (3) *authority* appropriate for the task; (4) a certain degree of *flexibility* for effective implementation, particularly on job assignments at the operating levels; and (5) *correlation* with other organizational plans, especially because of its heavy financial impact.

## PLANNING PROCESS

By definition, human resources planning is a process of determining future staffing requirements and developing action plans to meet them. In its basic form, human resources planning includes the following components: (1) an inventory of current personnel resources, (2) a forecast of the capabilities required on a given date in the future, (3) an analysis of internal and external influences or actions that will occur during the intervening period, (4) a forecast of the kinds of actions that will be required to achieve the desired capabilities, and (5) a comprehensive plan to implement these actions.

**Inventory of Current Resources**  This is the basic component. It is the starting point of the human resources plan since it establishes the takeoff point for all future actions. Depending upon ultimate requirements, the inventory can cover merely the number of workers in particular job titles on each shift in a particular plant or department, or it may also include breakdowns by race, sex, ethnic groups, age, length of service, degree or skill, promotional potential, educational background (and future plans for it), and the like. Off-job items may also be included, such as future career interests, outside leadership activities (in union, fraternal, civic, political, or professional organizations), and particular outside skills, interests, and hobbies. The list of possible items can be almost endless; those to be included in the inventory should be geared to the objectives of the planning exercise—the future requirements of the organization.

Much of the inventory data are already in the organization's records, noted on the employment applications and on payroll and other administrative records. Seldom, however, are *all* the desired data recorded, and rarely are they available or easily retrievable. As a result, a comprehensive data collection effort is usually required.

A broad-gauge employee questionnaire is often required: this will supersede or summarize *all* existing data on each employee to be included in the inventory. Alternatively, a smaller one may be sent out to pick up missing items after existing data have been consolidated. It is important, however, to be sure that the total requirements are known before the data collection is started. Not only are costs involved in the collection effort, but employee unrest may also be generated by concern as to how the information will be used. Thus, it is essential that the questionnaires collect *all* the necessary information initially, without requiring a second contact.

In an organization with several thousand employees—or where a large amount of data is being collected about each person—computer-based storage and retrieval may be appropriate because of the volume of data and frequency of use. (See Fig. H-2.)

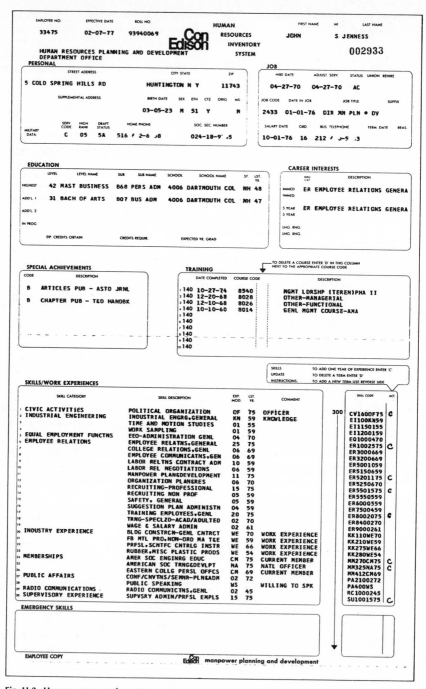

Fig. H-2. Human resources inventory system.

For smaller organizations or more limited data, a punch card system, such as McBee Card-Sort, may be adequate.

**Forecast of Future Requirements** This establishes the organization's goal that must be achieved by the human resources plan. This target may be established for one reason or several. Introduction of new machinery, a new product line, or a new facility often provides the requirement. It may come about through establishment of an affirmative-action plan to meet federal regulations, or it may result from the chief executive's wish to ensure that an appropriate program of succession planning is carried out.

In setting these goals, it is important that consideration be given to internal and external forces and that the ultimate goals be realistic and attainable. This is particularly true if the time frame covers 3 to 5 years or longer. General economic and local labor market forecasts, changing product demand, technological developments, and obsolescence fall into this category. Their implications should be considered thoroughly, and the final forecast revised if warranted.

Recommendations for human resources goals should be made by the planning staff, after obtaining input on the desired organization posture from the chief executive or key operating officers. These goals should then be refined into final statements by continuing discussion within top management between the "desired" and the "practical" or "possible."

**Analysis of Internal and External Factors** After current capabilities and future requirements are established, anticipated or possible changes must be determined before the actions of the human resources plan can be fully defined.

1. An analysis should be made of projected changes in the current work force that will affect the plan. This involves projected retirements, layoffs, terminations from all other causes, transfers or promotions into other specialties, and the like. Most of these losses will be factored directly into the plan since many times they will provide opportunity for reassignment and transfers that will assist in its operation.

2. An analysis of projected departmental expansions and contractions should be made. Short-term requirements, with resulting dips and peaks, could lead to layoffs or emergency transfers that would void longer-term opportunities required in the total plan.

3. Consideration should be taken of anticipated changes in the external labor force or market from which the organization draws. Relocation of major employers, either into or out of the labor market area, will affect an organization's ability to attract its desired candidates for employment. An increase or decrease in the number of engineers, accountants, scientists, or other specialists may have impact. Changes in legal [Equal Employment Opportunity (EEO)] requirements or in employment patterns of other concerns which draw from the same labor market must also be considered.

**Assessment of Potential Actions** The human resources plan will include a variety of personnel actions designed to fill the development or staffing gap between the current inventory and the required population and skills. These actions generally fall into two basic areas: (1) development of current employees and (2) employment and placement of persons not now employed. Prior to development of the actual plan, the planner should become familiar with these actions, their benefits, and implications.

*Development, or Training, of Present Employees.* This area covers a wide variety of actions, each with a varying cost. Among the most widely used techniques are:

1. On-the-job training on the new assignment. Under this approach, the individual learns necessary skills while functioning on the job. Assistance from the former jobholder, a "buddy" at the next machine or desk, or extra attention from the immediate supervisor is usually required for such action to be effective.

2. Job rotation. This is an extension of internal transfers. It may be a part of a job enlargement or enrichment program. It is particularly appropriate as a part in a long-range career development program.

3. Off-the-job "vestibule" or classroom training. It is often used to expose employees to new methods or ideas and provides an opportunity for practice within a classroom setting before trying them out in the workplace. This enables an organization to hire candidates who do not possess the necessary job skills, train them to an acceptable level in a simulated workplace, and then turn them over to operating supervisors in production units for final on-the-job training.

4. Formal apprenticeship programs. These are sophisticated techniques which combine on-the-job and vestibule training and also include off-the-job instruction, usually in a nearby evening vocational or trade school. These programs are usually offered to younger or recently hired employees.

5. Special programs conducted by universities, professional societies, or other organizations. These

assist middle and upper management personnel, in particular, to become better qualified for promotion within their organization.

6. Tuition aid. These are programs under which employees are reimbursed for certain costs involved in completing outside academic programs, usually on a university level, on their own time.

7. Correspondence courses. These may be particularly useful when potential participants are geographically isolated, work on rotating shifts, or are faced with other circumstances that impede attendance at other formal training programs.

*Preemployment Efforts.* At the preemployment level, several techniques are available for inclusion into a human resources plan.

1. Referrals. These can come from current employees or from organizations and agencies which specialize in identification of candidates with particular skills or attributes. This technique applies equally to using an executive search firm which specializes in placing top executives and to a community group which provides candidates with certain ethnic or racial backgrounds.

2. Employment advertising. This can be placed in general or specialized publications read by the target population.

3. Visitations. These may include active programs to selected academic and vocational high schools, junior and four-year colleges, and graduate schools.

4. Temporary or contract personnel. These are typically used to bridge a short-term gap, when it is undesirable or impossible to hire the kinds of employees desired under the long-term plan or to level out the workload and maintain a stable work force. This category most commonly includes clerical and secretarial temporaries, but organizations which will supply draftsmen, computer programmers, laborers, etc., can normally be found in major cities. (The common practice of contracting to outside organizations work that is expected to be short-term, nonrecurring, or requires skills not readily available within the organization is a varient of this technique.)

5. Comprehensive Employment and Training Act (CETA) participation. Involvement in this or other federally funded programs enables an organization to maintain its established standards for technical quality of new hirees while opening the door to members of disadvantaged groups in accordance with an affirmative-action program.

6. Purchase of another company or new product line to acquire an outstanding executive or an available work force. The converse is to develop, or buy, a new product line to more effectively utilize an existing work force, particularly if existing lines are strongly seasonal. Thus, a line of snow blowers for home driveways could provide a more constant workload for a manufacturer of power lawn mowers and reduce seasonal layoffs; addition of canvas and leisure shoes by a maker of winter overshoes and boots could do the same.

**Development and Implementation of Plan** A human resources plan can be a simple or complex document, covering the next 2 weeks or the next 5 years, depending on the criteria set down by top management.

The overall, or comprehensive, human resources plan is usually developed by a specialized staff in either the employee relations (personnel) or planning departments. To be more than a piece of paper, the plan requires approval by the chief executive and concurrency by both line management and the financial staff, since the line organization will have the responsibility for putting it into practice and the program costs will affect the organization's financial performance.

Within the framework of the comprehensive plan, the line organization will be responsible for implementation of several short-term plans. To implement the plan, the line will need authority to make short-term adjustments to meet its operating requirements. To this end key line managers need to be involved in all phases of the development of the plan, from the collection of raw data in the inventory to the agreement on the ultimate objectives of the plan. They may even be charged with the responsibility for developing the short-term document, with the requirement that it fit into the broad guidelines of the overall plan.

The plan should include specific subgoals, together with steps to achieve each goal within the requisite time period. Responsibility for accomplishment of each goal should be delineated, together with the necessary reporting and monitoring responsibilities.

It may be appropriate to construct individual (development) plans, within the overall plan, which spell out in fine detail various actions that will be required, both by an individual and the organization, for an employee to move from his or her present level of experience and skill to the desired level within the requisite period of time. Because these programs usually involve one or more organizational units, the staff personnel function usually has a major responsibility for final implementation, although involvement of the line organization is necessary to make them work effectively.

## FORECASTING, ESTIMATING AND CONTROL TECHNIQUES

In the analysis of internal and external factors (see above) three types of analysis were mentioned: (1) projected internal losses and/or lost time, (2) internal organizational changes, and (3) external changes (particularly in the local labor force). Within each area, data can be generated with varying degrees of accuracy and/or sophistication, depending upon the requirements of the plan. In most instances, comparison is required with a historical period that is considered to be either standard or similar to the actual period in question. Obviously, choice of the "correct" base period is of prime importance for accurate forecasting.

**Absenteeism**   Projections of lost time (absenteeism) are vital to ensure that operating supervisors have adequate workers each day to accomplish the assigned output of goods or services. A realistic human resources plan may include a staffing requirement of 115 to 120 percent of the daily work force to compensate for lost time (both scheduled and random) because of vacations, jury duty, illness, training time off the job, and other reasons. The actual percentage will depend on the age and length of service of the work force, the organization's vacation policies, etc., and should be based on historical analysis. However, if the rate is considered too high, one subgoal in the overall plan may be to reduce it.

**Turnover**   In estimating turnover, staff planners can calculate the loss rate from data for the previous 3 to 5 years. Separate categories should be set up for deaths, discharges, releases (layoffs), and resignations. Also, separate rates can be calculated for unskilled, semiskilled, and skilled workers or craftsmen, office workers, and lower, middle, and upper management. The rates should be adjusted for the influence of known nonrecurring external or internal pressures. For example, an economic downturn will reduce the resignation rate because outside employment will be difficult to obtain. On the other hand, it may increase the release or discharge rate if marginal performers are being replaced and the work force upgraded during this period. A major employer's move into, or out of, the labor market area can also have an impact on turnover, as can a change in management philosophy toward employee productivity.

In estimating turnover, it may be important to single out turnover caused by transfer and/or promotion within particular segments of the organization. Skills of such individuals are lost to their former supervisors and generally must be replaced just as if they had left the organization completely, yet they are additions to their new supervisors. Statistics on such turnover are often difficult to obtain but can be developed from payroll records and other documents. (A computerized system is of particular benefit here.)

As part of the turnover analysis, the human resources planner should also analyze the impact of organizational changes—growth or retrenchment—established or discontinued departments, sections, or units, etc. Layoffs due to temporary curtailment should be kept separate from other termination statistics, since this item is affected by the organization's marketing effectiveness and general market conditions. Layoffs may also be considered with organizational changes—the addition or elimination of a shift, product or product line, etc. Future production and marketing plans—and their staffing implications—are essential information at this point.

**External Factors**   In analyzing external factors for 5 or more years in the future, the human resources planner may be forced to resort to almost pure conjecture. For example, technological advances, either in the state of the art or by introduction of new machinery into the production process, may raise or lower the total staffing requirements, the skill levels of many members of the work force, or both. In the fast-changing political and economic world, massive infusions of federal funds or changes in EEO emphasis can cause unexpected tilts to the labor market.

The U.S. Bureau of Labor Statistics, the local and national Chambers of Commerce, the Engineers Joint Council, and other professional societies can provide local, statewide, or national labor market statistics and projections for particular job titles or categories.

**Control**   Effective implementation of a human resources plan requires a variety of control techniques to ensure compliance by all parts of the organization.

Staffing control is simple to initiate and flexible enough to be adapted to most requirements. A system of personnel requisitions, for management and/or nonmanagement positions, is a basic approach. It requires prior approval of a person or persons at higher levels than the supervisor to whom the additional employee will report. Thus, the requisition system provides control of both the number and quality (skill or other attributes) of new hires toward goals in the human resources plan. In the extreme, all such additions may require approval of a high operating executive if the goal is to shrink staffing in a particular department or plant, or certain jobs may be reserved for candidates with special desired qualifications.

One serious drawback occurs with strictly enforced hiring controls: line supervisors resist the elimination of poor or marginal performers without prior, ironclad assurances of approval for replacements. Their argument that "half a person is better than none" has a certain validity and can seriously impair a program to upgrade the effectiveness of a particular unit.

### OUTLOOK

Recognition of the need for formal human resources planning has been widespread. Within the planning hierarchy of most organizations, however, it still ranks at, or near, the bottom of the list. Few organizations have comprehensive human resources plans. Few companies fully recognize the savings that can be realized in this area, although all have fragmentary or rudimentary plans.

Looking toward the next decade, one can be certain that the cumulative effects of recent events, generally initiated by various branches of the federal government, will vastly increase the recognition and importance of this function.

Title VII of the Civil Rights Act of 1964 requires that most organizations set up affirmative-action programs dealing with employment and training of various minority groups, and the court decisions in the AT&T and other cases have forewarned industry of the cost of noncompliance. In its basic context, an affirmative-action plan *is* a human resources plan with circumscribed objectives.

Recent surpluses of engineers, teachers, and liberal arts college graduates and the shortages of doctors and other specialists point to the need for more effective communication on a national level to forecast surpluses and shortages. Such information can assist students in secondary schools to prepare for their future and calls for a human resources plan on the broadest possible level.

In the past, ambitious human resources plans such as President Johnson's Great Society programs were largely ineffectual because the goals tended to be imperfect. The programs provided for training, but the objectives fell short of the next step, placement in jobs. We must hope that the 1980s will not repeat that mistake.

*See also* ACCOUNTING, HUMAN RESOURCES ASSETS; AFFIRMATIVE ACTION; DEVELOPMENT AND TRAINING, EMPLOYEE; DEVELOPMENT AND TRAINING, MANAGE-MENT; FORECASTING BUSINESS CONDITIONS; PERSONNEL ADMINISTRATION; PLANNING, STRATEGIC MANAGERIAL; WORK DESIGN, JOB ENLARGEMENT, JOB ENRICHMENT, JOB DESIGN, AND AUTONOMOUS WORK GROUPS.

### REFERENCES

Burach, Elmer: *Strategies for Manpower Planning and Programming*, General Learning Press, 1972.

Famularo, Joseph J., ed.: *Handbook of Modern Personnel Administration*, McGraw-Hill Book Company, New York, 1972, chaps. 9 and 10.

French, Wendell: *The Personnel Management Process: Human Resources Administration*, Houghton Mifflin and Co., New York, 1964.

Patten, Thomas H., Jr.: *Manpower Planning and the Development of Human Resources*, John Wiley & Sons, Inc., New York, 1971, chaps. 2–6.

Vetter, Eric W.: *Manpower Planning for High Talent Personnel*, University of Michigan, Ann Arbor, 1967.

JOHN S. JENNESS *Consolidated Edison Company of New York, Inc.*

# Hygiene factors

*Hygiene factors* are those elements of workers' environment without which they will probably not attain job satisfaction and a positive attitude toward their jobs. Sometimes referred to as *maintenance factors*, hygiene factors include such elements as company policy and working conditions, money, status, relationships with supervisors, all essential for a psychologically sound, or "hygienic," working situation, free of unhealthy conditions.

Hygiene factors were defined by F. Herzberg and his associates, B. Mausner and B. B. Snyderman, in developing the theory of employee satisfaction and dissatisfaction known as the *motivation-hygiene theory* or the *dual-factor theory of work motivation*. Herzberg's studies at the Psychological Service of Pittsburgh in the late 1950s produced the theory in an attempt to extend and apply Maslow's need hierarchy to work motivation. It has produced considerable controversy since its proposal.

In his attempt to probe into what really motivates people, Herzberg asked his subjects to describe those elements of their jobs which made them happy and unhappy. His analysis convinced him that conditions relating to the working *environment* (hygiene factors) are essential to prevent dissatisfaction— they must be present to prevent absenteeism, low morale, and turnover. Factors relating to the job itself, however, are most critical in motivating workers to extend their efforts. It is these "motivators" which provide actual satisfaction in work, and they form the second element of the motivation-hygiene theory.

The presence of motivators (the work itself, recognition, advancement, possibility of growth, responsibility, etc.) can cause increased production, but lack of motivators would *not* cause people to complain. Motivators fill those human needs for power, competence, autonomy, etc., at the top of Maslow's hierarchy of self-actualization, while hygiene factors, on the other hand, meet needs clustered at the lower end of the scale. Examples of such "dissatisfiers" or "maintenance" factors are: (1) a superior who is nice, complimentary to subordinates; (2) a modern air-conditioned office; (3) coffee breaks; (4) tuition-refund programs; (5) elimination of personality frictions; (6) recognition of diligence and loyalty; (7) award of status symbols for seniority; (8) fringe benefits. While these lower needs must be met and cannot be ignored by management, such hygiene factors will *not* lead workers to make any more than the minimum effort needed to keep their jobs.

Herzberg's theory has proved so interesting that as many as 30 studies have attempted further validation. The bulk of the resulting evidence suggests, however, that this theory may not be a reliable model of worker motivation. Points of view from both sides of the controversy can be enumerated. Supporters acclaim the intrinsic contribution of the dual-factor theory to the study and understanding of job attitudes, as well as its application of Maslow's theory. Critics maintain, however, that Herzberg, like Maslow, oversimplifies the complexities of motivation. He fails to account for the differences between individuals, for the fact that the same factor may cause satisfaction for one worker and dissatisfaction for another, even within the same sample. His methods of obtaining and of analyzing and interpreting his information are central to the criticism, as is the narrowness of his sample (200 engineers and accountants from 11 industries), which may not be at all representative of the total work force. Additionally, there is doubt concerning Herzberg's claims that his results have been replicated in studies of varying worker groups. Indeed, other research has produced quite different results, in some cases indicating that hygiene factors such as wages or job security were considered by blue collar workers to be motivators. Finally, Herzberg is criticized for failing to define the relationship between the needs of the individual and those of the organization.

*See also* MOTIVATION IN ORGANIZATIONS; SYSTEM 4; THEORY X AND THEORY Y.

## REFERENCES

Herzberg, Frederick: *Work and the Nature of Man*, The World Publishing Company, Cleveland, 1966.
———, Bernard Mausner, and Barbara Syndeman: *The Motivation To Work*, 2d ed., John Wiley & Sons, Inc., New York, 1959.
House, R. J., and L. A. Wigdor: "Herzberg's Dual-Factor Theory of Job Satisfaction and Motivation: A Review of the Evidence and a Criticism," *Personnel Psychology*, vol. 20, pp. 369–389, winter 1967.
Whitsett, David A., and Erik K. Winslow: "An Analysis of Studies Critical of the Motivation-Hygiene Theory," *Personnel Psychology*, vol. 20, no. 4, pp. 391–415, winter 1967.

STAFF/HOKE

# I

**Ideation** (*See* PRODUCT PLANNING AND DEVELOPMENT.)

**Image, product** (*See* ADVERTISING CONCEPTS.)

**Imagination** (*See* MARKETING MANAGEMENT.)

**Imbalance, in scheduling** (*See* MATERIALS MANAGEMENT.)

**Implementation, policy** (*See* POLICY FORMULATION AND IMPLEMENTATION.)

**Importing** (*See* INTERNATIONAL TRADE.)

**Improvement, of costs** (*See* COST IMPROVEMENT.)

**Improvement, of profits** (*See* PROFIT IMPROVEMENT.)

**Improvement, work** (*See* WORK SIMPLIFICATION AND IMPROVEMENT.)

**Improvement methods and techniques** (*See heading in Table of Contents for complete listing.*)

**Improvement project review** (*See* INTERNATIONAL OPERATIONS AND MANAGEMENT IN MULTINATIONAL COMPANIES.)

**In-house courses** (*See* DEVELOPMENT AND TRAINING, MANAGEMENT.)

**Incentive plan** (*See* COMPENSATION, WAGE AND SALARY POLICY AND ADMINISTRATION.)

**Incentives, variable sales** (*See* COMPENSATION, SALES.)

**Income, marginal** (*See* MARGINAL INCOME ANALYSIS.)

**Income, personal** (*See* ECONOMICS MEASUREMENTS.)

**Income statement** (*See* ACCOUNTING, FINANCIAL; ACCOUNTING FOR MANAGERIAL CONTROL; FINANCIAL STATEMENT ANALYSIS.)

**Income tax accounting** (*See* ACCOUNTING, FINANCIAL; TAX MANAGEMENT, MANAGERIAL RESPONSIBILITY FOR FEDERAL INCOME TAX REPORTING.)

**Income taxes, federal** (*See* TAX MANAGEMENT, MANAGERIAL RESPONSIBILITY FOR FEDERAL INCOME TAX REPORTING.)

**Indexing, inverted** (*See* RECORDS MANAGEMENT.)

**Indicators, economic** (*See* ECONOMIC MEASUREMENTS; FORECASTING BUSINESS CONDITIONS.)

**Indicators, stock** (*See* MARKETS, STOCK INDICATOR SERIES.)

**Indices, economic** (*See* ECONOMIC MEASUREMENTS.)

**Industrial advertising** (*See* ADVERTISING MANAGEMENT, INDUSTRIAL.)

**Industrial dynamics** (*See* SYSTEM CONCEPT, TOTAL; SYSTEM DYNAMICS.)

**Industrial goods** (*See* MARKETS, CLASSIFICATIONS AND MARKET ANALYSIS.)

**Industrial management** (*See* MANAGEMENT, DEFINITIONS OF.)

**Industrial marketing** (*See* MARKETING, INDUSTRIAL.)

**Industrial relations management** (*See* PERSONNEL ADMINISTRATION.)

**Inflation accounting** (*See* ACCOUNTING, FINANCIAL.)

**Influence** (*See* POWER AND INFLUENCE.)

**Information, perfect** (*See* STATISTICAL ANALYSIS FOR MANAGEMENT.)

**Information classifications** [*See* INFORMATION SYSTEMS, MANAGEMENT (MIS), APPLIED.]

**Information processing** (*See* DATA PROCESSING PRINCIPLES AND PRACTICES.)

**Information retrieval system** (*See* RECORDS MANAGEMENT.)

## Information search

A wealth of information is already published and readily available to aid managers in analyzing problems and making decisions. The major sources of information are books and reference materials, periodicals and newspapers, United Nations and various governmental agency publications, and trade association data. Librarians can provide assistance in locating and utilizing these resources to satisfy information needs.

**Books and Reference Materials** A well-stocked library may offer thousands of individual titles. The card catalog serves as the index to the library's collection. Books can be located by looking up the author, title, or subject in the catalog. Books on a specific subject will be shelved together. Subject headings used in most libraries are those established in *Subject Headings Used in the Dictionary Catalogs of the Library of Congress.* If a desired title is not part of the library's collection, it can often be obtained by interlibrary loan.

Reference books cover a wide range of business interests. Biographical information can be found in sources such as *Poor's Register of Corporations, Directors, and Executives, United States and Canada* and *World Who's Who in Finance and Industry*. Directories such as *Thomas' Register of American Manufacturers,* which provides information on the manufacturers of more than 70,000 product items, are of particular value. Various business and financial services provide current reports through such publications as *Moody's Manuals of Investments (American and Foreign)*, which includes financial statements, stock issues, and other historical and financial information, and Standard and Poor's *Standard Corporation Records,* which supplies data on balance sheets, earnings and market prices for thousands of American and Canadian corporations. Both directories provide home office addresses and names of directors and principal officers for each firm listed.

**Periodicals and Newspapers** Periodicals and newspapers may provide the most up-to-date source of information. Periodicals may range from academically oriented journals to specific industry publications. Titles of periodicals published in a particular area of interest can be located through *Ulrich's International Periodicals Directory*. *Business Periodicals Index* indexes, by subject and by company name, articles which have appeared in a large number of business publications. If information on a specific subject, such as linear programming, is desired, locate that subject in the index and specific articles will be identified. In the same way, articles about a specific company can be located.

Newspapers provide sources of current happenings in industry and government, stock and bond quotations, and other data. The *Ayer's Directory of Newspapers and Periodicals* provides a comprehensive listing of newspapers, magazines, and trade publications printed in the United States. Indexes to articles in specific major newspapers are available, such as the *New York Times Index* and *Wall Street Journal Index*. Extensive coverage of back issues of periodicals and newspapers may be available on microfilm.

**United Nations and Governmental Agency Publications** The United Nations and various national, state, and local governmental agencies provide important sources of scientific, technical, and socioeconomic information. The *United Nations Document Index* may be helpful in locating specific publications of that body. A yearly checklist, "United Nations Publications in Print," is available free from United Nations Publications, LX-2300, New York, N.Y., 10017.

Large libraries may serve as depositories for United States government publications. The catalog which lists publications of all federal agencies is the *Monthly Catalog of United States Government Publications*. An index by subject, title, and the government agency which published the document appears in the back of each issue. Individual agencies may also provide an index to their publications. An index of specific articles which have appeared in 100 government-issued periodicals is provided by the *Index to U.S. Government Periodicals*.

A list of publications available through a specific agency can be obtained by writing directly to that agency. A monthly brochure, "Selected U.S. Government Publications," is available free from the Superintendent of Documents, U.S. Government Printing Office, Washington, D.C. 20402.

State agencies are sources of blue books, state statistical abstracts, and industrial and manufacturing directories. Some states offer checklist coverage of their publications, which may be available at your local library or may be obtained by writing the state library. A *Monthly Checklist of State Publications* is available, which lists all state publications received by the Library of Congress.

Information concerning a specific locality may be obtained by writing to the local chamber of commerce.

**Trade Associations** In many industries, corporations jointly sponsor trade associations to represent the industry and provide information to all member firms. Lists of available publications can be obtained by writing to the association. The *Encyclopedia of Associations* provides a list of such organizations, while the *Ayer's Directory of Newspapers and Periodicals* lists trade publications.

*See also* ASSOCIATIONS, TRADE AND PROFESSIONAL; ECONOMIC MEASUREMENTS; FORECASTING BUSINESS CONDITIONS; GOVERNMENT RELATIONS AND SERVICES; INFORMATION SYSTEMS, MANAGEMENT (MIS); MARKETING INFORMATION SYSTEMS; MARKETING RESEARCH; PLANNING, STRATEGIC MANAGERIAL; SMALL BUSINESS ADMINISTRATION.

## REFERENCES

*Business Periodicals Index*, The H. W. Wilson Company, New York, 1958– .

*Directory of Newspapers and Periodicals*, N. W. Ayer & Son, Inc., Philadelphia, 1880– .

*Discover and Use Your Public Library*, Small Business Administration, U.S. Department of Commerce, 1970.

*Encyclopedia of Associations*, Gale Research Company, Detroit, 1964– .

*Index to U.S. Government Periodicals*, Infordata International, Chicago, 1972– .

Levine, Sumner L.: *The Dow Jones-Irwin Business Almanac*, Dow Jones-Irwin, Inc., Homewood, Ill., 1977 and annually.

*Monthly Catalog of United States Government Publications,* 1895– .

*Moody's Manuals of Investments (American and Foreign),* Moody's Investors Service, New York, 1929– .

*New York Times Index,* New York Times, New York, 1913– .

*Poor's Register of Corporations, Directors, and Executives, United States and Canada,* Standard & Poor's Corporation, New York, 1928– .

*Standard Corporation Records,* Standard & Poor's Corporation, New York, 1914– .

*Thomas' Register of American Manufacturers,* Thomas Publishing Company, Inc., New York, 1910– .

*Ulrich's International Periodicals Directory,* Annual supplement, R. R. Bowker Company, New York, 1969.

*United Nations Document Index,* Dag Hammarskjöld Library, New York, 1950– .

U.S. Library of Congress: *Monthly Checklist of State Publications,* 1910– .

U.S. Library of Congress: *Subject Headings Used in the Dictionary Catalogs of the Library of Congress,* 1975.

*Wall Street Journal Index,* Dow Jones & Co., Inc., Princeton, 1961– .

*World Who's Who in Finance and Industry,* Marquis Who's Who, Chicago, 1936– .

INEZ L. RAMSEY, *James Madison University*

## Information system   (*See* SYSTEM CONCEPT, TOTAL.)

## Information systems   (*See heading in Table of Contents for complete listing.*)

## Information systems, management (MIS)

The term *management information systems* is a relatively recent addition to the vocabulary of management and was widely adopted following the accelerated use of computers in the early 1960s. Prior to that time *electronic data processing* (EDP) was the most frequently used term to describe computer usage. This earlier label reflected the view that the computer was little more than a fast calculator for large-scale, routine, clerical applications which had formerly been done manually. The notion has now emerged, and it is rather firmly established, that the computer can not only perform data processing but can also be a fine tool to improve the planning and control of operations by providing better information for decision making. This latter purpose is the

basis for the management information systems (hereafter abbreviated as MIS) concept.

### THE CONCEPT OF MIS

Definitions of MIS are about as numerous as the number of writers on the subject. The fundamental concept, however, remains essentially the same. In order to develop the concept of MIS it is useful to define the topic and then synthesize its parts.

**Definition**   A computer-based management information system (MIS) is a collection of data processing equipment, procedures, software, and people that integrates the subsystems of the organization and provides information for decision making on planning and controlling operations.

**The Concept**   The scope and purpose of MIS is better understood if each element of the term is described.

*Management.* This comprises activities of managers in operating their organization: planning, organizing, initiating, directing, and controlling operations. Because decision making is such a fundamental corequisite to each of these activities, the job of MIS is to facilitate the decisions that are necessary for planning, organizing, and controlling the work and the functions of the organization.

*Information.* Information must be distinguished from data, and this distinction is important. *Data* are merely facts and figures that have little to do with making decisions. They take the form of historical records such as files and source documents that constitute the backup for the financial statements. *Information,* on the other hand, is the essential raw material for making decisions. It consists of data that have been retrieved, processed, or otherwise used for planning and controlling operations. It is the essential job of MIS to turn data into information.

*Systems.* A system may be defined simply as a set of elements joined together for a common objective. (*See* SYSTEMS AND PROCEDURES.) For the purpose of MIS, the system is the organization and the elements are the parts (divisions, departments, functions, units, etc.) Although there is a high degree of *synergism* (joining together of subsystems) in scientific, mechanical, and factory manufacturing operations, the optimization of organizational elements by integration remains an elusive achievement. The systems concept of MIS is, therefore, one of optimizing the output of the organization by connecting the operating subsystems through the medium of information exchange. Sales must be integrated with design, production control with financial planning, and so on. The classic management information system, concerned almost totally with historical financial reporting, must be replaced with one that provides information, not data, for planning and controlling operations and synergistically integrates the subsystems of the organization in the process.

## BASIC MIS APPLICATIONS

The use of MIS ranges along a continuum. On the left are those common, widespread applications such as payroll and billing that are purely clerical in nature and whose objective is clerical displacement. On the right are those rare simulations in which the manager has a *cathode-ray tube (CRT)* with immediate access to the "big brain" of the company data base. This manager is an expert in information retrieval and simulation techniques, asking "what if" questions on a real-time basis for his or her entire world of problems and decisions.

The real world of MIS probably lies somewhere in the middle of the continuum. The typical company has developed or is in the process of developing the several operational information systems shown in Fig. I-1. In most cases, these represent basic data sources and have familiar names: order entry, production scheduling, sales planning, etc. All companies have some kind of financial information system, and this category of information is the

most widespread in use today. Objectives of selected subsystems can be illustrated:

| Subsystem | Objective(s) |
|---|---|
| Financial planning and control | Forecast variances to permit corrective action to maintain performance standards. |
| Purchasing | Determine Economic Order Quantity (EOQ) to purchase. Monitor buyer performance. Determine supplier performance. |
| Materials planning | Plan and control parts from a predetermined production schedule. |
| Sales analysis | Identify profitable accounts. Optimize product and customer mix. |
| Project control | Forecast variances by department in order to meet time, cost, and technical specifications. |
| Operation scheduling | Level production load by identifying orders to be rescheduled. Forecast equipment and tooling. Compute start dates and release dates for shop orders in order to meet delivery dates. |

**Integrated Information Systems and Data Banks** MIS has been conceptualized as a set of integrated subsystems. In practice, what is often obtained are "patchwork systems" or "islands of clerical mechanization." In most companies there is a heavy demand for *interfunctional communications*. For example, order entry is closely related to order processing in manufacturing, personnel systems are closely related to payroll, and so on.

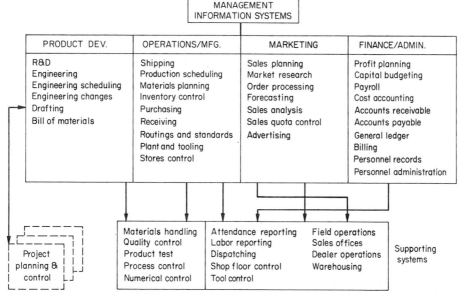

**Fig. I-1. Basic operational information systems. (Joel E. Ross, *Modern Management and Information Systems*, Reston Publishing Company, Reston, Va., 1976. Used by permission.)**

A major way to achieve integration of information subsystems is through the organization data bank. Data are accumulated in an information center where one set of books is maintained. This has the advantage of eliminating costly file duplication, and it has the capacity to integrate the separate functions and departments of the organization.

The *data bank*, or the *central data base* as it is sometimes called, is constructed to store and retrieve the information used in common by the various subsystems of the company. Using modern information-processing technology, a high-speed, random access, mass storage device is used to store large volumes of data concerning the various aspects of the firm and its environment. For example, in a manufacturing firm, a properly designed data bank could provide the information needs for a number of subsystems of a production information and control system. These might include: cost planning and control, engineering and production data control, customer order servicing, forecasting, master production schedule planning, inventory management, manufacturing activity planning, order release, plant monitoring and control, plant maintenance, purchasing, and receiving.

## DECISION MAKING AND MIS

If decision making is defined as the process of selecting from among alternatives a course of action to achieve an objective, the link between information and decision making becomes clear. Indeed, decision making and information processing, if not identical, are so interdependent that they become inseparable in practice. Therefore, considerations surrounding either information systems or decision making inevitably involve both topics.

Management information systems (MIS) can improve decision making in three ways.

**Upgrading Existing Clerical Systems** The overwhelming number of computer applications (some estimates range up to 98 percent) are of a clerical nature. It therefore becomes evident that an enormous potential exists for upgrading these systems for operational decision making. Historically, computers have been used for clerical displacement and administrative control. The illustrations below indicate how some of the widespread clerical applications can be upgraded into decision making and operational application.

| *Clerical System* | *Decision System* |
|---|---|
| Ledger accounting | *upgraded to* financial planning |
| Order entry and billing | *upgraded to* sales analysis |
| Inventory accounting | *upgraded to* inventory management |
| Production reports | *upgraded to* production planning and control |

**Programming Routine Decisions** Since routine and repetitive decisions constitute about 90 percent of the decisions that managers make, it is evident that an enormous potential exists for programming the decisions of the organization. There is no reason why a larger number of decisions cannot be programmed in the same way that production in the process of manufacturing has been automated.

The essential element in programming decisions is the *decision rule* (e.g., reorder if inventory declines below $X$ level). The objective is to design the information in such a way that the computer automatically makes the decisions. This is accomplished by the following steps:

1. Analyze the problem by means of management science and design a decision rule. A well-known example of a decision rule is economic order quantity (EOQ):

$$Qe = \sqrt{\frac{2RS}{I}}$$

where $Qe$ = economic order quantity
$R$ = total yearly requirements
$S$ = setup costs
$I$ = inventory carrying cost per item

2. Program the decision rule for the computer.

3. Design the input and output of the computer information system to provide for automatic decisions by the computer.

Figure I-2 illustrates some rather elementary applications (e.g., purchase order and shipment routing order) for programmed decision rules. Much more sophisticated applications exist, and the potential is limited only by time, expense, and the talents of the systems designer and user.

**Nonprogrammed Decisions** Most of the really important, and costly, decisions remain nonprogrammed and do not lend themselves to automatic solutions. Almost all top management decisions remain in this category. The problem is to furnish information that will help the manager make the unstructured, ill-defined, nonprogrammed decision. This might be called a *decision-assisting MIS*.

The information may be furnished to the manager independently (as in output reports) or in an interactive sense where there is a worker/machine relationship in a problem-solving communications network. Figure I-2 demonstrates both programmed and nonprogrammed, or decision-assisting, information. Notice that in this illustration

1. Some outputs are decisions; the computer has made a decision (e.g., the shipment order).

2. Some outputs are secondary information in the form of reports to be used by a human decision maker (e.g., variance analysis).

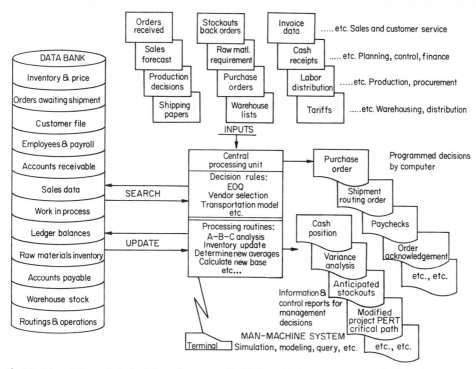

**Fig. I-2.** Integrated manufacturing information system. (Joel E. Ross, *Modern Management and Information Systems,* Reston Publishing Company, Reston, Va., 1976. Used by permission.)

3. Provisions are made for worker/machine interactions in the sense that the manager/decision maker can "model" his or her decisions prior to commitment.

4. Optimum solutions are provided by management science decision rules.

The simulation model is growing in use as a tool to assist decision makers at all levels. To the extent that the subsystems of the firm can be simulated, better information can be obtained for decision improvement. Typical application programs and analytical routines that are inexpensive and relatively easy to implement would include: asset payback schedule, direct-indirect labor cost by job, product break-even analysis, job-costing analysis, depreciation schedule, installment note payment schedule, forecasting trends, accounts receivable analysis, cash flow analysis, security portfolio analysis, inventory valuation, inventory turnover analysis, time series analysis, and statistical analysis.

## MANAGERIAL PARTICIPATION IN MIS DESIGN

Expert opinion is almost unanimous on two points: (1) computers are vastly underutilized for purposes of MIS, and (2) the number one reason is the lack of managerial involvement in the design process. Several surveys have concluded that substantially more profit from computers is made by companies who get managers involved in a hands-on way.

The minimum involvement for the user of an MIS can be described in terms of the six steps outlined below.

*Set System Objectives.* Most users understand the nature and need for objectives in other areas of company operations but find it difficult to state objectives for purposes of MIS design. Yet it is obviously essential to define objectives in terms of legitimacy of information demands. A common fallacy is to emphasize vague or platitudinous terms such as "reduce costs" or "improve efficiency." In neither case is the objective stated in terms that are specific enough to provide a measure of performance of the system or to design an information system to achieve the objective. Rather than defining the objective of the cost control system as "reducing costs," it might be better stated as "establish a system that can be used in manufacturing to forecast 48 hours ahead the labor costs, material costs, tool costs, and overruns by contract or customer order."

*Determine Information Needs.* It follows that if the objective of the system is to be achieved, information needs must be specifically stated. Once again, ambiguity must be avoided. Unless users of the proposed MIS can provide the specifications for what they want, the design effort will produce data, not information, because the systems analyst or computer technician will provide his or her objectives and information needs.

Two approaches are useful for eliciting information needs. The *first approach* involves having a list of the user's four or five major responsibilities and matching these with a list of specific items of information that are required to perform the responsibilities. A *second approach* is to let the user describe what occurs in the decision-making process and then identify the questions that are to be resolved in the activity for which the system is being designed.

*Establish System Constraints.* Sometimes called "problem boundaries" or "restrictions," constraints limit freedom of action in systems design and help ensure that the design effort is realistic. Constraints are both internal and external.

The most frequent *internal constraints* are those involving availability of a work force, cost, resource, and equipment availability, organization and policy restrictions, top management support, and any self-imposed constraints. *External constraints* include those imposed by requirements of the customer, the political and legal needs imposed by the government, and those imposed by a variety of other persons and organizations, such as the supplier.

*Determine Information Sources.* It is one thing to specify information needs and quite another to determine the sources. It is during this step that the form of the new system begins to take shape.

Sources of information include internal and external records, the development of new forms and reports, interviews with managers and operating personnel, and a number of sampling and estimating techniques. Following the identification of these sources, an information needs/sources matrix can be prepared as a summary.

*Develop the System Concept.* A description of the system concept includes essentially a flow chart or other documentation of the flow of information through the system, the inputs and outputs, and a narrative description of the operations. The objective is to provide a broad picture of the general system design before detailed analysis and design are undertaken. This picture is normally given by the general system flow, inputs, and outputs described below.

*General system flow chart* is a common method of indicating the general specifications of a computer-based MIS. It shows the description of the data-processing logic in general terms. A general systems flow chart is similar to that shown in Fig. I-2.

*System inputs* are determined mainly when information sources are listed. However, the task of designing the input format remains.

*System outputs* are by all measures the most important step in system design. These are the real purpose behind MIS design, because it is the output that provides the information needs to meet the objectives of the system: the information for making decisions regarding planning and controlling operations. Needless to say, this step should not be left to a computer technician.

*System Implementation.* Following the development of the general system concept and testing of the system, it is now ready for implementation: that herculean job of converting the system specifications into an operating system that achieves the objectives and information needs determined early in the design phase.

The organization and control of the many tasks involved in system implementation is best managed by the basic techniques associated with project planning and control.

## MIS DESIGN: THE APPROACH OF THE ANALYST

The manager should have some familiarity with the design process from the point of view of the systems analyst or other computer technician. A speaking knowledge of these activities will not only improve his or her chances of success due to better communications with the analyst but will also lend added expertise to the design effort so that the end product will better meet the manager's needs.

A detailed description of these steps is beyond the scope of this entry, but this list of steps represents the basics of systems analysis and design.

| Step | Description |
|---|---|
| Define the problem (system objective) | Make sure that the problem is defined or the objective established to ensure that the system does not provide the right solution to the wrong problem. |
| Feasibility study | Analyze whether it is technically practical and economically viable to change the method of handling information processing and install the proposed system. |
| Data gathering | Gather and document existing information about the present system and the information needs and interfaces be- |

| Step | Description |
|------|-------------|
| | tween related systems. The analyst must be familar with (1) what data to gather, (2) the sources of data, and (3) the techniques of data gathering. |
| Data analysis | Organize and analyze retained data, then analyze qualitatively and quantitatively the system activities, operation, and decision-making processes. |
| Determine alternative design concepts | Evaluate alternative designs involving different mixes of equipment, data bank organizations, processing steps, input-output combinations, and choose the best. |
| System controls | Establish controls for system and data security. These include manual controls, mechanical (machine) controls, operational controls for the EDP center, and personnel controls. |
| Documentation | This step is essential for subsequent system modification and for education. The documentation package may include the user's project request, a cost-benefit analysis of the proposed system, design specification controls, procedures, computer programming, and implementation summary. |
| Implementation | Plan, schedule, and control the tasks and work packages involved in bringing the system into operational status. |

## ROADBLOCKS TO MIS SUCCESS

Despite the potential for improving productivity through better management information systems, it simply has not happened. The enormous technological advances in computer hardware have not been accompanied by anything approaching similar advances in managerial applications. As one widely read survey concluded: "For the most part, third and fourth-generation equipment is being used on first-generation systems design."

In almost every case, MIS failure or suboptimization can be traced to one of seven basic causes. These causes and their cures are summarized below.

**Emphasis on Clerical Systems** This is sometimes known as the one-for-one changeover syndrome. It occurs when a technician takes an existing clerical system and converts or modifies it without upgrading or changing it. Although savings in clerical costs is a justifiable objective, this approach to MIS design does little for management. *The cure is to upgrade the clerical system to a management system.* (See the discussion under Decision Making and MIS in this entry.)

**Communications Gap** Most technicians speak "computerese" and have little appreciation for the process of management. The manager/user on the other hand is not generally prepared to speak the language of the computer. The result is frequently a design standoff. *The cure is management development for both the manager and the technician.*

**Reliance on a Consultant or the Manufacturer** Many consultants and manufacturers of computer equipment promise delivery of the "turnkey" system or the preprogrammed "off the shelf" design package that can quickly be adapted to meet your needs. Generally speaking, if the organization does not have the in-house talent to design its own systems, it does not have the talent to operate them. *The cure is to develop in-house design talent.*

**Lack of a Master Plan** Many surveys of computer usage among all types of organizations have concluded that the design of individual information systems usually proceeds without adequate attention to integration of subsystems. The result is a patchwork approach that not only is suboptimal but in the long run becomes very expensive to correct. *The cure is to design to a master plan.*

**Organization of the MIS Function** Historically, the computer was assigned to the chief accounting officer based on the rationale that the bulk of information in the ordinary firm was financial in nature. The result in too many cases has been an overemphasis on historical data for accounting purposes and not information for operational management decisions. *The cure is to make the MIS function independent so that it reports directly to top management.*

**Lack of Managerial Participation** This may be the foremost reason for MIS failure. Dozens of studies on hundreds of companies have concluded that the most striking characteristic of the successful company is that MIS development has been viewed as a responsibility of management. *The cure is top management support and a demand that managers participate in the design of their own MIS.*

**Overlooking Human Acceptance** It is necessary that people accept and utilize an information system if it is to be successful. Yet most systems designers admit to the unpleasant reality that the toughest part of designing and implementing the MIS is to gain the acceptance of the users. If the system is not accepted, people will resist it, work around it, continue to use the old system, and in extreme cases sabotage the new system. *The cure is to involve the users in the early stages of design and gain cooperation by demonstrating how their job will be affected in a positive way.*

*See also* ACCOUNTING FOR MANAGERIAL CONTROL; COMPUTER SYSTEMS; CONTROL SYSTEMS, MANAGEMENT; DATA PROCESSING PRINCIPLES AND PRACTICES; INFORMATION SEARCH; INFORMATION SYSTEMS, MANAGEMENT (MIS), APPLIED; INFORMATION SYSTEMS,

MANAGEMENT (MIS), IN LARGE ORGANIZATIONS; SYSTEMS AND PROCEDURES; WORD PROCESSING.

## REFERENCES

Burch, John G., Jr. and Felix R. Strater, Jr.: *Information Systems: Theory and Practice*, Hamilton Publishing Company, Santa Barbara, Calif., 1974.

*COPICS: Communications Oriented Production Information and Control System*, IBM Corporation, White Plains, N.Y., 1972.

Gross, Paul, and Robert D. Smith: *Systems Analysis and Design for Management*, Dun-Donnelley, New York, 1976.

Murdick, Robert G., and Joel E. Ross: *MIS in Action*, West Publishing Company, St. Paul, Minn., 1975. This is a collection of 58 recent articles concerned with management information systems.

Ross, Joel E.: *Modern Management and Information Systems*, Reston Publishing Company, Reston, Va., 1976.

Voich, Dan, Jr., Homer J. Mottice, and William A. Schrode: *Information Systems for Operations and Management*, South-Western Publishing Company, Incorporated, Cincinnati, 1975.

JOEL E. ROSS, *Florida Atlantic University*

# Information systems, management (MIS), applied

The term *management information systems* (MIS) has many interpretations, but it customarily refers to (1) the gathering of accounting, statistical, and related information through the use of computers and associated equipment, and (2) the summary and display of this information to management via computer reports (such as print-outs or hard copy), video display devices (e.g., cathode-ray terminals), telex messages, and so forth. A wide variety of computers and related equipment *(hardware)* is available for almost any budget or purpose, and this hardware can be operated by a wide variety of programmed instructions *(software)*. A vast array of terminology, slang or vernacular words, and descriptive phrases pertain to all that exists or is going on in the MIS area, and the uninitiated may have to devote some effort to learning the jargon of the trade.

**Basic Purposes**   From a practical viewpoint, an MIS can be thought of as performing two functions: (1) it provides management information (such as sales, production, and financial reports), and (2) it furnishes a mechanism for processing paper work transactions (such as the issuance of checks and invoices and the compilation of accounting data). Furthermore, the word *systems* customarily refers to all the procedures, hardware, software, methods, and communications arrangements that are necessary to produce information or process transactions, whereas the computer, or electronic data processing (EDP), function is largely thought of as the part devoted to day-to-day operations of the hardware and associated software. Programming refers to the area of writing detailed instructions *(programs)* that determine precisely how a computer processes data to produce the desired end result (e.g., report, check, invoice).

Along with marketing, production, finance, and research, MIS has emerged as a major organizational function. It must be regarded as such if its maximum value is to be obtained. MIS can permeate an entire organization and be used not only for gathering historical information or transaction processing but also for financial modeling and other simulation studies that attempt to show what might happen in the future.

## INFORMATION NEEDS

Every business must ask itself, "What is the optimum information required for running the business?" Since what is optimum is related to the cost of obtaining the information, it is fundamental to distinguish, function by function, the information that is absolutely necessary from that which may be desirable—with the latter perhaps broken down into two or more classes of desirability. In turn, the estimated cost—in terms of system development, programming, and projected operating expenses—must be developed. This will help to determine how far the company is willing to go to acquire the information. This study can lead to all sorts of incremental considerations since a certain size MIS may be able to provide additional information at a relatively low incremental cost, but there comes a time when the system is strained to the limit and only a costly jump to a much larger system will provide all the information that may be wanted. Determining what information needs are practically and economically attainable can be a major project in itself. It is usually desirable to identify the needs for each function, to correlate the needs between functions, and then to consolidate them to determine the overall needs. These needs, classified between necessary and desirable, provide the basis of a long-range plan—for they will be approached step-by-step, presumably in order of importance.

**Factors Affecting Needs**   Important factors to be considered when evaluating information needs and their costs include:

1. *Frequency*: Immediate (on request, on line), every few minutes, hourly, daily, weekly, monthly, quarterly, or annually?

2. *Scope and depth:* Summarized information (e.g., sales in a given market area)? Detailed information (e.g., sales for the most-detailed level of product classification to a particular customer destination)?

3. *Method of availability:* Computer print-outs (including number of copies and their distribution)? Video display screens?

4. *Elapsed time before information is available:* Daily? By what time the following day? Weekly, monthly, etc.? How long after the end of the period?

5. *Use of exception reporting:* Possible to have only exceptions (to a predetermined standard) reported, with quick access to detailed documentation for further information as necessary?

6. *Readability of information:* Descriptive captions? Numerical codes all right or are alphabetized descriptions needed? (If the latter, are abbreviations all right?) If on computer print-outs, is printed form needed or standard blank form all right?

**Information Need Classifications** While specific information needs tend to be related to the various functions of the business, many needs overlap the various functions. For MIS purposes, needs should be classified in groupings that relate more to the nature and availability of the data than to the separate functions of the business, such as sales, production, finance, research, and so forth. Many reports will ultimately be distributed, of course, to functional recipients. But grouping reports according to how they relate for MIS purposes permits easier control and resolution of information needs. A typical grouping of reports (and transaction processing output) for a manufacturing company might be along the following lines:

1. *Sales reports group.* Reports on sales, allocations, customers—by geographical location, product, responsibility, or other classification.

2. *Product profits group.* Reports by individual products, product groups, market areas, or producing or shipping locations.

3. *Production and cost accounting group.* Reports on production statistics and product costs.

4. *Orders-invoicing-inventory group.* Reports on orders, billings, inventories, and customer invoices.

5. *Prices-allowances-sales commissions group.* Reports on prices, allowances, and commissions; price lists.

6. *Receivables and collections group.* Reports on cash receipts and receivable trial balances; customer statements.

7. *Payroll group.* Payroll register, time reports, and government reports; payroll checks and government forms.

8. *Accounts payable group.* Voucher register, account distribution listings, payments by vendor, voucher checks, and check reconciliation listings.

9. *General ledger group.* Financial statements, general ledger trial balance, and expense listings—by account for various departments of the business.

10. *Fixed and leased property group.* Listings of fixed assets and long-term leases—by type and location.

## DESIGNING THE INFORMATION SYSTEM

Once the information needs are determined, it is necessary to design the information system (or change the existing system) to meet those needs. Designing the overall *business information system,* affecting as it does all the sources of input, communications, processing, and sources of output in the company, is a separate and distinct matter, of course, from designing *(configurating)* the *computer system* that will process the information. Design of the business information system involves systems people, users, and management. Configurating the computer system is largely the province of computer technicians, with some overview from the systems people to be sure that the computer system will be able to do the job required.

**Planning** A long-range plan must also be developed, with priorities assigned, for meeting the various information needs. It is not realistic to expect that all the needs are going to be met at a given time, or even in a short period of time following the development and completion of the necessary systems, programming, and EDP installation. Accordingly, the long-range plan must be broken down into what is attainable on a yearly (or more frequent) basis that is compatible with the budget, personnel resources, and the equipment that is to be available.

**Alternative Considerations** A staggering choice of alternatives is available, but the important considerations include:

1. Overall design of system.

*a.* Centralized, localized or some of each, depending on application?

*b.* Minicomputers used entirely or as supplements in certain situations?

*c.* Number and location of devices which originate data (input terminals) or produce data (output terminals).

*d.* Degree of automation in handling data. Will data originate from key punching of documents, card or tape entry, or machine-readable documents?

*e.* Transmittal of data. By mail, phone, leased wire, or facsimile transmission? How often?

*f.* Coding structure. Will it permit maximum flexibility? Compatible with data base?

2. Choice of equipment (including computer, peripheral, and communications equipment).

*a.* Reputation of manufacturer.

*b.* Cost.

*c.* Systems and programming assistance available.

*d.* Back-up equipment available.

*e.* Speed of processing and print-outs.

*f.* Risk of obsolescence.

*g.* Size of installation and capability of future expansion compatible with long-range plans.

*h.* Availability of maintenance service.

*i.* Staff training available from manufacturer.

*j.* Ability to handle all desired applications.

*k.* Data.

*l.* Storage or memory capacity.

*m.* Buy versus lease considerations.

3. Commitment of resources to MIS.

*a.* Operating budget per year.

*b.* Capability of MIS personnel.

*c.* Availability of users for involvement.

The foregoing considerations are not intended to be an inclusive checklist. They are simply representative of the many decisions that can only be made by thoroughly knowledgeable professional people on a case-by-case basis.

**Pitfalls to Watch For**   In designing the overall system and bringing specific applications into operation, a great deal of caution is advised. Experience indicates that many organizations are trapped by nine pitfalls common to MIS developments:

1. *Late completion dates.* These usually result from unforeseen interferences beyond the control of the MIS people.

2. *Temptation to proceed too fast.* There is a need for proceeding at a pace compatible with available resources and reasonable objectives.

3. *Temptation to be first.* There is a need for patience and for waiting to see what others do.

4. *Higher development costs than anticipated.* There is a need for a thorough, professional job of determining realistically the costs involved and for proper planning to reach the objectives.

5. *Higher operating costs than anticipated.* Ongoing costs of operations and hardware associated with each application must be realistically determined.

6. *Need for expensive machinery.* All alternatives should be thoroughly explored and the proper equipment secured at the best cost.

7. *Interference from unplanned projects.* This is going to happen in most businesses, and due allowance must be made.

8. *Problems arising from operating systems provided by computer manufacturers.* There is a need to be sure that the systems are as error-free as possible and that they will not be used or modified for purposes not intended by the manufacturer.

9. *Unproductive MIS staff.* There is a compelling need for sensitivity to the form of organization, staffing, training, salary levels, competency of employees, management attitudes, and other factors that typically affect the productivity of a staff group.

## DEVELOPING SPECIFIC APPLICATIONS

Once the basic business information system has been designed, planning can commence for the specific applications that will be necessary to attain the information needs of the business. The systems time and the programming time should be estimated carefully, with the expectation that it will be revised from time to time as experience and events suggest. Recognize, however, that an estimate of worker-days needed to complete an application does not necessarily mean that the project will be complete after the elapsed time. Unplanned interferences, waiting for decisions, and events beyond the control of the MIS people will usually postpone the target date suggested by the original estimate.

**Project Control**   For optimum results, the development of an MIS application must be tightly controlled, with written approvals and documentation supporting every step of the process. These steps normally involve (1) definition of a problem, (2) a preliminary survey, (3) study and preliminary design, (4) a design, (5) a detailed business system design, (6) a detailed computer system design, (7) programming specifications, (8) programming, (9) programming tests, (10) systems tests, (11) installation, and (12) a postcompletion audit.

**Extent of Detail**   The design of the information system should contemplate the use of the most detailed coding structure that is practical. For example, the use of one code classification for each product sold may not provide all the information that may ultimately be desired. It may be necessary to have codes for every grade of the product and for each variation for which a separate cost or selling price is in effect. With as detailed a coding structure as practical, it is a simple matter to summarize the data in any manner that is desired. This, incidentally, avoids expensive redesigns at a later time. The need to think through exactly what may be needed in any reasonably predictable set of circumstances cannot be overemphasized.

**Data Base** The computer system should be designed in such a way as to maximize the advantages of the data base. Data storage, access thereto, and computer processing should be brought together in such a way that related information can be furnished for various applications with a minimum of overlapping, backtracking, and duplication of effort. For example, MIS applications for order handling, invoicing to customers, and inventories are typically interrelated. One data base which provides all the information and transaction processing capabilities related to these three areas would normally be better than three separate groups of data and processing routines to satisfy the information needs of each area. The choice of hardware, software, peripheral, and communications equipment is so vast that the company must decide how far it is practical to go in examining various alternatives.

## INVOLVEMENT OF OTHERS

Successful operation of an MIS requires, like any other major organizational function, involvement of many people besides those who are developing and operating the system itself.

**Users** User involvement requires the assignment of one or more competent and knowledgeable people from the department using a particular MIS application to work with the systems people throughout the planning, development, and implementation phases. It often entails a substantial commitment of time and expense on the part of the user function. It means pinpointed responsibility every step of the way, with written requests and approvals at various stages which are signed personally by the company officer responsible for the user function. It requires seemingly endless meetings with systems personnel. Above all, it requires a thorough recognition of exactly what is wanted as early as possible and a constant awareness of all the contingencies and exceptions that, if not properly anticipated and programmed, may cause costly delays in bringing the application into full operational status. After implementation, the user must still be periodically involved as changes and modifications arise in response to the inevitable changing needs of the business. The axiom is inescapable, however: The greater the user involvement, the more likely early and continued success with a computer application will be.

**Executive Steering Committee** An executive steering committee is vital. It should be composed of the chief executive officer, the officers in charge of the principal user functions, the head of the systems-computer department, and the executives between him or her and the chief executive officer. Typically, this committee determines priorities, monitors progress on a periodic basis, and considers the relative merits of various proposed applications. Their meetings can be frequent or infrequent, depending upon all considerations pertinent to a particular company, but they should meet at least quarterly.

**Chief Executive Officer** The chief executive officer must also devote a certain amount of time to the information systems area. It is unrealistic to expect, however, with all the other demands, that the chief executive officer can be expected to be involved in day-to-day activities. Nevertheless, he or she should be involved in: (1) the periodic meetings of the executive steering committee (perhaps by chairing the meeting); (2) the budget for the activity (which would include major decisions to expand, contract, or rearrange the activity); and (3) such major decisions as buying versus leasing, converting from one computer manufacturer to another, etc. If the chief executive officer is not sufficiently involved, the information system normally will not be as good.

**Outsiders** Maintenance personnel from the computer manufacturer are always involved. Systems designers and analysts from the manufacturer are usually available—up to a point—to assist in developing and implementing various projects. Outside consultants may be used, although they are expensive and may not be an adequate substitute for an in-house team. If outside computers or time-sharing services are used, representatives from these organizations can be helpful.

## SYSTEM ORGANIZATION

The operation of a management information system should be regarded as a major function of any business, on a par with such time-honored functions as production, sales, finance, research, and so forth. Only when it is so recognized can a company expect to realize the optimum benefits inherent in the system. However, the inherently technical nature of an MIS suggests that in most instances the function should not report directly to the chief executive officer but rather to a knowledgeable high-level executive who can be the liaison between the technical staff and top management. Whether this person should be a financial executive, or someone else, can only be answered on a case-by-case basis. Whatever the background, however, the individual must possess the extreme disciplines (e.g., exactness, dedication to the job, ability to organize well, and ability to articulate problems to people outside the field) required for effective information systems management. The director of the MIS, or whatever title is used, should report to the executive between him or her and the chief executive officer.

**Internal Organization** Except in small installations where responsibilities may be combined, the business systems group—including systems designers, systems analysts, and programmers—is usually separate from the computer operations group that consists of computer operators, keypunch operators, data control clerks, and perhaps a librarian for the data files. Intermediate-level jobs, such as project managers in the business systems group and shift supervisors in the computer operations group, can be introduced as needed. Supervision of and responsibility for communications facilities (telephone, telex, input and output devices, etc.) may or may not be part of the overall responsibilities of the director of the MIS. In the MIS with communications facilities feeding directly into a centralized computer, it is usually desirable to place the communications system under the same direction as the rest of the MIS. In any event, the director of the MIS must be closely involved with all aspects of planning, operations, and control in the communications area that has a bearing on planning, operations, and control in the systems–data processing area.

**Business Systems Group** The day-to-day operations of the business systems people (designers, analysts, programmers), unless they are extremely experienced, need to be monitored carefully to be sure they are not going down the wrong road. Designers and analysts normally work closely with users or potential users of information to develop specific applications, but all too often the users do not understand (and sometimes do not want to understand) exactly how complicated it all may be. Furthermore, they may not be able to articulate exactly what they want. While the systems people have some responsibility to draw out of the users what they really want, many systems people have not had line experience in the user function, and so they, too, may not comprehend exactly what is wanted. Under such circumstances, the system may be poorly designed. It may be an unworkable system or a system that produces the wrong information and causes costly redesigns. Similarly, programming of the system may be done incorrectly if the programmer does not understand exactly what is wanted. The opportunities for communication failures between users and systems designer–analysts—and

between the latter and programmers—are so numerous that extra care must be taken to be sure that the proper road is being followed every step of the way. In addition, transfer of personnel (in both directions) between systems people and users can be very beneficial. The business systems group should also periodically review all output of the MIS (such as reports, print-outs, and documents) to be sure that the information (1) is still needed, (2) can be modified, or (3) permits reduction in the number of copies and distribution thereof. A master schedule of applications under study or in progress, with estimated worker-days to complete and operating target dates, should be maintained and revised as necessary.

**EDP Computer Group** The day-to-day operation of the computer installation is, of course, quite different from that for systems. All work orders or jobs should be numbered and scheduled. Operating logs (which may be computerized) of all activities should be maintained for planning, control, and audit trail purposes. Time must be made available to test the new and revised applications developed by the systems people. Down time and unproductive time, if any, should be carefully reviewed for possible reduction.

## SYSTEMS OPERATION

The day-to-day operation of MIS is probably more similar to the day-to-day operation of a production facility than anything else; the MIS produces *information*, whereas the production facility produces *products*. The nature of both is usually such that they must be geared up to handle unexpected emergencies in the most expeditious manner. A company cannot tolerate delayed information or processing capability for very long. Unfortunately, equipment failures, power outages, program "hang ups," communications difficulties, etc., can at times seemingly conspire to play havoc with the best of scheduled intentions. The MIS operating people (and, often, the vendor equipment maintenance people) should be expected to be available day and night until the problem is corrected. This is an occupational hazard and must be accepted as such by MIS personnel. Good planning and backup facilities may help to reduce the vulnerability to unexpected emergencies, but they will still happen, and so appropriate procedures should be on hand to deal with them.

## SYSTEMS JUSTIFICATION

Every management information system requires justification in the eyes of management, although a great deal of controversy can arise as to how much justification is needed. Certainly, computerized transaction processing applications (order handling, billing, accounts payable, etc.) should pay their own way as compared with such alternative methods as doing the job manually or with bookkeeping machines or other mechanical aids. At times, it may be better to perform some or all these applications with outside services rather than to use the company computer. This is particularly true where experience is sought before committing the company computer or where there is insufficient in-house capacity or too many other systems and computer priorities.

**Essential Information**   As to nontransaction processing applications, where basic information and reports essential to the operation of the business are sought, the need for detailed, documented economic justification is more debatable. Such information may be necessary regardless of cost—within reasonable bounds, of course. Often, the information simply could not be made available on a timely and economical basis except with the aid of a computer. To try to determine a theoretical economic benefit for each project may be more trouble than it is worth and perhaps not too accurate anyway. There have been many projects that have never gotten off the ground because they appeared to be too costly, yet the business will never know what it lost by not having the information available.

**Basic Cost Data**   To the extent that economic benefits are calculated, however (as for transaction processing applications), some basic data should be available to calculate such benefits. A sophisticated cost accounting system for MIS activities is not necessary, although—considering the funds expended—it might be worth working toward on a long-range basis. Such basic data as employee workhours (which can then be multiplied by an average hourly rate, including employee benefits, to product estimated labor cost), overhead costs, and equipment costs can be used to estimate costs (both development and operating) for specific applications.

**Cost Allocations**   Whether or not to charge the costs of an information systems department to the users is also a controversial matter. Many systems projects are interrelated with others in such a way that they benefit a number of users, and any single user accountability is impractical. Furthermore, some users balk at being accountable for heavy systems expenses and consequently deny themselves information which is vital to the operation of the business. In any event, it may be desirable to inform applicable users of MIS costs for projects in which they are involved even though such costs are not formally allocated to their budget.

## CONTROL AND EVALUATION

The investment in MIS, once made, is an investment from which there is no road back. Whether the monetary investment is large or small, the company has usually "severed the cord" from its ability to gather information or to process transactions in an alternative manner. If the business cannot process orders or bill customers or prepare accounting records or furnish needed information (depending on what has been computerized), it can get in trouble fast.

**Controls**   Thus, it is imperative that adequate controls be maintained to ensure the continued operation of the MIS. These controls consist of the following:

1. *Physical security.* This includes (a) restricted access of personnel, (b) freedom from exposure to hazardous risks, (c) fireproof storage of records, (d) back-up equipment with back-up programs, and (e) warning devices for heat, smoke, etc.

2. *Internal controls.* These include (a) review of all applications by knowledgeable auditors (inside and/or outside) to reduce exposure to employee manipulation of programs or output for personal gain and (b) maintenance of audit trails so all work can be reviewed and checked at a later time.

3. *Data control.* This covers separate balancing of control totals on all work being processed to ensure arithmetical accuracy.

4. *Operating records.* This covers maintenance of computer logs and systems-programming schedules, periodic review and follow-up thereof for identification of opportunities to do the job better.

5. *Vital-records duplication.* This includes off-premise duplicate storage of information which would be necessary to keep the business going in the event of a disaster affecting the computer. This could be duplicates of computer print-outs, tapes, discs, punched cards, etc. Such vital information would include accounting records (general ledger, accounts receivable, property records, payrolls, etc.), customer lists, and perhaps some sales and production data. In particular, duplicates should be maintained of the essential library of application programs to permit an easy restart in the event of a disaster.

6. *Disaster program.* This includes a program for alternative means of processing information in the event of a disaster, including availability and usage of basic sources of data and the processing thereof via back-up equipment, time sharing, outside services, bookkeeping, or similar machines, or manual methods.

**Evaluation** Only when an MIS is under good control, with alternative plans in the event of trouble, can company management be comfortable with an area that it usually does not know too much about. Only then can an intelligent evaluation be made of the worth of the system to the company. Adequate controls cost money to develop and sustain; without adequate controls, the costs of the MIS are incomplete, and the company may be exposing itself to risks which can be neither easily measured nor appreciated. If lack of controls permits employee fraud or exposure to unnecessary risks or cessation or postponement of vitally needed information or documents, the avoided investment in controls may result in far greater costs and, occasionally, threaten the survival of the business.

Even with adequate controls, however, the precise evaluation of the worth of MIS is a complicated exercise. Transaction processing operations (versus alternative means) should pay for themselves, but strictly informational output of the MIS will have to be evaluated in terms of whether the estimated cost of providing the information is balanced by benefits to the users and management. One rule of thumb states that the overall cost of an adequate, but not overly sophisticated, MIS should run somewhere between one-half and 1 percent of sales.

*See also* ACCOUNTING, FINANCIAL; ACCOUNTING FOR MANAGERIAL CONTROL; BUDGETS AND BUDGET PREPARATION; COMPUTER SYSTEMS; CONTROL SYSTEMS, MANAGEMENT; DATA PROCESSING PRINCIPLES AND PRACTICES; INFORMATION SYSTEMS, MANAGEMENT (MIS); INFORMATION SYSTEMS, MANAGEMENT (MIS), IN LARGE ORGANIZATIONS; PAPER WORK SIMPLIFICATION; RECORDS MANAGEMENT; SYSTEMS AND PROCEDURES; WORD PROCESSING.

CHARLES F. AXELSON, *Lawry's Foods, Inc.*

# Information systems, management (MIS), in large organizations

Scholarly research on the subject of management information systems (MIS) is usually directed to the most-advanced examples of computer hardware and computer systems design. It is difficult, against this background of MIS literature, to obtain an accurate picture of MIS techniques currently available to practicing managers. This entry summarizes the findings of a study of over 150 large business and government users of computer-based information systems.[1] In addition to state-of-the-art information,

the results provide a convenient yardstick for the evaluation of any organization's MIS.

Management information systems can be viewed as having two dimensions: technology and performance.

**Technology Dimension** Technology is commonly measured in terms of *computer generations.* Generations can be generically defined by attributes such as component technology (e.g., vacuum tube, transistor, integrated circuit, etc.), computational speed, storage capacity, input-output media and devices, and programming techniques. Over 91 percent of the organizations surveyed possess third-generation technology; 8.5 percent have what is considered to be fourth generation; and none have first- or second-generation technology. Government organizations tend to have the most-advanced technology, with financial institutions a close second. Retail/wholesale firms have the least-advanced technologies, while engineering, manufacturing, and service industries occupy intermediate positions.

**Performance Dimension** Performance is defined by characteristics such as the type of application, the nature of the data base, the degree to which the system supports organizational decision making, the organizational levels served, and the extent of interface with other organizational systems and elements. Systems performance is more difficult to measure than systems technology due to the lack of distinct performance generations. Nonetheless, a number of attempts have been made to classify MIS in a hierarchy based on the characteristics listed above.

*Performance Levels.* Although the terms used to describe levels of systems performance vary, most researchers consider four categories that trace the evolution of systems through (1) basic transaction processing, (2) operation and production control, (3) management support, and (4) strategic planning. The percentages of MIS in each category, for various types of organizations in the survey sample, are shown in Table I-1.

*Applications.* Although the application area is only one element considered in the determination of the performance level, it is the most discriminating factor and the one most easily used by non-ADP personnel in evaluating MIS. The extent to which different applications are used in MIS is shown in Table I-2. This table also shows the weight assigned each application by a panel of experts that judged performance characteristics for their relative sophistication.

*Decision Support.* Another important determinant of MIS performance is the capability to sup-

TABLE I-1  Systems Performance Levels by Category of Organization

| | Classification of systems | | | |
|---|---|---|---|---|
| | Basic transaction, % | Operation and production, % | Management support, % | Strategic planning, % |
| Engineering firms | 12 | 24 | 52 | 12 |
| Financial institutions | 0 | 25 | 75 | 0 |
| Manufacturing firms | 0 | 10 | 71 | 19 |
| Retail/wholesale firms | 12 | 47 | 35 | 6 |
| Service industries | 0 | 21 | 68 | 11 |
| Government agencies | 0 | 15 | 72 | 13 |
| All organizations | 3 | 20 | 65 | 12 |

TABLE 1-2  MIS Application Areas

| Application | Relative weight | Percent |
|---|---|---|
| Payroll | 1 | 60 |
| Inventory recordkeeping | 2 | 56 |
| General ledger accounting | 3 | 64 |
| Production scheduling | 4 | 43 |
| Sales forecasting | 4 | 32 |
| Capital budgeting | 5 | 35 |
| Production plant control | 5 | 31 |
| Long-range planning | 6 | 26 |
| Total weight | 30 | |

NOTE: The relative-weight column indicates the degree of sophistication of each application, as judged by a panel of experts.

The percent column shows the percentage of surveyed organizations utilizing the listed application in their MIS. For example, 60 percent have a payroll application, 32 percent have a sales forecasting application, and so on.

port organizational decision making. This factor is the second most discriminating characteristic of performance and ranges from no support at all to interactive managerial access of advanced mathematical and operations research models. Various MIS decision-support capabilities, the relative weights as-

TABLE I-3  MIS Decision-Support Capabilities

| Capability | Relative weight | Percent |
|---|---|---|
| None | 0 | 8 |
| Summary reports | 1 | 80 |
| Operational decisions | 2 | 35 |
| Management science methods | 3 | 22 |
| Manager-defined reports | 4 | 25 |
| Strategic planning | 5 | 25 |
| Manager access to mathematical models | 5 | 8 |
| Total weight | 20 | |

NOTE: The relative-weight column indicates the degree of sophistication of each capability, as judged by a panel of experts.

The percent column shows the percentage of surveyed organizations possessing the listed decision-support capability. For example, 25 percent support strategic planning with MIS.

signed them by the panel of experts, and the percentage of systems possessing each capability are shown in Table I-3.

**Evaluating MIS Performance**  Although other characteristics are considered in evaluating systems performance, applications and decision-support capabilities provide a good estimate of an organization's level of performance. Table I-4 shows, for each characteristic, the minimum score judged nec-

TABLE I-4  Systems Performance Scores

For Increasing Levels (or Degrees) of Performance Sophistication

| | Score ranges | | |
|---|---|---|---|
| | Application | Decision | Total |
| Basic transaction | 0–6 | 0–1 | 0–7 |
| Operation and production | 7–10 | 2–3 | 8–13 |
| Management support | 11–24 | 4–12 | 14–36 |
| Strategic planning | 25–30 | 13–20 | 37–50 |

Of Selected Industries

| | Score averages | | |
|---|---|---|---|
| | Application | Decision | Total |
| Engineering firms | 15.1 | 5.8 | 20.8 |
| Financial institutions | 10.3 | 4.0 | 14.4 |
| Manufacturing firms | 18.1 | 6.5 | 24.6 |
| Retail/wholesale firms | 10.9 | 4.5 | 15.4 |
| Service industries | 13.8 | 5.8 | 19.6 |
| Government agencies | 11.2 | 7.3 | 18.5 |
| All organizations | 13.6 | 6.0 | 19.6 |

essary to qualify a system for the various levels of systems performance. This table also shows how different categories of organizations scored in each performance area. To evaluate MIS performance, add the application score weight (from Table I-2) and the decision-support score weight (from Table I-3). The total can be converted to an overall level of systems performance and compared (in Table I-4) with the average for its particular industry. For example, suppose company A has an MIS application for payroll, inventory, general ledger accounting, and production scheduling. Its application score would be 10, which would place it in the second level. If it supported decision-making with summary reports and manager-defined reports, its decision score would be 5, or at the third level. And if A were a manufacturing company, it would find that its overall performance (15) is much lower than the industry average of 24.6.

*Balanced Systems.* In general, an organization can achieve maximum MIS efficiency with a balance of systems technology and systems performance; e.g., third-generation technology and management support performance. Just under two-thirds (65 percent) of the organizations surveyed have such a balanced MIS.

*Unbalanced Systems.* It is also possible to achieve high-level performance with comparatively lower technology (e.g., strategic planning performance with third-generation technology). There are only a few organizations (less than 8 percent of the survey sample) willing to undertake the risk and expense of such pioneering efforts. Most of these performance-intensive systems are found in government agencies or in very large manufacturing firms.

It is more likely that an unbalanced MIS will be of the technology-intensive variety; that is, third- or fourth-generation technology will be employed to achieve first- (basic transaction processing) or second- (operation and production control) level systems performance. The remaining 27 percent of the organizations surveyed have such systems. Although all categories of organizations have some technology-intensive systems, these systems are most common in businesses characterized by large volumes of transaction data, such as financial institutions and retail/wholesale firms. While the use of advanced technology for its sheer number-crunching ability may be cost effective, these organizations are not realizing the full potential of their computers.

For organizations that plan to upgrade systems performance, the survey suggested that the area most in need of improvement is decision support. The average MIS decision-support capability is only 30 percent of the maximum possible score, the lowest of all systems performance characteristics. It is particularly ironic that MIS, which were predicted by some to take over organizational decision making, should be the weakest in this most-important managerial function.

*See also* COMPUTER SYSTEMS; CONTROL SYSTEMS, MANAGEMENT; DATA PROCESSING PRINCIPLES AND PRACTICES; INFORMATION SYSTEMS, MANAGEMENT (MIS); INFORMATION SYSTEMS, MANAGEMENT (MIS), APPLIED; SYSTEM CONCEPT, TOTAL.

## NOTE

[1] From a study of 153 large organizations in an unpublished doctoral dissertation by Donald W. Kroeber, University of Georgia, 1976.

DONALD W. KROEBER, *James Madison University*

## Information systems, marketing  (*See* MARKETING INFORMATION SYSTEMS.)

## Informational conferences  (*See* CONFERENCE LEADERSHIP.)

## Injury frequency rate formula  (*See* SAFETY AND HEALTH MANAGEMENT, EMPLOYEE.)

## Injury severity rate formula  (*See* SAFETY AND HEALTH MANAGEMENT, EMPLOYEE.)

## Innovation  (*See* CONSUMER BEHAVIOR, MANAGERIAL RELEVANCE OF.)

## Innovation and creativity

A distinction can be made between innovation and invention that helps clarify the meaning of innovation.

An *invention* is literally a creation, a new device or method, or a new idea. Or, if one believes that there is no such thing as a truly new idea, an invention is a new application or a new way of using existing knowledge. The use of fluoride to prevent tooth decay was a new application—an invention.

*Innovation,* by contrast, is concerned with introduction. Innovation is the process of bringing a new idea or new application into general use. If the fluoride idea was an invention, then Crest toothpaste became an innovation.

**Distinguishing Characteristics** Innovation differs from invention in three important ways:

1. Innovation and invention are the same in that both are creative activities, but innovation is the more general activity. Invention is a creative *event;*

innovation is a creative *process*. Innovation begins with an invention and then introduces that invention into general use. The computer was an invention, but the application of that invention to handle the information needs of the firm has been an innovation.

2. Innovation applies to many areas in the organization. It is commonly thought of in connection with new product development, but it applies more broadly than this. It is common also, for example, in production, distribution, and financial management.

3. The importance of innovation, in contrast to invention, is often underestimated. In many organizational settings the challenge lies not in generating new ideas, but in finding and fostering the ability to introduce those ideas into general use. There is a saying among salespeople that "nothing happens until somebody sells something" that has its parallel in the invention/innovation field. No invention is worth much until someone persuades other people to use it. Innovation is the process of persuading people to adopt an invention.

**Innovation versus Sustaining Operations** Another insight into the problems involved in managing innovation is to contrast it with maintenance, or sustaining, operations. The dominant concern of most organizations is the sustaining of current operations rather than innovation. Sustaining operations are concerned with today—with generating profits or output to serve the needs of today. Innovation is concerned with tomorrow—with making sure that there is a continuing profit stream in the future. Innovation and sustaining operations are inextricably linked: the profits from sustaining today's operations ensure the survival of the organization and provide the resources that make innovation, tomorrow's activity, possible.

Innovation and sustaining operations, however, are different in important ways:

1. Innovation is a highly creative process, highly qualitative, highly unstructured; sustaining operations are disciplined and lend themselves to quantification.

2. Maintenance operations outcomes are more predictable than innovation. Innovation activities, because they do not lend themselves to precise forecasts, are far riskier.

3. Sustaining operations are immediate and create demands for immediate action. Innovation is postponable because it is concerned with tomorrow. Innovation and sustaining operations are often not compatible because of this difference; the immediacy of sustaining operations tends to crowd out or force postponement of innovation activities.

**Inherent Problems** The problem in managing innovation stems from the fact that most organizations are designed for management of maintenance or sustaining operations. This is only natural since business organizations are in business to do business and that usually means to take care of today's customer needs. The consideration of innovation is not meant to diminish the importance of maintenance management since it is absolutely essential to the survival of the firm that it efficiently manage its ongoing business. The problem arises when management attempts to impose that ongoing management approach on the *other* activity of the organization—innovation.

Maintenance management systems have characteristics that do not apply very well to problems of innovation.

1. Maintenance management systems are fairly rigid and have a rather well-defined structure. Jobs tend to be clearly and rather narrowly defined. Work is divided functionally so as to carry out the process of specialization to improve the efficiency of the firm.

2. Maintenance management systems establish an orderly process for handling work because the work is repetitive and predictable. To handle this kind of work, the organization tends to utilize people with orderly minds who can cope with repetitive activities. Survival demands that this work be efficiently performed, and this means that performance must be tightly controlled and work performance measured. This is possible because the work flows are predictable.

These systems do not work well when applied to management of innovation. Both the process and the people involved are different. It requires, therefore, a different management system attuned to the needs of the job to be done. This means a different structure and a different approach.

**Successful Management of Innovation** A management system designed to support the process of innovation must be attuned to the nature of innovation and the nature of innovators. Both the process and the people are creative. An effective system will include these 10 essential characteristics:

1. Less structure. The organization for innovation must have an open structure that encourages the creative process. Creativity is concerned with doing things differently and thinking about things differently. It must not be inhibited by the barriers of a maintenance management structure. This openness is consistent with the personality and style of the people—entrepreneurs—who must be supported by the innovative organization. Entrepreneurs, the people who carry out innovation in an

organization, are creative, work across disciplines, and are accustomed to dealing with uncertainty. Their efforts will not flourish in an inhibiting organization structure.

2. Separation from maintenance responsibilities. The innovation system must be separated from the sustaining organization. It is concerned with different tasks—one is concerned with today; the other with tomorrow—and it requires different skills. If the maintenance organization is joined with the innovative organization, the immediacy of maintenance problems will drive out the concern for building tomorrow.

3. An interdisciplinary, not functional, structure. The problems facing the innovator are highly complex and require the application of multiple disciplines. The innovative organization must be interdisciplinary in its makeup. This means more than just having multiple disciplines available when needed. The interdisciplinary approach requires the *simultaneous involvement* of all relevant disciplines so that each problem in the innovative process is considered and solved in the broadest light. As a practical guide, the innovative organization cannot be structured along functional lines; it must be a task-oriented structure containing each of the relevant disciplines.

4. Top management commitment. The biggest barrier to success in innovation is the lack of continuing commitment from top management. Top management must believe in the importance of innovation in shaping the future of the organization yet, at the same time, accept the risk that innovation efforts may fail. Acceptance of risk and the building of commitment can best be accomplished by continuing participation of top management in the process of innovation. This participation must go beyond the initial stages to a long-term involvement. To accomplish this, the innovation managers must have a direct and unhindered reporting relationship to the principal decision makers in the firm.

5. Continuity of senior professionals. The innovative organization must be staffed with senior professionals; it should not be treated as a training ground. The job demands experience both because of risks involved and the importance of success. Maintaining continuity of senior professionals in the innovative organization requires an incentive and advancement system that establishes long-term career potential for innovation positions.

6. Acceptance of qualitative control. The output of the innovation process rarely is predictable and does not lend itself to quantitative control. It is essential that the management system accept, par-

ticularly during the early stages of the innovation process, a control system that is qualitatively based. The control standards cannot be based on output, profit, or cost control. Instead, they should focus on the timeliness of decisions, the momentum of the process, and the quality of the development work.

7. Decision pressure. Despite the absence of quantitative control mechanisms, it is also essential that pressure for progress be maintained in the innovative organization. This is probably best accomplished by insisting that decisions be made and milestones reached according to compressed schedules. To accomplish this, decision-making ability must be located within the innovative organization so that communication lines are short and there is little opportunity to defer decisions by pushing them upstairs. The organization's ability to make timely decisions is an important incentive to the innovative group and an important measure of its productivity.

8. Entrepreneurial incentive. The successful system must attract entrepreneurs—professionals who are able to accept marketplace risk and who are committed to successful introduction. The management system must contain incentives that will attract these extremely rare, yet highly prized, innovators. While the innovative organization must recognize the high risk of failure, the innovative system must reward success and drive the entrepreneurs to the decisions that will bring inventions into general use.

9. Entrepreneurial leadership. The innovative organization needs strong leadership that will motivate, encourage, and push the professional innovators. The innovative organization needs a zealot, an individual committed to pressing forward, an individual who understands how to use persuasion to get decisions made and to sustain organizational commitment to innovation.

10. Consumer orientation. The system must recognize that products do not make markets: markets make products. The organization and the individuals in the organization must have strong marketing skills, sensitivity to the consumer, and a willingness to accept the risks of the marketplace. The innovative process must begin with the consumer or the user and work back to the drawing board to generate an idea or an application that will solve a real rather than a make-believe problem.

*See also* COMMUNICATIONS, ORGANIZATIONAL; CONFORMITY IN MANAGEMENT; DECISION-MAKING PROCESS; PRODUCT PLANNING AND DEVELOPMENT; PROJECT AND TASK FORCE MANAGEMENT; RESEARCH AND DEVELOPMENT MANAGEMENT.

## REFERENCES

Gee, Edwin A., and Tyler Chaplin: *Managing Innovation*, Interscience Publishers, a division of John Wiley & Sons, Inc., New York, 1976.

Kunstler, Donald A.: *Corporate Venture Groups: The Need, the Responsibility, the Organization, the Leadership*, American Marketing Association, Fall Conference Proceedings, Chicago, ser. 28, 1968, pp. 449–454.

Levitt, Theodore: *Innovation in Marketing*, McGraw-Hill Book Company, New York, 1962.

———: *The Marketing Mode*, McGraw-Hill Book Company, New York, 1969.

Rothberg, Robert R.: "Product Innovation in Perspective," in Robert R. Rothberg, ed., *Corporate Strategy and Product Innovation*, The Free Press, New York, 1976, pp. 3–13.

Schon, Donald R.: "Managing Technological Innovation," *Harvard Business Review*, vol. 47, no. 3, pp. 156–167, May–June 1969.

Schumpeter, J. A.: *Theory of Economic Development*, Harvard University Press, Cambridge, Mass., 1934.

Steiner, Gary A., ed.: *The Creative Organization*, The University of Chicago Press, Chicago, 1969.

DAVID W. NYLEN, *Booz·Allen Venture Management, Inc.*

# Input-output analysis

*Input-output analysis* is a technique developed by the Harvard economist Wassily Leontief for measuring the effect of interindustry transactions on (1) the economy and (2) individual industries.

Figure I-3*a*, shows a simplified input-output table in which each industry is designated by a number. (Only 15 are shown for purposes of illustration, whereas an actual table may cover several hundred.) *D* stands for total demand and *T* for total output; *H* designates household services, which are industry requirements other than those for products from suppliers—requirements for labor, for example. Inputs *I* are read from the vertical columns; outputs *O* are read from the horizontal columns.

Each industry uses part of its output for itself and delivers another part to final demand (which includes demand for export), while the remainder goes to the other industries appearing above it in the vertical column, as shown in Fig. I-3*b*, which is simply a rearrangement of Fig. I-3*a*. This rearrangement of the order in which the industries are listed will, in the case of an advanced industrialized country, produce the triangular pattern shown in Fig. I-3*b*, and from this it is possible to calculate how an increase in demand for the products of one industry will affect the demand for the products of its suppliers. Any increase in the demand for the

output of one industry "cascades," as Leontief has said, down the triangle, affecting all the industries below it. Thus, if the demand for the products of industry 9 increases, industry 4, which is its supplier, will experience an increase in demand and will, in turn, purchase more from industry 3, and so on.

Part A

| O\I | 1 | 2 | 3 | 4 | 5 | 6 | 7 | 8 | 9 | 10 | 11 | 12 | 13 | 14 | 15 | D | T |
|---|---|---|---|---|---|---|---|---|---|---|---|---|---|---|---|---|---|

Part B

| O\I | 9 | 4 | 3 | 10 | 13 | 5 | 11 | 1 | 12 | 7 | 14 | 2 | 6 | 15 | 8 | D | T |
|---|---|---|---|---|---|---|---|---|---|---|---|---|---|---|---|---|---|

**Fig. I-3. Examples of input-output tables. (Adapted from Wassily Leontief, "The Structure of Development," *Scientific American*, September 1963, pp 148–166. With permission of the copyright holder.)**

Of course, the increases in demand for the products of the supplier industries are not equal to the increases experienced by the customer industries above them, but coefficients have been developed to determine the effects on the supplier industries.

It has been found that all advanced economies, such as those of the United States and the industrialized countries of Western Europe, will exhibit a triangular pattern on an input-output table, whereas a table for a less-developed country will show a more-random design.

The U.S. Department of Commerce has developed input-output tables for the U.S. economy, and governments of other countries, including some of the less-developed countries, have also charted the interindustry patterns of their economies. These tables, of course, give industry names and the actual figures for the transactions.

*See also* ECONOMIC CONCEPTS; ECONOMIC MEASUREMENTS; FORECASTING BUSINESS CONDITIONS.

### REFERENCES

"The Input-Output Structure of the U.S. Economy: 1967," *Survey of Current Business*, February 1974, pp. 24–50.

Leontief, Wassily: *Input-Output Economics*, Oxford University Press, New York, 1966.

STAFF/SMITH

**Inputs, economic**  (*See* PRODUCTIVITY.)

**Inputs, production**  (*See* PRODUCTION/OPERATIONS MANAGEMENT.)

**Insecticide, Fungicide, and Rodenticide Act, Federal**  (*See* ENVIRONMENTAL PROTECTION LEGISLATION.)

**Inspection**  (*See* QUALITY MANAGEMENT.)

**Inspection symbol**  (*See* WORK SIMPLIFICATION AND IMPROVEMENT.)

**Installment sales accounting**  (*See* ACCOUNTING, FINANCIAL.)

**Institutional and public administration**  (*See heading in Table of Contents for complete listing.*)

**Institutional management**  (*See* HOSPITALITY MANAGEMENT.)

**Institutional managers**  (*See* MANAGER, DEFINITIONS OF.)

**Institutions, health**  (*See* HEALTH INSTITUTIONS, MANAGEMENT OF; HOSPITAL ADMINISTRATION.)

**Institutions, nonprofit**  (*See* NOT-FOR-PROFIT ORGANIZATIONS, MANAGEMENT OF.)

**Institutions, retail**  (*See* MARKETING CHANNELS OF DISTRIBUTION.)

**Instruction, programmed**  (*See* PROGRAMMED INSTRUCTION.)

**Insurance, group and employee**  (*See* COMPENSATION, EMPLOYEE BENEFIT PLANS.)

**Insurance, title**  (*See* REAL ESTATE MANAGEMENT.)

## Insurance and risk management

No matter how well management sets its goals and executes its plans, the goals may be thwarted by unplanned events such as fires, hurricanes, liability suits, embezzlement, and other fortuitous losses. It was to fit the management of these risks of loss into the larger framework of general management that the techniques of risk management have evolved.

**Risk Management Defined**  After initial opposition from those who felt its use would conflict with other concepts of business risks, the term *risk management* has now achieved general acceptance as referring to pure, rather than business, risks. It can be defined as the art of selecting methods of loss control, risk finance (including insurance), and internal administration which develop the lowest long-term total cost of risk to the organization.

*Loss control* refers to preventive measures taken by the organization under the direct or indirect supervision of the risk manager to control all fortuitous losses. It encompasses fire protection, personnel safety, security, and control of claims adjusting.

*Risk finance* refers to techniques used to fund known or anticipated losses. The most-common technique is insurance, but other techniques include bank lines of credit, formal or informal pooling of risks among members of a single industry, and chronological stabilization plans. The latter, sometimes referred to as "spread-loss plans," are similar to insurance but call for the insured to repay, over a period of years, claims which are paid. *Chronological stabilization* is thus a method of leveling high losses which occur in one year over subsequent years where losses may be lower, thus enabling concerns to assume a higher degree of risk than would be the case under pure insurance.

*Internal administration* of risk is concerned with (1) record-keeping of losses and values, (2) communications regarding claims and loss-prevention procedures, (3) preparation and administration of corporate policy and manuals, (4) allocation of risk costs among operating units, and (5) administrative aspects of insurance purchasing.

**Property** Risks of property loss are both direct and indirect.

*Direct loss* is (1) the amount the physical asset is diminished in value, as measured by the actual cash value (replacement cost less physical depreciation) or (2) the amount actually required to replace the destroyed property (replacement cost). To minimize cash-flow fluctuations, most organizations now insure on a replacement cost basis. Direct losses can occur to buildings, equipment, stock, vehicles, accounts receivable, valuable papers, boilers, cash, securities, cargo shipments, and any other tangible property.

*Indirect losses* include (1) loss of income, also known as business interruption, or the obsolescent term *use and occupancy;* (2) extra expenses (additional costs incurred to maintain activities as nearly normal as possible following destruction of property); and (3) loss of rent, loss of tuition fees, salesworker's commissions, power outage.

*Disaster control* is an element of risk management which establishes guides and procedures to follow when a fire, earthquake, airplane crash, or other disaster occurs. The risk manager should anticipate all possible cases and develop plans for immediate salvage and for communication with fire departments, police, the press, and important company officials. The plan should be followed up periodically to see that emergency supplies are intact and all parties are familiar with procedures.

**Personnel** The principal source of loss to personnel is on-the-job injuries, for which all states have statutory requirements for paying workers' compensation. Other sources of personnel loss are illnesses or off-the-job accidents, alcoholism, drug misuse, and strikes. Personnel safety is an important subject closely interwoven with government requirements (such as those from OSHA), labor relations (labor contracts often have references to safety), and insurance. Technical assistance is often available from insurance carriers and their agents or brokers. It is the risk manager's job to act as advisor and coordinator to all persons involved with the safety program to see that undue emphasis is not given to one aspect at the expense of others.

The safety function seems predominantly to be with the labor relations department of a large organization, although many are now placing it under the direction of the risk manager.

**Liability** The importance of public liability has grown enormously in recent years. The public has become increasingly aware that those whose negligence causes a loss can be held legally responsible. The courts have even gone beyond pure negligence and are holding many organizations legally responsible for damage where no negligence can be proved. This is reflected in the growing number of law suits and in the increasing amount of awards. Multimillion dollar judgments to single individuals are no longer rare.

The result has been to seriously undermine the stability of many important enterprises. The most prominent example is that of medical malpractice. Insurance companies underwriting this line have almost uniformly lost money and withdrawn from the field. Those few remaining must charge premiums so high that they are prohibitive to many doctors and hospitals. As a result many hospitals have formed their own insurance company, and a significant number of doctors have placed their assets in outside trusts and are going without any insurance.

*Product liability* seems to be following close behind medical malpractice. Manufacturers are being held to an almost absolute standard of care: suits are being judged against a manufacturer even if all reasonable precautions were used. Retailers and lessors who have no part to play in the safety of the product are also being held responsible. (*See* PRODUCT LIABILITY.)

*Municipal liability* is also growing at such a rate as to cause some cities and counties to go without insurance and others to form pools in which to handle their losses.

The conventional liabilities have to do with bodily injury and property damage. The increasing emphasis on professionalism has also caused increased liability for professional acts. Persons who hold themselves as experts in any recognized professional line have been held responsible for failure to carry out their professional duties in an acceptable manner. Engineers, architects, accountants, attorneys, and many other professionals have considerable exposures to such loss for which professional liability insurance may be, but is not always, available.

An important aspect of professional liability is that which directors and officers of corporations owe to stockholders and the public. Insurance on a limited basis for this type of claim is available, and most large corporations purchase the insurance.

**Insurance** Most of the risk manager's emphasis is placed on negotiating insurance within adequate limits, with coverage broad enough to include as many catastrophic losses as possible but not so complete as to insure minor losses which the organization could fund without insurance. Most organizations can readily absorb individual losses up to at least one-tenth of 1 percent of their annual revenues, but where the loss potential exceeds the tolerable level, insurance is desirable.

The risk manager's first step is to select a skilled agent or broker. The manager then communicates to the agent or broker (jointly called *producers*) just what the needs are. In this process, the manager may be given considerable assistance by the producer or specialized consultant.

*Property insurance* is normally placed in several different contracts: (1) fire and extended coverage (wind, explosion, hail, aircraft, riot, vehicles, and smoke); (2) boiler and machinery; (3) crime (including employee fidelity, money, securities, and forgeries); and (4) difference in conditions (extends coverage to all risks rather than named perils and may or may not include earthquake and flood).

*Liability insurance* is usually separated into primary and excess.

*Primary policies* cover all claims up to the primary limit, varying from about $100,000 to $500,000. Primary policies can be written for general premises, manufacturers and contractors, automobile, aircraft, professional (errors and omissions) liability, directors and officers, and many others. The most effective primary policy is the comprehensive

general automobile policy which provides the broadest coverage of any of the primary policies.

*The umbrella excess-liability policy* is then used to ride above all the primary policies, increasing their limits to the desired limit and providing even broader coverage than the primaries, subject to a major self-insured retention—at least $10,000. Most concerns are well advised to carry limits in excess of $5 million. Catastrophe protection is the most important function of insurance, and the higher limits are relatively inexpensive.

**Insurance Carriers** There are four kinds of insurance carriers: stock, mutual, reciprocal, and Lloyd's. The organizational form is of little concern to the risk manager because there are strong and weak companies in all categories. *Stock companies* are owned by private investors and constitute the greatest percent of insurers. *Mutual companies* are owned by the policy holders and usually pay dividends to the policy holders. *Reciprocal organizations* are similar to mutuals but act through an attorney in fact. The *Lloyd's organization* is one consisting of many individuals, by far the most prominent of which is Lloyd's of London, who operate worldwide in almost all lines.

Insurance carriers can also be subdivided into those who write only through agents and brokers and those who write directly with the policy holders. Most stock companies are agency companies, but some write direct. Many mutual companies are direct writers, but many also write exclusively through producers. Lloyd's works only through brokers.

Selection of the insurer is an important function which the risk manager must assume. Considerable help can be obtained from producers, and the insured may want to retain the producer for advice even when dealing directly with the insurer, in which case the insured pays the producer a fee in lieu of the commission he or she would normally receive.

**Self-insurance** The growing costs of insurance have directed management's attention to the fact that insurance is not an economical way to handle small losses. Interest in self-insuring the lower levels has grown. The most prominent subjects for self-insurance are workers' compensation (relatively high-frequency, low-magnitude losses), automobile physical damage, money and securities, plate glass, medical payments, and low-valued properties. Although property and workers' compensation were the first areas to receive self-insurance emphasis, growing interest in public liability self-insurance has led to the formation of many service firms whose sole function is to provide claims adjusting and other related services to self-insurers. The judicious selection of self-insurance service companies, loss-prevention specialists, and properly worded excess insurance is an increasingly important aspect of the risk manager's responsibility.

**Legal**  The risk manager works within a structure of statewide insurance regulations. United States insurance companies must meet varying state requirements for forms of coverage and rates they may charge. In some cases, this impedes their flexibility for the larger or more complex account, who then turns to the "surplus lines" or "nonadmitted" market. This consists of United States or foreign insurers not licensed in the state involved.

In large measure to by-pass this restrictive regulation, many large industrial firms have formed their own insurance companies—usually headquartered outside the United States, principally in Bermuda. These wholly owned insurance subsidiaries allow the risk manager direct access to the worldwide reinsurance market which offers more flexible terms. They also may assume reinsurance from other insurers and develop a profit center.

The risk manager frequently works in tandem with the firm's legal advisors in analyzing major contracts and leases. The manager is concerned with provisions which require insurance as well as indemnity (hold-harmless) agreements, whereby one party assumes liability of the other. These contract conditions must be carefully coordinated with insurance coverage.

**Summary**  Every organization has a risk manager whose duties may range from the simple purchase of property and liability insurance to the most complex arrangements of internal funding, captive insurance companies, contract claims, and loss-prevention services and worldwide accounting functions. In a small organization it may be the president who makes the decisions. In a larger organization it is usually the chief financial officer or a full-time risk manager reporting to the chief financial officer, though other orientations are used. The risk manager's work cuts across all lines of the organization. The manager must be aware of everything going on as well as plans for the future. The manager's background must be strong in insurance but should also include finance, accounting, engineering, and law. The goal of this responsibility is that of the organization itself: long-term conservation of assets and maximum profitability.

*See also* FINANCIAL MANAGEMENT; PRODUCT LIABILITY; REAL ESTATE MANAGEMENT, CORPORATE; RISK ANALYSIS AND MANAGEMENT.

## REFERENCES

Lenz, M., Jr.: *Risk Management Manual*, The Merritt Co., Santa Monica, Calif.

MacDonald, Donald L.: *Corporate Risk Control*, The Ronald Press Company, New York, 1966.

Mehr, R. I., and B. A. Hedges: *Risk Management: Concepts and Applications*, Richard D. Irwin, Inc., Homewood, Ill., 1974.

*Practical Risk Management*, Warren, McVeigh, and Griffin, San Francisco, Calif.

Williams, C. A., Jr., and R. M. Heins, *Risk Management and Insurance*, 3d ed., McGraw-Hill Book Company, New York, 1976.

DAVID WARREN, *Warren, McVeigh, and Griffin*

**Insurance management**  (*See* INSURANCE AND RISK MANAGEMENT.)

**Insurance plans, executive**  (*See* COMPENSATION, EXECUTIVE.)

**Integrational authority**  (*See* AUTHORITY, RESPONSIBILITY, AND ACCOUNTABILITY.)

**Intelligence, market**  (*See* MARKETING RESEARCH.)

**Interdependence, organizational**  (*See* ORGANIZATION STRUCTURES AND CHARTING.)

**Interest**  (*See* ECONOMIC MEASUREMENTS.)

**Interest rates**  (*See* CREDIT MANAGEMENT.)

**Interest tests**  (*See* TESTING, PSYCHOLOGICAL.)

**Interference, patent**  (*See* PATENTS AND VALUABLE INTANGIBLE RIGHTS.)

**Intergroup merging**  [*See* ORGANIZATION DEVELOPMENT (OD).]

### Intermediaries  (*See* MARKETING, CHANNELS OF DISTRIBUTION.)

### Intermodal (transportation) systems (*See* DISTRIBUTION, PHYSICAL.)

### Internal audit  (*See* AUDIT, MANAGEMENT.)

### Internal rate of return method  (*See* BUDGETING, CAPITAL.)

### International management, Japanese (*See* JAPANESE INDUSTRIES, MANAGEMENT IN.)

### International management, Western Europe  (*See* EUROPE, MANAGEMENT IN WESTERN.)

### International operations  (*See* heading in *Table of Contents for complete listing.*)

## International operations and management in multinational companies

A multinational company cannot operate effectively without a well-conceived philosophy to guide the people who manage its operations. Successful operations proceed from organizations that uniquely suit the individual company in its international market-place. A planning and reporting system consisting of a planning cycle and a development and reporting cycle is a most essential element. Four major functions—industrial relations, public relations, finance, and legal administration—deserve particular attention in international business. Finally, everything must be tied together by formulating written statements which set forth the various elements of the company's policy.

### AN INTERNATIONAL BUSINESS PHILOSOPHY STATEMENT

Managing and directing business operations on a worldwide basis is one of the greatest challenges confronting multinational corporations today. New and expanding markets offer opportunities for business growth on a global basis. Throughout much of

**536**

the world, rising economic and social goals, together with heightened levels of individual awareness and expectation, demand goods and services on an unprecedented scale. With these new opportunities have come new responsibilities both to the host countries and to their economic, political, and social institutions.

As a starting point for entering the international arena, a company must first develop an underlying philosophy. This philosophy statement sets forth the fundamental convictions and commitments the company will adopt in meeting its unique responsibilities in the worldwide market. Equally important, the statement provides sound, constructive guidelines for corporate management of its international operations. An example of one such statement, which could apply to almost any multinational or international company, appears in Table I-5.

### FORMS OF INTERNATIONAL ORGANIZATION

Selection of the proper form of organization is critical to the success of multinational operations. Before describing three possible forms of organization—out of a myriad of possibilities—it is important to recognize the following:

1. The organization form must be structured so as to meet the needs of the individual company in terms of its own philosophies, strategies, objectives, priorities, markets, products, and technologies.

2. The organization form is and must be dynamic and evolutionary in nature; i.e., it must be flexible enough to be adjusted as the aims of the company change and as market conditions change. As a result, the risks inherent in rigid adherence to a formal organization chart can be minimized.

3. In a multinational, multimarket, multitechnology company, the organization form must provide for and accommodate efficient, timely dissemination and flow of information.

4. The form of organization must be determined and built from the bottom up rather than from the top down.

Certain organization forms are used more often than others. Three, in particular, warrant consideration.

*International Company or International Profit Center.* This approach is best suited to the single product line company or to the company utilizing common fundamental technology across a number of product lines. The markets served are most often similar, if not identical, in nature. Typical characteristics of this form of organization are:

**TABLE I-5  Example of International Business Philosophy Statement**

1. *International business responsibilities*
    a. We are dedicated to search worldwide for new products, services, markets, joint ventures, and acquisitions that add to our capabilities to move the corporation forward. We recognize that operations on a worldwide basis will have an ever-increasing role in our future growth. Consequently, we are charged with the responsibility of developing our business planning, manufacturing, and marketing in the perspective of the global marketplace.
    b. We shall be aware of, and responsible to, the impact our operations have on host countries, and we shall promote a successful long-term relationship with the host nations in which we operate. We shall strive to contribute to their economic development through the introduction of advanced technology, management planning and control systems, marketing know-how, and the training and promotion of qualified national personnel.
    c. Within the framework of our organization, the operating groups have individual product and profit responsibility on a worldwide basis, unless otherwise assigned to a multiproduct, multimarket geographical organization. Corporate-level coordination and policy guidance will be provided by the office of the president, which must be informed at all times of matters which might affect the corporation's overall business practices or reputation.
2. *Investments*
    a. Based on sound economic planning, the corporation intends to make investments on a long-term basis. Where economically viable, we shall invest in productive facilities to enhance our opportunity for continued growth and expansion. Investment decisions will take into account such factors as opportunities within the host country markets, exports from host country operations, sources of supply, possibilities for volume production, operating economics, and the availability of a trained or trainable work force.
    b. Should it become impractical to continue an operation for whatever reason, we shall make every effort to minimize any adverse impact on the host country.
    c. The support and cooperation of host governments are prerequisites of long-range growth and development. We look to host governments to promulgate policies and regulations on a fair and nondiscriminatory basis, to establish sufficient opportunity for reinvestment and expansion, and to provide for repatriation of earnings on an equitable basis.
    d. We recognize our responsibility to accept reasonable obligations that are placed upon business enterprises in the national interest. We shall respect the sovereign rights, customs, laws, and regulations of our host governments. Our local managements will be expected to make full use of the legal facilities of the corporation to assure compliance with the host country's statutory requirements.
3. *Markets, customers, and suppliers*
    a. As we participate in new or expanding international markets, we shall endeavor to develop and market products and services which are specifically tailored for host country markets and which are produced in the most economical manner possible. Underlying this important responsibility is our firm obligation to take every step to maintain our high standards of product quality and design as well as to service our customers in a manner superior to our competition.
    b. We shall utilize host country suppliers to the greatest degree possible where price, quality, delivery, and service meet our requirements for being a low-cost manufacturer.
    c. In our dealings with customers, the only factors to be considered are quality, price, delivery, and service. It is not our policy to utilize the corporation's position as a purchaser to promote sales. Conversely, a supplier's position as a customer is not a factor to be considered when making purchases.
4. *Research and technology*
    a. A key element in achieving our corporate goal is a steady outflow of innovative, high-technology products for our worldwide markets. In technology, as in manufacturing and marketing, we recognize the global challenge we face in maintaining a competitive position. To realize the maximum advantage from our technical competency and experience, we shall exchange technology from operation to operation, without regard to location, wherever possible. When technology is exchanged between two countries, each operation should benefit by improved profitability. By sharing technical skills and experiences, all operating units are made stronger and better able to achieve their goals.
5. *Facilities*
    a. Our operations will be located wherever it is economically sound to do so, recognizing that facilities are constructed and expanded to support local market needs, as well as to provide an enlarging basis for export to regional and area markets. Where feasible, multiproduct plants that can manufacture products for more than one market will be utilized.
6. *Human resources*
    a. We consider our human resources the essential element in the continuing success of the corporation. Wherever in the world our men and women are located, we are pledged to the following standards:
        (1) We shall strive always to attract, develop, and motivate people who demonstrate willingness, intelligence, and strong moral fiber in carrying out their responsibilities.
        (2) We shall hire, train, and promote qualified national personnel at all levels of the operation to the greatest extent possible. Race, color, creed, national origin, age, and sex will not be factors influencing our decisions on employment and advancement.

*(Table continued on next page)*

TABLE 1-5  Example of International Business Philosophy Statement  (*Continued*)

 (3) One of our highest priorities is the development of our employees, at all levels, to enhance their personal opportunities for career development.

 (4) Mutual respect and trust, prerequisites of effective teamwork, are basic to our ability to compete. This means taking the initiative in developing wholesome and productive working environments which recognize the importance of human dignity in a person's satisfaction with job and life.

 (5) We shall encourage two-way communications with all employees. Employees should be informed about matters that affect them or their jobs, management's position on relevant issues, and corporate actions which materially influence their long-range interests.

 (6) Our objective is to establish and administer wage and benefit programs which are equal to or above industry practices and national norms.

7. *Finance*

 *a.* As a multinational corporation, we are necessarily involved in dealing in many of the world's currencies and in currency exchange. It is our policy to act to protect the corporation and its subsidiaries against exchange losses but not to seek speculative gains through currency transactions or similar activities unrelated to the nature of our business.

 *b.* Funds required for working capital and the growth of international operations should, where possible, be provided by borrowing in local currencies to protect against currency exchange losses and to avoid the complexity of currency conversions and exchange restrictions.

8. *Conflict of interest*

 Employees who are in a position to influence decisions must be aware of our policy concerning matters that may constitute a conflict of interest.

9. *Public responsibility*

 *a.* We believe our existence in the long term, and our role today in the many countries in which we operate, is dependent upon responsible citizenship in those societies. We have an obligation to use our resources in a manner which furthers an economically and socially healthy environment within our host countries.

 *b.* We shall conduct business in a manner which conveys the image of good neighbors and responsible, contributing citizens to our communities, governments, and the environment. Our objectives and accomplishments will be weighed by the measure of their contribution to the fulfillment of our social responsibility.

 *c.* In all cases, we shall abide by the spirit and letter of the local laws and customs of our host countries.

 *d.* Political contributions may be made only when permitted by the laws and regulations of the countries involved. All significant contributions must be approved in advance by the appropriate United States headquarters authority.

 *e.* Public positions on issues relating to business operations will be communicated only through appropriate channels and in a manner consistent with corporate policy. We shall refrain from any involvement in partisan politcal activity or interference with national political decisions.

1. Each international region has a senior operating executive in charge, reporting to the president who has responsibility for overall coordination.

2. The president has senior staff executives who provide specialized assistance to the regional executives as well as set and control policy in their respective functional areas. Senior staff executives report to the president.

3. Each region operates as a profit center within the company, and the company itself is an international profit center.

4. Finished products and components for the finished products often are transferred between regions on an intercompany basis.

5. The majority of the technology utilized is developed by the parent company. The same is true for systems and procedures; therefore, information flow and communication do not represent major problems, inasmuch as "common languages" are employed.

6. It is important to guard against duplicating functions in the international company where those functions are performed best in the parent company.

*Divisional Worldwide Profit and Product Responsibility.* This approach is best suited to the multiproduct, multimarket, multitechnology company where the application of the products is of paramount importance. Typical characteristics of this form of organization are:

1. The parent company is organized by product-oriented operating groups or divisions. The products in each division are related by technology and/or market.

2. Each operating division functions as a separate company, even though it is subject to overall corporate policy and broad directional control.

3. Each operating division has a worldwide responsibility for product and profit; therefore, it has its own international operations organization. It justifies and establishes its own international ventures and facilities.

4. The vast majority of the technology is developed at the home base.

5. Information flow and communications are facilitated because common products are dealt with on a worldwide basis.

6. An inherent problem in this form of organization is the tendency toward building excess productive and/or marketing capacity in a particular country or region.

*Geographic Area Administrative and Coordinating Organization.* This approach is best suited to the multiproduct, multimarket, multitechnology company which recognizes the need to provide overall guidance and policy control within each major geographic area to the various groups and divisions operating within that area. Typical characteristics of this form of organization are:

1. A relatively small group of highly competent executives are headquartered in a major geographic international area. These executives have the area product and profit responsibilities for the products produced by several of the corporation's divisions.

2. The products for which area executives have responsibility are common (or compatible) in the areas of technology and/or manufacturing and/or marketing and/or application.

3. Multiproduct marketing organizations are utilized.

4. Multiproduct manufacturing plants are utilized in order to minimize excess productive capacity.

5. Technology develops and flows both from the home base to the international geographic area and vice versa.

6. Communications and flow of information will be two of the most difficult—and yet two of the most important—aspects of the organization form.

## PLANNING AND REPORTING SYSTEM

The planning cycle, coupled with a development and reporting cycle, provides the basic framework for a planning and reporting system through which the international executive can manage the operations.

*Consistency and Comparability.* Two necessary factors which must be present to ensure that the planning and reporting system functions correctly are consistency and comparability between the reports from various countries. Accounting procedures vary greatly among countries, and it is necessary in most cases to maintain two sets of books. One set will follow the accounting requirements of the country in which the business is operating; and the other will follow the procedures of the country of the parent company. It is important that each operation maintain one set of books which is consistent in accounting procedure with the parent company. In this way, once the effects of translation are eliminated, the results from various countries will be comparable. An essential element in establishing these consistent procedures is to have a uniform chart of accounts to be utilized in the common financial statements.

With the advent of widespread use of floating exchange rates, the fluctuations in foreign exchange rates have caused considerable difficulties for companies with international operations. Accounting practices in the United States require that actual foreign exchange gains or losses be taken during the current period. This can have a significant effect on the planning process. A variety of methods are available to adjust for foreign currency fluctuations. These include (1) restating the original plan to current rates for comparison with current operating results or (2) providing a variance analysis to the original plan indicating the variance due to foreign exchange fluctuations. Regardless of the method used, the foreign exchange fluctuations should be taken into account for planning purposes.

**Planning Cycle**   As shown in the upper portion of Fig. I-4, both the long-term (5-year) growth plan and the short-term (annual) profit plan are dependent upon three separate annual reviews.

The purpose of the *cost/price review* is to project wage and material cost increases. This will lead in turn to the sales price increases and/or the manufacturing and engineering and product cost decreases necessary to maintain or increase profitabilty. The cost/price review provides input into the evaluation of prices and costs to be built into both the long-term growth plan and the short-term profit plan.

The *product development review* consists of a formal review of all major in-house product development projects. The review includes the project objectives; an evaluation of the product with reference to competitive products; and a market review, including projected sales trends for the next 5 years, market share, earnings, and return on investment, as well as a projection of the project expense plus associated capital required.

The purpose of the *departmental* (both operating and staff) *improvement project review* is to identify major areas of cost or expense and to develop programs to reduce the costs and/or to improve efficiency. Such programs name persons who are responsible for accomplishing definite project steps leading to specific results within a given period of time.

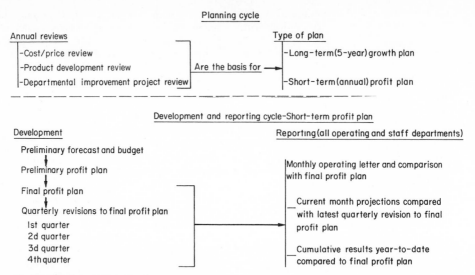

**Fig. I-4. Planning and Reporting System.**

The basic objective of the long-term growth plan is to develop strategic planning for the next 5 years. Each operation is required to submit in a standard format an analysis of the current position; matrix studies to identify product needs and acquisition opportunities; growth projects and sales growth analysis; prime tasks and operational requirements; and a financial summary, which includes major capital projects for the planning period and a cash-flow projection. This plan provides an opportunity to evaluate the logic built into the strategies for the next 5 years.

The short-term profit plan will be discussed in greater detail below.

**Development and Reporting Cycle—Short-Term Profit Plan**  As can be seen in the lower portion of Fig. I-4, the operations people begin the development of the short-term profit plan with the preparation of a *preliminary forecast and budget* which includes field-sales forecasts, expense projects, and departmental budgets. The forecasts are developed at the lowest realistic level of responsibility in order to give the individuals who are closest to the local market conditions and trends an opportunity to supply input.

The *preliminary profit plan* is prepared next. It serves as a basis for developing an area of agreement with top management on expected sales, profitability, capital requirements, and return on investment for the next fiscal year.

The *final profit plan* is submitted next and consists of the basic goals and objectives agreed upon in connection with the preliminary profit plan along with detailed analysis to support the plan. The supporting detail includes an analysis of each market and product with profitability evaluation, growth and improvement project studies, extensive financial statements, and detailed capital requirements. An important aspect of the final plan is an in-depth presentation of who has the responsibility in what time frame to accomplish each goal or objective incorporated in the plan.

At the completion of each quarter a revision to the final profit plan is submitted. Each *quarterly revision* projects the results for the year, based upon actual results experienced to date and upon the current outlook regarding business and market conditions.

In terms of reporting against the final profit plan and the latest quarterly revision to it, the "feedback loop" is the *monthly operating letter*. It deals with actual results versus planned results both for the current month and on a year-to-date basis.

## INTERNATIONAL INDUSTRIAL RELATIONS

In most cases, the organization of the international industrial relations function should follow closely the general organization structure of the company at large.

**Authority and Responsibility**  The role of the industrial relations executive abroad should be clearly defined, with specific areas of authority and responsibility carefully identified and agreed to by corporate operations and industrial relations officers. Time and thought given to function definition will be repaid many times over because the industrial relations executive and the executive's superiors know and understand the breadth and limitation of authority as well as the specific personnel policies and programs for which the activity is accountable. Line and staff relationships between international personnel managers and operating group and corporate industrial relations heads should receive the same careful attention.

**Staffing Practices** The selection, promotion, and retention of personnel in the international operation is especially crucial. There is no single policy that fits every company's needs or every situation within the full operation of a diverse multinational company. A uniform corporate staffing policy, however, applicable in most instances and under all but the most unusual conditions, is fundamental to sound international personnel management. As with organization style, the staffing of foreign operations is predicated largely on the company's general operational philosophy. Its choices range from developing a cadre of mobile international executives and functional specialists available for assignments throughout the world to employing exclusively local nationals at every level of the operation.

An emerging trend among many multinational companies is the utilization of local nationals in management and professional positions, thereby reducing or eliminating expatriate and third-country national personnel. While short-term indoctrination and training costs can be high, subsequent savings in expatriate and third-country national compensation and foreign service allowance costs can be substantial. Even more important in most cases, employment of host country nationals has cultural, social, and institutional benefits.

**Training and Development** The reality of the company's beliefs about its community and social responsibilities is often evidenced by its education and training practices. A clear definition of the organization's social philosophy is an important prerequisite to the development of a comprehensive training program. Selection of particular training and development techniques hinges on the company's staffing policies, the availability of experienced and knowledgeable job candidates in the employment market area, the stage of maturity of the local organization, and the organizational style of the firm. Core programs for supervisory, management, and executive personnel can be conducted at home or abroad by the corporate management development staff. Additional seminars and instructional programs can be continued by component operating organizations. These courses can provide concentrated study of supervisory and management methods or address technical and professional matters in detail.

**Compensation and Employee Benefits** Unquestionably, one of the most difficult and perplexing elements of international industrial relations management is the establishment and administration of compensation and benefit plans. The time, knowledge, and experience required in international compensation administration increases geometrically as the number of expatriates, nationals, and third-country nationals increases. This is compounded further by the increase in the number of countries in which the business operates. Subjects like tax equalization, foreign service allowances, moving and resettlement expenses, home leave practices, statutory benefit requirements, and host country customs and practices can be the bane of a salary and benefit plan designed for a domestic management structure. When operating abroad, a corporate policy of conforming to the host country's compensation customs and practices provides a logical basis for developing and administering specfic salary and benefit plans. Except for the most underdeveloped parts of the world, a comprehensive analysis of national and local pay rates, coupled with the company's general philosophy on remuneration levels, can be a principal tool for determining the basic wage and salary structure of the organization. Refinements to meet the more unusual compensation circumstances of expatriate and third-country national personnel can follow, but *the core structure is the local or national pay scale and the compensation customs, practices, and regulations of the host country.*

**Labor Relations** International labor-management relations remain one of the most unsettled areas of personnel management within the multinational business organization. The trend toward international unionism has accelerated with the internationalization of the business enterprise and with the formation of transnational management systems. At the same time, international management has become increasingly concerned with the rising power of organized labor abroad. By the same token, governmental regulations in such areas as wage-price controls, codetermination, and local ownership must be taken into account.

One of the essential questions facing multinational management, then, is the most effective way in which to administer the labor relations function. Should it be done at the local management level, by area or regional officials, or through representatives of the corporate industrial relations staff? Similarly, the multinational company must resolve the issue of the applicability of its basic labor relations policies, which frequently were developed to meet home country conditions, to a foreign environment.

In most industrial settings today, labor relations management can be delegated to the local organization, assuming that the necessary degree of competency has been developed. Generally, local management will be more familiar with shop conditions and competitive employment practices, as well as with the cultural, legal, and historic setting in which local labor relations are conducted.

With respect to the future, however, the placement of labor relations authority remains at question. The growing tendency to multinational unionism and international union cooperation may ultimately lead to the more frequent establishment of regional industrial relations offices that parallel the multinational union in authority and prestige.

## INTERNATIONAL PUBLIC RELATIONS

Today's international public relations management calls for a new perception of the world as countries develop their own resources and reach beyond their borders for materials, labor force, special skills, technology, and investment capital. As a consequence there are at least two ways to view public relations management on an international scale. One is from the standpoint of a company or operation intent on achieving a business objective in a foreign country. The other is through the eyes of the multinational corporation, whose commerce crosses many national boundaries and whose relationships with the public have a profound impact on the management of the world enterprise as well as on international trade itself.

**Evolution of Philosophy**  In tracing the evolution of public relations philosophy, it is accurate to say that, in the early days of the multinational company, overseas entities regarded themselves largely as islands, separate and distinct from both their parent companies and their counterpart subsidiaries in other countries. In those days, few companies recognized or acknowledged the public relations impact of their overseas activities. Those that did, confined their concerns to the countries in which they were located. Usually, the host countries were content to have them operate in this manner.

The advent of the European Common Market and the actions of the Organization of Petroleum Exporting Countries, the Organization for Economic Cooperation and Development, the agencies of the United Nations, international environmentalist and labor groups, and various other government and private-interest organizations have changed this situation. The result is that, if a change in corporate policy or an environmental problem or a violation of ethical standards is important enough to be reported by the press of one country, it is likely to be transmitted widely to other countries.

**Constituencies and Issues**  The first step, then, is for a company to know its constituencies. These can be identified as segments of the general public with which most companies have continuing interaction. They are the source of both criticism and support and are the objects of any well-planned public relations program. Generally speaking, they include public media, government and agencies, employees, conservationists, the financial community, churches, labor organizations, suppliers, distributors, customers, competitors, pressure groups, stockholders, academia, minority groups, plant communities, and the voting public.

The issues that surround these constituencies are multitudinous and must be well defined and understood before public relations planning begins. Typical of the issues are prices and profits, consumerism, demands, equal opportunities, nationalism, industrial democracy, industrial safety and health, truth in advertising, environment, energy and natural resources, exports-imports, taxes, incentives and restrictions, investments, employment, mergers and acquisitions, money and credit, business ethics, and the quality of management.

**Policies and Procedures**  Organizing a business for action on an international public relations front is essentially a three-phase procedure consisting of collection, evaluation, and dissemination or implementation: (1) in the collection phase, data, trends, and forecasts, such as customer's needs, market conditions, internal and external attitudes, and political, economic, and social projections form an information base; (2) the information is evaluated by a "think tank" comprised of top management, public relations professionals, specialists, and consultants; (3) the output, in the form of policy and approved action programs, is communicated to constituent groups.

The foregoing suggests these specific actions:

*Establish an Information Base.* Specifically, determine how your company's policies and practices are perceived by the public which is in a position to influence your future course of business. At the same time, assess the social needs and expectations of both home and host countries.

*Determine a Common Ground.* Do so based on your analysis of the information available. Make any nonpolicy changes that are indicated to accommodate local mores, customs, and traditions. Reevaluate other, broader policy questions with a view to making changes to improve the business environment.

*Develop Operational, Economic, and Ethical Guidelines.* These will assist your operating entities in their relationships with people inside and out of the corporation. Make it clear that a good business reputation, like bottom-line results, is an operating responsibility and that managers will be measured, promoted, and rewarded according to their results.

*Communicate Values to Your Constituents.* On an ongoing basis, show how your company's operations serve the needs of host countries. Do not neglect to report your efforts to shareholders, employees, citizens in the community, and other potential sources of support.

*Demonstrate an Interest in the Locales from Which You Draw Your Employees, Services, and Materials.* Do so by participating with others in efforts to improve these locales as places in which to live and work.

*Assign Specific Responsibility for Public Relations Management to Your Highest-Rank Operating Manager in Each Country.* Require that public relations problems, objectives, and strategies be included in the long-range planning cycle.

## INTERNATIONAL FINANCIAL MANAGEMENT

Financial activities outside the home country include essentially the same elements as those in the domestic area. The structure and methods used to perform the financial functions are dependent on, and must be consistent with, the organizational relationships established for all the functions of the company.

**Operation of a Typical System**  In this section, an international financial management system which is functionally centralized in the world headquarters is described. The system is patterned, however, to serve and to utilize, where appropriate, the company's operating organization which is decentralized on a product-line basis but centralized geographically in major international areas. Product line man-

agers in the home country have worldwide responsibility for product line profits.

Those groups with financial responsibilities who play major roles in this international management scheme are identified as field operating, field corporate, group operating, and home office corporate. Unit controllers or finance managers serving the operating divisions located outside the home country constitute *field operating* in this description. Their line reporting relationship is to operating division management.

*Field corporate* staff is provided only in countries or areas where two or more divisions conduct substantial business. Field corporate staffs are competent in both accounting and treasury matters. They report directly to home office corporate.

Under this management scheme, foreign operating units report to home country operating divisions which, in turn, report to home country operating groups. *Group operating*, as used in this section, refers to financial staffs in both operating divisions and operating groups in the home country. Group operating is responsible on a line basis to group management and functionally to home office corporate.

At the home office, financial functions include accounting, treasury, taxation, financial public relations, insurance, and other financial specialties. All these functions are included in *home office corporate* in this description.

*Forecasting and Accounting Practices.* These functions are performed by field operating under the direction and surveillance of group operating. The latter consolidates all operations of the operating group for reporting to group management and to corporate headquarters. Field operating also advises field corporate on all financial aspects of its forecast and its operating requirements. Accounting must conform to host country standards as well as to the parent company's requirements.

*Cash Management.*  Field corporate provides cash for all approved operating requirements in its geographic area, and it must invest or "dispose of" excess cash. It relies on forecasts from the operating units and manages cash within approved forecasts. It consults with home office corporate when significant deviations from forecast appear, and it works under the general surveillance of the home office corporate which has final responsibility for worldwide financial management.

In those areas where there is no corporate organization, field operating personnel are responsible for local cash management. In such instances, field operating reports to the home country group which looks to home office corporate to provide required financing for operating requirements.

*Bank Relations.* Responsibility for bank relations is shared by several of the financial groups. Field operating is responsible for relations with its own banks. Field corporate is responsible for relations with indigenous banks and local branches of the company's international banks used for corporate purposes. Home office corporate is responsible for establishing bank relations policy and for relations with the company's principal international banks.

Merchant bank contact and arrangements are the responsibility of home office corporate. Appropriate field corporate personnel, however, are made aware of any significant developments involving their local area merchant banks.

Contacts with important commercial and merchant banks are maintained in part by home office corporate visits with bank officials both in the corporate offices and in the bank offices in the home country and abroad. Home office corporate makes or approves major bank selections.

*Currency Control.* Control of currency exposure is a responsibility of home office corporate, although it is dependent on financial statements and supplemental currency reports from all field operations. The worldwide currency exposure position is visible only at home office corporate where final company consolidations are made. In making its currency judgments, however, home office corporate depends to an important extent on timely reporting and evaluation of the local economic and currency outlook by field operating and field corporate. Steps to remedy undesirable currency positions involve field operating through control of assets and liabilities, and may involve various field financial personnel if local loans are required. Hedging operations are directed and controlled by home office corporate.

*Taxation Coordination.* Home office corporate is responsible for coordination of taxation matters throughout the world. It relies on field operating and field corporate for preparation of local returns and routine relations with tax authorities. All significant tax returns are reviewed and all major tax negotiations are directed by home office corporate.

*Credit Management.* Credit matters are the direct responsibility of the various operating units. Home office corporate reviews credit performance, assists in negotiating special credit facilities, and provides other specialized credit services upon the request of operational units.

*Insurance.* Insurance matters worldwide are coordinated by home office corporate, and major insurance policies are arranged by it. Coverage requirements, employee benefit levels, pension funding, and similar matters are determined by home office corporate with the assistance of local management as required.

*Stockholder Relations.* These are the responsibility of home office corporate, although certain activities may take place in overseas areas with the assistance of local company personnel.

This financial management plan involves the financial staff at each level of the organization. The nature of services needed dictates this spread of responsibility. Furthermore, the multinational character of the financial community makes it necessary for the company to interface with the financial community on a worldwide basis. At the same time, the constraints of financial matters require worldwide compliance with company policy and effective surveillance by home office corporate.

## INTERNATIONAL LEGAL ADMINISTRATION

For the typical multinational company having manufacturing, marketing, and service facilities in many international countries, there are logistical problems in furnishing these operations with timely and effective legal services. Normally, these services are furnished either directly by in-house counsel, with assistance as required by outside foreign counsel, or through local foreign counsel. Aside from the careful selection and close monitoring of foreign counsel, it is essential that guidelines be established to distinguish (1) those matters which local operating personnel may handle directly with foreign counsel, without the necessity of reference to in-house counsel, from (2) those which must be referred first to in-house counsel. The fundamental premise underlying the determination of which matters must be referred first to in-house counsel is that such matters might involve legal or general corporate policy considerations, set a significant precedent, or involve unusual risk or significant loss exposure.

*Local Administration.* Examples of matters which might be handled directly by operating managers with foreign counsel are work permits, importation of products and supplies, immigration matters, limited currency control matters, collection matters where the amount involved is under $10,-000, and holding of shareholder and directors' meetings.

*Corporate Control.* Examples of matters which might be referred first to in-house counsel are all patent, trademark, and trade name matters; all income tax matters and, where the amount involved is over $10,000, all other tax matters; formation or dissolution of companies; registration or termination of branches; changes in charters and bylaws; capital revisions; changes in directors, officers, and branch managers; granting of broad powers of attorney; beginning new operations in a country; review and approval of shareholders and directors' meeting agenda prior to the meetings for both wholly owned and jointly owned companies; collection matters over $10,000 or if debtor is in a different country or where possible counterclaims are involved; trade regulation matters including antitrust and trading with restricted countries; licensing contracts; and product warranties which deviate from those previously approved.

*Legal Reviews.* A number of areas not listed above have legal aspects which must be examined by in-house counsel in support of other functional activities. The initial contact points, however, are with those departments having the prime responsibility. These matters could include such things as bank accounts, sales representatives and distributor agreements, insurance matters, purchase, sale, or lease of assets, and advertising and press releases.

**International Acquisition** Most multinational companies pursue growth both by internal development and by acquisition. To assist management in evaluating acquisitions, a checklist outlining the typical content of an acquisition proposal for presentation to corporate management is useful. Although such a checklist covers all elements of the operations of the company to be acquired, some of the important legal considerations are discussed below.

*Legal Checklist.* The essential information to be obtained is covered by 12 major headings. The following general guidelines apply to each of the categories:

1. *Corporate organization.* Assuming a stock acquisition as opposed to assets, is the entity to be acquired a parent corporation, a subsidiary of another corporation, or a division? Does the seller have the power and authority to consummate the transactions contemplated? This involves a review of corporate powers (e.g., charter, bylaws, corporate law, government controls) and contractual restrictions in bank or other loan agreements and stockholder arrangements.

2. *Stockholders of seller.* Will the transaction result in minority stockholders or provide dissenting stockholders with appraisal rights? Does a risk exist that the seller stockholders will attack the transaction?

3. *Creditors.* Is there a risk of attack by creditors, and are there any special laws to be compiled with?

4. *Antitrust.* Are there antitrust considerations? If so, what are they? (These basic questions should be supported by a detailed, specialized subchecklist.)

5. *Contracts.* To determine contractual exposure, the following types of agreements must be obtained and reviewed: licenses, consulting agreements, leases, suppliers' contracts, customer contracts, joint-venture agreements, distributor and other sales representation agreements, financing agreements or arrangements, and conditional sales contracts if not included in one of the above. It must also be determined whether the sellers' contracts are assignable or subject to prior assignment and whether the seller has benefits under any of the agreements or arrangements which would terminate or otherwise be jeopardized by reason of the acquisition.

6. *Employee-benefit plans.* The following plans or programs must be reviewed: profit sharing plans, contributory employee stock purchase or savings plans, stock option plans, pension plans, bonus plans, group insurance, and similar benefits, termination plans for employees, and vacation accruals. Generally it should be determined whether there are any local customs, laws, or contracts which would place an onerous obligation or duty on the buyer. An essential element is to determine whether employees have vested rights to employment or termination indemnity by virtue of contractual arrangement or governmental regulation.

7. *Real property.* A brief description of location and the general character of principal plants and offices must be obtained. With respect to property held in fee, a copy of the latest title policy or attorney's opinion should be obtained. With respect to leased property, copies of all leases which cannot be terminated on 30 days notice should be obtained. Lease-termination dates and termination penalties, including whether termination can occur merely by a change in ownership, should be analyzed. All major liens and encumbrances, restrictions on zoning, and any taxes which might result from the transfer of property must be determined.

8. *Personal property.* All leases of personal property, including those covering leased mobile equipment and/or airplanes, must be reviewed.

9. *Warranties.* The nature of product-warranty obligations, including the nature of any agreements to repurchase products, must be reviewed.

10. *Claims and litigation.* Copies of all injunc-

**TABLE 1-6  Example of International Joint-Venture Guidelines**

During recent years, we have entered into an increasing number of international joint-venture arrangements, and several new joint-venture opportunities are normally under study at any given time. Usually, joint ventures are entered into for one or more of the following reasons:

Local laws prohibit total ownership by foreign *or* foreign-owned companies.

The nature of the project, or the political or economic instability of the country in which the operation is located, makes it desirable to share risks with a local partner.

Growth potential is enhanced by the participation of local partners.

Partners can make a significant contribution by providing sources of raw materials, establishing marketing outlets, and, in some cases, technology.

It is important that all of us have a clear understanding of our corporate policy with respect to these arrangements. Therefore, the following general guidelines are set forth:

1. Sufficient equity is to be put into the joint venture to make it a viable economic entity. As a rule of thumb, equity capital should be equal to the investment in fixed assets, i.e., land, buildings, and equipment.

2. All joint-venture debt should be financed through local borrowing. Also, at times it may be desirable to finance a portion of our share of the equity capital through local borrowing. This is in keeping with our overall philosophy of providing funds required for growth of foreign operations in each major geographic area by borrowing in local currencies. By so doing, we are able to protect against currency exchange losses. In addition, debt can be serviced in the currency generated by the project without the complexity of currency conversions or exchange restrictions.

3. Any funds borrowed to finance fixed assets should be provided by long-term debt, preferably for a period of at least 10 years or a period corresponding to the useful life of the assets.

4. Working capital may be financed through short-term borrowing, such as bank overdraft facilities.

5. Joint-venture partners should have a controlling interest only where required by local law or when the partner is more critical to the success of the operation than is the parent company.

It is important to reemphasize that we want the joint venture to be a viable economic entity. Thus it should have sufficient equity to obtain working capital loans without partner guarantees. Also, in many countries, the ability to repatriate earnings in the form of dividends is directly related to the amount of equity investment.

We recognize that there may be extenuating circumstances which require deviation from one or more of the above guidelines. In order that we may properly coordinate operating unit objectives with overall corporate guidelines, all proposed capitalization and financing arrangements for joint ventures must be submitted to corporate headquarters for advance approval.

tions, orders, or decrees currently in effect, as well as a description of any present or threatened litigation or administrative proceeding which could affect the business or any of the property to be acquired, must be reviewed. Also, any allegations of patent infringement which have been made by or against others and the general attitude and pattern of compliance with various laws and regulations must be determined.

11. *Tax.* The status of taxes of all types must be reviewed and copies of all returns obtained. The tax aspect of the proposed method of acquisition on the acquirer and on the seller must be assessed. Is there a need for an appraisal?

12. *Proprietary rights.* How valid are the seller's property rights in any patents, trademarks, trade names, copyrights, and other intangible assets? Is the seller a party to any unusual confidential treatment, know-how, or secrecy agreements? Are invention agreements executed by employees assignable?

## FORMULATION OF INTERNATIONAL POLICY

The formulation of international policy in all its scope follows naturally from everything that has

been presented. Each company must examine the subject matter areas in which it feels policy statements are mandatory and/or desirable in the conduct of their international operations. An example of a statement in one such area of policy is shown in Table I-6.

*See also* CODETERMINATION AND INDUSTRIAL DEMOCRACY; DEVELOPING COUNTRIES, MANAGEMENT IN; EUROPE, MANAGEMENT IN WESTERN; EXCHANGE, FOREIGN, MANAGEMENT OF; INTERNATIONAL TRADE; JAPANESE INDUSTRIES, MANAGEMENT IN; TAX MANAGEMENT, MANAGERIAL RESPONSIBILITY FOR FEDERAL INCOME TAX REPORTING.

### REFERENCES

Dymsza, William A.: *Multinational Business Strategy*, McGraw-Hill Book Company, New York, 1972.

Fatemi, Nasrollah S., and Gail V. Williams: *Multinational Corporations: The Problems and the Prospects*, A. S. Barnes and Co., Inc., New York, 1975.

Fayerweather, John: *International Business Management: A Conceptual Framework*, McGraw-Hill Book Company, New York, 1969.

Guzzardi, Walter, Jr.: "An Unscandalized View of Those 'Bribes' Abroad," *Fortune*, July 1976.

"Multinational Business," *The Economist Intelligence Unit, Ltd.*, London, no. 4, 1975.

Powers, John J., Jr.: "International Business: The Multinational Corporation," in Peter F. Drucker, *Preparing Tomorrow's Business Leaders Today*, Prentice-Hall, Inc., Englewood Cliffs, N.J., 1969.

Prahalad, C. K.: "Strategic Choices in Diversified MNC's," *Harvard Business Review*, July–August 1976.

Sethi, S. Prakash, and Richard Holton, ed.: *Management of the Multinationals*, The Free Press, New York, 1974.

Stevens, Robert Warren: "Scanning the Multinational Firm," *Business Horizons*, June 1971.

REX A. SEBASTIAN, *Dresser Industries, Inc.*

# International trade

International trade is a trillion dollar opportunity available to the relatively efficient producers of primary and manufactured goods. In an increasingly interdependent world economy, the opportunities for profitable exchanges of goods grow far more quickly than do governmental efforts to protect domestic firms and workers from the shocks of unrestricted import competition. There is increasing recognition of the international benefits of an international specialization of labor. It is reflected in the continuing series of negotiations aimed at liberalizing the flow of trade. The successful outcomes of these negotiations have been a major factor in the unprecedented increase in the rate of world trade since 1950. Dynamic companies respect the need to come to grips with the specialized mechanics and jargon of trade in order to gain entry into the growing and profitable export sector.

## THE NATURE OF TRADE

International trade is the mutually profitable exchange of goods between citizens residing in different countries. Businesspeople are engaged in this practice for the same reason that they pursue domestic commerce: profits. Exports provide not only additional profits through increased sales, but the potential exists for introducing economies of scale to the production line. Importers, the international buyers, purchase foreign goods either for profitable resale or because foreign supplies provide cheaper or better raw materials and finished goods than those available domestically. In terms of export, companies are attracted to international trade when production and sales goals outgrow the potentials of the domestic market. Marketing strategies look upon foreign trade as an enormous extension of a finite home market. In many instances, foreign trade is the more appealing market in terms of size, growth, and profitability.

There are significant differences between international and domestic commerce, and the international trader must cope with new experiences and problems. Most important is the political reality that foreign trade is conducted among sovereign countries who jealously guard prerogatives to pursue national employment, price stability, economic growth, and industrial policies. Imports or exports may be arbitrarily controlled if they run askance of one or more of these policy priorities. Trade may be affected by foreign political policies or domestic health and safety standards. Sovereign countries also maintain proprietary laws and utilize different legal systems. National tastes differ widely in terms of needs and preferences. Language differences pose a number of problems in the marketing and distribution processes. Each country has its own currency. Accordingly, the price of all traded goods must be translated from the seller's currency into the comparable value of the buyer's currency. Floating exchange rates, the conversion and repatriation of foreign currencies, and the occasional use of exchange controls introduce additional complexities.

Except where state trading monopolies are involved, international trade is conducted by private business. Although transactions follow classic business patterns, international trade is specialized and specially structured. Transactions are routinely reported to the United States federal government for statistical purposes. In certain circumstances (e.g., strategic goods), exports must first acquire export license approval. In every case, imports must be appraised by customs officials to determine what, if any, entry duty—tariff—is to be applied and whether quotas or other local statutes ban the product from entry altogether. Tariffs are usually imposed on an *ad valorem* basis, which means at a specified percentage of the import's value. In a few cases, tariffs are assessed on a per unit basis, e.g., weight or volume. Only after the duty stipulated in the country's tariff schedule has been paid, can the importer legally take possession of the merchandise. Tariffs sometimes exceed 100 percent of the assessed value, which places the imports at a price disadvantage. Obviously, the importer must pass part or all of the tariff cost onto the consumer.

Historically, all nations have wanted to provide protection for domestically produced goods against those produced overseas. Thus, there is a correlation between tariff rates and a government's desire to encourage domestic production of a given product line. Conversely, raw materials and manufactured goods unavailable domestically will have little or no duty imposed on them. Finally, governments concern themselves with international freight rate schedules, lest a deviation from the norm discriminate favorably or unfavorably against the trade of a particular country.

## TRADE CONCEPTS

Countries engage in international trade because it is a mutually beneficial process. At the macro level, national welfare increases. At the micro level, individual exporters earn profits, provide an additional source of employment, and supply convertible foreign exchange (read *dollars*) which is used to pay for imported goods and services. For some politicians, this sell side is the only desirable end of foreign trade; exports provide jobs and capital, while imports provide *foreigners* with jobs and capital.

In terms of national welfare and economic common sense, imports are the ultimate rationale for trade. By definition, a good is unlikely to be imported unless it meets at least one of three criteria: (1) it is cheaper than domestically produced counterparts; (2) it is of better quality than its domestic competition; or (3) it is either unavailable or in short supply in the domestic market.

Obtaining goods from abroad at cheaper prices increases consumers' buying power, and, as a consequence, real incomes rise. This in turn means an increased standard of living in the importing country. High tariffs and other barriers to imports increase costs to consumers, lower real incomes, and reduce their freedom at the marketplace. One of the major sources of price disciplines and incentives for innovation by domestic industry is import competition. By absorbing domestic demand, imports are intrinsically deflationary. Furthermore, since one country's imports are another country's exports, failure to import by country A reduces the supply of foreign exchange needed by other countries to buy A's exports.

**Price Differentiation**   The ultimate basis for international trade is price differentiation. Each country is endowed with a different relative mixture of the factors of production. Traditionally, differences in the relative abundancy or scarcity of land, labor, and capital determined the domestic price structure and production possibilities. For example, a country with abundant labor and land tends to be an efficient producer of agricultural goods, whereas an abundance of capital and a scarcity of labor encourages efficiency in sophisticated manufacturing that requires laborsaving machinery. Since international trade today is much more sophisticated than in simpler times when wine was swapped for cloth, many economists now accept a fourth and even a

fifth factor of production: technology and managerial talent. The ability of a given country to be efficient in certain industrial products (e.g., Japan in electronics and the United States in computers) cannot be explained adequately only in terms of land, labor, and capital.

The theory of international trade is, therefore, dynamic. It must be continually modified to accommodate changes in business conditions. In the future, it will have to come to grips with the increasing role of foreign trade of multinational corporations. A growing volume of trade in manufactured goods is being done on the basis of an intracorporate transaction, not an arm's-length sale between nationals of two different countries.

**Comparative Advantage**   The essential elements of modern international trade theory are still intact. The theory holds that all countries have a *comparative advantage* in the production of certain goods, even if not an absolute advantage. World production, and therefore the world's welfare, will be increased if countries follow the dictum of an international division of labor: concentrate on production of goods in which you are *relatively* efficient, and import the goods in which you are *relatively* inefficient.

**Trade Restriction**   Economic theory clearly indicates that a sound foreign trade policy is one which allows a maximum freedom of movement for goods in the world marketplace so that desired foreign-made products may be imported as simply and cheaply as possible, not unlike the transfer of goods among the 50 states of the United States. In real life, this does not occur because politicians, not economists, promulgate trade policy. Visions of economic efficiency are subordinated to the domestic priorities of national security, full employment, etc.

The overriding international economic dilemma for national governments in today's sophisticated, interdependent world economy is how far to go in liberalizing the various barriers and distortions to world commerce that have been erected.

## TRADE LIBERALIZATION

The system of international trade which has evolved since the end of World War II has sought to reduce governmentally imposed trade barriers and distortions as fast as political sensitivities would allow. All industrialized countries have accepted in principle the advantages of freer trade. Subsequent to its creation in 1948, the General Agreement on Tariffs and Trade (GATT) has served as the negotiating and moral focal point for efforts at trade liberalization.

**GATT** GATT is literally nothing more than a treaty having a small international secretariat, with headquarters in Geneva, Switzerland, to support it. Yet as the world's premier treaty embodying reciprocal commercial rights and obligations, it is still the nucleus of international trade negotiations and consultations. The 80 plus signatory countries subscribe to three basic practices:

1. Nondiscrimination. Each country's negotiated concessions apply equally to all signatories; i.e., the products of all other countries receive the same treatment afforded to the most-favored nation.

2. Tariff protection. Tariffs, not quotas, are the sanctioned means of protecting domestic industries from foreign competition.

3. Consultations. Existing and potential trade disputes should be submitted for consultation. No new trade barriers should be implemented unannounced.

*Impact on Tariffs.* The international commitment to a rational utilization of the world's resources is mirrored in the results of six rounds of tariff-cutting negotiations completed thus far within GATT. With the successful conclusion of the Kennedy Round in 1967, the average tariff rates of the major industrialized countries, Western Europe, the United States, and Japan, fell to the 7 to 10 percent range. For most products, tariffs are now more of a nuisance than an effective barrier to trade.

In terms of tariffs on industrial goods, the work of GATT is almost completed. However, much progress needs to be made on other existing barriers. Agricultural trade continues to be restricted in deference to the political sensitivity of domestic farm-support systems practiced throughout the world. A wide variety of nontariff distortions to trade are still in place. Also referred to as nontariff barriers or measures, they include such devices as arithmetic quotas which arbitrarily limit imports to a certain level in complete disregard of price considerations. Governments employ a number of devices in their procurement procedures which discriminate in favor of domestic producers. In addition, safety, labeling, health, and antipollution requirements force foreign goods to conform to domestic specifications. Countries facing a balance of payments "emergency" may impose such financial requirements as advance deposits on imports or a special import surcharge tax.

On the export side, countries may adopt such diffuse measures as subsidies to increase exports or restrictive controls either to limit sales of goods in short supply or to attempt to increase the price paid by foreign buyers.

*Safeguards.* The transition beyond concern for reducing industrial tariffs is epitomized by the broadened agenda for the newest series of GATT-related trade negotiations. The so-called "Tokyo Round" began in earnest in 1974 with the broadest, most ambitious effort to come to grips not only with tariffs but also with nontariff distortions, agricultural trade, and other theory issues never before examined systematically. Among the latter is the question of a safeguard system, under which uniform rules would be established so that countries could take temporary import-restrictive measures to ease the adjustment impact of intense import competition.

Although GATT is the central international organization concerned with trade, a number of important regional organizations have come on the scene. In an effort to enjoy the fruits of freer trade and in recognition of the growing limits of the traditional nation-state as a viable market for large-scale industry, a number of countries have joined with their neighbors to form free trade areas and customs unions. The *free trade area* involves the negotiated elimination of all or most trade barriers among the member countries. The *customs union* carries the process one step further with the establishment of a common uniform tariff schedule for imports from all nonmember countries.

**Common Market** The most significant of these regional trade groups is the customs union formed by the European Economic Community (EEC), often referred to as the Common Market. The largest trading unit in the world, the EEC members consist of West Germany, France, Great Britain, Italy, the Netherlands, Belgium, Luxembourg, Denmark, and Ireland. Associate memberships of European and Mediterranean countries (e.g., Greece and Turkey), along with preferential market access agreements signed with developing countries (mainly former colonies of the full members), swell the number of countries affiliated with the EEC to well above 50. The member countries have nearly completed the process of developing a common international commercial policy (e.g., they negotiate as the Community in GATT, not as individual countries) and have committed themselves to the long-term process of full economic and monetary union. While the EEC is deeply committed to internal free trade, it is ambivalent in its policy toward outsiders. On the one hand, it consistently has lowered its common external tariff in GATT negotiations, but its common agricultural policy has had a significant impact on the farm trade of the Community, mainly in the form of excluding the competitive farm products of the United States and other efficient agricultural producers.

**United States Policy** Closer economic relations with the EEC have been the overall priority item of United States trade policy since the early 1960s. The attempt to keep the EEC "outward looking" was the basis of the United States initiatives to spawn the Kennedy Round of GATT talks in 1964 and the subsequent Tokyo Round. As these initiatives imply, the United States has played the leadership role in promoting trade liberalization ever since the passage of the Trade Agreements Program in 1934, a historic milestone in international trade policy. The disastrous effect of the Hawley-Smoot Tariff of 1930, the highest in the country's history, led to the unprecedented extension of tariff-cutting authority by the legislative branch to the President. Previously, Congress had set all tariffs, generally on purely political grounds, by virtue of the Constitution's specific extension of authority to it to regulate foreign commerce and levy duties.

*Trade Act of 1974.* American international trade policy to this day rests on the delegation of trade liberalizing authority to the President through periodic legislation. The current course of policy was charted in the Trade Act of 1974. In substance, the Trade Act does not affect the basic principles of policy: to reduce on a reciprocal basis American and foreign barriers to trade, to provide temporary protection to American firms and workers injured (or deemed about to be injured) by import competition, and to avoid discrimination among countries through application of the *most-favored-nation (MFN) principle.*

The statute is replete with provisions for congressional overrides of Presidential actions in trade policy. In addition, the statutory language by which Amercian workers and firms are eligible for relief from foreign competition has been eased considerably. The bill also authorized the United States to catch up with other industrialized countries by implementing tariff preferences, i.e., lower duties on imports of manufactured and processed goods produced by less-developed countries.

## MAGNITUDE OF WORLD TRADE

The recurring efforts to liberalize trade have accelerated the underlying economic trend of increased international interdependence. In terms of sales, the real growth market has been exports. The relative boom in international trade can be measured in two ways. In the 1960 to 1970 period, exports of the industrial countries grew at an average annual rate that was twice as fast as the value of real output, i.e., gross national product of 9.5 percent as opposed to 4.8 percent. In the 1971 to 1974 period, average annual real growth fell below 4 percent, but export growth remained slightly above 9 percent.

As Table I-7 demonstrates, the total value of international trade increased almost tenfold between 1955 and 1975. Although distorted by inflation and higher oil prices, total world exports doubled in value in just the 3 years after 1972, when total world exports amounted to $418 billion.

Increases in the value of trade experienced by the United States have also been drastic. From their twentieth century nadir in the early 1930s (when the average annual value was below $2 billion), American exports grew to $10 billion in 1950, and began doubling every 10 years thereafter: $20 billion in 1960 and $43 billion in 1970. Since then, it has taken less than 5 years to double again. Annual exports of the United States are now valued in excess of $110 billion. Imports are approximately of the same magnitude, having grown from a total of only $15 billion in 1960; nevertheless, the potential for further increases is still great. Despite these rapid increases in the value of trade, imports and exports, respectively, account for only 6 to 7 percent of total

**TABLE I-7   World Trade: Exports, in billions of U.S. dollars**

|  | 1955 | 1960 | 1965 | 1970 | 1975 | 1976* |
|---|---|---|---|---|---|---|
| United States† | 15.6 | 20.6 | 27.5 | 43.2 | 107.2 | 115.2 |
| Canada | 4.4 | 5.8 | 8.3 | 16.8 | 32.2 | 38.7 |
| Japan | 2.0 | 4.2 | 8.5 | 19.3 | 54.8 | 67.3 |
| European community | 28.3 | 51.5 | 78.2 | 136.9 | 360.2 | 399.5 |
| Other developed countries | 10.3 | 13.8 | 20.8 | 34.2 | 83.1 | 89.9 |
| Less-developed countries | 23.1 | 27.0 | 35.6 | 54.1 | 188.9 | 219.8 |
| Communist nations | 10.0 | 15.7 | 22.4 | 33.9 | 85.1 | 93.4 |
| Total | 93.7 | 138.6 | 201.3 | 338.4 | 911.5 | 1023.8 |

SOURCE: U.S. Department of Commerce
*Estimate
†Includes Department of Defense shipments

United States GNP, the lowest "pentration" of any industrialized noncommunist country. Potential on the export side is further demonstrated by the U.S. Department of Commerce estimate that only 8 percent of all American manufacturing corporations actually export and that 250 firms account for nearly 60 percent of total United States exports.

The commodity composition of United States exports has held fairly steady, with manufactured goods dominant. (See Table I-8). As can be seen in

**TABLE I-8  Composition of U.S. Exports by Major Sectors, in billions of U.S. dollars (excludes military grant-aid shipments)**

|  | Total | Manufacturing | Agricultural | Fuel | Minerals and metals |
|---|---|---|---|---|---|
| 1960 | 19.7 | 12.3 | 4.9 | 0.8 | 1.8 |
| 1970 | 42.7 | 29.1 | 7.2 | 1.6 | 3.5 |
| 1975 | 107.2 | 71.3 | 21.9 | 4.5 | 6.5 |

SOURCE: U.S. Department of Commerce

Table I-9, imports of manufactured goods have grown relatively quickly, and fuel imports have boomed.

The major commodities exported by the United States in 1975 were machinery, valued at $29.1 billion (of which $3.4 was power-generating ma-

**TABLE I-9  Composition of U.S. Imports by Major Sectors, in billions of U.S. dollars**

|  | Total | Manufacturing | Agricultural | Fuel | Minerals and metals |
|---|---|---|---|---|---|
| 1960 | 15.1 | 6.2 | 3.8 | 1.6 | 3.1 |
| 1970 | 40.0 | 24.5 | 5.8 | 3.1 | 5.3 |
| 1975 | 96.1 | 48.9 | 9.5 | 26.5 | 8.7 |

SOURCE: U.S. Department of Commerce

chinery, $2 billion in tractors and other agricultural machinery, and $2.2 billion in computers and parts); transport equipment, valued at $15 billion; chemicals, valued at $8.7 billion; coal, valued at $3.3 billion; pulp, paper, and paperboard, valued at $2.1 billion; iron and steel mill products, valued at $2.4 billion; and agricultural products, valued at $22 billion (of which wheat was $5.2 billion, corn was $4.4 billion, and soybean and soybean products, $3.8 billion).

Major American imports in 1975 were petroleum, valued at $25.3 billion; chemicals, $2.2 billion; iron and steel mill products, $4.6 billion; $24 billion in consumer goods, mainly automobiles, electronics, and clothing; capital goods, valued at $10.9 billion, mainly telecommunications apparatus and various machinery; and agricultural products of $9.6 billion.

The major trading partners of the United States are Canada, the European Economic Community, and Japan. The oil-exporting countries of OPEC are now as significant as Latin America among this country's trading partners in the less-developed category.

## IMPORTING AND EXPORTING

Few if any countries exert any official efforts on the import side other than to collect tariffs and administer various measures either to exclude imports altogether or place them at a competitive disadvantage in the domestic market. Imports, crudely speaking, are tolerated, not encouraged. Importers may be divisions of corporations or agents hired by exporting companies with active overseas sales programs. Occasionally businesspeople actively seek out the products of overseas companies through foreign travel or via contacts with commercial officers assigned to the embassies and consulates of foreign countries. In any event, the job of the importer is to assure the safe entry of goods through customs at approved ports of entry and to arrange for distribution to wholesale or retail purchasers.

**Protective Measures**  Domestic industries and workers in the United States and other industrialized countries are protected from injury caused by increases in imports through a number of devices, all recognized as valid elements of international trade law. First, there is protection against illegal or unfair trade practices. Antidumping legislation prevents exporters from selling goods at sales less than fair value (e.g., to quickly dispose of domestic production overruns or to drive competitors in the importing countries out of business). A sale at less than fair value is generally measured as being equivalent to selling goods in foreign markets at prices below those prevailing in the home market. Countervailing duty laws apply special rates on imports whose producers have been found to have received bounties or grants from their government that in effect subsidize the cost of the exports in question. Domestic business is supposed to compete only with foreign business, not foreign governments as well.

When American workers or firms feel threatened by completely fair foreign competition, they can petition for relief in the form of quotas or higher tariff rates under provisions of the "escape clause." Petitions for escape clause protection are made to the U.S. International Trade Commission (formerly the Tariff Commission) which conducts an investigation and renders a recommendation in conjunction with the law. Similarly, American workers or firms can petition for "adjustment assistance" in the form of government funds for retraining or plant modernization.

**Exporting Procedures** The profit potential of exporting invariably justifies the initial expense and energy required to gain a foreign foothold. Any company interested in overseas sales can produce a preliminary assessment of its capabilities simply by considering industry trends, the position of the firm in the domestic industry, the effects that additional sales will have on production costs and schedules, the status of the company's resources, and a "guesstimate" of the export potential of the company's products. Inevitably, export aggressiveness is a function of the size of the domestic market.

*Information and Assistance.* Foreign marketing intelligence can be obtained from a number of sources. The official American source is the series of data on United States exports published in varying detail by the Department of Commerce. The Department of Commerce regularly issues detailed reports on the American market share of major manufactured goods for all major foreign markets and on the economic and financial outlooks for foreign countries. Extensive marketing surveys are issued periodically for those industries targeted by the Department of Commerce as being areas where this country is highly competitive internationally. The Department of Commerce also provides a number of export promotion services, ranging from trade fairs to individual business counseling to providing data on potential foreign distributors or agents for an American company's products. The above mentioned publications and others, as well as information on all official export promotion efforts, are available at the Washington headquarters of the Department of Commerce or any of its 43 district offices. The U.S. government provides tax incentives for exporting companies, principally by the Domestic International Sales Corporation concept. For corporations that qualify, taxes may be deferred indefinitely on 50 percent of export earnings which are not distributed to shareholders.

Potential exporters can also obtain information and guidance from a number of private sources. These include local chambers of commerce, the international divisions of commercial banks, world trade clubs, trade associations, and export management companies.

*Direct and Indirect Selling.* Whether a company sells abroad on a direct or indirect basis will depend on marketing strategy, experience, size, and commitment to exporting. *Direct export selling* techniques are the same generically as domestic efforts. Utiliza-

tion can be made of sales representatives or agents, distributors, retailers, or state-controlled trading monopolies. *Indirect selling* efforts are expecially attractive to the novice or small exporter. In this category are export agents and commission agents located in the foreign market or *export management companies (EMCs)* located in the American market. Acting as the export departments of many companies simultaneously, EMCs solicit and transact business on behalf of the manufacturer in return for sales commissions or retainers.

## FINANCIAL ASPECTS

The financing of international trade is arranged through commercial banks. The two most common means of arranging payment between exporter and importer are drafts and letters of credit. The *draft* may be in the form of sight drafts for immediate payment or time drafts, requiring payment only after 30 or more days from the date in which the importer's bank receives all the requisite documentation. A *letter of credit*, when issued in irrevocable form by a bank in the buyer's country and confirmed by an American bank or when issued by an American bank on behalf of the importer, eliminates all credit risk for the seller. Unlike drafts, the exporter in this case is protected against the contingency that the buyer will suddenly be unable to pay for the goods upon delivery.

**Export-Import Bank** Commercial export financing is universally supplemented by official programs of export finance and insurance. The Export-Import Bank of the United States, with headquarters in Washington, operates two major programs:

1. *Direct loans.* Always in participation with commecial banks, these loans are for relatively large sales or for capital goods requiring longer-term financing; repayment terms vary from 5 years and longer.

2. *Guarantees and insurance.* On a medium-term basis, these guarantees protect the exporter (or the exporter's bank) against political and commerical risks. The privately operated Foreign Credit Insurance Association offers additional guarantees, particularly to exporters who, for competitive reasons, must sell on a deferred payment credit basis.

**International Monetary System** The conduct of trade is heavily influenced by the workings of the international monetary system. It is here that countries reconcile receipts and payments made to one another in their different currencies. A country's balance of payments is a complete accounting record of economic transactions between its citizens and residents of the rest of the world for a given period of time. If a country earns more abroad than it buys, it has a balance-of-payments surplus and, in effect, is a creditor country. A deficit results from net buying, produces a debtor status, and tends to diminish a currency's relative-value (exchange rate). A balance-of-payments surplus will tend to produce an upward movement on a currency's exchange rate as buyers exceed sellers in the world's foreign exchange markets.

*Fixed Rates.* The means by which exchange rates are managed goes to the very heart of the international monetary system. Under the fixed-rate system which prevailed from the end of World War II until 1973, countries were obligated to keep their exchange rates fixed by having their central banks intervene in foreign exchange markets to assure an equilibrium supply and demand situation for their own currency. By this means, the competitive exchange rate depreciations of the 1930s were to be avoided. Reluctance of countries to change their rates despite structural disequilibria and the increased activities of international currency speculators doomed the fixed-rate system.

*Float.* Under the existing exchange rate regime, monetary authorities are free to allow their currency's exchange rate to "float" in response to changes in free market pressures. In theory, a country could balance its external account simply by remaining aloof and allowing its exchange rate to move sufficiently high or low to find an equilibrium level. In practice, countries will not remain totally passive; they intervene in the foreign exchange markets whenever exchange rate movements are judged excessive. All this produces an element of uncertainty in international business. It is impossible to predict what the exchange rate is going to be between two currencies on that date in the future when the buyer is actually obliged to make payment to the exporter. Unless they are willing to gamble, international traders must *hedge* in the foreign exchange market. This is done by going to a commercial bank with a foreign exchange trading capability. An exporter will contract for the sale of a foreign currency (in which he or she expects eventual payment) on a specified future date for a specified rate. An importer will contract to purchase a foreign currency (the currency of the exporter's country) for delivery on a specified future date at a specified rate in terms of his or her own currency. By such an arrangement, no matter what exchange rate movements occur in the interim, international business executives will know beforehand the exact value of the foreign currency they are buying or selling in terms of their own currency. This is a potential business expense which must be taken into consideration in determining prices of internationally traded goods.

**Impact of Trade Balance** When a country's exchange rate depreciates (loses value) or appreciates (increases in value), a direct impact is felt on its trade balance in the medium to long term. A currency depreciation (or devaluation) makes a country's imports more expensive and its exports cheaper. Appreciation (or revaluation) has the opposite effect. This was the rationale for the two devaluations of the dollar in 1971 and 1973. American industry was losing its competitiveness because the dollar's exchange rate had become overvalued vis-à-vis most West European currencies and the Japanese yen. Very simply, those countries by then had recovered fully from the devastation of World War II. The devaluations led to a lowering of the price of American exports in these markets and an increase in the prices of our imports from those markets. The subsequent turnaround of the deteriorating American trade balance in 1975 was largely the result of the change in the dollar's exchange rate.

## EVALUATION

Engaging in international trade can be a burden, a luxury, a necessity, or a major profit center for companies. It depends on individual circumstances. A company with a unique product or one in worldwide short supply can sit back and wait for foreign buyers to come to its doors. Others must make a decisive first step into this profitable growing market. Assuming governments do not regress into protectionism and instead choose to reduce further the barriers to trade, companies will find it increasingly difficult and costly to ignore the opportunities of foreign markets. The very successes of the private sector in conducting international trade occasionally leads to temporary obstacles inflicted by governmental authorities anxious to avoid sudden domestic disruptions. However, for corporations with aggressiveness and persistence, the challenge of exporting is seldom insurmountable.

When an industry is unable to sell profitably overseas, it is likely to be losing ground in its own home market. Such an industry is a prime candidate to begin feeling stiff import competition from abroad. International trade flows are becoming a key barometer of efficiency and growth.

*See also* DEVELOPING COUNTRIES, MANAGEMENT IN; ECONOMIC SYSTEMS; EUROPE, MANAGEMENT IN WESTERN; EXCHANGE, FOREIGN, MANAGEMENT OF; IN-

TERNATIONAL OPERATIONS AND MANAGEMENT IN MULTINATIONAL COMPANIES; JAPANESE INDUSTRIES, MANAGEMENT IN; SMALL BUSINESS ADMINISTRATION.

## REFERENCES

Baldwin, Robert E.: *Nontariff Distortions of International Trade*, The Brookings Institution, Washington, 1970.

Daniels, John Earnest Ogram, and Lee Radebaugh: *International Business*, Addison-Wesley Publishing Company, Inc., Reading, Mass., 1976.

*Exporters' Encyclopedia*, Dun and Bradstreet Publications, Inc., New York, updated regularly.

Hess, John, and Philip Cateira: *International Marketing*, Richard D. Irwin, Inc., Homewood, Ill., 1975.

*International Economic Report of the President*, submitted annually to the Congress, U.S. Government Printing Office.

Meier, Gerald: *Problems of Trade Policy*, Oxford University Press, New York, 1973.

U.S. Department of Commerce, *A Basic Guide to Exporting*, 1976.

———: *Export Information Services for U.S. Business Firms*, 1976.

———: *Exporting to the United States*, 1971.

STEPHEN D. COHEN, *American University*

# Interpersonal relationships

Interpersonal relationships involve the content and quality of interaction between people and are defined by *both* the observable behavior that people exhibit in the interaction *and* the feelings that are associated with the interaction. These exchanges are typically personal, person-to-person, and usually involve verbal communication channels. These relationships are characterized by a substantial influence of affect, as experienced by the individuals involved, in determining the nature of the relationships. The quality and content of these relationships are also influenced over time by the cumulative effect of a series of exchanges.

Substantial parts of managers' jobs involve them in person-to-person contact with people within and outside of their organizations. In one study, for example, managers reported spending over half their time in these kinds of exchanges.[1] The quality and effectiveness of the managers' interpersonal relationships will directly bear on the quality and effectiveness of the managers' total performance, which, in turn, is highly influential in determining the effective performance of the organization unit.

Shortly after Frederick Taylor published *The Principles of Scientific Management*[2] and, in part, in response to Taylor's ideas, the human relations view of management began to take hold in American industry. An early study took place around 1930 in Western Electric's Hawthorne plant near Chicago. The Hawthorne Study investigated the effects of group and interpersonal relationships upon the productivity of workers.[3] It was found that informal relationships between workers can be a strong force in controlling the output of these workers, even, at times, inducing workers on an incentive pay scale to produce less than they might in order to obey the group's "rules." More than anything else, the Hawthorne Study made clear the importance of social variables such as group interpersonal relationships in the practice of management. If interpersonal relationships can have a profound effect on worker productivity, the question was posed, is it possible that responsible people can come to understand and manage that effect to everyone's benefit? This question intrigued many managers in the 1930s, and it continues to intrigue them today.

## PERSON PERCEPTION

What an individual senses and what that person perceives are not one and the same. Perceptions are impressions of others drawn in part from the input to the sense organs (eyes, ears, etc.) but reflected against past experiences and opinions. Every person is unique, yet the mind has its limits. One cannot think of all the unique characteristics of everyone encountered. In today's parlance, we tend to "put people in a bag." Social psychologists speak of creating invariances by which they mean sets that simplify the world with order and stability in our perceptions. An example of an invariance is the notion that good people do good deeds. The dual processes of "bagging" people and creating invariances are facts of the subjectivity of human perception of others. One might observe the same behavior in two individuals and yet perceive that behavior very differently. Further, one person's perception of a second person might be very different from the perception a third party may have of that same individual. For example, assume a long-haired, bearded young man is attempting to jar open a partially closed window of a parked limousine, with its headlights on high beam, at a country club's rear entrance. An older woman observes the behavioral act. The women perceives the behavior and concomitantly perceives the person. She might perceive the behavior as an act of vandalism and the person a good-for-nothing individual. These perceptions were derived from experiences and opinions as well as from what was observed. Suppose, too, that a young minister also observed the same behavioral act. Perhaps he might see it as a good deed: the efforts of a thoughtful young man to turn off the headlights before the car's battery is worn down. The young man is thus perceived as a good samaritan. The same behavioral act can result in different perceptions of things and people. Such is the legacy of person perception.

When we perceive others, we attribute intent to them; that is, we perceive they are motivated to try to get somewhere or do something. *Our perceptions of others are dominated by our assumptions of their directedness, of their motives*, not by what it is we actually see them doing or hear them saying.[4] Our attribution of motives to others depends heavily upon our own cognitive models, invariances, and the way we go about "bagging" others. Much of what we see in others is really within ourselves. The world we perceive is the one we create. The people we perceive are, in part, characters of our own mind.

As well as attributing motives to others, people attribute abilities, emotions, and powers to others. All these, too, grow in part from what is sensed and in part from individuals' cognitive models of the world. Often, just one trait in a person can cause others to imply that person's entire personality. The development of this *implicit personality* in others can be accurate or can be very inaccurate.

What implications does this hold for management? First, and most important, managers must recognize the existence of these dynamics. They must realize that their perceptions of others are far from objective; rather, perceptions are highly subjective. In a manager's work, each day he or she must judge other men and women and make decisions on their ability and desire to see a job done right. Managers may have an intuitive feel for people, and the high quality of that intuition may explain many of their successes as managers. It is possible, however, to sharpen intuition about people if the source of that intuition is examined to determine whether it comes from a cognitive model or from their behavior.

## AFFILIATION

A basic premise is that people are "needing" creatures and that their behavior reflects those needs. When things are denied us that we believe will satisfy a need we are experiencing, we become frustrated. (This unhappy sequence is discussed in more detail in the section on Conflict and Resolution in this entry. For the dynamics of relationships between needs, behavior, and outcomes, see MOTIVATION.) A simplified explanation of motivation suggests that a person behaves in a manner which satisfies a need that has been aroused. People's behavior, therefore, is not random nor capricious. Rather, it is goal directed and purposive.

This is of prime interest to managers because people's behavior can serve both their own individual goals *and* the objectives of the organization. The relative degree of overlap between individual and organizational goals is a variable over which managers exercise some control and influence.

**One-to-One Relationships**  One-to-one relationships are the fundamental basis of interpersonal relationships. Many of the dimensions of one-to-one relationships can be applied to more complex social situations involving three or more people. The essential point is that people engage in relationships with each other in attempts to satisfy their own particular needs. When satisfaction becomes reciprocal, the relationships can develop and flourish.

*Trust and Intimacy.*  People vary in their capacity to trust others. Similarly, people vary in the degree to which they are trustworthy. Positive interpersonal relationships require a minimum of mutual trust. To engage in genuine relationships requires that each person allow a degree of vulnerability to the other. This often occurs through the increasingly complete expression of one's true self in the relationships. As relationships mature and trust in the other person is proved to be well placed, increasing amounts of vulnerability and trust will permeate the relationship. Interpersonal trust is a fragile thing which cannot take many jolts without suffering serious fractures. Just as increasing levels of trust can be built up, the cycle can be reversed, often permanently, by a violation of trust. There are some people who have been sufficiently disappointed by other people that they trust no one. They have become convinced, or they have convinced themselves, that people are essentially bad. This conviction can result in behavior that is so self-protective and abrasive that their prophecies about others are fulfilled in their interpersonal relationships.

A manager can build a reputation among the people in the organization for being trustworthy. This reputation will provide a substantial base upon which fulfilling and effective interpersonal relationships can be constructed. Managers cannot condone illegal or inappropriate behavior, nor can they ignore it in their attempt to be trustworthy. However, by being open about one's position and by respecting confidences where appropriate, a manager can develop and maintain a reputation as a trustworthy person. This reputation will prove invaluable in furthering the quality of their interpersonal relationships.

*Empathy.* Empathy is a capacity to see, understand, and experience the world as another person is seeing, understanding, and experiencing it. Empathy is definitely not the same as sympathy or even understanding. The latter implies an intellectual process. Empathy includes understanding *plus* the emotional aspect of another person's life experience. An important characteristic of empathy is that it is not judgmental; it simply is the experiencing.

Empathy is a critical contributor to good interpersonal relationships because it fosters a situation in which one person can believe and genuinely feel that another human being knows what is going on inside oneself. Effective managers will have the capacity to empathize with others in the organization. At the same time, effective managers will not find themselves hamstrung and unable to act or decide because of that empathic understanding.

**Expression of Feelings** Interpersonal relationships that are on a good footing allow a wide range of feelings to be expressed. It is often the people to whom we are closest that we have the strongest emotional responses. Intense love, anger, joy, elation, or sorrow are seldom shared with strangers. Expression of extreme ranges of feelings is often considered unacceptable and unexpected behavior in organizations. The important point to recognize is that feelings are an unavoidable, real component of the human experience. To deny their existence or to require their complete suppression in the organizational setting is to ignore naively a powerful socioemotional force. Certainly, the unbridled expression of every fleeting emotion would not be likely to improve organizational performance. At the same time, denial that emotions exist about organizational issues is equally absurd.

**Perception** An important aspect of perception for one-to-one relationships involves the concept of selective perception. We engage in relationships to fulfill needs. Needs influence our perceptions so that what we perceive will reflect what we need. A manager's offhand comment about the responsibilities and rewards that come with a position soon to be vacant might be interpreted by an ambitious subordinate as a promise of the promotion. The manager may not have had that in mind at all.

When we perceive things, two different processes are taking place. There is (1) the physical sensing of data in the world and (2) the interpretation made on the basis of those data. Thus, what *is*, for a person, depends on the sensory data available and upon what meaning that person makes of the sensory data.

Managers will improve their one-to-one relationships when they are able to recognize that the other person's world is as the other person perceives it; it is not what the manager perceives or tells the other it is.

**Socioemotional Needs** These are a series of individual needs which people have and which involve relationships with others. The list presented here does not exhaust all the possibilities; it is intended to suggest the kinds of needs that are often associated with interpersonal relationships.

*Need for Affiliation.* People need other people. It is from other people that understanding, emotional support, friendship, and love come. It is to other people that these are extended. For most people, these needs are important and necessary.[5]

Within organizations, demands and changes are often required of peoples' loyalties, particularly when organizational changes are taking place. A promotion to a new department at a higher level in the hierarchy may call for new affiliations and loyalties. The new affiliations may make a continuation of earlier organizational and personal relationships awkward. Managers making moves of this sort will need to acknowledge and accept the required changes in the nature of earlier relationships while simultaneously not violating implicit levels of trust that had been developed.

*Need for Power.* Organizations create situations where one person has social power over others. Power implies the ability to influence another's behavior or the ability to resist another's efforts to alter one's own behavior.

A person's social power can be described as having its basis in one or more of the following categories:[6] (1) *reward* power, wherein the person has control of rewards for others; (2) *coercive* power, wherein the person has control over devices which make it sufficiently punishing for others not to conform; (3) *referent* power, wherein the person is positively perceived by others who try to identify with him or her; (4) *expert* power, wherein the person is believed to have special knowledge; and (5) *legitimate* power, wherein the person is seen to have the right to influence behavior by virtue of the others' acceptance of the person's organizational position.

Power, and the need for it, is central for managers and for their effective job performance. It has been suggested that this need is one which separates managers from nonmanagers.[7] While the power to reward and punish are the most commonly available bases for managers, it is short-sighted to overlook the other bases available.

Managers' decisions will unavoidably involve value judgments about the relative merits of means and ends used in the accomplishment of organizational goals. The issue of social power amplifies those value decisions. Should a popular but ineffective subordinate be fired? If so, how to do it? Should a bright, energetic, abrasive, insolent subordinate be stifled or brought under control? Managers must make these difficult choices and be prepared to live with the consequences and themselves.

*Need for Self-actualization.* Satisfaction of this need can often impinge on interpersonal relationships in a negative manner. Following Maslow's model,[8] as a person begins to fulfill self-actualizing needs, the needs that were fulfilled by social contact, respect of others, success, and status will have begun to diminish. As a consequence, self-actualized people will tend not to need interpersonal relationships as acutely as before and may even seem indifferent to them.

Managers will do well to remember that all people differ in their needs of friendship, love, closeness, and interaction with other people. It is particularly tempting to assume that most other people need social contact to the same degree and in the manner that we do. This is a dangerous assumption for managers to make, for it can lead to very inappropriate decisions. It is better to assume a wide range of difference and preferences among people, to observe carefully and to test for preferences before making decisions which impact on the interpersonal relationships of subordinates.

**Attitudes and Values** Attitudes are generally described as a person's thoughts, feelings, or predisposition to act in regard to things. Values are generally assumed to be a little more basic than attitudes and usually include a judgmental quality about basic rights and wrongs. People's attitudes and values exhibit a general kind of internal consistency. Attitudes are generally easier to change than values which are established early in life. Peer-group values will generally be included as a significant aspect of an individual's repertoire of values.

A dynamic relationship exists between behavior and attitudes. Generally, people try to keep them consistent with each other, so that if an attitude is changed, behavior will also alter to correspond. It also turns out that changing behavior can influence a change in attitude.

If people in an organization believe that the management is basically fair and trustworthy, then they will usually behave in a way that is consistent with those attitudes. On the other hand, an employee who has a bad attitude may believe that management is unconcerned, incompetent, and an antagonist. That employee's behavior and job performance will probably reflect those attitudes, which can become a problem for the manager involved.

By and large, a manager's chances of quickly changing a person's attitude or values are relatively slight. This is particularly true when the attitude is central to a person's self-concept. Rather than undertake to change very central attitudes and beliefs, a productive direction for a manager to take is first to understand what the subordinate's attitude really is. With that understanding, the manager can proceed to create an environment in which the attitude and associated behavior either are appropriate to organizational goals or, alternatively, do not conflict with them. For example, assume a supervisor is convinced that a high level of participation in decision making is tantamount to abdication of managerial responsibility. It would be folly to force that person to engage in a participatory kind of managerial behavior. Rather, that supervisor could be placed in an organizational setting with a task and situation that calls for strong, centralized decision making. In that way, the supervisor will not be required either to change the attitude or to behave in a way inconsistent with the attitude.

## JOINT GOAL ACCOMPLISHMENT

The relationship between managers and their immediate subordinates constitutes a major influence on the achievement of the group's goals. A central task of a manager is the coordination of the group's activities in the service of organizational goal achievement. It is essential, then, for managers to understand how groups function and to be able to use that understanding to promote achievement of organizational objectives. The problem for the manager is accentuated when a group's task calls for contributions by members whose skills, knowledge, and personal traits are very different. These differences will often lead to interpersonal difficulties. Management of such a group will require a firm understanding of the individual and group dynamics involved *and* an ability to apply those concepts effectively.

**Types of Groups** In general, a group is a collection of individuals who share a sense of relationship. The nature of the relationship can range from high levels of interdependence, as occurs on a basketball team, to substantial independence, as occurs on a golf team. Types of groups can be identified which differ in the manner in which they come into being, in their purposes, and in the manner in which they conduct their affairs. These differences are important because they constitute leverage points that managers can consider as they perform their coordination tasks.

*Formal and Informal Groups.* Formal groups come into being as a consequence of overt organizational action. Formal groups typically have a prescribed organizational hierarchy which defines expected relationships among its members. Further, this kind of group will usually have its mission or area of activity spelled out.

Informal groups, on the other hand, develop in response to the needs of the people making up the group. As a consequence, they do not have an explicitly stated set of goals nor are there institutionally defined positions of authority. These aspects of an informal group develop as a consequence of group and individual activities. Informal groups serve a number of functions which formal groups do not address, such as (1) filling voids and details in decisions made by the formal organization; (2) establishing expectations for interpersonal relationships; and (3) fulfilling members' individual needs not met by the formal organizations, particularly needs for social contact. An informal group's goals and organizational goals may coincide, but it is not always the case.

Managers have authority over a wide spectrum of activities in formal groups. Managers have no direct control over emergent informal groups. In the latter case, prudent managers will recognize a group member's need for informal groups and will not try to outlaw or banish the informal group. Rather, they will try to manage things so that the goals of the informal group complement organizational objectives.

*Committees.* Committees are common organizational groups. They often include representatives from several parts of the formal organization. They have the advantages and disadvantages of a membership with diverse backgrounds, interests, needs, and loyalties.

Committees are criticized as being inefficient and inept; nevertheless, they survive and are continually called upon to serve organizational objectives. Problems with committees can be reduced when their leaders skillfully assist the group in assessing its progress toward its goals as well as maintaining a clear understanding of those goals.

*Project Teams.* These groups are typically formed to complete a specific task; then they are disbanded. The members of project teams are usually assigned to the team because of special skills and knowledge they possess. The managers' task is to develop this group of individuals with their separate professional and personal ties into an effective working team.

Much of the success in managing a project team depends on effective communication channels and the unrestricted flow of information. People are not likely to feel they belong to a group when they do not know what is going on.

The team's approach to the project will have to be planned and then implemented. This critical planning phase often occurs so early in the group's development that the group has not had an opportunity to realize its potential as an effective working unit. Person perceptions have not been well established. Sources and bases of social need fulfillment have not been identified within the group. Both planning and implementation will require the coordinated application of individual team members' unique skills and knowledge. All other things being equal, the full and enthusiastic involvement of team members is highly desirable. Differences in approach, in personal style, and even in the definition of the problem at hand can be expected. Managers will use their best interpersonal skills as they nurture the development of a project team, work to resolve the inevitable conflicts, and see the project through to completion. This can be helped by (1) facilitating open communications with adequate levels of trust and (2) ensuring sufficient time and attention to individual and group maintenance needs.

**Dynamics of Groups**  Besides classifying groups into types, it is useful to identify issues and processes that occur in most groups. These issues are of interest to managers, for they are the critical aspects which influence group performance.

*Cohesiveness.* Groups differ in the degree to which the members are attracted to each other and value their membership in the group. This quality is known as group cohesiveness. In general, cohesiveness is higher (1) when group members are alike, sharing similar attitudes and values, (2) when they have ample opportunity to interact with each other, (3) when membership is relatively attractive, or (4) when the group is threatened from without. All other things being equal, a small group of four or five will interact more and be more cohesive than will a larger group.[9]

A highly cohesive group is a powerful social force

in an organization. Its influence is substantial in guiding and prescribing members' behavior. Work groups which stick together are helpful to managers when the groups' purposes align with organizational objectives. When that alignment does not occur, managers will need to understand and, when possible, alter the factors supporting the groups' antagonism to organizational goals. A work group which is not cohesive is a managerial problem in the sense that group pressures for excellence in job performance are not present.

*Norms.* A group norm is a powerful social force influencing group members' behavior. Norms are rules and standards that describe how a "good" group member should behave. Norms are developed informally in a group through the interaction of its members. Members may deviate some from group norms, but at some point more deviations will result in sanctions by the group. These sanctions have the objective of bringing a deviant member's behavior into line with the group's norms. Attempts to explain to the deviant member about "how things are done around here" are typical early warning devices used to bring a member's behavior into line. If the individual continues to violate norms, the group will isolate the person and, in the extreme, refuse to allow the deviant member to participate in the group's activities at all. Managers can expect that people will shape their behavior in a way that maintains their membership in desirable groups. If those behaviors happen to run counter to organizational goals, then the extreme trade off becomes group membership versus organizational goals. Managers will not help matters by forcing this dilemma or by denying its existence. Managers who recognize group norms and their impact on behavior will be able to create situations which (1) minimize the either-or quality and (2) capitalize on these very powerful social forces in the service of organizational goals.

*Decision Making in Groups.* It is often said that increased participation of group members in decision making results in greater acceptance of those decisions and an increased likelihood that the decisions will be successfully implemented. In some instances, research has supported the assertion, and in other instances, it has not.[10] In situations where a manager and a work group are involved, the powerful impact of the organizational hierarchy with its potential rewards and punishments cannot be ignored. Because of this, it has been suggested that it is unethical and improper for managers to expect or assert that true participation in decision making has taken place at all.[11]

As a practical matter, the amount of participation in group decision making can range along a continuum.[12] At one extreme, the manager makes all the decisions. At the other extreme, the group has substantial responsibility for decisions. No matter how the decision-making chores are divided, managers continue to be accountable within the formal hierarchy for the performance of their parts of the organization. This requires that managers be comfortable even when they do not have direct "hands-on" involvement in decisions.

The relative quality of group decisions is also of interest to managers. Whether or not a group makes a better decision than individuals do depends on (1) the nature of the problem, (2) the situation, (3) the availability of information, (4) the skills and knowledge of group members, and (5) their inclinations about involvement.

*Task and Maintenance Activities.* These two categories consume the major part of a group's time. *Task-related activities* have to do with the achievement of the group's goals and objectives. *Maintenance activities* are addressed to the social-emotional aspects that are necessary for the group to continue to function. At times, a third activity can gain a group's attention. This occurs when an individual captures the group's time and causes the group to deal with that person's own personal needs. The topics of these sorts of discussions have been termed *hidden agendas* since the individual involved often puts the issue in a way that does not directly identify the personal (unsatisfied) need that lies behind the public agenda being talked about.

Managers will be concerned with all three types of group activities at one time or another. The task and maintenance activities are of central importance since they will govern the quality of the group's goal attainment. Because groups serve a number of their members' social needs, and because social-emotional issues are generated as groups work, sufficient time and energy must be available to keep the group viable. While group maintenance activities, such as joking or humor, may seem inefficient and a waste of time, the severe denial or prohibition of these anxiety-reducing activities will reduce the effectiveness of the group over time. As with most managerial decisions, balance is the key. Both task *and* group maintenance activities are necessary for effective group performance.

## INFLUENCE AND CHANGE

A large measure of a manager's job is concerned with the influence of others. A manager must routinely ask an employee to change a work schedule in order to meet a new deadline. In the extreme, a manager may ask a person to move an entire family to another part of the country or across the sea. Each of these actions requires an ability and willingness to influence subordinates. A manager must also influence peers. Typically, managers find themselves in competition with other managers for the scarce resources of their company. In such cases, the manager must seek to modify the behavior of his or her associates. A manager often needs to influence superiors: the boss is about to make the wrong decision, or a situation should be reviewed one more time. In all of these, the same dynamics are at play. Insights to these dynamics are provided by the process and philosophy of change and influence which draw heavily from the work of H. J. Leavitt[13] and are developed here from that source.

From a broad perspective, the process of influence involves the person or people being changed and the person or people doing the changing. Conclusions drawn from person-to-person relationships are generally transferable to larger collectivities of change agents and changes.

Person A desiring person B to change must have a specific motive or reason for wanting B to change. Person A must also diagnose what B's current behavior is, as well as what B's motives happen to be, and what A wishes B's future behavior to be. Further, person B will impute motives to person A, which may or may not be the real reasons why A is trying to bring about a change in B. It is clear that both A and B may make errors in diagnosing each other's motives. Misdiagnosis on either side can cause difficulty and resistance in the change effort.

Once the changer A has diagnosed B's current behavior and motive constellation, a number of alternative philosophic approaches to influence and change B are open to A. Person A can (1) draw upon authority or (2) attempt to manipulate B or (3) engage in collaboration.

**Authority** This is the best-known approach to influence. In business relationships, it may be the most widely accepted philosophy. Authority means that A has the power to order B to change his or her behavior. When most employees join an organization, they agree psychologically (a psychological contract) to accept the authority of superiors. Thus, the use of authority is correct and proper. It is appropriate and is the most widely used means of influence and change between a superior and a subordinate. However, there are times when the influence and change can be less costly and the results

more productive if superiors select collaboration rather than authority as the philosophy behind their efforts of change. When, for example, the influence is directed at an activity close to the ego of B, A might do well to tell B of A's motive to change B and not order B to change. This approach allows the decision to change to be made by B after B has a full picture of the pros and cons of the change from A's perspective. Collaboration does not always work, but when appropriate, it can be more effective than authority for the boss and the organization.

**Manipulation** Unlike collaboration, manipulation is a philosophy of change in which A *does not* let B in on A's motives, including A's desire to change B. In an interpersonal relationship which is long term, manipulation is an irrational choice in that the costs of failure (even given a low probability of discovery and therefore failure) are so high as to make this an untenable alternative. In short-term interpersonal relationships, manipulation may be easier than collaboration, but it is still not recommended on the grounds that one's reputation and ability to deal in future interpersonal relationships may suffer irreparably.

**Collaboration** This is a philosophy of influence and change in which one seeks a candid and honest relationship with the person one wishes to influence. Suppose A makes known an intention to influence and change B's behavior *and* A's reasons for that intention. The next step is up to B. B must choose to change. If B so decides, A reinforces the decision by sharing the burden of change with B, including overcoming resistances to change from others. Collaboration is a time-consuming procedure. It takes time to communicate to B the motive and viewpoint for the change. B will have questions. These must be answered with care and consideration. But the outcome of collaboration is very productive: the change, if B chooses to make it, will be firm. Collaboration has another benefit: it provides a test of A's ideas. In the use of authority, A's ideas are not exposed to evaluation and criticism. Collaboration forces A to make disclosures and opens the way to constructive evaluation.

**Social Commitment** The dynamics of people working together in committees and groups open up one additional aspect of influence and change—that of social commitment. If A fully collaborates with a group of B's, tells them what A sees the cost and the benefits to be gained by the proposed change, of A's motive for that change, and of A's willingness to accept the group's decision—for or against A's proposal—then A is engaging in an act of collaborative group participation. Because so many B's have an input on the final decision, the change finally adopted may not be exactly as A had proposed. If A can take a flexible stand on the change issue, then collaborative group participation and change is the most desirable means of influence. Changes effected through collaborative means are supported by the social commitment of A and the group of B's. Their commitment to the change, to making it work, and to the relationship within which the change was designed gives the collaborative method its special value to managers. In the absence of managerial flexibility, however, this approach may be nonproductive and disfunctional.

## CONFLICT AND RESOLUTION

Conflict is a common occurrence in life. Conflict occurs when a desired goal or objective is not reasonably available. It takes place (1) within a person, (2) between people, (3) between organizational subunits, and (4) between organizations. The focus of this discussion is on the conflict issues of the first three levels.

**Conflict at the Individual Level** An individual will experience frustration when a barrier hampers the attainment of a desired objective. For example, a desired promotion or transfer which is denied because of budget limitations will result in frustration for the person. A number of common ways in which people behave when frustrated have been identified.

*Aggression.* The frustrated person may attack the barrier itself. For example, a vending machine which accepts quarters with abandon while refusing to produce a candy bar may receive all sorts of punches, slaps, kicks, and verbal abuse. In organizations, people often feel unable to attack the barrier directly, and so the aggression is displaced onto some other object or person. Raging at one's spouse, cat, or children might help relieve the immediate pressure caused by an uncooperative boss but does nothing toward reducing the real source of the internal conflict. In some extreme cases, people revert to infantile, maladaptive behavior—like plotting revenge or general negativism—when they have been severely frustrated.

Another alternative to being aggressive in response to frustration is to withdraw from the situation physically and/or psychologically. When this device is employed, people become withdrawn and apathetic. Clearly, this is behavior that managers will not want to encourage in subordinates. When this behavior is observed in an organization, it may

be a sign of a subordinate's frustration. Rather than try to cajole greater enthusiasm, the manager should seek to understand and change the organizational circumstances that lead to frustration and apathy.

*Internal Dilemmas.* Because people want different things and the wants themselves vary, people sometimes find themselves in conflict about their own goals. These internal conflicts can take one of three forms:

1. The person has two attractive goals which are mutually exclusive. When the attractiveness of the two choices is nearly equal, the tendency to be indecisive or to vacillate will be great. Choosing between taking a new job in a small firm with growth potential and high risk or staying in the present position with its built-up retirement benefits and predictable promotion sequence is an example of the approach-approach dilemma.

2. This combination involves conflicts over a goal which has both positive and negative aspects. A promotion which has all the rewards and gratifications normally associated with it *and* which requires a move to an undesirable geographical location is an example.

3. This combination involves a choice between two equally negative outcomes. An example is an organizational policy which calls for a pay reduction for failure to wear uncomfortable and unattractive protective goggles.

Reactions to internal conflict increase the levels of internal stress and tension. When managers see behavior that suggests such adaptive processes are occurring, they can take steps to alter relevant organizational factors. Energy not consumed in efforts to adapt to internal conflicts is potentially available for improving organizational performance.

**Conflict at the Organizational Level** Conflicts between people in organizations and between organizational units cannot be avoided. Furthermore, organizational conflict is not necessarily bad nor counterproductive to organizational goal achievement. Groups tend to behave in different but consistent ways, depending on whether they consider themselves winners or losers of a conflict. A winning group is apt to become complacent, relaxing in its victory. It will often begin to attend to the maintenance of its members' socioemotional needs at the expense of group-task performance. The losing group will tend to rationalize the defeat, or failing that, look inside the group for a cause of its loss. Fortunately, losing groups often are prepared to work harder to succeed and pay less attention to group members' individual needs.[14]

*Stages of Conflict.* [15] Organizational conflict proceeds through several distinct stages and stems from several unique sources. Identifying these stages and sources will assist the manager in designing an appropriate strategy for handling the situation.

1. Conflict has it genesis in an early latent state. The elements necessary for conflict are present in this stage, but they are not always visible. Where a latent conflict condition exists, one would probably find some combination of general uneasiness, perhaps apprehension, differences of opinion, different values, and limited resources.

2. The next stage occurs when the conflict is perceived and experienced by those involved. In this stage, people will feel more tense, hostile, and aggressive. They will begin to see the dimensions of the conflict taking shape. Battle lines are sketched out, and contingency plans are established. We-they distinctions become more important; good guys and bad guys are identified.

3. The final stage is one of manifest conflict where people are actually fighting. The fight will usually take place in the socially acceptable modes of verbal attack and defense and organizational intrigue. Occasionally, the fight gets to the physical aggression stage.

*Sources of Conflict.* Individuals and subunits in organizations may find themselves in disagreement about the facts of a situation, about the appropriate means and methods to be instituted, about the goals to be achieved, and about the relevant guiding values.

Competition for scarce resources is probably the most common source of organizational conflict. Conflict among claimants for resources can result in behavior and consequent resource distribution which is suboptimal for the organization. Winner-take-all battles can leave critical components of the organization with insufficient resources to operate properly. Management's concern is to achieve an orderly distribution of these limited resources and avoid the unnecessary costs of the competition.

A need for autonomy and independence will often spawn conflict within an organizational hierarchy. When a person joins an organization, some portion of autonomy and freedom of action is forfeited in deference to coordination and cooperation. Similarly, groups will have to subordinate some of their independence in deference to larger organizational objectives.

*Managing Conflict.* Resolution of conflict can take a number of different forms. Resolution will usually involve an investment of organizational time and energy. Avoiding unnecessary investments and disruptions is the critical managerial task. [16]

1. *Problem solving.* This technique for resolution relies on the open confrontation of differences among conflicting parties. It requires, at a minimum, open communications and that the parties be willing to try to resolve the issues. When the conflict is based on differences in values, the problem-solving model is not apt to be successful. When differences occur over facts, methods, or goals, the confrontation, open communication, and problem solving have potential for finding resolution.

2. *Smoothing.* This technique does not truly remove or reduce the basic conflict. By emphasizing positive aspects in the situation and avoiding sensitive areas of difference, it is sometimes possible to smooth the situation sufficiently for work to proceed. This technique is obviously a temporary solution.

3. *Referring to higher authority.* Resolutions of this sort will usually result in a winning and losing side. If production and sales cannot agree about the appropriate percentage of rejects per order, then the problem can be sent to the level of management that the two units have in common for resolution. When labor-management disputes are sent to arbitrators for solution, this general principle is being followed.

4. *Reduction in scarcity of resources.* Conflict based on competition for scarce resources can be resolved by increasing the pool of resources for all. Rather than fight over the relative size of portions, parties to the conflict can all enjoy increased portion size. This strategy will not be effective when there are status implications connected to relative amounts a given unit gains. Furthermore, managers are often constrained by organizational budgets so that making changes in the total pool of resources will often be a slow process.

5. *Avoidance.* This strategy is commonly found in interpersonal situations. One person, knowing another's sensitivities, can avoid a conflict by not bringing up topics in those areas. Nothing has changed, but a potential conflict has been avoided for a time during which progress may have occured in other dimensions.

6. *Compromise.* The difficulty with compromise solutions is that all parties lose a little. The final solution may not be a particularly good one from any of the parties' points of view. Compromise solutions do permit conflicting parties to move beyond a stalemated situation. Compromises tend not to be permanent solutions to underlying problems.

7. *Changing the people in conflict.* This solution is

not unanimously endorsed as practical by social scientists and organizational practitioners. People have a capacity for stubbornly clinging to their ways of being, believing, and behaving. To attempt to change people in the interest of conflict resolution is, at best, a long-term undertaking. By the time a conflict is manifest, people have usually taken positions publicly. To change one's position is to admit error and possibly lose face. Where conflict is based on an inaccurate view of the facts in the situation, changing people has some promise. New, or more complete, information may persuade people to alter their position. When conflicts are based in attitudes, beliefs, and values, hope for quick change in people is optimistic. Managers may occasionally be tempted to institute quick resolutions that do not address the basic sources of the conflict. In those cases, the manager is simply buying time; the conflict will remain and will require attention again.

## CONCLUSION

Interpersonal relationships are a key element in management. Scientific study of these relationships in the managerial context is less than a half-century old, however. This field is still in a state of search. There appears to be a taxonomy which allows us to order the key dynamics of interpersonal relationships in a meaningful way, but that is only the beginning. The condensation in this entry necessarily leaves very much unsaid. There is one general principle, however, to guide the study of interpersonal relationships: No person is a single entity; each person exists concomitantly in the other, and the study of management, as a substudy of humanity, is the study of that mutuality of existence.

*See also* ASSERTIVENESS TRAINING; CONFORMITY IN MANAGEMENT; CONTROL SYSTEMS, MANAGEMENT; HEALTH, MENTAL; HYGIENE FACTORS; LABORATORY (SENSITIVITY) TRAINING; LEADERSHIP; MANAGEMENT THEORY, SCIENCE, AND APPROACHES; MOTIVATION IN ORGANIZATIONS; ORGANIZATIONAL COMMUNICATIONS; TRANSACTIONAL ANALYSIS.

### NOTES

[1]R. A. Webber, *Time and Management*, Van Nostrand Reinhold Company, New York, 1972.

[2]Claude S. George, *The History of Management Thought*, Prentice-Hall, Inc., Englewood Cliffs, N.J., 1968.

[3]Committee on Work in Industry, National Research Council, *Fatigue of Workers: Its Relation to Industrial Production*, Reinhold Publishing Corporation, New York, 1941, pp. 77–86.

[4]A. Hastoff, Personal communication, 1968.

[5]See, for example, A. H. Maslow, *Motivation and Personality*, Harper Bros. and Co., New York, 1954; and S. Schachter, *The Psychology of Affiliation*, Stanford University Press, Stanford, Calif., 1959.

[6]J. R. P. French, Jr., and B. Raven, "The Bases of Social Power," in Dorwin Cartwright, ed., *Studies in Social Power*, University of Michigan Press, Institute for Social Research, Ann Arbor, 1959, pp. 150–167.

[7]David C. McClelland, and David H. Burnham, "Power Is the Great Motivator," *Harvard Business Review*, March–April 1976, pp. 100–110; Abraham Zaleznik, "Power and Politics in Organizational Life," *Harvard Business Review*, May–June 1970, pp. 47–60.

[8]Maslow, loc. cit.

[9]David R. Hampton, Charles E. Summer, and Ross A. Webber, *Organizational Behavior and the Practice of Management* rev. ed., Scott, Foresman and Company, Glenview, Ill., 1973, pp. 220–223.

[10]H. R. Bobbitt, et al., *Organizational Behavior: Understanding and Prediction*, Prentice-Hall, Inc., Englewood Cliffs, N.J., 1974, pp. 190–193.

[11]Harold J. Leavitt, "Applied Organizational Change in Industry: Structural Technological and Humanistic Approaches," in James G. March, ed., *Handbook of Organization*, Rand McNally & Company, Chicago, 1965, pp. 1152–1153.

[12]Robert Tannenbaum and Warren Schmidt, "How to Choose a Leadership Pattern," *Harvard Business Review*, vol. 51, p. 164, 1973.

[13]Harold J. Leavitt, *Managerial Psychology*, 3d ed., The University of Chicago Press, Chicago, 1972.

[14]Edgar Schein, *Organizational Psychology*, 2d ed., Prentice-Hall, Inc., Englewood Cliffs, N.J., 1970, pp. 96–103.

[15]L. R. Pondy, "Organizational Conflict: Concepts and Models," *Administrative Science Quarterly*, vol. 12, no. 2, pp. 296–320, September 1967.

[16]Stephen P. Robbins, *Managing Organizational Conflict: A Nontraditional Approach*, Prentice-Hall, Inc., Englewood Cliffs, N.J., 1974, pp. 59–74

ROBERT H. DOKTOR, *University of Hawaii at Manoa*
MARVIN D. LOPER, *University of Hawaii at Manoa*

## Interview, appraisal (*See* APPRAISAL, PERFORMANCE.)

## Interviewing, directed and nondirected (*See* PERSONNEL ADMINISTRATION.)

## Interviewing, employee

The employment interview is a conversation—a conversation with the particular purpose of determining qualifications for employment, keeping in mind the needs of the applicant as well as the employer. Insofar as qualifications are concerned, it is important to ask three basic questions: (1) *Can* the applicant do the job or be trained to do it? (2) *Will* the person do the job and continue to do it? (3) *How* will the communications and interpersonal skills of the applicant affect his or her success on the job?

A second, but important, objective of the employment interview is to promote good will regardless of whether or not an employment offer is made. Insufficient attention to this goal may discourage acceptance of a job offer, reduce the number of persons interested in seeking employment with a firm, make candidates for employment who are potential or current customers reluctant to purchase the product or services of that organization, and even precipitate legal action charging discrimination.

The costs of ineffective employment interviewing can be significantly high. Most studies indicate that it can easily cost several hundred dollars to place a nonexempt employee on the payroll and several thousand dollars for an exempt employee. These costs can be compounded when training and development are considered, particularly when the new employee is misplaced or turns out to be unmotivated, inept, or a troublemaker. Should an employer be found guilty, or even be accused of discrimination against a prospective employee because of race, color, age, sex, place of national origin, or religion, defense action and court-imposed costs can be many thousands, even millions, of dollars.

## THE INTERVIEWING PROCESS

Like any skill, interviewing requires that certain steps be taken or elements be included if the end results are to be achieved. These include preparing for the interview, establishing and maintaining rapport, gathering the necessary information, controlling the interview, and evaluating the data which have been collected in terms of the employer's and applicant's needs.

**Preparation**  No interviewer plans to fail, but by failing to plan, the chances of failure are increased. Some of the more important steps to be taken before the start of the interview are:

1. Develop your skills prior to any actual interviewing through supervised practice exercises, such as role-playing, where valuable feedback is given by knowledgeable and experienced interviewers.

2. Determine the essential job requirements by carefully studying the job description and specifica-

tions, talking with persons doing the job, and observing the job being done.

3. Arrange the physical environment so that it is pleasant, comfortable, quiet, private, and free from interruptions and undue distractions.

4. Be alert to fair and equal employment considerations so that legal requirements, as well as human and employment needs, are met.

5. Plan your action in a way that allows for time efficiency but provides for a thorough exploration of the candidate's qualifications as they relate to the demands of the job.

**Rapport**  The interview should be relatively free from stress, at least from the kind of stress that is deliberately induced. When the interviewee is placed under pressure, he or she becomes more concerned with protecting his or her ego, avoiding criticism, or attacking rather than communicating. Frequently, as a result of putting the applicant "on the spot" through cross-examination techniques, the relationship deteriorates, the information becomes more guarded and slanted, the good will lessened, and the interviewee is more inclined to feel discriminated against.

A friendly smile, a firm handshake, a warm greeting, and some small talk about travel, the weather, and some common interests can get the interview started in a way that will enhance the relationship and the communications.

Continued attention to the candidate's comfort-level needs (temperature, lighting, seating, furniture arrangement, beverages, rest room), displaying an animated and responsive countenance, actively listening to what is being said, and making sincere compliments when appropriate can help the interviewee feel that he or she is being regarded as someone of importance and dignity.

Although the interview should be sustained as a pleasant conversation, it should be remembered that the goal of the interview is to obtain, retain, and analyze data so that a proper employment decision can be made; it is not just to fill time with easy talk that is light and enjoyable but not necessarily meaningful.

**Gathering Information**  Most effective in encouraging the applicant to talk freely and responsively is the use of the *funnel approach;* that is, the questioning moves from the general to the specific, the public to the private knowledge area, and the impersonal to the personal. By gently probing in this manner, there is less possibility that the candidate will feel that the interviewer is moving too quickly and probing too deeply into background areas that are sensitive and personal.

Open-ended questions that begin with what, how, and why are most useful in enlarging upon and enriching the fund of knowledge already available through the person's résumé or completed application. Some examples are, "What were some of your more challenging responsibilities in your last position?" "How did you handle them?" "Why did you take the approach which you did?"

Least useful are direct, closed-ended questions that provoke a one-word or yes or no response. Yet, the majority of questions asked by most untrained interviewers are of this type. While not ruling out closed-ended questions, they should be used very sparingly. Not only do they reveal less in-depth information than open-ended questions, they often put words in the mouth of the interviewee. For example, "Did you do well in your last job?" "Would you say that you have a good personality?" "Do you think you can do this job?" What person who is interested in being offered a job would say no to these questions?

Too many questions in rapid-fire succession may turn the conversation into a grilling and reduce the flow of spontaneous replies and thus increase the number of distortions and untruths. To lessen the chances of this occurring, the interviewer can make use of nonverbal actions, such as smiling, raising the eyebrows, pausing, employing pertinent comments such as verbal pats on the back, reflection of feelings, and brief restatements of what the interviewee has said. These techniques not only reduce the threatening aspect of continuing questions, they provide for a change of pace, force the interviewer to listen to what is being said, and convince the applicant that an attempt is being made to understand what he or she is saying.

**Control** The interview should be a planned event, not a "happening." This not only keeps the interview on track, it reduces the possibility of forgetting or overlooking anything of importance. Additionally, the information obtained is sorted out in a systematic way so that the interviewer can absorb it more easily and make better sense out of it. There is more chance of a "happening" occurring where (1) the background data come forth at random without chronology and coherence, (2) control is weakened or lost, and (3) the interviewer becomes frustrated and confused.

After the initial greeting, welcome, small talk, and an opening question to learn what has transpired already and what the applicant's expectations are, broad-brush or lead statements can be used to describe to the candidate what is going to happen in the interview and the approach to be taken. These lead statements can be employed to introduce each major area, such as work, education, and even leisure if it appears relevant, as well as to summarize the highlights of the person's background and to close the interview.

**Closing** During the closing, the interviewer should thank the interviewee and determine whether there is anything else the interviewee would like to tell about himself or herself. The interviewer then presents information about the job, the organization, benefits and, finally, provides the applicant with an opportunity to ask questions.

The "sell" part of the closing should be based on the interviewer's evaluation of the candidate and directed to the personal and career needs of the applicant.

The applicant should leave feeling that he or she has been fully heard and fairly treated and that this has been a worthwhile investment of time and energy. If an offer is not made, the interviewee should clearly know what the next step is and when it will be taken.

**Interpretation** Interpretation is a mentally demanding task which is facilitated by learning the fundamentals of obtaining relevant and sufficient interview data. Once this is accomplished, the interviewer can concentrate on the process of evaluation.

As previously stated, the interviewer should ask three important questions when ascertaining a candidate's qualifications for employment. *Can* and *will* the candidate do the job, and *how* will he or she get along with superiors, coworkers, subordinates, and customers in terms of getting the job done?

*Can do* refers to the interviewee's abilities and work-related training, knowledge, skills, and experiences. *Will do* applies to motivation, initiative, drive, and aspiration. *How do* is concerned with communications and interpersonal effectiveness.

Based upon these considerations, four steps are necessary to determine the candidate's suitability for employment:

1. A decision must be reached as to what the job requirements are; i.e., what are the essential tasks that must be done.

2. It is important to decide what abilities, knowledge, skills, experience, and personal qualities a new employee must have in order to do what is required on the job.

3. One must select the most effective approach, method, or questions for eliciting the required evaluative data from the applicant.

4. In as comprehensive fashion as possible, the information collected from the applicant must be matched against the job demands.

The evaluation should take into account the overall view of what the candidate has done, the strengths, weaknesses, likes, and dislikes evidenced as related to the opening available. It should in every way possible justify the employment recommendation and the possibilities of mutual success and satisfaction for the employer and candidate.

*See also* COMMUNICATIONS, EMPLOYEE; COMMUNICATIONS, NONVERBAL; COUNSELING, EMPLOYEE; EMPLOYMENT PROCESS; PERSONNEL ADMINISTRATION.

### REFERENCES

Black, J. M.: *How to Get Results from Interviewing*, Mc-Graw-Hill Book Company, New York, 1970.

Drake, J. D.: *Intervieweing for Managers*, American Management Association, New York, 1972.

Fear, R. A.: *The Evaluation Interview*, McGraw-Hill Book Company, New York, 1973.

Hariton, T.: *Interview!*, Hastings House Publishers, Inc., New York, 1970.

Lopez, F. M., Jr.: *Personnel Interviewing: Theory and Practice*, 2d ed., McGraw-Hill Book Company, New York, 1975.

Morgan, H. H., and J. W. Cogger: *The Interviewer's Manual*, The Psychological Corporation, New York, 1973.

JOHN W. COGGER, *The Psychological Corporation*

## Intrinsic factors, Herzberg's    (*See* MOTIVATION IN ORGANIZATIONS.)

## Invention    (*See* INNOVATION AND CREATIVITY.)

## Inventory control, materials    (*See* MATERIALS MANAGEMENT.)

## Inventory control, physical and stock-keeping

The cost of carrying inventory is a major cost and is claimed to be anywhere from 15 to 60 percent of the value of the inventory. Of course, turnover makes these numbers more palatable. If the inventory can be turned 10 times each year, then inventory carrying costs might be the equivalent of 1.5 to 6 percent of sales. It all depends on the point of view. Regardless of how much it costs to carry inventory, however, most of the control problems relate to turnover. The more turnover required, the more likely warehousing will present serious control problems.

The ideal condition would be to synchronize supply and demand so that supply coming in the receiving door would always be matched with demand going out the shipping door. Such ideal conditions are unlikely. Instead, thousands of warehouses and storerooms are busily stocking supplies in anticipation of shipping orders that do not always match the inventory waiting to be shipped.

**Physical versus Accounting Control**    The ability to satisfy demand efficiently is directly related to the degree of control excercised by warehouse or storeroom personnel. Control is defined as physical control, as opposed to accounting control which is mainly concerned with financial responsibility and asset accounting. The firm's accounting department usually maintains a perpetual inventory control of some kind, and this inventory must be balanced periodically with the actual physical inventory. Balancing depends upon correctly accounting for receipts and withdrawals reported by the warehouse. This accounting normally takes place prior to issuing the shipping instructions, and entries are verifed after the shipping documents or reports relating to shipping and receiving have been comsummated. Periodically, physical inventories are taken to ensure that the actual inventory agrees with the perpetual book inventory. When discrepancies are found, adjustments must be made that will compensate for the overs and shorts detected, and the actual inventory is assumed to balance with the perpetual book inventory.

*Overs and Shorts.* In a very large warehouse where many stockkeeping units (SKUs) are stocked, all existing overs and shorts may not be detected, and new overages and shortages may be introduced unless careful attention is given to the establishment of a clean cut-off. Shortages and overages can also be introduced when verified counts are made of stacks in which all pallet loads are not uniformly loaded with the same number of warehousing units. In brief, a physical inventory cannot be assumed to be correct, because errors can be—and often are—found almost immediately following the completion of the inventory. Experience has also shown that errors can be made in adjustments; i.e., inventory is added that should be subtracted, and inventory is subtracted that should be added. It is a good practice to keep a file that includes *all* inventory adjustments, because this file can be used to account for both mysterious disappearances as well as appearances.

Many over and short errors occur in order selection. Checking does not catch all selection errors. Errors also occur in receiving. More or less inventory than was actually received may have been reported. Pilferage, or even large-scale theft, may account for some of the disappearances. Receiving may cooperate with inbound truck drivers and sign for more inventory than is actually received. Truck drivers may detect overages not caught at checking time and deliver only what the shipping order calls for, keeping the remainder or overage to be disposed of later. Receiving clerks are more apt to catch and report shortages and overlook overages, which go unreported. Order selectors may also make errors involving substitution of one product for another. For example, 12/12-ounce pack is ordered, and 12/21-ounce pack is shipped. Checkers may not catch such errors because they are "natural" errors. In warehouses located adjacent to production, the production-run quantity may become the record when the actual quantity is either greater or less than the production-run quantity reported.

The more infrequently physical inventories are taken, the more likely that errors in overs and shorts will create problems that cannot be effectively dealt with by a remote central order processing system.

## CENTRAL ORDER PROCESSING (COP)

In an effort to resolve many of these problems, more and more firms have moved inventory control out of the warehouse and set up a central order processing system (COP) to gain greater control over the inventory. Typically, adjustments in the perpetual book inventory are not permitted unless a physical inventory is taken and verified. Consequently, many firms adopt the policy that changes in the records made necessary by overages and shortages cannot be made except at the time an inventory of the entire warehouse takes place.

Under this policy, more errors are likely to creep into the records due to the increase in the number of "cuts" and/or reduced quantities associated with (1) shipping orders and (2) the method of reporting by exception which is used by many large firms that employ central order processing systems to control a network of inventory locations.

**Typical COP Process** In recent years, manual record-keeping systems which were used to maintain a perpetual inventory have been largely replaced by computers. COP is often designed to do away with this redundant record keeping on the grounds that costs are duplicated and no significant increase in accuracy or reliability is obtained. To understand the nature of the control problems encountered, it is necessary to describe briefly how

COP works in many firms that use this method of accounting.

1. Perpetual inventories are maintained by COP for each warehouse or storeroom in the network.

2. When purchase orders are placed, COP updates an open purchase-order file.

3. When inventory is received at the warehouse or storeroom, a report stating what has been received is prepared (usually punched tape) and transmitted to COP together with a report of shipments made.

4. When this report is received, COP updates the files, clears the purchase order from the open purchase-order file, and updates the inventory to reflect receipts and issues reported.

5. All shipping orders are transmitted to COP for processing. COP compares demand with supply, allocates inventory, and chooses the warehouse to satisfy each order as inventory dictates. Orders are then transmitted to the respective warehouses or storerooms. Each shipping order is assigned a serial number for reporting purposes so that all orders shipped in full need only to be confirmed by serial number. When orders cannot be shipped in full, the exceptions are reported together with the serial number.

6. Once each working day, or as frequently as service and volume requirements dictate, the warehouse calls COP and reports receipts and shipments. Upon completion of each cycle, the respective inventories are updated so that all receipts will be recorded to satisfy incoming shipping orders.

*Advantages.* When it is necessary to maintain a network of warehouses or storerooms, the main justification for COP is control. Customers frequently can be serviced from more than one location at little or no increase in cost, or as inventory conditions dictate. Centralized control allows for prompt invoicing and more-effective cash flow. The cost of carrying inventory can be reduced with the flexibility allowed by the ability to allocate or dispense inventory on the basis of the total inventory. Where inventory is sensitive to packaging changes, promotions, deals, short shelf life, etc., it is highly desirable to clear inventories so that obsolete inventory does not build up and create additional problems.

*Disadvantages.* While COP easily accounts for and gains greater control over the total inventory in the network of warehouses, the individual warehouses and storerooms become almost totally dependent on COP for information relating to the inventory in their care.

Some large firms have found a way around this

problem by partitioning COP so that individual warehouses can communicate directly with COP and retrieve information that might be needed between cycles. Still other firms have devised real-time systems in which the warehouse and storeroom can be continuously on line with the big computer. For many firms, however, this solution is either impractical or unaffordable. Here are some solutions that will prove helpful to large *and* small firms that cannot justify more elaborate or sophisticated systems of inventory control.

**Fixed-Slot Order Selection**  There is a practical rule called Pareto's law, or the 80-20 rule, that can help resolve many of the control problems encountered at the warehouse level when a perpetual inventory is maintained by COP. This rule can be used to demonstrate that about 80 percent of the items stocked in a warehouse are likely to account for about 20 percent of the volume of goods shipped. The remaining 20 percent of the items stocked account for as much as 80 percent of the volume, i.e., the bulk of the inventory handled through the warehouse. When one of these items is out of stock, everybody is likely to know it. Most of the problems relating to location are associated with the 80 percent of the items that account for 20 percent of the volume. The fixed-slot method can be used to resolve many, if not all, of the locator problems.

In this method a supply of each SKU (usually sufficient for one shift) is stored in a fixed location or slot. Each slot is numbered and chained to the product code number and/or description stored in the computer files. When shipping orders are processed by COP, items are arranged in slot sequence to facilitate sequential order selection and, thus, reduce travel and search time. This method allows each product to be stored in the selection line in the most efficient manner and facilitates order selection. For example,

1. Heavy items may be picked before lighter items.

2. Items can be arranged in the order of package height to facilitate loading pallets, containers, or carts.

3. Items can be arranged in order of dollar value to minimize the risk of loss, should one item be picked in place of another.

4. Items can be ranked by velocity, i.e., fast, medium, and slow movers.

5. Items can be categorized as being hazardous, perishable, fragile, etc., and grouped or sequenced to facilitate compliance with DOT, FDA, or OSHA requirements.

6. If cubic volume as well as weight is included in the master record, orders can be cubed for selection in terms of cart loads, pallet loads, etc. The computation of cubic volume on each shipping order can facilitate loading out and routing of shipments to minimize delivery cost and to comply with weight limits on carriers used.

All these benefits can be largely automatic once COP is programmed to accomplish these routine counting and computing tasks.

**Reserve-Stock Locator System**  When a fixed-slot system is used, it is seldom practical to keep all the stock of any given item in the pick-line or fixed-slot location. The reserve must therefore be stored elsewhere. The location of the reserve stock, however, must be readily available when needed.

*A Rudimentary System.* The most rudimentary system allows for chaining the reserve location to the fixed location as follows: (1) when stock is received, the fixed location is checked to determine if the stock is needed; (2) if the stock is needed and no older stock is available, the pick-line location is filled; (3) if the stock is not to be placed in the fixed slot, the lift truck operator records where the reserve stock is to be located and leaves a record chained to the fixed slot; and (4) should a pallet load be needed, the forklift driver checks the fixed slot for the location to be used to retrieve a pallet load and then goes to this location after checking off the withdrawal on a tally card maintained at the fixed-slot location. Alternatively, the order selector can call for restocking and give the location to the lift truck driver, who will check off the location after completing the move.

*Central Locator System.* A more sophisticated system may be indicated when the rudimentary system does not work for some reason. For example, the effectiveness of the rudimentary system depends on cooperation of personnel and on accuracy. If the desired level of cooperation and accuracy cannot be achieved, then a central locator system can be used. In this method, reserve stock is recorded on commodity cards or records, one record for each pallet load of a commodity or product stored in reserve. No records need to be kept for stock stored in fixed slots, since these locations are maintained by COP.

In this system, it may be practical to prepare records in the form of punched cards. A master record is created for each item that will be received and stored in reserve on pallets. A supply of these records is maintained in a tub file in the receiving office. When stock is received and palletized, or prepared for storage, the load specifications (cartons per course × courses per load) are checked, and a record corresponding to the SKU number is pulled from the tub file to be used by the forklift operator to take the pallet to storage. When the pallet is placed in storage, the lift truck driver records the location and returns the record to receiving. When receiving has been completed, the records are placed in the commodity tub file. If a keypunch is available in the receiving office and one master record has been prepared for each item to be handled on pallets, a copy of the master record can be duplicated as needed. The unit records are then used to keep track of location and at the same time serve as the instrument for (1) instructing the lift truck operator to retrieve a load to be used for replenishment or (2) shipping when full pallet loads are required.

## MINICOMPUTER APPLICATIONS

Another method for relieving COP problems would be to install a minicomputer at the warehouse. The minicomputer can be used as a stock locator system and warehouse controller. In this system, records relating to lot numbers, production codes, quality control information, quarantine, and other requirements can be integrated with the stock system, and a small printer can be used to prepare tickets referenced with warehouse locations. Cathode-ray-tube (CRT) terminals can be used to update records as inventory is received and to obtain location-referenced picking tickets for order entry when it is desired to ship orders. For example, if COP does not want to be bothered with the warehouse problems and is only concerned with network location problems, the minicomputer can be programmed to provide the auxiliary computer support the warehouse needs to cope with a growing variety of record-keeping requirements and physical inventory control problems. Some cost benefits may be realized by substituting the minicomputer for the terminal devices currently used by COP to transmit shipping orders to the warehouse and to retrieve information relating to receipts and data needed to maintain network control of the inventory.

**Complexity of Record Keeping.** The advent of many new regulations, such as those relating to the transportation and storage of hazardous materials, OSHA safety regulations, and FDA record-keeping requirements to facilitate product recall when products are found to endanger consumers, all combine to make record keeping a more detailed and costly function. The warehouse may be expected to keep more records relating to shipments. For example,

pesticides must be accounted for by lot number as they are shipped from the warehouse. Food and other products that are consumed or used by people must be accounted for in terms of lot numbers and destinations. Normally, these data must be captured at the warehouse and recorded on the shipping documents. COP is so busy performing other tasks, it should only be expected to be responsible for data processing relating to overall accounting, perpetual inventory control in the network, and functions relating to the control of credit and accounts receivable. The warehouse, on the other hand, needs to be relieved of these functions so that it can effectively deal with the increasing demand for more records and record keeping that can only be controlled at the warehouse level.

**Operational Control** Management at the local warehouse or storeroom level is just as concerned as COP with total inventory accountability. However, availability of the inventory to satisfy shipping orders is also of primary concern. Book inventory is not necessarily available inventory. Inventory can be damaged. Shelf life can have expired. Inventory may be in quarantine. Conditions not known to COP may make it impossible to ship orders which COP records indicate can be shipped. A more serious problem arises when COP transmits orders to the warehouse in anticipation of inventory being received. In this case, order selectors may search in vain for nonexistent stock.

*Stock Locator Systems.* When COP processes shipping orders, it generally arranges or sorts the items called for by the shipping order into product code-number sequence, which may not correspond to order selection or pick-line sequence. It is at this point that it would be useful to point out that the information contained on the shipping order has a great deal to do with labor productivity and the amount and quality of supervision required to manage the shipping function.

Order selector productivity is directly related to the design of the order selection system and the efficiency with which order selection or pick lines can be replenished. Computer-based COP systems can probably help the warehouse resolve some of the stock locator problems, provided its software can be modified to assign slot locations by warehouse when processing shipping orders.

*Space Management.* Invariably, every warehouse will find that it no longer has sufficient space to keep pace with the increased demand. A minicomputer or warehouse controller can be used to make more efficient use of the available warehouse space. Experience has shown that selection of a slot with the right capacity can make more effective use of the available space. Furthermore, with a warehouse controller, it will be practical to maintain an inventory of empty slots and capacities to (1) facilitate choosing the most appropriate empty location or (2) determine which items are candidates for rewarehousing to make room for incoming lots. As data is processed to account for receipts and issues, an algorithm can be used to compute turnover. These and other data relating to warehousing specifications can then be used to optimize the use of storage space as well as to control the quality of the warehouse performance.

*Performance Evaluation.* One final contribution that can be expected of a minicomputer or warehouse controller is the ability to measure and quantify the performance of individuals, groups, or departments. For example, productivity can be measured more accurately and at less cost as an automatic by-product of processing transactions in real time, as opposed to the arduous and time-consuming manual methods that must be employed when no computing power is available at the warehouse level.

**Partitioning the Large Computer** Many, if not all, of the benefits and control features described above can be obtained by partitioning the large computer. The same kind and quality of control can be achieved, but probably at a much higher cost than necessary. The determination of the practicality and benefits of any of the systems or combinations of systems outlined above must be made on the basis of record maintenance cost, product turnover, and the impact of inventory discrepancies on profits.

*See also* COMPUTER SYSTEMS; DATA PROCESSING PRINCIPLES AND PRACTICES; DISTRIBUTION, PHYSICAL; FACILITIES AND SITE PLANNING AND LAYOUT; INVENTORY CONTROL, PURCHASING AND ACCOUNTING ASPECTS; LOGISTICS, BUSINESS; MATERIAL HANDLING; MATERIALS MANAGEMENT; MATERIALS REQUIREMENTS PLANNING (MRP); PURCHASING MANAGEMENT.

### REFERENCES

Buffa, Elwood S.: *Basic Production Management*, 2d ed., John Wiley & Sons, Inc., New York, 1975, chap. 13.

Chase, Richard B., and Nicholas J. Aguilano: *Production and Operations Management*, Richard D. Irwin, Inc., Homewood, Ill., 1973, chaps. 8 and 9.

Greene, James H.: *Production and Inventory Control: Systems and Decisions*, Richard D. Irwin Inc., Homewood, Ill., 1974.

Killeen, Louis M.: *Techniques of Inventory Management*, American Management Association, New York, 1970.

Riggs, James L.: *Production Systems: Planning, Analysis and Control*, 2d ed., John Wiley & Sons, Inc., New York, 1976.

HOWARD WAY, *Howard Way and Associates, Inc.*

# Inventory control, purchasing and accounting aspects

In its broadest context, industry has two major components, fabrication (or manufacturing) and service. The past 15 years have seen an expansion of service industry in relation to manufacturing industry in terms of the distribution of employment. However, regardless of shifts in the resource makeup, common elements are reflecting major cost factors in each sector, i.e., labor, material, and capital. A study of 1972 to 1973 data from *Statistical Abstracts of the United States*[1] indicates the following cost relationship between these factors:[2]

| Industry | Labor, % | Material, % | Capital (Depreciation + Interest), % |
|---|---|---|---|
| Manufacturing | 28.0 | 65.0 | 7.0 |
| Retail | 16.7 | 82.6 | 0.7 |
| Wholesale | 6.6 | 93.0 | 0.4 |
| General service | 60.0 | 34.0 | 6.0 |

Further investigation of the manufacturing sector indicates that the distribution of material cost has a pattern, as indicated in Fig. I-5, when examined across various industries using standard industrial classification (SIC) codes. A study made of industry within one state,[3] for instance, indicates that approximately 3 to 5 percent of its manufacturers maintain approximately 50 percent of the material inventories. All these data point to the need for considerable attention to control inventories as a vital cost control measure.

Even if direct material utilization were 100 percent efficient, i.e., if all raw material was used in the final product sold, with no scrap loss, spoilage, deterioration, etc., considerable cost could be incurred in the production process if the right material were not in the right place, at the right time, and in the right quantity.

**Inventory Theory and Modeling** Proper control of inventory requires a delicate balance and careful, detailed planning. To the controller who sees funds tied up in material in the warehouse, work-in-process inventory, and finished goods not shipped, the natural reaction is that inventories are too high. To

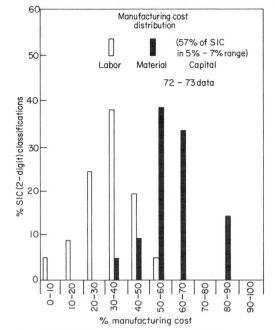

Fig. I-5. Distribution of manufacturing cost by SIC.

the production superintendent faced with the prospect of interrupted deliveries or silent production lines due to inadequate raw, in-process, or finished materials, the response must be that inventories are too low. Therefore, a balance is needed between holding large quantities to satisfy the latter and frequent stock replenishment to satisfy the former. This might be represented, as in Fig. I-6, if the replenishment quantity $q$ is represented on one axis

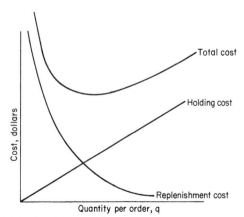

Fig. I-6. Cost-balance model.

and the total inventory cost in dollars is represented on the other.

Many reasons exist for keeping inventory. These include: to improve customer service, hedge against demand surges and variation of production level, take advantage of favorable prices, ensure against error and loss, and avoid production stoppage.

Overproduction for any of these reasons can, on the other hand, increase costs due to high investment and low capital turnover, material obsolescence, spoilage and deterioration, storage and handling excesses, and inefficient use of space due to overcrowding.

Inventory theory suggests that there are effective methods with which to do the careful planning necessary. The two most common approaches include (1) economic order quantity techniques and (2) a more recent control measure called material requirements planning. The former is discussed in this entry, while the latter is discussed in a separate entry. More commonly, these are intermixed to achieve the objective: cost control through material control.

**Factors in Inventory Control Modeling**  To develop models which can be used in determining proper inventory levels and replenishment quantities, basic information describing the inventory using system must be identified. These factors are represented in Fig. I-7 as cost, demand, and replenishment. Since numerous variations can exist, however, those conditions must be identified which most closely define the inventory system to be modeled.

The following illustrates the selection process for the identification of the appropriate characteristic.

*Costs.  Unit costs* may be constant within the planning period as reflected by accumulated manufacturing cost or purchase cost, or alternatively they may vary due to price discounting or economics of scale. *Storage cost* is an important factor and should reflect (1) the cost of capital invested in the stock item as well as (2) the physical costs to keep and protect the item. A third item of cost is *replenishment* (or ordering) *cost*. What is the cost of the clerical system to track the inventory use, initiate and process orders, set up production processes, and what are the costs to initiate a replenishment order? These occur only when a new order for replenishment is placed.

Finally, what is the penalty in terms of cost if the stock item should not be available when it is needed? This *stock-out cost* can be very high, but it is also more difficult to determine. It is not unusual to use a

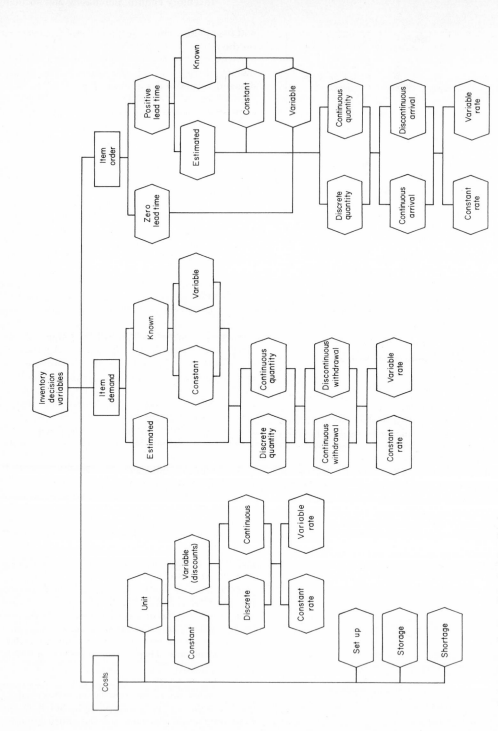

**Fig. I-7. Factors in determining inventory level.**

stock-out level as a planning factor, but this implies a certain cost. For example, a policy that "we will not exceed a stock-out factor of 1 percent" suggest that *safety stock* should be such that only 1 in 100 replenishment cycles will result in a stock shortage. This implies that the cost of running out is 100 times greater than that of storing the amount necessary to prevent a shortage. Attention to this cost element, though difficult, is extremely important.

*Demand.* Demand may be known and fixed or be highly variable and require forecasting techniques. In materials requirements planning (MRP), forecasts are necessary for the final product, but component parts are determined from bills of material. Consequently, a mixed system may frequently be necessary. Other demand variables that impact on inventory control systems include: (1) whether the item is bulk or the items are individually controllable; (2) frequency of use; and (3) regularity of use.

*Replenishment.* To replenish inventory stock requires some knowledge of order lead time and the variability of that lead time in order to build in the proper safeguards or safety stocks. The nature of delivery is also a factor in planning and controlling inventory, e.g., partial shipments, frequency of shipments, type of unit loads, etc.

*Use of Factors in Inventory Models.* It is often necessary to rely on economic order quantity concepts in order to develop and retain that balance between stocking too much (high investment cost) and not having enough (production down due to lack of material). The concept of economic order, or lot, quantities (EOQ) is based on knowledge of the previously discussed variables. An EOQ may be developed using (1) "quick and dirty" procedures and maintaining large safety stocks to accommodate error or (2) highly sophisticated techniques for close control. Needless to say, the former may be less costly to implement and can provide the necessary level of balance for some stock items, while very costly items would deserve the more costly control justified by the greater cost benefit. These concepts will be discussed further under ABC analysis in this entry.

Two basic concepts of control models need to be recognized: transaction reporting and periodic review.

*Transaction Reporting.* Transaction reporting requires continuous, accurate updating of stock records to determine when a replenishment order should be initiated. Frequent stock activity, high volume requirements, and identifiable individual units may make this type of a system more desirable. This may entail *perpetual* (or continuous) record

processing: e.g., reporting the use of each item and continuous monitoring of stock levels. When a predetermined reorder point is reached, an economic order quantity acquisition is initiated. This reorder point is set to ensure that sufficient stock is available to carry the production process until the replenishment supply is received.

*Periodic Review.* A second concept is that records will be reviewed periodically (weekly, monthly, quarterly, etc.), and if the level of inventory for that item has fallen below a certain target level, a new order will be placed. If it has not, the record will be returned to the file for review again at the end of the next period. Target levels, period lengths, and replenishment quantities are dependent on frequency of use, replenishment lead time, and criticality of item. This system is usually more difficult to establish but results in lower clerical cost to maintain stock control. Both transaction reporting and periodic review systems can be maintained manually or by computer, if the inventory system is of sufficient size to warrant computer control.

EXAMPLE: An example of a transaction system is represented by the following: A manufacturer uses wooden pallets for unit load shipping of the product. These pallets are used regularly at a rate of 100 per month and purchased from a vendor at $3.50 per pallet. They are stored in an unheated but covered shed until needed, and it is estimated that it costs 20 percent of the unit value to pay for the investment and storage costs. A fixed cost of $50 in clerical time and processing is incurred every time a replenishment order is processed. If pallets are available when needed, rehandling of the unit load of final product is necessary at a cost of $10 per unit. Delivery normally takes from 6 to 10 days from the time of order, and it is just as likely to take 6, 7, 8, 9, or 10 days.

To determine the EOQ, the following is considered:

| *Action* | *Result* |
| --- | --- |
| Frequent orders | Frequent replenishment cost |
| | Low average inventory and low storage cost |
| | More frequent risk of running out |
| Infrequent orders | Infrequent replenishment cost |
| | High average inventory and high storage cost |
| | Less risk of running out |

If $C$ = replenishment cost
$S$ = storage cost
$I$ = number of inventory turnovers per year
$T$ = total cost per year for storage and replenishment

$R$ = rate of demand
$Q$ = order quantity (EOQ)

then $Q$ can be calculated to be the order quantity which results in the lowest cost $T$

$$Q = \sqrt{\frac{2CR}{S}} = \sqrt{\frac{2(50)(100)}{(0.2)(3.50)}} = 120 \text{ pallets/order}$$

$$I = \frac{(R)(\text{number of months})}{Q}$$

$$= \frac{(100)(12)}{120} = 10 \text{ turnovers/year}$$

In this example, a transaction system is to be used, and a reorder point needs to be determined which will provide protection during the reorder period of 6 to 10 days. Since it is equally likely that delivery can be at any time between 6 and 10 days, inclusive, the reorder point will be selected at the point that gives a cost balance between overstocking during the lead time and understocking.

Each time period of days from 6 to 10 has 1 chance in 5 of occurring in the replenishment cycle. By weighting the chances of various delivery possibilities by the cost of overstocking versus understocking, a weighted average of delivery days can be computed which establishes a basis of the reorder points. In this example it may be computed as follows:

Number of items demanded per day = 100/20* = 5

*20 days assumes a 5-day workweek

Average cost of overstocking
$$= (5)(\$3.50)(1/5)(x - 5)$$

where $x$ = delivery period between 6 to 10 days

Average cost of understocking
$$= (\$10 \times 1/5)[10-(x - 5)]$$

solving for $x$ as the point where the weighted-average overstocking cost equals the weighted-average understocking cost:

$$(5)(\$3.50)(1/5)(x - 5) = (\$10)(1/5)(10 - x)$$
$$3.5x - 17.5 = 20 - 2x$$
$$5.5x = 37.5$$
$$x = 6.8$$

The weighted-average delivery period for the purpose of planning the reorder point is 6.8 days.

$$\text{Reorder point} = (100/20)(6.8) = 34.0$$

In summary, place an order for pallets when the pallet inventory drops to 34. This will provide an economical stock system for pallets as long as the costs and demand factors or the delivery time factors do not change.

**ABC Analysis**  It is not uncommon for an inventory system to have 30,000 line items in inventory control. These include supplies, packaging, maintenance parts, work in process, raw material, finished goods, and many other items. A *line item* includes an identifiable item and not the quantity of the item. For example, 500 rolls of 1-inch strapping tape for shipping purposes would be one line item for control purposes.

Clearly, a highly sophisticated inventory control system is not cost effective for all items. Some items simply do not warrant the detailed record keeping, order quantity monitoring, stores keeping, or handling, because the cost of the control system would far exceed the value of the item.

A rough classification to identify the line items which warrant a higher or lesser degree of control is commonly referred to as an ABC analysis. This analysis provides a method whereby the line items to be controlled can be classified according to *value* to provide indicators to the degree of control that can be justified. Characteristically, any inventory system will result in a relatively small percentage of the line items which constitute a large percentage of inventory value; e.g., 20 percent of the line items may constitute 95 percent of the inventory value. Thus, these items may justify a greater degree of control. Take, for example, the system of 10 line items A to J shown in Table I-10.

Figure I-8 presents the percent of total items and percent of total value of Table I-10 in graphic form. In this example, approximately 25 percent of the line item constitute approximately 55 percent of the value, and 55 percent of the items make up approximately 95 percent of the value. Subjectively, these could be classified as A class, B class, and C class items. The A class items may require individual control and will warrant greater expenditure in a control system. The B class items might be controlled more on a group (or family) of items basis,

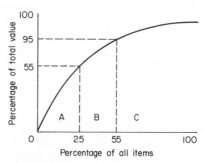

Fig. I-8. ABC curve.

**TABLE I-10**

| Line item | Annual usage | Unit value, in dollars | Annual value,* in dollars | Accumulated value, in dollars | Percent of total items | Percent of total value |
|---|---|---|---|---|---|---|
| A | 8000 | $2 | $16,000 | $16,000 | 10 | 26.7 |
| B | 400 | $32 | 12,800 | 28,800 | 20 | 48.0 |
| C | 50 | $200 | 10,000 | 38,800 | 30 | 64.7 |
| D | 100,000 | $0.10 | 10,000 | 48,800 | 40 | 81.3 |
| E | 500 | $10 | 5000 | 53,800 | 50 | 89.7 |
| F | 10,000 | $0.40 | 4000 | 57,800 | 60 | 96.3 |
| G | 5000 | $0.30 | 1500 | 59,300 | 70 | 98.8 |
| H | 100 | $5 | 500 | 59,800 | 80 | 99.7 |
| I | 200 | $0.90 | 180 | 59,980 | 90 | 99.9 |
| J | 10 | $2 | 20 | 60,000 | 100 | 100.0 |

*Computed by mulitplying the annual usage by the unit value.

and C class items could be controlled by a minimum expenditure system. Considerable care should be taken in the design of the total system to classify each line item and to establish proper control procedures to avoid paying $100 to control a $0.01 item or paying $0.01 to control a $100 item.

**Material Control** Imagination, ingenuity, and cost consciousness should go into the proper design of a control system.

*Simple.* A simple control, for example, is represented by a *two-bin* system. In this system small-value items may be stored in two containers. When one container is empty, replenishment is initiated, while the items in the second container are used.

*Complex.* A more complex system, however, is controlled by a basic inventory equation, as illustrated in Table I-11. The record balance necessary for various transactions is computed progressively from items 1 to 5.

In the two-bin case, minimal cost of control is required. In the latter case, elaborate procedures are necessary to maintain proper control.

**Productivity Measures for Inventory Control** A universal concept for productivity relates to labor productivity, i.e., units per labor hour. How-

ever, a concept of material productivity is equally important, as illustrated in the cost breakdown in the beginning of this entry. Some measures of material productivity include:

*Turnover:* The number of times per year inventory investment revolves

$$\text{Turnover} = \frac{\text{total annual material cost}}{\text{average inventory value on order and on hand}}$$

*Economic order quantity:* Equal to the size of the replenishment order to minimize total inventory control cost

*Average inventory value:* Equal to the average value of all inventory items in storage or on order

*Material productivity:*

$$\text{Material productivity} = \frac{\text{total material cost}}{\text{total manufacturing cost}}$$

*Work-in-process productivity:*

$$\text{Work-in-process productivity} = \frac{\text{average total material value in process}}{\text{average total inventory value}}$$

**TABLE I-11   Transaction Table**

| | Number on order + | Number on hand = | Number allocated to schedule production + | Number available |
|---|---|---|---|---|
| 1). Initial balance | $w$ | $x$ | $y$ | $z$ |
| 2). Order quantity when z reaches reorder point | + | | | + |
| 3). Order received | − | + | | |
| 4). Production order written allocating material | | | + | − |
| 5). Material issued to production floor | | − | − | |

*Finished-goods productivity:*

Finished-goods productivity
$$= \frac{\text{average total finished-goods inventory value}}{\text{average total inventory value}}$$

In establishing inventory value, two pricing policies are frequently used:

Last in, first out (LIFO): Establish value on the basis of the last quantity put in inventory.

First in, first out (FIFO): Establish value on the basis of the oldest item in the inventory.

The former tends to overvalue inventories in periods of inflating economies.

**Interdepartmental Relationships** Inventory control is normally a function of production control. The interactions between these organizational entities is crucial. Sales information is necessary to establish appropriate demand levels for planning purposes. Vendor pricing, lead times, and other replenishment information is equally vital to proper inventory planning and control. Production schedules become an integral part of the inventory controller's planning so that the *right materials* can be at the *right place* in the *right quantities*.

*See also* ACCOUNTING, FINANCIAL; DISTRIBUTION, PHYSICAL; FINANCIAL MANAGEMENT; FINANCIAL RATIO ANALYSIS; FINANCIAL STATEMENT ANALYSIS; INVENTORY CONTROL, PHYSICAL AND STOCKKEEPING; MATERIALS MANAGEMENT; MATERIALS REQUIREMENTS PLANNING (MRP); OPERATIONS RESEARCH AND MATHEMATICAL MODELING; PRODUCTION PLANNING AND CONTROL; PURCHASING MANAGEMENT; STATISTICAL ANALYSIS FOR MANAGEMENT.

### NOTES

[1] *Statistical Abstracts of the United States*, U.S. Department of Commerce, 1974.

[2] K. L. McRoberts, "Myths of Productivity," ASME publication 76-DET-103, June 1, 1977.

[3] K. L. McRoberts and S. H. Chung, "Technical Data Relating to the Small Manufacturing Industry in Iowa," *Final Report ISU-ERI-Ames-76022*, Department of Industrial Engineering, Iowa State University, Ames, Iowa, 1975.

### REFERENCES

Brown, R. G.: *Decision Rules for Inventory Management*, Holt, Rinehart and Winston, Inc., New York, 1967.

Greene, J. H.: *Production and Inventory Control Handbook*, McGraw-Hill Book Company, New York, 1971.

Orlicky, Joseph: *Materials Requirements Planning*, McGraw-Hill Book Company, New York, 1975.

Plossl, G. W., and O. W. Wight: *Production and Inventory Control*, Prentice-Hall, Inc., Englewood Cliffs, N.J., 1967.

KEITH L. McROBERTS, *Iowa State University*

**Inventory financing** (*See* FINANCIAL MANAGEMENT, SHORT-TERM, INTERMEDIATE, AND LONG-TERM FINANCING.)

**Inventory management** (*See* FINANCIAL MANAGEMENT.)

**Inventory turnover** (*See* INVENTORY CONTROL, PURCHASING AND ACCOUNTING ASPECTS.)

**Investment, capital** (*See* BUDGETING, CAPITAL.)

**Investment centers** (*See* ACCOUNTING FOR MANAGERIAL CONTROL.)

**Investment credit bureau managers** (*See* CREDIT MANAGEMENT.)

**Investment tax credit** (*See* ACCOUNTING, FINANCIAL; TAX MANAGEMENT, MANAGERIAL RESPONSIBILITY FOR FEDERAL INCOME TAX REPORTING.)

**Irrationality, cost of** (*See* STATISTICAL ANALYSIS FOR MANAGEMENT.)

**Issues, arbitrable** [*See* LABOR (TRADE) UNIONS.]

**Issues, negotiable** [*See* LABOR (TRADE) UNIONS.]

**Iteration** (*See* OPERATIONS RESEARCH AND MATHEMATICAL MODELING.)

# J

## Japanese industries, management in

The startling economic recovery of Japan since the end of World War II has been widely attributed to the effectiveness of Japanese management. The effective functioning of the Japanese management system can be credited to at least three major elements: a unique industrial relations system, unique methods of financing industries and business groups, and the unique role the Japanese government plays in business.

**Industrial Relations System**   One of the key elements in the management of Japan's major industrial firms is the permanent employment system. The basic features of the system are that employees (primarily male) enter a large firm after junior high, high school, or college graduation, receive in-company training, and remain employed with that firm until the age of 55.

Payment according to length of service is the basic practice which reinforces and maintains the permanence of employment among the workers within a firm. Usually only young recent graduates can afford to enter the system at beginning wages (in 1972, the monthly starting salary of college graduates was $179). Older workers cannot afford the loss of earnings a change of employer would entail. As a result, interfirm mobility is severely limited, and the vast majority of employees in large firms remain with the same employers throughout their careers.

The permanent employment system is the basic element providing the stability and continuity of human relationships essential to the behavioral effectiveness of the Japanese management style. Japanese permanent employees have reacted to their immobility by developing strong group loyalties, a system of shared obligations, heavy dependence on powerful superiors, and an intense competitive drive. Among these employees, who are associated more by location and situation than by any other common factor, such cohesiveness, coordination, and effectiveness are established by several powerful behavioral control mechanisms—a rigid, hierarchical structure based on seniority; intense emotional involvement in the group ethos; total fulfillment of security needs; and economic interdependence. Within this framework, certain limited areas of competition are permitted: among different firms within an industry, among separate work groups within a single firm, and among individuals for promotion within classes of employees who join a firm in the same year. This peculiar synthesis of cohesion and competition results in a remarkably effective work team.

The permanent employment system has other advantages as well. It makes extensive in-company training a profitable investment and provides large firms the stability they need for long-range planning. Employees find it easy to accept the organizational changes required by technological innovation and growth because their firms are committed to retain and retrain them. Further, since the wage levels of employees are determined by age and length of service, labor costs are related to the average age of the work force; therefore firms with higher growth rates, having high proportions of young starting workers, have lower wage bills. This cost advantage helps to keep firms vital by motivating them to grow and diversify.

*Extent of the Permanent Employment System.* One of the most widespread misconceptions about this system is that it pervades the management of Japanese industrial concerns. Actually, the system is seldom operative in any but the larger Japanese firms and applies to less than 30 percent of the nonagricultural labor force. In order to keep wage costs down, the number of new permanent recruits is kept at a cyclically justifiable minimum. Additional needs for labor are met by extensive use of temporary, subcontract, daily, and retired workers, whose wages are from 10 to 50 percent less than those of permanent workers. This arrangement is known as the dual wage structure and labor market of Japan.

*Role of the Labor Movement.* Japanese unions include manual as well as nonmanual workers and are organized on an enterprise basis, reflecting the structure of the enterprise entity and identifying with its interests. Most union members are permanent workers in large firms, while most untenured workers are outside the labor movement.

Union members are not differentiated by skills but by the employing firm, and thus many of the standard issues in the collective bargaining of other advanced countries—occupation-wide bargaining, jurisdictional disputes, rigid work rules, technological change, and job assignments—are nonissues in Japan. Japanese enterprise unions identify closely with the prosperity of the enterprise, and labor disputes are of short duration.

**Methods of Financial Management in Business Firms and Groups** Another unusual feature of the Japanese management system is that 80 to 90 percent of the capital requirements of Japanese companies are financed by debt. The major obligation of these firms in the area of capital financing is payment of debt servicing charges, which often equals or exceeds 5 percent of sales. Beyond this, there are few financial constraints on growth and diversification, as continuing expansion is simply financed by further debt.

*Role of the Japanese Government.* The apparent riskiness of this approach to finance is largely offset by the fact that the Japanese government essentially guarantees the debts of Japan's major firms. While individual firms obtain their loans from commercial banks, these banks usually have nearly all their deposits on loan and are heavily dependent for funds on the Central Bank of the Japanese government (Bank of Japan) and extremely vulnerable to its policies. When the Central Bank exercises influence by changing interest rates or required reserves for the commercial banks, the results are immediately felt by Japan's major firms. No large firm even requests a major loan without advance government approval. Because of its extensive control over the capital financing of Japanese industry, the Japanese government is able to play a major role in the direction and condition of those industries through its monetary policies and has the power either to salvage or eliminate troubled firms.

*Financing Within Business Groups.* The risks of such heavy debt financing are further minimized by the widespread tendency of Japanese firms to cluster together into groups. There are six major groups which dominate Japan's business world, among them are the familiar names Mitsubishi, Mitsui, and Sumitomo. Each of these groups embraces scores of companies and is continually expanding. Japan's Fair Trading Commission estimates that these six groups control approximately 40 percent of the nation's corporate capital and about 30 percent of Japan's corporate assets. Each group is headed by a central management council composed of a core group of top executives who exchange managerial resources, maintaining carefully cultivated personal relationships with each other, staying out of one another's established markets, and buying and selling to each other. They are joined together under the financial management of a major financial institution and borrow and lend to one another also. The diversified nature of the industries represented in a group virtually guarantees that the fortunes of all the firms involved will not fluctuate alike, which reduces risk for the group as a whole and supports a high-debt capacity among members.

*Cross-ownership of Stocks.* Another factor in the financial flexibility provided in the Japanese business group is the widespread cross-ownership of stocks among group members. As a rule, less than 10 percent of new capital comes from the external issue of new stocks. Unlike most American firms, Japanese corporations do not have to concern themselves with short-term shareholder interests and in this respect have a great deal of freedom to invest in long-term projects and outspend their competitors in promising new market situations.

*Subcontracting.* Yet another factor in the financial stability of large Japanese corporations is the extensive use of subcontracting. This serves the twofold purpose of providing large firms with a valuable cushion against fluctuations in the business cycle and enabling large firms to make higher profits by manufacturing goods at lower costs. These subcontracting arrangements often involve a pyramidal chain of relationships between a large master firm (usually part of one of the business groups) and a group of smaller firms, who may in turn subcontract with a group of even smaller firms. As was previously mentioned, the tenured employees of the master company enjoy higher wages and more benefits than the untenured employees of the many small firms involved in this hierarchy, reflecting a cost advantage to the master firm in maintaining the arrangement. Conversely, the small firms depend on the capital and market provided by the large firm and so must resist the trend toward higher wages among employees in order to produce at a price the large master firms are willing to pay. In the event of a recession, the master companies simply reduce their orders or reduce the limits on the prices they are willing to pay and allow the small firms to absorb the ill effects of the recession.

**Government and Industry** The relationships among various agencies of the Japanese government and related industries involve a degree of close interaction unrivaled among advanced nations. Apart from exerting influence through fiscal policy, as previously discussed, the government encourages compliance with its objectives through a complex system of tax incentives, an intricate network of personal interactions among individuals in government and industry, and sanctions controlling competition.

*Tax Structure.* The tax structure is utilized extensively by the Japanese government in influencing business outcomes, and tax incentives are carefully formulated to achieve desired ends. The government does not practice blind protectionism but rather offers tax incentives for the rationalization of production facilities in inefficient firms and grants tax benefits to export firms and promising young growing firms to encourage them to become competitive on the international market.

*Compliance Accomplished Through Consensus.* The Japanese government obtains compliance with its policies through consensus rather than enforcement, a process which is difficult for outsiders to understand. The government's Economic Planning Agency establishes Japan's official long-range economic plan, the objective of which is to establish what is the most efficient direction the economy should take. The plan is purely advisory in nature, with no powers of legal enforcement attached. It is primarily two government agencies—the Ministry

of International Trade and Industry and the Ministry of Finance—along with numerous consulting committees whose members consist of both government and business leaders, who work out the actual policies to be followed. A group prominently involved in this process is Keidanren, which is a federation of business organizations representing industry as a whole. As within business groups, as previously discussed, the members of these committees come from among the tenured elite, often having graduated from the same universities. They tend to maintain relationships at a personal level, constantly exchanging ideas and consulting with one another, so that each party knows the feelings of others on various issues and policy matters. There is a constant process of compromise and adjustment going on at this level, with government officials and top executives exchanging information and reactions on the economic plans of the major business corporations and proposed government policies that might affect the major corporations. Usually, through careful informal discussion, consensus is reached before government policies become law and corporate plans are put into effect, and so compliance is rarely an issue.

*Control of Competition.* The heavy emphasis on consensus does not preclude competition which is intense among different business groups and within industries, as when medium-small firms compete for the markets of the master companies. When the government determines that the competition furthers Japan's interests by strengthening the firms involved, the process is encouraged, but if the government establishes that the competition is having a harmful effect on the Japanese economy, it calls instead for cooperation. This peculiar coexistence of competition with cooperation and close interaction between government and industry can be attributed to the shared goals of both parties in furthering Japan's economic and national interests. The remarkable harmony with which the relationship is maintained can only be understood by the unique Japanese social patterns which heavily sanction the resolution of nearly every human conflict through the process of consensus rather than through enforcement imposed by a superior power.

Foreign business executives should take note that when they compete with Japanese firms, they face not only the firm itself and the resources of the group to which it belongs but also the Japanese government, with all its tax incentives, subsidies, and so forth. The close interaction between government and business in Japan has resulted in what is essentially a mega-conglomerate, often referred to as "Japan, Inc." This must be considered an important factor in the competitive position of Japanese in international business. When competition between Japanese and foreign firms occurs in third countries, probably the best way the foreign firm can compete with the enormous pool of invisible resources backing the Japanese firm is to attempt to replicate the Japanese situation by banding together with other firms to create its own business group. Foreign firms which seek to compete within Japan should not attempt a sole venture but should seek a joint venture with a Japanese firm so that they can benefit rather than suffer from the extensive government, managerial, and financial resources available to the Japanese.

*See also* DEVELOPING COUNTRIES, MANAGEMENT IN; EUROPE, MANAGEMENT IN WESTERN; INTERNATIONAL OPERATIONS AND MANAGEMENT IN MULTINATIONAL COMPANIES; INTERNATIONAL TRADE.

### REFERENCES

Abegglen, James C.: "The Economic Growth of Japan," *Scientific American*, vol. 222, no. 3, pp. 31–37, March, 1970.

Abegglen, James C.: *Management and Worker: The Japanese Solution*, Sophia University, Tokyo, 1973.

Ballon, Robert J., ed.: *The Japanese Employee*, Sophia University, Tokyo, 1969.

Barrett, M. Edgar, and Judith Ann Gehrke: "Significant Differences Between Japanese and American Business," *MSU Business Topics*, vol. 22, no. 1, pp. 41–49, Winter 1974.

Kaplan, Eugene J.: *Japan: The Government-Business Relationship; A Guide for the American Businessman*, U.S. Bureau of International Commerce, for sale by Superintendent of Documents, U.S. Government Printing Office, Washington, 1972.

Lockwood, William, ed.: *The State and Economic Enterprise in Japan*, Princeton University Press, Princeton, N.J., 1965.

Oh, Tai K.: "Japanese Management—A Critical Review," *Academy of Management Review*, vol. 1, no. 1, pp. 14–25, January 1976.

Yoshino, M. Y.: *Japan's Managerial System; Tradition and Innovation*, The M.I.T. Press, Cambridge, Mass., 1968.

TAI K. OH, *California State University at Fullerton*

# Job analysis

Job analysis involves (1) gathering information pertinent to the job and (2) defining the job by means of *job descriptions* which identify the job, outline work performed, and specify requirements for those who seek to fill the job.

Job analysis is usually performed as the first important step in the job evaluation process. Job analysis is necessary to justify higher pay for higher-level jobs based on job characteristics. Basic requirements for the job such as education, experience, inherent or acquired skills, working conditions which may be hazardous, and the supply-and-demand situation contribute to the differences in jobs which are systematically identified through job analysis.

In addition to wage-related use, job analysis can be used to improve work-force utilization by aiding in the assignment of time-consuming tasks to lower-paid jobs, by planning for worker-hours in order to ensure that all work assigned is essential, and by grouping tasks into efficient economic units. Job analysis is a managerial tool which can aid in the recruitment, selection, placement, and training of employees. It can be employed to help workers better understand their jobs, accept explanations for grievances, and agree to establish standards of job performance.[1]

The first step in job analysis is to obtain information about the job through interviews, observations, questionnaires, supervisory conferences, checklists, manuals, time-study reports, and descriptions of systems and organization charts. Job analysis may be performed by managers and employees trained by a professional job analyst, by outside consultants, or by committees of supervisors or workers, or both. The information gathered in job analysis is recorded in job descriptions.

**Job Description** The job description contains the following information:

*Identification.* Job titles, persons employed on the job, location in the organization chart, location defined by plant, department, machine, etc., and the number of personnel in the job category help identify the importance of the job to the organization.[2]

*Work Performed.* A concise description of what, how, and why a worker does a job defines the scope and purpose of the job. Detailed descriptions, including work assigned, specific tasks, area of responsibility, inherent authority, working relationships, specific methods, equipment and techniques, scope and impact, working conditions, and specific examples, are written in a chronological or functional basis.[3]

*Job Specifications.* Mental skills such as basic education, mental applications, and job knowledge and responsibility and physical requirements such as physical skills and working conditions constitute the basic factors of job specifications. Judgments regarding the presence of these attributes and their degree of importance are highly subjective since requirements are often inferred from duties.[4] Since the Equal Employment Opportunity Commission (EEOC) is making it difficult to substantiate these requirements as necessary for job performance, care must be taken when identifing jobs and hiring personnel on the basis of these requirements.

**Procedure** The principal steps in job analysis are:

1. Use current titles to list all positions in the organization.

2. Gather sufficient information about each position to permit identification of discrete jobs.

3. Prepare job descriptions and verify their accuracy through review and "sign-off" by selected incumbents and their supervisors.

4. Retitle and classify all positions.

*See also* COMPENSATION, WAGE AND SALARY POLICY AND ADMINISTRATION; DEVELOPMENT AND TRAINING, EMPLOYEE; EMPLOYMENT PROCESS; JOB EVALUATION; WORK DESIGN, JOB ENLARGEMENT, JOB ENRICHMENT, JOB DESIGN, AND AUTONOMOUS WORK GROUPS.

### NOTES

[1] Robert E. Sibson, *Wages and Salaries: A Handbook for Line Managers*, rev. ed., American Management Association, New York, 1967, p. 37.

[2] Charles W. Brennan, *Wage Administration*, rev. ed., Richard D. Irwin, Inc., Homewood, Ill., 1963, p. 101.

[3] David W. Belcher, *Compensation Administration*, Prentice-Hall, Inc., Englewood Cliffs, N.J., 1974, p. 125.

[4] Allan N. Nash and Stephen J. Carroll, Jr., *The Management of Compensation*, Brooks/Cole Publishing Company, Monterey, Calif., 1975, p. 115.

FREDERICK A. TEAGUE, *Booz·Allen and Hamilton, Inc.*

## Job description (*See* COMPENSATION, WAGE AND SALARY POLICY AND ADMINISTRATION; JOB ANALYSIS.)

## Job design (*See* WORK, CONCEPT AND IMPLICATIONS; WORK DESIGN, JOB ENLARGEMENT, JOB ENRICHMENT, JOB DESIGN, AND AUTONOMOUS WORK GROUPS.)

## Job enlargement (*See* MOTIVATION IN ORGANIZATIONS; WORK, CONCEPT AND IMPLICATIONS; WORK DESIGN, JOB ENLARGEMENT, JOB ENRICHMENT, JOB DESIGN, AND AUTONOMOUS WORK GROUPS.)

## Job enrichment (*See* WORK DESIGN, JOB ENLARGEMENT, JOB ENRICHMENT, JOB DESIGN, AND AUTONOMOUS WORK GROUPS.)

## Job evaluation

Job evaluation, which is used by companies to solve the wage-structure problem, emphasizes an organized and rational approach to determine the relative worth of jobs. The underlying principle that an employee should be paid in relation to the job-related contribution assumes that pay should be assigned in accordance with the difficulty and importance of the job. Equal pay for equal work and more pay for more important work support this basic principle. Application of this principle helps to establish equitable internal pay relationships.[1] Companies that adopt job evaluation have decided the wage-structure problem is important enough to justify the expense of undertaking a thorough and systematic study of job relationships. Participation in the program by representatives of all levels of the work force increases the possibility of good acceptance of salary differentials which, in turn, reduces a potentially serious source of employee dissatisfaction.[2]

**Prevalence of Job Evaluation** According to a survey conducted in 1972 by the Bureau of National Affairs, 60 percent of small organizations and 75 percent of large organizations stated that they used job evaluation to determine wage rates.[3] Wage rates for office, professional, technical, and managerial jobs were determined with job evaluation more frequently (75 percent of the time) than were the rates for plant and sales jobs (50 percent of the time). The increasing trend for using job evaluation for managerial- and professional-level jobs is reflected in these figures.[4] Office, managerial, and technical jobs in particular benefit from job evaluation since job attributes are not easily quantifiable. On the other hand, sales jobs can be measured by sales volume, and plant jobs can be measured by production output.

**Job-related Contributions** Job evaluation examines the job-related contributions which employers and employees accept as the basis for employment exchange. There is general agreement that certain jobs have higher value and that individuals performing these jobs should receive more pay than those who perform lower-valued jobs. Some jobs require more education, special skills (inherent or acquired), or specific experience—and thus call for higher pay to compensate individuals for spending time, energy, and money to acquire these qualifications.[5] Other jobs involve adverse working conditions, which also support higher pay. Although economics (supply and demand) and social (collective bargaining) factors enter into the determination of job worth, the compensable factors usually measured in job evaluation emphasize the administrative concept (importance and difficulty) of job worth.[6] Job evaluation plans are based on implicit or explicit acceptance of compensable factors related to job contributions.

Job evaluation involves the measurement of job duties against some kind of yardstick in order to assess relative job worth. The job, not the incumbent's performance, ability, background, potential, etc., is the quantity being measured.[7] Job evaluation attempts to compare the demands of normal performance of a worker in a particular job.

**Job Evaluation Process** Complete job evaluation consists of the development, application, and ongoing administration of a five-step process: (1) job analysis (described in another entry); (2) determination of compensable factors; (3) selection of an appropriate job evaluation plan; (4) pricing jobs internally and externally; and (5) implementation of the job evaluation plan and ongoing tuning and maintenance. This entry explains the second and third steps in the evaluation process and does not include pricing, implementation, and maintenance.

## DETERMINING THE COMPENSABLE FACTORS

The compensable factors (or elements) to be used to compare jobs in the hierarchy should be the mutually accepted, job-related contributions rewarded by the organization.[8] Workers presumably accept the fact that certain jobs require differing amounts of contributions and that the wage-structure hierarchy is based on these factors. Typically, three basic factors of responsibility, education, and experience can explain 80 percent of the variance in the worth of jobs in the wage structure, with the remaining 20 percent accounted for by working conditions, physical effort, and hazards factors.[9] Employees' acceptance of wage structure decisions is improved if more factors that they feel better represent their jobs are included.

Factors should apply to all jobs in the organization or to large groups or classes of jobs. Factors chosen should embody the following characteristics:

1. Factors must not overlap in meaning.

2. Employer, employee, and union must understand and accept the importance of the factors.

3. Factors selected must in some degree be found in all jobs and in varying amounts.[10]

4. Factors must be observable and measurable.

Factors frequently found in job evaluation systems for lower-ranking positions are education, su-pervision received, physical demand, working conditions, experience and training, complexity of duties, contact with others, and responsibility for equipment and tools.[11] For higher-level positions, additional factors include decision-making latitude, accountability for results, functional scope, and impact of discretionary actions.

## SELECTION OF METHOD

The third step in the job evaluation process is the selection of a system which will make it possible to list jobs according to the level of compensable factors present. There are four basic methods: ranking, classification, point system, and factor comparison. In ranking and factor comparison, jobs are compared with each other. In classification and the point system, jobs are measured against a scale. In the point system and factor-comparison method, elements or factors of the jobs are measured by quantitative point values. More complex plans are usually a hybrid of these plans. Ranking and classification plans are used less often than point system and factor comparison. A comparison of characteristics, advantages, and disadvantages of the four basic methods is found in Table J-1. Each method is explained below.

**Ranking** This plan places jobs in order of organizational importance on the basis of the whole job from highest to lowest. Ranking has been made more sophisticated by employing computers to facilitate raters' comparison. Since the system is so subjective, it is difficult to justify to employees and difficult to apply to large concerns.[12] It is not considered a very acceptable approach and is used by few companies.

*Procedure.* Steps in the ranking method include:

1. Obtain job information through job description and job specification employing compensable factors.

2. Select raters who know all jobs in the unit or specific departments.

3. Select compensable factors and outline a procedure for consistent application of factors.

4. Rank jobs by sorting or paired comparison. Sorting involves raters ranking jobs by ordering cards or lists on which job descriptions have been written. Paired comparison involves comparisons of each job with every other job (see Table J-2), either by comparing all possible combinations of two jobs or by checking the higher of two jobs indicated by the cells of a matrix. The rank is determined by the number of times the job is favorably compared.[13]

TABLE J-1   Job Evaluation Methods

| | Ranking | Classification | Point system | Factor comparison |
|---|---|---|---|---|
| **Characteristics** | | | | |
| Nonquantitative | X | X | | |
| Quantitative | | | X | X |
| Measure whole job | X | X | | |
| Measure job factors | | | X | X |
| Rank | X | | | X |
| Measure against yardstick | | X | X | |
| **Advantages** | | | | |
| Inexpensive and installation time short | X | X | | |
| Simple and easily understood | X | X | | |
| Not necessary to determine absolute value of job | X | X | | |
| Relative job differences determined without monetary considerations | X | X | X | |
| Consistent rating scales eliminate rater bias | | | X | |
| Employee acceptance aided by explanation of records of factors on point values | | | X | |
| Same job elements considered on all jobs | | | X | X |
| Factors limited to first or less avoids overlap | | | | X |
| Employee acceptance aided by easily understood job comparison scales | | | | X |
| Key job analysis ensures wage structure reflects the market | | | | X |
| Monetary units in comparison system permit rapid determination of wage scales | | | | X |
| Plan is tailormade for organization | | | | X |
| **Disadvantages** | | | | |
| Difficult to define overall job worth | X | X | | |
| Difficult to justify results to employees because no record of judgments | X | X | | |
| Raters may be inconsistent because factors not employed | X | X | | |
| Difficult to write grade comparison | | X | | |
| Difficult to develop points and weights which are easy to understand | | | X | X |
| Expensive, installation time long, maintenance costly | | | X | X |
| Monetary units introduce bias in evaluation of key jobs | | | | X |
| Few universal factors for all jobs is counter to concept of selecting factors which truly reflect job-related contributions | | | | X |

5. Average observations of all raters obtain a composite ranking.

**Classification**   In this method of job evaluation, classes or grades are defined verbally in terms of the types of jobs which fit into each class.[14] Jobs are classified by comparing each job with the descriptions.

The classification method has been used by the Civil Service Commission in the Classification Act of 1949, the Westinghouse Electric Company, and The Bell Telephone System.[15] The difficulty of explaining pay differentials based on the classification system has led to a decline in use.

*Procedure.* Steps in the classification method include:

1. Observe job analysis with job descriptions and job specifications.

2. Classify jobs into well-defined classes such as shop, sales, clerical, supervisory, and management.

TABLE J-2  Ranking Method

| Step 4: Paired Comparisons |
|---|

| Compare each job with every other job |
|---|

Keypunch—Stenographer
Stenographer—Typist
Typist—Keypunch

Summary of comparisons

| Job title | Times judged more difficult | Rank |
|---|---|---|
| Keypunch | 0 | 3 |
| Stenographer | 2 | 1 |
| Typist | 1 | 2 |

3. Select compensable factors.

4. Write grade descriptions that differentiate each class in terms of levels of compensable factors.[16]

5. Classify jobs by comparing job information with grade descriptions. (See Table J-3.)

**Point System**  The point system measures each job on a separate weighted scale for each factor. Point values assigned to each factor are summed for total job value. The popularity of the point system may be partly due to the fact that many ready-made plans of employer associations and consultants are available and can be adapted to a company's needs. The American Association of Industrial Management and the National Metal Trades Association have job rating plans for shop, service, office, technical, and managerial jobs. The plan of the National Electrical Manufacturers Association is widely used for factory jobs.[17]

*Procedure.*  Steps in the point-system method include the following:

1. Determine whether compensable factors should be applied to all jobs or job clusters and select the jobs to be evaluated.

TABLE J-3  Classification Method

| Step 5: Example of Grade Description |
|---|

*Grade 2:* Requires skill in handling relatively simple and precisely defined tasks. Requires general knowledge equivalent to a high school education plus skills in areas such as typing, blueprint reading, or operation of more complicated office or shop equipment. Position involves little or no administrative line responsibilities. Responsibilities require limited or no external contacts. Inadequate performance would have limited effect on cost of operations. Actions are reviewed regularly.

2. Analyze the job description for each job.

3. Select the proper compensable factors which reflect job-related contributions and are accepted by managers and workers.[18]

4. Establish factor degrees with appropriate divisions so that each degree is equidistant from the two adjacent degrees. Two-dimensional degrees are sometimes employed to obtain maximum flexibility.[19] (See Table J-4.)

5. Determine the relative value of factors by establishing factor weights. This may be done by statistical means, such as linear regressions, or by using committee judgment. Key jobs should be evaluated to determine the number of degrees necessary.[20]

6. Assign point values to degrees by arithmetic or geometric progression. These values may be checked by noting the effect produced on key jobs.[21]

7. Write a job evaluation manual to aid raters in evaluating jobs.

8. Rate all jobs by means of the manual, job descriptions, and job specifications.

**Factor Comparison**  The factor-comparison method, an extension of the ranking method, employs distinctive factors, such as mental requirements, physical requirements, skill requirements, responsibility, and working conditions, which have numerical values assigned to them. In the factor-comparison method, jobs are compared with one another one factor at a time to determine which jobs contain more of certain compensable factors.[22] Evaluators rank all jobs on the job-comparison scale and sum points to determine the value of the job. Separate job-comparison scales should be developed for each job cluster.

*Procedure.*  Steps in the factor-comparison method include:

1. Analyze the job and obtain job descriptions covering duties and job specifications based on factor definitions (30 to 40 percent of the jobs).

2. Select key jobs that are easily defined and compared and for which wage or salary data are clearly established.

3. Determine compensable factors and establish quantitative scales for factors, using either wage rates or point scores.

4. Rank key jobs by factors (see Table J-5).

5. Distribute wage rates by factors for all key jobs (see Table J-5).

6. Cross-check job-ranking judgment by comparing a company's difficulty rank with money rank to determine key jobs with consistent rankings (see Table J-5).

7. Construct the job-comparison scale by plac-

**TABLE J-4  Point-System Method**

Step 4: Two-Dimensional Degrees (Skills and Knowledge)

| Complexity of problem | General knowledge plus basic business skills | Knowledge plus competence in specialized fields | Scientific, professional, or management competence | Professional expertise | Extensive general management experience |
|---|---|---|---|---|---|
| Complex, loosely defined problem | 23 | 24 | 27 | 29 | 31 |
| Diverse and complex problem with solution by diverse principle | 17 | 19 | 21 | 23 | 25 |
| Difficult problem with solutions by diverse practices | 12 | 14 | 16 | 18 | 20 |
| Tasks with well-defined processes for solution | 8 | 10 | 12 | 14 | 16 |
| Simple, well-defined tasks | 5 | 7 | 9 | 11 | 13 |

ing key jobs opposite money positions or point values according to the factors (see Table J-6).

8. Evaluate the remaining jobs by placing them into the job-comparison scale one factor at a time.

9. Establish the wage structure by summing monetary or point values for all factors.

**Other Techniques**  Other methods for solving the wage-structure problem involve direct market pricing. The guideline method bases relative job value on marketplace values. Often 50 percent of the jobs are selected as key jobs, and the appropriate market rates are determined. Market rates of key jobs are matched against midpoints and are placed into grades. The remaining jobs are placed by relating them to key jobs.[23]

*See also* COMPENSATION, WAGE AND SALARY POLICY

**TABLE J-5  Factor-Comparison Method**

Step 4: Jobs Ranked by Factors

| Job title | Knowledge and skills | Administration responsibility | External relations |
|---|---|---|---|
| Keypunch | 3 | 2 | 3 |
| Stenographer | 1 | 1 | 1 |
| Typist | 2 | 3 | 2 |

Step 5: Wage-Rate Distribution

| Job title | Knowledge and skills | Administration responsibility | External relations | Wage rate |
|---|---|---|---|---|
| Keypunch | 2.25 | .30 | .20 | 2.75 |
| Stenographer | 3.10 | .40 | .65 | 4.15 |
| Typist | 2.70 | .20 | .40 | 3.30 |

Step 6: Comparison of Difficulty Ranking (D) and Money Ranking (M)

| Job title | Knowledge and skills | | Administration responsibility | | External relations | |
|---|---|---|---|---|---|---|
| | D | M | D | M | D | M |
| Keypunch | 3 | 2.25 | 2 | .30 | 3 | .20 |
| Stenographer | 1 | 3.10 | 1 | .40 | 2 | .65 |
| Typist | 2 | 2.70 | 3 | .20 | 1 | .40 |

**TABLE J-6  Factor-Comparison Method**

| | Step 7: Job-Comparison Scale | | |
| --- | --- | --- | --- |
| Cents | Knowledge and skills | Administration responsibility | External relations |
| 0.10 | | | |
| 0.20 | | Typist | Keypunch |
| 0.30 | | Keypunch | |
| 0.40 | | Stenographer | Typist |
| 0.50 | | | |
| 0.60 | | | Stenographer |
| 0.70 | | | |
| | | | |
| 2.10 | | | |
| 2.20 | Keypunch | | |
| 2.30 | | | |
| 2.40 | | | |
| 2.50 | | | |
| 2.60 | | | |
| 2.70 | Typist | | |
| 2.80 | | | |
| 2.90 | | | |
| 3.00 | | | |
| 3.10 | Stenographer | | |
| 3.20 | | | |

AND ADMINISTRATION; JOB ANALYSIS; PERSONNEL ADMINISTRATION; WORK DESIGN, JOB ENLARGEMENT, JOB ENRICHMENT, JOB DESIGN, AND AUTONOMOUS WORK GROUPS.

## NOTES

[1]David W. Belcher, *Compensation Administration*, adapted by permission of Prentice-Hall, Inc., Englewood Cliffs, N.J., © 1974, p. 87.

[2]Allan N. Nash and Stephen J. Carroll, Jr., *The Management of Compensation*, copyright © 1975 by Wadsworth Publishing Company, Inc. Adapted by permission of the publisher, Brooks/Cole Publishing Company, Monterey, Calif., p. 107.

[3]Nash, loc. cit.

[4]Nash, loc. cit.

[5]Charles W. Brennan, *Wage Administration*, rev. ed., Richard D. Irwin, Inc., Homewood, Ill., 1963, p. 64.

[6]Robert E. Sibson, *Wages and Salaries: A Handbook for Line Managers*, rev. ed., American Management Association, New York, 1967, p. 32.

[7]Sibson, op. cit., p. 31.

[8]Belcher, op. cit., pp. 134 and 136.

[9]Nash, op. cit., p. 123.

[10]Belcher, op. cit., p. 136.

[11]Nash, op. cit., p. 118.

[12]Nash, op. cit., p. 127.

[13]Belcher, op. cit., pp. 147 and 148.

[14]Belcher, op. cit., p. 149.

[15]Brennan, op. cit., p. 118.

[16]Belcher, op. cit., p. 151.

[17]Belcher, op. cit., p. 183.

[18]Belcher, op. cit., pp. 175 and 176.

[19]Belcher, op. cit., pp. 177 and 179.

[20]Belcher, op. cit., pp. 179, 180, and 181.

[21]Belcher, op. cit., p. 181.

[22]Belcher, op. cit., p. 155.

[23]Belcher, op. cit., p. 194.

## REFERENCES

Livy, Bryan: *Job Evaluation: A Critical Review*, Halstead Press, a division of John Wiley & Sons, Inc., New York, 1975.

Paterson, T. T., Jr.: *Job Evaluation: vol. I, A New Method*, Cahners Books, a division of Cahners Publishing Co., Inc., Boston, Mass., 1972.

FREDERICK A. TEAGUE, *Booz·Allen and Hamilton, Inc.*

## Job instruction training (JIT)  (*See* DEVELOPMENT AND TRAINING, EMPLOYEE.)

## Job order cost  (*See* ACCOUNTING, COST ANALYSIS AND CONTROL.)

## Job rating  (*See* COMPENSATION, WAGE AND SALARY POLICY AND ADMINISTRATION.)

## Job rotation  (*See* DEVELOPMENT AND TRAINING, EMPLOYEE.)

## Job shop  (*See* PRODUCTION PROCESSES.)

## Job specification  (*See* JOB ANALYSIS.)

## Joint utility theory  (*See* STATISTICAL ANALYSIS FOR MANAGEMENT.)

## Joint venture, international  (*See* INTERNATIONAL OPERATIONS AND MANAGEMENT IN MULTINATIONAL COMPANIES.)

## Jury duty  (*See* COMPENSATION, EMPLOYEE BENEFIT PLANS.)

# K

**Key terms**  (*See* RECORDS MANAGEMENT.)

**Keyboard outputs**  (*See* WORD PROCESSING.)

**Keynesian model**  (*See* ECONOMIC CONCEPTS.)

**Knowledge**  (*See* DEVELOPMENT AND TRAINING, EMPLOYEE.)

**L**

**Labor analysis sheet**  (*See* WORK MEASUREMENT.)

**Labor arbitration**  (*See* ARBITRATION, LABOR.)

**Labor contract**  (*See* LABOR-MANAGEMENT RELATIONS.)

**Labor force**  (*See* ECONOMIC MEASUREMENTS; EMPLOYMENT AND UNEMPLOYMENT.)

**Labor force, civilian**  (*See* ECONOMIC MEASUREMENTS.)

## Labor legislation

The mainstay of federal regulation of labor-management relations in the United States is the National Labor Relations Act (NLRA) of 1935. The NLRA seeks to balance the rights and obligations of unions and management while at the same time protecting the rights of individual employees. The NLRA was amended and augmented by the Taft-Hartley Act in 1947 and is now known as the Labor-Management Relations Act (LMRA). The Landrum-Griffin Act of 1959 made further changes in the law.

As presently implemented, the LMRA (1) permits employees to decide by secret ballot whether they wish representation by a labor union; (2) provides for rigid scrutiny by federal officials of the election process; (3) protects employees against unfair pressures from both management and unions with regard to their union participation; and (4) perhaps most important, encourages peaceful labor relations through the mechanism of collective bargaining. The achievement of a collective-bargaining agreement is probably the single most-important objective of United States labor laws. Subject to other legislation, these laws regulate hours, wages, working conditions, grievance procedures, employee benefits, and a host of other matters that are crucial to the employment relationship and to management planning. Thus, in general, labor relations in the United States are conducted with a mature regard for the health of the particular business or industry.

**Collective Bargaining**  Collective bargaining involves an effort to find solutions and live with agreements once they are made. There is of course a difference in style and emphasis among union leaders; some are more ideological than others. Many of the older leaders are basically nonideological. On the other hand, there is social-purpose rhetoric and some modest socialist bent in a few of the younger union leaders—particularly in the public sector. On the whole, however, the collective bargaining process is devoted to reaching economic solutions while agressively supporting the interests of the members. Political solutions are generally sought through the legislative process, but as one of the younger, more militant union leaders has put it,

The strange thing is that, unlike all the rest of the world's labor movements, ours is not an adversary of the system in terms of direction and philosophy. It is not socialistic: it wants to be part of the system.[1]

The absence of ideological commitment to an adversary posture is illustrated by the largely negative attitude of union leaders toward codetermination, which is a real issue in England and Germany. A top AFL-CIO executive observes:

Because American unions have won equality at the bargaining table, we have not sought it in corporate board rooms. . . . We do not seek to be a *partner* in management—to be, most likely, the junior partner in success and the senior partner in failure. *We do not want to blur in any way the distinctions between the respective roles of management and labor in the plant.*[2]

Thus, in general, social ideology is not a major issue among the leaders of organized labor in the United States, and the basic thrust of its labor laws toward promoting collective bargaining has been to a large extent successfully realized.

**Impact of Strikes**  The essence of the American collective bargaining arrangement is the preservation of the right to strike as well as the right of the employer to elect to sustain a strike. Strikes, however, are not a major problem in the American economy, although they hurt individual companies and industries at times. Some observers think that strikes may be even less of a problem in the future, and there is talk in some industries about pressing for further limitations on the right to strike. These developments suggest that the strike is becoming obsolete as labor's chief economic weapon in its dealings with management. Unions are increasingly more willing to cooperate to prevent strikes. In fact, George Meany, President of the AFL-CIO, frequently points out that strikes are becoming too costly for union members who have mortgage payments, car payments, college tuition payments— things that did not burden them 20 or 30 years ago.[3]

There is also a better understanding about the economics of world competition, for example, how the Japanese built some of their markets because of collective bargaining excesses in some American industries. One sign of the decline of the strike as

labor's chief weapon is the unprecedented agreement reached in 1974 between the steelworkers' union and steel companies. The agreement provides for binding arbitration of issues unresolved through negotiation in the industry's 1977 and 1980 contract discussions. The plan is still experimental, but, if successful, it will certainly appeal to other industries. A similar approach has already been developed in a few industries related to steel, such as the aluminum industry. Part of the union's willingness to abandon the use of the strike is no doubt attributable to the increasing number of members who are protected by cost-of-living clauses in their collective bargaining agreements.

**Impact on Nonunion Employees**  The effect of the federal labor laws is not confined to union members. Not only is the right to vote on whether to affiliate with a union preserved, but under the LMRA individual states may elect to pass right-to-work laws that preserve the right of individuals to refuse to join a union even after the union becomes the collective bargaining agent for that employee by winning a majority of the votes in a representation election. Furthermore, only one out of every four workers in the United States is a member of a union, and indications are that there will be a steady decline in the percentage of the labor force in union ranks. There are a number of reasons for this trend, including a pronounced shift in the value systems of many young people and in public attitudes toward unions.

Management, too, has been giving more attention to special needs and desires of nonunionized employees. The total industrial relations effort is under increased scrutiny and measurement; and more effective approaches to employee motivation have become top-priority management concerns. Another factor is the effort of employers to open new plants on a nonunion basis and to hope that employees will vote to remain nonunion. In many cases, this effort is made by employers in order to have a new plant start up without the presence of restrictive practices. Studies suggest that there may be productivity advantages of 20 percent or more in a nonunion type of operation.

**Governmental Influences**  With the growth in cooperation and understanding between employers and employees, whether or not unionized, the government has supplanted the unions in providing the major challenges in the area of employee relations, primarily as a result of new federal regulations concerning equal employment opportunity, occupational safety and health, and pension reform. Until a few years ago, government involvement in corporate human resource management was not a major concern to employers. Since passage of the Equal Pay Act of 1963, the Civil Rights Act of 1964, the Age Discrimination in Employment Act of 1967, the Vocational Rehabilitation Act of 1973, and the revival of civil rights statutes dating from the post-Civil War period, however, the issue of equal employment opportunity (EEO) has made government an increasingly active partner.

*Equal Employment Legislation.* Nearly every United States business with 15 or more employees is covered by extensive equal employment legislation. Virtually all federal contractors and subcontractors are required to perform extensive affirmative action pursuant to the provisions of Executive Order No. 11246. The issue affects more than personnel policy alone. Multimillion dollar awards, wide-ranging out-of-court settlements, and other conciliation agreements have set new patterns for future employment, training, and promotion. These have profoundly altered existing seniority systems in several industries and have made EEO considerations a major factor for management. This is a confused and rapidly changing area, and managers must take appropriate action to protect themselves and their organizations. Some of the confusion arises because government enforcement of the equal opportunity laws is not centralized but is divided among a large number of agencies. Consistent rules have yet to be developed to guide employers who seek to protect themselves from claims advanced by the government and by individuals who are protected under these laws and regulations. The equal employment opportunity area is made still more complex by the presence of state and local laws on the subject, many of them more stringent than the federal requirements.

*Occupational Safety and Health.* The business community has also found the Occupational Safety and Health Act (OSHA) to be very confusing, partly because its provisions and the standards to be enforced are quite unclear; it is a voluminous law which is almost impossible for the ordinary business manager to interpret. Unions, so-called "ad hoc groups" of workers in industries with safety or health problems, activist organizations, politicians, and even other federal agencies have been calling for harsher action by OSHA. It is clear that occupational health and safety matters must be given high priority in all business activities.

*ERISA.* Finally, the Employee Retirement Income Security Act of 1974 (ERISA) is unquestionably the most sweeping revision of rules applying to employee benefits ever enacted. It already affects the lives of more than 30 million workers under private pension plans and the handling of more than $200 billion in private pension funds. Obviously, its impact upon management policy making is broad. ERISA establishes new minimum standards for thousands of private employers, necessitating drastic revisions of existing benefit plans and applicable also to new plans as they are established. These standards include minimum requirements for (1) employee participation, (2) vesting of benefits, (3) the conduct of fiduciaries in connection with the plan, (4) funding, and (5) communication to the plan's participants and their beneficiaries. The new standards require complete disclosure of information about the pension plan to employees, who must be told everything they need to know about their pension and benefit plans in clear and simple language, readily understandable by the average plan participant. This communication requirement relates to on-the-job welfare benefits as well as to retirement benefits. Thus, employers must tell their employees fully and clearly about benefits such as hospital insurance, reimbursement for medical and surgical expenses, compensation for accident, disability, death, or unemployment, and other benefits. The law also sets up a new Pension Benefit Guaranty Corporation to protect the payment of vested benefits to the participants and beneficiaries of certain retirement plans. In the event of a plan termination, ERISA extends possible corporate liability to a maximum of 30 percent of the sponsoring company's net assets.

**Impact on Unions** In the future, membership in labor organizations will probably continue to grow with the expanding labor force (from a labor force of about 95 million in 1976 to 112 million in 1990), but the proportion of the labor force that is unionized (about 25 percent) is unlikely to grow. The greatest union growth is likely to come in the so-called "general workers unions" (the Teamsters and the Laborers) and in some public sector unions. There is likely to be a more rapid consolidation through mergers of national unions.

A significant trend within unions will be the adoption of professional managerial methods, particularly with respect to planning and decision making, decentralization of administration, and use of computer and communication technology and research tools. As the focus shifts to increased government regulation of matters traditionally controlled by collective bargaining agreements, the political efforts of unions will probably increase both with respect to efforts to gain public support on specific issues and to elect favored candidates. By seeking to become the determining force in elections, the unions hope to participate in shaping governmental policies and administrative regulations.

*See also* AFFIRMATIVE ACTION; ERISA; LABOR-MANAGEMENT RELATIONS; LABOR (TRADE) UNIONS; MINORITIES, MANAGEMENT OF AND EQUAL EMPLOYMENT OPPORTUNITY; PERSONNEL ADMINISTRATION; WAGES AND HOURS LEGISLATION; WOMEN IN INDUSTRY.

### NOTES

[1]Jerry Wurf, President of American Federation of State, County and Municipal Employees, *The New York Times*, sec. 3, page 1, September 5, 1976.

[2]Thomas Donahue, Executive Assistant to George Meany, John Herling's *Labor Letter, Inc.*, vol. 26, no. 32, August 7, 1976.

[3]Interview by six labor reporters with George Meany, President of AFL-CIO, in Washington, August 25, 1970.

VIRGIL B. DAY, *Vedder, Price, Kaufman, Kammholz and Day*

# Labor-management relations

The basic relationship between a company and a labor union is made up of many complex variables built on past practice. The relationship brings together individuals, groups, and institutions with different backgrounds, points of view, interests, and strengths. The balance of power is almost never equal; one party is usually dominant. These relative strengths will vary from time to time and situation to situation. Therefore, it is critically important that management establish, implement, and maintain a rational and objective approach for dealing with the union; one that considers both parties' needs and interests.

When business problems occur and any connection can be made to a deteriorating relationship with the union, the blame is often placed on *poor* labor relations. It is often said to be the union's fault. But serious business problems which result from strife and work stoppages, restrictive operating practices, etc., are in many cases just as much the fault of management as of the union. Unions can only make demands or try to take control; it is the company that must agree to the demands or allow them to happen. Hence, a need exists for a regular, careful, and critical review of the overall labor relations climate in an organization. Because it has such a significant impact on the business, professional management input is required.

Labor relations decisions should be based on research and planning, just as is done with a new product concept before designing, manufacturing,

and marketing it. Labor unions are staffed with members who have a high level of expertise and technical competence. Labor unions spend the necessary funds to research today's problems as well as to plan for the future. Management must do the same. These questions should be asked, "Are labor relations a mainstream operating activity in your company? Is the activity properly staffed? Is it held accountable for significant results? Does it know where the business is going?"

## FUNDAMENTAL FACTORS AFFECTING UNION-MANAGEMENT RELATIONS

The relations between the parties should not be allowed just to happen. They must be carefully thought through. They should develop as a result of planned actions and reactions.

**Basic Principles** A company's philosophy is the key factor that affects the relations between the company and union management. Several principles should guide the formulation of this philosophy.

*Conflict of Objectives.* The fundamental relationship between the union and the company is one of push and pull, most often in opposite directions, even though the company's continued success is essential for both parties. The union has as its primary objective the desire to obtain more in both economic (wages and benefits) and noneconomic (contract provisions and operating practices) areas. It expects to make these gains via the bargaining process, the grievance and arbitration procedure, and through management default. The company, on the other hand, resists all efforts of the union to restrict management's freedom to make decisions necessary to run the business. This conflict need not be personal in nature. In fact, it should not be. But one must be fully aware of the nature of the conflict involved in order to manage it properly.

*A Variety of Unions and Approaches.* The numbers and types of unions that are present in industry are many. There are simple single-plant unions, multiple unions in one plant, craft and trade unions, company-wide bargaining, industry-wide bargaining, coalition and coordinated bargaining, and multiple variations of the above. Management must know its own business and its objectives and needs and then, after critical and careful examination, must determine what relationship is best for each situation.

*Mutually Satisfactory Relationships.* Once a majority of employees in an appropriate unit vote to be represented by a union, the company must determine the type of relationship it wants. Since the relationship is usually of long duration, serious consideration should be given to the various factors affecting it. Over the long term, these relationships require give and take by both parties.

*Credibility.* The axiom of credibility is to say what we mean and mean what we say; it requires telling both the good and bad news. Management credibility does not interfere with hard bargaining. Experienced negotiators on both sides of the table can distinguish between bona fide bargaining on the one hand and vacillating uncertainty on the other. Credibility is absolutely essential to good labor-management relations, and the primary responsibility for attaining it rests with the company.

*Predictability.* Surprises and sudden changes are natural enemies of good labor relations. Union leaders should be informed in advance of changes in important employee relations policies or practices. Do not surprise union leaders. They should be able to predict with reasonable certainty how the company will react to specific situations.

*A Problem-Solving Approach.* Successful labor relations are not so much a matter of *who* is right as they are *what* is right. Management must consider the specific problem and alternative solutions. Frequently, the solution initially proposed either by the company or by the union is not the best one. It is important to search out mutually acceptable solutions which, in many cases, are found somewhere between the positions of the two parties.

*Open and Candid Communications.* Discussion between company and union representatives occurs in various degrees of formality. Usually the more formal the discussion, the less effective the result. Open and candid communication is necessary between the parties, in which the viewpoints of each party are freely expressed and heard. Effective communications usually can be improved by occasional informal business-related contacts between the parties. Such contact can lead to the development of mutual understanding and trust—essential factors in a continuing good relationship.

*Understanding of Union's Political Considerations.* One must accept the fact that unions are relatively political organizations and that most union officials want to be reelected. In order to secure cooperation from them in the consideration of the company's problems, management must be willing to consider the union's problems. At the same time, the union must be required to accept management's responsibility to manage the business.

*A Unified Management Front.* Unions understandably strive to whipsaw and divide manage-

ment. Operating management must be sufficiently informed of top management's position on any particular issue. Individually and collectively, all members of management must be able to defend that position in good conscience. Whenever management is divided in working with a union, it is an indication that management has not done its homework, an oversight which invariably is costly to the company.

*Carefully Thought-Out Negotiation Objectives.* The primary objective in union contract negotiations is to reach a fair and equitable settlement without a strike, within company-established cost limits and with contract terms that do not present unduly restrictive practices or obstacles to good management practices. One authority observes,

Once written into a contract, the life of a provision is all but everlasting. In those rare instances where a company has been able to negotiate a provision *out* of an agreement, it has had to pay a high trading price.[1]

*Fair and Consistent Practices.* Whether questions of contract interpretation, discipline, job evaluation, or enforcement of productivity standards are involved, it is essential that they be dealt with fairly and consistently. Similar circumstances must be consistently handled. Neither management nor the union can tolerate a failure to observe this principle.

**Fundamentals of Management Behavior** In addition to its philosophical tenets, a prudent management will also follow certain guidelines in its dealings with union matters and labor union representatives.

*Relationship Based on Mutual Respect.* Each must treat the other party with dignity and respect. This should be the case at all levels in both the company and the union. One need not tolerate personal attacks or abuses. Issues and resulting discussions should be based on facts of substance, never on personalities. If management representatives keep personal emotion to a minimum, union representatives will be apt to follow that lead.

*Basis for Change.* Constant change is a basic ingredient of business. When implementing changes that affect union relationships, management must try to have equity and moral forces working for it, not against it. Another authority comments,

Management in the performance of its function is primarily an instigator of change. Change is its way of life. The union, on the other hand, serves more as a restraint on management and a protector of security for its members; therefore it is frequently cast in the role of forestaller of change.[2]

This can be, and often is, the cause of conflict.

*Introduction of Change.* Changes should be introduced at a pace that the company can manage and that the union can accept, however reluctantly. If the pace is such that the company exceeds the union's ability to react in the most-rational way in which it is capable, the union will swamp the relationship with irrational behavior. Priorities for change should be based on operating needs and maximum long-range return. It is wasteful to spend a great amount of time and resources on things of little real business value.

*Proper Motivation.* In order to make changes, management should use both negative forces (e.g., discipline, loss of jobs) and positive forces (e.g., praise, reward) based on the situation at hand. If the use is consistent, union reaction may be more favorable than expected.

*Fairness and the Grievance Procedure.* The primary purpose of a grievance procedure is to settle disputes fairly. The technicalities of the procedure should not be allowed to prevent justice. Walter Baer, in his book *Grievance Handling*, writes that, "Grievance machinery is the formal process that enables the parties to attempt to resolve their differences in a peaceful, orderly, and expeditious manner."[3] The grievance procedure should be recognized and administered as a simple judicial process, not a political process. Thus, grievances should be adjusted on their merits, with concession by the company at an early stage if the evidence indicates the company was wrong.

Additionally,

Grievance machinery is really a system of communications extending from the bottommost layers of the plant to the top and back down again. To the extent that a management avails itself of this listening device, it is in a better position to anticipate problems and read the mood of the labor force.[4]

*Judge on Actions, Not Words.* It is a sound practice to judge the union not on what it says but on what it does, carefully observed and averaged over a period of time. Unions were designed for the offensive, because of their origin as reformers and agents of change. When they become more conservative, they rest more on the status quo. Management can now take the initiative for change, providing it follows such dos and don'ts as shown in Table L-1.

## LABOR RELATIONS CHARTER AND STRATEGY

In labor relations, just as in all other phases of business management, a company must know where it has been, where it is, and most important, where it is going. The company-union relationship is normally of long duration. It is established at both the bargaining table, where contracts are settled, and on the shop floor, where daily problems are resolved by understanding and/or conflict. As Blum says,

Unions are real; they affect the system and process of management. They influence day-to-day policy and programs. Managers face an obvious need to understand unions, the reasons why members join them, and the rationale of union policy and practice. Unions are an important fact in the daily lives of managers, whether or not they like it.[5]

In simple terms, a company must develop an overall union relations charter and strategy. Where more than one union exists, a separate strategy should be developed for each relationship. These strategies must be designed to supplement and fit the overall business plans and goals, both short and long term.

Once established, this basic approach must be documented, implemented, and revised as necessary. According to Dale Yoder, a labor relations

TABLE L-1 Management Dos and Don'ts

| Do | Don't |
|---|---|
| 1. Use muscle to obtain needed operating changes. | 1. Surprise your union. |
| 2. Solicit union inputs on changes. | 2. Use retaliation. |
| 3. Accept suggestions that will not compromise principles. | 3. Try to use union methods. |
| 4. Trade money for operating principles. | 4. Play the labor relations game; sound business practices should prevail. |
| 5. Bend over backwards to be fair. | 5. Say the company is going to do something unless it plans to do it; no idle threats. |
| 6. Keep employees informed on pertinent business information. | 6. Bribe good behavior. |
| 7. Preach and repreach the company's management principles. | 7. Buy off productivity—expect and require a fair day's work for a fair day's pay. |
| 8. Do a sound job of communicating with both management and employees. | 8. Corner the union or the company. |
| 9. Realize that politics are important to the union. | |

policy must rest on certain major "planks." Among these are the right and obligation to bargain, employer rights and responsibilities, and union rights and responsibilities.[6]

These must be taken into consideration in developing the strategy.

**Operating Goals and Strategy** Just as it is important for line management to establish business objectives, it is also important that these objectives be converted into specific labor relations goals. All activities on the part of the labor relations staff must be directed to providing operating management with the latitude it needs to run a competitive business. If close coordination of objectives is not achieved, line and staff may well be working at odds with each other or, at best, putting emphasis on the wrong issues.

The long- and short-range labor relations strategy must consider certain business factors:

1. Nature of the business and where it is going.

2. Impact of short- and long-range business plans on the contract and practices. This includes employee levels, skill requirements or changes, technological changes, product mixes, etc.

3. Nature of the competition.

4. Customers' needs and requirements in terms of their impact on practices and the contract and on the company's ability to meet schedules and deliveries.

5. Seasonality of business and customer requirements.

**Roles of Line and Staff** Primary responsibility for labor relations should rest with line-operating management. It sets the tone and, in fact, must run the facility. A high level of professional expertise must be provided by the employee relations staff, however, which is supportive of the line management's operating needs. Staff professionals must be knowledgeable in the contract and its administration, practices, negotiations, and legal considerations. They must be managers, tacticians, and strategists; not just administrators. A close working relationship must be established between and among various levels in operating management and their counterparts in the labor relations staff.

One of the union's favorite tactics is to whipsaw managers in one department against managers in another department; to ask the same question enough times and of enough different people to get the answer they want. Hence, the need exists for close coordination among management representatives. The respective roles of operating and staff management must be communicated to and understood by each of the parties.

**Erosion of Practices** What is gained in negotiations often is lost through poor practices, sometimes called "sleeping on your rights." What established practices and the labor agreement say a company can do is important, but more important is how the company has applied the agreements. Most arbiters look at what the company is actually doing and how it applies the contract, not at contract language alone. Unions spend considerable time and effort making inroads into a number of seemingly insignificant areas; before management knows it, the union "owns" a whole practice. Paradoxically these are often practices or principles which management would not have given up at the bargaining table. When erosion continues over an extended period of time, the union may well gain control. It is always costly to retrieve management rights which have slipped away.

**Multiple-Union Situation** If a company has multiple unions and/or multiple locations, consideration must be given to coalition bargaining or multiplant bargaining. Expiration dates of contracts are extremely important in such instances. Accordingly, the company may want to have a *lead* or *pattern* contract expire first in order to establish benchmarks for later negotiations. Decisions in these matters have high-level impact on the business and must be carefully evaluated.

**Past Relationships** Since so much of the future is dictated by the past, it is important that management maintain and review the past history of the company's union relationship. Meanwhile, the union will also be predicting the future based on the *company's* behavior. It wants to know where the company will stand firm and where it may give in to various levels of pressure. The company must know the same about the union as well as about itself. If management plans to change its basic relationship with the union, its position on important issues, its approach to the union and the relationship, then the union should be informed in advance, with detailed and understandable reasons for the change.

**The Union and its Leadership** Just as the future is to some degree predicted by the past, so the relationship with the union is influenced by past behavior patterns of the two parties. An analysis of this type includes an understanding of the philosophies and operating practices of the local union—such things as timing and method for electing officers, contract ratification procedure, involvement of the international union, etc. No two unions are the same. In fact, two locals of the same union or two business agents from the same local often differ considerably.

Management should have knowledge of the behavior pattern of the local membership, stewards and officers, and international representatives. It should know the union's approach to handling situations, hot issues, normal reactions, reactions under pressure, internal political pressures, etc.

**Union Decision Point**   It is imperative that management also know the decision point at the various levels of the union organization. It must determine what individual or group makes decisions at the various levels of issues or problems. Otherwise, management may find itself addressing the right questions for resolution to the wrong level of decision making. The result can be disastrous.

**Preparing the Written Policy**   With the above considerations in mind, an overall labor relations policy or strategy should be formulated and put into writing. It should include the following elements:

1. *Significant past business or company relationship factors affecting the relationship:* New management, pending negotiations, past strikes at contract expiration, wildcat strikes, changes in business direction, etc.

2. *Fundamentals of relationship:* The overall fundamentals of the relationship with union or unions, such as type and nature of communications, operation of grievance procedure, position on various management rights issues, etc.

3. *Current business strategies:* Priorities, timetables, and responsibilities of current business objectives which impact on labor relations, organization and manning level changes, product and technology changes, etc.

4. *Policy-making group:* The specific individuals responsible for various levels and types of decisions; also a list of union counterparts.

5. *Role of supervisors:* Types and level of problems they should handle and level of union representatives with whom they should work.

6. *Union leadership:* Control and decision points; types of actions or reactions that can be expected; role of officers, stewards, and international representatives; membership needs and attitudes, etc.

7. *Grievance and arbitration procedures:* Analysis of past utilization and responses; judicial approach or trading device; company and union positions on classes of grievances such as back pay, discipline, etc.

8. *Negotiations planning:* The role of negotiations as it relates to ongoing labor relations. (See next entry).

9. *Schedule of events:* Specific timetables, goals, and responsibilities necessary to implement strategies for the current year.

The policy should be used as a guideline for current actions and goals and long-range objectives. It should be a living document and control device. It should be revised and updated as necessary, but at least on an annual basis.

## COLLECTIVE-BARGAINING PROCESS

In terms of the business, stockholders, customers, employees, and public relations, no single employee relations event has as great an impact as contract negotiations. It is the culmination of all the activities, desires, needs, and frustrations of the past into a single finite point in time when the contract expires. Both parties position themselves and their constituents: for the union—its membership—and for the company—various levels of management. Both parties exchange thoughts and words, some logical and meaningful and other pure trivia and filler, which hopefully will result in a better contract for both. There is a certain ritual of collective bargaining, based on the particular situation.

The objective of collective bargaining, according to one authority, is

. . . to negotiate an agreement which will meet the needs of the company to remain competitive and profitable, while at the same time being creatively responsive to individual interests, situations, and concerns of employees.[7]

Another perspective is provided by Yoder, who states that, the

. . . *collective agreement or labor contract* is the charter on which employers and unions agree. It is a written statement of terms mutually accepted as defining the relationships and work conditions to be maintained in the bargaining unit. *Negotiation* is the process that creates and/or modifies the collective agreement.[8]

It is a foregone conclusion that, in most instances, unions will achieve and/or claim improvements for their members in direct wage and benefit areas. However, in the critical areas of noneconomic operating practices, management must protect, and sometimes regain, their rights to make basic decisions necessary to running a competitive business. Getting back such management rights short of a confrontation is difficult, if not impossible. It is difficult to convince the union leadership, and often more difficult for them to sell the membership, to give back those rights.

There are a number of steps necessary to plan for and manage effective negotiations. Each is discussed briefly below.

**Negotiations Schedule**   Approximately 9 months to a year before negotiations begin, a detailed negotiations schedule (see Table L-2) should

**TABLE L-2  Contract Negotiations Schedule**

| | Feb. | Mar. | Apr. | May | June | July | Aug. | Sept. | Oct. | Nov. |
|---|---|---|---|---|---|---|---|---|---|---|
| 1. Negotiations objective and plan | | | | | | | | | | |
|    *a.* Determine negotiations objectives | 2-2 | | | | | | | | | |
|    *b.* Strategy meetings | | 3-15 | | | | 7-18 | | 9-1 | | |
|       Status reviews—on task team | | | | | | | 8-3 Mtg. | | 10-5 Mtg. | 11-3 Implement |
| 2. Strike task force—facility | | First mtg. | | | 6-7 Mtg. | | 8-5 Mtg. | | | |
| 3. Customer protection contingency plan | | Approved plan 3-31 | | | | | | | | |
| 4. Communications program | | Draft 3-2 | | Review 5-4 | | | | | | |
| 5. Company negotiating committee | 2-9 | Determine 3-9 | | Define duties 5-11 | | | | | | |
|    *a.* Subcommittee | | | | | Rev. use | | | | | |
| 6. Company negotiating demands | | | | | | | | | | |
|    *a.* Development of plan | 2-19 | | | | | | | | | |
|    *b.* Line input | | | 4-14 | | | | | | | |
|    *c.* Draft demands | | | | | | | | | | |
|    *d.* Final demands | | | | | | 7-6 | 8-19 | | | |
| 7. Legal review of contract—corporate attorney | | 3-1 | | 5-3 | | | | | | |
|    *a.* Contract language—draft changes | | | | | | | | 9-9 | 10-7 | 11-2 |
| 8. Review side agreements to contract | | Start 3-31 | Fin. 4-28 | | | | | | | |
| 9. Contract data preparation | | | | | | | | | | |
|    *a.* 19___(last) negotiations results summary | | | Start 4-14 | Fin. 5-11 | | | | | | |
|    *b.* Market surveys | | | Determine structure 4-14 | | | Start 7-24 | Fin. 8-12 | | | |
|    *c.* Costing information | | | | | Start 6-9 | Start 7-10 | Fin. 8-19 | | | |
|    *d.* Employee data | | | | | Start 6-9 | Fin. 7-10 | | | | |
|    *e.* Grievance and arbitration data | | | | | | | | | | |
| 10. Union contract demands | | | | | | | | | | |
|    *a.* Anticipated demands—strike issues | | | | | Start 6-16 | Fin. 7-13 | Fin. 8-19 | | | |
|    *b.* Analyze actual demands | | | | | | 7-3 | 8-12 | | | |
| 11. Review role of local, district union officers, mediator | | | | | | | | Start 9-7 | Fin. 10-30 | |
| 12. Coordinated bargaining posture | | | | | | Decide 7-13 | 8-12 | | | |
| 13. Establish time, place, pay questions for negotiations | | | | | | 7-6 | | | | |
| 14. Federal mediating and conciliation service | | | | | First contact 6-16 | Co. mtg. 7-5 | | 60-day letter 9-1 | 10-10 Progress | |
| 15. Other contract settlements | | | | | | Review 7-18 | | | | |
|    *a.* Location A | | | | | | | | | | |
|    *b.* Location B | | | | | | | | | | |
| 16. Actual contract negotiations with union | | | | | | | Rev. 8-18 | | | |
|    *a.* Letter to union | | | | | | | | Send 9-1 | | |
|    *b.* Analyze—cost union demands | | | | | | | | Start 9-9 | 10-21 | |
| 17. Economic settlement—final package approval | | | | | | | | 9-23 | | Fin. 11-2 |
| 18. Expiration date | | | | | | | | | | 11-9 |

be prepared, setting forth each step to be taken, the individual responsible, and the completion date. This schedule, as revised, should become the control document for the preparation, execution, and follow-up of negotiations.

*Current Contract.* Negotiation preparations should begin with a thorough review of present contract language, supplemental agreements, and a knowledge of any problems relating to its application. Issues presented in grievance or arbitration and their resolution should be analyzed as an aid in identifying potential union demands or possible company proposals. Finally, existing plant practices should be carefully considered.

*Past Negotiations.* Past negotiations should be reviewed to determine what demands were made by the company and union, and the results. This information may indicate types of settlements and union areas of concentration which will be helpful in developing company negotiations strategy. The role of outside parties such as mediators or arbiters should be carefully reviewed.

*Status of Business.* Needless to say, the current status of business and future company operating plans that may affect employees must be known. It is often essential in countering points raised by the union, as well as in constructing company proposals, to know what is necessary for the accomplishment of business goals. Part of this review, of course, is obtaining information on current operating problems which are caused by present contract provisions or practices and which should be corrected in negotiations.

**Survey of Practices and Economic Trends** The formulation of company positions and rebuttal of union demands is greatly aided by knowledge of national, area, and competitive industry trends in the areas of wage and fringe benefits. Surveys on the present level of economic items and changes that have occurred in them during the term of the contract should be made and concluded at least 2 weeks prior to negotiations.

Care should be taken that a representative sample is obtained. Companies in the appropriate labor market, competitive companies, comparative industry, and national industry settlements and trends should be included.

**Bargaining Unit Information** Understanding and handling union demands, determining costs and effect on operations, and developing company policy and strategy can be properly done only with detailed knowledge of the work force and the union. Much of this required information, supplemented by personnel manuals, records, and reports, can be

obtained from payroll files. Table L-3 sets forth examples of the types of information you should analyze prior to the start of negotiations.

**TABLE L-3 Bargaining Unit Information**

1. Composition of the work force by
    a. Rate of pay
    b. Labor grade
    c. Sex
    d. Age
    e. Length of service
    f. Minority group status
    g. Job number and/or classification
    h. Breakdown of above information by seniority group
2. Participation figures in the following benefit plans (examples):
    a. Hospital insurance
    b. Life insurance
    c. Long-term disability
    d. Accidental death and dismemberment
    e. Major medical insurance
    f. Stock option or similar plans
    g. Dental
3. Computations
    a. Average straight time hourly rate by: grade, job number, length of service, etc.
    b. Average cents per straight time hour cost of fringe benefits
    c. Participation data expressed in percent
    d. Insurance premium figures
4. Data
    a. Shift populations and cost
    b. Number of downgrades, upgrades, and transfers
    c. Average overtime earnings
    d. Seniority group distributions
    e. Layoffs and number of persons with recall rights

**Review of Legal Requirements** Legal requirements make the presence or absence of certain practices mandatory, affecting various areas such as health and safety, equal employment, pensions, etc. Mandatory holidays, fringe benefits, working conditions, and required leave, termination, hiring, and promotion practices are examples. Such requirements, whether they are a product of legislation, regulations, or imposed as part of government contracts, change frequently and often vary widely between governmental authorities and industries.

*Legal Assistance.* It is essential that competent legal assistance be utilized throughout the early review of the current contract, proposed changes, the drafting of contract language, and as necessary to review legal questions on the bargaining process itself.

**Review of Union Negotiation and Ratification Practices** Most unions tend to follow a historical pattern in negotiation and ratification practices. While variances do occur, it is more likely that a union will act about the same as it has in previous negotiations rather than follow a significantly different course of conduct. Knowledge of and strategy based on a union's pattern of conduct can often mean the difference between obtaining a settlement without a strike or being struck.

*Union Negotiation Techniques.* At the outset it is important to review past demands against actual settlements. This provides some insight into how much room the union typically leaves for itself to move. It is also important to review the degree of importance which the union has attached to dropped demands which it may again bring up. Demands which are perennial but which the union does not really expect to get are often recognizable as such. However, if the union gave up on a demand only after hard bargaining, a repetition of the demand should be regarded as serious.

The pattern in which the union drops demands should be studied. A union may (1) rarely formally drop demands but simply stop talking about them; (2) make trades; (3) make few moves until the final hours of negotiations; (4) follow a fairly steady pace of movement from the start of negotiations; or (5) attempt to bluff through a "take it or leave it" position. The company must negotiate against the anticipated union conduct so that negotiations do not become prematurely deadlocked nor their end position arrived at too soon.

A related study should be made to determine if any traditional pattern exists by which the parties signal that they would be receptive to compromise proposals. If so, the company negotiator should be thoroughly familiar with the pattern so that he or she does not fail to perceive a union signal or inadvertently lead the union to believe the company is ready to move in an area when it, in fact, is not.

The negotiator should be aware, when the union stops talking about a demand, whether it is relatively certain that the issue has been dropped or whether there is a union practice of reviving a demand at the final hour. If so, a method of counteracting may be needed. Similarly, the negotiator must be aware of a tradition of bringing up new demands during the course of negotiations which were not in the original demands; some unions traditionally make significant last minute demands just as a settlement appears imminent.

*Obtaining Union Committee Agreement.* Obviously, the agreement of the union committee cannot be obtained unless the committee is convinced that the company has made its final offer. Traditionally certain words, circumstances, and events indicate to the union when this point has been reached—and a variance by the company from an anticipated pattern of conduct may result in disastrous confusion. It is, therefore, highly impor-

tant to know what previous negotiations have led the union to expect, who was involved, where, and when it was concluded. Further, mediation is traditionally a part of the final settlement process at some negotiations, and a final offer would not be credible unless it evolved from the mediation process; at others this is not necessary.

*Ratification.* Ratification practices, like negotiation practices, tend to follow traditional patterns. Members, like leaders, learn to expect certain things to occur before the company's final offer is credible. The company negotiators should be thoroughly familiar with past practices. In some situations the membership has historically been given a company offer some time before the contract expires, which it has traditionally rejected. Only the offer made at the time the contract expired or was about to expire is regarded as the final offer. In other situations, there is a tradition of settling early. The practice should be known if the final offer is to be timed correctly. It is also important to know if the members are accustomed to wait at the union hall while the negotiators work down to the last minute, or whether they typically hold a ratification meeting the day after the contract expires. The time of day the meeting is traditionally held and the group of employees who traditionally attend the meeting should also be known.

**Union Demands** It is important in planning company strategy and ascertaining the probable cost of reaching settlement to anticipate the demands the union may make in negotiations. Doing so can save valuable time later, particularly in costing, determining initial positions, and developing counter proposals. It can also give an indication of the support, or lack of it, for a union demand actually made in negotiations.

To most accurately anticipate union demands, the labor relations staff should (1) discuss the subject with supervisors who are in daily contact with bargaining unit employees; (2) attempt to get some advance hint from union officials; (3) review past grievances and past negotiation history; and (4) review settlements by other locals of the same union in the area or industry.

Once union demands have been received, each item should be analyzed and rated for (1) its impact on the business in terms of cost and operating restrictions and (2) the best appraisal of the priority which the union places on each demand.

Finally, a determination must be made of which union demands are strike issues. This cannot be taken lightly by either party. Once the company concludes and communicates that a demand is a strike issue, it must stand, or fall, with that position in order to protect its credibility in the future.

**Company Negotiating Team** One of the primary requisites of successful bargaining is the makeup of the company negotiating team. The team should be of manageable size, but sufficiently large to contain a cross section of management representatives who are knowledgeable in all aspects of plant operations, union relations, and contract administration. The representatives also should be of sufficient stature to be able to recommend effectively and assure the proper administration of the items to be negotiated. Selection should be made sufficiently in advance of actual negotiations so that members may participate in negotiation preparation, identification of company negotiating goals, and discussion of strategy.

*Committee Members.* The line manager responsible for the employees concerned in the negotiation should be a member of the team or available to the company spokesperson at all times during negotiations. Other members of the team should be selected from the lower levels of management responsible for managing the various areas to be affected by the contract.

*Company Spokesperson.* One individual should be identified as the company spokesperson. Normally he or she is the cognizant employee relations manager, although this is not a necessity. The individual must be articulate and have prestige with both the union and company representatives. The person should be of a stature to make decisions which the union knows are final and binding, of a level to be able to discuss any item with top management, and in some cases have the company's positions changed when he or she feels it is necessary. The individual has primary responsibility for conducting all aspects of negotiations both in terms of preparation and actual negotiating sessions, including company tactics, and at each stage must have the support of the negotiating committee. Negotiations have both conflict and crisis; the spokesperson must be able to handle the buildup of pressure.

*Training of Committee.* After selection, the team members should be thoroughly briefed by their spokesperson in the role each is to play in negotiations, as well as the overall strategy to be followed. It is essential that every member know the company's objectives and each step to be taken during negotiations; however, it is not necessary for all members of the company committee to know the details of the company's economic authorization.

*Conduct at Negotiating Table.* At the negotiating table, no other member of the committee should

speak unless pursuant to a plan worked out with the spokesperson in advance. It is often planned in advance that other members of the team will speak on certain subjects, but it must be understood that all discussion in the negotiating room is controlled by the company spokesperson. During meetings outside of the negotiating room or in caucuses, other members of the negotiating team should understand that they are to participate fully in discussing, objecting to, or advancing proposals according to what they feel is proper. Once an item is discussed and agreed upon, however, all members of the team must act of one accord when discussing it across the table with the union committee.

*Confidentiality of Negotiations.* All items discussed in preparation of and during the actual course of contract negotiations must be held confidential by the members of the negotiating team, unless specific authorization for certain types of communication is obtained from the company spokesperson.

*Power of Commitment.* Only the company spokesperson has the power to commit the company to an action. This must be clearly understood by the union negotiating committee as well as by the company committee members. The spokesperson in turn must receive approval from the designated higher-level manager.

**Formulation of Company Objectives and Proposals** Development of company proposals to be given to the union should be the *last* step in the process of determining management goals and objectives in negotiations. Indeed, after the process is completed, it may be decided *not* to make any company proposals.

However, sometimes the best defense is a good defense. Sloane and Witney, for example, view collective-bargaining sessions

. . . as productive in terms of protecting the basic interests of management as they are in protecting the legitimate job rights of employees. These results, however, cannot be accomplished when management remains constantly on the defensive.[9]

The process begins with a review of the strengths and weaknesses of current plant practices and contract provisions. After this, line management (including first-line supervision) should be solicited for their view of needed additions, deletions, or modifications to the contract; no evaluation of this input should be made until it is fully obtained. Simultaneously, top plant management should be requested to state what they desire the company to obtain in negotiations.

*Setting Priorities of Company Proposals.* After all this information is compiled, company objectives should be ranked in order of importance. Each should first be analyzed to determine whether a change in the contract is actually needed to achieve it. If not, it should be removed from consideration. It is not a good tactic to demand rights already assumed, or they may be lost if the union does not agree to the demand. Also, any items clearly impossible to negotiate should be deleted. Those items remaining should then be ranked (1) in order of importance to the company and (2) in order of the probability of obtaining union agreement. The list should then be pared to a manageable size. Items retained should be those that are the most important and have a reasonable probability of getting union agreement *provided* that a proposal not be made on any matter that, if unsuccessful, would put the company in a worse position than continuing the status quo—unless the company is willing to take a strike to get it. Some "droppable" proposals should be included purely for negotiating purposes.

*Presenting Company Proposals.* Company proposals are often stated in terms of the objective or as a discussion item, rather than in specific contract language, to provide more flexibility in negotiations. As indicated above, it is important not to ask for items or clarifications of things management believes it already has, unless it is very important to do so. Asking for something and then backing away from it may cause the company to forfeit an existing right. Also, any item considered to be a company strike issue should be clearly understood to be so before it is given such status in company negotiating strategy.

*Factual Support Proposals.* The negotiating team must be prepared to substantiate any proposal with facts. A weak presentation may mislead the union into thinking an important proposal is unimportant.

**The Final Offer** Two factors require careful preparation.

*Makeup.* In determining the makeup of the company's final offer, consideration must be given to a variety of external and internal factors. Consider the needs of company programs, union membership, union leadership, area pay and benefit practices, internal inequities, legal requirements, etc. These must be carefully studied and balanced. Normally, a final company offer should be allowed to go to the membership only if a majority of the union negotiating committee have recommended acceptance. The company should press for a unanimous recommendation. This will help increase the possibility of membership acceptance.

*Management Approval.* An unconditional offer made during negotiations by any member of the company's bargaining committee cannot readily be withdrawn (as a matter of negotiations reality or without running the risk of a refusal-to-bargain charge) even though the offer was not authorized by management. Therefore, it is essential to obtain approval *prior* to making any offers and to instruct all members of the company committee that they are not to make any proposals except as authorized and planned.

**Negotiating Process** The negotiating process is a ritual that is peculiar to the given situation, the times, and the parties. It is a give-and-take process, but above all else, the parties must be realistic. The company must understand the union leadership and the membership and their desires and needs. The union must also understand the company and its needs. Someone observed

The fact that collective bargaining is a two-way street is clearly evidenced in negotiation sessions. Some people hold the view that the collective bargaining process involves only the union's demanding and the company's giving. On the contrary, . . . the company frequently will resist and refuse to concede to some issues. And when the company believes that the stakes are extremely important it will take a strike rather than concede to a particular union demand.[10]

The problem is that both parties view those needs and expectations from their own position or point of view. The process then becomes one of lowering or adjusting expectations so that they, in fact, meet the other party's ability to deliver. This modulating of positions takes a great amount of time, discussion, and often patient waiting. For some bargaining tips, see Table L-4.

**Causes for Bargaining Breakdown** Bargaining that breaks down often results in conflicts or strikes. The causes for this breakdown include the following:

1. No real bargaining occurs; one party is not interested in negotiating; there is a failure to have give-and-take in position.

2. One party takes a strong intransigent position on an issue(s) critical to the other party. These are usually issues of principle. They are real problems to the party raising them.

3. It is the first contract, and the parties do not fully understand each other.

4. A dramatic change in style or procedure from past experiences occurs.

5. There is a failure to understand the situation; judgmental errors include not listening or miscalculating.

**TABLE L-4   Bargaining Tips**

1. Never give a false signal.
2. Never indicate you will consider a demand on which you do not intend to move.
3. Spend plenty of time listening.
4. Be sincere about your motives—do not attempt to conceal the fact that you are in business to make money.
5. Do not indicate you cannot afford or cannot compete if a demand is given unless you are willing to show your books or are sure they will not be demanded.
6. Do not index economic items on a percentage base; negotiate on fixed cost so that you can negotiate on the item in the future, and both company and union gain credit for improvements.
7. Do not indicate you will not negotiate on a subject unless you are sure that you have no legal duty to negotiate on it.
8. Let the union drop its demands gracefully.
9. Do not lose self-control or attack any member of the union committee personally.
10. Do not take or give abuse; adjourn the meeting until tempers have cooled.
11. Work from the company's language.
12. Make sessions as long as is necessary to obtain satisfactory understanding.

6. There is an inability to meet the other party's expectations.

## NEGOTIATIONS COMMUNICATIONS PROGRAM

The communication of information regarding negotiations, as well as communication in the event of a strike, is a very sensitive subject. Therefore, early in negotiations planning, it should be decided what, how much, when, how, and by whom such information is to be communicated to managers and supervisors, employees, and the public. Although a person who is not a member of the negotiating team may be responsible for administering a communications program, the content, form, and timing of communication releases must be controlled by the negotiations spokesperson so they will not conflict with overall strategy. Techniques to be reviewed are (1) letters to the home, (2) company newspaper, (3) bulletin-board notices, (4) supervisory meetings, (5) word of mouth, and (6) press releases.

Only *facts* and supporting arguments should be communicated; it is unwise to send up "trial balloons," engage in innuendo, or exaggerate. The key to any communications program is credibility. Further, consideration must be given to its effect on actual negotiations. If a past history of limited communications is dramatically or unexpectedly reversed, it may cause the union negotiators to view it as a pressure tactic or a violation of confidences. If the decision is made to change the approach to

communications, then the union should be told and given reasons for the change. Press releases should be issued through or coordinated with the cognizant public relations function.

## STRIKE PREPARATION AND CUSTOMER CONTINGENCY PLANNING

Major goals of strike preparation include maintaining the ability to meet customers' needs (to the greatest extent possible), preventing improper interference with company operations by striking employees, successfully concluding the strike, and resuming normal operations as quickly as possible. These goals require involvement of all management functions and close coordination with the labor contract negotiation process.

The company's preparations for a strike have the following main objectives, and a detailed written manual should be prepared as a guide should a strike occur. The objectives are:

1. To protect personnel, property, and maintain essential maintenance, production, and service; thereby to minimize financial losses to the company and personal losses to employees.
2. To maintain the good will of customers, the public, and employees to the maximum extent practical.
3. To enable the company to deal fairly in terms of its personnel policies with both striking and nonstriking employees.
4. To enable the company to resume normal operations when the strike ends within the shortest possible time.
5. To demonstrate to the union that the company will take a strike if necessary in order to continue to manage the business effectively.

**Critical Decisions**   The following critical decisions should be made before the strike begins. All of them, and any other policy decisions, should be reviewed with the company spokesperson before they are implemented. These decisions include:

1. Whether to build up inventory and/or make advance shipments.
2. Whether to contract out or divert work to other plants.
3. Whether to attempt to get agreement from the union that certain essential employees (maintenance persons, for example) will be issued union passes permitting them to cross picket lines and work.

4. Whether to lay off certain nonstriking employees. (If a decision is made to allow nonstriking employees to continue to work, plans should be made to assign the work force to assure its most effective utilization. Consideration should be given to providing training sessions for otherwise idle factory supervision.)

5. Whether to continue to operate nonstruck portions of the business.

6. Whether to attempt to operate struck areas of the business with nonstriking employees and/or temporary hires.

7. Whether, and if so, when, to replace the strikers with new hires.

8. Whether to receive or ship material during a strike. If so, how.

If a strike should occur, the strike plan should be implemented and managed by the strike committee. Competent legal assistance should be instantly available for possible injunctive purposes.

## SUMMARY

The primary goal in union relations is to establish an overall program, covering both daily contract administration and contract negotiations, which enables the company to remain profitable and competitive while providing employees with fair and equitable economic benefits and practices. Both parties, the union and the company, usually agree on this goal. A delicate balance comes into play since each party measures from its own point of view what is fair and equitable and what allows a company to remain profitable and competitive. A successful relationship takes years, not days to develop; it takes facts, not half truths; it takes ability to make a stand and not to vacillate; it takes an open mind, not arbitrary thinking; it takes a willingness to compromise, but not on an issue of principle. These actions and reactions must come from both parties, not just one.

Both the short- and long-run labor relations objective and strategies should be supportive of and complement the operating goals of the company. In order to ensure this achievement, the labor relations function must be a part of the overall management planning and goal-setting process. It must be involved in and actively participate in the give and take of the decision-making process.

*See also* HUMAN RESOURCES (WORK FORCE) PLANNING; LABOR LEGISLATION; *Labor-Management Relations;* LABOR (TRADE) UNIONS; NEGOTIATING; PERSONNEL ADMINISTRATION; PRODUCTIVITY; SAFETY AND HEALTH MANAGEMENT, EMPLOYEE; WAGES AND HOURS LEGISLATION.

### NOTES

[1] Dale Yoder, *Personnel Management and Industrial Relations*, Prentice-Hall, Inc., Englewood Cliffs, N.J., 1962, p. 482.

[2] H. D. Marshall and N. J. Marshall, *Collective Bargaining*, Random House, Inc., New York, 1971, p. 252.

[3] Walter Baer, *Grievance Handling*, American Management Association, New York, 1970, p. 2.

[4] A. A. Sloane and F. Witney, *Labor Relations*, Prentice-Hall, Inc., Englewood Cliffs, N.J., 1967, p. 169.

[5] A. Blum, "Collective Bargaining: Ritual or Reality," *Harvard Business Review*, vol. 39, pp. 63–69, November–December 1961.

[6] Yoder, op. cit., p. 491.

[7] Marshall and Marshall, op. cit., p. 252.

[8] Yoder, op. cit. p. 496.

[9] Sloane and Witney, op. cit., p. 169.

[10] Ibid.

PAUL W. BOCKLEY, *Honeywell, Inc.*

## Labor-management relations act  (*See* LABOR LEGISLATION.)

## Labor (trade) unions

The institution of unionism is rooted in the national concept of democracy. The principal distinctions that separate American and British democracies from autocracies may be subsumed into two basic concepts: (1) the participation of the governed in the formulation of the laws and regulations which accommodate individual freedom to group needs; and (2) the concept of *due process,* or a set of procedures instituted to resolve differences between the governed and the governors, with the added protection of a culminating decision vested in a judiciary that is completely independent of any pressure exercised by either group.

These concepts have been basic to political life in the United States since 1776 when the 13 colonies declared their independence from the British Crown. These concepts were institutionalized in the form of a national constitution in the last decade of the eighteenth century and in the various state constitutions at later dates. The Senate and the House of Representatives, the national legislative arms of the United States government, embody the participation of its citizenry in the legislative process.

*Political Citizens and Economic Subjects.* The judiciary resolves conflicts between citizens and their institutions and the executive branch of the political government in the event of conflict between individual citizens and the various areas of that government.

Paradoxically, the political citizen in the 1790s who was beginning to experience due process and participative decision making, albeit incomplete and rudimentary, in political life, was subjected to complete autocracy in his occupational role as an employee. If his employer was benevolent, he enjoyed benevolent despotism. If his employer was harsh, then he suffered harsh despotism.

From the very beginning of the Republic, some men revolted against this schizoid duality in their role as political citizen and economic subject if their labor was for hire. Their status as employee derived from the ancient law of master and servant. The contradiction between their political role and economic role led to the ultimate rejection of this status as servant. The vehicles which these workers created and which embodied the efforts at participation in deciding their fate became known as unions. They were industrial analogs of the legislature in the political domain.

*Wages and Conditions.* Because the economic demands which unions voiced were so much easier for the public to understand, their revolts were generally reported as a demand for a raise in wages. The demand for changes in rule making so that the workers could participate in the rules governing the workplace, received attention largely from specialized scholars; nevertheless, this second demand was present from the start as one of the twin pillars of the labor movement.

The first record of an American strike goes back to 1786 when the Philadelphia printers struck for a minimum income of $6 a week and indirectly for future participation in the determination of conditions of employment. They lost on both grounds.

Following this inconspicuous beginning, the labor movement waxed and waned throughout the years and assumed its modern form in 1881 with the formation of the Organized Trades and Labor Unions, renamed the American Federation of Labor (AFL) in 1886.

**Emergence of Collective Bargaining** In 1890 the United Mine Workers of America pioneered the concept of the collective agreement, an instrument achieved through collective bargaining with the employer and which represented a focusing of hitherto diffuse union tactics into an effective means of addressing their problems. Surprising as it may seem, many of the notions of a collective agreement, however natural it seems to contemporary Americans, represented a new departure in labor-management relations.

The process of collective bargaining has been defined as follows by the leading scholar in the field, Professor Sumner Slichter, late of Harvard.[1] He divides collective bargaining into two separate basic functions:

1. It is a method whereby labor as union and capital as management define the price of labor.

2. It is a method of introducing civil rights for labor into industry, that is, of requiring that management be conducted by rule rather than by arbitrary decision. In a sense, it is a method of introducing a system of jurisprudence into industry in very much the same manner that the glorious revolution of 1688 substituted Parliamentary Supremacy for the divine right of kings in political life. The labor movement extends this same constitutional concept to industrial life in very much the same manner that men instituted states in political life which define positive law, construct administrative procedures for carrying it out, and complement both statute law and administrative rule with a system of judicial review whose agent is *free* of any tie or obligation to either side.

The rise of the labor movement antedates the emergence of the institution of collective bargaining. The unions as a group within the labor movement *evolved collective bargaining after a long period of experimentation with other techniques.*

The unions first arose as a blind protest imbued with a purely adversary attitude. The progression from independent craft workers, owning and working with their own tools, to that of hired workers of faceless capital was stormy and had few precedents. It was only after a long period of experimentation with other devices and tactics that the institution of collective bargaining evolved. Earlier programs were predicated upon an antiprivate enterprise program.

*The Cooperative Movement.* The unions opposed the wage system as an institution and promoted producer cooperatives to escape the thralldom of the wage system. They rapidly became disenchanted with these cooperatives when they discovered that most of them failed because of lack of managerial competence. Those that succeeded presented an even more troublesome problem. Those who had pioneered the venture were loath to take on additional cooperators and give them the same ownership privileges enjoyed by the pioneers. Within a short time there was little to distinguish the enterprise that started as a producer's cooperative from any other private enterprise. For all purposes, the producer's cooperative had become a private partnership of the pioneers who then employed latecomers to the institution on the same basis as any other private enterprise. This historic progression has been repeated in some of the manufacturing-oriented kibbutzim in Israel in the last decade.

Similarly, attempts to solve problems via the political route by alliance with farmers and small businesses led working people to discover that when the coalition succeeded, small business resented organization even more bitterly than did big business because the former operated at such a close margin to survival.

*Management Under Law, or Work Rules.* Finally, the adoption of collective bargaining was predicated on the frank acceptance of capitalism as an institution and the desire to improve the workers' status under that economic system. This meant an abandonment of any class-war doctrine and the adoption of a creed that acknowledged a simultaneous (1) identity of conflict of interest with the employer and (2) identity of interest in the prosperity of the enterprise. In addition, it raised fundamental problems about the governance of the enterprise and the extent to which the employers participated in that governance. Management was acknowledged to be the industrial ruler, but this ruler was obliged to rule under law, or working rules, as they were called in industry. Conflicts over the interpretation of these laws, or rules, had to be resolved in accordance with the principle of due process.

This industrial law now pervades every facet of industrial management. Among the ideas are (1) entrance to the trade, (2) the method of production, and (3) the terms of the introduction of technological change. Each industry constitutes a local culture of its own and reflects the wide diversity of practices that fall under the rubric of industrial rights.

The American labor movement as we now know it can be dated from 1933 when President Roosevelt's election led to the revival of the labor organizations, many of which were left moribund by the Great Depression of the early 1930s.

The Norris-LaGuardia Act of 1932 had set the stage for this revival by sharply restricting the terms under which federal courts could issue labor injunctions—which had previously been capricious devices used by management to hobble labor.

Section 7a of the National Recovery Act of 1934, followed by the National Labor Relations Act of 1935, set the legislative climate in which unions could revive and flourish. The movement by and large confined itself to the private sector.

**Arbitrable and Negotiable Issues** From the very beginning, management generally has stood for a containing strategy designed to restrict the subjects about which it is willing to talk in collective bargaining. It has sought to restrict the area of collective bargaining to wages and hours, arguing that all remaining areas constitute management prerogative. The labor movement, on the other hand, has argued that management is obliged to negotiate in any area that exercises an impact on worker welfare.

*A Classic Confrontation.* Some years ago these points of view received a formal expression in a controversy between Mr. Phelps, at the time a Bethlehem Steel executive, and Mr. Goldberg, at the time the attorney for the United Steel Workers of America, later Secretary of Labor under President Kennedy, and still later Justice Goldberg of the United States Supreme Court. Phelps claimed that in the beginning all rights belonged to management, and management was therefore obligated to discuss only those areas which labor had managed to tear away and insert in the collective agreement.

Mr. Goldberg dissented, stating that in the beginning management was able to impose an absolute dictatorship on its workers, that collective bargaining broke this usurpation, and that equity had become the criterion for determining the area of collective bargaining upon which management was compelled to engage in joint decision making with the union.

*Landmark Legislation.* The conflict over the permissible areas of collective bargaining has resulted in a stormy history in the saga of United States industrial relations. Following World War I, President Wilson called an industrial relations conference in 1919 to head off a threatened outbreak of nationwide strikes. Management acknowledged the right of any individual worker to join a union but insisted that it remained management's right to deal with or refuse to deal with the union. After a series of bloody recognition strikes over the issue of whether management should or should not deal with the union, the U.S. government settled the controversy with the passage of the National Labor Relations Act of 1935. The act imposed upon management the obligation to bargain collectively with representatives of the workers who had been certified in an election procedure.

*Arbitrable Issues.* Now the controversy was transferred to the areas over which management was obligated to bargain. Almost every arbitration procedure over working conditions was bedeviled by management's claim that the dispute before the arbitrator was nonarbitrable because the areas were not specifically treated in the collective agreement.

A conference similar to the Wilson Industrial Relations conference of 1919 was called by President Truman in 1945 to avert anticipated post-World War II strikes. The conference foundered on the issue of management's insistence that labor must carefully restrict the collective bargaining subject area and recognize all other areas as management prerogatives. Labor demurred, insisting that such a move was impractical in a time when a rapidly changing economy disclosed that areas which had hitherto been management preserves had developed a powerful impact on working conditions.

In 1947 Arbitrator Harvey Shulman, late Dean of Yale Law School, was called upon to resolve a strike called by the United Automobile Workers (UAW) against the Ford Motor Company over an alleged speedup of the assembly line. Shulman resolved this problem by drawing a distinction between *absolute management rights* and *conditional management rights*. He defined the setting of production standards as a conditional management right, and management's right was restricted to initially proposing a standard over which the union could present grievances. As an example of an absolute management right, he listed the location of a plant.

*Narrowing Management Prerogatives.* Yet, even this apparently compelling management right was subject to question. The garment workers' union had a restriction in their agreement with the garment employers of ancient vintage even in 1947. It imposed upon the management the obligation not to move its plant outside the 5-cent fare zone of New York City. This provision had been prompted by the predilection of garment employers to sign an agreement on Friday and then escape the union by moving their plant out of town over the weekend.

The auto workers, who thought nothing of plant location in 1947, were concerned with it by 1958. This came about because, as a result of the decline in auto sales, the primary layoffs were in the older areas like Detroit where older plants were located. What work was being performed was in plants far from Detroit of a much more modern vintage. Plant location, a matter of no interest to the United Auto Workers in 1947, had become a major concern in the late 1950s. Thus, the nature and definition of what

constitutes a management prerogative is clearly changeable.

*Implicit as Well as Explicit Matters.* The matter of what areas are relevant to collective bargaining is generally linked to what is arbitrable under a collective agreement. The U.S. Supreme Court, in a trilogy of decisions,[2] struck down the strict construction that arbitrators are confined only to those issues specified in the contract. It defined the industrial relationship as a form of constitutional government in which the scope of arbitration is expanded to include contract implications as well as specific agreement subject areas.

**European Unionism** The system of industrial governance in United States collective bargaining is rooted in the shop or factory in which the worker participates in industrial government by means of the individual grievance. European unions, where organization does not reach into the shops, do not enjoy the same kind of rank-and-file participation in the everyday affairs of the union. For example, in Holland, as in Sweden, Norway, the German Federal Republic, and the United Kingdom, the labor unions play a much more publicly significant role in political matters than they do in the United States. Yet, as Professor Barbash put it in 1972 after observing the Dutch system of industrial relations, "When it comes to the shop, management's sovereignty is absolute."[3] European unions have been attempting to overcome some of these problems by voicing a demand for codetermination or participative management. By and large, United States labor has eschewed that approach, settling instead for participation in shop governance via the grievance procedure.

**Public Sector** Labor organizations in the United States developed later in the public sector. As early as 1912, the International Association of Machinists (among others) struck the Watertown Arsenal in the wake of efforts by the local management to introduce work measurements by time study into the plant. The result was that from that time to the 1940s all military appropriation bills carried a rider forbidding the expenditure of funds for any work-measurement purpose. However, the few unions that confined themselves to the governmental sector were relatively weak and ineffective with the possible exception of the postal employees. While all governmental unions eschewed the right to strike, the ubiquitous distribution of postal employees in every hamlet in the land gave them a lobbying influence in Congress that was more effective than any strike.

*Restrictive Attitudes.* The fundamental attitude toward labor unions in the public sector was laid down in 1919 by Calvin Coolidge, then the Governor of Massachusetts, later President, who broke the Boston police strike, declaring that, "There was no right to strike against the public any time, anywhere, any place."[4]

In 1937, President Roosevelt, who was largely responsible for the revival of unionism in the private sector, expressed himself on collective bargaining for public employees as follows:

"The process of collective bargaining as usually understood cannot be transplanted into the public service. It has its distinct and insurmountable limitations when applied to public personnel management. The very nature and purpose of government makes it impossible for administrative officials to represent fully or to bind the employer in mutual discussions with government employee organizations. The employer is the whole people who speak by means of laws enacted by their representatives in Congress. Accordingly, administrative officials and employees alike are governed and guided, and in many cases restricted by laws which establish policies, procedures or rules in personnel matters. Particularly, I want to emphasize my conviction that militant tactics have no place in the functions or any organization of government employees.[5]

Yet, some 30 years later a Republican administration in Pennsylvania, led by Governor Schaeffer, put into effect Act 195, which granted to state employees the statutory right to collective bargaining, including the right to strike. The only exceptions to Act 195 were police, fire fighters, and prison guards. They were covered by Act III, however, that eschewed strikes but invoked joint fact-finding and binding arbitration over issues which the parties could not resolve in collective negotiations.

*Facilitating Administrative Orders.* President Kennedy issued Executive Order 10988 which set forth the procedures to facilitate union recognition and negotiation in the federal service. It directly stimulated employee organization and negotiations, not only in the federal service but also indirectly at the state and local levels. The order provided somewhat the same impetus for public-sector labor relations that the Wagner Act of 1935 did in the 1930s for labor relations in the private sector. Executive Order 10988 was superseded by President Nixon's Executive Order 14197 which revised some procedures and amplified others. This, in turn, was followed by Executive Order 11616.

At the present time, local governments are increasingly becoming accustomed to dealing with their employees on the basis of the customs and procedures of collective bargaining. Many individual states have passed legislation to do for their employees what President Kennedy did for federal employees during his term of office.

*Public Process.* Public workers (who, it was expected, could never make use of such an instrument) are today engaged in collective bargaining. For example, the federal government has adapted collective bargaining to the very special circumstances of the government employee. Quite obviously, wages for Civil Service are set by the Congress. The degree to which the government employee can participate in setting government wages is the same as every other citizen who acts through his or her congressional representative. At the worksite, collective bargaining has been used to lend more reality to the appeals procedure, which Civil Service formerly furnished exclusively as a due process means of avoiding arbitrary, unreasonable behavior by the supervisory force. Although the Civil Service had long ago created an appeals procedure for individual federal workers, virtually all agree that the procedure was so weighted on the supervisor's side that the procedure left much to be desired in terms of a due process criterion.

*Unique Aspects.* What is unique about collective bargaining in the public sector is that the Civil Service worker is represented by a person independent of the Civil Service against whom the employee's supervisor can exercise no power. In this respect, the federal Civil Service problem with collective bargaining is very similar to those of any manager who must cope with the problem of due process enjoyed by his or her employees. In the last decade or so, collective bargaining has become a regular tool, increasingly available to the public employee. Local government representatives, as a matter of course, today meet with the Policemen's Benevolent Association, Fraternal Order of Police, and the International Association of Fire Fighters to determine the terms and conditions of employment for these public servants.

The railroad operating unions, the engineers, and conductors started mutual societies for insurance purposes. The hazard of their occupations banned them from ordinary commercial insurance at the time of organization. In a short time, their preoccupation with safety led them to demand certain working rules from railroad management as a part of working conditions.

The letter carriers' union likewise started as a mutual welfare organization for insurance and recreation. The organization of letter carriers' musical bands were undertaken for this purpose.

**Professional Organization** At times, professional organizations, organized for professional development, began by eschewing collective bargaining as a subprofessional activity, only to develop all the union functions under the pressure of the logic of events. The National Education Association (NEA), made up of teachers and administrators, was challenged by the American Federation of Teachers. The NEA found itself participating in election contests against the American Federation of Teachers for collective bargaining representation, an activity to which the association was allegedly opposed. NEA won the election, and before long, any differences between it and the American Federation of Teachers were reduced to a matter of rhetoric. In fact, both organizations have been discussing merger; the Los Angeles and New York State organizations have already merged. The administrators and principals, no longer comfortable in the teacher-dominated NEA, have organized their own association which is assuming on their behalf very much the same functions that the NEA continues to perform on behalf of the teachers.

Engineering organizations, shaken by the vulnerability of their constituents in the labor market, have moved to imitate certain aspects of unionism at the same time that they eschew unions as being subprofessional. The engineers' need for due process asserts itself despite the reiteration of symbolic ideological pretension.

Gunnar Myrdal, the Swedish social scientist, has observed that we are moving closer and closer to a completely organizational society in which each group will bargain with the greater collective to define the condition and limitation governing their contribution of goods and services to the commonwealth.

*See also* ARBITRATION, LABOR; EGALITARIANISM; EMPLOYMENT AND UNEMPLOYMENT; LABOR LEGISLATION; LABOR-MANAGEMENT RELATIONS; WAGES AND HOURS LEGISLATION.

### NOTES

[1]Sumner H. Slichter, *Union Policies and Industrial Management*, George Banta Company, Inc., Menasha, Wis., 1942.

[2]*USW v. American Manufacturing Company*, 363 U.S. 564 (1960); *USW v. Warrior and Gulf Navigation Company*, 363 U.S. 574 (1960); *USW v. Enterprise Wheel and Car Corporation*, 363 U.S. 593 (1950).

[3]Jack Barbash, *Trade Unions and National Economic Policy*, The Johns Hopkins Press, Baltimore, 1972.

[4]*The Public Papers and Addresses of Franklin D. Roosevelt*, 1937 vol., ed. Samuel Rosenman, The Macmillan Company, New York, 1941, p. 235.

[5]*Ibid.*

### REFERENCES

Bok, Dereck C., and John T. Dunlop: *Labor and the American Community*, Simon & Schuster, Inc., New York, 1970.

Chamberlain, Neil, and James W. Kuhn: *Collective Bargaining*, 2d ed., McGraw-Hill Book Company, New York, 1965.

Kuhn, Alfred: *Labor, Institutions and Economics*, Harcourt Brace Jovanovich, Inc., New York, 1967.

Slichter, Sumner, James S. Healy, and Robert E. Livernash: *Impact of Collective Bargaining on Management*, The Brookings Institution, Washington, 1960.

(This entry is adapted from the author's chapter in *Military Unions and the United States Armed Forces*, University of Pennsylvania Press, Philadelphia, 1977.)

WILLIAM GOMBERG, *The Wharton School, University of Pennsylvania*

# Laboratory (sensitivity) training

*Laboratory training*, also known as sensitivity training, is a form of leadership and personnel development which seeks to improve the ability of individuals to interact effectively with others by changing their attitudes through a strong emotional experience. This is accomplished by setting up training or T groups in a laboratory situation removed from the working environment and by encouraging confrontation between people and issues. This use of confrontation as a means of sensitizing participants to their own feelings and to those of others teaches them to accept these feelings consciously. By so doing, they are then able to understand and to promote the group process in order to achieve group goals.

Developed in the late 1940s and pioneered at the National Training Laboratories at Bethel, Maine, by Leland Bradford and his colleagues, laboratory training evolved from the experience of psychotherapists in treating individuals through group therapy. It is now a widespread practice throughout this country.

Laboratory training is characterized by (1) isolation from the work situation; (2) equal participation in leadership by all group members as peers; (3) no planned agenda or rules of procedure; (4) group sizes ranging from 10 to 16, with one or two trainers; (5) meetings lasting about 2 hours, twice daily, from 2 to 3 weeks. Experience has revealed a predictable pattern of the psychological states through which groups develop, although there is no guarantee that any group will progress through the entire pattern.

The disturbing vacuum created by the lack of

agenda and lack of group roles apparently causes frustrations which force participants to reexamine the process of working with groups or influencing people. Attempts to express leadership or to determine the group's direction generally lead to confrontation, often to expressions of hostility and conflict, and frequently to deep anxiety. The trainer observes and endeavors to communicate to the members the nature of these feelings and interactions so that the group eventually begins to perceive, analyze, and handle them for itself. Although trainers differ, probing into subconscious motivation is usually discouraged.

Recent innovations bring laboratory training closer to work realities: the introduction of specific management problems into the agenda and the increasing practice of forming T groups from members of one organization, either of peers or of vertical groupings.

Opinions vary widely: laboratory training has clearly changed the focus in organizations from that of management versus employees to a realization that people, filling different roles, are engaged together in an enterprise which requires mutual understanding. "Gut level" training is more likely to cause real behavior change than is intellectual training, change which can often be carried over into the work situation; sensitivity training groups from one enterprise often do develop into cohesive and more-efficient terms. The permanence of results has been questioned, however. Benefits are doubtful when the training attempts to prescribe behavior or attitudes and when it provokes deep anxieties and hostilities without resolving them. As a training tool, laboratory training needs further research and evidence before it can be objectively evaluated. It seems advisable that those who enter the experience be fully apprised of its intense, and even traumatic, nature.

*See also* HEALTH, MENTAL; INTERPERSONAL RELATIONSHIPS; MOTIVATION IN ORGANIZATIONS.

## REFERENCES

Argyris, Chris: *Integrating the Individual and the Organization*, John Wiley & Sons, Inc., New York, 1964.

House, R. J.: "T-Group Training: Good or Bad?," *Business Horizons*, vol. 12, no. 6, pp. 69–78, December 1969.

Katz, Daniel, and Robert Kahn: "Organizational Change," *Social Psychology of Organizations*, John Wiley & Sons, Inc., New York, 1966, pp. 390–391, 406–425.

Tannenbaum, R., I. R. Weschler, and F. Massarik: "Sensitivity Training for the Management Team," *Leadership and Organization*, McGraw Hill Book Company, New York, 1961, pp. 167–87.

STAFF/HOKE

**Last in, first out (LIFO)** (*See* ACCOUNTING, FINANCIAL; PROFITS AND PROFIT MAKING.)

**Law, business** (*See* GOVERNMENT REGULATIONS, BUSINESS LAW.)

**Law, corporation** (*See* LEGAL AFFAIRS, MANAGEMENT OF CORPORATE.)

**Law, preventive** (*See* LEGAL AFFAIRS, MANAGEMENT OF CORPORATE.)

**Laws affecting business** (*See* GOVERNMENT REGULATIONS, BUSINESS LAW.)

**Lawyers, inside and outside** (*See* LEGAL AFFAIRS, MANAGEMENT OF CORPORATE.)

**Layering on** (*See* PRODUCT PLANNING AND DEVELOPMENT.)

**Layoff** (*See* PERSONNEL ADMINISTRATION.)

**Layout** (*See* MATERIAL HANDLING.)

**Layout, cluster plan** (*See* OFFICE SPACE PLANNING AND DESIGN.)

**Layout, facilities** (*See* FACILITIES AND SITE PLANNING AND LAYOUT.)

**Layout, grid** (*See* OFFICE SPACE PLANNING AND DESIGN.)

**Layout, office** (*See* OFFICE SPACE PLANNING AND DESIGN.)

**Layout, open plan** (*See* OFFICE SPACE PLANNING AND DESIGN.)

**Layout, store**   (*See* RETAILING MANAGEMENT.)

**Layout, verticality**   (*See* OFFICE SPACE PLANNING AND DESIGN.)

**Layout, workplace**   (*See* PAPER WORK SIMPLIFICATION.)

**Leader-match concept**   (*See* LEADERSHIP.)

# Leadership

Leadership in business and industry is that part of management which deals with the direct supervision of subordinates. Given a reasonable equality in technical equipment and supplies, it is by far the single most-important factor in determining the effectiveness of a group or organization.

This entry is concerned with leadership in formal organizations. It concentrates on the problems of professional managers and supervisors who obtained their position primarily by appointment rather than by election or by the force of their personality in informal organizations. Emphasis here will be on the leader's role in determining productivity and effectiveness rather than on the personal growth and development of his or her employees, or their satisfaction with the job. This does not deny the rightful concern for these problems or the part the leader could or should play in furthering these goals. It simply is beyond the scope of this particular entry.

**Search for Traits**   Leadership holds an important place in philosophy and history for quite obvious reasons. The leadership of such men and women as Charles de Gaulle, Churchill, Golda Meir, Joan of Arc, Napoleon, Lincoln, Stalin, Mao Tse Tung, and Eisenhower made real differences. Similarly, the leadership of such men as the automobile manufacturer Henry Ford, the aircraft executive Boeing, or the film producer Samuel Goldwyn have made a critical impact on the success of their enterprises. It is not too surprising, therefore, that the ability to lead and direct has become identified in the popular mind with a personality type or a trait. In fact, most psychological research on leadership from about 1900 to 1950 was devoted to identifying magic leadership traits or personality patterns.

A moment of reflection will indicate why the trait approach is not likely to succeed. Practically all individuals are leaders on some occasions and followers most of the time. The person who might be singularly successful as chairperson of a Parent-Teacher Association committee will not necessarily succeed as the superintendent of a logging camp or the general manager of a savings and loan association. Leadership is not simply something within the individual. It is first and foremost an interpersonal relationship. Those who wish to know if they are leading need only to look behind to see if they have followers. This relationship which enables A to get B to do something in order to accomplish goal C is the essence of the leadership process. It is an everyday interaction which is learned. It is endowed neither with the mystic nor with the mysterious. It is, however, a very complex process.

The leadership-trait concept is, of course, seductively appealing. It goes back to the divine right of kings and the selection of military and political leaders from among those who by birth and bloodline are "ordained by God" to rule. It is a simple concept: "You either have it or you don't"; "Leaders are born and not made." It was only with the sudden need for managers which came with the upsurge of large organizations beginning with World War I that organizations began to search actively for methods which would allow them to select individuals who were able to handle the responsibilities of management. The thought was—if people could be classified on the basis of their intelligence and certain personality traits, why not also on the basis of some personality attributes which are related to the ability to manage?

*Absence of Evidence.* The trait approach was dominant until 1948 when Ralph Stogdill published a review of 43 years of research, including 124 empirical studies on leadership traits.[1] He was forced to conclude that there was no evidence of a single trait or characteristic that identified a person as a leader. Furthermore, he could find no constellation of personality attributes or traits which identified a leader in all situations. To be sure, leaders tended to be somewhat brighter than their followers, somewhat taller, somewhat more outgoing and socially adept, but these differences were slight. Stogdill's conclusions were subsequently confirmed by a number of other researchers, e.g., Mann.[2] Stogdill then surveyed an additional 163 studies[3] conducted since his earlier review and again came to the conclusion that there was nothing inherent in an individual's personality which would make him or her a leader, or a successful executive. A number of traits have indeed been listed as desirable, if not essential, for effective leadership. These include being fair, honest, loyal, thoughtful, judicious, etc. While these traits undoubtedly are admirable and praiseworthy, they would as easily qualify one to become Mother or Father of the Year as to be appointed to manage an organization or a department. The problem with this theory is not with the list of admirable traits which it produces but rather with the fact that this list is of little value to the practitioner, not to mention the sad fact that some highly effective leaders have not necessarily been fair, honest, truthful, or loyal. And yet, the search for the ideal leader has continued unabated.

## THEORIES OF IDEAL LEADER TYPES

If there are no personality traits which identify the successful leader, are there perhaps leader orientations or specific behaviors which make some individuals successful in directing others? The military services, for example, teach their officers and noncommissioned officers to act in certain ways; i.e., to prepare what they are going to say to a group; always to listen to both sides of the question; not to lose their temper; to plan a course of action; and to give praise when a job has been well done. Without a doubt, these are sensible ways of behaving, but they are certainly not sufficient to make a person a good leader. There are any number of leaders who have not always known ahead of time what they were going to say to their group, who have not always listened to both sides of the question, and who, on occasion, have given dazzling displays of temper. Still, the theories which have postulated an ideal leader type are popular within the business community.

**Theory X and Theory Y**  Among the best-known theories of management is McGregor's concept of leaders who fall roughly into two camps on the question of how to deal with their subordinates. The older and more orthodox approach, known as *theory X*, refers to managers who believe their workers to be naturally lazy, resisting change, requiring constant and close supervision, and unmotivated to perform well. McGregor sees this as being the natural set of assumptions of managers, and in fact, the assumptions by which most managers attain their managerial position.

The obvious consequence of these assumptions leads managers to believe that they must be authoritative and directive and that they must maintain a sufficient social distance from the employees to ensure their esteem. McGregor, in his well-known book, *The Human Side of Enterprise*[4] held that this approach hampers organizational performance since (1) it relies on a small and select group of people for decision making and judgment and (2) it absorbs a great deal of organizational time and resources in ensuring compliance with prescribed standards.

Accordingly, McGregor proposed another set of assumptions which he referred to as *theory Y*. This theory states that workers need to be seen basically as mature, desirous of being productive, wanting to identify with the job and contribute to its success, and willing to accomplish the organization's goals. Management must only remove the stumbling blocks to the workers' aspirations and provide the necessary organizational climate which will permit the employee to contribute meaningfully to organizational problem solving and goal attainment.

The implications of *theory Y* assumptions are that managers must be participative, democratic, and above all, must concern themselves with creating the conditions which permit the worker to find fulfillment in the job. The manager is, in effect, admonished to create a democratic industrial environment. This approach, which has had a tremendous impact on academic thinking, as well as on an important segment of business and industrial management, has been very influential in the philosophy of humanistic management. McGregor's theory, along with those of related thinkers,[5] has inspired a considerable amount of literature as well as some experimentation with industrial democracy which has become particularly prominent in the form of union participation in the managerial process in Europe. In some countries (for example, Germany and Sweden) union and worker participation in management is now mandated by law.

**Other Humanistic Approaches**  Several major theorists emerged during the late 1950s and early 1960s who capitalized on the humanistic approach to leadership development. Among the most important was Rensis Likert[6] who held that an employee-centered style of leadership (system 4) based on trust and participation will produce not only greater employee satisfaction but also increased organizational effectiveness.

*Stimulating Employee Action.* What, specifically, can the manager do to enhance employee contributions to organizational goal attainment? Sutermeister, in his book *People and Productivity*,[7] lists two dozen areas in which managers can take action to enhance employee contribution. Generally these fall into one of two categories.

1. The manager can initiate structural changes in the physical working conditions, such as facilitating employee interactions with managers (e.g., com-

mon lounge and eating spaces), attending to job content, and reducing hierarchical organizational structure.

2. The manager can make changes in the organizational process. These include the development of an organizational climate which recognizes and rewards employee contributions, the enhancement of interpersonal communication between superior and subordinate, acceptance of employee ideas, and the involvement of employees in decision making.

*Leader as Facilitator.* Likert[8] sees one important leader function as that of a "linking pin" between organizational levels. As such, the leader can act as a facilitator for the organization in planning, coordinating, identifying the needs of the organization at different levels, and translating these needs into task accomplishment by obtaining the employees' commitment to the organizational goals.

A major problem with this approach seems to be that many managers and organizations are not prepared to adopt such a philosophy of management, nor will such an approach be successful in every organization. In fact, McGregor had to abandon the style he espoused in his job as college president, and one of his strong supporters, Warren Bennis, likewise found that the theory Y assumptions do not apply in all situations. Moreover, recent studies show that most leaders tend to act on theory X assumptions at one time and theory Y assumptions at other times. In reviewing the literature on the subject, Stogdill concludes on the basis of several studies that the data " . . . do not support the hypothesis that group productivity and cohesion are higher under permissive, *Theory Y* types of leader behavior than under more restrictive, *Theory X* patterns of behavior."[9]

**T-Group Training** One important outgrowth of the humanistic management approach has been the so-called "laboratory, sensitivity, or T-group training." In large part as a response to a perceived need to humanize management, a number of well-known theorists and researchers in the leadership area, including among others, Warren Bennis, Edgar Schein, and Chris Argyris, developed the T (training)-group. A National Training Laboratory in Bethel, Maine, and similar residential training centers in other parts of this country and England, sprung up on the premise that managers could be taught to be employee-centered and to communicate better, as well as to acquire job-related interpersonal skills by a total immersion process in an unstructured group situation. Over the past 20 years, tens of thousands of managers have attended these and sim-

ilar training programs, which caught the imagination of leadership theorists and managers alike. Although different authors emphasize different goals of T-group laboratories, Bennis and Schein list their basic aims as follows:

(1) to effect a change in values so that *human factors and feelings come to be considered as legitimate* and (2) to assist in *developing skills among managers in order to increase interpersonal competence.*[10]

The T-group experience usually consists of a small, face-to-face group interaction for an extended period with no intended agenda or structure. The trainer, or facilitator, purposely avoids any semblance of group leadership, only providing such guidance as will focus the group on the here-and-now. Sessions rely heavily on the total involvement of emotion and feeling on the part of participants.

The proponents of T-group training stress that managers leave the sessions with a heightened awareness of the need for interpersonal skills, and personal testimony of attendees is usually equally supportive of that interpretation. On the other hand, several reviews have cast doubt as to the usefulness of this technique for developing leaders. Campbell and Dunnette summarize their findings by noting that "utility for the organization is not necessarily the same as utility for the individual."[11]

In his summary of the literature in the authoritative *Handbook of Leadership*, Stogdill, while acknowledging that T-group training does appear to change attitudes toward subordinates, is quick to point out that,

It is a contradiction of fact to call sensitivity training a method for building leadership. It is effective for its stated purpose of training in the "democratic" sharing of leadership with followers; however, it is a misnomer to call the resulting pattern of behavior a form of democratic leadership. The continuous examination of individual motives and group processes, and trainer refusal to provide structure or allow group members to provide structure, all combine to reinforce a laissez-faire pattern of behavior. Trainee reactions of confusion, frustration, anger, and emotional outburst are similar to children's reactions to laissez-faire leadership in the research of Lippitt and White (1943). . . . Not a single experiment analyzed for this report was designed to determine whether individuals are more or less effective in assuming or retaining the leadership role after sensitivity training. This is an incredible ommision. Even more incredible is the failure to employ legitimate criteria of the effects of training.[12]

**The Managerial Grid** A somewhat different approach was taken by Blake and Mouton[13] who popularized a method of leadership training which became widely used. Although equally prescriptive in the area of humanistic development, Blake and Mouton capitalized on the findings of the Ohio State studies of leadership[14] which demonstrated quite clearly that there are *two* fundamental dimensions of leader behavior in organizations. The first of these is *consideration of subordinates*, and consists of employee-centered behaviors. The second is *initiation of structure*, sometimes referred to as task-oriented behaviors.

*Consideration* measures the degree to which the leader "regards the comfort, well-being, status and contribution of followers." On the other hand, *structuring* behavior is defined as the degree to which the leader "clearly defines own role, and lets followers know what is expected."[15]

Unlike the proponents of the humanistic approach, Blake and Mouton stress that training in one dimension only, that is, in employee-centeredness, will not be sufficient to develop effective managers. Rather, the leader must also be trained in being concerned for getting the job done. This is not to say, of course, that Likert and others were unaware or unconcerned for task-related aspects of the leadership job, but they considered this concern largely as given.

The parallel between the Ohio State studies which led to the identification of the consideration and structuring behaviors and the managerial-grid approach can be seen in Fig. L-1*a* and *b*. Whereas the Ohio State research is descriptive, the managerial-grid approach is clearly prescriptive. Blake and Mouton posit that the 9-9, or team leadership, is the one best approach to yield maximum organizational output. This is done by first determining the manager's orientation on a self-assessment scale.[16] Once that is located on the grid, selected training techniques spanning a considerable length of time will provide the manager with the necessary skills to move toward the 9-9 style of leadership. Blake and Mouton (see Fig. L-1*b*) provide popular terms for each of the extremes on the grid. These are:

1. *Impoverished leadership* (1-1), which essentially represents no leadership at all.

2. *Country-club leadership* (1-9), which represents total concern for the needs of others and for creating a nonstressful work environment.

3. *Task leadership* (9-1), which represents total concern for production with minimum concern for the people of the organization.

4. *Middle-of-the-road* leadership (5-5), which reflects the maintenance of a satisfactory degree of concern for people and concern for production.

5. *Team leadership* (9-9), which, of course, reflects the criterion for successful leadership—accomplishing the organizational task with committed people through a relationship of trust and respect.

Although the managerial grid has been used with mixed results in a variety of organizations, the primary support for the model comes from a year-long study of a large petroleum corporation in which 800 managers underwent training designed to bring them to the 9-9 style of leadership.[17] At the conclusion of the study, the company showed a considerable increase in profit and decrease in costs which the authors interpreted as clear support for the grid approach. Interpretation of the study by others, however, has been negative. In particular, the study

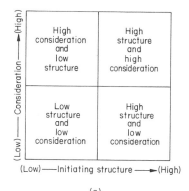

(a)

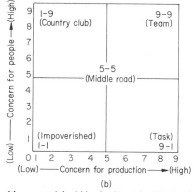

(b)

Fig. L-1. Comparison of the Ohio State quadrants (*a*) with managerial grid leadership styles (*b*). (*Paul Hersey and Kenneth H. Blanchard, Management of Organizational Behavior: Utilizing Human Resources, 2d ed.,* © *1972, pp. 74 and 75. Reprinted by permission of Prentice-Hall, Inc., Englewood Cliffs, N.J.*)

has been criticized because no control group was used upon which a comparison could be based. Consequently, other factors (e.g., a generally more-favorable economy) could have caused the increase in productivity.[18]

The simplicity of the grid approach presents somewhat of a paradox for managers bent on organizational improvement. In the first place, it is very easily conceptualized by the practitioner, and it is, therefore, very appealing. This same simplicity, however, brings to mind the many exceptions that may be generated by situational differences. Is 9-9 always the best set of behaviors for the leader to follow? The entry of one situational variable, *stress*, into the model clearly demonstrates its weakness. In times of high task stress, behaviors that typically reflect concern for people may not be most appropriate. In such a situation, the group members may expect the leader to reduce the stress, which may require extreme 9-1 types of behavior.

Kerr, Schriesheim, Murphy, and Stogdill point out that researchers have uncovered a number of other exceptions to the general rule that high consideration–high structuring leader behavior is to be preferred. They conclude that "the research suggests much more subtlety."[19]

In summary, therefore, prescriptive techniques that attempt to develop an ideal leader who will perform well in all situations leave much to be desired. General Patton was not notable for his consideration or his humanistic *theory Y* leadership approach, nor was Mahatma Ghandi known for his *theory X* approach. Different situations obviously call for different types of leadership.

## ASSESSMENT CENTERS

A development in the leadership area which merits considerable interest is the assessment center method. The primary purpose of the assessment center is the selection and the promotion of managers or organizational leaders by means of interviews, psychological tests, and such methods as role playing and work samples. The assessment center idea originated in the German armed services shortly before World War II and was adopted by the U.S. Office of Strategic Services for the selection of secret service agents. Subsequent studies, in particular, a major effort by the U.S. Veterans Administration to predict the success and performance of clinical psychologists and psychiatrists,[20] did not lead to impressive findings. Objective tests and occupational interest inventories predicted perfor-

mance as well as, if not better than, the more complex clinical techniques.

More recently, however, the assessment center concept has again become of interest in the management selection area. Several large corporations, notably AT&T, Sears, Roebuck and Co., Standard Oil (Ohio), IBM, and others have developed such centers.[21] The procedures are basically atheoretical in nature and simply ask, by means of interviews and tests, whether the center's assessment staffs are able to predict with reasonable accuracy the subsequent success of the assessee in the organization.

The most outstanding study along this line has been conducted by the staff of AT&T which followed the careers of executives for over 15 years and is continuing the program. The results of the AT&T program have been impressive, and correlations on the order of .50 have been reported between predictions and results. While the specific questionnaires and procedures have been kept confidential, Bray and Grant[22] have reported that their success is well above chance levels when evaluated on the basis of early promotion criteria and salary levels achieved after 5 and 10 year periods.

The assessment center has its problems. It is, above all, fairly expensive, and the success of the assessment is undoubtedly due in large part to a highly trained and professional assessment staff. Where such a staff cannot be maintained, the results are likely to be poor. This suggests that the assessment center is simply not practical for organizations which have fewer than 150 to 200 new managers per year.

The second problem is the unknown generality of the method. Does assessment work at AT&T because of the particular personnel requirements and expectations which this organization has of its managers, or would the same procedure also select as well the prospective managers of a candy factory or a hospital? The answers to these questions are unknown at this time but raise a serious doubt. Different organizational problems, different criteria of performance, and different standards and subcultures probably require different types of management.

Finally, the assessment center is a *management* selection procedure. It predicts the probable success of someone who moves into various management jobs within an organization, and these management jobs will range from line positions to staff responsibilities, from public relations to production. As emphasized earlier, leadership, as measured by the performance of the group or the organization, is only one aspect of the managerial job. The effectiveness of leaders is highly dependent on the particular situation in which they operate. It is, therefore, an important question whether the general-purpose leader can be selected by this or any other technique. At this time it simply cannot be confirmed to what extent the assessment center actually predicts leadership performance per se.

## SITUATIONAL THEORIES

A number of theories have been developed which are purely, or primarily, situational in character. These are basically theories of organizational structure and of management strategies rather than of leadership. In effect, these theories tell us the conditions or organizational structures in which *any* leader is likely to be more effective than he or she would be in different conditions or situational structures. An example of these theories comes from communication net studies[23] which showed that a centralized communication net under controlled laboratory conditions is more effective for decision making than a communication net which is circular, Y shaped, or in other ways decentralizes communication channels. Other examples are the classical writings by Barnard, Udy, Fayol, and others which prescribe a pyramidal organizational structure, proper span of control, or line-staff relationships. These are, however, not leadership theories in the usual sense and will not be discussed here.

## INTERACTIONAL AND CONTINGENCY THEORIES

The shortcomings of trait theories and the approaches which espouse one best type of leadership behavior or an ideal leader personality draw attention to the fact that a leader who excels under one condition might perform poorly, or even fail, under another condition. The leadership situation obviously has to be taken into account if one is to predict whether a particular leader will perform well or poorly. The first theory which provided a clear statement of the interaction between leader personality and situation was the contingency model, developed by one of the authors.[24] This theory is currently the most specific and articulated formulation of this approach.

The term *contingency* has become something of a buzzword in the leadership and management literature, and a wide variety of theoretical positions have been described as contingency theories. Among

these are House's path-goal theory, Hersey and Blanchard's life-cycle theory, and Vroom-Yetton's decision-making theory. Each of these will be described before examining the contingency model and a related leadership training program.

**Path-goal theory** This theory[25] constitutes an extension of motivation theory and in particular, the so-called "instrumentality theories." The theory is based on the premise that workers and employees have certain goals which are meaningful and important to them and that these goals can be either extrinsically or intrinsically related to the work itself. That is, either the work itself may be motivating (e.g., the challenging nature of the managerial job) or the rewards associated with the work may be seen as desirable. The hypothesis is that employees make subjective estimates of the probability of attaining these goals. For example, employees may estimate how likely it is that they will find the work challenging or that they will get a promotion or a raise in pay. If the likelihood is small, the employee will seek different, more attainable goals which may be unrelated to organizational aspirations. For example, the worker may see satisfaction in socializing with fellow workers rather than in trying to get the job done.

According to the path-goal theory, the leader has the task of providing the subordinates with either the goals themselves (the rewards they seek) or with the means for attaining these goals by training, coaching, removing roadblocks, or guidance. In a more comprehensive statement of the theory,[26] the effect which the leader has becomes *contingent* upon the psychological state of the subordinate and the situation in which leader and subordinate find themselves.

The critical variables with regard to the subordinate's psychological state, as they pertain to the theory, are not yet clear. However, House and Dressler cite an example of a subordinate who has a high need for affiliation and social approval, and they predict that this subordinate will find considerate behavior on the part of the leader to be a source of satisfaction.

The factors in the situational environment which determine the success of motivating subordinates consist of (1) the task to be performed, (2) the formality of the organization, and (3) the primary work group of the subordinate. Several studies seem to provide some support for this contingency approach, but the translation of the theory into a usable prescription for the practitioner is still unclear at this point.

**Life-Cycle Theory** Hersey and Blanchard[27] developed a model of leadership effectiveness that attempts to relate the maturity of the group to the prescribed leader behaviors. As in the path-goal theory, the important leader behaviors are defined by the two Ohio State dimensions of consideration and structuring.

Hersey and Blanchard hold that leaders must modify their behaviors as the maturity of their group changes. By maturity is meant (1) the group's capacity to set high and attainable goals, (2) the group members' willingness and ability to assume responsibility for their actions, and (3) the group's training or level of experience. Although the authors do not prescribe how to operationalize these maturity dimensions, life-cycle theory predicts a curvilinear relationship between group maturity and appropriateness of the leader's behavior. As can be seen in Fig. L-2, with an immature work group

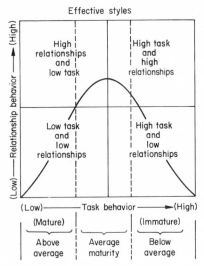

Effective styles

Fig. L-2. Maturity levels. *(Paul Hersey and Kenneth H. Blanchard, Management of Organizational Behavior: Utilizing Human Resources, 2d ed., © 1972, p. 142. Reprinted by permission of Prentice-Hall, Inc., Englewood Cliffs, N.J.)*

(perhaps a newly formed one with little or no training, which shows an unwillingness to assume responsibility and an incapacity to set its own goals) the appropriate behavior of the leader is to be very directive and authoritarian with very little concern for interpersonal maintenance. As the group begins to learn its job and mature along the listed dimensions, it is hypothesized that the leaders must maintain their concern with the task but must also begin to increase considerate behaviors. As maturity in-

creases even further, the need for both structure (task behavior) and consideration (relationship behavior) decreases until, when the group is fully matured, the need for both, in theory, subsides completely.

In this last case, the leader's function is primarily that of a linking pin, a point of contact between echelons, planning future group activities and coordinating with various outside agencies or peers in order to facilitate the smooth functioning of the group. Such organizational phenomena as personnel turnover, a reorganization, or a change of mission may of course reduce the group's maturity—again requiring leader-specific action.

Recently, Hersey and Blanchard have developed an instrument designed to give feedback on leadership style. By eliciting reactions to 12 written leadership situations, leader effectiveness and adaptability description (LEAD) purports to measure the individual's dominant leadership style based on the four quadrants of the Ohio State studies (see Fig. L-1*a*) as well as the associated "supporting style."[29]

While the theory and associated manual provide an attractive prescription for leader behavior, the critical concept, the maturity of the group, is not operationally defined, and it is, therefore, left to the leader's subjective judgment to determine how mature the group might be. Whether leaders are able to change their consideration or structuring behavior at will also remains a question. Above all, virtually no known empirical research supports the theory, and the prescriptions are highly speculative.

**Vroom-Yetton Decision-Making Theory** A quite different approach is taken by Vroom and Yetton[30] in their development of a normative theory of decision making. This is a highly detailed, real-world–oriented model which prescribes in detail the decisions which a manager must make under various conditions. The model spells out the most appropriate set of behaviors for carrying out effective organizational decision making. In fact, the authors have even developed a pocket calculator which indicates the most appropriate course of action, given the various conditions which the situation presents. Implicit in the Vroom-Yetton argument are the assumptions that better decision making on the part of the leader will result in greater productivity and that the leader is able to diagnose accurately the conditions in the situation which demand various types of reactions.

As is true for the path-goal theory, the Vroom-Yetton model predictions are *contingent* upon certain situational variables. The leader's motivation and cognitive attributes are ignored in this approach.

The leader's behavior associated with the implementation of decisions is, therefore, not related to such assumptions as those postulated by McGregor's theory X or theory Y. In fact, Vroom and Yetton prescribe totally nonparticipative procedures under some conditions and participation on the part of subordinates in others. In this respect, the Vroom-Yetton model is clearly superior to the many approaches which prescribe only one correct leadership behavior for all conditions.

The model is represented by a rather complex lattice or decision tree. It proposes five levels of leader-subordinate involvement in the decision-making process. These range from the totally authoritarian process in which the leader makes all the decisions on the basis of the information which is available (Type AI and AII in Fig. L-3) to the completely participative, consensus-oriented solution where the leader serves as the chairperson of the group, GII. In the intermediate modes of participation, called consultative, CI and CII, the leader asks for ideas and suggestions but makes the decision in a unilateral manner.

Ten considerations identify the appropriate use of

subordinates. These are reflected in the form of questions shown in Fig. L-3 (A thru H). In oversimplified form, if the problem at issue will have limited consequences on the people of the organization and the leader has all the information needed to solve the problem, he or she is advised to use an authoritative style of decision making. On the other hand, if the solution will have important consequences for subordinates, some degree of participation is required.

Another variable in the theory is time-efficient behavior. Essentially, the criterion for use of these decision-making behaviors (AI through GII) is the degree of pressure for a solution to the problem. Method AI, the authoritarian approach, is the most time efficient, while method GII, involving total group participation, is least time efficient. When time is not a critical factor, the leader may wish to invest time in team building which leads to long-term gains from decision making.

There are two fundamental problems with the Vroom-Yetton model:

1. While one would agree to the commonsense notion that decision making is an important leadership function, its relationship to overall organiza-

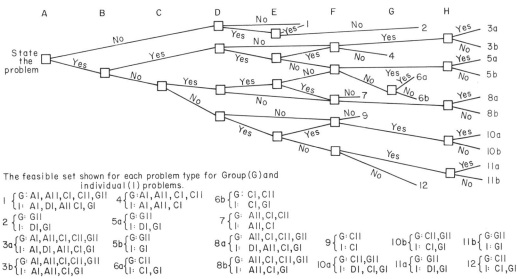

The feasible set shown for each problem type for Group (G) and individual (I) problems.

1 $\begin{cases} G: AI, AII, CI, CII, GII \\ I: AI, DI, AII CI, GI \end{cases}$   4 $\begin{cases} G: AI, AII, CI, CII \\ I: AI, AII, CI \end{cases}$   6b $\begin{cases} G: CI, CII \\ I: CI, GI \end{cases}$

2 $\begin{cases} G: GII \\ I: DI, GI \end{cases}$   5a $\begin{cases} G: GII \\ I: DI, GI \end{cases}$   7 $\begin{cases} G: AII, CI, CII \\ I: AII, CI \end{cases}$

3a $\begin{cases} G: AI, AII, CI, CII, GII \\ I: AI, DI, AII, CI, GI \end{cases}$   5b $\begin{cases} G: GII \\ I: GI \end{cases}$   8a $\begin{cases} G: AII, CI, CII, GII \\ I: DI, AII, CI, GI \end{cases}$   9 $\begin{cases} G: CII \\ I: CI \end{cases}$   10b $\begin{cases} G: CII, GII \\ I: CI, GI \end{cases}$   11b $\begin{cases} G: GII \\ I: GI \end{cases}$

3b $\begin{cases} G: AI, AII, CI, CII, GII \\ I: AI, AII, CI, GI \end{cases}$   6a $\begin{cases} G: CII \\ I: CI, GI \end{cases}$   8b $\begin{cases} G: AII, CI, CII, GII \\ I: AII, CI, GI \end{cases}$   10a $\begin{cases} G: CII, GII \\ I: DI, CI, GI \end{cases}$   11a $\begin{cases} G: GII \\ I: DI, GI \end{cases}$   12 $\begin{cases} G: CII \\ I: CI, GI \end{cases}$

A. Does the problem possess a quality requirement?
B. Do I have sufficient info to make a high quality decision?
C. Is the problem structured?
D. Is acceptance of decision by subordinates important for effective implementation?
E. If I were to make the decision by myself, is it reasonably certain that it would be accepted by my subordinates?
F. Do subordinates share the organizational goals to be attained in solving this problem?
G. Is conflict among subordinates likely in preferred solutions? (This question is irrelevant to individual problems.)
H. Do subordinates have sufficient info to make a high quality decision?

Fig. L-3. Decision-process flow chart. *(Reprinted from Victor H. Vroom and Philip W. Yetton, Leadership and Decision-Making, by permission of the University of Pittsburgh Press © 1973.)*

tional performance is not yet established. The evidence up to this point only shows that in retrospect managers describe themselves as having made decisions which are in conformance with the model. Whether the Vroom-Yetton model can predict group performance or teach leaders how to improve group performance by means of the prescribed decision process still needs to be shown.

2. The model assumes a great deal of flexibility on the part of leaders. Are they capable of changing their behavior as freely from an authoritative mode to a fully participative mode? Can all leaders effectively elicit the type of participative problem solving which the GII decision approach requires? Experience suggests that some people have a great deal of difficulty letting anybody else in on the decision-making act, while others find it very difficult to make their decisions without consultation and extensive discussion. The final verdict on this method must await convincing empirical studies that show improvement in organizational performance.

## THE CONTINGENCY MODEL

This theory holds that the effectiveness of a task group or of an organization depends upon two main factors: (1) the motivation of the leader (leadership style) and (2) the degree to which the situation gives the leader control and influence.

**Leader Motivation** The *relevant* aspect of the leader's personality is his or her motivational structure, that is, the basic or primary goals the leader seeks to satisfy in the work situation.

One type of person, called *relationship-motivated*, obtains self-esteem primarily through good interpersonal relationships with coworkers. This basic goal becomes apparent in uncertain and anxiety-provoking situations in which the individual seeks assurance that his or her really important goals are secured. Under these uncertain conditions, relationship-motivated leaders seek out group members and solicit their support. However, when these same leaders feel relaxed and secure because they already have group support and close interpersonal relationships with group members, they will also seek the esteem and admiration of those outside the group. In a leadership situation where task performance results in esteem and admiration from superiors, leaders will tend to concentrate on behaving in a task-relevant manner.

*Task-motivated* individuals obtain self-esteem primarily by the accomplishment of some tangible evidence of their worth. These persons get satisfaction from the task itself and from knowing that they have done well. In a leadership situation which is uncertain and anxiety provoking, the primary emphasis is on getting the job done. However, when leaders have considerable control and influence and feel assured of accomplishing the task, they can afford to relax and show concern for their group members' feelings and satisfactions. In other words, "business before pleasure, but business *with* pleasure if possible."

Both the relationship-motivated and the task-motivated persons may be pleasant and considerate toward their members under some conditions. However, task-motivated leaders tend to be considerate in situations in which their control is high; relationship-motivated leaders will tend to be considerate when their control is low and uncertainty is present.

*Least-Preferred Coworker Scale.* The leader's motivational structure (leadership style) is measured by the least-preferred coworker scale (LPC). This score is obtained by asking an individual to think of all people with whom he or she has ever worked and then to describe the *one* person who has been the *most* difficult to work with. The description of the least-preferred coworker is made on a short bipolar eight-point scale. The scale currently used has 18 items with a mean of 60. The LPC score is the sum of the 18-item scores, for example,

Friendly $\frac{}{8}$ $\frac{}{7}$ $\frac{}{6}$ $\frac{}{5}$ $\frac{}{4}$ $\frac{}{3}$ $\frac{}{2}$ $\frac{}{1}$ : unfriendly

Pleasant : $\frac{}{8}$ $\frac{}{7}$ $\frac{}{6}$ $\frac{}{5}$ $\frac{}{4}$ $\frac{}{3}$ $\frac{}{2}$ $\frac{}{1}$ : unpleasant

High LPC persons, that is, individuals who describe their least-preferred coworker in relatively positive terms, are primarily relationship-motivated. Low LPC persons, who describe their least-preferred coworker in very negative rejecting terms, are basically task-motivated. The LPC score is not a description of leader behavior since the behavior of high and low LPC people varies as their control of the situation changes. Rather, it is a measure of goals and motivation (leadership style) or the leader's approach to the management situation. Relationship-motivated people seem more open, more approachable, and more like McGregor's theory Y managers.[31] The task-motivated leaders tend to be more controlled and more controlling persons even though they are as well liked and as pleasant as their relationship-motivated colleagues.

Current evidence suggests that the LPC scores of mature adults in stable situations are about as reliable over time as many other personality measures.

That is, changes do occur, but in the absence of major upsets in the individual's life, changes tend to be gradual and relatively small.

**Leadership Situation**  The second variable, situational control or situational favorableness,[32] indicates the degree to which the situation gives leaders (1) control and influence and (2) the ability to predict the consequences of their behavior.[33]

Situational control is measured on the basis of three subscales. These are the degree to which

1. The leader is or feels accepted and supported by group members (leader-member relations).

2. The task is clear cut, programmed, and structured as to goals, procedures, and measurable progress (task structure).

3. The leader's position provides power to reward and punish and thus to obtain compliance from subordinates (position power).

Groups can then be categorized as being above or below the median (or the normative score) on these three dimensions. This leads to an eight-celled classification. The eight cells (or octants) are scaled from high control (octant I) to low control (octant VIII). Leaders obviously will have most control in situations which fall into octant I: that is, in which they have good leader-member relations, a structured task, and high position power. There will be somewhat less control in octant II, where they have good leader-member relations, a structured task, and weak position power, and so on to octant VIII in which they have poor leader-member relations, low task structure, and weak position power.

**The Leader-Situation Interaction**  A schematic description of the contingency model is shown in Fig. L-4. The leader's situational control is indicated on the horizontal axis, extending from high control on the left to low control on the right side of the graph. The vertical axis indicates the leader's or the group's performance. The solid line is the performance curve of the relationship-motivated (high LPC) leader, while the broken line indicates the performance of the task-motivated (low LPC) leader.

*Influence of Situations.*  These curves indicate that relationship-motivated as well as task-motivated leaders perform well under some conditions but not under others. It is, therefore, not accurate to speak of a good or a poor leader. Rather, a leader may perform well in one situation and poorly in another. Outstanding directors of research teams do not necessarily make good production supervisors, and good production managers may make poor advertising executives.

*Influence of Job Assignment.*  The second major implication of Fig. L-4 is that the performance of leaders depends as much on the situation to which the organization assigns them as on the leadership style which they bring to the job. Hence, organizational improvement can come about either by changing leadership style, which is at best a difficult and time-consuming process, or else by the much easier route of modifying the leader's situational control. As can be seen, certain leaders perform better with less rather than with more situational control. These are, for example, the people who constantly need the challenge of a new assignment in order to do well and who become stale and bored when they stay too long on the same job.

*Validity of Contingency Model Predictions.*  A considerable number of studies have tested the hypotheses derived from the contingency model. A review of the literature of various studies conducted up to 1972 showed that the relations were in the expected direction in 36 of 45 separate analyses.

The most convincing validation comes from a well-controlled field experiment conducted by Chemers and Skrzypek[34] at the U.S. Military Academy at West Point. LPC scores, as well as sociometric preference ratings to predict leader-member relations, were obtained several weeks prior to the study. Groups were assembled in advance on the basis of the leader's LPC score and the positive or negative feelings of group members toward one another. Leaders were given either high or low position power and assigned one structured and one unstructured task. The Chemers and Skrzypek study results were almost exactly as the contingency model predicted.

**Toward a Dynamic Theory of Leadership**  Leadership must be seen as a dynamic pro-

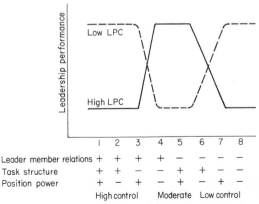

**Fig. L-4. Schematic representation of the contingency model.**

cess. Individuals change as they gain experience, training, and new perspectives about their job. Even more, however, organizations change. New personnel assignments, reorganization, and changes in the organizational mission demand a constant reassessment of a system in flux.

*Impact of Experience on Performance.* The schematic representation of the contingency model (Fig. L-4) illustrates the dynamic nature of the theory: As the leader's situational control changes, so will the match between leadership style and situational control and hence the performance of the leader. It is, therefore, possible to make various predictions about the changes in leadership performance which are likely to occur as a result of events which take place in the organization or as a consequence of changes in the leader's own ability to control the situation.

The latter typically occur with time on the job. Leaders learn the routines of the tasks they and their groups are to perform. They learn how to troubleshoot a machine, how to make sure that the supplies are available at the right time, and how to handle the various subordinates who are late or who need support and encouragement.

Figure L-4 also suggests what will happen when new leaders are placed in situations over which they at first have very little control. Under these conditions, task-motivated leaders are likely to perform better than the relationship-motivated leaders. However, as they gain in experience, the performance of task-motivated leaders should decline while that of relationship-motivated leaders should increase. When new leaders are placed in a situation in which they have moderate situational control as they begin the job, relationship-motivated leaders should perform well, but their performance should decline as they gain in experience. Task-motivated leaders, however, should perform poorly at first and then improve in their performance.

*Validation Studies.* The effect of experience on performance has been shown in a number of different studies. In one investigation by Bons and Hastings,[35] 28 infantry squad leaders were rated by two or more superiors, first at the time their units were organized and before the leaders had an opportunity to shape up their soldiers and the second time after 5 months of training. The situational control of the experienced leaders at time 2 is, of course, quite high. They have position power, highly structured tasks, and they are likely to have the support of their subordinates. Inexperienced squad leaders at time 1, however, have a less structured task as well as less assurance that they can rely on the effectiveness and

the support of their group. Hence, inexperienced leaders have moderate situational control.

The contingency model predicts that the relationship-motivated squad leaders will perform well initially, while they are inexperienced. Leaders with more experience will have higher situational control, and task-motivated leaders will perform better. That this is the case can be seen in Fig. L-5.

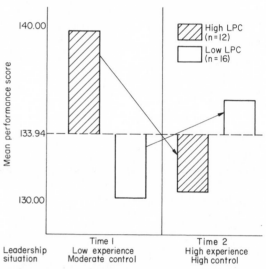

**Fig. L-5. Change in the performance of high and low LPC leaders as a function of increased experience and more structured task assignment over 5 months.**

Similar results were obtained in a study of general managers of a group of consumer cooperatives, where the performance measures consisted of the percent of net income and of operating expenses as a ratio to total sales.[36] The group of managers was subdivided into those with high and low LPC scores, and also into those with relatively high and low experience in the organization. Again in this study, the situation for experienced managers was rated as high in situational control, while that of the less-experienced leaders was moderate. Figure L-6 shows that the findings support the predictions of the contingency model

The contingency model thus explains, in large part, the lack of a consistent relationship between leadership experience and leadership performance.[37] It is not unusual, after all, for some young and aggressive managers and supervisors to get worse rather than better with each year of additional experience. The model suggests that some of these managers have been permitted to remain on their job too long and that they should have been rotated to a more challenging position which provides a better match between their leadership style and the situation.

*Impact of Task Training on Performance.* The model also predicts the effects of task training on leadership performance. This type of training should increase the structure of the task and hence the leader's situational control. A study by Chemers, Rice, Sundstrom, and Butler[38] supports this view. ROTC students and psychology students participated in an experiment which involved the following steps: (1) ROTC cadets were divided into those with high and with low LPC scores and assigned as team leaders; (2) the cadets who fell into the middle group, as well as the psychology students, were used as group members of the four-man teams; (3) half the high and half the low LPC leaders were randomly given task training, which consisted of directions for deciphering a series of coded messages similar to cryptograms. The training was simple but effective.

The group-climate scores, indicating leader-member relations, were poor, largely because of the mixed ROTC and psychology student membership and the unexpected pressure which the officers in charge of the ROTC unit brought to bear on the leaders to perform well. The position power of the leader was low since this was a volunteer group, and the task structure for the untrained leaders was also low, but it was high for those who had been given task training.

The theory predicts that the task-motivated leaders should outperform the relationship-motivated leaders in the low situational-control condition (no task training), while the relationship-motivated leaders should outperform the task-motivated leaders in the trained condition. As Fig. L-7 shows, this was the case.

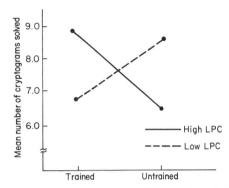

**Fig. L-7. Interaction of training and LPC on group productivity. (Reprinted by permission of the publisher from M. M. Chemers, R. W. Rice, E. Sundstrom, and W. M. Butler, "Leader Esteem for the Least Preferred Coworker Score, Training, and Effectiveness: An Experimental Examination," Journal of Personality and Social Psychology, vol. 31, no. 3, pp. 401–409, 1975.)**

*Leader Selection.* The contingency model also has some important implications in leadership selection. Obviously, if the performance of leaders changes as they gain in experience or acquire appropriate training, different selection policies must be adopted. Specifically, the organization must ask; (1) Do we want leaders who will perform well right now, but who may become less effective over time; (2) do we want leaders who may not do so well in the beginning but who will later become top performers? The theory provides a framework for the development of more rational policies and procedures in the field of work force utilization and planning.

**Shortcomings** As is true of the other models, the contingency model is not without valid criticism. Most of the criticism for this model, however, seems to stem from its derivation—its research base and Fiedler's interpretation of the meaning of the variables. Some authors question Fiedler's interpretation of LPC.[39] Others criticize the model because it is difficult to disprove[40] (e.g., the model is a data-built model rather than a conceptualized model). Others feel that LPC is not a personality variable at all[41] and that events such as training actually modify the leader and not the situation as Fiedler proposes.[42]

The contingency model, however, is a compel-

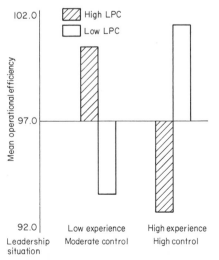

**Fig. L-6. Performance of high and low LPC company managers as a function of experience.**

ling concept for the practitioner who is bent on improving organizational performance by selectively training subordinate leaders and by modifying certain elements of the situation rather than by attempting to change the leader's personality. To this end, the contingency model has been translated into a practical training program.

### THE LEADER MATCH CONCEPT

Fiedler, Chemers, and Mahar[43] developed a self-paced leadership training manual based on the notion that it is difficult, if not impossible, for leaders to change their leadership style every time their leadership situation changes. In contrast, it is much easier (1) to teach leaders to diagnose the situations in which they are likely to perform best and (2) to modify aspects of the situation so that it appropriately matches their leadership style.

The training, which takes about 4 to 7 hours of reading and responding time, first asks the individual to complete an LPC scale which he or she scores and interprets. The trainee is then taught how to fill out various measures which indicate leader-member relations, task structure, and position power, and how to compute situational control. The final sections provide detailed instructions on (1) *modifying the situation* so that it matches leadership style and (2) *applying the training* to subordinate leaders by changing their situational control to match leadership style.

**Validation Studies**  The leader match training program has been tested in eight different studies.

*Six Basic Studies.*  In six studies, the organization was asked to furnish a list of managers or leaders who were considered eligible for training. That is, these leaders were expected to remain with the organization, their performance could be evaluated, and they could be spared for the amount of time required by the program. Approximately one-half the leaders were randomly chosen for training, with the other half serving as controls. In one study, trainees were simply mailed the manual and told to read it carefully. In most other studies, the organization provided time during work hours for the training. Specifically, the group to be trained was given a short introduction and then asked to go through the program in the time set aside. In part for training, in part to break the study time, they were also shown a movie about the contingency model, entitled *Leadership: Style or Circumstance* (CRM Productions, 1975).

The organizations studied included (1) a volunteer public health organization, (2) middle managers of a county government, (3) police sergeants, (4)

public works first- and second-level supervisors, (5) junior officers and chief petty officers at a naval air station, and (6) junior officers and petty officers on a Navy destroyer.

In all six studies, the trained group was rated as performing significantly and substantially better than the untrained group. In the Navy studies, leaders were rated as having improved significantly in performance from the time of the first performance rating prior to training to the final evaluation 6 months later.[44]

*Two Army Studies.*  Two further studies were conducted by Csoka and Bons[45] in an army service school. In one of these studies, one platoon leader in each of 27 training companies was randomly selected to receive training, while the two other platoon leaders served as controls. At the end of a 4-month period, an evaluation of all platoon leaders by their superiors showed that trained leaders were rated significantly more often as best or second best in their company than were untrained leaders. The second study involved 154 student leaders who were to be sent to various field units to act as platoon leaders. One-third of this group selected at random was given the training program to read prior to departure. At the end of the summer assignment, all student leaders were rated by their superiors. Again, those who had been given the program were ranked as significantly better than untrained leaders within the same unit.

These eight studies provide evidence that the contingency model is a theoretical framework which enables us to understand such previously puzzling findings as the fact that leadership experience typically does not correlate with leadership performance or that leadership training has not yielded the promised results. It also explains why rotation and transfer seem to improve the performance of some managers but decrease that of others.

Above all, the contingency model training demonstrates that it is possible to improve leadership performance by teaching the leaders to diagnose and modify the leadership situation to match their leadership style. In effect, if an organization can teach leaders how to avoid or modify situations in which they are likely to fail, they are bound to be successful. The contingency model training provides a method for doing just that at a cost the organization can afford.

### UNRESOLVED PROBLEMS

None of the theories examined here covers the entire range of leadership problems. Some positions concentrate on the growth, well-being, and satisfaction of group members;[46] others are more concerned with improving performance.[47] Yet, such positions as, for example, path-goal theory, the decision-making theory, and the contingency model are not essentially incompatible in their implications. In addition, other important issues are just now beginning to claim the attention of researchers. These include the part played by moral values, inspiration, and commitment[48] or intelligence and task abilities[49] in determining organizational performance. In time, perhaps, answers to these and similar questions will become integrated into a coherent theory of leadership and will increase the practical implications which leadership theory has for the professional manager.

*See also* ASSESSMENT CENTER METHOD; AUTHORITY, RESPONSIBILITY, AND ACCOUNTABILITY; COMMUNICATIONS, ORGANIZATIONAL; DELEGATION; INTERPERSONAL RELATIONSHIPS; MANAGEMENT THEORY, SCIENCE, AND APPROACHES; MANAGERIAL GRID; MOTIVATION IN ORGANIZATIONS; SYSTEM 4; THEORY X AND THEORY Y.

## NOTES

[1]R. Stogdill, "Personal Factors Associated with Leadership: A Survey of the Literature," *Journal of Psychology*, vol. 25, pp. 35–71, 1948.

[2]R. D. Mann, "A Review of the Relationships Between Personality and Performance in Small Groups," *Psychological Bulletin*, vol. 56, pp. 241–270, 1959.

[3]R. M. Stogdill, *The Handbook of Leadership*, The Free Press, New York, 1974.

[4]D. McGregor, *The Human Side of Enterprise*, McGraw-Hill Book Company, New York, 1960.

[5]C. Argyris, *Six Presidents: Increasing Leadership Effectiveness*, John Wiley & Sons, Inc., New York, 1976; W. G. Bennis, "Goals and Meta-Goals of Laboratory Training," in W. G. Bennis, D. E. Berlew, E. H. Schein, and F. I. Steele, eds., *Interpersonal Dynamics*, 3d ed., The Dorsey Press, Homewood, Ill., 1973.

[6]R. Likert, *New Patterns of Management*, McGraw-Hill Book Company, New York, 1961.

[7]R. A. Sutermeister, *People and Productivity*, 3d ed., McGraw-Hill Book Company, New York 1976, p. 107.

[8]Likert, op. cit.

[9]R. M. Stogdill, *The Handbook of Leadership*, p. 375.

[10]W. G. Bennis and E. H. Schein, "Principles and Strategies in the Use of Laboratory Training for Improving Social Systems," *Personal and Organizational Change Through Group Methods*, John Wiley & Sons, Inc., New York, 1965, p. 339.

[11]J. P. Campbell and M. D. Dunnette, "Effectiveness of T-Group Exercises in Managerial Training and Development," *Psychological Bulletin*, vol. 70, p. 97, 1968.

[12]R. M. Stogdill, *The Handbook of Leadership*, p. 199.

[13]R. R. Blake and J. S. Mouton, *The Managerial Grid*, Gulf Publishing Company, Houston, 1964; R. R. Blake and J. S. Mouton, *Building a Dynamic Corporation Through Grid Organizational Development*, Addison-Wesley Publishing Company, Reading, Mass., 1969.

[14]R. M. Stogdill and A. E. Coons, *Leader Behavior: Its Description and Measurement*, Ohio State University, Bureau of Business Research, Columbus, 1957.

[15]Stogdill, *The Handbook of Leadership*, p. 143.

[16]Blake and Mouton, *The Managerial Grid*, p. 1.

[17]R. R. Blake, J. S. Mouton, J. S. Barnes, and L. E. Greiner, "Breakthrough in Organizational Development," *Harvard Business Review*, vol. 42, p. 136, November–December 1964.

[18]O. Behling and C. Schriesheim, *Organizational Behavior: Theory, Research and Application*, Allyn and Bacon, Inc., Boston, 1967, pp. 330–336.

[19]S. Kerr, C. A. Schriesheim, C. J. Murphy, and R. M. Stogdill, "Toward a Contingency Theory of Leadership Based Upon the Consideration and Initiating Structure Literature," *Organizational Behavior and Human Performance*, vol. 12, p. 63, 1974.

[20]E. L. Kelly and D. W. Fisk, *The Prediction of Performance in Clinical Psychology*, The University of Michigan Press, Ann Arbor, 1951.

[21]W. C. Byham, "The Assessment Center as an Aid in Management Development," *Training and Development Journal*, December 1971.

[22]D. W. Bray and D. L. Grant, "The Assessment Center in the Measurement of Potential for Business Management," *Psychological Monographs*, vol. 80, (17), 1966.

[23]H. J. Leavitt, "Some Effects of Certain Communications Patterns on Group Performance" *Journal of Abnormal and Social Psychology*, vol. 46, pp. 38–50, 1951.

[24]F. E. Fiedler, "A Contingency Model of Leadership Effectiveness," in L. Berkowitz, ed., *Advances in Experimental Social Psychology*, vol. I, pp. 149–190, Academic Press, Inc., New York, 1964; F. E. Fiedler, *A Theory of Leadership Effectiveness*, McGraw-Hill Book Company, New York, 1967.

[25]R. J. House, A Path Goal Theory of Leader Effectiveness," *Administrative Science Quarterly*, vol. 16, pp. 312–338, 1971; R. J. House and G. Dressler, The Path-Goal Theory of Leadership: Some *post hoc* and *a priori* Tests," in J. G. Hunt and L. L. Larson, eds., *Contingency Approaches to Leadership*, Southern Illinois University Press, Carbondale, 1974.

[26]House and Dressler, Ibid.

[27]P. Hersey and K. H. Blanchard, *Management of Organizational Behavior*, Prentice-Hall, Inc., Englewood Cliffs, N.J., 1972.

[28]Ibid.

[29]P. Hersey and K. H. Blanchard, "Leader Effectiveness and Adaptability Description," in J. W. Pfeiffer and J. E. Jones, eds., *The 1976 Annual Handbook for Facilitators*, University Associates, Inc., LaJolla, Calif., 1976, pp. 87–99.

[30]V. Vroom and P. Yetton, *Leadership and Decision Making*, The University of Pittsburgh Press, Pittsburgh, 1973.

[31]L. K. Michaelsen, "Leader Orientation, Leader Behavior, Group Effectiveness and Situational Favorability: An Empirical Extension of the Contingency Model, *Organizational Behavior and Human Performance*, vol. 9, pp. 226–245, 1973.

[32]Fiedler, *A Theory of Leadership Effectiveness.*

[33]D. M. Nebeker, "Situational Favorability and Environmental Uncertainty: An Integrative Study," *Administrative Science Quarterly*, vol. 20, pp. 281–294, 1975.

[34]M. M. Chemers and G. J. Skrzypek, "An Experimental Test of the Contingency Model of Leadership Effectiveness," *Journal of Personality and Social Psychology,* vol. 24, pp. 172–177, 1972.

[35]F. E. Fiedler, P. Bons, and L. L. Hastings, "The Utilization of Leadership Resources," in W. T. Singleton and P. Spurgeon, eds., *Measurement of Human Resources*, Taylor and Francis, London, pp. 233–234, 1975.

[36]E. Godfrey, F. E. Fiedler, and D. M. Hall, *Boards, Management, and Company Success,* The Interstate Printers and Publishers, Inc., Danville, Ill., 1959; also cited in Fiedler, *A Theory of Leadership Effectiveness.*

[37]F. E. Fiedler, "Leadership Experience and Leader Performance—Another Hypothesis Shot to Hell," *Organizational Behavior and Human Performance*, vol. 5, pp. 1–14, 1970.

[38]M. M. Chemers, R. W. Rice, E. Sundstrom, and W. Butler, "Leader Esteem for the Least Preferred Coworker Score, Training and Effectiveness: An Experimental Examination," *Journal of Personality and Social Psychology*, vol. 31, pp. 401–409, 1975.

[39]Behling and Schriesheim, op. cit.

[40]G. Graen, D. Alvares, J. B. Orris, and J. A. Martella, "The Contingency Model of Leadership Effectiveness: Antecedent and Evidential Results," *Psychological Bulletin*, vol. 74, pp. 285–296, 1970.

[41]A. S. Ashour, "The Contingency Model of Leadership Effectiveness: An Evaluation," *Organizational Behavior and Human Performance*, vol. 9, pp. 339–355, 1973.

[42]S. Kerr and A. Harlan, "Predicting the Effects of Leadership Training and Experience from the Contingency Model: Some Remaining Problems," *Journal of Applied Psychology*, vol. 57, pp. 114–117, 1973.

[43]F. E. Fiedler, M. M. Chemers, and L. Mahar, *Improving Leadership Effectiveness: The Leader Match Concept*, John Wiley & Sons, Inc., New York, 1976.

[44]A. F. Leister, D. Borden, and F. E. Fiedler, "The Effect of Contingency Model Leadership Training on the Performance of Navy Leaders," *Academy of Management Journal*, 1977, in press.

[45]L. S. Csoka and P. M. Bons, "Manipulating the Situation to Fit the Leader's Style: Two Validation Studies of LEADER MATCH," *OML, USMA*, West Point, N.Y. 10996.

[46]Argyris, *Six Presidents: Increasing Leadership Effectiveness; Likert, New Patterns of Management;* Bennis, "Goals and Meta-Goals of Laboratory Training," in Bennis et al., *Interpersonal Dynamics.*

[47]Vroom and Yetton, *Leadership and Decision Making;* Fiedler, Chemers, Mahar, *Improving Leadership Effectiveness: The Leader Match Concept.*

[48]L. Porter, "Summary and Implications for Future Research," in B. King, S. Streufert, and F. Fiedler, eds., *Managerial Control and Organizational Democracy*, Winston and Sons, Washington, in press.

[49]J. W. Blades, *The Influence of Intelligence, Task Ability and Motivation on Group Performance*, unpublished doctoral dissertation, University of Washington, 1976; F. E. Fiedler and A. F. Leister, "Leader Intelligence and Task Performance: A Test of a Multiple Screen Model," *Organizational Behavior and Human Performance*, 1977, in press.

PAUL M. BONS, *United States Military Academy*
FRED E. FIEDLER, *University of Washington*

## Leadership theory, Gantt (See MANAGEMENT, HISTORICAL DEVELOPMENT OF.)

## Learning (experience) curves

Improvement is a way of life. As any task or activity is repeated, the individual or organization should become more proficient at it. In particular, the cost of performing the activity should decrease as the activity is repeated.

The learning curve (often called an experience, improvement, or manufacturing process curve) is a concept that quantitatively models the amount of cost reduction with increases in volume so that future costs can be predicted in advance and used for management decision making.

Although Wright[1] developed the learning curve in terms of manufacturing direct labor costs, the learning curve was later shown to apply to total manufacturing costs[2] and then to all costs.[3] Attempts to measure total cost reductions, including overhead costs, are often obscured by the accounting system, although Bhada[4] and Morse[5] have suggested useful approaches.

**Principles** The concept of the learning curve is straightforward: As the quantity of output is doubled, the cost per unit of output is decreased by a constant rate. That is, for an 80 percent learning curve, the cost of the ten-thousandth unit is 80 percent of the cost of the five-thousandth unit; the cost of the twenty-thousandth unit is 80 percent of the cost of the ten-thousandth unit, and so on.

An 80 percent learning curve for a hypothetical product is shown on an arithmetic scale in Fig. L-8 and on a double logarithmic scale in Fig. L-9. The log-log scale is a straight line, reflecting a constant decrease in cost, and is most useful for prediction.

A major question is the slope of the cost reduction line. Wright, in his original work, found an 80 percent rate.[6] Hirschmann suggested that the labor-machine ratio determined the slope; that is, a 75 percent labor–25 percent machine mix gave an 80 percent curve, a 50-50 mixture an 85 percent slope,

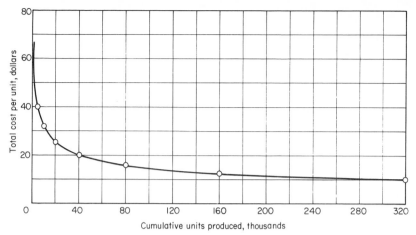

Fig. L-8. 80 percent learning curve: arithmetic scale.

and a 25-75 mixture a 90 percent slope.[7] For total costs, it is suggested that the slope is a function of both the product and the industry, with values varying in the 70 to 95 percent range.[8]

**Successful Applications**  The learning curve was first developed for aircraft assembly. It is so widely used in airframe manufacture that it is required by the United States government in dealing with prime contractors and by these contractors in dealing with their suppliers.[9] Abernathy notes its applicability in automobile manufacture[10] while Hirschmann details its occurrence in petroleum refining, large plant maintenance, electrical power generation, basic steel

output, and so on.[11] The Boston Consulting Group provides total cost data on 24 selected successful products, including transistors, diodes, integrated circuits, ethylene, polyvinylchlorides, aluminum, and others.[12] Additional applications have been widely noted in industrial and production engineering publications.

Successful application implies that the learning curve cost-reduction concept has been shown to apply to specific products. The firm's management may or may not recognize the fact and may or may not use it in formal future decision making such as price and profit planning.

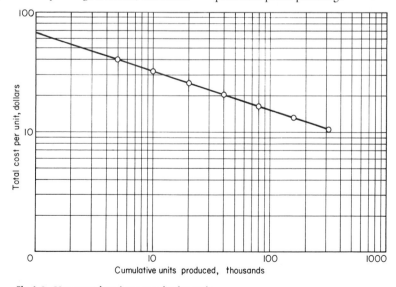

Fig. L-9. 80 percent learning curve: log-log scale.

## Application Opportunities and Techniques

The widespread use of the learning curve suggests its applicability to almost any product. The Boston Consulting Group goes so far as to note that "the relationship has been analyzed for virtually every client over the past five years. The evidence is overwhelming. The relationship always exists."[13] Failure to identify the effect, they note, is usually a result of poor product market segment identification, rapid shifts in the importance of cost factors, use of an allocation cost accounting system, and failure of management to recognize that cost reductions can be predicted.

A straightforward framework can be used to estimate a learning curve:

1. A specific product or product market is identified.

2. The cost accounting system is modified to identify specific costs associated with the product.

3. The slope of the cost reduction curve is determined by analyzing the product's past history, the history of other similar products of the firm, and by other industry data available.

4. A curve is drawn by plotting unit cost versus total volume. From this curve, future unit costs at any volume level can be estimated and used in price and profit planning.

## Evaluation

The learning curve is a valuable tool to predict future costs. As with any other tool, it should not be applied blindly. Although often used for small quantities of output (two or four aircraft), there are some suggestions that abnormal start-up costs may give a false cost picture. In addition, as a product is phased out, eliminating overhead costs and ending manufacturing costs may cause a curve variation.[14] Also, changes in product characteristics, manufacturing technology, and so on, over a long-lived high-volume product could result in a change in slope of the cost curve.[15]

Although learning assumes an inherent susceptibility of an activity to improve, no cost reduction will occur unless the cost reduction potential is exploited. Normal cost reduction techniques such as methods improvements, time studies, value engineering, and so on, are necessary to achieve these cost reductions. Most important, however, is a management environment aimed at stimulating employees to reduce costs by improving products and methods. In this context, the learning curve is a tool for estimating future costs for cost reduction goal setting as well as for price and profit planning.

*See also* DEVELOPMENT AND TRAINING, EMPLOYEE; LINE OF BALANCE (LOB); MARGINAL INCOME ANALYSIS; PRODUCT PLANNING AND DEVELOPMENT; PRODUCTION PLANNING AND CONTROL; PRODUCTION PLANNING AND DEVELOPMENT; PRODUCTIVITY; PURCHASING MANAGEMENT.

### NOTES

[1] T. P. Wright, "Factors Affecting the Cost of Airplanes," *Journal of Aeronautical Science*, February 1936, pp. 122–128.

[2] Winfred B. Hirschmann, "Profit from the Learning Curve," *Harvard Business Review*, vol. 42, no. 1, pp. 125–139, January–February 1964.

[3] *Perspectives on Experience*, Boston Consulting Group, Boston, 1972.

[4] Yezdi K. Bhada, "Dynamic Cost Analysis," *Management Accounting*, vol. 52, no. 1, pp. 11–14, July 1970.

[5] Wayne J. Morse, "Reporting Production Costs that Follow the Learning Curve Phenomenon," *The Accounting Review*, vol. 47, no. 4, pp. 761–773, October 1972.

[6] Wright, loc. cit.

[7] Hirschmann, op. cit., pp. 126–128.

[8] *Perspectives on Experience*, loc. cit.

[9] Wright, loc. cit.; Hirschmann, loc. cit.; William J. Abernathy and Kenneth Wayne, "Limits of the Learning Curve," *Harvard Business Review*, vol. 52, no. 5, pp. 109–119, September–October 1974.

[10] Abernathy, loc. cit.

[11] Hirschmann, loc. cit.

[12] *Perspectives on Experience*, op. cit., pp. 69–101.

[13] Ibid, p. i.

[14] Hirschmann, op. cit., pp. 127–129; Abernathy, op. cit., pp. 111–113.

[15] *Perspectives on Experience*, op. cit., pp. 70–101.

JACKSON E. RAMSEY, *James Madison University*

## Learning plateaus (*See* DEVELOPMENT AND TRAINING, EMPLOYEE.)

## Lease, key clauses (*See* OFFICE SPACE PLANNING AND DESIGN.)

## Lease-purchase analysis (*See* BUDGETING, CAPITAL.)

## Leases, real estate (*See* REAL ESTATE MANAGEMENT, CORPORATE.)

## Leasing (*See* FINANCIAL MANAGEMENT, SHORT-TERM, INTERMEDIATE, AND LONG-TERM FINANCING.)

# Leasing, equipment

This entry on modern equipment-leasing practices is based on a transaction in which a lessor (1) offers a lessee a lease arrangement for acquisition of new equipment or (2) offers to purchase existing equipment and lease it back. The transaction covers a period of several years, possibly as many years as the normal depreciable life of the equipment. Thus the term of the lease is longer than the usual rental contract, which may be by the day, week, or month.

The lease may be *financial*, in which the lessor furnishes only financing, or it may be *operating*, in which maintenance and repair of the assets may be included.

The leasing of capital assets has become popular both with those who use the assets and those who manufacture or distribute them. A lessor may offer a *pay-out lease*, in which the cost of the assets is returned in full by the lease payments, plus overhead and profit. Or the lessor may merchandise a non-pay-out lease, in which resale or the additional renting of assets returned from the lease provides new profits.

Lessors include banks, third-party leasing companies, finance companies, syndicated private investors, and manufacturers who offer leasing arrangements to stimulate sales. Lessees include any organizations which recognize the effect of leverage—the use of borrowed funds—on profitability of the enterprise.

## Advantages of Leasing to the User of Equipment

The dramatic growth of leasing is adequate testimony to its usefulness to the lessor and lessee. These advantages should be considered:

*Additional Source of Credit.* Those offering leasing service may have access to sources of financing which may not otherwise be available to the user. Insurance companies, pension trusts, syndicates of investors, and organizations with excess cash may be lease-financing sources. Leasing brokers and consultants specialize in guiding a potential lessor to contacts which may not be readily accessible to the financial executive.

*Cash Flow.* A properly negotiated lease permits full deduction of lease payments against income. The lease may be structured in a way that permits a greater deduction than would be given with depreciation associated with purchase of the asset.

*Investment Tax Credit.* Since the lessor will acquire the asset for the lessee, the lessor will be able to claim any investment tax credit (ITC) allowed under current legislation. The rules that were applicable in 1977 permitted the lessor the option of passing through the ITC to the lessor, or of retaining the ITC. The availability of this option is generally limited to corporate lessors. The lessee thus negotiates with the lessor, and if the lessee cannot absorb the passed-through ITC as a deduction against current taxes, it is possible that the lessor may be willing to reduce lease payments to reflect the lessor's additional profit which comes from retention of the ITC. Because of these negotiations, sometimes the effective cost of lease financing is below the prime bank-financing rate.

*Sale-Leaseback Considerations.* Many organizations have well-maintained equipment which has definite resale value. Such assets can be purchased by a lessor and leased back to the enterprise for a defined term. Professional managers realize that a productive asset employed in a business is useful regardless of its ownership status. Costs can be reduced by leased assets as well as by owned assets.

*Stabilization of Equipment Usage Costs.* Lease payments can be tailored to the particular need of the enterprise. Payments which vary with seasonal business volume can be arranged. Level payments can be scheduled over a period of many years. Some organizations which offer operating leases may include maintenance and parts supply at a fixed leasing cost determinable in advance. Or the lessee may negotiate for future maintenance at costs which will not be accelerated beyond levels associated with a government index, such as the cost of living. Leasing may thus simplify capital budgeting.

*Obsolescence Protection.* If the equipment being acquired via leasing has a past history of rapid technological obsolescence, the lessor and lessee can negotiate the contractual basis of trade-in and replacement of the leased asset prior to expiration of the agreed basic lease term.

*Purchasing and Lease Renewal Options.* If the lease is correctly drawn, the lessee may negotiate a purchase at the end of the basic lease term, or the lease may be renewed for stated periods.

*Simplified Asset Acquisition.* Most major lessors offer master leasing contracts covering the future equipment needs of the lessee. As other units of equipment are needed, simple schedules are executed under the terms of the master lease, thus decreasing paper work. Sometimes an operating manager is permitted to make equipment-acquisition decisions via leasing which involve yearly rental payments of a stated amount. Such arrangements simplify securing equipment needed for specific contracts, as payments can be tailored to contract terms. In contrast, purchase requests referred to a capital appropriations committee may involve lengthy consideration.

**Special Considerations for the Prospective Lessee**  A considerable body of leasing rules and administrative practices have been formulated by the Internal Revenue Service and the Financial Accounting Standards Board (FASB). Prior to entering into leasing arrangements, the lessee should consider these factors:

*Accounting Treatment.*  In the early days of leasing, lessees believed the leased asset could be treated as off-balance-sheet financing. As the asset was owned by the lessor, it did not need to be included among the lessee's fixed assets. This additional leverage improved earnings on the company's securities and eliminated capital acquisition requests to the board of directors or administrative committees. On December 2, 1976, FASB issued its "Statement of Financial Accounting Standards" on "Accounting for Leases." Rules were proposed which would have retroactive application to existing leases after a 4-year transition period. The announced rules, which will be followed by most of the accounting profession, are complex. In effect, any major lease commitment must be capitalized on the balance sheet. Full disclosure must likewise be made in balance sheet footnotes. Thus, the prospective lessee should discuss any substantial leasing transaction with professional accountants.

*Purchase and Renewal Options.*  Care should be taken to draw a contract which clearly shows that the intention of the lessor and lessee is to lease, not to purchase the asset. A nominal amount stated in a purchase option or a renewal amount which is priced at lower than the going market rates for leasing comparable used equipment may disqualify the deductibility of the basic lease payments. A *fair market value* purchase option, providing for third-party appraisal of the equipment's value at the end of the lease may help solve this problem.

*Maintenance, Taxes, and Insurance.*  As these items are usually considered indicia of ownership, the lessee should try to shift their payment to the lessor, adjusting rental rates accordingly. Otherwise, deductibility of lease payments may be questioned by the IRS.

*Length of the Lease.*  If a lease is written for a period materially shorter than the normal depreciable life of similar equipment, and if the lease provides that the lessee may retain the property on payment of some nominal renewal cost, the lease payments may be reclassified by the IRS as a combination of interest and a portion of the purchase price of the asset. Prior lease payment deductions would

have to be adjusted and taxes recalculated. However, if a business purpose is served by a short lease, such as completion of a specific contract, the lease may be an admirable vehicle to help concentrate proper costs into a period much shorter than the normal depreciable life of the assets involved.

*Local Taxes.*  In some states, sales and use taxes are added to each rental invoice by the lessee. If an asset should be returned to the lessor prior to the end of its useful life and a new lease contract negotiated for a replacement asset, there may be substantial savings in state taxes. This is because the entire tax on the original acquisition would have been payable on an outright purchase. Also, a knowledgeable lessee may negotiate payment of equipment personal property taxes by the lessor.

*Competition.*  Some of our country's largest banks have recognized the profit potential of acting as direct lessors of equipment. Similarly, major finance companies and financial conglomerates have competed vigorously for leasing business. Any prospective lessor should first contact the major bank of account and inquire about leasing service. Investment bankers will act as intermediaries in arranging large leasing transactions. Consultants and leasing brokers can assist. Insurance companies may be willing to talk directly to the corporate financial officer. Thus, competition is active; leasing specifications should be prepared and distributed for bid.

**Advantages of Leasing for the Manufacturer and Lessor**  Since equipment leasing first became popular in the early 1950s, lessors have proliferated. Any manufacturer that has a product which is durable, has a long life expectancy, and is sold at $500 or more per unit should add a leasing plan to its marketing strategy. This includes the following:

*Financing by the Manufacturer.*  All organizations recognize the effect of a substantial increase in unit sales on break-even points. A manufacturer who is substantially financed may wish to offer leasing or time-payment plans at financing rates that will cover paper work costs but which will be lower than those available from other financing sources. Such imaginative marketing may have a substantial effect on corporate profits. Many manufacturers have established captive finance companies which offer plans tailored to the specific needs of the customer group.

*Third-Party Leasing Companies.*  There are many leasing companies; some are subsidiaries of major conglomerates. These specialized firms work cooperatively with marketing representatives of the companies wishing to offer leasing plans. Attractive sales literature is developed; leasing experts from the third-party lessor will accompany marketing staff members on sales calls. Scientific techniques to upgrade sales to multiple units or more expensive units may be used, as a small increase in the monthly rental fee may permit the lessee to acquire a more-expensive machine, with profit to all.

*Forced Obsolescence.* When an asset is purchased, the owner tends to repair and maintain the machine just as long as possible. In contrast, the lessor has an opportunity to make a new "sale" at the end of the basic lease period. The original leased asset is taken back at a negotiated allowance; a new, improved unit is placed on another lease.

*Resale of Used Equipment.* If the lessee does not renew the lease or exercise the stated purchase option, the leased equipment will be returned to the lessor. The equipment can be reconditioned and leased again to a segment of the market which may not be able to afford new equipment. These marketing strategies have been particularly useful in computer leasing, as larger companies upgrade to newer generations of product development.

*Stabilizing Sales Revenue.* In certain capital goods industries, the business cycle alternately depresses and stimulates production. A carefully drawn lease-marketing plan can provide a steady source of lease revenue on a predictable basis, thus helping budget capital expenditures into the future.

*Profits on Renewals and Purchase Options.* If a true lease with fully deductible payments has been worked out by the lessor's lawyers and accountants, the cash flow from lease renewals may provide a welcome source of additional revenue. This is because cost and profit have been returned fully during the basic original lease term. A fair market value purchase option acted upon by the lessee constitutes an additional residual profit to the lessor.

*Additional Revenue from Investment Tax Credit.* As the lessor has the right to negotiate the retention or pass-through of the ITC, there is an opportunity for a substantial additional leasing profit if the ITC can be used by the lessor and if the lessee is willing to accept the lessor's lease rate.

*Discount from Manufacturer.* A third-party lessor may be able to negotiate special pricing arrangements when working with an equipment manufacturer, thus increasing the profit on the lease-marketing program.

## LEVERAGED LEASING

Some of the major third-party leasing organizations and investment bankers maintain special departments which arrange sizable leasing transactions of a million dollars or more, using leverage techniques.

Expressed simply, the objective is to invest as little equity money as possible and to borrow as much as possible.

As the lessor owns the leased asset, and as the asset is fully insured by the lessor or the lessee, there should be a substantial residual value at the end of the lease if the asset is durable and usable by another lessee or buyer should it be returned from the lease.

A participating financing institution has its lease loan collateralized by the assets, and its quoted financing rate to the lessor may reflect the asset's residual value and the general security of the loan. Procurement of 100 percent financing is not unusual when a financing institution is doing business with one of its own customers.

When a lease transaction is too large to be acceptable to a single financing institution, a number of financing sources may be brought together in a syndicated partnership. If an investor in the leasing syndication is a corporation, the corporate investors would be entitled to the investment tax credit. Both corporate and individual investors can use depreciation generated by the leased assets.

Thus, in leveraged leasing the lessee normally can negotiate a leasing rate which is well below the rate applicable to other long-term borrowing needs. The lessor receives valuable tax-shelter benefits, including eventual residual values on resale or re-lease of the asset. If an institutional lender is involved, the "basis points" on the lease loan usually are well in excess of the financing income from traditional mortgage loans.

The individual investor should consult with tax advisors before entering into a leasing transaction. Accelerated depreciation in excess of straight-line depreciation on personal property subject to a net lease is now considered a "tax preference" and may thus be subject to a minimum tax. Likewise, the interest cost on the individual's borrowing to finance the investment may be subject to limitations and thereby limit the deductibility of the interest shown on the individual's tax return. However, the limitations in effect in any particular year may still permit a substantial participation in the leasing venture.

The individual investor should also consider his or her tax position in future years when depreciation is less and profit from the transaction may be greater. If the individual's personal income will be less then because of retirement, the additional income may be welcome. If nonsalary income is equal to or greater than former income levels before retirement, then the individual investor may wish to sell his or her interest in the leasing transaction or give it to a family member who is in a lower tax bracket.

However, such disposition may still trigger a substantial tax cost.

Investors in syndicated transactions reduce income in the initial years by computing depreciation through use of accelerated methods. Also, they may arrange to incur substantial interest charges on highly leveraged transactions. Income generated in later years will be subject to ordinary tax rates, as will the profit on sale of the leased assets at the end of the lease.

As residual values cannot be estimated accurately in advance, most leveraged leasing arrangements are structured to provide an attractive return on the investor's equity without considering the residuals. Prospective users of leveraged leasing should note that the Tax Reform Act of 1976 substantially reduced the viability of syndicated leasing. This is because an investor's deductibility of losses from the partnership is now limited to his or her capital investment "at risk."

As this type of leasing transaction is arranged only for a lessee of the highest credit standards, the soundness of the investment is considerably more attractive than that of other tax shelters often used by individuals in high tax brackets. However, an investor should ask legal and tax advisors to fully evaluate any offered proposal.

## AUTOMOTIVE AND TRUCK LEASING

This specialized branch of equipment leasing has grown rapidly. Auto and truck lessors bring professional expertise to acquisition and disposal of automotive equipment needed by both large and small enterprises. Leases can be written which provide for automatic replacement of the fleet at specified time intervals, or flexible provisions may permit retention of low-mileage vehicles.

Leasing of cars for employees avoids arguments about fairness of mileage allowances. Mass purchasing power may decrease acquisition cost and save valuable time for corporate executives who must otherwise negotiate to replace individual cars as needed. Full-maintenance leases may bring overall economies by eliminating billings by employees for required repairs. Insurance costs may be less on a bulk basis. Major automotive lessors usually furnish fleet cost analyses to assist management in correct budgeting of corporate automotive expense.

Truck lessors provide everything but the driver, relieving the user of the need to establish expensive repair facilities for a comparatively small number of trucks. Replacement vehicles are furnished during maintenance work.

In some fleet management contracts, a specific percentage of monthly lease cost is credited to a depreciation reserve. At the end of an agreed lease period, the car is sold. Any excess of sale price over depreciation is refunded to the lessee; deficiencies are billed to the lessee. Insurance may be handled either by lessor or lessee, depending on purchasing skills and bulk rate possibilities. Discounts on tires and batteries normally are made available to the lessee drivers.

Car leasing by individuals, however, is rarely less expensive than the purchase and depreciation of an automobile over its useful life. Nevertheless, some lessors may offer executives personal leasing plans.

*See also* ACCOUNTING, FINANCIAL; FINANCIAL MANAGEMENT, SHORT-TERM, INTERMEDIATE, AND LONG-TERM FINANCING; REAL ESTATE MANAGEMENT, CORPORATE.

### REFERENCES

Griesinger, Frank K., and Harvey Greenfield: *Sale-Leasebacks and Leasing in Real Estate and Equipment Transactions*, McGraw-Hill Book Company, New York, 1959; available in microfilm edition from Frank K. Griesinger and Associates, Inc., Suite 1412, Superior Building, Cleveland, Ohio 44114.

Lee, Samuel J.: *Introduction to Leasing*, Coda Publications, Studio City, Calif., 1965.

Metz, Donald H.: *Leasing: Standards and Procedures*, Thomas Publications, Ltd., Kaukauna, Wis., 1968.

Vancil, Richard F.: *Leasing of Industrial Equipment*, McGraw-Hill Book Company, New York, 1963.

FRANK K. GRIESINGER, *Frank K. Griesinger and Associates, Inc.*

## Least-preferred coworker scale (LPC)
(*See* LEADERSHIP.)

## Least squares method (*See* ACCOUNTING FOR MANAGERIAL CONTROL.)

## Lecture (*See* DEVELOPMENT AND TRAINING, EMPLOYEE.)

## Legal administration, international (*See* INTERNATIONAL OPERATIONS AND MANAGEMENT IN MULTINATIONAL COMPANIES.)

# Legal affairs, management of corporate

The range of statutes and government regulations of business corporations, as well as their number, have increased substantially in recent years. The number of lawsuits brought against corporations by individuals, groups, and even other corporations has also multiplied. As a result, business executives find themselves spending substantial amounts of their time dealing with legal problems.

This increasing need for legal advice has resulted in the establishment of legal departments in almost all the larger corporations and the employment of one or more lawyers full time by many rather small corporations.

**Preventive Law** The primary objective of most consultations of business executives and lawyers is preventive law; that is, the corporation seeks to arrange its transactions so as to minimize legal risks. The corporation seeks not only to avoid legal liability but also to assure that its expectations will be realized even if things go awry or other parties wish to renege. This is the essence of management of the corporation's legal affairs. However, no one can really avoid becoming the target of a lawsuit; and if a corporation does not defend itself, a default judgment normally ensues.

Legal advice, whether rendered by corporate counsel (the term usually applied to inside counsel) or outside counsel, is not costless, either in the time of the lawyer or in the time of the business executives who seek advice and who furnish the business information upon which the legal opinion is based. Therefore, some sort of cost-benefit analysis must be made, rough as it is almost always bound to be, in determining when a lawyer should be consulted and how much time should be given to the problem.

It is common, however, for inside lawyers to be regularly in attendance at certain types of corporate meetings; for example, whenever new marketing or pricing programs are being considered and whenever union grievances are being reviewed. Even when the corporation has no law department, routines may be established requiring review by a lawyer of certain documents and transactions, such as all new product labels and all contracts not prepared on a previously approved form.

**Inside versus Outside Lawyers** There is no definitive answer to the question whether corporate counsel or outside lawyers render the best legal service. The answer in any given case depends on a number of variables; the most important are the nature of the legal problem and the background and competence of the lawyer.

In the practice of preventive law, the optimal solution to any legal problem requires a knowledge of the relevant facts and a knowledge of the law. It also includes an ability to imagine alternative ways to structure the desired transaction so as to accomplish the business objective with less legal risk than originally proposed. The business executive is usually the expert on the facts, and the lawyer is the expert on the law. But the more the lawyer knows of the business and the more the executive is aware of what sort of information is relevant to the solution of the problem, the better that solution is likely to be. Therefore, corporate counsel, after working within the corporation, is likely not only to know a great deal that otherwise needs to be learned fresh from the business executives but also to know the sources of information that would not occur to an outside attorney or be readily available to him or her. Also, effective legal advice requires a receptive and understanding executive as well as a competent lawyer; the inside lawyer is more likely to have the appropriate rapport with the executive, developed through frequent cooperative consultations. On the other hand, the corporate counsel may be biased in his or her view of the facts because of close association with the corporation and its executives, while a fresh study by outside counsel, particularly if informed by somewhat similar problems handled for other clients, may result in better advice. Although their relative degree of independence is the subject of controversy, outside counsel may be as dependent on the fee as the inside counsel is on the salary; independence of mind is probably more a matter of personal character than the pay arrangement.

Inside counsel can frequently perform many legal services more cheaply because (1) better knowledge of the potential use of their opinions may permit the corporation counsel to take shortcuts and (2) their acquaintance with the firm's executives and their work permits them to obtain necessary facts more quickly. Inside counsel may also have special expertise in certain areas of the law pertinent to the business of the corporation which, together with intimate knowledge of the situation, may permit them to give almost instantaneous advice. Generally, however, the establishment of a law department results in more frequent consultation with lawyers over a wider range of matters rather than in a reduction of cost of legal advice to the corporation.

The existence of even a very large law department will not eliminate the need to call on outside law firms. Most corporations do not use their corporate counsel to try lawsuits. Even if they do, local counsel would be required to assist if the suit is brought in a jurisdiction where the corporation's own trial lawyers are not admitted to practice. Then there are matters involving legal specialties that may be needed only infrequently, such as patents and trademarks or registration of securities, which can better be referred to outside counsel. Even when there is competency among corporate counsel, either the lawyer or the corporate executive may desire consultation with a highly regarded outside law firm because of the importance of the matter to the corporation or because of doubt or disagreement within the law department.

If outside counsel is to be relied upon entirely, better results are likely to be obtained if an ongoing relationship is developed with a particular lawyer of a given firm. That way, something approaching the broad knowledge of the business and the close counsel-client relationship typical of corporate counsel is developed. That particular lawyer can then refer matters outside his or her areas of competency to other lawyers in the firm or even to lawyers in other firms.

**Law Department Organization** There are two basic concepts for organizing the corporate law department: one is based upon specialization by legal field (antitrust, patents and trademarks, taxation, etc.) and the other on specialization by corporate function. In the latter system the lawyers are assigned to particular executives or divisions of the business, and this promotes the development of successful lawyer-client relationships. Some companies try to gain the advantages of both principles of organization by assigning one lawyer to each major executive but also expecting each lawyer to become expert in one of the legal specialities. To the extent possible, this area of expertise would be one related to the work of the assigned executive, but the lawyer would also serve as an expert consultant to the other members of the law department. In a very large law department, some members might serve only as specialists. In a law department of only one or a few lawyers, outside law firms would be relied upon for counsel in most legal specialties, and the corporate counsel would handle advice concerning the more repetitive activities of the corporation and those peculiar to its business.

**Utilization Procedure** Where the corporation has a law department, it is common to authorize the lawyers to deal directly with any employee who has responsibility to (1) prepare plans or (2) conduct transactions that might impose legal liabilities on the corporation. The goal of practicing preventive law is

generally well served by this policy because the lawyers are more likely to have the opportunity to give their inputs before plans are jelled to the point that they are difficult to change. Although this may result in apparently wasted effort by the lawyers on plans that will be changed or dropped at higher executive levels, it is likely to reduce corporate legal exposure.

If only outside counsel is used, and then relatively infrequently, it is advantageous to funnel legal matters through one or only a few executives in order to control costs and permit development of the mutual respect and cooperation necessary for a successful lawyer-client relationship.

Although sometimes corporate counsel are asked to give advice to top corporate executives or other personnel on their personal legal problems, this is likely to lead to conflict-of-interest situations—whether or not the lawyer charges a fee. A good way of handling such requests is for the corporate counsel to listen to the problem to determine whether legal assistance is needed but not to prepare the document or give the advice. If the employee has no previous contact with a lawyer competent in this area, corporate counsel can aid in selecting a lawyer.

**Problems in the Lawyer-Client Relationship** The role of corporate counsel is not always clearly understood by corporate executives or the lawyers, and this ambiguity may impede their effective use.

The business and legal aspects of a problem are often thoroughly intertwined. Some lawyers tend to sort them out as best they can and give advice only with respect to the law, even if this involves suggesting alternative ways of reaching the business objective. Other lawyers routinely advise with respect to the business aspects, without necessarily making this clear to the client. On the other hand, an executive may be aware that there is no serious legal problem but will come to the lawyer primarily to test out a business plan under consideration. The relationship usually works better and the corporation's welfare is promoted if the lawyer makes it clear to the client when an opinion is fundamentally a business rather than a legal judgment.

Another troubling problem is whether advice given to anyone other than the chief executive by the lawyer to the effect that a proposed course of action is legally hazardous is only advice or whether it is, in effect, a veto. It is better to view it only as advice, but the executive should feel bound to have the matter reviewed by a superior if the executive plans to disregard it.

Too many executives tend to view the lawyer as a

police officer to be duped rather than as an advisor to help in minimizing the corporation's legal risks. The executive client should realize that (1) the soundness of the lawyer's advice is dependent upon the accuracy and completeness of the information upon which it is founded, and (2) it is the executive's responsibility to provide that information. Often the lawyer, through his or her own sources, learns of additional or even inconsistent facts. Obviously, when the lawyer acts as an investigator within the corporation, pains should be taken to approach the search as a cooperative rather than an adversary endeavor. When this is done properly, mutual confidence is enhanced.

*See also* ARBITRATION, COMMERCIAL; ARBITRATION, LABOR; BOARDS OF DIRECTORS, LEGAL LIABILITY GUIDELINES; GOVERNMENT REGULATIONS, BUSINESS LAW; PATENTS AND VALUABLE INTANGIBLE RIGHTS; TAX MANAGEMENT, MANAGERIAL RESPONSIBILITY FOR FEDERAL INCOME TAX REPORTING.

### REFERENCES

Brown, Louis M.: "Corporate Counseling—in the Forefront of the Practice of Preventive Law," *California State Bar Journal*, vol. 42, p. 261, 1967.

Donnell, John D.: *The Corporate Counsel: A Role Study*, Bureau of Business Research, Graduate School of Business, Indiana University, Bloomington, 1970.

Donnell, John D.: "How to Use Your Business Lawyer," *Business Horizons*, Winter 1967, p. 37.

Hickman, L. E.: "The Emerging Role of Corporate Counsel," *The Business Lawyer*, vol. 12, p. 216, April 1957.

Maddock, Charles S.: "The Corporation Law Department," *Harvard Business Review*, vol. 30, p. 119, March–April 1952.

Ruder, David S.: "A Suggestion for Increased Use of Corporate Law Departments in Modern Corporations," *The Business Lawyer*, vol. 23, p. 341, January 1968.

Vogel, Harold: *Corporate Law Department Practice*, Prentice-Hall, Inc., Englewood Cliffs, N. J., 1972.

JOHN D. DONNELL, *Indiana University; former Editor in Chief, American Business Law Journal*

## Lesser-developed countries (LDC) (*See* DEVELOPING COUNTRIES, MANAGEMENT IN.)

## Letter of credit (*See* INTERNATIONAL TRADE.)

## Letter of intent (*See* ACQUISITIONS AND MERGERS.)

## Letters, management (*See* SHAREHOLDER RELATIONSHIPS.)

## Leverage, financial (*See* FINANCIAL MANAGEMENT; FINANCIAL MANAGEMENT CAPITAL STRUCTURE AND DIVIDEND POLICY.)

## Leveraged lease (*See* FINANCIAL MANAGEMENT, SHORT-TERM, INTERMEDIATE, AND LONG-TERM FINANCING; LEASING, EQUIPMENT.)

## Liabilities (*See* ACCOUNTING, FINANCIAL.)

## Liability, of boards of directors (*See* BOARDS OF DIRECTORS, LEGAL LIABILITY GUIDELINES.)

## Liability, product (*See* PRODUCT LIABILITY.)

## Liability, strict (*See* PRODUCT LIABILITY.)

## Liability insurance (*See* INSURANCE AND RISK MANAGEMENT.)

## Library searching (*See* INFORMATION SEARCH.)

## Licensing, patent (*See* PATENTS AND VALUABLE INTANGIBLE RIGHTS.)

## Life-cycle, product (*See* MARKET ANALYSIS.)

## Life-cycle concept, human (*See* MARKETING, CONCEPTS AND SYSTEMS.)

## Life-cycle factors (*See* PRODUCT PLANNING AND DEVELOPMENT.)

## Life-cycle theory    (*See* LEADERSHIP.)

## LIFO    (*See* ACCOUNTING, FINANCIAL; PROFITS AND PROFIT MAKING.)

## Lincoln incentive management plan
(*See* COMPENSATION, SPECIAL PLANS.)

## Line and staff    (*See* MANAGEMENT THEORY, SCIENCE, AND APPROACHES.)

## Line and staff functions, production    (*See* PRODUCTION/OPERATIONS MANAGEMENT.)

## Line and staff organization    (*See* ORGANIZATION ANALYSIS AND PLANNING.)

## Line balancing

*Line balancing* is arranging a production line so that there is an even flow of production from one work station to the next, that is, so that there are no delays at any work station that will leave the next station with idle time.

Balancing may be achieved by rearrangement of the work stations or by adding machines and/or workers at some of the stations so that all operations take about the same amount of time. In some cases, the balancing may be done by a computer program.

*See also* PRODUCTION/OPERATIONS MANAGEMENT; PRODUCTION PLANNING AND CONTROL; PRODUCTION PROCESSES; SYSTEM DYNAMICS.

### REFERENCES
Magee, John F., and David M. Boodman: *Production Planning and Inventory Control*, 2d ed., McGraw-Hill Book Company, New York, 1967, pp. 253–272.
O'Brien, James J.: *Scheduling Handbook*, McGraw-Hill Book Company, New York, 1969, pp. 256–278.

STAFF/SMITH

## Line managers    (*See* MANAGER, DEFINITIONS OF.)

## Line of balance (LOB)

A line of balance (LOB) is a charting device for planning and monitoring the progress of an order, project, or program to be completed by a target date. LOB contains elements of the program evaluation and review technique (PERT) in that the plan of operations is based upon establishment of critical dates at which materials must be on hand, contributing tasks accomplished, and subassemblies or subprojects completed. These tasks are represented by vertical bars of a length proportional to their production (or end point) requirements and are plotted sequentially on a Gantt-like vertical bar chart. The desired progress is the stairstep profile line derived by connecting the tops of the schedule bars: This profile line is the line of balance, shown in Fig. L-10. As the project is pursued, progress of each task is plotted on the LOB chart as a vertical bar (or

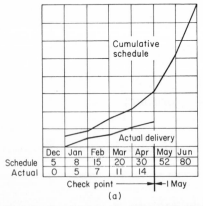

| | Dec | Jan | Feb | Mar | Apr | May | Jun |
|---|---|---|---|---|---|---|---|
| Schedule | 5 | 8 | 15 | 20 | 30 | 52 | 80 |
| Actual | 0 | 5 | 7 | 11 | 14 | | |

(a)

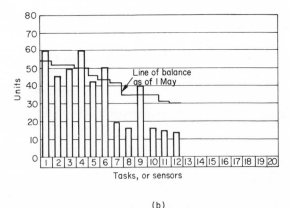

(b)

Fig. L-10. Line of balance charting. (a) Objective chart; (b) line of balance chart. (*Government Printing Office, Navy Special Projects Office.*)

sensor). At a particular check date (May 1 in Fig. L-10), the gap between the top of a bar and the line of balance shows where a delay, exception, or deficiency exists.

The LOB chart is usually studied in conjunction with an objective chart (Fig. L-10*a*), upon which is plotted the cumulative progress of the project (in terms of end units) toward its completion date. Figure L-10*a* shows that end units are far below schedule on May 1 (14 versus 30 units). Figure L-10*b* shows that tasks 2, 3, 5, 7, 8, 10, 11, and 12 are the critical reasons. A different line of balance is constructed for each check date and often for a number of closely related tasks (families).

*See also* GANTT CHARTS; NETWORK PLANNING METHODS; PRODUCTION PLANNING AND CONTROL.

### REFERENCES

O'Brien, James J.: *Scheduling Handbook*, McGraw-Hill Book Company, New York, 1969, pp. 246–255.
Schoderbek, and Lester A. Digman: "Third Generation PERT/LOB," *Harvard Business Review*, September–October 1967, pp. 100–110.
Whitehouse, Gary E.: "Project Management Techniques," *Industrial Engineering*, March 1973, pp. 24–28.

STAFF/SMITH

## Linear programming (*See* OPERATIONS RESEARCH AND MATHEMATICAL MODELING; PLANNING, STRATEGIC PLANNING MODELS.)

## Linking pins, in communications (*See* COMMUNICATIONS, ORGANIZATIONAL.)

## Loan applications (*See* FINANCIAL MANAGEMENT, BANK RELATIONSHIPS.)

## Loans, bank (*See* FINANCIAL MANAGEMENT, SHORT-TERM, INTERMEDIATE, AND LONG-TERM FINANCING.)

## Loans, credit (*See* CREDIT MANAGEMENT.)

## Location, store (*See* RETAILING MANAGEMENT.)

## Location strategy (*See* REAL ESTATE MANAGEMENT, CORPORATE.)

## Locator systems, central (*See* INVENTORY CONTROL, PHYSICAL AND STOCKKEEPING.)

## Logistics, business

The system of managing the flow of materials (raw materials, supplies, purchased parts, etc.) from the suppliers, through the company processes, to the customers is business logistics.

An effective logistics system will reduce costs by balancing such things as transportation costs, prices of materials, warehousing, and inventory costs in such a way as to achieve optimum flow.

*See also* DISTRIBUTION, PHYSICAL.

### REFERENCES

Ballou, Ronald H.: *Business Logistics Management*, Prentice-Hall, Inc., Englewood Cliffs, N.J., 1973.
Davis, Grant Miller: *Logistics Management*, Lexington Books, Lexington, Mass., 1974.
Farrell, Jack: "Managing Logistics: Service Contract," *Traffic Management*, January 1973, pp. 34–39.
Heskett, James L., and Peter F. Mathias: "The Management of Logistics in MNC's," *Columbia Journal of World Business*, Spring 1976, pp. 52–62.

STAFF/SMITH

## Logistics, distribution (*See* DISTRIBUTION, PHYSICAL; MARKETING, INDUSTRIAL.)

## Long-range planning, formal (*See* PLANNING, STRATEGIC MANAGERIAL.)

## Loss, direct and indirect (*See* INSURANCE AND RISK MANAGEMENT.)

## Loss, direct or insurable (*See* SAFETY AND HEALTH MANAGEMENT, EMPLOYEE.)

## Loss, indirect or hidden (*see* SAFETY AND HEALTH MANAGEMENT, EMPLOYEE.)

## Loss analysis (*See* STATISTICAL ANALYSIS FOR MANAGEMENT.)

## Loss control (*See* INSURANCE AND RISK MANAGEMENT.

# M

**Machine-center concept** (*See* AUTOMATION.)

**Macro economics** (*See* ECONOMIC CONCEPTS.)

**Mail-order house** (*See* MARKETING, CHANNELS OF DISTRIBUTION.)

**Maintenance, break-down** (*See* PLANT ENGINEERING MANAGEMENT.)

**Maintenance, contract** (*See* PRODUCTION/OPERATIONS MANAGEMENT.)

**Maintenance, routine** (*See* PLANT ENGINEERING MANAGEMENT.)

## Maintenance management

The prime objective of good maintenance management is the ability to analyze maintenance costs in order to maximize the value of the maintenance and repair dollar spent with minimum downtime of equipment and buildings. Maintenance operations cover diverse areas, including physical plant, production equipment, building service equipment, building structure, utilities, sanitation, grounds care, fleet, material handling equipment, and compliance with building safety and pollution codes, as well as the minimizing of energy expenditures.

**Organization** The demands placed on a large maintenance operation are so varied that they require the delegation of specific duties to those best qualified in each field.

The two basic approaches to organizing the maintenance functions are departmental maintenance and centralization.

*Departmental maintenance* is the philosophy of assigning maintenance personnel to specific production areas.

Generally speaking, the most efficient and practical organization is a *centralized* one. This system divides the maintenance responsibilities into specific functions headed by a specialist in each category. These specialists, in turn, report to one coordinator, typically the director of maintenance. Within the centralized organization a number of variations are possible. Some firms, for example, use a project engineer to coordinate specific projects. Appropriate tradespeople, materials, and equipment are assigned to the project engineer for the completion of the specific assignment. In some firms, the maintenance activity is so large that it requires several parallel structures. In such cases there are several area, zone, or section maintenance managers, each with their own staff. All the managers, however, report to the director of maintenance. (See Fig. M-1 for an example of a centralized maintenance organization.)

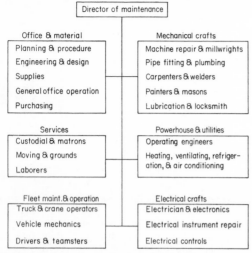

**Fig. M-1. Example of centralized maintenance organization.**

*Advantages of a centralized system*

1. The use of workers and materials can be directed more efficiently.

2. Training programs, the purchase of specialized tools, and the use of experts can be justified.

3. Costs and controls can be accounted for more readily.

4. Retaining higher-caliber maintenance managers can be justified.

*Disadvantages of a centralized system*

1. Time lost in travel can be substantial.

2. Since personnel are scattered throughout the plant, there will be less supervision.

3. Storage areas and tool cribs may be spread out, requiring excess time to complete a job.

4. A longer time elapses between breakdown and repair.

*Staffing.* The number of employees required in a maintenance division is affected by variations such as the age of the equipment and buildings, the economic importance of lost production time, and the individual company's own analysis of the quality and quantity of maintenance deemed necessary to assure the maximum return on investment.

A critical analysis should be made that will evaluate work force requirements for each subcategory within each department. It is essential that each

maintenance operation be carefully defined and time standards (time required) for each operation be determined. In addition, consideration must be given to peak loads, cost of equipment downtime, and specific industry requirements; for example, cleanliness must be considered in the food industry. It is imperative that the staff be sufficiently large to handle routine maintenance, emergency or breakdown maintenance, as well as preventive maintenance.

An example of maintenance work force requirements for 10 industries can be found in Fig. M-2. This figure presents the average ratios, by industry, of the number of total plant employees per maintenance hourly employee. The total plant employee category includes management and supervisory and technical employees. The maintenance hourly classification includes all craft and trades personnel but excludes janitorial and utilities employees.

One of the basic tools used to determine staffing and overtime requirements is the *backlog report*. This periodic report indicates, by priority, the number of work orders outstanding and the number of hours required to perform them.

**Planning** It is essential that each department within a company plan its maintenance needs for prescribed periods of time. Consideration must be given to production changes, plant expansions, changes in material handling techniques, and the like. Each proposed change affects the maintenance operation and should be planned for accordingly.

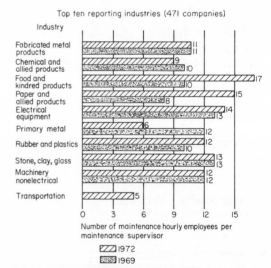

**Fig. M-2. How over 600 firms manage the maintenance force.** (*A summary report of a second survey of maintenance administrative ratios prepared by Albert Ramond and Associates, Inc., Research Planning Division, 1973.*)

Long-term plans and related cost and staffing will help to maximize the department's efficiency. Once the overall plan is operational, however, it is equally important to schedule each job precisely. This coordinates all activities such as labor, supervision, materials, equipment, and the method to be used in an appropriately convenient time. It is this coordinating function that assures that the plan of operation uses minimum work force and material, produces the least inconveniences, and results in minimum downtime.

*Estimating.* Several basic approaches can be used for estimating maintenance labor costs for any given job. The most common method is for supervisors to estimate the job based on their experience and knowledge. Another method is to analyze past experience as indicated in completed work orders; this is a historical approach based on past performance. Another common method is to use work sampling. Some companies use data based upon universal maintenance standards (UMS) or predetermined time measurements such as methods time measurements (MTM).

**Controlling Cost** Expenditures for maintenance are always subject to scrutiny since they are often the highest overhead item.

Management can utilize several tools to control its maintenance operation:

1. *The maintenance budget.* This is the most basic tool, and the allocation of funds through the budget procedure provides a positive control. The budget must be based on realistic company needs, however, which in turn should be based on the company's philosophy. If it becomes necessary to curtail expenditures during a budget period, an analysis should first be made of how these cuts will affect the total objective; otherwise, an across-the-board cut in appropriations can result in poor distribution of funds within a department, as well as loss of fundamental objectives and priorities.

2. *The work-order system.* This extremely important tool provides the foundation for control and analysis of all maintenance costs as well as a device for communicating information both horizontally and vertically. Approval for all work orders is the prime source of control. If a work order request does not fit into the objective and prevalent philosophy at the particular time, it can be denied. Once a work order is approved, requirements for material, labor, equipment, and supervision can be determined and priorities set. A good work-order system furnishes both the fiscal data and the necessary communications needed to fit maintenance activities into a company's total operational procedures.

3. *Industrial engineering techniques.* These include methods improvement, value engineering, work simplification, work measurement, and various cost control programs.

4. *Specifications and bidding procedures.* Administrators should evaluate and use appropriate specifications and bidding procedures to assure receipt of the best value for an expenditure. This includes continuing evaluation of the advantages and disadvantages of utilizing outside contractors versus in-plant personnel.

5. *Equipment and building records.* These records of cost, capability, care, and condition must be kept up to date in order to intelligently control the maintenance and replacement costs of individual pieces of equipment and buildings.

**Preventive Maintenance Programs** A company's philosophy determines the criteria used in establishing a *preventive maintenance* program. Management must first decide the extent to which the firm will be committed to a program that will (1) prevent premature failure and (2) reduce major production breakdown. Each category of buildings or equipment that is to be maintained should be analyzed. The cost of breakdown, the implication to the rest of production, safety, health, desired life expectancy of equipment, as well as the cost of repair or replacement, should be integral parts of these decisions.

The system itself involves maintenance aimed at preventing unpredicted breakdowns by systematically inspecting, adjusting, and lubricating and by scheduled repairs. Once installed, the program must be continually audited to ensure that the cost of the program is in line with the company's philosophy of replacement.

**Performance Evaluation** The tools to evaluate and measure the performance and quality of a maintenance department are as complex as the functions of the maintenance department are varied. One can find time standards for almost every maintenance task that is performed. These standards can be found in many maintenance handbooks and various trade publications. An excellent example of these labor standards can be found in the *Maintenance Engineering Handbook* by Higgins and Morrow (References). Administrators should measure these performances by using the objectives set by management. A criterion of performance must be part of a company's policy before effective evaluations can be made. Management must know what it wants, determine the level of performance desired, establish benchmarks, and then, at periodic intervals, measure achievement against objectives. Higher management should be concerned with the performance of the maintenance department as a whole. On the other hand, it is the responsibility of individual department heads, through their supervisors, to evaluate individual worker's performance. Realistic and specifically defined job descriptions that detail exact performance required should be established for each activity performed. It is especially helpful to prepare an evaluation sheet for each worker that charts his or her progress and is reviewed with the worker at specified intervals.

**Maintenance and the Community** Administrators caught in the continuous effort to justify expenditures and minimize cost often overlook the role that good housekeeping and a pleasing environment can play in establishing good company morale and community relations. It is difficult to measure the effect of a brightly painted wall or clean rest rooms on the overall plant performance, of course. There is no doubt, however, that an environment that encourages safety and promotes reasonable comfort will help reduce personnel turnover and improve employee morale. Moreover, attractive exterior appearances, including those of buildings and grounds, can sustain favorable community attitudes. This can also be enhanced when emphasis is placed through the maintenance department on such goals as water, air, and noise-pollution control, energy conservation, and preservation of natural resources.

*See also* FACILITIES AND SITE PLANNING AND LAYOUT; PLANT ENGINEERING MANAGEMENT; REAL ESTATE MANAGEMENT, CORPORATE; SAFETY AND HEALTH MANAGEMENT, EMPLOYEE.)

### REFERENCES

Cotz, V. J.: *Plant Engineer's Manual and Guide*, Prentice-Hall, Inc., Englewood Cliffs, N. J., 1973.

Cooling, W. Colebrook: *Low-Cost Maintenance Control*, American Management Association, New York, 1973.

Grothus, Horst: *Total Preventive Maintenance for Building Utilities*, Executive Enterprises Publications Co., Inc., New York, 1977.

Higgins, Lindley R., and L. C. Morrow, eds.: *Maintenance Engineering Handbook*, 3d ed., McGraw-Hill Book Company, New York, 1977.

Lewis, B. T., and J. P. Marron: *Facilities and Plant Engineering Handbook*, McGraw-Hill Book Company, New York, 1973.

Newbrough, E. T.: *Effective Maintenance Management*, McGraw-Hill Book Company, New York, 1967.

Staniar, W.: *Plant Engineering Handbook*, 2d ed., McGraw-Hill Book Company, New York, 1959.

SHELDON J. FUCHS, *Hofstra University*

## Make-or-buy decisions  (*See* PRODUCTION/ OPERATIONS MANAGEMENT.)

## Make ready  (*See* WORK SIMPLIFICATION AND IMPROVEMENT.)

# Management, definitions of

The most comprehensive definition views management as an integrating process by which authorized individuals create, maintain, and operate an organization in the selection and accomplishment of its aims. This basic concept has the advantage of denoting a process being carried out continuously over time. It includes the idea of a goal-oriented organization as the fundamental arena of managerial action, as well as the concept of persons specifically charged with managerial responsibility.

**Supporting Concepts** Other widely used definitions amplify the basic concept for use in practical settings:

1. *Management is getting things done through other people.* This definition stresses teamwork, delegation, and results.

2. *Management is partly an art and partly a science.* This definition recognizes the presence of intuitive, subjective skills in the management process and the growing importance of verified knowledge as a guide to managerial decision and action.

3. *Management is an academic and professional discipline.* This definition implies that a teachable body of knowledge is incorporated into the curricula of schools, colleges, and technical institutions. It includes the possibilities for the development of management as a profession.

4. *Management is a collective noun used to refer to the entire management group of an organization.* Used in this way, the term is convenient for designating a body of managers as a whole. For example, one may say, "the management of the Brown Corporation believes that. . . ."

5. *Management is the performance of the critical functions essential to the success of an organization.* This definition essentially holds that management *is* what managers *do* in performing their roles as managers.

The first four variations of the management concept listed above are limited in scope, partial in content, and handicapped by oversimplification. The fifth definition is the most fundamental. It will now be explained in greater detail.

Management can usefully be viewed as a network of interrelated functional responsibilities. They are not a sequence of activities but rather a set of interacting activities that constitute a whole. One can single out a particular function only for analytical or descriptive purposes, but it should be recognized that activity in one function has impact on one or more of the other functions.

The primary managerial functions are designated as planning, organizing, and controlling. Others include directing (leading), resourcing, activating, representing, coordinating, communicating, motivating, and, very important, decision making. Contributors to management knowledge do not agree on either the general or the relative importance of the various management functions. Some reject the functional approach on the grounds that the functions are only descriptive and are not precise enough for developing scientifically testable propositions. The concept of management, however, as a set of functional responsibilities performed by managers is an enduring one. Management scientists (operations researchers and decision theorists) stress decision making as the most important managerial function. Behavioral scientists focus on organization, organizational behavior, leadership, motivation, and communication. Other specialists in management utilize the traditional functions but draw upon management science and behavioral science contributors to extend and apply the functions.

The functions dramatize the differences between managerial and technical or other kinds of work. Planning, for example, is the manager's task because of the need to cope with change, but executing a plan to build a new plant also requires a grasp of technical elements such as layout, appearance, durability, and operating effectiveness. In almost every case, the manager's task is a mix of managerial (conceptual) behavior and the application of technical expertise. The higher the level of the manager, the greater is the proportion of managerial to technical content of the work.

**Variations** For practical purposes, the terms *management* and *administration* are used synonymously. The term *administration* is widely employed in associations and in governmental, service, and nonprofit organizations, whereas *management* is more often used in business firms.

The term *industrial management* connotes an industrial setting, such as manufacturing, mining, or construction.

The term *entrepreneurial management* describes a type of risk-taking management geared to the development of new business enterprises or highly diversified conglomerates.

**Management and Ownership** Business organizations are classified into three types according to their legal forms: (1) sole proprietorships, (2) partnerships, and (3) corporations. Management responsibilities and processes vary among the types.

In the sole proprietorship, the key manager is also likely to be the owner and execute the two roles simultaneously. In partnerships, the active partners are the key managers as well as the owners. Both proprietorships and partnerships are generally but not necessarily small firms, with the owners actively involved in the direct management of the organization.

The management group in a corporation functions in a *fiduciary* capacity—entrusted by owners with virtually complete responsibility for running the organization. Many corporation managers are also owners by virtue of holding shares of their company's stock, but their role remains essentially that of a managerial employee of the company.

*See also* ADMINISTRATIVE MANAGEMENT; AUDIT, MANAGEMENT; BOARDS OF DIRECTORS; COMMITTEES; MANAGEMENT THEORY, SCIENCE, AND APPROACHES; MANAGER, DEFINITIONS OF; NOT-FOR-PROFIT ORGANIZATIONS, MANAGEMENT OF; OFFICERS, CORPORATE; OWNERSHIP, LEGAL FORMS OF; PUBLIC ADMINISTRATION.

### REFERENCES

Davis, Ralph D.: *The Fundamentals of Top Management*, Harper & Row, Publishers, Incorporated, New York, 1951.

Koontz, Harold, and Cyril O'Donnell: *Management: A Systems and Contingency Analysis of the Managerial Functions*, 6th ed., McGraw-Hill Book Company, New York, 1976.

Lindemann, A. J., Earl F. Lundgren, and H. K. Von Kaas: *Encyclopaedic Dictionary of Management and Manufacturing Terms*, 2d ed., Kendall/Hunt Publishing Company, Dubuque, Iowa, 1974.

McFarland, Dalton E.: *Management: Principles and Practices*, 5th ed., The Macmillan Company, New York, 1979.

DALTON E. MCFARLAND, *University of Alabama in Birmingham*

# Management, future of

What will be the nature of the prevailing society and economy during the next decade? What management style and process will enable business institutions to survive and prosper? How should managers manage multinational and domestic business organizations through the 1980s so as to grasp opportunities, cope with problems, and meet the challenges that lie ahead? Managers will be engaged in the management of essential institutions in the future. Managers can predict with certainty that the future eventually will involve them. The pertinent question in the present is whether or not practicing and potential managers are preparing for the changing social, economic, political, and technological environments that are emerging as the 1980s approach.

An identification and analysis of the trends and forces in the managerial environment indicate that the United States may be involved in a periodic transformation in Western Civilization. Discernible signals in the post-industrial society point toward implications for the managers who will be responsible for the conduct of business enterprises. The practice of management in the next decade is being shaped by

1. The impact of social priorities and concerns on the objectives of business institutions.

2. The emergence of public-oriented managers who accept greater public responsibilities for private enterprises than professional managers or owner managers do.

3. The changing concept of the practice of management from a system of authority to management as a resource in society.

**Emerging Social Values and Objectives** The June 1971 statement by the Research and Policy Committee of the Committee for Economic Development entitled *"Social Responsibilities of Business Corporations"* is an indication of the concern for social priorities. The business leaders who formulated the policy statement wrote as follows:

There is now a pervasive feeling in the country that the social order somehow has gotten out of balance, and that greater affluence amid a deteriorating environment and community life does not make much sense.

The discontinuity between what we have accomplished as producers and consumers and what we want in the way of a good society has engendered strong social pressures to close the gap—to improve the way the overall American system is working so that a better quality of life can be achieved by the entire citizenry within a well-functioning community. The goals include:

Elimination of poverty and provision for good health care.

Equal opportunity for each person to realize his or her full potential regardless of race, sex, or creed.

Education and training for a fully productive and rewarding participation in modern society.

Ample jobs and career opportunities in all parts of society.

Livable communities with decent housing, safe streets, a clean and pleasant environment, efficient transportation, good cultural and educational opportunities, and a prevailing mood of civility among people.

This policy statement of the Committee for Economic Development presents the concept of a social philosophy that reflects prevailing social values and priorities. Inasmuch as business firms are expected to serve a wider range of human values and to contribute more to the quality of life than providing goods, services, and employment, the future role of private enterprise will depend upon the response of corporate managers to the changing values and anticipations of the producers and consumers.

**American Economic System** During the past century, owner managers and professional managers have operated business institutions to create wealth by the efficient production of goods and services. Wealth is the product of creative and imaginative economic processes. The American economic system is unchallenged as the best system in all history for the creation of wealth. The economic miracle of a trillion-dollar economy, as measured by gross national product and personal income, was achieved by American managers early in the 1970s. Employment levels, production, income, and spending—most of the economic indicators—were at historical high points. American managers were operating business firms as economic institutions and enjoying pinnacle performance. At a time of unprecedented economic success, however, signals of dissatisfaction appeared among the citizens. Instead of receiving appreciation for their brilliant economic performance, managers of business enterprises were served with an array of social problems:

1. Inflation and monetary devaluation

2. Rise of youth culture and a questioning of traditional values in society

3. Criticism of traditional institutions

4. Concern about poor quality of products and poor quality of work

5. Deterioration of the physical environment and mounting environmental concern

6. Cost of energy requirements

7. Dissatisfaction with the distribution of income

8. Concern about equal employment opportunities for minority workers and women

9. Dissatisfaction with work assignments and management styles

10. Disregard for law, order, and authority

11. Undesirable urban spread

12. Criticism of business institutions and business leadership

During this century, the managers who conducted the affairs of business firms as economic institutions contributed to increased prosperity for millions of workers and citizens. Yet dissatisfactions appeared with the economic values and priorities associated with business institutions. Never before in history had so relatively few people generated so much wealth and income with so much dissatisfaction caused by the prevailing attitudes, values, policies, institutions, and managerial styles and leadership.

**The People Variable**  Anticipating the future or analyzing the past requires an understanding of the changing value systems and priorities of people. Wealth, income, land, and property are inanimate. They are the factors in any situation that are dependent on how people value them and use them.

In the preconstitution period of development in what was to become the United States of America, the people were concerned with and motivated by their quest for religious freedom and their dissatisfaction with religious oppression. *Religious-oriented managers* established a foundation for religious freedom to support the desired life-style of the era. A foundation was prepared for future ethical considerations in the institutions to come. A viable religious philosophy was created to guide the destiny of the nation.

Subsequently, *politically oriented managers* embraced a new set of priorities and values. They were dissatisfied with the oppression of the monarchy and the crown of England. They were successful during the 1760-to-1860 period in attaining political freedom from England, Spain, and Mexico so as to live a life-style unfettered by political oppression. They created a political philosophy on the foundation of their religious philosophy which evolved as the Declaration of Independence and the Constitution.

Following the Civil War during the period that extended to the 1960s, *economic-oriented managers* came to the front in quest of wealth, income, land, and property. Economic managers were guided and motivated by an economic philosophy that (1) emphasized the importance of the individual, (2) considered property an extension of the individual and a source of economic and political legitimate authority, (3) permitted competition to determine the status of individuals and organizations, (4) placed government in a limited support role for competition in the marketplace, and (5) advocated specialization by individuals along channels of superior competency. It was assumed that proper attention to the parts of an economic system would result in the success of the whole system.

On the established foundations of the religious managers and political managers, economic managers have been successful in building the greatest industrial society in the world to decrease poverty by generating wealth and prosperity. The success in managing business firms as economic institutions has agitated dissatisfactions and generated several movements that are starting a state of transition or transformation in our post-industrial society, such as (1) the egalitarian movement with emphasis on equality of results; (2) the ecology movement for the preservation of natural resources; (3) the consumer movement that demands safety, quality, and performance of products; (4) the youth movement that seeks quality of life-style and participation in correcting economic ills; (5) the civil rights movement and the women's liberation movement to assure rights that have been denied in the past; and (6) the limits-to-growth or small-is-beautiful movement.

**Management of the Business Corporation as a Social Institution**  The American economic system is on a collision course with a developing social system that is characterized by a new and changing value system that will result in a period of transition for the mission of private enterprise.

*Impact of Social Values.*  Business has been considered and accepted as a dominant economic institution in society. Business may already be a dominant social institution, with social objectives pursued jointly with economic and political objectives. Prevailing social values merging with economic values are modifying old assumptions. New concepts of individual rights, private property, standards of business conduct, and social responsibilities, along with new attitudes toward growth and progress are establishing a different and more challenging environment for the management of business in the next decade.

*Impact of External Forces.*  Management of the future will be shaped by increasing external forces. Already managers of business organizations are guided and controlled by legislation that regulates most phases of business activities. Business-government relationships are approaching a state of symbiosis that is caused by the movements stemming from social forces and trends in society. For survival, future managers must learn to manage both the internal and external affairs of business institutions.

**Evolution of Public-Oriented Managers**  A new generation of managers is emerging to shape the future conduct of business and industrial enterprises. Public-oriented managers are developing a management style somewhat different from the characteristic practices of the owner managers and the highly successful professional managers. Public-oriented managers are advancing from (1) the professional manager positions of hired managers for shareholders to (2) positions of institutional leadership in behalf of multiple claimants on the outputs of their firms.

Public-oriented managers are maintaining the economic objective of business firms. They give primary emphasis to the economic interests of the owners of invested capital. In addition, though, they add objectives in the interests of employees, customers, and society in general. Corporate objectives are stated in both economic and social areas to satisfy both the economic and social demands of the economy in transition.

Typical of the stated corporate objectives of leading business institutions are these:

Aluminum Company of America, as a broadly owned multinational company, is committed to four fundamental objectives, all of which are essential to its long-term success. Alcoa intends to excel in all of these:
    Provide shareholders a return superior to that available from other investments of equal risk, based on reliable long-term growth in earnings per share.
    Provide for employees a rewarding and challenging employment environment with opportunity for economic and personal growth.
    Provide worldwide customers with products and services of quality.
    Direct its skills and resources to help solve the major problems of the societies and communities of which it is a part, while providing these societies with the benefits of its other fundamental objectives.

Public-oriented managers will be faced with the major responsibility of merging human values with the potential from technological advances to conserve human energy in the creation and distribution of goods and services for improved life-styles.

**Private and Public Responsibilities** No large business organization, whatever its formal ownership, will be able to escape social and public responsibilities. The environmental factors and forces at work, such as changing human priorities along with the growing size and complexity of organizational patterns, are blurring the traditional lines between what is private and what is public.

The future managers of private enterprise—profit or nonprofit—will gravitate toward the concept that they are responsible for people in general and will (although reluctantly) accept the government as a monitor of business affairs. Large complex business organizations, domestic and multinational, will operate under federal charters. The public-oriented managers will be guided by ethical codes of world-wide business conduct. Concurrently, the government will contract to the private enterprise firms a growing portion of public business because the public-oriented managers will be better-qualified managers in the public interest. A Public Management Commission may be created to assure the education and training of qualified managers who will serve the public interest with employment opportunities and the goods and services required for a growing population.

**Changing Concepts of Management** The managers in the 1980s will manage for desired results or predetermined multiple objectives within highly complex organizations laced together with effective information and communication systems. The organizational system will change from the hierarchical pyramid with its centralized decisions and most of the planning and control at the apex of the pyramid. Instead, the managers will design organizational mechanisms for achievement of objectives that will involve systems with interacting webs of tension caused by loose control of performance processes for desired results.

Power will be more diffused, with decisions decentralized through plural centers for decision making. As business organizations become more horizontal than vertical (through interacting systems), the style for managing them will become more collegial and consultive. The bigger the results to be accomplished and the more difficult the problems to be solved, the more authority and power will be diffused so that a larger number of capable people can work on the problems and objectives.

**Management as a Resource** The trend in management style is toward more informal, fluid work-ways of bargaining, brokerage, advice, and consent. Management will be practiced less as a system of authority in a vertical pyramid-type organization and more as a resource in a systems-type horizontal organization to achieve the satisfactions demanded by multiple claimants. The concepts and use of authority will be modified by the public-oriented manager in response to the increasing numbers of better-educated employees and the size and complexity of organizations. *The legitimacy of authority and management is in transition from ownership of capital and property to ownership of the benefits flowing from business organizations.* The concept of authority as the power to order or command subordinates is being modified by the qualification that obedience to authority can be expected only if those being ordered or directed can expect a satisfying result.

Managers in the future will realize that employees will be more inclined to accept authority from agreed-upon objectives and the nature of the work than from the dictation of an authoritarian boss. More than one mode of thinking can be utilized. The future managers will be dependent on the knowledge and skills of subordinates. They will be multipliers of the work of employees for mutual results rather than trying to manage activities or processes.

**Results Management Over Activities Management** The trend in management practice is to consider management as a resource for results achievement and not as an authoritarian manager operating from the apex of an organizational authority pyramid to control performance processes. The trend is toward an approach that has several descriptive names such as results management, goal-oriented supervision, or goal-setting for performance appraisal. Managers are oriented around *proacting* for future results instead of *reacting* to events and forces in the competitive situation.

Multiple management resources will be employed to determine first the strategic or long-range objectives and then the operational or short-range objectives of an enterprise. Objectives of the total organizational system will be translated into specific, quantifiable, realistic objectives for each subsystem or organizational unit. Employees will work to achieve definitive and satisfying results instead of following routine duties and procedures.

**Expectations for Future Managers** Managers in the future will be expected to create wealth, generate profits, and provide employment to produce goods and services for an expanding society in fulfillment of the public policy outlined in the Employment Act of 1946. Furthermore, they will be expected to utilize the human resources of the nation in accordance with the spirit of equal economic opportunity, civil rights, and the egalitarian quest for equality of human rights. Managers will also be expected to adhere to the clean-air and clean-water guidelines of the Environmental Protection Agency in compliance with the Occupational Health and Safety Act. A priority challenge for management in the 1980s will be to provide employment for an additional 2 million workers each year in a society that is developing into a nation of employees.

*See also* EGALITARIANISM; ETHICS, MANAGERIAL; MANAGEMENT, DEFINITIONS OF; MANAGEMENT, HISTORICAL DEVELOPMENT OF; MANAGEMENT THEORY, SCIENCE, AND APPROACHES; MANAGER, DEFINITIONS OF; SOCIAL RESPONSIBILITY OF BUSINESS; VALUE SYSTEMS, MANAGEMENT.

### REFERENCES

*Facts about Alcoa*, Aluminum Company of America, 1501 Alcoa Building, Pittsburgh, Pa., 15219, September 1974.

Mee, John F.: "Changing Concepts of Management," *Advanced Management Journal*, American Management Association, New York, October 1972.

———: "Debut of the Public Oriented Executive," *The Business Quarterly*, School of Business Administration, University of Western Ontario, London, Canada, Autumn 1975.

———: *Perspectives for the Future Manager and His Environment*, Committee for Future Studies, Indiana University, Bloomington, 1975.

*Social Responsibilities of Business Corporations*, Research and Policy Committee, Committee for Economic Development, 477 Madison Avenue, New York, N.Y., 10022, 1971.

JOHN F. MEE, *Indiana University*

# Management, historical development of

An awareness of the importance of management skills dates back beyond the beginning of written history. Most historians, however, generally mark the last two decades of the nineteenth century as the beginning of a recognized attempt to investigate systematically the development of basic management principles. This interest paralleled the growing economic and industrial development of the United States and Western Europe as major manufacturing centers. The forces of expanding technology and commerce, paired with new advances in transportation and communication, dramatically increased the scope and complexity of business undertakings. An unprecedented increase in the size of factories resulted in previously unexperienced problems of waste and inefficiency. These changes necessitated the formulation and investigation of new concepts regarding the scientific management of work.

The event most often referenced as the beginning of the search for a rational and systematic science of management came in 1886 with the presentation of a paper by Henry R. Towne, president of the Yale and Towne Manufacturing Company, on "The Engineer as Economist." His comments, delivered at a meeting of the American Society of Mechanical Engineers (ASME), stressed the importance of management as a field of independent study, equal to that of engineering. Noting the almost complete absence of management literature and the total lack of management associations, Towne urged that the ASME serve as a center for the development of an understanding of industrial management.

**Birth of Scientific Management** While Towne's presentation is recognized as marking the beginning of the search for a science of management, the birth of the scientific management movement is generally accredited to Frederick W. Taylor. His book, *The Principles of Scientific Management*, published in 1911, seriously questioned the traditional role of management. Synthesizing and refining the ideas and concepts developed in his earlier writings and experiments, Taylor envisioned a "mental revolution" whereby the concerns of both management and the worker would be based on a philosophy of "mutuality of interests." He conceived of management's new duties as involving (1) the development of a true science of managing, complete with clearly stated laws, rules, and principles to replace old rule-of-thumb methods; (2) the scientific selection, training, and development of workers; whereas in the past workers were randomly chosen and often untrained; (3) enthusiastic cooperation with workers to ensure that all work performed is done in accordance with scientific principles; and (4) the equal division of tasks and responsibilities between the worker and management.

Although the groundwork of Taylor's philosophy had been laid several years earlier, it was not until late 1910 that it began to receive widespread publicity. It was at this time that the Eastern railroads were seeking an increase in their freight rates to offset recent wage increases. Louis D. Brandeis, representing the opposing freight shippers, brought together a group of engineers in an attempt to have them agree upon a title to designate the principles and philosophy of Taylor's work. The term *scientific management* is said to have originated at this meeting.

As principal attorney for the freight shippers, it was Brandeis' strategy to prove by expert testimony that the railroads, by adopting the methods of scientific management, could not only considerably reduce their costs but could even further increase wages without increasing their rates. To this end, Brandeis presented a parade of expert witnesses, including Henry R. Towne, Henry L. Gantt, Frank B. Gilbreth, and Harrington Emerson. The high point of the hearings was reached with Emerson's testimony that the railroads could save at least a million dollars a day through the application of scientific management. Such testimony had a great appeal to the American press. The resulting widespread publicity served to provide the attention and support scientific management had previously lacked.

**Early Contributors** Paralleling the work of Taylor, numerous other early pioneers contributed to the emergence and development of management thought. Henry L. Gantt's major contributions included the task and bonus pay plan, the Gantt Chart

for production planning and control, and an early understanding of leadership theory. The most popular books of Gantt, a close associate of Taylor, were *Work, Wages, and Profits* (1910), *Industrial Leadership* (1916), and *Organizing for Work* (1919). His writings are characterized by a basic recognition of the human factor in industry and by his belief that workers should be provided with the means to find in their jobs a source of both income and pleasure. It was Gantt's belief that this ideal could only be achieved by providing each worker a task, with a bonus to be awarded for its accomplishment.

Although influenced by Taylor, Harrington Emerson worked independently as an early efficiency expert. His major contributions to the field of management are embodied in two books, *Efficiency as a Basis for Operation and Wages* (1911) and *The Twelve Principles of Efficiency* (1913). The main thrust of his efforts was aimed at the elimination of waste and the creation of wealth. He presented his "principles of efficiency" as forming an interdependent and coordinated management system. Emerson made a contribution to the early development of management by identifying and describing its activities. In 1912, Emerson helped found The Efficiency Society of New York City, and in 1933 he helped form the Association of Consulting Management Engineers.

The work of Frank B. and Lillian M. Gilbreth is significant for several reasons. Through their efforts, they created an understanding of motion study and the significance of increasing output by reducing effort. Perhaps more significantly, however, their work emphasized the importance of the relationship between management and the social sciences. Frank Gilbreth was primarily interested in the new field of motion study. His book *Motion Study* was published in 1911, followed by *Applied Motion Study* in 1917. He devised a system for classifying the motions of the hand into 17 basic divisions called *therbligs* ("Gilbreth" spelled backward with the *th* transposed). Lillian, his wife, a psychologist by training, pioneered in the new field of industrial psychology. Her book *The Psychology of Management*, published in 1916, is one of the most significant early contributions to the study of the human factor in industry.

**Through the Mid 1920s** As outlined by Mee, the period from 1910 through the mid 1920s witnessed the full blossoming of the management movement. During this period, some of the more significant events to occur were:[1]

1. Scientific management was recognized as a respectable university discipline. Courses in the

"new" management movement were offered at institutions such as Columbia University, Cornell University, Pennsylvania State University, and the Massachusetts Institute of Technology.

2. The first formal assembly on management, a gathering of some 300 educators, businessmen, and consultants, was called in 1911 at the Amos Tuck School of Administration and Finance at Dartmouth College. The proceedings of this meeting served to outline possible future courses of action for management thinking within the United States, and are considered by many historians as somewhat of a "charter" for the fledgling management movement.

3. The first professional management association came into being in 1914 with the founding of the Society to Promote the Science of Management. It was reestablished as the Taylor Society in 1916 and in 1930 evolved into the present Society for Advancement of Management. The National Industrial Conference Board was started in 1916, followed by organizations such as the American Management Association in 1923.

4. The first management textbooks began appearing as early as 1910. Hugo Diemer's *Factory Organization and Administration* (1910) was followed by volumes such as John C. Duncan's *The Principles of Industrial Management* (1911) and Dexter S. Kimball's *Principles of Industrial Organization* (1913).

5. Writing in 1916, Frenchman Henri Fayol was the first writer to classify the study of management into functional areas—such as planning, organizing, commanding, coordinating, and controlling. Unfortunately, Fayol's major contribution to management literature, *Administration industrielle et générale*, was not translated into English until 1930 and not widely distributed until a second English translation appeared in 1949.

6. In 1915, Horace B. Drury completed the first doctoral dissertation in management at Columbia University. It was entitled, "Scientific Management: A History and Criticism."

7. The first textbooks dealing with the topic of industrial psychology began to appear. Prominent early volumes included Walter Dill Scott's *Increasing Human Efficiency in Business* (1911), Hugo Munsterberg's *Psychology and Industrial Efficiency* (1913), and Lillian M. Gilbreth's *Psychology of Management* (1916).

8. The first journals and magazines devoted largely to management and industrial psychology began to appear. Periodicals with titles such as *Management and Administration*, *Factory and Industrial Management*, and *Journal of Applied Psychology* steadily grew in number.

**Hawthorne Studies** One of the most outstanding milestones in the historical development of management was passed in connection with a study launched in 1924 at the Hawthorne Plant of the Western Electric Company located near Cicero, Illinois. The study spanned a 12-year period. Initiated in collaboration with the National Research Council of the National Academy of Sciences, its original intent was to investigate the relationship between illumination and worker productivity. It had been hypothesized that as illumination was increased, productivity would increase. The researchers systematically varied and recorded the level of illumination within the study's test room, fully anticipating individual efficiency to vary directly with light intensity. The study's results, however, demonstrated no such pattern. Rather, individual output increased continually throughout the entire experiment without regard to level of illumination. While it seemed clear at this point that no predictable relationship existed between productivity and light intensity, it was entirely unclear why productivity increased throughout the study's duration.

*Phase 2.* The inconclusiveness of the illumination experiments stimulated additional research at the Hawthorne Plant. In 1927, Elton Mayo and Fritz J. Roethlisberger were asked to lead a group of researchers from the Harvard Business School to explore further the unanticipated worker reactions earlier encountered. The thrust of their efforts was designed to determine the effects of working conditions such as rest breaks and workday length on employee productivity. This phase of the experiment, known as the *relay-assembly test room study*, lasted 5 years. Like the illumination experiment, it also developed in quite an unexpected way. A test room was established, and six workers (five relay assemblers and a layout operator) were selected to participate in the experiment. In an effort to control test conditions more closely, careful measurements were made of variables such as the worker's blood pressure and vascular skin reaction, as well as factors such as the humidity and temperature of the test room. Throughout the first 2 years of the study, the length and frequency of rest pauses and the length of the workday and workweek were continually changed. Seemingly, however, without regard to experimental variation, just as in the illumination experiment, general productivity steadily increased. These results strongly suggested to the researchers that something a great deal more potent than test conditions had served to influence the productivity of the relay assemblers. Only in retrospect, however, were they able to determine that it was not test conditions but rather improved morale, a changed supervisory style, less worker control, and improved interpersonal relations that accounted for the largest portion of the increase in output. In both the illumination and relay-assembly test room experiments the workers were isolated from the regular factory floor in special test areas. Throughout the relay-assembly test room experiment, the workers assumed an increasing share of their own supervision. This resulted in a supervisory style that was less restrictive and more friendly. The change in supervisory style was accompanied by less-stringent control, with the relay-assemblers actually participating in decisions affecting their jobs. This change in orientation has since given rise to the concept of the *Hawthorne effect*, meaning essentially that the experimenters may have biased the outcome of the study through their own personal presence and the simple novelty of their efforts. Additional factors believed by the researchers to contribute to the increased output of the relay-assemblers were the formation of a cohesive group structure that stressed loyalty and cooperation and the general high morale that accompanied the entire experiment. The relay-assemblers enjoyed and drew a great deal of intrinsic satisfaction from the special roles they occupied in the study.

*Phase 3.* The final phase of the Hawthorne studies has become known as the *bank wiring observation* experiment. It essentially involved an analysis of spontaneous, informal social group behavior. An attempt was made to investigate the activities of a group of nine employees engaged in wiring switchboard equipment to determine the extent to which individual employee behavior was controlled by social groups that existed within each department. It was clear to the investigators from their early reports that several closely related phenomena were being encountered. In particular, it appeared that the group wage-incentive plan, in effect for the department, was being rendered ineffectual by collaborative group pressure to control output. The workers had established their own conception of a fair day's work and prevailed as a group upon one another not to exceed this predetermined level of output. In line with the behavior norms of the informal group, workers who exceeded the agreed-upon rate were known as "rate busters." Those workers whose production fell below the standard set by the group were known as "rate chiselers." The informal group enforced its norms of conduct through subtle forms of ridicule, sarcasm, and what came to be known as "binging." *Binging* was a practice in which a group member expressed displeasure with the actions of a coworker by hitting

the coworker as hard as possible on the upper arm. In short, the researchers had been previously unaware of the implications of informal group behavior on management practices. The bank wiring observation experiment highlighted the significance of the informal group as a powerful organizational force.

The outcomes of the Hawthorne experiments carried with them numerous important implications for the field of management. They stressed the importance of viewing the human element of an organization as part of a larger social system. They emphasized that the needs of employees are *both* physical and social in nature. They also underscored the existence of the informal social group as a natural outgrowth of the behavior patterns inherent in the formal structure of an organization.

In brief, the Hawthorne experiments, by emphasizing a new interpretation of work group behavior, ushered in the beginning of what was later to be known as the field of *human relations*.

**Mid 1930s**  By the mid 1930s, a change in the fundamental thinking of management, as expressed in the literature of the period, began to develop. Compared with the preceeding three decades, a more-mature philosophy of management had begun to emerge. Volumes such as Ordway Tead's *The Art of Leadership* (1935), Chester I. Barnard's *The Functions of the Executive* (1938), Charles P. McCormick's *Multiple Management* (1938), and Mary P. Follett's *Dynamic Administration* (1940) introduced concepts that replaced earlier, narrower themes and established the field of management within the total social framework of society in general.

**The 1940s Through Early 1950s**  The period of World War II and its aftermath may perhaps be best characterized by a refinement of known principles and techniques and a focus on the activities of top management.

One of the first empirical studies in the area of top management was released in 1941 by Paul Holden, Lounsbург S. Fish, and Hubert L. Smith. Published under the title *Top-Management Organization and Control*, the study reported the general management practices of 31 industrial corporations. Based on their findings, the authors concluded that the primary responsibilities of top management involved: (1) Long-range planning and the clear establishment of objectives; (2) the establishment of a sound organization structure; (3) the skillful training and development of all personnel; and (4) the establishment of effective control procedures. The significance of this conclusion lies in the fact that these are basically the same functions identified pragmatically by early writers such as Fayol. The Holden, Fish, and Smith study thus served to provide support for many earlier management theories that had been deduced through experience rather than through systematic research and experimentation.

Reflecting a broadening base of influence, significant contributions of this period included Burleigh B. Gardner's *Human Relations in Industry* (1945). Gardner, a veteran of 5-years experience as a director of employee relations research at the Hawthorne Plant of the Western Electric Company, drew upon his exposure to the ideas developed by Roethlisberger and Mayo to present a systematic discussion of the human element in industry. Published in 1947, Herbert A. Simon's *Administrative Behavior* represented a pioneering study of the basic concepts and framework of decision making as an organization process. Simon's work provided a foundation for the popularization of the quantitative techniques of the coming decade. Two additional books of this period that have enjoyed an enduring respect are Ralph C. Davis' *The Fundamentals of Top Management* (1951) and Peter F. Drucker's *The Practice of Management* (1954). The common objective of both Davis and Drucker was to present a general statement of business objectives and practices as they related to the basic business problems encountered by the practicing manager. It was in *The Practice of Management* that Drucker first introduced the widely accepted concept of *management by objectives*.

**Mid 1950s**  The mid 1950s gave rise to a tremendous increase in the number of books and periodicals devoted to the field of management. The trend in the development of management thought was reflected by the spreading multidisciplinary roots of study that initially began to spread in the late 1930s and in the years following World War II. *On one front*, the seeds of the Hawthorne experiments continued to grow as anthropologists, psychologists, and sociologists expressed a continuing interest in applying the tools of the behavioral sciences to management. Significant works of this period include William F. Whyte's *Money and Motivation* (1956), Reinhard Bendix's *Work and Authority in Industry* (1956), William H. Whyte, Jr.'s *The Organization Man* (1956), Chris Argyris' *Personality and Organization* (1957), Harold J. Leavitt's *Managerial Psychology* (1958), and James G. March and Herbert A. Simon's *Organizations* (1958).

*In a second direction*, management theory continued to evolve from an emphasis on general theory to a greater stress on the development of management principles. The emergence of the first principles-of-management textbooks in the first half of the 1950s is a reflection of this trend, William H. Newman's *Administrative Action* was published in 1951, George R. Terry's *Principles of Management* in 1953, and

Harold Koontz and Cyril O'Donnell's *Principles of Management: An Analysis of Managerial Functions* in 1955.

*A third direction* of growth was in the areas of management science and operations research. Building on advanced solutions to World War II operational problems in logistics and tactics, as well as on the theories of John von Neumann and Oskar Morgenstern (*Theory of Games and Economic Behavior*, 1944) and Norbert Wiener (*Cybernetics*, 1948), the areas of operations research and management science formally emerged in the early 1950s. Pioneer volumes in these areas include Phillip M. Morse and George E. Kimball's *Methods of Operations Research* (1951) and Joseph F. McCloskey and Florence N. Trefethen's *Operations Research for Management* (1954). *Operations Research*, the official journal for the Operations Research Society of America, was first published in 1953. *Management Science*, the journal of The Institute for Management Sciences, began publication in 1954.

**The 1960s**  As the 1960s unfolded, the various management thought streams that had developed in the preceeding 60-odd years began to converge slowly. The quantitative techniques which developed within the areas of management science and operations research contributed conceptual methods that were employed by a steady stream of social scientists conducting research into areas such as motivation, leadership, and group behavior. The work of researchers such as Douglas McGregor in the development of theories X and Y (*The Human Side of Enterprise*, 1960), Frederick Herzberg in the development of the motivation-hygiene theory, (*Work and the Nature of Man*, 1960), Rensis Likert in the differentiation of employee-centeredness and production-centeredness (*New Patterns of Management*, 1961, and *The Human Organization*, 1967), Victor Vroom in the development of the expectancy theory of motivation (*Work and Motivation*, 1964), and Fred Fiedler in the development of the leadership contingency model (*A Theory of Leadership Effectiveness*, 1967) particularly stand out. It is perhaps impossible to place these more-recent contributions into a clear perspective without the benefit of a greater lapse in time. Unknowingly, they may perhaps represent another shift in the continual evolution of management history.

*See also* MANAGEMENT, FUTURE OF; MANAGEMENT THEORY, SCIENCE, AND APPROACHES.

NOTE

[1]John F. Mee, *Management Thought in a Dynamic Economy*, New York University Press, New York, 1963.

**649**

## REFERENCES

George, Claude S., J.: *The History of Management Thought*, 2d ed., Prentice-Hall, Inc., Englewood Cliffs, N.J., 1972.

Mee, John F.: "A History of Twentieth Century Management," unpublished Ph.D. dissertation, Ohio State University, Columbus, Ohio, 1959.

Merrill, Harwood F.: *Classics in Management*, American Management Association, New York, 1960.

Pollard, Harold R.: *Developments in Management Thought*, Crane, Russak, Inc., New York, 1974.

Tillett, Anthony D., Thomas Kempner, and Gordon Wills, eds.: *Management Thinkers*, Penguin Books, Inc., Baltimore, 1970.

Wren, Daniel A.: *The Evolution of Management Thought*, The Ronald Press Company, New York, 1972.

ARTHUR G. BEDEIAN, *Auburn University*

## Management, of sales (*See* SALES MANAGEMENT.)

## Management, of small businesses (*See* SMALL BUSINESS ADMINISTRATION.)

## Management, strategic (*See* PLANNING, PLANNED MANAGEMENT OF TURBULENT CHANGE.)

## Management by anticipation [*See* OBJECTIVES, MANAGEMENT BY (MBO).]

## Management by commitment [*See* OBJECTIVES, MANAGEMENT BY (MBO).]

## Management by objectives [*See* OBJECTIVES, MANAGEMENT BY (MBO).]

## Management concepts and definitions (*See heading in Table of Contents for complete listing.*)

## Management consultants (*See* CONSULTANTS, MANAGEMENT.)

## Management development (*See* DEVELOPMENT AND TRAINING, MANAGEMENT.)

## Management information systems (MIS) [*See* INFORMATION SYSTEMS, MANAGEMENT (MIS); INFORMATION SYSTEMS, MANAGEMENT (MIS), APPLIED; INFORMATION SYSTEMS, MANAGEMENT (MIS), IN LARGE ORGANIZATIONS.]

## Management of marketing (*See* MARKETING MANAGEMENT.)

## Management process (*See* MANAGEMENT THEORY SCIENCE, AND APPROACHES.)

## Management science (*See* MANAGEMENT THEORY, SCIENCE, AND APPROACHES.)

## Management theory, science, and approaches

There may be no more important kind of human activity than managing. It is the basic task of all managers at all levels and in all kinds of enterprises to design and maintain an environment in which individuals, working together in groups, can accomplish preselected missions and objectives. In other words, managers are charged with the responsibility of doing those things which make it possible for individuals to contribute most effectively to attainment of group objectives.

In establishing this environment for group effort, the goal of all managers must logically and morally be conservation. In other words, whether managers are in a business or nonbusiness enterprise, whether they are presidents or supervisors, their principal task is to manage in such a way as (1) to accomplish objectives with a minimum input of money, materials, effort, time, or human dissatisfactions or (2) to accomplish as much of a mission or objective as possible with the available resources. Managers do so, of course, while being responsive to their entire external environment—economic, technological, political, social, and ethical. The purpose of an enterprise or department may vary, and these purposes may be more difficult to define in one situation than in another, but the basic managerial goal is the same.

In an activity as important and universal as management, the nature of the basic knowledge—concepts, theory, and techniques—underlying its practice holds tremendous significance for managers, for those being managed, and indeed, for the entire society.

## MANAGEMENT AS ART, SCIENCE, AND THEORY

In managing, as in any other field, unless practitioners are to learn only through trial and error, there is no other place they can turn to for meaningful guidance than the accumulated knowledge underlying their practice. Yet, in managing, much confusion remains about the nature of managerial knowledge. Questions are often raised whether management is a science or an art, what theory exists, and in what way it can be useful to managers, how technology fits into theory and science, and why there are so many schools or approaches to management theory and knowledge. What can managers believe, and how can this belief be useful to them?

**Both Art and Science** While these questions are often raised, a moment' reflection will indicate that they are really rather meaningless. Managing, like all other practices, is an art. It is know-how. It is doing things in the light of the realities of a situation. But the practice of managing must make use of underlying organized knowledge; and it is *this* knowledge, whether crude or advanced, whether exact or inexact, which, to the extent it is well organized, clear, and pertinent, constitutes a science. Thus, managing as practice is art; the organized knowledge underlying it may be referred to as science. Consequently, science and art are not mutually exclusive; they are complimentary.

As science improves, so should art, as has happened in the physical and biological sciences. To be sure, the science underlying managing is fairly crude and inexact. This is true partly because the multitude of variables which managers deal with are extremely complex and partly because relatively little research and development have been done in the field of management. But such management knowledge as is available can certainly be used to improve managerial practice. Physicians without the advantage of science would be little more than witch doctors. Executives who attempt to manage without such management science as is available today must trust to luck, intuition, or what they did in the past.

**Science and Theory** Science is organized knowledge. The essential feature of any science is that knowledge has been systematized through the application of the scientific method. Thus, the science of astronomy or chemistry, for example, involves clear concepts, theory, and other accumulated knowledge developed from hypotheses, experimentation, and analysis.

Scientific methods first require clarity of concepts. The meanings of words and terms must be clear, relevant to the phenomenon being analyzed, and meaningful to the scientist and practitioner alike. From this base, scientific method involves (1) determining facts through observation of events and verifying these facts through continued observation; (2) classifying and analyzing these facts; (3) identifying casual relationships which are believed to be true; and (4) testing these generalizations for accuracy and truth. When these generalizations appear to reflect or explain reality, and therefore to have value in predicting what will happen in similar circumstances, they are called *principles*. This does not always imply that these principles are unquestionably or invariably true; but it does imply that they are valid enough to be used for prediction.

Theory is a systematic grouping of interdependent concepts and principles which provides a framework or ties together a significant area of knowledge.

**Role of Management Theory** In the field of management, the role of theory is to provide a means of classifying significant and pertinent management knowledge. In the area of designing an effective organization structure, for example, a number of related principles are also dependent and have a predictive value for managers. There are principles, for example, that provide guidelines for delegating authority: delegating by results expected; the coincidence of authority and responsibility and the unity of command. Likewise, to comprehend the task of managerial planning, theory will disclose that decision making must be related to objectives sought, must be made in the light of the expected environment in which the decision will operate, and must involve proper analysis of the most promising alternatives.

It should be noted that principles in management, like those in physics, are descriptive or predictive and are not prescriptive. For example, the principle of unity of command states only that the more exclusively an individual reports to a single superior, the more likely that he or she will feel a sense of loyalty and obligation and the less likely that there will be confusion in instructions. The principle merely predicts. It in no sense prescribes that an individual should *never* report to more than one person. It does suggest, however, that if this is done, a manager must expect some possible disadvantages which should be taken into account in balancing the advantages, in some instances, of having multiple command.

In applying theory to managing, managers, like

engineers who apply physical principles to the design of a machine, must blend or compromise principles with realities. An engineer is often faced with the need to compromise considerations of weight, size, conductivity, and other factors in designing an instrument. Likewise, a manager may find that the advantages of giving a controller authority to prescribe accounting procedures throughout an organization outweigh the possible costs of disunity of command. By knowing the relevant theory, an informed manager will know that costs of disunity do exist and can undertake steps (such as making this functional authority crystal clear) to minimize the disadvantages.

**Management Techniques** Techniques are essentially reliable ways of doing things, methods for accomplishing a given result. In all fields of practice, techniques are important. This is true in management, too, even though relatively few vitally important managerial techniques have been invented. Among the most notable are budgeting, network planning, and control as in the program evaluation and review technique (PERT) or the critical-path method (CPM), rate-of-return-on-investment control, managing by objectives, and decision-tree analysis. As ways of doing things, techniques normally reflect theory and provide a means of helping managers undertake activities most effectively.

**Requirement of a Situational, or Contingency, Approach** By its very nature, managerial practice requires that managers take into account the realities of a situation when they apply theory or techniques. The task of science and theory is not to *prescribe* what should be done. Theories of management do not advocate the best way to do things in every situation, any more than the science of astrophysics tells an engineer how to design the single best rocket for all kinds of applications. The manner in which theory and science are applied in practice naturally depends on the situation.

*Contingency management* is akin to *situational management* and is often used synonymously. Some scholars distinguish between situational and contingency management on the basis that the latter implies an active interrelationship between the variables in a situation and the managerial solution devised, rather than merely implying modification of an approach in the light of a given situation. Thus, under a contingency approach, managers might look at an assembly-line situation and readily conclude that a highly structured organization pattern would best fit and interact with it. But whether a managerial approach is regarded as situational or contingency, the basic significance is the recognition that the application of science and theory to practice

must necessarily take into account a given set of circumstances. This view says that there is science and there is art; there is knowledge and there is practice. These are matters that any experienced manager has long known. One does not need much experience to understand that a corner grocery store could hardly be organized like General Motors.

**Requirement of a Systems Approach** Management theory and practice also require a systems approach. A system is essentially a set or assemblage of things interconnected, or interdependent, so as to form a complex unity. These things may be physical, as in the parts of an automobile engine; or they may be biological, as in the components of the human body; or they may be theoretical, as in the case of a well-integrated assemblage of concepts, principles, and techniques related to managing.

As can be seen in everyday life, while systems are given boundaries so that we can analyze them, there are no systems which are completely independent of others. Thus, while management theory arbitrarily sets as a boundary the knowledge underlying the managerial job—what managers actually do—this system must be related to many environmental variables. When managers plan, they have no choice but to take into account such external variables as markets, technology, social forces, laws, and regulations. When managers design an organizational system to help their people perform, they cannot help but be influenced by the pattern of behavior people bring to their jobs from a variety of external influences.

Systems also play an important part within the area of managing itself. There are such systems as organization systems, planning systems, control systems, and many others. And within these we can perceive subsystems, such as systems of delegation, network planning, and control feedback systems.

Perceptive practicing managers, accustomed as they are to seeing their problems and operations as a network of interrelated elements with daily interactions between environments inside and outside their enterprises or agencies, are often surprised to find that many academic observers regard the systems approach as something new. To be sure, conscious study of and emphasis on systems have forced managers and scholars to consider more perceptively the various interacting elements affecting management theory and practice. But that is all that is new.

## APPROACHES TO MANAGEMENT THEORY

Because of the extraordinary interest in management in recent years, a number of approaches, or "schools," have developed to explain the nature of the concepts, theory, and techniques underlying managerial practice. Although academic writers and theorists were notably absent from the study of management until the early 1950s, previous writing having largely come from practitioners, the past quarter century has seen a veritable deluge of writing from the academic halls. The variety of approaches to management analysis, the welter of research, and the divergence of views have resulted in much confusion as to what management is, what management theory and science are, and how managerial phenomena should be analyzed. As a matter of fact, some years ago the author called this situation "the management theory jungle."[1]

The various schools of, or approaches to, management are grouped here into the following categories: (1) the empirical, or case, approach; (2) the interpersonal behavior approach; (3) the group behavior approach; (4) the cooperative social systems approach; (5) the sociotechnical systems approach; (6) the decision theory approach; (7) the communications-center approach; (8) the mathematical, or management science, approach; and (9) the operational approach. Although not all the various nuances of each can be dealt with here, the nature of each can be sketched so that managers who wish to understand the present variety of writing and ideas can at least identify from what point of view they have probably been written.

**Empirical, or Case, Approach**    This school analyzes management by studying experience, usually through cases. It is based on the premise that, by studying managers' successes and mistakes in individual cases and their attempts to solve specific problems, students and practitioners will somehow come to know how to manage effectively in comparable situations.

Unless a study of experience is aimed at determining fundamentally why something happened or did not happen, however, this is likely to be a useless and even a dangerous approach to understanding management. The future is almost certain to be different. In other words, experience is not a helpful guide to knowledge unless it is distilled and different circumstances of the past considered.

If this distillation of experience takes place with a view to finding generalizations, the empirical, or case, approach can be a useful way to develop principles of management. Also, there can be no doubt that cases can provide a pseudo-laboratory situation for explaining and testing management knowledge. But the empirical approach has serious limitations simply because experience has definite limitations in a subject as complex and broad as management.

**Interpersonal Behavior Approach**    This school is based on the thesis that managing involves getting things done through people, and therefore its study should be centered on interpersonal relationships. Also called the human relations, leadership, or behavioral science approach, this school concentrates on the human aspect of management. Its advocates believe that when people work together to accomplish objectives, people should understand people.

Writers and scholars in this school are heavily oriented to individual psychology, and many are trained as psychologists. Their focus is the individual and his or her motivations as a sociopsychological being. Some supporters even seem to emphasize human relations as an art which a manager, perhaps even acting as an amateur psychologist, should understand and practice. There are those who focus attention on the manager as a leader and sometimes equate managing with leadership. Related to these are specialists who see leadership largely as a matter of understanding and developing means of obtaining response to human motivations.

That managing involves human behavior cannot be denied. That the study of human interactions, whether in the context of managing or elsewhere, is useful and important cannot be disputed. It would likewise be a mistake not to regard motivations and leadership as important for effective managing. Quite the contrary, effective managers do tend to become good leaders. In creating and maintaining an environment for performance, managers will almost surely develop situations where people will find it advantageous to follow them.

But it can hardly be said that the field of interpersonal behavior encompasses all there is to management. It is entirely possible for all the managers of a company to understand psychology and its nuances and yet not be effective in managing. Managers need to know something of planning, control and control techniques, and of devising a suitable organization structure, as well as other matters, in order to assure that the entire managerial task is accomplished.

Moreover, many of the more astute disciples of the interpersonal behavior school are finding that they must extend their views far beyond psychological phenomena. For example, in the area of leadership, research has shown that the entire organizational climate has much to do with effective leading. In understanding human motivations, psychologically oriented specialists are finding that such factors as meaningful and verifiable objectives and organization structures with clearly assigned responsibilities are also important stimulators of interest and effort.

**653**

**Group Behavior Approach** This approach, or school, is closely related to the interpersonal behavior approach and is often confused or intertwined with it. However, it is concerned primarily with behavior of people in groups rather than with strictly interpersonal behavior. It thus tends to be based on sociology, anthropology, and social psychology rather than on individual psychology.

The group behavior approach varies all the way from the study of small groups with their cultural and behavioral patterns to the behavioral composition of large groups. This latter approach is often called a study of organization behavior, where *organization* may mean the system or pattern of any set group relationships in a company, a government agency, a hospital, or any other kind of undertaking. But sometimes the term *organization* is used, as Chester Barnard used it, as the "cooperation of two or more persons,"[2] and the term *formal organization* is used to delineate conscious, deliberate, joint purpose.[3] Chris Argyris has even used the term *organization* to include "*all* the behavior of *all* the participants"[4] in a group undertaking.

This approach has made many worthwhile contributions to management. The recognition of any organized enterprise as a social organism made up, in turn, of many social organisms within it, with a complex of interacting attitudes, pressures, and conflicts arising from the cultural backgrounds of people, has been helpful to both the theorist and the practicing manager. Many of our problems in managing do arise from group behavior patterns, attitudes, and desires. Some problems arise from the enterprise as a group, but many come from the cultural environment of people outside a given company, department, or agency.

What is perhaps most disturbing about this school of thought is the tendency of its members to draw an artificial line between organization behavior and management. It does not appear to make sense to do this. In accumulating management knowledge, all behavioral sciences related to managing should be interwoven with management concepts, theory, and techniques in a eclectic way.

**Cooperative Social Systems Approach** An outgrowth of interpersonal and group behavior approaches has been an increased focus on the study of human relationships as cooperative social systems. This has been in part due to the vogue of looking at every kind of phenomenon from a systems point of view. It is also due to a desire to refine the group behavioral approach by giving emphasis to cooperation.

The idea of human relationships as social systems was early perceived by the great Italian sociologist

Vilfredo Pareto who published his famous *Treatise on General Sociology* in 1916. Pareto's work apparently affected modern social systems writings through his influence on Chester Barnard's *The Functions of the Executive*. In seeking to explain the work of executives, Barnard saw them as operating in and maintaining cooperative social systems which he referred to as "organizations." In other words, Barnard perceived social systems as the cooperative interaction of ideas, forces, desires, and thinking of two or more people.

The Barnard concept of a cooperative social system pervades the work of many social scientists concerned with management. For example, Herbert Simon at one time defined organizations as

. . . systems of interdependent activity, encompassing at least several primary groups and usually characterized at the level of consciousness of participants, by a high degree of rational direction of behavior towards ends that are objects of common knowledge.[5]

Simon and an increasing number of writers in recent years have expanded this concept to apply to any system of cooperative and purposeful group interrelationships or behavior and have given it the rather general title of *organization theory*.

The cooperative social systems approach does have pertinence to the study and analysis of management. All managers do, of course, operate in a cooperative social system. But managers are not truly in *all* kinds of cooperative social systems. A cooperating group of motorists sharing a main highway is not being managed. Nor would a family gathering to celebrate a birthday be thought of as managed. Organization theory is much broader in concept than management, but it also tends to overshadow many concepts, principles, and techniques that are important to managers.

**Sociotechnical Systems Approach** One of the newer schools of management identifies itself as the sociotechnical systems approach. This development is generally credited to E. L. Trist and his associates at the Tavistock Institute in England. In studies made of production problems in long-wall coal mining, this group found that it was not enough merely to study social problems.[6] Instead, it found that the technical system (machines and methods) had a strong and definite effect on the social system. In other words, personal attitudes and group behavior are influenced by the technical system in which people work. Thus, the sociotechnical systems approach to management emphasizes the interaction between social systems and technical systems and embraces the belief that they must be looked at together.

It is the position of this school of thought that social and technical systems must be made harmonious, and, if they are found not to be harmonious, changes could be made, usually in technical systems. Most of the work of this school has consequently been concentrated on production, office operations, and other areas where the technical systems have such a close connection to people. It tends, therefore, to be heavily oriented to industrial engineering.

As an approach to management, this school has made interesting contributions to management practice. It is doubtful, however, that any experienced manager could be surprised that technology affects individuals, groups, and organizations. For example, few people would be surprised that the technology of the automobile assembly line affects social systems and the way managing must be carried out. At the same time, particularly where technology has a great effect on group behavior patterns as it does in so much blue-collar and lower-level white-collar work, the orderly analysis and harmonization of social and technical systems can have great managerial benefits. But as promising as this approach is in such areas of operation, it is fairly safe to observe that there is much more to pertinent management knowledge than can be found in this approach.

**Decision Theory Approach** This approach to management has been based on the belief that, since it is the task of managers to make decisions, they must concentrate on decision making. Decision theorists focus on the making of decisions, on the persons or organized groups who are making decisions, and on an analysis of the decision process. The process of evaluating alternatives has become for many decision theorists a springboard for examining the entire area of enterprise activity, including the psychological and social reactions of individuals and groups, the nature of organization structure, the need and development of information for decisions, and the analysis of values. The result has been that decision theory tends no longer to be a neat and narrow concentration on decisions but has become a broader view of enterprises as social systems.

The decision theory school is apparently an outgrowth of economists' preoccupation with rationality in choosing among various economic alternatives. It has arisen out of such economic considerations as profit and utility maximization, indifference curves, marginal utility, and economic behavior under risks and uncertainties. It should be no surprise, then, that most members of this school are economists. It is likewise no surprise to find the content of this theory oriented to mathematics and model construction.

Decision making, as the central focus of management with the rest of management thought built around it, has a degree of reasonableness. But it does seem to overlook the fact that for most managers the actual making of a decision is relatively easy—if goals are clear, if the environment in which the decision will operate can be comprehended, if adequate information is available, if the organization structure provides a clear understanding of the responsibility for decisions and their interrelationships, if competent people are available to make decisions, and if many of the other prerequisites of the managerial task are present.

Important as it is in managing, decision making appears to be, at the same time, too narrow a focus on which to build a total theory of management, and, if its implications are considerably extended, too wide a focus.

**Communications-Center Approach** Closely related to decision theory is the suggestion made by a few management scholars that managers are communications centers and that the knowledge of managing can be constructed around this concept. This approach would see the managerial task as one of receiving information, processing it, and disseminating it. In this approach, the manager is sometimes likened to a telephone switchboard. By casting managers in the role of communications centers, it can be readily seen that the application of the computer to programmed and unprogrammed decision making falls neatly into place.

This approach does have some attractions. It furnishes a means for the growing information sciences built around the technology of the computer to be integrated into management thought and action. But it has certain deficiencies. As in the case of the decision theory approach, if defined narrowly, it is not realistically consistent with the entire sphere of pertinent management knowledge. If interpreted broadly to encompass managing, it would seem to be too general to furnish a basis for a practical science of management.

**Mathematical, or Management Science, Approach** Some theorists see managing as primarily an exercise in mathematical processes, concepts, symbols, and models. Perhaps the most widely known of these are the operations researchers, also called management scientists. The belief of this group is that if managing or organizing or planning or decision making is a logical process, it can be expressed in mathematical symbols and relationships. The primary focus of this school is, then, the mathematical model, since through this device, problems can be expressed in basic relationships. Where a given goal is sought, the model can often be expressed in terms of optimization. At the extreme, management scientists have an almost complete absorption with mathematics, and some members of this school have taken the position that "if you cannot express it mathematically, it is not worth expressing."

Many critics both inside and outside the ranks of the management scientists have observed that the narrow mathematical focus can hardly be called an approach to a true management science. Moreover, if one is to judge by the papers in *Management Science* and a similar journal, *Operations Research*, very few of the efforts of these management scientists are devoted to practical applications of their specialized mathematical techniques.[7]

On the other hand, no one interested in any scientific field can overlook the great usefulness of mathematical analyses. They force upon analysts the definition of a problem; they conveniently permit the insertion of symbols for unknown quantities; and they force consideration and inclusion of the more important variables in a situation. Additionally, the logical methodology of mathematics, developed over many years of scientific application, provides a powerful tool for simplifying and solving complex problems. Where mathematical approaches have been effectively used to help solve managerial problems, they have made a real contribution to orderly thinking and analysis. In these instances, mathematical techniques have forced on managers the means and desirability of seeing problems more clearly; they have compelled managers to see the need for defining goals and measures of effectiveness in reaching goals with greater precision; they have aided in seeing managing as a system of logical relationships; and they have on many occasions shown the need for developing information to quantify variables for which data had not theretofore been sought. Nevertheless, as promising as the potential of mathematical and simulation techniques is—the grist of the so-called management scientists—it is difficult to treat mathematics as a truly management science any more than astronomy.

**Operational Approach** The operational (also the management process) approach to management science and theory attempts to draw together the pertinent knowledge of management by relating it to the managerial job—what managers actually do. Like other operational sciences, it endeavors to place in a theoretical framework the concepts, principles, and techniques which underpin the task of managing.[8]

The operational approach recognizes that there is a central core of knowledge that exists only in man-

agement. Such matters as line and staff, departmentation, the limitations of the span of management, managerial appraisal, and various managerial control techniques involve concepts and theories only found where managers are involved. In addition, this approach is eclectic in that it draws on pertinent areas of knowledge derived from other fields. These include such matters as applications of systems theory, decision making, motivation and leadership, individual and group behavior, social systems, theories of cooperation and communication, and the application of mathematical analyses and concepts.

The nature of the operational approach can perhaps be best appreciated by reference to Fig. M-3. As this diagram shows, the operational management school recognizes a central core of science and theory peculiar to managing, but it also draws important contributions from various other schools and approaches. As the circumscribing circle is intended to show, the operational approach is not interested in *all* the important knowledge in these various fields, but only that which is deemed useful and relevant to managing.

Those who subscribe to the operational approach do so with the hope of developing a field of science and theory which has practical application to the field of managing and yet is not so broad as to encompass everything that might have any relationship to the managerial task. They recognize that managing is a difficult task with an immense number of variables affecting it. They realize that any field as complex as managing, which deals with the production and marketing of anything from bread to money to religion to government services, can never be isolated from the physical, biological, or cultural environment. But they recognize that some partitioning of knowledge is necessary and some boundaries must be set if meaningful progress is to be made in any field.

**Systems, Situational, and Contingency Approaches** Particularly among academics, much is made of the systems, situational, and contingency approaches to management. As noted at the outset, these do not really appear to be different schools of management thought. There are systemic interrelationships, for example, in all bodies of knowledge, and all the basic schools or approaches to management acknowledge this. No one would deprecate the importance of applying systems thinking and analysis to management, any more than one would in any other field.

Likewise, the situational and contingency approaches to management thought add little to fundamental management thought. Both are concerned

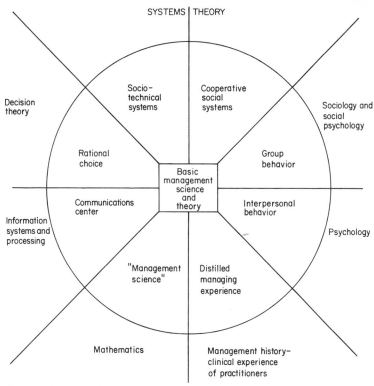

**Fig. M-3. The scope of operational science and theory as embraced by the operational approach to management.**

with managerial practice and the application of management concepts and science to the realities of given situations. The contingency approach, however, emphasizes some elements worthy of special note. It stresses the interaction of environmental factors in situations and as results of managerial action. For example, people in production, accounting, and sales departments tend to develop a mode of thinking and behavior reflecting their specialty. Thus contingency approaches aid in understanding managerial actions and deserve special attention by practitioners.

**Specialized Views of Specialists** One of the major reasons why there are so many different schools or approaches is the fact that various specialists who have studied the field have naturally tended to view it through the eyes of their specialty.

Practitioners see management as experience. Psychologists tend to view management as a matter of interpersonal relationships. Sociologists and social psychologists understandably concentrate on group behavior patterns, social systems, and phenomena of cooperation. Industrial engineers are inclined to

concentrate on technical systems and their relationship to social systems and have consequently given rise to the sociotechnical systems approach. Economists and those interested in rational processes have naturally been disposed to concentrate on decision making as at least an opening wedge in analyzing management. And mathematics and operations researchers, schooled in symbols, models, and abstractions, have stressed this aspect of managing.

It is not difficult to see the impact of specialist views. But unless specialists see the whole managerial situation and attempt eclectically to meld various views into an analysis of the whole, their analyses are likely to be myopic.

## INFLUENCE OF SEMANTICS AND TECHNOLOGY

Perhaps the major reason for the different schools of management thought is the matter of semantics. One might believe that in an occupation as common and universal as management, there would be a high degree of agreement in semantics and terminology.

Unfortunately, this is not true. This is one reason why a science of management has not developed faster. As Lord Wilfred Brown once remarked, electricity never became a science until certain definitions like volt, ohm, and ampere were made clear and were generally accepted; and management can hardly become a science until common terms have commonly accepted definitions.[9]

One of the great pioneers of management, Lt. Colonel Lyndall F. Urwick, has long pleaded for an accepted glossary of management concepts and terms.[10] In his opinion, this is the greatest single cause for the immaturity of management as a science. He feels that anything desiring to be called a discipline, as management should, must develop a standardized terminology.

Without attempting to exhaust all the semantic problems found in the analysis of management, it is worthwhile to mention a few. And, at the risk of suggesting a definition with which some specialists might not agree, definitions believed to be operational and practical will be made.

*Management and Managing.* It is not always agreed what even these two basic terms mean. Often they are used interchangeably. Sometimes management is regarded as the people who are managing. There does seem to be a fair degree of agreement that managing involves getting things done through people. But does it deal with all kinds of human relationships or just informally recognized enterprises, organizations, and institutions?

Rather than have the implication of managers as amateur psychologists manipulating people for whom they are responsible, managing is better regarded as the task of designing and maintaining an environment conductive to performance of individuals working in groups to accomplish preselected objectives. The implication, of course, is that managing does not in this sense deal primarily with materials and machines but with people. It also implies that managing only takes place where a formally and intentionally structured system of roles exists. This would include: (1) clear goals or objectives; (2) an understanding of the end result areas in which a person operates (for example, market research, district sales, or cost accounting); (3) an understanding of the degree of authority a role incumbent has, or, to put it another way, the degree to which discretion may be used in making performance possible; and (4) the availability of information, tools, and other resources necessary to accomplish given goals.

It would be helpful if the words *managing* and *management* were also used differently and clearly. Managing would appear to be best regarded as practice, while management would seem to be best used as applying to the body of science and theory—knowledge—underlying this practice.

*Organization and Organizing.* Perhaps the most important single semantic cause of confusion lies in the word *organization*. In the earlier years of management, an organization almost invariably referred to an intentional structure of roles in a formally organized enterprise. In more recent years, it has come to mean many different things. It may be used to mean an enterprise itself, like the General Motors Corporation or the Department of Defense. It has been used, particularly by behavioral scientists, to mean any pattern or system or set of human and group relationships in any kind of an operation or undertaking. There are even some behavioral scientists who would apply the term to any interpersonal relationship. In fact, *organization* has so many different meanings that readers today must first ascertain how the word is used if they are to understand the literature.

*Organizing,* on the other hand, tends to be used in a more exact way. While it can be used to denote the act of creating any system of human relationships, in professional managing it is likely to be more consistently used as the setting up of a formalized system of intentional roles.

Despite pleas that the present varied use of the term *organization* be made more precise and meaningful, the widespread differences with which this term is used are probably so ingrained that the word cannot be made more explicit. Perhaps the best way to handle this problem is to use the term *structural organization* when referring to the original managerial meaning and to insist that those writers who use the term otherwise define clearly how they are using it.

*Line and Staff.* The concepts of line and staff appear to be widely misused and misapplied. Moreover, these misapplications and misunderstandings have had much to do with the almost universal existence of wasteful frictions and difficulties in this area.

Perhaps the most widely held concepts of line and staff are to regard the *line* as those people and functions which have direct responsibility for accomplishing enterprise objectives and *staff* as those people and functions which merely help the line accomplish objectives. By so doing, it is common to regard production and marketing, and sometimes finance, as line functions and such activities as purchasing, accounting, personnel, quality control, and plant maintenance as staff functions.

The difficulty and confusion from this use of the terms are readily apparent. For example, it has been argued that purchasing, which is auxiliary to a main line activity such as production, is somehow not as essential as production. But can it be said that purchasing is any less important in accomplishing a manufacturing company's goals than production? Of course not. And can it be said that the so-called "staff" departments such as personnel, accounting, or maintenance are not directly related to accomplishment of enterprise goals?

The only really valid and logically precise concepts of line and staff are that these are not people, functions, or departments; they are simply relationships. A line relationship exists when a superior has a line of authority running to subordinates, a power to exercise discretion with respect to what they do, and a responsibility for the actions of those people reporting to the superior. A staff relationship exists when the relationship of one position to another is advisory; a person in a staff capacity can only offer counsel and advice, and not give instructions.

As a practical matter, many positions in an organization structure can be seen to have both line and staff relationships in them. A chief engineer, for example, will be responsible for an engineering department and will, as such, be in a line capacity. But a person in that position will also most certainly be a major source of engineering counsel and advice to people outside the engineering department; in this case, the relationship will be staff.

Obviously, it does make a difference whether a position bears a line or staff relationship. In a line relationship the incumbent has responsibility for the actions of subordinates; in a staff relationship the responsibility is purely advisory. These clearly imply two different behavioral patterns.

*Functional Authority.* One of the most misunderstood and confusing aspects of organizational relationships arises from the case of functional authority or functional supervision. Studies have disclosed almost uniform confusion in the understanding and application of this concept. Essentially, functional authority is the right which a position or department has had delegated to it over specified processes, practices, policies, or other matters relating to activities which are undertaken by personnel in positions or departments that do not generally report to the holders of this functional authority. This kind of authority is often assigned to positions that are primarily staff or to specialized service departments, in order to provide them with authority to issue instructions in their specialized areas.

As can be readily seen, functional authority is a case of bestowing a specialized and usually limited kind of line authority on a staff, service specialist, or operating department. While it does give rise to disunity of command, it is often regarded to be worth the cost. Many times it is quite necessary in order to assure uniform action in important areas like accounting, credit control, labor union contract administration, and quality control. In modern enterprise, functional authority appears to be unavoidable. Practicing managers should realize the nature of this concept and the difficulties its use can cause and should take steps, at least through clarification, to reduce the confusion and disunity involved.

*Service Departments.* Still another conceptual problem causing difficulty in managing is the common misunderstanding of service departments. Service departments are really a grouping of activities that might be carried on in other departments for purposes of efficiency, control, or both. Examples include such departments as purchasing, personnel, accounting, or maintenance. As noted above, they are often confused with staff. But a moment's reflection will disclose that they are really a kind of activity grouping and are as much operating departments in their specialized area as any manufacturing or sales department. Because they are groupings of specialists, however, they are often used for staff, or advisory, purposes. Also, they are often given functional authority.

*Authority and Responsibility.* These are also concepts that are commonly used inexactly. Managers often speak of delegating responsibility rather than authority. They do so probably because the word *authority* has a dictatorial tone to it and smacks of authoritarianism. It is true that earlier managers used the term *responsibility* to refer to a duty assigned with the implied authority to accomplish it. But, semantically this is wrong; responsibility is an obligation of subordinates to their superiors to perform; it cannot be delegated.

If by delegation a manager means giving someone the organizational power to undertake a job, then the manager is speaking of authority in the dictionary sense of "the right to command or act." It is perhaps more appropriate and exact, however, to use the term to mean the right to exercise discretion in carrying out a task, a right which implies creative use of power rather than authoritarianism.

Responsibility, then, becomes a matter of owing an obligation to a delegant to perform.

*Planning and Control.* There is some confusion and differences in these terms. Anthony of Harvard, for example, sees the managerial functions as strategic planning, management control, and operational control.[11] Within *strategic planning,* he would put the process of deciding on objectives of the enterprise, changes in these objectives, resources used to attain them, and policies to be applied in the acquisition, use, and disposition of resources. Within *management control,* Anthony would include planning associated with the ongoing management of an enterprise to assure that resources are used effectively and efficiently. He regards *operational control* as the process of assuring that specific tasks are carried out effectively and efficiently.

A slight different and more precise concept of planning is closer to what managers perceive and is perhaps more logical. *Planning* is probably best seen as the process of selecting from among alternative missions and objectives—and the strategies, policies, programs, and procedures for achieving them; thus, decision making lies at the core of planning. *Control,* on the other hand, may be best perceived as the process of measuring and correcting performance of activities of subordinates to assure that enterprise objectives and plans are being accomplished.

*Policies.* One of the most misused terms in practical managing is *policies.* If this concept is to have useful and consistent meaning, it should be defined as the establishment of a guide to *thinking* in decision making; the essense of policies is the existence of discretion, within certain bounds. Too often, what are called policies are really rules, implying that this or that *must* be done. Sometimes the term is used to cover *procedures,* which are accurately defined as a sequence of required actions or nonactions to assure that something is done in a precise way. While we do need rules and procedures in managing, it only makes sense to distinguish these from policies where we do expect people to use their discretion—but within certain bounds.

*Other Semantic Difficulties.* There are, of course, other semantic difficulties which interfere with the exactness and transferability of management knowledge. The use of decision making as ranging all the way from selecting a course of action to encompassing virtually all managing has been noted. Likewise, the pretensions of systems, situational, and contingency management specialists often confuse readers, largely because of the mixing of the concepts of management as a body of knowledge and managing as art or practice. But the most important semantic

difficulties that give rise to so much of the "management theory jungle" are perceptions of what managership is, how it may be distinguished from leadership, and the different meanings given to *organization.*

## MANAGEMENT KNOWLEDGE AND THE MANAGERIAL FUNCTIONS

A classification system is necessary to structure any field of knowledge. In management, a variety of first-order classifications could be used. It is believed, however, that it is both realistic and helpful to practitioners to use the *functions* of managers—planning, organizing, staffing, directing and leading, and controlling. A second-order classification might build knowledge in each function around its (1) nature and purpose, (2) structural properties, (3) manner of undertaking, (4) key concepts, (5) underlying theory and principles, (6) most useful techniques, (7) difficulties involved in application, and (8) development as an environment for performance.

This is usually the approach of the operational school of management. Because the functions of managers are used, this approach is often called the *management process* school. Inasmuch as the great management pioneer Henri Fayol first attempted to organize management knowledge around managerial functions, the school is often referred to as the *classical* or the *traditional* school. But it is really none of these. It is merely an approach that has been found useful and understandable to practicing managers. It likewise furnishes a means of distinguishing between managerial knowledge and such nonmanagerial—or technical—fields as marketing and production. It is also a way of being eclectic by integrating into management useful and pertinent knowledge from all the schools and approaches.

It is true that some people misunderstand this approach. For example, one highly regarded writer reported that a small sample of business executives he studied did not appear to plan, organize, coordinate, and control, and that, therefore, functions of managers were "folklore."[12] This author did not distinguish between an organized knowledge, or science, and practice. There is no such person as a 100-percent manager. All managers do things that are not managerial. What must not be obscured is that when managers make decisions, gather information, hold meetings, allocate resources, respond to forces external to an enterprise, and initiate changes, these activities almost certainly are evidence of practice in planning, organizing, staffing, leading, or controlling.

Moreover, the question of what managers actually do day by day and how they do it is really secondary to what makes an acceptable and useful classification of knowledge. Highly successful executives often overlook this point when trying to distinguish between theory and practice. Arrangement of knowledge with respect to managing is an indispensable first step. It makes possible the separation of managerial science from specialized techniques in operating areas like marketing, accounting, manufacturing, and engineering. It directs attention to those basic aspects of management which appear to have a high degree of universality. By utilizing the functions of managers as this first step, a logical start can be made in setting up pigeonholes for classifying managerial knowledge.[13] This approach recognizes, of course, that in management, as in all areas of knowledge, the classification is not airtight and that there are many interlocking and overlapping elements.

**Planning** Planning involves selecting from among alternative missions and objectives and the strategies, policies, procedures, and programs for achieving the objectives for the enterprise as a whole and for every department and section of the enterprise. As mentioned earlier, planning requires decision making, and it is quite proper to say that no plan exists until a decision has been made—a commitment of resources, direction, or reputation—to go in a certain direction. Before a decision is made, all that exists is a planning study, analysis, or proposal.

Planning is deciding in advance what to do, how to do it, when to do it, and who is to do it. Planning bridges the gap from where we are to where we want to be in a desired future. It strongly implies not only innovation but also rational and feasible innovation. It makes it possible for things to occur that would not otherwise occur. Although the future situation can seldom be predicted with accuracy and unforeseen events may interfere with the best-laid plans, unless plans have been made, actions of people tend to be random and left to chance.

There are many types of plans. If it is considered that plans involve a selected course of future action, the various types can be classified as follows:

Missions: the basic functions or purposes of an enterprise or agency or any department within it.

Objectives, or goals: the ends toward which organized activity is aimed—the endpoints of planning.

Strategies: objectives and major policies with an implied emphasis and allocation of resources in a given direction.

Policies: guides to thinking in decision making with the essential quality of permitting discretion, whether large or small, to people in the decision-making system.

Rules: required action or nonaction, allowing no discretion.

Procedures: chronological sequences of required actions detailing the exact manner in which an activity is to be accomplished.

Programs: a complex of goals, policies, procedures, rules, task assignments, steps to be taken, resources to be employed, and other elements necessary to carry out a given course of action, normally supported by capital and operating budgets.

Budgets: statements of plans and expected results expressed in numerical terms; numberized programs.

The *planning process*, being a practical exercise in rationality, logically involves the following steps:

1. Establishing objectives or goals.

2. Premising: establishing and obtaining the agreement of decision makers to utilize consistent planning assumptions—the expected environment in which plans will operate.

3. Searching for and examining alternative courses of action.

4. Evaluating alternative courses of action in the light of goals sought and planning premises adopted.

5. Selecting an alternative—the real point of decision making.

6. Formulating derivative plans necessary to support a major plan.

7. Numberizing plans through making budgets.

**Organizing** This area of managing has to do with the design of an intentional structure of roles and role relationships. It is within the connotation of defining and structuring roles that we think of organizing as involving the grouping of activities necessary to attain objectives, the assignment of each grouping to a managerial position with authority necessary to use discretion in helping subordinates achieve objectives, and the provision of coordination horizontally and vertically in the organization structure. An organization structure should be designed to clarify the task environment so that everyone knows who is to do what and who is responsible for what results; to remove obstacles to performance caused by confusion and uncertainty of assignment;

and to provide a decision-making communications network reflecting and supporting enterprise objectives. The organization structure is not, of course, an end in itself but a tool to help in accomplishing enterprise objectives.

*Span of Management.* An important problem in the sphere of organizing is determining the proper *span of management (or control)*. There is no single universally desirable number of people who should report to a given manager. The best span depends on a number of underlying variables in a given situation, such as the (1) clarity of plans and delegation, (2) pace of change, (3) extent to which subordinates are appropriately trained, (4) degree to which a superior can utilize efficient and objective control techniques, (5) effectiveness of a manager's communication techniques, and (6) amount of necessary personal contact with subordinates. Clearly, the fewer subordinates an individual manager can supervise, the more levels of organization there must be. Levels not only cost money but also make communications from the top to the bottom and from the bottom to the top of an enterprise more difficult since each level tends to be a communications filter.

*Patterns of Organization.* Another important aspect of organizing is selecting the appropriate patterns of departmentation. Managers must decide whether to organize on a functional basis or by territory, by product, by market channels or centers, by process or equipment, by customer, by setting up service departments, or by using a form of grid, or matrix, organization. Each has its advantages and disadvantages. By being aware of these, successful practitioners may adopt those patterns that promise to work best for them in a given situation.

*Line, Staff, and Functional Relationships.* The problem of establishing and clarifying line, staff, and functional authority relationships within a structure is also vital. Judging by the confusions so widely found in this area, this is also one of the more difficult aspects of practice. Authority delegation with clarity to the right degree and position, as well as decentralizing authority without loss of control by keeping the right decision-making power centralized, is often a major hallmark of good managing. As a matter of fact, inept delegation of authority is probably the most important single cause of managerial failures.

In addition, the area of organizing includes such important elements as the proper and effective use of committees, task forces, or other special group devices, as well as when and how to use grid, or matrix, devices. Moreover, since the organization structure gives the key to the kind of talent needed, organization planning can be an exceedingly important aspect of staffing.

**Staffing** Staffing entails manning positions provided for in the organization structure. It thus includes evaluating managerial jobs as a means of determining status and compensation, selecting persons to fill managerial positions, appraising managers, and giving them opportunities for development through desirable training.

Many theorists include the staffing function in organizing. There is, of course, a close relationship. In designing an organization structure, it is necessary to keep in mind that positions must be filled with people. But strong reasons exist for separating this function from organizing. In the first place, there is a tendency for managers to underestimate the importance of and their responsibility for staffing and to pass off too much of this responsibility to personnel departments. In the second place, a significant and growing body of knowledge and techniques exist in the field of staffing.

The function of staffing, like the other management functions, must be regarded as a system and, in turn, as a subsystem of the total system of managing. It is both logical and highly desirable to look upon the elements of staffing—especially selecting, appraising, and development as an interrelated system. Likewise, as can be easily perceived, staffing, as well as other functions of managing, must be regarded as requiring an open-systems approach. After all, it deals with people who are products of their cultural environment and continue to interact with this environment.

**Directing and Leading** This function encompasses the exceptionally significant interpersonal aspect of managing. All managers would agree that one of their most important problems arises from people, their desires and attitudes, their behavior patterns as individuals and in groups, and the need for effective managers also to be effective leaders. Thus, included in this function are such major subjects as motivation, leadership, and communication.

*Motivation.* As indicated in the discussion of approaches, or schools, of management, psychologists, sociologists, and social psychologists have given much attention to this area. Studies of motivation have, in recent years, disclosed that what gives rise to individual responses is a much more complicated matter than Maslow's hierarchy of needs (physiological, security and safety, affiliation or acceptance, esteem or status, and self-actualization) and even Herzberg's widely acclaimed motivator-hygiene approach (that certain satisfiers—all related to job content—motivate, and others—such as supervision, pay, and status—do not motivate, but their absence dissatisfies). Indeed most recent studies have disclosed that people are not only motivated by their needs but also by such factors as their perceptions and expectancy of rewards, their understanding of objectives, and the clarity of duties and responsibilities through good organization structuring. In other words, the entire managerial environment is important to motivation.

*Leadership.* Likewise, in the area of leadership, emphasis has shifted from traits and characteristics of leaders to such basic managerial elements as position power, task structures, the extent to which people like and trust a leader, and the environment for performance the leader creates. Thus, we begin to see a kind of coalescence between leadership and motivation and the manager's need to design and maintain an environment for performance.

*Communication.* Communication is coming to be perceived more as a matter of managers having something of value to communicate. This requires planning, knowing with whom to communicate and on what, effective organizing, and to see all social systems as communications networks, often with many "filters" and blockages which the successful manager must attempt to permeate or remove.

**Controlling** The function of controlling may be regarded as the measuring and correcting of activities of subordinates in order to make the accomplishment of intended objectives as certain as possible. Thus, it (1) involves measurement of actual performance as compared with goals and plans, and (2) where negative deviations exist, calls out the need for corrective action. To be sure, the correction of deviations may mean revising plans, reorganizing a department, improving staffing, or changing techniques of leadership. In this sense, controlling is often criticized as overlapping the other managerial functions. While this kind of overlap may exist, it really emphasizes that managing is a system, that the various functions of managers do interweave and interlock, and that controlling is in

part the function of closing the loop of managerial action.

Obviously, any meaningful control system or device requires two prerequisites. One is the existence of plans. Plans furnish the standards against which performance must be measured; and the clearer, more complete, and integrated plans are, the more effective controls can be. Another is the existence of a clear organization structure. Controlling can hardly be effective unless managers know precisely where the responsibility for deviations lies.

*Control Process.* The basic process of control is the same, regardless of the subject of control, whether cash, quality, morale, product development, costs, or anything else. Essentially, the control process, wherever it is found and whatever it controls, must encompass three steps: (1) establishing standards, (2) measuring performance against these standards, and (3) correcting deviations from standards and plans.

Controlling may be seen, then, as a cybernetic, or feedback, system, as indicated in Fig. M-4.

*Control Lag.* When control is seen as a system, it becomes apparent that the fastest information availability, even *real-time information* (information on what is happening now), will not remove the time lags in controls. Much time is typically spent in analyzing deviations and developing and implementing programs for correction. This suggests that truly effective management control requires techniques that make it reasonably possible for a manager to see the probable results of anticipated performance *before* the events actually occur. There are certain techniques that make this possible, such as cash forecasting, utilization of PERT and CPM network systems, and various devices of feedforward control.[14]

*Control Techniques.* There are a number of major techniques of control. Many are essentially techniques of both planning and control. Among the more traditional, the most important is budgeting. But other traditional devices include use of statistical data and analyses, break-even analyses, the regu-

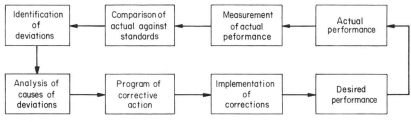

**Fig. M-4. The control process system.**

lar audit of operations, a rate-of-return-on-investment program, and, of course, personal observation by an astute manager.

Newer techniques of planning and control are built around systems approaches. Among these are the utilization of operations research simulation techniques, the use of time-event network analyses in the form of PERT or CPM, and following progress through the use of decision trees.

*Personal, or Direct, Control.* It cannot be overlooked that the most effective of all controls, one that might be regarded as the most direct of controls, is the assurance of high-quality managers and their subordinates. In a very strict sense, all other controls are indirect in that they are aimed at detecting and correcting deviations in such areas as goal performance, costs, worker-hours, machine hours, or sales. The higher the quality of managers and their subordinates, the less will be the need to rely on other, or indirect, controls. This is based on four grounds: (1) that qualified managers make a minimum of errors; (2) that competent managers will readily see and make corrections for deviations; (3) that managerial performance can be measured and appraised; and (4) that management concepts, theory, principles, and techniques are useful diagnostic standards to measure managerial performance.

*See also* AUTHORITY, RESPONSIBILITY, AND ACCOUNTABILITY; BUDGETS AND BUDGET PREPARATION; COMMUNICATIONS, ORGANIZATIONAL; CONTROL SYSTEMS, MANAGEMENT; INTERPERSONAL RELATIONSHIPS; LEADERSHIP; MANAGEMENT, DEFINITIONS OF; MANAGEMENT, HISTORICAL DEVELOPMENT OF; MANAGER, DEFINITIONS OF; MOTIVATION IN ORGANIZATIONS; ORGANIZATION ANALYSIS AND PLANNING; PLANNING, STRATEGIC MANAGERIAL; POLICY FORMULATION AND IMPLEMENTATION; STATISTICAL ANALYSIS FOR MANAGEMENT.

## NOTES

[1]Harold Koontz, "The Management Theory Jungle," *Journal of the Academy of Management*, vol. 4, no. 3, pp. 174–188, December 1961; Harold Koontz, "Making Sense of Management Theory," *Harvard Business Review*, vol. 40, no. 4, pp. 24ff, July–August 1962.

[2]C. I. Barnard, *The Functions of the Executive*, Harvard University Press, Cambridge, Mass., 1938, p. 65.

[3]*Ibid.*, p. 4.

[4]Chris Argyris, *Personality and Organization*, Harper & Brothers, New York, 1957, p. 239.

[5]"Comments on the Theory of Organizations," *American Political Science Review*, vol. 46, no. 4, p. 1130, 1952.

[6]E. L. Trist and K. W. Bamforth, "Some Social and Psychological Consequences of the Long-Wall Method of Coal Getting," *Human Relations*, vol. 4, no. 1, pp. 3–38,

1951; F. E. Emery, *Characteristics of Socio-Technical Systems*, Document 527, Tavistock Institute of Human Relations, London, 1959.

[7]See, for example, W. J. Gruber and J. S. Niles, "Problems in the Utilization of Management Science/Operations Research: A State of the Art Survey", *Interfaces*, vol. 2, no. 1, pp. 12–19, 1971. These authors found that only 2 percent of the articles in these two journals in 1962 and 3 percent in 1967 had any practical application.

[8]Referred to as "operational," following the logic and analysis in the classification of sciences outlined by P. W. Bridgman, *The Logic of Modern Physics*, The Macmillan Company, New York, 1938, pp. 2–32.

[9]See Lord Brown's discussion in Harold Koontz, ed., *Toward a Unified Theory of Management*, McGraw-Hill Book Company, New York, 1964, p. 105.

[10]See, for example, Lt. Colonel Hyndall F. Urwick, "That Word 'Organization,'" *Academy of Management Review*, vol. 1, no. 1, pp. 89–92, January 1976.

[11]Robert N. Anthony, *Planning and Control Systems: A Framework for Analysis* Harvard Graduate School of Business Administration, Boston, 1965, pp. 16–17.

[12]Henry Mintzberg. "The Manager's Job: Folklore and Fact," *Harvard Business Review*, vol. 53, no. 4, pp. 49–61, July–August, 1975.

[13]G. C. Homans, *The Human Group*, Harcourt, Brace & World, Inc., New York, 1958.

[14]For the theory and application of such devices, see Harold Koontz, "Managing Through Feedforward Control," *Business Horizons*, vol. 15, no. 3, pp. 25–36, June 1972.

(This entry draws much from the author's chapters in Harold Koontz and Cyril O'Donnell, *Management: A Systems and Contingency Analysis of the Managerial Functions*, 6th ed., McGraw-Hill Book Company, New York, 1976.)

HAROLD KOONTZ, *University of California, Los Angeles*

# Manager, definitions of

The term *manager* covers an enormous variety of persons because it is applied (1) in a variety of organizations, (2) at virtually every level within organizations, and (3) to persons who perform a wide range of duties and responsibilities.

A *manager* is best defined as a member of an organization whose tasks, duties, and responsibilities require the supervision of other people. Without subordinates, an organizational member works alone or, at best, cooperatively with others. The act of supervising others requires a reduction (but not elimination) of technical work and an increase in the relative importance of the managerial functions of planning, organizing, controlling, coordinating, and the like.

By delegating authority and responsibilities to subordinates, managers extend their personal influences and capabilities far beyond what they could accomplish alone. Only in this way can large-scale organizations be constructed and large-scale missions or tasks be pursued.

**Types of Organizations** By custom and for analytical convenience, organizations are classified into types based essentially on their main purpose. Managers and management practices and problems vary among the several types.

*Private-Sector Organizations.* These are predominantly profit-seeking organizations, such as business firms. Profits are partly retained by the firm and partly distributed to the owners. Managers are employees of the organization under mutually agreed-upon conditions of employment.

*Public-Sector Organizations.* These are government organizations at local, state and federal levels. Managers are often referred to as public servants. They are usually called administrators rather than managers. They are often subject to federal, state, county, or local civil service systems for purposes of personnel administration. They are subject to special constraints of the legislative mandates and missions which create the boards, jurisdictions, commissions, or government offices and bureaus they manage. *Military organizations* form a special category within the public sector.

*Not-for-Profit Organizations.* These include voluntary associations such as research foundations, mutual benefit societies, charitable organizations, fraternal groups, and a wide variety of community service organizations, such as the Red Cross, March of Dimes, or the YMCA. Managers in these organizations are professional specialists dedicated to the kinds of activities for which their associations are created. They usually collaborate with selected laypersons who serve as advisers, resource people, fund raisers, and in policy guidance.

*Institutional Organizations.* Many organizations in the service or public sectors are termed institutions. This is a general term nearly synonymous with the term organization. An organization tends to be referred to as an institution when it is enduring, well established, conforms to the typical features of its general class, has a history and tradition, and acquires a position of social importance in the culture of the society. Thus we speak of a particular hospital, school, or even a business firm, as an institution. It is possible to describe a business such as the General Motors Corporation as an institution, although this is a less-frequent use of the term. The managers in nonbusiness institutions are similar in their characteristics to those in not-for-profit or in public-sector organizations.

*Voluntary Associations.* An enormous group of organizations exist in which members are the clients rather than the employees of the organization. The Boy Scout organization is an example. Here the managers are few in number, and memberships are free or achieved informally at minimal cost. Voluntary associations are often, but not always, temporary or special-purpose groups. Managers are specialists or professionals with training and experience appropriate to the group's chosen areas of activity.

*Mixed.* Clearly the above categories are not mutually exclusive. All, however, have business problems in that they must obtain and husband scarce resources. All need managers of various types. Most voluntary associations are also not-for-profit organizations. An interesting type of mixed organization is *the quasi-public organization*—where the organization is a combination of government and private business ventures. An example is the U.S. Postal Service, which in 1970 was changed from a government bureau and set up separately from direct congressional control to operate more like an independent business, but subject to broad governmental directives and surveillance.

**Hierarchical Level** Managers occupy specific positions at the different levels of an organization. Their responsibilities, authority, and status are roughly commensurate with their level in the organization.

At the lowest level are first-line managers, often called supervisors. At the middle levels are section managers or department heads, plant or division superintendents, general managers, and professionals, such as industrial psychologists or engineers. At the top levels, managers are often referred to as executives, and they are in charge of major groups or units within the organization. These managers hold such positions as vice-president, division head, president, executive vice-president, etc. The term *senior vice-president* is often used to provide a special category between the vice-president and president. Some executives are also corporate officers, elected as such by the board of directors.

Some managers appear high up on organization charts but fill relatively minor subordinate roles. An example is an assistant to the president. The power and influence of assistants-to vary greatly depending upon their personalities, capabilities, and relationships with their superiors.

**Managerial Responsibilities** Managers can be classified according to the nature of their skills, functional responsibilities, duties, and professional interests.

One category is that of the *line managers*. They are typically in operations, close to the central purposes of the organization. They have command authority within their domain. Examples are the managers in finance, marketing, or production.

A second major category consists of *staff specialists* who work in a service or advisory capacity or in a function that cuts across other functions. Examples are the personnel director or the manager of public relations. They function as researchers, advisors, or idea people. They operate with a minimum of command authority. They work through planning, persuasion, and the application of specialized knowledge to the problems in their domain. Some staff groups may be delegated a control or other line-type function appropriate to their area of specialization, as in the case of a personnel officer who is expected to enforce safety rules.

Some managers belong to a *service* category, such as a data processing or computer services manager. Their chief source of authority is in their technical expertise.

Some managers are almost entirely *administrative*, such as those in central corporate headquarters, or, at a lower level, office managers.

*See also* AUTHORITY, RESPONSIBILITY, AND ACCOUNTABILITY; BOARDS OF DIRECTORS; COMMITTEES; LEADERSHIP; MANAGEMENT, DEFINITIONS OF; MANAGEMENT THEORY, SCIENCE, AND APPROACHES; NOT-FOR-PROFIT ORGANIZATIONS, MANAGEMENT OF; OFFICERS, CORPORATE; PUBLIC ADMINISTRATION; SUPERVISORY MANAGEMENT.

### REFERENCES

Drucker, Peter F.: *Management: Tasks, Responsibilities, Practices,* Harper & Row, Publishers, Incorporated, New York, 1974.

Duncan, W. Jack: *Essentials of Management,* The Dryden Press, Inc., New York, 1975.

Massie, Joseph L., and John Douglas: *Managing: A Contemporary Introduction,* Prentice-Hall, Inc. Englewood Cliffs, N.J., 1973.

Mintzberg, Henry: *The Nature of Managerial Work,* Harper & Row, Publishers, Incorporated, New York, 1973.

Newman, William H., Charles E. Summer, and E. Kirby Warren: *The Process of Management,* 3d ed., Prentice-Hall, Inc., Englewood Cliffs, N.J., 1972.

DALTON E. MCFARLAND, *University of Alabama in Birmingham*

**Managerial control**   (*See* CONTROL SYSTEMS, MANAGEMENT.)

**Managerial ethics**   (*See* ETHICS, MANAGERIAL.)

## Managerial grid

The *managerial grid*® is a two-dimensional model of the various styles of leadership. Based on the theory that managers can be simultaneously and to varying degrees both task- and people-oriented, the grid permits analysis on a scale of 1 to 9 of the degree of a leader's concern for people and for productivity. (See Fig. M-5.) The optimum position is usually considered to be 9,9—a maximum interest for both people and production.

The well-known managerial grid, registered, was developed by Robert R. Blake and Jane S. Mouton in 1962 in the course of research into leadership. They designed it as an alternative to the Ohio State University's quadrant model, which in its turn evolved from Rensis Likert's linear continuum model of leadership. (*See* SYSTEM 4.)

Blake and Mouton labeled the vertical axis of their managerial grid *concern for people*, the horizontal axis *concern for production*, and divided each into a scale of 9. Five basic leadership styles are highlighted in this conception. A 1,1 manager is abdicative, "impoverished," concerned neither for people nor production, only for maintaining the status quo. The 1,9 manager, fairly or not, has often been called the country club type, who shows great concern for people by emphasizing a friendly atmosphere and harmonious relationships but shows little interest in production. In contrast, the 9,1 manager is a slave driver, the autocratic task manager. The middle-of-the-road 5,5 manager shows a balanced concern for people and their morale and concern for production, but the middle-of-the-road manager also needs to move in the direction of the 9,9 team manager who evokes high production from people committed to the goals of the organization and relating to one another in trust and mutual respect.

Blake and Mouton have used the managerial grid both as a tool for the analysis of a leader's style and as an aid in setting goals and designing training for the development of effective managers. They have devised a six-stage training program to enable managers to move toward 7,7, 8,8, and 9,9 positions. The phases include laboratory-seminar training, team development, intergroup development, organizational goal setting, goal attainment, and stabilization, all factors to be measured in placing a manager on the grid.

The research findings of Blake and Mouton, as epitomized in the managerial grid, have changed the thinking of many theorists and led them to accept the concept that effective managers can be both hard and soft, both task- and people-oriented. Many companies have found the grid to be a practical tool for helping managers to increase their effectiveness, particularly in redirecting their orientation toward people, in the case of the 9,1 manager, or toward production, for the 1,9 manager. While the concept of the grid itself is widely accepted, it has not been established that most effective managers are indeed at 9,9, although the research of Blake and Mouton reveals that 99.5 percent of managers in their seminars do believe that this is the soundest way to manage. (The second most popular style among these managers is 9,1, and the third is 5,5.) Follow-up research 2 to 3 years later in companies using the grid finds managers retaining these opinions to the same degree. Blake and Mouton themselves, however, recommend the situational approach, using the style that works best in the particular situation.

*See also* INTERPERSONAL RELATIONSHIPS; LEADERSHIP; MOTIVATION IN ORGANIZATIONS.

### REFERENCES
Blake, Robert R., and Jane S. Mouton: *The Managerial Grid*, Gulf Publishing Company, Houston, 1964.
Blake, Robert R., Jane S. Mouton, Louis B. Barnes, and Larry E. Greiner: "Breakthrough in Organization Development," *Harvard Business Review*, November–December 1964, pp. 137–138.
Blake, Robert R., Jane Srygley Mouton, and Benjamin Fruchter: "A Factor Analysis of Training Group Behavior," *Journal of Social Psychology*, October 1962, pp. 121–130.
Hersey, P., and K. H. Blanchard: "So You Want to Know Your Leadership Style?" *Training and Development Journal*, vol. 28, no. 2, pp. 22–37, 1974.

STAFF/HOKE

## Managers, notable business

Many honors and awards programs exist for the recognition of those individuals who have made significant contributions to the field of management, either as practitioners or creative observers, or both. Typically, professional and trade associations and business or management publications and journals make such formal recognitions periodically. There are, however, two recognition programs that are

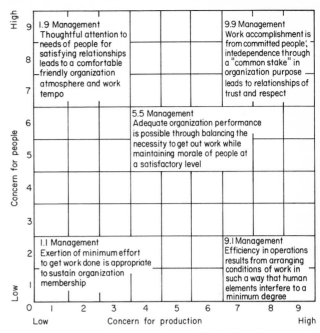

Fig. M-5. Managerial grid *(From Robert R. Blake and Jane S. Mouton, "Managerial Facades," Advanced Management Journal, July 1966, p. 31. Reprinted with permission.)*

particularly thorough and unbiased in their selection process and eclectic in the quality of their choices. These are (1) the Gantt Medal for "distinguished achievement in management as a service to the community" and (2) the Hall of Fame for Business Leadership. The former activity has been sponsored and conducted since 1929 jointly by the American Society of Mechanical Engineers and the American Management Association. The latter program began in 1975 and is sponsored by Junior Achievement, with selections made by the editors of *Fortune* magazine.

*See also* GANTT MEDAL AWARDS; HALL OF FAME OF BUSINESS LEADERSHIP; MANAGEMENT, HISTORICAL DEVELOPMENT OF.

### REFERENCES
Dale, Ernest: *The Great Organizers*, McGraw-Hill Book Company, New York, 1971.
Dale, Ernest: *Readings in Management: Landmarks and New Frontiers*, 3d ed., McGraw-Hill Book Company, New York, 1975.
Jennings, E. E.: *An Anatomy of Leadership: Princes, Heroes, and Supermen*, McGraw-Hill Book Company, New York, 1972.
Jennings, E. E.: *Routes to the Executive Suite*, McGraw-Hill Book Company, New York, 1976.

Merrill, Harwood F.: *Classics in Management*, American Management Association, New York, 1960.

Sizelove, Oliver J., and Marshall Anderson, eds.: *Fifty Years Progress in Management, 1910–1960*, The American Society of Mechanical Engineers, New York, 1960.

Urwick, L., ed.: *The Golden Book of Management*, Newman Neame, Limited, London, 1956.

Urwick, L., and E. F. L. Brech: *The Making of Scientific Management*, Management Publications, Trust, London, 1954.

STAFF/BITTEL

## Manipulation (*See* INTERPERSONAL RELATIONSHIPS.)

## Manuals, organization (*See* ORGANIZATION STRUCTURES AND CHARTING.)

## Manuals, personnel (*See* PERSONNEL ADMINISTRATION.)

## Manuals, policy and procedures

Policy and procedures manuals for an organization serve to record general and/or specific guidelines and operational elements and sequences for directive and/or reference purposes. Typically, these are active documents designed for ongoing managerial use and are subject to continual change and update.

Manuals are commonly prepared to include (and are often labeled as) the following:

*Policy*, covering general guidelines for major aspects of the organization's activities.

*Operations*, covering procedures for the central conversion processes of the particular organizations, such as manufacturing or production, construction, loans, credit, sales, accounting, data processing, and customer relations.

*Support*, covering the service or ancillary functions, such as maintenance, purchasing, inventory control, quality control, production control, research and development, advertising, and traffic.

*Administration*, covering office or clerically related procedures usually associated with accounting, sales and purchase-order processing, and data processing.

*Organization*, setting forth the organizational structure with specific attention to position titles and descriptions along with specifications of responsibilities and authorities, especially as they pertain to financial and legal activities for disbursing funds, approving sales and purchase commitments, signing contracts, and hiring and firing employees.

*Personnel*, dealing with the entire range of people-oriented activities, especially wages and hours, safety and health, promotions and separations, and employee benefits.

*Standards*, including—generally or separately—standard specifications for cost, time, processes and products, design and engineering.

**Content** Content of manuals varies widely according to their purpose, but all the following warrant consideration:

*Statement of policy*. For each item, a clear, concise delineation of the underlying policy provides the rationale for whatever specific implementation instructions follow.

*Implementation instructions*. These prescribe how the policy is to be carried out—the procedure or sequence—often in step-by-step order.

*Variations*. This acknowledges differences in application, as between home and branch offices, a main plant and a satellite, a domestic or a foreign operation.

*Explanations*. These anticipate problems of interpretation about critical or complex aspects and handle them in question and answer style or with examples.

*Forms*. Wherever a standard form is employed, it is helpful to reproduce it and to illustrate its use.

**Format** There are also common requirements of format that must be considered and resolved. These include:

*Physical format*. A looseleaf form is generally most suitable since it facilitates revision, but there is nothing wrong in issuing manuals periodically in bound form. Looseleaf format presupposes that holders of manuals routinely take care of the mechanics of updating, and this often does not occur.

*Readability*. Writing style, type selection, layout, and use of illustrations should aim toward the objective of clarity.

*Ease of reference*. Arrangement of material in the manual may be according to (1) function (assembly and finishing); (2) department (A shop and B shop); (3) problem (discipline and separation); or (4) any other way that conforms to the organization's typical way of thinking. Items and paragraphs may also be lettered and numbered, which helps in identifying material when revised. A comprehensive index and cross-index of terms and problems is especially useful.

*Cost*. The manual should not be designed to be a monument, and the cost of preparation and the format should be justified by the manual's intent and usage.

**Preparation**   In almost every instance, manual preparation is a costly, tedious, time-consuming, ongoing task. In its initial stages, a committee and subcommittee—at least for review purposes—are helpful. Usually, a single individual or department must be more or less permanently assigned to the task of assembling, integrating, rewriting, producing, distributing, monitoring, and updating.

**Distribution**   Two principal factors affect distribution: cost and control. The first is self-evident. The second depends upon both the degree to which information needs widespread dissemination and the degree to which the information is judged to be sensitive or privileged.

**Revision**   Policies need periodic review (annually is a good rule of thumb) in view of changing organizational objectives and strategies. Specific procedures need almost constant surveillance in view of the dynamic nature of most organizations and operations. On the one hand, revisions should be made as soon as a significant change in a critical element occurs. On the other hand, becoming aware of changes and making them accelerate the costs quickly. A determination of when or how often revisions should be made should relate to the true intent of the manual. If it is, in effect, a legal document, early change is probably warranted. If the manual deals with vital matters such as those affecting employee safety or product liability, early change is imperative. If, however, a particular matter is neither critical nor urgent and has been well communicated by other channels, it can wait for a periodic review.

*See also* COMMUNICATIONS, EMPLOYEE; COMMUNICATIONS, ORGANIZATIONAL; ORGANIZATION STRUCTURES AND CHARTING; POLICY FORMULATION AND IMPLEMENTATION; WRITING FOR BUSINESS.

### REFERENCES

"Financial Manuals," Report No. 510, The Conference Board, Inc., New York, 1971.
"How to Develop a Company Personnel Policy Manual," The Dartnell Corporation, Chicago, 1975.
"How to Prepare an Effective Company Operations Manual," The Dartnell Corporation, Chicago, 1974.
Lennox, Frederick E.: "Maintenance Manuals," in L. C. Morrow, ed., *Maintenance Engineering Handbook*, McGraw-Hill Book Company, New York, 1966.

STAFF/BITTEL

## Manuals, purchasing   (See PURCHASING MANAGEMENT.)

## Manufacturer's representatives   (See MARKETING, INDUSTRIAL.)

## Manufacturing, contract   (See PRODUCTION/OPERATIONS MANAGEMENT.)

## Manufacturing engineering   (See PRODUCTION PROCESSES.)

## Manufacturing management   (See PRODUCTION/OPERATIONS MANAGEMENT.)

## Manufacturing operations   (See PRODUCTION PROCESSES.)

## Manufacturing research   (See PRODUCTION PROCESSES.)

## MAPI, Machinery and Allied Products Institute   (See BUDGETING, CAPITAL.)

## Margin, contribution   (See ACCOUNTING FOR MANAGERIAL CONTROL.)

## Margin of safety   (See ACCOUNTING FOR MANAGERIAL CONTROL.)

## Marginal cost   (See PRODUCT AND SERVICE PRICING.)

## Marginal income analysis

Marginal income theory explains how to segregate costs according to the way in which they behave. The theory also explains the relationship between cost behavior and volume and resulting effects on profits.

In practice, marginal income analysis provides the professional manager with important insights into the business that are not possible under more traditional accounting and cost analysis techniques: (1) a quick, graphic way to determine break-even points; (2) an accurate measure of a product's true profitability; and (3) a sound basis for making pricing and marketing decisions. Beyond its usefulness as an analytical tool, marginal income provides a sound basis for cost control. By understanding the behavior pattern of costs, a manager can pinpoint responsibility and develop meaningful standards of performance.

## MARGINAL INCOME THEORY

The concept of marginal income, or direct costing upon which it is based, was not widely accepted until the early 1960s. In brief, marginal income theory holds that there is a natural and logical segregation of costs according to the pattern in which they behave. As illustrated in Fig. M-6, there are three categories of behavior:

*Variable costs:* those that vary directly with some measurable unit of production, such as the number of pieces produced or service transactions performed. The materials and labor used directly in manufacturing, shipping costs, and sales commissions are typically variable costs. (The examples cited here and below pertain to a manufacturing business, but the theory holds true for service-related enterprises and financial institutions equally well.)

*Fixed costs:* those that are measured by, or may change with, time. Supervisory salaries, insurance

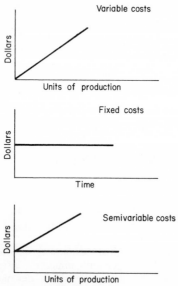

**Fig. M-6. Fixed versus variable costs.**

premiums, and property taxes are examples of fixed costs. They represent the cost of being in business and will not vary directly with the volume of the business. *Period costs* is a more accurate, but less generally used, definition of fixed costs.

*Semivariable costs:* those that contain both fixed and variable elements. Utilities are typically semivariable costs. There is generally a base charge for electricity whether you use 500 or 500,000 kilowatts. The incremental cost beyond the base charge moves up or down with usage.

This segregation of costs according to the way they behave enables an enterprise to look at some interesting and highly important facets of its business:

*Marginal income:* the amount of sales dollar left after variable costs are covered. If a company is selling a product for $20, and the total variable cost (labor, materials, expenses) of producing that product is $12, its marginal income is $8. Marginal income is used to pay fixed costs and to contribute to profits when sufficient volume has been reached.

*Marginal income ratio:* marginal income expressed as a percentage of sales dollars. For the product described above, the marginal income ratio is 40 percent ($8 ÷ $20).

*Break-even point:* the level of sales volume where marginal income equals the total of fixed costs. Sales above this level contribute to profits. Sales below this level result in a loss.

In short, marginal income seeks to separate the direct out-of-pocket costs that go into the product from the fixed costs of being in business.

## MARGINAL INCOME IN PRACTICE

As an example of the practical applications of marginal income, follow the hypothetical fortunes of The Orange Outdoor Grill Company, a manufacturer and distributor of fireplace grills. Examine how they use marginal income (1) in profit planning; (2) to measure the relative profitability of their product mix; and (3) to control costs.

**The Break-Even Chart** Unless a company systematically prepares a profit plan, it will simply be a matter of luck as to whether or not they obtain their profit objectives. The Orange Outdoor Grill Company, however, finds that the break-even chart based on marginal income principles provides them with a clear, concise look at their profit picture. The information needed to construct the chart is shown on the abbreviated marginal income statement in Table M-1.

**TABLE M-1  Example of an Abbreviated Marginal Income Statement**

THE ORANGE OUTDOOR GRILL COMPANY
Marginal Income Statement, January 1978

| | |
|---|---|
| Variable costs ............................ | $49,600 |
| Fixed costs ............................... | 43,100 |
| Total costs ............................... | 92,700 |
| Net sales.................................. | 139,000 |
| Net profit before taxes ................... | 46,300 |
| Marginal income .......................... | 89,400 |
| (Sales − variable costs) | |
| Marginal income ratio ..................... | 64% |
| (Marginal income ÷ sales) | |

A graph of the chart is shown in Fig. M-7. The horizontal axis represents sales dollars. (This can also represent units of production if a single product is charted.) The vertical axis represents fixed costs, or the dollar volume of loss from the midpoint downward and the dollar volume of net profit from the midpoint upward. The profit path begins at the point on the vertical axis representing total fixed

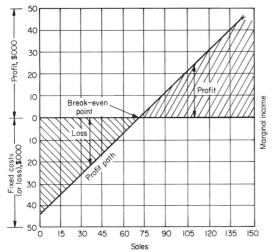

**Fig. M-7. Example of a break-even chart.**

costs, in this case $43,100. If the plant had been shut down for a month, it would have incurred no variable costs, received no revenue, and, therefore, taken a loss equal to the fixed cost of $43,100.

The slope of the profit path is predicated on the marginal income ratio or 64 percent. For every dollar of sales, 64 cents goes toward paying fixed costs and contributing to profits. The break-even point is where the profit path intersects the midpoint of the vertical axis. It represents the volume of sales where marginal income exactly equals fixed costs (64 percent × $67,300 = $43,100).

Another way to construct a break-even chart is illustrated in Fig. M-8. The information needed to construct it is the same, and the results are the same. The horizontal axis again represents sales and the vertical axis costs, profit, or loss. In this case, however, both axes begin at zero. The variable-cost line

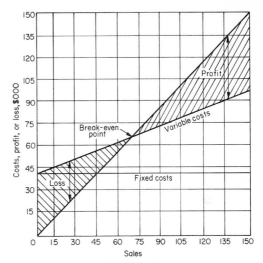

**Fig. M-8. Another example of a break-even chart.**

begins on the vertical axis at the point representing fixed costs—$43,100. The slope of the variable-cost line is determined by dividing variable costs by sales ($49,000 ÷ $139,000 = 36 percent). In other words, 36 cents of every sales dollar is spent for variable costs. It is the reciprocal of marginal income (64 percent). The break-even point occurs where the variable-cost line intersects the diagonal sales slope line [$43,100 + (36 percent × X) = $67,300].

The second method of constructing a break-even chart results in a somewhat more complicated graph. Doing it both ways, however, enhances an understanding of marginal income theory and helps ensure accuracy.

The break-even chart illustrates cost-volume-profit relationships graphically. With a profit objective in mind, a company can project alternative means to reach that objective. Here are some situations where break-even charts are useful:

1. *When considering a pricing change*, the break-even chart provides a means of determining the effects of the proposed change on profits and the break-even point. This is especially true where demand for the product has a high degree of elasticity, i.e., where the sales volume is sensitive to price changes. The break-even chart will not tell you how

elastic your market is, but it will help picture the profit potential as well as the risks to which you may be exposed.

    2. *During labor negotiations* the break-even chart helps to predict the effects on costs and profits of alternative bargaining proposals. An increase in fringe benefits will tend to increase fixed costs more heavily. A straight wage-rate increase will add to both fixed and variable costs proportionally.

    3. *When evaluating a proposed capital expenditure*, or alternative expenditures, the break-even chart will help evaluate the effects of the expenditure on the overall financial structure of the business.

**Product Profitability**  Marginal income theory provides the most accurate measure of the true profitability of various products. Absorption-based accounting systems that attempt to allocate overhead costs among various products frequently give misleading signals about the true worth of a product and its contribution to profits.

    Table M-2 shows the full marginal income statement for The Orange Outdoor Grill Company. The company sells three products—an economy grill, a standard grill, and the deluxe grill. At the bottom of Table M-2, the fixed costs of $43,100 are distributed among (or are "absorbed" by) the three products the company manufactures in proportion to the labor dollars expended on each product. This is the most common way of allocating overhead costs among absorption-based systems.

    Table M-3 compares the relative profitability of the three products on a full absorbed basis. It would appear that the deluxe grill has the better earning power of the three, enjoying a 38 percent return on

**TABLE M-2  Example of a Full Marginal Income Statement**

THE ORANGE OUTDOOR GRILL COMPANY
Marginal Income Statement, January 1978

| | Economy grill | Standard grill | Deluxe grill | Total |
|---|---|---|---|---|
| Variable costs | | | | |
|   Material | $6,000 | $9,500 | $10,700 | $26,200 |
|   Labor | 6,700 | 7,300 | 3,000 | 17,000 |
|   Expenses | 2,200 | 3,200 | 1,000 | 6,400 |
|   Total | 14,900 | 20,000 | 14,700 | 49,600 |
| Fixed costs | | | | 43,100 |
| Total costs | 14,900 | 20,000 | 14,700 | 92,700 |
| Net sales | 45,000 | 58,000 | 36,000 | 139,000 |
| Marginal income | 30,100 | 38,000 | 21,300 | 89,400 |
| Net profit before taxes | | | | 46,300 |
| Fixed costs absorbed | | | | |
|   on labor dollars | 16,800 | 18,500 | 7,800 | 43,100 |
| Net profit before taxes | 13,300 | 19,500 | 13,500 | 46,300 |

**TABLE M-3  Comparative Profitability of Products**

| | Economy grill | Standard grill | Deluxe grill |
|---|---|---|---|
| Sales | $45,000 | $58,000 | $36,000 |
| Fixed and variable costs | 31,700 | 38,500 | 22,500 |
| Net profit before taxes | 13,300 | 19,500 | 13,500 |
| Net profit/sales | 30% | 34% | 38% |

sales as compared with 34 and 30 percent, respectively, for the other two products.

    If one looks at marginal income ratios, however, and cuts through the fog of allocating unrelated overheads to individual products, a much different and clearer picture is shown in Table M-4. Based on actual, out-of-pocket costs, the economy and the standard grills are clearly the most profitable prod-

**TABLE M-4  Comparative Profitability with Marginal Income**

| | Economy grill | Standard grill | Deluxe grill |
|---|---|---|---|
| Sales | $45,000 | $58,000 | $36,000 |
| Variable costs | 14,900 | 20,000 | 14,700 |
| Marginal income | 30,100 | 38,000 | 21,300 |
| Marginal income/sales | 67% | 66% | 59% |

ucts, and the deluxe grill the least. If, for example, the company plans to spend $50,000 on a promotional campaign, the economy grill represents the most attractive investment opportunity. An increase in economy grill sales of $75,000 will cover the cost of the promotion. On the other hand, an increase in deluxe grill sales of $85,000 would be needed to cover the same promotional expenditure.

**Pricing Applications**  Marginal income provides a valuable insight into product profitability when faced with pricing decisions. Under the marginal income concept, the standard direct cost of a product includes all out-of-pocket costs for producing that product. This is the rock-bottom figure for pricing purposes. If unused plant capacity exists, *any* price set above the standard direct cost will generate marginal income to cover fixed costs and contribute toward profits.

    Assume that a national retailer approaches The Orange Outdoor Grill Company with an offer to buy 10,000 standard grills for delivery over the next 12 months under a private-label arrangement. Since it has the capacity to fill the order, the management at Orange thinks the offer represents an excellent opportunity—until it comes around to the question of price. The top price the retailer will pay is $30 a unit. Orange has produced 1160 standard grills in

January. If it looks only at the numbers generated by the traditional accounting systems (as shown in Table M-3), it would conclude that the cost of producing standard grills is slightly over $33 per unit ($38,500 ÷ 1160 = $33.19). As a result, it would appear that they would wind up losing over $30,000 on the order.

Marginal income (Table M-4), however, tells a completely different story. The variable out-of-pocket cost of producing a standard grill is actually $17.24 ($20,000 ÷ 1160), leaving a marginal income of $12.76 per unit on a selling price of $30. Instead of losing $32,000 on the deal, the company would gain an additional marginal income of $128,000 which would go toward covering fixed costs and contributing to profits.

**Marketing Applications** Analyzing marginal income, or cost-volume-profit relationships, at the production level tells one story for a manufacturing firm. When there are alternative distribution methods open to the firm, looking at marginal income ratios for merchandising costs also becomes important. A soft drink manufacturer, for example, has a wide variety of distribution outlets among which to choose: small grocery and confectionery stores, supermarkets, vending machines, taverns, and bars, among others. While the profit contribution of the product on the shipping dock is the same, each outlet is likely to show a different profit picture in the final analysis.

The Orange Outdoor Grill Company has two ways to merchandise its products: through volume sales to a national retailer under a private-label arrangement, or by direct sales through its own sales force. The best price it can get for the private-label sale is $30 a unit, while under its own brand name it can command a price of $50 a unit. Since manufacturing costs are the same in either case, it appears that sales through the company's own organization are far more attractive. By analyzing the comparative distribution costs, as shown in Table M-5, however, a different picture emerges. The final marginal income per unit is about the same. The marginal income ratio on the private-label sale is actually greater than through direct sales.

**Other Applications** The case studies described above illustrate the basic principles of the marginal income approach. There are many other situations that can be brought into clearer focus through the use of this technique:

1. *Product mix* has an important effect on profitability. This is especially true where there is a capacity constraint on production. Establishing the relationship between manufacturing run time and marginal income for each product provides the basis for planning the most advantageous product mix.

2. *Return on investment (ROI)*, or return on assets employed (ROA), analysis lends itself well to the marginal income approach. After establishing the percentage ROI desired, multiply that percentage by the average value of raw and finished inventories; by the average value of accounts receivable; and by the replacement value of your capital assets. To the sum of these three resultants, add the fixed and variable costs of manufacturing and distribution. The resulting figure is the sales goal you must reach to obtain the desired ROI. Adding in your ROI objectives as if they were a cost establishes a profit plan that both manufacturing and marketing can use to develop their strategies.

3. *The banking community* has found the marginal income approach to be a highly useful technique in improving their profitability. The "product" it deals with—money—differs in some respects from that of a typical manufacturing firm. But the techniques of segregating costs according to the way

**TABLE M-5  An Example of Merchandising Marginal Income Analysis**

| Per unit | Private label | Direct sales |
|---|---|---|
| Selling price | $30.00 | $50.00 |
| Standard variable manufacturing cost | 17.24 | 17.24 |
| Standard manufacturing marginal income | 12.76 | 32.76 |
| Standard manufacturing marginal income ratio | 43% | 66% |
| Standard variable distribution costs | | |
| Packing and loading | 0.65 | 2.33 |
| Freight | | |
| Truckload | 1.23 | |
| LTL | | 4.15 |
| Selling costs | | |
| Commissions | | 12.00 |
| Expenses | | 2.77 |
| Promotion and advertising | | 0.36 |
| Total standard variable distribution costs | 1.88 | 21.61 |
| Standard merchandising marginal income | 10.88 | 11.15 |
| Standard merchandising marginal income ratio | 34% | 22% |

in which they behave is just as appropriate. Take the installment loan department, for example. A marginal income ratio can be developed for each transaction at the branch office level where the loan originates. A secondary marginal income ratio can be developed after the loan has been processed through the centralized installment loan department. This same approach applies to all the services a bank offers to its customers.

## CONTROLLING COSTS WITH MARGINAL INCOME

Segregating costs according to the way in which they behave is not just a bookkeeping exercise: there are important corollaries from a cost-control standpoint.

*Variable costs* are controllable at the first level of supervision. It is first-level supervisors who see the direct labor and materials "going past their noses" every day. If effective control of those costs is to be obtained, it must be focused at that level of management.

*Fixed costs*, on the other hand, are controllable at higher levels in the organization. Supervisory salaries, depreciation, property taxes, insurance premiums, and the like, are costs that first-level supervisors have little, if any, influence over. Burdening lower levels of management with this information gains little and tends to distract them from their real mission—controlling variable costs.

**Performance Standards**  Gaining control over costs is a three-step process:

1. Determining what *should* happen
2. Identifying what *did* happen
3. Taking action to resolve the variances between the two

Most companies have reporting systems which portray what events *did happen* over some given time frame. It is determining what *should happen* over that time frame that is the trick. This is where performance standards are essential. Here are some observations on developing and using performance standards for control purposes:

1. Standards should be set for *all* costs, both fixed and variable. Fixed standards predict the hours or dollars that should be spent over some period of *time*, such as a week or a month; or that should be spent as the result of an *occurrence*, such as cleaning out a storage tank. Variable standards predict the hours or dollars that should be consumed as a consequence of some measurable unit of *activity*, such as pieces produced, hours of machine operation, or cases shipped.

2. There are two differing philosophical approaches to setting standards. The first is the engineered approach that seeks to develop the perfect standard which will only be attainable under ideal operating conditions. The engineered standards are set by using time and motion studies and other industrial engineering techniques. The second is a more empirical approach. It seeks to develop standards that can be met by the average performer under typical operating conditions. The standards are set by analyzing historical results and by consulting with supervisors who have responsibility for the activity under study.

Many companies have found that this latter approach will get the job done quicker and cheaper than going the engineered route. Further, involving the supervisor in the standard-setting process has positive motivational benefits. The standard becomes a personal goal that the supervisor has agreed can be met and is willing to be measured by.

3. Each standard should be traceable to that point in the organization where responsibility for controlling that cost resides. The standard should include only those costs over which the supervisor has direct control.

4. There are four elements of cost: labor, materials, expenses, and equipment utilization. Standards should be set for each element of cost independently. The individual standards can then be pulled together to measure a supervisor's full performance and to construct product cost standards.

**Control Reports**  The effort devoted to developing performance standards will be wasted if an effective means of looking at results is lacking. Everyone wants to do a good job. Everyone wants to know whether or not his or her performance is at an expected level. The overall objective of a control reporting system is to provide a "report card" on how well managers are performing at all levels in the organization.

Here are the fundamental criteria for an effective control system:

*Operations Orientation.*  By definition, a control system is primarily a tool for operating management. The language, terms, and phrases used should be those that operating management uses and feels comfortable with, not the lexicon of the accountant or industrial engineer.

*Timeliness.*  This is an essential point. Information must be made available consistent with management's opportunity and need to take action. Not all elements of cost have the same degree of urgency. Direct labor, for example, should be looked at each week; in a labor-intensive industry, perhaps daily. Fixed costs, such as insurance premiums and property taxes, on the other hand, need only be reviewed monthly or quarterly.

*Responsibility.*  Every cost must be associated with an individual in the organization where responsibility for controlling that cost resides. Where responsibility is not clearly established, there is no way to exercise control. Further, the arbitrary allocation of costs where no accurate measure of usage exists (utilities, for example) lessens rather than strengthens control.

*Standard versus Actual.* Every cost should be compared with a standard. Simply comparing costs with what happened last month or last year does not provide control. Where standards have not yet been developed, actual costs should be compared with a forecast, or budget, of what the costs should be for the current period of time. Budgets, however, are more valuable for planning purposes than for control purposes.

*Keeping Costs Pure.* Each element of cost (labor, materials, expenses, and equipment utilization) should be looked at independently and not in combination with one another. A first-level supervisor, for example, may have shown good results in equipment utilization, but may have done so by using

extra labor which exceeded the value of the increased output.

*Even Periods.* Operating people tend to think and plan in terms of weeks. For control purposes, a month has little significance. Dividing the year into 13 four-week periods provides greater comparability between reporting periods and avoids time-consuming midweek manipulations to meet a month-end closing. The financial system can be reconciled with the control system at the end of each quarter.

*Exception Reporting.* The well-designed control system provides information in diminishing detail at successively higher levels of management. The top-level summary report of even a billion dollar corporation should occupy no more than two or three pages. The virtue of comparing actual costs with standard costs allows managers at all levels to concentrate their energies on those areas most deserving of their efforts.

Table M-6 illustrates a typical control report embodying the principles described above. It portrays

**TABLE M-6   Example of a Typical Control Report**

THE ORANGE OUTDOOR GRILL COMPANY
Standard Grill Department Labor Control, dollars
Period 1: 4 weeks, ending 1/28/79
Responsibility: A. J. Miller

| Description | Resp. | Standard | | | Actual | Variance | % | O/T premium |
|---|---|---|---|---|---|---|---|---|
| | | Fixed | Variable | Total | | | | |
| 1 | 2 | 3 | 4 | 5 | 6 | 7 | 8 | 9 |
| Fabrication | | | | | | | | |
| Line 1 | H. K. | | 10,200 | 10,200 | 9,375 | 825 | 8 | 520 |
| Line 2 | S. M. | | 9,850 | 9,850 | 9,480 | 370 | 4 | 650 |
| Total | J. H. | | 20,050 | 20,050 | 18,855 | 1,195 | 6 | 1,170 |
| Finishing | | | | | | | | |
| Galvanizing | R. P. | | 9,820 | 9,820 | 13,176 | (3,356) | (34) | 1,275 |
| Painting | C. S. | | 14,730 | 14,730 | 15,319 | (589) | (4) | 850 |
| Total | W. E. | | 24,550 | 24,550 | 28,495 | (3,945) | (16) | 2,125 |
| Shipping | A. A. | 4,050 | 2,950 | 7,000 | 6,650 | 350 | 5 | |
| Maintenance | | | | | | | | |
| Equipment | C. A. | 7,250 | | 7,250 | 5,800 | 1,450 | 20 | 540 |
| Facilities | W. Z. | 3,250 | | 3,250 | 2,600 | 650 | 20 | |
| Total | C. H. | 10,500 | | 10,500 | 8,400 | 2,100 | 20 | 540 |
| Supervision | A. M. | 13,100 | | 13,100 | 12,600 | 500 | 4 | |
| Total department | A. M. | 27,650 | 47,550 | 75,200 | 75,000 | 200 | | 3,835 |

1—Description—The functional divisions of the standard grill department as defined by the organization structure of the department.

2—Resp.—The initials of the individual responsible for each function.

3—Fixed standard—The fixed portion of the standard applicable to this 4-week time period.

4—Variable standard—The variable portion of the standard based on the volume of activity. Fabrication, line 1, for example, consists of 460 grills x a standard of $22.17 labor dollars per grill = $10,200.

5—Total standard—The sum of columns 3 and 4.

6—Actual—The actual labor dollars spent by each functional area during the period.

7—Variance—The difference between standard (column 5) and actual (column 6). An unfavorable variance is enclosed in parentheses.

8—%—The variance (column 7) divided by the total standard (column 5).

9—O/T premium—The premium portion of overtime pay that is included in the actual dollars paid (column 6).

a labor control for the standard grill department, following a year of exceptional growth for The Orange Outdoor Grill Company.

The report gives Mr. A. J. Miller, the standard grill department manager, a quick, but comprehensive, picture of how his functional managers performed in controlling labor costs during the preceding 4-week period. The results did not come as a surprise. Mr. Miller, as well as his individual managers, had seen a report in identical format showing hours instead of dollars for each of the four preceding weeks. For operating people, the primary control over labor is in hours. The dollars simply show the economic consequences of their actions.

Overall, Mr. Miller sees that his department is on target with labor costs. Within the department, however, he has two trouble spots. First, his galvanizing line is having serious problems. The line had an unfavorable variance (actual costs exceeded standard costs) by $3356, or 34 percent. It also had the highest incidence of overtime in the department.

Mr. Miller's second problem is less apparent. His maintenance section had a favorable variance (actual costs were less than standard costs) by $2100, or 20 percent. Either his maintenance supervisors had discovered a means for accomplishing their tasks using less labor, or they are falling short on performing the required maintenance. If the latter is true, it spells future trouble.

Mr. Miller has diagnosed where his real and potential problem areas are. The next step is to take action to solve them.

**Variance Meetings** Just as developing performance standards is wasted effort without an effective reporting system, control reports by themselves do not result in control. A formal, systematic procedure is necessary for analyzing results and taking action.

Here are some key features of a successful variance meeting program:

1. Meetings should adhere to organizational lines. First-level supervisors meet with the group supervisor to whom they report; group supervisors meet with their superintendents, and so forth. The most productive size for a group is five or six, rarely more than 10.

2. There should be a regularly scheduled day, time, and place for each meeting.

3. The following agenda should be observed: (a) reports on prior unresolved assignments; (b) review of current control reports; (c) assignments for subsequent meetings.

4. Assignments should be specific: who will undertake them, what results are expected, and by what date they will be completed.

5. Brief one-page minutes of the meetings should be kept and copies distributed to those who attend.

6. In reviewing the current control reports, labor, materials, expenses, and equipment utilization should be looked at separately.

7. The meetings should last no more than an hour. If the agenda has not been covered, schedule a follow-up meeting.

*Philosophy of Variance Meetings.* There are two underlying philosophical objectives in holding variance meetings. On the surface the objectives appear to be contradictory. In practice they are not.

The first objective is to motivate the individual supervisors to improve performance. Almost everyone wants to do a good job. No one likes to show unfavorable variances that are visible to peers. The variance meeting sets up friendly competition among supervisors, exerting peer pressure toward better performance.

The second objective is to promote the team approach toward problem solving. The variance meeting brings together supervisors who face similar problems and who have had similar experiences. If one member of the group is having a problem, or if the group as a whole is facing a similar problem, the most workable solution is likely to result from collective rather than independent thinking about the problem.

Balancing friendly competition against the team approach requires management skill on the part of second-level supervisors and above. How well they exercise that skill to produce uniformly satisfactory results is the measure of their performance.

*See also* ACCOUNTING, COST ANALYSIS AND CONTROL; ACCOUNTING FOR MANAGERIAL CONTROL; BUDGETS AND BUDGET PREPARATION; EXCEPTION, MANAGEMENT BY; FINANCIAL MANAGEMENT; PROFIT IMPROVEMENT.

## REFERENCES

Batty, J.: *Standard Costing*, MacDonald and Evans, Ltd., London, 1975.

Dearden, John: *Cost Accounting and Financial Control Systems*, Addison-Wesley Publishing Company, Inc., Reading, Mass., 1973.

Livingstone, John Leslie: *Management Planning and Control: Mathematical Models*, McGraw-Hill Book Company, New York, 1970.

Maynard, H. B.: *Industrial Engineering Handbook*, 3d ed., McGraw-Hill Book Company, New York, 1971.

McCormick, Edmund J.: "Sharpening the Competitive Edge for Profits," *Financial Executive*, April 1975.

Wilson, R. M. S.: *Cost Control Handbook*, John Wiley & Sons, Inc., New York, 1975.

Woolsey, Samuel M.: *Direct Costing Techniques for Industry*, Prentice-Hall, Inc., Englewood Cliffs, N.J., 1967.

RANDOLPH B. MCMULLEN, *McCormick and Company, Consulting Engineers*

# Market, perfect (See ECONOMIC CONCEPTS.)

# Market analysis

Market analysis encompasses activities directed toward the systematic study of the nature of (1) consumer needs and wants, (2) product characteristics (to what extent they do or do not meet the needs), (3) competitive market structure, and (4) consumer characteristics. The objective of market analysis is to identify the consumer needs and wants, determine the degree to which the product characteristics meet these needs and wants, examine how the products may be modified or redesigned or new products created to increase the degree to which consumer needs and wants are met—while at the same time trying to minimize the impact of competing products/brands. After finding the characteristics of the buyers of the product, i.e., the target market, it is possible to estimate the potential of the market by estimating the expected demand based on the size and the income and expenditure characteristics of the target market.

Market analysis helps to reduce the degree of uncertainty associated with the outcome of alternative marketing strategies. It is instrumental in enabling management to develop and select viable strategies for product screening, positioning, maintaining, and, if necessary, phasing out.

Market analysis is interrelated with a wide variety of associated activities, such as marketing research. This entry, however, is organized around the central aspects of the subject. These are: (1) market opportunity analysis, (2) market segmentation analysis, and (3) market potential analysis.

## MARKET OPPORTUNITY ANALYSIS

The marketing manager faces threats due to the actions of rival companies, sudden changes in the economic environment, shifts in consumer life-styles, etc. Rather than reacting defensively, according to Kotler,[1] a more positive approach is to view these threats as veiled opportunities for revising ongoing marketing activities and examining alternatives. The process of the development and evaluation of alternatives is accomplished by means of market opportunity analysis. This process is characterized by (1) identification of alternatives; (2) determination of the value of the alternative relative to the objectives of the firm; (3) evaluation of the alternative with respect to the ability of the firm to adopt it and to take purposeful marketing action with a reasonable probability of success; and (4) formulation of feasible strategies for responding to the opportunity.

**Market Needs Analysis** This concept is central to the identification and generation of opportunities. It is based on the premise that all products satisfy certain needs that consumers have, and the performance of products is directly proportional to the salience of these needs and the degree to which they are satisfied. Market needs analysis is hence primarily concerned with the assessment of issues such as:

What are the needs of the consumers?

How important are these needs?

What is currently being done to satisfy these needs?

What would be an ideal solution?

What would be an acceptable solution?

What needs are likely to develop in the future as a result of technological breakthroughs or changes in life-styles?

Market needs analysis is usually performed at two levels. In conducting needs assessment at the *exploratory level*, all relevant inputs such as feedback from sales personnel, findings from ongoing marketing research, reports from the customer complaints and service departments, hunches, and expert opinions (to name a few) should be used. Techniques such as focus-group interviews, group discussions, and brainstorming are quite adequate because the objective at the exploratory level is to identify, speculate, and formulate hypotheses to be researched further. Subsequently, more *advanced* techniques of marketing research can be used to test these hypotheses with consumers, using approved methodologies for research design, survey methods, and statistical inference.[2]

**Product Position** In order to evaluate the attractiveness of any alternative, it becomes essential to examine market factors such as the ability of competitors to duplicate the product, the barriers to entry, and the trends that can be anticipated over the duration of the life of the product. A product's position, even the viability of its concept, depends on the needs of the consumer and the ability of the product (and its competitors) to satisfy those needs. Since both consumer needs and the nature of the competition are susceptible to changes over time, it is imperative to examine the profitability of products over their life span. This requires examination of the historical performance of the product and a projection of what may happen in the future.

**Product Life Cycle**   This is a related concept that addresses these issues. Basically, it is an attempt to identify distinct stages in the history of the product. Most examinations of sales histories of products yield four stages in the product life cycle: introduction, growth, maturity, and decline. Each stage characteristically faces relatively distinct problems with respect to marketing strategies due to distinct patterns of profit potential and competitive market structure. Accordingly, it is feasible to make better marketing plans if one can identify the stage the product is in or will be in.

Figure M-9 illustrates the typical sales and profit trends associated with the product life cycle. The theory of diffusion and adoption of innovations[3] lends support to the shape of the sales curve. In the introduction stage there is resistance from the consumers, and the firm has to create awareness, stimulate interest, etc. The product is adopted by a small proportion of potential customers (the innovators). Subsequently, as the product gains acceptability, there is a rapid increase in sales during the growth stage due to purchases by early adopters and early majority. The sales stabilize during the maturity stage when the major contribution to sales is due to replacement rather than initial purchase. Eventually, due to the emergence of new competing products, there is a decreasing interest in the product, leading to the decline stage.

Table M-7 contrasts some of the aspects of the four stages of the product life cycle that have impli-

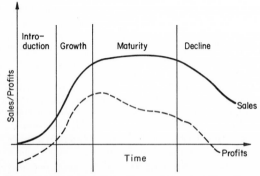

**Fig. M-9. Sales and profit trends over the product life cycle.**

cations for market opportunity analysis. Examination of Table M-7 reveals that products face varying levels of competition during their life cycle. The marketing manager will typically encounter different problem mixes over the four stages. Hence, at different stages of the product life cycle, different aspects of market analysis gain importance.

A key aspect in proceeding with analysis at this point is the concept of market segmentation which allows management to devise strategies to meet the differential demands of various segments of the market and, in addition, to uncover the presence of unfulfilled consumer needs that furnish future opportunities.

## MARKET SEGMENTATION ANALYSIS

The success of market segmentation approaches is centered on the validity of the following propositions: (1) consumers are different, and these differences are measurable; (2) differences among consumers are related to their differential behavior in the marketplace; and (3) segments of different consumers can be isolated in the market.[4]

Market segmentation in developed, competitive economies is an essentially viable strategy because it matches differential consumer needs with appropriate product characteristics or attributes. This by itself is not segmentation. Market segmentation also requires (1) the identification of homogeneous subsets of consumers that could be treated as target submarkets and (2) that these subsets be accessible with distinct marketing mixes.

*Advantages.* Market segmentation is associated with numerous advantages. Some of these are: (1) an understanding of the market, e.g., knowing who the customers are and why they purchase the product; (2) identification of new opportunities that may be exploited in the future; (3) enhancement of management's ability to identify and plan for changing market trends; (4) formulation of rational media plans; and (5) identification of strengths and weaknesses of competitors, and consequently the identification of segments that offer competitive advantages.

*Problems.* One of the main problems with segmentation is that it lends to product disaggregation, which adversely affects economies of scale. Also, management has to formulate and monitor marketing mixes for different segments which sometimes complicates decision making.

**Segmentation Variables**   A large number of variables, the choice of which is dictated by the product

**TABLE M-7    Some Aspects of the Product Life Cycle**

| Aspects \ Stages | Introduction | Growth | Maturity | Decline |
|---|---|---|---|---|
| Profit levels expected | Losses can be expected due to heavy costs of research and development, etc. | Increasing profits due to higher sales and decreasing unit costs for promotion and production. | Profits peak early in this stage and then start to decline due to more firms joining the "bandwagon," which results in intense competition, price cutting, etc. | Rapid decline in profits due to decreased sales, cut-throat competition, decreasing economics of scale. |
| Competitive market structure | Little competition unless rival firms are introducing similar products. Promotional efforts by competitors are likely to promote product class rather than brands. Since consumer preferences are not stabilized, market share fluctuates. | Competition is still limited, especially for products requiring greater technological know-how. However, if the technological barriers are low, promotional efforts play an important role in determining the market share that will ultimately result. | Competition becomes much more intense, and market share stabilizes due to the development of preferences based on earlier purchases. Because of a larger number of products with similar characteristics, price plays an important part in determining market share. | Because firms have sunk costs and market sales are declining, competitors are willing to cut prices almost to the level of marginal costs. Generally, only strongly entrenched firms can hold on to their market share. |
| Typical problem mixes—information needs for pertinent decisions | 1. Consumer resistance to adoption due to reluctance to change existing behavioral patterns, etc.<br>2. Uncertainty regarding the extent and nature of the market.<br>3. What product features are important to make it a success? How to emphasize them?<br>4. Distribution problems due to item 2. | 1. Estimation of the impact of competitors' strategies.<br>2. Should profit levels or market share be maximized?<br>3. Who are the customers? How should they be cultivated?<br>4. Are any product improvements necessary?<br>5. Is the distribution system adequate? | 1. How can we induce customers to use the product more frequently?<br>2. What are the characteristics of "heavy" users?<br>3. Can the product be modified or improved to stimulate sales?<br>4. Are there ways to increase the efficiency of the distribution system? Can profits of intermediaries be restricted without endangering market share?<br>5. Can we stress any attributes of our product to make inroads into competitors' market share? | 1. How rapid is the decline expected to be?<br>2. Should the firm withdraw from the market?<br>3. Is it worth the expense to try to reawaken interest?<br>4. What are the advantages of new competing products? Can these be offset? |

type and the objectives of the research, can be used to segment a market. These can be classified into six general categories: geographic, demographic, psychographic, product usage, perceptual, and brand loyalty variables.[5] The first three refer to consumer characteristics and the last three to consumer response. Table M-8 lists examples of these variables. Though not all variables are appropriate for every market, it is usually necessary to utilize a battery of measures of consumer characteristics (geographic, demographic, and psychographic variables) and response (product usage, perceptual, and brand loyalty variables).

**Types of Segmentation**    The type of market analysis employed depends on the type of information the researcher is seeking to aid in decision making. Correspondingly, the type of segmentation attempted depends on the objectives of the research.

Table M-8 lists some of the more common ways of segmenting a market, the variables used, the strategic implications, and the areas of market planning where they would be particularly useful. Depending on the complexity of the market situation, two or more of these ways of segmentation may have to be used. For example, the marketer may be interested in conducting market factor segmentation to develop promotional strategies and to effectively allocate resources for the marketing-mix variables. At the same time, the marketer may wish to conduct product-space segmentation to determine the need for product development and positioning.

As discussed earlier, the four stages in the product life cycle are characterized by different problem mixes that have varying information needs. Corresponding to these problem mixes, the various ways of segmenting a market will be differentially benefi-

**TABLE M-8  Types of Segmentation**

| Type of segmentation | Segmentation variables | Strategic implications | Relevant areas of marketing planning |
|---|---|---|---|
| *Geographic:* segmentation based on location of customers, sales territories, etc. | Geographic location regions, sales territories, rural/urban, etc. | Formulation of differentiated marketing strategies for dissimilar regions—could result in greater distribution efficiency and sales force effectiveness. | Physical distribution |
| *Demographic:* distinct groups are identified on the basis of demographic characteristics. | Age, sex, race, education, family size, stage in life cycle, income social class, etc. | Identification of target market in terms of salient demographic variables helps media selection; development of advertising copy to fit more desirable segments; choice of outlets to suit the desirable segments. | Media selection Advertising copy Retail store location |
| *Psychographic:* distinct groups are identified based on their personality life-styles. | Personality: leader/follower, introvert/extrovert, high/low achiever, conservative/radical, swinger/plain Joe, spender/thrifty, etc. | Identification of desired segments in terms of personality characteristics of the members allows the design of advertising copy—especially for image development. Also useful to conceptualize product improvements, package designs to suit different psychographic segments. | Advertising copy Product development Package design |
| *Benefit:* consumer groups identified on basis of the various benefits they are seeking from the product. Subsequently, these groups are identified in terms of demographic characteristics, when possible. | Preference for various product attributes. For example, in the case of automobiles, preference for roominess, miles per gallon, power, etc. | By estimating the sizes of the various market segments, the manufacturer may redesign the product to suit a potentially more viable segment; the approach also helps identify the advantages/disadvantages relative to competing products. Knowledge of benefits desired by consumers allows the producer to design the product and the advertising message to emphasize the relevant benefits. | Product development Product positioning Advertising |
| *Volume:* Consumers grouped in terms of their usage/consumption characteristics. Subsequently, an attempt is made to profile the segments on the basis of demographic data. | Usage rate: heavy users, medium users, light users, potential users, nonpotential users. | By identifying the heavy users and creating a profile for this segment in terms of demographic and/or personality variables, the marketer can develop viable advertising and media selection strategies. Also, if the size of the potential users (currently nonusers) segment is large, the manufacturer can conceivably tap this segment with a blend of promotion and product innovation. | Advertising copy Media selection Diffusion of innovation (penetration strategies) |
| *Product space:* Division of market into segments according to similarities in attributes and product characteristics as perceived by the consumer. Consumers with similar perceptions/preferences are grouped and then identified on the basis of demographics, etc. | Similarities or preferences between products. Either overall comparisons or comparisons along several attributes (dimensions) may be used. | Provides competitive advantages/disadvantages of product; identifies close competitors; may reveal areas in product space which have no competing products—i.e., lead to discovery of opportunities. Analysis of preferences will provide management guidelines for advertising. | Product development Idea generation (Identification of opportunities) Product positioning |
| *Market factor:* Division of market into groups susceptible to different mixes of marketing factors such as price deals, advertising, etc. Again, an attempt is made to profile the segments in terms of demographics. | Price, quality, service, packaging, advertising, etc. (Here either the consumers may be asked direct questions regarding their proneness to the marketing factors, or this susceptibility may be inferred through appropriate consumer choice models.) | Identification of segments based on their responsiveness to the different marketing factors enables the marketer to (1) develop strategies for each segment individually; (2) allocate resources according to the effectiveness of the marketing factors. | Promotional strategies Resource allocation for marketing-mix variables |

cial. For example, in the introduction stage we may be more interested in identifying adopters and nonadopters and in overcoming resistance to adoption. As such, the marketer could attempt to profile the adopters in terms of their demographic and psychographic characteristics, target communications toward this group, and subsequently achieve a higher rate of product adoption. Or, the opinion leaders may be identified, and the promotional campaign may be aimed at this group to obtain more effective dissemination of information. In the maturity stage, on the other hand, the marketer is interested in identifying the competitive advantages and disadvantages of the product and in spending the promotional dollars efficiently. Accordingly, product-space and market factor segmentation would be beneficial. If the product has too many disadvantages and few advantages, relative to the competitor's product, and is in the decline stage (or close to it), it is probably time to withdraw from the market. Product-space segmentation will provide such indications.

Notice in Table M-8 that the more complex types of segmentation analyses (product space, market factor, benefit segmentation) use a two-stage procedure, where segmentation is initially done on consumer response or buyer behavior variables, and subsequently the segments are described (*profiled*) in terms of demographic and psychographic variables. The main reason for this is that it is usually prohibitively expensive, if not impossible, to estimate the size and hence the potential of the segments on purely consumer response variables. Also, in order to use segmentation for media selection and to design advertising strategies, one has to know to whom the message is to be directed. Since demographic variables are the only measures on which comprehensive statistics are readily available, most segmentation studies ultimately attempt to classify segments according to demographics.

**Techniques Used in Segmentation Analysis** Since the use of market segmentation analysis entails the identification of groups (segments) of consumers who behave differently in the marketplace in terms of characteristic differences that are measurable, and the subsequent isolation of these segments in the market so that they can be reached by differentiated marketing strategies, the following techniques are typically used in segmentation:

1. Form groups or segments of consumers such that consumers exhibit similar buyer behavior within groups, while buyer behavior is distinctly different between groups.

2. Predict and classify into segments (above) on the basis of consumer characteristics that enable the marketer to identify and reach the different segments.

In step 1, the consumers are grouped together based on their behavior, as measured by the consumer response variables (product usage, brand loyalty, preference, etc.).[6] Subsequently, in step 2, consumer characteristics (geographic, demographic, and psychographic variables) are used to identify the composition of these segments so that the marketer can devise differentiated marketing strategies to reach and influence these groups and to estimate their size and potential.[7]

**Statistical Techniques** A host of mathematical techniques have been used at various stages of data analysis in segmentation studies. Factor analysis has been used to reduce the dimensionality; that is, to summarize the original variables by a smaller number of statistically independent variables while explaining a large proportion of the original data. Regression analysis has been used to predict group membership in instances where it is feasible to identify clusters based on an intervally scaled dependent variable. Nonmetric multidimensional scaling has been used to generate configurations of stimuli in product space, and these configurations can be subsequently used as input for cluster analysis to determine market segments.[8]

A combination of techniques may be used either sequentially (in tandem) or in parallel in segmentation studies. For example, cluster analysis may be used to classify consumers with similar preferences into segments. Subsequently, discriminant analysis may be used to find how these groups differ according to demographic and psychographic characteristics. The purpose of using a combination of multivariate techniques is not to go on a "fishing expedition." Rather, combinations of techniques, if used, furnish evidence that the results are not merely artifacts of the technique used or the algorithm employed.

The use of multivariate techniques in segmentation analysis requires that the researcher be conversant with marketing research literature and applications. Especially important are the statistical assumptions upon which the procedures are based, as it is only too easy to apply these techniques "correctly" while violating the data requirements.

Having identified the segments of the market, it is necessary to estimate the sizes of the segments and the income/expenditure characteristics of the consumers within them.

## MARKET POTENTIAL ANALYSIS

Market potential has been described as "the total amount of a product of a product class that would be sold to a market in a specified time period under a given set of conditions."[9] The conditions referred to are both *controllable* aspects of the market, such as promotion, distribution, etc., and *uncontrollable* factors, such as environmental and competitive influences.

The major use of market potential in market analysis is to evaluate opportunities that a product has to offer. For example, it is important for management to identify those segments that offer the greatest opportunities. *Market potential* represents the opportunities that are available to the entire set of producers. In order to determine *sales potential* (that portion of the market potential that a firm can expect to obtain), it is necessary to estimate the market share that the company expects. *Market share* reflects the extent of competition that a firm faces and also measures the *market penetration*, a concept essential to strategic market planning. By assessing the sales potential of different market segments, the firm may obtain an estimate of the total sales potential of a product by aggregating across the segments.

**Estimating Formula** In estimating the market potential of a product for a given segment, one examines the income/expenditure characteristics of the consumers in each segment. This estimation involves the following steps: (1) identification of market segments in terms of measurable consumer differences; (2) determination of the number of potential customers in segment $i$ ($= N_i$); (3) determination of the average income per customer in the $i$th segment ($= I_i$); and (4) determination of the proportion of the income spent on the product class ($= E_i$).

The market potential of the product for segment $i$ is

$$MP_i = N_i \times I_i \times E_i$$

If $m_i$ is the market share of the firm in segment $i$, the sales potential of the firm in segment $i$ is

$$SP_i = m_i \times MP_i$$

and the total sales potential of the firm is

$$SP = \sum_i SP_i$$

**Sources of Data** In step 1 emphasis is placed on the need to identify the segments in terms of measurable consumer differences. That way, the size and income/expenditure characteristics of the segments can be used to determine the market poten-

tial. Unfortunately, the availability of data for steps 2 through 4 is limited in cases where the segments have been identified in terms of either demographic or geographic characteristics. For example, if one can identify the segments in terms of sex, income, educational level, etc., one can use census data (see Table M-9) to estimate the size of the segments and the income/expenditure characteristics. If the segments are described in terms of psychographic or consumer response characteristics, no such convenient data bases are available. However, it is feasible to create customer profiles by a two-stage procedure, where (1) segments are identified in terms of psychographic and/or consumer response variables, and (2) techniques such as discriminant analysis are used to characterize these segments in terms of geographic and demographic variables.

**TABLE M-9   Sources of Segmentation Data**

| For determining size of segments |
| --- |
| U.S. Bureau of the Census, *County and City Data Book*. <br> Rand McNally & Company, *Commercial Atlas and Marketing Guide*. |

| For income data |
| --- |
| U.S. Bureau of the Census, *County and City Data Book*. <br> "Survey of Buying Power," *Sales and Marketing Management*, annually. <br> U.S. Department of Commerce, *Survey of Current Business*. |

| For expenditure data |
| --- |
| U.S. Department of Commerce, *Survey of Current Business*. <br> U.S. Bureau of Labor Statistics, *Survey of Consumer Expenditure*. |

## CONCLUSION

Application of the concepts discussed in this entry are not free from pitfalls. For example, segmentation analysis is not potentially productive if management has reasons to believe that the benefits of segmentation will be more than offset by the costs of reduced economies of scale. Also, market potential estimates are quite error-prone and sometimes must be tempered with managerial experience or expert opinions. The techniques and concepts suggested here merely *aid* decision making and are not substitutes for managerial experience. Indeed, the marketing manager must use all feasible and appropriate inputs such as market potential, competitive product advantages and disadvantages, the firm's ability to produce and distribute the product efficiently, etc., to screen the alternative opportunities that are available.

*See also* ECONOMIC MEASUREMENTS; FORECASTING

BUSINESS CONDITIONS; MARKETING INFORMATION SYSTEMS; MARKETING RESEARCH; MARKETS, CLASSIFICATIONS AND MARKET ANALYSIS; PRODUCT PLANNING AND DEVELOPMENT; STATISTICAL ANALYSIS FOR MANAGEMENT.

## NOTES

[1] Philip Kotler, *Marketing Management: Analysis, Planning, and Control*, 2d ed., Prentice-Hall, Inc., Englewood Cliffs, N.J., 1971, p. 58.

[2] Robert Ferber, ed., *Handbook of Marketing Research*, McGraw-Hill Book Company, New York, 1974; Gerald Zaltman and Philip Burger, *Marketing Research: Fundamentals and Dynamics*, The Dryden Press, Inc., Hinsdale, Ill., 1975.

[3] Everett Rogers and Floyd Shoemaker, *The Communication of Innovations*, The Free Press, New York, 1971.

[4] Wendell R. Smith, "Profit Differentiation and Market Segmentation as Alternative Marketing Strategies," *Journal of Marketing*, vol. 21, July 1956.

[5] J. F. Engel, H. F. Fiorillo, and M. A. Cayley, *Market Segmentation: Concepts and Application*, Holt, Rinehart and Winston, Inc., New York, 1972.

[6] R. E. Frank and P. E. Green, "Numerical Taxonomy in Marketing," *Journal of Marketing Research*, vol. 5, February 1968.

[7] R. E. Frank, "The Design of Market Segmentation Studies," in R. Ferber, *Handbook of Marketing Research*.

[8] D. A. Aaker, *Multivariate Analysis in Marketing: Theory and Application*, Wadsworth Publishing Company, Inc., Belmont, Calif., 1971.

[9] William R. King, "Estimating Market Potential," in Ferber, *Handbook of Marketing Research*.

RAJENDRA K. SRIVASTAVA, *University of Texas*

GERALD ZALTMAN, *University of Pittsburgh*

## Market demand   (*See* ECONOMIC CONCEPTS.)

## Market development   (*See* MARKETING, INDUSTRIAL.)

## Market method   (*See* MARKETS, CLASSIFICATIONS AND MARKET ANALYSIS.)

## Market penetration   (*See* MARKET ANALYSIS.)

## Market potential analysis   (*See* MARKET ANALYSIS.)

## Market segmentation   (*See* MARKETS, CLASSIFICATIONS AND MARKET ANALYSIS.)

## Market segmentation concept   (*See* MARKETING, CONCEPTS AND SYSTEMS.)

## Market share   (*See* MARKET ANALYSIS.)

## Market structure analysis   (*See* COMPETITION.)

# Marketing, channels of distribution

The distribution channel is composed of a linkage of institutions which collectively perform the essential functions in moving products from producers to consumers. In 97 percent of all product sales more than one firm participates. The concern that the company initiating the sale has for the product, while depending on other companies to cooperate, constitutes the heart of the channel problem. The task of channel management is to administer this collective effort in the interest of the product's favorable reception by the consumer. The initiating company cannot control the activities of other firms. However, by careful selection and by building and preserving effective relationships, it can influence the performance of these firms and achieve positive results.

**Two Basic Flows in the Channel**   There are two basic flows in the movement of the product through the channel: (1) the movement of the physical product from the point of production to consumption; (2) the informational flow both ways that precedes, accompanies, and follows the product. This flow can be of two classes: (*a*) deals with the purchase orders, bills of lading, invoices, payment for goods, and all other transactions essential to exchange; (*b*) relates to the promotional information about the product or institution.

The timing, economy, accuracy, and clarity with which these flows are administered measures the efficiency of the channel.

**Savings Achieved by Intermediaries**   Figure M-10 shows that firms using a retailing or wholesaling intermediary can serve five other companies with 20 transactions where it would require 50 transactions without the intermediary. A *transaction* includes an account receivable or payable, a purchase order,

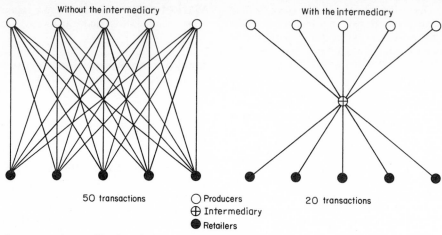

**Fig. M-10. Savings resulting from the use of intermediaries.**

invoice, bill of lading, and the servicing by a sales-person. This reduction in the transaction flow brought about by the re-sorting and shipment by the intermediary would be multiplied 20 times if there were 100 retailers.

In the *physical movement* of the product, the manufacturer ships in carload lots to intermediaries. Otherwise the manufacturer would have to break the shipment into many parcels at high transporation rates in order to deal directly with each retailer. The intermediary, by re-sorting the shipments, can combine many products for one retailer into a large and more economical shipment. The institutions participating in the channel are retailers, wholesalers, and producers, or manufacturers.

### RETAIL INSTITUTIONS

Retailers are the terminal link in the distribution channel which ultimately sells to the consumer.

*Competition.* Competition has been the arbiter of the retailers' success. Because of the increasing complexity, the growing volume of sales, and improved management practices, recent changes in the retail structure have been dramatic. Powered by the competitive spirit, retailers have capitalized on the fact that net unit costs and prices can be reduced and profits increased by volume sales.

*Nonprice Competition.* Retailers also compete in the nonprice area. They offer options of differentiated products and differing qualities of products at stores where the quality of surroundings also varies. Different combinations of these factors have broadened the spectrum of competition so that the retail structure includes all sizes and classes of stores—from the austere price-competitive institution to the luxurious retailer.

*Sale by Geographic Area.* Retail sales shares by region have corresponded to population shifts to the west and south. See Table M-10.

**TABLE M-10    Retail Sales and Population by Region for 1939, 1958, 1967, and 1972**

| Region | 1939 Percent population | 1939 Percent sales | 1958 Percent population | 1958 Percent sales | 1967 Percent population | 1967 Percent sales | 1972 Percent population | 1972 Percent sales |
|---|---|---|---|---|---|---|---|---|
| New England | 6.4 | 7.9 | 5.9 | 6.2 | 5.7 | 6.1 | 5.8 | 6.1 |
| Middle Atlantic | 21.1 | 24.5 | 19.3 | 20.2 | 18.6 | 18.7 | 18.0 | 17.7 |
| East North Central | 20.2 | 22.0 | 20.4 | 21.0 | 19.8 | 20.8 | 19.6 | 19.7 |
| West North Central | 10.3 | 9.8 | 8.6 | 9.1 | 8.1 | 8.6 | 8.0 | 7.6 |
| South Atlantic | 13.5 | 10.4 | 14.4 | 12.7 | 14.9 | 13.8 | 15.3 | 15.6 |
| East South Central | 8.2 | 4.4 | 6.7 | 4.9 | 6.5 | 5.1 | 6.3 | 5.5 |
| West South Central | 9.9 | 7.4 | 9.4 | 8.8 | 9.6 | 8.8 | 9.6 | 9.3 |
| Mountain | 3.1 | 3.4 | 3.7 | 4.0 | 4.1 | 3.9 | 4.3 | 4.6 |
| Pacific | 7.3 | 10.2 | 11.6 | 13.1 | 12.9 | 14.1 | 13.1 | 14.0 |

SOURCE; U.S. Census of Business, U.S. Department of Commerce.

*Sales by Legal Form.* In spite of tax benefits of partnerships and proprietorships, retailers favor the power of largeness, access to money markets, and limited liability that come with the corporate form.

**Retailer Classifications** The following classifications are most common:

*Specialty Stores.* Specialty stores that limit their offerings to one or a limited number of lines evolved with the general move to specialization. The census of business of 1972 indicates that since 1939 the categories which constitute specialty stores have increased proportionately in both number and size. The trends indicate continued growth in specializations within the respective categories by innovations in store decor, merchandise methods, and personalized customer services.

*Department Stores.* Department stores, classified with general merchandise stores, are stores offering a wide assortment of merchandise, with separate classifications divided into departments, each with a separate set of records. Department stores provide full services such as credit and delivery. Such stores have innovated constantly in design, services, and assortment of merchandise. Stores range widely in the clientele they seek. They have become big business: 94 percent of department store sales in 1972 were made by firms with sales of $25 million or more. They have also become chains or multiunit systems, with 88 percent of all department store sales credited to firms owning 11 or more stores.

*Mail-Order House.* Sears and Wards began, and still dominate, the mail-order business, even though many other firms have entered the field. Only 1 percent of total retail sales is done by mail. Reasons for this method not growing larger are (1) the availability of the automobile and hard surface roads to retail stores, (2) the inconvenience of filling out the order and waiting for the merchandise, as compared with picking merchandise up immediately from an attractive display, and (3) the expense of preparing catalogues in an age of rapid change when unit sales and sales per catalogue are small. Innovations such as in-store ordering desks and direct-wire service have firmed up the selling position of mail orders in the market, even though it is comparatively small.

*Chain Stores.* A chain or multiunit firm is defined as 11 or more retail stores under one owner. Advantages responsible for chain store success stems from (1) increased volume of sales which enables several establishments with one set of overhead cost to sell for less and to attract and hold better management; (2) an ability to achieve a greater impact in advertising both by professional preparation of advertising and by one advertisement benefiting collective stores; and (3) mass buying and large-volume transportation rates. Some independent managers, in responding to competition, achieve the same low cost and high satisfaction goals. See Fig. M-11 for comparative analysis by firm size.

*The Supermarket.* A supermarket is a complete departmentalized food store with a minimum sales volume of 1 million, with at least the grocery department being self-service. The supermarket concept is still evolving. Some large self-service units have remained food stores; others have popularized the one-stop shop concept and have organized massive distribution centers with virtually no limit to their offerings.

*The Discount House.* The discount house offers both hard and soft lines in a store of over 10,000 square feet at a cost structure below the traditional store. Its beginning was the result of merchandise shortages and high prices following World War II. Fair trade laws also sustained such high prices. Many states have now abandoned such laws; others ignore them. The discount houses succeeded because, with no services or guarantees and in austere store surroundings, they were able to cut prices dramatically and still realize a profit.

## WHOLESALING INSTITUTIONS

A wholesale sale is a sale that is not a retail sale, or it may be a sale made for business purposes and not to the ultimate consumer. The wholesaler is the institutional intermediary whose re-sorting economizes transaction and transportation costs. In spite of these savings, in some kinds of business and some lines of merchandise—such as furniture or ready-to-wear apparel—due to volume sales and importance of prompt delivery, the wholesale intermediary is bypassed, and sales are made by the manufacturer directly to the retailer or consumer.

The institutions which perform the wholesale functions are classified by the U.S. census as merchant wholesalers, manufacturer's sales branches, agents and brokers, and petroleum bulk–tank stations. The changes in comparative sales for these firms are shown in Table M-11. How these sales have been divided according to type of firms and goods sold in 1972 is illustrated in Fig. M-12.

*The Merchant Wholesaler.* Merchant wholesalers take title to the products they sell and assume the risks of ownership. They have innovated constantly with up-to-date warehousing, electronic data processing, and additional services. They have broadened their lines and increased in size to correlate with the one-stop shop trends in retailing. They

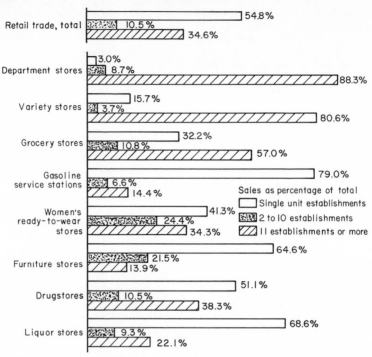

**Fig. M-11.** Percentage of distribution of sales by firm size in 1972 for selected kinds of business. Firm size is based on total number of retail establishments operated by the owning firm in the kind-of-business classification, group, or total for which data are presented. *(U.S. Department of Commerce, Social and Economic Statistics Administration, Bureau of the Census.)*

have evolved into large integrated systems in six general areas: (1) lumber and building materials; (2) paper goods; (3) automotive; (4) institutional sales to hospitals and restaurants and processors dealing with food, groceries, and paper supplies; (5) hard goods such as machinery, equipment, and industrial supplies; and (6) the wholesale grocer who carries diversified lines and deals with the grocery and supermarket trade. Like innovators in retailing, merchant wholesalers have decreased their cost margins dramatically.

*The Manufacturer's Sales Branch.* These firms are branches established by the manufacturer. They sell directly to dealers. Some perform the warehousing function. Sales branches are used by large firms where volume sales justify overhead, additional finance, and expanded management capacity. Firms such as Nabisco and General Electric are examples. They enjoy the following advantages: (1) product information and feedback is fast and dependable; (2) company gets suggestions for product and service improvements; (3) being close to the retailer enables the company to make accurate and short-term forecasts; and (4) as retailers get stronger, the company must stay close so as not to lose its influence. These reasons are considered by some firms as sufficient to offset the re-sorting and other advantages of the merchant wholesaler.

*Merchandise Agents and Brokers.* Merchandise agents and brokers buy and sell for the account of their principal. They do not take title or share the ownership risk. The brokers and manufacturers' agents represent the manufacturers to dealers by selling and arranging for shelf space and display. Their principal disadvantage is that they represent several manufacturers and must therefore dilute their efforts for one company. Their main advantage is that they work directly with dealers and retailers on a number of accounts and can therefore develop a closer relationship with them.

## CONDITIONS INFLUENCING CHANNEL RELATIONSHIPS

Usually one firm is dominant in taking the initiative to choose other firms for the channel and in planning the strategy. In the majority of cases, this dominant member is the manufacturer. There are instances, however, where initiative rests with the retailer (e.g., Sears) or the wholesaler (e.g., McKesson and Robbins).

**Confusion Arising from Differing Expectations**[1] As the result of competition, better communication, and improved management, the distribution channel is now perceived as a number of companies functioning as an interdependent unit. One company's performance influences all others. When serving a multitude of manufacturers, intermediaries have the problem of attempting to act

consistent with the collective expectations of the manufacturers. The manufacturer also frequently fails to satisfy the expectations of the intermediary. The most common of these differences is the relationship between a manufacturer of a few products and the promotional effort of the wholesaler who sells thousands of products. Other issues relate to maintenance of inventory, discount selling, bypassing intermediaries in selling large accounts, sales by factory-owned outlets, representational policies, national and private brands, promotional allowances, and service and warranty.

**TABLE M-11  Number of Establishments, Volume of Sales, and Percentage of Total Volume of Sales for Five Classes of Wholesale Establishments**

| | 1939 | | | 1948 | | | 1958 | | |
|---|---|---|---|---|---|---|---|---|---|
| | Sales, billion dollars | Percent sales | Establishments, 1000s | Sales, billion dollars | Percent sales | Establishments, 1000s | Sales, billion dollars | Percent sales | Establishments, 1000s |
| Total, all operations | 54 | 100 | 191 | 181 | 100 | 216 | 286 | 100 | 287 |
| Merchant wholesalers | 22 | 41 | 98 | 77 | 42 | 129 | 122 | 43 | 190 |
| Manufacturer's sales branches and offices | 14 | 26 | 18 | 51 | 28 | 24 | 88 | 31 | 25 |
| Petroleum bulk plants and terminals | 4 | 7 | 31 | 10 | 6 | 28 | 20 | 7 | 31 |
| Merchant agents and brokers | 12 | 22 | 21 | 33 | 18 | 18 | 47 | 16 | 27 |
| Assemblers | 2 | 4 | 23 | 10 | 6 | 17 | 9 | 3 | 14 |

| | 1963 | | | 1967 | | | 1972 | | |
|---|---|---|---|---|---|---|---|---|---|
| | Sales, billion dollars | Percent sales | Establishments, 1000s | Sales, billion dollars | Percent sales | Establishments, 1000s | Sales, billion dollars | Percent sales | Establishments, 1000s |
| Total, all operations | 357 | 100 | 305 | 459 | 100 | 311 | 697 | 100 | 371 |
| Merchant wholesalers | 157 | 44 | 208 | 206 | 45 | 213 | 344 | 49 | 279 |
| Manufacturer's sales branches and offices | 116 | 32 | 28 | 157 | 34 | 31 | 233 | 34 | 33 |
| Petroleum bulk plants and terminals | 21 | 6 | 30 | 25 | 5 | 30 | 33 | 5 | 26 |
| Merchant agents and brokers | 53 | 15 | 25 | 61 | 13 | 26 | 87 | 12 | 33 |
| Assemblers | 10 | 3 | 14 | 10 | 3 | 11 | * | * | * |

*Figures for this category are now included in the merchant wholesalers group.
SOURCE: U.S. Census of Business, U.S. Department of Commerce, 1939–1972.

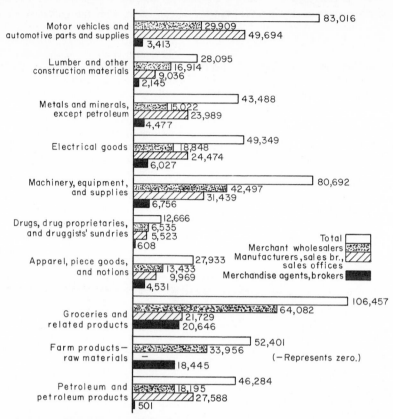

**Fig. M-12. United States wholesale trade in 1972 for sales by type of operation (in millions of dollars). Data are based on 1972 Standard Industrial Classification. (U.S. Department of Commerce, Social and Economic Statistics Administration, Bureau of the Census.)**

**Channel Noise** These frustrations are so common, the trade has called them channel "noise."[2] Channel noise may be minimized by (1) defining the company's target market, and selecting those intermediaries who will complement the need of the tarket market; (2) planning and executing a program that will keep the company's expectations of other channel members articulate and clear; (3) achieving market power with the consumer so the product will be in strong demand.

**Intensive, Exclusive, and Selective Plans** In achieving market coverage, firms usually choose one of three plans. An *intensive* plan is an arrangement which offers the product in as many retail outlets as possible. It is used when convenience and exposure to the public are important and high-volume sales are profitable (e.g., Coca-Cola). An *exclusive* plan is used when a company wishes to restrict the retail firms to a chosen few—and such firms will cooper-

ate in a promotion plan. It is often required that they will not stock competitive products. Such a plan enables a company to protect its product's image and get more cooperation from its dealers (e.g., Hart Schaffner & Marx). In the *selective* system, the manufacturer selects those dealers in a trading area who will represent the company products well, give them positive exposure, and respond positively to the company's goals for quality and market coverage (e.g., Cluett Peabody-Arrowshirts).

## TRADITIONAL DISTRIBUTION CHANNELS

Each firm selects and builds a channel for its line of products that is different from any other firm. The product line and its requirements, the competitive environment in which it sells, the characteristics of the other firms available with which to cooperate, and how the company wishes the product to be introduced to the target market are all relevant.[3] The most simple plan is a direct contact with the customer.

*Door to Door.* The advantages of the door-to-door plan are that the company has complete control of its product. There is no danger of channel noise or information distortion by intermediaries. The main disadvantage is the difficulty of maintaining a satisfactory sales force. The per-unit costs of this method compared with using other intermediaries is usually greater, since the costs of travel and shipment must be borne by a single line of products. Approximately 1 percent of total retail sales in the United States are sold door to door.

*Manufacturer to Wholesaler to Retailer.* This channel is typical; it offers the manufacturers a large coverage of the market at both the wholesale and the retail level. It places at their disposal representatives who have solid relationships with both retail and wholesale trade. Companies that have new, dynamic, and vigorous programs use this channel most frequently because of their freedom to change products and outlets at will.

*Manufacturer, Wholesaler, Broker, and Retailer.* Small firms, or new firms, that do not have the market power to command the attention of wholesalers and retailers, and some large firms, often employ a broker or a *manufacturer's agent* to provide contacts with the retailer and to take orders from the retailer for the wholesaler.

## VERTICAL DISTRIBUTION SYSTEMS

The two channels which include the wholesaler are those channels, unfortunately, that provide the base for role confusion and channel noise. In view of the facts that (1) the company gives up the ownership of its product to the wholesaler, and the wholesaler to the retailer and (2) these intermediaries deal in thousands of other products, there is always danger of confusion regarding the expectations of the initiating company. In solving this problem, progressive firms have built more reliable channels by adopting a vertical distribution system.

The vertical systems meet the problem of channel conflict by extending some control of the product through the channel. Formal arrangements with the wholesalers and retailers are often used. These vertical systems account for the sale of 64 percent of merchandise available for such sale. They are of three types: administrative, corporate, and contractual.[4]

**Administrative** Through administrative skills and unusual market power, some firms are able to win the cooperation of wholesalers and retailers by providing their products with administrative and selling support at each market level.

Procter & Gamble is an example. It holds the wholesalers and retailers into a unit by having its salespersons service and sell to the retailers but having all orders billed through the wholesaler. It sells directly to chain warehouses. It also sells directly to groups of large independent retailers if they will receive their goods in a single shipment. These shipments are billed through the wholesalers but are not warehoused. In addition to this program of *multiple channels* planned to satisfy the wants of the various channel members, the company advertises to the ultimate consumers and provides them with samples of new products and coupons redeemable at retail stores, thus creating a powerful consumer demand.

**Corporate** In the corporate vertical system, the initiating company owns all, or a significant portion of, the firms that make up the channel. Sears owns an interest in many of its manufacturers. Sherwin-Williams Paint owns 2000 retail outlets. Hart Schaffner & Marx owns over 200 retail stores and maintains the loyalty of other retailers by a carefully managed exclusive policy. In these instances the companys' need to have control of their product justifies, in their view, a major commitment of capital, management talent, and risk.

**Contractual** Cooperative voluntary groups and franchise systems provide a means of bringing greater harmony in channel communications.

*Cooperative Voluntary Groups.* In order to meet the competition and achieve the economies of the multiunit stores, some retail stores have formed groups which have adopted uniform improved management systems and have collectively warehoused, advertised, purchased, financed, and researched in the interest of increasing their market share. The wholesale intermediaries have taken the initiative in forming some of these groups (e.g., Independent Grocers Association); and in others, the retailers have set up a cooperative plan (e.g., Associated Grocers Association).

*Franchise Organization.* Under the franchise plan, successive stages of the production and distribution system are linked under one head, and franchises are granted by the franchisor to dealers who will conform to the franchisor's system. This concept is one of the fastest-growing areas of retailing.

There are three classes of franchise organizations: manufacturer-sponsored retailers (for example, the

Chevrolet franchise from General Motors); manufacturer-sponsored wholesalers (for example, Coca-Cola Bottlers); service firm-sponsored retailers (for example, McDonald's).

In each of these instances the franchisor establishes parameters which provide the control the system needs; yet there are many areas where the franchisee can use creative initiative and profit from extra effort. (*See* FRANCHISING.)

### EVALUATION[5]

In the interest of evaluating the effectiveness of the channel, management should frequently ask, does the channel (1) provide for the physical movement and storage of goods to achieve the greatest economy; (2) accommodate the distributional goals of the firm with a minimum of administrative transactional volume and confusion and maximum effectiveness; (3) guarantee an optimum amount and quality of promotional information to all prospective buyers and provide an adequate feedback; (4) have the flexibility to adapt creatively to company innovations; and (5) have sensitivity to each company's role as it relates to the expectations of the other channel members?

*See also* ADVERTISING CONCEPTS; CONSUMER BEHAVIOR, MANAGERIAL RELEVANCE OF; DISTRIBUTION, PHYSICAL; INTERNATIONAL TRADE; LOGISTICS, BUSINESS; MARKETING, INDUSTRIAL; MARKETING OF SERVICES; PRODUCT AND SERVICE PRICING; RETAILING MANAGEMENT.

### NOTES

[1]Bruce Mallen and Bernard Shuster, "Distribution Channel Relations," in Stewart Henderson Britt, ed., *Marketing Managers Handbook*, The Dartnell Corporation, Chicago, 1973, pp. 717–728.

[2]Louis W. Stern, Brian Sternal, and C. Samuel Craig, "Managing Conflict in Distribution Channels," *Journal of Marketing Research*, vol. X, pp. 169–179, May 1973.

[3]Philip Kotler, "Channel Decisions" *Marketing Management*, 2d ed., Prentice-Hall, Inc., Englewood Cliffs, N.J., 1972, pp. 552–574.

[4]Bert C. McCammon, Jr., "Perspectives for Distribution Programming," in Louis P. Bucklin, ed., *Vertical Marketing Systems*, Scott, Foresman and Company, Glenview, Ill., 1970, pp. 32–51.

[5]Weldon J. Taylor and Roy T. Shaw, Jr., *Marketing: An Integrated Analytical Approach*, 3d ed., South-Western Publishing Company, Incorporated, Cincinnati, 1975, pp. 67–189.

WELDON J. TAYLOR, *Brigham Young University*

# Marketing, concepts and systems

Market orientation—popularly referred to as the *marketing concept*—became a basic philosophy of American business during the 1950s and 1960s. Organizing a business to identify and serve the needs of the market was a necessary response to the rapid growth of the consumer economy which occurred during the 25 years following World War II.

Whether the marketing concept is adequate for the 1980s and beyond is a question that has been raised by marketing-thought leaders. Changes occurring during the 1970s—economic, environmental, social, and political—have posed new problems and challenges for the business community. Whether business response calls for a new concept or a revised marketing concept is not entirely clear. What is clear, however, is that business is operating under a different set of conditions than those that gave rise to the marketing concept.

## RISE OF THE MARKETING CONCEPT

*Marketing* has been defined in a number of ways, but central to most definitions is that it includes the performance of business activities that direct the flow of goods and services from the producer to the consumer or user. This definition is sound as far as it goes, but it does not necessarily convey the now generally accepted idea that the process begins with identification of market needs, wants, and preferences which in turn determine the goods and services the company should offer.

While it is axiomatic that for a company to succeed, it must satisfactorily supply some market demand, the marketing concept has served to emphasize the idea that markets do not exist to serve the needs of business but that business exists to serve the needs of the market.

Although the idea of market orientation predates World War II, it was the General Electric Company that provided impetus to the idea when in 1951 it publicly embraced the marketing concept. General Electric proceeded to reorganize its businesses—both consumer and industrial—so as to better identify and serve customer needs. Other leading companies followed the General Electric model. Although the marketing concept was simple and easily understood, implementation took longer and was more difficult than most managements had envisioned.

**A Response to Economic and Social Change** In retrospect the marketing concept can be seen as a response to an increasingly affluent society. Whereas the prewar economy concentrated primarily on providing basic essentials, the rapidly rising personal income of the postwar period provided dramatic changes in the nature of demand. Not only could consumers exercise more choice in supplying their basic wants, but their rising discretionary income enabled them to purchase many new products and services. Developments, such as more families in which both husbands and wives work and the shortening workweek, created demand for laborsaving devices, recreation, travel, education, and a variety of services. Services, for example, rose from 31 to 42 percent of the GNP between 1950 and 1970. Technological innovation was spurred by the new demands. New distribution systems evolved to serve the changing shopping patterns of a more mobile society.

The changes in life-styles resulting from higher income, technology, and mobility were more dramatic than for any other comparable time period. Naturally the impact was felt by the business community. Although benefiting from the increased demand, most companies also had to modify their product lines and methods of marketing to take advantage of the new opportunities. And they found it necessary to have far better knowledge of consumers than previously.

**Market Segmentation Concept** Nowhere was business practice more affected than by the growing consumer demand for variety. The relatively homogeneous markets of less-affluent times could be satisfied with limited product offerings. Increasing pruchasing power, however, caused markets to become more heterogeneous and to demand greater choice. Recognition of this change led to wide acceptance of the concept of market segmentation.

This concept assumes that the market for any product or service can be divided into segments, each with its own discrete needs, wants, or preferences. Marketing strategy calls for a company to determine which segment(s) it can serve most efficiently and profitably and to orient its product development, pricing, distribution, and communications policies to the preferred segment or segments. The automobile industry's wide offerings of brands, models, prices, and combinations of colors and accessories illustrate responsiveness to market segments.

The market segmentation concept should not be confused with the product differentiation concept. *Product differentiation* refers to how different brands are perceived by the consumer. This may stem from

real product differences or from purely perceived differences, which may be psychological in nature. Product differentiation is one means of appealing to a market segment.

## THE CHANGING MARKET ENVIRONMENT

While change in the 1950s and 1960s was stimulated by a rapidly growing economy, the 1970s have seen very different developments—a slower growing economy, public concern over the physical environment, dwindling raw material resources, and changing social values.

**Slower Economic Growth** A slower growing economy obviously affects overall market demand, but the nature of demand has been changing as well. Longer life expectancy increases demand for geriatric products and services, for example, while the lowering birth rate reduces demand for baby products and services. Less obvious, however, is the effect of the lowered birth rate on all family purchases. The concept of the human life cycle helps to explain why.

From a marketing standpoint the *human life cycle* can be classified by at least five stages: (1) single stage; (2) newlywed stage with no children; (3) full-nest stage—married with dependent children; (4) empty-nest stage—married with no dependent children; and (5) solitary survivor stage. While each stage shows different characteristics of demand, stage 3—the full-nest stage—provides the largest expenditures for a wide variety of goods, particularly among those families with younger children.

If family formations are postponed or if couples have fewer children, demand is affected not only for baby products but also for products such as housing, appliances, home furnishings, and automobiles. Knowledge of the characteristics of consumption by life-cycle stages, combined with census bureau population projections by age bracket, is useful in forecasting demand for many consumer products. Industrial goods producers supplying consumer goods companies are also affected since their demand is *derived* from the basic consumer demand.

**Environmental Concerns** There is growing awareness that the supply of most traditional raw materials and tillable land is insufficient to support the present world population and world economic growth over the long term. While new technology may resolve the problem before disaster overtakes us, the next few years seem certain to change many production and consumption patterns. Consumers and most industries will be affected either directly or indirectly. Rising petroleum prices provide an example of the worldwide economic disruptions that stem from an impending raw material shortage. Not to be ignored, however, are the new markets created within the Middle East oil-producing countries as the result of their new purchasing power.

Environmental factors that affect the quality of life have brought rising public concern, such as pollution, overcrowding, noise, public safety, crime, addictive drugs, and delinquency. Public and governmental pressures to alleviate these problems increase business costs and contribute to inflation, which in turn influences unit demand. Many industries, such as packaging and automotive, are affected directly. Opportunities, however, have been created for companies in a position to fulfill new needs, such as pollution control, safety, and noise-abatement equipment.

**New Social Values** The reasons for changing social values are involved and complicated, and their effects on marketing are apparent. Concern by some people over too much affluence, or over-consumption, has changed attitudes toward the purchase of many products. The choice of Volkswagens and blue jeans by people who can afford more prestigious purchases has brought into question Veblen's *theory of conspicuous consumption*. It is possible, of course, that the examples of the theory have merely switched from expensive cars and fur coats to stereo equipment, foreign travel, and where one's children go to college. Increased criticism of advertising results, at least in part, from an attitude that questions whether the good life really requires so many products.

Consumers support more government control of business, with legislation such as product safety, packaging, pricing, credit, warranties, service, and advertising claims. Increasing proportions of the GNP are being allocated to government, welfare, and education. Irrespective of their personal attitude toward changing social values, marketing executives need to understand and respond wherever social values affect products, services, and marketing methods.

**Modifying the Marketing Concept** In view of these new conditions, questions have been raised as to whether the marketing concept, which seemed so appropriate during the 1950s and 1960s, is right for the future. Some marketing authorities argue that what the customer wants may not always be good for society as a whole.

Examples of conflicts between individual consumer wants and the needs of the larger society are illustrated by the following types of questions: Should utilities promote the use of electricity in view of dwindling supplies of low-pollutant fuels? Should automobile companies promote the sale of larger cars in the face of scarce petroleum resources? Should container manufacturers promote disposable cans and bottles, or containers made of nonbiodegradable materials, in view of the problems of pollution and waste disposal? What benefit/safety criteria should determine whether a drug is to be sold? How should safety/cost issues be resolved? Should negative, as well as positive, product attributes be provided consumers by sellers?

Some argue that a societal-centered concept should replace the market-centered concept. Others point out that this would not work because in a free market economy the companies taking social leadership positions would be undercut by less-socially concerned competitors. Others argue that the answer lies in more government control over business.

Public support appears to be declining for a market system so free that companies may supply any product or service that someone is willing to pay for. Despite the basic soundness of organizing a business around the customer, it would seem that management must modify the concept of customer sovereignty with considerations of social (public) sovereignty. Such a modified concept might be stated as *the purpose of a business is to create and serve customers in a socially responsible manner*.

## ADAPTING TO FUTURE MARKET CHANGE

The central idea that should be apparent from the previous discussion is that business management—and particularly marketing management—must be concerned with change constantly occurring in the external environment. While a company may influence the environment to a limited extent, a major objective should be to recognize and adjust to environmental change. Four concepts appear useful in dealing successfully with environmental change.

**External Stimuli—Internal Response Concept** This concept proposes that several constantly changing external environments (stimuli) provide opportunities for the firm while at the same time exercising constraints over it. Each firm possesses a combination of resources (response mechanisms) which can be utilized to take advantage of the opportunities within the constraints imposed. This concept is sometimes discussed in terms of the noncontrollable elements (external environments) and the controllable elements (internal resources).

The external environments which the firm must deal with include the market, the economy, the industry, competition, legal and ethical, political, technological, and societal factors. The firm's resources are its facilities, technology, financial position, market position and reputation, personnel, and management.

Management identifies the opportunities and constraints and establishes tentative market objectives. It then proceeds to evaluate the strengths and weaknesses of its internal resources in relation to its market objectives. Resources may be strong in terms of one objective and weak in terms of another. For example, the firm's resources may be considered strong for maintaining market share in its traditional market but weak in one or more areas if the objective is to enter a new market. The weaker resources should be strengthened before the company attempts to enter the new market.

**Concept of the Marketing Mix**  This concept is similar to the one just described but directs attention to the marketing elements over which the firm has control. The concept of the marketing mix was developed by Neil Borden, although he gives credit for the idea to James Culliton.[1] Although Professor Borden listed some 12 elements of the mix, all but one (fact-finding and analysis) can be subsumed under the four major elements of product, price, distribution, and promotion.

The concept proposes that once market facts are known, marketing management can mix the four elements in proportions that will produce the most profitable marketing result. It assumes that the proportions of the mix will change as market conditions change or as the company's position in the market changes. Although the four internal marketing elements are controllable by the firm, it does not follow that marketing management may make decisions unconstrained by the external environment. Competitors' potential reactions, for example, limit the range of options open to a company.

**The Systems Concept**  The marketing process can be thought of as a system because the various functions and elements interrelate and interact. A change in one causes response in others. The elements of the marketing mix interact not only with the external environments but also with internal functions such as production, research and development, and finance. Interest in marketing as a system has developed for two reasons. First, it is useful in describing the intricate workings of an involved process. Second, systems models can be used as marketing planning and decision tools.

Systems analysts think in terms of macro, micro, and total marketing systems. Macro systems describe the larger external environment, while micro systems describe the internal environment of the firm. A total system links the two. See Fig. M-13 for a graphic model of a total marketing system. Analysts also think in terms of marketing subsystems such as a distribution system.

*Mathematical Models.*  While descriptions of marketing systems are useful in providing better understanding of the marketing process, operations researchers and management scientists translate the descriptive models into mathematical models for use in planning and decision making. Computer programmed models can be used to test various hypotheses by varying the inputs of the marketing mix and by using various assumptions about the likely reactions of the noncontrollable external factors. For example, the effect on sales of a change in price or a change in advertising expenditure can be projected in terms of several possible customer reactions and/or competitive reactions. A computer programmed model can quickly project the likely outcome of any number of combinations of internal and external variables from which management can choose the mix that appears best suited to its objectives.

Mathematical modeling has developed more slowly in marketing than in other business areas because of the large number of noncontrollable variables and the difficulty in predicting reactions from these variables to changes in the firm's marketing mix. A marketing subsystem, such as a distribution warehouse system, can be modeled more effectively, however, than a total marketing system because there is more factual data and the noncontrollable variables are more predictable.

**Strategic Marketing Planning**  Formalized marketing planning has developed concurrently with financial and other business planning necessary to support company sales forecasts, budgets, and profit forecasts. Until recently marketing planning dealt primarily with annual tactical plans, and more emphasis was given to the promotional mix—i.e., personal selling, advertising, sales promotion—than to the marketing mix. Some companies added longer-range marketing plans, although these usually ended up more as projections than as serious plans for achieving longer-range objectives.

The concept of strategic marketing planning is a more recent development that places emphasis on the means of achieving predetermined longer-range goals. In strategic planning, management determines where it wants to be at some future time in terms of sales and profits. If projections for its current businesses do not match these longer-range

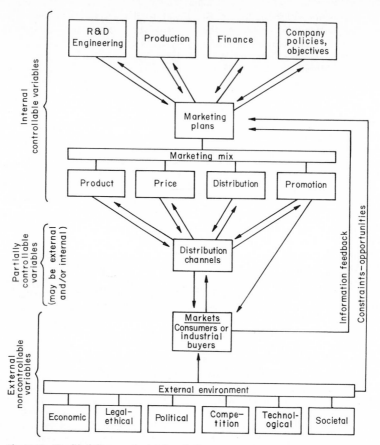

**Fig. M-13. Simplified diagram of a total marketing system.**

objectives, alternative means of filling the void are developed. These may include improvements in present businesses, new products, entering new markets, or diversification into new businesses.

Strategic plans cover major means of achieving major objectives. Consequently, they require more in-depth and profit-oriented thinking than do shorter-range tactical plans. In strategic marketing planning, tactical plans become the means for implementing the broader strategies. Tactical plans are developed annually, or more often if needed. Strategies are reviewed annually for updating as changing market conditions may require. Strategic marketing planning must be closely coordinated with total business planning.

*Product Life-Cycle Concept.* This concept has been used in shorter-range marketing planning and may now be one of the reasons more companies are adopting strategic marketing planning.

The concept assumes that every industry goes through four stages—*introduction*, *growth*, *maturity*, and *decline*. Industry profit rates rise during the growth period but decline during the maturity period as price cuts and higher promotional costs become common. Profits drop more severely during the decline stage. Realizing that their principal product lines were in maturing industries has caused some managements to turn to strategic marketing planning in search of additional means to profitable growth.

*Other Reasons for Strategic Planning.* The factors discussed in the section "The Changing Market Environment" have also focused attention on the need for longer-range strategies, as have declining trends in profit margins and return-on-invested capital experienced by many companies.

Another factor affecting strategic thinking has been the findings of the profit impact of marketing strategies (PIMS) project that return on investment increases as market share increases and vice versa.[2] This finding has caused some companies to reevaluate their strategies in industries where they have marginal market share positions.

## SUMMARY

The marketing concept remains a sound business philosophy, but business must increasingly consider the needs of society as well as the needs of the customer. Changes in the external marketing environment indicate an intensifying instability, and their impact on company operations requires continual surveillance. Every company faces marketing problems unique to itself. There are no prepackaged answers, and few marketing principles or techniques have universal application. Conceptual approaches provide a broader base and are proving helpful in analyzing problems, identifying opportunities, and developing profitable strategies.

*See also* CONSUMER BEHAVIOR, MANAGERIAL RELEVANCE OF; ECONOMIC SYSTEMS; MARKET ANALYSIS; MARKETING, CHANNELS OF DISTRIBUTION; MARKETING INFORMATION SYSTEMS; MARKETS, CLASSIFICATIONS AND MARKET ANALYSIS.

## NOTES
[1]Neil H. Borden, "The Concept of the Marketing Mix," *Journal of Advertising Research*, vol. 4, no. 2, June 1964.

[2]Sidney Schoeffler, Robert D. Buzzell, and Donald F. Heany, "Impact of Strategic Planning on Profit Performance," *Harvard Business Review*, vol. 52, no. 2, March–April 1974.

## REFERENCES
Adler, Lee: "A New Orientation for Plotting Marketing Strategy," *Business Horizons*, Winter 1964, pp. 37–50.

Bell, Martin L., and William Emory: "The Faltering Marketing Concept," *Journal of Marketing*, vol. 35, no. 4, pp. 37–42, October 1971.

Buell, Victor P.: *Handbook of Modern Marketing*, McGraw-Hill Book Company, New York, 1970.

Dhalla, Nariman K., and Winston H. Mahatoo: "Expanding the Scope of Segmentation Research," *Journal of Marketing*, vol. 40, no. 2, pp. 34–41, April 1976.

Forrester, Jay W.: "Modeling of Market and Company Interactions," *Marketing and Economic Development*, American Marketing Association, Fall 1965, pp. 363–364.

Greyser, Stephen A., and Steven L. Diamond: "Business is Adapting to Consumerism," *Harvard Business Review*, vol. 52, no. 5, pp. 38–58, September–October 1974.

Levitt, Theodore: "Exploit the Product Life Cycle," *Harvard Business Review*, vol. 43, pp. 81–94, November–December 1965.

McCarthy, E. Jerome: *Basic Marketing* 5th ed., Richard D. Irwin, Inc., Homewood, Ill., 1975.

Wells, William D., and George Gubar: "Life Cycle Concept in Marketing Research," *Journal of Marketing Research*, vol. 3, no. 4, pp. 355–367, November 1966.

VICTOR P. BUELL, *University of Massachusetts*

## Marketing, focused (*See* PRODUCT PLANNING AND DEVELOPMENT.)

## Marketing, hard-sell (*See* MARKETING OF SERVICES, PROFESSIONAL.)

## Marketing, industrial

Industrial marketing embraces those business activities which pertain to the flow of goods and services from producers or their agents to industrial organizations, institutions, associations, and government agencies, or to persons who use such goods and services in connection with the activities of these organizations. Buyers may be intermediaries or end users. As intermediaries they may absorb the identity of these goods and services into higher-level goods and services, or they may pass them on in substantially the same form. In the latter case they may be part of a broader package, or they may move these products to a nearer-to-utility position. It should be noted that it is the customer, not the product, that distinguishes industrial marketing from its other category, consumer marketing. For example, consumables such as paper and capital items such as furniture can be the medium for both industrial marketing and consumer marketing. It is the buyer or end user that distinguishes the kind of marketing that is involved.

**Industrial Products**   Certain products and services are principally identified with one or the other kind of marketing. Typically, industrial products can be classified into the following categories:

Capital goods, such as property, plant, and equipment

Raw and processed materials

Fabricated products and assemblies and component items

Manufacturing and processing services, including salvage

Operations supplies and support services

Engineering and administrative (including data processing) supplies and services

The task of marketing these goods and services to industrial markets is clearly a different matter from marketing either consumables or durables to consumer markets.

**Scope of Industrial Marketing**   Industrial marketing is concerned with those business activities which pertain to the flow of goods and services in typical industrial marketing situations. These activities include the following: (1) selling, sales training, and distributor management; (2) advertising, sales promotion, and publicity: (3) customer order service and proposal development; (4) product management and application engineering; (5) market development; (6) product service; (7) physical distribution and distribution logistics; (8) marketing information services; and (9) marketing administration.

Some activities in the foregoing list are arbitrarily combined. They imply a stereotype organizational structure which is never constant due to different organizational and operating situations and management philosophies.

**Influences In Industrial Purchasing**   It is important that the influencing participants in industrial purchasing also be identified. Typically, they and the products with which they are involved are as follows:

Purchasing personnel deal with all products. Usually these persons have singular influence over commodity items and maintenance and supply items.

Production personnel deal with production materials, component parts, and production equipment.

Engineering personnel deal with production materials and functional assemblies.

Quality assurance personnel deal with production materials, component parts, and functional assemblies.

Marketing personnel deal with resale items.

Top management deals with high-cost items, particularly capital equipment.

Outsiders who often influence industrial purchasing decisions and the products with which they are involved are as follows:

Architects and engineers are involved with equipment and materials for new and renovated facilities, and the services of building and trade contractors.

Construction and trade contractors are involved with supplies and materials for new and renovated facilities, and also with certain equipment.

Government contracting agencies are involved with materials and components used in products sold to these agencies.

Product design consultants are involved with product fabrication materials and components.

Consulting industrial engineers are involved with tooling, production equipment, and plant facilities.

Government agency inspectors and independent testing laboratories are involved with production facilities and equipment, product materials, and products.

Depending upon the particular industry, different combinations of the foregoing influences must be reached in order to consummate the industrial sale.

**Selling and Distribution**   In the large majority of industrial marketing situations the selling job relies heavily on personal attention and persuasion. Few industrial sales result from nonpersonalized, point-of-purchase merchandising. A relatively small number of industrial sales are consummated as a result of only advertising and mail promotion. While reorders are routinely placed by mail, periodic sales calls are essential to sustain these accounts. Industrial selling is achieved either directly or through wholesalers.

*Direct Selling.*   Direct sales are sales that are invoiced directly by the company to nondistributor customers. These sales are identified by producers with respect to product identity, quantity purchased, price, and customer identity. Direct selling is performed by the following categories of persons or organizational units:

Field salespeople. These are company professional sales personnel who are assigned geographic areas of responsibility and who usually are based in these areas.

National accounts sales executives. These are company professional sales personnel having high qualifications and who are assigned accounts that have multilocation operations, large purchasing potential, and some aspect of centralized purchasing or specifying influence. Usually these persons are based in headquarters.

Government market technical representatives. These are company professional sales personnel who have special technical qualifications and who are assigned sales responsibilities for government agencies and government contractors. They are known as technical representatives to accommodate the notion of objective government purchasing void of sales influence.

Service representatives. Many industrial products require occasional servicing by specially qualified personnel, often the manufacturer's service personnel. Frequently these persons sell their services independently of the field sales force.

Service parts-order personnel. A large number of repair and service parts sales are placed by mail or telephone. Persons who handle these orders will often solicit such sales by telephone to keep substitute parts made by independent suppliers from displacing the original manufacturer's parts.

Manufacturer representatives. These are independent businesspeople who are professional salespeople and work in behalf of particular manufacturing principals. In this capacity, they do not physically handle the products they sell, nor do they take title to products or collect payments for them.

*Indirect Selling.* Wholesalers exist in several forms in industrial channels of distribution. They are intermediaries in distribution in that they purchase goods from manufacturers in their own account and resell them in their geographical area. The role of wholesalers in the distribution system is as follows:

To serve as a bulk break point

To serve as a point of local inventory

To serve in local sales representation and communication

To serve as a local center for service

To take on the functions of customer credit risk, billing, and collection

In this role it is clear that sales by wholesalers to industrial markets are shielded from the view of the manufacturers that distribute through them. The wholesale channel can be one-step or two-step distribution. *One-step distribution* is one wholesaler between the producer and the industrial market customer. *Two-step distribution* would include the addition of large regional wholesalers who sell to local wholesalers who sell to the industrial market.

One-step wholesalers are known by a variety of titles: distributors, jobbers, supply houses, and merchant wholesalers. Occasionally, producers will also sell to dealers who function similarly to small, local store-front businesses. In two-step wholesaling, the first-level members are known as regional warehouses, warehouse distributors, and sometimes distributors. In the latter case, the second-step members in distribution are usually known as subdistributors and dealers.

**Advertising, Sales Promotion, and Publicity** The task of advertising and sales promotion in industrial marketing is best understood by studying the particular influences on industrial purchasing that must be considered and matching these with the appropriate materials. Typically the mix of tools and techniques available for this purpose are the following:

Catalogs

Product bulletins

Technical data sheets

Instruction sheets

Price lists

Newsletters

Media advertising

Direct mail

Reprints of technical conference papers and trade publication articles

Shows and exhibitions

Traveling displays

Sales aids

Remembrance advertising items—pencils, calendars

Publicity releases on new products, on personnel promotions, and on company financial reports

**Customer Order Service and Proposal Development** Customer order service in industrial marketing frequently calls for order editing before order entry.

1. Industrial products often have complex technical specifications or options that must be positively and correctly ascertained and priced before these orders can be entered. Many times, field sales personnel are not fully capable of doing the complete job.

2. Special designs, too, and system-related items often require special proposals. These proposals are prepared by order service or by market development when the complexity of the prospective order is beyond what might be handled by field sales personnel.

3. Drawings and bills of material of industrial products and systems are often submitted to customers for approval before production of these orders is authorized. Such administrative activity plus handling order-expediting requests are also done by customer-order service personnel.

**Product Management and Application Engineering** Product management is the source of recommendations on, and the administration of, marketing strategy and policy. It is here that the following aspects of marketing are looked after:

Product marketability—product market specifications, price, and functional packaging.

Product availability—finished inventory quantities and deployment, channels of distribution used, and density of coverage.

The marketing mix, promotional thrust, and the marketing plan.

Accounting of product line market performance and profitability.

Outside of the engineering department, the product manager is also the company's technical expert on his or her product line. Typically, applications and proposal engineers report to product management.

*Product versus Brand Manager.* As purchase decisions in industrial marketing situations are based most often upon expert examination of product specifications and values, the industrial marketing strategist is a product manager. By contrast, consumer purchase decisions are made more on brand claims and reputation. Hence, the consumer product marketing strategist is a brand manager. This difference notwithstanding, the role of product managers and brand managers is alike in that it is one of guiding marketing strategy.

**Market Development** Market development is not commonly organized separately from product management, but there are noteworthy exceptions. Persons assigned this responsibility are specialists in particular market segments, and they plan separate marketing programs for achievement in these segments. They provide market intelligence to product managers, who must balance product programs to meet the different needs of market development managers in the best way.

**Product Service** Product service is concerned with the installation, trouble shooting, and repair of products after they are shipped. In many cases, product service is established as a separate product line and profit center. For this reason, the product service department often adopts an active selling role (as opposed to a merely responsive one) in order to maximize (1) the company's total presence in the market and (2) the profit contribution of this activity.

**Physical Distribution and Distribution Logistics** Current organizational thinking is to look upon the activities of physical distribution as a part of operations rather than of marketing; nevertheless, many companies decentralize a number of marketing functions to the local warehouse level. In these cases, marketing personnel will manage order entry and will be in charge of planning warehouse inventories. Operating personnel will perform all material handling, storing, and movement work; and they will be in charge of the physical facility and of traffic operations.

**Marketing Information Services** This function includes market research, sales and performance analysis, marketing records and files, forecasts, marketing models (computerized), and the marketing department's representation on the company management information system committee. Marketing information services also undertake a wide variety of special marketing studies.

**Marketing Administration** Large industrial marketing organizations may include a marketing administration function. When this function is separately organized, it is involved in a variety of activities that vary according to the needs and management style of the chief marketing executive. Some of the more common areas of responsibility include the following: (1) marketing budgets; (2) profit and cost analysis; (3) marketing personnel administration; (4) incentives computation; (5) plans coordination; (6) procedures administration; (7) reports preparation; and (8) various assistant-to functions, special studies, and correspondence assistance.

**Summary** The foregoing discussion is organized along industrial marketing functional lines. Most organizations tend to structure and align these responsibilities in their own ways according to their particular circumstances. These different approaches are not important. What is important is (1) that all necessary functions be defined and assigned as responsibilities and (2) that there be effective harmony in carrying out all aspects of the total industrial marketing function.

*See also* ADVERTISING MANAGEMENT, INDUSTRIAL; MARKET ANALYSIS; MARKETS, CLASSIFICATIONS AND MARKET ANALYSIS; PURCHASING MANAGEMENT.

### REFERENCES

Alexander, Ralph S., James S. Cross, and Richard M. Hill: *Industrial Marketing*, Richard D. Irwin, Inc., Homewood, Ill., 1967.

Diamond, William T.: *Distribution Channels for Industrial Goods*, Bureau of Business Research, College of Commerce and Administration, Ohio State University, 1963.

Dodge, H. Robert: *Industrial Marketing*, McGraw-Hill Book Company, New York, 1970.

Fisher, Lawrence: *Industrial Marketing: An Analytical Approach to Planning and Execution*, Brandon/Systems Press, 1970.

Levitt, T.: *Industrial Purchasing Behavior*, Division of Research, Harvard Graduate School of Business Administration, Cambridge, Mass., 1965.

"1975 Survey of Industrial Purchasing Power," *Sales Management*, April 21, 1975.

Ward, John A.: "Markets and Their Effects on Marketing," in Russell F. Moore, ed., *AMA Management Handbook*, American Management Association, New York, 1970, p. 5-3.

Webster, F. E., Jr.: "Perceptions of the Industrial Distributor," *Industrial Marketing Management*, vol. 4, no. 5, October 1975, pp. 257–264.

Westfall, Ralph, and A. John Ward: "Sales Control Research," *Marketing Manager's Handbook*, The Dartnell Corporation, Chicago, 1973, p. 415.

A. JOHN WARD, *Management Research and Planning, Inc.*

**Marketing, minimal**  (*See* MARKETING OF SERVICES, PROFESSIONAL.)

**Marketing, retail**  (*See* RETAILING MANAGEMENT.)

**Marketing and sales practices**  (*See heading in Table of Contents for complete listing.*)

# Marketing information systems

A marketing information system is a specialized version of a management information system (MIS) which focuses on the marketing aspects of an organization. Ideally, it (1) monitors and searches a firm's total environment for activities and developments that may affect its marketing posture and (2) integrates this information into a form that will be useful in making marketing decisions at all related levels of management. In practice, these systems are more likely to be fragmented than integrative and to focus on the analysis of sales orders, salesperson's reports, informally gathered market data, and occasional market research.

**Users and Processors**  Those individuals and functions most commonly served by the marketing information systems are marketing management, brand and product managers, sales managers, new-product developments teams, advertising and promotion managers, market research and analysis specialists, and top management.

In the ultimate form, a marketing information system will utilize the talents of typical MIS developers such as information specialists, finance, accounting, and control departments, systems and procedures analysts, computer application specialists and programmers, and operations research and statistical people. The report forms may range from simple periodic typewritten reports to an array of daily or weekly computer print-outs or to almost instantaneous on-line visual displays.

**Scope of Search**  Search efforts typically scan (1) the general business environment and (2) the specific sales and market activities and conditions affecting a firm's particular product or service line. In the general environment, primary concerns are for economic forebodings; technological developments such as new materials to incorporate in the product or that may change a product's usage; cultural changes that affect consumer attitudes and habits generally; and political trends and the resultant legislation—either enabling or threatening. Concerns for developments that affect a firm's particular product line tend to focus on four areas: present and potential customers; present distributors and channels of distribution generally; present and potential suppliers; and the nature of present and potential competition.

**Search Methods**  Monitor and search techniques fall into three general categories:

1. Capture, storage, and analysis of routine sales order and control information handled in the firm's accounting or control processes. Typically, this effort may include analysis of sales and purchase orders, product and distribution costs, inventory levels and usage, credit and collections—by product, region, season, customer, and salesperson.

2. Informal and formal gathering, classifying, and analysis of general and specific market intelligence. This ranges from undirected, casual scanning by executives of "market tidings" discussed or observed at association meetings, trade shows, during sales negotiations, or gleaned from readings of trade and business publications. In a more formal fashion, it includes the preparation of sales call reports by salespersons, or warranty and service reports, and the analysis of the implications contained in them. In more sophisticated organizations, it includes the directed formal search analysis and dissemination of information and data collected from government census reports, selected business publications, and specialized reports such as those available from A. C. Neilsen Company, Market Research Corporation of America, Daniel Starch, and Brand Rating Index Corporation.

3. Marketing research conducted specifically for the firm. The objective of such research is to gain information about market characteristics and trends, consumer preferences, and sales force and advertising effectiveness. Studies typically conducted include (*a*) advertising research—motivational, copy, and media; (*b*) business trends forecasting affecting markets, both short and long term; (*c*) sales and market research—studies of market share and potential, distribution channels and costs studies, test markets, store audits, impact of coupons and other premiums, and the use of consumer panels; (*d*) product or service research—new product acceptance, impact of competitive products, product testing, and package research.

**System Optimizing**  As with any information system, a market information system must balance the cost of assembling, processing, disseminating, and analyzing the information against its value to the decision-making process. Information overkill is a distinct possibility. Timeliness, pertinence, and brevity are the system's most vital characteristics. This calls for personnel to perform the necessary abstracting, summarizing, and indexing. Additionally, the existence of good data begs for its further use in analyzing a firm's entire marketing system. Using quantitative techniques, progressive firms often build mathematical models of their total system in order to pretest decisions about pricing, packaging, and distribution methods, new products, and promotion techniques.

*See also* INFORMATION SYSTEMS, MANAGEMENT (MIS); MARKETING RESEARCH.

### REFERENCES

Aguilar, Francis J.: *Scanning the Business Environment*, The Macmillan Company, New York, 1967.

Amstutz, Arnold E.: "A Basic Market-Oriented Management Information System," paper presented to the American Marketing Association at Dallas, Texas, June 16, 1964.

Baker, George, ed.: *Effective Marketing Coordination*, American Marketing Association, Chicago, 1961.

Buzzel, Robert D., Donald F. Cox, and Rex V. Brown: *Marketing Research and Information Systems: Text and Cases*, McGraw-Hill Book Company, New York, 1969, chap. 12.

Frank, Ronald, Alfred A. Kuehn, and William F. Massy, eds.: *Quantitative Techniques in Marketing*, Richard D. Irwin, Inc., Homewood, Ill., 1962.

Greyser, Stephen A., ed.: *Toward Scientific Marketing*, American Marketing Association, Chicago, 1964.

Schaffer, Kurt H., and H. George Trentin: *Marketing Information Systems*, American Management Association, New York, 1973.

STAFF/BITTEL

# Marketing management

Marketing management is the sum of all the activities that convert the marketing concept into bottom-line results. It must rise a level above routine operation and administration, which is mainly concerned with extracting extra profit from an existing level of business. True marketing success hinges upon imagination and initiative coupled with rigorous analysis and planning. Specifically it requires (1) objectives, (2) strategies, (3) plans, and (4) implementation.

Clearly, the first three activities primarily involve analysis and thinking. In contrast, implementation requires much action and a great deal of time. In fact, most marketers probably spend 95 percent of their total work time implementing plans. Yet, unless an effective job is done in the first three "think" areas, even a superhuman implementation effort will fall short of otherwise attainable results.

**Objectives** Good marketing begins with a written statement of objectives for the product or service whose business is to be enlarged. Objectives should be (1) clear, (2) stated numerically whenever possible, and (3) imaginative, yet capable of attainment.

Clear objectives provide excellent targets against which marketing weapons can be aimed with precision. To illustrate, effective marketing objectives for brand X, the third-largest product in the widget category, might be written as follows:

Increase sales from $12.5 million to $15 million, while maintaining the current profit level of 10 percent before tax.

Increase market share from 13.7 to 17.0 percent.

By contrast, note how useless the following objectives are:

Increase sales and profits as much as possible.

Generate a significantly larger market share.

Each marketing activity, e.g., packaging, product formulation, advertising, promotion, etc., must also have its own set of objectives. Only in that way will each activity pull its required weight in contributing to the attainment of overall objectives.

**Strategy** The marketer must now describe broadly how the stated objectives are to be attained. To illustrate, consider again brand X in the widget category.

*To attain the above objectives, brand X will*

1. Persuade consumers of brands A and B, the two leading brands in the widget category, to switch to brand X. Those consumers will be persuaded that its new ingredient, Dura-Widge, enables brand X widgets to last twice as long as competitive items. Thus, brand X has a longer useful life and provides better value than competitive items, despite its premium price.

2. In general, promotion will be the primary tool used to attain the brand's objectives; advertising will be the secondary tool.

3. The price premium of brand X will be increased to 15 percent from its current 5 percent level over brands A and B.

**Marketing Plan** A marketing plan is the translation of brand objectives and strategies into a variety of activity areas.

*Activity Areas.* The following activity areas would be detailed in a typical product marketing plan:

Definition and description of product category

Recent category and own brand history

Competitive technological and regulatory environment

Strengths, limitations, and opportunities for own brand

Product formulation

Package design

Label design

Product name/trademark

Pricing

Consumer advertising
  Creative
  Media
Trade advertising
  Creative
  Media
Consumer promotion
Trade promotion
Field sales
Pro forma financial statements

For each activity area, objectives, strategies, and specific programs must be defined together with timetables, and the persons responsible for doing each job must be identified.

*Area Program.* A typical activity area section in a marketing plan might look like the following example for a "Consumer Advertising, Creative" section for brand X widgets:

OBJECTIVE: The objective of the advertising is to persuade current consumers of brands A and B (primarily those aged 18 to 39) that brand X widgets provide better value than other brands.

STRATEGY: To achieve the above objective, advertising will persuade other brand consumers that brand X widgets have a longer useful life than competitive items because of the new ingredient, Dura-Widge.

PROGRAM: To implement the above strategy, a cartoon character, King Dura-Widge, will be used in all advertising. He will be "stronger than strong or any other widget" and thus will be crowned King Dura-Widge. This symbol will be used to dramatize the greater power and longer life of Dura-Widge widgets.

SCHEDULE: This is the schedule of events leading to advertising release.

| Event | Completion Date | Person Responsible |
|---|---|---|
| Storyboards and layouts proposed | Jan. 15 | Jones |
| Storyboards and layouts revised | Feb. 7 | Jones |
| Production costs estimated | Feb. 14 | Smith |
| Storyboard and layouts: final approval | Feb. 21 | Jones and Smith |
| Production starts | Mar. 7 | Jones |
| Rough cuts | Apr. 21 | Jones |
| Mechanicals approved | May 1 | Jones |
| Answer prints | May 15 | Jones |
| Production prints approved | June 7 | Jones |
| Plates completed | June 15 | Jones |
| Prints to stations | June 15 | Green |
| Print released to September issues | July 1 | Jones |
| Air date | July 1 | Jones |

Note that while most of the above activities are actually performed by the advertising agency, a person within the client organization should always be assigned responsibility for completion on schedule.

## REQUIREMENTS FOR MARKETING SUCCESS

To achieve marketing success, the following are essential requirements:

**Scenario** In marketing, the toughest job is to develop an effective strategy. To do that, marketers must first develop a picture, or scenario, of both the consumer and the purchaser of the product. Then, all the information about the business must be condensed into a short description of "what makes the business go around." That is easier said than done. Routinely, the marketer is confronted with a vast quantity of information which invariably does not include some highly desired data. Additionally, the marketer is typically confronted with many colleagues, each of whom has a different view about "what makes the business go around."

To develop a unique viewpoint, the marketer must retreat to the quiet of his or her study and think. That is lonely and difficult work. The marketer who cuts this activity short or avoids it entirely, however, will see it reflected in an inferior strategy and reduced sales.

*Analytical Grid.* To aid in gathering their thoughts, many successful marketers use a simple grid such as the one shown below:

| | *Consumes/Uses* | *Buys/Purchases* |
|---|---|---|
| Who | | |
| What | | |
| When | | |
| Where | | |
| Why | | |
| How | | |

The columns refer to the product's consumers on the one hand, and to its buyers on the other. Sometimes, the same person is both consumer and buyer. More frequently, however, the consumer is different from the purchaser, as in the case of the child who eats the cereal the parent buys.

To use the grid, the marketer fills in the blanks, often, of necessity, by "guesstimating." For example, each of these *consumer* questions must be answered:

1. *Who* consumes the product? The marketer will write in his or her point of view about who consumes it. This should be as specific as possible. Appropriate demographic and psychographic data will be included.

2. *What* is consumed? It is important to be literal, but it is also important to be conceptual. If lipstick is being consumed, the consumer literally uses a product that puts chemicals on the lips. Conceptually, however, beauty is being applied.

3. *When* does the consumer use the product? This should be explicit—the time of day, year, etc.

4. *Where* is the product consumed? Here the marketer is concerned with both the in-house and out-of-house location of usage. Even more specifically, in which room and in what location within a room does consumption occur? Is one seated at the breakfast table, standing at the sink in the bathroom, etc.?

5. *Why* is the product consumed? This is often the most difficult area to sort out because it deals with basic motivations that affect the consumption of a product. Clearly, these will vary from one segment of consumers to another. Often several motivations can be identified, depending upon the particular consuming segment.

6. *How* is the product consumed? At this point the marketer is concerned with the way in which the product is actually consumed. Going back to the lipstick illustration: Does the consumer hold the lipstick in her hand; does she apply it with a brush; etc?

Next, the marketer goes down the list of *buyers or purchasers* and again asks the same kind of questions and seeks the same type of specificity.

Upon completion of the grid, the marketer will have a cohesive point of view—a scenario—about the key elements of the business and "what makes it go around." With that background, one is in a position to assess the point of view of colleagues and can accept or reject those points of view based upon the model which has already been developed. It is important that a marketer go through a grid analysis as quickly as possible. Otherwise, the marketer is likely to find his or her point of view changing after each exposure to an articulate colleague.

**Imagination** Based upon the scenario, the marketer must develop a specific, but imaginative, strategy. Again, there is no substitute for the hard work of quiet, private, and rigorous thinking. The marketer must ask, "What are the consumer's unmet needs; what is satisfying and what is not satisfying

current consumers and/or current purchasers; what needs are the products currently on the market fulfilling and not fulfilling?"

In this activity, it is not necessary for the marketer to possess a soaring imagination. Rather, it is vital that he or she be capable of recognizing a good idea when it is introduced or developed. Generally, marketers are surrounded by colleagues who, in total, generate more ideas than can possibly be used. The trick is to sort out those which are both economically sound and have the greatest consumer appeal.

**Consumer Orientation** Effective marketers are always concerned primarily with the consumer's wants and needs. The consumer is at the very core of a successful business. A manufacturer is in business to serve consumers' wants and needs. Although that may seem obvious, all too often marketers are diverted by other activities and unwittingly attach secondary importance to consumer orientation. For example, it is a rare marketer who has not been tempted, from time to time, to emphasize field sales aspects of the operation and to focus primarily on distributors as the key to marketing success. While such considerations are important, the consumer willl always be at the heart of a successful business. In short, the marketer must eat, sleep, and dream the consumer.

## ORGANIZATION

The line activities in marketing management encompass both planning and field sales. In some companies, the planning function is called *brand* or *product* management and may be separated organizationally from the sales activity.

As a rough guideline, *consumer* product manufacturers generally employ more people in the marketing planning area than do industrial companies. By way of contrast, field sales tend to be the larger activity within *industrial* product manufacturers: in these organizations, sales managers often do much of the marketing planning themselves.

In every company, however—either consumer or industrial—the two basic functions of planning and sales are always performed somewhere within the marketing department. Figure M-14 illustrates a typical organization chart for a consumer product company, and Fig. M-15 (page 704) shows a chart for an industrial product company.

**Think Time** One organization matter that deserves particular consideration is the necessity of allowing product managers and other marketing planners adequate time to think. Typically, these

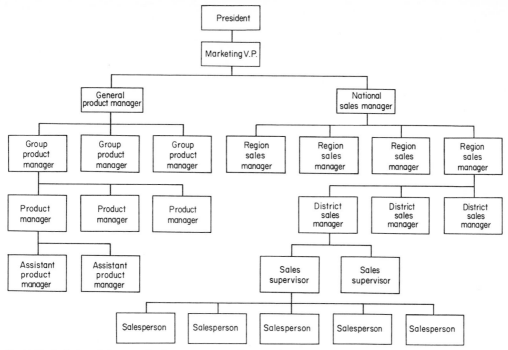

**Fig. M-14. Typical marketing organization: consumer product manufacturer.**

individuals are confronted with a tremendous workload of implementation tasks. Under such pressure the time available for analytical/creative thinking may be reduced to a highly counterproductive point. For this reason, if for no other, it is important to ensure that adequate staff resources, assistants, etc., are in a position to absorb some of the product manager/planners implementation workload.

*See also* ADVERTISING CONCEPTS; ADVERTISING MANAGEMENT, INDUSTRIAL; CONSUMER BEHAVIOR, MANAGERIAL RELEVANCE OF; INNOVATION AND CREATIVITY; MARKET ANALYSIS; MARKETING, CHANNELS OF DISTRIBUTION; MARKETING, CONCEPTS AND SYSTEMS; MARKETING, INDUSTRIAL; MARKETING INFORMATION SYSTEMS; MARKETING OF SERVICES; MARKETING RESEARCH; PRODUCT AND SERVICE PRICING; PRODUCT PLANNING AND DEVELOPMENT; RETAILING MANAGEMENT; SALES MANAGEMENT.

### REFERENCES

Boyd, Harper W., Jr., and William F. Massy: *Marketing Management,* Harcourt, Brace Jovanovich, Inc., New York, 1972.

Buzzell, R. D., R. E. M. Nourse, J. B. Matthews, and T. Levitt: *Marketing: A Contemporary Analysis,* 2d ed., McGraw-Hill Book Company, New York, 1972.

Carman, James M. and Kenneth P. Uhl: *Phillips and Duncan's Marketing: Principles and Methods,* 7th ed., Richard D. Irwin, Inc., Homewood, Ill., 1973.

Kotler, Philip: *Marketing Management: Analysis, Planning and Control,* 3d ed., Prentice-Hall, Inc., Englewood Cliffs, N.J., 1976.

McCarthy, E. Jerome: *Basic Marketing: A Managerial Approach,* 5th ed., Richard D. Irwin, Inc., Homewood, Ill., 1975.

Medcalf, G.: *Marketing and the Brand Manager,* Pergamon Press, New York, 1967.

RALPH W. ROGERS, *Rogers & Company, Strategic Planning*

## Marketing mix   (See MARKETING, CONCEPTS AND SYSTEMS.)

## Marketing mix for services   (See MARKETING OF SERVICES.)

## Marketing of services

Services are defined by the American Marketing Association as "activities, benefits or satisfactions

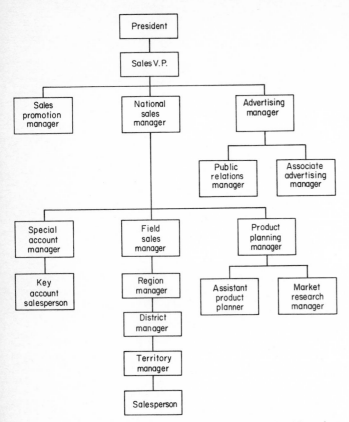

**Fig. M-15. Typical marketing organization: industrial product manufacturer.**

which are offered for sale, or are provided in connection with the sale of goods." Services, then, relate both to the sale of tangible goods and to intangible services themselves.

The marketing of services includes those activities which (1) accompany the sale of tangible goods and which are perceived to possess value for at least some of the customers (e.g., credit), and (2) are perceived to provide customer satisfaction without being tied to the sale of a tangible product (e.g., insurance).

**Size and Scope of Services** The importance of marketing services is clearly reflected in employment and expenditure figures. Roughly half the consumer work force and half the consumer expenditures are committed to providing and consuming services—private and public. Opportunities for employment and expanded service offerings in such areas as communications, health care, transporta-

tion, and recreation are strong. Between 1929 and 1965, the service sector employment of the economy increased by twice as much as the industry sector (20 million compared with 10 million).

One estimate of the magnitude of just one segment of the service industry—*utilities*, such as telephone and telegraph, electric and gas, and railroads—indicated sales of $42 billion in the mid 1960s. Of this amount, one-third was related to consumer service purchases and the remainder to industrial (including government, institutions, and agriculture) service purchases.

*Consumer* expenditures for services have received considerable attention and motivated such firms as Sears, Roebuck and Co. to offer traditional services such as insurance and interior decorating. The increase in spending for *business* services, however, has been even more impressive—although possibly less noticed. In one 5-year period during the past decade alone, business services were reported to increase by over 50 percent.

### PRODUCT-RELATED SERVICES

For the most part, most firms offer at least a limited number of services with the sale of a consumer good. Some of these, e.g., warranties, are required by law. Others are offered in an attempt to enhance sales and encourage selective demand for their product.

**Consumer Products** Four types of marketing services are readily related to consumer product sales.

*Credit.* Consumers in the United States increasingly live in a cashless society in which the ability to pay for the purchase during, or even after, consumption of part of or all the product is extremely important. Credit permits the buyer to consume without initial payment of the product's total economic purchase value—whether the buyer lacks the money to pay for the item or prefers to hold the money personally and pay the seller a fee (interest) for delayed payment. Credit also enables the seller to commit a buyer now to future payments and thus to avoid the possibility of that customer's spending those dollars elsewhere at a later time. Hence, when judiciously used, credit is a mutually advantageous marketing service that retailers can offer customers.

*Delivery.* In some cases, delivery service is purely a convenience; for example, delivery of a sterling-silver bottle stopper from a local department store minutes away. In other cases, delivery service is a necessity; for example, delivery of a refrigerator. Sometimes delivery is included in the price; at other times it is not. Regardless of the cost to the buyer, delivery is a service for which a cost is incurred not only in time and related expenses for transportation but also in terms of proper installation and use as related to the explicit and implied warranty.

*Warranty and Service.* Even though a firm may not have extended an express warranty, such obligations are now imposed by law. A product must be of average quality and fit the ordinary purpose for which the product is typically used. The seller also has an implied warranty that the goods sold for a particular use will be fit for such purpose. Hence, in the United States a consumer is entitled to a product which meets reasonable expectations for performance as intended by purchase.

To ensure that products do work properly and are repaired if they do not, firms typically offer some form of warranty and repair services. As noted above, delivery service and installation often are included in the purchase price to minimize warranty repair work. The range of warranty-repair service alternatives varies from simple replacement to complex service repair systems. When it is cheaper to replace a product than to repair it, the former is often selected. This covers most products in which the labor costs are higher than the materials involved; e.g., low-priced cameras, children's toys, or small appliances. Depending upon the time since purchase and the retailer from whom the product was purchased, the exchange can be made at the place of purchase, the manufacturer's service outlet, or the factory.

For moderately priced or expensive items, repair is usually attempted. If the product is portable, e.g., a sewing machine, repair is typically done at a service center which is owned or under contract with the manufacturer. If the product cannot be easily transported, e.g., a refrigerator, service at the user's home is required. At the extreme are products which become part of a system, such as home air-conditioning units or central vacuum cleaner systems, and must be completely serviced at the place of use.

The alternatives available to manufacturers include central factory repair services, a company or contracted (independent) network of repair stations located in areas of population concentration, or retailer-dealer repair arrangements. Each implies varying financial commitments, control potentials, and consumer satisfaction possibilities.

*User Instruction.* In many cases, instructions for product use are rarely needed or read by the purchaser, e.g., instructions for portable AM radios; however, as the complexity or hazard potential associated with use increases, e.g., hand tools and small appliances, the need for use instruction also increases, and elaborate instructions are included.

In some cases, doubt as to how to use an item inhibits purchase. For this reason, Litton Industries demonstrates its microwave ovens, and Cuisinart has distributor training sessions for its food mill operations.

Although the marketing services associated with consumer product offerings are frequently not sufficient in themselves to motivate continued selective demand, they are important in the overall product offering and marketing strategy.

**Industrial Products** Marketing services associated with industrial product sales are generally more numerous and significant than those for consumer products. In addition to the four service categories previously mentioned, five other services are typically offered.

*Financing.* In the case of consumer goods, financing typically is short term. The retail establishment either approves credit for the particular item to be purchased or arranges for a limited amount of credit over an indefinite period of time. In the operation of most businesses the purchase of equipment and supplies is vital. The availability of attractive financing (or credit)—long-term as well as short—is extremely important and can become the differentiating factor in determining which supplier is selected.

*Service Arrangements.* In many instances, it is the availability of convenient and inexpensive service which becomes the major reason for industrial customers to choose one brand over another. In large installations the costs associated with product failure can be disastrous for a firm; thus, service becomes a crucial factor in the purchase decision of the businessperson.

The firm providing the service must determine the true value that effective service adds to a product and the effect of varying service levels on profit and sales. This includes analysis of the types of service, e.g., order filling, installation and training, and repair and maintenance.

*Training.* Consumer training is typically limited to an instruction booklet, sales personnel instructions when considering the purchase, in-store demonstrations, or succinct installation directions of service personnel. For simple consumer goods, these methods are usually adequate. In the case of industrial goods, frequently they are not.

Training in the use of a product is imperative for some product's sales. For example, in the case of office machines, such as reproducing equipment and calculators, the individual's knowledge about the machine directly influences the output obtained. Since many of the machines are operated by individuals in positions where turnover is rather high, new operators must be trained to use the equipment properly if user satisfaction and continued use is to be expected. Thus, for many companies training is a necessary, ongoing process, and it represents a cost that must be considered by the seller as well as a desirable service by the purchaser.

*Order Filling and Processing.* Handling customer orders, processing the orders for subsequent production, shipping, and billing are services which can be offered as part of a sales program for industrial buyers. These services focus on the buyer and his or her needs. If they are properly administered, they lead to heightened customer satisfaction and long-term buyer-seller relationships. The strategy to supply such services represents a marketing orientation on the part of the seller, one in which the needs of the buyer are foremost in determining company policies. For example, where frequent deliveries are desirable for purchasers with limited inventory capabilities, product pricing which includes regular commercial carriers in place of company-owned truck deliveries every 10 days or so would be advantageous to the customer. So, too, could be supplier aid in proper inventory control and cost analyses.

*Installation and Application Assistance.* Unlike consumer goods, industrial equipment frequently involves installation procedures in the purchaser's plant. Installation may vary from delivery of an adding machine to a clerk's desk to installation of a complex and major piece of equipment. It could take only a few minutes, or months. Installation offers the seller an opportunity to build satisfying customer relationships—especially when the period of installation is extended, allowing auxilary applications to enhance the purchaser's operations. Installation and application services can be offered through the manufacturer's personnel or authorized representatives (dealers or independents). Ideally, company controlled and trained staff members are the most desirable alternative. However, geographic dispersion of purchasers and uneven demand rarely make it economically feasible to operate an in-house service organization to cover all customers.

In summary, industrial sales require strong service support. Consequently, the marketing services offered with industrial sales are the part and parcel key to product marketing strategy and corporate growth.

## ORGANIZATIONAL SERVICES

In the prior section, the discussion of marketing services was in terms of activities related to the sale of tangible products. In this section, emphasis shifts to the marketing of services per se, that is, the marketing of what is frequently referred to as intangibles, such as insurance, banking, or travel.

Where the service itself is the product, the tasks traditionally associated with product marketing are still relevant. That is, the marketing management tasks (1) of determining the marketing mix and (2) of planning for effective strategy and organization for action are critical to the total marketing effort.

**The Service Marketing Mix** The marketing mix—for services or for products—is comprised of four key elements: product, promotion, price, and distribution. Marketing managers dealing with services must develop effective strategies in each of these areas.

*Product.* With a service, the product is an intangible good. Most services cannot appeal to a buyer's sense of touch, smell, sight, taste, or hearing, e.g., insurance, investment services, or protection services. Services can be considered perishable; that is, if they are not utilized, the potential can never be recovered. For example, an unused seat on a train or an individual's unrequested time to entertain an audience can never reoccur, for time is itself perishable. Moreover, services themselves are sometimes difficult to distinguish from the seller or the provider of those services.

Because of the characteristics, the job of attaining effective sales revolves around astute use of the marketing mix in total. That includes, of course, the differentiation of the service offering (product) as well as a thorough understanding of the environmental (customer, competitive, etc.) conditions.

*Promotion.* An organization's promotion efforts include personal selling, advertising, publicity, public relations, and other sales promotional activities. Promotional activities are capable of creating perceived differences among service offerings, e.g., via imagery. Promotional activities are capable of directing the potential customer's attention toward the key attributes of the services as they relate to the potential buyer's needs, e.g., to sales or sales promotional literature. Promotional activities enable development of personalized relationships with the service organization, e.g., with sales people or public relations. Hence, promotional activities can be used by service organizations to (1) build a strong service image and (2) develop positively reinforcing personal relationships between the organization and its target market.

*Price.* Pricing objectives for a service organization are similar to those of product-oriented organizations, i.e., to enable goal attainment. The goal, of course, will vary with the organization. For a privately owned, profit-oriented organization, it would imply traditionally defined economic profits. For a government welfare organization, it might imply operating within the budget and servicing $x$ number of individuals. For a quasi-public–owned institution, it may mean perpetuation by covering costs and meeting the objectives established by the organizations's leaders.

In the private sector, pricing depends primarily upon supply and demand. Prices are critically reflected in the cost of labor in the case of services. Negotiation, however, is a realistic activity in which buyers and sellers engage to determine price—especially in highly individualized and specialized service areas.

In the case of some services, e.g., home contractors, negotiation is expected. In the case of others, e.g., medical or legal, general guidelines of what might be charged are established by the spokesgroup for the industry, e.g., by the Bar Association, although its legality is being questioned. In still other sectors, e.g., marketing research, proposals are prepared for prospective clients with details and cost of the services to be rendered.

Negotiation exists primarily because of the difficulty of tangibly differentiating one service offering from another and because of the individualization of the service offered to meet customer requirements.

On the other hand, very routine, organized service offerings that do not vary from one individual to another are often not subject to negotiation. For example, the services of a reducing gym, a dry cleaners, or a rug shampoo service typically have one-price (or multiple-service level) policies. In these cases, the price is determined by traditional cost plus return-on-investment, or target-return, pricing procedures.

*Distribution.* The distribution of services is influenced by the characteristics of a service. Its perishability with reference to time and its intimate tie with the providers of the service place restrictions on the proliferation of outlets possible, unless marked standardization can be achieved.

In the case of fast-food outlets, e.g., McDonald's, standardization of service levels and training, is possible which allows mass distribution of the convenience service. In the case of reducing salons, the standardization is tempered by the emphasis on personal contact with the operation's manager. At the other end of the scale, an organization such as a consulting operation requires special knowledge and personal attributes as keys to success rather than mass distributive efforts.

Regardless of the type of service—from fast-food operation to welfare organization to insurance company—the placement of contact points, e.g., offices, salespeople, places of operational contact, or the like, must meet the needs and desires of the population the organization hopes to serve. In this sense, they are no different from organizations offering products for sale.

## ORGANIZING THE SERVICE FUNCTION

Effective utilization of the total work force is especially critical in managing the service function, due to its high labor intensity and the difficulty in establishing performance standards.

**Standards of Performance** The traditional attitude has been that standards of performance can not be adequately set in the service industries. It may be difficult, but it is essential to have such standards. Alternative methods can be applied.

*Past Performance Records.* These are usually inadequate and inaccurate, since they use averages. They do, however, provide guidelines, which can be modified by experienced judgment.

*Time and Motion Study.* The contributions of industrial engineering to manufacturing industries are gradually being felt in the service field. There is no reason why such techniques as random sampling, time studies, workplace layout, work flow, etc., cannot equally be applied to service operations.

*Management by Objectives.* In management by objectives (MBO), the basic concepts of self-evaluation and setting one's own standards could have important applications to the service industry where individuals often have greater freedom of action than their industrial counterparts.

**Control** Burgeoning costs in the service industry demand more effective marketing control systems. Beyond simple cost and financial controls, an exhaustive cost-effectiveness analysis of the function to be performed is demanded:

1. Can steps in, or parts of, the service be modified or eliminated?

2. Can the type of labor be changed from professional to technical to semiskilled?

3. Are the control systems too elaborate; could they be replaced by simpler ones?

4. Are the costs allocated correctly?

5. Should some services be eliminated?

6. Is the supervisory structure too heavy or too expensive?

**Organization Structure** Recent experiments have shown that there can be higher productivity with less, rather than greater, specialization of labor.

*Organizing by Client or Geography.* This allows a combination of tasks for one individual or for one group. Successful applications occur in telephone companies.

*Autonomous Work Groups.* This approach features setting overall objectives for a group of workers and letting them control work assignments, working conditions, and even the managerial function.

*Flat Rather than Tall Structures.* Increasing the span of control reduces the number of supervisors.

*See also* MARKET ANALYSIS; MARKETING MANAGEMENT; MARKETING OF SERVICES, PROFESSIONAL; MARKETS CLASSIFICATIONS AND MARKET ANALYSIS.

### REFERENCES

Buell, Victor P., ed.: *Handbook of Modern Marketing*, McGraw-Hill Book Company, New York, 1970.

Fuchs, Victor R.: *The Service Economy*, National Bureau of Economic Research, Inc., New York, 1968.

George, William R., and Hiram C. Barksdale: "Marketing Activities in the Service Industries," *Journal of Marketing*, vol. 38, pp. 65–70, October 1974.

Green, Robert T., Eric Langeard, and Alice C. Favell: "Innovation in the Service Sector: Some Empirical Findings," *Journal of Marketing Research*, vol. 11, pp. 323–326, August 1974.

Judd, Robert C.: "The Case for Redefining Services," *Journal of Marketing*, vol. 28, pp. 58–59, January 1964.

Judd, Robert C.: "Similarities or Differences in Product and Service Retailing," *Journal of Retailing*, vol. 43, no. 4, pp. 1–9, Winter 1968.

*Marketing Definitions: A Glossary of Marketing Terms*, Committee on Definitions of the American Marketing Association, American Marketing Association, Chicago, 1960, p. 21.

Rathmell, John M.: "What is Meant by Services?" *Journal of Marketing*, vol. 30, pp. 32–36, October 1966.

Regan, William J.: "The Service Revolution," *Journal of Marketing*, vol. 27, pp. 57–62, July 1963.

Shapiro, Gerald: "Solving Management Problems in the Burgeoning Service Field," *SAM Advanced Management Journal*, April 1971, pp. 4–9.

DOUGLAS C. BASIL, *University of Southern California*

BURTON H. MARCUS, *University of Southern California*

# Marketing of services, professional

Marketing concepts and practices have been gradually moving into service industries. Their role in this broad area is still limited, however, having achieved greatest utilization in banks and airlines and much less attention in insurance, brokerage, and public transportation. Marketing has received the least attention in the professional service activities of law, accounting, management consulting, medicine, architecture, and engineering. Even marketing research firms and advertising agencies tend to underapply marketing concepts to the marketing of their own services. On the other hand, evidence implies that marketing can be a most important function in helping professional service firms meet the unprecedented challenges they face.

Professional practitioners must now cope with three increasingly significant forces:

1. *Assaults on professional codes of ethics.* The Supreme Court recently ruled that minimum fee schedules violate antitrust laws and stated, " . . . Federal law requiring price competition is applicable to legal services." Justice Douglas opined that, "For meaningful price competition the fees must be made known" rather than suppressed by rules against advertising.

2. *Changing expectations of clients.* Fewer clients today are in awe of the professional's credentials. Business executives are becoming more sophisticated in selecting, using, and—increasingly—in replacing professional firms. They insist on client-centered performance in contrast to technical-centered service.

3. *Increased competition.* In today's uncertain economy, it is not unusual to encounter situations in which as many as six to eight professional firms submit proposals for new work. Some firms are willing to "buy-in" to obtain off-season work; other firms are known to engage in questionable solicitation practices.

Professional service organizations are generally poorly equipped to cope with these forces due to three barriers to marketing:

1. *Disdain of commercialism.* Professionals do not like to think of themselves as business people. Many show hostility to any suggestion that they are motivated by money rather than service to their clients. Discussion of fees is usually distasteful to them.

2. *Associations' codes of ethics.* Professional associations have erected stringent rules against commercial behavior. In three professions—accounting, actuarial, and law—an absolute prohibition has

existed against anything resembling selling activity. Advertising, direct solicitation, and referral commissions have been banned. Other professional firms tend to adhere to certain standards of good practice, which tend to limit the use of effective marketing and sales techniques.

3. *Equating marketing with selling.* Because of the bars or bans against *selling*, professional service firms show little interest in the subject of *marketing*. They make a major error in equating *marketing* with *selling*. Marketing is a much larger activity than selling. By remaining ignorant of the concepts and practices that make up modern marketing, these firms are often without the skill to adapt smoothly to a rapidly changing environment and to grow to their potential. Professionalism may be a blind spot that keeps them from doing what they must do to achieve their goals. Their position grows more precarious as more of their sister firms begin to learn and apply modern marketing techniques. It is bad enough not to understand marketing in a strong market and when no one else does; it can be fatal to ignore it in a down market and when competitors are beginning to use it.

As a preliminary step in explicating the role of marketing in professional services firms, the following definition is proposed: Professional service marketing consists of organized activities and programs by professional service firms that are designed to retain present clients and attract new clients by sensing, serving, and satisfying their needs through delivery of appropriate services on a paid basis in a manner consistent with creditable professional goals and norms.

## STYLES OF MARKETING FOR PROFESSIONAL FIRMS

Professional firms, like other business firms, have three major objectives: sufficient demand, sustained growth, and profitable volume. They must turn to some form of marketing to achieve these objectives. In fact, three different styles of marketing can be distinguished.

**Minimal Marketing**  A large number of professional firms practice minimal marketing. They avoid or minimize conscious development of a marketing program. The firms feel that they will attain their objectives by rendering the best-quality service to existing clients. They reason that a high quality of service will lead to satisfied clients. Satisfied clients will place their new business with the firm. Furthermore, satisfied clients will recommend the firm to others, thus leading to a substantial inflow of new clients.

This logic is appealing and allows the firm to feel it is adhering to the spirit of the ethical canons prohibiting direct selling activity. Unfortunately, however, minimal marketing is a decreasingly tenable philosophy for professional firms.

1. It places too much confidence in the assumption that quality speaks for itself. In marketing circles, this is known as the "better mousetrap fallacy."

2. It assumes that the firm will deliver distinctively better quality than competitors. But when several firms pursue the same philosophy, no firm may strike the client as particularly exceptional in this respect.

3. It assumes that competitors are not using sophisticated marketing techniques. An increasing number of firms, however, are turning to aggressive or professional marketing, and it is questionable that a firm with a minimal marketing effort can compete effectively.

4. It is a reactive rather than a proactive approach to marketing opportunities. The firm does little to shape its future clients or services. Minimal marketing means that the clients choose the firm, rather than the firm choosing its clients.

**Hard-Sell Marketing**  A few professional service firms practice hard-sell marketing. They engage in glad handing, wining and dining, sharp pricing and discounting, slick brochures, partner bonuses for new clients, discreet badmouthing of competitors, and even some direct solicitation and possible referral commissions. There is a hustling for business that borders on, or is actually, a violation of the profession's code of ethics. Even if professional ethics are not violated, the majority of practitioners consider hard-sell marketing distasteful and predatory in nature.

Hard-sell marketing reflects a *sales orientation* rather than a *marketing orientation*. It may do more damage than good for the firm and the profession. It has two major faults:

It does not use a disciplined approach to identify and cultivate the market. It confuses sales (which is an outside job) with marketing (which is an inside job). It neglects the marketing process which is to choose targets, develop services, formulate plans, set up information systems, and establish controls.

Firms using this approach often get carried away with the problem of attracting new clients. This draws them into using more extreme techniques which begin to violate the ethical code. Worse still, it may result in acquiring marginal-type clients.

**Professional Marketing** This is a professional approach to the service/market opportunities of the firm that is consonant with the profession's canons of ethics. Its major attributes are listed here and developed later. It calls for the following:

1. Developing long-range marketing objectives and strategies

2. Developing annual volume, growth, and profit objectives, and detailed plans and budgets broken down into individual responsibilities

3. Holding regular training seminars to improve the professional person's effectiveness at marketing and personal selling

4. Assigning formal responsibility to one or a few people to organize, manage, and motivate the marketing activity

5. Allocating time and budget to support marketing activity

6. Setting up a system of controls and rewards tied to individual and group performance in attaining marketing goals

7. Making sure that the quality of professional work does not suffer as marketing activity is increased

8. Using only those marketing tools and procedures that are consonant with the industry's code of professional ethics.

## PROFESSIONAL MARKETING STRATEGIES

Six strategies are available to the professional firm that seeks disciplined growth.

*Expanding Service to Existing Clients.* Many professional firms see the key to growth in expanding their services to existing clients. A lawyer who prepares a client's taxes may uncover some poor asset management and propose estate planning. A public accountant may note an area of deficient performance and suggest that the client utilize the firm's management services division. Cross-selling of services is a major source of growth for the professional firm.

*Identifying and Cultivating High-Potential Prospective Clients.* This strategy calls for identifying eligible and attractive potential clients and laying plans for their cultivation. Each professional firm can identify specific prospective clients whom it would like to serve. The criteria for good prospects include high growth and profit potential, actual or potential dissatisfaction with their current firm, a

base for attracting further clients in that industry, and the availability of a good contact or referral source.

One firm divides the new client-development process into six stages: (1) generating and evaluating leads; (2) developing a plan for each good lead; (3) making contact with the prospect; (4) preparing and presenting the proposal; (5) closing the sale; and (6) follow-up work. Each stage is further modeled with specific procedures. For example, leads are evaluated with the following formula: Expected value of a prospect equals the probability of attracting the prospect with $C$ dollars of effort, times the value of the prospect if he or she becomes a client, minus the cost $C$ in dollars of trying to attract the prospect.

*Widening and Deepening Personal Referral Sources.* The professional firm also takes steps to cultivate key referral sources. Each professional firm has its own idea of which sources are most helpful. A lawyer in a medium-size law firm has ranked referral sources in the following way: Best sources for new business are bankers since bankers are often asked by their clients to recommend lawyers. Second-best sources are insurance agents; they recommend clients needing estate work and revised wills. Third-best sources are other lawyers with a high regard for this law firm's work in certain areas. Certified public accountants stand as a weak fourth in referral value to this law firm. This particular lawyer spends a lot of time with his referral sources, mostly in social settings. He practices reciprocity by recommending his clients to these firms when they need a bank, an insurance agent, a specialist lawyer, or an accountant. He carefully chooses his referral sources because he recognizes that his growth depends on their growth.

*Favorable Awareness Programs.* The professional firm also has to undertake steps to increase its overall market visibility and reputation. The first step is to assess its public image. Most professional firms have a distorted view of their image and are surprised to discover how they are actually perceived and talked about by competitors, referral sources, and clients. Figure M-16 shows the results of an image study of eight management consulting firms offering their services in France. The management consulting firms in the upper right quadrant are in the best position. On the other hand, a firm such as number 7 at the far left is seen to have fair quality but low awareness. Its task is to maintain quality and expand its public relations program to achieve higher visibility among French executives. Firm number 8, on the other hand, is seen as to have low quality and medium awareness. Its task is not to increase the market's awareness but rather to first upgrade its quality and then proceed to increase its visibility. Furthermore, image measurement is not confined to these two scales. The professional firm may also want to measure its image for integrity, innovativeness, size, experience, and friendliness.

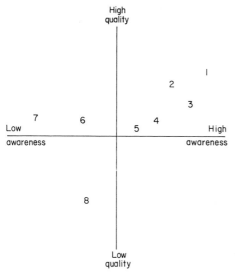

**Fig. M-16. Images of eight management consulting firms in France.**

Several methods are available to the professional firm seeking to increase its visibility and favorable image. The major method is *joining associations* by its members. Favored associations are business and trade groups, political parties, and charitable, religious, civic, and educational institutions.

A second method is that of *public speaking* and *writing*. Those partners who are effective at public speaking should seek out opportunities to speak to target industry groups, particularly those containing a high number of decision makers. Partners should be encouraged to write good articles for journals that reach a high number of potential clients.

A third method is *sponsoring seminars*. The professional accounting firm may build a seminar around a topical accounting subject, such as "Accounting for Inflation," or a seminar directed at a target industry, such as "New Directions in Bank Accounting," or an annual seminar to summarize new developments, such as "What's New in Auditing Practices." Invitations are sent out to current clients, important referral sources, existing contacts, and attractive prospects.

A fourth method is through *sponsoring scholarships,*

*awards, professional chairs, and professional training programs.* These goodwill gestures make a useful civic contribution and at the same time draw favorable attention to the firm.

A final way of achieving visibility is by *taking a controversial stand* on some public or professional issue. This brings immediate media attention and a flow of publicity to the firm. At the same time, this can be risky; a professional firm, in particular, must be on sure ground before staking out a role as iconoclast.

*Service and Market Specialization.* One of the major marketing errors of professional firms is to strike out in all directions for possible new clients. The partners join all kinds of associations, speak everywhere and anywhere, and accept all clients. This "total service" philosophy is counterproductive. It is an inferior strategy to that of service and market specialization. Specialization offers two distinct advantages to the professional firm: (1) it gives the firm a preferred position that places it automatically in contention for potential clients seeking that kind of expertise, and (2) it permits a greater profit on volume because the firm develops "cutting-edge" expertise and low-cost procedures for handling recurrent-type cases.

The management consulting department of a major accounting firm recently rated possible target industries on the basis of their growth potential, profit potential, specialized knowledge needs, degree of competition, and current available referral sources. On this basis, the department selected five industries for special attention: insurance, savings and loans, health care, banking, and real estate. A committee of partners was assigned to each industry to select the best target companies and to broaden exposure and contacts.

*Replacing Clients.* Replacing clients hardly sounds like a growth strategy, but under certain circumstances it is. Some of the clients of a professional firm are small, have little potential, require more attention during the "busy season," and may produce less than a normal rate of return. The firm needs an objective system to identify candidates for pruning. It also needs to know how to discontinue relationships with unattractive clients and discourage similar potential clients without damaging the reputation of the firm.

## IMPLEMENTING AN EFFECTIVE MARKETING PROGRAM

Professional marketing strategies are ineffective unless the professional service firm undertakes specific steps to train and motivate some of or all its practitioners to devote some time to business development. There are three alternatives for such implementation.

**Spontaneous Development**  The first is to leave business development to those in the firm who are most interested in it and effective at it. Every firm has certain partners, managers, and staff who have a flair for spotting market opportunities and converting them into realized business. If the firm, however, is lacking in "natural marketers," it should make a point of looking for this trait when it hires new staff. The natural marketers should meet from time to time as a marketing committee to exchange information and develop plans. The trouble with this alternative, however, is that it really does not improve the business growth rate that currently exists. While it has the merit of not foisting a role on the staff that is unnatural or uninteresting to them, it has the fault of leaving business growth to spontaneous, rather than organized, forces in the firm.

**A Specialized Marketing Office**  The second alternative is to develop a special office for business development headed by a partner or specialist in marketing. This *director of business planning* would have the following responsibilities: (1) guide the development of a long-range and an annual plan for business development; (2) search in a systematic way for new business opportunities; and (3) incentivize, assist, and train members of the firm to perform better in business development activities. The creation of this center of responsibility for business development is a necessary step in the evolution of a more effective business development procedure, but it is not a complete solution.

**A Pervasive Company-Wide Program**  The third alternative is to develop a firm-wide program for marketing training, incentivization, planning, and control. The firm's leadership decides that every professional in the firm—with the possible exception of junior practitioners and specialists—should receive training and incentives in business development. A large public accounting firm made the decision recently that practitioners should spend approximately one-fourth of their time in practice development. Management, however, realized that this would be a pious utterance unless backed by incentives and budget. Practitioners could not be expected to work a longer day, nor could they be expected to cut down their current billable time. The only solution was to create a budget account for business development which could support the practitioners' club memberships, luncheons, and charges to billable time. Furthermore, the desired

behavior still would not come about unless practitioners found that their effectiveness at business development was a factor in determing their annual bonuses. In addition, the firm created an office that, among other things, organized seminars to help practitioners improve their planning and sales skills. The office designed planning forms that are filled out by the practitioners each year with their plans in the areas of cross-selling, prospecting, referral source work, favorable awareness activities, and so on. These plans are reviewed quarterly for accomplishment and for replanning where necessary.

**Marketing Planning Model**  A firm with many branch offices must introduce further mechanisms to build up business development effectiveness. Consider the following marketing planning model used by a public accounting firm:

The planning process starts with the home office gathering information on the economy, market, and other factors that will influence its objectives for the year. The home office also carries on informal discussions with the business development coordinator in each branch office about possible growth goals. Based on its information, the home office adopts a 5-year growth objective and specific growth and profit objectives for the coming year. These objectives are communicated to the branch offices. Each branch office has a *business development committee* which looks at the firm-wide growth objectives and develops specific objectives for the branch office based on both the overall goals and local economic conditions. The *business development coordinator* in each office (who is a member of the business development committee) announces the branch's objectives to each department and practitioner. Each practitioner prepares an *individual business development plan* which states the individual's expected contribution in terms of fee objectives, expanded service to existing clients, potential new clients, planned work with referral sources, favorable awareness programs, and speaking, writing, and seminar work. The individual plans are reviewed by the business development committee, with suggested revisions through individual discussions. They are summarized for the branch office to make sure the time devoted to various marketing strategies is appropriate.

The branch office's business development plans are forwarded to the home office for review and approval. During the year, the home office receives branch office results and determines where consultation is desirable. The home office evaluates performance against objectives, using such measures as profitability, market share, the ratio of reported business development time to total hours, the hit ratio (ratio of successful proposals to total proposals), the percentage of lost clients, and the percentage of new clients.

*See also* CONSULTANTS, MANAGEMENT; ETHICS, MANAGERIAL; MARKETING OF SERVICES; PROFESSIONALISM IN MANAGEMENT; PUBLIC AND COMMUNITY RELATIONS.

### REFERENCES

Kotler, Philip: *Marketing for Nonprofit Organizations*, Prentice-Hall, Inc., Englewood Cliffs, N.J., 1975.

Rathmell, John M.: *Marketing in the Service Sector*, Winthrop Publishers, Inc., Cambridge, Mass., 1974. (See especially H. Justin Davidson, "Marketing by Consulting Firms," pp. 205–216.)

Turner, E. B.: "Marketing Professional Services," *Journal of Marketing*, October 1969, pp. 56–61.

Wilson, Aubrey: *Marketing of Professional Services*, McGraw-Hill Book Company, New York, 1972.

Wittreich, W. J.: "How to Buy/Sell Professional Services," *Harvard Business Review*, March–April 1966, pp. 127–138.

PHILIP KOTLER, *Northwestern University*

## Marketing plan (*See* MARKETING MANAGEMENT.)

RICHARD A. CONNOR, JR., *Professional Services Research Marketing*

## Marketing research

Marketing research is an all-inclusive term relating to the evaluation of any activity concerned with marketing. The scope is quite broad when it is understood that marketing includes all business activities required to move goods or services from the manufacturer or producer to the ultimate consumer. Proper marketing orientation focuses on the needs of the user, recognizing that user satisfactions must be met, as opposed to strictly those of the producer.

As a result of the increased awareness of the need to satisfy user requirements or needs as a prerequisite to success, there is an increased recognition that marketing goes beyond the traditional definition of moving a product or service from the producer into the hands of the consumer. When a company is concerned with moving an existing product through channels, it is operating under a product-oriented philosophy. Under a marketing-oriented philosophy, the company is concerned with the needs of the eventual users. As a result, there is a greater recognition that marketing, and therefore marketing research, comes into play long before a finished product or service is developed and remains in play after the product is delivered to the user.

A more appropriate definition of marketing research would encompass the study of the development, delivery, and consumption of a product or service rather than focus on delivery alone.

Marketing research is concerned with identifying and defining opportunity areas—to uncover customer needs and relate these to product ideas, market strategies, and programs that will satisfy these needs. It requires a continuous and imaginative analysis of business opportunities based on a systematic study of the whole business environment. The ultimate purpose of marketing research is to aid management decisions.

Marketing research must be distinguished from market research and market or marketing intelligence. *Market research* is the study of markets, usually in connection with existing products. (See MARKET ANALYSIS; MARKETS, CLASSIFICATIONS AND MARKET ANALYSIS.) Market or marketing intelligence is concerned with the collection of market or marketing data and provides information on how well the company is doing or what it is doing. The basic difference between marketing research and marketing intelligence is that marketing intelligence does not involve analytical comparisons or produce understanding of why something is happening or recommendations on future courses of action. These latter functions or activities are a part of marketing research.

Just two decades ago the techniques of marketing research were more limited than today, and almost any qualified researcher could effectively handle any type of marketing study. Today, the techniques available have increased in number and have become so sophisticated that specialists are usually consulted. It would be a rare researcher who would be highly qualified in all areas of marketing research—which can range from consumer needs analysis, through specialized economic forecasts, from motivation studies, to the various types of consumer behavior, or to the many faceted areas of advertising research.

**Proper Usage** While it is important to understand the complexities or broad scope of marketing research, where it can and cannot contribute, professional managers need not become preoccupied with the various techniques of marketing research. They should concern themselves with the problems or opportunities they see in marketing. The problem or opportunity defines the nature of the information that is needed, while the required information defines the technique that should be employed.

As a result, professional managers who feel there is a need for marketing research have the responsibility to define the problem or opportunity. Then through consultation with professional researchers the appropriate type of study can be instituted.

**Defining the Need**　Before managers can know there is a marketing problem or opportunity, or the intensity of such a problem or opportunity, they would have to have access to marketing intelligence. A review of the marketing intelligence will help define the existence and scope of the problem or opportunities. Therefore, it is recommended that a company establish a basic marketing intelligence program (a marketing information system) with systematic review to identify the existence and magnitude of potential marketing problems or opportunities. (*See* MARKETING INFORMATION SYSTEMS.) Evaluations of the problems or opportunities will then lead to an analysis of possible solutions—and possibly the recognition of the need for a marketing research study.

The standard procedure for management would be to

1. *Define the problem or opportunity*—including the full background of the factors that led to the recognition of the problem or opportunity and an overview of why a study is needed and what results might be expected.

2. *Define the objectives*—describing precisely what should be done in terms of the information areas that should be covered and a general overview of how the finding could aid in management decisions.

3. *Set up the organization* or project team that will conduct the required research.

4. *Follow up* to control the project and to ensure that it remains on track and is being successfully completed through the development of actionable results.

**Project Implementation**　For any marketing research project there is a recognized systematic approach that should be followed. The first step, problem definition, overlaps the first step of management's responsibility. But since the total marketing research project stems from the problem definition, a clear and unified understanding is critical. Therefore, the procedure for implementing and completing a marketing research project would include the following steps:

1. *Define the problem or opportunity.* This is a statement in specific terms of the problem or opportunity, including how the research is intended to be used to assist in solving the problem or opportunity.

2. *Develop specific research objectives.* These should be realistic in terms of what research can and

should be able to contribute. This step is instrumental in helping refine the problem relative to what research can realistically produce.

3. *Identify and define sources of information.* This is a review of secondary sources of information (published or otherwise available data) that might satisfy the objectives and the consideration of primary research sources.

4. *Develop the plan and forms for the collection of information.* Once the sources of information have been defined, it then becomes important to determine the methods to be employed in securing this information. This is a critical step in that what is done here will reflect directly in the results. Any shortcuts or oversights could greatly reduce the accuracy or completeness of the findings and resulting recommendations.

5. *Prepare sample design.* As in the above step, sample design is critical. Care must be exercised that key publics are defined and that the sample structure will reflect the needs stated in the research objectives.

6. *Execute plan and conduct fieldwork.* At this point the data collection phase of the study is instituted. Follow-up here is important to ensure that the plan is to be executed exactly as called for in steps 4 and 5 so that the accuracy and compliance can be verified.

7. *Analyze the data.* Once all the information has been collected, verified as to accuracy, and organized into a workable format, analysis begins. Analysis must be conducted in a way to reflect back to the research objectives. Without reference to the objectives, the analysis can stray from the intended purpose and therefore reduce the study's effectiveness and usefulness.

8. *Final report and recommendations.* The ultimate output of the research project is the final report. It should be a concise document outlining the procedures employed, the validity of the data, the analysis procedures used, and a summary of the results, including implications and recommendations. Again, the implications and recommendations must relate to the objectives if the project is to be on target and provide the management the insight intended.

This final step is what distinguishes marketing research from marketing information. Without implications and recommendations, the process would provide nothing more than additional marketing intelligence.

**Project Control**　To ensure the most effective and efficient use of the marketing research project team, a systematic approach that consolidates the thinking of all parties and pinpoints direction must be employed. To develop research programs that will answer the needs of a particular situation, a clear understanding of the problem or requirements must be communicated. Only then can a plan of action or research proposal be formulated.

*Research Proposal.* All research should be preceded by a written proposal which has been approved by the appropriate management personnel. Preparation of the proposal is the most crucial aspect of the research project. It is the blueprint for the research and must be agreed upon before study implementation. Once a proposal is approved and the research implemented, no deviations from the outlined procedure should be permitted. Therefore, a misdirected or incomplete proposal will result in misdirected or incomplete research. The proposal should fully cover the following areas:

1. *Background and/or problem.* A statement of the situation or problem should consist of a complete but concise description of the background and the circumstances that led to the realization that research was needed.

2. *Purpose.* A statement of what the research is intended to do—how the research is intended to reflect on the problem.

3. *Objectives.* A definition of what the study is to be designed to do in specific terms. The objectives would be stated in the proposal and final report.

4. *Scope.* Definition of the breadth of the study in terms of information sources to be consulted. For example, in sampling, the scope would define the limits—will the research cover a county, state, or be national in scope; will it consist of males or females; what age groups, job function, type of company, industry, etc.?

5. *Research procedure.* A detailed outline and justification of the exact methodology to be used, including sample-selection procedure, information-gathering techniques, information areas to be covered or a proposed questionnaire, information processing, method of reporting, and a list of any suppliers to be used.

6. *Cost estimate.* A firm estimate of total project cost with appropriate tolerances.

7. *Timing and reporting.* A realistic estimate of when the final report will be available and in what form the final report will be presented.

**Typical Studies** A number of studies could be considered standard in terms of a company's needs. Such studies have been termed as elements of a minimum program for marketing research. The first five types of research listed below (sales analysis, market penetration analysis, customer profiling, distribution research, and customer research) are basic

and within the reach of almost any company since the information sources are usually readily or easily available. These studies are first-step studies that will identify overall strengths and weaknesses within the company's competitive environment. They will signal the possible need for additional research by the nature and extent of problems or opportunities.

1. *Sales analysis.* The source information for a sales analysis is usually in existence with little or no revisions in sales-reporting procedures. A sales analysis would consist of a breakdown of sales by product for

*a.* Geographic regions—a market configuration consistent with the company's sales efforts. It could be by county, state, sales territory, sales district, market areas covered by media such as television ADI's (area of dominant influence), or plant locations, etc.

*b.* Customer type—classification of customers by Standard Industrial Classification (SIC), customer plant size by number of employees, or for consumer products by customer demographics such as age, income, sex, behavior patterns, or any characteristics that are unique to the particular product.

*c.* Time of year—any seasonal patterns where peaks or valleys in sales occur.

*d.* End use—where appropriate, how the product is used or consumed. It would include the application of the product and where and how it is used by the various customer types.

*e.* Purchase influences—who exerts what type of influence on the purchase of the product. What are the job functions of those involved, and what level of influence do they represent such as recommending the need for the basic product, initiating the purchase, selecting the suppliers, setting specifications, making the final authorization to purchase, etc.?

2. *Market penetration.* The next step in a basic research program, and one that grows out of the sales analysis, is research to determine the product's penetration or share of the market. This requires an understanding of the total sales of the product class against which the company's sales can be compared. This information, in conjunction with competitive penetration, identifies the relative importance of competitive companies as well. It also is a key factor in the realistic setting of sales goals or quotas.

Total industry or product-class sales or unit shipment data is not always readily available from secondary sources (previously published data from industry associations or government agencies, etc.) and may require original research.

3. *Customer profiling.* This type of study, again, is an outgrowth of the sales analysis. By defining the customer mix of the product class or company, concentrations by type of customer are usually observed. For example, a sales analysis for a product might show that 45 percent of the sales are to companies in a particular SIC with 100 or more employees. This process then defines a key market for the product. Potential sales or prospects can then be developed by identifying other companies that match the characteristics of the key customer group. In other words, this identifies all noncustomer companies in the same SIC group which employs 100 or more employees. This process, while explained quite generally here, can become quite sophisticated. It typically requires the services of an independent supplier specially equipped for such projects and who maintains industry census files. Such studies are routinely conducted, however, and are becoming a part of modern marketing information systems.

4. *Distribution research.* This form of research can and does take many directions, depending on the distribution procedures followed for a product class or industry. However, since distribution is the link between the manufacturer and seller, any weaknesses can have serious consequences. A periodic measurement of competitive distribution methods and performance should be conducted for management review. Many times, the recognition of a distribution problem will be uncovered by customer research.

5. *Customer research.* Earlier in this entry, emphasis was placed on the requirement to satisfy customer needs under the marketing-oriented philosophy. Customer research can measure how well the company *as well as* the product are satisfying the customer's needs. As can be imagined, customer needs can cover many areas, ranging from product performance requirements through company performance requirements. Customer studies can identify both the product and performance characteristics customers see as important and the perceived rating of the company *and its* competitors in meeting these requirements.

One of the most commonly conducted studies in this category is the company/product awareness and attitude study. Such studies generally measure target-audience awareness levels among competitive companies, comparative profile on pertinent characteristics, company/product associations, and brand preference. Also included in this category would be corporate image and corporate identity studies.

6. *New-product research.* New-product research is complex and, therefore, is treated separately in

another entry. A company should, however, establish a continuing new-product research program. This is considered by many to be the one type of research to which a company should be committed.

7. *Advertising research.* Advertising research is a term that covers all types of research concerned with the development, execution, and performance of advertising. It covers studies for the purpose of idea prospecting and needs analyses through use tracking, but is generally thought of in terms of the following:

*a. Concept testing*—the evaluation of an idea or the screening of several ideas before they have been formalized. The basic purpose and use of a concept test is to build a foundation for development by providing a relatively economical way of exploring the first stages of creative development.

*b. Copy testing*—sometimes referred to as ad or commercial testing, is concerned with the measurement of the ad or commercial execution. Pretesting—the evaluation of the ad or commercial prior to audience exposure and in some cases prior to final production—is conducted to ensure that the ad or commercial will perform as designed. By pretesting, revisions can be made before costly final production or media expenditures are invested.

*c. Benchmark and follow-up studies*—advertising-effectiveness tracking studies—a measurement prior to a campaign or advertising period and a second measurement after the period or at the conclusion of the campaign—are commonly used as a measure of performance. Such studies assume that the major variable during the test period is the advertising and, therefore, attribute any change in the market to the effects of the advertising. Controls can be applied to such studies to help reduce the influence of other variables and to determine a more accurate effect of advertising. This is commonly done by employing test and control markets, exposed and unexposed audiences, or test and control companies. In any type of tracking study, it is always advisable to track the major competitors in an industry so as to identify industry trends that might otherwise be attributed to some other influence.

*d. Ad readership research*—readership studies are probably one of the most easily available (often from the publisher) measurement tools for print advertising. They measure the relative memorability of ads in a studied issue and generally the portion of written material read. By tracking the readership scores of a program, first-stage or basic performance can be obtained.

*See also* ADVERTISING CONCEPTS; ADVERTISING

MANAGEMENT, INDUSTRIAL; MARKETING, CONCEPTS AND SYSTEMS; MARKETING INFORMATION SYSTEMS; STATISTICAL ANALYSIS FOR MANAGEMENT.

## REFERENCES

Bradford, Ernest S.: *Bradford's Directory of Marketing Research Agencies and Management Consultants in the United States and the World*, 11th ed., Bradford Company, Middlebury, Vt., 1966.

Buzzell, Robert D., Donald F. Cox, and Rex V. Brown: *Marketing Research and Information Systems: Text and Cases*, McGraw-Hill Book Company, New York, 1969.

Luck, David, Hugh G. Wales, and Donald A. Taylor: *Marketing Research*, 4th ed., Prentice-Hall, Inc., Englewood Cliffs, N.J., 1974.

Myers, James H., and Richard R. Mead: *The Management of Marketing Research*, International Textbook Company, Scranton, Pa., 1969.

Myers, James H., and A. Coskun Samli: "Management Control of Marketing Research," *Journal of Marketing Research*, August 1969.

Rummel, J. Francis, and Wesley C. Ballaine: *Research Methodology in Business*, Harper & Row, Publishers, Incorporated, New York, 1963.

J. WESLEY ROSBERG, *Meldrum and Fewsmith, Inc.*

BRUCE S. CHILDERS, *Meldrum and Fewsmith, Inc.*

# Marketing thrust (See PLANNING, PLANNED MANAGEMENT OF TURBULENT CHANGE.)

# Markets, classifications and market analysis

Market analysis is the derivation of sales opportunities, strategies, and controls for the firm or industry. Product-market classification is a tool that management applies in market analysis. It provides the analytical framework for the compilation of primary and secondary data, the interpretation of these data, and the evaluation of alternative marketing strategies. This entry sets forth the basic character of these concepts and discusses how they may be applied.

*Product-market classification* is a taxonomical technique designed to divide the vast range of heterogeneous goods and services provided by an economy into categories which are homogeneous in some meaningful way. Fundamentally, it is comparable to taxonomic procedures in other fields, such as biology or zoology, which serve a similar purpose—that of classifying living things into groups that are analytically meaningful.

The term *product-market* reflects the availability of two approaches to classification in marketing. The *product method* is based upon the intrinsic technical attributes of a good. The *market method* is derived from the purchasing patterns of buyers. To distinguish the two, a steel mill can produce steel plate, strip, sheet, galvanized sheets, pipes of varying diameters, rails and beams, etc., all from approximately the same technological base. For this reason the sales of these products and the operations of the mills that produce them, may be usefully combined into a single technical category. Alternatively, for any one of these products, significant competition from other technologies might exist. For example, galvanized steel for making liquid containers might compete with the technologies of aluminum, glass, plastic, and cardboard. Purchasing patterns of buyers for all these products will most likely be similar. The grouping of these products into a container-material category is a market-oriented means of classification.

## PRODUCT CLASSIFICATION

**Standard Industrial Classification System** The most important typology derived from the technical character of goods and services is the Standard Industrial Classification system (SIC). This approach, developed by the United States Bureau of the Census, categorizes the output of each commercial establishment (and some noncommercial establishments), e.g., factories, and stores in the country. Establishment output is identified by its chief product (if several are involved) and then grouped with others of similar technical character and composition. This aggregation process continues until the group reaches a point of significance in terms, for example, of number of establishments and wage earners, volume of business, and employment and payroll fluctuations. These groups are defined as industries. Some 470 such industries in manufacturing alone have been established.

Further aggregation in this analysis is achieved by combining the industries into (1) industry groups—in manufacturing there are about 150—and then (2) major groups—of which there are about 21. A final accumulation is made where all major groups are placed into divisions. There are about twelve of these:

Agriculture, forestry, and fishing
Mining
Contract construction
Manufacturing
Transportation
Communication

Electric, gas, and sanitary services
Wholesale and retail trade
Finance, insurance, and real estate
Services
Government
Nonclassifiable establishments

Each industry may also be subdivided into some finer components. Two such levels have been developed: the product class and the product line. The basis for these divisions may stem from wide disparities in the operating ratios of the industries because of differences in the (1) degree of vertical integration, (2) technology, (3) types of materials used, (4) methods of distribution, or (5) geographic location among the various establishments. For example, the bakery industry is further divided into wholesale bakeries, home-service bakeries, and retail multi-outlet bakeries. Unfortunately, however, published data on these finer divisions are typically limited to the value of shipments by geographic locations. The most extensive information is published for the industry category where data are available for the number of establishments, number of employees, payroll, annual sales, value added, and net worth, all by major geographical areas. Such data are derived from censuses taken every 5 years, and in annual supplements from sampling.

*Numerical Coding.* As an aid to distinguishing among these various levels of aggregation, the Bureau of the Census established a numerical coding system. Each of the industries was given a four-digit number. The industry groups were provided with three-digit identification and the major groups with two. At the finer level, the product class received a five-digit label and the product line seven digits.

To exemplify this procedure, consider the manufacturer of a brand of suntan lotion. The manufacturer is interested in the character of the market for his or her product and wishes to employ the SIC code for this purpose. Initially, this would involve finding the item in one of the two-digit groups in manufacturing. The 21 such groups have numbers ranging from 19 to 39. The suntan lotion falls within group 28, "chemicals and allied products." The major industry, or three-digit classification, is 284, "cleaning and toilet products." The basic industry, or four-digit group, is "toilet and cosmetic preparations," industry 2844. For the specific product, the five-digit product-class code 28445 of "other cosmetics and toilet preparations" encompasses the specific seven-digit product of "suntan lotions," number 2844515.

*Market Identification.* The use of the numerical designation may be seen to be a helpful device to enable a manufacturer to identify the scope of the market in terms of businesses which are related on a technological basis. For example, the first four digits of the product code, 2844515, identify a range of products which the manufacturer might well be able to manufacture within the plant and roughly within the familiar technology. By working with the available data and their related codes the manufacturer may readily identify patterns of market growth which will enable him or her to isolate opportunities for growth and expansion.

*Market Opportunities.* Alternatively, and perhaps even more importantly, the numerical codes may be employed as a means to seek market opportunities. For example, a manufacturer that sells a component or chemical used in the preparation of suntan lotions may find other manufacturers in the general industry interested in this product. Again by working through the codes, the scale, character, and general location of a variety of such customers may be located. These may be utilized to develop marketing plans and expected sales volumes.

*Strategic Building Blocks.* The SIC industries may also be employed as building blocks to develop product classifications useful in a somewhat different way. For example, industries may be classified in terms of the following:

Durable goods: tangible products normally not destroyed by consumption.

Nondurable goods: tangible goods normally destroyed by consumption.

Services: intangible products requiring immediate consumption for the transfer of value.

The marketing and sales characteristics of these products are often distinctive, providing useful insights as to possible marketing strategies and economic trends:

1. *Frequently purchased products*, such as many *nondurables*, are likely to require sale in convenient locations, be more susceptible to brand loyalty, and have a relatively stable sales pattern across business cycles.

2. *Durable goods*, on the other hand, are likely to require more personal selling and service, require more complex seller guarantees, involve shorter distribution channels, and possess relatively unstable sales patterns across the business cycle.

3. *Services*, because of their perishability and intangibility, often require totally different types of marketing programs. The close personal relationships typically involved in the provision of services has historically meant that relatively small business enterprises have typically been best able to survive. Because of the high labor intensity usually involved,

however, the service industry in recent years has been subject to reorganization to shift many tasks away from institutions at the point of sale and to mechanize others. The development of franchising in the service trades has been a powerful force moving in this direction.

## MARKET CLASSIFICATIONS

Market classifications are based upon the identity, characteristics, and purchasing patterns of the consumer. Numerous such classifications exist, and marketing strategies have increasingly required managers to develop more precise and finer measures. The concept of *market segmentation*, for example, is fundamentally a classification approach to categorize buyers in a manner which is strategically useful. (*See* R. Frank, W. Massy, and Y. Wind, *Market Segmentation*, Prentice-Hall, Inc., Englewood Cliffs, N.J., 1972.) Marketing segmentation is a process of dividing a market into subgroups and is directed at the development and pursuit of marketing programs for these subgroups. The consequence is that there are many alternative methods of market classification, and, in many instances, the individual industry or firm may find it appropriate to develop one that is unique to its own needs.

On a more general level, several broadly based market classification schemes have evolved through the years. These have come to distinguish basic elements to the field of marketing and represent formal elements of the vocabulary. Perhaps the most common of these is derived from the use made of the product by the buyer, distinguishing between (1) consumption for personal or household use and (2) consumption for intent to create new products and services for others. Products sold to buyers of the first category are referred to as consumer goods, those in the second as industrial goods.

This distinction typically reflects significant differences in the marketing strategies required to sell the two types of products. *Consumer goods* are sold to nonprofessional buyers who use more emotional than rational buying motives and who purchase in relatively small quantities. The result is that the channels of distribution and advertising for consumer goods tend to be more extensive than for industrial products. Companies engaged in selling *industrial goods* often find it difficult to market to householders, even where the product itself is not significantly different, e.g., cleaning compounds. As a consequence, there is a tendency for companies to specialize in one or the other. Where both are sold, then highly autonomous divisions are usually

established to permit the uninhibited development of the unique marketing strategies required by each market.

**Consumer Goods** Within both the consumer- and industrial-goods classifications, a number of additional typologies have been developed based upon buying patterns. The best known of these divides the field of consumer goods into convenience, shopping, and specialty categories.

1. *Convenience goods* are typically low in price; they are purchased frequently, often with limited search by the consumer. Ease of buying dominates the basis of choice, with brand preference and price being somewhat secondary. Products falling in this category are tobacco and gasoline. Marketing policies followed by sellers are typically characterized by intensive, widespread distribution and display, frequently buttressed by heavy advertising.

2. *Specialty goods* fall at the opposite extreme. They are usually highly expensive and infrequently purchased items. Consumers typically are willing to travel extensively to find precisely the brand or item they want. A product that might fall into this group is a high-fidelity musical system. Marketing will usually involved limited or exclusive distribution, more restricted advertising, and wide divergencies in prices due to differences, real or perceived, in quality or style.

3. *Shopping goods* include products for which a great deal of comparison shopping is typically required to identify the specific item desired. Consumers are looking not only for quality but often for best buys where prices have been specially lowered. A typical example is furniture. For such products, personal selling is often of substantial importance at the retail level, and selective distribution is employed. Advertising at the national, but especially the local, level is important to identify quality, price, and location of specific brands.

The essence of this classification scheme has been subjected to considerable debate in the marketing literature since its innovation in the early 1920s. Despite the development of somewhat more complex and alternative approaches to dividing consumer buying patterns, however, the integrity of the original ideas has held fast. They continue to provide the most clear-cut means for establishing the rationale for alternative marketing strategies.

**Industrial Goods** Regretfully, no classification of similar power has emerged in the area of industrial goods. Although to some extent the concepts of shopping and convenience goods have analogies in this category, these have not been useful in establishing meaningful differences in marketing strategies for industrial products. The classification approach most typically taken, therefore, is based upon alternative dimensions: the extent of processing through which the goods have already passed and their role in the buyer's production process.

*Processing-related Dimensions.* Here, five categories have been established. They are (1) raw materials, (2) fabricated parts and supplies, (3) operating supplies, (4) accessory equipment, and (5) installations. Raw materials are least complete in terms of prior production processing. Installations, such as large machine tools, computers, or bottling machines, are the most complex. The others lie in between. Raw materials are those most likely to be used up directly in the buyer's production process; installations provide services over a long period of time.

These characteristics do provide important clues as to the types of marketing strategies that are likely to prevail for industrial products:

1. *Raw materials* are likely to be purchased in substantial quantities and are relatively homogeneous across sellers. As a result, price competition is likely to be severe. Channels are likely to be short, with many purchases made on long-term contracts.

2. *Installations*, on the other hand, will be purchased irregularly, and products will be highly heterogeneous across sellers. Channels are likely to be short, not for logistic economies but for the provision of services. Personal selling as well as after-sales service will be important.

3. *Operating supplies* will typically involve relatively small purchases of a wide variety of product types. For such purposes, intermediaries such as merchant wholesalers are likely to be found in many channels. Although price competition will be of some importance, there will be many efforts made by marketers to obtain brand recognition as a means of offsetting the lack of direct sales contact.

4. *Fabricated parts* (e.g., spark plugs) will be purchased in varying quantities, depending upon their relative importance in the product line. Standardization will be significantly less than for raw materials, but price competiton will remain severe for all but the most unique items. Promotional efforts may be aimed not only at the buyers, often referred to as *original equipment manufacturers* (OEMs), but the ultimate consumer as well. Channels may be direct or through manufacturer agents.

5. *Accessory equipment* involves capital expenditures of less complexity and cost than installations. Included are typewriters, dictating equipment, duplicating equipment, forklift trucks, etc. Depending upon sales volume and complexity, these products may be sold direct or through exclusive distributors. Personal selling and brand recognition as well as after-sale service tend to be important. Standardization is less than in fabricated parts, but price competition is often an important element.

## STRATEGIC USE OF PRODUCT-MARKET CLASSIFICATIONS

In the development of the concepts of product-market classifications, product classifications are based largely on the technical characteristics of production, while market classifications are based upon consumer buying patterns. These distinctions provide useful bases for the development and control of marketing strategies.

1. Product classifications provide insight as to the level of demand, permitting the creation of effective sales forecasts, the establishment of useful sales quotas, and the identification of promising areas for expansion.

2. Market classifications provide insight as to the general types of marketing-mix strategies that are likely to be required in the sale of an item. Different marketing mixes require distinct types of distribution systems, and, often, a type of marketing department organization that is especially adapted to implementing the strategy.

**Long-Range Planning**  The general concepts of product-market classifications also provide the basis for long-run product planning. A firm may expand in roughly four ways. It may choose to exploit the product technology it has or move to alternative technologies. It may simultaneously sell to one type of consumer purchasing-pattern group or expand outside of this to other such groups. For example, the industrial product may be sold to the consumer market or vice versa. In the consumer market, the same technology may be adapted to sell in two or more of the categories described. For example, the same audio technology is capable of producing an inexpensive hand-held radio that would approach the convenience category, a table radio that might be a shopping good, and a high-fidelity receiver in the specialty field.

From these alternatives, the consumer goods firm could adopt a planning matrix involving six categories, as shown in Table M-12. If one assumes that category A is the original position of the firm, then the firm has its choice of expanding its market position there or moving to other markets and/or technologies. A vertical movement would imply devel-

TABLE M-12  Product-Planning Matrix

|  | Convenience | Shopping | Specialty |
|---|---|---|---|
| Technology 1 | A | B | C |
| Technology 2 | D | E | F |

oping technologies that would readily fit into the same type of marketing strategy that it is currently employing. Horizontal movement would involve shifting its existing technology into different markets with new strategies. A diagonal movement would imply altering both the technology and the market.

In this manner product-market technologies provide a basis for general long-run strategic planning, making clear the options to exploit the firm's technology or production capabilities or its market or marketing strategy skills.

*See also* ECONOMIC MEASUREMENTS; FORECASTING BUSINESS CONDITIONS; INTERNATIONAL TRADE; MARKET ANALYSIS; MARKETING, INDUSTRIAL; MARKETING OF SERVICES; MARKETING RESEARCH; MARKETS, PUBLIC; PRODUCT PLANNING AND DEVELOPMENT; RETAILING MANAGEMENT; STANDARD INDUSTRIAL CLASSIFICATIONS; STANDARD METROPOLITAN STATISTICAL AREAS.

### REFERENCES

Ansoff, H. I.: "A Model for Diversification," *Management Science*, vol. 4, July 1958.
Bucklin, L. P.: "Retail Strategy and the Classification of Consumer Goods," *Journal of Marketing*, vol. 27, January 1963.
Green, P. E., and F. J. Carmone, "Multidimensional Scaling: An Introduction and Comparison of Nonmetric Unfolding Techniques," *Journal of Marketing Research*, vol. 6, August 1969.
Holton, R. H.: "The Distinction Between Convenience Goods, Shopping Goods, and Specialty Goods," *Journal of Marketing*, vol. 23, July 1958.
Kernan, J. B.: "Product Planning and Control," in F. Sturdivant et al., eds.: *Managerial Analysis in Marketing*, Scott, Foresman and Company, Glenview, Ill., 1970, pp. 326–371.
Miracle, G. E.: "Product Characteristics and Marketing Strategy," *Journal of Marketing*, vol. 29, January 1965.

LOUIS P. BUCKLIN, *University of California, Berkeley*
MARCEL CORSTJENS, *University of California, Berkeley*

## Markets, commodities  (*See* COMMODITY MARKETS.)

## Markets, foreign exchange  (*See* EXCHANGE, FOREIGN, MANAGEMENT OF.)

## Markets for products and services  (*See heading in Table of Contents for complete listing.*)

## Markets, public

Although the government sector accounts for over 20 percent of the gross national product in the United States, there is very little actual physical production in government-owned facilities. Under the principle that government should buy from private industry whenever possible in order to prevent duplication of functions or the necessity for the maintenance of staff to perform infrequent functions, almost everything used by the government is purchased from firms in the private sector. This makes the public market the largest market in the United States, with government purchasing hundreds of billions of dollars worth of output every year. A list of suppliers in the public market includes the giants in virtually every industry in the economy. In addition, many small firms enter into supply or construction contracts with federal, state, or local governments. Governments are usually buyers in the public market; however, governments, in particular the federal government, also enter the market as sellers of surplus personal and real property as well as strategic and critical materials which have been stockpiled.

### SELLING IN THE PUBLIC MARKET

Although the federal government is the largest single buyer in the public market, the purchases of other jurisdictions—taken together—are larger. Preliminary estimates for 1975 indicate that governments purchased $331 billion of goods and services ($157 billion exclusive of wages and salaries). Federal government purchases were $123 billion, of which about 68 percent was for national defense purposes; the remaining $208 billion was purchased by state and local governments. As an indication of the scope of the public market, as of 1972, in addition to the federal government, there were 50 state governments, 3044 counties, 15,781 school districts, 18,517 municipalities, 16,991 townships, and 23,-

885 special districts, all buying in the public market. The relative volume of purchases in these markets can be seen in Table M-13.

Governments purchase thousands of items on both current and capital accounts. A classification of contracts according to what they will furnish might

**TABLE M-13  Direct General Expenditures of Governments 1971 to 1972\***

|  | Amount, millions of dollars | Percent of total |
|---|---|---|
| All governments | 323,000 | 100 |
| Federal | 154,516 | 48 |
| States | 62,051 | 19 |
| Counties | 22,757 | 7 |
| Municipalities | 35,400 | 11 |
| Townships | 3,853 | 1 |
| School districts | 38,893 | 12 |
| Special districts | 5,595 | 2 |

*Compiled from the 1972 *Census of Governments*, vol. 8, table 1, p. 155. These data are not directly comparable to those in 1975 because they are for a different year and a different concept of expenditures. The Vietnam War expenditures were also inflating the percentage of expenditures by the federal government during that period.

include, for example, the following items: supply, construction, transportation and communication, automatic data processing, maintenance, research and development, operation of facility, architecture, and engineering. Relative magnitudes of expenditures in different categories can be seen in Table M-14.

**General Procedures**  Operations in the public market are very much like those in any other market, with a few notable exceptions. The operations of the government are not normally guided by the profit motive, nor does it usually purchase for resale. The budget constraint which is faced by the government, and in particular by the federal government, is also quite different from that of a private firm. Finally, government purchases are subject to legal restrictions, especially in the case of the federal

government where procurement procedures are based on public law from initiation of bids to final inspection and acceptance. An example of a legal constraint within which public market activity is conducted is the *principle of local preference*. Many larger cities and counties operate under this principle in awarding contracts to suppliers or contractors. Similarly, the federal government standard contract includes a Buy America clause; in some cases there is a labor-surplus-area preference as well.

Typically, contracts in public markets are awarded on the basis of competitive bids. The federal government, in principle, invites bids from all known responsible suppliers who have an equal chance to compete for award of the contract. Procurement and construction intentions are publicized, and the federal government sends invitations for bids to all firms on its mailing lists. A bidder need not bid on the entire quantity.

In general, contracts are awarded to the lowest responsive bid by a responsible bidder, not necessarily the lowest bidder. A *responsive bid* is one which responds to the essential requirements of the invitation for bids. Each government jurisdiction is free to define a *responsible bidder* in any way it chooses. Most definitions would include reference to satisfactory past performance, dependability, quality of product, reliability of delivery dates, adequacy of plant, labor, and transportation facilities, and financial status. In selling to the federal government, a small firm which meets all the requirements except capacity or credit considerations may be issued a *certificate of competency* by the Small Business Administration.

There are some cases when bids are not taken, and governments negotiate for the items required. Many state and local governments will negotiate for very low-cost purchases, proprietary or patented items, and personal or professional services. The federal government also negotiates in these cases as well as in some special circumstances, such as (1) in

**TABLE M-14  Expenditures of Governments 1971 to 1972\***

|  | Current | | Capital | | Construction | | Equipment | | Land and existing structures | |
|---|---|---|---|---|---|---|---|---|---|---|
|  | Amount, millions of dollars | Percent of total | Amount, millions of dollars | Percent of total | Amount, millions of dollars | Percent of total | Amount, millions of dollars | Percent of total | Amount, millions of dollars | Percent of total |
| All | 226,953 | 100 | 55,446 | 100 | 33,223 | 100 | 18,039 | 100 | 4,183 | 100 |
| Federal | 100,130 | 44 | 20,816 | 38 | 4,801 | 14 | 14,810 | 82 | 1,205 | 29 |
| State | 39,790 | 18 | 15,286 | 28 | 13,022 | 39 | 892 | 5 | 1,369 | 33 |
| Local | 87,033 | 38 | 19,344 | 35 | 15,399 | 46 | 2,335 | 13 | 1,610 | 38 |

*Compiled from the 1972 *Census of Governments*, vol. 8, table 6, p. 158.

time of national emergency, (2) when there is an unusual time constraint, (3) for goods or services to be used outside the country, and (4) in some other special cases. In addition, negotiation is used if there is only one source of supply or if the bids are unreasonable or were determined to be not independent.

*Procurement Regulations.* The procurement regulations of the federal government are issued by the General Services Administration (GSA) or the Assistant Secretary of Defense for Installations and Logistics. The former agency issues the uniform procedures applicable to (1) procurement and construction by the executive agencies and (2) the "Federal Property Management Regulations," which describe the policies applicable to the management of federal government property and records. The "Armed Services Procurement Regulations" are issued by the Assistant Secretary. All these regulations are published in the *Code of Federal Regulations.* There is no uniform code for state and local government procurement.

*Specifications and Standards.* Specifications—describing the product, service, or construction item—and standards have been set for hundreds of items purchased by the federal government. GSA publishes a "Guide to Specifications and Standards of the Federal Government," which explains how to obtain copies of the specifications and standards. Specifications for state governments are found in *The Annual of State Specifications of Commodities.* Localities are influenced in their specifications and standards by the state and federal government requirements, but special requirements may exist in particular cases.

*Contracts.* Several types of contracts may be used in public markets. A contract may be for a nonrecurring purchase of a specific amount of a specified item. Or, the contract may be of a blanket nature concerning undetermined quantities of a product or service to be delivered as needed at a quoted price over a specific period of time or with no termination date stated. Most frequently, contracts are of a fixed-price type. These contracts may include a firm price statement or may allow for price adjustments according to an agreed-upon index or upon actual cost experience. In addition, incentive considerations may be included. Cost-type contracts are less often used.

Federal government contracts, in addition to the specific requirements pertaining to the contract, usually include a reference to general provisions. *Standard Form 32* contains the general provisions for supply and service contracts. The standard items cover such matters as inspection, payment procedures, assignment of claims and patents, and default and dispute settlement procedures. Also included are the relevant portions of the Buy America and Walsh-Healey Public Contract Acts.

Construction contracts are covered in *Standard Forms 19 and 23A.* The general provisions include specifications, inspection, and acceptance procedures for materials and workmanship, termination for default, damages for delays, time extensions, etc. Larger contracts contain Labor Standards Provisions, covering wages, hours, and employment conditions for labor. Copies of these standard contract forms can be obtained from the GSA Business Service Center.

**Becoming a Federal Government Supplier** By contracting the Regional Director of Business Affairs in a regional GSA office, a potential supplier of regular items purchased by the federal government can receive what is needed, i.e., "Bidders Mailing List Application" (Standard Form 129) and the "List of Commodities" (Standard Form 1382). Once on the mailing list, the potential supplier will receive invitations to submit bids for those items purchased through GSA. Since 1949 the GSA has been responsible for purchasing those items used in common throughout the government, including many items used by the military. A potential supplier of an item which is not being currently purchased by the government, such as a new product, should send a detailed description of the item to the Regional GSA Business Service Center, and an "Application for Presenting New or Improved Articles" will be sent. There is no uniform way of making a product known to all agencies of the federal government, although many agencies make use of the Bidders Mailing List Applications for soliciting bids.

Information about military procurement, including an alphabetical listing of the hundreds of products purchased in support of military operations and the addresses of procurement officers, is available in a Department of Defense publication, *Selling to the Military,* which is available from the U.S. Government Printing Office. A list of items purchased by the Defense Supply Agency reads, alphabetically, from "Accessories, Machine Tool" to "Yarn and Thread."

Bids for construction of buildings by the Public Building Service are solicited and opened by the GSA regional offices. Design contracts are solicited from architects or engineers who have filed with the GSA regional (and central) offices. Surveys, soil tests, etc., are usually subcontracted by the architect or engineer. Notice of opening of bids for construction contracts are publicized in the area where the construction is to take place and also in the *Commerce Business Daily*.

Notification of contract awards is normally sent by mail, along with directions to proceed. In the case of large contracts or those involving new departures or suppliers, notice of a contract award is delivered personally.

All items are inspected by the government before acceptance and final payment of the invoice.

**Becoming a State-Local Government Supplier** States, counties, and cities may be able to supply lists of products which they normally purchase. If a list exists, it may be obtained from the purchasing officer. If no list is maintained, a potential supplier can obtain the information about a particular product from the same source. There is no uniformity among governmental jurisdictions as to who is responsible for procurement. It may be the city or county clerk, the comptroller, or the engineer. Some jurisdictions have a contract officer, a director of procurement, or a purchasing agent.

One difference between private markets and the public market is that all transactions in the latter must be matters of public record. Therefore, the potential supplier has information available in the state capitol, county court house, or city hall which will allow an estimate of the volume of purchases of any particular item by a government as well as the names of all contractors, particularly construction contractors, who are a source of potential subcontracts for materials, supplies, or services.

### BUYING IN THE PUBLIC MARKET

The main sales outlets of the federal government are GSA and the Department of Defense (DOD). There are some exceptions; for example, houses obtained by mortgage foreclosure under G.I. loans are sold by the Veteran's Administration. In general, announcements of sales and catalogs of items to be sold are available to anyone who has expressed an interest in bidding. GSA maintains a separate mailing list for each geographical region; to get on the mailing list, a firm must contact the business service center in the relevant region. DOD has a centralized mailing list; contact the Defense Surplus Bidders Control Office. Information about government sales is summarized in Table M-15.

*See also* GOVERNMENT RELATIONS AND SERVICES; INTERNATIONAL TRADE; MARKETS, CLASSIFICATIONS AND MARKET ANALYSIS; PUBLIC ADMINISTRATION; SMALL BUSINESS ADMINISTRATION.

### SOURCES OF INFORMATION

An excellent source of general information about public markets is *The Businessman's Guide to Dealing with the Federal Government*, Drake Publishers, Inc., New York, 1973. Also see the pamphlet *Selling to the U.S. Government*, issued by the Office of Procurement Assistance, U.S. Small Business Administration, October 1975.

Other important information is available in *Commerce Business Daily* (Monday through Friday), and *U.S. Government Purchasing and Sales Directory*. Subscriptions to the former and copies of the latter are available through the Superintendent of Documents, U.S. Government Printing Office.

Many departments and agencies of the U.S. government publish documents called, "Selling to the Department of . . . ." A sampling of those available, giving specific information and procurement needs of the individual agencies, includes "Selling to the AEC," "Selling to the U.S. Department of Agriculture," "How to Sell to the U.S. Department of Commerce," "Selling to N.A.S.A," and "Selling to the Military."

An extensive bibliography is available in *Council of Planning Librarians Exchange Bibliography Number 980*, "Contractual Services in Government: Selected Bibliography on Practices in Federal, State, and Local Agencies, Education and Foreign Countries," Monticello, 1976.

EARL W. ADAMS, *Allegheny College*

## Markets, securities

The securities markets have much in common with markets of all kinds. A *market* is a means whereby

TABLE M-15  Government Sales*

| Category of good | How sold | To obtain information |
|---|---|---|
| Personal property | Sealed bid, public auction, or *spot bid*† | U.S. government publication, "Sale of Government Personal Property" |
| Real property | Sealed bid, public auction, or brokers | U.S. government publication, "Disposal of Surplus Real Property" |
| Strategic and critical materials | Sealed bid, negotiation, or fixed price | Contact Property Management and Disposal Services Administration (GSA) |

*Compiled from information in *The Bsuinessman's Guide to Dealing with the Federal Government*, pp. 116–121.
†The bidder writes the bid and places it in a bid box.

buyers and sellers are brought together to aid in the transfer of goods and/or services. Several aspects of this general definition seem worthy of emphasis:

1. It is *not* necessary that a market have a physical location. A market may be simply related by phones or some means of electronic communication. All that is necessary is that the buyers and sellers can communicate regarding the relevant aspects of the purchase or sale.

2. The market does *not* necessarily own the goods or services involved. There is no requirement other than to provide for the smooth and inexpensive transfer of goods and services. In the case of financial markets, those who establish and administer the market definitely do *not* own any of the assets; they simply provide a location for potential buyers and sellers and help the market to function.

3. A market can deal in any variety of goods and services—from fish and vegetables to stocks and bonds. Any commodity with a diverse clientele, however, will develop a market to aid in its transfer.

4. Typically, both buyers and sellers benefit from the existence of a market.

## PRIMARY AND SECONDARY SECURITIES MARKETS

The markets for securities—stocks and bonds—are classified two ways according to whether they deal in (1) new or (2) outstanding securities.

**Primary Markets**   The primary market is one in which new issues are sold by companies to acquire new capital for the corporation, through the sale of either corporate bonds, preferred stock, or common stock. These new issues are typically broken into two groups:

1. *Seasoned new issues.* These are issued by companies with existing public markets for their securities, such as General Motors selling a new issue of common stock in order to acquire additional external equity capital. In this case, there is an existing public market for General Motors stock, and the company is increasing the number of outstanding shares to acquire new equity capital.

2. *Initial public offerings.* This might take place when a small company sells common stock to the public for the first time. In this case, a public market does *not* exist for the stock; i.e., the company has been closely held.

*Underwriters.*   New issues (seasoned or initial offerings) are typically underwritten by investment bankers, or underwriters, who acquire the total issue from the company and, in turn, sell the issue to individual investors. The underwriter provides ad-

vice to the corporation on the general characteristics of the issue, the pricing of the issue, and the timing of the offering. The underwriter also accepts the risk of selling the new issue, after acquiring it from the corporation.

The arrangements between the company and the underwriter typically take one of three forms:

1. The most common arrangement is when a corporation *negotiates* with a specified underwriter regarding the pricing and the arrangements for the new issue. This arrangement is typical for existing industrial corporations who have an underwriter, or investment banker, they work with on a continuous basis. When they decide to come out with a new issue of securities, they seek the advice of the investment banker who helps them set up the issue and, subsequently, forms an underwriting syndicate for the sale of the issues.

2. An alternative arrangement is when a corporation specifies the characteristics of an issue it is contemplating and then solicits *competitive bids* from alternative underwriting firms. This is typically done by utilities, where, in many cases, they are required to submit their issues for competitive bids. It is contended that the cost of the issue is reduced in this manner, although it is acknowledged that there is a reduction in the services provided by the underwriter. Although less advice is provided, the investment banking firm still underwrites the issue in that they buy it from the firm and retail it through a syndicate.

3. A third arrangement is when an investment banker agrees to accept an issue and sell it on a *best-efforts basis*. This arrangement, which usually applies to a speculative new issue, arises when the investment banker is concerned with the possible success of the issue and will only become involved with the understanding that his or her best efforts will be used to sell the issue. The point is, the investment banker does *not* really underwrite the issue, since he or she does not buy the issue. In the best-efforts arrangement, the stock is owned by the company, and the investment banker acts more as a broker trying to sell what can be sold at the stipulated price.

**Secondary Markets**   These occur where there is trading in outstanding issues. In this market, the issue has already been sold to the public and is traded between current and potential owners of the outstanding securities. Secondary markets are typically broken down into three major groups:

1. Major national exchanges, which include the New York Stock Exchange and the American Stock Exchange.

2. Regional exchanges, which include the smaller exchanges in cities like Chicago, Boston, Philadelphia, Washington, and San Francisco.

3. The over-the-counter market, that includes trading in securities that are not listed on an organized exchange.

## SECONDARY EQUITY MARKETS

National exchanges and regional exchanges are similar in that they are referred to as listed securities exchanges; they differ because of size and geographic emphasis.

*Listed securities exchanges* are formal organizations that have a specified group of members who may use the facilities of the exchange and a specified list of securities (stocks or bonds) that have qualified for "listing" on the exchange. In addition to a limit on the membership and the securities eligible for trading, these exchanges also are similar in that prices are determined via an *auction* process, whereby interested buyers and sellers submit *bids* and *asks* for a given stock to a central location for that stock. The bids and asks are recorded by the specialist assigned to that stock, and the stock is sold to the highest bidder and bought from the individual with the lowest asking price (i.e., the lowest offering price).

**National Stock Exchanges** The New York Stock Exchange and the American Stock Exchange are considered national in scope because of the large number of securities listed, the geographic dispersion of these issues, and the national nature of their buyers and sellers.

*New York Stock Exchange (NYSE).* This is the largest organized securities market in the United States and dates back to a constitution in 1817. As of the late 1970s, there were over 1500 companies with stock listed on the NYSE, and there were over 2000 issues with a total market value of approximately $700 billion. The average number of shares traded on the exchange has increased steadily over time, with an increase in the number of issues listed and an increase in the turnover of shares listed. Average daily volume was about 5 million shares in the early 1960s, increased to about 10 million shares in the second half of the 1960s, and averaged about 15 million during the period from 1970 to 1974. During the latter part of the 1970s, trading increased to about 18 million shares a day, and during many days the volume exceeded 20 million shares.

The NYSE has consistently accounted for about 75 percent of all shares traded on listed exchanges, compared with about 10 to 20 percent for the American Stock Exchange (ASE), and about 10 percent for all the regional exchanges combined (the "other" category). Because the price of shares on the NYSE tends to be higher than prices on the ASE, the percent of value of the NYSE has averaged from 80 to 85 percent, with lower figures for the ASE, while the regional exchanges are comparable in shares and value.

*American Stock Exchange (ASE).* This exchange had its inception with the trading of unlisted shares at the corner of Wall and Hanover streets in New York City and was referred to as the Outdoor Curb Market. In 1911, formal trading rules were established, and in 1921, the members moved inside a building but continued to trade mainly in unlisted stocks. The dominance of unlisted stocks continued until 1946 when listed stocks finally outnumbered unlisted stocks. The current name was adopted in 1953.

While a small number of stocks are traded on both national exchanges, the overwhelming majority of stocks listed on the ASE are unique to that exchange.

*Innovation.* In addition to a different clientele of United States firms, the ASE has been innovative in listing foreign securities over the years. There were 68 foreign issues listed in 1972. Further, the ASE listed warrants for a number of years before the NYSE first listed them in 1970. The most recent innovation on the ASE has been the trading of call options on listed securities. This was introduced after option trading became widespread, following the establishment of the Chicago Board Options Exchange (CBOE). Because options were not traded on the NYSE, almost all the options traded on the ASE are for stocks listed on the NYSE.

At the end of 1976 there were approximately 1400 stock issues listed on the ASE. Average daily trading volume has fluctuated substantially over time as the demand for smaller and younger firms has changed. Prior to 1955 average daily volume was below 500,000 shares. Average daily volume reached its highest level of 6.3 million shares in 1968. Subsequently, it declined to about 2 million shares a day.

**Regional Exchanges** These have basically the same operating procedures as the NYSE and ASE but differ in their listing requirements and the geographic distribution of the firms listed. Their listing requirements are less stringent than for either of the national exchanges because the main incentive for many of these exchanges is to provide trading facilities for geographically local firms that (1) are not large enough or (2) do not have a national stockholder list to qualify for listing on one of the national exchanges. These exchanges also list stocks from the national exchanges that are of substantial interest to the members of the exchange, i.e., AT&T and General Motors.

The major regional exchanges are as follows: (1) Midwest Stock Exchange (Chicago), (2) Pacific Stock Exchange (San Francisco—Los Angeles), (3) PBW Exchange (Philadelphia–Pittsburgh), (4) Boston Stock Exchange (Boston), (5) Spokane Stock Exchange (Spokane, Washington), (6) Honolulu Stock Exchange (Honolulu, Hawaii), and (7) Intermountain Stock Exchange (Salt Lake City).

The fortunes of the regional exchanges have fluctuated substantially over time. They were popular during the late 1960s when there was strong interest in small, young firms. Their recent activity has been affected by institutional interest in stocks listed both on a national exchange and on a regional exchange.

**Over-the-Counter Market (OTC)**  This market includes the trading in all stocks not listed on one of the listed exchanges. (It can also include trading in stocks that are listed on an exchange in an arrangement referred to as the third market, which is discussed in detail below.) The OTC market is *not* a formal market organization with specific membership requirements or a specific list of stocks that are deemed eligible for trading. In theory, it is possible to trade *any* security on the OTC market as long as someone is willing to take a position in the stock. To *take a position* means that an individual or firm advertises its willingness to buy or sell the stock, i.e., to make a market in the stock.

*Size.*  Given the accessibility of the OTC market, it is not surprising that it is the largest segment of the secondary market in terms of the number of issues traded and the most diverse in terms of quality. Estimates of the number of issues traded on the OTC market run as high as 20,000. Many of these issues are very inactive, but at least 5000 issues are traded actively.

*Diversity.*  Since the OTC has no minimum requirements for listing, stocks traded on the OTC range from the smallest, most unprofitable company, to the largest, most profitable firms. It is notable that all U.S. Government Bonds are traded on the OTC market, and the vast majority of bank and insurance stocks are likewise not listed on any exchange but are traded only on the OTC. Finally, OTC handles some 150 dual-traded stocks of high quality, including AT&T and General Motors.

*Operation.*  Participants in the OTC market act as dealers because they buy and sell for their own account. This is in contrast to the listed exchanges where specialists generally act as the agents for other investors—i.e., specialists keep the books and attempt to match the buy and sell orders left with them. As such, the OTC market is referred to as a *negotiated* market where investors directly negotiate with dealers, in contrast to the exchanges that are auction markets with specialists acting as the intermediaries, or auctioneers.

*The NASDAQ System.*  NASDAQ is an acronym that stands for National Association of Securities Dealers Automatic Quotations. Briefly, it is an electronic quotation system that serves the vast OTC market. It is entirely possible to have 10, 15, or more market makers for a given stock, and it is common to have three to five dealers. Given an interest in an OTC stock, a major problem has always been to determine what the general market is and also what the markets of the specific market makers are. Prior to the introduction of NASDAQ it was necessary to make phone calls to three or four dealers to determine the best market, and then after such a "survey," go back to the one with the best market. In cases where there were 10 or 15 dealers, a dealer was not certain which made the best market. With NASDAQ *all* the quotes by market makers are available immediately, and the broker can make one phone call to the dealer with the best market, verify that the quote has not changed, and make the sale or purchase. There are three levels specified by the developers of the NASDAQ system to serve firms with different interests.

Level 1 is for firms that want current information on the OTC stocks but do not often buy or sell OTC stocks for their customers and are not market makers. Level 1 provides a median quote for all stocks on the system.

Level 2 is for firms that are serious traders in OTC stocks for themselves or their customers. This system provides all the quotes by all the individual market makers.

Level 3 is for investment firms that make markets in OTC stocks. It has the capability of level 2 plus the ability to change the quote on the market-makers' stocks.

**Third Market**  This term is used to describe the trading of shares listed on an exchange on the over-the-counter market. When a stock is listed on an exchange, members of that exchange are generally required to bring all buy and sell orders to the exchange to be executed. At the same time, there is no reason why an investment firm that is *not* a member of an exchange cannot make a market in a listed stock in the same way as a market in an unlisted stock. The success or failure of such a venture will obviously depend upon whether the

OTC market is as good as the exchange market and/or the relative cost of the transaction compared with the cost on the exchange. Volume on the third market grew consistently and dramatically from 1965 through 1972 (to better than 7 percent), followed by a decline in 1973 and 1974, and an increase in absolute terms but not in percent of trading during 1975. To understand this growth, two points must be known:

1. Almost all trading on the third market is by institutions. Most individuals do not even know that such a market exists, and if they know about it, they generally do not know how to use it.

2. Trading in the third market is concentrated in a limited number (less than 200) of stocks. The major stocks traded on the third market are the large active stocks of interest to financial institutions. Examples would be AT&T, General Motors, IBM, and General Electric.

**The Fourth Market** This term is used to describe the direct trading of securities between two parties with no broker intermediary. In almost all cases, the two parties involved are institutions. The main reason any investor takes a transaction to a broker and through the broker to a listed exchange is that it is faster and easier; and the owner of the stock is willing to pay a fee for this speed and convenience. This fee is the brokerage commission.

The fourth market evolved for institutions because at some point, with very large orders, the fee became so large that it became worthwhile for institutions to attempt to deal directly with each other to save the fee. The arrangements for bringing two interested parties together take one of two forms: (1) an electronic system or (2) a third-party system, where the third party works for a flat fee for a group of institutions.

The *electronic system* allows its subscribers (large institutions) to advertise on the system using a code number indicating that they want to buy or sell a certain number of shares of stock at a specified price. Nobody knows which institution is trying to buy or sell. Any other subscribing member who has an interest in completing the proposed transaction can teletype to the original party (by code); only after both parties have agreed to final terms are the names revealed. The electronic system enables the parties to come together anonymously, and there is no specific cost for the transaction—the only cost is a flat annual fee to be a subscriber. The *third-party system* works in about the same way except that the annual fee is paid to an individual who makes the contacts for his or her institutional clientele.

Obviously, the major advantage of the fourth market for the participants is substantially lower commission costs on large transactions compared with costs on the exchange and even the third market. A major disadvantage is that it is necessary to expose your potential interest in selling or buying a stock with the possible effect this may have on the price.

## ANALYSIS OF THE EXCHANGE MARKET

Because of the importance of the listed exchange market on national and international financial activities, this entry discusses in detail the several types of members on the exchange, the major types of orders used on the exchange, and the function of the specialist.

**Breakdown of Exchange Membership** Listed securities exchanges typically have four major categories of membership:

1. *Specialists,* who constitute about 25 percent of the total membership and are responsible for maintaining a fair and orderly market in the securities listed on the exchange.

2. *Odd-lot dealers,* who stand ready to buy and sell less than a round lot of a stock (typically 100 shares). When individuals want to buy less than 100 shares, the order is turned over to odd-lot dealers who will buy or sell from their own inventory. Notably, odd-lot dealers are *not* brokers, but dealers, and are buying and selling from their own inventory. Recently this function has been taken over by the exchange or by the specialist in the stock. In addition, some large brokerage firms (e.g., Merrill Lynch, Pierce, Fenner & Smith) have begun handling the odd-lot business for their own customers.

3. *Floor brokers,* who can be either members or partners of a brokerage house. They can be brokers who sell for their own customers, they can transact for other members too busy to trade, or they can buy and sell for brokers who are not members of an exchange. When a brokerage house such as Merrill Lynch, Pierce, Fenner & Smith advertises that it is a member of the New York Stock Exchange, this is what one of their members does—executes orders given to Merrill Lynch registered representatives.

4. *Registered traders,* who are allowed to use their membership to buy and sell for their own account. They are allowed to save the commission in their own trading, and observers feel they have an advantage because they are on the floor. The ex-

change and others feel they should be allowed these advantages because they provide added liquidity to the market—i.e., they will tend to trade against the crowd. At the same time, because of possible abuses, there are regulations regarding their conduct in terms of how they trade and how many registered traders can be in a trading crowd around a specialists' booth at a point in time.

**Types of Orders** To understand the specialists' role, one must first have a full understanding of the different types of orders available to individual investors and to the specialist in the dealer function.

*Market Order.* This is the most heavily used order and is an order to buy or sell a stock at the best prevailing price currently available. An investor who wants to sell some stock and uses a market order indicates that he or she is willing to sell immediately at the highest bid available at the time the order reaches the specialist on the exchange. In contrast, a potential buyer who uses a market order indicates that he or she is willing to pay the lowest offering price available at the time the order reaches the floor of the exchange. Market orders are used when an individual wants to effect a transaction quickly and is willing to accept the prevailing market price.

*Limit Order.* This specifies a definite price that the buyer will pay for the stock or the price at which the individual will sell the stock. As an example, an investor submits a bid to purchase 100 shares of stock at $48 a share, when the current market is 52 bid–52½ ask, with the expectation that the stock will decline to $48 in the near future. Such an order must also indicate *how long* the limit order will be outstanding. The alternatives, in terms of time, are basically without bounds—they can be for a part of a day, for a full day, for several days, a week, a month, or open-ended, which means the order is good until canceled (GTC). These limit orders are typically given to the specialist to execute. Rather than have the broker wait for a given price on a stock, the broker will give it to the specialist, who will put it in his or her book and act as the broker's representative. When, and if, the market reaches the limit order price, the specialist will execute the order and inform the broker.

*Short Sales.* While most investors purchase stock with the expectation that they will derive their return from an increase in value, there are instances when an investor may believe that a stock is overpriced and would like to invest in order to take advantage of an expected delcine in the price. The way to do this is to sell the stock short. A *short sale* is the sale of stock that is not owned with the intent of purchasing it later at a lower price. Specifically, the investor *borrows* the stock through a broker, from another investor, and sells it in the market. Subsequently, the investor will repurchase the stock (hopefully, at a lower price than he or she sold it at) and replace the stock borrowed. The investor who lent the stock has the use of the money paid for the stock, because it is left as collateral on the stock loan. While there is no time limit on the short sale, the lender of the stock may want to sell his or her shares, in which case the broker will find another investor who will lend the stock.

Two technical points in connection with short sales are important:

1. A short sale can only be made on an uptick trade. The reason for this restriction is because the exchanges do not want to make it possible for traders to be able to *force* a profit on a short sale by pushing the price down through continual short sales. Therefore, the transaction price for a short sale must be higher than the last trade price (an *uptick*). If there is no change in price, the previous price must have been higher than its previous price (a zero uptick).

2. The short seller is responsible for the dividends to the investor who lent the stock. The purchaser of the short sale stock receives the dividend from the corporation, and so the short seller must pay a similar dividend to the lender.

*Stop-Loss Order.* This is a conditional market order, whereby the investor indicates that he or she wants to sell a stock *if* the stock drops to a given price. As an example, an individual buys a stock at 50 expecting it to go up. At the same time, if the stock does not go up, the individual wants to make sure that the losses are minimized or limited. Therefore, he or she would put in a stop-loss order at 45. If the stock dropped to 45, then the stop-loss order would become a *market-sell order* and the stock would be sold at the prevailing market price. Notably, the order does not guarantee that the investor will get the $45. The investor can get a little bit more or a little bit less, because the order, as noted, is a conditional market order and becomes a market order only when a transaction takes place at 45. Because of the possibility of market disruption caused by a large number of stop-loss orders, the exchange, on occasion, has canceled all stop-loss orders on certain stocks.

*Stop-Buy Order.* A stop loss on the other side is called a *stop-buy order*. This is a conditional buy order by an individual who has engaged in a short sale. In this case, an investor has sold stock short and wants to minimize loss if a stock begins to increase in value rather than to decline as expected. This order makes it possible to place a conditional buy order at a price above the price at which the individual sold the stock short.

**The Specialist** The stock exchange specialist is often referred to as the "center of the auction market" for stocks. The specialist is a member of the exchange who decides to fulfill the specialist function and applies for such a position by requesting the exchange to assign stocks to him or her. It is necessary that the specialist possess substantial capital to carry out this function—either $500,000 or enough to purchase 5000 shares of the stock—whichever is greater.

*Specialist Functions.* The specialist has two major functions. The first is that of a *broker* who handles the limit orders or special orders placed with member brokers. As noted previously, the individual broker who receives a limit order to purchase a stock $5 below the current market does not have the time or inclination to constantly watch the stock to see when and if the decline takes place. Therefore, the individual broker leaves the limit order (or a stop-loss or stop-buy order) with the specialist who enters it in the book and executes it when appropriate. For this service the specialist receives a portion of the broker's commission on the trade.

The second major function is to act as a *dealer* in the assigned stocks in order to maintain a fair and orderly market. In this regard, the specialist is expected to buy and sell for his or her own account when there is insufficient public supply or demand to provide a continuous liquid market. As an example, if a stock is currently selling for about $40 per share, one could envision a situation in an auction market where the current bid and ask (without the specialist) might be 40 bid–41 ask. This means there is some public investor with a limit order on the books who is willing to buy stock at $40 per share, while another investor is willing to sell stock at $41 per share. If the specialist does not intercede and the market orders to buy and sell the stock come to the market in a random fashion, one would expect the price of the stock to fluctuate between 40 and 41 constantly—a movement of 2.5 percent between trades. Most investors would probably consider such a price pattern to be more volatile than desired; i.e., it would not be considered a very continuous market. The individual responsible for reducing the volatility and providing continuity in price changes

is the specialist. The specialist is expected to provide an alternative bid and/or ask that will narrow the spread and thereby provide greater price continuity over time. In the above example this would entail *either* entering a bid of $40\frac{1}{2}$ or $40\frac{3}{4}$ or an ask of $40\frac{1}{2}$ or $40\frac{1}{4}$ to narrow the spread to one-half point or one-quarter point.

*Specialist Income.* Specialists derive their income from both their major functions. The actual breakdown between income from acting as a broker for limit orders and income from acting as a dealer to maintain an orderly market will depend upon the specific stock. In the case of a very actively traded stock (e.g., American Telephone and Telegraph), there is not much need for the specialist to act as a dealer because the substantial public interest forms a pretty tight market. In such an instance, the major concern (and the main source of income) of the specialist is maintaining the limit orders for the stock. In contrast, in the case of stocks with low trading volume and substantial price volatility, specialists would be called upon to constantly interject themselves into the market to close the spread. In these cases, their major income would depend upon their ability to profitably trade in the stock.

*See also* AUDITING, FINANCIAL; FINANCIAL MANAGEMENT, CAPITAL STRUCTURE AND DIVIDEND POLICY; FINANCIAL MANAGEMENT, SHORT-TERM, INTERMEDIATE, AND LONG-TERM FINANCING; FINANCIAL RATIO ANALYSIS; FINANCIAL STATEMENT ANALYSIS; MARKETS, STOCK INDICATOR SERIES; SECURITIES AND EXCHANGE COMMISSION (SEC); SHAREHOLDER RELATIONSHIPS.

### REFERENCES

Armour, Lawrence A.: "Central Marketplace," *Barron's*, March 1972.

Eiteman, W. J., C. A. Dice, and D. K. Eiteman: *The Stock Market*, 4th ed., McGraw-Hill Book Company, New York, 1966.

Feuerstein, Donald M.: "Toward a National System of Securities Exchanges: The Third and Fourth Markets," *Financial Analysts Journal*, vol. 28, no. 4, pp. 57–59, 82–86, July–August 1972.

Friend, Irwin, and W. J. Winn: *The Over-the-Counter Securities Markets*, McGraw-Hill Book Company, New York, 1958.

Leffler, George L., and Loring Farwell: *The Stock Market*, 3d ed., The Ronald Press Company, New York, 1963.

Loll, Leo M., and Julian G. Buckley: *The Over-the-Counter Securities Markets*, 3d ed., Prentice-Hall Inc., Englewood Cliffs, N.J., 1967.

"NASDAQ and the OTC," National Association of Securities Dealers, New York, 1974.

New York Stock Exchange *Fact Books*.

Reilly, Frank K., ed.: *Readings and Issues in Investments,* The Dryden Press, Inc. Hinsdale, Ill., 1975. A number of the references in this chapter are reprinted in this book.

Robbins, Sidney: *The Securities Markets: Operations and Issues,* The Free Press, New York, 1966.

Sobel, Robert: *The Big Board,* The Free Press, New York, 1965.

"The Regional Stock Exchange's Fight for Survival," *Fortune,* November 1973.

Walter, James E.: *The Role of Regional Security Exchanges,* University of California Press, Berkeley, 1957.

West, Richard R.: "On the Difference Between Internal and External Market Efficiency," *Financial Analysts Journal,* vol. 31, no. 6, pp. 30–34, November–December 1975.

West, Richard R., and Seha M. Tinic: "Corporate Finance and the Changing Stock Market," *Financial Management,* vol. 3, no. 3, pp. 14–23, Autumn 1974.

West, Richard R., and Seha M. Tinic: *The Economics of the Stock Market,* Frederick A. Praeger, Inc., New York, 1971.

Frank K. Reilly, *University of Illinois at Urbana*

# Markets, stock indicator series

A stock market indicator series (or index) is a composite measure of stock prices in an aggregate market. Although stock portfolios are made up of individual stocks, most stocks tend to move with the aggregate market. If the overall market rises or falls, it is likely that an individual's portfolio will also rise or fall in value. Furthermore, investors generally wish to know what the aggregate state—or trend—of the market may be. To monitor these aggregate movements, financial publications and other interested parties have developed market indicator series. The purpose of these composite indicators is to provide an overall indication of aggregate market changes or market movements.

**Uses and Users**   There are at least three important uses for stock market indicator series:

1. *Benchmarks.* Market indicator series serve those who examine total market returns over some time period and use these derived market returns as a benchmark to judge the performance of alternative individual portfolios.

2. *Relationships.* Security analysts and portfolio managers in particular examine the factors that influence aggregate stock price movements in order to determine the relationship between alternative economic variables and aggregate stock market movements.

3. *Predictions.* Technicians study past price changes to predict future price movements.

## DIFFERENTIATING FACTORS IN CONSTRUCTION

Stock market indicator series are intended to indicate the overall movements for a group of stocks. Given this intent, it is necessary to consider what is important in computing any average intended to represent a total population.

**Sample**   The initial concern is the sample used to construct the market indicator series. Three factors must be considered: (1) the size of the sample, (2) the breadth of the sample, and (3) the source of the sample.

**Weighting**   The second concern is the weight given to each member in the sample. Three principal weighting schemes are used: (1) a price-weighted series, (2) a value-weighted series, and (3) an unweighted series, or what would be described as equally-weighted series.

**Computational Procedure**   The final consideration is the computational procedure used. There are three basic alternatives: (1) a simple arithmetic average of the various members in the series; (2) a derivation of an index with all changes, whether in price or value, reported in terms of a basic index; or (3) the incorporation of a geometric average rather than an arithmetic average.

## ALTERNATIVE INDICATOR SERIES

A number of widely used series warrant closer examination.

**Price-Weighted Series**   These include the oldest and certainly most popular stock market indicator series—the *Dow-Jones industrial average (DJIA).* The DJIA is a price-weighted average of 30 large industrial "blue chip" stocks listed on the New York Stock Exchange (NYSE). The value of this index is derived by adding the current prices of the 30 stocks and dividing that sum by a divisor that has been adjusted to take account of stock splits and changes in the sample average over time.

Because the series is price-weighted, a high-priced stock carries more weight in the series than a low-priced stock; i.e., a 10 percent change in a $100 stock ($10) will cause a larger change in the series than a 10 percent change in a $30 stock ($3).

In addition to a price series for industrial stocks, Dow-Jones also has a transportation average of 20 stocks and a utility average that includes 15 stocks.

**Value-Weighted Series**  A value-weighted index begins by deriving the initial total market value of all stocks used in the series (*market value* equals number of shares outstanding times current market price). This initial value is typically established as the base and assigned an index value of 100. A new market value is computed daily for all securities in the index. This new value is compared with the initial value to determine the percent change, and this percent change is applied to the beginning index value of 100.

There is an automatic adjustment for stock splits and other capital changes in a value index because the decrease in the stock price is offset by an increase in the number of shares outstanding. In a value-weighted index, the importance of individual stocks in the sample is determined by their relative market value; i.e., a given percent change in the value of a large company has a greater impact than a comparable percent change for a small company.

*Standard & Poor's Indexes.*  The first company to widely employ a market-value index was Standard & Poor's Corporation. It developed an index using 1935 to 1937 as a base period and computed a market-value index for 425 industrial stocks. It also computed an index of 60 utilities and 15 transportation firms. Finally, it developed a 500-stock composite index. Subsequently, the base period was changed to 1941 to 1943 and the base value to 10. In July 1976, the Standard & Poor's series underwent a major change. Prior to this time, all the stocks in the Standard & Poor's series were companies listed on the NYSE, and there was no index of financial firms. In July, 1976, Standard & Poor's revised the 500 index into four groups: 400 industrials, 40 public utilities, 20 transportation, and 40 financial. Several of the stocks added were from the OTC market. The net result of these changes is an index which is broader in terms of industry representation and of the total equity market.

In addition to its major market indicators, Standard & Poor's has constructed over 90 individual industry series that include from 3 to 11 companies within an industry group.

*New York Stock Exchange.*  Several other market indicators now employ the value-weighted index concept. In 1966, the NYSE derived a market-value index with figures available back to 1940. In contrast to other indexes, the various NYSE series are *not* based upon a sample of stocks. Specifically, the NYSE series include *all* the stocks listed on the exchange. As such, the NYSE is not concerned with the number of stocks in the sample nor its breadth because this series includes the total universe of stocks listed on the exchange. Nevertheless, because the index is value-weighted, the large companies still control the major movements in the index. As an illustration of this point, the 500 stocks in Standard & Poor's composite index represent *74 percent* of the market value of all stocks on the exchange although they are only about *28 percent* of the exchange in numbers.

*American Stock Exchange.*  The exchange originally developed a price-change series in 1966 in which the price changes during a given day were added, and then this sum was divided by the number of issues on the exchange. This average price change was then added to or subtracted from the previous day's index to arrive at a new index value. Unfortunately, this procedure eventually caused a distortion in the series because the price changes were influenced by the values. The ASE subsequently created a value-weighted series similar to that used by the NYSE that includes all the stocks on the exchange. This new series was released in September 1973. The index was set at 100 as of August 31, 1973. Subsequently the exchange made figures available for the new series back to 1969.

*NASDAQ Series.*  A relatively recent addition to the market indicator universe is the comprehensive price indicator series for the OTC market developed by the National Association of Securities Dealers (NASD). The NASDAQ-OTC price indicator series had an index value of 100 as of February 5, 1971. All active domestic OTC common stocks listed on NASDAQ are included in the indexes, as are new stocks added to the system. The 2359 issues included in the NASDAQ-OTC price indexes have been divided into the following seven categories:

1. Composite (2359 issues)
2. Industrials (1614 issues)
3. Banks (80 issues)
4. Insurance (133 issues)
5. Other finance (398 issues)
6. Transportation (56 issues)
7. Utilities (78 issues)

The indexes are value-weighted series similar to the Standard & Poor's series and the NYSE series. Because the composite index is value-weighted, it is heavily influenced by the largest 100 stocks on the NASDAQ system.

**Unweighted Price Indicator Series**  In an unweighted index, all stocks carry equal weight irrespective of their price and/or the value of the stock. Specifically, a $20 stock is as important as a $40 stock, and the total market value of the company is not important. Such an index is most appropriate for an individual who would randomly select stocks for his or her portfolio. One way to visualize what transpires in an unweighted series is to assume that equal dollar amounts are invested in each stock in the portfolio (e.g., an equal $1000 investment in each stock). Therefore, the investor would own 50 shares of a $20 stock, 100 shares of a $10 stock, and 10 shares of a $100 stock.

Probably the most well-known, unweighted, or equal-weighted stock market series are those constructed by Lawrence Fisher at the University of Chicago. Fisher and Lorie have carried out several studies examining the performance of stocks on the NYSE assuming that an investor bought equal amounts of each stock on the exchange. As suggested earlier, they concluded that the results in terms of appreciation or depreciation would be comparable to those derived by an investor who randomly selected a large sample of stocks from the NYSE.

Another unweighted price indicator series that has gained in prominence is the *Indicator Digest* index of all stocks on the NYSE. This series is more representative of all stocks on the exchange. In several instances, it reached a bottom earlier than other indicator series and continued to be depressed after some of the popular market indicator series resumed rising during a bull market. Such a difference indicates that the market rise only included the large popular stocks as contained in the DJIA or the Standard & Poor's market indicator series which are heavily weighted and influenced by the large well-known companies.

*See also* ECONOMIC MEASUREMENTS; FINANCIAL RATIO ANALYSIS; FINANCIAL STATEMENT ANALYSIS; FORECASTING BUSINESS CONDITIONS; MARKETS, SECURITIES; RISK ANALYSIS AND MANAGEMENT; SECURITIES AND EXCHANGE COMMISSION (SEC).

### REFERENCES

"Amex Introduces New Market Value Index System," *American Investor*, September 1973.

Balch, W. F.: "Market Guides," *Barron's*, September 19, 1966.

Carter, E. E., and K. J. Cohen: "Bias in the DJIA Caused by Stock Splits," *Financial Analysts Journal*, vol. 22, no. 6, December 1966.

Carter, E. E., and K. J. Cohen: "Stock Average, Stock Splits, and Bias," *Financial Analysts Journal*, vol. 23, no. 3, May–June 1967.

Cootner, Paul: "Stock Market Indexes—Fallacies and Illusions," *Commercial and Financial Chronicle*, Sept. 29, 1966.

Farrell, Maurice L., ed.: *Barron's Market Laboratory*, Dow-Jones Books, Princeton, N.J., published annually.

Farrell, Maurice L., ed.: *The Dow-Jones Investor's Handbook*, Dow-Jones Books, Princeton, N.J., published annually.

Fisher, Lawrence: "Outcomes for 'Random' Investments in Common Stock Listed on the New York Stock Exchange," *Journal of Business*, vol. 38, no. 2, April 1965.

Fisher, Lawrence: "Some New Stock Market Indexes," *Journal of Business*, supplement, vol. 39, no. 1, part II, January 1966.

Fisher, Lawrence, and James H. Lorie: "Rates of Return on Investments in Common Stock," *Journal of Business*, vol. 37, no. 1, January 1965.

Fisher, Lawrence, and J. H. Lorie: "Rates of Return on Investments in Common Stock, The Year-by-Year Record, 1926–65," *Journal of Business*, vol. 41, no. 3, July 1963.

Latane, Henry A., Donald L. Tuttle, and William E. Young: "Market Indexes and their Implications for Portfolio Management," *Financial Analysts Journal*, vol. 27, no. 5, September–October 1971.

Leuthold, S. C., and K. F. Blaich: "Warped Yardstick," *Barron's*, Sept. 18, 1972.

Milne, P. D.: "The Dow-Jones Industrial Average Reexamined," *Financial Analysts Journal*, vol. 22, no. 6, December 1966.

Molodovsky, Nicholas: "Building a Stock Market Measure—A Case Story," *Financial Analysts Journal*, vol. 23, no. 3, May–June 1967.

Reilly, Frank K.: "Evidence Regarding a Segmented Stock Market," *Journal of Finance*, vol. 27, no. 3, June 1972.

Reilly, Frank K.: "Price Changes in NYSE, AMEX and OTC Stocks Compared," *Financial Analysts Journal*, vol. 27, no. 2, March–April, 1971.

Schellbach, Lewis L.: "When Did the DJIA Top 1200?," *Financial Analysts Journal*, vol. 23, no. 3, May–June 1967.

Shaw, R. B.: "The Dow-Jones Industrials vs. the Dow-Jones Industrial Average," *Financial Analysts Journal*, vol. 11, no. 5, November 1955.

West, Stan, and Norman Miller: "Why the New NYSE Common Stock Indexes?," *Financial Analysts Journal*, vol. 23, no. 3, May–June 1967.

FRANK K. REILLY, *University of Illinois at Urbana*

## Markov chain (*See* OPERATIONS RESEARCH AND MATHEMATICAL MODELING.)

## Maslow's needs hierarchy (*See* MOTIVATION IN ORGANIZATIONS.)

## Mass production (*See* PRODUCTION PROCESSES.)

## Material handling

The most commonly held view of what material handling involves is that material handling concerns the handling of materials between the receiving and shipping activities in an enterprise. This is a narrow-minded view, however. Actually, "material handling is handling material"[1] from anywhere, to anywhere, in any type of enterprise or situation. The handling of material may vary from a mere 5 to 10 percent of productive activity to nearly 100 percent in some types of industries. On the average, it is thought that material handling in a typical manufacturing concern is judged to account for 40 to 60 percent of what goes on in the enterprise. The writer has estimated the total costs of handling in the United States to be $177 billion.[2] It is a gold mine of potential savings most worthy of close examination and analysis. A 10 percent reduction of material handling is not at all difficult to achieve.

**Scope** The scope of material handling in your business properly encompasses all handling involved in any of these activities:

Packaging (consumer) at supplier's plant
Packing (protective) at supplier's plant
Loading at supplier's plant
Transportation to user plant
External plant handling activities
Unloading activities
Receiving
Storage
Issuing materials
In-process handling
In-process storage
Work place handling
Intradepartmental handling
Interdepartmental handling
Intraplant handling
Handling related to auxiliary functions
Packaging
Warehousing of finished goods
Packing
Loading and shipping
Transportation to consumer
Interplant handling

**Benefits** Improved material handling may yield any of the following:

Improved material flow
Fewer unnecessary moves
Less unnecessary handling
Reduced manual handling
Increased production capacity
More efficient material flow
Increased space utilization
Increased work force utilization
Increased equipment utilization
Reduced employee fatigue
Reduced safety hazards

Better customer service
Controlled material flow
Improved housekeeping
Shorter production cycle
Reduced work in process
Higher inventory turnover
Reduced production cost
Increased profits

## PRINCIPLES OF MATERIAL HANDLING

As in many other areas of work, there is much to be learned from those who have worked in the field of material handling in the past. This experience has been summarized in the principles of material handling, as follows:[3]

**Related to Planning** Eight principles apply:

1. Planning principle: All handling activities should be planned.

2. Systems principle: Plan a *system* integrating as many handling activities as is practical and coordinating the full scope of operation.

3. Materials flow principle: Plan an operation sequence and equipment arrangement optimizing materials flow.

4. Simplification principle: Reduce or eliminate unnecessary movement and/or equipment.

5. Gravity principle: Utilize gravity to move material whenever practicable.

6. Space utilization: Make optimum utilization of the building cube.

7. Unit size principle: Increase quantity, size, and weight of load handled.

8. Safety principle: Provide for safe handling methods and equipment.

**Related to Equipment** Nine principles apply:

1. Mechanization/automation principle: Use mechanized or automated handling equipment when practicable.

2. Equipment-selection principle: In selecting handling equipment, consider all aspects of the *material* to be handled, the *move* to be made, and the *method(s)* to be utilized—all in terms of the lowest overall cost.

3. Standardization principle: Standardize methods as well as types and sizes of handling equipment.

4. Flexibility principle: Use methods and equipment that can perform a variety of tasks and applications.

5. Dead-weight principle: Reduce the ratio of equipment dead-weight to pay load.

6. Motion principle: Equipment designed to transport materials should be kept in motion.

7. Idle-time principle: Reduce idle, or unproductive, time of both handling equipment and work force.

8. Maintenance principle: Plan for preventive maintenance and scheduled repair of all handling equipment.

9. Obsolescence principle: Replace obsolete handling methods and equipment when newer methods or equipment will pay off in a reasonable time.

**Related to Operations**   Three principles apply:

1. Control principle: Use material handling equipment to improve production control, inventory control, and order handling.

2. Capacity principle: Use handling equipment to help achieve full production capacity.

3. Performance efficiency principle: Determine efficiency of handling performance in terms of expense per unit handled.

The principles, and their correlations, are most commonly used in check-sheet form, as shown in Fig. M-17.

## SURVEY PROCEDURES

In surveying material handling activities to uncover improvement opportunities, the following procedures and techniques may be helpful:[4]

1. Record the flow of material(s) by means of the following:

    Assembly chart
    Operation process chart
    Multiproduct process chart
    Process chart
    Flow diagram
    Flow process chart
    From-to (trip frequency) chart
    Activity relationship chart
    Activity relationship diagram
    Procedure chart (information flow)

2. Identify violations of good practice (improvement opportunities) using

    Charts listed above
    Walk-through
    Check sheets (indicators, symptoms)
    Flow-planning principles
    Material handling principles

3. List worst violations (best opportunities).

4. Identify causes of violations.

5. Analyze causes and define problems.

6. Translate problems (causes) into projects.

7. Develop evaluation criteria.

8. Evaluate potential benefits.

9. Select most-likely project(s) to begin with.

10. Establish project sequence.

11. Review interrelated projects to assure treatment from systems point of view.

12. Attack each problem.

13. Document and report all savings.

14. Periodically evaluate effectiveness of solution(s) for potential improvement.

## PROBLEM-SOLVING PROCEDURE

In attacking a specific material handling problem, it is beneficial to follow a systematic approach:

1. Identify the problem(s).

2. Determine the scope of the problem(s).

3. Establish objective(s).

4. Define problem(s).

5. Determine data to be collected.

6. Establish work plan and schedule.

7. Collect data.

8. Develop, weigh, and analyze data.

9. Develop improvements (and/or design proposed system).

10. Select equipment (see section below).

11. Prepare justification.

12. Obtain approvals.

13. Revise as necessary.

14. Work out procedure for implementation.

15. Supervise the installation.

16. Follow up.

## EQUIPMENT CONCEPTS

Inevitably, many solutions to material handling problems require the use of equipment. There are over 570 kinds, types, and varieties of handling equipment. Fortunately, they fall roughly into three major categories:

**Conveyors**   These are gravity or powered devices commonly used for moving uniform loads continuously from point-to-point over fixed paths, where the primary function is conveying. Conveyors are generally useful when (1) loads are uniform, (2) materials move continuously, (3) route does not vary, (4) load is constant, (5) movement rate is relatively fixed, (6) conveyors can by-pass cross traffic, (7) path to be followed is fixed, and (8) movement is from one fixed point to another point.

**Cranes and Hoists**   These are overhead devices usually utilized to move varying loads intermittently between points within an area fixed by the supporting and guiding rails, where the primary function is transferring. Cranes and hoists are most commonly used when (1) movement is within a fixed area, (2)

Material Handling Check Sheet

—Storage and Warehousing—

Plant _____     Location _____

Dept. _____     Operation _____

Observer _____     Date _____

| Indicators of Improvement Opportunities | CHECK | | Remarks |
|---|---|---|---|
| | Yes | No | |
| 1. Poor housekeeping | | | |
| 2. Lack of space | | | |
| 3. Traffic congestion | | | |
| 4. Excess storage at work areas | | | |
| 5. Stock bins (shelves, slots) overflowing | | | |
| 6. Stock bins, etc., empty | | | |
| 7. Unused overhead space | | | |
| 8. Small items in large space | | | |
| 9. Large items in small space | | | |
| 10. Materials piled on floor | | | |
| 11. Cluttered docks | | | |
| 12. Disorganized order accumulation area | | | |
| 13. Difficulty locating items | | | |
| 14. Difficult access to goods | | | |
| 15. Customer complaints | | | |
| 16. Damaged goods | | | |
| 17. Paperwork holding up production, storage, shipping | | | |
| 18. Unnecessary paperwork | | | |
| 19. Insufficient illumination | | | |
| 20. Aisles too narrow | | | |
| 21. Aisles too wide | | | |
| 22. Narrow-aisle equipment used in wide aisles | | | |
| 23. Wide-aisle equipment used in narrow aisles | | | |
| 24. Nonstandard containers, pallets | | | |
| 25. Pallets used when not needed | | | |
| 26. Wrong container and pallet sizes | | | |
| 27. Containers, etc., don't fit column spacing | | | |
| 28. Leaning stacks | | | |
| 29. Outdoor materials stored indoors | | | |
| 30. Indoor materials stored outdoors | | | |

Fig. M-17. Typical checklist for auditing material handling activities and conditions.

moves are intermittent, (3) loads vary in size or weight, (4) cross traffic would interfere with conveyors, and (5) units handled are not uniform.

**Industrial Trucks**   These are hand or powered vehicles (nonhighway) used for intermittent movement of mixed or uniform loads over various paths having suitable running surfaces and clearances, where the primary function is maneuvering or transporting. Industrial trucks are generally used when (1) material is moved intermittently, (2) movement is over varying routes, (3) loads are uniform or mixed in size and weight, (4) cross-traffic would prohibit conveyors, (5) clearances and running surfaces are adequate and suitable, (6) most of the operation consists of handling (or maneuvering, stacking, etc.), and (7) material can be put into unit loads.

## SELECTING EQUIPMENT

In selecting handling equipment (step 10 of the problem-solving procedure above) the analyst should:[5]

1. Review material handling equipment and problem factors.
2. Identify move(s) to be made.
3. Collect data.
4. Relate all factors.
5. Determine degree of mechanization.
6. Make tentative selection of equipment type.
7. Narrow the choice.
8. Evaluate alternatives.
9. Check each selection for compatibility with other equipment.
10. Select specific type of equipment.
11. Prepare performance specifications.
12. Consider lease or rent for trial period.
13. Develop tentative budget for implementation.
14. Prepare justification.
15. Obtain approvals.
16. Procure equipment.
17. Supervise installation.
18. Follow up.

**Selection Criteria**  It is important to review a number of criteria in selecting a specific piece of equipment. These criteria may be evaluated in the form of the following question: Does the equipment

1. Fit into the handling system?
2. Combine handling with other functions, (production, storage, inspection, packing, etc.)?
3. Optimize the flow of materials?
4. Provide simplicity as well as practicability?
5. Utilize gravity wherever possible?
6. Require a minimum of space?
7. Handle as large a load as is practical?
8. Make the move safely, in terms of both work force and material?
9. Use mechanization judiciously?
10. Offer flexibility and adaptability?
11. Have a low dead-weight to pay-load ratio?
12. Utilize a minimum of operator time?
13. Require a minimum of loading, unloading, and rehandling?
14. Call for as little maintenance, repair, power, and fuel as possible?
15. Have a long and useful life?
16. Facilitate capacity utilization?
17. Perform the handling operation efficiently and economically?

## TRENDS

In planning for better material handling, management should pay particular attention to these trends:

Increasingly wider scope of material handling activity.

Closer cooperation with and between manufacturers, carriers, vendors, customers.

Faster manufacturing cycles with resulting reduction of inventories.

Reduced handling by direct-labor employees.

Mechanization of indirect labor tasks.

Upgrading of job-skill requirements.

Vendor packing to customer specifications.

More attention to unit load handling methods.

Increased attention to receiving and shipping.

Layouts changed to improve material handling.

Increased emphasis on material handling at the workplace.

Higher integration of handling, processing, and information flow.

Greater use of continuous processing.

Greater use of handling equipment and higher degree of mechanization in warehousing.

Planned delivery to, and removal of materials from, the workplace.

Planning for flexibility, expansion, and growth.

Mechanized handling between departments.

Greater use of continuous processing.

Increase in number of production operations that are performed during handling operations.

*See also* DISTRIBUTION, PHYSICAL; FACILITIES AND SITE PLANNING AND LAYOUT; MATERIALS MANAGEMENT; OFFICE SPACE PLANNING AND LAYOUT.

### NOTES
[1] James M. Apple, *Material Handling Systems Design*, The Ronald Press Company, New York, 1972.
[2] James M. Apple, "The Emerging Importance of Material Handling in Industrial Engineering," Proceedings of the Fourth AIIE/MHI Seminar on Material Handling and the Industrial Engineer, March 1975.
[3] Apple, *Material Handling Systems Design*, chap. 4.
[4] J. M. Apple, *Productivity Improvement for Profit*, American Institute of Industrial Engineers, 1977.
[5] Apple, *Material Handling Systems Design*.

### REFERENCES
*Material Handling Engineering*, a monthly publication, Cleveland, Ohio.
*Modern Material Handling*, a monthly publication, Boston.

Muther, Richard: *Systematic Handling Analysis,* Management and Industrial Publications, 1969.

Sims, E. Ralph: *Planning and Managing Materials Flow,* E. R. Sims. Assoc., Lancaster, Ohio, 1968.

JAMES M. APPLE, *Georgia Institute of Technology*

## Materials control (*See* INVENTORY CONTROL, PURCHASING AND ACCOUNTING ASPECTS; MATERIALS MANAGEMENT.)

## Materials list (*See* MATERIALS MANAGEMENT.)

## Materials management

The concept of materials management involves a total overview of industrial logistics. Materials management can be dealt with on a micro basis within a particular manufacturing function, department, or plant or on a macro basis relating to the entire flow of materials from the mine or farm through the industrial process and physical distribution system to the ultimate consumer and, in some cases, through recycling and back into the manufacturing system. Materials managers who deal with the subject on a micro basis circumscribe their responsibilities with purchasing and shipping of finished goods. The macro system–oriented approach extends from commodity futures and mining and farming operations to physical distribution and retail marketing. This discussion looks at the business-oriented issues at both the micro and macro levels of the materials management configuration but restricts proscription of technique to the micro approach within the manufacturing organization.

**General Business Concepts** The flow of material through a business system is the physical manifestation of cash flow, and its control is essential to the fluidity and responsiveness of the business as a whole. One of the unique characteristics of the management of material flow is the fact that most materials change in shape, cube or volume, condition, and value as they move through the system. Thus the materials management system must control not only units and value but also space and time as it relates to facility capabilities, supplier lead time, seasonality, and marketing policy.

*Capital Allocation Options.* An additional factor in the material management concept is related to the allocation of capital. Management has three funda-mental options in dealing with the customer, and these options depend on a combination of market criteria and capital utilization. These options are the following:

1. *Manufacture product into finished-goods inventory* on a planned production schedule which levels operating cycles and optimizes the relationships between capital equipment, facilities, and the work force. In this case the flexibility factor is in the finished-goods inventory, and in some cases in the raw material and work-in-process inventory. The marketplace always has instant finished-goods support. Examples of this alternative can be found in the food industry, automotive supplies, and industrial hardware, where customers expect on-the-shelf finished inventory, and suppliers can develop reasonably reliable sales forecasts.

2. *Invest in excess productive capability* and then stock raw materials to permit manufacture on a real-time demand basis. Examples of this type of operation can be found in electric power generation, soft drink bottling, and construction operations.

3. *Make the customer wait.* In this type of operation the manufacturer builds to order and does not buy supplies or raw materials until the customer has made a firm commitment. The manufacturer schedules work and tells the customer when deliveries will be made. Examples of this type of business are found in aircraft and heavy machinery manufacturing, custom tailoring, and art.

As might be expected, each option requires slightly different policies concerning materials management. Each needs a different level of information and operational prediction. In the serialized-type business, which is represented by food, automobile, and appliance manufacture, management usually can make reasonably dependable projections of sales by product item. These forecasts can be exploded upstream and used as a material demand forecast in the procurement operation. In the case of the high capital, facility-oriented business, the commitment is made on the basis of speculative investment in (1) production capability and (2) either captive raw material supplies or a high inventory of production materials. This situation frequently leads to the purchase of mines and farms by the manufacturer.

In the case of custom manufacturing, it is not uncommon for the manufacturer to push the inventory-holding function upstream to a supplier in order to (1) ensure quick response and (2) minimize dollar lockup in raw materials and supplies. In such instances a manufacturer might buy metals fom a metal warehouse wholesaler, manufacturing hardware from a mill supply house, and other items from various wholesalers and jobbers. This would, of course, increase the price paid for these supplies, but at the same time it would reduce the manufacturer's cash lockup and assure rapid response at the supply end of the manufacturer's materials management system. In addition, the use of credit purchasing could have the effect of the supplier financing the production.

*Control versus Ownership Costs.* Another fundamental issue in the development of a materials management concept is the balance between the cost of the control system and the cost of owning inventory at fail-safe levels, which negates the need for precise control. Before the advent of the computer, the telephone, and the telegraph it was normal to buy inventories in large quantities relative to transactions. This was necessary in order to preclude production delays and to accommodate the long lead times which were normal in the days of horses and sails. Some companies have not yet learned to trust modern communications and logistics capabilities, and they still protect themselves with high safety stocks as a hedge against unreliable supply situations.

*Special Business Factors.* There are many other business issues which affect the philosophy and policy of a company's materials management system. For example, a toy manufacturer who must do 70 percent of the annual business in a six-week period cannot operate on the basis of economic lot quantities or marginal-inventory backup. The sales year of the toy manufacturer is short, and delivery must be guaranteed in time for Christmas sales. Conversely, a brewery can force the glass factory to deliver bottles and cartons on an hour by hour schedule and maintain as little as 4 hours of container inventory supply in the bottling plant, with the inventory guarantees in the hands of the glass company. Thus, the materials management philosophy and technique must be tailored to the manufacturing and marketing policy and business environment of the particular company.

## MATERIALS MANAGEMENT STRUCTURE

The starting point in the development of any materials management system must be in the development of a bill of materials for the particular product or products being manufactured. There are three basic classes of bills of material in current use, but only one of these has any significant value in the materials management structure. The three types are:

1. *A materials list* or takeoff, which is simply a list of the materials used to manufacture a product and is, more often than not, used primarily for purchasing and costing purposes.

2. *An engineering bill of materials,* which is generally structured according to engineering disciplines and is prepared by the designer. For example, an automotive engineering bill of materials could consist of no less than four or five separate engineering-discipline–type bills of materials. These might be mechanical or power train; structural, or frame and body; electrical and instruments; wiring and ignition; seating and upholstery; and appearance, or trim and paint.

3. *A manufacturing bill of materials,* in which the parts, materials, subassemblies, and components are arranged in level-by-level manufacturing or assembly sequence in the bill of materials. The stratified structure of the manufacturing bill of materials permits level-by-level manufacturing material control and production scheduling. *This bill of materials is the basis for any successful materials management system.*

**Parts Standardization and Coding** One of the key materials management issues concerns itself with the problem of parts and materials standardization. As a very fundamental example, the same $1/4$-20 one-inch socket head screw may be used at two or three levels in the manufacturing structure and in a whole variety of subassemblies at the same level. For example, this screw might be used to fasten the spring shackles to the frame on all four wheels of a motor vehicle, to fasten the steering column to the body, and to fasten the body to the chassis. This example, although a very mundane one, points up the need for item identification. It prevents multiple inventories or specifying of the same item, with the resulting increase in system complexity and product cost.

In order to achieve parts standardization it is essential to use some sort of worker-and-machine legible parts numbering system which will relate the part to its own identity, while at the same time providing a basis for level-by-level bill of materials structures and inventory control. Precise parts identification is essential for design retrieval, inventory control, scheduling, and procurement specifications. A good parts-number coding system, then, is the second element in the development of a modern materials management system.

**Inventory System and Data Bank** Production control is by definition level-by-level materials control or inventory management. Conversely, if level-by-level inventory control is in operation, then by definition, a degree of production control is in the system. Thus, the next building block in the materials control system is a sound level-by-level-inventory control procedure with an adequate data bank. This data bank can be on ledger cards or in a computer, but it must contain certain fundamental elements in order to be effective. When used in combination with a well-structured manufacturing bill of materials and a communicative parts-numbering system, the inventory management structure becomes a keystone of the materials management system. The *data bank* should have no less than the following elements:

1. *On order balance*—in units, dollars, handling modules (pallets, tote boxes, cartons, etc.), cubic feet, and period or date of scheduled arrival into inventory.

2. *On hand balance*—in units, dollars, handling modules (pallets, tote boxes, cartons, etc.), and cubic feet.

3. *Allocated or committed balance*—in units, dollars, handling modules (pallets, tote boxes, cartons, etc.), cubic feet, and scheduled commitment due date.

4. *Available balance*—in units, dollars, handling modules, and cubic feet currently available for commitment to scheduled use or sales.

5. *Miscellaneous information*—including dollar density (dollars per cubic foot), storage environment requirements (refrigeration, humidity control, security, red label, etc.), stackability, order picking location, and freight classification.

Each level of the inventory system from raw materials through finished goods (and in a captive distribution system, branch warehouses and retail stores) should have this same inventory system data bank. In each case all entries should be accompanied by the date of the entry, the identification or document number of the source of the entry, and any pertinent control date signals, such as projected out-of-stock date, engineering-change due date and configuration code, order arrival or scheduled completion date, etc. The master data bank (ledger card header or computer file) should also contain such information as a where-used list, vendor identity, vendor item number, specification codes, standard lot quantities, units per handling module (pallet, tote box, etc.), and standard costs.

If all these elements of information are properly built into the inventory control system, and if the system is based upon *a random access procedure* using either a random access computer or a ledger card technique, the inventory system can operate as the core or keystone of the overall materials manage-

ment structure. It will provide the basis for production scheduling, procurement, and materials control.

**Procurement Procedure**  The fourth element of the materials management system is the procurement procedure. It should be recognized that purchasing performs three separate, but interlocking, roles in most organizations. Only one of these roles is legitimately a part of the materials management system, but all are a part of the materials management function. These roles are:

1. *Material and supply research* to identify suppliers and products and to qualify products for use in the manufacturing or marketing system.

2. *Negotiation of terms and prices* and liaison with vendors in relationship to business practices, delivery schedules, and contract arrangements.

3. *Material and product acquisition* to assure the right product, at the right time, in the right quantity, and in the right place. This is an administrative function which is a fundamental element of the materials management system and procedure. The procurement function must anticipate the material requirement quantities and dates based upon inventory position, must anticipate demand or requisitions, must arrange for purchase and delivery of the materials, and must monitor the vendor to ensure the proper quantity, quality, and scheduling of the in-bound supplies.

Thus, the role of the procurement function in a materials management system is to interface requirements with the outside supplier and to ensure the vendor's proper response.

**Internal and External Transportation**  A fifth element of the materials management system is transportation. This function breaks into two primary elements: internal and external transport. The internal element is usually termed *materials handling,* and the external portion is generally known as *traffic.* The roles of these functions are basically the same, although they operate in different physical and business environments. Each has the responsibility to respond to schedule demand by having the right thing in the right place, at the right time, at the least cost, and in the right condition.

External movement is further broken down into inbound and outbound transportation. When private-vehicle fleets are involved, an additional breakdown is usually found in management, wherein the fleet operator is either separated and parallel to or under the direction of the traffic manager. The traffic manager usually performs the dual role of (1) transport purchasing and (2) movement scheduling and handles both inbound and outbound cargoes. In modern materials management systems, it is not uncommon to operate with inventories in transit in rail cars or in trucks and to include the transport timing in the materials management scheduling structure. This is particularly critical in international operations. It is also a part of the technique used in such serialized operations as automotive manufacturing, bottling, and perishable food operations.

**Shop-Loading Procedure** In the essential shop-loading portion of the system, material requirements, facility and labor capacity, inventory lot patterns, and time-related control elements are blended together to achieve an optimum balance between capital utilization, operating expense, supply availability, market demand, and the overall cash flow or financial structure of the business. The variety of production rates between machines, operations, and components and the varying assembly schedules and cube-impact factors make the scheduling and loading of the manufacturing process particularly critical. *Imbalance* or erratic machine scheduling can have a major impact on inventories, cash lockups, and market response. *Underscheduling* can generate shortages and delays, while *overscheduling* can absorb available capital, reduce liquidity, and generate facility congestion. Thus, the machine-loading procedures must recognize the economics of the production lot in terms of both (1) equipment and material utilization and (2) the relationship of a component to the schedule and the facility as a whole. Blind utilization of economic order quantities in facility scheduling or purchasing can result in disastrous distortions in the inventory/schedule pattern of the operation. Economic order quantities should be developed on a carefully researched local basis and should not be blindly based on the application of classical formulas or tables. The theory upon which these formulas are based depends upon academic assumptions which are nearly impossible to achieve in practice.

## MATERIALS REQUIREMENTS PLANNING

In its fundamental form the concept of materials requirements planning relates a sales forecast to a production and a materials procurement schedule. In order to make this conversion, however, one must start with basically sound data. It is unfortunate that sales-forecasting techniques are generally less than precise; therefore the system begins with

some built-in inadequacies which must be cushioned by inventories. The basic function of an inventory is to adjust the material flow between nonlinearly related activities, such as manufacturing and retailing, procurement and manufacturing, or different production rates in-process. Thus, if the sales forecast establishes a production schedule which is more optimistic than market performance, an inventory buildup occurs. Conversely, if the forecast is pessimistic and production schedules do not meet demands, inventory shortages will occur at many levels in the system. It follows that the first and key step in any materials management or materials requirements planning system is the establishment of a reasonably dependable sales forecast on a product-by-product basis. If a fairly reliable sales forecast is obtained, the next step in a materials requirements planning system is the process of (1) exploding the forecast into a product-level production schedule and (2) further exploding this into materials requirements.

**Multiple-Period Schedules** When the sales forecast is converted into a time-oriented product demand, it is then possible to establish completed product requirements on a period basis. The usual practice is to use either 12 or 13 months or periods, or in some cases to schedule on a weekly basis. Very few companies can achieve adequate precision for a daily schedule above the department level, and most product schedules are on a period or monthly basis. This approach allows for adjustments and slippages in the internal schedule to accommodate breakdowns, quality control problems, productivity variations, maintenance problems, and other unpredictable or difficult-to-anticipate occurrences.

**Consolidated Materials Requirements** When the product schedule is established for a given period, the manufacturing bill of materials for each product is exploded and extended to generate product and composite quantities of purchased materials and components and to identify parts manufacturing requirements. At this state lead-time factors and lot quantities are entered into the system, and the demand (or requirement) date for materials and purchased components is identified. By taking these data and applying them to the raw material and purchase component inventories, it is then possible to establish consolidated demands and procurement schedules for materials coming from outside vendors. At this stage appropriate safety stocks are also introduced into the system to cope with vendor reliability factors and unforeseen delays and shortages. The result of this calculation is modified by purchasing to achieve the optimum balance between requirements, schedules, price, and transport expense. Variations in quantity and schedule are absorbed into the raw material and supply inventory pattern.

**Balancing Schedules and Capacities** At the next level the machine-loading procedures are used to balance facility capacity against production schedules. Appropriate make-or-buy decisions are also made at this time. In many instances production-lot quantities and manufacturing order consolidation of common parts result in the development of work-in-process inventories. These inventories serve as the cushion between nonlinear manufacturing schedules. They also permit economies of scale to be applied to the fabrication and subassembly functions in serialized manufacturing, where common parts and components are used in a multiple of products. The economies of scale manifest themselves in more sophisticated tooling and more manufacturing-oriented part and component design.

The materials requirements planning concept adds greater control because it is based upon (1) the multiple-period approach to scheduling and (2) the consolidation of materials and parts orders into a level-by-level inventory and production scheduling procedure.

### SUMMARY

Materials management, as a total concept, encompasses all elements of the business system. The ability to control or schedule raw materials can be enhanced by owning the mine or the farm; but in the case of agricultural products, nature schedules production, and the consumer must be accommodated by the choice of processing and preservation techniques. The primary consideration in materials management is the control of cash flow and capital lockup without impinging upon facility utilization and customer service. The materials manager must recognize that the primary function of a manufacturing business is to support marketing and that effective decisions must be market-oriented first and facility-oriented only in support of that objective.

*See also* CONTROL SYSTEMS, MANAGEMENT; DISTRIBUTION, PHYSICAL; INVENTORY CONTROL, PHYSICAL AND STOCKKEEPING; INVENTORY CONTROL, PURCHASING AND ACCOUNTING ASPECTS; LOGISTICS, BUSINESS; MATERIAL HANDLING; MATERIALS REQUIREMENTS PLANNING (MRP); PURCHASING MANAGEMENT.

### REFERENCES

Orlicky, Joseph: *Material Requirements Planning*, McGraw-Hill Book Company, New York, 1975.

Plossl, G. W., and O. W. Wight: *Production and Inventory Control*, Prentice-Hall, Inc., Englewood Cliffs, N.J., 1967.
Pritzker, Robert A., and Robert A. Gring: *Modern Approaches to Production Planning and Control*, American Management Association, New York, 1960.
Tersine, Richard J.: *Materials Management and Inventory Systems*, American Elsevier, New York, 1976.

E. RALPH SIMS, JR., *E. Ralph Sims, Jr. and Associates, Incorporated*

# Materials requirements planning (MRP)

A computerized method of production scheduling that is designed to ensure that all materials and components needed are on hand when they are needed but no earlier is called *materials requirements planning*.

The first step is the preparation of a master production schedule made up of: (1) orders on the books, (2) forecasts of new orders, and (3) the dates on which the various products will be needed. The MRP program explodes the bills of materials to show the requirements and compares them with the materials in inventory to show what must be ordered and when.

The advantages of the system are said to be (1) lower inventories, since nothing is ordered earlier than necessary; (2) more realistic delivery promises (and early warning of delayed deliveries so that customers can be told of delays well before the promised delivery dates); and (3) better use of the time of machines and workers, for if there is a delay in the production of one component, the due dates for other components and the labor and equipment used for other jobs may be postponed.

*See also* INVENTORY CONTROL; PURCHASING AND ACCOUNTING ASPECTS; MATERIALS MANAGEMENT; PRODUCTION PLANNING AND CONTROL.

### REFERENCES

Miller, Jeffrey G., and Linda G. Sprague: "Behind the Growth in Materials Requirements Planning," *Harvard Business Review*, September–October 1975, pp. 83–91.
Ogden, William R.: "From Scratch to MRP," *Journal of Systems Management*, January 1974, pp. 8–11.
Orlicky, Joseph: *Material Requirements Planning*, McGraw-Hill Book Company, New York, 1975.
Putnam, Arnold O., and Romeyn Everdell: "ROP's and MRP in Perspective," *Production and Inventory Management*, third quarter, 1974, pp. 1–5.

STAFF/SMITH

**Mathematical modeling** (*See* OPERATIONS RESEARCH AND MATHEMATICAL MODELING.)

**Matrix, product-planning** (*See* MARKETS, CLASSIFICATIONS AND MARKET ANALYSIS.)

**Matrix organizations** (*See* ORGANIZATION ANALYSIS AND PLANNING; ORGANIZATION STRUCTURES AND CHARTING.)

**Maximax principle** (*See* RISK ANALYSIS AND MANAGEMENT; STATISTICAL ANALYSIS FOR MANAGEMENT.)

**Maximin principle** (*See* STATISTICAL ANALYSIS FOR MANAGEMENT.)

**Measured daywork system** (*See* WORK MEASUREMENT.)

**Measurement, work** (*See* WORK MEASUREMENT.)

**Measurements, accident** (*See* SAFETY AND HEALTH MANAGEMENT, EMPLOYEE.)

**Mechanization** (*See* AUTOMATION.)

**Media, advertising** (*See* ADVERTISING CONCEPTS.)

**Media audit** (*See* ADVERTISING MANAGEMENT, INDUSTRIAL.)

**Medicaid and Medicare** (*See* COMPENSATION, EMPLOYEE BENEFIT PLANS.)

**Medium-range planning** (*See* PLANNING, STRATEGIC MANAGERIAL.)

**Meetings, planning for** (*See* CONFERENCES AND MEETINGS, PLANNING FOR.)

**Memo-motion study** (*See* COST IMPROVEMENT.)

**Mercantile credit** (*See* CREDIT MANAGEMENT.)

**Merchandising management** (*See* RETAILING MANAGEMENT.)

**Mergers and acquisitions** (*See* ACQUISITIONS AND MERGERS.)

**Merit rating** (*See* APPRAISAL, PERFORMANCE.)

**Merit-rating systems** (*See* MOTIVATION IN ORGANIZATIONS.)

**Metatalk** (*See* COMMUNICATIONS, NONVERBAL.)

**Methods improvement** (*See* WORK SIMPLIFICATION AND IMPROVEMENT.)

**Metrology** (*See* QUALITY MANAGEMENT.)

**Microcomputer** (*See* AUTOMATION.)

**Microeconomics** (*See* ECONOMIC CONCEPTS.)

**Microprocessor** (*See* AUTOMATION.)

**Middle-level managers** (*See* MANAGER, DEFINITIONS OF.)

**Military managers** (*See* MANAGER, DEFINITIONS OF.)

## Minicomputer   (*See* AUTOMATION.)

## Minimax principle   (*See* RISK ANALYSIS AND MANAGEMENT; STATISTICAL ANALYSIS FOR MANAGEMENT.)

## Minorities, management of and equal employment opportunity

The management of equal employment opportunity (EEO) is a relatively new and specialized function by which a company, both voluntarily and to comply with federal law and regulations, systematically tries to provide fair and equal opportunity in hiring, promoting, and terminating minorities and women, and also the handicapped, veterans, and older people. In addition, the function includes affirmative action (or special efforts) to introduce more of these "affected classes" into all levels of the corporation where they are not proportionately represented.

**EEO Laws**   Management equal employment opportunity policies must now take account of a variety of laws, the most important one of which is the Civil Rights Act of 1964, amended in 1972. A manager should be familiar with its Title VII. Other major legal influences on EEO are the Fifth and Fourteenth Amendments of the United States Constitution, the Equal Pay Act of 1963, the Age Discrimination Act of 1967, the Rehabilitation Act of 1973, the Vietnam Era Veterans Act of 1974, and finally, state and city fair employment practice legislation. (*See* LABOR LEGISLATION.)

**Executive Orders**   A second and very important set of constraints and guidelines affecting management EEO policy and practices comes from the executive orders authorized by the President, especially Executive Order 11246, covering all government contractors and subcontractors and therefore including most companies of any size. Under EO 11246, Revised Order No. 4 calls for the reaffirmation of EEO policy "to recruit, hire, train and promote persons in all job groups, without regard to race, color, religion, sex or national origin, except where sex is a bona fide occupational qualification" (BFOQ). It also requires communication of that policy within the firm and to the general public, administration of EEO programs by a specific EEO manager, identification of problem areas by organizational units and job groups, establishment of goals and timetables, development and execution of pro-

grams to improve minority and female participation, internal audit reporting systems, and the support of community action programs.

Revised Order No. 14 attempts to standardize the compliance review among the dozen or so agencies. It gives detailed rules about the agencies' review of the contractor's EEO policies and practices, the desk audit, on-site review, off-site review, and use of confidential information. It provides a checklist of what is required of the contractor in practices and record keeping in every aspect of industrial relations, including the flow of applicants. It treats the compliance status of the contractor and possible remedial actions and sanctions.

**Supreme Court Rulings**   In 1971 the U.S. Supreme Court Griggs-Duke Power case led to a landmark decision also strongly affecting management EEO policy. The Court said that it was the consequences of an employer's action, not the employer's intention, that determined whether or not he or she was discriminating. If any practices or tests had an adverse effect or a differential effect on minorities, employers were guilty until they proved themselves innocent. An *adverse or differential effect* simply means that fewer minorities are included in the outcome of the test or the hiring and promotion practices than would be expected by their numerical proportion. The employer must show a "business necessity" for such an adverse effect; that is, the differential effect must be clearly justified by the need for satisfactory performance on the job. For example, a high school diploma and good grades on a general intelligence test were *not* clearly shown to have a demonstrable relationship toward successful performance on the job for Duke Power. If employers do not clear themselves in situations like this, they may be subject to charges for back pay and attorneys' fees.

However, in *I.B.T.—T.I.M.E. v. U.S.* (1977), the Court reinstated intent as one factor and ruled that seniority systems perpetuating past discrimination do not necessarily violate Title VII.

**Women's Movement**   Finally, the women's movement of the early seventies, plus the Equal Employment Opportunity Commission's guidelines against sex discrimination, gave an incentive so that not only minorities but also women would be protected and advanced. This new force culminated in the landmark AT&T consent decree of 1973 by which the nation's largest employer agreed to fundamentally change its personnel policies and to promote men and women into jobs from which they were traditionally excluded. In the decree, AT&T

agreed to pay over 50 million dollars in back pay and other costs in the first year alone.

A series of other consent decrees in the late seventies clearly showed the need for management to have intelligent and aggressive affirmative action plans in order to avoid expensive multimillion dollar fair employment practice suits.

**Enforcement Agencies** As it pursues these policies, management must be familiar with (1) the Equal Employment Opportunity Commission set up by the Civil Rights Act; (2) the Office of Federal Contract Compliance Programs of the Department of Labor which administers programs for all government contractors, both directly and through agencies such as the Department of Defense, the Treasury, the Department of Health, Education, and Welfare, and so forth; (3) the Wage and Hour Employment Standards Division of the Department of Labor; (4) the United States courts; (5) the National Labor Relations Board; and (6) state and municipal FEP commissions.

**Company EEO Staffs** Government contractors must now have a specialized EEO officer or director. Nearly all large corporations do have sizable staffs reporting directly to top management. One especially time-consuming staff problem is the amount and cost of record keeping. (Beginning in 1977 the Office of Federal Contract Compliance Programs tried to simplify its records requirements.) It is important, too, for EEO staffs to involve operating line management in carrying out affirmative action programs. As in other management areas, there is need to minimize friction and misunderstanding between line and staff.

**Communication of Policy** The 1974 EEOC guidelines give detailed suggestions to managers for communicating their policies to middle management, to employees who are affected, to the general public, and to potential recruits. Inadequate compliance is often rooted in poor communication to middle- and lower-level managers who have the task of implementing EEO policy. These operating managers must comprehend the federal pressures on their companies for EEO performance.

One key in communication is to factor into the annual performance appraisal of a manager his or her work toward facilitating greater participation of minorities and women in the work force. If a company is to secure change, performance on EEO must be part of the reward-penalty system for managers. Some companies (Sears, Roebuck and Co. and General Electric, for example) have explicit policies for factoring EEO performance into their reward and penalty systems. Many companies, especially smaller ones, do not as yet.

## NEW EEO STRATEGIES AND NEW PROBLEMS

Management is still moving down uncertain roads in attempting to comply with EEO requirements. Several effective administrative procedures and difficulties are emerging.

**Measurement** All companies with 100 employees or more must annually report to the federal government the number of their minorities and women on the nine steps of the employment ladder: officials and managers, professionals, technicians, sales workers, office and clerical, craftworkers, operatives, laborers, and service workers. Thanks to the computer, such data provide management and federal agencies with a vast amount of valuable information about human resources. But there are problems not as yet resolved.

**Problems**

1. The "snapshot approach." That is, there is a tendency to use the EEO-1 form in a rigid manner. A small number (or underrepresentation) of minorities and women at higher-level jobs or craft jobs may give suspicions of discrimination, but in no sense does this fact taken by itself prove discrimination. Even a second snapshot at a later date will not in itself tell whether or not there has been progress. Many other factors must be known—such as the supply of qualified people, the number of openings, the growth or decline of the business, the general business cycle, the location of the plant or office, and so forth.

2. Institutional racism or sexism. This may be defined as refusing to recognize that certain jobs have traditionally been reserved for men or for women or for certain races. To overcome this discriminatory practice, it is necessary to aggressively open up all jobs to all people who are qualified for them and who want them. As the EEO manager of a major retailing firm puts it, "We need to institutionalize the systems of change that will upset these institutionalized practices."

3. Variability of jobs that are included under a single EEO-1 category, such as "Officials and Managers." A branch bank might have *many* (lower-level) managers because they deal with the public. A large world bank might have *few* (higher-level) managers with more experience and education because they deal with major corporations. Thus, to compare the two banks at the "Officials and Managers"

level merely by their respective percentages of minorities and women, who tend to have less experience and specialized education, would be meaningless.

In a phrase: Numbers are definitely important and should not be ignored, but numbers must be interpreted intelligently and reasonably in line with the facts of business and personnel relations.

**Underutilization and Availability** Greater participation of minorities and women is furthered by the concept of underutilization. This is defined by Revised Order No. 4 as "having fewer minorities and women in a particular job group than would reasonably be expected by their availability"—an analysis made possible by the statistical data mentioned above. It is not always easy, however, to know who might reasonably be expected to be available since the supply of *qualified* and *willing* people is often difficult to determine not only within, but especially outside, the firm. Census and labor market data are not always up to date or adequate. Also, it may be costly to secure these data, though some companies form consortia to share the expense. Regardless of the difficulty of assessment, managers who find they are underutilizing minorities and women in their employ will be expected to remedy the situation.

**Targets, Goals, Quotas, and Timetables** Business is accustomed to using targets and goals for sales, profits, cost reduction, productivity, and so forth. The government now requires business to use targets and goals for improving minority and female participation in the work force. There is, at the very least, a semantic difference between targets and quotas. *Targets* have no precise floor and ceiling if there is good-faith effort toward achieving them; *quotas* have both rigid floors and ceilings. However, the difference can be very slight or negligible when setting or meeting certain requirements is rigidly interpreted. Rigidity makes a target or goal into a quota.

In Sears' Mandatory Achievement of Goals program (MAG), "the basic policy will be, at the minimum, to fill one out of every two openings with a minority man or woman of whatever races are present in your trading-hiring area." This may seem unduly rigid, but Sears does permit a manager to file for an exception. Sears' program is an aggressive way of building up minority and female participation according to certain timetables. The trouble with *timetables* is that it is not easy to predict future work force needs, especially when there are variations in the business cycle, such as the 1973 to 1975 recession.

In setting targets and goals, four options are often discussed:

1. The total minority and female work force should match the characteristics of the plant's relevant supply source within their standard metropolitan statistical area (SMSA). For example, if blacks make up 10 percent of the Peoria, Illinois, community, a company's Peoria plant and office might aim for the same mix in its total payroll.

2. The minority and female employees should be distributed evenly at each level of the organization according to their proportions in the relevant labor market.

3. Minorities and females should be represented at each level of the plant's organization by the same percentages as they appear in the plant's population.

4. Minorities and women should be represented in the professional and craft levels in about the same proportion in which they are found in the universities, professional schools, and trade schools preparing them for those levels.

Many people would accept option 1 if it were intelligently used. Options 2 and 3 are totally unrealistic unless they take into account the availability of qualified and willing people for those higher levels. Option 4 needs clarification of the *specific* qualities for each professional and craft level. No one of these options is adequate when taken alone, but all give pause for thought toward better human resource planning.

**Recruiting, Promoting, and Terminating** Revised Order No. 4 makes at least 25 innovative suggestions to management for recruiting, promoting, and building up minority participation. A manager, for example, must keep careful records of applicant flow, hirings, promotions, terminations—and be prepared to defend their fairness. Because of limited availability, especially of professionally and technically trained people among minorities and women, some companies have set up programs to increase the supply. [For example, General Electric's program to increase minority and female engineering graduates (PIMEG).] The national supply of qualified candidates will need to be greatly improved if the imbalances at higher-level jobs are to be corrected.

**Selecting and Testing** Company EEO staffs must be familiar with ways of keeping tests and selection procedures free from discriminatory bias. They should consult the newest federal guidelines for testing and test validation. *(See The Federal Register.)* *Validity* means that a test measures what it says it measures and does not exclude minorities or women in a discriminatory fashion. Consider two kinds of validity.

*Content Validity.* A certain part of the content of the job to be done may be put into the test; for example, typing ability may be tested in a job which will require typing. If a person is able to type in the test, presumably the person will be able to type later on the job. Technically, *content validity* is defined as the degree to which scores on a test may be accepted as representative of performance, within a specifically defined content domain, of which the test is a sample.

*Construct Validity.* Certain abilities that will be needed on the job may be artificially constructed in the test, such as intelligence or linguistic ability. Technically, *construct validity* is the degree to which scores obtained through a specified test or other assessment procedure may be interpreted as measuring some trait needed for the job. One special problem, of course, is that judgmental and evaluative interviews for higher management positions are hard, if not impossible, to validate in a precise way. Nevertheless, all selection procedures which have an adverse effect must be certified for validity if the company is to be in compliance with the law.

## MAJOR OBSTACLES

Progress toward full EEO and management's involvement in the process must clear two imposing obstacles.

**Preference versus Reverse Discrimination** The obvious and serious underrepresentation of minorities and women at higher-level positions and in skilled craft jobs in business has shown that merely opening doors is not enough. It is necessary to give special help for those groups which have been deprived or affected for so many years. Otherwise, it would take years, perhaps even centuries, to bring about equal participation at such jobs. The Civil Rights Act neither requires nor forbids preferential treatment for minorities and women. It explicitly excludes itself from requiring it. The act forbids preference only insofar as it forbids discrimination. But Revised Orders No. 4 and No. 14 do call for preferential practice even though they do not use the word. They call for special efforts. This is borne out in the consent decree of AT&T with its Goals-II program, requiring special percentages of females and minorities to be hired or promoted. The same is true in Sears' voluntary MAG program, saying that one out of every two openings must be filled with minority men or women. Open-track, or fast-track, promotions have become a common way to overcome imbalances.

However, some recent court decisions give conflicting and confusing guidelines, seeming to make out preferential practice to be reverse discrimination. The manager will need to follow court decisions carefully. Nor will *Bakke* (1978) settle the matter.

*Ethical Justification.* It is the author's position that preferential practice is justified under certain conditions, namely, that the minority person or the female must be qualified for the job, or qualifiable within a reasonable time. If the majority person or the male is slightly more qualified, the minority person or the female should be picked if it is necessary to do so to remedy underutilization, provided the gap in qualifications is small, and provided the urgency of the job is not great. For example, when choosing from applicants for an airline pilot's job, you would more readily consider merit over preference than when choosing from applicants for a flight attendant's job. One must consider safety, the rights of passengers, and so forth.

Preferring the qualified (but lesser qualified) minority person when the job importance and qualifications gap are high would be reverse discrimination. *Not* preferring the qualified (but lesser qualified) minority person when the job importance and qualifications gap are low would be *un*affirmative, or reverse affirmative, action.

Such preference is not necessarily reverse discrimination. Neither the qualified majority nor the qualified minority person has a right in commutative justice to a *specific* job or promotion. However, they should have "fair consideration" for the job. On the other hand, fair consideration does not always require the employer to hire or promote the *more*-qualified person. If the employer has a good and serious reason for employing the *qualified*, but *less*-qualified, person, this does not violate the rights in justice of the person passed over.

The author's ethical reasoning supporting carefully delimited preferential practice is this: Social justice requires just socioeconomic structures in institutions. When encrusted patterns of education, housing, and employment put individuals of certain *groups* at a special disadvantage just because they are members of such groups, it is within the context of social justice to give acceleration-preferential aid in employment to those individuals (if they are otherwise qualified) precisely because of their group membership. Not all groups need this special aid at this time, but those singled out by the Equal Employment Opportunity Commission, namely, blacks, Hispanics, Asians, American Indians, and women, do seem to need this help currently. The author believes that preferential practice as carefully defined above is not reverse discrimination. Management must await actions of the courts and of Congress. But the manager will also need to think this issue through. True, some white male backlash has arisen. This does not seem to be formidable, however, and can be dealt with by forthright management.

**Legalism and the Regulatory Agencies** Legalism and regulation are not the same thing. The Griggs-Duke Power case, for example, was generated quite independently of the regulatory agencies. On the other hand, the federal agencies can also be litigious and rule-conscious in the way they interpret the law and the Executive Orders.

There can be no doubt about the value of law. The Civil Rights Act of 1964 was a Magna Carta for minorities and women. At the same time, however, the manager will have to deal with legalism—the growing tendency to resolve problems by an excessive resort to tribunals, with high costs and delayed justice, as opposed to mediation, conciliation, and compromise between the parties themselves.

Legalism is not only a problem for government agencies. Private civil-rights lawyers sometimes broaden individual claims into class action suits that are based on sheer raw statistics, inadequately analyzed, with costly, sometimes frivolous, always time-consuming litigation. Legalism invites game-playing. It can draw corporate managers and attorneys away from positive efforts for working out creative affirmative action plans. Both the private sector and federal officials need to make greater use of conciliation. There have been some encouraging signs of such movements in the EEOC and the OFCCP. Companies, too, can minimize legalism by not discriminating and by developing creative affirmative action plans voluntarily.

Few people question the value of government agencies, especially the EEOC and the OFCCP, in making equal employment opportunities for minorities and women a reality. Yet the rapid growth of the agencies and their interagency rivalry has also brought many problems. Managers will have to learn to deal with those problems in the hope that future administrations, plus experience with these issues, will simplify the Washington tangle. Meanwhile, the EEO staff must guard against having its functions become totally controlled by their company's legal department.

**The Future** The future of equal employment opportunity in the United States depends on many factors independent of management: the leadership of the President as it affects the civil rights climate, the

actions of the House, the Senate, and of the courts, the problems of the city, white flight, inadequate education, and especially full employment. Managers have only moderate influence on some of these issues. Accordingly, managers must not promise too much. Progress will be slow. Normal progression takes many years. Realistically, there are relatively few openings for minorities and women at higher-level and craft jobs. Lack of professional and technical education plus the lack of desire for such jobs will keep many back. In all probability, special efforts on management's part will need to be continued at least to the year 2000. The author believes that the future will give us, however, more sophisticated human resource management systems that will benefit all employees, majority male as well as minority female, and thereby benefit the entire American economic system.

*See also* AFFIRMATIVE ACTION; EMPLOYMENT AND UNEMPLOYMENT; LABOR LEGISLATION; OLDER EMPLOYEES, MANAGEMENT OF; OMBUDSMAN; TESTING, PSYCHOLOGICAL; WOMEN IN INDUSTRY; WOMEN IN MANAGEMENT; YOUNGER EMPLOYEES, MANAGEMENT OF.

### REFERENCES

Ackerman, Robert W.: "How Companies Respond to Social Demands," *Harvard Business Review*, July–August 1973.

Andrews, Kenneth R.: " Can the Best Corporations Be Made Moral?," *Harvard Business Review*, May–June 1973.

Blodgett, Timothy B.: "Borderline Black Revisited," *Harvard Business Review*, March–April 1972.

Churchill, Neil C., and John K. Shank: "Affirmative Action and Guilt-Edged Goals," *Harvard Business Review*, March–April 1976.

*The Equal Employment Act of 1972*, The Bureau of National Affairs, Washington, 1973.

Glazer, Nathan: *Affirmative Discrimination: Ethnic Inequality, and Public Policy*, Basic Books, Inc., Publishers, New York, 1975.

Levitan, Sar A., William B. Johnston, Robert Taggert: *Still A Dream*, Harvard University Press, Cambridge, Mass., 1975.

Miner, Mary G.: *Equal Employment Opportunity Programs and Results*, The Bureau of National Affairs, Washington, PPF Survey No. 112, March 1976.

Purcell, Theodore V.: "The Case of the Borderline Black," *Harvard Business Review*, November–December 1971.

Purcell, Theodore V.: "How GE Measures Managers in Fair Employment," *Harvard Business Review*, November–December 1974.

Purcell, Theodore V., and Gerald F. Cavanagh: *Blacks in the Industrial World: Issues for the Manager*, The Free Press, New York, 1973.

Shaeffer, Ruth G.: "Non-Discrimination in Employment,

1973-1975," The Conference Board, Inc., New York, 1975.

Wallace, Phyllis A.: *Equal Employment Opportunity and the A.T.&T. Case*, The M.I.T. Press, Cambridge, Mass., 1976.

REV. THEODORE V. PURCELL, S.J., *Georgetown University*

## Missions (*See* MANAGEMENT THEORY, SCIENCE, AND APPROACHES; PLANNING, STRATEGIC MANAGERIAL.)

## Mix, marketing (*See* MARKETING, CONCEPTS AND SYSTEMS.)

## Mix, retailing (*See* RETAILING MANAGEMENT.)

## Model, deterministic (*See* STATISTICAL ANALYSIS FOR MANAGEMENT.)

## Model, for planning (*See* PLANNING, STRATEGIC MANAGERIAL.)

## Model, policy formulation and implementation (*See* POLICY FORMULATION AND IMPLEMENTATION.)

## Model, probabilistic (*See* STATISTICAL ANALYSIS FOR MANAGEMENT.)

## Model and models (*See* OPERATIONS RESEARCH AND MATHEMETICAL MODELING.)

## Model building (*See* SYSTEM CONCEPT, TOTAL.)

## Modeling, mathematical (*See* OPERATIONS RESEARCH AND MATHEMATICAL MODELING.)

## Models, causal (*See* FORECASTING BUSINESS CONDITIONS.)

## Models, econometric (*See* FORECASTING BUSINESS CONDITIONS.)

## Models, economic (*See* ECONOMIC CONCEPTS.)

## Models, mathematical (*See* OPERATIONS RESEARCH AND MATHEMATICAL MODELING.)

## Models, network (*See* NETWORK PLANNING METHODS.)

## Models, three-dimensional (*See* FACILITIES AND SITE PLANNING AND LAYOUT.)

## Monetary policy (*See* ECONOMIC MEASUREMENTS.)

## Monetary system, international (*See* INTERNATIONAL TRADE.)

## Money and banking (*See* ECONOMIC CONCEPTS.)

## Money and capital: sources and control (*See heading in Table of Contents for complete listing.*)

## Money supply (*See* ECONOMIC MEASUREMENTS.)

## Monopolist (*See* PRODUCT AND SERVICE PRICING.)

## Monopoly (*See* ECONOMIC CONCEPTS; GOVERNMENT REGULATIONS, FEDERAL REGULATION OF COMPETITION.)

## Monte Carlo analysis (*See* SYSTEM CONCEPT, TOTAL.)

## Morale surveys   *(See* ATTITUDE SURVEYS.*)*

## Motion economy   *(See* WORK SIMPLIFICATION AND IMPROVEMENT.*)*

## Motivation and leadership   *(See heading in Table of Contents for complete listing.)*

# Motivation in organizations

Motivation is a term that has been used frequently in many contexts. Thus, a precise unitary definition would be not only arbitrary but probably also dysfunctional. Generally speaking, however, persons who have thought and written about motivation have considered two distinct but interrelated sets of ideas.

1. One of these focuses on the environmental or personal characteristics that serve to energize, activate, or motivate the individual. These approaches have been referred to as *content* theories of motivation (Campbell, Dunnette, Lawler, and Weick, 1970, p. 341) since they aim at identifying classes of variables that serve to stimulate the individual.

2. A second approach has been concerned with explaining how the individual chooses to engage in a particular behavior. Campbell, et al. (1970, p. 341), refer to these orientations as *process* approaches since they focus on the mechanisms linking content variables to specific actions that the individual may perform.

A bit of reflection will suggest that knowledge of both motivational contents and processes is important if we are to understand and ultimately influence motivation. In an organizational context, for example, we must have information on the needs persons experience or the outcomes they seek (contents) in order to provide the types of rewards persons will find attractive. At the same time, however, these rewards must be administered so that persons will be encouraged to engage in the behaviors required by the organization. This requires knowledge of the motivational process.

This entry is concerned with motivation as it applies to organizational contexts. It is thus aimed at furthering understanding about motivational contents and processes as they apply to work-related behaviors such as job choice, job maintenance, and, particularly, job performance.

## MOTIVATIONAL CONTENTS

**Content Theories**  Motivational content can be viewed from two complementary perspectives (Cummings and Schwab, 1973, pp. 22–23). One is to view contents in terms of the deficiencies, deprivations, imbalances, or needs that activate the individual to behave. This is the traditional way of considering contents; it views them as internal to the individual. In this entry it will be referred to as the *needs* approach. A second, more recent, approach focuses on rewards or outcomes that serve to satisfy needs. Thus this approach considers contents in terms of consequences of the individual's behavior and will be referred to as the *outcomes* approach.

*Needs Approach.* A number of theories have emphasized taxonomies that purport to identify needs possessed by individuals. By far the best known of such theories to persons interested in organizational behavior is Maslow's (1970) *hierarchy of needs* theory. According to this theory, individuals may experience five classes of needs: (1) *physiological* (hunger and thirst); (2) *safety* (primarily bodily); (3) *social* (friendship and affiliation); (4) *esteem* (both self and the esteem of others); and (5) *self-actualization* (growth and realization of potential). These needs are hypothesized to be arranged in a hierarchy such that each lower-level need must be predominantly satisfied before the individual experiences higher-level needs. Moreover, Maslow hypothesized that as physiological-through-esteem needs are satisfied, they cease to motivate. Self-actualization needs, alternatively, are hypothesized to become more active as they are satisfied.

*Outcomes Approach.* Although explicitly aimed at identifying sources of satisfaction rather than motivation, Herzberg's *two-factor* taxonomy is the best-known attempt to identify motivating work outcomes (Herzberg, Mausner, and Snyderman, 1959). According to this approach, there are two types of work outcomes: (1) *intrinsic* factors, which have to do with promotion, recognition of one's work, and with the work itself; and (2) *extrinsic* factors, which have to do with the work environment including formal rewards other than promotion, such as salary, relations with coworkers, supervision and organizational administration, and working conditions. In subsequent writings regarding this taxonomy, Herzberg (e.g., 1966) has hypothesized that only the attainment of the intrinsic outcomes can initiate sustained motivation toward organizational goals.

**Evaluation** The content theories identified above, particularly the two-factor taxonomy, have stimulated much research. While findings from this research are not, on balance, favorable to the hypotheses of either Maslow or Herzberg, they have shed light on a number of important content issues.[1]

In all probability there are greater differences between individuals in the needs they experience, and hence in the outcomes they are motivated to seek, than either theory acknowledges. Except at the physiological level, needs depend substantially on the reinforcement environment one has been exposed to, particularly during the maturational years (Dawis, Lofquist, and Weiss, 1968). Since environmental experiences tend to be partially unique, so too will resulting individual need structures. Not surprisingly, therefore, studies investigating this issue have observed substantially greater individual differences in the relative salience of intrinsic versus extrinsic outcomes than hypothesized by Herzberg (e.g., Dunnette, Campbell, and Hakel, 1967).

As a corollary of the above, it should be noted that lower-level needs, or the value of extrinsic outcomes, are probably much more important than either Maslow's or Herzberg's analyses would suggest. *The importance of pay in the work environment has especially been understated.* There is an impressive amount of evidence indicating that pay is a very important outcome for individuals in a wide variety of occupational groups (Lawler, 1971, pp. 37–59). Moreover, the little evidence available does not support the idea that pay becomes less important as one has more of it (Giles and Barrett, 1971).

At present, less is known about how various needs or outcomes are connected to each other. There is little evidence, for example, supporting Maslow's hypothesis which states that satisfaction of needs decreases the importance of those needs. Indeed, some research findings tentatively indicate that needs strength and satisfaction are positively related. That is, the more satisfied one is with some need, the more important additional satisfaction is of that need (e.g., Lawler and Suttle, 1972).

Recently, a provocative hypothesis has been formulated suggesting that the association of extrinsic outcomes with an activity may decrease the intrinsic outcomes associated with the activity. In a work setting, this might mean that the use of extrinsic outcomes such as pay to motivate higher performance levels would be partially or wholly self-defeating since the very act of linking pay to performance might reduce the intrinsic value of performing the work itself. Indeed, Deci has conducted a series of experimental studies from which he concludes precisely this possibility (Deci, 1975). While the work of Deci is interesting, it should be noted that his conclusions have been severely criticized (e.g., Scott, 1976) and that reviewers have indicated the need for more carefully designed research on this issue (Campbell and Pritchard, 1976, p. 104).

**Implications** The typical organizational environment has four characteristics that may serve as sources of motivational outcomes:

1. The *work itself* can provide intrinsic or task-mediated outcomes.

2. *Personnel policies and practices* pertaining to rewards and discipline constitute a source of outcomes.

3. Interpersonal relationships with one's *supervisor* and the extent to which the supervisor provides recognition and allows for participation is an outcome source.

4. One's *coworkers* are typically a source of socially oriented outcomes.

Content theories and their interpretations have too often emphasized one of these sources of outcomes to the exclusion of the others.

A more appropriate interpretation of employee outcome preferences would take into consideration the following observations: (1) As stated earlier, substantial differences exist between individuals in their preferences for outcomes. (2) Organizations probably have little influence on the types of outcomes employees find motivating (Lawler, 1973, p. 38). (3) Employee preferences for outcomes, whatever the specific patterns, are likely to be fairly stable through time (Dawis, et al., 1968).

Organizations interested in providing motivating outcomes for a majority of employees would do well to heed the implications of these observations. In some respects, these observations put organizations in a passive role. Rather than attempting to change outcome preferences through communication or development programs, for example, these observations suggest the importance of identifying preexisting preferences. Attempts to change outcome preferences of employees probably have to come over time through selection procedures aimed at changing the labor force of the organization.

Most importantly, these observations suggest that organizations maintain a balanced approach to the administration of work outcomes. For example, while job enrichment may be appropriate for certain tasks and employees, it cannot by itself solve an organization's motivational problems. Attention must also be paid to the other sources of outcomes.

## MOTIVATIONAL PROCESSES

Practical considerations of motivation inevitably lead managers to the question of how needs or outcomes can be harnessed or linked to behaviors the organization wishes to encourage. That is, how can needs or outcomes serve to motivate certain types of behavior? This is the basic question about the *process* of motivation.

Over the years, many process theories have been proposed in several different branches of psychology. Interestingly, however, it was not until fairly recently that industrial psychologists and others interested in human behavior in organizations began to seriously consider and investigate theories that are essentially aimed at understanding motivational processes. While a number of theories have been proposed, Vroom's (1964) formulation of expectancy theory clearly has become dominant in recent years.

**Expectancy Theory** Expectancy theory has been used to explain choices between different actions, such as decisions about what job to accept. It has also been used to explain levels of intensity regarding a single activity—such as whether or not an employee will attempt to be a high, average, or low performer (Campbell and Pritchard, 1976, p. 74). The theory is thus obviously aimed at explaining behaviors of interest to organizations.

The theory is frequently referred to as a *cognitive* one in that it emphasizes the importance of the ability to think in determining voluntary activity. All told, one must consider three concepts that people presumably think about to understand the process of motivation according to this theory.[2]

*Valence of Outcomes.* One concept has to do with the attractiveness (or *valence*) of outcomes that may be associated with an activity. We have already discussed types of intrinsic and extrinsic outcomes that may occur in the work environment. Unlike the content theories discussed earlier, however, expectancy theory makes no a priori statements about what outcomes individuals will find valent or nonvalent.

*Instrumentality Perceptions.* A second concept has to do with individuals' beliefs about the connection or linkage between some activity and an outcome. These perceptions can be thought of as subjective probabilities and are referred to as *instrumentality* perceptions. In a work environment,

for example, individuals would be expected to have instrumentality perceptions regarding the link between performance and potential outcomes such as salary increases. Note that there is a potentially unique instrumentality perception for each outcome.

*Expectancy Perceptions.* A third concept pertains to the individuals' beliefs about the connection (or linkage) between one's effort to engage in an activity and the likelihood that the activity will be accomplished. These are called *expectancy* perceptions and may also be thought of as subjective probabilities. For example, an individual's expectancy perception regarding work performance might be thought of as his or her response to the question, "What is the likelihood of performing this task successfully if you exert a reasonable amount of effort?"

*Expectancy theory* states that motivation to engage in an activity will be high when an individual's expectancy perception regarding that activity is high and when instrumentality perceptions linking the activity to positively valent outcomes are high. Thus, we would expect an employee to be motivated to be a high work performer if that employee believed:

1. High performance was attainable through effort (high effort–performance expectancy).

2. High performance would lead to outcomes (high performance–outcome instrumentalities).

3. The outcomes were generally attractive (positively valent outcomes).

The major elements of the theory are diagrammed in Fig. M-18. Note that the motivational components of the theory speak only to the effort an individual may be expected to expend toward the accomplishment of some activity. Actual accomplishment depends not only on motivation but also on ability (Vroom, 1964, pp. 196–204). Thus, the complete theory states that behavior (e.g., performance) = motivation × ability.

**Evaluation** Since its formulation by Vroom in 1964, many studies have been conducted testing various aspects of the theory. For the most part, these studies have been conducted in actual public and private organizations. A wide variety of occupational groups have been investigated, including managers, professionals, and white- and blue-collar

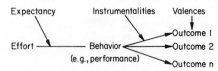

**Fig. M-18. Motivational components in expectancy theory.**

workers. Most of the research has been aimed at testing whether the theory can predict measures of employee performance or effort to perform. A few have used the theory in attempts to predict job choice.

By and large, findings from these studies have been favorable;[3] that is, it is frequently found that beliefs concerning valences of outcomes, and particularly concerning instrumentalities and expectancies, are associated with measures of effort and performance. Higher performers, or those exerting greater effort to perform, tend to have higher expectancies and higher instrumentalities that performance will lead to positively valent outcomes. While it is important to recognize that support for the theory has not been universal, nor always strong, it has been quite consistent.

**Implications for Practice** Expectancy theory is very rich in implications for administrative action. Motivation can be enhanced to the extent that the organization is able to appropriately influence valence, expectancy, or instrumentality perceptions of employees. Since we have already indicated that organizations have little influence over the types of outcomes employees find important (valent), the discussion which follows will focus on the latter two perceptions.

It should be noted at the outset that employees' perceptions are ultimately influenced most importantly by the objective state of affairs. Thus, administrative policies will be unsuccessful if they communicate expectancy or instrumentality linkages that are not consistent with the actual implementation of those policies.

At the same time, however, individuals taken singularly or as group members bring to the work environment a set of partially unique historical experiences. These experiences may tend to shade their feelings and beliefs regarding the important motivational components. Thus, majority relative to minority, rural relative to urban, female relative to male, advantaged relative to disadvantaged employees may hold somewhat different motivational perceptions regardless of organizational characteristics. Organizations must therefore show special sensitivity in establishing and implementing policy whenever persons of diverse backgrounds are employed.

*Influencing Instrumentality Perceptions.* There is little doubt that an organization can have the most immediate impact on motivation through its influence on instrumentality perceptions (beliefs regarding the links between behavior and outcomes). Instrumentality perceptions can be strengthened by making rewards contingent or dependent on desired behavior. Thus, if the organization wishes to encourage motivation to perform among its employees, it must reward the high performers with positively valent rewards. In addition, low performers must not be rewarded.[4] The key to establishing appropriate instrumentality perceptions is by *differentially* rewarding and not rewarding. Rewarding indiscriminately will not have positive motivational impacts.

Given the cognitive nature of expectancy theory, it follows that instrumentality linkages should be communicated. Employees need to be informed that behaving in desired ways will be rewarded. The more specific the organization is about the exact behavior desired and the exact rewards to be expected, the better. While contingent administration of rewards may influence behavior in any event, the impact can be more effective in a shorter time if it is explicitly communicated (e.g., Bandura, 1974).

There is substantial literature from reinforcement theory that has dealt with methods for linking rewards to desired behavior. This literature is frequently interpreted as suggesting that partial reinforcement schedules (i.e., where not every desirable behavior is rewarded) are most effective for motivation (e.g., Hamner, 1974, pp. 491–494). The evidence for this type of conclusion, however, has not been established on adults working in organizational settings. Field studies in the latter context suggest that continuous reinforcement (where every desirable behavior is rewarded) is at least as effective as partial reinforcement (Cummings, 1976). This latter observation is consistent with expectancy theory which would hypothesize that instrumentality perceptions would be maximized when every desirable behavior was rewarded.

In summary, organizations can have positive impacts on their employees' instrumentalities by

1. Communicating in specific terms the linkage between the behaviors and the rewards.

2. Implementing the communicated linkages, including withholding rewards from persons who do not engage in the desired behavior.

3. Where possible, offering the rewards for every or nearly every desired behavior.[5]

While the organization probably has the greatest impact on instrumentality perceptions through the processes described above, keep in mind that individuals also differ in how they respond to these processes.

*Influencing Expectancy Perceptions.* Expectancy perceptions (beliefs regarding the links between effort and behavior) can also be influenced by the organization. Since they pertain to an individual's feelings about his or her capabilities to perform some activity, they will depend mostly on the individual's perception of his or her ability *relative* to the ability requirements of the activity.[6] That is, expectancy perceptions depend jointly on the individual and the task to be done.

Such a formulation suggests that a number of organizational activities may have impacts on expectancy perceptions.

1. *Training and development programs* are an obvious method for attempting to change individuals. By sending employees through training programs, organizations typically attempt to increase their job skills. These changes, in turn, can frequently be expected to enhance expectancy perceptions.

2. *Selection* provides another method for changing, not individuals per se, but characteristics of the work force in the aggregate. By changing employment standards, organizations can influence the ability levels of those hired and consequently influence expectancy perceptions.

3. *Job simplification or enlargement* may also manipulate work content favorably. Simplification has been recommended as a mechanism for increasing productivity through an emphasis on employees' ability to perform. Recently, many persons have advocated enlarging or enriching jobs (i.e., making them more demanding and difficult). Emphasis has been placed on employees' *motivation* to perform. Here it is sufficient to indicate that manipulation of the job will likely influence the ability requirements of the job and hence employees' expectancy perceptions. Probable implications of job enrichment will be discussed in the last major section of this entry.

4. *The employee-job mix* may be changed by reallocation of persons within the organization. Transfers and promotions are frequently used as examples of this method for changing employees' relative ability to perform and hence their expectancy perceptions.

Viewing expectancy as proposed here suggests that it is a very dynamic construct. Employees change through time, jobs change, and hence expectancy perceptions change. It can frequently be expected that expectancy perceptions will be fairly low for employees starting on a job. With experience and/or training, these perceptions will likely increase. Changes in jobs, either through transfer or promotion or technological change, may dramatically alter expectancy perceptions of experienced employees, however. Thus, the organization must be continually alert to the implications of the congruence of worker abilities with job ability requirements for expectancy perceptions.

As with instrumentality perceptions, we can also expect individual differences in expectancy perceptions, primarily as a function of one's previous experience. Those who have a history of coping successfully with their environment in the past will probably have more positive expectancy perceptions than those who have been less successful.

## MOTIVATIONAL APPLICATIONS

A large amount of organizational effort is typically directed toward employee motivation: to join the organization, to remain with the organization, and particularly, to perform effectively. This suggests a brief review of issues relating to task redesign and compensation systems. Both have been suggested as strategies for enhancing employee motivation to perform. Moreover, both have been characterized in the literature by both successful *and* unsuccessful applications. By using expectancy theory, a manager can identify conditions when each of these strategies might be expected to be effective in motivating high performance.

**Task Redesign** The work itself, or the task, along with reward practices, supervisors, and co-workers, serves as a potentially important outcome source within the organizational environment. Recently, a large number of investigations have been conducted examining whether characteristics of the job itself influence employee attitudes and performance. Generally speaking, the results of those investigations have yielded ambiguous results. While there have been notable successes, so also there have been notable failures.[7]

The task is a potential source of so-called "intrinsic outcomes" such as feelings of achievement, accomplishment, and competence. To generate these feelings, however, the person performing the task must probably believe the task to be psychologically important. To be so, it has been suggested that the job must be seen as meaningful, requiring worker responsibility and providing knowledge about work results (Hackman and Oldham, 1976). These requirements tend to describe enlarged and enriched jobs more so than specialized jobs.

This then constitutes the major argument in favor of job enlargement or enrichment.[8] Enlarged or enriched jobs allow employees to experience intrinsic outcomes associated with doing the task. In expectancy theory terms, job enlargement or enrichment increases instrumentality perceptions linking successful performance to intrinsic outcomes. To this extent, job enlargement has a positive motivational impact.

Expectancy theory also tells us, of course, that instrumentality perceptions are of themselves not sufficient. The associated outcomes must also be positively valent for motivation to exist. Thus, organizations should not always expect that the outcomes of job enlargement or enrichment will be motivating to all its employees.[9]

Also, as has been suggested earlier, it is probable that changes in task scope will have an impact on expectancy perceptions. In the short run at least, broadening tasks through enlargement or enrichment programs will likely result in reduced expectancy perceptions. This, in turn, can be expected to reduce motivation to perform unless the organization offsets these dysfunctional impacts through careful planning, including, in all likelihood, formalized training programs to facilitate the transition.

**Compensation Systems** The impact of pay on motivation to perform has been controversial for reasons often not highly associated with the evidence. While there are plenty of examples showing pay systems failing, sometimes spectacularly so, it is typically not because pay fails to motivate. Indeed, sometimes pay motivates too well. Compensation systems have failed to anticipate how much employees can produce when motivated by a pay system, or how they can demoralize an administrative system to optimize their economic interests.[10]

The evidence, however, also shows that adequately administered compensation systems which have been designed to motivate performance, do so successfully (Nash and Carroll, 1975, pp. 199–202). A major reason for these successes is the high valence generally attached to pay (Lawler, 1971, pp. 37–42). High valence probably stems from the fact that pay is so generally transferable and frequently conveys other outcomes (e.g., recognition).

Since pay is generally valent to employees, the key to a motivating compensation system in terms of expectancy theory is to obtain high instrumentality perceptions that pay will be obtained if, and only if, the desired behavior is forthcoming. The closer the systems actually link pay to desired behaviors, the higher will be the instrumentality perceptions (Schwab, 1973). There is also evidence that employees with higher instrumentality perceptions regarding the link between pay and performance tend to be higher performers (e.g., Porter and Lawler, 1968; Schwab and Dyer, 1973).

If an organization desires to use compensation to motivate performance, a number of important conditions must be satisfied.

1. The organization must be sure that employees are responsible for their own performance. It makes little sense to link any reward to performance if performance is essentially out of the employees' control.

2. The organization must be able to *define* and *measure* performance. Two types of procedures are in general use. One, frequently associated with individual and group-incentive systems, is based on quantitative indicators of physical productivity measured against engineering-based standards. The second procedure for measuring is through some sort of evaluation or performance appraisal system. Such systems are typical for non managerial employees and involve the evaluation of one person by another.

3. The organization must actually link compensation outcomes to measured performance. This step is fairly direct in typical incentive systems using quantitative productivity measures. However, a frequent difficulty associated with such systems includes unnecessary complexity. Employees may not know how their pay is specifically determined, and instrumentality perceptions linking pay and performance will be lower than they could be.

Another major difficulty has to do with changing production standards. Attempts to raise standards as production increases will be met by employee resistance and probable output restriction. Employee instrumentality perceptions for the intermediate and long run will be low if they anticipate that standards will be raised as a consequence of increased productivity. This difficulty questions the advisability of incentive systems when production processes are subject to rapid technological change.

Performance appraisal procedures are generally connected to compensation through *merit-rating* systems. Policy regarding such systems frequently states that high performers can expect frequent and generous compensation increases, while low performers can expect infrequent and small, or nonexistent, increases. As Campbell, et al. (1971, pp. 51–54) have pointed out, however, organizations seldom follow through on these policies so that too often little difference exists between the salary increases obtained by individuals receiving the most-favorable evaluations and those receiving the least-favorable evaluations. The consequences, in terms of expectancy theory are predictable and necessarily dysfunctional. Pay-performance instrumentality will necessarily be weakened when salary increases are not differentially linked to evaluation results.

Undoubtedly, an important reason for unwillingness to differentiate more rigorously on the basis of appraisal results is a concern about the validity of those results. Typical appraisal procedures are permeated with errors. These errors occur substantially because the evaluator has no clear-cut standards against which to compare the evaluatees' performance.

*Management by Objectives (MBO).* This is one procedure which attempts to generate clear-cut performance standards. It establishes, frequently with the evaluatees' participation, explicit individualized standards as a basis for subsequent evaluation (Carroll and Tosi, 1973, pp. 1–16). Several elements of MBO have direct expectancy theory implications. One of the most consistent findings is that performance tends to increase as the goals established are made more specific (Steers and Porter, 1974). In all probability, specific goals help the employee clarify expectancy perceptions linking effort to performance. Management by objectives can thus provide a double-barreled motivational impact if the goal setting is combined with a system of linking goal accomplishment to financial rewards so that performance-pay instrumentality perceptions are high.

## CONCLUSION

Expectancy theory views motivation as a reasonably complex process involving multiple perceptions. As a consequence, analysis of administrative activities using this theory will yield multiple and sometimes conflicting impacts on organizational behavior. While this may seem initially frustrating to persons who desire to understand and/or influence behavior in organizations, it is realistic of the actual complexities. The alternative, attempting to understand organizational behavior in terms of unitary impacts, has always been doomed to failure.

*See also* BEHAVIORAL MODELS; DISCIPLINE; HYGIENE FACTORS; INTERPERSONAL RELATIONSHIPS; LEADERSHIP; SYSTEM 4; THEORY X AND THEORY Y; WORK, CONCEPT AND IMPLICATIONS; WORK DESIGN, JOB ENLARGEMENT, JOB ENRICHMENT, JOB DESIGN, AND AUTONOMOUS WORK GROUPS.

## NOTES

[1] Interested readers will find recent summaries regarding the hierarchy of needs in Campbell and Pritchard (1976, pp. 97–100); summaries regarding two-factor taxonomy will be found in Locke (1976, pp. 1309–1319, 1332–1333).

[2] Readers interested in the nuances of the theory are encouraged to read Vroom (1964, pp. 14–28) and Campbell and Pritchard (1976, pp. 74–84).

[3] A critical review of early research on expectancy theory has been performed by Heneman and Schwab (1972) and on the more recent research by Campbell and Pritchard (1976, pp. 84–95).

[4] This is not to suggest that low performers should be punished. Punishment does not generally influence behavior in a direction opposite to positive rewards and hence should not be thought of as falling on the opposite end of a continuum from positive rewards (e.g., Campbell and Pritchard, 1976, p. 71).

[5] This latter recommendation is the most tentative of the three because of the paucity of evidence from studies of humans in work organizations.

[6] The ideas expressed in this section have been substantially influenced by the theory of work adjustment (Dawis, England, and Lofquist, 1968).

[7] This literature has been reviewed by Hulin and Blood (1968) and Pierce and Dunham (1975).

[8] This analysis of task scope is based primarily on a paper by Schwab and Cummings (1976) which deals in greater depth with the issues discussed here.

[9] Hackman (1975) has suggested the intriguing hypothesis that the very possibility of receiving intrinsic outcomes makes them more valent. While this hypothesis is not universally accepted (Schwab and Cummings, 1976), if true, it would suggest that job enlargement and enrichment programs have broader applicability than previously thought.

[10] See Whyte (1955), pp. 90–96 for an illustration of the former and pp. 20–27 for an illustration of the latter.

[11] Much of what follows is based on Heneman and Schwab (1975).

## REFERENCES

Bandura, A.: "Behavior Theory and the Models of Man," *American Psychologist*, vol. 29, pp. 859–869, 1974.

Campbell, J. P., M. D. Dunnette, E. E. Lawler, III, and K. E. Weick, Jr.: *Managerial Behavior, Performance, and Effectiveness*, McGraw-Hill Book Company, New York, 1970.

Campbell, J. P. and R. D. Pritchard: "Motivation Theory in Industrial and Organizational Psychology," in M. D. Dunnette, ed.: *Handbook of Industrial and Organizational Psychology*, Rand McNally & Company, Skokie, Ill., 1976, pp. 63–130.

Carroll, S. J., Jr., and H. L. Tosi, Jr.: *Management by Objectives*, The Macmillan Company, New York, 1973.

Cummings, L. L.: "Reinforcement in Management: Principles and Cases," unpublished paper, Graduate School of Business, University of Wisconsin–Madison, 1976.

Cummings. L. L., and D. P. Schwab: *Performance in Organizations: Determinants and Appraisal*, Scott, Foresman and Company, Glenview, Ill., 1973.

Dawis, R. V., G. E. England, and D. J. Weiss: *A Theory of Work Adjustment: A Revision*, Minnesota Studies in Vocational Rehabilitation, Bulletin 47, Minneapolis, 1968.

Deci, E. L.: *Intrinsic Motivation*, Plenum Press, Plenum Publishing Corporation, New York, 1975.

Dunnette, M. D., J. P. Campbell, and M. D. Hakel: "Factors Contributing to Job Satisfaction and Job Dissatisfaction in Six Occupational Groups," *Organizational Behavior and Human Performance*, vol. 2, pp. 143–174, 1967.

Giles, B. A., and G. U. Barrett: "Utility of Merit Increases," *Journal of Applied Psychology*, vol. 55, pp. 103–109, 1971.

Hackman, J. R.: "On the Coming Demise of Job Enrichment," in E. L. Cass and F. G. Zimmer, eds.: *Man and Work in Society*, Van Nostrand Reinhold Company, New York, 1975.

Hackman, J. R., and G. R. Oldham: "Motivation Through the Design of Work: Test of a Theory," *Organizational Behavior and Human Performance*, vol. 16, pp. 250–279, 1976.

Hamner, W. C.: "Reinforcement Theory and Contingency Management in Organizational Settings," in H. L. Tosi and W. C. Hamner, ed.: *Organizational Behavior and Management: A Contingency Approach*, St. Clair Press, Chicago, Ill., 1974, pp. 86–112.

Heneman, H. G., III, and D. P. Schwab: "Evaluation of Research on Expectancy Theory Predictions of Employee Performance," *Psychological Bulletin*, vol. 78, pp. 1–9, 1972.

Heneman, H. G., III, and D. P. Schwab: "Work and Rewards Theory," in D. Yoder and H. G. Heneman, Jr., eds.: *Motivation and Commitment*, Bureau of National Affairs, Washington, 1975, pp. 1–21.

Herzberg, F: *Work and the Nature of Man*, World Book Company, Tarrytown-on-Hudson, N.Y., 1966.

Herzberg, F., B. Mausner, and B. B. Snyderman: *The Motivation to Work*, 2d ed., John Wiley Sons, Inc., New York, 1959.

Hulin, C. L., and M. R. Blood: "Job Enlargement, Individual Differences and Worker Responses," *Psychological Bulletin*, vol. 69, pp. 41–55, 1968.

Lawler, E. E., III: *Motivation in Work Organizations*, Brooks/Cole Publishing Company, Monterey, Calif., 1973.

Lawler, E. E., III: *Pay and Organizational Effectiveness: A Psychological View*, McGraw-Hill Book Company, New York, 1971.

Lawler, E. E., III, and J. L. Suttle: "A Causal Correlational Test of the Need Hierarchy Concept," *Organizational Behavior and Human Performance*, vol. 7, pp. 265–287, 1972.

Locke, E. A.: "The Nature and Causes of Job Satisfaction," in M. D. Dunnette, ed.: *Handbook of Industrial and Organizational Psychology*, Rand McNally &Company, Skokie, Ill., 1976, pp. 1297–1349.

Maslow, A. H.: *Motivation and Personality*, 2d ed., Harper & Row Publishers, Incorporated, New York, 1970.

Nash, A. N., and S. J. Carroll, Jr.: *The Management of Compensation*, Brooks/Cole Publishing Company, Monterey, Calif., 1975.

Pierce, J. L., and R. B. Dunham: "Task Design: A Literature Review," unpublished paper, Graduate School of Business, University of Wisconsin–Madison, 1975.

Porter, L. W., and E. E. Lawler, III: *Managerial Attitudes and Performance*, Richard D. Irwin, Inc., Homewood, Ill., 1968.

Schwab, D. P.: "Impact of Alternative Compensation Systems on Pay Valence and Instrumentality Perceptions," *Journal of Applied Psychology*, vol. 58, pp. 308–312, 1973.

Schwab, D. P., and L. L. Cummings: "A Theoretical Analysis of the Impact of Task Scope on Employee Performance," *Academy of Management Review*, vol. 1, no. 2, pp. 23–35, 1976.

Schwab, D. P., and L. D. Dyer: "The Motivational Impact of a Compensation System on Employee Performance," *Organizational Behavior and Human Performance*, vol. 9, pp. 215–225, 1973.

Scott, W. E., Jr.: "The Effects of Extrinsic Rewards on 'Intrinsic Motivation:' A Critique," *Organizational Behavior and Human Performance*, vol. 15, pp. 117–129, 1976.

Steers, R. M., and L. W. Porter: "The Role of Task-Goal Attributes in Employee Performance," *Psychological Bulletin*, vol. 81, pp. 434–452, 1974.

Vroom, V. H.: *Work and Motivation*, John Wiley & Sons, Inc., New York, 1964.

Whyte, W. F.: *Money and Motivation*, John Wiley & Sons, Inc., New York, 1955.

DONALD P. SCHWAB, *University of Wisconsin, Madison*

# Motivation research (See CONSUMER BEHAVIOR, MANAGERIAL RELEVANCE OF.)

# Motives (See OBJECTIVES AND GOALS.)

# Moving averages (See FORECASTING BUSINESS CONDITIONS.)

# Moving to new quarters (See OFFICE SPACE PLANNING AND DESIGN.)

# Multicolumn gang chart (See WORK SIMPLIFICATIONS AND IMPROVEMENT.)

# Multinational companies (See INTERNATIONAL OPERATIONS AND MANAGEMENT IN MULTINATIONAL COMPANIES.)

# Multiple-activity chart (See WORK SIMPLIFICATION AND IMPROVEMENT.)

**Multiple-criteria problem** *(See* STATISTI-
CAL ANALYSIS FOR MANAGEMENT.)

**Multiple management** [*See* COMPENSA-
TION, SPECIAL PLANS; ORGANIZATION DEVELOPMENT
(OD).]

**Multivariate arm models** *(See* FORECAST-
ING BUSINESS CONDITIONS.)

**Mutual companies** *(See* INSURANCE AND
RISK MANAGEMENT; OWNERSHIP, LEGAL FORMS OF.)

**NASDAQ system** (*See* MARKETS, SECURITIES.)

**National Emphasis Program (OSHA)** (*See* SAFETY AND HEALTH MANAGEMENT, EMPLOYEE.)

**National Labor Relations Act** (*See* LABOR LEGISLATION.)

**Need theory of negotiating** (*See* NEGOTIATING.)

**Negligence, product** (*See* PRODUCT LIABILITY.)

**Negligence doctrine** (*See* PRODUCT LIABILITY.)

## Negotiating

Every desire that demands satisfaction and every need that can be met potentially create an occasion for people to initiate the negotiating process. Whenever people exchange ideas with the intention of changing relationships, whenever they confer for agreement, they are negotiating. In the past, the study of negotiating was limited in that only certain areas were selected as germane to the subject. These areas consisted of collective bargaining, real estate, buying and selling, diplomacy, and interpersonal relations. All these and many more fields, however, serve as arenas for negotiation. Negotiating is a process, and parts of the same process occur in the same way in all the areas. The differences involve only a choice of strategies and an assessment of the risks and penalties, goals and counteractions available.

*A Life Process.* Segments that make up the negotiating process include making preparation (long and short term); understanding human behavior; receiving all forms of communication, including nonverbal and hidden verbal messages; making assumptions; asking questions; and negotiating philosophies.

As negotiating is a process, it has the same characteristics as other life processes, all of which are undergoing continuous change. Timing is critical for successful negotiations. How and where we deal with the process also make vital differences. These process characteristics suggest that strategies and tactics be classified into two groups: (1) "when" strategies, involving the proper sense of timing,

759

e.g., forbearance, surprise, fait accompli, etc.; and (2) "how and where" strategies, involving method and area of application, e.g., participation, association, disassociation, and crossroads.

*Negotiation as a Science.* At any given moment one, a group, or all of the behavioral and physical sciences may be brought to bear on a particular aspect of a negotiation. For example, game theory[1] techniques are applied to the negotiating process and are further amplified through the use of computers and mathematical models. Some shortcomings are acknowledged in this approach. Life situations have infinite numbers of variables; games are limited. In a life situation it is difficult to know the values and rules of all parties; in a game these are assumed. Computers and models are valuable, nevertheless, to use as a backup to one's judgment and in opening up possible alternatives.

In addition, theories concerning group dynamics are used to understand interpersonal and group interaction. Psychological studies have suggested many approaches such as conflict resolution, motivational determinants, and the need theory of negotiation, using Maslow's need hierarchy. Using psychological references, the negotiating process can be analyzed variously under role playing, anxiety and flexibility, cooperation/competition, trust/suspicion, and setting of climates.

Effective negotiation is a cooperative human process. Many managers, however, severely limit their techniques to those they believe produced successful results in the past. Since success to them is often equated with merely winning an advantage, negotiating is regarded not as an art but as a game of chance—win, lose, or draw. This is shortsighted. Managers should consider long-range objectives as well as short-term advantages. Negotiated solutions are likely to be longer lasting when each party gains something that is of value and has a stake in keeping it. Genuinely creative negotiating brings about conclusions that satisfy all parties.

*Negotiation as an Art.* Managers learn progressively from the negotiating process itself. Ordinarily the negotiator is thought to have little or no control over the complex variables and the innumerable strategies that the opposer may bring into the struggle. It is even more difficult to perceive the value structure upon which the opposer's strategy is based. No objective may be too small or too complex. No aspect of human behavior is irrelevant to the process. Thus, many managers view negotiation as an art.

*Need Theory of Negotiating.* Negotiating efforts can be focused, however, if both parties try to utilize the almost infinite alternatives available and to view the process as a cooperative enterprise in which each strives for shared goals. At first glance this may seem to limit possible agreements. In reality it does not. Two alternatives—you win or you lose—are exchanged for a virtually unlimited potential for satisfying human needs. The key to this approach lies in Abraham H. Maslow's pioneering work *Motivation and Personality.*[2] He presented a hierarchy of needs as basic factors in human behavior (homeostatic security, belonging, esteem, self-actualization, knowledge, and aesthetic needs). These in turn can provide a useful framework for studying needs in relation to negotiation. Such a framework for understanding the negotiating process is offered in Nierenberg's *Fundamentals of Negotiating.*[3]

Ultimately, needs and their satisfaction are the common denominator in negotiation. If people did not have unsatisfied needs, they would not negotiate. Effective negotiation presupposes that *both* the negotiator and the opposer want something; otherwise they would turn a deaf ear to each other's demands and there would be no bargaining. Careful consideration of human needs enables a manager to identify the needs involved on both sides of the bargaining table. Once identified and acknowledged, the relative strength and value of each need can be assessed and the negotiating techniques can be selected on the basis of need satisfaction. This highly structured need theory of negotiating helps to change a somewhat disordered and emotional process into a science-based art that can bring satisfaction to both sides of a negotiation.

*See also* COMMUNICATIONS, ORGANIZATIONAL; INTERPERSONAL RELATIONSHIPS; OPERATIONS RESEARCH AND MATHEMATICAL MODELING; PURCHASING MANAGEMENT.

### NOTES

[1] John Van Newmann and Oskar Morganstern, *Theory of Games and Economic Behavior*, Princeton University Press, Princeton, N.J., 1947.

[2] Abraham H. Maslow, *Motivation and Personality*, Harper & Brothers, New York, 1954.

[3] G. I. Nierenberg, *Fundamentals of Negotiating*, Hawthorn Books, Inc., New York, 1973.

GERARD I. NIERENBERG, ESQ., *Negotiation Institute, Inc.*

# Negotiation, labor (See LABOR-MANAGEMENT RELATIONS.)

# Negotiations, site  (*See* SITE SELECTION.)

# Net present value (NPV)  (*See* BUDGETING, CAPITAL.)

# Network, communications  (*See* COMMUNICATIONS, ORGANIZATIONAL.)

# Network chart  (*See* PAPER WORK SIMPLIFICATION.)

# Network planning methods

Network planning methods are a family of techniques specifically developed to aid in the management of projects. For purpose of definition, a *project* is a combination of interrelated activities that must be performed in a prescribed order to accomplish a specified goal. Some activities cannot start until others are completed. Activities require time and resources for completion. A due date may be prescribed for completion of the project.

Prior to recent developments, project planning and scheduling were accomplished using a method such as the Gantt bar chart, which specifies the start and finish times for each activity along a horizontal time scale. The Gantt chart is not suitable for use in planning large, complex projects, where there are numerous interdependencies between the activities and where time-cost trade-offs need to be investigated.

Network methods, on the other hand, are uniquely suitable for use in planning and scheduling projects. These methods construct arrow diagrams (or a network) representing the individual activities required to proceed from an initial event to an ultimate objective. The network shows all the interdependencies that exist among the individual activities. In modern management applications, a computer is utilized to assemble and sort the information on the precedence of activities, times, and costs to provide scheduled completion times and earliest and latest start dates of each activity, with associated time-oriented costs.

The network serves as both a model, or analogue, of the project as well as the representation of the master plan for controlling the project's activities. The network is a geometric representation or map of the project's activities, and may be "read" by the manager or the computer to yield important information for decision-making purposes. As in the case of maps, the network serves to identify the activities which are critical and require managerial review effort. These critical activities form the critical path requiring the most attention by the project manager. The noncritical, or slack, activities are those which do not affect the duration of the project and may be delayed or stretched out to obtain resources for the critical activities.

**Usefulness**  Network planning methods evolved as a management tool with the development of the critical path method (CPM) and the program evaluation and review technique (PERT). Both methods are time-oriented network planning methods; in CPM, activity durations are assumed to be known, and in PERT, activity durations are given by probability distributions.

CPM is useful in obtaining trade-offs between cost and completion dates. In this case a relationship is established between additional resources (such as labor, equipment, and facilities) to reduce the durations of activities and the increased costs of these resources. PERT is useful in planning projects where uncertainty is the underlying factor, such as in the case of R&D projects.

Network planning methods are useful at all levels of management:

1. At the first level of supervision, network planning methods are useful for identifying the need for the project and the "how or where" to better sequence the project and thereby reduce times and/or costs.

2. At the middle management level, network planning methods serve as a planning tool in formulating and integrating the activities of a project. The middle manager is able to determine whether or not a project can be accomplished within specified time and cost schedules.

3. At the top management level, network planning methods are a control device providing for status reporting and progress evaluation. The updated network and periodic status reports provide a continual comparison of expected or required performance with actual or predicted performance. Project time-cost problems are highlighted and may be ranked in order of importance in achieving overall program objectives.

The networking approach provides management with information which answers many of the questions occurring during the life of a project, such as:

How long the project will take and what it will cost

When parts and materials are needed

Where a project should be expedited to save money

Where overtime should and should not be used

How much equipment (by type) is needed and when

How far a subcontractor or material delivery can slip

How to maintain a level work force

The effect on schedule of late design changes

When funds will be required to pay subcontractors

Properly used, the networking approach provides advantages and benefits to management which may be summed up as follows:

1. Provides an integrated "big picture" of project management.

2. Forces a more logical and analytical approach to planning projects.

3. Guards against not considering important activities.

4. Facilitates coordination between prime contractors and subcontractors.

5. Permits analyzing the effects of changes and slippages on schedules.

6. Simplifies replanning and rescheduling.

7. Provides a means for project cost control.

8. Provides a means for compressing schedules to meet deadlines and to reduce total cost.

9. Provides a means to estimate cash flow requirements.

**Applications**  A variety of project types may use either CPM or PERT. The following are examples of applications: (1) space vehicle construction and launching, (2) building or highway construction, (3) oil refinery turnaround and maintenance, (4) computer system installation and data center operations, (5) new product introduction, (6) monthly, quarterly, and annual closing of accounting records, (7) broadway show opening, (8) electric generator manufacture and assembly, (9) contract bid preparation and submission, (10) medical patient examination and treatment, and (11) ship repair.

## BASIC DEFINITIONS

In project management, network planning emphasizes the scheduled completion time and resource allocation. Project management is concerned with the basic managerial tasks of planning, scheduling, and control.

The planning phase is initiated by breaking down the project into the distinct activities. Resource requirements in the form of labor, materials, equipment, and facilities are estimated. The time esti-

mates for these activities are then determined and a network (or arrow) diagram is constructed with each of its arcs (arrows) representing an activity. The entire network diagram gives a graphic representation of the interdependencies between the activities of the project. The construction of the network diagram as a planning phase has the advantage of analyzing the different activities in detail, perhaps suggesting improvements before the project is actually executed. Following the estimation of activity durations, costs are specified.

The ultimate objective of the scheduling phase is to determine the required start and finish times for each activity, as well as its relationship to other activities in the project, in order to achieve the project's anticipated completion date. In addition, the schedule must pinpoint the critical activities which require special attention if the project is to be completed on time. For the noncritical activities, the schedule must show the amount of slack (or float) times which can be used advantageously when such activities are delayed or when limited resources are to be used effectively.

The final phase in project management is project control. This includes the use of the network diagram and the time chart for making periodic progress reports. The difference between the scheduled and actual performance of each activity is reviewed. The network may thus be updated and analyzed and, if necessary, a new schedule determined for the remaining portion of the project.

A *project* is any operation with the following elements:

1. A scheduled list of component activities

2. A logical sequence or ordering of these activities

3. A statement of the time required to perform each activity

4. An indication of activity costs in the case of resource allocation problems

An example of a network representing a house construction project is given in Fig. N-1 and its accompanying table.

**Activities**  An *activity* is any portion of a project which consumes time and resources and has a specific starting and ending point. It is the work necessary to progress from one point in time to another point in time. Activities consume time, money, human energy, facilities, equipment, and/or materials. Examples of activities may be tasks involved in office paper work, processing plant machine operations, new highway construction, and corporate contractual negotiations. For each activity, the predecessor or successor activities must also be spec-

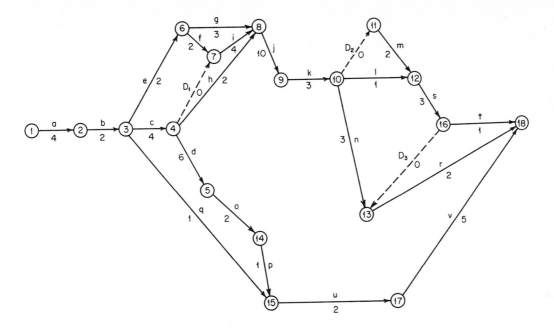

**House Construction Project**

| Job name | Alternate | Immediate predecessor | Time, days |
|---|---|---|---|
| a | (1,2) | — | 4 |
| b | (2,3) | a | 2 |
| c | (3,4) | b | 4 |
| d | (4,5) | c | 6 |
| e | (3,6) | b | 2 |
| f | (6,7) | e | 2 |
| g | (6,8) | e | 3 |
| h | (4,8) | c | 2 |
| $D_1$ (dummy) | (4,7) | c | 0 |
| i | (7,8) | $D_1$, f | 4 |
| j | (8,9) | g, h, i | 10 |
| k | (9,10) | j | 3 |
| l | (10,12) | k | 1 |
| $D_2$ (dummy) | (10,11) | k | 0 |
| m | (11,12) | $D_2$ | 2 |
| n | (10,13) | k | 3 |
| o | (5,14) | d | 2 |
| p | (14,15) | o | 1 |
| q | (3,15) | b | 1 |
| $D_3$ (dummy) | (13,16) | s | 0 |
| r | (13,18) | $D_3$, n | 2 |
| s | (12,16) | l, m | 3 |
| t | (16,18) | s | 1 |
| u | (15,17) | p, q | 2 |
| v | (17,18) | u | 5 |

**Fig. N-1. Typical network diagram.** *(J. D. Wiest and F. K. Levy, "A Management Guide to PERT/CPM," Prentice-Hall, Inc., Englewood Cliffs, N.J., 1969, pp. 18–19, reproduced with permission of the copyright holder.)*

ified. Graphically, an activity may be represented by an arrow with the descriptions and time estimates written alongside the arrow. The representation of an activity is as follows:

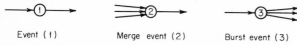

**Events** An *event* denotes either the beginning or the completion of an activity or a group of activities, and it occurs at a discrete point in time. Events do not consume time or resources and are normally represented by a numbered circle. The beginning and end points of an activity are described by two events. Synonymous with the term *events* are the terms *nodes* and *connectors*. An event denoting the joint completion of more than one activity is called a *merge* event while the event denoting the joint initiation of more than one activity is called a *burst* event, as shown in Fig. N-2.

An event is represented by a single number such as (1). An activity is represented by a pair of numbers such as (1,2). The direction of progress in each activity is specified by assigning a smaller number to the intiating event compared with the number of its ending event. The beginning and end points of an activity are described by two events.

**Fig. N-2. Types of events.**

**Dummy Activities** In many projects, such as in chemical processing, an activity cannot be undertaken unless the product of the preceding activity is available. Therefore, *dummy* activities are needed to represent the logical dependencies of the network. In the network these are generally represented by broken (dashed) lines. In effect, the line indicates an activity where no real work is represented, but rather a dependency relationship in the form of a *zero time* activity.

The following are examples of situations where dummy activities are required:

In a steel mill ingots cannot be sent to the rod mill before being sent into a 12- or 8-inch rolling mill.

In building construction involving concrete plastering, the plastering cannot start before the poured concrete is set.

In automobile assembly-line production, the carburetor cannot be adjusted before the engine is installed.

In the example shown in Fig. N-3*a*, activities A and B have the same end events. The procedure is to introduce a dummy activity either between A and one of the end events or between B and one of the end events. The modified representations, after introducing the dummy D, are shown in Fig. N-3*b*. As a result of using D, activities A and B can now be identified by unique end events. It must be noted that a dummy activity does not consume time or resources.

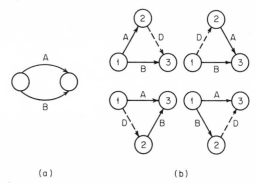

**Fig. N-3. Dummy activities. (a) activities with the same end events; (b) modified representations.**

Dummy activities are also useful in establishing logic relationships in the arrow diagram which otherwise cannot be represented correctly. Suppose in a certain project, activities A and B must precede C. On the other hand, activity E is preceded by activity B only; Fig. N-4*a* shows an incorrect version, since, although the relationship between A, B, and C is correct, the diagram implies that E must be preceded by both A and B. The correct representation using the dummy D is shown in Fig. N-4*b*. Since D consumes no time (or resources), the indicated precedence relationships are satisfied.

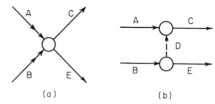

**Fig. N-4. Dummy events and logic relationships. (a) incorrect representation; (b) correct representation.**

## NETWORK CONSTRUCTION

A graphical representation of the project plan, showing the interrelationships of various activities and associated times, is called a *network*. The time phase plan for accomplishing the activities in the network is called a *project schedule*.

To plan a project means to identify the component activities necessary for the performance and to determine and express the logical order in which they will be carried out. This requires a thorough knowledge of the particular project concerned, a systematic procedure which may be followed in expressing any project as a network. The activities should be listed in the approximate order of their performance and referred to by the labels A, B, C, etc. The logical sequence should be expressed in a table as follows:

| Activity | Depends on (or is preceded by) |
|----------|-------------------------------|
| A | — |
| B | A |
| C | B |
| D | B |
| E | C |
| F | D,E |

The network may be drawn in the manner shown in Fig. N-5.

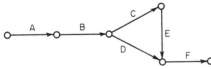

**Fig. N-5. Elementary diagramming.**

Another example of a network is shown in Fig. N-6. There are six events: (1), (2), (3), (4), (5), and (6). The reader should identify the nine activities and the associated pairs of numbers: (1,2), (1,3), (2,3), (2,4), (2,5), (3,5), (4,5), (4,6), and (5,6). The time for each activity is indicated above the activity.

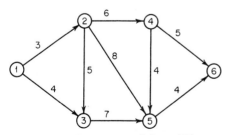

**Fig. N-6. Diagram with six events and nine activities.**

In the planning stage, while depicting the various interrelationships between the activities, the network will also reveal the factors which affect the timing of the accomplishment of any given activity or group of activities and the consequent effects on the project schedule. Networks are used for planning, plan integration, completion time analysis, and scheduling and resource analysis. The rules for constructing the network may be summarized as follows:

RULE 1: Each activity is represented by one and only one arrow in the network. No single activity can be represented twice in the network. This is to be differentiated from the case where one activity is broken down into segments. In this case, each segment may be represented by a separate arrow. For example, in laying down a pipe, this may be done in sections rather than as one job.

RULE 2: No two activities can be identified by the same initial and ending events. Such a situation may arise only when two or more activities can be performed concurrently.

RULE 3: In order to ensure the correct precedence relationship in the arrow diagram, the following questions must be answered when every activity is added to the network:

What activities must be completed immediately before this activity can start?

What activities must follow this activity?

What activities must occur concurrently with this activity?

This rule allows for checking (and rechecking) the precedence relationships in the development of the network.

EXAMPLE: Construct the arrow diagram comprising activities A, B, C, . . . , L such that the following relationships are satisfied:

1. A, B, and C, the first activities of the project, start simultaneously.
2. A and B precede D.
3. B precedes E, F, and H.
4. F and C precede G.
5. E and H precede I and J.
6. C, D, F, and J precede K.
7. K precedes L.
8. I, G, and L are the terminal activities of the project.

The resulting arrow diagram is shown in Fig. N-7. The dummy activities $D_1$ and $D_2$ are used to establish correct precedence relationships. $D_3$ is used to identify activities E and H with unique end events. The events of the project are numbered such that their ascending order indicates the direction of progress in the project.

**The Network Framework** The following elements are necessary to build a logical network to schedule activities:

*Network list:* name of the network and identifying codes of the work breakdown summary, etc.;

the organization carrying out the activities; and the individuals responsible for the planning and execution of the network.

*Event list:* listing of various events, their descriptions, and their importance; the scheduled occurrence dates, if any; and a temporary reference number for each of the events.

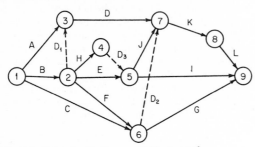

**Fig. N-7. Network with dummy activities inserted.**

*Activity list:* identification of specific activities with the following details: the activity description, the performing department, and tentative cost and resource estimates.

*The Network Logic.* Before the network is actually started the following requirements must be satisfied:

1. Before a certain activity begins all preceding activities must be completed.

2. Logical dependence must be signified by arrows.

**Time-Scaled Networks** A network may be represented in a line-scaled diagram, as shown in Fig. N-8. On a time scale the dashed arrows represent a slack. For example, both activities A and B must be completed prior to the initiation of C.

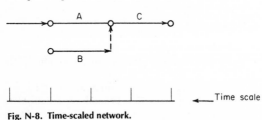

**Fig. N-8. Time-scaled network.**

## CRITICAL PATH METHOD (CPM)

In planning the project, it has been indicated that it is necessary to identify the associated activities, events, and activity times. Key management questions are: (1) How long will the project take? and (2) When may activities be scheduled? An important consideration in planning is the minimum time re-

quired to complete the project. It is necessary to find the longest path, or sequence of connected activities through the network, which is identified as the *critical path* in that it determines the duration of the project. The cumulative times of the activities along the critical path yield the length, or project duration.

As an example, consider the network in Fig. N-9, in which the direction of the arrows indicates the work to be accomplished and the time to perform each activity is indicated above the arrow. The problem is to find the (critical) activities on the critical path.

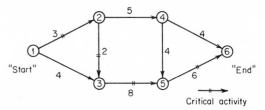

**Fig. N-9. CPM diagram construction.**

The possible sequences from starting event (1) to terminal event (6) are given by:

| Path Sequence | Path Length |
|---|---|
| (a) $1 - 2 - 4 - 6$ | $3 + 5 + 4 = 12$ |
| (b) $1 - 2 - 4 - 5 - 6$ | $3 + 5 + 4 + 6 = 18$ |
| (c) $1 - 2 - 3 - 5 - 6$ | $3 + 2 + 8 + 6 = 19$ (maximum) |
| (d) $1 - 3 - 5 - 6$ | $4 + 8 + 6 = 18$ |

The critical path is given by path (c), and the length of the critical path is 19. In the calculations below the results are systematized as a sequence of similar steps.

**Determination of the Critical Path** A critical path defines a sequence of critical activities, which connect the start and end events. The critical path identifies all the critical activities of the project. The method of determining such a path is illustrated by the example in Fig. N-10, which starts at node 1 and terminates at node 6. The time required to perform each activity is indicated on the arrows.

The critical path calculations include two phases. The first phase is called the *forward pass* where

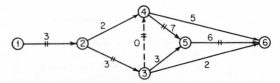

**Fig. N-10. Critical path determination.**

calculations begin from the start node and move to the end node. At each node a number is computed representing the earliest occurrence time of the corresponding event *(ES)*. The second phase, called the *backward pass*, begins calculations from the end node and moves to the start node, representing the latest occurrence time of the corresponding event *(LC)*. After the forward and backward pass computations are completed, the float (or slack) can be computed for each activity, the critical path determined, and the individual activity schedules determined.

*Forward Pass.* Let $ES_i$ be the *earliest start* time of all the activities emanating from event $i$. Thus, $ES_i$ represents the earliest occurrence time of event $i$. If $i = 1$ is the "start" event, then $ES_1 = 0$. Let $D_{ij}$ be the *duration* of activity $(i,j)$. The forward pass calculations are obtained from the equation

$$ES_j = \max_i\{ES_i + D_{ij}\}$$

for all defined $(i,j)$ activities which terminate with event $j$. To compute $ES_j$ for event $j$, $ES_i$ for the head events of all the incoming activities $(i,j)$ must be computed first.

The forward pass calculations applied to Fig. N-10 yield $ES_1 = 0$ as shown in row 1, column 3 of Table N-1. Since there is only one incoming activity (1,2) to event 2, with $D_{12} = 3$,

$$ES_2 = ES_1 + D_{12} = 0 + 3 = 3$$

This is entered in rows 2 and 3 of column 3 of the table. As the next event to be considered is (3),

$$ES_3 = ES_2 + D_{23} = 3 + 3 = 6$$

which is entered in rows 4, 5, and 6 of column 3. The value of $ES_4$ can now be obtained. Since there are two incoming activities, (2,4) and (3,4),

$$ES_4 = \max_{i=2,3}\{ES_i + D_{i4}\} = \max\{3 + 2, 6 + 0\}$$
$$= \max\{5,6\} = 6$$

This is entered in the rows associated with event 4 in column 3.

The procedure continues in the same manner until $ES_j$ is computed for all $j$. Thus,

$$ES_5 = \max_{i=3,4}\{ES_i + D_{i5}\} = \max\{6 + 3, 6 + 7\} = 13$$
$$ES_6 = \max_{i=3,4,5}\{ES_i + D_{i6}\}$$
$$= \max\{6 + 2, 6 + 5, 13 + 6\} = 19$$

These calculations complete the forward pass, and all values are entered in column 3.

*Backward Pass.* The backward pass starts from the "end" event. The objective of this phase is to compute $LC_i$, the *latest completion* time for all the activities coming into event $i$. Thus, if $i = n$ is the "end" event, $LC_n = ES_n$ initiates the backward pass. In general, for any node $i$,

$$LC_i = \min_j\{LC_j - D_{ij}\}$$
for all defined $(i,j)$ activities

The values of $LC$ entered in the sixth column of the table are determined as follows:

$$LC_6 = ES_6 = 19$$
$$LC_5 = LC_6 - D_{56} = 19 - 6 = 13$$
$$LC_4 = \min_{j=5,6}\{LC_j - D_{4j}\} = \min\{13 - 7, 19 - 5\}$$
$$= \min\{6, 14\} = 6$$
$$LC_3 = \min_{j=4,5,6}\{LC_j - D_{3j}\}$$
$$= \min\{6 - 0, 13 - 3, 19 - 2\} = 6$$
$$LC_2 = \min_{j=3,4}\{LC_j - D_{2j}\} = \min\{6 - 3, 6 - 2\} = 3$$
$$LC_1 = LC_2 - D_{12} = 3 - 3 = 0$$

This completes the backward pass calculations. In this backward procedure, note that $LC_6 = ES_6$. It would be possible to select another value for $LC_6$ as the target date of the project to provide for additional slack or whenever a due date is specified by other considerations.

The critical path activities can now be identified by using the results of the forward and backward passes. An activity $(i,j)$ lies on the critical path if it satisfies the following three conditions:

(i)     $ES_i = LC_i$
(ii)    $ES_j = LC_j$
(iii)   $ES_j - ES_i = LC_j - LC_i = D_{ij}$

These conditions actually indicate that there is no float or slack time between the earliest start (completion) and the latest start (completion) of the activity.

Activities (1,2) (2,3), (3,4), (4,5), and (5,6) define the critical path in Fig. N-10. This yields the shortest possible time to complete the project. Notice that activities (2,4), (3,5), (3,6), and (4,6) satisfy conditions (i) and (ii) for critical activities, but not condition (iii). Hence, they are not critical. Notice also that the critical path must form a sequence of connected activities which spans the network from initial event to final event.

*Determination of the Floats.* After the critical path has been determined, the floats for the noncritical activities must be computed. A critical activity must have a zero float.

Two new times are associated with each activity and must be defined. They are the *latest start (LS)*

767

and the *earliest completion* (EC) times, which are defined for activity $(i,j)$ by

$$LS_{ij} = LC_j - D_{ij}$$
$$EC_{ij} = ES_i + D_{ij}$$

There are two important types of floats: *total float* (TF) and *free float* (FF). The total float $TF_{ij}$ for activity $(i,j)$ is the difference between the maximum time available to perform the activity ($= LC_j - ES_i$) and its duration ($= D_{ij}$); that is,

$$TF_{ij} = LC_j - ES_i - D_{ij}$$
$$= LC_j - EC_{ij} = LS_{ij} - ES_i$$

The free float is defined by assuming that all the activities start as early as possible. In this case, $FF_{ij}$ for activity $(i,j)$ is the excess of available time ($= ES_j - ES_i$) over its duration ($= D_{ij}$); that is,

$$FF_{ij} = ES_j - ES_i - D_{ij}$$

The critical path calculations together with the floats for the noncritical activities are summarized in Table N-1. Columns 1, 2, 3, and 6 are obtained from the network calculations of the previous section. The remaining information can be determined from the equations given in this section.

The table gives a typical summary of the critical path calculations. It includes all the information necessary to construct the time chart. Notice that a critical activity, and only a critical activity, must have zero total float. The free float must also be zero when the total float is zero. The converse is not true, however, in the sense that a *noncritical* activity may have zero free float. Table N-1 shows that the total float is the same as the free float. This is accidental, since all the events of the project happen to be on the critical path. In general, this will not be true.

The positive values in the float columns of Table N-1 indicate the amount of time that the corresponding activity may be extended without affecting the duration of the project. For example, activity (4,6) may be extended from 5 to 13 without delaying the project, and the resources available for use in activity (4,6) may be partially utilized elsewhere.

## PROGRAM EVALUATION AND REVIEW TECHNIQUE (PERT)

Previously known as Polaris evaluation review technique, PERT was developed in 1958 to assist the U.S. Navy in development and production of the Polaris missile system. Since the existing facilities for integrated planning and control were not suitable for this assignment, Admiral W. F. Raborn sought the help of Lockheed Aircraft Corporation, the Navy Special Projects Office, and the consulting firm of Booz, Allen and Hamilton. This team evolved the PERT system from the consideration of techniques such as line of balance, Gantt charts, and "milestone reporting systems."

PERT involves considerations of duration times of activities which are subject to considerable variation. PERT provides the means to deal with these variations, making it possible to allow for choices in scheduling activities. PERT is used as a basis for determining the probability that the project, or key milestones in the project, are to be completed on or before scheduled date(s).

The sources of uncertainty in activity completion times may stem from uncertainties in personnel (absenteeism, vacations, strikes), equipment (breakdown, acquisitions), facilities (delays in installation), materials (supplier delays), utilities (energy shortages, power breakdowns), and environmental

**TABLE N-1**

| Activity $(i,j)$ (1) | Duration $D_{ij}$ (2) | Earliest | | Latest | | Total float $TF_{ij}$ (7) | Free float $FF_{ij}$ (8) |
|---|---|---|---|---|---|---|---|
| | | Start $ES_i$ (3) | Completion $EC_{ij}$ (4) | Start $LS_{ij}$ (5) | Completion $LC_j$ (6) | | |
| (1,2) | 3 | 0 | 3 | 0 | 3 | 0* | 0 |
| (2,3) | 3 | 3 | 6 | 3 | 6 | 0* | 0 |
| (2,4) | 2 | 3 | 5 | 4 | 6 | 1 | 1 |
| (3,4) | 0 | 6 | 6 | 6 | 6 | 0* | 0 |
| (3,5) | 3 | 6 | 9 | 10 | 13 | 4 | 4 |
| (3,6) | 2 | 6 | 8 | 17 | 19 | 11 | 11 |
| (4,5) | 7 | 6 | 13 | 6 | 13 | 0* | 0 |
| (4,6) | 5 | 6 | 11 | 14 | 19 | 8 | 8 |
| (5,6) | 6 | 13 | 19 | 13 | 19 | 0* | 0 |

*Critical activity.

conditions (temperature, snow, climatic conditions).

PERT uses probability theory in developing schedules to meet managerial objectives. Although the activities are specified, there is uncertainty in activity times. In the PERT system, three time estimates are obtained for each activity:

$a$ = the optimistic time, which will be required if execution goes extremely well.

$b$ = the pessimistic time, which will be required if everything goes badly.

$m$ = the most likely time, which will be required if execution is as expected.

The person most qualified to know, such as an engineer, a supervisor, or a worker, is requested to provide the estimates. The pessimistic estimate is based on the worst situation which may be encountered, where usual conditions are not likely to prevail. The optimistic estimate is based on the best possible situation, where everything goes right.

The range of times given by $(b-a)$ provides an indication of the degree of uncertainty associated with the time to perform an activity. The analyst is interested in deriving the probability distributions for the activity and project completion times. It is not possible to specify a definite time for the completion of a project; however, it is possible to state the probability of completing the project on or before a scheduled date. Utilizing the information on cost of not meeting a scheduled due date and the cost of expediting the project, managers are able to develop sound plans at the start of a project and to control the project once it is under way.

The expressions for the mean $\bar{D}$ and variance $V$ are

$$\bar{D} = \frac{a + 4m + b}{6} \quad \text{and} \quad V = \left(\frac{b - a}{6}\right)^2$$

The network calculations given in CPM can now be applied directly, with $\bar{D}$ replacing the single estimate $D$.

It is possible now to estimate the probability of occurrence of each event in the network. Let $\mu_i$ be the earliest occurrence time of event $i$. Since the times of the activities completed prior to $i$ are random variables, $\mu_i$ is also a random variable. Let us assume that all the activities in the network are statistically independent; then we obtain the mean and variance of $\mu_i$ as follows. If there is only one path leading from the "start" event to event $i$, $E\{\mu_i\}$ is given by the sum of the expected durations $\bar{D}$ for the activities along this path, and var$\{\mu_i\}$ is the sum of the variances of the same activities. Complications arise, however, where more than one path leads to the same event. In this case, if the exact $E\{\mu_i\}$ and var$\{\mu_i\}$ are to be computed, we must first develop the statistical distribution for the longest of the different paths (that is, the distribution of the maximum of several random variables) and then find its expected value and its variance. This is rather difficult in general, and a simplifying assumption is introduced which estimates $\{\mu_i\}$ and var$\{\mu_i\}$ as equal to those of the path leading to event $i$ and having the largest sum of expected activity durations. If two or more paths have the same $E\{\mu_i\}$, the one with the largest var$\{\theta_i\}$ is selected since it reflects greater uncertainty and hence more conservative results. To summarize, $E\{\mu_i\}$ and var$\{\mu_i\}$ are given for the selected path by

$$E\{\mu_i\} = \sum_k \bar{D}_k$$
$$\text{Var}\{\mu_i\} = \sum_k V_k$$

where $k$ defines the activities along the longest path leading to $i$.

As $\mu_i$ is the sum of independent random variables, according to the central limit theorem, $\mu_i$ is approximately normally distributed with mean $E\{\mu_i\}$ and variance var$\{\mu_i\}$. Since $\mu_i$ represents the earliest occurrence time, event $i$ will meet a certain schedule time $ST_i$, specified by management with probability

$$P\{\mu_i \leq ST_i\} = P\left\{\frac{\mu_i - E\{\mu_i\}}{\sqrt{\text{var}\{\mu_i\}}} \leq \frac{ST_i - E\{\mu_i\}}{\sqrt{\text{var}\{\mu_i\}}}\right\}$$
$$= P\{z \leq K_i\}$$

where $z$ is the standard normal distribution with mean zero and variance unity and

$$K_i = \frac{ST_i - E\{\mu_i\}}{\sqrt{\text{var}\{\mu_i\}}}$$

It is common practice to compute the probability that event $i$ will occur no later than its $LC_i$. Such probabilities will thus represent the chance that the succeeding events will occur within the $(ES_i, LC_i)$ duration.

**A PERT Example** Consider the project of the example given in Fig. N-10. To avoid repeating the critical path calculations, the values of $a$, $b$, and $m$ shown are selected such that $\bar{D}_{ij}$ will have the same value as its corresponding $D_{ij}$ in the example in Fig. N-10. The mean $\bar{D}_{ij}$ and variance $V_{ij}$ for the different activities are computed as shown in Table N-2.

The probabilities are given in Table N-3. The information in the $ST_i$ column is part of the input data.

**PERT Extensions: Alternative Near-Critical Paths** The estimate of completion time of a project, using the times along the critical path, may not be a valid estimate of the project duration. A non-critical path may become critical if it has a higher variance than the "original" critical path. Accordingly, it would be desirable to investigate alternate near-critical paths. In these cases, estimates based on a single path may seriously underestimate the actual completion time up to 20 percent.

**TABLE N-2**

| Activity $(i,j)$ | Estimated times $(a,b,m)$ | Activity $(i,j)$ | Estimated times $(a,b,m)$ |
|---|---|---|---|
| (1,2) | (2,8,2) | (3,6) | (1,3,2) |
| (2,3) | (1,11,1.5) | (4,5) | (6,8,7) |
| (2,4) | (0.5,7.5,1) | (4,6) | (3,11,4) |
| (3,5) | (1,7,2.5) | (5,6) | (4,8,6) |

| Activity | $\bar{D}_{ij}$ | $V_{ij}$ | Activity | $\bar{D}_{ij}$ | $V_{ij}$ |
|---|---|---|---|---|---|
| (1,2) | 3 | 1.00 | (3,6) | 2 | 0.11 |
| (2,3) | 3 | 2.78 | (4,5) | 7 | 0.11 |
| (2,4) | 2 | 1.36 | (4,6) | 5 | 1.78 |
| (3,5) | 3 | 1.00 | (5,6) | 6 | 0.44 |

Computer simulation is an excellent method for finding the expected completion time as well as the frequency distribution of completion times. In this case, activity times are randomly selected for each activity from the corresponding frequency distribution. The project path length and duration and critical path are then calculated in the usual (CPM)

**TABLE N-3**

| Event | Path | $E\{\mu_i\}$ | Var$\{\mu_i\}$ | $ST_i$ | $K_i$ | $P\{z \leqslant K_i\}$ |
|---|---|---|---|---|---|---|
| 1 | | | | | | |
| 2 | (1,2) | 3 | 1.00 | 2 | −1.000 | 0.159 |
| 3 | (1,2,3) | 6 | 3.80 | 5 | −0.512 | 0.304 |
| 4 | (1,2,3,4) | 6 | 3.80 | 6 | 0.000 | 0.500 |
| 5 | (1,2,3,4,5) | 13 | 3.91 | 17 | 2.020 | 0.978 |
| 6 | (1,2,3,4,5,6) | 19 | 4.35 | 20 | 0.480 | 0.584 |

way. The procedure is repeated several thousand times, using a computer program, and a record is kept of each run. An average project length and standard deviation are calculated on the basis of the simulation. The resulting simulation estimates are more reliable than the overly optimistic estimates produced by the standard (PERT) procedure, since the near-critical paths are considered in the simulation.

The simulation also provides a critical index for each activity. The critical index of an activity is the proportion of simulation runs in which the activity is critical. Although an activity may not be on the usual CPM critical path, it may have a critical index of, say, 0.5, indicating that 50 percent of the time it may be expected to be critical and therefore warrants managerial review. The simulation would also provide a probability estimation of slack values for each activity, again providing additional useful information for managerial review purposes.

## TIME-COST TRADE OFFS

Although PERT is able to schedule projects which allow for variations in activity times as a result of unpredictable situations, it is desirable to consider alternative project schedules which result from the planned use of resources at different levels. Activity times may be reduced if additional resources such as labor, machines, and money are allocated.

There may be increased costs associated with the *crashed* activities, which may result in a project being completed earlier, particularly in the case of critical activities. However, if the activity is not critical, and has slack (or total free float), then the activity should be accomplished at the most efficient rate, say in the normal time. Accordingly, only the critical activities need to be expedited, and in these cases, only those where the returns justify the additional expenditures.

The essential questions raised in time-cost trade offs for project scheduling are the following:

1. What is the optimal project duration and schedule?

2. Which activities should be expedited?

3. Of those activities to be expedited, what is their optimal completion times?

**Time-Cost Relationships** Project cost is composed of both direct and indirect costs. The direct costs are those associated with the individual activities, usually for elements such as labor, machine operation, and leased facilities. In addition, a project will have indirect costs such as managerial services, equipment rentals, and allocation of fixed expenses, which are affected adversely by the duration of the project. A project's contractor or customer may specify a due date, and delays beyond this date result in additional nonrecoverable costs to the project manager. For example, Lockheed's contract for the C-5A contained a $12,000-per-day late penalty clause, and General Dynamics received

$800,000 for flying the F-111 10 days ahead of schedule.

Project schedules may influence two kinds of costs: direct costs associated with individual activities, which *increase* if the activities are expedited, and indirect costs associated with the project, which *decrease* if the project is shortened.

**The Lowest Cost (Optimal) Project Schedule** From a managerial point of view, it is clear that there is an optimum project duration. The characteristic of the optimum is that it represents an intermediate schedule between one with excessive direct costs for shortening activities without a significant reduction in project duration and one with excessive indirect costs resulting in working many of the critical activities at their normal rates. The time-cost trade off analysis finds the optimum (least cost) schedule.

The general procedure involves defining the cost-time relationships and assigning the activities of the project their normal durations. The corresponding critical path is then computed and the associated costs are recorded. The next step is to consider reducing the duration of the project. Since such a reduction can be effected only if the duration of a critical activity is reduced, attention must be paid to such activities alone. In order to achieve a reduction in the duration at the least possible cost, one must compress as much as possible the critical activity having the smallest cost-time slope.

The amount by which an activity can be compressed is limited by its crash time. However, other limits must be taken into account before the exact compression amount can be determined.

The result of compressing an activity is a new schedule, perhaps with a new critical path. The cost associated with the new schedule must be greater than the immediately preceding one. The new schedule must now be considered for compression by selecting the (uncrashed) critical activity with the least cost-time slope. The procedure is repeated until all critical activities are at their crash times. The final result of the above calculations is a cost-time curve for the different schedules and their corresponding costs. A typical curve is shown in Fig. N-11 by a solid line, which represents the direct costs only.

As the duration of the project increases, the indirect costs also increase, as shown in Fig. N-11 by a dotted curve. The sum of these two costs (direct + indirect) gives the total cost of the project. The optimum schedule corresponds to the minimum total cost.

**Project Control: Review and Updating the Network Diagram** The network diagram should not be discarded when the time schedule is developed. In fact, an important use of the network diagram occurs during the execution phase of the project. It seldom happens that the planning phase will develop a time schedule that can be followed exactly during the execution phase. Quite often some of the activities are delayed or expedited. This naturally depends on actual work conditions. As soon as such disturbances occur in the original plan, it becomes necessary to develop a new time schedule for the remaining portion of the project.

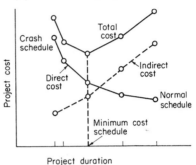

**Fig. N-11. Total cost chart.**

It is important to follow the progress of the project using the network diagram, rather than the time schedule alone. The time schedule is mainly used to check if each activity is on time. The effect of a delay in a certain activity on the remaining portion of the project can best be traced on the network diagram.

Suppose that as the project progresses over time, it is discovered that delays in some activities necessitate developing a completely new schedule. How can this be effected using the present network diagram? The immediate requirement is to update the network diagram by assigning zero values to the durations of the completed activities. Partially completed activities are assigned times equivalent to their unfinished portions. Changes in the network diagram such as addition or deletion of any future activities must also be made. By repeating the usual computations on the network diagram with its new time elements, one can determine the new time schedule and possible changes in the duration of the project. Such information is used until it is necessary to update the time schedule further. In real situations, many revisions of the time schedule are usually required at the early stages of the execution phase. A stable period then follows in which little revision of the current schedule is required.

## THE TIME CHART AND RESOURCE LEVELING

The end product of network calculations is the construction of the time chart (or schedule). The time chart can be converted easily into a calendar schedule.

The construction of the time chart must consider the limitations of the available resources, since it may not be possible to execute concurrent activities because of labor and equipment limitations. This is where the total floats for the noncritical activities become useful. Shifting a noncritical activity (back and forth) between earliest start (ES) and latest completion (LC) limits may make it possible to lower the project's maximum resource requirements. It is common practice to use total floats to level resources over the duration of the entire project, resulting in a steadier work force rather than one which varies drastically from one day to the next.

EXAMPLE: Figure N-12 shows a time chart corresponding to the data derived from a typical CPM analysis of Fig. N-10. The first step is to consider the scheduling of the critical activities. Next, the noncritical activities are considered by indicating their *ES* and *LC* time limits on the chart. The critical activities are shown with solid lines. The time ranges for the noncritical activities are shown by dashed lines, indicating that such activities may be scheduled anywhere within those ranges provided the precedence relationships are not disturbed. The dummy activity (3,4) consumes no time and hence is shown by a vertical solid line since

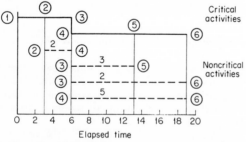

**Fig. N-12. Elapsed time chart.**

it is a critical activity. The numbers shown with the noncritical activities represent their durations. If resources are not an effective factor, each noncritical activity should be scheduled as early as possible.

This allows taking the utmost advantage of the float in case the execution of any of these activities is delayed unexpectedly.

In this example, suppose that the following labor requirements are specified for the different activities. It is necessary to develop a time schedule which will *level* these requirements during the project duration.

| Activity | No. of Workers | Activity | No. of Workers |
|----------|----------------|----------|----------------|
| (1,2) | 5 | (3,6) | 1 |
| (2,3) | 7 | (4,5) | 2 |
| (2,4) | 3 | (4,6) | 5 |
| (3,5) | 2 | (5,6) | 6 |

In Fig. N-13a, the labor requirements over time are shown, where the noncritical activities are scheduled as early as possible. In Fig. N-13b, the requirements are shown where these activities are scheduled as late as possible. The dotted line shows the requirements for the critical activities which must be satisfied if the project is to be completed on time.

The project requires at least 7 workers as indicated by the requirements of the critical activity (2,3). The earliest scheduling of the noncritical activities results in a maximum requirement of 10 workers, while the latest scheduling of the same

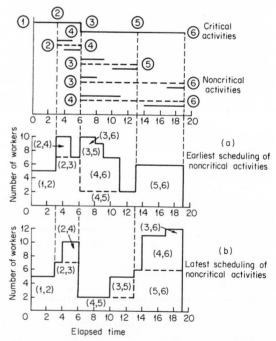

**Fig. N-13. Work force versus time schedule.**

activities sets the maximum requirements at 12 workers. This illustrates that the maximum requirements depend on how the total floats of the noncritical activities are used. However, regardless of how the floats are allocated the maximum requirement cannot be less than 10 workers. This follows since the range for activity (2,4) coincides with the time for the critical activity (2,3). The labor requirement using the earliest scheduling can be improved by rescheduling activity (3,5) at its latest possible time and activity (3,6) immediately after activity (4,6) is completed. This new requirement is shown in Fig. N-14. The new schedule has now resulted in a smoother allocation of resources.

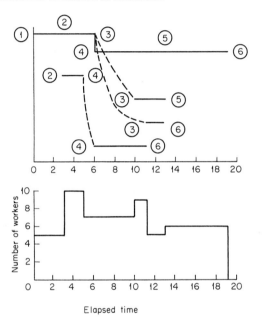

**Fig. N-14. Balancing work force versus time schedule.**

In some projects, the objective may be to keep the maximum resource utilization below a certain limit rather than merely to level the resources. If this cannot be accomplished by rescheduling the noncritical activities, it will be necessary to expand the time for some of the critical activities. This, however, may necessitate executing some activities in segments rather than as an entity.

## SPAR-1 RESOURCE ALLOCATION MODEL

A number of different resource allocation programs for scheduling large projects have been developed.

One of these, SPAR-1, illustrates how the basic model can be elaborated with additional heuristics.

SPAR-1 allocates available resources, period by period, to project jobs listed according to their early start times. Jobs are scheduled, starting with the first period, by selecting from the list of those currently available and sorted in order of their total slack (which is based on technological constraints only and normal resource assignments). The most critical jobs have the highest probability of being scheduled first, and as many of these jobs are scheduled as available resources permit. If an available job is not scheduled in that period, an attempt is made to schedule it the next period. Eventually, all jobs so postponed become critical and move to the top of the priority list of available jobs.

This basic program is modified by a number of additional scheduling heuristics (or subroutines) generally designed to increase the use of available resources and/or to decrease the length of the schedule. For simplicity in the description of these heuristics, we will refer to resources as *workers*, to the amount of resources applied to a job as the *crew size*, to a group of homogeneous resources as a *shop*, and to the scheduling period as a *day*. Any other units, of course, could be used in place of these.

**Crew Size**  With each job is associated a normal crew size, or the number of workers or other resources normally assigned to the job; a maximum crew size, or the maximum number of workers required for crashing the job; and a minimum crew size, or the smallest number of workers which can be assigned to the job. Normally, these three crew sizes will differ from one another. But in some cases two or all three of them may be equal, when jobs cannot be stretched out or crashed. The rules for crew size selection are as follows:

1. If a job to be scheduled is critical, it is placed on a priority list and given special treatment.

2. If sufficient workers are available, the job is scheduled at its maximum crew size; that is, it is crashed.

3. If insufficient workers are available to do so, or even to schedule the job at normal crew size, then an attempt is made to obtain the required workers by means of the "borrow and reschedule" routines described below.

4. If all efforts fail, however, and the job cannot be scheduled even at minimum crew size, then its early start date is delayed one period, and an attempt is made to schedule the job on the following day.

Jobs with sufficient positive slack (that is, noncritical jobs) are scheduled at normal crew size if the required number of workers are available; but if resources available are insufficient for scheduling even the minimum crew size, then the jobs are delayed for consideration until the next day.

**Augmenting Critical Jobs** Repeated attempts are made to speed up critical jobs—including those which become critical after being scheduled—which have crew sizes less than their maximum crew size. Before any new jobs are scheduled on a given day, jobs previously scheduled and still active are examined. If any of these is critical and has a crew size less than its maximum, and if resources are available, the job's crew size is increased as much as possible up to the maximum.

**Multiresource Jobs** Sometimes a job requires a number of different resources, such as workers of different skills, various machines, money, and so on, which may each be limited in quantity. For such multiresource jobs, separate jobs are created for each resource and the jobs are constrained to start on the same day with the same level of resource assignment—that is, normal, minimum, or maximum crew size.

**Borrowing from Active Jobs** If resources available are insufficient for scheduling some critical job J, then the model enters into a procedure for searching currently active jobs to see if sufficient workers can be borrowed from them for scheduling job J on that day. Workers are borrowed from a job only when the resultant stretching of the job will not delay the entire project.

**Rescheduling Active Jobs** Sometimes a critical job J can be scheduled if previously scheduled jobs which use the same resources have been postponed to a later time. The model scans the list of currently active jobs and picks out those which could be postponed without delaying the project due date. If sufficient workers can be obtained in this way and/or from the borrowing procedure described earlier, then job J is scheduled and the necessary adjustments are made in previous assignments.

**Adding on Unused Resources** After as many jobs as possible are scheduled on a given day, there still may be unused resources in some of the shops for that day. The model compiles a list of active jobs to which these resources may be assigned (that is, jobs which require these resources and which have assigned crew sizes less than the maximum crew size possible). It arranges these jobs in ascending order of their total slack. Proceeding down the list, the model increases the crew size of these jobs until the unused resources or the list of jobs is exhausted. The increment, however, is temporary; jobs supplemented in this way return to their assigned crew size the next day, unless unused resources are still available.

After going through the above scheduling routines each day, SPAR-1 records the results in a work force loading table which notes the number of workers assigned on each job and in each shop, and it updates the critical path data; that is, the early and late start times, early and late finish times, and total slack. Note that several of the above routines may alter a job's criticality; for example, when the maximum crew size is assigned to a critical job, the shortening of the job may result in its gaining positive slack and perhaps some other job or jobs becoming critical.

SPAR-1 is able to accommodate single or multiple projects, variable crew sizes, jobs that can be split, variable shop limits, shift or nonshift scheduling, and various criteria functions for evaluating a schedule.

## PERT/COST: A NETWORK COSTING METHOD

As described above, both PERT and CPM are time-oriented methods, which estimate the time required to complete a project. As scheduling techniques they provide a means of establishing time schedules for project activity. As control methods they allow managers to check scheduled time against actual times for activity durations or event occurrences. In CPM, a cost-time trade off is considered, where costs are considered as a means of finding optimal activity times. No provision is made for compiling activity costs, either for predicting or control purposes. Thus the output of CPM models are optimal activity times (durations), generally associated with early or late start schedules.

PERT/COST is a general method for controlling the costs of projects. The basic concept of the PERT and CPM cost systems is simple but importantly different from activities; they should be divided into a sequence of two or more subactivities, each of which has a relatively constant expenditure rate. Then the cost per period of an activity may be approximated by dividing its total cost by its duration in periods. A project cost schedule is then prepared by adding all activity costs, period by period, according to the activity time schedule.

The PERT/COST method utilizes the CPM calculations for early and late start schedules. A month-by-month summary of cost requirements is calculated for both early and late start schedules. A schedule graph, in which the network is plotted on a time scale and in which the horizontal length and placement of activity arrows indicate activity duration and schedule, facilitates cost calculation.

When plotted as in Fig. N-15, the cumulative cost figures illustrate graphically the budget implications of the early and late start schedules. The area between the two curves represents a range of budgets which are feasible from a technological

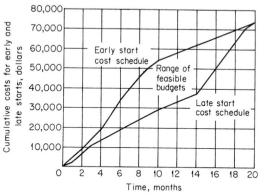

**Fig. N-15. PERT/COST budget projections.**

viewpoint. For budgetary or other reasons, it may be preferable to follow a relatively straight line of cumulative costs from start to finish. As long as this lies in the feasible region, it may be approximately achieved by juggling the scheduled starts of activities between their early and late start times.

The basic idea of the PERT/COST system is to measure and control costs in terms of the same entities of the project as are used for planning and scheduling purposes, that is, the activities. Actually, if a project has been broken down into activities small enough to be used for purposes of detailed planning and scheduling, many such activities will be too small to be used conveniently for cost control purposes. If so, several related activities may be grouped together into larger *work packages*, which represent particular units of work for which responsibility can be clearly defined and which are still small enough to be manageable for planning and control purposes.

**Applications**   For planning and budgeting purposes, it is useful for a manager to know what the time pattern of expenditures will be for a project. If costs are estimated for each activity or work package, then a projection of costs can easily be made, based upon an early start or a late start schedule or, for that matter, any other feasible schedule. To do this, the assumption is usually made that expenditures for an activity are incurred at a constant rate over the duration of the activity.

Project priority can also be viewed from a slightly different angle: How much is it going to cost if this project is not completed on time? How much can be saved or gained if it is completed ahead of time? The answers to these questions are crucial in the many areas of business where work projects are negotiated under bonus-penalty agreements.

Budget restrictions frequently limit the amount of expenditure in any one period, or certain critical resources; if workers, materials, machinery, and resource constraints are such that even the late start cost schedule cannot be met, then the finish date must be delayed and the activities must be scheduled according to methods such as those discussed for SPAR-1. Once a schedule has been found which is feasible in terms of both technology and resource availabilities, however, a cost schedule may be calculated and plotted as above. A computer may be used to advantage for large projects.

### RAMPS

This is a system for resource allocation and multiproject scheduling that incorporates the basic concepts of CPM; it uses the network for planning and relies on a careful analysis of the needs of each individual activity, but it also has unique features not found in CPM.

A unique feature of RAMPS is its ability to schedule more than one project *simultaneously*. The projects to be scheduled may differ in size, type of work, importance, and starting times. They are related only in their reliance on a common pool of resources.

RAMPS recognizes and responds to established priorities for the projects and competition among activities within all projects for limited quantities of available resources. The system also strives to meet established target completion dates by applying larger quantities of available resources to critical activities.

It should be emphasized that RAMPS attempts to complete each project as soon as possible by making the most efficient and appropriate use of time and resources. More specifically, RAMPS continually strives to:

1. Start and complete each activity at the earliest possible time.

2. Achieve a smooth rate of work accomplishment and resource utilization by "looking ahead" for possible bottlenecks.

3. Minimize idle resources.

4. Work simultaneously on as many activities as possible.

5. Give priority to critical activities.

6. Avoid interrupting work on an activity once it has been started.

In forming a schedule of work during a given time period, RAMPS is almost always confronted by conflicts among these objectives; rarely can they all be achieved at the same time. When there is conflict, the program must determine which of these objectives are to be satisfied at the necessary expense of excluding others.

## GERT NETWORK METHOD

PERT may be applied only in cases where (1) the activities to be performed are *known* in advance and (2) the project is completed only where *all* specified activities are performed. In some situations it is not possible or desirable to have these conditions satisfied. In these cases, such as in research and development (R&D) programs, the future work to be performed may be uncertain, and a rigid (deterministic) network should not be used in the planning process. It may be desirable to include optional or alternate activities in the planning process, where future choices may be made at an appropriate time.

Specifically, PERT imposes an assumption, which may be true in some cases, that *all* activities leading to an event must be completed prior to the event taking place. Also, PERT assumes that all activities following this event can be initiated only when all preceding activities have been performed. PERT does not permit the repetition of an activity, which may occur in many organizational projects: PERT deals only with *acyclic*, or nonrepetitive (noncyclic), projects. Finally, PERT permits the completion of the project to occur in only a single event and does not permit a multiplicity of possible outcomes or final states.

Because of PERT's shortcomings, the graphical evaluation and review technique (GERT) was introduced in 1966 as a network planning method to deal with situations satisfying the following requirements:

A network may be given as a stochastic (probabilistic) structure where some intermediate activities may not be successful.

An event may take place providing that only one of several activities be completed.

Repetition of an activity is permitted.

Parallel or sequential activities may be required to assure that the goal is reached.

Activity completion time depends on the successes and durations of sequential parallel activities.

Optional or choice activities may be available and specified.

A number of possible outcomes may occur.

A GERT network contains activities which (1) have a probability of occurrence, (2) have a choice of being performed, and (3) have variable completion times. GERT was introduced at the Rand Corporation in work performed for NASA on Project Apollo, the lunar landing program. It was found that the terminal countdown process on the launch of the Apollo space systems could be represented by a stochastic network utilizing GERT. Analytic methods were developed to handle the GERT networks.

**The GERT Approach** The properties of a stochastic network may be described as follows:

1. Each network consists of nodes denoting logical operations and arrows denoting activities.

2. An arrow has associated with it a probability that the activity represented by the network will be performed.

3. Other parameters describe the activities which the arrows represent. These parameters are usually additive, such as time or cost.

4. A realization of a network is a particular set of arrows and nodes which describes the network for one experiment.

5. If the time associated with an arrow is a random variable, then a realization also implies that a fixed time has been selected for each arrow.

GERT is used in planning the work undertaken in stochastic systems, in which both the realization of an activity and the time associated with it are probabilistic. The versatility of GERT as a networking technique is achieved, however, at the cost of increased mathematical complexity.

Areas of applications of GERT may be divided into two distinct categories:

1. GERT may be used as a framework for analysis of problems in the fields of probability, stochastic processes, and industrial engineering.

2. GERT may be used as a project management technique to analyze problems arising in various managerial settings, especially involving research and development. Figure N-16 illustrates a typical GERT construction.

Several applications have been identified for GERT in the field of marketing, including oil company sales negotiations and market research. For example, in planning a marketing research project using GERT, the activities and time distributions associated with each activity time are identified; using a simulation package, the completion time and

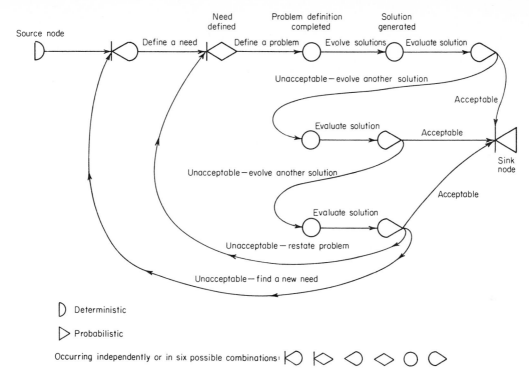

Fig. N-16. Example of GERT research planning model.

cost of the project, along with their corresponding distributions, are obtained. In another application, GERT was used in balancing resources and work load in a major jet engine overhaul unit at Kelly Air Force Base in Texas. In this case, the GERTS III QR simulator handled up to 10 different types of resources.

*See also* CONTROL SYSTEMS, MANAGEMENT; ENGINEERING MANAGEMENT; GANTT CHARTS; LINE OF BALANCE (LOB); PRODUCTION PLANNING AND CONTROL; PROJECT AND TASK FORCE MANAGEMENT.

## REFERENCES

Amiess, A. P., and W. A. Thompson: "PERT for Monthly Financial Closing," *Management Advisor*, January 1974, pp. 30–37.

Archibald, R. D., and R. L. Villoria: *Network Based Management Systems PERT/CPM*, John Wiley & Sons, Inc., New York, 1967.

Battersby, A.: *Network Analysis for Planning and Scheduling*, Macmillan & Co., Ltd., London, 1967.

Berman, E. B.: "Resource Allocation in a PERT Network under Continuous Activity Time-Cost Functions," *Management Science*, vol. 10, no. 4, July 1964, pp. 734–745.

Bird, Monroe M., et al.: "Sales Negotiation Cost Planning for Corporate Level Sales," *Journal of Marketing*, vol. 37, April 1973, pp. 7–13.

Branson, Michael H., and Bharat Shah: "On GERT Modeling of a Class of Finite Queuing Processes," *American Institute of Industrial Engineering Transactions*, vol. 4, no. 1, March 1972, pp. 43 and 47.

Charnes, A., W. W. Cooper, and G. L. Thompson: "Critical Path Analysis Via Chance Constrained and Stochastic Programming," *Operations Research*, vol. 12, no. 3, May–June 1964, pp. 460–470.

Clayton, Edward R., and Laurance J. Moore: "PERT vs. GERT," *Journal of Systems Management*, August 1972, pp. 18–21.

Crowston, W., and G. L. Thompson: "Decision CPM: A Method for Simultaneous Planning, Scheduling and Control of Projects," *Operations Research*, vol. 15, no. 3, May–June 1967, pp. 407–426.

Davis, E. W.: "Resource Allocation in Project Network Models—A Survey," *Journal of Industrial Engineering*, vol. XVII, no. 4, April 1966, pp. 177–188.

Dean, B. V.: *Applications of Operations Research in Research and Development*, John Wiley & Sons, Inc., New York, 1963.

Dean, B. V.: *Evaluating, Selecting, and Controlling R&D Projects*, American Management Association, Research Study 89, New York, 1968.

*DOD and NASA Guide, PERT COST Systems Design*, Secretary of Defense and National Aeronautics and Space Administration, Washington, June 1962.

Emaghraby, Salah E.: "The Theory of Networks and Management Science, Part I," *Management Science*, vol. 17, no. 1, September 1970, pp. 1–34.

Kelley, James E., Jr.: "The Critical Path Method: Resources Planning and Scheduling," in J. F. Math and G. L. Thompson (eds.), *Industrial Scheduling*, Prentice-Hall, Inc., Englewood Cliffs, N.J., 1963, chap. 21.

Levy, F. K., G. L. Thompson, and J. D. Wiest: "Multi-Ship, Multi-Shop, Workload Smoothing Program," *Naval Research Logistics Quarterly*, vol. 9, no. 1, March 1962, pp. 37–44.

Lukaszewicz, J.: "On the Estimation of Errors Introduced by Standard Assumptions Concerning the Distribution of Activity Duration in PERT Calculations," *Operations Research*, vol. 13, no. 2, March–April 1965, pp. 326–327.

MacCrimmon, K. R., and C. A. Ryavec: "An Analytical Study of the PERT Assumptions," *Operations Research*, vol. 12, no. 1, January–February 1964, pp. 16–37.

Maggard, Michael J. et al.: "Network Analysis with GERTS III QR," *Industrial Engineering*, May 1974, pp. 24–29.

Martino, R. L.: *Finding the Critical Path*, American Management Association, New York, 1964.

Martino, R. L.: *Resource Allocation and Scheduling*, American Management Association, Project Management and Control Series, vol. III, New York, 1965.

Miller, R. W.: *Schedule, Cost and Profit Control with PERT*, McGraw-Hill Book Company, New York, 1963.

Moder, J. J., and C. R. Phillips: *Project Management with CPM and PERT*, Reinhold Publishing Corporation, New York, 1970.

Moore, Laurence J., and Edward R. Clayton: *GERT Modeling and Simulation*, Fundamentals and Applications, Mason/Charter Publishers, Inc., New York, 1976.

Moshman, J., J. Johnson, and Madalyn Larsen: "RAMPS: A Technique for Resource Allocation and Multiproject Scheduling," *Proceedings of the 1963 Spring Joint Computer Conference*, New York.

Paige, H. W.: "How PERT-Cost Helps the General Manager," *Harvard Business Review*, vol. 41, no. 6, November–December 1963, pp. 87–95.

*PERT, Program Evaluation Research Task*, Phase I Summary Report, Special Projects Office, Bureau of Ordnance, no. 7, Department of the Navy, Washington, July 1958, pp. 646–669.

Pritsker, A. A. B.: "The Status of GERT," in H. Lombaers, ed., *Project Management by Network Analysis*, North-Holland Publishing Company, Amsterdam-London, 1970, pp. 147–153.

Robillard, P., and M. Traham: "The Completion Time of PERT Networks," *Operations Research*, vol. 25, no. 1, January–February 1977, pp. 15–28.

Samli, Coskun, and Carl Bellas: "The Use of GERT in the Planning and Control of Marketing Research," *Journal of Marketing Research*, vol. VIII, August 1971, pp. 335–339.

Sauls, Eugene: "The Use of GERT," *Journal of Systems Management*, February 1972, pp. 11–19.

Wiest, J. D.: "Some Properties of Schedules for Large Projects with Limited Resources," *Operations Research*, vol. 12, no. 3 May–June 1964, pp. 395–418.

Wiest, J. D., and F. K. Levy: *A Management Guide to PERT/CPM*, 2d ed., Prentice-Hall, Inc., Englewood Cliffs, N.J., 1977.

BURTON V. DEAN, *Case Western Reserve University*

## Noise, channel (*See* MARKETING, CHANNELS OF DISTRIBUTION.)

## Nondurable goods (*See* MARKETS, CLASSIFICATIONS AND MARKET ANALYSIS.)

## Nonstore retailing (*See* RETAILING MANAGEMENT.)

## Norm modification [*See* ORGANIZATION DEVELOPMENT (OD).]

## Norms, group (*See* INTERPERSONAL RELATIONSHIPS.)

## Norms for behavior (*See* CONFORMITY IN MANAGEMENT.)

## Not-for-profit managers (*See* MANAGER, DEFINITIONS OF.)

## Not-for-profit organizations, management of

All organizations, whether they are for-profit businesses, not-for-profit corporations, or government, have more in common in terms of management functions than they have differences. Of the three groups, the government has the most dissimilarities and will not be treated here. But the basic functions of managing any corporation—planning, organizing, financing, communications, etc.—are common to all organizations.

It is the author's view that management in a not-for-profit environment is the most difficult of the three possibilities. This tends to be true in many aspects, but in two functional areas in particular, communications and revenue management, this is quite clearly the case.

**Communications**　The communications function in a not-for-profit organization is more difficult than in a for-profit corporation for a number of reasons:

1. A large and diversified constituency.
2. Intangible nature of the results.
3. Broader and more diffuse objectives.
4. Volunteerism. The constituency is related to the institution in an avocational way rather than in a direct, formal way.

Nonprofit corporations are normally established to serve the secondary goals of a large number of organizations or individuals. Furthermore, they are not judged on the bottom line of a profit statement but on the *perception* of the effectiveness of their efforts in what is often an unending battle. Communications, therefore, are both more difficult and more critical.

**Revenue Management**　Income is important to any organization, since it determines the level of effort to be invested in the activity. For-profit corporations call the income-producing function *marketing* or *sales;* nonprofit organizations would be wise to do likewise. Selling memberships or otherwise generating operating funds takes the highest priority, and it is often the most difficult of all management assignments. The product being sold is among the most intangible. The benefits to the member are indirect at best and often very vague.

The mark of every successful not-for-profit organization is a well-organized and well-run marketing function. The sales staff is well paid, well managed, and well motivated.

There are tens of thousands of not-for-profit organizations in this country. Many are direct competitors. Many come and go, and many never get beyond a one- or two-person staff. Close examination will show that the key variable between the successful institutions and the also-rans is the ability to generate funds successfully and continuously.

Additionally, as a general rule, a continuous *growth* in revenue is almost essential. The many benefits associated with dynamic growth contrast sharply with stagnation or decline.

**Planning**　Planning begins with the statement of and understanding of the mission of the organization. Even the mission needs to be periodically reexamined in light of past success or failure and in light of change in the external environment. One thing that makes planning especially important in a not-for-profit organization is again the intangible nature of its goals and objectives. These goals and objectives are often unattainable in the short run. Therefore, the planning process becomes essential not only for determining a course of action but also for evaluating performance.

**Personnel Management**　Attracting and retaining good people is often made more difficult in the case of not-for-profits because of the "lowest common denominator syndrome." It is not unusual, for example, for the volunteer board of directors of a not-for-profit organization to set salary scales lower for that organization than they would accept in their own companies. This practice is rationalized by excuses such as, "Well, they are not really out there on the firing line, forced to meet a payroll and make a profit." The truth of the matter often is that the lowest common denominator becomes the benchmark because the directors do not want to insult any of their peers who come from a company where the salary scale is below average.

Fortunately, there are also many cases on the other side of that coin. Not-for-profit organizations that have a reputation for paying well are in the minority but are not rare. Usually in that minority, good managers who recognized the value of good people have stamped their imprint on the organization.

**Consensus-Building Skills**　The lowest common denominator syndrome also affects policy. As the constituency of, for example, a trade association grows larger and more diverse, the potential power of the organization's voice grows stronger. But at the same time, the increasing difficulty of achieving consensus makes it harder for the organization to say anything at all. Therefore, the manager of many not-for-profit's will have a greater need for the consensus-building skills of the politician than does the manager of a profit-oriented corporation.

**Staff Versus Volunteer Responsibilities**　The lowest common denominator syndrome does the most damage in those situations where the paid staff are unable or unwilling to make certain that the lines of division between the responsibilities of the staff and the responsibilities of the volunteers are clear and well enunciated. This, then, is a final function of the top management of a not-for-profit. While simple in concept, it can be complex in implementation and devastating if ignored. Volunteers serve on a part-time or once-in-a-while basis; the work goes on every day. The organization will fail miserably if careful attention is not paid to the matter of clearly dividing the responsibility and authority between the staff and the volunteers.

*See also* BUDGETS AND BUDGET PREPARATION; HEALTH INSTITUTIONS, MANAGEMENT OF HOSPITAL ADMINISTRATION; PUBLIC ADMINISTRATION.

REFERENCE

Fulmer, Robert M.: "Principles of Association Management," American Society of Association Executives and Chamber of Commerce of the United States, Washington, 1975.

RICHARD L. LESHER, *Chamber of Commerce of the United States*

**Numerical control** (*See* AUTOMATION; PRODUCTION PROCESSES.)

## Objectives  <small>(*See* MANAGEMENT THEORY, SCIENCE, AND APPROACHES.)</small>

## Objectives, management by (MBO)

The system of *management by objectives* (MBO) is a process whereby the superior and subordinate managers jointly identify the organization's common goals, define each individual's major areas of responsibility in terms of results expected, and use these measures as guides for operating the unit and assessing the contribution of each of its members.

Typically, MBO starts at the top of the organization, where a sequence is established for setting and reviewing objectives. This sequence comprises a rudimentary calendar of events that take place cyclically in 2-year periods.

### HOW TO SET STRATEGIC OBJECTIVES

The first step in goal setting is to determine the ordinary calendar of events which must be followed in the organization where MBO is to become the prevailing management system. This entails, as shown in Table O-1, some events that occur prior to the beginning of the target year and some events which will occur during that year.

**Management by Anticipation** This term is used to describe those goal-setting actions which are required of staff departments such as personnel, engineering, legal, traffic, finance, controller, and similar staff functions.

*Collect Audit Information.* This information, which includes program audits and overall reviews of the major strengths and weaknesses of each staff responsibility, should be reviewed to provide a basis for finding major opportunities and problems.

*Prepare 5-Year Plan.* The annual edition of the company's 5-year plan should be prepared for each of the major areas of responsibility. Thus the annual edition of the 5-year personnel plan, financial plan, technical plan, and the like should be prepared at a period about 3 months in advance of budget submission. For a company with a fiscal year starting in January, the close-off date for the annual 5-year plan would thus be about July 1 of the prior year. This permits an opportunity to revise budgetary plans, move resources to new uses, find new funding requirements, and make decisions about the abandonment of programs or plans.

*Issue Annual Budgets.* With audit information reviewed and the annual edition of the 5-year plan written and circulated, resources can be allocated. It permits more rational commitments of resources, including the use of zero-based budgeting for support services and cost-effectiveness methods for facility and program decisions.

**TABLE O-1   Calendar Illustrating the Rudimentary MBO Strategic Planning Cycle**
(For organizations on a calendar-year operating basis)

| Date | Event | Comments/responsibilities |
|---|---|---|
| July 1 | Prepare annual edition of the 5-year plan and review prior year's 5-year plan. | Responsibility of the top staff member and all major functional (staff) heads, assembled by planning department. |
| October 1 | Submit budget to budget decision group (for the following year). | Upward from all units, starting with sales forecast, cost estimates, and profit forecast to budgeteer. |
| | Review, revise, approve final budget figures. | Executive committee |
| January 1 | Start the new budget year; release resources. | Issue detailed, approved financial targets in final form. |
| January 15 to February 1 | Complete individual operational objectives at all levels. | Sets standards for managerial performance for the year. |
| | Annual goals conference by managers of departments. | To share goals and devise teamwork. |
| | Annual message of the president. | To give a challenge |
| April to July 1 October 1 | Quarterly reviews of individual results against goals; make adjustments as required. | All managers at all levels. |
| April 15 | Audits-including program | Staff departments |
| Monthly | Hold meetings of the executive and finance committee to note exceptions and make corrective moves. | |
| Passim (or throughout) | Circulate and discuss position papers and note policy committee actions as major issues. | By staff experts or any responsible manager or professional or functional group. |
| July 1 | Repeat the process. | |

**Strategic Objectives**   The three steps in management by anticipation are essential for the effective functioning of MBO. They assure that sound strategic objectives are in hand before operational objectives are chosen. *Without strategic objectives stated in advance, measurable operational objectives may not be valid. The organization may simply be running a well-run bankruptcy.*

In formulating strategic objectives, the following points should be considered:

Strategic objectives should be stated in advance of budgetary decisions.

Strategic objectives should define strengths, weaknesses, problems, threats, risks, and opportunities.

Strategic objectives should note trends and missions and define strategic options, including consequences of each option.

Good strategic objectives will answer the question, "Are we doing the right things?" in contrast to the operational objectives which define "how to do things right."

Strategic anticipation staff goals need not necessarily be measurable, but both words and numbers should be used with clarity to define long-run outcomes sought. Strategic goals are often established by groups such as the board of directors, the management committee, personnel policy committee, and the like. An example of a strategic goal statement might be: Apex Corporation will become the leading seller of solid-state monitoring devices in the field by 1983.

As shown in Table O-2, specific questions are answered or anticipated in the strategic goals statement of every staff department and major business unit.

## HOW TO SET OPERATIONAL OBJECTIVES

At the beginning of the operational year, each manager and subordinate manager conducts a formal dialogue on specific operational objectives for the coming year for the subordinate position. Prior to the discussion, each reviews the present situation, the results of the previous year, and some of the more likely requirements for change. Each thus comes to the discussion prepared to make commitments and to assume and delegate responsibilities.

*The superior* is armed with information about budget limitations, strategic goals which have been agreed upon, plus information about actual results obtained in the prior period.

*The subordinate* comes with some expectations and knowledge of his or her own performance strengths, weaknesses, and problems, as well as threats, risks, and opportunities.

**Management by Commitment** Operational management by objectives adds a new dimension to the previous management by anticipation, which is the subordinate's face-to-face relationship with the superior and, through that superior, with the organization itself. This is management by commitment.

---

**TABLE O-2  Format for Annual Strategic Objectives Statements**

Statement should
1. Be prepared 3 months in advance of budgeting decisions.
2. Come up from below as proposed alternative strategies.
3. Be prepared annually at *half-year*.

| OUTLINE FOR STATEMENT DEVELOPMENT | COMMENTS |
|---|---|
| 1.  Describe the present condition, statistically and verbally (and *add your professional opinion*) of:<br>　*a. Internal* strengths, weaknesses, and problems.<br>　*b. External* threats, risks, and opportunities.<br>2. Project today's trends: If we did not do anything differently in this area, where would we be in 1, 2, 5 years? (Do you like this possible outcome?)<br>3. What are we in business for? Who are our clients? What is our product? What should it be? | |

| 4. What are some optional strategies? | What would the consequences be? | | |
|---|---|---|---|
| | Contribution | Costs | Feasibility |
| *a.* Do nothing differently.<br>*b.* _____<br>*c.* _____<br>*d.* _____<br>*e.* _____<br>*f.* _____ | | | |
| (Press for multiple options) | | | |
| 5. Recommended action plan: To be turned into *strategic objectives*. | | | |

*Commitment* means making some promises of responsibility to somebody else whose opinion is important. This commitment is not general but specific, explicit, measurable, and worthwhile.

*Responsibility* means additionally the acceptance of full accountability for the outcomes produced during the commitment period, without reference to excuses or exculpatory explanations. Such a commitment does not guarantee that the responsible person will not fail for reasons beyond control. But regardless, this person assumes a "results" responsibility. This kind of responsibility implies adult behavior, professional effort, and mature self-control.

The superior is also committed. If the superior agrees in advance that the proposed operating goals are meritorious, then those objectives must also be accepted as the criteria for judging performance at the end of the period. Thus, committed objectives could also include salary adjustments and merit-pay recommendations, bonus awards, appraisal, promotability notations, and similar rewards for achievement. In accepting objectives in the beginning, the superior thus cannot apply capricious or ex post judgments.

*The key to management by commitment is that the hard bargaining about what constitutes excellence of performance is done up front, before the period begins, and not after a year or so of effort.*

The process by which the operating goals (commitments) are established consists of (1) a dialogue and (2) a memorandum. The dialogue is one in which each brings something. It is neither solely top down nor solely bottom up, but a genuine discussion. It is most satisfactory when it is conducted on an adult-adult level rather than a parent-child model. The memorandum confirms the dialogue in specific terms and written form.

## HOW TO WRITE OBJECTIVES FOR COMMITMENT

Operating objectives should constitute an ascending scale of excellence by which the manager can administer certain ongoing concerns in managing managers. For the subordinate it should be comprised of a series of levels of excellence. This is best accomplished when the superior has criteria for making year-end decisions for purposes of compensation, personnel records, defining promotability and assignments, coaching and training subordinates, and administering discipline and delegation.

For the subordinate, there are five questions to be answered or resolved:

What is expected of me? Let me know in advance.

What help and resources will be available to me in my work?

How much freedom may I expect, and what reporting times and form should I assume?

How can I tell how well I am doing in my work while I am doing it?

Upon what performance bases will rewards be issued?

Answers to these questions are best provided by placing them within a framework of three major goal categories. The commitment objectives should be written to cover all three.

*Category 1. Define* what the *regular responsibilities* of the position will be. These are the ongoing, recurring, repetitive, and measurable objectives of the job. These may range from dollar volume of sales at executive levels to units per shift at the supervisory level.

*Category 2. Identify the major problems* that should be attacked and solved in this position during the coming period. A problem can be a specific persistent deviation from a standard or simply something that somebody important wants to have fixed.

*Category 3. Specify the innovations* that will be attempted. These are not reactive but proactive goals. They are improvements, betterments, projects which will cause the organization under the subordinate's control to operate better, cheaper, faster, safer, at higher quality, or with greater dignity to people.

## SOME TYPICAL PERFORMANCE MEASURES

Starting with the regular objectives (category 1) of the general manager and his or her key subordinates, the goals chosen should lock the organization together through key indicators. Table O-3 shows a division general manager's sample objectives of an ongoing, recurring character together with related output indicators. Indicators of the regular category for this position include the following:

Dollar volume of revenue per month

Return on investment per quarter

Cash on hand at quarter end

Receivables, average age in days per quarter

Inventory, average dollar level over the quarter

Budget deviations as a percentage on capital budgets

Growth in dollar volume per quarter

Labor stoppages per year

**TABLE O-3   Example of Regular Objectives and their Key Output Indicators**

NAME _____ PERIOD _____

GENERAL MANAGER
REGULAR-BASIC INDICATOR OBJECTIVES

| Responsibility | | Level of Result Sought | | |
|---|---|---|---|---|
| Output indicator | Time period | Pessimistic | Normal realistic | Optimistic |
| 1. Dollar volume of revenue per month | Quarter | | | |
| 2. Profit: ROI<br>Dollar volume per month | Quarter<br>Quarter | | | |
| 3. Cash at month's end, dollars | Quarter | | | |
| 4. Receivables: Dollars at month's end<br>Days | Quarter<br>Quarter | | | |
| 5. Inventory: Dollars at month's end<br>Turn-over days | Quarter<br>Quarter | | | |
| 6. Capital budget, percent deviation | Quarter | | | |
| 7. Labor problems—Step 4 grievances | Quarter | | | |
| 8. Share of Market, percent | Quarter | | | |
| 9. Other _____ | _____ | | | |

RESULTS SCORE SHEET

| Target no. | First quarter | Second quarter | Third quarter | Fourth quarter | Total |
|---|---|---|---|---|---|
| 1 | | | | | |
| 2 | | | | | |
| 3 | | | | | |
| 4 | | | | | |
| 5 | | | | | |
| 6 | | | | | |
| 7 | | | | | |
| 8 | | | | | |
| | | | | | |
| | | | | | |
| | | | | | |

There are no standard indicators, but those listed were found to be common among a sample of 50 general managers. Further study of Table O-3 highlights several features of operating regular objectives.

1. They are stated as *outputs for a time period.* Statements of *activities* to be performed are not objectives; they are means.

2. The specific number chosen to quantify an objective should be stated as a range. Start by establishing the middle figure first to define *normal realities.* Let the subordinate set the optimistic, or stretch, objectives. The superior chooses the pessimistic figure. This lower figure fixes the *exception point* at which the subordinate knows that the superior should be notified that things are not going according to plan. The middle point is usually based upon history, estimates, or industrial engineering studies or sales forecasts.

3. When deviations occur, the subordinate should *(a)* know it before anyone else, *(b)* know why the deviation has occurred, *(c)* take corrective action where it is possible, and *(d)* notify a superior and request help at an early instance.

4. On the other hand, when the subordinate is attaining the middle-level (normal realistic) goals, he or she should be left alone to operate without interference.

Problem-solving objectives (category 2) might look like those illustrated in Table O-4. It is usually

**TABLE O-4   Requirements of Problem-Solving and Innovative Goals Statements**

Category 2. Statement of problem-solving objective

1. Present condition or situation
2. Desired condition or objective if the problem is solved satisfactorily
3. Time commitment (always state as a range: pessimistic, realistic, optimistic)

Category 3. Statement of innovative project commitment

1. Present condition or situation
2. Innovation to be attempted
3. Results sought (condition which would exist if the innovation were to work well)
4. Time commitment (always state dates: pessimistic, realistic, optimistic)

wise to limit these commitments to one or two major problems that define the following:

   Present level or condition
   Desired level or condition

Date when problem is to be corrected (brought to the desired level)

Examples of innovative objectives (category 3) are also shown in Table O-4. These goals provide a statement of the present condition, the desired condition, and some time frame for the proactive, innovative goals to be attained, perhaps including some stages of study or development.

**Organizational Objectives** The example given of the general manager's objectives must, of course, be supplemented (and complemented) by specific and explicit objectives for each of the key subordinates who report to the general manager. The manufacturing manager, for example, might have a commitment to these regular objectives (category 1) as measured by key output indicators:

   Average daily output per month
   Units per shift per month
   Indirect labor as a percent of direct labor per month
   Factory overhead as a percent of total overhead per month
   Average quality-reject rate per month
   Warranty and policy costs per month
   Number of step 4 grievances per quarter
   Overtime hours per week per quarter
   Hours of supervisory training per quarter

The sales manager, on the other hand, does not have the same objectives as either the general manager or the manufacturing manager except for a few key result areas. The sales manager's objectives might include the following indicators:

   Dollar volume per month and per quarter
   Costs of producing the revenue per month and per quarter
   New products introduced
   Dollar level of bad debts per quarter
   Days of sales training conducted per quarter
   New customers added per quarter
   Lost accounts per quarter

For each person reporting to the general manager, there are indicators which are unique to that position, but they follow a similar format: (1) Indicators of output for the time period, stated in ranges, and including (2) problem-solving and (3) innovative goals.

## AUDIT AND REVIEW OF OBJECTIVES

Two forms of systematic evaluation are important in MBO: periodic audits and continuing and annual reviews.

**Periodic Audit** The periodic audit is essentially a financial audit of a comprehensive nature, usually based upon a sampling of the numerically stated realities of the situation. It is closely related to the strategic objectives of the organization. It can be performed by professional internal auditors or by an outside audit group, such as a CPA firm. Program audits should be performed periodically not only for financial results and practices but for *program* operations as well.

Personnel audits and work force audits for such matters as affirmative action, replacements of key persons, compliance with company or organizational personnel policy, and similar matters, including labor relations, should be included in periodic audits. Safety audits performed internally against OSHA standards may prevent unfavorable audits by OSHA inspectors from enforcement agencies.

Other current practices of the best-run organizations include new forms of program audits such as the technical audit, community relations audit, public responsibility audit, purchasing practices audit, and legal compliance audit for antitrust or patent protection.

**Continuing Reviews** Each manager, having made commitments, should be conducting ongoing reviews of his or her own performance. These reviews consist of observations and notations of actual results as compared with the statements of objectives to which one is committed. These reviews are made frequently and relate to the shorter time periods, for example, daily, weekly, monthly, and quarterly, in which supervisory management gets reports of outputs.

*One of the major advantages of MBO is that it permits self-control by the manager against objectives agreed upon in advance.* Self-control has powerful motivational effects; the tightest and most perfect form of control is self-control. Commitment is a means of motivation, and it is considerably enhanced when self-correction is built into the system.

As shown at the bottom of Table O-3, a manager should be able to post his or her own actual outcomes for the original objectives and should send a copy to the superior. The function of the superior is to respond with help and resources when requested or when notified that exceptions are present.

*Annual Review.* At the end of each year, the superior and subordinate pull out the objectives prepared in advance and formally review actual results. This is a preface to defining new objectives for the coming year. Such discussions should be treated as important events. They should be done free from distraction and should deal with objectives, results, problems, deviations, and improvements needed. They should avoid personality discussions or a manner which is exacting, hostile, judgmental, or punitive.

With actual results against objectives in hand, the superior can then make such personnel decisions as are required.

*See also* APPRAISAL, PERFORMANCE; BUDGETS AND BUDGET PREPARATION; COMPENSATION, EXECUTIVE; CONTROL SYSTEMS, MANAGEMENT; EXCEPTION, MANAGEMENT BY; OBJECTIVES AND GOALS; PLANNING, STRATEGIC MANAGERIAL; POLICY FORMULATION AND IMPLEMENTATION.

### REFERENCES

Drucker, Peter F.: *Management: Tasks, Responsibilities, Practices,* Harper & Row, Publishers, Incorporated, New York, 1974, chaps. 7–9.

Jamieson, B. D.: "Behavioral Problems with Management by Objectives," *Academy of Management Journal,* vol. 16, no. 3, 1973.

Mali, F.: *Managing by Objectives,* John Wiley & Sons, Inc., New York, 1972.

Odiorne, George S.: *Management by Objectives,* Pitman Publishing Corporation, New York, 1965.

———: "The Politics of Implementing MBO," *Business Horizons,* June 1974.

Reddin, W. J.: *Effective Management by Objectives,* McGraw-Hill Book Company, New York, 1971.

GEORGE S. ODIORNE, *University of Massachusetts*

## Objectives, marketing (*See* MARKETING MANAGEMENT.)

## Objectives, strategic [*See* OBJECTIVES, MANAGEMENT BY (MBO).]

## Objectives and goals

No concern is more important to managing than goals. Objectives and goals (the terms will be used interchangeably) are the starting points of the logic that supports the idea of managing. It is in their contribution to efficient and effective goal achievement that managers find the fundamental rationale for their jobs.

"Think goals" is a useful dictum for managers to practice, but the emphasis needs to be as much on *think* as on *goals*. How does one think about goals? The approach in this entry is to examine five aspects of goals: terms, contributions, tests, classifications, and the goal-setting process. An overview follows:

*Terms.* Goals are desired ends toward which behavior is directed.In this entry, terms are defined and distinctions discussed.

*Contributions.* Goals contribute to managerial effectiveness by providing direction and motivation, by serving as standards, by providing a basis for the major jobs of managers, and by acting as a point of reference for evaluating change.

*Tests.* Goals that contribute to effective managing must be acceptable, precise, attainable, congruent, and compared against alternatives.

*Classifications.* Several bases for classifying goals are identified. Each of these bases provides a different but useful perspective on goals.

*Goal setting.* The goal-setting process in an organization translates broad organizational purposes into meaningful behavior guides for each level of the organization. The process is primarily a human behavior process and, as such, never works in a perfectly rational way.

## SOME BASIC TERMS

*Goals* are desired ends or results toward which behavior is directed. They are more than simply desired future states of affairs; goals are more than just "wouldn't it be nice" statements. The additional ingredient required of goals is evidence of behavior in support of the goal.

Suppose that an executive wants to become a vice-president of industrial relations by the age of 40. That is a goal, in the practical sense of the term, only to the extent that it is backed up by behavior that is consistent with obtaining that position.

The statements of goals that individuals and people who represent the organization make are sometimes called *stated* or *official goals.* These statements are public pronouncements about desired ends or results. They often appear in written form in a conspicuous place in offices and stores so that customers can see the goals. An important question to ask is, "Is behavior actually directed toward these goals?" If so, then the goals are not only official goals but also *operative goals.* They are goals supported by behavior. It is in the sense of operative goals that the term *goal* is used throughout this chapter.

For pragmatic purposes the terms *goals, objectives, aims,* and *purposes* are used interchangeably here. In practice, some firms find it useful to differentiate

between these terms. They base the distinction on the level of generality and the period of time represented by the term. Thus, an aim may be a very broad, ultimate desired state of affairs that is only achieved, if at all, over a long period of time. A purpose may be only slightly less specific. Objectives may be more immediate desired results that can be subdivided into subobjectives. These subobjectives can become goals or *targets.* The problem with this use of terms is that it is not uniform from firm to firm, and there is no particular need for uniform usage; the basic idea of each term is the same.

Goals are not the same as motives. *Motive* is a term used to identify the force inside a person that activates and directs behavior toward a goal. For example, 10 executives might be motivated by competition, but that competitive motive might be directed toward 10 different career goals. By the same token, the same goal can satisfy a variety of motives. Reaching a career goal, for example, might satisfy an executive's motives of competition, power, affiliation, and financial rewards.

## HOW GOALS CONTRIBUTE TO MANAGERIAL EFFECTIVENESS

All benefits of goals are only potential benefits; the mere presence of goals does not guarantee they will play any role in improving managerial effectiveness. Most managers are familiar with situations in which official goals are loudly and enthusiastically proclaimed, only to be quickly ignored and forgotten. When considering the potential benefits of goals to managers, keep in mind that the practical question for managers to ask themselves about these benefits is, "Are my goals actually achieving these benefits for my area of managerial accountability?"

All benefits of goals derive from their influence on behavior. This influence can take many forms, including providing a foundation for all other managerial functions and acting as a point of reference for evaluating change. Each of these potential influences on job behavior is discussed briefly below.

**Direction and Motivation** Goals can focus attention; they can tell what individuals should be doing; they can serve as targets for behavior. To the extent that goals do these things, job behavior can become more purposeful and productive. In a recent survey of 1275 company executives, the absence of well-defined organizational or departmental goals or objectives was cited by 50 percent of the executives as the *most common cause* of less-than-satisfactory executive productivity.[1] Such goals may not guarantee managerial effectiveness, but they are a necessary condition of it.

In addition to providing behavioral direction, goals can influence the level of motivation of managers and their employees. In order for goals to influence motivational levels, two conditions must be met. First, managers and employees must consider achieving the goals to be personally important or valuable. Second, they must consider that their level of job effort has some relationship to achieving the goals.

*Practical suggestions:* Think about how much of your behavior is actually directed toward achieving goals you say are important to you and your organization. Think about how many of the resources available for your use are being used to achieve those goals.

**Standards** Goals can serve as the standard against which to evaluate managerial and employee job behavior. By providing behavioral direction, goals suggest what should be done; as standards, goals are useful in determining *how well* actual job behavior matches desired behavior. It is reported that the new governor of a large state said, "I don't have any goals; they will evolve as we go along." That is a fairly effective way of eliminating the accountability for performing against a declared standard of performance. Of course, one reason executives are reluctant to use goals is that goals *do* hold them to a standard of performance.

The prevalence of the use of goals as standards is suggested by the frequency with which executives mention goals and objectives as the most effective yardstick for measuring productivity and by the frequency with which achievement of goals is mentioned as the definition of success.

*Practical suggestion:* Check your goals to see if they are, in fact, serving as standards against which job behavior is being evaluated.

**Foundation for Managerial Functions** What do managers do? A common reply is to say that they plan, organize, staff, direct, and control. This set of managerial functions or activities provides a general way of identifying some of the behaviors managers are supposed to engage in if they want to achieve goals efficiently and effectively. The entire rationale for this classification is that these managerial functions are essential activities that need to be performed if goals are to be achieved efficiently and effectively. In this widely accepted view of managerial functions, goals are the foundation on which all functions are built.

*Planning* has no meaning apart from goals; indeed, some authors and managers consider goal setting as a part of planning. The essence of planning is to determine the what, how, when, where, and who of action necessary to achieve goals. Since *controlling* is inseparable from planning, it, too, depends on goals for its rationale. Controlling is the function of assuring that actual behavior is contributing to goals.

The *organizing* function of managers has an influence on goals. On the one hand, the goals that guide behavior in organizations can have an influence on the way the organization is designed. On the other hand, the way the organization is designed can have an influence on what goals are selected to guide the behavior of the organization's members. In a similar way, the goals of an organization can influence the functions of *staffing* and *directing*. Who is hired and kept in an organization and how they are directed are partly determined by the organization's goals, but these goals are also influenced by the people in the organization that participate in formulating the goals.

The main point to consider is that goals can be a major influence on what managers do in terms of planning, organizing, controlling, staffing, and directing.

*Practical suggestion:* Evaluate your goals in terms of the actual impact they are having on the various managerial activities you perform.

**Evaluating Change** In the absence of goals and the plans and controls that support the goals it is difficult to evaluate proposed changes that might affect managerial and organizational effectiveness. The presence of such goals provides a point of reference that can be used in evaluating the impact of the proposed changes on the organization's people, markets, resources, structure, operational processes, and overall effectiveness.

Evaluating changes against goals may help managers and organizations avoid changes that have as their only or major justification that they *are* changes. Change for the sake of change may on occasion be necessary or desirable, but it is, in general, a weak rationale for committing organizational resources.

*Practical suggestion:* Analyze a recent implemented change in terms of its impact on goals and resources.

**Perspective** The four benefits of goals just discussed can be turned into obstacles to effective managing if goals are not kept in perspective. Goals that provide behavioral direction and focus attention can also become blinders. A kind of "goalopia" can set in that prevents managers from seeing the need for flexible, spontaneous behavior that may not be exactly consistent with goals but which is essential to overall effectiveness. "Goalopia" can hinder a manager's capacity to evaluate the continuing relevance of particular goals.

Goals that serve as standards may become obstacles to improved performance if they are not changed in response to actual performance appraisal. Goals that provide the foundation for other managerial functions can lead to overly mechanistic and programmed approaches to planning, organizing, staffing, directing, and controlling. Goals that are useful in evaluating change can also be used by managers as a basis for excessive resistance to change.

*Practical suggestion:* Examine each potential benefit periodically to avoid it from also contributing to your ineffectiveness.

Finally, it is possible to place too much emphasis on goals. Unfortunately, there is no single key to effective managing. Neither goals nor any other idea or managerial tool is *the* key to the task of effectively managing systems having human, technical, and economic dimensions. Goals are a necessary but not exclusive condition for managerial effectiveness.

*Practical suggestion:* Analyze your basic approach to managing with a view to determining if it overemphasizes goals, or any other managerial tool.

## TESTS THAT GOALS SHOULD MEET

If goals are going to be a useful tool for effective managing, they must meet certain criteria or tests.

**Acceptability** A certain minimum level of goal acceptance—enough to generate compliance behavior on the part of those responsible for achieving goals—is obviously essential. In short, no acceptance; no achievement. Beyond this minimum level, however, how much acceptance is necessary and/or desirable? How can this acceptance be acquired?

The "how much" question cannot be answered with specific terms. As a practical guide to goal acceptance, however, the idea of goal ownership is useful. *Goal ownership* reflects a good match between goals of the organization and the personal goals and aspirations of those who are involved in achieving the goals.

How can goal acceptance be achieved? One approach to achieving goal acceptance is to make sure goals are communicated, known, and understood. Although these steps do not guarantee acceptance, they are a necessary precondition of it. Another approach to achieving goal acceptance is to involve those who are going to be responsible for achieving the goals in the process of goal setting. This involvement or participation can range from an advisory or consultative role to one in which participants actually make goal decisions. The participation can occur at the beginning or end of the goal-setting process or at any point in between.

Participation in goal setting is *a* way of obtaining goal acceptance because the participation process, by virtue of the inputs of the participants, may result in goals that are in fact, or are perceived to be, more in line with the personal goals of those persons involved. In addition, the participative process—a process that gives one a sense of being ego-involved—may serve to raise the aspiration levels of those involved.

It should be stressed, however, that participation has no automatic positive impact on goal acceptance or performance. Participation may be a poor managerial strategy when analyzed from a cost-benefit viewpoint; for example, it is time consuming, and it does not necessarily lead to improved goals or to greater goal acceptance.

**Precision** There is an *appropriate degree* of precision or specificity for every goal, and it is imperative that goals be stated with that degree of precision—and no more. It is just as much of a mistake to impose on a goal more precision than it warrants as it is to undercut the usefulness of the goal by stating it with an insufficient degree of precision.

One of the most interesting and clear findings from studies—in the laboratory and in the real world—is that there is a definite positive relationship between job performance and the degree of precision in goals. In fact, both goal acceptance and goal precision consistently have been found to be positively related to performance.[2]

In a situation where managers and employees are given a very general goal (for example, to make a profit in this department) and told to do their best, goal precision is very low. Job performance is likely to suffer because the goals do not provide behavioral focus or motivation, nor do they provide an adequate basis for planning and controlling.

However, when goals are appropriately precise in terms of *quantity, quality, time,* and *cost* (for example, to earn a 10 percent rate of return on the book value of total assets in this department in each of the next 2 years), it is more likely that goals will provide a source of motivation and focus and will be a foundation for effective planning and controlling.

In goal setting it is necessary to strike a balance between too little and too much precision. Excessive precision can stifle motivation, lead to poor job attitudes, and adversely affect job performance. A preoccupation with precision may lead to adopting trivial goals *because* they can be stated precisely at the expense of adopting more meaningful and challenging goals. In short, precision can be carried too far.

In spite of cautions about balance, goal precision is crucial for effective managing. It is difficult to know whether a goal is being achieved unless it is stated in measurable, verifiable, specific terms of quantity, quality, time, and cost. Goals that can be so stated may be referred to as *operational goals*.

**Attainability** This test of goals is concerned with the level of goal difficulty. Goals that are set too high may demotivate behavior, create frustration and anxiety, lower job performance, and lead to performance appraisal difficulties. Goals that are set too low do not contribute much to the satisfaction people experience when they achieve them. Further, achievement of easy goals may not lead to a favorable performance appraisal; an anybody-could-have-done-that attitude may characterize the appraisal session.

Difficult goals might be made more attainable if they are divided into subgoals. People are more likely to accomplish difficult goals if they can achieve, and be rewarded for achieving, subgoals that represent progress toward the larger difficult goal. In addition, difficult goals may require more effort on the part of managers to gain goal acceptance. As noted above, increased goal acceptance may result in an increased commitment to achieve goals. There is some research support for the proposition that difficult, *but accepted*, goals lead to greater performance than do easy goals.[3]

The difficulty of goals is, in part, determined by the perception of managers and employees. One employee may see a goal as impossible, another may see it as challenging, and another as easy. Individual differences always enter into the relationship between a factor, such as goal difficulty, and job performance. Part of the skill of managing is in knowing how the differences between particular people enter into the resolution of managerial problems in specific concrete cases.

**Congruency** Congruency means that all the internal goals within an area of accountability must be consistent with each other (internal congruence) and with the goals of other organizational units with which the area interacts (external congruence). For example, if departmental performance goals are inconsistent or nonsupportive of personal development goals, good performance is unlikely. Addition-

ally, if goals of the production function, for example, are incompatible with goals of the marketing function, overall organizational effectiveness suffers.

A second meaning of goal congruence is that goals must be compatible with other characteristics of the organization. For example, a goal to increase the adaptability of an organization to changing environmental conditions may be inconsistent with the existing and rigid organizational structure. Goals that emphasize personal development and growth may be inconsistent with appraisal and reward systems that are based on subjective opinions and seniority. Human resource planning goals may be incompatible with current staffing practices. Congruency is a special case of a general management point: all elements—goals, plans, structure, controls, operating systems, etc.—of an organizational system must be compatible with each other.

Most complex organizations pursue so many different goals that it would be impossible for them all to be compatible with each other. It is not even possible to be aware of all goals being pursued. Thus, a certain amount of *goal conflict* is inevitable even in an organization whose members are committed to goal congruence.

**Comparison with Alternatives** Goals selected for use in managing must be evaluated against alternative goals that were not selected. It is useful to state explicitly those goals that were rejected. This exercise helps managers become more aware of the *opportunity cost* associated with goals. Every goal involves some trade off, and it is important for effective managers to be aware of what is being traded off. Quantity may be achieved at the expense of quality, quality may be possible only with higher costs, shorter customer delivery times may result in higher inventory carrying costs, and so on.

The trade offs involved by selecting a particular goal are not always as obvious as in the cases above. All that may be necessary to highlight trade offs, however, is the discipline of asking and answering this question, "What is the opportunity cost of this goal?"

*Practical suggestion:* Build into your goal-setting process procedures for assuring that your goals are acceptable, precise, attainable, congruent, and have been compared against alternatives.

## GOAL CLASSIFICATIONS

Professionals frequently refer to a number of goals. Each of these types can be placed into one of five primary classifications. The goals within each class may be regarded as *types* of goals.

**Time**   The time period covered by goals is one basis for classification. Although this period can range from a few minutes to a lifetime, the most common managerial practice is to refer to short-run or *tactical goals*, midrange or *intermediate goals*, and long-run or *strategic goals*. Typical, but arbitrary, time periods assigned to these goals are 1 year or less, 2 to 3 years, and over 3 years, respectively.

Managers should try to set goals for all time periods relevant to their specific area of accountability. Specific goals should be examined to see if they are stated in terms of the most appropriate time span. For example, *target rate-of-return goals*—goals that specify a percentage rate of return expected on an investment—need to cover a sufficient time period to allow the complete production and distribution exchange cycle to occur.

**Primary Beneficiary**   Organizations require goals for owners, employees, customers, suppliers, creditors, the local community, and society. Every organization has to achieve, in a satisfactory manner, a set of multiple goals. Each of these can be viewed as having a primary beneficiary, but none can be achieved unless all are satisfied to some extent. No one of these goals should be viewed as *the* goal of an entire organization, even though, at times, one goal may be given priority over others.

It is very common for *profitability* or *profit maximization* to be singled out as the goal of a business firm. A distinction needs to be made, however, between profitability as a goal and as a decision rule. As a goal, profitability is primarily the goal of the owners and key executives of a business firm; it is not *the* goal of the firm. As a decision rule, however, profitability is uniquely and critically important in business firms. It is the standard against which to evaluate many of the key decisions of business executives. It *is* the ultimate criterion for evaluating the effectiveness of business firms. It also provides the mechanism for assuring that the goals of all groups associated with the firm are satisfied.

**Priority**   All goals are not equally important. In the most fundamental sense, every organization exists for some primary purpose. For business firms, this primary purpose is to provide customers with goods and services in sufficient quantity, acceptable quality and cost, and at a time when the goods and services are needed. This is the societal justification for the existence of the business firm, and it is the distinct characteristic that distinguishes business firms from other types of organizations.

In a similar way, schools exist to educate, hospitals exist for the care of the sick, and so on. Every organization has a fundamental reason for existing that is, or should be, its highest priority goal.

This same line of reasoning applies to the smallest area of managerial accountability within an organization. Every such area has its primary objective(s). One of the manager's tasks is to identify the goal(s) from which all other goals derive their importance. Not only is it essential to assign priorities to these goals, the way in which priorities are assigned can differentiate effective from ineffective managers.

**Social Unit**   Goals range from individual or personal goals to organizational or system-wide goals, with a variety of social units between each of these two extremes. For convenience, we discuss goals of individuals, groups, and organizations. In a basic sense, every organization is a collection of individuals attempting to achieve their personal or *individual goals*. These individuals are members of the organization because they perceive membership in the organization as a vehicle for personal goal accomplishment. In terms of human behavior, the most essential task confronting organizational leaders is that of harmonizing or integrating the personal goals of members with those goals of larger social units. Without a satisfactory degree of integration, it is impossible to achieve those goals for which the organization was created.

*Group goals* are goals that the individual members of a group agree will serve as guides for the behavior of the group. Group goals are not identical to the individual goals of group members. Rather, they are goals agreed to by the individual members as behavioral guides for their role as members of the group.

A group can be any collection of two or more employees who interact on the job. The group can be an official or *formal group* such as a department or division, a project team, or a committee. Group goals also exist for *informal groups* in organizations— those groups that are not part of the formal organizational design but which exist to serve on-the-job needs of employees who are not served by formal organizational roles.

In connection with formal work groups it is common to identify the existence of two types of goals. *Task goals* are those goals that pertain to the assigned work role of the group. *Maintenance goals* are those goals that pertain to the way the members of the group get along with each other and the way the members function as a group. Both types of these goals are important to a group, and some time and effort needs to be devoted to achieving them.

*Organizational goals* are goals that serve to guide the decision behavior of key top managers on matters that impact the total organization or some major subsystem of the organization. The clearest example of such a goal in business firms is the profitability goal. This goal acts to constrain the decisions of top executives. Other constraints include growth and stability goals, goals dealing with management style and philosophy (centralization versus decentralization, tight versus loose structure, autocratic versus participative managerial styles), community and social goals, goals guiding decisions in the area of human resources development, product-innovation goals, and goals concerning market share.

**Performance Area**  Peter F. Drucker identifies the following eight key areas in which objectives are needed: (1) marketing, (2) innovation, (3) human organization, (4) financial resources, (5) physical resources, (6) productivity, (7) social responsibility, and (8) profit requirements. In listing these eight performance areas, Drucker's overall view is that objectives need to be set in all areas on which the economic performance of the firm depends. The specific objectives set in any one of these performance areas will depend on the strategy of the individual business, but the areas are common for all businesses because, Drucker suggests, "All businesses depend on the same factors for their survival."[4]

The most common performance area approach to grouping work in business firms is by function, such as finance, production, marketing, personnel, and engineering. In large firms, these functions are organized into departments, and the work of the departments is grouped into subunits. The marketing departments, for example, might include the subunits of sales, advertising, sales promotion, marketing research, and marketing services. The specific goals of each of these subunits are derived from and are supportive of the overall goals of the marketing department.

The idea of key performance areas can be applied to all types of organizations in which performance is critical. A university, for example, needs goals set in all performance areas crucial to its teaching, research, and community service purposes. A hospital needs goals in performance areas related to patient care, medical teaching and research, and community service. The message for managers of the performance-area idea is twofold: (1) identify key result areas and (2) establish goals in each area.

*Practical suggestion:* Analyze goals to determine (1) if all appropriate time periods and performance areas are represented; (2) if they have been ranked according to importance; and (3) if all appropriate

social units and primary beneficiaries have been considered.

## THE GOAL-SETTING PROCESS

Goals do not just appear; they are the result of a continuous organizational goal-setting process. What does this process involve? In the first place, it has an overall purpose, which is to translate broad organizational goals into meaningful behavioral guides for people at each level of the organization. In the second place, the goal-setting process is a human behavior process and, as such, is never perfectly rational or mechanistic.

**An Ends-Means Chain**  Every organization has to have some process by which it arrives at a *hierarchy of goals*. The goal-setting process starts with the organization's top management. This group formulates goals applicable to the organization's top level. For example, a top-level marketing goal might be to reach sales of $2 billion. This marketing goal provides the basis for goal setting in marketing functions at the middle level of the organization. For example, the sales function establishes specific goals by product to support the top-level sales goal of $2 billion. Thus, the goals at the middle levels of an organization are the means used for achieving the goals, or ends, of the top levels. This ends-means chain continues throughout the organization. The goals at each level are derived, more or less logically, from those of the level above, and they collectively form a hierarchy of goals.

The partial organization chart shown in Fig. O-1 illustrates the ends-means chain as it applies to the marketing function. Figure O-2 presents another view of the ends-means chain. For a few organizational units of an electric utility, Fig. O-2 shows how an end, or goal, at one level becomes a means for the level above. The numerical values shown in Fig. O-2 are hypothetical, and the goals have been abridged from the company's manual. The hierarchy of goals for the entire electric utility would, of course, require numerous ends-means staircases, such as that shown in Fig. O-2.

Every organization uses an ends-means chain for arriving at a hierarchy of goals. In some organizations the ends-means link between goals at different levels of the organization is very weak and indirect. In other organizations, this link is very strong and direct. Organizations differ in their need for congruence between goals. Nevertheless, the notion of an organization dictates the need for a hierarchy of goals—a set of goals linked together in an ends-means relationship.

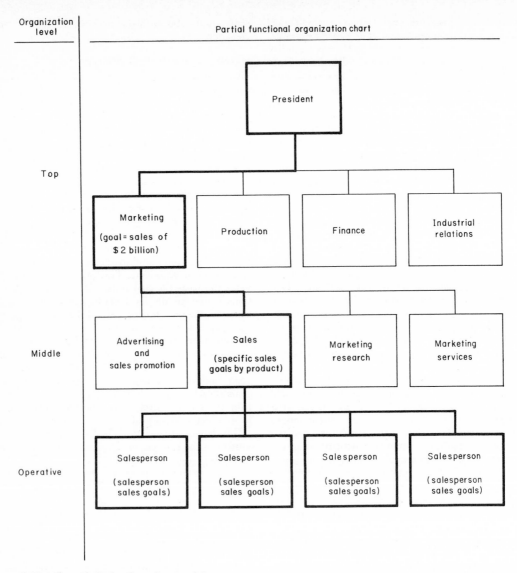

**Fig. O-1. The marketing function ends-means chain.**

**A Human Behavior Process**  Goal setting in organizations involves men and women in an interactive process in which they are looking out not only for the organization but for themselves as well. There is nothing wrong with this process; that is just the way it is. The key point is that goal setting cannot be viewed simply as a perfectly rational ends-means process that leads to a hierarchy of logically integrated goals. Rather, the hierarchy of goals results from an interactive human behavior process in which people have (1) a personal stake and (2) a limited perspective.

The personal stake involved concerns the perceived relationship between goals that are being set and the personal goals of the people involved. It is inevitable and very rational for individual organization members to watch out for their personal and organizational "selfish" interests. In its extreme form, such behavior can ruin an organization. More commonly, however, various nondestructive tactics are used by organization members to influence goals and the goal-setting process. Examples of these tactics include collective bargaining, informal negotiating, and forming temporary ad hoc groups or *coalitions* that push for particular goals.

These tactics may result in goals that are less than ideal or less than perfectly rational from a *total organization viewpoint*. The tactics may (will) generate conflict between individual members of the organization and between organizational units. The tactics and the conflict are an inevitable part of goal setting in organizations. They are part of the human behavior process that results in goals that are the *best compromises* that can be reached in efforts to integrate the diverse interests of organizational members.

Even if individual organization members had no personal stake in goals, goal setting would still be less than a perfectly rational process. That is because of the limited perspective of organizational members. Once again, this is neither good nor bad; it is just a reality of organizational life. Individual members of the organization view what is going on in their organization from their particular frame of reference. Their perspective is largely determined

by the scope of their responsibilities and by characteristics of their job specialization. This perspective, coupled with the limited ability of the human brain to process all the data that bombards it, means that every member brings a limited perspective to the goal-setting process. Some perspectives are more limited than others, of course, but all are limited.

It is not surprising that the various limited perspectives might be in conflict during the goal-setting process. There should be little surprise, either, about the line and staff conflicts that are common in organizations or at the conflicts between functions such as production and marketing. These conflicts are more than just conflicts about goals, of course. But differences that arise in the goal-setting process are an important ingredient of the conflict.

The goal-setting picture presented so far has two themes. One theme is the need for organizations to develop a hierarchy of goals that can be characterized as an ends-means chain. The other theme is that the hierarchy of goals comes about as a result of an interactive human behavior process in which individual organizational members have a personal stake and a limited perspective. One approach to the

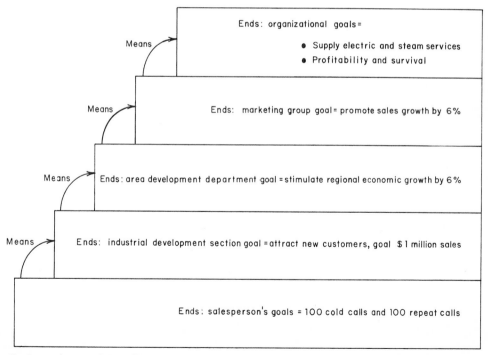

**Fig. O-2. Ends-means chain and hierarchy of goals for part of an electric utility.** *(Adapted from Don Hellriegel and John W. Slocum, Jr., Management: A Contingency Approach, Addison-Wesley Publishing Company, Inc., Reading, Mass., 1978.)*

goal-setting process that takes these two themes into account and that is widely used is management by objectives (MBO). [*See* OBJECTIVES, MANAGEMENT BY (MBO).]

Several of the ideas discussed in this entry on objectives and goals are brought together schemati-cally in Fig. O-3. Individuals and groups within organizations have needs, resources, and their own unique perspective that give rise to individual and group goals (box 1). Similarly, the organization has needs, resources, and a broad organizational per-spective that gives rise to organizational goals (box

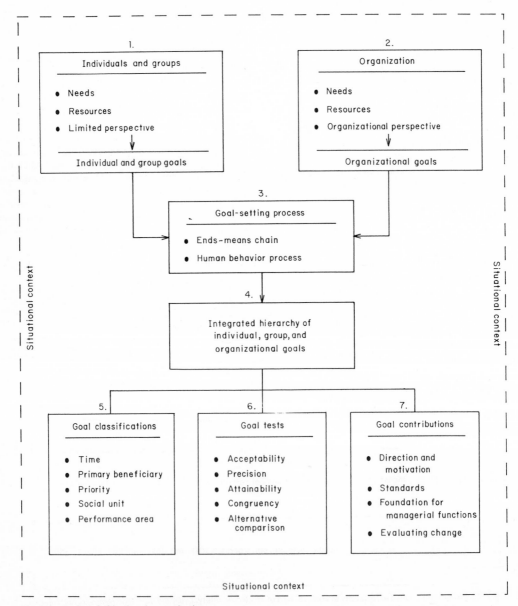

**Fig. O-3. Goals and objectives in organizations.**

2). By means of the goal-setting process (box 3) an integrated hierarchy of individual, group, and organizational goals is derived (box 4). Ideally, these goals will meet the organization's needs in terms of goal classifications (box 5), goal tests (box 6), and, most important, contributions to managerial and organizational effectiveness (box 7). The dashed line surrounding the seven boxes in Fig. O-3 conveys the idea that goal setting in organizations is influenced by situational factors, such as the type of organization, nature of the industry, degree of competition, environmental uncertainty, time available, and abilities and skills of personnel.

*See also* BUDGETS AND BUDGET PREPARATION; CONTROL SYSTEMS, MANAGEMENT; OBJECTIVES, MANAGEMENT BY (MBO); *Objectives and Goals;* PLANNING, STRATEGIC MANAGERIAL; POLICY FORMULATION AND IMPLEMENTATION.

### NOTES

[1] Herman S. Jacobs and Katherine Jillson, *Executive Productivity,* American Management Association, New York, 1974.

[2] Richard M. Steers and Lyman W. Porter, "The Role of Task-Goal Attributes in Employee Performance," *Psychological Bulletin,* vol. 81, no. 7, pp. 434–452, 1974.

[3] Gary P. Latham and Gary A. Yukl, "A Review of Research on the Application of Goal Setting in Organizations," *Academy of Management Journal,* vol. 18, no. 4, pp. 824–845, December 1975.

[4] Peter F. Drucker, *Management: Tasks, Responsibilities, Practices,* Harper & Row, Publishers, Incorporated, New York, 1974.

ROBERT ALBANESE, *Texas A & M University*

# Occupational Safety and Health Act of 1970 (OSHA) (*See* SAFETY AND HEALTH MANAGEMENT, EMPLOYEE.)

# Off-book financing (*See* FINANCIAL MANAGEMENT, SHORT-TERM, INTERMEDIATE, AND LONG-TERM FINANCING.)

# Offer, labor contract (*See* LABOR-MANAGEMENT RELATIONS.)

# Office landscape (*See* OFFICE SPACE PLANNING AND DESIGN.)

# Office management (*See* ADMINISTRATIVE MANAGEMENT.)

# Office space planning and design

In planning a major office facility, a logical sequence should be followed: plan the project; gather and analyze requirements data; select the solution (build, lease, renovate); design; build; move.

**Preliminary Planning** The project might require a few months for construction (for 20,000 square feet of leased space), 8 months (for a one-story simple structure on a suburban site), a year or year and a half (for 300,000 square feet of leased space), or 3 years (for a high-rise building on an urban site). Responsibility and authority should be defined and delegated from the start. An independent planning consultant and/or architect contribute greatly and should be selected as soon as possible. The consultant, architect, or some equally capable individual should have primary responsibility for setting up and monitoring the program and schedule.

*Creating the Project Team.* It is wise to select an in-house *project coordinator* who can devote full or part time to the project and who is competent to take day-to-day responsibility for coordination among all parties: planners, brokers, landlords, architects, contractors, and your own departments. Appoint a *facility planning committee* to have ultimate responsibility and to exercise final authority for all powers not delegated to the project coordinator. The facility planning committee should meet at least monthly to review progress and costs and should convene additionally whenever a major decision is needed: total requirements, budget, selection of space, approval of layout and design, and selection of major contractors. In a small company this committee might include the three or four top officers. In a large company it might include a senior vice-president (preferably for planning, finance, administration, or operations), the controller, personnel director, facility manager, and two or three key executives—particularly those who have expressed concern over the direction and cost of the project.

*Management's Preconceptions.* Top management will probably have preconceptions about the project. Valid preconceptions will set the project limits and goals; invalid ones must be tactfully refuted by the project team. Preconceptions include total growth, a schedule, maximum rent, total costs, buildings preferred, what is right or wrong with the present space, open versus enclosed space, new versus existing furniture, a design look, and relationship of office sizes to titles.

*Past Studies and Available Data.* Recent past studies concerning personnel growth, organization, functions, and space should be sought and reviewed. Data listing personnel by department, title, and pay grade will be a good starting point for determining personnel requirements. Inventories, particularly of major equipment, can be reused or updated. Measurements of the present departmental area can be used to compare present space use with projected space needs.

*Budget Factors.* Two types of costs affect the budget.

*One-time costs:* double rent, consultant's fees, construction, furniture, furnishings, art, telephone installation, EDP (electronic data processing), major utilities, audiovisual systems, move, move security, new office materiel, personnel relocation, personnel replacement and training.

*Recurring costs:* rent and rent escalation, electricity, telephone, cleaning and relamping, extra personnel, and extra services (not now required).

*Organizing Data.* Requirement data should be gathered and maintained in flexible increments. Restructure departments into *planning units.* Each unit should include those personnel and *special facilities* (conference rooms, food service, etc.) which must remain a physical unit to function effectively. A planning unit may be part of a department (e.g., an independent four-person group) or consist of an entire department. Assign an alpha code to each planning unit. (See Table O-5.) Select a series of

**TABLE O-5   Typical Planning Units**

| | | |
|---|---|---|
| A | Administration | |
| | AA | Executive group |
| | AB | Public relations |
| | AC | Government affairs |
| | AD | Office services |
| B | Finance | |
| | BA | Controller's office |
| | BB | Treasurer |
| | BC | General accounting |
| | BD | Payroll |
| C | Marketing | |
| | CA | Marketing administration |
| | CB | Product one |
| | CC | Product two |

planning units are unable to project needs beyond stage 2, the project team should anticipate stage 3 needs as a range of personnel and space requirements. The team should also identify *hard areas* (areas that are expensive to build or to move, such as food service, EDP, board rooms, print shops) based on phase 3 needs, even though *soft areas* (typical private office and general office areas) are based on stage 2 needs and might be relocated when stage 3 occurs.

*Review and Approval.* Establish a procedure for review and approval of major decisions by the facility planning committee. These items should be presented in written or graphic form and the fact of approval or redirection recorded in written minutes.

**Gathering and Analyzing Base Data**   The total space requirements (for a planning unit for a given planning stage) are comprised of several types of data. Express data in terms of functional needs and not in terms of area; area is determined only after the base data are analyzed and approved and after space standards are selected. Once a department head has said, "I need a 400-square foot office," it is difficult to assign space based on a uniform standard.

*Personnel.* Record personnel by work station categories related to a parity of function and/or status. The following categories and codings, listed in descending order of area normally required, are recommended:

*Private Stations*

| | |
|---|---|
| X | Chairman, president |
| A | Executive vice-president, senior vice-president |
| B | Vice-president, general manager |
| C | Manager, top professional |
| D | Assistant manager, top clerical supervisor, professional needing privacy |

*Nonprivate Stations* (*O* stands for open stations)

| | |
|---|---|
| OSX | Executive secretary |
| OA | Administrator, clerical supervisor, professional not needing privacy |
| OS | Secretary |
| OC | Clerk |

*Special-Facility Stations*

| | |
|---|---|
| N | Special-facility personnel |

Remember to include stations required by nonemployees: outside auditors, visitors, seasonal personnel, field persons.

*Files, Storage, and Special Equipment.* Files, bookcases, storage cabinets, and major machine requirements should be recorded if they are required in an open area since they require additional space

*planning stages* to determine the years for which personnel and area projections are needed. Stage 1 is the present. Stage 2 might be the move date plus 1,2, or 3 years (since the firm will not want to outgrow the space the day it moves in). Stage 3 would be the year more space is added, perhaps 5 to 7 years after the move. Even though the individual

(but not if they are required in a private office). When these occur in a special facility, they should be recorded under the special facility (e.g., engineering file room: 40 legal drawers, 60 plan drawers, one 36 by 72 by 18 cabinet). Remember, requirements are not the same as an inventory; many drawers and cabinets are empty or contain junk or inactive material that should be discarded or relocated to remote storage.

*Special Facilities.* Record the function, capacity needed, furniture and equipment to be accommodated, utilities and special construction, and special features for unique facilities. For example, conference-room requirements might be: to be used for client presentations; to seat 12 at single table; to seat 6 additionally; to have two working walls with pin-up surface and chart rails; to have one working wall with chalk surface; to have a motorized screen; to have a projection booth for a 16 mm film projector or 4 simultaneous slide projectors; to have variable lighting for wall display, screenings, and meetings; to have a smoke exhaust and temperature control; to have acoustical privacy; to have storage for 30 by 60 charts and 6 spare chairs.

*Utilities and Nonstandard Construction.* These requirements will mostly occur in the special facilities list. Some occur in general office areas (e.g., separate circuits, ventilation for machines, reinforced floors for files) and some in the X and A offices (e.g., ventilation, lighting, architectural features). These requirements affect the budget and must be considered when negotiating a lease.

*Special Studies.* Plans that affect long-range space needs should be reviewed in advance or simultaneously with your study of requirements. These include organization, automation, administrative support concept, word processing, records management, security, food service, private communications systems, methods, and work flow.

*Adjacency Priorities.* Determine adjacency priorities by asking planning unit managers to state these requirements or by analyzing the work flow. Work flow should consider actual task interrelationships (e.g., accounts payable hand delivering batches to disbursement) or the need for face-to-face contact (e.g., research with applications engineering). Plot these on a *bubble diagram* (see Fig. O-4), where a circle represents each planning unit, a rectangle each common-use special facility, and where adjacency priorities are shown by connecting lines and numbers:

1. Essential: must be adjacent.
2. Desirable: should be on the same floor or an adjacent floor.

3. Convenient: helpful if adjacent, but separation would not hurt function.

*Analysis and Approval of Base Data.* Base data should be tabulated by planning unit and by planning stage. These tabulations should be reviewed

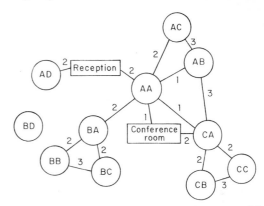

**Fig. O-4. Bubble diagram. Adjacency priorities: 1—essential; 2—desirable; 3—convenient. See Table O-5 for identification of planning units.**

by departments for their planning units, by divisions for their departments, and by top management for all divisions. Personnel totals should be confirmed. Parity in assigning space categories for similar functions and status should be positively checked; a single accidental deviation often results in charges of preferential treatment. Quantity of files and storage should be approved. Special facilities required should be compared with the size and capacity of present similar facilities.

**Computing Space Requirements** Compute space requirements by applying space standards to base data, by extending and adding areas for each planning unit and planning stage, and by applying a circulation factor. Establish an area standard for each space category (if a building has been selected or designed) or a range of areas for each category (if several buildings are being considered) (see Table O-6). Depending on the size of the company, the nature of its business, budget limitations, and the building's module, space standards can vary greatly. Establish area standards for files, storage units, and special equipment. Special facility areas should be based on a sketch for each. All standards should include access space (e.g., space to open a file drawer and stand in front of it) but not the pro rata share of common aisles.

*Circulation Factors.* Consider two kinds of circulation: *intraunit circulation*, or aisles connecting stations and special facilities within each planning

TABLE O-6   Computing Space Requirements

| Space type | Typical user | Range of area, square feet | |
|---|---|---|---|
| | | From | To |
| | Private Space Types | | |
| X | Chairman, president | 300 | 600 |
| A | Executive vice-president, senior vice-president | 275 | 400 |
| B | Vice-president, senior managers | 200 | 300 |
| C | Managers, top professionals | 130 | 165 |
| D | Assistant managers, other professionals | 81 | 144 |
| | General Office Space Types | | |
| OSX | Executive secretaries | 100 | 200 |
| OA | Administrators, clerical supervisors | 85 | 100 |
| OS | Secretaries, typists | 55 | 75 |
| OC | Clerks | 45 | 65 |

unit; *interunit circulation*, or aisles or corridors used by all planning units on one floor. The range of circulation factors to be applied to and added to basic space requirements could be the following:

*Intraunit Circulation*

| 12 percent | Many large stations and special facilities; rectilinear layouts |
| 18 percent | Many small stations, e.g., for clerks |
| 24 percent | All small stations; irregular or "landscape" layouts |

*Interunit Circulation*

| 10 percent | A few large planning units on a floor; deep space from window to core. |
| 15 percent | Many small planning units; shallow space from window to core |

As a practical matter, planners test layouts for three or four floors using typical requirements, compare the base requirements for all units accommodated with the usable area (see Usable and Rentable Area below) of each floor, and then select a combination of circulation factors to use for all planning units. If no test layouts are done, use 15 and 10 percent for typical rectilinear layouts; 20 and 12 percent for open-plan layouts that are not rectilinear.

*Computing Usable Area.* Table O-7 illustrates this computation for a typical planning unit.

*Stating Adjacency Requirements.* The adjacency data for each division (i.e., a group of departments) or for the entire company can be shown on one or two bubble diagrams. If a planning unit has significant interunit relationships, a separate bubble diagram or work-flow diagram should be made for that unit.

## SELECTING SPACE

Three options should be considered: build, lease, or renovate.

**Build a New Building**   This option involves a commitment to a particular site and a permanent facility of limited size, as well as the risks of building (cost and schedule) and ownership (operating costs and responsibilities and change in resale value). It provides benefits such as tax shelter, depreciation, and, if you lease part of the building, cash flow. A building can be refinanced advantageously if its value goes up.

**Lease Space**   When leasing space and evaluating alternative lease choices, a thorough analysis of each lease offer based on the company's requirements can reduce costs significantly. Using the space, utility, and construction requirements, negotiate with a landlord to provide specific needs at little or no cost. Understand the difference between usable and rentable area and match the available area to the needs of the company.

*Usable and Rentable Area.*  Landlords define *usable area* as the space within the glass line or exterior walls, less the enclosed areas within the core. Some of this, however, is not in fact usable; i.e., you cannot place furniture in the space required for convector enclosures, freight car and elevator lobbys, or corridors within the core line. For a tenant, the significant measure is the *assignable usable area* (AUA), which is the space within the line of the convector enclosure minus the entire core area. *Rentable area* is a term used by landlords to prorate all the areas within the core except stairs, elevators, and shafts to tenants. Thus rentable area includes toilets, lobbies, utility rooms, and sometimes air-conditioning equipment rooms. Landlords define this according to rules recommended by the Building Owners and Managers Association International (BOMAI) or, in New York State, by the Real Estate Board of New York (REBONY). Although the usable-rentable ratio (or *building efficiency*) depends on the plan of the particular building and the rules followed, this ratio is commonly 75 to 85 percent for floors with several tenants and 80 to 90 percent for floors with a single tenant.

*Floor Efficiency.* Module and floor features also affect the desirability of one building over another. A building with a 5-foot window module results in C and B offices being 10 or 15 feet wide; if the window module were 4 feet 6 inches, similar offices would be 9 feet 0 inches or 13 feet 6 inches wide. If there are many C or B offices, the larger module results in more spacious offices but requires more space for each.

*Work Letter.* This is the portion of the lease that specifies what construction the landlord will allow the tenant free or under a predetermined cost schedule. The standard work letter is usually a one or two page list giving the formulas for determining quantity allowances for necessary amenities: light fixtures, ceiling and floor tile, sheet-rock partitions, doors, electric and telephone wall outlets, and electric power. A general description of heating, ventilating, and air-conditioning service (HVAC) is stated. However, what is offered rarely covers everything needed but often covers some items or quantities that are not needed. It rarely provides a specification for quality. Negotiate for a work letter that gives you what is needed, e.g., metal partitions in place of sheet rock, additional floor outlets, etc. Insist on product names, or their equivalent, if specifications for material are omitted. To start negotiations, present your own version of an optimum work letter.

*Key Lease Clauses.* The lease should provide for changes in work letter allowances with credits for unused allowances; the right to substitute similar items in place of landlord's products; the cost basis for *additional work*, i.e., work beyond what the work letter offers (this should be at the *landlord's cost* plus a fixed profit-overhead factor, usually 10 to 21 percent); the right to use your own contractor for *tenant's installations* (e.g., cabinetwork, carpet, wall coverings). It should include a *rent commencement* clause, stating when rent begins (ideally, this should be when the landlord has completed all work that was undertaken for the tenant and when public areas and all building systems are complete). It should include terms for *rent escalation* (due to increases in operating cost and taxes), subleasing, options to cancel, options for more space, change to electric metering, hours and seasons for HVAC, and rights during construction and move-in (to power, trash removal, and use of elevators).

**Renovate Space** A major renovation requires more planning than new construction. Work must usually be done in two or more stages, moving part of the office to temporary quarters while that part is renovated. Basic systems (HVAC, plumbing, power capacity, elevator service, etc.) must be eval-

**TABLE O-7   Computation of Usable Area**

Planning Unit AA: Executive Group

| Title | Space type | Unit area | 19XX Person | 19XX Area | 19YY Person | 19YY Area |
|---|---|---|---|---|---|---|
| President | X | 500 | 1 | 500 | 1 | 500 |
| Executive vice-president | A | 300 | 1 | 300 | 2 | 600 |
| Vice-president | B | 225 | 2 | 450 | 2 | 450 |
| Administrative assistant | D | 100 | 1 | 100 | 2 | 200 |
| Executive secretary | OSX | 100 | 2 | 200 | 3 | 300 |
| Secretary | OS | 75 | 2 | 150 | 2 | 150 |
| Clerk | OC | 55 | | | 1 | 55 |
| Reception area | | | 1 | 500 | 1 | 500 |
| Board room | | | | 600 | | 600 |
| Subtotal | | | 10 | 2800 | 14 | 3355 |
| Intraunit Circulation, 15 percent | | | | 420 | | 503 |
| Subtotal | | | | 3220 | | 3858 |
| Interunit Circulation, 10 percent | | | | 322 | | 386 |
| Total | | | | 3542 | | 4244 |

uated and, if found inadequate for long-range needs, they should be replaced or corrected as part of the renovation. If more than one-third of the original construction must be replaced, it usually pays to gut the space and build a totally new interior—since the unit costs of renovation (e.g., replacing one light fixture, building one foot of partition) is far more than the unit costs for new construction in space that has been cleared of existing walls and ceilings.

## DESIGNING THE OFFICE FACILITY

If not done previously, it makes economic sense to retain professional help for the design phase. Secure top management's approval of cost and content before proceeding with each of the successive steps that follow.

*Design Concept and Scope Budget.* Determine the criteria that will affect design and budget: style or design look desired, luxurious or modest, need for flexibility, new versus existing furniture, open versus constructed layout. The planning consultant or architect should then prepare a design concept and scope budget. The design-concept presentation should include a layout system, sketches of typical design treatment, sketches of important special facilities, alternative color palettes, alternative furniture lines, alternative furnishing items (e.g., carpet, wall surfaces). The scope budget should include furniture, decorative items, art, directional signage (i.e., signs directing visitors to various departments), telephone, special facilities, special utilities, move, and security. Secure management approval before proceeding.

*Space Study.* First prepare a *stacking plan*, showing how departments will be assigned to floors, both for stage 2 and stage 3 growth. After approval, prepare a *blocking plan* for each floor, showing the approximate boundaries of departments on the floor and of any planning units that are separated from their departments. Next, prepare a preliminary *space study*, showing the exact boundaries of every planning unit, all constructed partition and door locations, each work station location (and as many titles or names as are needed to identify the use of the station), each special facility, and the location of major elements of open space (e.g., file groupings, reception areas, and copy and supply centers). For each typical space category (e.g., private spaces A, B, C, etc; open spaces OSX, OS, OA, and OC, etc.) show at least one complete furniture arrangement. Review the preliminary space study with department heads and key planning unit heads and

revise the space study until it is accepted. Secure signatures of approval from each department head on the final space study.

*Final Layout.* Develop the approved final space study into a *final layout*, showing types of partitions, all furniture and files, telephone locations, all equipment requiring special construction (i.e., special electrical, ventilation, plumbing, reinforcing work, etc.), and all titles (and some names if necessary to clarify). Secure signed approval of planning unit heads, then of department heads, then of top management. This document becomes the basis for all construction and procurement, and changes after this point might stop progress and result in extraordinary costs.

*Final Design and Budget.* These should be prepared simultaneously with the final layout. All three must be presented to top management at one time, since a change in layout or design affects the budget. The *final design* should include sketches and large-scale layouts of important areas, colored renderings of important design features, models or photos of models, perhaps full-size mock-ups of open plan work stations, a color palette and sample boards of every fabric or material, photos of every piece of new furniture, an exhibit of typical art proposed. The *final budget* should detail every cost, including allowances for delivery, storage, taxes, and contingencies. Following approval of these three final documents, documentation and procurement can proceed.

*Documentation.* A series of plans and related specifications must be submitted to the landlord or to your own contractors for costing. These could include plans for demolition, construction, electrical and telephone, reflected ceilings, sections, elevations, and other details (of construction). In addition, a separate set of plans and details is needed for cabinetwork, which frequently is contracted for separately from general construction. Special plans will be needed for audiovisual facilities, security systems, speaker systems (for masking sound, music, or announcements), communications networks, and any operations areas (EDP, dispatch centers, medical, kitchen, mail, print shops, etc.). New furniture should be documented by detailed specifications, suitable for getting competitive bids, by instruction to bidders, and (after selection of bidders) by purchase orders. Set up a cost control system at this time, covering budget amounts, amounts committed, construction revisions, field authorized work, and engineering changes. Document any controversies, changes, or delays that might become the basis for future claims.

## IMPLEMENTING THE DESIGN

There are four important aspects of design implementation: technical, bids and estimates, procurement, and supervision.

**Technical**  Plans and specifications must comply with fire and other local codes, and with the Office of Safety and Health Administration (OSHA), the national code on health and safety. A series of engineering reviews are needed: structural (for reinforced areas and stair openings), mechanical (for HVAC and plumbing), and electrical. Some design might be needed, and engineering plans must be prepared. A set of plans, based on the interior design and engineering plans, must be filed locally by a licensed architect or engineer and approved before construction can proceed. Since plans must be filed for renovation work, a seemingly minor renovation can invoke the latest codes and lead to more extensive work than was anticipated.

**Bids and Estimates**  The sum of all interior design and engineering plans, frequently called *tenant plans*, will be the basis for costing and construction by the landlord or the general contractor. Depending on how well the work letter was negotiated, some of this cost is the landlord's, the balance is yours. The landlord or general contractor must provide a firm, detailed estimate for approval or, if several contractors are considered, firm bids for all work. When the landlord has the exclusive right to perform all work, competitive bids are excluded. Estimates tend to be considerably higher when they are noncompetitive; a 20 to 100 percent differential is not uncommon.

**Furniture and Furnishings Procurement**  Written purchase orders, specifying all price elements, time, and terms for delivery are needed. Suppliers should acknowledge the price and delivery schedule for each order. A month before delivery is due, confirm that each shipment will be made on time. Delivery must be scheduled by floor. On each floor, furniture must follow carpet installation, which must follow painting, which must follow completion of construction. Furniture delivered ahead of schedule must be handled twice and is subject to damage and theft.

**Supervision**  The tenant's representative (interior planner or architect) must check all work specified by the tenant's interior plans, even though the landlord's architect has the ultimate responsibility for checking the work of the landlord's contractors. At the start of construction on the tenant's floors, field checks should be made every few days. When partition, lighting, electric outlet, and HVAC diffuser locations are being set, the tenant's representative should be on the job full time. A *punch list* should be prepared by room and by floor, listing errors, omissions, and defective work, and the list should be submitted to the landlord or general contractor weekly. The tenant's representative and the landlord's and general contractor's representatives should then meet at the job site, review and inspect each item, and determine what action will be taken.

The same process is required for all work performed by the tenant's own contractors and suppliers for cabinetwork, carpet, draperies, furniture, signage, audiovisual work, etc. When deliveries or installation are due, the tenant's representative should be on hand to observe the work.

## MANAGING THE MOVE

Several steps will enable the company to manage the move efficiently.

**Orientation of Personnel**  Executives and other employees should be familiarized with the project at three points: at the time the project starts, when a final design has been approved, and just before the move. The project must be sold to one's own company, particularly if new concepts are involved, e.g., open planning and administrative support systems. Everyone should be familiarized with the layout and with the new neighborhood. A series of group meetings, tours of the new premises, an orientation brochure, and a slide show can be helpful.

**Selecting a Moving Company**  Intrastate moves are state regulated, usually costed on numbers of loads, personnel, and time. Interstate moves are federally regulated and costed on weight and distance. For intrastate (and local) moves, competing movers will prepare estimates, using the same unit costs, but advance estimates are not binding. Therefore, select the mover based on past experience or on the recent experience of other companies of similar size.

**Logistics of the Move**  The mover, interior planner or architect, and your own staff should jointly plan the move (what to move, when and how to pack, how to tag, how to schedule) and arrange for partial moves (e.g., files and storage one weekend, balance the next). Prepare a move plan by coloring a copy of the final layout to distinguish new furniture and cabinetwork from items to be moved. Each space at the new location should have a wall-mounted sketch (or cut-out of the move plan) showing how each piece of furniture should be placed. Otherwise, someone must be on hand as each piece is placed, or everything will have to be shifted later.

Be certain the landlord will cooperate with your mover, that your schedule has been agreed to, that entrance doors are clear, elevators and building staff available, and loading docks clear. The cost of a poorly managed move can be double that of one that is well managed.

## CURRENT PLANNING CONCEPTS

The following developments indicate the dynamic nature of space planning concepts.

**Planning for Change**  Most companies grow, reorganize, and change functions on a continuing basis. It is not unusual for 20 percent or more of all personnel to be assigned new space each year. Renovation costs are high, and even a minor renovation disrupts the work of most of the floor's personnel. A good plan is one that accommodates change with the least amount of renovation.

**Hard Areas versus Soft Areas**  Identify the *hard areas*, i.e., those spaces that require unique or expensive construction: executive suites, food service, EDP, conference and training rooms, and medical facilities. Limit hard areas as much as possible; i.e., give vice-presidents better furniture and furnishings rather than custom lighting or cabinetwork: use a standard sized office for a secondary conference room. All other spaces are *soft areas;* i.e., they can be reassigned to any other location with little or no construction. Locate hard areas so that they do not inhibit expansion or contraction of space. Do not locate hard areas on floors that might be vacated in the future. Do not disperse them; try to group them all on just a few floors. If a floor must have a mix of hard and soft areas, group all hard areas adjacent to the core, or at one end of the floor.

**Flexible Layout Patterns**  If there are a large number of private spaces, changes in soft areas may be accommodated through a flexible layout pattern. This might require that all perimeter offices be two windows wide (a four-window office can be created by removing one wall and closing one door). Or set a rule that three-window offices will be permitted only in pairs (for easy conversion to 3 twos or to a four and a two). Require that all offices be the same depth. Insist on an overall ceiling pattern, i.e., one light fixture in every module (e.g., in every 5 by 5-foot module), on an underfloor electrical distribution system, and on a flexible air supply and return (e.g., through light fixtures). No planning system can be changed economically if the ceiling has to be modified or new outlets drilled in the floor whenever space is reassigned.

**Constructed versus Movable Partitions**  A rectilinear pattern of private spaces can be created with constructed partitions (e.g., sheet rock or gypsum board, constructed on site from floor to ceiling) or with movable partitions (e.g., prefabricated panels of sheet rock, metal, wood, fiber glass, plastics, etc.). Movable partitions costs 3 to 5 times as much as constructed partitions, but they can be moved and reused. Some companies claim that renovation with movable partitions costs only 5 to 10 percent as much as renovation with constructed partitions and can be done outside of working hours.

**Open Plans**  Frequently called *open landscape*, the term *open plan* covers several types of layout. The distinguishing feature of all the layouts is that there are few, or no, constructed or movable floor-to-ceiling partitions. These include the following:

*Grid Plan.*  This is a rectilinear plan using less-than-full-height partitions. It creates an open look, since the entire ceiling can be seen from any point, but it results in acoustical problems. It is an efficient use of space.

*Cluster Plan.*  This is a plan based on the pinwheel, where three or four work stations are built around a common point, sharing common partitions and power supplies. Each person works facing a partition, with his or her back to the traffic aisles. Although the area assigned each station is relatively small, the traffic aisles and common space are large. Space use is about the same as with the grid plan, but the space is less monotonous.

*Office Landspace.*  This layout is created by plotting traffic patterns among all work stations and all work groups, and then placing work stations at locations dictated by the traffic pattern. Screens are used to give visual privacy, but most work stations consist only of a surface and necessary storage units. Introduced to America in the 1960s by a German firm, the Quickborner Team, the term became a catchword and has been incorrectly used to describe all open plan systems (particularly by furniture manufacturers.)

*Verticality.*  With the development of the various open plan systems, manufacturers produced components to be used in combination with movable partitions to create grid and cluster layouts. A significant change from traditional office furniture (i.e., desks, credenzas, two-drawer files, and bookcases used in a few combinations), this new furniture consists of one or two vertical panels from which the components are supported. The basic work surface (traditionally 30 by 60 inches) can be made smaller since it no longer serves a storage function; storage can be hung over the surface.

Further, the employee faces the partition while working on a task, achieving some visual privacy. The employee turns to work with visitors, usually across a small extra table.

*Evaluation.* The private office with its rarely closed door has become a status symbol and reward for professionals and managers. The productivity of such persons is not measured in terms of work units performed but in terms of general effectiveness. Where top management has failed to give strong support to open planning, and where there has been no testing and orientation, professionals and managers often claim they are less effective in an open plan. As a result, the greater the number of older professionals and managers, the less successful open plan layouts have been. When a select few retain their private offices, it is particularly difficult to persuade other persons that *open* is equal to *closed*. Where there are large clerical groups, open plan systems have been most successful.

*See also* COST IMPROVEMENT; FACILITIES AND SITE PLANNING AND LAYOUT; HUMAN FACTORS ENGINEERING; MATERIAL HANDLING; REAL ESTATE MANAGEMENT, CORPORATE; RECORDS MANAGEMENT; SYSTEMS AND PROCEDURES.

### REFERENCES

Cumpston, Charles: "Accoustical Privacy: Key to Successful Open Office Planning," *Administrative Management*, July 1973.
Cumpston, Charles: "The 'Human Factor' Trade-off with Work Station Efficiency," *Administrative Management*, May 1973.
Hayden, Richard: "How to Look for a New Corporate Home," *Administrative Management*, May 1973.
King, John: "Contracting for Standards of Service in Leased Office Space," *Administrative Management*, February 1977.
Probst, Robert: *The Office—A Facility Based on Change*, The Business Press, Elmhurst, Ill., 1968.
Saphier, Michael: *Office Planning and Design*, McGraw-Hill Book Company, New York, 1968.
Shoshkes, Lila: *Space Planning: Designing the Office Environment*, Architectural Records Books, New York, 1976.
Stang, Claus D.: "Office Landscape Planning," *The Office*, October 1974.
Tierney, Ernest T.: "Five Steps to Better Office Layout," *Administrative Management*, September 1972.

HERBERT L. NEWMARK, *Planning Consultant Pompano Beach, Florida*

## Office systems   (*See* ADMINISTRATIVE MANAGEMENT.)

## Officer, chief financial (CFO)   (*See* FINANCIAL MANAGEMENT.)

## Officers, corporate

Corporate officers bear the company's heaviest responsibilities, for their decisions are legally binding on the corporation and they are the principle determinant of the company's destiny and performance. Since the officers are the top leadership group, their selection and performance are of critical importance.

State laws of incorporation without exception require boards of directors to elect the company officers. Corporate bylaws set forth the roles, duties, and titles of the corporate officers, together with procedures for their election or removal and other matters of governance. Bylaws, however, typically allow great flexibility in the board's determination of officer roles, duties, and titles. The specifications in bylaws are more general than typical job descriptions.

The titles and duties of officers are by no means standardized or uniform, but general patterns common to many enterprises have evolved. It is important to note that companies are empowered within the bylaws to change the roles and titles of officers to fit the changing status of people and the changing needs of the organization.

**Definition and Types of Officers**   The term *officer* is applied loosely, but it has come to be used to cover two main categories based on the focus of their responsibilities. The first is that of *officer of the board*, which includes officials who conduct the activities of the board itself or who come most closely under the direct authority of the board. The second category consists of *other officers* such as vice-presidents, whose primary responsibilities are in the operating sectors of the company.

**Officers of the Board**   Officers of the board typically include the chairman of the board, who serves primarily as the board's chief agent or representative, plus the chairmen of its various committees, and a secretary of the board.

*Chairman of the Board.*   Historically, the leadership of the board has been assigned to a chairman of the board. The chairman acts as the board's agent in the management of its own activities and also in the delegation of responsibilities to the top operations officers, principally the president or a person designated as the chief executive officer.

The chairman of the board may be on a full-time or a part-time basis, depending on the scope of the role assigned to the chairman compared with the roles of the other officers, especially that of the president. If the corporation decides to have only one top leadership position at the officer level, it is usually a full-time chairman of the board. If it chooses a dual leadership pattern, the president is usually designated as the other top officer. In this case the chairman of the board may be a part-time appointment, focusing on activities of the board itself and on the management of its retained powers and activities, while the president carries out operating responsibilities technically delegated by the board. In some companies, the selection of a chairman in addition to a president is mandatory; in others, it is optional.

*Chief Executive Officer.* The use of this title is confusing because it is used in various ways. Its primary use is in the designation of an officer attached to operations, mainly the president, as in the combined title of president and chief executive officer. The term, however, is occasionally used for an individual performing a wider role than that of president. It is sometimes combined, for example, with the chairman of the board.

The chief executive officer is the most important officer position, but the role varies widely from company to company. Some chief executive officers perform the dual roles of heading the board's activities with respect to powers it has reserved for itself and of carrying out the operational activities of the company. If the two top roles are separated, the chairman of the board takes the former role and the chief executive officer the latter. In practice, these distinctions are not always closely followed. The chief executive officer usually has a wide latitude for actions within the delegated scope of responsibilities. The chief executive officer makes recommendations to the board on basic policies but can take specific actions on subsidiary matters. Since chief executive officers have wide latitude in formulating proposals going before the board, they occupy a very powerful position. The chief executive officer also predominates in the selection of all other officers, though in theory they are also elected by the board.

*The President.* This role is usually combined with that of the chief executive officer, but it may be delegated to a separate officer. In either case, the president is a key link between the board itself and the other operating officers.

*Other Board Officers.* Under most bylaws the board is empowered to appoint other officers as are needed to manage the activities it retains and does not delegate. For example, the board may appoint a secretary of the board (not to be confused with the corporate secretary); it also elects the chairmen of its various committees.

**Other Officers** In addition to the positions described above, the board usually elects the following officers: the corporate secretary, the treasurer, and the vice-presidents of operating units.

The chief executive officer, except for the appointment of the officer who may be a possible successor, has a strong voice in choosing those who serve under him or her. This includes the other officers as well as nonofficer executives in top management. Boards, however, typically exercise careful control over the officer who is likely to succeed the chief executive officer—the president or an executive vice-president.

*Corporate Secretary.* The traditional role of corporate secretary has been to keep minutes of board and stockholder meetings, to keep registers of stockholders and stock certificates, to send out meeting notices, and to keep the corporate seal. Sometimes the corporate secretary also serves as board secretary, preparing agendas, distributing working documents, planning meeting arrangements, and the like. In practice, the role of secretary has been expanded to include a variety of other duties, such as records management, office management, financial work, liaison with stock exchanges, and supervision of transfer agents and dividend disbursement agents. Some corporate secretaries direct legal work associated with contracts, leases, patents, and trademarks. Often the secretary is also the corporation's legal counsel. The secretary usually reports to the company's chief executive officer.

*Treasurer.* The treasurer receives and has custody of corporate funds and keeps accounts thereof, prepares financial reports, and directs accounting policies and practices. Other duties, such as credit management or real estate development, are sometimes assigned. One important responsibility is to make financial reports directly to the board and to the chief executive officer. The treasurer may report directly to the chief executive officer, but more often reports indirectly through a vice-president for finance. The principal financial officer is often known as the chief financial officer (CFO).

*Vice-Presidents.* The principal vice-presidents in charge of the major functions or divisional units are usually elected officers. These include the vice-presidents of finance, marketing, and production, group vice-presidents, and senior vice-presidents. Less frequently, vice-presidents in staff functions such as personnel are elected as officers. In large, multidivisional firms, the chief executives of divisions or subsidiaries often hold the title of divisional president in addition to being elected vice-presidents of the corporation.

**Compensation of Officers** Full-time officers are compensated by a combination of salaries, bonuses, options, and other fringe benefits. (*See* COMPENSATION, EXECUTIVE.) Part-time officers may be compensated by prorated salaries or by fees. Most boards have a compensation committee which guides all executive compensation policies for the company.

The board of directors usually approves the salaries of full-time officers, as well as bonus, profit sharing, or stock option plans. To avoid conflicts of interest, bonus and option decisions are generally made by a committee consisting of directors, none of whom will themselves benefit.

A problem exists in cases where officers are also directors and therefore in the position of fixing their own compensation. Sometimes independent judgments are then sought from outside directors or even from majority stockholders. The salaries of officers who are not directors are largely influenced by their immediate supervisors, though board approval may be required by the bylaws.

*See also* BOARD OF DIRECTORS; BOARDS OF DIRECTORS, LEGAL LIABILITY GUIDELINES; COMMITTEES; COMPENSATION, EXECUTIVE; MANAGER, DEFINITIONS OF; ORGANIZATION STRUCTURES AND CHARTING.

### REFERENCES

Fever, Mortimer: *Handbook for Corporate Directors,* Prentice-Hall, Inc., Englewood Cliffs, N.J., 1965.

Juran, J. M., and J. Keith Louden: *The Corporate Director,* American Management Association, New York, 1966.

Koontz, Harold: *The Board of Directors and Effective Management,* McGraw-Hill Book Company, New York, 1967.

Mace, Myles L.: *Directors: Myth and Reality,* Harvard Business School, Division of Research, Boston, 1971.

Vance, Stanley: *Boards of Directors: Structure and Performance,* University of Oregon Press, Eugene, 1964.

DALTON E. MCFARLAND, *University of Alabama in Birmingham*

# Older employees, management of

Older employees, whether management or nonmanagement, whether men or women, present both advantages and inevitable problems to the manager. While it is a mistake to characterize older employees as a completely special breed, there are clear differences between them and employees, for example, in their late teens or early twenties. Definitions of *older* can vary, and deviations from any broad pattern are frequent, depending on specific industry practice, union arrangements, and cultural influences.

**Chronological Definition** By age 45, employees have become *older*. Typically, while in their twenties, they have completed their education or training and have made at least a tentative commitment to a career or trade or organization. In their thirties, they usually acquire both some solid experience in a field (depth) and some degree of variety in assignments (breadth). By their forties, they may take on major responsibilities associated with maturity and job seasoning. They already have family responsibilities, often heavy ones; signs of both physical aging and emotional wear are more evident. They are mature, settled, experienced, and usually well trained. Inevitably they are *older*.

**Characteristics** In 1976 there were 32.1 million people between the ages of 45 and 64 employed in United States nonagricultural industries—20.0 million men and 12.1 million women—or 42 percent of the nonagricultural work force. Among men in the labor force, 91.2 percent between the ages of 45 and 54 were working, as were 76.3 percent between the ages of 55 and 64. Among women the percentages were 54.3 and 40.4 percent, respectively.[1] During those age periods, unemployment rates were at the lowest levels of the adult working years, at about 2.5 percent for men and 3.5 percent for women (1974 figures).[2]

*Health.* Older employees' health records are consistently better, and men's health records are better than women's. This shows up in the following measures per 100 employed persons: (1) days lost from work; (2) days of restricted activity associated with acute conditions; (3) incidence of acute conditions; (4) days of bed disability; and (5) days of restricted activity. Only in the average *duration of disability* do older male employees show up worse than older female employees (8.4 days average versus 5.2 days average).[3] *Punctuality* records among older workers are also found to be better.

*Job Stability.* Older employees have considerable job stability but not significantly more than younger workers. A study of men 45 to 69 during the 3-year period 1966 to 1969 showed only 1 in 5 changing employers during that time, with 60 percent of the shifts occurring voluntarily.[4] Job changing was unrelated to race but closely tied to length of service, income, and occupation. Five years of service is a key stage in job stability, with men being 8 times as likely to shift voluntarily and 3 times as likely to shift involuntarily before that period. Blue-collar workers shift more readily than white-collar workers, and higher wages are a significant motivation in changing jobs. Men who reported themselves as "content" with their jobs were less likely to shift.

*Occupational Stability.* Older workers also have occupational stability, with career shifts being less likely with advancing age.[5] One result is an overrepresentation of older workers in receding or nonexpanding occupations, including management and administration. Earnings peak in the 45 to 54-year-old category for managerial employees and in the 35 to 44-year-old category for craftsworkers. *Educational differences* are narrowing rapidly, being most pronounced among those over 55.

**Legal Requirements** The Age Discrimination in Employment Act (ADEA) forbids discrimination against workers aged 40 to 64 who are working for commerce-related employers with 20 or more employees, for governmental units, in unions of 25 plus members or using hiring halls, or placed through employment agencies.[6] Discrimination based on age is forbidden in hiring, firing, promoting, classifying, paying, advertising, assigning, or eligibility for union membership. There are certain exceptions for apprenticeship programs, benefit plans, and clearly job-related age requirements. Sentiment is also growing for removal of mandated retirement at 65, either through an extension of this law beyond 64 or by court action. The law is hard to enforce, especially when employer action is linked to other factors, but government enforcement efforts are increasingly apparent. Equal Opportunity Laws can also apply in many of these situations.

**Comparisons with Younger Employees** Older employees can learn as well as younger workers and can be retrained as easily.[7] Except in very special circumstances, physical impairment is insignificant and safety statistics are better. Older managers are as effective information processors as younger managers and diagnose data more accurately although more slowly.[8] However, they have also been shown to have poorer short-term mental retention.[9] They are also less effective than younger managers in operating in groups and in using groups to accomplish a task, perhaps because of the exposure by younger managers to more group-oriented education.

*Job Satisfaction.* Job satisfaction appears to affect job performance to a considerable degree in terms described by Herzberg as performance, turnover, interpersonal relationships on the job, and mental health.[10] Herzberg also found job satisfaction high when people started their first job; it then declined until about age 30, when it began to rise for the remainder of the work career. Otherwise, the relationship of age to job satisfaction is not nearly as

clear as are, for example, the level of occupation, achievement, recognition, advancement, or the work itself.

**Midlife Problems** It is evident that something special takes place in midlife. A Massachusetts study of industry's reluctance to hire middle-aged managerial candidates noted that middle-aged candidates had poor general health and appearance, relied excessively on outdated experience, were reluctant to undertake training, and performed poorly in training undertaken.[11]

The midlife crisis is a common observance. The period after 35 is the time of greatest expansion of the human personality, when mature adults are in widest contact with their surroundings. Yet psychological and physical aging is evident to the older person who subtly gives up on competition, emphasizes personal relationships, and substitutes new motivations for living. Older employees begin to adjust to the limitations of their organizational prospects. When satisfaction with life and job is lowered, job effectiveness is also lowered; and the two satisfactions are inevitably linked. At the same time, mobility or a fresh start are discouraged by corporate and social "freeze-in" devices, such as fringe benefits. There are few significant problems in managing older employees, however, who are at high or rising positions in the organization, have authority and position, receive satisfying monetary and symbolic rewards, and clearly are considered vital parts of the organization. This is as true of blue-collar workers as it is of white-collar employees.[12] The problem for management comes when employees of whatever level no longer look to the organization for satisfaction of important elements of their aspirations. They then react similarly to employees in their mid twenties.

**Managerial Responses** Correct and positive approaches to the management of older employees fit a number of categories:

1. *Health.* Despite favorable absence and health statistics among older employees, management must be alert to overall general health, which can point to incipient problems (weight, blood pressure, alcoholism, etc.), and to psychological well being. Independent outside psychiatric consultants are recommended to handle midlife crises. The annual checkup is highly recommended.

2. *Obsolescence.* Executive development is widely used in industry and government, but it is often confined to rising or high-status managers. A full range of carefully considered programs make suitable provisions against obsolescence. If the employee *will not* adjust, there should be incentives to

mobility, including early pensions, severance pay, placement services, etc.

3. *Promotions, transfers, salary treatment, etc.* It is fatal to give the best treatment to younger employees. It symbolizes to older employees that their worst fears are essentially correct. Of course, there are cases justifying bias, but the reasons must be evident to all, including the employees involved.

4. *Fringe benefits.* These are too often mere satisfiers rather than dynamic aspects of employee growth. For example, tuition reimbursement should be granted only when the result of the schooling fits into the plans of both the employee *and* management. Health plans should have prevention and examination features. Pension plans should encourage leaving as well as staying, especially at management levels. Vacations are vital to both physical and mental well being: they are seldom managed other than routinely.

5. *Assignments.* Observers point out that older employees have a growing interest in other people. Japanese industry uses the "godfather" concept, linking older and younger employees rather than having them compete. The reward systems should encourage the development of the young to the benefit of the organization. It may be generally useful to downplay competition beyond a certain point in age or position.

6. *Leaves of absence.* In selected and carefully considered cases, a leave of absence can be the means of giving a new outlook to older employees. Academic sabbaticals are proven cases in point.

7. *Performance.* It is important that expectations of older employees be kept high, including level of output and quality of performance. There should be no rewards for age in terms of slackened performance, since experience and high-quality performance are precisely what older employees can give to the organization.

8. *Management attitude.* This will signal clearly whether the organization considers older employees valuable assets or burdens to be suffered. Younger employees will note this attitude in looking to their own commitment to the organization. Older employees will determine from it their own level of commitment.

*See also* MINORITIES, MANAGEMENT OF AND EQUAL EMPLOYMENT OPPORTUNITY; WOMEN IN INDUSTRY; YOUNGER EMPLOYEES, MANAGEMENT OF.

## NOTES

[1] *Employment and Earnings*, U.S. Department of Labor, Bureau of Labor Statistics, Washington, February 1976, p. 55.

[2] *Handbook of Labor Statistics*, U.S. Department of Labor, Bureau of Labor Statistics, Washington, 1975, p. 161.

[3] *Vital and Health Statistics*, U.S. Department of Health, Education, and Welfare, Public Health Service, Washington, 1974.

[4] *Monthly Labor Review*, U.S. Department of Labor, Manpower Administration, Washington, June 1973, pp. 60–61.

[5] Shirley H. Rhine, "The Senior Worker—Employed and Unemployed," *The Conference Board Record*, vol. 13, no. 5, pp. 7ff., May 1976.

[6] "Age Discrimination in Employment Act (ADEA)," *The CPA Journal*, vol. 45, no. 12, pp. 70–71, December 1975.

[7] Rhine, op. cit.

[8] Ronald N. Taylor, "Age and Experience as Determinants of Managerial Information Processing and Decision Making Performance," *Academy of Management Journal*, vol. 18, no. 1, pp. 74ff., March 1975.

[9] Wayne K. Kirchner, "Age Differences in Short-Term Retention," *Journal of Experimental Psychology*, vol. 55, no. 4, pp. 357–358, 1958.

[10] John W. Hunt and Peter N. Saul, "The Relationship of Age, Tenure, and Job Satisfaction in Males and Females," *Academy of Management Journal*, vol. 18, no. 4, pp. 690ff., December 1975.

[11] *The Aging Worker: Insights into the Massachusetts Problem*, John F. Kennedy Family Service Center, Inc., Older Worker Training and Employment Program, The Kennedy Center, Boston, 1969.

[12] Cyrus A. Altimus and Richard J. Tersine, "Chronological Age and Job Satisfaction: The Young Blue Collar Worker," *Academy of Management Journal*, vol. 16, no. 1, pp. 53ff., March 1973.

## REFERENCES

Criss, James C.: "The Out-Of-Date Employee in an Up-to-Date World," *Journal of Systems Management*, vol. 24, no. 10, October 1973.

Herzberg, Frederick, Bernard Mausner, and Barbara Block Snyderman: *The Motivation to Work*, John Wiley & Sons, Inc., New York, 1967.

Saleh, Shorekry, D., and Jay L. Otis: "Age and Level of Job Satisfaction," *Personnel Psychology*, vol 17, no. 4, Winter 1964.

Schultz, Duane: "Managing the Middle-Aged Manager," *Personnel*, vol. 51, no. 6, November–December 1974.

Webber, Ross A.: "The Relation of Group Performance to the Age of Members in Homogeneous Groups," *Academy of Management Journal*, vol. 17, no. 3, September 1974.

PHILIP T. CROTTY, *Northeastern University*

## Oligopolist (*See* PRODUCT AND SERVICE PRICING.)

## Oligopoly (*See* COMPETITION; ECONOMIC CONCEPTS.)

## Ombudsman

In Sweden and other countries, an official appointed by a legislative body to hear and investigate complaints by private citizens against government and government agencies is an *ombudsman*. In business, one who performs the same function for employees who have complaints about their superiors or company policies is an *ombudsman*. (An occasional firm also employs an ombudsman to represent the interests of the public it serves—as at the *Washington Post*.)

Business ombudsmen have no line authority but generally report to someone high in the corporate hierarchy (for example, the company president, a division manager, or a group vice-president). When they believe a complaint is justified, they may take it to higher and higher levels to get action. They may also recommend changes in company personnel policies.

Ombudsmen represent only nonunionized employees since complaints by union members will be handled under the usual grievance procedure.

*See also* ETHICS, MANAGERIAL; SOCIAL RESPONSIBILITY OF BUSINESS.

### REFERENCES
Dunn, Frederica H.: "The View from the Ombudsman's Chair," *New York Times*, Financial Section, May 2, 1976.

"How the Xerox Ombudsman Helps Xerox," *Business Week*, May 12, 1973, pp. 188 and 190.

Silver, Isadore: "The Corporate Ombudsman," *Harvard Business Review*, May–June 1967, pp. 77–87.

"Where the Ombudsmen Work Out," *Business Week*, May 3, 1976, pp. 114 and 116.

STAFF/SMITH

## Operating variables (*See* CONTROL SYSTEMS, MANAGEMENT.)

## Operation, large-scale (*See* PRODUCTION PROCESSES.)

## Operation chart (*See* PAPER WORK SIMPLIFICATION.)

## Operation symbol (*See* WORK SIMPLIFICATION AND IMPROVEMENT.)

## Operational approach (*See* MANAGEMENT THEORY, SCIENCE, AND APPROACHES.)

## Operational audit (*See* AUDIT, MANAGEMENT.)

## Operational management (*See* PLANNING, STRATEGIC MANAGERIAL.)

## Operations, sustaining (*See* INNOVATION AND CREATIVITY.)

## Operations management (*See* PRODUCTION/OPERATIONS MANAGEMENT.)

## Operations research and mathematical modeling

Since the early 1940s something called *operations research* in the United States and *operational research* in Great Britain (and *management science* in many university business admininstration or management schools) has emerged and developed to extraordinary dimensions. Operations research (commonly referred to as OR) has established itself as an activity that can and does bring new concepts, new ideas, new attitudes, and new approaches to the aide of management. Despite OR's rapid growth and increasing acceptance by all types of organizations, a great deal of confusion exists in many people's minds as to its nature and domain. In some aspects, it is similar to systems engineering and industrial engineering. It also depends heavily upon model building. applied mathematics, and applied economics. But these elements do not define OR. For example, *OR is not* (1) simply a collection of tools and/or mathematical techniques such as linear programming, theory of games, simulation, and queueing theory; (2) mathematical model building and manipulation, unless one wishes to conclude that all science is operations research; (3) utilization of interdisciplinary teams to study complex problems, although this approach is often followed; (4) a form of management. In fact, without the existence and participation of management, OR is a meaningless academic exercise.

**Nature and Domain of OR** Operations research defies easy definition because it uses the methodology and tools of various fields of science and engineering to study operations that are not conventionally the province of the scientist. A partial but circular definition is that operations research is research on operations. But this does not specify the type of research, its purpose, or on what operations. Accordingly, *operations research* can be defined broadly as the study of complex systems of people, equipment, money, and operational procedures for the purpose of understanding how they function, in order to improve their efficiency and effectiveness. Such studies are conducted through the use of the scientific method, utilizing tools and knowledge from the physical, mathematical, and behavioral sciences. Its ultimate purpose is to provide the manager with a sound, scientific, and quantitative basis for decision making.

*Purpose.* Operations research is concerned with determining (1) how a system behaves under a wide range of conditions; (2) the relationships between the components which explain why the system behaves in this manner; and (3) how the manager can improve and control the behavior and performance of the system to achieve the desired goals and objectives. Thus, OR is concerned with the solution of executive-type problems. Its goal is to provide management with better insight into and an understanding of the systems for which they are responsible. It is also concerned with providing management with a scientific basis for solving problems involving the interaction of the different functional units of the organization in terms of the best interests of the total organization.

*Technique.* Operations research accomplishes these goals by providing management with pertinent information upon which to make decisions. This information is obtained by utilizing the diverse skills of a mixed (academic and experience) group of appropriate researchers. This mixed team utilizes the scientific method and any or all available tools and techniques which are appropriate, to gather and process this information so as to analyze the operations of complex systems. The critical point in all of this is the purpose, not the methods. If an operations research study has not resulted in better decisions by the manager, it has failed, no matter how elegant its approach or technique. The end goal and criterion by which it must always be judged is results.

## AREAS OF APPLICATION

Operations research has been successfully applied in virtually every kind of business, industrial, and governmental organization.[1] When managers discuss decisions to be made, they often express a belief that their problems are different from those confronting other executives. They are correct in one sense. Problems can be viewed from two aspects—form and content. Two problems seldom have the same content, but they often have the same form. The following list illustrates some of the areas in which OR has been successfully applied.

**Production**  This includes: (1) production planning and scheduling, including decisions on product mixes, sequencing of jobs, overtime, scheduling, etc., (2) allocation of production orders to different plants or departments on the basis of production or transportation costs; (3) scheduling of maintenance (both preventive and corrective) and replacement of equipment; (4) assembly line balancing and allocation of facilities and personnel; (5) raw material and in-process inventory management; and (6) analysis of waiting lines and bottlenecks.

**Facilities Planning**  This includes: (1) number and location of factories, warehouses, tool cribs, service yards, retail outlets, fire stations, ambulances, schools, etc.; (2) internal allocation and layout of space; and (3) design of material handling systems.

**Purchasing and Procurement**  This includes: (1) development of rules for buying supplies with stable or significantly varying prices; (2) determination of quantities, timing, and source of purchase; (3) make-or-buy decisions of parts and components; (4) purchase-or-lease decisions on vehicles and equipment; and (5) spare-parts stocking requirements as well as problems associated with deterioration and shrinkage.

**Investment and Finance**  This includes: (1) cash-flow analysis, long-range capital requirements, alternative investments, and sources of capital; (2) development of automated dated processing systems, accounting systems, and auditing procedures; (3) diversification and acquisition decisions; (4) stock and bond portfolio selection; (5) budgeting, planning, and control; and (6) financial forecasting.

**Marketing**  This includes: (1) advertising strategies, including selection of media, frequency of advertising, and allocation of budget to various media; (2) product selection and timing of new products; (3) forecasting demand; (4) pricing and bidding strategies; (5) number of salespeople, size of territories, and allocation of sales effort; (6) salespeople's compensation and incentive plans; (7) warranty and customer service strategies; (8) company-owned outlets versus franchising decisions; and (9) space allocation for display and stock accessibility.

**Transportation and Physical Distribution** This includes: (1) multilevel inventory control systems; (2) worldwide logistics and supply systems; (3) development of transportation and support policies; and (4) determination of optimum routing of distribution and supply vehicles.

**Research and Development** This includes: (1) evaluation of alternative designs; (2) determination of areas of research needed and technological forecasting; (3) selection of individual projects; (4) allocation of resources between R&D projects; and (5) coordination and management control procedures for complex R&D projects.

**Personnel** This includes: (1) selection and recruiting policies of personnel, including determination of mixes of age and skills needed; (2) analysis of factors influencing labor turnover, absenteeism, and grievances; and (3) development of incentive, productivity improvement, and performance measurement schemes.

**Governmental** This includes: (1) analyses of air, rail, highway, and waterway transportation systems, including routes; (2) development of waste pickup and disposal strategies, including vehicle routing; (3) determination of school districts and school bus routings; (4) traffic control studies; (5) urban planning, including land use, transportation, and community facilities; (6) economic planning; (7) cost-benefit analysis; and (8) evaluation of military weapons and strategies.

## OR METHODOLOGY

Operations research emphasizes the application of the scientific method to the analysis and solution of decision problems. The *scientific method* is a rational, systematic method of approaching a problem and consists of the three phases of analysis, synthesis, and evaluation. Generally these consist of the following:

*Analysis Phase.* (1) Awareness and identification of needs; (2) definition in specific and detailed terms of the problem to be solved and the goals to be achieved; (3) gathering and structuring of information; (4) identification of the boundary conditions (i.e., what is and is not a part of the system); (5) identification of the relevant components of the system, including (*a*) input versus output variables, (*b*) controllable versus uncontrollable variables, and (*c*) decision makers and the decision-making process.

*Synthesis Phase.* (1) Determination of the criteria to be used for measuring effectiveness; (2) construction of an appropriate model; (3) data gathering; and

(4) search for and derivation of feasible solutions from the model.

*Evaluation Phase.* (1) Evaluation of solutions derived from the model; (2) making a decision; (3) implementing the decision; and (4) closure to see if the problem is really solved.

The phases and steps listed above are by no means completely definitive nor self-inclusive, nor do they always appear in the same order. All the steps represent continuing efforts throughout a study, with recurring interplay among the steps. There is an iterative nature to decision making, with a constant roving back and forth between generality and detail, as the practitioners continuously seek to improve their understanding and the description of the problem.

**Analysis** In the execution of an OR project, the problem formulation, or analysis, is often the most important phase of a study. It is comprised of the definition of the primary and subobjectives and the identification of the variables which significantly influence the performance of the system. Identification and consideration of uncontrollable variables such as the external business environment, competitors' actions, governmental regulations, and similar factors is also important. Another important aspect is that of determining the scope of the study in terms of long- or short-range planning.

**Synthesis** In the second phase, a model is usually developed. A *model* is a representation of an object, system, or idea in some form other than that of the entity itself. Its purpose is usually to aid in explaining, understanding, or improving the system under study. In most OR studies, a mathematical model is used.

*Mathematical models* consist of equations or formulas derived to show the relationships between important factors in the operation under study. Such models can be analyzed and manipulated more easily than the real system. Proposed changes or hypotheses can be tested and evaluated using the model without disrupting the real-world system. For those who seek to understand, control, or manipulate the infinite complexities of the real world, mathematics is a very powerful tool. It is not, however, just one more tool among many. It is a conceptual tool more powerful than most others. Mathematics is the most precise, unambiguous language devised by the human race.

*Underlying Principle.* A number of specialized mathematical techniques are used in constructing OR models. Many of these will be discussed later. Even though OR models can take on many forms, their underlying principle is relatively simple. In symbolic expression, the basic form of most OR models is

$$P = f(C_i, U_j)$$

where the system's overall performance $P$ is a function of a set of controllable aspects of the system $C_i$ and set of uncontrollable aspects $U_j$. This obvious oversimplification calls attention to the fact that the performance of the system is affected by variables outside the manager's control as well as those he or she can do something about. Once a model has been set up, one seeks those values of the controllable variables $C_i$ that maximize (or minimize) the performance $P$.

*Performance Measures.* The most difficult part of an OR study may be the development of an adequate measure of the system's performance. Unfortunately, there are usually several possible measures, and the right choice depends upon which question is being asked. The measure of performance must reflect the relative importance of the many (and often conflicting) objectives involved in every management decision. These objectives are of two types—retentive and acquisitive. *Retentive objectives* are those which deal with keeping or preserving either resources (for example, time, energy, and skills) or states (for example, comfort, safety, and employment levels). *Acquisitive goals* concern acquiring resources (for example, profits, personnel, and customers) or attaining states (for example, share of market and deterrent position) that the organization or manager seeks.

**Evaluation** The final phase involves an analysis of the sensitivity of proposed solutions to slight changes in assumptions, external and internal conditions, or levels of operation. It also consists of helping (1) to implement new policies and procedures and (2) to monitor the new system after implementation to ensure that the solution is correct and is solving the problem as anticipated.

## OR TOOLS AND MODELS

*Any* analytical, logical, or graphical methods that are helpful for solving problems are useful tools in operations research. Operations research uses techniques adopted from many fields such as physics, biology, chemistry, industrial engineering, electrical engineering, psychology, and most particularly symbolic logic, mathematics, and probability and statistics. In addition, new methods, techniques, and tools are continuously being developed espe-

cially for OR-type problems. Obviously, the rapid advances in analog and digital computer technology have greatly aided the growth and utility of operations research. (*See* COMPUTER SYSTEMS.)

An important aspect of almost every OR study is the development of a model. A model of an object may be an exact replica of the object (although perhaps executed in a different material and to a different scale), or it may be an abstraction of the object's salient properties.

**Types of Models** The various types of OR models can be classified in numerous ways. One common method is to first classify them as iconic, analog, or symbolic.

The distinguishing characteristic of an *iconic model* is that it in some sense looks like the entity being modeled. Iconic models may be full-scale mockups (such as trainers), scaled down (such as a model of the solar system), or scaled up (such as a model of an atom). They may also be two- or three-dimensional.

*Analog models* are those in which a property of the real object or system is represented by a substituted property that often behaves in a similar manner. The problem is sometimes solved in the substituted state, and the answer is translated to the original properties. An electronic analog computer in which the voltage through a network might represent the flow of goods through a system is an excellent example of an analog model. A *graph* can also be an analog model in which distance on the graph or a measured scale represents properties such as time, age, number, dollars, etc. A graph can also show the relationship between different variables, and can predict changes in some quantities when other quantities are changed.

*Symbolic* or *mathematical models* are those in which a symbol rather than a physical device is used to represent an entity. Thus, a mathematical model might use symbols such as X and Y to represent production volume and cost. Mathematical models are the most widely used models in OR studies. It is interesting to note that many of the mathematical models used in OR were originally derived by other sciences. For example, the same set of equations used to predict radioactivity and to attain equilibrium in cyclotron bombardment of a target can be used to predict the effect of advertising on sales. The same curves used to predict the growth of bacteria can be used to predict machinery breakdowns or the failure of electronic components.

In trying to model a complex system or operation, the researcher will usually resort to a combination of several types of models. Any system can be represented in several ways, which will vary in complexity and detail. Most OR studies will result in several different models of the same system. Usually, simple models lead to more complex models as the researcher analyzes and better understands the problem.

**Properties of Good Models**   The properties of a good OR model are that it be:

1. *Relevant.* It deals with problems of importance to the manager.

2. *Valid.* A high degree of confidence can be placed in any inferences drawn from it.

3. *Nontrivial.* It leads to insights into the system not readily perceivable by direct observation.

4. *Powerful.* It provides a large number of nontrivial insights.

5. *Usable.* It provides acceptable solutions that can be implemented.

6. *Flexible.* It can provide answers to "what if" type questions.

7. *Insensitive.* Large changes in the output variables do not result from small changes in the input variables.

8. *Elegant.* The structure is simple to understand, and it runs efficiently on a computer.

9. *Cost effective.* The improvements it makes possible exceed the expense of developing and applying the model.

10. *Timely.* It can provide the needed answers within the time frame needed.

**Structure of Mathematical Models**   Because of their importance and wide use in OR studies, a manager should understand the structure and form of mathematical models. Almost every mathematical model consists of the following ingredients: (1) components, (2) variables, (3) functional relationships, (4) constraints, and (5) criterion functions.

*Components.* These are the constituent parts that, when taken together, make up the system. Components may also be referred to as *elements* or *subsystems.* In a model of a city, for example, the components might be the educational system, health system, transportation system, etc. In an economic model, the components might be individual firms, individual consumers, etc. Components are the objects constituting the system of interest.

*Variables.* These are things in a system which are subject to change. There are two types of variables in a model of a system, exogenous and endogenous. *Exogenous variables* are also called input variables; i.e., they are variables originating or produced outside the system or resulting from external causes. *Endogenous variables* may be either status

variables (to indicate their state or condition within the system) or *output* variables (to indicate their state when they leave the system). Statisticians sometimes call exogenous variables *independent*, and endogenous variables *dependent*.

*Functional Relationships.* These describe how the variables are related and show their behavior within a component or between components. These relationships are either deterministic or probabilistic in nature. *Deterministic relationships* are identities or definitions that relate certain variables where a process output is uniquely determined by a given input (i.e., if $X$ occurs, then $Y$ occurs). *Probabilistic relationships*, on the other hand, are those in which the process characteristically has an uncertain output for a given input (i.e., if $X$ occurs, then either $Y$ occurs with a probability of $\frac{1}{2}$ or $Z$ occurs). Both types of relationships usually take the form of a mathematical equation relating the endogenous and status variables to the exogenous variables. Usually these relationships can only be hypothesized or inferred from statistical and mathematical analysis.

*Constraints.* These are limitations imposed on the values of the variables or on the way in which resources can be allocated or expended. These constraints can be self-imposed (i.e., setting minimum employment levels or setting an upper limit on funds available for capital expenditure) or system-imposed (i.e., one cannot sell more items than the system can produce).

*Criterion Function.* This is an explicit statement of the objectives or goals of the system (i.e., maximize profits or minimize costs) and how they are to be evaluated. The criterion function is a standard for judging and evaluating alternatives. *Optimizing* is determining what to do with the variables under management control in order to achieve the goal(s) specified by the criterion function.

## MATHEMATICAL MODELS

In general, mathematical models useful in OR studies can be categorized as being either deterministic or probabilistic in nature. This distinction is based upon what is known about the values of the variables. In a *deterministic* model, the values of the variables are known or assumed to be known. Thus, decision theorists refer to the use of such models as decision making under conditions of certainty. The assumption of certainty implies that the consequence of selecting a particular alternative is a uniquely determined outcome. On the other hand, *probabilistic* models assume that the values of the variables are not all known with certainty but that probability distributions can be associated with each of them. These probability distributions may be derived from theoretical, empirical (actual data), or subjective (expert opinion) considerations. Decision theorists refer to the use of such models as decision making under conditions of risk.

The purpose of a good mathematical model is to help managers understand and evaluate alternative policies efficiently. The procedure used to derive a solution to the problem from the model depends upon the characteristics of the model. These procedures are either analytical or numerical. *Analytical procedures* are those in which the equation or set of equations is solved directly. For example, the researcher might differentiate the equation, set it equal to zero, and then solve for the variables of interest—or plug the values of the variables directly into the equation and evaluate the function.

*Numerical procedures* are iterative in nature (trial and error) and are usually referred to as algorithms. An *algorithm* is a systematic step-by-step procedure for finding a solution. Numerical techniques consist essentially of substituting different numbers for the symbols in the model and finding which set of substituted numbers yield the maximum effectiveness. Usually some set of rules (algorithm) is used to determine which set of numbers will be tried next. Such a procedure (which might be thought of as directed trial and error) is called *iteration*. Analytic procedures are essentially deductive in character, whereas numerical procedures are essentially inductive in character.

**Classification of Mathematical Models** In order to discuss and understand the relationship between the various mathematical techniques and models, it is convenient to try to establish a framework or classification scheme. Any such attempt suffers, of course, from its inability to show models which fall into several categories.

I. *Deterministic models*
  A. Analytic (mathematical solution)
    1. Calculus
    2. Linear algebra
    3. Differential equations
  B. Numerical (iterative)
    1. Linear programming
      (*a*) Simplex algorithm
      (*a*) Transportation algorithm
      (*c*) Assignment algorithm
      (*d*) Goal programming
    2. Network optimization algorithms
      (*a*) Maximum flow
      (*b*) Shortest path
      (*c*) Longest path
      (*d*) PERT/CPM
    3. Integer programming
      (*a*) Branch and bound algorithm
      (*b*) Zero-one algorithm
    4. Nonlinear programming
      (*a*) Search techniques
      (*b*) Separable programming
      (*c*) Quadratic programming
      (*d*) Geometric programming
    5. Dynamic programming
    6. Heuristic algorithms
    7. Gaming theory
II. *Probabilistic models*
  A. Analytic (theoretical)
    1. Probability theory
    2. Queueing theory
    3. Markov processes
    4. Renewal processes
  B. Numerical (iterative and empirical)
    1. Simulation
    2. Expected value
    3. Decision trees
    4. Regression analysis

The characteristics of some of these models will be described below.

**Deterministic Models** Many decision problems lend themselves to direct solution through the use of classical mathematical techniques. The system being studied can often be represented by an equation or set of equations which can be solved directly by calculus, linear algebra, or the methods of differential equations. For example, deterministic inventory control problems can be modeled as an equation which can be differentiated, set equal to zero, and solved for the decision variables of interest. Likewise, many control problems can be represented by a set of differential equations which can then be solved directly.

*Mathematical programming* is perhaps the most highly developed and widely used area of operations research methodology. It is a generic term mainly covering the topics of linear programming, network analysis, nonlinear programming, and dynamic programming. It is used to help solve those problems in which the decision maker must allocate scarce or limited resources among various activities in order to optimize some specified goal.

*Linear programming* deals with allocation problems where the goal can be expressed as a linear function (equation) of the alternatives subject to a group of constraints which can also be expressed as linear equations.[2] If there are multiple goals, then the technique of *goal programming* can be utilized. Although there are several specialized linear programming methods (i.e., transportation and assignment methods) which can be used if the characteristics of the problem are correct, the most versatile (or general) is the simplex method devised by George C. Dantzig. The simplex method is a very powerful computational method which allows operations researchers to attack large-scale allocation problems. Commercial linear programming codes are available from most computer manufacturers and consulting firms. These computer programs will handle 16,000 or more constraints with no practical limit on the number of variables.

If there is the additional constraint, or requirement, that the resources can only be allocated as integers or whole numbers, then the problem is classified as one of *integer (linear) programming*. If the resources are such that they are either used or not used (i.e., go—no go) then it is a *zero-one linear programming* problem.

Many systems problems can be represented as a network. Transportation, communication, and distribution systems readily fall into this category. The analyst usually tries to find the shortest (or longest) path or the maximal flow through the network. The *program evaluation and review technique* (PERT) and the *critical path method* (CPM) are network techniques widely used in the planning, scheduling, and control of projects of various kinds. (*See* NETWORK PLANNING METHODS.)

*Nonlinear programming* methods are used when either the objective function (goal) and/or one or more of the constraints are expressed as nonlinear functions. Because many real-world problems contain nonlinearities, one might expect these techniques to be widely used. This is not the case, however, because of the computational difficulties inherent in solving nonlinear problems. A large family of *search* methods has been developed for seeking the solution to unconstrained nonlinear programming problems. Among the most widely used are the Fibonacci, golden section, Hooke-Jeeves, and gradient search techniques. These are sequential search methods which successively reduce the interval in which the maximum (minimum) value of a nonlinear function must lie. Although these search techniques usually work very well, their utility is limited by the fact that very few decision problems can be represented by a single equation with no constraints.

Since most real-world problems contain constraints on the decision variables, a number of techniques have been developed for problems where the objective function and/or the constraints are nonlinear, such as *separable programming*, *quadratic programming*, and *geometric programming*. Of these, sep-

arable programming is probably the most useful at the present time. The separable programming technique approximates the nonlinear functions with piecewise linear functions and then uses a modified simplex linear programming algorithm to solve the resulting problem.

*Dynamic programming* is a mathematical technique (whose development is due largely to Richard Bellman) used for solving sequential decision problems. Primarily, these models deal with multiperiod decisions—those which occur only at certain points of time called "stages." The basic objective of most dynamic programming models is to provide the manager with a policy. That is, if the system is found to be in a certain condition at a given time, then the derived policy tells which decision to make. Dynamic programming can also be used to solve problems which are single period in nature but which can be viewed as being solved through a sequence of decisions rather than a single decision; i.e., the decision-making process can be broken down into stages. This method is capable of handling either deterministic or stochastic (probabilistic) cases. In contrast to linear programming and other mathematical models, there is no standard form for dynamic programming models, nor is there a generalized computer program available. Thus although theoretically it is one of the more powerful analytic tools of OR, in practice its use is limited by difficulties in problem formulation and the computational limitations whenever problems with a large number of constraints are to be solved.

*Heuristic methods* are those which utilize some common-sense rules of thumb to search for an acceptable solution. Heuristic methods do not guarantee an optimum solution (although they often achieve one); instead they strive for a good or above-average solution. Heuristic techniques are most often used when the problem is of such size and complexity that exact optimizing algorithms are not available or not practical. The heuristic approach seeks solutions based upon acceptability characteristics rather than optimizing rules.

*Gaming theory* (developed by J. von Neumann) has been considered by some to be the most significant mathematical development of the past century. It is concerned with competitive situations in which two or more participants are in conflict. Each of the participants of the conflict controls some of, but not all, the actions which can take place. This is a situation where a decision maker wishes to achieve some objective. The individual selects a strategy from among the alternatives available. This strategy, together with the chance events or states of nature which occur and the competitive or counter strategy employed by the opponent, determines the degree to which the individual obtains or fails to obtain the chosen objective.

The most practical and significant contribution of gaming theory has been to provide a conceptual and rational framework for decision analysis. The very process of analyzing a competitive situation in a gaming theory context will serve to provide a logical approach and aid in understanding—even though it provides solutions for only very simple problems.

**Probabilistic Models**  Some of the most commonly applied OR techniques come from probability theory and statistics. They include discrete and continuous probability, combinatorial analysis, and renewal theory. By introducing the notions of confidence limits and probability of occurrence, rather than by using simple averages, a much more realistic view of probable outcomes is presented. (*See* RISK ANALYSIS AND MANAGEMENT; STATISTICAL ANALYSIS FOR MANAGEMENT.)

*Stochastic processes* are those in which the probabilities of certain events change dynamically with time, distance, or other parameters. One of the important offsprings of the increasing ability to deal with stochastic processes is queueing theory. *Queueing theory* deals with the study of waiting lines of every conceivable kind and the need to reduce bottlenecks and congestion. Queueing theory deals with the capacity of an operating unit to perform some service. The units, or elements of interest, arrive at the service facility, wait in line if necessary, receive the desired service, and leave the system. These models are characteristic of toll booths, sales counters, tool cribs, docking facilities, etc. They are also usable where the service is brought to the unit, such as where machines break down and await the arrival of a repair crew. The objective of studies using queueing theory is to determine the optimal number of personnel or facilities needed to service customers who arrive randomly—and to balance the cost of service with the cost of waiting or congestion.

In general, queueing theory offers information on the probability that a certain number of units (people, machines, etc.) will have to wait in line, how long these units can expect to wait, and the percent of idle time for the service facility. Such quantities can then be used to determine whether the size of the waiting space or speed of service should be increased.

Another useful form of stochastic models is the socalled "*renewal process.*" Studies related to the replacement of light bulbs according to their life expectancy or the overhaul of aircraft engines are examples. The studies of *renewal processes* involve the probability of failure or wearing out through time of some object. These renewal concepts are similar to those used by statisticians for life insurance acturial studies. System reliability studies are also closely related and utilize many of the same concepts.

When the probable future state of a system is dependent only upon the present state, it is called a *Markov process.* In a Markov-dependent sequence of events, knowledge of the present makes the future independent of the past. If the system is known to have reached a certain state, it is immaterial what chain of events is passed through on the way to this stage as far as predicting the state it will enter into next. In other words, the system has no *memory* that would allow it to modify its behavior. A sequence of events, each of which is subject to the above stated markovian property, is referred to as a *Markov chain.* Markov chains have been used to study brand loyalty, work force movement, and some types of financial analysis. The model involves several oversimplifying assumptions, however, which limit its utility.

Of all the modeling methodologies available, the most powerful and widely used is simulation.[3] A *simulation* model is one which imitates the behavior and exhibits the characteristics of the process or system of interest. Simulation consists of developing a model of the system that shows the logical relationships between the different components of the system and how they affect each other. The model must be capable of showing the connection between the successive states of the system being studied. The model developed can either be a physical (iconic) or a mathematical (logical) one which is computerized. The model is then used to conduct experiments for the purpose either of understanding the behavior of the system or of evaluating various strategies for the operation of the system.

*Physical simulation* models may be (1) full-scale mockups, such as those used for airline pilot or automobile driver training, or (2) reduced-scale models, such as those used for aircraft wind-tunnel testing. The widespread practice in the chemical industry of building a small pilot plant of a new process before going into full-scale production is an excellent example of simulation using physical models.

*Computerized simulation* models use mathematical and logical relationships to portray and imitate the behavior of components of the system being studied. Corporate planning models are usually computerized simulation models of the marketing and/or production aspects of their operations. Computerized simulation models can either be deterministic in nature or contain probabilistic variables. Simulation is used when (1) mathematical techniques are inadequate or do not exist; (2) there is a need to understand how a complex system operates and a need to know the effect of different decisions; and (3) potential problems and methods of dealing with them must be anticipated. (*See* PLANNING, STRATEGIC PLANNING MODELS; SYSTEM DYNAMICS.)

The *expected-value technique* is more of a decision-making criterion than a modeling method. The expected value of a particular decision or strategy is the sum of the values of each of the possible outcomes, each multiplied by its probability of occurrence. For example, if an individual were flipping a coin and received $1 for each head and forfeited $1 for each tail, then the expected value would be equal to .5($1) + .5(−$1) = 0. If the decision maker is considering several alternatives each with different payoffs and probability distributions, the expected value for each alternative can be calculated so as to select the one with the highest expected payoff.

*Decision trees* are a special case of dynamic programming used for representing problem situations which require a sequence of decisions. In a decision tree, there is a sequence of decisions for which, after every decision is made, there is a result which is probabilistic in nature; once that result is known, there is a need for a further decision. In diagrammatic form, this is represented by Fig. O-5. In the

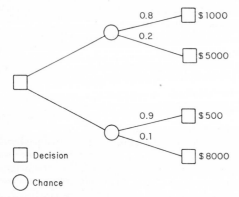

**Fig. O-5. Decision tree.**

tree there are two kinds of nodes: (1) decision points where the decision maker decides what to do next and (2) probabilistic nodes where someone or something else controls the outcome. A probability of occurrence is assigned to each branch at the probabilistic nodes. At the end of each of the branches of

the decision tree, a value is placed which represents the utility of arriving at that point.

The decision-tree approach then determines what decisions should be made by rolling back from the ends of the branches to the first decision point. An expected value for each decision alternative at a decision point is derived through the use of the expected-value technique.

*Regression analysis* is a widely used statistical technique to derive predictive equations from historical or empirical test data. It is essentially a line- or curve-fitting technique. If one suspects that the value of a variable is some function of one or more variables, regression analysis can be used to derive a predictive equation. Regression techniques are widely used by economists in econometric studies. (*See* STATISTICAL ANALYSIS FOR MANAGEMENT.)

## ORGANIZING FOR AN OR STUDY

The operations research group is essentially an internal consultant helping management to solve any type of problem which may occur. Its work, therefore, will impinge on that of almost every functional department and operation in the organization at one time or another. Since it is impossible to have an expert in every branch of the organization's activities within the OR department, it is necessary for practical as well as for sound psychological reasons to adopt the team (or task force) approach as standard practice.

**Task Force** For each specific project, an OR task force should be formed to carry out the study. The typical operations research department is relatively small; it is both necessary and desirable, therefore, that these professionals be augmented by others who are not regularly a part of the OR staff. The ideal team consists of the following:

1. *One or more operations research analysts.* These will be persons formally trained in OR methodology and can be either OR department staffers or outside consultants hired for the specific study.

2. *One or more computer scientists.* These may be the same persons as the OR analysts. They should not, however, be merely computer programmers. Typically, they would be an analyst and model builder, who can use the computer with confidence.

3. *One or more well-rounded nontechnical individuals.* They know the company, the organization, and particularly the problem area. These people should be directly involved with the operating function being studied. These are perhaps the most impor-

tant members of the team. They supply the necessary specific know-how and experience. They help in collecting and generating data, open doors for the OR team, and assist in working out the details of implementation. Their experience and knowledge assures that solutions generated are practical and implementable. They are also invaluable in selling the solution to the organization and following up during the implementation phase.

**Steering Committee** The task force should report to a steering committee consisting of the *managers* of those functions of the organizations most vitally connected with, and affected by, the study. The success of an operations research study usually depends as much on management as it does on the OR task team.

The management steering committee helps prevent errors of both omission and commission, provides additional know-how, and guides the team *during* the study. Throughout the study the task force should meet regularly with the steering committee. Such meetings should be held approximately two to four times per month, and even more frequently with individual members of the committee.

**Department Staffing** The average OR department has five to seven professionals with one or two secretary/clerk support personnel. Various surveys have shown that 13 percent hold a Ph.D. degree (one-third of the directors), 44 percent hold a master's degree, and the rest have a bachelor's degree or less. Engineering (predominately industrial) is the most common background, with business administration, economics, and mathematics degrees also common. A bachelor's degree in one of the above fields with graduate study in operations research is a desirable academic background.

**Use of Consultants** A survey conducted in 1974 among major corporations indicated that 67 percent of all studies were carried out in house without any outside assistance, 24 percent were developed in house with outside consultants, and only 8 percent were conducted entirely by an outside group. Outside consultants can be very helpful, of course, in that they add objectivity and specialized expertise. On the other hand, purchase of "off the shelf" or "canned" models from an outside vendor do not usually work out.

**Project Duration and Selection** The selection of projects is of vital importance, especially when an organization is just starting an OR group. The initial projects undertaken should have a relatively short time horizon with a high probability of success and a well-defined monetary return. Emphasis should be upon the pragmatic, demonstrable payoff and a reasonable return on the investment. After a period of successful operation for several internal clients, the group can then take on a mixture of long, short, and intermediate time horizon projects.

*See also* COMPUTER SYSTEMS; STATISTICAL ANALYSIS FOR MANAGEMENT; SYSTEM CONCEPT, TOTAL; SYSTEM DYNAMICS.

### NOTES

[1]E. S. Buffa, *Modern Production Management*, 4th ed., John Wiley & Sons, Inc., New York, 1973; R. I. Levin and C. A. Krikpatrick, *Quantitative Approaches to Management*, 3 ed., McGraw-Hill Book Company, New York, 1975; D. T. Phillips, A. Ravindran, and J. J. Solberg, *Operations Research, Principles and Practice*, John Wiley & Sons, Inc., New York, 1976.

[2]R. E. Machol, *Elementary Systems Mathematics: Linear Programming for Business and the Social Science*, McGraw-Hill Book Company, New York, 1976; Phillips et al., *Operations Research, Principles and Practice*.

[3]R. E. Shannon, *Systems Simulation: The Art and Science*, Prentice-Hall, Inc., Englewood Cliffs, N.J., 1975.

### REFERENCE

Loomba, N. P.: *Linear Programming: A Management Perspective*, 2d ed., The Macmillan Company, New York, 1976.

ROBERT E. SHANNON, *University of Alabama in Huntsville*

**Opinion surveys** (*see* ATTITUDE SURVEYS.)

**Opportunity analysis** (*See* MARKET ANALYSIS.)

**Opportunity profile, sales** (*See* SALES MANAGEMENT.)

**Optimization** (*See* SYSTEM CONCEPT, TOTAL.)

**Optimization, process of** (*See* PRODUCTION PROCESSES.)

**Optimizing** (*See* OPERATIONS RESEARCH AND MATHEMATICAL MODELING.)

## Options, executive stock  (*See* COMPEN-SATION, EXECUTIVE,)

## Order, market  (*See* MARKETS, SECURITIES.)

## Order, stop-loss and stop-buy  (*See* MARKETS, SECURITIES.)

## Order processing, central  (*See* INVEN-TORY CONTROL, PHYSICAL AND STOCKKEEPING.)

## Order selection, fixed slot  (*See* INVEN-TORY CONTROL, PHYSICAL AND STOCKKEEPING.)

## Orders, purchase  (*See* PURCHASING MAN-AGEMENT.)

## Organization  (*See* ORGANIZATION DEVELOP-MENT (OD).)

## Organization, geographic  (*See* INTERNA-TIONAL OPERATIONS AND MANAGEMENT IN MULTI-NATIONAL COMPANIES.)

## Organization, international operations  (*See* INTERNATIONAL OPERATIONS AND MANAGEMENT IN MULTINATIONAL COMPANIES.)

## Organization, marketing  (*See* MARKET-ING MANAGEMENT.)

## Organization, marketing of services  (*See* MARKETING OF SERVICES.)

## Organization analysis and planning

An organization may be thought of as the coordinated actions of two or more people for the purpose of meeting an objective. For example, two people arranging to meet for lunch at a particular time and location are engaged in organizing. The focus in this chapter, however, is upon *complex organizations,* so named because they involve groups of people differentiated by their work, physical space, or levels of authority. The purpose of these complex organizations is to transform something—materials, information, people—in a manner which adds value to the thing transformed and allows the organization to survive and prosper.

### ORGANIZATIONAL PURPOSE

An organization does a variety of things:

1. *It establishes a repetition of desired actions.* By making rules, procedures, and reporting relationships formal, the organization simplifies the processing of information required and ensures that necessary actions occur automatically. Attention may then be shifted to issues which are new or nonrepetitive. For example, a standing order, or rule, that all organization members will begin work at 9 A.M. eliminates the necessity of making a decision about starting time every day and permits the time and energy which would be used to make the decision to be applied to other issues.

2. *It ensures that actions by organization members will be coordinated.* The desired actions will fit together in a systematic way, ensuring an efficient and effective pattern of collective effort.

3. *It makes behavior predictable.* Organization members may act with reasonable assurance that other members will act in the same manner. Thus, members gain some degree of freedom since their actions need not be based on the unpredictable actions of others.

4. *It stores information.* Organizations "learn" in the course of their existence, and the information gained is added to their fund of standing orders. For example, a contingency plan may be discovered for dealing with shortages in raw materials and formalized as an alternative in the event that similar problems occur in the future.

5. *It establishes an identity independent of the people within it.* The organization becomes more or less free of members deemed indispensable as long as replacement people are available. Thus, it ensures its existence in spite of members who leave.

6. *It allocates rewards to contributors and claimants.* The organization contains a complex system of bargains between the people or groups who contribute to it or have claims upon it. It permits fair bargains to be struck for rewarding different kinds of work or levels of performance.

Thus, the failure to organize properly can result

in wasted energy and resources, the inability to accumulate knowledge, a dependency on the presence of certain people for existence, and a failure to provide incentives for contributions by its members.

## HOW KNOWLEDGE ABOUT ORGANIZATIONS IS OBTAINED

To understand and interpret information about organization design and analysis, a manager should have some basic understanding about how such information is derived. There are three elemental strategies for obtaining information: measures of events, measures of association, and measures of causation.

The first of these, *measures of events*, are "one shot" kinds of descriptions. An example of such a measure would be a case study of an organization. Such a case study would be useful in illustrating the characteristics of its structure and processes and could aid in understanding how these characteristics operate. However, it does *not* prove that it is the best form of organization. There is a great temptation on the part of those observing the organization of a successful enterprise to attribute its success to its design; that is, one may be tempted to move from saying "the organization has these features" to the statement that "the organization (and perhaps others as well) *should* have these features." This should be avoided. An example is not a proof of anything.

A second elemental strategy for research is the use of *measures of association*. Much of our information about organizations is derived with this research strategy. The association between two measures is determined and expressed as the extent of their correlation, and such correlation varies around 0, between plus and minus 1. For example, a survey of organizations might measure their size by the number of employees and measure the average satisfaction of their members by surveys of job satisfaction. If the results showed that as organization size increased, there was an equal, proportionate increase in job satisfaction, then the correlation would be +1.00. If the results showed absolutely no relationship between the two measures, then they would have a correlation of zero. The degree of association between two measures may thus be expressed by a correlation coefficient with a numerical value between +1.00 and −1.00. The correlation expresses the extent to which we can predict a change in job satisfaction by knowing size or vice versa.

The difficulty with such analyses is that they do not help much in understanding why such relationships exist, nor do they say anything about what

causes what. It would be wrong to say that organization size causes changes in satisfaction. Such might prove to be the case, but it is *not* demonstrated by measures of association. Indeed, both size and satisfaction might be the result of changes in some other variable.

The third elemental strategy in organization research is to use *measures of causation*. These are experimental procedures in which experimental groups or individuals are changed, like groups or individuals are not changed, and comparisons are made between the changed (experimental) and unchanged (control) individuals or groups. For example, suppose that we have two sets of work groups which have the same size and the same levels of job satisfaction among their members. Suppose further that we increase the size of one set of work groups but not the size of the other set. If we find that satisfaction decreases in the work groups which had their size increased, and remains the same in the groups whose size did not increase, then we could say that in these groups, increasing size caused a decrease in satisfaction. We would not know, necessarily, that such would always be the case in other kinds of groups. Nor would we know why the size change caused satisfaction to change.

The obvious difficulties involved in doing experiments with real organizations are that many such measures of causation are conducted with artificial groups in laboratories. Measures of causation are useful, however, because they permit a high degree of control over other elements which might affect the results and because they lead to a better understanding of what causes what.

In the remaining discussion in this entry we shall report facts about organizations derived from these methods and shall offer some tentative explanations about why relationships exist. Within the limits just described, the facts about organizations offer the organization planner some practical tools for improving organizational performance.

## ORGANIZATIONAL TYPES

Most discussions of organization design assume and encourage the development of professionally managed institutions with deliberate and conscious planning for survival and success. It may be noted, however, that there are at least three basic types of organization. Research by the author and others[1] has described and labeled these types as craft, promotion, and administrative.

*Craft* organizations are led by a chief executive who engages in technical rather than administrative duties and who seeks to make a comfortable living and to see the organization survive. Policies evolve by tradition, and the structure develops with little conscious planning. It is common for the organization to be layered by levels of power, with an elite group at the top, a group of long service and trusted employees in the middle, and a transient group of workers at the bottom. Members of craft organizations expect little change in their operations and, therefore, make minimal use of supervisory or indirect labor. They are not inclined to risk taking or innovation in their operations. Work technology is relatively uncomplex and tends to emphasize either an organization which sells something or an organization which makes something. Craft firms exist primarily at the mercy of a benevolent environment. They have great difficulty responding to important changes in technology, competition, or the market served.

In contrast, the *promotion* type of organization is strongly influenced by a chief executive who is charismatic to subordinates and a promoter of the firm's innovative advantage. Policies are fluid, changing from day to day at the discretion of the promoter, and the organization exists as an extension of the promoter's personality. He or she has contact and influence with most organization members. Middle management is by-passed by the promoter, and indirect labor provides technical or personal support for the chief executive. Basically, the organization exists to exploit a distinct market or product advantage, making planning or efficiency less important for organization survival and success. Such an advantage ends when competitors or imitators enter the field. Similarly, the enthusiastic support of the promoter by organization members early in the life of the promotion firm tends to diminish as the firm's competitive position changes. As implied, the promotion firm has a limited life. It must change or perish.

The third form of organization is *administrative*. This is the form described in this entry and, indeed, advocated by this Encyclopedia. It is managed professionally by a chief executive who directs a planned structure toward clearly defined goals. The organization becomes an institution with an absence of indispensable people. It is designed according to size and technological imperatives, to be described later, and it adjusts to changes in its market environment by means of planning.

**Organizational Change**  While craft firms may exist for many years in a stable market environment, a sudden shift in technology or competition may make survival dependent upon professional manage-

ment. In addition, a change in company goals from comfort and survival to growth and profitability may stimulate development of the administrative form to be described.

A change in the promotion form is more pronounced and dramatic. As the promotion form loses its unique market advantage and must compete with other firms which may be considerably more efficient, the promoter-dominated form of organization will no longer suffice. The annals of business history are filled with examples of promoters who built and promoted their enterprises at the beginning, and then led them to the brink of disaster as conditions changed.

The material which follows suggests how the craft or promotion organization may be redesigned along administrative lines and how existing administrative organizations may be analyzed for further improvement.

## KEY INFLUENCES ON STRUCTURE

In analyzing organization structure or in designing a structure, one might consider four basic influences which tend to shape it.

**Competitive Basis for Survival**  In general, there are two bases for organization survival: efficiency of operation or creativity and adaptability to client needs. Where the market for products is stable and predictable and where the company is providing products which are equal in quality to those of other suppliers, the organization will compete and survive on the basis of *efficiency*. Either its prices must be competitively favorable or else its prices must be equivalent to those of other suppliers, and the firm must be able to sell at those prices and make an adequate profit. Such organizations are designed to mass-produce standard items.

In contrast, where the market for the products is unstable or hard to predict and where the company is providing products which are more or less unique, the organization will compete and survive on the basis of its *unique service*. In such cases, there is a great deal about the product that is "made to order," and it must do what it is supposed to do. Customers pay a premium to ensure that they get the service desired. For example, such organizations are designed to produce houses, special tooling, fashion items, or highly technical products.

This trade off between efficiency and creativity in organization designs plays an important role within the organization as well. The efficiency and economy of some units within an organization will free the resources that can be devoted to creativity in other units. For example, by routinizing production or purchasing, creative efforts may be expended in research and development or in the top executive team.

**Technology**  The technology of an organization is related to its design, and it appears that there are proper designs for different technologies. One classification of technology is provided by Woodward[2] who grouped the manufacturing organizations she studied into three classes: (1) custom and small-batch production, (2) large-batch and mass production, and (3) process production. She demonstrated that there were distinctly different patterns of organization for successful and unsuccessful organizations in each class.

A second classification of technology is provided by Thompson.[3] He identified three types of technology: long-linked, mediating, and intensive.

*Long-linked technology*, such as that found in mass production, typically has a functional organization design with units like production, sales, and purchasing subordinate to central planning and scheduling activities. Such firms will expand through vertical integration, e.g., through control of suppliers and sources of raw materials and through control of market channels. Such firms are expected to be highly organized and will try to protect their production operations from disruption. As Thompson pointed out, "The constant rate of production means that, once adjusted, the proportions of resources involved can be standardized to the point where each contributes to its capacity; none need be underemployed."[4]

*Mediating* is a second form of technology. Such organizations link clients or customers who are or wish to be interdependent. Banks, insurance companies, the post office, and retail chains are examples. Mediating technology requires that an organization operate in standardized ways, relying upon fixed rules and procedures. In addition, the operations tend to be spread in time and space. These organizations will try to increase the population served by expanding the geographic area which they serve or by adding additional product lines. The central offices of such organizations will engage in the development of the necessary plans and schedules.

*Intensive* is the third form of technology. Such organizations combine a variety of skills and techniques to work upon a person or product in a special, unique, and customized way. Examples might include a hospital, a construction firm, or a research laboratory. It is important that intensive-technology organizations include the right skills and that the skills be available at the right time. Such organizations make frequent use of teams, project groups, or task forces.

**Size**  There are a number of somewhat unrelated but parallel forces that encourage an organization to increase its size.[5] As might be expected, as organizations increase their size, they also tend to become more formal and more complex. For example, Child[6] reviewed the relationship between size and organizational characteristics in several different groups of manufacturing companies, finding that as size increased, there were also increases in the number of divisions, the division of labor, the formalization of rules and regulations, and the number of levels in the companies.

In academic circles, a virtual battle has been raging about whether size or technology is the main determinant of organization design. Some researchers[7] have argued that technology, not size, is the more salient influence on structure. Others[8] have argued that size, not technology, is more important.

It seems likely that both technology and size affect organization design, perhaps in different ways. For example, if one distinguishes between the effect of size on *differentiation* (i.e., number of levels, number of departments, and number of job titles) and on complexity (i.e., degree of job skill, number of different occupations, and degree of professional orientation), then size might well have more impact on differentiation than on complexity[9]. For example, an increase in the size of a mass production firm would be expected to increase the number of levels and the division of labor without having much effect on the skill requirements of jobs involved. However, a shift in technology from mass production to specialty items could substantially alter the requirements for job design and skill requirements.

It may also be noted here that increases in size may be an advantage in some organizations but not in others. In long-linked technology, for example, size may be expected to provide potential benefits for efficiency and profit. In contrast, an increase in the size of firms with intensive technology can create difficulties in processing information which might, in turn, interfere with the ability of the firm to provide customized and effective service to clients.

**Markets or Environment Served**  The internal character of an organization also depends greatly upon the kind and degree of demands placed upon it by its environment. Where there are many changes in technology or many outsiders influencing or making claims upon the organization, the organization will be more differentiated. Where it can isolate or buffer itself from outside influences, the organization will be less differentiated. For example, Lawrence and Lorsch[10] compared firms in the plastics, food, and container industries. Plastics firms were most differentiated because of rapid changes in technology and needs to be creative. Food processing firms were less so. The container firms, operating in an environment of relative stability, were less differentiated and more structured to meet the demands for scheduling and efficiency.

Considered in another way, one may see that where the organization provides a product which is more or less made to order, the attention of organization members will be more concerned with client needs and with the output to meet those needs than where the organization mass produces a product. In the latter case, the organization will isolate its production processes so that it may produce a high volume of standard products without interruption or change.

In summary, four factors have been identified which influence the design of an organization. It may be seen that changes in organization design may be expected if the basis for survival changes from efficiency to creativity or the reverse, if size changes, if technology changes, or if the environment becomes more or less stable.

## DIMENSIONS OF ORGANIZATION DESIGN

The following design features provide the organizational pattern which affects the organization's success and survival.

**Functional and Goal-oriented Structures**
There are two fundamental designs for organizing which apply to a total organization or to the units within the total organization. The first pools relatively large numbers of people doing similar work in the same department or organizational unit, and it is called a functional structure. For example, the *functional organization* shown in Fig. O-6a contains production, sales, engineering, and personnel departments. One assumes that each department has enough production workers, salesworkers, etc., so that the people involved identify with their own functional interest rather than with the other departments or other people in the organization. This characteristic is quite important since it is generally associated with attention to the processing of people, information, materials, orders, or other products rather than with attention to the outcome or service of those products.

The second basic strategy for organizing is a goal-oriented organization. (Fig. O-6b). *Goal-oriented organizations* direct member attention to specific outcomes or client services. In many cases, they are teams of people with different specialties who work jointly to complete projects, to provide specialized services, or to solve unique problems. Thus, a project group doing a feasibility study on a new product or a small business in which the members work jointly to meet customer needs would be examples of goal-oriented units. In addition, the specialized adaptation of organization services to different industries or territories is also goal-oriented, since the design facilitates outcomes or services rather than processing.[11]

The functional or goal-oriented alternatives may be observed in many other kinds of organizations as well. For example, a public utility commission is commonly organized into departments of legal services, engineering, rate setting, etc., (functional structure) or into a utilities department and a transportation department (goal-oriented structure).

Different parts of an organization will be organized using either of the two alternatives. For example, a research and development division may be organized into departments of data processing, chemistry, and engineering (functional) or into project group A and project group B (goal-oriented). Secretarial services may be provided through a secretarial pool (functional) or through individual private secretaries (goal-oriented).

To emphasize, the essential logic of the two structures is that functional units contain enough people doing the same kind of work to have a departmental organization in which people identify principally with their own specialty and its processes. In contrast, the goal-oriented unit often contains a mixture of skills, and its emphasis is upon the outcomes of work effort for creativity and adaptiveness.

*Functional Analysis.* Consider the characteristics of the functional organization. Most importantly, it has great potential for efficiency. Resources are used fully. Personnel or equipment are typically added when they can be justified on the basis of full-time utilization. People within the department can be divided into subspecialties and can be advanced within their specialty. Relatively unskilled personnel may be employed and advanced as their skills increase. By working in the same department as others doing similar work, people can learn additional skills by contact with each other.

The supervision of functional departments is by specialists in the function, who can evaluate the professional or technical competence of people within the unit. However, the functional organiza-

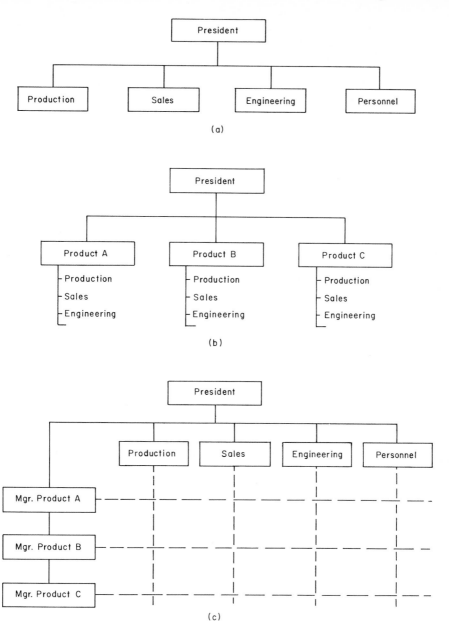

**Fig. O-6.** Alternative organization strategies. (*a*) Functional strategy; (*b*) goal-oriented strategy; (*c*) matrix strategy.

tion does not provide experience in general or professional management since only the chief executive is required to manage a variety of functional units.

Functional organizations typically have a very

formal organization and relatively inflexible operations. Employees are likely to take a short-term view of their work since they focus on day-to-day job requirements. Conflict between departments is common. Departments are mutually dependent

**825**

upon each other, and scheduling and coordination between them is difficult.

The functional organization is most appropriate where organizational survival is based upon efficiency, where technology is routine and relatively fixed, where size is great enough to permit standardized jobs and equipment, and where the market is stable and predictable.

*Goal-oriented Analysis.* The goal-oriented structure, on the other hand, has quite different characteristics. Unlike the functional organization, the goal-oriented structure is adaptive and creative, not especially efficient. Equipment and personnel may be duplicated between units and are present because of potential need rather than full-time use. Goal-oriented units require personnel who are talented in their specialty or profession, since they provide the complete resource base required. Because specialists are isolated from others in the same specialty, it is difficult to advance them within their specialty or subdivide them into subspecialties, nor can they learn from others within their specialties.

Where the goal-oriented unit contains a mixture of different specialties, supervision is by a generalist or professional manager who can integrate the efforts of the various specialties. Thus, the goal-oriented structure may provide a training ground for top management of the organization. Teams are typically informal in their interactions and creative in their efforts. If successful, they take a long-run view since the measure of their effectiveness is evaluated on the basis of an outcome—construction of a building, completion of a piece of equipment, release of an advertising campaign, etc.

Goal-oriented units tend to meet schedules effectively since they are less mutually dependent upon other units than functional organizations and because evaluation criteria include, importantly, the final accomplishment.

In terms of the key influences upon organization structure, the goal-oriented structure is most appropriate where organizational survival is based upon creativity and adaptiveness, where technology is relatively made to order, where unit size is small enough to permit informal and frequent interaction by unit members, and where the market is unstable and hard to predict.

*Size and Change Effects.* With these two designs clearly in mind, it is possible to identify some important consequences of size or change.

1. What happens with growth? A small organization making a piece of custom-designed industrial equipment may compete quite effectively with other larger firms since its existence is justified on the basis of its effectiveness in meeting client needs. Within obvious limits, the company may experience high profit margins on the product, if it can satisfy the customer. The small company functions as a single goal-oriented unit with informal operations, talented people, and common effort by everyone. As the company grows, it will begin to take on the characteristics of a functional structure. More people will be added, departments will begin to acquire a parochial view, and while the company will have potential for efficiency, its ability to adapt will diminish. In such cases, the firm may choose to develop standard lines to be produced in high volume, or it may wish to reorganize into smaller, goal-oriented units.

2. What happens if a large functional organization requires creativity? A large manufacturer of cardboard cartons may discover that a new plastic material has been developed which if applicable to the company products, could reduce production costs. A feasibility study is clearly warranted. If the president drops his or her normal duties, he or she might complete the study alone, at a cost of management necessary to the company. Or, the functional departments might be asked to report on the impact of the new material in their separate areas of interest. The cost of such effort is a fragmented collection of information. Still another alternative would be the creation of a project group—a goal-oriented unit—containing representatives of the various departments. The project group would conduct a feasibility study and, through the combined effort of its members, submit a report on the implications of the new material to the company's operations.

3. What is the effect of changes in the requirements for adaptability or efficiency on the organization's design? Suppose that in a large functional organization, the sales department has been subdivided into units serving different industries. A manufacturer of drive equipment might have different sales people serving the glass making, the automobile, and the lumber industries. This subdivision represents the application of a goal-oriented design within a single functional department. It assumes that special service and adaptation to client needs are in the interest of the company or department and that adaptability rather than economy is warranted. If the market changes, however, and the company is forced to survive on the basis of high-volume production of standard devices, it is not unlikely that it would consider using fewer, unspecialized sales people in its sales department.

*Matrix Organization Analysis.* In addition to functional and goal-oriented structures, there is also a third, hybrid form of organization structure which combines both organizing strategies. This strategy, a matrix organization, is illustrated in Fig. O-6c. As indicated, the *matrix organization* pools personnel and equipment within functional units, permitting subdivision in the specialties, advancement, effective use of resources, economies of scale, and the like. In addition, product responsibility is vested in product managers who coordinate and integrate the efforts in each department pertaining to a product. This goal-oriented strategy enhances adaptiveness and adherence to schedules, and it focuses on outcomes.

The matrix organization is well suited to situations where time constraints are more important than maximum economy. Thus, it has been used in many defense programs. It is also well suited to situations involving the use of temporary project groups which will terminate their existence once the projects are completed. It was widely used in NASA in the manned and unmanned space projects.[12]

Matrix organizations generally exhibit conflict between the functional administrators and the heads of goal-oriented units. One way to manage such conflict is to maintain a balance of power between the two groups by budgeting money to the projects and by having most of the personnel in functional units assigned to and employed by the projects. Thus, the goal-oriented units have the power of money which balances the functional units' power of expertise.

Matrix organizations also negate many of the old principles of management. Contrary to the principle that responsibility should equal authority, project or program managers have more responsibility than authority. In addition, contrary to the principle that each person should have only one boss, personnel assigned to goal-oriented units actually have two or more formal leaders—the heads of both the functional unit and the goal-oriented unit. The popular notion that each person should have only one boss is a convenience, not a necessity. Having one superior reduces potential role conflict on the part of an employee, but multiple bosses are possible, providing their authority is clearly defined.

**Centralization or Decentralization of Decision Making** A second design feature involves the extent to which key decisions are made in the top levels of the organization or whether they are delegated to lower levels of the organizational structure. For manufacturing organizations, such issues might include the following: capital acquisition, investment decisions, acquisition of subsidiaries, new-product development, marketing strategy, pricing, research and development, hiring and firing of key personnel, and changes in corporate policy. Delegation probably ranges from exclusive control by the board of directors or top executive at one extreme to complete responsibility vested in a level below the chief executive without executive review at the other extreme.

A study of 79 manufacturing firms[13] considered the relationship between the technology of the firms, the degree of vertical integration involved, the size, the extent of decentralization, and the use of sophisticated controls. In addition, the study contrasted the patterns of organization in high-profit and low-profit firms.

The results showed that the more the technology of the firm was characterized by high volume and mass production and the larger the firm's size, the more it was vertically integrated. Further, the more vertically integrated, the greater was the decentralization of decision making. Finally, the more decentralized, the more the firm used sophisticated controls for quality, costing, inventory, scheduling, finances, and evaluation of executive performance. Equally important, the more-profitable firms tended to follow this pattern more than less profitable firms.

In addition, as one would expect, the more standardized the technology, the more the firms were organized functionally instead of using some goal-oriented structure such as product, territory, or customer.

Considered from the standpoint of a more made to order, or customized, technology, or from smaller firm size, this information suggests that such firms should not integrate vertically and should contain more centralized control by top management. Customized product firms would not expect to have sophisticated controls like mass production firms.

**Line and Staff Organization** A third design feature has to do with the assignment and use of auxiliary services, generally called *staff*. In contrast to staff services, activities which are directly concerned with the creation or sale of a product are generally called *line*. The distinction between line and staff is clearest and most useful in manufacturing organizations.

Both size and technology are major determinants of staff use. Technology influences staff use through its influence on the application of sophisticated controls. Successful high-volume manufacturers use elaborate planning and control techniques,[14] and such planning and control is the primary responsibility of staff personnel. Size is also a factor since the use of such specialized personnel is or is not feasible on a cost effectiveness basis, and small size may not permit employment of staff personnel.

Staff units may be identified as one of two types: general and specialist.

1. *General staff.* These units are most readily identified in the corporate offices of large companies. For example, Fig. O-7 shows corporate staff units reporting to the president of a company with three large product divisions. These corporate staff offices generally develop policies which affect all divisions of the organization and probably serve an adaptive function in an organization which is deeply embedded in a functional structure. As a study of 76 divisionalized companies for the National Industrial Conference Board reported,[15] virtually all corporate staff units fall within nine functional areas: finance, legal-secretarial, personnel, marketing, manufacturing, public relations, research and development, purchasing and traffic, and corporate planning.

Another form of general staff is the personal assistant, usually identified by an "assistant-to" title. Such positions do not have responsibility identified by function as do other corporate staff offices. Instead, assistants perform a variety of duties within the responsibility and authority of the person whom they serve, expanding the administrative capacity of that person. The addition of one or more personal assistants tends to increase the number of people who may be supervised effectively.

General staff units, whether corporate staff or personal staff, report to the principal whom they serve. They provide a goal-oriented, adaptive function at the top of the organization, taking a long-run view, even though the rest of the organization is organized into functional units.

2. *Specialist staff.* These units are identified as engaging primarily in service, advice, or control activities. *Service staffs* are added when it becomes economical to employ a specialist rather than have the same functions performed by a line unit. A purchasing agent, a maintenance person, or a mar-

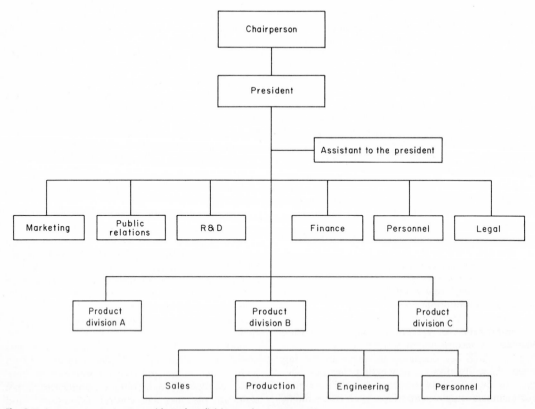

**Fig. O-7. Large corporate structure with product divisions and corporate staff.**

ket research analyst are examples. *Advisory staffs* aid in problem solving by providing specialized information, such as legal advice or retirement counseling. Finally, *control staff* units provide special planning and control activities. Production control, cost control, and quality control are examples of the latter.

Specialist staff units typically report to the level of authority above the area of their service. For example, the personnel manager in product division B in Fig. O-7 is shown reporting to the head of that division, suggesting that the personnel function serves sales, production, and engineering units in that division. If the personnel manager engaged in selection, training, and other personnel matters only for the production unit in division B, then he or she would normally report to the head of the production department.

In addition, where a specialist staff unit engages in control over another unit, the head of the staff and the head of the unit controlled will report to a common superior. A quality control manager might not report to the head of a manufacturing department, for example, since a manufacturing department is evaluated by production volume and might bring pressure to bear against a quality control department to reduce its standards.

While the design questions regarding staff assignment or staff use are not difficult to answer, the question regarding how much staff to use is not easily answered. The latter depends upon issues of resource allocation. In other words, the creation of a staff unit depends upon whether staff functions are better performed by line managers themselves or by being assigned to a new or existing staff unit. In addition, some staff services may be purchased, instead of employing people who provide the service internally. The most specific guidelines regarding the proper amount of staff to use may be obtained from staffing surveys in a single industry, broken down by company size and technology.

*Extent of Staff Use.* A few generalizations regarding the level of staff use are possible, however.

1. The distinction between line and staff and the emphasis on staff services will be greatest in high-volume mass production technologies. As indicated earlier, that type of technology requires decentralization of decision making and use of sophisticated controls. Those controls are provided by specialist staffs engaged in planning and control. Woodward[16] reported that firms with large-batch or mass production had one staff employee for each $5\frac{1}{2}$ direct production employees. Where unit or small-batch production was employed, the ratio dropped

to one staff employee for eight production employees. The ratio for process firms was 1 to 2.

2. As small organizations grow, the percentage of staff utilized will increase to some point and then remain at about the same percentage of total employment. For example, a study by DeSpelder[17] of 155 automobile parts manufacturers reported that staff as a percentage of line employment grew to about 550 direct production employees and then remained at about 57 to 51 percent of line (production) employment. The early growth of staff seems to occur as company size permits the economical use of fully employed staff units. Before such use is economical, the activities are performed by line managers or purchased externally. Finally, it is clear that the failure to use staff when needed can be a serious false economy. For example, Filley[18] investigated the historical growth of staff in five companies. In one of these, a large batch manufacturer with sales of $4.7 million, staff remained at about 10 percent of total employment. Company policy precluded the use of indirect labor, and it was not until new top management took over and profits were absent that the company employed the necessary internal staff to ensure efficient, profitable operations.

*Line and Staff Authority.* A manager's authority refers to the way in which the organization intends for him or her to influence others in the organization. Where a direct, formal reporting relationship is present, the superior is identified as having line authority over the subordinate. Thus, both the production manager and the personnel manager have *line* authority over their immediate subordinates. In contrast, where a manager is expected to provide service or advice or control outside the immediate reporting relationship, the authority is labeled *staff*.

Staff authority varies. At one extreme, a manager is empowered to give advice to others where it is requested. Next, where compulsory staff advice is a company policy, organization members are expected to ask for advice from designated sources before taking action, though they do not have to follow the advice. Such a policy ensures that appropriate sources of information are used. Next, some organizations require that concurrent agreements take place between two units before actions are taken. For example, this policy gives a finance department the opportunity to veto a capital expenditure by a production manager. Finally, a manager may have functional authority over other units in the organization. Functional authority is a limited right to give orders and expect compliance outside the normal chain of command. For example, a safety engineer may be empowered to stop an unsafe operation or an inspector may have the right to reject products which do not meet quality standards.

Since staff executives generally have a great deal of power or informal influence in an organization even though they have relatively little formal authority, it is not uncommon for conflicts to occur between line and staff executives. This difficulty may be reduced by planning the degree of staff authority which executives may exercise over each other.

**Organization Shape** The shape of an organization is influenced by the number of levels used and the span of control (number of people supervised) of each manager. Other things being equal, an organization with many levels will have smaller spans of control. Conversely, if the same number of people are organized into broad spans of control, the number of levels required will be reduced.

*Number of Organization Levels.* An analysis of organization design should consider the number of levels used. With too many levels of management, the organization experiences unnecessary administrative expense and channels of communication are lengthened. With too few levels, supervisory effectiveness is hampered and spans of control become too great.

*Levels and Size.* As one might expect, the number of levels in an organization is related to its size. In addition, in the smaller size range it takes a smaller increase in organization size to generate new levels than it does in size ranges of large organizations. Studies of business organizations consistently show high correlations between size and the number of levels. To illustrate, studies[19] of 128 business organizations indicated that they had roughly four levels complete in firms with 100 employees, six levels in firms of 1000 employees, and between seven and eight levels in firms with 10,000 employees.

*Levels and Technology.* The number of levels is also influenced by technology, though not as clearly as size. At least one study has shown that the number of levels of supervision increases with technological complexity. In her study of firms with more than 100 employees, Woodward[20] reported that firms with unit or small-batch production had a median of three levels of management, while large-batch and mass production firms had a median of four levels, and process firms had a median of six levels. Less successful firms deviated from those averages.

In contrast, another study[21] focused on the same three classes of technology and found just over five levels for unit production (average plant size, 421), mass production (average plant size, 631), and process production (average plan size, 326). It is difficult to explain this finding, since one would expect unit production firms to be less structured than mass production and to require fewer levels of supervision.

*Levels and Employee Attitudes.* While there is no clear and direct relationship between employee satisfaction and employee performance, there is a frequent relationship between satisfaction and the behavior of coming to and staying at work. That is, turnover and absenteeism rates are more favorable for satisfied employees than for dissatisfied employees. This being the case, it is useful to determine the effect of the number of levels upon measures of satisfaction.

Two extensive literature reviews have addressed this question.[22] Both clearly indicate that there is a tendency for satisfaction to increase with each higher level in the organization.

Of particular interest for present purposes, El Salmi and Cummings[23] considered the shape of the organization as well. Comparing satisfaction by organizational level in tall, intermediate, and flat organizations, they found that top managers in tall organizations reported more satisfaction of their needs than top managers in intermediate or flat organizations. However, middle and lower-level managers in intermediate and flat organizations had higher need satisfaction than similar managers in tall organizations.

It is possible that the differences in shape were due to different organizing strategies or different technologies. However, if shape differences do reflect differences in the number of levels per se, then they suggest that one cost of unnecessary levels is lower satisfaction by lower-level managers.

*Spans of Supervision.* Another specific design issue involves the number of people supervised by any manager. As suggested earlier, the shape of the organization will be influenced by the spans used, affecting the cost of supervision and the quality of management exercised. Consider, for example, the difference between a span of control of 10 and a span of control of five. With one supervisor for 10 employees there is one level of supervision and the necessary expense of one supervisor. But, if the same 10 employees have two supervisors, each with a span of control of five, then someone must be added to coordinate their work, and the result is two levels of supervision and the expense of three managers.

*Executive Span of Supervision.* The proper span of control for a chief executive depends upon his or her particular style of management and the organizing strategy of the company. Unlike the span of lower-level managers, it is not much influenced by the organization's size or technology. The organizing strategy plays a part because where units reporting to the executive are self-contained, many can be supervised without detracting from organizational effectiveness. Such is the case, for example, in a retail chain or a large divisionalized manufacturing firm.

The executive's personal style is particularly important in determining his or her span. Patterns vary considerably, with some having a span of one, with an executive vice-president at the next level. Others seem to have a collective executive, with several people sharing the executive duties. Still others may prefer a corporate staff and direct line management.[24] There are no clear correlations between organization size and the span of the chief executive.[25]

Since technology and organizing strategy are related, there does seem to be some influence of technology. It is not uncommon for chief executives in mass production firms to have about seven subordinates and for spans in process firms to be greater than this.[26] Perhaps most important is the earlier indication that, whatever the span, the chief executive in a small-batch or custom technology should arrange to have more centralized control of operations than in other forms of technology.

*Supervisory Spans.* Supervisory spans seem to vary more systematically than those of higher-level executives. They are less subject to the personal style of the manager and more influenced by the imperatives of size and technology. Blau et al.[27] report significant correlations between size and spans of first-line supervision but not between degree of technology and supervisory spans. If the type of technology is considered, however, some patterns become apparent. Spans of production supervisors in Woodward's study averaged between 21 and 30 for unit and small-batch production, between 41 and 50 for large-batch and mass production, and between 11 and 20 for process firms. With a similar pattern, the firms in the Blau et al. study averaged 19.63 persons, 25.40 persons, and 13.46 persons for each type of technology, respectively. In both cases, the spans of supervision were greatest for high-volume mass production technology.

The reason for this difference seems to be that in large-batch or mass production the work of the *people* involved in production is standardized. In contrast, in unit or small-batch production, the work is less standardized. Finally, in process firms, while the mechanical processes are highly standardized and automated, the people involved are relatively free to use judgment and the work is nonroutine. Where the work that people do is relatively fixed and routine, effective spans will be greater.

To illustrate the way in which the relative spans within a single organization may be determined, the experience of the Lockheed Missiles and Space Company, a division of Lockheed Aircraft, is instructive.[28] Lockheed's organizational analysts selected seven factors which appeared to influence spans of supervision:

1. Similarity of function—the degree to which functions performed by the various components are alike or different (more similar = broader span).

2. Geographic contiguity—the physical location of the components and personnel reporting to a principal (more contiguous = broader span).

3. Complexity of functions—the nature of the duties being performed by the organization components or personnel. This takes into account the skills necessary to perform satisfactorily (simple duties = broader span).

4. Direction and control—the nature of the personnel reporting directly to a principal. This includes the degree of the principal's attention required for proper supervision of subordinates' actions (little supervision = broader span).

5. Coordination—the extent to which the principal must exert time and effort in keeping actions properly correlated and in keeping his or her activities keyed in with other activities in the company (independent activity = broader span).

6. Planning—the importance, complexity, and time required to review and establish future programs and objectives (little planning = broader span).

7. Organizational assistance—the help received by the principal from direct-line assistants, staff activities, and asssistants-to (more staff support = broader span).

The factors mentioned were weighted, scaled, and used to analyze the relative differences in spans required. Stieglitz reported that one unit expanded the average span from 3.8 people to 4.2 and reduced supervisory levels from five to four. Another broadened the average span of middle managers from 3.0 to 4.2 and cut levels from six to five. While no performance data are available, it is reported that reductions in administrative expenses were substantial.

In summary, while executive spans seem to have little systematic variation with organization size or technology, the spans of supervision at lower levels do seem to vary with size, technology, and other characteristics of the job. If jobs are relatively routine and repetitive, then broad spans may be used effectively.

**Task Design and Worker Values**  A fifth dimension in organizational analysis and design includes the job characteristics involved and the values of people holding the jobs. An important purpose of organizational analysis, therefore, is to establish congruence between the design of the organization, the design of jobs within the organization, and the values of job holders. If these three parts can be properly matched, then the result should be more effective performance by the organization and greater satisfaction for its members.

*Job Design.*  At the turn of the century, industry developed a major emphasis upon the use of mass production technology. It was felt, in many cases correctly, that if jobs could be routinized and made repetitive, the result would be high efficiency and low cost of operation. These benefits could occur because repetitive performance of simplified jobs would permit the use of relatively unskilled labor, ease of training and replacement, less physical effort, and predictable rates of production.

Such proved to be the case. However, the simplification of jobs was not without difficulty. For some workers, the routinized jobs were boring and monotonous, resulting in dissatisfaction and poor performance. High rates of absenteeism and turnover increased costs because of requirements for additional labor and the necessary expense of training and replacement.

In an effort to have the best of both worlds—efficient production and satisfied labor—a number of remedies have been tried. Human relations training, participative management, and job enlargement are examples of such remedies. In some cases, these actions did what they were supposed to do: satisfaction and worker performance increased. In other cases, they were obvious failures. The reason for success or failure is now becoming clear. If productivity and satisfaction are to be achieved, then job design and worker values should match. This requires an objective assessment of job characteristics and the matching of different job designs with different kinds of employees.

One example of the assessment of job designs is the job diagnostic survey (JDS) developed by Hackman and Oldham.[29] Like other similar measures, JDS determines employee perception of the following job dimensions:

*Skill variety*—the extent to which a number of different skills or talents are required.

*Task identity*—the extent to which the job requires the completion of a whole and identifiable piece of work.

*Task significance*—the extent to which the task has impact on the lives of work of others.

*Autonomy*—the extent to which the job provides freedom and independence in scheduling or determining work methods.

*Feedback*—the extent to which knowledge of results is fed back to the job holder.

This assessment does not measure "goodness" or "badness" of job design. It merely assesses perceptions of job design.

*Employee Values.*  A further contribution to successful job design efforts has been the assessment of employee values and the proper matching of employee values with different kinds of job design. Assessment of values about work has been of interest in recent years, following a discovery that workers from small towns and rural areas seemed to respond favorably to jobs high in such things as task identity, task significance, autonomy, and the like, while workers from large urban settings often did not.[30]

Further investigation has revealed that geographic location was merely a rough indicator of certain worker values that are compatible with different job designs.[31] Workers who are most likely to respond to jobs with much responsibility and autonomy seem to believe that hard work is a virtue and that jobs which provide opportunities for personal growth, accomplishment, and achievement are preferable. For example, one such measure of values developed by Hackman and Lawler[32] assesses "higher order need strength." In it, the respondent is asked to make a series of choices between two types of jobs. Respondents with higher-order need-strength prefer jobs in which they work alone over jobs which offer no challenge; jobs which provide opportunity for creativity over jobs which have good pay; jobs which allow one to make important decisions over jobs with pleasant people to work with, to cite a few illustrations.

Research to date indicates that employees—particularly blue-collar workers—who have higher-order need-strength will probably respond favorably to challenging job designs. In contrast, employees low in higher-order need-strength will respond less favorably, or perhaps even negatively, to challenging jobs. If this is true, then it suggests that employers should take pains to match different kinds of job designs with different kinds of employee values. Employees with higher-order need-strength should be rewarded with opportunities for interesting and varied and challenging jobs. In contrast, employees low in such need-strength may be more productively and satisfactorily utilized in jobs where the performance requirements are clear and routine, and where employees can be rewarded with money and free time once standards are met.

## MATCHING ORGANIZATIONAL DESIGN, JOB DESIGN, AND EMPLOYEE VALUES

It should be apparent at this point that an organization which seeks high levels of performance with satisfied employees should find a proper fit between the design of its structure, the design of its jobs, and the values of its job holders. As indicated in Fig. O-8, the requirements for efficiency or adaptability, the nature of technology, the size of the organization, and the relative stability of the environment all influence the kind of organization design which will be appropriate.

This organization design will, in turn, influence the character of job design. For example, large functional organizations competing on the basis of efficiency will probably have fairly routinized jobs in many organizational units. It would appear that these jobs would be performed best by workers who do *not* seek challenge and autonomy in their work. Where the proper fit between job and values does not occur, it may be possible to redesign the jobs to provide needed challenge, to find new workers with requisite values, or, perhaps, to change worker values.

*See also* AUTHORITY, RESPONSIBILITY, AND ACCOUNTABILITY; INTERPERSONAL RELATIONSHIPS; OBJECTIVES AND GOALS; ORGANIZATION DEVELOPMENT (OD) ORGANIZATION STRUCTURES AND CHARTING; POLICY FORMULATION AND IMPLEMENTATION; PROJECT AND TASK FORCE MANAGEMENT; WORK DESIGN, JOB ENLARGEMENT, JOB ENRICHMENT, JOB DESIGN, AND AUTONOMOUS WORK GROUPS.

## NOTES

[1] A. C. Filley and R. J. Aldag, "Implications of an Organization Typology," Paper presented at the meetings of the Midwest Academy of Management, St. Louis, April 1976, *Proceedings of the 19th Annual Conference of the Midwest Division of the Academy of Management*, 1976, pp. 1–12; Alan C. Filley, Robert J. House, and Steven Kerr, *Managerial Process and Organizational Behavior*, 2d ed., Scott, Foresman and Company, Glenview, Ill., 1976, chap. 22.

[2] J. Woodward, *Industrial Organization: Theory and Practice*, Oxford University Press, London, 1965.

[3] J. D. Thompson, *Organizations in Action*, McGraw-Hill Book Company, New York, 1967.

[4] Ibid., p. 16.

[5] Daniel Katz and Robert L. Kahn, *The Social Psychology of Organizations*, John Wiley & Sons, Inc., New York, 1966.

[6] John Child, "Predicting and Understanding Organization Structure," *Administrative Science Quarterly*, vol. 18, no. 2, pp. 168–185, 1973.

[7] Howard E. Aldrich, "Technology and Organizational Structure: A Re-examination of the Findings of the Aston Group," *Administrative Science Quarterly*, vol. 17, no. 1, pp. 26–43, 1972; Woodward, *Industrial Organization: Theory and Practice;* William L. Zwerman, *New Perspectives on Organization Theory*, Greenwood Publishing, Westport, Conn., 1970.

[8] Peter M. Blau, Cecilia McHugh Falbe, William McKinley, and Phelps K. Tracy, "Technology and Organization in Manufacturing," *Administrative Science Quarterly*, vol. 21, no. 1, pp. 20–40, March 1976; John Child and Roger Mansfield, "Technology, Size and Organization Structure," *Sociology*, vol. 6, pp. 369–393, 1972; D. S. Pugh, D. J. Hickson, C. R. Hinings, and C. Turner, "Dimensions of Organization Structure," *Administrative Science Quarterly*, vol. 13, no. 1, pp. 65–105, June 1968.

[9] R. Dewar and J. Hage, "Size, Technology, Complexity and Structural Differentiation: Towards a Theoretical Synthesis," unpublished manuscript.

[10] P. Lawrence and J. Lorsch, *Organization and Environment*, Division of Research, Harvard Graduate School of

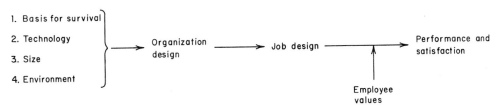

Fig. O-8. Balancing organization design, job design, and employee values.

Business Administration, Boston, 1967.

[11]Filley, House, and Kerr, *Managerial Process and Organizational Behavior;* Walter R. Mahler, *Structure, Power and Results: How to Organize Your Company for Optimum Performance,* Dow Jones-Irwin, Inc., Homewood, Ill., 1975.

[12]Andre Delbecq and Alan Filley, "Program and Project Management in a Matrix Organization: A Case Study," *Monograph No. 9,* Bureau of Business Research and Service, The University of Wisconsin Press, Madison, January 1974.

[13]P. N. Khandwalla, "Mass Output Orientation of Operations Technology and Organizational Structure," *Administrative Science Quarterly,* vol. 19, no. 1, pp. 74–97, March 1974.

[14]Ibid.

[15]Howard Stieglitz and Allen R. Janger, *Top Management Organization in Divisionalized Companies,* National Industrial Conference Board, Inc., New York, 1965.

[16]Woodward, *Industrial Organization: Theory and Practice.*

[17]B. DeSpelder, "Ratios of Staff to Line Personnel," *Research Monograph No. 106,* Bureau of Business Research, Ohio State University Press, Columbus, 1962.

[18]A. C. Filley, "Decisions and Research in Staff Utilization," *Academy of Management Journal,* vol. 5, no. 3, pp. 220–231, September 1963.

[19]Child, "Predicting and Understanding Organization Structure."

[20]Woodward, *Industrial Organization: Theory and Practice.*

[21]Blau et al., "Technology and Organization in Manufacturing."

[22]Chris J. Berger and L. L. Cummings, "Organizational Structure, Attitudes, and Behaviors," The University of Wisconsin Press, Madison, unpublished manuscript, 1975; L. L. Cummings and C. J. Berger, "Organization Structure: How Does it Influence Attitudes and Performance?" *Organizational Dynamics,* vol. 5, no. 2, pp. 34–39, Autumn 1976; Lyman W. Porter and Edward E. Lawler, III, "Properties of Organization Structure in Relation to Job Attitudes and Job Behavior," *Psychological Bulletin,* vol. 64, no. 1, pp. 23–51, 1965.

[23]A. M. El Salmi and L. L. Cummings, "Managers' Perception of Needs and Need Satisfactions as a Function of Interactions Among Organizational Variables," *Personnel Psychology,* vol. 21, no. 4, pp. 465–477, 1968.

[24]Stieglitz and Janger, *Top Management Organization in Divisionalized Companies.*

[25]E. Dale, "Planning and Developing the Company Organization Structure," *Research Report No. 20,* American Management Association, 1952; J. H. Healey, *Executive Coordination and Control,* Bureau of Business Research, Ohio State University Press, Columbus, 1956; A. Janger, "Analyzing the Span of Control," *Management Record,* vol. 22, nos. 7 and 8, pp. 7–10, 1960.

[26]Blau et al., "Technology and Organization in Manufacturing"; Woodward, *Industrial Organization: Theory and Practice.*

[27]Blau et al., "Technology and Organization in Manufacturing."

[28]J. Stieglitz, "Optimizing Span of Control," *Management Record,* vol. 24, no. 9, pp. 25–29, September 1962.

[29]J. Richard Hackman and Greg R. Oldham, "The Job Diagnostic Survey: An Instrument for the Diagnosis of Jobs and the Evaluation of Job Redesign Projects," *Technical Report No. 4,* Department of Administrative Sciences, Yale University, May 1974.

[30]C. L. Hulin and M. R. Blood, "Job Enlargement, Individual Differences, and Worker Responses," *Psychological Bulletin,* vol. 69, no. 1, pp. 41–55, 1968.

[31]Jon Pierce and R. Dunham, "Task Design: A Literature Review," *Academy of Managment Review,* vol. 1, no. 4, pp. 83–97, October 1976.

[32]J. R. Hackman and E. E. Lawler, "Employee Reactions to Job Characteristics," *Journal of Applied Psychology,* Monograph 55, pp. 259–286,1971.

The author wishes to thank Larry L. Cummings and André Delbecq for their useful comments on this section.

ALAN C. FILLEY, *University of Wisconsin*

## Organization behavior (*See* MANAGEMENT THEORY, SCIENCE, AND APPROACHES; MOTIVATION IN ORGANIZATIONS.)

## Organization design and work structure (*See* WORK, CONCEPT AND IMPLICATIONS.)

## Organization development (OD)

Organization development deals with organizational aspects of the behavioral sciences and may be known as, or associated with, human resource development, organization behavior, organization psychology, and organization renewal. OD also tends to overlap such fields as employee relations, sociology, anthropology, management, training, education, human relations, clinical psychology, and probably every other social and behavioral science.

Definitions of OD are many and varied. A particularly useful one is: *Any planned activity directed toward helping the members of an organization to interact more effectively in pursuit of the organization's goals.* Some practitioners insist that other provisions be stipulated, such as: *must be an organization-wide effort; must be directed toward more participative management; must provide for integrating the individual's goals with the organization's; must be considered an ongoing process—not an activity.* The real difference between OD activities and those technologically, economically, or administratively imposed is that OD is intentionally based on a scientific awareness of human behavior and organization dynamics.

*The Promise of OD.* The great promise of OD lies in its ability to merge the interests of individuals and the organization and make both more successful. Much personal unhappiness can be traced to feelings of being inadequately integrated in organizations—particularly in work organizations. Similarly, much organizational inefficiency can be traced to member disinterest in, or even hostility to, the organization. In the past, organizations have been successful due largely to the intuitive talent of leaders or the fortuitous combinations of the many contributing factors. In the future, organizations will owe more of their success to those who aptly use OD concepts and techniques. While OD will not overcome such deficiencies as outdated technology, inadequate financing, or hostile and overwhelming external forces, it will enable organizations to cope more effectively with these negative influences. OD does this by releasing the power of people to work willingly together for the common good.

**Background Theory and Assumptions** The definition of an organization, as used in this entry, is two or more persons interacting within some mutually recognized power relationship for some common purpose. This definition is intentionally broad in order to include all sizes and types of organizations, formal or informal, of either a temporary or more permanent nature. The power relationship may be hierarchical or that of equals.

Organizing is one of the oldest human activities. It is a phenomenon that will continue to be important to people. OD is based on the assumption that organizations influence human behavior and individuals influence an organization's behavior. OD also assumes that both individual behavior and organizational behavior can be modified and done so with favorable results—if based on proper diagnosis and skillful interventions. The terms *climate* and *spirit (Orgeist)* are sometimes used in describing the mixture of individual and group feelings. Those who claim some professional expertise in positively influencing the behavior of an organization based on OD knowledge and skills are called *change agents*, practitioners, or consultants. Internal consultants are those who are also members of the organization, and external consultants are those who are independently contracted to serve the organization.

Organizations may be classified in many ways to fit the proclivities and motivations of the individual studying or working with them. One way to classify an organization is in terms of how it relates to its interest groups. The four interest groups are the owners, clients or customers, members, and the encompassing society. The same individuals may be part of two or more interest groups. Ideally, organizations should never be expected to serve one interest at the expense of the others. Most of today's leaders recognize the interdependence of the interests and consider each to various extents when making decisions. Quite often, the actual behavior of the members is at variance with the purpose of the organization. Cases like these are the proper targets for OD efforts.

Another way to classify organizations is on the basis of how the members are used to make and implement decisions. At one end of the continuum would be a plantation or slave camp where the members' decision-making skills are not used at all and behavior is motivated by deprivation, fear, or force. Next along the continuum would be highly structured organizations demanding member conformity to the wishes of those higher on the power ladder. Motivation in such organizations is effected through combinations of threats against nonconformity and rewards for cooperation. The source of the punishment and reward may be the leaders and peer group in either the formal or informal structure. Further along the continuum would be organizations of equals who make decisions based on the will of the majority. Here the majority is influenced by subgroups, factions, and powerful individuals. Motivation is usually based on anticipation of personal gain, be it selfish or altruistic in intent. At the farthest extreme of the continuum would be those organizations that strive for consensus of all members and interested parties in the decision-making process. The decision-making process is usually slower in such organizations, but implementation is faster because the members "own" the decision. While the value of any type of organization along the continuum may be relative, the consensus-seeking organization is superior in using members as a resource for solving problems. Most OD practitioners tend to view their mission as that of helping client organizations become more participative and consensus seeking.

**OD Interventions and Techniques** The members of the organization are the primary target of the OD practitioner, even though they may ultimately be serving the interests of the owners or clients or society at large as well. While the practitioner knows the target group is influenced by technological and economic factors and that he or she is partly responsible for influences on these subsystems, the primary concern is with the social system—how people interrelate.

**Consultant/Client Contract** The OD practitioner may intervene at any level or any process in the organization, but most prefer to start with the most powerful person. Without the support of the most powerful figures in the organization, an OD effort is severely handicapped and limited. The client/consultant contract may take many meetings to assume form, and it may end in failure. When the negotiations are successful, the consultant and the one or more powerful figures and their agents agree on the goals of the effort, the roles to be played by the OD team, and the strategies to be used. They also reach consensus on how the OD process can be evaluated with hard data at specific points in time.

The client and consultant should strive to build a relationship of trust in which both can level with each other in an open, risk-taking atmosphere without fear of being used, and in which both will grow in response to the challenges facing them. To accomplish this, the executive must avoid using the OD practitioner to take a problem off his or her hands. The executive must also avoid considering the OD practitioner as a temporary employee who must be closely supervised. Further, the OD practitioner must be supported during the early stages and beyond, when resistance to change, a natural by-product in the client system, is encountered. The OD practitioner, in turn, should be guided by professional standards, as illustrated by this excerpt from the code of ethics of one professional society.

As a member of the Chicago Organization Development Association and as an O.D. practitioner I strive to:

Maintain a stance of concerned objectivity in all relations with my clients, keeping in mind the confidence and trust they place in me and the power my professional background gives me to influence their welfare.

Serve the interests of both client organizations and those who are members of the organization, but not to serve one at the expense of the other.

Help my clients understand and accept the ultimate responsibility for solving their own problems and realizing their own opportunities and never allow my clients to become dependent upon our continuing relationship.

Help my clients reach meaningful and measureable objectives in the shortest possible time for the lowest possible cost.

**Diagnostic Efforts** In the diagnostic stage of their work, OD practitioners use what seem to be well-known and commonplace tools: surveys, interviews, and direct observation methods. They also look at the traditional indicators of member dissatisfaction such as slumping production figures, delayed shipments, absenteeism, turnover, pilferage, poor housekeeping, grievances, and strikes.

In addition, they observe the *norms* operating within the organization—those unwritten rules of behavior that may be working contrary to official policy. They note the degree of openness among members communicating upward, downward, and with peers. They look for efficiency-sapping rivalries between groups within the organization or between members of the same group. They ascertain the extent to which individuals are matched by personality to those they report to and to those who report to them and the extent of the imposed or natural structure in their jobs and in the entire organizational climate.

Ideally, the OD process is organic rather than mechanical. The change agent helps the process grow in the organization and avoids imposing an externally developed system. As a technical resource for an emerging technology, however, OD practitioners tend to rely on a proven set of interventions. Some interventions have their origins in methods of clinical psychology, particularly those with a group orientation. Others have their origins in the fields of training and management. The former tend to be more people-centered and the latter more organization-centered.

*Team building (or group development)* encompasses a broad range of activities directed toward helping the members of a specific group work together. Team building applies to the initial conract between the consultant and the client executive. It can also apply to the relationship between a leader and one or all the followers, or to any group of any size that works together on a regular basis, such as executive committees or project-oriented groups of peers that are ad hoc in nature. The purpose of team building is to help the members become more effective as a problem-solving or project-planning/directing group.

*Leader/follower team building* may be illustrated through the use of a model called the *Org concept.* This model depicts both the leader's and follower's perception of the leader's style, the follower's style, and the follower's job situation, all in terms of structure. Leaders and followers use the model to communicate perceptions and make mutual decisions regarding modifying interpersonal elements in order to foster working harmony and greater productivity.

*Group team building* usually involves instruction in distinguishing between problem content, procedures, and processes. The *problem content* refers to the technical details of the group's concern; *procedures* refer to the steps involved in problem solving; and *processes* refer to the subconsciously motivated behaviors that tend to help or inhibit the ability of the group to work effectively on problems. Through the aid of a facilitator, the members are made aware of the processes influencing their behavior. The group strives to become self-facilitating.

*Performance factor analysis* is a method for focusing attention on the variables that influence organization behavior, particularly work performance. The factors are communication—understanding what is expected; training—knowing how to do what is expected; motivation—wanting to do what is expected; and freedom—being equipped and permitted by officials and unofficial forces to do what is expected. The above may be expressed as: $C \times T \times M \times F = P$.

*Reward system analysis* is a systematic study of (1) all the formal and informal rewards and punishments to which an organization member is exposed and (2) how these rewards and punishments promote positive or negative behavior in terms of the organization's goals.

*Management by objectives* (MBO) is perhaps the most famous OD strategy which has been widely adopted. It has not been applied uniformly, and its results are very mixed. While the logic is perfect, the application is often mismanaged. MBO maximizes member participation in setting and integrating organization and individual goals. All participators theoretically know where they are going, why they are going there, their rate of progress, and how their efforts integrate with the efforts of other members. [*See* OBJECTIVES, MANAGEMENT BY (MBO).]

*Norm modification* is an OD strategy that starts with a view of the organization in terms of the norms that govern the behavior of the members. *Norms* are those unwritten behavioral rules that group members follow which may or may not be in tune with official organization policy. When negative norms, such as, "Everybody starts late around here," can be identified and replaced with positive ones, such as "We all put in a full day's work here," the members and the entire organization benefit.

*Force field analysis* is a technique for systematically reviewing the elements of power working for and against a given issue or a proposed course of action. By identifying the potential trouble spots, it is possible to bring them into line with the project's goals before battle lines are clearly drawn and before peace, in the eyes of those involved, becomes secondary in importance to being right or winning. Intelligent use of this technique can help promote "win-win" situations where all power bases in an organization cooperate and benefit.

*Conflict resolution* strategies are those directed toward helping individuals or groups in conflict

within the organization to surface their feelings and expectations about each other and to deal with them in an open, problem-solving way.

*Intergroup merging* is a technique for encouraging the members of merged groups to integrate through recognizing the new power relationships, acceptance standards, norms, and functional expectations of all.

*Feedback*, in an OD context, is an interpersonal communications technique originally used in encounter groups. Its purpose is to sensitize members to their own feelings and to those of others. The technique involves reacting to others by discussing their behavior with them, and giving a personal assessment of the significance—and the results—of their behavior. Feedback is given in the spirit of welcoming feedback in return in order to promote mutual growth and understanding.

*OD team development* is the process of identifying those members of the organization who seem to have a natural proclivity for OD-type efforts. The process also includes recruiting and training those individuals to become either direct or indirect agents for positive changes in the organization's processes.

*Multiple management* is a relatively old organization design for fostering better communications and utilizing human resources. While the traditional pyramid structure is maintained to distribute responsibility and authority, peer-level councils are also used. The councils solve interdepartmental problems informally and provide a two-way channel of communication for policies, ideas, and general feedback among the power levels.

*Training* is not usually considered an OD strategy, mainly because it has been in use so much longer than OD. Indeed, the training field was one of the major fonts from which OD has sprung. Perhaps it would be truer to say that OD sprang from a recognized weakness in management and human relations training programs. All too often, changes made in an individual through traditional training methods are lost in a very short time once he or she returns to the original work environment.

Training given within a systematic framework of an OD program tends to be more lasting. When all members in the organization receive the same general training, they have a common frame of reference from which they can constantly reinforce one another in their day-to-day interactions.

Training efforts such as those specifically designed to train supervisors or managers in handling their subordinates can readily be fitted into the broad definition of OD. So can those programs for members who must work effectively with many individuals in various departments or sections of the organization. Such programs have traditionally been called human relations programs but are currently being updated with behavioral science techniques. The most popular model for such training programs is TA—*Transactional analysis*—which enables trained persons to identify and deal with their own and others' ego states (parent, child, or adult) as they interact. (*See* TRANSACTIONAL ANALYSIS.)

Some other traditional organization activities that can justifiably be considered as OD strategies include:

*Brainstorming:* a group idea-producing technique that also teaches individuals to work with each other in a noncritical, noncompetitive atmosphere.

*Program evaluation review technique (PERT):* a way of planning complex projects and also of showing the interdependence of all persons involved. It can be used to foster cooperation.

*Planned meetings:* used for the traditional reason of giving and getting information; may also be engineered through format and seating to foster feelings of mutual respect and equality among the participants. Schoolroom-like meetings, for example, promote teacher and pupil attitudes, whereas round table meetings tend to promote peer attitudes.

*Career planning:* an organization-sponsored effort to help individuals plan their long-range and short-range goals; tends to foster loyalty and openness and thereby strengthens individual/organization bonds.

*Communications systems analysis:* a method for looking at the way messages are formally transmitted through regular channels and informally transmitted through linking pins in the organization. What messages are sent, how they are sent, who sends them, and who receives them all influence the organization in an integrative or disintegrative way.

**Summary** OD is a relatively new, but very promising, science/art/profession that holds great promise for management. People still have the age-old need to be considered individuals. They must also be members of one or more organizations. Organizations are the vehicles through which people can improve their lot in the world. Executives have always recognized the importance of the organization phenomenon and have struggled, more than other people, with its problems. At present, only a small percentage of organization leaders are consciously employing the OD strategies described above. In the near future, however, these strategies and those still being developed will be common tools of the successful executive.

*See also* CONSULTANTS, MANAGEMENT; COUNSELING, EMPLOYEE; INTERPERSONAL RELATIONSHIPS; OBJECTIVES, MANAGEMENT BY (MBO); ORGANIZATION ANALYSIS AND PLANNING; ORGANIZATION STRUCTURES AND CHARTING; TRANSACTIONAL ANALYSIS.

### REFERENCES

Beckhard, R.: *Organization Development: Strategies and Models*, Addison-Wesley Publishing Company, Inc., Reading, Mass., 1969.

Bennis, W. G.: *The Nature of Organization Development*, Addison-Wesley Publishing Company, Inc., Reading, Mass., 1969.

Burke, W. W., and H. A. Hornstein, eds.: *The Social Technology of Organization Development*, NTL Learning Resources Corp., Fairfax, Va., 1972.

Dalton, G. W., P. R. Lawrence, and L. E. Greiner: *Organization Change and Development*, Irwin-Dorsey, Homewood, Ill., 1970.

Fordyce, J. D., and R. Weil: *Managing With People*, Addison-Wesley Publishing Company, Inc., Reading, Mass., 1971.

French, W. L., and C. H. Bell: *Organization Development*, Prentice-Hall, Inc., Englewood Cliffs, N.J., 1973.

Grossman, Lee: *The Change Agent*, American Management Association, New York, 1974.

Huse, E. F.: *Organization Development and Change*, West Publishing Company, St. Paul, Minn., 1975.

Lawrence, P. R., and J. W. Lorsch: *Organization and Environment*, Harvard Business School, Division of Research, Boston, 1967.

Lippitt, G. L.: *Organization Renewal*, Appleton-Century-Crofts, Inc., New York, 1969.

Margulies, N., and A. P. Raia: *Organization Development: Values, Process and Technology*, McGraw-Hill Book Company, New York, 1972.

Tagliere, D. A.: *People, Power and Organization*, American Management Association, Saranac, N.Y., 1973.

Tagliere, D. A.: "What an Executive Should Know About O.D.," *ASTD Journal*, July 1975.

DANIEL A. TAGLIERE, *Organization Development Services, Inc.*

# Organization structures and charting

Structures are the functions, rules, relationships, and responsibilities which serve as the framework for carrying out organizational activities. Structures are purposeful in the sense that they facilitate reaching organizational goals and objectives through the activities of organizational members. The concern here is with *formal* structures and with those features which are the result of deliberate strategies or designs. Unfortunately a considerable number of structures in contemporary organizations emerge on a haphazard basis, often without rhyme or reason. Equally as bad are those situations where structural design approaches have been poorly thought out and thus give rise to unexpected or unwanted consequences.

**Structural Purposes**   Structure is neutral; by itself, it is neither good or bad. Yet, for many organization members, structure has come to mean rules or functions which restrict individual creativity. Many also think of structure as synonymous with bureaucracy, as a substitute for thinking, planning, or rational action. None of these negative meanings needs to be attached to structure. Structure is what the policy maker, manager, or organization designer makes it or allows to happen.

*Traditional View.*   The negative flavor often assigned to structure is not without foundation. Generations of organization members have been exposed to principles of organization structure which meant certain ratios of subordinates to supervisors, centralization of responsibilities, prescribed channels of communication, and fixed lines of authority relationships. In the traditional view, structure sought to lessen dependence on people and to substitute mechanisms for coordinating and controlling member activity for the purpose of high productivity and performance.

*Contemporary View.*   Many social, economic, and environmental forces have combined to lessen reliability on pursuing purely structural approaches to performance. Organization members have witnessed the seeming adherence to (or dogmatic determination to abide by) the rules of the structural principles with growing dysfunctions, lackluster performances, and the growing estrangement of organization members. In short, newer and older generations of organization members have witnessed structural principles which have not delivered valued performances—if they ever did. It is little wonder that structure has been viewed with skepticism and dismay by many.

The point, of course, is that the intended purpose of structure and the actual result are often quite different. Structure is neutral. It is the position of most contemporary designers of organization structure that structure facilitate both institutional *and* social processes. Thus the assessment of the functionality of organization structure will involve various economic performance measures (e.g., profits, costs, return on investment, productivity) and human performance measures (e.g., job-related satisfaction). The greater the complexity of organiza-

tional environments and activities, the greater is the influence of human or social performance on economic performance.

## STRUCTURAL FEATURES

Certain general considerations establish the overall structural features, or external shell, of an organization. A wide variety of authority structures emerge within the external shell, and subsequent sections of this entry will deal with some of their more important considerations. At this point, however, the basic concerns are: (1) What general factors shape the overall characteristics of the organization? (2) What dimensions underlie these general factors so that general guidelines can be developed?

**General Descriptive Factors**   Some general, and thus imprecise, factors impart a basic flavor to structure. When considered in combination, they make a greater anticipation of structural specifics possible. They are of a descriptive nature, however, and offer only a low power in prediction.

1. *Nature of the industry.* Basic steel, for example, indicates the presence of coking, hot melt, and basic rolling units—of which each suggests an organization segment. Intercity transportation systems (bus, air, rail) suggest some form of geographic decentralization in organization structure.

2. *Size, maturity, degree of physical decentralization.* Size (measured in dollars, assets, or people) provides a sense of the scope of operations, the complexity of organization structure, and some idea of the proportions of worker, administrative, or staff groups. Many industry associations have worked out desirable ratios or proportions for member organizations. Yet it is difficult to go beyond this point.

Maturity may provide structural guidelines, indicating characteristic forms at different points in the growth cycle: for example, single product/single line (at an early point); increasing size of basic lines and maturing of appropriate internal organizations; multiproduct structures; and finally for some, conglomeration. The degree of physical decentralization lends some degree of specification to structure, such as the number of field units, plants, or establishments.

3. *Legal considerations and restraints.* Federal and state laws, plus various regulating commissions, have established the limits to size (e.g., in the area of economic competition) or branching (e.g., in banking).

**Structural Determinants**   Structure emerges in response to a wide variety of needs, environmental developments, and resource, market, and individual considerations. Structure is dynamic and responds to various situations which present themselves. As changes occur over a period of time, structure provides a vehicle on which to capitalize on opportunity, to consolidate past growth, and to base future growth. At a general level, the circumstances and factors shaping structure include:

1. Institutional goals and the particular work niche or product-service market segment to be serviced by the organization.

2. Functional work activities to secure the goals and product-service segment established for the organization.

3. Scope and sequence of functional steps in performing work and/or functional activities.

4. Economic size, physical dispersion of facilities or resources, and local, regional, national, or international character of operations.

5. Organizational maturity and development, where structure stands in time and space by way of consolidating past gains, stability of markets, capability and depth of management, and financial position.

6. Complexity of circumstances, as this emerges from diversity of business and work activities, number and type of employees, diversity of relevant environmental forces (including competition), and legal demands and constraints.

7. Uncertainty and the managerial, administrative, and analytical activities needed to deal with this situation.

8. Capability, depth, and limitations of the organization's management and professional members.

9. Prominence and relative importance of work and/or information technologies. Where production facilities or information processing are major aspects of the organization, they shape overall structural features.

10. Philosophical and social considerations, where the ambitions or interests of the owner or the organization's desire to better-meet individual motivational and growth needs impart further characteristics to structure.

Some of these points require little additional elaboration since they fall within the general experience of a large number of managers and officials. Others require more detailed explanation, and these follow.

**Organizational Maturity and Development** Many institutions fail to see the connection between structural evolution and business development and success (see Chandler and Greiner in References below). The point is simply that many organization structures grow and develop in systematic fashion.

One theme (Greiner) is that companies develop through alternate stages of prolonged growth (evolution) and considerable turmoil (revolution). Marketing opportunities and needs largely determine organization strategies, and these strategies determine structure (Chandler). On the other hand, structure may influence strategy to the extent that existing functions, hierarchy, and deployment of facilities may greatly influence strategy (Greiner).

Viewing structure as a central feature of a developing organization leads to the identification of five dimensions which provide some degree of predictability regarding future directions: (1) organization size, (2) organization age, (3) evolutionary stages, (4) revolutionary stages, and (5) industry growth rate.

Greiner used these five dimensions to identify five typical stages of general organization development, as summarized in Table O-8. Organizations which are in fast-growth industries or are growing rapidly in size are likely to encounter all the indicated stages in a comparatively short period of time. Smaller companies or those that are part of slower-paced industries are not likely to progress through all the indicated stages.

Organizations experience widely different needs for structure, depending on the more immediate circumstances of size, stage of development, maturity, and general growth pace of their industry. At an early point (stage 1) ownership is often completely taken up with getting work done. Structures are informal (often in disarray), and survival is a major concern. The preconditions for stage 2 emerge where growth has taken place, and continued informality of structures and direction create growing confusion and uneconomic action. Thus, stage 2 structure emerges as a logical management response to the growing turmoil of stage 1, and further structural adjustments come into view.

**Philosophy of Management** A sense of personal competency, at times combined with a lack of high-talent people, can lead to a high level of centralized control. Under some conditions, the distinction between highly centralized control (e.g., in decision making and planning) and autocratic management may be only a fine line. Highly centralized control can be expressed in an organization in several different ways—through the allocation of responsibilities and/or structural form.

In one extreme in this approach, the boss makes all the important decisions. In smaller organizations, the president or general manager makes decisions on such matters as budget, capital expenditure, new products, or hiring of key people. Where the organization is of substantial size and organized along

**TABLE O-8   Stages of Structural Development***

| Stage | Main focus | Structure | Communication, coordination, and control | Growing or central challenge | Founder, top management role |
|---|---|---|---|---|---|
| 1 | Birth, creativity, continuity | Informal | Informal and reactive to immediate needs | Resolving leadership and management growth needs | Make, sell, or deliver product or service |
| 2 | Growth | Growing formalization: functionalization; centralized direction, budgets, standards | Growth of functional structures—accounting, inventory, formalization of communications | Centralized directions versus growing needs for flexibility in response to complexity | Professional management and direction |
| 3 | Decentralization and delegation | Decentralized by product, geographic area | Greater control and direction from officials of decentralized limits—decentralization of information processing | Budget control by top management in face of autonomy of decentralized officials | Professional management—top management guidance, policy |
| 4 | Coordination and integration | Product groups, divisions | Expansion of centralized staff for analysis, coordination, control, growing centralization of information processing | Credibility gap between headquarters and field, staff and field or line personnel | Strengthen policy, planning and review |
| 5 | Collaboration and conflict resolution | Preserve previous authority structures but greater emphasis on processes such as matrix design | Group processes, conflict resolution, greater flexibility | | Mediator, coordinator, moderator |

*Based on the study of Larry E. Greiner, "Evolution and Revolution as Organizations Grow," *Harvard Business Review*, vol. 50, no. 4, pp. 37–46, July–August 1972.

divisional or departmental lines, the boss may be a division (or department) head. At times, the centralization of decision making may include the chief executive and divisions heads; little but routine responsibilities are left for the rest of the organization.

**Environmental and System Dimensions**   Several newer research directions indicate promising results in accounting for *overall structural features* through environmental and systems analyses. For example, uncertainty (see Burack, Burns and Stalker, Van deVen and Delbecq, Lawrence and Lorsch in References below) has been considered as a characteristic of an organization's (external) environment and a feature of the work task. Interdependence is a systems notion, which suggests the intensity of relationships between units.

*Environmental Uncertainty.* This refers to the variability and relative instability of the forces surrounding an organization; e.g., unpredictable competitive tactics, world tension, and sources of change that cannot be fully identified. The greater the uncertainty, the greater the turbulence and unpredictability of events.

Under turbulent conditions, organizations are forced to develop flexible and contingent approaches. Where environmental conditions are more stable and predictable (low uncertainty), more traditional structures will usually suffice. Structural characteristics typically found under these two conditions are shown in Table O-9. Where environmental uncertainty can be ascribed to more specific factors, greater preciseness becomes possible in specifying its structural effects. For example, for a manufacturing firm, great uncertainty from technological innovations (of competition and new scientific breakthroughs) might lead to the creation of a department for technology.

*Task Uncertainty.* According to Van deVen, this concept refers to the variability and difficulty of the work performed. Variability occurs where a number of exceptional or unexpected situations emerge. The difficulty may involve (1) the clarity of steps that must be followed, (2) the predictability of knowing which is right or wrong, and (3) the time required to develop an approach. High task uncertainty forces the exercise of individual judgment or discretion (as opposed to predetermined rules) and pushes down (decentralizes) decision making in the

TABLE O-9  Effects of Environmental Uncertainty on Structure

| | Environmental Uncertainty Feature | |
|---|---|---|
| | Low uncertainty | High uncertainty |
| Overall form | Traditional bureaucratic model, featuring specialization, division of labor, hierarchy | Organic with a good degree of interaction and permitting flexibility for needed changes |
| Coordination control | Rules, procedures, and dependency of allocation of responsibility | May require use of integrator to coordinate various elements of structure or system |
| Information gathering | Routine | Crucial in assessing appropriate shifts (affects, technology monitoring, market research, financial forecasting, etc.) |

organization. The practical result of high task uncertainty is to lower the amount of supervisory decision making and to increase nonsupervisory, or colleague, decision making.

*Interdependence.* This characteristic relates to the extent that organizational units are dependent upon one another for performance resulting from the flow between units of work, materials, or information. A general relationship appears to exist between interdependence and the type and source of decision making. According to Galbraith, as interdependence grows, more complex communications structures are required and more mutual accommodation and adjustment must take place. Rules and regulations will be depended on to take care of some of the arising situations. As contingencies grow, communication needs go beyond programming (i.e., rules), and hierarchy (higher authority) must be involved to resolve the arising issues. Additionally, as interdependency grows, group discussions and decision making will have to be relied on.

## A STEP-WISE APPROACH IN DESIGN

If there is anything which has been learned from the efforts of organization theorists and designers, it is that there is no one best way of designing structures. Few modern organizations of any size are simple enough, or of such singular purposes, that a single design guide could be employed. Fortunately, however, few design problems involve a total organization. It is much more common to deal with matters confined to a particular department or division. Additionally, various portions of an organization must be handled in a way appropriate to (contingent upon) the needs of its situation. Two, three, or even four design concepts may be used in different areas of a given organization. Moreover, traditional approaches are not necessarily bad, and contemporary models are not necessarily good. Thoughtful structural designs use both contemporary and traditional approaches.

Another realization which has emerged is that a specific design or overall approach is best described as satisfactory and not optimum. The number of goals and/or criteria which must be satisfied simultaneously—combinations of economic and social considerations, complex environments, and varying degrees of uncertainty which are a result of change—rule out precise solutions. As a result, prudent organizations follow a contingency strategy, which incorporates flexibility or adaptability features in proportion to the unknowns or unexpected factors.

**General Specifications**  Various general specifications are employed in most structures regardless of the particular needs involved. It seems unwise to label these specifications as principles, but these generalizations do provide some general criteria to guide most design effort, as shown in Table O-10. The six points in Table O-10 are interrelated and cover points often ignored, although they may appear to be mostly a matter of common sense. Situations that confront organizations are constantly changing; a particular matter may be no problem today but a major problem tomorrow. Thus, adaptability and flexibility are exceedingly important.

*The Contingency Concept.* Contingency structuring focuses on management's main tasks and the relationships between these. Drucker has visualized these as the (1) work task, which is focused on today's activities and work performance; (2) innovative task, which provides the ideas, products, and work accomplishments for tomorrow's organization; and (3) task of ownership or top management, which provides the vision and guidelines for joining today's reality with tomorrow's possibilities.

A particular structural design serves organizational needs. It emerges only after various central issues have been resolved. Clarity of organizational purposes, identification of the key tasks to be accomplished and evolution of a strategy for achieving institutional goals and purposes come *before* design procedures. Structural design follows strategy. It focuses first on tasks and work activity, not the individual who performs them. The final design, however, must meet the needs of both the organization *and* the individual, and some structural adjustments may have to be made.

*The Contingency Approach.* There is no one best way to organize, yet alternative approaches are not equally effective. For any situation, contingency analysis presupposes that a relatively modest number of variables (of the many present) will be relevant to the problem at hand. The relevant variables will be found as a part of the environments (external and internal), work systems, people, organization and/or institutional philosophy "surrounding" the design matter. For example, the greater the environmental uncertainty is, the greater the need for information processing by decision makers prior to rendering decisions. Thus organizations must be flexible and display an ability to adapt to unplanned-

**TABLE O-10   General Structural Specifications***

| Clarity of purposes | Organizations have multiple rather than single goals, and these are acknowledged and understood by its members. |
| Adaptability | Change is pervasive and affects all organizations so that the question is one of degree of needed adaptation rather than whether it is needed. |
| Flexibility | Structure displays the ability to shift or blend, avoiding rigidities which negate adaptability and build internal pressures. |
| Efficiency | Economy of effort for efficiency needs is met through joint economic and social objectives. |
| Stability | Structures (and the organization as a whole) incorporate mechanisms which seek to continually establish relationships, activities, and processes which are vulnerable to disruption because of change—stability represents a condition to be met by adaptability. |
| Organization renewal | Structural mechanisms, functions, and design incorporate needed change to permit survival and future growth. |

*Based in part on Peter F. Drucker, "New Templates for Today's Organizations," *Harvard Business Review*, vol. 52, no. 1, pp. 45–51, January–February 1971.

for occurrences. A step-by-step contingency approach to organization design follows:

1. Review organizational goals: economic, social, long range and short range. Note also the niche the organization is to occupy in the future; the owner's philosophy; public regulatory restrictions; and historical criteria of performance.

2. Examine the firm's external environment: describe major forces, trends, and likely future occurrences; identify international, national, regional, and/or local forces for change which are likely to affect the organization, its customers, clients, mode of doing business, etc.; and determine those functional areas of the organization likely to sustain change and their general approaches for coping.

3. Identify key end accomplishments and means of achieving these; indicate major work accomplishments and major work system.

4. Identify key (internal) subenvironments of the organization necessary for securing its niche. Determine the influence of key parameters such as size (number of people), geographic location, and physical dispersion on the scope and dispersion of the key subenvironments.

5. For each key subenvironment, determine (*a*) the pace of change, uncertainty, and complexity confronting it and (*b*) the quality and quantity of information and feedback vital to its functioning. Determine also the nature of communications: What has existed? Problems/dysfunctions? Future needs?

6. Formulate systems or work-flow models that relate the key subenvironments, indicating the step-by-step flow of major activities and key relationships. Also, determine organizational arrangements and functions (coordination, control, flexibility, etc.) needed to cope with change.

7. Determine the general organizational or structural requirements to achieve (*a*) *key functional activities* of planning, control, coordination, and direction; (*b*) *key offices*—research and development, finance, engineering, etc.; and (*c*) *key internal climate* features—reward, communications, and interaction. Utilize the models and prescriptions of the worker machine model, bureaucratic structure and Rensis Likert's "system 4" organization.

8. Consider jointly (*a*) the organization's integration needs to coordinate activities and (*b*) the requirements for differentiation, which serve to strengthen areas of specialized expertise.

9. Examine job features, especially the motivational climate.

10. Modify structural design based on a review of general design specifications and/or factors assigned high priority or urgency yet not fully acknowledged previously.

The 10-step contingency design procedure may also be diagrammed schematically as in Fig. O-9.

*Available Structural Designs.* Although literally hundreds of variations of structural concepts and theories may apply to particular situations, these applications tend to draw from a comparatively

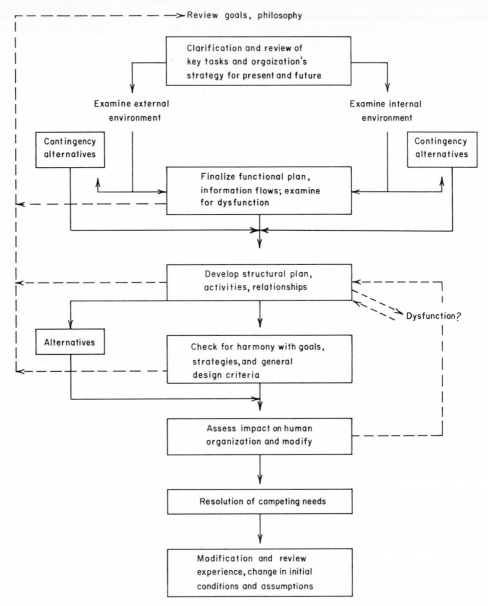

**Fig. O-9. Step-wise contingency procedure for structural design.**

small number of forms and concepts. Key models which have gained widespread usage follow.

*Traditional designs* include:

1. Centralized decision making and the functional format (e.g., marketing, finance, production, etc.).

2. Divisionalization and decentralization of op-

erating authority and responsibility to heads of divisions (or departments), with the corporation or headquarters unit retaining general policy, capital allocation, coordination, and overall strategy responsibilities. Decentralization is commonly accomplished along product/service or geographic lines.

*Contemporary designs* include:

1. Project, or team, approaches (involving multiple technical and social abilities) which are used in addition to, or beyond, traditional structural designs. This is not so much an independent design as it is a construct to meet difficult or complex technical situations, one-time projects, etc. (*See* PROJECT AND TASK FORCE MANAGEMENT.)

2. Colleague management which visualizes situations of overall management among peers. A "president's" office may be created (or something similar), and a highly participative style may emerge among a small group of "equals."

3. A matrix organization which combines both vertical authority relationship and horizontal or diagonal work relationships for dealing with complex work environments (as in medical units, teaching situations, social welfare groups, architectural-engineering units, etc.).

*Underlying concepts* include:

1. Specialization—gathering together or differentiating common skills or areas of knowledge to gain the benefit of concentrated effort.

2. Division of labor—the classical ideas of Adam Smith or Charles Babbage, in which work efforts are viewed in elementary form and so arranged or combined as to maximize overall economic performance.

3. Systems development, which emphasizes work/information flow and relationships. Where these flows or relationships are critical, traditional structural or hierarchical relationships are subordinated to these considerations.

4. Bureaucratic or structural nomenclature such as hierarchy, span of command, etc., which have tended to become more descriptive of a situation rather than definitive.

Contingency and classical models for structural design differ greatly in concepts, approaches, and specifics. Table O-11 summarizes the differences.

*Organization Goals.* Organization goals that reflect a philosophy of organizational creation, stockholder profit motives, growth needs, personal development of organization members, social objectives, and organizational renewal provide the ultimate criteria for testing any design. It is also worth noting Drucker's observation (1974) that (1) individual sub-unit success must be subordinated to overall success and that (2) structures are fragile and sustain changes "based on the demands of the situation."

*Contingency Example.* Examine the case of Globe Petroleum (name is fictitious), an integrated producer, which elected diversification into related fields as one of its major goals for the future. This goal was in support of a general profit objective and

in recognition of various longer-run profit limitations from purely petroleum operations. One of the strategies for this longer-range goal was the development of a family of petrochemical products, utilizing a common petroleum base stock but requiring different chemical processes and marketing strategies.

FUNCTIONAL PLAN, INFORMATION NEEDS, STRUCTURE: The fact that the chemical lines would entail differentiation of chemical processes and marketing approaches (at least initially) suggested the building of strong, largely autonomous companies. Considerable flexibility would be needed in these chemical organizations for some years to come, as new chemical processes were established and new markets cultivated.

Consequently, the initial functional plan and

**TABLE O-11 Contingency versus Traditional Approaches in Designing Organization Structures**

| Contingency approach | Traditional approach |
|---|---|
| **Direction of Relations** | |
| Develops relationships, communications, and interactions, whether horizontal, vertical, or diagonal | Places primary stress on hierarchical structure and vertically oriented authority |
| **Number of Supervisors** | |
| Designs will sometimes involve multiple relationships with various supervisors assessing different aspects of individual performance | Emphasis on unity of command and only one boss for an individual |
| **Locus of Decision Making** | |
| Considers centralization or decentralization dependent on such things as individual abilities, available technology, and personal realizations | Focus on centralization of decision making |
| **Span of Control** | |
| Depends on the situation which encompasses people involved, communications needs, needed assistance time | Largely fixed, considering specific limits based on level of authority or point in hierarchical structure |
| **Overall Orientation** | |
| Takes into account environmental, organizational, technological, and individual considerations; social, technical, and economic features | Basic focus on control and assumption of the inadequacies of people—when in doubt, rely on technology or structure but not on people |

structural approach was "divisionalization," with three essentially independent operating-marketing companies being established.

HARMONY, RESOLVING COMPETING NEEDS: At the same time, the initial plan proposed the use of corporate staff units in engineering, research, and information processing. Subsequent analysis indicated that engineering would entail too many specifics in process development, and a decision was made to decentralize this function while attempting to keep research and information processing as centralized activities. It was thought that specialization in research and information processing would entail much less overall costs while capitalizing on skills thought to be common in the three companies.

MODIFICATION, REVIEW, REASSESSMENT: After almost 3 years of experience with the (decentralized) divisionalized companies, it appeared that the overall organization format was functional. Yet the presidents of two divisions were insistent concerning the dilution of their efforts by positioning research and information processing in the corporate unit (centralization).

They claimed that: (1) research chemists and engineers did not understand client problems and were not responsive enough to information supplied by field personnel; (2) information analysis and problem solving were seriously hampered by time delays and mistakes because systems personnel were too far removed from source information and problems. As a result of these difficulties, research and information processing functions were relocated to the (decentralized) divisional organizations.

## TRADITIONALLY IMPORTANT STRUCTURES

Hierarchy, specialization, control, and impersonality are among the key principles by which organizations have been structured in the past. Hierarchy is the vertical dimension of differentiated authority levels and responsibility. Horizontal differentiation distinguishes the departments, divisions, or functional units organized by product, activity, process, or location. Horizontal differentiation assumes that organizational effectiveness is best brought about through the grouping of like abilities, skills, or mission. Hierarchy is inherently pyramidal in overall shape, with a gradient from top to bottom of diminishing authority and responsibility.

**Classic Design Principles**   Five traditional principles of organizational structure still apply to many common design problems.

1. *Unity of command.* A participant should receive orders from only one individual.

2. *Commensurate authority and responsibility.*

3. *Limited span of command* (control). The number of subordinates that can be controlled by a supervisor or official was thought to be largely fixed; at times, precise numbers or ranges of figures have been recorded as a function of the level of hierarchical authority.

4. *Centralization of major responsibilities.* This approach also called for delegation of routine responsibilities. In this context, centralization called for control over charting the future course of the firm, preserving and regulating economic resources, and formulating guidelines for daily operations.

5. *Line-staff organization.* Staff groups were to be organized around specialized areas of knowledge and ability to support the line operations of the work organization. Clear lines of responsibility were established among the two groups in order to avoid authority conflicts.

**Structural Form: Tall, Flat**   Top management's philosophy of the appropriate model for organization may lead to structural modifications, at times affecting overall organization features. One strategy, which assumes almost dramatic proportions, is the creation of a tall or flat structure.

In the *flat structure*, an attempt is made to reduce the number of authority levels, and considerable responsibility is laid at the door of middle management. In the *tall structure*, authority levels tend to be increased, spans of command reduced, decision making more centralized, and upper management's influence on control extended.

Sears, Roebuck and Co. is probably the best-known example of a structural strategy as an outgrowth of philosophy of organization. It created an essentially flat structure (Fig. O-10) to decentralize major operating responsibilities into the hands of its area and store managers, promote managerial development, and shorten the communications distance (authority levels) between customer, store management, and top management. Given the size of the Sears organization, the flat structure created extremely large spans of command at the middle management level of the structure. Middle-level managers were encouraged to develop self-reliance and to run their own shows. This structural strategy was a contributing factor in the growth of Sears as it far outstripped its early rival, Montgomery Ward, in sales. Yet the decentralization of responsibilities and creation of a flat authority structure may well have outlived its utility at Sears—for the recentralization of authority was being considered by top level Sears planners.

**Example of Centralization Strategy**   A large integrated petroleum firm provides an example of es-

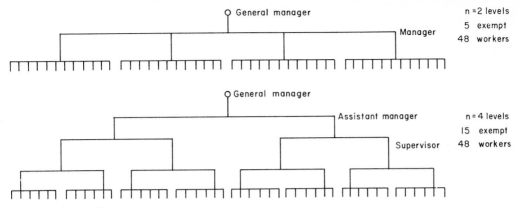

**Fig. O-10. Tall versus flat structures.**

tablishing the level of responsibilities as a corporate strategy. The company originally operated as a divisionalized organization with largely autonomous operating units. Each division was largely self-contained, even to the extent of possessing extensive computer facilities, financial accounting management, and various staff units. Organizational units were dispersed physically over many states, and even in foreign nations. Corporate headquarters functioned largely as a holding company—providing policy guidelines, exercising major financial and budget options, and carrying out long-range plans.

*Problems of Decentralization.* The benefits of flexibility and autonomy of decentralized business operations were increasingly challenged by performance weaknesses and omissions such as the following:

Excess costs of duplicated facilities, information processing capabilities, and staff.

Great unevenness in the exercise of organizational, product, work force, and cost controls.

Large variations in the organizational concepts, effort, and personal dedication.

Added information, reporting, and regulating requirements because of legislation.

Changes in the role and deployment of staff and a need to develop their strengths further.

*Problems of Centralization.* As a reply to the problems of uncontrolled autonomy, the company decided to centralize.

Almost from the start, it was clear that communications and coordination would provide major challenges to subsidiary and corporate management. Moving staff and information capabilities from their point of application and need was bound to create problems. What was not clear was when and where the stresses would develop. Neither was it apparent as to how much restructuring would have to take

place. It was also feared that additional coordinating personnel would reduce the planned economies of consolidation. Consequently, centralization (or recentralization) was carried out as an evolutionary tactic.

*Coordination.* It soon became clear that a formal role of coordinator would have to be created to tie together subsidiary and headquarters organizations. The role of the coordinator required knowledge of the internal organization, staff capabilities, and skills in working with senior managers and technical personnel. Specialized knowledge was not required, but the coordinator had to know where particular knowledge or abilities could be secured and how communications and areas of responsibility could be clarified.

Coordinators (at headquarters) were established in each of the major staff areas (such as accounting and personnel) for activities previously carried out in subsidiary operations. Also, coordinators were established to relate to each of the four main subsidiaries. In total, eight coordinators were eventually established.

Table O-12 summarizes the benefits sought for in the petroleum firm's centralization strategy. These are contrasted with key advantages gained from the decentralization approach. Clearly the advantages of either approach are contingent upon the specific organizational situation being considered—identification of the relevant variables and the priority or importance assigned to these variables.

**Product Versus Functional Organization**  One of the oldest controversies in structural design concerns the choice between a product and a functional form of organization. There are genuine arguments which can be advanced in favor of each.

*Growth and Change.* Viewing structure as a historical, evolutionary process suggests that both

**847**

TABLE O-12  Centralization versus Decentralization as an Organizational Strategy

|  | Centralization | Decentralization |
|---|---|---|
| Flexibility in field decisions |  | X X X |
| Field conditions diverse |  | X X X |
| Technology is standardized | X X X |  |
| Monitoring and interpretation of broad trends in innovation and creativity | XXX |  |
| Developing middle-level managers |  | X X X |
| Broad-based competition | X X |  |
| Narrowly focused competition |  | X X |
| Legally (governmentally) mandated information gathering, processing, reporting | X X X |  |
| Economies of computer use | X X |  |
| Overall control accessible | X X |  |
| Overall coordination need | X X |  |
| Uniformity in policies, plans, and programs | X X X |  |

Key: xxx strong consideration
xx moderate consideration
x some consideration

product and functional forms may be legitimate structural strategies. Similarly, it suggests that progress should be in evolutionary steps (from the functional form to the product form) as structural changes modify complexity. The recognition of these critical points for change is facilitated through size measures—the observance of general economic indicators (e.g., sales)—product-line diversification, geographic or organizational decentralization, and behavioral analyses of internal stress and conflict.

*Traditional Arguments.* Specialization of skills, equipment, products, or activities was frequently a basic guide for designing organization structures using traditional approaches (see Walker and Lorsch). For the most part, psychological and social consequences were ignored in favor of an approach which (1) optimized the use of technical knowledge and equipment and (2) facilitated the needed coordination and control. The major trade offs implicit in these arguments are the benefits of functional specialization versus the strengthening of coordination and control. The latter assure greater integration of work-related or administrative functions.

If the contingency approach is utilized, the introduction of situational considerations of environment and work may assist in resolving this design problem (see Walker and Lorsch). Functional organization is the logical choice where performance is relatively stable and administration assumes (or can assume) a relatively routine basis. In other words, where integration can be achieved through preconceived plans and conflict routinely handled through hierarchical arrangement, the functional model appears adequate for organizational needs. Conversely, the more unstable the environment and the

less predictable the task, the greater is the need for flexibility and innovative planning and problem-solving approaches. The latter appears more feasible for the product-type structural model. Where both stable and unstable conditions exist simultaneously within different areas of a given organization, new structural roles may be indicated: committees, coordinators, or the use of a matrix-type organization.

**Impact of Size**  The sheer impact of size can outweigh technology, philosophy, and a great number of other forces already identified. For illustration consider a commercial bread unit—say one producing 200,000 loaves of bread per day. A plant for producing 400,000 loaves would involve many more people, and the pieces of equipment would almost double; the organization structure would expand. However, in a different type of production unit, for example, in petroleum refining, increased size would only mean *larger* equipment rather than *more* equipment. Under these conditions, various personnel-supervisory relationships might remain the same despite the doubling of capacity.

*Manner of Growth.* Size is reflected in such measures as number of employees, dollar sales, and assets. Yet the structural form to achieve larger size varies greatly in each industry. For example, in some insurance companies and banks, growth in size is accomplished through the addition of more regional divisions or branches, while others in the same industry add to the work force and product line at a centralized headquarters unit. In basic steel operation, greater size may mean added capacity and/or integration (into the company) of related production operations. By definition, the conglomerate grows through acquisition of newer business enter-prises, often unrelated to the initial core units.

*Size Generalizations.* Growth in size is typically accompanied by greater *formalization* of procedures and relationships and the need for better, more thorough *integration* of activities for control and coordination. The question of whether greater size truly requires more centralization or decentraliza-tion of decision making, planning, etc., is far more complex to resolve. The answers are probably re-lated to the following:

1. How organizations conceive of their com-petitive environment and work tasks (viz., uncer-tainty, turbulence, complexity).

2. The interdependencies between system ele-ments, including organization, administrative, and work units.

## RECENT STRUCTURAL APPROACHES

Historically, two major organizational models evolved to meet competitive and survival needs while delivering the amounts of internal coordina-tion and control adequate for existing needs. In smaller organizations and simpler environments, the functional form of Henry Fayol proved adequate. As organizations grew in size and complexity, Alfred P. Sloan, Jr., of General Motors proposed and developed the divisionalized structure, which decentralized authority but retained overall corpo-rate control centrally. Both models were copied widely and find extensive use even today.

**Trends**  The continuing pace of technical eco-nomic and social change, however, has brought about the needs for newer structural arrangements, either in combination with traditional structure or as independent self-standing arrangements. In brief, the newer trends include:

1. Growth in service-type organizations (hos-pitals, schools, universities), where the work pro-cesses, assumptions, and relationships of manufac-turing prototypes are inappropriate.

2. Conglomeration, where organizations com-pete in various markets simultaneously and also contain multiple and distinct technologies, product lines, support facilities, and managements.

3. Multinational operation, where the distance considerations are compounded by multiproduct and/or multitechnology considerations.

4. Reduction in the relative proportion of blue-collar workers with a corresponding growth in num-ber and proportion of white-collar workers or professional staff.

5. Growth in environmental or organizational complexity, which has parlayed information needs to meet the requirements of multiproduct, physi-cally decentralized, and/or multinational operations. Thus, the need for new information technologies, integration, coordination, and control present them-selves as major challenges to policy makers and organizational designers.

**Contemporary Structural Models**  Highly com-plex organizational environments and problems have spawned the development of various flexible, adoptive structural arrangements to cope with these situations. Two structural models which have emerged in response to these needs are project orga-nization (known for some years in technical or capi-tal-intensive industries), and the newer matrix organization.

**Project Organization**  The essence of project or-ganization emerges from the need for (1) considera-ble planning, (2) coordination or research to deal with a complex problem or task goal, and (3) com-pletion in a specified length of time (say several months to several years). It also assumes that routine organization procedures and formal structure are unable to deal with the situation in efficient or economic fashion. A temporary group is formed, combining and integrating diverse physical and so-cial science talents with whatever equipment and procedures are needed to secure task goals. Group members return to their respective departments and positions at the completion of the project or their particular phase of the project.

Project organization departs from traditional structure-authority arrangements in that it com-bines horizontal, vertical, and diagonal communica-tions, work, and liaison interactions.

The utility and capability of the project group resides with the requisite self-containment and flexi-bility to meet project goals. The conceptualization and planning of newer-generation computers, con-struction projects, area redevelopment, energy from waste matter, new products, feasibility, etc., are examples of wide ranging project situations which, for success, must combine diverse social and techni-cal skills plus various resources in flexible and crea-tive fashion. The wide variety of capabilities that may reside within a project group are illustrated in Fig. O-11.

*Role of the Project Manager.* Project managers play a unique role for they assume responsibility for successful project completion in conjunction with personnel who typically have no direct or formal authority relationship with them. A given project team may have engineers, architects, estimators,

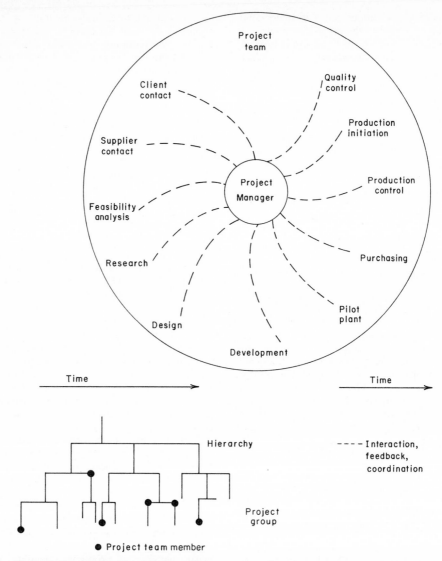

Fig. O-11. Dynamic character of the the project group.

systems people, and a cost accountant—easily representing four or five different functional departments; even six or seven would not be unusual. Thus, the project group superimposes a work and communications structure on top of a traditional hierarchical structure. The project manager evaluates individual performance on the task while the individual's formal supervisor assesses other personal performance or activity features and assumes responsibility for preparation of an overall evaluation. Understandably, the ground conditions exist here for great conflict, and these become acute in the matrix design. Formal authority within the project team is largely on a colleague basis, which involves persuasion and demonstration of correctness. One's reputation is constantly put on the line in carrying out project functions such as goal accomplishment, efficiency, creativity, and timeliness. Project management and participation call for training in modes of communication and interaction which go far beyond the normal assertion of formal authority in traditional structures.

*Staffing the Project Team.* From a technical viewpoint, the group must encompass the full range of social and technical abilities needed to conduct the project. Frequently, all the members will not be needed at the same time; they will phase in at appropriate stages or as needed (posing orientation and integration problems at these points). The feasible number of team members requires a contingency response. Member size could range from as few as three to upwards of 40. Members' technical ability is assumed; in practice, the assumption may be unrealistic and force much higher integration, technical assistance, or coordination efforts by the project manager. The slack in project management efforts is often drawn up in the number of different projects assigned to project managers, often a class of specialists onto themselves. As project complexity, technical difficulties, or coordination problems go up, the project manager increasingly focuses on a single project undertaking where still more project assistance is required.

**Matrix Organization**   This structure is related to the project structure in the sense of flexibility, capabilities, work, and communication relationships but involves multiple and simultaneous undertakings in an organization. Additionally, a matrix organization may combine some project groupings having a temporary character with other arrangements having semipermanent working arrangements.

As an example, Fig. O-12 depicts a matrix organization involving three different groups (A, B, and C) which involve three organizational units and seven different departments. Team members are drawn from all departments, and the composition of each team is unique. Consider, for example, team medicine. In this case each department represents a specialty such as urology, opthalmology, geriatrics, etc. The scientific developments in one specialty involve the contributions of sister disciplines. The practice

of a concept or technique may be most easily conveyed by seeking to integrate (for the patient in various treatment units) diverse bodies of knowledge. The elements of complexity, diverse knowledge, requirement to integrate, and continuing (semipermanent) need set out key elements of the matrix design. Needless to say, integration of knowledge domains involves far more than a mechanical mixing of (knowledge) fields.

Table O-13 summarizes features and problems of the matrix organization, some of which also apply to project-type organizations.

**Office of the President**   Although actual usage is quite infrequent, this structural form incorporates several ideas that promise utility in future organizational structures. The office of the president is part of a broader set of ideas based on *colleague management.* This approach represents a highly participative management style, often among individuals considered to be peers based on educational preparation, business and organizational skills, experience, and potential contribution to the organization's welfare. The office of the president may be simply two people who share the responsibilities of the office and reach consensus on important issues. Clearly, the effectiveness of this structure depends on participant understanding of underlying assumptions, abilities brought to the office, and development of a good working relationship.

The concept of the office of the president has been used in various types of corporations, companies, and partnerships. Where legal constraints exist, the office is used as a concept to broaden the participative base rather than as a structural rearrangement. Ordinary functional titles are assigned to top officials, yet the operating mode and structural style is one of an office of the president.

*Limitations.* Such arrangements may impose significant limitations on organizational responsibilities

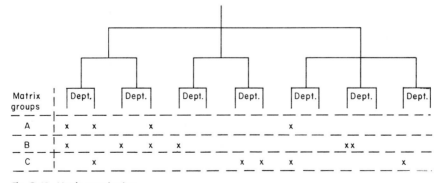

Fig. O-12. Matrix organization.

TABLE O-13  Features and Problems Associated with Matrix Organizations

| Features | Problems, issues |
|---|---|
| Combine diverse skills. | Conflict in authority between formal roles and those assumed in matrix mode. |
| Excellent basis for broadening participation and developing leadership. | Effective performance dependent on group processes involving leadership, working relationships, and communications. |
| Vehicle and framework for developing and presenting diverse bodies of knowledge and information. | Leadership may not be accepted by group members. |
| Greater opportunity for individual job enrichment. | Traditional roles may be taken with growth in size, and so lead to problems of traditional structures. |
| Flexible format permitting ready change of membership and adaptability to a variety of situations. | Flexibility and, at times, transient composition difficult for some to accept. |
| Presents a good fit with the increasingly complex environments (internal and external) in modern organizations. | Matrix design may bleed-off key performers from functional departments. |
| An effective basis to override traditional hierarchical relationships while permitting the preservation of this structure for other purposes. | Some view participation as added duties or responsibilities. |
| | To the extent design is successful, people may be reluctant to dissolve the matrix team. |

assigned to participants. This would be especially true, for example, where a divisionalized form of structure exists, units are relatively independent, and division heads are a part of a colleague arrangement. The greater the interdependency among organizational subunits, the greater is the reliance on coordinative activities—and this calls for frequent interaction of unit heads. When such interdependency exists, conflict is much more likely.

**Structure and Production Technology**  It appears that a general relationship exists between structural characteristics and technology. For example,

1. Structural characteristics involve such features as number of authority levels, ratio of first-line supervisors to subordinates, and the proportion of indirect to direct production workers.

2. The relationship exists because it reflects both economic and technical considerations. Yet, it is debatable how closely a particular firm has studied these relationships and thus how aware it might be of possibilities in this area.

This relationship is more evident in a production organization (e.g., a manufacturing plant) and less so where the organization includes marketing and administration. In short, the greater the organizational focus on production and directly related activities, the closer are the expected relationships.

*Concepts and Relationships.*  The theme is relatively simple: structural features are related to the level of technology. The *level of technology* generally represents the degree of sophistication and controlability. A scale reflecting the level of technology would appear as shown in Table O-14.

An English study completed by Joan Woodward in the early 1960s is probably the largest and most representative study conducted of technology and structure. It involved 100 manufacturing companies. American studies appear generally to support the findings *except* where (1) larger units are included

TABLE O-14  The Technology Scale (Continuum)

| Level of technology | Low level | | Intermediate level | | | Advanced level |
|---|---|---|---|---|---|---|
| Description of technology | Unit production | Small-batch production | Large-batch production | Mass production (Detroit type) | Automatic, near-continuous processing | Continuous processing |
| Control features | Manual | Mechanical | Semi-automatic controls | Automatic | Feedback, manual adjustment | Feedback, automatic adjustment |

that involve nonproduction elements or (2) many different technologies are involved. The Woodward study provides three important measures of structural features which are related to the level of technology. Average (median) figures from this study (also reflecting firms with good profit performance) are as follows:

| | Low level | Intermediate level | High level |
|---|---|---|---|
| Authority levels | 3 | 4 | 6 |
| Subordinate-supervisory ratio (first level) | 21–30 | 41–50 | 11–20 |
| Proportion of indirect workers to total (approximately), % | 5 | 15 | 30 |

These figures serve as general guidelines for a wide variety of production units. The specific figures are not so important as the recognition that structure should be responsive to the level of technology.

*Effects of Mixed Technologies.* Few work systems consist of a single type of technology. Typically, they contain a mixture of small-batch and mass production elements. Some plants may have large-batch and continuous-process elements. An automotive assembly plant, for example, contains many different work systems in addition to the final assembly line. The point is that structural features involving the first-line supervisory ratio (subordinates to supervisor), the relative proportion of indirect workers, and even authority levels will differ among departments. Structural planning for an entire plant is quite different from that required for an individual department. The policy maker who studies the organizational-structural requirements for a whole unit really looks at a number of different suborganizations (departments) and must gather these together into the overall design.

*Size and Technology.* Advances in production technology result in curvilinear relationships with various aspects of plant structure (see Blau et al.) Mass production work is more routine than most small-batch work: this leads to lower worker skill levels and changes in activity of plant staff. In updating mass production systems (i.e., units assuming greater process characteristics), further changes take place. Complex equipment must be maintained, monitoring functions are increased, and complex administrative structures emerge. Highly mechanized production technologies discourage decentralization by reducing the autonomy of plant managers in favor of higher authority levels and various staff support units. Centralization or decentralization, however, is still a matter of managerial philosophy

and strategic choice. Thus, in some corporations, authority has remained *de*centralized (along with the provision of requisite staff) to encourage individual development and leadership growth—despite economic benefits which seem to indicate centralization.

The impact of plant organization size and corporate affiliation are intertwined with these trends. For the most part, mass production-type plants tend to be larger than either batch or process-type plants (excepting petroleum) so that both size and level of technology may change simultaneously. Also, process-type plants tend to have (relatively) smaller direct labor components and total numbers of plant workers relative to mass production units.

Relationships between production technology and plant structure are further complicated by corporate form and disposition of corporate management and administrative staffs. In the United States, many manufacturing plants are a part of larger corporate systems. As such, substantial support staffs will often be found within corporate units, while plant staffs are adequate only to meet day-to-day operating needs.

Advances made in computer technology have provided new options in strategic choices of structural form. Aside from their use in upgrading production processes (see Burack and McNichols), the computer's impact on administrative structure permits choices between centralization and decentralization. When computers are provided at the plant level, their ability to support administrative control and coordinate activities permit the (re)establishment of plant management autonomy. However, one consideration which has worked heavily against the decentralization choice has been the multiplication (and duplication) of computers across units of a given corporation. The author observed one case in which the installation of over 50 computers in plant units became one of the compelling reasons for centralization and consolidation of these activities.

## ORGANIZATION MANUALS AND CHARTS

Manuals and charts are central records in the documentation of organizational procedures and relationships.

**Drawbacks** Through abuse, neglect, and misinterpretation, manuals and charts, however, have probably caused as many problems as they have solved. Probably the greatest "sin" in procedural circles is that of allowing manuals and charts to get out of date. Thus they are relegated to dusty corners or desk drawers, infrequent reference, or complete disregard. A "sin" of almost equal magnitude—and a major area of abuse—is slavish adherence to manuals or charts when common sense and very little imagination suggest a modified approach to a situation. Out-of-date material or charts force people to seek their own means of getting things done: they evolve a livable policy and work out relationships regardless of what the chart says. Overly detailed material often tries to answer everything and ends up answering little, if anything at all.

**Manuals** Many companies have successfully devised manuals that bring together organizational policies, procedures, goal statements, and related documents. Manuals can provide an outstanding codification of what an organization stands for. They can provide needed guidelines for dealing with various situations without emotion or recourse to (high) authority figures. Additionally, memories are fragile, facilities are dispersed, and a myriad of situations arise in modern organizations which require reference to policy—all of which argue for useful manuals. In this sense, the manual is neutral and impersonal—if the contents are thoughtful, timely, and permit imaginative actions for the unexpected or contingencies. Thoughtful, timely manual material is excellent for matters ranging from orientation of new employees to resolving issues among managers. The utility of a particular manual is measured by its usefulness to organization members. Its importance is signaled by the active support and referenced usage by managers and officials.

**Charts** A number of companies are known to the author where change in managerial offices is so frequent that charts are maintained on magnetic boards. Additions, movements, or quits are readily disposed of by quick adjustments, snapping a picture, and producing a newly revised chart. Unfortunately, a preoccupation with mechanics may cause one to lose sight of the basic purposes of charting. Charts, like manuals, can (1) promote understanding of communication problems, (2) orient newer people to structural relationships and complexities, and (3) provide a graphic picture of the full sweep of organizational activities, services, and the units and personnel central to these.

Charts in their simplest form display only functional units and relationships. In their most complex state, job of office holder, major responsibilities, committees, and even communication relationships can be added. However, many modern organizations are so large and complex that only key positions or organizational segments are visible.

Decades of exposure to organizational principles and hierarchical authority have resulted in charts being interpreted in both an organizational and social/power sense. For example, if one job happens to be positioned slightly above another, for example, a director of nursing higher than a medical director, adverse consequences are almost guaranteed. Thus, in chart construction, status, equity, power, and authority may be part of a *hidden agenda* in a particular organization—and in most organizations at least one of these notions might be involved. No general rules can deal with these types of interpretations. Thus charts must be developed with an eye to situations that exist in particular organizations. In some organizations, these matters have led to so much difficulty or a sense of inflexibility that charts are prohibited.

## TOWARD THE FUTURE

Structural design in the not-too-distant future will involve more comprehensive, precise, and systematic approaches than those in evidence today.

**Analytical Techniques** These new approaches will require more powerful analytical and behavioral theories and further advances in the application of contingency modeling. For example, the use of various multiple-regression models reflects the reality that numerous structure-related variables will have to be dealt with simultaneously to deal with complex environments featured by various interacting variables. At the same time, these more powerful analytical methods will have to capitalize on behavioral and structural theories which jointly involve structural, technological, and behavioral considerations.

**Participation Models** Another near-term trend appears to be the use of structural models which further individual participation. As educational levels continue to increase, greater stress will be placed on colleague-type models and organic relationships which favor participation. The concept of the office of the president seems likely to be extended as a participation format into other areas of existing organizations. Also, communications considerations will further affect structural designs by encouraging types which stimulate multidirectional flows and two-way interchange.

**Design Constructs** Environmental and systems descriptions appear slated to receive much greater attention because of their potential power to systematize design and offer broad latitude of application. Constructs such as environmental uncertainty, turbulence, and complexity are suggestive of one area of development. Systems-related notions with considerable promise include interdependence and various features of information processing. In conjunction with these constructs, organizations will direct more attention to developing their own data files of information on (1) factors shaping their structures, (2) response of organization members to various designs, (3) economic performance under alternative structures, and (4) work force and career planning.

**Structural Alternatives** Advances in computer technology promise to (1) relieve organizations of reliance on traditional structural approaches such as rules and procedures and (2) offer greater flexibility in positioning the locus of authority and responsibility. The ability to capture and transmit process information will provide new options regarding the placement of decision making, planning, coordination, and control.

*See also* BOARDS OF DIRECTORS; MANAGEMENT THEORY, SCIENCE, AND APPROACHES; OFFICERS, CORPORATE; ORGANIZATION ANALYSIS AND PLANNING; ORGANIZATION DEVELOPMENT (OD); PROJECT AND TASK FORCE MANAGEMENT.

## REFERENCES

Aldrich, Howard: "Technology and Organizational Structure: A Reexamination of the Findings of the Action Group," *Administrative Science Quarterly* vol. 17, no. 1, pp. 24–43, March 1972.

Bell, Gerald D.: "Determinants of Span of Control," *American Journal of Sociology*, vol. 73, pp. 100–109, 1967.

Blau, Peter M., Cecilia McHugh Falbe, William McKinly, and Phelps K. Tracy: "Technology and Organization in Manufacturing," *Administrative Science Quarterly*, vol. 21, no. 1, pp. 20–40, March 1976.

Blau, Peter M., and Richard A. Schoenherr: *The Structure of Organizations*, Basic Books, Inc., Publishers, New York, 1971.

Burack, Elmer H.: "Industrial Management in Advanced Production Systems: Some Theoretical Concepts and Preliminary Findings," *Administrative Science Quarterly*, vol. 12, no. 4, pp. 479–500, December 1967.

Burack, Elmer H.: *Organization Analysis: Theory and Applications*, Dryden Publishing Co., Hinsdale, Ill., 1975, especially chaps. 2–4, 7.

Burack, Elmer H., and Thomas J. McNichols: *Human Resource Planning: Technology, Policy, Change*, Comparative Administration Research Institute, Center for Business and Economic Research, College of Business, Kent State University, Kent, Ohio, 1973, especially chaps. 3 and 5.

Burack, Elmer H., and Anant Negandhi: *Organization Design: Theory, Research and Applications*, Kent State University Press and College of Organization and Administrative Sciences, Kent, Ohio, 1978.

Burns, Tom, and G. Stalker: *The Management of Innovation*, Tavistock Institute of Human Relations, London, 1961.

Chandler, Alfred D., Jr.: *Strategy and Structure*, The M.I.T. Press, Cambridge, Mass., 1962.

Child, John: "Predicting and Understanding Organization Structure," *Administrative Science Quarterly*, vol. 18, no. 2, pp. 168–185, June 1973.

Clewett, Richard M., and Stanley F. Stasch, "Shifting Role for the Product Manager," *Harvard Business Review*, vol. 53, no. 1, pp. 65–73, January–February 1975.

Donaldson, Lex, John Child, and Howard Aldrich: "The Ashton Findings on Centralization: Further Discussion," *Administrative Science Quarterly*, vol. 20, no. 3, pp. 453–460, September 1973.

Drucker, Peter F.: "New Templates for Today's Organizations, *Harvard Business Review*, vol. 52, no. 1, pp. 45–53, January–February 1974.

Duncan, Robert B.: "Characteristics of Organizations Environment and Environmental Uncertainty," *Administrative Science Quarterly*, vol. 17, no. 3, pp. 319–327, September 1972.

Galbraith, Jay: "Designing Complex Organization," Addison-Wesley Publishing Company, Inc., Reading, Mass., 1973.

Goggin, William C.: "How the Multidimensional Structure Works at Dow Corning," *Harvard Business Review*, vol. 52, no. 1, pp. 54–65, January–February 1974.

Greiner, Larry E.: "Evolution and Revolution as Organizations Grow," *Harvard Business Review*, vol. 50, no. 4, pp. 37–46, July–August 1972.

Grimes, Andrew J., Stuart M. Klein, and Frement A. Shull: "Matrix Model: A Selective Empirical Text," *Academy of Management Journal*, vol. 15, no. 1, pp. 9–31, January 1972.

Hellriegel, Donald, and John Slocum: *Organizational Behavior: Contingency Views*, West Publishing Company, St. Paul, Minn., 1976, especially pp. 62–73 and chaps. 8 and 11.

Hughes, Everett C.: "Preserving Individualism on the R&D Team," *Harvard Business Review*, vol. 46, no. 1, pp. 72–82, January–February 1968.

Jurkovich, Ray: "A Core Typology of Organizational Environments," *Administrative Science Quarterly*, vol. 19, no. 3, pp. 380–394, September 1974.

Khandwalla, Pradik N.: "Viable and Effective Organizational Designs of Farms," *Academy of Management Journal*, vol. 16, no. 3, pp. 481–495, September 1973.

Lawrence, Paul R., and Jay W. Lorsch: "New Management Job: The Integrator," *Harvard Business Review*, vol. 45, no. 6, pp. 142–151, November–December 1967.

Lawrence, Paul R., and Jay W. Lorsch: *Organization and Environment*, Harvard Graduate School of Business Administration, Boston, 1967.

Louis, Arthur M.: "An Awesome Mind Was Fletcher Byrom's Secret Weapon," *Fortune*, vol. 44, no. 1, p. 112, July 1976.

McCaskey, Michael B.: "An Introduction to Organizational Design," *California Management Review*, vol. 17, no. 2, pp. 13–20, Winter 1974.

McMillan, Charles J., David J. Hecksin, Christopher R. Henings, and Rodney E. Schneck: "The Structure of Work Organizations Across Societies," *Academy of Man-*

*agement Journal*, vol. 16, no. 4, pp. 555–569, December 1973.

Mansfield, Roger: "Bureaucracy and Centralization: An Examination of Organizational Structure," *Administrative Science Quarterly*, vol. 18, no. 4, pp. 477–488, December 1973.

Ouchi, William G., and James B. Dawling: "Defining the Span of Control," *Administrative Science Quarterly*, vol. 19, no. 3, pp. 357–365, September 1974.

Pfeffer, Jeffrey: "Size and Corporation of Corporate Boards of Director: The Organization and its Environment," *Administrative Science Quarterly*, vol. 17, no. 2, pp. 218–228, June 1972.

Pugh, D. S., D. J. Hecksin, C. R. Henings, and C. Turner: "Dimensions of Organization Structure," *Administrative Science Quarterly*, vol. 13, no. 1, pp. 65–105, December 1968.

Reeves, Tom Kynaston, and Barry A. Turner: "A Theory of Organization and Behavior in Bolet Production Factories," *Administrative Science Quarterly*, vol. 17, no. 1, pp. 81–98, March 1972.

Reimann, Bernard D.: "On the Dimensions of Bureaucratic Structure: An Empirical Reappraisal," *Administrative Science Quarterly*, vol. 18, no. 4, pp. 462–476, December 1973.

Tosi, Henry, Raman Aldag, and Ronald Slorey: "On the Measurement of the Environment: An Assessment of the Lawrence and Lorsch Environment Uncertainty Questionnaires," *Administrative Science Quarterly*, vol. 18, no. 1, pp. 27–36, March 1973.

Van de Ven, Andrew: "Structural Design Alternatives in Public Organization," in Burack and Negandhi, op. cit.

Van de Ven, Andrew, and Andre Delbecq: "Nominal Versus Interacting Group Processes for Committee Decision Making Effectiveness, *Academy of Management Journal*, vol. 14, no. 2, pp. 203–212, June 1971.

Walker, Arthur H., and Jay W. Lorsch: "Organizational Choice: Product vs. Function," *Harvard Business Review*, vol. 46, no. 6, pp. 129–138, November–December 1968.

Wieland, George F., and Robert A. Ullrich: *Organizations: Behavior, Design, and Change*, 2d ed., Richard D. Irwin, Inc., Homewood, Ill., 1976, especially chaps. 2, 4, and 13.

Woodward, Joan: *Industrial Organization, Theory and Practice*, Oxford University Press, London, 1965.

The author acknowledges the help of various organization planners in providing resource material, in particular, that of Robert A. Dinerstein, Standard Oil Company (Indiana).

ELMER H. BURACK, *University of Illinois,*
*Chicago Circle*

## Organization theory (*See* MANAGEMENT THEORY, SCIENCE, AND APPROACHES.)

## Organizing and organizations (*See heading in Table of Contents for complete listing.*)

## Orientation training (*See* DEVELOPMENT AND TRAINING, EMPLOYEE.)

## Outcome, optimum (*See* STATISTICAL ANALYSIS FOR MANAGEMENT.)

## Output, economic (*See* PRODUCTIVITY.)

## Outputs, production (*See* PRODUCTION/OPERATIONS MANAGEMENT.)

## Outside directors (*See* BOARDS OF DIRECTORS.)

## Overhead budgets (*See* BUDGETS AND BUDGET PREPARATION.)

## Overhead costs (*See* ACCOUNTING, COST ANALYSIS AND CONTROL.)

## Over-the-counter market (*See* MARKETS, SECURITIES.)

## Overtime premiums (*See* COMPENSATION, EMPLOYEE BENEFIT PLANS.)

## Owner's equity (*See* ACCOUNTING, FINANCIAL.)

## Ownership (*See heading in Table of Contents for complete listing.*)

# Ownership, legal forms of

In a private enterprise system, economic decisions related to what shall be produced, how it shall be produced, and for whom, are usually determined by organizations known as businesses. Generally speaking, businesses are economic organizations developed by individuals for the purpose of providing some good(s) or service(s) for a profit. Moreover, the majority of profit-oriented businesses operating in the American enterprise system can be classified as either sole proprietorships, partnerships, or corporations. The advantages, disadvantages, and unique characteristics of each of these forms of business organization will be examined in this entry.

## UNINCORPORATED BUSINESSES

Unincorporated businesses are primarily of two types: sole proprietorships and partnerships. Unincorporated businesses are the most popular form of business structure in the American enterprise system. The average size of unincorporated businesses is substantially smaller, however, than the average size of incorporated businesses. Consequently, unincorporated businesses constitute a smaller percentage of total business assets than incorporated businesses.

**Sole Proprietorship**  The sole proprietorship is the oldest, and yet most popular, form of business organization. Indeed, there are approximately 3 times as many sole proprietorships in the United States as there are partnerships and corporations combined. The respective advantages and disadvantages of the sole proprietorship form of organization are discussed in more detail below.

*Advantages of the Sole Proprietorship Organization.*  There are four primary advantages associated with the sole proprietorship form of organization. The first of these, that of ease of entry and exit, is probably best epitomized by the very nature of sole proprietorships. Sole proprietorships are, by definition, businesses composed of one owner, or proprietor. Such businesses are usually small and usually operate in the services or retail goods business. One typical sole proprietorship is probably the "mom and pop" grocery store found in abundance throughout America. (See Table O-15.)

Organizing and starting a sole proprietorship involves fewer obstacles than most other business forms. Other than the obvious start-up problems common to all businesses, the sole proprietor has few other obligations. In some communities and in

**TABLE O-15   Characteristics of Sole Proprietorships**

| Advantages | Disadvantages |
|---|---|
| Ease of entry and exit | Limited life-span |
| Full managerial powers | Limited size |
| Right to all profits | Unlimited liability |
| Taxation benefits | |

some areas of business (for example, the retail liquor business) special licenses may be required by the local authorities, but such is not normally the case. In similar fashion, exit from business is a more simplified process for the sole proprietor than for other forms of organization. A sign in the window, a bolt on the door, and the business is closed.

A second advantage of the sole proprietorship is the right to full managerial say-so on the part of the proprietor. This advantage is usually a major factor cited by those who begin sole proprietorships. People, it seems, like to be their own boss. Nonetheless, this advantage contains a strong qualification, for it is one thing to desire full managerial authority and another to be a truly qualified manager. Indeed, statistics have shown that the major reason for the failure of small businesses has involved managerial incompetence in one or more areas vital to a business' success.

A third advantage to the sole proprietorship form of business enterprise is the right to all the profits of the business. Inherent with this advantage, however, is the undeniable fact that all losses also accrue to the sole proprietor. While all proprietors enter business with the expectation of making profits, there always looms the risk that such profits may not materialize and that instead losses will result.

Should, however, profits result from the proprietorship, yet another benefit may result. This benefit relates to the tax treatment accorded sole proprietorship profits. The law does not distinguish between profits earned by the sole proprietor or the business. For tax purposes, all such incomes are treated as belonging to the individual proprietor and are thus taxed at the individual rate. For most proprietorships, this has the effect of taxing business profits at a lower rate than would be the case if the business were incorporated.

*Disadvantages of the Sole Proprietorship Organization.*  Despite the many significant advantages inherent in sole proprietorships, certain disadvantages exist which tend to mute some of the overall attractiveness of this form of business organization. To begin with, sole proprietorships have the unfortunate characteristic of possessing a limited life-span. Because the sole proprietorship has only one owner, the life-span of the business cannot exceed that of the proprietor.

The limited life-span of sole proprietorships tends to lead to yet another disadvantage, namely, the characteristic of limited size. Businesses become large only with the benefit of two factors: time and capital. Because a sole proprietorship's life-span is limited, most such organizations lack sufficient time to grow large. Additionally, only one owner exists to provide the capital necessary to attain large size. When these two items are combined, the reason for the generally small size of most sole proprietorships becomes clear.

Finally, the sole proprietorship possesses the discomforting attribute of conveying unlimited liability to the proprietor. In essence, this means that under the sole proprietorship form of organization, the sole proprietor is personally responsible for all the debts and obligations accruing to the business. This liability extends to the full personal asset position of the sole proprietor and is indeed a major drawback to this form of business organization.

**Partnership**  The second major type of unincorporated business is the partnership. The partnership form of organization is characterized by the existence of two or more owners, or partners, at least one of whom must accept unlimited liability for the acts and obligations of the partnership. In addition to possessing characteristics unique only to this form of organization, partnerships possess advantages and disadvantages that can be clearly identified.

As noted, partnerships are distinguished by the existence of two or more owners, at least one of whom has unlimited liability for the debts of the business. Those partners who agree to accept unlimited liability are known as *general partners*. They enjoy all the benefits of the partnership and are generally active in the management of the partnership. Unless specifically stated otherwise in the partnership agreement, all partners are assumed to be general partners.

On occasion, other types of partners (besides general partners) may partake in a partnership. *Limited partners* are individuals whose contribution to the management of the firm is restricted to a particular facet of the firm's operations. For example, a lawyer or an accountant may be a limited partner. Because the managerial role of limited partners is restricted, these partners are not subject to unlimited liability for the debts of the firm.

Similarly, *silent partners* and *secret partners* enjoy limited liability for the debts of a partnership. Silent partners are partners who do not play an active role

in the management of the partnership but who allow the partnership to list their names as partners in the firm. Secret partners are partners who, although active in the management of the firm, are not recognized as partners by the general public. If for some reason the partnership status of the secret partner becomes known, that partner becomes a general partner and loses the limited liability status previously enjoyed. (See Table O-16.)

**TABLE O-16  Characteristics of Partnerships**

| Unique characteristics | Advantages | Disadvantages |
|---|---|---|
| Type of partners | Ease of entry  Division of labor  Tax benefits | Limited life  Unlimited liability  Personality conflicts |

*Advantages of the Partnership Form of Organization.*  Like the sole proprietorship, partnerships are relatively easy to form. Generally, a written agreement, known as the *Articles of Copartnership*, is drawn up by the various parties, outlining the duties, responsibilities, capital contributions, and profit sharing relationship of each of the partners. No other extensive legal formalities need to be undertaken (except in isolated industries) to begin the business.

A second advantage of the partnership form of organization is the possibility of achieving a division of labor in the management of the firm. With multiple partners in the firm, it is conceivable that one partner could assume responsibility for, say, marketing efforts, another could handle personnel, etc. By dividing responsibilities among the various partners, improved business management can be achieved.

Finally, partnerships possess the same tax advantages that accrue to sole proprietorships. That is, profits earned by the partnership are assumed to be earned by the various owners in proportion to the arrangement agreed on in the *Articles of Copartnership*. Usually, this means the profits of the firm are taxed at a lower rate than would be the case if the business incorporated.

*Disadvantages of the Partnership Form of Organization.*  Generally speaking, partnerships suffer from many of the same disadvantages that are found in sole proprietorships. For example, partnerships tend to have a very limited life. If any of the general partners dies or becomes unable to function as a partner, the partnership comes to an end. Indeed, even the death of a special partner can, under some circumstances, terminate a partnership.

Another disadvantage is that all general partners are fully liable for all the debts of the business. As we have noted, this unlimited liability feature may even extend to secret partners, should word ever spread about their ownership position.

Finally, partnerships suffer from what can be called a "personality crisis." It is difficult to find a group of people who trust one another so much that they allow each other the freedom to commit acts which could result in a creditor suing them for the full extent of their wealth. It has often been said that a partnership is much like a marriage, in that the trust one partner must have in the others must be complete and total. Unfortunately, such trust is not easy to find.

## INCORPORATED BUSINESSES

The second major type of business organization in America is known as incorporated business. To create an incorporated business, it is necessary to obtain the permission of the appropriate legal authorities. Such permission, however, may obligate the incorporated business to follow certain rules, regulations, and possibly regulatory agencies in the course of doing business.

**Corporation** Perhaps the most important, and yet least understood, business structure in America is the corporation. By definition, a corporation is "an artificial being, invisible, intangible, and existing only in contemplation of law." (*Dartmouth College v. Woodward*, 17 U.S. 518.) This definition, handed down by Chief Justice John Marshall in 1819, decrees that a corporation is, in fact, a legal person, possessing many of the rights and obligations of ordinary people. Thus, a corporation can sue or be sued, it pays taxes on its earnings, and in some ways, it even possesses abilities not radically different from marriage and divorce. The characteristics—advantages and disadvantages—of the corporate business organization, are noted below. (See Table O-17.)

When individuals desire to form a corporation, they must submit a charter to the state in which the corporation will be domiciled. This charter specifies the objectives of the corporation, the nature of its business, names of the owners or organizers, the number of shares of ownership stock that will be issued, etc. Approval of the charter by the state government is necessary before the corporation can be created.

A second significant feature of the corporation is the existence of stockholders. By definition, the *stockholders* of a corporation are the owners of the firm. Such ownership is signified by possession of a certificate of ownership, known commonly as a *stock certificate*. Each shareholder's ownership consists of the percent of the total shares of stock owned by that shareholder. Perhaps an example will clarify the situation.

Suppose a group of people desire to form a corporation. They submit a charter to the state, which gets approved. In that charter, assume the company asked for authorization to issue 1000 shares of stock at a price of $10 per share. Upon approval of the charter, the company offers the stock to the general public. Eventually, all 1000 shares are sold. The company has received a total of $10,000 (its initial capital) with which to begin business. Each of the people who bought the stock becomes known as a shareholder of the firm.

Because shareholders may live all over the world, it is impossible for them to engage in day-to-day management of the firm. As a consequence, the shareholders elect a team of professional managers to run the corporation for them. This team is known as the *board of directors*. The board has the responsibility of choosing a president and a vice-president and watching over the interests of the shareholders who elected them.

A third unique characteristic of corporations is their diversity. For example, corporations may be public or private creations. *Private* corporations are typified by the large industrial corporations like General Motors. *Public* corporations, such as TVA or many large cities in the country, are less common. Recently, *quasi-public* corporations (Amtrak, for example) have also come into being. These are corporations created jointly by public and private interests.

Additionally, corporations can be classed as open or closed. An *open* corporation is one whose stock is widely owned and in which it is generally possible to buy shares from existing shareholders. *Closed* corporations are owned by only a few individuals who rarely sell their stock. Thus, the investing public has little opportunity to buy stock in these firms. An example of a closed corporation might be

**TABLE O-17  Characteristics of Corporations**

| Unique characteristics | Advantages | Disadvantages |
|---|---|---|
| Corporate charter | Transfer of ownership | Organizational expense |
| Stockholders | Unlimited life | |
| Types of corporations | Ease of expansion | Lack of privacy |
| | Division of labor | Double taxation |
| | Limited liability | |

any of the professional sports teams operating in the country.

Corporations can also be classed as profit or nonprofit institutions. Most private, industrial corporations are *profit*-oriented concerns. By contrast, most hospitals, churches, foundations, and some schools are *nonprofit*-oriented institutions.

Finally, corporations can be classified as being either domestic, foreign, or alien corporations. A *domestic* corporation is one which is operating in the state in which it received its charter. A *foreign* corporation is defined as one operating in a state other than the one in which it was chartered. An *alien* corporation is one that received its charter in a foreign country. Volkswagen, Toyota, and Datsun are all examples of alien corporations in the United States.

*Advantages of the Corporate Form of Organization.* The corporate form of business organization enjoys many advantages over the unincorporated businesses. First, the corporation is the only business institution that allows for easy transfer of ownership from one person or institution to another. To transfer ownership, the two parties (the selling party and the purchasing party) need only make contact, agree on a price, make the sale, and notify the company of the sale. The company then removes the name of the selling party from its ownership records and replaces it with the name and address of the new shareholder. Moreover, for most of the large, public, industrial corporations, the securities markets provide an easy and efficient means for the transfer of ownership.

Because of this ease of transferability of ownership, yet another advantage accrues to the corporation, that is, the potential for an unlimited life. The corporation, by virtue of its status as a "legal person," enjoys a life all its own. It is not dependent upon the life of its shareholders, since the demise of any shareholder merely transfers those ownership rights to his or her legal heirs.

A third advantage is the ease with which most corporations can expand and grow. A corporation can raise new capital by amending the charter and asking permission to issue more shares. If the state and the existing shareholders agree, the corporation may then offer more stock to the investing public and thus raise the desired new capital.

A fourth advantage of the corporation is the ability to enjoy a real division of labor. The owners of the corporation normally do not actively manage their business. Rather, this managerial task is assigned to a board of directors who are authorized to hire all those people they feel necessary to accomplish the goals of the firm. As a result, most corporations have well-defined organizational structures, with vast reservoirs of expertise available to run the business.

Finally, the corporation provides its shareholders with one final advantage, namely, the right of limited liability. Because the corporation is a "legal person," it, and it alone, is responsible for its debts. The shareholders of the corporation can lose no more than their investment in the stock of the company.

*Disadvantages of the Corporate Form of Organization.* Although significant advantages exist with the corporate organizational structure, several major weaknesses are found with this form. First is the problem of organizational expense. Forming a corporation involves lengthy legal proceedings, the cost of which can often run into thousands of dollars.

Yet a second disadvantage is the loss of privacy of business operations. Because corporations are creations of the state, they must file regular reports and financial statements to the state of incorporation. These reports become part of the public record and are available for anyone, including competitors, to see.

Finally, corporations are subject to what is commonly known as "double taxation." When a corporation earns a profit, it pays taxes—at a rather high corporate tax rate—on those profits. From its after-tax profits, the corporation may then pay dividends to its shareholders. These dividends are considered to be income to the shareholder and, to the extent that they exceed presently allowed exclusions, are subject to personal income taxes. Thus, some of the profits earned by the corporation are taxed twice; once when earned by the corporation and again when earned by the shareholder.

**Other Incorporated Businesses** Although sole proprietorships, partnerships, and corporations constitute the majority of business organizations, a few other types exist which deserve mention.

*Cooperatives.* Cooperatives are variations of corporations. An incorporated business, they differ from corporations in that (1) each shareholder is an active member of the co-op; (2) each shareholder has only one vote in co-op affairs, regardless of the size of his or her investment; and (3) in many cases they are not profit-oriented. Co-ops are not overly popular in America. The few that do exist are primarily in the agricultural fields.

*Mutual Companies.* Mutual companies are companies, organized under state law, which are usually found in the banking or insurance fields. These companies are owned by the policyholders or depositors of the firm. Profits earned from the business are returned to the members (policyholders or depositors) as a dividend. Participants in mutual companies may also be liable for debts incurred by the company, although the extent of that liability is usually limited.

*See also* BOARDS OF DIRECTORS; CONSORTIUM; ECONOMIC SYSTEMS; INTERNATIONAL OPERATIONS AND MANAGEMENT IN MULTINATIONAL COMPANIES; OFFICERS, CORPORATE; ORGANIZATION STRUCTURES AND CHARTING; SYNDICATES.

### REFERENCES

Acharya, S., and T. V. Rao: "On Profits and Profitabilities of Small Scale Firms," *Economic Affairs*, vol. 20, no. 7, July 1975.

"The Board: It's Obsolete Unless Overhauled," *Business Week*, Special Report, May 22, 1971.
McEachern, William A.: *Managerial Control and Performance*, Heath, Lexington Books, Lexington, Mass., 1975.
Perlick, Walter W., and Raymond V. Lesikar: *Introduction to Business: A Societal Approach*, Business Publications, Inc., Dallas, 1975.

WALTER W. PERLICK, *Colorado State University*

# Ownership capital (*See* FINANCIAL MANAGEMENT.)

# P

## Paired comparison appraisal method

(*See* APPRAISAL, PERFORMANCE.)

## Paper, commercial (*See* GOVERNMENT REGU-
LATIONS, BUSINESS LAW; and FINANCIAL MANAGE-
MENT, SHORT-TERM, INTERMEDIATE, AND LONG-
TERM FINANCING.)

## Paper work simplification

Paper work simplification is the organized application of common sense to eliminate waste and establish more effective and efficient ways of doing paper work. It includes analytical techniques and a participative approach to applying them. One of the most widely used and productive of the techniques, procedure flow charting, is presented in this entry to illustrate the paper work simplification approach. The rest of the techniques are simply enumerated with a few words of explanation.

### PRINCIPLES

The definition, as stated above, includes the basic concepts of organization, common sense, waste reduction, effectiveness, and efficiency. These concepts, in turn, establish the basic principles of paper work simplification:

1. Organize the facts of the work for examination with analytical techniques, charts, and diagrams.
2. Utilize the common sense of people who are involved in and affected by the procedures under examination (the users).
3. Carefully review the procedures step by step and eliminate waste of any kind, such as of time, energy, space, material, and equipment.
4. Reorganize the procedure, reflecting the best judgment of the involved users and participating specialists.

### A TYPICAL IMPROVEMENT PROJECT

**Project Definition and Team Formation** Paper work simplification projects begin for many reasons, such as to speed up processing, to ferret out and correct causes of processing errors, to adapt a procedure to meet new reporting requirements, to clean up a procedure for automation, or to clarify and document a procedure.

Projects are initiated by management. First the scope and objectives are agreed upon and users from the affected areas are formed into a project team. One team member is elected or assigned as team leader and another as recorder. These people are expected to participate 4 to 6 hours per week assisted by an analyst (referred to as coordinator) who is trained in the techniques and works on the project full time. The team also receives assistance from specialists when their expertise is needed (i.e., in areas such as forms analysis, records management, computer systems, communications systems, word processing, microform, etc.).

**Training and Data Collection**  A brief orientation is usually conducted by the coordinator, outlining project methods and the techniques to be used. This is often reinforced with films depicting the paper work simplification process and with short improvement exercises.

Data collection involves interviewing people at each step of the procedure. When procedure flow charting is employed, the data is collected on procedure data charts (Fig. P-1), one for each document involved in the procedure.

It is important to interview the people who do the work rather than people who may be unaware of

details or may not be up to date about them. Managers' descriptions are often incomplete and occasionally erroneous. Using written procedures as a source, without checking them out, also risks being unrealistic. The objective is to record the facts accurately as they exist. It is necessary to "get it straight" from people who know.

**Organizing the Facts**  People involved in paper work simplification are often surprised to discover that their existing procedures are far more complex than anticipated. Each step of the procedure had seemed so simple. Then as the many facts pour in, they become overwhelming. This is the main reason why so many things go wrong with paper work. There are so many details that pieces are often overlooked. When troubles surface, however, the solutions may be embarrassingly simple.

Since the problem is one of massive detail, the appropriate solution is to organize that detail, put-

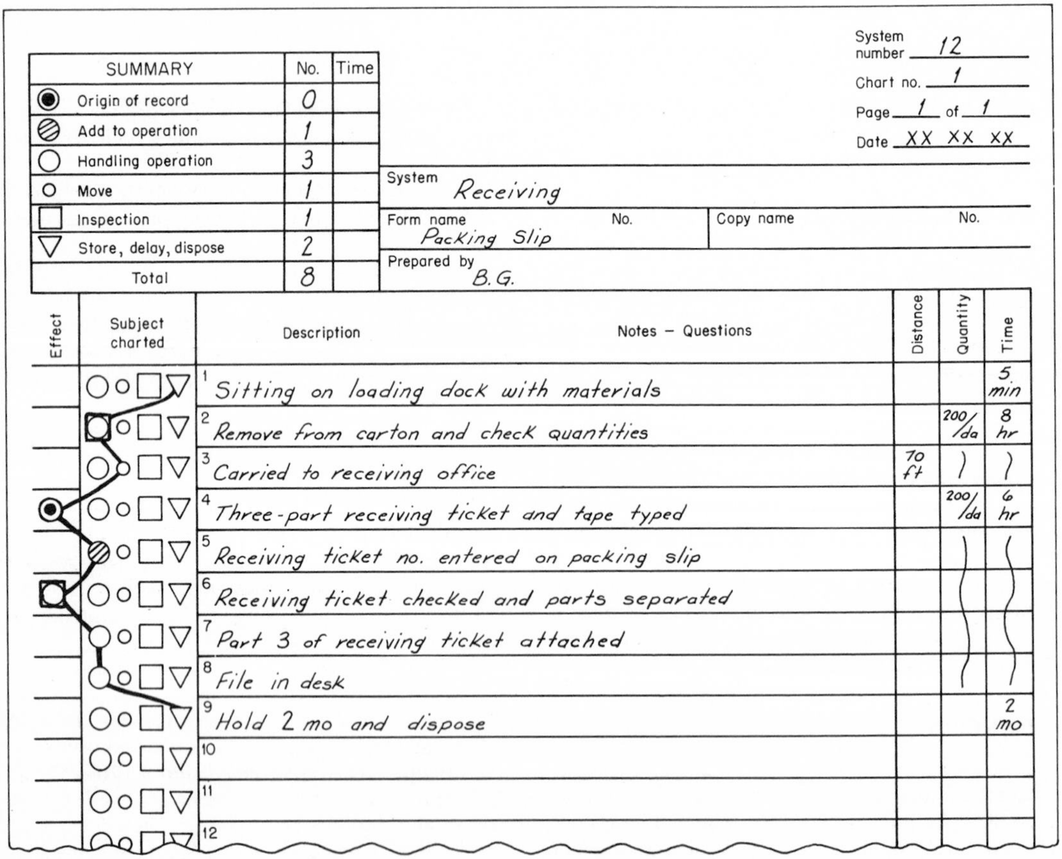

**Fig. P-1. Procedure data chart.**

ting all the pieces in their places with a chart or diagram, usually prepared by the analyst. The alternative of ignoring the detail invites an unrealistic solution, mistakes of omission, and a lack of coordination. On the other hand, when people take the time to chart their procedures in detail, alternatives become apparent as they see for the first time how the parts fit together. (*See* Fig. P-2.)

**Analyzing the Facts**   Before the team can effectively study the facts and produce recommendations, it must become familiar with the charts. The analyst first explains the charts, step by step, and the team members may go over the charts several times. At the close of this familiarization session, team members may be given reduced copies of the charts to study and to mark up with ideas before the next meeting.

The actual improvement meetings begin with the team leader reviewing the project objectives. Then the team begins a careful analysis of each step of the procedure. As each step comes under scrutiny it is questioned: what is done and why, where is it done and why there, when is it done and why at that time, who does it and why that person, and finally, how is it done and why in that way. When the answers to these questions do not satisfy the team's common sense, alternatives are suggested, and these are recorded by the team recorder as possible recommendations. It is important to record all recommendations whether they appear feasible or not. Selection among alternatives will follow.

Frequently, more information is needed, such as how often this happens, whether there is a legal retention period, etc. To find answers to these questions, assignments are made by the team leader.

**Preparing the Proposal**   In a few weeks the team has enough recommendations to begin preparing a proposal. To accomplish this, the analyst prepares a new set of charts which incorporate the selected recommendations. Then, armed with two sets of charts, the analyst reviews the procedure (1) as it is and (2) as the team feels it should be. A reconciliation is then performed, listing step by step all the differences between the charts. These differences are analyzed in terms of costs and benefits, and together they make up the proposal.

**Presentation of the Proposal and Approval**   The proposal is presented, by the project team, to the managers and officials whose approval is needed. If the analysis has been carefully undertaken, the specific recommendations and their costs and benefits can be listed on three to five pages. This list is distributed to the authorities at the start of the presentation. Each of the recommendations is ex-plained by a team member, usually from the area affected. Typically, about half the recommendations are approved immediately, while others require questions and discussion. Several issues must be worked out after the meeting.

**Installation**   When it is agreed which recommendations are approved, the charts of the proposal are adjusted to reflect those which were disapproved. Those which were approved are broken down into details for installation (i.e. forms, equipment, training, floor plans, policy statements, procedure manuals, etc.). These become the activities of the installation that will be organized in a network planning chart.

## TECHNIQUES

Many techniques, charts, and devices are employed by the paper work simplification analyst, including the following:

*System study sheet.* This is also known as a project definition sheet, project request, etc. It is a form used to define the scope and objectives of a project.

*Flow process chart.* This chart shows the flow of a single item, which can be studied autonomously.

*Flow diagram.* This is a floor plan on which has been superimposed the route of a process or a procedure.

*Operation chart.* This is a chart showing the details of the methods of work done at a single work place.

*Right- and left-hand chart.* This chart shows step by step the activities of the two hands.

*Work place layout.* This is a work place diagram, drawn to scale, showing location of materials, equipment, etc.

*Procedure data chart.* This chart is used to record the flow of a single document.

*Procedure flow chart.* This chart shows the flow of all the documents involved in a procedure.

*Gantt chart.* This is a chart plotting activities of work against a time scale.

*Network chart.* This is a PERT- or CPM-type chart showing work activities arranged in the sequences in which they must occur (particularly useful where activities are highly interdependent).

*Recurring data chart.* This chart shows recurrence of entries on various forms and records.

*Forms analysis checklist.* This is a list of questions which suggest alternatives to existing forms.

*Entries check-off list.* This is a check list employed when interviewing users about a form, entry by entry.

*Typewriter analysis sheet.* This sheet is used to develop efficient typewritten forms.

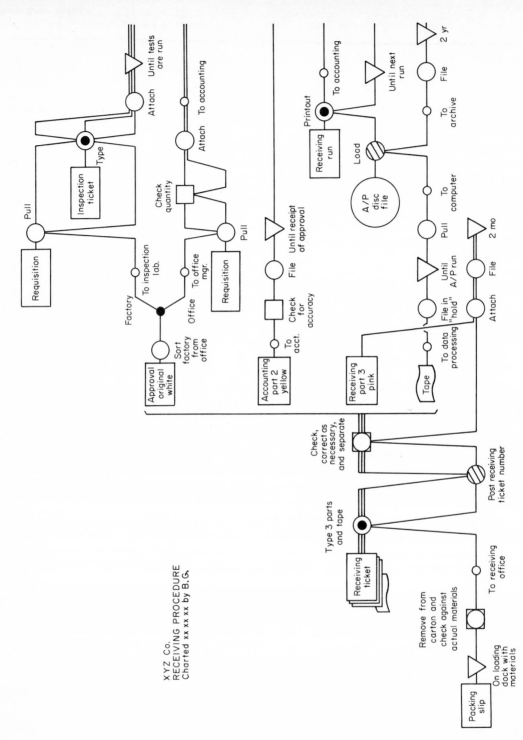

**Fig. P-2. Procedure flow chart.**

*Print-cycle analysis sheet.* This sheet is used to develop efficient forms for high-speed printers.

*Responsibility chart.* This detailed chart displays how individual responsibilities are aligned in a procedure.

*Task data sheet.* This is a form used to collect data on the time required to perform tasks.

*Work distribution chart.* This chart displays how much time is spent on each of the activities in a work unit.

*Cost-benefit work sheets.* These work sheets enable project teams to calculate costs and benefits of their recommendations in terms of work force, materials, machines, processing time, error reduction, etc.

## BENEFITS

Many organizations have used paper work simplification charting and analysis techniques to achieve benefits typified by the following examples.

Personnel of the Federal Bureau of Drugs studied the procedures of reviewing, approving, and monitoring new drugs. In 5 months' time they prepared a proposal that resulted in doubling productivity, reducing access time for documents from 2 days to 15 minutes, and eliminating two-thirds of the forms and records.

State Farm Insurance Companies use this approach with their agents and increased suggestions from this source over a hundredfold.

Abbott International trained project leaders from their Latin American affiliates and saved over $200,-000 in a little over a year.

Hundreds of other organizations have recorded benefits such as doubling operating capacity with no increase in administrative staff; reducing the number of forms required by factors as large as 7 : 1; redesigning forms for faster typing or printing, easier mailing, filing, etc.; cutting process time to less than half; discovering and removing serious error sources; and reorganizing offices, files, work places, mail service, etc.

## LIMITATIONS AND PITFALLS

The basic limitation is the judgment and experience of the users. Analytical techniques, however, tend to extend their effectiveness. Nevertheless, there are always a number of potential pitfalls.

Management may believe that employees lack sufficient judgment and experience (an opinion which is often self-fulfilling as it allows employees little opportunity to demonstrate more than routine performance).

Management may be unwilling to support a participative effort, fearing this will be construed as blanket approval of recommendations. Proper support means endorsing the study and listening to the recommendations. Beyond that, it is up to the teams to develop sound proposals and present them clearly.

The coordinator may take over the project, leading the users to lose interest or even become resistant.

The team may jump to conclusions without carefully reviewing the facts. As a result, problems which could have been resolved in weeks may hang on for years.

Interdepartmental rivalries and jealousies often interfere. Improvement requires responsible, adult behavior.

*See also* COST IMPROVEMENT; DATA PROCESSING PRINCIPLES AND PRACTICES; FORMS DESIGN AND CONTROL; INFORMATION SYSTEMS, MANAGEMENT (MIS); RECORDS MANAGEMENT; SYSTEMS AND PROCEDURES; THERBLIGS; WORK SIMPLIFICATION AND IMPROVEMENT.

## REFERENCES

Forster, Michael: "Paperwork Simplification at the State of Washington Health Service," *Newsletter*, no. 68, p. 256, Improvement Institute, Largo, Fla., February-March 1976.

Graham, Ben S.: "The Blue Book of Paperwork Simplification," The Ben Graham Corporation, Tipp City, Ohio, undated.

Graham, Ben S., Jr.: "Work Simplification—It Still Pays Off," *Ideas for Management*, Interstate Printers and Publishers, Inc., Danville, Ill., 1969, p. 1.

Mathies, Leslie H., and Ellen Mathies: "How Important Are People?" *Journal of Systems Management*, vol. 26, no. 7, p. 26, July 1975.

*Methods Improvement Management*, a film produced and distributed by Kinotek Corp., Washington, 1971.

Miller, O. Owen: "Office Work Simplification," in Carl Heyel (ed.), *Handbook of Modern Office Management and Administrative Services*, McGraw Hill Book Company, New York, 1972.

*Paperwork Simplification*, a film produced and distributed by Improvement Institute, Largo, Fla., 1976.

Weaver, R. F., and Ben Graham, Jr.: "A Policy for Your Paperwork Complex," *The Office*, vol. 79, no. 1, p. 80, January 1974.

"Work Simplification in Systems," *Systemation Letter*, no. 290, Systemation, Inc., Colorado Springs, Colo., 1974.

Zaiden, Dennis J.: "An Introduction to Paperwork Simplification," Dartnell Office Administration Service, Chicago, December 1971.

BEN S. GRAHAM, JR., *The Ben Graham Corporation: Paperwork Simplification Division*

## Pareto's law  (*See* INVENTORY CONTROL, PHYSICAL AND STOCKKEEPING.)

## Participation models, organization
(*See* ORGANIZATION STRUCTURES AND CHARTING.)

## Participator, active  (*See* HEALTH, EXECUTIVE, MANAGING STRESS AND JOB TENSION.)

## Partnership  (*See* GOVERNMENT REGULATIONS, BUSINESS LAW; OWNERSHIP, LEGAL FORMS OF.)

## Partnership management  (*See* MANAGEMENT, DEFINITIONS OF.)

## Patent contracts  (*See* PRODUCT PLANNING AND DEVELOPMENT.)

## Patent monopoly  (*See* PRODUCT PLANNING AND DEVELOPMENT.)

## Patent value  (*See* PRODUCT PLANNING AND DEVELOPMENT.)

## Patents and valuable intangible rights

A *patent* is a limited monopoly right conferred by the government of a country in accordance with its own laws and regulations. Since a patent is issued by a government, it provides protection only within the territory of that government. A patent consists essentially of a specification and possibly drawing(s) to describe the invention and one or more claims. In the United States, claims set forth the metes and bounds of the invention just as a property deed sets forth the property lines. This is important so that third parties understand when and where they will be trespassing.

A patent is not a privilege to use an idea or invention, but rather an exclusionary right, i.e., the right to exclude others from using the idea or invention described and claimed by that patent, at least within the territory of the government that issued

the patent. The patent owner can exclude others from using the invention even if the owner is not using it. The owner may choose to manufacture directly or set up a joint venture or license third parties or employ a combination of these possibilities. In the United States a patent lasts for 17 years from the date it is issued.

**Utility Versus Design**  The function and the design of an invention are subject to separate patents. Take a lamp, for example. Its electric circuitry, the switch, or other functional features relating to the lamp's use would be the subject matter of a utility patent. On the other hand, ornamental features of the lamp would pertain to a design patent. That is, a *utility* patent is concerned with functionality of either a process, a machine, a manufactured item, or a composition of matter; a *design* patent is concerned with ornamental features of an article of manufacture.

**Valuable Intangible Rights**  In addition to patents, there are other valuable, protectable types of ownership rights.

*Trademarks.* If a lamp happens to have a brand name identifying its manufacturer, that brand name is said to be its trademark. Because a trademark is synonomous with a brand name, it need not be registered to be protected. The only way to actually acquire trademark rights in the United States is by *use* of the trademark in connection with goods. That use can consist of either selling or advertising the goods under that trademark.

The trademark can be a word, name, symbol, device, or a combination of them. Trademarks are the means by which (1) manufacturers and merchants can identify their goods and distinguish them from others and (2) consumers can identify the source of the products they buy or of the services rendered them.

*Copyrights.* A copyright is the exclusive right to prevent the unauthorized use or copying of what the United States Constitution and the common law call *writings* of authors. Writings not only refer to literature but apply as well to photographs, musical compositions, labels, sound recordings, and works of art and their reproductions. A copyright does not relate to and does not protect ideas; it protects the *expression* of ideas. The ornamental features of a lamp may be protected by a design patent. However, a copyright can be obtained for the *artistic* features of the design on the lampshade and the artistry of the base of the lamp. Thus there may be some instances where the right to a design patent and the right to a copyright overlap and both can be obtained. The patent is for the tangible embodiment of the "idea" involved; the copyright is for the artistic expression of that idea.

*Know-How and Trade Secrets.* Trade secrets constitute subject matter which is not generally known to the trade and which provides a competitive advantage. These may or may not be patentable. Trade secrets also can include business information, sources of supply, customer lists, and almost anything which is not known to competitors and which gives a competitive edge. Trade secrets are technically protected by common law. Know-how can be thought of as generic to trade secrets. It includes, as well, information which technically is not protectable as a trade secret because it is generally known to competitors, e.g., business acumen, but which may be valuable to a purchaser anyway. The purchaser might otherwise need months, if not longer, to acquire the same, albeit "public," information. A court will enjoin the disclosure of trade secrets but not after publication. Contracts for the transfer of "public" information in the form of know-how, however, are enforceable in the absence of fraud.

When should one file for patent protection rather than rely on the common law of trade secrets? The classic case, of course, is Coca-Cola syrup, whose formula has successfully been maintained as a trade secret. For each such case, however, there are literally thousands of instances where information which was once a trade secret became public knowledge. Whether it is a disgruntled former employee, a slip of the tongue, or reverse engineering on the part of competitors, the fact remains that it is the exception, not the rule, that information can be maintained in secrecy. If the idea is patentable, then as a general rule, patent protection is preferable. Exceptions can be made but only after the risks have been fully evaluated.

**Application Requirements** In the United States, a patent application must be filed by the inventor within 1 year of the date that the inventor publicly uses or publishes the invention. Otherwise, the inventor forfeits the right to a valid patent. On the other hand, if the use or public disclosure was by some third party, then the inventor will have a chance to prove that he or she was the first to conceive the invention and reduced it to practice with appropriate diligence. Keep in mind, however, that a patent is invalid in the United States if the invention was published or publicly known or used by others more than a year prior to the date that the application was filed.

**Interference Contests** The United States system is a "first to invent" patent system as opposed to "first to file" systems commonly found overseas. Accordingly, when there are two conflicting patent applications, an "interference" contest is held to determine who is the first inventor. The Patent and Trademark Office will inform an applicant when there is a conflict with one or more other applications claiming the same invention (or that there is a partial overlap of claimed subject matter) and will request information to help it decide who is the first inventor. The parties may take testimony and cross-examine each other's witnesses as well as submit affidavits and research records in an effort to establish prior right to the claimed invention. The need for detailed research records is apparent.

**Obtaining Patents in Other Countries** Since patent rights are limited to those particular rights and privileges conferred by the country that granted the patent, separate applications have to be filed in each country in which patent protection is sought. There is an international convention, however, whereby the priority date of an application can be protected by filing in one member country, e.g., the United States, and then filing in other member countries within 1 year after the original filing. Safeguarding that filing date is important for asserting and enforcing foreign patent rights. The patent owner can look to the original filing date in the United States should a dispute arise as to whether the invention had been known or used in another nation before the owner applied there.

*Where to Apply.* Deciding where to apply for a patent is closely related to the inventor's objectives. It is wise to consider patent protection in every country in which one can reasonably anticipate doing business to a significant extent. Sometimes it is desirable to file in a particular country because of the legitimate concern that a third party will start manufacturing in that country and take advantage of trade pacts which favor the free flow of goods across borders, exporting their goods into the patent owner's prime markets.

**Patent Licensing or Assignment (Sale)** Deciding whether to grant a license or self-exploit is largely a business decision. Licensing is not mandatory. While counsel can provide input as to the likelihood of enforcing the patent, the business philosophy and marketing strategy of the patent owner should take precedence. It is not always desirable to license, particularly where the patent owner would like to be alone in the market for a period of time and it appears that the patent position is a good one. There are times, however, when the patent owner will take a hard look at the situation and decide that the cost of manufacturing and distribution, transportation, and, when selling overseas, customs and tariff duties, etc., are such that it is more economical to license rather than to attempt to do business directly.

Not every patent owner wants, or is financially able, to set up manufacturing facilities, particularly overseas. Often the initial capital investments are substantial, and the financial risk coupled with other business uncertainties or legal restrictions may prohibit self-exploitation of the patent. In some nations the law requires that citizens of that country own half or even a controlling interest in businesses exploiting patent and trademark rights. In some instances, nations block or restrict the transfer of their currency outside their country. Thus a decision to license or self-exploit requires a careful analysis of the objectives and capabilities of the patent owner in the light of the potential marketplace and the financial and legal risks in each case.

**Tax Implications and Transfer of Ownership Rights**  Licenses can take different forms, and each may have different tax consequences. For example, a nonexclusive license is essentially an agreement that the patent owner will not sue the licensee. Since the licensee acquires no "title" rights beyond freedom from a lawsuit, nothing has been transferred in the eyes of the U.S. Internal Revenue Service (IRS) and any royalty (or other consideration) is treated as ordinary income.

In an exclusive license, the owner parts company with the right to grant further licenses and, therefore, the royalty (consideration) can qualify as capital gains. This is sometimes called parting with equitable title and retaining bare legal title. But note that the IRS imposes additional criteria to determine whether all substantial rights have been parted with. IRS reasoning is that if the patent owner can terminate the exclusive license at will (without default by the licensee) or retains other rights indicative of true ownership, then the transfer of ownership rights is more apparent than substantive and, therefore, the transaction should not qualify for capital gains treatment.

A patent assignment is the "sale" of a patent. Since legal as well as equitable title is transferred from the patent owner, the transaction will ordinarily qualify for capital gains treatment. This will be true even if the owner (inventor) retains a right to part of the royalties derived from subsequent licensing by the assignee. Once more, the IRS looks beyond what the parties name the agreement to determine the true nature of the transaction from the terms of the agreement. Thus, the tax consequences can only be determined by examining the full agreement.

**Royalty Charges**  There is no legal restriction on the size of the consideration for a license, but discriminatory royalties have been challenged by the Federal Trade Commission as a form of unfair competition. In some industries there are accepted guidelines for the size of a royalty, but in any given case the consideration for a license will be determined primarily by the contribution of that technology to the licensee's business. For example, in the case of a process that saves a licensee a substantial sum in manufacturing costs, it would not be unusual to ask for anywhere from one-fourth to one-half the savings realized by the licensee. Generally, one intelligent approach to negotiating a fair royalty is to determine the probable benefit to the licensee and gear the royalty toward a portion of that benefit.

**Major Licensing Terms**  In addition to royalties, among the most important considerations are whether to (1) insist on minimums, (2) ask for grantback rights to any improvements made by the licensee, (3) provide for technical assistance and know-how in addition to patent rights, (4) insist upon confidentiality with regard to that know-how (which should survive termination of the agreement), (5) provide for appropriate warranties and indemnities, (6) define the responsibility for prosecuting third party infringers, (7) define the licensee's right to subcontract or sublicense or specify the absence of such right, (8) provide for payment of taxes (particularly in foreign licenses), (9) depending upon the circumstances, allow for transportation and shipping charges, and (10) provide for conditions under which the agreement can be terminated. Obviously there are many other considerations which should be worked out to make for a clear understanding. A detailed agreement is sometimes not appreciated at the time a transaction is entered into, but in the event of a dispute, it will often help determine who was to do what as well as the rights of the parties. If the transaction cannot withstand the test of being specific (with all rights and obligations clear and in writing) at the time the agreement is first entered into, then it is not likely to withstand the test of enforceability later on. While some understandings based on a handshake have lasted, most wind up in the courtroom.

**Patent Validity and Infringement**  A patent, once granted, is presumed valid until proved otherwise. This gives the patent owner an advantage in a lawsuit since the burden of proof is on the one claiming its invalidity. A patent owner can seek a court-ordered injunction against third-party infringement on his or her patent and can seek damages (and sometimes costs) for losses sustained because of the infringement. Conversely, any member of the public who is threatened by the patent owner can challenge the patent and seek a judgment declaring it invalid. The challenger can also seek damages and sometimes costs.

Before bringing a lawsuit, the patent owner or challenger should have a validity study made of the patent. The U.S. Patent and Trademark Office, of course, performs a search of related subject matter to determine novelty and unobviousness before granting a patent. But the number of pending applications, coupled with limitations in staff and time, necessarily result in a limited search. A thorough validity study sometimes turns up relevant previous publications (prior art) that the patent examiner did not consider during evaluation of the application. The newly discovered prior art can be used to challenge the patent's validity in court and it is often a persuasive means of overcoming the presumption of validity. If so, this shifts the burden of proof back to the patentee, who now must convince the court that the patent is still valid.

**Antitrust Considerations** Treble damages can be obtained when it is shown that an antitrust violation occurred, such as fraud in obtaining the patent (e.g., the basis for more than 10 years of multimillion-dollar litigation in the tetracycline cases) or misuse of the patent (e.g., tying sale of the patented product to the purchase of unpatented goods.) Thus, care should be taken when obtaining a patent to advise the Patent and Trademark Office of the best prior art known to the applicant. When licensing a patent or selling patented products, avoid the temptation to use the patent as leverage for some extraneous purpose. A patent grants its owner the right for a period of time to exclude others from using the claimed invention without his or her permission. The patent's use should be confined within the limits of that grant.

See also BRANDS AND BRAND NAMES, GOVERNMENT REGULATIONS, BUSINESS LAW; INNOVATION AND CREATIVITY; INTERNATIONAL TRADE; LEGAL AFFAIRS, MANAGEMENT OF CORPORATE; PRODUCT PLANNING AND DEVELOPMENT; RESEARCH AND DEVELOPMENT MANAGEMENT; TECHNOLOGY EXCHANGE.

### REFERENCES

Finnegan, M. B., and Goldsheider, R.: *The Law & Business of Licensing*, 2 vols., Clark Boardman Company, Ltd., New York, 1975.

Goldstein, P., *Copyright, Patent, Trademark and Related State Doctrines*, Callaghan & Co., Chicago, 1973.

Kintner, E. W., and Lahr, J. L.: *An Intellectual Property Law Primer*, Macmillan Publishing Co., Inc., New York, 1975.

Pollzien, G. M., and Langen, E.: *International Licensing Agreements*, 2d ed., The Bobbs-Merrill Company, Inc., Indianapolis, 1965.

Stiefel, M., *European Patent Law and Practice*, Practising Law Institute, New York, 1971.

STANLEY H. LIEBERSTEIN, *Ostrolenk, Faber, Gerb and Soffen*

**Path-goal theory**   (*See* LEADERSHIP.)

**Pay-as-you-go requirements**   (*See* TAX MANAGEMENT, MANAGERIAL RESPONSIBILITY FOR FEDERAL INCOME TAX REPORTING.)

**Pay practices**   (*See* COMPENSATION, WAGE AND SALARY POLICY AND ADMINISTRATION.)

**Payback method**   (*See* BUDGETING, CAPITAL.)

**Payoff and loss tables**   (*See* STATISTICAL ANALYSIS FOR MANAGERS.)

**Pegging**   (*See* EXCHANGE, FOREIGN, MANAGEMENT OF.)

**Perception**   (*See* INTERPERSONAL RELATIONSHIPS.)

**Perceptions, instrumentality**   (*See* MOTIVATION IN ORGANIZATIONS.)

**Performance appraisal**   (*See* APPRAISAL, PERFORMANCE.)

**Performance dimension, MIS**   [*See* INFORMATION SYSTEMS, MANAGEMENT (MIS), IN LARGE ORGANIZATIONS.]

### Performance factor analysis  [*See* ORGA-
NIZATION DEVELOPMENT (OD).]


### Performance profile, sales  (*See* SALES
MANAGEMENT.)


### Performance standards  (*See* DEVELOP-
MENT AND TRAINING, MANAGEMENT.)


### Periodicals and publications  (*See* IN-
FORMATION SEARCH.)


### Perquisites  (*See* COMPENSATION, EMPLOYEE
BENEFIT PLANS; COMPENSATION, EXECUTIVE.)


### Person-centered appraisal  (*See* AP-
PRAISAL, PERFORMANCE.)


### Personal file, employee  (*See* PERSONNEL
ADMINISTRATION.)


### Personal health  (*See* HEALTH INSTITUTIONS,
MANAGEMENT OF.)


### Personality tests  (*See* TESTING, PSYCHOLOGI-
CAL.)


## Personnel administration

Although all managers are intimately involved with and held responsible for "people" problems in their areas, it is generally agreed that for consistency, equity, and efficiency a central unit provides supporting personnel services and guidelines for carrying out management's personnel function. The unit is termed the personnel department, employee relations department or, more recently, the human resources department. Unionized companies usually call this unit the industrial relations department.

The need for a central unit becomes increasingly apparent as the employee count passes 20, at which time the job is often assigned as an additional duty. The volume of related tasks, however, forces consideration of a full-time personnel staff as the employee count nears 200.

The many tasks which are comprised by the general term *personnel administration* may be divided into broad categories, such as the following cited by the American Society for Personnel Administration in its accreditation program: (1) employment, placement, and personnel planning; (2) training and development; (3) compensation and benefits, (4) health, safety, and security; (5) employee and labor relations; (6) personnel research.

### PERSONNEL POLICIES

All corporate policy is mangement's saying to itself, "Here is how we are going to approach things in order to reach our corporate goals." Practice and procedure spell out the implementation of the approach. The importance of personnel policies is that they are management's way of saying, "Here are the guidelines to be followed in personnel matters in order to achieve maximum utilization of our human resources." Personnel practice and procedure provide the details.

Personnel policies exist in every organization. The difference is the extent to which they are written, communicated, and consistently applied. Organizations interested in maintaining the trust and confidence of their employees strive to score high on these three counts.

The chief executive often insists that the personnel executive submit written personnel policies for adoption as corporate policies. The reasons for this include the following: (1) to confirm that the policies to be implemented are acceptable to the corporation; (2) to assure the clarity, feasibility, and adequacy of the policies; and (3) to indicate to all concerned that the policies have been seriously considered and adopted as the policies of top management.

**Personnel Manual**  Personnel policies are best communicated to all levels of management by the issuance of a personnel policy manual. The manual provides a ready reference and facilitates consistent handling of similar situations throughout the organization. A common technique is to devote a separate section of the manual to each policy statement and a suitably detailed treatment of the personnel practices and procedures which are currently being utilized to implement the policy. Many firms consider it equally important to issue to all nonmanagement personnel an employee handbook which contains an appropriately written condensation of the same information. Both publications lend themselves to being published in loose-leaf binders in order to accommodate frequent changes in practice and procedure.

## IMPACT OF REGULATORY AGENCIES

Compliance with the Fair Labor Standards Act (Wage-Hour Act) of 1938 was the primary legal concern of the personnel administrator for a number of years. Its provisions, applicable to employers engaged in interstate commerce, covered minimum wage standards, overtime pay, employment of minors, and definitions of exempt employees. The relatively simple administration of the act was assigned to the personnel staff for implementation; thus the provisions were of slight concern to top management. Only the section that prohibited unequal pay for equal work because of sex did not take hold to the point that another act, the Equal Pay Act of 1963, was necessary to reiterate the provision.

That almost placid era came to an end in 1964 with the passage of the Civil Rights Act, or more specifically, Title VII of that act. The Civil Rights Act and its attendant executive orders, guidelines, and court decisions at the federal, state, and local levels (combined with several other major acts which have emanated from congressional concern with safety in the work place, privacy, pension reform, and other social issues) have had an enormous effect on every organization's personnel operations. Virtually every personnel activity is now influenced by governmental regulation. If ever there was doubt that personnel administration was the concern not only of the personnel manager but of every manager in the organization, it has been dispelled since 1964. Legal penalties can be equally heavy for discriminatory acts by line supervisors or personnel executives.

Many organizations train all management personnel in the requirements and implications of personnel-related regulations. Among those regulations are the following:

*Title VII, Civil Rights Act of 1964* (as amended), is applicable to private employers of 15 or more persons engaged in interstate commerce, educational institutions, state and local governments, employment agencies, and labor unions with 15 or more members. It prohibits discrimination based on race, color, religion, sex, or national origin in any term, condition, or privilege of employment (e.g., hiring, promotion, demotion, transfer, layoff or termination, rate of pay, benefits, and selection for training).

*Executive Order 11246* (1965) as amended by Executive Order 11375 (1967) is applicable to federal contractors and subcontractors and requires affirmative action programs to implement Title VII. The programs of firms with contracts over $50,000 and having 50 or more employees must be written and are monitored by an assigned federal agency.

*OFCC Revised Order No. 4* (1971) details the steps to be taken by firms required to implement affirmative action programs. Included in the steps are the identification of areas in which minorities and women are underutilized and the establishment of hiring and promotion goals.

*Equal Employment Opportunity Act of 1972* (an amendment to Title VII of the Civil Rights Act of 1964) strengthens the power of the Equal Employment Opportunity Commission (EEOC) to enforce Title VII. EEOC receives, from individuals or organizations representing them, job discrimination complaints and attempts to conciliate them. When conciliation fails, EEOC may go directly to court to enforce the law.

*Age Discrimination in Employment Act* (1967) is applicable to employers of 25 or more persons. It prohibits discrimination in any aspect of employment against persons aged 40 to 65.

*Vietnam Era Veterans' Readjustment Assistance Act* (1974) requires federal contractors and subcontractors with contracts of $10,000 or more to take affirmative action in hiring and promoting qualified disabled veterans and Vietnam era veterans.

*Title V of the Rehabilitation Act* (1973) requires affirmative action of federal contractors and subcontractors with contracts of $2500 or more to hire and promote qualified individuals who have physical or mental handicaps which substantially limit one or more major life activities or have records of such impairments or are regarded as having such impairments.

*Occupational Safety and Health Act (OSHA)* (1970) authorizes the Secretary of Labor to establish mandatory safety and health standards in businesses engaged in interstate commerce.

*Employee Retirement Income Security Act (ERISA)* (1974), also called the Pension Reform Act, establishes and protects numerous employee benefit rights. Disclosure, eligibility, vesting, and fiduciary requirements for pension plans are provided.

In addition, there are state and local laws, often patterned after federal law. Hence, many small employers or those without federal contracts are facing the same requirements but from a different source.

## COSTS AND BUDGETS

In addition to the normal overhead expenses, the personnel unit's budget often provides for the organization's total recruiting costs (e.g., advertising, agency fees, applicant expenses, and moving expenses) training and development expenses, and employee service expenses (e.g., recreation, physical examinations, cafeteria, and service awards). Although salary administration and employee benefits may be engineered by the personnel staff, salary and benefit costs are normally budgeted by all departments in order to facilitate functional cost analysis.

A 1976 study conducted by the American Society for Personnel Administration and Bureau of National Affairs reported the average personnel budget to be $256 per employee. The budgets of companies surveyed ranged from $47 to $2121 per employee. The same study showed the personnel unit's budget for 1975 to range from .007 to 32.5 percent of the company's total operating budget. The median was 1.1 percent.

## PERFORMANCE MEASURES AND STANDARDS

It is highly desirable that performance standards exist for all segments of the personnel function against which current performance can be measured. They are, however, subject to questions of validity and relevance. This stems from the fact that many personnel activity measures are influenced by uncontrollable factors, including the unpredictability of people and events. A recruiting time standard, for example, should consider job level, skills required, and availability of applicants among other factors.

Personnel measures must also take into account the influence of related personnel policies. A wage policy that results in paying less than going rates is apt to affect a recruiting time standard, for example.

The following are among the commonly utilized measures of the personnel functions:

1. Payroll as a percent of total costs
2. Average wage rate, by several employee categories
3. Average annual percentage wage increase, by several employee categories
4. Employee benefit costs as a percent of payroll
5. Selection ratio (number of hires per 100 applicants)
6. Recruiting lag (average number of days required to fill a job opening)
7. Personnel ratio (number of personnel workers per 100 employees)

The standards against which these and other measures are compared are based on in-house experience or on intercompany surveys.

## RECORDS AND REPORTS

Personnel records are essential for many reasons and are often required by law. Yet unless controlled they can become redundant and unfairly damaging to the employee. Computerized record keeping is a means of greatly reducing the time and effort devoted to maintaining records and producing reports, but it is not until the work force approaches 500 that computerization is considered economically feasible. The microfilming of inactive records is another means of reducing the paper load.

Among the myriad of conceivable records, the following are essential:

An *employee personal file* is a folder containing papers related to an employee's affiliation with the organization. It may contain the employment application, physical examination results, attendance record, past performance appraisals, employee benefit records, payroll deduction authorizations, and correspondence. A common practice is to purge the file every 2 to 3 years to remove obsolete material, including adverse appraisal comments which are no longer applicable. The Privacy Act of 1974 gives everyone the right to examine records pertaining to themselves held by any federal agency or educational institution and to demand the correction of any erroneous information. Legislation has been proposed to extend that right to include examination of records held within private industry.

A *master employee record* is a quick reference device consolidating frequently needed employee information from other sources. It is often a computerized record or on cardstock. It shows personal data, employment and earnings history, test scores, special training, and skills data as well as attendance history and benefit entitlements.

*Record of time worked*, commonly called a time card, is legally required to be maintained for employees who are not exempt from provisions of the Wage and Hour Act of 1938. Although time clocks are still the most common means of recording time worked, they are giving way rapidly, especially in offices, to an honor system whereby the employee completes a time sheet by hand. Another method, approved by many local Department of Labor offices, is the exception method, requiring the employee to make time card entries only when time other than published normal working hours is worked or when normal hours are not worked.

The U.S. Department of Labor requires employee information records to be retained for 3 years following separation. IRS requires earnings records to be kept 4 years after tax due date. ERISA, however, seems to supercede all other employee record retention regulations. Without specifying a required retention period, ERISA requires maintenance of employee records sufficient to determine benefits due or which may become due. Benefit vesting rights assured by ERISA for separated employees could require record retention for up to 50 years. EEOC regulations require records pertaining to hiring (applications, tests, etc.), promotion, termination and other placement changes to be retained for 6 months from the date of record or action, whichever is later.

*Reports* can be divided into two groups: (1) those required for regulatory compliance and (2) those required by management. Federal and state laws, e.g., EEOC, OSHA, and ERISA, should be closely followed for changing report requirements. Management is interested in reports of such measures as those discussed in the preceding section. Many personnel executives originate an annual personnel report, which serves as an excellent future reference in their own area and presents a comprehensive report of the year's personnel activities to top management. In addition to abbreviated discussions of projects undertaken during the year, the report provides and analyzes annual statistics on such matters as employment, training, job evaluation, salary administration, benefits, attendance, turnover, and grievances.

## EMPLOYMENT

In defining *employment* as the utilization of a person's services and paying for those services, it follows that the employment function goes beyond recruiting and placement. It includes the justification for employment, the most advantageous use of the person's services through promotion or transfer, and the termination of employment.

*Employment Office.* A designated employment office is highly desirable for several reasons including avoidance of overlapping efforts, cost savings, and consistent application of employment policies and regulatory requirements. This does not imply an infringement on the line manager's "right to hire": the final employment decision is usually made by the line manager. It does imply the value of a trained employment staff.

The employment office is often staffed by one or more interviewers and a receptionist whose duties may include providing applicants with employment forms, administering tests, and conducting prescreening interviews. The prescreening interview is a brief exchange to determine whether or not the applicant possesses the most obvious qualifications for an available job. Totally unqualified applicants are usually released at this point, but a notation of the visit is made to assure complete applicant flow information.

*Employee Requisitions.* The employee requisition is a written request by a responsible manager for assistance in filling a specific job. A form is often used for the purpose of eliciting the job title, labor grade, rate of pay, desired starting date, and qualifications required. The employee requisition is looked upon as the employment office's authority to recruit and hire. It is the responsible manager's statement that an authorized job is vacant and that help is requested to fill it. Candidates for the job are then presented by the employment office to the manager. When the manager determines which candidate is to be offered the job, it is usually desirable for the employment office to make the job offer in order to assure consistency, clarity, and adherence to corporate policy and practice in all terms of the employment agreement.

It is not unusual to have the employment office hire a person for a job without referring that person to the manager for consideration, especially for entry-level or junior jobs. This is particularly true in large organizations or in firms committed to the hiring provisions of a labor contract. When feasible, however, the mutual benefits gained by the applicant-manager interview make it a desirable step in the employment process.

**Recruiting**   Recruiting is the process of soliciting the interest of potentially qualified people in an employment opportunity. It is not selective except to the extent that recruiting activity is limited and that published qualification requirements discourage inquiries. A number of sources of applicants are available to the employment office. Their use depends on the job level being recruited, recruiting policy, and costs.

*In-House.* The most obvious recruiting source is from within the organization. An internal search is usually the first recruiting step taken in a firm committed to a policy of promotion from within. A common tool for internal recruiting is job posting, which is the publication, often via bulletin boards, of openings within the company. A posting normally indicates the labor grade of the available job, qualifications required, and an invitation for employees on lower labor grades to apply. Critics of job posting cite the multiple training costs resulting from departmental turnover due to the program.

*External Recruiting.* Review of applications already on file is a logical first step in external recruiting. It is also a recommended one by EEOC as an affirmative action step.

*Referral* of applicants by employees is an excellent source. It can be a delicate one, however, in view of the EEOC opinion that it may be a discriminatory practice in a dominantly white organization. The offering of incentives for employment referrals in a largely white firm compounds the possibility of EEOC action.

*Advertising* a job opening in newspapers or trade journals is another common practice. The ad may be blind or open. A blind ad is one that does not identify the employer; a box number is provided for responses. Its advantages are that resentment by present employees is avoided and that responses to the ad need not be acknowledged. Open or signed ads are considered by some as a screening device; time is not wasted on those who prefer not to work in the employer's location, industry, or company. Radio, television, and billboard advertising are other lesser-used media. In any case, the advertising message must be carefully worded to avoid any semblance of discrimination.

*Campus recruiting* at high schools and colleges is commonplace. Appointments are made through the guidance counselor or placement director on campus. The most promising students are invited to the firm, normally at company expense, for further interviews.

*Employment agencies,* which may be public or commercial, are of considerable assistance. Public agencies do not charge a fee for their service. In some states, employers are required to list all job openings with their local state employment service. Commercial agency fees, payable when an agency-referred applicant is hired , can run quite high and the trend is strong toward the employer paying the fee rather than the applicant. It is not unusual for the fee to range from 7 percent of annual salary for junior jobs up to 25 percent of annual salary for senior positions. Many employers build a close relationship with selected agencies to the extent that the agencies are, in effect, the recruiting arm of the organization for specified jobs. Listing an important position with an employment agency, like use of the blind ad, tends to assure the confidentiality of the search.

*Executive search firms* distinguish themselves from employment agencies in that they consider the employer, not the applicant, to be their client. All expenses and fees are borne by the employer rather than the applicant, who might otherwise be expected to pay the fee of an employment agency. This distinction becomes increasingly blurred, however, as employers pay more of the agency fees. Another difference remains in that executive search firms often provide consultant services in connection with the company's search for top management candidates. The services may include a study of the company's history, organization, and objectives as well as extensive interviews to determine the personalities of company executives in an effort to introduce only the best-suited candidates for consideration. The process is attractive as a means of reaching into other firms for top people who are not actively seeking new employment and luring them away. If the employer were to do this directly at any level, it would be called pirating. *See* SEARCH AND RECRUITMENT, EXECUTIVE.

Finally, *temporary help agencies* should be noted as an excellent source of short-term help, especially when the need is urgent and time does not permit normal recruiting methods. These agencies maintain a call list of people with widely diverse skills and qualifications. Temporary workers obtained through this source are not employees of the company. They remain employees of the agency and are paid by the agency. In many cases, it is less expensive to pay the fees of an agency for temporary help than to put a temporary person on the payroll because of the savings in Social Security and other benefit payments.

**Selection**   Selection is the process of narrowing down the field of applicants to the one person to be offered the job. It has become in many cases a highly controversial activity as governmental agencies pursue claims of discrimination in hiring based on race, sex, age, and handicap. The common selection policy to hire the "best qualified" person is being challenged as a form of systemic discrimination against the Title VII–protected classes. Conversely, reverse discrimination cases are growing against firms who have struck the word *best* from their policy statements as an affirmative action measure. A clearly stated selection policy announced by top management with every manager held accountable for its implementation is an important step many organizations are taking to resolve the conflicting pressures present in the selection process today.

Opinions vary as to the proper sequence of selection steps in the employment office. Some insist that every applicant complete an application form prior to an interview. Others have the application completed only by those who interview favorably. Testing, physical examination, and reference checks are also inserted before, between, or after interviews. Regardless of the sequence utilized, good practice calls for (1) every applicant to be recorded for compliance and corporate statistical purposes; (2) each step to be clear of discriminatory implications toward Title VII–protected classes; (3) courteous, considerate behavior toward the applicant; (4) testing and interviewing facilities which are quiet and free from interruption; and (5) referring to line managers only those applicants considered to be reasonably qualified for the available job.

*Application Form.* An early step in the selection process is a study of the candidate's application form or résumé. EEOC-related laws require that questions which have a disproportionate negative effect on Title VII–protected classes not be asked on the application form or in interviews unless there is strong evidence of their job-relatedness or business necessity. Courts have upheld the banning of not only questions dealing with race, sex, national origin, age, and religion, but also those dealing with non-job-related educational requirements, arrest and conviction records, credit rating, marital and family status, physical and experience requirements, and other potential areas of discrimination.

*Résumés.* A résumé is a nonstandardized, written presentation of one's qualification for employment. Since it is originated by the applicant, its content is not restricted by law. Résumés are commonly requested of, or volunteered by, applicants for senior-level positions.

*Interviewing.* This is the most influential step in the selection process. To minimize bias, many firms use the patterned, guided, or *directed* interview in the employment office. This method fosters a uniform approach to eliciting pertinent responses by providing a guide list of questions to be asked. An application form may be the basis of the directed interview, or a separate interview form may be provided. In either case, employment office interviews are normally designed to elaborate upon the application form information and to correlate that information with the job requirements. *See* INTERVIEW, EMPLOYMENT.

The unpatterned, unguided, or *nondirected* interview is essentially unplanned, and the interviewee's comments are unrestricted. Although its use is most appropriate in exit, grievance, or counseling interviews, a semblance of the unguided interview is frequently used by the line manager in an employment situation, especially for higher-level jobs. The line manager is interested in the applicant's work methods, attitudes, and ambitions which can best be learned by asking brief questions which invite extended answers. It is a difficult technique to use effectively. The untrained interviewer can easily talk too much or ask leading, improper, or illegal questions.

*Group* interviews, in which several interviewers question the applicant in the same meeting, are common when filling a senior-level position. They offer the advantages of introducing the candidate to several prospective associates and allowing an exchange of opinion among the interviewers.

The *stress* interview should not be used by the untrained, nor is it applicable in the great majority of employment situations. Designed to test emotional control under trying circumstances, the stress interview calls for the interviewer to be openly hostile and irritating to the applicant. The technique may be applicable for police, sales, investigative, or clandestine work, but it is generally undesirable for common use.

*Physical Examination.* A physical examination today is more apt to be geared toward appropriate placement than toward a hire-or-reject decision. Many jobs can be performed by employees with physical limitations. This premise is given substance and the power of law by the Rehabilitation Act of 1973 (Title V), which affects federal contractors, and by several state laws.

*References.* The checking of an applicant's references, especially of former employers, is an important step. The value of a friend's, neighbor's, or minister's comment may be questionable. Face-to-face contact with the reference is most desirable. Telephone contact must often suffice. Written contact is least desirable because of the time element, most people's unwillingness to put unfavorable comments in writing, and the inability to pursue specific points of interest. In no case should the applicant's current employer be contacted without the applicant's consent. A most telling question to be asked at the end of a reference check is: Is this person eligible for rehire at your firm, and if not, why?

*Credit Checks.* These and other commercial investigative reports are utilized frequently when hiring a senior person. The Fair Credit Reporting Act, which became effective in 1971, provides that the applicant must be informed that such a procedure may be used and if so, that the name and address of the reporting agency be provided to the applicant if as a result of the report the applicant is deprived employment.

*Tests.* The use of tests in selection has always been controversial and has become more so since the advent of Title VII. *See* TESTING, PSYCHOLOGICAL.

**Placement** Placement begins with the acceptance of a job offer and does not end until termination of employment. It is the assignment of an individual to a job and, ideally, to the job best fitting his or her abilities and interests. It is the result of hiring, promotion, demotion, or transfer.

The job offer and its acceptance constitute a verbal contract. Because an understanding of its terms is so important, many firms put the offer in writing and ask for a written acceptance, especially for higher-level jobs. The job offer should include the job title, salary, starting date, name of immediate superior, exceptions to published employee benefits, special compensation terms, and any other unique terms of employment.

Affirmative action plans, whether legally required or voluntarily implemented, have a strong influence on placement. The legal and moral implications of equal employment opportunity impose an obligation on every manager to cooperate with efforts to place qualified minorities, women, individuals aged 40 to 65, and the handicapped at all levels in the organization. In meeting that obligation, many managers have been forced to realize that many traditional selection and placement criteria have been counterproductive. Excessive educational requirements, test cutoff scores, marital status, and sex and race preclusions are a few of the idols that have toppled.

**Promotion, Transfer, Demotion**  A promotion is an advancement to a position of increased status and responsibility. Increased earnings are usually associated with promotions, but this is not essential.

A transfer is the lateral movement of an employee to another job of essentially the same status but usually with different duties. The transfer may be initiated by the employer because of shifting production needs or requested by the employee because of changing career goals or personal reasons.

A demotion denotes movement to a position of lesser status and responsibility. The use of demotion as a disciplinary penalty is generally considered inadvisable. A demotion may, however, be occasioned by circumstances wherein it is acceptable to the employee. A major reduction in work force with consequent bumping based on seniority is one such situation. Stepping down because of health reasons is another. A third is a situation where poor performance can be attributed to placement in a job that is beyond the employee's capacity. A reduction in earnings may or may not take place in a demotion, but if not, they are often frozen until other factors bring them in line.

**Separations**  *Separation* is a general term which encompasses all forms of termination of employment.

*Resignation*, or voluntary termination, is normally initiated by the employee. It is also offered at times as a face-saving device to spare a person from the stigma of a discharge. *Exit interviews* with resigning employees, conducted in the personnel department,

are widely used as an indicator of employee morale and perceptions. Popular opinion is that comment from a resigning person is more apt to be frank and honest than that obtained under normal conditions. Others believe that either possible bitterness or a desire to leave with no ill feelings are apt to color exit interview comments. In any case, the exit interview is an appropriate means of delivering all final payments to the employee, explaining the disposition of benefits, and assuring the return of company property.

*Layoff* is a temporary or permanent involuntary termination due to a production cutback or stoppage. The order of layoff and recall back to work in a unionized organization is commonly based on seniority. Other labor contract provisions may provide supplemental unemployment benefits, accrued vacation pay, and other benefits to laid-off workers.

*Discharge* is a permanent involuntary termination usually due to a serious rule-infraction or unsatisfactory performance. Because of its severity and finality, many firms follow a prescribed warning system prior to discharge in all but the most extreme cases. Solutions to performance problems are also sought prior to discharge.

*Retirement* may be a voluntary or involuntary termination of employment. Legislation is expected to change the mandatory retirement age stated in many plans from age 65 to 70. Plans may, however, permit working beyond that age and/or voluntary retirement at an earlier age. An increasing number of firms offer preretirement counseling, seminars, and publications in an effort to assist in the transition to retired status.

**Status Changes**  The status changes resulting from promotions, transfers, demotions, and impending separations are reported promptly to the personnel department to assure proper salary payment and accurate employee records. In many cases, these status changes are made in consultation with the personnel staff to guarantee conformance with company policy and EEOC-related guidelines.

The following are other status changes that can result in confusion, extra cost, and embarrassment if not reported promptly: (1) transfer from or to permanent, temporary, full-time, or part-time employment; and (2) changes of name, marital status, address, telephone number, and other personal information required for benefit purposes.

## PERSONNEL PROBLEM INDICATORS

The personnel department is expected to be alert to signs of employee discontent, problems generated by company practice, and other hindrances to productivity in order that appropriate action may be taken to overcome them. A number of indicators are used for this purpose. Among them are the following:

*Grievances.* A grievance is an employee's expression to management of discontent or of a belief that an injustice is being suffered in a job-related matter. A formal system for handling grievances is followed in most companies. A periodic analysis of grievances to determine departmental frequency, the nature of the grievances, and the step at which each grievance was resolved is a prime problem indicator.

*Disciplinary Actions.* As used here, *discipline* is a negative term referring to the use of penalties to discourage unacceptable behavior. The exercise of discipline is a line manager's responsibility but because it is a sensitive matter subject to corporate, legal, and union guidelines, personnel staff consultation is commonly sought. Penalties may include oral and written reprimands, loss of privileges, fines, suspension, demotion, and discharge. Discipline practices often outline offenses which warrant penalties, the sequence of penalties, and senior management concurrence requirements.

*Turnover.* Turnover, or separation rate, is the number of separations during a period of time expressed as a percentage of the average employee count during that period. A degree of turnover must be expected and is healthy for the organization. It is also costly and therefore employers are interested in keeping turnover in line with expectations as reflected by turnover surveys and in-house past experience. Turnover statistics are commonly analyzed by departments, employee levels, length of service, and cause of separation to determine problem areas. Exit interview data is used to supplement turnover analysis.

*Absence.* Job dissatisfaction sometimes results in excessive absence. Hence, departmental and company absence rates are analyzed periodically. Absence rates are computed and expressed in a variety of ways. A preferred method by some is to speak of average days absence per employee per period of time. It is found by dividing the total days of absence recorded by the group by the average size of the group during the period. Others choose to express the rate as a percentage: the number of days lost during the period is divided by the average number of employees times the number of work days in the period, and the result is multiplied by 100. Because lengthy illnesses may distort the absence rate, periods of absence rather than days of absence are also analyzed by some firms. The definition of excessive absence also varies widely be-

tween firms and industries—from as low as 9 days per year to as high as 3 days per month. Absence rates may also be analyzed by age, sex, years of service, reasons given, days of the week, and type of work assigned to uncover problems. Lateness, which is a partial day's absence, is often similarly analyzed.

*Suggestion Boxes.* Designed as a means of receiving productive or cost-saving ideas from employees, suggestion systems often reveal employee gripes, attitudes, or specific complaints. When they examined for such content, problem areas can be uncovered.

*Attitude Surveys.* An attitude survey is an effort by management to determine employee perceptions of designated job-related factors. The survey may be accomplished by interview or questionnaire and may include a random sample of employee opinion or responses from the total work force. In all cases, anonymity of responses is assured. When interviews are used, outside consultants are usually utilized. Questionnaires are unsigned and sent to a central location. Survey content varies depending on the subjects management wants to explore. It might include questions related to job satisfaction, working conditions, supervision, training, opportunity for advancement, recognition, job security, pay, benefits, communications, company image, and personnel policies. It is generally agreed that survey findings should be reported back to the group surveyed and that the best method of doing so is through a series of meetings conducted by immediate supervisors. Feedback of unfavorable results is essential if employee trust is to be maintained. Equally essential is a commitment by management to take action based on the results. A well-conducted survey can be an extremely valuable tool to uncover and respond to employee concerns.

*See also* AFFIRMATIVE ACTION; APPRAISAL, PERFORMANCE; ATTITUDE SURVEYS; COMMUNICATIONS, EMPLOYEE; DEVELOPMENT AND TRAINING; EMPLOYMENT PROCESS; JOB EVALUATION; INTERVIEWING EMPLOYEE; LABOR LEGISLATION; MINORITIES, MANAGEMENT OF AND EQUAL EMPLOYMENT OPPORTUNITY; OLDER EMPLOYEES, MANAGEMENT OF; *Personnel Administration;* SAFETY AND HEALTH MANAGEMENT, EMPLOYEE; SEARCH AND RECRUITMENT, EXECUTIVE; SUGGESTION SYSTEMS; TEMPORARY HELP; WAGES AND HOURS LEGISLATION; WOMEN IN INDUSTRY; WORK HOURS, FLEXIBLE; YOUNGER EMPLOYEES, MANAGEMENT OF.

## REFERENCES

*Affirmative Action and Equal Employment: A Guidebook for Employers*, vols. 1 and 2, U.S. Equal Employment Opportunity Commission, Washington, January 1974.

*ASPA Accreditation Program*, American Society for Personnel Administration Accreditation Institute, Berea, Ohio, 1976.

Austin, Robert B.: "Payroll-Personnel Records," *Records Management Quarterly*, vol. 10, no. 3, pp. 15–20, Association of Records Managers and Administrators, Bradford, R.I., July 1976.

Beach, Dale S.: *Personnel: The Management of People at Work*, 3d ed., Macmillan Publishing Co., Inc., New York, 1975.

Flippo, Edwin B.: *Principles of Personnel Management*, 4th ed., McGraw-Hill Book Company, New York, 1976.

Miner, John B., and Mary Green Miner: *Personnel and Industrial Relations: A Managerial Approach*, 2d ed., Macmillan Publishing Co., Inc., New York, 1973.

*The Personnel Department: Budgets and Staffing Policies*, Bureau of National Affairs, Bulletin to Management, no. 1371, Washington, May 20, 1976.

Yoder, Dale: *Personnel Management and Industrial Relations*, 6th ed., Prentice-Hall, Inc., Englewood Cliffs, N.J., 1970.

DAVID G. MULLER, *Ohio National Life Insurance Company*

## Personnel subsystem (*See* HUMAN FACTORS ENGINEERING.)

## PERT/COST (*See* NETWORK PLANNING METHODS.)

## PERT/CPM (*See* NETWORK PLANNING METHODS; PRODUCTION PLANNING AND CONTROL.)

## Philosophy statement (*See* INTERNATIONAL OPERATIONS AND MANAGEMENT IN MULTINATIONAL COMPANIES.)

## Physical environment (*See* ENVIRONMENT, PHYSICAL.)

## Placement, employee (*See* PERSONNEL ADMINISTRATION.)

## Plan, marketing (*See* MARKETING MANAGEMENT.)

## Planning (*See* MANAGEMENT THEORY, SCIENCE, AND APPROACHES.)

## Planning, community (*See* COMMUNITY PLANNING LEGISLATION.)

## Planning, intuitive-anticipatory (*See* PLANNING, STRATEGIC MANAGERIAL.)

## Planning, planned management of turbulent change

Management is the creative and error-correcting activity that gives a firm its purpose and cohesion and assures an effective return on the investment. Thus, it can be said that the essence of management is creation, adaptation, and coping with change.

Change management occurs on all levels of the firm, from a first-line supervisor resolving a personnel conflict to a top management strategist contemplating a bold new venture. While respective problems, perspectives, approaches, and solutions are distinctive and different at each level, the focus here is on general management: the levels of management charged with guiding the behavior of the firm as a whole in its environment.

Seen from the viewpoint of general management, there are two basic types of change. One type is fluctuation in the operating levels and conditions: in sales, profits, inventory, labor force, budgets, productive capacities, etc. This kind of change expands and contracts the activities of the firm but leaves the nature of the firm intact. The other type transforms the firm: its products, its markets, its technology, its culture, its systems, or its structure. It is this enterprise-transforming or *strategic* change that will be analyzed here.[1]

### MANAGEMENT OF CHANGE IN A HISTORICAL PERSPECTIVE

**Focus on Adaptation to Environment** In his classic book, A. D. Chandler[2] studies the strategic change in American firms during the first part of this century. His results show a general relationship between changes in the environment; the adaptation of the firm through new products, markets, and technology; and subsequent internal adaptation of the internal culture, structure, and systems.

Chandler's results suggest that early in the century, a majority of firms did not really manage change but rather were managed by it: changes in the environment forced changes in the external strategy and these, in turn, forced changes in the internal configuration. Since the middle fifties this *lag time adaptation* became increasingly ineffective, because of the accelerating pace of environmental change. In response, some firms began to develop know-how and technology for managing change through anticipating and preparing for it.

It is necessary to recognize that throughout the history of the American firm there have been change-creating managers who made their firms into trailblazers of progress. Behind the few trailblazers, however, come the majority of followers, and it is to them that this analysis is addressed.

The early focus was on planning the external strategy in the expectation that the internal configuration did not need major modifications and that new strategies could be chosen so as to capitalize on the firm's existing strengths and avoid its weaknesses. But since the 1970s it has become increasingly clear that both external strategy and internal "structure" need to change substantially as the envi-

ronment becomes more turbulent. It is also becoming evident that the historical sequence of "structure" following changes in strategy is frequently too slow and inefficient in the modern environment.

Today's problem of managing strategic change can be stated as follows: (1) what strategy to develop to enable the firm to succeed in a changing environment, (2) what "structure" to install to support the strategy, and (3) how to relate and sequence the development of the strategy and the "structure." Answers to these questions must be given against the background of the firm's environment, which in recent years has been growing increasingly complex and turbulent.

**Changing Nature of Change**  Table P-1 illustrates the evolution of the firm's environment, starting from 1900 and projecting into the 1990s. The upper part of the table shows that the commercial challenges during the first half of the century were intense but simple: first to exploit the vast untapped primary demand and later to develop sophisticated marketing approaches to the increasingly affluent and discriminating customers.

**TABLE P-1  Environmental Challenges in a Historical Perspective**

| Time / Dimensions of challenge | 1900 | 1930 | 1950 | 1970 | 1990 |
|---|---|---|---|---|---|
| Product—markets | Basic demand | Differentiated demand | Saturation of demand / Technological turbulence / Multinational markets / Government markets / Leisure markets / Technology-created industries | | Loss of control over environment / Sociopolitical impact on market behavior / Strategic surprises / Constraints on growth / Constraints on resources / Socialist markets / Developing country markets |
| Geographic perspective | Nation-state | Developed nations | | | Socialist and third world |
| Internal environment | "Honest day's work for fair day's pay" / Management by authority | Management by concensus | Enrichment of work / Local participation | | Redesign of work / Participation in strategic decision / Management by conflict |
| External sociopolitical environment | Laissez-faire | | Loss of social immunity / Consumerism / Pressures for social responsibility / Reaction to "pollution" / Reaction to business power | | New ideological raison d'etre: / Socialism / Neocapitalism |

As the table shows, since World War II the challenges have become increasingly frequent, complex, and numerous. One consequence was a growing incidence of new and unfamiliar threats and opportunities. Another was a progressive loss of control by the firm over its environment. This was caused in part by a growing unpredictability of environmental change and in part by increasing difficulty in predicting the consequences of initiatives undertaken by the firm.

An equally important reason for loss of control has been a loss of immunity from governmental and social influence, illustrated in the lower part of the table. Both inside and outside the firm, new sources of power, with conflicting demands and ideologies, progressively influence all aspects of the firm's behavior.

**Evolution of Management Systems** Table P-1 conveys an impression of increasing turbulence, a continual "heating up" of the environment, which manifests itself through diversity of novel challenges, increasing frequency of their occurrence, acceleration of their evolution, and the growing dif-

ficulties of anticipating them. These characteristics are summarized in Table P-2, which suggests that the environment has developed through a series of states of increasing turbulence, which are given descriptive titles at the top of the table. The table shows that until the 1950s, past experience was a reliable guide to the future. Recognition of familiar patterns, or extrapolation of familiar trends, enabled the firm to see the future clearly. The need to anticipate was not urgent, because change evolved at rates slow enough to permit organized and measured response.

But after the 1950s the change became increasingly discontinuous from the past. Some changes were identifiable through analysis of the underlying forces, but their occurrence was uncertain. Yet other changes remained hidden in the complexity of the environment until the moment of their impact on the firm and thus emerged as unpredictable strategic surprises.

As the environment changed, management developed systematic approaches to handling the increasing turbulence and complexity. As the future be-

**TABLE P-2  Growing Environmental Turbulence**

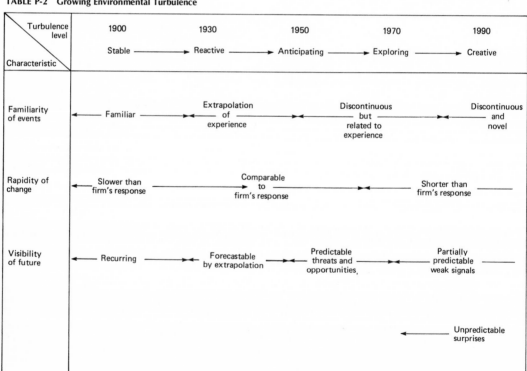

TABLE P-3  Evolution of Management Systems

| Environment / Future | 1900 Stable | 1930 Reactive | 1950 Anticipating | 1970 Exploring | 1990 Creative |
|---|---|---|---|---|---|
| Recurring | • Systems and procedures manuals | | | | |
| Forecastable by extrapolation | | • Financial control | | | |
| | | • Short-term budgeting | | | |
| | | | • Capital budgeting | | |
| | | | • Management by objectives | | |
| | | | • Long-range planning | | |
| Predictable threats and opportunities | | | | • Periodic strategic planning | |
| | | | | | • Periodic strategic management |
| | | | | • Issue analysis | |
| Partially predictable weak signals | | | | | • Real time strategic management |
| Unpredictable surprises | | | | | • Surprise management |

came more turbulent and less foreseeable, systems became increasingly sophisticated, each complementing and enlarging the earlier ones.[3]

The evolution of systems for general management is shown in Table P-3. The earlier systems, up to and including long-range planning, are now widely used. Periodic strategic planning, invented back in the mid 1950s, has been widely discussed but is only now emerging in practice. Systems beyond strategic planning shown in the table are not yet a practical reality; they are forecasts of the likely evolution. Since the older systems are now generally understood and practiced in a majority of firms, we shall focus the remainder of our discussion on the emerging systems.

## STRATEGIC MANAGEMENT

**Evolution of Managerial Response**  To the challenges shown in Table P-1, management developed appropriate responses. These are summarized in

Table P-4. As the table shows, managerial attention has alternated between the outside and the inside of the firm. Early in the century, focus was internal, on perfecting the mass production "machine." As basic demand approached saturation, attention shifted outside to mass marketing: the annual model change, artificial obsolescence, enlargement of the product line, promotion, advertising, and the art of consumer influence.

After World War II external preoccupations became even more intense. Firms began to venture in many directions, away from their traditional businesses: diversification into other industries, adoption of new technologies, expansion into the Common Market and the third world, and trade with the socialist countries. Until recently the dominant focus of external attention has been on the markets of the firm, but, as Table P-4 shows, the petroleum crisis, stagflation, environmental pollution, and potential exhaustion of natural resources are forcing management attention toward problems of con-

883

TABLE P-4   Evolution of Managerial Response

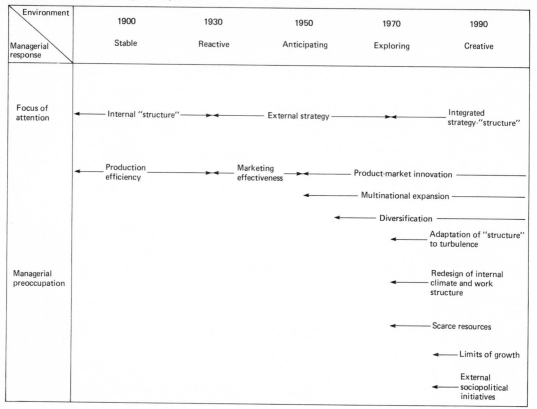

| Environment<br>Managerial response | 1900<br>Stable | 1930<br>Reactive | 1950<br>Anticipating | 1970<br>Exploring | 1990<br>Creative |
|---|---|---|---|---|---|
| Focus of attention | ←— Internal "structure" —→ | | ←— External strategy —→ | | ←— Integrated strategy-"structure" |
| Managerial preoccupation | ←— Production efficiency | | ←— Marketing effectiveness —→ | ←— Product-market innovation —→ | |
| | | | | ←— Multinational expansion —→ | |
| | | | | ←— Diversification —→ | |
| | | | | | ←— Adaptation of "structure" to turbulence |
| | | | | | ←— Redesign of internal climate and work structure |
| | | | | ←— Scarce resources | |
| | | | | | ←— Limits of growth |
| | | | | | ←— External sociopolitical initiatives |

trolled growth and availability of strategic resources. Further, the firm has been forced to abandon its exclusive preoccupation with the "business of business" and engage increasingly in sociopolitical interactions with consumers, public, and governments.

In addition, firms are increasingly finding that strategic adaptation to the environment is not possible without a simultaneous adaptation of the internal culture and capability. The historical practice of letting "structure" eventually catch up with strategy is no longer feasible, given the rapid environmental change.

As a result, management will be increasingly planning internal "structure" rather than letting it evolve through trial and error. This inward refocusing of attention, however, does not mean abandoning of the growing external preoccupations. As the first entry in Table P-4 suggests, the two will proceed side by side toward an integrated approach, which balances growth ambitions against resource availabilities and matches external strategies to internal capabilities. This global approach is just emerging and has no generally accepted name. We shall refer to is as *strategic management.*[4]

**Choice of the Strategic Thrust**   A key element in strategic management is the firm's strategic thrust, which determines the extent and the rate of change of its products, markets, and technology. One extreme is to stick to tried and true product-markets, as Henry Ford I did when he instructed his marketeers to "give it [the model T] to them in any color so long as it is black." Another extreme is to innovate continuously both by changing the strategy of approach to the markets and by creatively enlarging the product mix.

Strategic thrusts which fall between the two extremes are illustrated in Table P-5. Two dimensions of strategy are shown: (1) entrepreneurial innovation which changes the product-market mix and (2) marketing strategy which defines the competitive behavior. A firm's choice of its strategic thrust is

**884**

determined by both internal and environmental factors.

The internal factors are the following:

1. The degree of departure from present product-markets is determined, on the one hand, by the aggressiveness of the firm's objectives and, on the other hand, by the potential for growth offered by the present product-markets. If the firm's objectives can be met within the present position (as Henry Ford I succeeded in doing between 1900 and 1925) the firm is best advised to "stick to its last" and to continue to exploit its current position. If the pres-

**TABLE P-5   Types of Entrepreneurial and Marketing Strategies**

| Marketing \ Entrepreneurial | | Continuity | | | Discontinuity | |
|---|---|---|---|---|---|---|
| | | S | R | A | E | C |
| Continuity | S | Fixed products—markets / Making product available to markets | Expansion of familiar markets / Incremental product adaptation | Expansion to related markets / Related product innovation based on known technology | Expansion to foreign markets / Novel product concepts / Adoption of new technologies | Opening of novel markets / Pioneering of products / Creation of novel technologies |
| | R | Defensive maintenance of market share | | | | |
| | A | Aggressive search of market share | | | | |
| Discontinuity | E | Adoption of new marketing concepts | | | | |
| | C | Pioneering marketing concepts | | | | |

ent position cannot meet the growth objectives, or if it is actually deteriorating, a more venturesome strategic thrust is indicated.

2. In deciding how far to venture, management must make a trade off: by choosing a continuous strategy the firm can transfer its capabilities and experience to the new ventures and thus both maximize the chances of success and minimize costs; by choosing a discontinuous strategy the firm opens wide the field of opportunities and enhances the changes of entry into growth fields. The rule might be: Choose the most continuous strategy which still meets the objectives of the firm.

3. On the other hand, this rule, while economically valid, is frequently disregarded because managers are driven not only by growth and profits but by their personal styles and preferences. Technologically oriented managers who "grew up" in the business will typically prefer a continuous strategy. Professional entrepreneurs, financially or legally trained, will prefer low synergy, discontinuous strategies. Thus, in recent years, a number of firms have followed a conglomerate strategy of unrelated acquisitions primarily because of the personal drive of the controlling manager. (For example, it is Harold Geneen's personality that transformed the slumbering ITT into a growth-bent conglomerate.)

The external pressures on the choice of strategy are the following:

1. Whatever the managerial objectives and preferences, the firm must remain in step with the environment. Failing to do so means stagnation and eventual decline. When the environment becomes turbulent (as it did for Henry Ford I in the period 1925–1935), the firm must shift to a more venturesome and aggressive strategic thrust.

2. The environment is increasingly unpredictable; the result is "strategic surprises": technological, political, social, and competitive discontinuities which can suddenly and drastically affect (positively or negatively) the firm's prospects. To avoid getting caught with "all its eggs in one basket," a firm must select a strategic thrust which will position it in several different industries that do not share strategic vulnerabilities.

The choice of the strategic thrust can be summarized as follows: Other things being equal, the firm will produce better profits and incur smaller risks by doing what it does best, that is, maintaining its historical strategic thrust. But "other things" are typically unequal. Therefore, the problem is to select a strategy which simultaneously meets the objectives of management, protects the firm from strategic vulnerability, and takes maximum possible

advantage of the firm's competencies and capabilities.

**Adaptation of "Structure" to Strategy**  In the early thinking about strategy it was assumed that a new suitable strategy could always be found to match the existing capability. The idea was to choose a strategy which took advantage of the firm's strengths and avoided its weaknesses. As the environment "heated" up, however, firms increasingly found that their traditional capabilities had few strengths in the newly turbulent world. For example, when competition began to shift in the 1930s from an emphasis on mass production to mass marketing, production-oriented firms found themselves lacking in both marketing and product development capability.

Today it is clear that different strategies require significantly different capabilities. Continuous strategies require stable internal environments based on advantages of routine, repetition, division of labor, and mass production. Discontinuous strategies require the firm to be perceptive and open to the environment and capable of rapid, effective innovation. A matching of typical capabilities to the strategy types of Table P-5 is shown in Table P-6. Table P-6 explains why this author has consistently placed the word *structure* in quotation marks. The formal organizational structure (line 7) is seen to be only one of eight attributes which, together, constitute the managerial capability of the firm. If one or more attributes is out of line with the others, the capability becomes unbalanced, resulting in inefficient and dysfunctional behavior. Thus an entrepreneurially oriented top manager will find himself or herself at loggerheads with an organization whose capability is reactive. If a modern strategic planning system is introduced into a stable firm, it will be resisted by the organization which has neither the competence nor the motivation to use it.[5]

If an environment remains on a fixed level of turbulence long enough, each well-managed firm will adapt its strategy to the turbulence and then match the capability to the strategy. But if the firm is poorly managed, or the environmental turbulence changes frequently, it will frequently turn out that *both* the strategy and the capability are out of tune with the environment. When this occurs, the firm must simultaneously choose the new strategic thrust and the new managerial capability.

To enable the reader to make a quick diagnosis of his or her own firm, the corresponding columns in Tables P-2, P-5, and P-6 have been identically labeled. Thus, a reactive environment as inferred from Table P-2 requires the reactive strategies

**TABLE P-6   Profile of Managerial Capability**

| Attributes \ Types | Stable | Reactive | Anticipating | Exploring | Creative |
|---|---|---|---|---|---|
| (1) Culture | "Don't rock the boat" | "Roll with the punches" | "Plan ahead" | "The world's our oyster" | "New is good" |
| (2) Attitude to change | Reject | Accept when necessary | Seek familiar change | Seek novel change | Create change |
| (3) Success criterion | Stability and survival | Efficiency | Synergistic effectiveness | Global effectiveness | Effectiveness through innovation |
| (4) Locus of power | Production | Marketing | Marketing and R&D | Entrepreneurs | Creators |
| (5) Problem solving | Trial and error | Diagnostic | Optimization | Ill-structured | Creative |
| (6) Information system | Precedent | Historical performance | Extrapolated | New futures | Latent opportunities |
| (7) Organization structure | Functional | Functional | Divisional | Multinational matrix | New venture contigent structure |
| (8) Management system | Systems and procedures | Control | Long-range planning | Periodic strategic planning | Venture management real-time strategic planning |

shown in Table P-5 and the reactive capability shown in Table P-6.

The process is simple. Using Table P-2, identify the state of the firm's environment. In Table P-5, identify the present strategy of the firm. The difference between this strategy and the state of the environment is the strategic gap to be closed. Next identify the present capability in Table P-6. The gap between it and the state of the environment is the capability gap.

For some firms this analysis will show that only one of the aspects needs changing: either the capability must be brought in line with the present strategy, or a more aggressive strategy must be built on the already existing capability. But frequently both need changing.

When this arises the problem is no longer to find a new strategy while keeping the firm's strengths and weaknesses intact. The new strategy and the new capability must be developed side by side. The complexion and the difficulty of this problem depend on whether the firm chooses to develop the new strategic posture using its own resources or whether it embarks on a merger/acquisition route. The choice between the two depends on urgency and synergy.

Internal development makes sense under two conditions: when there is sufficient time to effect the change and when the firm's new strategic position is synergistic with the present (in other words, when the present capabilities and competitive srengths carry over to the new position). Acquisition of other firms becomes a necessity when the desired markets, products, and technologies are outside the competencies of the firm. But acquisition may be preferred also when the environment is pressing and the change is urgent.

If the acquisition route is followed, both the new

strategic position and the capability are purchased in a package, necessitating a minimum disturbance to the existing organization. If a do-it-yourself approach is used, the timing and priorities of the strategy and capability need to be established.

If there is sufficient time, the least-cost route is to develop the new capability and new strategy in parallel, gradually, and step by step, so that they continue to support and reinforce each other. If failure to change strategy promptly will mean serious losses, strategy must take priority. In the initial stages, the lack of capability can be made up by recourse to external resources such as consulting firms. As the new strategy is installed some capability will develop in the process; the rest can be built up after the new market position has been secured.

**Strategic Management and Strategic Planning** The analysis of the preceding sections aligns the firm with the environment through selection of the general strategic thrust and of the capability needed to support it. It remains to elaborate the thrust and the capability into specific strategies.

*Strategic planning,* which made its appearance in the mid 1950s, is a system designed for elaborating the strategic thrust. This is accomplished by translating the entrepreneurial thrust into an *entrepreneurial strategy,* which is also sometimes called the *product-market scope,* the *position* strategy, the *what* strategy, or *the business we are in* strategy. This strategy specifies the scope of the markets, type of products, and technologies in which the firm intends to do business. It also specifies the common threads among them, which bind the firm into an integrated whole.

The marketing thrust is similarly elaborated. The result is called the *competitive* strategy, the *competitive niche,* or the *how* strategy. It defines the manner by which the firm will distinguish itself in the eyes of the customer, how it will outmaneuver the competition, and how it will take advantage of its relative strengths and weaknesses.

Strategic planning has been widely discussed in a number of books and periodicals.[6] It is useful here to show how strategic planning fits into the larger perspective of strategic management, as illustrated in Table P-7.

The starting concerns in strategic management are two: (1) whether the firm's strategic behavior is aggressive enough and far-ranging enough for the environment in which it finds itself; and (2) whether the firm's values, managerial skills, motivation, information base, systems, and organizational structure are sufficiently open and flexible to enable the

firm to behave effectively. The output of this stage of analysis is to pinpoint the appropriate strategic thrust and the appropriate capability.

At the lower left of Table P-7, "conventional" strategic planning takes over. Objectives and goals are established, threats and opportunities are identified, strengths and weaknesses are analyzed. The output are (1) a specification of the areas in which the firm wishes to do business—a statement of the "business we are in," and (2) a specification of the competitive approaches to each distinctive area of the business. At the right of Table P-7 the mode of change (acquisition or do-it-yourself) is determined and translated into strategic programs and budgets.

It can be seen that, if the level of environmental turbulence does not change significantly over time, the strategic thrust need not change and the pattern of strengths and weaknesses remains relatively constant. Under these conditions the early stages of analysis shown in Table P-7 become unnecessary and strategic management collapses into strategic planning. Put differently, strategic planning needs to be expanded into strategic management when the intensity of environmental turbulence is changing.

## MANAGEMENT IN UNPREDICTABLE ENVIRONMENTS

**Strategic Issue Management** Both strategic planning and strategic management are organization-wide processes, lasting several months and involving many levels of management. These systems are too slow and cumbersome to cope with unanticipated midyear surprises, originating from government, foreign competitors, breakthroughs in R&D, etc., which develop rapidly and which cannot wait until the next planning cycle.

To deal with such fast-moving challenges some firms have begun to use a technique, called *strategic issue analysis,* which enables them to react as soon as the change becomes visible and to respond quickly. The technique is simple to install and manage and does not interfere with the existing structure and systems. Briefly, the ingredients of issue analysis are the following:

1. A continuous surveillance is instituted over business-economic-social-political trends.

2. The impact of the trends is interpreted, and the findings are presented as key strategic issues to top management at frequent meetings and whenever a new major threat or opportunity is perceived.

**TABLE P-7   Decision Flow in Strategic Management**

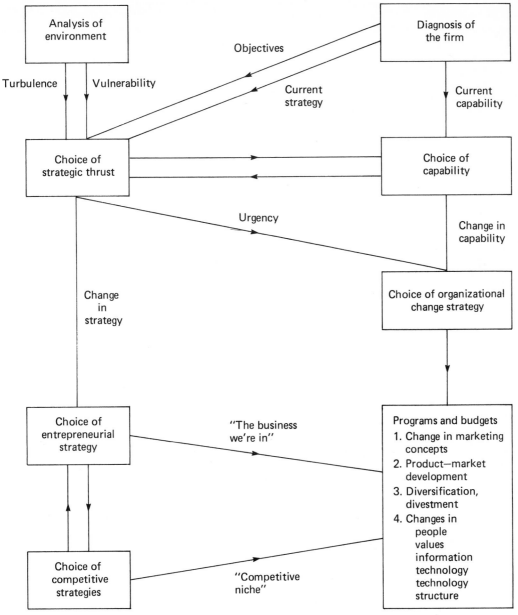

3. Together with the planning staff, top management analyzes the impact of the issues and assigns them into one of three categories:

 *a.* Those that require immediate and urgent attention.

 *b.* Those that need to be resolved during the next planning cycle.

 *c.* Those that require continuous monitoring.

4. The urgent issues are assigned for study and

resolution, either to existing organizational units or, whenever rapid crossorganizational response is essential, to special task forces.

5. The resolution of issues is monitored by top management both for strategic and tactical implications.

6. The list of the issues and their priorities is kept up to date through periodic review by the top management.

**Weak Signals and Graduated Response**  The issues included in the active list will have different visibility. Some will be definite and clear, permitting specific response; others will be vague, ill-defined, and uncertain. If the latter are not urgent, they can be monitored until information improves. But some among them will develop so fast that their impact will be felt before their implications become clear. If the firm waits too long for improved information, it will be hit by a strategic surprise. A way to avoid such surprises is to monitor weak and uncertain information and to develop appropriate "weak" responses which minimize the likelihood of a surprise.

A method for doing this is illustrated in Table P-8. The left column identifies five stages in the evolu-

tion of a new issue. Proceeding from top to bottom, the originally weak signals become progressively stronger. At the top the only information available is a certainty that the environment holds potential surprises. At the bottom enough is known to compute the profit consequences of both the impact and the response. Just above this strongest signal, on level 4, enough is known to launch a concrete response to the threat, even though the firm is not able to estimate its financial consequences. At levels 3 and above information is not adequate for devising a direct response.

The column headings of Table P-8, from left to right, show progressively stronger responses. The weakest response is to start environmental surveillance and interpretation. At the other extreme, the strongest response is to deal directly with the threat. The responses between the two extremes become progressively more costly and irreversible, as one progresses from left to right.

The shaded areas inside the table show that as the signals gain strength, progressively stronger responses become possible. By the time the source of threat is identified (but not yet its actual shape), a substantial program can be launched which will

**TABLE P-8  Weak Signals and Graduated Response**

| Graduated response / Strength of signal | A Environmental surveillance | B Identification of relative strengths and weaknesses | C Reduction of external strategic vulnerability | D Increase of internal strategic flexibility | E Capability plans and response | F Action plans and response |
|---|---|---|---|---|---|---|
| I Sense of threat | | | | | | |
| II Source of threat is known | | | | | | |
| III Shape of threat is concrete | | | Feasible region | | | |
| IV Response strategies are understood | | | | | | |
| V Outcome of response is forecastable | | | | | | |

reduce the firm's vulnerability, increase flexibility, and enhance readiness for response to the change in whatever form it materialized eventually.

The approach of Table P-8 can be used to refine the strategic issue analysis to include response to weak signals. This requires encouraging the environmental surveillance staff to report early warning signals of emerging issues. But it also requires that the general management and other participants develop an attitude which welcomes change, a decision-making behavior which accepts unfamiliar risks, and a problem-solving approach which forgoes reliance on experience in favor of new learning.

**Strategic Surprise Management**  Just as in a radar surveillance system, some issues, in spite of the best efforts, will slip by the environmental surveyors and become strategic surprises. This means four things:

1. The issue arrives suddenly, unanticipated.

2. It poses novel problems in which the firm has little prior experience.

3. Failure to respond implies either a major financial reversal or loss of a major opporutnity.

4. The response is urgent and cannot be handled promptly enough, either by the normal systems and procedures or by the strategic issue analysis.

The combination of the four factors creates major problems. The previous strategies and plans do not apply, the challenge is unfamiliar, and there is a flood of new information to process and to analyze. Thus the firm is in danger of developing an information overload. The suddenness and the prospects of a major loss, usually widely perceived throughout the organization, create a threat of widespread panic. Perhaps most importantly, decentralized initiatives, which normally can expedite response, become ineffective and even potentially dangerous in a strategic surprise. Lacking a coherent strategy of response, local managers are likely to move the firm in "all directions at the same time" and create havoc. Finally, preoccupation with morale and the surprise are likely to divert attention from the continuing operations of producing, selling, and distributing.

If the firm wants to minimize the disorganization it needs to invest in yet another system, a strategic surprise management system. The characteristics of such a system are the following:

1. When a strategic surprise occurs, an emergency communications network goes into effect. The network crosses normal organizational boundaries, filters the information, and rapidly communicates it to the entire organization.

2. For the duration of the emergency, the responsibilities of top management are repartitioned:

   *a.* One group devotes its attention to control and maintenance of organizational morale.

   *b.* Another group assures continuance of business as usual with a minimum of disruptions.

   *c.* A third group takes charge of response to the surprise.

3. For dealing with the surprises, a strategic task force network is activated.

   *a.* Leaders and task force members cross normal organizational lines and constitute strategic action (not just planning!) units.

   *b.* The communications network is star-shaped, with lines directly between the task forces and the central top management group.

   *c.* The top management group formulates the overall strategy, assigns implementation responsibilities, and coordinates the implementation.

   *d.* The decentralized task forces implement their components of the new strategy.

4. The task force and communications networks are predesigned and trained.

   *a.* Several networks may be predesigned: one to deal with surprises in the marketplace, another with technological surprises, a third for political surprises, etc.

   *b.* The task forces are trained in prompt response to novel problems, which combines creativity with analytic techniques.

5. The networks are exercised under noncrisis conditions in addressing real strategic issues, *as if* they were surprises.

## CHOICE OF MANAGEMENT SYSTEMS

When the environment turns turbulent a first reaction on the part of some observers is to proclaim that the technology of long-term anticipation and planning is no longer applicable and that it is time to return to seat-of-the-pants management, based on intuition and and experience.[7,8] Such a reaction is naïve and unrealistic, in view of the novelty of the problems and complexity of the issues. What is needed instead are more supple and flexible systematic approaches which can bolster intuition at a time when problems are unfamiliar and seat-of-the-pants experience is just as likely to be wrong as right.

This entry has outlined several such approaches. Significantly, the complexity and responsiveness of the appropriate systems depend on the turbulence of

**TABLE P-9   Management System Selection Matrix**

| Characteristics of environment | | | Management system | | | | |
|---|---|---|---|---|---|---|---|
| Basic trend | Continuity of change | Visibility of change | Long-range planning | Periodic strategic planning | Periodic strategic management | Real time issue management | Strategic surprise management |
| (1) Acceptable | Continuous | Forecastable | • | | | | |
| (2) | Discontinuous | Weak signals | • | | | • | |
| (3) | | Surprises | • | | | • | • |
| (4) Unacceptable | Continuous | Forecastable | • | • | | | |
| (5) | Familiar discontinuity | Predictable | • | • | • | | |
| (6) | Unfamiliar discontinuity | Weak signals | • | • | • | • | |
| (7) | | Surprises | • | • | • | • | • |

their environment. Table P-9, a management system selection matrix, provides guidelines for choosing the most appropriate system.

To use the matrix, management first needs to diagnose in column 1 whether the basic trends in the firm's environment are promising enough to be acceptable to the firm. If they are, a diagnosis of columns 2 and 3 identifies the degree of environmental turbulence. This will locate the firm in line 1, 2, or 3. The right part of the table will then indicate the desirable combination of management systems. If the basic growth prospects are not acceptable, a similar analysis in the lower part of the table will lead to the choice of a more complicated system.

*See also* AUDIT, MANAGEMENT; INNOVATION AND CREATIVITY; MARKET ANALYSIS; PLANNING, STRATEGIC PLANNING MODELS; POLICY FORMULATION AND IMPLEMENTATION; PRODUCT PLANNING AND DEVELOPMENT.

### NOTES

[1] H. Igor Ansoff, *Corporate Strategy*, McGraw-Hill Book Company, New York, 1965.

[2] A. D. Chandler, Jr., *Strategy and Structure*, The M.I.T. Press, Cambridge, Mass., 1962.

[3] H. Igor Ansoff, "The State of Practice in Management Systems," European Institute for Advanced Studies in Management, Working Paper, no. 75-11, Brussels, April 1975.

[4] H. I. Ansoff, R. P. Declerck, and R. L. Hayes, *From Strategic Planning to Strategic Management*, John Wiley & Sons, Ltd., London, 1976.

[5] H. I. Ansoff, R. P. Declerck, and R. L. Hayes, "From Strategic Planning to Strategic Management," in H. I. Ansoff et al., *From Strategic Planning to Strategic Management*, John Wiley & Sons, Ltd., London, 1976.

[6] Ansoff, *Corporate Strategy*.

[7] Henry Mintzberg, "Planning on the Left Side and Managing on the Right," *Harvard Business Review*, vol. 54, no. 4, July–August 1976.

[8] Francois de Witt, "Quand les Entreprises perdent la boussole," *L'Expansion*, November 1975.

H. IGOR ANSOFF, *European Institute for Advanced Studies in Management, Brussels; Stockholm School of Economics*

## Planning, policy formulation   (*See* POLICY FORMULATION AND IMPLEMENTATION.)

## Planning, product   (*See* PRODUCT PLANNING AND DEVELOPMENT.)

## Planning, production (*See* PRODUCTION PLANNING AND CONTROL.)

## Planning, strategic managerial

Strategic managerial planning systems, called by many different names, have developed and spread rapidly around the world during the past 15 to 20 years among both profit and nonprofit organizations. The volume of literature on the subject is truly mountainous. This entry will summarize from the literature and from practice the essential conceptual and operational aspects of these planning systems.[1] Emphasis will be placed on definitions, the fundamental nature of planning, processes in organizing and doing planning, and problems of implementation. The following discussion of six overarching aspects of comprehensive managerial planning will provide an initial perspective.

*Planning and Management.* Long-range planning is inextricably woven into the entire process of management. The role of a manager as planner is meshed with his or her other roles in a seamless web of management. To oversimplify, there are two fundamentally different types of management. One is strategic management, which is done at the top of organizations. Everything else is operational management. The planning systems discussed here constitute a central foundation for strategic management. But just as strategic management is directly concerned with operational management, so strategic planning systems deal with both aspects of management.

*Each Organization is Unique.* There is no such thing as a single planning model that fits all organizations. The comprehensive planning system must fit the characteristics of each organization for which it is designed. Since each organization is unique, the operational details of any one planning system will differ from that of all other organizations.

*Lessons of Experience for Success.* Although planning systems will differ, experience points out the fundamental dos and don'ts in organizing and doing planning that must be understood if successful planning is to be achieved. Successful planning systems do have common fundamental characteristics despite differing operational details.

*Incidence of Usage.* It is rare to find anywhere in the world a large corporation that does not have some type of formal long-range planning system. Increasingly, also, smaller corporations and nonprofit organizations are developing formal planning systems.

*Problems of Implementation.* The fundamental concepts of comprehensive planning are rather simple. Their implementation, however, is deceptively difficult. At its heart, planning is a creative as well as a systematic effort. As a result, it requires the integration of two antithetical approaches.

*Intuitive-Anticipatory versus Formal Long-Range Planning.* Fundamentally, there are two types of comprehensive long-range corporate planning. The first is intuitive-anticipatory planning. While no one really knows the precise mental processes by which it is done, it has several major discernible characteristics. Generally it is the work of one person. It may, but often does not, result in a written set of plans. It generally has a short time horizon and reaction time. It is based upon past experience, the "gut" feeling, the judgment, and the reflective thinking of a manager. Many managers have an extraordinary intuitive ability to devise brilliant strategies and methods to carry them out.[2] If an organization is managed by intuitive geniuses, there is no need for formal planning. But how many organizations are so blessed? And even if the managers are geniuses, how many times are they incorrect in their judgments?

In contrast, a formal planning system is organized and developed on the basis of a set of procedures. It is explicit in the sense that people know what is being done. It is research-based, involves the work of many people, and results in a set of written plans.

The two systems of planning often clash. A manager who has made successful intuitive judgments is not likely to accept completely the constraints of a formal system. He or she may be uneasy with some of the new language and methods incorporated by a sophisticated staff in a formal planning system. Or the manager may feel that his or her authority is challenged as others engage in the decision-making process. Furthermore, the manager's thought processes may conflict with the requirements of formal planning.

For such reasons, and because of cognitive differences between intuitive and systematic thinkers, some believe that with intuitive thinkers there can be no formal planning.[3] This either-or conclusion is not correct. Limited empirical observation will show that the two approaches are indeed meshed in many organizations. There is often conflict, to be sure, but each can be and often is adapted to the requirements of the other. They can and should complement one another.

In a fundamental sense, formal planning is an effort to duplicate intuitive planning. But formal planning cannot be really effective unless managers at all levels inject their judgments and intuition into the planning process.

### FORMAL LONG-RANGE PLANNING DEFINED

In its early history, the words *long-range planning* were used to describe the system that is the subject of this entry. Other names have subsequently been coined. Long ago, for reasons which will be developed below, this author abandoned the exclusive use of the words *long-range planning* to describe the system. Instead, he uses synonymously these words: comprehensive corporate planning, comprehensive managerial planning, total planning, long-range planning, integrated planning, formal planning, overall planning, corporate planning, strategic planning, and other combinations of these words.

Corporate long-range planning should be defined in at least four ways, each of which is needed to understand it.

First, long-range planning deals with the futurity of current decisions. This means that long-range planning looks at the cause-and-effect consequences over time of manager's actual or intended decision. A manager who does not like the prospective picture will change the decision. Long-range planning also looks at the alternative courses of action that will be open in the future. When choices are made, they become the basis for making current decisions. The essence of long-range planning is a systematic identification of future opportunities and threats, which, in combination with other relevant data, provides a basis for making current decisions to exploit the opportunities and avoid the threats.

Second, comprehensive corporate planning is a process. It is a process which begins with the development of objectives, defines strategies and policies to achieve objectives, and develops detailed plans to make sure that the strategies are carried out. It is a process of deciding in advance what is to be done, when it is to be done, how it is to be done, and who is going to do it.

Third, it is a philosophy. Many businesspeople talk about corporate planning as being a way of life. Executives speak of assuring the proper climate in their enterprise to do the most effective corporate planning. This climate is a function of many forces among which is an attitude of wanting to do effective planning.

Fourth, comprehensive corporate planning may be defined as a structure of plans. It is a structure which integrates strategic with short-range operational plans. At all levels of this structure are inte-

grated the major objectives, strategies, policies, and functions of an enterprise.

### WHAT STRATEGIC PLANNING IS NOT

Strategic planning does not attempt to make future decisions. Rather, planning involves choosing the more desirable future alternatives open to a company so that better current decisions can be made.

Comprehensive corporate planning is not forecasting. It is not forecasting product sales and then determining what should be done to fulfill the forecasts, with respect to material purchases, facilities, labor, and so on. Corporate planning goes beyond present forecasts of current products and markets and asks such questions as: Are we in the right business? What are our basic objectives? When will our present products become obsolete? Are our markets accelerating or eroding? For most companies there is a wide gap between a simple forecast based on present sales and profits and what top management would like its sales and profits to be. If so, there is a gap to be filled by comprehensive corporate planning.

Comprehensive long-range planning does not attempt to blueprint the future. It is not the development of a set of plans which are cast in bronze to be used day after day into the far distant future. Most companies revise plans periodically, usually once a year.

### THE PLANNING MODEL

Figure P-3 shows the author's conceptual model of the structure and process of corporate planning. It further elaborates the meaning of comprehensive planning and explains how the process can be carried out. Over a number of years the author has examined planning systems of many companies and concludes that the companies that do effective comprehensive planning follow this model explicitly or implicitly. Yet, paradoxically, the author has never found an operational system diagramed in precisely the same way as in Fig. P-3. Operational flow charts vary depending upon differences among companies but, underneath, the basic elements shown in the figure are found in the better systems. If one element of the model is missing, either explicitly or implicitly, the system will not operate effectively. Conceptual models of leading authors in the field are quite comparable to this model.[4]

In the following exposition Fig. P-3 is used to explain the planning process. It should be pointed

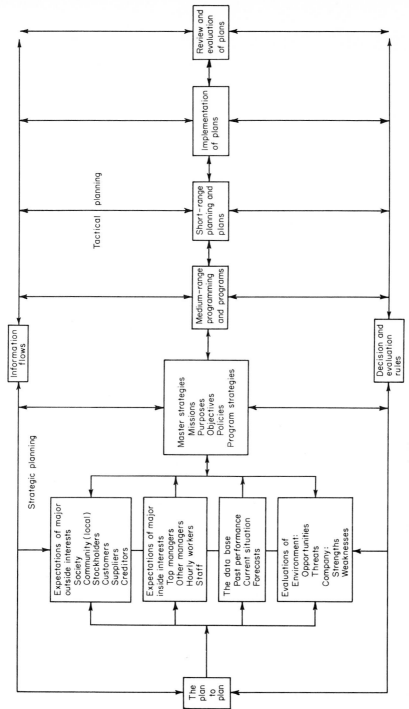

**Fig. P-3. Structure and process of company-wide business planning.**

895

out, however, that in actual practice the process is iterative and may begin at different points. In practice there is much back-and-forth analysis before decisions are made.

Conceptually, the information collected and the decisions made in the four stacked boxes to the left of Fig. P-3 provide the basis for making the strategic decisions identified in the box labeled *master strategies*. This, then provides a foundation for making medium-range program plans. These are then translated into current budget numbers. Then follows implementation and periodic review.

**The Plan to Plan** It is wise to have a plan to plan, or a planning guide. Sometimes this is called a planning manual. It ranges from two or three double-spaced typewritten pages in some companies to a printed book of several hundred pages. Conceptually the guide should contain the following: a strong statement of the chief executive officer's commitment to effective formal planning as an essential managerial need, a glossary of terms, specification of data required from the planning system, specification of who is to supply what data, a schedule of data flow, and any special planning rules, such as whether pricing used in the planning process will be on a constant or current basis.

**Nomenclature Problems** There is no consensus about the meaning of terms used in planning. Words mean different things to different writers and practitioners. Furthermore, some words are interchangeable and can stretch in different contexts. The semantic problem in this field complicates an understanding of planning.[5] It is desirable, therefore, to establish common definitions of terms.

To illustrate, consider the use of the word *strategy* and its derivations. Strategic planning, according to Fig. P-3, includes those elements in the stacked boxes to the left, plus a box of master strategies. To make matters more confusing, this box also contains something called *program strategies*. Furthermore, the entire figure represents the strategic planning process because it is designed to translate strategies decisions into current actions. Clearly there is a need for new words to define different aspects of comprehensive long-range planning.

Organizational missions, purposes, philosophies, policies, and long-range objectives are master strategies. Program strategies refer to decisions concerning the acquisition, use, and disposition of resources to pursue specific functions and activities such as facility construction, penetration of the European market, or the development and marketing of a new product. The process involved in making these decisions is strategic planning.

Planning decisions range from strategies at one end of the spectrum to tactics at the other. Tactical planning refers to courses of action to implement strategic plans. At the extremes there are clear distinctions between the two, but as they move closer to one another they may be indistinguishable.[6]

**The Situation Audit** The situation audit includes what is collected in the stacked boxes shown in Fig. P-3. There is no unanimity about this definition, nor is there agreement on the words used to describe the process. It is sometimes called planning premises, corporate appraisal, position audit, or assessment of current position. What is done is more important than the words to describe it.

No organization, no matter how large or profitable, can thoroughly examine all the elements which conceivably could be included in its situation audit. Each organization, therefore, must identify those elements—past, present, and future—which are most significant to its growth, prosperity, and well-being and concentrate thought and effort on understanding them.

*Expectations of Major Outside Interests.* All organizations have constituents with varying degrees of interest in the enterprise, and management must consider them. Planning begins with an assessment of such interests. Up to a few years ago, a business was said to have only one socioeconomic purpose and that was to use the resources at its disposal as efficiently as possible in producing the goods and services that consumers wanted at prices they were willing to pay. If this was done well, it was reasoned that profits would be maximized. Since corporations are owned by stockholders, the idea flourished that management owed its sole responsibility to stockholders. More and more people in and out of business, however, think that the socioeconomic purpose of a business is not so narrow. For example, Edward N. Cole, when president of General Motors Corporation, wrote:

The big challenge to American business—as I see it—is to carefully evaluate the constantly changing expressions of public and national goals. Then we must modify our own objectives and programs to meet—as far as possible within the realm of economic and technological feasibility—the new demands of the society we serve.[7]

Any large company that begins its long-range planning with the profit maximization principle as its only objective will inevitably wind up in trouble.

*Expectations of Major Inside Interests.* Managers and employees of organizations have interests which also must be appraised and addressed in the planning process. Especially important are the interests of top executives which are derived from their value systems. They are basic and fundamental premises in any comprehensive planning system. Sometimes executive values are written, but most of the time they are not written or even articulated. The correctness of many of these values cannot be proved or disproved on the basis of numbers or even logic; yet they may determine the basic long-range aims of a company. For instance, a chief executive may say: "I want my company to be the biggest in our industry in 10 years." Or "I want my company to be the technologically best in the industry." Or "My goal is to make my company the biggest and the technically best company in my industry in the next decade." Each of these aims provides a very different frame of reference for doing corporate planning.

*The Data Base.* Included in the data base, as shown in Fig. P-3, is information about past performance, the current situation, and the future. A company should look at its past track record as a base for evaluating current performance and as a guide to the future. Illustrative of the types of information that may be collected are data on sales, profits, return on investment, market share, employee productivity, public relations, and product development capability.

Data about the current situation may include financial information, resource use efficiencies, managerial capabilities, employee skills and productivity, competition, corporate image, social demands on the company, and so on.

Data about the future should certainly include forecasts of markets, sales, and selected economic trends of prime interest to the company. Forecasts of competition should definitely be added. To these traditional projections more companies today are making future estimates of technology developments likely to affect the company, changing social expectations, and other trends of particular concern to the organization (e.g., population, international turbulence, government regulations, and so on).

In appraising the current situation some companies prepare forms which vertically list specific items to be appraised, such as financial ratios, production measures, marketing criteria, technology situation, and so on. Each item is then evaluated in terms such as (1) superior, or better than any other company in the industry; (2) better than average; (3) average, acceptable, or about equal to the competition; (4) below average, situation not acceptable, or situation deteriorating and must be changed; or (5) real cause for alarm, situation poor, action must be taken to improve.[8] Some companies set forth a list of key questions concerning critical elements in a com-

pany's position. For example, for products, questions such as these may be raised: Are our products competitive? What are the margins for each of our products? Are any margins too low? Where is each product in its life cycle? What are our current plans for improving our products? Do we know what our competitors are planning? Key questions are raised about other major areas such as customers, research, finance, and management.[9]

*WOTS Up Analysis.* This is an acronym for weaknesses, opportunities, threats, and strengths. This is a critical phase of the situation audit for, among other things, the identification of these elements suggests specific strategies and also provides useful data for evaluating strategies.

There are many ways to make a WOTS Up analysis. Brainstorming is sometimes employed. At the other extreme is rigorous staff research concerning specific questions. In between is thoughtful response of selected managers and staff about their suggested opportunities, threats, strengths, or weaknesses, which should be considered in developing strategies. Some companies use a simple form to get this information. In any event, the number of environmental forces and internal factors of importance to a company, either as opportunities, threats, strengths, or weaknesses, is so great that there must be careful selection of those which will be studied at any length.

It is hardly necessary to comment that a company should maximize its strengths and avoid its weaknesses, and it should understand that a strength today may become a weakness in tomorrow's environment. Yet it is observable that companies often fail because they blindly assumed that an existing success syndrome was based upon a strength which would continue. Not enough companies systematically examine their strengths; fewer systematically study their weakenesses.

This is a much too brief and inadequate examination of how a manager can identify the right problem, opportunity, and threat. The literature on how to solve a problem once it is discovered is mountainous. The literature on how to be sure to identify the right problem and how to recognize the best opportunity is extremely small. This is too bad because a businessperson runs a far greater risk in not finding the right problem or opportunity than in determining how to solve the problem or how to exploit the opportunity once it is identified.

**The Network of Organizational Aims** On the basis of premises developed in the above steps, the strategic planning process then hammers out basic missions, long-range objectives, and policies and program strategies to achieve them. Each of these will be treated in turn. But first it is useful to point out that, contrary to so many elementary economic textbooks, there is no such thing as a single goal or objective of a company. Each firm has a network of aims as shown in Table P-10.[10] Each of these is different, has a different purpose in the planning process, and is developed in a different fashion.

*Missions and Purposes.* A surprising number of companies have developed creeds, philosophies, or statements of purpose for general distribution. These statements frequently include, as shown in Table P-10, not only basic economic and social ends which are sought by top management but also the moral and ethical principles which should govern personal actions of all employees in achieving them.[11]

Missions are statements about the underlying design, aim, or thrust of a company. If expressed as a grand design at a high level of abstraction, and in generalities, they may be considered basic purposes or philosophies, as noted in Table P-10.

Basic missions should be stated in both product and market terms. A company may say that it is in the business of producing air conditioners. It will be in entirely different businesses, however, if it chooses to make air conditioners for office buildings or for home cooling or for automobiles. Deciding upon a basic mission is a fundamental step in planning. If the Baldwin Locomotive Works had said its mission was to make tractive power for railroads, instead of solely making steam locomotives, it probably would still be in business. A company that says it is not in the business of making bricks for construction but is in the clay products business for construction widens its opportunities. The company also increases its threats, however, and too broad a mission, may be dangerous. For instance, it is doubtful whether a company making lead pencils should say its mission is changed to making communications equipment. There is an iron law of product-market development that says the further a company gets from its present products and markets, the less likely it will make a profit. But if the product and market are very narrow, growth and prosperity can be enhanced by a judicious widening of the mission.

*Objectives.* Objectives are desired results to be achieved, usually in a specific time. They are very important in the planning process because they are guides to the development of actions to assure their fulfillment. Behavioral scientists also conclude that they are important motivators of people in organizations, because people generally like to try to achieve the objectives set for the organization. The more people in organizations participate in the objective-setting process, the greater is their motivation to achieve them. Objectives can be used effectively, of course, as standards for measuring performance.

Objectives may be expressed for every element of a business which is considered important enough to be the subject of plans. There is no standard classification of objectives or of the number of objectives which a company should have.

Companies that have a planning process generally set objectives for profits and sales. In addition, in planning systems of larger companies one often finds objectives for the following: marketing (e.g., share of market), finance (e.g., sales, profits, employment), personnel (e.g., developing managers, working conditions, employment levels), and research and development. This does not exhaust the list, and many subobjectives are possible in each category.

Peter Drucker says that objectives are needed in every area of a business where performance and results directly and importantly affect the survival and prosperity of the enterprise. The areas where he says objectives ought to be set are these: market standing, innovation, productivity, physical and financial resources, profitability, manager performance and development, worker performance and attitude, and public responsibility.[12]

Objectives can be based on different considerations. They may be dictated by top management without any research analysis, or they may be based upon thorough analysis. They may be extrapolated from the past or set to exploit a foreseen opportunity or avoid a perceived threat. They may be derived from a settled strategy or designed to support other objectives.

Objectives, however derived, should exhibit a few major characteristics. First, they should be able to lead and motivate, and the more concrete and specific they are, the more likely they are to have directive power. To say that "our company seeks to make a good profit" is far less suitable for planning than to say, "Our objective is to make $4 million in profits 3 years from today." Second, objectives should be actionable. Goals which are far too high or far too low do not lead to action. Objectives should be a little aggressive and require imagination and hard work to achieve. Third, objectives should be understood by those who are to develop means to achieve them. Fourth, objectives should conform to ethical and social codes accepted by society and by the business. Finally, objectives should correlate and be mutually supporting, to the extent possible.

**TABLE P-10    The Network of Organizational Aims**

| Classification of aim | Illustration |
|---|---|
| 1. Personal aims (CEOs) | "Have challenging problems to solve."* <br> "Become financially independent." <br> "Satisfy creative urge and talent." |
| 2. Governing philosophy, creed, and purpose for the organization | "Become the most profitable company in the industry." <br> "Become the largest company in the industry." <br> "Become the technical standard of the industry." <br> "Make profits sufficiently large to meet the expectations of stockholders and employees." <br> "Be a good citizen in all communities where the organization operates." <br> "Observe the highest possible level of ethical and moral conduct in all dealings." <br> "Treat all employees fairly with justice and dignity." |
| 3. Underlying mission <br>    *a.* Grand design | "Our business is service." <br> "Better things for better living through chemistry." <br> "Maintain global leadership through new products and research, supported by aggressive marketing." <br> "Provide guidance and coordination to all federal agencies concerned with and relative to their emergency preparedness and resource management responsibilities." |
|    *b.* Specific thrust | "Be a producer of fabricated steel shapes and forms for worldwide markets." <br> "Produce light airplanes for the general aviation market." <br> "Maintain a viable, growing business by developing, producing, and marketing engineered products and services to satisfy selected needs of utility, construction, and manufacturing industries." <br> "Deal profitably in beef and purified animal by-products." |
| 4. Specific objectives for key result areas <br>    *a.* Core objectives <br>       Sales <br>       Profits <br>       ROI <br>       Margin <br><br>    *b.* Other <br>       Market share <br>       Product development <br>       Productivity <br>       Diversification <br>       Minority hiring <br>       Facility replacement <br>       Labor content of product <br>       Social responsibilities | "Increase sales from $25 million this year to $50 million in 5 years." <br> "Increase sales by 15 percent per year." <br> "Increase profit margin from 7 percent this year to 12 percent in 5 years." <br><br> "Raise market share from 5 percent this year to 25 percent in 5 years." <br> "Establish within 2 years a fully operative plan by means of which each employee may develop a personal career path with the organization." |
| 5. Departmental, divisional, and personal objectives <br>    *a.* Core objectives <br>       Sales <br>       Profits <br>       Etc. <br>    *b.* Other <br>       Market share <br>       Product development <br>       Etc. | |
| 6. Program objectives | "Penetrate Europe by acquiring a small advertising firm." <br> "Sell the Brazilian subsidiary." <br> "Market a low-priced digital watch." |
| 7. Short-term budget targets <br>       Material purchases <br>       Machinery purchases <br>       Production goals <br>       Sales goals <br>       Etc. | |

*For all groups illustrative only.

For instance, if the objective is to achieve a return on investment of 15 percent, after taxes, by the end of 5 years, the target is much more likely to be achieved if subobjectives and subsubobjectives are linked to it. For instance, subobjectives might be to increase sales to $10 million in 5 years, raise gross profits to $2.5 million in 5 years, build modern facilities and operate them at capacity over the next 5 years, and upgrade and maintain a skilled work force in specified ways. These objectives might also be linked to subsubobjectives. For example, an increase in sales might be sought by setting specific objectives for market share, advertising expenditures, market penetration, new products, and research and development in specific directions.

**Developing Policies and Strategies**   Once objectives are established, the logical sequence is to develop policies and program strategies to achieve them. *Policies* are broad guides to action, such as a decision to allow divisions to acquire other companies, after approval of headquarters, or a decision not to require one division of a company to buy the products of another division unless it wishes to do so. When speaking of major decisions of top management, what is a policy in contrast to a *strategy* may be indistinguishable. At this level the author uses the words synonomously.[13]

Most of what follows is directed principally at program strategies in functional areas. There is no classification of program strategies that has common acceptance. Strategies can be associated with all sorts of activities of an organization, such as markets, products, financing, diversification, pricing, and so on. The most successful strategies turn out to be clusters of strategies.

*Approaches to Identifying Program Strategies.* A systematic strategic planning process in a formal planning system is the preferred approach to the identification of effective program strategies. Other specific approaches that can be accommodated in a formal planning process or can be conducted in the absence of a formal system are as follows:

1. Ask what today's strategies are and whether they ought to be changed. This is called making a strategic profile.

2. Examine the present product-market mix and ask whether it is acceptable for tomorrow.

3. Identify the stages in the life cycle of specific products.

4. If possible, use computer simulation and econometric models to identify strategies.

5. Use intuition, which, as pointed out earlier, is an excellent approach if it is brilliant.

6. For some activities, such as acquisitions, try the ad hoc, trial and error approach.

7. Invent. (A successful invention is an unexcelled strategy.)

8. Determine the really significant factors that are important in the success of a particular business and concentrate major decisions on them. For instance, a new imaginative toy is a critically strategic factor in the success of a toy company, but superior technical and fail-safe qualities are of dominant importance to the success of an airplane manufacturer.[14]

9. Find a particular spot, a propitious niche, where the company can give a customer an irresistible value that is not being satisfied and at a relatively low cost. This strategy has made many companies rich.[15]

10. Use a WOTS Up analysis, as noted previously.

11. Don't discount luck, opportunism, brainstorming, and following the lead of another company.

Two concluding points should be added about identifying program strategies. What is a successful strategy for one company may turn out to be another's poison. Chances are that if Avon changed strategies with Revlon, neither would do as well as they now are. Also, timing is very important. The Edsel filled a niche for the Ford Motor Company, but the timing was bad and the product failed.

*Evaluating Strategies.* Once strategies are identified they must, of course, be evaluated. There is no single way to do this. Managers should be careful to make sure that appropriate tests are applied and that the evaluations are appropriate to the nature and significance of the program strategies under review. Both quantitative and qualitative measure must be applied. To help managers in this process the author has prepared 25 major tests, which are presented in Table P-11. Not all questions are appropriate to every company and proposed strategy. The list illustrates the point that a key method of measurement is to ask the right questions.

**Other Aspects**   Several characteristics of the strategic planning process should be observed. First, the time spectrum covered ranges from the very short term to the infinite. While the general thrust and content of strategic planning is long range, a decision can be made in this process to stop making product X tomorrow or to start building a new plant tomorrow to make product Y.

Another important characteristic is that while the process may produce a written document on a peri-

**TABLE P-11   Twenty-five Major Tests for Your Strategies**

1. Is your strategy identifiable and understood by all those in the company with a need to know?

2. Is your strategy consistent with the environment of your company?

3. Is your strategy consistent with the internal strengths, objectives, policies, resources, and personal values of managers and employees?

4. Does your strategy balance the acceptance of minimum risk with the maximum profit potential consistent with your company's resources and propsects?

5. Does your strategy fit a niche in the market which is not now filled by others? Is this niche likely to remain open to you for a long enough time to return your capital investment plus a required profit?

6. Does the strategy under review conflict with other strategies in your company?

7. Is the strategy under evaluation divided into substrategies which interrelate properly?

8. Has the strategy been tested by developing subplans for an extended period of time in the future which appear to be acceptable and doable?

9. Has the strategy been tested with appropriate criteria such as consistency with past, present, and prospective trends; risk analysis; return on investment criteria; and so on?

10. Does strategy fit the life cycle of each product?

11. Is the timing of your strategy correct?

12. Does your strategy pit you against a powerful competitor? If so, reconsider very carefully your position.

13. Does your strategy leave you vulnerable to the power of one major customer? If so, reconsider very carefully.

14. Does your strategy involve the production of a new product for a new market? If so, reconsider very carefully.

15. Does your strategy follow that of a strong competitor? If so, reconsider carefully.

16. Are you rushing a revolutionary product to market? If so, reconsider carefully.

17. Do you really have an honest and accurate appraisal of your competition? Are you underestimating your competition?

18. Is your market share (present and/or prospective) sufficient to be competitive and make an acceptable profit?

19. Does your company have the financial resources to achieve a targeted market share? If it does not have the resources now, can it get them at an acceptable cost?

20. If your strategy seeks an enlarged market share, is it likely to be stopped by the Antitrust Division of the Department of Justice?

21. Is it possible that other federal government agencies will prevent your achieving the objectives sought by your strategy?

22. Is your organizational structure consistent with your strategy?

23. Can the strategy be implemented in an efficient and effective fashion?

24. Is your strategy acceptable to the major constituents of your company?

25. Is your strategy legal and in conformance with moral and ethical codes of conduct applicable to your company?

odic basis, such as once a year, the process is a *continuous* activity of top management, as illustrated in Fig. P-8. Top management cannot, of course, develop a strategic plan once a year and forget strategy in the meantime.

Another important characteristic of strategic planning, as compared with medium-range and short-range planning, is that the results are not usually neatly incorporated in a prescribed form. Medium-range and short-range planning results in numbers for specific functions for a prescribed period of time, as shown in Fig. P-4. Strategic planning covers any element of the business which is important at the time of analysis and embodies details which are of sufficient scope and depth to provide the necessary basis for implementation. The format for strategic plans generally is much more flexible, and varying in content from time to time, than for other types of plans.

**Medium-Range Programming and Programs** Medium-range programming is the process whereby specific functional plans are related for specific numbers of years to display the details of how strategies are to be carried out to achieve long-range objectives and company missions. There are two general methods employed in this process:

1. Functional plans for an entire department or division are interrelated for a specific number of years. The typical planning period is 5 years, but there is a tendency for more technically advanced companies to plan ahead for 7 or more years. Also, as environments become more uncertain and turbulent, there is the reverse tendency to reduce the number of years for functional integrated planning. In most companies the medium-range plans cover only a few major functions and are quantified on comparatively simple forms, as shown in Fig. P-4. In most companies the functional plans are translated into financial terms on a pro forma profit and loss statement, as shown in Fig. P-5. Sometimes a pro forma balance sheet is also prepared.

2. A second approach is to develop medium-range or tactical plans in detail only for major specific program strategies, such as the development of a new product or the penetration of a new market.[16] For new construction, detailed forms are often completed to show specific tactical plans related to it.

**Short-Range Planning and Plans** The next step, of course, is to develop short-range plans on the basis of the medium-range plans. In about half the companies that do formal planning the numbers for the first year of the medium-range plans are the same as in the short-range yearly operational budget summaries. Some companies feel that tightly linking budgets and medium-range plans will help to make long-range plans realistic. Others feel that a close relationship will divert attention from the long-range to current matters, such as return on invest-

| Item | Last year | This year forecast | Next five years | | | | |
|---|---|---|---|---|---|---|---|
| | | | First year | Second year | Third year | Fourth year | Fifth year |
| Sales | | | | | | | |
| Marketing expenditures | | | | | | | |
|    Advertising | | | | | | | |
|    Distribution | | | | | | | |
| Unit production | | | | | | | |
| Employees | | | | | | | |
|    Total | | | | | | | |
|    Direct | | | | | | | |
|    Indirect | | | | | | | |
| R&D outlays | | | | | | | |
|    New products | | | | | | | |
|    Product improvement | | | | | | | |
|    Cost reduction | | | | | | | |
| New facilities (total) | | | | | | | |
|    Expansion of present product | | | | | | | |
|    New products | | | | | | | |
|    Cost reduction | | | | | | | |
|    Maintenance | | | | | | | |

**Fig. P-4. Matrix for development of a divisional five-year plan.**

ment. This is especially so if a manager's compensation is based principally on yearly return-on-investment performance.

The current operating budgets will, of course, be in very great detail compared with the numbers in the medium-range plans. Many more subjects will be covered according to what management wishes to control in the short run.

While strategic and medium-range plans provide the framework within which short-range planning is done, the different types of short-range plans that can be affected cover a wide range, including plant location, layout of facilities, work methods, inventory plans and control, employee training, job enrichment, management education, and negotiations with unions.

**Translating Strategic Plans into Current Decisions** Figure P-6 shows that corporate strategies can be reflected immediately in current plans or used as a basis for the development of medium-range plans, which in turn are the basis for annual or shorter plans. In a divisionalized company where there is decentralized authority, the general manager will be obliged to make studies of the environment for his or her product. This information will be used, with whatever directions received from headquarters about objectives and strategies, to make medium-range plans. Thus there should be a close linkage between top management objectives and strategies, and subobjectives and substrategies forged by the division manager.

Details of the 1-year budget are considerably different from the main categories of the 5-year plans. The two can be the same, but the budget is more concerned with coordination and control of critical internal flows of resources.

**Planning Studies and Feasibility Testing** Planning studies can, of course, be made throughout the planning process. Such studies, essential in examining the environment, are also important in analyzing matters of current inventory replacement policy or suitability of the present organization for planning.

Feasibility testing takes place throughout the planning spectrum. For instance, when lower-level managers are examining different alternative choices, one may comment, "Method A has great profit potential, but I do not think top management would like to use this method." The manager is obviously applying a feasibility test by appraising an alternative against the values of top management, as the manager understands them. At lower levels, the testing can become completely quantitative and sometimes very sophisticated, as for instance in the use of a linear programming model to test distribution routes for products to their markets.

**Review and Evaluation** There is nothing that produces better plans on the part of subordinates than for the top managers to show a keen interest in the plans and the results that they bring. When comprehensive formal planning was first developed, there was a tendency to make written plans and not redo them until they became clearly obsolete. Now, the great majority of companies go through an annual cycle of comprehensive planning in which the plans are reviewed and revised.

**Planning Tools** The range of tools available for making "rational" decisions in the planning process is very broad. It covers a spectrum from nonquantitative tools, such as intuition, judgment, and hunches, to very complex and highly sophisticated methods such as systems analysis and computer simulation. In between are older quantitative tools such as conventional accounting techniques and newer quantitative methods such as probability theory and linear programming.

There are several points about the use of planning tools that should be emphasized. First, the applicability of different tools varies greatly depending upon where and when they are applied in the planning process. For example, a sophisticated quantitative forecasting technique, such as exponential smoothing, is not very effective in making a forecast with great unknowns, such as the market for aspirin in China. Second, it is very important for technicians to use their methods to solve major business problems for managers rather than to try to find problems which their tools can solve easily. Third, there is growing use of more sophisticated quantitative tools at higher levels of corporate planning. For

Division: _____

| | This year | 19__ | 19__ | 19__ | 19__ | 19__ |
|---|---|---|---|---|---|---|
| Sales—units Gross sales—dollars Allowances | | | | | | |
| Net sales | | | | | | |
| Cost of goods sold | | | | | | |
| Gross profit on sales | | | | | | |
| G & A expense Selling expense Advertising expense R & D expense | | | | | | |
| Total operating expense | | | | | | |
| Other charges, net | | | | | | |
| Interest on long—term obligations Other | | | | | | |
| Income before depreciation Depreciation | | | | | | |
| Income before overhead allocation | | | | | | |
| Allocation of general overhead | | | | | | |
| Net income before taxes | | | | | | |
| Rate of return on assets | | | | | | |

**Fig. P-5. Form for income statement projection.**

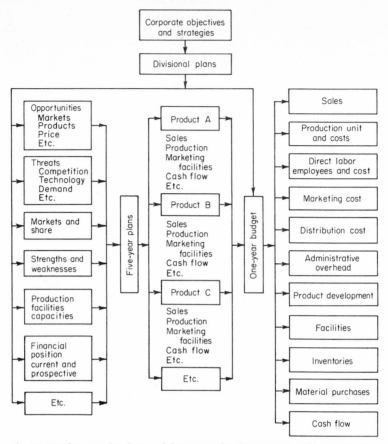

**Fig. P-6. Development of medium- and short-range plans from strategic and long-range plans.**

instance, computer simulation and risk analysis is being used widely in strategic planning.[17] Most of the computer simulation models are deterministic: they answer "what if" types of questions. But, increasingly, probability theory is being used in top-level decision making, as for instance David Hertz's risk analysis.[18] Fourth, the higher up the management level a decision is made and the more important that decision is to the organization, the more significant, generally, the nonquantifiable criteria are in making the decision. Finally, there is no substitute for the ability to ask the right question.

## ORGANIZING THE FORMAL PLANNING PROCESS

There is no single method, formula, or standard way to start and conduct a formal corporate planning system. What is done is a function of such factors as managerial style, size of organization, whether the firm is centralized or decentralized, managerial authority extended to decentralized managers, types of problems the company faces, managerial knowledge, types of products, and other comparable factors. So each system is fitted to each company.

**Four Approaches to Systems Design** There are four fundamentally different approaches to doing formal planning.

*Top-Down Approach.* Comprehensive planning in a centralized company is done at the top of the corporation, and departments and outlying activities develop plans, if any, within specific constraints. In a decentralized company the flow of activity is shown in Fig. P-7. The president gives guidelines to the divisions and asks for plans. The plans are reviewed at headquarters and sent back to the divisions for modification or with a note of acceptance.

If the division plans do not achieve objectives sought by top management, additional plans are made at the corporate level for acquisitions, divestment, or refinancing.

*Bottom-Up Approach.* In this approach, the top management gives the division no guidelines and asks them to submit plans. Information such as the following may be requested: major opportunities and threats, major objectives, strategies to achieve the objectives, and specific data on sales, profits, market share sought, capital requirements, and number of employees for a specified number of years. This then is reviewed at top management levels and the same process as noted above is followed.

*Combination Approach.* A third method is a mixture of the top-down and bottom-up approach. This is the method used in most large decentralized companies. Top management gives guidelines to the divisions: generally, they are broad enough to permit the divisions a good bit of flexibility in developing their own plans. Sometimes a top management may hammer out a basic objective by dialogue with division managers. Such objectives as return on investment may be derived in this way, especially if the performance of the division manager is measured upon the basis of this standard.

*Line Managers as Staff.* In smaller, centralized companies the chief executive will often use his or her main line managers as staff in helping to develop formal plans. In some very large companies the president will use line managers in the same fashion. In many companies the president meets with a group of executives on a regular basis to deal with all the problems facing the company. In some companies, part of the time of this group is spent on strategic planning. Over time the group will develop written long-range plans.

**Design Alternatives** Within each of these basic systems there are many alternatives which illustrates that there is great flexibility in designing systems to fit particular organizational characteristics. Ten major alternatives are as follows:

1. *Completeness of the system.* To follow the complete model shown in Fig. P-3 would be very demanding. When first starting formal planning, a company might decide only to develop a list of major opportunities and threats and then devise strategies to exploit the opportunities and avoid the threats. It might go a bit further and, skipping over medium-range planning, jump to making current budgets in light of these strategies.

2. *Depth of analysis.* When first starting a planning system, it is easy to overload the managerial and staff system with overdemanding analysis. This should not be done. For many planning data inputs and evaluations the best judgments of managers may be acceptable without rigorous staff research.

3. *Degree of formality.* Systems can be highly formalized and ritualistic or very informal. Designers have this choice.

4. *Linkage.* As noted earlier, the current budget numbers can be the same as the numbers in the first year of a 5-year plan. Or they can simply "reflect" the 5-year plan.

5. *Time horizons.* This choice is obvious.

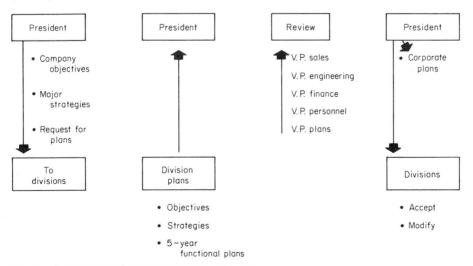

Fig. P-7. Planning systems design in a decentralized company.

6. *The corporate planner.* Organizations can determine whether or not a corporate planner is needed and what the functions of the job should be. If a corporate planner is appointed, he (or she) should report to the top management. His basic functions are to help others, particularly line managers, to do an effective planning job and to coordinate the plans developed by different parts of the organization when that is desirable. He may help top management formulate goals, policies, and strategies to guide the planning process. When plans are received from others he may help top management evaluate them. He may make forecasts for others to use, help weak divisions make plans, show others how to develop effective plans, assist top management in making current decisions on the basis of long-range planning, and make recommendations concerning product development. He does not assume responsibility for doing the planning for either the top management or other line managers. Long-range planning is a line function and cannot be delegated to staff.[19]

7. *Getting the system started.* It is not necessary to start the planning process as described in Fig. P-3. It can begin at many different points—a problem, a new product from research, a flash of managerial intuition, a study of the company's strategic profile, identification of a new opportunity or threat, systematic forecasting, and so on. But, however started, sooner or later all the blocks in Fig. P-3 should be explicitly or implicitly covered.

8. *Participation of people.* There are obviously many choices here about how people, whether line managers or staff, should get involved and what they should be doing in the planning system. Staff should not make plans for line managers, but there are degrees to which management may rely on staff help in making plans.

9. *The role of the chief executive officer.* Comprehensive planning is the responsibility of the chief executive officer. He or she can delegate parts of it but not the responsibility for it. How the chief executive officer does it, however, depends much upon personal managerial style. The design of a planning system will differ significantly depending upon whether the chief executive officer is authoritarian or permissive. Some top managers are their own corporate planners. Some managers welcome a cooperative atmosphere in decision making, while others are "loners."

10. *Time schedule.* The schedule for planning, of course, offers the opportunity for many choices. Figure P-8 shows a typical time schedule for comprehensive planning in a large decentralized company.

**Other Major Determinants of Systems Design**  Many other considerations influence systems design:

First, whenever an organization attempts to develop its first formal planning system every effort should be made to make the system very simple. After an organization, especially a large one, has had experience with formal planning the system can be more sophisticated.

Second, the formality of a system ranges from practically none (e.g., in a very small company with few employees and a manager who has neither the time nor the inclination to formalize planning) to a great deal (e.g., in a large decentralized corporation with much planning experience).

Third, corporations go through life cycles and, other things being equal, the planning system will

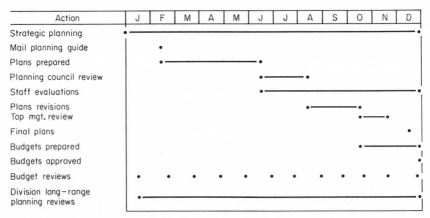

**Fig. P-8. Typical time schedule for planning in a comprehensive company.**

vary depending upon which stage it is in. To over-simplify, at first there will be very little, if any, formal planning. Then, as sales increase, it will be necessary to watch cash flows carefully, especially the changes taking place in current assets and liabilities. Later, with more growth, it may be necessary to integrate major functions more carefully to assure efficient production. Then additional products may be added to the line and divisions established. This will require a different management style and planning system.

Fourth, highly technical companies making products with long lead times will tend to have more formal systems than those producing fashion products with short life cycles.

Fifth, the more a manager depends on intuition and judgment and resists help in decision making, the less formality a system will have, assuming there is one.

Sixth, environment is a significant design determinant. Other things being equal, the more stable and certain the envisioned future environment for an organization is, the more formal and comprehensive the planning system may be. The more turbulent and uncertain the perceived environment is, the less formal and comprehensive the system will be and the more its managers will rely upon their intuition and judgment.

*Contingency Theory.* Each organization is unique, and each planning system differs from all others. The design of the system depends upon dominating characteristics in each situation. This is called the contingency theory.

**Principles in Starting Planning** There are also many important lessons of experience which bear consideration when starting a formal strategic planning system:

1. Do not start without a clear understanding of what long-range planning is and what you want it to do for your organization.

2. Prepare a planning guide.

3. Be sure the climate is appropriate for the first effort. This involves many things as, for example, a determination and commitment to get something useful out of the first effort. Managers should be encouraged to keep an open mind and to be willing to face unpleasant facts and have their judgments challenged. They should be persuaded that planning is valuable and necessary. Every effort should be made to provide a climate that encourages creativity and imagination. Stifling ritual and procedure should be avoided.

4. Make haste slowly. Do not try to do too much too quickly.

5. Make sure the system meets the critical needs of the chief executive officer and his or her top managers.

6. Make sure the system is tailored to the unique characteristics of the organization.

7. Plan for the real world: forget perfection.

8. Make sure the line managers, the doers, are dominant. Do not place too heavy reliance on staff.

9. Take care to avoid the 10 pitfalls which practitioners have identified as being most lethal to effective planning (*see* Table P-12).

## PLANNING AND PEOPLE

Planning collides with people when they are conceiving the idea to plan, organizing to do it, doing it, and implementing plans. Understanding and resolving people problems is a major key to successful planning. This is a large and complicated subject that has been underestimated in planning literature.[20] What follows is meant only to be illustrative.

**Antiplanning Forces** Newton's law that "for every force there is a counterforce" is applicable to planning. People resist planning with such excuses as: It is impossible to see the future so planning is futile. I do not have enough time to do my regular work, let alone planning. Long-range planning is too complicated for me.

Such excuses are often manifestations of deeper responses. Planning can give rise to vague feelings of discontent, inadequacy, and hostility. These forces can arise from many sources, such as changes that planning may bring about. For example, planning involves group activity and new groups may be formed, the relationships among which may not be clear. Planning may change the patterns of decision making, the flow of information, and the distribution of power. Dealing with ambiguities in planning may frustrate some people. Planning may alter the visions of people about the future of the company and their role in it. Many people are uneasy when dealing with unpleasant facts that planning may uncover, and considering these facts may be uncomfortable.

**Advancing the Interests of People** On the other hand, planning can improve, reinforce, and advance the interests of people. For example, in doing planning people have an opportunity to participate in the decision-making process, to deal with major problems of their organization which are of concern to them, to help in formulating objectives to be achieved, and to utilize their capabilities in a creative fashion. As a result of the planning process people in an organization may better understand the

A.    PITFALLS IN GETTING STARTED:

[1]*    1.    Top management's assumption that it can delegate the planning function to a planner.

2.    Rejecting planning because there has been success without it.

3.    Rejecting formal planning because the system failed in the past to foresee a critical problem and/or did not result in substantive decisions that satisfied top management.

4.    Assuming that the present body of knowledge about planning is insufficient to guide fruitful comprehensive planning.

5.    Assuming that a company cannot develop effective long-range planning in a way appropriate to its re-sources and needs.

6.    Assuming that comprehensive corporate planning can be introduced into a company and overnight miracu-lous results will appear.

7.    Thinking that a successful corporate plan can be moved from one company to another without change and with equal success.

8.    Assuming that a formal system can be introduced into a company without an "agonizing reappraisal" of current managerial practices and decision-making processes.

9.    Ignoring the power structure of a company in organiz-ing the planning process.

10.    Failure to develop a clear understanding of the long-range planning procedure before the process is actually undertaken.

[6]    11.    Failure to create a climate in the company which is congenial and not resistant to planning.

12.    Failing to locate the corporate planner at a high enough level in the managerial hierarchy.

13.    Failure to make sure that the planning staff has the necessary qualities of leadership, technical expertise, and personality to discharge properly its responsibili-ties in making the planning system effective.

B.    PITFALLS RELATED TO A MISUNDERSTAND-ING OF THE NATURE OF LONG-RANGE PLANNING:

14.    Forgetting that planning is a political, a social, and an organizational, as well as a rational, process.

[7]    15.    Assuming that corporate comprehensive planning is something separate from the entire management process.

16.    Failure to make sure that top management and major line officers really understand the nature of long-range planning and what it will accomplish for them and the company.

17.    Failing to understand that systematic formal planning and intuitive (opportunistic, or entrepreneurial) plan-ning are complementary.

18.    Assuming that plans can be made by staff planners for line managers to implement.

19.    Ignoring the fact that planning is and should be a learning process.

20.    Assuming that planning is easy.

21.    Assuming that planning is hard.

22.    Assuming that long-range planning can get a company out of a current crisis.

23.    Assuming that long-range planning is only strategic planning, or just planning for a major product, or simply looking ahead at likely development of present product. (In other words, failing to see that compre-hensive planning is an integrated managerial system.)

C.    PITFALLS IN DOING LONG-RANGE PLANNING:
*Managerial involvement*

[2]    24.    Top management becomes so engrossed in current problems that it spends insufficient time on long-range planning, and the process becomes discredited among other managers and staff.

25.    Long-range planning becomes unpopular because top management spends so much time on long-range prob-lems that it ignores short-range problems.

[4]    26.    Failure to assure the necessary involvement in the plan-ning process of major line personnel.

27.    Too much centralization of long-range planning in the central headquarters so that divisions feel little respon-sibility for developing effective plans.

*The Process of planning*

[3]    28.    Failure to develop company goals suitable as a basis for formulating long-range plans.

29.    Assuming that equal weight should be given to all elements of planning (i.e., that the same emphasis should be placed on strategic as on tactical planning, or that the same emphasis should be accorded to major functional plans).

[8]    30.    Injecting so much formality into the system that it lacks flexibility, looseness, and simplicity, and restrains creativity.

31.    Inability to avoid over-optimism and/or over-cautious-ness in committing resources.

32.    Extrapolating rather than rethinking the entire process in each cycle (i.e., if plans are made for 1972 through 1976, adding 1977 in the 1973 cycle rather than redoing all plans from 1973 to 1977).

33.    Developing such a reverence for numbers that irrever-ence for intuition and value judgments predominates the thinking going into planning.

34.    Seeking precision of numbers throughout the planning horizon.

35.    Assuming that older methods to choose from among alternatives should be discarded in favor of newer techniques.

36.    Assuming that new quantitative techniques are not as useful as advertised.

37.    Doing long-range planning periodically and forgetting it in between cycles.

*Creditability of results*

38.    Failure to develop planning capabilities in major oper-ating units.

39.    Failure of top management, and/or the planning staff, to give departments and divisions sufficient informa-tion and guidance (e.g., top management interests, environmental projections, etc.)

40.    Attempting to do too much in too short a time.

41.    Failure to secure that minimum of system and informa-tion to make the process and its results creditable and useful.

D.    PITFALLS IN USING LONG-RANGE PLANS:

[9]    42.    Failure of top management to review with departmen-tal and divisional heads the long-range plans which they have developed.

43.    Forgetting that the fundamental purpose of the exer-cises is to make better current decisions.

44.    Assuming that plans once made are in the nature of blueprints and should be followed rigorously until changed in the next planning cycle.

[10]    45.    Top management's consistently rejecting the formal planning mechanism by making intuitive decisions which conflict with the formal plans.

46.    Assuming that, because plans must result in current decisions, it is the short-term that counts and planning efforts should concentrate on the short-run.

[5]    47.    Failing to use plans as standards for measuring manage-rial performance.

48.    Forgetting to apply a cost-benefit analysis to the system to make sure advantages are greater than costs.

49.    Failing to encourage managers to do good long-range planning by basing reward solely on short-range per-formance measures.

50.    Failing to exploit the fact that formal planning is a managerial process which can be used to improve man-agerial capabilities throughout a company.

*Indicates this is the most important pitfall to be avoided. [2] is the second most important one to avoid, and so on.

thinking of top managers and their part in implementing major policy and strategy decisions.

**Offsetting Antiplanning Biases** There are many things that can be done to assure that people overcome their planning biases and show acceptance and perhaps enthusiasm. Observers have noted a close correlation between top-management involvement and successful planning. Management should also make sure that the process of planning is suitable to the unique characteristics of the organization, that planning achieves benefits greater than the costs, that the requirements of planning are achievable without excessive frustrations and work load, and that there is widespread understanding and acceptance of the process.

Many companies have found that a top-level planning committee is effective in meeting some of these requirements. Such committees are composed of main line and staff managers. The head of the committee is the top executive or the next in command, and the secretary is a director of corporate planning, if the organization has such a person.

It should be noted, finally, that successful comprehensive corporate planning is not likely where the management, overall, is weak and ineffective. Poor managers do not make strong planners.

## CONTINGENCY PLANS

Contingency plans are advance preparations for dealing with emergencies not considered in the regular planning process. The regular planning process is based upon the most probable events. Events considered less probable, however, may take place without warning, can visit disasterous consequences upon an organization, and demand swift and sure management action.

The approach is to ask the question, "What if . . . ?" What if our major competitor unexpectedly makes a 25 percent cut in the price of the product with which we directly compete? What if the only plant we have producing one-of-a-kind ball bearings for our fractional horsepower motors is completely destroyed by fire?

Contingency planning should identify possible emergency situations which management can and should do something about. Feasible defensive strategies should be determined. The most desirable strategies should then be identified and any desired tactical plans should be made.

There is no uniform content of contingency plans. The Conference Board surveyed corporations concerning their contingency plans and has reproduced several different types.[21]

## BENEFITS FROM LONG-RANGE PLANNING

Comprehensive formal long-range planning has been growing in use throughout the world simply because managers find that it is valuable. There are many reasons why this is so.

1. The times demand it. Business environment is changing faster and becoming much more turbulent. In the product area, for instance, the typical life cycle is shrinking rapidly; but the average research and development time is lengthening and the costs to prototype are increasing. Technological threats to products are growing in numbers and coming from areas other than the industry to which they are related. Everyone is aware of shifting population movements, more and highly complex government regulations, changing consumer demands, and many other forces which make the evolving environment at one and the same time a world of opportunity and threat to every company.

2. Long-range planning is essential to discharging top management's responsibilities. Some companies, with job descriptions for their chief executive officer, say explicitly the chief executive is the chief planner of the company.

3. Planning enables a company to make a written simulation of the future. If the company does not like what it sees it erases and starts over. This is much less expensive than letting the future evolve on an ad hoc basis. It forces a company to set objectives and clarifies future opportunities and threats. It links decision making between top and lower-level managers. It sets standards of performance.

4. Formal planning asks and answers some very significant questions for a manager, such as: What is our basic line of business? What are the company's long-range objectives? What products are or are not going to be obsolete? How shall we replace these products and when? What will our cash flow be over the next few years? What and where are our markets? What share of the market do we wish to get? How will we get it?

5. Long-range planning is a new and significant communications system. It permits people to participate in the decision-making process. People are more adaptable to change because they participate in making the change. It is a learning and mind-stretching exercise that increasingly is being recognized as a major tool for training managers.

6. Recent studies are providing concrete evidence that long-range planning helps produce superior performance.[22] Of course, superior perfor-

mance is not directly attributable to formal long-range planning but is the result of the entire range of managerial capabilities. In general terms, however, superior managements know how to develop planning systems to suit their needs. When this is done, the entire process of management is strengthened.

In sum, there are two types of benefits derived from comprehensive long-range planning—substantive and behavioral. Either set should be sufficient to convince management of its value. When both are considered it is easy to see why formal long-range planning has been introduced into most medium-sized and larger companies.

## LIMITS OF FORMAL PLANNING

Comprehensive corporate planning is not, of course, without its shortcomings. There are intrinsic shortcomings of planning. For example, long-range plans may not turn out well sometimes because of unexpected changes in the environment. Of fundamental importance, also, is the fact that long-range planning is virtually worthless in getting a company out of a major current crisis. Planning requires a certain type of creative talent, which must exist in an organization for it to be effective. Planning initiates antiplanning biases. Finally, planning cannot replace intuitive brilliance.

## PITFALLS IN COMPREHENSIVE FORMAL PLANNING

There are also imposed shortcomings of formal planning. Most of them can be described in terms of 50 major common pitfalls to be avoided in starting, doing, and implementing long-range planning (Table P-12). A survey of 215 respondents concluded that these were, indeed, the most important pitfalls to be avoided if planning was to be effective. This survey asked correspondents to identify the 10 most important pitfalls to be avoided. Their rankings are shown in brackets in Table P-12. Respondents were asked whether their organizations had fallen in a significant way into any of the listed pitfalls. They were also asked whether they were satisfied or dissatisfied with their planning process. There was a high correlation between dissatisfaction with planning and having fallen into one or more of the top most lethal traps to be avoided.[23]

## STRATEGIC PLANNING IN NOT-FOR-PROFIT ORGANIZATIONS

A substantial part of what has been presented here is applicable to planning in the not-for-profit sector. There are significant similarities among organiza-

910

tions in both sectors. There are, however, major differences, and no comparison of the two will be made here. As in business, however, each situation is unique and, therefore, the planning system will be unique.

Introducing and maintaining a strategic planning system in a typical public not-for-profit organization is considerably more complex and difficult than in the typical private profit organization. But lessons of planning in the private sector have been applied to the public sector, for example, the planning-program-budgeting system of the federal government,[24] a town,[25] a church,[26] and hospitals.[27] The methodology can be applied to personal lifetime planning.[28]

*See also* AUDITS, MANAGEMENT; BUDGETS AND BUDGET PREPARATION; DECISION-MAKING PROCESS; NETWORK PLANNING METHODS; OBJECTIVES AND GOALS; PLANNING, PLANNED MANAGEMENT OF TURBULENT CHANGE; PLANNING, STRATEGIC PLANNING MODELS; POLICY FORMULATION AND DEVELOPMENT; PROGRAM PLANNING AND IMPLEMENTATION.

## NOTES
[1]This entry is adapted from George A. Steiner, *Comprehensive Managerial Planning*, Planning Executives Institute, Oxford, Ohio, 1971; and ———, "Comprehensive Managerial Planning," in Joseph W. McGuire, (ed.), *Contemporary Management: Issues and Viewpoints*, Prentice-Hall, Inc., Englewood Cliffs, N.J., 1974, chap. 12.

[2]George A. Steiner, *Top Management Planning*, The Macmillan Company, New York, 1969, pp. 353–355.

[3]Henry Mintzberg, "Planning on the Left Side and Managing on the Right," *Harvard Business Review*, July–August 1976.

[4]See, for example, Robert N. Anthony, *Planning and Control Systems: A Framework for Analysis*, Graduate School of Business, Harvard University, Boston, 1952; Frank Gilmore and R. G. Brandenberg, "Anatomy of Corporate Planning," *Harvard Business Review*, vol. 40, November–December 1962, pp. 61–69; and Robert F. Stewart, "A Framework for Business Planning," Stanford Research Institute, Long Range Planning Service, Report No. 162, Menlo Park, Calif., February 1963.

[5]Bertram M. Gross, "The Matrix of Purposes," *The Managing of Organizations*, vol. II, The Free Press, New York, 1964, chap. 19.

[6]Steiner, *Top Management Planning*, pp. 37–41.

[7]Edward N. Cole, "Management Priorities for the 1970's," *Michigan Business Review*, vol. XXII, July 1970, p. 1. *See also Social Responsibilities of Business Corporations*, Committee for Economic Development, New York, June 1971; and George A. Steiner, *Business and Society*, 2d ed., Random House, Inc., New York, 1975, chap. 10.

[8]Marritt L. Kastens, *Long-Range Planning for your Business*, American Management Association, New York, 1976, pp. 52–53.

[9]Theodore Cohn and Roy A. Lindberg, *Survival & Growth: Management Strategies for the Small Firm*, American Management Association, New York, 1974, pp. 52–53.

[10]Charles H. Granger, "The Hierarchy of Objectives," *Harvard Business Review*, May–June 1964.

[11]Stewart Thompson, *Management Creeds and Philosophies*, American Management Association, 1958.

[12]Peter F. Drucker, *The Practice of Management*, Harper & Brothers New York, 1954, p. 63.

[13]George A. Steiner, and John B. Miner, "The Nature of Policy/Strategy," *Management Policy and Strategy*, Macmillan Publishing Co., Inc., New York, 1977, chap. II.

[14]George A. Steiner, *Strategic Factors in Business Success*, Financial Executives Research Foundation, New York, 1969.

[15]William H. Newman, "Shaping the Master Strategy of Your Firm," *California Management Review*, Spring 1967.

[16]Rochelle O. O'Connor, *Corporate Guides to Long-Range Planning*, The Conference Board Inc., New York, 1976.

[17]James B. Boulden, *Computer-Assisted Planning Systems*, McGraw-Hill Book Company, New York, 1975.

[18]David B. Hertz, *New Power for Management*, McGraw-Hill Book Company, New York, 1969.

[19]George A. Steiner, "Rise of the Corporate Planner," *Harvard Business Review*, vol. 48, September–October 1970, pp. 133–139; and Richard F. Vancil, "So You're Going to Have a Planning Department!" *Harvard Business Review*, vol. 45, May–June 1967, pp. 88–96.

[20]A major exception is David W. Ewing, *The Human Side Of Planning*, The Macmillan Company, New York, 1969.

[21]O'Connor, op. cit.

[22]Stanley S. Thune and Robert J. House, "Where Long-Range Planning Pays Off," *Business Horizons*, August 1970; H. Igor Ansoff et al., "Does Planning Pay?" *Long Range Planning*, December 1970; L. W. Rue and R. M. Fulmer, "Is Long-Range Planning Profitable?" *Proceedings of the Business Policy and Planning Division of the Academy of Management*, Annual Meeting of the Academy of Management, Boston, 1968; Delmar Karger, "Long Range Planning and Organizational Performance," *Long Range Planning*, December 1975.

[23]George A. Steiner and Schollhammer, "Pitfalls in Comprehensive Long-Range Planning: A Comparative Multi-National Survey," *Long Range Planning*, April 1975.

[24]W. DeWoolfson, Jr., *Pitfalls in Planning-Programming-Budgeting Systems*, Doctoral Dissertation, Graduate School of Administration, University of California, Irvine, 1974.

[25]Roger E. Paine, "Corporate Planning for a Town—A Case History," *Long Range Planning*, October 1975.

[26]David E. Hussey, "Corporate Planning for a Church," *Long Range Planning*, April 1974.

[27]Joseph P. Peters, *Concept/Commitment/Action*, A joint publication of the United Hospital Fund of New York and the Health and Hospital Planning Council of Southern New York, Inc., 1974.

[28]George A. Steiner, "Invent Your Own Future," *California Management Review*, Fall 1976.

## REFERENCES

Ackoff, Russell L.: *A Concept of Corporate Planning*, Wiley-Interscience, a division of John Wiley & Sons, Inc., New York, 1970.

Argenti, John: *Corporate Planning: A Practical Guide*, Dow Jones-Irwin, Inc., Homewood, Ill., 1969.

Bower, Marvin: *The Will to Manage*, McGraw-Hill Book Company, New York, 1966.

Cleland, David I. and William R. King: "Developing a Planning Culture for Effective Strategic Planning," *Long Range Planning*, June 1974, p. 70.

Drucker, Peter F.: *Management: Tasks, Responsibilities, Practices*, Harper & Row, Publishers, Incorporated, New York, 1974.

Harrison, E. Frank: *The Managerial Decision-Making Process*, Houghton Mifflin Company, Boston, 1975.

Hofer, Charles W.: "Research on Strategic Planning: A Survey of Past Studies and Suggestions for Future Efforts," *Journal of Economics and Business*, Spring–Summer 1976.

Hofer, Charles W.: "Toward A Contingency Theory of Business Strategy," *Academy of Management Journal*, December 1975.

Hussey, David E.: *Corporate Planning: Theory and Practice*, Pergamon Press, New York, 1974.

Jones, Harry: *Preparing Company Plans*, Gower Press Limited, Epping, Essex, England, 1974.

Mockler, Robert J.: *Business Planning and Policy Formulation*, Appleton-Century-Crofts, Inc., New York, 1972.

Steiner, George A.: *Pitfalls in Comprehensive Long-Range Planning*, Planning Executives Institute, Oxford, Ohio, 1972.

Special reference should be made to *Long Range Planning*, published by Pergamon Press Ltd. on behalf of the Society for Long Range Planning, Terminal House, Grosvenor Gardens, London. It is the only journal in the world devoted exclusively to long-range planning.

GEORGE A. STEINER, *University of California, Los Angeles*

## Planning, strategic marketing (*See* MARKETING, CONCEPTS AND SYSTEMS.)

## Planning, strategic planning models

Strategic planning involves an examination of a company's current operations and a determination of where the company wants to be 2, 3, 5, or even 10 years in the future. It is a means of assuring that a company will be viable over the long term and that current short-term efforts are consistent with long-term objectives.

Many variables, both internal and external to the company, can affect future planning. This makes it extremely difficult to consider them in a realistic time frame using conventional techniques. As a result, more and more companies are turning to computer models to assist them in the planning process.

## THE STRATEGIC PLANNING MODEL

A strategic planning model is a representation of actual or projected conditions reduced to computer format; it is used to answer "what if" questions and to test the effects of alternative courses of action. Such models can represent worldwide conditions such as the controversial Club of Rome model which forecast an early depletion of world resources; they can be national in scope such as the Wharton School and other United States econometric models; or they can be restricted to a specific market segment, company, or area of business within a company.

**Coping with Complexity**   Planning is a prerequisite to effective management. There are countless examples of well-known companies neglecting this basic precept; most no longer exist. The interrelationships of the many variables found in the business environment today are difficult to visualize and evaluate with normal analytical techniques. The cost of trial and error is, of course, prohibitive. Consequently, because of time constraints and the great amount of internal and external data that must be manipulated, companies turn frequently to the computer as a tool to assist in the evaluation of alternative courses of action.

**Basic Requirements**   There are a number of basic guidelines that should be considered. The following are critical:

1. Management must actively participate in model development with regard to such things as (*a*) understanding fully what is being done; (*b*) identifying specific questions that must be answered; (*c*) identifying expected results and the types of recommendations that might be forthcoming; (*d*) establishing basic assumptions, limits to the analysis, and realistic possibilities for changes in policy; (*e*) determining the practicality of study results; and (*f*) understanding the implications of study results.

2. The type of strategic planning model that is selected must be appropriate to the problem under study and the decision-making environment.

3. The model selected must fit the needs of the company. These needs should not be modified significantly to fit a specific model. This means, in many instances, that a "canned" model cannot be utilized, or if one is utilized, it must be drastically altered to meet the specific requirements of the company.

4. In choosing a model, the company must be careful not to "reinvent the wheel." It must determine what has been done before by others and build from there.

5. Realistic time and cost parameters must be established for completion of the analysis. These must be reasonable in view of the results that are expected.

## MODELING TECHNIQUES

Computer analytical (or modeling) techniques differ, of course, but all of them can be placed into three basic categories: (1) simulation, (2) linear programming, and (3) heuristic or specialized analytical techniques. The following describes each of these and its potential.

**Simulation**   This technique is aimed at depicting a given system and determining how it will operate under various conditions. It converts a system or operation to computer format. In effect, a simulation model represents a specific system and tests how it might vary under actual operating conditions. The major drawback of simulation is that it does not provide an optimal answer for the problem being studied. It does, however, permit evaluation in greater detail over time than almost any other modeling technique available.

Problems associated with simulation also include:

1. Difficulty in answering "what if" questions.

2. The length of time required to establish a truly useful model. It can take 6 months or more to solve a typical problem.

3. It can be more costly than other techniques.

4. Even after the analysis is completed, the user cannot be sure that the best answer has been found.

Computer simulations have been used to test such things as automated warehouse material handling systems, complex plant operations, and the market impact of various promotional strategies.

Some of the simulation models available include general purpose systems simulation (GPSS) and distribution system simulation (DSS), both available from IBM, and long-range environmental planning simulator (LREPS).[1,2]

**Linear Programming**   This technique includes such variations as mixed integer programming and separable programming. It has been applied in a practical way to strategic planning problems by a number of companies. One of its main attractions is that it can achieve an optimum solution and evaluate the sensitivity of the solution to changes in various factors. Linear programming can also be utilized to describe fairly accurately costs and other factors that are nonlinear. An example of this would be in warehouse applications where cost per unit of throughput typically decreases as volumes through a warehouse increase.

Some of the major drawbacks with linear programming and its allied techniques are:

1. Difficulty in understanding why a given solution is optimum.

2. The need for an "expert" to formulate the problems, who may not fully understand management needs.

3. The high cost of obtaining a solution. Typical solutions for distribution problems can cost as much as $500 to $800 per run.

4. Limitations to the size of the problem it can solve.

Within these limitations, linear programming has been used successfully for such varying applications as facility planning (described in Case No. 1 at the end of this entry), classical product-ingredient mix problems, and allocation of company resources such as advertising dollars.[3,4,5]

**Heuristic and Other "Customized" Methods**  Heuristic and related empirical techniques provide a trial and error extension of management thinking and can incorporate all significant parameters required to solve specific problems. While they do not always result in a strictly optimal solution, they generally provide a solution that is optimal within the practical limits of the available data. Models using these techniques can be designed to fit a particular business need and can be readily understood by management because of the way they are constructed. These methods have certain other advantages. They are:

1. Excellent for addressing "what if" questions.

2. Usable with nonlinear data.

3. Interactive with the user so that modifications can be made to basic parameters for evaluating sensitivity.

4. Relatively easy to construct and change basic parameters.

5. Cheap and quick to run. Typical runs of simple models will cost $25 to $75 on a large computer (i.e., IBM 370-158). Consequently, many different assumptions and variations can be evaluated at a minimum cost.

6. Capable of being combined, where required, with simulation and linear programming. For example, the output from a heuristic program can be used as input to a simulation to obtain more detail on the effect of the proposed solution on the system. The output can also be used as input to a linear program to further refine the data. While such combinations will increase the running cost, this cost is generally less than the cost of a straight linear programming solution.[6]

## APPLICATION PRINCIPALS

Development and application of strategic models will generally achieve a high degree of success if the following basic rules are adhered to:

1. Keep the program simple. Do not incorporate anything in the model for which the answer is obvious.

2. Develop the program in modules—do not create one large monster.

3. Where possible, tie in with other programs in the company.

4. Be sure managers and other users realize that they must be continually involved. For example, anticipate the need for verification of data and other factors before they are utilized by the model.

5. Define the areas where the model is to be applied. Include a precise list of questions to be answered. Check continually during the model development phase to be sure these questions have not changed or should not be changed. If it appears that change is required, be sure management concurs.

6. Schedule specific progress review dates. Prepare satisfactory explanations for any modifications.

7. Be sure output formats are readily understandable and in conformance with general company practice for similar reports.

8. Develop exception reports where feasible.

9. Be sure there is a complete audit trail for all information put into the model and coming from it.

10. Be sure to document (a) the objective and scope of what is to be done, (b) major assumptions, (c) design, (d) project schedule, (e) any interim changes or modifications to basic rules, and (f) each step of the process so that others can use them in the future.

## SPECIFIC USES OF STRATEGIC PLANNING MODELS

As noted previously, strategic planning models have been used for everything from analysis of the national economy under various assumptions to evaluation of market strategy including competitive reactions, the effect of new product introductions, and the likely effectiveness of alternative strategies to increase market share. The most widespread use of models, however, occurs in facility planning and related activities. This is the area in which modeling has most nearly achieved maturity. The balance of this entry describes two typical applications in this general area.

**Case No. 1: Distribution Facilities**  A heuristic model of this type has been used for a number of companies that have these basic characteristics:

> 10 to 15 plants
> 50 to 200 warehouses
> 10 to 25 product groups
> 120 customer demand areas
> Up to 7 different transportation modes

*Model Objectives.*  A typical objective would be to determine the number and location of production and distribution facilities, required inventory levels at each location, and the distribution patterns necessary to meet customer service objectives at minimum operating cost. Figure P-9 shows a generalized picture of this kind of model.

This type of model frequently answers questions such as the following:

Where should manufacturing plants be located? How many plants should there be?

Which products should be manufactured at each plant?

How many warehouses should there be in the system?

Where should these warehouses be located?

Which plants should service each warehouse with which products?

Which plants and warehouses should service which customers with which products?

How much inventory of each product is required at each point in the system (i.e., at plants and warehouses)?

Which modes of transportation should be utilized from plants to warehouses and from warehouses to customers?

Which costs are involved in moving products from plants to warehouses to customers?

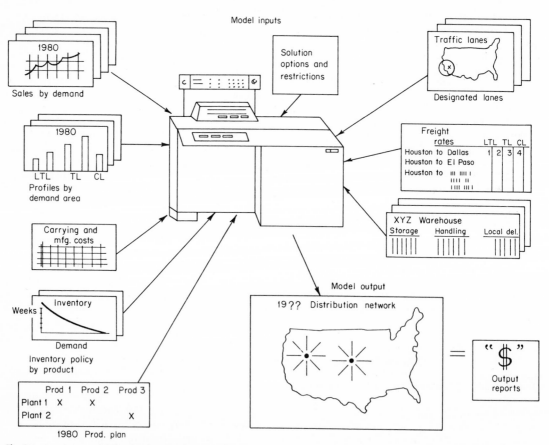

**Fig. P-9. A systems model for planning distribution facilities.**

What effect might capacity limitations at plants and warehouses have on the optimal solution and what alternatives are practical considering such limitations?

*Cost Elements.* In general, such models consider the following cost elements:

1. Manufacturing costs of each product at each plant as these costs vary over a range of throughput volumes

2. Inventory carrying costs by product at plants and warehouses

3. Handling costs by product at plants and warehouses

4. Storage costs at stocking points

5. Freight costs from plants to warehouses and from plants to warehouses and customers

These costs are generally nonlinear; that is, unit costs are lower for higher volumes, as shown in Fig. P-10.

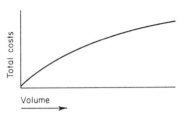

**Fig. P-10. Example of nonlinear warehouse costs.**

*Options.* A number of options are available with this type of model. These include:

Allowing or disallowing individual products to be produced at specific plants

Allowing or disallowing individual products to be stocked at specific warehouses

Establishing different capacity limitations by product at each plant and warehouse

Establishing different customer service levels at individual distribution points

Specifying different customer-demand volumes of individual products by area to measure the effect of growth on costs

Varying unit costs with changes in volume for handling and storage of inventory and for inventory carrying costs

*Output Reports.* Model output reports typically include (1) recommended plant-to-warehouse flows by product; (2) recommended warehouse-to-customer flows by product; (3) cost summaries, by product, for the optimum system and the next most optimal system; (4) inventory requirements of individual products by location; and (5) summary reports of costs, inventories, product flows, and other key factors.

*Typical Results.* Such evaluations of facility requirements have yielded savings of from 10 to 20 percent of total system operating costs. In one instance, the number of warehouses was reduced from over 150 to 20 by combining seven separate systems into one market-oriented distribution operation. In another instance, the model determined the best location for a new plant to service projected sales volume over the following 10 years, and a distribution center that had been planned for a major metropolitan area was found to have significant cost penalties.

**Case No. 2: Transportation System**  As transportation costs increase, more and more companies are considering the use of their own truck fleets as an alternate to common carriers. The feasibility of such a private fleet depends to a large extent on the company's ability to keep the trucks loaded and minimize empty miles.

Typically, a truck will go from its starting point to three or four other points before returning to its starting point at the end of a trip. The individual movements from point A to points B, C, and D and back constitute a transportation loop or route. In general, as the number of individual points served by a route increases, the cost savings potential also increases because empty point-to-point legs become a smaller proportion of total route mileage. However, the complexity of dispatch and the difficulty of maintaining multiple stop routes also increases.

Recognizing the increasing need to assess the feasibility of private carriage, A. T. Kearney developed a private fleet feasibility planning system (PFFPS). This system enables the computer to determine optimally which routes or loops should be handled by the company and which ones should be handled by common carriers in order to maximize company profit.

*Model Objectives.* The objective of the PFFPS is to enable a company to determine where it should be using its own fleet. The model is useful for looking at long-range overall strategic considerations; it is not a tool for scheduling day-to-day operations. The questions the model might answer include:

On what routes should the company operate its own fleet?

What are the savings on each route versus common carrier cost?

How big should the fleet be if the company's objective is to obtain a certain rate of return (e.g., 5, 10, 20, 25, or 30 percent or more) on its investment?

Where should drivers and equipment be domiciled?

What products should be carried on each private fleet segment?

If a company is operating a number of separate divisional fleets, what might be the savings if the fleets were consolidated?

What size, number, and types of vehicles should the company utilize if a private fleet is feasible?

*Cost Elements.* Cost elements usually considered in such a model include:

Common carrier cost by leg

Private fleet cost by leg

Fixed domicile operating costs

*System Description.* The basic system utilized in the program is a combination of heuristic and linear programs, as shown in Fig. P-11.

1. The first module (loop finder) considers such data as point-to-point freight volumes, common carrier costs for each traffic lane, private fleet costs, empty mileage, and other factors to generate

potential private fleet loops. (In one recent situation, the total number of these loops amounted to 80,-000.) Loops are then screened against such parameters as maximum driving speed, percent loaded miles, percent empty miles, and the number of stops per loop.

2. Each acceptable loop is then passed on to the second module, a linear program, along with driving hours, common carrier costs, private fleet savings, total miles, and empty miles. Loops are then segregated by percent savings (that is, whether a loop provides a 5, 10, 15, 20, 25, 30, 35 percent, or more savings against common carrier costs).

3. The linear program module maximizes savings based upon the loops selected and the various constraints imposed.

*Output Reports.* These include (1) the volume of traffic flow by origin and destination, (2) detailed shipment listings, (3) detailed loop listing, and (4) cost analysis summaries.

*Typical Results.* This model has enabled many companies to identify opportunities in which a private fleet could save 20 percent or more as compared to the use of common carriers. The model has also served as a bargaining tool with common and contract carriers.

*See also* OPERATIONS RESEARCH; PLANNING, STRATEGIC MANAGERIAL; POLICY FORMULATION AND IMPLEMENTATION; STATISTICAL ANALYSIS FOR MANAGEMENT.

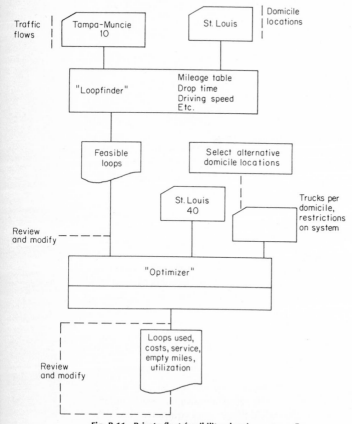

Fig. P-11. Private fleet feasibility planning systems flow.

### NOTES

[1] D. J. Bowersox, O. K. Helferich, E. J. Marien, P. Gilmour, et al., *Dynamic Simulation of Physical Distribution Systems*, Michigan State University Business Systems, East Lansing, 1972.

[2] "General Purpose Simulation System V (GPSSV), GPSS-VOS (GH20/0825), GPSS-VDOS (GH20/0826)," *IBM General Information Manual.*

[3] A. M. Geoffrion, "Mathematical Programming," *Management Science*, vol. 20, no. 5, January 1974.

[4] A. Charnes, W. W. Cooper, and A. Henderson, *An Introduction to Linear Programming*, John Wiley & Sons, Inc., New York, 1953.

[5] D. J. Sweeney and Ronald L. Tatham, "Improved Long-Run Model for Multiple Warehouse Location," *Management Science*, vol. 22, no. 7, March 1976.

[6] A. A. Kuehn and J. J. Hamburger, "A Heuristic Program for Locating Warehouses," *Management Science*, vol. 9, no. 4, July 1963.

ARTHUR S. GRAHAM, JR., *A. T. Kearney, Inc., Management Consultants*

**Planning and control** (*See* MANAGEMENT THEORY, SCIENCE, AND APPROACHES.)

# Planning horizon   (*See* PRODUCTION PROCESSES.)

# Planning and policy making   (*See heading in Table of Contents for complete listing.*)

# Planning report, plant engineering
(*See* PLANT ENGINEERING MANAGEMENT.)

# Planning stages, office   (*See* OFFICE SPACE PLANNING AND DESIGN.)

# Planning under uncertainty

Uncertainty can be defined as a condition not subject to the laws of probability. In a strategic sense, it means that predictions (certainties) about the environment facing the business firm cannot be made with precision. Causes of uncertainty, from acts of God to government regulations, have always loomed on the business horizon. But in recent years, the degree and extent of uncertainty have exponentially increased over the golden age of the 1950s and 1960s. All too often the response has been the ostrich syndrome.

**Planning Gaps**   Can a firm do strategic planning under uncertainty? The answer is a qualified "yes," since it depends upon the degree of uncertainty. A look at planning gaps will further elaborate this point.

*Environmental Scanning Deficiencies.* Firms often do not predict either the consequences of a failure to take action or the results of actions they have taken. General Motors failed to consider the possibility of utilizing the Wankel engine and had to purchase the rights to manufacture the engine from Curtiss-Wright, the owner of the United States rights. The packaging industry in the United States copes with over 350 restrictive bills which might have been modified or even eliminated had the industry scanned the trend to pollution control and the husbanding of natural resources.

*Organizational Inflexibility.* A firm may do an adequate job of environmental scanning but find itself unable to make an adequate response to the need for change. An example of such organizational inflexibility (as well as other factors) is the failure of either RCA or General Electric to succeed in computer manufacturing, even though both firms are well managed and successful in their own fields of endeavor.

*Insufficient Environmental Support.* The gap here lies in governmental failures to take appropriate action to ensure the viability of its institutions and its organizations, public and private. An example is the action of the Civil Aeronautics Board in continuing to grant more and more routes to airlines in competition with Pan American Airlines, which resulted in massive losses for the country's major flag carrier on many international routes.

*Resource Inapplicability.* Strategic planning requires an assessment of the resources of the firm available to implement any strategic plan. Many such resource inapplicabilities have occurred in acquisitions, where subsequent failures are often the result of a disregard for the applicability of the firm's resources. Economies of scale in the brewing industry, for example, favor large firms: over 100 smaller breweries have disappeared in the last decade. Schlitz, one of the largest brewers, produces 4.4 million barrels of beer with 483 production workers. Falstaff, the seventh largest, produces 4.1 million with 1800 workers. The disparity is ominous.

*Oversimplification of Strategic Planning.* The tendency to develop strategies based upon an oversimplification of the issues has resulted in even very large and successful companies making errors of unbelievable magnitude. The aircraft manufacturing industry has been guilty of this time after time from General Dynamics' manufacture of the Convair 880 and 990 to the Concorde. General Dynamics lost $425 million, and the Concorde has already lost over $2 billion.

*Ignoring Change Signals.* If a firm can predict the need for new strategies early enough, then usually it can adjust to most changes. The automobile industry has seen many change signals—but often too late to adjust quickly enough to the changes. Volkswagen's fantastic success with its Beetle seemingly blinded the company to the changing tastes of the consumer, with the result that Japanese small cars soon started to fill the market niche left by Volkswagen's late start in producing other types of cars.

**Classification of Change**   There is no doubt that change is accelerating both in magnitude and rate. Can such changes be predicted? Although there was evidence that the Organization of Petroleum Exporting Countries (OPEC) resented the price cut imposed on them by the international oil companies in the 1960s, that the United States was rapidly depleting its oil reserves, that oil reserves were finite, it would be irresponsible to say that one could

917

have predicted the fourfold price increase in petroleum exacted by OPEC. But the devaluation of the United States dollar and the inflationary spiral was predictable by examination of such factors as the United States budget deficit, the growth of the Euro-dollar market, and the United States balance of payments deficit.

These six planning gaps resulted from the inability of firms to deal effectively with uncertainty. In some instances, the uncertainty was external to the firm and in others internal. But in all cases the uncertainty was related to change.

Individual companies may not always be able to identify consequences, but they have no alternative to tracking environmental changes that will impact on their strategic plans. Three broad categories of change can be utilized as a framework.

*Technological Change.* It is quite possible that the pivotal technological change may occur not within the company's own industry but in quite a different industry. Examples include the impact of a commercial version of the Lockheed C5A aircraft on the trucking and railroad industries. The major technological changes in the can industry came from (1) the aluminum industry, which developed an aluminum can, and (2) the food processing industry where frozen foods eliminate the need for cans.

*Social/Behavioral Change.* This affects the firm in three ways:

*Employee attitudes and work ethics.* The demand for greater self-determination and fulfillment, higher education levels, and value shifts require that the internal organization and management of the firm be responsive to these changes or face a catastrophe such as the worker sabotage in General Motors' plant in Lordstown, Ohio.

*Consumer tastes and preferences.* Over 90 percent of the products on the shelves of a supermarket did not exist 10 years ago. Inexpensive hand-held calculators, small economy cars, and jumbo jets are as much shifts in consumer tastes and preferences as they may be products of technological change.

*Government regulations stemming from changed aspirations and needs of society.* Government regulation belongs more appropriately in the third category of change (structural/institutional), but its basis must be recognized in social/behavioral change.

*Structural/Institutional Change.* The whole gamut of government action and international actions such as those by the European Economic Community (EEC) have major impact on a firm's strategic posture. But there are structural changes that result from technological and social/behavioral change as well. For example, there is a major shift of population to the sun belt in the South and West, and demographics change as families have fewer children.

**Identifying Change**  First, the firm must recognize the need for research and classification as well as impact analysis of the change on its strategic options. There are already "change-identifying specialists" (such as *Business International*), which function as an industrial intelligence system specializing in identifying environmental change.

The major classifications of technological, social/behavioral, and structural/institutional change need subclassifications as a starting point for planning under uncertainty. The development of a data bank could start with the work of Herman Kahn and the Hudson Institute and that of other futurists. Special studies could be commissioned with organizations such as the Center for Future Research of the University of Southern California or the Stanford Research Institute. Forecasting techniques such as Delphi and Cross Impact are valuable tools for providing a broad framework of the future.

It is critical that the search for change signals be not too limited or parochial. The industrial intelligence system must monitor widely enough and deeply enough not to miss events outside of the normal planning horizon of the organization. Information is readily available which a very small trained staff could analyze for change signals to assist a business to predict and deal with uncertainty.

Short- and long-range planning are obsolete terms. The critical issue is to adjust the planning time horizon to the degree of uncertainty. Furthermore, different divisions or even products have different planning horizons. It is inappropriate to utilize one time frame for all parts of a business or to use an arbitrary "3-year" or "5-year" business planning cycle. What is essential is to adjust commitments of time, investment funds, and management to the appropriate cycle. Traditional methods of calculating investment payback can be utilized once the planning horizons are determined.

## PLANNING FOR CHANGE

What can a firm do once it tracks the environmental changes?

1. Establish a planning horizon. It can decide upon its planning horizon depending upon its ability to control its environment as shown in Fig. P-12.

2. Predict the range of uncertainty. For example, what will the prime interest rate be over the next 2 or 3 years? Basic data on government bud-

gets, balance of payments, and various economic factors provide the background for an anlysis. This could provide a range prediction as shown in Fig. P-13.

If the range is 7 to 12 percent, most firms can develop strategic plans with some degree of cer-

Fig. P-12.  **Planning horizons.**

tainty. However, if the range were 5 to 25 percent, the firm might be unable to develop any effective strategic plans; instead it might follow an opportunistic path with very short planning horizons.

3. Develop contingency plans. This requires highly documented premises underlying each plan and a monitoring-evaluating system to trigger the implementation of contingency plans.

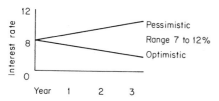

Fig. P-13.  **Ranges of uncertainty.**

Since the primary causes creating uncertainty are external to the firm, monitoring the environment becomes critical during the implementation of the plan. Changes in the premises and assumptions projected for the environment will obviously invalidate the plan. Limits to environmental changes should be predetermined to allow computer or staff tracking to trigger top management examination of the plan's validity as environmental change takes place. Decisions to implement contingency plans or subplans could also be predetermined to allow a proactive rather than reactive planning process.

**Summary**  Every firm follows a strategic plan, since everyday decisions are made that in some way are based upon a prediction, regardless of how unconsciously or imperfect, of future events. Strategic planning, even under conditions of uncertainty, is better done consciously than by merely assuming that today's decisions affect only today.

*See also* PLANNING, PLANNED MANAGEMENT OF TURBULENT CHANGE; PLANNING, STRATEGIC MANAGERIAL; PLANNING, STRATEGIC PLANNING MODELS;

POLICY FORMULATION AND IMPLEMENTATION; RISK ANALYSIS AND MANAGEMENT.

### REFERENCES

Basil, Douglas C., and Curtis W. Cook: *Management of Change*, McGraw-Hill Publishing Company, Ltd., London, New York, 1974.

Cook, Curtis W.: *Organization, Environment, and Strategy*, unpublished doctoral dissertation, University of Southern California, Los Angeles, 1974.

Greiner, L. E.: "Evolution and Revolution as Organizations Grow," *Harvard Business Review*, vol. 50, no. 4, pp. 37–46, 1972.

Hellriegel, D., and J. W. Slocum, Jr.: "Integrating Systems Concepts and Organizational Strategy," *Business Horizons*, vol. 15, no. 2, pp. 71–78, 1972.

Moos, R. W.: "Conceptualizations of Human Environments," *American Psychologist*, vol. 28, pp. 652–665, 1973.

DOUGLAS C. BASIL, *University of Southern California*

## Plans, contingency  (*See* PLANNING, STRATEGIC MANAGERIAL.)

## Plant engineering management

Plant Engineering is that branch of engineering which embraces the installation, operation, maintenance, modification, modernization, and protection of physical facilities and equipment used to produce a product or provide a service. It requires the special competency to assume liaison or control responsibility for coordinating multidisciplinary engineering activities such as contractual engineering services, facility design, equipment selection and procurement and construction.[1]

Plant Engineers are defined as those exercising responsible charge of, or supervisory or executive responsibility for the engineering associated with all or some phase of design, layout, construction, maintenance and/or control of fixed and mobile facilities or plant; or those who, by high standards of technical knowledge and experience, qualify to practice the profession.[2]

Plant engineers are both engineers and managers. They combine the technical skill of engineering discipline with the managerial skills of a professional manager. Those who manage plant engineers must deal with the engineering aspect of the plant engineer in a professional, technical manner and with the management aspect with professional management methods.

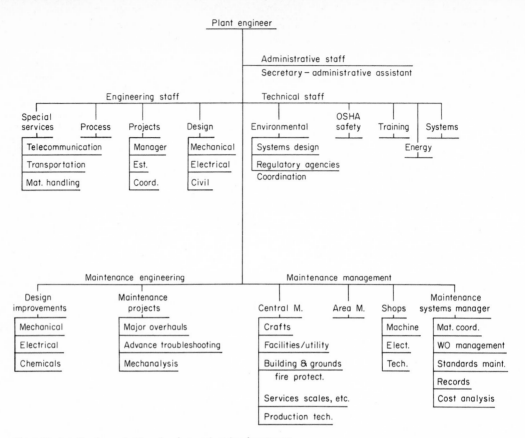

**Fig. P-14. Functional organization of a plant engineering department.**

## OBJECTIVES

The objectives of plant engineering will vary with the company objectives and the size of the organization. The objectives should be set by the responsible management in consultation with the plant engineer.

A typical general objective is that all plant engineering objectives be consistent with the corporate objectives and reflect similar priorities and emphases. These objectives should provide an efficient engineering organization and service of sufficient quality and quantity (1) to maintain the facilities of the corporation; (2) to keep abreast of technological progress; (3) to design and manage installation of physical properties necessary for the expansion, modification, or replacement of physical facilities of the corporation; (4) to meet the requirement of the corporation operating at a stated per year sales (or production); and (5) to provide a maintenance orga-

nization at the lowest cost and highest efficiency necessary to ensure continuous operation of plant equipment.

## ORGANIZATION

The plant engineering department should be organized around functional responsibilities (*see* Fig. P-14). Basically, plant engineering is a service organization that provides two major functions: engineering and maintenance. To provide these two services, however, it is necessary for the department to include an administrative or management section.

**Engineering Staff**   The engineering staff's function is to provide the technical expertise for layout, design, modification, management, and improvement of the physical properties of the company. It may be a one-person engineering section or a multidisciplinary section, depending on the size and requirements of the organization it serves. Functions

920

or assignments may be combined within the section to provide full work assignments such as projects and design or safety and training; or it may be necessary to divide a single function to maintain control. Engineers or technical people within the section may vary in qualifications necessary to satisfy the requirements of the position.

**Maintenance Staff**  The maintenance staff provides the technical expertise and supervision of the maintenance functions. This includes engineering design, project management, supervision of technicians and crafts, program maintenance, cost control, and facilities management. The size of the maintenance staff will be determined by the number of functions it contains and the frequency of the application of these functions. Generally, a maintenance supervisor should control no less than 3 subordinates and no more than 20. No supervisor should control more than three functions without assistance. A convenient way to determine the number of staff people needed and the functions performed by each is to have the plant engineer prepare a responsibility assessment chart (*see* Fig. P-15).

**Maintenance Programs**  There are three basic maintenance programs which will cover most maintenance functions.

*Routine Maintenance Programs.* These are the functions necessary to keep a machine operating without major expenditures or repairs. Maintenance functions at this level are basic in nature such as lubrication, drive tension, cleaning, fluid level, etc. These functions can be performed without interfering with the equipment running time. Routine maintenance will account for approximately 30 percent of the total maintenance cost.

*Breakdown, or Controlled, Maintenance Programs.* These functions are performed when a part or operation of a piece of equipment fails and must be repaired to resume proper operation. Generally, an inspection program is performed to check wear and determine when the part has failed. It may be economically desirable to let a part wear completely out before replacement so that the condition of the part is the determining factor for replacement rather than time or schedule. Usually these are parts that will not cause major damage or long shutdowns when they fail. Breakdown or controlled maintenance accounts for approximately 35 percent of the total maintenance cost.

*Preventive, or Planned, Maintenance Programs.* These maintenance functions and programs are prescheduled and performed to prevent the failure of a part or the loss of machine time. Such functions include daily routine monitoring or inspecting to anticipate wear or need of repair, planned stoppage for test or inspections, and major overhauls.

The degree of intensity of any maintenance program is determined by the results produced by the program. The two main measures of the efficiency of a maintenance program are cost and reduction of downtime. The minimum cost and maximum efficiency is a balance of these programs as shown in Fig. P-16.

## PLANT ENGINEERING MANAGEMENT CONTROLS

**Budget**  The preparation and maintenance of a departmental budget is probably the best control tool for plant engineering management. The budget should contain a breakdown by line-item of each controllable item for which the plant engineer is responsible. People, material, equipment, and services are the major items. Because it is a service organization, all cost incurred by the department should be charged back to the organization being served.

The two primary budgets controlling the plant engineering functions are the operating budget and the capital expenditure budget.

An *operating budget* is determined by the level of operation to be maintained, personnel requirements, and equipment involved. It can be made by updating historical records with current requirement and cost data.

A *capital expenditure budget* includes all new money for new work, improvements, and replacements. It can best be made by making an estimate on all projects included. Most organizations require an estimate of material cost, labor, service, and maintenance required. Also, the cost of money, taxes, and return on investment should be included.

| Responsibility assessment | | | | | | | |
|---|---|---|---|---|---|---|---|
| Function | Purpose | Value | Time and frequency | Skill | Responsible to | Review by | Performed by |
| | | | | | | | |

**Fig. P-15. Responsibility assessment chart.**

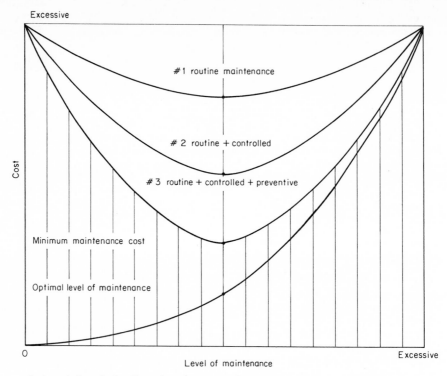

Cost = cost of required routine maintenance + cost of controlled maintenance + cost of p.m.

Cost included: direct cost + indirect cost

Direct cost: time and materials

Indirect cost: overhead, production losses, and loss of sales

**Fig. P-16. Maintenance program measurement of efficiency.**

Reports will keep the manager informed on the efficiency of the plant engineering organization. The manager should first determine the standard by which the department will be measured. Typical standards are:

1. Plant engineering cost as a percent of the total operating cost

2. Plant engineering cost as a percent of total sales

| Daily downtime report | | | | | Date: |
|---|---|---|---|---|---|
| Machine no. | Time down | Date 1st down | Reason for downtime | Parts status | Estimated comp. date |
| | | | | | |
| | | | | | |

**Fig. P-17. Daily downtime report.**

3. Plant engineering cost per unit of production produced

4. Rate of production downtime to running time

5. Comparison to predetermine work standards

None of these will give a complete, accurate measure of the efficiency of plant engineering, but all can be used as a barometer to indicate the level of functioning of the department. The plant engineer uses numerous systems and reports to control the activities supervised. Summaries of these reports will give the manager a good indication of the departmental efficiency. Figures P-17, P-18, P-19, and P-20 illustrate four particularly useful reports.

*See also* ENERGY RESOURCES, MANAGEMENT OF; FACILITIES AND SITE PLANNING AND LAYOUT; MAINTENANCE MANAGEMENT; MATERIAL HANDLING; OFFICE

SPACE PLANNING AND DESIGN; REAL ESTATE MANAGEMENT, CORPORATE; SAFETY AND HEALTH MANAGEMENT, EMPLOYEE; SITE SELECTION.

NOTES

[1]American Institute of Plant Engineers, Barrington, Ill.
[2]Ibid.

REFERENCES

Higgins, L. R., and L. C. Morrow: *Maintenance Engineering Handbook*, 3d. ed., McGraw-Hill Book Company, New York, 1977.
Lewis, Bernard T.: *Management Handbook for Plant Engineers*, McGraw-Hill Book Company, New York, 1977.
Lewis, Bernard T., and J. P. Marron, eds.: *Facilities and Plant Engineering Handbook*, McGraw-Hill Book Company, New York, 1974.
Staniar, William, ed.: *Plant Engineering Handbook*, 2d ed., McGraw-Hill Book Company, 1959.

FRANK HOLLADAY, *Southwire Corporation*

## Point system

(*See* JOB EVALUATION.)

## Policies

(*See* MANAGEMENT THEORY, SCIENCE, AND APPROACHES; PLANNING, STRATEGIC MANAGERIAL.)

## Policies, insurance

(*See* RISK ANALYSIS AND MANAGEMENT.)

| Monthly downtime—production analysis | | | | | | | Date: |
|---|---|---|---|---|---|---|---|
| Machine | Scheduled hours | Total hours downtime | % downtime | Units produced | Units std. prod. | % efficiency | % + change− |
| | | | | | | | |
| | | | | | | | |

Fig. P-18. Monthly downtime—production analysis.

## Policies, personnel

(*See* PERSONNEL ADMINISTRATION.)

## Policy, manufacturing

(*See* PRODUCTION/OPERATIONS MANAGEMENT.)

## Policy, system

(*See* SYSTEM DYNAMICS.)

## Policy formulation, international

(*See* INTERNATIONAL OPERATIONS AND MANAGEMENT IN MULTINATIONAL COMPANIES.)

## Policy formulation and implementation

Policy formulation and implementation can be broadly or narrowly treated. The term *policy* can

| Engineering priority list | | | | | | | | | |
|---|---|---|---|---|---|---|---|---|---|
| Dept. job number | Capital job no. | Title | Initiation | Priority | Estimated % completed | Budget | Cost to date | Cost to completion | Completion date |
| | | | | | | | | | |

Fig. P-19. Engineering priority list.

Plant engineering planning report

Section ____________ Date ____________

| | | |
|---|---|---|
| No. of employees ______ | No. of hours worked ______ | No. of projects worked ______ |
| No. of new employees ______ | No. of hours lost ______ | No. of projects completed ______ |
| No. of employees term. ______ | No. of hours vac. ______ | No. of new projects ______ |
| Total no. of employees ______ | | Total no. of projects ______ |

| Section | Capital | Job title | Initiator | Responsible | Job status/goals | Ref. |
|---|---|---|---|---|---|---|
| | | | | | | |
| | | | | | | |

Fig. P-20. Plant engineering planning report.

mean anything from a top management decision to a first-line supervisor's policy on late arrivals at work. It is important, therefore, to focus on a single definition or perspective.

## DEFINITIONS AND MODELS[1]

There are a number of ways to define the policy process. One is with words. Another is with a model.

*Policy formulation and implementation* is the process by which the enterprise and its leaders develop an effective strategy to meet the enterprise objectives. A *strategy* is the unified comprehensive plan the enterprise develops to reach these objectives. The subsidiary plans and policies are those which make the strategy applicable and meaningful to the managers and employees of the enterprise.

Figure P-21 is a model of this process. The objectives are at once the beginning and the end of policy formulation. They are what is sought in operating the enterprise, and they are modified by the realities of the environment in which the enterprise operates.

The policy makers are three groups of executives: (1) the top managers of the enterprise (such as the president and/or chief operating officer) and corporate-wide top executives; (2) a corporate planning staff (in larger enterprises) which assists the top managers in detailed planning, and (3) middle managers (division heads and major department heads). The shaded areas of Fig. P-21 indicate which group of executives is involved in the various facets of the policy process.

The policy process consists of four elements: (1) appraisal of the current state, (2) choice of future states, (3) implementation of the policy-strategy choice made, and (4) evaluation of the choice and its implementation.

**Importance of the Policy Process[2]**  Policy making, specifically, and planning, more generally, are important to the effectiveness of an enterprise and its managers. But there is a special irony in policy making. Even if a manager realizes the importance of it, and even if he or she is competent to perform it, most managers do not enjoy it. Why? Managers are busy people. They are rewarded for doing things. At first glance, policy making looks like thinking and paper work. Managers prefer immediate activity because it provides immediate feedback and reward. Policy making is future-oriented, and the rewards come later—perhaps to someone else. Nevertheless, managers who get involved in policy making enjoy these advantages:

1. Policy making leads to success. Common sense indicates that if a manager plans to anticipate likely future problems and makes decisions while there is time to consider alternatives (instead of making last-minute decisions), effectiveness will follow. A number of good, solid research studies support this conclusion. The best known ones are by Ansoff et al., Eastlack and McDonald, Stagner, Thune and House, and Herold.

2. Policy making helps the manager cope with change. Change is characteristic of our society. Effective planning based upon prepared policies and strategic decisions helps to anticipate and manage the change in our environment.

3. Policy making helps employees focus on the key objectives of the enterprise. Effective policy making helps employees see the forest and the trees. Without it, employees do the job and do the work, but without understanding why. Policies focus on why as well as how.

4. Policy making is essential for an effective control system. Since the enterprise exists in an imperfect but perfectible world, control is necessary. Control holds employees accountable for resources and evaluates to see if they are well or poorly used. This leads to effective reward systems. Policies and standards provide the basis for this employee evaluation and control.

## POLICY FORMULATION AND OBJECTIVES[3]

Enterprise objectives are those ends the enterprise seeks to accomplish. Every enterprise had objectives when it came into existence. Since its creation, those beginning objectives could be the same or different. The degree of specificity of objectives varies, however, with the size of the organization, its age, and the sophistication of the enterprise's managers.

**Evolutionary Stages**  An enterprise's objectives appear to evolve through five stages of development.

STAGE 1: no formal objectives. In some organizations, the objectives are vague and verbal. Nowhere will one find written objectives. General feelings that the enterprise "exists to make a profit" or should "serve our customers" are typical managerial views at this stage. In general, they don't think much about objectives at this point.

STAGE 2: formulation of general objectives. They are usually not in written form. At this stage, the manager begins to think about objectives and realizes there should be some, but they still remain in verbal form.

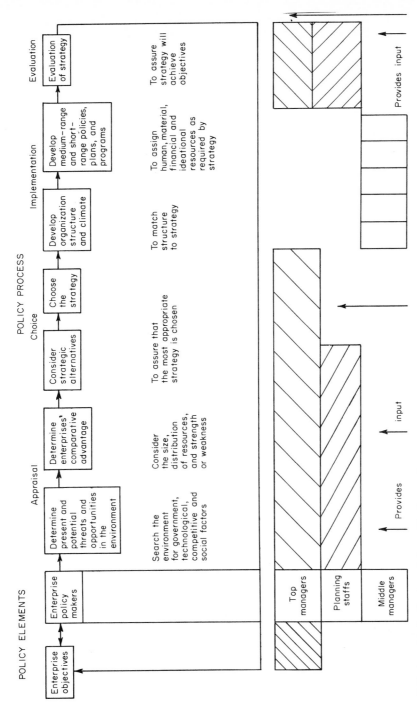

**P-21. A model of policy formulation and implementation.**

STAGE 3: formulation of general objectives in written form. When the manager sees the need for formalizing the process of policy making and control, a set of written objectives is drawn up. Typical objectives at this stage include phrases such as "increased profit" and "increased market share."

STAGE 4: formulation of specific objectives in written form. At this stage, the manager takes the stage 3 objectives and puts the numbers to them. "Increased profit" becomes "increase ROI from 4 to $4\frac{1}{2}$ percent"; "increase market share" becomes "increase market share nationally from 21 to 23 percent by increasing our market share in Western regions by 2 percent and Southeastern region by 4 percent."

STAGE 5: formulating a ranking of specific objectives. The final and most difficult step is for management to compute trade offs between objectives. This requires them to say, for example, "ROI is more important than market share; market share is more important than satisfied employees." This step is found only in the most sophisticated firms—perhaps in less than 1 percent of the firms in the United States and Canada.

**Management by Objectives** There are various techniques for moving the firm through these stages. One of the more popular is management by objectives (MBO). MBO attempts to develop an enterprise philosophy by requiring top managers to proceed through step 5 in formulating objectives. Then middle and lower management are expected to translate these objectives into specific targets and plans.

**Specificity of Objectives** As time goes on, objectives tend to get more specific. Nonspecific objectives allow less effective management to get by with lower performance longer. So they fight against specificity, too. A difficult question always is: How specific *should* objectives be? The answer is: As specific as the nature of the objective *can* be. Generally, the lower the level in the enterprise, the greater the specificity.

**Ranking of Objectives** Management's ranking of objectives is influenced by:

1. The realities of the environment. If an enterprise is powerful in the marketplace, it can attain its objectives more easily than if it is weak.

2. The realities of the enterprise's internal power relationship and its resource base. In both these factors are the political realities of the management relative to other groups involved. Does the management have full support of the stockholders? Has the management developed the support of employees and key employee groups, such as the

professional employees or lower and middle management? If so, the management can set higher objectives that employees will help to achieve. Or the management can act to force employees to meet the objectives and receive support from owners if they wish to take drastic sanctions to assure success.

3. The values and preferences of the managers. These are developed from their education, experience, and the information they receive in their jobs. Enterprises with strong value systems or ideologies will attract and retain managers whose values are similar. And the reverse is also true. These values are essentially a set of attitudes about what is good or bad, desirable or undesirable. It is easy to see how one set of executives with certain values emphasizes one set of objectives; another group, another set of objectives.

Management does not begin over again each year to establish objectives; it starts from the most recent set. These objectives may have been laid down by strong leaders in the past. Then the present leaders make small changes in that set. Given the current environment and current demands of the conflicting groups in the enterprise, managers develop ideas of what the objectives ought to be in a future period. By "muddling through," they set the current objectives to satisfy as many of the demands as they can.

In sum, objectives are formed for an enterprise when its top managers react to the complex interplay of demands from groups in the environment and inside the enterprise. The managers then incrementally adjust the objectives considering these demands and their own values and aspirations.

*Changes in Objectives.* Organizational objectives change as a result of:

1. Increased demands from coalition groups that make up the enterprise.

2. Change in the expectation levels of managers. As managers begin to examine past achievements, they expect the enterprise can do more. Or they look at what competitors and other enterprises have achieved and decide to match, or achieve, that level of objectives.

3. A crisis or the attainment of an ultimate goal. The National Foundation for Infantile Paralysis went through a crisis when a cure was found for the disease. NASA went through a crisis when men were placed on the moon. When the ultimate goal is attained or a crisis arises, objectives must be changed. In successful organizations, they are changed.

**Basic Objectives** Businesses typically embrace five varieties of objectives:

Survival, i.e., to stay in business

Production of goods/services that customers continue to buy

Efficiency objectives, i.e., maximum production at minimum costs

Employee satisfaction and development

Adaptiveness to changing circumstances

Finally, objectives are the beginning point of the policy formulation and implementation process. They are why the enterprise exists and continues. They are the basis for the whole process.

## ENTERPRISE APPRAISAL[4]

The policy formulation phase consists of two major parts: appraisal and choice, as shown in Fig. P-21.

**External Appraisal** In an appraisal, managers examine the environment for future happenings: (1) opportunities for gain and (2) threats to current progress or even to the enterprise's existence. In its search, management utilizes information gathering, spying, and forecasting/modeling. Managers gather information on the market, suppliers, technological change, and government actions, usually obtaining verbal accounts from subordinates and friends in the industry. Outside information often comes unsolicited. Formal forecasting and modeling are talked about more than done, and when done, often are rarely used by top managers in making significant decisions. Spying is not a well-researched topic and is clothed in mystery. It probably is used more in volatile industries than in others.

*Information Search.* An effective manager searches for information on the environment by putting his or her emphasis on the critical factors in the industry. Propositions 1 to 6 describe how a manager determines this.

PROPOSITION 1: The greater the power of the enterprise is relative to its competitors, the less it will focus on the competitive sector of the environment.

PROPOSITION 3: The less dependent the enterprise is on the government for subsidies and the less regulated the enterprise is by the government, the less it will focus on the political sector of the environment.

PROPOSITION 4: The less dependent the enterprise is on one or a few suppliers, the less it will focus on the supplier sector.

PROPOSITION 5: The greater the volatility of the technological environment, the more the managers of an enterprise will focus on the technological sector.

PROPOSITION 6: The smaller the geographic area served by the enterprise, the less widely it will search the environment.

If after analysis the manager realizes that the enterprise's critical factors are its volatility and a few customers and suppliers, the external focus centers on these factors. This search enables the manager to anticipate likely future events, which may be classified as positive (opportunities) and negative (threats).

*Internal Appraisal.* This is required for managers to realize the particular abilities the enterprise has to take advantage of the opportunities and meet the threats. The process of internal appraisal has as its outcome a profile of the strategic advantages of the enterprise: its particular strengths and weaknesses. These then can be matched with the external threats and opportunities to determine the crucial decisions the manager must make in the upcoming period. Many factors can be turned to, ranging from marketing to operations to finance to organization to top management itself. When the external and internal analyses are complete, the appraisal phase is also complete.

## STRATEGIC CHOICE[5]

The final phase of policy formulation entails (1) consideration of strategic alternatives and (2) choice of the strategy or guiding policy for the enterprise.

The range of available choices is wide. The strategy chosen can be an active exploitation of opportunities or the meeting head on of threats. It can also be passive, such as a "wait and see" defensive strategy.

**Business Definition** The essence of the strategic choice decision is the definition (really redefinition) of the business. Strategic alternatives always involve answering questions such as:

Should we stay in the same business(es)?

Should we get out of this business entirely or some subparts of it?

Should we stay in this business but get more efficient at it?

Should we get into new businesses?

**The Four Strategic Alternatives** Viewed systematically, there are four strategic alternatives always available to top managers:

*Stable Growth.* This is (1) a continuation of serving the same or similar product/service sectors in the business mission statement (2) the pursuit of the same or a similar level of objectives.

*Growth.* This alternative calls for significant increases in the level of objectives sought by the enterprise and/or increases the number of product/service sectors served. Growth is accomplished by internal growth, external growth (mergers), or a combination of both.

*Retrenchment.* Conversely, retrenchment represents a significant reduction in level of objectives sought and/or reduction in the number of product/service sectors served. (Examples of retrenchment strategies are cutting back, becoming a captive company, divesting of "losers," and liquidating.)

*Combination.* Two or more of the grand strategies (stable growth, growth, retrenchment) can be pursued simultaneously in different parts of the enterprise; or two or more grand strategies can be used over time (for example, stable growth for 2 years, then growth).

All these strategies are effective when chosen to match the opportunities and threats faced by the business and given the internal strategic advantages. The top managers choose the strategy. Their choice is affected by several factors:

1. Top management's perception of the power of the enterprise relative to the environment
2. Top management's willingness to take or avoid risk
3. The tendency of top management to continue past strategies
4. The internal power politics of the top management group

If a coalition of key top managers favors one choice, this strongly influences the decision. These factors are illustrated in Fig. P-22. The most probable choice is shown in the choice zone, including the past strategy.

## POLICY IMPLEMENTATION

Implementation is the process by which top managers assure that (1) policies are communicated, (2) the organization of people and resources reinforce the choice, and (3) subsidiary policies are consistent and reinforce the basic policy choice.

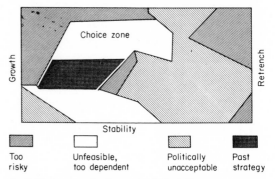

Fig. P-22. An example of strategic choice influences.

**Roles of Middle and Supervisory Management** After the strategic policy decision, middle management takes over. It develops the plans to break down the big decisions into meaningful decisions for divisions, departments, and units. Plans developed by middle managers are (1) policies, (2) procedures, (3) rules, (4) intermediate level budgets, and (5) organizational changes. Supervisors also get involved, as shown in Table P-13. The table describes how all levels of managers institute a multilevel set of plans to help achieve the enterprise objectives. Each level prepares its set of plans and policies derived from the higher level so as to fit

TABLE P-13 Types of Plans and Policy Decisions Made by Three Levels of Managers

| Management level | Type of plan | General content |
|---|---|---|
| Top<br>Board of directors, president, operating division vice-presidents | Strategic planning<br>Top-level budgets | Objective of enterprise<br>Basic mission<br>Basic strategies<br>Total budget |
| Middle<br>Staff departments, Department heads, regional executives, etc. | Policies, rules, procedures, intermediate-level budget | Quarterly plans<br>Standing plans<br>Subdivisions of budget |
| First level<br>Supervisors, etc. | Schedules, programs, short-run budgets | Daily and weekly plans<br>Unit budgets |

them to the needs of its own employees (and those below).

*Top management* sets objectives and makes the major policy decisions as to how the enterprise will respond to its environmental threats and opportunities.

*Middle management* translates these strategic decisions and long-range plans into specific terms, both financially and organizationally. This sets up a system of quarterly and yearly targets and budgets.

*Lower middle management* factors these plans into monthly plans.

*Supervisors* then set daily, weekly, and biweekly (possibly monthly) plans, as monitored by middle management.

All these plans are designed to help achieve the objectives of the enterprise. This description implies that plans only cascade downward. Obviously, adjustments and recommendations flow upward as necessary.

**Implementation: Subsidiary Policies** A policy is not a specific directive. It provides only *general guidance* for middle and supervisory managers and their employees in a particular decisions area. It is middle and lower-level management's responsibility to develop subsidiary policies, procedures, rules, budgets, and schedules and to implement them.

Suppose, for example, top management has set a strategic policy: growth. To implement this decision, middle managers must develop subsidiary policies to make this decision a reality. Typically, subsidiary policies cover these areas:

Operations/production
Finance/accounting
Personnel
Marketing/logistics
Research and development

Here are examples of *possible* policies:

*Personnel Policies*

1. Promotion policy: As the enterprise grows, managers should be promoted from within. Normally, the enterprise hires only supervisory managers from the outside.

2. Managerial selection policy: In selecting potential supervisory managers, normally we will hire college graduates.

*Marketing Policies*

1. Internal growth policy: Normally, the major avenue of growth is to increase the sales of present products. Merger will be a rarely used method of growth.

2. New product policy: Normally, when new products are added they will fit our current product line by increasing the number of sizes of the product offered or the number of quality levels of the product offered.

Clearly, an enterprise could develop hundreds of policies to cover the important areas of the business. Note that a policy does not tell too specifically how to handle a specific promotion or to add a specific product. It is a *general* guide to action. It limits the choice in most cases (for example, it implies: Don't expect to lure a new vice-president from another firm; don't expect to get new products from a merger). But it does not totally limit a manager's choices.

**Policy Purpose and Principles** Policies are developed to assure that:

1. The strategic choice is implemented.

2. A basis for control is provided.

3. Relative consistency and coordination of work are ensured.

4. The amount of time executives spend on making decisions is reduced.

Without a policy development, managers would make the same decisions over and over. Different managers might choose different directions on, for example, promotion from within, and this could lead to personnel and motivation problems. Policies should never be so inflexible as to prevent exceptions for good reasons, but it is useful to develop policies for the reasons given.

In smaller and many medium-sized enterprises, subsidiary policies are generally understood and verbal. In large and some medium-sized firms, subsidiary policies are often in written form.

**Procedures and Rules** After the broadest policies are developed, many enterprises push the planning process further and develop procedures or rules. These are the more specific plans that limit the choices of middle and supervisory managers further than policies do. Procedures and rules are developed for the same reasons as policies. They focus on areas where problems have been severe in the past or in areas where management wishes to prevent certain problems from arising in the future.

Procedures or rules are specific guides to action. A procedure tells a manager how to do a particular activity. In larger organizations, procedures are collected and put into manuals often called standard operating procedures (SOPs).

Procedures or rules or methods (all about the same) exist to make sure the policy decisions are carried out. Consider again the managerial selection policy described above (in selecting potential supervisory managers, normally we will hire college graduates). If the management feels this is an important area in developing the growth strategy, it will develop procedures based on enterprise experience to get the best manager. Some procedures to implement this might be:

PROCEDURE 1. Hire only graduates of business and engineering schools.

PROCEDURE 2. Give all potential managers a full-day site visit and have them be interviewed by at least 10 supervisory and middle managers.

PROCEDURE 3. Give preference to veterans.

PROCEDURE 4. Give preference to individuals who worked their way through school.

PROCEDURE 5. Give preference to the top 5 percent of a graduating class.

**Procedure Purpose and Guidelines**  There is a danger in an enterprise's having procedures for everything: managers may barely be able to find them, much less remember or effectively use them. In government, the military, or very large organization, procedures tend to slow down operations and decision making. A balance between initiative and consistency must be struck. In general, only truly critical decision areas warrant formal procedural plans.

This does not mean to imply that procedures and rules only restrict managers' actions. In many cases, they also free managers from making decisions in areas where they have (1) less competence or (2) no desire to become involved. In this sense, rules and procedures help managers to concentrate on more important issues and on decisions for which they have greater competence.

## EVALUATION OF POLICIES

In an enterprise with a completely developed planning system, an evaluation should take place several times each year. The strategic managers should review the success and/or failures of their plans and policy decisions with a view toward improving future plans and the planning process itself. Although this is desirable, there is little hard evidence to show how this is done or how frequently and effectively. More often, it can be presumed that evaluation is integrated into the enterprise's routine control process.

## SUMMARY

The policy planning process is continuous and iterative. For convenience, this discussion has treated the phases as if they were separate and distinct. In actual practice, the phases overlap and blend together. They cannot be separated.

Policy formulation and implementation makes good sense—when managers are really interested in effectiveness. But the *irony* is that to perform other than superficially, managers must do what they have rarely been rewarded for doing: taking time out from daily pressures and rewards, stepping back and looking at where the enterprise is now and what is in store for it tomorrow, and then anticipating these implications and taking steps to do something about them.

Policy formulation and implementation requires that executives (1) formalize objectives, (2) formally assess what is coming up from the environment, (3) formally figure out where their firm's strengths and weaknesses are, (4) systematically compare several choices, (5) choose the best one, (6) implement it, and (7) take time to evaluate and make changes. These steps can be taken in many different sequences. This entry has presented a formal, normative way of going about it. Whatever way it is accomplished, so long as policy making is formalized, it will improve organizational effectiveness.

*See also* ACQUISITIONS AND MERGERS; AUDIT, MANAGEMENT; OBJECTIVES AND GOALS; OBJECTIVES, MANAGEMENT BY (MBO); PLANNING, STRATEGIC MANAGERIAL; PLANNING, PLANNED MANAGEMENT OF TURBULENT CHANGE; PLANNING UNDER UNCERTAINTY.

## NOTES
[1]This section is partly based on the following: William F. Glueck, *Business Policy: Strategy Formation and Management Action*, 2d ed., McGraw-Hill Book Company, New York, 1976; William F. Glueck, *Management*, Dryden Press, Div. of Holt, Rinehart & Winston, Hinsdale, Ill., 1977, especially chap. 11.

[2]H. Igor Ansoff et al., *Acquisition Behavior of U.S. Manufacturing Firms, 1946–65*, Vanderbilt University Press, Nashville, Tenn., 1971; Joseph Eastlack, Jr., and Philip McDonald, "CEO's Role in Corporate Growth," *Harvard Business Review*, May-June, 1970, pp. 150–163; William F. Glueck, *Management*, chap. 11; David Herold, "Long Range Planning and Organizational Performance: A Cross Validation Study," *Academy of Management Journal*, March 1972, pp. 91–102; Ross Stagner, "Corporate Decision Making," *Journal of Applied Psychology* vol. 53, no. 1, February 1969, pp. 1–13; and Stanley Thune and Robert House, "Where Long Range Planning Pays Off," *Business Horizons*, August 1970, pp. 81–87.

[3]Richard Cyert and James March, *Behavioral Theory of the Firm*, Prentice-Hall, Inc., Englewood Cliffs, N.J., 1963; James Dent, "Organizational Correlates of the Goals of Business Managers," *Personnel Psychology*, vol. 12 no. 3, 1959; George England, "Organizational Goals and Ex-

pected Behavior of American Managers," *Academy of Management Journal*, June 1967; David Sills, *The Volunteers*, The Free Press of Glencoe, Inc., New York, 1957, pp. 253–368.

[4]Francis Aguilar, *Scanning the Business Environment*, The Macmillan Company, New York, 1967; Robert Collings, *Scanning the Business Environment for Strategic Information*, unpublished DBA thesis, Harvard Business School, Cambridge, Mass., 1968; Warren Keegan, *Scanning the International Business Environment*, unpublished DBA thesis, Harvard Business School, Cambridge, Mass., 1967; Jerry Wall, "What the Competition is Doing: Your Need to Know," *Harvard Business Review*, November-December, 1974.

[5]Joseph Bower, *Managing the Resource Allocation Process*, Harvard University Press, Cambridge, Mass., 1970; E. Eugene Carter, "The Behavioral Theory of the Firm and Top Level Corporate Decisions," *Administrative Science Quarterly*, vol 16, no. 4, 1971, pp. 413–428; Jules Schwartz, "The Decision to Innovate," unpublished DBA thesis, Harvard Business School, Cambridge, Mass., 1973.

WILLIAM F. GLUECK, *The University of Georgia*

# Politically oriented managers (*See* MANAGEMENT, FUTURE OF.)

# Pollution control and abatement (*See* ENVIRONMENT, PHYSICAL.)

# Pollution protection legislation (*See* ENVIRONMENTAL PROTECTION LEGISLATION.)

# Populism (*See* EGALITARIANISM.)

# Portal-to-Portal Act (*See* WAGES AND HOURS LEGISLATION.)

# Position strategy (*See* PLANNING, PLANNED MANAGEMENT OF TURBULLENT CHANGE.)

# Positioning, product (*See* ADVERTISING CONCEPTS.)

# Potential problem analysis (*See* DECISION-MAKING PROCESS.)

# Power and influence

Power is generally viewed as the ability to compel obedience or cooperation. In its narrower sense, it is a delegated right or privilege, usually assigned legally and/or formally by an organization in the form of authority. In its broader sense, power is spoken of as the ability to prevail. Hence, organizational behaviorists prefer the term *influence* to *power*.

Power or influence may reside in an individual, or it may be a characteristic of a group as perceived by individuals within or outside of the group. In the individual sense, power is associated with leadership and the requirement of management to plan and organize and especially to direct and control others. In the organizational sense, power represents the influence a group, such as a work group or entire company, exerts upon its members to obtain participation and conformance while seeking its objectives.

Power may be described in several ways, according to its source, and be either real or as perceived by another individual:

*Reward power* is dependent upon the ability to provide incentives in the form of rewards such as pay increases, promotions, attractive assignments, and job security.

*Coercive power* reflects the ability to impose sanctions in the form of criticism, dismissal, unattractive assignments, and withheld rewards.

*Referent power* is a function of an individual's ability to project a personal form of appeal to followers and is based more upon faith and charisma than upon reward or coercion or identifiable logic.

*Expert power* stems from the possession of specialized knowledge or skills perceived by others to be valuable to them in their organizational activities and relationships.

*Legitimate power* is that conveyed by the organization to the various managers throughout its hierarchy in the form of designated titles and positions.

**Perceptive Aspect** Power and influence is a two-way entity. There is, on the one hand, the power an individual holds as a result of personal qualities and/or those conferred legitimately upon him or her. On the other hand, there is the power that another individual *perceives* that the person holds for whatever reasons. In many organizational circumstances, there may be significant differences between the intrinsic power of an individual and the perception others have of this power. It is for this reason that organizations often strive so hard to establish the legitimacy of authority and to build up the reward and coercive prerogatives invested in its managers. It is also for this reason that legitimate, reward, coercive, and even expert power fall far short of being enough for managers lacking in referent power.

**Power Needs**  Individuals vary in their need for personal power. Individuals also vary according to their response to the power of others. Some are influenced by one sort of power, such as charisma, and rebel against another, such as coercion. Others respond mainly to rewards and punishment. A bureaucrat may respect only legitimacy; a specialist, only expertise. Obviously, there may be followers and nonfollowers for each manager according to the needs of his or her organizational subordinates and associates.

**Effect of Power**  It is not certain how legitimate power will affect the individual who holds it and how he or she will use it. Some persons become more compassionate; others exploit their power. It appears that two factors may encourage the latter tendency. Many organizations seem to reward those who hold power so the struggle to attain this valuable commodity can become rapacious. Furthermore, the larger the gap is between those who exert power and those who feel powerless, the easier—and thus greater—the exploitation is likely to be. Paradoxically, the feeling of powerlessness and overdependence often induces noncooperative behavior, perhaps because the less powerful individual no longer perceives benefits to be derived from his or her participation.

Typically, those who hold power in organizations resist the removal of that power. They do so by direct and indirect intimidation and by isolation of others who try to take it from them. Thus, the so-called "power struggle" is evident in many organizations where some degree of power equalization has not been developed.

**Exercise of Power**  While the mere possession or nonpossession of power has an effect on an individual, the manner in which power is exercised and the kind of power employed can affect an organization's goals. Traditionally, organizations have depended upon the right of the supervisor to require certain behavior (legitimate power) and the capability of the supervisor to impose sanctions (coercive power). While the use of legitimate power may elicit compliance from the subordinate, the compliance is likely to produce only "acceptable" levels of performance and is unlikely to produce increases in performance

levels. The use of coercive power produces those feelings of powerlessness and overdependence on the part of the subordinate that may lead to alienation and noncooperative behavior. The use of expert or referent power correlates most strongly with organizational effectiveness, employee satisfaction, and higher levels of performance.

Ideally, then, the supervisor's attempts to influence subordinates should be based upon expert or referent power. It should be emphasized, however, that in spite of a manager's belief that his or her influence attempts are based upon expert or referent power, the employee's perception of this basis may be more important. While the manager may, in fact, possess specialized knowledge and skills, the employee may comply mainly because he or she perceives the manager's ability to impose sanctions or grant rewards, or simply because the employee acknowledges the authority vested in the supervisor to require certain behavior. If an employee maintains either of these attitudes, then the results of the compliance may be the same as if the manager had overtly used sanctions, rewards, etc., in the first place. Briefly, what is important in the influence attempt is the employee's perception of the basis of power and not the superior's. Since superiors do in fact possess legitimate, reward, and coercive power, it is very difficult for the employee in any given situation to perceive correctly the kind of power the supervisor intends to use.

**Exchange Relationships**  Students of organization behavior view social behavior as an exchange. They contend that an understanding of this concept will minimize power conflicts and maximize cooperation. Effective managers, they observe, recognize this implicit exchange in management-employee relations and seek the employ power from various sources accordingly. The employee or subordinate, in effect, trades certain prerogatives for certain privileges in relationship to personal and organizational values. Participative management approaches are based upon this view that power relationships are mutually determined. The offer of participation by a manger to subordinates is a sharing of power. It seeks a balance between (1) generally accepted managerial prerogatives and (2) freedom of the employee to develop his or her own expert power. In the eyes of Richard Boyatzis, this promotes "efficacy" wherein "an individual builds . . . his perceived ability to influence his future and his environment through interaction with the people who have the ability to influence him."[1]

*See also* AUTHORITY, RESPONSIBILITY, AND ACCOUNTABILITY; DISCIPLINE; INTERPERSONAL RELA-

TIONSHIPS; LEADERSHIP; MOTIVATION IN ORGANIZA-
TIONS.

## NOTES

[1]Richard E. Boyatzis, "Building Efficacy: An Effective Use of Power," *Industrial Management Review*, no. 1, Fall 1969.

## REFERENCES

Bachman, Jerald G., David Bowers, and Philip M. Marcus: "Bases of Supervisory Power: A Comparative Study in Five Organizational Settings," in Arnold Tannenbaum (ed.), *Control in Organizations*, McGraw-Hill Book Company, New York, 1968.

Boyatzis, Richard E.: "Building Efficacy: An Effective Use of Power," *Industrial Management Review*, no. 1, Fall 1969.

French, John R. P., Jr., and Bertram Raven: "The Bases of Social Power," in Dorwin Cartwright (ed.), *Studies in Social Power*, Institute for Social Research, Ann Arbor, Mich., 1959.

Kipnis, David: *The Powerholders*, The University of Chicago Press, Chicago, 1976.

Patchen, Martin: "The Locus and Basis of Influence on Organizational Decisions," *Organizational Behavior and Human Performance*, April 1974.

Schopler, John: "Social Power," in Leonard Berkowitz, (ed.), *Advances in Experimental Social Psychology*, vol. 2, Academic Press, New York, 1965.

D. KENT ZIMMERMAN, *James Madison University*

**Power needs** (*See* INTERPERSONAL RELATIONSHIPS.)

**Predetermined time systems** (*See* WORK MEASUREMENT.)

**Prerogatives, management** [*See* LABOR (TRADE) UNIONS.]

**Present value method** (*See* BUDGETING, CAPITAL.)

**President, corporate** (*See* OFFICERS, CORPORATE.)

**President, office of** (*See* ORGANIZATION STRUCTURES AND CHARTING.)

**Preventive maintenance** (*See* MAINTENANCE MANAGEMENT.)

**Price of services** (*See* MARKETING OF SERVICES.)

**Price differentiation** (*See* INTERNATIONAL TRADE.)

**Price discrimination** (*See* PRODUCT AND SERVICE PRICING.)

**Price fixing** (*See* PRODUCT AND SERVICE PRICING.)

**Price index** (*See* ECONOMIC MEASUREMENTS.)

**Price leadership** (*See* PRODUCT AND SERVICE PRICING.)

**Price maintenance, retail** (*See* PRODUCT AND SERVICE PRICING.)

**Price theory** (*See* ECONOMIC CONCEPTS.)

**Price war** (*See* PRODUCT AND SERVICE PRICING.)

**Prices** (*See* ECONOMIC MEASUREMENTS.)

**Pricing, incremental** (*See* PRODUCT AND SERVICE PRICING.)

**Pricing, intracompany** (*See* ACCOUNTING FOR MANAGERIAL CONTROL.)

**Pricing, product and service** (*See* PRODUCT AND SERVICE PRICING.)

**Pricing, retail**   (*See* RETAILING MANAGEMENT.)

**Pricing, special order**   (*See* PRODUCT AND SERVICE PRICING.)

**Pricing, straight markup**   (*See* PRODUCT AND SERVICE PRICING.)

**Pricing, target-rate-of-return**   (*See* PRODUCT AND SERVICE PRICING.)

**Pricing, transfer**   (*See* ACCOUNTING FOR MANAGERIAL CONTROL.)

**Principal, loan**   (*See* CREDIT MANAGEMENT.)

**Principle, management**   (*See* MANAGEMENT THEORY, SCIENCE AND APPROACHES.)

**Principle of local preference**   (*See* MARKETS, PUBLIC.)

**Principles, organizational design**   (*See* ORGANIZATION STRUCTURES AND CHARTING.)

**Print-cycle analysis**   (*See* PAPER WORK SIMPLIFICATION.)

**Priority list, engineering**   (*See* PLANT ENGINEERING MANAGEMENT.)

**Private sector managers**   (*See* MANAGER, DEFINITIONS OF.)

**Probability assessment methods**   (*See* FORECASTING BUSINESS CONDITIONS.)

**Problem analysis**   (*See* DECISION-MAKING PROCESS.)

**Problem-solving conferences**   (*See* CONFERENCE LEADERSHIP.)

**Problem solving with economics**   (*See* ECONOMIC CONCEPTS.)

**Procedure data chart**   (*See* PAPER WORK SIMPLIFICATION.)

**Procedure flow chart**   (*See* PAPER WORK SIMPLIFICATION.)

**Procedures**   (*See* MANAGEMENT THEORY, SCIENCE, AND APPROACHES; POLICY FORMULATION AND IMPLEMENTATION.)

**Procedures, administrative**   (*See* SYSTEMS AND PROCEDURES.)

**Procedures manual**   (*See* MANUALS, POLICY AND PROCEDURES.)

**Process**   (*See* PRODUCTION PROCESSES.)

**Process, continuous**   (*See* PRODUCTION PROCESSES.)

**Process, production**   (*See* PRODUCTION/OPERATIONS MANAGEMENT.)

**Process approaches to motivation**   (*See* MOTIVATION IN ORGANIZATIONS.)

**Process cost systems**   (*See* ACCOUNTING, COST ANALYSIS AND CONTROL.)

**Process optimization** *(See* PRODUCTION PROCESSES.*)*

**Process selection** *(See* PRODUCTION PROCESSES.*)*

**Processing** *(See* PRODUCTION PROCESSES.*)*

**Processing-related dimensions, industrial** *(See* MARKETS, CLASSIFICATIONS AND MARKET ANALYSIS.*)*

**Procurement, materials** *(See* PURCHASING MANAGEMENT.*)*

**Procurement procedure** *(See* MATERIALS MANAGEMENT.*)*

**Product analysis** *(See* PRODUCTION PROCESSES.*)*

**Product attributes** *(See* PRODUCT PLANNING AND DEVELOPMENT.*)*

**Product branding** *(See* PRODUCT PLANNING AND DEVELOPMENT.*)*

**Product cost, variable** *(See* PRODUCT AND SERVICE PRICING.*)*

**Product development review** *(See* INTERNATIONAL OPERATIONS AND MANAGEMENT IN MULTINATIONAL COMPANIES.*)*

**Product differentiation** *(See* MARKETING, CONCEPTS AND SYSTEMS.*)*

**Product leadership** *(See* PRODUCT PLANNING AND DEVELOPMENT.*)*

# Product liability

The change in legal philosophy in the United States from *caveat emptor*, buyer beware, to *caveat venditor*, seller beware, has significant implications for the business executive. Nowhere has this change been more readily apparent than in the area of product liability. Product liability refers to the legal responsibility of a manufacturer or seller of a product to compensate a buyer who has been injured by the product. In recent years, the courts, regulators, and legislatures have extended liability to a wide range of product situations where it did not exist before. In 1976, United States companies had over 1 million product liability claims filed against them seeking some $50 billion in total damages. In 1965, claims totaled only $500,000. More important from the firm's standpoint, the average award granted increased to $79,940 in 1973 from $11,644 in 1965.[1] Compounding this problem is the fact that insurance companies, even with premium increases of 300 to 500 percent in 5 years, find it difficult to support the inflated awards and open-ended risk trend, and thus are becoming increasingly reluctant to provide product liability insurance. Although numerous reasons can be presented for the increase in the number of product liability cases, most experts recognize that it is primarily the result of the consumer's increasing awareness of his or her right to sue and the increasing willingness to exercise that right. All evidence indicates that product liability as a critical concern for business is here to stay; therefore, it behooves the executive to acquire an appreciation of the contemporary legal concepts, the situations in which they are applicable, the defenses available, and, specifically, what each firm can do organizationally to reduce its exposure to product liability and the associated claims and costs.

**Widespread Vulnerability** Legislation such as the Consumer Product Safety Act and the Magnuson-Moss Warranty–Federal Trade Commission Improvement Act, tends to give the impression that only firms manufacturing and distributing consumer products need to be concerned with product liability. This impression is erroneous, since an estimated 85 percent of all product liability suits have involved industrial rather than consumer products. In addition, the present application of legal doctrines by the courts has expanded product liability to the distributor as well as the manufacturer. In certain instances, legal suits may even include firms that are peripheral members of the channel of distribution, such as advertising agencies, endorsing firms, and testing firms.

Further compounding the product liability problem is the fact exposure to liability is not a function of firm size. In fact, a small firm is at a decided disadvantage, and it is more likely to be forced out of business because it may be less able to satisfy a liability claim or unable to pay the high cost of liability insurance. Differences in risk, however, are related to types of products. Although some products such as drugs, foods, chemicals, and selected types of machinery present a greater risk for the firms that produce them, product liability presents a critical challenge for *all* firms.

## CONTEMPORARY LEGAL DOCTRINES

In recent years, the liability of the manufacturer and seller for injury caused by defective products has increased substantially. In bringing suit against a manufacturer or distributor, legal doctrines of negligence, breach of warranty, or strict liability in tort are usually at issue. Negligence and strict liability have their basis in tort law (law of personal injury or property damage), whereas breach of warranty is in contract law. Even though differences among these three doctrines exist, it is not uncommon to find all three doctrines of liability at issue in a product liability suit.

**Negligence Doctrine** The basis of liability for negligence is the failure of a manufacturer to design, manufacture, or market a product with reasonable care. Failure to exercise reasonable care allows buyers, users, and others within the foreseeable scope of product use to seek recovery for damages. Until the early 1900s, negligence was the only doctrine of liability available to an injured buyer. The courts protected manufacturers from these claims, however, by adopting a rule that required the injured person to be in privity of contract before he or she could bring suit. *Privity of contract* means that there must exist a direct contractual relationship between the consumer (injured person) and the manufacturer. Since consumers do not usually purchase directly from a manufacturer, the cases were dismissed by the courts for lack of privity. The privity requirement in negligence cases was abolished by Judge Cardoza in the 1916 case *MacPherson v. Buick Motor Company*.[2]

Today, negligence still remains a major basis for product liability suits. Court decisions indicate that most negligence cases in product liability are based upon faulty production, poor product design, improper packaging, or inadequate warnings or instructions relating to dangers associated with the product.

Distributors may also be held liable for negligence by failing to inspect and give warnings for products, such as lawnmowers and chain saws, which may be inherently dangerous in their normal or foreseeable use. The duty to give a warning out of a foreseeable danger of injury arises from the normal or probable use of the product and the likelihood that unless warned the user will not ordinarily be aware of such danger.

**Breach of Warranty Doctrine** Breach of warranty refers to a failure by a manufacturer or seller to satisfy a contractual promise made in connection with the sale of a product.[3] Most managers only consider the express promises or warranties presented as a provision in a contract of sale, a statement in an advertisement or label, or in certain circumstances, the oral representation made by a salesperson at the time of sale. The sale of products, however, may also be covered by implied promises or warranties which require that the seller's product is either merchantable or fit for a particular purpose as expressed by the buyer.

For a product to be merchantable, it must be fit for the "ordinary" purpose for which it is used. For example, a package of hot dogs that contains glass fragments and causes injury to a consumer is not fit for human consumption (its ordinary purpose).

The implied warranty of fitness for a particular purpose is different in that it is an indication by the seller that a product is suitable for a buyer's particular need, and the buyer relies on the seller's skill or judgment in making a purchase. For example, if a distributor sells a vehicle to a buyer knowing that he intends to use it as an off-the-road vehicle and the buyer is injured when the steering mechanism fails during off-the-road use, then the seller is liable because the vehicle was not fit for the particular use.

Implied warranties do not apply to contracts for services. Any injuries incurred as a result of improper services must be based on negligence. However, it is not always easy to determine what is a product and what is a service.

Since breach of warranty as a basis for product liability is a contract action, it requires privity of contract and can work to the advantage of the manufacturer. Recently though, the courts either have stretched the privity concept to a meaningless point or have chosen to abandon it altogether when dealing with implied warranties arising out of the sale of certain inherently dangerous products. For example, in the case *Henningsen v. Bloomfield Motors, Inc.*,[4] an auto manufacturer was held liable for injuries caused by a defective steering wheel not only to the purchaser of the automobile but also to injured passengers and bystanders.

**Strict Liability in Tort Doctrine** The doctrine of strict liability has evolved from the doctrine of negligence. It imposes liability on a seller of defective products that cause injury to users or consumers even though due care has been exercised in their manufacture and sale. A manufacturer is also strictly liable for injuries caused by defective components purchased from others and merely assembled into the final products. In addition, courts have imposed liability on distributors and retailers—including those selling used products. At present, strict liability has normally only been applied to firms regularly engaged in the business of manufacturing, selling, or leasing products, but courts could expand application to include advertising agencies, product testing agencies, etc. Strict liability differs from negligence in that recovery does not require proof of negligence. Therefore, an individual injured by a defective product may recover damages if he or she is able to prove the following:

1. The product was defective.
2. Injury resulted from a defect in the product.
3. The defect existed at the time the product left the manufacturer's/supplier's control.

It is important to emphasize that although all reasonable care was exercised in the manufacturing and selling of a product, the courts may find it defective if it is not safe for expected use and an adequate warning is not provided. *Foreseeable product defects* are dangers that should have been anticipated by the seller, and either the product should have been redesigned or buyers should have been given adequate warnings. The critical factor to be determined in situations where foreseeability is an issue is the limit to what a manufacturer/seller is expected to foresee. At present, there is little guidance for the courts to make the final judgment. In all probability, there will continue to be an increase in the use of strict liability by injured parties in product liability cases because it frees them from many of the requirements under the doctrines of negligence and breach of warranty.

## MANUFACTURER/DISTRIBUTOR DEFENSES

As noted above, a manufacturer of a defective product, or the distributor who sold it, may be held liable to the injured person based upon breach of warranty, negligence, or strict liability in tort. It is critical to establish which basis of liability is to be relied upon because such determination will govern the defenses available. The legislatures in their interpretation of statutes and the courts in their interpretation of statutes and legal doctrines have broadened the concept of what makes a product defective. In so doing, they not only have substantially increased the likelihood of product liability claims against manufacturers and distributors but have also limited many of the available defenses. The affirmative defenses that must be proven by manufacturers or distributors to avoid liability are identified below.

**Defenses to Breach of Warranty** There are a number of defenses available to the manufacturer of allegedly defective products in breach of warranty cases under the Uniform Commercial Code. However, the manufacturer must be aware that under breach of warranty, unlike negligence, the exercise of due care in the manufacture of a product is not a relevant issue. In effect, a manufacturer's liability is absolute if a defect in the product is proven in a breach of warranty case.

*Disclaimer of Warranty.* One of the principal defenses available to the manufacturer is that no warranties, either express or implied, were given. However, a disclaimer of warranty defense will be unacceptable if a prior agreement during negotiations indicated that express warranties existed. In addition, to effectively exclude liability for implied warranties, specific language must be used in the disclaimer. First, in order to exclude the warranty of merchantability, the disclaimer must mention the term *implied warranty of merchantability* and if in writing, it must be conspicious. Second, to exclude the implied warranty of fitness, it is sufficient to use a general disclaimer indicating that no warranties are given.

Both types of implied warranty are excluded when expressions comparable to "as is" or "with all faults" are used in the disclaimer. Implied warranties are also excluded if the buyer has had the opportunity to identify discoverable defects by examining the product or a sample of the product. Additionally, exclusion of implied warranties may exist if past and present contracts between parties exclude all implied warranties or it is industry custom to exclude all implied warranties.

*Notice of Breach.* A second defense available to the manufacturer is notice of breach to the seller. Under this defense, the buyer has a duty to notify the seller of a breach of warranty within a reasonable time after discovery of a defect.

*Statute of Limitations.* A third defense is the statute of limitations. Generally, this requires the injured product user to bring suit within 4 years after delivery of the product.

**Defenses to Negligence** The most common defense used in negligence cases is contributory negligence. *Contributory negligence* refers to conduct by an injured product-user which is a contributing cause of the injuries because the user failed to exercise due care. For example, contributory negligence was successfully established in a case against a nightgown manufacturer. An individual suffered severe burns when a combustible nightgown caught fire while she was smoking in bed "in a semi-conscious state induced by . . . a highly potent sleeping pill." The court ruled in favor of the firm because the injured party's conduct contributed to the cause of the accident.[5] It is important to recognize that in most states, the proving of contributory negligence on the part of the injured person prevents recovery of any damages for negligence of the manufacturer. This is true even though the manufacturer's negligence may be much greater than that of the injured product-user.

To avoid the seemingly harsh results of the strict application of contributory negligence on an injured product-user, some states have adopted the concept of *comparative negligence*. Under this concept, a jury will determine the percentage of each party's negligence and then allow recovery accordingly.

Another major defense available to the manufacturer in negligence cases is *assumption of risk*. Under this defense, an injured product-user may be denied recovery if he or she assumes the risk of any damage created by a manufacturer's negligence. However, in most cases, this requires the manufacturer to

prove not only that the injured party knew of the defect creating the danger but also that he or she realized the full extent of the danger.

**Defenses to Strict Liability in Tort**   The only affirmative defense available to the manufacturer under strict liability in tort is one also available in negligence cases: the assumption of risk. As stated previously, a manufacturer is not liable under this defense if an injured product-user had knowledge of the existence of a dangerous defect and voluntarily continued to use the product. The assumption of risk defense is strengthened if the manufacturer shows that adequate warnings were given for all foreseeable uses or misuses of the product.

In contrast to the breach of warranty statute of limitations, an action based on the doctrine of strict liability and negligence must begin within a given period from the time of injury. This period of time is usually shorter than that provided in product liability cases based upon warranty.

### AN ACTION PROGRAM

A prudent firm can take positive action to minimize at least and perhaps even eliminate losses. It requires, however, a commitment by the firm to provide a comprehensive program—one that considers product safety from the perspective of the firm as a whole. The mere fact that the majority of product liability suits are due to defective design, faulty production or assembly, improper packaging, or inadequate warnings or instructions relating to product use should be evidence enough to support this view (*see* Fig. P-23). Since suits normally cut across many functions in the firm, every department must play a key role in contributing to a corporate product safety program—including engineering (research and development), production, purchasing, quality control, advertising, sales, and sales service. In addition, this program must be concerned with the entire life cycle of the product—including both the internal cycle (under the manufacturer's control) and the external cycle (after leaving the manufacturer's control).

The following is a framework and list of factors to be considered by a firm when establishing an action program to deal with the product liability challenge:

**Establish Objectives**   Specific objectives must be established in order to provide sufficient coverage and direction in approaching the product liability challenge. These should include the following:

1. Creation of a safe product
2. Assurance that the product will perform safely under ordinary circumstances
3. Assurance that the product will perform

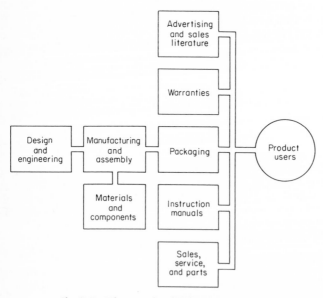

Fig. P-23. Where product liability suits arise. (Adapted from "How to Control Product Liability Losses," Journal of American Insurance, vol. 52, no. 2, p. 21, Summer 1976.)

safely under extraordinary circumstances (foreseeable misuse)

4. Assurance of accurate and complete information to the buyer concerning the following:

   *a.* Product attributes

   *b.* Product usage

   *c.* Product warning

5. Assurance of coordination with channel members to provide the following:

   *a.* Accurate information

   *b.* Accurate training with regard to (1) transportation and handling, (2) demonstration, (3) installation, and (4) service

6. Acquisition of accurate product-market experience records

7. Assurance that when a product safety problem is identified, a contingency plan exists to take action with regard to (1) customers (users), (2) product, (3) channel members, and (4) government agencies

8. Active support of constructive steps that can be taken to remove inequities relating to product liability (safety)

**Assign Organizational Responsibility** The placement of organizational responsibility for product safety is critical to its success. It must be placed in the organization where those assigned responsibility can be held accountable. The foregoing comments suggest the following:

1. Responsibility for product liability must rest with top management, since it cuts across all functions and can arise at every stage of the product's development, manufacture, and service life.

2. Responsibility for product liability may be vested in one individual or a number of individuals brought together as a product safety committee (the size and structure of the committee must be adapted to the particular needs of the company).

3. The size and complexity of the organizational structure responsible for product liability is dependent upon the particular needs of the company. However, it must enable the firm to achieve its established product liability program objectives.

4. The product liability program actually assumes the appearance of a product liability audit. It is not a one-time affair, but rather a continuous process used to isolate areas where additional work is needed. For example, it is necessary to evaluate not only new product designs but also older designs to ensure they incorporate current safety standards. Thus, the responsibility for accomplishment must be given organizational permanency.

**Operationalize the Objectives** In order to achieve the established objectives, a plan of action must be developed that will identify these goals and describe how they are to be accomplished. The tasks include the following:

1. A written corporate policy on product safety should be communicated to all employees, stressing the company's commitment to design, develop, manufacture, and market safe products (product safety must be an integral part of all product decision areas).

2. Company standards should be developed for product design, development, and quality control. These standards should meet or exceed federal, state, local, or industry-recommended or mandatory safety standards.

3. Quality standards should be stated in writing for all production-related tasks, including the purchase of raw materials and components, manufacture, assembly, packaging, and shipping.

4. Carefully supervised product-use tests should be performed, representing use of the product under both ordinary and extraordinary circumstances (foreseeable but unintended use).

5. Product information generated by the firm should be reviewed for clarity, accuracy, and completeness. This information includes technical manuals, instructions and directions, warranties, labels, advertisements, service manuals, and product claims (printed information must include complete disclosure of product information and must not overstate or misstate the product's capabilities).

6. Information intended to warn the user about hazards that cannot be eliminated by design should be conspicuously placed on the product, presented in understandable language and symbols, and last the life of the product.

7. Close relationships with channel members should be promoted and maintained by providing:

   *a.* Relevant product literature to channel members (training sessions should be provided if necessary). Distributors, however, must *not* modify service or advertise a product without authorization.

   *b.* Skilled salespeople.

   *c.* Skilled field-service technicians.

8. The company should maintain a vital record file for each product including sales records, sales literature, design specifications and drawings, purchase orders, technical manuals, instruction and training manuals, modification releases, performance tests, inspection controls, field service reports, recall campaigns, and packaging and shipping instructions.

9. The company should monitor relevant environments, including:

*a.* Product/customer environment by (1) reviewing submitted quality control reports; (2) receiving warranty card purchase data and comments from customers; (3) reviewing customer complaints (a follow-up when an accident or near accident related to the product is reported); and (4) reviewing information gathered from salespeople, channel members, customers, and competitors.

*b.* External environment by (1) reviewing professional and trade association reports; (2) reviewing industry journals; and (3) reviewing reports of government agencies (i.e., Consumer Product Safety Commission, Federal Trade Commission, etc.).

**Prepare for Contingency Events** Implementation of programs in product liability does not eliminate entirely the risk of costly suits; it will, however, reduce the impact of suits. A successful program requires anticipating future events by:

1. Investing in adequate liability insurance written through a reliable company by a knowledgeable agent or broker.

2. Establishing a plan for quickly notifying distributors and customers when a defect is identified and specifying what procedure should be followed in order to have the product replaced or repaired. This information must also be relayed to meet the requirements of relevant government agencies.

3. Establishing a predetermined and tested product recall plan for a defective product, which includes the following:

*a.* Task force responsible for product recall.

*b.* Information systems for identifying sources and types of product-market information.

*c.* Recall strategy for identifying, contacting distributors and customers, and picking up products.

*d.* Financing strategy consistent with the company's resources and the potential costs of recall.

*e.* Promotional program to minimize the effects of the product recall.

4. Establishing a plan for using corporate counsel not only in the development of product liability prevention programs but also as a defender of the company's existing law suits. (In the latter role, the corporate counsel is the liaison officer with the insurance carrier, assistant to trial counsel, and investigator and coordinator within the company.)

5. Supporting legislation that establishes time limits on product liability claims, dollar limits on certain types of damages, and limits on lawyers'

contingent fees that are linked to the size of the settlement.

## CONCLUSION

The trend of public policy as seen in new legislation and court decisions has established that the marketing of defective products results in a major risk of injury to customers. The trend has also established that the manufacturer and distributor are better able than the consumer to assume or insure against the risk of loss arising from defective products. The critical issue management must recognize is that product liability is here to stay as a major and expensive risk of doing business. Given the diversity of business firms, the complexity of their product lines, and the varying level of resources available to them, only a general framework regarding product liability has been outlined above. To deal with this issue demands that each firm develop an intelligent, creative, and carefully planned program. Only through such an approach can management hope to establish an integrated and effective strategy to meet the challenge of product liability.

*See also* CONSUMERISM AND CONSUMER PROTECTION LEGISLATION; DESIGN, INDUSTRIAL; GOVERNMENT REGULATION, UNIFORM COMMERCIAL CODE; PRODUCT PLANNING AND DEVELOPMENT; QUALITY MANAGEMENT.

### NOTES

[1]"Calculating Your Liability Risk," *Modern Packaging,* vol. 48, October 1975, p. 10.

[2]First court decision which held that the privity requirement afforded no protection to a negligent manufacturer or seller if the product which caused injury was the type of product that is reasonably certain to be dangerous if negligently manufactured. *MacPherson v. Buick Motor Co.,* 217 N.Y. 382, 111 N.E. 1050 (1916).

[3]All warranties in the sale of goods arise from the Uniform Commercial Code–Article on Sales, enacted by essentially all states.

[4]*Henningson v. Bloomfield Motors, Inc.,* 32 N.J. 358, 161 A.2d 69 (1960).

[5]*Dallison v. Sears, Roebuck and Co.,* 313 F.2d 343 (Colorado Law) (1962).

### REFERENCES

Gray, Irwin, with Albert L. Bases, Charles H. Martin, and Alexander Sternberg: *Product Liability: A Management Response,* American Management Association, New York, 1975.

*Safety in the Marketplace,* Washington.

Many associations have made available for a nominal charge product liability awareness pamphlets and program manuals, such as the following:

*Product Liability Manual*, American Mutual Insurance Alliance, 20 North Wacker Drive, Chicago, Ill. 60606. $2.
*Product Liability Pamphlet*, Defense Research Institute, 1100 West Wells Street, Milwaukee, Wis. 53233. $.50.

LONNIE L OSTROM, *Arizona State University*

# Product life cycle (*See* MARKETS CLASSIFICATIONS AND MARKET ANALYSIS; MARKETING, CONCEPTS AND SYSTEMS.)

# Product-line policy (*See* PRODUCT PLANNING AND DEVELOPMENT.)

# Product management (*See* MARKETING, INDUSTRIAL.)

# Product-market classifications (*See* MARKETS, CLASSIFICATIONS AND MARKET ANALYSIS.)

# Product-market scope (*See* PLANNING, PLANNED MANAGEMENT OF TURBULENT CHANGE.)

# Product method (*See* MARKETS, CLASSIFICATIONS AND MARKET ANALYSIS.)

# Product mix (*See* PRODUCT PLANNING AND DEVELOPMENT.)

# Product organization (*See* ORGANIZATION STRUCTURES AND CHARTING.)

# Product planning and development

Product planning is both a fundamental and a strategic business function that generates profit by identifying customer wants and needs and translating them into product and/or service specifications. Product planning also translates newly developed specifications into the language of the customer, production, and finance to determine the profit potential.

**Two-Thirds Fail** Most companies do not realize the impact of their poor product decisions on the profitability of their firm. Surveys show conclusively that the present nonsystematic methods of developing product plans are only one-third effective and that two-thirds of all new products (and businesses) fail.[1] This bad record stems from either a single, strong personality or a committee (formal or ad hoc) that makes all the product planning decisions. (The function is always performed, but the performance of the function usually goes unmeasured.) On the other hand, some companies with good planning are over 80 percent effective.[2] That is why many managements are rethinking the product planning function and are attempting to make it more effective.

**Rethinking Product Planning** The first step in rethinking the product planning function is to admit that a great many managers do not really know what this fundamental and strategic function is. Professors have given it a name, just as doctors give their treatments names, but the product planning function is rarely well understood. Furthermore, this discussion is too general and necessarily short to be able to provide the depth of understanding necessary to increase significantly the effectiveness of product planning within a specific company. Something better and more permanent than a short course is usually needed.

The second step is to admit that few individuals (including top managers) have *both* the breadth and the depth of technical capability to be good product planners. Thus, since something better than the usual committee is needed, serious consideration must be given to establishing a multidisciplined product planning activity (or hiring a qualified consultant) that is rewarded primarily for increasing the effectiveness of planning, rather than for increasing sales, reducing costs, or submitting reports on time.

The third step is the most difficult. It is to concede that a large amount of both real and potential profit has been lost as a result of poor product planning. Reviewing records and talking with people may provide an indication of the losses. Then it is time to rethink product planning.

**Organizing Effectively** Because the losses resulting from poor product planning can be very large (remember the $250 million lost on the Edsel), it is often wisely proposed that product planning should appear on the organization charts at a level *equal* to the conventional functions of marketing, engineering, production, and finance. Today, product planning is normally found several levels below. Furthermore, many managements expect too little from product planning. Rather than expecting meaningful integrated strategic plans with clearly identified contingencies, they are satisfied with non-strategic projects that are merely reactions to competitive moves. This is due, in part, to the location of the function in the organization. A few companies such as General Electric and Ford Motor Company, of course, have rethought product planning and have reorganized so that the function reports to top management. These companies are exceptions.

## PRODUCT PLANNING: A STRATEGIC FUNCTION

**Definition of *Strategy*** A great amount of careful thinking already has been done about the subject of strategy. In spite of all this work, strategy remains hard to define. Debates rage as to whether it can be both inward and outward looking or whether it must restrict itself to being outward looking only. To address such problems, some companies call the outward-looking plans *strategies*—and the inward-looking plans *policy*. Each type of plan must be supported with resource allocation commitments in the form of detailed schedules (PERT, CPM, milestones) and budgets. Other companies have tried to define clearly the nuances between strategy and policy, but while useful for learning, such activity has little practical value in the business world. Thus, a simple and useful definition of *strategy* is a fundamental plan of action that is intended to accomplish the company's objectives.

Since strategic product planning must address itself to fundamental concepts, it is appropriate to review some of the strategic concepts that must be considered by product planners.

**The Experience Curve** The Boston Consulting Group has published the book *Perspectives on Experience*,[3] which indicates that costs (in constant dollars), relative to the value added by the company, decrease by about 20 percent every time the total (cumulative) volume doubles. To support this insight, they document examples ranging from transistors to appliances, from plastics to beer, and from cleansing tissue to power generation. The strategic importance of the concept is that the company with the greatest market share automatically gains the greatest experience, and therefore can have the lowest costs (assuming good management).

The Boston Consulting Group also discusses the following:

A way to calculate the investment necessary to "catch up" on experience.

A rationale that indicates that the best time to increase market share is during rapid market growth.

The observation that the impact of vertical integration might be less than anticipated because the experience available in the "new" business lags significantly behind competitors. This has a marked impact on make versus buy decisions.

Since the real competitive advantage results from total accumulated experience, the value of patents lies in their ability to provide a headstart on total experience. This concept suggests that royalty payments might be preferable to the delays encountered while the company seeks a way to circumvent a patent.

**Market Share Importance** The experience curve phenomenon has recently been confirmed by a group of Harvard professors who studied over 600 different businesses using computerized regression analysis techniques. Their study indicated that market share was the single biggest measurable factor affecting profits.[4]

The key variable in the study was the definition of the market. Thus, a hardware store might have a market that is purely geographic. It prospers because it dominates its particular geographic segmentation. If another hardware store moved in, both might barely survive.

Realistic market segmentation is vital to the success of product planning. Thus, while Kodak dominates the low and middle end of its camera market, the high end is available. While IBM dominates the main frame business computer market, competition can do quite well in small and/or scientific markets. While General Motors dominates the car market in the United States, other companies dominate the markets in other countries.

**Reasons People Buy** Psychogenic reasons for buying products are not very useful to product planners. Rather, those needs must be translated into product attributes, which in turn can be translated into product specifications. The following list of product attributes has been gradually developed by the author over the past 15 years and is quite serviceable, although it must not be considered complete.

*Price* is a clear product-planning variable. What is not clear is affordability. Xerox and IBM lease their equipment to make it affordable. Polaroid sells low-priced cameras to create a large market for its profitable film. Many companies use a build/sell/lease-back arrangement to improve their return on investment on buildings. Homes are mortgaged, cars financed, education funds borrowed, etc.

*Performance* will vary with price. Thus, either a trade off or a line of products is required. Obviously, each product (or service) has unique performance criteria. For a food chain it might be salad crispness, and for an automobile it might be interior space versus fuel economy. Each company must carefully define performance for each of its markets.

*Quality* is a subjective term. Only the market can define the expected performance that it has for a product. The product planner must find what that definition of quality is for each product in each market segment.

*Reliability and durability* are often thought of as quality. However, quality refers to performance problems that cannot be corrected by service, while reliability and durability problems can be corrected through proper maintenance. Specifically, reliability refers to infant mortality (serviceable problems that occur in the first weeks of ownership). Durability refers to the product's performance as measured by mean time between failures.

*Appearance* is a very important factor in many markets. Thus, Hershey chocolates have used the appearance of their package so effectively that little added advertising is needed. Mercedes Benz has distinctive styling to communicate their quality image. Car companies still use styling to sell new products. The message is apparent: In some markets, people buy style.

*Conspicuousness* is still an important factor in planning products. Sometimes only a brand name provides the conspicuousness; for instance, a Cadillac and a Chevrolet share a remarkably large number of parts, ranging from engines to fasteners. A common technique of planning new products is to make a new feature conspicuous to help communicate its newness to the customer. Thus, many citizens band radios have a public address switch that is never used.

Probably the easiest way to think about conspicuousness is to ask how easy something is to see. If a feature must be identified, it is not very conspicuous. If the feature is apparent when the product is in use, that is good. But the best situation is to have the product conspicuous even when not in use.

Occasionally a product has a conspicuous feature when it becomes inconspicuous. Thus, automobile manufacturers invested a great deal of money to make a stereo tape player look exactly like a conventional in-dash car radio because customers had a major problem with tape deck theft. To the customer, the inconspicuous styling is a conspicuous advantage.

*Ease of usage* is another customer benefit—but this one has a "hooker." If the pattern of usage is different from normal practice, the benefit may become a disadvantage.

For example, Ford developed a new steering wheel in the early sixties. It was called "wrist twist steering," and it consisted of two hand grips that rotated by merely turning them with a normal wrist action. The market survey results were outstanding. Over 70 percent of those surveyed thought the system was a definite advantage. About 27 percent thought the system was as good as conventional power steering. Police departments that used the vehicles thought the system was clearly superior for their exacting driving requirements. Only about 3 percent of the hundreds surveyed did not like the new option. The downfall of the idea came when *one* man panicked and tried to drive the test car using only one of the grips as though it were a normal (two-handed) steering wheel. Despite the fact that the system was to be optional and was believed to be safer (according to the police in several states), the reaction of one customer to the unfamiliar (yet "easier") method of operation caused Ford to reject the feature.

*Safety* must always be considered. More precisely, the consequences of an error and the ease of making the error must be evaluated. The competitive advantage that can be gained by making a product safer is much smaller now than it has been historically. There are a large number of federal, state, and local agencies and laws that are intended to protect the customer's safety. The challenge of the product planner is to find a way to do it for less cost than the competition or to provide additional safety features.

*Service* has long been a major competitive advantage used by industry giants. That is why all the successful import car distributors started out by emphasizing service. It is one reason why Sears, Roebuck and Co. is so strong in retailing.

Many planners argue that it is better to make a product that is service-free rather than make servicing easier and/or develop a service network. Obviously, an economic trade off is involved that balances the extra cost for a completely trouble-free product versus the extra cost for a service network, and balances a product that is easy to service versus the costs associated with customer satisfaction.

*Availability* of a product is often critical. Many believe that George Eastman's basic strategy was merely to make film available on Sunday (when the workweek was 6 days) by selling it through pharmacies (the only stores that were open). Sears, Roebuck and Co. located stores in shopping centers to make its products available to the newly mobile public. McDonald's located in neighborhoods to make its burgers more available than ever before. Calculators can be bought in food stores as can panty hose, motor oil, and electric switches. Banks have earlier and later hours. Even cars can be bought (at lower prices) via a company store or by mail order. Thus, new channels of distribution to reach the same market, or a new market, are frequently used to gain a competitive advantage. This often means that both the product and its package must be designed to permit the new distribution. Similarly, service businesses must review their distribution requirements or relinquish a potential advantage to competition.

*Other product factors* that can be used to obtain a competitive advantage are:

Nationalism

Patents

Legal monopolies (utilities, air routes, etc.)

Ease of service or ease of installation (which are of interest to the intermediate customer)

Strong guarantees and/or liberal warranty policies

Built-in social advantages (quietness, biodegradability, etc.)

*Credibility* is the last item. A firm can design a new product that has exactly the benefits the market says it wants, yet the product can fail. Years ago, a food mixer survey indicated a need for a more powerful yet quieter product. One company introduced the new mixer and it sold poorly. A new survey indicated, "It doesn't sound powerful." The company wisely added some gear noise, and the product sold well.[5] Benefit credibility is quite important.

**Supply/Demand**   After an examination of a long list of product characteristics, any of which can interact with price, it becomes obvious that the concept of supply and demand is not a fundamental factor in pricing. Thus, the price for ice cream might be 15 percent higher at the convenient local store that is open 24 hours a day than at a conventional store. The price for a Sunday dental repair might be 100 percent more than on a weekday. The price for a Rolls Royce might be 10 times that of a Cadillac, which might be twice that of a full-size Plymouth. The point is that there are so many other product factors that the product planner can utilize to "shift" the supply and demand curve—that the real importance of conventional economic analysis is uncertain. What is certain is that the planner must focus on obtaining a significant share (over 30 percent) of each target market that has been selected. The price versus competition in that specific segment is important, but obviously not as important as the sum of the other factors.

Even a commodity product can be marketed at higher prices if a different channel of distribution is used. Thus, natural food stores obtain premium prices for herbs and grains. White eggs can be priced higher than brown. Whipped butter gets a premium price.

**Life Cycle Factors**   Recently the concept of product life cycle has come under attack. It is pointed out that, while technological obsolescence does occur, the basic functional requirement continues to grow. To illustrate: fashions change but clothing sales increase; tubes have been replaced by transistors, which are being replaced by integrated circuits; Studebaker faded as Volkswagen prospered; mechanical calculators cannot be sold, yet the sale of calculators has increased a thousandfold. On the other hand, more radios have been sold since television was introduced than ever before. The conclusion is that, from a very fundamental viewpoint, product and brand mismanagement cause life cycles, not the fundamental market demand.

At a less theoretical level, the fact is that the Frisbee has replaced the hula hoop, Xerox machines have replaced mimeographs, plastics have replaced castings, and electronic calculators have replaced slide rules. The conclusion is obvious: *Individual models* have life cycles. Strategically, this is important because different model characteristics are important at different stages of the life cycle.

*Introduction*.   The new model must have good reliability and durability to survive the introduction stage. Severe quality problems will undoubtedly kill any new product. Furthermore, new model quality problems need to be minimized by a liberal warranty program. Also, the product is helped significantly if it has features that are easily advertised, conspicuous, or easy to talk about, thereby making the market aware of the new offering.

*Growth*.   Advertising and the ability to talk about the product assume prime importance at this stage. The model needs conspicuous features to maximize its growth rate. Obviously, quality is still very important since market position has not yet been established.

*Maturity*.   This is defined as the time when sales begin leveling off, profit margins peak and begin declining, and pricing (along with advertising) becomes more critical. Thus, the product planner must emphasize cost reduction programs which should be completed by this stage of the product life cycle to keep the product competitive.

*Saturation*.   This sets in when sales peak, when new models are introduced by competition, and when many companies repackage their existing models to generate increased sales. This is also the period when the product planner should be introducing the next generation of product in order to regenerate the entire market. Frequently this is accomplished using a technique called *layering on*. This technique merely introduces a new model that utilizes most of the components and subsystems of the existing product, but either adds or deletes features to increase sales by appealing to a different segment. Frequently, this approach will delay the saturation of the market by causing a market rejuvenation to occur.

*Decline.* The sales of existing models decline as a result of new model inroads. Some competitors drop out, and those remaining often emphasize advertising, durability, and service in order to maximize profits.

*Summary.* It is important to remember that different stages of the model life cycle require different product characteristics. The ones discussed are often found, but the emphasis will shift from market to market as well as within markets. The product planner who fully understands the strategic impact of the life cycle will recognize that product changes are necessary, then find out what the best ones are.

**Focused Marketing** The concept of focused marketing is rarely overlooked by product planners. Thus, if a company has distribution strength to discount stores, a model should not be introduced that purports to be the very best available. A strong guarantee should not be given if the service capability is weak or nonexistent. A production-limited company should not emphasize price. A company with a "no advertising" policy should not develop consumer products. A low-priced item should not be chrome-trimmed. A new feature should be advertised. Better performance should be demonstrable.

The concept of a focused image is sometimes overlooked, however. The highest-quality product should by all means be packaged in molded foam protection inside a four-color printed package, have instructions written on slick paper, etc. But if the image is one of rugged, low-cost dependability, the product should have a single-color, corrugated package, a guarantee printed on a postage-paid, no-nonsense card, instructions on a piece of heavy plain white paper, and simple, effective packing material. The low-cost product can be packaged six to a carton in a blister pack or shrink package that has the instructions printed on it, and the customer takes the product home from the store in a paper bag.

In other words, be consistent in the product focus.

**Resource Focus** It is appropriate always to plan products that use the resources of the firm—unless those resources are becoming technically obsolete. Thus, the maker of a food mixer might profitably focus on blenders and can openers because they use the same size motors. But radio tube makers have been technologically obsoleted and need to revise their technical capabilities.

Stated another way, a focus on the firm's resources might maximize sales per unit of engineering effort, but profits will gradually decrease if the inroads of a new technology cause a decline in market share.

**Market Research Problems** Another area where the focus on internal resources often causes problems is that of market research. Stripped of all the mathematics, questionnare design techniques, and test marketing demographics, market research gets its information in only four ways:

By analyzing what people have done
By asking people what they will do
By asking experts what people will do
By finding out what people do (test marketing)

A truly new product can rarely build on past history. However, it is usually possible to forecast new *model* sales using historic information since the new model often substitutes for the old (as with "new" cars).

If the product is new, questionnaires are often used to determine the market demand. However, this type of market research usually lacks five basic elements:

Time (to do the survey properly)
Talent (to design and analyze the survey)
Money (to do the job right)
Objectivity (of the researcher, especially a company researcher)
Courage (to present unpopular views)

When salespeople are asked to act as experts on what is needed, they often respond with answers that amount to one word: more! They want more performance for less money, more features, more models, more speed in delivery; more! That does not mean that sales inputs are not important, because they are. It does mean that they should not be regarded as the only source of marketing information. A product planner should always remember that many developments often came from outside the field of the specialists who "know" the market. For instance:

Electronic calculators were not developed by computer companies.
The Swiss did not develop electronic watches.
Kodak did not introduce instant pictures.
Printers did not develop holography.
Jazz did not come from concert halls.
General Motors did not develop compact cars.
The motel was not supported by the hotel industry.

945

IBM did not develop minicomputers.

Movie producers did not pioneer TV movies.

The automakers did not develop the recreation vehicle business.

The telephone company did not develop many of the telephone accessories that people buy.

The transistor was not developed by a tube maker.

Car stereo tape was not developed by a tape-recorder maker.

The list can go on and on. The point is that each of the businesses will never be the same, and the "experts" in the existing companies did not identify the customer needs and/or act on them. The result was predictable. The existing companies lost market share—and profits—and many decided to play the costly game of catch up.

Always ask: What new product could effectively destroy my market position? If you do not come up with any, think again. Even the steel industry has felt the impact of compact cars, plastics, aluminum, etc.

Market researchers rarely go to consumers to search for potential new products that have not been listed previously. This "hypothesis seeking," however, is what helps to give a company true product leadership by allowing it to introduce products that the customers really want but did not know they could have. Product leadership is important because, according to the experience curve theory, it gives a company a real head start in reducing costs, obtaining a market franchise (a large share), and increasing profits. Studies by the Brookings Institution have indicated that product leadership is a key item in estimating the profitability of a company.[6]

The need for product leadership is clear, but too few companies take the time necessary to develop their organizations in such a way that they readily accept change—the change implicit in a product leadership role. Thus, the inward-looking focus on the company's resources often thwarts true progress.

Similarly, a narrow view of competition can be dangerous. For one thing, it assumes that the company knows who its competitors are. Yet every consumer knows that a good camera may be competing with a new stereo for his or her dollar; a new boat with a camper; a new car with a swimming pool or a patio; chips with crackers; furniture with a vacation trip; wine with beer; a ball game with a museum; or a box of candy with flowers. The real competition is for the customer's dollar, not for a percentage of the existing market. A good product planner always tries to expand the existing market, because profits climb faster when markets expand than at any other time.

Similarly, good market research always tries to determine the real competitors for the customer's dollar, rather than simply identifying similar products.

## PERFORMANCE CRITERIA

After listing a large number of strategic concepts, it is necessary to translate these into measurable criteria. This is one of the hardest ideas to communicate, yet good product planning requires that top management quantify its performance criteria. It forces a large company to decide whether or not it is interested in very small opportunities; and if it is, then product planning acts as a catalyst to make the necessary organization changes to allow the small business to survive among the existing "giants." Conversely, it makes a small company fully evaluate the real constraints on its growth rate—sometimes even recommending delays in new product introduction to allow time for marketing to strengthen itself or for new plants to be completed.

Unfortunately, most managers do not like to quantify their new product evaluation criteria for fear that it will stifle creativity. Yet, criteria must be established and communicated if the product planning process is to have a chance to improve the effectivity of new product development. Usually planners do this on an ad hoc basis, by either using management's inputs or inferring the criteria by examining past decisions.

One of the most difficult (and important) criteria which must be quantified is that of profit. Most managers think of profit as return on sales or return on investment (or assets, net assets, or equity). Few have adopted Peter Drucker's view that profit is the cost of doing business in the future. Not many view it in terms of asset growth. Yet an entire nation has adopted the philosophy that people are their greatest asset and that job security is the least a company should guarantee in order to retain its assets. The country is Japan, and when that "philosophy" on profit is combined with a good work ethic and access to low-cost (3 percent) money (to buy more productive plants and equipment), a very capable competitor is created. Japanese companies will reduce prices (to maintain employment) to levels at which United States businesses would judge "profits" to be too low. Yet the Japanese view the same profits as reasonable.

Different cultures are not necessary to produce a fundamental difference in the concept of profit. For instance, if company A makes its product decisions based on 5-year profit forecasts and company B makes its decisions on the basis of 10-year profit forecasts, company A will be more likely to design its products for low-cost labor whereas company B will be more likely to automate (simply because it can afford to mechanize). Then, as worldwide inflation takes its toll, company B will become more competitive. Company A may react by mechanizing, but tooling costs will be higher because of inflation. Thus company B will continue to have lower costs and greater profits.

The entire scenario would be reversed if company B based its mechanization on a design or manufacturing technology that was changing. Thus, while mechanized foundries can compete with other foundries, they cannot compete with certain plastics and rolled metal forms. While automated radio tube manufacturing is very efficient, it cannot compete with integrated circuits. While automated dry cleaning is great, permanent press clothes do not need dry cleaning. Large capital investments should be *avoided* if the technology is changing.

There are a large number of other criteria that must be considered, including the strategic issues already discussed. Each company must decide for itself which factors are critical and quantify them. In order to do this, a company should clearly understand the product planning and development process.

## THE PRODUCT PLANNING AND DEVELOPMENT PROCESS

This process starts with an analysis of the business and all its aspects, then objectives and goals are established. Various ways to satisfy the objectives are generated, screened, and finally submitted to a detailed business analysis during which strategies are finalized. Finally, product development begins, based on well-defined cost, timing, and performance goals. Figure P-24 illustrates the entire process.

Note that there are many double-ended arrows, indicating many feedback loops. For instance, during the development of a product, a new discovery might be made that causes a reevaluation of the objectives of the company, that requires a new technology forecast, etc.

To be complete, there could be a feedback connection between every item. Regrettably, many companies do not even identify many of the items.

Many more do not provide the necessary feedback communication capabilities. The lack of these characteristics is one basic reason why so many products fail.

**Analysis** The activities of diagnosis and prognosis are usually called analysis. Yet they are quite different. One monitors, and the other forecasts. One indicates where we are, and the other tries to say where we are going. One deals with facts and history, the other with probabilities and the future.

Typical diagnostic activities include monitoring the social environment to become sensitive to potential new products; monitoring the industry and business environment to become aware of new trends, long before they are generally recognized; and monitoring the company situation to know better when to sell a new idea.

Probably the most common type of forecasting merely quotes an outside expert whose forecasts coincide with the company's opinion. Unfortunately, this usually means that little attention is given to developing a systematic program for early identification of new trends, the trend of the company, or of new social, business, or customer needs. Technology forecasting is often spotty.

But most importantly, there is often no system to tie the analysis together. Thus, in most companies, the *process* is missing.

As a result of not having a process, company needs are not identified, new opportunities are not systematically developed and explored, acquisitions are not sought in a unified manner, and outside talent is not hired to enable a company to be better and more professionally staffed.

Figure P-24 shows these various factors, with many feedback loops identified. The key problem with managing such a system is clear: many inexperienced product planners only analyze and never get around to *doing* things that generate profit. Regardless of how profit is measured, profit maximization is the primary objective of product planning and development.

**Objectives and Goals** While profit is almost always indicated in any list of objectives and goals, as are sales (or sales growth), the list thereafter gets more difficult. Some topics that frequently are the subject of objectives are shown in Fig. P-24. If a company has developed a strong social conscience, it may talk about job security or supplemental unemployment schemes. If it has succeeded as a follower, it may talk about engineering's ability to quickly respond to the needs of the market (to competition's latest new product).

## Product planning and development

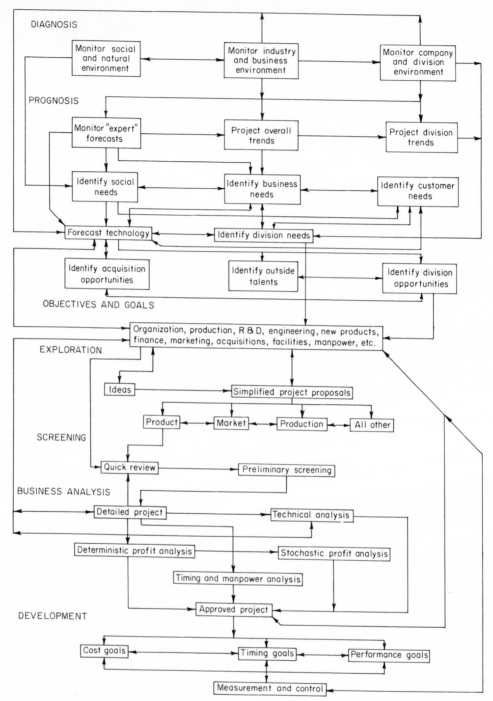

Fig. P-24. The planning system.

Regardless of what the objectives are, they should accurately reflect the organization's capability as it really is—unless the "do differently" objectives are clearly supported with detailed work plans that change the company's ability to compete. All too often objectives are written to please the stockholders or the president or the market analysts. The results are uniformly useless.

**Exploration** The next step in the product planning development process is usually skipped. Because exploration is omitted, the effectivity of the resulting programs is probably cut by as much as 50 percent. This is the stage of the process where creativity needs to be given full reign. There should be no criticism, no judgments, no censure. All ideas, new and old, should be brought forth. Nothing should be taboo.

Idea processing should not be relegated to private log books. That is the place for all the calculations and other back-up data. Rather, a highly visible idea-gathering system is needed. It should be simple to use—so simple that engineers will come to regard the forms as scrap paper and have no qualms about tearing one up. However, when it is completed, the idea form should provide adequate legal protection for all potential patent rights. Thus, there should be at least one dated witness signature (and preferably two) on each idea. The date of the disclosure is also helped by identifying each idea received with a sequential number. The sequential numbers also help to establish the disclosure dates. Finally, someone is needed to categorize, circulate, and file the ideas. The circulation aspect is vital because it helps one idea spawn another.

**Project Proposals** Simplified project proposals are the next output. A fairly large number should be generated to develop the same new product. However, each should be distinctive. They rarely need to be over a page long, with a sketch or two (or the idea sheet) to explain the concept. The simplified project proposal should indicate what the product or service is, what market segment it is believed to satisfy, and what production processes would be required. It must also indicate all critical assumptions, such as where the new inventions are needed.

**Screening** Figure P-25 is an example of a quick screening form that was used at Motorola in one of its divisions. (It has since been updated to better reflect current screening criteria.) The way it is used is by *always* filling in the center column with a highlighting marker—then continuing to mark to the left or right in response to the question. Table P-14 identifies each item.

While it is simple to use, the quick screening form is based on the strategic and fundamental concepts discussed previously. However, the screening form must always be modified to reflect the realities faced by a particular company.

The quick screening form is not merely a convenient checklist; it is also an effective visual display. All the favorable items are listed to the right of the center column, and all the unfavorable ones to the left. Thus, the potential viability of a new product can be seen from 10 paces away.

In addition to its communication ability, the form is also valuable in emphasizing the fact that each product has trade offs. A number of checks and balances have been built into the questionnaire. For instance, improved performance generally requires more product cost and a higher price than the competition's, not the same price or one that is lower. Besides, even if the price could be lower, if there is a strong technological advantage, reducing the price would only reduce profits. However, if the strategy is to increase the share of market (especially in an expanding market), then a price reduction might be justified. There are always trade offs, and they should be clearly identified.

Most importantly, the form helps to plan the proposed product. Thus, if used by R&D, the new idea would be quickly screened then revised to eliminate some of the negatives in the technical area. Marketing would then have a chance to evaluate the idea (before a project was approved). They too could suggest ideas to make it better from a marketing standpoint.

If the system is given active support by top management, the company should soon find itself in the enviable position of having "too many" good ideas. Furthermore, because of the discipline imposed by criteria evaluation, each of the proposed products will have a higher probability of success than was historically true.

The reason that the quick screening works so well is that it effectively quantifies management's judgment criteria. It does not attempt to weight the criteria, since experiments have indicated that changing circumstances, different products, and competitive actions would automatically change weights. However, the small box at the left-hand side of the form, next to each item, can be used to indicate those factors that are weighted heaviest.

**Business Analysis and Strategy Development** After the simplified project proposals have been screened, one or more are selected to be expanded into a detailed project proposal. This pro-

# Product planning and development

SCREENING FORM                                                                    SCORE ☐

**TITLE**

| Technical screening | BAD | POOR | OK | GOOD | BEST |
|---|---|---|---|---|---|
| **Legality** | Illegal | Publicly?? | | Unrest | Known legal |
| Safety | Decrease | Slight decrease | | Slight improvement | Improvement |
| Charter | Conflict | Questions | | ///////// | ///////// |
| Confidence in success | <40% | 40–60% | | 60–80% | >80% |
| **Exclusivity** | ///////// | ///////// | ///////// | ///////// | ///////// |
| Company's patent position | Open or none | Unknown | | Limited pat. | Patentable |
| Technological advantage | No advantages | Slight advantage | | Good advantage | Breakthrough |
| Competition: Now | Strong competition | Moderate competition | | Nonprice | None |
| Later | Strong competition | Moderate competition | | Nonprice | None |
| **Customer benefits** | ///////// | ///////// | ///////// | ///////// | ///////// |
| Performance | Decrease | Minor decrease | | Some improvement | Obvious improvement |
| Ease of usage | Instructions | Demonstrate | | Familiar | Easier |
| Convenience/comfort | Decrease | Minor decrease | | Some improvement | Obvious improvement |
| Economy of operation | Decrease | Minor decrease | | Some improvement | Obvious improvement |
| Reliability/durability | Decrease | Minor decrease | | Some improvement | Obvious improvement |
| Ease of service | Decrease | Minor decrease | | Some improvement | Obvious improvement |
| Credibility of: Benefits | Little | So-so | | Good | Very high |
| Liabilities | Very high | Good | | So-so | Little |
| **Other company benefits** | ///////// | ///////// | ///////// | ///////// | ///////// |
| Product cost vs. comp.: Now | Disadvantage | Slight disadvantage | | Slight advantage | Advantage |
| Later | Disadvantage | Slight disadvantage | | Slight advantage | Advantage |
| Equipment & plant | New plant | New equipment | | Some equipment | Tooling only |
| Manufacturing process | All new | Some new | | Familiar | Routine |
| Fixed invest. vs. competition | Disadvantage | Slight disadvantage | | Slight advantage | Advantage |
| Equipment & methods | >6 years old | 3–6 years old | | New | Latest |
| Vert. integration: Mature mkt. | Little/none | Some | | Good | Significant |
| Growth mkt. | Significant | Good | | Some | Little/none |
| Cost of warranty | Increase | Slight increase | | Slight decrease | Decrease |
| Internal follow-on | None | Need men | | Budgeted | ///////// |
| Champion | R & D | Mkt./eng. | | Profit center | 2 corp. VPs |

| Overall technical rank | –3 | –2 | –1 | | +1 | +2 | +3 |
|---|---|---|---|---|---|---|---|

| Market & business screening | BAD | POOR | | GOOD | BEST |
|---|---|---|---|---|---|
| **Market data** | ///////// | ///////// | ///////// | ///////// | ///////// |
| Market growth rate | Decline | 0–5% | | >10% | >20% |
| Potential—Worldwide | <$25 million | $25-50 million | | $50-100 million | >$100 million |
| Motorola | <$ 6 million | $ 6-15 million | | $15- 30 million | > $30 million |
| Motorola est. sales | <$ 2 million | $ 2- 5 million | | $ 5- 10 million | > $10 million |
| Time to achieve sales | >4 years | 3-4 years | | 2-3 years | <2 years |
| Price ($ /Units) | Declining | Stable | | Rising | Rising rapidly |
| Confidence in above | Good <80% | Very good 80-90% | | High 90-95% | Very high >95% |
| **Exclusivity** | ///////// | ///////// | ///////// | ///////// | ///////// |
| Market share: Now | <15% | 15–25% | | 25–35% | >35% |
| Later | <15% | 15–25% | | 25–35% | >35% |
| Next 2 competitors vs. Motorola | Twice Motorola | Greater than Motorola | | Less than Motorola | Half of Motorola |
| Product leadership | Disadvantage | Slight disadvantage | | Advantage | ///////// |
| Product "important" to customers | Critical | "A" item | | "B" item | Minor |
| **Customer benefits** | ///////// | ///////// | ///////// | ///////// | ///////// |
| Appearance | Not styled | Conventional | | Good | Wow |
| Conspicuousness | None | Identifiable | | When in use | Easily seen |
| Market differentiation | None | Minor | | Can advertise | Good ad copy |
| Social value | Antisocial | Questionable | | Some improvement | Obvious improvement |
| Service availability | Factory only | Training | | Parts & instructions | Available |
| Price vs. competition | Disadvantage | – Slight disadvantage | | Slight advantage | Advantage |
| **Other company benefits** | ///////// | ///////// | ///////// | ///////// | ///////// |
| Distribution | Other new | New OEM dist | | Need men | Suitable |
| Present product sales | Replaces | Some replace | | Compliments | Increased |
| New product life | <3 years | 3-5 years | | 5-7 years | >7 years |
| Similarity to present | All new prod. | Mostly new | | Fits line OK | Fits well |
| Customers | All old | Mostly old | | Mostly new | All new |
| Change in mkt. share: Mature | Increase | Slight increase | | Slight decrease | Decrease |
| Growth | Decrease | Slight decrease | | Slight increase | Increase |
| Marketing effort vs. competition | Disadvantage | Slight disadvantage | | Advantage | Significant advantage |
| R & D to marketing ratio | One emphasized | Unbalanced | | Balanced | ///////// |
| Estimated asset turnover | <1.2 | 1.2-2.0 | | 2.0-2.8 | >2.8 |
| Form of reward: Mature | >Share | Share | | Profit | >Profit |
| Growth | >Profit | Profit | | Share | >Share |

| Overall market rank | –3 | –2 | –1 | | +1 | +2 | +3 |
|---|---|---|---|---|---|---|---|

**Description and comments**



| PREPARED BY: | DATE: | ENDORSED BY: | DATE: |
|---|---|---|---|

**Fig. P-25. Screening form.**

## TECHNICAL SCREENING

- LEGALITY: If there is talk that the product might be illegal but it has not been discussed in the media, then the ranking should be in the unrest area rather than the publicly questioned area.
- SAFETY: Self-explanatory.
- CHARTER: If the product fits the charter of the division, then the ranking is in the OK section. However, if questions relative to the charter have arisen or if there is conflict over who should have the charter, then the ranking should be appropriately decreased. Note that charter issues never affect a product screening in a positive manner, only in a negative manner.
- CONFIDENCE IN SUCCESS: Refers to the confidence in technical success.
- COMPANY'S PATENT POSITION: Self-explanatory.
- TECHNOLOGICAL ADVANTAGE: Relative to competition.
- COMPETITION NOW AND LATER: Self-explanatory.
- PERFORMANCE: Relative to competition (including products it replaces).
- EASE OF USAGE: Also includes the concept of ease of error and relates directly to the safety issue with respect to the consequences of an error.
- CONVENIENCE/COMFORT: Relative to competition.
- ECONOMY OF OPERATION: Relative to competition.
- RELIABILITY/DURABILITY: Relative to competition.
- EASE OF SERVICE: Relative to competition.
- CREDIBILITY OF BENEFITS: Self-explanatory.
- CREDIBILITY OF LIABILITIES: Reverse of credibility of benefits in order to provide a proper visual display for screening purposes. In each case either the benefits or the liabilities will be applicable to the particular ranking.
- PRODUCT COST VS. COMPETITION, BOTH NOW AND LATER: Self-explanatory.
- EQUIPMENT AND PLANT: Self-explanatory.
- MANUFACTURING PROCESS: Self-explanatory.
- FIXED INVESTMENT VS. COMPETITION: Would competition have to make less investment in order to get into the same market or product area?
- EQUIPMENT AND METHODS: Relates directly to anticipated product cost versus competition.
- VERTICAL INTEGRATION IN A MATURE MARKET is recommended in order to provide potential for profit.
- VERTICAL INTEGRATION IN A GROWTH MARKET is *not* recommended because of the instability in emerging technologies and market segments.
- COST OF WARRANTY: Self-explanatory.
- INTERNAL FOLLOW-ON: Unless the workers are actually budgeted the ranking can be no better than OK.
- CHAMPION: Ideas require a champion, and the more important the champion is, the more likely a success will be.
- OVERALL TECHNICAL RANK: Note that the best category is divided into two halves in order to differentiate products more precisely.

## MARKET AND BUSINESS SCREENING

- MARKET GROWTH RATE: Per year.
- POTENTIAL MARKET, both worldwide and for Motorola refers to the total market to be served. The Motorola potential volume refers to that volume which is "available to us."
- MOTOROLA ESTIMATED SALES: Per annum in a mature market.
- TIME TO ACHIEVE THE SALES LEVEL: This is the time necessary to penetrate the market after the product has been introduced on the market. The longer it takes to achieve full penetration, the lower the overall ranking will be.
- PRICE: The selling price per unit is identified. The ranking indicates that it is more profitable to have products in a market where the price is rising than it is to have products where prices are stable or declining.
- CONFIDENCE IN MARKET DATA: Refers to the confidence that the marketing department places on meeting the estimated sales level in the estimated time at the estimated price.
- MARKET SHARE NOW AND LATER: Companies with less than 15% market share are rarely profitable and companies with over 35% market share are rarely unprofitable. The market segment can be defined precisely but should not be overly restrictive.
- NEXT 2 COMPETITORS VS. MOTOROLA: If the total sales of the next two competitors were added together would they be twice the size of Motorola (bad)?—or would Motorola be twice the size of the next two competitors (i.e., they would be half of Motorola)?
- PRODUCT LEADERSHIP: Product leadship is an assymetrical ranking since an advantage is good, but a disadvantage can be disastrous.
- PRODUCT IMPORTANCE TO CUSTOMERS: If the item is critical, the customer will pay close attention to it and attempt to develop strong competition. "A" items are that 10% of the items that account for 80% of the total cost of material in many companies. ("B" items are not subjected to as much competitive pressure as critical items, or "A" items.)
- APPEARANCE: Self-explanatory.
- CONSPICUOUSNESS: Self-explanatory.
- MARKET DIFFERENTIATION: Self-explanatory.
- SOCIAL VALUE: Self-explanatory.
- SERVICE AVAILABILITY: Self-explanatory.
- PRICE VS. COMPETITION: Self-explanatory.
- DISTRIBUTION: Self-explanatory.
- PRESENT PRODUCT SALES: Self-explanatory.
- NEW PRODUCT LIFE: Self-explanatory.
- SIMILARITY TO PRESENT PRODUCTS: Self-explanatory.
- CUSTOMERS: Self-explanatory.
- CHANGE IN MARKET SHARE IN A MATURE MARKET: Increases in market share in a mature market cause a decline in profits. Conversely, harvesting of profits in a mature market can result in a decrease in market share.
- CHANGE IN MARKET SHARE IN A GROWTH MARKET: An increase in market share in a growth market (to provide a base for profits in the future) is highly desirable. Thus, the rankings are the reverse of those for the mature market.
- MARKETING EFFORT VS. COMPETITION: Self-explanatory.
- R&D TO MARKETING RATIO: If both are emphasized, you have a product leader strategy. If both are deemphasized, you have a product follower strategy. You can make money either way. What you cannot do is make money when there is an imbalance between R&D and marketing.
- ESTIMATED ASSET TURNOVER: As investment increases (thereby increasing assets), the ROI decreases. Thus, asset turnover becomes a critical factor in anticipating the level of ROI to be attained. Asset turnover is obtained by dividing the anticipated sales by the anticipated assets. Another way of estimating asset turnover is to ask the question, How large does our investment have to be? If the answer is that your business will have heavy capitalization, then the asset turnover will probably be low.
- FORM OF REWARD IN A MATURE MARKET: Here, profits should be emphasized.
- FORM OF REWARD IN A GROWTH MARKET: Here, share of market should be emphasized in order to obtain a strategic position for harvesting profits later.
- OVERALL MARKET RANK: The extreme rankings are divided into two parts in order to better differentiate products.

## GENERAL

- SCORE: At the upper right-hand corner of the form is a box titled *Score*. The score is calculated by adding the overall technical rank to the overall market rank.
- DESCRIPTION AND COMMENTS: A brief description of the product should be written here and comments relative to the technical, market, and business screening should be made.

posal must quantify cost and performance goals; clearly identify the schedule, the work force loading, and timing of management progress reports; and establish an early warning system for potential problems. A good market forecast (as good as possible) is also needed at this time.

The information is used to project total revenues and profits prior to approving the project. If the project is large, some companies will perform a stochastic market and financial analysis. The only difference between this type of analysis and the normal analysis is that the 10th, 50th, and 90th percentile estimates are given for key factors. This "probabilistic" forecast thereby quantifies the very real fact that the future is truly unknown.

Stochastic forecasting models can be very simple or quite complex. Key factors that are estimated often include the total market; market growth; market share; material and labor costs; investment in engineering, plant, equipment, and tools; marketing costs; other costs (general and administrative, purchasing, etc.). The system works very well but needs to be tailored for each company. Regrettably, because it is unfamiliar to most managements, even though the information is readily available, such systems are not normally used.

**Product Development**   Once the project is approved, development can begin.

Sometimes an excellent manufacturer will employ no design engineers. This happens routinely in the electronics industry of Japan, where consulting engineers design the same product for several companies, often using the same components and assemblies, thereby providing a reliable and low-cost product at an engineering investment that is lower than the cost of an internal engineering staff.

Typically, engineering is done internally. The key here is tight control and early warning of the problems. This is often accomplished with a simple, easy to understand, milestone schedule. However, more complex engineering programs require network planning such as PERT or CPM. A major problem often occurs with resource allocation. For instance, six programs can be moving quite well until three of them need a week of surface-grinding work in the model shop, all at the same time. When this happens, one project is automatically 1 week late and another is 2 weeks late. A similar situation occurs daily in drafting, test labs, model shops, engineering labs, etc.

There are two common solutions to the preceding problem: computerized scheduling techniques and task force approaches. Computerization is becoming more widely used, but it is still complex and re-

quires a knowledgeable scheduling activity to obtain the necessary information from engineering and the necessary priorities from management. Even when the infrastructure is available, difficult policy issues remain. For example, should the development program having the No. 1 priority be finished first, or should the first two programs be finished in the shortest total time? Should total engineering output be maximized? Should overtime be minimized?

By assigning individuals within a department to a task force, part of the record keeping of the scheduling activity is eliminated. However, even the task force technique often has serious engineering support problems.

## OTHER USEFUL PRODUCT PLANNING TECHNIQUES

After briefly describing the process of product planning, it is useful to comment on more specific techniques that can be used.

**Technology Forecasting**   The idea of technological leadership is often thought to be critical. Yet, as indicated earlier, its true purpose is to obtain a market franchise and/or retain it. Probably the most useful technique for generating a technological forecast is the delphi approach (see also FORECASTING BUSINESS CONDITIONS). It works like this:

1. A list of questions is prepared and sent to the technology panel selected. The questions are designed to probe both the evolution and the revolution that might impact the design, manufacture, and sale of a product, including the assessment of any adverse consequences.

2. The answers are reviewed for consensus, and the people having the most divergent views are asked to state their reasons.

3. Their answers are sent out with the next questionnaire (without identifying who held the opinions).

4. The procedure continues until either a concensus is reached or a clear split occurs. At all times the responses are kept anonymous so that neither peer pressure nor hierarchic pressure can influence the results.

The delphi technique usually requires about 3 months to complete, which is very reasonable if it reveals a major opportunity for the business or a major threat to the business for which contingency plans can be prepared.

**Analysis of the Business Climate**   Monitoring of the outside environment can cause some planners never to get anything else done. To avoid that, and to focus on the key factors, the following technique has been successfully used:

1. A two-page questionnaire is made up and distributed to all the key executives. It asks:

PAGE 1: What are the five most important outside factors that help the business? Are they increasing or decreasing in importance? What is the ranking of each of the five items?

PAGE 2: For each item, what actions, policies, and strategies have been taken? How effective have they been? What new actions, etc., might be taken?

2. A week later the same two-page questionnaire is sent out again. This time it focuses on outside factors that *threaten* the business.

3. The following week a two-page questionnaire focusing on internal positive factors (strengths) is sent.

4. And finally, a two-page questionnaire on internal negative factors (restraints on success, weaknesses) goes out.

5. Meantime, during the second week, the results of the first survey are published in summary form, and all participants are asked to rank the items from 1 to 10, regardless of their original ranking.

6. The same review of results and ranking process takes place the week following each survey.

7. Finally, during the sixth week, everyone is brought together to review the results and agree on the major factors impacting the business both from within and without. (Alternatively, a delphi approach could be used from this point forward.)

The virtue of the technique is that little time is required by each participant, social pressures are minimized, and a clear timetable is established for the product planner, thereby preventing the work of analysis from consuming excessive amounts of time.

**Analysis of Competition**  Competition must always be assessed when planning a product. The simplest competition research is catalog research, in which a competitor's catalog is reviewed and the key attributes are listed.

The simplest form of product planning merely indicates, "Make it the same as our competition, except add this feature." The only virtue of this approach is economy. Profits will remain low because the company will always be a follower.

A better approach is to identify thoroughly the competitor's strengths and weaknesses with respect to market segments, products, finances, engineering, marketing, etc. In this manner insights into the competition's strategies can be obtained and alternative strategies developed.

**Ideation**  Creative activity is necessary to obtain enough alternatives to ensure a high probability of success. Four techniques for generating ideas are:

Attribute listing
Forced relationships
Brainstorming
Synectics

*Attribute listing* is useful for individuals because it focuses attention on the problem(s) to be solved. The danger is that the wrong attributes may have been listed, as was the case with all the industries identified above that did not make the major breakthroughs.

*Forced relationships* occur when two different products are forced to become one. For example, a lamp and a birdcage make a unique pull-down lamp. However, a wall and a table become a marketable new product, and one that is currently finding acceptance.

*Brainstorming* is a group creativity effort that requires no criticism and rapid give and take within a group. Alex Osborn in his book *Applied Imagination* describes some of the techniques of brainstorming as these: Make it larger, make it smaller, turn it upside down, divide it, multiply it, reverse it, keep the ideas flowing, and above all, don't criticize.[7]

*Synectics* is a technique that asks the group to withdraw from the specific problem to a more general problem.[8] As an example of synectics, consider the problem of closure. What is there in nature that closes? One list might include a flower, an eyelid, a mouth, a pore, a hand, the iris of the eye, a Venus's-flytrap, a honeycomb cell, a heart valve, etc. Once the problem is described using terms remote from the problem at hand, it is then possible to return to the main problem. In this case it was to develop a closure device for a thermos bottle. A unique design was developed using the principle of the iris. Unfortunately, when this was analyzed for potential new problems, the design had to be dropped because of foreseeable problems associated with a knife cutting or a fork puncturing the closure.

**A Sick Product Identification**  A simplified view of a portfolio of products indicates that there are four basic categories:

Stars: products with high growth and good margins.

Cows: products with low growth but good margins.

Dogs: products with low growth and low margins.

Unknowns: products that haven't yet proven themselves.

The theory of product portfolio management is to move the questionable products to become stars, which ultimately mature (according to the life-cycle theory) and become cows, before eventually degenerating and becoming dogs. The challenge of product planning is either to convert the dogs into stars (or cows) or to eliminate them.

Trend analysis is one technique for accomplishing this. Here graphs of industry sales, company sales, company share of market, company profits, company margins, etc., are charted. Often trends become very apparent, and corrective actions can be taken.

Comparison to competition is one of the most valuable approaches when the market is mature. Remember, however, that the real challenge is to rejuvenate the market through new product introductions.

**Product Simplification**   Value engineering is product simplification; so is the reduction of the number of models in a line; and so is a well-developed standardization program. Salespeople are the biggest opponents of product simplification. They want to provide a specifically tailored product for each customer; yet that is normally impossible. A broad product line can attract more customers, but it must be justified on an economic basis. Regrettably, the discipline of an economic analysis is often skipped in order to obtain increased sales with reduced but adequate profits.

Probably the best example of product simplification in industry is IBM's Endicott, N.Y., operation. At that plant, they have eliminated 95 percent of the drawings by converting all the necessary information to computer files. To make a product (including sample parts for completely new products), the information is fed from a central information system to the appropriate numeric control machines. These machines will drill, mill, cut, punch, insert, or solder the product, as required. IBM has effectively eliminated set-up costs through the use of standard manufacturing interface technology. The result is that they can produce 1 unit of a product almost as efficiently as they can produce 1000; yet they can produce thousands of different products using the standardized processes. This is a dramatic example of product simplification without sacrificing the customer requirements for unique features.

**Legal Considerations**   Regulations that must be met vary from industry to industry, country to country, state to state, city to city. Because of the proliferation of regulations, it is necessary for product planners to have good legal counsel.

An emerging legal area is that of technological assessment. For instance, 5 years ago, the idea of a biodegradable cooking pouch for vegetables was not an issue; today it is.

Patent committees are common within most companies. They usually consist of the chief engineer, the general manager, the sales manager, and the patent lawyer. These individuals are expected to review each new idea not only for patentability but also for their impact on technology, markets, and overall business strategy. In general, patent committees work fairly well, yet few companies end up with a true patent monopoly unless they set out to create that monopoly.

To create a patent monopoly requires a focused engineering program, a training program for employees so that they know the proper way to reveal ideas to obtain patents, and (of course) very creative engineers.

The U.S. Patent Office grants a 17-year exclusive right to use a patent. Normally, employees sign an agreement when hired that assign patents to the company for payment of a nominal fee. However, many companies are finding that increasing the fee is necessary in order to attract the engineering talent necessary to obtain a patent monopoly.

Contracts can be made between the owner of an outside patent and those who wish to use it. These contracts (licenses) can be granted according to terms agreed to at the discretion of the parties involved.

Foreign patents often require simultaneous filing with United States filing, or the technology becomes available to the foreign country.

Because of the complex nature of both domestic and foreign patent law, a company should have good legal advice on this subject. If the objective is to obtain a patent monopoly in a certain area of technology, then an internal staff of patent lawyers is often valuable to expedite the development of a complete portfolio.

**Product Line Policy**   By now it should be apparent that product line policy is a complex subject requiring the utilization of the entire product-planning process. However, there are a few added concepts that can be mentioned.

*Segmentation versus differentiation* is a basic decision. The planner who elects to segment the market aims a product at a specific group of customers who (preferably) are not being served by competition. The planner who elects to differentiate a product tries to provide unique characteristics that will make it more attractive to customers who are already being served by competition. Segmentation is focused on customers while differentiation is focused on competitors.

*Product mix* must be justified by economics rather than by emotional statements such as, We will serve the entire market!

*Branding* is a critical decision for the product planner. The name should not invoke any negative reactions. Rather, it should be neutral (such as the name *Sanka*), or it should invoke a positive reaction (for example, the name *Maverick*). The brand, like the product, should continuously project a focused market image. Thus, Cadillac does not produce a car that competes with Pinto.

Brand management can be used to increase sales. For example, the Hoover company sold its vacuum cleaners under the Penncrest name for many years. The Mercury and the Ford are the same product except for styling items. In these, and other examples, sales were increased by using another brand name.

*Guarantees* must also be consistent with the image projected by the product line. The concept of focus is extremely important.

**Financial Analysis**   Since the objective of product planning is to maximize both customer satisfaction and company profits, financial analysis plays a large role in the everyday activities of planning. Perhaps the most valuable tool to the planner is the variance analysis work sheet. Such a technique can analyze P&L and balance sheet items to identify the change in profitability and cash flow as a result of changing product decisions. At Ford Motor Company they are called road maps because they clearly show management the impact of their decisions on all aspects of the financial operation of the company.

### CONCLUSION

Good product planners are experts in their business. They know the market and the competition. They know the rules and regulations governing their business. They know the common practices, the importance of patents, branding, copyrights, warrantees, technology, production techniques, and so forth.

But most of all, product planners know the process of planning and have developed a set of pragmatic techniques that allow them to quickly evaluate new product ideas and sense potential advantages.

*See also* BRANDS AND BRAND NAMES; CONSUMER BEHAVIOR, MANAGERIAL RELEVANCE OF; FORECASTING BUSINESS CONDITIONS; INNOVATION AND CREATIVITY; MARKETS, CLASSIFICATIONS AND MARKET ANALYSIS; MARKETING RESEARCH; PATENTS AND VALUABLE INTANGIBLE RIGHTS; PLANNING AND POLICY MAKING; PRODUCT AND SERVICE PRICING; PROJECT AND TASK FORCE MANAGEMENT; RESEARCH AND DEVELOPMENT MANAGEMENT.

### NOTES

[1]*Management of New Products*, Booz-Allen & Hamilton, Chicago, Ill., 1968, p. 2.
[2]Ibid.
[3]*Perspectives on Experience*, The Boston Consulting Group, Boston, Mass., 1972.
[4]Schoeffler, Buzzell, and Heany, "Impact of Strategic Planning on Profit Performance," *Harvard Business Review*, March–April 1974, p. 137.
[5]Author's personal knowledge.
[6]Leo Burnett, "Marketing Snags and Fallacies," *Journal of Marketing*, July 1966, p. 1.
[7]Alex Osborn, *Applied Imagination*, Charles Scribner's Sons, New York, 1963.
[8]William J. Gordon, *Synectics: The Development of Creative Capacity*, The Macmillan Company, New York, 1968.

### REFERENCES

Gorle, Peter, and James Long: *Essentials of Product Planning*, McGraw-Hill Book Company, New York, 1973.
*Perspectives on Experience*, The Boston Consulting Group, Boston, Mass., 1972.
Steiner, George A.: *Top Management Planning*, The Macmillan Company, New York, 1969.
Weber-Teal-Schillinger, ed.: *Technology Forecast for 1980*, Van Nostrand Reinhold Co., New York, 1971. See especially Herman Kahn: "Speculations on the Emergent U.S. Post-Industrial Society," pp. 21–45.

CHARLES J. MATHEY, *The Futures Group, Glastonbury, Connecticut*

## Product position   <small>(See MARKETS, CLASSIFICATIONS AND MARKET ANALYSIS.)</small>

## Product screening form   <small>(See PRODUCT PLANNING AND DEVELOPMENT.)</small>

## Product service   <small>(See MARKETING, INDUSTRIAL.)</small>

## Product and services development
<small>(See heading in Table of Contents for complete listing.)</small>

## Product and service pricing

Price is the result of many influences. Effective pricing takes the combined skills of the economist, the accountant, the psychologist, the sociologist, the market researcher, and the lawyer. Many pricing concepts cross discipline lines, but for the sake of simplicity they have been assigned in this entry to four groups: economic pricing concepts, accounting pricing concepts, marketing pricing concepts, and legal pricing concepts.

## ECONOMIC INPUTS TO PRICING

There is no pricing idea more basic in economics than the concept of a *demand curve*. This is an expression of the relationship between various prices a firm might set and the quantity of goods or services it can sell at those prices. This expression can be a table, a graph, an algebraic equation, or a verbal description. Firms usually have some idea about their demand curve.

With few exceptions, however, these curves are not nearly so well defined as traditional economic analysis would require. Therefore, another economic concept is more useful in most pricing situations. To change price, a firm must consider its product's demand elasticity. *Demand elasticity* explains how a firm's quantity sold will change if it changes price. More precisely, it can be defined in terms of how revenue (price × quantity sold) changes when price changes. Will revenue go up? That is, does quantity sold change only slightly if price goes up? Will revenue stay the same? Or will it drop?

The reaction of buyers to price changes in part depends on several other concepts in the area of economics. The economist identifies at least four types of markets a pricer may face: perfect competition, monopolistic competition, oligopoly, and monopoly. These market structures exist because of reactions by competitors and because of characteristics of a firm's products.

**Perfect Competition Conditions** In the perfectly competitive market a firm is one of many relatively small sellers. Each firm's product is similar enough so that forms of promotion, such as advertising, are of little importance. In this type of market, prices tend to be low enough so that extended price competition would gain little for any firm. In addition, the reaction of customers to a price rise by any one firm would be to buy elsewhere. The nature of the product is such that little brand loyalty exists.

The relatively small size of each firm in this type of market suggests another characteristic of the products that are sold: usually they require little, if any, specialized skills or equipment. In other words, products or services requiring large inputs of equipment suitable for a specific production process or of highly trained people tend not to be sold in perfectly competitive markets. Generally, products or services sold in these markets permit two decisions:

1. If our firm is losing money, should we sell at the existing price or should we cease operations immediately?

2. Should our firm look for other ways to use the capital we have invested in this product?

The answer to the first question depends on whether or not the firm will do better by shutting down immediately. To the extent a firm wishes to base an evaluation of "better" on income statement effects, the action chosen depends on whether the revenue it receives from operating exceeds the incremental cost (defined below) of operating. Most firms have some commitments, such as rent or guaranteed wages to employees, which they cannot avoid by shutting down. Therefore, a firm which shows a net loss from operations should not necessarily shut down immediately.

The second question is a longer-range decision. Since the firm's equipment and/or skills are not unique to one product or service, the firm should frequently consider if it is earning enough income to warrant staying with the existing product or service. Other potential uses of a firm's abilities should be considered.

**Monopolistic Competition** The monopolistic competitor faces a slightly more responsive situation. Some brand loyalty can be created in markets of this type so that some price differences can exist between successful firms selling virtually the same physical product or service. Factors such as convenience of location, quality differences perceived by customers, and minor service differences can result in a monopolistic competitive market. In addition to the questions faced by the perfect competitor, the monopolistic competitor also must attempt to balance price adjustments unique to its firm with product differentiation.

**Oligopoly Situations** The most complex pricing situation is faced by the oligopolist, which is one of few firms in a market where other competitors can and will retaliate to price adjustments. Having few firms in a market frequently means that the equipment is too costly and/or specialized for other firms to produce the product. Auto and steel manufacturers and petroleum refiners are classic examples. The costliness of the equipment makes it financially difficult to enter the market. The specialized nature of the equipment makes entering the market quite risky. If the venture fails, the entering firm cannot easily dispose of the equipment.

Because of the potential for retaliation, price adjustments are few and rigid. Oligopolists often resort to price leadership. By voluntary action, one firm's price adjustments are followed by all other firms in the industry. No formal agreement exists. In fact there are cases in which a would-be price leader has had to recall an announced price change because others have failed to follow. Price leaders often announce their price changes in response to major events which tend to affect all firms in the industry, such as signing a new labor contract. A popular pricing technique for the price leader is target-rate-of-return pricing (defined below). Price followers do not need a price computation method per se. Instead they need a method to evaluate the proposed change by the price leader.

**Monopoly Situations** The monopolist is almost like the price leader. Although the only firm in an industry, the monopolist still faces possible retaliation. One generally thinks of the monopolist as being created by the government and hence, as being severely regulated. A monopolist can also exist, however, because of geographic factors. In this case the monopolist is the only firm close enough to supply the product or service. A TV repairperson in an isolated community may be a monopolist.

Government-regulated monopolies face the retaliation of the regulating body if price adjustments are unreasonable. Geographic monopolies face the threat of competitors entering the market and destroying the monopoly position. Both of these possibilities have to be considered when the monopolist sets a price.

The economist also provides definitions for intermarket reactions. In addition to the effect of the pricing decision on the firm's own markets, it must be aware that other markets may also be affected. The terms *complementary product* and *substitute product* describe two potential situations. Complementary products are those products whose unit sales respond in the same way to a price change in either one. Hamburger and hamburger buns may be an example of complementary products. If the price of hamburger rises, the quantity of hamburger sold tends to drop. Quite possibly people will also buy fewer hamburger buns, too, because they plan to make fewer hamburgers. This situation creates several important problems. First, a firm may find price changes in other markets influencing its sales. Second, if the firm makes products that are complements (such as automobiles and auto parts), the impact of a change in one segment of the business on the other segment must be carefully considered.

The effect of shutting down an unprofitable segment may be devestating. Suppose an auto manufacturer quits providing spare parts. One would expect a serious decline in the sales of that automobile.

Substitute products prompt the opposite behavior. A price rise in one product causes an increase in sales of a substitute product because buyers will switch to it. Once again, interfirm and intrafirm reactions to price changes must be evaluated.

## PRICING INPUTS FROM ACCOUNTING

Among the key inputs to pricing provided by the accountant is product cost information. The role of product cost varies from market to market. For example, the perfect competitor may wish to know a cost representing a minimum below which production should be shut down. The price leader may use a cost as the base on which to set a price. For these different purposes different costs are appropriate. In this section, several product costs that firms might use in various situations are described. Also, two price-setting methods which build directly on the accountant's cost figures are discussed.

**Basic Accounting Methods** The first three cost terms—marginal cost, variable product cost, and incremental cost—have some definite similarities. *Marginal cost* is usually considered to be an economics concept, but it is a figure which a firm's accountant might approximate. It is the increase in total cost which will occur if the firm produces one additional unit. Two important points concerning marginal cost are (1) marginal cost is concerned with one-unit changes in output, and (2) marginal cost is dependent on the level of activity at which it is measured. A product's marginal cost may vary significantly over the levels of activity at which a firm usually operates. Since it is not usually the case that a firm is attempting to decide whether to produce just one more unit or how to price just one of their units, the next two product costs are more useful in product pricing.

A *variable product cost* is a per-unit cost computed by adding together those unit cost items such as material, labor, and certain overhead items which are incurred in increasing amounts as activity increases. For a merchandising firm, this would include such items as the cost of the product it sells plus the shipping cost incurred to obtain the product. There are two key differences between variable product cost and marginal cost. First, if, at a given level a firm must incur a large cost to increase capacity, that unusual increase will be considered part of the marginal cost. It is not a part of the variable product cost. Only costs that respond to unit-by-unit changes in production over broad ranges are considered variable costing product costs. Second, variable product costs are usually averages; therefore, the variable product cost is assumed to be the same for each unit over broad ranges of activities. This assumption is usually reasonable.

The *incremental cost* is the total amount of cost increase expected for a significant change in production. It, like the marginal cost, depends on the level from which a firm begins to measure the incremental cost. Unlike the marginal cost, it is the cost change resulting from a change of more than one unit.

*Example of Differences.* A brief example clarifies these differences. Suppose a firm faces the following situation:

| Production, units | Total cost, dollars |
|---|---|
| 400 | 4000 |
| 401 | 4010 |
| 402 | 5020 |
| 403 | 5030 |

The marginal cost of producing the 401st unit is $10 ($4010 − $4000), the change in total cost due to producing one more unit when the firm already produces 400 units. The marginal cost of the 402nd unit is $1010 ($5020 − $4010). The variable product cost appears to be $10, which is the average increase observed except from unit 401 to 402. The incremental cost of producing two additional units when the firm already produces 401 is $1020 ($5030 − $4010).

For various forms of pricing, these costs represent minimums below which price should not be set. The result of pricing below these figures is receiving less from selling the product than the firm must incur to obtain the product to sell. Pricing below this level is the basis of the old joke of the retailer saying, "I sell my widgets for $1 and I buy them from my wholesaler for $1.10, but I make up for that in volume." Each unit sold increases the firm's net loss. There is no way volume can improve this situation.

**Below-Minimum Pricing** There are, however, several situations in which a firm may rationally price below this minimum. One such situation occurs when a firm has dropped a product and is trying to get rid of existing stock. Here the firm has no intention of acquiring additional units, and the only question faced is how to get rid of the units at the best price. Even if the price is below the minimum, the firm is concerned with getting rid of the units, and any price received is usually better than not disposing of the units.

A second below-minimum pricing situation can exist with complementary goods. If the firm prices below minimum on one good, it does so because its complementary good sells for well above its minimum. In this case, it has assumed that the low price of the below-minimum good increases the sales volume of the above-minimum good. One still needs to ask if the sales of the above-minimum good are increased enough to justify selling its complement at all.

A third below-minimum situation exists when a firm temporarily prices low to gain sales from customers who are expected to develop brand loyalty. In this case the firm must be sure that it will be able to successfully raise prices later to compensate for the temporary below-minimum price.

If a firm is pricing a group of units, such as a special order or a unique job to be bid upon, the incremental cost is the appropriate minimum to consider. For products part of their normal product line, the variable product cost, often increased by nonproduction variable costs such as commissions and shipping costs, is the appropriate minimum.

These costs do not, however, assure that the firm will earn a profit or that the firm should continue to stay in the product any longer than it takes to terminate existing production commitments such as rent or salaries. The full cost is a better figure for that purpose.

**Full-Cost Pricing** The *full cost* is a unit cost which includes the variable product cost, variable nonproduction costs, and an allocation of fixed costs. It is an average operating cost. A price above this figure means the firm is earning a profit. Over the long run, this is the minimum a firm must receive if it is to consider remaining in the current product.

*Markup Pricing.* Two common pricing policies use the full cost as a basis for setting price. The most common policy is straight markup pricing. In straight markup pricing, the pricer adds an amount to the full cost which is felt to represent a sufficient amount of income per unit sold. This markup can either be a fixed dollar amount or a percent of cost.

In some cases, the markup is added to a product cost, such as an absorption-costing product cost or a variable product cost, instead of the full cost. These product costs include fewer cost items than does the full cost. The fewer the costs included in the product cost, the higher the necessary markup. For example, if a firm uses a product cost which does not include the cost of shipping its product, the markup must represent not only an average profit per unit but also an average shipping cost per unit.

*Target Rate-of-Return Pricing.* The second method built on full cost is a refinement of straight markup pricing and tends to be used by larger firms. In target-rate-of-return pricing, the markup is a per-unit average of a desired firm return. The firm determines what rate of return it wishes to earn on its assets. This return is multiplied by the assets it uses in its operations. This amount is then divided by the projected annual sales or by an average of projected annual sales for several years to obtain the desired markup. When the markup is added to full cost, this yields the target-rate-of-return price.

These two pricing methods yield a computed price for price leaders and firms whose sales volume is only slightly affected by price. Further, these figures may be used as long-range targets. If a firm cannot, on the average, sell at this price, it may wish to consider dropping the product line or making other major modifications in its operations. In making this decision, the firm should, of course, consider the effects of the decision on complementary products.

**Incremental Pricing** Special order or incremental pricing is done when the firm is approached to provide a batch of units outside its normal market. Two important points are the following: (1) multiple units are being sold, and (2) these units are not being sold through the normal distribution channel. Such a situation would exist if a large department store chain such as Sears, Roebuck and Co. approached a major tire manufacturer to purchase a large quantity of tires similar to those made for the manufacturer's own brand but to be sold under the department store brand name.

The pricer must consider a number of consequences of providing goods for the special order. Can the order be filled with existing capacity without giving up current sales? If not, what is the cost of giving up current sales or of obtaining additional production capacity both now and in the future? Will the special order goods affect existing sales? They might, for example, be sold to customers who would otherwise buy the manufacturer's product. If sales will be reduced, what chance is there that another manufacturer will take on the order? This would have the same effect except that someone else would sell the special-order goods. Does the buyer of the special order intend to request other special

orders in the future? Will these special orders grow in size until they require expanded capacity? What success will be had in raising the price on future special orders?

The answers to all these questions affect how low a price on a special order the firm should be willing to set. Frequently, the buyer comes to the manufacturer with a suggested price. In this case, the manufacturer is in the position of either accepting or rejecting an offered price. Under almost all circumstances, a price below incremental cost should not be accepted. Perhaps the only situation in which a below-incremental cost price is acceptable is a case in which the buyer will be making subsequent orders and the manufacturer is relatively sure of getting the future business and will be able to raise the price on future orders.

Special orders which require increased capacity or which in some way disturb existing sales have higher incremental costs than special orders that do not have these effects. The cost of increasing capacity or the contribution margin on existing sales given up for the special order is part of the incremental cost of the special order.

*Bid pricers* face many of the same problems as special-order pricers. The main difference seems to be that a bid pricer has to worry about bid prices developed by other firms. Therefore, the bid pricer must attempt to outguess other firms' bids and offer the lowest bid, but not bid so low as to be below the incremental cost of the bid. Probability assessments are particularly appropriate here.[1]

A specialized form of bid pricing exists when one deals with the government. The problems of this area are highly specialized, and the reader is directed to *Negotiation and Management of Defense Contracts* (especially Chapter 3).[2]

## MARKETING CONCEPTS IMPORTANT TO THE PRICER

Among other factors one needs to keep in mind when pricing are the relationship of price and quality, the lure of prestige lines, brand loyalty, the public affinity for odd prices, and the danger of price wars.

**Price-Quality Relationships** For some products, there seems to be some consumer belief that high price means high quality. This is certainly not the case for all products. If one is considering a small price reduction, however, one should be aware that instead of producing the desired result—increased sales volume—this could result in reduced sales if the public perceives the price cut to be associated with a quality cut.

**Prestige Factor** This price-quality relationship also has a parallel in high-priced prestige lines. It appears that some of the status associated with high-priced lines of any product is due to the high price. For this reason, a firm may find it desirable to use higher markups on items that it views as top of the line in an attempt to add status appeal to the product rather than popular appeal. Having a status line sometimes can increase sales of the firm's cheaper lines also. This is undoubtedly why many firms label their cheaper lines with the tag: "By the makers of _____." Some status rubs off from the prestige line to the less-expensive, high-volume line.

**Product Images** Brand loyalty has been indirectly described earlier. It is simply the public belief that one product is better or more desirable than similar or identical products available from competitors. Brand loyalty is frequently created by advertising. It can manifest itself in the public paying higher prices for physically equivalent products. It appears that Bayer aspirin has successfully created brand loyalty for their product. If all brands of aspirin are chemically the same and are all subject to the same purity requirements, brand loyalty must explain the higher price received by Bayer. Another interesting example of an attempt to establish brand loyalty involves the Dole banana. Bananas are not a product one would expect to be bought by brand. One does not buy fresh tomatoes or celery by brand, but Dole, through television and magazine advertising, has attempted—with some success—to encourage the public to prefer Dole bananas.

**"Right" Prices and "Odd" Prices** Associated with what people believe about a product is what they believe about price. Studies have demonstrated that some products have a price people associate with it as the "right" price. For other products, they have no idea what the price of the item should be or normally is.

Some prices are set to capitalize on the public's believed love of odd prices, set at $1.99, $3.09, and so on. It is generally felt that these prices are more effective than $2.00, $3.10, and so on. Whether the public feels it is getting a bargain or that it is attracted to the unusualness of the price as they might be attracted to a hot orange–colored package is not certain. In fact, it may be that the odd price does nothing for the product sales but that pricers believe it does. Although frequently used, the real impact of odd pricing is unclear.

**Price Wars** Price changes can result in unwanted competitor reaction and culminate in a price war. It is for this reason that competitor as well as customer reaction should be considered. A price war is a period of heavy and potentially destructive price cutting. In a price war, prices frequently drop to or below the minimum price. Continuation of prices at such a low level usually means that some firms can no longer stay in business. Gasoline price wars are the most common example. It is usually the case that several stations fall victim to a price war and are forced to close.

The initial reaction to a price war might be to shut down temporarily until the war is over and one's competitors have been severely weakened or forced out of business. But the difficulty in regaining lost customers usually keeps most participants in a price war until it ends or until they must cease business altogether. Since a price war is temporary in nature, prices will rise again. The firm that finds itself in a price war must hope that it can hold on until prices rise and that they rise enough to make up for the losses suffered during the price cutting.

Even after contending with the complexities discussed above, the pricer has still not solved all the problems. He or she must also consider the legal limitations imposed on pricers by various governmental bodies.

## LEGAL LIMITATIONS ON PRICING

Under the guise of promoting competition, the government has passed numerous restrictions which influence the way a pricer may set price. For this reason, a pricer may find a lawyer's input most useful when product pricing.

Of the many terms which could be discussed in this section, three are most important: price fixing, price discrimination, and resale price maintenance. Firms have, on occasion, made explicit agreements concerning prices they will charge for their products. Such *price fixing* between supposedly competing firms is generally held to be illegal under the provisions of the Sherman Antitrust Act. The fines and damages provided for under the act can be extremely high and include a provision of triple damages to parties injured by price fixing. One of the classic recent examples of a suit under this act involved various electric equipment manufacturers and resulted in company fines of $11,787,000 and 30-day jail sentences for seven executives.[3]

Provisions of the Robinson-Pattman Act restrict various forms of price discrimination. *Price discrimination* is the selling of the same product to different customers at a different price. The statute declares price discrimination on "commodities of like grade and quality" to be illegal "where the effect of such discrimination may be 'substantially to lessen competition or tend to create a monopoly in any line of commerce, or to injure, destroy, or prevent competition."

This part of the act seems designed to protect small retailers from large retailers who might be able to command significant price concessions from suppliers. Various states have also passed laws designed to protect the small store by requiring large stores to sell at no lower than cost. The overall intent of such legislation is to prevent large firms from forcing small firms out of business.

The Robinson-Pattman Act also provides for resale price maintenance in states with fair trade laws. *Resale price maintenance* is the practice whereby manufacturers and sellers agree to the price the consumer will pay for a product and agree to enforce that price on all other sellers dealing in that product.

### PRICING IN REVIEW

There are no easy answers for the pricer, who must balance many inputs in order to be successful. The pricer must be aware of the market in which his or her product is sold and of the potential reaction of customers and competitors to price changes. He or she must be sure that the price is not "too low" as determined by various cost figures. Or, if the price is below the minimums suggested in this entry, then there should be a reason for the low price. Finally, the pricer must be careful not to violate the law.

*See also* ACCOUNTING FOR MANAGERIAL CONTROL; BRANDS AND BRAND NAMES; CREDIT MANAGEMENT; ECONOMIC CONCEPTS; MARKETING, CHANNELS OF DISTRIBUTION; PRODUCT PLANNING AND DEVELOPMENT; REGULATED INDUSTRIES, MANAGEMENT IN.

### NOTES

[1]Mark I. Alpert, *Pricing Decisions*, Scott, Foresman and Company, Glenview, Ill., 1971.

[2]Dean F. Pace, *Negotiations and Management of Defense Contracts*, John Wiley & Sons, Inc., New York, 1970.

[3]Donald V. Harper, *Price Policy and Procedure*, Harcourt, Brace & World, Inc., New York, 1966.

### REFERENCES

Brooks, Douglas G.: "Cost-Oriented Pricing: A Realistic Solution to a Complicated Problem," *Journal of Marketing*, April 1975, pp. 72–74.

Corr, A. V.: "The Role of Cost in Pricing," *Management Accounting*, November 1974, pp. 15–18.

Fuss, Norman H.: "How to Raise Prices—Judiciously—to Meet Today's Conditions," *Harvard Business Review*, May 1975, pp. 10, 12, 164.

Lere, John C.: *Pricing Techniques for the Financial Executive*, John Wiley & Sons, Inc., New York, 1974.

Lynn, Robert A.: *Price Policies and Marketing Management*, Richard D. Irwin, Inc., Homewood, Ill., 1967.

Oxenfeldt, Alfred R.: *Pricing Strategies*, American Management Association, New York, 1975.

JOHN C. LERE, *University of Minnesota*

## Production control (*See* MATERIALS MANAGEMENT; PRODUCTION PLANNING AND CONTROL.)

## Production/operations management

*Production* is any process or procedure used to create goods or services which have utility or value. A given process can be simultaneously physical, human, and economic, and it is designed to transform a given set of input elements into a specified set of output elements.

A *production system* is any cohesive collection of elements that are dynamically related for the purpose of production. Any such system has three distinguishable component parts: the inputs, the process, and the outputs.

By these definitions, production and production systems exist in hospitals, supermarkets, educational institutions, insurance companies, airlines, as well as in manufacturing plants. *Inputs* may be materials, labor, and energy as found in the manufacturing setting, but under this broader definition they could also be standard paper work forms, clients, patients, or entire communities as found in service settings. The production *process* involves one or more separate operations, which might be mechanical, chemical, assembly, movement, personal contact, or the administration of help or treatment. The *outputs* may be completed parts, finished products, bulk chemicals, completed reports, serviced customers, or treated patients.

Production management deals with decision making as related to the design and control of production processes. In the managing process the production manager is responsible for meeting (1) quality requirements, (2) established delivery or completion dates, (3) quality levels placed on the outputs, and (4) the selection and application of the most economical methods for accomplishing these. This holds true for profit and nonprofit organizations, private concerns, and forms of government, whether the output is tangible or intangible, a product or a service.

The knowledge of production management developed in the factory setting; hence the traditional association of production management with manufacturing management. This same methodology, however, applies to production systems as found in hospitals, railroads, consulting firms, airlines, insurance companies, and so on, thus explaining the modern viewpoint which includes under production management *any* management concerned with *any* system whose function is to create tangible or intangible utility.

The term *production management* is being gradually replaced with the more general term *operations management*, or *production/operations management (POM)*, thereby transcending the manufacturing setting. Emphasis is on applicability to any type of production system.

## MANUFACTURING (PRODUCTION) POLICIES

A *policy* is a code, guide, or general rule which stipulates the preferred procedure to follow in handling a recurring situation or in exercising a delegated authority. It serves as a guide to decision making as it defines a range wherein decisions may be made; as such it enables top management to delegate authority while maintaining control through the policy statement. Theoretically the underlying purpose of all policies is to ensure that decisions support organizational objectives and desired plans in a coordinated and consistent manner.

**Characteristics of a Good Policy** A good policy has the following characteristics: (1) It reflects the objectives and plans of top management; (2) it represents a consistent pattern of thought; (3) it is stable, but subject to change when change is needed; (4) it is sufficiently flexible to accommodate conditions which are unusual or unforeseen; (5) it is carefully thought out and clearly written; (6) it is well communicated and understood by those to be guided by it; and (7) it is controlled and consistently enforced. There are certain circumstances where it is advisable not to have a policy formalized in writing, such as when certain highly confidential matters are involved; however, control is very easily lost with informal policies, and so written policies should be the general rule. A good policy program requires that policies be reviewed on a regular basis to determine whether or not they need updating, if they are complete and support current objectives, if they are understood, and if they are being complied with. Some large companies will assign this duty to a special group, department, or committee.

**Hierarchy of Policies** Policies are needed at all levels of management; thus there is a hierarchy of policies. The basic policies, which represent the prerogatives of top management, are at the top, with the lesser ones beneath but in harmony with and reflecting the former. The matter of vertical integration is a basic policy issue, and the decision here will establish the confines of the total activity in which the firm will be engaged. Will the firm push ownership back to raw materials by acquiring its own sources of materials? Will it reach out toward the market by acquiring its own retail outlets? Horizontal integration is another basic issue, which deals with the question of whether or not duplicate plants, each doing the same job, will be used to supply the firm's markets, or whether a single, general purpose plant will be used. Other basic issues are the level of ownership of assets (owning versus renting or leasing), ground rules for guiding capital investments, and make-or-buy guidelines. Policies closer to operating management cover such matters as the following:

*Inventory:* Location of inventories; mix of items to be stocked; customer service–level targets; amount of allowed forward buying in anticipation of price increases or material shortages; limits on the use of inventories to level production; inventory turnover targets.

*Equipment replacement:* Interest rates to be used in various types of capital replacement requests; service life estimates for classes of machinery, equipment, buildings, or other assets; sources of final approvals for various types and sizes of expenditures.

*Quality control:* What type of checking will apply to specific outputs; the permissible level of risk for producing and shipping defective items and also for scrapping acceptable ones; application of quality control, whether during production or afterward in the form of 100 percent inspection.

*Production control:* Percent goal of on-time delivery to customers and also from vendors; investment in inventory; degree of employment stability; process improvment program; cost reduction programs.

Policy statements are also needed on purchasing, plant maintenance, plant security, safety habits, and housekeeping as well as on such common points as hours worked, attendance, overtime regulations, and so on.

## PRODUCTION ECONOMICS

The fundamental concept of production economics is that of utility of goods and services produced and either sold or dispensed. Utility in this sense is synonymous with the economic value assigned to these goods and services. While financial management is responsible for utility in terms of monetary value (i.e., cost and prices), production management sees utility as product availability in terms of quantity, timing, location, and the reliability of performance built into the product. The underlying premise is that the utility or value of the output is greater than the sum of the utilities or values of the inputs plus that of the investment in the production process when appropriately amortized.

Economics concentrates on the ways in which resources are or can be allocated to meet human needs, whereas economics of business concerns the allocations of organizational resources to meeting business needs. Production economics is a further refinement to production system needs where the allocation decisions arise from two broad areas of responsibility, namely, the designing of the production system and the operating and controlling of the system.

**Capital Investment**  A particular economic decision may involve a capital investment to replace worn out or obsolete equipment, to expand facilities in accordance with growing market demand, to introduce capacity for a new product, or to improve quality, plant efficiency, or general working conditions. In each case an economic appraisal is required, which is based on the requested capital, operating costs, income, profit or loss, and the intangible factors which characterize the proposal. A particular appraisal's structure and scope will depend not only on the nature and size of the investment but also on the type of enterprise. Thus a manufacturer may emphasize costs, consistent with quality and delivery requirements, whereas a hospital would tend to place more emphasis on reliability and service, consistent with cost objectives.

**Investment Appraisal**  The required investment is related to its associated profit or loss (i.e., the yield of the investment), and this is compared to the return which the company expects from this type of investment (normally specified in a policy). If the return calculated from the proposal falls below this benchmark, it is rejected. The two most popular measures of return are the internal rate of return and the discounted value of cash flow for an imputed cost of capital (i.e., the present value method). The internal rate of return has the advantage of providing an index number, without the need for estimating a cost of capital, which can be used as a criterion for comparing alternative capital requests: to arrange requests with respect to profitability one

places them in descending order of magnitude of their rates of return. The present value method is often used in making a single decision as to whether equipment replacements should be made and comparing alternative candidates.

## MAKE-OR-BUY DECISIONS

Many manufacturers have the option of either making a particular material, component part, or finished product or buying it from outside suppliers. An automobile manufacturer can buy tires or develop its own facilities for making them, just as a pharmaceutical firm can make or buy its basic chemical ingredients or the bottles, boxes, and cartons it uses. This also applies to buildings, special tooling and equipment, and even process designs.

A particular firm may make a portion of its need for a certain component part and buy the rest outside, thereby avoiding plant expansion. It may choose to send out those requirements needing special technology that it does not have internally, thereby forgoing hiring specialists. It may be in the best interests of the firm to ensure that a particular vendor stays in business. Or it may simply be that the outside source makes it cheaper or can deliver against a tighter schedule than inside. This is another area where top management must spell out the basic policy it wants followed. What factors are to be included in the comparison? What specific calculations and formulas are to be used? What is the division of responsibility among the management team?

**Costing Practices**  Normally, all direct material, labor, and any other out-of-pocket costs are included in the make cost: if making requires subcontracting, this cost is included in the direct variable cost. It is usually not adequate to use only out-of-pocket costs as the criterion. Incremental costs, overhead absorption, and any other factors which appear pertinent to the particular decision should also be included. Indirect labor, overtime premiums, hourly supervision, special training of skills, additional material handling, and the like are elements of direct variable overhead which may be pertinent to the decision.

If the decision is one of short term, then basing it on direct variable costs may be appropriate. If it is long term, then certain semivariable and fixed costs should be included since these will inevitably change over the long term. A definition of long and short term is needed, and an adequate one can be devised on the basis of a representative allocation of direct labor standard hours. If the production hours involved in the decision exceed this value, then it constitutes a long-term decision; otherwise, it is short term.

A given firm may locate the responsibility for make-or-buy decisions in the accounting function or the purchasing function or even make it the responsibility of the cost center most directly concerned. But regardless of where the responsibility may reside, there are profit improvement opportunities connected with these decisions, and attention to them should be established as part of the firm's routine activities.

## TRADE-OFF ANALYSIS

A trade-off problem is a decision problem in which the objective is to select the balancing point among two or more conflicting factors. The conflict may arise because the factors work in opposite directions or because they work at different rates in the same direction. Thus, one set of cost factors may increase with increases in equipment size, while another set decreases as size is increased. The problem is to find the size that balances the two sets of costs, i.e., that produces the minimum of their sum.

Trade-off problems arise where there are multiple objectives on the one hand and limited resources on the other, thus creating the need to balance off the objectives. This may lead to the fulfillment of one objective at the expense of the other, but most often neither objective is fully achieved; instead, a blend of the two results.

The area of inventory control is a common one for the application of trade-off analyses. The economic order quantity is a trade off of inventory investment against ordering costs; while the level of safety stock held is a trade off of inventory investment against customer service or stock-out costs. The same idea is applied when capital equipment is substituted for labor (i.e., mechanization or automation), when repair crews are sized by finding the minimum of the sum of the cost of equipment downtime and the cost of repair crew idle time, or when the level of quality and product reliability is selected on the basis of costs.

In formalizing a trade-off problem one starts by identifying the *decision variable*. This is either the variable which is inherent in the decision or a reflection of it (which is used owing to the ease with which it can be calculated or manipulated). This might be the size of inventory to hold as safety stock, the number of repairpeople in the crew, or the number of units to order in an economic order. In general, it is that factor which, when appropriately specified, will achieve the optimum trade off.

There may be more than one variable directly involved, in which case one speaks of a *decision vector*.

The other element one must identify is the *measure of effectiveness* to be used. This is simply the scale against which each potential decision (i.e., each value of the decision variable) will be measured and in terms of which the optimum point is selected. Most often this is total cost or total variable cost; however, it can also be gross profit or a physical measure such as process yield, elapsed time, or a flow rate such as patients seen per day. The objective is to find the value of the decision variable which will give the maximum measure of effectiveness (as would apply to profits or flow rates) or the minimum value (as in costs or elapsed time). In short, the objective is to optimize the measure of effectiveness in accordance with the logic of the decision. In many situations there is not complete freedom in setting values for the decision variable; i.e., there are constraints which are imposed and which limit the range of decisions. The objective is therefore to optimize the measure of effectiveness as much as possible within these constraints.

**Economic Balance** The economic balance may be determined by analytical or graphical (tabulation) means. In the former, one must be able to write down mathematical expressions which explicitly relate the decision variable to the measure of effectiveness. At this point the tools and techniques of mathematical analysis are applied to determine the optimum value of the decision variable. The key here is the ability to formulate these expressions and then to find the optimum value analytically. In the graphical approach, one calculates the measure of effectiveness for various values of the decision variable and then plots these against the latter. The optimum value is then estimated from the graphical plot when interpreted in terms of the objective. This approach is used when the problem is very straightforward and of small dimension, but most often when the analytical approach is not possible. It is important to recognize the service which is being provided by management scientists and operations researchers in the development of methods and techniques for performing such analytical analyses. Of particular importance are mathematical programming and simulation, which along with data processing devices, have opened up areas to analysis which were previously closed to production management.

## CONTRACT MANUFACTURING

Contract (custom) manufacturing involves a contractual agreement whereby a firm engages an outside company to perform productive or service work that can be identified as the main line of business of the purchaser. It is becoming very popular with firms as part of their global production program and is a way of obtaining low-cost component parts or having a production base for final products. Thus, a pharmaceutical firm may manufacture a chemical or other primary ingredient for one of its products and employ contract manufacturing to formulate and package the finished product using ingredients which it supplies to the contractor. The contractor may be given the complete manufacturing job or only the technical know-how or product specifications. This option is frequently used when the firm needs to buy capacity (or time) to release capacity in-house (or to enable it to get onto the market while its own facilities are being constructed). Conversely, many companies that find they have excess capacity are putting themselves on the market for contract manufacturing.

*Advantages.* Some of the advantages to using contract manufacturing are (1) it enables a firm to establish a production base locally where the current market size does not justify any sizable investment (this can be critical in foreign countries which have tight controls on imports); (2) it may provide components or materials of lower cost and higher quality because of the expertise of the contractor; (3) it avoids the problems connected with maintaining a stable work force when product demand is highly seasonal; and (4) it enables the firm to avoid the labor problems it might face if it manufactured internally.

*Disadvantages.* The main disadvantages are (1) manufacturing profit is lower because of the profit margin of the contractor; (2) it may transfer critical technology, which in turn may mean that the contractor can become a competitor after the contract expires; and (3) it releases control of product quality and thereby places the firm's image in the hands of a disinterested party.

## SUBCONTRACTING

Subcontracting also involves a contractual agreement for the performance of work, but in this case the work is usually in the areas which are peripheral to the main line of business of the purchaser. Thus, a company may subcontract its major maintenance or overhaul projects or the final distribution of its products but not the actual manufacturing of its products.

Subcontracting is highly developed in the construction industry, often to the point where the ultimate responsibility lies in the hands of a broker. It is also prevalent in continuous flow or highly mechanized process industries such as chemical and chemical products, food and beverages, metal fabrication, and petroleum.

There are certain crafts and occupations which are most frequently affected by subcontracting arrangement. These are construction crafts such as painting, masonry, electrical work, carpentry, plumbing, sheet metal, and iron work trades, and service occupations such as trucking, janitorial, and security. Typically, complete reliance on outside help is used in the case of cafeteria operations and frequently in trucking and security occupations. The installation, service, and repair of specialized equipment, such as refrigeration units, office equipment, or computers, is another popular area for subcontracting.

Subcontracting of maintenance work is most common in process industries, where only routine maintenance and minor jobs are performed internally. There is, however, increasing use of contract maintenance, which, like contract manufacturing, is usually a broad program whereby the entire maintenance of all equipment is contracted out, including maintenance management.

The decision to subcontract or not is analogous to the make-or-buy decision—more appropriately termed *do or buy*—and must be evaluated accordingly.

## FUNCTIONS OF PRODUCTION

Except for the most basic type of system, the modern production system is organized as a combination of line and staff functions.

*Line operative functions* are directly concerned with the primary objectives of the firm, and to define *line* one must know these objectives. In a manufacturing enterprise, where the primary objectives are to make and sell products, the two basic lines are production and selling (and sometimes finance), whereas in a retailing setting the elements directly concerned with buying and selling constitute the line. The line production functions are directly responsible for the actual output of the firm through the operation of the production processes. The specific definition and character of a given line function are corollaries of the outputs to be made, the technology to be used, as well as the type and size of the organization of which it is a part.

*Staff functions* provide services to the line operative functions by advising, developing plans, counseling, coordinating, or performing specific tasks. A staff cannot order a line function to perform a specific task, nor is it ever directly responsible for the production performance, quality of output, timing of availability, or cost of production—these are line responsibilities.

The usual services-to-production functions which are provided by staffs are designing outputs, designing processes, providing materials and supplies, planning and controlling production, controlling quality (error), maintaining and repairing process components, and controlling cost. In the broad sense, the functions listed above, both line and staff, constitute production management.

## RELATIONSHIPS

Since firms are traditionally organized in accordance with the principles of specialization and the division of labor, primary functional groups have evolved, such as marketing, finance, and manufacturing. Each function tends to be organized and managed as a separate activity, promoting functional traditions, methodologies, and points of view. The major concern of each function also tends to be the efficiency in performing its own tasks and responsibilities. In the past top management assumed that if each function operated at top efficiency, then the total organization would also operate at maximum effectiveness. Modern management recognizes that this assumption is not necessarily true and usually is not. Conflicts arise when functional efficiency takes precedence over overall enterprise effectiveness. Such efficiency-based conflicts must be resolved in accord with the firm's objectives. There must be an explicit structure of decision rules under which conflicting efficiency objectives will be traded off. There must be conditions under which exceptions to the rules will be allowed and an indication of the allowable extent of these exceptions. There must be a means for deciding whether or not the trade offs are worthwhile from the organizational point of view. Finally, it must be assured that the component which is suboptimized, or whose local efficiency is curtailed, is not penalized for having yielded to the good of the total enterprise.

**Relations with Marketing** Marketing interprets the demand for future periods, translates these into units of production output, and establishes desired delivery dates. Production management in turn provides production facilities (plant, personnel, and equipment) and acceptable quality, in addition to promoting growth in process improvement, technological advancement, and improvement in economic viability.

Conflicts arise between these two functions from their local efficiency viewpoints. Production management would like long design leadtimes, long production runs with few models, long and inflexible ordering leadtimes, strict production schedules, and infrequent model changes. On the other hand, marketing would prefer short design leadtimes, short production runs with many models, short order leadtimes, scheduling to meet emergency orders, and frequent model changes.

**Relations with Finance** Financial management's concern is with the efficient use of the firm's capital resources. The design and operation of a production system entails various needs for capital for reducing operating costs, increasing yields, or otherwise improving processes. Conflict arises from questioning the value of these investments as well as the general availability of capital to production. Again, one turns to policy statements which establish procedures by which such conflict is to be resolved: the form of capital cost, the expected return, specific measures of merit, and so on.

*See also* ACCOUNTING, COST ANALYSIS AND CONTROL; AUTOMATION; BUDGETING, CAPITAL; COST IMPROVEMENT; LEARNING (EXPERIENCE) CURVES; MATERIAL HANDLING; PRODUCTION PLANNING AND CONTROL; PRODUCTION PROCESSES; SCHEDULING, SHORT-INTERVAL; WORK SIMPLIFICATION AND IMPROVEMENT.

### REFERENCES

Gold, B.: *Explorations in Managerial Economics*, Basic Books, Inc., Publishers, New York, 1971.

Hopeman, R. J.: *Production Concepts: Analysis-Control*, 2d ed., Charles E. Merrill Books, Inc., Columbus, Ohio, 1971.

Levin, R. I., et al.: *Production/Operations Management: Contemporary Policy for Managing Operating Systems*, McGraw-Hill Book Company, New York, 1972.

Mantell, L. H., and F. P. Sing: *Economics for Business Decisions*, McGraw-Hill Book Company, New York, 1972.

Mayer, R. R.: *Production and Operations Management*, 3d ed., McGraw-Hill Book Company, New York, 1975.

Moore, F. G.: *Production Management*, Richard D. Irwin, Inc., Homewood, Ill., 1973.

Starr, M. K.: *Production Management: Systems and Synthesis*, 2d ed., Prentice-Hall Inc., Englewood Cliffs, N.J. 1972.

JAMES A. PARSONS, *American Cyanamid Company*

# Production/operations and manufacturing (*See heading in Table of Contents for complete listing.*)

# Production planning and control

*Production planning* focuses on the bringing together of the optimal choice of raw material under the optimal technology to create the optimal product. *Production control* consists of the continued adjustments which are required to accomplish the plan and infers the existence of (1) an information system by which the actual state of the system is compared against the planned state and (2) the existence of a feedback mechanism by which adjustments can be made into the production planning phase.

The function of production is to create the right product of acceptable quality at the correct point in time and at minimum cost. This means planning and controlling capacity, priorities, quality, and costs. The long-range decisions select the product and the technology. The ongoing decisions require continual forecasts of demand to develop the master production schedule. The master schedule then determines the production activities and their timing.

Production planning infers choices and trade offs among various alternative actions. Optimization techniques to assist in planning have been developed within such disciplines as operations research, decision science, operations management, managerial economics, and industrial engineering.

Production control depends upon processing adequate amounts of accurate and timely information regarding the current status of the production plan, the work in process, inventories, human and physical resource availability, and requirements projections. Rapid recent development in electronic data processing machinery and techniques have had profound impact upon practical approaches to production control.

## MANUFACTURING PROGRESS (LEARNING CURVES)

The production decision overlaps the marketing strategy in deciding price and penetration and the choice of manufacturing methods. The manufacturing progress function, or the learning curve, consists of the observation that progressively less labor is required per unit of production as experience in producing this item accumulates. The learning curve reflects both the learning by workers and operators and also engineering changes and redesign of production methods over time.

The relationship has been found to be $L = cx^a$, where $a = (\log f/\log 2)$ is a negative exponent. $L$ is the labor costs per unit produced, $c$ is the labor cost to produce the first unit at the start of time, $x$ is the number of the unit now being produced at current time, and $f$ is the learning factor.

Learning factors range in value from 1.0 (denoting no learning) toward zero, and often are about 0.9 to 0.8 down to perhaps 0.6, which would indicate rapid learning.

The above equation has a negative exponent corresponding to the situation that the required labor decreases very rapidly with $x$ at first, then more slowly as experience accumulates. The learning curve has an equivalent logarithmic form which is useful for fitting the empirical data and performing calculations:

$$\text{Log } L = \log c + \frac{\log f}{\log 2} \log x$$

Sometimes the learning curve labor is defined somewhat differently from the above. Instead of $L$ being defined as the labor cost for the $x$th unit, $L$ is defined as the cumulative average labor required to produce all the units up to and including the $x$th unit. Either definition is acceptable provided that one is consistent in always employing the same definition when gathering the empirical data, calculating the parameters, and using the equations. *See* LEARNING (EXPERIENCE) CURVES.

**An Indicator of Production Scale** The long-range production and marketing plan should include consideration of the observed value of the learning factor, $f$, of the item. If $f$ is not known, it may be estimated, since similar products generally have similar learning factors.

For example, if the value of $f$ for a proposed product is much less than unity, denoting that rapid learning is anticipated during its manufacture, and if at the same time the potential market size is large and is responsive to price (elastic), then the long-range production strategy is influenced in favor of mass production of a standardized product to give the firm deep penetration and an early advantage over potential competitors. (Standardized production might be made consistent with marketing variety by using modularized design.) Conversely, a product with $f$ closer to unity would denote less potential learning and suggest perhaps job-shop manufacture rather than production line, less standardization, lower volume, and higher profit margin per unit.

**Calculation Technique** To illustrate the calculation, the first task is to estimate the value of $f$. Assuming that the firm has some preliminary production experience with this (or a similar) product, $f$ may be determined by linear regression using the above logarithmic equation for $L$ versus the logarithms of $x$, with $x = 1$ denoting the first unit of production for which records are at hand. The slope of the regression line is therefore $a$, which is log $f$/log 2, and the $y$-intercept of the regression is log $c$, and the antilogs may then be found from log tables or a calculator having a log key.

For example, if $c$ were found to be 90 minutes

and $f$ equal to 0.8, then the time to produce the 100th unit could be calculated:

$$\text{Log } L = \log 90 + \frac{\log 0.8}{\log 2} \log 100$$

$$= 1.9542 - \frac{.09691}{.3010} (2.00)$$

$$= 1.31028$$

then

$$L = \text{antilog } (1.31028)$$

$$= 20 \text{ minutes}$$

Similar calculations show that the 200th unit should require about 16 minutes and the 500th unit should require roughly 12 minutes of production time.

**Cumulative Average and Total Times** Since $L$ was defined as the time required for the individual $x$th unit, a method or equation is needed to calculate the cumulative average time up to and including the $x$th unit. This cumulative average is useful for price and profit estimations.

One method to calculate the cumulative average would be simply to add up all the unit times and divide by $x$, although this would be tedious. A second method is to use standard tables of the cumulative average versus the unit number $x$ and the learning factor $f$.

A third method, which is precise enough for practical purposes, is to estimate the cumulative times by the equation

$$\text{Cumulative total time} = \frac{cx^{a+1}}{a+1}$$

To illustrate, if the learning factor is 0.8 and the value of $c$ is 90, then the total time to produce the first 100 units could be estimated:

$$\text{Cumulative total} = \frac{90(100)^{1+\log 0.8/\log 2}}{1 + \log 0.8/\log 2}$$

$$= \frac{90(100)^{0.678}}{1 - 0.322}$$

$$= 3013 \text{ minutes, or 50 hours}$$

The expected total time for the first 200 units could similarly be calculated to be about 4820 minutes, or 80 hours. Thus the total time for the *second batch* of 100 units would be about $(4820 - 3013) = 1807$ minutes, or 30 hours. Therefore the second batch of 100 required an average time of 0.3 hour per unit, compared to 0.5 hour per unit for the first batch. This is a drastic cost difference.

**Uses** Part of what the economist calls *economies of scale* can be interpreted in light of the learning curve. The learning factor for an operation should be kept in mind when making decisions on capacity, production run lengths, make versus buy decisions, standard costs, and production technology.

## MASTER FORECASTING AND PLANNING

The master production planning consists of the creation of the schedule of the items to be produced over the planning time horizon. The horizon is typically several months to 1 year ahead, but it must be at least as long as the longest production and lead time of any item produced. Major tasks of master planning include (1) predicting sales demand using forecasting techniques; (2) deciding how much of the potential demand to produce; and (3) developing the master production schedule from which resource needs with time can be determined, coordinated, and implemented. All production activities should be based on the master schedule.

**Forecasting** The term *forecasting* is often ambiguously used to mean either prediction or else that part of prediction which rests upon formalized techniques. Assorted formal techniques, tempered by intuition, can generally be combined to yield better predictions of the future than can intuition alone. Useful techniques include statistical time series analysis, surveying industry and other "expert" opinion, econometric forecasting models which are maintained by several universities and institutions, and other business and economic forecasts. *See* FORECASTING BUSINESS CONDITIONS.

Several measures are popularly employed for determining how closely the forecasts coincide with the realized production demand. One statistical measure is the mean squared error of the forecast or standard deviations (sigmas). In production management, however, errors are more often measured in mean absolute deviations (MADs). The MAD is simpler to calculate than sigma, and between them exists the relationship that one MAD is about 0.8 sigma. Thus it is expected that 89 percent of the observations should fall within $\pm 2$ MAD of the forecasts, and 98 percent within $\pm 3$ MAD.

*Use of Time Series.* Statistical time series forecasting is based upon the notion that past data usually can be extrapolated to obtain a base forecast upon which to predict the future. The simplest extrapolation consists of plotting the time series (sales demand, for example) versus time and drawing a freehand trend line through the data points. At the other extreme of sophistication and complexity lie such techniques as spectral analysis and Box-Jenkins modeling, which seek to discover the statistical structure of the time series to obtain clues regarding the nature of the process which is generating the data.

In production and inventory control, the objective is often to compute reasonably smoothed forecasts for many items on a routine basis. For this, the technique of exponential smoothing has proved very popular. Exponential smoothing computes a weighted moving average forecast with minimal data manipulation and minimal storage of information. The weights are easily modified. Forecasts can be automatically maintained by computer, with human intervention occurring only on an exceptions basis.

*Exponential Smoothing.* The exponentially smoothed average of past data at any point $t$ in time is

$$F_t = \alpha D_t + (1 - \alpha)F_t - 1$$

where $D_t$ is the most recent data point and $F_{t-1}$ is the smoothed average which was calculated the period previous to $t$ and was the basis by which $D_t$ was forecasted before $D_t$ became known.

The smoothing constant is $\alpha$ (alpha) which is a constant set at whatever value is found to give on the average the best forecasts. Alpha always lies between zero and 1, and is often found to be in the range of 0.1 to 0.3. The exponentially smoothed average can be made approximately equivalent to a moving average of any particular length by suitable choice of alpha.

The smoothed average, $F_t$, may simply be extrapolated and called the forecast for the next period, or the trend and seasonality may be brought into the forecast by more complicated kinds of exponential smoothing, using additional smoothing factors. Usually either the above simple model (called first-order smoothing) is adequate, or a trend factor is added (second-order smoothing).

The calculation of the forecast for each period requires carrying forward only the last forecast and alpha to combine with the new data point, so it requires very little computer memory to routinely update many forecasts for large inventory and production systems. Although $F_{t-1}$ is only one number, it actually contains all the past history on a weighted basis, since it is calculated recursively from the data

$$F_{t-1} = \alpha D_{t-1} + \alpha(1 - \alpha)D_{t-2} + \alpha(1 - \alpha)^2 D_{t-3} + \cdots + \alpha(1 - \alpha)^n F_o$$

where $F_o$ is the first forecast which was made $n$ periods ago. Thus we discard history more slowly with a small value of alpha, or we can choose to weight the recent past more heavily with a larger alpha.

*Tracking Signals.* If the system which is generating the time series data (such as sales demand) is not changing with time, then we can predict the percentage of observations that should fall within plus-or-minus some number of MADs (sum of the mean absolute deviations) of the forecasts. Too many observations falling outside of this range would signal that the model is not forecasting properly. Therefore a tracking signal is generally built into the calculations, which can be set at any degree of sensitivity to generate exception reports. The tracking signal equals the sum of forecast errors divided by the MAD.

**Master Scheduling** The master schedule consists of a listing of the forecasted production requirements over time. The production forecast reflects the sales forecast, inventory adjustments, backlogs, and production leveling adjustments. One format is depicted in Fig. P-26, where the end items to be produced are listed down the left margin, production time periods across the top, and the actual quantities to produce in each period (time bucket) are entered in the squares of the matrix.

Alternative formats include that of one page per end item, which may include information on inventories and breakdown of the sources of the demand, to serve also as a work sheet for the master scheduler.

The master schedule is the plan from which all production activities are developed and coordinated, as distinguished from assembly schedules or work schedules. It must be updated as frequently as fluctuations occur in demand, priorities, raw material availability, and plant capacity in order to keep the master schedule credible and not be circumvented by informal scheduling. A master schedule should not, for example, show production backlog, since nothing can be produced yesterday. Instead, it is revised and reissued as often as necessary to remain the basic planning document for each period.

Universal Widget Corp.
Master production schedule                Page 7

| End item | Current | Production period 10/22 | 10/29 | 11/5 | 11/12 |
|---|---|---|---|---|---|
| 27-135 | 2000 | 2000 | 2000 | 3000 | 3000 |
| 28-136 | 1000 | 1000 | 1000 | 0 | 0 |
| 17-206 | 500 | 0 | 500 | 0 | 500 |
| 05-721 | 10 | 10 | 10 | 10 | 10 |

**Fig. P-26. A master production schedule.**

The master schedule shows the production plan to a time horizon that is at least as distant as the most lengthy production or procurement time for any end item or component. Time buckets may be of any suitable interval and typically consist of weekly periods for the present and near future, then monthly and quarterly periods for the more remote future.

Each item listed on the master schedule is described by a specific bill of material number. The item number may describe either an actual end product or, to reduce the length of the master schedule, describe product groups which have forecastable demands as groups. ("modular bills").

A *bill of material* (BM) is a complete listing of the quantities of all the components of an end item. The end item may be a finished good or a component of a higher-level end item. In various industries, the bill of material may be called the furnish, formula, specification, or procedure.

Various formats exist for manufacturing bills of materials. One example is the single-level explosion format depicted in Fig. P-27. Here the end-item product 27-135 is constructed of three component parts. Each one of these components might in turn have a bill of material.

End item 27-135

| Part no. | Description | Quantity |
|---|---|---|
| 219 | Frame | 1 |
| 526 | Bracket | 5 |
| 735 | Fastener | 12 |

**Fig. P-27. A bill of material (single-level explosion).**

Many firms have their bills of material stored on computer disk files which are accessed by the bill of materials processor, a computer software package. The multiple levels of bills may then be quickly "chained" by computer to obtain a listing of all components and subcomponents of an end item.

The BMs are prepared from engineering drawings and parts lists, but often should be numbered differently from the engineering parts and assemblies. The reason is that every unique production end item should have its unique production bill of material number, but production end items may not correspond to physical end items. For example, a subassembly manufactured for in-process inventory might be a production end item, but would only be a collection of components from the engineering viewpoint.

The details of the manufacture are specified on a routing sheet, as depicted in Fig. P-28. The routing

Part name: Housing base plate HP 72-19
Usage: Assembly A 735X
Date issued: 10/24

| Operation no. | Operation description | Machine | Setup (hr) | Rate per/hr | Tools |
|---|---|---|---|---|---|
| 10 | Rough grind edges | 521 | 0.7 | 100 | |
| 20 | Drill 6 holes 0.500 ± 0.001 | D17 | 0.1 | 260 | |
| 30 | Deburr | D15 | 0.1 | 200 | Jig #491 |

**Fig. P-28. A routing sheet.**

sheet contains a heading of general information, followed by sequencing information which shows the work centers into which to route the job, and contains space on the sheet for each work center to record the progress history of the job. Route sheets often are prepared and updated by punched cards and computerized systems.

The master schedule is the basic plan from which the material requirements plan and the capacity requirements plan are developed. If capacity and material are inadequate to supply demand, then either additional resources must be procured or else the master schedule must be reduced to less than demand. An iterative process may be performed to reconcile objectives to feasibility through simulation. One form of simulation consists of creating a tentative master schedule from which materials and capacity requirements are estimated and then adjusting the plan until it becomes feasible. This improves the leveling of the loading of the work centers and assigns more valid priorities to work in the queue.

## INVENTORY OPTIMIZATION AND MATERIAL REQUIREMENTS PLANNING

The basic principle of inventory optimization and materials management is to minimize the competing costs of having either too little or too much in inventories of raw material, work in process, or finished goods. Inventories provide indispensible buffers to improve the leveling of production activity, but they constitute a major investment of the funds of most firms. *See* INVENTORY CONTROL, PHYSICAL AND STOCKKEEPING; MATERIALS MANAGEMENT.

The total costs of inventory policy (TC) are generally taken to include the following as the most important cost elements:

TC = value of goods + procurement costs
    + holding costs + stock-out costs

The mathematics for minimizing these costs has been worked out for many situations. Under the simplest assumptions, this model gives rise to the well-known EOQ and EPQ, or square-root formulas. If stock-out costs are important, then the statistics of replenishment and demand during order lead time must be considered to derive more complicated $R,Q$ models, which simultaneously make best estimates of both the reorder point ($R$) and the reorder quantity ($Q$). Inventory strategy for items subject to independent demand, such as finished goods or service parts, should begin by determining the optimal ($R,Q$) policy.

The advent of low-cost electronic data processing has created an improved framework for maintaining inventories of goods subject to dependent demand. Component parts and manufacturing subassemblies are examples of dependent demand items. Forecasting the demand for the end product automatically forecasts the demand for all the components of that end item. This framework is called material requirements planning (MRP). MRP is an inventory optimization system and is also a framework for planning, scheduling, and controlling production activities.

**EOQ/EPQ Models** The square-root inventory models are well known, but their nature is often misunderstood by practitioners. The models are derived from the above total cost relationship by making certain simplifying assumptions. By solving for the EOQ or EPQ batch size and being aware of the nature of the simplifying assumptions, one can make reasonable ball-park estimates of the least-cost policy.

A first approximation to the cost categories of the above equation is to specify the total cost to be

$$TC = Dp + \frac{cD}{Q} + \frac{ipQ(1 - d/r)}{2}$$

for an item that is never out of stock and has an annual forecasted demand for $D$ units at a value of $p$ per unit. The procurement or setup cost is $c$ dollars per order, and the order or production run amount is $Q$ units per batch. If the item is produced then it is at a daily rate of $r$ and depleted at a daily rate of $d$. The value for the effective rate of interest, $i$, is often taken to be about 30 percent, to include the opportunity cost of capital, insurance, obsolescence, and other costs of holding.

*Economical Order Quantity (EOQ).* If the demand-depletion rate, goods cost, and effective interest rate are constant, and the unit is ordered rather than produced, then the above equation can be solved by the methods of calculus to give the EOQ formula

$$EOQ = \sqrt{\frac{2Dc}{ip}}$$

The EOQ is a first estimate of the quantity to time an order is placed with a vendor or supplier. It seeks the best trade off between ordering costs and carrying costs. Since costs increase more rapidly if too little is ordered versus too much, and also since stock-out costs are ignored in the above equation, the proper procedure is to calculate the EOQ and then order somewhat more than the EOQ amount.

*Economical Production Quantity (EPQ).* The above TC equation can be solved for producing instead of ordering. If the trade off between machine setup costs versus carrying costs is to be optimized, the TC equation is minimized when

$$EPQ = \sqrt{\frac{2Dc}{ip(1 - d/r)}}$$

This equation is for the case of setting up a machine to run the item to a certain inventory level, then running that machine on another item until stocks are nearly depleted.

The EPQ is the approximate optimal value for $Q$ in units per batch to manufacture in such instances as a finished good where demand is fairly uniform but insufficient to dedicate a work center to that item on a constant basis. Like the EOQ, the EPQ is often adjusted upward by a small arbitrary amount.

Certain costs which can sometimes be important are not taken into account in the EPQ formula. More complicated formulas are useful for considering optimizing setups over a cycle of different products, for including statistical shortage costs of the item being produced, or if logistics or learning or economies of scale are important.

Particularly if the item being produced is a component part of another item, the shortage costs for an item may easily be so great as to overwhelm the other cost considerations. This does not invalidate the cost minimization concept but shifts it into the format which is called material requirements planning.

**MRP and Dependent Demand Inventory** Material requirements planning (MRP) is an information and planning system to time the arrival of material and production so that stock-outs should never occur [*see* MATERIALS REQUIREMENTS PLANNING (MRP)]. MRP uses the data of the master schedule, the current inventory status report, and the bills of material of the items to be produced to determine the time phasing and priorities of production activity. Each end item (or group) that is to be produced is contained in the master schedule as to its time of need and its bill of material number. In the MRP procedure, each bill of material is broken down or "exploded" into a list of all the subassemblies and component parts (including the raw materials and purchases) which are required for the production of the end items. Manufacturing and procurement lead times are then estimated and controlled so that raw material and in-process inventories will be at the correct levels at the correct times.

MRP specifically minimizes two of the principal costs of the total inventory cost equation, namely, the holding costs and the stock-out or shortage costs. Holding costs are reduced both by reducing the average value of goods on hand at times they are not needed and by reducing the effective interest rate factor which contains allowance for obsolescence and losses. The third principal cost, which is ordering or procurement costs, is treated in MRP by various lot-sizing techniques. MRP is ideally suited to an electronic data processing system, which can in itself reduce the procurement costs per transaction with respect to records and information processing.

MRP is more than an inventory control technique. It can be an element of a total data-based planning and production control system. Although the principles of MRP are not new, widespread interest in MRP as a practical approach has developed only since about 1970, stimulated by the advent of more generally available computer software, notably the PIC and then the COPICS systems of IBM, and the vigorous promotion of the concept by APICS (American Production and Inventory Control Society).

Just as the master schedule "drives" the MRP system, an MRP system can drive a capacity planning system. The MRP system displays the requirements for all raw materials and components in aggregate which are necessary for the production of the various end items. By inspection of this listing, management can ascertain whether the resources and the lead times are adequate to meet the master schedule or whether more capacity is required to meet objectives. The material capacity planning system is also implicitly a personnel planning system.

**ABC Analysis** The ABC concept is based upon the observation that the bulk of the dollar sales volume (say, 80 percent) involves relatively few items (say, 15 percent) of the stock numbers. By carefully managing these high-volume A items, or perhaps both the A and the B items, the C items, which constitute most of the items stocked, can be relegated to only occasional periodic maintenance. An ABC system might have A items on continuous or daily records and reordering, while C items are reviewed quarterly or when stock-out is realized.

The ABC concept is useful for systems with independent demands. For dependent demand, however, the MRP system supplants the ABC for all the items which are contained in the bills of material. The reason is that the low-turnover C items are no longer unimportant if their stock-out prevents the timely completion of the end item of which they are a component. Also all inventory can readily be monitored with an electronic data processing system without the need for distinction by usage level.

## CAPACITY PLANNING

Capacity planning on the operational level consists of using the resources at hand to the best advantage. Planning provides for the timely accomplishment of work in the correct priorities, minimization of idleness of each aspect of the work centers, and utilization of the least-cost techniques for performing the tasks.

Capacity planning is performed by maintaining adequate data on the status of the production system and continually applying various heuristic rules of thumb, simulations, and mathematical and graphical techniques to attempt to determine the best procedures in the face of complex interaction.

**Capacity Requirements Planning** Manufacturing production systems using material requirements planning should use the information which is generated to perform capacity requirements planning. The procedure is to use the demand forecasts to develop a tentative master schedule, from which the material requirements planning is computed. This tentative MRP determines the tentative priorities of production and the capacities required to accomplish the production schedule. If these tentative capacity requirements are available and feasible, then the (simulated) tentative master schedule becomes the actual master schedule for production. If these tentative capacity requirements are not available, then the tentative master schedule must be revised until the plan is feasible.

Capacity requirements planning typically employs the assistance of electronic data processing to maintain the files of information needed and to prepare the tabulated plans. This data processing capability allows revision of the production plan as frequently as desired (e.g., daily or weekly) to reflect current priorities and capacity changes adequately.

This approach is a move toward central planning by removing production backlogs from the shop floor and replacing informal scheduling and control procedures by a formalized procedure. Difficulties include (1) the need for accurate data systems and (2) human factors, which tend to replace formal systems by informal ones.

**Linear Programming**   Linear programming (LP) is a general technique for optimally allocating resources. It is particularly useful for determining how to schedule various kinds of tasks through multiple work centers, where each work center has only a finite capacity.

The various tasks might be, for example, the daily production of many different dimensions of lumber (1 × 12s, 2 × 4s, etc.) through work centers which included trucking in the logs, several sawing operations, multiple planing operations, and kiln drying and warehouse handling. Linear programming could quickly determine which operations are most efficiently performed on which of alternative machines and then identify the real process bottlenecks.

The calculations would also automatically determine the additional profit contribution generated by scheduling more capacity and the potential profits due to changing the product mix. The LP solution would provide top management with information regarding the payoff of possible long-range capital expansion of facilities.

In a manufacturing flow environment, linear programming analyses should be performed from time to time to determine whether the standard procedures are efficiently utilizing capacity and other resources. In a job-shop or project-oriented environment, LP can be useful on a more regular basis as one of various techniques which are embodied in the scheduling.

**Simulation**   The essence of simulation is to calculate the sequence of details of a possible situation before actually encountering it. By simulating, various scenarios can be investigated to see which courses of action would be best to implement. One form of simulation, in which the master schedule is simulated through the MRP system, is outlined above in the discussion of capacity requirements planning.

Other modes of simulation are also useful in capacity planning. Models can be constructed to represent complex interaction of production situations.

Monte Carlo simulation refers to models where probabilities of interacting events are considered, and the model is recalculated many times on a computer to find the probabilities of the possible outcomes of a decision or situation. Deterministic simulation refers to calculating through a mathematical or computer model which does not include probabilities, but which is usually too complex for routine analysis by intuition.

Simulation can be one of the most powerful tools for better understanding a system (*see also* SYSTEM DYNAMICS). Its importance has lead to the creation of several computer languages designed especially for simulation, such as GPSS, GASP, SIMSCRIP, and DYNAMO. Of course, other more general languages such as FORTRAN can also be used, and very simple models can be simulated by hand calculation.

**Queuing Models**   The time that a job spends in a manufacturing process typically consists of waiting in a queue for the first operation, then setup, then machine operation time, then move time to the next queue of the second operation, and so forth through many operations.

One's tendency is to predict job completion times by summing the times for each work center operation. Usually, however, the time spent in the many queues is far greater than the actual operation times. This is one reason why most facilities are found to have chronic backlogs and why expediting work can have dramatic results.

Queuing theory consists of the study of systems in which there are arrivals into the system bearing probability distributions, and service with (usually) different statistical features. Queuing theory provides for understanding of how waiting lines lengthen or shorten as functions of system statistics.

Until recently, queuing theory was too couched in mathematics for practical use in routine study of multiple-server, multiple-queue production processes. With the advent of high-speed computing, however, and with languages tailored for simulation modeling, queuing modeling is beginning to be a capacity planning tool for the practitioner.

**PERT/CPM**   Program evaluation and review technique (PERT) and critical path method (CPM) are network planning techniques for project management. These are most suited for complex extensive tasks, such as the production of a building or a ship. PERT and CPM differ from each other in their fine points, with PERT providing probability estimates of all the completion times for a job but CPM restricting its focus to the control of the critical paths of the project.

The principal value of PERT/CPM is often the project definition and planning which occurs during the development of the chart of sequential and parallel tasks which constitute the proposed project. This planning is usually much more critical than the updating control capability. Computer libraries are commonly available for the periodic updating of the PERT/CPM network of a project for management control. *See* NETWORK PLANNING METHODS.

**Job-Shop Loading Techniques** Various approaches have been pursued for better allocating capacity to work flow. These include operations research techniques, heuristic rules, and computer-based methods.

Allocation and scheduling problems can be studied by operations research techniques such as branch-and-bound methods, dynamic programming, and integer programming. These are more specialized approaches because of their technical complexities.

Practitioners often use standard rules of thumb for scheduling work flow. Rules that operations researchers have shown to be "good" or "optimal" should be adopted where possible. One such example is the job-shop scheduling algorithm, which has been worked out for certain situations.

Computer-based scheduling algorithms have been under active development. As knowledge in this area expands, software is becoming available to place more sophisticated scheduling on a user level.

## PRODUCTION CONTROL

Production control begins with techniques for organizing and conceptualizing information about the plan and the current status of events in pursuing the plan. The subsequent task of causing the system to react to this information rests upon the skill of the manager in interpreting the information that is presented and in reducing any variance between the plan and the actual status.

**Charting Techniques** A simple but useful control technique is to use a calendar or time graph or bar chart of some sort to visually present each task to be performed and the time schedule relationships. Examples include PERT and CPM, which can be displayed in different formats stressing milestones events and time-scaled activities. Other techniques include Gantt charts, line of balance charts, and combinations of these.

*Gantt Charts.* For assembly line operations, the simple Gantt chart is still often used to provide management with a quick impression of job status, priorities, and interdependencies. For project man-

agement, the Gantt chart has generally been supplanted by PERT/CPM. The Gantt chart is a bar chart which lists the different tasks to be performed and shows the task time as horizontal bars drawn to represent calendar times for execution (*see* GANTT CHARTS).

*Line of Balance.* The line of balance (LOB) technique is a more detailed management-oriented charting technique for monitoring assembly line progress. The four inputs which are required for an LOB chart are (1) the production plan, showing the key "milestone" events of the production process; (2) the cumulative schedule of time to reach each milestone; (3) the production progress, recorded on a vertical Gantt bar chart; and (4) the line of balance, which is a stairstep line obtained by calculating the cumulative number of units which must be completed to meet the schedule for each milestone. LOB charts may be maintained by hand or computerized. *See* LINE OF BALANCE (LOB).

**Critical Ratios** Critical ratios are often maintained on work flowing through the shop to signal by exception reports which jobs should be expedited. Various formulas have been invented for critical ratios, which yield a number indicating the ratio of the time in which the job should be finished divided by the projected time in which the job will actually be finished. If the calculated critical ratio for a job is greater than 1.0, it indicates that the job is ahead of schedule; if it is equal to 1.0, the job is exactly on schedule; if it is less than 1.0, the job is behind schedule ("critical"). One way of ordering priorities might thus be to process in order of the smallest critical ratio.

The use of critical ratios is controversial and is possibly obsolete for manufacturing environments which have MRP-based capacity requirements planning systems. One reason is that strict attention to expediting according to the ratio can cause erratic "hurry-and-wait" behavior, particularly for "lumpy-demand" items. Another reason is that better information systems allow better priority control than by ratios.

**Dispatch Lists** A dispatch list is a regular (usually daily) listing of the tasks to be done by each work center in order of priority. Firms with on-line computer inquiry terminals even allow the work centers to inquire at any moment regarding current job priorities. Jobs are taken from the top of the list, and as work is completed the work center creates a report to update the status.

A difficulty of this technique is in making it reflect true priorities and in not having persons bypass it. Supervisors or operators do not always prefer to perform tasks in the order listed, particularly if they are not convinced of the validity of the list.

## SOURCES OF ADDITIONAL INFORMATION

Techniques which concentrate on the general optimization concepts and on the long-range or strategic aspects of production planning are found in textbooks on operations research, operations management, decision science, and managerial economics. Production planning overlaps in depth the other functional areas of the firm, including the finance, marketing, personnel, and accounting functions. Production management draws heavily upon industrial engineering techniques.

Textbooks aimed at business schools use tend to stress the longer-range considerations and the viewpoint of top management and generally lean toward methodology. Methodological journals include *Management Science*, *Operations Research*, and *Decision Sciences*.

A principal source of literature on shorter-range production planning and control from the viewpoint of operating management is through the American Production and Inventory Control Society (APICS), which distributes educational material, a journal *Production Management*, and bound proceedings of the annual conferences of the society. The society maintains a national examination and certification program in production and inventory management. APICS sponsored the *Production and Inventory Control Handbook*.

*See also* CONTROL SYSTEMS, MANAGEMENT; GANTT CHARTS; INVENTORY CONTROL, PHYSICAL AND STOCKKEEPING; LEARNING (EXPERIENCE) CURVES; LINE BALANCING; LINE OF BALANCE (LOB); MATERIALS MANAGEMENT; MATERIALS REQUIREMENTS PLANNING (MRP); NETWORK PLANNING METHODS; OPERATIONS RESEARCH AND MATHEMATICAL MODELING; PRODUCTION/OPERATIONS MANAGEMENT; SCHEDULING, SHORT-INTERVAL; SYSTEMS CONCEPT, TOTAL; SYSTEM DYNAMICS; WORK SIMPLIFICATION AND IMPROVEMENT.

### REFERENCES

Buffa, Elwood: *Operations Management—Problems and Models*, John Wiley & Sons, Inc., New York, 1972.

Fabrycky, W. J., P. M. Ghare, and P. F. Torgersen: *Industrial Operations Research*, Prentice-Hall, Inc., Englewood Cliffs, N.J., 1972.

Greene, J. H., (ed.), *Production and Inventory Control Handbook*, McGraw-Hill Book Company, New York, 1970.

Hillier, F. S. and G. J. Lieberman: *Operations Research*, Holden-Day, Inc., Publisher, San Francisco, 1974.

Moder, J. J., and C. R. Phillips: *Project Management with CPM and PERT*, Van Nostrand Reinhold Company, New York, 1970.

Orlicky, Joseph: *Material Requirements Planning*, McGraw-Hill Book Company, New York, 1975.

Tersine, R. J.: *Materials Management and Inventory Systems*, North-Holland Publishing Company, New York, 1976.

Wight, Oliver W.: *Production and Inventory Management in the Computer Age*, Cahners Books International, Inc., Boston, 1974.

JAMES W. RICE, *University of Wisconsin, Oshkosh*

# Production processes: analysis, selection, and optimization

A *process* can be broadly defined as a way of "converting" a "raw material" into a "product" that is desired by a customer or user. The quotation marks are used to emphasize the fact that each of those terms must in each instance be very broadly defined. The raw material, the process, and the product are dependent upon the type of industry.

## PROCESS VARIATIONS BY TYPE OF INDUSTRY

Most physical raw materials are made available by an extractive industry. Two examples of extractive industries are mining and oil production. In mining, the process involves the removal of the ore from the earth and its preparation for the next stage, which is refining at a mill.

In the construction industry, the process is the building of the physical structure, such as a building or a road. In construction, each job is generally different from the previous one; frequently the time span is long, and the product is usually built at the location where it will be used.

Service industries, such as banks, insurance companies, hotels, restaurants, and dry cleaning establishments, for example, also involve processes by which they provide their service.

In banks and insurance companies, the process is essentially one of handling paper work in such a way as to provide service to clients. In hotels, the process provides a service. The hotel customer arrives without a physical product and leaves without a physical product but usually consumes products or services while there. In some service industries, such as dry cleaning, the process operates on a customer's product in a way that makes it more valuable to the customer.

The process in the transportation industry provides a service by moving people or products. The process in wholesaling and retailing provides an interface or buffer between the producer and the consumer. There are also industries which can be categorized as institutions, for example, hospitals and schools. Institutions use processes to make customers or users more valuable to themselves and to society.

## PROCESSES IN MANUFACTURING INDUSTRIES

Processing in the traditional sense tends to focus on the manufacturing industries, where processes have received the most extensive study. Manufacturing processes involve the conversion of a raw material into a finished product. The raw material is often the end product of another plant or industry. The raw material for the steel mill, for example, is the end product of the iron ore mining industry.

It is also possible to define conversion in a more restricted sense such that it implies a change in nature of the product. The refinery converts crude oil into gasolines, oils, and tars, for instance. When the manufacturing process changes the physical shape of the raw material, the process can be called *fabrication;* a bolt is fabricated from bar stock. An *assembly process,* on the other hand, combines a group of discrete parts into a whole. The automobile is an assembled product.

**Classification by Size and Volume of Output**    A manufacturing operation may be called a *large-scale* operation if it involves large quantities of product requiring extensive resources. Large-scale operations may also be termed *mass production* operations. Mass-produced items are usually made on highly specialized equipment. The automobile industry is an example of a large-scale, mass production industry. Sometimes, the term *large scale* is used in reference to large items that may be produced in small quantities. One example is the manufacture of large turbine-generators for power stations. A mass production operation need not, however, be a large-scale operation. Paper clips are mass-produced, but they do not require a large-scale operation.

*Custom manufacture* refers to the manufacture of an item to a customer's specification. Sometimes, the options available to the customer are constrained by the manufacturer. The automobile industry has an aspect of custom manufacture since it is possible to order an automobile to a customer's specification, but the customer is constrained to a list of options that have been predetermined by the maker. The housing industry has an aspect of custom building

since the home buyer can frequently choose the floor plan, etc., from a fixed set of plans. At the most liberal extreme, a buyer can even have a house custom-built to a set of specifications established by an architect of the customer's choosing. Therefore, custom manufacture implies a degree of customer control over the output of the process.

A *job shop* is a custom manufacturing operation in the broader sense of the term. Most, or all, of the work in a job shop is done to the buyer's design or specification. The tool and die making industry consists mostly of job-shop activities. Job shops usually make items in very small quantities (frequently the quantity is one) on general purpose machines.

In some industries, such as small appliance manufacture, the demand for a standard product may be such that economies can be obtained by using mass production techniques as contrasted to using general purpose equipment. The potential production rate of the equipment, however, exceeds the demand rate, and the product is made in lots several times during a planning horizon. (A *planning horizon* is the length of time covered in a production plan.) When small lot manufacture is used, the production line is frequently designed to be easily modified to make several products. For example, a manufacturer of small appliances could make three models of toasters on the same facilities by slight alteration of the setup. Each model would then be made in lots.

**Classification by Type of Process**    Manufacturing processes can also be classified as continuous, intermittent, or batch process. A *continuous* process is one in which there is a continuous input of raw material and a continuous output of finished goods. The output may be in discrete units, such as washing machines, or in a continuous flow, such as gasoline from a refinery. In *intermittent* manufacture, the product is not made continuously. A job shop is an example of intermittent manufacture. *Batch* processes are those in which a predetermined quantity of product is made at one time. Paint manufacture is an example of a batch process. The paint is made in limited amounts between the minimum and maximum amount that can be handled and processed by the equipment at the same time. Usually each batch is identified as a *lot* for record-keeping and control purposes.

## PRODUCTION PROCESSES

Production processes within the manufacturing industries can be classified in many ways since there are many distinguishable processes, machines, and methods. The following set of processes is not all inclusive but identifies the primary processes by which discrete products are made. There are only three basic ways in which a discrete part can be made. It can be (1) formed directly by solidification from the liquid state, (2) shaped by plastic flow without the removal of chips, or (3) shaped by a cutting or removal operation.

**Casting and Forging**   A foundry makes parts by *casting*: a metal is melted in a crucible or similar device and the molten (liquid) metal is poured into a cavity in a mold where it solidifies. This is identical to the process used in the "manufacture" of ice cubes. The water is analogous to the molten metal. The ice cube tray is the mold with cavities for the ice cubes, and the solidification process is the freezing of the water into ice. The range of sizes, shapes, weights, and precision of cast parts is highly variable. The weight of a casting may vary from a fraction of an ounce to many tons. Materials include a large number of metals, alloys, plastics, or ceramics. Castings have certain properties that make them desirable for many applications.

Many products and parts of products are formed or forged. Sometimes a distinction is made between the several processes or subprocesses that result in a shaped part by plastic flow. A part is said to be *formed* if it is bent to shape. If the shaping process involves any stretching of the material from its original flat shape, it is said to be *drawn*. An automobile fender is drawn. Other processes in this general category are stamping (cutting a shaped part in a single stroke of a press), piercing (making a hole), and shearing (cutting to shape).

*Forged* parts are shaped by extensive plastic flow. Everyone has shaped clay by a process not unlike forging. Forged parts generally have better properties than cast parts and, depending on the forging process and the shape of the part, have directional properties. The forging of heavy metals typically takes place at elevated temperatures. There is, however, a trend toward cold forging which sometimes provides better properties and may be energy conservative. Forged parts generally require additional processing such as machining or grinding.

**Cutting and Machining**   The development of *flame-cutting* techniques and equipment has led to their increased use as a method for cutting plate materials into outline shapes. The process "cuts" with heat from a gas flame, possibly with additives for the controlled melting of metals to provide shapes. Flame cutting has been refined to a point where some parts can be cut to finish size, requiring no additional processing.

*Chip removal* processes such as machining and grinding are used to shape an unlimited variety of parts. *Machining* processes remove metal in the form of microscopic chips either by the motion of a cutter against a workpiece or the reverse or some combinations thereof. Two common machining processes are *turning* (on a lathe) and *milling* (on a milling machine or miller). The cutting edge used in a machining operation is usually continuous although there may be several cutting edges (teeth) on a milling cutter.

**Surface Finishing**   Machining operations produce moderately smooth surfaces. The surface finish, a measure of the quality (or smoothness) of a surface, depends on the material and on the conditions during the cutting operation. The surface finish of a part may be improved by grinding. In *grinding* (also used to obtain precise shapes from hard materials), a rotating abrasive wheel removes very small chips by a series of thousands of irregular cutting edges (grains). The cutting edges are continually changing during the grinding process because of breakage of the grits or grains. Existing edges are broken and new ones are formed. Grinding wheels come in many sizes, with many grit sizes and many bonding materials. *Honing* and *lapping* are similar processes that employ a grit to finish a metallic surface.

**Powder Metallurgy**   When metal parts are required to have a certain amount of controlled porosity, they can be made from powdered metals. In the *powder metallurgy* process, the metal is usually ground into fine particles of controlled size and shape. The powder is then compacted in a mold with sufficient pressure so that it will retain its shape when removed from the mold or die. This is called *briquetting*. The part is then sintered by heating and holding (*soaking*) at an elevated temperature for a specified time. The particle size of the powder, the briquetting pressure, and the sintering time and temperature determine the properties of the end product. Most oil-impregnated bearings are made by powder metallurgy. The powder metallurgy process is also used to make parts from metals that are difficult to cast or form by other techniques. This is particularly so for materials with very high melting temperatures. Recent advances permit the manufacture of large powdered metal logs or rounds that are useful for the manufacture of tools and dies. A major advantage of powdered metal parts is the lack of directionality in their physical properties, such as strength. Powdered metal parts may be more expensive than parts of the same shape made by other processes and thus should be specified only where necessary and economically advantageous.

**Plastic Processes**   *Plastics* are polymers in which the basic building units, mers, are linked together by a process called polymerization. There are two broad classifications of plastics: *thermoplastic*, which can be melted and reformed, and *thermosetting*, which cannot be melted and formed. The range of properties—hardness, strength, chemical resistance, temperature resistance, etc.—is very wide, and a plastic material should be specifically chosen for a given application. While plastics are generally shaped by a casting process, some are extruded and others are rolled or pressed. Thermoplastic materials can be reformed by heating and shaping and joined by welding. Partially polymerized plastics are used for heat-shrinkable tubing.

**Ceramic Processes** *Ceramics* are materials that usually involve silicon in some form. They are generally very hard and brittle and provide electrical and thermal insulation. They are shaped while in a plastic state, then fired to form strong bonds between atoms. Some of the better cutting tool materials are ceramics.

**Heat Processes** *Heat treatment* is a thermal process used to alter the atomic structure of a material (usually a metal) in order to affect its physical properties. Heat treatment may harden the material, relieve stresses caused by a forming or forging process (to cause grain growth), or achieve a specified hardness and strength. There is a high positive correlation between hardness and strength and a high negative correlation between hardness and ductility.

In some cases, only the surface of the metal is heat-treated. Such surface hardening is used on the teeth of gears or the hasps of padlocks. For some materials, the surface is rapidly heated and quenched to form a hard wear-resistant surface and a soft, ductile inner core. The ductile inner core serves to make the part shock resistant. The surface of a low-carbon steel can be hardened by heat treatment in a carbonaceous atmosphere.

**Joining Processes** Parts may be permanently joined by welding, brazing, soldering, using adhesives, riveting, and press or shrink fitting and semipermanently joined by using bolts or screws. In *welding*, there is some fusion of the parts and usually, but not necessarily, the addition of a filler metal that is quite similar in composition to the parent metal. In *brazing*, the filler material has a lower melting temperature than the parent material, and there is no fusion of the parent metal even though a strong mechanical bond and some alloying occur. *Soldering* uses a low melting point alloy, usually an alloy of tin and lead. The composition of the solder alloy affects its melting and solidification properties. Some alloys solidify at a constant tem-

perature (such alloys are used in electronics) while other alloys solidify over a range of temperatures (the transformation is from liquid to a semisolid or mushy state to a solid state). Such solders are sometimes called wiping solders and are used by plumbers. The bond between parts, when soldered, is a mechanical joint. *Adhesives* also form a joint which is partly mechanical and/or partly the attraction of atoms or molecules. *Riveting* joins parts by a mechanical bond. The rivet is inserted through holes in the parts, and a head is formed at both ends. Riveting is a strong, permanent method of joining parts, but the joint is usually not airtight or smooth and therefore use of the method is declining. Bolts and screws make strong, semipermanent joints and are used where part replacement is anticipated. In a *press fit*, one part is forced into another. Parts are *shrunk fit* by either heating or cooling one part. Upon return to room temperature the parts are rigidly mated. Press and shrink fits are usually used between cylindrical surfaces (for example, between a pulley and a shaft) where alignment is critical. As other manufacturing techniques improve in accuracy and precision, there is less need for press and shrink fitting.

**Finishing Processes** Finishes may be added to a surface for decorative purposes, for environmental protection, or for wear resistance. A surface is usually painted for environmental protection and for decorative purposes. *Electroplating* is used to provide some physical protection as well as for decorative purposes and environmental protection. *Hard surfacing* can be used to improve the surface properties of an item subject to wear. With aluminum surfaces, protection can be obtained by forming a surface oxide with a process called *anodizing*.

**Special Processes** There are a number of processes that have been developed for special purposes or to solve special problems. *Electrodischarge machining (EDM)* uses a spark between a shaped tool and a workpiece submerged in an electrolyte to remove metal. The process is capable of cutting shaped holes or cavities in hard metals where other processes cannot be used. Its primary advantage is that it is often easier to machine the tool than the cavity.

Another process used to make holes of any shape in very hard materials is ultrasonic machining. *Ultrasonic machining* uses a tool, vibrating at approximately 20,000 cycles per second, and an abrasive slurry to "wear" holes in hard materials, even glass.

*Chemical milling (CM)* uses controlled erosion to shape parts. Usually the shape is a cutout of limited depth in a piece of sheet material. The sheet is masked with a corrosion-resistant material, selected areas of the mask are removed, and the part is immersed in an acid bath of known strength for a predetermined time. The erosion process, in the absence of impurities, is uniform, but there will be some undercutting of the masked areas. *Electrochemical milling (ECM)* uses a chemical erosion process supplemented by an electric current between a tool (electrode) and the workpiece. No masking is necessary. *Electrolytic grinding* is similar to ECM except the tool is a grinding wheel.

Two new, dual-purpose processes are (1) *laser machining* and *laser welding* and (2) *electron-beam machining* and *electron-beam welding*. Their primary application has been to make very small cuts and welds, although size is becoming less of a limiting factor.

Hard-to-shape parts can sometimes be made economically by electroforming. *Electroforming* is an electroplating process in which the parent shape is removed at the completion of the electrodeposition phase. The form may be an electrically conductive plastic, which is chemically or thermally removed, leaving the electrodeposited material as the finished part.

High explosives and high-voltage electric spark discharges have been used to form difficult shapes. They have been called *high energy rate forming (HERF)* processes. Since they employ either high explosives, whose storage and use is legally constrained, or high-voltage discharges (25,000 volts) with an element of danger, they have limited use.

A process that is rapidly changing and that has a major impact on our daily lives is *electronics manufacture*. This process uses the deposition of materials or ions to form electrically different regions within a very small area on a silicon, sapphire, or similar crystalline material. This technology is changing so rapidly that a state-of-the-art description might be totally obsolete at the time of reading. Its impact, however, is very significant.

## PROCESS CONTROLS

Processes can be controlled manually, automatically, numerically, or digitally. In most cases the control is a combination of more than one type. Manual process control is used mostly for job-shop operations where only one, or a few, items of a given design are made. The operator who interprets the specifications and the results of the operations provides the necessary control. As processes become more complex or quantities become larger, there may be advantages in automatic controls such as cams, relays, solenoids, switches, etc. Frequently

such control systems become large and complex, with high maintenance costs. Furthermore, these systems do not involve arithmetic capability, only logic.

**Numerical Control** Numerical control (NC) systems were developed and became common—especially in the aerospace industry—during the 1950s and 1960s. NC systems comprise a machine control unit and a tape reader. The tape reader provides instructions to the machine control unit, which in turn controls the process. The advantages of a NC system are flexibility and uniformity. A punched tape is prepared by a parts programmer. The tape consists of a set of instructions that will be performed sequentially. More sophisticated systems use a computer to do much of the part programming. A novel feature of NC systems is that they can easily be programmed to make mirror-image parts, such as right- and left-hand parts for furniture.

**Machine Controllers** By the late 1960s and early 1970s, electronic technology had advanced to a point where relays and switches could be replaced by their solid state counterparts, thus eliminating some mechanical actions which are slow, noisy, and subject to failure. The machine controller which incorporates these solid state devices may also have a read-only memory (ROM) that is somewhat comparable to the punched tape of NC. Once programmed, ROM cannot easily be changed. Machine controllers, like NC and the older electromechanical systems, are logic-only systems. They have no arithmetic capability; i.e., they can not add, subtract, etc.

**Computer Control** When a digital computer is added to the control system, there exists a capability of changing a process during a cycle. For example, it can compensate for actual tool wear by measuring the part or the tool and calculating changes in process settings. The computer, when properly programmed, can also calculate the path to be taken by a cutter if given data or a description of the part to be made. The control rests with the computer programmer and computer operator. Many process control applications employ minicomputers. These are small computers, with *small* implying small size, relatively low cost, or perhaps limited capability. Generally they can do all the things a large computer can do except that they are slower and have less memory and less precision. The minicomputer is being replaced by the microcomputer, which has capabilities and capacities comparable to the minicomputer but is very much smaller, usually contained on one or only a few chips. This is a result of developments in a technology called *large-scale integration (LSI)*, where many (thousands) of electronic devices are manufactured on a single chip. The heart of the microcomputer is the microprocessor, which is usually on a single chip. The microprocessor can be programmed to perform certain functions such as to control a machine or to control the fuel injection system in an automobile so as to minimize emissions. Minicomputers and microcomputers provide the capability to sense a phenomena, to make calculations based on the inputs, and thus to determine the correct outputs. It is within the realm of possibility that as many as 1 or 2 billion microprocessors will be in use in the next decade. The cost of a unit is under $5, so that applications are limited only by our ability to find ways to use them. *See* AUTOMATION.

## MASS PRODUCTION TECHNIQUES

Most mass production systems are organized as lines so that the flow of product is unidirectional from the start of processing to the completion of the product. In mass machining operations the part, such as an engine block, may be produced on a transfer machine or line. Each work station performs certain operations, and the part moves sequentially to the next station. A similar type of movement occurs on an assembly line, where the parts of a product are joined to form the finished product. A major problem in setting up a production line or an assembly line is to balance the work load at each work station. This is commonly called the *line-balancing* problem (*see* LINE BALANCING). The overall cycle time, or production rate, of the line is dependent on the longest times taken at each work station. The assignment of operations to individual work stations is thus constrained by the time needed to perform each operation, the cycle time, and the required assembly or production sequence. The line balancing problem is further compounded when several models of product are made on the same line, such as on auto assembly lines.

## MANUFACTURING POLICY

Management policies dramatically affect manufacturing and the production process. Make-or-buy decisions will determine the equipment, tooling, and personnel needed. The expected volume of product and the stability of the design also affect the manufacturing engineering for a product. Decisions relative to monetary policies, such as rates of return or whether the company is to be labor intensive or capital intensive, affect the production system.

**Manufacturing Research** Manufacturing research should be directed toward (1) developing new processes to make new products, (2) developing new processes to make old products, (3) modifying old processes to make better products, less expensive products, or new products, and (4) understanding existing processes better. In addition, energy and material shortages place emphasis on finding processes that make products with less energy and from more abundant materials.

**Manufacturing Engineering** Manufacturing engineering encompasses nearly everything the two words imply. Activities primarily associated with manufacturing engineering, however, are product analysis, process analysis, process selection, system design, and process optimization. The primary emphasis during product analysis is to determine the most producible design that meets all product specifications. This activity, therefore, represents a joint effort of marketing, design engineering, and quality assurance. The process analysis activity can apply either to a reexamination of existing processes or to the evaluation of new processes. Process selection involves the choice of the process for a new part or product. Care should be given here to manufacturing policies, energy and material usage, capital costs versus labor costs, production rate, expected life of the product and the process, and other uses for the same process. Systems design integrates the various processes, equipments, etc., into a unified, efficient system including controls. Process optimization, which seeks the highest level of balance between all contributing factors, should always be considered at the process selection and systems design stages, but every process should always be considered to be a candidate for further improvement and optimization.

*See also* AUTOMATION; COST IMPROVEMENT; ENGINEERING, INDUSTRIAL; LEARNING (EXPERIENCE) CURVES; MATERIAL HANDLING; PRODUCTION/OPERATIONS MANAGEMENT; PRODUCTION PLANNING AND CONTROL; QUALITY MANAGEMENT; SYSTEMS DYNAMICS; WORK SIMPLIFICATION AND IMPROVEMENT.

## REFERENCES

Bolz, Roger W.: *Production Processes, The Productivity Handbook*, Conquest Publications, Novelty, Ohio, 1974.
*Metals Handbook*, 8th ed., American Society for Metals, Metals Park, Ohio:
Vol. 1, *Properties and Selection*, 1961.
Vol. 2, *Heat Treating, Cleaning and Finishing*, 1964.
Vol. 3, *Machining*, 1967.
Vol. 4, *Forming*, 1969.

Vol. 5, *Forging and Casting*, 1970.
Vol. 6, *Welding and Brazing*, 1971.

Moore, Harry D., and Donald R. Kibbey: *Manufacturing: Materials and Processes*, Grid, Inc., Columbus, Ohio, 1975.

Niebel, Benjamin W., and Alan B. Draper: *Product Design and Process Engineering*, McGraw-Hill Book Company, New York, 1974.

Society of Manufacturing Engineers: *Tool and Manufacturing Engineers Handbook*, 3d ed., McGraw-Hill Book Company, New York, 1976.

JOHN E. BIEGEL, *Syracuse University*

# Productivity

*Productivity* is generally defined as the relationship between output and any or all associated inputs measured in real (physical volume) terms. It may be measured for producing organizations (business firms, government agencies, or private nonprofit institutions) or their components for which separate records are maintained (divisions, departments, plants, cost centers). Likewise, it may be measured for industries, sectors, or entire economies. Early concepts and measures of productivity related mainly to the macroeconomic level. Since the late 1940s, there has been increasing emphasis on measuring productivity in plant units or companies. The underlying concepts and measurement techniques are the same, however, regardless of the level of aggregation, although the uses of the measures differ. At the macroeconomic level, the measures are used (1) to analyze the sources of productivity advances and their economic impacts as background for projections of outputs or input requirements and (2) for formulation of policies to promote relatively stable economic growth. In a particular company, productivity measures are used as a management tool (1) for promoting productivity and (2) for budgeting and longer-term projections. The following discussion focuses on productivity measures for the firm.

**Concepts and Meaning**  When output is related to all associated inputs (usually in ratio form converted to index numbers for successive time periods), the resulting *total productivity measures* reflect the net reduction of real costs per unit of output and thus the increase in productive efficiency. *Output* is generally a weighted aggregate of physical units of the various products of the firm. *Inputs* consist of the three major cost categories: labor, "intermediate products" (materials, supplies, energy, and purchased outside services), and capital—likewise expressed in real, constant dollars. *Partial productivity*

measures are the ratios of output to individual classes of inputs. These reflect not only changes in productive efficiency but also changes in the mix of inputs, or factor substitutions. Thus, the most usual partial productivity ratio, output per worker-hour, reflects increases in capital and other inputs per worker-hour, as well as general efficiency changes.

A variant measure *is total factor productivity* (TFP), for which the constant-dollar intermediate product purchases are deducted from the real value of gross output to yield a measure of real value added. This real product measure is then related to the inputs of the basic factors of production, labor and capital (including developed land). The advantage of TFP measures is that they are consistent among firms and coordinate with macroeconomic measures, since value added sums up to gross product of the business sector, by industry. Nevertheless, total productivity measures seem preferable for company management purposes, since (1) all inputs must be considered in seeking least-cost combinations and (2) over time managers try to reduce inputs of purchased goods and services, as well as of labor and capital factors, per unit of output.

Changes in total productivity in the short run reflect changes in rates of utilization of capacity over the business cycle. Over the longer run, productivity increase reflects technological and organizational advances resulting from cost-reducing innovations in the ways and means of production. These, in turn, derive from (1) research and development activities in the given firm and by suppliers of producers' goods; (2) the tangible investments in the capital goods in which technological improvements are embodied; and (3) intangible investments in education and training required to produce and apply advancing technology and in health, safety and mobility of workers. In addition, economies of scale, changes in allocative efficiency, and changes in the average inherent quality of resources may affect productivity.

**Measurement**  Measurement of productivity involves converting estimates of the value and costs of production into constant prices. Since values represent price times quantities ($V = P \times Q$), measurement of the output numerator and the input denominator of productivity ratios involves separating the $P$'s and $Q$'s in a detailed operating statement, then recombining the $Q$'s in successive periods by multiplying (weighting) them by the constant prices of a single *base* period. Alternatively, the values and costs of production may be divided (deflated) by index numbers of average prices received for the firm's output, and prices paid for the inputs. By and large, the underlying data for productivity estimates can be obtained from the company's information systems. Various problems will be encountered, such as adjusting outputs for model or quality changes or determining the degree of detail to be used for the categories of outputs and of inputs.[1] Since each firm is unique, the estimator must still use his or her best judgment in applying general principles to special situations.

**Applications** In the late 1940s, the U.S. Bureau of Labor Statistics conducted a series of studies comparing levels and rates of change in labor productivity among plants in a variety of industries. The estimates were used to analyze causes of differences, but they had the side effect of stimulating some firms to measure their own productivity. A number of private investigators also measured productivity of various firms in selected industries. Kendrick's manual,[2] in particular, further promoted company efforts to measure productivity, total as well as partial. Another flurry of activity was stimulated by phase 2 of the wage and price control program in 1971–1972, which initially required company productivity estimates as part of the cost justification in applications for price increases. Since 1970, productivity has been measured in U.S. federal government agencies covering more than half of all their civilian workers. An increasing number of state and local governments are also applying productivity measurement at various organizational and/or functional levels.

*Programs.* A major benefit of organizational productivity measurement is the promotion of "productivity-mindedness." To have maximum impact, the periodic results must be circulated beyond management circles and be linked to company-wide productivity improvement programs. Beginning in 1975, the U.S. National Center for Productivity and Quality of Working Life began publishing the series *Improving Productivity, A Description of Selected Company Programs.* These programs, initiated by top management to help meet special challenges or to reinforce continuing cost-reduction efforts, involved workers at all levels in programs featuring work measurement and simplification, special incentive schemes, job redesign, value engineering, waste reduction, salvage, improved quality, and (where unions were strong) joint labor-management productivity committees. These productivity improvement programs were generally linked to measurement systems which (1) provided psychological reinforcement and (2) enabled quantification of the program results.

*Diagnosis.* Productivity measures themselves, as a part of broader management information systems, serve as a tool for identifying adverse situations or trends requiring further investigation and possibly corrective action. This function of the measures is enhanced if they are prepared in considerable detail with respect to types of inputs and organizational units. Thus when plants producing the same range of products are being compared with each other or with industry averages, lower productivity ratios or smaller rates of increase become red signal flags. The ratios may also be used to set goals for reducing input requirements per unit of output during a specified future period.

*Projections.* Productivity measures are particularly valuable as a background for projection. Past trends should not be mechanically extrapolated, however, but should be modified to take account of new investments and other planned cost-reduction measures, as well as of projected sales, output, and consequent changes in rates of utilization of capacity. When divided into projected output, the total and partial productivity projections provide projections of labor, materials, and capital input requirements. These are helpful in planning recruitment, purchasing, and investment policies. When multiplied by projected average hourly labor compensation and other input prices, the input projections yield cost estimates for the future period. They are thus a useful ingredient for budgeting as well as for longer-term projections.

*See also* ECONOMIC MEASUREMENTS; PROFIT IMPROVEMENT; VALUE-ADDED TAX; WORK MEASUREMENT.

### NOTES

[1] For detailed explanations of measurement techniques, *see* John W. Kendrick and Daniel Creamer, *Measuring Productivity: Handbook with Case Studies, Studies in Business Economics No. 89*, The Conference Board, New York, 1965.

[2] Ibid.

### REFERENCES

Carr, J. J.: *Measuring Productivity.* Undated. May be obtained at no charge from Charles E. Beall, Director of Publications; Arthur Anderson & Co.; 69 W. Washington St.; Chicago, Ill. 60602.

Cocks, D. L.: "The Measurement of Total Factor Productivity for a Large U.S. Manufacturing Corporation," *Studies in Business Economics*, The Conference Board, New York, September 1974.

Craig, C. E., and R. C. Harris: "Total Productivity Measurement at the Firm Level," *Sloan Management Review*, Massachusetts Institute of Technology, E 52-062, Cambridge, Mass., Spring 1973.

Greenberg, Leon: *A Practical Guide to Productivity Measurement*, Bureau of National Affairs, Inc., Washington, 1973.

*Improving Productivity, A Description of Selected Company Programs, Series 1*, National Center for Productivity and Quality of Working Life, Washington, December 1975.

JOHN W. KENDRICK, *George Washington University*

## Products, complimentary   (*See* PRODUCT AND SERVICE PRICING.)

## Products, industrial   (*See* MARKETING OF SERVICES.)

## Products, substitute   (*See* PRODUCT AND SERVICE PRICING.)

## Profession   (*See* PROFESSIONALISM IN MANAGEMENT.)

## Professional orientation   (*See* HOSPITAL ADMINISTRATION.)

## Professional services, marketing of
(*See* MARKETING OF SERVICES, PROFESSIONAL.)

## Professional societies   (*See* SOCIETIES, PROFESSIONAL.)

## Professionalism in management

"Modern life ever to a greater extent is grouping itself into professions."[1] The words are those of the distinguished philosopher, Alfred North Whitehead, written in 1933. Today, almost every field involving career preparation has its proponents claiming a measure of professionalism. Such claims run the gamut of careers from those of the established professions, theology, medicine, and law to those fields with perhaps more tenuous claims to true professionalism.

This entry explores the topic of professionalism and examines the extent to which management may be deemed a profession. The concept of profession and professional standards will be considered, utilizing, to some extent, the model of established professions, and professionalizing activity will be discussed including present-day certification efforts. Additionally, the practical obstacles to management becoming a profession in the traditional sense will be outlined, and the challenge and opportunity to management will be presented.

**Profession versus Professionalizing**   The question of professionalism is one replete with emotion-laden issues, stemming as often from semantic misinterpretation as from reasoned disagreement. No one would argue with the notion that a competent manager behaves professionally; yet it is a large step from regarding certain behavior as professional to classifying the work as a profession. Traditionally, a *profession* may be defined as a calling often requiring extensive academic preparation, while the term *professionalizing* refers to the process of improving the various aspects of a field of endeavor to bring that field closer to the ideal model of a profession. We see, then, a distinction between the thing (profession) and the process (professionalizing).

The lists of criteria for a profession are as numerous as writers on the subject; however, the following criteria are common to most listings: an organized body of knowledge, client recognition of the authority of the profession, community approval of the profession's authority, a code of ethics, and a professional culture nurtured by professional associations.[2] The criteria may be considered as constituting an ideal model to which no field fully measures up. One can readily see that the field of management does meet all these standards to some degree, but the issue is precisely a question of degree. On the other hand, while management may not meet the standards as fully as the traditionally accepted professions, there is much evidence of professionalizing activity.

**The Work of Professionalizing**   The work of professionalizing management may be attributed to internal and external forces. The internal forces consist of the managers of organizations and members of the academic community, as well as the representative associations of these individuals. Many are engaged in better defining the work itself, the body of knowledge, and the role of the manager.[3] Others are engaging in activity to arrive at a consensus regarding standards of conduct.[4] Such activity is also going on in other countries, as evidenced by the codes of the British Institute of Management, the Greek Management Association, and the RKW of the Federal Republic of Germany.[5]

Another movement to professionalize is the attempt to certify managers. A model certification program, based upon present-day certification efforts, might include the following five phases: an evaluation of the manager's experience and education credentials, participation in an intensive workshop or seminar, an examination of management knowledge, the acceptance of a code of ethics, and provision for continuing education and development. The assumptions of certification are that universal standards may be developed and applied to the field and/or examination performance of a manager. The arguments for certification are that the process will improve the individual manager and the work of managing. Those opposed to certification cite the traditional argument that a good manager is a generalist and that certification is more appropriate for specialists, whose minds are in a "groove." Since most certification efforts appear best-suited for the supervisory level and possibly the middle-management level, the latter argument may bear some weight. Despite the possible limitations of certification, the work being done is one important piece of the larger professionalizing mosaic.

The external forces may be discerned almost daily in the news media. Stories of the exposures of corporate difficulties, government legislation, and employee aspirations for greater involvement are reported frequently and are all a form of pressure to which an increasingly professional management must respond.

**The Many Obstacles**   The obstacles to regarding management as a profession are many. Because of the diversity of their backgrounds, work responsibilities, and the levels at which managers operate within organizations, there is no single professional association which could attract and represent all managers as well as validate managerial practices. Without such a central, professional body, entry into the work of managing can occur without the application of any standards. Furthermore, the work of management, involving as it does individual, group, and organizational process and behavior, falls within the behavioral and social sciences. And the knowledge of human behavior and organizational processes will never advance to such a stage that one can be as confident about the outcome of adding a new sales manager and six salespeople to a territory to increase market share as one can be about the effects of administering a dosage of penicillin to counteract a bacterial infection. Further-

more, the manager does not possess the equivalent of a code of law and legal precedent to determine an appropriate course of action. With respect to codes of ethics and the enforcement of standards of conduct, there is no counterpart in the management field to the processes of disbarment, revocation of licenses to practice medicine, or defrocking. The import of these conclusions is that the work of managing is not a profession in the traditional sense of that term; however, this is not the issue. The point of consequence is that managers continue to engage in activities which professionalize their work. It is the process of professionalizing which is critical to management in the future. As was suggested earlier, the model of profession is an ideal. Even in the established professions, advancements which add to the body of knowledge continue to be made. Entrance standards undergo continual review, and the development of codes of ethics is never a completed task. The same truths hold for management. The professionalizing work must continue.

**The Challenges and Opportunities**   The work of the manager becomes increasingly important in our society of organizations. If the multifold form of the futurologists, Kahn and Weiner, is an accurate reflection of what the future holds, management will become especially critical and challenging.[6] The work of professional associations, interested managers, and management scholars assists all managers in better understanding the nature of their work and the role they play in organizations and society. Management is not presently a profession, nor may it ever be a profession in the traditional sense; however, the responsible actions of countless individuals continue to professionalize the critical work called management. And this is the key to success in the future.

*See also* AUDIT, MANAGEMENT; ETHICS, MANAGERIAL; MANAGEMENT, DEFINITIONS OF; MANAGEMENT, FUTURE OF; MANAGEMENT, HISTORICAL DEVELOPMENT OF; MANAGEMENT THEORY, SCIENCE, AND APPROACHES; MANAGER, DEFINITIONS OF; SOCIAL RESPONSIBILITY OF BUSINESS.

### NOTES

[1] Alfred North Whitehead, *Adventures of Ideas*, The Macmillan Company, New York, 1933.

[2] Ernest Greenwood, "The Elements of Professionalization," in Howard M. Vollmer and Donald L. Mills (eds.), *Professionalization*, Prentice-Hall, Inc., Englewood Cliffs, N.J., 1966, p. 9.

[3] *See* Henry Mintzberg, "Managerial Work: Analysis from Observation," *Management Science*, vol. 18, no. 2, October 1971, p. B-97.

[4]Terry P. Brown, "Craft-Minded Chief at Bendix Tries to Set a Businessman's Code," *Wall Street Journal*, vol. CLXXXVI, no. 99, Nov. 18, 1975.

[5]Nancy G. McNulty, "And Now, Professional Codes for the Practices of Management," *The Conference Board Record*, vol. XII, no. 4, April 1975.

[6]Herman Kahn and A. J. Weiner, *Year Two Thousand.* The Macmillan Company, New York, 1967.

ANTHONY F. JURKUS, *Louisiana Tech University*

# Professionalizing  (*See* PROFESSIONALISM IN MANAGEMENT.)

# Profit center, international  (*See* INTERNATIONAL OPERATIONS AND MULTINATIONAL COMPANIES.)

# Profit centers  (*See* ACCOUNTING FOR MANAGERIAL CONTROL.)

# Profit improvement

The key factor for a successful profit-improvement effort is the determination of the organization's chief executive. Voluntary programs initiated by the chief executive officer or down-the-line managers rarely achieve results interesting enough to write about. Although approaches to profit improvement vary from applying basic principles of good management to changing fundamental management tenets, individuals who have successfully implemented major profit-improvement programs seem to agree on three major steps:

1. Identifying specifically what has to be done and where, and securing a commitment from upper-level management

2. Building an environment for change

3. Implementing a number of profit-improvement projects and monitoring their progress

### IDENTIFYING WHAT HAS TO BE DONE

Too many managers wait for problems to develop. Especially in new assignments, they tend to let valuable time slip by in get-acquainted meetings with colleagues and subordinates, visits to plant locations, and talks with customers. They read company literature and reports and gain familiarity with major activities, processes and operations. But once the fire fighting starts, they wish they had done more.

**Starting from Scratch** The new executive should try to get a handle on an assignment in the first 30 to 90 days. This will require four key steps:

1. Assess the company's present operations and outlook for future growth, and pinpoint overall industry and company problems.

2. Identify major profit-building opportunities for significantly improving near-term company performance while maintaining or strengthening longer-term goals.

3. Evaluate the company's organization structure and its individual skills in terms of what is needed to realize the opportunities identified.

4. Reach agreement with the boss or the board of directors on specific improvement recommendations.

STEP 1: Develop an economic and financial perspective. As a first step, the executive should develop a financial and economic perspective of his or her industry and company. This will lay the groundwork for other steps that should be taken during this period.

For example, to establish an information base for this analysis, the executive of a large metal-fabricating company gathered financial and economic data by using *Thomas Register, Standard & Poor's Industry Surveys, Value Line* industry and company reports, *Wall Street Transcripts, Predicast* industry surveys, trade association material, and recent industry investment studies by securities brokerage firms and banks.

For industry data, he referred to *Census of Manufacturers, U.S. Industrial Outlook,* and *SEC-FTC Quarterly Reports of Manufacturing Corporations.*

For company data, he used *Moody's* and *Standard & Poor's Stock Reports,* his own company's and competitors' prospectuses, SEC's detailed Form 10 KS and annual reports for the last 5 years, and available division, product line, and plant financial statements.

With this information, the executive was able to develop an initial understanding of the industry, e.g., product line characteristics, degree of vertical-horizontal integration, cyclical and seasonal influences, and four to six key factors for success broken down into their profit-making components. For example, if marketing effectiveness is a key success factor, the profit-building components might be a strong distributor organization, high market share, and a profitable product mix sold.

Many successful executives advocate conducting

this profit-improvement analysis personally instead of relying on staff work. One marketing head used this approach and then invited the controller to participate in financial perspective meetings. These meetings included brainstorming sessions where "wild" ideas for improvement were encouraged with evaluation postponed to keep the discussion on a positive note. Subsequently, the marketing chief classified the improvement ideas by functional responsibility and assigned the appropriate individuals to evaluate them.

STEP 2: Identify profit-building opportunities. The next step is to evaluate the improvement ideas identified as part of the economic and financial analysis and to discard those that are obviously not feasible. The profit-improvement potential of each idea is assessed, including the assignment of a dollar value to less tangible benefits. Implementation costs are estimated, and next steps to be taken are outlined along with responsibility assignments and timing for complicated changes. Profit-improvement recommendations are then developed and classified as near or long term. Finally, priorities are established on the basis of profit-building impact.

*Selection of High-Impact Projects.* Faced with the need to improve near-term performance, the critical skill is to pinpoint and take action on those high-impact or dramatic and highly visible changes that can be accomplished quickly. In addition to their profit-building impact, these "quick and easy" changes both encourage subordinates to initiate a momentum for change and bolster senior management's confidence in the executive's ability to bring about change.

Another advantage of these actions is that they can often be taken in the absence of a well-formulated strategy, which is generally difficult (and usually not imperative) to define at the early stages of one's exposure. Thus, the executive can make some essential near-term improvements while wrestling with overall strategy.

*Example of Short-Term Plans.* One new marketer, for example, who was selling production items to off-road equipment manufacturers, had sound concerns about his company's capacity to compete in a particular product area in terms of costs and technology. While he gave this major strategic question due recognition, he resisted letting it obscure current improvement possibilities. These four immediate projects became the main elements of his plan for marketing improvements:

1. Raise prices 5 percent across the board on June 1 and again on December 1. It was felt that higher prices had a good chance of sticking without loss in volume because of the few sources of supply and the lengthy new source approval processes followed by customers. The decision was made to have two rounds of smaller increases because one large increase might really invite new competition.

2. Institute minimum order quantities on June 1. Demand for replacement parts, in particular, had drifted downward to the point that the plant was choking with uneconomical runs.

3. Shift promptly the burden of following major new business inquiries from the field sales force to the research and development laboratory. The technical skills of the sales force were not adequate to work with customer engineering. Training would take time. As volume was needed, the best stopgap measure was to make development personnel responsible for key inquiries.

4. Ask research to explore the feasibility of lowering raw material costs by December 1. This was clearly a longer-range project that would have a major bearing on strategy; moreover, it could have a sizable influence on second-year results. The point now was to get it started.

This simple plan was straightforward and proved effective. It was not cloaked in an all-encompassing strategy. It dealt with immediate issues, yet it provided for input from research for strategy resolution.

STEP 3: Evaluate the organization structure and personnel. The next step in the initial stage is to evaluate the company's organization structure and the skills and capabilities of its personnel in relation to the opportunities identified. This step is essential to develop a complete business plan.

*Organization.* In serious turnaround situations where (as is often the case) structure is often conspicuously absent, it is imperative to establish one even if it is only temporary. If a formal organization is in place, it is still worthwhile to consider modification since the structure is probably designed to maintain the status quo rather than to bring about change.

One good way to start is by removing as many layers as possible between top management and first-line supervisors. In one situation, seven layers were cut to three with immediate benefits of improved communications and a better feel for what was going on. It also improved the executive's own use of time because he now had more things to do than were feasible and had to decide which were vital and which could be put off. Span of control is also an area for organizational improvement. Where a great deal of change has to be managed, additional supervision is usually needed; where little change is required, span of control can typically be increased. In one company, for example, where product quality had eroded significantly, the newly appointed executive cut work sections of 20 to 30 people down to 12 to 14; sections where a great deal of change was required were reduced to eight people. In another company, however, the manufacturing vice-president found that his lower-level managers were supervising only 5 to 10 people. Investigation showed that this setup originated a few years back when the organization was expanding rapidly and new supervisors were scrambling simply to meet their basic responsibilities. But as in any position, there is a learning curve over time, and the supervisors now knew their jobs. By increasing the span of control of some supervisors and assigning others to vital profit-improvement projects, work force utilization was greatly improved.

It should be cautioned, however, that wholesale organizational changes, particularly involving the field sales force, should be considered only as a last resort. It takes at least a year for most organizational changes to be effective—even when skilled managers are on board. One chemical company consolidated its autonomous selling units and soon found that volume in certain areas was dropping. The reason: There had been a sweeping change in customer contact continuity which eroded a substantial number of account positions where personal selling relationships were vital.

*Personnel.* Especially in the case of a new assignment, the executive should make an early evaluation of personnel. Many newly appointed—and incumbent—executives have difficulty coming to grips with an organizational evaluation of this nature. This indecision stems from the absence of three sets of guidelines:

1. Established standards for the specific management skills needed to accomplish demanding objectives

2. Objective appraisals of the individuals involved against these standards, asking the question, "Can the organization and its people do significantly more to improve results than is now being done?"

3. A consideration of all the alternatives to replacing personnel, such as training and job restructuring

Once an evaluation is made, it is wise to determine through all available sources if any key lieutenants considered vital to a profit turnaround are thinking of leaving, since continuity is essential for success. Organizational change often gives rise to career evaluation on the part of the incumbent staff. It behooves the top executive to seek feedback and to take proper actions to hold good people.

Bringing in new people poses three problems. First, it takes time for a new manager to learn the operation, decide what has to be done, and begin doing it. Someone hired from a competitor could take 6 months to get up to speed; someone hired from a different industry could require twice that long. Second, the newly appointed executive will need all the inside knowledge available, and present members of his or her staff have valuable knowledge in their heads, not on paper. It was impossible, for example, for the president of a major publisher to replace his otherwise incompetent financial vice-president at the outset of his appointment because he was completely dependent on the latter's knowledge. The larger the organization is, the more this becomes a factor. Third, the farther afield one looks for talent, the higher the risk is that the people brought in (1) will not meet expectations and (2) may damage the morale of the existing management team. In *The Will to Manage*, Marvin Bower, the former managing director of McKinsey & Company, Inc., supports this view:

Although I can't prove it, I believe that the insider who seems 65 percent qualified for the job is likely to outperform the typical outsider who seems 90 percent qualified. Such assessments are apt to be unbalanced, because the weaknesses of the insider are known, while those of the outsider are hard to learn accurately in advance. Since an insider's success will improve the morale and productivity of the executive group generally, it is usually worth taking a substantial risk on an insider, particularly if the only count against him is youth or lack of experience for the job.[1]

STEP 4: Present the business plan to superiors. At this final step of the initial phase, the new executive must let his or her superior or the board know in what direction he or she is going—and why. There are two good reasons for this:

1. A logical formal action plan is a good indicator of likely results and, if it is approved, will help buy time for accomplishing objectives. The plan can similarly be used by the chief executive or the board, which may be under pressure from external sources, e.g., the financial press, stockholders, customers, to explain what is being done, what can be expected, and by when.

2. The superior officer may have some special insight as a result of more experience with the organization and its environment. For example, one

newly appointed marketing chief failed to tell his superior of an important downward price that was planned. A competitor not only followed but went one step further—a reaction that the marketer's superior would have fully anticipated because of his familiarity with the competitor's market strategy.

## BUILDING AN ENVIRONMENT FOR CHANGE

When an organization is in profit trouble, its down-the-line managers are typically backed into a corner, defending themselves and the system. Their response to pressures for change is: "It worked in the past, it should work now; just give us a little more time and staff." In this situation, unless the incumbent can change the tone of the organization and get it off the defensive, there will be little chance for making improvements.

To build this climate for change, the executive in charge must assure the organization that they are with a winner and that the new directions are both sound and reasonable. The executive should plan steps to take charge, to gain the cooperation of other top executives, to motivate line managers, to win the confidence of rank and file employees, and to initiate profit-improvement actions.

**Taking Charge**   In every business, there are key decisions in which the executive must be directly involved. These must be firmly established so that subordinate managers know on what and when to check before they move ahead. These "management guides" should cover such topics as work force levels, replacement of managerial or technical staff; compensation changes; organization changes, either in terms of structure or promotion of key personnel; capital expenditure approval; changes in terms of sale; pricing; movement into new distribution channels; deferment of expenses; ethical conduct on the part of managers; and a host of other topics. Management guides will save a great deal of time and frustration and give down-the-line managers a clear idea of their freedom to act in the months ahead.

**Motivating Executives**   An operating chief must review the company's business situation in depth with his or her key executives, using facts and figures while carefully avoiding opinions and criticism. If the objective is a turnaround, the manager must explain what has to be done to return to performance levels of prior years and specify monthly profit goals for the next 6 months. There is a critical need to convince key people of the reasonableness of objectives and to indicate clearly what is

expected of each staff member. Once this framework for action is established, its motivational impact can be maintained by:

1. Providing for daily, weekly, and monthly personal guidance to staff members as they give progress reports.

2. Helping them develop projects to increase profits. The job of any manager, including the chief executive officer, is largely one of teaching others how to attain objectives. In a turnaround situation, it may be assumed that staff members need extra coaching.

3. Motivating them through pride, compensation, stock options, growth, or survival in the job and with the company.

**Motivating Middle Managers**   One of the most powerful motivators is the opportunity to advance on merit. To this end, a mandatory annual performance review should be established for every managerial position in the company. Such a program ensures that responsibilities have been clearly assigned and authority properly delegated. In effect, it is a vehicle for planning each individual's job objectives so that they are in line with company objectives. That way, each manager knows what is specifically expected and can measure his or her own progress against these expectations.

The sooner the down-the-line managers are convinced that results will determine their future compensation increases and promotions, the sooner the cobwebs will disappear. Performance reviews open lines of communications that often do not (but should) exist, especially in an organization with significant turnaround opportunities. Every higher-level executive should read as many managers' performance reviews as possible and provide his or her own personal counsel on how to improve each review. Down-the-line managers should be expected to do the same with their staff members.

Another means of motivating managers is taking a one-on-one approach, instead of a committee approach, to problem solving. Executives should encourage subordinate managers to do the same in their problem-solving efforts. In committees, people may be reluctant to call a spade a spade, whereas on an individual basis they will talk more freely and openly.

Stock options can also serve as powerful motivators, not only for top executives but also for supervisors. These managers will recognize the degree of importance placed on their thoughts and the results they produce.

Finally, there should be a careful review of the

company's compensation plan, especially as it applies to the managerial group. More than one company has been hampered by an unfair plan. Raises may be in order for certain top performers. The existing incentive plan may need to be sweetened or even replaced.

**Gaining Employee Confidence**  Effective executives stress the importance of developing organizational "reach," that is, getting to know all, or as many as possible, of the people in the organization. Employees get a tremendous boost from talking directly to the company president and, better yet, from being addressed by name. Some newly appointed executives find that contact can be made with up to 1000 or more employees within the first 6 months on the job and is well worth the investment in time and effort.

**Initiating Profit-Improvement Actions**  A quick way to change the organizational environment is to initiate tangible profit-improvement actions such as the following:

*Freezing Employment Levels.* Establishing a holding action on costs is a straightforward task. In a labor-intensive operation, it means controlling head counts and wage increases. To control head count, the key executive should require that all requisitions for additional personnel bear his or her signature. This will reduce the number of requests by 90 to 95 percent. In terms of controlling pay rates, an executive will have less leverage if the operation is unionized. It is possible, however, to put a lid on the costs of promotions by requiring that all salary increases due to promotion include the name of the person being replaced and his or her new assignment. This prevents the promotion of people to new jobs created solely for the purpose of increasing their salaries.

Another sound approach is to have an analysis prepared of the work force levels as of the end of the month and on the same date for each year as far back as 4 years. This analysis should be developed on a department-by-department basis to see where head counts have risen in relation to the sales level, production level, or some other indicator of business activity appropriate to each department. This information should be presented to the managers, with the request that they achieve former levels of employment in relation to the activity or (for those who have done a good job) with congratulations and encouragement to find new ways to increase the productivity of their organization.

*Discontinuing Uneconomical Projects.* This action requires sorting the work being performed in the company into two categories: (1) maintenance of the day-to-day business and (2) project work, such as that designed to develop new products, reduce costs, increase sales, improve employer-employee relations, and improve the company's computer system.

Obviously business maintenance activities must go on, and steps should be taken to reduce the costs of performing these activities. One note of caution: The current selling expense level will be a very sensitive area to tamper with. Selling activities are close to the customer, and many an emotional case has been presented for not cutting selling expenses for that reason. One approach is to establish a specific dollar amount that is to be spent and make sure that the marketing managers spend all of it in the most effective manner possible. Their job is to produce income, not to save on the budgeted amount for selling expense.

On the other hand, projects can be started or stopped without affecting the day-to-day business maintenance work, although they can affect the long-term levels of effectiveness and costs of performing the day-to-day activities. Each project should be evaluated on a cost-benefit basis. Too often, managers get carried away with projects that have little or no tangible benefits. Careful analysis will reveal many projects not worth doing, and such projects can generate substantial unanticipated extra costs once they are under way. Likewise, the potential benefits identified are often never realized for one reason or another.

## IMPLEMENTING CHANGE

Once the right environment has been established, implementation of change should begin without delay. Many executives in turnaround situations rely upon change through sound project management, from the installation of a new piece of machinery to the development of a new data processing system. The value in the project management approach is that it forces the participants to focus on the end results. Successful project management follows two principles: (1) Keep track of *what* you want to do, *whom* you want to do it, and the *date* you want it done; and (2) decide which of these three parameters you can afford to use as a safety valve.

**Project Guidelines**  In setting up projects, several guidelines should be kept in mind:

1. Make sure that if the project is successful, it will move the company toward a solution to the major problem outlined in the business plan.

2. Be careful not to saddle an individual with responsibility for more than one major project at a time. Within one key executive's area of responsibility, however, it is not uncommon for 20 to 30 major and minor projects to be going on simultaneously.

3. Offer assistance, and work with managers on projects. When managers and others see that mistakes can be made without prejudice, it reinforces their feeling that change is acceptable with minimum personal risk and maximum potential gain.

4. Keep in mind that 99 percent of the projects undertaken will never adhere to the original plan. In introducing change, there is usually very little historical (i.e., empirical) evidence on which to base a plan; therefore, executives should allow a little leeway and be prepared to give the project as much time and money as they think will be required. These are one-time expenditures that will soon be forgotten if the technical quality of the project is outstanding. For example, one executive implemented the first major real-time teleprocessing computer system for controlling work in process. Instead of winding up the project once it had met the original specifications, his staff spent several additional months redefining and reworking it. As a result, they were able to reduce related employment by 5 percent (approximately a 200 percent return on their investment) and gain much greater acceptance of the system on the part of down-the-line managers.

5. Accept the fact that things will get worse before they get better. This is true whether computer software is modified, new equipment is introduced, or manual procedures are changed. The key executive should warn superiors, subordinates, and peers to expect additional problems and to avoid prejudice during a critical transitional period.

## TRACKING PROGRESS AND TAKING CORRECTIVE ACTION

The basic reason for setting up a monitoring system is to enable an executive to take corrective action when required. Another reason is to establish a baseline—before and after measures for each activity—against which to report progress.

*Indicators.* Every time a major change is made, an indicator should be installed that will show whether the change (1) is being implemented and (2) is accomplishing its objective. Initial performance indicators need not be sophisticated or minutely accurate. The information does not have to be summarized, which causes delays and makes the infor-

mation stale. Nor does it have to be machine-generated, which often takes too long to get under way.

*Overreaction.* When a performance indicator identifies an impending problem, it is wise to avoid a drastic reaction that might destroy the fragile environment for change. If the indicators have been carefully set up, the problem area can be spotted before others outside the operation are aware of it. This is a decided advantage and enables the executive to attack the problem in an orderly manner.

*Pace of Change.* In tracking progress, the pace of change is also important. If a change is not moving as fast as it should, perhaps managers are being asked to do too many things. If members of a management team are assigned more improvement projects than they can handle, they are likely to balk and retreat into their old roles and habits.

*Reinforcing Successes.* Although many executives spend a great deal of their time modifying changes that are not effective, each change should be held up to appropriate members of the management team as an example of what can be done. In addition, some kind of visible reward should be provided for those responsible for implementation to reinforce the value of risking change.

*Fine Tuning.* Finally, executives should avoid fine-tuning improvements. When 80 percent of the targeted results are achieved, hand the project over to the appropriate down-the-line manager and concentrate on the remaining opportunity areas. Otherwise, it will be difficult if not impossible to achieve overall improvement objectives in the allocated time span.

## SUMMARY

Executives entering new positions charged with the responsibility for significantly improving earnings per share or activities assigned to them often lack a sound concept of what they should be doing and how and when to do it during their initial 6 to 12 months on the job. Many tend to forgo formal planning and are satisfied in spending the initial "quiet period" on the job getting the feel of things, meeting other executives and subordinates, taking a look at some operations, and learning the business by osmosis before becoming forced into fire fighting, attending meetings, and serving on project committees.

Without a sound and demanding concept of what they should accomplish during their initial months, executives may lose the opportunity to gain a clear understanding of the economics of the company within its industry, identify the significant profit-improvement opportunities, develop hypotheses, and determine sound concepts of what is achievable by when. Without this background, the newly appointed executive is not in a position to evaluate his or her organization effectively against a demanding standard; i.e., whether the organization and its people can do significantly more to improve results than is being done—a key ingredient for accomplishing the turnaround objectives.

*See also* ACCOUNTING, COST ANALYSIS AND CONTROL; AUDIT, MANAGEMENT; BUDGETS AND BUDGET PREPARATION; COST IMPROVEMENT; PLANNING, PLANNED MANAGEMENT OF TURBULENT CHANGE; WORK SIMPLIFICATION AND IMPROVEMENT.

### NOTES
[1] Marvin Bower, *The Will to Manage*, McGraw-Hill Book Company, New York, 1966, p. 170.

### REFERENCES
Buffa, E. S.: *Modern Production Management*, John Wiley & Sons, Inc., New York, 1969.
De Bono, Edward: *Lateral Thinking for Management*, American Management Association, New York, 1971.
Eisenberg, Joseph: *Turnaround Management*, McGraw-Hill Book Company, New York, 1972.
Maynard, H. B.: *Top Management Handbook*, McGraw-Hill Book Company, New York, 1960.
Schaffer, Robert H.: "Demand Better Results—And Get Them," *Harvard Business Review*, vol. 52, no. 6, p. 91. Boston, Mass., November–December 1974.

Much of the information presented here is based on the successful profit-improvement experiences of E. Joseph Bensler, Citibank; Frederick J. Mancheski, Echlin Manufacturing Company; and John W. Priesing, Phelps Dodge Industries. Their help and advice are greatly appreciated.

JOSEPH EISENBERG, *Profit-Improvement, Inc., Management Consultants*

## Profit and loss statement    (*See* ACCOUNTING FOR MANAGERIAL CONTROL.)

## Profit maximization    (*See* OBJECTIVES AND GOALS.)

## Profit plans    (*See* INTERNATIONAL OPERATIONS AND MANAGEMENT IN MULTINATIONAL COMPANIES.)

## Profit sharing    (*See* COMPENSATION, SPECIAL PLANS.)

## Profit Sharing Council of America
(*See* COMPENSATION, SPECIAL PLANS.)

## Profitability, product    (*See* MARGINAL INCOME ANALYSIS.)

## Profitability index    (*See* BUDGETING, CAPITAL.)

## Profitability ratios    (*See* FINANCIAL RATIO ANALYSIS.)

## Profits and profit making

Profits may be loosely defined as the excess of sales revenue over the cost of providing a product or service to buyers. If the total cost of providing a product or service exceeds the amount for which it can be sold, the firm incurs a loss instead of a profit. Unfortunately, this simple, intuitive definition must not be used without thought of its implications.

**Accounting Profit**    The term *profit* is applied by accountants to the results of a firm's past performance. This accounting concept tells about the business history of the enterprise. From knowledge of past performance, managers and investors may draw conclusions about future performance, as well as gain clues about what changes in the firm's policies may be called for.

Accounting profit is not always a hard-and-fast, clearly defined concept, because there are many options about how to calculate it. For example, a firm may set aside reserves or take special write offs during a given year which reduce profits in that year but increase it in other years. Profit rates are also affected by methods of inventory valuation. During periods of inflation, prices of items used to produce products or services are rising; consequently, the inventory valuation method employed by the firm will affect accounting profits. If the firm assumes that the items sold first are those last added to the inventory (LIFO), the inventory level will be frozen at historical costs and the items costing more will be sold first. In that way current profits would be lower during periods of rising prices than if the firm assumed that the lower-cost items were sold first (FIFO).

Taxes affect both apparent and actual profitability. For example, a firm financing with bonds is permitted by law in the United States to deduct the bond interest from its taxable income before computing corporate income taxes. A firm that finances through common stock, however, is not permitted to deduct dividends to stockholders before computing income tax. Since stockholders individually pay taxes on dividends, use of the stock alternative means that the stockholders and the firm combined pay higher income tax than if the bond alternative were used, other things being equal.

**Profits and Decision Making** The term *profit* also applies to the criteria used by businesses and economists in making such *business* decisions as which price to set, where to locate a new branch, and whether to invest in a prospective opportunity. The simple, intuitive accounting concept of profit as the amount of revenue left after paying all expenditures does not suffice for business decisions. For example, assume that a publishing firm has been selling a book for several years, but sales have now tapered off to the point at which the publisher is almost ready to take the book out of print. Another firm comes along and offers to buy 2000 copies at $2 each for a total of $4000. The "out-of-pocket" printing, binding, and other production expenditures for the lot of 2000 books would be about $2200. The publisher refuses the deal, however, because the accountant rules that the sale would not be profitable, on the grounds that when the original expenditures for editing and typesetting are allowed for, the cost of 2000 books comes to more than $2 apiece. Of course, the publisher would be better off accepting the deal, as is intuitively obvious to you. The editing and other overhead costs are all in the past. They cannot be affected by *this* sale, and hence they are not longer relevant. That is, the deal truly is profitable, even though the accountant says it is not.

*Contribution to Profit Concept.* To get around this difficulty, the concept of *contribution to profit* was invented. This is really a redefinition of profit. Any decision that can be expected to lead to a higher end-of-year profit in the present year, taking into account only the *relevant* costs, is said to make a positive contribution to profit. Suppose, for example, a firm has unused capacity equal to 25 percent of its total capacity. Assume further that the variable costs (the additional costs from selling and producing an additional unit of output) are equal to $1 per unit, and overhead costs, if allocated, would raise the costs per unit to $3. This firm should not price the product *of this additional production* over $3 if market forces do not support a price of that magnitude. Instead, the firm should be content to

sell the additional units at any price greater than $1 because the sale revenue would contribute to the profits of the whole organization; the particular price level should be set only after considering market pressure from competition. The essential point is that the profit-making process calls for price setting at something lower than full costs, but greater than the additional cost of the sale, if that lower price is required to make the sale. It must be understood, however, that this profit strategy could not be employed for *all* products produced by a firm; overhead costs must finally be covered by the firm's operation. Obviously, if a firm sold all its output at a price only slightly over variable costs, then the firm would suffer a loss on operations. Overhead must be covered in some market segments.

It should be noted that the contribution-to-profit concept itself presents problems. A major difficulty is the determination of which costs are relevant to a given activity of the firm. For example, is the sales manager's salary relevant to the proposed book deal mentioned above? One *can* get around the problem of figuring relevant or incremental costs by looking at the total revenues or total expenditures for a firm under the various alternatives, to see which alternative yields the greatest overall difference between revenues and expenditures.

Another major difficulty of the contribution-to-profit concept is that it refers only to the firm's revenues and expenditures in the present period. It is a fundamental fact of business life that all important decisions have ramifications far beyond the present year. There is no satisfactory simple way, therefore, to represent the future impacts in terms of this year's revenues and costs; normal accounting concepts are often misleading if one tries to do so. Hence, it is necessary to use a more general criterion.

*The Appropriate Profit Criterion.* The appropriate criterion for decision where impacts are spread over time (and this includes most business decisions) is the *discounted net present value* of the alternative, or simply, *present value*. This may be defined in two ways:

1. Described in words, the present value of an alternative equals the sum of the net revenues of the entire firm in each future year under this alternative, after each year's net revenue is adjusted (discounted) to reflect the fact that a sum of money in the future is worth less than the same sum in hand at the present moment.

2. Stated algebraically, the present value of an alternative is determined as follows:

$$V_{T=0} = (S_{t=0} - E_{t=0}) + (S_{t=1} - E_{t=1}d$$
$$+ (S_{t=2}d^2 - E_{t=2}d^2)$$
$$+ (S_{t=3}d^3 - E_{t=3}\overline{d}^3)$$
$$+ \cdots + (S_{t=k}d^k - E_{t=k}d^k)$$
$$+ (W_{t=k}d^k - W_{t=0})$$

where $V_{T=0}$ = present value of alternative $i$ at time $T$

$S_t$ = expected gross sales revenue from alternative $i$ in period $t$

$E_t$ = total expenditure in period $t$

$W_t$ = market value of firm's productive assets in period

*Comparison of Accounting and Decision-Making Concepts.* The accountant's concept looks *backward* at history, to evaluate what happened. The purpose is to hold individuals and organizations "accountable" for auditing purposes and to judge whether they performed well or poorly. Although the information on past performance can be useful in the prediction of future performance, it is not in itself a good framework for making business decisions. In contrast, the business criterion is *forward-looking*. Its task is to evaluate what will happen in the future and then to choose the best among the available alternatives.

In line with its own purposes, the accountant's concept of profit applies to a limited time period, such as a quarter of a year or a year. The concept of present value, however, refers to the entire future life of an alternative. Furthermore, accounting profit refers to what actually happened, whereas present value refers to what is *expected* to happen. The expected and actual outcomes do not always coincide. Also, the present value notion assumes that available sums of money are invested at the appropriate rate of return, whereas the accountant's one-period concept of profit does not need to make such an assumption.

**Sources of Profits** How do opportunities for profits exist? Why does not competition squeeze firms to the point that no profits can be made? One part of the answer is that ordinary profits may be considered simply as a return to the invested capital, including returns to the ordinary risks involved. But sometimes a firm can make out-of-the-ordinary profits.

Unusually high profits may emerge from three possible sources: (1) a reward for risk taking, (2) a reward for successful innovation, and (3) a consequence of frictions and imperfections in the dynamic economy.

1. Profits as a reward for risk taking accrue to businesses when they invest resources in special purpose assets such as unique machinery and equipment to provide a specific product or service to consumers. To the extent that providing the item to buyers results in sales revenues which exceed costs, the firm has generated a profit. The profit stems from the firm's willingness to assume the risks of investing in the special-purpose equipment, which is not as liquid as cash and is riskier than an investment in, say, government notes.

2. Profits may also come from innovation, such as a purposeful change in production method which increases productivity or provides a superior product. Innovation can give a firm an edge over competition and thus increase profits. Profits from innovation may often be protected by a patent, which prevents others from providing the same item in competition with the original producer.

3. Another source of profits is frictions and imperfections. Profits of this type occur when market forces are such that demand for a product or service grows faster than firms are able to supply the product. The resulting "friction" drives up prices and profits. Conditions may also exist where a firm faces weak competition from rivals, and this permits it to reap larger profits than if the firm had to reduce prices and revenue to meet the market prices of stiffer, more perfect competition.

**Limiting Profits** Though businesses prefer larger over smaller profits, circumstances may sometimes make it seem wise to limit profits, in the short run at least. High profits attract competition; therefore, a firm may limit profits to discourage entry of additional rivals. Similarly, a firm may provide better working conditions than required in order to attract and hold superior employees; this will also reduce profitability. A firm may also limit profits so as not to attract antitrust pressure. Anticipation of labor demands may also be another reason for limiting profits; large profit levels sometimes signal labor to increase wage demands. Another reason for limiting profits is to maintain customer good will. If profits appear too large, there is the possibility that customers may view the firm unfavorably and seek other suppliers. A distinction must be made, of course, between long-run and short-run profitability. Many firms sometimes forgo short-run profits in order to attain larger, long-run profits.

*See also* ECONOMIC CONCEPTS; EGALITARIANISM; PROFIT IMPROVEMENT; *Profits and Profit Making*.

## REFERENCES

Dean, Joel: *Managerial Economics*, Prentice-Hall, Inc., Englewood Cliffs, N.J., 1951.

Friedman, Milton: "The Social Responsibility of Business Is to Increase Its Profits," *The New York Times Magazine*, Sept. 30, 1970.

Haner, F. T.: *Business Policy, Planning, and Strategy*, Winthrop Publishing Co., Englewood Cliffs, N.J., 1976.

Haynes, W. W., and W. R. Henry: *Managerial Economics*, Business Publications, Inc., Dallas, Tex., 1974.

Newman, William H., and James P. Logan: *Strategy, Policy, and Central Management*, South-Western Publishing Company, Incorporated, Cincinnati, Ohio, 1976.

Simon, Julian L.: *Applied Managerial Economics*, Prentice-Hall, Inc., Englewood Cliffs, N.J., 1975.

Some material in this entry was drawn from Simon, pages 11–12, cited above.

WALTER J. PRIMEAUX, JR., *University of Illinois at Urbana*

JULIAN L. SIMON, *University of Illinois at Urbana*

# Program budgeting (PPBS)

Program budgeting, or the planning-programming-budgeting system (PPBS), can be described in a number of ways. For example, Charles Schultze, former director of the Bureau of the Budget, in a 1966 statement to the U.S. Senate Committee on Government Operations said:

PPBS is really a system that starts with planning about objectives, develops programs through analysis on the basis of those objectives and translates those programs into budgetary requirements. So, PPBS is a system which attempts to relate policy planning on the one hand to resource use, and budgets on the other.[1]

Joon Chien Doh in an empirical study of the experience in the National Aeronautics and Space Administration, the Department of Agriculture, and the Department of Health, Education and Welfare put it this way:

Program Budgeting's objectives can be summarized as:

A. Identification and clarification of program objectives.
B. Assessment of whether or not program outputs are fulfilling these objectives.
C. Determination of full costs of programs.
D. Long-range planning.
E. Analysis of program alternatives as an integral part of budget process, and
F. Budget as the instrument for implementing policy and program decisions produced by analytic efforts.[2]

Frederick Mosher wrote in *Public Administration Review* (March–April 1970):

The system known as planning-programming-budgeting (PPBS) . . . future historians may consider the most significant administrative innovation of the 1960s. PPBS in some form and to some degree is now installed in most federal agencies—all the large ones—in the majority of states, and in many of the largest cities and counties. It is doubtful that any definition would satisfy all students and practitioners of PPBS, but most would agree that a central feature is the objective analysis of the probable costs and effectiveness of alternative courses of action to achieve goals, independent of political considerations (in the narrow sense of "Political"), bureaucratic considerations, and personal wishes or hunches. In the words of one federal official "PPBS is simply a means to make public decision-making more rational."

Mosher, Doh, Schultze, and a host of others were trying to define the product of the McNamara Revolution in the Department of Defense and President Johnson's bombshell announcement of program budgeting for the entire federal establishment on August 25, 1965. Both of these actions had their origin in the ideas set out in *Efficiency and Economy in Government* (Rand Corporation, 1953) and related publications by this writer.[3]

The theme in all these publications was: Make the budget useful to decision makers instead of making it a comptroller's document for financial control as in pre-1961 government practice.

Despite its initial acceptance, by 1971 there was less activity in program budgeting in the United States and other countries than there had been in the mid 1960s. In the enthusiasm that followed President Johnson's announcement of the new management concept, there was an obvious desire in the United States to jump on the bandwagon and take advantage quickly of what sometimes was described as a miraculous cure-all for managements' ills. In 1969 B. M. Gross put it this way:

As with many new managerial techniques, PPB was initiated in a burst of grandiose claims of "breakthroughs" and exaggerated applications to irrelevant situations. It has been pioneered by many technical specialists with little understanding, less interest, and no experience in general management.[4]

Because of the "little understanding and no experience" in many of the applications of program budgeting, by 1971 a great many strange and inappropriate activities were labelled PPBS. For this reason, a studied effort was made to define program budgeting properly. The product of that effort was published in 1973, and at this date it still seems the most satisfactory. Now, as then, so many different ideas and management systems are labelled or justified or explained as PPBS that it is again essential to define "What Program Budgeting Is and Is Not."[5]

**Distinctive Features** Program budgeting is a management system that has 10 distinctive major features. These are:

1. Definition of an organization's objectives in terms as specific as possible

2. Determination of programs, including possible alternatives, to achieve the stated objectives

3. Identification of major issues to be resolved in the formulation of objectives and/or the development of programs

4. An annual cycle with appropriate subdivisions for the planning, programming, and budgeting steps to ensure an ordered approach and to make appropriate amounts of time available for analysis and decision making at all levels of management

5. Continuous reexamination of program results in relationship to anticipated costs and outcomes to determine need for changes in stated programs and objectives as originally established

6. Recognition of issues and other problems that require more time than is available in the annual cycle so that they can be explicitly identified and set apart from the current period for completion in 2 or more years, as the subject matter and availability of personnel require

7. Analysis of programs and their alternatives in terms of probable outcomes and both direct and indirect costs

8. Development of analytical tools necessary for measuring costs and benefits

9. Development each year of a multiyear program and financial plan with full recognition of the fact that in many areas resource allocations in the early years (e.g., years 1 through 5) require projections of plans and programs and their resource demands for 10 or more years into the future

10. Adaptation of existing accounting and statistical reporting systems to provide inputs into planning and programming, as well as continuing information on resources used in and actions taken to implement programs

**What Program Budgeting Is Not** Program budgeting is *not* a system (even when called PB or PPBS) if it does not deal with choosing objectives and developing plans through systematic analysis of costs and effectiveness, resource allocation, and other major decision areas. The false labeling includes:

1. Reorganization plans justified on the basis that the organization must fit the program structure

2. New accounting or statistical systems that identify program elements

3. Management-information systems undertaken as a substitute for major program budget features

4. Elaborate new personnel recruiting, education, or training undertaken without developing the PB organization and procedures which will utilize them effectively

5. Extensive use of the words *program* and *program budgeting* in existing documents and procedures in lieu of developing and introducing the PB concepts and required changes

6. Treating performance budgeting, management by objectives (MBO), and other methods for improving administration of specific tasks as a substitute for PB treatment of major decision-making problems

**Business Applications** Obviously, all the foregoing has been in terms of public sector applications. This should *not* be taken to mean that PPBS is used only there. In private business, management tools of the program budgeting type were developed first by E. I. du Pont de Nemours & Co., around the time of World War I, and in General Motors in the early 1920s.[6] When Henry Ford II came into control at Ford Motor Company at the end of World War II and faced very serious financial problems, among his emergency actions was the hiring of several new executives from General Motors. They brought with them the General Motors management methods. According to Professor Christenson of the Harvard Business School, this transfer from General Motors to Ford extended to the point where "for a while, Ford actually used the same forms . . . in its system."[7] At that time, Henry Ford II also hired a group of ex–air force officers known as the Whiz Kids, to work on his company's management problems. One of them was Robert S. McNamara; another was C. B. ("Tex") Thornton.

When the Chrysler Corporation was in financial difficulty in 1958, there were reports that it, too, had repeated what Ford had done earlier in terms of borrowing both brainpower and management methods from General Motors (and Ford). The only publicly available document on program budgeting at Chrysler is *PROBE*, which appeared in 1967.[8] The acronym stands for program review of budgeted expenses. Chrysler's paper refers to program budgeting and claims for PROBE some of the same management improvements that usually are attributed to program budgeting. It cites the application of the methodology at Ford and in the U.S. federal government in its support.

Just as managerial personnel moving from one auto company to another in Detroit carried program budgeting with them, so did executives going from the automotive giants to corporations in other lines of business. Apparently, however, all these companies treat their management concepts and methods as proprietary. They do not make their manuals available to outsiders or authorize publication of information on their methods. As a result, published accounts of experience in business are limited. One is Alfred P. Sloan's reference in *My Years with General Motors*. Another is the application of program budgeting to research and development at General Electric.[9] Still another is the 1968 to 1970 development of program budgeting for the John Hancock Mutual Life Insurance Company.[10]

Some of the concepts used in program budgeting have had significant application in business under such terms as strategic planning, project management, and the like (*see* PLANNING, STRATEGIC MANAGERIAL). When such experience is included, a substantially larger part of the business picture can be identified as utilizing the major features of program budgeting.

In the private and public sectors, the words *program budgeting, planning-programming-budgeting system,* or *PPBS* appear less frequently today than 10 or even 5 years ago. As a senior official of the Office of Management and Budget remarked to this writer, "This is one case when the substance survives after the name is gone." The occasion was when Director Roy Ash threw out PPBS and installed MBO in 1972.[11] It is worth noting that the Federal Energy Agency (which did not exist in 1972) in the summer of 1976 requested proposals for assistance in "development of required program, planning, and budget documentation . . . within FEA that . . . properly reflects the elements of a PPBS process."

Despite that action, the Five Year Defense Program carries on with PPBS terminology in the Department of Defense. Even when the forbidden symbols have been dropped in other agencies, the emphasis on analysis and the development of issues for policy and budget decisions continues. In business, activities are following a pattern that is the reverse of the one for the federal government. This is a gradual development of strategic planning, issue identification, and other major features of objective analysis of the probable costs and effectiveness of alternative courses of actions to achieve objectives. In short, management is tying together business policy planning, decision making, and budget making, as is done in program budgeting or PPBS.

*See also* BUDGETS AND BUDGET PREPARATION; HEALTH SERVICES, PLANNING FOR; HEALTH INSTITUTIONS, MANAGEMENT OF; NOT-FOR-PROFIT INSTITUTIONS, MANAGEMENT OF; OBJECTIVES, MANAGEMENT BY (MBO); PROGRAM PLANNING AND IMPLEMENTATION; PROJECT AND TASK FORCE MANAGEMENT; PUBLIC ADMINISTRATION.

## NOTES

[1]Charles Schultze, *Planning, Programming, Budgeting,* U.S. Senate, Committee on Government Operations, Washington, 1970, p. 196.

[2]Joon Chien Doh, *The Planning-Programming-Budgeting System in Three Federal Agencies,* Praeger Publishers, Inc., New York, 1971, pp. 17–18.

[3]David Novick, "Which Program Do We Mean in 'Program Budgeting'?" *Newsletter,* Armed Forces Management Association, August 1954; ——— *A New Approach to Military Budget,* The Rand Corp., June 1956; ——— *New Tools for Planners and Programmers,* The Rand Corp., November 1960; ——— *The Executive,* Harvard Business School, September 1961; ——— "Origin and History of Program Budgeting," *Program Budgeting,* 2d ed., Harvard University Press, Boston, 1966.

[4]B. M. Gross, "The New Systems Budgeting," *Public Administration Review,* March–April 1969.

[5]David Novick, (ed.), *Current Practice in Program Budgeting (PPBS),* Crane, Russak & Co., Inc., New York, 1973.

[6]A. H. Swayne and Donaldson Brown, "Tuning Up General Motors," *Management and Administration,* vol. 7, nos. 1–4, The Ronald Press Company, New York, 1924.

[7]"Some Lessons in Business from PPBS, Analysis for Planning-Programming-Budgeting," WORC, Potomac, Md., 1968, p. 58.

[8]"Program Review of Budgeted Expenditures," Chrysler Corp., Detroit, 1967.

[9]Novick, *Current Practice in Program Budgeting (PPBS),* chap. 18.

[10]Novick, *Current Practice in Program Budgeting (PPBS),* chap. 19.

[11]An interesting application of program budgeting is its increasing use by United Funds, Church Missionary Hospitals, and other quasipublic organizations, particularly since 1972.

DAVID NOVICK, *David Novick Associates*

# Program planning and implementation

Planning is a process by which future actions are decided upon in terms of specific organizational or institutional goals. Program planning is a specialized planning process which is output-oriented and involves sets of resources encompassing a broader range of objectives than more traditional planning efforts. It combines long- and short-range planning while emphasizing the use of budgets in establishing priorities and in selecting alternatives. It is, in essence, a systematized way for organizations to deal with large-scale resource use and at the same time deal with dynamic, rapidly changing economic, political, social, and technological environments.

Program planning has been used for some time in the federal government of the United States, in particular, the Department of Defense. Other agencies of the federal government have adopted program planning and implementation as a part of a formal planning-programming-budgeting system (PPBS). Although the concept was adopted from industry, indications are that program planning has been generally limited to the federal, and recently state, government organizations. This may be shortsighted. Traditional planning tools are increasingly restrictive. Although PPBS systems are more complex than the needs of modern business organizations, program planning can provide a highly useful approach to restructuring a firm's total planning effort.

One must not confuse program planning with project planning, product planning, or brand management. Project planning is finite, dealing with a specific set of objectives. It ends when the project has been completed. Product management is tied to a specific product or product family and does not include the interrelationships between that particular product and other aspects of the firm's operation. Brand management is more narrow, dealing mainly with a very specific product or product line. Although these three terms are often used synonymously with program planning, they are not the same.

The most important aspect of program management is that it is not tied to any specific period of time. Additionally, it (1) involves a significant amount of the firm's resources and (2) focuses on program interactions with a number of the organization's activities. A single functional area of the firm for example, such as accounting or production, may be committed to a number of the firm's programs. Hence, the firm's goal setting, structure, resource allocation, and decision-making processes must take on a "systems view" in order to deal with the demands of program planning and implementation.

## THE ORIGINS OF PROGRAM PLANNING

Program planning has its roots in the PPBS system developed in the U.S. federal government during

the mid 1960s. Even earlier evidence is found during World War II when the National Defense Advisory Commission was formed in an attempt to expand American production efforts to support war efforts on both the Atlantic and Pacific fronts. Major goals were established for combat needs, essential civilian requirements, aid to friendly nations, and economic warfare. The analytical methods developed to deal with these resource allocation problems set the stage for later RAND Corporation efforts with the United States Air Force.

For a number of years, RAND analysts worked with Air Force planners developing systems analyses for strategic bombers. Then in 1961, an effort was launched under the Kennedy administration to define the United States military budget in more understandable terms. A program budget was defined, such that all the defense functional areas (Air Force, Navy, Army, Marine Corps) would work toward common defense objectives. Thus each specific program was identified, and all defense resources were allocated to one or more of these specific programs. The organization of this first major program planning effort is contained in Fig. P-29.

Program planning's goal was to understand and allocate more systematically the vast resources of the Defense Department. The result was to eliminate dual missions, minimize misallocation of resources,

**Fig. P-29. Planning-programming-budgeting systems (PPBS) in the Department of Defense.**

and most important, help each of the services to understand its contribution to the overall defense effort. Planning in this manner has withstood the test of time. It appears to have developed a better understanding of the military mission in terms of these broader goals rather than the separate desires of each of the military services.

A number of points became clear from the defense experience: (1) Each functional head has to become committed to the PPBS system, (2) full-time staffs representing each of the functional agencies must be formed to ensure close cooperation and coordination, and (3) a previous emphasis on input definition (i.e., dollars available for defense) is turned to quantifiable measures of output. This gave defense planners a goal orientation, a concept that has long been common to industrial organizations.

At the same time, PPBS reaped benefits which the planners had not proposed. People in government now look at results. More importantly, this goal orientation was extended from a fiscal year perspective to an evaluation of programs over an extended period of time, in some cases up to 10 or 20 years.

Along with the benefits came new problems. The most important of these was an inability to quantify or measure organizational outputs. For example, it is difficult for planners to fully document "success" with respect to strategic retaliatory forces. Many programs simply do not have dollar benefits that can be measured. Nonetheless, planners developed surrogate measures to evaluate goal achievement in each of the nine program areas. The success of the defense experience spilled over to all government agencies, and in 1965 all federal agencies were required to adopt a PPBS system.

Other federal agencies using program planning techniques include the National Aeronautics and Space Administration, which adopted PPBS in early 1959. The program to land a man on the moon is the most notable example of this agency's attempt to use program planning. Similar success was enjoyed by the Department of Transportation when it developed five specific programs: general development of freight and passenger transportation in the United States, provision of better access to rural and remote towns and cities, relief of urban traffic congestion problems, creation of standby transportation capacity for war and other national emergencies, and promotion of national prestige and international trade.

Program planning was readily accepted by these agencies because of the size of their efforts, diversity of resources, and multiplicity of goals.

## PROGRAM PLANNING IN INDUSTRY: A HISTORICAL PERSPECTIVE

Program planning in industry can be traced back to the mid 1920s with the General Motors Corporation. Its programs were developed not along product lines, but rather in terms of price classes and categories of cars to be offered. Resources were allocated to each of the divisions so that certain models of Chevrolets could compete with Pontiac and Buick, for example. As a result, GM's objectives focused on a major segment of the market but without respect to a specific automobile product line. Further, because of the lead time in tooling for automobiles, program planning extended up to 5 years in the future. Interchangeability of parts and the need to allocate materials such as rubber, steel, and glass necessitated long lead times and allocation choices from among a number of different alternatives.

Other companies that developed program planning were the Bell Laboratories, which introduced the concept of systems planning in the 1920s, and later the Ford Motor Company under Robert McNamara, which introduced systems analysis into Ford planning in the 1950s.

The major thread running through each of these examples is that program planning and implementation was first used by very large organizations having a variety of resources and difficult allocation decisions. Given today's economy, the number of choices available to consumers, and the increased complexity of routine decision-making, program planning has become a viable tool for a much broader range of industrial and nonindustrial organizations.

## IMPLICATIONS FOR TODAY'S MANAGERS

Program planning provides new ways to look at a very old problem: how to evaluate the future. It structures the planning problem in such a way as to force the manager to consider all the environmental impacts on the organization's decisions. Finally, it provides alternative ways in which an executive can structure organizational decision making to deal more effectively with the complex future uncertainties.

1. Program planning forces a firm to reexamine its goals. In many organizations, goals have existed for a long time. Typically, they are expressed as some form of profit or growth. As a result, economic retrenchment or rapid advances in technology have

caught many firms short. Today's plans become obsolete quickly. A manager must not be totally influenced by the past or even the present. Instead he or she must take a look at the opportunities available in the scenario of the future. Is a national firm in the business of selling soap, or is it involved with the methods of cleaning clothes, dishes, walls, etc.? The crux of the program planning method is to force the organization to ask such questions as "Will there be a *need* for soap in the foreseeable future?" "How might we clean clothes in the future?" "Will we be using dishes by the year 2000?" In essence, program planning asks "What business are we *really* in?" Goal definition is often the most difficult task top management faces in constructing a program plan.

2. In evaluating alternatives goals, a firm must study the rapidly changing economic, political, and social environments. The soap company above would look at alternatives to today's chemicals, the economic viability of synthetic substitutes, and the social, political, and legal demands for nonpollutant ingredients. This way, attention is not focused on the competitiveness of a single product or product line, but on the firm's ability to deal with the program of supplying economically useful, competitive cleansing alternatives for the home and industry.

3. The organization must modify or adapt its structure to match the purpose of its program. Traditional hierarchies, functional organizations, project groups, and product or brand structures are increasingly found to be too myopic in dealing with environmental change. Because of the tremendous value of resources that enter today's technology,

(consumer or industrial), the cost of a mistake is similarly high. On one hand, the organization's response may be to take fewer risks. But in doing so, the company may lose its competitive edge. On the other hand, taking risks without systematically evaluating *all* the alternatives increases the chance of failure. Often, the organization form that emerges is one that focuses on the interrelationship between the functional support and the company's programs: a matrix form, where operational responsibility for a company goal rests with the program manager. An example is shown in Fig. P-30.

4. By carefully defining a firm's goals and arranging the resource allocation in a program structure, a manager can develop more precise ways of obtaining feedback and control. When resource use is assigned against a specific program, cause and effect relationships are more clearly understood. Adjustments to the program plan are more easily identified and better defined.

## RISKS, PROBLEMS, AND LIMITATIONS

Many managers have great difficulty in reevaluating or redefining an organization's goals. Because business is so output-oriented, profit, whether short or long range, seems the most likely alternative. Reexamining a company's goals with respect to other alternatives such as survival or social welfare is time-consuming and difficult to articulate. Nonetheless, the process of asking the right question helps to understand the changing nature of organization goals. The clustering of common goals into program choices is often the result.

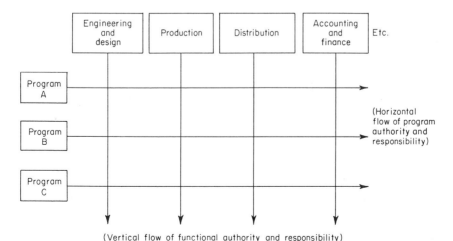

**Fig. P-30. Matrix form of organization structure for program management.**

A second problem and perhaps one of more import, is the use of annual or fiscal budgeting common to most organizations. Because programs extend over a number of years, budgets are really long-range projections. This not only includes capital expenditures but involves all expenditures associated with program forecasts. It is difficult for many firms to define operating budgets for a period longer than a year, and resistance to program planning often focuses in this area.

A third problem involves resistance to structural changes. Although aerospace firms have used such concepts as project management and matrix management structures for a number of years, shared managerial responsibility and authority are relatively uncommon in the industrial and nonindustrial sectors. Tradition emphasizes the principles of "unity of command" and "one person—one boss." Because there is no one to blame when things go wrong, the concept of sharing resources and decision-making authority is difficult for many managers to accept. One popular alternative, committee management, rarely results in quick decisions. As a result, this alternative, too, is often discarded. Paradoxically, shared responsibility and resources are actually more definitive. Activities are directed toward specific program objectives; thus control is greater, and the effects of management actions are more clearly defined.

Finally, it is difficult to establish a thorough control system that accurately identifies critical deviations from the planned program. The tendency is to develop controls for all program activities. Experience has shown that feedback and control in the Department of Defense and other federal agencies often turns out to be cumbersome and unwieldy. A major management task is to design a useful control system and feedback process to support the program without it becoming the program itself.

## IMPLEMENTING THE PROGRAM

In order to ensure a systematic program development, four specific steps are required. These are the establishment of goals, the definition of objectives, the allocation and structuring of resources, and the creation of a feedback and control mechanism. The relationship between these elements is portrayed in Fig. P-31.

STEP 1: Goal setting. The organization must decide upon its long-range goals and the timing of goal achievement. This requires asking and answering the question, "What business are we in now, and what business do we want to be in in the future?"

Top management must identify common sets of goals in such a way that clusters emerge and programs are identified. An example of how this was done in one chemical firm is shown in Fig. P-32.

Goals that are similar, with respect to home chemicals, pharmaceuticals, and industrial chemicals, are identified and grouped according to the firm's program emphasis. When a long-range perspective is taken, this kind of goal identification can be done for almost any firm.

STEP 2: Definition of objectives. For each of the programs, alternative strategies must be identified. At this stage planners seek answers to the question, "How will the firm meet its requirements in the next 5 years with respect to the home chemical industry or pharmaceuticals?" This avoids homing in on a short-term profit objective and encourages the firm to opt for a longer-term program development to meet the projected needs. Thereby it concentrates on the future rather than on the present. The alternative strategies are, in essence, a set of program opportunities. They are evaluated with respect to the firm's long-range development criteria. New product lines, market expansion, and new product technologies are program opportunities that can be achieved in many different ways. The firm must evaluate present and projected resources, markets, and the competitive environment to select the strategy having the best complement of risk and return over the life of the program. A strategy can then be defined and short-run objectives established. These objectives become the goals for the immediate future that fit into the long-range program. For example, the hypothetical firm portrayed in Fig. P-32 might decide that vitamins will play an increasingly important role in the pharmaceutical industry and choose to concentrate on the development of synthetic vitamins for home use. Meanwhile, as a part of its overall pharmaceutical program, it will monitor the environment for replacement of alternative opportunities.

STEP 3: Joint allocation of resources. To meet the defined objectives, both near and long term, resource allocation must be applied in such a way as to meet all defined programs. Manufacturing capacity is not the initial consideration, for example. Rather, the needs of each of the firm's programs must be established and the firm's manufacturing capacity must be allocated accordingly. Targets for each of the programs must be controlled by the program manager. Production, finance, marketing, engineering, and other functional managers must work to support the program managers in the accomplishment of their objectives. In the hypothetical firm,

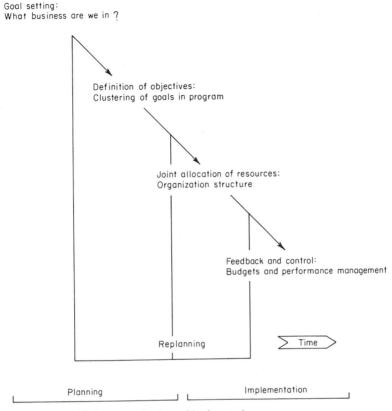

**Fig. P-31. A model of program planning and implementation.**

the decision to make a production run for household cleaning chemicals versus dish detergents would not be a production decision alone; it would be formulated in a joint meeting with the program manager. At that meeting, all aspects of this decision would be evaluated: production changeover problems, finance problems, raw materials availability, demand for the product, etc. Rather than suboptimizing this production decision, the firm optimizes its activities with respect to the organization. Typically, this joint meeting will produce a decision that neither the program manager nor the chief of production would have made independently. Typically, neither had all the information necessary; joint planning

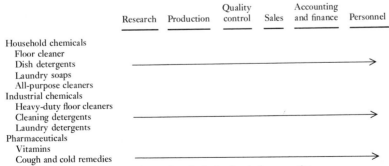

**Fig. P-32. Program structure in a hypothetical chemical corporation.**

forces organizational goal considerations in the chemical program.

STEP 4: Feedback and control. The final step in program implementation is the establishment of a feedback and control mechanism. A management information system may provide a great deal of computerized data, but unless it provides the right information quickly, it may be ineffective. Accordingly, an essential part of the program plan is to establish specific, quantifiable, and verifiable objectives. Milestones that identify when these objectives are to be accomplished are necessary, along with a specific measure that reflects the accomplishment of the goal. Thus, it is not the quantity of information available to the manager that is necessary, but the quality needed to make useful decisions.

The most important control mechanism is the budget. Inherent in the entire program planning procedure is a concern for financial administration. Cost estimating, revenue generation, and profit guides are integral to planning and control. Program budgets must be closely coordinated; they are at the heart of the entire process.

Replanning at frequent intervals is a necessary part of program implementation. The program plan is a long-term effort, and the environment changes rapidly. A good manager must not be afraid to start over again whenever environmental constraints make the current plan ineffective or obsolete.

### PROGRAM PLANNING: A TOOL FOR ANY ORGANIZATION

Program planning and implementation is not an ominous task, nor is it merely an academic exercise. It is a way of planning mostly applied in public organizations that are characterized by an absence of accurate output measures or by requirements to budget from an output standpoint. Success in these organizations has led a number of business firms to adopt the tenets of program planning with substantial benefits.

Program planning and implementation involves time, managerial talents, and most important, organizational focus on the future. There are but four steps to the process, but these four steps imply a fresh understanding and a total restructuring of organizational planning. For those organizations that adopt program planning, the benefits far outweigh the costs.

*See also* ACCOUNTING, COST ANALYSIS AND CONTROL; BUDGETS AND BUDGET PREPARATION; CONTROL SYSTEMS, MANAGEMENT; COST-BENEFIT ANALYSIS; ORGANIZATION STRUCTURES AND CHARTING; PLANNING, STRATEGIC MANAGERIAL; PROGRAM BUDGETING (PPBS); PROJECT AND TASK FORCE MANAGEMENT; PUBLIC ADMINISTRATION.

#### REFERENCES
Anthony, Robert N.: *Planning and Control Systems: A Framework for Analysis* Harvard University Graduate School of Business Administration, Boston, Mass., 1965.

Cleland, David I., and William R. King: "Organizing for Long-Range Planning," *Business Horizons*, vol. XVII, no. 4, pp. 25–32, August 1974.

Hussey, D. E.: *Corporate Planning: Theory and Practice*, Pergamon Press, Oxford, 1974.

King, William R., and David I. Cleland: "A New Method for Strategic Systems Planning," *Business Horizons*, vol. XVIII, no. 4, August 1975, pp. 55–64.

Novick, David, ed., *Program Budgeting* Holt, Rinehart and Winston, Inc., New York, 1969.

Sayles, Leonard R., and Margaret K. Chandler: *Managing Large Systems: Organizations for the Future* Harper & Row, Publishers, Incorporated, New York, 1971.

ROBERT L. TAYLOR, *United States Air Force Academy, Colorado*

## Program strategies (*See* PLANNING, STRATEGIC MANAGERIAL.)

## Programmed instruction

*Programmed instruction* is sequenced self-instruction that does not require a human instructor. It utilizes specially designed textbooks or any of a variety of devices ranging from simple teaching machines to audiovisual systems to computer-assisted instruction (CAI).

The use of programmed instruction exploded suddenly in the 1960s after the publication in 1954 of B. F. Skinner's famous paper "The Science of Learning and the Art of Teaching," advocating machine teaching designed around the needs of the learner. After a "glamor" period, the method appears to be stabilizing as a reliable means of training motivated employees.

It is characterized by these principles: (1) Sequenced subject material is presented in very small steps (frames) building upon preceding learned material; (2) the trainee participates actively by responding to a question or performing a task at each step; (3) continuous learner self-evaluation is provided by immediate feedback: each wrong answer is corrected, and right answers are reinforced; (4) the learner proceeds at his or her own pace; and (5) difficulty of the material increases gradually.

Programmed self-instruction is often motivating to employees; learning is frequently faster and retention higher than in conventional teaching. It is effective for training large numbers of employees or those needing to assimilate large amounts of material frequently. It is also very effective in developing mechanical, spatial, abstract, and logical skills. In the future the increased sophistication of CAI may make it also effective in developing management and creative competencies. The only major disadvantage to the use of programmed instruction lies in the cost of developing in-house programs.

*See also* DEVELOPMENT AND TRAINING, EMPLOYEE.

### REFERENCES

Lysaught, Jerome P., and Clarence M. Williams: *A Guide to Programmed Instruction*, John Wiley & Sons, Inc., New York, 1963.

*Programmed Learning: A Bibliography of Programs and Presentation Devices*, 5th ed., Dr. Carl H. Hendershot, 4114 Ridgewood, Bay City, Mich., 48706.

Skinner, B. F.: "The Science of Learning and the Art of Teaching," *Harvard Educational Review*, Spring 1954.

STAFF/HOKE

## Programming [*See* INFORMATION SYSTEMS, MANAGEMENT (MIS), APPLIED.]

## Programs (*See* MANAGEMENT THEORY, SCIENCE, AND APPROACHES.)

## Progress review (*See* PROJECT AND TASK FORCE MANAGEMENT.)

## Project (*See* PROJECT AND TASK FORCE MANAGEMENT.)

## Project, improvement (*See* PAPER WORK SIMPLIFICATION.)

## Project coordinator, office (*See* OFFICE SPACE PLANNING AND DESIGN.)

## Project management (*See heading in Table of Contents for complete listing.*)

## Project organization (*See* ORGANIZATION STRUCTURES AND CHARTING.)

## Project planning (*See* PROGRAM PLANNING AND IMPLEMENTATION.)

## Project and task force management

A *project* is an organized program of investigation and activity carried out to reach a defined goal, often of a nonrecurring nature, with a specified terminal point. This entry is devoted to technoeconomic aspects of projects associated with product and process development, which are the chief objectives of research and development (R&D) in industry and mission-oriented public agencies. The same principles and procedures can be used for management of other types of projects, such as the design of quality control systems, production planning, sales campaigns, corporate or regional development, and social improvement programs.

Managements are flooded with ideas for new projects from both internal and external sources. Experience shows that only a very small number of these, probably less than 1 percent in most companies and agencies, will reach full-scale implementation. Screening is necessary to avoid dissipation of skilled workers and other resources. The criteria used should eliminate unlikely concepts as soon as possible without excluding innovative ideas that may lead to breakthroughs in the use of technology or other assets.

Various forms of network analysis have been developed for implementation and control of very large and complex projects with inputs from multiple independent sources. These are more elaborate than are commonly required for typical R&D, but the network philosophy should guide the management of these less exotic problems.

**Project Definition** Organizations of all types have adopted project systems to expose ideas to consistent screening and programming. For this purpose they use some form of project outline to describe the work to be done and the expected benefits.

Some exploratory effort is necessary to prepare a project outline. There is always a strong tendency to prolong exploration after sufficient information is available for a formal summary. Because this practice is likely to waste skills by delaying critical managerial review, many organizations impose limits on the amount of exploratory work permitted, for example one worker-month, before the concept must be presented in a formal way.

Public agencies often set a prescribed form for project proposals. Private organizations use forms suitable for their own criteria, using headings similar to the model shown below.

Large and complicated projects are typically broken down into a series of subprojects covering major stages to be conducted separately, often in succession because the findings of each serve as a basis for planning the next. The scope of a subproject should have a workable degree of homogeneity in skills required and scale of work. Figure P-33 illustrates a common type of subdivision for a product development project; it shows also the nature of evaluation of feasibility appropriate to each major phase. There may be justification for some overlapping of stages, but the findings of each should be reviewed critically to make sure there are no obvious bars to ultimate success of the idea.

**Model Project Outline** The following list of headings illustrates the areas of analysis included by many successful companies for evaluating project proposals.

*Title:* A short descriptive name for identification, filing, and control; a serial number is often used for convenience.

*Object:* A concise statement of the general purpose of the investigation.

*Background:* A brief summary of available information on technology and economics on which the proposal is based.

*Justification:* A preliminary estimate of the benefits if the total project is successful.

*Program:* An outline of the work to be carried out, including the organizational units to be involved.

*Duration:* An estimate of completion date.

*Personnel:* Proposed amount of effort by participants in the program.

*Cost:* A forecast of the total expense of the work, including salaries and wages, with overheads, and items of direct expense.

*Future work:* A summary of additional work to carry the project to completion, preferably prepared in consultation with other groups to be involved later.

*Cost-benefit:* As soon as feasible, a comparison of project costs with expected benefits.

*Authorization:* Signatures and dates of signing by project leader and supervising executive.

**Project Personnel and Activities** After formal approval of the outline, work moves forward according to the plan under supervision of the leader.

*Project Leader.* As much responsibility and authority as are consistent with organizational policy are delegated to the project leader. This encourages managerial development and builds morale. Managers at higher levels will be wise to leave details to the leader and to confine their supervision to general overseeing.

*Other Personnel.* Other team members, either from the same group or from some other units, are selected by the team leader and should agree to the roles he or she assigns. They should be briefed thoroughly on the project outline and its implications for their activities.

*Reporting.* The project leader installs and controls a reporting system on a need-to-know basis. Weekly reports by each key participant are a wise procedure. The writers themselves derive major benefit by systematizing their findings as a basis for planning future work. Well-prepared interim summaries facilitate the writing of more comprehensive reports.

*Review of Progress.* The team leader reviews progress and program periodically with the individuals or groups involved. Difficulties and obstacles should be overcome in such a manner as to prevent wasted effort by other, later participants. Visual aids, such as bar charts, are helpful for evaluating progress.

*Adjustment of Project Outline.* When circumstances warrant a material change in program or schedule, appropriate alteration in the project outline, as the governing document for the work, should be made and disseminated.

*Coordination with Other Functions.* It is essential that other departments, particularly those to be involved at later stages, be kept informed of progress so that they may adjust their schedules accordingly.

*Unwarranted Delays.* Perfectionists tend to hold on to their assignments too long in an effort to attain maximum performance. To counteract this inertia, the leader must decide arbitrarily to freeze the program at a satisfactory point in order that later stages may be begun.

*Abandonment of Projects.* When a decision is reached to stop a project, there is often resistance from some participants, frequently as "bootleg" work. The easiest way to terminate is to transfer their efforts to atttractive and more promising assignments. A plea is often made to do more work to round out a final report for future use; the fallacy is that if the project is later revived, the new status of technology and economics may greatly reduce the value of earlier findings.

| Criteria → / Stages ↓ | Product | Process | Marketing | Managerial interest | Raw materials | Facilities | Manufacturing | Cost-benefit | Legal aspects |
|---|---|---|---|---|---|---|---|---|---|
| Product concept | General description | Probably feasible | Probably salable | *Exploratory stage* | | | | | |
| Product development | Initial prototype | Preliminary appraisal | Preliminary approach | Conformance with plans | Preliminary selection | | | Preliminary estimate | Initial review |
| Process development | Possible modification | Basic design | | | Preliminary specifications | Initial concept | Feasibility review | Revised estimate | Preliminary review |
| Market projection | Performance evaluation | Reliability review | Specific opportunities | Confirmation of interest | | | | Revised estimate | |
| Process confirmation | Possible modification | Final design | Acceptability of product | Review of specifications | Review of specifications | Complete flow diagram | Confirmation of practicality | Semifinal estimates | Interim approval |
| Market confirmation | Firm specifications | | Confirmed opportunities | Critical review | | | | Semifinal estimates | |
| Comprehensive review | Final specifications | Confirmed design | Marketing plan | Coordination | Firm specifications | Final design | Manufacturing plan | Final estimates | Final approval |
| Management action | | | | Decision to commercialize | | | | | |
| Manufacturing mobilization | Consultation | Consultation | Information | General supervision | Procurement | Construction | Primary responsibility | Financing and costing | Patents licenses |
| Marketing mobilization | Consultation | Consultation | Primary responsibility | General supervision | Information | Information | Scheduling | Costing | Contracts |
| Commercial operation | Improvements | Improvements | Sales operations | Overseeing | Purchasing control | Adjustment | Plant operation | Cost control | Continuing review |

*(Stage groupings noted in the Managerial interest column: Exploratory stage; Development stages; Confirmation stages; Implementation stages.)*

Fig. P-33. **Progressive application of technoeconomic criteria.** *(Reproduced with permission of the publisher from Lawrence W. Bass, "Management by Task Forces: A Manual on the Operation of Interdisciplinary Teams," Lomond Books, Mt. Airy, Md., 1975.)*

**Progressive Appraisal of Feasibility** For innovative products or processes, evaluation of the probability of commercial success should be carried out periodically, particularly at the end of each major stage (cf. Fig. P-33). In conventional cellular organizations, this process requires a very effective communication system, but when interdisciplinary teams are used, the conclusions of different specialists have already been interwoven into consolidated conclusions.

When new products or processes involve customary operations of the company, the course of appraisal is simpler because of similarity to existing commercial experience. Even in these cases, however, it is recommended that the procedure of comprehensive review be carried out to avoid the delay and expense of premature commercialization.

For projects to create new product lines to serve new groups of customers, technological factors require the usual course of investigation. But marketing demands a new commercial system, with very different patterns of distribution channels, sales and promotion techniques, and trade practices.

*Defensive versus Aggressive Projects.* A valuable concept for judging the balance of the total R&D program is to classify all projects as defensive or aggressive. Defensive work is aimed at strengthening the competitive position of the present product line; it includes quality and process control, technical service, product and process improvement, and development of products and processes using modifications of current technology and marketing. Aggressive work is concerned with serving customers in new ways or in entering new commercial fields; it includes development of innovative products or processes, new product lines, and oriented long-range research.

Many executives are unaware of this distinction and assume that the major part of the technical program is devoted to glamorous new products. Actually, even progressive companies in rapidly changing fields of technology seldom devote more than 20 percent of their technical budgets to aggressive research. There are practical limits to the number of innovations they can commercialize. Other companies, feeling there is ample opportunity to expand the use of their present technology, may devote practically all their efforts to defensive activities.

**Major Stages in Development** The following tabulation of major stages describes the status of projects at critical points in development. Failure to meet all the criteria at any stage gives a sharp warning that the project should be abandoned or radically altered.

*Exploratory:* The idea appears to be sufficiently sound to undertake product development work.

*Product development:* Small-scale work demonstrates that a promising product can be made by a process that seems to be practical.

*Process development:* Work on large laboratory, or prepilot, scale confirms probable feasibility of the operation.

*Market research:* Analysis of the needs of potential customers indicates an attractive market.

*Process confirmation:* Pilot or small commercial operation confirms the earlier view of feasibility.

*Market confirmation:* Large-scale tests with industrial users or retail customers confirm market suitability of the product.

*Comprehensive review:* Coordinated opinions regarding all technical and economic facets are favorable for final management decision to commercialize. A review of this type should be carried out on all projects.

*Manufacturing mobilization:* Coordination of facilities, materials, process, operating and control procedures, and training of personnel for start-up of the plant.

*Marketing mobilization:* Coordination of all training, sales, and promotional activities to start distribution to customers as production begins.

*Commercial operation:* Activation of all programs to begin operations and sales with proper allowances for readjustment as experience requires.

**Interdisciplinary Teams** Management at all stages of project operation is greatly improved and progress is sped up by the use of interdisciplinary teams. Many organizations have successfully used task forces to meet emergencies. When the crisis is passed, however, they forget the impact of a coordinated company-wide effort and lapse into the customary pattern of isolated cells of expertise with all the disadvantages of slow, circuitous feedback of information. Experience shows that it is practical to use interdisciplinary principles as a general tonic to focus the range of skills within the organization.[1]

*Team Composition.* Each team is composed of a team leader with a collection of experts from the disciplines most appropriate to the particular stage of the investigation. He or she is subject to minimum direct supervision and has wide latitude in selecting and using the talents assembled for the task. The inertia of large groups is avoided by the device of a key group of three to five members who cover those skills which are dominant in planning and carrying out the program, coordinating the findings, and bringing the study to a practical conclusion. For a product development project, the key team might, for example, consist of a technologist as leader, with experts in quality evaluation, process engineering, and market research as associates.

*Team Leadership.* The leader should be an experienced specialist with a broad understanding of the techniques and usefulness of the other disciplines represented. He or she must function as a leader, not as a dictatorial director or manager; if the leader were a master of all component skills, no team would be needed. The leader should be given responsibility and authority for running the program with only general overseeing by superiors, except as advisers who do not intervene directly in the managerial functions.

The team leader is responsible for formulating the project, subject to executive approval, selecting and indoctrinating other team members, overseeing their performance, establishing a communications system, and coordinating the findings into official reports. He or she represents the composite talents of the team in later stages to which their work can contribute. The leader must maintain planning and budgetary control. Success depends on his or her ability to marshal the skills into a unified effort.

*Team Membership.* The other members may be from different groups or departments, and the leader may have no direct organizational authority over them; they are in a sense volunteers responsible to him or her only for the purpose of the project. The leader recruits them, with concurrence of their supervisors, for an agreed amount of effort, which is likely to be on a part-time basis for the duration of the project. Some of them serve only as consultants when needed. They are all free to seek information or advice from others, so long as they do not infringe upon the responsibilities of the leader.

*Introduction of the System.* Interdisciplinary teams obviously represent a radical departure from the usual cellular line and staff operations. They involve two channels of management: (1) the formal, hierarchial system to accommodate the individual to his or her role in the organization and (2) the informal team structure by means of which the individual applies his or her talents to problem solving as a member of a close-knit group.

**Cost of Projects and Implementation**  For critical evaluation of the merits of a project proposal, it is necessary to compare the expense of the investigation with the financial benefit expected. Social improvements are very difficult to reduce to meaningful monetary terms.

*Project Costs.* To determine the cost of carrying out a study, some measure of effort expended must be instituted. The common practice is to compile the amount of time spent by the participants in conducting their assignments. This is not, of course, a direct measure of the quality of their work, but unfortunately there is no reliable yardstick for doing this.

The recommended practice is for each project worker to keep a running record of the time spent on different projects, usually in hours although some organizations use shorter or longer intervals. The amount of time is then converted into money equivalent, preferably including all appropriate overheads. These records of effort expended and the cost thereof give project leaders a means of controlling the professional inputs devoted to the projects for which they are responsible.

Experience of many companies indicates that the cost of small-scale R&D (product and process development and market research) usually amounts to only 5 to 10 percent of the total cost of implementation. The wisdom of doing investigation on as small a scale as feasible is evident; more costly stages should be employed chiefly to confirm these initial findings, not to experiment.

The time card system may be extended to both overhead activities and to routine repetitive work (e.g., quality control), the latter summarized under collective projects. In this way the total available time of each staff member is accounted for, so that managers can schedule optimum use of the skills of the people reporting to them.

It is astounding how few organizations have realistic knowledge of the cost of carrying out their various functions. While the expense of hourly labor and clerical help is carefully analyzed, the effective use of higher-priced employees, whose contributions to the business are highly significant, is lightly passed over.

*Plant Investment.* Estimation of the cost of the completed plant is usually done by process engineers. There is extensive literature on the procedures; a few monographs are listed below. A common cause of complaint by top management is failure to provide adequately for escalation due to inflation.

*Operating Costs.* The projected expense of running a manufacturing operation is in the province of production and accounting departments.

*Marketing Costs.* Distribution expense is normally estimated by the sales department.

*Cost-Benefit.* Evaluation of expected benefits from projects compared with cost is often carried out in large organizations by special groups or departments reporting to top management.

*See also* CONTROL SYSTEMS, MANAGEMENT; ENGINEERING MANAGEMENT; NETWORK PLANNING METHODS; ORGANIZATION STRUCTURES AND CHARTING; RESEARCH AND DEVELOPMENT MANAGEMENT.

## NOTES

[1]Lawrence W. Bass, *Management by Task Forces: A Manual on the Operation of Interdisciplinary Teams*, Lomond Books, Mt. Airy, Md., 1975.

## REFERENCES

Archibald, Russell: *Managing High-Technology Programs and Projects*, John Wiley & Sons, Inc., New York, 1976.

Bass, Lawrence W.: "Industrial Research Institutes: Guidelines for Evaluation," United Nations Industrial Development Organization, New York, 1971.

Baumgartner, Stanley S.: *Project Management*, Richard D. Irwin, Inc., Homewood, Ill., 1963.

Beattie, C. J. and R. D. Reader: *Quantitative Management in R&D*, Halsted Press, New York, 1971.

Burman, P. J.: *Precedence Networks for Project Planning and Control*, McGraw-Hill Book Company, New York, 1972.

Flippo, E. B.: *Management—A Behavioral Approach*, Allyn and Bacon, Inc., Boston, 1966.

Johnson, Richard A., Fremont E. Kast, and James E. Rosenzweig: *The Theory and Management of Systems*, 3d ed., McGraw-Hill Book Company, New York, 1973.

Martin, Charles C.: *Project Management: How to Make It Work*, American Management Association, New York, 1976.

Ryan, J. Corboy: *Management and Research Management: Robert E. Krieger Pub. Co., Inc.*, Huntington, N.Y., 1972.

Sayles, Leonard R.: and Margaret K. Chandler: *Managing Large Systems*, Harper & Row, Incorporated, Publishers, New York, 1971.

Silverman, Martin: *Project Management*, John Wiley & Sons, Inc., New York, 1976.

LAWRENCE W. BASS, *Arthur D. Little, Inc.*

## Project teams (*See* INTERPERSONAL RELATIONSHIPS.)

## Projective techniques (*See* CONSUMER BEHAVIOR, MANAGERIAL RELEVANCE OF.)

## Projects, aggressive (*See* PROJECT AND TASK FORCE MANAGEMENT.)

## Projects, defensive (*See* PROJECT AND TASK FORCE MANAGEMENT.)

## Promotion (*See* PERSONNEL ADMINISTRATION.)

## Promotion, retail (*See* RETAILING MANAGEMENT.)

## Promotion of services (*See* MARKETING OF SERVICES.)

## Promotion organization (*See* ORGANIZATION ANALYSIS AND PLANNING.)

## Property, real and personal (*See* GOVERNMENT REGULATIONS, BUSINESS LAW.)

## Proprietorship, sole (*See* OWNERSHIP, LEGAL FORMS OF.)

## Proprietorship management (*See* MANAGEMENT, DEFINITIONS OF.)

## Proxy fight (*See* SHAREHOLDER RELATIONSHIPS.)

## Psychoanalytical theory (*See* CONSUMER BEHAVIOR, MANAGERIAL RELEVANCE OF.)

## Psychological tests (*See* TESTING, PSYCHOLOGICAL.)

## Public administration

The administration of government and of public affairs generally has existed since the beginnings of government. As a self-conscious profession and field of study, however, the origins of public administration lie in the last decades of the nineteenth century, principally in the United States. In practical applications, some key American cities were the centers of activity by the 1880s. Reorganization of state governments became a thrust of the movement by the Progressive Era. The central government became a focus in World War I and, much more, during and after the Great Depression. After World War II, activity extended to international and comparative administration, and by then its applications also encompassed many dimensions of public affairs which are tangential to government.

In intellectual terms, the origin of American public administration is most often identified with an 1887 essay by Woodrow Wilson, *The Study of Public Administration*, followed by Frank J. Goodnow's *Politics and Administration* (1900) and a few early treatises and texts, most notably Leonard D. White's *Introduction to the Study of Public Administration* (1st ed., 1926). From these beginnings, one conclusion merits foremost attention: Public administration has been and remains heavily dependent upon its varied and complex environment; consequently, it is a broad profession, drawing on many disciplines and based in a variety of models or paradigms, integrated in the United States by some generally accepted public interest values of constitutional democracy.

## OCCUPATIONAL SPECIALTIES

The most influential delineation of program specialties and subject matter areas in public management was adopted in 1974 by the National Association of Schools of Public Affairs and Administration (NASPAA). Part II of that matrix lists program specializations at four levels of government: urban/local, state/regional, national, and international.

**Competencies** The elaborately detailed Part I of the NASPAA matrix lists the following five broad subject areas of professional competencies to be attained by public managers:

Political, social, and economic context
Analytical tools: quantitative and nonquantitative
Individual/group/organizational dynamics
Policy analysis
Administrative/management processes

For each of these five areas, the matrix identifies characteristics of a public manager in terms of four basic elements: (1) knowledge, (2) skills, (3) public interest values, and (4) behavior.

**Occupations** Of the 12½ million employees of state and local governments and the 2¾ million federal government employees in 1977, only a small fraction would normally identify themselves with the profession of public administration. Indeed, only a fraction of 1 percent of the new entrants into public service are products of academic programs in public administration, while many who initially enter government as professionals in various program specialties or who begin as nonprofessionals later engage in midcareer training and/or education for more responsible administrative responsibilities.

The "PA professionals" are typically (1) general managers, such as city or county managers; (2) staff specialists in such fields as (*a*) budget, finance, or audits, (*b*) personnel and/or labor relations, (*c*) property and general services management, and (*d*) information systems; (3) policy/program analysts, often with program evaluation specialties; and (4) program managers, either out of other specialties, such as ballistics or health services, or with preparation as generalists in varied program areas.

**Specialization** Although academic public administration has often stressed generalist functions, government in the United States has characteristically relied on specialists, even at the highest career levels. In the federal government, for example, 41 percent of the top career executives (the *supergrades*) are in scientific and engineering specialties, and about three-fourths of the total are program managers, commonly drawn from the specialties managed (with obvious overlap of these groupings).

**Executives** Typically, top executive positions in government in the United States represent a smaller percentage of total employees than the ratio in private enterprise. For example, only 0.5 percent of the federal government positions are at executive levels. Noncareer political appointees typically fill the highest-level positions in the federal government and in state governments and in some politically managed local governments. In the federal government, for example, in 1977 there were about 625 positions at Executive Levels I through V (I = Secretary of Defense; III = Chairman, U.S. Civil Service Commission; V = an Assistant Secretary or Bureau Director), nearly all of them political appointees. There were about 10,600 executives in the supergrade equivalents (GS-16, 17, 18), and from 12 to 25 percent of those positions have generally been filled politically.

## THE PUBLIC ENVIRONMENT

The governmental/public affairs environment of public administration accounts for distinctions in its ideas and practices from "generic" administration. Changing social, economic, and technological contexts also condition the field, in many respects just as in business or other administration.

When government in the United States was relatively limited in powers and small in fact, "administration" per se was of little concern. By the 1800s, however, administration of government became a topic of some interest; by the 1920s public administration was a recognized field of study and practice; and by the 1970s, with over one-third of U.S. gross national product consumed through governments, the field had become a dominant concern.

**Constitutional Basis**  The most basic values of American public administration are inherited from the ideas of constitutional democracy which define the political system. Those are the classic values of human dignity and rule of law, dynamic values which have been defined by changing aspiration and experience, but which remain essential imperatives. American constitutional concepts designed to advance those values are likewise most fundamental: popular sovereignty and limited government, separation of powers, federalism, and judicial review.

Although the above values and concepts are basic to American public administration, the field drew heavily on the ideas and practices of business at its beginnings, and it was deliberately moved in that direction by Leonard White and other leaders of the 1920s. With the emergence of a mixed private-public enterprise system in the United States by the post–World War II period, generic administration came to be common to much of business, government, and other organizations, with extensive exchange of ideas and practices.

**Bureaucratic Context**  The principal ideas of public administration from the 1880s through its first 60 years were centralization, economy and efficiency, and separation of politics from administration. Centralization became the bureaucratizing thrust of the field, most evident by the close of the Progressive Era in the city management movement and in state reorganization efforts. The field was then dominated by the ideas of scientific management, which likewise influenced business and engineering, and by aspirations to become a clear discipline. It thus sought to discover and to implement the "one best way" in government administration. The traditional bureaucratic model of public administration was born out of those efforts, with the following "principles" of organization more or less prescribed as guides by the 1930s:

1. External policy direction and control
2. Hierarchical conformation and executive leadership
3. Coordinated staff services under a chief executive
4. Departmentalization according to functions
5. Merit selection and protection of personnel—and objective detachment
6. Organizational compliance based on internalization of society's basic values

Academic study of public administration at first relied heavily on case studies and comparison. The field also drew early on bureaucratic theory in sociology and law. The Human Relations Movement,

which swept business after the Hawthorne Studies, also influenced public administration. Behavioral theory from the social sciences likewise influenced the field enormously in the 1950s and 1960s.

**Performance Effectiveness**  One most important practical dimension of contemporary public administration began to emerge in the 1940s—a concern with effectiveness as an administrative responsibility, along with the traditional concerns of efficiency and economy. In effect, this was a reflection of increasing limits on the practicality of separation of politics (and policy making) from administration. In line with this changing orientation, budgeting and related management developments shifted from simple control and line-item budgeting to performance budgeting, beginning as an idea in the late 1930s and coming into general practice in the late 1950s. Program budgeting followed in the 1960s, often as a formal planning-programming-budgeting system (PPBS). More varied, situational orientations followed in the early 1970s, with the adoption of an open approach to management by objectives (MBO) in the federal government. Program evaluation next became the dominant orientation, in part as a dimension of MBO, but also as a principal congressional concern. Zero-base budgeting and "sunset" provisions for periodic review of needs for public programs thus became possible. Policy analysis supported these developments, drawing particularly on the discipline of economics and on information technologies and knowledge capabilities of cybernetics. By the 1970s, social indicators were being developed to add to economic indicators for macroperspectives on social problems and government policies.

**Modern Concepts**  At the organizational level, modifications or alternatives to elements of the traditional bureaucratic model came into practice in the 1960s, with some of these open-systems or dispersed-authority concepts found in government:

1. Dispersion of power and responsibility
2. Greater emphasis on processes and on fluid functional relationships than on hard-boundary structures
3. Open systems with widely shared information and access to expertise and technical services
4. Inability of closed elites to block entry into organizational systems
5. Recognized interdependence—such linkages as to resolve conflicts with minimal dissonance and to promote generation and accomplishment of changing goals
6. Organization on a real-time basis, open to the future, in a system of institutionalized, generated change

## TRENDS

The future of public administration will be conditioned by its changing and varied contexts, as it has been from its beginnings, with the following dimensions among the likely important influences on the last decades of the twentieth century in the United States:

1. Work force, productivity, and consumption trends, such as the shift between 1947 and 1976 from over one-half of United States workers producing tangibles to two-thirds producing intangibles, and the federal budget changes between 1960 and 1976 from over 50 percent to less than 28 percent for defense, space, and foreign affairs and from less than 25 percent to more than 50 percent for human resources activities.

2. Scientific, technological, and cybernetic trends, such as the knowledge and information processing revolutions between the 1950s and 1970s.

3. Domestic social forces, such as the racial and sexual equality movements since World War II and the unionization movement, which has become much stronger in government than in the private sector, with over two-thirds of federal employees in exclusive units in the mid 1970s.

4. International forces, such as the past moves of the United States from isolationism to internationalism to world supremacy to a position in the 1970s of international economic interdependence without supremacy.

5. Probably most important, the nation's political and value frameworks. In the United States, as long as constitutional democracy survives, the most important of these will remain the concept of popular sovereignty and limited government to facilitate people seeking human dignity and rule of law or reasonableness in social relationships.

*See also* COLLEGE AND UNIVERSITY ADMINISTRATION; EGALITARIANISM; GOVERNMENT RELATIONS AND SERVICES; HEALTH INSTITUTIONS, MANAGEMENT OF; HOSPITAL ADMINISTRATION; NOT-FOR-PROFIT ORGANIZATIONS, MANAGEMENT OF.

### REFERENCES

*Guidelines and Standards for Professional Masters Degree Programs in Public Affairs/Public Administration,* National Association of Schools of Public Affairs and Administration, Washington, 1974.

Mosher, Frederick, C., (ed.): *American Public Administration: Past, Present, Future,* University of Alabama Press, University, 1975.

*Public Administration Review,* bimonthly journal of the American Society for Public Administration, 1225 Connecticut Ave., N.W. Washington, D.C. 20036. *See* especially "Special Bicentennial Issue: American Public Administration in Three Centuries," vol. 36, no. 5, September–October 1976.

*United States Organization Manual,* Washington. Annual.

Waldo, Dwight: *The Administrative State,* The Ronald Press Company, New York, 1948.

CHESTER A. NEWLAND, *University of Southern California*

# Public and community relations

"Public Relations is the management function which evaluates public attitudes, identifies the policies and procedures of an individual or an organization with the public interest, and plans and executes a program of action to earn public understanding and acceptance." This is the official definition given in *Public Relations News,* the pioneer weekly newsletter in the field of public relations.

Organizations must communicate to survive. On the positive side, good communications can help sell products, improve worker productivity, maintain good relations with local, state, and federal governments, and enhance an organization's ability to attract capital needed to grow. On the other hand, poor communications can make the company more vulnerable to increasing external pressures from government, consumers, community groups, and the press.

Despite impressive progress and acceptance by a great many forward-thinking companies, public relations is frequently misused and underutilized. Often, there is resistance to giving public relations (PR) the full recognition and application that it deserves. This is not necessarily a conscious decision, but rather the result of insufficient understanding and appreciation of underlying values. Over and over, PR capabilities are used randomly in defensive, crisis-oriented situations.

Many managers have yet to perceive how public relations can be utilized to *avoid* crises. A case in point is the delayed and generally inadequate response of industry to environmental pollution criticisms. Proper PR perspective would have disclosed long in advance the public's impending ecological challenges. Furthermore, even after environmental activists created massive public concern, industry generally adopted a low-key defensive posture. Even though many companies (voluntarily or otherwise) do an effective environmental job and have spent billions in the process, they fail, for the most part, to bring their accomplishments before the public.

The world often perceives a significant difference between two otherwise evenly matched competitors. One company seems to do everything right and get all the credit. The other produces raised eyebrows and quizzical looks when its name is mentioned. Such quick evaluation of organizations goes on all the time, and it can and does affect the bottom line. Public relations, therefore, is often a major factor in the development of what has come to be called *the corporate image*. For this reason, if no other, corporate management expects its key people to practice the art of public relations in the plant, in the community, among customers and suppliers, with government, and special interest groups of all kinds. This responsibility can be carried out with varying degrees of success, dependent on three chief elements: sensitivity, communications resources, and management leadership.

## SENSITIVITY

Much has been written in the field of industrial relations on how management can "keep its ear to the ground," how to set up early warning systems to detect employee trouble before it happens, ways and means of taking periodic morale readings, and so on. These constitute mechanisms for listening, a crucial component of the communications process. Listening helps isolate and define both the problems and the opportunities among the various publics important to the organization.

**Surveillance Systems** In order to listen better, it makes sense to set up a structure for assessing the level of corporate acceptance among internal and external groups. This, in turn, helps define communications needs and opportunities.

In small companies, there is no need for an elaborate system. The top executive need only put the subject of "public relations" on the agenda periodically in operating committee meetings. In the smaller organizations, top management is also far less insulated by layers of management. Good and bad "vibrations" come through without much distortion—except where executives feel constrained about revealing imperfections in their areas of responsibility. To guard against this, top management must work hard to encourage straight talk rather than cover up. Unfortunately, some managers deny the existence of communications problems until they are about ready to explode.

For the medium and larger-sized organization, it has become fairly common to conduct periodic attitude surveys, performed with the assistance of an outside firm. The attitudes surveyed are most often those of employees, but the same technique can be used effectively to determine the attitudes of community leaders, local press, and various levels of government. It is a truism that the very act of making an attitude survey is a mark per se of good public relations, since it suggests that the organization cares about its acceptance.

**Communications Assessment** There should also be a continuing sensitivity to the need for better communications. When these needs come to the surface, either via some early warning technique or formal surveys, they should be analyzed and approached as major potential roadblocks to the forward movement of the organization. It is important to distinguish between words (what the company says) and deeds (what the company does) in the business of communicating. Deeds are often the best communicators in terms of getting the attention of an audience, but they do not necessarily tell the full story by themselves. Consider a negative example of the company that suddenly must close down one of its two plants in town, and then refuses to explain its action in anything more than a terse statement on the plant bulletin board. Typically, the community goes into a state of shock. Then come the rumors. Before the situation can be rescued, morale and productivity in the remaining plant have plummeted.

**Corporate Visibility** Words and deeds must work together, one in support of the other. When there are deeds without words, there is incomplete communications, which can lead to a variety of misunderstandings. When there are words without deeds, the enterprise can eventually lose its credibility. It is also important to acknowledge that a firm is constantly communicating something, whether it is aware of it or not. Organizations have visibility from a number of different sources:

1. From the physical presence: what people see of a company's buildings, parking lots, smokestacks, architectural and environmental impact.

2. From how an organization treats its people: employees, customers, suppliers.

3. From what the media say about the organization: in the local and regional press, newspapers and magazines, professional publications, radio and television, house organs and club publications.

4. From how a company discloses itself: through printed reports, bulletins, press releases, speech-making, films, and participation in community activities.

5. From the reputation an organization has earned on the professional, political, industry, and consumer levels: how those people whose good will and approval are essential to an organization are talking about it.

**Internal Insights**  Management must also give thought to its own attitudes and be sensitive to these at all times. It must ask such questions as: What kind of organization do *we* operate? What do we think of external groups? Do we simply want to use them as part of our plan to achieve corporate objectives? Or do we think they have something important to contribute? Do we say one thing and do another? Do we feel a real sense of responsibility to employees and the community? Answers to these questions help form the basis for external judgment of a company and how people react to the company and to its management.

**Press Relationships**  Excellent sources of insights about a company's management are the press people locally and the trade press nationally. Public relations professionals often start with an audit of local press attitudes, because it is the local reporter who can draw a graphic picture of community opinion, and sometimes even employee opinion, of the organization. It is true that editors and reporters sometimes see a company with bias. For example, a company may spend a lot of money to clean up emissions and be criticized by the press for not spending more. In being sensitive, however, it helps to listen to these critics and try to hear what they are really saying. Often what they really mean is something like the following:

"You have *not* been a good neighbor, historically."

"Neither you nor your people take an active interest in community betterment."

"You don't ever give us the bad news, so we have to get it elsewhere."

"You try too hard to get your good stories printed, as if they were full-page advertisements."

"You didn't tell the truth several times in the past.

"Your top people are inaccessible."

"You simply don't care."

The press is not the enemy. The real enemy is management's sense of frustration over its inability to convert the press to the company point of view. Yet there are few situations where press relations did not improve significantly when a sincere effort was made by an organization to improve them.

## COMMUNICATIONS RESOURCES

A perceptive management quickly recognizes the importance of good communications, organizes its people to meet the needs, and supports them with appropriate budgets. There is no good rule of thumb to suggest what kind of public relations staff or outside counsel may be needed. Some very small organizations employ an internal staff and an outside agency as well. Some fairly large organizations may have neither. Both may say that they are doing just fine.

The important point to make is that there should be at least one person in the company whose prime responsibility is: (1) to assess communications on a continuing basis, (2) to make recommendations for improvement, (3) to develop the capability of executing such programs with or without help, and (4) to insist upon and justify the budget needed to support them. This individual needs the attention and full support of the chief executive. Without it, any program is doomed.

**The Plan**  Once such a person is on staff, management should demand an annual review of past activity, a critical evaluation of the company's relationship with its key publics, and a very specific public relations plan or program for the year ahead. From this kind of planning come the set of corporate public relations objectives, the strategy for achieving them, the tactics for carrying them out effectively, and the budgets and timetables that are required. The making of the plan forces management at least once a year to give due consideration to communications problems and opportunities.

**Internal Expertise**  The internal executive must try to understand the style or personality of the company and seek to project it in a variety of ways. There is more to public relations than publicity and more to publicity than press releases. This person often comes to the company from a newspaper, magazine, radio, or television background, but this is by no means the sine qua non of a successful public relations executive. Journalism experience, however, is sound evidence of interest in, and awareness of, the art and science of communications.

Many companies, of course, function without internal staff by assigning certain communications responsibilities to key staff people. For example:

1. Responsibility for employee and community relations including local press may be assigned to the chief of personnel.

2. The chief financial officer may deal with the financial community and with the financial press.

3. The sales manager (together with the advertising manager) may handle publicity about the company's products and/or services.

4. The president might typically speak for the company on larger questions, both within the industry and in the total business environment.

Unless this arrangement is coordinated by a single executive, however, this approach may result in community relations and publicity activities that are inconsistent or even counterproductive.

**Outside Expertise**   The use of outside counsel offers several advantages whether or not there is an internal public relations staff. This counsel, under any circumstances, however, needs access to management.

*Program Responsibility.* Outside counsel can relieve internal work loads by taking on full responsibility. If so, it makes an assessment of the company's needs, drafts the public relations objectives and program, implements it, and evaluates performance continually in the light of changing corporate requirements.

*Audit Responsibility.*  Sometimes a company retains outside counsel solely for the purpose of (1) performing an objective audit of corporate communications and (2) preparing a specific long-range program for improving the entire spectrum of communications. Part of any agency assignment can be an evaluation of the existing communications structure, recommendations on the type of internal staffing required, and, sometimes, even going out and finding the right people.

*Specialized Skills.*  In many cases, it is too costly for a firm to employ on its own payroll PR specialists such as speech writers, financial relations experts, television placement people, researchers, arts counselors, and specialists in government relations, social affairs, and other vital areas. The full-service PR agency typically has a battery of such specialists immediately available for client assignments.

## MANAGEMENT LEADERSHIP

It is worth repeating that a PR program without the interest and participation of top management is doomed to failure. This is true because the chief executive officer personalizes the company and projects the attitudes, style, and personality of the organization. It is the chief executive officer who provides the impetus for serious public relations programs and then passes his or her standards, style, and enthusiasm down the line to other managers in the organization.

Top management typically recognizes its responsibility for the total communications function. Many company presidents spend the great majority of their time communicating—to their employees and managers, bankers and security analysts, mayors and city councils, engineers and suppliers, customers and potential customers. These corporate

executives do so because they recognize quickly enough that the public relations program supports short- and long-range corporate goals.

**Reactive or Proactive?**   Some companies are content to handle public relations in a reactive manner so as to "keep a low profile" or "not to make waves." Obviously, these companies are often on the defensive in communications.

Other top managers refuse to sit still waiting for events to which they can respond. In contrast, they use creative means to generate news about their ideas, their company, and their products. These are the companies that want to "lead the pack" and to become industry leaders.

Both kinds of companies exist successfully. Regardless of approach, however, it is important to remember that public relations should not be turned on and off like a faucet. It is neither effective nor economical to bring in public relations people to solve a problem and then send them packing once the problem is solved. Use of PR for emergencies only paves the way for more crises. In the long run, it is less expensive and more efficient to accept the vital importance of the public relations function, to invite public relations thinking at key corporate meetings, and to support positive and continuing programs designed to help the company reach its objectives. In this way, an organization has a better chance to create a real deterrent to communications troubles and costly surprises for management.

**Effective Guidelines**   Managers who are sophisticated in public relations follow certain fundamental practices. These are some of them:

1.  Have a key person inside the company who is designated to outsiders and insiders as the information contact person. That person becomes the conduit for receiving and disseminating information. Without some centralization of control, there can be chaos.

2.  When outsiders such as reporters or local groups get in touch directly with executives other than the contact person, those executives should immediately report the nature of the discussion to the contact person. The information specialist should be kept apprised of all external contacts made with corporate executives. That way, he or she can perform more effectively. A single responsible person can better evaluate the company's position in the community, can help capitalize on public relations opportunities, can coordinate company statements, and can clarify, when necessary, remarks that may have been confusing or in any way in need of improvement.

3.  Maintain an early warning system to detect

communications problems. This can take several forms:

*a.* Regular meetings with local, national, and trade press are used by sophisticated executives just as much to get information as to give it.

*b.* Monitoring of letters and evaluation of calls from customers and critics, while often disregarded, provide indicators of trouble trends.

*c.* Visits to Washington and to appropriate state capitols can provide signals of upcoming legislation that can affect the organization positively or negatively.

*d.* Regular sessions with investment bankers, commercial bankers, and security analysts are essential. Not only can the company story be presented to this vital public, but management can also listen to assessments of the organization, its performance and its prospects. It is the job of the financial community to worry about its investments, and if it is worried about a firm, that firm has ample cause to be worried about itself.

*e.* Sensitivity to rumors is essential. Sometimes, in listening, management will hear nothing more than vague rumors. Rumors left alone, however, can assume the substance of fact. Skilled information specialists need to deal immediately and forcefully with these kinds of problems.

4. Make all executives aware of their public information responsibility. Are they allowed to speak directly to the press? Can they accept dates for speeches? Do they need to clear statements in advance of delivery? Are there company positions on certain crucial matters? The communications role of each executive should be clearly defined.

5. Do not try to "use" the press to solve company problems. Many executives feel that the only time to talk to journalists is when the company needs *them*—to help sell its products or to explain its position or to correct misconceptions on the part of customers, employees, or the community. While these are certainly excellent reasons to be in touch with the press, it is also vital that there be continuing contact with reporters and editors to keep them informed of what the company is doing even if there is no important news to report. This provides an ongoing opportunity to create a better understanding of the company in an easy, relaxed atmosphere.

6. When trouble hits, try to get the whole thing over fast. Everyone knows about the Watergate scandal. It was a disaster made worse by the attempt to cover up. This triggered an almost endless succession of new discoveries, which made bigger and bigger headlines and destroyed the credibility of government spokesmen. Let good news linger as long as possible, but expel bad news—*all* of it—fast.

7. Do not forget the importance of communications to *all* employees. There *is* a jungle telegraph that tells them what is really going on inside the company, so it makes a lot of sense to carry out an employee communications program that carefully explains the rationale of corporate policies and programs. If employees are on the company's side, it is a big help, with everything from productivity to publicity. If employees are disaffected, the company can be in deep trouble, regardless of its external PR effort.

8. Continuing contact is also the secret of improving labor-management relations, customer relations, financial relations, etc. The corporate organization must be out there telling its story in good times and in bad. If the key publics understand what the company is doing and why, the company will more often than not find that it has some friends out there when it needs them most.

*See also* ATTITUDE SURVEYS; ASSOCIATIONS, TRADE AND PROFESSIONAL; COMMUNICATIONS, EMPLOYEE; COMMUNICATIONS, ORGANIZATIONAL; CONFERENCE LEADERSHIP; CONFERENCES AND MEETINGS, PLANNING FOR; CONSUMERISM AND CONSUMER PROTECTION LEGISLATION; GOVERNMENT RELATIONS AND SERVICES; MARKETING OF SERVICES, PROFESSIONAL; SHAREHOLDER RELATIONS; SOCIAL RESPONSIBILITY OF BUSINESS.

## REFERENCES

Canfield, Bertrand R., and H. F. Moore: *Public Relations Principles*, 6th ed., Richard D. Irwin, Homewood, Ill., 1973.

Center, Allen H.: *Public Relations Practices*, Prentice-Hall, Inc., Englewood Cliffs, N.J., 1975.

Marston, John: *The Nature of Public Relations*, McGraw-Hill Book Company, New York, 1963.

Norton, Alice, (ed.): *Public Relations Information Sources*, Gale Research Company, Detroit, 1970.

*Public Relations and Publicity Style Book*, 4th ed., N. W. Ayer & Son, Inc., Philadelphia, 1973.

Stephenson, Howard, (ed.): *Handbook of Public Relations*, 2d ed., McGraw-Hill Book Company, New York, 1971.

Wilkens, Henry T.: "Positive Approaches to Negative News," *Public Relations Journal*, January 1977.

NORMAN WEISSMAN, *Ruder and Finn, Inc.*

# Public environment (*See* PUBLIC ADMINISTRATION.)

**Public health**  (*See* HEALTH INSTITUTIONS, MANAGEMENT OF.)

**Public health service**  (*See* HEALTH SERVICES, PLANNING FOR.)

**Public markets**  (*See* MARKET, PUBLIC.)

**Public-oriented managers**  (*See* MANAGEMENT, FUTURE OF.)

**Public relations, international**  (*See* INTERNATIONAL OPERATIONS AND MANAGEMENT IN MULTINATIONAL COMPANIES.)

**Public sector, management in**  (*See* PUBLIC ADMINISTRATION.)

**Publicity**  (*See* PUBLIC AND COMMUNITY RELATIONS.)

**Purchasing, industrial**  (*See* MARKETING, INDUSTRIAL.)

**Purchasing, inventory, and materials management**  (*See heading in Table of Contents for complete listing.*)

**Purchasing, speculative**  (*See* PURCHASING MANAGEMENT.)

## Purchasing management

Emphasis placed on purchasing shifts constantly among various aspects of total procurement management, depending on which stage of the business cycle purchases are made in. Purchasing has been one of the last management functions to be handled by professionalized practitioners because it was one of the last responsibilities management delegated as companies grew in size. Previously the function was retained at the very top because major buying decisions greatly affected profitability. Purchasing still has this tremendous leverage on profitability, but increasingly, top managers have had to let go of buying decisions. Yet, to one degree or another, management is always involved, especially on major procurements.

**Resource Acquisition**  One term frequently used for the procurement function is *resource acquisition*. Vendors or suppliers are "extensions" of a company's production line, manufacturing process, or service operation. A business can be thought of as acquiring its work force, its materials, its finances, and the like; and it is in this sense that the materials acquired have been termed *resources acquisitioned*.

The complete process, from the development of need to the end user, might more properly be termed *economic supply assurance*, because purchasing has a long-range objective of both supply continuity and economic supply. Regardless of terminology and scope, with material costs at about 53 percent of many companies' sales dollar, recurring profit squeezes have focused greater emphasis on the savings potential in prudent purchasing and control of materials.

### ORGANIZATIONAL POSITION

There is no typical purchasing organization, but there are hybrids of all kinds. For purchasing personnel to perform successfully, the department must be well integrated within its parent organization. Much of purchasing's activities, however, occur in the marketplace in confrontation with conflicting interests. Thus the place of purchasing within the organization has considerable impact on the function's effectiveness.

An example of an organization for a complex purchasing operation spending $200 million is depicted in Fig. P-34.

Initially, purchasing was the domain of the chief executive. As companies grew in size, however, the buying function was often assigned to the production department because it consumed most materials purchased. While some companies follow this practice today, there has been a clear trend since World War II to separate purchasing from production. By the late 1950s, independent purchasing departments had become commonplace. Today, most purchasing officials report to top management.

Corporate, or headquarters, purchasing is typically organized quite differently from plant or divisional purchasing. In simple, one-plant companies, purchasing can be a small department with one head

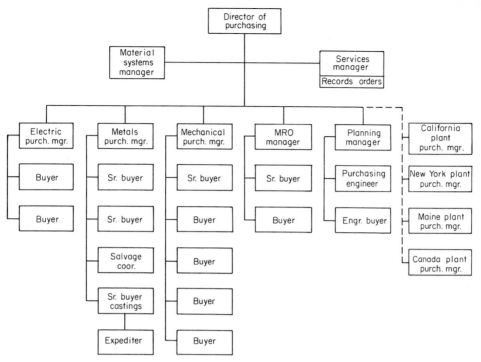

**Fig. P-34. Organization chart of central purchasing operation located at headquarters with decentralized buying at branch plants.**

reporting to either the president, manufacturing vice-president, or plant manager. Or it can be considered part of a materials organization and can report to a materials manager. Some authorities who study the system of decision making pertaining to materials systems prefer to group all activities that play a role within one total system and under the control of one head. Other advocates extend the procurement scope to include physical distribution, traffic, warehousing, and stores and use the term *materials* or *logistics management*. Considerable controversy exists as to whether this is desirable. Proponents claim conflicts are lessened and control improved. Opponents argue that purchasing, representing the vendor interface, has more than enough in handling material acquisition alone. Usually, the determining factor is the magnitude of impact of purchased material on profitability, although inventory may sometimes be the more important area to be controlled.

Organization of the purchasing activity often depends on how management "sees" the purchasing function within its total operation. Purchasing does not exist in a vacuum; it operates within the frame-

work determined by management. In practice, it reports to various management levels depending upon whether the company is large or small, centralized or very diverse and decentralized. In short, purchasing mirrors management's philosophy and structure of its operations. At the same time, however, the purchasing function often affects other departments' performance. Accordingly, production frequently prefers purchasing under its control; others see it as part of the financial function. For this reason, it is not unusual to find purchasing reporting almost anywhere in an organization. As a general rule, where the purchasing dollar spent is a large percent of expenditures, purchasing reports at a very high level.

**Relationships with Other Functions** It is doubtful that any other function has greater interrelationships than purchasing, not only within its own company but with the outside supplier organization. A variety of influences affect every buy. They range from one extreme where the buyer exerts total influence to one where the buyer has very little influence. This spectrum of buying influences properly reflects the composite needs of the operating concern. But this reality causes misunderstanding and ambiguity as to how purchasing operates and affects its relationships with other functions.

*Settlement of Conflicts.* Purchasing, on the fringe of the production sphere yet usually independent, might be described as being in conflict with two worlds: that of the company it represents and of the supplying interests. It must frequently settle material disputes such as disagreements between requesting departments and vendors as to whether quality is acceptable and whether the delivery requirement can be met and at what cost. Rejected purchases must be adjusted, costs controlled, and replacements made. While many operating functions have a large stake in what purchasing does, it often represents a very narrow interest to the vendor. Purchasing, then, must balance the interest of its own company with that of the vendor to protect long-range availability and to maintain its company's integrity. This is a role that may never completely satisfy everyone, neither management nor supplier. Yet, if purchasing is to adjust disputes, it has to find a common ground for settlement.

*Impact on Performance.* Purchasing cuts across every major function. As a result, purchasing capability greatly influences the performance of others. This makes its contributions and problems more apparent. Failures of purchasing to perform are immediately visible, and the information top management receives too often appears to be negative. Purchasing's relationships are numerous and include those with the comptroller, finance, legal, plant management, production control, data processing, information systems, quality control, top management, traffic, logistics, audit, receiving department, engineering, stores, sales or marketing, international, government liaison, administration, and personnel. Each involvement is different. Engineering needs help with its new materials search and expects cost reduction cooperation and guidance when seeking samples. The comptroller is interested in accurate estimates of cash discounts earned, what dollars of commitment need to be covered, and predictions as to future material cost trends, etc. Production control expects prompt processing of its needs: it wants vendor deliveries on time and assistance in keeping the inventories down. And so it goes. In turn, purchasing must secure maximum cooperation from all other departments in order to represent the company successfully. Purchasing is always responsible for supplier performance. How well purchasing serves others will to a large degree determine how much authority purchasing really can exert in buying control.

*With Engineering.* While the major interrelationship is with the production operation, the most vital relationship is usually with engineering. In the area of controlling material costs, the engineer plays a vital role by creating specifications and influencing source selection. There is no substitute for effective liaison between purchasing and engineering.

*With Vendor Sales.* A buyer must be firm when dealing with outside suppliers and vendor salespeople, but he or she must also be fair. A buyer must build a reputation for fair dealing and integrity and must give competition a chance. A buyer has to be open, making unbiased judgments and giving consideration to seller's difficulties in trying to perform.

## PERFORMANCE MEASURES

Purchasing performance can and should be measured. Experience indicates, however, that comparisons with other purchasing operations can be misleading. A better, more useful measure is to record the *trend* of performance with respect to past performance.[1] Trend measurements cover three basic areas: conceptual, behavorial, and resultant. Conceptual and behavorial measures are those associated with management-by-objective goals. Resultant measurements are the statistical ones: dollars saved, reductions of purchase orders issued, work load reductions, etc. No composite index seems to suffice or to replace interpretive judgment when using specific measurement information. Data for over at least a 5-year period should be used. Table P-15 illustrates some of the more useful data which can be incorporated as measurements of purchasing performance.

Standard cost performance as it pertains to material costs is also useful as a measurement of purchasing performance. Purchasing's control of its material expenditures provides another meaningful measurement. A variance report, chart form, is useful for indicating the trend of material costs. When this trend is compared to material indexes such as the Wholesale Price Index (WPI), it gives some indication as to whether expenditures are greater or less than the general material price changes.

Purchasing's contribution to return on invested capital for the company overall provides an interesting measurement. Calculations of the company's income statement with and without known purchasing savings shows the effect of a purchase saving dollar on the ROI. It is magnified manyfold. A reduced cost of material purchased reflects in both the profit margin and the investment turnover, so there is a double-barreled effect on return on investment.

**TABLE P-15  Data Chart on Indicators of Purchasing Efficiency**

| No. | Factor | Year | | | | |
|---|---|---|---|---|---|---|
| | | 1 | 2 | 3 | 4 | 5 |
| 1 | Purchases per year, $ mill. | 12.4 | 16.6 | 20.4 | 16.8 | 18.0 |
| 2 | Sales per year, $ mill. | 24.3 | 33.0 | 41.5 | 33.6 | 35.7 |
| 3 | $\dfrac{\text{Purchases}}{\text{Sales}}$ (%) | 51.0 | 50.2 | 49.0 | 50.0 | 50.5 |
| 4 | No. of purchase orders | 24,909 | 25,530 | 25,655 | 26,230 | 26,000 |
| 5 | $\dfrac{\text{Purchasing employees}}{\text{Total employees}}$ | $\dfrac{1}{124}$ | $\dfrac{1}{122}$ | $\dfrac{1}{126}$ | $\dfrac{1}{131}$ | $\dfrac{1}{146}$ |
| 6 | Cost of purchasing dept., $ | 120,000 | 140,000 | 153,500 | 150,000 | 152,000 |
| 7 | Cost per purchase order, $ | 4.83 | 5.69 | 5.97 | 5.73 | 5.85 |
| 8 | Saving per year, $ | 125,200 | 127,000 | 321,000 | 353,000 | 295,000 |
| 9 | $\dfrac{\text{Saving}}{\text{Purchases}}$ (%) | 1.01 | 0.77 | 1.58 | 2.10 | 1.64 |
| 10 | Purchased material price index % increase (Base = 100) | 50.1 | 51.2 | 55.3 | 58.1 | 61.0 |

## PURCHASING ETHICS

Because of the nature of the work, purchasing personnel are often confronted with questions of ethics. Buying decisions must stand scrutiny, especially where price discrimination may be an issue or where other legal technicalities prevail. And because the behavior of purchasing people is always subject to challenge, it should be above suspicion. High personal integrity and moral conviction are prerequisites in dealing with ethical buying questions. As in most ethical matters, there are no absolute guidelines. There *are* legitimate business expenditures for trade promotions, sales, and advertising; and many of these are aimed at the purchasing professional. Rightfully, a salesperson's purpose in contacting buyers is to influence the buyer's choice. Hopefully, this influence is based mainly on the superior features, price or service, or other legitimate inducements. The gray area involving ethics occurs when side inducements are offered the buyer. Vendor influence, such as gifts or entertainment, is discouraged and frequently forbidden by company policy. When money is involved, it is generally illegal. Bribery or "kickback" is not condoned by any responsible company. Conflict of interest is generally avoided by requiring key employees to sign affidavits that they are not involved in investments with, or otherwise tied to, any supplier.

Unquestionably, the best answer for anyone involved in the buying profession is to stay away from situations judged by others to be an influence in reaching buying decisions. All business relationships should be conducted in such a manner that no one has an opportunity to assume improper influence.

## PURCHASING SPECIFICATIONS

Without purchase specifications, and a related identification code, the purchasing department would be doomed to verbal descriptions. Purchases would be either impossible to audit or a nightmare of detailed wordage. Specification sheets enable an item to be purchased repetitively and economically through a system of codes. Additionally, without concise, accurate, and complete specifications the process of receiving and checking incoming shipments for quality would be ineffective.

Basically, a *specification* is simply a description of what is required. It may take the form of (1) a brand or trade name, (2) reference to explicit mechanical and/or chemical properties, (3) written description, (4) method by which the item is produced, or (5) end use intended and how it is to perform. It may refer to certain industrial or society standard specifications already established, such as by ASME, ASTM, SAE, and the like. Another method of specification is by a sample that is to be reproduced.

Buying by brand or trade name places the trust entirely with the supplier's ability to produce quality. Preferably two brands will be specified so there is some competition available.

Specifications are typically supported and detailed by code sheet and/or blueprint. These are the best specifications in that they illustrate the item precisely and in great detail. Detailed specifications are mandatory for such items as forgings, castings, dies, and special machine parts.

Specification by performance is very desirable because it holds the supplier liable for operation. This also leaves the vendor free to furnish whatever he or she deems desirable so long as it works. This is often necessary if the buying company has little experience or knowledge as to how to specify what is required.

Specification by sample should be avoided if possible; it can be confusing as to what sample was submitted. There are times, however, when sample buying is the only method available.

A proper specification should be as simple and concise as possible to allow the supplier to provide what is required. It should have an identification so that it can be referred to. It should have reasonable tolerances that do not inhibit the supplier unnecessarily, causing increased cost. It should allow at least several companies to participate in the business. Above all it should be capable of allowing inspection when the material is received.

## SOURCES OF SUPPLY

Other than negotiating for the actual price, source selection is unquestionably purchasing's most vital function. It is the buyer's knowledge as to *who* can furnish the item to be procured that initiates the inquiry. A request for quotation may be initiated formally in writing or by phone or personal visit.

**Vendor Selection** Factors to be considered in vendor selection and evaluation include the following:

*Quality Factors.* These include (1) consistent ability to meet specifications, (2) technical capability (including research), (3) performance, and (4) life expectancy.

*Cost Factors.* These include (1) total cost of using product, (2) price, (3) price stability, (4) freight, (5) financial stability, and (6) ability to remain competitive and profitable.

*Service Factors.* These include (1) repair service availability, (2) delivery performance, (3) location, as affects transportation cost and transit time, (4) accuracy of information on progress of orders, (5) operation control (quality and inventory systems), (6) desire for business, (7) warranties and claims adjustments for faulty goods, (8) technical aid, and (9) compliance with needs.

*Miscellaneous Factors.* These include (1) production facilities and capacity, (2) ability to handle seasonal volume, (3) management, (4) reputation, and (5) performance history.

A vendor who serves well over an extended period makes potentially a better source of supply than one untried. On the other hand, there is a powerful need for alternate or multiple sources. When a company buys from one source only, competition is eliminated. Without warning, an act of God may render a particular vendor inoperative; a strike may idle the facilities; another supplier may develop a superior product. Without multiple sources, the buyer loses a powerful leverage on material costs—the ability to change sources quickly.

## STANDARDIZATION

An excellent way to control material costs is through standardization: simply the reduction of the number of different items purchased. If two will do the job of three, inventory control is simplified, obsolescence is reduced, and the entire administrative cost of purchasing, receiving, stores, etc., also decreases. Standardization is relatively simple. It is a matter of (1) listing all like items purchased and then (2) having engineering and technical people determine if some of the lesser-used items can be cut out. For example, a firm uses five different bolts. One of these is bought in lots of 50 per year whereas others are bought in 10,000 piece lots. The application for the 50 could use one of the other bolts but at a cost penalty. It would pay the company to eliminate the fifth bolt and inventory four items, thus reducing operating costs. Without standardization, over a period of time a company may end up with a multiplicity of items which are totally unnecessary.

Standardization also results from reducing the number of suppliers. This may be especially effective where costly setups occur.

## PURCHASING NEGOTIATIONS

If there is one key personal quality the professional buyer must possess, it is an ability to handle purchasing negotiations. The framework must first, however, exist for price analysis or other means for determining whether the price is fair, should be reduced, or perhaps even increased. The buyer then has at his or her option several techniques which will be examined individually below.

**Purpose** Negotiations vary depending on their purpose. Negotiations may be carried on to (1) establish a specific contract at a specific price, (2) revise prices either upward or downward, (3) change prices to meet adverse costs or operating changes, and (4) settle problems not covered nor anticipated in the purchase.

**Price Analysis** This comes through cost analysis or a breakdown of component costs. A simple analysis of price applies the formula that price is equal to material plus labor plus labor burden costs, plus selling and general administration costs, plus a profit. An illustration of that follows.

Manufacturing cost

Price = material + labor + labor burden
+ selling & general administration cost + profit

| | |
|---|---|
| Material | $1.00 |
| Labor | .40 |
| Labor burden | .80 |
| Manufacturing cost | $2.20 |
| Selling & GA @ 14% | .31 |
| | $2.51 |
| Profit at 10% | .25 |
| Price | $2.76 |

Tooling and engineering costs may be itemized separately; so may many other items according to buyer or seller preferences.

Such analysis provides grist for negotiations.

**Learning Curve** This is a sophisticated mathematical form of price versus cost analysis. It is based on the fact that for a specific quantity, repetitive production can be produced with a percentage (example 80 percent) of previous labor cost, thus producing a *learning curve*, showing lower future costs with increased experience. *See* LEARNING (EXPERIENCE) CURVES.

**Bids** These connote a formal buying approach. Bids may be closed or open. *Closed* bids indicate that the buyer reserves to himself or herself the opening and study of these bids in private so that competitive prices may not be revealed. In *open* bids, the buyer declares bids will be opened, with all bidders free to attend the bid opening so as to know all prices submitted.

Not to be confused with bids are *quotations*, which in effect represent the price a vendor *asks* for a product or service. A bid is what the supplier *feels* that the price shall be.

An approved bid list is sometimes kept for major construction or repair work. A firm is placed on the list by its previous or known performance or by meeting strict conditions. Bids are commonly used for governmental and publicly controlled buying. Quotations are more commonly used in industry.

**Blanket Orders** These are the means by which administrative and paper work costs can be greatly reduced. By issuing a blanket order on an annual basis, a buyer can be freed of issuing routine releases and repetitive purchase orders. Blanket orders facilitate central buying and negotiations and enable multiplant decentralized operations to release their needs against the contract source and at the agreed price. The user may "release" a shipment from a supplier simply by specifying what quantity is wanted on what date. This method of buying frees the buyer of the releasing and expediting work

load and allows the plant to control more directly its own input flow of materials.

So-called "basket purchases" occur when a grouping of items are negotiated and bought in toto. For example, all fasteners for a particular job might be bought at one lump sum. This is similar to taking the list of lumber required to build a home and having it priced in one basket. Often, a better price can be achieved than by buying each item for the house individually.

**Contracts** This is a general term and may include not only purchase orders, which are themselves contracts, but also other formal legal contracts used to purchase. Contracts may be signed by the supplier or vendor and agreed to by the buyer. More often the buyer simply uses the buyer's own purchase order form. When a contract is to exist for a period longer than a year or is more detailed in nature than can be covered through a normal purchase order, a formal legal contract is more desirable. For example, if there is a forklift truck lease of 5 year's duration, details may be far too involved to put on a standard purchase order form. In the case of special buying, such as in procuring private branded products, a legal contract may be preferable to the purchase order.

**Systems Contracting** This is a technique commonly used for maintenance, repair, and/or operating purchases. It greatly reduces the administrative costs of purchasing. It is accomplished by negotiating all of a like commodity from available suppliers at a fixed mark-up. For example, all plumbing supplies are shopped with several plumbing supply houses. Frequently, the buyer will negotiate a supplier's profit. Upon agreement, a catalog of items to be purchased will be attached and made part of the systems contract. The buyer delegates to the using department authority to release directly from the supplier within the scope of the contract. A simplified format exists for releasing and invoicing, which cuts down the longer format of a formal purchase order. A systems contract pins down source and price: the requisitioner releases what he or she needs when it is needed.

**Forward Buying** This occurs when a buy is made in advance, with full knowledge of what a future price will be since it has already been announced. It often requires reserving material well before needed. From this information an economic analysis of holding costs, carrying costs, and the like can be made to determine whether or not the buy should be made.

**Speculative Purchasing** This is essentially an investment purchase of a speculative nature and has no place in ordinary industrial procurement. A speculative purchase is one made on the belief that prices might go higher; so it would be better to buy ahead. This should not be confused with a forward buy defined above; otherwise a speculation exists, and that is not the intent of good material supply.

**Hedging**   A hedge position may assure that key costs are determined. For example, a food processor sells its output of canned pears in advance of the season. Prior to canning, if sugar costs rise sharply, no profit results. By buying sugar *futures* contracts on the Commodity Exchange, the processor covers its required sugar tonnage. The processor "fixes" this cost since (in theory) the physical price of sugar and the futures price advance or decline an equal amount. While a decision to take physical delivery of sugar from the Commodity Exchange can be made, usually the processor will sell off its contracts prior to delivery time, while continuing to buy from regular sources. If the physical price of sugar advances 5 cents per pound, the processor pays extra when it receives sugar from suppliers but makes 5 cents per pound when it sells an equal amount of its commodity futures. Conversely, if sugar prices decrease 5 cents, the processor spends 5 cents less but loses 5 cents on its futures. In either case, the two transactions cancel out, producing a no change position for the processor's costs. This action thus hedges the costs.

In practice, no purchasing operation can hedge without management and financial involvement as to the business profit objective.

**Capital Goods Procurement**   This applies to the acquisition of buildings, equipment, or large items which may be negotiated in a manner different from other types of goods. For example, in this type of procurement, final price may be achieved through final negotiations after preliminaries are out of the way. This contrasts with open bids, where the best price is presented the first time. The contractual terms are specific and applied in greater depth for repetitive purchases.

**Discounting**   This can apply to most of the purchases listed above. It is a term for the percent deducted from the list price. It can be negotiated depending on volume and other economic factors. A company may price a motor at list price, for example, but very few people pay the list. An original equipment manufacturer will allow one discount to another equipment manufacturer and a different discount to the end user.

**Reciprocity**   This exists when there is a relationship which ties what is bought to what is sold and is part of the negotiation or agreement to do business.

It is now illegal. In past years, companies would frequently make buying and selling arrangements based on the volume given in exchange for purchases. The last decade has seen a trend away from trade relations and toward sales and purchases kept completely separate, with sales (and purchases) made on the basis of merit and value, but not tied together.

## PURCHASING OPERATIONS

Every purchasing operation is supported and facilitated by certain documents, records, ordering systems, and procedures.

Documents in common use include address books and/or vendor profiles listing addresses, phone numbers, key personnel, labor unions at suppliers' plants, plant locations, number of employees, and a variety of other statistical information which may be of some assistance in knowing a vendor company and in working with it.

Records most frequently kept include purchase price paid for items purchased together with a listing of alternate vendor's prices. Such records are often kept by the buyer's secretary. On the other hand, some companies can justify data processing systems that make this data available for immediate recall at the buyer's request. There is really no such thing as a standard system, and many computer programs have been evolved to suit the needs of a particular corporation.

**Expediting**   In smaller organizations this may be done by the buyer who places the order. In larger companies, there is a tendency to set up special expeditors who spend all their time on this activity. When buyers place blanket orders and a plant releases against those blankets, the plant does the expediting. Regardless of who does the expediting, the buyer can never be totally divorced from responsibility for expediting. Since delivery of the goods is a condition of the contract agreement, the buyer must always be held accountable ultimately for delivery performance.

**Purchasing Manuals**   Most progressive purchasing operations are guided by their own purchasing manual. If there is a headquarters (or divisional) purchasing staff, the manual will be maintained and updated at central headquarters and distributed to decentralized plants. A manual generally consists of (1) general policies and procedures laid down by the purchasing head and (2) specific details of carrying out various purchasing routines.

Policies in the manual might cover such items as responsibilities and objectives of the purchasing function, relationships with other departments, gifts and ethical considerations, and the duties and organization structure with position guides. In particular, the policy as to authority to commit the company should be clearly detailed and approved by top management.

Procedures explain such things as how buys are made, how long purchase orders are kept on file, what contracting forms to use, and special procedures, reports, and statistics deemed desirable.

## PURCHASING INVENTORY CONTROL

Whether inventory controls are placed within purchasing or controlled elsewhere depends on organizational policy and structure of the company or group served. Purchasing inventory controls, however, are essentially the same as inventory controls (see INVENTORY CONTROL, PURCHASING AND ACCOUNTING ASPECTS). It is useful nonetheless to consider some necessary purchasing inputs to the inventory control process.

**Forecasting** A vital input in determining inventory levels (whether from a standard cost base or actual cost base) can be provided by the purchasing department. Financial people know current prices paid, but they cannot project ahead except on a straight inflationary percent basis provided by economic forecasts. The purchasing department can provide specific material cost forecasts either for each major item or for the overall material budget. These forecasts are based on the buyer's market knowledge and latest estimate of future cost trends. Many companies calculate their own material price index, which is weighted from the Industrial Wholesale Price Index.

**Stockless Purchasing** This technique is similar to systems contracting and is used when purchasing people have persuaded suppliers to carry in stock sufficient quantities of items so that the purchaser may operate its production processes without considerable inventory of its own. These stocking programs are usually negotiable and produce savings by reducing the actual physical space needed for, and dollar value of, the inventory required to run the business.

## VENDOR RELATIONS

Purchasing's relationship with vendors deserves particular attention. Newly initiated buyers often can be identified by an attitude of trying to "sock it to them." After operating through all levels of a business cycle, a purchasing professional learns that the best results come from relating well to the supplier. People make up organizations; if there is no one within the supplier's plant to speak well of the buyer, it may turn out that the vendor will not be able to meet the buyer's demanding delivery schedule. Sensitive areas that affect vendor relations include treatment of supplier's personnel during visits for sales or problem-solving purposes; unreasonable tolerances or specifications; late payment for goods; unreasonable delivery demands, especially after not allowing lead time; and method of handling complaints and rejections. In short, anything which allows friction to irritate or fester between supplier and consumer lessens a department's effectiveness. Diplomacy and tact are required.

**Evaluation** Proper evaluation of vendor performance can assist suppliers to maintain required quality levels. The act of reviewing a supplier's performance tells the vendor his or her performance is important and watched, and it provides an incentive to do better. A high evaluation can be a source of pride and satisfaction, a low one a prod to improve (or lose out). Methods of evaluation include the use of control charts, standard deviation calculations, and audit inspections.

Mathematical formulas and rating systems have been utilized. Figure P-35 illustrates one such system. The consolidated index is flawed by judgment, which renders it questionable. But the indexes on (1) quality, (2) cost, and (3) services and delivery are most constructively used.

**Selecting Vendors** Source selection should result from controlled decision making: otherwise it will happen haphazardly. To a large extent the vendors selected determine the effectiveness of the purchasing job itself. As discussed above, the sourcing decisions stem from previous experience on delivery, quality, and price. Then, too, current financial strength of the vendor and his or her potential profitability on the sale are important. Technical and service support lead the other variables in the selection process.

**Supplier Quality Programs** Purchasing should support every effort by suppliers to maintain effective quality assurance programs. Four basic responsibilities of the vendor's quality system are to (1) be of assistance to the engineering department so as to establish reasonable quality standards, (2) determine how well the standards are attained, (3) see that corrective action is taken when required, and (4) achieve improvements in quality when needed. Quality control efforts should be sufficient not only to specify the sampling plans and degree of protec-

| QUALITY RATING | | | | | | | | | |
|---|---|---|---|---|---|---|---|---|---|
| Kind and class: iron CL 2.   Period reported: 1st quarter | | | | | | | | | |
| Vendors | 3 | 16 | 21 | 27 | 35 | | | | |
| Factors | X | X | X | X | X | X | X | X | X |
| Received | 126 | 243 | 132 | 98 | 57 | | | | |
| Rec. insp. rej. | 10 | 28 | 31 | 36 | 2 | | | | |
| Line rej. | 5 | 12 | 3 | 4 | 1 | | | | |
| Total rej. | 15 | 40 | 34 | 40 | 3 | | | | |
| % accept | 88.1 | 83.5 | 74.2 | 59.2 | 94.7 | | | | |
| Rating (% acc. x 40) | 35.2 | 33.4 | 29.7 | 23.7 | 37.9 | | | | |

| COST RATING | | | | | | |
|---|---|---|---|---|---|---|
| Kind and class: iron CL 2.   Period reported: 1st quarter | | | | | | |
| Vendors | 3 | 16 | 21 | 27 | 35 | |
| Factors | X | X | X | X | X | X |
| Price 1 lb. | .19 | .18 | .16 | .16 | .20 | |
| +Discount (10%) | .019 | .018 | .016 | .016 | .020 | |
| | .171 | .162 | .144 | .144 | .180 | |
| +Trans. | .021 | .046 | .051 | .039 | .032 | |
| +Variance chgs. | .033 | .056 | .123 | .142 | .011 | |
| net | .235 | .264 | .318 | .325 | .223 | |
| Rating | 33.2 | 29.6 | 24.5 | 24.0 | 35.0 | |

| SERVICE RATING | | | | | | |
|---|---|---|---|---|---|---|
| Kind and class: iron CL 2.   Period reported: 1st quarter | | | | | | |
| Vendors | 3 | 16 | 21 | 27 | 35 | |
| Factors | X | X | X | X | X | X |
| Promises kept | 97 | 93 | 89 | 86 | 100.0 | |
| Rating | 24.3 | 23.3 | 22.3 | 21.5 | 25 | |

| VENDOR RATINGS (consolidated) | | | | | | |
|---|---|---|---|---|---|---|
| Kind and class:  iron CL 2.   Period reported: 1st quarter | | | | | | |
| Vendors | 3 | 16 | 21 | 27 | 35 | |
| Factors | X | X | X | X | X | X |
| Quality | 35.2 | 33.4 | 29.7 | 23.7 | 37.9 | |
| Cost | 33.2 | 29.6 | 24.5 | 24.0 | 35.0 | |
| Service | 24.3 | 23.3 | 22.3 | 21.5 | 25.0 | |
| Consolidated rating | 92.7 | 86.3 | 75.5 | 69.2 | 97.9 | |

**Fig. P-35. Examples of numerical vendor ratings. These charts depict quality, cost, and service ratings, with an additional rating combining the three.**

tion against failures but to determine where improvements need to be made. In similar fashion, they will identify good performance. Vendors should make use of such tools as statistical control charts, audit inspection, and reliability test laboratories, depending on the purchased item. Vendors should also identify the longevity of any item or its shelf life. In turn, purchasing must encourage its own quality people to assist vendors. They have a mutual concern, since supplier's quality affects the buyer's end product quality.

Failure of the vendor to maintain an adequate quality program affects the buyer when failures disrupt the production schedule and tie up vital floor space where units must be replaced or repaired. It is generally true also that the cost of repairs or replacements will not be totally recovered from the vendor. The vendor may replace a bolt, but the vendor will not be responsible for the repeated tests, the teardown, and many of the auxiliary functions that have to be performed to overcome the vendor's defect.

**Vendor Visitations**   Visist to a vendor's offices, plants, and warehouses provide an excellent means of buyer education, supplier awareness of the importance of the customer, an exchange of information, and an aid to improved relationships. Over a period of time, the purchasing department that makes it a practice to visit vendors—not solely to handle delivery problems when they occur but also to discuss how well the business is going—will

outperform one that mails the order and uses the telephone exclusively. An observant visiting buyer can determine whether the vendors need new business and how well they are operating. The buyer can also make it a point to note the key people who control quality, pricing, and the like. Visits represent an extra cost to the buying company, but they repay in expertise, general business acumen, and better relations with suppliers' managements.

*See also* INVENTORY CONTROL, PHYSICAL AND STOCKKEEPING; INVENTORY CONTROL, PURCHASING AND ACCOUNTING ASPECTS; LOGISTICS, BUSINESS; MATERIALS MANAGEMENT; MATERIALS REQUIREMENTS PLANNING (MRP); PRODUCTION PLANNING AND CONTROL; QUALITY MANAGEMENT.

### NOTES

[1] Victor H. Pooler, "Measuring the Purchasing Man," *TREND: Journal of Purchasing*, November 1973, p. 74.

### REFERENCES

Aljain, G. W.: *Purchasing Handbook*, 3d ed., McGraw-Hill Book Company, New York, 1973.

Ammer, Dean S.: *Materials Management*, 3d ed., Richard D. Irwin, Inc., Homewood, Ill., 1973.

Dowst, Somerby: *Basics for Buyers*, 3d ed., Cahners Books International, Inc., Boston, 1973.

Englund, W. B., and M. R. Leenders: *Purchasing and Materials Management*, 6th ed., Richard D. Irwin, Inc., Homewood, Ill., 1975.

Heinritz, E. F., and P. V. Farrell: *Purchasing: Principles and Applications*, 5th ed., Prentice-Hall, Inc., Englewood Cliffs, N.J., 1971.

*Journal of Purchasing and Materials Management*, National Association of Purchasing Management, New York. Periodic.

Kudrna, Dennis A.: *Purchasing Manager's Decision Handbook*, 1st ed., Cahners Books International, Inc., Boston, 1974.

Lee, L. and D. W. Dobler: *Purchasing and Materials Management*, 2d ed., McGraw-Hill Book Company, New York, 1971.

*National Association of Purchasing Management: Guide to Purchasing*, vols. 1 and 2, National Association of Purchasing Management, New York, 1965–1973.

Pooler, Victor H.: *The Purchasing Man and His Job*, American Management Association, New York, 1964.

Pooler, V. H., and R. G. Johnson: *Fundamentals of Effective Purchasing (Programmed Instruction)*, Preston Publishing Company, Inc., New York, 1967.

*Purchasing Magazine*, Cahners Publishing Co., Inc., Boston.

*Purchasing World*, Technical Publishing Co., Barrington, Ill.

Westing, J. H., I. V. Fine, and G. J. Zenz: *Purchasing Management—Materials in Motion*, 4th ed., John Wiley & Sons, Inc., New York, 1976.

VICTOR H. POOLER, *Carrier Corporation*

# Purchasing power reporting, general (GPPR) (*See* FINANCIAL STATEMENT ANALYSIS.)

# Put away (*See* WORK SIMPLIFICATION AND IMPROVEMENT.)

## Quality control (*See* QUALITY MANAGEMENT.)

## Quality control and management
*(See heading in Table of Contents for complete listing.)*

## Quality management

Quality management is the functional management discipline responsible for defining and implementing professionally developed programs of (1) quality improvement, (2) error control, and (3) defect prevention within an organization for the purpose of assuring that its products and services will conform to their requirements, that customers will be protected and satisfied, and that the cost of quality will be continually reduced.

A prudent company makes certain that its products and services are delivered to the customer by a management system that does not condone rework, repair, waste, or nonconformance of any sort. These are expensive problems and must be not only detected and resolved at the earliest moment but, if possible, prevented. To forestall these problems and accomplish these tasks it is necessary to establish a quality management function to assure that the required professionally designed and implemented programs are conducted. These programs range from training new employees to inspecting current products, conducting quality improvement, performing design reviews, and calculating the cost of quality.

Organizationally, quality management must report to the senior executive of the company. This is to make certain that the judgment of those involved cannot be adversely influenced by reporting arrangements. The basic rule is that no one should ever work for someone he or she is charged with evaluating. In its broadest sense the quality function serves not only as the "conscience" of the company but also as a compelling force for continual improvement from within. Utilizing planned communication activities, the quality operation attacks conventional mind sets such as "error is inevitable" and "that is as good as we can get."

**Essential Definitions** A number of terms and concepts underlie the proper implementation of quality management. These are defined briefly below:

*ASQC:* American Society for Quality Control.

*Audit:* A planned evaluation (or inspection) of any operation for the purpose of determining compliance with published procedures, processes, or requirements. Audits are usually conducted by personnel trained for that purpose and are not routinely assigned to the unit being audited. Reports of audits are supplied to senior management as well as to the management being audited. *Product* audits may include disassembly of the product for measurement of individual components and parts. *Process* audits include chemical analysis of fluids or ingredients used. *Procedural* audits include subjective evaluations; all subjective analysis should be reported as such.

*Communications:* The part of quality training involved with continually reminding all individuals of their personal responsibility to the quality program of the company and of the concepts and data that may be useful to them in this effort.

*Complaint handling:* Processing complaints communicated from customers and requiring that (1) they are satisfactorily resolved externally, (2) the cause of the complaint is eliminated by the organization responsible for the problem, (3) accurate records are kept, and (4) the results are followed up to verify effectiveness. It is necessary to be certain that all complaints are treated objectively.

*Consumer affairs:* Programmed activities (discussed in detail below) designed to assure that the customers of a company receive proper consideration when they need to complain or to seek information; also concerned with evaluating the effect of any company action on customers or other consumers; serves as ombudsman for consumers.

*Corrective action:* The systematic action taken to identify, evaluate, and resolve problems of nonconformance. This is usually considered to have two stages: (1) immediate handling of the current nonconformance in order to resume operations, and (2) longer-range actions to prevent the recurrence of the problem. Corrective action is the prime responsibility of the quality engineer.

*Cost of quality:* A calculation of the expenses involved in measuring product or service conformance, preventing errors, and dealing with failures. This includes all professional quality actions such as (1) inspection, test, qualification, quality engineering, etc.; (2) scrap, rework, service after service, warranty, customer services; and (3) quality training, qualification testing, audits, etc. The cost of quality serves as a management tool when used to measure the success of quality improvement actions and goal attainment.

*Design review:* Evaluating a completed or planned design by presenting it to a team representing all functional operations that will have to deal with the product, such as manufacturing, quality, applications, etc. The purpose of the design review is to verify the producibility of the product and to identify preventable errors that might be observed because of past experience.

*Environmental quality:* Concerned with (1) evaluating company performance against regulations concerning pollution created by company facilities, (2) preventing violations in new facilities, (3) increasing employee awareness, and (4) establishing communication between the company and the public.

*Make certain:* An awareness program oriented toward white-collar functions in manufacturing plants and everyone in service industries. The program is conducted primarily between the supervisor and the employee. The key part of the program is helping the individuals to recognize that "most of the mistakes we commit are our own fault." This encourages all employees to make defect prevention suggestions since those who cause the problems are the most qualified to offer ideas to prevent them in the future.

*Measurement:* The planned recording of inspection, test, or other appraisal results in a systematic manner that enables management to determine status of conformance in any given area or operation.

*Metrology:* The general term encompassing the broad spectrum of the science of measurement.

*Procedure proving:* The verification of a new procedure, such as how to total the hotel cashier's receipts at the end of the shift, by having the procedure conducted exactly as it reads.

*Process proving:* The act of taking a new process, such as printed circuit board coating, and accomplishing the process exactly as described. The results are then subjected to environmental and other tests to determine that complying with the exact process will produce a conforming product.

*Product acceptance:* Sometimes called *appraisal*, this term refers to all the planned inspections, tests, and other measurement actions conducted to verify that the product conforms to its requirements at various stages in its development. The actions are planned by quality engineering and conducted by professionally trained personnel. Part of product acceptance is the recording of results according to a prescribed procedure.

*Product qualification:* The planned conducting of tests and inspections (including environmental) to determine if new or redesigned products will comply with all the requirements of performance and configuration attributed to them.

*Product recall:* The systematic process of identifying potentially harmful or nonconforming product already delivered to customers and retrieving all such material for replacement with a conforming product or repair to their satisfaction. Recalls are formally handled and recorded.

*Product safety:* The professional discipline dedicated to the continual evaluation of products for conditions that may cause harm to the user even when the product is misused. Product safety is primarily oriented toward prevention of unsafe characteristics but is heavily involved in internal communication and the formal handling of problems such as product recall.

*Quality:* Conformance to requirements.

*Quality engineering:* The portion of quality management concerned with prevention planning and the correction of nonconformances within the production or service cycle. This function establishes all necessary measurement, analysis, and reporting actions and is continually concerned with getting things done right the first time.

*Quality improvement program:* The planned, long-range implementation by a company or organization of a formal program for (1) systematic reduction in the cost of quality, (2) improvement of the company's quality reputation, (3) increasing employee awareness of the importance of quality in their jobs, and (4) eliminating nonconformance in product and services. The program (discussed in detail below) contains specific actions requiring participation by all levels of management and employees.

*Quality training:* The planned process of informing every individual in the organization about the quality concepts and methods being utilized and their personal role in implementing them. Training activities include new employee orientation, executive training, quality engineering techniques, and company-wide quality improvement programs.

*Reliability:* The evaluation function concerned with calculating the performance life of a product at the earliest possible stage in its development. Practices are oriented toward prevention of system failures by assuring the competence of the components and subsystems.

*Software qualification:* A system of testing software to determine that it contains no errors and will cause the desired computer programs to operate.

*Statistical quality control (SQC):* The application of statistical concepts and specifically developed techniques to the control of processes and mass-produced products. It is also utilized as the basis for sampling plans and problem evaluations.

*Statistical quality control chart:* Typical example of $\bar{X}$ (average of sample results) and R (range of sample results) charts to control the output of a machine or process. X marks the spot where the process or machine went "out of control." At this point, work is stopped until the assignable cause is discovered and corrected. In a different example, the range (R) might have been the indicator of an out-of-control condition or it might have followed the mean and been out on the same sample. See Fig. Q-1.

*Status reporting:* The planned action of publishing evaluated measurement results in an agreed for-

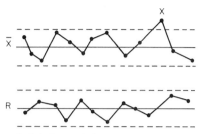

**Fig. Q-1. Statistical control chart.**

mat so management can know the status of the product or service in terms of conformance to requirements with particular emphasis on problems, and the actions being taken to resolve them. *See* Fig. Q-2.

*Supplier quality:* Most companies spend a third or more of their sales dollars on purchased material. Some actions involved are clearly spelling out the conformance requirements of a purchase, assisting the supplier in clarification or technology, conducting appraisal activities at the supplier's plant or in your own, and directing corrective action where applicable.

*Zero defects (ZD):* The phrase used in expressing the management standard: Do the job right the first time. The ZD concept states that people expect errors to occur in their jobs because management expects them to happen; however, individuals have higher standards in their personal life. Management cannot use vague phrases when it establishes performance standards, or it will get vague results. The test is: "What standard would you set on how many babies nurses are allowed to drop?" ZD should be used in improvement programs to establish the goal of the programs clearly. It is not a "motivational" program.

## IMPLEMENTING QUALITY MANAGEMENT

There are six specific actions necessary for installing a mature quality management program: (1) quality improvement, (2) supplier quality, (3) product acceptance, (4) service quality management, (5) quality engineering, and (6) consumer affairs.

**Strategy** The primary problem most professionals face, however, is not so much determining the

Special programs

| Item | Status or results |
|---|---|
| 1. Quality department budget performance ($000) | 1. YTD—$482.3 actual vs. $480.0 budget |
| 2. Corrective action | 2. New problems opened −29<br>Problems closed −32<br>Balance still open −28 |
| 3. Zero Defects program | 3. QIT meeting this month reviewed and reached agreement on Marketing Department ZD goals. |

Cost of quality summary

| Months | Monthly data – actual cost of quality, $(000) | | | | | | | | | | | | Year end |
|---|---|---|---|---|---|---|---|---|---|---|---|---|---|
| | J | F | M | A | M | J | J | A | S | O | N | D | Previous years<br>Actual |
| Prevention | 38.3 | 39.4 | 46.5 | | | | | | | | | | |
| Appraisal | 107.0 | 111.8 | 139.3 | | | | | | | | | | 9.9 |
| Failure | 73.1 | 81.3 | 93.2 | | | | | | | | | | |
| Total cost of quality | 218.4 | 232.5 | 279.0 | | | | | | | | | | Year-end-target |
| Percentage of sales | 9.1 | 9.3 | 9.0 | | | | | | | | | | 8.9 |

Basic quality measurements (percent defective)

| Area/Criteria | Previous year act. | J | F | M | A | M | J | J | A | S | O | N | D | Year-end goal |
|---|---|---|---|---|---|---|---|---|---|---|---|---|---|---|
| Recv. Insp. | 8.7 | 9.5 | 8.5 | 7.0 | 6.0 | | | | | | | | | 5.0 |
| Fabrication | 0.75 | 0.50 | 0.70 | 0.60 | 0.45 | | | | | | | | | 0.3 |
| PCB Insp. | 12.5 | 12.0 | 14.0 | 13.5 | 11.5 | | | | | | | | | 6.0 |
| Sub.assy.insp. | 5.0 | 3.0 | 1.8 | 1.9 | 1.7 | | | | | | | | | 1.0 |
| PCB test | 11.0 | 10.0 | 10.0 | 8.5 | 9.5 | | | | | | | | | 6.0 |
| Sub.assy.test | 14.5 | 13.0 | 9.0 | 12.0 | 9.0 | | | | | | | | | 4.0 |
| System test | 9.6 | 7.0 | 6.0 | 8.0 | 4.0 | | | | | | | | | 2.0 |
| | | | | | | | | | | | | | | |
| | | | | | | | | | | | | | | |

Major items contributing to quality costs

| Items | Responsibility and action plan |
|---|---|
| 1. PCB rework approx. $4500.00/mo. | Industrial engineering continues a major task effort to incrementally improve the processes, parts control, instructions, and training aids. |
| 2. Sub assy. test rejections $15,000.00/mo | Three (3) controlled lots of accepted PCBs are being carefully monitored to determine the cause of module rejections traced to PCBs. |

Customer complaint summary

| Items | Actions being taken |
|---|---|
| 1. Customer rejections of lots of submitted reached zero (144 submissions) for the first time (average for 19XX was 0.3%). | 1. Action not required. |
| 2. Customer deficiency reports (from system audit results) continue below the goal of 2 per month or less. | 2. Action taken on (1) QDR received. |

**Fig. Q-2. Quality status report.**

content of their programs as it is creating support of both management and employees for quality. To make that happen, it is necessary to involve all personnel in a deliberate quality improvement program so they can experience the value of such activities. Participation creates support for the establishment of the permanent programs of control and prevention.

Installation of defect detection and defect prevention programs in a company requires a genuine understanding of a complete strategy and the actions to implement it. Whether the "product" of a company is cast iron fittings or clean hotel rooms, the foremost quality management actions take place with people. Employees, customers, and suppliers are all involved as individuals and as corporate entities. Even in the most integrated manufacturing companies, half the people are involved in service and administrative functions. They never lay hands on the product itself during the manufacturing cycle. The only difference between programs in manufacturing and service is in what results are measured. Paper work measurement requires special techniques, of course, but all things are measurable.

**Three Basic Actions** To install a complete quality program in any organization, three basic actions are necessary.

1. Calculate the cost of quality. This can be done by estimate to show the top management that reducing this cost is an attractive option. This calculation is made by adding together the full cost of (*a*) all efforts involved in doing work over, including clerical work, (*b*) all scrap, (*c*) warranty, (*d*) after-service warranty, (*e*) complaint handling, (*f*) inspection and test, and (*g*) other nonquality costs. It is normal to underestimate this cost of quality by two-thirds. With experience, each additional search will find more costs exposing themselves.

To make this cost more meaningful, it should be related to a significant base, such as a percent of sales revenue. (In a business with high distribution costs—such as bread baking—it can be related to cost of production.) A proper quality program costs around 2 percent of sales. All other quality costs are probably waste that is redeemable from the process. These numbers should be presented to management with the advice that it is possible to install a quality program that is practical, produces real cost savings while not increasing operating costs, involves everyone, and is comfortable to work with. The typical top executive welcomes this positive approach to a problem that is often viewed negatively.

2. Install the quality improvement program. A step-by-step procedure is detailed below. This program gets everyone involved with quality improvement, produces satisfying results quickly, and provides a solid base for installing the completely professional quality system.

3. Continually remember that improvement never ends and programs can never be assumed to be completed. The dangers to quality become most active when it looks as if everything is doing well. That is the time when people relax their vigilance or reduce the demand for error-free performance. Status reporting must be continuous; corrective action must be insisted upon even when the seriousness of defects lessens; new people must be continually oriented to the program, and older ones retrained.

## QUALITY IMPROVEMENT PROGRAM

There are 14 steps to follow in an effective program.

STEP 1: Management commitment

*Action.* Discuss the need for quality improvement with management people with an emphasis on the need for defect prevention. There are plenty of movies, visual aids, and other material available to support this communication. (Do not confuse this with *motivation*. Communication is long lasting; motivation tends to be shallow and short-lived.) Prepare a quality policy that states that each individual is expected to "perform exactly according to the requirement or cause the requirement to be officially changed to what we and the customer really need." Agree that quality improvement is a practical way to profit improvement.

*Accomplishment.* Helping management to recognize their personal requirement to participate raises the level of visibility for quality and assures everyone's cooperation so long as there is some progress.

STEP 2: Quality improvement team

*Action.* Bring together representatives of each department to form the quality improvement team. These should be people who can speak for their department in order to commit that operation to action. Preferably, the department heads should participate—at least on the first go around. Orient the team members as to the content of the program, its purpose, and their role, which is to cause the necessary actions to take place in their department and in the company.

*Accomplishment.* All the tools necessary to do the job are now together in one team. It works well to appoint one of the members as the chairperson of the team for this phase.

STEP 3: Quality measurement

*Action.* It is necessary to find out the performance status of quality throughout the company. Quality measurements for each area of activity must be established where they do not exist and reviewed where they do. Quality status is recorded to show where improvement is possible and where corrective action is necessary and to document actual improvement later on.

Nonmanufacturing measurements, which are sometimes difficult to establish can include the following:

Accounting:
Percentage of late reports
Computer input incorrect
Errors in specific reports as audited
Data processing:
Keypunch cards thrown out for error
Computer downtime due to error
Rerun time
Engineering:
Change orders due to error
Drafting errors found by checkers
Late releases
Finance:
Billing errors (check accounts receivable overdues)
Payroll errors
Accounts payable deductions missed
Hotel front desk:
Guests taken to unmade rooms
Reservations not honored
Manufacturing engineering:
Process change notices due to error
Tool rework to correct design
Methods improvement
Marketing:
Contract errors
Order description errors
Plant engineering:
Time lost due to equipment failures
Callbacks on repairs
Purchasing:
Purchase order changes due to error
Late receipt of material
Rejections due to incomplete description

There are innumerable ways to measure any procedure. The people doing the work will respond with delight to the opportunity to identify some measurements for their work. A supervisor who says his or her area is completely immeasurable can be helped by asking how he or she knows who is doing the best work, whom to keep, and whom to replace.

*Accomplishment.* Formalizing the company measurement system strengthens the inspection and test functions and assures proper measurement. Getting the paper work and service operations involved sets the stage for effective defect prevention where it counts. Placing the results of measurement in highly visible charts establishes the foundation of the entire quality improvement program.

STEP 4: Cost of quality evaluation

*Action.* Initial estimates are likely to be shaky (although low), so it is necessary now to get more accurate figures. The comptroller's office must do this. It should be provided first with detailed information as to what constitutes the cost of quality. The cost of quality is not an absolute performance measurement: it is an indication of where corrective action will be profitable for a company. The higher the cost, the more corrective action to be taken.

*Accomplishment.* Having the comptroller establish the cost of quality removes any suspected bias from the calculation. More important, a measurement of quality management performance has been established in the company's system.

STEP 5: Quality awareness

*Action.* It is time now to share with employees these measurements of what nonquality is costing. This is done by training supervisors to orient employees and by providing visible evidence of the concern for quality improvement through communication material such as booklets, films, posters, and similar actions. This should not be confused with motivation. There is no intent to manipulate people. It is a sharing process. This is an important step; it may be the most important. Service and administrative people should be included on a first-class basis.

*Accomplishment.* The real benefit of communications is that it gets supervisors and employees in the habit of talking positively about quality. It aids the process of changing, or perhaps clarifying, existing attitudes toward quality. And it sets the basis for the corrective action and error-cause identification steps.

STEP 6: Corrective action

*Action.* As people are encouraged to talk about their problems, opportunities for correction come to light. These problems include not only the defects found by inspection, audit, or self-evaluation, but also situations that require attention—as seen by the working people. The problems must be brought to the supervision meetings at each level, and the ones that cannot be resolved are formally passed up to the next level of supervision for review at their regular meeting. If a specific functional area does not hold such meetings, the team should take action to establish them in that department.

*Accomplishment.* Individuals soon see that the problems brought to light have the opportunity to be resolved on a regular basis. The habit of facing problems and correcting them is developing.

STEP 7: Ad hoc committee for the zero defects program

*Action.* Three or four members of the team are selected to investigate the zero defects (ZD) concept and ways to implement the program. The quality manager must establish in his or her mind at the start, and then transmit to the team, a clear understanding that ZD is *not* a motivation program. Its purpose is to *communicate* to all employees the literal meaning of the words and the thought that everyone should do things right the first time. In particular, the ad hoc group should seek out ways to match the program to the company's personality.

*Accomplishment.* Improvement comes with each step of the overall program. By the time ZD day is conducted, as much as a year may have gone by and the initial improvement will be flattening out. At that point the new commitment to an explicit goal takes over and starts the improvement again. Setting up this committee to study and prepare the implementation actually installs the program with the thought leaders of the company.

STEP 8: Supervisor training

*Action.* A formal orientation with all levels of management should be conducted prior to implementation of the next steps. All managers must understand each step well enough to explain it to their people; that is the test.

*Accomplishment.* Eventually all supervision will be tuned into the program and realize the value themselves. Then they will concentrate their action on the program.

STEP 9: Zero defects day

*Action.* When zero defects is established as the performance standard of the company, it should be done in one day. That way everyone has the same understanding of it. Supervisors should explain the program to their people and *do* something different in the facility so that everyone will recognize it is a "new attitude" day.

*Accomplishment.* Making a "day" of the zero defects commitment provides an emphasis and a memory that will be long lasting.

STEP 10: Goal setting

*Action.* During meetings with employees each supervisor requests that they establish the goals they would like to strive for against their measurement. Usually, goals should be for 30-, 60-, and 90-day periods. All should be specific and relate to numbers.

*Accomplishment.* This phase helps people learn to think in terms of meeting goals and accomplishing specific tasks as a team.

STEP 11: Error cause removal (ECR)

*Action.* Using a simple one-page form, individuals are asked to describe any problem that keeps them from performing error-free work. This is not a suggestion system in that all each must do is to list the problem; the appropriate functional group (i.e., industrial engineering) will develop the answer. It is important that ECRs are acknowledged quickly—within 24 hours.

Typical inputs on the form might be:

1. "This tool is not long enough to work right with all the parts."
2. "The sales department makes too many errors on their order entry forms."
3. "We make a lot of changes in response to telephone calls, and many of them end up having to be done all over again."
4. "I do not have any place to put my pocketbook."

*Accomplishment.* People now know that their problems can be heard and answered. Once employees learn to trust this communication, the program can go on forever.

STEP 12: Recognition

*Action.* Award programs are established to recognize those who meet their goals or perform outstandingly. It is wise not to attach a value to the problem identifications. They should all be treated the same since they are not suggestions. The prizes or awards should not be expensive. The recognition is what is important.

*Accomplishment.* Genuine recognition of performance is something people really appreciate. They will continue to support the program whether or not they, as individuals, participate in the awards.

STEP 13: Quality councils

*Action.* The quality professionals and team chairpersons should be brought together regularly to communicate with each other and to determine actions necessary to upgrade and improve the solid quality program being installed.

*Accomplishment.* These councils are the best source of information on the status of programs and ideas for action. It also brings the professionals into a close affiliation.

STEP 14: Do it over again

*Action.* The typical program takes 1 year to 18 months to perform. By that time turnover and changing situations will have wiped out much of the education effort. Therefore, it is necessary to set up a new team of representatives and begin again. ZD day, for instance, should be marked as an anniversary. Nothing more than the notification and special lunch for all employees is necessary. But the program is never over.

*Accomplishment.* Repetition makes the program perpetual and thus "part of the woodwork." If quality is not that ingrained in the organization, then it will never happen.

## SUPPLIER QUALITY

The purpose of a supplier quality program is to eliminate the flow of unacceptable or unusable material from supplier to user. The service that supplier quality provides to the purchasing function may include any or all of the following: (1) surveys of supplier quality capabilities, (2) reviews of purchase order technical requirements, (3) itinerant or resident source inspection, (4) receiving inspection and test, (5) supplier corrective action, and (6) quality rating systems. *See* PURCHASING MANAGEMENT.

## PRODUCT ACCEPTANCE

A company or organization producing a product or service must know that its output conforms to the requirements of the technical design, advertising literature, government regulations, and/or customer standards. Product acceptance, or the *appraisal* of a product, includes all the planned inspections, tests, and other measurement actions conducted to verify that the product conforms to its requirements during each phase of its development and production. Its primary purpose is to assure product readiness for proceeding into the next phase right up to its individual acceptability for delivery to a customer.

The extent of inspection in any given area is established by quality engineering. Inspection plans will normally be based on (1) those product characteristics that are critical to end-product performance, (2) those characteristics that are controlled by tooling, and (3) the extent of risk based on recent past performance.

Testing is an important part of the overall acceptance function for many companies. Its importance lies in its significant effect on the performance of a company's products. Its expense arises from the high level of skills and costly test equipment often involved. Testing starts with qualification testing of new designs and continues through the testing of purchased products, manufactured subassemblies and final product testing. Like inspection, testing is always conducted by the quality department in accordance with specific plans and procedures.

For any acceptance measurement, there is always the possibility that nonconforming material will be discovered. When this occurs, acceptance cannot be achieved and the responsibility of the acceptance function becomes one of clearly defining and recording the exact conditions of nonconformance. This documentation is absolutely basic to effective corrective action.

## SERVICE QUALITY MANAGEMENT

Service quality management pertains to the service and administrative areas of manufacturing companies as well as to the entire "service" industry. Its specific objective is the prevention of errors in service and administrative activities and the continuous improvement of service operations. There is no basic difference between manufacturing and service management except that one has tangibles as its product and the other does not. Both require people to perform.

Service quality management is accomplished through the formal application of a quality improvement program. The improvement cycle will begin when each service activity center looks at itself as an individual entity with suppliers and customers. This examination will help to identify incoming, internal, and outgoing errors or deficiencies, which then become the basis for measuring the performance of this service activity. Measuring performance is the first step of improvement, and this measurement can be anything from the number of actual paper work errors, such as wrong shipments, to a determination of the percentage of directly serviced customers who indicate satisfaction with the service.

## QUALITY ENGINEERING

The purpose of quality engineering might be briefly described as the application of the technology of quality systems to the specific technologies of a company's business. It is intended to supply the necessary engineering base to allow the fruits of quality improvement to achieve the maximum desirable effect on product or service quality. Organizationally, quality engineering embodies (1) activities of inspection and test planning, (2) data analysis and corrective action, and (3) the quality interface actions with marketing and engineering. In this capacity, quality engineers are responsible for continued state-of-the-art improvements in quality documentation systems, statistical techniques, testing systems, failure analysis techniques, reliability programs, vendor quality techniques, and many others.

**Quality Planning** The first task of quality engineering is quality planning, which has the following purposes:

1. To provide the basic plan for the maintenance and improvement of product or service quality

2. To judiciously place available controls where they offer the most protection or prevention for the dollars spent

3. To exert maximum influence on the planning of others in an effort to make conformance to requirements and prevention of errors an inherent part of each company operation

4. To review and analyze results periodically and present them to management in such a way that improvements can be forthcoming

Visible evidence of the work of quality planning can be found in inspection and test plans, documentation systems, quality status reports, procedures for the control of quality, and the attitude of other planning groups with respect to the importance of quality.

**Corrective Actions** For companies that deal in products, quality engineering's contribution to product quality improvement will be directly related to its ability to cause corrective actions. Without corrective changes, there can be no improvement. Opportunities for improvement begin with the first rejects or with nonconforming material found on the production floor. Quality engineers will (1) guide the acceptance function in requiring correction for obvious errors; (2) perform failed-product analyses to determine the causes of not-so-obvious errors, (3) direct supplementary investigative efforts for more complex product problems, and (4) ultimately require the commitment of responsible activities for specific corrective actions. Experience in this area of quality engineering is what qualifies them for doing customer problem analysis and making valuable contributions to the marketing and design engineering efforts.

## CONSUMER AFFAIRS

Companies will become more responsible to the needs and expectations of their customers through the implementation of a formal consumer affairs program. This extension of the quality management function is directed toward providing to ultimate consumers products and services which conform to agreed or implied requirements and reasonable expectations. The responsibility of this function is to promote and coordinate all efforts necessary to es-

tablish and improve consumer communications, complaint handling, consumer and company education, and compliance with applicable consumer-oriented laws, regulations, and standards. The consumer affairs manager can then act as an internal consultant for consumer matters (the consumer's advocate). *See* CONSUMERISM AND CONSUMER PROTECTION LEGISLATION; PRODUCT LIABILITY.

**Guidelines** Typical guidelines for the consumer affairs program include the following:

1. Products manufactured, imported, exported, sold, or distributed must be in conformance with all requirements and in compliance with all applicable laws, regulations, and standards established for protection of users of such products.

2. Services provided must be (*a*) responsive to consumer needs and expectations and (*b*) in compliance with applicable government regulations, codes, and standards.

3. Complaint handling must be swift and courteous and provide fair settlement of just claims.

4. Company activities which could have a significant impact on consumer satisfaction (such as marketing, advertising, product development, manufacturing, and others) should be monitored by the consumer affairs activity.

5. The consumer affairs manager should prepare a manual containing written procedures to describe the activities required by all functions in the company necessary to carry out the consumer affairs program and to measure the status of the program at that particular point in time.

6. All the information processed by the consumer affairs activity should routinely be analyzed for identification of problems and system weaknesses, and these results will become an important input to the corrective action system.

*See also* CONSUMERISM AND CONSUMER PROTECTION LEGISLATION; CONTROL SYSTEMS, MANAGEMENT; DESIGN, INDUSTRIAL; PRODUCT LIABILITY; PRODUCT PLANNING AND DEVELOPMENT; PRODUCTION PLANNING AND CONTROL.

### REFERENCES

Crosby, P. B.: *The Art of Getting Your Own Sweet Way,* McGraw-Hill Book Company, New York, 1972.

———: *Quality Is Free,* McGraw-Hill Book Company, New York, 1978.

———: *Cutting the Cost of Quality,* Woodsdale, Inc., Greenwich, Conn., 1969.

Duncan, Acheson J.: *Quality Control and Industrial Statistics,* 4th ed., Richard D. Irwin, Inc., Homewood, Ill., 1974.

Grant, E. L., and R. S. Leavenworth: *Statistical Quality*

*Control*, 4th ed., McGraw-Hill Book Company, New York, 1972.

Groocock, J. M., *The Cost of Quality*, Pitman Publishing Corporation, New York, 1974.

*A Guide To Zero Defects*, Department of Defense, Quality and Reliability Assurance Handbook, no. 4114.12H, Washington, November 1965.

Hagan, J. T.: *A Management Role for Quality Control*, American Management Associations, New York, 1968.

Juran, J. M., and Frank M. Gryna, Jr.: *Quality Planning and Analysis: From Product Development Through Usage*, McGraw-Hill Book Company, New York, 1970.

Kirkpatrick, Elwood G.: *Quality Control for Managers and Engineers*, John Wiley & Sons, Inc., New York, 1970.

*Quality Motivation Workbook*, American Society for Quality Control, Milwaukee, Wis., May 1967.

*Quality Program Requirements, Mil-Q-9858A*, Washington, Dec. 16, 1963, pp. 1–9.

PHILIP B. CROSBY, *ITT*

## Quality programs, supplier (*See* PURCHASING MANAGEMENT.)

## Quantitative methods and management sciences (*See heading in Table of Contents for complete listing.*)

## Quasipublic managers (*See* MANAGER, DEFINITIONS OF.)

## Queuing theory (*See* OPERATIONS RESEARCH AND MATHEMATICAL MODELING.)

## Quotas, minority (*See* MINORITIES, MANAGEMENT OF AND EQUAL EMPLOYMENT OPPORTUNITY.)

## Quotas, sales (*See* SALES MANAGEMENT.)

## Quotations (*See* PURCHASING MANAGEMENT.)

# R

**Raid, corporate** (*See* ACQUISITIONS AND MERGERS.)

**Ramps** (*See* NETWORK PLANNING METHODS.)

**Random access for inventory control** (*See* MATERIALS MANAGEMENT.)

**Rank order appraisal method** (*See* APPRAISAL, PERFORMANCE.)

**Ranking of jobs** (*See* JOB EVALUATION.)

**Rate making in regulated industries** (*See* REGULATED INDUSTRIES, MANAGEMENT OF.)

**Rates, full and floating** (*See* EXCHANGE, FOREIGN, MANAGEMENT OF.)

**Ratification, contract** (*See* LABOR-MANAGEMENT RELATIONS.)

**Ratio, marginal income** (*See* MARGINAL INCOME ANALYSIS.)

**Ratio analysis, financial** (*See* FINANCIAL RATIO ANALYSIS; FINANCIAL STATEMENT ANALYSIS.)

**Ratio delay** (*See* WORK SAMPLING.)

**Rational thought process** (*See* DECISION-MAKING PROCESS.)

**Ratios, activity** (*See* FINANCIAL RATIO ANALYSIS; FINANCIAL STATEMENT ANALYSIS.)

**Ratios, financial** (*See* FINANCIAL MANAGEMENT; FINANCIAL RATIO ANALYSIS; FINANCIAL STATEMENT ANALYSIS.)

## Ratios, leverage and coverage (*See* FI-NANCIAL RATIO ANALYSIS; FINANCIAL STATEMENT ANALYSIS.)

## Ratios, liquidity (*See* FINANCIAL RATIO ANALYSIS; FINANCIAL STATEMENT ANALYSIS.)

## Ratios, profitability (*See* FINANCIAL RATIO ANALYSIS; FINANCIAL STATEMENT ANALYSIS.

## Reactor, passive (*See* HEALTH, EXECUTIVE, MANAGING STRESS AND JOB TENSION.)

## Real estate management, corporate

Almost all enterprises, whether they provide goods or services or are of an institutional nature, use real estate in some manner. Many organizations face decisions on real estate matters only infrequently; others must cope with realty matters regularly. In either instance, sound real estate decision making is often crucial to corporate profitability or institutional durability. Important aspects of real estate management requiring decisions include location strategy, leasing, development, appraisal, financing, law, taxation, maintenance, insurance, and disposition.

**Location Strategy** For many organizations, location is the most critical aspect of real estate planning. Corporate income statements are sure to reflect the higher product cost due to poorly located manufacturing and distribution facilities and/or lower sales due to poor choices of store location. On the other hand, the location of some businesses is dictated by the location of something else. For example, a mining company must place operations where there are minerals; a hydroelectric company must be at a dam. For most businesses, however, the choice of a location is far more complex. Judgment and analysis are imperative.

*Manufacturing.* In selecting a site for manufacturing operations, important matters to be considered at state and local levels include the following:

1. Labor force availability and wage rates
2. Ad valorem and income tax rates
3. Municipal services: roads, police, and fire protection
4. Utilities: availability and cost of water, sewerage, gas, and electricity, both in the general area and at the specific site

5. Proximity and adequacy of transportation facilities: streets, highways, airports, railways, etc.
6. Transportation costs to and from customers and suppliers
7. Land and construction costs
8. Building codes, land use restrictions, and zoning
9. Ecological considerations
10. Political climate and policies

*Retailing.* For retail store location, considerations include area population, income levels, consumer buying habits, traffic and site accessibility, the location of competitors, and shifts that may take place in these matters.

*Offices.* Office space users should consider the proximity to necessary services such as parking and banking facilities and the location of legal and accounting counsel. Corporate managers must also decide whether a prestige address is important for some or all of the office operations.

*Expansion.* Regardless of the type of use, the availability of space for expansion must not be overlooked. Without adequate room for expansion at a given site, inefficiencies will be realized; obtaining larger facilities and moving to them may not be economically feasible.

**Leasing** A lease is a device that transfers possession, but not ownership, for a period of time. Leases are usually categorized as net or gross. Under a *net* lease, the tenant must pay operating expenses; with a gross lease, operating expenses are the property owner's obligation. Since any provision may be written into a lease as long as it is legal, reading each lease is an essential step that prevents a misunderstanding of rights and obligations. For example, under some leases the property owner is obligated for insurance; yet the lease may be called net. Also, a gross lease may have *stop* clauses (also known as *escalation* clauses) that pass along operating expense increases to the tenant.

Provisions that allow the assignment of leases and the subletting of space should be in the original lease. Though these features do not relieve the tenant of his or her primary obligation, they will allow some flexibility in the use of space when it is no longer needed.

Since an established tenant often has more at stake in a particular location than the property owner has, provisions for the distribution of condemnation awards should be described in the lease. Renewal options and purchase options give the tenant the to remain if he or she chooses; income tax implications of these clauses should not be overlooked.

Some leases require level rents throughout the lease term; others have step-up or step-down rental rates. Fledgling corporations often seek low rental rates in early years; thus a step-up lease can be satisfactory. Prestige space may be leased with step-down rates which acknowledge that the space will not be so valuable in coming years.

*Percentage* leases are typically used in conjunction with retail stores. The rental rate is a fixed percentage of retail sales, though a minimum base rental is also specified. Percentage overrides give a property owner incentive to properly maintain and promote a shopping center.

**Development** An organization that elects to develop property typically seeks expert assistance. After choosing the best possible location with respect to the items noted previously, corporate managers must consult attorneys, architects, real estate brokers, accountants, and contractors. Selection of capable and reputable people for a development team is essential.

An agreement for the purchase of land should not be lightly entered into. Contingencies should be stated, such as "subject to rezoning for industrial use" or "contingent upon results from soil boring tests that indicate that the land can support the intended improvements."

It is not uncommon for local attorneys and architects to be hired in addition to those on retainer to the corporation. Local professionals are more likely to be aware of peculiarities unique to their area and can often help to overcome public and political resistance.

Contractors may submit competitive bids based upon detailed project plans. A knowledgeable attorney should review all construction contracts. A performance bond provides important protection for the corporate developer. Contractor *draws* with holdback provisions assure that the contractor has a financial interest in seeing the project to fruition. A certificate of occupancy is needed to occupy a building; without one, property is useless. A corporate manager must therefore have assurances that one will be obtained for each building and must continually monitor the structure to assure maintenance of the certificate.

**Appraisal** Before entering into an agreement for the purchase, sale, or lease of real property, it is a good policy to have the property appraised. An *appraisal* is a professionally derived estimate of value. The term *value* can take on many meanings. Most appraisals are estimates of fair market value, but, to many corporations, value in use or investment value may be more significant.

*Value in use* is an estimation of property value to a user, given a specific type of use. A vacant structure intended for light manufacture may not be worth the same if it were intended for use as a warehouse. *Investment value* refers to the worth to a specific owner, considering the owner's individual investment needs. An appraiser must be advised of the type of value estimate sought.

There are three approaches to appraising:

1. Income, predicated upon the philosophy that present property value lies in the worth of anticipated future income
2. Market (comparison), based on recent sales of comparable property
3. Cost (summation), based on replacement cost (less depreciation) for improvements, plus the land value

Appraisers often estimate value using all three approaches, then arrive at a final value estimate by weighting amounts from each approach. Greater weight is applied to the approach considered the most meaningful under the circumstances.

**Financing** Long-term financing is available for most improved realty. Thinly capitalized corporations, especially those that require special-purpose buildings, may encounter difficulty in this respect. Real estate financing can be tailored to the company's needs and philosophy, of course. Some companies prefer to minimize fixed obligations, while others prefer to minimize the amounts tied up in realty.

Mortgage bankers and brokers specialize in originating mortgage loans, including those on corporate realty. During the 1970s, investment bankers began to offer financing for pools of corporate real estate, which obviates the need for single-project financing. Sale-leasebacks, whereby property is sold to an investor then leased back under a long-term lease, can be used to free working capital for other purposes. Industrial revenue bonds, popular in the 1960s, serve to pass on the benefit of tax-exempt interest rates to corporations that bring industry to a local area. Tax law changes have limited the use of this type of financing, however. Corporate managers should also be mindful of property refinancing or secondary financing, which can provide additional long-term funds at favorable rates.

**Real Estate Law** Each state in the United States has real estate laws peculiar to it. That and the fact that such laws have evolved over many centuries make the practice of real estate law a challenge, even to practicing attorneys. Corporate managers should be aware, however, of two provisions of real estate law that set the tone for transactions. The principle of *caveat emptor* (let the buyer beware) states that the buyer is duty-bound to examine the property and he or she assumes responsibility for defects except those that are hidden. The other provision is the Statute of Frauds, which renders verbal real estate contracts unenforceable. Corporate managers must therefore make a careful physical inspection of the property under consideration and are admonished not to accept the other party's word for anything—to be enforceable, agreements must be in writing. When in doubt, a buyer should consult an attorney; it is better to get legal advice before entering into a contract than to risk costly error.

**Taxation**    Income and ad valorem taxes will be imposed almost everywhere. Careful planning can help to minimize these expenses. Since corporations strive for income, income taxes (though costly) are preferable to genuine financial losses. Real estate ownership can help reduce a corporation's income tax burden.

Owners of depreciable property may claim a tax deduction for depreciation; the deduction requires no cash outlay and can reduce, postpone, or eliminate some taxes. Depreciation deductions, however, also apply to financial reporting, which is a matter that requires attention as well. Rent on a bona fide lease is tax deductible, but only the interest portion of mortgage loan payments is tax deductible. The trade offs of buying as compared to leasing can be rapidly analyzed on an aftertax–present-value basis using a computer.

Ad valorem taxes are applied by municipalities against the value of property. The product of the millage rate and the fraction of value assessed establishes the effective rate of taxation. Local governments may woo a corporation into constructing a plant in their jurisdiction by offering reduced or deferred taxation. Corporation managers should remember, however, that the corporation does not vote for new schools, libraries, or other services; the public does this. It is best, therefore, to establish firmly the term and amount of tax reduction being offered before entering into an irrevocable location decision.

**Maintenance**    Proper maintenance is essential to retain property values. It is important to physically inspect facilities for necessary repairs and replacements. Periodic deposits into a replacement reserve account can smooth out income flows caused by events that occur irregularly. The curing of functional obsolescence is also necessary to keep up with competitors who have more modern facilities.

A periodic review of operating expenses is often rewarded. Expense-saving opportunities can be pin-

pointed by comparing current amounts of various expenses—oil, gas, electricity, water—to amounts paid the previous month and the same month of the previous year. Substantial changes in amounts offer clues to rate and/or consumption increases. A follow-up to detect reasons for the change can disclose worthwhile cost-saving opportunities.

**Insurance**    The soundness of a company rests heavily on the amount and type of real estate insurance coverage it has. Two important kinds of insurance for real estate are title insurance and hazard insurance.

*Title Insurance*    Whenever real estate is financed, the mortgagee will require title insurance to protect his or her interest. The property owner bears the cost of this insurance, which protects against valid claims of property ownership. The cost of title insurance is proportional to the value of the property; owners may also purchase title insurance to cover their equity.

*Hazard Insurance*.    Insurance brokers offer hazard insurance. The simplest form is fire insurance; extended coverage covers other risks. But even policies that are called *all-risk* have exclusions written into them. Nearly all hazard insurance policies include 80 percent coinsurance clauses. These clauses require the insured to maintain insurance of at least 80 percent of the property value. To the extent that such a ratio is not maintained, the insured shares the risk of loss. Though some policies include automatic upward adjustments for inflation, coverage may be inadequate for the current property value; so the adequacy of hazard insurance should be reviewed periodically.

**Disposition**    The disposition of industrial, commercial, or office space requires the assistance of specially trained personnel who know that particular market. To locate a substitute tenant and/or owner for a special-purpose building is often difficult. Extra efforts are necessary to reach potential users; creativity as to possible alternative building uses may also be needed. It is not unlikely that losses will be sustained upon the disposition of special-purpose buildings, even though gains and losses are measured against the depreciated book value.

Perhaps the best method of avoiding dispositions and potential losses is to analyze needs carefully and choose a suitable location and facility at the outset so that the likelihood of a disposition is reduced.

*See also* BUDGETING, CAPITAL; FACILITIES AND SITE PLANNING AND LAYOUT; INSURANCE AND RISK MANAGEMENT; LEASING, EQUIPMENT; OFFICE SPACE PLANNING AND DESIGN; SITE SELECTION; TAX MANAGE-

MENT, MANAGERIAL RESPONSIBILITY FOR FEDERAL INCOME TAX REPORTING.

## REFERENCES

*The Appraisal of Real Estate*, 6th ed., American Institute of Real Estate Appraisers, 1973.

Cribbet, John E.: *Principles of the Law of Property*, The Foundation Press, Inc., 1975.

*The Dollars and Cents of Shopping Centers*, The Urban Land Institute.

*Federal Taxes Affecting Real Estate*, Partners Arthur Andersen & Co.

McMahan, John: *Property Development: Effective Decision Making in Uncertain Times*, McGraw-Hill Book Company, New York, 1976.

Maisel, Sherman J., and Stephen E. Roulac: *Real Estate Investment and Finance*, McGraw-Hill Book Company, New York, 1976.

Ring, Alfred A.: *Real Estate Principles and Practices*, 7th ed., Prentice-Hall Inc., Englewood Cliffs, N.J., 1972.

Smith, Halbert C., et al.: *Real Estate and Urban Development*, Richard D. Irwin Inc., Homewood, Ill., 1973.

ELBERT W. HUBBARD, *Georgia State University*

JACK P. FRIEDMAN, *The University of Texas at Arlington*

# Reality principle   (*See* HEALTH, MENTAL.)

# Receivables, aging   (*See* CREDIT MANAGEMENT.)

# Receivables financing   (*See* FINANCIAL MANAGEMENT OF SHORT-TERM, INTERMEDIATE, AND LONG-TERM FINANCING.)

# Receivables management   (*See* FINANCIAL MANAGEMENT.)

# Receivables turnovers   (*See* CREDIT MANAGEMENT.)

# Reciprocal companies   (*See* RISK ANALYSIS AND MANAGEMENT.)

# Reciprocity   (*See* PURCHASING MANAGEMENT.)

# Records, personnel   (*See* PERSONNEL ADMINISTRATION.)

# Records management

The growing complexity of business operations, modern technology, and increasing government regulation have created massive paper work problems. Typical indicators are the following:

U.S. government agencies print over 10 billion sheets of paper a year to be completed by businesses.

Businesses with 50 employees or less complete approximately 75 types of forms annually.

One major oil company annually files 400 reports to 45 different federal agencies, excluding tax reports.

A typical small business with a gross income under $30,000 is required to file 53 tax forms each year.

Official records stored around the country total 11.6 million cubic feet.

**Impact of Technology**   The modern filing system is indebted to Johann Gutenberg, whose invention of the printing press in the fifteenth century gave the world movable type. This meant that people could produce quickly and easily several copies of an original, without having to resort to laborious copying by hand. The first typewriter was manufactured in the United States in 1874. The invention of carbon paper helped to generate more paper; and more paper meant that new filing methods would have to be found. At the turn of the century, Melvil Dewey created the system now used to classify knowledge. He divided learning into ten "100" categories, from 000 to 900. Each category divided into 10s, the 10s into 1s, and the 1s into an infinite number of figures stretching to the right of the decimal point. The invention of the punch card system in the 1920s provided machines that are able to file automatically, when fed the right information. The tiny punch marks on a telephone billing or a check represent a language which the machine understands. Today's high-speed filing systems enable clerks to retrieve information in a few seconds. A modern elevator file contains electrically powered shelves that operate in 3-second intervals. The file clerk presses a button and a mechanical "traffic cop" determines priority and routes the desired information by the shortest distance, reducing travel time to a minimum. This new file stretches from floor to ceiling, conserving valuable office space.

The extent to which modern technology has

tamed the paper work monster is a moot point. Through micrographics, we can reduce 3000 letters to a 100-foot roll of 16 mm microfilm. An entire document file can be stored on a 4- by 5-inch sheet of film or microfiche. Engineering drawings can be reduced to a 35 mm chip and mounted on an aperture card, a tabulating card capable of machine sorting, selection, and printout. Automatic typewriters and text-editing equipment are able to produce printed output at speeds from 100 to 450 words per minute. In time-shared or minicomputer-based systems, a separate high-speed line printer is often located at a central location and used for high-volume work (direct mail labels, envelopes, form letters) at speeds often exceeding 20,000 words per minute. The electromechanical technology available is astounding, but it does not deal with the source of the problem.

## INFORMATION RETRIEVAL

It is the effectiveness of the information retrieval system that determines the difficulty of the records management problem. Planned well, with the users' needs in mind, an information retrieval system can be a highly effective corporate tool. It provides a company with a continuing capability to find, recognize, and utilize business intelligence—a major factor in how strongly a firm can compete for its share of the market. If poorly planned, the retrieval system may be a complex, glamorous toy, expensive yet of little help. The key to retrieval usefulness is not the machine used but the design of the system. For the average business firm, the problem is not one of machines at all, but how to identify and select information to be indexed and then how to file it so it can be found when needed.

**Documents in Subject Files** There are two basic types of records: transaction and reference. *Transaction* documents, such as invoices, checks, requisitions, and purchase orders, lead themsleves readily to simple patterns of numeric or alphabetic filing. *Reference* documents, however, are difficult to file and find again. It was for these documents—which account for about 10 to 15 percent of the paper work load—that the retrieval system was developed.

There are two principal types of subject files: dictionary and functional. The *dictionary* pattern is a simple, straight alphabetic arrangement, self-indexing in nature and requiring a minimum of thought for filing and retrieving information. It is a perfectly valid system, but it becomes cumbersome when related documents get too widely separated, thus decreasing the speed and convenience of access.

When the dictionary approach becomes unwieldy, most firms turn to a *functional* breakdown as a means of classifying, filing, and retrieving documents. Many functional approaches are possible; they vary with the size, complexity, and operations of a company. Functional systems are a hierarchical arrangement of related functional organization terms or subjects, i.e., Personnel, *a.* Benefits, *b.* Pension Plan, etc. Furthermore, most subject classifications are hierarchical; that is, each major subject is, in turn, divided into subordinate subjects. These, in turn, may be further subdivided. The Dewey decimal system used by many libraries is a hierarchical breakdown.

*Drawbacks of Functional or Subject Files.* The functional approach is excellent for retrieval in many cases; it is a logical breakdown, easy to understand. It does not require intensive training of personnel in indexing techniques if they already know the company's functions. It is a familiar type of breakdown to most people and helps those who classify information understand where each piece fits. Yet functional files also have severe retrieval disadvantages. Most important is their inherent inflexibility. By prescription, a functional classification is set up in advance; it is a closed system. New subdivisions may be added, but time has a devastating effect.

Imagine a scientific classification set up 500 years ago, and then picture the adjustment required to accommodate the new subjects of today—electronics, nuclear fission, ionic propulsion, etc. Not only must a classification be adjusted, but the shift of thinking over a period of time reduces the chance of finding information of value. For example, consider a searcher trying to retrieve information in a subject he or she thinks of in today's terminology. What is the likelihood that the subject will be defined in the same terms that an unknown indexer used years ago?

**Concept Coordination** One possible alternative to subject or functional classification is to allow the document to classify itself through key terms used in the title or text. Another is to apply a number of descriptors, using a combination of them to help define the document. Either way, whether external descriptors or internal terms are used, the system is known as *concept coordination* or *inverted indexing.*

*Comparison with Subject Files.* Simply expressed, in a subject classification, an item of information (a document) is indexed by a subject heading. This is an item entry because the basic record is the item itself. In a library catalog, the cards for a given book are filed under the author's name, the title, and subject headings. Inverted indexing merely makes the key term or descriptor the basic record; items or documents are listed on cards bearing applicable terms.

*Applications.* Inverted indexing, or concept coordination, is a fast, effective way to provide many retrieval handles for such items as reference documents, slides and photographs, specifications and samples, patents, legal precedents, directors' minutes and resolutions, laboratory notebooks, policies and procedures, personnel skills, inventories, and survey data. It also permits in-depth indexing of the contents or language of a document by means of relevant descriptors, which serve as convenient avenues of retrieval for other documents as well.

Under conventional indexing conditions, a separate index card is created and filed for each of the various concepts contained in a document. Yet in a typical situation, you may want to provide many such retrieval handles. In a marketing research information center, for example, you may wish to retrieve a document by any of the following avenues: title, corporate author or issuing organization, individual author, geographic areas, date of issue, industries or products, type of promotional programs, markets, brand names, type of selling outlet, subject content, and so forth. Using conventional techniques, it is not at all unusual to create as many as 10 or even 20 index cards for each input document. This means that if 10,000 reports and documents are fed into the collection, the index can contain 100,000 or more index cards. Thus it is difficult, from a retrieval point of view, to search the whole index.

Careful analysis of a file of conventional index cards will reveal that many basic subjects or concepts are repeated again and again. In other words, there are many more index cards than there are subjects. Using an inverted indexing system, an index card is created for each subject or concept rather than for each document. As documents are processed into the system, they are identified on the relevant concept cards. This method greatly reduces the number of index cards; a system containing 10,000 documents may be thoroughly indexed with less than 1000 index cards.

Broad retrieval requests can be answered by producing all the documents listed on any one card. Specific requests are answered by matching two or more cards to determine documents that relate to both.

*Variations.* The *uniterm* approach is one type of concept coordination; the terms used in this approach are extracted directly from either the titles or texts of documents. Another approach is IBM's keyword-in-context (KWIC) index, developed by H. P. Luhn, which relies on identification of keywords in the title as a means of indexing. The main advantage of KWIC is that cross references on all keywords are machine-produced. The computer is programmed to ignore insignificant words in the title of the article and index the rest. The efficiency of the index depends on how relevant the words in the title are; if either the author or the publication uses a title to attract the reader rather than to describe the article accurately, the index will be less effective.

*Mechanization.* Concept coordination systems are easily mechanized. Devices and systems available for mechanizing concept coordination include the following:

1. *Optical coincidence (or "peek-a-boo") systems.* These consist of large cards, one for each term or descriptor. Holes are punched in a matrix form, each hole identifying a document for that term. By superimposing several cards, a visual inspection shows which documents contain the required terms.

2. *Magnetic storage.* Indexing can be done on tapes, disks, or other computer memory devices. This is a high-speed machine approach to retrieval and can be used in conjunction with other searching techniques.

3. *Photographic systems.* These use film chips, microfilm in roll form, microfilm cards, sheets of film miniatures, or "aperture" punched cards. Like magnetic storage media, photographic devices can be used in combination with other systems.

The number and variety of available devices call for a good fit between the user and the equipment. Specific user needs are of the utmost importance in selecting equipment.

*Advantages.* Some of the main advantages of the concept coordination approach, whether mechanized or manual, are the following:

*Unlimited expansion capability.* The inverted index is much more flexible than a hierarchical functional classification where the subjects must be defined in advance. It can be more easily expanded to include new subjects, new products, and new ideas.

*Fewer subject classification decisions.* Term systems require less knowledge of the subject; documents almost index themselves. Hence, they do not require indexing personnel with as extensive an education as do hierarchical systems.

*Adaptability to mechanization.* Most of the mechanical information retrieval marvels on the market and the drawing boards manipulate documents (or document images). They rely on concept coordination for programming input and providing document addresses for fast retrieval. Conversion to a manual system of inverted indexing provides a building block for future mechanization.

*Limitations.* In addition to the advantages of faster information input, faster search and response, and higher degree of use, concept coordination has these limitations:

*False drops.* When a search is requested based on any combination of several terms or descriptors, a number of documents having two or more of the descriptors will drop out. Some of these drops will be false; that is, they will not describe the concept the searcher is looking for.

For example, a search for copper-plated nickel is likely to retrieve false drops describing nickel-copper; hence there is a word order difficulty. False drops also occur because of differing word meanings. The searcher looking for documents about outer space may receive those on advertising space if only space is specified. The viewpoint may cause false drops: does the searcher's interest in alcohol pertain to its use as a chemical, as a beverage, as an antiseptic, or as a fuel?

*Specifics required.* In requesting a search, the user must specify what terms apply. One must clarify the meaning of these terms; if information is requested about the substance *pitch*, the user's need must be identified in order to eliminate false drops about motion, acoustics, and angle.

*Links and role indicators.* To eliminate false drops due to syntactics or word order may require the use of links (for example, aluminum casting, casting aluminum; clock radios, radio clocks). Essentially, links define groups of words or ideas that are linked with one another in the original article. A dictionary or thesaurus may also provide role indicators, that is, a code showing the role or part each word plays in the concept of the original article.

## STEPS IN DEVELOPING A RETRIEVAL SYSTEM

The basic objective is to file information for effective recall. A poor filing system is costly in terms of personnel, space, equipment, and information feedback. Most companies would be well advised not to jump into information retrieval immediately. First, they should develop a sound information program. They can start by taking these basic steps:

1. Clean up the company's overall filing system and develop a common filing language. "Clean up" includes destroying obsolete records and removing noncurrent records to storage.

2. Start with a manual process. Both the company and the people will gain experience; make requirements and adjustments along the way. This approach is a form of insurance that what works manually will mechanize easily. It avoids the limitations of a prematurely mechanized system.

3. Become aware of the company's unique information requirements. What do you need to know about your market, your competition, your products, and your industry? Which information is essential, which only "nice to have"? How do your users go about asking for information?

4. Learn about techniques and devices to see what might help you. Avoid a "canned" approach. Your people need information, not machines.

5. Inquire of other companies to learn what has worked for them. But do not build your system based on someone else's needs—this is an expensive shortcut.

6. Discuss your information needs with a management consulting firm that has sound experience in records, filing, and information retrieval. Advice from this source may be the least expensive path to effective information retrieval in your organization.

7. Bear in mind what the basic problem has been and continues to be: how to find relevant information in a reasonable time at a reasonable cost.

8. Whatever your filing or indexing system, train your employees; impress upon them the high cost of error. In a five-drawer file cabinet, 99 percent accuracy means 150 documents misfiled—possibly lost beyond retrieval.

9. Avoid complacency about what you have now, or what you install in the future. It pays to monitor an information program periodically and to inquire who uses it, why, and how much.

10. Recognize that in an information system, the user is the customer. Give your users information about how the system works and what is in it. Provide the language needed to articulate requests. Table R-1 is a useful list against which to audit present and future plans.

**Integration with Management Information Networks** Records management increasingly assumes a vital management role in structuring and managing a company-wide information network. This information network (or management information system) under the most advanced concept is a service designed to provide, at a single point of inquiry, access to all records, information, and data anywhere in the company, including selected outside sources such as subscription information services,

**TABLE R-1  Audit Procedures List**

PART 1.: GENERAL INFORMATION
Name of file.
Location.
Type of service rendered, e.g., engineering, executive, etc.
No. of people serviced.
No. of file drawers and cabinets.
History of files.
No. of items filed per day.
No. of references found per day or week.
No. of requests not found per day or week.
No. of folders prepared each day.
Analysis of references:
    Requester.
    What requested.
    Date.
    Material provided.
No. of file personnel and salaries.
Cost of file space per year.
Retention period.
Check quality of classification system.
Check folder captions against approved subject headings.
Check folders for proper arrangement.
Check records within folders for classification markings, misfiles, and duplicates.
Is there a procedure for disposing of obsolete material? If so what?
Are duplicate copies filed? If not, how is it avoided?
Is each filed item recorded?

PART 2: FILES—CONDITIONS AND ACTIVITY
General appearance.
    Good housekeeping: no papers on top of files.
    Uniform equipment.
    Arrangement of file room.
    Legible labeling on drawers.
    Total number of cabinets or drawers.
File drawers.
    Check for overcrowding (about 3 inches free).
    Check for guides (10 to 15 per drawer).
    Check amount of material in folder (not more than 1 inch).
    Check labels for consistency in typing.
    Check for out cards.
    Check general condition of folders (old or new).
    Check for dust.
General Information
    How many items are filed per day?
    How many references per day?
    What type of system is used? (Dictionary Classified)
    If more than one system is used, how many?
    Ask to see their subject heading list and card file.
    What system is used to follow up charge-outs?
    Is there any difficulty in locating material, and if so, what type especially?
    How many file clerks and supervisors are there?
    Determine whether other copies are being filed elsewhere.
    What is the time period covered?
    Check follow-up system for charge-outs.
    Determine the distance of file from users.
    What is the method of delivery?
    Interview users for comments, suggestions, and degree of satisfaction.

PART 3: FILES SERIES AND ANALYSIS
Status analysis.
    Series name.
    Items composing series (forms nos., color, size, etc.).
    Product (purpose).
    Arrangement (primary, secondary, tertiary, etc.).
    Volume.
    Dates (range).
    Cutoff period.
    Retention (office and total).
    Uses.
    Equipment (type and amount).
    Space.
    Supplies (supplier's name and style).

    Labeling practices.
    Guiding practices.
    Paid worker-hours (includes all paid time including sick leave and vacations).
    Operating costs.
    Duplicate items.
    Number of people.
    Housekeeping.
Accession analysis.
    List of contribution (dictators and secretaries).
    Frequency of incoming collections.
    Volume (postings and/or pieces of paper).
    Age (when received, range).
    Classifying (coding-marking) practices.
    Indexing practices.
    Cross referencing practices.
    Sorting practices.
    Filing practices.
    Worker-hours, accession activities.
    Number of people.
Reference analysis.
    Number of requests.
    Methods of request receipts (phone, visit, writing).
    Methods of request answers (phone, visit, copy, charge-out).
    Requests not answerable.
    Age of requested material.
    Request record.
    Requestors ranked by frequency.
    Charge-out practices.
    Follow-up practices.
    Request interrogation technique (phone particularly).
    Reuester problems (user interviews).
    Worker-hours referencing activities.
    Number of people.
    Average charge-out time retained.
    Refile practices.

PART 4: RECORDS STORAGE FACILITIES
Physical conditions.
    Description of building or space in use.
    Shipping and receiving facilities.
    Fire protection.
    Office space.
    Floor load.
    Elevator facilities.
    Sanitary and health facilities.
    Lighting conditions.
Equipment.
    Type of containers used for storing records, evaluated on the basis of the activity of records stored therein.
Storage system (description of records storage area):
    Height of files.
    Aisle space.
    Records accessibility.
    Area location system.
    Arrangement and control of record containers.
    Labels.
Use of records.
    How are records referred to?
    What control is there for charged-out records?
    What types of service are provided by the records center?
    How is information transmitted?
    What types of information are provided?
Square footage of storage space.
Cost per square foot.
Volume of records stored per square foot.
Number of employees.
Salaries.
Personnel costs per square foot.
Cost for storing and maintaining each cubic foot of records:

$$\frac{\text{Space} + \text{equipment} + \text{personnel} + \text{maintenance}}{\text{Cubic feet of records}} = \frac{\text{cost per}}{\text{cubic foot}}$$

Reference activity: number of references per cubic foot of records maintained.

outside data banks, and the like. The network links available information resources—customer and product information, technical information, market and financial information, etc. The format of the information resources linked to the network ranges from original documents to tab cards, tapes, "real-time" computerized information systems both in-house and on-line, and the newer "public utility" type of data processing service centers.

Given this complexity of relationships, there is no clear-cut pattern of organizational position and reporting for the records management function—beyond the fact that it has acquired a much greater status than it had a short decade ago. Whether or not a company recognizes information management by formal title, the records management function will increasingly assume integrated information management responsibilities.

## RECORDS RETENTION

There can be no quick and easy solution to the records retention problem. An effective schedule is as individual as a prescription for eyeglasses. However, some general rules or guideposts can be given.

**Retention Schedule**   Here are the basic factors to consider in the light of your own operations and experience:

*Legal Requirement.* Pay primary attention to what records must be kept for specified lengths of time in order to comply with federal, state, or local requirements. Also, there are instances where certain records should be kept even in the absence of a specific rule because of statutes of limitation. These laws prescribe the length of time after an action during which legal proceedings can be taken against a company or any of its personnel. Note that it is the information contained in a record that must be kept, not a record as such.

*Administrative Requirements.* In the main, your own operating needs should prevail. Your schedule must take into account your current practices. There are advantages to continuing procedures which are found to be satisfactory and with which your employees are familiar. Also, records of historical value, especially those indicating why certain decisions or policies were adopted in the past, may provide valuable future administrative guidance.

*Administrative Discretion.* It is management's discretion that dictates which records will best satisfy all requirements. For example, the regulations of the Interstate Commerce Commission concerning certain carriers and freight forwarders contain retention clauses stipulating from 2 years to perma-

nent retention for information about property. In addition, payrolls and material distribution sheets must be kept permanently, except when the data is transcribed to other permanent records. But whole series of records frequently contain this information—time cards, vouchers, job tickets, payroll work sheets—and it is within management's discretion to designate one or two of these for permanent retention. In this way, much space and equipment can be saved. Many statutes of limitation also leave room for discretion. In several states, the statute on open accounts is 6 years. Therefore, based on your own past experience, you may decide that it will be sufficient to keep vouchers for small sums (say under $50) for only 3 years.

*Specific Record Groups.* The following typical groups summarize some important factors to watch in setting a retention period for each type of record.

*Accounting, general* (journals, ledgers, trial balance). Journals and ledgers mean different things to different companies. The general ledger, as the basic summary accounting record, is usually retained permanently. The subsidiary journals and ledgers are required only for internal administration and need be retained only through periods of actual use by the accounting department, auditors, or top management. Trial balances are working papers that need be retained only through final audit.

*Accounts payable* (general canceled checks, canceled payroll checks, vouchers). While general canceled checks may be retained for the number of years defined in each state's statute of limitations (average of 6 years), some companies keep payroll checks for only 2 years. Canceled payroll checks can create a volume problem. Activity is greatest in the first few weeks after issuance, and it usually falls to next to nothing after the first year. Vouchers are always a bulk problem. Rather than keep them all for 6 to 20 years, breaks can be made between plant vouchers (retained permanently), operating vouchers (retained for an average of 6 years), and petty cash vouchers (retained for an average of 1 to 2 years). This holds for originals only. Further breaks may be made by dollar value. It pays to limit retaining copies of these vouchers for a minimum number of weeks or months.

*Accounts receivable* (billing copies of invoices, credit-memo invoices, accounts receivable ledger). Management's chief concern is with the unpaid invoices. Paid invoices, particularly large-volume, small-dollar-volume items, may often be disposed of within 6 months to 2 years. Most complaints on payment or amount of payment are received within this period. Equally important is minimum retention of any invoice files that duplicate the basic record (arranged by customer or by invoice number). Only those invoices connected with items of new design or the first item of a patentable product require long, indefinite retention. The accounts receivable ledger, as a basic summary of credit sales, needs to be kept only so long as it is a ready index to invoices or total daily sales. Where there is no other summary of sales, it may be useful to retain the ledger indefinitely for historical purposes.

*Legal* (contracts, copyrights, patents, trademarks, suits). Copyrights, patents, and trademarks are usually retained permanently. Contracts are more often kept for 6 years after expiration, but when renewed annually are generally kept for shorter periods. Records on lawsuits are typically kept for 6 to 10 years after settlement. Bulky work papers and routine notes connected with contracts and suits should be cleaned out as soon as the matter is legally completed.

*Payroll* (earnings records, payrolls, pension records). The basic legal requirements are (1) Internal Revenue Service: 4 years for earnings records (Federal Insurance Contributions Act and Federal Unemployment Tax); (2) Department of Labor, Wage and Hour Divison: 3 years for payrolls, 2 years for earnings records; and (3) the Department of Labor, Divison of Public Contracts: 4 years for wage and hour records. Pension records are usually retained permanently and may often serve as the earnings record as well.

*Personnel* (applications for employment, attendance records, time clock cards, employee history records, personnel folders). Where a company maintains both employee history cards and personnel folders, the history cards may be destroyed within 1 year after termination of employment. An exception to the latter might be the top executive personnel data. Employment applications should be kept only for jobs or persons where the company anticipates action in the near future. Attendance records, time clock cards, and related data should be handled as a package. Where this information is summarized on project or payroll records, the bulky initial records may be discarded within 1 to 6 months.

*Production* (job tickets, maintenance records, operating reports, production orders). Job tickets and production orders are really only of value in processing the order through the factory or when the customer raises questions on delivery or quality. These points come up in the initial months after shipping. Actual production orders are the only ones that warrant retention beyond 1 year. And of all the records for one order (e.g. job ticket, shipping ticket, bill of lading) only one needs to be retained in the original. Most information is repeated from one form to the next. Maintenance records are usually retained for the life of the equipment on which the data are compiled. Monthly operating reports on production are valuable up to 2 years. Annual operating reports should be kept permanently for historical and management purposes.

*Purchasing* (bids, purchase orders, receiving reports, purchase requisitions). Purchase orders should be broken down into categories for retention purposes: major equipment, expendable supplies and materials, and so forth. Major purchase records, particularly where specifications are included, might be kept for 6 years. The retention period for routine items may be cut to 3 years and still stay within legal requirements on proof of local purchase and on records of use for tax purposes. Purchase requisitions need to be retained only until the items are received, since the data are covered on the purchase order. Receiving reports are usually supporting documents for the accounts payable vouchers and are retained accordingly. Bids are kept after a contract is let out only so long as management wants them for postaudit purposes, and so long as purchasing agents may need them as references for the next contract for the same service or items.

*Real estate* (deeds, leases). Deeds, rights of way and easements are usually retained permanently; leases for 6 years after expiration. If leases are renewed annually, they may be kept only for the current year plus 1 additional year.

*Sales* (correspondence, customer orders, sales staff reports). Sales correspondence on deliveries, acknowledgements, bids, and so on need only be kept at the most 30 to 60 days for possible answer and follow-up policy. Policy letters should be segregated and retained permanently. Customer orders in sales departments are only copies of accounts receivable files and should be kept, if at all, for minimum periods. Sales staff reports on individual sales and expenses are important only for immediate review. They warrant keeping for only a few months.

*Secretarial* (annual reports, bylaws, minutes of stockholders meetings, canceled stock certificates). The first three items are usually kept permanently. Canceled stock certificates are not governed by any federal legal requirement (except for regulated companies) and may be destroyed at the discretion of the company. However, most firms keep a formal certificate of destruction.

*Tax* (purchase-and-use tax returns, state and federal tax returns). Regulations on purchase-and-use taxes usually state that a city must announce its intentions to act on a company's returns within 3 years. There is no limitation, however, in cases of fraud. The same holds true for state and federal returns. The purchase-and-use tax statements are usually retained for 3 years. State and federal returns, being more involved, are retained at least 6 years, and often permanently. Work papers may be destroyed within the minimum periods.

*Traffic* (bills of lading, freight bills, packing lists). The only legal requirement on these items is on "order, shipping and billing records" (Department of Labor, Wage and Hour Division) for 2 years. However, there is rarely need for more than one official record to cover any one shipment (*see also* section above on production).

**Operating under a Retention Schedule** While the core of a sound record-keeping program is an accurate retention schedule, an efficient system also means the following:

1. Know what records and how many of them you have. A physical inventory should be taken of all your records, preferably under the direction of the person who is responsible for the entire operation. It is not necessary to examine every single piece of paper, only the different groups of records. Using a separate sheet of paper for every record type, record the following facts: (*a*) type of record (checks, accounts payable, employment applications, and the like); (*b*) period covered, beginning and closing dates; (*c*) department that has jurisdiction over the record, such as sales, shipping, or accounting; (*d*) location of the record; (*e*) kind of equipment the record is in; (*f*) volume in cubic feet: letter-size drawers usually contain 1.6 cubic feet, legal-size 2 cubic feet; and (*g*) amount of space occupied by files and by shelving for records.

2. Learn how much use is made of each record type. Have a reference analysis made over 3 to 6 months to see how frequently a given type of record is actually used. This information will give you a factual basis for earmarking records for retention, destruction, or storage in a low-cost records center.

3. Set up a low-cost records center. Once you know what records you have, how often they are used, and how long to keep them, you are prepared to realize substantial dollar savings in equipment, space, and personnel by scheduling inactive records for transfer to a new type of records center. Such a center can ensure both better reference service and economy if you locate it in low-cost space away from the office and institute a reference system. You can use the center for records that must be kept permanently and for those not yet old enough to be destroyed or sold as waste paper.

1048

*Essentials of a Records Center.* An effective records center should include the following elements:

*Shelving.* Space-saving shelves, preferably of metal, are used to store cartons of records. Ordinarily, 12 cartons can be stored satisfactorily on a 32 × 42 inch shelf.

*Cartons.* Corrugated cardboard containers having 10 × 12 × 15 inch dimensions are ideal. They may be used for either letter- or legal-size documents. Economical and sturdy, they may be obtained from a number of manufacturers.

*Index.* Records should be indexed as they are boxed for storage. Each cardboard box should have a number which designates the permanent location assigned to it in the records center and an inventory sheet showing the contents of the box.

*System.* A system for obtaining information on records from the center should be established. It should include procedures for finding material rapidly and for returning it to its proper place after use.

**Conclusion** Paper work and miles and piles of files are not like the weather—you can do something about them!

*See also* ADMINISTRATIVE MANAGEMENT; COMPUTER SYSTEMS; DATA PROCESSING PRINCIPLES AND PRACTICES; FORMS DESIGN AND CONTROL; INFORMATION SEARCH; INFORMATION SYSTEMS, MANAGEMENT (MIS); PAPER WORK SIMPLIFICATION; SYSTEMS AND PROCEDURES; WORD PROCESSING.

### REFERENCES

*Administrative Management*, Geyer-McAllister Publications, 51 Madison Avenue, New York, N.Y. 10010.

Bassett, Ernest, D., and David G. Goodman: *Business Filing and Records Control*, South-Western Publishing Company, Incorporated, Cincinnati, 1974.

*Information and Records Management*, Information and Records Management, Inc., 250 Fulton Road, Hempstead, N.Y. 11550.

Johnson, Mina M., and Norma F. Kallaus: *Records Management*, 2d ed., South-Western Publishing Company, Incorporated, Cincinnati, 1974.

Maedke, Wilmer, Mary F. Robek, and Gerald F. Brown: *Information and Records Management*, Glencoe Press, Beverly Hills, Calif., 1974.

*The Office*, Office Publications, Inc., 1200 Summer Street, Stamford, Conn. 94305.

*Records Management Quarterly*, Association of Records Managers and Administrators, P.O. Box 281, Bradford, R.I. 20808.

ROBERT A. SHIFF, *Naremco Services, Inc., Management Consultants*

**Recruiting** (See EMPLOYMENT PROCESS.)

**Recruiting, employee** (*See* PERSONNEL ADMINISTRATION.)

**Recruiting, executive** (*See* SEARCH AND RECRUITMENT, EXECUTIVE.)

**Recurring data chart** (*See* PAPER WORK SIMPLIFICATION.)

**References, employment** (*See* EMPLOYMENT PROCESS.)

**Regression analysis** (*See* FORECASTING BUSINESS CONDITIONS; MARKET ANALYSIS; OPERATIONS RESEARCH AND MATHEMATICAL MODELING.)

# Regulated industries, management of

All industries are regulated to some extent. Regulation of financial reports, occupational safety, environmental impact, and employment conditions is ubiquitous, but there are groups of companies that are also subject to regulatory control over the prices they charge for their products and the way they operate their businesses. These are companies serving a public interest of a type that can best be satisfied if competition is limited.

**The Regulated and Regulators** The scope of companies that are subject to price and operating regulation for this purpose is quite broad. The major groups are (1) energy distribution companies such as electric and gas utilities and natural gas pipelines; (2) transportation companies such as airlines, railroads and truckers; (3) communications companies such as telephone, telegraph and cable TV systems; and (4) financial companies such as banks and insurance underwriters.

The agencies responsible for regulating prices and operating conditions for these companies are numerous. Each state has its own, as does the federal government. On the state level, energy distribution, transportation, and communications companies are usually regulated by a public utilities commission and financial companies are usually regulated by banking and insurance commissions. The jurisdiction of these agencies over prices and conditions of service does not extend to activities over which the federal government claims jurisdiction, such as transactions in interstate commerce. Authority over such activities rests with federal agencies such as the

Federal Power Commission, the Interstate Commerce Commission, the Civil Aeronautics Board, the Federal Communications Commission, the Federal Reserve Board, and the Comptroller of the Currency. The split between state and federal regulation sometimes produces conflicts.

**Regulatory Intent** Regulated companies can be placed in two categories. The transportation companies and the financial companies are regulated to avoid the type of competition that would disrupt the vital services provided by these industries. In these industries price competition is restricted and similar companies charge similar rates. The cost for assurance that service will be available even to individuals who are difficult or costly to serve is generally reflected in regulated prices that are higher than would result from unrestrained competition.

Modern regulation of electric and gas utilities, telephone systems, and pipelines (the public utilities) is based on the prevention of competition that would result in unnecessary duplication by competitors of very expensive facilities. Regulated prices are based on the costs in each individual company and may vary widely from company to company. Price competition is avoided by granting each company an exclusive service territory. This type of regulation holds prices lower than would result from unrestrained competition.

Because of declining markets for their services, railroads are a special case, but may be classified most readily with the other transportation industries. This is not so much because of the type of service they offer as it is that the goal of railroad regulation is to maintain railroad service; nevertheless, railroads have a number of the characteristics of the public utilities.

The rationale that regulation is a substitute for competition is only partially true in the real world of business. Competition is generally only restricted or prohibited between similar types of companies, such as telephone companies. It is not always restricted between different types of regulated companies within the same industry group, e.g., between an electric utility and a gas utility. In some cases the restriction is in one direction only, as when a natural gas utility that is prohibited from promoting sales of its product competes with an oil company that has no such restrictions.

The situation is even less clear outside the public utilities. In the transportation and financial industries competition on a basis other than price is common, such as passenger services offered by airlines and coverages offered by insurance companies. In the banking industry, interest rates paid to business depositors are severely restricted by regulation while interest rates charged to business borrowers are established largely by competitive factors. Managements of regulated companies will, therefore, sometimes be operating in the same competitive climate facing any industrial firm and sometimes in a closely controlled noncompetitive atmosphere.

**Regulatory Outlook** It is possible that some regulation of prices and operations will be extended to other industries in the future, but this is not necessarily so. New industries that develop within or in competition with one of the already regulated industries may find it difficult to escape such regulation. Other than this, however, it does not seem likely that other industries face possible price and operations regulation unless they have some of the characteristics of public utilities. The antitrust laws should be adequate to take care of other circumstances.

Any industry, however, that believes it requires some protection from competition is a candidate for regulation, particularly if disruption of its service or product would have a widespread economic impact. In other countries, this set of circumstances has resulted in nationalization of industries such as coal mining or steel. In the United States regulation is more likely than nationalization.

**Impact of Regulation on Management** To the extent that regulation replaces competition, it does so by protecting the customers from undue exercise of monopoly power. In the financial industries this is accomplished in the traditional way of limiting expansion by individual companies and encouraging new companies. This is not much different from the impact of the antitrust laws in other industries. In practice, of course, regulations concerning competition in the financial industries do differ from specific antitrust laws, but a discussion of the distinctions is beyond the scope of this entry.

In other regulated industries protection from monopoly power is accomplished by requiring the regulated company to provide a certain level of service and by regulating the prices that can be charged for such service to levels that reflect only a regulated company's or industry's cost to provide such service. These restrictions have significant impacts on management that are not felt by other industries.

*Financial Aspects.* The requirement to provide a certain level of service imposes financial as well as operating burdens on management. Public utilities have an obligation to provide service to anyone who applies for it. This imposes on utility management the burden of raising funds to provide facilities for that purpose regardless of economic, money market, or corporate financial condition at the time the funds are required. Some regulated companies, such as

airlines, have considerable flexibility in meeting the levels of service required since they can phase their purchase of aircraft and rearrange schedules. Others, such as natural gas pipelines, have little flexibility because every major investment in new facilities must be approved by the Federal Power Commission as being required to serve customers. However, all publicly owned nonfinancial regulated companies spend much of their management time raising money and maintaining good relations with the financial community. These activities are particularly important because most major nonfinancial regulated industries tend to be capital intensive. For example, the average electric utility sells $1 of electricity each year for every $4 it has invested in fixed assets. In most industries, sales of $1 of product are backed by less than $1 of investment. This makes a regulated company's earnings and financial stability more sensitive to capital structure policies and cash flow management than is true in most businesses. The adequacy of a company's earnings in a given year often depends on the success of management in setting and implementing policies in these two areas. It is not surprising that in many regulated companies the chief financial officer has more authority and influence than anyone but the president.

*Visibility.* Price regulation also creates unique problems for the transportation and public utility industries. Since such regulation is based on costs, anything necessary to determine those costs must be disclosed to the regulators. Once disclosed, it usually becomes available to the public. Such information often covers management policies, operating practices, financial transactions, and plans for the future. It is the type of fishbowl atmosphere that requires significant management effort and expertise in external relations. It is important that senior management, particularly the chief executive, have a sensitivity to key public policy issues and be able to explain positions on them to the press and citizens groups that may be hostile.

*Accounting Standards.* Although financing and public affairs may be of more importance in regulated industry than in industry as a whole, the reverse is true in other areas, such as accounting for financial transactions. Each regulated industry has a uniform system of accounts that has been specified by its regulatory agencies and which it must follow in recording financial transactions. This reduces the opportunities for "creative accounting" that are open to manufacturers. It also adds to the need for good, open, candid relationships with the financial community since uniform accounting invites superficial comparisons between regulated companies.

*Pricing Structure.* In all but the financial companies, price regulation is exercised through a process called *rate making*. Rates are complex price structures. A separate rate or series of rates is usually established for each type of service provided, e.g., for residential customers of a utility or for dry bulk shipments on a railroad. The rates are established to recover all costs associated with providing such service. The rates are generally structured, however, so that incremental or marginal costs, competitive influences, desired disincentives, and other factors are properly reflected in the final prices charged to individual customers; therefore, rates usually result in different unit prices for similar service to different customers. Designing such rates is a complex process that does not exist to anywhere near the same extent in other industries. Each major regulated company engages specialists in this field, but it is important for management to have a basic understanding of the economics and mechanics of rate making if rational pricing policies are to be established.

*Regulatory Lag.* New rates must be approved by the appropriate state and/or federal regulatory agencies after there has been a full opportunity to examine the basis for them in open hearings. The support for the new rates is based most commonly on past experience and known facts, although there has been some recent movement by some regulatory agencies toward looking to the future. The hearings can be quite lengthy, which leads to management problems not faced by other industries. By the time hearings are completed and a decision rendered, the costs and economic conditions that were used to justify the rates are generally out of date. This regulatory lag not only ensures that a regulated company's rates will not be designed to match current economic conditions but also prohibits rapid adjustment of rates or prices to reflect rapidly changing costs. Past experiences have led to some attempts by regulators to speed up the process of rate adjustments especially for costs over which the regulated industry has no control, such as fuel costs in utilities and airlines. Nevertheless, regulatory lag places a heavy burden on company managements to forecast future conditions accurately and to stand ready to take appropriate action to cut costs and file for new rates early enough to compensate for these changes.

*Information Exchange.* Not all the impacts of price regulation are burdensome. Companies within a regulated industry are generally much freer to exchange information and to discuss policies and business practices among themselves. Trade associations for regulated industries have active committees, made up of industry executives, for exchange of information and discussion of matters that would be prohibited by antitrust laws in other industries. Even pricing information is exchanged, and the committees concerned with rate making are often among the most active. In fact, exchange of information among regulated companies is so widespread that it is possible that legal questions could be raised if one or more companies in a given industry were excluded from the exchange of information in that industry.

*See also* CONSUMERISM AND CONSUMER PROTECTION LEGISLATION; ECONOMIC CONCEPTS; ECONOMIC SYSTEMS; EGALITARIANISM; ENERGY RESOURCES, MANAGEMENT OF; ENVIRONMENTAL PROTECTION LEGISLATION; FINANCIAL MANAGEMENT, BANK RELATIONSHIPS; NOT-FOR-PROFIT INSTITUTIONS, MANAGEMENT OF; PUBLIC ADMINISTRATION; SOCIAL RESPONSIBILITY OF BUSINESS.

### REFERENCES

Black, Kenneth, Jr., and S. S. Huebner: *Life Insurance,* 7th ed, Appleton-Century-Crofts, Inc., New York, 1969.

Bonbright, James, C.: *Principles of Public Utility Rates,* Columbia University Press, New York and London, 1961.

Clemens, Eli Winston, *Economics and Public Utilities,* Appleton-Century-Crofts, New York, 1950.

Dauten, Carl A., and Merle T. Welshans: *Principles of Finance,* South-Western Publishing Company, Incorporated, Cincinnati, 1958.

Garfield, Paul J., and Wallace F. Lovejoy: *Public Utility Economics,* Prentice-Hall, Inc., Englewood Cliffs, N.J., 1964.

Howard, R. Hayden, and Harry M. Trebing, eds.: *Rate of Return under Regulation: New Directions and Perspectives,* MSU Public Utilities Studies, Institute of Public Utilities, East Lansing, Mich., 1969.

Rowe, J. Z.: *The Public-Private Character of United States Central Banking,* Rutgers University Press, New Brunswick, N.J., 1965.

PETER J. McTAGUE, *Green Mountain Power Corporation*

## Regulatory agencies and commissions, United States (*See* GOVERNMENT RELATIONS, FEDERAL REGULATION OF COMPETITION.)

## Relationship chart, layout (*See* FACILITIES AND SITE PLANNING AND LAYOUT.)

**Relationships, lawyer-client**  (*See* LEGAL AFFAIRS, MANAGEMENT OF CORPORATE.)

**Reliability**  (*See* QUALITY MANAGEMENT.)

**Reliability, test**  (*See* TESTING, PSYCHOLOGICAL.)

**Religious-oriented managers**  (*See* MANAGEMENT, FUTURE OF.)

**Replacement cost accounting**  (*See* ACCOUNTING, FINANCIAL; FINANCIAL STATEMENT ANALYSIS.)

**Report, annual**  (*See* SHAREHOLDER RELATIONSHIPS.)

**Report, business**  (*See* WRITING FOR BUSINESS.)

**Reports, control**  (*See* CONTROL SYSTEMS, MANAGEMENT; MARGINAL INCOME ANALYSIS.)

**Reports, exception**  (*See* CONTROL SYSTEMS, MANAGEMENT.)

**Requisitions, employee**  (*See* PERSONNEL ADMINISTRATION.)

**Requisitions, purchase**  (*See* PURCHASING MANAGEMENT.)

**Research, applied**  (*See* RESEARCH AND DEVELOPMENT MANAGEMENT.)

**Research, basic**  (*See* RESEARCH AND DEVELOPMENT MANAGEMENT.)

**Research, catalog**  (*See* PRODUCT PLANNING AND DEVELOPMENT.)

**Research, market**  (*See* MARKETING RESEARCH.)

# Research and development management

Definitions of research and development (R&D) vary and are often controversial. The following will provide a basis for this examination of the subject.

**Research:**  The two kinds of research consist of:

*Basic:* Searches for the understanding of a process or subject, with little expectation of a direct payoff.

EXAMPLE: Studies aimed at a better understanding of the mechanism by which detergents function.

*Applied:* Probes of the unknown for a specific goal or reason.

EXAMPLE: Studies to develop leather substitutes.

**Development:**  Application of science and technology to take a successful applied research project to a commercial scale. Applied research often follows on the heels of basic research. Development is almost always preceded by applied research.

EXAMPLE: Transformation of applied research on leather substitutes to a commercially available product.

**Discovery:**  An innovation—something new or a new application. Research and development are the search for discovery. Through discovery one can implement research or development.

**Application:**  Engineering; the application of science, technology, art, and economics to the definition and solution of real problems.

## OBJECTIVES AND POLICIES

While most sophisticated organizations have objectives and policies, they often are not clearly stated nor do they relate to the concerns of research and development. In such far from uncommon instances, the practical answer for R&D is to generate its own objectives and policies. It can be done without rocking the corporate boat too much. In fact, such action is frequently taken by R&D without recognizing it as such. The act of questioning where the company is going can lead toward a set of priorities for research and development.

**Interdependency of Company and R&D Goals**
R&D may be its own best counsel in the establish-

ment of specific goals. As a group it has more opportunity and time to contemplate the future than do operating divisions. Company objectives can be defined by active discussion in an atmosphere as open as possible with a minimum of "put-downs" for different ideas. In fact, R&D can lead a company to a set of goals—at the very least for the R&D group. Research staffers should meet, argue, and confer to establish an informal set of objectives. The group will then ask for comment and agreement on those goals. While probability of success is limited on the first attempt, perseverance can pay off later. Consider the alternative: Research sits on its thumbs while top management does the forward planning. Clearly research input is needed. Research objectives and policies ought to be in agreement with the parent organization, but research cannot wait for a set of objectives to be formulated for it. It must be an active part of and often the initiator of the planning dialogue.

## R&D ORGANIZATION

Organizational arrangement can enhance or retard R&D progress and productivity. While organization principles obviously apply to R&D, some are particularly pertinent:

1. Whatever the organizational arrangement is, its purpose is to bring workers together to get jobs done.

2. The overall purpose is to improve operations rather than to classify and categorize work.

3. The most effective organizational groups are frequently informal ones set up by research workers themselves, not by management.

4. Matrix-type systems can be effective, but they require extensive communication to operate well. *See* PROJECT AND TASK FORCE MANAGEMENT.

5. Whatever the organization, communication should be free and open, and it should be encouraged to take place at the lowest possible level.

**Informal Groups and Communication**   Workers must feel free to consult with other researchers across organizational lines. Informal groups (not shown on any organizational charts) develop from these contacts. From this can come good cross-fertilization of ideas, innovations, and problem solutions. This is one of the underlying reasons for adopting matrix management.

Whenever organizations impede communications across lines, there is an inherent risk of lost opportunity. For example: Research is asked to solve a certain plant problem. Initial communication may take Path A shown in Fig. R-1. Future communica-

tion can take several paths, from worst to best. One of the attributes of the "best" solution is that the plant problem will in fact be communicated to the researcher for his or her consideration. That does not necessarily follow for the other two arrangements. Additionally the best solution enables the researcher to obtain a fuller picture of the plant problem. The solution to the plant problem may lie in a domain only uncovered by the dialogue between engineer X and researcher Y.

All communication channels, including the "best" arrangement, have their problems. Engineer X and researcher Y, supervisors A and B, the plant manager, and the research director can all be operating on three different channels, and confusion can result. For example, researcher Y finds out from her manager that there is a plant problem involving product quality. A specific kind of solution is proposed by management which Y is asked to pursue. Y talks to X. In the course of their dialogue Y finds that the quality problem has its origin elsewhere in the plant and that the proposed solution is not only costly, but not as good as an alternative one. Here Y has to be sure to tell her boss what is going on and so does X. If that is done, then all the participants can agree on the new solution. What often happens, though, is that plant manager A finds out from another source about the new solution. He calls research manager B and asks what is going on. B feels embarrassed at not knowing; he thinks he should tell researcher Y not to talk to engineer X so there will be less confusion. While such a move to control communication may be tempting, it should be resisted. Too much is lost by cutting the communication lines between X and Y. The problems which arise periodically from the "best" solution are generally not significant compared to the benefits derived from it.

## BUDGETS

Budgets for R&D vary from industry to industry and from company to company within an industry group. Like those for other functions, the R&D budget reflects:

1. How much available money a company has

2. What a company feels it needs to accomplish its objectives

3. What its competition is spending

Typically, budget preparation starts some 3 to 6 months before the end of the fiscal or planning year. Actual methods differ from one firm to another, but most involve estimates of capital requirements and necessary expenses. These go hand in hand with the

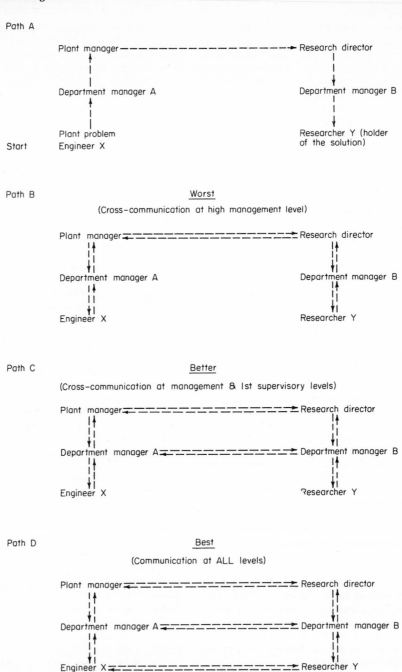

Fig. R-1. R&D communications paths.

R&D program and are useful for historical perspective. They are also helpful in preparation of the next year's budget to the extent that there are no large changes in the scope of the R&D program. Since budgets are only projections, it is important not to get caught up in endless detail about the accuracy of forecasts. It is wise to keep a good perspective about the budget; once the budget is approved, the spending rules are generally less stringent than those used in formulation.

**Comparative Allocations** Recent changes in accounting rules make it possible to see what various companies and industries are doing. Prior to 1975, data were scarce, and there was no uniformity of reporting. Currently, there are restrictions as to what cannot be listed as R&D. These include routine product improvements, seasonal style changes, patent and licensing costs, and others. Reported figures show no distinction between research and development, but this is understandable since one person's applied research is another's product development. R&D expenditures by industry group are shown in Table R-2 as a percent of sales and on a per employee basis. Range within the group is given as well as the industry composite.

## PROJECTS

Ideally, research money should be spent on projects where there is a good chance for a positive payoff. This is easier said than done. The research staff itself, however, may be the best source for sound project ideas. Unfortunately, some research people are uncomfortable with the notion that they are a valuable resource for future company activities. Nonetheless, the R&D staff itself is an excellent starting place. Good research ideas often come from unexpected sources, too. Consequently, management often has to force itself to be open to suggestions that come from seemingly unqualified sources. It is costly to think that those well versed in a specialty have a monopoly on all the good ideas in that specialty. Often the reverse is true; people outside the specialized area may have the most objectivity. They are not constrained by the knowledge of the specialty.

Marketing, for example, can be a fertile source for research projects. By its very nature, marketing contacts people with problems to be solved. These should be thought of as research opportunities. Management, generally, is a good source for research ideas. While research, marketing, and management constitute the major sources of research ideas, they are by no means the only sources.

**TABLE R-2 R&D Expenditures by Industry Group**

| Industry group | 1975 expenditures | | | |
| | % sales | | Per employee | |
| | Range | Av. | Range | Av. |
|---|---|---|---|---|
| Aerospace | 0.4–22.7 | 3.2 | 105–7535 | 1324 |
| Appliances (including trucks and parts) | 0.7–2.9 | 1.2 | 181–1188 | 369 |
| Automotive | 0.8–3.8 | 2.7 | 198–1796 | 1340 |
| Beverages | 0.1–0.6 | 0.3 | 94–397 | 253 |
| Building materials | 0.1–3.9 | 1.2 | 68–2098 | 527 |
| Chemicals | 0.1–7.5 | 2.6 | 109–4626 | 1570 |
| Conglomerates | 0.1–2.9 | 1.5 | 31–1503 | 571 |
| Containers | 0.1–1.5 | 1.1 | 80–677 | 495 |
| Drugs | 0.9–8.9 | 4.7 | 357–4646 | 2016 |
| Electrical/electronics | 0.5–16.5 | 3.0 | 219–3390 | 1038 |
| Food | 0–2.5 | 0.5 | 0–2439 | 303 |
| General machinery | 0.3–4.6 | 1.7 | 113–2955 | 673 |
| Instruments | 0.1–15.2 | 5.4 | 81–5676 | 1990 |
| Leisure time | 0.2–3.3 | 1.7 | 73–1391 | 620 |
| Metals and mining | 0–7.1 | 1.2 | 168–2646 | 698 |
| Misc. manufacture | 0.1–2.8 | 1.8 | 22–1828 | 770 |
| Fuels (oil/coal) | 0–.9 | 0.4 | 0–2346 | 1008 |
| Office equipment, computers | 0.3–15.2 | 5.6 | 202–4973 | 2260 |
| Oil service and supply | 0–4.5 | 1.2 | 0–2490 | 396 |
| Paper | 0.1–2.0 | 0.8 | 50–1203 | 432 |
| Personal care products | 0.1–6.4 | 1.6 | 16–4916 | 1074 |
| Service industries | 0–11.6 | 0.3 | 0–5271 | 170 |
| Special machinery | 1.0–3.3 | 1.0 | 537–1821 | 1360 |
| Steel | 0.1–2.4 | 0.6 | 158–1576 | 294 |
| Textiles/apparel | 0–4.3 | 0.4 | 0–2125 | 103 |
| Tire and rubber | 0.5–6.5 | 1.9 | 190–1223 | 740 |

SOURCE: "Survey of Corporate Research & Development Spending: 1975," *Business Week*, June 28, 1976, pp. 62–84.

**Project Selection** Successful research effort comes from the proper selection of projects—provided there are good projects proposed. No culling process can produce good fruit from a poor lot. Selection of projects is typically done through a quasiformal procedure of project proposal, with backup data prepared on the proposed project for review by research management. Project selection is based on an assessment of payoff. Accordingly, there are critical questions to ask of a proposal:

1. What are the probabilities of success? Low? Medium? High?

2. What is the specific nature of the payoff if the project is a success?

3. What kind of resources must be committed by the research group to support the proposal? What will they cost?

4. Will the company exploit the project if successful? How?

5. Will there be a market for the invention if successful?

6. Is the competition ahead or behind? Many

companies may be working on obvious needs; e.g., "What this country needs is a good 5-cent cigar" or "Won't someone invent a really good gloss latex paint?" Thus an assessment of a sure market with a big payoff should be tempered by the thought that others are searching, too.

**Backlogs and Timing** There has been deemphasis of longer-range, less-specific research in American industry. This poses real challenges. Pure research has lost its glamour; concrete results are being demanded. Technical service and short-term development have replaced longer-range work. While this may be good for next year's balance sheet, it can spell long-term trouble. There is probably no good formula for the correct mix of long- and short-term research. Nor is there a sure-fire method to achieve a given program. What seems clear is that research, itself, must support long-term research and argue in its own behalf. Even in companies where long-term goals are not popular, research must keep them in view while working on short-term projects.

One of the best ways to alleviate overemphasis on the short term is to conduct early exploratory work on a small scale. Cast project objectives in as general a way as possible. Keep a sufficiently low profile and do the work necessary to get lead time on those who think only on the short term.

Structuring the R&D function so that research people have designated areas of long-range interest can help in this regard. Such a commitment has several advantages:

1. It indicates to the researcher that the company supports some longer-term objectives.

2. It lends perspective to the research and development program.

3. It is not a hard concept to sell to higher management. For example, to obtain commitment for research on new energy sources may not be difficult. After all, new energy sources are sorely needed. It is a broadly stated objective and easily accepted. On the other hand, a long-term, specifically delineated research project on fuel cells may elicit only corporate wrath because the same executives who encourage energy research may feel that fuel cells have little potential.

With the right research mix—both long and short term—there should be no problem with having a full docket of projects. If there is a problem of too few project proposals, then several questions need to be asked:

1. Has management inhibited its people so they are reluctant to propose new work?

2. Has management force-fed its research group so much that they expect to be told what they will do next?

3. Is the work program so crash-and-crisis–oriented that no one has time or energy to contemplate the future?

4. Has the research group progressed with time? Have the innovators left and the dullards remained?

5. Are all the above true?

**Program and Project Control** It is no easy task to keep a R&D program on a relevant path. Some never get on a good course; once there, it is easy to fall off it. Review measures are necessary for all programs. These are often accomplished through periodic progress (monthly) reports. The frequency of those reports, however, makes them less effective as an overall control than semiannual reports of a more general nature. Periodic reviews of areas of research are excellent for both control and information. For the semiannual report and/or related critique sessions some questions are appropriate:

1. Do the writers of project review reports really know why they are writing them? Do they know the intended audience? All too often the researcher is not aware of either. Management, in turn, may respond negatively to a report if it is written primarily for research specialists.

2. Is the principal investigator invited to the review meetings about his or her project and perhaps to other closely associated ones? If not, a valuable resource is not being put to full use.

3. Is the management group getting out of its offices to talk to the R&D group face to face in an informal manner? Discussions held in the researcher's territory can be much more informative than those held in the manager's office.

**Project Termination** Deciding when to stop a project is sometimes more difficult than determining when to start one. If there are regular program review sessions, the answer will be easier. Workers generally want to continue their projects; they cannot·be relied on for an objective evaluation. Nonetheless, they should be asked their opinions; they should know more about their project than anyone else in the company. Negative answers to any of four key questions may help in making the termination decision.

1. Have the major objectives been accomplished? Is the project really finished but still hanging on because of inertia?

2. Have the major objectives been reduced as work has progressed? That is, "Six months ago we

were aiming for Mars; now it is the moon. Perhaps we should throw in the towel."

3. Has the marketplace undergone changes that will cut the scope dramatically? A better "bias" tire has far less chance for success if the public wants radial tires.

4. Has the company itself undergone a change in philosophy, making an area of R&D not as vital? This is one time when quitting probably hurts the most. R&D may think it has a winner, but company attitudes have changed. It may be that the company position was never well defined to begin with; the definition came only when confronted with a real prospect for a new venture.

## EVALUATION OF R&D MANAGEMENT PERFORMANCE

Over the long haul, management of research and development must be judged by what the function accomplishes:

1. Is there a good flow of technology from the laboratory to operations?

2. Do operations personnel view R&D as an asset?

3. Does operations seek help from R&D or does it go outside the company for support?
Answers provide objective estimates of R&D performance and are good indicators of the quality of R&D management.

R&D management can also be evaluated by staff turnover and salary administration. Low turnover does not necessarily mean good management. The reverse may be true. A mediocre staff with mediocre management will have very low turnover. The clue is to look at who is leaving and why. Salary administration should provide similar indications. Some people should be expected to complain about salaries. Are they the low achievers? Are they leaving? Or are the high performers unhappy and moving on? What is important is *who* is unhappy and *why*.

Other indicators of management's influence on R&D performance involve a look outside the organization. Do R&D people participate regularly in conferences and professional activities? Is their organization highly regarded by other companies?

Finally, in evaluating research managers these questions might be asked:

1. Are the people under each manager's supervision growing as professionals? Are their skills increasing? Are their job assignments and projects changed from time to time?

2. Does the manager look ahead to new chal-

lenges, new ways to do old things, and increases in productivity?

3. Does the manager represent his or her people well? Does the manager understand the projects they are doing? Will the manager stand up for these people when the going gets rough?

4. Does the manager anticipate or play catch-up? Are there future-oriented departmental goals? Is the manager interested in tomorrow or yesterday?

*See also* ENGINEERING MANAGEMENT; INNOVATION AND CREATIVITY; NETWORK PLANNING METHODS; PRODUCT PLANNING AND DEVELOPMENT; PROGRAM PLANNING AND IMPLEMENTATION; PROJECT AND TASK FORCE MANAGEMENT; WRITING FOR BUSINESS.

### REFERENCES
Cook, C. F.: "Troubled Life of the Young Ph.D. in an Industrial Research Lab," *Research Management*, vol. 18, May 1975, pp. 28–31.
Horwood, R. M., and R. Hinden: "Supreme Court Adopts Liberal Definition of R&D Deductibility under Section 174," *Journal of Taxation*, vol. 41, July 1974, pp. 2–5.
"How GM Manages Its Billion Dollar R&D Program," *Business Week*, June 1976, pp. 54–58.
Souder, W. E.: "Achieving Organizational Consensus with Respect to R&D Project Selection Criteria," *Management Science*, vol. 21, February 1975, pp. 669–681.
"Where Private Industry Puts Its Research Money," *Business Week*, June 28, 1976, pp. 62–83.

CARLE C. ZIMMERMAN, JR., *Marathon Oil Company*

## Reserve stock locator systems   (See INVENTORY CONTROL, PHYSICAL AND STOCKKEEPING.)

## Resources, energy   (See ENERGY RESOURCES, MANAGEMENT OF.)

## Resources, physical   (See ENVIRONMENT, PHYSICAL.)

## Responsibility   (See AUTHORITY, RESPONSIBILITY, AND ACCOUNTABILITY.)

## Responsibility, management   [See OBJECTIVES, MANAGEMENT BY (MBO).]

**Responsibility accounting** (*See* AC-COUNTING, COST ANALYSIS AND CONTROL.)

**Responsibility chart** (*See* PAPER WORK SIMPLIFICATION.)

**Responsive bid** (*See* MARKETS, PUBLIC.)

**Results from training** (*See* DEVELOPMENT AND TRAINING, MANAGEMENT.)

**Results management** (*See* MANAGEMENT, FUTURE OF.)

**Retail credit** (*See* CREDIT MANAGEMENT.)

**Retailer** (*See* RETAILING MANAGEMENT.)

**Retailer classifications** (*See* MARKETING, CHANNELS OF DISTRIBUTION.)

**Retailers** (*See* MARKETING, CHANNELS OF DISTRIBUTION.)

## Retailing management

Retailing management includes all business activities associated with selling goods and services to an ultimate or final user for personal consumption. A *retailer* is an independent merchant who stands between a producer and the consumer and, in effect, is the one who serves as the consumer's purchasing agent. The essence of a retailer's operation is the active and prominent role he or she plays as a supplier of the right merchandise at the right time, at the right place, and at the right price. Many functions such as buying, bulk breaking, warehousing, financing, and risk bearing are performed by the retailer, and the success of any retail store depends upon the efficiency with which these functions are performed and how well management has planned for them.

A *retailing mix* is a combination of the store's goods and services, promotion, prices, merchandising, location, sales personnel, reputation, and image, which when blended, create an atmosphere in which the retailer conducts business. Retail store managers must be perceptive in determining what the best retailing mix is for that particular store.

**Decision Influences** Certain social, economic, technological, and competitive factors influence the everyday decisions of a retail manager.

*Social Forces.* These include (1) the general level of the economy, (2) interest rates, (3) income, (4) purchasing power, and (5) inflation.

*Technological Advances.* These include (1) electronic computers, (2) data processing systems, and (3) modern cash registers which aid in inventory control.

*Competitive Forces.* In response to increasingly severe competition, many retailers are forced to change store policies, practices, and procedures and alter their retailing mix in order to remain competitive.

**Forms of Retailing** In adjusting to decision influences, retailing takes a variety of forms. *Warehouse retailing* usually involves a warehouse or barnlike structure. Merchandise samples are displayed in a showroom, and a retailer's entire inventory is located in a storage room adjacent to the showroom. Typically, the warehouse retailer sells only a single line of merchandise, using price appeal to sell only national brands right from the carton.

*Discount retailing* emphasizes the sale of name-brand merchandise with price as the main appeal. Discount retailers, unlike warehouse retailers, carry a reasonably complete line of hard and soft goods with well-known, presold brand names, and this merchandise is consistently sold somewhat below the advertised or manufacturer's suggested retail price. The discount retailing concept is simplicity itself: a one-stop shopping center selling only fast-moving, branded merchandise at cut-rate prices. The discount retailer is often located in a free-standing store, and the rate of inventory turnover is much faster than for traditional retailers selling the same merchandise.

*Department stores* are large retail institutions handling many different product lines. Generally, department store management is divided into four functions: (1) operations, (2) sales promotion, (3) merchandising, and (4) control.

*Chain stores* are retail institutions consisting of two or more units that are centrally owned and managed. Chain stores are usually large-scale retailers and often enjoy competitive advantages associated with their relative size. These advantages may include greater price discounts on buying merchandise for resale, financial strength, a greater number of resources, the ability to spread risks, and in some instances, the ability to sell goods at lower retail prices than some independents. One reason for the latter may be that chains sell many house brands rather than national or producer's brands.

*Specialty stores* specialize in a given line of merchandise and provide consumers with a wide choice in that product line. The specialty store merchant is able to buy a larger assortment of goods than is possible when the same amount of money is invested in several lines of merchandise. By specializing, he or she may have a greater knowledge of consumer brand preferences, prices, styles, and fashion responsiveness than other types of retailers possess.

*Nonstore retailing* consists of mail order, door-to-door, and automatic vending. *Mail-order retailing* allows the consumer to purchase merchandise from a catalog at his or her leisure. Mail-order retailing generally benefits from lower operating costs than in-store retailing incurs. Delivery times, returning goods, and the inability to inspect the merchandise are major disadvantages for the consumer. Probably the oldest method of retailing involves a meeting between the buyer and the seller in the buyer's home. *Door-to-door retailing* is usually associated with producers, although many retailers also sell door to door.

*Automatic vending retailing* lends itself to an amazingly wide variety of products, usually low–unit-value items such as cigarettes, candy, soft drinks, hosiery, cosmetics, etc. Automatic vending retailing is expensive for the retailer because of mechanical breakdowns, theft, and initial equipment investment.

*Franchise retailing* has become an accepted and proven way of operating a retail business. A franchise is a contract which gives the retailer the right to do business under the name and image of a manufacturer or wholesaler. The party granting the license is called the franchisor; the party purchasing the license is called a franchisee. A franchise contract is an agreement between a franchisor (parent company) and a franchisee (individual) whereby the franchisee is provided with an opportunity to conduct a business according to a definite plan. The contract probably includes the franchisor's name and method of operation, inventory requirements, record-keeping, etc. Franchise retailing has encouraged the growth of small independent retailers by providing them with managerial techniques, skills,

training, and know-how. Through a franchise arrangement, the small independent retailer is provided with a proven system of business with the franchisor overseeing the operation of the retail store. For this guidance, aid, and instruction, the franchisee usually pays an initial fee and, in some instances, a percentage of the profits of the business. In essence, the franchisor and the franchisee become partners in business although the franchisee often appears as an independent retailer. *See* FRANCHISING.

**Retail Segmentation** Retailers cannot possibly cater to all markets; thus there must be some division or segmentation of them. Market segmentation consists of dividing a market which has different characteristics into one which has similar characteristics. In retailing, consumer products are classified according to three broad categories and patterns:

1. *Convenience goods* are those products which are usually low in cost and are purchased with a minimum of effort.

2. *Shopping goods* are those products for which the consumer will shop and compare different product features, prices, warranties, colors, styles, and other characteristics.

3. *Specialty goods* are those products which a consumer will make a considerable effort to find. Usually there is a strong brand preference for specialty goods, and the consumer has full knowledge of the product.

Every retailer needs to know why consumers purchase or do not purchase certain goods and services. An understanding of consumer purchasing behavior is the retailer's foundation for developing a proper retailing mix—a combination of goods and services, price, promotion, image, prestige, location, and other characteristics which blended together will result in optimum sales and profits for the retailer. The disciplines of psychology, sociology, and social psychology will aid the retailer in better understanding consumers. *See* CONSUMER BEHAVIOR, MANAGERIAL RELEVANCE OF.

## RETAIL PLANNING

Retail business planning is a process whereby a retailer decides at present what to do in the future. It encompasses a determination of objectives and includes the necessary procedures for accomplishing those objectives. The procedures for attaining goals are referred to as retailing strategies and tactics. From these strategies and tactics, the retailer can select the best alternative for a certain set of market conditions.

In a planning approach to retailing management,

one visualizes a retailing institution as a total system of interacting and related activities, each of which influences and affects the profitability of that business enterprise. In other words, managerial decisions in any one area of a retail business will directly or indirectly affect and influence all other activities within that institution.

**The Retail Business Plan**    A retail business plan is a written document which specifies systematic, orderly, and integrated procedures for achieving certain predetermined objectives within a specified period of time. Briefly, the plan should state what is to be done, how it is to be done, by whom the work will be performed, and when the work is to be completed. Retail business planning has a number of benefits:

1. Objectives for the business are put in writing.

2. It leads to improved coordination of retailing activities.

3. It provides for an effective control system.

4. It results in a more effective utilization of personnel, money, and physical facilities.

*Common Elements.*  Although each retail business plan is tailored to the store, most contain the following common elements:

1. A written statement of a retailer's goals and objectives

2. A determination of a retailer's potential market and a sales forecast for the ensuing year(s)

3. An evaluation of the retail store's location, new or existing

4. A determination of the store's interior layout and exterior design

5. A resolution of the number of resources or vendors from which a retailer will purchase merchandise for resale to the consumer

6. The negotiations with resources (suppliers) for the terms of sale

7. A provision for handling incoming merchandise (receiving, checking, marking, and the movement of goods)

8. A general pricing policy and pricing strategies and tactics to be used by the store to stimulate profitable sales volume

9. The promotional policies and strategies to be used by the store

10. The management's policies and practices for handling a store's personnel

11. A complete financial analysis of the business (including an analysis of sales, expenses, and profits)

12. A merchandise control system (inventory control procedures)

13. An expense control system (accounting procedures)

14. A system for the control of stock losses

**Statement of Goals**    A retailer's objectives must be succinct and specific; e.g., the store will have $1 million in sales next year; the store or firm will increase last year's sales by 11 percent; the store will sell 750 units; or the business will obtain a 10 percent rate of return on investment.

**Potential Market**    A contributing factor toward the failure of many retail stores is management's error in estimating the market potential of a trade area. A proper analysis leads to improved decisions all along the line. For example, assume that a department store chain is attempting to decide in which of serveral suburbs it should locate a branch store. An analysis of market potential and expected sales volume in terms of gross sales in each suburb will be a helpful and guiding factor. There are three basic trade areas: (1) primary, (2) secondary, and (3) fringe. One of the most widely used devices to estimate market potential in a trade area is the index-of-buying-power method. This is based upon (1) the number of people living in a trade area and (2) the amount of purchasing power held by these people. Additionally, the trade area for a particular kind of retail store should be researched and analyzed from several points of view: (1) social considerations, (2) economic conditions, (3) extent and aggressiveness of competition, (4) location and ease of access, and (5) potential sales volume.

**Store Location**    The location of a retail business is of paramount importance since the quality of a location does not remain static; it either improves or deteriorates. Many retail businesses fail because of poor locations, and the store site should be selected carefully. It must be justified by its ability to serve a segmented consumer group.

**Interior Layout and Exterior Design**    Every retail institution has a "personality" which either attracts or repels consumers. The basic purpose of interior store layout and design is to promote profitable sales volume. Accordingly, merchandise arrangement, fixtures, space allocation, and decorations not only should be functional but should create the proper atmosphere for the type of customer served. A store's exterior should be an invitation to the consumer to enter and browse.

**Resource Determination**    There is an adage that states, "One cannot do business from an empty wagon." In other words, a retailer must have the correct merchandise at the proper time and at the right price for the customer if the business is going to be successful. Generally, there are two main sources of supply: producers and distributors. A retailer may purchase from both supply sources, but care should be exercised so that purchases are not spread out between too many sources offering the same type of merchandise. By limiting the number of sources, a retailer will be better able to (1) take advantage of both quantity and cash discounts, (2) establish rapport with suppliers, and (3) stock the latest merchandise for the store's customers.

**Negotiations with Vendors** Before the actual purchases are made, a retailer must negotiate with suppliers on a number of factors. One major point is price, which will vary depending upon the quality, quantity, and various discounts allowed by the vendor. Also, a retailer is concerned with the period of time allowed before payment must be made. This time period is often referred to as *dating*, and together with the price of the merchandise, is called the *terms of sale*. Other negotiable factors include guarantees against a price decline, return of merchandise, and transportation charges.

**Incoming Merchandise** Purchased goods must be received, checked, marked, and placed on the selling floor. A shipment of merchandise should be inspected as it is received from the carrier and a record made. Merchandise should be checked against the invoice for any discrepancies in price, quantity, or quality.

**Pricing** A general policy should underly all prices, although specific prices may be marked on the merchandise as it is received. A general pricing policy may follow one of the three possible routes: (1) pricing above the competition, (2) pricing below competitive levels, or (3) meeting competition with pricing strategies and tactics. Although general price levels of merchandise are determined by many factors, specific retail prices are under the control of the retailer. *See* PRODUCT AND SERVICE PRICING.

**Promotion** Promotional policy should be determined in part by the image that the retailer wishes to project to the consumer. Sales promotion in retailing includes advertising, personal selling, displaying of merchandise, and any other strategy and tactic which induces a profitable sales volume. The mix should attract customers to the store and entice them to make purchases.

**Store Personnel** Staffing may be one of the most important functions of retail store management. Employees must perform retailing activities to the satisfaction of both owner and customer.

**Financial Planning and Analysis** There is no substitute for proper financial planning for either a new or an existing retail business. Inadequate financial planning is not limited to small retailers. Large chains also miscalculate their revenues and expenses.

*Financial planning* focuses on budgeting for the operation of the retail business while *financial analysis* is concerned with controlling sales, expenses, and profits.

1. Sales analysis may show that some products or product lines should be eliminated because they are not profitable. Retail sales transactions are often vital indicators of a store's current performance and can be checked against past or anticipated sales for more effective financial planning.

2. Expenses typically include costs of merchandise, delivery charges, wages, rent, insurance, promotional expenditures, equipment costs, and depreciation. Since these operating costs affect profits, they must be controlled by management.

3. Profits should be analyzed and compared with return on investment by similar retail operations and product line(s). Profit analysis provides the ultimate basis for attaining greater control and efficiency within a store.

**Merchandise Control Systems** Merchandise control systems are designed to aid management by providing precise information on the movement of merchandise into and out of warehouses, stockrooms, display areas, and the store itself. These systems vary from store to store because of factors such as size, type of merchandise, and management philosophy and should be tailored to each store's requirements.

**Expense Control and Analysis** An analysis of operating expenses should determine not only the dollar amount but also their classification. This helps to determine which expenditures should be modified. Whether retail expenses should be reduced or increased depends, of course, on the results expected in the retail business plan. Since expenses vary considerably by the type of business (e.g., self-service to full-service stores) and are affected by other factors (e.g., size, location, and assortment of merchandise), expense control should concentrate on methods by which certain types of expenses can be controlled and/or reduced as opposed to outright elimination of essential operations.

**Control of Stock Losses** Stock, or merchandise, losses vary by the type of retail store and the efficiency of retailing management. Stock losses may range from about 0.5 percent of sales for a well-managed store to approximately 6 percent for those retail stores which are not well controlled.

There are two main classifications of merchandise losses: (1) shoplifting and (2) employee theft. Other reasons for stock shortages include breakage, cash register mistakes, and a failure to correctly weigh or measure certain types of goods. Although a retailer cannot completely eliminate merchandise losses, positive steps can be taken to keep stock losses at a minimum, and the key to low stock losses is proper managerial control.

*See also* ADVERTISING CONCEPTS; CONSUMER BEHAVIOR, MANAGERIAL RELEVANCE OF; CREDIT MANAGEMENT; FRANCHISING; MARKETS, CLASSIFICATIONS AND MARKET ANALYSIS; MARKETING, CHANNELS OF DISTRIBUTION; MARKETING MANAGEMENT; PRODUCT AND SERVICE PRICING; SITE SELECTION; STANDARD METROPOLITAN STATISTICAL AREA (SMSA).

## REFERENCES

Bearchell, Charles A.: *Retailing; A Professional Approach*, Harcourt Brace Jovanovich, Inc., New York, 1975.

Dickinson, Roger A.: *Retailing Management, A Channels Approach*, Wadsworth Publishing Company, Inc., Belmont, Calif., 1974.

Duncan, Delbert J., Charles F. Phillips, and Stanley C. Hollander: *Modern Retailing Management, Basic Concepts and Practices*, Richard D. Irwin, Inc., Homewood, Ill., 1972.

Hartley, Robert F.: *Retailing, Challenge and Opportunity*, Houghton Mifflin Company, Boston, 1975.

James, Don L., Bruce J. Walker, and Michael J. Etzel: *Retailing Today An Introduction*, Harcourt Brace Jovanovich, Inc., New York, 1975.

Marquardt, Raymond A., James C. Makens, and Robert G. Roe: *Retailing Management*, The Dryden Press, 1975.

Rachman, David J.: *Retail Strategy and Structure*, 2d ed., Prentice-Hall, Inc., Englewood Cliffs, N.J., 1975.

Redinbaugh, Larry D.: *Retailing Management: A Planning Approach*, McGraw-Hill Book Company, New York, 1976.

Shipp, Ralph D., Jr.: *Retail Merchandising, Principles and Applications*, Houghton Mifflin Company, Boston, 1976.

LARRY D. REDINBAUGH, *University of Montana*

## Retention schedule, records   (*See* RECORDS MANAGEMENT.)

## Retirement   (*See* PERSONNEL ADMINISTRATION.)

## Retirement benefit plans   (*See* COMPENSATION, EMPLOYEE BENEFIT PLANS.)

## Retirement counseling   (*See* COMPENSATION, EMPLOYEE BENEFIT PLANS.)

## Retirement security   (*See* ERISA.)

## Retrenchment strategy   (*See* POLICY FORMULATION AND IMPLEMENTATION.)

## Return on investment (ROI) analysis   (*See* BUDGETING, CAPITAL; FINANCIAL MANAGEMENT; FINANCIAL MANAGEMENT, CAPITAL STRUCTURE AND DIVIDEND POLICY.)

## Revenue management   (*See* NOT-FOR-PROFIT INSTITUTIONS, MANAGEMENT OF.)

## Revised Order IV   (*See* WOMEN IN INDUSTRY.)

## Right- and left-hand chart   (*See* PAPER WORK SIMPLIFICATION.)

## Risk   (*See* INSURANCE AND RISK MANAGEMENT; RISK ANALYSIS AND MANAGEMENT; STATISTICAL ANALYSIS FOR MANAGERS.)

## Risk, assumption of   (*See* PRODUCT LIABILITY.)

## Risk, perceived   (*See* CONSUMER BEHAVIOR, MANAGERIAL RELEVANCE OF.)

## Risk analysis and management

Outcomes, or consequences, of human actions are rarely predictable with perfect knowledge. Because management decisions do not have inevitable outcomes, these decisions are essentially wagers involving risk or uncertainty. At times, consequences of a particular course of action may be truly inevitable, but decision makers cannot include them in their plans because they do not have adequate knowledge of them. Decisions made under these circumstances are characterized as risky or uncertain.

Technically, risk and uncertainty do not mean the same thing. A situation is *risky* when a complete list of all possible outcomes and the associated chance of their occurence is known in advance. When these conditions—knowledge of possible outcomes and the chance of their assurance—are not met, the situation is characterized as *uncertain*. The decision process under risk involves both the measurement of and attitude toward risk. The decision process under uncertainty involves listing the economic outcomes under differing conditions for every decision alternative and selecting the decision without weighting different outcomes by the chance of their occurence. As will be demonstrated later, the original distinction revolving around measurement is no longer regarded critical; hence, the distinction between risk and uncertainty is practically ignored. The methods proposed for dealing with uncertainty are, however, of interest to managers, and they will be briefly described below.

## MEASUREMENT OF RISK

Risk is measured in terms of probabilities, reflecting relative changes of occurence of possible outcomes. For instance, if one rolls a die 1200 times, the number 6 is likely to appear 200 times. Thus the probability of number 6 appearing upon a roll of a die is $^{200}/_{1200}$ or $^1/_6$. The same holds true for numbers 5, 4, 3, 2, and 1. Because probabilities are ratios or relative numbers, it follows that when probabilities of all possible outcomes are summed, the sum equals 1. Although the notion of probabilities seems clear and straightforward, it involves one controversial issue. Instead of a detailed discussion of the issue, the description here will be limited to its practical significance.

**Objective versus Subjective Views**   The issue is what happens when the die is rolled only once. In that case, either the number 6 appears or it does not. Is the notion of probability valid? Two different answers are provided. Those who believe in the *objective approach* regard probabilities irrelevant in this instance. They argue that "valid" probabilities can be obtained only if the die is rolled a large number of times. In business situations, such large numbers of trials are obtained when one deals with, say, insurance problems or machine replacement needs. The objectivists also maintain that probabilities are valid only when one additional condition is fulfilled: If the die is rolled the first time and the number 6 is obtained, that should not create a bias for or against obtaining the number 6 in subsequent rolls. In other words, results obtained in earlier rolls or trials should not influence the outcomes in the subsequent rolls or trials. Those who believe in

*subjective probabilities* regard this condition of a *large number* of *unrelated* trials as too restrictive. They believe that even when these conditions are not met, probabilities can be computed by considering the decision maker's experience, intuition, and judgment. Indeed, the probabilities thus obtained are considered by them a valuable tool for systematic decision making. The following example illustrates the conflicting viewpoints.

A firm is considering introduction of a new product in the marketplace. This is the first new product that the firm has developed, and the firm does not think it can introduce another such product in the foreseeable future. The industry experience, however, is that 1 in every 10 new products succeeds. The objectivist is very likely to reject the idea of probability application in this situation because new products are not supposed to come on stream, and thus there is a violation of condition regarding a large number of trials. On the other hand, the subjectivist may take the probability of success being $^1/_{10}$ or .10 on the basis of the industry experience as a starting point, and depending upon the manager's confidence in the new product, revise it, say, up to .20 or down to .05.

Suppose the subjectivist comes up with the figure of .20 as the probability of success of the new product. How does he or she do that? The procedure is somewhat complex,[1] but essentially it boils down to the following proposition. Suppose the manager is offered a choice between two alternatives: (1) Sell the new product development to another firm in the industry for $X, or (2) charge $X to a gambler who gets the same payoff as the successful new product if the gambler draws a white ball from a jar containing 2 white balls and 8 red balls of equal size, and nothing otherwise. If the manager is indifferent toward these two alternatives with equal payoffs for success or failure, then the probability of success or failure to these alternatives should be identical.

**Expected Value**   No matter how the probabilities are determined, it is clear that the larger the probability of an outcome, the more certain the occurence of the outcome. The extreme values are 1 and 0. When an outcome is certain, the probability of its occurence is 1. When the outcome is impossible, its probability is 0. This being the case, it is reasonable to weigh each uncertain outcome with the associated probability—to discount, so to speak, the uncertainty contained in the outcome. When all possible outcomes are thus adjusted with their associated probabilities and summed, the resulting number is defined as the *expected value*, or mean. Because the expected value represents a discount for certainty, it is often a reasonable practice to compare two decision alternatives in terms of the expected value of the possible outcomes and regard as superior the alternative with a higher expected value.

**Variance**   Although the expected value can be an excellent index of risk, it may not always accurately reflect the riskiness of future outcomes. For example, alternative A in the situation shown in Table R-3 has the same expected value ($50) as alternative B. The decision maker may, however, regard alternative B as riskier than alternative A, because the spread from the expected outcome is much smaller for alternative A than for B. To put it differently, the losses and the gains would be much greater for alternative B than for A, if the expected outcome did not occur.

This idea is systematically reflected in the measure of variance. The *variance* measures the difference between an outcome and the expected value. Since this may be positive or negative and since one's interest is in the spread, this difference is squared (a squared number is always positive). The squared difference is weighed with the probabiity of the outcomes so that a remotely possible outcome may not be weighed unduly just because of its large magnitude of difference from the expected value. The sum of the weighted squared difference is the variance. Often, the square root of the variance, called the *standard deviation,* is used as an alternative in place of the variance. It follows from the above description that the larger the possibility that an outcome would differ from the expected value, the larger the variance or the standard deviation. And the greater the risk, the larger the variance (or the standard deviation). Often, a "relative" measure of risk is employed in the form of the ratio of the standard deviation to the expected value. This ratio is known as the *coefficient of variation.*

**Distributions**   Although the measure of variance adequately reflects risk under normal circumstances, it suffers from a conceptual problem as well as a practical difficulty. Conceptually, the measure is likely to be appropriate for symmetrical distributions (Fig. R-2a), but when the distribution is skewed (Fig. R-2b), other measures are called for.

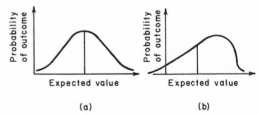

Fig. R-2. Two distributions. (a) symmetrical; (b) skewed.

This discussion will ignore these refinements. The practical problem is in terms of the requirement that the manager will be called upon not only to determine future outcomes possible for each decision alternative but also to assess associated probabilities. Even when the task is feasible, it is questionable whether the effort is worthwhile in terms of time or cost. In this instance, a shortcut to measure both the expected value and the standard deviation may be taken as follows. The manager is asked (1) what is the most likely outcome, M; and (2) what is the highest possible outcome, H, and the lowest possible outcome, L. In that case:

$$\text{Expected value} = \frac{2M + (H + L)/2}{3}$$
$$\text{Standard deviation} = \frac{H - L}{6}$$

Sometimes the measurement is computed along the following lines:

$$\text{Expected value} = M$$
$$\text{Standard deviation} = \frac{H - L}{4}$$

These approximations are based on a *normal* distribution, one of the most widely used distributions. In a normal distribution, if the expected value is taken as a benchmark, say 0, 99 percent of the deviations from the expected value fall in the range $0 \pm 3$ (standard deviation), as shown in Fig. R-3.

In brief, dealing with risk requires measurement of either probabilities or probability-derived measures such as expected value and standard deviation (or variance).

**TABLE R-3**

| (1) Alternative | (2) Probability of outcome | (3) Outcome, in dollars | (4) = (2) × (3) Probable weighted outcome, in dollars |
|---|---|---|---|
| A | .25 | 49 | 12.25 |
|   | .50 | 50 | 25.00 |
|   | .25 | 51 | 12.75 |
|   |     |    | 50.00 |
| B | .25 | −50 | −12.50 |
|   | .50 | 50 | 25.00 |
|   | .25 | 150 | 37.50 |
|   |     |     | 50.00 |

## ATTITUDE TOWARD RISK

As was shown above, sole reliance on the expected value may not lead to a choice of the most desirable alternative. The decision maker who strictly relies on the expected value is described as *risk-neutral*. The decision maker who prefers risk is called a *risk lover* or *speculator*. Most decision makers, however, do not fall into either of the above two categories; instead they are risk averters. A *risk averter* may be defined as a person who prefers higher returns for a given amount of risk (or less risk for a given expected return). Since the attitude of risk aversion is most commonly encountered, this discussion will deal only with that attitude.

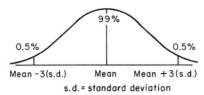

**Fig. R-3. Normal distribution.**

**Risk Aversion** When the probability distribution is specified, the simplest possible way of arriving at a decision is to choose the alternative which has the smallest chance of acceptable adverse results. For instance, avoiding stock-out in inventory management may be too expensive or even impossible. Hence, the manager has to indicate a willingness to take, say, 1 in 20 chances of being out of stock. In terms of the probability distribution, this means that the probability of stock below zero should be .05 or less. Suppose the current inventory policy leads to 1 in 10 chances of being out of stock, as shown by the cross-hatched axis in Fig. R-4*a*. If an alternative policy (with minimum cost increase) provides 1 in 20 chances, as shown in Fig. R-4*b*, the alternate policy should be selected by the manager. Decisions along this line can also be made for optimal debt in the capital structure of the company.[2]

**Outcome Utilities** Although a variety of decisions can also be made along the above line, the decision process is awkward and at times does not lead to the most desirable decision. Suppose an investor is looking at two securities, each having a 5 percent chance of providing zero or even negative return. Should the investor remain indifferent toward the choice of the security? It is possible that the expected return is 10 percent on one security but 17 percent on the other. Thus the choice may

not be a matter of indifference or of purely noneconomic considerations.

One way out is to assign "utilities" to the value of outcomes, and weigh the utilities with probabilities associated with the outcome. The sum of all "weighted" utilities for a decision is the expected utility of that decision. The decision alternative which has the highest utility is the most desirable alternative. How to measure utilities is the critical consideration in this decision process. One way is to define the worst possible and the most desirable outcomes. Suppose −$500,000 and $10 million are two such outcomes. Attach 0 utility units, or *utiles*, to −$500,000 and 1 utile to $10 million. The decision maker is told that a gamble has .10 probability of winning $10 million and .90 probability of losing $500,000; how much would he (or she) be willing to pay for such a gamble? The decision maker's reply is, say, $400,000. In that case

$$\text{Utilities of } \$400,000 = .9 \, [\text{utility } (-\$500,000)]$$
$$+ .1 \, [\text{utility } (\$10 \text{ million})]$$
$$= .9 \times 0 + .1 \times 1$$
$$\text{Utility } (\$400,000) = .10$$
$$= .10$$

Now the decision maker is asked how much he would be willing to pay for a gamble with payoffs of $400,000 and −$500,000 with the respective probabilities of .3 and .7 (these probability figures are not pertinent except in the calculation of the utility of the price that the decision maker is willing to pay

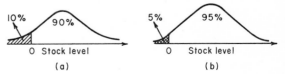

**Fig. R-4. Alternative inventory policies.**

for the gamble). Suppose the decision maker's answer is that he is not willing to pay a single penny for the gamble. After some query, he admits that were he to be *paid* $250,000 for playing the gamble, he would consider it. In that case,

$$\text{Utility } (-\$250,000) = .7 \, [\text{utility } (-\$500,000)]$$
$$+ .3 \, [\text{utility } (\$400,000)]$$
$$= .7 \times 0 + 0.3 \times .1$$
$$= .03$$

Thus the decision maker attaches .03 utiles to the loss of $250,000 and .10 utiles to the profit of $400,000.

In the above example, the range of the scale for

1065

utilities covers the values from 0 to 1. It does not matter if the scale, instead, is $-10,000$ to $+500,000$. What is critical is the ranking of the outcomes in terms of relative desirability. So long as that does not change, the final choice will remain the same irrespective of the scale. Of course, utile assignment does not necessarily remain identical for two individuals; it depends on the individual's attitude toward risk.

One caution should be taken when utilities are determined in the above way. The net utility of two outcomes combined together is not the same as the sum of the utilities of each outcome considered separately. In other words,

$$\text{Utility } (A + B) \neq \text{utility } A + \text{utility } B$$

Thus, when several capital projects are being considered, their evaluation should not be made individually. Similarly, because capital projects are typically added to the existing pool of assets of the firm, they cannot be evaluated without considering the characteristics of the current mode of operations.

**Certainty-Equivalent Values** One of the biggest limitations of the utility approach is the complexity of figuring out not only the probabilities but also the utility associated with each outcome. If, for measurement purposes, the probability distribution can be conveniently collapsed into two numbers, expected value and standard deviation, as shown earlier, the question is whether an effective way can be employed to reflect attitude toward risk in terms of these two numbers. When a decision maker is a risk averter, preferring higher returns for a given amount of risk, it is possible to determine his (or her) risk-return trade-off and thereby arrive at certainty-equivalent values adjusted for risk. If returns are designated by the expected value, EV, and risk by the variance, VAR, the certainty-equivalent value, CE, may be expressed as

$$CE = EV - a \cdot VAR$$

where $a$ reflects the decision maker's attitude toward risk. The larger the value of $a$, the greater the decision maker's aversion toward risk. Determination of $a$ can be shown graphically with the help of Fig. R-5. Suppose the decision maker faces a risky outcome with $EV_1$ and $VAR_1$ as the expected value and the variance respectively. This is designated as point A in the figure. The decision maker is asked to give the maximum price (certain amount) he would be willing to pay for this outcome. Equivalently, if he were to own a business with risk-return characteristics of A, what would be the smallest offer he would accept for selling the business? This amount

is designated by point $C_A$ in Fig. R-5. Amount $C_A$ is the certainty-equivalent amount (note that it is on the vertical axis with variance 0). The line $C_A A$ represents an indifference curve on which the expected utility is constant (any point on line $C_A A$ has the certainty-equivalent value $C_A$). If there is any other risky outcome, say B, its certainty-equivalent value $C_B$ is easily found by drawing a line $C_B B$ parallel to $C_A A$ and passing through the point B. The value of $a$ is provided by the slope of the line $C_A A$ or $C_B B$.

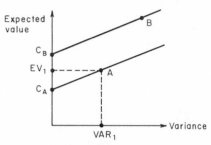

Fig. R-5. Risk-return trade-off and certainty-equivalent values, in terms of expected value and variance.

It is also possible to obtain the certainty-equivalent values in terms of the expected value and the standard deviation, as shown in Fig. R-6. The only difference is that the straight lines are now replaced by the curves.

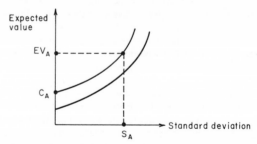

Fig. R-6. Risk-return trade-off and certainty-equivalent values, in terms of expected value and standard deviation.

In brief, the attitude toward risk can be incorporated in decision making in several ways. One way focuses on deviations from the expected value on the downside without explicitly considering the expected value. Another way considers utilities of possible outcomes and adjusts them for the probability of occurence of outcomes. The third way described here is a special case of the second approach in that it takes into account two surrogates of the probability distribution, viz., the expected value and the variance (or the standard deviation). Two major areas of finance where these techniques have been extensively employed are securities selection and capital budgeting. In the next section, some applications in these two fields will be described.

**Application: Securities Selection** When the choice is between a risk security and riskless investment, say, a treasury bond, the decision can be undertaken exactly along the line of reasoning suggested in the previous section. The certainty-equivalent rate of return on the risky security is thus compared with the return on the treasury bond, and whichever provides the higher return will be the choice of the investor.

When the number of risky securities is larger than one, the analyst cannot select these securities in terms of their *individual* risk (variance). This is because the risk of *all* securities combined is not necessarily the same as the sum of their individual risk measures. The variance of two securities, A and B combined, for instance, is given by VAR(A + B) where

$$VAR(A + B) = VAR(A) + VAR(B) + 2COV(A,B)$$

and COV(A,B) = covariance of A with B

In turn, the covariance is defined as follows:

$$COV(A,B) = \text{correlation coefficient } (A, B) \times [VAR(A)]^{1/2} \times [VAR(B)]^{1/2}$$

Thus if returns on two securities are highly positively correlated (the correlation coefficient approximately equal to +1), the covariance will be positive and large. On the other hand, if they are unrelated (with 0 correlation coefficient), the covariance will be 0. Finally, when the returns on the two securities are highly negatively correlated (the correlation coefficient in the neighborhood of −1), the covariance will be negative. Hence,

$$VAR(A + B) = VAR(A) + VAR(B)$$

only when returns on two securities are unrelated. When they are negatively correlated, the *overall* risk—VAR(A + B)—will be smaller than the sum of the individual security risk.

It follows then that individual securities should not be selected in terms of their *own* risk but in terms of their contribution to the risk of the bundle of the securities. A practical problem immediately arises. If there are *two* securities, then *two* expected values, *two* variance, and *one* covariance need to be estimated. If there are three securities, then three each of expected value, variance, and covariances are to be estimated. As the number of securities

increases, the number of covariances to be estimated increases even faster; when there are 50 securities, the number of covariances to be estimated will be 1225!

An ingenious shortcut has been suggested by Sharpe, whereby he links the return on an individual security with a market index such as Standard and Poor's, and the linkage relationship in turn provides the covariance between two securities.[3] For different bundles of securities—portfolios—the overall expected return and the associated variance (or standard deviation) can be estimated. The portfolio that has the highest certainty-equivalent return (along Fig. R-5 or R-6) is the most desirable for the investor.

**Application: Capital Budgeting** Capital expenditures involve cash flows over several time periods. Hence, their evaluation requires adjustment not only in terms of time but also for risk. A widely prescribed decision rule is in terms of the *net present value*, NPV, defined as

$$NPV = \text{cash flow } (0) + \frac{\text{cash flow } (1)}{(1 + d)^1}$$
$$+ \frac{\text{cash flow } (2)}{(1 + d)^2} + \frac{\text{cash flow } (N)}{(1 + d)^N}$$
$$= \sum_{t=0}^{N} \frac{\text{cash flow } (t)}{(1 + d)^t}$$

where cash flow $(t)$ = positive or negative cash flow in period $t$ associated with the project under consideration

$d$ = discount rate

$N$ = economic life of the project

*Risk Adjustment.* Risk involved in the project is adjusted in one of the three ways:

1. Shorten the economic life. If, for instance, a project has a 10-year life, cash flows for only, say, a 7-year time-span are considered in decision making because beyond the seventh year the estimates are deemed too unreliable to be taken into account. The popular payback method is one extreme example where risk is reflected in the shortened life-span of the project.

2. Modify the discount rate. Many companies, for instance, employ a 12 percent discount rate for replacement expenditures, 16 percent for plant expansions, 18 percent for new products, and 24 percent for research and development.

A major problem with the above two methods is that adjustments in the life-span of the discount rate are arbitrary. Thus they are hardly related to the goals of the firm. Further, the payback method ignores not only cash flows beyond the payback period but also the *timing* of flows within the payback period. Similarly, risk adjustment in the discount rate requires it to reflect both the timing and risk considerations. As a result, a constant risk-adjusted discount rate implies that the inherent risk in the capital project increases at a constant rate over time. Introduction of a new product may have substantial risk for the first 2 years, but as the dust settles, the risk may not be as high as at the initial level. Thus, application of a high discount rate such as 18 percent may not accurately reflect the risk inherent in the new product.

3. Adjust the relevant cash flows for risk. This avoids the problems associated with the first two methods. Basically, the technique of the certainty-equivalent value is applied. There are, however, some interesting wrinkles in such an application. Although probabilities associated with the future periods may reflect substantial risk in isolation, they may have smaller risk once resolution of uncertainty *in the interim* is considered. For instance, if one were to estimate cash flows in the fifth year of a new product, the range of outcome may vary, say, from −$2 million to $1 million. However, an ability of the firm to debug or modify the product within 3 years, to increase the advertising budget substantially if the expected demand does not materialize in 4 years, or to modify the price as well as gain better knowledge of the market in the first 4 years may mean that *conditional* outcome in the fifth year would become more certain. A *decision-tree framework* is employed to consider risk modification over time to reflect not only better knowledge of the future but also the manager's ability to modify the eventual outcomes.[4]

The decision-tree method is, however, extremely cumbersome to reflect the basic risk characteristic of the capital expenditure decision: it has to consider not only the risk embodied in the variability of cash flows *within* each period, but also the covariability of flows *between* two periods. The simulation method is reasonable for tackling such a job.[5] However, the tremendous effort required in carrying out such work is economically justifiable only for big projects.

In a nutshell, none of the methods suggested for risk adjustment is perfect for *all* situations. For an important project, where the stakes are high, cash flow modification provides a great deal of flexibility. For routine projects, risk-adjusted discount rates are reasonably adequate. When a manager does not trust his (or her) ability to assess risk or does not believe in the discount mechanism, he (or she) utilizes a payback period—although its justification is hard to demonstrate in a typical situation.

## UNCERTAINTY AND DECISION MAKING

A manager who is ignorant of or unwilling to make subjective estimates of probabilities can still make decisions in a systematic way. The theory of games describes two such ways: the *minimax* (or *maximin*) principle and the *maximax* principle.

Suppose a decision maker is pondering over the alternatives of plant expansion or the status quo. For simplicity, he (or she) thinks that the economy will either prosper if the government aggressively undertakes deficit financing or will have price stability but miniscule growth if the government tries to balance the budget. Further suppose that he chooses not to estimate the probability of the economy being in state 1 (prosperity and inflation) or state 2 (stability and slow growth), because the government action is likely to depend on his decision as well as decisions of other businesspeople like him. Finally suppose that he determines the payoff of each decision corresponding to the two states, as shown in the following table.

| Decision | State 1 (Prosperity) | State 2 (Stability) |
|---|---|---|
| Expansion | +$500 | −$150 |
| No expansion | +$200 | −$ 70 |

**Minimax**  Under the minimax principle, the decision maker will choose the alternative that has the smallest worst loss. The worst outcome of the expansion decision is −$70. Since a loss of $70 is smaller and less painful that a loss of $150, the decision maker will choose not to expand. He has thus minimized the maximum loss.

**Maximax**  Under the maximax principle, he will choose the decision alternative that has the maximum most favorable outcome. In this instance, his strategy would be to opt for expansion (having the most favorable outcome of $500 versus that of $200 under the no-expansion alternative).

**Mixed Strategies**  A further refinement in the form of the *mixed strategies* principle is sometimes introduced. Suppose $P_1$ is the (as yet unknown) probability of prosperity, and $P_2$, the probability of stability. The outcomes have the *same value* when

$$500P_1 + (-150)P_2 = 200P_1 + (-70)P_2$$
$$300P_1 = 80P_2$$
$$P_1 = \frac{80P_2}{300}, \text{ or } .2667P_2$$

Since the sum of the probabilities is unity,

$$P_1 + P_2 = 1$$

Hence    $.2667P_2 + P_2 = 1$

or                $P_2 = 1/1.2667$, or $.79$

Hence, if the probability of stability were to be .79, the likely loss for the decision maker is the same as to what the government does. If the probability of stability is greater than .79, the likely loss is larger for the decision of expansion, and hence it should be rejected. Notice that the minimax solution is obtained for the extreme case where the probability of stability is 1.0. On the other hand, if the probability of stability is less than .79, the expansion decision is preferred to the nonexpansion decision. Again, the extreme case of probability of stability being 0 is the same as the maximax principle. In this sense, the mixed strategy is only a generalization of the minimax and maximax principles.

The example can be easily extended to more than two states and/or decision alternatives. The procedure is cumbersome but does not involve any significant modification.

A question is reasonable at this juncture. Uncertainty was introduced because estimation of objective or subjective probabilities was ruled out, and yet the mixed strategy procedure showed that probabilities were called for, either directly or indirectly. Then why not introduce probabilities from the start and follow the procedures suggested earlier? The answer lies in the calculation of probabilities. In the case of risk, it was implicitly assumed that the decision maker's action would not elicit any hostile response from the opponent so as to modify the probabilities of outcomes. In other words, the nature of the opponent was assumed passive. When the decision maker is faced with a hostile opponent, who is, so to speak, out to wreck the decision maker's plan, the decision maker does not form the decision proceeding from probabilities but instead calculates the probabilities implicit in decision alternatives and reacts to them by making a choice.

*See also* BUDGETING, CAPITAL; DECISION-MAKING PROCESS; FORECASTING BUSINESS CONDITIONS; OPERATIONS RESEARCH AND MATHEMATICAL MODELING; POLICY FORMULATION AND IMPLEMENTATION; SIMULATIONS, BUSINESS AND MANAGEMENT; STATISTICAL ANALYSIS FOR MANAGEMENT; SYSTEM CONCEPT, TOTAL.

### NOTES

[1] Howard Raiffa, *Decision Analysis: Introductory Lectures on Choices under Uncertainty*, Addison-Wesley Publishing Company, Inc., Reading, Mass., 1968.

[2] Gordon Donaldson, "New Framework for Corporate Debt Policy," *Harvard Business Review*, vol. 40, March-April 1962, pp. 117–131.

[3] William F. Sharpe, "A Simplified Model for Portfolio Analysis," *Management Science*, January 1963, pp. 277–293.

[4] John F. Magee, "How to Use Decision Trees in Capital Investment," *Harvard Business Review*, vol. 42, September-October 1964, pp. 79–86.

[5] David B. Hertz, "Risk Analysis in Capital Investment," *Harvard Business Review*, vol. 42, January-February 1964, pp. 95–106.

DILEEP R. MEHTA, *Georgia State University*

## Risk aversion    (*See* RISK ANALYSIS AND MANAGEMENT.)

## Risk finance    (*See* INSURANCE RISK AND MANAGEMENT.)

## Robinson-Patman Act    (*See* GOVERNMENT REGULATIONS, FEDERAL REGULATION OF COMPETITION.)

## Rollback method    (*See* STATISTICAL ANALYSIS FOR MANAGEMENT.)

## Routing sheet    (*See* PRODUCTION PLANNING AND CONTROL.)

## Royalty    (*See* VALUABLE INTANGIBLE RIGHTS.)

## Rucker plan

The Rucker plan is a group incentive or profit-sharing plan developed by the consultant Allen W. Rucker of the Eddy-Rucker-Nickels Company.

The amount available for bonuses is determined by the ratio of the wage bill to the value added to the raw materials by manufacturing. The normal ratio is ascertained from past history, and a reduction in the proportion of the value added accounted for by wages is considered extra profit. Then the proportion of the value added that can be considered the result of labor is ascertained, and that proportion of the extra profit is the amount available for the bonuses.

*See also* COMPENSATION, SPECIAL PLANS; SCANLON PLAN.

## REFERENCES

Geare, A. J.: "Profitability from Scanlon-Type Plans," *Academy of Management Review*, July 1976, p. 101.

Rucker, Allen W.: *A Dynamic Wage Policy for Industry's Coming Growth*, Eddy-Rucker-Nickels Company, Cambridge, Mass., 1953.

Von Kaas, H. K., in collaboration with A. J. Lindemann: *Making Wage Incentives Work*, American Management Association, New York, 1971, pp. 24–25, 64, 66, 70.

STAFF/SMITH

**Rules** (*See* MANAGEMENT THEORY, SCIENCE, AND APPROACHES; POLICY FORMULATION AND IMPLEMENTATION.)

**Rules, safety** (*See* SAFETY AND HEALTH MANAGEMENT, EMPLOYEE.)

**Sabbaticals** (*See* COMPENSATION, EMPLOYEE BENEFIT PLANS.)

# Safety and health management, employee

*Safety engineering* is a multidisciplinary area of concern not only in the United States but throughout the world. Interpretations of *safety* are as varied as the interests of people defining the word. In a broad sense, it includes the reduction, control, or elimination of all hazardous conditions which pose a threat to person or property. In the past, safety activities were directed at physical improvement of machinery and buildings, emphasizing physical aspects of accident prevention such as good housekeeping. These are and will continue to be important. The current trend emphasizes the development of a safety-conscious attitude on the part of individuals toward eliminating accident-prone habits. The theory is that contented and unworried workers will have fewer accidents.

Since workers, under concerned management, are becoming more involved with their own welfare, they perform the vital functions of participating in the detection and reporting of potential danger or accident-producing areas. Employees and employee organizations are progressively placing greater emphasis on the safety of the work force. The majority of labor contracts now contain provisions concerning safety and health. Employers have been similarly active in supporting the safety movement and providing safer facilities and equipment for the protection of employees. Many employers today have upgraded their operations so as to exceed the minimum requirements of legislative action.

## OCCUPATIONAL SAFETY, HEALTH, AND SANITATION LEGISLATION

The Occupational Safety and Health Act (OSHA) of 1970 became a law on December 29, 1970. Its purpose is:

To assure safe and healthful working conditions for working men and women; by authorizing enforcement of the standards developed under the Act; by assisting and encouraging the States in their efforts to assure safe and healthful working conditions; by providing for research, information, education, and training in the field of occupational safety and health; and for other purposes.

The Occupational Safety and Health Standards are composed of national consensus standards and established federal standards. These standards are applicable to industry in general and are known as Part 1910—Occupational Safety and Health Standards. Part 1910 amended Chapter XVII of Title 29 of the Code of Federal Regulations established on April 13, 1971. This amendment was made pursuant to the authority designated in Sections 6(a) and 8(g) of the Williams-Steiger Occupational Safety and Health Act (OSHA) of 1970.

The Secretary of Labor is authorized by OSHA to enforce the safety and health standards through official inspections and investigations and to cite violations, penalizing according to the magnitude of noncompliance. On September 4, 1971, Part 1903 of Title 29 CFR Chapter XVII was published in the Federal Register. The 20 parts of this section outlined the specifics of the enforcement portion of this final version of the act.

**Standards**  Part 1910 classifies the standards of OSHA. These subparts are as follows: A—General; B—Adoption and Extension of Established Federal Standards; C—Reserved; D—Walking and Working Surfaces; E—Means of Egress; F—Powered Platforms, Manlifts and Vehicle-Mounted Work Platforms; G—Occupational Health and Environmental Control; H—Hazardous Materials; I—Personal Protective Equipment; J—General Environmental Controls; K—Medical and First Aid; L—Fire Protection; M—Compressed Gas and Compressed Air Equipment; N—Materials Handling and Storage; O—Machinery and Machine Guarding; P—Hand and Portable Powered Tools and Other Hand-held Equipment; Subpart Q—Welding, Cutting and Brazing; Subpart R—Special Industries; Subpart S—Electrical; Subpart Z—Toxic and Hazardous Substances.

*Sanitation.* Sanitation requirements are contained in Part 1910.141 of Subpart J—General Environmental Controls. Areas covered are general requirements for housekeeping, such as keeping all places of employment as clean as possible. Containers for waste disposal must be available and be of a type which will not leak and can be sanitized. Extermination programs must be in effect for vermin control. Food and beverage consumption on the premises is dealt with in this section. Wastes contaminated in the laboratory and animal carcasses must be placed in impervious containers that are closed and decontaminated before removal.

Washrooms, toilet facilities, and water supplies are also covered in Subpart J. Provision must be made for clearly labeling potable and nonpotable water supplies. Toilet facilities are required with a minimum number of water closets in accordance with the number and sex of employees. Covered receptacles must be provided in women's lavatories. Construction and sanitation requirements for these facilities are indicated in this section. Showers,

change rooms, and clothes drying facilities must be provided in those instances where required.

**Implementation Targets**  In the early stages of the act, OSHA officials reviewed accidents to determine which industries should be given priority. Their review became known as the target industry program. The industries chosen were:

Roofing and sheet metal work
Meat products
Lumber and wood products
Miscellaneous transportation equipment
Water transportation services

This program was then expanded by OSHA into a national emphasis program. This project involved safety and health inspectors in a joint effort and emphasized training and cooperation. The industrial classifications included in this program were:

Gray iron foundries
Malleable iron foundries
Steel foundries
Metal stamping
Aluminum casting
Bronze, brass, copper, and copper bronze alloy casting

The first industries to be inspected by the more than 1000 compliance officers and 100 industrial hygienists were selected on the basis of severity of accidents, employee exposure to toxic substances, and industrial and geographical concentration. The hazards involved included electrical shock, machinery exposures, strains, and health hazards.

**Record-Keeping Requirements**  The data giving OSHA the insight to formulate these emphasis programs come from another section of the act, the record-keeping requirements section, calling for mandatory maintenance of records of occupational injuries and illnesses.

OSHA Form No. 100 is the log of occupational injuries and illnesses which classifies and notes the extent of each qualifying injury or illness. This form is to be completed on each incident, although most workmen's compensation insurance reports are acceptable if they contain the required data called for on the form.

The Summary Form No. 102 is used at the end of each calendar year to tabulate all incidents that occurred during the year as taken from the log OSHA Form No. 100. The summary must be posted no later than February 1 and remain in place until March 1, situated so that all employees are likely to see it. All these records must be kept for 5 years after the applicable year. As of January 1, 1978, Forms 100 and 102 were combined into a single Form 200.

OSHA standards require that additional specialized records be maintained by employers. Equipment records are to be kept on such items as scaffolding, platforms, manlifts, fire extinguishers, respirators, cranes, derricks, and power presses. These records should include maintenance and inspection dates. Other records that are required concern radiation exposure, flammable and combustible liquids inventories, and monitoring logs of toxic and hazardous substances. Each employer must also display a poster explaining the act to employees.

## SAFETY RULES, REGULATIONS, AND ENFORCEMENT

Today every facet of existence is scrutinized with a view toward protecting people individually and collectively from unnecessary risks in business as well as private life. In addition to OSHA, there are the Consumer Product Safety Commission and the National Fire Prevention and Control Administration; new regulatory agencies are being formed all the time. State and local safety agencies involved in issuing safety regulations are also proliferating. Each of these agencies has its own enforcement program to ensure compliance with its regulations.

**Voluntary Standards**  In private industry, safety rules are emphasized according to interest. The Manufacturing Chemists Association issues data sheets concerning the proper and safe handling of chemicals. The National Fire Protection Association prepares material relating to the prevention of fire. Another recognized contributor to fire safety is the Factory Mutual Engineering Corporation which issues loss prevention data sheets. The American Industrial Hygiene Association recommends safe practices on exposures to toxic materials. The American National Standards Institute has prepared specifications for safety on nearly any industrial exposure imaginable.

There are 6500 American National standards on safety and health covering such areas as agricultural safety, occupational safety and health, highway and traffic safety, fire safety, construction, and recreational safety. More than 200 of these ANSI-approved national consensus standards have been adapted or referenced by the U.S. Department of Labor under the Occupational Safety and Health Act.

Probably the most pragmatic attack on the industrial injury exposure comes from individual company efforts. A well thought out, efficiently operated, safety program produces the least number of accident-producing situations.

## ACCIDENT PREVENTION PROGRAMS

Successful accident prevention programs depend upon employer leadership, the provision of safe and healthful working conditions and environment in all operations, and the development by the company of an employee awareness and responsibility toward practicing safety on the job. The employer or chief executive must set the establishment's safety policies, stimulate safety awareness in all subordinates, and show his or her own interest if all employees are to cooperate in making for a safe and healthful working environment.

Management support of the accident prevention program should be clear. Management should provide active direction through specific delegation of responsibility and mandate accountability from those individuals charged with this responsibility.

While many individuals consider the supervisor the key person in safety activities, this is true only when much is expected of the supervisor and comparatively little of higher levels of management. With clear delineation of responsibility and accountability, no one level of management has a more vital role in safety activities than any other level. Each member of management has a function accompanied by personal responsibilities and is accountable for results.

**Integration with Other Activities**  The safety activities of each member of management must be carried on as a normal, natural part of supervising and directing the work force. Accident prevention is not separate from nor is it a supplement to good supervision. Safety is the foundation of good supervision and is a required management responsibility revolving around the administrative, control, and training functions vested in each level of management. These functions naturally vary by level of management, and when each of these functions is performed systematically and continuously by each level of the organization, then acceptable safety performance standards are met. Thus, in effect, each member of management is accountable for the complete fulfilment of responsibilities in each of these areas.

## ACCIDENT MEASUREMENT AND REPORTING

Two basic measurements of accident occurrences are the *injury frequency rate* and *injury severity rate*. The frequency rate indicates how often accidents have occurred. Its traditional formula is as follows:

Frequency rate

$$= \frac{\text{number of disabling injuries per year} \times 1{,}000{,}000}{\text{total number of hours worked per year}}$$

= number of injuries (lost-time accidents) per million hours worked

The injury severity rate provides a measure of how long injured persons have been disabled. Its traditional formula follows:

Severity rate

$$= \frac{\text{total number of days lost} \times 1{,}000{,}000}{\text{total number of hours worked per year}}$$

= number of days lost (due to lost-time accidents) per million hours worked

OSHA insists on its own version of these formulas:

Frequency rate

$$= \frac{\text{number of incidents} \times 200{,}000}{\text{number of hours worked}}$$

Severity rate

$$= \frac{\text{number of lost days} \times 200{,}000}{\text{number of hours worked}}$$

These yield rates per year; 200,000 is 100 employees working 40 hours per week, 50 weeks per year.

**Experience Records**  One of the tools of accident prevention is knowledge of past accident experience, which, when analyzed properly, provides considerable aid in preventing accidents. Statistical printouts can give clues to trends by showing a total loss picture. Indications are then evaluated for further action. A plant's loss experience can be compared with a company average so as to highlight areas where the number of accidents is excessive. Insurance company loss printouts will show cost figures by plant, identifying plants with abnormally high accident costs.

Further examination of accident experience can depict the predominant type of accident, part of body injured, department, age, sex, day and time of week, whether new or long-term employee, etc. Accident analyses can be as refined as time and money permit, but a basic analysis is necessary to formulate a method of attack to minimize injuring the 1 out of every 10 workers hurt annually.

Many analogies have been made concerning the costs in money of accidents in the workplace. Probably the most revealing type of analogy concerns the number of tasks businesses must perform to overcome the losses incurred as a result of employee accidents as compared with $100 of work accident loss. For example, the sales volume needed to generate enough profit to overcome a small $100 work

accident in a restaurant would be to serve 1351 $2 lunches. A supermarket has to generate 500 $20 sales; a bakery must bake over 37,000 loaves of bread; a publisher must sell 20,000 newspapers; and a department store must sell over 5000 pairs of boys' socks.

**Direct and Indirect Losses**  Industrial accidents result in two separate and distinct types of loss. One is the direct or insurable loss which is the most obvious and consists of medical care, weekly compensable benefits, and perhaps a scheduled award depending upon the nature and seriousness of the injury. The other type is the indirect loss which includes hidden accident costs that are not reimbursable through compensation insurance. Hidden costs of accidents generally exceed the direct costs.

Monies lost due to nonproductive hidden accident costs can be attributed to a multitude of causes. Production downtime; machinery or property damage; material spoilage; time lost by supervisors to attend the injured employee and prepare accident reports; time needed to hire and train replacement employees, and overtime required to make up lower production output are some examples of indirect accident costs.

*Accident reports* and accident investigation reports record conditions and practices as they occur in the workplace. Accidents are the result of unsafe work practices and/or unsafe working conditions. The objective and factual recording of accidents provides data which can be used to avert future occurrences of a similar nature. As with any management function in efficient control of production, cost, quality, and the like, factual records are necessary for successful accident prevention efforts. Collection and analysis of records related to causes of accidents are the foundation of a good management approach to accident prevention.

## SAFETY TRAINING

Operating supervisors are responsible for identifying safety training requirements as part of their regular function. Safe work procedures must be taught not only during indoctrination of a new employee but as an ongoing program. Hazards are associated with every job in the industrial environment and should be evaluated by each supervisor in a hazard recognition program. The program can then be incorporated into on-the-job training for safe operating procedures to be practiced by employees.

Compliance with safe work procedures must be continuously monitored, and reinstruction given to employees who violate safety rules. Periodic meetings must be arranged for instruction and reinstruction in the factors of the safety program. Among these factors might be the proper observance of general safety regulations, the routing for emergency egress, accident and injury treatment and reporting, and fire and explosion emergency activity.

**OSHA Requirements** While most employers are aware of the need to comply with the standards promulgated under OSHA, many may not be familiar with the standards requiring that training be provided to employees. Employers must show that each employee has been given training based on an analysis of the tasks as performed by the employee. The job evaluation must itemize the actual as well as the potential hazards associated with each function and the equipment and procedures that an employee should use to minimize the injury risk.

Initial training requirements of the OSHA have been put forth under Part 1910 which relates to general industry, Parts 1915–18 concerning maritime, and Part 1926 on construction. The general industry training requirements include the following subparts: G—occupational health and environmental control; H—hazardous materials; I—personal protective equipment; J—general environmental controls; K—medical and first aid; L—fire protection; N—materials handling and storage; O—machine and machine guarding; Q—welding, cutting, and brazing; R—special industries. Parts 1915–18 cover the safety and health training standards for maritime equipment as follows: Subpart D—welding, cutting, and heating; F—general working conditions; H—tools and related equipment; I—personal protective equipment. In construction, the training requirements may be found in Part 1926 concerning these subparts: C—general safety and health provisions; D—occupational health and environmental controls; E—personal protective and lifesaving equipment; F—fire protection and prevention; J—welding and cutting; S—tunnels and shafts, caissons, cofferdams, and compressed air; U-blasting and use of explosives.

## SAFETY EDUCATION

Promotional activities depend greatly upon finding a common sphere of interest among people and then discovering a method of communication for message transferral. People want to know, "What is in it for me?" To instill safety-mindedness, management must direct its efforts toward creating and maintaining interest in the merits of an accident prevention

program. Employees are interested in job security, opportunity, dignity, earnings, etc. When workers are convinced that the accident prevention efforts of a company represent stepping-stones toward their personal goals, it follows that safety awareness by employees will be enhanced.

**Communication and Promotion** Safety attitudes will not develop by merely allowing the accident record to speak for itself. Employees must continuously be reminded and stimulated to work safely and observe safety rules and regulations. Such efforts may be termed *safety promotion* which includes displays, publicity, posters, awards, incentives, contests, as well as many of the other techniques normally associated with advertising a product.

Bulletin boards, posters, signs, displays, and the like are effective means of calling attention to various phases of a safety program. Publications covering safety talks, safe driving habits, first aid, proper lifting, etc., are available from a variety of sources. Trade associations put forth specific safety bulletins covering appropriate industries. Other outside sources of material include safety councils, state and federal labor departments, the government printing office, and insurance carriers and brokers.

Many employers get the message across through the use of contests and incentives. The National Safety Council sponsors the National Safety Council General Industry Competition and Safe Driver Contests.

*Plant safety committees* are a useful vehicle for disseminating information. These committees meet regularly to discuss accident and illness prevention methods, safety and health promotion, providing information on safe working practices, and, in general, promoting safety and health programs for all employees. It must be remembered that safety promotional activities do not of themselves constitute a safety program but supplement basic accident prevention activities such as sound safety engineering.

## SPECIALIZED SAFETY PROGRAMS

Depending upon the type of operation and its inherent exposures, specialized programs concentrating on specific loss prevention activities must be formulated.

**Emergency Organizations** One such activity is an emergency (or disaster) organization set up to respond to fires, bomb threats, explosions, etc. The size of this group varies with the size and sophistication of the facility and personnel in need of protection. It might include medical staff, rescue squads, special equipment drivers, a fire squad, a salvage squad, etc. Each of these people must be trained for a specific purpose with retraining on a continuous basis to ensure an efficient well-trained organization.

**Motor Vehicle Safety** Another specialized safety program concerns itself with motor vehicles. Many companies will have a fleet of vehicles ranging anywhere from a few cars or trucks to thousands of salespersons operating company cars scattered across the nation. As maintenance, repair, and insurance costs are skyrocketing, it becomes mandatory to implement a fleet safety program to hold these vehicle expenses to a practical minimum. Driver selection, driver training, vehicle maintenance control, etc., all play a large role in a fleet accident prevention program.

**Program Sponsorship** Sophisticated safety programs have been developed and are in force in a multitude of industries. Nuclear safety programs, laboratory accident prevention activities, and safety/health programs in such diverse areas as offices, forklift truck operations, construction, shipping, security, data processing, printing, and schools are an ongoing operational requirement.

However, the best accident prevention program in the world is worth no more than the paper it is printed on if it has no sponsor. The higher and the stronger the support of management, the more effective will be a safety program.

*See also* COMPENSATION, EMPLOYEE BENEFIT PLANS; HEALTH, MENTAL; LABOR LEGISLATION; PERSONNEL ADMINISTRATION; SOCIAL RESPONSIBILITY OF BUSINESS.

### REFERENCES

*Accident Prevention Manual for Industrial Operations*, 7th ed., National Safety Council, 425 North Michigan Avenue, Chicago, Ill., 60611, 1974.

*Advanced First Aid and Emergency Care*, American National Red Cross, 17th and East Streets, N.W., Washington, 20006, 1973.

*Approval Guide Equipment, Materials, Services for Conservation of Property*, Factory Mutual System, 1151 Boston-Providence Turnpike, Norwood, Mass., 02062, annual.

*Best's Safety Directory*, A. M. Best Co., Park Avenue, Morristown, N.J. 07960, annual.

*Fundamentals of Industrial Hygiene*, National Safety Council, 425 North Michigan Avenue, Chicago, Ill., 60611, 1970.

*Guidebook to Occupational Safety and Health*, Commerce Clearing House, 4025 West Peterson, Chicago, Ill., 60646, annual.

Heinrich, H. W., *Industrial Accident Prevention*, 4th ed., McGraw-Hill Book Company, New York, 1959.

Strobl, Walter M., *Security*, The Industrial Press, Inc., New York, 1973.

*Supervisors Safety Manual*, 4th ed., National Safety Council, Chicago, 1973.

*System Safety Techniques*, American Society of Safety Engineers, 850 Busse Highway, Park Ridge, Ill., 60068, 1971.

Watt, John H., and Wilford I. Summers, *NFPA Handbook of the National Electrical Code*, 4th ed., McGraw-Hill Book Company, New York, 1975.

FRED L. SCHMIDT, *Bristol-Myers Company*

## Safety margin, in accounting (*See* ACCOUNTING FOR MANAGERIAL CONTROL.)

## Safety stock (*See* INVENTORY CONTROL, PURCHASING AND ACCOUNTING ASPECTS.)

## Sale and lease back (*See* LEASING, EQUIPMENT; REAL ESTATE MANAGEMENT, CORPORATE.)

## Sale (legal) (*See* GOVERNMENT REGULATIONS, BUSINESS LAW.)

## Sales, in government market (*See* MARKETS, PUBLIC.)

## Sales bogeys (*See* COMPENSATION, SALES.)

## Sales bonus (*See* COMPENSATION, SALES.)

## Sales compensation plans (*See* COMPENSATION, SALES.)

## Sales forecasts (*See* COMPENSATION, SALES.)

## Sales management

Sales management is responsible for adding value to the organization by attaining financial objectives, contributory objectives, and market position. It achieves this added value by investing and managing the corporate resources of money, machines, materials, people, and time. The investment and management must take place within the definition of the organization's business, the policies governing the business, the overall marketing strategy of the business, and via a coordinated and cooperative team effort with all other organization functions from production to engineering to research and development.

## PLANNING SALES GROWTH

Sales planning is the continuous process (a series of risk-taking activities) of investing corporate resources in the ongoing business marketplace in order to satisfy client/customer needs and exploit opportunities so as to achieve the enterprise's long-range and short-range objectives. The sales planning process consists of four action-oriented components: (1) Structuring the planning base; (2) developing the sales organization's profiles; (3) writing the sales plan of action; (4) implementing and controlling. A sales organization, whether industrial, consumer, or service, cannot operate efficiently without a comprehensive, relevant sales plan.

**Structuring the Planning Base** This component involves collecting and analyzing all the relevant data about the marketplace necessary for sales planning and decision making. The data are arrived at by a six-step environmental examination. Sensitivity and response to the enterprise's environment appear in the written sales plan.

STEP 1: IDENTIFY BOTH THE HEAVY-USE CUSTOMERS OF THE ENTERPRISE'S PRODUCTS AND THE LIGHT, OR PERIODIC, USERS. The 80-20 rule, which states that generally 80 percent of a company's profitable sales can come from as few as 20 percent of the customers, remains valid. "Your heavy-user customers must determine two aspects of your sales growth planning: (1) your sales growth objectives, which will be largely dependent on the penetration you can make into heavy-user demand, and (2) your sales growth strategies, which must offer the highest value-to-price benefits to your heavy users."[1]

STEP 2: PROVIDE A MARKETING OFFERING THAT HEAVY-USER CUSTOMERS ARE WILLING TO PAY FOR. The starting point is to recognize the needs of the key customers the company serves. Each customer segment (there is generally more than one) may have 15 to 25 needs that it wants satisfied. Sales management and its sales force must resist the temptation of condensing the need list. Instead, the need list should be extended and a value placed on each need as perceived by the customer. For example, does the

need have high, medium, or low value in the eyes of the heavy user? Answers provide management with directional guidelines for planning, organizing, developing, and managing its sales force.

STEP 3: CONDUCT A COMPETITIVE AUDIT. This is a comparison of the company's marketing offering with that of the major and minor competitors. The objective is to determine the strengths, weaknesses, and uniquenesses of the company's offering—versus that of the competitors—as seen in the eyes of the marketplace.

STEP 4: SEARCH FOR CHANGES IN THE MARKETPLACE. Changes within an industry present the company with either an opportunity to pursue or a threat to defend against. Leaders in an industry *cause* change; followers *react* to change. Sales management and its sales force are the first to feel the impact of change. They play the important role of sounding a company's "change alarm."

STEP 5: IDENTIFY ENVIRONMENTAL INFLUENCES. These are the changes that take place outside the industry over which sales management has no control. They are economic, political, technical, and social in character. Outside influences also come in two forms: opportunity or threat. Recognition of them will aid in the sales planning process and the development of a profitable sales plan of action.

STEP 6: DETERMINE INDUSTRY DIMENSIONS. This is accomplished by diagnosing the following: total size of the industry of which the company is a member; company's share of the market in which it competes; company's share trend versus industry trend; competitor's share of market; competitor's share versus industry trends; industry trends for the various products being marketed; company's product performance versus that of the industry versus that of competition; and any other trend data that should be tracked on an ongoing basis. Until all the facts relative to the six planning steps are dug out, the sales plan of action cannot be written.

**Developing the Sales Department's Three Profiles** These encompass three critical factors: capability, opportunity, and performance.

*The capability profile* shows the sales department's strengths, limitations, and uniquenesses. Capabilities can be measured in terms of product performance, product availability, pricing, customer service, application technology, raw materials position, distribution system, financial status, personnel, etc.

*The opportunity profile* describes the opportunities that exist in the marketplace and those that the enterprise is capable of pursuing with a high achievement probability. Successful sales planning is always based on maximizing opportunities. Emphasis must focus on opportunity planning, which is offensive in nature. Caution: pursuit of an opportunity without the required resource and/or capabilities can only result in poor performance.

*The performance profile* states the sales department's record of opportunity achievement. Poor performance can be caused by one or more of the following: (1) Inaccurate designation of opportunities, (2) deficiency in capabilities, and (3) ineffective management of capabilities.

Inability to assess realistically the sales department's three profiles versus those of the competition leads to the setting of unsound objectives, poorly designed sales strategies, and weak sales programming. Objective self-appraisal is a vital requirement of planning.

**Writing the Sales Plan of Action**  Diagnosis of the company's sales situation provides the platform on which to develop the sales plan of action.

*Objectives.*  As the income-producing facts about the company's business are studied, sales objectives will come to light.

There are three kinds of objectives that can add value to your sales growth. (See Fig. S-1.) *The first is financial.* These objectives are the numbers that tell you how profitably you are managing your business. For this reason, financial objectives are primary objectives. *The second kind are sales objectives,* which underlie financial objectives. Sales objectives make financial objectives possible and for this reason can be regarded as contributory objectives. *Another contributory objective is the market position objective,* which underlies sales objectives.[2]

*Qualitative targets* such as "improve sales force communication," "gather pertinent sales intelligence," "change sales service policies," and "introduce new credit policy" can also be established.

---

*Primary Objectives*
  1. Financial objectives
    1.1 Profit on sales
    1.2 Return on investment

*Contributory Objectives*
  2. Sales objectives
    2.1 Dollar sales volume
    2.2 Unit sales volume
    2.3 Share of market penetration
  3. Market position objectives
    3.1 Key customer's image of company

---

Fig. S-1. Hierarchy of objectives. (*From Mack Hanan, Howard Berrian, James Cribbin, and Jack Donis, Take-Charge Sales Management, AMACON—a Division of American Management Associations, New York, 1976. Reprinted with permission.*)

*Criteria.*  When the final selection is made from a lengthy list of objectives, arriving at a manageable number is important. This can be done by considering the following criteria: (1) Cost, (2) resource requirements, (3) long-term versus short-term payoff, (4) probability of achievement, (5) company's life-cycle position, and (6) competitive obstacles.

*Assumptions.*  A statement of assumptions follows the setting of objectives. Assumptions are agreed-upon forecasts about the future selling environment of the company. These assumptions become guidelines for anticipating developments that will have either positive or negative impact on the sales department's ability to achieve its objectives. Assumptions also reduce the risk of planning in a vacuum. They dictate that sales management focus on the future and also "look from the outside in" when planning.

*Sales Strategies.*  These provide direction for sales management and the sales team. Strategies are developed by focusing attention on the company's heavy-user customers and their needs while anticipating competitive marketing actions. Sales strategies, to produce results, must:

1. Be fixed firmly enough to operate over relatively long periods of time.

2. Be identifiable and made clear in words and practice.

3. Capitalize on the sales department's competence and resources, both present and projected.

4. Exploit competitive weaknesses when and where possible.

5. Speak to the significant needs of customers and have the customers recognize that its needs are being spoken to.

6. Project whatever "branded" image and posture the company wishes.

7. Motivate a high degree of commitment from the personnel who have to implement them.

8. Take advantage of marketplace opportunities.

9. Be consistent with policies and systems of the company.

*Programs.*  The heart of the sales plan of action is the programs and actions that must be implemented to achieve the sales department's objectives. Each stated sales program encompasses four components: (1) What is it? (Description of the program.) (2) Who is to do it? (People involved and their tasks.) (3) When is it to be done? (Completion dates.) (4) What is the estimated cost? (Price tag for the program.)

Dynamic and distracting business conditions, more than any other cause, require that the sales plan of action be committed to writing. Specifically, the program plan should include all the following:

1. Return-on-resource investment target.

2. Individual and team responsibilities.

3. Time scale for attainment of privacy and contributory objectives.

4. Specified control measurement quantified in numbers and on a time scale.

5. Costs established prior to investment on the basis of realistic estimates of the potential return.

6. Accurate sales budgeting, the price tag placed on all the action plan programs.

**Implementing and Controlling**  The sales plan of action should be monitored every 30-day period, every quarter, and, finally, at the year-end performance review. At each monitoring point, four controlling questions are asked: (1) What was the performance? (2) What are the reasons for plus or minus variances from the plan? (3) Was the budget adhered to? (4) What changes, if any, in the plan are called for?

Each monthly and quarterly evaluation session is also a key decision-making point. Planning decision possibilities at each review include: (1) No action required; (2) changes in environment require close 30-day surveillance; (3) adjust objectives; (4) implement contingency strategies; (5) adjust objectives and implement contingency strategies; (6) adjust, add, or eliminate tactical sales programs; and/or (7) revise the total plan.

## ORGANIZING THE SALES FORCE

There are three prime ways of organizing a sales organization: line concept, line and staff concept, and functional concept. In order to increase the effectiveness of any of the three types of sales organizations, many companies also extend the concept according to geographical coverage, product line, market served, or type of customer served.

**Line Organization**  In the line organization (Fig. S-2) authority flows directly from the chief sales executive to his or her subordinate and so on down the line.

**Line-Staff Organization**  The line-staff organization (Fig. S-3) evolves from the line organization in order to extend its effectiveness. Staff assistants are added in key speciality areas. They act in an advisory or service capacity only and have no direct line authority over the sales force. Authority still flows from the chief sales executive through the field sales manager to the sales force.

**Functional Organization**  The functional organization (Fig. S-4) looks like the line-staff organization. The difference is that in a functional organization there may be a number of managers who give direct orders to the sales force. The functional orga-

nization is generally used in conjunction with a product structure, or a geographic, market-served, or customer-type structure. It is an organizational structure that is used when line management may lack special expertise, when time-saving is vital,

**Fig. S-2. Line organization.**

when heavy-user needs require special services and abilities, and/or when only a small part of the sales staff is involved with the line sales force.

## DEVELOPING THE SALES FORCE

Management know-how and leadership must be brought into play by the chief sales executive in the development of the men and women who actually make the sales. Specifically, sales management must assist each salesperson to:

1. Diagnose individual strengths.

2. Diagnose individual weaknesses to reduce the development gap between performance and capability.

3. Construct a development program that maximizes strengths and minimizes weaknesses.

4. Commit himself or herself to a customized program work.

Simultaneously, sales management must monitor and evaluate the program's effectiveness and dem-

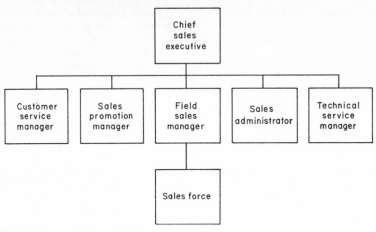

Fig. S-3. Line and staff organization.

onstrate to each salesperson a high degree of concern for his or her personal growth.

**Development Needs**   Each member of the sales force has three sets of development needs: (1) Technical skills (product application, technical advisor, product problem solver, trainer, service consultant, intelligence supplier); (2) interacting skills (understanding personalities, training people, reading interaction behavior, negotiating, building a climate of confidence, motivating individuals, handling groups); (3) management skills (time and territory management, budget and expense administration, customer sales planning, customer relations development, new business supervision, and self-management of talent, time, thinking, and energy).

**Selling Needs**   A sales force has to sell productively. The chief sales executive has the responsibility to develop this skill in the sales force. Selling effectively is a two-sided coin: one side is consultative salesmanship, the other is consultative selling.

*Consultative Salesmanship.*   This is the process of selling in a face-to-face sequential process that carries throughout the total sales transaction. It works in the following manner:

First, client needs are revealed.

Second, perceptual differences are reduced between customer and sales representative by the sales representative putting himself or herself in the customer's place and assessing the sales situation from the customer's standpoint.

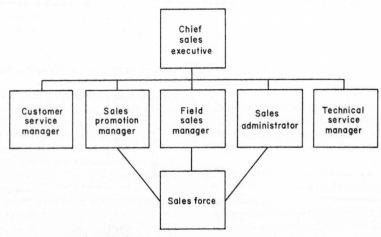

Fig. S-4. Functional organization.

Third, customer needs are satisfied by demonstrating that the company's product/service system is superior to that of the competition and that the sales representative is a value adder.

Fourth, total customer satisfaction with the company's product/service system and with the sales representative's service are assured.

*Consultative Selling.* This is an operating behavior implemented by a sales representative in heavy-user customer situations. It is based upon the concept that the ultimate customer benefit provided by a company and its sales team is profit improvement of the customer's business by reducing the customer's cost of doing business and/or increasing the customer's revenues. The sales representative accomplishes this by the application of six operating principles:

(1) Regards self as the manager of his or her own personal service business; (2) concerns self with the sum total of the customer's needs which his or her combined personal and corporate expertise can help make more efficient and/or more economical; (3) considers self as a marketeer knowing the markets of his or her key accounts, plus knowing the business of his or her customer's customer; (4) concentrates on profitable sales; (5) operates with a plan of action for all key accounts, and (6) provides the customer with innovative business development ideas based upon the customer's needs for new products, new service systems and new markets.[3]

## MANAGING THE SALES FORCE

The sales plan of action is translated into (1) external actions that are applied in key account situations and (2) internal actions, those management processes that the chief sales executive uses in managing the sales force. External and internal actions are: (1) organizing territories, (2) assigning quotas, (3) establishing call patterns, (4) supervising, (5) evaluating performance, and (6) training.

**Organizing Sales Territories** "Heavy-user customers are the focal point for territory organization making the best resolution of four factors: (1) types of accounts to be developed, (2) number of key accounts of each type, (3) profit value and gross sales volume of each key account, and (4) cumulative call time required to develop the full profit value of each key account."[4]

**Quota Assignment** Every sales territory should carry an assigned quota indicating its contribution to profit and volume and its sales activity requirements. The three types of quotas for a territory are: (1) Profit quota by product line or by service, (2) dollar sales volume quota by product line or by service, and (3) activity quota in terms of demonstrations, tests, seminars, sampling, trade shows, etc.

**Establishing Call Patterns** The number of calls per month is not the most important criterion in setting up territory call patterns. The best rule of thumb is to respect the 80-20 rule and call more frequently on heavy-user accounts that have high actual and potential profit value. Key accounts require intensive cultivation if full profit potential is to be realized. Sales representatives have to penetrate upward, downward, and horizontally in key accounts to achieve profit objectives. This requires a cumulative time investment plan per key account. It must reflect the time required to reach and influence all decision makers and their influencers. To supplement the pattern of in-person calls, sales management and the sales representative can use telephone calls, direct mail support, letters, second-party assistance, service support calls, technical support calls, etc.

**Supervising** Personal supervision, if properly applied, has high motivational value. The chief sales executive, field sales manager, and lower echelon sales management all play a supervisory role. Personal supervision aids monitoring of individual sales performance and is a major educational tool for improving individual sales performance. A personal supervision mix can include personal praise letters, on-the-job coaching, personal counseling sessions, telephone conferences, informal get-togethers, and performance review sessions.

**Evaluating Performance** Evaluation of sales performance has one main objective—to help the sales representative improve. When setting performance objectives, from both a psychological and operational viewpoint each salesperson has to: (1) participate in setting the objectives; (2) accept the objectives as being reasonable and attainable; (3) commit himself or herself to achieving these objectives and adhering to a plan of personal development.

Sales performance is measured from two aspects, effectiveness and efficiency. *Effective* performance accomplishes objectives within the allocated resources. *Efficient* performance achieves objectives profitably in terms of the time, materials, money, and efforts invested. Effectiveness can be evaluated by establishing: (1) a sales revenue target per salesperson; (2) a sales revenue target per salesperson per day; and (3) an annual share-of-market objective. Efficiency can be evaluated by establishing: (1) a monthly expense/volume ratio; (2) a monthly profit/volume ratio; and (3) a return on sales expenditure ratio (total margin of sales revenue over total sales budget).

**Training**  On-the-job training is a required complement to on-the-job experience. Training a sales representative in self-development requires a seven-component system: (1) One-on-one counseling, (2) job rotation, (3) special outside assignments, (4) teach-self programs, (5) training and teaching assignments, (6) club/association participation, and (7) job enrichment via increasing responsibilities and rewards.

*See also* COMPENSATION, SALES; CONSUMER BEHAVIOR, MANAGERIAL RELEVANCE OF; MARKETING, CHANNELS AND DISTRIBUTION; MARKETING MANAGEMENT; PRODUCTION PLANNING AND DEVELOPMENT; RETAILING MANAGEMENT.

### NOTES

[1] Mack Hanan, Howard Berrian, James Cribben, and Jack Donis, *Take-Charge Sales Management*, American Management Association, New York, 1976, p. 80.

[2] *Ibid*, p. 107.

[3] Mack Hanan, James Cribben, and Herman Heiser, *Consultative Selling*, American Management Association, New York, 1973, pp. 8–10.

[4] Hanan, Berrian, Cribben, and Donis, *op. cit.*, p. 83.

### REFERENCES

Aspley, J. C.: *The Sales Manager's Handbook*, The Dartnell Corporation, Chicago, 1968.

Davis, Kenneth R. and Frederick E. Webster, Jr.: *Sales Force Management*, The Ronald Press Company, New York, 1968.

Downing, George D.: *Sales Management*, John Wiley & Sons, Inc., New York, 1969.

Shapiro, Benson P.: *Managing the Sales Program*, McGraw-Hill Book Company, New York, 1977.

Stanton, William J. and Richard H. Buskirk: *Management of the Sales Force*, Richard D. Irwin, Homewood, Ill., 1969.

Stroh, Thomas F.: *Training and Developing the Professional Salesman*, American Management Association, New York, 1973.

HOWARD A. BERRIAN, *Berrian Associates, Inc.*

## Sales potential  (*See* MARKET ANALYSIS.)

## Sales and volume budgeting  (*See* BUDGETS AND BUDGET PREPARATION.)

## Sales quotas  (*See* COMPENSATION, SALES.)

## Salespeople, field  (*See* MARKETING, INDUSTRIAL.)

## Sampling, work  (*See* WORK SAMPLING.)

## Sampling probabilities  (*See* STATISTICAL ANALYSIS FOR MANAGEMENT.)

## Sanitation  (*See* SAFETY AND HEALTH MANAGEMENT, EMPLOYEE.)

## Satisfaction, job  (*See* OLDER EMPLOYEES, MANAGEMENT OF.)

## Satisfiers and dissatisfiers  (*See* HYGIENE FACTORS.)

## Scaling, nonmetric multidimensional  (*See* MARKET ANALYSIS.)

## Scanlon plan

The Scanlon plan is a group incentive or profit-sharing plan developed for the Adamson Company, makers of steel tanks, by Joseph Scanlon, originally an official of the United Steelworkers Union, later with the Massachusetts Institute of Technology. The plan was subsequently adopted by a number of other companies.

Bonuses are based on reductions in the ratio of employee compensation to the value of the output produced. If, for example, the compensation bill in the base year amounted to 25 percent of the value of the goods produced, any reduction in that percentage would mean a bonus for the employees.

A second feature of the plan is a suggestion system through which employees submit ideas for increasing productivity. There are no individual awards; instead, the employee profits because increased productivity increases everyone's bonus. Suggestions applicable to a single department are evaluated by a departmental committee made up of representatives of management and the union, and in some cases the ideas may be put into effect at once. Rejected suggestions and those applicable plantwide are evaluated by top management and union leadership.

See also COMPENSATION, SPECIAL PLANS; RUCKER PLAN.

### REFERENCES

Geare, A. J.: "Productivity from Scanlon-type plans," *Academy of Management Review*, July 1976, pp. 99–108.

Goodman, Robert K., J. H. Wakely, and R. H. Ruh: "What Employees Think of the Scanlon Plan," *Personnel*, September–October 1972, pp. 22–29.

Lesieur, Frederick G., ed.: *The Scanlon Plan: a Frontier in Labor-Management Cooperation*, Industrial Relations Section, Massachusetts Institute of Technology, Boston, 1968.

Ross, Timothy L. and Gardner Jones: "An Approach to Increased Productivity: The Scanlon Plan," *Financial Executive*, February 1972, pp. 23–29.

STAFF/SMITH

## Scattergraph (See ACCOUNTING FOR MANAGERIAL CONTROL.)

## Scenario, marketing (See MARKETING MANAGEMENT.)

## Schedule, for planning (See PLANNING, STRATEGIC MANAGERIAL.)

## Scheduling, production (See PRODUCTION PLANNING AND CONTROL.)

## Scheduling, short-interval

*Short-interval scheduling* (SIS) is a system of scheduling work in small, timed batches. In each case the employee is told when the batch should be finished, and a record is kept of performance.

The first step in development of a system is the preparation of *activity reports*—a form of work measurement—showing how each employee spends the working day. (Fig. S-5 is an activity report for a

| Department: Sales order | | | Position: Typist | | Lunch Hour | Individual: Amy Bittel   Date: Aug. 25 | | |
|---|---|---|---|---|---|---|---|---|
| Description of activity performed | How often performed | Unit of measure | 8:00 A.M. to 10:00 A.M. | 10:00 A.M. to 12:00 A.M. | Lunch Hour | 1:00 P.M. to 3:00 P.M. | 3:00 P.M. to 5:00 P.M. | Totals |
| | | | | | OUTPUT | | | |
| Type receipt forms | Daily | One page | /// | | | | | 3 |
| Type inquiry letters | Daily | Form letter | / | // | | | | 3 |
| Type envelopes | Daily | 10 business envelopes | / | | | | ‖‖ | 6 |
| Handle telephone calls | Daily | Call | | | //// | | | 4 |
| Type order record cards | Weekly | 10 cards | | ‖‖ /// | | ‖‖ ‖‖ / | | 19 |
| File order record cards | Weekly | 100 cards | | | | | / | 1 |
| Cut form-letter stencils | Monthly | Stencil | | | | | | 0 |
| Make copies on copying machine | Daily | 1 piece 5-10 copies | / | // | | | | 3 |
| | | | | | | | | |
| | | | | | | | | |

Fig. S-5. Activity report for short-interval scheduling.

typist. The tally marks are entered by the employee.) When all employees have completed daily activity reports for a month, the amount of work each employee may reasonably be expected to complete in a given time period and the total workload for each section can be determined. (The time allowed is "pure" working time: delays not attributable to the employee are excluded.)

Once reasonable time estimates have been determined, work is assigned in batches, each one accompanied by a *batch ticket* which indicates a scheduled time and upon which the employee records the start, stop, and elapsed times. In the case of clerical employees, a batch may amount to an hour's work; for others it may be larger. The supervisor checks on progress every 2 hours and enters the amount of work on the *schedule control form* which follows each employee's daily progress according to the planned output of work that is actually completed. A fourth form, the *schedule-miss chart*, shows at the end of the day which scheduled assignments were missed by each employee, the reason (e.g., shortage of supplies, poor instructions, a calculator that breaks down), and corrective action taken.

Short-interval scheduling is most often applied to clerical work, but it has been used also for production and especially for maintenance.

*See also* FORMS DESGN AND CONTROL; PAPERWORK SIMPLIFICATION; PRODUCTION PLANNING AND CONTROL; RECORDS MANAGEMENT; SYSTEMS AND PROCEDURES.

### REFERENCES

Batie, B. N.: "Short-Interval Scheduling," *Management World*, June 1973, pp. 22–23.

Carver, John O.: "Short-Interval Maintenance Scheduling," *Plant Engineering*, June 10, 1971, pp. 95–97.

Fein, Mitchell: "Short Interval Scheduling: A Labor Control Technique," *Industrial Engineering*, February 1972, pp. 14–21.

Smith, Martin R.: "Control through Short-Interval Scheduling," in Carl Heyel (ed.), *Handbook of Modern Office Management and Administrative Services*, McGraw-Hill Book Company, New York, 1972, pp. 5-111–5-125.

———: *Short-Interval Scheduling: A Systematic Approach to Cost Reduction*, McGraw-Hill Book Company, New York, 1968, p. 238.

STAFF/SMITH

## Schedules, multiple-period (*See* MATERIALS MANAGEMENT.)

## Scholarships (*See* COMPENSATION, EMPLOYEE BENEFIT PLANS.)

## Schools of management (*See* MANAGEMENT THEORY, SCIENCE, AND APPROACHES.)

## Science, management (*See* MANAGEMENT THEORY, SCIENCE, AND APPROACHES.)

## Scientific management, principles of (*See* MANAGEMENT, HISTORICAL DEVELOPMENT OF.)

## Scientific method (*See* MANAGEMENT THEORY, SCIENCE, AND APPROACHES; OPERATIONS RESEARCH AND MATHEMATICAL MODELING.)

## Screening, employment (*See* EMPLOYMENT PROCESS.)

## Search, information (*See* INFORMATION SEARCH.)

## Search, site (*See* SITE SELECTION.)

## Search and recruitment, executive

Executive recruiting as an identifiable profession grew rapidly in the post-World War II period, and it is now an accepted business practice. In 1975 *Business Week* estimated that the field had doubled in size in the preceding decade, with its worth rising from $50 million to well over $100 million. There are two principal reasons for this phenomenon:

The practice of management has been made steadily more sophisticated and complex, not only because of advances in technology and technique, but also because of the increasingly difficult environment in which businesses must operate.

The low birth rate of the 1930s limits the size of the management pool in relation to the business community's growing needs.

Both combine to require sustained and time-consuming efforts to locate superior executives—and persuade them to consider new opportunities. Successful searches for executives often take 3 to 6 months and usually involve special recruiting strategies and techniques. For that reason many companies, from the small and medium-sized to major multinationals, now engage professional search firms to do this work. Organizations should interview several search firms before making their final choice. An alphabetical listing of member firms may be obtained by writing the Association of Executive Recruiting Consultants, Inc., 30 Rockefeller Plaza, New York, N.Y., 10020. The AERC was formed in 1959 for the purpose of establishing and maintaining professional standards and ethical conduct in the search field. Member firms serve a wide range of business, industrial, and financial institutions. They also assist trade organizations, scientific, educational, medical, and nonprofit groups, and all levels of government in filling management positions.

**Guiding Principles** Executive recruiters who follow professional standards accept assignments only from corporate and institutional clients, never from individuals. A search firm should be judged according to four main considerations: (1) The quality of its client list, (2) the esteem in which the clients hold the firm, (3) the percentage of the firm's searches undertaken on behalf of its regular clients, and (4) the firm's general reputation in the business community, as judged by bankers, lawyers, accountants, management consultants, and other professional people.

The three reasons for organizations to engage recruiting firms cited most often are: (1) Senior management does not want to sap its strength by recruiting, particularly at a time when the company may well be understaffed at the top and competition is increasing; (2) recruiters have wide access to the business community, including competitors, and as third parties are adept at determining the executives who really are responsible for outstanding performances, and (3) executives believe that secrecy is better maintained by recruiters, an important consideration, for example, at a time when the organization is searching for a new sales vice-president to remedy sagging sales, and does not want its competition and its customers to know about its weakness.

**Typical Procedures** An executive search begins with detailed discussions between the recruiter and the client, leading to a precise definition of the position to be filled and a carefully drawn description of the most desirable candidate (see Table S-1). Typically, this involves conferences on the client's home ground to enable the recruiter to meet all company executives participating in the selection process. In this way the recruiter develops an accurate description of the position and learns as much as possible about the organizational chemistry involved. The initial task of both recruiter and client is to reach a mutual understanding of the true requirements of the search. Of course, these requirements may be modified during the course of the search, as circumstances dictate.

When the position description has been drawn up by the recruiter and approved by the client, it is presented—in complete confidence—to the other members of the search firm, so that the full resources of the firm are brought to bear.

In seeking qualified potential candidates, the recruiter consults on a highly confidential basis with selected sources—industry, government, education, or trade and professional associations, accounting and law firms, banks, and management consulting organizations.

In addition, the recruiter undertakes thorough reviews of business directories and related reference

**TABLE S-1 Example of a Desirable Candidate Description**

| | Materials manager, precision metal manufacturing company |
|---|---|
| Client | A well-known large precision metal manufacturing company. We are concerned with a multiplant division specializing in bearings. Annual sales approach $100 million. |
| Location | Eastern United States. |
| Position and responsibilities | Reporting to the division president, the materials manager will be responsible for the flow of all material into, through, and out of the plants. This will include purchasing, raw material inventory, work-in-process, finished goods inventory, all production control, and shipping and receiving. Responsibilities will entail very close coordination with the factory managers, the marketing department, and vendors (including subcontractors). Since this is a new position and a new concept in this company, the proper staffing and training of employees will be an important consideration. |
| Necessary background | The right person for the position will be a well-organized manager who has had experience in sophisticated material requirement planning, including *master scheduling, purchasing, inventory control,* and *production control.* This experience will have been gained in a plant or plants engaged in metalworking where many parts and sizes are involved. We seek practical experience at the factory management level. Although this person's department will make heavy use of the EDP department, we do not wish a person who has dealt with scheduling only at arm's length using computers. This will be the type of person who gets fully involved in all aspects of an operation. |
| Education | College degree. |
| Compensation | A base salary of up to $40,000 depending on past experience and present compensation. There is an excellent chance for growth. |

works, as well as of other sources of information, in order to secure additional leads.

The recruiting firm, assisted by its support staff, also examines its own records containing the classified and coded resumes of thousands of executives from all industries and disciplines.

These activities usually result in a lengthy list of candidates who are interviewed in depth by the recruiter. The client sees only those few who are best matched to the particular requirements. Regular reports are submitted to the client during this period, keeping the contact informed but taking up no more of his or her time than necessary.

The process continues until the client makes a decision, subject to final reference checks by the recruiter.

**Rules of an Effective Search** Experience has shown clearly that search firms and their clients must meet five important conditions if executive searches are to be carried out efficiently and effectively.

*First*, there is a compelling need for mutual trust and candor. The recruiter should not hesitate to call to a client's attention any factors that may make it difficult to complete searches successfully. By the same token, the client must be as candid as the internal situation permits in discussing assignments.

*Second*, it is essential that the search firm have an exclusive arrangment with the client on each assignment. The confusion and ill will that can result from having more than one firm working to fill an executive opening are obvious.

*Third*, a professional search firm will not take assignments on a contingency basis. Fees charged by members of the Association of Executive Recruiters are billed monthly and are not refundable in the event a client terminates a search. Charges for professional time spent, however, are stopped immediately if an assignment is canceled. A client might cancel an assignment for unforeseen reasons, such as a change in plans or the unexpected availability of a competent executive within the company.

*Fourth*, recruiters believe that in most situations the client's identity should not be revealed until necessary and appropriate. Premature disclosure may cause internal embarrassment, start awkward rumors, and give competitors a temporary advantage. In return, search firms will insist that clients do not conduct premature reference checks, however informally, on attractive candidates. Recruiters must be able to assure such candidates that they can explore openings at no risk to themselves.

*Fifth*, recruiters ask that clients cooperate to the fullest extent possible in arranging to meet recommended candidates promptly. While company di-

rectors and officers have many other demands on their time, experience has shown that failure to set aside reasonable amounts of time for interviewing often results in the loss of top-flight candidates.

**Examples of Differing Approaches** Two model searches exemplify the range of basic techniques employed by executive recruiters.

The first illustrates the *inductive* approach. A high percentage of the high-fire whiteware ceramic insulators produced by three major porcelain companies for aircraft jet engines were cracking, and the U.S. Navy was extremely disturbed. One of the companies advertised in trade journals for 2 years but could not locate a technician who had mastered the art of making the insulators, a process that has been compared with baking bread. A recruiter was called in, and he spent over 80 hours in libraries, compiling lists of more than 2000 ceramic engineers from source books. In addition, he interviewed professors at four universities offering ceramic courses in this country and wrote to others in the United Kingdom, Germany, and Japan. Descriptions of the position were mailed to the 2000 engineers, and 112 of them responded. The recruiter then secured a set of highly technical questions from the company and mailed it to the respondents. Six of them answered the questions correctly, and one of the six was chosen for the job. Within months the problem of the cracked ceramic insulators was cleared up.

The second model case is regarded as a classic in *deductive* reasoning within the recruiting field. A major brewer was concerned about the possibility of losing ground to its chief competitor and assigned a recruiter to search for someone to revise and strengthen marketing procedures. The recruiter first determined that the percentage of beer sold in food stores had risen from 30 percent to 70 percent, largely at the expense of tavern sales. So the recruiter went to several supermarkets and methodically listed all nonfood products on the shelves. He next listed the foremost company in each product grouping and identified the executive most responsible for that leadership. One of these executives was the president of a paint company whose sales of mix-it-yourself color paints were rising rapidly on supermarket sales charts. Interestingly enough, the president was on leave at the Harvard Business School, doing a depth study on the XYZ brewing company and why it was in danger of losing ground to its principal competitor. The study, which by coincidence included a detailed examination of nonfood product sales in supermarkets, made so much sense that the author was selected marketing vice-president of the company.

*See also* COMPENSATION, EXECUTIVE; CONSULTANTS,

MANAGEMENT; EMPLOYMENT PROCESS; MANAGER, DEFINITIONS OF; PERSONNEL ADMINISTRATION.

### REFERENCES

*Guidelines for Executive Recruiters*, Association of Executive Recruiting Consultants, Inc., New York, 1976.

Jennings, Eugene E.: *Routes to the Executive Suite*, McGraw-Hill Book Company, New York, 1976.

Kennedy, James H.: *The Handbook of Executive Search*, Consultants News, 1974.

*What Every Executive Should Know about Executive Recruiting*, Association of Executive Recruiting Consultants, Inc., New York, 1976.

WARDWELL HOWELL, *Ward Howell Associates, Inc.*

## Secretary, corporate   (*See* OFFICERS, CORPORATE.)

## Securities Act of 1933   (*See* BOARDS OF DIRECTORS, LEGAL LIABILITY GUIDELINES.)

## Securities and Exchange Commission (SEC)

The *Securities and Exchange Commission* (SEC) is a government agency set up to ensure that companies provide the fullest possible disclosure of information on their securities and to protect the public, especially investors, against malpractices in the securities and financial fields. It polices observance of federal laws covering this area, including the Securities Act of 1933 (requiring registration of new offerings) and the Securities Exchange Act of 1934. It may obtain court orders enjoining improper acts and, in cases of fraud, initiate prosecution.

*See also* FINANCIAL STATEMENT ANALYSIS; MARKETS, SECURITIES; MARKETS, STOCK INDICATOR SERIES.

### REFERENCE

*U.S. Government Manual 1975/1976*, Office of the Federal Register, National Archives and Records Service, General Services Administration, pp. 567–573.

STAFF/SMITH

## Securities Exchange Act of 1934   (*See* BOARDS OF DIRECTORS, LEGAL LIABILITY GUIDELINES.)

## Securities exchanges   (*See* MARKETS, SECURITIES.)

## Securities market   (*See* MARKETS, SECURITIES.)

## Security management

*Security management* concerns the protection against theft in three areas vital to any company: (1) physical plant, properties, and cash; (2) marketing and product information (company secrets); and (3) computers and computer-stored data. Today security planning must also include measures against sabotage and vandalism.

*Physical security* against both vandalism and theft, although still lax in many vulnerable enterprises, has received markedly increased attention and funding in recent years. Fencing, uniformed guards, rigid procedures to control and limit access of personnel and vehicles to plant or building areas, and increasingly sophisticated technology are being employed. Important to security are sequence lock and master key lock systems and computer-controlled locks. Closed-circuit television to act not only as an extension of the guard but also as a silent intrusion alarm system and recorder (on videotape) of intrusions is utilized. Management must now also be highly conscious of providing security against personal violence for employees, particularly those working at night or on weekends.

*Industrial espionage* and counterespionage, particularly in certain highly competitive industries, are rarely publicly revealed but are rampant, often highly refined, and may skirt perilously close to illegality.

*Computer security*, against both physical destruction and illegal modification or access to data, must now be of overriding importance even to small companies relying on computers in an era often characterized by extremism and extortion and the concentration into an increasingly smaller physical area of a company's vital data. Destruction by fire, storm, or disgruntled employees can result in the potential collapse of the company itself, not to mention the personal legal vulnerability of top management shown to be imprudent in security planning. Highly sophisticated defense systems are also now required to provide maximum protection (which can never be 100 percent) against large-scale computer-assisted fraud (CAF), which amounts to many millions of dollars and is growing at an alarming rate. An addi-

**1087**

tional concern must be the privacy of proprietary data.

Assistance of consulting experts from the complex new science of computer protection is a common recourse. The basic rule for computer security: plan for what *could* happen, and make the trade-off decision—how much security is essential, and at what cost?

*See also* COMPUTER SYSTEMS; MAINTENANCE MANAGEMENT; PLANT ENGINEERING MANAGEMENT.

## REFERENCES

*Approaches to Privacy and Security in Computer Systems: Proceedings of Conference, National Bureau of Standards, March 4–5, 1974*, Clark R. Renninger (ed.), Superintendent of Documents No. C13.10:404, National Bureau of Standards, U.S. Department of Commerce.

"Business Sharpens Its Spying Techniques," *Business Week*, Aug. 4, 1975.

Carlson, Bud: "The New Power Blackout: A Couple of Thoughts on the Vulnerability of Our Electric Utilities," *Video Systems*, July–August 1976.

"Espionage in the Computer Business," *Business Week*, July 28, 1975.

Healy, Richard J., and Timothy J. Walson: *Industrial Security: A Cost-Effective Approach*, American Management Association, New York, 1971.

Krauss, Leonard: "Complete Checklist of "Do's and Don'ts" To Guard against CAF," Ernst & Ernst, 140 Broadway, New York, 10005.

Palme, Jacob: "Software Security," *Datamation*, January 1974.

Pantages, Angeline: "The Price of Protection," *Datamation*, March 1976.

Strobl, Walter: *Security: Theft Protection, Security Development, Fire Protection, Emergency and Disaster Planning and Guard Organization*, The Industrial Press, New York, 1975.

Weiss, Harold: "Computer Security: An Overview," *Datamation*, January 1974.

STAFF/HOKE

## Segmentation, retail   (*See* RETAILING MANAGEMENT.)

## Segmentation analysis, market   (*See* MARKET ANALYSIS.)

## Segmentation concept, marketing   (*See* MARKETING, CONCEPTS AND SYSTEMS.)

## Selection, employee   (*See* PERSONNEL ADMINISTRATION.)

## Selection, minority   (*See* MINORITIES, MANAGEMENT OF AND EQUAL EMPLOYMENT OPPORTUNITY.)

## Self-actualization   (*See* INTERPERSONAL RELATIONSHIPS.)

## Self-improvement for managers   (*See* heading in Table of Contents for complete listing.)

## Self-insurance   (*See* INSURANCE AND RISK MANAGEMENT.)

## Selling   (*See* SALES MANAGEMENT.)

## Selling, direct industrial   (*See* MARKETING, INDUSTRIAL.)

## Selling, indirect industrial   (*See* MARKETING, INDUSTRIAL.)

## Selling, international, direct   (*See* INTERNATIONAL TRADE.)

## Selling, international, indirect   (*See* INTERNATIONAL TRADE.)

## Sensitivity analysis   (*See* BUDGETING, CAPITAL.)

## Sensitivity training   [*See* LABORATORY (SENSITIVITY) TRAINING.]

## Separations, employee   (*See* PERSONNEL ADMINISTRATION.)

## Series, stock, price and value   (*See* MARKETS, STOCK INDICATOR SERIES.)

**Service award, bonus**   (*See* COMPENSATION, EMPLOYEE BENEFIT PLANS.)

**Service category managers**   (*See* MANAGER, DEFINITIONS OF.)

**Service Contract Act of 1965**   (*See* WAGES AND HOURS LEGISLATION.)

**Service departments**   (*See* MANAGEMENT THEORY, SCIENCE, AND APPROACHES.)

**Service representatives**   (*See* MARKETING, INDUSTRIAL.)

**Service-type organizations**   (*See* ORGANIZATION STRUCTURES AND CHARTING.)

**Services, market classification**   (*See* MARKETS, CLASSIFICATIONS AND MARKET ANALYSIS.)

**Services, marketing of**   (*See* MARKETING OF SERVICES.)

**Services, marketing of professional**   (*See* MARKETING OF SERVICES, PROFESSIONAL.)

**Services, organizational**   (*See* MARKETING OF SERVICES.)

**Services, product-related**   (*See* MARKETING OF SERVICES.)

**Set-asides, for small businesses**   (*See* SMALL BUSINESS ADMINISTRATION.)

**Severance pay**   (*See* COMPENSATION, EMPLOYEE BENEFIT PLANS.)

# Shareholder relationships

Shareholder relationships are an essential management function for publicly held companies. Although communication is the most visible part of this function, the appropriate foundation for a valuable relationship is an attitude that shareholders are important and that management is operating in the shareholders' interests.

The majority of a company's investor communications are often directed at professional investors, such as security analysts, portfolio managers, and others in financial institutions and funds who represent the investments of individuals. Most corporations are well versed in conducting these relationships, usually having a clear picture of the needs of this audience and how to respond to them. This discussion will concentrate on communication to and from that segment of corporate ownership more difficult to identify and understand—individual shareholders.

**A Declining Population**   The individual shareholder is often ignored in these days of heavy emphasis on institutional trading, and some executives question the need to pay any attention at all to this segment of their shareholder population. After all, their reasoning runs, the individual investor is, and has been, leaving the market on a steady basis since 1970. The New York Stock Exchange reported that from early 1970 to mid 1975, the U.S. shareowner population dropped from 30.8 million individuals to 25.3 million, an 18 percent decline. Stock held by individuals as of mid 1975 accounted for only 52.7 percent of the total market value of all shares, down from 64.1 percent in 1970.[1]

**Benefiting from Successful Shareholder Relations**   In view of the importance of institutional investors, management might ask, "Why pay attention to the individual shareholder?" To a large extent the answer lies in the role individual investors often can play in a corporation's stability and well-being. The need to raise capital has become a significant concern for U.S. businesses, and the individual shareholder's role in this arena is significant. The individual is one of the best prospective investors for a company's stock because the individual shareholder can provide liquidity in the marketplace, serve as a loyal resistance in the case of unfriendly raids, provide important additional capital, and be a good customer, a more loyal employee, and a supporter in the political and economic arena.

Many companies have instituted active programs to communicate with this vital financial audience. Unfortunately, far too many companies wait too long to start such a shareholder program. They find themselves in a proxy or tender fight and then do not understand why shareholders are not more loyal to the company. Others are not sure how to communicate with their shareholders when a crisis arises because they do not know anything about them.

A basic concept in any well-thought-out shareholder relations program is to treat shareholders in the same way that important customers are treated. To do this, management must find out who they are, why they are interested in the company, and what makes them happy and/or unhappy, then make an effort to gain their trust and regard.

**Identifying Stockholder Population** Corporations that ignore their shareholders do not know enough about them, cannot reach them, capture their interest, or hold their attention when it is most needed. A report by the American Society of Corporate Secretaries indicates that fewer than 10 percent of U.S. corporations have undertaken stockholder research studies, although many companies do not hesitate to undertake studies of their important customers.

Many alert companies attempt to build a profile of their shareholder community. They want to know, for example, whether it is a dominantly professional group or mostly unsophisticated individuals, its geographic distribution, its stability, and its turnover. A company might consider the following data important in efforts to improve its shareholder communications program:

What makes owners buy, sell, and hold stock in the corporation—for example, do they have specific investment goals or price objectives?

How do they feel about the company's management—its dividend policies, products, and communications? Do they have misconceptions in these areas that can and should be corrected?

To whom do the shareholders listen for advice on their investment?

How are answers found to these questions? One simple approach is to ask the stockholders. Stockholder surveys have grown in importance and vary in sophistication, length, and cost.

One method is to employ questionnaires tailored to a company's specific situation and mailed to a random sample of stockholders, followed by random telephone interviews in more depth. The sample size is important. It must be large enough to ensure representative and reliable results but not so large as to unduly increase the time required to complete analysis. Questions should be objective and, in more sophisticated approaches, can be analyzed by computer. More refined approaches may allow for correlation between different data, provid-

ing answers to such questions as, "Do large shareholders feel differently about certain issues than do small shareholders?"

A less costly and much simpler procedure is to include a stockholder reply card or questionnaire in regular written communications, particularly the annual report. While this approach is less expensive, it produces results that are less statistically valid. In addition, simply asking shareholders their opinion often has a salutary effect on their view of the management and the company.

These techniques help to identify misunderstandings about the company and management and provide input for future policy decisions (such as dividend policy and diversification).

*Reaching Street Name Holders.* Probably the segment of the shareholder population most difficult to reach is the group termed *street name holders*—that is, those stockholders whose stock is held in the name of a brokerage house. A sizable number of holders prefer either the anonymity or the convenience—or both—that this arrangement provides. Seventeen percent of all outstanding corporate stock is now held in street name, a frustration for companies seeking more knowledge about their stockholders.

Because these individuals cannot be identified, companies have no way of communicating with them, except through the holder of record. This often means a delay in communications, which is not only frustrating, but can be a major problem in proxy or tender contests. In fact, some experts in investor relations suspect that material intended for street name holders never reaches them, except for annual reports, proxies, and materials that legally must be forwarded. Many executives seek ways to communicate with these stockholders directly. One technique is to include a return postcard in regular material (annual or quarterly reports) mailed to street name holders. These cards ask the owners to identify themselves to the company in order to receive information directly and may ask the number of shares held and date of purchase. In some cases banks and brokerage firms have been reluctant to mail such reply cards for various reasons. One is that they cannot mail one kind of material to street name shareholders (i.e., material with a return card) and another kind of material to other shareholders (material without a card). Most companies have been willing to mail the material to all shareholders to avoid this complaint—although the subsequent sorting has, in some cases, been costly to the company.

*Transfer Sheet Analysis.* One way to gain insight into those who are buying and selling shares is to study the transfer sheets (supplied to the company by the registrar) on a regular basis. *Caution:* The review of these sheets should be the responsibility of someone who can quickly spot trends and can analyze the situation; otherwise this is a costly, time-consuming process. The Depository Trust Company (CEDE) will supply a corporation with a monthly printout of the stock held by its depositors for a fee.

**Proxy Fights and Tender Offers** Perhaps the most valuable benefit of an effective shareholder relations program is experienced in a proxy fight or contested tender offer. The impulse is to develop a check list of things to do, lawyers to call, and boiler plate copy for advertisements and letters to stockholders. Many companies, before a fight or raid, regard their stockholders as adversaries. Other companies maintain a stereotyped image of their stockholders as irrelevant or as cranks who write fractious notes in the margins of proxy cards. To try to communicate in a crisis with these stereotypes in mind invites, rather than solves, problems. The fact is, of course, that such owners make up only an insignificant minority of the shareowner group as a whole.

A positive program of shareholder relations is the best opportunity a company has to build a reservoir of support for such occasions, especially if it cannot boast an unbroken string of dividend payments. If management has built a good relationship with its shareholders, if it has taken the time and effort to know who the owners are and what their aspirations and expectations are, the company will be more successful in winning shareholder support in a crisis.

**Dividend Reinvestment** One excellent step offered by more than 400 companies is a stockholders dividend reinvestment program—the option of automatically investing their dividends in additional shares. In some cases, shareholders pay a service charge for the transaction to the bank administering the plan. Where companies administer their own plans, stockholders usually purchase their additional shares at no cost—an attractive savings for investors. A few firms offer added enticements such as permitting shareholders to reinvest cash dividends in new stock at a discount below market price or allowing the shareholder to add some personal cash toward the purchase of shares. For corporations, such plans offer two advantages: (1) they help to regain part of the money paid out as dividends and (2) they promote shareholder goodwill.

Participation in such plans ranges from 5 percent to as high as 21 percent of a stockholder population and is usually favored by the small shareholder who owns 100 to 300 shares, to whom the investing

convenience and commission savings are most attractive.

**Communicating Effectively with Shareholders** Modern business reporting is complex and demanding; management has the responsibility to get across the most important facts to its shareholders in order of importance. It is not enough simply to fulfill the regulatory requirements. In fact, recent requirements instituted by the SEC on a corporation's communications are directed at increasing disclosure so that individual shareholders receive the same information as professional investors. The emphasis is on presenting the information in a straightforward, readable manner.

The channels of communication also must be open—giving the bad news as well as the good. Companies that communicate clearly, accurately, and thoroughly when things are bad find it easier to win support and influence with stockholders in a lasting way.

*Annual Reports.* Most experts on investor relations consider the annual report to be the most important communication document a corporation puts out on itself. And the cost can range up to tens of thousands of dollars. The last few years have seen an evolution in the contents of this report required by the SEC and the Financial Accounting Standards Board. The rules are complex and changing, and there is no attempt to review them here.

Of more concern is the effectiveness of these reporting documents as communications tools. Many reports neglect the individual investor and instead are aimed at the analysts and other professional investors, a group with whom the planners and writers usually are better acquainted. The result is that the individual does not understand the report or is turned off by it. Yet preparing an annual report that presents easily absorbed data in plainly written prose is not impossible. Unique approaches to increase effectiveness and readability include:

1. Use of the report as an educational tool on (*a*) financial statements, (*b*) the free enterprise system, or (*c*) current national issues such as environment or government regulation.

2. Combination of the annual report with the form 10-K [the annual report a company files with the Securities and Exchange Commission (SEC)] and issuance of supplementary statistical publications.

3. Interviews with members of such key audiences as security analysts, stockholders, and customers.

Management must, of course, ask itself if its annual report reflects an honest desire to communicate with investors about how the company is really doing. Does the report show real concern for the owners? Does it present the material in a credible manner?

Although studies disagree on which section of annual reports shareholders consider of greatest importance, most indicate that the amount of time a shareholder spends on a report is very limited. All agree, however, that at the top of the list of most frequently read sections are the financial highlights and the president's letter. The president's letter is a good opportunity to present the company's story. It should be brief and easy to read. More importantly, it should be candid and informative. For those who will not take the time to read on, it should provide the important data and leave the reader with a feeling that problems are being dealt with and the company is well directed. It should set forth the company's objectives for the next year and how management views the company's future.

*Interim Reports.* Traditionally, quarterly reports disclose only limited information to investors. Although there are no rules stating that a company must issue a quarterly report to stockholders, the SEC has expanded the requirements for the quarterly form 10-Q (the report a company must file with the commission). As the 10-Q form has gained more attention from the SEC, the quarterly report to stockholders has grown in importance. Stockholders no longer are willing to wait for year-end results; they seek interim data that are detailed and informative. No longer is this publication destined to be a three-fold document to go along with the dividend check. New approaches include (1) preparing quarterly features on new products and developments, (2) utilizing the four quarterly reports together to yield an annual, (3) adding questions and answers from analyst meetings, and (4) reprinting management speeches.

*Management Letters.* Just as companies write letters to potential customers promising savings and offering service, a company might consider a similar effort to gain stockholder trust and regard. A company going through a difficult time, for example, can write brief letters to stockholders describing problems and outlining plans to solve them. Companies seeking approval from stockholders for a merger have sent out "thank you" notes to shareholders who return proxies. Such unorthodox approaches receive surprisingly favorable comments from stockholders.

"Welcome" letters to new shareholders offer another effective communication tool for management. These letters should be short, thank the individual for his or her support, and enclose the latest informational material about the company.

*Personal Contact.* In a stockholder relations program, there is no substitute for direct meetings with the stockholders. The company's regular annual meeting presents one important opportunity for such personal contact. Some companies hold their annual meeting in a different location each year in an effort to reach more shareholders. The cities are chosen according to their concentration of stockholders and location of operational facilities. Another approach is to hold special regional stockholder meetings—inviting both street name and beneficial owners whenever possible. One interesting device used to ensure a good turnout for these meetings is to engage retirees to make invitation follow-up calls. Incidentally, the retiree group has another value; it can be mobilized easily in the future for proxy solicitation.

AT&T takes the personal touch even further. Representatives from the company have been making house and office calls on shareholders since 1956—some 50,000 calls a year. The objective is to answer questions about the company and foster a feeling of belonging among its owners. Telephone contact is a way for any company to maintain personal contact with its significant shareholders. A convenient time for calls is after the regular annual meeting or following the announcement of a major development—such as an increase of dividend or a stock split. Stockholders can be asked if they (1) are satisfied with the company's communications efforts, (2) have any questions, and (3) resent company performance and direction.

*See also* BOARDS OF DIRECTORS; FINANCIAL MANAGEMENT; FINANCIAL MANAGEMENT, CAPITAL STRUCTURE AND DIVIDEND POLICY; FINANCIAL STATEMENT ANALYSIS; MARKETS, SECURITIES; OWNERSHIP, LEGAL FORMS OF; PUBLIC AND COMMUNITY RELATIONS; SECURITIES AND EXCHANGE COMMISSION (SEC).

## NOTES

[1] *Shareownership 1975*, The New York Stock Exchange, Inc., New York, 1976.

[2] *1974 Corporate Communications*, survey conducted by the American Society of Corporate Secretaries, New York.

## REFERENCES

"Annual Reports Awards," *Financial World* (published annually in October).

"Annual Reports Survey," *Financial World* (published annually, last issue in June).

*National Investor Relations Institute*, Washington (periodic programs and publications on general subjects of investor relations).

*The New York Stock Exchange Fact Book*, New York, published annually.

*Public Relations Society*, Investor Relations Section, quarterly newsletter.

Roalman, Arthur, ed.: *Investor Relations Handbook*, American Management Association, New York, 1974.

*The SEC, the Stock Exchange and Your Financial Public Relations*, Hill and Knowlton, Inc., New York, 1972.

RICHARD E. CHENEY, *Hill and Knowlton, Inc.*

CAROL A. RUTH, *Hill and Knowlton, Inc.*

# Sherman Act (*See* GOVERNMENT REGULATIONS, FEDERAL REGULATION OF COMPETITION.)

# Shopping goods (*See* MARKETS, CLASSIFICATIONS AND MARKET ANALYSIS; RETAILING MANAGEMENT.)

# Short-interval scheduling (*See* SCHEDULING, SHORT-INTERVAL.)

# Short-range planning (*See* PLANNING, STRATEGIC MANAGERIAL.)

# Simplification, paper work (*See* PAPER WORK SIMPLIFICATION.)

# Simplification, product (*See* PRODUCT PLANNING AND DEVELOPMENT.)

# Simplification, work (*See* WORK SIMPLIFICATION AND IMPROVEMENT.)

# Simulation (*See* PLANNING, STRATEGIC PLANNING MODELS; SIMULATIONS, BUSINESS AND MANAGEMENT; SYSTEM CONCEPT, TOTAL; SYSTEM DYNAMICS.)

# Simulation, computer (*See* SYSTEM DYNAMICS.)

# Simulation model (*See* OPERATIONS RESEARCH AND MATHEMATICAL MODELING.)

# Simulations, business and management

The management (or business) game is essentially a pedagogical device that enables the individual to learn by participation and involvement. The simulation—or game—is a contest among participants, either as individuals or as teams, who must follow a set of rules and who aim to win the contest. The game is successful when the participants have obtained a better understanding of that portion of reality simulated within the game model. Learning involves three successive steps:

1. Acquiring the *common language* and the facts expressed in the game
2. Learning the *process* simulated within the game model, including restrictions
3. Understanding the relative tradeoffs—the costs, the advantages and disadvantages—required of the different *strategies* and *alternatives*

Games are usually conducted in three phases: (1) Preplay description and briefing of the rules; (2) play itself—in sequential, discrete, and compressed periods of time; and (3) postgame critique of the decisions and consequences, possibly with participant suggestions to improve the realism of the game. Because of the competitive nature of the game, participants are usually motivated to learn by their desire to win.

### EARLY DEVELOPMENTS

Gaming has been used for some time to facilitate training in the military. From simple chesslike games employed in India many centuries ago to week-long simulated worldwide games employed today, military gaming provides a rich antecedent to management and business gaming.

From the beginning, war games involved two or more teams of participants competing for the control of an area. By the mid 1800s all the elements of modern war gaming had been developed: the inclusion of environmental factors, the passage of time, and the detailed simulation of activities.

The first business game, using a mathematical model and a computer to facilitate calculation, was conceived in the mid 1950s by Frank M. Ricciardi, who was then manager of the finance division of the American Management Association (AMA). Following a visit to the Naval War College at Newport, Rhode Island, to see an existing war game facility, he secured a commitment within the AMA to develop a "business war game." The first model of the AMA game evolved early in 1956 and was tested for a year by staff members.

On May 2, 1957, under the aegis of the AMA, 20 company presidents took part in the first management game ever staged for corporate executives. Each team received some initial basic operating information, including the dollar resources available for expenditure. The five companies were assumed to manufacture a single identical product whose price was specified within the $5 to $10 price range in direct competition against one another. At the outset, each team had exactly one-fifth of the market, identical dollar value in assets, and the same range of available choices. Each team made decisions on a quarterly basis and decided how much to spend over the next period for production, marketing, research and development, and additional plant investment. The price for the product was also specified. After making its decisions, each team received a quarterly operating statement indicating the number of units sold and the costs incurred. They repeated the cycle, quarter by quarter, until the equivalent of three business years had elapsed. This initial game, like many games still in use today, concluded with a critique session wherein each group had the opportunity to compare its results with those of its competitors and to contrast strategies. In the initial AMA game, no winner was named, although the team which was most successful in increasing its assets was generally considered to have won.

Within a year, several games following the AMA simulation were introduced in various universities and other settings across the country. The University of California (Los Angeles) and the International Business Machines Corporation developed and made extensive use of two noteworthy games.

## FEATURES AND TYPES OF GAMES

A management game incorporates a mathematical model or replica of reality which establishes a set of relationships. These should and can be as simple as possible. But the game must also be intuitively sound and credible to the participants.

**Features** Games usually reproduce reality through a compression of time. Like earlier games, some present-day games require decisions which then project over a quarter. Four such decisions obviously represent a year in the existence of the firm. These four decisions can be made in sequential ½-hour periods and the total game, representing 4 or 5 years in the existence of the firm, can be completed within 1 day. The choice of the simulated time period depends upon the function in question

and can reflect a day, a week, a month, or even a year.

Games differ in their use of interactive or noninteractive relationships. Games that attempt to reproduce the competitive aspects of business and that include, in particular, a marketing component are likely to be interactive. Within this framework, the action taken by one team or firm may affect the results of an action taken by one or more opponents, as well as the action of the team in question. An interactive game is analogous to tennis where the tactics and success of an individual depend upon the strokes of the opponent. In golf, by contrast, all participants compete against a benign opponent, i.e., the golf course, and except for some psychological pressures introduced by a competitor through a particularly well-placed shot, no interaction of shots (or decisions) is possible. It should be obvious that it is not necessary to include interaction in order to introduce competition. The model itself can represent the golf course against which all participants compete, some with more success than others.

Games may or may not employ a computer. The advantages of using a computer are much the same as the advantages of using a computer for any day-to-day processing task: speed, accuracy, and comprehensive reports. The computer-based game is likely to be more complex because more complex relationships can be modeled and mathematically manipulated. However, the noncomputer game has the flexibility of being carried into the classroom or on the road without concern for computer accessibility and compatibility.

**Types** Management games are conveniently classified by subject matter. While the earliest games were the so-called general management or total enterprise games, in recent years functional games and specialized or industry games have been developed either to meet a more specific pedagogical objective or to characterize the uniqueness of a business, industry, or other organizational entity. These three types will be discussed in turn.

*General Management Games.* The general management game is typically competitive, interactive, computer-scored, predominantly deterministic, and designed for team play. The players are usually divided into teams, each to represent the top management group of one of several competing companies. Each company starts in the same financial position with the same options available to it and is in direct competition with every other company in the manufacture of a single, identical product for sale in the same market. The players are provided financial data and an overview of the economic conditions which will influence the results of their decisions. They are usually asked to make quantitative decisions and, typically, must allocate dollars among the group of alternative expenditures—production, additional plant investment, research, advertising, or marketing effort—and they must designate the price for their product. The allocation of sales among the companies is in accordance with the model formulation and relates causally the implications of all decisions made by each team. The players are given the results in the form of financial statements representing the period in question.

Some of the general management games incorporate unique features. One provides for four marketing areas instead of one, permitting the use of different prices in sales expenditure strategies in each area. A second includes provision for bank loans and corporate dividends, and a third requires labor negotiations. Still another general management game requires raw material purchases as a decision. Some games provide for a depreciation in production capacity and a corresponding investment just to maintain capacity. Further investment is needed to increase capacity. Finally, one game separates the process engineering expenditures from product development instead of grouping them under research and development. All general management games operate from the perspective of a top management team within the organization.

*Functional Games.* Games have also been designed to develop skill in the performance of specific functions, e.g., inventory control, production scheduling, and quality control, while being aimed at the middle or lower level of management. These games tend to vary greatly in complexity and may be manual or computer-based, deterministic or random, interactive or noninteractive, and with team or individual participation. The university course in quality control might easily accommodate a simple exercise in which the participants are required to design a single sampling plan by attributes and then to test that plan against the simulated arrival of lots of materials of varying quality. Similarly, class participants might be required to schedule production in the face of a probabilistic sales requirement. Games as diverse as those requiring job-shop scheduling, machine loading, the scheduling of maintenance activities, and even the bidding of jobs in a construction industry lend themselves to the explicit reinforcement of the concepts to be developed within a more theoretical framework in the classroom. Through the game, the participants have the opportunity to test theory against a simulated requirement.

*Industry or Specialized Games.* The third class of games might be called "specialized." These games are either general management, developed to meet the requirements of an individual company or companies in a specific industry, or functional, designed to display the uniqueness of a given situation. Numerous retail industry games have been developed, as have games involving service-station operations and automobile dealerships. A game requiring scheduling and work loading within the maintenance department of an urban mass transit authority is more functional than management-oriented, but is unique to that industry. Finally, a number of games have been developed which capture banking, transportation, agribusiness, and even university functions.

## THE USES OF GAMES

The use and potential value of games may be illustrated in the context of a specific, specialized game. In the Academic Department Head game, participants are presumed to be directing a department of statistics within a large state university. Decisions are required on a semester-by-semester basis for 10 periods, simulating 5 years in the existence of this academic department. The game participant is provided with an initial roster of eight faculty members, including a personal sketch of each individual, as well as an insight into his or her professional interests and abilities. Then, at any time during the game, these faculty members may choose to resign or, if nontenured, may be terminated. Additional faculty must then be secured, and it is not unusual for a department to change in composition over the 5 years of its existence. In the game, as in reality, the objectives of the department have to be achieved through the faculty. As a result, the critical decisions in this simulation exercise focus upon the recruitment and retention of faculty and the assignment of faculty to teaching and research. The game participant is required to assign faculty to courses, which are diverse in number and level, and the subdiscipline within the field of statistics. The department head provides salary increases in varying amounts in accordance with his or her assessment of faculty productivity and is also able to recommend promotions and/or tenure, where warranted, or nonreappointment, if the individual is not tenured. If vacancies occur or the department increases in size, the department head (game participant) can recruit from an available pool of applicants. The measure of departmental progress is seen in the composite criteria which include some proportion of teaching effectiveness, scholarship and research, and service to both the institution and the profession. The Academic Department Head game has been designed as both an orientation and a training device for the new or the aspiring department head. It can also be used to orient others, either within or outside the university, who might profit from a better understanding of some of the significant decisions required in the administration of an academic department. Obviously the game excludes many decision situations that confront the department on a daily basis; for example, the situation in which a group of students complains about the length of the homework assignment required by a new assistant professor. Further, the department head is not required to respond to the query of the faculty member who cannot find a parking place and is habitually late for the first class. But the game does provide for a review of the more profound decisions required of a manager within this unique organizational setting. The game can be used as a vehicle for discussing the "real-world" situation.

The business game, in contrast to the more traditional teaching techniques, requires a pattern of decision, feedback, and new response. Not only do players have to live with the consequences of their decisions, but they also operate within a recurring pattern which represents a "dynamic" case study. Participants become highly motivated to do well in the game and will often hotly debate the merits of alternate strategies. In particular, games motivate the players to attempt to identify clearly what is to be maximized—what is important—and then attempt to devise mini-experiments to ascertain which few of the many controllable (and uncontrollable) factors seem to influence results. Gaming is potentially a powerful teaching tool. Whether all games do, in fact, teach is difficult to measure.

Games, by necessity, tend to ignore qualitative factors in order to permit the manipulation of a quantitative mathematical model which can easily be scored. With the exception of such recent games as the Academic Department Head game, the human element is entirely omitted. As a result, games tend to reproduce the idealized situation rather than the actuality of missed deadlines, equipment breakdowns, sales requirements lost owing to the inadvertent delivery of the product to the wrong market area, and so forth. Games are not usually offered within the framework of teaching the "correct decision." Rather they are offered as a framework within which discussion can proceed. Just as one seeks a solution to a case study, so, too, the winning strategy in a gaming situation is only a reference for

discussion and the more general understanding of the real-world situation contained within the game model.

*See also* ASSESSMENT CENTER METHOD; DEVELOPMENT AND TRAINING, MANAGEMENT; OPERATIONS RESEARCH AND MATHEMATICAL MODELING; STATISTICAL ANALYSIS FOR MANAGERS.

### REFERENCES

Abt, C. C.: *Serious Games*, The Viking Press, Inc., New York, 1970.
Belch, Jean: *Contemporary Games*, vols. I and II, Gale Research Company, Detroit, 1973.
Bittel, L. R.: "A Model of Simulated Management Experience for Engineering Managers, "Winter Annual Meeting ASME, Houston, Nov. 30–Dec. 4, 1975, 75-WA/Mgt-5.
Carlson, John G. H., and Michael J. Misshauk: *Introduction to Gaming: Management Decision Simulations*, John Wiley & Sons, Inc., New York, 1972.
Ricciardi, Frank M., et al.: *Top Management Decision Simulation*, American Management Association, 1957.
Shubik, Martin: "Gaming: Costs and Facilities," *Management Science*, July 1968, pp. 736–751.
Torgersen, Paul E., and Taylor, Robert E.: "The Department Head in Facsimile," *Engineering Education*, January 1974, pp. 245–249.

PAUL E. TORGERSEN, *Virginia Polytechnic Institute and State University*

# Site planning  (*See* FACILITIES AND SITE PLANNING AND LAYOUT.)

# Site selection

Within the field of industrial site selection, two sets of criteria exist: (1) general or geographical factors and (2) specific or local factors. The former category concerns itself with comparisons of continents, countries, regions, states, counties, cities, and towns. The latter category comes into focus after a preferred general area has been identified and site selection is reduced to the comparison of the qualities of individual land parcels. The following discussion will deal with both general and specific site selection factors.

**Acquisition Costs and Procedure**  Total costs include those for land acquisition and preparation, construction, and interest on borrowed funds. If the new facility is to be leased instead of owned, lease terms are included under total costs.

*Search.*  In assembling a land site, a good policy usually is to seek the assistance of a reputable industrial real estate broker who knows the land available and the prices being asked. This does not preclude, of course, using railroad industrial development departments, banks, utility companies, chambers of commerce, and area, state, and local industrial development commissions. All these can be very helpful, especially in narrowing down the area of search.

*Negotiations.* Assembling an industrial site can be a sensitive matter. If more than one parcel is involved, each owner must be approached individually. At this time the industrial or land broker, serving as an agent, can explore whatever problems exist in each parcel of land while simultaneously maintaining the anonymity of the principal. If word leaks out during the investigative stage that a well-known company is interested in the site, the price almost automatically jumps upward as each succeeding land owner is approached. This problem may be successfully combatted, however. If the agent lets it be known that the principal is, indeed, interested in the land but has established a rigid budget for acquisition, hard-bargaining land owners may be willing to accept the argument. The best policy, of course, is to keep the principal anonymous as long as possible so as to hold the acquisition price at its lowest possible level.

**Site Configuration and Quality**   The site should be large enough to permit an efficient operation at the outset, as well as to allow for future expansion. A land-to-building ratio, of from 3 to 5, i.e., three to five times as much land as building, is usually adequate for modern one-story facilities.

*Requirement Specifications.* More specifically, the size of the new structure will be determined by expansion requirements; code setbacks; employee and visitor parking; required truck dock areas; railroad sidings, number and length of cars to be handled daily and radius of the track siding; and requirements for outside storage of raw materials, work-in-process, or finished products.

*Topographical Considerations.* The site's topography, soil, and subsoil conditions are important considerations. Land should never be purchased without prior inspection of a United States Geological Service survey and the results of soil testing. It can become very costly to rectify substandard conditions in a land site so that it will accept aboveground improvements. The costs associated with correcting a poor site can often amount to more than the initial sale price of the land.

**Deed Restrictions**   The current, or previous, owner of the land site often has entered restrictions to the parcel in an attempt to guarantee the value of the property for future owners. Restrictions of this kind are a form of zoning that goes beyond ordinary local codes and ordinances. They usually concern themselves with aesthetic considerations, but sometimes are a whim of the owner. Some examples of private deed restrictions are: a requirement of approval of building plans by a developer or architectural review board, prohibition of certain materials for use in exterior walls, denial of truck-dock construction facing a street or a demand that docks be enclosed, prohibition of outside storage, and a stipulation that extensive landscaping be undertaken.

**Zoning**   Building codes and other controls on land and building use are designed to protect industry from encroachment by commercial and residential development and to guarantee equitable and uniform enforcement. Some of the more common zoning ordinances deal with lot coverage or land-to-building ratio, setbacks from lot lines, uses permitted, parking requirements, and height restrictions. Almost all local building codes make reference to the requirements set forth by the Building Officials Conference of America or the National Association of Insurance Underwriters. With only minor variations, both codes cover the same items.

**Utilities and Other Requirements**   The following should be carefully investigated:

1. *Electric power.* Most suppliers construct lines free of charge up to the new industrial facility. Sometimes, however, there is an extra charge if service requirements go beyond a certain standard. The charge must be borne by the owner of the site, developer, landlord, or industrial user.

2. *Natural gas.* If gas for heating or power is required, an early inquiry to determine its availability is vital. Except for a few areas, a natural gas shortage exists which forces utilities either to put applications on a waiting list or to allot usage to those that are granted.

3. *Water supply.* Important items to check are main size, pressure per square inch, reliability of service, flow tests, mineral content, tap-on charges, and off-site extension costs. In most areas, environmental protection agencies make judgments as to water utility plant capacities and quality.

4. *Sprinkler systems.* The degree of hazard involved in storing particular types of goods will determine whether ordinary or high-density sprinkler heads should be used. The height of the proposed structure will also have a bearing on whether sprinklering will be necessary within storage racking. The Factory Mutual Association (FMA) and similar insurance rating agencies insist on certain requirements for a preferred rating. In areas where water pressure is low, FMA or another group will also

require the installation of a pump or pumps to guarantee a proper water pressure.

5. *Sewer requirements.* These include many of the same factors as with water supply. Main sizes, capacity of the local plant, the very important approval of the Environmental Protection Agency, and type of effluent permitted are the prime concerns.

6. *Storm drainage.* This can be handled by storm sewers, an open ditch, swale, underground piping and drains, or natural runoff. The topography of the site will determine which method is best. Storm sewers are expensive, but they add to the value of the industrial property.

**Transportation Facilities** It is the rule, rather than the exception, that proposed manufacturing and/or distribution facilities will require dependable and reliable railroad and trucking services tendered by local and interstate carriers.

*Rail.* It is usually wise to locate the new operation at a site where rail service can be accepted from a long-haul carrier or from a belt or switching line. *Other important points* are the number and frequency of daily car spots; direction of the turnout to avoid overshooting and backing-up of cars for placement; ability of smaller belt or switching lines to handle the projected volume; eligibility of the site for reciprocal switching and favorable rate privileges; elevation of the site to the grade of the rail service roadbed—a 2 percent gradient or a 2-foot increase or decrease in elevation per 100 feet is allowable; ability of the proposed structure to accept a rail spur at the side or rear with no more than a turning radius curve of 12° or 475 lineal feet; and the policy of the rail carrier on acceptance of less-than-carload shipments.

*Truck.* Trucking requirements are equally important in the planning of a new manufacturing and/or distribution operation. Management must determine whether the proposed location is within the commercial zone of a municipality or at least enjoys the rate basis of the nearby metropolitan area. If the proposed site is in a rural area, there probably will be additional freight charges on inbound and outbound shipments. The additional freight charges quite likely will be offset by other more favorable factors—a trade-off.

Load limits and height restrictions on arterial roads, highways, and bridges, must be examined. In many cases, state, country, and local governing bodies will cooperate on these matters. Also of extreme importance are such factors as road widths, traffic congestion, rush-hour problems, and possible tie-ups at railroad crossings. If access roads must go through residential areas, problems can arise. A site

**1098**

should be chosen that will allow direct access to roads and highways on which truck traffic is accepted.

**Labor Supply** Even with increasing automation, the availability and quality of the labor supply is important. Generally, 30 miles is the maximum distance workers can be expected to commute by automobile. Personnel managers of nearby industrial firms can shed light on such conditions as degree of difficulty in hiring labor, pirating of employees, wage levels, and aggressiveness of local unions. Routine investigation of help-wanted signs and advertisements and local employment agencies will also provide a valuable insight into prevailing labor conditions.

**Taxes** Local real estate, personal property, and inventory taxes should be carefully considered. Present rates should be examined along with close scrutiny of the trend over a 5- to 10-year period. On real estate taxes, it is vital to investigate carefully previous years' changes in the assessed valuation percentage, rate per $100 of valuation, and, if applicable, the state's equalization factor for the area.

**Community Services** If a site is selected in an established community, the nature and quality of public services are important. Fire and police protection, road maintenance, and, in a northern climate, snow removal should be evaluated. Of course, if a site is selected in an unincorporated area because of other favorable features, the company itself may be required to provide some form of these services at the new facility. An important point to remember is that the quantity and quality of these community services have a great effect on insurance rates and coverage.

**Proximity to Sources of Supply and Markets** It should be self-evident that for any site to be considered for development, that site must optimize the relationship between these two factors.

**Expressway or Highway Identity** To many enterprises there is a substantial public relations value in having a modern, attractive facility located adjacent to a major expressway or highway. This is especially true when a firm produces and distributes consumer goods. To other companies, such a location can be a hiring aid because employees like to be close to expressways for easy access in their daily traveling to and from work—and it extends the employment area.

**Traffic Congestion** If a site or sites are near a metropolitan area, vehicular congestion (automobile, bus, truck, and railroad) must be investigated. It is important, not only in the inbound and outbound movement of goods, but also in the hiring and keeping of personnel.

**Neighborhood** In a rural area, the surrounding neighborhood may not be a great factor. If the proposed site is located near a metropolitan area, however, a positive prognosis for the future is important. Barring unusual overgrowth or unforeseen market conditions, the company should view the site as one that will take care of its needs for many years.

**Cultural, Educational, and Recreational Facilities** These factors vary in importance according to the nature of employees' interests and expectations. If the site chosen is in a small community or rural area, the company may feel a responsibility for establishing some of these facilities for its employees—especially those it wishes to attract from metropolitan areas.

*See also* COMMUNITY PLANNING LEGISLATION; DISTRIBUTION, PHYSICAL; FACILITIES AND SITE PLANNING AND LAYOUT; REAL ESTATE MANAGEMENT, CORPORATE.

### REFERENCES

Boblett, Robert P.: "Factors in Industrial Location," Society of Industrial Realtors *Newsletter*, July–August 1968.

Gross, Sheldon A.: "A Model for Selective Site Selection," *Real Estate Today*, May–June 1975.

Kinnard, William N., Jr., and Stephen D. Messner: *Industrial Real Estate*, 2d ed., Society of Industrial Realtors, 1971.

Linane, William E.: "Basics of Site Selection for the Distribution Manager," *Transportation and Distribution Management*, August 1973.

Marsh, W. Y.: "Selecting an Industrial Site," *Journal of Property Management*, Spring 1963.

Mitchell, Richard E.: "Industrial Site Selection Outside of Urban Centers," *The Appraisal Journal*, October 1966.

Speir, William B.: "The Common Denominator in Selecting New Sites," *Industrial Development*, January–February 1969.

Vaughn, Stuart H.: "Engineering Aspects of Industrial Site Selection," *Industrial Development*, January–February 1969.

WILLIAM E. LINANE, *Linane & Company, Inc.*

## Situation appraisal (*See* DECISION-MAKING PROCESS.)

## Situation audit (*See* PLANNING, STRATEGIC MANAGERIAL.)

## Situational control (*See* LEADERSHIP.)

## Situational management (*See* HEALTH INSTITUTIONS, MANAGEMENT OF.)

## Skill (*See* DEVELOPMENT AND TRAINING, EMPLOYEE.)

## Skills inventory (*See* DEVELOPMENT AND TRAINING, EMPLOYEE.)

## Small Business Administration

The Small Business Administration (SBA) of the United States was created in 1953 and directed by law to aid, counsel, assist, and protect insofar as possible the interests of small business concerns. Congress prescribed that the role of the federal government would (1) be supportive rather than dominant and (2) be geared to encourage rather than to regulate and control. Thus, a basic feature of the original legislation of 1953 was a lending program under which the SBA would undertake to make loans with public funds to small firms in circumstances where such loans would not otherwise be made. In this way, the formerly submarginal loan applicant would receive funds with the loan risks shared by private banks and the federal government.

The SBA is unique in concept and design because it is the only independent federal government agency with programs specifically designed to promote and protect the welfare of the 13 million or more small businesses. The services it provides are authorized by the Small Business Act and the Small Business Investment Act. The agency strives to carry out this mandate by ensuring that small business concerns receive a fair proportion of government purchases, contracts, and subcontracts, as well as of the sales of government property; making loans to small business concerns, state and local development companies, and victims of floods or other catastrophes; licensing, regulating, and lending to small business investment companies; improving the management skills of established and potential small business owners; conducting studies of the economic environment, and acting as advocate for the small business community.

The concept of a *small business* is rather flexible, but as the term is currently being applied to SBA loans, the following standards of definition have been adopted:

Retailing: annual sales or receipts of not over $2 million to $7.5 million

Services: annual receipts not exceeding $2 million to $8 million

Wholesaling: yearly receipts not over $9.5 million to $22 million

Manufacturing: up to 1500 employees

Note that all definitions are dependent on the industry in which the applicant is primarily engaged.

## FINANCIAL ASSISTANCE

The Small Business Administration provides loan guarantees and makes direct or lender-participation loans to small business concerns to help them finance plant construction, conversion, expansion, acquisition of equipment, facilities, machinery, supplies or materials and, if necessary, provide working capital, if the financing is not otherwise available on reasonable terms.

SBA can make a direct loan for as much as $150,000 if money is available, or will consider either participating with a bank in a loan or guaranteeing up to 90 percent of an amount of up to $350,000 (or $500,000 in special situations).

Financing may also be available to firms which have sustained substantial economic injury from a major or natural disaster, or have been economically injured by a federally aided urban renewal or highway construction program or by any construction program conducted with federal funds.

**Physical Disaster**  The Small Business Administration can help victims of storms, floods, earthquakes, or other catastrophes to repair physical damage in times of disasters. In these cases, the agency makes loans to individuals, churches, business concerns of all sizes, and nonprofit organizations to repair or replace damaged structures, lost or damaged furnishings, business machinery, equipment, and inventory.

**Economic Injury**  Firms that have suffered substantial economic injury because they cannot process or market a product for human consumption because of disease or toxicity resulting from either natural or undetermined causes may receive financial assistance. Other loans made under the disaster loan programs are those to concerns that must make changes in their equipment, facilities, or operations in order to meet the standards set by the Federal Coal Mine Health and Safety Act of 1969; the Egg Products Act; the Wholesome Meat Act of 1967; the Occupational Safety and Health Act of 1970; the Federal Water Pollution Control Act; the Clean Air Act; or the closing by the federal government of a major military installation, if it is determined that they will suffer substantial economic injury without the financing. Loans are also made available to small firms that have suffered economic injury as the result of shortages of fuel, electrical energy, or energy-producing resources, or by a shortage of raw or processed material resulting from such shortage.

In addition to the compliance loans to meet various federal standards, SBA provides similar financial assistance to help small firms meet requirements imposed by any federal law, any state law enacted as a result of the federal law, or any regulations of a federal law. Financing is also offered to nonprofit organizations employing 75 percent handicapped persons in the production of goods and services and to small businesses owned or to be owned by handicapped individuals; and to veterans of the Vietnam war and socially or economically disadvantaged persons.

**Ineligible Applications**  Because it is a public agency using taxpayer's funds, SBA has an unusual responsibility as a lender. It therefore will not make loans:

If the funds are otherwise available on reasonable terms.

If the loan is to (1) pay off a loan to a creditor or creditors of the applicant who are inadequately secured and in a position to sustain loss, (2) provide funds for distribution or payment to the principals of the applicant, or (3) replenish funds previously used for such purposes.

If the loan allows speculation on any kind of property.

If the applicant is a nonprofit enterprise (with the exception noted above)

If the applicant is a publisher of a newspaper, magazines, or books, or similar enterprise.

If any of the gross income of the applicant (or of any of its principal owners) is derived from gambling activities, except for those small firms which obtain less than one-third of their income from the sale of state lottery tickets under a state license, or from gambling activities in those states where such activities are legal within the state.

If the loan provides funds to an enterprise primarily engaged in lending or investing.

If the loan finances real property that is, or is to be, held for investment.

If the loan encourages monopoly or is inconsistent with the accepted standards of the American system of free competitive enterprise.

If the loan is used to relocate a business for other than sound business purposes.

**Community Development**  In order to assist the planned economic growth in communities needing assistance that will promote the development of small business concerns in their areas, the SBA will make loans to state and local development companies to assist identified small business. A *state development company* is a corporation organized by a special act of the state legislature to operate statewide in assisting the growth and development of business concerns, including small firms in its area. *Local development companies* are composed of local citizens who form a corporation with at least 75 percent of its ownership vested in persons living or doing business in the community. It may be profit or nonprofit and must have a minimum of 25 stockholders or members.

**Bonding**  SBA is authorized to guarantee to a qualified surety up to 90 percent of losses incurred under bid, payment, or performance bonds issued to contractors for construction, supplies, or services provided by either a prime or subcontractor for governmental or nongovernmental work.

**Financing for Investment Companies**  For the purpose of improving and stimulating the national economy and the small business segment, the SBA licenses, regulates, and provides financial assistance to regular *small business investment companies* (SBICs), which are privately owned and supply venture capital and long-term financing to small firms, and those licensed under Section 301(d) of the Small Business Investment Act for the purpose of providing management and advisory services and venture capital in the form of equity financing and long-term loans to small firms owned by the socially or economically disadvantaged. SBICs must operate within SBA regulations, but their transactions with small firms are private arrangements.

## BUYING FROM AND SELLING TO THE U.S. GOVERNMENT

Each year, the U.S. government does billions of dollars worth of business with private companies, both in buying needed goods and services and disposing of surplus government property. The SBA is charged with assisting small businesses to secure a fair share.

Also, while it is comparatively easy for large companies to keep informed on government activities and to deal directly with the government, it has been traditionally difficult for small businesses to learn what the government is in the market to buy and what it has to sell. The Small Business Administration tries in various ways to minimize the disadvantages the small business faces when dealing with the government.

SBA's government liaison staff works closely at the policy level of federal agencies. The staff reviews government procurement policies and proposed policy changes, analyzes the effect on small business, prepares the SBA position on such policies, and presents this position to the various federal agencies. The staff informs the directors of SBA procurement assistance programs of procurement policy changes of federal agencies and informs government agencies of SBA procurement assistance policy changes.

**Procurement Assistance**  SBA provides assistance to small firms so they can secure a fair share of the government's prime contracts and subcontracts. Specialists in SBA field offices advise small businesses which government agencies are prospective customers, how they can have their names placed on bidders lists, and how to obtain drawings and specifications for specific contracts.

An SBA publication, *The U.S. Government Purchasing and Sales Directory*, lists principal goods and services bought by each government agency. The directory is available from the Superintendent of Documents, U.S. Government Printing Office, Washington, 20402. Another pamphlet, *Selling to the U.S. Government*, explains how to sell to the government and how to find subcontract opportunities. It is available free from SBA field offices.

**Small Business Set-Asides**  Government procurement officials at military and civilian purchasing offices review proposed prime contracts to determine which ones can be set aside for competitive bidding by small business. Before a purchase may be set aside, there must be a reasonable expectation that a sufficient number of small firms will bid so the government is ensured of receiving a fair and reasonable price.

Contracts may be either totally set aside for small business participation or partially set aside. On a *total set-aside*, small businesses participate on an equal basis. Under the *partial set-aside*, all firms large and small may bid on the unrestricted portion of the contract. Small business firms that wish to participate in the set-aside portion indicate this in their bid. Negotiations for award of the set-aside portion of the contract are conducted only with responsible small business concerns who have submitted responsible bids or proposals on the non-set-aside portion.

**Subcontract Program**  The SBA develops subcontract opportunities for small businesses by encouraging prime contractors to increase their subcontracting to small concerns. In addition, SBA informs small firms of these opportunities and assists them in properly presenting their capabilities to contractors.

In an effort to secure a larger percentage of subcontracts for small firms, SBA continually works with the largest contract awarding agencies, the

Department of Defense and the General Services Administration, to develop contractual provisions whereby prime contractors will provide greater opportunities for subcontract awards to small concerns.

**Locating Additional Suppliers** SBA representatives review proposed government purchase contracts for which there has been inadequate small business competition. If the representatives believe small firms are capable of performing the contracts, they have SBA offices find small companies that want to bid on them through searching the procurement source file, and they recommend that contracting officials solicit the firms for bids. Another source of information and guidance to those who want to buy and sell to the government is the government purchasing and sales directory mentioned above which lists principal goods and services bought and sold by military and civilian agencies and the purchasing offices which buy them.

**Certificates of Competency** A Certificate of Competency (COC) is a statement issued by the Small Business Administration that a small business is technically and financially capable of carrying out a specific government contract.

On occasion, when a small business submits the lowest competitive bid, the government contracting officer refuses to award the contract because of a negative finding as to the production or financial capacity of the firm. After rejecting the lowest bidder for such reasons, the contracting officer advises SBA. The agency, in turn, contacts the small firm to find out if it wishes to apply for a certificate of competency. If the firm applies, SBA specialists make an on-site study of the company's resources, management, performance record, and financial status. The company's plans to secure financing, personnel, and equipment to perform the contract are reviewed. At times, the company may submit an application for an SBA loan with its request for a certificate of competency and the agency takes this into consideration.

If SBA is convinced that the company has the necessary credit or productive capacity to perform the contract, the agency issues a certificate of competency that is binding on the contracting officer. The certificate is valid only for the specific contract involved.

When a company is awarded a contract as the result of a COC, the SBA requires the company to report regularly on the performance of the contract. If the firm has difficulty performing, SBA can assist by providing aid in obtaining financing, technical advice, and assistance, and by locating scarce materials and equipment.

**Procurement Source Search** The Small Business Act empowers SBA to make a complete inventory of all productive facilities of small business concerns. In carrying out this activity, the agency maintains a facility register of small business productive capabilities. This inventory is used principally in assisting the registered companies in their efforts to obtain prime and subcontracts, in locating new sources for government purchasing offices, and in locating scarce or specialized machine tools or equipment when calls are received for them.

**Prime Contract Referral** Small firms interested in selling to the government should have their names placed on contracting agencies bidders lists so they will receive notices of government solicitation for bids directly from the contracting office.

**Government Property Sales Assistance** Each year the U.S. government sells, leases, and otherwise disposes of considerable amounts of real and personal property and natural resources. It is the responsibility of the Small Business Administration to advise and assist small businesses in obtaining a fair portion of the total sales. The agency in cooperation with federal sales offices may set aside appropriate sales for bidding by small businesses only. Property of almost every kind and variety, from machine tools to minerals to timber, may be found in the government's stockpile and inventory.

**Technology Assistance** Under this program, SBA will assist small businesses to obtain the benefits of research and development (R&D) performed under government contracts. One objective is to shorten the time gap between discovery of new technology and its use in the marketplace.

**Research and Development** The SBA has specialists located in each area office who maintain close working relationships with procurement and technical personnel at the major R&D purchasing offices. The specialists obtain procurement information for the purpose of aiding qualified small business concerns in obtaining an opportunity to bid on R&D contracts.

SBA maintains a listing of qualified R&D firms which is made available upon request to government procurement offices and major prime contracts. In addition, these specialists counsel small firms on the procurement offices most likely to need their services and disseminate general information of the latest state of the art in given scientific fields.

## BUSINESS DEVELOPMENT PROGRAM

Section 8(a) of the Small Business Act authorizes the SBA to enter into contracts with the U.S. government in departments, agencies, and offices having procurement powers and, in turn, to subcontract to small business concerns for the performance of those contracts. This authorization is used by SBA to assist in the expansion and development of existing, newly organized, or prospective profit-oriented small business concerns owned and controlled by eligible disadvantaged persons.

In this business development effort, contracting opportunities offered by federal procuring agencies are utilized in conjunction with measured inputs of the full range of assistance generated by SBA, to assist approved companies to achieve the ability to survive and prosper in a competitive environment. Such assistance includes financial assistance for eligible concerns as well as management and technical assistance.

Participation in the program is contingent upon: (1) the review and approval of SBA of a long-term development plan, prepared and submitted by the applicant, (2) a reasonable likelihood of the availability of government contract support, and (3) a reasonable likelihood of the existence of a commercial market for the applicant company's goods or services.

## MANAGEMENT ASSISTANCE

It is estimated that managerial deficiencies cause 9 out of 10 small business failures. A major objective of the SBA is to remedy this situation. Through the programs of the Office of Management Assistance, SBA works to improve and strengthen the management capabilities of small business.

**Counseling** Management counseling emphasizes (1) the expansion of assistance to current and prospective clients, and (2) continuous, or long-term, in-depth counseling. Although the preponderance of business ills can be traced to lack of management skills on the part of owners/managers, every case is different, and every applicant for counseling requires—and receives—individual, personalized assistance.

**SCORE and ACE** The Service Corps of Retired Executives (SCORE), is a volunteer group of retired men and women who provide free management counseling to small business owner/managers and those who are considering starting a business. Sponsored by the SBA, SCORE was developed in 1964 as a means of tapping the business expertise of the growing ranks of top-notch retired executives for the benefit of America's small business community. Currently, there are some 7500 dedicated SCORE volunteers working out of nearly 332 SCORE chapters in all 50 states and Puerto Rico. In conjunction

with the Active Corps of Executives (ACE), SCORE has aided more than 300,000 small businesses in all parts of the nation. ACE was established in 1969 as a supplement to SCORE. It is composed of more than 3500 executives who are still active in the business world but have volunteered their time and talents to help the small business community.

**Small Business Institute Program** The Small Business Institute (SBI) program, a three-way cooperative between universities, members of the nation's small business community, and the SBA, is a relatively new source of management assistance. Under the supervision of university faculty and SBA staff, senior and graduate students of business administration work directly with owners of small firms.

The program began in 1972 with 36 schools of business administration around the country. Since then, it has grown to include 400 participating universities. More than 7500 small businesses receive counseling from 20,000 students each year.

**Call Contracting Program** This program authorizes SBA to place contracts with qualified individuals and businesses in order to provide management and technical aid to SBA clients who meet the eligibility requirements of Section 7(i) and 7(j) of the Small Business Act, as amended in 1974. This service is provided to the socially and economically disadvantaged. It also allows SBA to initiate, organize, and maintain this management counseling service for small firms as required.

**Training** The training program utilizes cosponsors such as Chambers of Commerce, trade associations, community colleges, and SCORE to provide practical training for prospective and existing small business owner/managers. The types of training (workshops, problem clinics, etc.) and the subjects (financial management, marketing, crime prevention, etc.) are selected according to local needs by SBA's 103 field offices. Supporting this effort are substantive training materials and a film library.

**Publications** The publications program provides reliable, unbiased business information to help small business owner/managers and prospectives solve problems and make wise decisions. Included in the four series of leaflets and booklets are marketing aids, management aids, bibliographies, and checklists. Some are sold through the Government Printing Office, with the most popular ones ranging in price from 75 cents to $1.35. Most are distributed free through SBA field offices, often in conjunction with counseling or training efforts.

**International Trade Program** The SBA's International Trade Program consists of: (1) cosponsored international trade training with other government agencies and educational institutions, and (2) a program of individual counseling in basic international trade procedures and overseas marketing opportunities. This counseling is provided by SCORE and ACE executives and representatives of various trade and professional associations.

The SBA, in its International Trade Program, works very closely with the U.S. Department of Commerce, the Export-Import Bank, and other government agencies.

### MINORITY SMALL BUSINESS PROGRAM

The purpose of the Minority Small Business Program is to open the doors of business opportunity to all minority members who want to enter the economic mainstream on their own and who have the capability for business ownership. This program brings together all SBA's services and those of private industry, banks, local communities, and other Government agencies to substantially increase the number of minority-owned businesses.

Through this program, potential or established minority business owners can apply for financial assistance under relaxed eligibility criteria, with emphasis on the applicant's character and ability to repay the loan and other obligations from the profits of the business.

The agency assists minority groups to form local development companies; helps minority-owned or managed firms to perform government contracts; guarantees surety bonds on construction contracts; offers a revolving line of credit to minority contractors with assignable contracts; sponsors a system called the Minority Vendors Program whereby the needs of major private concerns are matched with the services of qualified minority vendors; and gives management assistance separately or in conjunction with the programs mentioned.

### ADVOCACY AND PUBLIC COMMUNICATIONS

SBA champions the cause of small business before other government agencies. It tries to ensure that these other agencies consider the welfare and interests of small business firms in their policies, programs, regulations, and actions.

The advocacy office serves as a focal point for receiving complaints, criticisms, and suggestions regarding the SBA and other federal agencies' policies and activities which affect small firms. It counsels small businesses on resolving problems concerning their relationship with the federal government. Under this program proposals are developed to bring about changes in the policies and activities of the federal government as they relate to the small business community. In carrying out these responsibilities, the advocacy office enlists the cooperation and assistance of public and private agencies, businesses, and other organizations. It develops agency guidelines for making information and/or records available for public use in conformance with the Freedom of Information and Privacy Acts, and it serves as coordinator for the agency regarding the cost and availability of information and/or records requested by the public.

*See also* COMPETITION; FINANCIAL MANAGEMENT, SHORT-TERM, INTERMEDIATE, AND LONG-TERM FINANCING; GOVERNMENT RELATIONS AND SERVICES; MARKETS, PUBLIC; OWNERSHIP, LEGAL FORMS OF; PROFIT IMPROVEMENT.

MARIAN W. BYERS and PAUL A. LODATO,
*United States Small Business Administration*

## Small business investment corporation (SBIC) (*See* SMALL BUSINESS ADMINISTRATION.)

## Smoothing methods (*See* FORECASTING BUSINESS CONDITIONS.)

## Social, civic, and ethical responsibilities (*See heading in Table of Contents for complete listing.*)

## Social responsibility of business

The social responsibility of business is whatever society decides that it is. In recent years society has been exceptionally ambivalent. Both its needs and its boundaries are uncertain.

The fundamental purpose of business in all societies is to produce and to distribute goods and services in such a manner that income exceeds costs. Communities at different times and in different places establish different constraints within which business is expected to fulfill this purpose. These constraints concern, for example, the nature and quality of goods and services, the characteristics and forms of production and distribution, the definition of a "cost," the allowable excess of income over costs (profits), and the allocation of that excess.

**Situational Differences** These constraints reflect various situations: different characteristics of the real world within which business operates. In a situation of scarcity, for example, waste is a crime; in one of surplus, it is acceptable. Hevrat Ovdim, the business end of the Israeli Federation of Labor which accounts for about 20 percent of Israel's national product, is constrained and formed by a dedication to the growth, development, and independence of a Jewish state. Similarly, the structure and behavior of Japanese trading companies reflect the needs of that society. In the United States business activity has reflected a particular situation at a particular time, and as that situation changes so do the constraints on business. It is the change that raises the issues of social responsibility.

**Society's Needs** The social responsibility of business is a function of the needs of the communities which the business serves and affects. These needs may be defined by individual consumers expressing their desires in an open marketplace, by investors seeking to maximize the return on their investments in capital markets, by the membership of the business—its managers and its managed, by government allocating capital, natural, and sometimes human resources to those economic activities which the government decides are most urgent, or, of course, by some mixture of these methods.

If a community's needs are clear and explicit, social responsibility is scarcely an issue; it is a well-understood given. When Thomas Acquinas told the medieval bankers that the maximum permissible interest which they could charge was 5% and no more, their social responsibility was clear. Similarly, in World War II business in America was proudly dedicated to the fulfillment of a well-defined need; social responsibility was not an issue.

**Changing Constraints** Today in the United States and elsewhere, social responsibility is a very real issue because the definition of the needs of the different communities which business serves and affects is as unclear as is the matter of who decides those needs and by what procedures. Consumer desires expressed in the marketplace are increasingly distinct from a variety of community needs for such things as clean air, pure water, and natural beauty. Old management-labor hierarchies, acceptable in an earlier time in which one worked to survive, are less well suited to a situation in which survival is in essence a right of membership in the community. Layoffs in bad times to sustain dividend payments

were once acceptable; today they are less so. The assembly line, once the glorious achievement of efficiency-minded production managers, is less acceptable as new human dimensions of cost are counted. The very idea of growth is in question. Some growth is acceptable as, for example, in world food production. Other growth is obnoxious if it fractures ecological integrity and wastes increasingly valuable energy. And what is acceptable in one place may be unacceptable in another. The definitions of "development" in Brazil's Amazon jungle and in New Jersey are plainly different. There are a host of unmade trade offs which obscure the constraints within which business activity can properly take place, particularly in the United States. The old rules which reflected the old situation are no longer acceptable. The new ones are neither clear nor explicit.

**Multiple Relationships** The term *social responsibility* embraces a multitude of internal and external relationships of the corporation (and we are speaking here of the large, publicly held corporation, not the corner grocery store). Concern with social responsibility has risen as society's expectations of corporate activity have become increasingly ambivalent. Obeying the law has become at once vastly more complicated and at the same time insufficient. A multiplicity of interest groups bombard the corporation with complaints about which it is uncertain because society as a whole is uncertain. On many issues the community has not spoken with a clear voice.

**Corporate Response** In the midst of this uncertainty corporations have taken a variety of actions. First, they have sought to improve their internal machinery for complying with new laws, especially those regarding racial and ethnic minorities, women, ecological effects of production, consumers, employee welfare, and their own general impact on the community. This machinery has included so-called "social audits" and other more or less formal procedures for monitoring corporate compliance with changing social demands. Second, business has attempted through advertising and public relations activity to explain and accentuate its consistency with various social objectives. And, finally, it has made an effort to increase its sensitivity to current and future pressures for changes in social expectations.[1]

Corporate efforts to cope with the question of social responsibility are greatly complicated by three factors:

1. The large corporation serves and affects a number of very diverse communities: shareholders,

debt holders, employees, consumers, Detroit, New York, Brazil, France, and more.

2. There is considerable confusion about what the needs and rights of each of those communities are. What are the criteria for accountability, for legitimacy, for authority? The old notions of property rights, the bond of contract, competition to satisfy consumer desires, the limited state, and the glories of technological innovation and growth for its own sake are wearing thin. New ones are coming but they are unclear.

3. In the meantime who has the right and the competence to decide what these different communities need? Who has the right and the competence to determine, in short, the social responsibility of business? The answer does not seem to be business. It must be the community, acting through the political order in one way or another. It may be through government or through the pulling and hauling of interest groups. Business has some choice here, and it is probable that it will prefer government because it is somewhat more orderly and predictable. It is not surprising that concerns are rising about alliance of big corporations and big government, corporate-statism as it were. But is there any real alternative? Do not the real issues revolve around what sort of an alliance? How open is it? Can everyone inspect and control it?

As we speculate about the future, it is useful to remember that we are discussing here age-old questions of *authority* and *control*.

**Sources of Authority**   The managers of business have no God-given rights. Their rights may derive from three sources. The *first* is property rights. This continues satisfactorily to provide authority to managers of small, clearly owned enterprises. But with respect to great, publicly held corporations, the notion of property is a myth. Nobody "owns" them in any real sense. Consequently their managers are extremely vulnerable. Their authority is weak because their legitimacy is questionable. At the same time, it is as unlikely as it is impractical to return to a simpler day when shareholders actually did own the companies in which they invested. Shareholder democracy attracts little enthusiasm from shareholders or anybody else. A *second* source of managerial authority is all the members of the enterprise—the managed. This is somewhat more promising, and we see a wide variety of forms of worker participation in management, with or without unions, being tried throughout the Western world. *Finally*, there is the state. Whether we like it or not, it is difficult to deny that, increasingly, managerial rights are indeed deriving from government at var-

ious levels. The issues here are ones of degree, of centralization versus decentralization of forms of participation by business and other groups in governmental decision making. These three sources are the ones and the only ones from which managers may choose for the future.

**Sources of Control**   With respect to control we are back to the matter of community need. Who decides and how? There are three ways.

*Marketplace Reactions.* The *first* is competition among a number of preferably small proprietors to satisfy individual consumer desires in an open marketplace. This is the way preferred in the United States; it lies at the heart of the antitrust laws. In practice, however, it presents difficulties. An increasing number of consumer desires may be irrelevant to or inconsistent with community need. Consumers also may not know what is good for them: in the days of Upton Sinclair's "jungle," business put rats in the hot dogs and consumers had no way of knowing that they were there. More recently, consumers in the mid 1960s had no special concern about increasing the safety of automobiles. They had been conditioned to desire other qualities: power, luxury, tail fins, and the like. Ralph Nader came along and said in effect, "It doesn't make any difference what consumers want. The community needs safety." Congress enacted stringent new safety regulations. Similarly with respect to air and water pollution and other community needs, the old laws of competition are less reliable. In addition, efficiency may dictate bigness. The necessity of huge capital investments for research, development, and new plant and equipment; the economy of large production runs; the efficiency of managing worldwide production and distribution systems—all these tend to intensify the trend toward large, coordinated, and concentrated firms. Japan and Europe have accepted this trend ideologically long ago; for the United States it is still something of a shock and contributes to the debate about social responsibility.

*Government Regulation.* Where traditional marketplace competition does not work, a *second* alternative is regulation by government. But there are many difficulties here, too. From what level of government does the regulation emanate—the city, the state, the nation, or from many nations? Social and political pressures appear to be tending to push regulation up the governmental ladder. But government is unready. There is little multinational government of any sort, and national government in the United States has traditionally approached the problem of regulation in an ad hoc fashion, responding to separate crises as they occur. The result is that there is a good deal of regulation but little planning or coordination among the regulators, considerable intervention, and much visionless flailing. In such circumstances large corporations have naturally devoted considerable time and effort to seeking to influence government. The Watergate investigations revealed that in many cases this effort was illegal; society judged it irresponsible as well. Many corporate executives were removed from office.

Disappointment with regulation as a means of controlling business has caused increasing attention to be paid to the *third* means of control, which is through the corporate charter or some sort of partnership between government and business. The Tennessee Valley Authority and the Communications Satellite Corporation (COMSAT) are examples of corporations which are controlled through their charter. Large defense contractors and the major oil companies reflect partnership arrangements.

*Charter Revision.* In the early days of the republic the normal source of corporate control was its charter. Corporations were created by state legislatures to do things that needed doing, mostly public works. As time went by this process became both undemocratic and corrupt. Corporate charters tended to go to those who had the power and the influence to get them. Furthermore, growing America saw in the corporation an unquestionably efficient means of mobilizing capital growth and expansion, both of which were unquestionably good things. Every effort was, therefore, made to encourage the formation of corporations for vitually any purpose whatsoever. The corporate charter became a lifeless document generally kept in Delaware. Recently, however, attention is once again being focused on the charter as a means of stipulating the terms and conditions under which the nation will allow a corporation to exist. The presumption of proponents of federal chartering schemes is that the nation knows what those terms and conditions should be. In the mid 1970s, however, there still was some confusion and doubt; society seemed to be having difficulty defining what it wanted its corporations to do or to be, what, in fact, responsible behavior was.

One of the most vexing problems accompanying a closer connection between great corporations and national government has arisen from the extent to which those corporations had become global undertakings upon which the world depended for such vital resources as oil and food. As a consequence it would seem likely that pressures for multination or world governance of global corporate activity will

increase. The definition of social responsibility must fit society, and society is evidently less national and more global as spaceship Earth continues its perilous course.

*See also* COMMUNITY PLANNING LEGISLATION; CONSUMERISM AND CONSUMER PROTECTION LEGISLATION; EGALITARIANISM; ENVIRONMENTAL PROTECTION LEGISLATION; ETHICS, MANAGERIAL; GOVERNMENT REGULATIONS, FEDERAL REGULATION OF COMPETITION; MANAGEMENT, HISTORICAL DEVELOPMENT OF; OMBUDSMAN; PRODUCT LIABILITY; VALUE SYSTEMS, MANAGEMENT: SOCIAL AND CULTURAL.

### NOTES
[1] Robert Ackerman and Raymond Bauer, *Corporate Social Responsiveness: The Modern Dilemma*, Reston Publishing Co. Inc., Reston, Va., 1976, pp. 3–42.

### REFERENCES
Anshen, Melvin, ed.: *Managing the Socially Responsible Corporation*, The Free Press, Glencoe, Ill., 1974.

Farmer, Richard N. and W. Dickerson Hogue: *Corporate Social Responsibility*, Science Research Associates, Inc., Chicago, 1973.

Silk, Leonard, and David Vogel: *Ethics and Profits: The Crisis of Confidence in American Business*, Simon & Schuster, Inc., New York, 1976.

GEORGE C. LODGE, *Harvard University*

## Socialism   (*See* ECONOMIC SYSTEMS.)

## Societies, professional

Professional organizations have played an integral part in the advancement of management thought and practice particularly since the emergence of the professional managers and their ties to the professional associations.

**Industrialization and Management**[1]   After the United States won its independence, the country began a gradual shift from a predominantly agricultural economy to include an emerging industrial economy. Industrialization was aided and encouraged by developments of the means of production to support transportation, machinery manufacture, and the provision of industrial supplies. The increased industrial activity meant that greater numbers of men with engineering skill and administrative ability were required to staff and manage the new enterprises.

With the changes in manufacturing and administration, structural changes came about in the nature of organizations to accomplish the more complex task of managing the larger organizations. The corporate form of business organization was necessitated because of the large scale of business operations. And with the corporate form of management came the professional manager.

There also came problems of administration of operations, integration, and control of complex structures that management had not encountered previously. In their quest for solutions, the managers of these industrial complexes looked for help among their own colleagues. The professional engineer, with a grounding in the hard sciences and a training in the scientific method, frequently was identified as the most likely candidate for upper management positions. As these professionals became involved in operational and general management, they realized that their technical backgrounds did not provide solutions to pressing organizational and human problems. When respected speakers with successful experiences in management began to write papers and to make presentations at the American Society of Mechanical Engineers, they found a receptive audience. Management papers during this era were few in number and were published almost exclusively in engineering journals.

Internationally, the professional organizations were serving a similar function. For example, Henry Fayol first presented his ideas about a system of management to his colleagues in France in 1916. Speaking before the Societe de l'Industrie Minerale, he presented his now classic principles of management. Later, this presentation was reworked as a book in 1925[2] on general and industrial management.

If the changing industrialization had spawned the demand for competent, nonowner general and operating managers, the associations clearly contributed to the increasing recognition of the professional managers and opened opportunities to share problems and ideas for solution among the members.

**The Professional Manager** The professional manager may be characterized as a new type in charge of the management of the enterprise on behalf of the owners, the stockholders.[3] The single business unit, because of its increased size, now needed a number of managers at the several levels of administration. Levels of managerial executive tasks evolved in the composite structure. With specialization of managerial tasks, there arose the need for collegial associations where problems could be examined and solutions proposed. The professional manager, although not clearly identified as such at

the time, was expected to bring to the office most of the following qualifications:

Adequate formal preparation in his field

A quieting spirit that will drive him to search for and apply new knowledge

Imbuement with a strong sense of ethics and social responsibility[4]

During the latter part of the 1860–1900 period, the engineering schools were the early sources of formal preparations for management, if any was to be had. The formal education provided was predominantly technical with some industrial management concepts taught in the course of the discussions. It was through the association meetings of the established engineering profession, however, that the widest range of information needed by the emerging professional managers first became available.

**Association Impact on Management Education** Before 1900, only three universities in the United States offered a curriculum in management education, and this was most limited in scope. Courses in economics dealing with economic theory and principles of trade and commerce were deemed beneficial. Practical solutions and needed guidance for day-by-day operating problems were not, however, transmitted at the college level.

Although it is difficult to pinpoint the role of professional associations in the early development of curricula in business management in colleges and universities, it may be inferred that there was an influence. Source information for teaching business administration courses was drawn from the business organizations. Published papers, association journals, presentations by speakers, and courses in management and administration taught by business persons served as sources of information for building business programs. The persistence of associations pressing for formal instructional programs leading to degrees in their special interest areas is felt even now in colleges and universities.

**Role of the Professional Management Organization** The major contributions of the professional management organizations are to:

1. Provide a forum where current problems and new ideas may be proposed, evaluated, and reviewed by the professionals in management.

2. Provide channels for the distribution of information dealing with management problems and solutions. Papers presented at meetings are available for review by an audience which reaches beyond the organization membership. The journals of the professional management organizations alert the readers to impending problems, workable solutions,

and new ideas. The Academy of Management, in particular, has performed this role exceedingly well for the academic area.

3. Maintain the collegial interaction that characterizes the professions. Associations give the specialists an opportunity to get together with their peers. Members may mingle with leaders in their profession who have similar interests.[5]

4. Provide a special library service for the technical and professional areas of management. The American Management Association, for example, for years has maintained a professional library for the lending of books, magazine articles, and related publications pertinent to members' areas of interest.

5. Conduct seminars for management development. The Association for Systems Management, for example, is notable in this respect.

6. Provide the means for transmitting organizational needs for management skills to colleges and universities. The American Banking Association was an early leader in arousing interest in the promotion of higher education for business in the United States during the last decade of the nineteenth century.

7. Furnish an opportunity to conduct surveys and management science research, coordinated with the interests of the associations. Financing of research by professional organizations, or accessibility to selected business firms by the academic researcher, is frequently facilitated when endorsed by the local or national association officers.

8. Alert the profession to impending action by government or other power groups or influences which could have a significant impact on the management practices of members.

**Status of Professional Associations** The contributions of the professional organizations can be clearly established historically. The role of the professional management associations indicates a strong potential for continued service to the members and to society. But recent experience of the professional organizations and attitudes expressed by members raise troubling issues.

*Optimistic View.* In 1974 *Nations Business* surveyed the trade and professional associations and reported its findings. In general, it was found that, "Trade and professional associations activities pay off for their members; but some of the extra benefits these groups provide may surprise you."[6] The article observed that the main purpose of any trade or professional association was to serve its members and professional or commercial benefits occupy an important role in the continuation of membership.

*Pessimistic View.* A penetrating analysis of the current values of the strictly professional association was reported by Berkwitt.[7] He stated that after years of growth, professional societies are on the decline. He indicated that for many professionals, the typical benefits of membership are no longer significant or even relevant. Among the factors that may explain the decline in memberships in professional management associations are these implied from Berkwitt's study.

1. Needs of members are changing, but the associations are not. Membership benefits, such as attendance at meetings, journals, seminars, and related publications are no longer regarded as compelling reasons to retain membership.

2. Changing expectations of members that the associations should play a more active role in the individual professional's concerns—locating jobs, protecting rights, or undertaking some such functions as the unions perform for their constituents.

3. Salespeople, consultants, and others who use the associations primarily as a place to do business have infiltrated them and monopolized their programs. Consequently, many of the "pros" have stopped attending because they refuse to be accosted by such practitioners. Additionally, members are bombarded with mail and solicitation from opportunists using the association roster to promote their interests.

4. Memberships are often used primarily as a source of making commercial, rather than professional, contacts. Firms spend thousands of dollars in membership fees for its members just so the "right" people are identified for the commercial follow-up.

5. Industry no longer is so certain the professional association has a valuable contribution to make to the development and professionalization of its management people. There is a noticeable cutting back in association memberships paid by employers since 1970. Companies cutting expenses where value cannot be pinpointed identify memberships in the associations as among the first to go.

6. Attendance is down in the local meetings owing to dull, lackluster, or irrelevant programs. The annual meeting is a showy, expensive affair that only a small percentage of the total membership does, or can, attend. The journals are boring, containing theoretical pieces written by professors who must publish or perish. Articles frequently fail to meet the needs of the readers.

7. Officers at the national level control the incoming national officers, and the "club" perpetuates itself for its own benefit rather than representing the

membership's interests. At the local level, it is a struggle to find someone willing to run for office, with dwindling membership taking its toll of effective candidates.

**Outlook** After proliferating since the 1900s to some 1000 organizations today, professional associations will decline in the specialities which are duplicated among the societies and associations. Some 12 professional management associations may be identified among the hundreds of currently listed societies and trade associations.[8] Several of the current management associations evolved from mergers with smaller or single-purpose associations which were declining in their ability to attract and hold members. Others have survived by changing in those ways that were attractive to members and prospective members. Name changes, along with changes in organizational structure and types of services offered, seem to fortell the pattern for survival and growth. Mergers will continue as a means of survival for some associations. The shakeout caused by the recession and declining memberships at both national and local levels will strengthen the excellent associations and, one hopes, encourage them to emphasize professional aspects and reduce commercialization to a bare minimum. There is irrefutable evidence that the professional management organizations must contribute to the benefits professional managers expect from their associations if they are to occupy the role that the membership perceives they must fulfill.

*See also* ASSOCIATIONS, TRADE AND PROFESSIONAL; DEVELOPMENT AND TRAINING, MANAGEMENT; ETHICS, MANAGERIAL; PROFESSIONALISM; SOCIAL RESPONSIBILITY OF BUSINESS; VALUE SYSTEMS, MANAGEMENT: SOCIAL AND CULTURAL.

## NOTES

[1] Meeri Marjatta Saarsalmi, "Some Aspects of the Thought Underlying Higher Education for Business in the United States," unpublished D.B.A. dissertation, Indiana University, School of Business, Bloomington, Ind., 1955. Concepts from which the statements are derived are contained in chap. II, pp. 31–49.

[2] Henry Fayol, *General and Industrial Management*, Pitman Publishing Company, London, 1949.

[3] Saarsalmi, op. cit., p. 40.

[4] Theodore Harriman, *Professional Management*, Houghton Mifflin Company, Boston, 1962, p. vii.

[5] George J. Berkwitt, "Are Professional Societies Dead?" *Dun's* Review, vol. 99, p. 46, March 1972.

[6] "Professional Associations Busily Helping Business and Society," *Nations Business*, vol. 62, pp. 47–52, December 1974.

[7] Berkwitt, op. cit., pp. 44ff.

[8] Encyclopedia of Associations, vol. 1, National Organizations of the U.S., 10th ed. Gale Research Company, Detroit, 1976.

LOREN E. WALTZ, *Indiana University at South Bend*

# Socioeconomic and demographic factors (SED) (*See* CONSUMER BEHAVIOR, MANAGERIAL RELEVANCE OF.)

# Socioemotional needs (*See* INTERPERSONAL RELATIONSHIPS.)

# Sociotechnical system (*See* MANAGEMENT THEORY, SCIENCE, AND APPROACHES.)

# Software [*See* INFORMATION SYSTEMS, MANAGEMENT (MIS), APPLIED.]

# Source document (*See* DATA PROCESSING PRINCIPLES AND PRACTICES.)

# Space management (*See* INVENTORY CONTROL, PHYSICAL AND STOCKKEEPING.)

# Space requirements, office (*See* OFFICE SPACE PLANNING AND DESIGN.)

# Space study (*See* OFFICE SPACE PLANNING AND DESIGN.)

# Space utilization (*See* MATERIAL HANDLING.)

# Span of management (*See* MANAGEMENT THEORY, SCIENCE, AND APPROACHES.)

# Span of supervision (*See* ORGANIZATION ANALYSIS AND PLANNING.)

**SPAR-1** (*See* NETWORK PLANNING METHODS.)

**Specialist, market** (*See* MARKETS, SECURITIES.)

**Specialty goods** (*See* MARKETS, CLASSIFICATIONS AND MARKET ANALYSIS; RETAILING MANAGEMENT.)

**Specialty stores** (*See* MARKETING, CHANNELS OF DISTRIBUTION.)

**Specialty stores, retailing** (*See* RETAILING MANAGEMENT.)

**Specifications, purchasing** (*See* PURCHASING MANAGEMENT.)

**Spread-loss plans, insurance** (*See* INSURANCE AND RISK MANAGEMENT.)

**Staff authority** (*See* AUTHORITY, RESPONSIBILITY, AND ACCOUNTABILITY.)

**Staff responsibility** (*See* NOT-FOR-PROFIT ORGANIZATIONS, MANAGEMENT OF.)

**Staff and service functions** (*See heading in Table of Contents for complete listing.*)

**Staff specialists** (*See* MANAGER, DEFINITIONS OF.)

**Staffing** (*See* MANAGEMENT THEORY, SCIENCE, AND APPROACHES.)

**Stand-alone text editors** (*See* WORD PROCESSING.)

# Standard industrial classifications

*Standard industrial classifications* (SIC) are a numbering system developed by the U.S. Office of Management and Budget to facilitate collection and analysis of data on economic establishments and to ensure that statistics on activities in various economic areas are comparable. In this instance, an "establishment" is not necessarily, perhaps not even usually, a company. Rather it is defined as "an economic unit, generally at a single physical location where business is conducted or industrial operations are performed." Thus a single factory or a store would constitute an establishment.

Establishments are classified first into divisions, then into major groups, then into finer subdivisions. The divisions and the numbers used for the major groups in each one are as follows:

Division A: Agriculture, forestry, and fishing, 01–09

Division B: Mining, 10–14

Division C: Construction, 15–17

Division D: Manufacturing, 20–39

Division E: Transportation, communications, electric, gas, and sanitary services, 40–49

Division F: Wholesale trade, 50–51

Division G: Retail trade, 52–59

Division H: Finance, insurance, real estate, 60–67

Division I: Services, 70–89

Division J: Public administration, 91–97

Division K: Nonclassifiable establishments, 99

The system of numbering the major groups and the subdivisions within the groups may be explained by some examples. An establishment manufacturing wood household furniture (except upholstered) would be numbered 2511. The 2 indicates a manufacturing establishment; the 5 the major group, furniture and fixtures; the first 1 household furniture; and the second 1 wood except upholstered. The number 2512 indicates wood upholstered furniture. Office furniture numbers are 2521 for wood and 2522 for metal.

This system enables companies to identify the areas in which customers for their products exist, because the numbers are used in reports from the Census of Manufactures and the Census of Business, which show the number of establishments in each area, their size, and other facts about them. Thus they can help a firm to determine the areas to which marketing efforts should be directed.

*See also* ECONOMIC MEASUREMENTS; FORECASTING BUSINESS CONDITIONS; MARKETING RESEARCH; MAR-

KETS, CLASSIFICATIONS AND MARKET ANALYSIS; STANDARD METROPOLITAN STATISTICAL AREAS.

## REFERENCES

Harding, Murray: "SIC Unlocks Packaging Market," *Industrial Marketing*, May 1967, pp. 55–57.

Hill, Michael: "The ABC's of Using Your Market SIC's," *Industrial Marketing*, May 1967, pp. 58–61.

*Standard Industrial Classification Manual, 1972*, Office of Management and Budget, Statistical Policy Division, Washington, 1972.

STAFF/SMITH

# Standard metropolitan statistical areas

A *Standard metropolitan statistical area* (SMSA) is an urban market of the United States as defined by the U.S. Office of Management and Budget. An SMSA is generally a city with a population of 50,000 or more and the county in which it is situated, although territory in contiguous counties may be included if it is socially and economically integrated with the city. Other tests are used in some cases. For example, a city of 25,000 and its environs may be an SMSA if the surrounding area meets certain criteria of population size and density.

Currently, there are 281 SMSAs in the United States. See Fig. S-6 (pp. 1114–1115). The number changes constantly because of population growth and population shifts. Generally the number has been growing, but some areas have been dropped from the count because they have lost population.

A large amount of census data on these areas exists for use in pinpointing markets—data on the ages and incomes of the population, for example, and on the number of establishments in each of the industrial classifications of the Bureau of the Budget.

In addition, the Bureau of Economic Analysis (BEA) of the Department of Commerce has divided the whole country into what are called "BEA economic areas," and a large amount of government data on these exists as well.

*See also* ECONOMIC MEASUREMENTS; FORECASTING BUSINESS CONDITIONS; MARKETING RESEARCH; MARKETS, CLASSIFICATION AND MARKET ANALYSIS; STANDARD INDUSTRIAL CLASSIFICATIONS.

## REFERENCES

*Area Economic Projections 1990* (by states, regions, BEAs and SMSAs), Department of Commerce Bureau of Economic Analysis, Washington.

"BEA Economic Areas: Structural Changes and Growth 1950–1973," *Survey of Current Business*, November 1975.

Goeldner, C. R., and Laura M. Dirks: "Business Facts: Where To Find Them," *MSU Business Topics*, Michigan State University, Graduate School of Business Administration, Summer 1976, pp. 23–36.

"Now It's the Supermetros," *Sales Management*, Sept. 8, 1975, pp. 18 and 20.

*Standard Metropolitan Statistical Areas*, Federal Information Processing Standards Publication, FIPS Pub. 127, rev. ed. 1975, Washington, 1976.

STAFF/SMITH

## Standard and Poor's index (*See* MARKETS, STOCK INDICATOR SERIES.)

## Standard time data (*See* WORK MEASUREMENT.)

## Standardization (*See* PURCHASING MANAGEMENT.)

## Standardization of parts (*See* MATERIALS MANAGEMENT.)

## Standards, fixed cost (*See* MARGINAL INCOME ANALYSIS.)

## Standards, organizational (*See* OBJECTIVES AND GOALS.)

## Standards, performance (*See* DEVELOPMENT AND TRAINING, MANAGEMENT.)

## Standards, personnel (*See* PERSONNEL ADMINISTRATION.)

## Standards, safety (*See* SAFETY AND HEALTH MANAGEMENT, EMPLOYEE.)

## Standards, variable cost (*See* MARGINAL INCOME ANALYSIS.)

# Standards and standardization programs

Industry and business use standards to solve problems that occur again and again and to facilitate internal and external communications with everyone involved in an activity or operation. Application of standards increases profits, improves efficiency and safety of operations, and enhances the dependability and quality of products.

Companies adopt or adapt national, international, or industry standards to meet their needs and those of their customers. They also develop standards, as required, to solve unique problems. Formal standardization programs are generally established within companies to handle the development and adoption/adaptation processes; to promulgate and revise standards accepted for company use; to supervise application of standards on assignment; and to coordinate participation in external standards-developing activities at industry, national, and international levels.

## APPLICATION AND BENEFITS OF STANDARDS

Standards cover almost every field and discipline. They are invaluable to industry in design, production, quality control, procurement, materials handling, and construction and maintenance of plants and offices.

Dimensional and rating standards enable equipment produced by different manufacturers to be used together in individual and interconnected systems. Standards for parts and components reduce variety, thus resulting in longer production runs, reduced setup time, and rapid training of personnel. Other advantages are reduced inventory, decrease in purchasing transactions, and the freeing of engineering talent for innovative work. Application of standards for materials opens up new sources of supply and reduces manufacturing costs. Uniform levels of product performance, reliability, and safety result from the use of standards for processing, inspection, and testing. By making mass production possible, standards reduce costs and selling price. Industrial workers are protected by the application of standards for construction and use of machinery, protective clothing, and ventilation, among many examples.

Manufacturing is, of course, not the only user of standards. Business uses them for information processing, purchasing, and establishing procedures; government, for procurement, to provide for safety and health of the public, to effect economies, and in providing for transportation and communication.

## COMPANY STANDARDS PROGRAMS

Some type of formal standards program is required within a company to coordinate activities and supervise the application of standards. Uncoordinated development, selection, and use by various departments or divisions, acting independently, will result in waste and confusion and compound the problems that application of standards is intended to solve.

**Organization** How a standards program is organized and administered depends on the needs of the company and its organizational structure. Whatever the organizational mode, adherence to certain principles is essential to the success of the standards activity:

1. The program should be made applicable to all company functions.

2. The program should be established by, report to, and have the active support of top management.

3. Standards approved for company use should be acceptable to all affected departments.

In small companies, administration of the standards program may be assigned to the head of a division or department—engineering or design, for example. Larger companies may establish a separate standards department, which should be coequal with other functional departments. Some companies assign administration of the program to a standards policy committee composed of department heads, chaired by a corporate-level executive, and supported by a standards department, which serves as secretariat.

**Procedures** The first step in implementing a company standards program is to identify the problems that application of standards will solve. The next is to locate or develop standards that will meet these needs, achieve acceptance of the various departments that will be affected, and promulgate the standards for company use.

More than 8000 national consensus standards covering virtually every field and discipline are available in the United States. A search and evaluation should be made to determine if any fulfill the stated need, either as promulgated or with modifications. International standards or, on occasion, the national standards of other countries should be sought by a company that is multinational or engaged in export/import. If no applicable national (or international) standard can be located, a similar search and evaluation should be made of industry standards. If this search also proves fruitless, development work on a company standard should be considered. Another alternative, time permitting, is to petition the national/international coordinating organization to initiate a standards development project. If the pro-

posed standard will affect more than one company, industry, or sector, this approach is essential.

Before a standards-writing project is initiated by a company, certain questions should be answered: Is the standard technically feasible? Is the development effort timely? What will be the overall costs of

**Fig. S-6. Standard metropolitan statistical areas of the United States, 1977.**
*(© 1977 by Sales & Marketing Management Magazine.)*

developing the standard, maintaining it, converting to it, and implementing it? What are the long-term benefits of application? Will application be useful within the user's business environment?

The choice of who is to develop the standard—the standards department, standards policy com-

mittee, or designated subgroup—depends on the organization of the function within the company. Regardless of who develops the standard, extensive cooperation and consultation with affected departments are essential during the development process and reconciliation of differences. Also of vital im-

portance is final acceptance of the standard for company use by all affected groups, whether the standard is developed internally or adopted or adapted from those available from outside sources.

When a standard has been accepted, it is issued to all affected departments. Distribution is usually carried out by the standards department, which serves as the clearinghouse for all company standards. Duplicate sets may be located in various departments or divisions. Ensuring that they are kept up-to-date is another responsibility of the standards department. Supervision of the application of standards within the company may be the responsibility of the standards department or may be handled through the company's normal management system.

## SOURCES OF STANDARDS

**Company Standards**   Development of standards in the United States is a complex, interrelated process. Standards may be developed by a company to fulfill an individual need. If a particular standard is also found to serve the needs of many companies or industries or other affected sectors, it may be elevated to, or serve as the basis for, an industry or a national or international standard.

Thousands of standards also originate at the industry or national or international levels.

**Industry Standards**   Industry standards are developed and promulgated through trade, technical, professional, or scientific associations and societies that serve particular industries or disciplines and, in general, produce standards applicable to their particular fields.

In the United States most of these organizations cooperate within the federated national standards system coordinated by the American National Standards Institute (ANSI). They submit to ANSI standards developed under their own procedures for recognition as national consensus standards. In many cases they also cooperate in the development of standards within national standards committees that operate under ANSI procedures.

**National Standards**   ANSI provides and administers the only recognized system in the United States for establishing standards—no matter what their origin—as American National (consensus) Standards. Its approval procedures ensure that all concerned interests have had an opportunity to participate in a standard's development or to comment on its provisions. They further ensure that the standard has achieved general recognition and acceptance for use. To date ANSI has approved more

than 8000 national standards encompassing virtually every field and discipline.

Other major ANSI functions are to coordinate the voluntary development of national standards and of U.S. participation in nongovernmental international standards efforts, and to serve as the source of information on availability of national and international standards.

**International Standards**   Two major nongovernmental organizations coordinate the development and approve a large proportion of the voluntary international standards used throughout the world. They are the International Organization for Standardization (ISO) and the International Electrotechnical Commission (IEC), located in Geneva, Switzerland. The IEC is responsible for standards in the electrical and electronics fields; ISO, for all other fields. Both maintain close liaison with each other and with other international organizations engaged in standardization. ISO and IEC have approved nearly 5000 standards which affect product acceptance throughout the world because they are adopted by many countries as the basis of product inspection, approval, and certification systems. These standards are available in the United States through ANSI, the U.S. member of these organizations.

*See also* INVENTORY CONTROL, PURCHASING AND ACCOUNTING ASPECTS; PRODUCTION/OPERATIONS MANAGEMENT; PRODUCTION PROCESSES; PURCHASING MANAGEMENT; QUALITY MANAGEMENT; VALUE ANALYSIS.

### REFERENCES

*ABCs of International Standardization*, American National Standards Institute, New York, 1975.

*ANSI Progress Report*, American National Standards Institute, New York (annual).

*Catalog of American National Standards*, American National Standards Institute, New York.

Chumas, Sophie J., ed.: *Directory of United States Standardization Activities*, National Bureau of Standards Special Publication 417, Catalog No. C13.10:417, Government Printing Office, 1975.

Glie, Rowan, ed.: *Speaking of Standards*, Cahners Publishing Company, Boston, 1972.

Ollner, Jan: *The Company and Standardization*, Swedish Standards Institution, Stockholm, 1973. Available in the United States from the American Society for Testing and Materials, 1916 Race St., Philadelphia 19103.

Sanders, T. R. B., ed.: *The Aims and Principles of Standardization*, International Organization for Standardization, Geneva, 1972. Available in the United States from the American National Standards Institute, 1430 Broadway, New York, 10018.

Verman, Lal: *Standardization, A New Discipline*, The Shoe String Press, Hamden, Conn., 1973.

DOROTHY HOGAN, *American National Standards Institute, Inc.*

## Stations, personnel (*See* OFFICE SPACE PLANNING AND DESIGN.)

## Statistical analysis for management

Successful managing and planning in an increasingly complex environment requires more than intuitive, reactive approaches to decision making. Greater emphasis is now placed on analysis that applies mathematical and statistical techniques to the process. Experience and knowledge of operations still are essential, but they are being used with greater discipline.

*Decision Theory.* A wide range of quantitative techniques can be used to reduce an otherwise complex problem to manageable dimensions. The collection of these techniques has become loosely known as "decision theory," although there certainly is no such thing as an integrated theory of how to make decisions. Nevertheless, the ultimate impact of these methods extends far beyond the decision tools themselves. In fact, there is a large body of opinion that believes that the greatest impact of the quantitative approach will be not in the area of problem solving but rather in problem formulation. It will radically alter the way managers think about their problems—how they analyze them, gain insights, relate them to other problems, communicate them to other people, and gather information for solving them.

### DECISION MAKING UNDER UNCERTAINTY

When all information relevant to a particular problem is gathered so that the outcome of each alternative action available to the decision maker can be predicted accurately, the analyst is said to be operating under conditions of *certainty*. The mathematical formulation used to help analyze such problems is called a *deterministic model*. For example, a purchasing agent might evaluate different suppliers on the basis of minimizing total acquisition costs or shipping miles. In either case, the criterion for the best solution is expressed in known units. A wrong decision would be caused by either excessively difficult computations or errors in the formulation of the problem.

It is frequently necessary to make decisions when any one of several different outcomes could possibly occur following the selection of a particular course of action. These decisions are said to be made under conditions of *uncertainty* or risk. (Some statisticians draw a technical distinction between the terms *uncertainty* and *risk*. There is not a consensus on how or whether to differentiate, however, and the two terms will be used interchangeably in this discussion.) In some cases, all the possible outcomes of a particular course of action cannot be specified. In other cases, all outcomes can be specified, but nothing is known about the relative likelihood of the occurrence of each. Most quantitative techniques cannot be employed to analyze these situations. Formal analysis of a decision that can result in any one of several different consequences generally requires that each consequence and its associated probability of occurrence be specified. Probability assignments can be based on subjective judgment, historical data, or empirical forecasts. Analysis is conducted using what are commonly referred to as *probabilistic models*.

### THE DECISION MATRIX

When decisions are made under uncertainty, any one of several different outcomes can follow the decision to take a given action. The particular outcome that actually occurs will depend on what state of nature exists after the decision is made. For example, the return on an investment in a new product is dependent on the level of demand experienced after it is put on the market.

The outcomes of possible combinations of alternative decisions and ensuing states of nature can be shown concisely in a *decision matrix*. The alternatives available to the decision maker are referred to as *actions*, and the possible states of nature that can exist following the choice of a decision are *events*. The outcome associated with each action-event combination is referred to as a *payoff* (or *loss*).

A decision matrix portraying a situation with three alternative actions and four possible events is shown in Table S-2. Actions that can be taken by the decision maker are denoted by numbers; events that can occur following the selection of an action are denoted by letters. [It is generally, although not necessarily, assumed that the event which occurs is independent of the action which is taken. For exam-

TABLE S-2    Decision Matrix

| Events | Actions, in dollars | | |
|---|---|---|---|
| | 1 | 2 | 3 |
| A | 4 | −2 | 7 |
| B | 0 | 6 | 3 |
| C | −5 | 9 | 2 |
| D | 4 | −1 | 3 |

ple, the possibility (event) of having a fire is not affected by the decision (action) of whether to purchase fire insurance.]

In a decision matrix, the payoff (outcome) of a particular action depends on the event that occurs. Because of this relationship, a decision matrix is sometimes termed a *conditional payoff table*. It specifies the payoff that will occur for each event *given*, or *conditional on*, the specification of a particular action. In Table S-2, for example, the payoff is a gain of $3 *if* action 3 is selected and event B occurs. This outcome is called a *conditional payoff*; i.e., it is conditional on selecting action 3 and having event B occur.

Models constructed to represent such problems are called *probabilistic models*. Since a multiplicity of outcomes can result from the choice of a particular action, the decision maker—in effect—is forced to gamble. Regardless of the quality of the analysis upon which the decision is based, the decision may turn out, after the fact, to have been wrong. No strategy will consistently lead to objectively correct decisions. Thus a strategy for making decisions under uncertainty cannot be formulated until the manager first specifies what is meant by a "best" decision. While a "best" decision might mean different things to different people, the individual should devise a strategy that is consistent with the decision maker's personal judgment and preferences. Several different strategies are frequently used.

### THE MAXIMIN, MINIMAX, AND MAXIMAX PRINCIPLES

The best decision generally is not readily apparent. With the advantage of hindsight, it can be seen from Table S-2 that action 3 would have been the best decision if event A occurred, action 2 would have been the best decision if either of events B or C occurred, and action 3 would have been the best if event D occurred.

Unfortunately, at the time a decision must be made, it is not known which event will occur.

**Maximin**   One possible strategy is to select that action which would *maximize* the *minimum* gain, or

payoff. This is the "maximin" principle, which is the basis for a conservative decision strategy. The decision maker behaves as though nature—or whoever or whatever else determines which event will occur—is acting as an adversary and will choose the most adverse event possible given the action that has been selected. The worst possible outcomes for actions 1, 2, and 3 are, respectively, $−5, $−2, and $2. According to the maximin criterion, therefore, action 3 would be selected; that is, the worst possible outcomes for actions 1 and 2 are less desirable than the worst possible outcome for action 3.

**Minimax**   An alternative decision strategy would be for the decision maker to select the action that would *minimize* the *maximum* loss (the "minimax" criterion) rather than maximize the minimum gain. *Loss* is defined as the difference between the minimum payoff for a given action and the highest minimum payoff for any of the actions available. The losses for the actions described in Table S-2 would be $7 for action 1, $4 for action 2, and $0 for action 3. Thus, action 3 would be best according to the minimax criterion.

Two general observations can be made from the example: (1) The maximin and minimax criteria will always give the same result; (2) the loss of the "best" action would be zero.

**Maximax**   A related decision strategy can be formulated from the opposite perspective of the maximin principle. That is, rather than minimize the minimum gain, the decision maker could select the action that would *maximize* the *maximum* gain (the "maximax" principle). This criterion would be used by a gambler or someone who expected nature to respond benevolently. Since the maximum payoffs for actions 1, 2 and 3 are, respectively, $4, $9, and $7, application of the maximax principle would lead to the selection of action 2.

**Caution**   Sometimes the blind application of decision rules such as the maximin or maximax criteria can lead to poor decisions. Suppose, for example, an investor is trying to decide whether to invest in a bond or a stock. The percentage returns on these two alternative investments, conditional on one of two possible states of the economy ($E_1$ or $E_2$) are given in Table S-3 The maximin principle would lead to investment in the bond, but this would not

TABLE S-3    Investment Returns

| | Bond, % | Stock, % |
|---|---|---|
| $E_1$ | 8 | 20 |
| $E_2$ | 8 | 7 |

be a good decision unless the investor strongly felt that economic condition $E_2$ would occur. On the other hand, the use of the maximax principle would not be appropriate given the possible investment returns in Table S-4, unless a high probability of occurrence can be attached to economic condition $E_1$.

**TABLE S-4   Investment Returns**

|        | Bond, % | Stock, % |
|--------|---------|----------|
| $E_1$  | 8       | 10       |
| $E_2$  | 8       | −5       |

## EXPECTED VALUE

It is generally appropriate to regard nature as being neutral, not malevolent or benevolent. An event will not be chosen in response to the selection of a given action. In fact, the probability of each event's occurring should not be affected by the choice of a particular action. It is therefore desirable to devise a decision strategy which, based on the neutrality of nature, will maximize benefits in the long run. Selecting the action with the largest expected value is such a strategy. The expected value is a weighted average of the conditional values. The weights are the probabilities that each conditional value actually will be received (or that each associated event will occur). Thus the expected value of a given action is the average outcome that would occur if the same action were repeated a large number of times under identical circumstances. An example of the calculation of an expected value is given in Table S-5.

**TABLE S-5   Calculation of Expected Value**

| Event | Probability | Conditional value, dollars | Expected value, dollars |
|-------|-------------|----------------------------|-------------------------|
| X     | .2          | 10                         | 2                       |
| Y     | .5          | 14                         | 7                       |
| Z     | .3          | 20                         | 6                       |
|       | 1.0         |                            | Expected value = 15     |

*Long-Run Averages.*   It should be obvious that no alternative action could provide greater total payoffs in the long run than the action with the highest expected value. (This is not to deny that alternative actions may, after the fact, have been superior for *some* decisions.) Note that the actual outcome will never equal the expected value. The expected value is simply the long-run average outcome that will result if the same situation is repeated a large number of times. Thus, maximizing the expected value

on each occasion will maximize the long-run average payoff. It is also true, however, that applying maximum expected value criteria to nonrepetitive decisions is the strategy that will maximize the expected total payoffs to the firm in the long run. Any other strategy might result in occasional spectacular gains but would be a suboptimal strategy over a prolonged period of time.

*Assignment of Probabilities.*   The use of expected value to select from actions 1, 2, and 3 in Table S-2 requires that a probability of occurrence be assigned to each of the four possible events. Suppose the following probability distribution is assumed:

| Event       | A | B | C | D |
|-------------|---|---|---|---|
| Probability | .3 | .2 | .1 | .4 |

*Optimum Outcome.*   The objective is to determine which action leads to the optimum outcome (highest expected value). This is accomplished by calculating the expected payoff for each possible action. The expected payoff for an action is determined by summing the products of each conditional outcome and its associated probability of occurrence. The individual products and their sums are given in Table S-6. The table indicates that the

**TABLE S-6   Calculation of Expected Values**

| Events | Probability | Actions, dollars | | |
|--------|-------------|------|------|------|
|        |             | 1    | 2    | 3    |
| A      | .3          | 1.20 | −.60 | 2.10 |
| B      | .2          | 0    | 1.20 | .60  |
| C      | .1          | −.50 | .90  | .20  |
| D      | .4          | 1.60 | −.40 | 1.20 |
|        | Expected value: | 2.30 | 1.10 | 4.10 |

decision maker's best alternative is action 3. This strategy has an expected value of $4.10, greater than the expected payoff of the other two available actions.

*Loss Analysis.*   The same decision can be reached by means of a loss analysis (just as the minimax principle leads to the same decision as the maximin principle). The conditional loss table given in Table S-7 can be obtained directly from the decision matrix, or conditional payoff table, given in Table S-2.

**TABLE S-7   Conditional Loss Table**

| Events | Actions, dollars | | |
|--------|------|---|---|
|        | 1    | 2 | 3 |
| A      | 3    | 9 | 0 |
| B      | 6    | 0 | 3 |
| C      | 14   | 0 | 7 |
| D      | 0    | 5 | 1 |

The first step is to find the highest conditional payoff corresponding to each event. This payoff corresponds to the best action that could have been taken given that a particular event has occurred. The next step is to subtract all conditional payoffs in the event row from the optimal. Notice that all conditional losses will have values that are either zero (corresponding to the maximum payoffs for each event) or positive.

An expected loss table can be calculated for each possible action using the same procedure employed to calculate expected payoffs. An expected loss table is presented in Table S-8. The appropriate decision criterion is now to select an action with the minimum expected loss. This criterion leads to the selection of action 3.

**TABLE S-8   Calculation of Expected Losses**

| Events | Probability | Actions, dollars | | |
|---|---|---|---|---|
| | | 1 | 2 | 3 |
| A | .3 | .90 | 2.70 | 0 |
| B | .2 | 1.20 | 0 | .60 |
| C | .1 | 1.40 | 0 | .70 |
| D | .4 | 0 | 2.00 | .40 |
| | Expected loss: | 3.50 | 4.70 | 1.70 |

**Analysis of Payoff and Loss Tables**   The expected opportunity loss of action A is $1.70. This is the smallest possible expected loss that can be achieved on the basis of available information, even though, over the long run, action A will turn out to have been the best choice only 30 percent of the time. That is, 70 percent of the time events B, C, or D will occur, and, on those occasions, either action 1 or 2 will give a smaller conditional loss (or larger conditional payoff) than action 3. Nevertheless, action 3 will give the smallest expected, or average, loss over time.

*Cost of Uncertainty.*   Action 3's expected loss could be eliminated only if one knew in advance which event was going to occur—so that the appropriate action could be taken. Since this information is not available, the minimum expected loss can be thought of as the "cost of uncertainty." In this example, the cost of uncertainty is $1.70 and, in the absence of additional information, it is an irreducible cost.

*Perfect Information.*   Suppose, however, that it is possible to determine in advance which event will occur. Given the availability of this perfect information, it would be possible to select an action so that the conditional loss would always turn out to be zero. Action 1 would be taken 40 percent of the time (when it is known in advance that event D will

1120

occur); action 2 would be taken 30 percent of the time (when it is known that either event B or C will occur), and action 3 would be taken 30 percent of the time (when event A will occur). The expected, or average, payoff under conditions of certainty would be $5.80, as shown in Table S-9.

**TABLE S-9   Expected Payoff under Perfect Information**

| Event | Probability | Appropriate action | Conditional payoff, dollars | Expected payoff, dollars |
|---|---|---|---|---|
| A | .3 | 3 | 7 | 2.10 |
| B | .2 | 2 | 6 | 1.20 |
| C | .1 | 2 | 9 | .90 |
| D | .4 | 1 | 4 | 1.60 |
| | | | Expected payoff = | 5.80 |

The computations in Table S-9 show that the average payoff over a long period of time would be $5.80 if perfect advance information were available as to which event would occur. In the absence of perfect information, the expected payoff would be $4.10. The difference between these amounts is the *expected value of perfect information* (EVPI). In this instance a merchant could pay up to a maximum of $1.70 ($5.80 − $4.10) to obtain a perfect forecast of which event would occur. The $1.70 represents the increase in expected payoff that could be achieved if perfect advance information were available.

Notice that the EVPI and the cost of uncertainty are equal. They represent the same quantity interpreted in slightly different ways. It should also be noted that the sum of the expected payoff and the expected loss is $5.80 for all alternative actions.

The EVPI can be used as a quick check of the advisibility of sampling to obtain additional information. If the cost of sampling would be in excess of the EVPI, it clearly would not be worthwhile. If sample information can be obtained very inexpensively, and if it would greatly improve the decision maker's ability to forecast the actual event that will occur, proceeding would definitely be advantageous. But if the cost of taking a sample would be relatively expensive (although less than the EVPI) and/or the potential value of sample information is questionable, a more formal analysis should be conducted.

*Cost of Irrationality.*   Suppose that, in the absence of perfect information, the decision maker selected action 2 instead of the optimal action 3. The expected loss due to this alternative is $4.70. The decision maker is using a suboptimal strategy and is therefore incurring a higher expected loss than would be necessary. The difference between this expected loss and the cost of uncertainty is called the "cost of irrationality." In this example the cost of irrationality is $3.00 ($4.70 − $1.70). This is the *additional* loss, over and above the cost of uncertainty, incurred by the decision maker as a result of choosing a suboptimal, or irrational, action.

From the expected payoff table (Table S-6) the expected payoff of action 3 is $4.10. This is the highest expected payoff that can be achieved. A decision to select any other action will result in a lower expected payoff. For example, the expected payoff for action 2 is $1.10. The difference in the two payoff values is $3.00 ($4.10 − $1.10), or the cost of irrationality. This will always be true. The cost of irrationality is equal to both the increase in the expected loss and the decrease in the expected payoff that results from selecting a suboptimal action. Thus the cost of irrationality of action 1 is $1.80 ($3.50 − $1.70 = $4.10 − $2.30).

## BAYESIAN ANALYSIS

The cost of uncertainty can generally be reduced if information can be obtained which allows the decision maker to better forecast the event that will occur. This explains why market surveys, investment analysis, sales forecasts, and other related activities are undertaken. Technically, from the view of decision theory, new information is collected to allow the reassessment of probability assignments in order to reduce the cost of uncertainty.

The initial probability assignments are called *prior* (before new information) *probabilities*. The probabilities determined on the basis of new information are called *posterior probabilities*. Thus a mechanism is needed to revise the initial probabilities, given new information. The mechanism is called Bayes' rule. It can be written as:

$$P\frac{A_i}{B} = \frac{P(A_i)P(B/A_i)}{\sum\limits_{i=1}^{n} P(A_i)P(B/A_i)}$$

where $A_i \ldots A_n$ is the set of possible events and $B$ is the new or sample information.

Bayes' rule can best be illustrated by tabular analysis. Consider the situation where one feels that the probability a stock is a good buy is .4. That is, the prior (before new information) probabilities are $P$ (good buy) = .4 and $P$ (bad buy) = .6. Now an investment service that has a record of being right 80 percent of the time recommends purchase of the stock. What then should be the revised or posterior (after new information) probability that the stock is a good buy, i.e., $P$ (good buy/investment service recommendation)?

The basic data can be structured as shown in Table S-10, since there are only two possible outcomes for the stock. Based on past records, the sample result "recommend" would occur 80 percent of the time when a stock is actually a good buy and 20 percent of the time when it is actually a bad buy. Such conditional probabilities of the sample result are called the *sampling probabilities*.

**TABLE S-10   Information Necessary for Solution of Bayes' Rule**

| $A_i$ Possible outcomes | $P(A_i)$ Prior probabilities | $P(B/A_i)$ Sampling probabilities |
|---|---|---|
| $A_1$ = good buy | .4 | .8 |
| $A_2$ = bad buy | .6 | .2 |

The first step is to multiply each element in column 2 by its respective element in column 3, as shown in Table S-11. Each element in the new column (column 4) represents a joint probability, which is one of the terms in the numerator of the foregoing equation representing Bayes' rule. Thus, each element represents the probability of the row's outcome and $B$, and the sum of the column values equals the value of the denominator. Finally, division of the individual column entry by the column sum represents the conditional probability $P(A_i/B)$. Hence using the Bayesian tabular analysis, one finds that the revised or posterior probabilities are 32/44 that the stock is a good buy and, conversely, 12/44 that it a bad buy.

**TABLE S-11   Tabular Analysis of Example**

| $A_i$ | $P(A_i)$ | $P(B/a_i)$ | $P(A_i)p(B/A_i)$ | $P(A_i/B)$ |
|---|---|---|---|---|
| $A_1$ = good buy | .4 | .8 | .32 | $\frac{32}{44}$ |
| $A_2$ = bad buy | .6 | .2 | $\frac{.12}{.44}$ | $\frac{12}{44}$ |

In analyzing the use of Bayes' rule to revise prior probability estimates in light of new information, the following relationship should be noted. The stronger the initial prior probabilities, the less effect the new information has on changing the probabilities. Conversely, the more conclusive the new information, the greater the impact on the revised probabilities. For example, if the prior probabilities are .99 and .01 for a good buy and a bad buy, respectively, the revised probabilities would be 792/794 and 2/794, respectively. If the investment service is right 99 percent of the time, the revised probabilities would be 198/201 and 3/201, respectively.

### DECISION TREES

The alternative courses of action that will be available in the future are frequently determined by the decisions that are made today. Sometimes the interrelationships between current and future actions are known, and so strategies can be devised that will lead to an optimum sequence of decisions. Future decisions will be based on future events, certainly, but a well-devised strategy will indicate which action should be taken given the event (or sequence of events) that has occurred.

A situation may require a series of actions, and several different sequences (or strategies) can be followed. For example, the introduction of a new product or a new manufacturing process may require the construction of new plant facilities. The size of plant that will be needed will depend on the success of the new product or process. Three alternatives initially are open to the firm. A large plant can be constructed immediately, a small plant can be constructed, or the firm can decide to maintain the status quo and do nothing. The construction of a small plant would be a cautious decision. If future events are favorable, larger facilities could be provided by an expansion of the small plant.

A similar problem could be involved in marketing a new product. A strong national marketing effort could be undertaken immediately. Alternatively, the product could be test marketed in one or more regions and, if successful, brought out nationally at a later date. Or the firm could decide not to market the product at all. If cost figures and probability estimates of future demand are available, decision trees can be utilized in solving these problems.

**Definition**  A *decision tree* is a network representation of sequences of action-event combinations that are available to the decision maker. Each possible sequence of decisions and consequences is shown by a different path through the tree. Although some of the problems that are solved through the use of decision trees are very complex, the fundamental solution techniques are relatively straightforward. In fact, one of the major advantages of decision trees is that the problem is structured clearly. This makes possible a systematic and logical attack on the problem of solving for the optimum strategy.

Just about any problem that can be solved using decision trees can also be solved with payoff tables. The two techniques have much in common. Payoff tables generally are used when only one decision must be made (or where a situation—and therefore decision—is to be repeated), whereas decision trees are used most often when a series of interrelated decisions must be made over time. Payoff tables quickly become unwieldy when used for the latter type of problem.

**Application**  Suppose a decision maker has identified two attractive projects (denoted by $X$ and $Y$) but lacks the capital necessary to undertake both of them simultaneously. Because the two projects are independent, however, it is possible to undertake $X$ first and then, if $X$ is successful, undertake $Y$, or vice versa. Project $X$ requires an outlay of $10,000, while $Y$ requires an outlay of $12,000. Neither project will return anything if it is unsuccessful. Successful completion of $X$ will return $8000 (over cost); of $Y$, $11,000 (over cost). The probability of success for $X$ is .7 and for $Y$ is .6.

*Strategies.*  A full analysis of this problem would evaluate five alternative strategies: (1) Do nothing; (2) undertake $X$ and then stop regardless of the outcome; (3) undertake $Y$ and then stop regardless of the outcome; (4) undertake $X$ and, if successful, undertake $Y$: (5) undertake $Y$ and, if successful, undertake $X$.

In a decision tree each decision, including components of an overall strategy, is analyzed individually. A decision tree depicting the above problem is presented in Fig. S-7. Notice that the tree consists of alternating *action-event areas*. The "action" area represents a time of decision for the decision maker. The "event" area that follows indicates the various consequences that can follow the action that is taken. These areas are also called "areas of choice and chance." The probabilities of success or failure are shown on the tree following actions that can result in these two outcomes.

**Rollback Method**  A solution is obtained by working backward through the tree, i.e., from the most distant decisions sequentially back to the initial decision. This is sometimes called the "rollback" method. It is assumed that different decision points in the tree have been reached and, for each, the optimal decision is determined conditional on having reached the decision point being analyzed. Once a decision point has been analyzed, the next step in the procedure is to move backward along the path and analyze the preceding decision point. Each decision point is analyzed, taking into account both the immediate possible outcomes and the expected consequences of subsequent decisions.

The procedure for solving a decision tree can be illustrated with the problem concerning projects $X$ and $Y$. The decision tree for the problem is given in Fig. S-7 where, for reference purposes, each decision point is identified by a circled number. Deci-

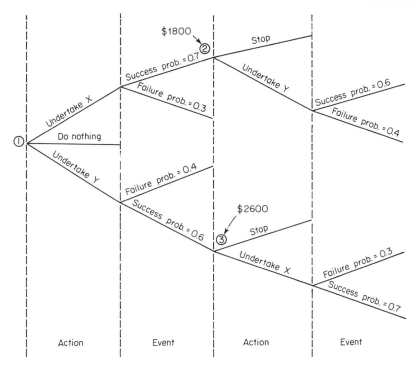

**Fig. S-7. Decision tree.**

sion 3 will be evaluated first. This point is reached only after successful completion of project $Y$. The expected values of the two alternatives—stop or undertake $X$—are given in Table S-12. The expected value of stopping is $0 and the expected value of undertaking $X$ is $2600. On the basis of the criterion of maximizing expected value, $X$ should be accepted if $Y$ is successful. Accordingly, a value of $2600 is assigned to the position corresponding to reaching decision point 3.

Decision point 2 will be evaluated next. (Since points 2 and 3 are not points along the same path, the order in which they are evaluated is arbitrary.)

TABLE S-12   **Evaluation of Decision Point 3**

1. Undertake $X$

| Event | Probability | Conditional payoff, dollars | Expected payoff, dollars |
|-------|-------------|----------------------------|--------------------------|
| Success | .7 | 8000 | 5600 |
| Failure | .3 | −10,000 | −3000 |
| | | | 2600 |

2. Stop
   Expected value = $0

The alternative actions and their expected values are given in Table S-13. On the basis of the calculated expected values, the best decision would be to undertake $Y$. Thus the expected value of successfully completing $X$ and being in a position to undertake $Y$

TABLE S-13   **Evaluation of Decision Point 2**

1. Undertake $Y$

| Event | Probability | Conditional payoff, dollars | Expected payoff, dollars |
|-------|-------------|----------------------------|--------------------------|
| Success | .6 | 11,000 | 6600 |
| Failure | .4 | −12,000 | −4800 |
| | | | 1800 |

2. Stop
   Expected value = $0

is $1800. This potential expected gain is shown in Fig. S-7 by assigning a value of $1800 to the point corresponding to decision 2.

Two conditional decisions have been made: That $X$ should be undertaken following successful completion of $Y$ and that $Y$ should be undertaken if $X$ is successfully completed. The final step, shown as decision point 1, is to decide whether to first undertake $X$, first undertake $Y$, or do nothing. The expected values of these three alternatives are given in Table S-14. The procedure is similar to that used above, but one additional factor must now be considered. Successful completion of $X$ brings an immediate cash benefit of $8000 *plus* the opportunity to undertake investment $Y$. The expected value of accepting investment $Y$ is $1800, so the total payoff of successfully investing in $X$ is $8000 plus $1800, for a total of $9800. Likewise, if $Y$ is accepted first and is successful, the total payoff is $13,600. This amount consists of $11,000, the immediate and direct benefit, plus $2600, the expected value of being able to continue and accept $X$.

**TABLE S-14   Evaluation of Decision Point 1**

1. Undertake $X$ and then $Y$

| Event | Probability | Conditional payoff, dollars | Expected payoff, dollars |
|---|---|---|---|
| | | (8000 + 1800) = | |
| Success | .7 | 9,800 | 6860 |
| Failure | .3 | −10,000 | −3000 |
| | | | 3860 |

2. Undertake $Y$ and then $X$

| | | (11,000 + 2600) = | |
|---|---|---|---|
| Success | .6 | 13,600 | 8160 |
| Failure | .4 | −12,000 | −4800 |
| | | | 3360 |

3. Do nothing
   Expected value = $0

On the basis of the computations in Table S-14, the best initial decision is to undertake $X$. The best overall strategy is to accept $X$ and, if successful, then to undertake $Y$. The path through the tree that corresponds to this strategy has an expected value of $3860.

This example illustrates the usefulness of the rollback procedure. Although most problems are much more complicated than the one discussed above, the use of the decision tree approach enables a final solution to be obtained from the systematic solution of a series of small, individual subproblems. The computations become more time-consuming than difficult as the size and complexity of the decision tree grow.

## MULTIPLE CRITERIA

Up to this point the exposition has always assumed that the objective was to maximize or minimize some single measurable outcome. Hence, the consequence at the end of each decision tree branch was a single numerical value. Most frequently in routine business problems, one is minimizing costs or expected costs or maximizing the net present value of a profit stream or expected net present value of a profit stream. However, the concept of maximizing profit may be an oversimplification to top management. Business decisions are often made on the basis of consideration of various objectives. For example, an investor may wish to select the portfolio which maximizes expected return but minimizes risk. Here there are two objectives or decision criteria; moreover, they tend to be conversely related. Another example is to minimize costs and maximize the quality of service. Still another is to decide where to build a new plant. The objectives may be to (1) minimize total construction costs, (2) minimize employee disruption due to the necessity of transfer to a new building, (3) maximize the availability of a qualified labor force, (4) minimize necessary transportation costs of goods received and shipped, and (5) maximize the environmental aspects for employee moral.

In sum, the *multiple-criteria problems*, often called *complex value problems*, are those where the consequences of a decision cannot be adequately described objectively by a single value such as dollars.

The multiple-criteria problem can be divided into two general parts. The first is the proper definition and measurement of the various criteria and the second is the proper method of evaluating the importance and trade-offs of the various criteria to make the best decision.

**Definition and Measurement**   With respect to the first, the tasks are (1) to define objectives upon which an alternative action will be evaluated and (2) to measure the success of an alternative action with respect to each objective. Such measurements are called *attributes*. Attributes might be *direct measures* (cost per unit produced), *proxy measures* (a direct measure of something correlated to the objective but not directly the objective), *subjective index of success* (the common social indices for quality of life), or *direct preference measures* (the assignment of the expected utility of the outcome). These tasks are, of course, similar to that of a single-criterion problem, differing only in the number of objectives and attributes which must be defined. However, since one must ultimately evaluate jointly the various objectives through the attributes, a new dimension has been added to the task: that of structuring a set of attributes which are (1) *complete*, or cover all the important criteria; (2) *operational*, in a form that can be meaningfully used to assess trade-offs between objectives; (3) *decomposable*, such that the evaluation process can be simplified by breaking it down into parts; (4) *nonredundant*, so that double counting of impacts is avoided, and, (5) *minimal*, so the dimensions of the task are as small as possible.

**Evaluation** Three systematic approaches to finding an optimal action evaluated against multiple criteria are possible, as described below.

*Cost-Effectiveness.* Here, no attempt is made to combine the criteria into a single composite measure to be maximized or minimized. One typically lists *aspiration levels* for each attribute and searches for a solution which meets the levels. If it cannot be found, the aspiration levels are decreased selectively until a solution is found. If a solution is found, investigation must proceed to determine whether any aspiration level can be increased such that a better solution can be found. This approach requires simulation and has two serious weaknesses: (1) It begs the question of what the aspiration levels should be and the appropriate trade-offs among the attributes; (2), it does not permit the introduction of uncertainty into the problem.

*Cost-Benefit Analysis.* In this approach one combines the attributes into a single composite benefit measure by weighting the value of each attribute. The trick is to find suitable conversion factors which convert to commensurable units and reflect the appropriate trade-offs. In practice, the conversion is usually obtained by objective market mechanisms or by subjectively imputing dollar prices of monetary worth to each attribute. Cost-benefit is preferable to cost-effectiveness in that it makes arriving at an "optimal" solution easier—that is, the action which maximizes total benefits for a given cost constraint. Its weaknesses, however, are that pricing many attributes such as goodwill or customer satisfaction is often very difficult and introducing uncertainty into the process is also difficult. Nevertheless, it is the most common approach used.

*Joint Utility Theory.* Here, the decision maker must, in essence, assign a utility or develop a function for ordering the utilities for each possible set of attribute outcomes. Hence, the optimal action is the one which maximizes overall utility. This approach is theoretically appealing, especially since it can systematically and effectively handle uncertainty. However, this approach is extremely complex and difficult (if not impossible in some cases) to use. Consequently, it is rarely used in practice.

*See also* CONTROL SYSTEMS, MANAGEMENT; OPERA-

TIONS RESEARCH AND MATHEMATICAL MODELING; RISK ANALYSIS AND MANAGEMENT; SYSTEM CONCEPT, TOTAL.

### REFERENCES

Jedamus, Paul, Robert Frame, and Robert Taylor: *Statistical Analysis for Business Decisions*, McGraw-Hill Book Company, New York, 1976.

Johnson, Rodney D., and Bernard R. Siskin: *Quantitative Techniques for Business Decisions*, Prentice-Hall, Inc., Englewood Cliffs, N.J., 1976.

Parsons, Robert: *Statistical Analysis: A Decision-Making Approach*, Harper & Row, Publishers, Inc., New York, 1974.

Reichard, Richard S.: *The Numbers Game: Uses and Abuses of Managerial Statistics*, McGraw-Hill Book Company, New York, 1972.

Shag, Stephen P.: *Statistics for Business and Economics*, 3d ed., Charles E. Merrill Books, Inc., Columbus, Ohio, 1967.

Snedecor, George W., and William G. Cochran: *Statistical Methods*, 6th ed., Iowa State University Press, Ames, 1967.

RODNEY JOHNSON, *Deputy Director of Finance, City of Philadelphia*
BERNARD R. SISKIN, *Temple University*

## Statistical decision making   (*See* DECISION-MAKING PROCESS.)

## Statistical methods   (*See* STATISTICAL ANALYSIS FOR MANAGEMENT.)

## Statistical quality control (SQC)   (*See* QUALITY MANAGEMENT.)

## Status change, employee   (*See* PERSONNEL ADMINISTRATION.)

## Status variables   (*See* CONTROL SYSTEMS, MANAGEMENT.)

## Statute of limitations   (*See* PRODUCT LIABILITY.)

## Stochastic processes   (*See* OPERATIONS RESEARCH AND MATHEMATICAL MODELING.)

**Stock, common** (*See* FINANCIAL MANAGE-MENT; FINANCIAL MANAGEMENT OF SHORT-TERM, INTERMEDIATE, AND LONG-TERM FINANCING.)

**Stock, cross-ownership** (*See* JAPANESE INDUSTRIES, MANAGEMENT IN.)

**Stock, performance shares** (*See* COMPEN-SATION, EXECUTIVE.)

**Stock, phantom** (*See* COMPENSATION EXECU-TIVE.)

**Stock, preferred** (*See* FINANCIAL MANAGE-MENT; FINANCIAL MANAGEMENT, SHORT-TERM, IN-TERMEDIATE, AND LONG-TERM FINANCING.)

**Stock certificate** (*See* OWNERSHIP, LEGAL FORMS OF.)

**Stock companies** (*See* INSURANCE AND RISK MANAGEMENT.)

**Stock control, retail** (*See* RETAILING MAN-AGEMENT.)

**Stock dividends** (*See* FINANCIAL MANAGE-MENT, CAPITAL STRUCTURE AND DIVIDEND POLICY.)

**Stock market indicators** (*See* MARKETS, STOCK INDICATOR SERIES.)

**Stock ownership plans, employee (ESOP)** (*See* COMPENSATION, EMPLOYEE BEN-EFIT PLANS.)

**Stock repurchases** (*See* FINANCIAL MAN-AGEMENT, CAPITAL STRUCTURE AND DIVIDEND POLICY.)

**Stock rooms** (*See* INVENTORY CONTROL, PHYSI-CAL AND STOCKKEEPING.)

**Stock splits** (*See* FINANCIAL MANAGEMENT, CAPITAL STRUCTURE AND DIVIDEND POLICY.)

**Stockholder relationships** (*See* SHARE-HOLDER RELATIONSHIPS.)

**Stockholders** (*See* OWNERSHIP, LEGAL FORMS OF.)

**Stockless purchasing** (*See* PURCHASING MANAGEMENT.)

**Storage symbol** (*See* WORK SIMPLIFICATION AND IMPROVEMENT.)

**Strategic issue analysis** (*See* PLANNING, PLANNED MANAGEMENT OF TURBULENT CHANGE.)

**Strategic management** (*See* PLANNING, STRATEGIC MANAGERIAL.)

**Strategic marketing planning** (*See* MAR-KETING, CONCEPTS AND SYSTEMS.)

**Strategic planning models** (*See* PLAN-NING, STRATEGIC PLANNING MODELS.)

**Strategies, advertising** (*See* ADVERTISING CONCEPTS.)

**Strategy** (*See* POLICY FORMULATION AND IMPLE-MENTATION.)

**Strategy, entrepreneurial** (*See* PLANNING, PLANNED MANAGEMENT OF TURBULENT CHANGE.)

**Strategy, for labor relations**   (*See* LABOR-MANAGEMENT RELATIONS.)

**Strategy, marketing**   (*See* MARKETING MANAGEMENT.)

**"Street name" holders**   (*See* SHAREHOLDER RELATIONSHIPS.)

**Stress**   (*See* HEALTH, EXECUTIVE, MANAGING STRESS AND JOB TENSION.)

**Stress potential**   (*See* HEALTH, EXECUTIVE, MANAGING STRESS AND JOB TENSION.)

**Strike preparation**   (*See* LABOR-MANAGEMENT RELATIONS.)

**Structure, flat**   (*See* ORGANIZATION ANALYSES AND PLANNING; ORGANIZATION STRUCTURES AND CHARTING.)

**Structure, tall**   (*See* ORGANIZATION ANALYSIS AND PLANNING; ORGANIZATION STRUCTURES AND CHARTING.)

**Structure of work**   (*See* WORK, CONCEPT AND INDICATIONS.)

**Structures, organization**   (*See* ORGANIZATION ANALYSIS AND PLANNING; ORGANIZATION STRUCTURES AND CHARTING.)

**Subcontracting**   (*See* PRODUCTION/OPERATIONS MANAGEMENT.)

**Suboptimization**   (*See* SYSTEM CONCEPT, TOTAL.)

# Suggestion systems

A *suggestion system* is a formal program under which employees are encouraged to submit written suggestions to management and are rewarded for those which are adopted. Rewards are usually financial, either a set sum or a percentage of savings to the company effected by adoption of the suggestion.

Now firmly established as an effective management tool, formal suggestion systems started in industry after 1900 but were first widely applied during World War II when Ezra S. Taylor of the Pullman Company was asked to design a system for civilian personnel in the War Department. Today they are used by many hundreds of companies and by every department of the federal government. In a 1973 survey of about 1400 companies with approximately 7½ million employees, over 3½ million suggestions were received, over $42 million in awards paid.

An effective system requires that management: (1) define precise objectives; (2) set a time frame for their attainment; (3) demonstrate prominent, widely communicated, and continual commitment; (4) provide prompt feedback to all suggesters (30 days for processing, 60 days at most for action); (5) publicize awards widely, in-house and locally; (6) thoroughly train middle management and supervisors (the critical elements in a suggestion system); (7) provide thorough and tailored communication to all employees about the system and its rules; (8) allocate sufficient budgeting for expert administration and complete record keeping (using data processing if more than 1500 files per year are generated); (9) specify in detail the evaluation process; (10) receive reports at least quarterly; (11) check on legal aspects of all steps before implementing a system; (12) lean over backwards to ensure that rewards are adequate (typical and recommended: a minimum of $25 or 15 to 25 percent of net savings earned the first year).

Effective systems average impressive net returns on investment: 600 to 700 percent. They are a proved cost-reduction/profit-improvement tool, serve to locate both problem areas and talent, increase productivity and work quality, improve employee-management relationships, and develop employee motivation by providing direct communication upward and a medium for self-expression, achievement, and recognition—thus a feeling of involvement and responsibility to the company. A cautionary note: Experts warn that casual or half-hearted support of a suggestion system by management can actually harm the company by causing employee dissatisfaction and frustration.

*See also* ATTITUDE SURVEYS; COMMUNICATIONS, EMPLOYEE; COMMUNICATIONS, ORGANIZATIONAL; WORK SIMPLIFICATION AND IMPROVEMENT.

### REFERENCES

Hein, John E.: "Employee Suggestion Systems Pay," *Personnel Journal*, March 1973.

Mathis, R. L., and J. H. Jackson: *Personnel: Contemporary Perspectives and Applications*, West Publishing Company, St. Paul, Minn., 1976.

National Association of Suggestion Systems, 435 North Michigan Ave., Chicago, 60611. This is a nonprofit organization founded in 1942 as a center for suggestion systems development and information exchange. It provides a wide variety of services to members in the development, implementation, and administration of systems.

Tatter, Milton A.: "Turning Ideas into Gold," *Management Review*, March 1975.

STAFF/HOKE

## Sunset budgeting   (*See* ZERO-BASE BUDGETING.)

## Supermarket   (*See* MARKETING, CHANNELS OF DISTRIBUTION.)

## Supervisor   (*See* SUPERVISORY MANAGEMENT.)

## Supervisory boards   (*See* CODETERMINATION AND INDUSTRIAL DEMOCRACY.)

## Supervisory management

Perhaps more than any other individual, the person who directly supervises the nonmanagement employees is the key ingredient in the overall organizational success. Although every individual who has managerial responsibility can be viewed as a supervisor, the term is generally applied to the first level of managerial responsibility. As such, the supervisor is a vital link between the plans of an organization and their execution. This is especially true in regard to cost reduction and productivity. Supervisors are also the vital link between top management and the worker. Approximately one-eighth of all employed persons serve in some supervisory capacity.

**Definition**   According to the Labor Management Act (Taft-Hartley) of 1947, a supervisor is a person who has formal authority to:

> . . . hire, transfer, suspend, lay off, recall, promote, discharge, assign, reward, or discipline other employees, or responsibility to direct them, or to adjust their grievances, or effectively to recommend such action, if in connection with the foregoing the exercise of such authority is not a merely routine or clerical nature, but requires the use of independent judgment.

The Fair Labor Standards Act of 1938 considers employees supervisors if they spend no more than 20 percent of their time performing the same kind of work that their subordinates do and if they are paid a salary with no compensation for overtime.

**Job Responsibilities**   In a 1970 study conducted by Purdue University, 4250 supervisors were asked to identify their most important job functions. The results clearly indicated that interpersonal demands of working with subordinates were judged more important by the supervisors than some of their more traditional responsibilities in labor relations or cost control.[1]

| Supervisory Functions | Performed by Supervisors, % |
|---|---|
| Employee direction and supervision | 91 |
| Safety | 53 |
| Training | 42 |
| Production machinery surveillance | 30 |
| Quality control and inspection | 24 |
| Labor relations | 21 |
| Cost and financial control | 15 |

**Time Allocations**   In attempting to identify the actual demands on a supervisor's time, the challenge of meeting standards of "getting out the work" seems to predominant. Chester Evans, a consulting psychologist and professor at Wayne State University has studied the percentages of time allocated to various job functions.[2] The result of his and other studies confirms the fact that the two key challenges of the supervisor's job are people and production.

| Supervisor's Activity | Time Distribution in Approximate percent |
|---|---|
| Production supervision | 25 |
| Personnel administration and grievances | 20 |
| Concern with machines and equipment | 15 |
| Appraising worker performance | 8 |
| Concern with materials | 8 |
| Planning and scheduling work | 5 |
| Meetings and conferences | 3 |
| Other | 16 |
| | 100 |

Generally, supervisors are promoted to their positions from the ranks of line workers, and experi-

ence is a primary consideration. Men or women are seldom hired directly as supervisors from educational institutions or training programs. For these reasons, a new supervisor may be familiar with the technical aspects of getting the work out without having acquired the necessary interpersonal skills required to motivate and lead others in meeting production goals.

**Increased Professionalization** As an aid to helping supervisors and their employers concentrate on the important skills of supervision, two of the largest organizations of first-level managers (the National Management Association and the International Management Council affiliated with the YMCA) have created the Institute of Certified Professional Managers. This institute attempts to provide direction and evaluation of a supervisor's efforts at personal growth and development in management. Experience, skills, and knowledge in human relations, administration, and personal skills are viewed as the basis for successful growth in this important dimension of management.

*See also* LEADERSHIP; MANAGER, DEFINITIONS OF.

### NOTES

[1]W. Richard Plunkett, *Manpower Report 70-2*, "Foremen in Indiana Industries: Their Characteristics, Job Functions, and Educational Requirements," C. Brown Company Publishers, Dubuque, Iowa, 1975, p. 41.

[2]Lester R. Bittel, *What Every Supervisor Should Know*, 3d ed., McGraw-Hill Book Company, New York, 1974, p. 10.

### REFERENCES

Bittel, Lester R.: *Improving Supervisory Performance*, McGraw-Hill Book Company, New York, 1976.

Boyd, Bradford B.: *Management-Minded Supervision*, 2d ed., McGraw-Hill Book Company, New York, 1976.

———: *Supervisory Training: Approaches and Methods*, American Society for Training and Development, Madison, Wis., 1976.

Eckles, Robert W., Ronald L. Carmichael, and Bernard R. Sarchet: *Essentials of Management for First-Line Supervision*, John Wiley & Sons, Inc., New York, 1974.

Ficker, Victor B.: *Effective Supervison*, Charles E. Merrill Publishing Company, Columbus, Ohio, 1975.

Fulmer, Robert M.: *Supervision: Principles of Professional Management*, Glencoe Press, Beverly Hills, Cal., 1976.

Haimann, Theo, and Raymond L. Hilgert: *Supervison: Concepts and Practices of Management*, South-Western Publishing Company, Cincinnati, 1972.

Reber, Ralph W., and Gloria E. Terry: *Behavioral Insights for Supervision*, Prentice-Hall, Inc., Englewood Cliffs, N.J., 1975.

Rudkin, Donald A., and Fred D. Veal, Jr.: *Principles of Supervision*, Auerbach Publishers, Inc., Philadelphia, 1973.

Steinmetz, Lawrence L., and H. Ralph Todd, Jr.: *First-Line Management*, Business Publications, Inc., Dallas, 1975.

Van Dersal, William R.: *The Successful Supervisor: In Government and Business*, 3d. ed., Harper & Row, Publishers, Inc., New York, 1975.

ROBERT M. FULMER, *Memphis State University*

## Supplementary unemployment benefits (SUB) (*See* COMPENSATION, EMPLOYEE BENEFIT PLANS.)

## Supplier quality (*See* QUALITY MANAGEMENT.)

## Suppliers, for government purchases (*See* MARKETS, PUBLIC.)

## Supply, economic (*See* ECONOMIC CONCEPTS.)

## Supply and demand (*See* PRODUCT PLANNING AND DEVELOPMENT.)

## Support systems, work (*See* WORK, CONCEPT AND IMPLICATIONS.)

## Survivor protection plans (*See* COMPENSATION, EMPLOYEE BENEFIT PLANS.)

## Syndicates

A syndicate is a temporary association of two or more investors or investing companies formed to participate in a joint venture or to carry out a single business undertaking for profit. Members usually share in any profits or losses in proportion to their individual contributions.

One of the oldest kinds of partnership, the syndicate is typically formed to reduce individual investors' risk in a project such as the development and sale of real estate or the underwriting by a group of investment firms of a large new capital issue. In some cases a cartel or trust is called a syndicate. Although occasionally ongoing, the syndicate typically is dissolved at the completion of the transaction.

*See also* CONSORTIUM; LEASING, EQUIPMENT; OWNERSHIP, LEGAL FORMS OF.

STAFF/HOKE

## Synectics   (*See* PRODUCT PLANNING AND DEVELOPMENT.)

## System   (*See* SYSTEM CONCEPT, TOTAL.)

## System, production   (*See* PRODUCTION/OPERATIONS MANAGEMENT.)

## System concept, total

The total system concept is concerned with a holistic view of interacting components in dynamic, complex situations. It offers perspective to understand the interrelationships among these components and their contribution to the performance of the whole. The concept also allows study of the impact between the system of interest and the environment in which it functions.

The word *total* is somewhat confounding since all systems, except an ultimate universe, are limited to some degree. Since the concept represents a way of thinking rather than a precise methodology, the author will emphasize the "systems approach" which is closely linked with modern ideas on organization and information.

### SYSTEM PRINCIPLES

**System Defined**   Few words are so overworked and so often defined as *system*, which means:

*A set of interrelated components that function together within constraints toward a common purpose.*

The term *total system* suggests components which interact dynamically to create a synergistic whole that is greater than the mere sum of its parts. The concept indicates that performance of a component cannot be evaluated by viewing it in isolation. It must be seen in context of contiguous functions and must be judged by its contribution to the achievement of the overall system objectives. A component may be either an individual element or an aggregation of them, known as a *subsystem*. Subsystems may be arranged in a *hierarchy*, in which components are layered to form a complex network. Complexity characteristic of business and industrial activities may be expressed in terms of product or service variety, market diversification, organizational interaction, geographic distribution, and a plethora of external influences. Another important dimension of the total system concept is the time horizon over which it evolves.

*Theoretical Aspects.* Systems theory addresses the establishment of order and regularity in dealing with the nature and representation of systems and their components. Ludwig von Bertalanffy has made considerable contribution in his writings on *general systems theory* in which he extrapolates from study of biological systems. The theory deals primarily with intrinsic aspects of systems and involves abstraction and mathematical representation in order to identify principles and to foster communication among disciplines. *Cybernetics*, the science of communication and control, provides a framework for considering system functions, particularly the notion of feedback. Cybernetic principles have been extended from traditional mechanical and electrical processes to be applied to the management of political, social, and business activities.

*Empirical Aspects.* More pragmatic views are concerned with observing and describing the characteristics and performance of functioning systems. The prime consideration is generally control of the functions utilizing organization, information processing, and decision structure principles. An observer of functioning systems must be concerned with the loose coordination, redundancy, and contradiction prevalent in complex, dynamic systems. External influences are important, and controls may include the capability for human override of system operation on an intuitive basis.

**Nature of Systems**   Business and industry have become increasingly aware of the external influences upon their organizations. Traditional organization theory assumed that it dealt with closed systems in the sense that destinies and performance were relatively deterministic and controlled from within. The modern concept is to view an organization as an *open system* which has significant interactions with the environment, depending upon it for resources and being constrained by its influences. The open system usually involves humans as developers, operators, and users who contribute to the uncertainty in function and results. While the open system has control guidance, it involves qualitative judgment and probabilistic performance. The general characteristics of an organization viewed as an open system are illustrated in Fig. S-8 and explained below.

*Mission.* The unifying force for the components of a system is a common purpose. The mission is expressed in terms of objectives and products, including both goods and services. The objectives are often general and subjective in nature, being concerned with such things as profit, growth, productivity, human need satisfaction, and public benefit. They are also concerned with the quantity and quality of the system output. A major point about the total system concept is that the hierarchy of subsystems exists solely to provide functions required to achieve the system purpose. Subsystem goals must be subordinate, and performance should be evaluated primarily on the subsystem contribution to the whole.

*Environment.* For a closed system, it is relatively easy to determine components necessary to achieve a given purpose. These components lie within a defined boundary and are under control of the system. All activities outside this boundary and control are classified as the environment. An open system is more interactive with the environment, making the boundary more difficult to define in terms of purpose, components, and manageability. External constraints, such as those listed in Fig. S-8, become important parts of the definition of the system boundary.

*Resources.* The inputs to the open system are the various resources, illustrated in Fig. S-8, which must be transformed into the products or services to achieve system purpose. Generally, the resources are described in terms of value and dimension of raw materials for the system process. More subjective inputs may include new opportunities and increased management skills.

*Process.* The functions needed to transform resources into desired output comprise the system process. Control over component operation is achieved by monitoring the state of activity; sensing output attributes; comparing actual results with those intended; and providing feedback to adjust inputs as necessary. Negative feedback makes corrections to return to an intended output characteristic, or essentially steady state. Positive feedback is utilized to change direction toward new goals.

*Structure.* Each system requires organization and procedures to define relationships among components and to provide channels for flow of communications. Centralized authority is implied by the need to coordinate component performance. But broad understanding of objectives coupled with effective communication gives latitude for decentralizing both authority and responsibility. Adaptation to changes in purpose or environment is a management function crucial to the continued success of the system.

**Modular Approach**  The total systems approach is susceptible to a challenge of what is manageable in

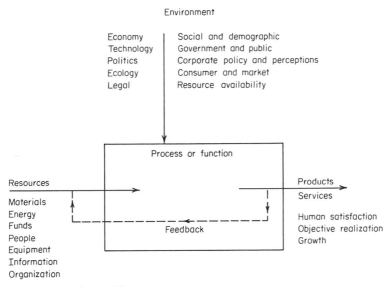

Fig. S-8. System characteristics.

the "total" perspective. A modern industrial plant, commercial enterprise, or government agency may be beyond the limits of individual comprehension. Literature abounds with "total" labels for such limited functions as materials flow in a hospital or facility control in a factory. The degree to which one can integrate functions and still control operation is countered by the ability to describe functional modules without sacrificing objectives. In physical systems, we have learned to design modules that can be plugged together to form an effective system. In open systems of business and industry, we must learn to specify accurately enough to allow a network of linked modules, each of which is susceptible to individual development and management but becomes part of the illusory total system.

## APPLICATION OF SYSTEM PRINCIPLES

**Life Cycle** Advocates of the systems approach imply that it applies equally to all activities. Experience tells us, however, that the approach has different ramifications for each phase of the life cycle of a system. This reinforces the time influence ascribed to the total systems concept by indicating that relevance varies from inception to replacement.

*Planning.* The planning stage is marked by efforts to define behavior of the systems of interest in future time periods. Analyzing the continuing present situation, forecasting effect of proposed alternatives, and assessing opportunities are the concerns. Efforts must be expended to define the scope and to classify objectives of a prospective system. The systems approach militates that an overview of dominant objectives provides the focus for this stage. Also, it suggests concentration on organizational goals and measures of effectiveness rather than limited analysis on a piecemeal approach.

*Design.* Design of a system entails the specification of means to accomplish performance required to meet identified purposes. The systems approach suggests that this be done in a "top down" manner, i.e., the design proceeds from the general overview to the lower-level details. *Systems engineering* is a deductive design process which develops specifications for an optimal system. Well-defined modules provide a means to accommodate change.

*Development.* Development is a creative stage which translates the design into an operational entity. Elegance of design may be compromised to ensure a workable product in a confounding environment. Acceptance and reliability of the system usually dominate consideration of methods to achieve the system mission. Project management, a special application of the systems approach, assumes prominent significance during this phase. Well-designed tests are of particular importance. Each component must be assessed to determine whether it performs its intended function effectively. Even more important, however, interactive effects among components must be tested in dynamic situations.

*Implementation.* After a system has performed satisfactorily in a test environment, its success is determined in live circumstances. People must accept and energize the new business, industry, or government system. Generally this means organizational development to assist people in effecting change, particularly involving training for new duties. Conversion from existing files and procedures requires significant effort because current records are almost sure to be inaccurate and/or insufficient relative to need in the new procedures. Implementation obviously must proceed from a foundation; one cannot expect the spire of a bridge or the roof garden of a building to be the first component in place. Implementation is an orderly process of assembling the developed modules and subsystems in accordance with a preconceived architectural plan to achieve the designed benefits.

*Operation.* During the operational stage, the systems approach assumes the form of problem solving, decision making, and control functions. *Systems analysis* is a methodical, reproducible way to identify significant problems from symptoms and to evaluate alternative solutions for situations in existing systems. In the process, resources are utilized in a way to optimize the time, cost, and quality issues. Output is sensed and compared with objectives, and feedback is generated to control the process. Decisions are made toward improving productivity and maintaining the process through repair and minor alteration of components.

*Evaluation.* System evaluation focuses on the overall performance using criteria established during design. The measures of effectiveness for an organization normally aggregate into multicriteria objective functions which contain both quantitative and qualitative factors. It is common to stress evaluation of the process rather than the outcome of an activated system. The process in a complex, dynamic open system is highly probabilistic, making cause-effect relationships difficult to identify and quality of outcome highly influenced by fluctuations in the state of the system. Evaluation procedures should be developed as a by-product of normal operation during design in order to minimize cost. Unintended side effects should also be expected in the form of problems to be solved or windfall benefits to be exploited in continued operation. Evaluation often leads to redesign to modify the system or to planning toward a major revision or replacement.

**Activity Levels**  The different phases of system life are frequently encountered in project-oriented situations. Ongoing business, industry, and government institutions are more concerned with sustaining operation and adapting to changing conditions and opportunities. Evolution is usually accomplished while the organizational mission is performed rather than through complete replacement of obsolescent units, an approach common in physical systems. Table S-15 summarizes characteristics and implications of the systems approach for different levels of activity normally associated with a business organization. All levels are usually extant simultaneously in parts of a typical institution.

**Management Style**  Many managers have been heavily exposed to the system approach through education and/or experience. Frequently they overreact toward using the concept as a sole approach for all situations. Others feel that reported or experienced shortcomings are universal and that success depends upon a combination of factors that far outweigh a systems approach. Some managers utilize

quantitatively detailed estimates as a basis for decisions. Others are more comfortable dealing with intuition to generate new ideas, to assume risk, or to resolve subjective issues. The systems approach should be hardy enough to support these differing roles and attitudes.

## METHODOLOGY

**The Systems Approach**  As we have mentioned earlier, the total system concept is a perspective rather than a prescribed methodology. Conceiving the entire system as an entity is often construed to mean that it must be treated as a monolithic structure. Only the smallest of organizations, however, can be considered without factoring integral functions into subsystems or modules. Therefore, the systems approach must embrace the means to specify functions during design of the system and to assemble them into a unified whole at implementation. Because of the adaptive nature of organizations, heuristic decision processes are appropriate. Algorithms, or procedures that ensure solution to mathematical problems in a finite number of steps, have limited application in the situations typical of management systems. The involvement of humans

**TABLE S-15  Activity Level Considerations**

| Activity levels | System implication | | Performance measure examples |
| | Organization | Information | |
|---|---|---|---|
| Strategic | Planning, future time periods<br>Policy, mission-oriented<br>Heuristic decision process<br>Open system; probabilistic | Predictive models, representative samples<br>Relevance<br>Intuitive, qualitative, uncertainty<br>Environmental influence | Satisfaction<br>Share of market<br>Change in risk |
| Tactical | Resource allocation proximate time period<br>Flexible, adaptive; choice among alternatives<br>Revision of objectives<br>Nonprogrammed decisions | Optimization models sufficiency, conciseness, management decision<br>Summary and analysis of functional performance | Delivery time<br>Unit cost<br>Utilization %<br>Scheduled task completion |
| Operational | Control of ongoing events and resource use<br>Goal seeking, continuity of process or function<br>Programmed decisions | Normative models<br>Monitoring during operation cycle<br>Reliability<br>Feedback, output comparison | Downtime<br>Time between failures<br>Frequency of service requests<br>Quality % |
| Clerical | Productivity, cost displacement<br>Conditioned reaction to input transactions<br>Closed system, near deterministic | Descriptive models<br>Data recording<br>Accuracy | Error rate<br>Capacity use<br>Throughput volume<br>Handling cost |

as decision makers stresses the need to apply modern ideas of organization and information systems. The *information system* is a set of rules and procedures designed to transform data into information which has utility in planning, organizing, and controlling activity. Such procedures do not require a computer, but its advent has made possible the handling of more variables and interactions. Thus, the systems approach has become more meaningful with the escalation of computer capability, especially data storage and management.

**Models**   *Model building* is the construction of a physical or abstract representation of all or part of a process. For management decision processes, the model is nearly always mathematical and/or logical in form and describes performance, either actual or ideal, or predicts potential outcomes. The models are intended to simplify and reduce complexity of operational situations for added perspective and insight, rather than to provide explicit solutions to dynamic problems. In addition to the validity of a model itself, the data utilized must be accurate and represent the actual situation if the results are to be relevant.

*Optimization.* The choice of the best alternative, making trade offs among conflicting or constraining objectives, is called *optimization*. To be consistent with the total system concept, the objective function and relationships for the entire system should be considered in effective utilization of such a model or technique. *Suboptimization* is the result of considering separately the subsystem goals or isolated functions performed within the system. For example, minimization of materials cost or maximization of revenue for a marketing region refers to specific management responsibilities, but neither guarantees success of the entire organization.

In general, models deal with suboptimization at lower activity levels. The manager is usually less concerned with optimality than with *feasibility* of proposed solutions. The latter involves ability to meet objectives in light of technical, economic, and operational considerations. *Satisficing* involves a decision criterion based on acceptance by concerned parties, usually by meeting a few dominant factors rather than seeking an optimal solution.

*Simulation.* A comprehensive system description involves multiple performance criteria, complex interrelationships, uncertainty about cause and effect, and dynamic change over time. *Simulation* is operation of a model with such characteristics in order to estimate the outcome of different combinations of factors and events. This manipulation "creates experience" through a series of tests or experiments with possible decision alternatives, compressing the time for results and by-passing need for trials in the actual situation. *Monte Carlo analysis* is used to approximate the effects of probabilistic elements over a period of time. *Industrial dynamics* provides a means to view organizational performance with feedback components.

*Operational gaming* is another form of simulation in which humans assume roles and make decisions involving conflicts among interests. Business and management games are effective for learning or team building in competitive situations. The gaming approach is also used to develop individual skills and to condition people regarding conformance to procedure, e.g., in-basket exercises. Gaming is highly relevant to the systems approach during evaluation of performance, experimentation with new methods, and training toward implementation.

## STATE OF THE ART

Examples of successful application of the total system concept are limited indeed. Weapons systems often illustrate classic systems engineering. Even for such a well-defined system, the objective function is concerned with qualitative factors such as probable deterrence or denial of target area, rather than just quantitative measures of destruction. The National Aeronautics and Space Administration is an organizational example, having been created to perform a relatively specific mission. Components were assembled in regard to their contribution to the overall mission. However, as the mission was modified and reduced, suboptimization became more prevalent.

Literature is full of references to "total systems" experiences which are too small in scope to qualify in terms of this presentation. Much has also been written about the seeming lack of success or acceptance of the systems approach. Some of the influences which affect the form and results of applying the concept were pointed out earlier. Clearly, the systems approach does not guarantee success for every endeavor in all circumstances. However, its thoughtful application can improve significantly the odds for success in most situations.

Definition of an open system is a major challenge, in that clear and logical description of boundaries is difficult. Should customers be included in the marketing subsystem or vendors in the materials acquisition subsystem? If they are included, how does the system exercise control over their activities? If not, in what sense are we dealing with a "total system"? Assume that boundaries can be initially established to define the system of interest and to segregate it from other systems or suprasystems in a hierarchy. How can one accommodate the continual changes of state within the system and adapt to the influences which are associated with the environment? Expansion, variant inputs, transient functions all cause overlaps and gaps among subsystems and also among those interacting systems which make up the environment. Indeed, one never deals with a "total system"; consideration of the whole or its parts in isolation is always a matter of degree.

The systems approach must support compromise in perspective, but it should also promote an overview that keeps major corporate goals dominant. Even when components are isolated for manageable study, the assessment criteria should stress contribution to the whole rather than efficiency of the part.

*See also* COMPUTER SYSTEMS; CONTROL SYSTEMS, MANAGEMENT; OPERATIONS RESEARCH AND MATHEMATICAL MODELING; PLANNING, STRATEGIC MANAGERIAL PLANNING; SIMULATIONS, BUSINESS AND MANAGEMENT; STATISTICAL ANALYSIS FOR MANAGEMENT; SYSTEM DYNAMICS.

### REFERENCES

Churchman, C. West: "Perspectives of the Systems Approach,"*Interfaces*, vol. 4, no. 4, pp. 6–11, August 1974.
————: *The Systems Approach*, Dell Publishing Co., Inc., New York, 1968.
Johnson, Richard A., Fremont E. Kast, and James E. Rosenzweig: *The Theory of Management Systems*, 3d ed., McGraw-Hill Book Company, New York, 1973.
Optner, Stanford I.: *Systems Analysis for Business Management*, 3d ed., Prentice-Hall, Inc., Englewood Cliffs, N.J., 1975.
Payne, Eugene E., Joel E. Ross, and Robert G. Murdick: *The Scope of Management Information Systems*, Computer and Information Systems Monograph no. 1, American Institute of Industrial Engineers, Norcross, Ga., 1975.
Schoderbek, Peter P.: *Management Systems*, 2d ed., John Wiley & Sons, Inc., New York, 1971.

WILLIAM A. SMITH, JR., *North Carolina State University*

# System dynamics

System dynamics (formerly called industrial dynamics) is a methodology for analyzing the dynamic behavior of industrial and other social systems. Modes of dynamic behavior include growth, unstable growth, stagnation, decay, and cyclical instability. In industry symptoms of problem behavior include loss of market share, declining profitability, and fluctuating production and employment. The system dynamics approach organizes the structure, information flows, and policies of a system into a computer model. Because many causes of behavior lie in the interactions between parts of a system, the system dynamics model generally incorporates the interactions between functional areas such as finance and production and between the firm and the market. Simulation of the model is used to gain an understanding of the cause of the problem behavior and thereby to design new corporate policies which improve behavior. System dynamics is a tool for the clarification of corporate goals and for the design of policies and strategies to achieve those goals.

## SYSTEM DYNAMICS APPROACH

**General Approach** The system dynamics approach to the design of corporate policies starts with a statement of corporate goals and an identification of the dynamic behavior of interest. One must then detect and describe the nature of, and the relationships between, the factors deemed important to the behavior being studied. Such a description is termed a *verbal (or written) model* of the system. A straightforward translation from the verbal description to a mathematical notation then creates a *mathematical model* which can be used to simulate operation of the actual system. Such model experimentation reveals the implications of the policies and relationships which have been stated in the model. Moreover, the experimentation can point out inconsistencies and trade-offs in corporate goals. The verbal and mathematical model descriptions of the actual system are revised until the model adequately represents the important behavior characteristics of the real system. Policy changes which might be made in an actual system are then tried in the model system to determine how the performance characteristics of the system can be improved. As a result, controlled laboratory experiments are possible as aids in the design of industrial and social policy.

**Background Threads** The system dynamics approach is perhaps best described in terms of the background threads on which it builds. In Fig. S-9, three earlier developments—traditional management of social systems, feedback theory, and computer simulation—combine to become system dynamics. Traditional management is the process used to govern social systems throughout history. Feedback theory or cybernetics is a body of methods and principles developed during the last hundred years dealing with the way decisions, and the way they are imbedded in information channels, cause the dynamic behavior of systems. Computer simulation allows one to determine the time-varying behavior implicit in the complex structure of a system.

*Traditional Management.* Traditional management is the general process through which people arrive at decisions. The process starts with an observation of the world about, notation of the pressures

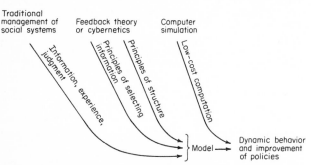

**Fig. S-9. Background of system dynamics.**

and reactions of people and groups, and detection of the linkages and flows of information and influence. From these observations, mental images or models of the structure of a social system are formed. Finally, the mental images are used to anticipate what will happen next and to take actions to alter that behavior, if necessary.

Traditional management, based on observation and judgment, has great strengths. One derives from the wealth of information available from the separate observations and experiences of people. In their mental stores of knowledge are probably a thousand or a million times more information than has been converted to written form in libraries. In turn, written descriptions cover a thousand or a million times the scope and richness of information that is available in measured and numerical form. A second strength of traditional management, which makes the first usable, is that people accurately perceive first-order cause and effect linkages within a system. As noted below, errors in translating this information into action generally create problem behavior. In past system dynamics studies, a model based on the cause and effect linkages as perceived by system participants recreates system behavior. Management error has been not so much in perceiving the individual linkages as in translating the multitude of individual linkages into an understanding of the way the system as a whole behaves.

As a result, the system dynamics approach builds on the comprehensive, reasonably accurate information base of the traditional management process. But

system dynamics goes further to overcome several weaknesses of traditional management.

*Feedback Theory.* The first weakness in traditional management arises from the very wealth of information that is its greatest strength. In fact, we have too much information—we are flooded and overwhelmed with it. The traditional processes contain no general principles or organized philosophy for picking the relevant from the extraneous information. As indicated in Fig. S-9, in the system dynamics approach principles drawn from feedback theory assist in choosing from the excess of information that which is relevant to the behavior modes of interest. Feedback theory provides guidelines for the construction of verbal models.

A second weakness of traditional management arises from lack of organizing principles for the structuring of information. Even if the first weakness is overcome and the relevant information and relationships are chosen, no guidelines exist for organizing the chosen assumptions into a structure that explains the observed system behavior. Again, feedback theory offers principles for simplifying and organizing the structure of a system, that is, principles for translating the verbal model into the mathematical model.

*Computer Simulation.* But even if information is effectively selected and usefully organized into a relevant model, traditional management encounters a third weakness. Although assumptions may be explicitly stated, the human mind is not well adapted to determining the future time-varying consequences of those assumptions. Different people may accept the same assumptions and structure, then draw contrary conclusions. A consensus is hard to reach, and even a majority opinion may be incorrect. As suggested in Fig. S-9, computer simulation can be used to determine, without doubt, the future dynamic implications of a specific set of assumptions.

**Summary** System dynamics starts from the practical world of normal industrial and economic management. It does not begin with abstract theory, nor is it restricted to the limited information available in numerical form. Instead it uses the descriptive knowledge of the operating arena about structure, along with available experience about decision making. Such inputs are augmented where possible by written description, theory, and numerical data. Feedback theory is used as a guide for selecting and filtering information to yield the structure and numerical values for a computer simulation model. Because the resulting models are too complex for either intuitive or mathematical solution, a computer simulates, or plays the roles, of the many participants in the system to determine how they interact with one another to produce changing patterns of behavior as time progresses.

## SYSTEM DYNAMICS PRINCIPLES

**Structure of Systems**   Feedback theory has demonstrated that, for the purpose of understanding dynamic behavior, systems are best viewed as having a structure consisting of two elements:

1. A set of interconnected feedback loops of causal forces within a closed system boundary

2. Variables of two basic types—*levels*, or accumulations, and *rates*, or flows, which alter the levels

These two elements provide the necessary framework for organizing information about a system so as to determine its dynamic behavior.

A causal feedback loop, as illustrated in Fig. S-10a, is any circular chain of causally related variables. This figure indicates that variable A influences

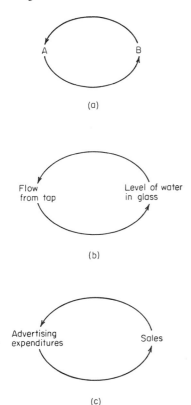

(a)

(b)

(c)

**Fig. S-10. Feedback loops.**

variable B and that variable B in turn affects variable A.

The concept of feedback is extremely important because it underlies all dynamic behavior. Yet most discussion and analysis stops with the statement that an action leads to a result; for example, the flow of water from a tap fills a glass (Fig. S-10b), or changes in advertising expenditures change sales (Fig. S-10c). But it is as correct to say that the increasing level of water in the glass turns off the tap, or that changes in sales induce changes in advertising. The other portion of a system, the policy statement which changes the action, is always present. A complete model of a system includes both the way the action determines a result and the way changes in the result lead to further action. Such a model thereby describes the process of change in a system.

The behavior or direction of change in a system depends on whether the controlling feedback loop is positive or negative. A *positive feedback loop* exists whenever action A increases result R (as indicated by the plus sign at the end of the arrow in Fig. S-11a) and the increase in R leads to further increase in action A. Figure S-11b gives an example: Interest payments, the action, increase bank balance, the result; an increase in bank balance further increases interest payments. Exponential growth is the dynamic behavior pattern of this interest–bank balance system, and of any positive feedback loop acting in isolation.

At this point it is useful to introduce the second element of the model structure of system dynamics—levels and rates. In Fig. S-11c, bank balance is a level variable (denoted by the rectangular symbol) or an accumulation of the rate or flow of interest payments (denoted by the valvelike symbol). The action flow is denoted by a solid arrow, moving dollars from a level outside the system (a source or sink represented by the cloudlike symbol) into the bank balance. An information flow, which does not alter the bank balance level, is denoted by a dashed arrow. In Fig. S-11c, information about bank balance is combined with information about interest rate (here a constant as represented by a solid line under the variable name) to determine interest payments.

A *negative feedback loop* exists whenever an increase in action A increases result R, but the increase in R then causes a decrease in further action (denoted by the negative sign at the end of the arrow in Fig. S-12a). Figure S-12b gives an example in which the firm strives to maintain a desired cash balance, borrowing (or investing) to correct any discrepancy between desired and actual cash balance. Negative feedback loops are goal-seeking. Action is stimulated whenever actual system conditions differ from desired system conditions. Figure S-12c depicts the level-rate structure of the cash balance system.

In summary, a system dynamics model consists of the set of interconnected feedback loops of causal

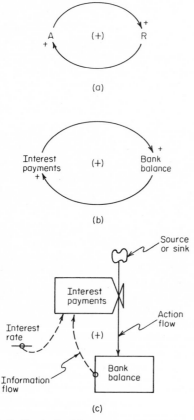

(a)

(b)

(c)

**Fig. S-11. Positive feedback loop.**

forces believed to underlie the dynamic behavior of interest. Within the model (and the system), positive feedback loops are responsible for any growth tendencies and can also contribute to any deviations from desired conditions. Negative feedback loops strive to achieve a goal and in the process can create instability or stagnation. Each feedback loop consists of one or more levels and rates. Equations describing these levels and rates are simulated on a digital computer to determine the dynamic behavior of the model. Policies are changed so as to improve the behavior of the models (and systems). Simulation and policy design are discussed further below.

**Features of System Dynamics Methodology** In addition to the theory of structure just discussed, the system dynamics methodology embodies several other features and underlying viewpoints which distinguish it from other modeling approaches. These features include (1) an emphasis on understanding the causes of dynamic behavior; (2) inclusion of all variables relevant to the problem behavior; (3) a focus on policy design rather than decision making or forecasting. Although other modeling techniques embody some of these features, system dynamics appears to be unique in combining all these aspects into a single approach.

*Understanding Behavior.* A system dynamics model is constructed in order to gain insight into the causes of a particular mode of behavior. Modes of behavior include growth, unstable growth, stagnation, decay, and cyclical instability. A model might also be constructed to gain insight into the causes of a shift in behavior mode, say, from growth to stag-

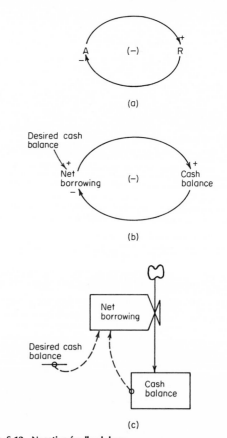

(a)

(b)

(c)

**Fig. S-12. Negative feedback loop.**

nation. [The behavior of population, industry, and housing in older cities exhibits a time pattern of growth giving way to a period of stability or even slight decline (stagnation). Some industries, for example the railroad industry, and some companies exhibit similar growth-to-stagnation behavior.] Once such insight is obtained, the model is then used to explore changes in system structure which improve behavior in the model and might do so when implemented in the real system.

*Inclusion of All Variables.* The emphasis on understanding and changing behavior necessitates that all variables relevant to the problem behavior be included in the model. Consequently, a system dynamics model may include causal feedback loops which cross departmental or functional boundaries and which interrelate the firm, competitors, and the market for its product. Problems of loss of market share and fluctuating employment often stem from such interactions. Moreover, the model may contain variables which have not or cannot be objectively measured (for example, expectations, perceptions, and attitudes). If these variables contribute to dynamic behavior, they must be included in a model which aims to understand the causes of such behavior; omission of these variables would be equivalent to saying that they exert no impact of significance. As a result, a system dynamics model is drawn more from descriptive information about the way people act and the way decisions are made under different circumstances, pressures, and motivations than from the much smaller and limited collection of numerical data.

*Focus on Policy.* An important objective of the modeling process is to produce a set of policy recommendations that are internally and mutually consistent and which lead to desired behavior. It is important to distinguish here between policy and decisions. A *policy*, as analyzed in a system dynamics model, is a general rule or guideline that states the way decisions are made, under all circumstances, on the basis of available information. For example, a policy might state the way a firm's dividend payments depend on earnings, earnings growth rate, return on equity, and cash availability. In contrast, a *decision* is the result of application of the policy to a specific set of information; for example, it would be a decision to pay $2 per share in dividends if earnings per share are $3, earnings growth rate 3 percent per year, return on equity 10 percent, and cash equal to desired cash. In some cases policies are written and explicit (as for travel expense reimbursement), while in others they are unwritten and implicit, based on habit, conformity, social pressures, ingrained concepts of goals, awareness of power centers within an organization, and personal interest (as for dividend payments). A system dynamics model provides a vehicle for testing the effects of various policies on the behavior of the overall system.

The policy focus of a system dynamics model can also be contrasted with the objective of predicting the exact future state of the system 1 or 2 years hence. Social systems, such as a firm or industry, are subject to numerous random influences. The presence of such random disturbances tends to preclude forecasting the state of the firm far enough ahead to allow time for effective action. Moreover, the behavior of the system is dependent on the forecasting process—because forecasting is part of the feedback loop structure. On the other hand, even if the future condition of the firm cannot be forecast accurately, effective policies can still be designed to improve the overall mode of behavior. Thus, for example, a model might be used to design policies that would minimize fluctuations in production and employment triggered by random disturbance.

**Simulation** The term *simulation*, as used here, refers to the process of step-by-step solution for the values of model variables. In the simulation process, the values of the level variables at the next future time (say, time 1) are calculated by adding to the present values of the level variables (at time 0) the rates of flow over the solution interval (from 0 to 1). The rates of flow over the next solution interval (from 1 to 2) are then calculated, as specified by the model equations, on the basis of the value of the levels at time 1. The process is repeated until the desired simulation length is reached.

Table S-16 gives an example. In Table S-16*a*, model equations for the cash balance model of Fig. S-12*c* are given. Equation 1, a level equation, states that cash balance $CB$ at time $t$ plus $\Delta t$ equals cash balance at time $t$ plus the solution interval $\Delta t$ multiplied by net borrowing $NB$, as calculated at time $t$. Cash balance at time zero is arbitrarily set to zero. Equation 2 is a rate equation defining net borrowing $NB$. Here $NB$ is set equal to the difference between desired cash balance $DCB$ and cash balance $CB$, divided by the time to adjust cash balance $TACB$. $DCB$ and $TACB$ are arbitrarily set at $100 and 4 days, respectively.

Table S-16*b* gives the simulation output for five periods. At time zero, cash balance $CB$ is zero. Consequently, net borrowing $NB$ at time zero (and over the interval from zero to 1) equals $25 per day. At time 1, $CB(1)$ is calculated to $CB(0)$ plus $NB(0)$,

**TABLE S-16  Simulation Example**

(a) Model equations for Fig. S-12c

(1) $CB(t + \Delta t) = CB(t) + [\Delta t)(NB(t)]$  
$CB(0) = 0$                 Cash balance, \$

(2) $NB(t) = \dfrac{DCB - CB(t)}{TACB}$        Net borrowing, \$/day

where   $DCB = 100$        Desired cash balance, \$  
        $TACB = 4$ days      Time to adjust cash balance  
        $\Delta t = 1$ day        Delta time, simulation solution interval

(b) Simulation output

| Time periods | CB, dollars | NB, dollars |
|---|---|---|
| 0 | 0 | 25 |
| 1 | 25 | 18.75 |
| 2 | 43.75 | 14.06 |
| 3 | 57.81 | 10.55 |
| 4 | 68.36 | 7.91 |
| 5 | 76.27 | 5.93 |

or $0 + 25 = 25$; $NB(1)$ is then calculated as 18.75. The reader is urged to execute the additional steps.

Simulation, therefore, is a relatively simple procedure which can be carried out by hand. The computer, however, makes the simulation of social system models practical.

## SYSTEM DYNAMICS APPLICATIONS

Industrial applications of system dynamics take two forms: generic studies of problems common to many firms and studies of specific companies or industries. System dynamics has also been applied to biological, economic, and urban systems.

*Generic industrial studies* provide material for (1) the understanding of the behavioral problems created by the interactions among the parts of the firm and between the firm and the market, (2) the teaching of top management policy issues, and (3) the development of models and policies in specific applications. The generic studies deal with two major problem areas: production and employment instability, and corporate growth. Production and employment studies illustrate the manner in which inventory ordering, employment, and production policies, either individually or in consort, can create a regular cyclic behavior pattern in the face of random variations in such inputs as normal sales rate. Corporate growth studies examine the way policies for the acquisition of production resources (labor, parts and materials inventory, machinery, floor space), financial resources, and professional resources (marketing, research and development, and management)

affect the firm's growth pattern. Different realistic policies can create such varied patterns as rapid, smooth growth, growth intermixed with periods of leveling off or decline, and stagnation. In the generic studies, policies which alleviate the problem behavior are developed.

*Corporate studies* using system dynamics have dealt with production and employment instability, loss of market share, commodity price fluctuations, declining profitability, inventory cycles, and personnel fluctuations, as well as many more dynamic behavior problems. A short list of firms which have in some way used system dynamics includes: Coca-Cola Company, Cummins Engine Company, Digital Equipment Corporation, IBM Corporation, Eastman Kodak Company, Polaroid Corporation, and Sprague Electric Company. Model details and policy conclusions in most corporate studies are proprietary and, therefore, have never been published.

Because the ideas of feedback loops and level-rate structure are universal in describing the process of change, system dynamics has been applied to many seemingly diverse areas: blood sugar regulation in the human body (focusing on treatments for diabetes), fluctuations in commodity markets, the growth and stagnation of urban areas, the interactions between major population and industrial forces on a worldwide basis, and the problem of heroin addiction. Most recently, system dynamics is being applied to the analysis of the various business cycles: the 3- to 7-year business cycle, the 18- to 20-year Kuznet cycle, and the 50-year Kondratieff cycle, or long-wave cycle.

## IMPLEMENTATION PROBLEMS

System dynamics has been applied successfully in many diverse areas. Yet, successful applications are not easily developed, or two reasons. First, despite its apparent simplicity and ease of communication (system dynamics has been taught at the elementary school level), system dynamics models (particularly models which will result in corporate or social system policy change) are difficult for the novice to construct, analyze, and improve. One can pick up an understanding of system dynamics in several weeks of intensive study and begin to develop simple models within several months, but several years of practice are required before one is capable of developing complex models in a new area.

Second, system dynamics models require significant managerial input for their development (recall the primary information source for a system dynamics model). Moreover, implementation of change in corporate policy will not occur until management "believes" the model, a "belief" which will not result until the manager understands the model. But how much managerial time is spent on the long-range, strategic policy design questions which system dynamics is suited for? In many firms, very little. Managers, including top management, are too often involved in day-to-day operating decisions and "fire fighting," rather than in the design of policies to prevent future fires. Without a significant input from top management, the system dynamics study will produce little in terms of implemented results.

*See also* COMPUTER SYSTEMS; CONTROL SYSTEMS, MANAGEMENT; OPERATIONS RESEARCH AND MATHEMATICAL MODELING; PLANNING, STRATEGIC MANAGERIAL; PLANNING, STRATEGIC PLANNING MODELS; STATISTICAL ANALYSIS FOR MANAGEMENT; SYSTEM CONCEPT, TOTAL.

### REFERENCES

*Methodology:*
Forrester, Jay W.: *Industrial Dynamics*, The M.I.T. Press, Cambridge, Mass., 1961.
————: *Principles of Systems*, Wright-Allen Press, Cambridge, Mass., 1968.
Goodman, Michael R.: *Study Notes in System Dynamics*, Wright-Allen Press, Cambridge, Mass., 1974.
Pugh, Alexander L., III: *DYNAMO II User's Manual*, 4th ed., The M.I.T. Press, Cambridge, Mass., 1973.

*Generic Industrial Applications:*
Lyneis, James M.: "Introduction to Industrial Dynamics," System Dynamics Group Memorandum D-2764-1, M.I.T. System Dynamics Group, Cambridge, Mass., 1976. (Will be in book form within 2 years.)
Roberts, Edward B.: *The Dynamics of Research and Development*, Harper & Row, Publishers, Inc., New York, 1964.

*Corporate Industrial Applications:*
Roberts, Edward B.: *Managerial Applications of System Dynamics*, the M.I.T. Press, Cambridge, Mass., 1978.
*System Dynamics Newsletter*, M.I.T. System Dynamics Group, Cambridge, Mass. (yearly).

*Other Applications:*
Forrester, Jay W.: *Urban Dynamics*, The M.I.T. Press, Cambridge, Mass., 1969.
Mass, Nathaniel J.: *Economic Cycles: An Analysis of Underlying Causes*, Wright-Allen Press, Cambridge, Mass., 1975.
Meadows, Donella H., Dennis L. Meadows, Jorgen Randers, and William W. Behrens III: *The Limits to Growth*, Universe Books, New York, 1972.
Roberts, Edward B., Gary B. Hirsch, and Gilbert Levin: *The Persistant Poppy: A Computer Aided Search for Heroin Policy*, Ballinger Publishing Company, Cambridge, Mass., 1975.

JAMES M. LYNEIS, *Massachusetts Institute of Technology*

# System 4

System 4 is the designation given by Rensis Likert to a participative-democratic style of management. Also known as *participative-group management*, it is highly employee-centered. Likert considers it to be the best style of leadership, one which over time will bring the highest improvement in goal performances as well as the greatest satisfaction of subordinates. Its crucial components are the complete confidence of management in subordinates and the decentralization of decision making within a mutually trusting, friendly environment.

In the early 1960s, after conducting leadership research in hundreds of organizations, Rensis Likert, director of the Institute for Social Research at the University of Michigan, discovered four basic management styles. He labeled them systems 1, 2, 3, and 4. These designations can be applied to both individual managers and an organization as a whole.

In the course of attempting to measure those intervening variables which he believed inevitably affect the casual variables of managerial behavior, Likert discerned a continuum of four managerial styles. System 1, at one extreme, is exploitive-authoritative; system 2, benevolent-authoritative; system 3, consultative-democratic, and system 4, at the other end the continuum, is participative-democratic. It is characterized by: (1) communication initiated at all levels; (2) full use by management of economic, ego, and other motives; (3) high performance goals; (4) a feeling of responsibility by personnel for the organization's goals; (5) decision makers being well aware of problems; (6) widespread responsibility for review and control; (7) formal and informal organizations usually identical; (8) control data used for problem solving, not punishment. In these assumptions system 4 closely approximates theory Y, as system 1 similarly approximates theory X, as developed by McGregor.

Likert and his associates concurrently developed an instrument to evaluate the leadership style of a manager or of a group. Used periodically, the instrument provides a profile of style which can also serve to predict end results, such as profits and costs, of human performance.

Research tends to support the reports of Likert that most managers believe that high-producing departments use a system 4 style. There is some question concerning the objectivity and the relative crudity of the measuring instrument, which clearly needs further validation by research. In sum, however, widespread opinion generally accepts system 4 as the embodiment of good management practice.

*See also* HYGIENE FACTORS; LEADERSHIP; MOTIVATION IN ORGANIZATIONS; THEORY X AND THEORY Y.

### REFERENCES
Harrison, Roger: "Understanding Your Organization's Character," *Harvard Business Review*, May–June 1972, p. 119.

Likert, Rensis: *The Human Organization*, McGraw-Hill Book Company, New York, 1967.

———: *New Patterns of Management*, McGraw-Hill Book Company, 1961.

Stogdill, R. M.: *Handbook of Leadership: A Survey of Theory and Research*, Free Press, New York, 1974.

STAFF/HOKE

## System study sheet (*See* PAPER WORK SIMPLIFICATION.)

## Systems, analysis of (*See* SYSTEM CONCEPT, TOTAL.)

## Systems, balanced and unbalanced, MIS [*See* INFORMATION SYSTEMS, MANAGEMENT (MIS), IN LARGE ORGANIZATIONS.]

## Systems, hierarchy of (*See* SYSTEM CONCEPT, TOTAL.)

## Systems, integrated (*See* DATA PROCESSING PRINCIPLES AND PRACTICES.)

## Systems, marketing (*See* MARKETING, CONCEPTS AND SYSTEMS.)

## Systems analysis and control techniques (*See heading in Table of Contents for complete listing.*)

## Systems approach (*See* MANAGEMENT THEORY, SCIENCE, AND APPROACHES.)

## Systems design (*See* PRODUCTION PROCESSES.)

## Systems performance levels, MIS [*See* INFORMATION SYSTEMS, MANAGEMENT (MIS), IN LARGE ORGANIZATIONS.]

## Systems and procedures

Systems and procedures analysis, which had its origins in the study and improvement of information, communications, and paper work flow within an organization, has gradually extended its scope to include just about any kind of integrated analysis and improvement of the various functional aspects of an organization. Responsibility for it may be the domain of a separate systems (or systems and procedures) department, it may fall under the wing of an industrial engineering department, or it may be wholly the work of a management information systems activity. A fully operative systems function will include the talents of systems specialists such as operations research and statistical people, industrial and methods engineers, forms designers, records management analysts, and data processing and equipment experts. These talents may be those of full-time employees, or they may be obtained on a periodic consultative basis.

**Activities** Systems analysis, design, and implementation draw from a wide range of activities and from many fields. Typically these encompass a number of stages such as the following, but not necessarily in this order.

1. *Objectives verification.* Akin to strategic planning, a starting point for most systems studies is the identification of a company's long-term goals together with its implementation strategies. This study ranges downward from broad organizational goals to specific, functional, and departmental goals.

In many instances, it focuses on the administrative aspects of information processing and management.

2. *Implementation analysis.* An effort is made to relate (*a*) the various processes and functions performed by the company to (*b*) its cbosen goals. This helps to uncover overlapping and superfluous activities as well as gaps in necessary coverage. The underlying questions are: Does every activity now performed contribute to identifiable objectives? In the most effective manner? While not omitting anything that is absolutely necessary? Industrial engineers are especially effective in this phase.

3. *Information analysis.* Presuming that the existing, or revised, operating system is effective, a determination must be made of the information needed at all decision points to keep it operative. Key questions are: What kind of information is needed? At what points? When? In what form?

4. *Communications analysis.* Each organization adapts itself to its own best communication channels, and information flow must respect these channels, although it may by-pass some channels and be redundant in others. Organization development specialists can make great contributions to phases 3 and 4.

5. *Systems design.* At some stage of analysis, it becomes imperative to put together—as well as possible, perfection being rarely possible—the implementation process activities (and structure), the communication channels, and the required information. The system must fit the restraints of all three elements. This is the stage in which operations research experts are best utilized.

6. *Systems transformation.* Only after the unifying system has been designed can data processing specialists convert the system to an information processing system. At this phase those with know-how about hardware and software make their greatest contribution.

7. *Forms design.* This calls for a determination of the best form or format upon (or with) which to collect information, transmit it through the system, and present it to the various decision makers. This is a specialty requiring knowledge ranging from that of human perceptions to the extensive mechanics of reproduction materials and devices.

8. *Records procedures.* The line between forms and records is indistinct, but the former tends to emphasize physical considerations while the latter is more concerned with the sequences of information flow and with establishing policy about records dissemination, retention, and retrieval.

9. *Equipment specification.* Systems design recognizes the ubiquitous interface between person and machine and the need to delineate exactly what each will do. Ideally, the machine will be required to perform that portion of the work that it can do better, faster, or more economically than human beings. Therein lies the critical aspect of equipment specification and selection, a field of expertise dominated by equipment manufacturers and consultants.

10. *Electronic adaptation.* Electronic equipment—the computer and its ancillaries—is especially suitable for the data processing required by complex systems. Most systems ultimately must depend upon the computer's capabilities, and few systems should be accepted that do not acknowledge that eventuality.

11. *Work measurement.* Presuming that there is concern for the effectiveness of administrative systems (as distinguished from production systems, although a total system approach would not view them separately), operating procedures and work requirements should be based upon a systematic study of the human work involved. This can be obtained by such techniques as time and motion study, predetermined time standards, activity charting, and work sampling.

12. *Work standardization.* The publication of procedures to be followed by those who operate the system requires that work be defined and routinized along with the specification of quantitative time and/or cost standards.

13. *Work simplification.* Somewhere along the line of system study and specification, thought should be given to improvement in—or simplification of—work methods, especially those related to paperwork and administrative services such as mail handling, word processing, key punching, and reproduction functions.

14. *Procedures preparation.* This is the phase that joins procedures to systems and in which all the previous decisions about design, forms, and equipment are formalized into a prescribed (and written) set of policies, standards, and procedures.

15. *Procedures publication.* Most organizations find it useful, if not absolutely necessary, to publish their policies and procedures in the form of manuals that are distributed to management and/or operations personnel in the various functional areas. These are used for instruction, training, and reference and must be updated periodically as the system itself evolves or is redesigned. Communications specialists are especially useful in phases 14 and 15.

16. *Organization development.* In its ultimate form, systems and procedures analysis may begin with a study and redevelopment of the company's organization relationships and basic structure. This involves the defining of new goals and the establishment of new strategies beginning at the top and

cascading downward throughout the organization. If a company chooses this route, only after this phase is completed would the other 15 phases be considered. Organization development (OD) is typically conducted under the guidance of organizational and behavioral specialists.

Systems work, by its very designation, implies unification rather than fragmentation. It would be short-sighted, however, to suggest that the principles can be applied only to a company's total system. In many instances, because of internally or externally imposed restrictions, the systems approach can be applied effectively to the system that exists within a department or even a small work group. It is better to first design the overall system, of course, and then integrate the smaller system, but the work of any single function or department can be attacked independently.

*See also* ADMINISTRATIVE MANAGEMENT; DATA PROCESSING PRINCIPLES AND PRACTICES; FORMS DESIGN AND CONTROL; GANTT CHARTS; MANUALS, POLICY AND PROCEDURE; OFFICE SPACE PLANNING AND LAYOUT; PAPER WORK SIMPLIFICATION; POLICY FORMULATION AND IMPLEMENTATION; RECORDS MANAGEMENT; SCHEDULING, SHORT INTERVAL; SYSTEM CONCEPT, TOTAL; WORK DESIGN; WORK MEASUREMENT; WORK SIMPLIFICATION AND IMPROVEMENT.

### REFERENCES

Daniels, Alan, and Donald Yeates, ed.: *Systems Analysis*, Science Research Associates, Inc., Chicago, 1971.

Glans, Thomas B., Burton Grad, and David Holstein: *Management Systems*, Holt, Rinehart and Winston, Inc., New York, 1968.

Heyel, Carl, ed.: *Handbook of Modern Office Management and Administrative Services*, McGraw-Hill Book Company, New York, 1971.

McFarlan, F. Warren, Richard L. Nolan, and David P. Norton: *Information System Administration*, Holt, Rinehart and Winston, Inc., New York, 1973.

Martino, R. L.: *Management Information Systems*, McGraw-Hill Book Company, New York, 1970.

STAFF/BITTEL

## Systems psychology  (*See* HUMAN FACTORS ENGINEERING.)

**T**

**T-group training** (*See* LEADERSHIP.)

**Target industrial program (OSHA)**
(*See* SAFETY AND HEALTH MANAGEMENT, EM-
PLOYEE.)

**Target rate of return goals** (*See* OBJEC-
TIVES AND GOALS.)

**Targets** (*See* OBJECTIVES AND GOALS.)

**Tariffs** (*See* INTERNATIONAL TRADE.)

**Task analysis** (*See* HUMAN FACTORS ENGI-
NEERING.)

**Task data sheet** (*See* PAPER WORK SIMPLIFI-
CATION.)

**Task force management** (*See* PROJECT
AND TASK FORCE MANAGEMENT.)

**Task method** (*See* ADVERTISING MANAGE-
MENT, INDUSTRIAL.)

**Task redesign** (*See* MOTIVATION IN ORGANI-
ZATIONS.)

**Task uncertainty** (*See* ORGANIZATION STRUC-
TURES AND CHARTING.)

**Tax department, corporate** (*See* TAX
MANAGEMENT, MANAGERIAL RESPONSIBILITY FOR
FEDERAL INCOME TAX REPORTING.)

**Tax management, managerial respon-
sibility for federal income tax
reporting**

Management responsibilities for federal income tax
accounting are examined here from the standpoint
of some of the critical topics and policy issues of
concern to the generalist corporate manager. Emphasis is placed on what a manager should look for,
be alert to, and identify in ongoing business transac-

tions and planning as constituting either turning points for policy decisions or managerial danger signs. The tax law is and has been undergoing constant changes; hence there is a need for caution in using any publication addressing substantive topics. Subjects included, however, have a fairly high degree of fundamental stability, and the principles highlighted should have a continuing applicability. Constraints imposed by space cause the content here to be highly selective and, as to the substantive areas, only illustrative.

## THE CORPORATE TAX DEPARTMENT

An effective tax department must be directed toward the objective of meeting corporate tax obligations with a minimum of friction with the Internal Revenue Service (IRS) in the compliance areas that can be described as "no win."

The "no win" area means that failure to comply can result only in a disservice to the corporation; there can be no real benefits. Examples are failure to file required returns, failure to meet advance payment requirements, failure to make timely elections, and failure to properly execute tax and related forms so they will process through the IRS data processing system. Not only are interest and penalties significantly high for these kinds of failures, but the resulting deluge of computer-generated correspondence will be time-consuming and can result in compounding the error.

The managerial task of making certain the department is meeting the many recurring tax requirements imposed by government is, indeed, substantial. While this entry is concerned with federal income tax accounting, the multistate corporate operation must meet filing requirements in many states, as well as municipalities, townships, and counties. In terms of volume, these state requirements can exceed the federal by as much as 50 times in even the medium-sized multistate operation. Thus, more department personnel must be assigned to state returns than to federal requirements.

One key to effective handling of these numerous recurring responsibilities is the use of a master tax calendar. The calendar carries due dates for every type of requirement that will have to be met during the year. In addition to the calendar, various cross-checks are maintained, including the alert provided by receipt of blank forms from the IRS or state tax agency, calendars offered by various commercial publications, and the use of a computer to provide workload schedules.

## THE TAX AUDIT

Management does have a responsibility to set the climate in terms of relationships between the corporation and IRS, the administering agency. Management may unwisely abdicate this responsibility and leave it to the tax department, or worse, may establish the climate by bad example: i.e., consistently skirting the edge of compliance or engaging in practices that smack of evasion. The best atttiudinal stance is one of enlightened self-interest, vigorously asserting and protecting the corporate rights on the basis of "what's right" and, when necessary, disagreeing without being disagreeable.

Management can gain insight as to both the efficiency and attitudinal stance of the corporate tax department as a result of an examination of corporate records by internal revenue agents. Normally, all the very large corporations are audited each year. The "team audit" concept is used; the team consists of various experts such as engineers who are skilled in depreciable equipment, pension trust specialists, computer specialists who are able to cope with computerized records, and one or more revenue agents who are generalists in corporate examinations. If a corporate taxpayer is found to be in substantial compliance, the service may forgo an audit for one or more years.

**Impact on Operations**  An effective tax department will keep management apprised throughout the course of the audit as to the issues being raised. The audit may well proceed for several months, and, to the extent practicable, issues may be disposed of concurrently to avoid bunching at the conclusion. The issues are often those which involve shifts of income or deductions between or among years. The benefit of a deduction usually will not be lost but rather postponed. As to larger items of this kind which are conceded, management will be concerned with (1) what causal factors are responsible for the adjustment, and (2) what will be the impact of the deficiency on cash flow.

Other issues will have an adverse, irretrievable tax impact on the corporation or its officers or shareholders. If the amount is large, management usually regards these adjustments quite seriously and will carefully consider the likelihood of prevailing through further administrative and judicial action.

**Audit Process**  For various reasons, evaluation of the tax department and other related corporate functions, i.e., accounting, data processing, and internal audit, on the basis of results of an IRS audit can be difficult and frustrating. First, the issue list is often very long; it will change in the course of conferences at the agent level and, if protested, at higher administrative and/or judicial levels. Second, the procedure usually takes a great deal of time. Thus, even with current briefings, the manager will have difficulty tracking the process.

Additionally, the results of prior audits are only a partial guide to the current or future audits. This circumstance is the product of a number of factors: (1) while audits have become more thorough and more penetrating under the "large case" program, the effectiveness will vary among agents or "teams"; (2) the IRS is constantly gaining new insights into old problems, e.g., the computer-assisted audits have ensured that a mass of transactions recorded on magnetic tape are no longer free from scrutiny; and (3) new issues are constantly being identified which have industry-wide significance.

Nonetheless, it is important that, to the extent feasible, the evaluation referred to above be undertaken. The effort may lead to routines within the accounting department where classification between repair and capital are the subject of inadequate instruction or where cost-accounting procedures have fragmentized transactions to the end that major capital items may be buried or in-house construction is not properly classified as to repairs and new structures.

Management of the larger corporate entity must think in terms of internal and/or external audit entirely aside from IRS. This kind of tool can provide a realistic cross-check by professionals skilled in their function. Reports can be produced which provide management with an opportunity for corrective action. Whether such action will be taken depends on the quality of management itself.

**Criminal Aspects** The corporate entity which has been indifferent to IRS oversight can be in for a major shock where an IRS audit uncovers proscribed campaign contributions, major executive use of corporate facilities for personal use, and expenditures to influence potential buyer-representatives. These kinds of transactions, once identified, can rather readily lead to a criminal investigation.

The criminal investigation of a major corporate entity can pose numerous problems for the IRS, such as the difficulty of identifying the responsible official and showing that the conduct was with knowledge of its wrongful nature. Responsible management, however, will never want to reach the point where its security rests on the difficulties such an investigation and successful prosecution pose.

Tax executives of major companies are fully aware that IRS has a strong internal security program and that attempting to bribe an agent is "not

worth it." Agents are constantly indoctrinated as to methods of handling the bribe proffer. Some managers, however, may obtain an erroneous idea that the sophisticated way to handle a difficult issue is through bribing the agent. To those, we can say that even the amoral are deterred when the risk of detection is substantial. Regardless of whether it seems to have worked in the past, or the agent seems receptive, such a course should never be adopted. Entertainment of the agent(s), even in modest ways, is proscribed by the IRS.

## TRUST FUND DEPOSITORIES

The delinquent trust fund problem is endemic to the corporation with a serious "cash flow" problem. The sizeable amounts of money involved in withholding of federal income taxes and the ever-increasing rates and ceiling of salaries subject to the Federal Insurance Contribution Act (Social Security) involve a constant temptation for hard-pressed management to pay only the net salaries to employees and defer the trust fund amounts for resolution at a future time. Under the prodding of various administrations, Congress has enacted an increasingly stringent series of remedies for failure of the taxpayer to make trust fund deposits.

In overall terms, management needs to be aware of the following provisions: (1) failure-to-file penalty, (2) failure-to-pay penalty, (3) interest rates on delinquent amounts, (4) mandatory deposit of trust funds, (5) the 100 percent penalty, and (6) criminal sanctions.

**Pay-As-You-Go Requirements** The concept of "pay-as-you-go," so well illustrated by individual withholding of federal income tax and Social Security tax (FICA) and their companion piece, the declaration of estimated tax (form 1040ES) for current payment of an individual's tax, has over the years not only been spread through nearly the entire system of federal tax liabilities, but it has often been accelerated so that now the funds are remitted to the Treasury at the earliest practicable date.

In general, corporations are required to deposit estimated tax payments with an authorized commercial bank depository or Federal Reserve Bank during the taxable year if the corporation's estimated tax can be expected to be $40.00 or more. No estimated return as such is required, but the depository receipts are listed on the U.S. Corporation Income Tax Return, form 1120, filed for the taxable year.

With very limited exceptions, the corporation will, as an employer, also be liable for federal unemployment tax (FUTA). The return (form 940) is to be filed on or before January 31 following the calendar year, and during each year the corporation must make a computation to determine whether it is liable for quarterly deposits of the tax to an authorized commercial bank or Federal Reserve Bank.

From a managerial standpoint, however, the most crucial depository requirements are those referred to above, involving income tax and social security tax withheld for employees, plus the employer's share of the latter. These are *crucial* because in any organization with a number of employees large amounts will be involved, and the remedies available to the government for the corporation's failure to comply are, at least, extraordinary.

Deposits must also be made to an authorized commercial bank or Federal Reserve Bank for these "collected" taxes. The return itself, form 941, Employer's Quarterly Federal Tax Return, is due quarterly. The timing of the deposit requirement, however, depends on the amount of taxes currently involved and ranges from quarter-monthly (approximately weekly) to monthly to quarterly.

**Delinquency Penalties**  Civil penalties for failure to deposit, failure to pay, failure to file the return when due, plus an interest rate which is now tied to the prime rate quoted by commercial banks, can have a significant combined dollar impact on the corporation. From a tax policy perspective, the penalties and interest are designed to take any profit out of diverting resources to other applications in lieu of meeting the various depository and payment requirements.

Now management must give consideration throughout the operating year to the requirements for cash flow to meet these depository responsibilities. In earlier years, the corporation could have the benefit of trust funds for the full calendar quarter and to the actual filing of the quarterly employer's return. Similarly, corporate income tax liabilities and federal unemployment tax were payable annually as contrasted to the current "pay-as-you-go" system, which is also without benefit of interest to the corporation for money so deposited.

Management that is seriously hard pressed for cash and opts to paying only net salaries of employees while putting off the inevitable day of payment of the trust fund liabilities needs to be alert to the following extraordinary remedies available to the government.

Statutory authority and administrative procedure exist to require the corporation or other business entity which has employees, collects withholding of federal income taxes and social security taxes therefrom, and has a history of delinquency, to pay over, within 2 banking days, to a designated depository such collections in trust for the United States. Failure of a corporate officer or other responsible person to comply can subject such person to a fine and imprisonment (misdemeanor).

The result of the imposition of the 100 percent penalty is usually the insolvency and bankruptcy of the corporation as either a "no-asset" case or liquidation without full discharge of outstanding trust fund liabilities. In these situations the Internal Revenue Code authorizes the use of a penalty equal to the trust fund taxes unpaid—hence, the term 100 percent penalty.

The penalty can be assessed only against responsible officials who "willfully" failed to collect and pay over to the United States such trust funds. It is usually not too difficult to show that one or more responsible officials had such knowledge. Against an individual's personal estate, these assessments are often so large as to be devastating. The assessment also will be joint and several against all responsible officials who willfully failed in their duty.

## MANAGERIAL ASPECTS OF TAX QUESTIONS

It is customary for proposed corporate undertakings to be submitted to the tax department for an opinion when the tax significance is not clear or the exact monetary impact is unknown. In order to formulate a sound opinion, the tax department may need to consult specialists for various facets of the problem.

At the same time, the tax department should, at its own initiative, be submitting staff papers, perhaps a quarterly report, and similar material to top management. In addition, however, the generalist executive can obtain an effective conceptual grasp of the tax significance involved in various projects, plans, and functions. This kind of viewpoint may actually contribute more to the quality of the managerial decision than the expert's opinion. Some examples follow of the methodology which can be used by the generalist in developing skill in this area.

**Depreciation Policy**  While there is a substantial volume of rules governing the treatment of depreciation of assets used in trade or business, in the context of financial planning the following information should meet the manager's needs. Over the last 1½ decades, Congress (following initial action by the executive branch) moved to liberalize depreciation allowances for tax purposes, largely to make U.S. manufacturing more competitive internationally. The liberalization occurred principally in the shortening, unifying, and stabilizing of estimated useful lives and enforcement by IRS through what became known as the Asset Depreciation Range System plus the most generous allowances for depreciation during the initial years of acquisition of business property having a useful life of at least several years. Generically, the latter can be described as fast writeoff provisions such as double-declining balance, additional first-year 20 percent depreciation bonus, and sum of the years digits.

Depreciation can, of course, be deducted only once. Thus, for any major acquisitions of business assets, the manager needs to make a conscious decision as to whether to elect the accelerated write-off provisions. Management may decide to use the fast write-off for all qualifying acquisitions on the ground that neither profits nor taxes will diminish to any degree in the future and, thus, a current maximum deduction is wise. Where the new business involves a substantial outlay for equipment, management may conclude that the taxes saved in the early years will be of great help in improving cash flow for operational needs and/or reducing the need for financing.

*Impact on Capital Gains.* Lastly, the manager should proceed on the premise that depreciated business property sold or disposed of at a gain will probably be taxable at ordinary rather than capital gain rates. Earlier the reverse was true, but along with depreciation liberalization, depreciation recapture rules were enacted to tax at ordinary income tax rates gain attributable to depreciation previously claimed. The distinctions between real and personal property, phase-in rules, and exceptions to depreciation recapture are properly left to the experts, but the above generalizations should be adequate to guide the generalist executive.

**Investment Tax Credit**    The tax policy objective of investment tax credit has been to provide an economic incentive of some consequence to U.S. business; managers, in turn, are concerned with ways to achieve the maximum benefit from the credit, consistent with their business objectives.

*Limitations and Restrictions.* The investment credit is remarkable for the host of limitations and qualifications applicable in order to obtain this valuable direct subtraction from the corporate tax liability otherwise computed. These limitations affect the kind of property acquired, whether new or used, useful life of the property, the type of business

entity acquiring the property, the manner in which it was acquired, the maximum dollar credit in any one year, and a credit recapture for early property disposition.

The restrictions are ameliorated by provisions for the carry-back and carry-forward of unused (or unusable) investment credit and, in general, the pour-through of the credit to a lessee as it relates to new qualifying property.

*Guidelines.* Out of this complex web, there are certain facts the manager may usefully keep in mind. Depending on the applicable law in a given year, the credit ranges from 10 to 11.5 percent of the cost of tangible personal property subject to depreciation; of such credit, generally, the maximum deductible in any year is $25,000 plus 50 percent of the tax liability in excess of the $25,000. Unused credit can be carried back 3 years and forward 7 years. For property with a useful life of less than 3 years, the credit is zero; for a useful life of at least 3 and less than 7 years, the credit is graduated or less than the full percentum.

On close questions relative to the acquisition of equipment, the management may be influenced as to whether the corporation already has unused investment credits available. Similarly, whether a property considered for acquisition is new or used may be important since only up to $100,000 of the cost of the latter may be used for investment credit purposes.

**True and Accurate Accountability**    The objective manager's responsibility for a true and accurate accountability for federal taxes can be sorely tested in the closely held corporation. This is particularly true where such manager reports to a strong, dominate majority shareholder-officer, either by virtue of outright holdings or family relationship among stockholders, and the majority shareholder is either hostile or indifferent to the strictures imposed by the federal tax laws.

It is not practical to cover in detail the numerous statutory, regulatory, and ruling provisions designed to control relevant transactions so as to preclude defeating the federal tax liabilities of corporations, shareholder-officers, and non–shareholder-officers. The manager can be alert, however, to certain categories of business practice which can result in an issue being raised by the IRS:

1. Classification of corporate disbursements as business expense which are in fact dividends in whole or in part, or additional compensation to a non–shareholder-officer.

2. Classification or handling of corporate re-

ceipts or disbursements so as to evade any corporate or individual tax liability.

3. Classification of transactions with the corporation so as to provide the appearance of a capital gain rather than a dividend.

4. Classification of corporate disbursements in violation of public policy as ordinary business expenses.

*Examples of Requirements.* In some instances, by proper planning and execution certain of these transactions can warrant the favorable tax treatment sought. But as the four categories imply, that is generally not the case.

*1. Personal Expenses.* There is a long history of abuses by some shareholder-officers and, in the larger corporations, non–shareholder-officers, of charging personal expenses to the corporation, usually under the heading of travel and entertainment. The current code does require adequate and complete documentation of these expenses; in the absence of records, the deduction will be denied. Personal and business expenses often will be commingled so as to provide a facade of "all business." Civil adjustments by IRS will be either in the form of a simple disallowance of the deduction claimed by the corporation or, in addition, for more blatant cases, the inclusion of the amount as a dividend in the income of the shareholder-officer.

*Excessive compensation* paid to a shareholder-officer is a potential issue where there is a question involving the reasonableness of the salary. This can occur where the shareholder-officer of a profitable corporation disburses funds from the corporation for personal use and classifies the total amount as salary, for which the corporation can obtain a deduction, in lieu of classifying a portion as dividends, wherein the corporation cannot obtain a deduction. In a civil tax case, the burden is on the corporation to show that the salary was reasonable. Where a shareholder has a personal interest in the underlying asset, other expenses of the corporation, such as rents and royalties, can raise a similar question as to reasonableness of the amount, i.e., whether there is really a dividend element involved in the claimed business expense.

Where the corporation is the obligor and a shareholder the obligee, the use of *interest-bearing debt* can be a device for obtaining an interest deduction for the corporation in lieu of a nondeductible dividend; the issue is generally described as "thin incorporation," where the debt greatly exceeds the stock, and IRS will contend that the corporation is undercapitalized.

*2. Common Evasion Schemes.* When the shareholder-officer siphons off corporate gross receipts, thus evading both corporate and individual tax liability, IRS is presented with criminal conduct, and the burden of proof shifts to the government. This kind of conduct is more commonly found in the small closely held corporation in which internal control is either nonexistent or ineffectual. Two examples are these:

The larger corporate entity may be misused by a corporate officer to *deflect miscellaneous receipts,* such as scrap sales, to his or her personal use or to require *kickbacks from suppliers* who are highly dependent on a single corporate vendee.

A potential civil issue is withdrawal of corporate funds by a shareholder as a *non-interest-bearing loan* from the corporation where the loan is not bona fide but simply an undeclared dividend.

*3. Capital Gains.* A shareholder's stock may be redeemed by the corporation, and the shareholder may obtain the benefit of capital gains treatment on the gain; conversely, the transaction may be a mere dividend. Assuming an ongoing corporation, one of the distinctions is whether the shareholder's relative standing as to control is the same after the transaction as before; if it is, a dividend is involved; if some change occurred, the rules must be consulted to determine whether it was a sufficient change to warrant capital gain treatment. If the transaction appears to the manager to be essentially equivalent to a dividend, an expert should be consulted as to the probable tax consequences if, in fact, capital gain treatment is being sought.

*4. Payments to Public Officials.* In recent years extensive publicity of indictments and prosecutions of business executives has created a widespread awareness of the consequences of making proscribed payments to public officials or their agents. From a tax standpoint, deductions for the payoff, bribe, or campaign disbursements by a corporation are denied when they contravene some public policy, usually a state or federal law. When the proscribed payment is deducted and concealed or disguised, both civil and criminal sanctions can be applied to the corporation and the knowledgeable, responsible officers. Nontax statutes may also be applicable. A corporation can be convicted of a crime, although no confinement is possible.

**Accumulated Earnings Tax** Since corporate dividends are nondeductible by the payer corporation and, in general, taxable to the shareholders, writers and speakers will often say corporate earnings are subject to "double taxation." As a consequence, corporate transactions may be shaped so as to avoid or evade such double taxation. Tax laws and enforcement efforts are designed to counter such tactics or require that the objective be achieved only in certain ways.

In this regard, one of the important statutory controls is the accumulated earnings tax. Directors need to know that they may be personally liable to the corporation for any imposition of such tax, which is in addition to the regular corporate income taxes. This additional tax applicability turns on the answer to the question of whether earnings are available, and, if so, whether dividends have been declared, or, if not, whether the accumulated earnings have been appropriately applied to further the business purposes. The directors are responsible for the corporate dividend policy.

Leaving aside the many technical provisions, if the corporation has net income for the taxable year and earned surplus at the beginning of the year is more than $150,000, the manager should make note of whether the dividends declared or to be declared, plus earnings applied or to be applied to expansion, replacement, and similar business purposes will be about equal to the net earnings available for the year. If the answer is no, management should consult its counsel.

Loans to shareholders, investments in securities, and the absence of any concrete plans for the application of earnings are additional flags which should spur the manager to check on the possibility of an accumulated earnings tax and ways to avoid it.

**Carry-Back and Carry-Forward** Congress has recognized the need to ameliorate the result of treating, for tax purposes, each taxable year as an isolated unit. The situation is aggravated by the use of a graduated rate concept in taxing individuals and a surtax rate for the taxation of corporations. Income averaging was adopted to provide relief for the fluctuating income of individuals, and the net operating loss deduction was provided for trade or business. The latter has been made available to most business entities.

The financial manager is generally more concerned with the provisions relating to net operating loss. The basic concept, again, subject to certain exceptions, involves a 3-year carry-back and a 7-year carry-forward for a net operating loss. The net operating loss is basically the excess of allowable deductions over gross income with some adjustments; in the carry-back, carry-over process, the income of the profit year also requires some adjustments. In general, the adjustments are designed to

make certain that only a true operating loss is used to reduce taxable income.

*Acquisitions.* The acquisition of loss corporations, in a rather long-term climate of interest in growth-through-merger-and-reorganization, has been a matter of continual managerial interest. A successor corporation can obtain the benefit of unused net operating losses as a carry-over, but there is a requirement of continuity of ownership from the acquired loss corporation to the new entity. The Tax Reform Act of 1976 adopted new and generally tighter rules to determine whether all, part, or none of a net operating loss carry-over of an acquired corporation will be allowed. Where management anticipates obtaining the benefit of an acquired operating loss, it should consult its experts for an opinion of the impact of the limitations on its use.

**Business Form** Perhaps the majority of managers will have little interest in business forms, e.g., proprietorship, partnership, corporation, owing to the popularity and general suitability of the corporate form of operation for the larger activity. The number of factors involved in exercising a choice as to business form are considerable; only the dominate aspects are discussed here.

From a tax standpoint, proprietorship and partnership net income are reflected directly in the individual or partner's personal federal income tax return. Under the federal income tax laws the partnership is not a taxable entity, but the partnership is required to file an information return.

In contrast, the corporate form does permit alternative choices which involve both advantages and disadvantages. If the owners feel most of the net income will need to be distributed to them to meet their current personal needs, the corporate structure will yield a tax result to the owners substantially similar to a partnership, provided the corporate distribution to the owners is in the form of salaries. If the distribution will need to be some combination of dividend and salaries, the traditional form of corporate operation will be less favorable than a partnership because the dividends are nondeductible in computing corporate income. In the latter situation the Subchapter S corporation is available for most small businesses with not more than 10 shareholders (although in some circumstances the number can be as high as 15) and accords the benefits of both the corporate and partnership arrangement.

If, however, the corporation involves a thriving activity with growth potential, the owners are willing to apply a good portion of retained earnings to attain such growth, and the owners are in higher tax brackets, the lower normal and surtax corporate rates, coupled with a number of fringe benefits the corporate form can offer to owners, can combine to make the corporate format a very viable choice for operations.

Lastly, it must be remembered that nontax considerations may well constitute the turning points in any decision as to which business form is most suitable.

**Caution** Generalist managers can understand, consider, and decide the policy issues inherent in complicated tax questions as they can with any other managerial problem. But, as a practical matter, to do so they must insist that the tax department or tax counsel provide the relevant information in such a fashion that the policy questions are identifiable.

*See also* ACCOUNTING, FINANCIAL; ACCOUNTING, WHOLE-DOLLAR; AUDITING, FINANCIAL; FINANCIAL STATEMENT ANALYSIS.

### REFERENCES

*Employer's Tax Guide*, Circular E, Publication 15, Internal Revenue Service.

*Federal Tax Course*, Prentice-Hall, Inc., Englewood Cliffs, N.J., 1976.

*Income Tax Regulations*, 26 Code of Federal Regulations, part 1.

*Internal Revenue Code of 1954*, Title 26, United States Code.

*Standard Federal Tax Reporter*, 63d ed., Commerce Clearing House, Inc.

*Tax Reform Act of 1976*, Public Law 94-455, Oct. 4, 1976.

DEAN J. BARRON, *Attorney at Law*

## Taxes, ad valorem (*See* REAL ESTATE MANAGEMENT, CORPORATE.)

## Taylor, Frederick W. (*See* MANAGEMENT, HISTORICAL DEVELOPMENT OF.)

## Team building [*See* ORGANIZATION DEVELOPMENT (OD).]

## Teams, interdisciplinary (*See* PROJECT AND TASK FORCE MANAGEMENT.)

## Techniques, management (*See* MANAGEMENT THEORY, SCIENCE, AND APPROACHES.)

## Technology, management implications

Technology and technological change have their most direct impact on human affairs through the development, conversion, management, and use of natural resources—food, water, materials, energy—for the benefit of human life. The enormous benefits of technology—and also, of course, the sometimes damaging side effects—so pervade modern society that it is almost impossible to imagine living otherwise, even so recently as a century or two ago. "No one in his senses," said the British historian J. H. Plumb, "would choose to have been born in a previous age unless he could be certain that he would have been born into a prosperous family, that he would have enjoyed extremely good health, and that he could have accepted stoically the death of the majority of his children."

**Impact on Organizations** Great as is the impact of technology on individuals, it is even greater on men and women as social animals—on the organizations and institutional systems under which they live. In this arena managers face a powerful challenge that to so many seems wholly new. In one sense, in the perspective of recent history, there is nothing new about today's problems *themselves*, but there is a great deal that is new about their size, their complexity, and their implications. These problems require mixed solutions that are not only technical, economic, and managerial, but political and social as well. The great failing of the solutions in the past—and a deficiency that is becoming dangerous in the present—is that they are victims of partial definition. There is too much emphasis first on one aspect of the problem and then another so that momentum related to a balanced definition and solution cannot be sustained. It is the interconnections of technology and human systems that make for the complications. One always returns, however, to the central role played by technology in developing the resources on which every contemporary industrial society is based. But what of technology in the future? Will its importance diminish? How will it be managed? These are questions for which the answers are so relevant to our own history, character, and mission. In reflecting on these questions, in the context of our own society, my principal associates at Massachusetts Institute of Technology and I have said this:

Today, modern technology has for the first time brought us the power to achieve that just world, free of fear, disease, and hunger of which men and women have long dreamed. We have turned to our use a remarkable range of materials and other resources from the environment in which we live; we have developed an effective economic system to spur technical and social development; we have a high standard of living; and we have made major commitments to social justice and welfare.

Yet the world is beset with threatened scarcity of resources; and as a result, with frustration and uncertainty. Many of our aspirations are yet unfulfilled; many of their implications are inadequately understood. Our efforts to solve old problems often create new ones, and some of these appear to be even more complex and intractable than those they displace. Problems increasingly cross national borders so that solutions are not under control of one nation, and actions taken far away for local reasons may have important effects close at home. In fact, the growing importance of the international dimension of the major issues of our society has served to complicate these effects even more.

Thus many people feel adrift, caught up in a system that seems to emphasize material goods beyond humanism. They fear that even today's standards of life cannot be brought equitably to everyone, or perhaps even sustained for the more affluent. Everything seems related to everything else in a web of such complexity as to defy our understanding and management. We are puzzled about next steps, and while we ponder them, we seem to find ourselves surrounded by constraints and complications that sap much of our momentum and confidence and freedom of action.

If today's problems are the consequences of our earlier successes and accomplishments, shall we solve them by renouncing those achievements and abandoning our technological society? Such a course is inconceivable; no clock can be turned back to an earlier era of history.

Clearly our purpose must be to direct our energy toward a more intelligent application of existing and new knowledge and toward a wiser and more responsible management of our technology. It is our conviction that there still can be major advances in the human condition, and that the best ingredients for the future remain those which have brought us so far in the past—free human beings and innovative private industrial organizations functioning in a democratic society under a responsive government. We can do far more than we have done to improve people's lives. And we can strengthen the technological base that undergirds the whole by exploiting our technology more effectively and efficiently and by managing it more wisely.

In short, many of the problems facing the world are bound up with technology; and such issues cannot be understood adequately and dealt with effectively unless there is a deep and pervasive appreciation of this technology and of its impacts. For the future, then, the technology-relatedness of social and organizational problems can only increase.

**The Largest Resource** Technology itself is, in a sense, the largest resource available to human beings. Most informed managers are convinced that the continued development of technology, of the great resources of research, of the ongoing advancement of science will continue to provide a major key to the world's future. People must have more science and engineering, not less, and have in addition the trained management to employ them to meet human needs if expectations for the enhancement of the quality of life, for the conservation and improvement of the environment, and for using efficiently and well our physical and human resources are to be met.

*Growth or No-Growth.* This optimistic view of the human capacity to cope with its problems contrasts with the gloomier prophets of the limits of growth. Prophecy, of course, is extremely difficult—especially in regard to the future! Whatever the answer to our problems may be, it is assuredly *not at this time* a policy of no-growth. This is not to say that there is not somewhere a limit to our useful natural resources. But an absolute policy of no-growth now would be simplistic and probably unwise.

Putting the problem most starkly, the questions are, "How much will nations of the world do without now for the rest of the world tomorrow? Or for the human race 200 years from now? Or 2000 years hence?" That horizon is limitless. No-growth policies, as Roland McKean and others have stressed, "would undoubtedly reduce aggregate success in research and development and diminish the chances of solving particular technological problems. This sacrifice of knowledge might be terribly important . . . because technological developments, especially those pertaining to energy and biology, might reduce problems of pollution and exhaustible resources and contribute enormously to the well-being of posterity."[1]

*Influence of Market Mechanisms.* The arguments of the limits of growth school should not be taken lightly, of course. Management cannot deny their relevance; they have made a great contribution in focusing sharp attention on the basic problems of planning, of allocation, and of affording opportunity to the longer-range market mechanism to price scarce resources. In spite of projections of near-term limits, however, the market mechanism can continue to be a primary way in which further advance—and not only material advance—can be made. The record speaks eloquently to this point. Accordingly, present proponents of the limits of growth should pay attention to the mechanism of the market, and corporate capitalism must be equally concerned with the arguments of limits.

*Role of Managerial Leadership.* Businesses quite naturally tend to establish strong growth plans for their own futures. Thus most organizations hope that they will grow at some significant rate over the years ahead. In these plans, unfortunately, many have not faced up to the fact that sheer economic growth, unrestrained by other influences, will probably become incompatible with the goal of achieving a proper balance between the effective use of the earth's resources and the needs of the earth's expanding population. This is a difficult and challenging domain. Society at large, as well as business, needs new explorations and new designs for the proper conservation and optimization of use *over the generations* of the whole of our resources for the future.

In these explorations the leadership firms in business and industry have the responsibility to *lead* in thinking through the strategies society must adopt. Management must not shrink from this task. As Schumpeter often pointed out, the genius of capitalism is that it is flexible. It knows when to revise, and because it does not hesitate to change and adapt, it keeps the system vigorous. In that sense it is a mechanism of humanism.

**Managed Technology**   If a continued and growing technology will be a requisite for handling future problems, it will have to be a new kind of managed technology. Tomorrow's technology must be defined differently from today's. Technology in the new era must take into larger account basic human, social, and environmental concerns, at a new level of awareness, and with a longer time frame in mind. The new definition will need to take into account also the international interconnections of technology and the aspirations of developing nations, as well as any given country's immediate and domestic present.

*Requirements in Private and Public Sectors*. Such a definition will place a much larger emphasis on the research base for technology, on understanding the scientific outcomes—biological, physical, and social—of the applications of technology, and in monitoring the ongoing effects of technology. Such a definition will place more emphasis, too, on the best ways to stimulate and encourage needed new technologies. In the longer run, such a definition will encourage a greater understanding on the part of developed countries for expanding wealth distribution beyond their borders and at the same time encourage the developing countries to understand the need for capital growth and wise expansion of technology within their own boundaries.

The development of an enlightened, managed technology will necessarily require better perfor-

mance from both the public and private sectors. Private companies—multinational companies—are likely to be the most effective mechanisms for the spread and development of useful technology in the sense used here. That kind of private development should be encouraged, and it must be monitored by a constructive governmental and, in some situations intergovernmental, framework.

Large-scale technology requires the wise balancing of inputs from both private and public sources. Private effort, in the absence of effective competition, becomes too easily self-pressed for short-run gains. Government, on the other hand, left to its own bureaucratic tendencies uncontrolled by private standards of performance, slips too easily into the role of delayer, frustrator, inhibitor. What is needed to make managed technology useful, then, is a new spirit of positive leadership in both sectors.

*Applications*. The world's problems are manifold. They encompass the huge dilemmas of energy—its sources, storage, transmission—and, in general, of the allocation of other natural resources. They include the problems of the cities and their underachieving systems of housing, transportation, protection, education, and quality of life. And they cover the complex of problems related to medicine and health, to food and population. Yet we *can* bring these problems closer to solution, and technologies, old and new, can lead the way.

DEVELOPING COUNTRIES: Food supply is an example. Technologically, much can be done to improve the world food situation, but the attack on this problem should be enlarged. Particularly, there is a need to focus on increased food production in the developing countries through higher yields and new methods of efficient distribution. Even in the United States, which is the Saudi Arabia of food, important areas of research vital to strengthening food protein supply are either inadequately funded or entirely neglected. Priorities include application of new developments in biology and food technology to conventional agriculture, better identification of human protein needs, more comprehensive assessment of the protein value and safety of foods, and the long-range development of such novel protein resources as those from green leaves, yeast, bacteria, fungi, and chemical synthesis.

DEVELOPED COUNTRIES: For the developed countries, energy is almost as vital as food—and a problem of perhaps greater complexity. These countries have all obviously entered a difficult period of transition in their methods of energy supply and utilization. Life-styles and productive technology have evolved on a basis of abundant and relatively cheap energy. Easily accessible domestic fuel resources have been exploited, and the national supply system has become vulnerable to outside control.

As with food, research must be accelerated over a broad spectrum of energy alternatives including more vigorous efforts at conservation. The research effort should include unconventional sources, such as solar energy, and continuing economic and technical feasibility studies of synthetic fuels. It should include also second- and third-generation potentialities, such as fusion, because if the basic research is not done now, energy-dependent nations will be caught just as short some years from now as they are today.

*Interactive Relationships.* With every opportunity for technological advance come problems of fallout and side effects that often loom large. For example, there are issues of privacy, of health effects, of environmental impact, and the like. They are an integral part of every technological assessment, of every advance. Typical questions demanding our attention are these.

Assuming that nuclear energy is a requirement, where do we site the plant and with what safeguards?

If some of the facts of citizens' lives are to be put into a computer, what facts should be chosen and who will have access to them?

As medical technology advances and becomes more specialized, when do we call a halt?

In genetic engineering, what is the next step and who will decide?

Such questions can become difficult and deep, and dealing with them—whether they be profound or mundane—is one of the requirements of managed technology. Governments, and in some cases international bodies, must have a primary responsibility for building the research base that permits better understanding of such dangers and what to do to ensure that they do not materialize.

Private companies must be concerned on their own, in the development of technology, to understand and to prevent disastrous side effects. Companies should encourage their managers first to examine and think through the kind of regulation that serves the purpose and common good of all. Corporations entering upon this process could then propose to government, and expect of government, wise and effective regulation. The potential pollution of rivers, contamination of air, and production of unsafe devices are the proper concern of the manufacturers involved.

To make such a concern effective, important new ground must be broken. There is a growing need to define levels of safety or danger in many areas in the next decade. Though this is a rich world, it cannot afford zero risk; but since we live in an impulsive world, we cannot afford all risk. The range of safety is a human decision based on good research data. No self-interest group or firm should make that decision on its own. Methods and mechanisms must be developed nationally where that is effective and proper—as they have been in the United Kingdom and in the Federal Republic of Germany—and internationally for the oil spill, the ozone layer, and the like, if progress in the management of technology is to be achieved.

**Management's Responsibility**  If progress is to be achieved, understanding and managing the complex interactions of technology and society are the very heart of the matter. There is a need, in this requirement for management, for human talent of breadth and quality. Assume that the world can develop a sense of the priorities arrived at on a basis of broad understanding. Assume, too, that with an appropriate research base the world can develop the requisite technologies. There will still be the need for the quality of management—for the people, for the trained leadership—to make the system function.

The constraints on an effective, functioning system by the twenty-first century will likely be more human than technical. There will, of course, be changes in the natural constraints upon the system. But the most difficult constraints will relate to the need for managers in all sectors of any society who can make the largest strategic judgments in positions that carry great visibility. Legal requirements, governmental pressures, and the decisive interests of many more people will combine to place extraordinary demands upon this management. Of all the factors that relate to the wise and humane future development of society, this requirement is the most complex. And at the heart of the complexity lies the question of incentives: making it worthwhile to get the extra level of performance. These must be people with the highest sense of standards and values for the advance of our human society. There must be a clearer understanding in the leadership cadres of the world that wealth is the material basis of human advance and the crucial issue is not the wealth itself but the uses we are able to make of it.

Technological advance will not deal with all the world's problems. There remain the human problems of prejudice, greed, and sloth, the political problems engendered by nationalism, and the spiritual decay that people inflict upon themselves. But technological advance can provide the optimum setting of the material and social world in which human growth can be protected and encouraged, and in which it can, in fact, take place.

*See also* DEVELOPING COUNTRIES, MANAGEMENT IN; ECONOMIC SYSTEMS; ETHICS, MANAGERIAL; SOCIAL RESPONSIBILITY OF BUSINESS; TECHNOLOGY EXCHANGE.

### NOTE
[1]*Daedalus*, fall 1973, p. 222.

### REFERENCES
Edison Electric Institute: *Economic Growth in the Future: The Growth Debate in National and Global Perspective*, McGraw-Hill Book Company, New York, 1976.

Tuve, George L.: *Our Four Interdependent Crises: Energy, Environment, Populations & Food*, Interscience Publishers, a division of John Wiley & Sons, Inc., New York, 1976.

HOWARD W. JOHNSON, *Massachusetts Institute of Technology*

## Technology dimension, MIS [*See* INFORMATION SYSTEMS, MANAGEMENT (MIS), IN LARGE ORGANIZATIONS.]

## Technology exchange

*Technology exchange* is the transfer of technology developed by government research to industry and the exchange of technology among industries.

The most important source of data developed by government research is the National Technical Information Service of the U.S. Department of Commerce, located in Springfield, Virginia. It collects technological reports from most government agencies, including the Department of Defense, the National Aeronautics and Space Administration (NASA), the Environmental Protection Agency, and the National Science Foundation, and from some universities and other institutions engaged in research. Among the services it provides is an on-line search (known as NTISearch) of an enormous number of reports and other analyses. This provides summaries of the research and, if needed, complete texts of the reports on microfiche. There is a charge for this service, and others provided by NTIS, but the service's catalog (see References below) is free and can be obtained from most Department of Commerce offices. The NTIS also publishes *Weekly Government Abstract* newsletters (26 in all, each dealing with a different subject), which are obtainable by subscription.

In addition, there are various centers around the country which issue reports and will help in the location of data. Examples are the Metals and Ceramics Information Center, sponsored by the Department of Defense, at the Battelle Laboratory in Columbus, Ohio, and the Plastics Technical Evaluation Center at the Picatinny Arsenal in Dover, New Jersey.

Other sources of technological information are trade associations, universities, and, in some cases, companies. The Library of Congress has published a directory of sources, which includes these institutions (see References below).

*See also* INFORMATION SEARCH; INNOVATION AND CREATIVITY; MARKETING RESEARCH; PLANNING, PLANNED MANAGEMENT OF TUBULENT CHANGE; PLANNING, STRATEGIC MANAGERIAL PLANNING; RESEARCH AND DEVELOPMENT MANAGEMENT.

### REFERENCES
*A Directory of Information Sources in the United States: Physical Sciences and Engineering*, Library of Congress, Science and Technology Division, National Referral Center, Washington, 1971.

Hough, Granville W.: *Technology Diffusion: Federal Programs and Procedures*, Lomond Systems, Inc., Mt. Airy, Md., 1976.

*NTIS General Catalog*, no. 4, Springfield, Va., January 1976.

Rosenbloom, Richard S., and Francis Wolek: *Technology and Information Transfer: A Survey of Practice in Industrial Organizations*, Harvard University, Graduate School of Business Administration, Division of Research, Cambridge, Mass., 1970.

*Special Technology Group Catalog*, U.S. Department of Commerce, National Technical Information Service, Springfield, Va., 1975. (Services provided free by government information centers around the country.)

STAFF/SMITH

## Technology of organizations (*See* ORGANIZATION ANALYSIS AND PLANNING.)

## Telecommunications

In the sense used in this entry, *telecommunications* refers to the transmission or reception of writing, sounds, or intelligence of any nature by wire, radio, microwave, satellite, or other electromechanical means. The observations that follow relate chiefly to administrative telecommunications in either voice or written mode.

In managing this activity, management must contrast the cost of the service with its utility. Accordingly, this entry emphasizes the practical aspects and provides use-tested suggestions for saving money, improving service, and enhancing the public image of an enterprise. For the sake of brevity, the following abbreviations are used: AT&T, American Telephone & Telegraph Company; FCC, Federal Communications Commission; and Telco, your local telephone company.

## LONG-DISTANCE TOLL CHARGES

When a person calls a point outside the metropolitan area of the originating city, the call travels over a long-distance circuit. Some callers may rent special circuits furnished by private common carriers, which give access to certain geographic areas. Others may secure special facilities from their telephone company, which give "wholesale" rates for large quantities of calls. These services will be discussed later. The following suggestions apply to the long-distance toll call, called *message telephone service (MTS)* by AT&T.

MTS rates are based on airline mileages between the areas involved. AT&T sets rates; the Federal Communications Commission approves or disapproves them. The various Bell System and independent telephone companies agree to a complicated "separations" formula which divides MTS revenue between the various telephone utilities involved. Consumers should be alert for announcements of MTS rate increases and let the state or federal officials know their position on such matters. Long-distance rates for calls which travel within a state are set by the telephone utilities operating in that state, and these are regulated by the state public utility commission.

The typical user of telecommunications services makes many long-distance calls. The following explanations and suggestions will help to reduce their cost.

**Interstate and Intrastate Calls**   An interstate long-distance call terminates in a state different from that in which it begins. An intrastate call begins and terminates within the same state. Interstate long-distance directly dialed calls are subject to a 1-minute minimum charge. Intrastate directly dialed calls may have a 1-, 2-, or 3-minute minimum charge, depending on the rules of that state's public utility commission. In most states the cost per minute of the intrastate call traveling a given distance is considerably higher than that of the interstate call traveling a similar distance. If a call requires the assistance of a telephone company operator, a 3-

minute minimun charge will apply whether it is an interstate or intrastate call.

**Types of Calls**   The cost of a long-distance call is determined by the type of call, the time of day, the day of week when the call is made, and the airline mileage to the distant point.

*Directly Dialed Calls.*  A directly dialed call is one made without the assistance of a telephone company operator. In some smaller communities, older telephone exchanges still require that an operator ask the caller's telephone number. The lowest rate applies to calls directly dialed in those communities, as it does when an operator's assistance is not required.

*Operator-Handled Calls.*  If a caller dials 0 and asks the operator for certain kinds of assistance, a much higher rate will apply to the first 3 minutes of conversation. A minimum charge for 3 minutes is made even if elapsed conversation time is shorter. No "time-of-day" discounts apply to the first 3 minutes of conversation. The rate is the same on a 24-hour, 7-day basis. If the call is placed at a time when discounts apply to directly dialed calls, those discounts will likewise apply to the fourth and succeeding minutes of the operator-handled call.

Just as long-distance directly dialed rates increase with distance, the operator-handling surcharge similarly increases.

Person-to-person calls are a variation of operator-handled calls. They carry the most expensive rate of all. If the caller asks the operator for:

Name of person wanted

Title of person wanted

Name of department wanted

Interior station number (e.g., extension 493)

an additional surcharge will be added. In 1978, a 3-minute coast-to-coast person-to-person call was billed at $3.55. A 3-minute operator-handled station-to-station call, in which the caller was willing to talk to anyone answering, was billed at $2.25. A 1-minute directly-dialed call cost 54 cents.

**Time Periods**   Substantially reduced rates for directly dialed calls are available at times that are usually listed in the front pages of the telephone directory's white pages. In 1978, a 35 percent discount applied to directly dialed calls placed between 5 and 11 P.M. Monday through Friday and on Sunday. A 60 percent discount applied daily from 11 P.M. to 8 A.M., from 8 A.M. to 11 P.M. on Saturday, and from 8 A.M. to 5 P.M. on Sunday. The effective time is that in effect in the city where the call originates.

The 5 P.M. discount is useful when calling to time zones west of the originating point, as people there are still working during normal business hours. Late working shifts can concentrate on after-hours calling for sales promotion, credit and collection, and similar projects.

The 60 percent discount can be used effectively by people calling from west to east. If a call originating in Los Angeles is answered in New York City before 8 A.M. Los Angeles time, the 60 percent discount applies to the entire conversation or data transmission, regardless of call length.

Those placing long-distance calls from hotels or motels should try to have their calls connected before 8 A.M. or after 5 P.M.. While a higher operator-handled rate will apply to the first 3 minutes of a call, the fourth and succeeding minutes will be billed at the discounted rates.

**Types of Operator-Handled Calls**  The professional manager must learn how to reduce the use of operator-handled call classifications, which add as much as 30 percent to call cost. Cost-reduction suggestions include the following:

*Credit Card Calls.*  A telephone credit card can be issued to any person or organization with proper credit standing. Major corporations have discontinued corporate telephone credit cards. Instead, they ask their employees to apply for individual credit cards billed to residence telephone numbers. Reimbursement for business calling is made via the monthly expense account. Result: less personal calls made at corporate expense. Credit card holders should not use their credit card at home or at any facility where direct dialing can be done.

*Hotel-Motel Calls.*  Major hotels and motels now use an automated system in which the guest dials the area code and telephone number desired; the telephone company operator asks for the room number; the call is then processed. Some hotels add a second surcharge to *intrastate* long-distance calls charged to room numbers. Such extra profit is permitted by some state public utility commissions. To avoid the special hotel surcharge, the caller should give the intercepting operator a credit card number, or charge the call to a home or corporate telephone number. The FCC prohibits the placement of hotel surcharges on interstate calls.

*Coin Station Calls.*  A small saving may be made by using a credit card number instead of dropping coins, as call costs are rounded upward or downward to the nearest nickel.

*Collect Calls.*  Callers should be trained to call only by main telephone number, saying they will speak to anyone. The receiving organization operator can be given a list of approved collect callers. The operator accepts the call and then directs it to the department or individual wanted. This procedure eliminates the collect person-to-person call, which would be billed at a substantially higher rate.

Any organization that makes a large volume of collect calling should investigate inward Wide Area Telecommunications Service (WATS), which utilizes a number with 800 prefixed. Cost per call should be reduced substantially if the new service is properly controlled.

*Zenith* and *Enterprise* services are variations of collect calling systems. Special directory numbers are printed in the telephone directory white pages. A monthly charge is made for each directory listing, and the call is billed at operator-handled rates. These services are very expensive in comparison with station-to-station collect calling or inward WATS and are now considered obsolete.

*Remote Call Forwarding (RCF) Service.*  This new AT&T service is initially available in 315 cities in 40 states. Independent telephone utilities may also offer RCF. The organization wishing to establish toll-free inward calling rents a special telephone number in the city where customers are located. The number may or may not be listed in local directories. The caller pays only the cost of a local call to reach the sponsoring organization. In 1978, only interstate calls were being handled by RCF. Intrastate service was not available.

RCF requires an Electronic Switching System (ESS) telephone company central office. The ESS computer directly dials the call to the sponsor's office. Charges are at the direct-dial rate in effect at the time the call is placed. A listing charge is made for the special number, whether or not it appears in directories.

RCF is helpful if there is need for toll-free service, but not enough quantity of calling to justify "800" inward WATS service. The telephone company can assist in providing comparative costs.

*Third-Number Calls.*  The telephone number of a residence or organization may be given to a telephone company operator as a charging number when the caller does not wish to call collect or have the call charged to the telephone being used. When such calls appear on the monthly telephone bill, they should be carefully examined. Strangers could be charging calls to the organization. Telco business office personnel can provide the name of those renting the telephone circuit at both ends of the conversation. If this information does not help, Telco's investigative staff will usually try to determine who is charging the calls. Unidentified calls should be deducted from payment for long-distance service until Telco proves that the call is yours.

## "WHOLESALE" TELEPHONE SERVICES

The cost of long-distance service can be decreased substantially by the use of "wholesale" services. Sales representatives of operating telephone companies and the private telecommunications carriers can provide costs and details. Descriptions and suggestions about popular services which can be used when there is a sufficient volume of long-distance calling are as follows.

**Wide Area Telecommunications Service** WATS, properly designed, installed, and *controlled* can bring about a dramatic reduction in long-distance expense, sometimes as much as 30 to 50 percent of the former cost for long-distance calls. In 1978, interstate and intrastate WATS lines were available for either inward or outward long-distance calls. The service is furnished in a "package" of hours on a minimum-charge basis. No refund is made if fewer hours are used than were purchased. If more hours are required, they are available at an hourly rate which decreases as usage increases. Each WATS line, inward or outward, is a separate billing entity and must be justified by the amount of traffic placed on the specific circuit.

Each WATS line covers a defined zone and can reach any telephone number within that zone. Each interstate zone is inclusive of less-expensive zones. Thus, if the entire United States is covered by WATS zone C, a WATS line secured for that zone would likewise cover the telephones reached in lower-cost zones A and B. Zone B would similarly include the telephones in zone A. The interstate WATS zones never include the state in which the calls originate. Intrastate WATS service must be purchased separately. Interstate WATS service is priced by AT&T and regulated by the FCC. Intrastate service is priced by the state's operating telephone utilities and regulated by the state public utility commissions.

**Foreign Exchange Service (FX)** With service termed *foreign exchange* the user calls over a trunk which is brought to the user's telephone or switchboard and dial equipment from an exchange which is foreign or distant from the user's own telephone exchange. The line may come from another part of the city or from across the country. The user rents the line at the rate in effect in the distant community and also pays a monthly mileage charge calculated on the distance between the distant exchange and the user's exchange.

An FX line can reduce the cost of long-distance calls for a company whose personnel make many calls to many different numbers in a specific distant city. People in the distant city can likewise dial the company's office toll-free if they know the FX number. The more calls placed on a single line, the more money is saved. The line can be used 24 hours daily, 7 days weekly.

**Tie-Line Service** A tie line is a circuit which connects two or more telephone systems. A mileage charge applies, plus charges for any switching equipment required so that callers can dial those at the distant end without requiring help from the switchboard operator. Tie-line circuits cost less than WATS circuits, as only a few points are connected. However, the caller may ask the switchboard operator at the distant point to dial local calls for other numbers in that city. If there is a dial PABX system at the distant point, the user may be able to dial 9 and then dial a local or long-distance call without operator assistance.

**Off-Premise Extensions** The off-premise extension (OPS or OPX) is a station of a company's own telephone system. However, it is located in a different place than the one which houses the switchboard and switching equipment. The person who uses the distant OPS telephone instrument hears the company's dial tone. Any station in the company's system can be dialed directly without operator assistance, and outside calls can be made by dialing 9. The switchboard operator can give the caller a WATS or FX line. No message-unit charges apply to the call between the instrument used and the switchboard location. The OPS is often used to eliminate charges for local calls between two locations in the same city. It can be practical as a tie line between two cities if the person in the distant city needs speedy communication with many different people at headquarters. The OPS circuit is billed as a station of the headquarters system, plus a mileage charge.

**Local Private Lines (LPL)** Two telephones can be connected by a "hot line" so that the distant phone rings as soon as the receiver is lifted by the call originator. No dialing or operator assistance is required.

**Circuits Furnished by Private Common Carriers** Many organizations offer private-line circuits between major cities. Cost per airline mile may be less than that quoted by the long lines department of AT&T. A local "land line" must be furnished by Telco to bring the circuit from the private carrier's facilities to the user's office. Circuits are furnished on a full-time or measured-time basis. The private common carriers use microwave and satellite circuits as well as traditional wired circuits. In 1978 a

New York-Chicago full-time satellite circuit was billed at $500 monthly plus land line charges. At a monthly line usage figure of 8300 minutes, which is 70 percent of theoretical capacity during a 9-hour daily, 22-day working month, cost for such conversation or data transmission would be about 6 cents a minute. This figure is well below the usual cost for long-distance calling.

## MANAGING LONG-DISTANCE EXPENSE

The professional manager must make sure that long-distance usage is carefully controlled. If company policy permits an executive to secure immediate access to a long-distance circuit, automatic accounting equipment may be employed to charge the call to the originating station or account number. The term *automatic identification of outward dialing (AIOD)* is applied to such hardware or software. Calling activity is recorded magnetically; software programs translate the recording into any type of report desired by management. Hardware can be purchased to do the recording in the user's office, or shared-time services can be used. Costs for such services are substantial, but equipment may provide valuable traffic statistics which permit better management of long-distance facilities. Expensive units can also provide call queuing, least-cost routing, and priority awarding.

Before a substantial capital investment or rental commitment for AIOD is made, management should attempt to control long-distance calling *before the call is made*. The suggestions which follow have substantially decreased the cost of long-distance calling in the author's client group.

*Restrict Telephones*. Telco can wire the switching system so users can make local calls but not long-distance or operator-assisted calls. In some systems the wiring can be done selectively. Other systems require total toll restriction.

*Use Operator Control*. Users phone their long-distance request to a reservation clerk or directly to the switchboard operator. The call is ticketed, routed, timed. Specialist operators select the least-cost circuit, upgrading the call to a more expensive circuit if necessary. Long talkers are controlled by management and may be given long-distance toll circuits. Operators extend priorities in emergencies. They can immediately connect calls which must use long-distance circuits to secure distant unknown telephone numbers from "information," international, "800" toll-free, or prepaid "operator 6" calls.

*Use Call Ticket as Accounting Input*. There is no need to employ expensive recording equipment when the call ticket provides all needed information for accounting and control.

*Avoid Dial Access Circuits*. If daytime users are permitted to dial a long-distance circuit directly, personal calls multiply to as much as 30 percent of calling volume. Also, random access to circuits produces multiple busy signals, which encourage frustrated people to by-pass the system via the expensive long-distance toll call.

*Use Dial Access after Switchboard Closes*. If a full-time special long-distance circuit is employed, dial access may be used to secure the circuit after the switchboard closes. The user should be careful to calculate the cost per minute of the wholesale circuit, contrasting it with the cost of long-distance calling during the 35 and 60 percent discount periods available in off-peak periods. In 1978, toll discounts made the 10-hour WATS service more expensive than a long-distance call except for the hours 8 A.M. to 5 P.M. Monday through Friday.

*Constantly Evaluate "Mix" of Wholesale Services*. Cost per minute must be calculated regularly on all services and contrasted against the cost of similar or competing services. Once a facility is installed, the quantity of traffic in calls and minutes must be measured regularly. Complimentary analyses of long-distance calling patterns are available from all telecommunications common carriers. Users should request them regularly.

## TELEPHONE SWITCHING SYSTEMS FOR THE SMALL BUSINESS

The simplest system is a six-button telephone. The telephone instrument accommodates five telephone lines and a hold button. An incoming call is held by a secretary, the person called is dialed on a simple dial intercom, the secretary identifies which line to depress; the call is picked up by the person called.

## TELEPHONE SWITCHING SYSTEMS FOR THE LARGER BUSINESS

A majority of businesses still use older step-by-step and crossbar switching. These systems have many useful features. They are long-lived and relatively inexpensive. If a telephone system must be replaced or expanded, the user should insist that Telco quote on several alternatives, not just on a single system. For instance, for the medium-sized enterprise, a crossbar system may be 30 percent less expensive than an electronic system. In other instances, expansion of the step-by-step system may be the least expensive alternative.

Telcos and vendors of private telephone systems are aggressively marketing electronic "stored-program" switches. Such systems give the user as many as 70 helpful features or services which cannot be furnished by older generations of equipment.

The acquiring user should determine whether the newer features are genuinely helpful and worth their higher cost or whether most users of the new system will quickly forget their detailed training on feature operation and settle on only a few features which might be furnished by less expensive equipment.

In general, electronic equipment is flexible, dependable, easily maintained, and sometimes less expensive than older electromechanical systems. There is a wide variety of choice from many well-known manufacturers which supply similar systems to the operating telephone utilities. Regulations of the Federal Communications Commission permit connection of private systems to the central office facilities of all telephone companies.

To combat outright purchase of switching systems by users and the interconnection of those switches to their networks, Telcos have adopted new pricing policies. While major utilities still do not permit their customers to own equipment outright, they now permit prepayment of capital expense in a lump sum, or they may offer time payment plans for capital portions of equipment cost. The plans typically offer payment periods of 36 to 144 months. Such plans are not subject to rate escalation. A second pricing tier covers maintenance and rental of trunks and key systems and is subject to rate escalation. These pricing plans, with known effective maintenance service, are providing private vendors with effective competition.

## THE TELECOMMUNICATIONS REGULATORY SCENE

In 1976 and in 1977, bills were introduced into both houses of Congress which would effectively eliminate or greatly reduce competition to the existing telephone utilities. In 1978, most observers believe these bills will not be brought to vote. However, while the legislation is pending, users should be very cautious in acquiring systems or terminals from a vendor of weak financial or marketing background. Should interconnection of certain equipment become illegal in some states, there would be a considerable mortality among manufacturers and dealer/distributors now marketing telecommunications equipment.

On the other hand, many excellent companies now sell direct to the end user as well as to telecommunications utilities. By utilizing those manufacturers' service schools, and by stocking spare parts, a systems user can furnish in-house maintenance and eliminate the continuing capital outlay for rental of telecommunications facilities.

## WESTERN UNION DOMESTIC SERVICES

Space permits only a brief description of four Western Union services which move the written word or data over public Western Union networks.

*Telex.* Telex is a service timed in one-tenth minute increments. Speed is 66 words per minute. Cost in 1978 varied from $22\frac{1}{2}$ to $52\frac{1}{2}$ cents a minute. A three-row teleprinter is used which is compatible with all similar equipment throughout the world. Telex is ideal for many short messages which must move speedily to destination. Cost, for example, was as little as 6 cents in 1977 for a 15-word message moving from Boston to Pittsburgh.

*TWX.* TWX is a service timed in 1-minute increments. Speed is 100 words per minute. Cost for interstate transmissions in 1978 varied from 30 to 52 cents a minute. A four-row teleprinter is used with a typewriter keyboard. TWX is used for transmissions that consistently exceed 1 minute in length. If time-sharing computer terminals are employed in an enterprise, they can be equipped with an "alternative use" key which makes them usable on the public TWX network.

*Mailgram.* This joint venture between the Postal Service and Western Union moves a telegraph-type message from originating city to destination city overnight for delivery in the first mail delivery the following day. Service is dependable and is achieving popularity among those formerly using telegrams and night letters, which have become obsolete because of substantially higher costs. In 1978, a 100-word Mailgram telephoned to a Western Union "800" number was billed at $2.95. A 15-word delivered telegram cost $7.95. A Mailgram dispatched over a Telex or TWX teleprinter would be billed at $1.00 plus the Telex charge for the transmission time used.

*Infomaster.* This Western Union computer service is available to either Telex or TWX users. Telex language can be translated to TWX language and vice versa, and so the user needs only one dispatching teleprinter. Other services are provided, such as acceptance of same-text, multiple-address messages, storage of mailing lists, collect message sending, and similar items. Western Union offices can furnish full details.

Users of these services should be alert to possibilities for sending written traffic at very low cost as a substitute for one-way or "request for information" voice messages.

### FACSIMILE TRANSMISSION SERVICES

Services transmitting facsimile material, known as "fax," have achieved great popularity among telecommunications users. Fax traffic moves over voice telephone lines by means of special modems. Speed has been increasing consistently. In 1977 as little as 35 seconds was required for transmitting an 8½ by 11 inch sheet of typed or drawn material. Management must carefully inspect fax traffic. Material may be moving over expensive voice circuits which should be sent via regular or express mail. Secretaries may produce triple-spaced material which takes 3 times as long to transmit as single-spaced material. Machines likewise tend to proliferate unless management controls their use.

### INTERNATIONAL COMMUNICATIONS

Many new developments have taken place in international message transmission for voice and data. Satellite circuits have supplemented cable and radio services. Costs have been reduced. Brief suggestions for usage include the following:

*International Direct Distance Dialing.* Most major cities offer this service, which eliminates usage of the international operator. AT&T publishes booklets giving full instructions and showing the rate reductions which are possible to certain countries equipped for direct-dialing service.

*International Telex.* Using the 66 word-per-minute teleprinter, this service provides immediate connection to the world's Telex network at minimum cost. In 1977, the cost per minute to most European countries from the United States was $2.55.

*Cablegrams.* Added facilities move cablegrams faster. They are dispatched by telephoning Western Union's "800" number or routing messages to a specific international carrier via Telex or TWX equipment. Every word may count in a cablegram, including address and signature. Cost can be reduced by 50 percent if overnight service is used instead of full rate service; the symbol LT should be put before the first word of the cablegram address.

*See also* COMMUNICATIONS, ORGANIZATIONAL; COMPUTER SYSTEMS; COST IMPROVEMENT; DATA PROCESSING PRINCIPLES AND PRACTICES; INFORMATION SYSTEMS, MANAGEMENT (MIS); INFORMATION SYSTEMS, MANAGEMENT (MIS), APPLIED.

### REFERENCES

*Periodicals:*
*Administrative Management*, Geyer-McAllister Publications, Inc., New York.
*Business Communications Review*, Box 302, Downers Grove, Ill. 60515.
*Communications News*, Brookhill Publishing Co., Wheaton, Ill. 60187.
*Telecommunications*, 610 Washington Street, Dedham, Mass. 02026.
*Telephone Engineer and Management*, Brookhill Publishing Co., Wheaton, Ill. 60187.
*Telephony*, 53 West Jackson Boulevard, Chicago, Ill. 60604.
*Books:*
Griesinger, Frank K.: *How To Cut Costs and Improve Service of Your Telephone, Telex, TWX, and Other Telecommunications*, McGraw-Hill Book Company, New York, 1974.
Kuehn, Richard A.: *Cost-Effective Telecommunications*, American Management Association, New York, 1975.

FRANK K. GRIESINGER, *Frank K. Griesinger and Associates, Inc., Suite 1412, Superior Building, Cleveland, Ohio*

## Telephone usage (*See* TELECOMMUNICATIONS.)

## Temporal method (*See* EXCHANGE, FOREIGN, MANAGEMENT OF.)

## Temporary help

The term *temporary help* is used for employees supplied by an outside agency to (1) fill in for regular employees who are absent or on vacation, (2) assist during peak loads, or (3) handle work for which the regular employees do not have the skills.

Many contracting firms supply temporary clerical

employees on demand, and some of them have offices in more than one city. Other types of workers may be obtained as well, often from firms that specialize in providing one particular skill or group of skills.

Temporary workers are often used by maintenance departments, especially for cleaning work. In these cases, the company has a contract with the supplier which runs for a year or more. Generally, the agreement will set forth the frequency with which various cleaning jobs will be performed and the standards of cleanliness.

Other types of contracts cover different kinds of work: construction and electrical work of various kinds, for example. It is also quite common for oil refining plants to have contractors supply people to handle their "turn-arounds," periodic overhauls of major equipment. In a few cases, oil refineries have all their maintenance performed by an outside contractor.

Companies that use temporary help or contract labor generally pay a flat fee, sometimes an hourly or per diem rate to the contractor for each employee. The contractor then pays the employees and provides their fringe benefits.

In some cases companies hire people for special types of work on a temporary basis and contract with the individual rather than with a firm for services at a per diem rate.

*See also* HUMAN RESOURCES (WORK FORCE) PLANNING; MAINTENANCE MANAGEMENT; PLANT ENGINEERING MANAGEMENT; WAGES AND HOURS LEGISLATION; WORK HOURS, FLEXIBLE.

### REFERENCES

Feldman, Edwin B.: "Contract Cleaning—Pro and Con," in Alice Smith, ed., *Techniques of Plant Engineering and Maintenance*, Clapp & Poliak, Inc., New York, 1969, pp. 30–32.

Gannon, M. J.: "Profile of the Temporary Help Industry and Its Workers," *Monthly Labor Review*, May 1974, pp. 44–49.

Jordan, James H.: "Research in Contract Maintenance," in Alice Smith, ed., *op cit.*, pp. 253–254.

STAFF/SMITH

## Temporary help agencies  (*See* PERSONNEL ADMINISTRATION.)

## Tenant plans  (*See* OFFICE SPACE PLANNING AND DESIGN.)

## Tender offer  (*See* SHAREHOLDER RELATIONSHIPS.)

## Tension, job  (*See* HEALTH, EXECUTIVE, MANAGING STRESS AND JOB TENSION.)

## Terminology, management  (*See* MANAGEMENT, DEFINITIONS OF.)

## Testing, concept  (*See* MARKETING RESEARCH.)

## Testing, copy  (*See* MARKETING RESEARCH.)

## Testing, minority  (*See* MINORITIES, MANAGEMENT OF AND EQUAL EMPLOYMENT OPPORTUNITY.)

## Testing, psychological

Although an estimate is difficult to make, there are at least 50,000 organizations in the United States that use psychological tests to help make decisions about people they plan to hire or promote. Obviously there are abuses in these ranks, but generally managers apply these tests in good faith to upgrade skills found in their work forces. Every organization wants to hire or promote the most qualified individuals, and a properly developed and executed testing program can contribute substantially to this goal.

Psychological tests are widely used but at the same time are quite misunderstood, not because testing is a mysterious or complicated subject, but because most people lack the basic knowledge to answer key questions. What makes a test good or bad? Can tests be used within the framework of the law? How can an organization benefit from using psychological tests? Which tests should be used for employment selection or evaluation?

### LEGAL ISSUES

Sometime within the last decade, word spread throughout industry in the United States that to use psychological tests was illegal. This is not now true, nor has it ever been true. This idea is promoted somewhat by conservative lawyers and organizations who thought, erroneously, that suits could be avoided by doing away with testing. The rumors were also fed by impractical federal agencies with unworkable testing guidelines. These agencies were so inconsistent in their enforcement practices that many multiunit organizations felt that they had to abide by a different set of regulations in each region of the country. With all this confusion it is no wonder that many organizations dropped psychological testing.

The facts are that any organization has the right to use psychological tests, and there has never been a law prohibiting this right. Section 703 (h) of Title VII of the 1964 Civil Rights Act, also known as the Tower Amendment, states quite clearly: "Nor shall it be an unlawful employment practice for an employer to give and act upon the results of any professionally developed ability test provided that such test, its administration or action upon the results is not designed, intended or used to discriminate because of race, color, religion, sex or national origin." The Uniform Guidelines on Employee Selection Procedures published in the Federal Register by the Equal Employment Opportunity Co-ordinating Council states the following: "In addition, the guidelines are based upon the recognition that properly developed and validated tests can significantly aid in the development and maintenance of an efficient work force and in the effective utilization of human recource."

**Two Basic Issues** *Griggs et al. v. Duke Power Company* is the most important court case to date regarding the use of psychological tests. Minority workers of the company involved in this case were employed solely in the maintenance department; the other four departments employed only Caucasians. In order to advance to a higher level, an individual had to pass a test of general intelligence, pass a mechanical aptitude test, and have a high school diploma. These requirements made it difficult for black employees to advance since few had high school diplomas. The company felt that it was not discriminating since it applied all three criteria equally, but the Supreme Court disagreed. The Court said that the issue was not that the promotion and hiring criteria were being applied equally, but that these criteria were rejecting a disproportionate number of black applicants. According to the Court, the selection program may have been "fair in form" but it was "discriminatory in practice." The Court went on to say that the criteria were not job related, since several white employees in advanced positions had never passed the tests nor achieved a high school

diploma, but were able to function adequately on the job. Thus, two issues emerged from this case and became the overriding concern of government agencies and many organizations engaged in testing: tests should (1) be job related and (2) not have an adverse impact on members of minority groups. Government guidelines now call for a company to show evidence of job relatedness only when adverse impact exists. A test has adverse impact when it rejects a disproportionate number of minority group members. A company proves job relatedness through validation of its tests.

Government testing guidelines spell out exactly what psychologists have maintained for years. Preselection tests or other data used to make employment decisions should be related to job duties.

It is important to realize that any selection criterion can have an adverse impact and can trigger the requirement of proof of job relatedness. The selection interview, education, and training requirements and physical requirements are but a few of the many preselection criteria that could adversely affect minority groups or women.

## CHARACTERISTICS OF PSYCHOLOGICAL TESTS

Psychological tests are measuring instruments that must possess certain characteristics in order to be useful. A good test must be both *reliable* and *valid*. If a test or other screening device does not possess these characteristics, it is useless. Publishers are required to present reliability and validity evidence in test examiners' manuals, and when such data are lacking, the tests should be avoided.

Many companies have attempted to devise their own tests. This is not advisable unless expert advice is available. The vast majority of in-house tests have not been researched well enough to justify their use. Test development is a long, involved, and expensive process which should be left to professionals.

**Reliability** A prerequisite to validity, *reliability* refers to the consistency of a test in terms of measuring a trait. An examinee's test score should not vary a great deal over a number of testings unless, of course, the trait being measured was improved upon by experience or special training. The examinee's actual raw score would not be exactly the same each time the test was taken, but would vary within acceptable tolerances. In practice, people usually take a test only once or twice; therefore, reliability is a theoretical concept that is verified with basic research and becomes an assumption upon which the test is used.

A notorious example of unreliable preemployment measure is the selection interview. Judging people by the same standards is difficult from interview to interview. An interviewer may evaluate or interpret the data differently with each interview, stressing the importance of one factor in one interview and deemphasizing or ignoring the importance of that same factor in the next interview. When this is the case, it makes the interview a useless measure of future job performance.

**Validity**  Validity simply means that a test measures what it is supposed to measure. When a test is published, the developer uses a variety of techniques to demonstrate that the test is a valid measure of the trait in question. Validity coefficients are generated in order to answer questions. Does the intelligence test measure intelligence? Does the mechanical aptitude test measure mechanical aptitude? This type of validity evidence is somewhat different from the type of evidence used to define a test as having job relatedness or validity in regard to federal guidelines. When a company tries to validate a mechanical aptitude test to be used in the selection of maintenance mechanics, its purpose is not to prove that the test measures mechanical aptitude. The publisher has already accomplished this. What it must prove is that mechanical aptitude is needed to succeed as a maintenance mechanic in this particular company.

## VARIETIES OF PSYCHOLOGICAL TESTS

Psychological tests can be categorized as measures of general ability (intelligence), aptitude or achievement, personality and interest. Each type of test may be used in an industrial setting depending upon existing needs. Personality and interest tests, however, are not used to make predictions regarding job performance but are used when personality or certain patterns of interest are known to be related to performance in a particular setting.

Tests can be administered to either groups or single individuals. Group tests can be given to groups of any size and to single individuals, but individual tests can be administered to only one person at a time. Group tests are common in industry, since they are usually less expensive and less time-consuming than individual tests.

**General Ability Tests**  These vary in their complexity and function. The best example of a sophisticated and comprehensive intelligence test is the *Wechsler Adult Intelligence Scale* (WAIS). This test must be administered and interpreted by a trained psychologist, and it yields the traditional intelligence quotient (IQ) score. It is a very detailed test upon which many shorter tests are based. The WAIS is usually administered to executive and management personnel in order to assess particular styles and qualities of intellectual functioning. It should not be used as an absolute measure in deciding whether a person will be hired or promoted.

There are many shorter, less comprehensive tests of general ability. The *Otis Self Administering Test of Mental Ability, Wonderlic Personnel Test, SRA Verbal,* and *Thurston Test of Mental Alertness* are a few of the most popular. These tests estimate intellectual functioning and generally do not yield IQ scores.

**Aptitude and Achievement Tests**  These are often hard to differentiate. The way in which a test is used often indicates whether it is a measure of aptitude or achievement. Theoretically, an *aptitude test* measures ability to perform a particular kind of task and is used to predict future performance on the job or in training. The *achievement test* is a measure of present functioning and is used to determine to what extent a given trait has been learned or mastered through training or job experience.

**Personality Tests**  These should be administered by properly trained personnel; a master's degree in psychology is usually a minimum requirement, a doctorate is preferable. Personality tests measure abstract concepts such as aggressiveness, independence, support, conformity, passivity, and the like. More controversy is generated by personality tests than any other kind. The reality is that personality testing is the most difficult area of psychological testing, especially in terms of development. Even the best personality tests are often criticized for lack of technical support, and for this reason it is so very important to scrutinize carefully the use of these tests and to have trained personnel administer and interpret them.

Personality tests, as well as intelligence tests, should not be used as the sole measure to hire or promote anyone; no test should. They should be used as diagnostic tools to help form a picture of the total person in order to evaluate how he or she might function under certain circumstances.

**Interest Tests**  These are seldom used to make predictions regarding job performance. They are, instead, inventories of a person's likes and dislikes and are generally used for career and vocational guidance. The best-known and most widely used interest tests are the *Strong-Campbell Vocational Interest Blank* and the *Kuder Preference Record.* These tests tell how a person's interests compare with the interests of others in various occupational groups. The assumption is that a person will be more satisfied working among those with similar likes and dislikes.

## CONCLUSION

It is management's prerogative to use and act upon the results of professionally developed psychological tests. No law or government regulation can prohibit any organization from using psychological tests when those tests measure traits that are significantly related to job performance.

It is important to choose tests or any other selection device very carefully. The selection should be based upon a complete analysis of job requirements. The procedure must have proved reliability and validity. A testing program is not an absolute answer to all personnel problems. A properly developed and executed testing program, however, can contribute substantially to the development and utilization of human resources.

*See also* AFFIRMATIVE ACTION; ASSESSMENT CENTER METHOD; DEVELOPMENT AND TRAINING, EMPLOYEE; EMPLOYMENT PROCESS; INTERVIEWING, EMPLOYEE; MINORITIES, MANAGEMENT OF AND, EQUAL EMPLOYMENT OPPORTUNITY; PERSONNEL ADMINISTRATION.

### REFERENCES

Anastasi, A.: *Psychological Testing*, 4th ed., The Macmillan Company, New York, 1976.
Campbell, J. P., M. D. Dunnette, E. E. Lawler, and K. E. Weick: *Managerial Behavior, Performance, and Effectiveness*, McGraw-Hill Book Company, New York, 1970.
Cronbach, L.: *Essentials of Psychological Testing*, 3d ed., Harper & Rowe, New York, 1970.
Dunnette, M. D.,: *Handbook of Industrial and Organizational Psychology*, Rand-McNally & Company, Chicago, 1975.
——: *Personnel Selection and Placement*, Brooks/Cole Publishing Company, Belmont, Calif., 1966.
Ghiselli, E. E.: *The Validity of Occupational Aptitude Tests*, John Wiley & Sons, Inc., New York, 1966.
Guion, R. E.: *Personnel Testing*, McGraw-Hill Book Company, New York, 1965.
Kirkpatrick, J. J., R. B. Ewen, R. S. Barrett, and R. A. Katzell: *Testing and Fair Employment*, New York University Press, 1968.

STEVEN J. STANARD, *Personnel and Management Consulting*

## Tests, psychological (*See* TESTING, PSYCHOLOGICAL.)

## Theories of management (*See* MANAGEMENT THEORY, SCIENCE, AND APPROACHES.)

## Theory, management (*See* MANAGEMENT THEORY, SCIENCE, AND APPROACHES.)

## Theory X and Theory Y

*Theory X* and *Theory Y* are two theories of management which are based on antithetical assumptions about human nature and work. Theory X, the traditional, work-centered, authoritarian approach, assumes that employees dislike work and must be coerced by management. Theory Y believes that people can and will enjoy fully productive work if permitted to participate significantly in decision making. It is as such a people-centered, democratic, human relations approach.

Douglas McGregor first enunciated the two theories in 1960 in an attempt to explain the inadequacies of authoritarian types of management and to devise a better type on the basis of modern behavioral science and Maslow's definition of human needs and motivation.

The implicit assumptions of the managers of an organization will determine its modus operandi, down to the smallest action. Theory X management assumes: (1) there is no intrinsic satisfaction for people in work; (2) humans will avoid work as much as possible; (3) therefore, management must direct, control, coerce, and threaten workers in order to achieve management goals; (4) the average human seeks to avoid responsibility, lacks ambition or imagination, craves direction and, above all, security. On the basis of these assumptions, theory X management must, to achieve its goals, apply external motivating force, or authority, which in turn determines that: (1) the *locus of decision* will be solely in the nominal head of the organization; (2) the *structure of the organization* will be pyramidal, with authority flowing from the top down; (3) the *supervisor's* main functions are to transmit orders (not to make decisions) and to emphasize production; (4) *the role of the worker* is that of an isolated cog in the machine, communicating only with his or her supervisor.

Theory Y, at the opposite end of the continuum, assumes: (1) expenditure of effort in work and play is natural to humans; (2) external control and threat are not essential to bring about effort toward organizational goals to which humans are committed; (3) the satisfaction of individual ego and self-actualization needs can be direct products of efforts toward organizational goals; (4) the average human learns, under proper conditions, not only to accept but to seek responsibility; (5) the capacity for creativity is widely distributed in the population; (6) modern industry rarely utilizes the intellectual potentialities of the average human. Theory Y assumptions thus lead to a *participatory* organization in which authority is accepted by workers, not imposed on them. Accordingly, (1) the *locus of decision* may be widespread, at any level; (2) the group, including its supervisor, becomes the *primary organizational unit;* (3) the *supervisor* deals with groups; (4) the *worker* has become a group member who participates in setting organizational goals and therefore works willingly, intelligently. In sum, theory X management will rationalize problems by blaming the nature of its human resources, but a theory Y management assumes responsibility for the attitudes and productivity of its employees.

The concepts of theory X and theory Y have been of great service in defining the limits of the approaches to organization theory and in focusing attention on their opposing assumptions. Criticism centers on their extreme and rather sweeping generalizations. The theories pay insufficient attention to the specifics of interrelationships between particular jobs, to the great variety of conditions and of human individuals. Finally, neither theory X nor theory Y seems to be consistently supported by research findings.

*See also* HYGIENE FACTORS; LEADERSHIP; MOTIVATION IN ORGANIZATIONS; SYSTEM 4.

### REFERENCE

McGregor, Douglas: *The Human Side of Enterprise*, McGraw-Hill Book Company, New York, 1960.

STAFF/HOKE

## Therbligs

A *therblig* is the lowest indivisible work movement operation of the body; it is one of the 18 elementary subdivisions, physical, visual, or mental, which are supposedly common to all kinds of industrial manual work. The term *therblig* (Gilbreth spelled backwards, phonetically) was coined by Frank Bunker Gilbreth, 1868–1924, in his pioneering work in motion study. The concept is in active use today in the highly developed science of time and motion study. While not a totally pure concept, it is very useful to the skilled industrial operations analyst.

In an effort to find the most economical (and least fatiguing) way of using the worker in combination with his or her tools or machine, the concept of the therblig is used as filmed motions performed by the worker in a manual operation are charted graphi-

cally and minutely analyzed. Examples of therbligs are "search"—during which the worker's hands or eyes are seeking the tool or object needed—and "find/select," the therblig which follows "search" and which may be either a mental or visual operation.

*See also* HUMAN FACTORS ENGINEERING; WORK MEASUREMENT; WORK SIMPLIFICATION AND IMPROVEMENT.

### REFERENCES

Barnes, Ralph M.: *Motion and Time Study*, 5th ed., John Wiley & Sons, Inc., New York, 1963.
Gilbreth, Frank K.: *Motion Study*, D. Van Nostrand Company, Inc., New York, 1911.

STAFF/HOKE

## Third market, securities (*See* MARKETS, SECURITIES.)

## Third world countries (*See* DEVELOPING COUNTRIES, MANAGEMENT IN.)

## Third world management (*See* DEVELOPING COUNTRIES, MANAGEMENT IN.)

## Time chart (*See* NETWORK PLANNING METHODS.)

## Time/cost trade-off (*See* NETWORK PLANNING METHODS.)

## Time management

Time is the universal measure. It can be applied to each of an organization's inputs. The time value of facilities and equipment is rent. The time value of electrical energy is kilowatt-hours. The time value of money and materials is interest. The time value of labor is worker-hours. Similarly, output is valued in the number of units per minute, per hour, per week, per month, per year. Profits, too, are sized for a year's period of time. In almost all instances, time costs money.

Time is also an unforgiving measure of an organization's—and a manager's—effectiveness. It sets the restrictions on every operation and process. Time's two persistent questions are "How long will it take?" and "Was it finished on time?"

Time is a resource, too. As the late Ralph Cordiner, president of General Electric Company and architect of its massive reorganization in the 1950s, observed, "Time is an asset that all competitors share in common, but the management of time can be one of the decisive elements in success or failure." It follows that time can be wasted, or it can be conserved. An executive must manage time wisely whether it is the time allotted to processes or the limited personal time available for overseeing responsibilities. These two charges can be classified as time commitments and management of personal time.

**Time Commitments**  Specifically, three kinds of situations press a manager for a time commitment. These situations appear in almost all kinds of enterprises, regardless of the exact nature of the manager's responsibility.

*Production Schedules.* Whether managers are held responsible for a product or service, they are routinely asked to meet certain production schedules which usually call for a specific number of units of output per day, per week, or per month. These schedules act like a "go-no go" gauge of a manager's capability. Allowances will be made for interruptions and delays beyond the manager's control, but repeated failures will be held against the manager. The presumption is that a manager will alert the schedule makers to factors which contribute to delays so that the schedules incorporate enough time to allow for them. Put another way, if a manager regularly has problems meeting the schedules, initiative for corrective action must be provided by either (1) finding ways to meet schedules or (2) seeing that the schedules are adjusted beforehand.

*Promised Delivery Dates.* Routine schedules cover the great majority of time commitments; nevertheless, there are a number of nonroutine situations in which a manager is asked to see that the product or service is ready for delivery (or shipment) by a specific date. These promised delivery dates may be derived by the sales department, which has already made a commitment to a customer. They may be imposed upon the manager with apparent good reason by someone else in higher authority. The manager may also simply volunteer. In any event, most of these promises are binding. Thus, a manager should try not to accept delivery dates that appear unreasonable without first making his or her own time estimates. If such promises imply that previously scheduled priorities must be rearranged, the proper time to speak of this is when the commit-

ment is accepted; after, it is usually too late to complain about disruptions to routine schedules. The same advice goes for added costs—the costs of interrupting assembly runs, of overtime, or of expediting. These considerations should be brought up early in the negotiation rather than after the promise has been exacted.

*Project Completion Deadlines.* Many deadlines can best be described as *project completion dates*. These may be associated with such matters as: (1) construction of a facility which must be ready for occupancy at a certain date; (2) installation of a new machine which must be in operation when the seasonal rush begins; (3) development of a paper work system which must be operative before the next accounting period begins; (4) preparation of a study or a report which is due when it is time to file appropriation requests; and (5) test of a proposed process which must be completed before design plans are firmed up.

Project completion deadlines, like promised delivery dates, may be imposed upon a manager from above, or they may represent free choice. In either instance, the prudence and care the manager takes in establishing these deadlines go a long way toward ensuring that they can be met.

**Factors Affecting Time Estimates**  In cases where time measurements and calculations of the time needed to complete a task or an assignment are precise, many variable factors may reduce even the most careful approaches to rough estimates. In order to understand how this can be so, the variable time factors are examined one by one.

*Inherent Time.* Inherent in the conversion or production process are a number of nonproductive essentials. An order or instruction must be received and noted, for example. An individual or a machine (frequently both) must work on the material or paperwork form involved. The material or form must be moved from work station to work station. Finally, the finished product or form is ready for shipment or delivery. Industrial engineers call this total process the *order-delivery cycle* or the *manufacturing cycle*. This cycle has the following inescapable elements:

Labor time or worker-hours needed to perform the recording, fabricating, transcribing, transmitting, assembly, finishing, inspecting, calculating, and packaging functions.

Machine time or machine hours to perform, or assist in performing, functions listed under labor time.

Handling time needed to move materials, supplies, parts, paper work, and communications from one operation to another.

*Setup Time.* This is also known as "make-ready" time or, when it includes the beginning and the end of an operation, "setup and tear-down" or "get-ready and put-away" time. It is, of course, the time always needed to prepare an operation and to clean up after it is finished. The more often a schedule calls for a change in setups, the more time the department consumes in nonproductive work. Setup times may be necessary and unavoidable, but they consume time without actually producing a product or service. The best ways to attack this particular problem are to try to minimize the number of instances in which a line must be changed over and to direct work simplification efforts to that end.

*Learning Time.* Learning time can be viewed as a special version of setup time because it is typically associated with starting up—a new process, a new product, a new operation, a new organization, or a new employee. Output rates are always slower when starting up than after things are running smoothly. Employees have to learn the new operation or the new machine. "Bugs" show up that must be eliminated. Operations have to be coordinated. Unanticipated problems must be solved. Statistically, when anyone is learning, there is a uniform percent drop (such as 10 percent) in the time needed to produce a single unit of output every time the total number of units of output is doubled. [*See* LEARNING (EXPERIENCE) CURVES.]

*Lost Time.* A manager's time plans must also accept the fact that the operations will lose time in two ways: (1) Personal time lost from a scheduled 8-hour day for washup, rest periods, lunch periods, plus the time lost from the schedule for vacations, holidays, and sickness; (2) technical time delays caused by machine breakdowns, material shortages, and open spots on the schedule.

*Costly Time.* Certain practices often cause a manager to buy time in a costly fashion. These situations come about through:

1. Crash time or "red rush" when a product or service is forced into a schedule out of turn and hastened through the process with special attention and handling. Such instances usually arise from attempts to mollify favored customers, meet a competitor's delivery offer, or make good on a delay caused by improper scheduling or oversight. In any event, rush jobs always cost more to produce because they do not move through normal channels.

2. Expediting time which employs the use of a manager or clerk to trace down so-called "lost" orders and/or "walk" them through the shop. Obviously this is a costly use of valuable time. It often occurs in conjunction with crash time and rush jobs.

3. Overtime which entails the use of costly worker-hours beyond 8 in a day or 40 in a week to complete schedules.

**Managing Personal Time** Almost everything that can be said about conservation and utilization of operation and process times can also be said of a manager's own time. In many ways, this time is more valuable than all the other time put together. This is because a manager's interest, attention, and initiative are almost constantly needed to direct and maximize the total conversion process. Only a very determined person can maintain time headway each day in the face of distractions that come from every corner.

*Personal Time Analysis.* The best starting point in managing personal time is to find out where it goes. To do so, a work-sampling study should be made, similar to Fig. T-1. Observations should also be made at the same time each day in order to determine when these activities and functions take place. On the basis of the facts revealed in this study, a manager can prepare a fairly standardized personal time budget.

*Personal Time Budget.* This time budget may be basic, or it may be as complex as the individual feels is necessary. In a basic time budget (Fig. T-2) a manager's time is classified four ways.

1. *Routine paper work.* This includes checking time cards, filling out pay sheets, checking log books and tally sheets, and answering mail. While this activity should be held to a minimum, most budgets allocate between 10 and 20 percent of time to it.

2. *Supervisory duties.* These make up the core of most management jobs and are often the most important part. They include, first and foremost, supervising employees and all that attends that task—assigning work, training, checking performance, counseling. Most managers should try to function in this capacity for at least 50 percent of the time.

3. *Special assignments.* For a manager who is well regarded, these extra activities will eat into the available time and also stretch the normal day from 8 to 9 or 10 hours. While it may be good for a manager's record to serve on safety and cost reduction committees, or to be the person tagged for research on special projects, it does not pay to be too eager. Special assignments may erode the supervisory performance that is basic to a manager's survival. Generally, these special activities should be limited to about 10 to 20 percent of a manager's time.

4. *Planning and creative work.* These are the things managers do on their own initiative to smooth out the work flow, to improve layout and methods in operations, to train the staff for new assignments,

| Personal Time Analysis Sheet | | | | | | | | | | | | |
|---|---|---|---|---|---|---|---|---|---|---|---|---|
| | | | | | | | | | Date: | | | |
| Observed activity and function | Observation times | | | | | | | | | | | Percent of all observations |
| | 7:45 | 8:15 | 8:45 | 9:15 | 9:45 | | 3:15 | 3:45 | 4:15 | 4:45 | 5:15 | Totals | |
| **Activity** | | | | | | | | | | | | | |
| A. Personal contacts | | | | | | | | | | | | | |
| B. Telephone | | | | | | | | | | | | | |
| C. Paperwork | | | | | | | | | | | | | |
| D. Meetings | | | | | | | | | | | | | |
| E. Personal (travel, lunch, etc.) | | | | | | | | | | | | | |
| F. Other | | | | | | | | | | | | | |
| **Function** | | | | | | | | | | | | | |
| 1. Assigning work | | | | | | | | | | | | | |
| 2. Reviewing subordinate performance | | | | | | | | | | | | | |
| 3. Expediting orders and supplies | | | | | | | | | | | | | |
| 4. Preparing and analyzing reports | | | | | | | | | | | | | |
| 5. Preparing plans and schedules | | | | | | | | | | | | | |
| 6. Organizational development | | | | | | | | | | | | | |
| 7. Sales/customer development | | | | | | | | | | | | | |
| 8. Product development | | | | | | | | | | | | | |
| 9. Creative/self-improvement | | | | | | | | | | | | | |
| 10. Other | | | | | | | | | | | | | |

Fig. T-1. Personal time analysis sheet. For each observation time, place a mark in the activity and function group.

and to make the most of the time available to all. Planning time also includes time for thought and reflection and for self-improvement. At a minimum, a manager ought to allot 15 percent of the time to planning and creative work.

**Conserving Personal Time** Personal time has a way of finding the leaks in the system. It drains away far more easily than it is utilized. There are, however, a number of ways in which an alert manager can plug these leaks.

1. *Control the telephone.* There is probably no demon more apt to chew up personal time than the telephone. Often, what begins as a brief exchange of business information degenerates into 15 minutes of irrelevant gossip. Time also is wasted when a manager accepts a nonurgent call during a meeting or when the manager is conducting business with a

subordinate. Such calls can be handled by saying, "Please call back later," or "I'll return your call in 15 minutes."

2. *Limit chitchat.* There is nothing like a 20-minute conversation about the weekend's ski trip to put a manager behind schedule the first thing Monday morning. It is difficult, of course, to sense when to lend an interested ear and when to cut a conversation short. It is probably best to develop a routine way of handling such situations by saying, "I'd love to hear about it at lunch," or "Let's get together during the coffee break, if we can, so that I can hear the whole story."

3. *Decide quickly on small matters.* Most problems do not require a lot of time for a decision. On small matters, especially, there is rarely justification for asking for time to think them over. A prompt

"yes" or "no" saves time since it enables a manager to dispose of the matter without having to return to it later.

4. *Start early.* Many personal time problems can be avoided by beginning the workday a few minutes early. A great number of successful executives can testify to this. They say that they can accomplish more by getting to work ½ hour early in the morning than they can during any 2 or 3 hours during the day. Obviously, this is a good time for disposing of routine paper work.

5. *Discourage interruptions.* If managers develop and follow time budgets, they can be justifiably firm about asking that their routines not be disturbed except in an emergency. They can do so because enough time has been allotted for the major duties. In this way, subordinates and others have a designated time during which they and their supervisors are free to discuss any problems which may arise during a day.

6. *Avoid overcommitting personal time.* A manager has an obligation to contribute to the organization's overall welfare but must avoid carrying these activities too far. Quite simply, a manager has to learn to say "no" when the time budget is overloaded.

7. *Utilize travel time.* A manager deserves rest and relaxation, of course. It makes good sense, however, to consider that the working day begins when a manager leaves home in the morning and ends upon reaching home at night. Many solutions can be effected quicker by using extra times such as commuting hours, lunch periods, and waiting times in airports to think over problems encountered during the day.

*See also* DELEGATION; LEARNING (EXPERIENCE) CURVES; WORK MEASUREMENT; WORK SAMPLING; WORK SIMPLIFICATION AND IMPROVEMENT.

### REFERENCES

Bittel, Lester R.: *Improving Supervisory Performance*, McGraw-Hill Book Company, New York, 1976, chap. 9.
McCay, James T.: *The Management of Time*, Prentice-Hall, Inc., Englewood Cliffs, N.J., 1973.
Mackenzie, R. Alec.: *The Time Trap*, McGraw-Hill Book Company, New York, 1972.

STAFF/BITTEL

**Time series** (*See* FORECASTING BUSINESS CONDITIONS.)

| | Monday | Tuesday | Wednesday | Thursday | Friday |
|---|---|---|---|---|---|
| 8 | Routine | Routine | Routine | Routine | Routine |
| 9 | Inspection and supervision of operations | Individual work with staff  Regular | Inspection and supervision of operations | Individual work with staff  Regular | Special work |
| 10 | | Inspection and supervision of operations | Regular | Control studies and reports | Inspection and supervision of operations  Regular |
| 11 | Regular | Regular | Division staff meeting  Regular | Regular | Staff meeting  Regular |
| 12 | L | U | N | C | H |
| 1 | Interviews and contacts  Regular | Interviews and contacts  Regular | Interviews and contacts  Regular | Interviews and contacts  Regular | Creative work |
| 2 | Planning and organizing | Inspection and supervision of operations | Special work | Inspection and supervision of operations | |
| 3 | | | | | |
| 4 | Regular | Regular | | Regular | |
| 5 | Routine | Routine | Routine | Routine | Routine |

**Fig. T-2. Personal time budget.**

**Time study**  (*See* WORK MEASUREMENT.)

**Timetables, affirmative action**  (*See* MI-NORITIES, MANAGEMENT OF AND EQUAL EMPLOYMENT OPPORTUNITIES.)

**Title VII of Civil Rights Act of 1964** (*See* WOMEN IN INDUSTRY.)

**Top-down planning**  (*See* PLANNING, STRATEGIC MANAGERIAL.)

**Top-level managers**  (*See* MANAGER, DEFINITIONS OF.)

**Torts**  (*See* GOVERNMENT REGULATIONS, BUSINESS LAW.)

**Towne, Henry R.**  (*See* MANAGEMENT, HISTORICAL DEVELOPMENT OF.)

**Toxic Substances Control Act**  (*See* ENVIRONMENTAL PROTECTION LEGISLATION.)

**Trade, international**  (*See* INTERNATIONAL TRADE.)

**Trade associations**  (*See* ASSOCIATIONS, TRADE AND PROFESSIONAL.)

**Trademarks**  (*See* BRANDS AND BRAND NAMES; PATENTS AND VALUABLE INTANGIBLE RIGHTS.)

**Trade names**  (*See* BRANDS AND BRAND NAMES.)

**Trade-off analysis**  (*See* PRODUCTION/OPERATIONS MANAGEMENT.)

**Trade-offs, in control**  (*See* CONTROL SYSTEMS, MANAGEMENT.)

**Trade secrets**  (*See* PATENTS AND VALUABLE INTANGIBLE RIGHTS.)

**Trade unions**  [*See* LABOR (TRADE) UNIONS.]

**Traditional school**  (*See* MANAGEMENT THEORY, SCIENCE, AND APPROACHES.)

**Traffic management**  (*See* DISTRIBUTION, PHYSICAL.)

**Traffic manager**  (*See* MATERIALS MANAGEMENT.)

**Training and development, career paths**  (*See* DEVELOPMENT AND TRAINING, CAREER PATH PLANNING FOR MANAGERS.)

**Training and development, employee**  (*See* DEVELOPMENT AND TRAINING, EMPLOYEE.)

**Training and development, management**  (*See* DEVELOPMENT AND TRAINING, MANAGEMENT.)

**Training needs analysis**  (*See* DEVELOPMENT AND TRAINING, EMPLOYEE.)

**Training programs, employee**  (*See* DEVELOPMENT AND TRAINING, EMPLOYEE.)

**Transaction reporting**  (*See* INVENTORY CONTROL, PURCHASING AND ACCOUNTING ASPECTS.)

# Transaction table    (*See* INVENTORY CONTROL, PURCHASING AND ACCOUNTING ASPECTS.)

# Transactional analysis

*Transactional analysis* (TA) is the term used to describe both a theory and the application of that theory in the description and understanding of human behavior and interpersonal relations ("transactions"). It is used by management to heighten a trainee's ability to manage his or her own behavior and that of others and to build an atmosphere of mutual respect and trust.

Derived largely from Freud, developed and popularized by Dr. Eric L. Berne *(Games People Play)* and Dr. Thomas A. Harris *(I'm Okay, You're Okay)* in the 1950s, TA has been used by scores of corporations to train thousands of employees at all levels to use their rational abilities for problem solving and decision making more effectively. It is seen also as a management tool for improving in-house communication.

TA is a simplified approach to psychological therapy. The professional consultant teaches it as a basic language and trains small groups to use it to recognize and describe the "child," "parent," or "adult" ego state predominating in each participant in a simulated interaction. Trainees become aware of the consequences to other people of various behaviors and practice suggesting alternative behaviors in the optimal rational ("adult") mode of transaction, thus leading to improved individual and group effectiveness and communication.

Although its effectiveness is still difficult to measure, many corporations see positive benefits from TA training in improved customer relations, sharply decreased resignations (owing to improved managerial insights in handling subordinates—and bosses), increased enthusiasm for monotonous jobs, and in its uses as a nonthreatening "gripe method." TA gives supervisors improved tools for selecting new hires, evaluating performance, and promoting. It sharply improves teams' abilities to perceive and manage their own processes. Conversely, as a technique that gives autonomy to people as a means toward productivity, it is not attractive to strongly autocratic managements. As a relatively shallow theory, it also needs a much stronger base in research than has yet been provided. When used in a firm, it sometimes causes new problems to surface, makes new demands on managers. Employees may suspect management of playing God or "big brother"; nevertheless, the popularity of TA is symptomatic of the intense interest of people in their own behavior, and its future in business is probably assured.

*See also* INTERPERSONAL RELATIONSHIPS; LABORATORY (SENSITIVITY) TRAINING.

## REFERENCES

Berne, Eric L.: "Ego States in Psychotherapy," *American Journal of Psychotherapy*, 1957, 11, 293.
——: *Games People Play*, Grove Press, Inc., New York, 1964.
——: *Principles of Group Treatment*, Oxford University Press, New York, 1966.
——: *The Structure and Dynamics of Organizations and Groups*, J. P. Lippincott Company, Philadelphia, 1963.
Harris, Thomas A.: *I'm OK—You're OK: A Practical Guide to Transactional analysis*, Harper & Row, Publishers, Incorporated, New York, 1967.

STAFF/HOKE

# Transfer    (*See* PERSONNEL ADMINISTRATION.)

# "Transfer sheet" analysis    (*See* SHAREHOLDER RELATIONSHIPS.)

# Translation    (*See* EXCHANGE, FOREIGN, MANAGEMENT OF.)

# Transportation, internal and external    (*See* MATERIALS MANAGEMENT.)

# Transportation industry management    (*See* REGULATED INDUSTRIES, MANAGEMENT OF.)

# Transportation symbol    (*See* WORK SIMPLIFICATION AND IMPROVEMENT.)

# Transportation systems    (*See* PLANNING, STRATEGIC PLANNING MODELS.)

**Treasurer, corporate**    (*See* OFFICERS, COR-
PORATE.)

**Trend analysis, financial**    (*See* FINANCIAL
MANAGEMENT; PRODUCT PLANNING AND DEVELOP-
MENT.)

**TREND measures, purchasing**    (*See* PUR-
CHASING MANAGEMENT.)

**Trends, management**    (*See* MANAGEMENT,
FUTURE OF.)

**Trusteeship**    (*See* BOARDS OF DIRECTORS;
BOARDS OF DIRECTORS, LEGAL LIABILITY GUIDE-
LINES.)

**Trust fund depositories**    (*See* TAX MAN-
AGEMENT, MANAGERIAL RESPONSIBILITY FOR FED-
ERAL INCOME TAX REPORTING.)

**Truth-in-lending regulation Z**    (*See*
CREDIT MANAGEMENT.)

**Turnover, employee**    (*See* PERSONNEL AD-
MINISTRATION.)

**Two-factor taxonomy of motivation**
(*See* MOTIVATION IN ORGANIZATIONS.)

**Typewriter analysis**    (*See* PAPER WORK SIM-
PLIFICATION.)

# U

**Uncertainty** (*See* RISK ANALYSIS AND MANAGEMENT; STATISTICAL ANALYSIS FOR MANAGEMENT.)

**Underutilization, minorities** (*See* MINORITIES, MANAGEMENT OF AND EQUAL EMPLOYMENT OPPORTUNITY.)

**Unemployment** (*See* EMPLOYMENT AND UNEMPLOYMENT.)

**Unemployment, cyclical** (*See* EMPLOYMENT AND UNEMPLOYMENT.)

**Unemployment, frictional** (*See* EMPLOYMENT AND UNEMPLOYMENT.)

**Unemployment, structural** (*See* EMPLOYMENT AND UNEMPLOYMENT.)

**Unemployment compensation** (*See* COMPENSATION, EMPLOYEE BENEFIT PLANS.)

**Unemployment rate** (*See* EMPLOYMENT AND UNEMPLOYMENT.)

**Uniform commercial code** (*See* GOVERNMENT REGULATIONS, UNIFORM COMMERCIAL CODE.)

**Union negotiations** (*See* LABOR-MANAGEMENT RELATIONS.)

**Unions, labor** [*See* LABOR (TRADE) UNIONS.]

**Unit, bargaining** (*See* LABOR-MANAGEMENT RELATIONS.)

**Units, office planning** (*See* OFFICE SPACE PLANNING AND DESIGN.)

**Unity of command** (*See* MANAGEMENT THEORY, SCIENCE, AND APPROACHES.)

**University executive programs** (*See* DEVELOPMENT AND TRAINING, UNIVERSITY EXECUTIVE PROGRAMS.)

**University management** (*See* COLLEGE AND UNIVERSITY ADMINISTRATION.)

**Utility industry management** (*See* REGULATED INDUSTRIES, MANAGEMENT OF.)

**Utility, economic** (*See* ECONOMIC CONCEPTS.)

**Utility patent** (*See* PATENTS AND VALUABLE INTANGIBLE RIGHTS.)

# V

**Vacations**  (*See* COMPENSATION, EMPLOYEE
BENEFIT PLANS.)

**Validity, construct**  (*See* MINORITIES, MAN-
AGEMENT OF AND EQUAL EMPLOYMENT OPPORTU-
NITY.)

**Validity, content**  (*See* MINORITIES, MANAGE-
MENT OF AND EQUAL EMPLOYMENT OPPORTUNITY.)

**Validity, test**  (*See* TESTING, PSYCHOLOGICAL.)

**Valuation**  (*See* ACQUISITIONS AND MERGERS.)

**Value, expected**  (*See* STATISTICAL ANALYSIS
FOR MANAGEMENT.)

**Value, present**  (*See* PROFITS AND PROFIT
MAKING.)

## Value-added tax

Value-added tax (VAT) is a multistage sales tax
computed by adding to the net value of a taxable
product the algebraic sum of wages, interest, profits, rent, and all sums paid to other firms in purchasing inputs. Essentially, it is a sales tax on the increased value of goods as they go from producer
through distributors to the consumer.

Never widely utilized in the United States, although imposed by Michigan, the VAT was proposed and rejected by the president's Special Tax
Task Force in 1970 as a partial substitute for the
corporate income tax in order to make the price of
United States products more competitive in foreign
markets. In 1954 the VAT was instituted by France
and has since been widely adopted by other Western
European countries. In Europe, the VAT has been
used to overcome the inequities of the multistage
turnover tax, since it offers the political advantage of
spreading the tax base among nearly all firms. Also,
a low tax rate can bring in great sums. It is regarded
as punitive by many in the United States since it is
proportional and paid by all, regardless of ability to
pay.

*See also* ECONOMIC CONCEPTS.

### REFERENCES

*A Better Balance in Federal Taxes on Business*, Committee for
Economic Development, New York, 1966.
Summerfield, Ray M., Hershel M. Anderson, and Horace
R. Brock: *An Introduction to Taxation*, 2d ed., Harcourt
Brace Jovanovich, Inc., New York, 1972.

STAFF/HOKE

# Value analysis

Value analysis is a proven management tool for profit assurance, but to be effective it must be part of the daily life of operating management. Many factors must be considered by management before a decision can be made concerning the establishment of a value program. There is no standard solution that will satisfy all corporate requirements, and there are as many variables as there are types of companies. One of the variables having considerable effect on the ultimate decision is the type of industry—whether it is a typical manufacturing plant heavily engaged in fabrication and assembly operations or an industry engaged in a continuous process. Those companies heavily oriented toward design and manufacture of "hardware" have excellent potential for sizable cost avoidance during the design phase as well as cost reduction resulting from value-analyzing their products and components already in production.

Value analysis has proven to be highly successful in many areas in addition to manufacturing companies. Substantial cost reductions have been achieved in hospital administration, banking, and construction and by state and local governments.

## DEFINITION OF TERMS

Value programs have grown so rapidly in recent years that the terms *value analysis, value engineering, value control, value assurance, value management* and almost any program with the word *value* in the title can be found in effect somewhere. The predominant term is the one coined in 1948 by Larry D. Miles at General Electric, Schnectady, where he pioneered the technique. *Value analysis* is an organized, creative approach to the problem of identifying and eliminating unnecessary cost, especially of a product or service. When applied to the design function, the activity is more commonly known as *value engineering*. In many cases, value analysis and value engineering are used interchangeably, as will be done in this entry.

Elimination of unnecessary cost causes no adverse affect on quality, reliability, maintainability, or salability. The problem, however, is to identify what element of cost is unnecessary. The value analysis program is the technique for accomplishing this objective. All costs connected with the product design, material, manufacturing processes, and especially the specifications and requirements are subjected to the value analysis study. Specifically the characteristics of value analysis are (1) it is an orga-

nized, creative approach to cost reduction, (2) it places emphasis on function rather than method, (3) it identifies areas of excessive or unnecessary costs, (4) it improves the value of the product, (5) it provides the same or better performance at a lower cost, and (6) it reduces neither quality nor reliability. *Value* is the lowest cost needed to reliably accomplish the essential function.

**Value Engineering Study** A value engineering study is an objective appraisal of all the elements of the design, construction, procurement, installation, and maintenance of equipment, including the specifications, to achieve the necessary functions, maintainability, and reliability at the lowest cost. Value engineering entails a detailed review of product designs and specifications, placing a total dollar value on the costs of production and maintenance and relating these costs to the functional value of each part and assembly. Alternative designs, materials, processes, and methods of fabrication, together with standard products available from specialty suppliers, are explored to find the lowest-cost way to achieve required functions.

**Function** Function is that which makes a product work or sell. The function should be defined in two words, a verb and a noun; for example, "support cable." There are two reasons for restricting analysis to such a definition of function:

1. The use of two words avoids the possibility of combining functions and attempting to define more than one simple function at a time.

2. The use of two simple words will assure the achievement of the lowest level of abstraction possible with words; the identification of the function should be as precise as possible.

**Primary or Basic Function** The primary or basic function is the most important essential function without the peformance of which the product would be virtually worthless. If a function can be eliminated without preventing the achievement of the basic function, then this function is secondary.

## VALUE ENGINEERING TECHNIQUES

The primary concern in any design is the function. Too often, however, the subject of cost is pushed into the background and then forgotten. Most of the key value engineering techniques are not new or revolutionary; they are elements of good engineering practice applied in a systematic sequence to achieve maximum value. The following are 21 techniques used in value engineering:

1. Set up the value engineering job plan. The job plan consists of five phases: (*a*) information, (*b*) speculation, (*c*) analysis, (*d*) decision, and (*e*) execution.

2. Get all available facts. As a first step in reducing costs, it is necessary to become completely familiar with the product by factual review. This consists of determining: What is the primary function? What are the secondary functions? Why was it designed this way? How is it made? How much does it cost? What does it weigh? What are the specifications? How many units will be used? What is the lead time for fabrication or procurement of each part? Only after you are armed with all the facts can you approach the problem intelligently.

3. Get information from the best sources. Contact people who can provide needed information accurately and quickly. For example, contact production engineering for information on materials, processes, and finishes; manufacturing planning for fabrication methods; and material procurement for vendor information and cost estimates of purchased parts.

4. Know costs. To make a complete analysis of any component, it is necessary to know not only the total cost of the component but the breakdown of the total cost. This breakdown will include materials, labor, and overhead. Each operation eliminated will then remove that portion of the cost.

5. Define each function. This technique consists of describing the function of each part with a verb and a noun. For example, a diaphragm (*a*) holds pressure, (*b*) seals holes, (*c*) provides reliability, and so on.

6. Evaluate each function. After defining each function, set up the relative importance of each function in dollars and cents. Eliminate those functions not essential for adequate use of the component, thus eliminating that portion of the cost. Use the following outline in the evaluation: What is it? What does it do? What does it cost? What else will do the job? What does that cost?

Value is measured by comparison. Compare the cost of an item with the costs of other familiar, commonplace products that perform similar functions. For comparison purposes, attempt to obtain design data produced by other companies. A number of differences will exist, but a comparison of end-product costs can be made.

7. Work on specifics; avoid generalities. This technique can be used effectively with the preceding one. Work on each function individually before attempting to combine them into a single, multifunctioning product. By using this technique, hidden costs can be more easily removed from the overall assembly. Recognize that if a generality exists, it has probably deferred effective action in the past.

8. Think creatively. Use as many creative techniques as necessary to get a fresh point of view. One accepted technique has been aptly named *brainstorming*. While applying this technique, do not evaluate ideas. Turn the evaluation part of your brain off and become a dreamer. Make short statements to express your ideas. Do not attempt to develop your ideas. Once you have expressed the idea, record it, forget it, and go on to the next idea. Do not limit yourself to the conventional approach. The main purpose is to accumulate as many different approaches to the problem as possible before evaluating any of them.

9. Blast and create, then refine. When first attempting to remove costs from a product or process, it is helpful to blast away all thought of the existing concept. Attempt to remove 50 to 75 percent of the cost, as opposed to 5 to 10 percent. Removal of such a large percentage requires new methods, possibly a completely different design concept or fabrication procedure, but always without changing the primary function.

As an example, each of the four main wing tanks in the C-130 fuel system contains an electric booster pump. To ensure that the booster pump is adequately supplied in all flight attitudes, an electric scavenger pump was provided to transfer fuel continuously from the opposite side of the tank to the surge box surrounding the booster pump. By blasting away the concept of a "pump," it was suggested that an eductor, with no moving parts, would accomplish the transfer of fuel with high reliability. Reliability was increased, weight was reduced 16 pounds per plane, maintenance was simplified, and the cost of spares was reduced. Production and installation costs were reduced by more than 85 percent.

Begin to refine only after creating ideas that promise to remove 50 percent or more of the cost. In the refining process, it may be necessary to add 10 to 15 percent to ensure that essential secondary requirements are met. The net gain should amount to a minimum of 30 percent. It is easier in the long run to go through this procedure and remove 30 percent of the cost than to refine the present component and remove 10 percent.

10. Put a dollar sign on each main idea. Prior to launching a thorough investigation into the whys and wherefores of ideas, estimate their worth. Use a dollar sign in setting up a priority on which ideas merit first and most serious consideration. Before

evaluating these ideas, try to estimate the possible dividends in return for your invested time.

In an oil filter circuit, for example, analysis pointed up the fact that two filters accounted for more than two-thirds of the total cost and therefore merited first consideration. Combining the functions of the two filters into a single filter that could be produced in quantity saved 65 percent.

11. Use company specialists and services. During the analysis and decision phases of idea development, make full use of the many and varied company services available to you. Consult company specialists or service groups. They are competent and readily available sources of information.

12. Use standard items. Wherever possible, use standard components. This reduces cost by increasing competition, eliminating proprietary information or processes, eliminating tooling costs, and ensuring quality products.

13. Bring new information into each functional area. Use specialists when investigating unfamiliar fields. A theoretical approach may lead to previously untried approaches which, when developed, can be great cost savers. Technical breakthroughs and financial breakthroughs usually go hand in hand.

14. Use industry and vendor specialized knowledge. Many firms specialize in limited fields. Their ability to stay in business depends on their being in the forefront of the technology in those fields. Approach appropriate specialty suppliers with a problem, not with a detailed drawing of a solution. Explain the function that must be achieved and ask for recommendations. Frequently, the specialist will suggest solutions which are new to the design engineer and will offer to furnish the hardware at a greatly reduced price as compared with in-plant manufacture of the design engineer's solution.

15. Use specialty processes. The tried and proved processes are often overused because they require the least investigative work. They also give the least financial return. Using new methods can reduce costs. For example, tape-indexed, three-dimensional machining is replacing forging, machining, welding, heat treating, final contouring, and stress relieving. Precision molding minimizes the high cost of machining, cuts rejection rates, and simplifies assembly procedures.

16. Use specialty products and materials. Specialty products are those that are not necessarily covered by a design or blueprint but could be covered by a specification-controlled drawing. A specialty product could be an item which is unlike what you might design, but which would fit the part or assembly and perform the desired function with no sacrifice in quality or reliability—and in most cases at a fraction of the cost of a specially designed part.

17. Put dollar signs on key tolerances. Do this, whether they are on dimensions, chemical constituents, weights, or surface variations. It is often difficult during development to relax initial tolerances, because so little is known of their importance to the final assembly.

18. Use personal judgment. Although the analyst should ask the advice of specialists and other designers, do not jump to use the suggestions of others. Use your own judgment. After having come this far, you are the expert on a particular project. You have most of the information, and your design sense and your common sense are your greatest aids.

19. Spend the company's money as you would your own. The analyst's decisions commit the company's money. It should be spent exactly the way the individual would his or her own. Ask, "What would I do if it were my money?" or "If it were my money, would I be willing to pay that much for it?" This criterion can be very effective in eliminating overdesign.

20. Identify and overcome roadblocks. Roadblocks are considered to be anything that impedes progress or progressive thinking. They commonly evolve from negative thinking, fear (particularly of personal loss), ignorance, laziness, self-defense, or undesirable habits. Your first hint of danger in confronting one of these roadblocks will be the sound of phrases such as, "We have always done it this way." "Why change it? It works." "It is company policy." When your progress is impeded, clearly define the obstacle. Overcoming the obstacle then becomes the problem. To do this, more facts must be brought to bear.

21. Use better human relations. A high percentage of failures can be charged to poor human relations. The analyst should stress asking, not demanding; suggesting, not criticizing; helping, not hindering; and interest, not boredom. This enlists voluntary aid and makes contacts that can be useful in future assignments.

### FIVE-PHASE JOB PLAN

The first and perhaps the most important technique of value engineering is the organized approach—the value engineering job plan. If outstanding results are to be achieved in getting better value, and 30, 50, or even 75 percent of the original costs are to be removed, there must be a systematic plan of attack. The job plan consists of the following five phases:

**The Information Phase**  Each problem requires a phase in which all the facts are clearly determined.

Get complete information concerning costs, inventory, usage, specifications, development history, material, manufacturing methods, and processes. Get drawings, manufacturing operation sheets, and actual samples. Define the primary function and secondary functions. Collect too much rather than too little information. Exhaust all possible sources of information. Separate facts from opinions. Do not "stack" the evidence.

**The Speculation Phase**   Here is where you put to use the creative approach. Try to answer the question, "What else will do the job?" Blast away old concepts. Make use of the brainstorming method. Exclude negative thoughts. Avoid analysis of ideas at this stage. Record all ideas; then forget them for the time being. To start the ideas flowing, try asking simple, suggestive questions such as:

In what form could this be?

How would I make it in my home workshop?

Should it slide instead of rotate?

What other layout might be better?

What if it were turned upside down? Inside out?

Record all ideas for achieving the function regardless of specifications, interchangeability, and so on. Many times, good ideas come from trying to develop others that obviously would not work.

Set a target to take out at least one-half of the cost from functional areas and nine-tenths of the cost from some of the components. By so doing, you will be forced into new areas—areas not previously explored.

**The Analysis Phase**   The primary objective here is to analyze and weigh the ideas generated with regard to cost, function, and feasibility. Establish a dollar value of each idea. Challenge each idea by applying the following tests for value:

Does its use contribute value?

Is its cost proportionate to its usefulness?

Can it or some of its features be eliminated?

Can its required function be achieved in a simpler manner?

Can a usable standard product be found?

Is it made on proper tooling, considering quantities used?

Will another supplier provide it for less?

Is anyone buying it for less?

Refine all ideas that show promise of providing improved value. Evaluate these ideas by comparison. Select for further consideration those ideas that have weathered the storm of evaluation.

Do not try to eliminate ideas. Instead, try to analyze ideas to see how they can be made to work. A positive approach must be used. Ideas emanating from a brainstorming session are not going to spring to life correct in all details. They are concepts only. Do not let an obvious fault hide the merits of a proposal and thus prevent its thorough analysis. With a small modification, it may become a promising idea.

**The Decision Phase**   Take the best ideas and plan a program to obtain the information needed to develop these ideas into sound, usable suggestions. What must be done is to recognize the problem and search for the person who can help. There are many specialists in a company, and the services of every specialist in industry are available on request. In drawing help from outside the company, from suppliers or specialists, do not just hand them a drawing and specifications and say, "What can you do with this?" Instead, inform them of the function you want, draw out their ideas on the problem, and give them some latitude to work in.

Certain ideas will develop and promise a future. Each idea should be reviewed with the thought, "Is this really the best idea?" "With this new information could a better job be done?" Now is the time to use your best judgment. Select those ideas showing the most promise, and plan your campaign for selling your proposals to top management.

**The Execution Phase**   In this phase, the idea must be sold. Be prepared to meet and triumph over considerable resistance. To do so, present a clear and concise picture of exactly what is proposed and what the proposal will mean to top management, their project, and the company. When making recommendations, always be prepared to give and take. Have an alternate plan ready in the event the primary proposal is rejected. Stress the technical capability of the proposal, and use cost reduction as an incentive.

## ORGANIZATION AND STAFFING

Location of the value engineering function within a company is dependent upon the type of industry. With complete backing of top management, location of the function is not as important as the personnel selected to staff the organization. Most companies tend to place the value engineering operation within their engineering branch if the company is heavily design-oriented. Process-type industries more than likely will place the value operation within the procurement branch, where it is most often called value analysis. The reasoning behind this approach is based upon the higher percentage of dollar expenditure allocated to the procurement of materials in contrast to the cost of design fabrication and assembly operations. When value analysis is applied to manufacturing operations or to clerical systems and procedures, it is typically supervised by the industrial engineering organization.

Selection of the value engineering staff should be based upon the experience and educational background most suitable to the type of industry. The nature of the value engineering task makes certain personality and character traits very important. The job requires extensive personal contact with people at all levels of management and in all areas of the company organization. The need for the value engineer to deal with these contacts in a positive, constructive manner cannot be overemphasized. The value engineer must possess sufficient initiative to undertake difficult tasks in previewing unexplored areas, and he or she must be sensitive to the personal views of those contacted. Obviously, the analyst must be articulate in presenting findings in both oral and written presentations. He or she must possess a degree of maturity and should not become easily discouraged when proposals are rebuffed. An engineering degree, or the equivalent in experience, is almost a necessity for value engineers assigned to work on design projects. The formal education requirements are not as stringent in those areas not involving technical design work.

Experience has shown that it is normal to expect a 10:1 return on value engineering effort. In other words, there should be approximately a $10 net saving for every dollar spent on value engineering investigations. In a design organization, it has been found that a ratio of 1 value engineer to each 30 technical designers is sufficient to obtain good cost reduction through value engineering efforts.

## PROGRAM CONTROL

Six factors warrant control:

**Target Costs**  An excellent program control is the use of a target-cost procedure which measures production costs as a function of design and provides a system of program control whereby value engineering personnel continuously monitor the progress of design as it relates to the base configuration. The costs of design deviations from the base configuration are determined and reflected on a target chart of the appropriate item to indicate the under- or over-cost condition. Potential cost increases alert affected management to the problem areas, and prompt action can then be initiated.

**Technical Requirement Reviews**  Technical engineering requirement reviews should be initiated in the early phases of design and development. These reviews, conducted with the value engineer, serve as

the means for identifying the necessary functions, isolating those design requirements necessary to satisfy the functions, and documenting the design-requirement justification. Alternatives for obtaining the functional requirements are determined and evaluated in relation to functional performance lists, subsystem interrelationships, and system cost.

**Value Engineering Studies**  These are formal reports utilized to conduct and document functional analyses of design requirements and parameters. They are initiated when multiple approaches are proposed for accomplishing functional requirements. Detailed evaluations of the technical requirements are made and their effect on total system performance determined. Concurrently, the effect on system cost of each alternative is determined and related to the individual technical requirements. Areas of both high cost and high-cost sensitivity are identified, and the associated requirement is examined in relation to its contribution to system effectivenss. The requirements identified by these high-cost areas are examined in detail from a cost-effectiveness standpoint. These elements of disproportionate high cost then become the subject of further investigation.

**Design Value Reviews**  Verification that functional requirements are satisfied at minimum cost is established by design value reviews prior to final engineering release. Value reviews are composite studies of designs, technical requirements, and specifications which lead to formal approval of designs, specifications, and procurement. The value engineer makes a continual review from concept to hardware to achieve complete verification of low-cost objectives. He or she is a member of the design review team and provides cost-target information of the base-line configuration and generates alternative considerations. The designer is given guidance on the least costly material, production technique, tooling, test, and the cost effect of spares, reliability, and maintainability for the given application. These costs are equated to system productivity. Consideration of these design recommendations is verified by the value engineer's signature on the drawing or specification prior to release.

**Total Systems Control**  Value engineering techniques should also be employed in the areas of testing procedures and testing equipment, facilities, tooling, purchasing, packaging, production operations, and information systems. Cost methodology employed in the analyses of design alternatives should be organized to develop a total system cost in terms of acquisition cost plus the operation over a period of years equivalent to the service life of the product. Cost models are used when determining total system cost. After the total system cost has been determined for a particular design consideration, a cost optimization process is employed to determine the best combination of cost measures.

The elements of the value engineering program are separate and identifiable portions of the total tasks associated with the design, development, and production of a system for which value engineering has primary responsibility. These include a target cost and tracking system.

**Monitoring** Monitoring elements, on the other hand, comprise those tasks which are controlled outside the value engineering organization, but which are implemented and assessed by value engineering review. These include procurement and the value engineering effort of subcontractors, engineering developmental testing, and manufacturing-operations value engineering.

*See also* COST IMPROVEMENT; DESIGN, INDUSTRIAL; ENGINEERING, INDUSTRIAL; PAPER WORK SIMPLIFICATION; PRODUCT PLANNING AND DEVELOPMENT; SYSTEMS AND PROCEDURES; WORK SIMPLIFICATION AND IMPROVEMENT.

### REFERENCES

Grove, John W., ed.: *Value Engineering in Manufacturing*, Prentice-Hall, Inc., Englewood Cliffs, N.J., 1967.

Miles, L. D.: *The Techniques of Value Analysis and Value Engineering*, 2d ed., McGraw-Hill Book Company, New York, 1972.

*Proceedings of 1962 Third EIA Conference on Value Engineering*, Electronics Industries Association, New York, 1962.

Ridge, Warren F.: *Value Analysis for Better Management*, American Management Association, New York, 1969.

*Value Engineering*, U.S. Department of Defense Handbook H-111, Washington, Mar. 29, 1963.

Adapted from Frank J. Johnson, "Value Analysis," in H. B. Maynard (ed.), *The Handbook of Business Administration*, McGraw-Hill Book Company, New York, 1967, by permission of the publisher.

FRANK J. JOHNSON, *Johnson Management Corporation*

# Value engineering   (*See* VALUE ANALYSIS.)

# Value systems, management: social and cultural

Management is a major agent of change in present-day society. Because it must adapt sensitively to sociocultural change in order to remain authentic and economically viable, management—as it changes—brings about further social and cultural change.

An example of this circular feedback process is what has happened in technology. Organizations have fostered the development of vastly increased technical specialization, supported by the computer. This has contributed to a quick, sharp rise in the educational level of the labor force. (According to Likert,[1] in 1940, 39.1 percent of workers had a high school or college education; by 1959 that figure had increased to 62 percent.) More highly educated workers, however, become restive with routine or repetitive jobs. Job dissatisfaction is a matter of serious concern to management, which now launches experiments in job enrichment and methods attempting supervision with minimal pressure.

**Special Concerns** Management has a self-interest in a healthy society, as Drucker[2] has pointed out. Management faces several new elements, besides the high educational level, on which its self-interest must be focused:

*Special Need Groups.* There has been rapid change in the status of blacks. Equal Opportunity Employment and affirmative action programs may reduce management options and require the attention of all types of organizations. The young black worker who challenges and denounces a statement of his or her supervisor at a departmental meeting may be making a valid analytic comment about the matter at hand. The worker is also reacting, in part at least, to history and to situations outside the organization. The point, of course, is that this sort of challenge would probably not have happened before Selma, and management is still inexperienced with it. The issue is not so much that new ideas are abroad in the land as that there is a new atmosphere of greater attention to old ideas of civil rights.

There has been an increase in the number of women in the work force, owing to limitations of family size, decreased housework load with better mechanical appliances, and the organization of women's movements. Working mothers often need different job arrangements and more flexibility because of their children's needs. They present an important new set of considerations for management. When a local business organization provides start-up support for a day-care center so that employees who take care of small children can work the day shift, the community has achieved a change, and management has been the agent of change.

Youths, since the upheavals of the 1960s, tend to be better educated, better informed, and sometimes impatient with employers' explanations. They often test the authority of their own knowledge against the authority of position and seek reform through democratic processes. Because the younger generation will constitute 30 percent of the nation's population within the next 10 years,[3] they are a force to be reckoned with.

If management can find some innovative solutions to the special needs of workers who are black, female, or young, it can make a major contribution to the lubrication of the social gears and thereby enhance the quality of life in society generally.

*Rising Tensions of Daily Life.* Contributing to this social element are increased costs of food and services, rising taxes, unemployment, speed, noise, and the continued threat of wars and nuclear annihilation. Responding to the latter threat are the organized peace movements. These were especially vocal during the Vietnam war and had some effect in restricting the scope of United States participation in the war, undoubtedly cutting the earnings—and therefore the management options—of some war-related businesses. At times, the greatest tensions and fears are that the struggle against all these threats may be futile. Television sometimes seems to compound and propagate these tensions by the very immediacy of the violence it brings into the living room, instantly and from anywhere in the world.

*Government Regulations and Consumerism.* Industrial and service institutions are subject to more and more regulation. The record-keeping procedures necessary to meet government requirements are costly and cumbersome. Consumer advocate groups protest rising costs and, unwittingly, often raise costs by pushing for new controls.

*Tighter Health, Safety, and Environmental Standards.* These all impinge on organizations, increase costs, limit options, and sometimes impose such strains on management that its self-interest in a healthy society is severely tested. Harassed industry has retaliated and brought some change in the health system by persuading government to place limits on the charges for the health benefits purchased by management employees. If federal legislation is passed directing a broad-scale national health insurance, management will have participated in bringing about a profound social change.

*Liability Judgments.* Increases in the number of suits and in the sizes of the awards, especially in the health field, have curtailed research and development of new ideas. This has sometimes required an extramanagerial solution, as in the case of the production of swine-influenza vaccine in 1976.

**Outlook** Likert sees social science research as "pointing the way to an appreciably more effective system of management than now exists. . . . One important source of increased productivity will be the full development and skillful application of the form of social organization which the highest-producing managers are using increasingly." Citing Argyris, Likert points out, however, the problem management has in attempting to follow management principles and at the same time meet the personality needs of emotionally mature people. An example of that complexity is the finding that high-producing employees do not necessarily want their wage increases linked to performance ratings. This seems to be due, Likert says, to a "desire to have no conditions superimposed on the work group which cause competition and discriminatory cleavages among members of the group. To have a friendly, supportive relationship . . . with one's colleagues is more important to most people than relatively minor financial rewards."[4]

Recent attention to social, psychological, and cultural factors in management has produced an expansion of efforts to change organizations by changing the personalities of key individuals or by shifting individuals within the organization to match specific administrative tasks with personalities deemed the most appropriate for those tasks. But Whyte reminds us that "it is well nigh impossible to change a mature personality" and warns against concentration on social and psychological factors at the expense of structure. Although this orientation "may lead to a kind of catharsis every now and then as people talk out their problems and relieve their tensions and sometimes develop new insights in the process, . . . unless those insights lead to *structural* changes, you will be stuck with the same problem you had before."[5]

Etzioni is concerned about the potential effect of uncontrolled expansion of technology: "At present, scientists in various laboratories explore chemical means of controlling behavior; psychological research is being conducted that could lead to effective subliminal advertising; drugs are being developed that will enable parents to choose the sex of their children. The societal forces that will promote the introduction of these new technologies . . . are already present"[6] (and are not disinterested). He suggests that one societal agency systematically attempt to explore the implications of new technologies.

Drucker suggests that the managers of the major institutions, and especially business, should do this monitoring:

Social responsibility cannot be evaded. . . . the fact remains that in modern society there is no other leadership group but managers. If the managers of our major institutions, and especially of business, do not take the responsibility for the common good, no one else can or will. . . .

Social impacts and social responsibilities are areas in which business—and not only big business—has to think through its role, has to set objectives, has to perform. *Social impacts and social responsibilities have to be managed.*[7]

*See also* ETHICS, MANAGERIAL; MINORITIES, MANAGEMENT OF AND EQUAL EMPLOYMENT OPPORTUNITY; OLDER EMPLOYEES, MANAGEMENT OF; SOCIAL RESPONSIBILITY OF BUSINESS; TECHNOLOGY, MANAGEMENT IMPLICATIONS OF; WOMEN IN INDUSTRY; YOUNGER EMPLOYEES, MANAGEMENT OF.

### NOTES

[1]R. Likert, *New Patterns of Management*, McGraw Hill Book Company, New York, 1961, p. 2.

[2]P. Drucker, *Management: Tasks, Responsibilities, Practices*, Harper & Row, Publishers, Incorporated, New York, 1974, p. 327.

[3]A. Bennett, "Effective Management Centers on Human Values," *Hospitals, J.A.H.A.*, vol. 50, no. 14, July 16, 1976, p. 73.

[4]R. Likert, *op. cit.*, pp. 1–25.

[5]W. Whyte, "Conversation with William F. Whyte," *Organizational Dynamics*, Spring 1975, p. 54.

[6]A. Etzioni, *The Active Society*, The Free Press, New York, 1968, p. 209.

[7]P. Drucker, *op cit.*, p. 325.

WILLIAM P. CAMP, M.D., *Director, Friends Hospital*

---

**Values, personal**   (*See* INTERPERSONAL RELATIONSHIPS.)

**Variable cost budgets**   (*See* BUDGETS AND BUDGET PREPARATION.)

**Variance**   (*See* RISK ANALYSIS AND MANAGEMENT.)

**Variance analysis**   (*See* PRODUCT PLANNING AND DEVELOPMENT.)

**Variance meeting**   (*See* MARGINAL INCOME ANALYSIS.)

**Velocity of money**   (*See* ECONOMIC CONCEPTS.)

**Vending, automatic**   (*See* RETAILING MANAGEMENT.)

**Vendor**   (*See* PURCHASING MANAGEMENT.)

**Vendor negotiations**   (*See* RETAILING MANAGEMENT.)

**Vendor relations ratings**   (*See* PURCHASING MANAGEMENT.)

**Vertical distribution systems**   (*See* MARKETING, CHANNELS OF DISTRIBUTION.)

**Vestibule training**   (*See* DEVELOPMENT AND TRAINING, EMPLOYEE.)

**Vice-president, corporate**   (*See* OFFICERS, CORPORATE.)

**Visual aids**   (*See* CONFERENCES AND MEETINGS, PLANNING FOR; DEVELOPMENT AND TRAINING, EMPLOYEE.)

**Voluntary association managers**   (*See* MANAGER, DEFINITIONS OF.)

**Volunteer responsibility**   (*See* NOT-FOR-PROFIT ORGANIZATIONS, MANAGEMENT OF.)

W

## Wage and salary administration (*See* COMPENSATION, WAGE AND SALARY POLICY AND ADMINISTRATION.)

## Wages and hours legislation

Virtually every business in the United States is subject to legislative regulation of wages and working hours. As federal regulations do not preempt state action in the wage and hour area, most enterprises are within the ambit of overlapping statutes which generally mandate a minimum wage, equal pay for equal work, and payment of time and one-half after an employee has worked a certain number of hours. In the case of a conflict between federal and state requirements, the stricter wage and hour regulations always apply. The principal wage and hour law is the federal Fair Labor Standards Act [(FLSA) 29 U.S.C. 201 *et. seq.*]. FLSA requires the payment of minimum wages and overtime pay for employees not specifically exempt who are (1) engaged in (interstate) commerce; (2) engaged in the production of goods for commerce; or (3) employed by an enterprise engaged in commerce or the production of goods for commerce.

Separate statutes provide somewhat more demanding wage standards for businesses which enter into government contracts. However, federal laws *do not* (1) limit the number of hours worked per week; (2) require payment for holidays, vacations, or sick leave or (3) require different rates of pay for weekends or holidays.

Complaints that an employer has failed to pay minimum wage or overtime entitlements generally may be brought to a regulatory agency or to court either by employees or by governmental agencies (such as the Department of Labor's Wage and Hour Division) on the employees' behalf. Certain employees are exempt from wage and hour requirements. Objective, accurate job descriptions and evaluations help to (1) avoid liability for underpaying workers who are nonexempt, and (2) develop compensation programs which go beyond the requirements of law and aid the enterprise to gain the greatest return for its payroll dollar.

Employer liability for back wages and liquidated damages can be substantial. Basic steps for avoiding liability include (1) keeping accurate records in the format required and (2) using honest and prudent judgment in determining employee exemptions.

### LEGISLATION AND REGULATION

Before the groundswell of social welfare and labor legislation during the Depression years, states and the federal government made some attempts to mandate a minimum wage and maximum hours of work. It was not until the enactment of the Walsh-Healey

Public Contracts Act in 1936, however, that base wage rates and overtime payment requirements for broad classes of workers became a part of American law. Legislative regulation of wages and hours has generally been prompted by the conclusion that a living wage is a means toward securing an acceptable standard of living. A wage floor is usually viewed as a desirable alternative to an extensive transfer payment system, where the government would pay some percentage of the difference between the cost of living and an employee's wages. The social welfare laws of the 1930s, which are the foundation for most subsequent wage and hour acts, also reflect concern that certain baseline conditions of employment must be mandated by statute.

*The Fair Labor Standards Act*, which is frequently amended and updated by Congress, is the most significant of all wage and hour laws. It establishes minimum wage, overtime, equal pay, child labor, and record-keeping standards for covered employment, unless a specific exemption applies.

**FLSA Coverage** The coverage of FLSA is quite extensive, and its provisions affect the employees of almost every conceivable commercial entity. The act is an exercise of the Congressional power to regulate interstate commerce, and employees are protected by the act, either because of their individual involvement in commerce or by reason of their employer's relationship with commerce. Any worker who is engaged in commerce or in the production of goods for commerce is within FLSA's *individual employee coverage*. *Enterprise coverage* adds those workers who are employed by an entity which performs related activities with other businesses which are under common control and which operate for the common business purpose of engaging in interstate commerce or the production of goods for commerce. *All* employees of an enterprise are covered, regardless of the relationship between their jobs and interstate commerce.[1] Coverage under the FLSA is broad. For example, the use of the interstate mails qualifies secretarial personnel as workers who are engaged in commerce. Coverage of all the workers of an enterprise may require that at least two workers be covered individually. Thus, enterprise coverage is somewhat keyed to the innumerable traditional coverage decisions.[2] Even an extremely limited interstate operation has put businesses within the reach of enterprise coverage. A newspaper's out-of-state circulation was only 1/2 percent, and yet on the basis of the limited interstate contact, the newspaper was deemed an enterprise engaged in production of goods for commerce. The Courts and the Wage Hour Administrator have al-

lowed some exceptions, but exceptions are usually esoteric or obtuse and are becoming less common. Accordingly, no employer should assume an exception in the absence of prudent legal advice.

*Minimum wage.* Under FLSA, covered employees must be paid at least the minimum hourly wage. In setting standards under wage and hour laws, legislators try to avoid the disappearance of marginal jobs which might occur if the minimum wage were set too high. The history of the statute shows differential minimum wages for employees in different industries. However, in 1978 the minimum wage is now the *same* for all covered employees—$2.65 per hour. Minimum wage figures will, however, be subject to constant revision. A telephone call to the Department of Labor's Wage and Hour Office can yield information on the current minimum, and regional administrators are usually familiar with proposed legislation which could affect payroll planning.

*Overtime.* The overtime provisions of FLSA stipulate that covered employees must be paid time and one-half for all hours worked in excess of 40 during a *workweek*. A workweek may begin at any hour of any day set by the employer and is a period of 168 hours running during seven consecutive 24-hour periods. The hours worked during two or more workweeks cannot be averaged to minimize overtime payments, except in certain exceptional occupations such as seamen and hospital employees. In computing overtime, the employer must pay $1\frac{1}{2}$ times the employee's regular rate of pay. The regular rate is the employee's total weekly remuneration for work, minus statutory exclusions, divided by the total weekly hours worked for which such compensation was paid. "*Premiums* for regularly scheduled hours of work outside of the normal daytime shift are considered part of an employee's regular rate for the purpose of computing overtime."[3] For example, if a factory pays $3.00 per hour for the day shift and $3.10 per hour for the night shift, the night shift worker's overtime must be $1\frac{1}{2}$ times $3.10, or $4.65 per hour.

Employers often incur substantial overtime liability merely by permitting work which they do not really want. For example, a nonexempt sales clerk who stays past official quitting time of his or her own accord to put away stock must be paid overtime if such extra efforts bring the hours of work over 40 per week. "Work not requested but offered or permitted is work time." [29 C.F.R. 785.11]. *The Portal-to-Portal Act* [29 U.S.C. 251 *et. seq.*] more precisely defines what time an employee must be paid for. A shorthand rule is that any time spent by a worker for the benefit of the business must be paid for—as in the case of a factory hand who is preparing a machine for the day's work. Rather complicated rules control the inclusion or exclusion of bonuses from regular wage rates. On occasion, employers have intended a bonus as largess and yet have incurred disconcerting overtime liability because of the bonus payments. To avoid this result, the employer should maintain a maximum amount of discretion as to the payment and amount of any bonus.[4] Additionally, since exemption status is determined on a weekly basis, an employee can be exempt one week and nonexempt the next. This is particularly true in the case of exemptions from overtime. Under certain conditions, workers employed at piece rates, workers who do two or more jobs for which different hourly or piece rate schedules have been established, and workers who have negotiated a special rate to be used expressly for overtime purposes may be paid on an alternative basis. The use of any of these alternative methods of overtime calculation requires the employee's consent.

*Child Labor.* FLSA prohibits "oppressive child labor"—that is, the employment of minors under the legal minimum ages. Sixteen is the basic minimum age for employment in any nonagricultural occupation not specifically designated *hazardous* by the Secretary of Labor. Sixteen year olds may work in hazardous agricultural occupations; a worker must be 18 to work in other hazardous jobs. Persons 14 years of age may work in specified occupations outside of school hours. The act provides certain child labor exemptions for minors employed by their own parents, for juvenile actors, and for apprentices and students. Of course, unless an exemption applies, covered minor employees have to be paid the minimum wage and are entitled to overtime. Violations of the child labor strictures of FLSA may result in fines of up to $10,000, imprisonment, and injunctions. A plethora of state laws on child labor supplement FLSA by regulating conditions, employment during school hours, and the like. Usually, cautious employers can protect themselves from either state or federal liability by obtaining work permits from the federal or state Department of Labor showing minor employees to be of the age established by law for their occupation.

*Equal Pay Act.* Section 6(d) of FLSA, which was grafted on to the statute as the *Equal Pay Act of 1963*, is rapidly becoming one of the act's most important sections. The equal pay section requires that men and women performing jobs requiring equal skill, effort, and responsibility under similar working conditions be paid equal wages. Allegations of illegal wage discrimination based on sex have been on the rise during the past few years. Equal pay rules apply even to executive, administrative, and professional employees and to outside salespeople who are *otherwise* exempt from FLSA's minimum wage and overtime provisions. The Equal Pay Act expressly permits wage differentials which are based on (1) seniority, (2) merit, (3) measurement of earnings by quality or quantity of production, or (4) any factor other than sex. The crux of equal pay requirements is that male and female workers must be paid equally if the jobs they are doing are substantially equal. *Substantial equality* is a phrase that is usually quite broadly construed, casting suspicion on many pay differentials.[5]

*Exemption Structure.* The exemption structure of the FLSA is one of its most crucial and complex provisions. Any relatively complex question regarding an employee's exemption status is likely to require the advice of legal counsel. It is possible for an employee to be exempt from both the minimum wage and overtime dictates of the act, or exempt only from the act's overtime requirements. Of course, determination of the exempt or nonexempt status of employees has vital ramifications for compensation planning.

One of the most common and important exclusions from both minimum wage and overtime coverage is that for executive, administrative, and professional employees and outside salespeople. Academic administrative personnel and teachers are included in this category. Tests for exemption status have been devised to aid businesses in determining which of their employees qualify for these important exemptions. A bona fide *executive* must meet all the following criteria: (1) the executive's primary duty must be the management of an enterprise or a department thereof; (2) the executive must customarily direct the work of two or more employees; (3) the executive must have the authority to hire and fire, or to give important recommendations regarding hiring and firing; (4) the executive must regularly exercise discretionary powers; (5) the executive must devote no more than 20 percent of his or her hours to nonmanagerial functions[6] and (6) the executive must be paid at least $155 a week on a salary basis.[7]

*Administrative employees* are exempt if they (1) perform responsible office or nonmanual work; (2) exercise independent discretion and judgment and have the authority to make important decisions; (3) regularly assist a proprietor or executive; (4) perform specialized or technical work or execute special assignments under only general supervision; (5) do not spend 20 percent of the workweek on nonexempt work; and (6) are paid at least $155 per week.[8]

The *professional employees* category includes the learned, artistic, and teaching professions. The law requires that exempt professional work (1) require advanced knowledge in a recognized field of learning, usually obtained by a specialized course of study, or (2) be original and creative in character in a recognized artistic field; (3) be exercised with discretion and judgment; (4) be intellectual and varied, rather than routine and mechanical; (5) consist of nonprofessional duties for no more than 20 percent of the workweek; and (6) pay a salary of at least $170 a week. The salary requirement does not apply to doctors, lawyers, or teachers. An *outside salesperson* is exempt if (1) he or she is employed for the purpose of working, and customarily and regularly works, away from the employer's place of business; (2) he or she is selling tangible or intangible items such as goods, insurance, stocks, bonds, or real estate; (3) he or she is obtaining orders or contracts for services or the use of facilities, such as advertising, radio time, or typewriter repair; and (4) the hours spent in nonoutside work do not exceed 20 percent of the hours worked in the workweek by nonexempt employees of the employer.

Streamlined tests for exemption status are available in the cases of high-salaried executive, administrative, and professional employees, which may be found either in wage and hour handbooks or in federal publications.[9]

The remaining exemptions from minimum wage and overtime, or simply from overtime, are many. Learners, apprentices, handicapped workers [section 13(a) (2)], seamen on foreign vessels [section 13(a) (12)], and fishing and fish processing at sea employees [section 13(a) (5)] are among the several groups exempted from both minimum wage and overtime. Motor carrier [section 13(b) (1)], railroad [section 13(b) (2)], and airline [section 13(b) (3)] workers are exempt from overtime, along with many other workers. Perhaps the only fair advice that can be given about the FLSA's exemption structure is that Congress is *constantly* altering it, and that it is wise to consult sections 6, 7, and 13 of the act. Conflicts over the interpretation of the exemption structure generate hundreds of thousands of dollars worth of litigation every year. Caution and recourse to expert advice should be the executive's watchwords in making exemption decisions.

*Trends.* The trend in legislation for some years has been to extend coverage and to phase out exemptions. For example, the 1974 Amendments extended statutory coverage to employees of federal and state government(s) and their political subdivisions, to domestics, and to the employees of many retail and agricultural "conglomerates." But, state and local government employees (including those of state-run hospitals, institutions, and school systems), however, are *not* covered. The Supreme Court (5–4) in *National League of Cities v. Usery*—426 U.S. 833 (Nos. 74-878, 879)—(1976), ruled that Congress unconstitutionally usurped state sovereignty by extending coverage to them. So, state and local governments are not bound by the federal wage and hour laws. Nevertheless, it is not yet clear that state and local governments can unilaterally set wage and hour standards for their employees.

Importantly, an FLSA exemption does *not* mean that the minimum wage does not have to be paid if another statute requires it. Section 18 of the act states that no FLSA provision shall excuse noncompliance with a federal or state law or city ordinance requiring a higher minimum wage or a shorter maximum workweek. An employee might be exempt under the FLSA but entitled to a base wage and overtime under state law.

To resolve troubling exemption questions, an employer should (1) consult the full text of applicable federal and state statutes; (2) obtain legal advice; and (3) solicit a written opinion from the Wage and Hour Administrator of the Department of Labor.

**Enforcement**  The enforcement of wage and hour laws is uaually the function of federal and state Departments of Labor. The enforcement of the Fair Labor Standards Act is the responsibility of the Department of Labor's Wage and Hour Division. The statute provides for three modes of assuring adherence: (1) the Secretary of Labor may seek an injunction to compel compliance with the statute and the payment of back wages to the agrieved employee; (2) the Justice Department can bring criminal charges against *willful* violators; (3) employees themselves may sue for back wages due plus an equal amount in liquidated damages and reasonable attorney's fees. The statute of limitations for nonwillful violations is 2 years; it is 3 years for willful infractions. There is no statute of limitations applicable to injunctions. The Wage and Hour Administrator is empowered to issue interpretive bulletins construing the act, but has no power to simply issue compliance orders when violations seem evident.

**Other Federal Laws**  Business relations with the federal government are controlled by a number of special wage and hour laws.

1. *The Walsh-Healy Public Contracts Act* [41 U.S.C. 35 *et. seq.*] sets basic standards for work

done on United States government contracts greater than $10,000 in value. Minimum wages to be paid are set by the Secretary of Labor, based on standards in the industry. Overtime must be paid for all work over 8 hours a day or 40 hours a week, whichever number of overtime hours is greater. As under FLSA, in some situations subminimum wages may be paid to beginners, apprentices, student learners, and handicapped workers. Executive, administrative, and professional employees are exempt, and Walsh-Healy does not cover contracts for utility services, common carriers under published tariffs, perishable agricultural products, or rentals. Violators of the Walsh-Healy Act are liable to injured employees through the government. Additionally, violations may result in contract cancellation, and a violator's firm may be denied any government contracts for 3 years.

2. *The Davis-Bacon Act* [40 U.S.C. 276(a) *et. seq.*] applies to federal construction contracts of about $2000 in value. The Secretary of Labor sets minimum wage rates and *required fringe benefits* based on similar work in the locality. It is not a valid defense for contractors to show that their employees accepted rates of pay below those set by the Secretary, and the government may withhold payments from any violating firm, for the benefit of the employees who have not been paid the required wages.

3. *The Miller Act* [40 U.S.C. 270 *et. seq.*] stipulates that any firm entering into a government contract for the contruction, alteration, or repair of any public building or work in the United States valued at over $2000 must execute a payment bond with a surety to protect the wages of all persons supplying labor. A worker who is not paid within 90 days after the last labor performed may sue the contractor's surety in any federal district where the contract was to be performed and executed.

4. *The Work Hours Act of 1962* [5 U.S.C. 673(c); 28 U.S.C. 1499; 40 U.S.C. 327 *et. seq.*] provides an 8-hour workday and a 40-hour workweek, with overtime at 1½ times the basic rate, for all work involving the employment of laborers or mechanics, including security and guards: (1) on any federal public work; (2) for any contract to which the federal government is a party; or (3) for any contract financed in whole or in part by federal loans or grants and to which federal wage standard laws apply. The 1962 act is not applicable where the federal assistance is only in the nature of a loan guarantee or insurance.

5. *The Service Contract Act of 1965* [41 U.S.C. 351 *et. seq.*] stipulates that contracts for services entered into by any federal instrumentality must provide a minimum wage and certain fringe benefits. The wage/benefit package is established by the Secretary of Labor, based upon "standards prevailing in the community." Administrative, executive, and professional employees are exempt, and the Service Contract Act does not apply to several types of transportation, communication, and public utility contracts. Contracts within the purview of Davis-Bacon and Walsh-Healy are also exempt. Examples of covered contracts are those for laundry and dry cleaning, mail transport, custodial and janitorial, packing and crating, food service, warehousing and storage, and support service arrangements for military personnel. The sanctions available to the government against violators parallel those of Walsh-Healy and Davis-Bacon.

6. *The Consumer Credit Protection Act of 1968* [15 U.S.C. 1671 *et. seq.*] gives wage earners protection from harassment or loss of work due to indebtedness. The act provides that *no* state or federal court may issue any order garnishing the aggregate disposable earnings of any individual for any workweek which is above the *lesser* of (1) 25 percent of disposable earnings for that workweek; or (2) the amount by which disposable earnings per week exceed 30 times the minimum wage under section 6(a)(1) of FLSA. The act does not apply to support orders, court orders under chapter XIII of the Bankruptcy Act, or to any debt due for any state or federal tax. States may not garnish above these rates, but if state law provides for a lower rate of garnishment, the state law must be applied. No employee may be discharged for being subjected to garnishment for any one indebtedness.

**State Laws**  State wage and hour laws often set minimum wages and require overtime payments. The requirements in the applicable jurisdiction should always be checked, because section 18 of the FLSA requires that if a state law establishes more generous wage and overtime levels, or a different set of coverage criteria, the state law must be followed. Most states have statutes establishing additional pay practice requirements. Commonly, regular paydays are required, usually at least semimonthly. In many cases, employees must be paid in lawful money, and scrip is prohibited. Requirements that workers be promptly paid in the event that they are discharged, quit, or leave work due to a labor dispute are also common. In many states, persons who have not been paid wages due them may assign their back wage claims to a state agency, which will prosecute the claims for the aggrieved employees.[10]

**Fringe Benefits**  A general trend in both federal and state law is to require certain employee (or fringe) benefits. A case in point is the Davis-Bacon Act, which makes employers match fringe benefits to those of prevailing area standards. Noncash compensation often subject to such regulation includes medical care, pensions, myriad varieties of insurance, and vacation and holiday pay. In some cases, if benefits are not matched in kind, cash value must be added to the hourly rate for straight time work, but not for overtime work.[11]

## RECORD KEEPING

Fortunately, the various wage and hour laws have similar record keeping requirements. Usually, no particular form for the records is stipulated. The record-keeping requirements for FLSA are illustrative, and adherence to them will generally satisfy the provisions of other statutes. To satisfy FLSA, an employee's records must include:

1. The employee's full name and address.
2. The employee's birth date, especially if he or she is under 19 years of age.
3. The sex of the employee and the occupation in which employed.
4. The day of the week and time of that day when the employee's workweek begins.
5. The basis on which wages are paid (e.g., $3.75 per hour, $150 per week).
6. The regular hourly pay rate for any week in which overtime is worked. (If the employee is paid on a salary basis, the salary figure must be converted to an hourly rate for this purpose.)
7. The amount and nature of each payment excluded from the regular rate.
8. Total daily or weekly straight time earnings.
9. Total overtime earnings for the workweek.
10. All additions to or deductions from the employee's wages for each pay period.
11. Total wages paid each pay period.
12. Dates of payment and the pay period covered by the payment.[12]

The record-keeping checklist for executive, administrative, and professional employees and outside salespeople is as follows:

1. The employee's full name and address.
2. The employee's sex and occupation.
3. His or her date of birth, if under 19.
4. The time of day and day of the week when the employee's workweek begins.
5. Data on fringe benefits, so that the employee's total remuneration for the position may be calculated.[13]

Records for all employees subject to the minimum wage provisions of the act must be kept, even if the employee is not subject to the law's overtime requirements. Records of hours worked must be kept, regardless of whether the worker is paid by the piece, hour, week, month, in tips, through commissions, or otherwise. Any complete and accurate timekeeping plan is permissible. Production workers may be paid on a salary basis, but for regulatory purposes, records indicating their compensation per hour must be kept.[14]

The minimum wage need not be paid completely in cash, but employers may not make a profit on noncash payments. Tips will be credited up to 50 percent of the minimum wage rate. The cost of facilities primarily for the benefit of the employer, such as tools, may not be credited toward the minimum wage.

All information required by the Wage and Hour Department's regulations must be retained for 3 years. All data on which wage and hour computations are based must be kept for 2 years. Any enterprise having employees subject to the provisions of federal wage and hour laws must post a special poster, which is available free from the Department of Labor.

## RELATIONS WITH REGULATORY AGENCIES

Successful relations with regulatory agencies require as a baseline an awareness of statutory wage, hour, and ancillary requirements *and* accurate, complete, and up-to-date records. The precise powers of different regulatory agencies at various governmental levels are somewhat dissimilar. However, the practices of the Department of Labor's Wage and Hour Division are again illustrative. Wage and hour compliance officers are empowered to investigate any business employing persons subject to the act. A complaint is *not* needed to trigger their inquiries. The Wage and Hour Office would like to direct the thrust of their enforcement effort so as to spend as much time as possible conducting field investigations and disseminating information. In practice, though, independent investigations usually take a back seat to the servicing of complaints.[15]

The Department of Labor also conducts a program of planned litigation to encourage compliance in the wage and hour area and to increase employer awareness of the law's various provisions. Allegations of sex discrimination in wage rates, in violation of the Equal Pay law, have been especially prevalent recently. It is imperative that employers formally determine that their pay structure is not sex-typed.

Questions regarding exceptions, records, and the like are the subject of comment by the Wage and Hour Administrator in special bulletins. Written inquiries to the Administrator's office could yield information helpful in coping with the law's subtle points. An employer has a defense to wage and hour charges where the employer pleads and proves that he or she acted in good faith, relying upon a written administrative regulation, interpretation, ruling, order, practice, or enforcement policy. In the case of the FLSA, the ruling relied upon must have been issued by the Wage and Hour Administrator. Under Davis-Bacon, an employer may rely upon a ruling by the Secretary of Labor. Reliance on rulings made by the Secretary of Labor or any federal officer utilized by the Secretary in the administration of the act will suffice as a defense to charges brought under the Walsh-Healy Act.

Wage and Hour compliance officers are alert for employer's allowing "work off the clock" and for inflated job titles which overstate a job's responsibilities in order to claim an exemption. The nonpayment of overtime to nonexempt salaried retail sales personnel is also a common violation.

## THE IMPACT OF WAGE AND HOUR LAWS

The plethora of wage and hour laws tend to encourage traditional pay and hour practices—such as the 5-day workweek.[16] More importantly, the occasional complexity and the pervasiveness of these laws suggest that employers evaluate their entire compensation structure to make sure that it not only meets legal nuances but also advances company goals. Government regulations which require that certain employees be paid $X$ dollars in $Y$ fashion can never be more than a *component* of an enterprise's total compensation challenge. A good way for a company to help itself adhere to the law *and* to achieve its other employee reward goals is to obtain an objective evaluation of its compensation programs.[17] (See Fig. C-3 in COMPENSATION, SALES.) Reliance on a sophisticated job evaluation system helps in giving a wage and hour compliance officer a clear, reasonable explanation of why one position has been treated as exempt and another as nonexempt.[18] Job evaluations serve as a defense to allegations of wage and hour violations. In fact, in some equal pay cases, courts have intimated that job evaluations may provide the employer with a powerful tool for the defense of pay differentials.[19]

Once enterprise objectives have been defined and jobs formally evaluated, an executive can go about making wage and hour compliance a part of the organization's total compensation package. Refinements in pay and benefit structure may be considered at this point. Some companies, for example,

may wish to develop incentive plans for nonexempt workers.[20] Some employers find it helpful to pay overtime to certain exempt employees.[21] Often, equity adjustments between some exempt and nonexempt workers must be made. In short, professional job evaluation is an excellent tool for linking wage and hour compliance efforts to the overall development of a company compensation program.

Compliance with wage and hour regulations generally requires few pay scales or record-keeping methods that any company which adheres to good business practices would ignore. Classification of jobs so as to conform to statutory strictures should be only a part of a precise, formal job evaluation program. Accurate job evaluations can provide a baseline for a compensation system which pays what employees *ought* to be paid, as well as what the law says they *must* be paid.

*See also* COMPENSATION, EMPLOYEE BENEFIT PLANS; COMPENSATION, WAGE AND SALARY POLICY AND ADMINISTRATION; FOUR-DAY WEEK; LABOR LEGISLATION; JOB ANALYSIS; JOB EVALUATION; PERSONNEL ADMINISTRATION; WORK HOURS, FLEXIBLE.

## NOTES

[1] An employee engaged in commerce or in the production of goods for commerce during a workweek is entitled to protection under the act for that entire workweek regardless of the small amount of time that was devoted to interstate work. Mack A. Player, "Enterprise Coverage Under the Fair Labor Standards Act—An Assessment of the First Generation," 28 VAND. L. REV. 283 (1975), at 308. See also 29 C.F.R. 776.4.

[2] Ibid. pp. 286–287.

[3] Russell L. Greenman and Eric J. Schmertz, *Personnel Administration and the Law*, Bureau of National Affairs, Inc., Washington, 1972, pp. 24–25.

[4] *Guidebook to Federal Wage-Hour Laws*, Commerce Clearing House, Inc., Chicago, 1974, p. 25.

[5] *Brennan v. Houston Endowment* 7 EPD 9204. Female janitors who used vacuums were held to be engaged in work substantially equal to that male janitors who used large power-driven machines such as floor buffers and carpet pile lifters.

[6] Less than 40 percent, if employed by a retail or service establishment.

[7] $130 per week in Puerto Rico, the Virgin Islands, and American Samoa, exclusive of board and lodging.

[8] Notes 6 and 7 apply.

[9] See *Guidebook to Federal Wage-Hours Laws*, Commerce Clearing House, Inc., Chicago, 1974; U.S. Department of Labor, *Executive, Administrative, Professional, and Outside Salesmen Exemptions Under the Fair Labor Standards Act*, WH Publication 1363.

[10] U.S. Department of Labor, *Growth of Labor Law in the United States*, 1967, pp. 101–114.

[11] Ibid. p. 119.

[12] 29 C.F.R. 516.

[13] 29 C.F.R. 516.3.

[14] Robert D. Hulme and Richard V. Bevan, "The Blue Collar Worker Goes on Salary," *Harvard Business Review*, vol. 53, March–April 1975.

[15] U.S. Department of Labor, *Minimum Wage and Maximum Hours Standards Under the Fair Labor Standards Act*, 1976.

[16] Janice Neipert Hedges, "How Many Days Make a Workweek?" *Monthly Labor Review*, vol. 98, p. 20, April 1975. The author discusses the contribution of FLSA to the prevailing 5-day 40-hour workweek.

[17] See Milton L. Rock, ed., *Handbook of Wage and Salary Administration*, McGraw-Hill Book Company, New York, 1972, especially parts 1 and 2.

[18] See Jon Laking and Robin Roark, *Retailing Job Analysis and Job Evaluation*, National Retail Merchants Association, New York, 1975.

[19] See Corning Glass Works v. Brennan, 417 U.S. 188 (1974); Marsh W. Bates and Richard G. Vail, "Job Evaluation and Equal Employment Opportunity: A Tool for Compliance—A Weapon for Defense," *Employee Relations Law Journal*, Spring 1976, p. 535; Murphy, "Female Wage Discrimination: A Study of the Equal Pay Act 1963–1970," 39 U. CIN. L. REV. 615, 634–637 (1970).

[20] Don R. Marshall, "Merit Pay without Headaches: How to Design a Plan for Nonexempts," *Compensation Review*, second quarter, 1975, p. 32; H. W. Lieber and Frederic L. Taylor, "Designing Incentives for Hourly Personnel," in Milton L. Rock, ed., *Handbook of Wage and Salary Administration*, McGraw-Hill Book Company, New York, 1972, pp. 7–14.

[21] Dennis S. Kennedy and H. Paul Abbott, "Establishing the Clerical Pay Structure" in Rock, *Handbook of Wage and Salary Administration*, pp. 4–44; David A. Weeks, *Overtime Pay for Exempt Employees*, National Industrial Conference Board, Inc., New York, 1967.

## REFERENCES

Elder, Peyton: "The 1974 Amendments to the Federal Minimum Wage Law," *Monthly Labor Review*, July 1974, pp. 33–38.

Feder, Gerald M.: *Highlights of the New Wage and Hour Law*, Bureau of National Affairs, Inc., Washington, 1974.

Greenman, Russell Q., and Eric J. Schmertz: *Personnel Administration and the Law*, Bureau of National Affairs, Inc., Washington, 1972.

*Guidebook to Federal Wage-Hour Laws*, Commerce Clearing House, Inc., Chicago, 1974.

Hedges, Janice Neipert: "How Many Days Make a Workweek?" *Monthly Labor Review*, April 1975, pp. 29–35.

Player, Mack A.: "Enterprise Coverage Under the Fair Labor Standards Act: An Assessment of the First Generation," 28 VAND. L. REV. 283, 283–347 (1975).

Rock, Milton L., ed.: *Handbook of Wage and Salary Administration*, McGraw-Hill Book Company, New York, 1972.

J. ROBIN ROARK, *Hay Associates, Management Consultants*

## Walsh-Healy public contracts act
(*See* WAGES AND HOURS LEGISLATION.)

## War game, business
(*See* SIMULATIONS, BUSINESS AND MANAGEMENT.)

## Warehouse automation
(*See* AUTOMATION.)

## Warehouse retailing
(*See* RETAILING MANAGEMENT.)

## Warehouses, public, private, and contract
(*See* DISTRIBUTION, PHYSICAL.)

## Warehousing
(*See* INVENTORY CONTROL, PHYSICAL AND STOCKKEEPING.)

## Warranties, consumer
(*See* CONSUMERISM AND CONSUMER PROTECTION LEGISLATION.)

## Warranty
(*See* GOVERNMENT REGULATIONS, BUSINESS LAW.)

## Warranty, breach of
(*See* PRODUCT LIABILITY.)

## Warranty, implied
(*See* PRODUCT LIABILITY.)

## Wash up, clean up
(*See* COMPENSATION, EMPLOYEE BENEFIT PLANS.)

## Water Pollution Control Act, Federal
(*See* ENVIRONMENTAL PROTECTION LEGISLATION.)

## Weighted-average method, for inventories
(*See* ACCOUNTING, FINANCIAL.)

**Wholesalers** (*See* MARKETING, CHANNELS OF DISTRIBUTION.)

**Wholesalers, industrial** (*See* MARKETING, INDUSTRIAL.)

**Wide area telecommunications service (WATS)** (*See* TELECOMMUNICATIONS.)

**Withdrawal response** (*See* HEALTH, MENTAL.)

# Women in industry

American women are found in almost all organizations and job categories. Their work history outside the home parallels United States industrial development. As industry replaced home manufacture, as compulsory education spread, and as the typewriter and telephone were developed, women have increasingly assumed larger work roles in the labor force.

## HISTORICAL PROFILE

The role of women today can be more fully understood against a background of major changes in "women's work" and in societal attitudes in the last century. During the colonial and frontier era, women were active partners in home industry as well as housekeepers, nurses, and teachers for their families. Participation of middle- and upper-class women in family economic activities, however, diminished as factories began to produce goods.[1] A job outside the home was inconsistent with social status and negatively reflected on husbands as providers. Marriage, motherhood, and homemaking became a full-time profession. As young girls graduated from the new colleges for women, however, some of them began to pioneer business and professional occupations. Many of these women, viewing suffrage as a way toward equal working status with men, thought that the Nineteenth Amendment in 1920 was the beginning of sex equality.[2]

**Employment Impact of World Wars I and II** The typewriter, adding machine, telephone, lightening and simplification of many industrial operations, as well as the need for "womanpower" during World War I created new white-collar opportunities for women. Although more than one-fifth of all women responded to the country's labor needs during World War I, the greatest impact of the war was in the type of work women did. White-collar employment of women increased from 28.2 percent before World War I to 45 percent by 1940.[3]

Few women moved into positions competitive with or superior to those of men, however. In fact, in 1940 only 12.3 percent (compared with 12 percent in 1920) of the working women were professionals. Of those who were, nearly three out of four were elementary school teachers or nurses. Moreover, female workers rarely earned more than 50 to 65 percent of what men did, even when they held the same jobs as men. The assumption was that women worked for "pin money" while men, as fathers and husbands, provided support. The U.S. Women's Bureau studies showed that, in actuality, at least 90 percent of these working women were supporting themselves and their families.

Probably World War II was the most decisive turning point in the overall work history of American women. The war urgently summoned women for jobs that demanded skills, responsibility, and intelligence. Women of all ages worked in about every type of job and at pay never before offered them. "Rosie the Riveter," "Winnie the Welder," "Carrie the Crane Operator," and "Tillie the Truck Driver" were familiar heroines.

By the end of the war, women were 36 percent of the total civilian working population.[4] They had proved their brainpower and stamina in handling operative, executive, and professional jobs; and many of them had no intention of returning home, as most women did at the end of World War I. They discovered not only that their homes did not fall apart but also that their children had not become juvenile delinquents. Moreover, they had grown used to their paychecks and independence. Between 1940 and 1950, 2.5 million women over 33 entered the labor force.

**Postwar Employment Participation** Not only did the wars legitimatize employment for middle-class and married women, but clerical and white-collar positions became consistent with their status. During the fifties, employment of women increased 4 times faster than that of men. By the mid seventies, 45 percent of all women over 16 and more than half of all women between 35 and 54 years old worked.

The proportion of married women in the labor force increased from 15 percent in 1940 to 30 percent in 1960 to 40 percent in 1970. During the sixties and early seventies, however, the greatest increase in the female labor force took place among younger women. The 20 to 24 age group increased from 50 percent in 1964 to 61 percent in 1973; and the 25- to 35-year-old group rose from 37 to 50 percent. Moreover, between 1959 and 1974, the employment rate more than doubled for mothers with children under three (from 15 to 31 percent).

World War II marked the beginning of a new and massive impetus in women's participation and realization of their own ambitions in the economic mainstream of society. In the postwar period, new patterns began to emerge to transform the direction of women and, therefore, the lives of men. These patterns culminated in the women's movement and a significant decade of change in the sixties.

## WOMEN'S MOVEMENT

Better pay and the equal right to employment in other than menial jobs as well as more and better education for women were advocated long before the women's movement—in fact, as long before as 1792.[5] Also, the second Women's Rights Convention in 1848 voted for new employment fields for women, admission to all educational institutions, and equal pay for equal work. But deeply rooted social attitudes—as noted by a Presidential Task Force on Women's Rights and Responsibilities in 1970—are slow to change. Not until the struggle for Negro rights in the sixties highlighted discrimination on the basis of physical characteristics did the women's movement gather momentum.

Inspired by the civil rights model, many middle-class business and professional women pushed for equality by joining organizations like the National Organization for Women (NOW). By 1974, women's liberation was reported by pollster Daniel Yankelovich to be favored for the first time by more than half the 18-and-over population. The issue closest to universal approval was equal pay for equal work.

Movements succeed when they become economically and sociologically feasible. More than likely, the women's movements in the sixties could not have had any greater impact than it had more than a century and a half before if several significant environmental forces unique to the last half of the twentieth century had not been involved:

**Technology** Technological advances had not only reduced household demands but also lessened physical strength requirements for most jobs. Most heavy-lifting jobs had been converted into meter-watching or button-pushing activities. Technology also widened the employment scope for women through development of new areas with no tradi-

tional male history (e.g., information retrieval, computer data processing).

**Science** Advances in science had brought women not only predictable birth control but also a longer and healthier life. The average female in 1976 could expect a life-span of 76 years, nearly 8 years longer than the average male.

**A Service Economy** More than half of all American jobs were in the service industries where mental and other skills are more important than physical strength.

**Education** In 1976, 7.1 million women were college graduates, and many wanted to use their education. Overall, four out of five women between 25 and 34 years old had at least a high school education, and one in six had a college degree (up from one in ten the decade before). More women 35 years and older in middle- and upper-income groups were enrolled in college programs for career preparation. Perhaps because of shared educational experiences, more men appeared increasingly supportive of the career needs of women, also.

**Attitudes** Attitudes were more liberal about combining marriage, family, and a career. A working wife no longer stamped a poor-provider stigma on her husband. More than half (58 percent) of all women workers in 1976 were married. The woman was no longer considered to be a bad mother if she worked (13.6 million women with children under eighteen years worked); also families were smaller and responsibility to family demands shorter. More than one married woman in six in the 18 to 24 age group expected to remain childless or to have only one offspring. Seventy-five percent expected to have no more than two or three children.

Attitudes had changed toward single women, too. In the 20 to 24 age bracket, two out of every five women were unmarried. Moreover, 7.2 million United States families—or one in eight—were headed by women (a 45 percent increase—from 5 million, one in ten—from 10 years before).

**Rising Costs** Higher living costs motivated more couples to want two incomes. In 1976, almost half of all families were reported to have had more than one source of income. The U.S. Labor Department has predicted that within 20 years, 75 percent of all women between the ages of 25 and 54 will have a job outside the home.[6] This development of the family as an economic unit brings us full circle to an earlier period of family industry. The difference is that family members now work outside the home in the paid labor force.[7]

**Work Force** Statisticians see labor shortages in the population between the ages of 35 and 45 for the managerial, professional, technical, and skilled trade areas. Women present a large unused reserve in these categories.

**Legislative Suport** A firm's management is now legally pressured to hire and promote women into jobs traditionally reserved for males only. United States federal laws enacted or modified during the sixties and early seventies to prohibit sex discrimination in employment include the Equal Pay Act, Title VII of the Civil Rights Act, Executive Order 11246, and Revised Order IV.

*The Equal Pay Act* (June 1963) amended the Fair Labor Standards Act (1938) to require the same pay for men and women doing similar work.

*Title VII (of the Civil Rights Act of 1964)* prohibits employers, unions, and employment agencies from sex discrimination in hiring; in wages, terms, conditions, or privileges of employment; in classifying; assigning, or promoting employees, and extending or assigning use of facilities; and in training, retraining, and apprenticeship.

*Executive Order 11246*, as amended by Executive Order 11375, prohibits discrimination in employment by contractors and subcontractors (including colleges and universities) who have $10,000 or more in federal contracts with the federal goverment. These government contractors and subcontractors must institute affirmative action programs. Specifically, they cannot

Make any distinctions based on sex in employment opportunities, wages, hours, or other conditions of employment, including fringe benefits and pension plans.

Distinguish between married and single persons of one sex and not the other.

Advertise in sex-segregated help-wanted columns unless sex is a bona fide occupational qualification.

Deny employment to women with young children unless the same policy applies to men with young children.

Terminate an employee of one sex upon reaching a certain age, but not an employee of the other sex.

Penalize women because they require time away from work for childbearing (childbearing is justification for a leave of absence for a reasonable period of time whether or not an employer has a leave policy).

Maintain seniority lists based solely on sex.

Deny a female employee the right to a job for which she is qualified because of state "protective" legislation.

*Revised Order IV* (effective December 4, 1971) strengthened these guidelines. It requires that contractors (1) analyze their company work force to determine if women are underemployed and (2) set numerical goals and timetables by job classification and organizational unit to correct any deficiencies. Goals, however, are to reflect the characteristics of the female work force in the relevant labor market and should not be used to force hiring of unqualified persons. Failure to meet certain goals is not noncompliance *if* good faith is demonstrated.

In summary, then, the U.S. Department of Labor can demand under present guidelines: (1) equality of opportunity in hiring and placement: (2) recruitment of women for all jobs at all levels, skills, and pay rates; (3) equality of opportunity in transfers, promotions, upgrading, and protection from layoffs; (4) equality of opportunity for training; (5) equal application of seniority and retirement policies; and (6) special protection of women who need maternity leave. A problem is that, in many situations, it is not easy to make clear-cut cases to prove sex discrimination. In white-collar jobs, for example, equal work or precise reasons for promoting one person over another are difficult to define.

An *Equal Rights Amendement* passed by the U.S. Senate in March, 1972 is before the states for ratification. To become law, 38 states must ratify it.

## EMPLOYMENT OF WOMEN AND MEN: A COMPARISON

Over the last 20 years, nearly 17 million women entered the work force, compared with less than 12 million men. Particularly in the last 10 years, the greatest growth in job holders has been among females. For instance, the number of men in the labor force increased by 16.8 percent, compared with a 42.3 percent increase for women. Female job holders increased by almost 2 million between 1975 and 1976 alone. (See Table W-1.) In 1976, nearly half of all women—37.4 million women; 47 percent aged

**TABLE W-1 Number of Civilian Labor Force Workers, by Sex (1966–1976)**

| Year | Male | Female |
|------|------|--------|
| 1966 | 48,471,000 | 27,299,000 |
| 1967 | 48,987,000 | 28,360,000 |
| 1968 | 49,533,000 | 29,204,000 |
| 1969 | 50,221,000 | 30,513,000 |
| 1970 | 51,195,000 | 31,520,000 |
| 1971 | 52,021,000 | 32,091,000 |
| 1972 | 53,265,000 | 33,277,000 |
| 1973 | 54,203,000 | 34,510,000 |
| 1974 | 55,186,000 | 35,825,000 |
| 1975 | 55,615,000 | 36,998,000 |
| 1976 | 56,631,000 | 38,856,000 |

SOURCE: John O'Riley, "Review of Current Trends in Business and Finance," *Wall Street Journal*, Sept. 20, 1976.

**TABLE W-2  Employment by Occupation, Total and Women Workers, 1962 and 1974**

| Occupational group, numbers in thousands | 1962 | | | 1974 | | |
|---|---|---|---|---|---|---|
| | | Women | | | Women | |
| | Total | Number | Percent of total | Total | Number | Percent of total |
| Total employed | 67,972 | 23,029 | 33.9 | 85,936 | 33,417 | 38.9 |
| Professional and technical | 8,050 | 2,890 | 35.9 | 12,338 | 4,992 | 40.5 |
| Accountants | 518 | 97 | 18.7 | 803 | 190 | 23.7 |
| Lawyers and judges | 247 | 7 | 2.8 | 359 | 25 | 7.0 |
| Librarians | 105 | 90 | 85.7 | 180 | 147 | 81.7 |
| Chemists | 93 | 8 | 8.6 | 121 | 12 | 14.0 |
| Personnel and labor relations workers | 113 | 31 | 27.4 | 321 | 112 | 34.9 |
| Pharmacists | 125 | 13 | 10.4 | 127 | 21 | 16.5 |
| Physicians, medical and osteopathic | 238 | 13 | 5.5 | 346 | 34 | 9.8 |
| Registered nurses | 591 | 582 | 98.5 | 904 | 886 | 98.0 |
| Psychologists | 12 | 5 | 41.7 | 58 | 24 | 41.4 |
| Social workers | 118 | 71 | 60.2 | 300 | 184 | 61.3 |
| College and university teachers | 172 | 33 | 19.2 | 518 | 160 | 30.9 |
| Elementary schoolteachers | 976 | 844 | 86.5 | 1,297 | 1,094 | 84.3 |
| Drafting workers | 266 | 11 | 4.1 | 298 | 23 | 7.7 |
| Designers | 57 | 15 | 26.3 | 129 | 31 | 24.0 |
| Editors and reporters | 111 | 42 | 37.8 | 156 | 68 | 43.6 |
| Painters and sculptors | 123 | 50 | 40.7 | 149 | 62 | 41.6 |
| Public relations specialists and publicity writers | 35 | 7 | 20.0 | 104 | 30 | 28.8 |
| Managers and administrators, except farm | 7,421 | 1,138 | 15.3 | 8,941 | 1,650 | 18.5 |
| Purchasing agents and buyers, not elsewhere classified | 122 | 13 | 10.7 | 189 | 33 | 17.5 |
| Salesworkers | 4,374 | 1,715 | 39.2 | 5,417 | 2,265 | 41.8 |
| Hucksters and peddlers | 129 | 85 | 65.9 | 201 | 151 | 75.1 |
| Insurance agents, brokers, and underwriters | 356 | 36 | 10.1 | 466 | 62 | 13.3 |
| Newspapers carriers and vendors | 284 | 9 | 3.2 | 75 | 19 | 25.3 |
| Real estate and brokers | 179 | 51 | 28.5 | 394 | 151 | 38.3 |
| Clerical and kindred workers | 10,054 | 6,918 | 68.8 | 15,043 | 11,676 | 77.6 |
| Bank tellers | 123 | 88 | 71.5 | 351 | 321 | 91.5 |
| Bookkeepers | 1,094 | 934 | 85.4 | 1,690 | 1,508 | 89.2 |
| Cashiers | 543 | 448 | 82.5 | 1,111 | 974 | 87.7 |
| Collectors, bill and account | 33 | 7 | 21.2 | 63 | 29 | 46.0 |
| Dispatchers and starters, vehicle | 66 | 6 | 9.1 | 91 | 22 | 24.2 |
| Insurance adjusters, examiners, and investigators | 53 | 5 | 9.4 | 125 | 54 | 45.6 |
| Mail carriers, post office | 206 | 6 | 2.9 | 267 | 20 | 7.5 |
| Messengers and office helpers | 74 | 11 | 14.9 | 76 | 18 | 23.7 |
| Office machine operators | 399 | 291 | 72.9 | 662 | 472 | 71.3 |
| Payroll and timekeeping clerks | 135 | 83 | 61.5 | 204 | 158 | 77.4 |
| Postal clerks | 245 | 36 | 14.7 | 293 | 82 | 28.0 |
| Secretaries | 1,655 | 1,630 | 98.5 | 3,187 | 3,165 | 99.2 |
| Shipping and receiving clerks | 331 | 25 | 7.6 | 465 | 74 | 15.9 |
| Stock clerks and storekeepers | 368 | 64 | 17.4 | 488 | 123 | 25.2 |

16 and over—worked, holding two out of every five jobs in the United States. (See Table W-2 for the total employment by occupation in relation to women workers between 1962 and 1974.) If the trend continues, there could be as many women as men in the work force by the year 2000.

**Blue Collar**  Between 1960 and 1970 the number of women in the skilled trades increased dramatically. For example, in 1970 almost one-half million women (495,000) worked in skilled occupations, up from 277,000 in 1960 and 85 times the increase for men in the skilled trades.[8]

Of all women workers, however, less than one-sixth (about 16 percent) are in blue-collar occupations, compared with about 21 percent of the males.

**White Collar**  More than three-fifths (about 62 percent) of all women workers are in white-collar jobs. In fact, most women employees are likely to be in retail sales and office work—e.g., secretaries, typists, bookkeepers, receptionists, file clerks, telephone operators, bank tellers, and sales clerks.

Women account for more than three-fourths of all clerical workers. Not only is it the largest occupational group employing women, it has been one of

| Occupational group, numbers in thousands | 1962 | | | 1974 | | |
| --- | --- | --- | --- | --- | --- | --- |
| | | Women | | | Women | |
| | Total | Number | Percent of total | Total | Number | Percent of total |
| Telephone operators | 327 | 315 | 96.3 | 390 | 366 | 93.8 |
| Ticket, station, and express agents | 95 | 20 | 21.1 | 121 | 46 | 38.0 |
| Typists | 600 | 569 | 94.8 | 1,038 | 999 | 96.2 |
| Craft and kindred workers | 9,214 | 232 | 2.5 | 11,477 | 511 | 4.5 |
| Bakers | 93 | 17 | 18.3 | 107 | 44 | 41.1 |
| Compositors and typesetters | 160 | 10 | 6.3 | 166 | 33 | 19.9 |
| Decorators and window dressers | 48 | 24 | 50.0 | 101 | 63 | 62.4 |
| Painters, construction and maintenance | 394 | 10 | 2.5 | 454 | 12 | 2.6 |
| Operatives | 13,093 | 3,392 | 25.9 | 13,919 | 4,331 | 31.1 |
| Checkers, examiners, and inspectors (manufacturing) | 518 | 235 | 45.5 | 757 | 383 | 50.6 |
| Garage workers and gas station attendants | 390 | 6 | 1.5 | 397 | 21 | 5.3 |
| Graders and sorters, manufacturing | 31 | 17 | 54.8 | 44 | 33 | 75.0 |
| Packers and wrappers, except meat and produce | 536 | 323 | 60.3 | 661 | 417 | 63.1 |
| Photographic process workers | 51 | 21 | 41.2 | 83 | 39 | 47.0 |
| Weavers, textile | 58 | 26 | 44.8 | 42 | 25 | 59.5 |
| Welders and flame cutters | 366 | 22 | 6.0 | 646 | 32 | 5.0 |
| Bus drivers | 177 | 21 | 11.9 | 265 | 99 | 37.4 |
| Delivery and route workers | 492 | 8 | 1.6 | 595 | 26 | 4.4 |
| Taxicab drivers and chauffeurs | 162 | 6 | 3.7 | 174 | 20 | 11.5 |
| Laborers, except farm | 3,549 | 94 | 2.6 | 4,380 | 354 | 8.1 |
| Farmers and farm managers | 2,577 | 132 | 5.1 | 1,643 | 98 | 6.0 |
| Farmers (owners and tenants) | 2,421 | 13 | 0.5 | 1,610 | 97 | 6.0 |
| Farm laborers and supervisors | 2,286 | 732 | 32.0 | 1,405 | 385 | 27.4 |
| Farm laborers and wage workers | 1,377 | 232 | 16.8 | 983 | 144 | 14.6 |
| Farm laborers and unpaid family workers | 880 | 501 | 56.9 | 376 | 239 | 63.6 |
| Service workers, except private household | 6,461 | 3,457 | 53.5 | 6,145 | 5,955 | 58.7 |
| Bartenders | 139 | 16 | 11.5 | 233 | 76 | 32.6 |
| Cooks, except private household | 571 | 363 | 63.6 | 955 | 562 | 53.8 |
| Food counter and fountain workers | 163 | 110 | 67.5 | 351 | 299 | 85.2 |
| Waiters | 913 | 798 | 87.4 | 1,182 | 1,085 | 91.8 |
| Attendants, recreation and amusement | 87 | 13 | 14.9 | 142 | 51 | 35.9 |
| Hairdressers and cosmetologists | 387 | 341 | 88.1 | 498 | 460 | 92.4 |
| Guards and watch workers | 300 | 15 | 5.0 | 473 | 29 | 6.1 |
| Nursing aides, orderlies, and attendants | 509 | 382 | 75.0 | 959 | 833 | 86.9 |

*Note:* Data for 1962 are not strictly comparable with 1974 figures because of definitional changes in occupational categories, and because 14- and 15-year-olds are included in 1962 and excluded from 1974 data.

SOURCE: *Monthly Labor Review,* vol. 98, no. 11, November 1975.

the fastest growing occupational groups for women—increasing by about 68 percent between 1960 and 1973. In 1973, salaries in these jobs were low, averaging $4700 for salesclerks and $6400 for clerical workers. Advancement to mangement or administrative levels has been rare, and little social status has been attached to the work.[9] By contrast, less than 7 percent of all male workers held clerical jobs in 1973.

**Professional** More than 4.7 million women—or one out of seven working women—are in professional and technical occupations. About 2 million more women were employed in professional occupations in 1973 than in 1960. Teaching and health fields account for about one-fifth of the professional and technical workers. The number of women in the traditionally male-dominated areas, however, is increasing.[10]

Conversely, the number of men is increasing in the so-called "women's professions"—librarians, registered nurses, and elementary school teachers.[11] The U.S. Department of Labor reports that in the eighties, new jobs will open faster for professional and office workers than for blue-collar employees. (See Table W-3 for the projected changes.)

## INCOME: A COMPARISON

The 1974 reported median annual income was $12,-152 for men and $6957 for women. In fact, the

TABLE W-3  Projected Changes for 1985 in White- and Blue-Collar Workers

|  | 1975 jobs, in millions | 1985 jobs (projected), in millions | Change |
|---|---|---|---|
| White-collar workers | 42.2 | 53.2 | Up 26% |
| Professional, technical | 12.7 | 16.0 | Up 26% |
| Managers, administrators | 8.9 | 10.9 | Up 22% |
| Salesworkers | 5.5 | 6.3 | Up 15% |
| Clerical workers | 15.1 | 20.1 | Up 33% |
| Blue-collar workers | 28.0 | 33.7 | Up 20% |
| Craft and kindred workers | 11.0 | 13.8 | Up 25% |
| Operatives | 12.9 | 15.2 | Up 18% |
| Nonfarm laborers | 4.1 | 4.8 | Up 17% |
| Service workers | 11.7 | 14.6 | Up 25% |

*Note:* Details may not add to totals because of rounding.
SOURCE: *U.S. News & World Report,* Oct. 11, 1976, p. 60.

overall pay gap between men and women has widened since 1955 when women earned nearly 67 percent of a man's salary. By 1970 this ratio had fallen to 59 percent and by 1974 to 57 percent.[12] (See Table W-4 for a comparison of median incomes between men and women from 1956 to 1974 and Table W-5 for the average weekly earnings for full-time women workers as a percentage of men's earnings.)

Part of the difference in median income between men and women may be explained by the fact that women have not made substantial inroads into the most valued market occupations.[13] They have been mostly in low-status, low-paying jobs with little advancement potential. Other reasons that have been traditionally given for the income disparity include lack of continuous full-time employment, job inexperience, limited vocational and training skills, lower educational levels, and inability to work full time. Institutional and attitudinal barriers— i.e., well-intentioned protective laws (overtime, weightlifting) as well as attitudes toward women's place and value of women's work[14]—have been ex-

TABLE W-4  Comparison of Median Earnings of Full-Time Male and Female Workers, 1956–1974

|  | 1956 | 1964 | 1974 |
|---|---|---|---|
| Men | $4,462 | $6,283 | $12,152 |
| Women | 2,828 | 3,710 | 6,957 |
| Women's pay as a percentage of men's | 63% | 59% | 57% |

SOURCE: U.S. Department of Commerce.

tremely significant factors in the participation and marketable worth of women in labor market. Pressures of changing social and economic conditons will cause these factors, however, to be examined and reexamined in the future.

## IN PERSPECTIVE

Biology and the need for survival in our preindustrial environment created roles for men and women. These cultural ideas of "man's work" and "woman's work"—what is masculine and what is feminine— have survived long after the need has disappeared.

In perspective, however, preindustrial women— except perhaps those in the upper social strata— were not full-time wives and mothers, as the twentieth-century American women became. They were productive partners on farm and craft teams with their husbands and other adult kin. The world came into their homes—customers, farmhands, and relatives. While preindustrial women had had a significant economic role, twentieth-century women did not. They—and society—began in the sixties and early seventies to face the question of who they are besides wife and mother.

TABLE W-5  Average Weekly Earnings of Full-Time Women Workers and Percentage of Men's Average Weekly Earnings

| Occupation | Average weekly earnings | Percentage of men's average weekly earnings |
|---|---|---|
| Professional, technical | $208 | 73 |
| Managers, administrators | 173 | 58 |
| Clerical | 138 | 65 |
| Craft workers | 138 | 61 |
| Laborers | 116 | 73 |
| Factory workers | 115 | 61 |
| Service workers | 103 | 64 |
| Salesworkers | 102 | 44 |
| Farm workers | 95 | 84 |

SOURCE: U.S. Department of Labor.

Although the traditional system continues to work well for many men and women, it does not work for an increasing number of others. Consequently, more and more women will pursue careers in both the traditionally feminine areas and in those formerly for men only. In fact, more women work today than ever before. In 1900, women made up only 18 percent of all workers; in 1940, about 25 percent. During World War II, the proportion reached 36 percent; and, significantly, in 1976, almost half of all women between the ages 18 and 64 worked. Importantly, too, where the average woman worker was 28 years old and single in 1920, today she is 39 years old and married with children.

Most women are still employed in the traditional women's jobs (e.g., secretary, retail salesworker, bookkeeper, elementary school teacher, waitress, typist, cashier, and nurse). Jobs traditionally held by males, however, are opening to women. Apprentice programs in a number of trades show a growing acceptance toward women. In the professions, more women are becoming physicians, lawyers, dentists, engineers, architects, and mangers. This trend is expected to accelerate.

In final summary, economics—industrialization, World War II, and such postwar factors as industrial expansion, the Korean and Vietnam conflicts, and work force shortages in scientific-technical fields—has contributed to fuller acceptance and use of women at all levels. The thrust in the eighties may come from the need for management talent at all functional levels, both line and staff. Statistical evidence suggests that industry, government, and the professions may have to draw increasingly on women to fill work force shortages. Certainly, more intelligent use of career women represents one of the greatest potentials for productivity improvement.

*See also* EGALITARIANISM; LABOR LEGISLATION; MINORITIES, MANAGEMENT OF AND EQUAL EMPLOYMENT OPPORTUNITY; OLDER EMPLOYEES, VALUE SYSTEMS, SOCIAL AND CULTURAL; MANAGEMENT OF; WOMEN IN MANAGEMENT; YOUNGER EMPLOYEES, MANAGEMENT OF.

## NOTES

[1] The 1900 census showed that most of the 1 million women who worked in the factories were not covered by middle-class norms. Forty-one percent of all nonwhite women worked, while most of the 17 percent of the white women who worked were immigrants.

[2] Evelyn Acworth, *The New Matriarchy*, Victor Gollanez, Ltd., London, 1965, pp. 143 and 147.

[3] Unless otherwise indicated, the statistics in this entry are from various U.S. Department of Labor reports.

[4] National Manpower Council, *Womanpower*, Columbia University Press, New York, 1957, pp. 143-146.

[5] Mary Wollstonecraft, *A Vindication of the Rights of Women*, Peter Edes for Thomas and Andrews, Boston.

[6] "Working Wives and Family Finances," *The Plain Dealer*, Dec. 9, 1976, p. E-2.

[7] Ibid.

[8] For example, the number of women in the following crafts reportedly increased between 1960 and 1970: from 8000 carpenters to 11,000; 2500 electricians to 7000; 1000 plumbers to 4000; 2300 auto mechanics to 11,000; 6400 painters to 13,400; 1100 tool and die makers to 4200; 6700 machinists to 11,800; and 15,500 compositors and typesetters to 24,000.

[9] "A Powerful New Role in the Work Force, But . . . ," *U.S. News and World Report*, Dec. 8, 1975, pp. 58–62.

[10] Between 1960 and 1970 the number of women lawyers was reported to have increased from 5000 to 12,000; physicians from 16,000 to 26,000; dentists from 1900 to 3100; engineers from 7000 to 19,600; and accountants from 80,400 to 183,000.

[11] "The American Woman: On the Move—But Where?," *U.S. News and World Report*, Dec. 8, 1975, p. 54.

[12] Howard J. Ehrlich, *Selected Differences in the Life Changes of Men and Women in the United States*, The Johns Hopkins Press, Baltimore, 1973, pp. 70–72.

[13] U.S. Department of Labor, *Underutilization of Women Workers*, Women's Bureau Workplace Standards Administration 1971, p. 71.

[14] Juanita M. Kreps, "The Value of Women's Work," *Sex in the Marketplace: American Women at Work*, The Johns Hopkins Press, Baltimore, pp. 70–72.

ELEANOR BRANTLEY SCHWARTZ, *Cleveland State University*

# Women in management

While World War II and Title VII[1] were decisive breakthroughs for working women in general, Revised Order Four[2] may be the most significant turning point for women in management. For the first time in history, women must be recruited, hired, and promoted into management jobs. As a result, many changes in company policies and practices can be expected in the next decade.

## STATUS OF WOMEN MANAGERS

Women make up almost half the labor force, but few of them are in management. The United States Census Bureau reports that women totaled 18.5 percent of all managers and administrators in 1974. One out of five of these women managers were either self-employed or an unpaid family employee.

Other reports also substantiate that few women have advanced to the more responsible jobs. Of 2500 presidents, key vice-presidents, and chairpersons who direct major corporations, *Business Week* reported "only 15 or so top-level women executives."[3] This figure excluded entrepreneurs and inheritors who never competed for their corporate jobs.

Among 20 major corporations employing nearly 2 million people, less than 1 percent of the officials, managers, and professionals were women—most of whom were at the supervisory or first-management level.[4] In another survey of the top 500 United States corporations, men outnumbered women 600 to 1 at the corporate executive level.[5] Moreover, many of the women executives had titles more important than their functions.

**Traditional Misconceptions** An overall labor force comparison shows nearly one out of seven men in managerial/administrative occupations, compared with one out of twenty women.[6] Social norms have kept women out of positions either competitive with or superior to those of men. Attitudes still range from one extreme of, "qualified women can perform adequately in any job," to the other extreme, "women are excellent for handling details, but never for management." By 1982, however, the number of women in management can be expected to triple. Meanwhile, a number of beliefs must be overcome, particularly the following traditional assumptions that:

*Women Do Not Work Long Enough to Justify Management Training.* A common argument against women in management has been that their turnover is too high. Comparisons with turnover of men in similar occupations, however, show almost no difference. Both unreliability and job-hopping appear to be related more to job satisfaction, salary, occupational level, and age than to one's gender. Polaroid Corporation, for example, reported not only that turnover rates were highest in its lower-level jobs but also that the rates were the same for both sexes.[7]

Upward mobility, equal pay, and various social factors—such as more female heads of households and acceptability of career-oriented mothers—have stimulated higher career aspirations and stability.[8] With female life expectancy now over 75 years, the average family size barely two children, many women who interrupt their careers return to the work force by their forties with a quarter of a century left to contribute. The more attractive the job and the more valued she is, the more she wants to return.

*Women Lack Skills, Training, and Education for Management.* Because women are disporportionately concentrated at the lower occupational levels, the education of many women is not fully utilized. As pointed out in a Department of Labor report, 7 percent of employed women with 5 or more years of college work as services workers (including household), operatives, sales workers, or clerical workers. Nearly one-fifth of employed women with 4 years of college also work in these occupations, as do about two-thirds of those who had 1 to 3 years of college.[9]

Educated women have tended traditionally to cluster in the so-called "helping professions"—e.g.,

secretarial, nursing, teaching, social work, psychology, and occupational and physical speech therapy. Although commonly said that this work was the most appropriate for, or congenial to, women, the reality has been that only these professions have been open to women in any large numbers until recently.

*Women Do Not Want Increased Responsibility.* The general contention has been that, since marriage was their primary career, women work only to get away from home or for pin money rather than for intrinsic achievement or economic needs. The women's movement, legal changes, and recent legal actions (e.g., against AT&T, Bank of America, Bank of California, and the American Tobacco Company) strongly indicate women are interested in assuming organizational responsibility. Few women were found in managerial positions prior to the seventies because these roles were socially unacceptable for them. Before the legal pressures, few employers would put women in a managerial job. Few women trained for or applied for jobs in management out of realism about the prospects for payoff of the training and application than from reluctance to assume management responsibility.[10]

*Woman Are Absent from Work More than Men.* Many employers have felt that absenteeism is complicated by women's home responsibility. Actually, men and women lose about the same number of days from work, including days lost because of pregnancy and childbirth. A Public Health Survey found that women tend to miss 5.9 days a year because of illness, whereas men tend to miss 5.2 days a year. Responsibility level appears to be the significant factor in absenteeism.

Moreover, younger women, while not choosing between marriage and career as perhaps many of their mothers did, are choosing between "being a super working Mom and not mothering at all."[11] Many husbands of women with career aspirations find their wives rejecting pregnancy unless they get an assurance of partnership parenting—an agreement to help run the house and raise the children.[12]

*Women Are Usually Unwilling to Transfer.* Among most couples, geographic mobility has traditionally depended upon the male's career. Among many couples today, however, the male no longer arbitrarily determines where they will live. Some companies have begun to hire "executive couples" and to relocate them in concert. For other couples, a compromise is often made between two careers. Some husbands, for example, will accept a job transfer only if their wives' career will not be adversely affected. Some recent studies also show that many men with nonworking wives increasingly do not want to relocate because the wife has no job status of her own and suffers with each move.

*Woman Should Not and Usually Do Not Want to Travel.* Willingness to travel depends on the individual, not one's gender. The trip is business, regardless of whether both men and women are involved. Traveling together does not automatically mean intimacy.

## TOP MANAGEMENT CHALLENGE

Although there is no convincing evidence that one sex is brighter or more creative than the other or that there are innate differences in cognitive functioning, many people, nevertheless, still believe that women are different in ways that affect their managerial performance.[13] A *Harvard Business Review* survey of 1500 subscribers revealed that social and psychological barriers still affect the employment, promotion, and effectiveness of women managers.[14] For example, women managers have been perceived to have different skills, habits, and motivations that make them undesirable leaders. The idea that neither men nor women like to work for women and that women have lower career aspirations than men, less commitment to work, more concern with friendships than with work itself, and make poor leaders because they are not assertive—or if they are assertive, they are too dictatorial and bitchy—is prevalent in literature on women executives. This has been perceived this way because management has been viewed as a masculine occupation requiring traits more commonly thought to be masculine.

The organization's culture operates on perceptions that reflect conventional male and female behavior.[15] When a woman steps out of her traditional role, she upsets the balance of both roles for traditionally oriented people.

Probably the greatest initial problem for the woman manager is that few people can forget she is a woman—and different from a man. But if women are to be accepted as professional peers and managerial superiors, it is critically important that we come to truly believe that management skills are asexual and to recognize that few men or women learn to apply them effectively.

There are probably as many definitions of management as there are managers. But in its final analysis, the major responsibility of a manager is to direct, organize, and abet the activities of other people toward achievement of the objectives of the company that employs them. Thus, the function of a manager is to work with other people, developing their skills so that they grow more useful to themselves and to the company for which they work.

But women are generally not perceived as having management skills. The paradox is that the skills that women have socialized into them from early life are the very same skills required for success in the managerial sphere of activity. Females are socialized to be affiliative rather than independent; to give nurturance and support to others rather than to remain aloof; to find satisfaction in the achievement of others and to stimulate the achievement of others (e.g., children and husband). These same characteristics of affiliation, nurturance, and facilitation of the achievement of others are what most managers need in their moment-to-moment interaction with those whom they supervise.

The picture that emerges with respect to women as managers, then, is that they have the intelligence and motivation to assume and fulfill the managerial role; and equally important, by virtue of the socialization process which has feminized them, women have the interpersonal skills requisite to being effective managers. The same personality characteristics and skills that have made women excellent students, homemakers, and rearers of children are the skills managers desperately need. Indeed, many industrial corporations are trying to teach their male managers these same skills.

Of course, the setting for the application of these skills is different, and that makes a difference. Undoubtedly, the expectations placed on managers in the business world are different than expectations on students, wives, or mothers. And because the setting and the expectations of the business world are different, the female managers cannot be expected to make an immediate and direct application of their problem-solving and nurturance skills. But those skills are there. The organization has moved into a postauthoritarian age where emphasis is upon growth, nurturance, creativity, communication, and the ability to mediate between forces that must work together but differ in purpose and approach. Women are particularly suited to meet these needs.

Management's challenge is to create an organizational climate in which male and female managers, along with their support teams, can effectively collaborate. To do this, top management must help people at all organizational levels to break through the sex-role stereotypes to develop professional relationships based on competency, personality, and a mutual commitment to the well-being of the organization.

## WHAT TOP MANAGEMENT CAN DO

The least-tried work relationships are women managing men and men working with women peers. Also, most male managers have supervised women who work in traditional women's jobs. Now, however, men face working for and with women; and some men must supervise and facilitate the development of women managers and help integrate them into male management groups.

How can an organization alter its culture? William H. Chafe[16] observed that people do not change from edict but from successful examples of people who do something which breaks the old cycle and starts a new one. To do this, top management must reflect in its policies, procedures, and *practices* a commitment to draw on the resources of *every* individual who wants and has the capacity and qualifications to make a management contribution. Direction from the top lowers role conflict and *by example* gradually increases comfortableness in the new working relationships with women as colleagues and superiors. Certainly, clear-cut patterns for guidance do not exist yet in most organizations. The following actions, however, can be a good beginning:

1. *Select the right person for the job.* Taking "cosmetic" action and moving women too fast are two dangers in hiring and promoting women as managers. Selection and promotion criteria should be the same for both men and women. This is easier said than done, however. Many men, for instance, feel they can spot technical and professional capabilities in another man but doubt their judgment about women.

2. *Sensitize male managers to the ambitions and potentials of women managers.* While male managers may be supportive of women managers who assume nontraditional roles, they may not see some of the more subtle forms of discrimination or know how to help women set goals, analyze their interests and abilities, or evaluate career alternatives. The manager of a woman manager, for example, needs to be aware of how male behavior can reinforce and perpetuate sex-role stereotyping; i.e., the informal behaviors that treat women as special or different (references to the woman's appearance during a business meeting, exaggerated chivalry—chair holding, cigarette lighting, introductions such as "our *woman* manager"). On the other hand, some well-educated and talented women who have been taught to play dumb or to hide their light may have to be encouraged to raise their professional aspirations.

The goal is to realize that few differences exist between men and women managers.[17] A number of recent comparative studies indicate that men and women managers have similar managerial styles, attitudes, and temperaments.[18] For instance, women can be as objective, decisive, and pragmatic in their decision making and can tolerate uncertainty and ambiguity as well as men.[19] The focus should be upon job demands and how a person's qualities will or will not enable him or her to meet them.

3. *Define her role.* If a woman's role is vaguely defined, she can never be sure of the extent and authority of her position, how she is evaluated, or exactly what she must achieve to be promoted or otherwise rewarded. Moreover, no one else can see the effects of her efforts, presence, and input. This affects not only others' evaluation of her performance but also their acceptance of her as well as her own self-concept and motivation.

4. *Announce new responsibilities.* When a man is given new responsibilities and authority, it is usually announced to subordinates and others in the organization. Women, again and again, report that when they are given similar assignments, rarely is it formally or informally announced. As a result, subordinates and peers often resist her intrusion. Publicizing her role legitimatizes her and shows top management's support. It clarifies her place in the hierarchy and helps ensure that her male peers treat her as equal.

5. *Expect competency.* A woman manager's supervisor should expect the same performance from her as from her male counterparts. She should also receive the same help in areas where she needs help that would be given a male subordinate. Her superior should level with her, tell her the facts straight, what is good, what is bad—anything that affects her job performance. Competent, qualified, hard-working female managers *want* objective performance evaluation. Those who are not, *need* it.

6. *Identify and sponsor women who have management potential.* Many companies use assessment centers to identify men as candidates for management positions Some of the methods developed are proving to be accurate predictors among men over time. Little assessment center information, however, is available on women. Nevertheless, management might examine how men get ahead and compare this with how women are advanced. For instance, women have not been a part of the informal sponsorship system. A young man more often than not is

a protegé of an older, established person. Executives have tended to identify a bright young man rather than a bright young woman as a protegé. This hesitancy toward women as protegés has been a major problem for women. Because a woman also tends to be seen as an assistant rather than as a colleague, her superior may fail to introduce her to his colleagues or sponsor her for jobs.

7. *Provide management training.* A woman cannot function as a good manager without appropriate training anymore than a man can. She must develop her skills through higher levels of in-service training, related job rotation, and cross-functional assignments. She must be put into progressively more responsible positions where she can use her capabilities and be held accountable for the results.

Most women have advanced into management through specialized skills in a technical or staff area rather than through the general management training and development route through which most men have progressed. As a result, management skills most women managers reportedly need to improve tend to be in finance and budgeting, planning, and effective decision making.[20] Organizational skills that tend to need improvement are policy and budget-making guidelines.[21]

Lack of involvement in budget development and budget management may have special overtures for the woman manager. Some men who fail to involve women in budget activities may have fallen prey to the sexual stereotype that women are inherently inept at dealing with numbers and money. If that is the case, it is bad enough on the face of it, but at least there is hope for changing the stereotype from which the behavior derives. Another reason women may not have been involved in budgeting and financial management is far more important. Money is power. Whoever controls the money through the budgeting process exerts considerable power in any organization. If some males resist women assuming managerial positions, it would seem logical that the very last bastion of resistance would focus on the process of budgeting since that is a locus of power.

## SUMMARY

After more than 3 years of federal legislation, relentless efforts from women, and shifts in public attitudes, women are beginning to move into corporate management. Within the next decade, it will not be an anomaly to see a woman walk down a corporate hallway with a briefcase.

People will adjust to women managers—if they are given the same training, responsibility, authority, staff, and other support that male managers receive.

To be an effective leader, every manager—man or woman—needs support from above and below in the organization. This support, more than sex or leadership style, determines one's effectiveness or ineffectiveness. It is needed to back up one's demands and decisions which, in turn, ensures the confidence and loyalty of subordinates—for if the boss has no influence, the department has no influence; so subordinates' attitude, more often than not, is one of "why go all out?"

Women are capable of risk taking, decision making, and other managerial behavior usually attributed to men. These qualities describe *self-confident people* and are not confined to one sex or the other. By taking advantage of an exceptionally underutilized management resource, a firm can broaden its managerial base and, therefore, its competitive edge. Certainly, as highly motivated and qualified women directly compete with men on the way up, top management can come closer to eliminating mediocrity from its ranks. As this happens, top management will find its investment in talented women is worth that extra effort.

*See also* LABOR LEGISLATION; MINORITIES, MANAGEMENT OF AND EQUAL EMPLOYMENT OPPORTUNITY; WOMEN IN INDUSTRY.

## NOTES

[1] Title VII of the Civil Rights Act of 1964.

[2] *See* WOMEN IN INDUSTRY.

[3] "The Corporate Woman: Up the Ladder Finally," *Business Week*, Nov. 24, 1975, pp. 58–68.

[4] Survey by *Harvard Business Review*, Harvard Graduate School of Business Administration, Boston, September–October 1973.

[5] Wyndham Robertson, "The Ten Highest Ranking Women in Big Business," *Fortune*, April 1973, p. 81.

[6] U.S. Department of Labor, *1975 Handbook on Women Workers*, Employment Standards Administration, Bulletin 297, p. 86.

[7] Mike Tharp, "Improved Image: Women in Work Force Post Better Records for Stability in Jobs," *The Wall Street Journal*, Nov. 20, 1974, pp. 1 and 34.

[8] Ibid.

[9] U.S. Department of Labor, *Underutilization of Women Workers*, Women's Bureau Workplace Standards Administration, 1971, p. 17.

[10] B. R. Bergmann and Irma Adelman, "Economic Role of Women," *The American Economic Review*, vol. 63, no. 4, p. 510, September 1973.

[11] Ellen Goodman, "Working Wives in 30s Shape New Generation," *The Plain Dealer*, Dec. 12, 1976, p. 15.

[12] Ibid.

[13] William E. Reif, John W. Newstrom, and Robert M. Monczka, "Exploding the Myths About Women Man-

agers," *California Management Review*, vol. XII, No. 4, pp. 72–79, Summer 1976.

[14] *Harvard Business Review*, March–April 1974.

[15] Eleanor Brantley Schwartz and Walter B. Waetjen, "Improving the Self-Concept of Women Managers," *The Business Quarterly*, University of Western Ontario, Canada, Winter 1977.

[16] William H. Chafe, *The American Woman*, Oxford University Press, New York, 1972.

[17] D. R. Ray and R. M. Stodgill, "Leader Behavior of Male and Female Supervisors; A Comparative Study," *Personnel Psychology*, vol. 25, pp. 353–360, 1972.

[18] W. E. Rosenbauch, R. C. Dailey, and C. P. Morgan, "Differences Among Women in Perceptions of Their Jobs," *Proceedings of the 36th Annual Meeting of the Academy of Mangement*, 1976, pp. 472–476.

[19] W. E. Rosenbauch, R. C. Dailey, and C. P. Morgan, "Dispelling Some Myths and Stereotypes About Women in Business Management," *Colorado Business Review*, vol. XLIX, no. 9, pp. 2–4, September 1976.

[20] Martha G. Burrow, *Women: A Worldwide View of Their Management Development Needs*, American Management Association, New York, 1976, pp. 15–16.

[21] Ibid.

### REFERENCE

Lynch, Edith: *The Executive Suite: Feminine Style*, American Management Association, New York, 1973.

Eleanor Brantley Schwartz, *Cleveland State University*

Walter Bernhard Waetjen, *Cleveland State University*

# Word processing

Word processing is the production of written communications through the combined use of systems management procedures, automated technology, and accomplished personnel. As a concept, word processing represents an advanced attempt to introduce production technology into the office environment. It requires a substantive change in office structure and procedures.

Only recently has management begun to recognize the cost of managing information.[1] Generally, the cost of managing information in an organization is exceeded only by personnel, material, and transportation costs. In government and some service-type organizations, the percent of the budget devoted to information management is frequently second only to that of personnel.

The spiraling costs of written communications are the result of several conditions: (1) there are more people generating paper work; (2) there are relatively fewer office workers to do it; (3) clerical productivity has not risen perceptibly for the last two decades; and (4) salaries of office workers continue to increase.

Word processing has made it possible not only to reduce office costs but to improve the quality and reduce the turnaround time of the work produced. Potential savings from word processing range from 15 to 40 percent in secretarial and typing costs—depending on the degree to which the office is systematized and automated.[2] Although savings accruing to the professional staff from word processing have not been adequately verified, indications are that these savings dwarf those associated with the support staff.

**Systems Approach** Automated equipment can be placed in the traditional unstructured office, words can be processed, and savings can accrue; however, approximately 80 percent of the savings associated with word processing are attributable to an integrated systems design, while only 20 percent are attributable to automated equipment. In word processing, the systems approach is applied when the written communications functions and highly skilled specialists are placed in a structured environment to assume responsibility for specific functions, as shown in Fig. W-1.

Personnel working in *written communications* are specialists in grammatical construction, correspondence procedures, and the conceptualization and operation of electronic equipment. Personnel working in *administrative support* are specialists in the other various support areas, such as filing and retrieval, scheduling of travel, receptionist duties, conference preparation, telephone service, duplication and distribution, or mail service.

As a rule of thumb, an office producing from 3500 to 6000 pages per year will find it economically feasible to consider automated equipment. If the total volume is 15,000 pages or more per year and other considerations are conducive, it is feasible to consider a systems approach to word processing.

**Applications** The seven basic applications of word processing are:

1. *Transcription of materials.* The originator of the document dictates onto a magnetic medium, and the information is later transcribed by a word processing specialist. This saves the time of both the originator and the support staff. With proper equipment, the originator can dictate in the office or away from the office. There is no secretarial time consumed in taking dictation, and materials can be scheduled for transcription on a systematic basis.

2. *Repetitive communications.* Perfect original copies of communications, such as form letters, are

processed on automated equipment. These copies do not vary.

3. *Combination of repetitive and variable communications.* Personalized communications are produced by automatically adding variable information such as names, dates, or amounts to stored paragraphs.

4. *Text preparation.* Documents such as manuals, long reports, proposals, contracts, and other extensive communications that require editing, additions, deletions, and revisions are input onto the word processor. The material may be called up for review and revision, and a hard copy is produced. This procedure is repeated as many times as is necessary.

5. *Communications requiring immediate turn-around time.* Materials are keyboarded at rough-draft speed, and the computer is given instructions for formatting. The material is reviewed on the video scanner, and the output mechanism produces a review copy or final copy.

6. *Composition and typesetting.* The word processor is used to record copy for setting and arranging type, along with the instructions. The material, recorded on magnetic media or paper tape, goes to a composing typewriter, photocomposition device, or typesetter.

7. *Systems use.* The word processor produces information according to preprogrammed procedures, performs basic information retrieval functions, automatically produces documents, or performs limited calculations in conjunction with the production of communications.

**Organizational Structure** Word processing may be implemented anyplace in an organization where it effectively raises productivity.[3] Word processing fits efficiently in a large center, in satellite centers, in work groups, or in one-machine situations. The determinants are (1) the nature and volume of work and (2) the way people and organizational components are structured. Word processing is a flexible concept, not a single stereotyped approach. It is necessary to analyze the administrative and correspondence support required by management, then design and implement a means of doing the work more efficiently than can be done by traditional methods.

**Equipment** Equipment used in word processing includes dictation, or input, equipment and keyboard, or output, equipment. Copiers, facsimile transmission equipment, and communications devices for accessing computers are also used, depending on the complexity and the sophistication of the system.[4]

*Input, Dictation.* There are three basic categories of dictation equipment: (1) portable, (2) desktop, and (3) remote or central recorders. A variety of media is used with this equipment, including magnetic cassettes, tapes, small disks, and belts.

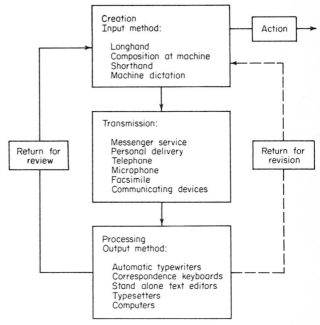

Fig. W-1. The word processing system.

*Output, Keyboard.* There are five basic categories of word processors or keyboard equipment: automatic typewriters, correspondence keyboard, stand-alone text editors, composition and typesetting, and computers. Description and evaluation follow:

1. The least sophisticated of the word processors are the *automatic typewriters.* They are designed to handle high-volume typing and repetitive correspondence.

2. The *correspondence keyboards* have more capability than the automatic typewriters but less than the stand-alone text editors. This equipment is used primarily in processing short documents, repetitive correspondence, and statistical documents.

3. The *stand-alone text editors* will do everything the automatic and correspondence keyboards will do and more. Most of the market today centers around this category of word processors. The storage medium is largely magnetic card, cassette, cartridge, or disk; although some models have buffer memories, and a few still use paper tape. These machines

provide a wide range of features for correcting, revising, inserting, deleting, centering, aligning, and formatting.

4. In a system using *composition and typesetting,* the word processor is used to record copy, along with instructions for setting and arranging type. The material recorded on magnetic disks, cassettes, cartridges, cards, or paper tape goes to a composing typewriter, photocomposition device, or typesetter that produces camera-ready copy.

5. Two approaches are available for *computerized word processing:* (*a*) a dedicated minicomputer or (*b*) a time-sharing system, which may be either user-supplied or vendor-supplied.

The advantages of using *minicomputers* include the variety of documents that can be processed, the ability to develop broader systems approaches by including several subdivisons of an organization in one system through the use of terminals, and the ability to produce massive quantities of material at a very low cost per document.

A *time-sharing computer system,* either user-supplied or vendor-supplied, allows a number of users to gain access to its facilities through terminals. There are several text-editing programs that can be used in conjunction with a user's in-house computer system. User-supplied or in-house computer systems are practical, however, only when text editing requirements are extensive and when many typewriter terminals and other peripheral devices such as video display units and printers are linked to the central computer.

**Trends** Word processing is in its infancy. All indications are that word processing will be an integral part of the office of the future. There will be less need for manual skills; but people entering the field will need a knowledge of management techniques, an understanding of the structure and operation of the organization, some background in the fundamentals of electronic data processing, and familiarity with the machines and systems used in word processing.

The technological forecasts are far-reaching:

Communication typewriters or terminals connected to computers in even the small office

Increasingly flexible word processing systems, with the telephone used to interface over great distances and to link networks of word processing systems

Automatic typing systems with increased self-contained intelligence and faster print-out capabilities

Common use of interface with photo typesetting and optical character recognition.

*See also* ADMINISTRATIVE MANAGEMENT; DATA PROCESSING PRINCIPLES AND PRACTICES; FORMS DESIGN AND CONTROL; INFORMATION SYSTEMS, MANAGEMENT (MIS); PAPER WORK SIMPLIFICATION; RECORDS MANAGEMENT; SYSTEMS AND PROCEDURES.

### NOTES

[1] Thomas J. Anderson and William R. Trotter, *Word Processing,* American Management Association, New York, 1974, pp. 2–4.

[2] Army found clerical support savings to range from 15 to 30 percent. U.S. Department of Army, *A Management Introduction to Word Processing,* 1975, p. 2-1.

[3] Walter A. Kleinschrod, *Word Processing, an AMA Management Briefing,* American Management Association, New York, 1974, pp. 10–11.

[4] Walter A. Kleinschrod, *Management's Guide to Word Processing,* The Dartnell Corporation, Chicago, 1975, pp. 149–182.

L. RUTH THOMAS, *United States Immigration and Naturalization Service*

## Work-centered appraisal (*See* APPRAISAL, PERFORMANCE.)

## Work, concept and implications

Dramatic changes are occurring in the ideas people have about the kind of work they will do and the role work should play in their lives. Unfortunately, some trends in the nature and organization of work run counter to changing worker values. Inevitably, these differences cause frustration, conflict, reduced productivity, and lowered quality in products and services. To relieve these frictions, work—its design, its organization, and its human resources impact—must come to the center of any effective management strategy. It now seems clear that the evolving technology of work and organization design, critically and conscientiously applied, can contribute significantly to corporate results as well as to fullfillment of specific employee needs.

### THE STRUCTURE OF WORK AND ITS IMPACT

At its most abstract, work is any physical or mental effort performed in a purposeful activity. In the strictest modern sense, work is not solely a human function: it is also a function of the machine. In fact, one of the primary goals of mechanization and automation is to transfer work from the human to the machine. Critical in such technology are the decisions about which work to allocate to the machine and which to the person.

Good allocation decisions result in compatability between person and machine—not only in tailoring the machine to the physical capabilities and characteristics of the human being but also in creating a person/machine system consistent with the workers' psychological requirements. Poor allocation decisions result in work that is fragmented, with little significance to the worker and with minimal requirements for choice and decisions by the worker. The corporate penalty for designing such human work is at least as great as the penalty to the individual worker.

**Payoffs and Penalties** Application in a wide variety of work situations has repeatedly demonstrated favorable outcomes of work designed to accommodate some of the motivational requirements of the worker. In AT&T for example, redesign of human work has yielded these results: (1) After service-order *typist jobs* were redesigned, service orders completed on time jumped from 27 to 90 percent within a month. For that same group, absence dropped from 2.5 to 0.6 percent, and errors from 4.6 to 2.9 percent. (2) In an engineering organization of about 80 people, a reduction in *supervisory jobs* resulted in a loaded salary savings of about $250,000 a year. In that same group, the percentage of engineering estimates submitted on time increased from 57 to 76 percent after work redesign. (3) In a *manufacturing setting*, work redesign contributed to the elimination of back orders valued at $226,100 plus orders valued at $26,700 shipped ahead of schedule.

Work redesign as practiced at AT&T can apparently be applied in all work situations: management and nonmanagement work, line and staff work, work with and without equipment, and independent as well as interdependent jobs. Applying the approach to new work as it is designed requires a slightly different technique from that described in the next section, but the underlying principles are similar. The opportunities for effective design of new work systems are almost limitless, beginning in the very early stages of new system design where functions are first being allocated between the human and the machine.

On the other hand, work which is poorly designed for the person typically results in less than optimum performance—errors, waste, unproductive time, negative attitudes, mental health problems, and turnover—especially when the economic and employment conditions allow the worker a choice.

**Structure of Work.** There are several dimensions along which work can be designed to meet worker motivational needs and thus to produce effective performance in support of corporate goals. Here are six of particular concern:

*Functional completeness.* Degree to which a job provides opportunities to perform whole functions, from beginning to end, toward a clearly identifiable product or service

*Direct, consistent relationship.* Degree to which a job allows for an ongoing relationship and direct contact with a user, client, customer, or geographical area

*Skill and task variety.* Degree to which a job requries the worker to use several skills in a number of different tasks or activities

*Autonomy.* Degree to which a job allows the worker independence and choice in planning and carrying out the work

*Direct feedback from work.* Degree to which performing the job directly yields information to the worker about the effectiveness of his or her performance

*Opportunity for work-related growth.* Degree to which the job provides opportunities for the worker to increase work-related skills on an ongoing basis

Measurement and enhancement of these work dimensions are fundamental to the work design technology described later.

**Worker Differences** As with all physical and psychological qualities, workers differ in their preferences for the work dimensions and in their performance when those dimensions are present. Research and experience suggest that most people perform more effectively with at least a moderate degree of these dimensions. Furthermore, a number of surveys and other indicators show that workers place increased importance on well-designed work. Even though everyone will not respond in the same way to work designed along the work dimensions, the odds are high for double payoff—corporate and individual—if the work design process gives weight to them.

**Work and Organization** In any organization, work is the functional core around which all other aspects of organization and management must be built. The work itself is represented by tasks and functions, arranged in a work flow, assigned to specific jobs, and constrained by the equipment used, the physical environment, the detailed procedures and methods, and the standards to be achieved.

**Problem Solving** The organization is designed around the work core with consideration of such variables as total size, decision-making needs, specialization, standardization, and coordination among organizational components. Once that organizational structure is defined, the many programs and systems in support of human performance must be provided: job description and evaluation, selection and placement, training, supervisory and management methods, performance evaluation, compensation, benefits, and so on. Problem solving, in many organizations, typically begins by attacking elements in the outer structure, such as training or management methods. Many problems, however, cannot be solved at that level or even at the level of organization structure. Only by attacking the inner structure—the work and its constraining elements—can many critical problems be solved and new objectives established.

## A TECHNOLOGY OF WORK AND ORGANIZATION DESIGN

In an attempt to keep work and its structure central for organizational performance, staff members at AT&T have been developing and implementing a technology of work and organization design. The strategy, as applied to existing work systems among the corporation's internal "clients," consists of four basic phases:

**Phase 1: Definition of Problems and Objectives**  Since objectives for the work design study must be geared to valid problems and needs, this first phase may require preliminary data gathering and analysis to arrive at *statements of objectives* on which both the client and the work team can agree.

On each project, all the initial agreements on objectives, information to be collected, the strategy for evaluating results, resources required, and schedules are crystalized in a proposal for final negotiation with the internal clients.

**Phase 2: Diagnosis of Work and Organization Design**  Work design technology at AT&T emphasizes measurement and evaluation at several steps. The most-critical data collection and analysis occur during the diagnostic phase. Three kinds of information are gathered: *baseline data*, for diagnosing work design problems as well as for establishing a baseline against which effects of redesign can be measured; *work and organizational process data*, the detailed information about how work currently gets accomplished and where various kinds of work-related problems occur; and *individual and demographic data*, which help to identify worker characteristics that may affect the design of work and organization.

Most projects require either individual or group *work-flow interviews* geared to the project's objectives. *Detailed time records* can collect information on activity frequency, length, and job loading. *Questionnaires* may be administered to determine worker perceptions of the work dimensions in their current jobs, their reactions to specific issues unique to the project, and their satisfaction with various facets of their jobs and the organization.

**Phase 3: Redesign of Work, Organization, and Support Systems**  If the diagnostic data indicate a need for changing the work or organization design, redesign steps are initiated. These activities are carried out largely by the organization and workers involved, aided by the coaching and assistance of work design experts. The redesign strategy is to attack specific work design problems identified, using the desired work dimensions together with performance expectations as criteria for deciding on changes. In one study, for example, a key problem was that work was highly fragmented among two or more jobs (low functional completeness, in work dimension terms). One of the agreed-upon project goals was to reduce the overall time to complete a specific work function. This objective was partly accomplished by reducing fragmentation.

Changes in the organization structure may emerge from the redesign of the work. Attention is also given to organizational and work support system features such as span of control, departmentalization, staff and line division of responsibilities, job descriptions, communications and feedback channels, and training for the redesigned job.

**Phase 4: Tryout, Evaluation, Implementation, and Tracking**  The keystone in this phase—as for much of this technology—is evaluation and measurement. After tryout, data are collected and compared with the baseline established in phase 2. As implementation progresses, an ongoing tracking and monitoring period ensues. Data are periodically gathered during tracking to watch trends in results, especially after the novelty of change wears off.

## ENCOURAGEMENTS AND CAUTIONS

Experience with processes, referred to by such terms as job enrichment, work restructuring, and work redesign, has been accompanied by a vast amount of commentary ranging from unconditional endorsement to unqualified disparagement. Most of the positions on this continuum are based more on personal opinion than on hard data. Nor is it likely that definitive data will ever be available to unequivocally support the benefits and costs of work design. This is so, partly because work design is a strategy which can be applied with tremendous variation in technique, in situation, and in skill. This is true, of course, of other strategies such as management by objectives and organization development.

The question to ask therefore is not, "Is work design a successful management strategy?" but rather, "What conditions make work design more successful as a strategy?" Conditions described in the four-phase approach—establishing clear objectives, negotiating at key points, involving the workers, etc.—are essential to the success of the strategy.

Implementation of any work design methodology with disregard of such requirements is a highly speculative approach. When these conditions can be met, however, work design is one of the most valuable management strategies available today, since it is geared to meeting both the corporate demands for effective performance and the employee's needs for something more than just a job.

*See also* HUMAN FACTORS ENGINEERING; HYGIENE FACTORS; JOB ANALYSIS; MOTIVATION IN ORGANIZATIONS; ORGANIZATION DEVELOPMENT (OD); PRODUCTIVITY; THEORY X AND THEORY Y; WORK DESIGN, JOB ENLARGEMENT, JOB ENRICHMENT, JOB DESIGN, AND AUTONOMOUS WORK GROUPS; WORK MEASUREMENT; WORK SIMPLIFICATION AND IMPROVEMENT.

### REFERENCES

*Trends in attitudes and concepts about work:*
Rosow, J. M., ed.: *The Worker and the Job: Coping with Change*, Prentice-Hall, Inc., Englewood Cliffs, N.J., 1974.
Report of a Special Task Force to the Secretary of Health, Education, and Welfare, "Work in America," The M.I.T. Press, Cambridge, Mass., 1973.
Davis, L. E., and A. B. Cherns, eds.: *The Quality of Working Life (vol. I): Problems, Prospects, and the State of the Art*, The Free Press, New York, 1975.

*Human factors in systems design:*
Meister, D.: *Human Factors: Theory and Practice*, John Wiley & Sons, Inc., New York, 1971.

*Diverse positions on work, its design, and its impact on the worker:*
Cass, E. J., and F. G. Zimmer, eds.: *Man and Work in Society*, Van Nostrand Reinhold Company, New York, 1975.

*Job enrichment and work design strategies:*
Hackman, J. R., G. Oldham, R. Janson, and K. Purdy: "A New Strategy for Job Enrichment," *California Management Review*, vol. 17, no. 4, p. 57, Summer 1975.
Peterson, R. O., and B. H. Duffany: "Job Enrichment and Redesign," in Craig, R. L., ed.: *Training and Development*

*ment Handbook*, McGraw-Hill Book Company, New York, 1976.
Also see references at the end of WORK DESIGN, JOB ENLARGEMENT AND JOB ENRICHMENT.

*Cases and results:*
Davis, L. E., and A. B. Cherns, eds.: *The Quality of Working Life (vol. 2): Cases and Commentary*, The Free Press, New York, 1975.
Katzell, R. A., D. Yankelovich, et al.: *Work, Productivity, and Job Satisfaction*, The Psychological Corporation, New York, 1975.
Ford, R. N.: *Motivation Through the Work Itself*, American Management Association, New York, 1969.

H. WESTON CLARKE, JR., *AT&T*
RICHARD O. PETERSON, *AT&T*

## Work concepts and job design  *(See heading in Table of Contents for complete listing.)*

## Work content  *(See* WORK MEASUREMENT.*)*

## Work councils  *(See* CODETERMINATION AND INDUSTRIAL DEMOCRACY.*)*

## Work design  *(See* COST IMPROVEMENT.*)*

## Work design, job enlargement, job enrichment, job design, and autonomous work groups

All the terms described below refer to techniques for expanding the content of jobs by adding new functions and/or responsibilities. These techniques rest on the following common assumptions:

Many employees have more capability than their jobs require.

Many of them desire to use that capability.

Greater utilization of employee capabilities would benefit both the employees and the organization.

*Job Design.* Of the terms considered here, job design has enjoyed the longest period of use. It is best understood as a generic term under which all the others fit. Job design denotes exactly what it says: the design of jobs. The specific connotative meaning of the term has shifted with time and changes in management philosophy. F. W. Taylor[1] advocated a scientific approach to the design of jobs which involved simplifying the work and specifying in great detail what was to be done and how it was to be done. Currently, the term *job design* is used to refer to any of a variety of approaches aimed at increasing the level of satisfaction with work by making jobs more challenging and interesting to do.

Most of the practitioners of job enlargement, job enrichment, and the establishment of autonomous work groups would be comfortable with having their efforts included under the heading of job design.

*Job Enlargement.* This emphasizes the expansion of a job to include other related tasks of approximately the same level of difficulty. Its basic thrust is horizontal in that it involves combining into a single job, tasks that may have been performed by several different employees at the same level. It has the effects of reducing specialization and increasing the variety of tasks performed by the worker.

*Job Enrichment.* This approach is most often associated with the motivation theories of Frederick Herzberg[2] and involves altering job content to give the worker more control and decision-making opportunity as well as improved feedback on performance. It may or may not include the addition of new tasks, as in the case of job enlargement.

The objectives of job enrichment are: (1) to build clearly defined and complete pieces of work (sometimes called *modules* of work); (2) to give the worker substantial opportunity to decide how that piece of work will be completed; (3) to give the worker appropriate information to help in making those decisions.

In Scott Myers'[3] terms, job enrichment is intended to offer workers an opportunity to *plan* and *control* their work in addition to *doing* their work.

*Autonomous Work Groups.* These are an outgrowth of the sociotechnical systems approach to the design of work.[4] This approach has been advocated by those associated with the Tavistock Institute of Human Relations in London, England. The basic premise is that the social (human) system and the technical (machine and work technology) system are, in reality, *one* highly interlocked system which is labeled a *sociotechnical system.*

The goal is to build relatively independent work groups (autonomous work groups) that can assert control over the technology involved in their work. This is accomplished by allowing the work group to decide for itself how its objectives will be established and met and which group member will do what and when. Depending on how the group decides to structure its work, the result may include aspects of job enlargement, job enrichment, job rotation, or all three.

**Application Opportunities** Job design techniques have their greatest impact under the following conditions:

When top management is knowledgeable about and willing to support experimentation with the design of the work.

When there is a feeling among many supervisors and managers in the area in question that things need to be improved or that some type of change is called for.

When many of the employees have more capability than their current jobs require.

When many of the employees indicate an interest in and desire for more challenging work.

When the basic needs of the employees for reasonable pay, benefits, working conditions, and fair treatment are being met.

Where the current structure of the jobs offers the opportunity to make significant improvements in their design.[5]

**Application Procedures** The design, or redesign, of work can be and is accomplished in a variety of ways. Listed below, however, is a set of steps that are broadly representative of most approaches currently in use. Application procedures are most often carried out by task forces consisting of staff people trained in the processes of redesigning work (such as representatives of personnel or industrial engineering departments) and members of line management who are familiar with the jobs in question. In some cases, representatives of union groups and/or other employees who perform the jobs being studied are also involved in the planning.

*Step 1: Feasibility Study.* The feasibility study determines whether redesigning the work will be an effective activity in a particular organization or work unit. A complete study will usually require an examination of existing data on production, quality, absenteeism, turnover, etc.; an analysis of the work flow; interviews with employees to learn how they do their work and what they like and dislike about it; questionnaires to measure employees' satisfaction with the work;[6] interviews with supervisors and managers to determine their interest in and support for changes in work design; and the gathering of data concerning prospective changes in management, equipment, sales forecasts, etc., that might affect the advisability of becoming involved in an effort to redesign the work. A report is then written, based on this information, and a decision is made whether or not to proceed with the work design effort. Obviously, the following steps will occur only if a positive decision is reached.

*Step 2: Planning the Work Design Changes.* The planning often begins with a workshop or seminar that may last anywhere from a few hours to a few days. The workshop typically features a discussion of job design principles and illustrations to stimulate the participants' thinking. In the case of job enrichment and job enlargement, a brainstorming approach is often used at this point. Its objective is to generate ideas for changes in the design of the work. In building autonomous work groups, an analytical procedure designed to identify sources of variance in the technological system is most often employed.[7]

When a pool of ideas has been generated, the next step is to decide which changes merit implementation. This process is usually begun in the initial workshop, but most often it cannot be completed there because of the time involved as well as the necessity to gather additional information needed to assess feasibility of the proposals. As a result, the usual procedure is to set up a series of follow-up meetings to continue the planning. These meetings (from 1 to 3 hours each) are generally held on a weekly basis and may continue for a period of a few weeks to several months, depending upon the complexity of the work being designed.

Once a complete design has been agreed upon, a schedule of implementation must be laid out. If (as is usually the case) the changeover to the new work design is to be accomplished in phases rather than all at once, plans must specify which workers will be involved at which points, how and when any training will be accomplished, etc.

Quite often, in order to test the effectiveness of the new design, a pilot study is implemented. This involves trying out the new work methods with a small group of employees (1) to make certain the plan will work and (2) to anticipate potential difficulties.

*Step 3: Implementation.* During the implementation period it is important for the task force to meet regularly. Its function now is to monitor the progress of the change and to make corrections as necessary. Depending on the number of unforeseen difficulties experienced, implementation may take from as little as a few weeks to as long as 3 years. An average implementation period ranges from 6 months to 1 year.

*Step 4: Evaluation.* Results of a work design change are usually of two kinds. First, there are often shifts in the job attitudes of employees. These can be measured by readministering the questionnaires used in the feasibility study, by reinterviewing some of the people, and by measuring shifts in such indicators as grievances, absences, and turnover. Second, there may be changes in the organization's effectiveness which can be measured by data on productivity, quality, customer complaints,

waste, downtime, and unit costs. In all these measures, it is important that data be gathered *before* any changes are made and then again *after* the bulk of the change has been accomplished.

**Examples of Successful Work Design**  In the United States, companies that have successfully implemented work design changes include Texas Instruments, General Foods, Prudential Insurance, American Telephone and Telegraph, PPG Industries, IBM, Cryovac Division of W. R. Grace, Procter & Gamble, and Monsanto, among many others. In other countries, organizations such as Olivetti, Volvo, Hallstavik Paper, Saab-Scania, Phillips, and Imperial Chemical Industries have been active in this area. Three brief examples follow.

*Prudential Insurance* is a company that has implemented these ideas very broadly. It has been actively involved in job enrichment (Prudential's term is *job design*) since 1970. It has more than 25 full-time job designers (internal consultants whose assignment is to implement job design concepts in the company). Over 100 divisions of the company have implemented job design changes, and the jobs of over 2000 employees have been restructured. These jobs include those of claims clerks, underwriters, personnel department employees, and data processing people.

Prudential believes that well-designed jobs should have

1. An identifiable beginning and end, as well as identifiable "customers" or receivers of the work.

2. A significant amount of decison-making opportunity.

3. Built-in feedback so that workers can tell how well they are doing.

Prudential's results indicate that staff has been reduced in 33 percent of the divisions affected; service to policyholders has improved in 52 percent of the work units; quality of performance has improved in 47 percent of the work units; job attitude and morale is up in 52 percent of the work units; productivity has improved in 46 percent of the work units; attendance has improved in 26 percent of the work units; and turnover has decreased in 33 percent of the work units.

*General Foods* implemented a major change in work design at its pet-food plant in Topeka, Kansas, that opened in 1971. A work force of about 70 employees is organized into six autonomous work groups. Each group is composed of from seven to fourteen members and a team leader. The work groups decide for themselves how to divide up their work, screen and select new team members, and counsel with those members who do not meet team standards. Staff units and specialized jobs are avoided. Each team has responsibility for performing its own quality tests and for ensuring quality standards.

In this plant, pay increases are geared to an employee's progress in mastering an increasing number of tasks, beginning with those in his or her own team and then in the rest of the plant. Thus compensation is offered for what one knows, rather than for what one does.

There are no supervisors. Each team selects its own team leader whose major responsibilities are team development and group decision making.

The physical environment of the plant emphasizes the equality discussed above. There is a single open parking lot, a single entrance for all members of the organization, and one decor scheme throughout.

Results are generally favorable. Original staffing estimates called for a work force of about 110 employees as compared with the actual work force of 70. Overhead costs are about one-third less than in the company's older plant. Quality figures are especially strong, indicating 92 percent fewer rejects.

Employees in the plant appear to be strongly supportive of the system. Absenteeism is 9 percent below the industry average, turnover is quite low, and interviews with workers indicate high morale and interest in their work.

*Volvo's* auto assembly plant at Kalmar is the innovation in Swedish industry that has attracted the most attention since it opened in 1974. It is the first auto plant in the world to be designed without a fixed-speed assembly line. In this plant, Volvo has made a major effort to adapt technology to human needs.

The most obvious difference between this plant and more conventional ones is in the shape of the building itself. It is constructed of seven hexagons (four on one level and three on another) joined at the center. Each corner of the factory is occupied by one of 20 autonomous work groups of 15 to 25 workers. Each group has its own entrance, dressing rooms, and break area. Large windows provide an outdoor view. Noise level is extremely low.

As attractive as the physical environment may be, the most impressive aspect of this plant is the work provided. To replace the usual conveyor/assembly line technology, Volvo developed battery-operated unmanned carriers which (1) move silently about the plant bearing both body and engine assemblies and (2) carry them to and from preprogrammed points.

Within each work group's area there is room for approximately six of these carriers at a time. Each group is responsible for one homogeneous collection of tasks and can organize its work as it wishes. An individual's work cycle can be as long as 20 minutes or as short as under 1 minute, depending on the work group's preferences.

Most groups develop tasks involving significant decision making with an emphasis on quality. A highly developed information system provides feedback to group members as to how their part of the auto makes out at subsequent quality check points.

This plant cost about 10 percent more to build than a conventional plant of the same capacity. Volvo is confident that it will recover this cost and more through the long-term results obtained.

Attitudes of most workers in the plant appear positive. Absenteeism and turnover rates are lower than in other Swedish auto plants. In terms of actual cost of operation, the plant appears to be doing well when compared with more conventional plants. Exactly how well is, as yet, uncertain.

**Requirements for Success** As noted above, changes in the design of work have the potential to produce clear improvements in both workers' attitudes and organizational effectiveness. In addition, there are often benefits such as improved quality of supervision, greater cross-function cooperation, and improved customer relations. It is also important to note, however, that such benefits are frequently obtained only with significant difficulty.

The implementation of this type of change requires a great deal of time, patience, and follow-up support. This, of course, can be said of any attempt to change an organization, but it seems to be even more applicable to attempts to alter the design of work.

Specifically, this type of program fails in the absence of long-term support (for a period of *years*) on the part of top management. It also fails when it is not coordinated with a variety of other functions such as job evaluation and pay systems, career-planning systems, supervisory and managerial appraisal programs, and developments in data systems and machine technology.[8]

Changes in work design or structure create ripples throughout an organization. For this reason they should be undertaken with great caution and careful planning. Significantly, the failures in work design programs are generally not of the type that create great organizational difficulty: it is just that *nothing* happens. The potential benefits are great, but anything less than complete commitment appears unlikely to reap them.

*See also* HUMAN FACTORS ENGINEERING; HYGIENE FACTORS; JOB ANALYSIS; MOTIVATION IN ORGANIZATIONS; ORGANIZATION DEVELOPMENT (OD); PRODUC-

TIVITY; THEORY X AND THEORY Y; WORK, CONCEPT AND IMPLICATIONS; WORK MEASUREMENT; WORK SIMPLIFICATION AND IMPROVEMENT.

### NOTES

[1]F. W. Taylor, *The Principles of Scientific Management*, Harper & Row, Publishers, Incorporated, New York, 1911.

[2]F. Herzberg, *Work and the Nature of Man*, New American Library, Inc., New York, 1973.

[3]S. Myers, *Every Employee a Manager*, McGraw-Hill Book Company, New York, 1970.

[4]L. Davis, and J. Taylor, *Design of Jobs*, Penguin Books, Inc., Baltimore, 1972.

[5]D. A. Whitsett, "Where Are Your Enriched Jobs?" *Harvard Business Review*, January–February 1975.

[6]The two most widely used questionnaires are the job Reaction Survey (See R. N. Ford and E. Borgatta, "Satisfaction with the Work Itself," *Journal of Applied Psychology*, April 1970.) and the Job Diagnostic Survey (See J. R. Hackman and G. Oldham, *Technical Report No. 4*, Department of Administrative Sciences, Yale University, 1974.)

[7]For a concise description of how these two approaches have been combined successfully, see J. Powers, "Job Enrichment: How One Company Overcame the Obstacles," *Personnel*, May–June 1972.

[8]For a more complete listing and discussion of the obstacles, see D. Sirota and A. Wolfson, "Job Enrichment: What Are the Obstacles?" *Personnel*, May–June 1972.

### REFERENCES

Davis, L., and A. Cherns: *The Quality of Working Life*, 2 vols., The Free Press, New York, 1975.

Ford, R. N.; *Motivation through the Work Itself*, American Management Association, 1969.

Schappe, R. H.: "Twenty-Two Arguments against Job Enrichment," *Personnel Journal*, February 1974.

Yorks, L.: *A Radical Approach to Job Enrichment*, American Management Association, New York, 1976.

DAVID A. WHITSETT, *University of Northern Iowa*

## Work-distribution chart (See COST IMPROVEMENT; PAPER WORK SIMPLIFICATION.)

## Work force planning [See HUMAN RESOURCES (WORK FORCE) PLANNING.]

## Work hours, flexible

*Flexitime* (flexible work hours) is a schedule that permits employees to choose their own working hours to some extent, provided they work the normal number of hours.

Flexitime schedules generally include several (perhaps 6) hours of "core time" during which all employees must be on the job. However, an employee may choose to come to work a ½ hour or an hour late and make up the time after the normal closing time. Conversely, employees may start earlier and leave earlier if they prefer.

In some cases, the working time may be averaged over a week or even over several weeks. Thus an employee might work fewer than the normal hours some days and make up the time later.

Flexitime started in Europe and seems to be most widely used in Switzerland. It has even been adopted in cases where a group must operate as a team—in that case, team members agree each day on the next day's starting time, and all work the same hours.

Most companies find that employees like the system and the greater freedom it allows them. In any case, except where the work is entirely a team effort, nothing prevents an employee from working normal hours if he or she wants to. In the United States, of course, payment for hours worked must conform to requirements of wages and hours legislation, regardless of the individual's preferences.

*See also* FOUR-DAY WEEK; TEMPORARY HELP; WORK DESIGN, JOB ENLARGEMENT, JOB ENRICHMENT, JOB DESIGN, AND AUTONOMOUS WORK GROUPS.

### REFERENCES

"Europe Likes Flexi-Time Work," *Business Week*, Oct. 7, 1972.

Fleuter, Douglas L.: *The Workweek Revolution: A Guide to the Changing Workweek*, Addison-Wesley Publishing Company, Inc., Reading, Mass., 1975.

*Flexitime*, U.S. Civil Service Commission, Code 101, Ext. 25604, May 15, 1974.

"The Flexitime Concept Gets a Wider Test," *Business Week*, May 24, 1976.

Hedges, Janice Neipert: "New Patterns of Working Time," *Monthly Labor Review*, February 1973.

Wade, Michael: *Flexible Working Hours in Practice*, Gower Press Ltd., Epping, Essex, England, 1973.

Werther, William B.: "Good News and Bad News of Flexible Hours," *Administrative Management*, November 1973.

STAFF/SMITH

## Work hours act of 1962 (See WAGES AND HOURS LEGISLATION.)

## Work letter, contract (See OFFICE SPACE PLANNING AND DESIGN.)

# Work measurement

*Work measurement* assesses the content of work, primarily physical work, although, in this context, work may include decisions or a series of thoughts usually regarded as mental activities. Work measurement also includes analysis and use of certain relevant data, i.e., machine and equipment operating rates and limitations.

*Work content* is usually stated in terms of time per physical unit, i.e., minutes per piece, pound, or foot, although it is sometimes expressed in unrelated form, i.e., per occurrence. *Work*, as examined in this entry, usually refers to those activities performed within a manufacturing or processing facility. It also includes, of course, those activities of clerical and other skilled and semiskilled office workers that are susceptible to analysis and measurement by direct visual observation and/or certain written records of a particular character and kind.

## CONCEPTS

Several concepts underlie work measurement and its applications.

**Fair Day's Work**[1] This term, which is commonly used throughout industry, is a primary objective of work measurement and related techniques. In particular, it is related to compensation through the usual wording in a labor contract which includes the obligation to perform "a fair day's work for a fair day's pay."

A fair day's work is usually and best illustrated by motion picture films of common operations, i.e., walking, case handling, shoveling. These operations are physical in nature, and the apparent rate of work is easily judged, even by untrained observers. Films of many manufacturing, clerical, and other jobs and activities are available from a number of sources, such as the Society for the Advancement of Management. They are useful in providing supervisory, staff, and technical personnel with the approximate level of effort and skill associated with reasonable performance.

Various definitions of a fair day's work exist, but they are subjective in nature and employ terms such as *average* and *normal* without further definition.

**Standard Time Data** The concept of standard time data, or standard data, is important to an understanding of work measurement. It is defined as a number of individually derived standards that are condensed into a tabular array to facilitate their storage, referral, and further use.

The array is generated by graphical or statistical analysis of elemental times and physical attributes of the operation/product, to ascertain valid existing relationships or functions. (See Fig. W-2.) These can be expressed in equation form, usually derived by fitting a scattergraph to a straight line, when done manually. The computer has made it possible to handle massive data inputs and, through regression techniques, to improve accuracy.

Standard time data also improve consistency, in that human error inherent in the leveling—or judgment—process is, in some degree, reduced. Additionally, these data reduce the time spent in observation of the task, once the relationship of time to physical attribute is established and verified. Interpolation can be employed to establish a time for an operation on a specific product without making an actual observation.

## TECHNIQUES AND PROCEDURES

Selection of the work measurement technique to be used is an important decision, with serious cost implications, and involves significant considerations of a less-tangible nature.[2]

**Time Study** Basically, all time-study procedures are alike in that they constitute a time record of what, when, how, where, and by whom work was performed. Typically, the task is broken into smaller logically sequenced subtasks, referred to as *elements*, for which the time is recorded.

The technique of time study is usually accompanied by the estimates of the worker's effectiveness during observation: This involves assigning a level-of-performance index, usually on a scale of 0 to approximately 150, with 100 being designated as normal or average. Among a dozen or so other terms, this mental comparison is often referred to as *leveling*, *accomplishment rating*, or *pace rating*.

In addition to the effort-leveling procedure, other allowances are usually added to time-study–derived data. These usually cover fatigue and personal needs, although the amount of delay judged to be inherent is sometimes factored similarly.

*Enforced attention time* involves an interrelationship between workers and machine(s), which then removes, in varying proportion, control of workers' performances from the individual or group. The amount of enforced attention time during which the operator must stay in the immediate area to tend to the equipment must be found and incorporated in the standard time.

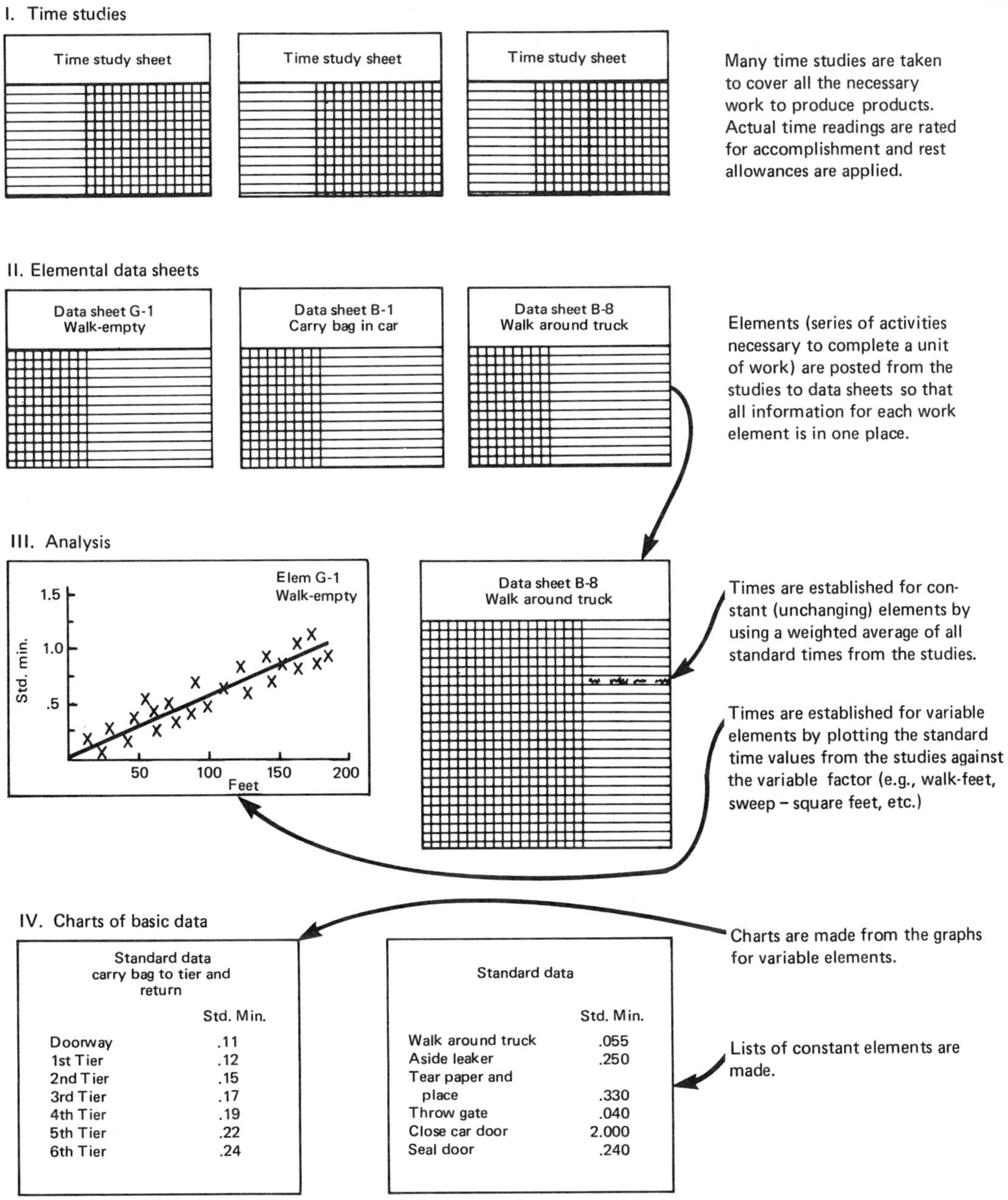

I. Time studies

| Time study sheet | Time study sheet | Time study sheet |

Many time studies are taken to cover all the necessary work to produce products. Actual time readings are rated for accomplishment and rest allowances are applied.

II. Elemental data sheets

| Data sheet G-1 Walk-empty | Data sheet B-1 Carry bag in car | Data sheet B-8 Walk around truck |

Elements (series of activities necessary to complete a unit of work) are posted from the studies to data sheets so that all information for each work element is in one place.

III. Analysis

Elem G-1
Walk-empty

Std. min.
1.5
1.0
.5

50   100   150   200
Feet

Data sheet B-8
Walk around truck

Times are established for constant (unchanging) elements by using a weighted average of all standard times from the studies.

Times are established for variable elements by plotting the standard time values from the studies against the variable factor (e.g., walk-feet, sweep – square feet, etc.)

IV. Charts of basic data

Charts are made from the graphs for variable elements.

Lists of constant elements are made.

| Standard data carry bag to tier and return | |
|---|---|
| | Std. Min. |
| Doorway | .11 |
| 1st Tier | .12 |
| 2nd Tier | .15 |
| 3rd Tier | .17 |
| 4th Tier | .19 |
| 5th Tier | .22 |
| 6th Tier | .24 |

| Standard data | |
|---|---|
| | Std. Min. |
| Walk around truck | .055 |
| Aside leaker | .250 |
| Tear paper and place | .330 |
| Throw gate | .040 |
| Close car door | 2.000 |
| Seal door | .240 |

Fig. W-2. Standard data derivation.

*Fatigue* is the more variable and least understood of allowances. It is usually expressed as a factor to be multiplied by the leveled time for the element. It can range from a minimum of 1.05 to 1.10 to 2.00 or higher under extreme conditions. Less often, fatigue is accommodated in specified minutes per hour, ranging from a low of five to a high of twelve or more. Various tables exist which can be used. (See Table W-6.)

*Personal allowances* involve an estimate of the time needed to perform the human functions of elimination, quenching thirst, and related necessities. Washing, or clean-up, may or may not be included in this portion. If not, where it is significant and time-consuming, involving travel to facilities or very dirty working conditions, it is usually expressed as a flat allowance in minutes.

In continuous operations, lunch may be included in this allowed time. Recently, OSHA-promulgated regulations have brought about a spate of state laws affecting both rest and personal allowances. However, the main impact has been in the areas of extremes, e.g., the maximum weights that can be lifted under specified circumstances or the allowable exposure to certain environments for specified lengths of time.

**Predetermined Time Systems**   Since the beginning of detailed motion study, microelemental systems have proliferated. Essentially, these systems are constructed on the principles first articulated by Gilbreth. The principal objective is to reduce all human movement to its most fundamental discernible components. These can then be combined as necessary to synthesize a standard operational time. In addition, the task of estimating performance during time studies is eliminated.

Several of these systems have become well established and are extensively installed, often concentrating in particular industries. They are known by both public and proprietary terms. Each possesses certain features considered by the originators and/or proprietors to make them uniquely valuable. Basically, all deal in very small (micro) elements, with times expressed in decimal portions of minutes or hours, and are given a name.

The basic *microelemental time values* for elemental motions are often combined into clusters or modules to facilitate derivation and application of standards. This loses some degree of accuracy, but administration and application to written records of operations is simplified.[3]

It is common for practitioners very familiar with these techniques to check the derived time values by using a stopwatch or other means. This is intended to ensure that they have not misinterpreted the description of the operation under consideration or in some other way erred in the development of standard times.

**Work Sampling**   It has been found to be useful as well as reliable to observe human work activities in a noncontinuous mode, most often referred to as sampling.[4] This technique is capable of deriving standard times and/or allowances or delays for elements. (*See* WORK SAMPLING.)

Work sampling is often performed using random numbers as the basis for the time interval at which the work shall be observed; however, its validity when using fixed intervals has also been established.

Sampling is a convenient method by which the activities of many individuals can be observed readily and translated into meaningful information. It has advantages, mainly cost advantages, over the detailed recording of work by orthodox time-study procedures. It is easily applied to (1) personnel visible within a particular area and (2) those who provide service to direct operations. It is also useful in examining the activities of personnel who are spread out over a much larger area, such as maintenance employees who may cover vast spaces of plants and grounds.[5]

**Historical Data**   Lacking any other reference materials or direct observational information, work content can be approximated, using past historical data related to rates of output, if these data are available in sufficient detail. This usually necessitates factoring by operations or groups, intended to correct historical rates or bring them into line.

**Frequency Distribution Analysis**   It is possible to plot standard times for elements as well as operations and from these to develop histograms and frequency distributions. The shape of the distributions, skewing, and other characteristics indicate the time for an operation which could be designated as standard. It is a useful technique for comparing (1) operator with operator or (2) similar methods for consistency, range, and other aspects of working times.

**Multiple Regression**   Some operations are of such nature that the length of time to perform them is reflected in more than one variable, sometimes several. The manual derivation of the influence of any one of several factors which influence the time necessary is laborious. The technique of multiple regression isolates and quantifies the independent variables.

Multiple regression often entails the development of exponential polynomial equations. Software programs have been developed and are available under

**TABLE W-6   Schedule of Fatigue and Personal Allowances for Factoring Elements**

### Selection Key for Handling Operations

| From | Above head | Chest | Waist | Knee | Floor |
|------|-----------|-------|-------|------|-------|
| Above head | 4 / 1.18 | 5 / 1.15 | 4 / 1.12 | 3 / 1.12 | 3 / 1.14 |
| Chest | 5 / 1.23 | 5 / 1.12 | 3 / 1.13 | 3 / 1.12 | 3 / 1.14 |
| Waist | 5 / 1.18 | 5 / 1.17 | 1 / 1.10 | 2 / 1.15 | 2 / 1.15 |
| Knee | 4 / 1.19 | 4 / 1.18 | 3 / 1.22 | 3 / 1.14 | 3 / 1.19 |
| Floor | 4 / 1.22 | 3 / 1.22 | 3 / 1.25 | 3 / 1.33 | 2 / 1.20 |

*LEGEND**

Load RF key no. / Basic rest factor*

### Rest Factors for Transporting Operations

| Element | Load RF key no. | Basic rest factor* | Load limit |
|---------|-----------------|--------------------|------------|
| Walking on level | 1 | 1.10 | 75# |
| Ascending stairs | 3 | 1.50 | 50# |
| Descending stairs | 2 | 1.20 | 50# |
| Ascending rung ladder | 3 | 1.60 | 25# |
| Descending rung ladder | 2 | 1.40 | 25# |
| Walking up grade | 3 | $1.10 + [(.001) \times (\% \text{ up grade})^2]$ | 10% grade-75# |
| Walking down grade | 2 | $1.10 + [(.0005) \times (\% \text{ down grade})^2]$ | 10% grade-75# |

### Load Rest Factors

| Load, pounds | Load rest factor key number | | | | |
|--------------|-----|-----|-----|-----|-----|
| | 1 | 2 | 3 | 4 | 5 |
| 5 | .01 | .02 | .02 | .02 | .03 |
| 10 | .03 | .04 | .04 | .05 | .06 |
| 15 | .05 | .06 | .07 | .08 | .09 |
| 20 | .06 | .08 | .10 | .11 | .13 |
| 25 | .09 | .11 | .13 | .15 | .17 |
| 30 | .11 | .14 | .16 | .19 | .22 |
| 35 | .13 | .17 | .20 | .23 | .27 |
| 40 | .16 | .20 | .24 | .28 | .32 |
| 45 | .19 | .24 | .28 | .33 | .38 |
| 50 | .22 | .28 | .33 | .39 | .44 |
| 55 | .25 | .32 | .38 | .44 | .51 |
| 60 | .29 | .36 | .43 | .50 | .57 |
| 65 | .32 | .40 | .48 | .57 | .65 |
| 70 | .36 | .46 | .55 | .64 | .73 |
| 75 | .40 | .51 | .61 | .71 | .81 |

*Note:* Rest factor = basic rest factor + load rest factor.
*Use basic rest factor for no load.
SOURCE: Copyright 1946 by Albert Ramond and Associates, Inc., Chicago, Ill.

proprietary ownership from several sources, facilitating the handling of cumbersome data inputs and derivation. (*See* STATISTICAL ANALYSIS FOR MANAGEMENT.)

**Other Techniques** In special circumstances, linear programming, critical path methodology, and simulation are used in the general area of work measurement. Within a limited context, other terms and compilations are in use to indicate a rate of work which has been arrived at through a rational process such as *reasonable expectancy*, a task time used in conjunction with short-interval scheduling or incremental work assignment/loading; *ZIP standard data*, a block-type standard used when application expense is to be minimized and accuracy is of minimal importance; and *commerical-industrial estimating manuals*, in which dollar estimates can be converted to useful standard time data.

## APPLICATIONS

Work measurement has a wide variety of practical uses, including the following:

**Labor Utilization** The most frequent, and often the most productive, use of standard times derived from work measurement is the development of information for management control which reflects the rate of labor utilization.[6] This can be collected over various periods of time and for various size groups of personnel ranging from total plants to individuals.

The classical definition of labor utilization is efficiency. *Efficiency* is the ratio of the earned hours generated by an employee, divided by the actual hours, i.e., clock hours, recorded during the time the corresponding work was performed. Thus, the above corresponds directly to the engineering definition, output divided by input.

*Earned hours* is the term used to describe the product of the standard time(s) for operation(s) multiplied by the number of times the operation was performed. The term *earned hours* is generally used, although it may be designated otherwise.

It is customary for most organizations to calculate the labor efficiency for any particular group on a continuing basis. It is not always possible for employees, however well motivated, to be at all times gainfully employed at desirable efficiencies. It is also impractical for work to be made available to all employees at all times. As a consequence, pure calculations of earned hours and actual hours cannot always be made.

*Labor Analysis Sheets.* In practice, workers report actual hours spent in other classifications, some

of which are delay time, lost time, personal time, and union time. These classifications are recorded on labor analysis sheets, in various formats, and distributed at periodic intervals (daily, weekly, monthly) as local procedures and needs may dictate. These displays of the performance of labor are provided to the various echelons of management for their information, analysis, and action. (See Fig. W-3.)

**Standard Costs** Labor standards are widely used in the build-up of standard costs. These are usually posted on a card, or other format, by operations and also by product as the basis, together with material, upon which burden and other costs are allocated.

**Production Control/Planning** In this area, labor standards are used in conjunction with production quantity requirements as these reflect sales demand. To order or release work to the manufacturing facility, incoming sales data are assembled and translated into internal operating orders. The production control/planning function combines the standards for labor performance and the customary or past performances of labor. This enables planners and schedulers to anticipate the completion of known product quantities and the sequence in which these will become available.

**Methods/Equipment Analyses** Labor standard data are useful, and often essential, in the development of accurate cost comparisons directed toward the selection of equipment and methods.

**Labor Disputes/Arbitrations/Grievances** It is very difficult to enforce labor performance clauses (as stated in labor contracts) unless the data gathered in the analysis of the situation are supported in adequate detail by labor standard times. Labor arbitrators have upheld the right of management to specify and to expect certain established levels of performance. Moreover, it has become possible to discipline and ultimately to discharge employees for failure to accomplish a certain defined level of performance, if this can be demonstrated by an adequate and complete documentation of their work performance history.

**Wage Incentive Systems** Work measurement, accompanied by adequately developed supporting systems, is the best foundation for incentive wage payment. In certain instances, standard times are supplemented by other factors, e.g., quality or yield parameters.

The labor content is used to establish a standard time which then becomes the norm—or that level of output which must be attained in order to earn above a certain level of pay in conformance with the

| Period | | Actual labor-hours | | | | Performance | | | | | | | Savings | |
|---|---|---|---|---|---|---|---|---|---|---|---|---|---|---|
| | As designated | Daywork hours unmeasured | On standard hours | Lost time hours | Total labor-hours | Earned std. hours | % measured hrs. Excluding noncoverable | Total labor-hours | % work perf. | % pay perf. | Cost per std. dollar | | This week | To date |
| | Reference | | | | | | | | | | | | | |
| | Last quarter | | | | | | | | | | | | | |
| 1 | Feb.8 | 729.5 | 2155.2 | 57.1 | 2941.8 | 2218.9 | 85.0 | 73.3 | 103.0 | 119.0 | 1.18 | | 3,987 | 3,987 |
| 2 | 15 | 793.7 | 2299.6 | 57.7 | 3151.0 | 2598.8 | 85.7 | 73.0 | 113.0 | 124.0 | 1.12 | | 5,218 | 9,905 |
| 3 | 22 | 743.5 | 2462.8 | 57.5 | 3263.8 | 2857.4 | 88.6 | 75.5 | 116.0 | 125.5 | 1.10 | | 5,948 | 15,153 |
| 4 | Mar. 1 | 903.6 | 2345.4 | 54.6 | 3303.6 | 2602.3 | 85.9 | 71.0 | 111.0 | 123.0 | 1.13 | | 5.124 | 20,277 |
| | Month | 3170.3 | 9263.0 | 226.9 | 12660.2 | 10277.4 | 86.1 | 73.0 | 111.0 | 123.0 | 1.13 | | – | 20,277 |
| 5 | Mar. 8 | 924.7 | 2173.4 | 54.3 | 3152.4 | 2427.1 | 82.7 | 68.9 | 111.7 | 123.5 | 1.13 | | 4,784 | 4,784 |
| 6 | 15 | 780.5 | 2130.4 | 39.3 | 2950.2 | 2404.3 | 85.3 | 72.2 | 112.9 | 124.0 | 1.12 | | 4,791 | 9,575 |
| 7 | 22 | 852.0 | 2459.5 | 55.3 | 3366.8 | 2798.3 | 86.2 | 73.1 | 113.8 | 124.5 | 1.11 | | 5,582 | 15,157 |
| 8 | 29 | 745.2 | 2010.8 | 34.6 | 2790.6 | 2166.1 | 84.8 | 72.1 | 107.7 | 121.5 | 1.15 | | 4,055 | 19,212 |
| 9 | Apr. 5 | 796.3 | 2072.4 | 43.8 | 2912.5 | 2300.3 | 84.3 | 71.2 | 111.0 | 123.0 | 1.13 | | 4,437 | 23,649 |
| | Totals | | | | | | | | | | | | | |
| | | 1 | 2 | 3 | 4 | 5 | 6 | 7 | 8 | 9 | 10 | | 11 | 12 |

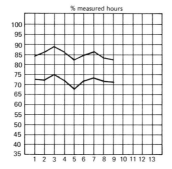
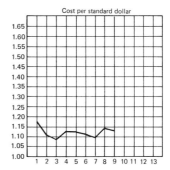

**Fig. W-3. Labor analysis sheet.**

governing clauses in the labor contract or incentive manual.

**Budgeting** Standard labor hours serve as an accurate means of predicting certain variable costs, usually allocated to cost-center burden accounts. Expenditure levels are adjusted above or below the planned level of activity as measured by earned standard hours produced over a specified period of time. These summaries are usually prepared on a monthly and accumulated (year-to-date) basis. Those accounts running over and below budgeted amounts are readily identified and analyzed.

## SUCCESSFUL APPLICATIONS— WORK MEASUREMENT

The following three cases illustrate some of the fundamental uses of work measurement:

### Manufacturer of Hydraulic Components

*Focus:* Scheduling and productivity.

*Period of observation:* Over 20 years, with growth from 500 to over 3000 employees.

*Purpose and techniques:* Original program was a measured daywork system for all machining and assembly operations. A measured daywork system is simply the application of work measurement without wage incentives. Its primary purposes were (1) improvement of scheduling by means of standards and (2) improvement of productivity through a system of measurement and evaluation.

*Administration:* The system emphasized basic time-study standards and strong, comprehensive production controls. A methods evaluation and improvement activity used standards as a basis for identifying problem areas and corrective action. A follow-up system utilized decentralized dispatch booths strategically located throughout the plant for job-by-job and day-by-day review, evaluation, reporting, and control of work assignments.

*Results:* Before, performance averaged 70 percent on measured work. After, performance increased to 90 percent at current operating levels. Savings were over $2 million per year, after deducting annual costs of system administration. Production output capacity for the existing plant facilities rose 28 percent.

### Medium-Sized Steel Producer

*Focus:* Cost control and profit improvement.

*Period of observation:* Covers a 12- to 13-year period.

*Purpose and techniques:* Original program was a work measurement system for all direct labor and indirect labor operations, including plant maintenance. Its primary purposes were to establish an accurate cost control and profit improvement system based on utilization of engineered standards for all operations.

*Administration:* This was designed to form the basis for a comprehensive standard cost system in which the labor and overhead costs were derived from engineered operating standards. These were developed using a variety of industrial engineering techniques. Profit improvement evaluation and review systems for decision making and corrective action were based on continual monitoring and an analysis of standard cost variances by all levels of management and supervision. An industrial engineering group, assigned by areas in the plant, maintained timely analysis and monitoring of day-by-day operations in support to line management.

*Results:* Before, overall effectiveness was 75 percent. One year after installation, and consistently thereafter, audits indicated performance averages of 92 percent. Yearly savings of over $2.5 million have been sustained. Production output increased 12 percent within existing plant facilities.

### Specialty Rubber Goods Producer

*Focus:* Direct labor.

*Period of observation:* Three years; approximately 300 employees.

*Purpose and techniques:* The primary objective of the program was to develop standard time data for all direct operations as the basis for a wage incentive system. These were developed by time study and reduction to standard time data, motion-time measurement, and equipment capacity analysis.

The wage incentive system was implemented to motivate employees to increase their performance, thereby raising plant capacity. Also, very high turnover and absenteeism had become intolerable.

*Administration:* Efforts centered on the attainment of equitable pay-performance relationships, despite considerable hostility from hourly employees. Supervisors were oriented to understand and support the standards published and released to the hourly employees. Monitoring by management identified potential troublesome areas. Communications were intensified.

*Results:* Before, performance was controlled at a level of approximately 70 percent. Since, performance has attained a plant-wide average of 120 percent. Net financial impact has stabilized in the middle six figures per year. Absenteeism and turnover have been reduced by over 80 percent.

## OUTLOOK FOR WORK MEASUREMENT

The main stream of effort in work measurement has shifted from the development of techniques for the derivation of work content to the following major areas of activity:

1. Simplified, cost-effective procedures concerning the application of standard times to production records.

2. Improvement of management, supervisory, and staff roles in the administration of work measurement.

3. Use of the computer and peripheral equipment in reporting time and production, processing data, and generating meaningful information for executive and operating action.

4. Development, modification, and use of computer-oriented software systems incorporating standard time data.

**Administration**   The day-to-day maintenance of reliable and accurate work measurement—related files, records, and reports—is that task which is most often defaulted. Employee pressures and understaffed functions often combine to erode well-conceived systems. This then induces a tendency to eliminate work rather than to demonstrate changes of lesser magnitude to unwilling employees. Thus, the phrase *engineered out* has come into common usage. This avenue, which emphasizes the development and installation of tooling, equipment, and capital goods is less offensive (than work measurement) to unions and/or employees.

**State of Development**   While many examples of the successful development and use of work measurement exist, many executives ignore the subject completely and/or give it less than its rightful amount of attention.[7] Improvement, or the development, of techniques which overcome the persistent resistance to work measurement do not appear to be materializing. Admittedly, the behavioral sciences continue to contribute to an understanding of work and its management. It seems fair to conclude, however, that there is as yet no real agreement among leading observers and practitioners as to the degree of applicability feasible through various techniques.

Neither does there appear to be a resolution of the

basic conflicts which revolve around (1) assessing the rate of work performance by direct time-study observation and (2) synthesizing the amount of work contained within a task through other avenues of approach, mainly those associated with predetermined motion-time systems.

**Industry Variations**   Without doubt, work measurement has had its greatest impact in the hourly work force within the factory. Acceptance of work measurement varies widely. In some industries, such as steel and garment making, work measurement and, further, incentive wage payment are traditional, common, and accepted in some large measure by the work force affected. In other industries, neither is tolerable. Any measurement approach other than the crudest estimating procedure is sufficient to create a furor and often results in severe disruption.

The application of work measurement in those industries where it is little used still holds promise of great benefit. Process industries, for example, are increasingly using work measurement in any of several forms to increase the productivity of their facilities as engineering technology (with its large capital requirement) begins to approach the point of diminishing return.

**Scope of Application**   There is a pervasive feeling which makes many managers feel that work measurement is most useful, and indeed most accurate and trouble-free, when it is employed to assess the content of standardized work, specifically and especially with direct labor. There is also a conviction that indirect or unstandardized work cannot be measured adequately or properly controlled. This notion is probably derived from the early orientation of work measurement activists. They held that work must be very closely specified and analyzed in order to establish the one best way in which it must be performed. As a result, they left a vast area of unstandardized or peripheral work areas uncovered, normally designated as indirect or burden labor, or simply, services. Indirect or burden labor is meant to include those activities normally covered by the terms *maintenance*, *material handling*, *distribution* (shipping and receiving), *repair operations*, *janitorial work*, etc. Industry and management today suffer from this limiting, inaccurate view of the suitability of the application of work measurement. Much work is nonrepetitive and filled with variations from task to task and day to day. It is true that other activities, e.g., purchasing and engineering, have been measured with some degree of success, but these extensions of the concepts have been made on an extremely limited basis.[8]

*See also* COMPENSATION, WAGE AND SALARY POLICY AND ADMINISTRATION; COST IMPROVEMENT; ENGINEERING, INDUSTRIAL; JOB ANALYSIS; JOB EVALUATION; THERBLIGS; WORK, CONCEPT AND IMPLICATIONS; WORK DESIGN, JOB ENLARGEMENT, JOB ENRICHMENT, JOB DESIGN, AND AUTONOMOUS WORK GROUPS; WORK SAMPLING; WORK SIMPLIFICATION AND IMPROVEMENT.

NOTES
[1] B.W. Niebel, *Motion and Time Study*, Richard D. Irwin, Inc., Homewood, Ill., 1967, p. 192.
[2] John G. Hutchinson, *Managing a Fair Day's Work*, Bureau of Industrial Relations, The University of Michigan Press, Ann Arbor, 1963, pp. 58–59.
[3] K. B. Zandin, "Better Work Management with Most," *Management Review*, American Management Association, July 1975.
[4] G. Salvendy and G. P. McCabe, "Auditing Standards by Sample," *Industrial Engineering Magazine*, September 1976, p. 25.
[5] H. F. Allard, "Work Sampling, Valuable Maintenance Management Aid," *Plant Engineering*, Sept. 19, 1968.
[6] M. Fein, "Work Measurement and Wage Incentives," *Industrial Engineering Magazine*, September 1973, p. 49.
[7] Frank DeWitt, "Productivity and the Industrial Engineer," *Industrial Engineering Magazine*, January 1976, p. 21.
[8] C. N. Berton and J. E. Martin, "Work Measurement of Purchasing," *Industrial Engineering Magazine*, January 1976, p. 31.

ROY ABEL, *Albert Ramond and Associates, Inc.*

# Work methods improvement   (*See* WORK SIMPLIFICATION AND IMPROVEMENT.)

# Work order system   (*See* MAINTENANCE MANAGEMENT.)

# Work rules   (*See* LABOR (TRADE) UNIONS.)

# Work sampling

Work sampling is a fact-finding technique which measures directly the overall activities of people or machines. It is of interest to the professional manager primarily because it can provide the answers to basic questions such as what percent of their time maintenance craftworkers spend in actual craft work or what the utilization pattern for the fork trucks is in the warehouse. Work sampling is a form of work measurement but does not carry with it demand for the heavy involvement of trained personnel, nor is it related to problems of wage rate structures and incentives. It can be a means of supervisory development and is particularly applicable as a first analysis technique in attacking the cost of service and indirect labor activities.

**Study Technique** A work sampling study consists of a series of snap, or instantaneous, observations of each of the people or machines making up the group under study. The observer classifies whatever activity he or she sees into a predefined series of categories. These categories may be as simple as classifying a typist as either typing or other activity. Usually, for an initial study, there are fewer than 10 categories. As an example, in the case of an analysis of typists, the categories might be as follows:

1. Typing
2. Taking dictation
3. Transcribing from a dictating machine
4. Clerical activity at desk
5. Away from desk, but in office
6. Talking, telephoning
7. Personal
8. Not in office

Each of these categories will be defined in writing and discussed with the supervisors and typists before sampling. The procedure for taking the observations is straightforward. At randomly selected times during the workday, the observer looks at each of the typists in turn and decides for each individually which category of activity best describes what is being done (or not done) at that particular moment. The observer then writes down the number of the category for each typist on a form similar to that shown in Fig. W-4. The names of the

| Name of typist | Random observation times | | | | | | | | |
|---|---|---|---|---|---|---|---|---|---|
| | 9:07 | 9:53 | 11:21 | 1:17 | 2:46 | 3:38 | 3:49 | 4:22 | 4:31 |
| Cain | 7 | 8 | 1 | 1 | 3 | 5 | 6 | 3 | 1 |
| Yeager | 2 | 1 | 6 | 4 | 1 | 3 | 7 | 6 | 2 |
| Cooke | 7 | 4 | 5 | 1 | 8 | 1 | 1 | 3 | 8 |
| Dooley | 7 | 8 | 7 | 4 | 1 | 1 | 2 | 1 | 8 |
| Macy | 4 | 1 | 2 | 5 | 7 | 5 | 1 | 4 | 1 |
| | | | | | | | | | |

Date ___7/16___   Supervisor ___Hartke___
(Observer)

Categories:
1. Typing          5. Away from desk
2. Taking dictation   6. Talking
3. Transcribing     7. Personal
4. Clerical at desk   8. Not in office

**Fig. W-4. Example of work sampling observation sheet.**

typists appear on the form for ease of recording but usually are not carried forward in any report. If there are five typists in the group, there will be five observations for each round of observations. Random times are used to determine the start of each round. Several rounds are made each day, perhaps eight or ten in an office and only three or four when studying widely dispersed groups such as maintenance craftworkers.

The results of a work sampling study are given as a set of percentages or proportions for each category. These reflect the overall activity. Suppose in the example that for a group of five typists, the observer makes nine rounds per day and that the study extends over a month of 22 working days. The total number of observations would then be five observations per round, times nine rounds per day, times 22 days, or a total of 990 observations. Suppose the distribution of observations and the percentages of the total are as shown in Table W-7.

**TABLE W-7**

| Category | Number of observations | Percent of observations |
|---|---|---|
| Typing | 487 | 49.2 |
| Taking dictation | 23 | 2.3 |
| Transcribing from machine | 86 | 8.7 |
| Clerical activity at desk | 71 | 7.2 |
| Away from desk, in office | 36 | 3.6 |
| Talking, telephoning | 68 | 6.9 |
| Personal | 113 | 11.4 |
| Not in office | 106 | 10.7 |
| | 990 | 100.0 |

These results are in a form easily understood by all. The reliability (possible error) due to sample size can be calculated very simply. Although a work sampling study does not provide much detail, it is a direct measurement which does give a form of bottom-line analysis that is of practical value to the executive. This is true because the end result of personnel practice, motivation, planning, scheduling, and control many times can be measured if management knows how people really spend their time.

**Inputs versus Outputs** Work sampling, then, measures input in terms of hours spent at various activities. The other important element, output, must be measured also. Together, input and output measures enable management to determine unit costs and thus establish a *benchmark* for evaluating improvement. Organizations typically keep records of output in the form of an administrative measure. In the example, the number and classification of documents typed represent measures of output. Depending on the results of an initial analysis, the observer may make a more detailed analysis. In cases of studies made of indirect and service activities, work sampling and the concommitant analysis of units of output often provide the executive with the first truly structured approach to cost improvement.

**Work Sampling Compared with Work Measurement** It is appropriate here to distinguish between work sampling as a form of work measurement and the more traditional work measurement techniques of stopwatch time study and of the use of predetermined human work times [such as Methods Time Measurement (MTM) or Work Factor]. These other techniques are all similar in the sense that each determines a standard time to perform a particular task. The term *standard* is the key, however, since the time to do a task depends directly on the method, tools, and equipment, the skill and motivation of the operator, and on environmental factors. All these must be standardized for conventional work measurement. When this is done, it provides a time per unit of output, which is extremely useful for management purposes.

*Technique for Improvement.* Work sampling, in contrast, does not directly yield a time per unit. Nor does it provide the basis for methods improvement of a direct nature. It is not really an appropriate tool for the measurement of repetitive work. Instead, work sampling is most effective as a broad survey-type measurement technique. It can provide, for example, the first form of measurement in indirect cost areas. In such uses it is common to find an unstructured pattern of activity. Methods may not be specified, and record keeping of units of output may be in terms of very gross units only; thus there may be very little real control of cost. Under these conditions, overstaffing is common, and great reliance is placed on the judgment of the individual who actually does the work. Managers are understandably uneasy in such situations. Without some sort of standards, managers cannot truly manage. Frederick W. Taylor observed that, "To manage we first must measure." This statement has withstood the test of time. Work sampling provides a means of taking the first important step in the management process where the absence of measurement is typical.

*Technique for Development.* One of the positive features of work sampling is that it can serve as an effective means of supervisory development. The supervisor is a logical candidate to act as the observer in those cases where a work sampling study is made of indirect work. The supervisor knows the work and knows the people. Further, the supervisor is the one who is central to any steps taken toward work improvement. No matter who conducts the study, the supervisor must be convinced of its reliability. When supervisors take an active part in the study, it is much easier for them to accept the results and to explain the implications to their employees.

Many refinements have been made in the technique of work sampling, but it is only one of a series of measurement techniques, and the executive should devote more thought to being sure that it is used in an appropriate application than to the details of the study method.

*See also* COST IMPROVEMENT; STATISTICAL ANALYSIS FOR MANAGEMENT; WORK MEASUREMENT; WORK SIMPLIFICATION AND IMPROVEMENT.

### REFERENCES

Brisley, Chester L.: "Work Sampling for Work Measurement," *IMS Clinic Proceedings*, Des Plaines, Ill., 1974, pp. 127–130.

Buese, Frank A.: "Continuous Work Sampling," *IMS Clinic Proceedings*, Des Plaines, Ill., 1975, pp. 93–96.

Gesler, E. E., Jr.: "Work Sampling and Cost Control," *Chemical Engineering Progress*, June 1967, pp. 29–35.

Gibson, D. F.: "Work Sampling Monitors Job Shop Productivity," *Industrial Engineering*, June 1970.

Lindenmuth, John: "Effective Work Sampling," *IMS Clinic Proceedings*, Des Plaines, Ill., 1973, pp. 112–119.

Richardson, Wallace J.: *Cost Improvement, Work Sampling, and Short Interval Scheduling*, Reston Publishing Co., Inc., Reston, Va., 1976, pp. 87 and 153.

Schmid, Merle D.: "Work Measurement Sampling," *IMS Clinic Proceedings*, Des Plaines, Ill., 1970, pp. 32–38.

WALLACE J. RICHARDSON, *Lehigh University*

# Work simplification and improvement

Work simplification stems from the concept first expressed by the author in 1930, "that the person doing a job knows more about that job than anyone else, and is therefore the one person best fitted to improve that job." It is further extended by the observation of Dr. Lillian M. Gilbreth, "We spend far too much time studying operations that should not be done at all!" Originally called motion economy, the concept was later designated as work simplification by Erwin H. Schell, of M.I.T. Since 1937, the concept and practice have been refined in the Work Simplification Conferences held annually at Lake Placid, N.Y., and at Sea Island, Ga.

### PHILOSOPHY

Work simplification (WS) consists of three parts: (1) the philosophy, (2) the pattern, and (3) a plan of action. Basic to the philosophy is a genuine belief in people. The furor today over job enrichment simply reflects the WS belief in people which was best expressed by Peter F. Drucker in his book *Management: Tasks, Responsibilities, Practices* (page 202*n*):

The fact remains, however, that scientific management or industrial engineering has been content to stop where Taylor stopped. Few of its scholars and practitioners have concerned themselves with working: i.e., with the synthesis of operations into a job. An important exception was one of Taylor's disciples, Allan Mogensen, who in the 1920's, pioneered what he called 'work simplification'—startlingly similar to what is now being rediscovered as 'job enrichment', if not way ahead of it.

**Job Involvement**   WS philosophy says that there are three ways of getting results through people. You can *tell them*, using force, fear, or authority. You can *sell them*, using persuasion or monetary rewards. Or you can *involve them in improvement*, thus providing people with the satisfactions they are looking for in their work. These satisfactions are found through a challenging job which allows a feeling of achievement, responsibility, growth, advancement, enjoyment of work itself, and earned recognition. The factors that most often dissatisfy workers are those that are peripheral to the job—work rules, lighting, coffee breaks, titles, seniority rights, wages, fringe benefits, and the like.

**Confidence and Desire**   Before one can put WS to work, one must sincerely believe that there is a vast, widespread, and largely untapped resource of ingenuity and creativity among almost all those in the work force. Most managers have little idea of how to go about unleashing this powerful force. As has been demonstrated by the widespread failure of the conventional suggestion system with its boxes and prizes, it takes more than hoopla to bring forth substantial ideas that pay off on the bottom line.

**Training**   Unless *all* employees are given basic training in the principles and tools of WS, a company will wind up with results typical of a suggestion plan with only 25 percent acceptance of the ideas submitted. Under a good WS program it is not unusual to *install*, not accept, 60, 70 and 80 percent. One large company has received 3,054,814 WS ideas in over 33 years and has implemented 2,799,-547. This is an implementation rate of nearly 92 percent. Training is the underlying success factor. At the Maytag Company, where WS began in

1948, every new employee receives this basic training.

**Management Attitudes**   Managers and supervisors must be given an opportunity to develop their capacity for handling the human relations problems involved. There is still a tendency to promote those people who have demonstrated skill in the technology of their job. The result is that these people spend the majority of their time on the technological problems and only a small portion of time working on human problems.

Texas Instruments Company, in one of its management directives, *Three Management Approaches*, has attempted to suggest a progression toward more effective management.

*Traditional Approach*. This causes the following:

ASSUMPTIONS
1. People dislike work.
2. People work only for money.
3. Few people are capable of self-direction.

POLICIES
1. Keep jobs simple and repetitive.
2. Supervise closely.
3. Set rules and routines.

EXPECTATIONS
1. If closely controlled, people will meet standards.
2. If firm but fair, supervisor will be respected by employees.

*Human Relations Approach*. This causes the following:

ASSUMPTIONS
1. People want to feel important.
2. People want to be recognized.
3. People want to be consulted.

POLICIES
1. Discuss plans and listen to objections.
2. Allow self-control on routine tasks.

EXPECTATIONS
1. Participation increases satisfaction and morale.
2. Subordinates will willingly cooperate.

*Human Resources Approach*. This causes the following:

ASSUMPTIONS
1. People want to contribute.
2. People will exercise broad self-direction and self-control.
3. People represent untapped resources.

POLICIES
1. Create a climate where all can contribute fully.

2. Develop full participation on important problems.

3. Continually broaden the area of self-direction and control.

EXPECTATIONS

1. Direct improvements in decision making and control.

2. Satisfaction increases as a by-product.

The reader will recognize the thinking of Maslow, McGregor, Likert, and other behavioral scientists in this succinct listing, as well as the contributions of M. Scott Myers.

**Basic Problems**  The two most vexing causes of many problems associated with WS are

1. People resist change.

2. People resent criticism.

For years the author has put these two statements on the board in front of many thousands of people all over the world and asked, "Do you believe them to be true?" The question never fails to get unanimous agreement. After discussion, however, some dissidents appear. Finally, they modify the two problems to read:

1. People resist *being* changed.

2. People resent *being* criticized.

When the work force becomes involved in improvement, the ideas become theirs and they will work very hard to see that they succeed. This is contrary to the traditional approach where new ideas and new methods are *imposed* upon people.

One more caution should be added: *Every time you criticize a method, someone takes it as personal criticism.* A manager may sincerely believe that he or she is being helpful and is criticizing a method, but someone will take it as personal criticism.

**Commitment and Pledge**  To ensure success with WS, it is essential to build *trust* in your organization. This requires a statement of policy on the part of the chief executive officer *and* the continuing demonstration of support. In most companies, it is customary to assure employees that no one will lose his or her *employment* as a result of a WS improvement.

## PATTERN

The pattern of WS develops the tools and techniques that make the difference between getting ideas that are flash improvements based on snap judgment and using an organized approach. The most commonly used pattern for improving methods follows five steps:

1. Select a job to improve.
2. Get all the facts.
   Make a process chart.
3. Challenge every detail.
   What—*Why?*
   Where—*Why?*
   When—*Why?*
   Who—*Why?*
   How—*Why?*
   List possibilities: Can we
      Eliminate
      Combine
      Change: Sequence; place; person
   Improve necessary details.
4. Develop the preferred method.
5. Install it—check results.

## FLOW PROCESS CHART

The first and basic tool used within the framework of the WS pattern is the flow process chart. The beginning point is to examine critically the problem *as a whole.* Ask *what* is the *purpose?* What function is to be carried out? What is to be accomplished? The entire process might be eliminated. It may be outmoded. If so, why look at details? Perhaps a technical development has made it obsolete. Is a new machine, process, or material now available that will make a better product or service at a lower cost? A plant making precision castings, for example, found that a centrifugal process would eliminate several machining operations. Another found that welded steel stampings could replace cumbersome castings. A plastic plant adopted high-frequency heating, and a fixture plant, electrostatic paint spraying. An office noted that punch cards would eliminate many sortings, tabulating, and calculating operations. Perhaps the product itself can be eliminated as part of an assembly. The guide is to look at the overall objective first. Perhaps the chart of the details will not be necessary.

*Symbols.* Frank Gilbreth invented a sign language to visualize the steps on his flow process chart. Like the symbols a secretary uses in Pitman or Gregg, Gilbreth's shorthand symbols make it easy to pack a lot of information in a small place. The original Gilbreth set included about 40 symbols. As WS programs developed, the list was simplified to five basic symbols. In 1946, under the leadership of David B. Porter, the ASME standardized on the symbols shown on the next page. They are used for steps performed on a material or by a person.

OPERATION

○

to CHANGE

When something is intentionally changed in any of its physical or chemical characteristics, is assembled or disassembled from another object, or is arranged or prepared for another OPERATION, TRANSPORTATION, INSPECTION, or STORAGE. Also when information is given or received, or when planning or calculating takes place.

TRANSPORTATION

⇨

to MOVE

When something is moved from one place to another. If the movement is part of an OPERATION, or if it involves an operator moving about a workplace, the step is not called TRANSPORTATION, but it is included in the description of the OPERATION or INSPECTION.

INSPECTION

☐

to VERIFY

Whenever something is examined for identification, or is verified for quantity or quality in any of its characteristics. It should either accept or reject.

DELAY

◗

to WAIT

When something waits for the next planned action, except when this waiting is for the purpose of conditioning the material, i.e., seasoning, cooling, drying, curing; then it is an OPERATION.

STORAGE

▽

to PROTECT

When something is kept and protected against unauthorized removal or is stored in a file.

COMBINED

ACTIVITY

⬚

When two activities are performed concurrently, or at the same work station, the symbols may be combined. The example shown combines OPERATION and INSPECTION.

*Information.* To make a clear picture, the chart should show the TIME, DISTANCE, PERSON, and PLACE for each important step. The description should be as brief as a telegram. For a *person*-type chart, the action should be in the *active* form: drills, taps, grinds, types, posts, checks, etc. For a *material*-type chart, the action should be in the *passive* form: drilled, tapped, ground, typed, posted, checked, etc.

*Pick an Important Problem.* To get worthwhile results from a flow process chart, it is wise to pick an important problem. When a stockholder complimented President Schwab on his management skill which produced dividends for Bethlehem Steel, President Schwab replied, "Madam, it takes the same management skill to run Bethlehem Steel or a peanut stand. The difference is that, in one case you have big dividends, and in the other case peanuts." So decide now if you want dividends or peanuts.

*Decide on Person or Material.* The chart can follow either one person or one material. In general, the person-type chart will be useful where the same person carries the action from place to place. This is the case of a maintenance person, a bank teller, or a messenger. The material-type chart is recommended where one material carries the action from place to place. This would happen in most factory operations on a product or in clerical operations on some work paper in a procedure. For more than one person or one material, additional charts are made.

*Beginning and Endings.* Pick a clear-cut starting point, where the action begins, and a clear-cut ending point. If an individual conducts the study, both points should be within his or her department. If the study is conducted by a team, the chart can include all the departments involved.

**Making the Chart** Fill in the headings at top of the chart (Fig. W-5). Walk from station to station where each step is performed. Do not depend on memory. Discuss each step with the person on the job, as if you were a newspaper reporter. Avoid any criticism, but note any suggestions made by the operator or clerk. Make them a partner in the search for the *one best way.* If the activity is important, try to estimate an average time for each work station. Count the steps to the next operation and convert them into feet traveled.

*Flow Lines.* To visualize the flow (or change of action) from step to step, and as an aid to analysis, a flow line is traced on the chart. The original Gilbreth charts were on a large roll of paper, the symbols made with a template. In 1940 the preprinted symbol chart was developed. This simplifies the construction job. A line is drawn from the bottom of one symbol to the top of the next, as shown in Fig. W-5.

DO *Operations.* Operations are classified as MAKE READY or DO or PUT AWAY. The DO operations are those that alter the product or carry out the function of the process or procedure. The preparatory steps are called MAKE READY, and the clean-up or disposal steps are called PUT AWAY. On the chart, blacken in the symbols for the DO operations. In this way they can be analyzed first. If a DO operation is eliminated, this automatically eliminates both the MAKE READY and the PUT AWAY associated with it.

*Summary.* Now count the operations, inspections, etc., along with the time and distance where shown, and post the total in the SUMMARY at the top of the chart. This will provide an overall picture of the process or procedure that the individual plans to improve.

No. 1
Page 1 of 1

Summary

| | Present No. | Present Time | Proposed No. | Proposed Time | Difference No. | Difference Time |
|---|---|---|---|---|---|---|
| ○ Operations | 15 | | | | | |
| ⇨ Transportations | 2 | | | | | |
| □ Inspections | 2 | | | | | |
| D Delays | 5 | | | | | |
| ▽ Storages | 1 | | | | | |
| Distance traveled | 600 ft. | | ft. | | ft. | |

Job Fill out and approve form X

☐ Person or ☐ Material

Chart begins In A's desk drawer

Chart ends In A's out box

Charted by AHM Date Oct 8

| | Details of (Present ~~Proposed~~) method | Operation / Transport / Inspection / Delay / Storage | Distance in feet | Quantity | Time | Possibilities: Eliminate / Combine / Seque. / Place / Person / Improve (Change) | Notes |
|---|---|---|---|---|---|---|---|
| 1 | In A's desk drawer | ○⇨□D▽ | | | | | No definite location |
| 2 | Removed and placed on desk | ○⇨□D▽ | | | | | Cluttered desk |
| 3 | Filled out | ●⇨□D▽ | | | | | Original & 5 copies |
| 4 | Placed in OUT box | ○⇨□D▽ | | | | | Long reach |
| 5 | Waits | ○⇨□D▽ | | | | | For messenger pickup |
| 6 | Picked up by messenger | ○⇨□D▽ | | | | | Difficult grasp |
| 7 | To B's office | ○⇨□D▽ | | | | | Delay in rest room |
| 8 | Placed in IN box | ○⇨□D▽ | | | | | |
| 9 | Waits | ○⇨□D▽ | | | | | |
| 10 | Picked up by B | ○⇨□D▽ | | | | | Difficult grasp |
| 11 | Examined | ○⇨□D▽ | | | | | |
| 12 | Signed | ●⇨□D▽ | | | | | |
| 13 | Placed in OUT box | ○⇨□D▽ | | | | | Long reach |
| 14 | Waits | ○⇨□D▽ | | | | | For pickup |
| 15 | Picked up by messenger | ○⇨□D▽ | | | | | Difficult grasp |
| 16 | Back to A | ○⇨□D▽ | | | | | |
| 17 | Placed in IN box | ○⇨□D▽ | | | | | Location of box bad |
| 18 | Waits | ○⇨□D▽ | | | | | |
| 19 | Picked up by A | ○⇨□D▽ | | | | | |
| 20 | Read | ○⇨□D▽ | | | | | |
| 21 | Paper clips removed | ○⇨□D▽ | | | | | |
| 22 | Carbons and copies separated | ○⇨□D▽ | | | | | |
| 23 | Reassembled | ○⇨□D▽ | | | | | |
| 24 | Placed in OUT box | ○⇨□D▽ | | | | | Long reach |
| 25 | Waits | ○⇨□D▽ | | | | | For messenger pickup |

**Fig. W-5. Flow process chart.**

### THE FLOW DIAGRAM

In studies where the person or material moves from place to place, a picture of the movement may be shown on a *flow diagram*. This is done on a layout, or floor plan, that shows the location of the workplaces. The movement from station to station is shown by dotted lines. The action, such as operations, inspections, etc., is shown by symbols with a number enclosed, to match the flow process chart. To avoid confusing details, only the *important* operations are shown. Delays are usually omitted. The direction is shown by the head of the transportation arrow.

When a flow process is drawn for either a person or material, it is usually evident that attention must be paid to the work space layout. Unless the operation is such that it will be repeated many times over a long period or is one that involves large numbers of operators, it is not necessary to go to the detail of making an operator chart, or right- and left-hand chart, as it is sometimes called.

**Motion Economy** WS at this stage is vitally concerned with proper design of workplaces, in factory, home, and office. The basic concepts of motion economy apply, as developed by William R. Mullee from the original Gilbreth principles:

1. Begin each element simultaneously with both hands.

2. End each element simultaneously with both hands.

3. Use simultaneous arm motions in opposite, symmetrical directions.

4. Use hand motions of lowest classification for satisfactory operation.

5. Keep motion paths within the normal work areas.

6. Avoid sharp changes of direction, with a smooth curved motion path.

7. Slide or roll; do not lift and carry.

8. Locate tools and materials in proper sequence at fixed work stations.

9. Use method with fewest work elements, for shortest time with least fatigue.

10. Use rhythm and automaticity to increase output and reduce fatigue.

11. Relieve hands with foot pedals whenever practical.

12. Do not hold; use a vise or fixture, freeing hands to move pieces.

13. Provide foot-operated ejectors to remove finished product.

14. Use drop delivery to dispose of the finished product.

15. Shorten all transports and provide gravity-feed hoppers.

16. Preposition tools for quick grasp.

17. Preposition product for next operation.

18. Locate machine controls for convenience and ease of operation.

19. Design workplace height for sitting-standing operation, with posture seat and adjustable backrest and footrest.

20. Provide pleasant working conditions: illumination, air, noise, color, orderliness.

Each job should be checked against this list of principles to see what changes may be made to improve the method and reduce fatigue in the search for the one best way.

### MACHINE-CONTROLLED OPERATIONS

Many of the details of a flow process chart are performed by groups of people or by people and machines. The coordinated breakdown of their respective activity as a team, represented graphically according to a time scale, becomes a *multiple activity chart*. Such a chart may portray the detailed activity of one person running a machine, one person operating several machines, or several people working together as a team. In its simplest form, the multiple activity chart is made up of two columns, one headed *Person* and the other *Machine*. The *person* column shows on a time scale the operations, transportations, and waits that occur in the work done by the operator. Under the *machine* heading, the starts, stops, machining operations, and idle time in relation to the movements of the operator are shown.

**Time Delays** Whenever machines or equipment are used, there are three ways to lose time: (1) operator waiting time, (2) machine waiting time, or (3) a combination of 1 and 2.

There is often a tendency to purchase a new piece of equipment without asking, "Can the job be done more effectively with the equipment already on hand?" It is a mistake to authorize purchase of elaborate or automatic equipment without thoroughly verifying its justification beforehand. Of particular concern are the time delays, as they affect expensive equipment, where the loss of time on the part of the operator is less significant. As machines become more complex, the cost of idle time may spell the difference between profit and loss. Frequently, these idle times occur at intervals throughout their operating cycle, and are not readily apparent.

**Machine Work Classifications**  There are three classes of work which usually occur with machines—make ready, do, and put away.

1. *Make ready* is part of the operation in preparation for doing the work. It may include getting instruction, getting and checking materials, loading, setting up, and adjusting the machine. It includes all the work done before actually setting the machine in motion to do the specific task for which it was designed. Generally, the machine is idle while operators are making ready.

2. *Do* is the productive work done by the machine, such as winding, cutting, mixing, writing, computing, printing, etc. The operator is usually waiting while the machine is doing its work.

3. *Put away* covers the details necessary to remove the finished work and dispose of it, replace tools, and inspect. The machine is generally idle while operators are putting away.

**Improvement Analysis**  To analyze the chart for improvement, follow the same WS pattern as applied in the previous charts. Challenge every detail, asking questions, "What?" and "Why?", which leads to *elimination;* "Where?" and "Why?", which leads to a *combination* of details, *changes of sequence,* and possible *changes in work space;* "Who?" and "Why?", which leads to the possibility of having the machine perform details which the operator now does or having the operator perform details now performed by the machine. In the case where several operators are involved, it leads to the possibility of changing the person or the place with the work area. Finally, ask "How?" and "Why?", which leads to the possibilities of *improvement* (1) in tooling on the part of the machine and (2) in method on the part of the operator.

When all improvements have been listed, rearrangements of the make ready, do, and put away have been placed into their final sequence, the proposed or preferred method chart is completed as step 4 of the pattern.

**Installation of Improvements**  As in the case of our other charts, the final step is actually to try out the job and put the improvements into effect. It is often assumed that workers will oppose such improvements because they will be regarded as "speed-up." If operators are taught how to use this tool and have been involved in the improvement, the feared opposition rarely materializes.

## TEAM OPERATIONS

With increased mechanization and the advent of automation, much production work, formerly manual, is now done by machine. Manual work now consists mainly of servicing machines, handling materials, providing maintenance, erecting, receiving, shipping, and storing. A considerable amount of work is done by groups of two or more people who work in teams, or gangs.

The simplest team is the operator and helper arrangement, common to maintenance operations. Typically, one person spends much time waiting for a helper. Unplanned activity means excess walking, rearrangement of materials, or looking for equipment. Simple changes can make substantial savings in labor, with reduced fatigue.

Development of larger material handling units, portable power tools, etc., has expanded the two-person team into three, four, and larger crews. Accordingly, some visual device is needed to show clearly what each person is doing in relation to other gang members.

The *multicolumn gang chart* was designed to show the activity of each member of a crew at regular intervals, in a series of mental snapshots. Each snapshot shows all members simultaneously. The chart can handle two or more people working as a team or several people and machines whose work is related, in regular work cycles. If the people are working independently, a regular flow process chart is used instead of a gang chart.

The gang chart offers a picture similar to "memo-motion" study, but without the need for camera, film, video tape, and accessories. Unlike *work sampling,* where data are taken over a number of days at random intervals, the gang chart gets the data in a few cycles, with observations taken at regular intervals.

Since work of this nature is often best planned on the job instead of from the office, the gang chart is designed for use by supervisors or crew leaders. It encourages participation by members of the team, using their ideas for improvement of the method, layout, tools, and equipment. Changes can be tried out on the job. Rearrangements of personnel and transfers come by common consent rather than by edict from above. Management and workers together seek a common goal in the one best way. (*See* PAPER WORK SIMPLIFICATION.)

## APPLICATION

Appreciation of and training in the use of the five-step pattern and the basic tools of WS are of no avail unless they are followed by a plan of action. Far too many companies have trained supervisors and workers to use these tools, only to have the whole effort go down the drain because their program never moved over into the application phase. (See Fig. W-6.) Only when the whole effort is directed to this final and most important phase will WS be other than just another program and become a way of life in the organization.

One of the most successful continuing improvement programs is that of the Procter & Gamble Co.

Its program, which started in 1946 with training in WS, is called "A Program of Deliberate Methods Change." Annual net profit improvement has now run on the order of more than $300 million in *new* savings. Arthur Spinanger, who headed this activity at Procter & Gamble for over 25 years, said, "At Procter & Gamble, the Methods Change Program produces one of our most attractive payouts. The

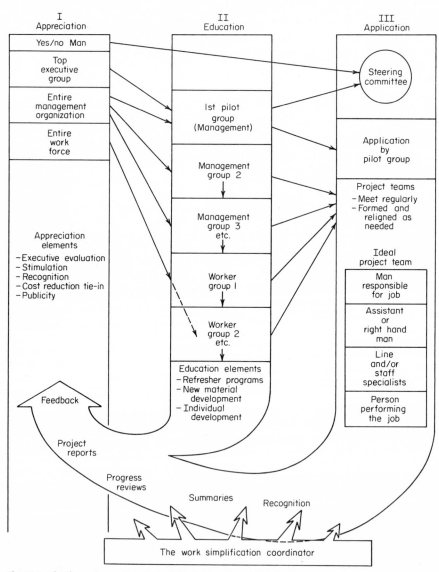

**Fig. W-6. The three phases of work simplification, as pictured in the chart: Appreciation—stimulation of interest in and understanding of objectives, approach, and need. Education—internal development of philosophy, pattern, and program. Application—deliberate scheduling of time for improvement activity as a routine managerial function.**

rate of return—using first-year profit increase only—has been between 500 to 1000 percent. In other words, $5 to $10 of profit is returned for every $1 spent. I know of no other portion of management effort that can match this."

*See also* COST IMPROVEMENT; ENGINEERING, INDUSTRIAL; JOB ANALYSIS; MATERIAL HANDLING; PAPER WORK SIMPLIFICATION; PRODUCTION PROCESSES; SYSTEMS AND PROCEDURES; THERBLIGS; WORK MEASUREMENT.

### REFERENCES
Barnes, R. M.: *Motion and Time Study*, 4th ed., John Wiley & Sons, Inc., New York, 1958.
Bittel, Lester R.: *Improving Supervisory Performance*, McGraw-Hill Book Company, 1976, chap. 13.
Drucker, Peter F.: *Management: Tasks, Responsibilities, Practices*, Harper & Row, Publishers, Incorporated, New York, 1974.
Kobayashi, Shigeru: *Creative Management*, American Management Association, New York, 1971.
Maynard, H. B., ed.: *Industrial Engineering* Handbook, 2d ed., McGraw-Hill Book Company, New York, 1963, sec. 2, chaps. 1–10; sec. 5, chap. 3; sec. 10, chaps. 10 and 16.
Myers, M. S.: *Every Employee A Manager: More Meaningful Work Through Job Enrichment*, McGraw-Hill Book Company, New York, 1970.
———: *Managing with Unions*, Addison-Wesley Publishing Company, Inc., Reading, Mass., 1978.
———: *Managing Without Unions*, Addison-Wesley Publishing Company, Inc., Reading, Mass. 1976.
Neibel, B. W.: *Motion and Time Study*, Richard D. Irwin, Inc., Homewood, Ill., 1955.
Reilly, William J.: *The Law of Intelligent Action*, Harper & Row, Publishers, Incorporated, New York, 1950.
Vough, Clair F.: *Tapping the Human Resource*, American Management Association, New York, 1975.

ALLAN H. MOGENSEN, *Work Simplification Conferences*


# Worker-machine interrelationships
(*See* HUMAN FACTORS ENGINEERING.)


# Workers' compensation (*See* COMPENSATION, EMPLOYEE BENEFIT PLANS.)


# Working capital management (*See* FINANCIAL MANAGEMENT, WORKING CAPITAL CONTROLS.)


# Working capital method (*See* EXCHANGE, FOREIGN, MANAGEMENT OF.)


# Workplace democracy (*See* CODETERMINATION AND INDUSTRIAL DEMOCRACY.)


# WOTS UP analysis (*See* PLANNING, STRATEGIC MANAGERIAL PLANNING.)


# Writing for business

Managing other people's writing is a vital, but rarely formalized, function of most managers. It includes all forms of written communications, from informal memos to sales letters and call reports to formal project proposals and policy statements. Managers in all types of organizations might, therefore, approach the function of written communications by asking themselves these leading questions:

Are you satisfied with the quality of reports, proposals, letters, and memos written by your subordinates or by others in your organization?

Do you find that you waste too much of your valuable time struggling through these written communications to be sure you fully understand the problem, the facts, and the recommendations?

Must you spend too many evenings and weekends wading through poorly written reports which are an essential part of your management information system, and on the basis of which you must make decisions?

Are letters and proposals to customers, clients, and the public too often written without a clear recognition of the reader's needs and problems, as distinguished from the writer's needs and problems?

If a manager answers yes to any of these four questions, then he or she faces a problem common to many managers, particularly those in larger organizations. This entry analyzes the problems, suggests some practical solutions, and demonstrates an efficient format for business communications. In so doing, it follows a unique format. The format is intended to suggest a visually, and conceptually, effective style for developing written communications in complex organizations. Note, also, the frequent use of the second person (you)—either literally or implied: This helps to make the communication more personal and direct.


## SUMMARY

SUBJECT: This entry describes how to manage other people's writing.

OBJECTIVE: The objectives of this entry are:

- Demonstrate an efficient format for the writing of letters, memos, reports, and proposals.

- Identify basic causes for poor writing in organizations.

- Recommend practical solutions.

BACKGROUND:

1. Senior managers in many organizations complain that the quality of written communications reaching their desks is poor. They must therefore waste time in analyzing these communications to be sure they understand all the facts so that they can reach an intelligent decision.

2. Clear written communications are an essential part of an efficient management information system, particularly in larger organizations. Clear written communications are equally important in dealing with customers, clients, and the public.

3. Line managers are often action-oriented and thus prefer verbal rather than written communications. But there is no way that the verbal communication alone can do the job, as the organization becomes larger and more complex.

4. Furthermore, in some organizations or units within organizations, the written communication is itself the final work product. This is particularly true in government agencies (regulations and reports), insurance companies (the insurance policy and the many communications explaining and interpreting it), and in any staff job involving analytical study or research which is ultimately described in a report (analysts and researchers frequently fail to see that they have not finished a project until they have written a report on it).

FINDINGS:

1. There are five basic causes for poor writing in organizations:

- The modern educational system largely fails to teach the essential skills of clear communication, particularly written communication.

- When writing is taught in school or college, the wrong principles are often emphasized. The principles for efficient business writing are not the same as those for academic writing or creative writing.

- Managers have no generally accepted standards by which to judge the quality of the written communications they must read.

- Writers seldom receive useful feedback in regard to the quality of their writing, as distinguished from feedback on the substantive correctness of what they say.

- Managers fail to realize the benefits the organization can realize from clear writing. These include greater efficiency, better service to customers, increased sales, and improved morale.

2. Poor writing in an organization is a management problem, not just a writing problem. The manager who wants to improve the quality of writing in his or her organization must look at the entire process of which the written communication is a part, not just at that part of the process which involves one writer putting words on paper.

3. The best style for written business communications is almost always one that is simple, clear, direct, logical, carefully organized, and carefully structured. To develop and use this style, the writer must develop the skills of careful planning and clear thinking. The intuitive thinking skills which the writer may have found valuable in solving the problem must not be allowed to interfere with a logical, orderly presentation in the communication.

RECOMMENDATIONS: To improve the quality and efficiency of written communications in an organization, a manager should follow these steps:

- Require, whenever possible, the use of a reporting format similar to that illustrated in this encyclopedia entry.

- Develop a checklist or set of standards by which the quality of writing can be measured.

- Provide writers with regular feedback about the quality of their writing.

- Train writers how to use the format and checklist.

(The balance of this entry, under the Discussion heading, explains how to accomplish each of these four steps.)

## DISCUSSION

1. *Use a standard reporting format.*

The first of the four steps for improving the quality and efficiency of written communications is to require the use of a standard reporting format, whenever possible. This entry, particularly the headings under the Summary above, illustrates a widely used standard format for internal reporting. With appropriate modifications, this format is also useful for proposals, for letters to customers and the public, and for oral presentations.

This format is designed to answer quickly and efficiently for each reader six key questions. The list below presents the six questions, followed by typical standard headings for each.

| QUESTION | STANDARD HEADINGS |
|---|---|
| • What am I reading? What is the subject? | Subject, Purpose |
| • Why was this written? What problem or objective led to this communication? | Problem, Objective, Issue, Policy, Scope, Mission |
| • What key background facts do I need in order to understand the problem or objective, or the findings or recommendations.? | Background, Highlights, Alternatives, Assumptions, Criteria |
| • What are the key findings of this communication? | Findings, Conclusions |
| • What are the key recommendations or proposals? | Recommendations, Proposals |
| • Who must take what action? How does this affect me? | Action |

(Note that the Summary section of this article illustrates the use of all headings except Action.)

Not all questions need to be answered for each reader in each case; but the writer should always stop to consider whether he or she has answered promptly and in a clear format those questions that are pertinent.

When does the writer use separate Summary and Discussion sections, and when does he or she use the standard format but omit the headings?

- If the report is long, use a separate Summary, with headings, which summarizes the answers to the key questions in not more than two pages. Follow this Summary with a detailed Discussion section. Expand as appropriate in the Discussion on each heading in the Summary, following the same order as the Summary. Do not hesitate to repeat the brief statement in the Summary; it can be a useful lead-in to the detailed Discussion.

- If the report is shorter but you wish to expand on certain points (as in this article), then use a Summary plus a Discussion covering those points only.

- If the report is too short to require a separate Discussion section, then present all information in order under the standard headings. Omit the use of Summary or Discussion headings.

- Finally, omit the standard headings when you are writing to an audience that is unfamiliar with them or when their use seems inappropriate (as in a sales proposal). It is often helpful in these cases to use special headings appropriate for this particular communication.

*2. Develop a checklist to measure writing quality.*

Most experienced writers and reviewers have developed mental checklists for reviewing their own or other's writing. But mental checklists are not enough. Writers, reviewers, and senior managers need to reach agreement on a basic set of principles against which the quality of writing can be judged.

When this is done, the writer need not reinvent the wheel each time he or she faces a difficult writing job, or, worse still, go to the files and slavishly copy a format and style that may have originated 50 years ago (thus perpetuating the errors of the past).

Here are some suggestions of basic principles for clear business writing that should be on any checklist—it can undoubtedly be edited to suit each organization's needs:

- Plan carefully before you write. Clear writing requires clear thinking first.

- Use a standard format, such as that illustrated in this entry.

- Write for your audience, not for yourself. Define your audience broadly and write for the broader audience. Repeatedly ask yourself, "Will all my audience clearly understand what I am trying to say?"

- Be sure your instructions and data are adequate. Be sure you have carefully defined your objective.

- Anticipate resistance and decide how to meet it. Stress the benefits to your audience of acting the way you want them to act.

- Keep your sentences and paragraphs short. In general, avoid sentences of over 25 words and paragraphs of over 75 words.

- Use a step-by-step listing format (as illustrated by this list) to present any series of facts, causes, conditions, opinions, alternatives, etc.

- Let the verb carry the weight of the sentence; prefer active action verbs and avoid weak passive verbs.

- Prefer the short, simple, direct, clear, declarative sentence. You are not a novelist or storyteller; leave the unusual sentence structures to them.

- Avoid pompous polysyllables, gobbledygook, and in-house jargon; once again, to communicate clearly—keep it simple!

3. *Provide writers with regular feedback.*

Few writers in an organization receive any regular feedback as to the quality of their writing. If management wants to improve the quality of writing, it must develop a system that provides regular feedback to the writer. Preferably, do this in a face-to-face meeting. Aim for prompt, specific, constructive criticism. If a checklist or other standards have been developed, it will be much easier to provide writers with specific, objective feedback; only then can you be sure the quality of their writing will improve.

The basic goal is to increase efficiency by improving the quality of written communications. To the extent that written communications are an important work product, the organization will benefit if objective, generally accepted standards are developed for producing this work product.

4. *Train writers how to use your format and checklist.*

After a standard format and checklist have been developed and after a means for providing regular feedback to writers has been established, plan to train writers in this process. This should not just be writing training, it should be training in the entire process of preparing written communications in your organization.

Depending on the number of writers and the volume and complexity of their communications, such training may range from formal workshop programs to informal meetings. Do not expect real improvement, however, unless you plan for some kind of training sessions that bring everyone concerned together in a meeting room. Then the new approach can be presented, tested, and ample opportunity allowed for questions.

Be sure, as you plan the training, to include everyone who might resist or block the changes you are proposing.

*See also* DATA PROCESSING PRINCIPLES AND PRACTICES; INFORMATION SEARCH; INFORMATION SYSTEMS, MANAGEMENT (MIS); MANUALS, POLICY AND PROCEDURES; PAPER WORK SIMPLIFICATION; RECORDS MANAGEMENT; SYSTEMS AND PROCEDURES.

## REFERENCES

Brock, Luther A.: *How to Communicate by Letter and Memo,* McGraw-Hill Book Company, New York, 1974.

Flesch, Rudolf: *How to Write, Speak, and Think More Effectively,* Signet Books, New American Library, Inc., New York, 1963.

Gilbert, Marilyn B.: *Clear Writing,* John Wiley & Sons, Inc., New York, 1972.

*Managing Correspondence: Plain Letters,* Records Management Handbook, General Services Administration, National Archives and Records Service, Office of Records Management, Federal Stock No. 7610-205-1091, U.S. Superintendent of Documents, 1973.

Mandel, Siegfried, and David L. Caldwell: *Proposal and Inquiry Writing,* The Macmillan Company, New York, 1963.

Morris, John O.: *Make Yourself Clear!* McGraw-Hill Book Company, New York, 1972.

"Preparation of Papers for ASME Meetings and Publications," *ASME Manual MS-4,* American Society of Mechanical Engineers, New York, September 1974.

Tichy, H. J.: *Effective Writing for Engineers, Managers, and Scientists,* John Wiley & Sons, Inc., New York, 1975.

JOHN O. MORRIS, *Siegel & Gale, New York*

# Y

## Younger employees, management of

To develop and maintain high levels of motivation and productivity among younger employees require understanding and sometimes different techniques than managers have typically used. Although the problems of integrating those under 25 years into the organization are not entirely unique to this group, it is increasingly apparent that young people cannot be supervised, motivated, or trained in traditional ways without creating substantial difficulties both for them and for the organization.[1]

### ORGANIZATION PROBLEMS

Organizations report a growing number of problems with managing younger employees, including the following:

As much as a 50 percent turnover rate after their first year of work

A divisive generation gap between young employees and older managers

A loss of creativity, innovativeness, and energy during their first years of employment

Naïveté and unrealistic expectations[2]

Kotter's research indicates that early experiences on the job can have a major effect on careers as well as job satisfaction, employee attitudes, productivity levels, and turnover. Kotter believes that better management of the process of integrating the individual into the organization can result in greater organizational effectiveness by making employees more efficient faster; by increasing job satisfaction, morale, and productivity; by decreasing turnover; by increasing creativity; by decreasing superior-subordinate conflict and tension, and by increasing the number of members of the organization who are achieving their true potential.[3]

### INSIGHT INTO YOUNGER EMPLOYEES

There seem to be four general characteristics or traits which young employees bring to their first full-time, formal job:

1. Greater mobility, which makes them potential candidates for turnover. They have fewer financial commitments. They are typically less affected by family considerations and less constrained by employee benefits based on length of service.

2. Changing attitudes and values, which cause them to expect more from an organization. They seem less tolerant of what they believe are imperfect managerial practices.

3. A relatively optimistic idea of what they can immediately contribute to an organization in terms of skills and abilities. They expect their talents to be utilized quickly. This is especially true of recent college graduates.

4. An inclination to seek satisfaction of higher-order needs on the job, such as the psychological and self-fulfillment needs.

5. A desire to participate in decisions which affect their jobs and working conditions.

**Job Expectations** Berlew and Hall have listed 13 expectations which new employees bring to the job. They are as follows: a sense of meaning or purpose in the job; personal development opportunities; extent of work that stimulates curiosity and induces excitement; challenge; power and responsibility; recognition and approval for good work; status and prestige; friendliness and congeniality of the work group; salary; a minimum of discipline and regimentation; a degree of security; advancement opportunities; and greater frequency of feedback and evaluation.[4]

**High School Students** Scanlan surveyed high school students between the ages of 17 and 19, who expressed interest in the following job aspects in descending order of importance: (1) interesting work, (2) wages, (3) pleasant working conditions, (4) advancement possibilities, (5) work associates, (6) job security, (7) recognition for a job well done, (8) tactful discipline, (9) good initial training, and (10) job importance.[5]

**Blue-Collar Workers** Altimus and Tersine surveyed blue-collar workers and found the following differences between the younger workers (25 and under), middle-aged workers (26 to 35), and older workers (36 and over):

Younger workers were more dissatisfied with their work than older workers.

Younger workers exhibited a significantly greater dissatisfaction with the extent to which their esteem and self-actualization needs were met on the job than did the oldest age group.

Younger workers expressed greater dissatisfaction with pay, supervision, coworkers, and promotional opportunities than older workers.

Younger workers reported considerably less satisfaction than both middle-aged and older workers in the fulfillment of their security needs.

Younger workers indicated that their needs for esteem, autonomy, and self-actualization were higher than those of the older workers.

Younger workers tried to meet higher-level needs on the job (esteem, autonomy, and self-actualization), while older workers considered social needs more important.

Younger workers were more highly motivated by individually applied incentives, while older workers were more highly motivated by group incentives.[6]

**College Students** Yankelovich surveyed college students and made the following observations:

The number of students who did not mind being bossed on the job has steadily dropped to 36 percent.

An ever-growing number of students find it harder to accept outward conformity for the sake of career advancement and to abide by rules with which they do not agree.

Students rank the opportunity to make a contribution, job challenge, the ability to find self-expression, and free time for outside interests as the most important influences on their career choices.

Some 69 percent of all students no longer believe hard work will pay off. A majority do not regard work as very important, ranking it well behind love, friendship, education, self-expression, family, and privacy.[7]

**Graduate Students** Schein surveyed students in MIT's Master's Degree in Management program and found that these students want the following:

To have an opportunity to test themselves to find out if they can do anything worthwhile and to make a meaningful contribution

To have an opportunity to learn and grow and make use of their abilities and education

To be able to retain their integrity and individuality and not be forced to conform to a company pattern or organization-employee mentality

To work for a company that is dynamic and exciting, receptive to new ideas, and run according to rational business principles[8]

Kotter surveyed a similar group and compared graduate student expectations with those of organizations. He found the following significant differences in descending order of magnitude: (1) organizations expected to give greater job security than the students wanted; (2) organizations wanted greater acceptance of corporate values and goals than the graduates were expecting to give; (3) graduates wanted greater personal development opportunities than the organizations intended to provide; (4) organizations wanted greater conformity than the graduates believed was necessary; (5) organizations believed an ability to work with groups was more important than did the students; (6) students wanted more interesting work than the organizations thought they needed; and (7) students wanted jobs with a greater sense of meaning or purpose than the organizations were willing to provide.[9]

It seems obvious from the various research studies that younger workers have different perceptions, needs, expectations, and values than older workers and most managers. Even within the younger workers group, there are substantial differences depending on age and education.

## PRACTICAL GUIDELINES FOR MANAGING YOUNGER EMPLOYEES

To begin with, managers need to understand the differences among employees. These differences appear to be most acute in comparisons between younger and older employees. A really effective manager must also have insight into the differences between different groups of younger employees. Admittedly, this is a complex job and requires substantial efforts from organizations and their managers. A failure to do this, however, results in a lowering of organizational effectiveness through reduced employee efficiency; lower productivity; higher absenteeism and turnover; reductions in creativity; increased superior-subordinate conflict, tension and miscommunication; and further erosion of the employee-employer relationship.

**General Approaches** Scanlan suggests that managers consider the following general approaches:

1. Provide knowledge of what is expected. Jobs must be defined in terms of results expected. Knowing what to do is not enough; the individual must also know how performance will be measured.

2. Provide an opportunity to perform. Individuals should be given the freedom to exercise initiative and ingenuity in determining how to achieve objectives.

3. Provide feedback. Employees should be given continual appraisals of performance to maximize learning.

4. Provide assistance and support. Managers need to provide their subordinates with the necessary interdepartmental and intradepartmental coordination and guidance.

5. Provide rewards for results achieved. Both financial and nonfinancial rewards need to be distributed on the basis of performance. Accomplishment and improvement need to be recognized by the reward system in order to stimulate employee achievement.[10]

**For Young Adults** Scanlan[11] further suggests the following as means to motivate young adults:

1. Provide interesting work. Job enrichment is a promising means to challenge the young adult as is the opportunity to participate as much as possible in decisions relating to how work should be performed.

Generally, the more ability the individual possesses, the greater his or her desire is to perform varied and challenging tasks. Thus managers must assess the individual's capabilities and needs, as people vary greatly as to what they consider to be challenging and interesting.

2. Provide a clearly understood wage system. Young adults, especially, are concerned about equity in their wage plans. Satisfaction may result as much from a feeling of being treated fairly as from receiving an exceptionally high wage.

3. Provide good physical surroundings. Young people like to have a feeling of pride about the places where they work; a gloomy atmosphere is not conducive to such an attitude. Pleasant working conditions have been classified as a hygiene factor which has no motivational effect on employees, yet the absence of which can cause dissatisfaction.

4. Provide advancement opportunities. Most workers become unhappy with their jobs when advancement opportunities narrow or disappear. The young adult, particularly, finds it disconcerting to be in a dead-end job. Managers should make the ambitious young employees aware of advancement possibilities, yet care should be taken to avoid making promises which cannot be kept.

5. Provide opportunities for socialization. Most young adults prefer to work with other young adults, preferably ones with whom they have common interests and with whom they feel comfortable.

6. Provide job security. Although surveys do not show job security to be a primary concern of young adults, a sustained decline in business is likely to result in a motivation slump among all employees—youthful ones included. Rumors of layoffs and dismissals invariably cause restlessness. Only an exceptionally skillful supervisor will be able to keep the young employee contented when a loss of job appears imminent.

7. Provide recognition. Young people often feel the need for recognition with particular acuteness because they feel they are performing an "invisible" job.[12] Recognition may come in varied forms— it may be positive, such as an increase in salary or oral or written appreciation from the individual's supervisor, or it may be negative in the form of correction. Improperly used as cheap praise, however, it accomplishes nothing. If appreciation is to be an effective tool in managing the young adult, the manager must believe it and what it will accomplish.

8. Provide training. Young people appreciate the employer who spends time with them in training; the instruction they receive gives them self-confidence and the ability to perform their jobs more accurately.

9. Provide a sense of job importance. A person who feels that his or her job is important is a much more effective employee than one who does not.

10. Be careful when criticizing and disciplining. Tactful discipline will produce good results, whereas inconsiderate discipline often results in defensive behavior on the part of the rebuked employee and a loss of respect for the manager.

11. Communicate with employees. If one word were to be chosen as the key to effective management of young adults, that word would have to be *communication*. Young people need this even more than older employees do. They must have some feedback on their performance in their jobs. Morgan suggests several worthwhile elements in communicating with young adults: Communicate frequently, even if it is no more than to ask how things are going; when complex instructions are to be given, explain one portion at a time; recognize that minor problems may seem major to the young adult, and be willing to provide reassurance; make no promises that cannot be kept, and act on those made; when criticism is necessary, give it as impersonally as possible; be specific in instructions; and solicit questions and feedback, thus maintaining an open-door policy.[13]

**For College Graduates**  Schein suggests the following techniques for recent college graduates:

1. Provide opportunities for them to test their abilities with work that is clearly important.

2. Recognize the importance of the influence of the graduate's first supervisor. Select supervisors who are mature and secure in their knowledge as supervisors of new college graduates. Provide training for these supervisors so that they will be prepared to understand and work with these people.

3. Reform current approaches to the recruitment of college graduates to shift the emphasis from selling the student and in the process building up high and often unrealistic expectations to a more realistic dialogue. Also recruit on the basis of specific matches of talents to needs rather than just hiring "good people."[14]

Kotter adds the following:

1. Make sure that supervisors are rewarded for effective and efficient integration of the new employee into the organization.

2. Select the first job assignment very carefully so that it contributes to the new employee's feelings of accomplishment, purpose, and self-confidence coupled with meaningful learning about the job and the organization.[15]

Drucker further suggests that benefits should be structured to the needs of the employee, particularly to the needs of specific groups within the employ-

ees. He also recommends the Japanese "godfather" system, an informal network of senior middle-management people who are given responsibility for young people during the first 10 years of their careers in the company. Godfathers are expected to keep in close touch with their godchildren—to know them, to see them fairly regularly, to be available for advice and counsel, and to assist their early learning and career development.[16]

*See also* MINORITIES, MANAGEMENT OF AND EQUAL EMPLOYMENT OPPORTUNITY; MOTIVATION IN ORGANIZATIONS; OLDER EMPLOYEES, MANAGEMENT OF; WOMEN IN INDUSTRY.

## NOTES

[1] *See* Cyrus A. Altimus, Jr., and Richard J. Tersine, "Chronological Age and Job Satisfaction: The Young Blue Collar Worker," *Academy of Management Journal*, March 1973, vol. 16, no. 1, pp. 55–66.

[2] John Paul Kotter, "The Psychological Contract: Managing the Joining-Up Process," *California Management Review*, Spring 1973, vol. XV, no. 3, pp. 91–99.

[3] Ibid., p. 91.

[4] David E. Berlew and Douglas T. Hall, "The Socialization of Managers: Effects of Expectations on Performance," *Administrative Science Quarterly*, September 1966, pp. 207–223; David Cherrington, "The Values of Younger Workers," *Business Horizons*, December 1977, vol. 20, no. 6, pp. 18–29.

[5] Burt K. Scanlan, "Motivating Young Adults in Retailing," *Journal of Small Business Management*, vol. 4, no. 2, April 1976, pp. 46–54.

[6] Altimus and Tersine, op. cit., pp. 64–65.

[7] Daniel Yankelovich, "The Student Revolution Permeates All Our Lives," *The Detroit News*, Apr. 2, 1971, p. 1E, cited in "The Real Meaning of the Student Revolution," *Conference Board Record*, March 1972.

[8] Edgar H. Schein, "The First Job Dilemma: An Appraisal of Why College Graduates Change Jobs and What Can Be Done About It," *Psychology Today*, March 1968, pp. 26–37.

[9] Kotter, op. cit., p. 95.

[10] Burt K. Scanlan, *Principles of Management and Organization Behavior*, John Wiley & Sons, Inc., New York, 1973, pp. 428–429.

[11] Scanlan, "Motivating Young Adults in Retailing," pp. 50–54.

[12] John S. Morgan, *Managing the Young Adult*, American Management Association, New York, 1967, p. 107.

[13] John S. Morgan, "Communicating with Young Workers," *Supervisory Management*, May 1967, pp. 21–25.

[14] Schein, op. cit., pp. 36–37.

[15] Kotter, op. cit., pp. 98–99.

[16] Peter F. Drucker, *Management: Tasks, Responsibilities and Practices*, Harper & Row, Publishers, Incorporated, New York, 1974, p. 254–257.

BURT K. SCANLAN, *University of Oklahoma*

ROGER M. ATHERTON, JR., *University of Oklahoma*

# Z

## Zero accounts, bank  (*See* FINANCIAL MANAGEMENT.)

## Zero-base budgeting

Zero-base budgeting (ZBB) is an operating, planning, and budgeting process which requires each manager to justify his or her entire budget request in detail from scratch (hence, zero-base) and shifts the burden of proof to each manager to justify why any money should be spent at all, as well as how the job can be done better. This approach requires that (1) all activities be identified in "decision packages" (or programs) that relate inputs (costs) with outputs (benefits), (2) each one be evaluated by systematic analysis, and (3) all programs be ranked in order of performance.

ZBB is becoming increasingly popular as a management tool in public and private sectors. Peter Pyhrr initiated ZBB at Texas Instruments, Inc., in 1970, where the staff and research departments faced a budget decrease without a clear understanding of where and how the budget should be allocated. Pyhrr instituted a planning and budgeting methodology termed zero-base budgeting, using a concept previously employed at the U.S. Department of Agriculture.[1] Zero-base budgeting was then expanded throughout all divisions of Texas Instruments to prepare the 1971 budget.

As a consequence of a Pyhrr article in the *Harvard Business Review*,[2] Jimmy Carter, with the assistance of Pyhrr, implemented ZBB in Georgia in 1971[3] with considerable success. Logan Cheek initiated ZBB in Xerox in the personnel function in 1971.[4]

ZBB has proved effective in state governmental operations. A study by Allen Schick and Robert Keith of the Congressional Research Service found that most states using ZBB were pleased with the results.[5] Other early users of ZBB were Southern California Edison, Dillingham Corporation, and United California Bank.[6-10] In 1976, it was asserted that ZBB had 100 users.[11] Over 20 cities were using ZBB by 1977.[12,13]

ZBB was implemented in the federal government in 1977. In 1976, the U.S. Senate Committee on Government Operations stated:[5]

It is necessary to challenge the traditional assumption of budgeting—because a program was funded last year, it deserves to be funded again.

The zero-base review concept . . . has a very different assumption as its foundation—that programs are not entitled automatically to continued funding once they are created; rather, that a case must be made for continued funding.

Depending on how well that case is made, programs can be funded at the current level or at lower or higher levels; or revised to reflect the findings of the zero-base review.

If they fail to meet the test for reauthorization, they will be terminated.

The key element in zero-base budgeting legislation is a requirement that all federal programs come under the review procedure over a fixed cycle.

Furthermore, in establishing a ZBB procedure, each individual program would be reviewed in detail in 1979–1983. The review would permit Congress to determine whether an individual program is working as intended. In April 1977, the Office of Management and Budget issued guidelines for the use of ZBB in the federal government in preparing the FY 1979 budget.[14]

ZBB is important because it reflects recent thinking in budgeting methodology. ZBB is not just a method of budget cutting; it is a planning and budget control system as well. Not only is there an accounting of funds but also a description of how those funds will be used for the organization's goals and functions. Managers can be held accountable for both the planning and the use of funds.

The core concept of ZBB, building a budget up from ground zero, is not new in the budgeting literature.[15] What is new is the methodology by which the ZBB system is implemented in an organization.[16–18]

## BASIC ELEMENTS OF THE PROCESS

ZBB is a bottoms-up planning and budgeting process that requires every manager or supervisor to reexamine each program or activity from the ground up each fiscal year before funds are allocated.[19] The manager begins with the assumption that *all* resource needs must be justified. This is accomplished through a formal process of developing decision units, decision packages, and ranking.

The four basic elements in the ZBB system are:

*Decision units*. Each significant program, individual department, or level of an organization is identified.

*Decision packages*. Each decision unit manager draws up, in priority order, a number of packages, which together make up the total budget request for that unit.

*Ranking process*. All decision packages are ranked in order of decreasing benefits to the organization. The ranking process establishes priorities on the basis of functions described in each decision package.

*Allocation of organizational resources*. This is arrived at by the actual allocation of the organization's resources using rank ordering at successively higher budget cutoff levels in the organizational structure and the preparation of detailed line item budgets.

The corporate budget is derived from the establishment of a cutoff budget at the highest level of the organization, which in turn establishes the cutoff budgets at each lower level. The corresponding decision packages to be approved are above the cutoff budgets.

The use of decision units provides the organization with the identification of the specific organizational units or programs to be included in the ZBB process. Through decision packages, each manager identifies, reviews, evaluates, and justifies all programs, projects, and activities. The manager is required to consider the alternative *ways* of performing each identified activity and must also consider the different *levels* of effort and resource requirements that might be needed. Thus, in addition to reexamining the current level of service, the manager develops minimum (highest priority) and incremental decision packages that relate the costs and benefits of stepwise increased expenditure levels.

In ranking, each manager rates each decision package relative to all other packages and selects those packages to be included in the budget (resource) request. Decision packages are then consolidated and ranked by each succeeding level of hierarchal management. The final budget comprises a prioritized list of those packages proposed to be funded and selected from the total list of packages. During the fiscal year, each decision unit manager is responsible for achieving the specified performance objectives indicated in the decision package description, accomplishing this within the corresponding budget levels. ZBB provides an excellent cost control system.

**Applicability of ZBB**  The budget for an organization often signifies a quantification of objectives, and the allocation of limited resources, the framework from which top management works. ZBB helps link together top management's strategic planning activities with the programming and control functions performed by all levels in the management hierarchy.

In general, ZBB can be used in any function or operation of the organization where it is possible to perform cost-benefit analyses. However, it has also been observed that ZBB is not easily adaptable to direct manufacturing operations, where the budget is usually determined on the basis of the units of output and standardized costs.[2] Although ZBB may not be easily used in direct manufacturing, it has been widely employed in manufacturing support and services, such as maintenance, supervision, production planning, inventory control, and industrial engineering. More generally, ZBB may be used in all services, support, and overhead activities such as accounting, data processing, personnel, and R&D. Some firms have used ZBB in capital project budgeting.

In industry, ZBB has been used primarily in staff areas as follows:

*Manufacturing*
Manufacturing control
Manufacturing engineering
Procurement
Production planning
*Marketing and Sales*
Product development
Product management
Marketing research
Advertising and sales promotion
*Distribution*
Inventory control
Freight and traffic staff
Research and engineering
*Corporate*
Personnel administration
Accounting and finance
Legal administration

ZBB is useful in budgeting those activities which provide the greatest leverage in determining short-term profitability and long-range development.[1,20] ZBB is used for those activities where management typically has the most difficulty in evaluating and allocating resources in administrative, technical, and commercial areas. It is also used for those activities which can be varied substantially in the short term and those activities which determine future growth, such as R&D and marketing. In governmental operations, ZBB is useful in all activities at city, state, and federal levels.[1,13,14,21,22]

**Planning Assumptions and Requirements** As ZBB deals with a total budget request, not just an increase (decrease) over the previous year, the existing activities are reviewed as closely as any proposed new activities. The emphasis is on the choice between alternative ways of providing a service as well as alternative funding levels for each proposed service. However, ZBB is not a strategic planning or corporate planning procedure.

The ZBB process requires the prior development of planning assumptions and objectives for the forthcoming fiscal period. Assumptions are provided to each of the operating or service departments for use in their individual budget preparation

efforts. Each manager requires guidelines concerning inflation rates, fringe benefits, and salary increases. In addition, managers require information concerning service-level requirements of related activities and departments.

Finally, planning information and guidelines are required concerning (1) the overall purpose of the organization, (2) specification of both short-term and long-range goals and plans, (3) definition of the organization's performance objectives, and (4) development of department, division, and subunit objectives.

## DECISION UNITS

The initial step in a ZBB process is the identification and analysis of decision units. A decision unit is an activity that can be analyzed for discretionary decisions and funding. A decision unit may be a program, an organizational unit, an activity, a cost center, an appropriation item, or a line item.

**Identification and Definition** The decision unit should correspond to a specific responsibility for the preparation of budgets. In each case, the decision unit should have an identifiable manager. The decision unit may correspond to a budget unit in those organizations with a detailed budget-unit or cost-center structure.[11] In some cases, the budget-unit manager may wish to separate different functions or operations within the budget unit that are significant in size and that require separate analysis. In such a case, several decision units may correspond to a budget unit. Decision units can also be defined as major projects, special work assignments, or capital projects. In practice, top management usually determines the organization or program level at which decision units must be defined, leaving it to the discretion of each manager to identify additional decision units that are appropriate.

In defining decision units, it is necessary to consider the size of the unit. If too small a decision unit is selected, considerable detail is required with little payoff in the budget process. If too large a decision unit is derived, the alternatives may not be properly evaluated. Typical decision units include between 5 and 15 people and a total annual budget of about $150,000–$400,000.[23]

The following are examples of some typical decision units:

| Department | Decision Units |
| --- | --- |
| Engineering | Drafting |
| | Maintenance |
| | Project design |

| Plant | Customer service |
|---|---|
| | Production scheduling |
| Finance | Accounting |
| | Data processing |
| Personnel | Fringe benefits |
| | Employee training |
| Marketing | Direct sales |
| | Advertising |

**Analysis** In the analysis of decision units the following information is required: (1) definition of objectives, (2) documentation of current operations and available resources, (3) definition of work load and measures of performance, (4) analysis of alternative means of achieving objectives.

*Objectives and Performance Measures.* The decision unit manager specifies the objectives and purpose of the decision unit and describes current operations and available resources. Work load and measure of performance are presented, as in the following examples:

Production control: number of orders processed weekly and on-time delivery performance

Regional sales manager: number of customer requests for cancellation and customer service levels

Internal audit: number of accounts audited and cycle for audit coverage of reporting units

Materials engineering: number of failure analyses performed; quality control and assurance

*Operating Alternatives.* The manager considers alternative ways of operating a decision unit.[24] Examples of different operational modes are centralizing the function, decentralizing the function, contracting for the function, combining the function with other activities, or eliminating the function. The selection of the best method of operating the decision unit is made on the basis of an analysis showing the advantages and disadvantages of each alternative, as evaluated by the performance measurements.

**Documentation Statement** Documentation of the statement and description of a decision unit is prepared so as to include the following items:

Identification of the decision unit—name, organizational unit, and cost center

Statement of the objectives of the decision unit

Description of how the decision unit currently operates

Description of the personnel requirements and associated functions

Description of the program by means of which the goals are to be achieved

Identification and evaluation of alternative means of accomplishing the decision unit's objectives

Identification and evaluation of incremental levels of service and their related costs; determination of how the decision unit's objectives are accomplished with each increment and the levels of additional benefits

Identification of work load and performance measurements for the decision unit

Identification and evaluation of all alternatives including the current method of operations

## DECISION PACKAGES

A decision package is a discrete program with goals, activities, and resources along with a document that identifies and describes the program as follows:

Statement of goals of the program

Activities by means of which the goals are to be achieved

Benefits to be expected from the program

Alternatives to the program

Consequences of not approving the program

Expenditures of funds and personnel which the program requires

**Formulation** In formulating decision packages it is necessary that each decision unit's budget request be made up of a sum of a series of discrete decision packages. Furthermore, each decision package specifies a prescribed set of performance measures, activities, and resources. The first package, the one that is given the highest priority, represents a minimum level of funding, usually substantially less than the current level, say 20 to 40 percent less. At a higher cost level, corresponding to the previous year's budget, two or more decision packages are considered. It is also possible to formulate additional decision packages which have total costs above the current level. The number of decision packages per decision unit may vary, say from 3 to 10.

**Documentation** In documenting the decision packages, it is necessary to list the services to be provided, the resources required for this package and any cumulative packages below it, measures of performance of this package and cumulative ones, and any additional background information necessary for a cost-benefit analysis. Organizations have developed specific forms for compiling such information, which are illustrated in a number of references.[1,2,5,14,22,23,25]

A form provides the following information concerning a decision package:

An identification of the decision package, as a decision unit increment

A description of the services which are to be provided or activities to be performed if the package is funded

The resource requirements of the package and their costs

A quantitative expression of work-load output or results anticipated if the package is funded

An evaluation of the effects of changes if the package is not funded

**Types of Decision Packages** There are two types of decision packages:[1]

1. *Mutually exclusive packages*, which identify *alternative means* of performing the same function. In this case, the best alternative is selected, where the other packages are discarded.

2. *Incremental packages*, which reflect *different levels* of funding that may be expended on a specific organizational function. An initial package may represent the action of *not funding* the unit at all, with the associated costs of this action identified. The next level may reflect a *base* package, which is a minimum level of activity. Other levels may indicate the current and increased activities.

**Alternative Methods and Level of Effort** The key to developing decision packages lies in formulating meaningful alternatives. Two alternatives are illustrated by the mutually exclusive and incremental packages. Two additional alternatives should also be examined:

*Alternative methods of accomplishing the objectives or performing the operation.* Managers should identify and evaluate all meaningful alternatives and choose the alternative method of accomplishing the objective or performing the operation that is considered best. If an alternative to one currently being funded is chosen, the recommended one should be shown in the decision package and mention made that the current method was not selected.

*Different levels of effort of performing the operation.* Once the best method of accomplishing the operation has been chosen from among the various methods being evaluated, a manager must identify alternative levels of effort and funding to perform that operation. Managers must establish a minimum level of effort (which should be significantly below the current level of operation), then identify additional levels or increments as separate decision packages. If appropriate, these incremental levels may bring the operation up to and above its current level.

The identification and evaluation of different levels of effort probably represent the two most difficult aspects of ZBB, yet they are key elements of the process. If only one level of effort were analyzed (probably reflecting the funding level desired by the manager), and the request from the manager for funds exceeded funding availability, management would have no choice but to do one of four things: It could fund the activity at the requested level, thus reducing profits; eliminate the program; make arbitrary reductions; or recycle the budgetary process.

## RANKING OF DECISION PACKAGES

The *ranking process* is the listing of decision packages in order of decreasing benefit or importance to the organization so that management can optimally allocate its resources by determining the following:

What are the key objectives which must be achieved?

How much should be budgeted to all packages?

Where should the resources be allocated?

The ranking process identifies and recommends where money can best be spent. Management decides on the overall budget by determining the *cutoff level* of funding (i.e., packages 1 through 50 are funded, package 51 and all lower ranked packages are not funded).

In ZBB, ranking has a key role in selecting the most effective decision packages for funding. In fact, ZBB has arisen at the time when the U.S. economy has entered a lowered growth phase and there is a greater need to select the most profitable alternatives. The decision packages are ranked in order of decreasing benefits to the organizational decision unit. The ranking process establishes priorities on the basis of functions described in the decision packages.

**The Ranking Form** A ranking form is a document which lists the ranked decision packages, in order of importance from the top line, along with information on the proposed, current, cumulative, and percentage charge of resources such as amount of expenses and number of employees. Ranking forms are illustrated in the literature.[1,5,14,20,21,23] Pyhrr has defined top level managers' needs for a ranking form as:[26]

Identifying cumulative funding levels so that top management can judge the budget impact of approving any given number of packages

Allowing top management to skim the rankings to get a feel for the types of activities as well as the dollars and people involved, and to selectively pick the packages they want to review in detail

Identifying the trend between the current year's effort and the minimum level of effort identified for the budget year (if we follow the convention of showing the current year's expense in the minimum level of effort package), so that top management can readily flag for further review those minimum level of effort packages showing increased effort or no reduction in effort

Providing a work sheet that top management can use to make funding decisions among several rankings, readily adjusting the funding levels during the decision making by varying the number of packages funded in each ranking

Following completion of the decision unit summary and individual decision package increments, the ranking manager should review these documents, focusing on the importance to the objectives of the decision unit of each higher increment and the measure used to describe work load and performance. The corporate budget is derived on the basis of establishing a cutoff level at the highest level in the organization. This in turn establishes cutoff levels at each lower level of the organization and corresponding decision packages to be approved above the cutoff levels.

During the fiscal year each manager is responsible for achieving the specified performance levels indicated in the decision package description and accomplishing this within the corresponding proposed budget levels.

**Methods of Ranking** A ranking method to be used should be adapted to satisfy organizational needs.[1,20,27] There is no ranking method that is universally valid. However, the following are general types of approaches, where an organization may select one to be followed:

*Single Criterion.* All packages are evaluated on the basis of one and only one criterion. Examples of economic criteria are return on investment, cost savings, net present value, discounted cash flow, cost-benefit ratio, and payback period.

In this case the ranking procedure would involve the following steps:

1. Agree on the single criterion to be used.

2. Rank all packages from top to bottom, using the criterion in 1 above.

3. Determine the cutoff point, based on available funds and/or personnel.

4. Recommend to fund all packages above the cutoff level, and defer or eliminate all others.

5. Communicate the decision to the appropriate managers.

*Voting System.* Although the single-criterion approach is conceptually sound, problems associated with conflicting multiobjectives make it nonapplicable.[2] Pyhrr developed a voting system for use by a committee in ranking a large number of packages, as follows:[28]

1. Each committee member is provided with a complete set of decision packages and ranking sheets.

2. The committee discusses each package to obtain a thorough understanding of it, then votes on

a fixed scale with either the average or the total points determining the ranking.

3. The committee reviews and discusses the ranking, resolves the principal differences, and reorders the packages.

4. Final ranking is achieved and passed on to the next higher level for consolidation.

*Major Categories.* It is possible to obviate the purposes of ZBB by ranking poorer packages higher than worthwhile packages so as to increase the budget.[22] To prevent the likelihood of this happening, it is worthwhile to classify packages by major categories in order of importance.[2]

1. All efforts that are explicitly required by law

2. All efforts that pay for themselves in the first year

3. All packages that require a core management group

4. All packages that have a substantial long-term economic impact

5. All other packages

*Multiple Standards.* Cheek has applied a multiple-standard approach to Xerox personnel and planning areas.[4] Five criteria are used to rank order packages:

Is the package legally required? (Legal Requirement)

Does the organization have the necessary technical skills? (State-of-the-Art)

Will line management accept and execute the package? (Ease of Implementation)

Is the package cost-effective? (Net Economic Benefits)

Can the organization afford not to select the package? (Economic Risks)

Decision tables and program-ranking schedule forms are given by Cheek.[4,20]

The process of decision package ranking becomes difficult when benefits cannot be dollar-quantified. Comparability among decision packages on the basis of benefits is compromised because of the differing units of measurement; thus, the ranking procedure becomes more complex. Instead of ranking packages on the basis of cost-benefit ratios, or return on investment ratios, other criteria must be used. As previously mentioned, some of these other criteria include:

Perceived importance of service

Potential consequences of not providing service

Statutory or contractual agreements

Informal assessments

Political reasons

The rigorousness of the ZBB methodology begins

to deteriorate when these other ranking criteria are employed. Likewise, the prioritization feature of ZBB is undermined and the benefits of ZBB are not fully realized.[29]

**Procedural Problems in the Ranking Process** The ranking process as described encounters three problems:[2]

The large number of potential decision packages generated overwhelms top management's ability to evaluate them thoroughly and rank them in the allotted time.

Managers have conceptual difficulty in ranking packages they consider to be operationally obligatory.

Managers express concern about their own ability to judge the relative importance of dissimilar activities, especially in areas where packages require subjective evaluation and ranking.

In application, the total volume of packages is often found to increase greatly with each consolidation, at each successive level. To reduce the number of packages to be reviewed in detail by successively higher levels of management and to concentrate top management's attention on the lower-ranked activities, a cutoff expense line is established at each organizational level. Management at that level then reviews in detail and ranks only the decision packages involving expenditures below that cutoff line in any detail.

Packages above the cutoff level are reviewed at each successive level to give management a feel for the entire operation and to allow top management to verify to its own satisfaction the relative importance of the packages above the cutoff line versus the ones below it—that is, the ones being studied in detail and ranked. Since the total number of packages to be reviewed does increase at each higher level, the cutoff level must be made more stringent at the lower level if the volume of packages to be reviewed at successive levels is to be kept under control.

**Setting the Cutoff Levels** In practice, it is best to establish the cutoff level at the highest consolidation level first and then establish the cutoff level for the lower levels. The most effective way to establish this first cutoff is for management at the highest consolidation level to estimate the expense that will be approved at the top level and then set the cutoff far enough below this expected expense figure to allow the desired trading-off between the divisions whose packages are being ranked. Lower consolidation levels then set less stringent cutoffs for their own use. It is important to note that these cutoffs must be set before consolidation at any level begins.

At the lower level, assume a cutoff line of 50 percent had been set. When the lowest level had handed up its rankings, management at the lower level would have glanced over all the packages, approved the top ones up to a total value of 50 percent of last year's expenditures in the areas in question, checked these for reasonableness, and then evaluated and consolidated the rest in its own, new ranking to be handed up to the higher level.

The ability to achieve a list of ranked packages at any given organizational level allows management to evaluate the desirability of various expenditure levels throughout the budgeting process. Also, this ranked list provides management with a reference point to be used during the operating year to identify activities to be reduced or expanded if allowable expenditure levels change or if the organization is over or under budget during the year.

## PREPARATION OF DETAILED BUDGETS

The ranking process culminates in the allocation decisions and the cutoff level, or total budget, being specified. The final step in the ZBB process is the preparation of detailed budgets, incorporating the organization's account codes and descriptions.[30]

A decision-unit summary budget form is used to provide information on projected operating expenses by line item for each increment of effort and is the basis for the detailed budgets. This form is filled out in accordance with the organization's established policies on accounting procedures and is subject to accounting audit. Major categories of expense should be listed on the form. All expenses must be accounted for, even if some are miscellaneous. Each expense is recorded across from the departmental suffix, which is appropriate, and beneath the column of appropriate increment.

The final budget is prepared from the detailed budget form.[23] Although the budget may be prepared using the ZBB process, it is similar in format to the final product as prepared in the usual way. The cost breakdowns such as salaries, supplies, and travel are entered into the organization's existing budgetary and control system. ZBB demonstrates how each line item of expenditures relates to final goods or services.

Although the primary responsibility for the successful implementation of a ZBB system lies with the effectiveness of decision unit managers and the efficiency of the ranking process, the management accountants play an integral role in ensuring that the ZBB system is properly implemented and operated.[21] Specific areas where the accountant provides assistance are:

Determining the appropriate areas within a company in which to apply ZBB, as ZBB is most effective in controlling discretionary cost centers where there is considerable flexibility in funding levels.

Integrating the ZBB system with the firm's existing budget system. For example, will ZBB replace, complement, or be totally separate from the normal budget process? It is difficult to envision a case where it would be totally separate. A typical situation is one where a ZBB system would be installed to complement and improve upon an existing budget system.

Developing procedures and forms for use in system implementation.

Training of decision unit managers and continued assistance to these managers in operating the ZBB system.

Monitoring and recommending improvements to the ZBB process after its implementation.

## MANAGING THE ZBB IMPLEMENTATION PROCESS

Initial implementation of ZBB is often accomplished by a task force of operating and financial managers who are responsible for the design and administration of the process in the organization. The inclusion of operating managers in the task force is essential, since they are the most knowledgeable about operating needs and problems, will be largely responsible for implementing the ZBB process, and will add credibility to the proposed zero-base implementation plan.

The task force manages the process by:[23]

Designing the process to fit the specific needs and character of the organization

Preparing a simple, straightforward budget manual that illustrates the ZBB process and explains the decision unit, decision package, and ranking concepts

Presenting the process to management and teaching operating managers responsible for ZBB analysis of a decision unit how to apply the technique

Working with decision unit managers to improve and expedite the ZBB process

If required, designing, developing, and operating a computer system for ZBB

An important requirement in instituting a sound ZBB process is to manage carefully and efficiently the implementation of ZBB. The following are typi-

cal activities that must be performed in implementing ZBB:

1. Establish a ZBB task force responsible for the implementation of ZBB.

2. Develop a work plan and time schedule for implementation.

3. Review and document all current planning, budgeting, and control procedures.

4. Design a ZBB process that is adaptable to the organization's needs.

5. Prepare a manual that documents the ZBB process in simple, straightforward terms.

6. Conduct a training presentation to introduce decision unit managers to the ZBB process.

7. Assist decision unit managers in defining and formulating decision packages.

8. Work closely with decision unit managers to (a) specify current methods of operation, (b) specify performing measures, (c) develop alternative methods of operation, and (d) develop incremental cost-benefit analysis.

9. Assist decision unit managers to develop a procedure for ranking decision packages and to prescribe cutoff budget levels.

10. Assist in consolidating and summarizing the plan and detailed budgets.

*See also* ACCOUNTING FOR MANAGERIAL CONTROL; BUDGETS AND BUDGET PREPARATION; HEALTH SERVICES, PLANNING FOR; PROGRAM BUDGETING (PPBS); PROGRAM PLANNING AND IMPLEMENTATION.

## NOTES

[1]Peter A. Pyhrr, *Zero-Base Budgeting, A Practical Management Tool for Evaluating Expenses,* John Wiley & Sons, Inc., New York, 1973.

[2]Peter A. Pyhrr, "Zero-Base Budgeting," *Harvard Business Review,* November–December 1970, pp. 111–121.

[3]Jimmy Carter, *Why Not the Best,* Broadman Press, Nashville, 1975, chap. 11.

[4]Logan M. Cheek, "Cost Effectiveness Comes to the Personnel Function," *Harvard Business Review,* May–June 1973, pp. 96–105.

[5]*Compendium on Zero-Base Budgeting in State Governments,* Report of Committee on Governmental Operations, January 1977.

[6]Donald N. Anderson, "Zero-Based Budgets Offer Data, Spending Control," *Industry Week,* Jan. 12, 1976, p. 49.

[7]Donald N. Anderson, "Zero-Based Budgeting: How to Get Rid of Corporate Crabgrass," *Management Review,* October 1976, pp. 4–16.

[8]Donald N. Anderson, "Zero-Based Budgeting: Weeding Out Corporate Crabgrass," *Manager's Forum,* May 1976.

[9]Thomas H. Murray, "The Tough Job of Zero Budgeting," *Dun's Review,* October 1974, pp. 71–72, 128.

[10]James D. Suver and Ray L. Brown, "Where Does Zero-Base Budgeting Work?" *Harvard Business Review*, November–December 1977, pp. 76–84.

[11]Peter A. Pyhrr, "Zero-Base Budgeting: Where to Use It and How to Begin," *Advanced Management Journal*, Summer 1976, pp. 4–14.

[12]Scott Cowen, "Zero-Base Budgeting in the Municipalities," ORSA/TIMS Sessions, November 1977 and May 1978.

[13]"ZBB," *The Bureaucrat*, April 1977, vol. 6, no. 1.

[14]"Zero-Base Budgeting," OMB Guidelines, Executive Office of the President, Washington, April 1977.

[15]Aaron Wildavksy, *Budgeting—A Comparative Theory of Budgetary Processes*, Little, Brown and Company, Boston, 1975.

[16]Paul J. Stonich, "Zero-Base Planning—A Management Tool," *Managerial Planning*, July–August 1976, vol. 25, no. 1, pp. 1–4.

[17]Paul J. Stonich and William H. Steeves, "Zero-Base Planning and Budgeting for Utilities," *Public Utilities Fortnightly*, Sept. 9, 1976.

[18]"Zero-Base Budgeting—A Way to Cut Spending, or a Gimmick," *U.S. News & World Report*, Sept. 20, 1976, pp. 79–82.

[19]"Zero-Base Budgeting," IMAGES, Case Western Reserve University, October 1977.

[20]Logan M. Cheek, *Zero-Base Budgeting Comes of Age*, AMACOM, New York, 1977.

[21]Scott Cowen and Burton V. Dean, "Zero-Base Budgeting as a Management Tool," *Michigan State Business Review*, Spring 1978.

[22]Burton V. Dean, "Problems in Implementing Zero-Base Budgeting," *American Association for Budget and Program Analysis*, March 1977.

[23]Paul J. Stonich, *Zero-Base Planning and Budgeting*, Dow-Jones Irwin, Inc., Homewood, Ill., 1977, p. 21.

[24]Ibid., p. 23.

[25]Ronald E. Dunn, "Zero-Base Budgeting at Commercial Credit Company," *Cash Management Forum*, vol. 2, no. 1, March 1976, pp. 4, 8.

[26]Pyhrr, *Zero-Base Budgeting, A Practical Management Tool for Evaluating Expenses*, p. 79.

[27]Burton V. Dean, "Evaluating, Selecting, and Controlling R&D Projects," *American Management Association*, Research Study 89, 1968.

[28]Pyhrr, *Zero-Base Budgeting, A Practical Management Tool for Evaluating Expenses*, pp. 94, 95.

[29]Burton V. Dean, "Zero-Base Budgeting in Industry," ORSA/TIMS Sessions, November 1977 and May 1978.

[30]Stonich, *Zero-Base Planning and Budgeting*, p. 31.

Burton V. Dean, *Case Western Reserve University*

## Zero-base planning (*See* BUDGETS AND BUDGET PREPARATION.)

## Zero defects (*See* QUALITY MANAGEMENT.)

## Zip standard data (*See* WORK MEASUREMENT.)

## Zoning (*See* COMMUNITY PLANNING LEGISLATION; SITE SELECTION.)

# Index

# Index

# Index

# Index

# Index

# Index

# Index

# Index

# Index

# Index

# Index

# Index

# Index

# Index

# Index

# Index

# Index

# Index

# Index

# Index

# Index

# Index